W9-BPJ-377

ProQuest Statistical Abstract of the United States 2014

ProQuest Statistical Abstract of the United States 2014

Issued December 2013

Published in the United States of America by Bernan, a wholly owned subsidiary of Rowman & Littlefield
4501 Forbes Boulevard, Suite 200 Lanham, Maryland 20706

Bernan
800-865-3457
www.bernan.com

ISBN 13: 978-1-59888-639-9

Suggested Citation:
ProQuest LLC. *ProQuest Statistical Abstract of the United States, 2014.* (2nd ed.) Bethesda, MD, 2013

Preface

The *Statistical Abstract of the United States*, published since 1878, is the best-known statistical reference publication in the country. As a comprehensive collection of statistics on the social, political, and economic conditions of the United States, it is a snapshot of America and its people. In the spring of 2011, the Census Bureau announced that the edition published that year would be the last one produced at government expense. Beginning in 2012, ProQuest took on responsibility for updating and releasing this publication, the most used statistical reference tool in U.S. libraries.

The editors at ProQuest have endeavored to continue the tradition established by the Census Bureau Statistical Compendia Branch. Like its predecessors, the *ProQuest Statistical Abstract of the United States* is designed to serve as a convenient volume for statistical reference and as a guide to other statistical publications and sources. The latter function is served by the introductory text to each section, the source note appearing below each table, and Appendix I, which is comprised of the *Guide to Sources of Statistics*, the *Guide to State Statistical Abstracts*, and the *Guide to Foreign Statistical Abstracts*.

This volume includes a selection of data from many statistical sources, both government and private. Publications cited as sources usually contain additional statistical detail and more comprehensive discussions of definitions and concepts. Data not available in publications issued by the contributing agency, but obtained from the Internet or unpublished records are identified in the source notes. More information on the subjects covered in the tables may generally be obtained from the source.

Except as indicated, figures are for the United States as presently constituted. Although emphasis in the *ProQuest Statistical Abstract* is primarily given to national data, many tables present data for regions and individual states and a smaller number for metropolitan areas and cities. "Appendix II, Metropolitan and Micropolitan Statistical Areas: Concepts, Components, and Population," presents explanatory text, a complete current listing, and population data for metropolitan and micropolitan areas defined as of February 2013. Statistics for the Commonwealth of Puerto Rico and for Island Areas of the United States are included in many state tables and are supplemented by information in Section 29.

Statistics in this edition are generally for the most recent year or period available, as of early September 2013. Each year over 1,400 tables are reviewed and evaluated, new tables of current interest are added, continuing series are updated, and less timely data are condensed or eliminated. Text notes and appendices are revised as appropriate.

Changes in this edition—This year ProQuest introduces 55 new tables, presenting new material on a variety of topics, including firearm-related violence and deaths, homeless population, prevalence of allergies among children, sexual assault in the military, student loans of bachelor's degree recipients, and online course enrollment. For a complete list of new tables, see "New Tables," p. xi.

ProQuest Statistical Abstract is also available in an online edition. This dynamic edition features table-specific capabilities for narrowing results by source, data date, subject, and type of data breakdown. Importantly, the online edition is updated with new statistical content on a monthly basis, enabling users to regularly access new and revised data. The online product functions as a repository for additional back year's data that cannot fit into the print publication. Users will find spreadsheets that correspond to each table in the book. In many cases, these spreadsheets present expanded coverage of the data shown in print. It is available as a stand-alone product or a fully integrated component of *ProQuest Statistical Insight*.

Limitations of the data—The contents of this volume were taken from many sources. All data from censuses, surveys, and administrative records are subject to error arising from a number of factors including the following: sampling variability (for statistics based on samples), reporting errors in the data for individual units, incomplete coverage, nonresponse, and imputation and processing errors. (See also Appendix III). ProQuest cannot accept responsibility for the accuracy or limitations of the data presented here. However, selection of the material and its proper presentation is the responsibility of ProQuest.

For additional information on data presented—Please consult the source publications available in local libraries and on the Internet, or contact the agency or organization indicated in the source notes.

Contents

[Numbers following subject are page numbers]

New and Deleted Tables in 2014 Edition

New Tables for 2014

See footnotes at end of table.

New Tables for 2014-Continued.

See headnote on page 11.

Tables Deleted From the 2013 Edition of the Statistical Abstract

[Tables are deleted for several reasons, including: source data has been discontinued, source data was monographic and new data is not expected to be available, data is believed to no longer be reliable, and data was previously unpublished and cannot be replicated. Many tables have been replaced with tables illustrating similar content. Where applicable, please see reference to new table number]

Table Number	Section/Table Title	Replaced by Table Number
	Section 1: Population	
Table 75...............	Same-Sex Couple Households by Legal Recognition of Same-Sex Couple Marriages and Unions: 2010	
	Section 2: Births, Deaths, Marriages, and Divorces	
Table 102.............	Infants Who Were Ever Breastfed by Maternal Age and Race-Ethnicity: 1999 to 2006	
Table 110.............	Expectation of Life and Expected Deaths by Race, Sex, and Age: 2008	
Table 132.............	Deaths—Life Years Lost and Mortality Costs by Age, Sex, and Cause: 2009	
	Section 3: Health and Nutrition	
Table 147.............	Medicare Disbursements by Type of Beneficiary: 1990 to 2010	Table 155
Table 152.............	Medicare Benefits by Type of Provider: 1990 to 2010	
Table 157.............	Persons Enrolled in Health Maintenance Organizations (HMOs) by State: 2007 and 2008	
Table 172.............	Visits to Office-Based Physicians and Hospital Outpatient Departments by Diagnosis: 2003 and 2008	Table 186 and Table 187
Table 199.............	Insufficient Rest or Sleep by Number of Days and selected Characteristics: 2008	Table 226
Table 211.............	Cumulative Percent Distribution of Population by Height and Sex: 2007 to 2008	Table 217
Table 212.............	Cumulative Percent Distribution of Population by Weight and Sex: 2007 to 2008	Table 218
Table 213.............	Age-Adjusted Percent Distribution of Body Mass Index (BMI) Among Persons 18 Years Old and Over by Selected Characteristics: 2007 to 2008	Table 219
	Section 4: Education	
Table 233.............	Students Who Are Foreign Born or Who Have Foreign-Born Parents: 2009	
Table 249.............	Public Elementary and Secondary Schools and Enrollment—States: 2008 to 2009	
Table 263.............	Public School Districts Offering Various Technology Resources to All or Some Students by District Characteristics: 2008	
Table 273.............	Employment Status of High School Graduates and Dropouts Not Enrolled in School by Sex and Race: 1980 to 2010	
	Section 5: Law Enforcement, Courts, and Prisons	
Table 320.............	Forcible Rape—Number and Rate: 1990 to 2009	
Table 353.............	Child Abuse and Neglect Cases Reported, Investigated, and Number of Child Victims by State: 2010	Table 361
Table 355.............	Adults Under Correctional Supervision: 2000 to 2010	Table 369
	Section 6: Geography and Environment	
Table 382.............	Emissions of Greenhouse Gases by Type and Source: 1990 to 2009	Table 393
Table 383.............	Carbon Dioxide Emissions by Sector and Source: 1990 to 2009	Table 394
	Section 12: Labor Force, Employment, and Earnings	
Table 618.............	Persons on Flexible Schedules: 2004	
Table 654.............	Average Hours Per Week Spent Doing Unpaid Household Work and Paid Work by Sex and Age: 2003 to 2007	
Table 672.............	Workplace Violence Incidents and Security Measures: 2005	Table 690
	Section15: Business Enterprise	
Table 775.............	Establishment Births, Deaths, and Employment by Sector and Firm Type—Startups, Young, and Mature Firms: 2010	
	Section 16: Science and Technology	
Table 829.............	Employment, Mean Earnings, and Growth in Science and Engineering (S&E) Occupations: 2004 to 2008	
Table 830.............	Research and Development (R&D) Scientists and Engineers—Employment and Cost by Industry: 2005 to 2007	
	Section 17: Agriculture	
Table 845.............	Certified Organic Farmland, Crops, and Livestock: 2000 to 2008	
Table 859.............	Civilian Consumer Expenditures for Farm Foods: 1990 to 2008	Table 871
Table 875.............	Fresh Fruits and Vegetables—Supply and Use: 2000 to 2011	Table 903
	Section 18: Forestry, Fishing, and Mining	
Table 927.............	Oil and Gas Extraction Industry—Establishments, Employees, and Payroll by State: 2009	Table 948 and Table 941
	Section 19: Energy and Utilities	
Table 957.............	Solar Collector Shipments by Type, End Use, and Market Sector: 1980 to 2009	
	Section 20: Construction and Housing	
Table 982.............	New Privately Owned Housing Units Started—Selected Characteristics: 1970 to 2011	
	Section 21: Manufactures	
Table 1049............	U.S. Aircraft Shipments: 1990 to 2010	Table 1062
	Section 23: Transportation	
Table 1114............	Speeding-Related Traffic Fatalities by Road Type, Speed Limit, and State: 2009	Table 1133
	Section 24: Information and Communication	
Table 1157............	Telephone Systems—Summary: 1990 to 2008	
Table 1160............	Cable and Other Programming Distribution—Estimated Revenue: 2006 to 2010	
	Section 28: Foreign Commerce and Aid	
Table 1309............	U.S. Businesses Acquired or Established by Foreign Direct Investors—Investment Outlays by Industry of U.S. Business Enterprise and Country of Ultimate Beneficial Owner: 2000 to 2008	
	Section 30: International Statistics	
Table 1351............	Births to Unmarried Women by Country: 1980 to 2008	
Table 1352............	Marriage and Divorce Rates by Country: 1980 to 2008	
Table 1353............	Single-Parent Households: 1980 to 2009	
Table 1354............	Percent Distribution of Households by Type and Country: 1980 to 2009	
Table 1392............	EU and U.S. Organic Land and Farm Sector: 2007 and 2008	
Table 1402............	Commercial Nuclear Power Generation by Country: 1990 to 2010	

Guide to Tabular Presentation

Example of Table Structure

Table 1269. Top 20 U.S. Gateways for Nonstop International Air Travel: 2009 and 2010

[151,324 represents 151,324,000. International passengers are residents of any country traveling nonstop to and from the United States on U.S. and foreign carriers. The data cover all passengers arriving and departing from U.S. airports on nonstop commercial international flights with 60 seats or more]

Gateway airport	2009 [1]	2010	Percent change 2009–2010	Gateway airport	2009 [1]	2010	Percent change 2009–2010
Total..............................	**151,324**	**160,018**	**5.7**	Washington (Dulles), DC.......	5,986	6,170	3.1
Total, top 20.....................	**136,317**	**144,724**	**6.2**	Dallas-Ft. Worth, TX............	4,667	5,050	8.2
Top 20, percentage of total...	**90.1**	**90.4**	**0.4**	Philadelphia, PA.................	3,738	3,799	1.6
				Boston, MA......................	3,472	3,647	5.0
New York (JFK), NY..............	21,487	22,783	6.0	Honolulu, HI.....................	3,276	3,609	10.2
Miami, FL.......................	15,836	16,734	5.7	Fort Lauderdale, FL.............	2,932	3,328	13.5
Los Angeles, CA.................	14,833	15,518	4.6	Orlando, FL.....................	2,815	3,078	9.3
Newark, NJ......................	10,676	11,376	6.6	Detroit, MI......................	2,738	2,884	5.3
Chicago (O'Hare), IL..............	10,184	10,444	2.5	Guam Island, GU................	2,333	2,732	17.1
Atlanta, GA......................	8,764	9,124	4.1	Charlotte, NC....................	2,344	2,690	14.8
San Francisco, CA...............	7,889	8,479	7.5	Seattle-Tacoma, WA.............	2,528	2,672	5.7
Houston (G. Bush), TX............	7,605	8,323	9.4	Minneapolis-St. Paul, MN......	2,213	2,283	3.1

[1] Data have been revised.

Source: U.S. Department of Transportation, Research and Innovative Technology Administration, Bureau of Transportation Statistics, Office of Airline Information, T-100 International Segment data, September 2011 <http://www.transtats.bts.gov/>.

Headnotes immediately below table titles provide information important for correct interpretation or evaluation of the table as a whole or for a major segment of it.

Footnotes below the bottom rule of tables give information relating to specific items or figures within the table.

Unit indicators show the *specified quantities* in which data items are presented. They are used for two primary reasons. Sometimes data are not available in absolute form and are estimates (as in the case of many surveys). In other cases we round the numbers in order to save space to show more data, as in the case above.

When a table presents data with more than one unit indicator, they are found in the headnotes and column headings (Tables 2 and 27), spanner (Table 38), stub (Table 22), or unit column (Table 164). When the data in a table are shown in the same unit indicator, it is shown as the first part of the headnote (Table 2). If no unit indicator is shown, data presented are in absolute form (Table 1).

Vertical rules are used to separate independent sections of a table (Table 1), or in tables where the stub is continued into one or more additional columns (Table 2).

Averages—An average is a single number or value that is often used to represent the "typical value" of a group of numbers. It is regarded as a measure of "location" or "central tendency" of a of numbers.

The *arithmetic mean* is the type of average used most frequently. It is derived by summing the individual item values of a particular group and dividing the total by the number of items. The arithmetic mean is often referred to as simply the "mean" or "average."

The *median* of a group of numbers is the middle number or value when each item in the group is arranged according to size (lowest to highest or visa versa); it generally has the same number of items above it as well as below it. If there is an even number of items in the group, the median is taken to be the average of the two middle numbers.

Per capita (or per person) quantities—a per capita figure represents an average computed for every person in a specified group (or population). It is derived by taking the total for an item (such as income, taxes, or retail sales) and dividing it by the number of persons in the specified population.

Index numbers—An index number is the measure of difference or change, usually expressed as a percent, relating one quantity (the variable) of a specified kind to another quantity of the same kind. Index numbers are widely used to express changes in prices over periods of time, but may also be used to express differences between related subjects for a single point in time.

To compute a price index, a base year or period is selected. The base year price (of the commodity or service) is then designated as the base or reference price to which the prices for other years or periods are related. Many price indexes use the year 1982 as the base year; in tables this is shown as "1982 = 100." A method expressing the price relationship is: The price of a set of one or more items for a related year (e.g. 1990) **divided by** the price of the same set of items for the base year (e.g. 1982). The result multiplied by 100 provides the index number. When 100 is subtracted from the index number, the result equals the percent change in price from the base year.

Average annual percent change—Unless otherwise stated in the *Abstract* (as in Section 1, Population), average annual percent change is computed by use of a *compound interest formula*. This formula assumes that the rate of change is constant throughout a specified compounding period (1 year for average annual rates of change). The formula is similar to that used to compute the balance of a savings account that receives compound interest. According to this formula, at the end of a compounding period the amount of accrued change (e.g., school enrollment or bank interest) is added to the amount that existed at the beginning of the period. As a result, over time (e.g., with each year or quarter), the same rate of change is applied to a larger and larger figure.

The *exponential formula*, which is based on continuous compounding, is often used to measure population change. It is preferred by population experts, because they view population and population-related subjects as changing without interruption, ever ongoing. Both exponential and compound interest formulas assume a constant rate of change. The former, however, applies the amount of change continuously to the base rather than at the end of each compounding period. When the average annual rates are small (e.g., less than 5 percent) both formulas give virtually the same results. For an explanation of these two formulas as they relate to population, see U.S. Census Bureau, *The Methods and Materials of Demography,* Vol. 2, 3d printing (rev.), 1975.

Current and constant dollars—Statistics in some tables in a number of sections are expressed in both current and constant dollars (see, e.g., Table 695 in Section 13, Income, Expenditures, Poverty, and Wealth). Current dollar figures reflect actual prices or costs prevailing during the specified year(s). Constant dollar figures are estimates representing an effort to remove the effects of price changes from statistical series reported in dollar terms. In general, constant dollar series are derived by dividing current dollar estimates by the appropriate price index for the appropriate period (e.g., the Consumer Price Index).

The result is a series as it would presumably exist if prices were the same throughout, as in the base year—in other words, as if the dollar had constant purchasing power. Any changes in this constant dollar series would reflect only changes in real volume of output, income, expenditures, or other measure.

Explanation of Symbols

The following symbols, used in the tables throughout this book, are explained in condensed form in footnotes to the tables where they appear:

— Represents zero or rounds to less than half the unit of measurement shown.

B Base figure too small to meet statistical standards for reliability of a derived figure.

D Figure withheld to avoid disclosure pertaining to a specific organization or individual.

NA Data not enumerated, tabulated, or otherwise available separately.

P Data are preliminary.

S Figure does not meet publication standards for reasons other than that covered by symbol B, above.

X Figure not applicable because column heading and stub line make entry impossible, absurd, or meaningless.

Z Entry would amount to less than half the unit of measurement shown.

In many tables, details will not add to the totals shown because of rounding.

Population

This section presents statistics on the growth, distribution, and characteristics of the U.S. population. The principal source of these data is the U.S. Census Bureau, which conducts a decennial census of population, a monthly population survey, a program of population estimates and projections, and a number of other periodic surveys.

Decennial censuses—The U.S. Constitution provides for a census of the population every 10 years, primarily to establish a basis for apportionment of members of the House of Representatives among the states. For over a century after the first census in 1790, the census organization was a temporary one, created only for each decennial census. In 1902, the Census Bureau was established as a permanent federal agency, responsible for enumerating the population and also for compiling statistics on other population and housing characteristics.

Historically, the enumeration of the population has been a complete (100 percent) count. That is, an attempt is made to account for every person, for each person's residence, and for other characteristics (sex, age, family relationships, etc.). In the twentieth century, the questions were divided between a "short" and "long" form. Only a subset of the population was required to answer the long-form questions. The most recent census consisted of a short form, which included basic questions about age, sex, race, Hispanic origin, household relationship, and owner/renter status. After the 2000 Census, the long form became the American Community Survey (ACS) and continues to collect long-form-type information. The ACS includes not only the basic short-form questions, but also detailed questions about population and housing characteristics. It is a nationwide, continuous sample survey designed to provide communities with reliable and timely demographic, housing, social, and economic data every year. Since its start, the ACS has been providing a continuous stream of updated information for states and local areas. Sample data may be used with confidence where large numbers are involved and assumed to indicate trends and relationships where small numbers are involved.

Current Population Survey (CPS)—This is a monthly nationwide survey of a scientifically selected sample representing the noninstitutionalized civilian population. The sample is located in 824 areas with coverage in every state and the District of Columbia and is subject to sampling error. At the present time, about 60,000 occupied households are eligible for interview every month; of these, about 8 percent are, for various reasons, unavailable for interview.

While the primary purpose of the CPS is to obtain monthly statistics on the labor force, it also serves as a vehicle for inquiries on other subjects. Using CPS data, the Census Bureau issues a series of publications under the general title of *Current Population Reports*.

Estimates of population characteristics based on the CPS will not agree with the counts from the census because the CPS and the census use different procedures for collecting and processing the data for racial groups, the Hispanic population, and other topics. Caution should also be used when comparing estimates for various years because of the periodic introduction of changes into the CPS. Beginning in January 1994, a number of changes were introduced into the CPS that affect all data comparisons with prior years. These changes included the results of a major redesign of the survey questionnaire and collection methodology and the introduction of 1990 census population controls, adjusted for the estimated undercount. Beginning with the 2001 CPS Annual Demographic Supplement, the independent estimates used as control totals for the CPS are based on civilian population benchmarks consistent with Census 2000. In March 2002, the sample size of the Annual Demographic Supplement was increased to approximately 78,000. In 2003 the name of the March supplement was changed to Annual Social and Economic Supplement. Beginning with the 2012 March CPS supplement the estimates are based on Census 2010 population controls. These changes in population controls had relatively little impact on derived measures such as means, medians, and percent distribution, but did have a significant impact on levels.

Population estimates and projections—Estimates of the United States population are derived by updating the resident population enumerated in Census 2010 with information on the components of population change: births, deaths, and net international migration. The population estimates base reflects changes to the decennial census population due to the Count Question Resolution (CQR) program and geographic program revisions.

Registered births and deaths are estimated from data supplied by the National Center for Health Statistics. The net international migration component consists of four parts: (1) the net international migration of the foreign born, (2) the net migration of natives to and from the United States, (3) the net migration between the United States and Puerto Rico, and (4) the net overseas movement of the Armed Forces population. Data from the ACS are used to estimate the annual net migration of the foreign-born population. Estimates of the net migration of natives and net migration between Puerto Rico and the United States prior to 2005 are derived from the Demographic Analysis and Population Estimates (DAPE) project (see Population Division Working Paper Series, No. 63 and No. 64). Estimates for net migration between Puerto Rico and the U.S. for 2005 and later years are derived from the ACS and the Puerto Rico Community Survey. Estimates of the net overseas movement of the Armed Forces are derived from data collected by the Defense Manpower Data Center.

Estimates for state and county areas are based on the same components of change data and sources as the national estimates with the addition of net internal migration. Estimates of net internal migration are derived from federal income tax returns from the Internal Revenue Service, group quarters data from the Federal-State Cooperative Program, and Medicare data from the Centers for Medicare and Medicaid Services.

The population by age for April 1, 1990, reflects modifications to the 1990 census data counts. The review of detailed 1990 information indicated that respondents tended to report age as of the date of completion of the questionnaire, not as of April 1, 1990. In addition, there may have been a tendency for respondents to round up their age if they were close to having a birthday. A detailed explanation of the age modification procedure appears in 1990 Census of Population and Housing, Data Paper Listing CPH-L74.

Population estimates and projections are available on the Census Bureau Web site, see <http://www.census.gov>. These estimates and projections are consistent with official decennial census figures with no adjustment for estimated net census coverage. However, the categories for these estimates and projections by race have been modified and are not comparable to the census race categories (see section below under "Race"). For details on methodology, see the sources cited below the individual tables.

Immigration—Immigration (migration to a country) is one component of international migration; the other component is emigration (migration *from* a country). In its simplest form, international migration is defined as any movement across a national border. In the United States, federal statistics on international migration are produced primarily by the U.S. Census Bureau and the Office of Immigration Statistics of the U.S. Department of Homeland Security (DHS).

The Census Bureau collects data used to estimate international migration through its decennial censuses and numerous surveys of the U.S. population.

The Office of Immigration Statistics publishes immigration data in annual flow reports and the *Yearbook of Immigration Statistics*. Data for these publications are collected from several administrative data sources including the DS-230 Application for Immigrant Visa and Alien Registration, the DS-260 Electronic Application for Immigrant Visa and Alien Registration of the U.S. Department of State (used by applicants living abroad), and the I-485 Application to Register Permanent Residence or Adjust Status (U.S. Citizenship and Immigration Services—USCIS) for applicants living in the United States.

An immigrant, or legal permanent resident (LPR), is a foreign national who has been granted lawful permanent residence in the United States. New arrivals are foreign nationals living abroad who apply for an immigrant visa at a consular office of the Department of State, while individuals adjusting status are already living in the United States and file an application for adjustment of status to lawful permanent residence with USCIS. Individuals adjusting status include refugees, asylees, and various classes of nonimmigrants. A refugee is an alien outside the United States who is unable or unwilling to return to his or her country of nationality because of persecution or a well-founded fear of persecution. Asylees must meet the same criteria as refugees, but are located in the United States or at a port of entry. Refugees are required to apply for adjustment to legal permanent resident status after one year of residence in the United States. Asylees are eligible to apply one year after they are granted asylum.

Nonimmigrants are foreign nationals granted temporary entry into the United States. The major activities for which nonimmigrant admission is authorized include temporary visits for business or pleasure, academic or vocational study, temporary employment, and to act as a representative of a foreign government or international organization. DHS collects information on the characteristics of a proportion of nonimmigrant admissions, those recorded on the I-94 Arrival/Departure Record.

U.S. immigration law gives preferential immigration status to persons with a close family relationship with a U.S. citizen or legal permanent resident, persons with needed job skills, persons who qualify as refugees or asylees, and persons who are from countries with relatively low levels of immigration to the United States (diversity immigrants). Immigration to the United States can be divided into two general categories: (1) classes of admission subject to the annual worldwide limitation and (2) classes of admission exempt from worldwide limitations. Numerical limits are imposed on visas issued and not on admissions. In 2012, the annual limit for preference visas subject to limitation was 370,951, which included a family-sponsored preference limit of 226,000 and an employment-based preference limit of 144,951.

The Diversity Visa Program is available to nationals of countries with fewer than 50,000 persons granted LPR status during the preceding five years in the employment- based and family-sponsored preferences and immediate relative classes of admission. The annual diversity visa limit has been 50,000 since 1999.

The number of persons who may be admitted to the United States as refugees each year is established by the President in consultation with Congress. The ceiling was 76,000 for 2012. There is no numerical limit on the number of persons who can be granted asylum status in a year.

Classes of admission exempt from the worldwide limitation include immediate relatives of U.S. citizens, refugees and asylees adjusting to permanent residence, and other various classes of special immigrants.

Metropolitan and micropolitan areas—Metropolitan and micropolitan statistical areas (metro and micro areas) are geographic entities delineated by the U.S. Office of Management and Budget (OMB) for use by Federal statistical agencies in collecting, tabulating, and publishing Federal statistics. These areas are the result of the application of published standards to Census Bureau data. Generally, the areas are delineated using the most recent set of standards following each decennial census. Between censuses, the delineations are updated annually to reflect the most recent Census Bureau population estimates. Areas based on the 2010 standards and Census Bureau data were delineated in February of 2013.

The term "Core Based Statistical Area" (CBSA) is a collective term for both metro and micro areas. A metro area contains a core urban area of 50,000 or more population, and a micro area contains an urban core of at least 10,000 (but less than 50,000) population. Each metro or micro area consists of one or more counties and includes the counties containing the core urban area, as well as any adjacent counties that have a high degree of social and economic integration (as measured by commuting to work) with the urban core.

Urban and rural—For Census 2000 and 2010, the Census Bureau classified as urban all territory, population, and housing units located within urbanized areas (UAs) and urban clusters (UCs). A UA consists of densely settled territory that contains 50,000 or more people, while a UC consists of densely settled territory with at least 2,500 people but fewer than 50,000 people. For the 1990 census, the urban population consisted of all people living in UAs and most places outside of UAs with a census population of 2,500 or more.

UAs and UCs encompass territory that generally consists of:

1 A cluster of one or more block groups or census blocks each of which has a population density of at least 1,000 people per square mile at the time.

2 Surrounding block groups and census blocks each of which has a population density of at least 500 people per square mile at the time.

3 Less densely settled blocks that form enclaves or indentations, or are used to connect discontiguous areas with qualifying densities.

They also may include an airport located adjacent to qualifying densely settled area if it has an annual enplanement (aircraft boarding) of at least 10,000 people. "Rural" encompasses all population, housing, and territory not included within an urban area. For Census 2010, many more geographic entities, including metropolitan areas, counties, and places, contain both urban and rural territory, population, and housing units.

Residence—In determining residence, the Census Bureau counts each person as an inhabitant of a usual place of residence (i.e., the place where one lives and sleeps most of the time). While this place is not necessarily a person's legal residence or voting residence, the use of these different bases of classification would produce the same results in the vast majority of cases.

Race—Census 2000 and 2010 adhere to the federal standards for collecting and presenting data on race and ethnicity as established by the OMB in October 1997. Starting with Census 2000, the OMB requires federal agencies to use a minimum of five race categories: White, Black or African American, American Indian or Alaska Native, Asian, and Native Hawaiian or Other Pacific Islander. Additionally, to collect data on individuals of mixed race parentage, respondents were allowed to select one or more races. For respondents unable to identify with any of these five race categories, the OMB approved and included a sixth category—"Some other race" on the Census 2000 and 2010 questionnaire. The Census 2000 and 2010 question on race included 15 separate response categories and three areas where respondents could write in a more specific race group. The response categories and write-in answers can be combined to create the five minimum OMB race categories plus "Some other race." People who responded to the question on race by indicating only one race are referred to as the *race alone* population, or the group that reported only one race category. Six categories make up this population: White alone, Black or African American alone, American Indian and Alaska Native alone, Asian alone, Native Hawaiian and Other Pacific Islander alone, and Some other race alone. Individuals who chose more than one of the six race categories are referred to as the *Two or More Races* population, or as the group that reported more than one race. Additionally, respondents who reported one race together with those who reported the same race plus one or more other races are combined to create the race alone or in *combination* categories. For example,

the *White alone or in combination group* consists of those respondents who reported only White or who reported White combined with one or more other race groups, such as "White and Black or African American," or "White and Asian and American Indian and Alaska Native." Another way to think of the group who reported White alone or in combination is as the total number of people who identified entirely or partially as White. This group is also described as people who reported White, whether or not they reported any other race.

The *alone or in combination* categories are tallies of *responses* rather than *respondents*. That is, the alone or in combination categories are not mutually exclusive. Individuals who reported two races were counted in two separate and distinct alone or in combination race categories, while those who reported three races were counted in three categories, and so on. Consequently, the sum of all alone or in combination categories equals the number of races reported, which exceeds the total population.

The racial categories included in the census questionnaire generally reflect a social definition of race recognized in this country and not an attempt to define race biologically, anthropologically, or genetically. In addition, it is recognized that the categories of the race item include racial and national origin or sociocultural groups. Additionally, data are available for the American Indian and Alaska Native tribes. A detailed explanation of race can be found at <http://www.census.gov/prod/cen2010/doc/sf1.pdf>.

Data for the population by race for April 1, 2000 and 2010, (shown in Tables 6 and 10) are modified counts and are not comparable to Census 2000 and 2010 race categories. These numbers were computed using Census 2000 and 2010 data by race and had been modified to be consistent with the 1997 OMB's "Revisions to the Standards for the Classification of Federal Data on Race and Ethnicity," (Federal Register Notice, Vol. 62, No 210, October 1997). A detailed explanation of the race modification procedure appears at <http://www.census.gov/popest/data/historical/files/MRSF-01-US1.pdf>.

In the CPS and other household sample surveys in which data are obtained through personal interview, respondents are asked to classify their race as: (1) White; (2) Black, African American, or Negro; (3) American Indian or Alaska Native; (4) Asian; or (5) Native Hawaiian or Other Pacific Islander. Beginning January 2003, respondents were allowed to report more than one race to indicate their mixed racial heritage.

Hispanic population—People who identify with the terms "Hispanic" or "Latino" are those who classify themselves in one of the specific Hispanic or Latino categories listed on the decennial census questionnaire and various Census Bureau survey questionnaires – "Mexican, Mexican American, Chicano" or "Puerto Rican" or "Cuban" – as well as those who indicate that they are "another Hispanic, Latino, or Spanish origin." Origin can be viewed as the heritage, nationality group, lineage, or country of birth of the person or the person's ancestors before their arrival in the United States.

Traditional and current data collection and classification treat race and Hispanic origin as two separate and distinct concepts in accordance with guidelines from the OMB. Race and Hispanic origin are two separate concepts in the federal statistical system.

People who are Hispanic may be any race and people in each race group may be either Hispanic or Not Hispanic. Also, each person has two attributes, their race (or races) and whether or not they are Hispanic. The overlap of race and Hispanic origin is the main comparability issue. For example, Black Hispanics (Hispanic Blacks) are included in both the number of Blacks and in the number of Hispanics. For further information, see <http://www.census.gov/population/www/socdemo/compraceho.html>.

Foreign-born and native populations—The Census Bureau separates the U.S. resident population into two groups based on whether or not a person was a U.S. citizen or U.S. national at the time of birth. Anyone born in the United States, Puerto Rico, or a U.S. Island Area (such as Guam), or born abroad to a U.S. citizen parent is a U.S. citizen at the time of birth and consequently included in the *native population*. The term *foreign-born population* refers to anyone who is not a U.S. citizen or a U.S. national at birth. This includes naturalized U.S. citizens, legal permanent resident aliens (immigrants), temporary migrants (such as foreign students), humanitarian migrants (such as refugees), and people illegally present in the United States. The Census Bureau provides a variety of demographic, social, economic, geographic, and housing information on the foreign-born population in the United States at <http://www.census.gov/population/foreign/>.

Mobility status—The U.S. population is classified according to mobility status on the basis of a comparison between the place of residence of each individual at the time of the survey or census and the place of residence at a specified earlier date. Nonmovers are all persons who were living in the same house or apartment at the end of the period as at the beginning of the period. Movers are all persons who were living in a different house or apartment at the end of the period than at the beginning of the period. Movers are further classified as to whether they were living in the same or different county, state, region, or were movers from abroad. Movers from abroad include all persons whose place of residence was outside the United States (including Puerto Rico, other U.S. Island Area, or a foreign country) at the beginning of the period.

Living arrangements—Living arrangements refer to residency in households or in group quarters. A "household" comprises all persons who occupy a "housing unit," that is, a house, an apartment or other group of rooms, or a single room that constitutes "separate living quarters." A household includes the related family members and all the unrelated persons, if any, such as lodgers, foster children, or employees who share the housing unit. A person living alone or a group of unrelated persons sharing the same housing unit is also counted as a household. See text, Section 20, Construction and Housing, for definition of housing unit.

All persons not living in housing units are classified as living in group quarters. These individuals may be institutionalized, e.g., under care or custody in juvenile facilities, jails, correctional centers, hospitals, or nursing homes; or they may be residents in noninstitutional group quarters such as college dormitories, group homes, or military barracks.

Householder—The householder is the person, or one of the people, in whose name the home is owned, being bought, or rented. If a home is owned or rented jointly by a married couple, either the husband or the wife may be listed first. Two types of householders are distinguished: a family householder and a nonfamily householder. A family householder is a householder living with one or more people related to him or her by birth, marriage, or adoption. The householder and all people in the household related to him or her are family members. A family household may contain people not related to the householder, but those people are not included as part of the householder's family in census tabulations. Thus, the number of family households is equal to the number of families, but family households may include more members than do families.

Nonfamily—A nonfamily householder is a householder living alone or with nonrelatives only.

Subfamily—A subfamily consists of a married couple (with or without children) or an unmarried parent with one or more never-married children under 18 years old residing with the householder, but not including the householder's spouse. Subfamilies are divided into "related" and "unrelated" subfamilies. A related subfamily is related to, but does not include, the householder or the spouse of the householder. Members of a related subfamily are also members of the family with whom they live. The number of related subfamilies, therefore, is not included in the count of families. An unrelated subfamily may include persons such as guests, lodgers, or resident employees and their spouses and/or children; none of whom is related to the householder.

Married couple—A married couple is defined as a husband and wife living together in the same household, with or without children and other relatives.

Statistical reliability—For a discussion of statistical collection and estimation, sampling procedures, and measures of statistical reliability applicable to Census Bureau data, see Appendix III.

Figure 1.1
Percent Change in Population for States: April 1, 2000 to April 1, 2010

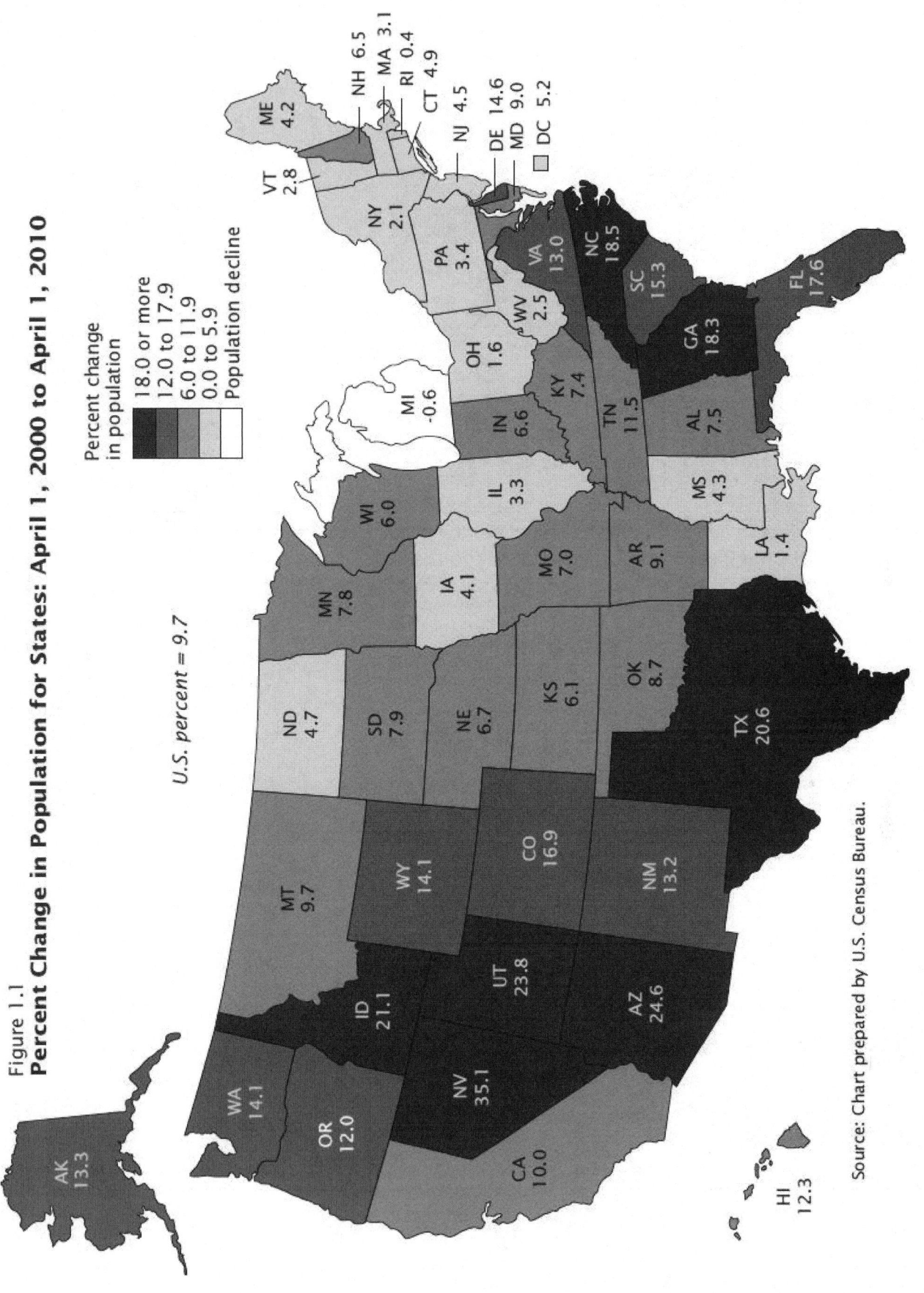

Percent change
in population

- 18.0 or more
- 12.0 to 17.9
- 6.0 to 11.9
- 0.0 to 5.9
- Population decline

U.S. percent = 9.7

Source: Chart prepared by U.S. Census Bureau.

Mean Center of Population for the United States: 1790 to 2010

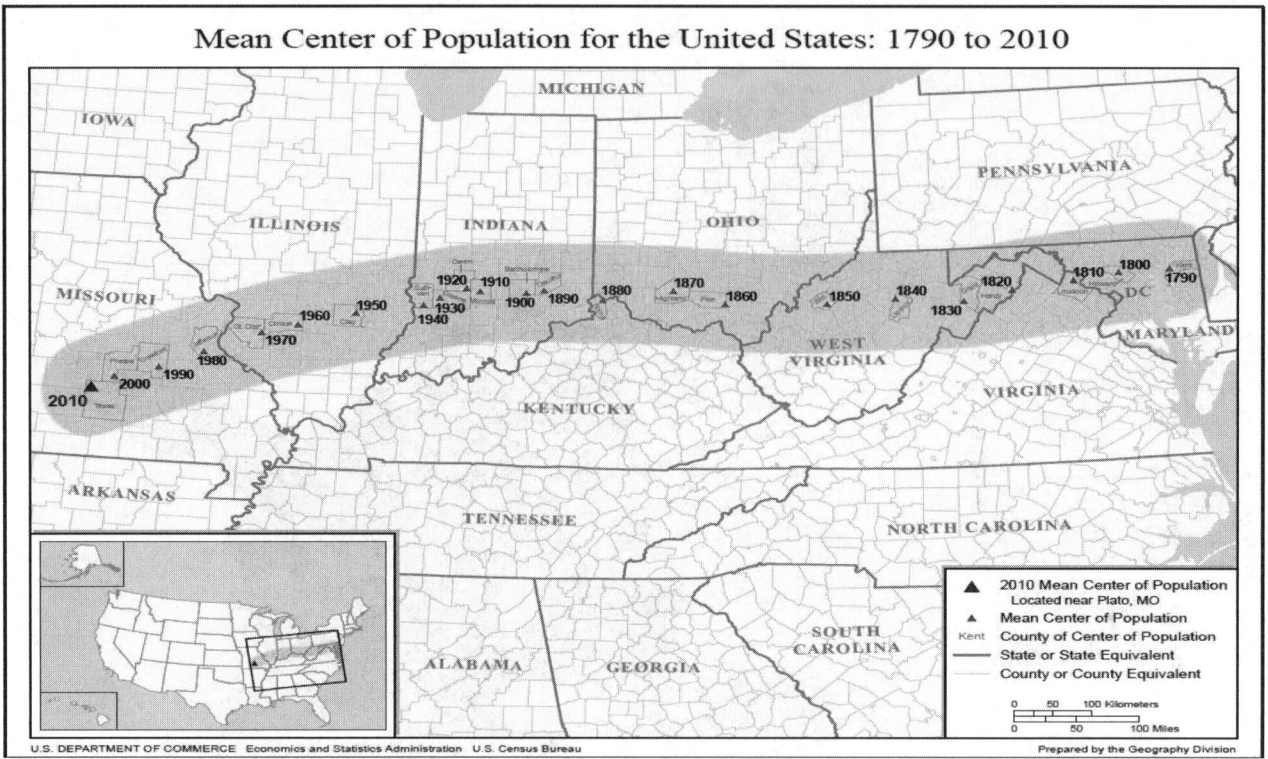

U.S. DEPARTMENT OF COMMERCE   Economics and Statistics Administration   U.S. Census Bureau

Prepared by the Geography Division

Median Center of Population for the United States: 1880 to 2010

U.S. DEPARTMENT OF COMMERCE   Economics and Statistics Administration   U.S. Census Bureau

Prepared by the Geography Division

Table 1. Population and Area: 1790 to 2010

[Area figures represent area on indicated date including in some cases considerable areas not then organized or settled, and not covered by the census. Area data include Alaska beginning in 1870 and Hawaii beginning in 1900. Total area figures for 1790 to 1970 have been recalculated on the basis of the remeasurement of states and counties for the 1980 census, but not on the basis of subsequent censuses. The land and water area figures for past censuses have not been adjusted and are not strictly comparable with the total area data for comparable dates because the land areas were derived from different base data, and these values are known to have changed with the construction of reservoirs, draining of lakes, etc. Density figures are based on land area measurements as reported in earlier censuses]

| Census date | Resident population | | | | Area (square miles) | | |
| | Number | Per square mile of land area | Increase over preceding census | | Total | Land | Water [1] |
			Number	Percent			
1790 (Aug. 2).......	3,929,214	4.5	(X)	(X)	891,364	864,746	24,065
1800 (Aug. 4).......	5,308,483	6.1	1,379,269	35.1	891,364	864,746	24,065
1810 (Aug. 6).......	7,239,881	4.3	1,931,398	36.4	1,722,685	1,681,828	34,175
1820 (Aug. 7).......	9,638,453	5.5	2,398,572	33.1	1,792,552	1,749,462	38,544
1830 (June 1)......	12,866,020	7.4	3,227,567	33.5	1,792,552	1,749,462	38,544
1840 (June 1)......	17,069,453	9.8	4,203,433	32.7	1,792,552	1,749,462	38,544
1850 (June 1)......	23,191,876	7.9	6,122,423	35.9	2,991,655	2,940,042	52,705
1860 (June 1)......	31,443,321	10.6	8,251,445	35.6	3,021,295	2,969,640	52,747
1870 (June 1)......	[2] 39,818,449	[2] 11.2	8,375,128	26.6	3,612,299	3,540,705	68,082
1880 (June 1)......	50,189,209	14.2	10,370,760	26.0	3,612,299	3,540,705	68,082
1890 (June 1)......	62,979,766	17.8	12,790,557	25.5	3,612,299	3,540,705	68,082
1900 (June 1)......	76,212,168	21.5	13,232,402	21.0	3,618,770	3,547,314	67,901
1910 (Apr. 15).....	92,228,496	26.0	16,016,328	21.0	3,618,770	3,547,045	68,170
1920 (Jan. 1).......	106,021,537	29.9	13,793,041	15.0	3,618,770	3,546,931	68,284
1930 (Apr. 1).......	123,202,624	34.7	17,181,087	16.2	3,618,770	3,554,608	60,607
1940 (Apr. 1).......	132,164,569	37.2	8,961,945	7.3	3,618,770	3,554,608	60,607
1950 (Apr. 1).......	151,325,798	42.6	19,161,229	14.5	3,618,770	3,552,206	63,005
1960 (Apr. 1).......	179,323,175	50.6	27,997,377	18.5	3,618,770	3,540,911	74,212
1970 (Apr. 1).......	203,302,031	57.5	23,978,856	13.4	3,618,770	3,536,855	78,444
1980 (Apr. 1).......	[3] 226,542,199	64.0	23,240,168	11.4	3,618,770	3,539,289	79,481
1990 (Apr. 1).......	[4] 248,718,302	70.3	22,176,103	9.8	[5] 3,717,796	3,536,278	[5] 181,518
2000 (Apr. 1).......	[6] 281,424,603	79.6	32,706,301	13.1	3,794,083	3,537,438	256,645
2010 (Apr. 1).......	[7] 308,745,856	87.4	27,321,253	9.7	3,796,742	3,531,905	264,837

X Not applicable. [1] Data for 1790 to 1980 cover inland water only. Data for 1990 comprise Great Lakes, inland, and coastal water. Data for 2000 and 2010 comprise Great Lakes, inland, territorial, and coastal water. [2] Revised to include adjustments for underenumeration in southern states; unrevised number is 38,558,371 (10.9 per square mile). [3] Total population count has been revised since the 1980 census publications. Numbers by age, race, Hispanic origin, and sex have not been corrected. [4] The April 1, 1990, census count includes count question resolution corrections processed through December 1997, and does not include adjustments for census coverage errors. [5] Data reflect corrections made after publication of the results. [6] Reflects modifications to the Census 2000 population as documented in the Count Question Resolution program. [7] Reflects modifications to the Census 2010 population as documented in the Count Question Resolution program (updated August 27, 2013).

Source: U.S. Census Bureau, *Notes and Errata, 2010 Census of Population and Housing*, SF/10-1, 2013; 2000 Census of Population and Housing, *Population and Housing Unit Counts, United States Summary*, Series PHC-3-1, and *Notes and Errata*, (2000), SF/01-ER; *Areas of the United States: 1940*; Area data for 1990: unpublished data from TIGER ®; and Davis, Warren, personal correspondence, U.S. Census Bureau, 23 June 2006.

Table 2. Population: 1970 to 2012

[In thousands, except as indicated (205,052 represents 205,052,000). Estimates as of July 1. Civilian population excludes Armed Forces. For basis of estimates, see text, this section]

Year	Resident population, including Armed Forces overseas	Resident population	Civilian population	Year	Resident population, including Armed Forces overseas	Resident population	Civilian population
1970........	205,052	203,984	201,895	1992........	256,894	256,514	254,929
1971........	207,661	206,827	204,866	1993........	260,255	259,919	258,446
1972........	209,896	209,284	207,511	1994........	263,436	263,126	261,714
1973........	211,909	211,357	209,600	1995........	266,557	266,278	264,927
1974........	213,854	213,342	211,636	1996........	269,667	269,394	268,108
1975........	215,973	215,465	213,789	1997........	272,912	272,647	271,394
1976........	218,035	217,563	215,894	1998........	276,115	275,854	274,633
1977........	220,239	219,760	218,106	1999........	279,295	279,040	277,841
1978........	222,585	222,095	220,467	2000........	(NA)	282,162	(NA)
1979........	225,055	224,567	222,969	2001........	(NA)	284,969	(NA)
1980........	227,726	227,225	225,621	2002........	(NA)	287,625	(NA)
1981........	229,966	229,466	227,818	2003........	(NA)	290,108	(NA)
1982........	232,188	231,664	229,995	2004........	(NA)	292,805	(NA)
1983........	234,307	233,792	232,097	2005........	(NA)	295,517	(NA)
1984........	236,348	235,825	234,110	2006........	(NA)	298,380	(NA)
1985........	238,466	237,924	236,219	2007........	(NA)	301,231	(NA)
1986........	240,651	240,133	238,412	2008........	(NA)	304,094	(NA)
1987........	242,804	242,289	240,550	2009........	(NA)	306,772	(NA)
1988........	245,021	244,499	242,817	2010........	309,746	309,326	308,091
1989........	247,342	246,819	245,131	2011........	312,005	311,588	310,370
1990........	250,132	249,623	247,983	2012........	314,250	313,914	312,674
1991........	253,493	252,981	251,370				

NA Not available.

Source: U.S. Census Bureau, Population Division, data prior to 2010, <http://www.census.gov/popest/data/historical/index.html>; and 2010 to 2012: "Monthly Population Estimates for the United States: April 1, 2010 to March 1, 2013 (NA-EST2012-01)," <http://www.census.gov/popest/data/national/totals/2012/index.html>, accessed April 2013.

Table 3. Resident Population Projections: 2015 to 2060

[In thousands, except as indicated (321,363 represents 321,363,000). As of July 1. Projections are based on the July 1, 2011 population estimates, which are based on the 2010 Census, and assumptions about future births, deaths, and net international migration. More information on methodology and assumptions is available at <http://www.census.gov/population/projections/files/methodology/methodstatement12.pdf>]

Year	Population	Percent change [1]	Year	Population	Percent change [1]	Year	Population	Percent change [1]
2015.........	321,363	0.8	2031.........	360,792	0.6	2046.........	391,902	0.5
2016.........	323,849	0.8	2032.........	363,070	0.6	2047.........	393,869	0.5
2017.........	326,348	0.8	2033.........	365,307	0.6	2048.........	395,841	0.5
2018.........	328,857	0.8	2034.........	367,503	0.6	2049.........	397,818	0.5
2019.........	331,375	0.8	2035.........	369,662	0.6	2050.........	399,803	0.5
2020.........	333,896	0.8	2036.........	371,788	0.6	2051.........	401,796	0.5
2021.........	336,416	0.8	2037.........	373,883	0.6	2052.........	403,798	0.5
2022.........	338,930	0.7	2038.........	375,950	0.6	2053.........	405,811	0.5
2023.........	341,436	0.7	2039.........	377,993	0.5	2054.........	407,835	0.5
2024.........	343,929	0.7	2040.........	380,016	0.5	2055.........	409,873	0.5
2025.........	346,407	0.7	2041.........	382,021	0.5	2056.........	411,923	0.5
2026.........	348,867	0.7	2042.........	384,012	0.5	2057.........	413,989	0.5
2027.........	351,304	0.7	2043.........	385,992	0.5	2058.........	416,068	0.5
2028.........	353,718	0.7	2044.........	387,965	0.5	2059.........	418,161	0.5
2029.........	356,107	0.7	2045.........	389,934	0.5	2060.........	420,268	0.5
2030.........	358,471	0.7						

[1] Percent change from immediate preceding year. 2015, change from 2014.

Source: U.S. Census Bureau, Population Division, "2012 National Population Projections," December 2012, <http://www.census.gov/population/projections/data/national/2012.html>, accessed March 2013.

Table 4. Components of Population Change: 2010 to 2012

[In thousands, except as indicated (308,748 represents 308,748,000). Resident population]

Period	Population as of beginning of period	Net increase		Births	Deaths	Net international migration [2]	Population as of end of period
		Total	Percent [1]				
April 1, 2010 to July 1, 2010 [3]....................	308,748	579	0.2	988	599	190	309,326
July 1, 2010 to July 1, 2011.....................	309,326	2,262	0.7	3,977	2,491	776	311,588
July 1, 2011 to July 1, 2012.....................	311,588	2,326	0.7	3,954	2,513	886	313,914

[1] Percent of population at beginning of period. [2] Net international migration includes the international migration of both native and foreign-born populations. Specifically, it includes: (a) the net international migration of the foreign born, (b) the net migration between the United States and Puerto Rico, (c) the net migration of natives to and from the United States, and (d) the net movement of the Armed Forces population between the United States and overseas. [3] The April 1, 2010, population estimates base reflects changes from the Count Question Resolution program and geographic program revisions.

Source: U.S. Census Bureau, Population Division, "Population, population change, and estimated components of population change: April 1, 2010 to July 1, 2012 (NST-EST2012-alldata)," <http://www.census.gov/popest/data/national/totals/2012/index.html>, accessed June 2013.

Table 5. Components of Population Change by Race and Hispanic Origin: 2010 to 2012

[In thousands (5,167 represents 5,167,000). Resident population. Covers period April 1, 2010 to July 1, 2012. The April 1, 2010 population estimates base reflects changes to the Census 2010 population from the Count Question Resolution program and geographic program revisions. Responses of "Some Other Race" from the 2010 Census are modified. This results in differences between the population for specific race categories shown for the 2010 Census population in this table versus those in the original 2010 Census data]

Race and Hispanic origin	April 1, 2010 to July 1, 2012				
	Net increase	Natural increase	Births	Deaths	Net international migration [1]
Total..	**5,167**	**3,316**	**8,918**	**5,603**	**1,851**
One race..	4,648	2,829	8,386	5,557	1,818
White..	2,557	1,687	6,434	4,747	870
Black or African American......................	953	713	1,366	653	240
American Indian and Alaska Native..............	118	105	145	40	13
Asian..	986	301	415	114	685
Native Hawaiian and Other Pacific Islander.....	33	23	26	3	9
Two or more races................................	519	486	532	46	33
Race alone or in combination: [2]					
White..	3,038	2,140	6,924	4,784	898
Black or African American......................	1,242	986	1,654	668	256
American Indian and Alaska Native..............	210	190	254	64	21
Asian..	1,179	480	608	129	699
Native Hawaiian and Other Pacific Islander.....	68	56	65	9	12
Hispanic [3]......................................	2,550	1,975	2,309	335	575
White alone, not Hispanic.........................	386	25	4,466	4,441	361

[1] See footnote 2, Table 4. [2] In combination with one or more other races. The sum of the five race groups adds to more than the total population because individuals may report more than one race. [3] Hispanic origin is considered an ethnicity, not a race. Hispanics may be of any race.

Source: U.S. Census Bureau, Population Division, "Estimates of the Components of Resident Population Change by Race and Hispanic Origin for the United States: April 1, 2010 to July 1, 2012," <http://factfinder2.census.gov>, accessed June 2013.

Table 6. Resident Population by Sex, Race, and Hispanic-Origin Status: 2000 to 2012

[281,425 represents 281,425,000. Data shown are modified race counts; see text, this section]

Characteristic	Number (1,000)				Percent change	
	2000 [1] (April)	2010 [1] (April)	2011 (July)	2012 (July)	2000 to 2010	2010 to 2012
BOTH SEXES						
Total	**281,425**	**308,748**	**311,588**	**313,914**	**9.7**	**1.7**
One race	277,527	301,763	304,317	306,411	8.7	1.5
White	228,106	241,938	243,342	244,496	6.1	1.1
Black or African American	35,705	40,251	40,775	41,205	12.7	2.4
American Indian and Alaska Native	2,664	3,740	3,805	3,857	40.4	3.2
Asian	10,589	15,160	15,702	16,146	43.2	6.5
Native Hawaiian and Other Pacific Islander	463	675	693	707	45.9	4.8
Two or more races	3,898	6,984	7,271	7,503	79.2	7.4
Race alone or in combination: [2]						
White	(NA)	248,069	249,738	251,107	(NA)	1.2
Black or African American	(NA)	43,214	43,897	44,456	(NA)	2.9
American Indian and Alaska Native	(NA)	6,138	6,255	6,349	(NA)	3.4
Asian	(NA)	17,677	18,325	18,855	(NA)	6.7
Native Hawaiian and Other Pacific Islander	(NA)	1,332	1,370	1,400	(NA)	5.1
Not Hispanic	246,118	258,270	259,707	260,886	4.9	1.0
One race	242,712	252,665	253,882	254,883	4.1	0.9
White	195,577	197,320	197,530	197,706	0.9	0.2
Black or African American	34,314	37,923	38,365	38,727	10.5	2.1
American Indian and Alaska Native	2,097	2,263	2,289	2,309	7.9	2.0
Asian	10,357	14,662	15,188	15,620	41.6	6.5
Native Hawaiian and Other Pacific Islander	367	497	510	521	35.4	4.7
Two or more races	3,406	5,604	5,825	6,004	64.5	7.1
Race alone or in combination: [2]						
White	(NA)	202,231	202,646	202,988	(NA)	0.4
Black or African American	(NA)	40,284	40,849	41,312	(NA)	2.6
American Indian and Alaska Native	(NA)	4,042	4,096	4,139	(NA)	2.4
Asian	(NA)	16,795	17,410	17,912	(NA)	6.7
Native Hawaiian and Other Pacific Islander	(NA)	1,020	1,047	1,069	(NA)	4.8
Hispanic [3]	35,306	50,478	51,881	53,028	43.0	5.1
One race	34,815	49,098	50,435	51,528	41.0	4.9
White	32,530	44,618	45,813	46,790	37.2	4.9
Black or African American	1,391	2,328	2,411	2,478	67.4	6.4
American Indian and Alaska Native	566	1,476	1,516	1,548	160.6	4.9
Asian	232	498	513	526	114.2	5.6
Native Hawaiian and Other Pacific Islander	95	177	182	187	85.9	5.1
Two or more races	491	1,380	1,446	1,499	180.8	8.7
Race alone or in combination: [2]						
White	(NA)	45,838	47,093	48,119	(NA)	5.0
Black or African American	(NA)	2,930	3,048	3,144	(NA)	7.3
American Indian and Alaska Native	(NA)	2,097	2,159	2,210	(NA)	5.4
Asian	(NA)	881	915	943	(NA)	7.0
Native Hawaiian and Other Pacific Islander	(NA)	312	323	331	(NA)	6.2
MALE						
Total	**138,056**	**151,783**	**153,261**	**154,492**	**9.9**	**1.8**
One race	136,146	148,357	149,688	150,800	9.0	1.6
White	112,478	119,700	120,466	121,109	6.4	1.2
Black or African American	16,972	19,206	19,472	19,695	13.2	2.5
American Indian and Alaska Native	1,333	1,890	1,922	1,949	41.8	3.1
Asian	5,128	7,218	7,476	7,687	40.8	6.5
Native Hawaiian and Other Pacific Islander	235	343	352	360	45.8	4.9
Two or more races	1,910	3,426	3,573	3,692	79.4	7.8
Race alone or in combination: [2]						
White	(NA)	122,717	123,619	124,373	(NA)	1.3
Black or African American	(NA)	20,634	20,981	21,270	(NA)	3.1
American Indian and Alaska Native	(NA)	3,055	3,114	3,161	(NA)	3.5
Asian	(NA)	8,468	8,780	9,035	(NA)	6.7
Native Hawaiian and Other Pacific Islander	(NA)	668	687	703	(NA)	5.2
Not Hispanic	119,894	126,164	126,923	127,562	5.2	1.1
Hispanic [3]	18,162	25,619	26,338	26,930	41.1	5.1
FEMALE						
Total	**143,368**	**156,964**	**158,326**	**159,422**	**9.5**	**1.6**
One race	141,381	153,406	154,629	155,611	8.5	1.4
White	115,628	122,238	122,877	123,386	5.7	0.9
Black or African American	18,733	21,046	21,303	21,510	12.3	2.2
American Indian and Alaska Native	1,331	1,850	1,883	1,909	39.0	3.2
Asian	5,461	7,941	8,226	8,459	45.4	6.5
Native Hawaiian and Other Pacific Islander	227	332	340	348	45.9	4.8
Two or more races	1,987	3,558	3,698	3,811	79.0	7.1
Race alone or in combination: [2]						
White	(NA)	125,352	126,119	126,734	(NA)	1.1
Black or African American	(NA)	22,580	22,916	23,186	(NA)	2.7
American Indian and Alaska Native	(NA)	3,084	3,142	3,188	(NA)	3.4
Asian	(NA)	9,208	9,545	9,820	(NA)	6.6
Native Hawaiian and Other Pacific Islander	(NA)	665	683	698	(NA)	4.9
Not Hispanic	126,224	132,105	132,783	133,324	4.7	0.9
Hispanic [3]	17,144	24,859	25,543	26,098	45.0	5.0

NA Not available. [1] The April 1, 2000 and 2010 population estimates base reflects changes to the Census 2000 and 2010 population from the Count Question Resolution program and geographic program revisions. [2] In combination with one or more races. The sum of the five race groups adds to more than the total population because individuals may report more than one race. [3] See footnote 3, Table 5.

Source: U.S. Census Bureau, Population Division, "Table 2. (US-EST00INT-02)," September 2011, <http://www.census.gov/popest/data/intercensal/national/nat2010.html>; and "National Population Estimates for the 2010s," <http://www.census.gov/popest/data/national/asrh/2012/2012-nat-res.html>; accessed June 2013.

Table 7. Resident Population by Sex and Age: 2000 to 2012

[In thousands, except as indicated (281,425 represents 281,425,000). As of April 1, except 2011 and 2012 as of July 1. Excludes Armed Forces overseas. For definition of median, see Guide to Tabular Presentation]

Age	2000 [1]			2010 [1]			2011			2012		
	Total	Male	Female	Total	Male	Female	Total	Male	Female	Total	Male	Female
Total.................	281,425	138,056	143,368	308,748	151,783	156,964	311,588	153,261	158,326	313,914	154,492	159,422
Under 5 years........	19,176	9,811	9,365	20,201	10,319	9,882	20,128	10,282	9,846	19,999	10,216	9,783
5 to 9 years..........	20,550	10,523	10,026	20,349	10,390	9,959	20,336	10,385	9,951	20,476	10,459	10,016
10 to 14 years........	20,528	10,520	10,008	20,677	10,580	10,097	20,711	10,590	10,121	20,669	10,567	10,102
15 to 19 years........	20,219	10,391	9,828	22,040	11,304	10,737	21,648	11,118	10,531	21,361	10,963	10,398
20 to 24 years........	18,963	9,688	9,275	21,586	11,014	10,572	22,155	11,308	10,847	22,583	11,549	11,034
25 to 29 years........	19,382	9,799	9,583	21,102	10,636	10,466	21,284	10,757	10,528	21,398	10,845	10,553
30 to 34 years........	20,511	10,322	10,189	19,962	9,997	9,966	20,514	10,281	10,233	20,911	10,494	10,417
35 to 39 years........	22,707	11,319	11,388	20,180	10,042	10,138	19,596	9,760	9,836	19,488	9,715	9,774
40 to 44 years........	22,442	11,130	11,313	20,891	10,394	10,497	21,038	10,463	10,575	21,028	10,459	10,569
45 to 49 years........	20,093	9,890	10,203	22,709	11,209	11,500	22,164	10,954	11,210	21,689	10,727	10,963
50 to 54 years........	17,586	8,608	8,978	22,298	10,934	11,365	22,567	11,069	11,498	22,579	11,080	11,499
55 to 59 years........	13,469	6,509	6,961	19,665	9,524	10,141	20,260	9,817	10,443	20,773	10,068	10,704
60 to 64 years........	10,806	5,137	5,669	16,818	8,078	8,740	17,813	8,544	9,269	17,814	8,534	9,279
65 to 74 years........	18,391	8,303	10,088	21,713	10,097	11,617	22,486	10,477	12,009	23,985	11,203	12,783
75 to 84 years........	12,361	4,879	7,482	13,061	5,477	7,584	13,172	5,571	7,601	13,273	5,648	7,624
85 years and over.................	4,240	1,227	3,013	5,493	1,790	3,704	5,715	1,886	3,829	5,887	1,964	3,923
5 to 13 years.........	37,026	18,964	18,062	36,860	18,834	18,026	36,916	18,864	18,052	37,009	18,911	18,099
14 to 17 years........	16,093	8,285	7,808	17,120	8,792	8,328	16,867	8,645	8,221	16,719	8,563	8,156
18 to 24 years........	27,141	13,873	13,268	30,672	15,662	15,010	31,067	15,891	15,176	31,360	16,065	15,295
18 years and over....	209,130	100,996	108,133	234,566	113,838	120,728	237,677	115,470	122,207	240,186	116,802	123,383
55 years and over....	59,267	26,055	33,212	76,751	34,964	41,787	79,445	36,294	43,151	81,732	37,418	44,314
65 years and over....	34,992	14,410	20,582	40,268	17,363	22,905	41,373	17,934	23,438	43,145	18,815	24,330
75 years and over....	16,601	6,106	10,495	18,555	7,266	11,288	18,887	7,457	11,430	19,160	7,612	11,548
Median age (years)..............	35.3	34.0	36.5	37.2	35.8	38.5	37.3	36.0	38.7	37.4	36.1	38.8

[1] The April 1, 2000 and April 1, 2010 population estimates bases reflect changes to the Census 2000 and Census 2010 population from the Count Question Resolution program and geographic program revisions..

Source: U.S. Census Bureau, "Intercensal Estimates of the United States Population by Age and Sex, 1990-2000: All Months," September 2002, <http://www.census.gov/popest/data/intercensal/national/index.html>; and "Annual Estimates of the Resident Population for Selected Age Groups by Sex for the United States, States, Counties, and Puerto Rico Commonwealth and Municipios: April 1, 2010 to July 1, 2012," <http://factfinder2.census.gov>; accessed July 2013.

Table 8. Intercensal Resident Population by Age: 2001 to 2009

[In thousands, except as indicated (284,969 represents 284,969,000). As of July 1. Excludes Armed Forces overseas. For definition of median, see Guide to Tabular Presentation]

Age	2001	2002	2003	2004	2005	2006	2007	2008	2009
Total...................	284,969	287,625	290,108	292,805	295,517	298,380	301,231	304,094	306,772
Under 5 years...........	19,298	19,429	19,592	19,786	19,917	19,939	20,126	20,271	20,245
5 to 9 years..............	20,173	19,872	19,621	19,454	19,389	19,545	19,715	19,930	20,182
10 to 14 years...........	20,979	21,261	21,415	21,412	21,213	21,033	20,841	20,707	20,661
15 to 19 years...........	20,456	20,610	20,797	21,103	21,486	21,808	22,068	22,211	22,193
20 to 24 years...........	19,757	20,244	20,592	20,846	20,960	21,036	21,078	21,181	21,384
25 to 29 years...........	18,819	18,691	18,772	19,107	19,535	20,110	20,543	20,903	21,078
30 to 34 years...........	20,652	20,658	20,472	20,160	19,724	19,285	19,171	19,305	19,645
35 to 39 years...........	22,236	21,751	21,264	20,875	20,799	20,941	20,964	20,817	20,508
40 to 44 years...........	22,816	22,889	22,890	22,926	22,707	22,303	21,832	21,375	20,980
45 to 49 years...........	20,699	21,252	21,723	22,065	22,417	22,715	22,800	22,821	22,862
50 to 54 years...........	18,687	18,740	19,097	19,565	20,079	20,571	21,140	21,639	22,005
55 to 59 years...........	13,969	15,143	15,815	16,607	17,503	18,397	18,455	18,815	19,281
60 to 64 years...........	11,136	11,560	12,194	12,698	13,138	13,533	14,674	15,342	16,125
65 to 74 years...........	18,384	18,389	18,501	18,668	18,882	19,203	19,699	20,506	21,233
75 to 84 years...........	12,594	12,765	12,896	12,990	13,075	13,095	13,087	13,076	13,023
85 years and over.......	4,312	4,369	4,466	4,546	4,693	4,866	5,040	5,196	5,367
5 to 13 years............	37,093	37,001	36,814	36,458	36,248	36,269	36,296	36,438	36,657
14 to 17 years...........	16,280	16,506	16,694	17,054	17,358	17,549	17,597	17,395	17,232
18 to 24 years...........	27,993	28,481	28,917	29,302	29,442	29,603	29,808	30,194	30,530
18 years and over.......	212,298	214,689	217,007	219,508	221,993	224,622	227,212	229,989	232,637
55 years and over.......	60,396	62,226	63,872	65,509	67,291	69,094	70,954	72,935	75,029
65 years and over.......	35,290	35,522	35,864	36,203	36,650	37,164	37,826	38,778	39,623
75 years and over.......	16,906	17,134	17,363	17,536	17,768	17,961	18,127	18,272	18,390
Median age (years).....	35.6	35.8	35.9	36.1	36.3	36.5	36.7	36.9	37.1

Source: U.S. Census Bureau, "Table 1. Intercensal Estimates of the Resident Population by Sex and Age for the United States: April 1, 2000 to July 1, 2010 (US-EST00INT-01)," September 2011, <http://www.census.gov/popest/data/intercensal/national/nat2010.html>.

Table 9. Resident Population Projections by Sex and Age: 2015 to 2050

[In thousands, except as indicated (321,363 represents 321,363,000). As of July 1. Projections are based on the July 1, 2011 population estimates, which are based on the 2010 Census, and assumptions about future births, deaths, and net international migration. More information on methodology and assumptions is available at <http://www.census.gov/population/projections/files/methodology/methodstatement12.pdf>]

Age	2015 Total	2015 Male	2015 Female	2020	2025	2030	2035	2040	2045	2050	Percent distribution 2015	2020	2025	2050
Total	321,363	158,362	163,001	333,896	346,407	358,471	369,662	380,016	389,934	399,803	100.0	100.0	100.0	100.0
Under 5 years	21,051	10,763	10,288	21,808	22,115	22,252	22,516	23,004	23,591	24,115	6.6	6.5	6.4	6.0
5 to 9 years	20,422	10,434	9,988	21,307	22,104	22,451	22,611	22,886	23,387	23,983	6.4	6.4	6.4	6.0
10 to 14 years	20,508	10,475	10,033	20,616	21,534	22,365	22,728	22,893	23,175	23,682	6.4	6.2	6.2	5.9
15 to 19 years	20,940	10,722	10,218	20,806	20,972	21,946	22,801	23,174	23,350	23,642	6.5	6.2	6.1	5.9
20 to 24 years	22,580	11,603	10,977	21,651	21,646	21,940	22,979	23,863	24,263	24,463	7.0	6.5	6.2	6.1
25 to 29 years	22,352	11,392	10,960	23,366	22,579	22,712	23,081	24,151	25,065	25,493	7.0	7.0	6.5	6.4
30 to 34 years	21,589	10,870	10,719	22,906	24,019	23,340	23,532	23,924	25,015	25,949	6.7	6.9	6.9	6.5
35 to 39 years	20,277	10,140	10,137	21,869	23,247	24,423	23,788	24,002	24,411	25,513	6.3	6.5	6.7	6.4
40 to 44 years	20,109	9,987	10,122	20,361	21,988	23,403	24,611	24,000	24,234	24,655	6.3	6.1	6.3	6.2
45 to 49 years	20,752	10,293	10,459	20,008	20,293	21,935	23,368	24,595	24,011	24,262	6.5	6.0	5.9	6.1
50 to 54 years	22,266	10,938	11,328	20,467	19,769	20,083	21,731	23,176	24,419	23,866	6.9	6.1	5.7	6.0
55 to 59 years	21,771	10,586	11,186	21,747	20,039	19,393	19,737	21,384	22,839	24,094	6.8	6.5	5.8	6.0
60 to 64 years	19,050	9,118	9,932	21,017	21,052	19,454	18,864	19,242	20,888	22,348	5.9	6.3	6.1	5.6
65 to 69 years	16,036	7,585	8,451	18,052	19,980	20,077	18,611	18,090	18,512	20,144	5.0	5.4	5.8	5.0
70 to 74 years	11,459	5,287	6,172	14,744	16,666	18,516	18,669	17,374	16,941	17,410	3.6	4.4	4.8	4.4
75 to 79 years	8,102	3,600	4,502	10,010	12,955	14,722	16,431	16,640	15,569	15,243	2.5	3.0	3.7	3.8
80 to 84 years	5,792	2,406	3,386	6,470	8,061	10,513	12,025	13,501	13,753	12,963	1.8	1.9	2.3	3.2
85 to 89 years	3,870	1,439	2,430	3,934	4,453	5,616	7,404	8,555	9,693	9,958	1.2	1.2	1.3	2.5
90 to 94 years	1,860	585	1,275	2,008	2,079	2,402	3,083	4,138	4,865	5,594	0.6	0.6	0.6	1.4
95 to 99 years	498	125	373	645	714	760	903	1,191	1,644	1,985	0.2	0.2	0.2	0.5
100 years and over	78	14	64	106	143	168	188	230	310	442	(Z)	(Z)	(Z)	0.1
5 to 13 years	36,772	18,784	17,988	37,769	39,511	40,366	40,790	41,190	41,936	42,951	11.4	11.3	11.4	10.7
14 to 17 years	16,695	8,541	8,153	16,582	16,565	17,730	18,203	18,427	18,558	18,852	5.2	5.0	4.8	4.7
18 to 24 years	30,983	15,908	15,075	30,028	30,180	30,605	32,125	33,199	33,680	33,967	9.6	9.0	8.7	8.5
16 years and over	255,161	124,529	130,631	266,024	276,558	286,967	297,259	306,634	315,152	323,314	79.4	79.7	79.8	80.9
18 years and over	246,845	120,273	126,572	257,737	268,218	278,123	288,153	297,395	305,850	313,885	76.8	77.2	77.4	78.5
16 to 64 years	207,466	103,488	103,977	210,055	211,506	214,193	219,944	226,915	233,864	239,575	64.6	62.9	61.1	59.9
55 years and over	88,516	40,745	47,771	98,733	106,142	111,621	115,915	120,345	125,014	130,181	27.5	29.6	30.6	32.6
65 years and over	47,695	21,041	26,654	55,969	65,052	72,774	77,315	79,719	81,288	83,739	14.8	16.8	18.8	20.9
75 years and over	20,200	8,169	12,030	23,173	28,405	34,181	40,034	44,255	45,834	46,185	6.3	6.9	8.2	11.6
85 years and over	6,306	2,163	4,143	6,693	7,389	8,946	11,579	14,115	16,512	17,978	2.0	2.0	2.1	4.5
Median age (years)[1]	37.7	36.4	39.1	38.3	38.9	39.6	40.2	40.4	40.6	40.6	(X)	(X)	(X)	(X)

X Not applicable. Z Less than 0.05 percent. [1] For definition of median, see Guide to Tabular Presentation.

Source: U.S. Census Bureau, "2012 National Population Projections," December 2012, <http://www.census.gov/population/projections/data/national/2012.html>, accessed March 2013.

Table 10. Resident Population by Race, Hispanic Origin, and Age: 2010 and 2012

[In thousands, except as indicated (308,748 represents 308,748,000). 2010, as of April 1, and 2012, as of July 1]

Age	Total 2010[1]	Total 2012	White alone 2010[1]	White alone 2012	Black or African American alone 2010[1]	Black or African American alone 2012	American Indian, Alaska Native alone 2010[1]	American Indian, Alaska Native alone 2012	Asian alone 2010[1]	Asian alone 2012	Native Hawaiian, Other Pacific Islander alone 2010[1]	Native Hawaiian, Other Pacific Islander alone 2012	Two or more races 2010[1]	Two or more races 2012	Hispanic origin[2] 2010[1]	Hispanic origin[2] 2012	Not Hispanic White alone 2010[1]	Not Hispanic White alone 2012
Total..........	308,748	313,914	241,938	244,496	40,251	41,205	3,740	3,857	15,160	16,146	675	707	6,984	7,503	50,478	53,028	197,320	197,706
Under 5 years...	20,201	19,999	14,691	14,424	3,055	3,046	330	325	948	979	59	60	1,119	1,166	5,114	5,155	10,307	10,023
5 to 9 years...	20,349	20,476	15,044	15,020	3,013	3,030	321	329	972	1,014	56	58	944	1,024	4,791	5,025	10,885	10,679
10 to 14 years...	20,677	20,669	15,399	15,310	3,154	3,135	318	320	922	968	54	55	829	881	4,525	4,694	11,449	11,221
15 to 19 years...	22,040	21,361	16,346	15,855	3,573	3,359	340	326	999	993	60	57	723	770	4,532	4,581	12,387	11,846
20 to 24 years...	21,586	22,583	16,246	16,749	3,240	3,562	319	339	1,149	1,219	66	67	566	647	4,322	4,585	12,467	12,746
25 to 29 years...	21,102	21,398	16,061	16,169	2,912	2,996	300	307	1,284	1,346	64	66	488	514	4,311	4,369	12,268	12,332
30 to 34 years...	19,962	20,911	15,184	15,842	2,743	2,884	275	289	1,334	1,376	56	61	420	459	4,124	4,302	11,534	12,047
35 to 39 years...	20,180	19,488	15,473	14,808	2,707	2,633	261	262	1,188	1,359	49	52	357	375	3,856	3,983	12,018	11,256
40 to 44 years...	20,891	21,028	16,341	16,295	2,752	2,770	251	257	1,105	1,319	45	48	314	340	3,442	3,666	13,250	13,007
45 to 49 years...	22,709	21,689	18,103	17,104	2,901	2,831	255	251	1,004	1,156	43	44	302	302	3,022	3,206	15,387	14,225
50 to 54 years...	22,298	22,579	18,008	18,150	2,753	2,815	228	239	863	1,050	37	40	268	285	2,441	2,683	15,813	15,739
55 to 59 years...	19,665	20,773	16,144	16,920	2,246	2,442	177	198	703	946	28	32	207	234	1,841	2,089	14,476	15,037
60 to 64 years...	16,818	17,814	14,089	14,753	1,715	1,920	134	149	483	793	21	24	156	174	1,372	1,546	12,839	13,350
65 to 69 years...	12,435	13,977	10,564	11,853	1,181	1,317	89	103	361	564	14	17	105	124	949	1,100	9,693	10,847
70 to 74 years...	9,278	10,008	7,910	8,510	865	928	60	68	255	409	9	11	72	82	700	768	7,265	7,803
75 to 79 years...	7,318	7,490	6,341	6,426	625	667	39	44	171	289	6	7	51	56	511	556	5,867	5,912
80 to 84 years...	5,743	5,783	5,079	5,074	430	445	25	27	94	194	4	4	35	38	351	390	4,751	4,711
85 to 89 years...	3,620	3,755	3,244	3,337	248	267	13	15	35	112	2	4	20	22	185	219	3,071	3,134
90 to 94 years...	1,448	1,655	1,300	1,477	101	116	5	6	9	46	1	2	7	9	65	85	1,240	1,398
95 to 99 years...	371	416	328	366	31	34	1	2	1	12	(Z)	1	2	2	18	21	312	346
100 years and over...	53	62	45	51	7	8	(Z)	(Z)			(Z)	(Z)	(Z)	(Z)	3	4	42	48
5 to 13 years...	36,860	37,009	27,331	27,260	5,530	5,532	576	585	1,707	1,791	99	102	1,617	1,738	8,426	8,808	20,002	19,624
14 to 17 years...	17,120	16,719	12,724	12,436	2,732	2,567	263	255	756	776	45	44	601	641	3,591	3,635	9,581	9,259
18 to 24 years...	30,672	31,360	22,980	23,238	4,718	4,987	459	474	1,579	1,626	92	91	844	943	6,154	6,442	17,605	17,608
16 years and over...	243,277	248,626	193,649	196,658	30,359	31,362	2,706	2,820	12,130	12,992	495	523	3,939	4,271	35,153	37,249	162,304	163,491
18 years and over...	234,566	240,186	187,193	190,375	28,935	30,060	2,571	2,692	11,749	12,599	471	501	3,647	3,959	33,347	35,430	157,430	158,799
16 to 64 years...	203,009	205,481	158,839	159,563	26,871	27,581	2,474	2,555	10,720	11,363	459	481	3,646	3,938	32,372	34,105	130,063	129,290
55 years and over...	76,751	81,732	65,042	68,768	7,449	8,143	543	613	2,976	3,368	85	99	656	741	5,995	6,779	59,556	62,587
65 years and over...	40,268	43,145	34,810	37,095	3,487	3,781	232	266	1,410	1,628	36	42	293	333	2,782	3,144	32,241	34,200
75 years and over...	18,555	19,160	16,335	16,733	1,442	1,536	83	94	566	655	13	15	116	128	1,133	1,275	15,282	15,550
85 years and over...	5,493	5,887	4,916	5,232	386	424	19	22	140	172	3	3	30	34	271	329	4,664	4,926
Median age (years)[3]...	37.2	37.4	39.0	39.3	32.0	32.5	29.0	29.7	35.1	35.7	28.3	29.3	19.1	19.4	27.3	27.8	42.0	42.6

Z Less than 500. [1] The April 1, 2010 population estimates base reflects changes to the Census 2010 population from the Count Question Resolution program and geographic program revisions. [2] Hispanic origin is considered an ethnicity, not a race. Hispanics may be of any race. [3] For definition of median, see Guide to Tabular Presentation.

Source: U.S. Census Bureau, Population Division, "National Characteristics: Vintage 2012, Median Age and Age by Sex, Race, and Hispanic Origin," <http://www.census.gov/popest/data/national/asrh/2012/index.html>, accessed July 2013.

Table 11. Resident Population by Race, Hispanic Origin, and Single Years of Age: 2012

[In thousands, except as indicated (313,914 represents 313,914,000). As of July 1. For derivation of estimates, see text, this section]

| Age | Total | Race | | | | | | Hispanic origin [1] | Non-Hispanic White alone |
		White alone	Black or African American alone	American Indian, Alaska Native alone	Asian alone	Native Hawaiian and Other Pacific Islander alone	Two or more races		
Total......................	313,914	244,496	41,205	3,857	16,146	707	7,503	53,028	197,706
Under 5 years old............	19,999	14,424	3,046	325	979	60	1,166	5,155	10,023
Under 1 year old............	3,943	2,840	602	64	188	12	237	1,024	1,967
1 year old..................	3,982	2,864	610	64	196	12	236	1,039	1,978
2 years old.................	3,980	2,868	601	65	198	12	236	1,027	1,993
3 years old.................	3,982	2,877	606	65	194	12	228	1,016	2,009
4 years old.................	4,112	2,975	626	67	203	12	229	1,049	2,076
5 to 9 years old.............	20,476	15,020	3,030	329	1,014	58	1,024	5,025	10,679
5 years old.................	4,133	3,004	626	68	201	12	222	1,049	2,103
6 years old.................	4,099	2,997	611	67	200	12	212	1,026	2,112
7 years old.................	4,086	2,998	602	66	204	12	204	1,004	2,130
8 years old.................	4,094	3,018	598	65	205	11	197	982	2,168
9 years old.................	4,064	3,003	594	64	203	11	188	963	2,166
10 to 14 years old...........	20,669	15,310	3,135	320	968	55	881	4,694	11,221
10 years old................	4,046	2,992	604	63	194	11	182	949	2,166
11 years old................	4,145	3,063	625	64	200	11	181	955	2,231
12 years old................	4,207	3,112	644	65	196	11	179	955	2,280
13 years old................	4,136	3,073	629	64	187	11	173	923	2,268
14 years old................	4,135	3,071	633	64	191	11	167	911	2,275
15 to 19 years old...........	21,361	15,855	3,359	326	993	57	770	4,581	11,846
15 years old................	4,144	3,083	632	63	193	11	162	905	2,293
16 years old................	4,174	3,112	634	63	196	11	158	903	2,322
17 years old................	4,266	3,171	668	65	197	11	154	916	2,369
18 years old................	4,354	3,222	701	67	201	12	151	926	2,411
19 years old................	4,423	3,267	723	69	206	12	145	931	2,451
20 to 24 years old...........	22,583	16,749	3,562	339	1,219	67	647	4,585	12,746
20 years old................	4,544	3,358	741	71	219	12	144	949	2,527
21 years old................	4,628	3,417	750	70	238	14	138	941	2,598
22 years old................	4,624	3,423	737	69	250	14	130	930	2,612
23 years old................	4,444	3,298	689	65	257	14	121	885	2,526
24 years old................	4,345	3,253	645	64	255	13	114	880	2,483
25 to 29 years old...........	21,398	16,169	2,996	307	1,346	66	514	4,369	12,332
25 years old................	4,275	3,217	619	62	255	13	109	870	2,454
26 years old................	4,299	3,248	608	62	263	13	105	878	2,477
27 years old................	4,340	3,284	605	62	273	13	103	885	2,506
28 years old................	4,207	3,182	578	60	275	13	99	860	2,426
29 years old................	4,278	3,239	586	61	280	13	99	877	2,468
30 to 34 years old...........	20,911	15,842	2,884	289	1,376	61	459	4,302	12,047
30 years old................	4,283	3,244	586	60	284	13	97	881	2,468
31 years old................	4,242	3,219	581	59	276	12	95	870	2,452
32 years old................	4,332	3,275	606	60	283	13	95	897	2,483
33 years old................	4,066	3,075	565	56	270	12	88	829	2,345
34 years old................	3,988	3,029	545	55	263	11	84	825	2,299
35 to 39 years old...........	19,488	14,808	2,633	262	1,359	52	375	3,983	11,256
35 years old................	3,951	3,000	539	54	265	11	82	818	2,275
36 years old................	3,836	2,911	518	52	267	10	77	804	2,196
37 years old................	3,959	3,012	532	53	278	10	75	812	2,286
38 years old................	3,839	2,920	514	51	273	10	71	779	2,222
39 years old................	3,903	2,965	530	51	276	10	70	769	2,277
40 to 44 years old...........	21,028	16,295	2,770	257	1,319	48	340	3,666	13,007
40 years old................	4,084	3,127	550	52	276	10	70	762	2,444
41 years old................	4,325	3,345	574	53	271	10	72	758	2,666
42 years old................	4,384	3,403	575	53	272	10	71	755	2,726
43 years old................	4,159	3,245	534	50	256	9	65	704	2,612
44 years old................	4,076	3,175	537	49	244	9	62	687	2,558
45 to 49 years old...........	21,689	17,104	2,831	251	1,156	44	302	3,206	14,225
45 years old................	4,085	3,206	536	48	226	9	60	660	2,613
46 years old................	4,166	3,263	557	49	228	9	59	653	2,677
47 years old................	4,421	3,482	585	52	233	9	61	658	2,890
48 years old................	4,508	3,571	581	51	235	9	61	632	3,003
49 years old................	4,510	3,583	573	51	234	9	60	603	3,042
50 to 54 years old...........	22,579	18,150	2,815	239	1,050	40	285	2,683	15,739
50 years old................	4,506	3,608	567	50	213	9	59	580	3,087
51 years old................	4,566	3,673	569	49	209	8	59	557	3,172
52 years old................	4,610	3,691	583	50	219	8	59	557	3,190
53 years old................	4,460	3,590	557	46	204	8	55	508	3,133
54 years old................	4,438	3,588	540	45	204	7	53	480	3,156
55 to 59 years old...........	20,773	16,920	2,442	198	946	32	234	2,089	15,037
55 years old................	4,393	3,559	534	44	198	7	52	464	3,142
56 years old................	4,240	3,435	511	42	196	7	49	442	3,038
57 years old................	4,208	3,421	497	40	195	6	47	427	3,035
58 years old................	4,040	3,305	465	37	182	6	44	391	2,951
59 years old................	3,891	3,199	435	35	175	6	41	365	2,869
60 to 64 years old...........	17,814	14,753	1,920	149	793	24	174	1,546	13,350

See footnotes at end of table.

Table 11. Resident Population by Race, Hispanic Origin, and Single Years of Age: 2012-Continued.

See headnote on page 13.

Age	Total	Race						Hispanic origin [1]	Non-Hispanic White alone
		White alone	Black or African American alone	American Indian, Alaska Native alone	Asian alone	Native Hawaiian and Other Pacific Islander alone	Two or more races		
60 years old..................	3,745	3,092	412	32	166	5	38	338	2,786
61 years old..................	3,635	2,997	406	31	160	5	36	326	2,701
62 years old..................	3,554	2,923	394	30	167	5	35	315	2,637
63 years old..................	3,455	2,871	364	28	154	5	33	290	2,607
64 years old..................	3,424	2,871	344	27	146	4	32	278	2,618
65 to 69 years old............	13,977	11,853	1,317	103	564	17	124	1,100	10,847
65 years old..................	3,571	3,048	325	27	136	4	32	264	2,807
66 years old..................	2,641	2,216	260	21	116	4	24	229	2,007
67 years old..................	2,609	2,193	257	20	112	3	24	217	1,994
68 years old..................	2,547	2,159	240	19	104	3	22	200	1,976
69 years old..................	2,610	2,237	235	18	97	3	21	190	2,063
70 to 74 years old............	10,008	8,510	928	68	409	11	82	768	7,803
70 years old..................	2,280	1,940	210	16	93	2	19	171	1,782
71 years old..................	2,088	1,772	196	15	86	2	17	161	1,624
72 years old..................	1,980	1,675	189	14	84	2	17	156	1,531
73 years old..................	1,868	1,592	171	12	75	2	15	144	1,460
74 years old..................	1,793	1,532	162	12	72	2	14	136	1,406
75 to 79 years old............	7,490	6,426	667	44	289	7	56	556	5,912
75 years old..................	1,658	1,416	150	10	67	2	13	126	1,300
76 years old..................	1,588	1,358	145	10	62	2	12	120	1,247
77 years old..................	1,528	1,312	136	9	58	1	11	115	1,206
78 years old..................	1,378	1,185	122	8	52	1	10	101	1,091
79 years old..................	1,338	1,155	115	7	50	1	9	94	1,068
80 to 84 years old............	5,783	5,074	445	27	194	4	38	390	4,711
80 years old..................	1,284	1,118	104	7	45	1	9	90	1,035
81 years old..................	1,228	1,077	95	6	42	1	8	85	998
82 years old..................	1,184	1,038	92	6	40	1	8	81	962
83 years old..................	1,075	947	81	5	35	1	7	71	881
84 years old..................	1,012	895	74	4	32	1	6	64	836
85 to 89 years old............	3,755	3,337	267	15	112	2	22	219	3,134
90 to 94 years old............	1,655	1,477	116	6	46	1	9	85	1,398
95 to 99 years old............	416	366	34	2	12	(Z)	2	21	346
100 years old and over.......	62	51	8	(Z)	2	(Z)	(Z)	4	48
Median age (years) [2]........	37.4	39.3	32.5	29.7	35.7	29.3	19.4	27.8	42.6

Z Less than 500. [1] Hispanic origin is considered an ethnicity, not a race. Hispanics may be of any race. [2] For definition of median, see Guide to Tabular Presentation.

Source: U.S. Census Bureau, Population Division, "National Characteristics: Vintage 2012, Median Age and Age by Sex, Race, and Hispanic Origin," <http://www.census.gov/popest/data/national/asrh/2012/index.html>, accessed July 2013.

Table 12. Resident Population Projections by Race, Hispanic Origin, and Age: 2015

[In thousands (321,363 represents 321,363,000). As of July 1. Projections are based on the July 1, 2011 population estimates, which are based on the 2010 Census, and assumptions about future births, deaths, and net international migration. More information on methodology and assumptions is available at <http://www.census.gov/population/projections/files/methodology/methodstatement12.pdf>]

Age group	Total	White alone	Black or African American alone	American Indian /Alaska Native alone	Asian alone	Native Hawaiian /Other Pacific Islander alone	Two or more races	Hispanic origin [1]	Not Hispanic White alone
Total	321,363	248,725	42,532	4,042	17,009	749	8,306	57,075	198,449
Under 5 years	21,051	15,036	3,229	348	1,049	65	1,323	5,609	10,270
5 to 9 years	20,422	14,790	3,085	332	1,025	60	1,131	5,236	10,298
10 to 14 years	20,508	15,124	3,025	323	1,026	57	953	4,899	10,869
15 to 19 years	20,940	15,554	3,177	321	996	55	838	4,693	11,451
20 to 24 years	22,580	16,681	3,604	344	1,153	62	735	4,884	12,393
25 to 29 years	22,352	16,653	3,331	326	1,392	70	581	4,644	12,577
30 to 34 years	21,589	16,306	2,955	303	1,464	66	495	4,508	12,332
35 to 39 years	20,277	15,350	2,775	278	1,391	58	426	4,248	11,587
40 to 44 years	20,109	15,355	2,690	260	1,397	50	357	3,913	11,849
45 to 49 years	20,752	16,199	2,712	248	1,232	46	314	3,466	13,087
50 to 54 years	22,266	17,730	2,824	249	1,121	43	298	3,019	15,017
55 to 59 years	21,771	17,586	2,651	222	1,012	37	264	2,431	15,400
60 to 64 years	19,050	15,651	2,134	170	864	28	202	1,823	14,002
65 to 69 years	16,036	13,441	1,600	126	698	21	150	1,340	12,222
70 to 74 years	11,459	9,745	1,056	81	466	13	98	900	8,920
75 to 79 years	8,102	6,915	735	52	328	9	64	635	6,331
80 to 84 years	5,792	5,022	484	31	209	5	41	427	4,627
85 to 89 years	3,870	3,420	286	17	120	3	24	258	3,180
90 to 94 years	1,860	1,660	131	7	51	1	10	109	1,558
95 to 99 years	498	442	39	2	13	(Z)	3	28	417
100 years and over	78	67	8	(Z)	2	(Z)	1	5	62
5 to 13 years	36,772	26,841	5,485	591	1,847	106	1,903	9,170	18,935
14 to 17 years	16,695	12,370	2,532	258	791	44	699	3,795	9,058
18 to 24 years	30,983	22,937	4,875	472	1,561	84	1,055	6,746	17,017
16 years and over	255,161	200,653	32,548	2,973	13,710	556	4,721	40,366	164,732
18 years and over	246,845	194,477	31,286	2,845	13,322	534	4,381	38,500	160,185
16 to 64 years	207,465	159,942	28,210	2,655	11,823	504	4,331	36,664	127,415
55 years and over	88,517	73,948	9,124	710	3,763	116	856	7,956	66,719
65 years and over	47,695	40,711	4,339	318	1,887	51	390	3,702	37,317
75 years and over	20,200	17,526	1,683	111	722	17	142	1,462	16,175
85 years and over	6,306	5,588	464	27	185	4	38	400	5,217

Z Less than 500. [1] Hispanic origin is considered an ethnicity, not a race. Hispanics may be of any race.

Source: U.S. Census Bureau, "2012 National Population Projections," December 2012, <http://www.census.gov/population/projections/data/national/2012.html>, accessed March 2013.

Table 13. Resident Population Projections by Race/Ethnicity and Hispanic Origin: 2015 to 2050

[In thousands, except as indicated (321,363 represents 321,363,000). As of July 1. Data shown are modified race counts; see text, this section. Projections are based on July 1, 2011 population estimates, which are based on the 2010 Census, and assumptions about future births, deaths, and net international migration. For more information on methodology and assumptions, see <http://www.census.gov/population/projections/files/methodology/methodstatement12.pdf>]

Characteristic	2015	2020	2025	2030	2035	2040	2045	2050
Total	**321,363**	**333,896**	**346,407**	**358,471**	**369,662**	**380,016**	**389,934**	**399,803**
One race	313,057	324,192	335,165	345,542	354,882	363,201	370,895	378,360
White	248,725	255,346	261,761	267,604	272,493	276,438	279,798	282,959
Black or African American	42,532	44,810	47,064	49,246	51,348	53,412	55,474	57,553
American Indian and Alaska Native	4,042	4,328	4,613	4,889	5,154	5,407	5,650	5,881
Asian	17,009	18,884	20,830	22,833	24,849	26,838	28,798	30,726
Native Hawaiian/Other Pacific Islander	749	824	898	969	1,039	1,107	1,174	1,241
Two or more races	8,306	9,704	11,243	12,929	14,780	16,814	19,039	21,443
Race alone or in combination: [1]								
White	256,085	264,012	271,872	279,305	285,944	291,821	297,300	302,756
Black or African American	46,246	49,338	52,512	55,727	58,987	62,350	65,859	69,525
American Indian and Alaska Native	6,673	7,194	7,719	8,238	8,744	9,241	9,732	10,217
Asian	20,007	22,384	24,878	27,482	30,159	32,876	35,628	38,407
Native Hawaiian/Other Pacific Islander	1,496	1,661	1,832	2,006	2,185	2,372	2,568	2,772
Not Hispanic	**264,288**	**270,111**	**275,434**	**279,816**	**283,003**	**285,140**	**286,675**	**288,072**
One race	257,665	262,414	266,560	269,668	271,472	272,104	272,005	271,648
White	198,449	199,313	199,557	198,817	196,886	193,887	190,221	186,334
Black or African American	39,850	41,776	43,660	45,452	47,141	48,769	50,376	51,988
American Indian and Alaska Native	2,377	2,481	2,576	2,657	2,725	2,781	2,830	2,872
Asian	16,441	18,246	20,118	22,044	23,979	25,881	27,749	29,583
Native Hawaiian/Other Pacific Islander	548	599	649	697	743	786	829	871
Two or more races	6,623	7,698	8,873	10,148	11,531	13,036	14,669	16,423
Race alone or in combination: [1]								
White	204,313	206,187	207,541	208,009	207,392	205,830	203,729	201,526
Black or African American	42,805	45,372	47,980	50,576	53,157	55,777	58,483	61,294
American Indian and Alaska Native	4,284	4,518	4,743	4,949	5,133	5,301	5,460	5,615
Asian	18,965	21,175	23,487	25,889	28,339	30,803	33,274	35,748
Native Hawaiian/Other Pacific Islander	1,132	1,245	1,360	1,475	1,590	1,706	1,826	1,950
Hispanic [2]	**57,075**	**63,784**	**70,973**	**78,655**	**86,659**	**94,876**	**103,259**	**111,732**
One race	55,392	61,778	68,604	75,874	83,410	91,097	98,890	106,712
White	50,276	56,033	62,204	68,787	75,608	82,551	89,577	96,625
Black or African American	2,681	3,034	3,404	3,794	4,207	4,643	5,098	5,565
American Indian and Alaska Native	1,665	1,848	2,037	2,232	2,429	2,626	2,820	3,009
Asian	568	639	712	789	870	957	1,049	1,144
Native Hawaiian/Other Pacific Islander	201	225	248	272	296	321	346	370
Two or more races	1,683	2,006	2,369	2,781	3,249	3,779	4,370	5,020
Race alone or in combination: [1]								
White	51,772	57,825	64,331	71,296	78,552	85,990	93,571	101,230
Black or African American	3,442	3,966	4,532	5,151	5,830	6,572	7,376	8,231
American Indian and Alaska Native	2,389	2,676	2,976	3,289	3,611	3,939	4,271	4,602
Asian	1,042	1,209	1,391	1,593	1,820	2,073	2,354	2,659
Native Hawaiian/Other Pacific Islander	364	416	471	531	595	665	741	822
PERCENT DISTRIBUTION								
Total	**100.0**	**100.0**	**100.0**	**100.0**	**100.0**	**100.0**	**100.0**	**100.0**
Not Hispanic	**82.2**	**80.9**	**79.5**	**78.1**	**76.6**	**75.0**	**73.5**	**72.1**
One race	80.2	78.6	76.9	75.2	73.4	71.6	69.8	67.9
White	61.8	59.7	57.6	55.5	53.3	51.0	48.8	46.6
Black or African American	12.4	12.5	12.6	12.7	12.8	12.8	12.9	13.0
American Indian and Alaska Native	0.7	0.7	0.7	0.7	0.7	0.7	0.7	0.7
Asian	5.1	5.5	5.8	6.1	6.5	6.8	7.1	7.4
Native Hawaiian/Other Pacific Islander	0.2	0.2	0.2	0.2	0.2	0.2	0.2	0.2
Two or more races	2.1	2.3	2.6	2.8	3.1	3.4	3.8	4.1
Hispanic [2]	**17.8**	**19.1**	**20.5**	**21.9**	**23.4**	**25.0**	**26.5**	**27.9**
One race	17.2	18.5	19.8	21.2	22.6	24.0	25.4	26.7
White	15.6	16.8	18.0	19.2	20.5	21.7	23.0	24.2
Black or African American	0.8	0.9	1.0	1.1	1.1	1.2	1.3	1.4
American Indian and Alaska Native	0.5	0.6	0.6	0.6	0.7	0.7	0.7	0.8
Asian	0.2	0.2	0.2	0.2	0.2	0.3	0.3	0.3
Native Hawaiian/Other Pacific Islander	0.1	0.1	0.1	0.1	0.1	0.1	0.1	0.1
Two or more races	0.5	0.6	0.7	0.8	0.9	1.0	1.1	1.3

[1] In combination with one or more other races. The sum of the five race groups adds to more than the total population because individuals may report more than one race. The original race data from Census 2010 are modified to eliminate the "some other race" category. [2] Persons of Hispanic origin may be of any race.

Source: U.S. Census Bureau, Population Division, "2012 National Population Projections," December 2012, <http://www.census.gov/population/projections/data/national/2012.html>.

Table 14. Resident Population—States: 1990 to 2012

[In thousands (248,791 represents 248,791,000). 1990, 2000, and 2010 data as of April 1, data for other years as of July 1. Insofar as possible, population shown for all years is that of present area of state. See Appendix III]

State	1990, estimates base [1]	2000, estimates base [2]	2005	2007	2008	2009	2010, estimates base [3]	2011	2012
United States..........	**248,791**	**281,425**	**295,517**	**301,231**	**304,094**	**306,772**	**308,748**	**311,588**	**313,914**
Alabama..................	4,040	4,447	4,570	4,673	4,718	4,758	4,780	4,804	4,822
Alaska....................	550	627	667	680	687	699	710	724	731
Arizona...................	3,665	5,130	5,839	6,168	6,280	6,343	6,392	6,467	6,553
Arkansas.................	2,351	2,673	2,781	2,849	2,875	2,897	2,916	2,939	2,949
California................	29,811	33,872	35,828	36,250	36,604	36,961	37,254	37,684	38,041
Colorado.................	3,294	4,302	4,632	4,804	4,890	4,972	5,029	5,116	5,188
Connecticut.............	3,287	3,406	3,507	3,527	3,546	3,562	3,574	3,587	3,590
Delaware.................	666	784	845	872	884	892	898	908	917
District of Columbia.....	607	572	567	574	580	592	602	619	632
Florida...................	12,938	15,983	17,842	18,368	18,527	18,653	18,803	19,082	19,318
Georgia..................	6,478	8,187	8,926	9,350	9,505	9,621	9,688	9,812	9,920
Hawaii...................	1,108	1,211	1,293	1,316	1,332	1,347	1,360	1,378	1,392
Idaho....................	1,007	1,294	1,428	1,505	1,534	1,554	1,568	1,584	1,596
Illinois...................	11,431	12,420	12,610	12,696	12,747	12,797	12,831	12,860	12,875
Indiana..................	5,544	6,081	6,279	6,380	6,425	6,459	6,484	6,516	6,537
Iowa.....................	2,777	2,927	2,964	2,999	3,017	3,033	3,047	3,064	3,074
Kansas...................	2,478	2,689	2,745	2,784	2,808	2,833	2,853	2,870	2,886
Kentucky.................	3,687	4,042	4,183	4,257	4,290	4,317	4,339	4,367	4,380
Louisiana................	4,222	4,469	4,577	4,376	4,436	4,492	4,533	4,575	4,602
Maine....................	1,228	1,275	1,319	1,327	1,331	1,330	1,328	1,329	1,329
Maryland.................	4,781	5,297	5,592	5,653	5,685	5,730	5,774	5,840	5,885
Massachusetts...........	6,016	6,349	6,403	6,432	6,469	6,518	6,548	6,607	6,646
Michigan.................	9,295	9,939	10,051	10,001	9,947	9,902	9,884	9,877	9,883
Minnesota...............	4,376	4,920	5,120	5,207	5,247	5,281	5,304	5,347	5,379
Mississippi...............	2,575	2,845	2,906	2,928	2,948	2,959	2,967	2,977	2,985
Missouri.................	5,117	5,597	5,790	5,888	5,924	5,961	5,989	6,009	6,022
Montana..................	799	902	940	965	976	984	989	998	1,005
Nebraska.................	1,578	1,711	1,761	1,783	1,796	1,813	1,826	1,842	1,856
Nevada...................	1,202	1,998	2,432	2,601	2,654	2,685	2,701	2,720	2,759
New Hampshire..........	1,109	1,236	1,298	1,313	1,316	1,316	1,316	1,318	1,321
New Jersey..............	7,748	8,415	8,652	8,678	8,711	8,756	8,792	8,835	8,865
New Mexico.............	1,515	1,819	1,932	1,990	2,011	2,037	2,059	2,079	2,086
New York................	17,991	18,977	19,133	19,132	19,212	19,307	19,378	19,502	19,570
North Carolina...........	6,632	8,046	8,705	9,118	9,309	9,450	9,535	9,651	9,752
North Dakota............	639	642	646	653	658	665	673	685	700
Ohio.....................	10,847	11,353	11,463	11,500	11,515	11,529	11,537	11,541	11,544
Oklahoma................	3,146	3,450	3,549	3,634	3,669	3,718	3,751	3,784	3,815
Oregon...................	2,842	3,422	3,613	3,722	3,769	3,809	3,831	3,868	3,899
Pennsylvania.............	11,883	12,281	12,450	12,564	12,612	12,667	12,702	12,744	12,764
Rhode Island............	1,003	1,048	1,068	1,057	1,055	1,054	1,053	1,051	1,050
South Carolina..........	3,486	4,012	4,270	4,444	4,529	4,590	4,625	4,673	4,724
South Dakota............	696	755	775	792	799	807	814	824	833
Tennessee...............	4,877	5,689	5,991	6,176	6,247	6,306	6,346	6,400	6,456
Texas....................	16,986	20,851	22,778	23,832	24,309	24,802	25,146	25,632	26,059
Utah.....................	1,723	2,233	2,458	2,598	2,663	2,723	2,764	2,814	2,855
Vermont..................	563	609	621	623	624	625	626	627	626
Virginia..................	6,189	7,079	7,577	7,751	7,833	7,926	8,001	8,104	8,186
Washington..............	4,867	5,894	6,257	6,462	6,562	6,667	6,725	6,823	6,897
West Virginia............	1,793	1,808	1,820	1,834	1,840	1,848	1,853	1,855	1,855
Wisconsin...............	4,892	5,364	5,546	5,611	5,641	5,669	5,687	5,710	5,726
Wyoming.................	454	494	514	535	546	560	564	567	576

[1] The April 1, 1990 census counts include corrections processed through August 1997, results of special censuses and test censuses, and do not include adjustments for census coverage errors. [2] The April 1, 2000 population estimates base reflects changes to the Census 2000 population from the Count Question Resolution program, legal boundary updates, and other geographic program revisions. [3] The April 1, 2010 population estimates base reflects changes to the Census 2010 population from the Count Question Resolution program and geographic program revisions.

Source: U.S. Census Bureau, "Table CO-EST2001-12-00 - Time Series of Intercensal State Population Estimates: April 1, 1990 to April 1, 2000," April 2002, <http://www.census.gov/popest/data/intercensal/st-co/files/CO-EST2001-12-00.pdf>; "Table 1. Intercensal Estimates of the Resident Population for the United States, Regions, States, and Puerto Rico: April 1, 2000 to July 1, 2010 (ST-EST00INT-01)," September 2011, <http://www.census.gov/popest/data/intercensal/state/state2010.html>; and "Table 1. Annual Estimates of the Population for the United States, Regions, States, and Puerto Rico: April 1, 2010 to July 1, 2012 (NST-EST2012-01)," December 2012, <http://www.census.gov/popest/data/state/totals/2012/index.html>.

Table 15. State Population—Rank, Percent Change, and Population Density: 1990 to 2012

[As of April 1, except 2012 as of July 1. Insofar as possible, population shown for all years is that of present area of state. For area figures of states, see Table 376. Minus sign (-) indicates decrease. See Appendix III]

State	Rank				Percent change			Population per square mile of land area [1]		
	1990	2000	2010	2012	1990–2000	2000–2010	2010–2012 [2]	2000	2010	2012
United States.........	**(X)**	**(X)**	**(X)**	**(X)**	**13.1**	**9.7**	**1.7**	**79.7**	**87.4**	**88.9**
Alabama.................	22	23	23	23	10.1	7.5	0.9	87.8	94.4	95.2
Alaska...................	49	48	47	47	14.0	13.3	3.0	1.1	1.2	1.3
Arizona.................	24	20	16	15	40.0	24.6	2.5	45.2	56.3	57.7
Arkansas...............	33	33	32	32	13.7	9.1	1.1	51.4	56.0	56.7
California..............	1	1	1	1	13.8	10.0	2.1	217.4	239.1	244.2
Colorado...............	26	24	22	22	30.6	16.9	3.1	41.5	48.5	50.1
Connecticut............	27	29	29	29	3.6	4.9	0.5	703.3	738.1	741.4
Delaware...............	46	45	45	45	17.6	14.6	2.1	402.1	460.8	470.7
District of Columbia. ...	(X)	(X)	(X)	(X)	-5.7	5.2	5.1	9,370.6	9,856.5	10,357.5
Florida..................	4	4	4	4	23.5	17.6	2.7	298.0	350.6	360.2
Georgia.................	11	10	9	8	26.4	18.3	2.4	142.3	168.4	172.5
Hawaii..................	41	42	40	40	9.3	12.3	2.4	188.6	211.8	216.8
Idaho...................	42	39	39	39	28.5	21.1	1.8	15.7	19.0	19.3
Illinois..................	6	5	5	5	8.6	3.3	0.3	223.7	231.1	231.9
Indiana.................	14	14	15	16	9.7	6.6	0.8	169.7	181.0	182.5
Iowa....................	30	30	30	30	5.4	4.1	0.9	52.4	54.5	55.0
Kansas.................	32	32	33	33	8.5	6.1	1.1	32.9	34.9	35.3
Kentucky...............	23	25	26	26	9.6	7.4	0.9	102.4	109.9	110.9
Louisiana..............	21	22	25	25	5.9	1.4	1.5	103.4	104.9	106.5
Maine...................	38	40	41	41	3.8	4.2	0.1	41.3	43.1	43.1
Maryland...............	19	19	19	19	10.8	9.0	1.9	545.6	594.8	606.2
Massachusetts.........	13	13	14	14	5.5	3.1	1.5	814.0	839.4	852.1
Michigan...............	8	8	8	9	6.9	-0.6	(-Z)	175.8	174.8	174.8
Minnesota.............	20	21	21	21	12.4	7.8	1.4	61.8	66.6	67.6
Mississippi.............	31	31	31	31	10.5	4.3	0.6	60.6	63.2	63.6
Missouri................	15	17	18	18	9.3	7.0	0.6	81.4	87.1	87.6
Montana................	44	44	44	44	12.9	9.7	1.6	6.2	6.8	6.9
Nebraska...............	36	38	38	37	8.4	6.7	1.6	22.3	23.8	24.2
Nevada.................	39	35	35	35	66.3	35.1	2.2	18.2	24.6	25.1
New Hampshire........	40	41	42	42	11.4	6.5	0.3	138.0	147.0	147.5
New Jersey............	9	9	11	11	8.9	4.5	0.8	1,144.2	1,195.5	1,205.4
New Mexico............	37	36	36	36	20.1	13.2	1.3	15.0	17.0	17.2
New York...............	2	3	3	3	5.5	2.1	1.0	402.7	411.2	415.3
North Carolina.........	10	11	10	10	21.4	18.5	2.3	165.6	196.1	200.6
North Dakota...........	47	47	48	48	0.5	4.7	4.0	9.3	9.7	10.1
Ohio....................	7	7	7	7	4.7	1.6	0.1	277.8	282.3	282.5
Oklahoma..............	28	27	28	28	9.7	8.7	1.7	50.3	54.7	55.6
Oregon.................	29	28	27	27	20.4	12.0	1.8	35.6	39.9	40.6
Pennsylvania...........	5	6	6	6	3.4	3.4	0.5	274.5	283.9	285.3
Rhode Island...........	43	43	43	43	4.5	0.4	-0.2	1,014.0	1,018.1	1,015.9
South Carolina.........	25	26	24	24	15.1	15.3	2.1	133.5	153.9	157.1
South Dakota..........	45	46	46	46	8.5	7.9	2.4	10.0	10.7	11.0
Tennessee.............	17	16	17	17	16.7	11.5	1.7	138.0	153.9	156.6
Texas..................	3	2	2	2	22.8	20.6	3.6	79.8	96.3	99.8
Utah....................	35	34	34	34	29.6	23.8	3.3	27.2	33.6	34.7
Vermont................	48	49	49	49	8.2	2.8	(Z)	66.1	67.9	67.9
Virginia.................	12	12	12	12	14.4	13.0	2.3	179.2	202.6	207.3
Washington............	18	15	13	13	21.1	14.1	2.6	88.7	101.2	103.8
West Virginia...........	34	37	37	38	0.8	2.5	0.1	75.2	77.1	77.2
Wisconsin..............	16	18	20	20	9.6	6.0	0.7	99.0	105.0	105.7
Wyoming...............	50	50	50	50	8.9	14.1	2.3	5.1	5.8	5.9

X Not applicable. Z Less than 0.05 percent. [1] Persons per square mile were calculated on the basis of land area data from the 2010 census. [2] Based on 2010 population estimates base that reflects changes to the Census 2010 population from the Count Question Resolution program and geographic program revisions.

Source: U.S. Census Bureau, United States Summary: 2000 (PHC-3-1), <http://www.census.gov/prod/cen2000/phc3-us-pt1.pdf>; "2010 Census Briefs, Population Distribution and Change: 2000 to 2010," March 2011, <http://www.census.gov/prod/cen2010/briefs/c2010br-01.pdf>; and "Table 2. Cumulative Estimates of Resident Population Change for the United States, Regions, States, and Puerto Rico and Region and State Rankings April 1, 2010 to July 1, 2012 (NST-EST2012-02), December 2012, <http://www.census.gov/popest/data/state/totals/2012/index.html>.

Table 16. State Resident Population—Components of Change: 2010 to 2012

[Covers period April 1, 2010 to July 1, 2012. Minus sign (-) indicates net decrease or net outflow]

State	Numeric population change [1]	Births	Deaths	Natural increase (births minus deaths)	Net migration Total	Net migration International [2]	Net migration Domestic
United States	**5,166,532**	**8,918,468**	**5,602,865**	**3,315,603**	**1,850,929**	**1,850,929**	**(X)**
Alabama	42,278	137,514	109,105	28,409	13,545	12,288	1,257
Alaska	21,218	25,889	7,589	18,300	2,638	4,471	-1,833
Arizona	161,240	193,899	106,658	87,241	73,049	24,790	48,259
Arkansas	33,212	85,342	64,590	20,752	12,111	6,627	5,484
California	787,474	1,159,112	537,016	622,096	172,716	276,809	-104,093
Colorado	158,386	147,515	71,725	75,790	80,587	18,291	62,296
Connecticut	16,250	83,174	65,102	18,072	-811	33,660	-34,471
Delaware	19,158	25,491	17,482	8,009	11,278	5,097	6,181
District of Columbia	30,600	20,537	10,593	9,944	20,369	6,199	14,170
Florida	514,878	476,020	392,110	83,910	431,042	212,039	219,003
Georgia	232,282	297,798	160,842	136,956	90,782	54,699	36,083
Hawaii	32,012	41,798	22,275	19,523	13,124	17,361	-4,237
Idaho	28,076	50,637	26,175	24,462	3,100	3,914	-814
Illinois	44,623	369,642	228,958	140,684	-95,069	61,128	-156,197
Indiana	53,534	189,041	129,580	59,461	-5,532	18,806	-24,338
Iowa	27,329	85,272	63,778	21,494	5,995	9,269	-3,274
Kansas	32,789	91,020	54,764	36,256	-3,599	10,693	-14,292
Kentucky	41,058	125,523	96,274	29,249	12,051	13,127	-1,076
Louisiana	68,521	142,118	93,427	48,691	19,435	13,470	5,965
Maine	831	29,066	28,931	135	1,014	2,348	-1,334
Maryland	111,011	162,714	98,598	64,116	47,519	55,059	-7,540
Massachusetts	98,515	163,810	119,214	44,596	56,572	66,293	-9,721
Michigan	-275	254,152	198,341	55,811	-56,325	37,043	-93,368
Minnesota	75,214	151,960	88,548	63,412	12,156	27,231	-15,075
Mississippi	17,627	89,282	66,148	23,134	-6,610	5,782	-12,392
Missouri	33,064	169,040	123,646	45,394	-12,326	16,273	-28,599
Montana	15,724	26,740	19,636	7,104	8,447	1,136	7,311
Nebraska	29,184	59,344	34,073	25,271	3,977	6,485	-2,508
Nevada	58,379	81,640	43,829	37,811	20,711	17,973	2,738
New Hampshire	4,249	28,428	23,334	5,094	-389	3,951	-4,340
New Jersey	72,692	230,222	154,982	75,240	-1,594	101,658	-103,252
New Mexico	26,358	63,673	36,198	27,475	-1,069	4,229	-5,298
New York	192,157	543,408	333,712	209,696	-14,551	209,917	-224,468
North Carolina	216,602	270,488	178,941	91,547	122,575	50,439	72,136
North Dakota	27,037	20,393	13,299	7,094	19,506	2,117	17,389
Ohio	7,723	305,848	245,688	60,160	-51,037	33,491	-84,528
Oklahoma	63,466	114,749	79,477	35,272	27,256	10,896	16,360
Oregon	68,280	101,333	71,781	29,552	38,753	14,374	24,379
Pennsylvania	61,157	320,606	283,295	37,311	26,819	54,466	-27,647
Rhode Island	-2,275	24,409	20,912	3,497	-5,712	7,547	-13,259
South Carolina	98,359	128,897	95,175	33,722	63,360	16,276	47,084
South Dakota	19,174	26,110	15,876	10,234	8,822	1,875	6,947
Tennessee	110,130	179,801	135,379	44,422	65,779	19,160	46,619
Texas	913,642	856,583	381,060	475,523	432,773	142,419	290,354
Utah	91,402	115,478	33,363	82,115	9,173	10,049	-876
Vermont	270	13,415	11,827	1,588	-1,134	1,269	-2,403
Virginia	184,836	228,798	134,908	93,890	88,259	65,960	22,299
Washington	172,469	194,307	109,513	84,794	88,104	47,019	41,085
West Virginia	2,414	45,849	49,008	-3,159	5,665	1,925	3,740
Wisconsin	39,412	153,924	106,191	47,733	-8,256	12,797	-21,053
Wyoming	12,786	16,657	9,937	6,720	5,881	734	5,147

X Not applicable. [1] Total population change includes a residual. This residual represents the change in population that cannot be attributed to any specific demographic component. [2] Net international migration includes the international migration of both native and foreign-born populations. Specifically, it includes: (a) the net international migration of the foreign born, (b) the net migration between the United States and Puerto Rico, (c) the net migration of natives to and from the United States, and (d) the net movement of the Armed Forces population between the United States and overseas.

Source: U.S. Census Bureau, Population Division, "Table 4. Cumulative Estimates of the Components of Resident Population Change for the United States, Regions, States, and Puerto Rico: April 1, 2010 to July 1, 2012 (NST-EST2012-04)," December 2012, <http://www.census.gov/popest/data/state/totals/2012/index.html>.

Table 17. Resident Population by Age and State: 2012

[In thousands, except percent (313,914 represents 313,914,000). As of July 1]

State	Total	Under 5 years	5 to 14 years	15 to 24 years	25 to 34 years	35 to 44 years	45 to 54 years	55 to 64 years	65 to 74 years	75 to 84 years	85 years and over	Percent 65 years old and over
U.S.......	313,914	19,999	41,145	43,944	42,309	40,516	44,269	38,586	23,985	13,273	5,887	13.7
AL.........	4,822	305	627	677	618	607	673	615	403	217	80	14.5
AK.........	731	55	102	110	111	92	106	93	41	16	5	8.5
AZ.........	6,553	440	912	922	878	826	839	765	559	299	114	14.8
AR.........	2,949	194	399	404	384	364	397	364	253	136	54	15.0
CA.........	38,041	2,541	5,086	5,634	5,483	5,161	5,232	4,304	2,539	1,407	654	12.1
CO.........	5,188	338	696	705	762	707	725	642	358	178	77	11.8
CT.........	3,590	193	453	485	435	458	567	467	282	163	88	14.8
DE.........	917	56	114	128	116	111	132	118	81	43	17	15.3
DC.........	632	39	54	99	140	85	76	68	40	21	11	11.4
FL.........	19,318	1,071	2,229	2,493	2,401	2,403	2,746	2,464	1,895	1,132	483	18.2
GA.........	9,920	675	1,404	1,428	1,367	1,378	1,395	1,135	687	329	123	11.5
HI.........	1,392	89	165	186	199	175	186	181	112	64	35	15.1
ID.........	1,596	116	241	226	211	194	203	192	123	63	27	13.3
IL.........	12,875	816	1,714	1,789	1,786	1,694	1,824	1,558	923	523	248	13.2
IN.........	6,537	426	895	934	836	825	920	813	494	274	122	13.6
IA.........	3,074	196	405	436	390	359	424	394	241	152	77	15.3
KS.........	2,886	203	403	415	387	343	389	351	207	125	62	13.7
KY.........	4,380	280	570	593	568	566	627	563	355	186	73	14.0
LA.........	4,602	315	621	658	653	560	634	567	342	183	71	12.9
ME.........	1,329	67	150	165	148	162	210	201	126	70	30	17.0
MD.........	5,885	365	746	800	802	775	896	737	431	226	106	13.0
MA.........	6,646	366	782	939	892	854	1,005	850	508	297	153	14.4
MI.........	9,883	576	1,279	1,411	1,178	1,222	1,454	1,322	796	443	204	14.6
MN.........	5,379	348	714	721	737	667	787	675	392	225	113	13.6
MS.........	2,985	204	417	435	389	370	403	363	232	125	47	13.5
MO.........	6,022	379	786	832	792	731	857	763	487	276	120	14.7
MT.........	1,005	61	123	136	126	113	140	147	90	47	21	15.7
NE.........	1,856	132	257	260	252	221	249	227	133	84	41	13.9
NV.........	2,759	183	368	367	392	380	377	331	223	103	35	13.1
NH.........	1,321	66	156	179	149	167	220	190	110	58	26	14.7
NJ.........	8,865	528	1,139	1,145	1,134	1,199	1,366	1,104	671	390	189	14.1
NM.........	2,086	144	287	292	277	245	279	267	170	90	35	14.1
NY.........	19,570	1,167	2,341	2,752	2,757	2,540	2,840	2,415	1,481	862	414	14.1
NC.........	9,752	620	1,291	1,348	1,267	1,312	1,366	1,199	782	406	160	13.8
ND.........	700	46	84	112	99	77	93	88	50	33	17	14.4
OH.........	11,544	695	1,502	1,575	1,435	1,428	1,675	1,530	924	538	244	14.8
OK.........	3,815	262	525	542	521	463	506	462	302	166	66	14.0
OR.........	3,899	233	480	513	533	506	521	533	331	169	82	14.9
PA.........	12,764	720	1,527	1,756	1,577	1,550	1,881	1,710	1,063	658	322	16.0
RI.........	1,050	55	122	160	131	129	158	137	82	49	28	15.1
SC.........	4,724	296	605	663	607	593	653	611	417	202	76	14.7
SD.........	833	59	112	117	110	94	113	107	62	40	20	14.7
TN.........	6,456	404	838	877	844	842	911	823	536	276	106	14.2
TX.........	26,059	1,942	3,913	3,814	3,764	3,536	3,451	2,800	1,644	860	336	10.9
UT.........	2,855	258	497	461	445	357	306	261	154	84	33	9.5
VT.........	626	31	70	90	71	74	98	94	56	29	14	15.7
VA.........	8,186	510	1,036	1,135	1,143	1,092	1,202	1,006	616	314	132	13.0
WA.........	6,897	443	876	933	976	911	964	885	523	261	125	13.2
WV.........	1,855	103	215	237	220	232	264	272	176	98	38	16.8
WI.........	5,726	351	740	781	734	699	851	746	440	260	124	14.4
WY.........	576	39	75	80	81	68	79	79	44	23	9	13.1

Source: U.S. Census Bureau, "Annual Estimates of the Resident Population for Selected Age Groups by Sex for the United States, States, Counties, and Puerto Rico Commonwealth and Municipios: April 1, 2010 to July 1, 2012," <http://factfinder2.census.gov>, accessed July 2013.

Table 18. Age Dependency Ratios by State: 2000 to 2012

[As of April, except 2012 as of July]

State	Age dependency ratio [1]			Child dependency ratio [2]			Old-age dependency ratio [3]		
	2000	2010	2012	2000	2010	2012	2000	2010	2012
United States	**61.6**	**58.9**	**59.3**	**41.5**	**38.2**	**37.4**	**20.1**	**20.7**	**21.9**
Alabama	62.1	59.9	60.8	40.9	37.9	37.5	21.1	22.0	23.3
Alaska	56.5	51.8	51.8	47.6	40.0	38.8	8.9	11.7	13.0
Arizona	65.7	64.7	65.5	44.2	42.0	40.9	21.6	22.7	24.5
Arkansas	65.1	63.4	64.2	42.0	39.9	39.6	23.1	23.5	24.6
California	61.1	57.1	57.2	44.0	39.2	38.2	17.1	17.9	19.0
Colorado	54.5	54.6	55.2	39.5	37.7	36.8	14.9	16.9	18.3
Connecticut	62.7	58.8	58.6	40.2	36.3	35.0	22.5	22.5	23.5
Delaware	60.8	59.5	60.5	39.9	36.6	35.9	20.9	23.0	24.6
District of Columbia	47.8	39.3	40.2	29.7	23.3	24.3	18.1	15.9	15.9
Florida	67.7	62.9	63.6	38.3	34.7	33.9	29.5	28.2	29.7
Georgia	56.5	57.2	57.7	41.5	40.4	39.6	15.0	16.7	18.1
Hawaii	60.4	57.9	58.5	39.2	35.3	34.5	21.3	22.7	24.0
Idaho	66.1	66.1	66.8	47.4	45.5	44.6	18.7	20.6	22.2
Illinois	61.8	58.6	58.6	42.3	38.7	37.7	19.5	19.9	20.9
Indiana	62.0	60.7	61.1	41.9	39.9	39.2	20.1	20.8	21.9
Iowa	66.6	63.3	63.4	41.8	39.0	38.4	24.8	24.3	25.0
Kansas	66.0	63.0	63.3	44.0	41.5	41.0	22.0	21.5	22.3
Kentucky	59.0	58.5	59.4	39.1	37.4	37.1	19.9	21.1	22.4
Louisiana	63.6	58.6	59.3	44.6	39.1	38.7	18.9	19.5	20.6
Maine	61.3	57.6	58.8	38.1	32.6	31.8	23.2	25.0	27.0
Maryland	58.5	55.5	55.8	40.6	36.4	35.6	17.9	19.1	20.2
Massachusetts	59.2	54.9	55.1	37.6	33.6	32.7	21.6	21.4	22.4
Michigan	62.3	60.0	60.1	42.4	37.9	36.7	19.9	22.0	23.4
Minnesota	61.9	59.0	59.5	42.4	38.5	37.8	19.6	20.5	21.6
Mississippi	64.8	62.0	62.6	44.9	41.3	40.6	19.9	20.8	22.0
Missouri	64.0	60.8	61.2	41.8	38.3	37.6	22.1	22.5	23.6
Montana	63.7	59.8	60.9	41.7	36.1	35.5	21.9	23.7	25.3
Nebraska	66.3	63.0	63.5	43.8	41.0	40.8	22.6	22.0	22.7
Nevada	57.6	57.8	59.1	40.4	38.9	38.3	17.3	19.0	20.8
New Hampshire	58.8	54.7	55.0	39.8	33.8	32.3	19.0	20.9	22.7
New Jersey	61.4	58.7	58.6	40.0	37.3	36.3	21.4	21.4	22.4
New Mexico	65.6	62.4	63.4	46.3	40.9	40.3	19.3	21.5	23.1
New York	60.3	55.8	55.9	39.6	34.8	34.0	20.7	21.1	22.0
North Carolina	57.3	58.4	59.4	38.4	37.9	37.4	19.0	20.5	22.0
North Dakota	66.0	58.2	57.4	41.6	35.2	34.8	24.4	22.9	22.7
Ohio	63.2	60.6	60.9	41.5	38.0	37.1	21.7	22.6	23.8
Oklahoma	64.1	62.0	62.8	42.4	40.2	40.0	21.7	21.9	22.8
Oregon	60.1	57.6	58.7	39.6	35.6	35.0	20.5	21.9	23.7
Pennsylvania	65.1	59.8	59.9	39.3	35.1	34.3	25.8	24.6	25.6
Rhode Island	61.8	55.5	55.6	38.2	33.1	32.1	23.5	22.4	23.5
South Carolina	59.4	58.8	60.2	40.1	37.1	36.6	19.3	21.7	23.6
South Dakota	70.0	64.5	64.4	45.6	41.0	40.3	24.4	23.6	24.1
Tennessee	58.6	58.8	59.7	39.0	37.4	36.9	19.6	21.4	22.7
Texas	61.7	60.4	60.5	45.7	43.8	43.0	16.1	16.6	17.5
Utah	68.6	68.2	68.4	54.3	53.0	52.4	14.4	15.2	16.0
Vermont	58.6	54.3	55.1	38.4	31.9	30.7	20.2	22.5	24.4
Virginia	55.6	54.7	55.4	38.2	35.9	35.3	17.4	18.9	20.2
Washington	58.5	55.8	56.6	40.7	36.6	36.0	17.8	19.2	20.6
West Virginia	60.2	58.6	60.0	35.6	33.2	33.1	24.5	25.5	26.9
Wisconsin	62.9	59.3	59.8	41.6	37.5	36.8	21.3	21.8	23.0
Wyoming	60.7	57.4	57.7	41.9	37.8	37.1	18.8	19.6	20.7

[1] The age dependency ratio is derived by dividing the combined under 18 and 65-and-over populations by the 18-to-64 population and multiplying by 100. [2] The child dependency ratio is derived by dividing the population under 18 by the 18-to-64 population and multiplying by 100. [3] The old-age dependency ratio is derived by dividing the population 65 and over by the 18-to-64 population and multiplying by 100.

Source: U.S. Census Bureau, Census 2010 Briefs, "Age and Sex Composition: 2010," May 2011; and "Annual Estimates of the Resident Population for Selected Age Groups by Sex for the United States, States, Counties, and Puerto Rico Commonwealth and Municipios: April 1, 2010 to July 1, 2012," <http://factfinder2.census.gov>, accessed July 2013.

Table 19. Resident Population by Hispanic Origin and State: 2012

[In thousands, except as indicated (313,914 represents 313,914,000). As of July 1. Hispanic origin is considered an ethnicity, not a race. Persons of Hispanic origin may be of any race]

State	Number (1,000)				Percent		
	Total population	Hispanic or Latino	Total Non-Hispanic	Non-Hispanic White alone	Hispanic or Latino	Total Non-Hispanic	Non-Hispanic White alone
U.S.........	313,914	53,028	260,886	197,706	16.9	83.1	63.0
AL............	4,822	196	4,626	3,210	4.1	95.9	66.6
AK............	731	45	687	461	6.1	93.9	63.1
AZ............	6,553	1,976	4,577	3,739	30.2	69.8	57.1
AR............	2,949	200	2,749	2,181	6.8	93.2	73.9
CA............	38,041	14,538	23,504	14,971	38.2	61.8	39.4
CO..........	5,188	1,089	4,099	3,608	21.0	79.0	69.6
CT............	3,590	511	3,080	2,523	14.2	85.8	70.3
DE............	917	79	838	592	8.6	91.4	64.6
DC............	632	63	570	224	9.9	90.1	35.5
FL............	19,318	4,484	14,833	11,008	23.2	76.8	57.0
GA............	9,920	910	9,010	5,470	9.2	90.8	55.1
HI............	1,392	132	1,261	318	9.5	90.5	22.8
ID............	1,596	185	1,411	1,332	11.6	88.4	83.5
IL............	12,875	2,101	10,774	8,115	16.3	83.7	63.0
IN............	6,537	413	6,125	5,296	6.3	93.7	81.0
IA............	3,074	163	2,911	2,706	5.3	94.7	88.0
KS............	2,886	317	2,569	2,235	11.0	89.0	77.5
KY............	4,380	142	4,238	3,761	3.2	96.8	85.9
LA............	4,602	208	4,394	2,756	4.5	95.5	59.9
ME..........	1,329	19	1,311	1,251	1.4	98.6	94.1
MD..........	5,885	512	5,373	3,170	8.7	91.3	53.9
MA..........	6,646	674	5,972	5,038	10.1	89.9	75.8
MI............	9,883	456	9,427	7,534	4.6	95.4	76.2
MN..........	5,379	264	5,115	4,430	4.9	95.1	82.4
MS..........	2,985	85	2,900	1,720	2.9	97.1	57.6
MO..........	6,022	225	5,797	4,856	3.7	96.3	80.6
MT............	1,005	32	974	877	3.1	96.9	87.2
NE............	1,856	180	1,676	1,510	9.7	90.3	81.4
NV............	2,759	752	2,007	1,458	27.3	72.7	52.9
NH............	1,321	40	1,281	1,213	3.0	97.0	91.9
NJ............	8,865	1,641	7,223	5,162	18.5	81.5	58.2
NM............	2,086	980	1,106	830	47.0	53.0	39.8
NY............	19,570	3,553	16,017	11,272	18.2	81.8	57.6
NC............	9,752	851	8,901	6,310	8.7	91.3	64.7
ND............	700	17	682	616	2.5	97.5	88.1
OH..........	11,544	377	11,167	9,321	3.3	96.7	80.7
OK............	3,815	356	3,459	2,589	9.3	90.7	67.9
OR............	3,899	474	3,425	3,034	12.2	87.8	77.8
PA............	12,764	781	11,982	10,054	6.1	93.9	78.8
RI............	1,050	139	912	797	13.2	86.8	75.9
SC............	4,724	250	4,474	3,021	5.3	94.7	64.0
SD............	833	26	808	699	3.1	96.9	83.8
TN............	6,456	313	6,144	4,849	4.8	95.2	75.1
TX............	26,059	9,961	16,098	11,584	38.2	61.8	44.5
UT............	2,855	379	2,476	2,282	13.3	86.7	79.9
VT............	626	10	616	589	1.6	98.4	94.0
VA............	8,186	687	7,498	5,246	8.4	91.6	64.1
WA..........	6,897	808	6,089	4,936	11.7	88.3	71.6
WV..........	1,855	25	1,831	1,723	1.3	98.7	92.9
WI............	5,726	355	5,371	4,742	6.2	93.8	82.8
WY..........	576	55	522	488	9.5	90.5	84.6

Source: U.S. Census Bureau, "Annual Estimates of the Resident Population by Sex, Race, and Hispanic Origin for the United States, States, and Counties: April 1, 2010 to July 1, 2012," <http://factfinder2.census.gov>, accessed July 2013.

Table 20. Resident Population by Race and State: 2012

[In thousands, except as indicated (313,914 represents 313,914,000). As of July 1]

| State | Number (1,000) — One race | | | | | | | Percent distribution — One race | | | | | |
	Total population	White alone	Black or African American alone	American Indian, Alaska Native alone	Asian alone	Native Hawaiian and Other Pacific Islander alone	Two or more races	White alone	Black or African American alone	American Indian, Alaska Native alone	Asian alone	Native Hawaiian and Other Pacific Islander alone	Two or more races
U.S.	**313,914**	**244,496**	**41,205**	**3,857**	**16,146**	**707**	**7,503**	**77.9**	**13.1**	**1.2**	**5.1**	**0.2**	**2.4**
AL	4,822	3,374	1,280	34	60	5	70	70.0	26.5	0.7	1.2	0.1	1.5
AK	731	493	27	108	42	9	52	67.5	3.7	14.8	5.7	1.2	7.1
AZ	6,553	5,522	298	346	205	17	166	84.3	4.5	5.3	3.1	0.3	2.5
AR	2,949	2,360	460	28	41	7	53	80.0	15.6	0.9	1.4	0.3	1.8
CA	38,041	28,034	2,516	640	5,294	188	1,370	73.7	6.6	1.7	13.9	0.5	3.6
CO	5,188	4,572	225	82	155	9	144	88.1	4.3	1.6	3.0	0.2	2.8
CT	3,590	2,942	401	18	151	4	75	82.0	11.2	0.5	4.2	0.1	2.1
DE	917	654	202	6	32	1	22	71.4	22.0	0.7	3.5	0.1	2.4
DC	632	271	316	3	24	1	16	42.9	50.1	0.6	3.8	0.2	2.5
FL	19,318	15,120	3,206	95	512	20	364	78.3	16.6	0.5	2.7	0.1	1.9
GA	9,920	6,232	3,092	51	352	11	183	62.8	31.2	0.5	3.5	0.1	1.8
HI	1,392	364	30	6	533	140	321	26.1	2.1	0.4	38.3	10.1	23.0
ID	1,596	1,497	12	27	22	3	35	93.8	0.8	1.7	1.4	0.2	2.2
IL	12,875	10,029	1,901	76	638	8	224	77.9	14.8	0.6	5.0	0.1	1.7
IN	6,537	5,660	616	25	116	4	116	86.6	9.4	0.4	1.8	0.1	1.8
IA	3,074	2,852	97	14	60	3	49	92.8	3.2	0.5	2.0	0.1	1.6
KS	2,886	2,518	179	34	75	3	78	87.2	6.2	1.2	2.6	0.1	2.7
KY	4,380	3,883	354	12	55	3	72	88.6	8.1	0.3	1.3	0.1	1.6
LA	4,602	2,930	1,491	34	77	3	66	63.7	32.4	0.7	1.7	0.1	1.4
ME	1,329	1,267	18	9	15	1	21	95.3	1.3	0.7	1.1	(Z)	1.5
MD	5,885	3,579	1,767	32	352	6	148	60.8	30.0	0.5	6.0	0.1	2.5
MA	6,646	5,560	526	31	388	6	135	83.7	7.9	0.5	5.8	0.1	2.0
MI	9,883	7,920	1,415	70	260	4	215	80.1	14.3	0.7	2.6	(Z)	2.2
MN	5,379	4,654	298	69	235	3	120	86.5	5.5	1.3	4.4	0.1	2.2
MS	2,985	1,789	1,116	18	28	2	32	59.9	37.4	0.6	0.9	0.1	1.1
MO	6,022	5,050	706	32	107	8	120	83.9	11.7	0.5	1.8	0.1	2.0
MT	1,005	901	6	65	7	1	25	89.7	0.6	6.5	0.7	0.1	2.5
NE	1,856	1,669	89	24	36	2	35	89.9	4.8	1.3	2.0	0.1	1.9
NV	2,759	2,128	244	45	217	20	104	77.1	8.9	1.6	7.9	0.7	3.8
NH	1,321	1,247	18	4	31	1	20	94.4	1.4	0.3	2.4	(Z)	1.5
NJ	8,865	6,538	1,299	52	795	8	172	73.8	14.7	0.6	9.0	0.1	1.9
NM	2,086	1,735	51	213	34	3	49	83.2	2.4	10.2	1.6	0.2	2.4
NY	19,570	13,931	3,423	187	1,566	25	439	71.2	17.5	1.0	8.0	0.1	2.2
NC	9,752	7,013	2,148	151	239	11	191	71.9	22.0	1.5	2.5	0.1	2.0
ND	700	630	11	38	8	(Z)	12	90.1	1.5	5.5	1.1	0.1	1.8
OH	11,544	9,631	1,440	31	211	6	227	83.4	12.5	0.3	1.8	(Z)	2.0
OK	3,815	2,882	292	342	73	6	221	75.5	7.6	9.0	1.9	0.2	5.8
OR	3,899	3,445	78	69	156	16	136	88.3	2.0	1.8	4.0	0.4	3.5
PA	12,764	10,656	1,457	42	384	8	217	83.5	11.4	0.3	3.0	0.1	1.7
RI	1,050	902	77	9	34	2	26	85.9	7.3	0.9	3.2	0.2	2.5

See footnotes at end of table.

Table 20. Resident Population by Race and State: 2012-Continued.

See headnote on page 23.

| State | Number (1,000) | | | | | | | Percent distribution | | | | | |
| | Total population | One race | | | | | Two or more races | One race | | | | | Two or more races |
		White alone	Black or African American alone	American Indian, Alaska Native alone	Asian alone	Native Hawaiian and Other Pacific Islander alone		White alone	Black or African American alone	American Indian, Alaska Native alone	Asian alone	Native Hawaiian and Other Pacific Islander alone	
SC	4,724	3,229	1,323	25	68	4	75	68.4	28.0	0.5	1.4	0.1	1.6
SD	833	718	14	74	9	1	17	86.2	1.7	8.9	1.1	0.1	2.1
TN	6,456	5,117	1,098	27	103	6	105	79.3	17.0	0.4	1.6	0.1	1.6
TX	26,059	21,001	3,216	266	1,095	34	447	80.6	12.3	1.0	4.2	0.1	1.7
UT	2,855	2,621	37	42	64	28	64	91.8	1.3	1.5	2.2	1.0	2.3
VT	626	597	7	2	9	(Z)	11	95.4	1.1	0.4	1.4	(Z)	1.7
VA	8,186	5,819	1,613	44	488	9	214	71.1	19.7	0.5	6.0	0.1	2.6
WA	6,897	5,625	269	127	531	46	299	81.6	3.9	1.8	7.7	0.7	4.3
WV	1,855	1,744	66	4	14	1	27	94.0	3.5	0.2	0.7	(Z)	1.5
WI	5,726	5,052	373	62	141	3	95	88.2	6.5	1.1	2.5	(Z)	1.7
WY	576	536	9	15	5	1	11	93.1	1.5	2.6	0.9	0.1	1.8

Z Less than 500 or 0.05 percent.

Source: U.S. Census Bureau, "Annual Estimates of the Resident Population by Sex, Race, and Hispanic Origin for the United States, States, and Counties: April 1, 2010 to July 1, 2012," <http://factfinder2.census.gov>, accessed July 2013.

Table 21. Large Metropolitan Statistical Areas—Population: 2000 to 2012

[As of April 1, except 2012 as of July 1. In thousands, except as indicated (695 represents 695,000). Covers metropolitan statistical areas with 250,000 and over population in 2012, as delineated by the U.S. Office of Management and Budget as of February 2013. For definitions and components of all metropolitan and micropolitan areas, see Appendix II. Minus sign (-) indicates decrease]

Metropolitan statistical area	2000	2010, estimates base [1]	2012	Change 2000–2010 [2] Number	Change 2000–2010 [2] Percent	Change 2010–2012 Number	Change 2010–2012 Percent	Rank, 2012
Akron, OH.........................	695	703	702	8	1.2	-1	-0.1	77
Albany-Schenectady-Troy, NY..............	826	871	875	45	5.4	4	0.5	61
Albuquerque, NM.....................	730	887	902	157	21.6	15	1.6	59
Allentown-Bethlehem-Easton, PA-NJ..........	740	821	827	81	10.9	6	0.7	68
Amarillo, TX........................	229	252	258	23	10.2	6	2.2	180
Anchorage, AK......................	320	381	393	61	19.2	12	3.1	134
Ann Arbor, MI.......................	323	345	351	22	6.8	6	1.8	147
Asheville, NC.......................	369	425	432	56	15.1	8	1.8	118
Atlanta-Sandy Springs-Roswell, GA.	4,263	5,287	5,458	1,023	24.0	171	3.2	9
Atlantic City-Hammonton, NJ.............	253	275	275	22	8.7	1	0.3	167
Augusta-Richmond County, GA-SC.........	508	565	576	57	11.2	11	2.0	93
Austin-Round Rock, TX.................	1,250	1,716	1,834	467	37.3	118	6.9	35
Bakersfield, CA.....................	662	840	856	178	26.9	17	2.0	63
Baltimore-Columbia-Towson, MD..........	2,553	2,710	2,753	157	6.2	43	1.6	20
Baton Rouge, LA.....................	706	802	815	97	13.7	13	1.6	69
Beaumont-Port Arthur, TX..............	400	403	404	3	0.8	1	0.2	129
Birmingham-Hoover, AL................	1,052	1,128	1,137	76	7.2	9	0.8	48
Boise City, ID.......................	465	617	638	152	32.6	21	3.5	83
Boston-Cambridge-Newton, MA-NH........	4,391	4,552	4,641	161	3.7	88	1.9	10
Boulder, CO [3].....................	270	295	305	25	9.2	11	3.6	161
Bremerton-Silverdale, WA..............	232	251	255	19	8.3	4	1.5	184
Bridgeport-Stamford-Norwalk, CT.........	883	917	934	34	3.9	17	1.9	57
Brownsville-Harlingen, TX..............	335	406	416	71	21.2	9	2.3	126
Buffalo-Cheektowaga-Niagara Falls, NY......	1,170	1,136	1,134	-35	-3.0	-1	-0.1	49
Canton-Massillon, OH.................	407	404	403	-3	-0.6	-1	-0.2	130
Cape Coral-Fort Myers, FL..............	441	619	645	178	40.3	27	4.3	82
Cedar Rapids, IA.....................	237	258	262	21	8.7	4	1.5	177
Charleston-North Charleston, SC..........	549	665	697	116	21.1	33	4.9	78
Charlotte-Concord-Gastonia, NC-SC........	1,717	2,217	2,297	500	29.1	80	3.6	23
Chattanooga, TN-GA..................	477	528	538	52	10.8	10	1.8	99
Chicago-Naperville-Elgin, IL-IN-WI.........	9,098	9,461	9,522	363	4.0	61	0.6	3
Cincinnati, OH-KY-IN..................	1,995	2,115	2,129	120	6.0	14	0.7	28
Clarksville, TN-KY....................	220	261	274	41	18.7	14	5.3	169
Cleveland-Elyria, OH..................	2,148	2,077	2,064	-71	-3.3	-14	-0.7	29
Colorado Springs, CO.................	537	646	668	108	20.1	23	3.5	79
Columbia, SC.......................	647	768	785	120	18.6	17	2.2	72
Columbus, GA-AL....................	282	295	311	13	4.6	16	5.3	156
Columbus, OH......................	1,675	1,902	1,944	227	13.5	42	2.2	32
Corpus Christi, TX....................	403	428	437	25	6.2	9	2.1	115
Dallas-Fort Worth-Arlington, TX..........	5,204	6,426	6,701	1,222	23.5	275	4.3	4
Davenport-Moline-Rock Island, IA-IL........	376	380	383	4	1.0	3	0.8	135
Dayton, OH........................	806	799	801	-7	-0.8	2	0.2	71
Deltona-Daytona Beach-Ormond Beach, FL......	493	590	595	97	19.7	5	0.8	90
Denver-Aurora-Lakewood, CO [3].........	2,179	2,543	2,645	364	16.7	102	4.0	21
Des Moines-West Des Moines, IA..........	481	570	589	88	18.3	19	3.4	91
Detroit-Warren-Dearborn, MI............	4,453	4,296	4,292	-156	-3.5	-4	-0.1	14
Duluth, MN-WI......................	275	280	279	4	1.6	(-Z)	-0.1	166
Durham-Chapel Hill, NC................	426	504	523	78	18.3	18	3.7	102
El Paso, TX........................	683	804	831	121	17.7	27	3.3	67
Erie, PA...........................	281	281	281	(-Z)	-0.1	(Z)	(Z)	164
Eugene, OR........................	323	352	355	29	8.9	3	0.8	146
Evansville, IN-KY....................	296	312	313	15	5.2	2	0.6	154
Fayetteville, NC.....................	337	366	375	30	8.8	8	2.2	141
Fayetteville-Springdale-Rogers, AR-MO.........	347	463	482	116	33.5	19	4.1	107
Flint, MI...........................	436	426	418	-10	-2.4	-7	-1.7	125
Fort Collins, CO.....................	251	300	310	48	19.1	11	3.6	157
Fort Smith, AR-OK...................	255	280	281	25	9.8	(Z)	(Z)	165
Fort Wayne, IN......................	390	416	421	26	6.7	5	1.2	122
Fresno, CA.........................	799	930	948	131	16.4	17	1.9	56
Gainesville, FL......................	232	264	268	32	13.7	4	1.5	172
Grand Rapids-Wyoming, MI.............	931	989	1,006	58	6.3	17	1.7	52
Greeley, CO [3].....................	181	253	264	72	39.7	11	4.3	174
Green Bay, WI......................	283	306	311	24	8.4	5	1.6	155
Greensboro-High Point, NC.............	643	724	736	80	12.5	12	1.7	73
Greenville-Anderson-Mauldin, SC.........	726	824	843	98	13.6	19	2.3	65
Gulfport-Biloxi-Pascagoula, MS...........	364	371	380	7	1.8	9	2.4	138
Hagerstown-Martinsburg, MD-WV..........	208	252	256	44	21.1	5	1.9	182
Harrisburg-Carlisle, PA................	509	549	554	40	7.9	5	0.8	96
Hartford-West Hartford-East Hartford, CT.........	1,149	1,212	1,214	64	5.6	2	0.2	46
Hickory-Lenoir-Morganton, NC...........	342	365	364	24	6.9	-2	-0.5	144
Houston-The Woodlands-Sugar Land, TX.........	4,693	5,920	6,177	1,227	26.1	257	4.3	5
Huntington-Ashland, WV-KY-OH...........	362	365	365	3	0.7	(-Z)	-0.1	143
Huntsville, AL......................	342	418	431	75	22.0	13	3.1	120
Indianapolis-Carmel-Anderson, IN.........	1,658	1,888	1,929	229	13.8	41	2.2	33
Jackson, MS........................	525	567	577	42	8.0	10	1.7	92
Jacksonville, FL.....................	1,123	1,346	1,378	223	19.8	32	2.4	40
Kalamazoo-Portage, MI................	315	327	330	12	3.7	3	1.1	151
Kansas City, MO-KS..................	1,811	2,009	2,039	198	10.9	29	1.5	30
Kennewick-Richland, WA...............	192	253	268	62	32.1	15	5.9	171
Killeen-Temple, TX...................	331	405	420	75	22.6	15	3.7	124
Kingsport-Bristol-Bristol, TN-VA..........	298	310	309	11	3.7	-1	-0.2	160
Knoxville, TN.......................	748	838	848	89	11.9	11	1.3	64
Lafayette, LA.......................	425	467	474	42	9.8	8	1.6	108

See footnotes at end of table.

Table 21. Large Metropolitan Statistical Areas—Population: 2000 to 2012-Continued.

See headnote on page 25.

Metropolitan statistical area	2000	2010, estimates base [1]	2012	Change 2000–2010 [2] Number	Percent	Change 2010–2012 Number	Percent	Rank, 2012
Lakeland-Winter Haven, FL	484	602	616	118	24.4	14	2.3	87
Lancaster, PA	471	519	527	49	10.4	7	1.4	101
Lansing-East Lansing, MI	448	464	466	16	3.6	2	0.4	109
Laredo, TX	193	250	259	57	29.6	9	3.5	178
Las Vegas-Henderson-Paradise, NV	1,376	1,951	2,001	576	41.8	49	2.5	31
Lexington-Fayette, KY	408	472	485	64	15.6	13	2.7	106
Lincoln, NE	267	302	310	35	13.3	8	2.7	158
Little Rock-North Little Rock-Conway, AR	611	700	718	89	14.6	18	2.6	75
Los Angeles-Long Beach-Anaheim, CA	12,366	12,829	13,053	463	3.7	224	1.7	2
Louisville/Jefferson County, KY-IN	1,121	1,236	1,251	115	10.2	16	1.3	43
Lubbock, TX	256	291	298	35	13.5	7	2.4	163
Lynchburg, VA	229	253	255	24	10.5	3	1.1	183
Madison, WI	535	605	621	70	13.1	15	2.5	86
Manchester-Nashua, NH	381	401	403	20	5.2	2	0.5	131
McAllen-Edinburg-Mission, TX	569	775	807	205	36.1	32	4.1	70
Memphis, TN-MS-AR	1,213	1,325	1,342	112	9.2	17	1.3	41
Merced, CA	211	256	262	45	21.5	7	2.5	176
Miami-Fort Lauderdale-West Palm Beach, FL	5,008	5,565	5,763	557	11.1	198	3.6	8
Milwaukee-Waukesha-West Allis, WI	1,501	1,556	1,567	55	3.7	11	0.7	39
Minneapolis-St. Paul-Bloomington, MN-WI	3,032	3,349	3,422	317	10.5	73	2.2	16
Mobile, AL	400	413	414	13	3.3	1	0.2	127
Modesto, CA	447	514	522	67	15.1	7	1.4	103
Montgomery, AL	347	375	377	28	8.1	3	0.7	139
Myrtle Beach-Conway-North Myrtle Beach, SC-NC	270	377	395	107	39.6	18	4.7	133
Naples-Immokalee-Marco Island, FL	251	322	332	70	27.9	11	3.4	150
Nashville-Davidson--Murfreesboro--Franklin, TN	1,381	1,671	1,727	290	21.0	56	3.3	36
New Haven-Milford, CT	824	862	863	38	4.7	(Z)	(Z)	62
New Orleans-Metairie, LA	1,338	1,190	1,227	-148	-11.1	37	3.1	45
New York-Newark-Jersey City, NY-NJ-PA	18,945	19,567	19,832	623	3.3	264	1.4	1
North Port-Sarasota-Bradenton, FL	590	702	720	112	19.0	18	2.5	74
Norwich-New London, CT	259	274	274	15	5.8	(Z)	(Z)	170
Ocala, FL	259	331	335	72	28.0	4	1.2	149
Ogden-Clearfield, UT	485	597	612	112	23.0	15	2.6	88
Oklahoma City, OK	1,095	1,253	1,297	158	14.4	44	3.5	42
Olympia-Tumwater, WA	207	252	258	45	21.7	6	2.4	179
Omaha-Council Bluffs, NE-IA	767	865	886	98	12.8	20	2.3	60
Orlando-Kissimmee-Sanford, FL	1,645	2,134	2,224	490	29.8	89	4.2	26
Oxnard-Thousand Oaks-Ventura, CA	753	823	836	70	9.3	13	1.5	66
Palm Bay-Melbourne-Titusville, FL	476	543	547	67	14.1	4	0.7	98
Pensacola-Ferry Pass-Brent, FL	412	449	461	37	8.9	12	2.7	110
Peoria, IL	367	379	380	12	3.3	1	0.3	137
Philadelphia-Camden-Wilmington, PA-NJ-DE-MD	5,687	5,965	6,019	278	4.9	53	0.9	6
Phoenix-Mesa-Scottsdale, AZ	3,252	4,193	4,330	941	28.9	137	3.3	13
Pittsburgh, PA	2,431	2,356	2,361	-75	-3.1	4	0.2	22
Portland-South Portland, ME	488	514	518	27	5.4	4	0.8	104
Portland-Vancouver-Hillsboro, OR-WA	1,928	2,226	2,290	298	15.5	64	2.9	24
Port St. Lucie, FL	319	424	433	105	32.8	9	2.0	117
Providence-Warwick, RI-MA	1,583	1,601	1,601	18	1.1	1	(Z)	38
Provo-Orem, UT	377	527	551	150	39.8	24	4.6	97
Raleigh, NC	797	1,130	1,189	333	41.8	58	5.1	47
Reading, PA	374	411	413	38	10.1	2	0.5	128
Reno, NV	343	425	434	83	24.1	8	2.0	116
Richmond, VA	1,056	1,208	1,232	152	14.4	24	2.0	44
Riverside-San Bernardino-Ontario, CA	3,255	4,225	4,350	970	29.8	125	3.0	12
Roanoke, VA	288	309	310	20	7.1	1	0.5	159
Rochester, NY	1,062	1,080	1,082	17	1.6	3	0.2	51
Rockford, IL	320	349	346	29	9.1	-3	-1.0	148
Sacramento--Roseville--Arden-Arcade, CA	1,797	2,149	2,196	352	19.6	47	2.2	27
St. Louis, MO-IL [4]	2,675	2,788	2,796	112	4.2	8	0.3	19
Salem, OR	347	391	396	44	12.5	6	1.4	132
Salinas, CA	402	415	427	13	3.3	12	2.8	121
Salisbury, MD-DE	313	374	382	61	19.6	8	2.2	136
Salt Lake City, UT	939	1,088	1,124	149	15.8	36	3.3	50
San Antonio-New Braunfels, TX	1,712	2,143	2,234	431	25.2	91	4.3	25
San Diego-Carlsbad, CA	2,814	3,095	3,177	281	10.0	82	2.6	17
San Francisco-Oakland-Hayward, CA	4,124	4,335	4,456	212	5.1	120	2.8	11
San Jose-Sunnyvale-Santa Clara, CA	1,736	1,837	1,894	101	5.8	57	3.1	34
San Luis Obispo-Paso Robles-Arroyo Grande, CA	247	270	275	23	9.3	5	1.9	168
Santa Cruz-Watsonville, CA	256	262	267	7	2.7	4	1.7	173
Santa Maria-Santa Barbara, CA	399	424	431	25	6.1	7	1.7	119
Santa Rosa, CA	459	484	492	25	5.5	8	1.6	105
Savannah, GA	293	348	362	55	18.6	14	4.1	145
Scranton--Wilkes-Barre--Hazleton, PA	561	564	564	3	0.5	(-Z)	(-Z)	94
Seattle-Tacoma-Bellevue, WA	3,044	3,440	3,552	396	13.0	112	3.3	15
Shreveport-Bossier City, LA	418	440	447	22	5.3	7	1.7	112
South Bend-Mishawaka, IN-MI	317	319	319	3	0.8	-1	-0.2	152
Spartanburg, SC	284	313	317	30	10.4	4	1.2	153
Spokane-Spokane Valley, WA	470	528	532	58	12.4	5	0.9	100
Springfield, MA	608	622	626	13	2.2	4	0.7	85
Springfield, MO	368	437	445	68	18.6	8	1.8	113
Stockton-Lodi, CA	564	685	703	122	21.6	17	2.5	76
Syracuse, NY	650	663	661	12	1.9	-2	(-Z)	80

See footnotes at end of table.

Metropolitan statistical area	2000	2010, estimates base [1]	2012	Change				Rank, 2012
				2000–2010 [2]		2010–2012		
				Number	Percent	Number	Percent	
Tallahassee, FL	320	369	375	47	14.7	7	1.8	140
Tampa-St. Petersburg-Clearwater, FL	2,396	2,783	2,843	387	16.2	60	2.1	18
Toledo, OH	618	610	609	-8	-1.3	-1	(-Z)	89
Trenton, NJ	351	367	368	16	4.5	2	0.5	142
Tucson, AZ	844	980	992	137	16.2	12	1.2	53
Tulsa, OK	860	937	952	78	9.1	14	1.5	55
Urban Honolulu, HI	876	953	976	77	8.8	23	2.4	54
Utica-Rome, NY	300	299	298	(-Z)	-0.2	-1	-0.4	162
Vallejo-Fairfield, CA	395	413	421	19	4.8	7	1.8	123
Virginia Beach-Norfolk-Newport News, VA-NC	1,580	1,677	1,700	97	6.1	23	1.4	37
Visalia-Porterville, CA	368	442	452	74	20.2	10	2.2	111
Waco, TX	232	253	256	21	8.9	4	1.4	181
Washington-Arlington-Alexandria, DC-VA-MD-WV	4,837	5,636	5,860	799	16.5	224	4.0	7
Wichita, KS	580	631	636	51	8.8	5	0.8	84
Wilmington, NC	201	255	263	53	26.6	9	3.4	175
Winston-Salem, NC	569	641	648	71	12.5	7	1.1	81
Worcester, MA-CT	860	917	924	57	6.6	7	0.7	58
York-Hanover, PA	382	435	438	53	13.9	3	0.7	114
Youngstown-Warren-Boardman, OH-PA	603	566	558	-37	-6.2	-8	-1.3	95

Z Less than 500 or .05 percent. [1] The April 1, 2010 population estimates base reflects changes to the Census 2010 population from the Count Question Resolution program and geographic program revisions. [2] Based on census data. [3] Broomfield County, CO, was formed from parts of Adams, Boulder, Jefferson, and Weld Counties, CO, on November 15, 2001, and is coextensive with Broomfield city. For purposes of defining and presenting data for metropolitan statistical areas, Broomfield city is treated as if it were a county at the time of the 2000 census. [4] The portion of Sullivan city in Crawford County, Missouri, is legally part of the St. Louis, MO-IL MSA. Data shown here do not include this area.

Source: U.S. Census Bureau, "CPH-T-5. Population Change for Metropolitan and Micropolitan Statistical Areas in the United States and Puerto Rico (February 2013 Delineations): 2000 to 2010", March 2013, <http://www.census.gov/population/www/cen2010/cph-t/cph-t-5.html>; and "Table 1. Annual Estimates of the Population of Metropolitan and Micropolitan Statistical Areas: April 1, 2010 to July 1, 2012 (CBSA-EST2012-01)", and "Table 7. Cumulative Estimates of Population Change for Metropolitan Statistical Areas and Rankings: April 1, 2010 to July 1, 2012 (CBSA-EST2012-07)", March 2013, <http://www.census.gov/popest/data/metro/totals/2012/index> .

Table 22. Population in Coastal Counties: 1980 to 2012

[1980 to 2010 as of April 1, beginning 2011 as of July 1 (3,537 represents 3,537,000). Areas as defined by U.S. National Oceanic and Atmospheric Administration, 1992. Covers 675 counties and equivalent areas with at least 15 percent of their land area either in a coastal watershed (drainage area) or in a coastal cataloging unit (a coastal area between watersheds). See Appendix III]

Year	Total	Counties in coastal regions					Balance of United States
		Total	Atlantic	Gulf of Mexico	Great Lakes	Pacific	
Land area, 2010 (1,000 sq. mi.)	3,537	886	147	114	115	510	2,649
POPULATION							
1980 (mil.)	226.5	119.8	53.7	13.1	26.0	27.0	106.7
1990 (mil.)	248.7	133.4	59.0	15.2	25.9	33.2	115.3
2000 (mil.)	281.4	148.3	65.2	18.0	27.3	37.8	133.1
2010 (mil.)	308.7	159.6	70.2	20.8	27.2	41.4	149.1
2011 (mil.)	311.6	161.1	70.9	21.1	27.2	41.9	150.5
2012 (mil.)	313.9	162.3	71.4	21.3	27.2	42.4	151.6
1980 (percent)	100	53	24	6	11	12	47
1990 (percent)	100	54	24	6	10	13	46
2000 (percent)	100	53	23	6	10	13	47
2010 (percent)	100	52	23	7	9	13	48
2011 (percent)	100	52	23	7	9	13	48
2012 (percent)	100	52	23	7	9	13	48

Source: U.S. Census Bureau, *U.S. Summary, 1980 Census of Population,* Vol. 1, Chapter A (PC80-1-A-1); *1990 Census of Population and Housing (CPH1)*; "Annual Estimates of the Resident Population for Counties: April 1, 2000 to July 1, 2009," March 2011, <http://www.census.gov/popest/data/counties/totals/2009/CO-EST2009-01.html>; and "County Totals Datasets: Population, Population Change and Estimated Components of Population Change: April 1, 2010 to July 1, 2012," March 2013, <http://www.census.gov/popest/data/counties/totals/2012/CO-EST2012-alldata.html>.

Table 23. Metropolitan Statistical Areas With More Than 750,000 Persons in 2010—Population by Age: 2010

[In thousands (871 represents 871,000). As of April 1. Covers metropolitan statistical areas as defined by the U.S. Office of Management and Budget as of December 2009. All geographic boundaries are defined as of January 1, 2010. For definitions and components of all metropolitan and micropolitan areas, see Appendix II]

Metropolitan statistical area	Number (1,000)						Percent under 18 years	Percent 65 years and over
	Total	Under 18 years	18 to 44 years	45 to 64 years	65 to 74 years	75 years and over		
Albany-Schenectady-Troy, NY....................	871	186	313	249	62	60	21.4	14.0
Albuquerque, NM...............................	887	218	323	237	61	48	24.6	12.3
Allentown-Bethlehem-Easton, PA-NJ...........	821	187	275	234	62	63	22.8	15.2
Atlanta-Sandy Springs-Marietta, GA.............	5,269	1,396	2,076	1,325	283	189	26.5	9.0
Austin-Round Rock-San Marcos, TX.............	1,716	435	750	392	81	58	25.3	8.1
Bakersfield-Delano, CA.........................	840	254	324	186	44	32	30.3	9.0
Baltimore-Towson, MD..........................	2,710	623	992	753	183	159	23.0	12.6
Baton Rouge, LA...............................	802	198	313	205	50	37	24.7	10.7
Birmingham-Hoover, AL.........................	1,128	270	409	304	80	66	23.9	13.0
Boston-Cambridge-Quincy, MA-NH..............	4,552	983	1,721	1,252	306	290	21.6	13.1
Bridgeport-Stamford-Norwalk, CT...............	917	227	309	256	62	62	24.8	13.5
Buffalo-Niagara Falls, NY.......................	1,136	245	388	323	87	92	21.6	15.7
Charlotte-Gastonia-Rock Hill, NC-SC...........	1,758	456	688	437	102	76	25.9	10.1
Chicago-Joliet-Naperville, IL-IN-WI..............	9,461	2,378	3,574	2,429	579	501	25.1	11.4
Cincinnati-Middletown, OH-KY-IN...............	2,130	531	761	578	140	120	24.9	12.2
Cleveland-Elyria-Mentor, OH...................	2,077	481	682	598	159	157	23.2	15.2
Columbia, SC.................................	768	180	299	201	50	37	23.5	11.4
Columbus, OH................................	1,837	455	720	468	108	86	24.8	10.6
Dallas-Fort Worth-Arlington, TX.................	6,372	1,774	2,506	1,532	328	233	27.8	8.8
Dayton, OH...................................	842	193	290	233	66	60	23.0	14.9
Denver-Aurora-Broomfield, CO..................	2,543	634	987	666	144	112	24.9	10.0
Detroit-Warren-Livonia, MI.....................	4,296	1,044	1,471	1,215	296	271	24.3	13.2
El Paso, TX..................................	801	241	301	177	44	38	30.1	10.3
Fresno, CA..................................	930	278	356	204	49	44	29.8	10.0
Grand Rapids-Wyoming, MI.....................	774	200	281	202	48	43	25.9	11.7
Hartford-West Hartford-East Hartford, CT.......	1,212	270	420	348	87	87	22.3	14.3
Honolulu, HI..................................	953	211	358	246	69	70	22.1	14.5
Houston-Sugar Land-Baytown, TX...............	5,947	1,662	2,329	1,444	303	208	28.0	8.6
Indianapolis-Carmel, IN........................	1,756	460	653	453	105	86	26.2	10.9
Jacksonville, FL...............................	1,346	321	493	369	93	70	23.8	12.1
Kansas City, MO-KS...........................	2,035	522	730	540	130	113	25.6	12.0
Las Vegas-Paradise, NV........................	1,951	489	762	480	135	86	25.0	11.3
Los Angeles-Long Beach-Santa Ana, CA........	12,829	3,139	5,126	3,148	756	659	24.5	11.0
Louisville/Jefferson County, KY-IN..............	1,284	308	455	356	90	75	24.0	12.8
McAllen-Edinburg-Mission, TX..................	775	268	294	140	40	33	34.7	9.3
Memphis, TN-MS-AR...........................	1,316	350	487	340	79	60	26.6	10.5
Miami-Fort Lauderdale-Pompano Beach, FL.....	5,565	1,206	2,001	1,471	443	444	21.7	15.9
Milwaukee-Waukesha-West Allis, WI............	1,556	383	560	417	97	99	24.6	12.6
Minneapolis-St. Paul-Bloomington, MN-WI......	3,280	820	1,232	879	188	162	25.0	10.7
Nashville-Davidson—Murfreesboro—Franklin, TN.	1,590	388	619	413	98	72	24.4	10.7
New Haven-Milford, CT.........................	862	193	308	238	61	63	22.4	14.4
New Orleans-Metairie-Kenner, LA...............	1,168	273	431	322	79	63	23.4	12.2
New York-Northern New Jersey-Long Island, NY-NJ-PA.	18,897	4,312	7,132	4,980	1,288	1,185	22.8	13.1
Oklahoma City, OK.............................	1,253	313	477	315	82	66	25.0	11.8
Omaha-Council Bluffs, NE-IA....................	865	227	323	219	51	45	26.3	11.1
Orlando-Kissimmee-Sanford, FL................	2,134	499	830	542	146	117	23.4	12.3
Oxnard-Thousand Oaks-Ventura, CA............	823	212	298	217	51	45	25.7	11.7
Philadelphia-Camden-Wilmington, PA-NJ-DE-MD.	5,965	1,391	2,160	1,622	405	388	23.3	13.3
Phoenix-Mesa-Glendale, AZ.....................	4,193	1,108	1,581	989	289	226	26.4	12.3
Pittsburgh, PA................................	2,356	475	778	696	195	212	20.2	17.3
Portland-Vancouver-Hillsboro, OR-WA...........	2,226	527	854	593	138	114	23.7	11.3
Providence-New Bedford-Fall River, RI-MA......	1,601	346	578	447	113	117	21.6	14.4
Raleigh-Cary, NC..............................	1,130	296	453	280	60	42	26.2	9.0
Richmond, VA.................................	1,258	294	462	350	85	68	23.3	12.1
Riverside-San Bernardino-Ontario, CA...........	4,225	1,215	1,589	981	244	196	28.8	10.4
Rochester, NY................................	1,054	238	370	298	76	72	22.6	14.1
Sacramento—Arden-Arcade—Roseville, CA.......	2,149	535	797	559	138	120	24.9	12.0
St. Louis, MO-IL [1]...........................	2,813	671	990	777	196	179	23.8	13.3
Salt Lake City, UT.............................	1,124	331	455	241	54	43	29.4	8.6
San Antonio-New Braunfels, TX.................	2,143	576	808	524	131	104	26.9	11.0
San Diego-Carlsbad-San Marcos, CA...........	3,095	724	1,259	760	181	171	23.4	11.4
San Francisco-Oakland-Fremont, CA............	4,335	921	1,689	1,179	289	258	21.2	12.6
San Jose-Sunnyvale-Santa Clara, CA...........	1,837	446	726	463	109	93	24.3	11.0
Seattle-Tacoma-Bellevue, WA..................	3,440	786	1,353	929	203	169	22.8	10.8
Tampa-St. Petersburg-Clearwater, FL...........	2,783	590	943	770	249	231	21.2	17.2
Tucson, AZ..................................	980	225	350	254	82	70	23.0	15.4
Tulsa, OK....................................	937	239	333	245	67	54	25.5	12.8
Virginia Beach-Norfolk-Newport News, VA-NC.	1,672	394	648	436	107	86	23.6	11.6
Washington-Arlington-Alexandria, DC-VA-MD-WV.	5,582	1,332	2,212	1,480	320	238	23.9	10.0
Worcester, MA................................	799	187	282	227	51	51	23.4	12.8

[1] The portion of Sullivan city in Crawford County, Missouri, is legally part of the St. Louis, MO-IL MSA. Data shown here do not include this area.

Source: U.S. Census Bureau, USA Counties, <http://censtats.census.gov/usa/usa.shtml>, accessed June 2011.

Table 24. Metropolitan Statistical Areas With More Than 750,000 Persons in 2010—Population by Race and Hispanic or Latino Origin: 2010

[In thousands (871 represents 871,000). As of April 1. Covers metropolitan statistical areas as defined by the U.S. Office of Management and Budget as of December 2009. All geographic boundaries are defined as of January 1, 2010. For definitions and components of all metropolitan and micropolitan areas, see Appendix II]

Metropolitan statistical area	Total	White alone	Black or African American alone	American Indian and Alaska Native alone	Asian alone	Native Hawaiian and Other Pacific Islander alone	Two or more races	Hispanic or Latino origin [1]
Albany-Schenectady-Troy, NY	871	739	67	2	27	(Z)	21	36
Albuquerque, NM	887	618	24	52	18	1	38	414
Allentown-Bethlehem-Easton, PA-NJ	821	694	41	2	20	(Z)	19	107
Atlanta-Sandy Springs-Marietta, GA	5,269	2,920	1,708	18	254	3	126	547
Austin-Round Rock-San Marcos, TX	1,716	1,250	127	13	82	1	55	538
Bakersfield-Delano, CA	840	500	49	13	35	1	38	413
Baltimore-Towson, MD	2,710	1,684	779	9	123	1	68	124
Baton Rouge, LA	802	480	286	2	14	(Z)	10	27
Birmingham-Hoover, AL	1,128	753	318	3	14	1	13	49
Boston-Cambridge-Quincy, MA-NH	4,552	3,588	331	11	295	1	118	411
Bridgeport-Stamford-Norwalk, CT	917	686	99	2	42	(Z)	24	155
Buffalo-Niagara Falls, NY	1,136	927	139	8	26	(Z)	21	46
Charlotte-Gastonia-Rock Hill, NC-SC	1,758	1,145	421	9	55	1	39	173
Chicago-Joliet-Naperville, IL-IN-WI	9,461	6,184	1,646	37	533	3	230	1,957
Cincinnati-Middletown, OH-KY-IN	2,130	1,766	256	4	40	1	39	55
Cleveland-Elyria-Mentor, OH	2,077	1,538	417	4	41	(Z)	42	98
Columbia, SC	768	464	255	3	13	1	15	39
Columbus, OH	1,837	1,424	274	4	57	1	46	66
Dallas-Fort Worth-Arlington, TX	6,372	4,161	962	43	342	6	180	1,752
Dayton, OH	842	673	126	2	15	(Z)	19	17
Denver-Aurora-Broomfield, CO	2,543	1,983	143	25	94	3	91	571
Detroit-Warren-Livonia, MI	4,296	3,011	980	15	141	1	95	168
El Paso, TX	801	657	25	6	8	1	20	658
Fresno, CA	930	515	50	16	89	1	42	468
Grand Rapids-Wyoming, MI	774	643	62	4	15	(Z)	21	65
Hartford-West Hartford-East Hartford, CT	1,212	932	132	3	47	(Z)	30	151
Honolulu, HI	953	199	19	2	418	91	213	77
Houston-Sugar Land-Baytown, TX	5,947	3,581	1,026	38	389	4	180	2,099
Indianapolis-Carmel, IN	1,756	1,353	263	5	40	1	38	108
Jacksonville, FL	1,346	940	293	5	46	1	35	93
Kansas City, MO-KS	2,035	1,597	255	10	46	3	56	167
Las Vegas-Paradise, NV	1,951	1,188	204	14	169	14	99	569
Los Angeles-Long Beach-Santa Ana, CA	12,829	6,767	908	91	1,885	35	567	5,701
Louisville/Jefferson County, KY-IN	1,284	1,037	176	3	20	1	26	50
McAllen-Edinburg-Mission, TX	775	682	5	3	7	(Z)	10	702
Memphis, TN-MS-AR	1,316	631	601	3	24	1	18	65
Miami-Fort Lauderdale-Pompano Beach, FL	5,565	3,914	1,169	16	126	2	140	2,313
Milwaukee-Waukesha-West Allis, WI	1,556	1,147	261	8	46	1	36	148
Minneapolis-St. Paul-Bloomington, MN-WI	3,280	2,657	243	23	188	1	91	176
Nashville-Davidson—Murfreesboro—Franklin, TN	1,590	1,222	242	5	36	1	33	105
New Haven-Milford, CT	862	645	110	2	30	(Z)	23	130
New Orleans-Metairie-Kenner, LA	1,168	680	397	5	32	1	23	92
New York-Northern New Jersey-Long Island, NY-NJ-PA	18,897	11,178	3,363	93	1,878	9	613	4,328
Oklahoma City, OK	1,253	901	131	51	35	1	65	142
Omaha-Council Bluffs, NE-IA	865	714	68	5	18	1	22	78
Orlando-Kissimmee-Sanford, FL	2,134	1,494	345	9	85	2	69	539
Oxnard-Thousand Oaks-Ventura, CA	823	566	15	8	55	2	37	332
Philadelphia-Camden-Wilmington, PA-NJ-DE-MD	5,965	4,068	1,242	16	296	2	139	468
Phoenix-Mesa-Glendale, AZ	4,193	3,059	208	99	139	9	146	1,236
Pittsburgh, PA	2,356	2,069	197	3	41	(Z)	37	30
Portland-Vancouver-Hillsboro, OR-WA	2,226	1,804	64	21	127	10	91	242
Providence-New Bedford-Fall River, RI-MA	1,601	1,342	78	8	41	1	49	164
Raleigh-Cary, NC	1,130	763	228	6	50	(Z)	27	115
Richmond, VA	1,258	780	375	5	39	1	29	63
Riverside-San Bernardino-Ontario, CA	4,225	2,488	322	46	259	14	207	1,996
Rochester, NY	1,054	855	123	3	27	(Z)	24	65
Sacramento—Arden-Arcade—Roseville, CA	2,149	1,390	158	22	256	16	127	434
St. Louis, MO-IL [2]	2,813	2,153	516	7	60	1	51	72
Salt Lake City, UT	1,124	922	17	10	35	16	35	187
San Antonio-New Braunfels, TX	2,143	1,617	141	17	45	3	70	1,158
San Diego-Carlsbad-San Marcos, CA	3,095	1,981	158	26	336	15	158	991
San Francisco-Oakland-Fremont, CA	4,335	2,240	364	25	1,006	32	240	939
San Jose-Sunnyvale-Santa Clara, CA	1,837	872	47	14	572	7	90	510
Seattle-Tacoma-Bellevue, WA	3,440	2,475	192	37	393	28	184	309
Tampa-St. Petersburg-Clearwater, FL	2,783	2,193	329	10	81	2	73	452
Tucson, AZ	980	729	35	33	26	2	36	339
Tulsa, OK	937	665	79	77	17	1	60	78
Virginia Beach-Norfolk-Newport News, VA-NC	1,672	997	522	7	58	2	57	90
Washington-Arlington-Alexandria, DC-VA-MD-WV	5,582	3,059	1,438	23	517	4	206	771
Worcester, MA	799	683	33	2	32	(Z)	19	75

Z Less than 500. [1] Persons of Hispanic origin may be of any race. [2] The portion of Sullivan city in Crawford County, Missouri, is legally part of the St. Louis, MO-IL MSA. Data shown here do not include this area.

Source: U.S. Census Bureau, USA Counties, <http://censtats.census.gov/usa/usa.shtml>, accessed June 2011.

Table 25. Population by Core Based Statistical Area (CBSA) Status and State: 2012

[As of July 1. (313,914 represents 313,914,000). Covers core based statistical areas (metropolitan and micropolitan statistical areas) as delineated by the U.S. Office of Management and Budget as of February 2013. For definitions and components of all metropolitan and micropolitan statistical areas, see Appendix II. Minus sign (-) indicates decrease]

State	Total popula-tion, 2012 (1,000)	Inside Core-Based Statistical Area (metropolitan or micropolitan statistical area), 2012				Outside CBSA, 2012		Percent change, 2010–2012		
		Total		Metro-politan (1,000)	Micro-politan (1,000)	Number (1,000)	Percent	Metro-politan	Micro-politan	Outside CBSAs
		Number (1,000)	Percent							
U.S.....	313,914	294,881	93.9	267,664	27,217	19,033	6.1	2.0	0.2	-0.6
AL........	4,822	4,191	86.9	3,658	533	631	13.1	1.4	0.2	-1.4
AK.......	731	539	73.7	493	46	192	26.3	3.0	3.5	2.8
AZ........	6,553	6,451	98.4	6,206	245	102	1.6	2.6	-0.3	1.8
AR........	2,949	2,368	80.3	1,791	576	582	19.7	2.2	(-Z)	-0.9
CA........	38,041	37,769	99.3	37,205	564	273	0.7	2.2	-0.8	-1.6
CO........	5,188	4,883	94.1	4,502	382	304	5.9	3.7	0.1	-0.6
CT........	3,590	3,590	100.0	3,403	188	0	0.0	0.6	-1.3	0.0
DE.......	917	917	100.0	917	0	0	0.0	2.1	0.0	0.0
DC.......	632	632	100.0	632	0	0	0.0	5.1	0.0	0.0
FL........	19,318	18,969	98.2	18,614	355	349	1.8	2.9	-0.4	-0.5
GA........	9,920	9,131	92.0	8,145	987	789	8.0	2.9	0.5	-0.5
HI........	1,392	1,392	100.0	1,135	258	0	0.0	2.4	2.2	0.0
ID........	1,596	1,458	91.4	1,052	405	138	8.6	2.9	0.2	-1.3
IL.........	12,875	12,258	95.2	11,362	896	617	4.8	0.5	-0.9	-1.0
IN.........	6,537	6,074	92.9	5,063	1,011	463	7.1	1.2	-0.2	-0.6
IA.........	3,074	2,280	74.2	1,782	497	795	25.8	2.0	-0.3	-0.8
KS.......	2,886	2,486	86.1	1,928	558	400	13.9	1.7	0.9	-1.0
KY.......	4,380	3,382	77.2	2,541	841	998	22.8	1.7	0.6	-0.6
LA........	4,602	4,238	92.1	3,830	408	364	7.9	1.9	(Z)	-0.9
ME.......	1,329	901	67.8	779	122	428	32.2	0.5	-0.2	-0.6
MD.......	5,885	5,802	98.6	5,731	71	83	1.4	2.0	0.4	-0.7
MA.......	6,646	6,636	99.8	6,547	89	10	0.2	1.5	0.8	1.2
MI........	9,883	9,211	93.2	8,077	1,134	672	6.8	0.1	-0.1	-1.2
MN.......	5,379	4,798	89.2	4,140	657	581	10.8	1.9	0.2	-0.8
MS.......	2,985	2,313	77.5	1,354	959	672	22.5	2.0	-0.2	-1.0
MO.......	6,022	5,184	86.1	4,465	719	838	13.9	0.8	0.5	-0.9
MT.......	1,005	650	64.7	356	295	355	35.3	1.7	1.9	1.2
NE.......	1,856	1,511	81.4	1,184	327	344	18.6	2.7	0.3	-0.7
NV.......	2,759	2,725	98.8	2,489	236	34	1.2	2.4	0.3	0.3
NH.......	1,321	1,273	96.4	825	448	48	3.6	0.7	-0.3	-0.5
NJ........	8,865	8,865	100.0	8,865	0	0	0.0	0.8	0.0	0.0
NM.......	2,086	1,989	95.4	1,391	598	97	4.6	1.5	1.3	-2.0
NY.......	19,570	19,168	97.9	18,157	1,011	402	2.1	1.1	-0.4	-0.9
NC.......	9,752	9,111	93.4	7,541	1,569	641	6.6	2.8	0.8	-0.6
ND.......	700	507	72.5	344	164	192	27.5	3.7	6.6	2.4
OH.......	11,544	11,090	96.1	9,164	1,926	455	3.9	0.2	-0.6	-0.6
OK.......	3,815	3,270	85.7	2,472	798	545	14.3	2.4	1.0	-0.6
OR.......	3,899	3,802	97.5	3,248	555	97	2.5	2.2	-0.1	-0.8
PA........	12,764	12,347	96.7	11,263	1,084	417	3.3	0.6	-0.6	-0.7
RI........	1,050	1,050	100.0	1,050	0	0	0.0	-0.2	0.0	0.0
SC........	4,724	4,410	93.4	3,968	443	313	6.6	2.7	-0.3	-2.0
SD........	833	616	74.0	391	225	217	26.0	3.6	1.7	0.9
TN.......	6,456	5,807	89.9	4,966	841	649	10.1	2.2	0.6	-0.4
TX........	26,059	24,655	94.6	23,038	1,617	1,404	5.4	4.1	0.9	0.2
UT........	2,855	2,713	95.0	2,547	166	142	5.0	3.4	3.6	0.6
VT........	626	462	73.8	214	248	164	26.2	1.2	-0.7	-0.2
VA........	8,186	7,398	90.4	7,121	277	787	9.6	2.8	-1.2	-0.5
WA.......	6,897	6,744	97.8	6,186	558	153	2.2	2.8	1.0	0.1
WV.......	1,855	1,445	77.9	1,138	306	411	22.1	0.5	(-Z)	-0.8
WI........	5,726	5,000	87.3	4,221	779	726	12.7	1.0	0.1	-0.4
WY.......	576	417	72.3	173	244	159	27.7	3.5	2.5	0.6

Z Less than .05 percent.

Source: U.S. Census Bureau, "Metropolitan and micropolitan statistical area population and estimated components of change: April 1, 2010 to July 1, 2012 (CBSA-EST2012-alldata)"; March 2013, <http://www.census.gov/popest/data/metro/totals/2012/index.html>.

Table 26. The 50 Largest Metropolitan Statistical Areas in 2012— Components of Population Change: 2010 to 2012

[Covers period April 1, 2010 to July 1, 2012 (171 represents 171,000). Covers metropolitan statistical areas as delineated by the U.S. Office of Management and Budget as of February 2013. For definitions and components of all metropolitan and micropolitan areas, see Appendix II. Minus sign (-) indicates decrease or outmigration]

| Metropolitan statistical area | Number (1,000) | | | | | | | Percent change |
| | Total change [1] | Natural increase | | | Net migration | | | |
		Total	Births	Deaths	Total	International	Domestic migration	
Atlanta-Sandy Springs-Roswell, GA..........................	171	92	165	73	77	40	37	3.2
Austin-Round Rock, TX...	118	38	57	19	78	12	66	6.9
Baltimore-Columbia-Towson, MD.............................	43	24	75	51	19	19	(Z)	1.6
Birmingham-Hoover, AL..	9	10	35	25	-1	3	-4	0.8
Boston-Cambridge-Newton, MA-NH........................	88	39	116	77	51	51	1	1.9
Buffalo-Cheektowaga-Niagara Falls, NY..................	-1	(Z)	27	26	-1	5	-6	-0.1
Charlotte-Concord-Gastonia, NC-SC......................	80	29	66	37	50	12	37	3.6
Chicago-Naperville-Elgin, IL-IN-WI.........................	61	132	283	151	-70	52	-122	0.6
Cincinnati, OH-KY-IN...	14	21	62	41	-7	7	-14	0.7
Cleveland-Elyria, OH...	-14	6	52	46	-19	8	-27	-0.7
Columbus, OH...	42	26	59	32	16	10	5	2.2
Dallas-Fort Worth-Arlington, TX..............................	275	132	217	85	141	43	99	4.3
Denver-Aurora-Lakewood, CO................................	102	43	78	35	57	10	47	4.0
Detroit-Warren-Dearborn, MI..................................	-4	24	112	87	-29	22	-50	-0.1
Hartford-West Hartford-East Hartford, CT...............	2	5	27	23	-2	11	-13	0.2
Houston-The Woodlands-Sugar Land, TX................	257	131	208	76	125	54	71	4.3
Indianapolis-Carmel-Anderson, IN..........................	41	28	61	33	13	8	5	2.2
Jacksonville, FL..	32	14	39	25	18	8	10	2.4
Kansas City, MO-KS..	29	27	62	35	2	7	-4	1.5
Las Vegas-Henderson-Paradise, NV.......................	49	31	61	30	19	15	3	2.5
Los Angeles-Long Beach-Anaheim, CA...................	224	217	391	173	10	113	-102	1.7
Louisville/Jefferson County, KY-IN.........................	16	10	36	25	5	5	1	1.3
Memphis, TN-MS-AR..	17	18	43	25	-1	4	-5	1.3
Miami-Fort Lauderdale-West Palm Beach, FL...........	198	43	148	104	155	111	44	3.6
Milwaukee-Waukesha-West Allis, WI......................	11	17	46	29	-6	5	-11	0.7
Minneapolis-St. Paul-Bloomington, MN-WI..............	73	53	100	47	21	23	-2	2.2
Nashville-Davidson--Murfreesboro--Franklin, TN.......	56	22	51	29	33	8	25	3.3
New Orleans-Metairie, LA......................................	37	12	36	23	24	6	18	3.1
New York-Newark-Jersey City, NY-NJ-PA................	264	251	563	312	16	269	-254	1.4
Oklahoma City, OK..	44	18	41	23	25	5	20	3.5
Orlando-Kissimmee-Sanford, FL.............................	89	25	59	33	64	32	32	4.2
Philadelphia-Camden-Wilmington, PA-NJ-DE-MD.......	53	49	166	117	6	38	-33	0.9
Phoenix-Mesa-Scottsdale, AZ................................	137	69	132	63	66	19	47	3.3
Pittsburgh, PA..	4	-7	53	60	13	6	7	0.2
Portland-Vancouver-Hillsboro, OR-WA....................	64	28	62	35	36	12	24	2.9
Providence-Warwick, RI-MA...................................	1	6	38	32	-5	9	-14	(Z)
Raleigh, NC..	58	21	35	14	37	8	29	5.1
Richmond, VA..	24	11	33	21	12	7	6	2.0
Riverside-San Bernardino-Ontario, CA....................	125	83	143	60	42	13	29	3.0
Sacramento--Roseville--Arden-Arcade, CA..............	47	29	63	34	19	14	4	2.2
St. Louis, MO-IL [2]...	8	22	77	55	-13	9	-22	0.3
Salt Lake City, UT...	36	29	43	14	7	6	2	3.3
San Antonio-New Braunfels, TX..............................	91	37	70	33	54	8	46	4.3
San Diego-Carlsbad, CA..	82	56	100	44	27	26	1	2.6
San Francisco-Oakland-Hayward, CA......................	120	54	117	64	68	49	19	2.8
San Jose-Sunnyvale-Santa Clara, CA.....................	57	35	56	22	24	30	-7	3.1
Seattle-Tacoma-Bellevue, WA................................	112	50	100	50	63	36	27	3.3
Tampa-St. Petersburg-Clearwater, FL.....................	60	4	69	65	56	20	36	2.1
Virginia Beach-Norfolk-Newport News, VA-NC..........	23	22	51	29	1	13	-12	1.4
Washington-Arlington-Alexandria, DC-VA-MD-WV......	224	108	179	70	115	80	35	4.0

Z Less than 500 or .05 percent. [1] Total population change includes residual. This residual represents the change in population that cannot be attributed to any specific demographic component of change. [2] The portion of Sullivan city in Crawford County, Missouri, is legally part of the St. Louis, MO-IL MSA. Data shown here do not include this area.

Source: U.S. Census Bureau, "Table 11. Cumulative Estimates of the Components of Population Change for Metropolitan and Micropolitan Statistical Areas: April 1, 2010 to July 1, 2012 (CBSA-EST2012-11)," March 2013, <http://www.census.gov/popest/data/metro/totals/2012/index.html>.

Table 27. States With Coastal Counties—Population and Housing Units, Establishments, and Employees by Coastal Region and State: 2010 to 2012

[308,748 represents 308,748,000. 2010 as of April 1, 2012 as of July 1. 2010 data reflect population estimates base. See headnote, Table 22. Minus sign (-) indicates decrease]

Coastal region and state	Population					Housing units			Private nonfarm [2]	
		2012				Number				
	2010 (1,000)	Number (1,000)	Percent of total state popu-lation	Percent change, 2010–2012	Per square mile, 2012 [1]	2010 (1,000)	2012 (1,000)	Percent change, 2010–2012	Establish-ments, 2011 (1,000)	Employees, 2011 (1,000)
United States, total......	**308,748**	**313,914**	**(X)**	**1.7**	**89**	**131,705**	**132,452**	**0.6**	**7,354**	**113,426**
Interior U.S................	149,149	151,586	(X)	1.6	57	64,704	65,164	0.7	3,438	54,830
Coastal counties, total...	**159,599**	**162,328**	**(X)**	**1.7**	**183**	**67,001**	**67,288**	**0.4**	**3,916**	**58,596**
Atlantic......................	70,217	71,416	(X)	1.7	486	29,908	30,042	0.5	1,824	26,792
Connecticut.................	3,574	3,590	100.0	0.5	741	1,488	1,488	(Z)	88	1,443
Delaware....................	898	917	100.0	2.1	471	406	410	1.1	24	360
District of Columbia.........	602	632	100.0	5.1	10,357	297	300	1.2	22	478
Florida......................	10,894	11,230	58.1	3.1	603	4,940	4,960	0.4	303	3,695
Georgia.....................	945	970	9.8	2.6	82	414	418	0.8	19	262
Maine.......................	1,239	1,241	93.4	0.2	61	667	669	0.4	37	452
Maryland....................	5,288	5,392	91.6	2.0	717	2,176	2,191	0.7	121	1,917
Massachusetts..............	6,318	6,415	96.5	1.5	976	2,712	2,714	0.1	164	2,838
New Hampshire..............	1,073	1,080	81.7	0.6	257	485	487	0.4	30	433
New Jersey..................	8,683	8,757	98.8	0.8	1,251	3,509	3,529	0.6	224	3,282
New York....................	13,952	14,149	72.3	1.4	1,831	5,601	5,614	0.2	400	5,394
North Carolina..............	2,233	2,263	23.2	1.3	116	1,069	1,084	1.3	46	604
Pennsylvania................	6,108	6,168	48.3	1.0	899	2,512	2,514	0.1	142	2,509
Rhode Island................	1,053	1,050	100.0	-0.2	1,016	463	463	-0.2	28	406
South Carolina..............	1,932	1,983	42.0	2.6	130	953	962	1.0	44	585
Virginia.....................	5,426	5,578	68.1	2.8	403	2,216	2,239	1.0	131	2,135
Gulf of Mexico..............	20,763	21,312	(X)	2.6	187	9,229	9,340	1.2	455	6,733
Alabama....................	765	772	16.0	1.0	89	363	366	0.9	17	240
Florida......................	7,436	7,613	39.4	2.4	244	3,832	3,853	0.6	177	2,166
Georgia.....................	98	98	1.0	0.1	61	43	43	0.2	2	26
Louisiana...................	3,548	3,611	78.5	1.8	142	1,533	1,551	1.2	82	1,274
Mississippi..................	629	638	21.4	1.5	94	280	285	1.7	12	182
Texas.......................	8,288	8,580	32.9	3.5	214	3,178	3,242	2.0	165	2,846
Great Lakes.................	27,190	27,227	(X)	0.1	236	12,128	12,119	-0.1	628	10,388
Illinois......................	5,898	5,933	46.1	0.6	4,272	2,441	2,435	-0.2	147	2,501
Indiana.....................	1,433	1,433	21.9	0.1	352	607	608	0.2	31	532
Michigan....................	8,797	8,804	89.1	0.1	173	4,050	4,044	-0.2	196	3,003
Minnesota..................	252	252	4.7	(Z)	24	132	132	0.1	7	95
New York....................	3,635	3,637	18.6	(Z)	170	1,647	1,648	0.1	82	1,340
Ohio........................	4,326	4,303	37.3	-0.5	409	1,967	1,965	-0.1	101	1,729
Pennsylvania................	281	281	2.2	(Z)	351	119	119	0.2	6	114
Wisconsin...................	2,569	2,584	45.1	0.6	168	1,165	1,168	0.2	58	1,072
Pacific......................	41,429	42,373	(X)	2.3	83	15,737	15,787	0.3	1,009	14,684
Alaska......................	598	616	84.3	3.0	2	255	256	0.3	17	220
California...................	32,259	32,977	86.7	2.2	424	11,803	11,822	0.2	763	11,320
Hawaii......................	1,360	1,392	100.0	2.4	217	520	524	0.9	31	486
Oregon.....................	1,982	2,017	51.7	1.8	96	895	899	0.4	58	743
Washington.................	5,229	5,370	77.9	2.7	218	2,264	2,285	0.9	139	1,914

X Not applicable. Z Less than .05 percent. [1] Calculated on the basis of land area data from the 2010 census. [2] Covers establishments with payroll. Excludes most government employees, railroad employees, and self-employed persons. Employees are for the week including March 12.

Source: U.S. Census Bureau, "County Totals Datasets: Population, Population Change and Estimated Components of Population Change: April 1, 2010 to July 1, 2012," March 2013, <http://www.census.gov/popest/data/counties/totals/2012/CO-EST2012-alldata.html>; and "Annual Estimates of Housing Units for the United States, Regions, Divisions, States, and Counties: April 1, 2010 to July 1, 2012" and "County Business Patterns"; <http://factfinder2.census.gov>, accessed July 2013.

Table 28. Population of Incorporated Places With 175,000 or More Inhabitants in 2012: 1990 to 2012

[In thousands, except as indicated (223 represents 223,000). As of April 1, except beginning 2011, as of July 1. Estimates are based on the 2010 Census and reflect changes to the April 1, 2010 population due to the Count Question Resolution program and geographic program revisions. All geographic boundaries for the 2012 population estimates series are defined as of January 1, 2012. For 1990 and 2000, the counts relate to places as defined on January 1, 2000. Data for 1970 and 1980 refer to boundaries in effect for those censuses. Minus sign (-) indicates decrease. See Appendix III]

City	Number (1,000)					Percent change		Rank, 2012
	1990	2000 [1]	2010	2011	2012	2000 to 2010 [1]	2010 to 2012	
Akron, OH	223	217	199	199	199	-8.3	-0.3	114
Albuquerque, NM	385	449	547	552	555	21.7	1.6	32
Amarillo, TX	158	174	191	194	195	9.8	2.4	119
Anaheim, CA	267	328	336	341	343	2.5	2.1	55
Anchorage, AK	226	260	292	296	299	12.1	2.3	63
Arlington, TX	262	333	365	371	376	9.8	2.8	50
Atlanta, GA	394	416	420	432	444	0.8	5.6	40
Augusta–Richmond County, GA [2]	186	200	196	196	198	-2.0	1.0	117
Aurora, CO	222	276	325	332	339	17.6	4.4	56
Aurora, IL	100	143	198	199	200	38.4	1.1	112
Austin, TX	466	657	791	817	843	20.4	6.6	11
Bakersfield, CA	175	247	348	354	359	40.6	3.2	52
Baltimore, MD	736	651	621	620	621	-4.6	0.1	26
Baton Rouge, LA	223	228	229	229	230	0.7	0.2	90
Birmingham, AL	265	243	212	212	212	-12.6	-0.1	100
Boise City, ID	126	186	206	209	212	10.7	3.0	99
Boston, MA	575	589	618	628	636	4.8	3.1	21
Brownsville, TX	114	140	175	178	180	25.3	2.9	131
Buffalo, NY	328	293	261	260	259	-10.7	-0.7	73
Chandler, AZ	90	177	236	240	246	33.7	4.0	80
Charlotte, NC	428	541	736	756	775	35.2	5.4	17
Chesapeake, VA	152	199	222	226	228	11.6	2.8	92
Chicago, IL	2,783	2,896	2,696	2,705	2,715	-6.9	0.7	3
Chula Vista, CA	135	174	244	248	252	40.5	3.5	76
Cincinnati, OH	364	331	297	296	297	-10.4	-0.1	65
Cleveland, OH	506	478	397	393	391	-17.1	-1.5	48
Colorado Springs, CO	280	361	416	426	432	15.4	3.7	41
Columbus, GA	[2] 179	[2] 186	190	194	198	1.9	4.5	116
Columbus, OH	633	711	789	799	810	10.6	2.7	15
Corpus Christi, TX	258	277	305	308	312	10.0	2.3	60
Dallas, TX	1,008	1,189	1,198	1,218	1,241	0.8	3.6	9
Denver, CO	468	555	600	619	634	8.2	5.7	23
Des Moines, IA	193	199	204	206	207	2.4	1.2	104
Detroit, MI	1,028	951	714	706	701	-25.0	-1.7	18
Durham, NC	137	187	228	234	239	22.1	4.8	83
El Paso, TX	515	564	649	664	673	15.2	3.6	19
Fayetteville, NC	76	121	201	201	202	65.7	0.8	107
Fontana, CA	88	129	196	200	202	52.1	2.9	110
Fort Wayne, IN	173	206	254	254	255	23.3	0.3	74
Fort Worth, TX	448	535	742	762	778	38.6	4.8	16
Fremont, CA	173	203	214	218	222	5.2	3.7	96
Fresno, CA	354	428	496	501	506	15.7	2.0	34
Garland, TX	181	216	227	230	234	5.1	2.9	86
Gilbert, AZ	29	110	208	214	221	90.0	6.1	97
Glendale, AZ	148	219	226	229	232	3.6	2.5	87
Glendale, CA	180	195	192	193	194	-1.7	1.4	122
Grand Prairie, TX	100	127	175	179	182	37.6	3.6	129
Grand Rapids, MI	189	198	188	189	190	-4.9	1.3	123
Greensboro, NC	184	224	270	273	277	20.4	2.7	69
Henderson, NV	65	175	258	260	266	47.0	3.1	71
Hialeah, FL	188	226	225	230	232	-0.8	3.2	88
Houston, TX	1,631	1,954	2,097	2,126	2,161	7.5	3.0	4
Huntington Beach, CA	182	190	191	193	195	0.2	1.9	121
Huntsville, AL	160	158	180	182	184	13.8	2.0	126
Indianapolis, IN [2]	731	792	820	828	835	3.6	1.8	13
Irvine, CA	110	143	212	221	230	48.4	8.5	91
Irving, TX	155	192	216	220	225	12.9	4.2	93
Jackson, MS	197	184	174	175	175	-5.8	1.1	135
Jacksonville, FL	635	736	822	829	837	11.7	1.8	12
Jersey City, NJ	229	240	248	252	254	3.1	2.8	75
Kansas City, MO	435	442	460	462	464	4.1	1.0	37
Knoxville, TN	165	174	179	181	182	2.9	1.9	128
Laredo, TX	123	177	236	241	245	33.7	3.7	81
Las Vegas, NV	258	478	584	588	596	22.0	2.2	31
Lexington–Fayette, KY	225	261	296	301	305	13.5	3.3	62
Lincoln, NE	192	226	258	262	265	14.5	2.7	72
Little Rock, AR	176	183	194	195	197	5.7	1.6	118
Long Beach, CA	429	462	462	465	468	0.2	1.2	36
Los Angeles, CA	3,486	3,695	3,793	3,823	3,858	2.6	1.7	2
Louisville/Jefferson County, KY [2]	[3] 270	[3] 256	597	602	605	(X)	1.3	27
Lubbock, TX	186	200	230	234	236	15.0	2.8	84
Madison, WI	191	208	233	237	240	12.1	3.0	82
Memphis, TN	610	650	647	651	655	-0.5	1.3	20
Mesa, AZ	288	396	440	445	452	10.8	2.8	38
Miami, FL	359	362	400	410	414	10.2	3.6	44
Milwaukee, WI	628	597	595	598	599	-0.4	0.7	30
Minneapolis, MN	368	383	383	388	393	0.0	2.7	47
Mobile, AL	196	199	195	195	195	-1.9	-0.1	120
Modesto, CA	165	189	201	202	204	6.5	1.2	106
Montgomery, AL	188	202	206	208	205	2.1	-0.1	105

See footnotes at end of table.

City	Number (1,000)					Percent change		Rank, 2012
	1990	2000 [1]	2010	2011	2012	2000 to 2010 [1]	2010 to 2012	
Moreno Valley, CA.............	119	142	193	197	200	35.8	3.2	113
Nashville–Davidson, TN [2].............	488	570	604	612	624	5.5	3.5	25
New Orleans, LA..................	497	485	344	360	369	-29.1	7.4	51
New York, NY..................	7,323	8,008	8,175	8,270	8,337	2.1	2.0	1
Newark, NJ..................	275	274	277	278	278	1.3	0.2	68
Newport News, VA..................	171	180	181	180	181	0.3	-0.1	130
Norfolk, VA..................	261	234	243	244	246	3.6	1.2	79
North Las Vegas, NV..................	48	115	217	219	223	87.9	3.0	95
Oakland, CA..................	372	399	391	396	401	-2.2	2.6	45
Oklahoma City, OK..................	445	506	580	589	599	14.6	3.3	29
Omaha, NE..................	336	390	410	416	422	4.9	2.9	43
Orlando, FL..................	165	186	238	243	250	28.2	4.7	77
Overland Park, KS..................	112	149	173	176	179	16.3	3.2	133
Oxnard, CA..................	143	170	198	200	202	16.2	1.8	111
Philadelphia, PA..................	1,586	1,518	1,526	1,539	1,548	0.6	1.4	5
Phoenix, AZ..................	983	1,321	1,448	1,464	1,489	9.4	2.8	6
Pittsburgh, PA..................	370	335	306	306	306	-8.6	0.2	61
Plano, TX..................	128	222	260	267	272	17.0	4.7	70
Portland, OR..................	439	529	584	594	603	10.3	3.3	28
Providence, RI..................	161	174	178	178	178	2.5	0.2	134
Raleigh, NC..................	212	276	404	414	423	46.3	4.8	42
Reno, NV..................	134	180	226	229	231	24.8	2.2	89
Richmond, VA..................	203	198	204	206	210	3.2	3.0	102
Riverside, CA..................	227	255	304	310	314	19.1	3.2	59
Rochester, NY..................	230	220	211	211	211	-4.2	(Z)	101
Sacramento, CA..................	369	407	466	472	476	14.6	1.9	35
Salt Lake City, UT..................	160	182	186	188	189	2.6	1.5	124
San Antonio, TX..................	935	1,145	1,328	1,358	1,383	16.0	4.2	7
San Bernardino, CA..................	165	185	210	212	213	13.2	1.6	98
San Diego, CA..................	1,111	1,223	1,302	1,320	1,338	6.9	2.8	8
San Francisco, CA..................	724	777	805	814	826	3.7	2.6	14
San Jose, CA..................	782	895	953	970	983	5.7	3.2	10
Santa Ana, CA..................	294	338	325	328	331	-4.0	2.0	57
Santa Clarita, CA..................	111	151	176	178	179	16.7	1.5	132
Scottsdale, AZ..................	130	203	217	220	224	7.2	2.8	94
Seattle, WA..................	516	563	609	622	635	8.0	4.3	22
Shreveport, LA..................	199	200	200	202	202	-0.4	0.7	109
Spokane, WA..................	177	196	209	209	210	6.8	(Z)	103
St. Louis, MO..................	397	348	319	319	318	-8.3	-0.4	58
St. Paul, MN..................	272	287	285	289	291	-0.7	2.0	66
St. Petersburg, FL..................	240	248	245	245	247	-1.4	0.7	78
Stockton, CA..................	211	244	292	296	298	19.7	2.1	64
Tacoma, WA..................	177	194	198	200	202	2.5	1.8	108
Tallahassee, FL..................	125	151	181	183	187	20.4	3.1	125
Tampa, FL..................	280	303	336	346	348	10.6	3.6	53
Toledo, OH..................	333	314	287	286	284	-8.4	-1.1	67
Tucson, AZ..................	405	487	520	523	524	6.9	0.8	33
Tulsa, OK..................	367	393	392	392	394	-0.3	0.5	46
Urban Honolulu CDP, HI [4]..................	(NA)	(NA)	337	342	346	(NA)	2.5	54
Virginia Beach, VA..................	393	425	438	443	447	3.0	2.1	39
Washington, DC..................	607	572	602	619	632	5.2	5.1	24
Wichita, KS..................	304	344	382	384	386	11.1	0.8	49
Winston–Salem, NC..................	143	186	230	232	234	23.6	2.1	85
Worcester, MA..................	170	173	181	182	183	4.9	0.9	127
Yonkers, NY..................	188	196	196	198	198	-0.1	1.3	115

NA Not available. X Not applicable. Z Less than .05 percent. [1] Based on 2000 Census numbers as tabulated. [2] Represents the portion of a consolidated city that is not within one or more separately incorporated places. [3] Data are for the incorporated place of Louisville city before consolidation of the city and county governments. [4] CDP=Census Designated Place.

Source: U.S. Census Bureau, 1990 data: *1990 Census of Population and Housing, Population and Housing Unit Counts*, and *1990 CPH-L-157 Corrected Counts*; 2000 Census data: *2000 Census of Population and Housing, Population and Housing Unit Counts PHC-3* and *Census of Population and Housing, 2010, CPH-2. Population and Housing Unit Counts*; and beginning 2010: "Annual Estimates of the Resident Population for Incorporated Places Over 50,000, Ranked by July 1, 2012 Population: April 1, 2010 to July 1, 2012," May 2013, <http://www.census.gov/popest/data/cities/totals/2012/index.html>.

Table 29. Incorporated Places by Population Size: 1990 to 2012

[153.1 represents 153,100,000. See Appendix III]

Population size	Number of incorporated places				Population (mil.)				Percent of total			
	1990	2000	2010	2012	1990	2000	2010	2012	1990	2000	2010	2012
Total.....................	19,262	19,452	19,540	19,516	153.1	173.5	192.0	196.3	100.0	100.0	100.0	100.0
1,000,000 or more.........	8	9	9	9	20.0	22.9	23.6	24.1	13.1	13.2	12.3	12.3
500,000 to 999,999.........	15	20	24	25	10.1	12.9	16.1	17.1	6.6	7.4	8.4	8.7
250,000 to 499,999.........	41	37	40	42	14.2	13.3	14.0	14.6	9.3	7.7	7.3	7.4
100,000 to 249,999.........	131	172	200	213	19.1	25.5	30.2	31.9	12.5	14.7	15.7	16.3
50,000 to 99,999...........	309	363	432	437	21.2	24.9	30.1	30.4	13.8	14.4	15.7	15.5
25,000 to 49,999...........	567	644	723	720	20.0	22.6	25.2	25.1	13.1	13.0	13.1	12.8
10,000 to 24,999...........	1,290	1,435	1,542	1,545	20.3	22.6	24.2	24.4	13.3	13.0	12.6	12.4
Under 10,000...............	16,901	16,772	16,570	16,525	28.2	28.7	28.7	28.7	18.4	16.5	14.9	14.6

Source: U.S. Census Bureau, *1990 Census of Population and Housing, Population and Housing Unit Counts (CPH-2-1)*; *Census 2000 PHC-3, Population and Housing Unit Counts*; *2010 Census Redistricting Data (Public Law 94-171) Summary File*; and "Annual Estimates of the Resident Population for Incorporated Places Over 50,000, Ranked by July 1, 2012 Population: April 1, 2010 to July 1, 2012", May 2013, <http://www.census.gov/popest/data/cities/totals/2012/index.html>.

Table 30. Urban and Rural Population by State: 2000 and 2010

[222,361 represents 222,361,000. As of April 1. Resident population. Based on current urban definitions, see text, this section]

State	2000		2010			State	2000		2010		
	Urban (1,000)	Rural (1,000)	Urban Number (1,000)	Urban Percent	Rural (1,000)		Urban (1,000)	Rural (1,000)	Urban Number (1,000)	Urban Percent	Rural (1,000)
U.S. total....	222,361	59,061	249,253	80.7	59,492						
						MO.........	3,883	1,712	4,218	70.4	1,771
AL.........	2,466	1,981	2,822	59.0	1,958	MT.........	488	414	553	55.9	436
AK.........	411	216	469	66.0	241	NE.........	1,194	518	1,336	73.1	491
AZ.........	4,524	607	5,741	89.8	651	NV.........	1,829	170	2,544	94.2	157
AR.........	1,404	1,269	1,638	56.2	1,278	NH.........	732	503	794	60.3	523
CA.........	31,990	1,882	35,374	95.0	1,880	NJ.........	7,939	475	8,324	94.7	468
CO.........	3,633	668	4,333	86.2	696	NM.........	1,364	456	1,594	77.4	465
CT.........	2,988	418	3,145	88.0	429	NY.........	16,603	2,374	17,028	87.9	2,350
DE.........	628	156	748	83.3	150	NC.........	4,849	3,200	6,302	66.1	3,234
DC.........	572	0	602	100.0	0	ND.........	359	283	403	59.9	270
FL.........	14,270	1,712	17,140	91.2	1,661						
						OH.........	8,782	2,571	8,990	77.9	2,547
GA.........	5,864	2,322	7,272	75.1	2,416	OK.........	2,255	1,196	2,485	66.2	1,266
HI.........	1,108	103	1,250	91.9	110	OR.........	2,694	727	3,104	81.0	727
ID.........	859	434	1,106	70.6	461	PA.........	9,464	2,817	9,991	78.7	2,711
IL.........	10,910	1,510	11,354	88.5	1,477	RI.........	953	95	955	90.7	98
IN.........	4,304	1,776	4,697	72.4	1,787	SC.........	2,427	1,585	3,068	66.3	1,558
IA.........	1,787	1,139	1,950	64.0	1,096	SD.........	391	363	461	56.7	353
KS.........	1,921	768	2,117	74.2	736	TN.........	3,620	2,069	4,213	66.4	2,133
KY.........	2,254	1,788	2,533	58.4	1,806	TX.........	17,204	3,648	21,298	84.7	3,848
LA.........	3,246	1,223	3,318	73.2	1,216	UT.........	1,970	263	2,504	90.6	260
ME.........	513	762	514	38.7	815						
						VT.........	232	376	243	38.9	382
MD.........	4,559	738	5,034	87.2	739	VA.........	5,170	1,909	6,037	75.5	1,964
MA.........	5,801	548	6,022	92.0	526	WA.........	4,831	1,063	5,652	84.1	1,073
MI.........	7,419	2,519	7,370	74.6	2,514	WV.........	833	976	903	48.7	950
MN.........	3,490	1,429	3,886	73.3	1,418	WI.........	3,664	1,700	3,990	70.2	1,697
MS.........	1,387	1,457	1,464	49.4	1,503	WY.........	321	172	365	64.8	199

Source: U.S. Census Bureau, 2000 Census of Population and Housing, *Population and Housing Unit Counts PHC-3*; 2010 Census of Population and Housing, *Population and Housing Unit Counts, CPH-2-1, United States Summary*; and "Percent Urban and Rural in 2010 by State," <http://www2.census.gov/geo/ua/>, accessed March 2013.

Table 31. Mobility Status of the Population by Selected Characteristics: 1981 to 2012

[As of March (221,641 represents 221,641,000). For persons 1 year old and over. Based on comparison of place of residence in immediate prior year and year shown. Excludes members of the Armed Forces except those living off post or with their families on post. Based on Current Population Survey, Annual Social and Economic Supplement. See text, this section and Appendix III. For composition of regions, see map, inside front cover]

Mobility period and characteristic	Total (1,000)	Non–movers	Movers (different house in United States) Total	Same county	Different county Total	Same state	Different state	Movers from abroad
1981	221,641	83	17	10	6	3	3	1
1991	244,884	83	16	10	6	3	3	1
2001	275,611	86	14	8	6	3	3	1
2011	302,005	88	11	8	4	2	2	–
2012, total	**304,924**	**88**	**12**	**8**	**4**	**2**	**2**	**–**
1 to 4 years old	16,207	81	19	13	6	3	2	1
5 to 9 years old	20,416	86	14	10	4	2	2	–
10 to 14 years old	20,605	88	11	8	3	2	1	–
15 to 19 years old	21,239	88	11	8	4	2	1	–
20 to 24 years old	21,878	75	24	16	8	4	3	1
25 to 29 years old	20,893	75	24	15	8	4	4	1
30 to 44 years old	60,253	86	13	9	4	3	2	–
45 to 64 years old	81,926	93	7	4	2	1	1	–
65 to 74 years old	23,383	96	4	2	2	1	1	–
75 to 84 years old	13,117	97	3	2	1	-	1	–
85 years old and over	5,006	97	3	2	1	1	1	–
Northeast	54,373	92	8	5	3	1	1	1
Midwest	65,311	89	11	7	4	2	1	–
South	113,565	87	13	8	5	3	2	–
West	71,675	86	13	9	4	2	2	1
Persons 16 years old and over	243,538	89	11	7	4	2	2	–
Civilian labor force	154,213	87	12	8	4	2	2	–
Employed	140,970	88	12	8	4	2	2	–
Unemployed	13,243	81	18	11	7	3	3	1
Armed Forces	936	71	26	9	17	4	13	3
Not in labor force	88,390	91	8	6	3	2	1	–
Employed civilians, 16 years old and over	140,970	88	12	8	4	2	2	–
Management, business, and financial	22,054	90	9	6	4	2	2	–
Professional	31,103	89	11	6	4	2	2	–
Service	25,373	85	15	11	4	3	2	–
Sales	15,180	87	13	8	5	3	2	–
Office and administrative support	18,058	88	11	8	3	2	1	–
Farming, fishing, and forestry	927	86	13	10	4	1	2	1
Construction and extraction	6,754	88	12	9	3	2	1	–
Installation, maintenance, and repair	4,628	90	9	6	3	2	1	–
Production	8,502	88	12	8	3	2	1	–
Transportation and material moving	8,390	87	13	9	4	2	1	–
Tenure:								
Owner occupied units	204,716	95	5	3	2	1	1	–
Renter occupied units	96,608	73	26	18	8	5	4	1
No cash renter occupied units	3,600	82	17	11	6	3	3	2

– Represents or rounds to zero.

Source: U.S. Census Bureau, "Geographical Mobility: 2011 to 2012," December 2012, <http://www.census.gov/hhes/migration/data/cps/cps2012.html> and previous reports.

Table 32. Movers by Type of Move and Reason for Moving: 2012

[As of March (36,488 represents 36,488,000). For persons 1 year old and over. Based on comparison of place of residence in 2011 and 2012. Excludes members of the Armed Forces except those living off post or with their families on post. Based on Current Population Survey, Annual Social and Economic Supplement. See text, this section and Appendix III]

Reason for move	All movers	Intra-county	Inter-county	From abroad	Reason for move	All movers	Intra-county	Inter-county	From abroad
Total (1,000)	**36,488**	**23,493**	**11,842**	**1,154**	Housing–related reasons	49.4	58.8	32.9	28.0
PERCENT DISTRIBUTION					Wanted to own home/ not rent	4.7	6.1	2.3	0.8
Total	100.0	100.0	100.0	100.0	New/better house/ apartment	15.9	21.0	7.3	1.4
					Better neighborhood/less crime	3.4	3.8	2.8	0.4
Family–related reasons	29.3	30.3	27.4	29.2	Cheaper housing	8.9	11.4	4.9	0.8
Change in marital status	6.3	6.6	6.1	3.2	Foreclosure/eviction	2.2	2.5	1.5	1.1
To establish own household	10.7	13.0	6.1	10.5	Other housing	14.4	14.0	14.1	23.5
Other family reasons	12.3	10.7	15.2	15.5	Other reasons	1.9	1.5	2.6	4.0
Work–related reasons	19.3	9.5	37.1	38.6	Attend/leave college	0.5	0.3	0.8	2.4
New job/job transfer	9.5	2.2	22.5	25.5	Change of climate	–	–	0.1	–
To look for work/lost job	1.8	0.9	3.1	6.8	Health reasons	0.3	0.2	0.4	–
Closer to work/easier commute	5.5	5.2	6.4	2.3	Natural disaster	0.2	0.1	0.2	–
Retired	0.5	0.2	1.0	0.9	Other reason	0.9	0.8	1.1	1.6
Other job–related reason	2.1	1.0	4.1	3.1					

– Represents or rounds to zero.

Source: U.S. Census Bureau, "Geographical Mobility: 2011 to 2012," December 2012, <http://www.census.gov/hhes/migration/data/cps/cps2012.html>.

Table 33. Mobility Status of Households by Household Income: 2012

[As of March (121,107 represents 121,107,000). Covers householders 15 years old and over. Based on comparison of place of residence in 2011 and 2012. Excludes members of the Armed Forces except those living off post or with their families on post. Based on Current Population Survey, Annual Social and Economic Supplement. See text, this section and Appendix III]

| Household income in 2011 | Total (1,000) | Non–movers | Movers (different house in United States) | | Different county | | | Movers from abroad |
			Total	Same county	Total	Same state	Different state	
Householders, 15 years and over	**121,107**	**88**	**11**	**7**	**4**	**2**	**2**	–
Under $5,000 or loss	4,270	77	21	14	7	4	3	2
$5,000 to $9,999	4,974	83	17	13	4	2	2	–
$10,000 to $14,999	7,127	86	14	10	4	2	2	–
$15,000 to $24,999	13,977	86	14	10	4	2	2	–
$25,000 to $34,999	13,260	87	13	9	4	2	2	–
$35,000 to $49,999	16,877	87	13	9	4	3	2	–
$50,000 to $69,999	17,688	89	10	7	3	2	1	–
$70,000 to $99,999	17,511	91	8	5	3	2	1	–
$100,000 and over	25,423	93	7	4	3	2	1	–

– Represents or rounds to zero.

Source: U.S. Census Bureau, "Geographical Mobility: 2011 to 2012," December 2012, <http://www.census.gov/hhes/migration/data/cps/cps2012.html>.

Table 34. Mobility Status of Resident Population by State: 2011

[In percent, except as indicated (307,900 represents 307,900,000). Based on comparison of place of residence in 2010 and 2011. The American Community Survey universe includes the household population and the population living in institutions, college dormitories, and other group quarters. Based on a sample and subject to sampling variability. See text, this section and Appendix III]

| State | Population 1 year old and over [1] (1,000) | Same house in 2010 | Different house in United States in 2010 | | State | Population 1 year old and over [1] (1,000) | Same house in 2010 | Different house in United States in 2010 | |
			Same county	Different county				Same county	Different county
U.S.	**307,900**	**84.8**	**9.2**	**5.4**	MO	5,938	83.6	9.0	7.0
AL	4,745	84.8	9.3	5.6	MT	987	83.9	9.1	6.7
AK	712	80.3	11.4	7.7	NE	1,817	82.8	10.3	6.5
AZ	6,402	79.8	14.1	5.5	NV	2,688	77.5	17.0	5.0
AR	2,907	83.3	10.5	5.8	NH	1,306	87.4	7.1	5.1
CA	37,223	83.9	11.3	4.1	NJ	8,720	89.7	5.9	3.7
CO	5,048	80.2	9.9	9.2	NM	2,055	85.3	8.8	5.4
CT	3,549	88.5	7.0	3.9	NY	19,249	88.6	6.7	3.9
DE	897	86.4	8.3	4.7	NC	9,539	84.6	8.7	6.2
DC	612	80.1	10.9	7.9	ND	675	82.9	8.6	8.0
FL	18,864	83.5	10.0	5.6	OH	11,419	85.5	9.5	4.7
GA	9,700	83.5	8.4	7.7	OK	3,743	82.5	9.9	7.1
HI	1,358	85.5	8.5	4.8	OR	3,829	81.7	10.8	6.8
ID	1,560	82.4	10.0	7.2	PA	12,610	88.0	7.3	4.3
IL	12,718	87.1	8.2	4.1	RI	1,040	86.9	8.2	4.2
IN	6,437	85.1	9.1	5.5	SC	4,624	84.3	8.8	6.4
IA	3,028	85.0	8.3	6.2	SD	814	84.6	7.8	7.2
KS	2,834	83.7	9.5	6.3	TN	6,333	84.4	9.4	5.8
KY	4,316	85.4	8.4	5.9	TX	25,327	82.9	10.6	5.8
LA	4,519	85.5	8.5	5.7	UT	2,770	82.9	10.5	6.1
ME	1,316	85.1	8.6	6.0	VT	621	86.5	7.6	5.4
MD	5,759	87.0	7.0	5.2	VA	7,997	84.9	6.5	7.8
MA	6,515	86.9	7.4	4.8	WA	6,748	82.5	10.8	5.9
MI	9,767	85.4	8.9	5.2	WV	1,837	87.6	6.9	5.2
MN	5,277	85.4	7.5	6.6	WI	5,647	85.8	8.7	5.2
MS	2,943	86.1	7.6	6.0	WY	561	82.4	9.1	8.2

[1] Includes persons moving from abroad, not shown separately.

Source: U.S. Census Bureau, 2011 American Community Survey, B07003, "Residence 1 Year Ago by Sex," <http://factfinder2.census.gov/>, accessed April 2013.

Table 35. Persons 65 Years Old and Over—Characteristics by Sex: 2000 to 2012

[As of March, except as noted (32.6 represents 32,600,000). Covers civilian noninstitutional population. Excludes members of Armed Forces except those living off post or with their families on post. Data for 2000 data based on 1990 Census population controls; data for 2005 and 2010 based on 2000 Census population controls; data for 2012 based on 2010 Census population controls. Beginning 2005, data based on an expanded sample of households. Based on Current Population Survey. See text, this section and Appendix III]

Characteristic	Total				Male				Female			
	2000	2005	2010	2012	2000	2005	2010	2012	2000	2005	2010	2012
Total (million).........................	**32.6**	**35.2**	**38.6**	**41.5**	**13.9**	**15.1**	**16.8**	**18.3**	**18.7**	**20.0**	**21.8**	**23.2**
PERCENT DISTRIBUTION												
Marital status:												
Never married............................	3.9	4.1	4.3	4.4	4.2	4.4	4.1	4.5	3.6	3.9	4.5	4.3
Married....................................	57.2	57.7	57.6	59.1	75.2	74.9	74.5	74.6	43.8	44.7	44.5	46.7
Spouse present.......................	54.6	54.8	55.2	56.8	72.6	71.7	71.7	72.1	41.3	42.0	42.4	44.6
Spouse absent [1]...................	2.6	2.9	2.4	2.3	2.6	3.2	2.8	2.5	2.5	2.7	2.1	2.1
Widowed...................................	32.1	30.3	28.1	25.7	14.4	13.7	12.7	11.5	45.3	42.9	39.9	36.9
Divorced..................................	6.7	7.9	10.0	10.9	6.1	7.0	8.7	9.4	7.2	8.5	11.1	12.0
Educational attainment:												
Less than ninth grade...................	16.7	13.4	10.2	9.0	17.8	13.2	10.2	9.0	15.9	13.5	10.1	9.0
Completed 9th to 12th grade, but no high school diploma............	13.8	12.7	10.3	9.9	12.7	11.9	9.7	9.0	14.7	13.3	10.8	10.6
High school graduate....................	35.9	36.3	36.4	35.6	30.4	31.6	32.0	30.6	39.9	39.9	39.8	39.5
Some college or associate's degree....................................	18.0	18.7	20.6	21.3	17.8	18.4	19.7	21.2	18.2	19.0	21.2	21.4
Bachelor's or advanced degree....................................	15.6	18.9	22.5	24.3	21.4	24.9	28.4	30.2	11.4	14.3	18.0	19.6
Labor force participation: [2]												
Employed.................................	12.4	14.5	16.2	17.3	16.9	19.1	20.5	22.1	9.1	11.1	12.9	13.5
Unemployed..............................	0.4	0.5	1.2	1.2	0.6	0.7	1.6	1.5	0.3	0.4	0.9	0.9
Not in labor force.......................	87.2	84.9	82.6	81.5	82.5	80.2	77.9	76.4	90.6	88.5	86.2	85.6
Percent below poverty level [3]...........	9.7	9.8	8.9	8.7	6.9	7.0	6.6	6.2	11.8	11.9	10.7	10.7

[1] Includes separated. [2] Annual averages of monthly figures. Source: U.S. Bureau of Labor Statistics, "Labor Force Characteristics," <http://www.bls.gov/cps/lfcharacteristics.htm#laborforce>. See footnote 2, Table 613. [3] Poverty status based on income in preceding year.

Source: Except as noted, U.S. Census Bureau, Current Population Reports, "The Older Population in the United States: March 2000 Detailed Tables," <http://www.census.gov/population/age/data/2000.html>; "Educational Attainment," <http://www.census.gov/hhes/socdemo/education/>; "Families and Living Arrangements," <http://www.census.gov/hhes/families/data/cps.html>; and "Detailed Poverty Tabulations from the CPS," <http://www.census.gov/hhes/www/cpstables/032012/pov/toc.htm>; accessed April 2013.

Table 36. Persons 65 Years and Over—Living Arrangements and Disability Status: 2011

[In thousands (41,385 represents 41,385,000), except as indicated. Based on the American Community Survey (ACS). Disability data limited to civilian noninstitutionalized population. Based on a sample and subject to sampling variability; see text, this section and Appendix III]

Relationship by household type	Number	Percent distribu- tion	Type of disability	Total	65 to 74 years old	75 years old and over
Total................................	**41,385**	**100.0**	**Persons with any disability**........	**14,659**	**5,660**	**8,999**
In households...........................	39,912	96.4				
In family households.................	27,603	66.7	With a hearing difficulty................	6,030	2,004	4,026
Householder.........................	13,686	33.1	With a vision difficulty.................	2,728	909	1,819
Spouse..............................	9,861	23.8	With a cognitive difficulty.............	3,784	1,212	2,572
Parent...............................	2,308	5.6	With an ambulatory difficulty..........	9,470	3,543	5,927
Other relatives......................	1,549	3.7	With a self-care difficulty.............	3,550	1,039	2,512
Nonrelatives........................	199	0.5	With an independent living difficulty...	6,492	1,820	4,672
In nonfamily households.............	12,309	29.7				
Householder.........................	11,719	28.3				
Living alone........................	11,112	26.9				
Not living alone....................	607	1.5				
Nonrelatives........................	590	1.4				
In group quarters.....................	1,473	3.6				

Source: U.S. Census Bureau, 2011 American Community Survey, B09017, "Relationship by Household Type (Including Living Alone) for the Population 65 Years and Over;" B18101, "Sex by Age by Disability Status;" B18102, "Sex by Age by Hearing Difficulty;" B18103, "Sex by Age by Vision Difficulty;" B18104, "Sex by Age by Cognitive Difficulty;" B18105, "Sex by Age by Ambulatory Difficulty;" B18106, "Sex by Age by Self-Care Difficulty;" and B18107, "Sex by Age by Independent Living Difficulty;" <http://factfinder2.census.gov>, accessed April 2013.

Table 37. Selected Characteristics of Racial Groups and Hispanic or Latino Population: 2011

[In thousands (206,472 represents 206,472,000), except as indicated. The American Community Survey universe includes the household population and the population living in institutions, college dormitories, and other group quarters. Based on a sample and subject to sampling variability; see text, this section and Appendix III]

Characteristic	Total population	White alone	Black or African American alone	American Indian, Alaska Native alone	Asian alone	Native Hawaiian and Other Pacific Islander alone	Some other race alone	Two or more races	Hispanic or Latino origin [1]	White alone, not Hispanic or Latino
EDUCATIONAL ATTAINMENT										
Persons 25 years old and over, total	**206,472**	**158,845**	**23,898**	**1,502**	**10,242**	**290**	**8,153**	**3,542**	**28,158**	**140,304**
Less than 9th grade	12,318	7,714	1,210	120	902	14	2,120	239	6,175	3,886
9th to 12th grade, no diploma	16,772	11,289	2,984	197	620	30	1,346	306	4,189	8,639
High school graduate (includes equivalency)	58,653	45,797	7,537	472	1,603	105	2,281	860	7,625	40,826
Some college, no degree	43,822	33,893	5,797	394	1,320	76	1,266	896	4,894	30,612
Associate's degree	16,016	12,722	1,790	120	674	24	372	314	1,551	11,649
Bachelor's degree	36,915	29,763	2,841	134	3,005	30	552	591	2,560	27,906
Graduate degree	21,975	17,667	1,560	65	2,117	13	216	337	1,164	16,786
OCCUPATION										
Employed civilian population, 16 years old and over, total	**140,400**	**107,791**	**15,137**	**918**	**7,305**	**215**	**6,331**	**2,702**	**21,331**	**93,916**
Management, business, science, and arts occupations	50,509	40,611	4,272	240	3,544	52	922	867	4,089	37,700
Management, business, and financial occupations	20,103	16,603	1,527	93	1,150	23	387	319	1,667	15,417
Computer, engineering, and science occupations	7,362	5,562	467	27	1,055	6	104	141	489	5,210
Education, legal, community service, arts, and media occupations	15,181	12,352	1,488	86	647	16	315	276	1,393	11,372
Healthcare practitioners and technical occupations	7,863	6,094	790	34	691	7	116	130	541	5,700
Service occupations	25,740	17,787	3,936	228	1,273	55	1,850	611	5,700	14,247
Sales and office occupations	34,448	26,797	3,843	210	1,543	57	1,293	705	4,732	23,636
Natural resources, construction, and maintenance occupations	12,749	10,261	822	114	242	18	1,075	216	3,256	8,204
Farming, fishing, and forestry occupations	1,059	787	46	12	15	1	183	14	538	448
Construction and extraction occupations	7,002	5,620	425	65	95	11	667	119	1,954	4,401
Installation, maintenance, and repair occupations	4,688	3,854	350	37	133	6	225	82	763	3,355
Production, transportation, and material moving occupations	16,955	12,335	2,264	126	703	33	1,191	304	3,554	10,130
Production occupations	8,399	6,165	937	63	460	13	624	138	1,816	5,048
Transportation occupations	4,972	3,694	754	34	144	9	249	88	798	3,184
Material moving occupations	3,583	2,476	574	29	99	11	317	78	940	1,898
FAMILY INCOME IN THE PAST 12 MONTHS										
Total families	**76,084**	**58,947**	**8,726**	**557**	**3,446**	**101**	**3,026**	**1,280**	**10,541**	**51,980**
Less than $10,000	3,871	2,250	1,044	64	138	7	272	96	847	1,733
$10,000 to $19,999	5,824	3,738	1,190	73	217	10	459	136	1,437	2,835
$20,000 to $29,999	7,077	5,024	1,136	72	237	10	458	141	1,545	4,014
$30,000 to $39,999	7,136	5,297	980	64	254	11	402	129	1,309	4,451
$40,000 to $49,999	6,783	5,220	820	54	241	10	319	118	1,088	4,506
$50,000 to $59,999	6,338	4,999	694	44	237	7	252	104	885	4,412
$60,000 to $74,999	8,375	6,771	789	52	339	10	283	130	1,013	6,092
$75,000 to $99,999	10,561	8,698	882	61	463	12	285	161	1,051	7,987
$100,000 to $124,999	7,259	6,066	513	34	383	12	147	104	600	5,647
$125,000 to $149,999	4,252	3,577	280	16	250	5	68	56	306	3,357
$150,000 to $199,999	4,374	3,676	245	13	328	6	51	54	275	3,464
$200,000 or more	4,234	3,630	153	10	359	3	30	50	187	3,481
Median family income in the past 12 months (dol.)[2]	61,455	66,025	40,140	40,962	77,742	54,485	37,430	51,603	40,982	69,715
POVERTY STATUS IN THE PAST 12 MONTHS [3]										
Persons below poverty level	48,452	29,261	10,543	725	1,888	106	4,122	1,808	13,126	21,123
Families below poverty level	8,939	5,330	2,101	136	331	18	794	229	2,443	3,815
HOUSING TENURE										
Total households	**114,992**	**89,717**	**13,879**	**814**	**4,644**	**130**	**3,841**	**1,965**	**13,369**	**80,687**
Owner-occupied	74,264	62,594	6,027	437	2,680	52	1,488	985	6,299	58,071
Renter-occupied	40,727	27,123	7,852	377	1,964	78	2,353	980	7,070	22,615

[1] Persons of Hispanic origin may be of any race. [2] For definition of median, see Guide to Tabular Presentation. [3] For explanation of poverty level, see text, Section 13.

Source: U.S. Census Bureau, 2011 American Community Survey, Tables B15002, B24010, B19101, B19113, B17001, B17010, and B25003, <http://factfinder2.census.gov/>, accessed April 2013.

Table 38. Social and Economic Characteristics of the Hispanic Population: 2011

[As of March, except labor force status, annual average (49,972 represents 49,972,000). Excludes members of the Armed Forces except those living off post or with their families on post. Based on Current Population Survey; see text, this section and Appendix III]

Characteristic	Number (1,000)					Percent distribution				
	His-panic, total [1]	Mexi-can	Puerto Rican	Central Ameri-can [2]	South Ameri-can [2]	His-panic, total [1]	Mexi-can	Puerto Rican	Central Ameri-can [2]	South Ameri-can [2]
Total persons	**49,972**	**32,539**	**4,625**	**4,205**	**2,830**	**100.0**	**100.0**	**100.0**	**100.0**	**100.0**
Under 5 years old	5,542	3,965	461	386	247	11.1	12.2	10.0	9.2	8.7
5 to 14 years old	9,360	6,620	865	630	373	18.7	20.4	18.7	15.0	13.1
15 to 44 years old	23,597	15,476	2,002	2,280	1,336	47.3	47.6	43.3	54.2	47.1
45 to 64 years old	8,616	5,024	917	741	654	17.2	15.4	19.8	17.7	23.1
65 years old and over	2,857	1,454	380	167	221	5.7	4.5	8.2	4.0	7.8
EDUCATIONAL ATTAINMENT										
Persons 25 years old and over	**26,672**	**16,300**	**2,564**	**2,476**	**1,835**	**100.0**	**100.0**	**100.0**	**100.0**	**100.0**
High school graduate or more	17,158	9,498	1,962	1,351	1,568	64.3	58.3	76.5	54.6	85.5
Bachelor's degree or more	3,759	1,616	461	263	581	14.1	9.9	18.0	10.6	31.7
LABOR FORCE STATUS [3]										
Civilians 16 years old and over	**34,438**	**21,519**	**3,201**	**(NA)**	**(NA)**	**100.0**	**100.0**	**100.0**	**(NA)**	**(NA)**
Civilian labor force	22,898	14,360	1,893	(NA)	(NA)	66.5	66.7	59.1	(NA)	(NA)
Employed	20,269	12,697	1,627	(NA)	(NA)	58.9	59.0	50.8	(NA)	(NA)
Unemployed	2,629	1,663	266	(NA)	(NA)	7.6	7.7	8.3	(NA)	(NA)
Unemployment rate [4]	11.5	11.6	14.1	(NA)	(NA)	(X)	(X)	(X)	(NA)	(NA)
Male	11.2	11.2	14.7	(NA)	(NA)	(X)	(X)	(X)	(NA)	(NA)
Female	11.8	12.2	13.5	(NA)	(NA)	(X)	(X)	(X)	(NA)	(NA)
Not in labor force	11,540	7,159	1,307	(NA)	(NA)	33.5	33.3	40.8	(NA)	(NA)
HOUSEHOLDS [5]										
Total	**13,665**	**8,231**	**1,510**	**1,122**	**875**	**100.0**	**100.0**	**100.0**	**100.0**	**100.0**
Family households	10,659	6,669	1,096	877	658	78.0	81.0	72.6	78.2	75.2
Married-couple families	6,725	4,293	566	527	481	49.2	52.2	37.4	46.9	55.0
Male householder, no spouse present	1,180	744	126	125	56	8.6	9.0	8.3	11.2	6.4
Female householder, no spouse present	2,754	1,632	405	225	121	20.2	19.8	26.8	20.1	13.8
Nonfamily households	3,006	1,562	414	245	217	22.0	19.0	27.4	21.8	24.8
Male householder	1,635	905	203	135	117	12.0	11.0	13.4	12.0	13.3
Female householder	1,371	657	212	110	100	10.0	8.0	14.0	9.8	11.5
Size:										
One person	2,197	1,106	336	175	148	16.1	13.4	22.3	15.6	16.9
Two people	3,166	1,686	445	209	232	23.2	20.5	29.5	18.6	26.5
Three people	2,546	1,434	309	226	209	18.6	17.4	20.4	20.2	23.9
Four people	2,647	1,736	240	223	150	19.4	21.1	15.9	19.9	17.1
Five or more people	3,109	2,269	181	289	136	22.7	27.6	12.0	25.7	15.5
FAMILY INCOME IN 2010										
Total families	**10,659**	**6,669**	**1,096**	**877**	**658**	**100.0**	**100.0**	**100.0**	**100.0**	**100.0**
Less than $5,000	406	271	59	27	8	3.8	4.1	5.4	3.1	1.2
$5,000 to $14,999	1,025	667	129	72	31	9.6	10.0	11.8	8.3	4.6
$15,000 to $24,999	1,494	1,007	149	135	61	14.0	15.1	13.5	15.5	9.3
$25,000 to $34,999	1,502	977	147	149	64	14.1	14.7	13.4	16.9	9.8
$35,000 to $49,999	1,732	1,124	143	158	88	16.2	16.8	13.0	18.0	13.3
$50,000 to $74,999	2,005	1,252	180	171	151	18.8	18.8	16.4	19.5	22.9
$75,000 to $99,999	1,099	654	120	74	101	10.3	9.8	11.0	8.5	15.3
$100,000 and over	1,396	719	170	90	155	13.1	10.8	15.5	10.2	23.6
POVERTY STATUS IN 2010										
Persons below poverty level [6]	**13,243**	**9,282**	**1,241**	**1,152**	**396**	**26.6**	**28.6**	**26.9**	**27.4**	**14.0**
HOUSEHOLD TENURE										
Total occupied units	**13,665**	**8,231**	**1,510**	**1,122**	**875**	**100.0**	**100.0**	**100.0**	**100.0**	**100.0**
Owner occupied	6,359	3,957	589	387	448	46.5	48.1	39.0	34.5	51.2
Renter occupied [7]	7,306	4,274	921	735	427	53.5	51.9	61.0	65.5	48.8

NA Not available. X Not applicable. [1] Includes other Hispanic groups not shown separately. [2] Refers to people whose origin is from Spanish-speaking Central or South American countries. Central American totals exclude Mexican and Cuban. [3] Source: U.S. Bureau of Labor Statistics, "Employment and Earnings Online," January 2013, <http://stats.bls.gov/opub/ee/home.htm>. [4] Total unemployment as percent of civilian labor force. [5] Household type is shown by the Hispanic origin of the householder. [6] Excludes unrelated individuals under 15 years old. For explanation of poverty level; see text, Section 13. [7] Includes no cash rent.

Source: Except as noted, U.S. Census Bureau, "The Hispanic Population in the United States: 2011, Detailed Tables," November 2012, <http://www.census.gov/population/hispanic/data/2011.html>.

Table 39. Native and Foreign-Born Population by State: 2011

[271,214 represents 271,214,000. The American Community Survey universe includes the household population and the population living in institutions, college dormitories, and other group quarters. Based on a sample and subject to sampling variability; see text, this section and Appendix III. See headnote, Table 43]

State	Native population (1,000)	Foreign-born population Number (1,000)	Foreign-born population Percent of total population	Foreign-born population Percent entered 2000 or later	State	Native population (1,000)	Foreign-born population Number (1,000)	Foreign-born population Percent of total population	Foreign-born population Percent entered 2000 or later
U.S........	271,214	40,378	13.0	35.7	MO.........	5,767	243	4.0	48.0
AL..........	4,640	163	3.4	49.7	MT..........	978	20	2.0	38.8
AK..........	671	52	7.1	38.3	NE..........	1,727	116	6.3	49.3
AZ..........	5,611	872	13.4	33.0	NV..........	2,201	522	19.2	33.3
AR..........	2,809	129	4.4	45.8	NH..........	1,244	74	5.6	36.4
CA..........	27,497	10,195	27.0	28.5	NJ..........	6,928	1,893	21.5	36.4
CO..........	4,622	495	9.7	40.1	NM..........	1,871	211	10.1	35.1
CT..........	3,102	478	13.4	37.0	NY..........	15,147	4,318	22.2	33.4
DE..........	831	76	8.4	46.3	NC..........	8,948	708	7.3	44.9
DC..........	534	84	13.5	46.3	ND..........	667	17	2.4	62.1
FL..........	15,355	3,703	19.4	36.1	OH..........	11,089	456	4.0	43.8
GA..........	8,872	943	9.6	43.3	OK..........	3,583	209	5.5	46.7
HI..........	1,129	246	17.9	33.3	OR..........	3,494	378	9.8	37.5
ID..........	1,490	95	6.0	37.9	PA..........	11,986	756	5.9	39.7
IL..........	11,070	1,799	14.0	33.7	RI..........	910	142	13.5	33.2
IN..........	6,210	307	4.7	49.3	SC..........	4,457	222	4.7	45.6
IA..........	2,929	134	4.4	48.5	SD..........	802	22	2.7	59.6
KS..........	2,672	199	6.9	44.9	TN..........	6,097	307	4.8	48.8
KY..........	4,229	140	3.2	54.6	TX..........	21,473	4,202	16.4	37.2
LA..........	4,401	174	3.8	46.8	UT..........	2,579	238	8.4	40.0
ME..........	1,285	43	3.2	31.4	VT..........	602	24	3.9	28.7
MD..........	5,017	812	13.9	42.8	VA..........	7,196	900	11.1	43.0
MA..........	5,604	983	14.9	39.3	WA..........	5,921	909	13.3	38.4
MI..........	9,272	604	6.1	37.0	WV..........	1,832	24	1.3	43.6
MN..........	4,956	389	7.3	46.4	WI..........	5,442	270	4.7	40.9
MS..........	2,913	65	2.2	49.1	WY..........	550	18	3.2	55.6

Source: U.S. Census Bureau, 2011 American Community Survey, C05002, "Place of Birth by Nativity"; and C05005, "Year of Entry by Nativity in the United States"; <http://factfinder2.census.gov>, accessed July 2013.

Table 40. Nativity and Place of Birth of Resident Population— 25 Largest Cities: 2011

[821 represents 821,000. The American Community Survey universe includes the household population and the population living in institutions, college dormitories, and other group quarters. Based on a sample and subject to sampling variability; see text, this section and Appendix III. See headnote, Table 43]

City	Total population (1,000)	Native population Total (1,000)	Native population Born in United States (1,000)	Native population Born outside United States (1,000)	Foreign born Total Number (1,000)	Foreign born Total Percent of total population	Foreign born Entered 2000 or later Number (1,000)	Foreign born Entered 2000 or later Percent of foreign-born population
Austin, TX....................	821	665	651	14	155	18.9	75	48.5
Boston, MA..................	625	460	438	22	165	26.5	70	42.6
Charlotte, NC...............	751	642	635	7	109	14.5	50	46.3
Chicago, IL..................	2,707	2,128	2,081	47	579	21.4	204	35.3
Columbus, OH..............	796	716	709	7	80	10.0	48	60.1
Dallas, TX...................	1,223	913	905	8	310	25.4	126	40.7
Denver, CO..................	620	519	511	8	101	16.3	42	41.4
Detroit, MI...................	707	672	666	5	35	5.0	13	35.8
El Paso, TX..................	666	497	481	16	169	25.4	47	27.6
Fort Worth, TX..............	761	634	624	10	127	16.7	45	35.9
Houston, TX.................	2,146	1,553	1,530	23	593	27.7	252	42.4
Indianapolis, IN [1].........	824	757	751	6	67	8.2	38	56.2
Jacksonville, FL............	828	747	723	24	80	9.7	33	41.5
Los Angeles, CA...........	3,820	2,330	2,290	40	1,490	39.0	428	28.8
Memphis, TN................	652	609	604	5	43	6.6	22	50.4
Nashville–Davidson, TN [1].........	610	535	529	6	74	12.2	38	50.6
New York, NY...............	8,245	5,178	4,866	312	3,067	37.2	1,054	34.4
Philadelphia, PA...........	1,536	1,345	1,291	54	192	12.5	87	45.2
Phoenix, AZ.................	1,469	1,173	1,157	16	297	20.2	92	31.1
San Antonio, TX............	1,360	1,170	1,142	28	190	14.0	68	35.7
San Diego, CA..............	1,326	975	950	25	351	26.4	109	31.1
San Francisco, CA.........	813	512	497	15	301	37.0	100	33.1
San Jose, CA...............	967	589	577	11	379	39.2	120	31.8
Seattle, WA.................	621	502	489	12	119	19.2	52	43.5
Washington, DC............	618	534	524	10	84	13.5	39	46.3

[1] Represents the portion of a consolidated city that is not within one or more separately incorporated places.

Source: U.S. Census Bureau, 2011 American Community Survey, C05002, "Place of Birth by Nativity"; and C05005, "Year of Entry by Nativity in the United States"; <http://factfinder2.census.gov>, accessed July 2013.

Table 41. Native and Foreign-Born Populations by Selected Characteristics: 2010

[In thousands (304,280 represents 304,280,000). As of March. The foreign-born population includes anyone who is not a U.S. citizen at birth. This includes legal permanent residents (immigrants), temporary migrants (such as students), humanitarian migrants (such as refugees), and persons illegally present in the United States. Based on Current Population Survey, Annual Social and Economic Supplement which includes the civilian noninstitutional population plus Armed Forces living off post or with their families on post; see text, this section, and Appendix III]

Characteristic	Total population	Native population	Foreign-born population			
			Total	Natural-ized citizen	Not U.S. citizen	Year of entry: 2000 to March 2010
Total............................	**304,280**	**266,674**	**37,606**	**16,024**	**21,581**	**13,085**
Under 5 years old.....................	21,434	21,162	272	53	219	272
5 to 14 years old.....................	40,678	39,028	1,651	314	1,337	1,415
15 to 24 years old....................	42,240	38,433	3,807	878	2,929	2,345
25 to 34 years old....................	41,085	33,507	7,577	1,974	5,603	4,106
35 to 44 years old....................	40,447	31,905	8,542	3,323	5,219	2,570
45 to 54 years old....................	44,387	37,611	6,776	3,546	3,230	1,303
55 to 64 years old....................	35,395	31,003	4,391	2,747	1,643	624
65 to 74 years old....................	20,956	18,294	2,663	1,795	868	263
75 to 84 years old....................	12,964	11,499	1,466	1,048	419	151
85 years old and over.................	4,693	4,233	460	347	114	35
Median age (years) [1]................	36.7	35.4	41.3	48.9	36.2	31.0
Male.................................	149,485	130,728	18,758	7,470	11,288	6,690
Female...............................	154,795	135,946	18,849	8,555	10,294	6,395
MARITAL STATUS						
Persons 15 years old and over......	**242,168**	**206,485**	**35,683**	**15,658**	**20,025**	**11,398**
Married..............................	124,219	102,435	21,784	10,300	11,484	6,316
Widowed..............................	14,356	12,605	1,751	1,078	673	267
Divorced.............................	23,758	21,374	2,384	1,322	1,062	409
Separated............................	5,541	4,348	1,193	455	738	355
Never married........................	74,294	65,723	8,570	2,503	6,067	4,052
EDUCATIONAL ATTAINMENT						
Persons 25 years old and over......	**199,928**	**168,052**	**31,876**	**14,780**	**17,096**	**9,052**
Not high school graduate..............	25,711	16,212	9,499	2,802	6,697	2,799
High school graduate/some college.....	114,376	101,203	13,174	6,785	6,389	3,359
Bachelor's degree.....................	38,784	33,016	5,769	3,296	2,473	1,831
Advanced degree......................	21,056	17,620	3,434	1,897	1,537	1,062
EARNINGS IN 2009 [2]						
Persons 15 years old and over with earnings......	**99,270**	**83,790**	**15,480**	**7,459**	**8,020**	**4,524**
Under $15,000........................	5,685	4,290	1,394	426	969	525
$15,000 to $24,999...................	14,845	11,294	3,551	1,075	2,475	1,422
$25,000 to $34,999...................	17,553	14,528	3,025	1,415	1,610	845
$35,000 to $49,999...................	21,591	18,931	2,660	1,522	1,138	586
$50,000 to $74,999...................	21,131	18,706	2,425	1,461	964	561
$75,000 and over.....................	18,465	16,040	2,425	1,561	864	584
Median earnings (dollars) [1].........	41,480	42,283	32,932	41,339	27,170	27,198
HOUSEHOLD SIZE [3]						
Total households..................	**117,538**	**102,039**	**15,499**	**7,834**	**7,665**	**3,978**
One person...........................	31,399	28,615	2,784	1,626	1,158	578
Two persons..........................	39,487	35,720	3,767	2,172	1,595	931
Three persons........................	18,638	15,736	2,902	1,346	1,556	885
Four persons.........................	16,122	13,121	3,001	1,383	1,618	833
Five persons.........................	7,367	5,709	1,658	776	882	412
Six persons..........................	2,784	2,010	774	312	463	179
Seven persons or more................	1,740	1,128	612	218	394	160
INCOME IN 2009 [3]						
Total family households...........	**78,833**	**66,840**	**11,993**	**5,952**	**6,041**	**3,066**
Under $15,000........................	6,030	4,769	1,261	410	851	431
$15,000 to $24,999...................	6,968	5,500	1,469	520	949	418
$25,000 to $34,999...................	7,795	6,274	1,522	613	908	439
$35,000 to $49,999...................	10,881	9,187	1,694	819	875	451
$50,000 to $74,999...................	15,633	13,387	2,246	1,194	1,052	534
$75,000 and over.....................	31,525	27,724	3,801	2,395	1,406	794
Median income (dollars) [1]..........	61,265	63,231	50,341	61,333	39,542	41,507
POVERTY STATUS IN 2009 [4]						
Persons below poverty level..........	43,569	36,407	7,162	1,736	5,425	3,350
Persons at or above poverty level....	260,251	229,815	30,435	14,288	16,147	9,727
HOUSEHOLD TENURE [3]						
Total households..................	**117,539**	**102,039**	**15,500**	**7,834**	**7,666**	**3,978**
Owner occupied unit..................	78,780	70,687	8,092	5,261	2,831	1,121
Renter occupied unit [5].............	38,759	31,352	7,408	2,573	4,835	2,857

[1] For definition of median, see Guide to Tabular Presentation. [2] Covers only year-round, full-time workers. [3] Based on citizenship of householder. [4] Persons for whom poverty status is determined. Excludes unrelated individuals under 15 years old. [5] Includes occupiers who paid no cash rent.

Source: U.S. Census Bureau, "Current Population Survey - March 2010 Detailed Tables, Characteristics of the Foreign-Born Population by Nativity and U.S. Citizenship Status," <http://www.census.gov/population/foreign/data/cps2010.html>.

Table 42. Foreign-Born Population—Selected Characteristics by Region of Origin: 2010

[In thousands (37,606 represents 37,606,000). As of March. The term foreign-born refers to anyone who is not a U.S. citizen at birth. This includes naturalized U.S. citizens, legal permanent residents (immigrants), temporary migrants (such as foreign students), humanitarian migrants (such as refugees), and persons illegally present in the United States. Based on Current Population Survey, Annual Social and Economic Supplement; see text, this section and Appendix III]

Characteristic	Total foreign-born	Europe	Asia	Latin America Total	Carib-bean	Central America [1]	South America	Other areas
Total	**37,606**	**4,509**	**10,126**	**20,419**	**3,649**	**14,400**	**2,370**	**2,553**
Under 5 years old	272	35	100	83	4	76	2	54
5 to 14 years old	1,651	151	466	892	152	667	73	142
15 to 24 years old	3,807	296	848	2,390	351	1,822	217	273
25 to 34 years old	7,577	544	1,868	4,620	536	3,648	436	545
35 to 44 years old	8,542	778	2,190	5,005	637	3,805	563	569
45 to 54 years old	6,776	742	1,927	3,661	805	2,329	527	446
55 to 64 years old	4,391	695	1,405	2,036	523	1,244	268	255
65 to 74 years old	2,663	683	753	1,071	352	534	184	156
75 to 84 years old	1,466	412	457	515	233	205	77	82
85 years old and over	460	171	111	147	55	69	23	31
EDUCATIONAL ATTAINMENT								
Persons 25 years old and over	**31,876**	**4,026**	**8,712**	**17,054**	**3,142**	**11,834**	**2,078**	**2,083**
Less than ninth grade	5,906	302	618	4,844	394	4,273	177	142
9th to 12th grade (no diploma)	3,593	154	438	2,909	331	2,405	173	92
High school graduate	8,138	1,102	1,836	4,725	967	3,055	703	475
Some college or associate's degree	5,035	814	1,259	2,436	748	1,245	443	526
Bachelor's degree	5,769	996	2,753	1,554	500	682	372	466
Advanced degree	3,434	659	1,807	586	202	176	209	382
High school graduate or more	22,377	3,570	7,655	9,301	2,417	5,157	1,728	1,851
Bachelor's degree or more	9,204	1,654	4,561	2,141	702	857	582	848
INCOME IN 2009								
Total family households	**11,993**	**1,444**	**3,365**	**6,362**	**1,218**	**4,439**	**705**	**821**
Under $15,000	1,261	87	241	834	167	614	53	100
$15,000 to $24,999	1,469	128	249	1,035	171	798	66	57
$25,000 to $34,999	1,522	152	276	995	169	753	74	99
$35,000 to $49,999	1,694	165	373	1,050	190	768	92	107
$50,000 to $74,999	2,246	292	633	1,191	200	806	185	130
$75,000 and over	3,801	621	1,595	1,257	322	700	235	328
Median income (dol.) [2]	50,341	64,340	70,856	38,785	41,972	35,789	56,963	55,758
POVERTY STATUS IN 2009 [3]								
Persons below poverty level	7,162	442	1,325	4,957	689	3,984	285	438
Persons at or above poverty level	30,435	4,067	8,801	15,455	2,960	10,409	2,085	2,112

[1] Includes Mexico. [2] For definition of median, see Guide to Tabular Presentation. [3] Persons for whom poverty status is determined. Excludes unrelated individuals under 15 years old.

Source: U.S. Census Bureau, "Current Population Survey - March 2010 Detailed Tables, Characteristics of the Foreign-Born Population by Nativity and U.S. Citizenship Status," <http://www.census.gov/population/foreign/data/cps2010.html>.

Table 43. Foreign-Born Population by Citizenship Status and Place of Birth: 2011

[The term foreign-born refers to anyone who is not a U.S. citizen at birth. This includes naturalized U.S. citizens, legal permanent residents (immigrants), temporary migrants (such as foreign students), humanitarian migrants (such as refugees), and persons illegally present in the United States. The American Community Survey universe includes the household population and the population living in institutions, college dormitories, and other group quarters. Based on a sample and subject to sampling variability; see text, this section and Appendix III]

Region	Foreign-born population, total	Naturalized citizen	Not U.S. citizen Number	Not U.S. citizen Percent of foreign-born
Total [1]	**40,377,860**	**18,140,192**	**22,237,668**	**55.1**
Latin America	21,245,344	7,099,001	14,146,343	66.6
Caribbean	3,776,783	2,050,675	1,726,108	45.7
Cuba	1,094,811	(NA)	(NA)	(NA)
Central America	14,758,017	3,771,564	10,986,453	74.4
Mexico	11,672,619	2,815,812	8,856,807	75.9
Other Central America	3,085,398	955,752	2,129,646	69.0
El Salvador	1,264,743	(NA)	(NA)	(NA)
South America	2,710,544	1,276,762	1,433,782	52.9
Asia	11,562,022	6,707,954	4,854,068	42.0
China, excluding Taiwan	1,866,225	(NA)	(NA)	(NA)
India	1,856,777	(NA)	(NA)	(NA)
Korea	1,082,613	(NA)	(NA)	(NA)
Philippines	1,813,597	(NA)	(NA)	(NA)
Vietnam	1,259,317	(NA)	(NA)	(NA)
Europe	4,889,987	3,098,694	1,791,293	36.6
Africa	1,664,414	(NA)	(NA)	(NA)
Northern America	794,779	(NA)	(NA)	(NA)
Oceania	221,211	(NA)	(NA)	(NA)

NA Not available. [1] Includes persons born at sea.

Source: U.S. Census Bureau, 2011 American Community Survey, B05002, "Place of Birth by Citizenship Status"; C05006, "Place of Birth for the Foreign-Born Population"; and B05007, "Place of Birth by Year of Entry by Citizenship Status for the Foreign-Born Population"; <http://factfinder2.census.gov>, accessed July 2013.

Table 44. American Indian Reservations and Alaska Native Village Statistical Areas With Largest American Indian and Alaska Native Populations: 2010

[As of April. Rankings of the American Indian reservations and Alaska Native village statistical areas are based on the American Indian and Alaska Native alone-or-in-combination population]

Area	Total population	American Indian and Alaska Native			Not American Indian and Alaska Native alone or in combination [1]
		Alone or in combination [1]	Alone	In combination [1]	
American Indian Reservation					
Navajo Nation Reservation and Off-Reservation Trust Land, AZ–NM–UT....................	173,667	169,321	166,824	2,497	4,346
Pine Ridge Reservation, SD–NE....................	18,834	16,906	16,580	326	1,928
Fort Apache Reservation, AZ....................	13,409	13,014	12,870	144	395
Gila River Indian Reservation, AZ....................	11,712	11,251	10,845	406	461
Osage Reservation, OK....................	47,472	9,920	6,858	3,062	37,552
San Carlos Reservation, AZ....................	10,068	9,901	9,835	66	167
Rosebud Indian Reservation and Off-Reservation Trust Land, SD....................	10,869	9,809	9,617	192	1,060
Tohono O'odham Nation Reservation and Off-Reservation Trust Land, AZ....................	10,201	9,278	9,139	139	923
Blackfeet Indian Reservation and Off-Reservation Trust Land, MT....................	10,405	9,149	8,944	205	1,256
Flathead Reservation, MT....................	28,359	9,138	7,042	2,096	19,221
Alaska Native Village Statistical Area					
Knik Alaska Native village statistical area....................	65,768	6,582	3,529	3,053	59,186
Bethel Alaska Native village statistical area....................	6,080	4,334	3,953	381	1,746
Kenaitze Alaska Native village statistical area....................	32,902	3,417	2,001	1,416	29,485
Barrow Alaska Native village statistical area....................	4,212	2,889	2,577	312	1,323
Ketchikan Alaska Native village statistical area....................	12,742	2,605	1,692	913	10,137
Kotzebue Alaska Native village statistical area....................	3,201	2,585	2,355	230	616
Nome Alaska Native village statistical area....................	3,681	2,396	1,994	402	1,285
Chickaloon Alaska Native village statistical area....................	23,087	2,373	1,369	1,004	20,714
Dillingham Alaska Native village statistical area....................	2,378	1,583	1,333	250	795
Sitka Alaska Native village statistical area....................	4,480	1,240	855	385	3,240

[1] In combination with one or more other race groups.

Source: U.S. Census Bureau, 2010 Census Briefs, *The American Indian and Alaska Native Population: 2010*, January 2012. See also <http://www.census.gov/2010census/data/>.

Table 45. American Indian and Alaska Native Population by Selected Tribal Groupings: 2010

[As of April. Data shown for American Indian and Alaska Native tribes alone or in combination of tribes or races]

Tribal grouping	American Indian and Alaska Native tribal grouping alone or in any combination [1]	Tribal grouping	American Indian and Alaska Native tribal grouping alone or in any combination [1]
Total [2]....................	**5,220,579**	Navajo....................	332,129
American Indian Tribes		Osage....................	18,576
Apache....................	111,810	Ottawa....................	13,033
Arapaho....................	10,861	Paiute....................	13,767
Blackfeet....................	105,304	Pima....................	26,655
Canadian and French American Indian.....	14,822	Potawatomi....................	33,771
Central American Indian....................	27,844	Pueblo....................	62,540
Cherokee....................	819,105	Puget Sound Salish....................	20,260
Cheyenne....................	19,051	Seminole....................	31,971
Chickasaw....................	52,278	Shoshone....................	13,002
Chippewa....................	170,742	Sioux....................	170,110
Choctaw....................	195,764	South American Indian....................	47,233
Colville....................	10,549	Spanish American Indian....................	19,951
Comanche....................	23,330	Tohono O'Odham....................	23,478
Cree....................	7,983	Ute....................	11,491
Creek....................	88,332	Yakama....................	11,527
Crow....................	15,203	Yaqui....................	32,595
Delaware....................	18,264	Yuman....................	10,089
Hopi....................	18,327	**Alaska Native Tribes**	
Houma....................	10,768	Alaskan Athabascan....................	22,484
Iroquois....................	81,002	Aleut....................	19,282
Kiowa....................	13,787	Inupiat....................	33,360
Lumbee....................	73,691	Tlingit-Haida....................	26,080
Menominee....................	11,133	Tsimshian....................	3,755
Mexican American Indian....................	175,494	Yup'ik....................	33,889

[1] The numbers by American Indian and Alaska Native tribal grouping do not add to the total American Indian and Alaska Native population. This is because the American Indian and Alaska Native tribal groupings are tallies of the number of American Indian and Alaska Native responses rather than the number of American Indian or Alaska Native respondents. Respondents reporting several American Indian or Alaska Native groups are counted several times. [2] Includes other tribal groupings not shown separately.

Source: U.S. Census Bureau, 2010 Census Briefs, *The American Indian and Alaska Native Population: 2010*, January 2012. See also <http://www.census.gov/2010census/data/>.

Table 46. Persons Obtaining Legal Permanent Resident Status: 1901 to 2012

[8,795 represents 8,795,000. For fiscal years ending in year shown; see text, Section 8. Rates based on Census Bureau estimates as of July 1 for resident population through 1929 and for total population thereafter (excluding Alaska and Hawaii prior to 1959)]

Period	Number (1,000)	Rate [1]	Year	Number (1,000)	Rate [1]
1901 to 1910	8,795	10.4	1990	1,536	6.1
1911 to 1920	5,736	5.7	1995	720	2.7
1921 to 1930	4,107	3.5	2000	841	3.0
1931 to 1940	528	0.4	2005	1,122	3.8
1941 to 1950	1,035	0.7	2006	1,266	4.2
1951 to 1960	2,515	1.5	2007	1,052	3.5
1961 to 1970	3,322	1.7	2008	1,107	3.6
1971 to 1980	4,399	2.0	2009	1,131	3.7
1981 to 1990	7,256	3.0	2010	1,043	3.4
1991 to 2000	9,081	3.4	2011	1,062	3.4
2001 to 2010	10,501	3.5	2012	1,032	3.3

[1] Annual rate per 1,000 U.S. population. Rate computed by dividing sum of annual immigration totals by sum of annual U.S. population totals for same number of years.

Source: U.S. Department of Homeland Security, Office of Immigration Statistics, "2012 Yearbook of Immigration Statistics," <http://www.dhs.gov/yearbook-immigration-statistics>, accessed May 2013.

Table 47. Refugee Arrivals and Individuals Granted Asylum by Country of Nationality: 2010 to 2012

[For year ending September 30. Data shown provide information on the number of persons admitted to the U.S. as refugees or granted asylum in the United States in the year shown. In cases with no country of nationality, the applicant's last country of residence is assigned. For definitions of refugee and asylee, see text, this section. Based on data from the Bureau of Population, Refugees, and Migration of the U.S. Department of State and the Executive Office for Immigration Review of the U.S. Department of Justice]

Country of nationality	Refugee arrivals			Country of nationality	Asylees		
	2010	2011	2012		2010	2011	2012
Total	73,293	56,384	58,179	Total	21,084	24,873	29,484
Bhutan	12,363	14,999	15,070	China	6,693	8,585	10,151
Burma	16,693	16,972	14,160	Egypt	531	1,026	2,882
Iraq	18,016	9,388	12,163	Ethiopia	1,086	1,068	1,122
Somalia	4,884	3,161	4,911	Venezuela	648	1,103	1,099
Cuba	4,818	2,920	1,948	Nepal	639	742	974
Congo, Democratic Republic of the	3,174	977	1,863	Russia	551	661	728
Iran	3,543	2,032	1,758	Iran	481	474	716
Eritrea	2,570	2,032	1,346	Haiti	834	872	682
Sudan	558	334	1,077	Guatemala	460	480	536
Ethiopia	668	560	620	Eritrea	360	633	472
Other countries [1]	6,006	3,009	3,263	Other countries [1]	8,801	9,229	10,122

[1] Includes unknown.

Source: U.S. Department of Homeland Security, Office of Immigration Statistics, *Annual Flow Report, Refugees and Asylees: 2012*, April 2013. See also <http://www.dhs.gov/yearbook-immigration-statistics>.

Table 48. Estimated Unauthorized Immigrants by Selected States and Countries of Birth: 2000 and 2011

[In thousands (8,460 represents 8,460,000). As of January. The unauthorized resident immigrant population is defined as all foreign-born non-citizens who are not legal residents. Most unauthorized residents either entered the United States without inspection or were admitted temporarily and stayed past the date they were required to leave. Unauthorized aliens who have applied for but have not yet received approval to lawfully remain in the United States are considered to be unauthorized. These estimates were calculated using a "residual method," whereby estimates of the legally resident foreign born population were subtracted from the total foreign-born population in order to derive the unauthorized immigrant population. All of these component populations were resident in the United States on January 1, 2011, and entered during the 1980–2010 period. Persons who entered the United States prior to 1980 were assumed to be legally resident. Estimates of the legally resident foreign-born were based primarily on administrative data of the Department of Homeland Security, while estimates of the total foreign-born population were obtained from the American Community Survey of the U.S. Census Bureau. Estimates for 2000 are based on the same methodology, assumptions, and definitions with the exception that data from Census 2000 were used to estimate the foreign-born population in 2000 that entered the United States from January 1, 1980 through December 31, 1999]

State of residence	2000	2011	Country of birth	2000	2011
United States, total	8,460	11,510	Total	8,460	11,510
California	2,510	2,830	Mexico	4,680	6,800
Texas	1,090	1,790	El Salvador	430	660
Florida	800	740	Guatemala	290	520
New York	540	630	Honduras	160	380
Illinois	440	550	China	190	280
Georgia	220	440	Philippines	200	270
New Jersey	350	420	India	120	240
North Carolina	260	400	Korea	180	230
Arizona	330	360	Ecuador	110	210
Washington	170	260	Vietnam	160	170
Other states	1,750	3,100	Other countries	1,940	1,750

Source: U.S. Department of Homeland Security, Office of Immigration Statistics, "Estimates of the Unauthorized Immigrant Population Residing in the United States: January 2011." See also <http://www.dhs.gov/xlibrary/assets/statistics/publications/ois_ill_pe_2011.pdf>.

Table 49. Immigrant Orphans Adopted by U.S. Citizens by Sex, Age, Region, and Country of Birth: 2012

[For year ending September 30]

Region and country of birth	Total	Male	Female	Under 1 year old	1 to 4 years old	5 years old and over
REGION						
Total...............	**8,619**	**3,993**	**4,626**	**860**	**5,053**	**2,706**
Africa...................	2,556	1,326	1,230	455	1,191	910
Asia.....................	4,007	1,627	2,380	305	2,905	797
Europe..................	1,411	738	673	35	750	626
North America...........	321	144	177	6	123	192
Oceania.................	30	15	15	22	5	3
South America...........	293	142	151	37	79	177
Unknown.................	1	1	0	0	0	1
COUNTRY						
Total [1]...............	**8,619**	**3,993**	**4,626**	**860**	**5,053**	**2,706**
Armenia.................	19	5	14	9	(D)	(D)
Bangladesh.............	17	7	10	8	5	4
Brazil...................	24	13	11	0	8	16
Bulgaria................	124	54	70	0	46	78
China...................	2,709	872	1,837	167	2,004	538
Colombia................	191	93	98	35	54	102
Congo, Democratic Republic of the...........	168	74	94	45	91	32
Congo, Republic of the...................	54	25	29	12	31	11
Ethiopia................	1,540	836	704	317	705	518
Ghana...................	173	81	92	(D)	(D)	104
Guyana..................	36	20	16	(D)	(D)	32
Haiti....................	166	72	94	(D)	(D)	88
Hungary.................	24	14	10	0	13	11
India...................	164	46	118	3	105	56
Jamaica.................	38	20	18	0	14	24
Japan...................	22	19	3	17	5	0
Korea, South............	621	446	175	3	607	11
Latvia..................	74	39	35	0	(D)	(D)
Liberia.................	34	18	16	0	4	30
Marshall Islands........	19	8	11	(D)	0	(D)
Mexico..................	21	10	11	0	5	16
Morocco.................	58	42	16	33	20	5
Nicaragua...............	20	8	12	(D)	(D)	12
Nigeria.................	187	77	110	13	108	66
Pakistan................	27	12	15	21	0	6
Peru....................	26	10	16	0	9	17
Philippines.............	137	72	65	0	39	98
Poland..................	35	16	19	0	15	20
Russia..................	759	398	361	30	609	120
Rwanda..................	26	15	11	11	9	6
Taiwan..................	176	90	86	69	65	42
Thailand................	58	32	26	0	37	21
Uganda..................	239	122	117	19	141	79
Ukraine.................	365	202	163	5	55	305

D Data withheld to limit disclosure. [1] Includes unknown and other countries not shown separately.

Source: U.S. Department of Homeland Security, Office of Immigration Statistics, "2012 Yearbook of Immigration Statistics," <http://www.dhs.gov/yearbook-immigration-statistics>, accessed May 2013.

Table 50. Petitions for Naturalization Filed, Persons Naturalized, and Petitions Denied: 1990 to 2012

[For years ending September 30. Naturalizations refer to persons 18 and over who become citizens of the United States]

Year	Petitions filed	Persons naturalized				Petitions denied
		Total	Civilian	Military	Not reported	
1990............	233,843	267,586	245,410	1,618	20,558	6,516
1995............	959,963	485,720	472,518	3,855	9,347	46,067
1998............	932,957	461,169	437,689	961	22,519	137,395
1999............	765,346	837,418	740,718	711	95,989	379,993
2000............	460,916	886,026	812,579	836	72,611	399,670
2001............	501,643	606,259	575,030	758	30,471	218,326
2002............	700,649	572,646	550,835	1,053	20,758	139,779
2003............	523,370	462,435	449,123	3,865	9,447	91,599
2004............	662,796	537,151	520,771	4,668	11,712	103,339
2005............	602,972	604,280	589,269	4,614	10,397	108,247
2006............	730,642	702,589	684,484	6,259	11,846	120,722
2007............	1,382,993	660,477	648,005	3,808	8,664	89,683
2008............	525,786	1,046,539	1,032,281	4,342	9,916	121,283
2009............	570,442	743,715	726,043	7,100	10,572	109,813
2010............	710,544	619,913	604,410	9,122	6,381	56,994
2011............	756,008	694,193	677,385	8,373	8,435	57,065
2012............	899,162	757,434	745,932	7,257	4,245	65,874

Source: U.S. Department of Homeland Security, Office of Immigration Statistics, "2012 Yearbook of Immigration Statistics," <http://www.dhs.gov/yearbook-immigration-statistics>, accessed May 2013.

Table 51. Persons Obtaining Legal Permanent Resident Status by Class of Admission: 2000 to 2012

[For years ending September 30. For definition of immigrants, see text, this section]

Class of admission	2000	2005	2009	2010	2011	2012
Total	**841,002**	**1,122,257**	**1,130,818**	**1,042,625**	**1,062,040**	**1,031,631**
New arrivals	407,279	383,955	463,042	476,049	481,948	484,072
Adjustments	433,723	738,302	667,776	566,576	580,092	547,559
Family-sponsored preferences	235,092	212,970	211,859	214,589	234,931	202,019
Unmarried sons/daughters of U.S. citizens and their children	27,635	24,729	23,965	26,998	27,299	20,660
Spouses, unmarried sons/daughters of alien residents and their children	124,540	100,139	98,567	92,088	108,618	99,709
Married sons/daughters of U.S. citizens [1]	22,804	22,953	25,930	32,817	27,704	21,752
Brothers or sisters of U.S. citizens age 21 and older [1]	60,113	65,149	63,397	62,686	71,310	59,898
Employment-based preferences	106,642	246,865	140,903	148,343	139,339	143,998
Priority workers [1]	27,566	64,731	40,924	41,055	25,251	39,316
Professionals with advanced degrees or aliens of exceptional ability [1]	20,255	42,597	45,552	53,946	66,831	50,959
Skilled workers, professionals, unskilled workers [1]	49,589	129,070	40,398	39,762	37,216	39,229
Special immigrants [1]	9,014	10,121	10,341	11,100	6,701	7,866
Employment creation (investors) [1]	218	346	3,688	2,480	3,340	6,628
Immediate relatives of U.S. citizens	346,350	436,115	535,554	476,414	453,158	478,780
Spouses	196,405	259,144	317,129	271,909	258,320	273,429
Children [2]	82,638	94,858	98,270	88,297	80,311	81,121
Parents	67,307	82,113	120,155	116,208	114,527	124,230
Refugees	56,091	112,676	118,836	92,741	113,045	105,528
Asylees	6,837	30,286	58,532	43,550	55,415	45,086
Diversity (lottery) [3]	50,920	46,234	47,879	49,763	50,103	40,320
Cancellation of removal	12,154	20,785	8,156	8,180	7,430	6,818
Parolees	3,162	7,715	2,385	1,592	1,147	758
Children born abroad to alien residents	(NA)	571	587	716	633	643
Nicaraguan Adjustment and Central American Relief Act (NACARA)	20,364	1,155	296	248	158	183
Haitian Refugee Immigration Fairness Act (HRIFA)	435	2,820	552	386	154	93
Other	2,955	4,065	5,279	6,103	6,527	7,405

NA Not available. [1] Includes spouses and children. [2] Includes orphans. [3] The Diversity Visa Program is a lottery available to nationals of countries with fewer than 50,000 persons granted legal permanent residency status during the preceding 5 years in the employment-based and family-sponsored preferences and immediate relative classes of admission. Includes categories of immigrants admitted under three laws intended to diversify immigration: P.L. 99-603, P.L. 100-658, and P.L. 101-649.

Source: U.S. Department of Homeland Security, Office of Immigration Statistics, "2012 Yearbook of Immigration Statistics," <http://www.dhs.gov/yearbook-immigration-statistics>, accessed May 2013.

Table 52. Persons Obtaining Legal Permanent Resident Status by Selected Country of Birth and Selected Characteristics: 2012

[For year ending September 30]

Age, marital status, class of admission	All countries [1]	Mexico	China	India	Philippines	Dominican Republic	Cuba	Vietnam	Haiti
Total	**1,031,631**	**146,406**	**81,784**	**66,434**	**57,327**	**41,566**	**32,820**	**28,304**	**22,818**
Under 18 years old	202,118	27,201	12,798	7,460	11,802	13,639	6,001	5,205	6,933
18 to 24 years old	141,061	24,910	9,821	4,539	7,003	6,577	3,803	5,017	3,310
25 to 34 years old	249,111	32,455	16,894	24,570	10,018	7,032	5,560	5,385	3,549
35 to 44 years old	187,101	28,202	17,953	14,547	9,615	5,704	6,478	4,156	3,346
45 to 54 years old	117,397	16,686	11,667	5,331	7,478	4,250	5,054	4,537	2,104
55 to 64 years old	79,206	9,237	7,336	5,377	7,057	2,578	2,998	2,966	1,736
65 years old and over	55,628	7,714	5,314	4,610	4,352	1,785	2,926	1,038	1,840
Unknown	9	1	1	0	2	1	0	0	0
Single	374,559	47,305	25,327	12,195	22,810	23,502	13,739	9,870	14,121
Married	600,961	92,344	52,511	51,292	31,256	16,267	14,063	16,836	7,877
Other	51,281	5,976	3,719	2,719	3,147	1,678	4,849	1,561	729
Unknown	4,830	781	227	228	114	119	169	37	91
Family-sponsored preferences	202,019	41,724	17,789	11,433	17,735	19,427	971	14,309	8,447
Employment-based preferences	143,998	7,858	19,930	33,408	9,250	377	13	(D)	(D)
Immediate relatives of U.S. citizens	478,780	92,053	25,714	20,497	30,229	21,629	3,402	12,930	11,495
Diversity programs	40,320	7	44	27	10	3	74	(D)	(D)
Refugees and asylees	150,614	508	18,167	895	31	61	28,346	620	2,348
Other	15,900	4,256	140	174	72	69	14	113	395

D Data withheld to avoid disclosure. [1] Includes other countries not shown separately.

Source: U.S. Department of Homeland Security, Office of Immigration Statistics, "Profiles on Legal Permanent Residents: 2012," <http://www.dhs.gov/profiles-legal-permanent-residents-2012-country>, accessed July 2013.

Table 53. Persons Obtaining Legal Permanent Resident Status by Country of Birth: 1991 to 2012

[In thousands (9,080.5 represents 9,080,500). For years ending Sept. 30. Persons by country prior to 1996 are unrevised]

Region and Country of birth	1991–2000, total	2001–2010, total	2011	2012	Region and Country of birth	1991–2000, total	2001–2010, total	2011	2012
All countries [1]	9,080.5	10,501.1	1,062.0	1,031.6					
Europe [1]	1,226.0	1,263.9	83.9	81.7	Vietnam	420.8	306.1	34.2	28.3
Albania	26.2	50.5	3.6	3.4					
Belarus	[2] 28.9	25.7	2.0	1.7	Africa [1]	382.5	860.4	100.4	107.2
Bosnia and Herzegovina	[2] 38.8	89.0	0.9	0.8	Egypt	46.7	73.1	7.8	9.0
Bulgaria	23.1	39.2	2.7	2.4	Ethiopia	49.3	109.7	13.8	14.5
France	27.4	39.6	3.7	3.9	Ghana	35.6	65.3	8.8	10.6
Germany	67.6	77.7	6.1	5.8	Kenya	14.0	59.7	7.8	7.0
Ireland	58.9	15.5	1.4	1.5	Liberia	16.0	45.2	4.2	4.1
Poland	169.5	116.8	6.9	6.3	Morocco	20.0	44.4	4.4	3.7
Romania	57.5	53.6	3.9	3.7	Nigeria	67.2	111.2	11.8	13.6
Russia	[2] 127.8	139.7	7.9	10.0	Somalia	20.1	64.2	4.5	5.2
Serbia and Montenegro [3, 4]	25.8	46.2	1.4	0.8	South Africa	22.6	32.9	2.6	2.8
Soviet Union [3]	103.8	37.5	3.7	1.3					
Ukraine	[2] 141.0	149.3	8.3	7.6	Oceania	47.9	58.1	5.0	4.7
United Kingdom	135.6	153.5	11.6	12.0	North America [1]	3,910.1	3,605.1	333.9	327.8
Asia [1]	2,973.2	3,784.6	451.6	429.6	Canada	137.2	168.2	12.8	12.9
Armenia	[2] 26.6	29.9	3.0	2.7	Mexico	2,250.5	1,693.2	143.4	146.4
Bangladesh	66.0	106.7	16.7	14.7	Cuba	178.7	318.4	36.5	32.8
Burma	11.0	45.0	16.5	17.4	Dominican				
China	424.4	662.7	87.0	81.8	Republic	340.8	329.1	46.1	41.6
Hong Kong	74.0	40.8	2.3	2.1	Haiti	181.7	213.8	22.1	22.8
India	383.0	662.5	69.0	66.4	Jamaica	173.4	180.7	19.7	20.7
Iran	112.5	125.9	14.8	12.9	Trinidad				
Iraq	40.7	65.0	21.1	20.4	and Tobago	63.2	61.8	5.0	5.2
Israel	31.9	46.6	3.8	4.2	El Salvador	217.3	252.8	18.7	16.3
Japan	61.4	76.1	6.2	6.1	Guatemala	103.0	160.7	11.1	10.3
Jordan [5]	39.7	38.7	3.9	4.1	Honduras	66.7	65.4	6.1	6.9
Korea, South [6]	171.1	221.5	22.8	20.8	Nicaragua	94.6	60.9	3.4	3.0
Laos	43.5	16.5	1.0	0.9	South America [1]	539.3	906.0	86.1	79.4
Lebanon	43.4	39.5	3.3	2.9	Argentina	24.3	50.5	4.5	4.4
Pakistan	124.5	157.0	15.5	14.7	Brazil	52.2	123.8	11.8	11.4
Philippines	505.3	587.2	57.0	57.3	Colombia	130.8	251.3	22.6	20.9
Taiwan	106.3	87.9	6.2	5.3	Ecuador	76.3	112.5	11.1	9.3
Thailand	48.4	68.3	10.0	9.5	Guyana	73.8	76.2	6.6	5.7
Turkey	26.3	41.1	4.4	4.2	Peru	105.6	145.7	14.1	12.6
Uzbekistan	[2] 22.9	36.0	5.1	4.7	Venezuela	29.9	84.4	9.2	9.4

[1] Includes other countries not shown separately. [2] Covers years 1992–2000. [3] Prior to 1992, data include independent republics; beginning in 1992, data are for unknown republic only. [4] Yugoslavia (unknown republic) prior to February 7, 2003. [5] Prior to 2003, includes Palestine; beginning in 2003, Palestine included in Unknown. [6] Prior to 2009, includes a small number of cases from North Korea.

Source: U.S. Department of Homeland Security, Office of Immigration Statistics, "2012 Yearbook of Immigration Statistics," <http://www.dhs.gov/yearbook-immigration-statistics>, accessed May 2013.

Table 54. Refugees and Asylees Obtaining Legal Permanent Resident Status by Country of Birth: 2001 to 2012

[For years ending September 30]

Country of birth	2001–2010, total	2011	2012	Country of birth	2001–2010, total	2011	2012
Total [1]	1,325,365	168,460	150,614	Thailand	22,405	5,247	4,935
				Uzbekistan	14,047	472	531
Europe [1]	296,794	4,760	4,096	Vietnam	36,990	1,703	620
Albania	10,905	415	291	Africa [1]	242,839	23,523	26,312
Belarus	9,310	356	300	Cameroon	7,564	1,653	1,150
Bosnia and Herzegovina	82,485	251	167	Congo,			
Croatia	9,498	20	22	Democratic Republic of the	5,643	1,446	2,462
Moldova	10,813	601	445	Egypt	7,987	746	934
Russia	32,819	892	811	Eritrea	4,534	1,346	1,820
Serbia and Montenegro [2]	25,422	226	174	Ethiopia	31,900	3,352	4,669
Ukraine	57,186	833	695	Kenya	15,351	1,961	2,071
				Liberia	28,808	1,615	1,387
Asia [1]	389,469	97,031	82,680	Sierra Leone	10,369	364	286
Afghanistan	13,533	501	503	Somalia	59,069	3,622	4,154
Armenia	12,408	767	521	Sudan	23,580	1,428	943
Bhutan	6,762	10,119	10,171	Oceania	1,453	49	74
Burma	32,904	14,833	15,883	North America [1]	326,846	38,022	32,964
China	111,632	27,097	18,167	Cuba	276,331	33,129	28,346
India	24,010	1,217	895	Guatemala	7,399	794	718
Indonesia	7,618	489	354	Haiti	29,824	2,388	2,348
Iran	45,515	5,386	3,430	South America [1]	65,912	4,868	4,310
Iraq	40,789	19,104	15,421	Colombia	40,321	1,920	1,464
Nepal	6,000	5,299	5,987	Peru	7,258	509	362
Pakistan	8,339	512	713	Venezuela	10,726	1,348	1,528

[1] Includes other countries and unknown not shown separately. [2] Data are for unknown republic only. Yugoslavia (unknown republic) prior to February 7, 2003.

Source: U.S. Department of Homeland Security, Office of Immigration Statistics, "2012 Yearbook of Immigration Statistics," <http://www.dhs.gov/yearbook-immigration-statistics>, accessed May 2013.

Table 55. Population by Selected Ancestry Group and Region: 2011

[In thousands (311,592 represents 311,592,000), except percent. Covers single and multiple ancestries. Ancestry refers to a person's ethnic origin or descent, "roots," or heritage; or the place of birth of the person, the person's parents, or ancestors before their arrival in the United States. The American Community Survey universe includes the household population and the population living in institutions, college dormitories, and other group quarters. Based on a sample and subject to sampling variability; see text, this section, and Appendix III. For composition of regions of the United States, see map, inside front cover]

Ancestry group	Total, (1,000)	Percent distribution by region — North-east	Mid-west	South	West	Ancestry group	Total, (1,000)	Percent distribution by region — North-east	Mid-west	South	West
Total population [1]	311,592	18	22	37	23	Irish	34,521	26	24	32	18
						Israeli	143	41	10	20	28
Afghan	89	17	7	17	59	Italian	17,446	45	17	22	17
Albanian	196	55	27	12	6	Latvian	87	27	25	24	24
American	24,145	12	21	53	14	Lithuanian	654	38	27	20	15
Arab [1]	1,769	25	26	27	22	Northern European	275	13	22	23	42
Egyptian	216	38	12	24	26	Norwegian	4,399	6	49	12	33
Iraqi	112	8	37	22	33	Pennsylvania					
Lebanese	491	26	28	29	18	German	331	58	25	11	5
Moroccan	87	37	11	35	18	Polish	9,448	33	37	18	12
Palestinian	97	20	28	34	19	Portuguese	1,379	47	3	13	37
Syrian	153	34	21	23	22	Romanian	465	26	27	19	28
Arab	330	20	32	26	23	Russian	2,995	36	17	21	26
Armenian	483	21	8	9	62	Scandinavian	567	7	32	18	42
Assyrian/						Scotch-Irish	3,144	12	17	51	20
Chaldean/Syriac	111	5	50	2	43	Scottish	5,413	17	20	37	27
Australian	90	20	17	25	37	Serbian	177	20	45	15	20
Austrian	684	31	23	23	24	Slavic	129	30	28	21	21
Belgian	345	11	55	17	16	Slovak	730	44	33	15	8
Brazilian	371	46	6	35	13	Slovene	167	17	55	13	15
British	1,194	16	17	40	28	Sub-Saharan					
Bulgarian	101	17	27	27	28	African [1]	2,928	21	19	44	16
Cajun	105	3	4	83	10	Cape Verdean	103	89	0	8	3
Canadian	705	27	16	27	29	Ethiopian	191	9	21	41	29
Croatian	412	22	39	15	23	Ghanian	108	42	14	36	8
Czech	1,508	12	44	28	17	Nigerian	271	22	15	50	13
Czechoslovakian	297	21	32	25	22	Somalian	132	8	49	20	24
Danish	1,336	8	31	14	46	African	1,771	17	19	49	15
Dutch	4,440	15	36	26	23	Swedish	4,002	13	38	17	32
Eastern European	506	42	13	22	23	Swiss	916	16	34	20	30
English	25,696	17	21	38	25	Turkish	199	35	14	34	17
European	3,651	13	20	33	34	Ukrainian	958	39	20	18	23
Finnish	649	12	47	14	27	Welsh	1,773	20	22	30	28
French						West Indian [1,2]	2,716	46	3	46	5
(except Basque)	8,596	25	22	33	20	British					
French						West Indian	84	67	3	28	3
Canadian	1,972	41	19	25	15	Haitian	908	41	2	55	2
German	47,384	16	38	26	19	Jamaican	1,030	45	5	45	5
Greek	1,281	33	22	25	19	Trinidadian and					
Guyanese	209	75	2	20	2	Tobagonian	196	61	2	33	5
Hungarian	1,415	31	31	22	17	West Indian	308	61	3	32	5
Iranian	470	13	9	25	53	Yugoslavian	297	18	30	22	30

[1] Includes other groups, not shown separately. [2] Excludes Hispanic-origin groups.

Source: U.S. Census Bureau, 2011 American Community Survey, B04006, "People Reporting Ancestry," <http://factfinder2.census.gov/>, accessed April 2013.

Table 56. Language Spoken at Home and English Speaking Ability: 2011

[See headnote Table 55.]

Language	Number	Percent who speak English less than "very well"	Language	Number	Percent who speak English less than "very well"
Total population 5 years old and over	291,524,091	(X)	Other Indic languages	815,345	39.4
Speak only English	230,947,071	(X)	Other Indo-European languages	449,600	34.9
Spanish or Spanish Creole	37,579,787	43.7	Chinese	2,882,497	55.7
French (including Patois, Cajun)	1,301,443	20.4	Japanese	436,110	42.5
French Creole	753,990	43.2	Korean	1,141,277	55.5
Italian	723,632	26.5	Mon-Khmer, Cambodian	212,505	52.9
Portuguese or Portuguese Creole	673,566	38.2	Hmong	211,227	43.3
German	1,083,637	17.1	Thai	163,251	56.6
Yiddish	160,968	31.6	Laotian	140,866	49.1
Other West Germanic languages	290,461	22.4	Vietnamese	1,419,539	60.2
Scandinavian languages	135,025	9.4	Other Asian languages	855,303	30.7
Greek	304,928	24.7	Tagalog	1,594,413	32.8
Russian	905,843	47.7	Other Pacific Island languages	428,476	38.4
Polish	607,531	40.0	Navajo	169,369	21.2
Serbo-Croatian	269,624	38.3	Other Native North American languages	195,407	14.6
Other Slavic languages	336,062	37.9	Hungarian	93,102	29.0
Armenian	246,915	46.2	Arabic	951,699	36.7
Persian	407,586	37.3	Hebrew	216,343	15.3
Gujarathi	358,422	36.2	African languages	884,660	31.9
Hindi	648,983	23.0	Other and unspecified languages	153,777	43.7
Urdu	373,851	30.0			

X Not applicable.

Source: U.S. Census Bureau, 2011 American Community Survey, B16001, "Language Spoken at Home by Ability to Speak English for the Population 5 Years and Over," <http://factfinder2.census.gov/>, accessed July 2013.

Table 57. Language Spoken at Home by State: 2011

[In thousands (291,524 represents 291,524,000), except percent. The American Community Survey universe includes the household population and the population living in institutions, college dormitories, and other group quarters. Based on a sample and subject to sampling variability; see text, this section, and Appendix III]

State	Population 5 years and over (1,000)	English only (1,000)	Language other than English Number (1,000)	Language other than English Percent of population 5 years and over	State	Population 5 years and over (1,000)	English only (1,000)	Language other than English Number (1,000)	Language other than English Percent of population 5 years and over
U.S.	291,524	230,947	60,577	20.8	MO	5,629	5,267	362	6.4
AL	4,504	4,268	236	5.2	MT	938	894	44	4.7
AK	669	557	111	16.6	NE	1,712	1,536	176	10.3
AZ	6,035	4,405	1,630	27.0	NV	2,538	1,784	755	29.7
AR	2,740	2,536	205	7.5	NH	1,251	1,153	97	7.8
CA	35,158	19,768	15,390	43.8	NJ	8,286	5,765	2,521	30.4
CO	4,776	3,977	799	16.7	NM	1,938	1,230	708	36.5
CT	3,385	2,660	724	21.4	NY	18,308	12,801	5,507	30.1
DE	852	736	116	13.6	NC	9,030	8,063	966	10.7
DC	582	494	88	15.0	ND	638	605	32	5.1
FL	17,983	13,024	4,959	27.6	OH	10,837	10,115	722	6.7
GA	9,141	7,926	1,215	13.3	OK	3,527	3,198	329	9.3
HI	1,287	963	324	25.2	OR	3,633	3,093	540	14.9
ID	1,466	1,314	153	10.4	PA	12,022	10,784	1,238	10.3
IL	12,042	9,312	2,730	22.7	RI	996	785	211	21.2
IN	6,089	5,587	502	8.2	SC	4,377	4,088	289	6.6
IA	2,864	2,656	208	7.3	SD	766	715	50	6.6
KS	2,669	2,365	304	11.4	TN	6,004	5,589	415	6.9
KY	4,090	3,893	197	4.8	TX	23,721	15,500	8,221	34.7
LA	4,262	3,890	372	8.7	UT	2,555	2,175	380	14.9
ME	1,262	1,178	84	6.6	VT	596	566	29	4.9
MD	5,465	4,551	914	16.7	VA	7,588	6,456	1,132	14.9
MA	6,225	4,855	1,370	22.0	WA	6,391	5,204	1,187	18.6
MI	9,293	8,446	847	9.1	WV	1,751	1,711	40	2.3
MN	4,992	4,452	541	10.8	WI	5,363	4,895	468	8.7
MS	2,773	2,668	105	3.8	WY	529	495	34	6.4

Source: U.S. Census Bureau, 2011 American Community Survey, C16005, "Nativity by Language Spoken at Home by Ability to Speak English for the Population 5 Years and Over," <http://factfinder2.census.gov/>, accessed July 2013.

Table 58. Language Spoken at Home—25 Largest Cities: 2011

[In thousands (763 represents 763,000), except percent. The American Community Survey universe includes the household population and the population living in institutions, college dormitories, and other group quarters. Based on a sample and subject to sampling variability; see text, this section, and Appendix III]

City	Population 5 years and over (1,000)	English only (1,000)	Language other than English, total [1] Number (1,000)	Language other than English, total [1] Percent of population 5 years and over	Language other than English, total [1] Speak English less than "very well" (1,000)	Spanish (1,000)	Other Indo-European languages (1,000)	Asian and Pacific Island languages (1,000)
Austin, TX	763	503	260	34.1	116	204	23	29
Boston, MA	591	375	217	36.6	100	97	63	45
Charlotte, NC	695	556	139	20.0	60	83	28	21
Chicago, IL	2,518	1,598	920	36.5	425	639	162	81
Columbus, OH	735	639	96	13.0	40	32	21	20
Dallas, TX	1,123	623	500	44.6	265	444	20	20
Denver, CO	574	416	159	27.6	69	121	15	15
Detroit, MI	656	593	63	9.6	27	39	11	3
El Paso, TX	615	179	436	70.9	182	422	6	6
Fort Worth, TX	694	477	216	31.2	103	184	13	16
Houston, TX	1,973	1,064	909	46.1	470	753	57	77
Indianapolis, IN [2]	761	669	93	12.2	45	62	13	9
Jacksonville, FL	770	665	105	13.7	39	49	25	24
Los Angeles, CA	3,571	1,402	2,169	60.7	1,061	1,531	270	318
Memphis, TN	602	543	59	9.9	29	40	8	9
Nashville–Davidson, TN [2]	565	473	92	16.3	46	51	16	12
New York, NY	7,711	3,926	3,785	49.1	1,796	1,900	1,037	647
Philadelphia, PA	1,431	1,129	303	21.2	136	138	75	71
Phoenix, AZ	1,353	868	485	35.8	185	398	33	30
San Antonio, TX	1,257	693	564	44.9	166	523	16	16
San Diego, CA	1,243	740	503	40.5	217	291	53	139
San Francisco, CA	777	420	357	46.0	180	91	51	207
San Jose, CA	900	391	508	56.5	231	211	61	225
Seattle, WA	588	446	142	24.1	61	25	25	71
Washington, DC	582	494	88	15.0	24	42	26	9

[1] Includes other language groups, not shown separately. [2] Represents the portion of a consolidated city that is not within one or more separately incorporated places.

Source: U.S. Census Bureau, 2011 American Community Survey, C16005, "Nativity by Language Spoken at Home by Ability to Speak English for the Population 5 Years and Over," <http://factfinder2.census.gov/>, accessed July 2013.

Table 59. Marital Status of the Population by Sex, Race, and Hispanic Origin: 2000 to 2012

[In millions, except percent (201.8 represents 201,800,000). As of March. Persons 18 years old and over. Excludes members of Armed Forces except those living off post or with their families on post. Beginning 2005 based on an expanded sample of households. Data for 2005 and 2010 based on population controls from Census 2000. 2012 data based on population controls from Census 2010. Based on Current Population Survey, see text, this section and Appendix III]

Marital status, race and Hispanic origin	Total				Male				Female			
	2000	2005	2010	2012	2000	2005	2010	2012	2000	2005	2010	2012
Total [1].............	**201.8**	**217.2**	**229.1**	**234.6**	**96.9**	**104.8**	**111.1**	**113.2**	**104.9**	**112.3**	**118.0**	**121.4**
Never married................	48.2	53.9	61.5	64.5	26.1	29.6	33.7	34.5	22.1	24.3	27.8	30.1
Married [2]..................	120.1	127.4	129.5	131.1	59.6	63.3	64.4	65.2	60.4	64.0	65.1	65.9
Widowed.....................	13.7	13.8	14.3	14.1	2.6	2.7	3.0	2.9	11.1	11.1	11.4	11.2
Divorced....................	19.8	22.1	23.7	24.9	8.5	9.2	10.0	10.7	11.3	12.9	13.7	14.2
Percent of total............	100.0	100.0	100.0	100.0	100.0	100.0	100.0	100.0	100.0	100.0	100.0	100.0
Never married................	23.9	24.8	26.9	27.5	27.0	28.2	30.4	30.4	21.1	21.6	23.6	24.8
Married [2]..................	59.5	58.6	56.4	55.9	61.5	60.4	57.9	57.5	57.6	56.9	55.1	54.4
Widowed.....................	6.8	6.4	6.3	6.0	2.7	2.6	2.7	2.5	10.5	9.9	9.6	9.2
Divorced....................	9.8	10.2	10.4	10.6	8.8	8.8	9.0	9.4	10.8	11.5	11.7	11.7
White, total [3]...........	**168.1**	**177.5**	**185.7**	**187.1**	**81.6**	**86.6**	**91.2**	**91.4**	**86.6**	**90.9**	**94.5**	**95.6**
Never married................	36.0	39.7	45.1	46.2	20.3	22.6	25.7	25.6	15.7	17.0	19.4	20.5
Married [2]..................	104.1	108.3	109.4	109.1	51.8	54.0	54.7	54.5	52.2	54.2	54.7	54.6
Widowed.....................	11.5	11.5	11.8	11.5	2.2	2.3	2.5	2.4	9.3	9.2	9.3	9.1
Divorced....................	16.5	18.1	19.4	20.2	7.2	7.6	8.3	8.8	9.3	10.4	11.1	11.4
Percent of total............	100.0	100.0	100.0	100.0	100.0	100.0	100.0	100.0	100.0	100.0	100.0	100.0
Never married................	21.4	22.3	24.3	24.7	24.9	26.1	28.2	28.0	18.1	18.7	20.6	21.5
Married [2]..................	62.0	61.0	58.9	58.4	63.5	62.4	60.0	59.7	60.3	59.7	57.9	57.1
Widowed.....................	6.8	6.5	6.3	6.2	2.7	2.6	2.7	2.7	10.8	10.2	9.8	9.5
Divorced....................	9.8	10.2	10.4	10.8	8.8	8.8	9.1	9.7	10.7	11.5	11.7	11.9
Black, total [3]............	**24.0**	**25.2**	**27.3**	**28.5**	**10.7**	**11.2**	**12.3**	**12.8**	**13.3**	**13.9**	**15.0**	**15.7**
Never married................	9.5	10.2	11.7	12.3	4.3	4.7	5.5	5.6	5.1	5.5	6.2	6.7
Married [2]..................	10.1	10.3	10.6	11.0	5.0	5.0	5.2	5.5	5.1	5.2	5.3	5.5
Widowed.....................	1.7	1.7	1.8	1.7	0.3	0.3	0.4	0.3	1.4	1.4	1.5	1.4
Divorced....................	2.8	2.9	3.2	3.4	1.1	1.1	1.2	1.4	1.7	1.8	2.0	2.0
Percent of total............	100.0	100.0	100.0	100.0	100.0	100.0	100.0	100.0	100.0	100.0	100.0	100.0
Never married................	39.4	40.6	42.8	43.4	40.2	42.0	44.5	44.2	38.3	39.5	41.4	42.8
Married [2]..................	42.1	41.0	38.8	38.6	46.7	45.5	42.7	42.7	38.3	37.4	35.6	35.1
Widowed.....................	7.0	6.6	6.7	6.1	2.8	2.7	2.9	2.4	10.5	10.0	9.8	9.1
Divorced....................	11.5	11.7	11.7	11.9	10.3	9.8	9.9	10.6	12.8	13.3	13.2	13.0
Asian, total [3]............	**(NA)**	**9.4**	**10.7**	**12.4**	**(NA)**	**4.5**	**5.1**	**5.8**	**(NA)**	**4.9**	**5.6**	**6.6**
Never married................	(NA)	2.3	2.7	3.3	(NA)	1.3	1.5	1.8	(NA)	1.0	1.2	1.6
Married [2]..................	(NA)	6.2	7.0	8.1	(NA)	2.9	3.3	3.7	(NA)	3.3	3.7	4.3
Widowed.....................	(NA)	0.4	0.5	0.5	(NA)	0.1	0.1	0.1	(NA)	0.3	0.5	0.4
Divorced....................	(NA)	0.5	0.5	0.5	(NA)	0.2	0.2	0.2	(NA)	0.3	0.3	0.3
Percent of total............	100.0	100.0	100.0	100.0	100.0	100.0	100.0	100.0	100.0	100.0	100.0	100.0
Never married................	(NA)	24.8	25.1	26.9	(NA)	29.7	29.8	30.9	(NA)	20.3	20.8	23.4
Married [2]..................	(NA)	65.6	65.5	64.8	(NA)	64.7	65.5	64.8	(NA)	66.5	65.7	64.9
Widowed.....................	(NA)	4.3	4.9	3.9	(NA)	1.3	1.3	1.1	(NA)	6.7	8.1	6.4
Divorced....................	(NA)	5.3	4.5	4.3	(NA)	4.1	3.4	3.2	(NA)	6.4	5.4	5.2
Hispanic, total [4]..........	**21.1**	**27.5**	**31.8**	**34.7**	**10.4**	**14.1**	**16.4**	**17.4**	**10.7**	**13.4**	**15.4**	**17.2**
Never married................	5.9	8.6	10.9	12.2	3.4	5.2	6.5	7.0	2.5	3.4	4.4	5.2
Married [2]..................	12.7	15.6	17.1	18.4	6.2	7.8	8.6	9.1	6.5	7.8	8.5	9.3
Widowed.....................	0.9	1.0	1.2	1.2	0.2	0.2	0.3	0.3	0.7	0.8	0.9	1.0
Divorced....................	1.6	2.2	2.6	2.9	0.7	0.9	1.1	1.1	1.0	1.3	1.5	1.7
Percent of total............	100.0	100.0	100.0	100.0	100.0	100.0	100.0	100.0	100.0	100.0	100.0	100.0
Never married................	28.0	31.3	34.2	35.2	32.3	36.7	39.3	39.9	23.4	25.6	28.7	30.4
Married [2]..................	60.2	57.0	53.8	53.0	59.7	55.6	52.2	52.1	60.7	58.7	55.6	54.1
Widowed.....................	4.2	3.7	3.8	3.5	1.6	1.5	1.8	1.4	6.5	6.1	5.8	5.6
Divorced....................	7.6	7.9	8.2	8.2	6.4	6.3	6.7	6.6	9.3	9.7	9.9	9.9
Non-Hispanic White, total [3]...........	**(NA)**	**151.9**	**156.2**	**155.9**	**(NA)**	**73.4**	**75.9**	**75.7**	**(NA)**	**78.5**	**80.3**	**80.2**
Never married................	(NA)	31.8	35.2	35.4	(NA)	17.8	19.8	19.5	(NA)	13.9	15.5	16.0
Married [2]..................	(NA)	93.5	93.3	92.3	(NA)	46.6	46.6	46.2	(NA)	47.0	46.7	46.1
Widowed.....................	(NA)	10.6	10.6	10.4	(NA)	2.1	2.2	2.2	(NA)	8.5	8.4	8.2
Divorced....................	(NA)	16.0	17.0	17.7	(NA)	6.8	7.3	7.8	(NA)	9.2	9.7	9.9
Percent of total............	100.0	100.0	100.0	100.0	100.0	100.0	100.0	100.0	100.0	100.0	100.0	100.0
Never married................	(NA)	20.9	22.6	22.7	(NA)	24.3	26.0	25.7	(NA)	17.7	19.3	19.9
Married [2]..................	(NA)	61.5	59.7	59.2	(NA)	63.5	61.4	61.0	(NA)	59.7	58.1	57.5
Widowed.....................	(NA)	6.9	6.8	6.7	(NA)	2.8	2.9	2.9	(NA)	10.8	10.5	10.3
Divorced....................	(NA)	10.6	10.9	11.4	(NA)	9.3	9.7	10.3	(NA)	11.7	12.1	12.3

NA Not available. [1] Includes persons of other races not shown separately. [2] Includes persons who are married with spouse present, married with spouse absent, and separated. [3] Beginning 2005, data represent persons who selected this race group only and exclude persons reporting more than one race. The CPS in 2000 only allowed respondents to report one race group. See also comments on race in the text for this section. [4] Hispanic persons may be of any race.

Source: U.S. Census Bureau, Current Population Reports, P20-537, 2001; and "America's Families and Living Arrangements," <http://www.census.gov/hhes/families/data/cps.html>, accessed April 2013.

Table 60. Marital Status of the Population by Sex and Age: 2012

[As of March (113,213 represents 113,213,000). Excludes members of Armed Forces except those living off post or with their families on post. Population controls based on Census 2010. Based on Current Population Survey, see text, this section, and Appendix III]

Sex and age	Number of persons (1,000)					Percent distribution				
	Total	Never married	Married [1]	Widowed	Divorced	Total	Never married	Married [1]	Widowed	Divorced
Male	**113,213**	**34,471**	**65,190**	**2,864**	**10,688**	**100.0**	**30.4**	**57.5**	**2.5**	**9.4**
18 to 19 years old	4,172	4,051	106	4	12	100.0	97.1	2.6	0.1	0.3
20 to 24 years old	10,982	9,800	1,102	9	70	100.0	89.2	10.0	0.1	0.6
25 to 29 years old	10,430	6,620	3,494	10	305	100.0	63.5	33.5	0.1	2.9
30 to 34 years old	10,028	3,924	5,493	8	602	100.0	39.1	54.8	0.1	6.0
35 to 39 years old	9,418	2,294	6,240	38	847	100.0	24.4	66.2	0.4	9.0
40 to 44 years old	10,252	2,057	6,957	27	1,212	100.0	20.1	67.8	0.3	11.8
45 to 54 years old	21,463	3,202	14,961	208	3,093	100.0	14.9	69.7	1.0	14.4
55 to 64 years old	18,137	1,707	13,157	446	2,826	100.0	9.4	72.6	2.5	15.6
65 to 74 years old	10,980	541	8,471	690	1,278	100.0	4.9	77.2	6.3	11.6
75 years old and over	7,352	275	5,210	1,425	444	100.0	3.7	70.9	19.4	6.0
Female	**121,385**	**30,061**	**65,926**	**11,190**	**14,208**	**100.0**	**24.8**	**54.4**	**9.2**	**11.7**
18 to 19 years old	4,083	3,938	121	11	14	100.0	96.4	2.9	0.3	0.3
20 to 24 years old	10,888	8,850	1,890	23	124	100.0	81.3	17.4	0.2	1.1
25 to 29 years old	10,459	5,338	4,625	33	463	100.0	51.0	44.2	0.3	4.4
30 to 34 years old	10,284	3,055	6,365	28	836	100.0	29.7	62.0	0.3	8.1
35 to 39 years old	9,714	1,953	6,560	80	1,122	100.0	20.1	67.4	0.8	11.5
40 to 44 years old	10,530	1,580	7,342	144	1,464	100.0	15.0	69.7	1.4	13.9
45 to 54 years old	22,459	2,628	15,313	709	3,810	100.0	11.7	68.2	3.2	17.0
55 to 64 years old	19,808	1,716	12,881	1,622	3,588	100.0	8.7	65.0	8.2	18.1
65 to 74 years old	12,393	588	7,160	2,717	1,929	100.0	4.7	57.8	21.9	15.6
75 years old and over	10,767	415	3,670	5,823	860	100.0	3.9	34.1	54.1	8.0

[1] Includes persons who are married with spouse present, married with spouse absent, and separated.

Source: U.S. Census Bureau, "America's Families and Living Arrangements: 2012, Table 1A. Marital Status of People 15 Years and Over, by Age, Sex, Personal Earnings, Race, and Hispanic Origin: 2012," <http://www.census.gov/hhes/families/data/cps2012.html>, accessed April 2013.

Table 61. Living Arrangements of Persons 15 Years Old and Over by Age and Sex: 2012

[As of March (247,573 represents 247,353,000). See headnote, Table 60]

Living arrangement	Total	15 to 19 years old	20 to 24 years old	25 to 34 years old	35 to 44 years old	45 to 54 years old	55 to 64 years old	65 to 74 years old	75 years old and over
NUMBER (1,000)									
Total	**247,573**	**21,230**	**21,870**	**41,201**	**39,914**	**43,921**	**37,944**	**23,373**	**18,120**
Alone	33,188	110	1,269	4,082	3,455	5,552	6,903	5,198	6,620
With spouse	117,898	102	2,120	17,518	24,233	27,125	23,886	14,709	8,205
With other persons	96,487	21,018	18,481	19,601	12,226	11,244	7,155	3,466	3,295
Male	119,877	10,836	10,982	20,458	19,670	21,463	18,137	10,980	7,352
Alone	14,835	58	596	2,323	2,137	3,052	3,206	1,829	1,633
With spouse	58,949	33	763	7,872	11,888	13,425	12,123	7,994	4,852
With other persons	46,093	10,745	9,623	10,263	5,645	4,986	2,808	1,157	867
Female	127,695	10,393	10,888	20,743	20,244	22,459	19,808	12,393	10,767
Alone	18,354	51	673	1,758	1,319	2,501	3,697	3,369	4,987
With spouse	58,949	69	1,355	9,649	12,344	13,701	11,765	6,716	3,352
With other persons	50,392	10,273	8,860	9,336	6,581	6,257	4,346	2,308	2,428
PERCENT DISTRIBUTION									
Total	100.0	100.0	100.0	100.0	100.0	100.0	100.0	100.0	100.0
Alone	13.4	0.5	5.8	9.9	8.7	12.6	18.2	22.2	36.5
With spouse	47.6	0.5	9.7	42.5	60.7	61.8	63.0	62.9	45.3
With other persons	39.0	99.0	84.5	47.6	30.6	25.6	18.9	14.8	18.2
Male	100.0	100.0	100.0	100.0	100.0	100.0	100.0	100.0	100.0
Alone	12.4	0.5	5.4	11.4	10.9	14.2	17.7	16.7	22.2
With spouse	49.2	0.3	6.9	38.5	60.4	62.5	66.8	72.8	66.0
With other persons	38.5	99.2	87.6	50.2	28.7	23.2	15.5	10.5	11.8
Female	100.0	100.0	100.0	100.0	100.0	100.0	100.0	100.0	100.0
Alone	14.4	0.5	6.2	8.5	6.5	11.1	18.7	27.2	46.3
With spouse	46.2	0.7	12.4	46.5	61.0	61.0	59.4	54.2	31.1
With other persons	39.5	98.8	81.4	45.0	32.5	27.9	21.9	18.6	22.6

Source: U.S. Census Bureau, "America's Families and Living Arrangements: 2012, Table A2. Family Status and Household Relationship of People 15 Years and Over, by Marital Status, Age, and Sex: 2012," <http://www.census.gov/hhes/families/data/cps2012.html>, accessed April 2013.

Table 62. Households, Families, Subfamilies, and Married Couples: 1990 to 2012

[In thousands, except as indicated (93,347 represents 93,347,000). As of March. Excludes members of Armed Forces except those living off post or with their families on post. Beginning 2005, based on an expanded sample of households. 2005 and 2010 data based on Census 2000 population controls. Beginning 2011, based on Census 2010 population controls. Based on Current Population Survey, see text, this section and Appendix III. Minus sign (-) indicates decrease]

Type of unit	1990	2000	2005	2010	2011	2012	Percent change 1990 to 2000	Percent change 2000 to 2010	Percent change 2010 to 2012
Households	**93,347**	**104,705**	**113,343**	**117,538**	**119,927**	**121,084**	**12**	**12**	**3**
Persons per household	2.63	2.62	2.57	2.59	2.56	2.55	(X)	(X)	(X)
White [1]	80,163	87,671	92,880	95,489	96,306	96,964	9	9	2
Black [1]	10,486	12,849	13,809	14,730	15,265	15,583	23	15	6
Asian [1]	(NA)	(NA)	4,123	4,687	5,212	5,374	(NA)	(NA)	15
Hispanic [2]	5,933	9,319	12,178	13,298	14,435	14,939	57	43	12
Family households	66,090	72,025	76,858	78,833	79,539	80,506	9	9	2
Married couple	52,317	55,311	57,975	58,410	58,656	58,949	6	6	1
Male householder [3]	2,884	4,028	4,901	5,580	5,648	5,888	40	39	6
Female householder [3]	10,890	12,687	13,981	14,843	15,235	15,669	17	17	6
Nonfamily households	27,257	32,680	36,485	38,705	40,388	40,578	20	18	5
Male householder	11,606	14,641	16,543	18,263	18,968	19,195	26	25	5
Female householder	15,651	18,039	19,942	20,442	21,420	21,383	15	13	5
One person	22,999	26,724	30,137	31,399	33,020	33,188	16	17	6
Families	**66,090**	**72,025**	**76,858**	**78,833**	**79,539**	**80,506**	**9**	**9**	**2**
Persons per family	3.17	3.17	3.13	3.16	3.14	3.13	(X)	(X)	(X)
With own children [4]	32,289	34,605	36,211	35,218	35,060	34,989	7	2	-1
Without own children [4]	33,801	37,420	40,647	43,615	44,479	45,517	11	17	4
Married couple	52,317	55,311	57,975	58,410	58,656	58,949	6	6	1
With own children [4]	24,537	25,248	25,919	24,575	24,112	23,704	3	-3	-4
Without own children [4]	27,780	30,062	32,056	33,835	34,544	35,245	8	13	4
Male householder [3]	2,884	4,028	4,901	5,580	5,648	5,888	40	39	6
With own children [4]	1,153	1,786	2,021	2,224	2,247	2,415	55	25	9
Without own children [4]	1,731	2,242	2,880	3,356	3,401	3,473	30	50	3
Female householder [3]	10,890	12,687	13,981	14,843	15,235	15,669	17	17	6
With own children [4]	6,599	7,571	8,270	8,419	8,701	8,869	15	11	5
Without own children [4]	4,290	5,116	5,711	6,424	6,534	6,799	19	26	6
Unrelated subfamilies	534	571	515	484	(NA)	604	7	-15	25
Married couple	68	37	62	93	(NA)	108	(B)	(B)	16
Male reference persons [3]	45	57	61	44	(NA)	75	(B)	(B)	(B)
Female reference persons [3]	421	477	392	347	(NA)	421	13	-27	21
Related subfamilies	2,403	2,984	3,427	4,300	(NA)	4,353	24	44	1
Married couple	871	1,149	1,336	1,881	(NA)	1,990	32	64	6
Father-child [3]	153	201	387	313	(NA)	315	31	56	1
Mother-child [3]	1,378	1,634	1,704	2,106	(NA)	2,048	19	29	-3
Married couples	**53,256**	**56,497**	**59,373**	**60,384**	**(NA)**	**61,047**	**6**	**7**	**1**
With own household	52,317	55,311	57,975	58,410	58,656	58,949	6	6	1
Without own household	939	1,186	1,398	1,974	(NA)	2,098	26	66	6
Percent without	1.8	2.1	2.4	3.2	(NA)	3.4	(X)	(X)	(X)

B Base less than 75,000. NA Not available. X Not applicable. [1] Beginning with the 2003 Current Population Survey (CPS), respondents could choose more than one race. Beginning 2005, data shown represent persons who selected this race group only and exclude persons reporting more than one race. The CPS prior to 2003 only allowed respondents to report one race group. See also comments on race in the text for this section. [2] Persons of Hispanic origin may be of any race. [3] No spouse present. [4] Under 18 years old.

Source: U.S. Census Bureau, "Current Population Survey Data on Families and Living Arrangements," <http://www.census.gov/hhes/families/data/cps.html>, accessed April 2013.

Table 63. Interracially Married Couples by Race and Hispanic Origin of Spouses: 1980 to 2012

[In thousands (49,714 represents 49,714,000). As of March. Persons 15 years old and over. Persons of Hispanic origin may be of any race. Population controls for 2010 and 2011 based on Census 2000; population controls for 2012 based on Census 2010. Based on Current Population Survey; see headnote, Table 62 and Appendix III]

Race and origin of spouses	1980	1990	2000	2010	2011	2012
Married couples, total [1]	**49,714**	**53,256**	**56,497**	**60,384**	**60,155**	**61,047**
Interracial married couples, total	651	964	1,464	2,413	2,393	2,599
White [2]/Black [2]	167	211	363	558	515	537
Black husband/White wife	122	150	268	390	356	381
White husband/Black wife	45	61	95	168	159	156
White [2]/other race [3]	450	720	1,051	1,723	1,748	1,923
Black [2]/other race [3]	34	33	50	132	130	139
HISPANIC ORIGIN						
Hispanic/Hispanic	1,906	3,085	4,739	6,166	6,255	6,730
Hispanic/other origin (not Hispanic)	891	1,193	1,743	2,289	2,363	2,531
All other couples (not of Hispanic origin)	46,917	48,979	50,015	51,928	51,536	51,787

[1] Includes other married couples not shown separately. [2] See footnote 1, Table 62. [3] "Other race," is any race other than White or Black, such as American Indian, Japanese, Chinese, etc. This total excludes combinations of other races by other races.

Source: U.S. Census Bureau, "Families and Living Arrangements, Table MS-3. Interracial Married Couples: 1980 to 2002;" and "America's Families and Living Arrangements, Table FG3. Married Couple Family Groups, By Presence Of Own Children Under 18, And Age, Earnings, Education, And Race And Hispanic Origin Of Both Spouses," <http://www.census.gov/hhes/families/data/cps.html>, accessed April 2013.

Table 64. Households and Persons Per Household by Type of Household: 2000 to 2012

[As of March (104,705 represents 104,705,000). See headnote, Table 62]

Type of household	Households						Persons per household		
	Number (1,000)			Percent distribution					
	2000	2010	2012	2000	2010	2012	2000	2010	2012
Total households................................	104,705	117,538	121,084	100	100	100	2.62	2.59	2.55
Family households................................	72,025	78,833	80,506	69	67	66	3.24	3.24	3.21
Married couple family..............................	55,311	58,410	58,949	53	50	49	3.26	3.24	3.20
Male householder, no spouse present........	4,028	5,580	5,888	4	5	5	3.16	3.24	3.20
Female householder, no spouse present.....	12,687	14,843	15,669	12	13	13	3.17	3.23	3.24
Nonfamily households.............................	32,680	38,705	40,578	31	33	34	1.25	1.26	1.24
Living alone..	26,724	31,399	33,188	26	27	27	1.00	1.00	1.00
Male householder.................................	14,641	18,263	19,195	14	16	16	1.34	1.35	1.32
Living alone..	11,181	13,971	14,835	11	12	12	1.00	1.00	1.00
Female householder..............................	18,039	20,442	21,383	17	17	18	1.17	1.18	1.17
Living alone..	15,543	17,428	18,354	15	15	15	1.00	1.00	1.00

Source: U.S. Census Bureau, Current Population Reports, P20-537, 2001; and "America's Families and Living Arrangements," <http://www.census.gov/hhes/families/data/cps.html>, accessed April 2013.

Table 65. Households by Age of Householder and Size of Household: 1990 to 2012

[In millions (93.3 represents 93,300,000). As of March. Based on Current Population Survey; see headnote, Table 62]

Age of householder and size of household	1990	2000	2010	2012					
				Total [1]	White [2]	Black [2]	Asian [2]	Hispanic [3]	Non-Hispanic White [2]
Total........................	93.3	104.7	117.5	121.1	97.0	15.6	5.4	14.9	83.6
15 to 24 years old............	5.1	5.9	6.2	6.2	4.5	1.1	0.4	1.3	3.4
25 to 29 years old............	9.4	8.5	9.4	9.2	7.0	1.3	0.5	1.6	5.6
30 to 34 years old............	11.0	10.1	9.8	10.6	8.1	1.5	0.6	1.9	6.3
35 to 44 years old............	20.6	24.0	21.5	21.2	16.3	3.1	1.3	3.6	13.1
45 to 54 years old............	14.5	20.9	24.9	24.2	19.2	3.2	1.1	2.9	16.6
55 to 64 years old............	12.5	13.6	20.4	22.8	18.6	2.9	0.8	1.9	16.9
65 to 74 years old............	11.7	11.3	13.2	14.5	12.3	1.5	0.4	1.0	11.4
75 years old and over........	8.4	10.4	12.1	12.3	10.9	1.0	0.3	0.6	10.3
One person...................	23.0	26.7	31.4	33.2	26.2	5.2	0.9	2.5	24.0
Male......................	9.0	11.2	14.0	14.8	11.7	2.3	0.4	1.3	10.6
Female....................	14.0	15.5	17.4	18.4	14.5	2.9	0.5	1.3	13.4
Two persons.................	30.1	34.7	39.5	41.0	34.3	4.2	1.5	3.4	31.3
Three persons...............	16.1	17.2	18.6	19.2	14.9	2.6	1.1	2.9	12.3
Four persons................	14.5	15.3	16.1	16.0	12.6	1.9	1.1	2.9	10.0
Five persons................	6.2	7.0	7.4	7.3	5.6	0.9	0.4	1.8	4.0
Six persons.................	2.1	2.4	2.8	2.7	2.1	0.4	0.2	0.8	1.4
Seven persons or more.....	1.3	1.4	1.7	1.6	1.1	0.3	0.1	0.6	0.6

[1] Includes other races, not shown separately. [2] Represents persons who selected this race group only and excludes persons reporting more than one race. See also comments on race in the text for this section. [3] Hispanic persons may be of any race.

Source: U.S. Census Bureau, Current Population Reports, P20-537, and earlier reports; "Table HINC-01. Selected Characteristics of Households, by Total Money Income in 2011," and "Table HINC-02. Age of Householder--Households, by Total Money Income in 2011, Type of Household, Race and Hispanic Origin of Householder," <http://www.census.gov/hhes/www/cpstables/032012/hhinc/toc.htm>, accessed April 2013.

Table 66. Unmarried-Partner Households by Region and Sex of Partners: 2011

[The American Community Survey universe includes the household population and the population living in institutions, college dormitories, and other group quarters. For composition of regions, see inside front cover. Based on a sample and subject to sampling variability; see text, this section and Appendix III]

Item	Total	Northeast	Midwest	South	West
Total households...	114,991,725	20,914,732	25,877,131	42,703,311	25,496,551
Unmarried-partner households......................	6,715,374	1,249,124	1,528,181	2,241,677	1,696,392
Male householder and male partner......................	284,295	57,751	50,579	95,729	80,236
Male householder and female partner.....................	3,074,955	557,162	707,291	1,030,932	779,570
Female householder and female partner..................	321,177	65,492	65,443	104,702	85,540
Female householder and male partner....................	3,034,947	568,719	704,868	1,010,314	751,046
All other households....................................	108,276,351	19,665,608	24,348,950	40,461,634	23,800,159

Source: U.S. Census Bureau, 2011 American Community Survey, B11009, "Unmarried-Partner Households by Sex of Partner," <http://factfinder2.census.gov/>, accessed April 2013.

Table 67. Family Households by Number of Own Children Under 18 Years of Age: 2000 to 2012

[As of March (72,025 represents 72,025,000). Based on Current Population Survey; see headnote, Table 70]

Race, Hispanic origin, and year	Number of families (1,000)					Percent distribution				
	Total	No children	One child	Two children	Three or more children	Total	No children	One child	Two children	Three or more children
ALL FAMILIES [1]										
2000	72,025	37,420	14,311	13,215	7,080	100	52	20	18	10
2010	78,833	43,615	15,149	12,947	7,122	100	55	19	16	9
2012, total	**80,506**	**45,517**	**15,033**	**12,999**	**6,957**	**100**	**57**	**19**	**16**	**9**
Married couple	58,949	35,245	9,215	9,442	5,047	100	60	16	16	9
Male householder [2]	5,888	3,473	1,419	704	293	100	59	24	12	5
Female householder [2]	15,669	6,799	4,399	2,853	1,618	100	43	28	18	10
WHITE FAMILIES [3]										
2000	60,251	32,144	11,496	10,918	5,693	100	53	19	18	9
2010	64,120	36,464	11,856	10,275	5,525	100	57	18	16	9
2012, total	**64,614**	**37,653**	**11,445**	**10,149**	**5,368**	**100**	**58**	**18**	**16**	**8**
Married couple	50,054	30,577	7,470	7,774	4,233	100	61	15	16	8
Male householder [2]	4,348	2,506	1,113	532	198	100	58	26	12	5
Female householder [2]	10,211	4,570	2,862	1,843	936	100	45	28	18	9
BLACK FAMILIES [3]										
2000	8,664	3,882	2,101	1,624	1,058	100	45	24	19	12
2010	9,358	4,502	2,142	1,608	1,106	100	48	23	17	12
2012, total	**9,651**	**4,731**	**2,255**	**1,597**	**1,067**	**100**	**49**	**23**	**17**	**11**
Married couple	4,361	2,454	801	672	434	100	56	18	15	10
Male householder [2]	956	568	213	107	68	100	59	22	11	7
Female householder [2]	4,334	1,710	1,242	818	565	100	39	29	19	13
ASIAN FAMILIES [3]										
2010	3,592	1,794	777	754	267	100	50	22	21	7
2012, total	**4,149**	**2,189**	**859**	**859**	**242**	**100**	**53**	**21**	**21**	**6**
Married couple	3,298	1,620	698	782	199	100	49	21	24	6
Male householder [2]	320	250	44	19	6	100	78	14	6	2
Female householder [2]	531	318	118	58	36	100	60	22	11	7
HISPANIC FAMILIES [4]										
2000	7,561	2,747	1,791	1,693	1,330	100	36	24	22	18
2010	10,412	4,173	2,344	2,269	1,626	100	40	23	22	16
2012, total	**11,585**	**4,673**	**2,649**	**2,517**	**1,747**	**100**	**40**	**23**	**22**	**15**
Married couple	7,222	2,855	1,513	1,686	1,168	100	40	21	23	16
Male householder [2]	1,277	772	285	142	78	100	60	22	11	6
Female householder [2]	3,086	1,046	851	689	501	100	34	28	22	16
NON-HISPANIC WHITE FAMILIES [3]										
2010	54,445	32,569	9,691	8,173	4,012	100	60	18	15	7
2012, total	**54,146**	**33,356**	**9,098**	**7,889**	**3,802**	**100**	**62**	**17**	**15**	**7**
Married couple	43,376	27,909	6,086	6,212	3,169	100	64	14	14	7
Male householder [2]	3,231	1,832	864	411	124	100	57	27	13	4
Female householder [2]	7,539	3,615	2,148	1,266	509	100	48	28	17	7

[1] Includes other races and non-Hispanic groups, not shown separately. [2] No spouse present. [3] Beginning with the 2003 Current Population Survey (CPS), respondents could choose more than one race. Beginning 2010 data represent persons who selected this race group only and exclude persons reporting more than one race. The CPS prior to 2003 only allowed respondents to report one race group. See also comments on race in the text for this section. [4] Hispanic persons may be of any race.

Source: U.S. Census Bureau, Current Population Reports, P20-537; and "America's Families and Living Arrangements," <http://www.census.gov/hhes/families/data/cps.html>, accessed April 2013.

Table 68. Family Households With Own Children Under 18 Years of Age by Type of Family, 2000 to 2012, and by Age of Householder, 2012

[As of March (34,605 represents 34,605,000). See headnote, Table 70]

Age of Householder	Family households with children		Married couple households with children		Male householder with children [1]		Female householder with children [1]	
	Number (1,000)	Percent of all family households	Number (1,000)	Percent of all married couple households	Number (1,000)	Percent of all male householder families [1]	Number (1,000)	Percent of all female householder families [1]
2000, total	34,605	48	25,248	46	1,786	44	7,571	60
2010, total	35,218	45	24,575	42	2,224	40	8,419	57
2012, total	**34,989**	**43**	**23,704**	**40**	**2,415**	**41**	**8,869**	**57**
15 to 24 years old	1,737	52	597	56	171	21	970	67
25 to 34 years old	9,996	74	6,153	71	765	53	3,077	90
35 to 44 years old	13,458	80	9,643	81	804	70	3,010	82
45 to 54 years old	8,093	46	6,048	45	514	46	1,531	49
55 to 64 years old	1,428	10	1,079	9	124	16	224	11
65 years old and over	277	2	183	2	37	6	57	3

[1] No spouse present.

Source: Current Population Reports, P20-537, 2001 and earlier reports; and "America's Families and Living Arrangements," November 2012, <http://www.census.gov/hhes/families/data/cps.html>.

Table 69. Families by Type, Race, and Hispanic Origin: 2012

[In thousands (80,506 represents 80,506,000). As of March. Excludes members of Armed Forces except those living off post or with their families on post. Population controls based on Census 2010 and an expanded sample of households. Based on Current Population Survey; see text, this section and Appendix III]

Characteristic	All families	Married couple families						Female family householder [4]						Male family householder, [4] all races
		All races [1]	White [2]	Black [2]	Asian [2]	Hispanic [3]	Non-Hispanic White [2]	All races [1]	White [2]	Black [2]	Asian [2]	Hispanic [3]	Non-Hispanic White [2]	
All families	**80,506**	**58,949**	**50,054**	**4,361**	**3,298**	**7,222**	**43,376**	**15,669**	**10,211**	**4,334**	**531**	**3,086**	**7,539**	**5,888**
Age of householder:														
Under 25 years old	3,333	1,059	905	88	24	241	674	1,456	917	406	61	423	547	819
25 to 34 years old	13,511	8,658	7,196	608	586	1,668	5,689	3,420	2,041	1,115	87	806	1,335	1,433
35 to 44 years old	16,782	11,954	9,733	1,009	916	2,031	7,863	3,672	2,369	1,045	120	811	1,691	1,156
45 to 54 years old	17,547	13,299	11,175	1,065	785	1,653	9,631	3,136	2,089	823	114	540	1,630	1,111
55 to 64 years old	14,902	12,093	10,415	905	567	959	9,524	2,013	1,331	540	84	296	1,064	795
65 to 74 years old	8,924	7,596	6,708	494	285	452	6,286	1,010	726	223	35	126	607	317
75 years old and over	5,508	4,290	3,922	192	136	218	3,709	962	737	182	30	85	664	256
Without own children under 18	45,517	35,245	30,577	2,454	1,620	2,855	27,909	6,799	4,570	1,710	318	1,046	3,615	3,473
With own children under 18	34,989	23,704	19,477	1,907	1,678	4,367	15,467	8,869	5,641	2,625	212	2,040	3,924	2,415
One own child under 18	15,033	9,215	7,470	801	698	1,513	6,086	4,399	2,862	1,242	118	851	2,148	1,419
Two own children under 18	12,999	9,442	7,774	672	782	1,686	6,212	2,853	1,843	818	58	689	1,266	704
Three or more own children under 18	6,957	5,047	4,233	434	199	1,168	3,169	1,618	936	565	36	501	509	293
Age of own children:														
Of any age [5]	47,912	30,882	25,323	2,559	2,199	5,332	20,409	13,397	8,739	3,782	371	2,639	6,481	3,633
Under 25 years old	41,601	27,929	22,998	2,233	1,962	4,943	18,452	10,693	6,814	3,162	266	2,325	4,853	2,978
Under 18 years old	34,989	23,704	19,477	1,907	1,678	4,367	15,467	8,869	5,641	2,625	212	2,040	3,924	2,415
Under 12 years old	25,601	17,530	14,351	1,398	1,287	3,387	11,231	6,368	3,980	1,949	152	1,559	2,661	1,703
Under 6 years old	15,343	10,676	8,728	831	813	2,121	6,780	3,636	2,276	1,119	75	970	1,444	1,031
Under 3 years old	8,606	6,104	5,003	473	471	1,157	3,934	1,884	1,192	567	37	504	763	618
Under 1 year old	2,802	2,015	1,665	136	149	339	1,353	559	353	175	14	127	239	228
Members 65 and older:														
Without members 65 and older	62,167	44,413	37,340	3,425	2,621	6,192	31,638	12,965	8,258	3,771	407	2,720	5,917	4,788
With members 65 and older	18,339	14,535	12,715	936	677	1,031	11,738	2,703	1,954	563	124	366	1,622	1,101
Marital status of householder:														
Married, spouse present	58,949	58,949	50,054	4,361	3,298	7,222	43,376	(X)	(X)	(X)	(X)	(X)	(X)	(X)
Married, spouse absent	910	(X)	(X)	(X)	(X)	(X)	(X)	647	398	163	73	183	233	263
Widowed	2,731	(X)	(X)	(X)	(X)	(X)	(X)	2,229	1,662	412	96	258	1,429	502
Divorced	7,007	(X)	(X)	(X)	(X)	(X)	(X)	5,174	3,935	939	132	806	3,225	1,833
Separated	2,033	(X)	(X)	(X)	(X)	(X)	(X)	1,547	1,015	418	35	456	634	486
Never married	8,876	(X)	(X)	(X)	(X)	(X)	(X)	6,071	3,207	2,406	194	1,386	2,019	2,805

X Not applicable. [1] Includes other races and non-Hispanic groups, not shown separately. [2] Beginning with the 2003 Current Population Survey (CPS), respondents could choose more than one race. Data represent persons who selected this race group only and exclude persons reporting more than one race. See also comments on race in the text for this section. [3] Persons of Hispanic origin may be of any race. [4] No spouse present. Data by race, Hispanic origin and marital status based on tabulations from CPS Table Creator. While tabulations may be conceptually the same as published estimates, in many cases they will not exactly match published estimates because the Table Creator uses the CPS public use file. [5] Children are included regardless of their marital status.

Source: U.S. Census Bureau, "America's Families and Living Arrangements: 2012," <http://www.census.gov/hhes/families/data/cps2012.html> and tabulations from "CPS Table Creator," <http://www.census.gov/cps/data/cpstablecreator.html>, accessed April 2013.

Table 70. Family Groups With Children Under 18 Years of Age by Race and Hispanic Origin: 2000 to 2012

[As of March. In thousands (37,496 represents 37,496,000). Family groups comprise family households, related subfamilies, and unrelated subfamilies. Excludes members of Armed Forces except those living off post or with their families on post. Beginning 2005, based on an expanded sample of households. Data for 2005 and 2010 based on Census 2000 population controls. Data for 2012 based on Census 2010 population controls. Based on Current Population Survey, see text, this section and Appendix III]

Race and Hispanic origin of householder or reference person	Number (1,000)				Percent distribution			
	2000	2005	2010	2012	2000	2005	2010	2012
All races, total [1]	**37,496**	**39,317**	**38,768**	**38,582**	**100**	**100**	**100**	**100**
Two-parent family groups [2]	25,771	26,482	27,082	26,304	69	67	70	68
One-parent family groups	11,725	12,835	11,686	12,278	31	32	30	32
Maintained by mother	9,681	10,366	9,924	10,322	26	26	26	27
Maintained by father	2,044	2,469	1,762	1,956	5	6	5	5
White, total [3]	**30,079**	**30,960**	**30,186**	**29,492**	**100**	**100**	**100**	**100**
Two-parent family groups [2]	22,241	22,319	22,457	21,437	74	72	74	73
One-parent family groups	7,838	8,641	7,729	8,055	26	28	26	27
Maintained by mother	6,216	6,747	6,396	6,566	21	22	21	22
Maintained by father	1,622	1,894	1,333	1,489	5	6	4	5
Black, total [3]	**5,530**	**5,495**	**5,555**	**5,621**	**100**	**100**	**100**	**100**
Two-parent family groups [2]	2,135	2,065	2,275	2,262	39	38	41	40
One-parent family groups	3,396	3,430	3,280	3,359	61	62	59	60
Maintained by mother	3,060	3,037	2,977	3,035	55	55	54	54
Maintained by father	335	393	303	324	6	7	5	6
Asian, total [3]	**1,469**	**1,757**	**1,986**	**2,166**	**100**	**100**	**100**	**100**
Two-parent family groups [2]	1,184	1,472	1,694	1,845	81	84	85	85
One-parent family groups	285	285	292	321	19	16	15	15
Maintained by mother	236	222	235	265	16	13	12	12
Maintained by father	49	63	57	56	3	4	3	3
Hispanic, total [4]	**5,503**	**6,752**	**7,355**	**7,990**	**100**	**100**	**100**	**100**
Two-parent family groups [2]	3,625	4,346	4,856	5,264	66	64	66	66
One-parent family groups	1,877	2,406	2,499	2,726	34	36	34	34
Maintained by mother	1,565	1,964	2,186	2,381	28	29	30	30
Maintained by father	313	442	313	345	6	7	4	4
Non-Hispanic White, total [3]	**24,847**	**24,730**	**23,368**	**22,347**	**100**	**100**	**100**	**100**
Two-parent family groups [2]	18,750	18,253	17,911	16,641	75	74	77	74
One-parent family groups	6,096	6,476	5,457	5,706	25	26	23	26
Maintained by mother	4,766	4,984	4,404	4,521	19	20	19	20
Maintained by father	1,331	1,492	1,053	1,185	5	6	5	5

[1] Includes other races and non-Hispanic groups, not shown separately. [2] Beginning 2007, includes children living both with married and unmarried parents. [3] Beginning with the 2003 Current Population Survey (CPS), respondents could choose more than one race. Beginning 2005, data represent persons who selected this race group only and exclude persons reporting more than one race. The CPS prior to 2003 allowed respondents to report only one race group. See also comments on race in the text for this section. [4] Hispanic persons may be of any race.

Source: U.S. Census Bureau, *Families and Living Arrangements,* Current Population Reports, P20-537, 2001; and "America's Families and Living Arrangements," November 2012, <http://www.census.gov/hhes/families/data/cps.html>.

Table 71. Parents and Children in Stay-At-Home Parent Family Groups: 1995 to 2012

[In thousands (22,973 represents 22,973,000). Family groups with children include those families that maintain their own household (family households with own children); those that live in the home of a relative (related subfamilies); and those that live in the home of a nonrelative (unrelated subfamilies). Stay-at-home family groups are married-couple family groups with children under 15 where one parent is in the labor force all of the previous year and their spouse is out of the labor force for the entire year with the reason 'taking care of home and family.' Only married couples with children under 15 are included. Based on Current Population Survey; see Appendix III]

Year	Married-couple family groups with children under 15 years old			Children under 15 years old in married-couple family groups		
	Total	With stay-at-home mothers	With stay-at-home fathers	Total	With stay-at-home mothers	With stay-at-home fathers
1995	22,973	4,440	64	41,008	9,106	125
1996	22,808	4,633	49	40,739	9,693	115
1997	22,779	4,617	71	40,798	9,788	140
1998	22,881	4,555	90	41,038	9,432	196
1999	22,754	4,731	71	41,003	9,796	143
2000	22,953	4,785	93	41,860	10,087	180
2001	22,922	4,934	81	41,862	10,194	148
2002	23,339	5,206	106	41,802	10,573	189
2003	23,209	5,388	98	41,654	11,028	175
2004	23,160	5,571	147	41,409	11,205	268
2005	23,305	5,584	142	41,111	11,224	247
2006	23,232	5,646	159	41,259	11,372	283
2007	23,507	5,563	165	41,559	11,193	303
2008	22,445	5,327	140	41,037	11,132	234
2009	22,523	5,095	158	41,208	10,934	290
2010	22,138	5,020	154	41,026	10,833	287
2011 [1]	21,689	4,976	176	40,592	10,763	343
2011 [2]	21,852	5,051	178	39,827	10,465	340
2012	21,334	5,091	189	39,222	10,675	369

[1] Based on Census 2000 population controls. [2] Based on Census 2010 population controls.

Source: U.S. Census Bureau, "Families and Living Arrangements, Table SHP-1. Parents and Children in Stay-At-Home Parent Family Groups: 1994 to Present," <http://www.census.gov/hhes/families/data/families.html>, accessed April 2013.

Table 72. Children Under 18 Years Old by Presence of Parents: 2000 to 2012

[As of March (72,012 represents 72,012,000). Excludes persons under 18 years old who maintained households or family groups and their spouses. Based on Current Population Survey; see headnote, Table 70]

Race, Hispanic origin, and year	Number (1,000)	Both parents [1]	Percent living with—							
			Mother only						Father only	Neither parent
			Total	Divorced	Married, spouse absent [2]	Never married	Widowed			
ALL RACES [3]										
2000	72,012	69.1	22.4	7.9	4.5	9.2	1.0		4.2	4.2
2005	73,494	67.3	23.4	7.9	4.6	10.1	0.8		4.8	4.5
2010	74,718	69.4	23.1	7.1	5.1	10.1	0.8		3.4	4.1
2011	74,630	68.9	23.6	7.2	4.7	10.8	0.9		3.5	3.9
2012	73,817	68.1	24.4	7.3	4.9	11.3	0.8		4.0	3.6
WHITE [4]										
2000	56,455	75.3	17.3	(NA)	(NA)	(NA)	(NA)		4.3	3.1
2005	56,234	73.5	18.4	7.9	4.0	5.8	0.7		4.7	3.4
2010	56,416	74.9	18.3	6.9	4.5	6.1	0.8		3.5	3.4
2011	56,319	74.6	18.7	7.1	4.1	6.6	0.9		3.6	3.2
2012	54,259	73.8	19.3	7.3	4.4	6.8	0.8		4.0	2.9
BLACK [4]										
2000	11,412	37.6	49.0	(NA)	(NA)	(NA)	(NA)		4.2	9.2
2005	11,293	35.0	50.2	8.7	8.1	32.0	1.3		5.0	9.8
2010	11,272	39.2	49.7	8.6	8.4	31.5	1.2		3.6	7.5
2011	11,155	37.7	51.3	8.6	8.2	33.5	1.0		3.5	7.6
2012	11,166	38.1	50.9	8.4	7.7	34.0	0.8		4.2	6.7
ASIAN [4]										
2005	2,843	83.6	10.2	4.0	2.3	2.7	1.3		3.6	2.5
2010	3,300	85.5	10.1	3.8	3.7	2.1	0.6		2.2	2.1
2011	3,297	87.4	9.1	3.5	2.8	2.1	0.6		1.3	2.3
2012	3,628	85.1	10.6	2.9	3.8	3.1	0.8		2.3	2.0
HISPANIC [5]										
2000	11,613	65.1	25.1	(NA)	(NA)	(NA)	(NA)		4.4	5.4
2005	14,241	64.7	25.4	6.1	7.1	11.4	0.8		4.8	5.2
2010	16,941	67.0	26.3	5.8	8.1	11.7	0.7		2.7	4.0
2011	17,418	66.9	26.5	6.2	6.7	12.8	0.7		2.8	3.9
2012	17,570	65.7	28.0	6.8	7.5	13.0	0.7		3.1	3.2
NON-HISPANIC WHITE [4]										
2005	43,106	75.9	16.4	8.5	3.1	4.2	0.7		4.8	2.9
2010	41,089	77.5	15.5	7.5	3.1	4.2	0.8		3.8	3.1
2011	40,616	77.2	15.9	7.6	3.1	4.3	0.9		4.0	3.0
2012	39,062	76.5	16.4	7.6	3.3	4.7	0.9		4.3	2.8

NA Not available. [1] Beginning in 2007, includes children living both with married and unmarried parents. [2] Includes separated. [3] Includes other races and non-Hispanic groups, not shown separately. [4] Beginning with the 2003 Current Population Survey (CPS), respondents could choose more than one race. Beginning 2005, data represent persons who selected this race group only and exclude persons reporting more than one race. The CPS prior to 2003 allowed respondents to report only one race group. See also comments on race in the text for this section. [5] Hispanic persons may be of any race.

Source: U.S. Census Bureau, "America's Families and Living Arrangements," November 2012, <http://www.census.gov/hhes/families/data/cps.html>.

Table 73. Grandparents Living With Grandchildren by Race and Sex: 2011

[In thousands (7,059 represents 7,059,000) except percent. Covers both grandparents living in own home with grandchildren present and grandparents living in grandchildren's home. The American Community Survey universe includes the household population and the population living in institutions, college dormitories, and other group quarters. Based on a sample and subject to sampling variability; see text, this section, and Appendix III]

Race, Hispanic origin, and sex	Grandparents living with own grandchildren, total	Grandparents responsible for grandchildren		
		Total	30 to 59 years old	60 years old and over
Grandparents living with own grandchildren under 18 years old (1,000)	**7,059**	**2,732**	**1,818**	**914**
PERCENT DISTRIBUTION				
Total	100.0	100.0	100.0	100.0
White alone	63.3	64.2	64.0	64.6
Black or African American alone	17.7	22.2	22.2	22.1
American Indian and Alaska Native alone	1.5	2.1	2.0	2.1
Asian alone	7.7	3.0	2.2	4.6
Native Hawaiian and Other Pacific Islander alone	0.4	0.3	0.4	0.3
Some other race alone	7.5	6.2	7.2	4.2
Two or more races	2.0	2.0	2.0	2.1
Hispanic origin [1]	25.3	20.5	23.1	15.4
White alone, not Hispanic	46.6	51.0	49.3	54.5
Male	35.9	37.4	35.0	42.2
Female	64.1	62.6	65.0	57.8

[1] Persons of Hispanic origin may be of any race.

Source: U.S. Census Bureau, American Community Survey 2011, Subject Table S1002, "Grandparents," <http://factfinder2.census.gov/>, accessed April 2013.

Table 74. Nonfamily Households by Sex and Age of Householder: 2012

[In thousands (19,196 represents 19,196,000). As of March. See headnote, Table 79]

Item	Male householder					Female householder				
	Total	15 to 24 yrs. old	25 to 44 yrs. old	45 to 64 yrs. old	65 yrs. old and over	Total	15 to 24 yrs. old	25 to 44 yrs. old	45 to 64 yrs. old	65 yrs. old and over
Total............................	**19,196**	**1,420**	**6,589**	**7,407**	**3,778**	**21,383**	**1,427**	**4,204**	**7,119**	**8,635**
One person (living alone).....	14,835	654	4,460	6,258	3,462	18,354	724	3,077	6,198	8,356
Nonrelatives present..........	4,361	766	2,129	1,149	316	3,029	703	1,127	921	279
Never married...................	9,578	1,361	4,920	2,699	599	7,214	1,355	3,161	2,085	616
Married spouse absent........	671	10	229	264	169	475	16	94	229	135
Separated.......................	1,070	16	303	588	161	813	20	205	433	155
Widowed........................	1,943	5	23	381	1,534	7,020	19	65	1,155	5,781
Divorced........................	5,934	30	1,115	3,474	1,315	5,860	17	678	3,217	1,948

Source: U.S. Census Bureau, "America's Families and Living Arrangements, Table A2. Family Status and Household Relationship of People 15 Years and Over, by Marital Status, Age, and Sex," November 2012, <http://www.census.gov/hhes/families/data/cps2012.html>.

Table 75. Group Quarters Population by Type of Group Quarter and Selected Characteristics: 2011

[In percent, except as indicated (8,006 represents 8,006,000). The American Community Survey universe includes the household population and the population living in institutions, college dormitories, and other group quarters. Based on a sample and subject to sampling variability; see text, this section, and Appendix III]

Characteristic	Total group quarters population [1]	Adult correctional facilities	Nursing facilities/ skilled nursing facilities	College/ university housing	Characteristic	Total group quarters population [1]	Adult correctional facilities	Nursing facilities/ skilled nursing facilities	College/ university housing
Total population (1,000)...................	**8,006**	**2,268**	**1,502**	**2,530**	One race (1,000).............	7,758	2,184	1,490	2,444
					Two or more races (1,000)...	248	83	12	86
PERCENT DISTRIBUTION					PERCENT DISTRIBUTION				
Male.........................	60.7	91.5	33.6	45.5	One race.....................	100.0	100.0	100.0	100.0
Female......................	39.3	8.5	66.4	54.5	White......................	67.8	50.0	82.7	75.7
					Black......................	23.1	40.3	13.8	13.1
Under 15 years old........	1.0	(X)	(X)	(X)	American Indian and				
15 to 17 years old.........	1.8	0.3	(X)	1.2	Alaska Native...............	1.2	2.1	0.4	0.5
18 to 24 years old.........	41.1	16.9	0.2	96.1	Asian......................	3.9	0.9	1.6	8.7
25 to 34 years old.........	13.1	32.7	0.6	2.2	Native Hawaiian/				
35 to 44 years old.........	9.8	24.8	1.5	0.3	Pacific Islander.............	0.2	0.2	0.1	0.2
45 to 54 years old.........	9.1	18.1	4.6	0.1	Some other race............	3.8	6.5	1.4	1.9
55 to 64 years old.........	5.8	5.9	9.5	0.1					
65 to 74 years old.........	4.0	1.1	14.6	0.0	Hispanic origin [2].............	12.0	20.6	4.8	7.3
75 to 84 years old.........	5.9	0.2	27.4	(X)	Not Hispanic.................	88.0	79.4	95.2	92.7
85 years old and over.....	8.5	0.0	41.6	(X)	White alone, not Hispanic..	58.7	35.8	79.0	68.6

X Not applicable. [1] Includes other types of group quarters, not shown separately. [2] Persons of Hispanic origin may be of any race.

Source: U.S. Census Bureau, 2011 American Community Survey, S2601A, "Characteristics of the Group Quarters Population;" S2601B, "Characteristics of the Group Quarters Population by Group Quarters Type," <http://factfinder2.census.gov/>, accessed April 2013.

Table 76. Population in Group Quarters by State: 2000 to 2012

[In thousands (7,780 represents 7,780,000). As of April, except 2012 as of July. For definition of group quarters, see text, this section]

State	2000 [1]	2010 [2]	2012	State	2000 [1]	2010 [2]	2012	State	2000 [1]	2010 [2]	2012
U.S......	**7,780**	**7,989**	**8,029**	KS........	82	79	79	NC........	254	257	255
AL........	115	116	115	KY........	115	126	126	ND........	24	25	26
AK........	19	26	27	LA........	136	127	128	OH........	299	306	307
AZ........	110	139	149	ME........	35	36	36	OK........	112	112	110
AR........	74	79	81	MD........	134	138	141	OR........	77	87	86
CA........	820	820	816	MA........	221	239	248	PA........	433	426	428
CO........	103	116	116	MI........	250	229	227	RI........	39	43	41
CT........	108	118	117	MN........	136	135	137	SC........	135	139	139
DE........	25	24	25	MS........	95	92	93	SD........	28	34	34
DC........	36	40	40	MO........	164	174	174	TN........	148	153	153
FL........	389	423	425	MT........	25	29	29	TX........	561	581	586
GA........	234	253	265	NE........	51	51	51	UT........	40	46	46
HI........	36	43	44	NV........	34	36	36	VT........	21	25	25
ID........	31	29	30	NH........	36	40	40	VA........	231	240	244
IL........	322	302	299	NJ........	195	187	187	WA........	136	139	141
IN........	178	187	188	NM........	36	43	43	WV........	43	49	49
IA........	104	99	100	NY........	581	586	584	WI........	156	150	148
								WY........	14	14	14

[1] The April 1, 2000, Population Estimates base reflects changes to the Census 2000 population from the Count Question Resolution program and geographic program revisions. [2] The April 1, 2010 population estimates base reflects changes to the Census 2010 population from the Count Question Resolution program and geographic program revisions.

Source: U.S. Census Bureau, "Annual Resident Population Estimates, Estimated Components of Resident Population Change, and Rates of the Components of Resident Population Change for States and Counties: April 1, 2000 to July 1, 2009," <http://www.census.gov/popest/data/counties/totals/2009/files/CO-EST2009-ALLDATA.csv> and "Population, population change and estimated components of population change: April 1, 2010 to July 1, 2012 (CO-EST2012-alldata)," <http://www.census.gov/popest/data/counties/totals/2012/index.html>, accessed April 2013.

Table 77. Same-Sex Couple Households by Sex, Partner Status and Presence of Children—States: 2010

[As of April. These preferred figures revise earlier estimates of same-sex unmarried partners released from the 2010 Census Summary File 1 because Census Bureau staff discovered an inconsistency in the responses in the 2010 Census summary file statistics that artificially inflated the number of same-sex couples. Statistics on same-sex couple households are derived from two questions on the census: relationship to householder and the sex of each person. When data were captured for these two questions on the 2010 Census door-to-door form, the wrong box may have been checked for the sex of a small percentage of opposite-sex spouses and unmarried partners. Because the population of opposite-sex married couples is large and the population of same-sex married couples in particular is small, an error of this type artificially inflates the number of same-sex married partners. After discovering the inconsistency, Census Bureau staff developed another set of estimates to provide a more accurate way to measure same-sex couple households. The revised figures were developed by using an index of names to re-estimate the number of same-sex married and unmarried partners by the sex commonly associated with the person's first name]

State	Same-sex households			Male householder			Female householder		
	Total	With own children under 18 years [1]	Without own children under 18 years	Total	Same-sex unmarried partner	Reported same-sex spouse	Total	Same-sex unmarried partner	Reported same-sex spouse
United States..............	646,464	111,033	535,431	313,577	249,354	64,223	332,887	265,381	67,506
Alabama......................	6,582	1,341	5,241	2,985	2,190	795	3,597	2,688	909
Alaska........................	1,228	284	944	466	331	135	762	619	143
Arizona.......................	15,817	2,608	13,209	7,521	6,315	1,206	8,296	7,237	1,059
Arkansas....................	4,226	898	3,328	1,914	1,371	543	2,312	1,815	497
California....................	98,153	15,698	82,455	52,490	38,093	14,397	45,663	31,748	13,915
Colorado....................	12,424	1,975	10,449	5,366	4,567	799	7,058	6,239	819
Connecticut................	7,852	1,338	6,514	3,473	2,329	1,144	4,379	2,819	1,560
Delaware....................	2,646	412	2,234	1,250	1,069	181	1,396	1,197	199
District of Columbia..........	4,822	419	4,403	3,583	3,086	497	1,239	991	248
Florida.......................	48,496	6,453	42,043	26,625	23,040	3,585	21,871	18,672	3,199
Georgia.....................	21,318	4,179	17,139	10,703	8,882	1,821	10,615	8,775	1,840
Hawaii.......................	3,239	513	2,726	1,715	1,417	298	1,524	1,242	282
Idaho........................	2,042	455	1,587	801	592	209	1,241	1,004	237
Illinois.......................	23,049	3,831	19,218	12,068	10,253	1,815	10,981	9,189	1,792
Indiana......................	11,074	2,090	8,984	4,838	4,050	788	6,236	5,421	815
Iowa.........................	4,093	761	3,332	1,730	1,179	551	2,363	1,541	822
Kansas......................	4,009	873	3,136	1,694	1,272	422	2,315	1,904	411
Kentucky....................	7,195	1,328	5,867	3,230	2,570	660	3,965	3,297	668
Louisiana...................	8,076	1,611	6,465	3,659	2,847	812	4,417	3,498	919
Maine........................	3,958	547	3,411	1,497	1,309	188	2,461	2,242	219
Maryland....................	12,538	2,544	9,994	5,320	4,260	1,060	7,218	5,957	1,261
Massachusetts...............	20,256	3,459	16,797	8,683	5,332	3,351	11,573	6,061	5,512
Michigan....................	14,598	2,650	11,948	6,314	5,262	1,052	8,284	7,134	1,150
Minnesota..................	10,207	1,681	8,526	4,658	4,031	627	5,549	4,846	703
Mississippi.................	3,484	895	2,589	1,459	992	467	2,025	1,442	583
Missouri.....................	10,557	1,828	8,729	4,953	4,127	826	5,604	4,838	766
Montana.....................	1,348	297	1,051	525	373	152	823	689	134
Nebraska...................	2,356	462	1,894	1,040	801	239	1,316	1,045	271
Nevada......................	7,140	1,217	5,923	3,768	3,087	681	3,372	2,801	571
New Hampshire...............	3,260	538	2,722	1,186	818	368	2,074	1,426	648
New Jersey..................	16,875	3,323	13,552	8,097	5,962	2,135	8,778	6,466	2,312
New Mexico.................	5,825	1,038	4,787	2,222	1,844	378	3,603	3,123	480
New York....................	48,932	8,025	40,907	26,681	21,572	5,109	22,251	17,235	5,016
North Carolina..............	18,309	3,380	14,929	8,037	6,461	1,576	10,272	8,624	1,648
North Dakota...............	559	121	438	247	169	78	312	244	68
Ohio.........................	19,684	3,480	16,204	8,987	7,643	1,344	10,697	9,380	1,317
Oklahoma...................	6,134	1,280	4,854	2,778	2,092	686	3,356	2,707	649
Oregon......................	11,773	1,920	9,853	4,622	3,746	876	7,151	6,025	1,126
Pennsylvania................	22,336	3,543	18,793	10,519	8,989	1,530	11,817	10,119	1,698
Rhode Island................	2,785	432	2,353	1,215	961	254	1,570	1,232	338
South Carolina.............	7,214	1,360	5,854	3,160	2,400	760	4,054	3,218	836
South Dakota...............	714	151	563	313	219	94	401	320	81
Tennessee.................	10,898	1,968	8,930	5,054	4,099	955	5,844	4,840	1,004
Texas........................	46,401	9,191	37,210	22,412	18,137	4,275	23,989	19,867	4,122
Utah.........................	3,909	786	3,123	1,841	1,405	436	2,068	1,695	373
Vermont.....................	2,143	399	1,744	718	463	255	1,425	925	500
Virginia......................	14,243	2,279	11,964	6,990	5,731	1,259	7,253	6,038	1,215
Washington.................	19,003	2,998	16,005	8,636	7,139	1,497	10,367	8,792	1,575
West Virginia................	2,848	507	2,341	1,330	974	356	1,518	1,194	324
Wisconsin...................	9,179	1,505	7,674	3,936	3,334	602	5,243	4,651	592
Wyoming....................	657	162	495	268	169	99	389	309	80

[1] The "own children" category includes any child under 18 years who is a son or daughter by birth, a stepchild, or an adopted child of the householder.

Source: U.S. Census Bureau, "Same-sex Couple Household Statistics from the 2010 Census," September 2011, <http://www.census.gov/hhes/samesex/>.

Table 78. Household Characteristics of Opposite-Sex and Same-Sex Couple Households: 2011

[In percent, except as indicated (55,520 represents 55,520,000). The American Community Survey universe includes the household population and the population living in institutions, college dormitories, and other group quarters. Based on a sample and subject to sampling variability. See text, this section and Appendix III]

Household Characteristics	Married opposite-sex couples	Unmarried opposite-sex couples	Unmarried same-sex couples		
			Total	Male-male couples	Female-female couples
Total households (1,000)	**55,520**	**6,110**	**605**	**284**	**321**
Age of householder:					
15 to 24 years old	1.4	13.2	3.9	3.0	4.7
25 to 34 years old	13.6	35.3	16.5	15.0	17.8
35 to 44 years old	20.6	21.3	20.8	21.4	20.2
45 to 54 years old	23.4	16.3	29.1	30.5	27.9
55 to 64 years old	21.0	9.3	17.2	18.5	16.0
65 years old and over	20.0	4.6	12.6	11.6	13.5
Average age of householder (years)	51.3	38.3	47.7	48.0	47.5
Average age of spouse/partner (years)	50.3	37.5	45.8	45.8	45.8
Race of householder:					
White	82.8	76.5	85.3	86.9	83.8
Black or African American	6.9	11.6	7.0	5.9	8.1
American Indian or Alaska Native	0.6	1.2	0.7	0.5	0.8
Asian	5.0	2.2	2.4	2.6	2.1
Native Hawaiian or Pacific Islander	0.1	0.2	0.2	0.2	0.3
Some other race	3.2	5.9	2.3	2.2	2.5
Two or more races	1.4	2.4	2.1	1.8	2.4
Percent of interracial couples	6.4	12.7	13.9	15.1	12.8
Hispanic origin of householder:					
Hispanic [1]	11.8	18.3	9.8	10.2	9.4
White alone, not Hispanic	74.7	65.2	78.6	79.5	77.9
Educational attainment:					
Householder has at least a bachelor's degree	35.8	21.7	48.8	52.3	45.7
Both partners with at least a bachelor's degree	22.3	11.2	31.0	32.4	29.8
Employment status: [2]					
Householder employed	67.5	75.0	73.2	74.4	72.2
Both partners employed	47.2	54.7	58.0	58.4	57.6
Children in the household:					
Children in the household [3]	40.7	41.8	17.5	11.0	23.2
Own children in the household	40.6	38.6	16.4	10.5	21.6
Household income:					
Less than $35,000	17.2	32.5	16.4	13.1	19.3
$35,000 to $49,999	12.5	16.6	10.7	9.4	11.9
$50,000 to $74,999	20.5	21.3	17.3	16.1	18.4
$75,000 to $99,999	16.3	12.8	15.8	15.9	15.7
$100,000 or more	33.5	16.7	39.8	45.5	34.7
Average household Income (dollars)	95,506	64,562	106,753	120,786	94,333
Housing Tenure:					
Owner occupied	80.7	42.3	70.1	71.5	68.9
Renter occupied	19.3	57.7	29.9	28.5	31.1

[1] Persons of Hispanic origin may be of any race. [2] Employed or in the Armed forces. [3] Includes own children and nonrelatives of the householder under 18 years.

Source: U.S. Census Bureau, American Community Survey, "Table 1. Household Characteristics of Opposite-Sex and Same-sex Couple Households: ACS 2011," <http://www.census.gov/hhes/samesex/data/acs.html>, accessed April 2013.

Table 79. Persons Living Alone by Sex and Age: 2000 to 2012

[As of March (26,724 represents 26,724,000). Excludes members of Armed Forces except those living off post or with their families on post. Beginning 2005, based on an expanded sample of households. Data for 2005 and 2010 based on Census 2000 population controls. Data for 2012 based on Census 2010 population controls. Based on Current Population Survey, see text, this section and Appendix III]

Sex and age	Number of persons (1,000)						Percent distribution				
				2012					2012		
	2000	2005	2010	Total	Male	Female	2000	2010	Total	Male	Female
Total	**26,724**	**30,137**	**31,399**	**33,188**	**14,835**	**18,354**	**100**	**100**	**100**	**100**	**100**
15 to 24 years old	1,144	1,521	1,367	1,379	654	724	4	4	4	4	4
25 to 34 years old	3,848	3,836	3,917	4,082	2,323	1,758	14	12	12	16	10
35 to 44 years old	4,109	3,988	3,453	3,455	2,137	1,319	15	11	10	14	7
45 to 64 years old	7,842	10,180	11,345	12,455	6,258	6,198	29	36	38	42	34
65 to 74 years old	4,091	4,222	4,709	5,198	1,829	3,369	15	15	16	12	18
75 years old and over	5,692	6,391	6,608	6,620	1,633	4,987	21	21	20	11	27

Source: U.S. Census Bureau, Current Population Reports, P20-537, 2001, and "America's Families and Living Arrangements," November 2012, <http://www.census.gov/hhes/families/data/cps.html>.

Table 80. Self-Described Religious Identification of Adult Population: 1990, 2001, and 2008

[In thousands (175,440 represents 175,440,000). The methodology of the American Religious Identification Survey (ARIS) 2008 replicated that used in previous surveys. The three surveys are based on random-digit-dialing telephone surveys of residential households in the continental U.S. (48 states): 54,461 interviews in 2008, 50,281 in 2001, and 113,723 in 1990. Respondents were asked to describe themselves in terms of religion with an open-ended question. Interviewers did not prompt or offer a suggested list of potential answers. Moreover, the self-description of respondents was not based on whether established religious bodies, institutions, churches, mosques or synagogues considered them to be members. Instead, the surveys sought to determine whether the respondents regarded themselves as adherents of a religious community. Subjective rather than objective standards of religious identification were tapped by the surveys]

Religious group	1990	2001	2008
Adult population, total [1]	**175,440**	**207,983**	**228,182**
Christian, total [2]	151,225	159,514	173,402
Catholic	46,004	50,873	57,199
Baptist	33,964	33,820	36,148
Methodist	14,174	14,039	11,366
Lutheran	9,110	9,580	8,674
Presbyterian	4,985	5,596	4,723
Episcopalian/Anglican	3,043	3,451	2,405
Orthodox (Eastern)	502	645	824
United Church of Christ	438	1,378	736
Disciples of Christ	144	492	263
Reformed/Dutch Reform	161	289	206
Quaker	67	217	130
Christian unspecified	8,073	14,190	16,834
Nondenominational Christian [3]	194	2,489	8,032
Protestant unspecified	17,214	4,647	5,187
Evangelical/Born Again [3]	546	1,088	2,154
Independent Christian Church	25	71	86
Pentecostal unspecified	3,116	4,407	5,416
Assemblies of God	617	1,105	810
Church of God	590	943	663
Holiness/Holy	610	569	352
Church of the Nazarene	549	544	358
Foursquare Gospel	28	70	116
Churches of Christ	1,769	2,593	1,921
Jehovah's Witness	1,381	1,331	1,914
Apostolic/New Apostolic	117	254	970
Seventh-day Adventist	668	724	938
Mennonite	235	346	438
Christian Reform	40	79	381
Christian Science	214	194	339
Church of the Brethren	206	358	231
Mormon/Latter-Day Saints	2,487	2,697	3,158
Other Christian [4]	105	254	206
Other religions, total [2]	5,853	7,740	8,796
Jewish	3,137	2,837	2,680
Buddhist	404	1,082	1,189
Hindu	227	766	582
Sikh	13	57	78
Muslim	527	1,104	1,349
Unitarian/Universalist	502	629	586
Spiritualist	(NA)	116	426
Wiccan	8	134	342
Pagan	(NA)	140	340
Native American [3]	47	103	186
Other unclassified [4]	991	774	1,030
No religion specified, total [2]	14,331	29,481	34,169
Agnostic	[5] 1,186	991	1,985
Atheist	[5]	902	1,621
Humanist	29	49	90
No Religion [4]	13,116	27,486	30,427
Other No Religion [4]	(NA)	57	45
Refused to reply to question	4,031	11,246	11,815

NA Not available. [1] Refers to the total number of adults in all fifty states. All other figures are based on projections from surveys conducted in the continental United States (48 states). [2] Includes other groups, not shown separately. [3] Because of the subjective nature of replies to open-ended questions, these categories are the most unstable as they do not refer to clearly identifiable denominations as much as underlying feelings about religion. Thus they may be the most subject to fluctuation over time. [4] Estimates for subpopulations smaller than 75,000 adults are aggregated to minimize sampling errors. [5] Atheist included in Agnostic.

Source: 1990 data, Barry A. Kosmin and Seymour P. Lachman, "One Nation Under God: Religion in Contemporary American Society, 1993;" 2001 data, Barry A. Kosmin and Ariela Keysar, *Religion in A Free Market: Religious and Non-Religious Americans, Who, What, Why, Where, 2006*; and 2008 data, Barry A. Kosmin & Ariela Keysar, *American Religious Identification Survey (ARIS 2008) Summary Report*, 2009, Institute for the Study of Secularism in Society and Culture, Trinity College, Hartford, CT <http://www.trincoll.edu/Academics/centers/ISSSC/Pages/ARIS-Data-Archive.aspx> and <www.AmericanReligionSurvey-ARIS.org> ©.

Table 81. Religious Adherents and Jewish Population - States: 2010 to 2013

[137,450 represents 137,450,000. Adherents were defined as "all members, including full members, their children and others who regularly attend services." The Jewish population includes Jews who define themselves as Jewish by religion as well as those who define themselves as Jewish in cultural or ethnic terms. Data on Jewish population are based on scientific studies and informant estimates provided by local Jewish communities]

State	Number (1,000)			Percent of population [3]		
	Christian adherents [1], 2010	Other religious adherents [2], 2010	Jewish population, 2013	Christian adherents [1], 2010	Other religious adherents [2], 2010	Jewish population, 2013
United States..............................	**137,450**	**10,890**	**6,722**	**44.5**	**3.5**	**2.1**
Alabama.........................	2,948	52	9	61.7	1.1	0.2
Alaska............................	200	40	6	28.1	5.7	0.8
Arizona...........................	1,894	466	106	29.6	7.3	1.6
Arkansas.........................	1,573	40	2	53.9	1.4	0.1
California.........................	15,021	1,530	1,221	40.3	4.1	3.2
Colorado.........................	1,684	199	92	33.5	4.0	1.8
Connecticut.....................	1,735	48	116	48.6	1.3	3.2
Delaware.........................	349	22	15	38.9	2.5	1.6
District of Columbia...........	298	16	28	49.6	2.7	4.4
Florida............................	6,829	400	639	36.3	2.1	3.3
Georgia...........................	4,702	186	127	48.5	1.9	1.3
Hawaii............................	421	140	7	31.0	10.3	0.5
Idaho.............................	384	417	2	24.5	26.6	0.1
Illinois............................	6,529	486	298	50.9	3.8	2.3
Indiana...........................	2,793	69	17	43.1	1.1	0.3
Iowa..............................	1,592	46	6	52.3	1.5	0.2
Kansas...........................	1,375	61	18	48.2	2.1	0.6
Kentucky.........................	2,182	49	11	50.3	1.1	0.3
Louisiana........................	2,688	50	11	59.3	1.1	0.2
Maine............................	345	19	14	26.0	1.4	1.0
Maryland.........................	2,214	118	238	38.3	2.0	4.0
Massachusetts..................	3,546	122	278	54.2	1.9	4.2
Michigan.........................	3,910	211	82	39.6	2.1	0.8
Minnesota........................	2,894	69	46	54.6	1.3	0.8
Mississippi.......................	1,709	33	2	57.6	1.1	0.1
Missouri..........................	2,806	123	59	46.9	2.0	1.0
Montana..........................	326	50	1	33.0	5.0	0.1
Nebraska.........................	974	38	6	53.3	2.1	0.3
Nevada...........................	725	196	76	26.8	7.3	2.8
New Hampshire..................	444	14	10	33.7	1.1	0.8
New Jersey.......................	4,321	272	509	49.1	3.1	5.7
New Mexico......................	940	87	13	45.6	4.2	0.6
New York.........................	8,529	611	1,760	44.0	3.2	9.0
North Carolina...................	4,372	140	32	45.9	1.5	0.3
North Dakota.....................	443	8	(Z)	65.9	1.2	0.1
Ohio..............................	4,861	146	149	42.1	1.3	1.3
Oklahoma........................	2,148	75	5	57.3	2.0	0.1
Oregon...........................	998	187	41	26.1	4.9	1.0
Pennsylvania....................	6,530	206	295	51.4	1.6	2.3
Rhode Island.....................	558	10	19	53.1	0.9	1.8
South Carolina...................	2,337	70	14	50.5	1.5	0.3
South Dakota....................	464	13	(Z)	57.0	1.6	(Z)
Tennessee.......................	3,425	82	20	54.0	1.3	0.3
Texas.............................	13,062	872	139	51.9	3.5	0.5
Utah..............................	256	1,929	6	9.3	69.8	0.2
Vermont..........................	199	9	5	31.8	1.4	0.8
Virginia...........................	3,206	351	95	40.1	4.4	1.2
Washington.......................	1,945	364	46	28.9	5.4	0.7
West Virginia.....................	635	22	2	34.3	1.2	0.1
Wisconsin........................	2,973	62	28	52.3	1.1	0.5
Wyoming.........................	158	65	1	28.0	11.5	0.2

Z Fewer than 500 or less than 0.05 percent. [1] Comprises evangelical Protestants, Black Protestants, mainline Protestants, Orthodox and Catholic groups. [2] Includes counts of Jain, Shinto, Sikh, Tao, National Spiritualist Association, Church of Jesus Christ of Latter Day Saints, Unitarian Universalist, Jehovah's Witnesses, Church of Christ Scientist, Bahá'í, three Buddhist groupings, four Hindu groupings, Muslims, and Zoroastrians. Excludes four Judaism groups. [3] Based on U.S. Census Bureau data for resident population enumerated as of April 1, 2010 and estimated as of July 2012.

Source: Religious adherents: Clifford Grammich, Kirk Hadaway, Richard Houseal, Dale E. Jones, Alexei Krindatch, Richie Stanley, and Richard H. Taylor, *2010 U.S. Religion Census: Religious Congregations & Membership Study*, 2012, ©, Association of Statisticians of American Religious Bodies. See also <http://www.asarb.org>. Jewish population: Ira M. Sheskin and Arnold Dashefsky, "Jewish Population in the United States, 2013," in Arnold Dashefsky and Ira M. Sheskin. (Editors) *The American Jewish Year Book, 2013, Volume 113* (2013) (Dordrecht: Springer) © in press. See also <http://www.jewishdatabank.org>.

Table 82. Religious Bodies—Selected Data: 1988 to 2010

[Includes the self-reported membership of religious bodies with 750,000 or more as reported to the Yearbook of American and Canadian Churches. Groups may be excluded if they do not supply information. The data are not standardized so comparisons between groups are difficult. The definition of "church member" is determined by the religious body]

Religious body	Year reported	Churches reported	Membership
African Methodist Episcopal Church	2009	4,100	2,500,000
African Methodist Episcopal Zion Church	2010	(NA)	1,400,000
American Baptist Churches in the USA	2010	5,366	1,308,054
Assemblies of God	2010	12,457	3,030,944
Catholic Church	2010	18,199	68,202,492
Christian Churches and Churches of Christ	1988	5,579	1,071,616
Christian Methodist Episcopal Church	2006	3,500	850,000
Church of God in Christ	1991	15,300	5,499,875
Church of God (Cleveland, Tennessee)	2010	6,481	1,074,047
Church of Jesus Christ of Latter-day Saints	2010	13,601	6,157,238
Churches of Christ	2006	13,000	1,639,495
Episcopal Church	2010	6,794	1,951,907
Evangelical Lutheran Church in America	2010	9,995	4,274,855
Greek Orthodox Archdiocese of America	2006	560	1,500,000
Jehovah's Witnesses	2010	13,021	1,184,249
Lutheran Church—Missouri Synod	2010	6,158	2,278,586
National Baptist Convention of America Inc	2000	(NA)	3,500,000
National Baptist Convention, U.S.A., Inc.	2010	10,358	5,197,512
National Missionary Baptist Convention of America	1992	(NA)	2,500,000
Pentecostal Assemblies of the World, Inc.	2010	2,550	1,800,000
Presbyterian Church (U.S.A.)	2010	10,560	2,675,873
Progressive National Baptist Convention, Inc.	2009	1,500	1,010,000
Seventh-day Adventist Church	2010	4,916	1,060,386
Southern Baptist Convention	2010	45,727	16,136,044
United Church of Christ	2010	5,227	1,058,423
United Methodist Church	2009	33,583	7,679,850

NA Not available.

Source: National Council of Churches of Christ in the USA, *2012 Yearbook of American and Canadian Churches* ©. See also <http://www.ncccusa.org/>.

Table 83. Religious Adherents by Metropolitan Area Status and Religious Groups: 2010

[Groups shown have 500,000 adherents or more. Adherents were defined as all members, including full members, their children and the estimated number of other participants who are not considered members. Based on a study of 236 religious bodies sponsored by the Association of Statisticians of American Religious Bodies. Participants included 217 Christian denominations, associations, or communions (including Latter-day Saints, Messianic Jews, and Unitarian/Universalist groups); counts of Jain, Shinto, Sikh, Tao, and National Spiritualist Association congregations, and counts of congregations and individuals for Bahá'í, three Buddhist groupings, four Hindu groupings, four Jewish groupings, Muslims, and Zoroastrians. For definition of metropolitan and micropolitan areas, see Appendix II]

Religious group	Total adherents (1,000)	Percent		
		In metropolitan area	In micropolitan area	Outside metro/micro area
U.S. population, total	308,746	83.7	10.0	6.3
Total adherents	**150,686**	**83.5**	**10.0**	**6.5**
Catholic	58,929	90.5	6.2	3.3
Southern Baptist Convention	19,897	69.3	17.2	13.5
Non-denominational Christian Churches	12,241	88.7	7.8	3.5
United Methodist Church	9,948	73.6	15.3	11.1
Church of Jesus Christ of Latter-day Saints	6,145	82.8	11.6	5.6
Evangelical Lutheran Church in America	4,181	70.4	16.0	13.6
Assemblies of God	2,945	82.7	11.0	6.3
Muslim Estimate	2,600	97.4	2.0	0.6
Presbyterian Church (U.S.A.)	2,452	82.5	11.4	6.1
Lutheran Church—Missouri Synod	2,271	72.7	13.7	13.6
Episcopal	1,952	88.2	8.1	3.7
National Baptist Convention, USA, Inc	1,881	90.3	7.0	2.7
Churches of Christ	1,584	69.8	17.1	13.1
American Baptist Churches in the USA	1,561	83.8	9.8	6.4
Christian Churches and Churches of Christ	1,453	72.6	15.9	11.5
United Church of Christ	1,284	79.3	13.5	7.2
Seventh-day Adventist Church	1,195	87.7	8.2	4.1
Church of God (Cleveland, Tennessee)	1,110	72.2	17.5	10.3
African Methodist Episcopal Church	1,010	77.7	12.3	10.0
Orthodox Judaism	947	99.6	0.0	0.4
Church of the Nazarene	894	76.2	15.6	8.2
Christian Church (Disciples of Christ)	786	70.3	17.7	12.0
Reform Judaism	766	98.3	1.3	0.4
Mahayana Buddhism	733	92.8	6.8	0.4
Church of God in Christ	624	87.8	7.3	4.9
Conservative Judaism	502	99.5	0.4	0.1

Source: Clifford Grammich, Kirk Hadaway, Richard Houseal, Dale E. Jones, Alexei Krindatch, Richie Stanley, and Richard H. Taylor. *2010 U.S. Religion Census: Religious Congregations & Membership Study*, 2012 ©. Association of Statisticians of American Religious Bodies.

Section 2
Births, Deaths, Marriages, and Divorces

This section presents vital statistics data on natality, mortality, marriages, and divorces, as well as factors that help explain fertility, such as, use of contraception, sexual activity, and prevalence of abortions and fetal deaths. Vital statistics are collected and disseminated for the nation through the National Vital Statistics System by the National Center for Health Statistics (NCHS) and published annually in *Vital Statistics of the United States, National Vital Statistics Reports (NVSR),* and other selected publications. Reports are also issued by various state bureaus participating in the National Vital Statistics System. Factors influencing fertility are collected in NCHS's National Survey of Family Growth and the U.S. Census Bureau's American Community Survey and Current Population Reports (published in *Fertility of American Women*). Data on abortions are published by the Alan Guttmacher Institute in selected issues of *Perspectives on Sexual and Reproductive Health.*

Registration of vital events—The registration of births, deaths, fetal deaths, and other vital events in the United States is primarily a state and local function. There are 57 vital registration jurisdictions in the United States: the 50 states, five territories (Puerto Rico, etc.), District of Columbia, and New York City. Each of the 57 jurisdictions has a direct statistical reporting relationship with NCHS. Vital events occurring to U.S. residents outside the United States are not included in the data.

Births and deaths—The live-birth, death, and fetal-death statistics prepared by NCHS are based on vital records filed in the registration offices of all states, New York City, and the District of Columbia. The annual collection of death statistics on a national basis began in 1900 with a national death-registration area of ten states and the District of Columbia; a similar annual collection of birth statistics for a national birth-registration area began in 1915, also with ten reporting states and the District of Columbia. Since 1933, the birth- and death-registration areas have comprised the entire United States, including Alaska (beginning 1959) and Hawaii (beginning 1960). National statistics on fetal deaths were first compiled for 1918 and annually since 1922. Prior to 1951, birth statistics came from a complete count of records received in the Public Health Service (now received in NCHS). From 1951 through 1971, they were based on a 50-percent sample of all registered births (except for a complete count in 1955 and a 20- to 50-percent sample in 1967). Since 1972, they have been based on a complete count for states participating in the Vital Statistics Cooperative Program (VSCP) (for details, see the technical appendix in *Vital Statistics of the United States*) and on a 50- percent sample of all other areas. Beginning in 1986, all reporting areas participated in the VSCP. Mortality data have been based on a complete count of records for each area (except for a 50-percent sample in 1972). Beginning in 1970, births to and deaths of nonresident aliens of the United States and U.S. citizens outside the United States have been excluded from the data. Fetal deaths and deaths among Armed Forces abroad are excluded. Data based on samples are subject to sampling error; for details, see annual issues of *National Vital Statistics Reports.*

Mortality statistics by cause of death are compiled in accordance with World Health Organization regulations according to the *International Classification of Diseases* (ICD). The ICD is revised approximately every 10 years. The tenth revision of the ICD was employed beginning in 1999. Deaths for prior years were classified according to the revision of the ICD in use at the time. Each revision of the ICD introduces a number of discontinuities in mortality statistics; for a discussion of those between the ninth and tenth revisions of the ICD, see *National Vital Statistics Reports,* Vol. 61, No. 4. Preliminary mortality data are based on a percentage of death records weighted up to the total number of deaths reported for the given year; for a discussion of preliminary data, see *National Vital Statistics Reports,* Vol. 61, No. 6. Information on tests of statistical significance, differences between death rates, and standard errors can also be found in the reports mentioned above. Some of the tables present age-adjusted death rates in addition to crude death rates. Age-adjusted death rates shown in this section were prepared using the direct method, in which age-specific death rates for a population of interest are applied to a standard population distributed by age. Age adjustment eliminates the differences in observed rates between points in time or among compared population groups that result from age differences in population composition.

Fertility and life expectancy—The total fertility rate, defined as the number of births that 1,000 women would have in their lifetime if, at each year of age, they experienced the birth rates occurring in the specified year, is compiled and published by NCHS. See *Births: Final Data for 2010, National Vital Statistics Reports,* Vol. 61, No. 1. Data on life expectancy, the average remaining lifetime in years for persons who attain a given age, are computed and published by NCHS. For details, see *Deaths: Final Data for 2010, National Vital Statistics Reports,* Vol. 61, No. 4 and <http://www.cdc.gov/nchs/deaths.htm>.

Marriage and divorce—In 1957 and 1958 respectively, the National Office of Vital Statistics established marriage- and divorce-registration areas. Beginning in 1957, the marriage-registration area comprised 30 states, plus Alaska, Hawaii, Puerto Rico, and the Virgin Islands; it currently includes 42 states and the District of Columbia. The divorce-registration area, starting in 1958 with 14 states, Alaska, Hawaii, and the Virgin Islands, currently includes a total of 31 states and the Virgin Islands. Procedures for estimating the number of marriages and divorces in the registration states are discussed in *Vital Statistics of the United States, Vol. III—Marriage and Divorce.* Total counts of events for registration and nonregistration states are gathered by collecting already summarized data on marriages and divorces reported by state offices of vital statistics and by county offices of registration. The collection and publication of detailed marriage and divorce statistics was suspended beginning in January 1996. For additional information, contact the National Center for Health Statistics online at <http://www.cdc.gov/nchs/mardiv.htm>.

Vital statistics rates—Except as noted, vital statistics rates computed by NCHS are based on decennial census population figures as of April 1 for 1960, 1970, 1980, 1990, 2000, and 2010; and on midyear population figures for other years, as estimated by the Census Bureau (see text, Section 1).

Race—Data by race for births, deaths, marriages, and divorces from NCHS are based on information contained in the certificates of registration. The Census Bureau's Current Population Survey obtains information on race by asking respondents to classify their race as (1) White, (2) Black, (3) American Indian or Alaska Native, (4) Native Hawaiian or Other Pacific Islander, and (5) Asian. Beginning with the 1989 data year, NCHS has tabulated birth data primarily by race of the mother. In 1988 and prior years, births were tabulated by race of the child, which was determined from the race of the parents as entered on the birth certificate. Trend data by race shown in this section are by race of mother beginning with the 1980 data. Hispanic origin of the mother is reported and tabulated independently of race. Thus, persons of Hispanic origin may be any race. The majority of women of Hispanic origin are reported as White.

Statistical reliability—For a discussion of statistical collection, estimation, and sampling procedures and measures of reliability applicable to data from NCHS and the Census Bureau, see Appendix III.

Table 84. Live Births, Deaths, Marriages, and Divorces: 1960 to 2011

[4,258 represents 4,258,000. Rates for 2001-2009 have been revised using population estimates based on the 2010 Census. Beginning 1970, excludes births to, and deaths of nonresidents of the United States. See Appendix III]

Year	Number					Rate per 1,000 population				
	Births (1,000)	Deaths		Mar-riages [2] (1,000)	Divorces [3] (1,000)	Births	Deaths		Mar-riages [2]	Divorces [3]
		Total (1,000)	Infant [1] (1,000)				Total	Infant [1]		
1960	4,258	1,712	111	1,523	393	23.7	9.5	26.0	8.5	2.2
1970	3,731	1,921	75	2,159	708	18.4	9.5	20.0	10.6	3.5
1971	3,556	1,928	68	2,190	773	17.2	9.3	19.1	10.6	3.7
1972	3,258	1,964	60	2,282	845	15.6	9.4	18.5	10.9	4.0
1973	3,137	1,973	56	2,284	915	14.8	9.3	17.7	10.8	4.3
1974	3,160	1,934	53	2,230	977	14.8	9.1	16.7	10.5	4.6
1975	3,144	1,893	51	2,153	1,036	14.6	8.8	16.1	10.0	4.8
1976	3,168	1,909	48	2,155	1,083	14.6	8.8	15.2	9.9	5.0
1977	3,327	1,900	47	2,178	1,091	15.1	8.6	14.1	9.9	5.0
1978	3,333	1,928	46	2,282	1,130	15.0	8.7	13.8	10.3	5.1
1979	3,494	1,914	46	2,331	1,181	15.6	8.5	13.1	10.4	5.3
1980	3,612	1,990	46	2,390	1,189	15.9	8.8	12.6	10.6	5.2
1981	3,629	1,978	43	2,422	1,213	15.8	8.6	11.9	10.6	5.3
1982	3,681	1,975	42	2,456	1,170	15.9	8.5	11.5	10.6	5.1
1983	3,639	2,019	41	2,446	1,158	15.6	8.6	11.2	10.5	5.0
1984	3,669	2,039	40	2,477	1,169	15.6	8.6	10.8	10.5	5.0
1985	3,761	2,086	40	2,413	1,190	15.8	8.8	10.6	10.1	5.0
1986	3,757	2,105	39	2,407	1,178	15.6	8.8	10.4	10.0	4.9
1987	3,809	2,123	38	2,403	1,166	15.7	8.8	10.1	9.9	4.8
1988	3,910	2,168	39	2,396	1,167	16.0	8.9	10.0	9.8	4.8
1989	4,041	2,150	40	2,403	1,157	16.4	8.7	9.8	9.7	4.7
1990	4,158	2,148	38	2,443	1,182	16.7	8.6	9.2	9.8	4.7
1991	4,111	2,170	37	2,371	1,187	16.2	8.6	8.9	9.4	4.7
1992	4,065	2,176	35	2,362	1,215	15.8	8.5	8.5	9.3	4.8
1993	4,000	2,269	33	2,334	1,187	15.4	8.7	8.4	9.0	4.6
1994	3,953	2,279	31	2,362	1,191	15.0	8.7	8.0	9.1	4.6
1995	3,900	2,312	30	2,336	1,169	14.6	8.7	7.6	8.9	4.4
1996	3,891	2,315	28	2,344	1,150	14.4	8.6	7.3	8.8	4.3
1997	3,881	2,314	28	2,384	1,163	14.2	8.5	7.2	8.9	4.3
1998	3,942	2,337	28	2,244	[4] 1,135	14.3	8.5	7.2	8.4	[4] 4.2
1999	3,959	2,391	28	2,358	(NA)	14.2	8.6	7.1	8.6	[4] 4.1
2000	4,059	2,403	28	2,315	[5] 944	14.4	8.5	6.9	8.2	[5] 4.0
2001	4,026	2,416	28	2,326	[5] 940	14.1	8.5	6.9	8.2	[5] 4.0
2002	4,022	2,443	28	2,290	[6] 955	14.0	8.5	7.0	8.0	[6] 3.9
2003	4,090	2,448	28	2,245	[7] 927	14.1	8.4	6.9	7.7	[7] 3.8
2004	4,112	2,398	28	2,279	[8] 879	14.0	8.2	6.8	7.8	[8] 3.7
2005	4,138	2,448	28	2,249	[9] 847	14.0	8.3	6.9	7.6	[9] 3.6
2006	4,266	2,426	29	2,193	[9] 872	14.3	8.1	6.7	[10] 7.5	[9] 3.7
2007	4,316	2,424	29	2,197	[9] 856	14.3	8.0	6.8	7.3	[9] 3.6
2008	4,248	2,472	28	2,157	[9] 844	14.0	8.1	6.6	7.1	[9] 3.5
2009	4,131	2,437	26	2,080	[9] 840	13.5	7.9	6.4	6.8	[9] 3.5
2010	3,999	2,468	25	2,096	[9] 872	13.0	8.0	6.2	6.8	[9] 3.6
2011	3,954	(NA)	(NA)	2,118	[9] 877	12.7	(NA)	(NA)	6.8	[9] 3.6

NA Not available. [1] Infant mortality rate; infants under 1 year, excluding fetal deaths. [2] Marriages and marriage rates are by place of occurrence. Beginning 1991 data are provisional. Includes estimates for some States through 1965 and also for 1976 and 1977 and marriage licenses for some states for all years except 1973 and 1975. Beginning 1978, includes nonlicensed marriages in California. [3] Divorces and divorce rates are by place of occurrence. Includes reported annulments and some estimated state figures for all years. Beginning 1991 data are provisional. [4] Excludes data for California, Colorado, Indiana, and Louisiana. [5] Excludes data for California, Indiana, Louisiana, and Oklahoma. [6] Excludes data for California, Indiana, and Oklahoma. [7] Excludes data for California, Hawaii, Indiana, and Oklahoma [8] Excludes data for California, Georgia, Hawaii, Indiana, and Louisiana. [9] Excludes data for California, Georgia, Hawaii, Indiana, Louisiana, and Minnesota. [10] Excludes Louisiana.

Source: U.S. National Center for Health Statistics, *Births: Final Data for 2011*, June 2013; *Deaths: Final Data for 2010*, May 2013; and "National Marriage and Divorce Rate Trends," <http://www.cdc.gov/nchs/nvss/marriage_divorce_tables.htm>, accessed September 2013.

Table 85. Live Births, Birth Rates, and Fertility Rates by Hispanic Origin: 2000 to 2010

[Births in thousands (4,059 represents 4,059,000). Represents registered births. Excludes births to nonresidents of the United States. Data are based on Hispanic origin and race of mother. Persons of Hispanic origin may be of any race. See Appendix III]

Hispanic-origin status and race of mother	Number of births (1,000)				Birth rate per 1,000 population [5]				Fertility rate [1, 5]			
	2000	2005	2009	2010	2000	2005	2009	2010	2000	2005	2009	2010
Total [2]	4,059	4,138	4,131	3,999	14.4	14.0	13.5	13.0	65.9	66.7	66.2	64.1
Hispanic	816	986	1,000	945	23.1	22.9	20.3	18.7	95.9	96.4	86.5	80.2
Mexican	582	693	645	598	25.0	24.5	19.8	18.1	105.1	104.5	84.8	77.8
Puerto Rico	58	63	68	66	18.1	17.0	15.5	14.6	73.5	69.8	63.7	61.7
Cuban	13	16	17	17	9.7	10.2	9.5	9.0	49.3	49.1	46.0	44.1
Central and South American [3]	113	151	149	143	21.8	22.7	25.5	24.0	85.1	90.5	107.5	100.0
Other and unknown Hispanic	49	62	120	121	([3])	([3])	([3])	([3])	([3])	([3])	([3])	([3])
Non-Hispanic [4]	3,200	3,123	3,101	3,027	13.2	12.5	12.2	11.8	61.1	60.8	61.6	60.4
White	2,363	2,280	2,213	2,162	12.2	11.6	11.2	10.9	58.5	59.0	59.6	58.7
Black	604	584	610	590	17.3	15.8	15.7	15.1	71.4	67.2	68.9	66.6

[1] Live births per 1,000 women aged 15 to 44 years in specified group. [2] Includes all races and Hispanic origin status not stated. [3] Rates for the Central and South American population include other and unknown Hispanic. [4] Includes other races not shown separately. [5] Rates for 2005 and 2009 have been revised using population estimates based on the 2010 census and may differ from rates previously published.

Source: U.S. National Center for Health Statistics, National Vital Statistics Reports, *Births: Final Data for 2010*, Vol. 61, No. 1, August 2012. See also <http://www.cdc.gov/nchs/births.htm>.

Table 86. Births, Birth Rates, and Fertility Rates by Race, Sex, and Age: 1980 to 2010

[Births in thousands (3,612 represents 3,612,000). Except as indicated, births by race of mother. Excludes births to nonresidents of the United States. For population bases used to derive these data; see text, this section and Appendix III]

Item	1980	1990	2000	2003	2004	2005	2006	2007	2008	2009	2010
Live births [1]	**3,612**	**4,158**	**4,059**	**4,090**	**4,112**	**4,138**	**4,266**	**4,316**	**4,248**	**4,131**	**3,999**
White	2,936	3,290	3,194	3,226	3,223	3,229	3,310	3,337	3,274	3,173	3,069
Black	568	684	623	600	616	633	666	676	671	658	636
American Indian or Alaska Native	29	39	42	43	44	45	47	49	50	48,665	47
Asian or Pacific Islander	74	142	201	221	229	231	241	254	253	251,089	247
Male	1,853	2,129	2,077	2,094	2,105	2,119	2,184	2,208	2,173	2,114	2,047
Female	1,760	2,029	1,982	1,996	2,007	2,019	2,081	2,108	2,074	2,017	1,952
Males per 100 females (sex ratio)	105	105	105	105	105	105	105	105	105	105	105
Age of mother:											
Under 20 years	562	533	478	421	422	421	442	451	441	415	372
20 to 24 years	1,226	1,094	1,018	1,032	1,034	1,040	1,081	1,082	1,052	1,006	952
25 to 29 years	1,108	1,277	1,088	1,086	1,104	1,132	1,182	1,208	1,196	1,167	1,134
30 to 34 years	550	886	929	976	966	951	950	962	957	955	962
35 to 39 years	141	318	452	468	476	483	499	500	489	474	465
40 to 44 years	(NA)	(NA)	90	101	104	105	106	105	106	106	107
45 to 54 years	(NA)	(NA)	4	6	6	6	7	7	7	8	8
Mean age of mother at first birth (years)	22.7	24.2	24.9	25.2	25.2	25.2	25.0	25.0	25.1	25.2	25.4
Birth rate per 1,000 population	**15.9**	**16.7**	**14.4**	**14.1**	**14.0**	**14.0**	**14.3**	**14.3**	**14.0**	**13.5**	**13.0**
White	15.1	15.8	13.9	13.7	13.6	13.6	13.8	13.8	13.5	13.0	12.5
Black	21.3	22.4	17.0	15.7	15.9	16.1	16.7	16.7	16.3	15.8	15.1
American Indian or Alaska Native	20.7	18.9	14.0	13.0	12.8	12.6	13.0	12.9	12.5	11.8	11.0
Asian or Pacific Islander	19.9	19.0	17.1	16.4	16.4	15.9	16.0	16.4	15.7	15.1	14.5
Age of mother:											
10 to 14 years	1.1	1.4	0.9	0.6	0.6	0.6	0.6	0.6	0.6	0.5	0.4
15 to 19 years	53.0	59.9	47.7	41.1	40.5	39.7	41.1	41.5	40.2	37.9	34.2
20 to 24 years	115.1	116.5	109.7	102.3	101.5	101.8	105.5	105.4	101.8	96.2	90.0
25 to 29 years	112.9	120.2	113.5	116.7	116.5	116.5	118.0	118.1	115.0	111.5	108.3
30 to 34 years	61.9	80.8	91.2	95.7	96.2	96.7	98.9	100.6	99.4	97.5	96.5
35 to 39 years	19.8	31.7	39.7	43.9	45.5	46.4	47.5	47.6	46.8	46.1	45.9
40 to 44 years	3.9	5.5	8.0	8.7	9.0	9.1	9.4	9.6	9.9	10.0	10.2
45 to 54 years [2]	0.2	0.2	0.5	0.5	0.5	0.6	0.6	0.6	0.7	0.7	0.7
Fertility rate per 1,000 women [3]	**68.4**	**70.9**	**65.9**	**66.1**	**66.4**	**66.7**	**68.6**	**69.3**	**68.1**	**66.2**	**64.1**
White [3]	65.6	68.3	65.3	66.4	66.5	66.8	68.7	69.4	68.3	66.4	64.4
Black [3]	84.9	84.8	70.0	66.0	67.2	68.5	71.4	71.7	70.6	68.8	66.3
American Indian or Alaska Native [3]	82.7	76.2	58.7	55.0	54.3	53.6	55.4	55.6	54.1	51.7	48.6
Asian or Pacific Islander [3]	73.2	69.6	65.8	64.2	64.5	63.0	63.6	65.3	63.3	61.3	59.2

NA Not available. [1] Includes other races not shown separately. [2] The number of births shown is the total for women aged 45–54 years. The rate is computed by relating the births to women aged 45–54 years to women aged 45–49 years. [3] Number of live births per 1,000 women, 15 to 44 years old in specified group.

Source: U.S. National Center for Health Statistics, National Vital Statistics Reports, *Births: Final Data for 2010*, Vol. 61, No. 1, August 2012, and earlier reports. See also <http://www.cdc.gov/nchs/births.htm>.

Table 87. Births and Multiple Births by Race and Hispanic Origin of Mother: 1990 to 2010

[Represents registered births. Excludes births to nonresidents of the United States. Data are based on Hispanic origin and race of mother. Persons of Hispanic origin may be of any race. See Appendix III]

Birth order	1990 [1]	2000	2005	2008	2009	2010
All births, total number [2]	4,158,212	4,058,814	4,138,349	4,247,694	4,130,665	3,999,386
Twin births	93,865	118,916	133,122	138,660	137,217	132,562
Triplet and higher order multiple births	3,028	7,325	6,694	6,268	6,340	5,503
Multiple birth rate [3]	23.3	31.1	33.8	34.1	34.8	34.5
Twin birth rate [4]	22.6	29.3	32.2	32.6	33.2	33.1
Triplet and higher order multiple birth rate [5]	72.8	180.5	161.8	147.6	153.5	137.6
Non-Hispanic White births, total number	2,626,500	2,362,968	2,279,768	2,267,817	2,212,552	2,162,406
Twin births	60,210	76,018	82,223	82,903	81,954	79,728
Triplet and higher order multiple births	2,358	5,821	4,966	4,493	4,457	3,842
Multiple birth rate [3]	23.8	34.6	38.2	38.5	39.1	38.6
Twin birth rate [4]	22.9	32.2	36.1	36.6	37.0	36.9
Non-Hispanic Black births, total number	661,701	604,346	583,759	623,029	609,584	589,808
Twin births	17,646	20,173	21,254	22,924	23,159	21,804
Triplet and higher order multiple births	306	506	616	569	644	574
Multiple birth rate [3]	27.1	34.2	33.8	37.7	39.0	37.9
Twin birth rate [4]	26.7	33.4	32.2	36.8	38.0	37.0
Hispanic births, total number	595,073	815,868	985,505	1,041,239	999,548	945,180
Twin births	10,713	16,470	21,723	23,266	22,481	21,359
Triplet and higher order multiple births	235	659	761	834	835	721
Multiple birth rate [3]	18.4	21.0	22.8	23.1	23.3	23.4
Twin birth rate [4]	18.0	20.2	22.0	22.3	22.5	22.6

[1] Data by Hispanic-origin status exclude data for New Hampshire and Oklahoma, which did not report Hispanic origin. [2] Includes other races not shown separately. [3] Number of live births in all multiple deliveries per 1,000 live births. [4] Number of live births in twin deliveries per 1,000 live births. [5] Births in greater than twin deliveries per 100,000 live births.

Source: U.S. National Center for Health Statistics, *Births: Final Data for 2010*, Vol. 61, No. 1, August 2012. See also <http://www.cdc.gov/nchs/births.htm>.

Table 88. Births—Number and Rate by State and Island Areas: Preliminary 2011

[Number of births, except rates. Registered births by place of residence. Excludes births to nonresidents of the United States. Based on race and Hispanic origin of mother. Preliminary data are based on 100 percent of registered vital records occurring in calendar year 2011. See Appendix III]

State	All races [1]	Non-Hispanic White	Non-Hispanic Black	American Indian or Alaska Native	Asian or Pacific Islander	Hispanic [2]	Birth rate [3]	Fertility rate [4]
United States...............	3,953,593	2,150,926	583,079	46,536	253,864	912,290	12.7	63.2
Alabama........................	59,347	35,687	17,983	196	1,016	4,474	12.4	61.8
Alaska..........................	11,455	6,081	437	2,842	1,040	757	15.8	78.5
Arizona.........................	85,543	38,987	4,083	5,989	3,553	33,255	13.2	67.3
Arkansas.......................	38,713	26,407	7,231	280	755	3,957	13.2	67.8
California.......................	502,118	144,583	29,901	3,461	70,418	250,031	13.3	63.4
Colorado.......................	65,055	40,439	3,054	675	2,546	18,077	12.7	62.7
Connecticut....................	37,280	21,541	4,777	255	2,289	8,388	10.4	54.3
Delaware.......................	11,257	6,221	3,031	23	552	1,416	12.4	62.9
District of Columbia..........	9,314	2,637	4,817	20	560	1,373	15.1	56.1
Florida..........................	213,344	97,250	49,070	435	7,291	58,735	11.2	59.6
Georgia.........................	132,488	60,672	44,667	339	6,200	18,671	13.5	63.8
Hawaii..........................	18,957	4,861	508	80	12,247	3,038	13.8	71.9
Idaho...........................	22,305	17,869	192	414	440	3,475	14.1	72.3
Illinois..........................	161,312	87,952	27,183	218	9,727	35,765	12.5	61.5
Indiana.........................	83,702	64,490	9,831	157	2,021	7,180	12.8	65.0
Iowa............................	38,213	31,927	1,844	266	1,208	3,114	12.5	66.1
Kansas.........................	39,642	28,814	2,934	380	1,342	6,294	13.8	71.2
Kentucky.......................	55,377	46,200	5,202	86	1,195	2,781	12.7	64.7
Louisiana.......................	61,889	33,114	23,607	381	1,340	3,607	13.5	66.4
Maine...........................	12,704	11,746	395	112	212	207	9.6	53.1
Maryland.......................	73,086	33,261	23,844	205	5,722	10,330	12.5	61.3
Massachusetts.................	73,225	50,918	7,887	279	6,211	6,764	11.1	54.4
Michigan.......................	114,004	79,604	21,774	793	3,991	7,628	11.5	59.9
Minnesota......................	68,411	50,296	6,473	1,540	5,115	4,629	12.8	65.5
Mississippi.....................	39,856	20,499	17,302	282	427	1,319	13.4	66.0
Missouri........................	76,117	57,811	11,435	395	2,007	4,114	12.7	64.8
Montana........................	12,069	9,934	75	1,486	143	449	12.1	66.7
Nebraska.......................	25,720	19,301	1,708	514	723	3,646	14.0	72.0
Nevada.........................	35,295	15,259	3,695	468	2,980	13,049	13.0	64.2
New Hampshire................	12,852	11,403	235	23	515	524	9.7	51.9
New Jersey.....................	105,886	49,664	16,049	182	11,853	28,010	12.0	61.3
New Mexico....................	27,289	7,719	473	3,615	525	15,061	13.1	68.2
New York.......................	241,290	117,198	39,158	1,183	24,794	56,698	12.4	59.8
North Carolina.................	120,385	67,685	28,598	1,982	5,164	18,219	12.5	61.5
North Dakota..................	9,527	7,759	218	1,036	172	307	13.9	72.4
Ohio............................	137,916	104,505	22,836	273	3,509	6,337	11.9	62.1
Oklahoma......................	52,274	33,361	4,815	6,186	1,474	6,684	13.8	70.4
Oregon.........................	45,157	31,768	1,170	873	2,687	8,742	11.7	59.4
Pennsylvania...................	143,148	100,767	21,024	383	6,290	14,180	11.2	58.8
Rhode Island...................	10,960	6,758	961	149	597	2,417	10.4	51.5
South Carolina.................	57,368	32,960	18,283	241	1,205	4,747	12.3	61.8
South Dakota..................	11,849	8,862	266	2,094	230	505	14.4	77.1
Tennessee......................	79,588	54,131	16,557	234	1,933	7,022	12.4	62.3
Texas...........................	377,449	133,890	43,211	1,106	17,289	182,510	14.7	69.8
Utah............................	51,223	40,860	568	770	1,683	7,686	18.2	83.6
Vermont........................	6,078	5,728	89	17	158	71	9.7	51.8
Virginia.........................	102,648	60,369	21,942	121	7,643	12,473	12.7	61.9
Washington....................	86,976	55,084	4,303	2,234	9,444	15,976	12.7	63.7
West Virginia...................	20,720	19,521	724	19	185	207	11.2	60.7
Wisconsin......................	67,811	50,500	6,593	975	3,141	6,525	11.9	62.0
Wyoming.......................	7,398	6,071	65	268	102	864	13.0	69.1
Puerto Rico....................	41,065	1,148	133	(NA)	(NA)	39,765	11.1	53.6
Virgin Islands..................	(NA)	(NA)	(NA)	(NA)	(NA)	(NA)	(NA)	(NA)
Guam...........................	3,294	198	25	6	3,031	52	20.6	95.9
American Samoa...............	1,216	(NA)	(NA)	–	1,212	(NA)	22.0	92.2
Northern Marianas.............	(NA)	(NA)	(NA)	(NA)	(NA)	(NA)	(NA)	(NA)

– Represents zero. NA Not available. [1] Includes persons of other groups, not shown separately. [2] Persons of Hispanic origin may be of any race. [3] Per 1,000 estimated population. [4] Number of births per 1,000 women aged 15 to 44 years.

Source: U.S. National Center for Health Statistics, National Vital Statistics Reports (NVSR), *Births: Preliminary Data for 2011*, Vol. 61, No. 5, October 2012. See also <http://www.cdc.gov/nchs/births.htm>.

Table 89. Total Fertility Rate by Race and Hispanic Origin: 1980 to 2010

[Based on race of mother. Excludes births to nonresidents of United States. Data for 2001-2009 has been revised using population estimates based on the 2010 Census. The *total fertility rate* is the number of births that 1,000 women would have in their lifetime if, at each year of age, they experienced the birth rates occurring in the specified year. A total fertility rate of 2,100 represents "replacement level" fertility for the total population under current mortality conditions (assuming no net immigration). See Appendix III]

Race and Hispanic origin	1980	1990	2000	2005	2007	2008	2009	2010
Total [1]	1,840	2,081	2,056	2,057	2,120	2,072	2,002	1,931
White	1,773	2,003	2,051	2,079	2,137	2,087	2,017	1,948
Black	2,177	2,480	2,129	2,062	2,145	2,102	2,035	1,957
American Indian or Alaska Native	2,165	2,185	1,773	1,587	1,626	1,574	1,499	1,404
Asian or Pacific Islander	1,954	2,003	1,892	1,785	1,850	1,797	1,743	1,689
Hispanic [2]	(NA)	2,960	2,730	2,792	2,840	2,706	2,532	2,350

NA Not available. [1] For 1980 and 1990, includes births to races not shown separately. Beginning 1992, unknown race of mother is imputed. [2] Persons of Hispanic origin may be of any race.

Source: U.S. National Center for Health Statistics, National Vital Statistics Report, *Births: Final Data for 2010*, Vol. 61, No. 1, August 2012. See also <http://www.cdc.gov/nchs/births.htm>.

Table 90. Teenagers—Births and Birth Rates by Age, Race, and Hispanic Origin: 1990 to 2010

[Birth rates per 1,000 women in specified group. Based on race and Hispanic origin of mother. Birth rates for 2005-2009 have been revised using population estimates based on the 2010 census. See text this section]

Item	Number of births					Birth rate				
	1990	2000	2005	2009	2010	1990	2000	2005	2009	2010
All races, 15 to 19 years	[1] 521,826	468,990	414,593	409,802	367,678	59.9	47.7	39.7	37.9	34.2
15 to 17 years	183,327	157,209	133,191	124,247	109,173	37.5	26.9	21.1	19.6	17.3
18 to 19 years	338,499	311,781	281,402	285,555	258,505	88.6	78.1	68.4	64.0	58.2
White	354,482	333,013	295,265	288,709	259,058	50.8	43.2	36.7	35.3	31.9
Black	151,613	118,954	103,905	105,725	94,950	112.8	77.4	60.1	56.4	51.1
American Indian or Alaska Native	(NA)	8,055	7,807	8,315	7,408	81.1	58.3	46.0	43.8	38.7
Asian or Pacific Islander	(NA)	8,968	7,616	7,053	6,262	26.4	20.5	15.4	12.6	10.9
Hispanic [2]	(NA)	129,469	136,906	136,263	121,798	100.3	87.3	76.5	63.6	55.7
Non-Hispanic White	(NA)	204,056	165,005	159,579	144,102	42.5	32.6	26.0	25.7	23.5
Non-Hispanic Black	(NA)	116,019	96,813	98,448	88,329	116.2	79.2	59.4	56.7	51.5

NA Not available. [1] Includes races other than White and Black, not shown separately. [2] Persons of Hispanic origin may be of any race.

Source: U.S. National Center for Health Statistics, National Vital Statistics Reports, *Births: Final Data for 2010*, Vol. 61, No. 1, August 2012, and previous reports. See also <http://www.cdc.gov/nchs/births.htm>.

Table 91. Births to Unmarried Women by Race, Hispanic Origin, and Age of Mother: 1990 to 2010

[1,165 represents 1,165,000. Excludes births to nonresidents of the United States. Persons of Hispanic origin may be of any race. Marital status is inferred from a comparison of the child's and parents' surnames on the birth certificate for those states that do not report on marital status. No estimates included for misstatements on birth records or failure to register births. Based on race and Hispanic origin of mother. See also Appendix III]

Race and age of mother	Number (1,000)				Percent distribution				Birth rate [1]			
	1990	2000	2005	2010	1990	2000	2005	2010	1990	2000	2005 [5]	2010
Total live births [2]	1,165	1,347	1,527	1,633	100.0	100.0	100.0	100.0	43.8	44.1	47.2	47.6
White	670	866	1,023	1,102	57.5	64.3	67.0	67.5	32.9	38.2	43.2	44.5
Black	455	427	439	459	39.1	31.7	28.7	28.1	90.5	70.5	67.2	65.3
American Indian or Alaska Native	(NA)	(NA)	28	31	(NA)	(NA)	1.9	1.9	(NA)	(NA)	(NA)	(NA)
Asian or Pacific Islander	(NA)	(NA)	37	42	(NA)	(NA)	2.4	2.6	(NA)	20.9	22.8	22.3
Hispanic [2]	[3] 219	348	473	504	[3] 18.8	25.8	31.0	30.9	[3] 89.6	87.2	96.2	80.6
Non-Hispanic White	[3] 443	522	578	628	[3] 38.0	38.7	37.8	38.4	[3] 24.4	28.0	30.4	32.9
Non-Hispanic Black	(NA)	415	408	428	(NA)	30.8	26.7	26.2	(NA)	(NA)	(NA)	(NA)
Under 15 years	11	8	7	4	0.9	0.6	0.4	0.3	(NA)	(NA)	(NA)	(NA)
15 to 19 years	350	369	345	324	30.0	27.4	22.6	19.8	42.5	39.0	33.9	31.1
20 to 24 years	404	504	585	601	34.7	37.4	38.3	36.8	65.1	72.2	74.5	70.0
25 to 29 years	230	255	332	385	19.7	18.9	21.7	23.6	56.0	58.5	71.5	69.2
30 to 34 years	118	130	162	203	10.1	9.7	10.6	12.5	37.6	39.3	50.4	56.3
35 to 39 years	44	65	76	91	3.8	4.8	5.0	5.6	17.3	19.7	24.5	29.6
40 years and over [4]	9	16	21	25	0.7	1.2	1.4	1.5	3.6	5.0	6.2	8.0

NA Not available. [1] Rate per 1,000 unmarried women (never-married, widowed, and divorced) estimated as of July 1. Total rate and rates by race cover women 15 to 44 years old. [2] Includes races other than White and Black, not shown separately. [3] Excludes data for New Hampshire and Oklahoma, which did not report Hispanic origin. [4] Beginning in 1997, birth rates computed by relating births to unmarried mothers aged 40 years and over to unmarried women aged 40–44 years. [5] Birth rates for 2005 have been revised using population estimates based on the 2010 Census.

Source: U.S. National Center for Health Statistics, National Vital Statistics Reports, *Births: Final Data for 2010*, Vol. 61, No. 1, August 2012, and earlier reports. See also <http://www.cdc.gov/nchs/births.htm>.

Table 92. Percent of Births to Teens, Unmarried Mothers, and Births With Low Birth Weight: 1990 to 2010

[Represents registered births. Excludes births to nonresidents of the United States. Data are based on race and Hispanic origin of mother. See Appendix III]

Characteristics	1990	1995	2000	2005	2008	2009	2010
Percent of births to teenage mothers [1]	**12.8**	**13.1**	**11.8**	**10.2**	**10.4**	**10.0**	**9.3**
White	10.9	11.5	10.6	9.3	9.5	9.2	8.5
Black	23.1	23.1	19.7	16.9	17.0	16.4	15.2
American Indian or Alaska Native	19.5	21.4	19.7	17.7	18.0	17.3	16.1
Asian or Pacific Islander	5.7	5.6	4.5	3.3	3.0	2.8	2.6
Hispanic origin [2]	16.8	17.9	16.2	14.1	14.1	13.8	13.1
Mexican	17.7	18.8	17.0	14.9	14.8	14.5	13.8
Puerto Rican	21.7	23.5	20.0	17.4	17.3	16.5	15.3
Cuban	7.7	7.7	7.5	7.7	7.8	7.0	6.2
Central and South American	9.0	10.6	9.9	8.6	8.4	7.8	7.2
Other and unknown Hispanic	(NA)	20.1	18.8	17.1	17.1	17.3	16.3
Non-Hispanic	(NA)	(NA)	10.7	8.9	9.1	8.8	8.1
White	(NA)	(NA)	8.7	7.3	7.5	7.3	6.7
Black	(NA)	(NA)	19.8	17.0	17.1	16.4	15.2
Percent of births to unmarried mothers	**26.6**	**32.2**	**33.2**	**36.9**	**40.6**	**41.1**	**40.8**
White	16.9	25.3	27.1	31.7	35.7	36.0	35.9
Black	66.7	69.9	68.5	69.3	71.8	72.3	72.1
American Indian or Alaska Native	53.6	57.2	58.4	63.5	65.8	65.4	65.6
Asian or Pacific Islander	13.2	16.3	14.8	16.2	16.9	17.2	17.0
Hispanic origin [2]	36.7	40.8	42.7	48.0	52.6	53.2	53.4
Mexican	33.3	38.1	40.7	46.7	51.3	51.8	52.0
Puerto Rican	55.9	60.0	59.6	61.7	64.6	65.2	65.2
Cuban	18.2	23.8	27.3	36.4	44.2	46.0	47.0
Central and South American	41.2	44.1	44.7	49.2	52.3	52.4	51.8
Other and unknown Hispanic	(NA)	44.0	46.2	48.6	54.4	55.8	56.3
Non-Hispanic	(NA)	(NA)	30.8	33.4	36.7	37.1	36.9
White	(NA)	(NA)	22.1	25.3	28.7	29.0	29.0
Black	(NA)	(NA)	68.7	69.9	72.3	72.8	72.5
Percent of births with low birth weight [3]	**7.0**	**7.3**	**7.6**	**8.2**	**8.2**	**8.2**	**8.1**
White	5.7	6.2	6.5	7.2	7.1	7.1	7.1
Black	13.3	13.1	13.0	13.6	13.4	13.3	13.2
American Indian or Alaska Native	6.1	6.6	6.8	7.4	7.4	7.3	7.6
Asian or Pacific Islander	(NA)	6.9	7.3	8.0	8.2	8.3	8.5
Hispanic origin [2]	6.1	6.3	6.4	6.9	7.0	6.9	7.0
Mexican	5.5	5.8	6.0	6.5	6.5	6.5	6.5
Puerto Rican	9.0	9.4	9.3	9.9	9.9	9.6	9.6
Cuban	5.7	6.5	6.5	7.6	7.8	7.5	7.3
Central and South American	5.8	6.2	6.3	6.8	6.7	6.6	6.5
Other and unknown Hispanic	(NA)	7.5	7.8	8.3	8.2	8.3	8.4
Non-Hispanic	(NA)	(NA)	7.9	8.6	8.6	8.5	8.5
White	(NA)	(NA)	6.6	7.3	7.2	7.2	7.1
Black	(NA)	(NA)	13.1	14.0	13.7	13.6	13.5

NA Not available. [1] Mothers under 20 years. [2] Hispanic persons may be of any race. [3] Births less than 2,500 grams (5 pounds–8 ounces).

Source: U.S. National Center for Health Statistics, National Vital Statistics Reports, *Births: Final Data for 2010*, Vol. 61, No. 1, August 2012, and earlier reports. See also <http://www.cdc.gov/nchs/births.htm>.

Table 93. Births by Race, Hispanic Origin, and Method of Delivery: 1990 to 2010

[In thousands (4,111 represents 4,111,000), except rate. Persons of Hispanic origin may be of any race. See Appendix III]

Method of delivery	1990 [1]	2000	2005	2009	2010			
					Total [2]	Hispanic	Non-Hispanic White	Non-Hispanic Black
Births, total	**4,111**	**4,059**	**4,138**	**4,131**	**3,999**	**945**	**2,162**	**590**
Vaginal	3,111	3,108	2,874	2,764	2,681	644	1,455	380
Cesarean deliveries	914	924	1,249	1,354	1,309	300	703	209
Not stated	85	27	16	13	9	1	5	2
Cesarean delivery rate [3]	22.7	22.9	30.3	32.9	32.8	31.8	32.6	35.5

[1] 1990 excludes data for Oklahoma, which did not report method of delivery on the birth certificate. [2] Includes other races, not shown separately. [3] Percent of all live births by cesarean delivery.

Source: U.S. National Center for Health Statistics, *Births: Final Data for 2010*, Vol. 61, No. 1, August 2012, and earlier reports. See also <http://www.cdc.gov/nchs/births.htm>.

Table 94. Induction of Labor by Gestational Age: 1990 to 2010

[In percent. Data are for singleton births]

Gestational age	1990 [1]	1995	2000	2003	2004	2005	2006	2007	2008	2009	2010
All gestations............	**9.2**	**15.9**	**19.7**	**20.5**	**21.2**	**22.2**	**22.5**	**22.7**	**22.9**	**23.1**	**23.3**
Under 20 weeks............	8.2	11.3	13.9	11.9	12.0	12.0	11.2	11.8	10.0	10.2	12.5
20-27 weeks................	4.1	5.7	6.5	5.4	5.7	5.5	5.4	5.3	5.6	5.7	5.7
28-31 weeks................	4.6	7.8	9.0	8.2	8.3	8.7	8.6	8.7	8.8	8.8	9.0
32-35 weeks................	6.4	11.1	13.8	13.1	13.5	13.9	13.9	13.8	13.8	13.8	14.0
36 weeks....................	7.5	12.8	16.3	16.2	16.7	17.3	17.3	16.9	17.0	16.6	16.7
37-39 weeks................	7.6	14.2	18.7	19.7	20.5	21.6	21.8	21.8	22.0	21.8	21.9
40 weeks....................	8.6	16.1	20.6	22.7	23.2	24.9	25.5	26.0	26.1	27.1	27.3
41 weeks....................	13.0	22.4	26.9	28.7	29.4	30.7	31.4	31.8	32.2	32.9	33.6
42 weeks and over.........	14.4	21.1	24.1	24.2	25.2	26.0	26.6	26.7	27.2	27.8	28.2

[1] Oklahoma did not report induction of labor.

Source: U.S. National Center for Health Statistics, "VitalStats," <http://www.cdc.gov/nchs/vitalstats.htm>, accessed September 2012.

Table 95. Percent of Births to Teenage Mothers, Unmarried Women, and Births with Low Birth Weight by State and Island Areas: 2000 to 2010

[In percent. By place of residence. Excludes nonresidents of the United States. Data for 2010 have been revised]

State and Island Area	Births to teenage mothers [1] 2000	Births to teenage mothers [1] 2010	Births to unmarried women 2000	Births to unmarried women 2010	Births with low birth weight [2] 2000	Births with low birth weight [2] 2010	State and Island Area	Births to teenage mothers [1] 2000	Births to teenage mothers [1] 2010	Births to unmarried women 2000	Births to unmarried women 2010	Births with low birth weight [2] 2000	Births with low birth weight [2] 2010
U.S. [3]	**11.8**	**9.3**	**33.2**	**40.8**	**7.8**	**8.1**	NE............	10.2	7.6	27.2	33.6	7.2	7.1
AL..............	15.7	12.4	34.3	41.9	9.9	10.3	NV............	12.7	9.7	36.4	44.3	7.5	8.3
AK..............	11.8	8.4	33.0	37.6	5.8	5.7	NH............	6.8	5.6	24.7	33.2	6.3	6.9
AZ..............	14.3	10.9	39.3	44.9	6.8	7.1	NJ............	7.1	5.5	28.9	35.4	8.0	8.2
AR..............	17.3	13.8	35.7	45.3	8.6	8.8	NM............	17.4	14.1	45.6	52.3	8.0	8.7
CA..............	10.6	8.5	32.7	40.5	6.4	6.8	NY............	8.2	6.3	36.6	41.7	7.9	8.2
CO..............	11.7	8.3	25.0	23.9	8.9	8.8	NC............	13.0	10.2	33.3	42.0	9.0	9.1
CT..............	7.8	6.1	29.3	37.4	7.8	8.0	ND............	9.2	7.3	28.3	32.7	6.3	6.7
DE..............	12.3	8.7	37.9	47.4	9.9	8.9	OH............	12.1	10.0	34.6	43.8	8.3	8.6
DC..............	14.2	10.6	60.3	54.8	11.6	10.2	OK............	15.9	12.4	34.3	41.8	8.0	8.4
FL..............	12.6	9.0	38.2	47.5	8.4	8.7	OR............	11.3	7.7	30.1	35.7	5.8	6.3
GA..............	13.9	10.9	37.0	45.8	8.9	9.7	PA............	9.9	8.5	32.7	41.5	8.2	8.3
HI..............	10.3	7.1	32.2	37.8	8.3	8.3	RI............	10.2	8.0	35.5	45.0	7.9	7.7
ID..............	11.6	8.1	21.6	26.5	6.1	6.8	SC............	15.3	11.9	39.8	47.6	10.0	9.9
IL..............	11.4	9.1	34.5	40.5	8.2	8.3	SD............	11.6	8.3	33.5	37.6	7.2	6.8
IN..............	12.5	10.4	34.7	43.0	7.6	8.0	TN............	14.7	11.8	34.5	44.1	9.2	9.0
IA..............	10.0	7.9	28.0	34.2	6.6	7.0	TX............	15.3	12.5	30.5	42.4	7.7	8.4
KS..............	12.0	9.6	29.0	37.8	7.0	7.1	UT............	8.9	5.9	17.3	19.2	6.4	7.0
KY..............	14.1	12.1	31.0	41.2	8.6	9.0	VT............	8.0	6.5	28.1	39.2	6.4	6.1
LA..............	17.0	12.5	45.6	53.3	10.4	10.7	VA............	9.9	7.2	29.9	35.5	7.9	8.2
ME..............	9.4	7.1	31.0	41.2	6.3	6.3	WA............	10.2	7.0	28.2	33.0	5.9	6.3
MD..............	9.9	7.4	34.6	41.9	9.0	8.8	WV............	15.9	12.8	31.7	43.9	9.0	9.2
MA..............	6.6	5.4	26.5	34.7	7.5	7.7	WI............	10.2	7.5	29.3	36.7	6.6	7.0
MI..............	10.5	9.6	33.3	41.8	8.0	8.4	WY............	13.5	9.6	28.8	34.0	8.4	9.0
MN..............	8.3	5.9	25.8	33.2	6.3	6.4	PR............	(NA)	(NA)	49.7	65.5	11.5	12.6
MS..............	18.8	15.5	46.0	54.8	11.2	12.1	VI............	(NA)	(NA)	66.7	71.6	11.8	9.0
MO..............	13.1	10.1	34.6	40.2	8.0	8.2	GU............	(NA)	(NA)	54.8	59.7	8.0	8.6
MT..............	11.6	9.5	30.8	36.4	6.8	7.5	AS............	(NA)	(NA)	35.5	35.4	3.9	3.7
							MP............	(NA)	(NA)	(NA)	56.6	6.9	(NA)

NA Not available. [1] Defined as mothers who are 20 years of age or younger. [2] Less than 2,500 grams (5 pounds–8 ounces). [3] Excludes data for the territories.

Source: U.S. National Center for Health Statistics, National Vital Statistics Reports (NVSR), *Births: Final Data for 2010, Supplemental Tables*, Vol. 61, No. 1, August 2012, and earlier reports; and "VitalStats - Births," <http://www.cdc.gov/nchs/data_access/vitalstats/VitalStats_Births.htm>, accessed May 2013.

Table 96. Women Who had a Child in the Last Year by Living Arrangement, Age, and Educational Attainment: 2010

[In percent except total. (480 represents 480,000). As of June. Based on Current Population Survey. See headnote Table 97]

Living arrangement	Less than high school 15 to 29 years old	Less than high school 30 to 44 years old	High school graduate 15 to 29 years old	High school graduate 30 to 44 years old	Some college 15 to 29 years old	Some college 30 to 44 years old	Bachelor's degree or more 15 to 29 years old	Bachelor's degree or more 30 to 44 years old
Total (1,000)...................	**480**	**141**	**723**	**281**	**681**	**336**	**347**	**697**
PERCENT								
Total.........................	**100.0**	**100.0**	**100.0**	**100.0**	**100.0**	**100.0**	**100.0**	**100.0**
Married spouse present........	29.7	71.1	40.7	68.2	46.7	81.2	85.0	91.3
Cohabiting.....................	17.8	9.7	19.7	7.2	16.9	6.2	8.0	3.7
Not living with spouse or partner.........................	52.5	19.2	39.6	24.5	36.4	12.7	6.9	5.0

Source: U.S Census Bureau, Current Population Survey, "Fertility of American Women," <http://www.census.gov/hhes/fertility/>.

Table 97. Women Who Had a Child in the Last Year by Selected Characteristics: 1990 to 2010

[58,381 represents 58,381,000. As of June. Covers civilian noninstitutional population. Since the number of women who had a birth during the 12-month period was tabulated and not the actual numbers of births, some small underestimation of fertility for this period may exist due to the omission of: (1) Multiple births, (2) Two or more live births spaced within the 12-month period (the woman is counted only once), (3) Women who had births in the period and who did not survive to the survey date, (4) Women who were in institutions and therefore not in the survey universe. These losses may be somewhat offset by the inclusion in the Current Population Survey (CPS) of births to immigrants who did not have their children born in the United States and births to nonresident women. These births would not have been recorded in the vital registration system. Based on June supplement, Current Population Survey. The 2003 Current Population Survey allowed respondents to choose more than one race. Beginning 2003 data represent persons who selected this race group only and exclude persons reporting more than one race. The Current Population Survey in prior years allowed respondents to report only one race group. See also comments on race in Section 1]

Characteristic	Total women (1,000)	Percent childless	Women who had a child in the last year			
			Total births		First births	
			Number (1,000)	Per 1,000 women	Number (1,000)	Per 1,000 women
1990........................	58,381	41.6	3,913	67.0	1,540	26.4
2000........................	60,873	42.8	3,934	64.6	1,626	26.7
2010, total [1]................	**61,481**	**47.1**	**3,686**	**60.0**	**1,467**	**23.9**
Age:						
15 to 19 years old..............	10,273	94.6	301	29.3	229	22.3
20 to 24 years old..............	10,493	70.5	916	87.3	462	44.0
25 to 29 years old..............	10,501	47.6	1,014	96.6	405	38.6
30 to 34 years old..............	9,923	29.7	820	82.7	225	22.7
35 to 39 years old..............	9,917	19.7	503	50.7	126	12.7
40 to 44 years old..............	10,374	18.8	131	12.6	20	1.9
Race and Hispanic origin:						
White alone....................	47,186	47.6	2,763	58.6	1,135	24.1
White alone, non-Hispanic......	37,271	49.9	2,069	55.5	868	23.3
Black alone....................	9,035	43.3	574	63.5	186	20.6
Asian alone....................	3,353	48.8	237	70.6	93	27.6
Hispanic [2]....................	10,845	39.0	756	69.7	296	27.3
Marital status:						
Married, husband present.......	25,018	18.6	2,250	89.9	765	30.6
Married, husband absent [3]......	2,298	25.4	124	54.1	29	12.4
Widowed or divorced...........	4,518	21.3	152	33.6	48	10.6
Never married.................	29,648	76.8	1,160	39.1	625	21.1
Educational attainment:						
Not a high school graduate......	12,380	64.1	621	50.2	230	18.6
High school, 4 years...........	14,763	35.9	1,004	68.0	398	27.0
Some college, no degree........	12,463	50.3	667	53.6	291	23.4
Associate's degree.............	5,498	33.5	349	63.5	139	25.3
Bachelor's degree..............	11,527	48.0	688	59.7	254	22.0
Graduate or professional degree...	4,851	42.7	356	73.3	154	31.7
Labor force status:						
In labor force.................	41,467	45.8	2,026	48.9	851	20.5
Employed....................	36,983	45.5	1,771	47.9	748	20.2
Unemployed.................	4,484	48.7	256	57.0	103	22.9
Not in labor force..............	20,014	49.7	1,660	82.9	616	30.8
Family income:						
Under $10,000.................	3,810	40.4	374	98.3	127	33.3
$10,000 to $19,999.............	5,327	40.3	398	74.7	156	29.3
$20,000 to $24,999.............	2,879	43.2	179	62.1	50	17.5
$25,000 to $29,999.............	3,039	45.5	202	66.4	82	26.8
$30,000 to $34,999.............	3,066	41.8	208	67.9	87	28.5
$35,000 to $49,999.............	7,336	47.9	403	55.0	171	23.3
$50,000 to $74,999.............	9,893	49.7	549	55.5	220	22.2
$75,000 and over..............	15,714	51.1	862	54.8	340	21.6

[1] Includes women of other races and women with family income not reported, not shown separately. [2] Persons of Hispanic origin may be of any race. [3] Includes separated women.

Source: U.S. Census Bureau, Current Population Reports, "Fertility of American Women," <http://www.census.gov/hhes/fertility/>; and unpublished data.

Table 98. Women Who Had a Child in the Last Year by Age: 1990 to 2010

[3,913 represents 3,913,000. As of June. Based on Current Population Survey. See headnote Table 97]

Age of mother	Women who had a child in last year (1,000)			Total births per 1,000 women			First births per 1,000 women		
	1990	2000	2010	1990	2000	2010	1990	2000	2010
Total...................	**3,913**	**3,934**	**3,686**	**67.0**	**64.6**	**60.0**	**26.4**	**26.7**	**23.9**
15 to 29 years old...........	2,568	2,432	2,231	90.8	85.9	71.4	43.2	43.1	35.1
15 to 19 years old..........	338	586	301	39.8	59.7	29.3	30.1	38.7	22.3
20 to 24 years old..........	1,038	850	916	113.4	91.8	87.3	51.8	47.1	44.0
25 to 29 years old..........	1,192	996	1,014	112.1	107.9	96.6	46.2	43.7	38.6
30 to 44 years old...........	1,346	1,502	1,454	44.7	46.1	48.1	10.6	12.5	12.3
30 to 34 years old..........	892	871	820	80.4	87.9	82.7	21.9	27.5	22.7
35 to 39 years old..........	377	506	503	37.3	45.1	50.7	6.5	9.6	12.7
40 to 44 years old..........	77	125	131	8.6	10.9	12.6	1.2	2.3	1.9

Source: U.S. Census Bureau, Current Population Reports, "Fertility of American Women," <http://www.census.gov/hhes/fertility/>; and unpublished data.

Table 99. Women With Births in the Past 12 Months by Citizenship Status, Educational Attainment, and Poverty Status, by State: 2011

[In percent, except for total. For women 15 to 50 years old. Based on 2011 American Community Survey (ACS). The ACS universe includes the household population and the population living in institutions, college dormitories, and other group quarters. Based on a sample and subject to sampling variability; See Appendix III]

State	Total (number)	Citizenship status		Educational attainment					Below poverty [2]
		Native born	Foreign born [1]	Less than high school graduate	High school graduate (includes equivalency)	Some college or associate's degree	Bachelor's degree	Graduate or professional degree	
United States......	4,113,472	**79.3**	**20.7**	**16.4**	**22.9**	**31.5**	**18.8**	**10.4**	**27.7**
Alabama.............	70,601	92.9	7.1	18.6	21.5	36.8	14.6	8.5	31.9
Alaska................	12,883	93.7	6.3	7.1	24.9	42.2	16.8	9.0	21.1
Arizona..............	84,696	77.5	22.5	22.0	20.2	34.5	15.7	7.7	33.3
Arkansas............	36,586	89.8	10.2	18.1	28.5	30.5	15.5	7.5	36.0
California............	518,722	63.0	37.0	21.2	20.6	29.8	18.1	10.3	26.7
Colorado............	75,261	80.5	19.5	15.7	19.2	32.9	20.8	11.4	24.6
Connecticut.........	39,770	77.4	22.6	13.7	20.4	24.7	22.9	18.3	20.9
Delaware............	10,066	85.5	14.5	7.9	26.1	35.4	13.1	17.5	21.6
District of Columbia...	7,070	73.2	26.8	11.7	22.2	24.7	12.5	28.9	27.3
Florida...............	206,786	73.3	26.7	15.0	25.2	34.2	18.1	7.6	27.3
Georgia.............	135,886	83.3	16.7	16.2	26.1	32.6	15.5	9.7	29.1
Hawaii...............	22,942	76.8	23.2	8.0	27.5	41.0	18.1	5.4	21.6
Idaho................	27,418	84.0	16.0	13.1	29.2	37.0	16.1	4.6	29.9
Illinois...............	161,456	77.8	22.2	15.1	21.6	29.0	22.2	12.2	25.6
Indiana..............	88,441	89.0	11.0	18.2	21.4	35.6	16.3	8.5	29.3
Iowa.................	37,621	89.2	10.8	10.9	19.7	33.4	25.5	10.5	22.2
Kansas..............	43,443	84.5	15.5	15.0	19.5	32.1	23.0	10.4	23.0
Kentucky............	56,213	94.1	5.9	16.8	23.7	35.2	15.9	8.4	33.8
Louisiana............	65,280	94.2	5.8	17.3	28.7	34.7	13.5	5.7	33.2
Maine................	13,843	96.5	3.5	8.3	26.2	29.1	22.5	13.9	26.2
Maryland............	78,351	74.8	25.2	15.2	20.8	26.2	23.2	14.5	20.0
Massachusetts.......	79,641	74.7	25.3	9.8	21.1	26.4	22.7	19.9	19.1
Michigan............	122,324	90.0	10.0	13.6	22.8	35.4	18.7	9.6	31.1
Minnesota...........	74,548	84.0	16.0	11.1	16.3	33.3	26.5	12.7	21.5
Mississippi..........	36,711	95.6	4.4	15.9	27.2	38.4	12.6	5.8	33.0
Missouri.............	78,269	91.5	8.5	13.4	21.2	33.5	19.3	12.6	29.2
Montana.............	12,558	95.2	4.8	9.8	24.7	32.6	24.2	8.7	18.7
Nebraska............	25,777	85.8	14.2	10.7	18.6	40.7	21.1	8.9	18.3
Nevada..............	35,270	71.5	28.5	26.2	22.4	28.9	16.4	6.2	29.5
New Hampshire.......	14,182	91.2	8.8	3.5	19.4	24.3	31.4	21.4	5.2
New Jersey..........	108,843	68.0	32.0	10.1	21.1	27.1	25.8	15.9	19.1
New Mexico..........	29,765	84.4	15.6	20.4	25.7	34.8	12.1	7.0	35.5
New York............	247,202	69.4	30.6	16.8	22.2	25.7	18.3	16.9	27.1
North Carolina.......	133,512	83.9	16.1	17.3	22.0	33.1	18.1	9.4	32.6
North Dakota.........	10,400	96.6	3.4	7.2	18.1	42.8	25.8	6.1	20.2
Ohio.................	142,781	92.8	7.2	15.4	22.7	31.1	19.6	11.2	32.1
Oklahoma............	53,718	90.2	9.8	17.2	28.5	34.4	14.8	5.2	32.5
Oregon...............	49,012	79.5	20.5	13.0	28.6	31.8	17.1	9.6	29.9
Pennsylvania.........	147,720	89.6	10.4	13.6	27.1	26.9	20.1	12.3	26.6
Rhode Island.........	13,199	79.5	20.5	16.2	17.7	38.1	20.0	7.9	33.7
South Carolina.......	68,937	89.8	10.2	17.2	25.4	32.4	17.3	7.7	33.5
South Dakota.........	11,258	95.0	5.0	13.0	22.0	39.8	17.0	8.3	31.5
Tennessee...........	85,632	90.6	9.4	15.1	27.5	31.8	17.0	8.7	33.5
Texas................	384,330	72.3	27.7	23.4	25.0	29.4	15.1	7.2	33.1
Utah.................	51,272	84.9	15.1	10.4	20.4	40.9	24.8	3.5	20.1
Vermont.............	6,255	92.2	7.8	4.6	25.9	31.9	25.7	11.9	15.4
Virginia..............	110,163	79.7	20.3	11.7	19.1	31.6	24.8	12.8	18.2
Washington..........	92,152	75.0	25.0	14.6	20.4	35.2	19.2	10.5	23.3
West Virginia.........	18,305	98.0	2.0	12.2	28.9	31.5	20.2	7.2	27.1
Wisconsin............	69,390	92.3	7.7	10.6	23.8	35.1	20.4	10.1	23.7
Wyoming.............	7,011	95.2	4.8	15.7	37.7	33.9	10.4	2.3	35.0

[1] Foreign born excludes people born outside the United States to a parent who is a U.S. citizen. [2] The population universe used when determining poverty status excludes institutionalized people, people in military group quarters, people in college dormitories, and unrelated individuals under 15 years old.

Source: U.S. Census Bureau, 2011 American Community Survey, B13008, "Women 15 to 50 Years Who Had a Birth in the Past 12 Months by Marital Status and Nativity;" B13010, "Women 15 to 50 Years Who Had a Birth in the Past 12 Months by Marital Status and Poverty Status in the past 12 Months;" and B13014, "Women 15 to 50 Years Who Had a Birth in the Past 12 Months by Marital Status and Educational Attainment;" <http://factfinder2.census.gov>, accessed February 2013.

Table 100. Births by Whether Pregnancy Intended at Conception and Selected Characteristics of Mother: 2006 to 2010

[Data based on 2006-2010 National Survey of Family Growth, which included in-person interviews with 12,279 women aged 15-44]

Characteristic	Total Births (1,000)	Percent intended [1]	Percent unintended Total	Unwanted	Mistimed
Total [2]	**21,161**	**62.9**	**37.1**	**13.8**	**23.3**
Age:					
15-19 years	2,283	22.8	77.2	19.3	57.9
20-24 years	5,243	49.9	50.1	16.5	33.6
25-44 years	13,635	74.6	25.4	11.8	13.7
Race/Ethnicity:					
Hispanic or Latina	4,546	57.1	42.9	18.1	24.8
White (Not Hispanic or Latina)	11,600	69.3	30.7	9.3	21.4
Black or African American	3,256	46.5	53.5	22.9	30.6
Marital/cohabitating status:					
Married	12,635	76.6	23.4	7.2	16.2
Unmarried, cohabitating	4,950	49.3	50.7	20.4	30.3
Unmarried, not cohabitating	3,576	33.1	66.9	27.7	39.2
Education:					
Less than high school diploma	3,409	58.9	41.1	23.2	17.9
High school diploma or GED	4,973	59.9	40.1	17.3	22.8
Some college	4,897	63.3	36.7	12.6	24.1
College degree	5,604	83.3	16.6	4.0	12.6

[1] Includes birth with intendedness reported as "don't know." [2] Includes women of other or unknown race and ethnic groups not shown separately.

Source: U.S. National Center for Health Statistics, *Intended and Unintended Births in the United States: 1982-2010*, July 2012. See also <http://www.cdc.gov/nchs/births.htm>.

Table 101. Current Contraceptive Use by Women by Age, Race, and Hispanic Origin: 2006 to 2010

[61,755 represents 61,755,000. Based on the National Survey of Family Growth conducted from June 2006 to June 2010. Contraceptive use reported by women 15–44 years of age during heterosexual vaginal intercourse. Women using more than one method of contraception are classified by most effective method reported]

Contraceptive status and method	All women [1]	Age 15 to 19 years old	20 to 24 years old	25 to 29 years old	30 to 34 years old	35 to 39 years old	40 to 44 years old	White only, Non-Hispanic	Black only, Non-Hispanic	Hispanic [2]
All women (1,000)	**61,755**	**10,478**	**10,365**	**10,535**	**9,188**	**10,538**	**10,652**	**37,384**	**8,451**	**10,474**
PERCENT DISTRIBUTION										
Using contraception (contraceptors) [3]	62.2	30.5	58.3	65.3	69.7	74.6	75.3	65.6	54.2	59.7
Female sterilization	16.5	(S)	1.5	10.7	20.9	27.9	38.1	15.5	20.2	18.9
Male sterilization	6.2	(S)	0.5	2.7	6.6	12.4	15.1	8.7	0.9	3.3
Pill	17.1	16.2	27.4	21.5	17.7	12.7	7.4	21.0	9.9	11.8
Other hormonal methods	4.5	4.9	7.1	7.4	3.9	2.0	1.4	3.5	7.2	5.5
Implant, Lunelle™	0.9	0.7	1.1	1.5	0.9	0.5	(S)	0.5	1.0	1.5
3-month injectable (Depo-Provera™)	2.3	3.5	3.3	3.4	1.7	1.0	0.6	1.6	4.6	2.9
Contraceptive ring	1.3	0.7	2.7	2.4	1.4	0.5	0.4	1.4	1.6	1.0
Intrauterine device (IUD)	3.5	0.8	3.3	4.7	4.9	4.8	2.4	3.6	2.6	4.0
Condom	10.2	6.1	14.9	13.6	10.8	9.0	6.8	9.2	10.5	10.8
Periodic abstinence-calendar rhythm	0.6	(S)	0.2	0.5	0.8	1.0	1.1	0.6	0.2	0.8
Periodic abstinence-natural family planning	0.1	–	–	–	0.4	(S)	(S)	0.1	(S)	(S)
Withdrawal	3.2	2.1	3.3	4.1	3.2	4.1	2.6	3.1	2.4	3.4
Other methods [3]	0.3	0.2	(S)	0.3	0.5	0.6	0.4	0.3	0.1	0.7
Not using contraception	37.8	69.5	41.7	34.7	30.3	25.4	24.7	34.4	45.8	40.3
Surgically sterile-female (noncontraceptive)	0.4	(S)	(S)	0.2	(S)	0.4	1.5	0.3	0.4	0.7
Nonsurgically sterile-female or male	1.7	0.5	1.4	1.4	1.8	2.0	3.1	1.5	2.3	1.6
Pregnant or postpartum	5.0	3.2	8.1	8.4	7.2	2.3	1.4	4.5	6.1	6.7
Seeking pregnancy	4.0	0.6	4.0	6.3	6.0	4.8	2.4	3.6	4.7	4.5
Never had intercourse	11.8	51.4	11.6	3.1	1.9	1.1	0.6	11.3	11.8	12.4
No intercourse in 3 months before interview	7.3	7.1	7.9	7.0	6.6	6.5	8.6	6.4	9.2	7.5
Had intercourse in 3 months before interview	7.7	6.7	8.7	8.4	6.7	8.4	7.1	6.9	11.2	7.0

– Represents zero. S Figure does not meet publication standards. [1] Includes other races not shown separately. [2] Persons of Hispanic origin may be of any race. [3] Includes diaphragm, emergency contraception, female condom or vaginal pouch, foam, cervical cap, Today™ sponge, suppository or insert, jelly or cream, and other methods.

Source: U.S. National Center for Health Statistics, National Survey of Family Growth, *Current Contraceptive Use in the United States, 2006-10, and Changes in Patterns of Use Since 1995*, National Health Statistics Reports, No. 60, October 2012. See also <http://www.cdc.gov/nchs/nsfg.htm>.

Table 102. Women Who Had a Child in the Last Year by Age and Labor Force Status: 1980 to 2010

[3,913 represents 3,913,000. As of June. Based on Current Population Survey. See headnote, Table 97]

Year	Total, 15 to 44 years old			15 to 29 years old			30 to 44 years old		
		In the labor force			In the labor force			In the labor force	
	Number (1,000)	Number (1,000)	Percent	Number (1,000)	Number (1,000)	Percent	Number (1,000)	Number (1,000)	Percent
1990...........	3,913	2,068	53	2,568	1,275	50	1,346	793	59
1995...........	3,696	2,034	55	2,252	1,150	51	1,444	884	61
2000...........	3,934	2,170	55	2,432	1,304	54	1,502	866	58
2006...........	3,974	2,221	56	2,399	1,273	53	1,576	948	60
2008...........	3,960	2,261	57	2,372	1,299	55	1,587	962	61
2010...........	3,686	2,026	55	2,231	1,114	50	1,454	912	63

Source: U.S. Bureau of the Census, Current Population Reports, "Fertility of American Women," <http://www.census.gov/hhes/fertility/>; and earlier reports and unpublished data.

Table 103. Persons Who Have Ever Had Sexual Contact by Selected Characteristics: 2006 to 2008

[In percent except as indicated (62,199 represents 62,199,000). Based on the National Survey of Family Growth conducted from July 2006 through December 2008. See Appendix III]

Characteristic	Number (1,000)	Number of opposite-sex partners in lifetime							Any same-sex sexual contact [3]
		Any [1]	One	Two	3 to 6	7 to 14	15 or more	Median number [2]	
Males, 15 to 44 years old [4]............	**62,199**	**88.8**	**15.0**	**7.6**	**26.5**	**18.1**	**21.4**	**5.1**	**5.2**
15 to 19 years old...........................	10,777	58.0	21.2	9.4	17.6	5.4	3.1	1.8	2.5
20 to 24 years old...........................	10,404	85.7	19.1	8.0	26.1	18.1	14.2	4.1	5.6
25 to 44 years old...........................	41,019	97.7	12.3	7.0	28.9	21.5	27.9	6.1	5.8
25 to 29 years old...........................	10,431	96.2	11.8	8.9	29.5	22.9	23.1	5.7	5.2
30 to 34 years old...........................	9,575	96.9	14.2	6.1	26.6	21.7	28.3	6.4	4.0
35 to 39 years old...........................	10,318	98.7	13.3	5.6	29.7	19.6	30.6	6.2	5.7
40 to 44 years old...........................	10,695	98.8	10.3	7.2	29.7	21.6	30.0	6.4	8.1
Hispanic..	11,724	92.0	12.5	10.2	32.6	17.8	19.1	4.6	3.8
Non-Hispanic White.........................	37,374	88.5	16.1	7.3	25.7	18.4	20.9	5.1	6.0
Non-Hispanic Black.........................	7,186	90.7	8.3	5.0	25.6	21.6	30.0	6.9	2.4
Currently married...........................	24,763	100.0	19.1	7.5	30.7	20.7	22.1	4.9	3.5
Currently cohabiting........................	7,301	100.0	10.3	7.6	24.4	25.9	31.8	7.3	3.2
Never married, not cohabiting..............	27,012	74.2	14.1	8.2	23.6	12.9	14.9	4.1	7.2
Formerly married, not cohabiting...........	3,123	100.0	1.4	2.2	23.9	25.1	47.4	11.9	6.4
Females, 15 to 44 years old [4]............	**61,865**	**89.0**	**22.2**	**10.7**	**31.6**	**16.0**	**8.3**	**3.2**	**12.5**
15 to 19 years old...........................	10,431	53.0	22.7	8.2	15.7	4.1	1.1	1.4	11.0
20 to 24 years old...........................	10,140	87.7	24.5	12.5	31.6	11.7	7.2	2.6	15.8
25 to 44 years old...........................	41,294	98.4	21.4	10.9	35.6	20.1	10.4	3.6	12.0
25 to 29 years old...........................	10,250	96.6	20.0	12.4	31.0	20.4	12.8	3.6	15.0
30 to 34 years old...........................	9,587	98.1	20.9	10.6	31.9	21.3	13.4	4.2	14.2
35 to 39 years old...........................	10,475	99.1	22.2	9.9	38.3	20.8	7.9	3.5	11.5
40 to 44 years old...........................	10,982	99.7	22.4	10.8	40.5	18.0	8.0	3.4	7.9
Hispanic..	10,377	89.5	35.0	16.7	26.6	6.6	4.4	1.6	6.3
Non-Hispanic White.........................	37,660	88.4	19.2	9.7	31.4	18.9	8.9	3.7	14.6
Non-Hispanic Black.........................	8,452	90.2	12.3	8.3	40.9	16.7	11.3	4.4	11.3
Currently married...........................	27,006	100.0	32.2	12.3	34.4	15.0	6.1	2.5	8.3
Currently cohabiting........................	6,821	100.0	12.8	11.6	37.0	24.9	13.7	4.6	20.5
Never married, not cohabiting..............	22,847	70.1	16.4	9.1	25.2	11.9	6.9	3.2	13.4
Formerly married, not cohabiting...........	5,190	100.0	6.8	8.7	37.7	28.0	18.8	5.3	19.6

[1] Includes vaginal, oral, or anal sex. [2] Excludes those who have never had sexual intercourse with a person of the opposite sex. For definition of median, see Guide to Tabular Presentation. [3] For females includes oral sex or any sexual experience. For males includes oral or anal sex with male partners. [4] Includes persons of other or multiple race and origin groups, not shown separately.

Source: U.S. National Center for Health Statistics, National Health Statistics Report, No.36, *Sexual Behavior, Sexual Attraction, and Sexual Identity in the United States: Data From the 2006–2008 National Survey of Family Growth*, March 2011. See also <http://www.cdc.gov/nchs/nsfg.htm>.

Table 104. Number and Type of Sexual Partners in the Past 12 Months: 2006 to 2008

[In percent except as indicated (62,199 represents 62,199,000). Based on the National Survey of Family Growth conducted from July 2006 through December 2008. See Appendix III]

Sex and age	Number (1,000)	Sexual partners in last 12 months [1]				
		No partner in last month	Any same-sex partners	One opposite-sex partner, but no same-sex partners	Two or more opposite-sex partners, but no same sex-sex partners	Did not report
Males 15 to 44 years old....................	**62,199**	**16.0**	**4.3**	**60.2**	**17.6**	**2.0**
15 to 19 years old...............................	10,777	48.9	1.5	25.1	21.2	3.3
20 to 24 years old...............................	10,404	18.3	4.6	48.0	27.2	1.9
25 to 44 years old...............................	41,019	6.8	4.9	72.4	14.2	1.7
25 to 29 years old...............................	10,431	7.6	4.8	65.7	20.3	1.6
30 to 34 years old...............................	9,575	6.6	3.6	75.3	13.0	1.4
35 to 39 years old...............................	10,318	5.1	5.0	73.7	14.2	2.0
40 to 44 years old...............................	10,695	7.7	6.2	75.2	9.3	1.6
Females 15 to 44 years old................	**61,865**	**15.9**	**11.7**	**61.3**	**9.4**	**1.7**
15 to 19 years old...............................	10,431	51.3	9.5	24.2	13.5	1.6
20 to 24 years old...............................	10,140	15.8	15.2	49.5	17.7	1.8
25 to 44 years old...............................	41,294	7.0	11.4	73.6	6.3	1.8
25 to 29 years old...............................	10,250	7.6	14.3	65.1	10.6	2.4
30 to 34 years old...............................	9,587	5.2	13.6	73.8	6.0	1.5
35 to 39 years old...............................	10,475	6.8	10.8	76.2	4.2	2.0
40 to 44 years old...............................	10,982	8.3	7.1	79.0	4.5	1.1

[1] Includes vaginal, oral, or anal sex.

Source: U.S. National Center for Health Statistics, National Health Statistics Report, No.36, *Sexual Behavior, Sexual Attraction, and Sexual Identity in the United States: Data From the 2006–2008 National Survey of Family Growth*, March 2011. See also <http://www.cdc.gov/nchs/nsfg.htm>.

Table 105. Sexual Identity Among Men and Women: 2006 to 2008

[In percent except as indicated (55,556 represents 55,556,000). For men and women 18 to 44 years of age. Based on the National Survey of Family Growth conducted from July 2006 through December 2008. See Appendix III]

Characteristic	Number (1,000)	Sexual identity				Did not report
		Heterosexual or straight	Homosexual or gay	Bisexual	Something else	
Males, 18 to 44 years old [1]..............	**55,556**	**95.7**	**1.7**	**1.1**	**0.2**	**1.3**
18 to 19 years old..........................	4,134	96.6	1.6	1.1	(S)	0.6
20 to 24 years old..........................	10,404	95.1	1.2	2.0	0.4	1.3
25 to 29 years old..........................	10,431	96.3	1.7	0.8	0.5	0.8
30 to 34 years old..........................	9,575	96.2	1.5	0.6	(S)	1.8
35 to 44 years old..........................	21,013	95.2	2.1	1.0	0.2	1.5
Hispanic......................................	10,618	93.4	1.2	0.9	0.6	3.9
Non-Hispanic White.........................	33,573	96.6	1.8	1.1	0.1	0.4
Non-Hispanic Black.........................	6,208	97.8	1.2	(S)	(S)	0.4
Females, 18 to 44 years old [1]...........	**56,032**	**93.7**	**1.1**	**3.5**	**0.6**	**1.1**
18 to 19 years old..........................	4,598	90.1	1.9	5.8	(S)	(S)
20 to 24 years old..........................	10,140	90.4	1.3	6.3	0.9	1.2
25 to 29 years old..........................	10,250	91.9	1.2	5.4	0.6	0.9
30 to 34 years old..........................	9,587	94.4	1.1	2.9	0.8	1.0
35 to 44 years old..........................	21,457	96.6	0.7	1.1	0.2	1.3
Hispanic......................................	9,272	92.1	0.9	2.2	0.7	4.1
Non-Hispanic White.........................	34,410	94.2	0.9	4.1	0.5	0.4
Non-Hispanic Black.........................	7,520	93.3	1.6	3.0	1.5	0.7

S Figure does not meet publication standards. [1] Includes person of other or multiple race and origin groups, not shown separately.

Source: U.S. National Center for Health Statistics, National Health Statistics Report, No. 36, *Sexual Behavior, Sexual Attraction, and Sexual Identity in the United States: Data From the 2006–2008 National Survey of Family Growth*, March 2011. See also <http://www.cdc.gov/nchs/nsfg.htm>.

Table 106. Outcomes of Assisted Reproductive Technology (ART) Procedures: 2000 to 2009

[In 1996, Centers for Disease Control (CDC) initiated data collection regarding Assisted Reproductive Technology (ART) procedures performed in the United States, as mandated by the Fertility Clinic Success Rate and Certification Act. ARTs include those infertility treatments in which both eggs and sperm are handled in the laboratory for the purpose of establishing a pregnancy (i.e., in vitro fertilization and related procedures)]

Year	Procedures started [1]	Number of pregnancies	Live birth deliveries [2]	Live born infants
2000.........................	99,629	30,557	25,228	35,025
2003.........................	122,872	43,503	35,785	48,756
2004.........................	127,977	44,774	36,760	49,458
2005.........................	134,260	47,651	38,910	52,041
2006.........................	138,198	50,571	41,343	54,656
2007.........................	142,435	(NA)	43,412	57,569
2008.........................	148,055	(NA)	46,326	61,426
2009.........................	146,244	56,399	45,870	60,190

NA Not available. [1] Excludes procedures for which new treatments were being evaluated. [2] A live-birth delivery is defined as the delivery of one or more live born infants.

Source: U.S. Centers for Disease Control and Prevention, *Assisted Reproductive Technology Surveillance - United States, 2009*, November 2012, and earlier reports. See also <http://www.cdc.gov/art/index.htm>.

Table 107. Abortions—Number and Rate by Race: 1990 to 2009

[In thousands (58,700 represents 58,700,000), except rate. Data for 2000-07 have been revised based on Census Bureau intercensal population estimates, as of October 2012]

Year	All races			White			Black			Other		
		Abortions			Abortions			Abortions			Abortions	
	Women aged 15 to 44	Number (1,000)	Rate per 1,000 women [1]	Women aged 15 to 44	Number (1,000)	Rate per 1,000 women [1]	Women aged 15 to 44	Number (1,000)	Rate per 1,000 women [1]	Women aged 15 to 44	Number (1,000)	Rate per 1,000 women [1]
1990 [2].............	58,700	1,609	27.4	48,224	1,039	21.5	7,905	505	63.9	2,571	65	25.1
1991.............	59,305	1,557	26.2	48,560	982	20.2	8,053	507	62.9	2,692	68	26.2
1992.............	59,417	1,529	25.7	48,435	943	19.5	8,170	517	63.3	2,812	69	24.4
1993 [2].............	59,712	1,495	25.0	48,497	908	18.7	8,282	517	62.4	2,933	70	23.9
1994 [2].............	60,020	1,423	23.7	48,592	856	17.6	8,390	492	58.6	3,039	76	23.7
1995.............	60,368	1,359	22.5	48,719	817	16.8	8,496	462	54.4	3,153	80	25.3
1996.............	60,704	1,360	22.4	48,837	797	16.3	8,592	483	56.2	3,275	81	24.6
1997 [2].............	61,041	1,335	21.9	48,942	777	15.9	8,694	479	55.1	3,405	79	23.1
1998 [2].............	61,326	1,319	21.5	49,012	762	15.5	8,785	476	54.2	3,528	81	23.1
1999.............	61,475	1,315	21.4	48,974	743	15.2	8,851	485	54.8	3,650	87	24.0
2000.............	61,642	1,313	21.3	48,939	733	15.0	8,911	488	54.8	3,792	92	24.3
2001 [2].............	61,795	1,291	20.9	48,877	717	14.7	8,977	476	53.0	3,941	99	25.1
2002 [2].............	61,856	1,269	20.5	48,735	706	14.5	9,034	468	51.8	4,088	96	23.4
2003 [2].............	61,888	1,250	20.2	48,570	695	14.3	9,092	458	50.4	4,227	97	23.0
2004.............	61,969	1,222	19.7	48,438	674	13.9	9,168	453	49.4	4,364	95	21.8
2005.............	62,071	1,206	19.4	48,321	662	13.7	9,246	452	48.9	4,504	92	20.5
2006 [2].............	62,190	1,242	20.0	48,205	681	14.1	9,335	464	49.7	4,649	97	20.8
2007.............	62,292	1,210	19.4	48,082	668	13.9	9,421	448	47.6	4,789	93	19.5
2008.............	62,360	1,212	19.4	47,943	664	13.8	9,499	458	48.2	4,918	90	18.4
2009 [2].............	62,373	1,152	18.5	47,772	621	13.0	9,560	445	46.6	5,042	86	17.0

[1] Aged 15–44. [2] Total numbers of abortions in (1983, 1986, 1989), 1990, 1993, 1994, 1997, 1998, 2001-2003, 2006, and 2009 have been estimated by interpolation.

Source: R.K. Jones and K. Kooistra, "Abortion Incidence and Access to Services in the United States, 2008," *Perspectives on Sexual and Reproductive Health*, 43.1 (2011) ©; and unpublished data from the Guttmacher Institute ©. See also <http://www.guttmacher.org/>.

Table 108. Abortions—Number and Rate by State of Occurrence: 2000 to 2008

[Number of abortions by state of occurrence from surveys of hospitals, clinics, and physicians identified as providers of abortion services conducted by the Guttmacher Institute. The Guttmacher Institute reallocates abortions to the woman's state of residence for survey years. Abortion rates are computed per 1,000 women 15 to 44 years of age on July 1 of specified year. Estimates for 2000-07 have been revised based on Census Bureau intercensal population estimates, as of October 2012]

| State | State of occurrence | | | | | | State | State of occurrence | | | | | |
| | Number | | | Rate [1] | | | | Number | | | Rate [1] | | |
	2000	2005	2008	2000	2005	2008		2000	2005	2008	2000	2005	2008
U.S.	**1,312,990**	**1,206,200**	**1,211,500**	**21.3**	**19.4**	**19.6**	MO	7,920	8,400	7,440	6.6	7.0	6.3
AL	13,830	11,340	11,270	14.3	11.9	11.7	MT	2,510	2,150	2,230	13.5	11.9	12.3
AK	1,660	1,880	1,700	11.8	13.3	12.1	NE	4,250	3,220	2,840	11.6	9.0	8.0
AZ	17,940	19,480	19,500	16.5	16.3	15.5	NV	13,740	13,530	13,450	32.1	26.8	24.5
AR	5,540	4,710	4,890	9.8	8.3	8.6	NH	3,010	3,170	3,200	11.2	11.9	12.4
CA	236,060	208,430	214,190	31.1	26.8	27.4	NJ	65,780	61,150	54,160	36.2	34.2	30.9
CO	15,530	16,120	15,960	15.9	16.3	15.8	NM	5,760	6,220	6,150	14.7	15.7	15.5
CT	15,240	16,780	17,030	21.1	23.6	24.4	NY	164,630	155,960	153,110	39.1	37.9	37.7
DE	5,440	5,150	7,070	31.3	28.9	39.3	NC	37,610	34,500	33,140	21.1	18.7	17.1
DC	9,800	7,230	4,450	68.2	50.2	29.1	ND	1,340	1,230	1,400	9.9	9.5	11.0
FL	103,050	92,300	94,360	31.9	26.2	26.4	OH	40,230	35,060	33,550	16.5	15.0	14.8
GA	32,140	33,180	39,820	16.9	16.7	19.2	OK	7,390	6,950	7,160	10.1	9.6	9.8
HI	5,630	5,350	5,630	22.2	20.7	21.6	OR	17,010	13,200	12,920	23.5	18.1	17.2
ID	1,950	1,810	1,800	7.0	6.2	5.9	PA	36,570	34,150	41,000	14.3	13.7	16.7
IL	63,690	50,970	54,920	23.2	19.1	20.7	RI	5,600	5,290	5,000	24.1	23.2	22.9
IN	12,490	11,150	10,680	9.4	8.6	8.2	SC	8,210	7,080	7,300	9.3	7.9	7.9
IA	5,970	6,370	6,560	9.8	10.8	11.3	SD	870	790	850	5.5	5.1	5.6
KS	12,270	10,410	9,770	21.4	18.6	17.6	TN	19,010	18,140	19,550	15.2	14.5	15.3
KY	4,700	3,870	4,430	5.3	4.5	5.1	TX	89,160	85,760	84,610	18.7	17.2	16.2
LA	13,100	11,400	14,860	13.0	11.6	16.1	UT	3,510	3,630	4,000	6.6	6.5	6.8
ME	2,650	2,770	2,800	9.9	10.7	11.2	VT	1,660	1,490	1,510	12.7	11.9	12.5
MD	34,560	37,590	34,290	29.0	31.1	28.7	VA	28,780	26,520	28,520	18.1	16.2	17.3
MA	30,410	27,270	24,900	21.4	19.8	18.4	WA	26,200	23,260	24,320	20.2	17.7	18.1
MI	46,470	40,600	36,790	21.6	19.7	18.6	WV	2,540	2,360	2,280	6.8	6.7	6.6
MN	14,610	13,910	13,060	13.5	13.0	12.4	WI	11,130	9,800	8,230	9.6	8.6	7.4
MS	3,780	3,090	2,770	6.0	5.0	4.6	WY	100	70	90	1.0	0.7	0.9

[1] Rate per 1,000 women, 15 to 44 years old on July 1 of specified year.

Source: R.K. Jones et al., "Abortion in the United States: Incidence and Access to Services, 2005," *Perspectives on Sexual and Reproductive Health*, 40.1 (2008) ©; R.K. Jones and K. Kooistra, "Abortion Incidence and Access to Services in the United States, 2008," *Perspectives on Sexual and Reproductive Health*, 43.1 (2011) ©; and unpublished data from the Guttmacher Institute ©. See also <http://www.guttmacher.org/>.

Table 109. Abortions by Selected Characteristics: 1990 to 2009

[1,609 represents 1,609,000. Number of abortions from surveys conducted by source; characteristics from the U.S. Centers for Disease Control's (CDC) annual abortion surveillance summaries, with adjustments for changes in states reporting data to the Centers for Disease Control each year. Data for 2000 have been revised based on Census Bureau intercensal population estimates, as of October 2012]

| Characteristic | Number (1,000) | | | Percent distribution | | | Abortion rate per 1,000 women | | |
	1990	2000	2009	1990	2000	2009	1990	2000	2009
Total abortions	**1,609**	**1,313**	**1,152**	**100.0**	**100.0**	**100.0**	**27.4**	**21.3**	**18.5**
Age of woman:									
Less than 15 years [1]	13	9	6	0.8	0.7	0.5	7.9	4.3	2.8
15 to 19 years	351	235	179	21.8	17.9	15.5	40.6	23.9	16.6
20 to 24 years	532	430	376	33.1	32.7	32.7	56.7	45.9	36.0
25 to 29 years	360	303	281	22.4	23.0	24.4	34.0	31.7	26.9
30 to 34 years	216	190	170	13.4	14.5	14.7	19.7	18.6	17.3
35 to 39 years	108	110	102	6.7	8.4	8.8	10.7	9.7	9.9
40 years and over [2]	29	37	38	1.8	2.8	3.3	3.2	3.2	3.6
Race/ethnicity of woman:									
White	1,039	733	621	64.6	55.8	53.9	21.5	15.0	13.0
Black	505	488	445	31.4	37.2	38.7	63.9	54.8	46.6
Other	65	92	86	4.0	7.0	7.5	25.1	24.3	17.0
Hispanic	195	261	252	12.1	19.8	21.9	35.1	30.3	21.8
Non-Hispanic White	852	479	383	52.9	36.5	33.3	19.7	11.7	10.2
Marital status of woman: [3]									
Married	341	246	173	21.0	19.0	15.0	10.6	7.9	6.0
Unmarried	1,268	1,067	979	79.0	81.0	85.0	47.7	35.0	29.1
Number of prior live births:									
None	780	533	465	49.0	41.0	40.3	32.0	20.2	(NA)
One	396	361	312	25.0	28.0	27.1	36.9	32.5	(NA)
Two	280	260	219	17.0	20.0	19.0	20.5	18.9	(NA)
Three	102	104	99	6.0	8.0	8.6	15.6	14.8	(NA)
Four or more	50	56	58	3.0	4.0	5.0	14.7	16.5	(NA)
Number of prior induced abortions:									
None	891	699	617	55.0	53.0	53.6	(NA)	(NA)	(NA)
One	443	355	302	28.0	27.0	26.2	(NA)	(NA)	(NA)
Two or more	275	259	233	17.0	20.0	20.2	(NA)	(NA)	(NA)
Weeks of gestation:									
Less than 9 weeks	825	749	720	51.3	57.1	62.5	(NA)	(NA)	(NA)
9 to 10 weeks	416	269	192	25.8	20.5	16.7	(NA)	(NA)	(NA)
11 to 12 weeks	195	138	111	12.1	10.5	9.6	(NA)	(NA)	(NA)
13 weeks or more	173	156	129	10.8	11.9	11.2	(NA)	(NA)	(NA)

NA Not available. [1] Denominator of rate is women aged 14. [2] Denominator of rate is women aged 40–44. [3] Separated women are included with married.

Source: R.K. Jones and K. Kooistra, "Abortion Incidence and Access to Services in the United States, 2008," *Perspectives on Sexual and Reproductive Health*, 43.1 (2011) ©; S.K. Henshaw and K. Kost, *Trends in the Characteristics of Women Obtaining Abortions, 1974–2004*, ©; and unpublished data from the Guttmacher Institute ©. See also <http://www.guttmacher.org/>.

Table 110. Percent of Babies Breastfed by Selected Characteristics of Mother: 1972 to 2007

[Data are based on household interviews of samples of women aged 15-44 from the National Survey of Family Growth]

Mother's Characteristics	1972-1974	1986-1988	1989-1991	1992-1994	1995-1998	1999-2001	2002-2004	2005-2007
PERCENT OF BABIES EVER BREASTFED								
Total......................................	**30.1**	**54.1**	**53.3**	**57.6**	**64.4**	**66.5**	**69.5**	**68.8**
Age at baby's birth								
Under 20 years..........................	17.0	28.4	34.7	41.0	49.5	47.3	60.0	50.7
20-24 years..............................	28.7	48.2	44.3	50.0	55.9	59.3	61.4	64.3
25-29 years..............................	38.7	58.2	56.4	57.4	68.1	63.5	71.1	70.6
30-44 years..............................	43.1	68.6	66.0	70.2	72.8	80.0	77.1	76.2
Race and Hispanic origin [1]:								
Not Hispanic or Latina:								
White only.............................	32.5	59.1	58.4	61.7	66.5	68.7	73.8	72.3
Black or African American only........	12.5	22.3	22.4	26.1	47.9	45.3	42.3	46.2
Hispanic or Latina.......................	33.1	55.6	57.0	63.8	71.2	76.0	76.6	73.7
Education [2]:								
No high school diploma or GED........	14.0	31.8	36.5	44.6	50.6	46.6	56.3	58.7
High school diploma or GED............	25.0	47.4	45.5	51.1	55.9	61.6	61.2	55.4
Some college, no bachelor's degree....	35.2	62.2	61.4	64.3	70.1	75.6	68.1	72.7
Bachelor's degree or higher............	65.5	78.4	80.6	82.5	82.0	81.3	89.6	88.3
Region								
Northeast................................	29.9	51.3	53.5	56.5	61.6	66.9	73.0	72.4
Midwest..................................	22.3	52.3	49.6	51.7	61.7	61.9	66.0	66.2
South....................................	30.6	44.6	43.6	48.6	58.1	60.9	62.2	62.6
West.....................................	47.1	71.4	69.5	77.3	78.1	78.9	83.3	79.0
PERCENT OF BABIES EVER BREASTFED 3 MONTHS OR MORE								
Total......................................	**62.3**	**34.6**	**31.8**	**33.6**	**45.8**	**48.4**	**50.6**	**46.6**
Age at baby's birth								
Under 20 years..........................	50.0	18.5	(S)	(S)	30.0	30.0	37.6	26.6
20-24 years..............................	57.7	26.1	24.1	25.1	36.6	41.8	38.0	38.6
25-29 years..............................	68.3	36.9	32.3	35.6	46.3	43.7	50.2	49.0
30-44 years..............................	79.4	50.1	46.8	46.7	57.5	62.4	63.9	56.3
Race and Hispanic origin [1]:								
Not Hispanic or Latina:								
White only.............................	62.1	37.7	35.2	36.6	47.8	49.7	54.5	49.5
Black or African American only........	47.8	11.6	11.5	13.3	29.6	33.7	29.2	26.3
Hispanic or Latina.......................	64.7	38.2	33.9	35.0	49.7	54.3	55.9	49.4
Education [2]:								
No high school diploma or GED........	54.4	21.8	17.6	25.2	33.9	37.0	39.9	41.3
High school diploma or GED............	53.7	28.2	28.0	27.4	36.9	43.1	41.9	36.8
Some college, no bachelor's degree....	69.5	38.7	33.1	38.7	49.6	52.8	43.2	48.7
Bachelor's degree or higher............	69.2	55.0	56.1	59.3	64.5	64.1	75.9	65.8
Region								
Northeast................................	64.6	29.9	37.2	36.4	48.2	48.8	59.9	51.5
Midwest..................................	44.4	30.3	31.5	30.1	42.0	42.8	46.8	41.6
South....................................	72.6	27.7	20.1	26.2	38.9	44.4	42.7	40.5
West.....................................	69.0	52.4	42.9	45.3	58.2	59.2	62.6	57.8

S Figure does not meet publication standards. [1] Starting with 1995 data, race-specific estimates are tabulated according to 1997 Revisions to the Standards for the Classification of Federal Data on Race and Ethnicity and are not strictly comparable with estimates for earlier years. Starting with 1995 data, race-specific estimates are for persons who reported only one racial group. Prior to data year 1995, data were tabulated according to the 1977 Standards. Estimates for single-race categories prior to 1995 included persons who reported one race or, if they reported more than one race, identified one race as best representing their race. [2] Educational attainment is presented only for women aged 22-44, as of year of interview.

Source: U.S. National Center for Health Statistics, *Health, United States, 2012*, May 2013. See also <http://www.cdc.gov/nchs/hus.htm>.

Table 111. Life Expectancy by Sex, Age, and Race: 2010

[Average number of years of life remaining. Excludes deaths of nonresidents of the United States]

Age	Total [1]			White			Black		
	Total	Male	Female	Total	Male	Female	Total	Male	Female
0.....................	78.7	76.2	81.0	78.9	76.5	81.3	75.1	71.8	78.0
1.....................	78.1	75.7	80.5	78.4	76.0	80.7	75.0	71.8	77.8
5.....................	74.2	71.8	76.6	74.4	72.1	76.7	71.1	67.9	73.9
10.....................	69.3	66.8	71.6	69.5	67.1	71.8	66.1	62.9	69.0
15.....................	64.3	61.9	66.6	64.5	62.1	66.8	61.2	58.0	64.0
20.....................	59.5	57.1	61.7	59.7	57.3	61.9	56.4	53.3	59.1
25.....................	54.7	52.4	56.9	54.9	52.7	57.0	51.7	48.8	54.3
30.....................	50.0	47.8	52.0	50.1	48.0	52.2	47.1	44.3	49.5
35.....................	45.2	43.1	47.2	45.4	43.3	47.4	42.4	39.7	44.7
40.....................	40.5	38.5	42.4	40.7	38.7	42.6	37.8	35.2	40.1
45.....................	35.9	33.9	37.7	36.0	34.1	37.9	33.4	30.8	35.5
50.....................	31.4	29.6	33.2	31.6	29.7	33.3	29.1	26.6	31.1
55.....................	27.2	25.4	28.8	27.3	25.5	28.8	25.1	22.7	27.0
60.....................	23.1	21.5	24.5	23.1	21.6	24.5	21.3	19.2	23.0
65.....................	19.1	17.7	20.3	19.2	17.8	20.3	17.8	15.9	19.3
70.....................	15.5	14.2	16.5	15.5	14.2	16.4	14.6	12.9	15.8
75.....................	12.1	11.0	12.9	12.1	11.0	12.8	11.6	10.2	12.5
80.....................	9.1	8.2	9.7	9.0	8.2	9.6	9.0	7.8	9.6
85.....................	6.5	5.8	6.9	6.5	5.8	6.9	6.8	5.9	7.1
90.....................	4.6	4.1	4.8	4.5	4.0	4.8	5.0	4.4	5.2
95.....................	3.2	2.9	3.3	3.2	2.8	3.3	3.7	3.3	3.8
100.....................	2.3	2.1	2.3	2.3	2.0	2.3	2.8	2.5	2.8

[1] Includes races other than White and Black.

Source: U.S. National Center for Health Statistics, National Vital Statistics Reports (NVSR), *Deaths: Final Data for 2010*, Vol. 61, No. 4, May 2013. See also <http://www.cdc.gov/nchs/deaths.htm>.

Table 112. Expectation of Life at Birth, 1960 to 2010, and Projections, 2015 to 2060

[In years. Beginning in 1970, excludes deaths of nonresidents of the United States. See Appendix III]

Year	Total			White			Black		
	Total	Male	Female	Total	Male	Female	Total	Male	Female
1960......................	69.7	66.6	73.1	70.6	67.4	74.1	(NA)	(NA)	(NA)
1970......................	70.8	67.1	74.7	71.7	68.0	75.6	64.1	60.0	68.3
1980......................	73.7	70.0	77.4	74.4	70.7	78.1	68.1	63.8	72.5
1981......................	74.1	70.4	77.8	74.8	71.1	78.4	68.9	64.5	73.2
1982......................	74.5	70.8	78.1	75.1	71.5	78.7	69.4	65.1	73.6
1983......................	74.6	71.0	78.1	75.2	71.6	78.7	69.4	65.2	73.5
1984......................	74.7	71.1	78.2	75.3	71.8	78.7	69.5	65.3	73.6
1985......................	74.7	71.1	78.2	75.3	71.8	78.7	69.3	65.0	73.4
1986......................	74.7	71.2	78.2	75.4	71.9	78.8	69.1	64.8	73.4
1987......................	74.9	71.4	78.3	75.6	72.1	78.9	69.1	64.7	73.4
1988......................	74.9	71.4	78.3	75.6	72.2	78.9	68.9	64.4	73.2
1989......................	75.1	71.7	78.5	75.9	72.5	79.2	68.8	64.3	73.3
1990......................	75.4	71.8	78.8	76.1	72.7	79.4	69.1	64.5	73.6
1991......................	75.5	72.0	78.9	76.3	72.9	79.6	69.3	64.6	73.8
1992......................	75.8	72.3	79.1	76.5	73.2	79.8	69.6	65.0	73.9
1993......................	75.5	72.2	78.8	76.3	73.1	79.5	69.2	64.6	73.7
1994......................	75.7	72.4	79.0	76.5	73.3	79.6	69.5	64.9	73.9
1995......................	75.8	72.5	78.9	76.5	73.4	79.6	69.6	65.2	73.9
1996......................	76.1	73.1	79.1	76.8	73.9	79.7	70.2	66.1	74.2
1997......................	76.5	73.6	79.4	77.1	74.3	79.9	71.1	67.2	74.7
1998......................	76.7	73.8	79.5	77.3	74.5	80.0	71.3	67.6	74.8
1999......................	76.7	73.9	79.4	77.3	74.6	79.9	71.4	67.8	74.7
2000......................	76.8	74.1	79.3	77.3	74.7	79.9	71.8	68.2	75.1
2001 [1, 3]...............	77.0	74.3	79.5	77.5	74.9	80.0	72.0	68.5	75.3
2002 [1, 3]...............	77.0	74.4	79.6	77.5	74.9	80.1	72.2	68.7	75.4
2003 [1, 2, 3]...........	77.2	74.5	79.7	77.7	75.1	80.2	72.4	68.9	75.7
2004 [1, 2, 3]...........	77.6	75.0	80.1	78.1	75.5	80.5	72.9	69.4	76.1
2005 [1, 2, 3]...........	77.6	75.0	80.1	78.0	75.5	80.5	73.0	69.5	76.2
2006 [1, 2, 3]...........	77.8	75.2	80.3	78.3	75.8	80.7	73.4	69.9	76.7
2007 [1, 2, 3]...........	78.1	75.5	80.6	78.5	76.0	80.9	73.8	70.3	77.0
2008 [1, 2, 3]...........	78.2	75.6	80.6	78.5	76.1	80.9	74.3	70.9	77.3
2009 [1, 2, 3]...........	78.5	76.0	80.9	78.8	76.4	81.2	74.7	71.4	77.7
2010 [1, 2]...............	78.7	76.2	81.0	78.9	76.5	81.3	75.1	71.8	78.0
Projections: [4]									
2015...................	79.5	77.1	81.8	80.1	77.7	82.3	75.8	72.7	78.7
2020...................	80.2	77.9	82.5	80.7	78.5	83.0	76.8	73.8	79.5
2030...................	81.5	79.3	83.7	82.0	79.9	84.1	78.6	75.9	81.0
2040...................	82.7	80.6	84.8	83.1	81.1	85.2	80.2	77.7	82.4
2050...................	83.8	81.8	85.9	84.2	82.2	86.2	81.6	79.3	83.8
2060...................	84.8	82.8	86.8	85.2	83.2	87.2	82.9	80.6	84.9

NA Not available. [1] Life expectancies for 2001–2010 were calculated using a revised methodology and may differ from those previously published. [2] Multiple-race data were bridged to the single-race categories of the 1977 OMB standards for comparability with other reporting areas. [3] Data for 2001-2009 have been re-estimated using new 2001-2009 intercensal population estimates and may differ from data previously published. [4] Based on mortality assumptions; for details, see source: U.S. Census Bureau, 2012 National Population Projections, "Table 10: Projected Life Expectancy at Birth by Sex, Race, and Hispanic Origin for the United States: 2015 to 2060 (NP2012-T10)," December 2012, <http://www.census.gov/population/projections/>.

Source: Except as noted. U.S. National Center for Health Statistics, National Vital Statistics Reports (NVSR), *Deaths: Final Data for 2010*, Vol. 61, No. 4, May 2013. See also <http://www.cdc.gov/nchs/deaths.htm>.

Table 113. Selected Life Table Values: 1959 to 2008

[Decennial life tables are based on population data from a decennial census and reported deaths of the 3-year period surrounding the census year; the census year is the middle year. The annual tables are based on deaths in a single year, and except for census years, on postcensal population estimates. Beginning in 1970, data exclude deaths of nonresidents of the United States. See Technical Notes, source]

Age and sex	All races						White						Black [1]					
	1959–1961	1969–1971	1979–1981	1989–1991	1999–2001	2008 [3]	1959–1961	1969–1971	1979–1981	1989–1991	1999–2001	2008 [3]	1959–1961	1969–1971	1979–1981	1989–1991	1999–2001	2008 [3]
EXPECTATION OF LIFE IN YEARS																		
Male by age:																		
At Birth	66.8	67.0	70.1	71.8	74.1	75.6	67.6	67.9	70.8	72.7	74.7	76.1	61.5	60.0	64.1	64.5	68.1	70.6
Age 20	49.8	49.5	51.9	53.3	55.2	56.6	50.3	50.2	52.5	54.0	55.7	56.9	45.8	43.5	46.5	46.7	49.8	52.2
Age 40	31.4	31.5	33.6	35.1	36.6	38.0	31.7	31.9	34.0	35.6	37.0	38.3	28.7	27.6	29.5	30.1	32.1	34.2
Age 50	23.0	23.1	25.0	26.4	27.8	29.1	23.2	23.3	25.3	26.7	28.1	29.3	21.3	20.7	22.0	22.5	24.1	25.7
Age 60	15.9	16.0	17.5	18.5	19.7	21.0	16.0	16.1	17.6	18.7	19.9	21.2	15.3	14.9	15.9	16.0	17.1	18.5
Age 70	10.3	10.4	11.4	12.1	12.8	13.9	10.3	10.4	11.4	12.1	12.9	13.9	10.8	10.4	10.9	10.9	11.4	12.6
Female by age:																		
At Birth	73.2	74.6	77.6	78.8	79.5	80.6	74.2	75.5	78.2	79.5	80.0	80.9	66.5	68.3	72.9	73.7	75.1	77.2
Age 20	55.6	56.6	59.0	59.9	60.3	61.3	56.3	57.2	59.4	60.4	60.7	61.6	50.1	51.2	54.9	55.5	56.5	58.4
Age 40	36.6	37.6	39.8	40.7	41.0	42.0	37.1	38.1	40.2	41.0	41.3	42.2	32.2	33.3	36.3	37.0	37.7	39.4
Age 50	27.7	28.8	30.7	31.4	31.7	32.8	28.1	29.1	31.0	31.7	32.0	32.9	24.3	25.5	27.8	28.4	29.0	30.6
Age 60	19.5	20.6	22.3	22.9	23.1	24.1	19.7	20.8	22.5	23.1	23.2	24.1	17.8	18.7	20.4	20.7	21.2	22.6
Age 70	12.4	13.4	14.8	15.4	15.4	16.2	12.4	13.4	14.9	15.5	15.5	16.2	12.5	13.0	14.1	14.3	14.4	15.4
PERCENT SURVIVING OUT OF 1,000 BORN ALIVE																		
Male by age:																		
At Birth	100.0	100.0	100.0	100.0	100.0	100.0	100.0	100.0	100.0	100.0	100.0	100.0	100.0	100.0	100.0	100.0	100.0	100.0
Age 20	95.5	96.1	97.3	97.9	98.4	98.6	95.9	96.5	97.5	98.1	98.6	98.8	93.1	94.1	96.1	96.3	97.3	97.6
Age 40	91.6	91.5	93.3	93.8	95.4	95.7	92.4	92.6	94.0	94.6	95.9	96.0	85.7	83.4	88.5	87.9	91.9	93.1
Age 50	86.2	86.1	89.0	89.9	91.8	92.4	87.4	87.7	90.1	91.1	92.6	92.9	77.2	73.3	80.1	80.0	85.6	88.4
Age 60	73.9	74.0	79.0	81.4	84.5	85.4	75.5	76.0	80.6	83.2	85.7	86.3	61.7	57.5	65.0	66.3	73.4	77.4
Age 70	52.2	52.3	59.7	64.1	69.4	72.3	53.8	54.1	61.4	66.2	70.9	73.4	39.9	36.9	44.2	45.7	53.9	59.3
Female by age:																		
At Birth	100.0	100.0	100.0	100.0	100.0	100.0	100.0	100.0	100.0	100.0	100.0	100.0	100.0	100.0	100.0	100.0	100.0	100.0
Age 20	96.8	97.3	98.2	98.6	98.9	99.0	97.1	97.6	98.4	98.9	99.0	99.1	94.7	95.7	97.2	97.6	98.1	98.4
Age 40	94.6	95.1	96.5	97.0	97.5	97.7	95.3	95.8	96.9	97.5	97.8	97.9	89.7	90.8	94.1	94.4	95.6	96.3
Age 50	91.3	91.9	94.1	94.9	95.4	95.6	92.5	92.9	94.7	95.6	96.0	96.0	83.0	84.2	89.6	90.3	91.7	93.0
Age 60	84.4	85.1	88.4	89.7	90.7	91.3	86.3	86.7	89.5	90.8	91.6	91.9	69.9	72.8	80.3	81.9	84.0	86.2
Age 70	70.1	72.0	76.7	78.5	80.2	82.0	72.5	74.1	78.1	80.0	81.3	82.9	51.3	54.9	64.7	66.3	69.6	73.9

[1] Prior to 1970, data for the black population are not available. Data shown for 1959–1970 are for the non-white population. [2] The number of persons from the original synthetic cohort of 1,000 live births, who survive the beginning of each age interval. [3] Data have been revised.

Source: U.S. National Center for Health Statistics, National Vital Statistics Reports (NVSR), *United States Life Tables, 2008,* Vol. 61, No. 3, September 2012. See also <http://www.cdc.gov/nchs/products/life_tables.htm>.

Table 114. Life Expectancy at Birth by Sex, Race, and State: 1989 to 2001

[Average number of years of life remaining. Excludes deaths of nonresidents of the United States. Decennial life tables are based on population data from a decennial census and reported deaths of the 3-year period surrounding the census year; the census year is the middle year. The annual tables are based on deaths in a single year, and except for census years, on postcensal population estimates]

State	Total, 1989–1991	1999-2001						
		Total	Male			Female		
			Total	White	Black	Total	White	Black
United States................	**75.37**	**76.83**	**74.10**	**74.74**	**68.08**	**79.45**	**79.97**	**75.12**
Alabama.......................	73.64	74.80	71.32	72.85	66.42	78.34	79.14	74.94
Alaska.........................	74.83	76.63	74.18	75.45	(B)	79.41	80.10	(B)
Arizona........................	76.10	78.15	75.25	75.51	70.95	81.16	81.64	77.70
Arkansas......................	74.33	75.43	72.05	73.17	67.30	78.99	79.59	73.58
California......................	75.86	78.80	76.02	76.11	69.97	81.63	81.36	76.67
Colorado......................	76.96	78.72	76.29	76.23	71.71	81.16	81.31	76.59
Connecticut...................	76.91	78.90	76.13	76.73	71.73	81.63	81.92	77.71
Delaware......................	74.76	77.04	74.24	75.05	70.27	79.78	80.55	75.21
District of Columbia...........	67.99	73.09	68.57	78.94	64.59	77.59	84.31	74.46
Florida.........................	75.84	78.10	74.97	75.64	68.98	81.40	82.14	75.53
Georgia........................	73.61	75.27	72.28	73.88	68.29	78.22	79.53	76.16
Hawaii.........................	78.21	80.23	77.17	78.40	(B)	83.65	83.31	(B)
Idaho..........................	76.88	78.29	76.18	76.46	(B)	80.50	80.53	(B)
Illinois.........................	74.90	77.06	73.91	75.33	66.81	80.26	80.78	74.20
Indiana........................	75.39	76.47	73.55	74.24	67.47	79.45	79.69	76.55
Iowa...........................	77.29	78.76	76.11	76.19	70.81	81.39	81.35	75.16
Kansas........................	76.76	77.78	74.84	75.46	68.47	80.88	81.00	75.02
Kentucky......................	74.37	75.20	72.25	72.73	69.01	78.20	78.42	74.46
Louisiana......................	73.05	74.28	71.12	73.47	66.45	77.44	79.41	75.30
Maine..........................	76.35	77.46	75.23	75.59	(B)	79.63	80.88	(B)
Maryland.......................	74.79	76.36	73.55	75.58	68.41	79.08	80.66	75.78
Massachusetts.................	76.72	78.76	75.79	76.35	73.14	81.68	81.63	79.33
Michigan.......................	75.04	76.90	73.98	75.26	67.38	79.83	80.59	75.95
Minnesota.....................	77.76	79.26	76.74	77.03	71.59	81.80	82.61	76.60
Mississippi....................	73.03	73.88	70.30	72.25	66.72	77.62	79.13	73.68
Missouri.......................	75.25	76.52	73.59	74.29	67.22	79.46	79.93	74.50
Montana.......................	76.23	77.74	75.18	75.07	(B)	80.56	81.24	(B)
Nebraska......................	76.92	78.37	76.00	76.17	69.15	80.78	81.14	74.67
Nevada........................	74.18	76.05	73.34	73.49	70.56	79.24	78.97	74.75
New Hampshire................	76.72	78.79	76.24	76.46	(B)	81.40	81.30	(B)
New Jersey....................	75.42	77.58	74.77	75.82	68.85	80.32	81.32	75.54
New Mexico....................	75.74	77.26	74.52	75.19	71.63	80.06	80.69	74.37
New York......................	74.68	78.20	75.13	75.78	70.13	81.16	81.49	77.84
North Carolina.................	74.48	76.27	73.05	74.27	66.33	79.56	80.34	76.68
North Dakota..................	77.62	79.06	75.96	76.65	(B)	82.61	82.67	(B)
Ohio...........................	75.32	76.49	73.94	74.58	68.60	78.95	80.01	74.91
Oklahoma.....................	75.10	75.61	72.75	73.00	68.97	78.59	78.75	74.34
Oregon........................	76.44	78.09	75.82	75.72	70.67	80.37	80.20	78.24
Pennsylvania..................	75.38	77.02	74.09	75.03	67.26	79.90	80.65	75.34
Rhode Island..................	76.54	78.65	75.83	76.06	72.18	81.42	81.60	77.39
South Carolina.................	73.51	75.04	71.68	73.76	67.34	78.49	79.77	75.41
South Dakota..................	76.91	78.34	75.19	76.35	(B)	81.79	82.61	(B)
Tennessee.....................	74.32	75.29	71.98	73.31	66.86	78.66	79.28	74.16
Texas..........................	75.14	77.04	74.12	74.74	69.18	80.05	80.35	74.76
Utah...........................	77.70	78.89	76.84	76.95	(B)	80.95	80.93	(B)
Vermont........................	76.54	78.24	76.18	76.30	(B)	80.29	80.90	(B)
Virginia........................	75.22	76.95	74.48	75.62	69.37	79.34	80.69	76.20
Washington....................	76.82	78.64	76.18	76.10	71.90	81.14	80.98	77.11
West Virginia..................	74.26	75.28	72.75	72.75	69.87	77.84	78.36	72.65
Wisconsin......................	76.87	78.56	75.61	76.12	68.41	81.64	81.87	74.34
Wyoming.......................	76.21	76.64	74.83	75.33	(B)	78.55	80.41	(B)

B Base figure too small to meet statistical standards for reliability.

Source: U.S. National Center for Health Statistics, National Vital Statistics Reports (NVSR), *U.S. Decennial Life Tables for 1999-2001: State Life Tables*, Vol. 60, No. 9, September 2012, and earlier reports. See also <http://www.cdc.gov/nchs/products/life_tables.htm>.

Births, Deaths, Marriages, and Divorces

Table 115. Deaths and Death Rates by Sex, Race, and Hispanic Origin: 1970 to 2010

[1,921 represents 1,921,000. Rates are per 1,000 population for specified groups. Excludes deaths of nonresidents of the United States and fetal deaths. Rates are based on population enumerated as of April 1 for census years and estimated as of July 1 for all other years. Rates for 2001-2009 have been revised using population estimates based on the 2010 Census. Data for Hispanic origin and specified races other than White and Black should be interpreted with caution because of inconsistencies between reporting Hispanic origin and race on death certificates and censuses and surveys]

Sex and race	1970	1980	1990	2000	2004	2005	2006	2007	2008	2009	2010
Deaths [1] (1,000)	**1,921**	**1,990**	**2,148**	**2,403**	**2,398**	**2,448**	**2,426**	**2,424**	**2,472**	**2,437**	**2,468**
Male [1] (1,000)	1,078	1,075	1,113	1,178	1,182	1,208	1,202	1,204	1,226	1,217	1,232
Female [1] (1,000)	843	915	1,035	1,226	1,216	1,240	1,224	1,220	1,246	1,220	1,236
White (1,000)	1,682	1,739	1,853	2,071	2,057	2,098	2,078	2,074	2,120	2,086	2,115
Male (1,000)	942	934	951	1,007	1,007	1,028	1,022	1,024	1,046	1,037	1,052
Female (1,000)	740	805	902	1,064	1,049	1,070	1,055	1,050	1,074	1,049	1,063
Black (1,000)	226	233	265	286	287	293	290	290	289	287	287
Male (1,000)	128	130	145	145	146	149	149	148	147	146	146
Female (1,000)	98	103	120	141	141	144	141	141	142	140	141
American Indian or Alaska Native (1,000)	6	7	8	11	13	14	14	14	15	15	16
Male (1,000)	3	4	5	6	7	8	8	8	8	8	9
Female (1,000)	2	3	3	5	6	6	6	6	7	7	7
Asian or Pacific Islander (1,000)	(NA)	11	21	35	41	43	45	46	48	49	51
Male (1,000)	(NA)	7	12	19	21	23	23	24	25	26	27
Female (1,000)	(NA)	4	9	16	19	20	21	22	23	24	25
Hispanic origin [2]	(NA)	(NA)	(NA)	107	122	131	133	136	139	142	144
Male (1,000)	(NA)	(NA)	(NA)	60	69	74	74	76	77	78	80
Female (1,000)	(NA)	(NA)	(NA)	47	54	57	59	60	62	63	65
Non-Hispanic, White (1,000)	(NA)	(NA)	(NA)	1,960	1,933	1,967	1,945	1,940	1,981	1,945	1,970
Male (1,000)	(NA)	(NA)	(NA)	945	938	954	948	949	969	959	972
Female (1,000)	(NA)	(NA)	(NA)	1,015	995	1,013	997	991	1,012	986	998
Death rates [1]	**9.5**	**8.8**	**8.6**	**8.5**	**8.2**	**8.3**	**8.1**	**8.0**	**8.1**	**7.9**	**8.0**
Male [1]	10.9	9.8	9.2	8.5	8.2	8.3	8.2	8.1	8.2	8.1	8.1
Female [1]	8.1	7.9	8.1	8.6	8.2	8.3	8.1	8.0	8.1	7.8	7.9
White	9.5	8.9	8.9	9.0	8.7	8.8	8.7	8.6	8.7	8.5	8.6
Male	10.9	9.8	9.3	8.9	8.6	8.7	8.6	8.6	8.7	8.6	8.7
Female	8.1	8.1	8.5	9.1	8.8	8.9	8.7	8.6	8.7	8.5	8.6
Black	10.0	8.8	8.7	7.8	7.4	7.5	7.3	7.2	7.0	6.9	6.8
Male	11.9	10.3	10.1	8.3	7.9	8.0	7.8	7.7	7.5	7.4	7.3
Female	8.3	7.3	7.5	7.3	7.0	7.0	6.8	6.7	6.6	6.5	6.4
American Indian or Alaska Native	(NA)	4.9	4.0	3.8	3.8	3.9	3.8	3.8	3.7	3.6	3.7
Male	(NA)	6.0	4.8	4.2	4.2	4.3	4.1	4.1	4.1	3.9	4.0
Female	(NA)	3.8	3.3	3.5	3.5	3.5	3.5	3.4	3.3	3.3	3.3
Asian or Pacific Islander	(NA)	3.0	2.8	3.0	2.9	3.0	3.0	2.9	3.0	3.0	3.0
Male	(NA)	3.8	3.3	3.3	3.2	3.3	3.2	3.2	3.2	3.2	3.3
Female	(NA)	2.2	2.3	2.6	2.7	2.7	2.7	2.7	2.8	2.7	2.8
Hispanic origin [2]	(NA)	(NA)	(NA)	3.0	3.0	3.0	3.0	2.9	2.9	2.9	2.9
Male	(NA)	(NA)	(NA)	3.3	3.2	3.4	3.3	3.2	3.2	3.1	3.1
Female	(NA)	(NA)	(NA)	2.7	2.7	2.7	2.7	2.6	2.7	2.6	2.6
Non-Hispanic, White	(NA)	(NA)	(NA)	9.9	9.7	9.9	9.8	9.7	9.9	9.7	9.8
Male	(NA)	(NA)	(NA)	9.8	9.6	9.8	9.7	9.7	9.9	9.8	9.9
Female	(NA)	(NA)	(NA)	10.1	9.8	10.0	9.8	9.8	10.0	9.7	9.8
Age-adjusted death rates [1, 3]	**12.2**	**10.4**	**9.4**	**8.7**	**8.1**	**8.2**	**7.9**	**7.8**	**7.7**	**7.5**	**7.5**
Male [1]	15.4	13.5	12.0	10.5	9.7	9.7	9.4	9.2	9.2	8.9	8.9
Female [1]	9.7	8.2	7.5	7.3	6.9	6.9	6.7	6.6	6.6	6.4	6.3
White	11.9	10.1	9.1	8.5	8.0	8.0	7.8	7.6	7.7	7.4	7.4
Male	15.1	13.2	11.7	10.3	9.5	9.5	9.3	9.1	9.1	8.8	8.8
Female	9.4	8.0	7.3	7.2	6.8	6.8	6.6	6.5	6.5	6.3	6.3
Black	15.2	13.1	12.5	11.2	10.4	10.4	10.0	9.7	9.5	9.1	9.0
Male	18.7	17.0	16.4	14.0	13.0	12.8	12.4	12.0	11.7	11.2	11.0
Female	12.3	10.3	9.8	9.3	8.7	8.6	8.3	8.1	7.9	7.6	7.5
American Indian or Alaska Native	(NA)	8.7	7.2	7.1	6.9	7.0	6.8	6.6	6.4	6.2	6.3
Male	(NA)	11.1	9.2	8.4	8.1	8.2	7.8	7.8	7.6	7.1	7.3
Female	(NA)	6.6	5.6	6.0	5.9	6.0	5.9	5.7	5.5	5.4	5.4
Asian or Pacific Islander	(NA)	5.9	5.8	5.1	4.6	4.6	4.5	4.4	4.4	4.2	4.2
Male	(NA)	7.9	7.2	6.2	5.6	5.6	5.4	5.3	5.2	5.1	5.1
Female	(NA)	4.3	4.7	4.2	3.9	3.9	3.8	3.7	3.7	3.6	3.6
Hispanic origin [2]	(NA)	(NA)	(NA)	6.7	6.2	6.3	6.0	5.9	5.8	5.6	5.6
Male	(NA)	(NA)	(NA)	8.2	7.5	7.7	7.3	7.1	7.0	6.8	6.8
Female	(NA)	(NA)	(NA)	5.5	5.1	5.1	5.0	4.8	4.8	4.7	4.6
Non-Hispanic, White	(NA)	(NA)	(NA)	8.6	8.1	8.1	7.9	7.8	7.8	7.6	7.6
Male	(NA)	(NA)	(NA)	10.4	9.6	9.6	9.4	9.2	9.2	8.9	8.9
Female	(NA)	(NA)	(NA)	7.2	6.9	6.9	6.7	6.6	6.7	6.4	6.4

NA Not available. [1] Includes other races not shown separately. [2] Persons of Hispanic origin may be of any race. [3] Age-adjusted death rates are better indicators than crude death rates for showing changes in the risk of death over time when the age distribution of the population is changing, and for comparing the mortality of population subgroups that have different age compositions. All age-adjusted death rates are standardized to the year 2010 population.

Source: U.S. National Center for Health Statistics, National Vital Statistics Reports (NVSR), *Deaths: Final Data for 2010*, Vol. 61, No. 4, May 2013. See also <http://www.cdc.gov/nchs/deaths.htm>.

Table 116. Death Rates by Age, Sex, and Race: 1950 to 2010

[Rates per 100,000 population. Data for 2001-2009 has been revised using population estimates based on the 2010 Census]

Characteristic	All ages [1]	Under 1 year	1 to 4 years	5 to 14 years	15 to 24 years	25 to 34 years	35 to 44 years	45 to 54 years	55 to 64 years	65 to 74 years	75 to 84 years	85 years and over
MALE												
1950	1,106	3,728	152	71	168	217	429	1,067	2,395	4,931	10,426	21,636
1960	1,105	3,059	120	56	152	188	373	992	2,310	4,914	10,178	21,186
1970	1,090	2,410	93	51	189	215	403	959	2,283	4,874	10,010	17,822
1980	977	1,429	73	37	172	196	299	767	1,815	4,105	8,817	18,801
1990	918	1,083	52	29	147	204	310	610	1,553	3,492	7,889	18,057
2000	853	807	36	21	115	139	255	543	1,231	2,980	6,973	17,501
2010	812	680	30	15	98	142	213	506	1,076	2,275	5,694	15,414
White:												
1990	931	896	46	26	131	176	268	549	1,467	3,398	7,845	18,268
2000	888	668	33	20	106	124	234	497	1,163	2,906	6,933	17,716
2005	874	665	32	17	111	136	232	512	1,061	2,512	6,278	16,693
2008	871	636	31	15	102	139	218	505	1,044	2,325	5,938	15,923
2009	858	611	28	15	95	136	217	502	1,032	2,245	5,737	15,362
2010	866	584	27	14	92	136	207	492	1,033	2,232	5,704	15,640
Black:												
1990	1,008	2,112	86	41	252	431	700	1,261	2,618	4,946	9,130	16,955
2000	834	1,568	55	28	181	261	453	1,018	2,080	4,254	8,486	16,791
2005	796	1,479	49	26	171	265	394	923	1,878	3,607	7,675	16,769
2008	751	1,343	48	23	156	236	342	791	1,723	3,348	7,084	15,380
2009	735	1,357	42	22	143	226	337	760	1,707	3,250	6,728	14,563
2010	725	1,207	43	20	143	217	308	716	1,662	3,206	6,722	14,715
Asian or Pacific Islander: [2]												
1990	334	605	45	21	76	80	131	287	789	2,041	5,009	12,446
2000	333	529	23	13	55	55	105	250	642	1,661	4,328	12,125
2005	327	439	20	14	51	55	97	242	540	1,389	3,875	11,343
2008	320	444	17	12	42	51	89	219	516	1,273	3,596	10,493
2009	321	412	19	11	41	50	94	227	510	1,219	3,457	10,477
2010	327	434	19	8	43	53	84	214	519	1,226	3,439	10,825
American Indian, or Alaska Native: [2]												
1990	476	1,057	77	33	220	256	365	620	1,211	2,462	5,389	11,244
2000	416	700	45	20	136	179	295	520	1,090	2,478	5,351	10,726
2005	428	601	50	20	127	192	305	542	1,077	2,244	4,878	11,842
2008	409	600	35	15	122	171	263	535	962	2,128	4,730	9,881
2009	390	549	31	16	121	155	276	487	941	1,970	4,342	9,175
2010	398	543	34	18	116	156	258	496	951	1,971	4,452	10,268
FEMALE												
1950	824	2,855	127	49	89	143	290	642	1,405	3,333	8,400	19,195
1960	809	2,321	98	37	61	107	229	527	1,196	2,872	7,633	19,008
1970	808	1,864	75	32	68	102	231	517	1,099	2,580	6,678	15,518
1980	785	1,142	55	24	58	76	159	413	934	2,145	5,440	14,747
1990	812	856	41	19	49	74	138	343	879	1,991	4,883	14,274
2000	855	663	29	15	43	64	143	313	772	1,921	4,815	14,719
2010	787	564	23	11	36	64	129	311	644	1,528	4,138	13,219
White:												
1990	847	690	36	18	46	62	117	309	823	1,924	4,839	14,401
2000	912	551	26	14	41	55	126	281	731	1,868	4,785	14,891
2005	888	536	24	13	42	59	131	292	660	1,688	4,526	14,438
2008	875	525	24	11	38	59	127	296	633	1,578	4,353	13,869
2009	849	502	23	11	37	63	128	302	625	1,518	4,191	13,133
2010	857	488	22	11	36	61	123	295	618	1,505	4,165	13,419
Black:												
1990	748	1,736	68	28	69	160	299	639	1,453	2,866	5,688	13,310
2000	733	1,280	45	20	58	122	272	588	1,227	2,690	5,697	13,941
2005	699	1,203	38	19	50	110	248	562	1,083	2,301	5,279	14,184
2008	662	1,105	36	16	49	97	218	515	1,000	2,102	4,843	13,178
2009	646	1,070	38	17	47	98	208	501	984	2,041	4,694	12,379
2010	643	994	33	15	43	93	199	481	972	2,021	4,581	12,590
Asian or Pacific Islander: [2]												
1990	234	518	32	13	29	38	70	183	483	1,089	3,128	10,254
2000	262	434	20	12	22	28	66	156	391	996	2,882	9,052
2005	271	374	16	11	23	27	58	140	343	896	2,613	8,769
2008	277	361	19	8	19	30	48	130	310	836	2,531	8,859
2009	274	374	13	10	21	26	51	122	295	777	2,472	8,685
2010	277	342	16	8	17	27	49	128	299	789	2,446	8,590
American Indian, or Alaska Native: [2]												
1990	330	689	38	26	69	102	156	381	806	1,679	3,073	8,201
2000	346	492	40	18	59	85	172	285	772	1,900	3,850	9,118
2005	355	500	31	15	62	81	171	339	676	1,770	3,813	9,752
2008	333	437	36	13	49	84	178	300	626	1,528	3,473	9,024
2009	332	444	24	16	56	82	172	347	604	1,472	3,333	8,619
2010	332	366	24	11	44	86	147	326	624	1,482	3,392	9,278

[1] Figures for age not stated are included in "All ages" but not distributed among age groups. [2] The death rates for specified races other than white and black should be interpreted with caution because of inconsistencies between reporting race on death certificates and censuses and surveys.

Source: U.S. National Center for Health Statistics, "Health, United States 2011, web updates," <http://www.cdc.gov/NCHS/hus.htm>, accessed May 2013.

Table 117. Age-Adjusted Death Rates by Sex, Race, and Hispanic Origin: 1970 to 2010

[Age-adjusted rates per 100,000 population. Data for 2001-2009 has been revised using population estimates based on the 2010 Census. Age-adjusted death rates are better indicators than crude death rates for showing changes in the risk of death over time when the age distribution of the population is changing, and for comparing the mortality of population subgroups that have different age compositions. Populations enumerated as of April 1 for census years and estimated as of July 1 for all other years. Excludes fetal deaths and deaths of nonresidents of the United States. Data for Hispanic-origin and specified races other than White and Black should be interpreted with caution because of inconsistencies reporting race on death certificates and on censuses and surveys. See text this section and Appendix III]

Sex, race, and Hispanic origin	1970	1980	1990	2000	2005	2006	2007	2008	2009	2010
ALL RACES [1]										
Total	1,223	1,039	939	869	815	792	775	775	750	747
Male	1,542	1,348	1,203	1,054	972	944	923	919	891	887
Female	971	818	751	731	692	672	658	660	637	635
WHITE										
Total	1,193	1,013	910	850	801	779	764	767	743	742
Male	1,514	1,318	1,166	1,029	953	926	907	907	881	879
Female	944	796	729	715	681	662	649	654	631	631
BLACK										
Total	1,518	1,315	1,250	1,121	1,035	998	972	948	913	898
Male	1,874	1,698	1,645	1,404	1,281	1,240	1,205	1,168	1,123	1,104
Female	1,229	1,033	975	928	863	828	808	792	763	753
AMERICAN INDIAN OR ALASKA NATIVE										
Total	(NA)	867	716	709	701	677	661	644	616	628
Male	(NA)	1,112	916	842	825	781	780	757	709	730
Female	(NA)	662	562	605	602	589	565	549	536	542
ASIAN OR PACIFIC ISLANDER										
Total	(NA)	590	582	506	460	451	436	435	425	424
Male	(NA)	787	716	624	561	545	526	519	509	512
Female	(NA)	426	469	417	385	381	369	372	361	359
HISPANIC ORIGIN [2]										
Total	(NA)	(NA)	(NA)	666	628	604	586	580	560	559
Male	(NA)	(NA)	(NA)	818	771	732	711	695	676	678
Female	(NA)	(NA)	(NA)	546	514	500	484	485	466	463
NON-HISPANIC, WHITE										
Total	(NA)	(NA)	(NA)	856	810	789	775	779	755	755
Male	(NA)	(NA)	(NA)	1,035	962	936	918	920	894	893
Female	(NA)	(NA)	(NA)	722	691	672	661	665	643	643

NA Not available. [1] For 1970 to 1990 includes deaths among races not shown separately. [2] Persons of Hispanic origin may be of any race.

Source: U.S. National Center for Health Statistics, National Vital Statistics Reports (NVSR), *Deaths: Final Data for 2010*, Vol. 61, No. 4, May 2013. See also <http://www.cdc.gov/nchs/deaths.htm>.

Table 118. Death Rates by Hispanic-Origin Status, Sex, and Age: 2000 to 2010

[Rates per 100,000 U.S. standard population. Rates are based on populations enumerated as of April 1 for census years and estimated as of July 1 for all other years. Rates for 2005 have been revised using population estimates based on the 2010 Census. Excludes deaths of nonresidents of the United States. Data for Hispanic-origin should be interpreted with caution because of inconsistencies between reporting Hispanic origin and race on death certificates and censuses and surveys]

Age	Hispanic male			Hispanic female			Non-Hispanic White male			Non-Hispanic White female		
	2000	2005	2010	2000	2005	2010	2000	2005	2010	2000	2005	2010
Age adjusted [1]	818	771	678	546	514	463	1,035	962	893	722	691	643
Crude [2]	331	336	311	275	273	261	979	978	988	1,007	1,000	981
Under 1 year	637	638	557	554	526	463	659	656	576	531	522	480
1 to 4 years	32	33	25	28	24	20	32	31	28	24	23	22
5 to 14 years	18	15	11	13	12	9	20	18	14	14	13	11
15 to 24 years	108	112	79	32	35	26	104	108	93	43	43	38
25 to 34 years	120	123	101	43	41	39	123	138	144	57	63	67
35 to 44 years	211	189	146	101	89	75	234	238	219	128	138	133
45 to 54 years	439	422	352	224	214	194	498	519	508	285	299	308
55 to 64 years	966	880	815	548	489	450	1,171	1,071	1,046	742	673	632
65 to 74 years	2,288	2,052	1,775	1,423	1,285	1,086	2,931	2,536	2,257	1,891	1,715	1,536
75 to 84 years	5,395	5,097	4,462	3,625	3,465	3,067	6,978	6,330	5,770	4,819	4,577	4,233
85 years and over	13,086	12,746	11,780	11,203	10,770	10,237	17,853	16,841	15,817	14,972	14,561	13,544

[1] Age-adjusted death rates are better indicators than crude death rates for showing changes in the risk of death over time when the age distribution of the population is changing, and for comparing the mortality of population subgroups that have different age compositions. [2] The total number of deaths in a given time period divided by the total resident population.

Source: U.S. National Center for Health Statistics, *Health, United States, 2012*, May 2013. See also <http://www.cdc.gov/nchs/hus.htm>.

Table 119. Deaths and Death Rates by State: 1990 to 2010

[2,148 represents 2,148,000. Rates for 2001-2009 have been revised using population estimates based on the 2010 Census. By state of residence. Excludes deaths of nonresidents of the United States. Caution should be used in comparing death rates by state; rates are affected by the population composition of the area. See also Appendix III]

State	Number of deaths (1,000)						Death rate per 1,000 population [1]						Age-adjusted rate 2010 [1,2]
	1990	1995	2000	2005	2009	2010	1990	1995	2000	2005	2009	2010	
United States	**2,148**	**2,312**	**2,403**	**2,448**	**2,437**	**2,468**	**8.6**	**8.7**	**8.5**	**8.3**	**7.9**	**8.0**	**7.5**
Alabama	39	42	45	47	47	48	9.7	10.0	10.1	10.3	10.0	10.1	9.4
Alaska	2	3	3	3	4	4	4.0	4.2	4.6	4.8	5.2	5.2	7.7
Arizona	29	35	41	46	46	47	7.9	8.4	7.9	7.8	7.2	7.3	6.9
Arkansas	25	27	28	28	29	29	10.5	10.8	10.6	10.1	9.9	9.9	8.9
California	214	224	230	237	233	234	7.2	7.1	6.8	6.6	6.3	6.3	6.5
Colorado	22	25	27	30	31	31	6.6	6.7	6.3	6.4	6.3	6.3	6.8
Connecticut	28	29	30	29	29	29	8.4	9.0	8.8	8.4	8.0	8.0	6.5
Delaware	6	6	7	7	8	8	8.7	8.8	8.8	8.8	8.4	8.6	7.7
District of Columbia	7	7	6	5	5	5	12.0	12.4	10.5	9.7	8.2	7.8	7.9
Florida	134	153	164	171	170	174	10.4	10.8	10.3	9.6	9.1	9.2	7.0
Georgia	52	58	64	67	70	71	8.0	8.1	7.8	7.5	7.2	7.4	8.5
Hawaii	7	8	8	9	10	10	6.1	6.4	6.8	7.1	7.4	7.1	5.9
Idaho	7	9	10	11	11	11	7.4	7.3	7.4	7.4	7.1	7.3	7.3
Illinois	103	108	107	104	100	100	9.0	9.2	8.6	8.2	7.8	7.8	7.4
Indiana	50	53	55	56	56	57	8.9	9.2	9.1	8.9	8.7	8.8	8.2
Iowa	27	28	28	28	28	28	9.7	9.9	9.6	9.4	9.1	9.1	7.2
Kansas	22	24	25	25	24	25	9.0	9.3	9.2	9.0	8.5	8.6	7.6
Kentucky	35	37	40	40	41	42	9.5	9.6	9.8	9.6	9.6	9.7	9.2
Louisiana	38	40	41	44	40	41	8.9	9.1	9.2	9.7	9.0	9.0	9.0
Maine	11	12	12	13	13	13	9.0	9.5	9.7	9.8	9.5	9.6	7.5
Maryland	38	42	44	44	44	43	8.0	8.3	8.3	7.8	7.7	7.5	7.3
Massachusetts	53	55	57	54	52	53	8.8	9.1	8.9	8.4	8.0	8.0	6.7
Michigan	79	84	87	87	86	88	8.5	8.8	8.7	8.6	8.7	8.9	7.9
Minnesota	35	38	38	38	38	39	7.9	8.1	7.7	7.3	7.2	7.3	6.6
Mississippi	25	27	29	29	28	29	9.8	10.0	10.1	10.0	9.6	9.8	9.6
Missouri	50	54	55	55	54	55	9.8	10.2	9.8	9.4	9.1	9.2	8.2
Montana	7	8	8	9	9	9	8.6	8.8	9.0	9.1	8.9	8.9	7.5
Nebraska	15	15	15	15	15	15	9.4	9.3	8.8	8.5	8.2	8.3	7.2
Nevada	9	13	15	19	19	20	7.8	8.2	7.6	7.8	7.2	7.3	8.0
New Hampshire	8	9	10	10	10	10	7.7	8.0	7.8	7.9	7.7	7.7	6.9
New Jersey	70	74	75	72	68	69	9.1	9.3	8.9	8.3	7.9	7.9	6.9
New Mexico	11	13	13	15	16	16	7.0	7.4	7.4	7.8	7.7	7.7	7.5
New York	169	168	158	152	146	146	9.4	9.3	8.3	8.0	7.6	7.6	6.7
North Carolina	57	65	72	75	77	79	8.6	9.0	8.9	8.6	8.2	8.3	8.0
North Dakota	6	6	6	6	6	6	8.9	9.3	9.1	8.9	8.9	8.8	7.0
Ohio	99	106	108	109	107	109	9.1	9.5	9.5	9.5	9.3	9.4	8.2
Oklahoma	30	33	35	36	36	37	9.7	10.0	10.2	10.2	9.6	9.7	9.2
Oregon	25	28	30	31	32	32	8.8	9.0	8.6	8.6	8.3	8.3	7.2
Pennsylvania	122	128	131	130	125	125	10.3	10.6	10.7	10.4	9.9	9.8	7.7
Rhode Island	10	10	10	10	9	10	9.5	9.8	9.6	9.4	8.9	9.1	7.2
South Carolina	30	34	37	39	40	42	8.5	9.1	9.2	9.1	8.8	9.0	8.5
South Dakota	6	7	7	7	7	7	9.1	9.5	9.3	9.1	8.6	8.7	7.2
Tennessee	46	51	55	57	58	60	9.5	9.8	9.7	9.6	9.2	9.4	8.9
Texas	125	138	150	156	163	167	7.4	7.4	7.2	6.9	6.6	6.6	7.7
Utah	9	11	12	13	14	15	5.3	5.6	5.5	5.5	5.2	5.3	7.0
Vermont	5	5	5	5	5	5	8.2	8.5	8.4	8.2	8.1	8.6	7.2
Virginia	48	53	56	58	59	59	7.8	8.0	8.0	7.6	7.4	7.4	7.4
Washington	37	41	44	46	48	48	7.6	7.5	7.5	7.4	7.2	7.2	6.9
West Virginia	19	20	21	21	21	21	10.8	11.1	11.7	11.4	11.6	11.5	9.3
Wisconsin	43	45	46	47	46	47	8.7	8.8	8.7	8.4	8.1	8.3	7.2
Wyoming	3	4	4	4	4	4	7.1	7.7	7.9	8.0	7.7	7.9	7.8

[1] Rates based on enumerated resident population as of April 1 for 1990, 2000, and 2010; estimated resident population as of July 1 for all other years. [2] Age-adjusted death rates are better indicators than crude death rates for showing changes in the risk of death over time when the age distribution of the population is changing, and for comparing the mortality of population subgroups that have different age compositions. See text this section.

Source: U.S. National Center for Health Statistics, CDC WONDER Online Database, "Compressed Mortality File 1999-2010," <http://wonder.cdc.gov/>, accessed September 2013.

Table 120. Fetal and Infant Deaths: 1990 to 2006

[The term "fetal death" defined on an all inclusive basis to end confusion arising from the use of such terms as stillbirth, spontaneous abortion, and miscarriage have been adopted by the National Center for Health Statistics (NCHS) as the nationally recommended standard. Fetal deaths do not include induced terminations of pregnancy. See also Appendix III]

Year	Fetal deaths [1]			Infant deaths		Fetal mortality rate [2]			Perinatal mortality rate	
	Total [1]	20 to 27 weeks [3]	28 weeks or more [3]	Less than 7 days	Less than 28 days	Total [1]	20–27 weeks [3]	28 weeks or more [3]	Defi-nition I [4]	Defi-nition II [5]
1990.....	31,386	13,427	17,959	19,439	23,591	7.49	3.22	4.30	8.95	13.12
1995.....	27,294	13,043	14,251	15,483	19,186	6.95	3.33	3.64	7.60	11.84
1996.....	27,069	12,990	14,079	14,947	18,556	6.91	3.33	3.60	7.43	11.64
1997.....	26,486	12,800	13,686	14,827	18,507	6.78	3.29	3.51	7.32	11.51
1998.....	26,702	13,229	13,473	15,061	18,915	6.73	3.35	3.41	7.21	11.50
1999.....	26,884	13,457	13,427	14,874	18,700	6.74	3.39	3.38	7.12	11.44
2000.....	27,003	13,497	13,506	14,893	18,733	6.61	3.31	3.32	6.97	11.19
2001.....	26,373	13,122	13,251	14,622	18,275	6.51	3.25	3.28	6.90	11.02
2002.....	25,943	13,072	12,871	15,020	18,791	6.41	3.24	3.19	6.91	11.05
2003.....	26,004	13,348	12,656	15,152	18,935	6.32	3.25	3.08	6.78	10.92
2004.....	26,001	13,068	12,933	14,836	18,602	6.28	3.17	3.14	6.73	10.78
2005.....	25,894	13,327	12,567	15,013	18,782	6.22	3.21	3.03	6.64	10.73
2006.....	25,972	13,270	12,702	15,148	19,041	6.05	3.10	2.97	6.51	10.49

[1] Fetal deaths with stated or presumed gestation of 20 weeks or more. [2] Rate per 1,000 live births and fetal deaths in specified group. [3] Not stated gestational age proportionally distributed. [4] Infant deaths of less than 7 days and fetal deaths with stated or presumed period of gestation of 28 weeks or more, per 1,000 live births and fetal deaths. [5] Infant deaths of less than 28 days and fetal deaths with stated or presumed period of gestation of 20 weeks or more per 1,000 live births and fetal deaths.

Source: U.S. National Center for Health Statistics, National Vital Statistics Reports (NVSR), *Fetal and Perinatal Mortality, U.S., 2006*, Vol. 60. No. 8, August 2012. See also <http://www.cdc.gov/nchs/fetal_death.htm>.

Table 121. Fetal, Infant, Neonatal, and Maternal Mortality Rates by Race: 1980 to 2010

[Deaths per 1,000 live births, except as noted. Data based on death certificates, fetal death records, and birth certificates. Excludes deaths of nonresidents of the United States. See also Appendix III]

Race and year	Infant [1]	Neonatal [1]		Post-neonatal [1]	Fetal mortality rate [2]	Late fetal mortality rate [3]	Perinatal mortality rate [4]	Maternal mortality rate [5]
		Under 28 days	Under 7 days					
ALL RACES								
1980..............	12.6	8.5	7.1	4.1	9.1	6.2	13.2	9.2
1990..............	9.2	5.8	4.8	3.4	7.5	4.3	9.0	8.2
1995..............	7.6	4.9	4.0	2.7	7.0	3.6	7.6	7.1
2000..............	6.9	4.6	3.7	2.3	6.6	3.3	7.0	9.8
2005..............	6.9	4.5	3.6	2.3	6.2	3.0	6.6	[6] 15.1
2006..............	6.7	4.5	3.5	2.2	6.1	3.0	6.5	13.3
2007..............	6.8	4.4	3.5	2.3	(NA)	(NA)	(NA)	12.7
2008..............	6.6	4.3	3.4	2.3	(NA)	(NA)	(NA)	(NA)
2009..............	6.4	4.2	3.3	2.2	(NA)	(NA)	(NA)	(NA)
2010..............	6.1	4.0	3.2	2.1	(NA)	(NA)	(NA)	(NA)
WHITE [7]								
1980..............	10.9	7.4	6.1	3.5	8.1	5.7	11.8	6.7
1990..............	7.6	4.8	3.9	2.8	6.4	3.8	7.7	5.4
1995..............	6.3	4.1	3.3	2.2	5.9	3.3	6.5	4.2
2000..............	5.7	3.8	3.0	1.9	5.6	2.9	5.9	7.5
2005..............	5.7	3.8	3.0	1.9	5.3	2.7	5.7	[6] 11.1
2006..............	5.6	3.7	2.9	1.8	5.2	2.7	5.6	9.5
2007..............	5.6	3.7	2.9	1.9	(NA)	(NA)	(NA)	10.0
2008..............	5.5	3.6	2.9	1.9	(NA)	(NA)	(NA)	(NA)
2009..............	5.3	3.5	2.8	1.8	(NA)	(NA)	(NA)	(NA)
2010..............	5.2	3.5	2.7	1.7	(NA)	(NA)	(NA)	(NA)
BLACK [7]								
1980..............	22.2	14.6	12.3	7.6	14.7	9.1	21.3	22.4
1990..............	18.0	11.6	9.7	6.4	13.3	6.7	16.4	22.4
1995..............	15.1	9.8	8.2	5.3	12.7	5.7	13.8	22.1
2000..............	14.1	9.4	7.6	4.7	12.4	5.4	13.0	22.0
2005..............	13.7	9.1	7.3	4.7	11.4	4.9	12.1	[6] 36.5
2006..............	13.3	8.8	7.0	4.5	10.8	4.6	11.5	32.7
2007..............	13.2	8.6	6.9	4.6	(NA)	(NA)	(NA)	26.5
2008..............	12.7	8.2	6.6	4.5	(NA)	(NA)	(NA)	(NA)
2009..............	12.6	8.2	6.6	4.5	(NA)	(NA)	(NA)	(NA)
2010..............	11.6	7.5	6.0	4.1	(NA)	(NA)	(NA)	(NA)

NA Not available. [1] Infant (under 1 year of age), neonatal (under 28 days), early neonatal (under 7 days), and postneonatal (28 days–11 months). [2] Number of fetal deaths of 20 weeks or more gestation per 1,000 live births plus fetal deaths. [3] Number of fetal deaths of 28 weeks or more gestation (late fetal deaths) per 1,000 live births plus late fetal deaths. [4] Number of late fetal deaths plus infant deaths within 7 days of birth per 1,000 live births plus late fetal deaths. [5] Per 100,000 live births from deliveries and complications of pregnancy, childbirth, and the puerperium. Beginning 2000, deaths are classified according to the tenth revision of the International Classification of Diseases; earlier years classified according to the revision in use at the time; see text, this section. [6] Increase partially reflects the use of a separate item on the death certificate on pregnancy status by an increasing number of states. [7] Infant deaths are tabulated by race of decedent; fetal deaths and live births are tabulated by race of mother.

Source: U.S. National Center for Health Statistics, *Health, United States, 2012*, May 2013, and earlier reports. See also <http://cdc.gov/nchs/hus.htm>.

Table 122. Infant Mortality Rates by Race, States, and Island Areas: 1980 to 2010

[Deaths per 1,000 live births, by place of residence. Represents deaths of infants under 1 year old, exclusive of fetal deaths. Excludes deaths of nonresidents of the United States]

State	Total [1]				White				Black			
	1980	1990	2000	2010	1980	1990	2000	2010	1980	1990	2000	2010
United States....	**12.6**	**9.2**	**6.9**	**6.2**	**10.9**	**7.6**	**5.7**	**5.2**	**22.2**	**18.0**	**14.1**	**11.6**
Alabama...........	15.1	10.8	9.4	8.7	11.6	8.1	6.6	6.6	21.6	16.0	15.4	13.7
Alaska............	12.3	10.5	6.8	3.8	9.4	7.6	5.8	3.3	19.5	(B)	(B)	(B)
Arizona...........	12.4	8.8	6.7	6.0	11.8	7.8	6.2	5.5	18.4	20.6	17.6	12.1
Arkansas..........	12.7	9.2	8.4	7.3	10.3	8.4	7.0	6.7	20.0	13.9	13.7	10.3
California.........	11.1	7.9	5.4	4.7	10.6	7.0	5.1	4.6	18.0	16.8	12.9	9.8
Colorado..........	10.1	8.8	6.2	5.9	9.8	7.8	5.6	5.6	19.1	19.4	19.5	13.1
Connecticut.......	11.2	7.9	6.6	5.3	10.2	6.3	5.6	4.5	19.1	17.6	14.4	11.6
Delaware..........	13.9	10.1	9.2	7.7	9.8	9.7	7.9	6.4	27.9	20.1	14.8	11.9
District of Columbia........	25.0	20.7	12.0	7.9	17.8	(B)	(B)	(B)	26.7	24.6	16.1	10.5
Florida...........	14.6	9.6	7.0	6.5	11.8	6.7	5.4	5.0	22.8	16.8	12.6	11.3
Georgia...........	14.5	12.4	8.5	6.4	10.8	7.4	5.9	5.1	21.0	18.3	13.9	9.1
Hawaii............	10.3	6.7	8.1	6.2	11.6	6.1	6.5	3.9	(B)	(B)	(B)	(B)
Idaho.............	10.7	8.7	7.5	4.8	10.7	8.6	7.5	4.8	(NA)	(B)	(B)	(B)
Illinois...........	14.8	10.7	8.5	6.8	11.7	7.9	6.6	5.4	26.3	22.4	17.1	13.6
Indiana...........	11.9	9.6	7.8	7.6	10.5	7.9	6.9	6.7	23.4	17.4	15.8	15.0
Iowa..............	11.8	8.1	6.5	4.9	11.5	7.9	6.0	4.6	27.2	21.9	21.1	11.2
Kansas............	10.4	8.4	6.8	6.2	9.5	8.0	6.4	5.7	20.6	17.7	12.2	12.4
Kentucky..........	12.9	8.5	7.2	6.8	12.0	8.2	6.7	6.4	22.0	14.3	12.7	11.1
Louisiana.........	14.3	11.1	9.0	7.6	10.5	8.1	5.9	4.9	20.6	16.7	13.3	11.8
Maine.............	9.2	6.2	4.9	5.4	9.4	6.7	4.8	5.4	(B)	(B)	(B)	(B)
Maryland..........	14.0	9.5	7.6	6.8	11.6	6.8	4.8	4.4	20.4	17.1	13.2	11.6
Massachusetts.....	10.5	7.0	4.6	4.4	10.1	6.1	4.0	4.0	16.8	11.9	9.9	7.2
Michigan..........	12.8	10.7	8.2	7.1	10.6	7.4	6.0	5.5	24.2	21.6	18.2	14.1
Minnesota.........	10.0	7.3	5.6	4.5	9.6	6.7	4.8	4.2	20.0	23.7	14.6	6.4
Mississippi........	17.0	12.1	10.7	9.7	11.1	7.4	6.8	6.6	23.7	16.2	15.3	13.8
Missouri..........	12.4	9.4	7.2	6.6	11.1	7.9	5.9	5.8	20.7	18.2	14.7	11.8
Montana...........	12.4	9.0	6.1	5.9	11.8	6.0	5.5	5.9	(NA)	(B)	(B)	(B)
Nebraska..........	11.5	8.3	7.3	5.3	10.7	6.9	6.4	4.7	25.2	18.9	20.3	13.4
Nevada............	10.7	8.4	6.5	5.6	10.0	8.2	6.0	4.8	20.6	14.2	12.7	13.8
New Hampshire....	9.9	7.1	5.7	4.0	9.9	6.0	5.5	3.9	22.5	(B)	(B)	(B)
New Jersey........	12.5	9.0	6.3	4.8	10.3	6.4	5.0	3.6	21.9	18.4	13.6	10.4
New Mexico........	11.5	9.0	6.6	5.6	11.3	7.6	6.3	5.5	23.1	(B)	(B)	(B)
New York..........	12.5	9.6	6.4	5.1	10.8	7.4	5.4	4.2	20.0	18.1	10.9	9.2
North Carolina.....	14.5	10.6	8.6	7.0	12.1	8.0	6.3	5.4	20.0	16.5	15.7	12.3
North Dakota.......	12.1	8.0	8.1	6.8	11.7	7.2	7.5	5.4	27.5	(B)	(B)	(B)
Ohio..............	12.8	9.8	7.6	7.7	11.2	7.8	6.3	6.3	23.0	19.5	15.4	14.8
Oklahoma..........	12.7	9.2	8.5	7.6	12.1	9.1	7.9	6.3	21.8	14.3	16.9	12.4
Oregon............	12.2	8.3	5.6	4.9	12.2	7.0	5.5	4.7	15.9	(B)	(B)	(B)
Pennsylvania.......	13.2	9.6	7.1	7.3	11.9	7.4	5.8	6.3	23.1	20.5	15.7	12.6
Rhode Island.......	11.0	8.1	6.3	7.1	10.9	7.0	5.9	6.7	(B)	(B)	(B)	(B)
South Carolina.....	15.6	11.7	8.7	7.4	10.8	8.1	5.4	5.3	22.9	17.3	14.8	11.3
South Dakota......	10.9	10.1	5.5	6.9	9.0	8.0	4.3	6.0	(NA)	(B)	(B)	(B)
Tennessee.........	13.5	10.3	9.1	7.9	11.9	7.3	6.8	6.6	19.3	17.9	18.0	13.3
Texas.............	12.2	8.1	5.7	6.1	11.2	6.7	5.1	5.6	18.8	14.7	11.4	11.2
Utah..............	10.4	7.5	5.2	4.9	10.5	6.0	5.1	4.5	27.3	(B)	(B)	(B)
Vermont...........	10.7	6.4	6.0	4.2	10.7	5.9	6.1	4.4	(B)	(B)	(B)	(B)
Virginia...........	13.6	10.2	6.9	6.8	11.9	7.4	5.4	4.8	19.8	19.5	12.4	14.3
Washington........	11.8	7.8	5.2	4.5	11.5	7.3	4.9	4.0	16.4	20.6	9.4	8.2
West Virginia......	11.8	9.9	7.6	7.3	11.4	8.1	7.4	7.1	21.5	(B)	(B)	(B)
Wisconsin..........	10.3	8.2	6.6	5.8	9.7	7.7	5.5	4.9	18.5	19.0	17.2	14.6
Wyoming..........	9.8	8.6	6.7	6.8	9.3	7.5	6.5	6.4	25.9	(B)	(B)	(B)
Puerto Rico.......	(NA)	(NA)	9.7	8.1	(NA)	(NA)	10.2	8.8	(NA)	(NA)	(B)	(B)
Virgin Islands.....	(NA)	(NA)	13.4	(B)	(NA)	(NA)	(B)	(B)	(B)	(B)	(B)	(B)
Guam.............	(NA)	(NA)	5.8	14.1	(NA)	(NA)	(B)	(B)	(B)	(B)	(B)	(B)
American Samoa..........	(NA)	(NA)	(B)	(B)	(B)	(B)	(B)	(B)	(B)	(B)	(B)	(B)
Northern Marianas........	(NA)	(NA)	(B)	(B)	(B)	(B)	(B)	(B)	(B)	(B)	(B)	(B)

B Base figure too small to meet statistical standards for reliability. NA Not available. [1] Includes other races, not shown separately.

Source: U.S. National Center for Health Statistics, National Vital Statistics Reports (NVSR), *Deaths: Final Data for 2010*, Vol. 61, No. 4, May 2013, and earlier reports. See also <http://www.cdc.gov/nchs/nvss.htm>.

Table 123. Age-Adjusted Death Rates by Major Causes: 1960 to 2011

[Age-adjusted rates per 100,000 population. Rates for 2001-2009 have been revised using population estimates based on the 2010 Census. Age adjusted death rates were prepared using the direct method, in which age specific death rates for a population of interest are applied to a standard population distributed by age. Age adjustment eliminates the differences in observed rates between points in time or among compared population groups that result from age differences in population composition. Beginning 1999, deaths classified according to tenth revision of International Classification of Diseases; for earlier years, causes of death were classified according to the revisions then in use. Changes in classification of causes of death due to these revisions may result in discontinuities in cause-of-death trends. See Appendix III]

Year	Diseases of the heart	Malignant neoplasms (cancer)	Cerebrovascular diseases	Chronic lower respiratory diseases	Accidents [1]	Alzheimer's disease	Diabetes mellitus	Influenza and pneumonia	Chronic liver disease and cirrhosis	Intentional self-harm (suicide)
1960.....	559.0	193.9	177.9	12.5	63.1	(NA)	22.5	53.7	13.3	12.5
1961.....	545.3	193.4	173.1	12.6	60.6	(NA)	22.1	43.4	13.3	12.2
1962.....	556.9	193.3	174.0	14.2	62.9	(NA)	22.6	47.1	13.8	12.8
1963.....	563.4	194.7	173.9	16.5	64.0	(NA)	23.1	55.6	14.0	13.0
1964.....	543.3	193.6	167.0	16.3	64.1	(NA)	22.5	45.4	14.2	12.7
1965.....	542.5	195.6	166.4	18.3	65.8	(NA)	22.9	46.8	14.9	13.0
1966.....	541.2	196.5	165.8	19.2	67.6	(NA)	23.6	47.9	15.9	12.7
1967.....	524.7	197.3	159.3	19.2	66.2	(NA)	23.4	42.2	16.3	12.5
1968.....	531.0	198.8	162.5	20.7	65.5	(NA)	25.3	52.8	16.9	12.4
1969.....	516.8	198.5	155.4	20.9	64.9	(NA)	25.1	47.9	17.1	12.7
1970.....	492.7	198.6	147.7	21.3	62.2	(NA)	24.3	41.7	17.8	13.1
1971.....	492.9	199.3	147.6	21.8	60.3	(NA)	23.9	38.4	17.8	13.1
1972.....	490.2	200.3	147.3	22.8	60.2	(NA)	23.7	41.3	18.0	13.3
1973.....	482.0	200.0	145.2	23.6	59.3	(NA)	23.0	41.2	18.1	13.1
1974.....	458.8	201.5	136.8	23.2	52.7	(NA)	22.1	35.5	17.9	13.2
1975.....	431.2	200.1	123.5	23.7	50.8	(NA)	20.3	34.9	16.7	13.6
1976.....	426.9	202.5	117.4	24.9	48.7	(NA)	19.5	38.8	16.4	13.2
1977.....	413.7	203.5	110.4	24.7	48.8	(NA)	18.2	31.0	15.8	13.7
1978.....	409.9	204.9	103.7	26.3	48.9	(NA)	18.3	34.5	15.2	12.9
1979.....	401.6	204.0	97.1	25.5	46.5	(NA)	17.5	26.1	14.8	12.6
1980.....	412.1	207.9	96.4	28.3	46.4	(NA)	18.1	31.4	15.1	12.2
1981.....	397.0	206.4	89.5	29.0	43.4	0.9	17.6	30.0	14.2	12.3
1982.....	389.0	208.3	84.2	29.1	40.1	1.3	17.2	26.5	13.2	12.5
1983.....	388.9	209.1	81.2	31.6	39.1	2.2	17.6	29.8	12.8	12.4
1984.....	378.8	210.8	78.7	32.4	38.8	3.1	17.2	30.6	12.7	12.6
1985.....	375.0	211.3	76.6	34.5	38.5	4.1	17.4	34.5	12.3	12.5
1986.....	365.1	211.5	73.1	34.8	38.6	4.6	17.2	34.8	11.8	13.0
1987.....	355.9	211.7	71.6	35.0	38.2	5.5	17.4	33.8	11.7	12.8
1988.....	352.5	212.5	70.6	36.5	38.9	5.8	18.0	37.3	11.6	12.5
1989.....	332.0	214.2	66.9	36.6	37.7	6.1	20.5	35.9	11.6	12.3
1990.....	321.8	216.0	65.3	37.2	36.3	6.3	20.7	36.8	11.1	12.5
1991.....	312.5	215.2	62.9	37.9	34.7	6.3	20.7	34.7	10.7	12.3
1992.....	304.0	213.5	61.5	37.7	33.2	6.3	20.7	32.8	10.4	12.0
1993.....	308.1	213.5	62.7	40.7	34.2	7.1	21.9	35.0	10.2	12.1
1994.....	297.5	211.7	62.6	40.3	34.2	7.7	22.6	33.6	10.1	11.9
1995.....	293.4	209.9	63.1	40.1	34.4	8.4	23.2	33.4	9.9	11.8
1996.....	285.7	206.7	62.5	40.6	34.5	8.5	23.8	32.9	9.7	11.5
1997.....	277.7	203.4	61.1	41.1	34.2	8.7	23.7	33.3	9.5	11.2
1998.....	267.4	202.1	62.8	43.8	35.6	8.6	24.2	24.2	9.6	11.1
1999.....	266.5	200.8	61.6	45.4	35.3	16.5	25.0	23.5	9.6	10.5
2000.....	257.6	199.6	60.9	44.2	34.9	18.1	25.0	23.7	9.5	10.4
2001.....	249.5	196.5	58.4	43.9	35.7	19.3	25.4	22.2	9.5	10.7
2002.....	244.6	194.3	57.2	43.9	37.1	20.8	25.6	23.2	9.4	10.9
2003.....	236.3	190.9	54.6	43.7	37.6	22.1	25.5	22.6	9.3	10.8
2004.....	221.6	186.8	51.2	41.6	38.1	22.6	24.7	20.4	9.0	11.0
2005.....	216.8	185.1	48.0	43.9	39.5	24.0	24.9	21.0	8.9	10.9
2006.....	205.5	181.8	44.8	41.0	40.2	23.7	23.6	18.4	8.8	11.0
2007.....	196.1	179.3	43.5	41.4	40.4	23.8	22.8	16.8	9.1	11.3
2008.....	192.1	176.4	42.1	44.7	39.2	25.8	22.0	17.6	9.2	11.6
2009.....	182.8	173.5	39.6	42.7	37.5	24.2	21.0	16.5	9.1	11.8
2010.....	179.1	172.8	39.1	42.2	38.0	25.1	20.8	15.1	9.4	12.1
2011 [2].....	173.7	168.6	37.9	42.7	38.0	24.6	21.5	15.7	9.7	12.0

NA Not available. [1] Unintentional injuries. [2] Preliminary data.

Source: U.S. National Center for Health Statistics, National Vital Statistics Reports, *Deaths: Preliminary Data for 2011*, Vol. 61, No. 6, October 2012; and *Health, United States, 2012*, May 2013. See also <http://www.cdc.gov/nchs/products/nvsr.htm>.

Table 124. Leading Causes of Deaths by Race: 2009

[Cause of death based on International Classification of Diseases, Tenth Revision (ICD-10)]

Cause of death	White Rank[1]	White Deaths	White Per-cent	Black Rank[1]	Black Deaths	Black Per-cent	American Indian/ Alaskan Native Rank[1]	American Indian/ Alaskan Native Deaths	American Indian/ Alaskan Native Per-cent	Asian/ Pacific Islander Rank[1]	Asian/ Pacific Islander Deaths	Asian/ Pacific Islander Per-cent
All causes..............	(X)	2,086,355	100.0	(X)	286,623	100.0	(X)	14,960	100.0	(X)	49,225	100.0
Diseases of heart............	1	515,587	24.7	1	69,687	24.3	1	2,764	18.5	2	11,375	23.1
Malignant neoplasms........	2	486,995	23.3	2	64,649	22.6	2	2,710	18.1	1	13,274	27.0
Chronic lower respiratory diseases....................	3	126,733	6.1	7	8,530	3.0	6	610	4.1	7	1,480	3.0
Cerebrovascular diseases...	4	108,764	5.2	3	15,878	5.5	7	561	3.8	3	3,639	7.4
Accidents (unintentional injuries)...................	5	102,170	4.9	4	12,074	4.2	3	1,733	11.6	4	2,044	4.2
Alzheimer's disease........	6	72,696	3.5	12	5,090	1.8	13	193	1.3	9	1,024	2.1
Diabetes mellitus............	7	54,113	2.6	5	11,960	4.2	4	786	5.3	5	1,846	3.8
Influenza and pneumonia. . .	8	46,432	2.2	11	5,290	1.8	9	402	2.7	6	1,568	3.2
Nephritis, nephrotic syndrome and nephrosis......	9	38,758	1.9	6	8,808	3.1	10	307	2.1	8	1,062	2.2
Intentional self harm (suicide).................	10	33,425	1.6	16	2,084	0.7	8	429	2.9	10	971	2.0
Septicemia..................	11	28,609	1.4	9	6,179	2.2	11	275	1.8	12	576	1.2
Chronic liver disease and cirrhosis.................	12	26,820	1.3	15	2,560	0.9	5	714	4.8	13	464	0.9
Assault (homicide)..........	18	8,323	0.4	8	7,874	2.7	12	254	1.7	16	348	0.7
Human immunodeficiency virus (HIV).................	24	3,896	0.2	10	5,377	1.9	19	64	0.4	28	69	0.1

X Not applicable. [1] Rank based on number of deaths.

Source: U.S. National Center for Health Statistics, National Vital Statistics Reports (NVSR), *Deaths: Leading Causes for 2009*, Vol. 61, No. 7, October 2012. See also <http://www.cdc.gov/nchs/deaths.htm>.

Table 125. Leading Causes of Deaths by Hispanic Origin: 2009

[Race and Hispanic origin are reported separately on death certificate. Persons of Hispanic origin may be any race. Cause of death based on International Classification of Diseases, Tenth Revision (ICD-10)]

Cause of death	Hispanic Rank[1]	Hispanic Deaths	Hispanic Per-cent	Non-Hispanic Rank[1]	Non-Hispanic Deaths	Non-Hispanic Per-cent	Non-Hispanic White Rank[1]	Non-Hispanic White Deaths	Non-Hispanic White Per-cent	Non-Hispanic Black Rank[1]	Non-Hispanic Black Deaths	Non-Hispanic Black Per-cent
All causes..............	(X)	141,576	100.0	(X)	2,289,999	100.0	(X)	1,944,606	100.0	(X)	282,982	100.0
Malignant neoplasms.......	1	29,935	21.1	2	536,814	23.4	2	457,189	23.5	2	63,967	22.6
Diseases of heart...........	2	29,611	20.9	1	568,378	24.8	1	485,779	25.0	1	68,811	24.3
Accidents (unintentional injuries).....................	3	10,654	7.5	5	106,812	4.7	5	91,416	4.7	5	11,810	4.2
Cerebrovascular diseases....................	4	7,065	5.0	4	121,540	5.3	4	101,703	5.2	3	15,718	5.6
Diabetes mellitus............	5	6,311	4.5	7	62,250	2.7	7	47,851	2.5	4	11,833	4.2
Chronic liver disease and cirrhosis....................	6	4,303	3.0	12	26,160	1.1	12	22,520	1.2	15	2,518	0.9
Chronic lower respiratory diseases....................	7	4,026	2.8	3	133,095	5.8	3	122,605	6.3	7	8,444	3.0
Influenza and pneumonia...	8	3,679	2.6	8	49,905	2.2	8	42,752	2.2	11	5,214	1.8
Assault (homicide)..........	9	3,179	2.2	17	13,456	0.6	22	5,163	0.3	8	7,733	2.7
Nephritis, nephrotic syndrome and nephrosis.....	10	3,107	2.2	9	45,729	2.0	9	35,670	1.8	6	8,727	3.1
Alzheimer's disease........	11	2,986	2.1	6	75,932	3.3	6	69,695	3.6	12	5,042	1.8
Intentional self harm (suicide)..................	13	2,573	1.8	10	34,188	1.5	10	30,813	1.6	16	2,034	0.7
Septicemia..................	14	2,077	1.5	11	33,491	1.5	11	26,533	1.4	9	6,131	2.2
Human immunodeficiency virus (HIV).................	17	1,263	0.9	20	8,071	0.4	25	2,640	0.1	10	5,307	1.9

X Not applicable. [1]Rank based on number of deaths.

Source: U.S. National Center for Health Statistics, National Vital Statistics Reports (NVSR), *Deaths: Leading Causes for 2009*, Vol. 61, No.7, October 2012. See also http://www.cdc.gov/nchs/deaths.htm>.

Table 126. Deaths and Death Rates by Selected Causes: 2010 and Preliminary 2011

[Rates per 100,000 population. Figures are weighted data rounded to the nearest individual, so categories may not add to total or subtotal. Excludes deaths of nonresidents of the United States. Deaths classified according to tenth revision of International Classification of Diseases (ICD). See also Appendix III]

Cause of death	2010			2011 [1]		
	Number	Rate	Age-adjusted rate [2]	Number	Rate	Age-adjusted rate [2]
All causes [3]	2,468,435	799.5	747.0	2,512,873	806.5	740.6
Major cardiovascular diseases [3]	780,213	252.7	234.2	778,503	249.8	227.1
Diseases of heart	597,689	193.6	179.1	596,339	191.4	173.7
Acute rheumatic fever and chronic rheumatic heart disease	2,987	1.0	0.9	3,070	1.0	0.9
Hypertensive heart disease	33,678	10.9	10.0	33,383	10.7	9.6
Hypertensive heart and renal disease	2,807	0.9	0.8	3,598	1.2	1.0
Ischemic heart disease	379,559	122.9	113.6	374,601	120.2	109.0
Acute myocardial infarction	122,071	39.5	36.5	119,732	38.4	34.9
Other heart diseases	178,658	57.9	53.7	181,686	58.3	53.1
Heart failure	57,757	18.7	17.3	59,544	19.1	17.3
Essential (primary) hypertension and hypertensive renal disease	26,634	8.6	8.0	27,477	8.8	8.0
Cerebrovascular diseases	129,476	41.9	39.1	128,931	41.4	37.9
Atherosclerosis	7,230	2.3	2.2	7,011	2.3	2.0
Malignant neoplasms [3]	574,743	186.2	172.8	575,313	184.6	168.6
Malignant neoplasms of lip, oral cavity, and pharynx	8,474	2.7	2.5	8,625	2.8	2.5
Malignant neoplasms of esophagus	14,490	4.7	4.3	14,413	4.6	4.1
Malignant neoplasms of stomach	11,390	3.7	3.4	10,995	3.5	3.2
Malignant neoplasms of colon, rectum and anus	52,622	17.0	15.8	52,243	16.8	15.3
Malignant neoplasms of liver and intrahepatic bile ducts	20,305	6.6	6.0	21,519	6.9	6.1
Malignant neoplasms of pancreas	36,888	11.9	11.0	37,371	12.0	10.9
Malignant neoplasms of trachea, bronchus and lung	158,318	51.3	47.6	156,614	50.3	45.9
Malignant melanoma of skin	9,154	3.0	2.8	9,126	2.9	2.7
Malignant neoplasm of breast	41,435	13.4	12.4	41,271	13.2	12.0
Malignant neoplasm of ovary	14,572	4.7	4.4	14,312	4.6	4.2
Malignant neoplasm of prostate	28,561	9.3	8.7	27,929	9.0	8.3
Malignant neoplasms of kidney and renal pelvis	13,219	4.3	3.9	13,520	4.3	4.0
Malignant neoplasms of bladder	14,731	4.8	4.5	14,969	4.8	4.4
Malignant neoplasms of meninges, brain and other parts of central nervous system	14,164	4.6	4.3	14,492	4.7	4.3
Malignant neoplasms of lymphoid, hematopoietic and related tissue [3]	55,590	18.0	17.0	56,263	18.1	16.8
Non-Hodgkins' lymphoma	20,294	6.6	6.2	20,221	6.5	6.0
Leukemia	22,569	7.3	6.9	22,982	7.4	6.9
Accidents (unintentional injuries)	120,859	39.1	38.0	122,777	39.4	38.0
Transport accidents [3]	37,961	12.3	12.1	37,275	12.0	11.7
Motor vehicle accidents	35,332	11.4	11.3	34,677	11.1	10.9
Nontransport accidents [3]	82,898	26.8	25.9	85,502	27.4	26.2
Falls	26,009	8.4	7.9	26,631	8.5	7.8
Accidental drowning and submersion	3,782	1.2	1.2	3,555	1.1	1.1
Accidental exposure to smoke, fire and flames	2,782	0.9	0.9	2,621	0.8	0.8
Accidental poisoning and exposure to noxious substances	33,041	10.7	10.6	33,554	10.8	10.7
Chronic lower respiratory diseases [3]	138,080	44.7	42.2	143,382	46.0	42.7
Emphysema	10,034	3.2	3.1	9,418	3.0	2.8
Asthma	3,404	1.1	1.0	3,311	1.1	1.0
Influenza and pneumonia [3]	50,097	16.2	15.1	53,667	17.2	15.7
Pneumonia	49,597	16.1	14.9	52,136	16.7	15.2
Septicemia (blood poisoning)	34,812	11.3	10.6	35,539	11.4	10.5
Viral hepatitis	7,564	2.4	2.1	7,794	2.5	2.1
Human immunodeficiency virus (HIV) disease	8,369	2.7	2.6	7,638	2.5	2.4
Anemias	4,852	1.6	1.5	4,956	1.6	1.5
Diabetes mellitus	69,071	22.4	20.8	73,282	23.5	21.5
Nutritional deficiencies	2,948	1.0	0.9	3,177	1.0	0.9
Malnutrition	2,790	0.9	0.8	2,993	1.0	0.9
Parkinson's disease	22,032	7.1	6.8	23,107	7.4	7.0
Alzheimer's disease	83,494	27.0	25.1	84,691	27.2	24.6
Chronic liver disease and cirrhosis	31,903	10.3	9.4	33,539	10.8	9.7
Alcoholic liver disease	15,990	5.2	4.7	16,634	5.3	4.8
Nephritis, nephrotic syndrome, and nephrosis [3]	50,476	16.3	15.3	45,731	14.7	13.4
Renal failure	44,362	14.4	13.4	43,682	14.0	12.8
Intentional self-harm (suicide)	38,364	12.4	12.1	38,285	12.3	12.0
Intentional self-harm (suicide) by discharge of firearms	19,392	6.3	6.1	19,766	6.3	6.1
Assault (homicide)	16,259	5.3	5.3	15,953	5.1	5.2
Assault (homicide) by discharge of firearms	11,078	3.6	3.6	11,101	3.6	3.6
Events of undetermined intent	4,908	1.6	1.6	4,446	1.4	1.4
Drug-induced deaths [4]	40,393	13.1	12.9	40,239	12.9	12.8
Alcohol-induced deaths [4]	25,692	8.3	7.6	26,256	8.4	7.6

[1] Data for 2011 are preliminary. [2] See text, this section. [3] Includes other causes, not shown separately. [4] Included in selected categories.

Source: U.S. National Center for Health Statistics, National Vital Statistics Reports, *Deaths: Preliminary Data for 2011*, Vol. 61, No. 1, October 2012, and earlier reports. See also <http://www.cdc.gov/nchs/deaths.htm>.

Table 127. Deaths by Age and Selected Causes: 2010

[Deaths are classified according to the tenth revision of the International Classification of Diseases. See Appendix III]

Cause of death	All ages[1]	Under 1 year	1 to 4 years	5 to 14 years	15 to 24 years	25 to 34 years	35 to 44 years	45 to 54 years	55 to 64 years	65 to 74 years	75 to 84 years	85 years and over
All causes[2]	2,468,435	24,586	4,316	5,279	29,551	42,259	70,033	183,207	310,802	407,151	625,651	765,474
Septicemia	34,812	215	62	67	141	312	767	2,333	4,604	6,545	9,931	9,834
Human immunodeficiency virus (HIV) disease	8,369	–	–	3	147	741	1,898	3,123	1,822	486	124	23
Malignant neoplasms[2]	574,743	62	346	916	1,604	3,619	11,809	50,211	109,501	144,635	157,025	95,010
Malignant neoplasm of esophagus	14,490	–	–	–	2	32	222	1,483	3,683	3,953	3,517	1,598
Malignant neoplasms of colon, rectum, and anus	52,622	–	–	4	54	312	1,345	5,052	9,453	11,459	13,846	11,096
Malignant neoplasms of liver and intrahepatic bile ducts	20,305	4	19	20	31	90	315	2,493	5,819	4,814	4,569	2,130
Malignant neoplasm of pancreas	36,888	–	–	3	8	64	468	2,869	7,382	9,658	10,452	5,984
Malignant neoplasms of trachea, bronchus, and lung	158,318	–	–	7	31	162	1,351	12,093	31,147	48,606	46,658	18,262
Malignant neoplasm of breast	41,435	–	–	1	7	323	2,045	5,915	9,104	8,710	8,385	6,945
Malignant neoplasm of ovary	14,572	–	–	1	22	97	345	1,510	3,104	3,724	3,722	2,046
Malignant neoplasm of prostate	28,561	–	–	2	2	1	20	493	2,555	5,866	10,135	9,488
Malignant neoplasm of bladder	14,731	–	–	–	–	17	90	602	1,731	3,019	5,027	4,244
Malignant neoplasms of lymphoid, hematopoietic and related tissue[2]	55,590	28	115	286	533	771	1,261	3,439	8,002	12,789	17,069	11,297
Non-Hodgkins lymphoma	20,294	2	3	30	103	204	429	1,316	2,912	4,621	6,223	4,451
Leukemia	22,569	25	112	253	376	439	608	1,377	2,973	4,914	6,883	4,609
Diabetes mellitus	69,071	3	4	26	165	606	1,789	5,610	11,677	14,687	18,822	15,682
Parkinson's disease	22,032	–	–	–	3	5	7	80	489	2,567	9,769	9,112
Alzheimer's disease	83,494	–	–	–	–	–	7	121	750	4,291	24,099	54,226
Major cardiovascular diseases[2]	780,213	468	213	282	1,286	4,012	13,313	45,149	83,886	114,483	205,180	311,910
Diseases of heart[2]	597,689	329	159	185	1,028	3,222	10,594	36,729	68,077	88,851	153,080	235,407
Hypertensive heart disease	33,678	–	2	2	47	371	1,358	4,097	5,369	4,567	6,330	11,529
Ischemic heart diseases	379,559	20	5	9	113	1,023	5,330	23,008	46,291	60,934	100,056	142,754
Acute myocardial infarction	122,071	14	2	4	61	353	2,053	8,862	17,680	22,219	32,058	38,763
Heart failure	57,757	26	13	9	42	107	298	1,116	2,912	5,864	15,094	32,274
Essential (primary) hypertension and hypertensive renal disease	26,634	3	1	2	21	110	394	1,384	2,672	3,636	6,763	11,648
Cerebrovascular diseases	129,476	130	50	90	190	517	1,904	5,910	10,693	17,736	37,659	54,595
Influenza and pneumonia	50,097	195	91	71	181	385	773	1,926	3,627	6,066	13,369	23,411
Pneumonia	49,597	179	78	59	150	341	720	1,823	3,543	6,027	13,325	23,350
Chronic lower respiratory diseases[2]	138,080	37	51	133	149	272	709	4,452	14,242	31,777	48,309	37,945
Emphysema	10,034	1	–	2	2	9	44	411	1,264	2,650	3,556	2,095
Pneumonitis due to solids and liquids	17,011	18	13	9	42	69	142	487	1,005	1,869	4,990	8,367
Chronic liver disease and cirrhosis	31,903	3	2	3	34	487	2,423	8,651	9,764	5,720	3,620	1,195
Nephritis, nephrotic syndrome, and nephrosis[2]	50,476	105	13	22	68	243	726	2,222	5,082	8,541	15,118	18,335
Renal failure	44,362	110	10	16	65	220	668	2,057	4,698	7,824	13,395	15,308
Accidents (unintentional injuries)[2]	120,859	1,110	1,394	1,643	12,341	14,573	14,792	19,667	14,023	9,407	13,853	18,040
Transport accidents	37,961	81	469	956	7,549	6,090	5,124	5,955	4,806	2,942	2,620	1,366
Motor vehicle accidents	35,332	79	449	890	7,250	5,746	4,745	5,392	4,335	2,676	2,458	1,309
Nontransport accidents	82,898	1,029	925	687	4,792	8,483	9,668	13,712	9,217	6,465	11,233	16,674
Falls	26,009	10	24	28	211	299	493	1,283	2,011	2,988	7,249	11,412
Accidental poisoning and exposure to noxious substances	33,041	6	34	54	3,183	6,767	7,476	9,662	4,451	837	338	227
Intentional self-harm (suicide)	38,364	–	–	274	4,600	5,735	6,571	8,799	6,384	2,974	2,052	968
Assault (homicide)	16,259	311	385	261	4,678	4,258	2,473	1,997	1,065	452	250	112
Assault (homicide) by discharge of firearms	11,078	11	43	165	3,889	3,331	1,673	1,097	533	207	90	34
Enterocolitis due to clostridium difficile	7,298	2	–	4	6	6	27	149	426	1,063	2,462	3,153

– Represents zero. [1] Includes persons with age not stated, not shown separately. [2] Includes other causes, not shown separately.

Source: U.S. National Center for Health Statistics, National Vital Statistics Reports, *Deaths: Final Data for 2010*, Vol. 61, No. 4, May 2013. See also: <http://www.cdc.gov/nchs/deaths.htm>.

Table 128. Deaths and Death Rates by Leading Causes of Death and Age: 2009

[Rates per 100,000 population in specified group. Data are based on International Classification of Diseases, Tenth Revision (ICD-10). See Appendix III]

Age and cause of death	Number	Rate	Age and cause of death	Number	Rate
ALL AGES [1]			**20 TO 24 YEARS**		
All causes	2,437,163	793.8	All causes	18,896	87.7
Diseases of heart	599,413	195.2	Accidents (unintentional injuries)	7,651	35.5
Malignant neoplasms	567,628	184.9	Assault (homicide)	2,943	13.7
Chronic lower respiratory diseases	137,353	44.7	Intentional self-harm (suicide)	2,702	12.5
Cerebrovascular diseases	128,842	42.0	Malignant neoplasms	992	4.6
Accidents (unintentional injuries)	118,021	38.4	Diseases of heart	700	3.2
Alzheimer's disease	79,003	25.7	Influenza and pneumonia	255	1.2
Diabetes mellitus	68,705	22.4	Congenital malformations, deformations		
Influenza and pneumonia	53,692	17.5	and chromosomal abnormalities	227	1.1
Nephritis, nephrotic syndrome and			Pregnancy, childbirth and		
nephrosis	48,935	15.9	the puerperium	169	0.8
Intentional self-harm (suicide)	36,909	12.0	Cerebrovascular diseases	133	0.6
			Human immunodeficiency virus (HIV)	127	0.6
1 TO 4 YEARS			**25 TO 34 YEARS**		
All causes	4,450	26.1	All causes	42,502	102.3
Accidents (unintentional injuries)	1,466	8.6	Accidents (unintentional injuries)	14,062	33.8
Congenital malformations, deformations			Intentional self-harm (suicide)	5,320	12.8
and chromosomal abnormalities	464	2.7	Assault (homicide)	4,222	10.2
Assault (homicide)	376	2.2	Malignant neoplasms	3,659	8.8
Malignant neoplasms	350	2.1	Diseases of heart	3,174	7.6
Diseases of heart	154	0.9	Human immunodeficiency virus (HIV)	881	2.1
Influenza and pneumonia	146	0.9	Influenza and pneumonia	807	1.9
Septicemia	71	0.4	Diabetes mellitus	604	1.5
Chronic lower respiratory diseases	66	0.4	Cerebrovascular diseases	537	1.3
Certain conditions originating in the			Chronic liver disease and cirrhosis	459	1.1
perinatal period	58	0.3			
In situ neoplasms, benign neoplasms			**35 TO 44 YEARS**		
and neoplasms of uncertain or			All causes	74,665	179.8
unknown behavior	53	0.3	Accidents	15,102	36.4
			Malignant neoplasms	12,519	30.1
			Diseases of heart	11,081	26.7
5 TO 9 YEARS			Intentional self-harm (suicide)	6,677	16.1
All causes	2,523	12.2	Assault (homicide)	2,762	6.7
Accidents (unintentional injuries)	773	3.8	Chronic liver disease and cirrhosis	2,481	6.0
Malignant neoplasms	477	2.3	Human immunodeficiency virus (HIV)	2,425	5.8
Congenital malformations, deformations			Cerebrovascular diseases	1,916	4.6
and chromosomal abnormalities	195	0.9	Diabetes mellitus	1,872	4.5
Assault (homicide)	119	0.6	Influenza and pneumonia	1,314	3.2
Influenza and pneumonia	106	0.5			
Diseases of heart	97	0.5	**45 TO 54 YEARS**		
Chronic lower respiratory diseases	64	0.3	All causes	187,568	420.6
In situ neoplasms, benign neoplasms			Malignant neoplasms	50,616	113.5
and neoplasms of uncertain or			Diseases of heart	36,927	82.8
unknown behavior	40	0.2	Accidents (unintentional injuries)	19,974	44.8
Septicemia	33	0.2	Intentional self-harm (suicide)	8,598	19.3
Cerebrovascular disease	32	0.2	Chronic liver disease and cirrhosis	8,377	18.8
			Cerebrovascular diseases	6,163	13.8
			Diabetes mellitus	5,725	12.8
			Chronic lower respiratory diseases	4,664	10.5
10 TO 14 YEARS			Human immunodeficiency virus (HIV)	3,388	7.6
All causes	3,128	15.7	Influenza and pneumonia	2,918	6.5
Accidents (unintentional injuries)	916	4.6			
Malignant neoplasms	419	2.1			
Intentional self-harm (suicide)	259	1.3	**55 TO 64 YEARS**		
Assault (homicide)	186	0.9	All causes	303,307	871.9
Congenital malformations, deformations			Malignant neoplasms	106,829	307.1
and chromosomal abnormalities	169	0.8	Diseases of heart	67,261	193.4
Influenza and pneumonia	122	0.6	Chronic lower respiratory diseases	14,160	40.7
Diseases of heart	120	0.6	Accidents (unintentional injuries)	12,933	37.2
Chronic lower respiratory diseases	59	0.3	Diabetes mellitus	11,361	32.7
In situ neoplasms, benign neoplasms			Cerebrovascular diseases	10,523	30.2
and neoplasms of uncertain or			Chronic liver disease and cirrhosis	9,154	26.3
unknown behavior	45	0.2	Intentional self-harm (suicide)	5,808	16.7
Cerebrovascular diseases	42	0.2	Nephritis, nephrotic syndrome and		
			nephrosis	4,792	13.8
			Septicemia	4,628	13.3
15 TO 19 YEARS					
All causes	11,520	53.5	**65 YEARS AND OLDER**		
Accidents (unintentional injuries)	4,807	22.3	All causes	1,761,937	4,452.6
Assault (homicide)	1,919	8.9	Diseases of heart	479,150	1,210.9
Intentional self-harm (suicide)	1,669	7.7	Malignant neoplasms	391,035	988.2
Malignant neoplasms	644	3.0	Chronic lower respiratory diseases	117,098	295.9
Diseases of heart	335	1.6	Cerebrovascular diseases	109,238	276.1
Congenital malformations, deformations			Alzheimer's disease	78,168	197.5
and chromosomal abnormalities	230	1.1	Diabetes mellitus	48,944	123.7
Influenza and pneumonia	163	0.8	Influenza and pneumonia	43,469	109.9
Chronic lower respiratory diseases	86	0.4	Nephritis, nephrotic syndrome and		
Septicemia	61	0.3	nephrosis	40,465	102.3
Cerebrovascular diseases	60	0.3	Accidents (unintentional injuries)	39,111	98.8
			Septicemia	26,763	67.6

[1] Includes deaths under 1 year of age.

Source: U.S. National Center for Health Statistics, National Vital Statistics Reports (NVSR), *Deaths: Leading Causes for 2009*, Vol. 61, No. 7, October 2012. See also <http://www.cdc.gov/nchs/deaths.htm>.

Table 129. Age-Adjusted Death Rates for Major Causes of Death—States and Island Areas: 2010

[Age adjusted rates per 100,000 resident population based on the 2010 Census, as of Apr. 1. By place of residence. Excludes nonresidents of the United States. Causes of death classified according to the tenth revision of International Classification of Diseases (ICD)]

State and Island Areas	All causes of death	Diseases of heart	Malignant neoplasms	Cerebro-vascular diseases	Chronic lower respira-tory disease	Accidents Total	Accidents Motor vehicle acci-dents	Alz-heimer's disease	Diabetes mellitus	Influ-enza and pneu-monia	Inten-tional self-harm (suicide)
U.S.	**747.0**	**179.1**	**172.8**	**39.1**	**42.2**	**38.0**	**11.3**	**25.1**	**20.8**	**15.1**	**12.1**
AL	939.7	236.0	191.7	51.6	55.4	49.6	19.4	31.2	25.0	18.7	14.0
AK	771.5	151.5	176.9	40.9	41.5	58.7	10.4	25.9	19.6	15.8	22.8
AZ	693.1	146.7	154.2	31.9	43.1	46.7	12.3	35.3	20.3	11.4	17.0
AR	892.7	222.5	194.7	53.8	53.5	49.4	20.7	29.6	25.8	19.9	15.5
CA	646.7	161.9	156.9	38.1	37.0	27.8	7.7	30.1	19.7	16.4	10.3
CO	682.7	132.8	149.5	36.1	49.7	43.5	9.5	31.1	15.2	12.3	16.8
CT	652.9	155.7	163.4	29.4	29.4	33.6	9.1	17.1	15.4	12.1	9.4
DE	769.9	175.7	185.7	40.7	44.0	39.2	12.5	21.9	19.2	13.8	11.3
DC	792.4	222.4	178.3	32.7	25.7	35.1	6.0	18.7	24.9	13.5	6.9
FL	701.1	162.3	165.6	32.8	40.1	43.1	13.0	18.1	20.1	8.9	13.7
GA	845.4	192.6	174.8	46.3	46.7	40.7	13.9	28.3	23.1	18.3	11.7
HI	589.6	134.7	140.9	35.8	18.0	29.6	9.1	10.5	16.6	17.0	15.0
ID	731.6	159.3	159.9	42.0	47.0	42.1	13.8	26.8	22.5	13.5	18.8
IL	736.9	181.7	178.6	39.2	39.3	30.4	7.9	20.9	18.5	16.1	9.0
IN	820.6	191.8	188.6	44.5	55.3	38.5	11.8	27.8	22.7	16.8	13.1
IA	721.7	173.3	171.9	38.0	44.7	37.2	12.7	32.9	19.3	13.7	12.1
KS	762.2	164.9	171.3	41.2	50.0	44.0	16.6	24.2	20.5	16.4	13.9
KY	915.0	210.1	208.3	44.1	60.0	60.5	18.8	33.5	26.0	21.0	14.2
LA	903.8	229.4	197.6	44.9	43.6	44.4	15.8	30.7	26.4	20.2	12.3
ME	749.6	151.1	187.9	34.5	47.4	36.5	12.2	28.5	21.8	13.4	13.2
MD	728.6	182.2	171.2	38.8	35.0	24.7	8.8	16.8	19.9	15.7	8.3
MA	675.0	150.0	171.3	31.3	31.0	28.5	5.5	21.2	13.3	16.0	8.8
MI	786.2	204.2	182.9	39.5	45.6	36.2	10.3	24.0	24.0	13.6	12.5
MN	661.5	119.4	167.2	36.1	35.1	36.7	9.5	23.4	17.7	9.7	11.2
MS	962.0	251.1	201.4	51.2	55.2	56.8	22.9	32.6	30.3	19.2	13.0
MO	819.5	201.8	185.6	44.0	52.6	47.9	14.4	28.8	21.2	17.4	14.0
MT	754.7	154.2	161.0	41.8	51.3	53.2	19.6	25.2	19.1	13.6	21.8
NE	717.8	154.2	167.4	40.5	48.8	35.8	11.3	24.9	21.7	11.9	10.4
NV	795.4	197.3	174.2	33.3	49.5	41.3	10.7	14.2	13.8	19.8	19.8
NH	690.4	152.7	167.9	33.5	41.7	37.2	10.1	26.9	16.1	12.6	14.1
NJ	691.1	182.0	169.5	33.3	31.4	26.7	6.5	17.7	21.0	11.0	7.7
NM	749.0	151.2	152.4	38.4	47.7	60.7	16.4	16.8	29.8	14.2	20.1
NY	665.5	199.9	163.1	27.9	31.4	24.2	6.6	11.3	16.7	20.6	7.7
NC	804.9	174.9	179.0	44.7	46.1	43.2	14.5	30.3	20.5	17.7	12.0
ND	704.3	158.0	157.1	42.9	43.1	38.8	14.5	37.2	22.2	13.9	15.6
OH	815.7	192.4	187.7	42.6	50.5	42.4	10.6	29.7	25.8	14.6	12.2
OK	915.5	235.2	191.3	50.0	67.4	60.3	19.0	26.1	26.9	19.7	16.5
OR	723.1	137.9	173.9	40.1	45.3	37.8	8.1	28.5	23.7	9.2	17.1
PA	765.9	187.0	181.6	39.3	37.9	41.1	11.0	20.0	20.0	13.6	11.9
RI	721.7	167.1	178.3	31.4	38.5	40.0	8.2	22.6	16.0	13.8	12.3
SC	854.8	189.9	183.6	47.9	46.3	48.9	17.5	34.7	22.6	15.9	13.5
SD	715.1	155.2	171.0	39.9	46.0	44.5	17.3	35.9	24.5	15.8	17.5
TN	890.8	217.4	195.7	48.7	52.7	54.9	17.1	38.5	24.7	20.5	14.6
TX	772.3	181.1	165.9	44.4	43.0	39.0	13.4	26.8	21.6	14.6	11.7
UT	703.2	143.2	133.7	37.1	33.1	40.6	10.6	19.3	22.7	17.1	18.3
VT	718.7	153.6	183.2	35.3	45.3	42.7	11.8	30.8	20.7	7.9	15.7
VA	741.6	168.5	172.4	42.1	38.1	31.6	9.0	24.4	18.8	15.5	11.7
WA	692.3	151.5	170.5	37.0	40.4	37.6	7.9	43.6	21.6	8.3	13.9
WV	933.6	211.2	198.0	47.8	62.7	63.7	16.2	26.0	32.9	19.0	14.1
WI	719.0	165.1	174.5	38.7	38.0	40.8	10.6	25.3	17.7	13.3	13.4
WY	778.8	169.8	172.6	37.2	59.5	59.8	23.1	27.2	18.5	19.5	22.4
PR [1]	712.8	124.9	123.3	36.4	26.5	25.9	9.1	46.0	70.2	19.9	7.6
VI [1]	663.2	149.7	109.3	33.4	(S)	22.5	(S)	(S)	42.3	(S)	(S)
GU [1]	810.6	254.9	133.6	71.6	24.5	36.7	(S)	(S)	37.1	(S)	19.2
AS [1]	932.9	168.9	152.5	94.5	(S)	(S)	(S)	(S)	104.2	(S)	(S)
MP [1]	863.3	167.0	123.0	(S)	(S)	(S)	(S)	(S)	(S)	(S)	(S)

S Figure does not meet standards of reliability or precision. [1] Age-adjusted death rates for Puerto Rico, Virgin Islands, Guam, American Samoa, and Northern Marianas are based on the 2010 Census, estimated as of July 1, 2010.

Source: U.S. National Center for Health Statistics, National Vital Statistics Reports, (NVSR), *Deaths: Final Data for 2010*, Vol. 61, No. 4, May 2013. See also <http://www.cdc.gov/nchs/deaths.htm>.

Table 130. Death Rates From Heart Disease by Selected Characteristics: 1980 to 2010

[Rates per 100,000 population. See headnotes, Table 132. Rates for 2005-2009 have been revised using population estimates based on the 2010 Census. See Appendix III]

Characteristics	1980	1990	2000	2005	2006	2007	2008	2009	2010
All ages, age adjusted [1]	**412.1**	**321.8**	**257.6**	**216.8**	**205.5**	**196.1**	**192.1**	**182.8**	**179.1**
All ages, crude rate	**336.0**	**289.5**	**252.6**	**220.7**	**211.7**	**204.5**	**202.8**	**195.4**	**193.6**
Under 1 year	22.8	20.1	13.0	8.9	8.6	10.2	9.6	9.6	8.3
1 to 4 years	2.6	1.9	1.2	0.9	1.0	1.1	1.2	0.9	1.0
5 to 14 years	0.9	0.9	0.7	0.6	0.6	0.6	0.6	0.5	0.5
15 to 24 years	2.9	2.5	2.6	2.6	2.5	2.5	2.5	2.4	2.4
25 to 34 years	8.3	7.6	7.4	8.3	8.4	8.1	8.1	7.8	7.8
35 to 44 years	44.6	31.4	29.2	29.2	28.5	27.7	26.9	26.7	25.8
45 to 54 years	180.2	120.5	94.2	89.7	88.0	85.2	85.2	82.3	81.6
55 to 64 years	494.1	367.3	261.2	212.8	205.1	197.8	195.3	190.0	186.6
65 to 74 years	1,218.6	894.3	665.6	512.3	483.0	454.8	441.4	422.8	409.2
75 to 84 years	2,993.1	2,295.7	1,780.3	1,458.5	1,378.0	1,308.6	1,271.7	1,210.8	1,172.0
85 years and over	7,777.1	6,739.9	5,926.1	5,188.3	4,877.6	4,668.1	4,598.4	4,316.9	4,285.2
Male, age adjusted [1]	**538.9**	**412.4**	**320.0**	**268.2**	**254.9**	**243.7**	**238.5**	**229.4**	**225.1**
White	539.6	409.2	316.7	264.8	251.1	240.3	235.8	226.6	222.9
Black	561.4	485.4	392.5	338.8	328.3	312.4	301.2	289.0	280.6
American Indian, Alaska Native	320.5	264.1	222.2	191.7	186.1	175.5	163.5	162.2	158.7
Asian, Pacific Islander	286.9	220.7	185.5	149.4	145.4	134.4	133.0	130.2	127.2
Hispanic origin [2]	(NA)	270.0	238.2	210.5	193.7	183.1	171.2	169.4	165.1
Non-Hispanic, White [2]	(NA)	413.6	319.9	267.9	254.6	244.0	240.0	230.4	226.9
Male, crude rate	**368.6**	**297.6**	**249.8**	**222.3**	**215.3**	**209.2**	**208.2**	**203.7**	**202.5**
Under 1 year	25.5	21.9	13.3	9.6	9.1	11.2	10.3	10.5	9.8
1 to 4 years	2.8	1.9	1.4	1.0	1.1	1.0	1.2	0.9	1.1
5 to 14 years	1.0	0.9	0.8	0.6	0.7	0.6	0.6	0.5	0.5
15 to 24 years	3.7	3.1	3.2	3.5	3.2	3.2	3.3	3.1	3.2
25 to 34 years	11.4	10.3	9.6	11.2	11.6	10.9	10.8	10.6	10.7
35 to 44 years	68.7	48.1	41.4	41.3	40.1	39.2	37.4	37.5	36.0
45 to 54 years	282.6	183.0	140.2	131.6	128.9	124.6	122.9	119.8	117.8
55 to 64 years	746.8	537.3	371.7	303.9	293.4	285.1	280.8	274.1	269.5
65 to 74 years	1,728.0	1,250.0	898.3	680.1	646.9	610.0	594.0	571.1	553.0
75 to 84 years	3,834.3	2,968.2	2,248.1	1,815.1	1,722.7	1,631.9	1,584.3	1,514.8	1,475.7
85 years and over	8,752.7	7,418.4	6,430.0	5,713.2	5,359.2	5,154.3	5,083.6	4,862.8	4,833.6
Female, age adjusted [1]	**320.8**	**257.0**	**210.9**	**177.5**	**167.2**	**159.0**	**155.9**	**146.6**	**143.3**
White	315.9	250.9	205.6	173.2	163.4	155.4	152.5	143.4	140.4
Black	378.6	327.5	277.6	234.5	218.1	209.8	202.5	191.0	185.3
American Indian, Alaska Native	175.4	153.1	143.6	129.3	126.1	112.2	106.8	104.6	103.5
Asian, Pacific Islander	132.3	149.2	115.7	97.5	93.7	88.5	88.5	83.6	81.2
Hispanic origin [2]	(NA)	177.2	163.7	139.9	130.1	123.2	117.6	109.6	107.8
Non-Hispanic, White [2]	(NA)	252.6	206.8	174.8	165.2	157.3	154.6	145.4	142.5
Female, crude rate	**305.1**	**281.8**	**255.3**	**219.0**	**208.2**	**199.9**	**197.7**	**187.3**	**184.9**
Under 1 year	20.0	18.3	12.5	8.2	8.0	9.2	8.8	8.8	6.8
1 to 4 years	2.5	1.9	1.0	0.9	0.9	1.2	1.1	1.0	0.9
5 to 14 years	0.9	0.8	0.5	0.6	0.6	0.5	0.5	0.5	0.4
15 to 24 years	2.1	1.8	2.1	1.7	1.8	1.8	1.6	1.6	1.5
25 to 34 years	5.3	5.0	5.2	5.3	5.1	5.3	5.4	5.0	4.9
35 to 44 years	21.4	15.1	17.2	17.2	17.1	16.2	16.4	16.0	15.6
45 to 54 years	84.5	61.0	49.8	49.1	48.4	47.1	48.8	46.0	46.5
55 to 64 years	272.1	215.7	159.3	128.0	122.8	116.4	115.6	111.6	109.3
65 to 74 years	828.6	616.8	474.0	369.5	342.8	321.4	309.7	294.2	284.2
75 to 84 years	2,497.0	1,893.8	1,475.1	1,213.8	1,139.0	1,082.0	1,050.4	993.3	952.7
85 years and over	7,350.5	6,478.1	5,720.9	4,955.1	4,659.1	4,443.3	4,370.0	4,056.0	4,020.3

NA Not available. [1] Age-adjusted death rates were prepared using the direct method, in which age-specific death rates for a population of interest are applied to a standard population distributed by age. Age adjustment eliminates the differences in observed rates between points in time or among compared population groups that result from age differences in population composition. [2] Persons of Hispanic origin may be of any race. Prior to 1997 excludes data from States lacking an Hispanic-origin item on their death certificates. See text, this section.

Source: U.S. National Center for Health Statistics, "Health, United States 2011, web updates," <http://cdc.gov/nchs/hus.htm>, accessed May 2013.

Table 131. Death Rates From Cerebrovascular Diseases by Sex and Age: 1990 to 2010

[Rates per 100,000 population. See headnote, Table 132. See Appendix III]

Characteristics	Total				Male				Female			
	1990	2000	2009	2010	1990	2000	2009	2010	1990	2000	2009	2010
All ages, age adjusted [1]	**65.3**	**60.9**	**39.6**	**39.1**	**68.5**	**62.4**	**39.9**	**39.3**	**62.6**	**59.1**	**38.8**	**38.3**
All ages, crude rate......	57.8	59.6	42.0	41.9	46.7	46.9	34.5	34.5	68.4	71.8	49.2	49.1
Under 1 year.............	3.8	3.3	3.7	3.3	4.4	3.8	4.4	3.2	3.1	2.7	3.0	3.4
1 to 4 years.............	0.3	0.3	0.3	0.3	0.3	(B)	0.3	0.3	0.3	0.4	0.3	0.3
5 to 14 years............	0.2	0.2	0.2	0.2	0.2	0.2	0.2	0.3	0.2	0.2	0.1	0.2
15 to 24 years...........	0.6	0.5	0.4	0.4	0.7	0.5	0.5	0.5	0.6	0.5	0.4	0.4
25 to 34 years...........	2.2	1.5	1.3	1.3	2.1	1.5	1.5	1.3	2.2	1.5	1.2	1.2
35 to 44 years...........	6.4	5.8	4.6	4.6	6.8	5.8	5.1	5.0	6.1	5.7	4.2	4.2
45 to 54 years...........	18.7	16.0	13.7	13.1	20.5	17.5	15.3	14.9	17.0	14.5	12.2	11.4
55 to 64 years...........	47.9	41.0	29.7	29.3	54.3	47.2	35.0	34.7	42.2	35.3	24.8	24.3
65 to 74 years...........	144.2	128.6	82.8	81.7	166.6	145.0	94.2	92.0	126.7	115.1	72.9	72.8
75 to 84 years...........	498.0	461.3	294.9	288.3	551.1	490.8	300.9	295.2	466.2	442.1	290.6	283.4
85 years and over.........	1,628.9	1,589.2	992.2	993.8	1,528.5	1,484.3	891.6	892.0	1,667.6	1,632.0	1,040.2	1,043.0

B Figure too small to meet statistical standards for reliability. [1] See footnote 1, Table 130.

Source: U.S. National Center for Health Statistics, "Health, United States 2011, web updates," <http://www.cdc.gov/NCHS/hus.htm>, accessed May 2013.

Table 132. Death Rates From Malignant Neoplasms by Selected Characteristics: 1990 to 2010

[Rates per 100,000 population. Rates for 2005-2009 have been revised using population estimates based on the 2010 Census. Excludes deaths of nonresidents of the United States. Beginning 1999, deaths classified according to tenth revision of International Classification of Diseases (ICD); for earlier years, causes of death were classified according to the revisions then in use. Changes in classification of causes of death due to these revisions may result in discontinuities in cause-of-death trends. For explanation of age adjustment, see text, this section. See Appendix III]

Characteristic	1990	2000	2005	2007	2008	2009	2010
All ages, age adjusted [1]	**216.0**	**199.6**	**185.1**	**179.3**	**176.4**	**173.5**	**172.8**
All ages, crude rate	**203.2**	**196.5**	**189.3**	**186.9**	**186.0**	**185.0**	**186.2**
Under 1 year..............	2.3	2.4	1.9	1.7	1.7	1.8	1.6
1 to 4 years..............	3.5	2.7	2.4	2.3	2.4	2.2	2.1
5 to 14 years.............	3.1	2.5	2.5	2.4	2.2	2.2	2.2
15 to 24 years............	4.9	4.4	4.0	3.8	3.8	3.8	3.7
25 to 34 years............	12.6	9.8	9.2	8.7	8.8	9.0	8.8
35 to 44 years............	43.3	36.6	33.5	31.0	30.1	30.2	28.8
45 to 54 years............	158.9	127.5	118.6	114.2	113.4	112.8	111.6
55 to 64 years............	449.6	366.7	323.9	311.4	304.7	301.7	300.1
65 to 74 years............	872.3	816.3	733.2	702.9	688.4	668.2	666.1
75 to 84 years............	1,348.5	1,335.6	1,272.8	1,250.1	1,230.9	1,213.0	1,202.2
85 years old and over......	1,752.9	1,819.4	1,778.2	1,739.4	1,724.6	1,699.3	1,729.5
DEATH RATES FOR MALIGNANT NEOPLASM OF BREASTS FOR FEMALES							
All ages, age adjusted [1]	**33.3**	**26.8**	**24.2**	**23.0**	**22.6**	**22.3**	**22.1**
All ages, crude rate	**34.0**	**29.2**	**27.4**	**26.5**	**26.3**	**26.1**	**26.1**
Under 25 years............	(B)	(B)	(B)	(B)	(B)	(B)	(B)
25 to 34 years............	2.9	2.3	1.8	1.7	1.6	1.7	1.6
35 to 44 years............	17.8	12.4	11.4	10.1	10.1	10.5	9.8
45 to 54 years............	45.4	33.0	28.7	26.7	26.2	26.2	25.7
55 to 64 years............	78.6	59.3	54.0	50.7	49.2	47.9	47.7
65 to 74 years............	111.7	88.3	78.5	76.3	75.6	73.4	73.9
75 to 84 years............	146.3	128.9	119.6	116.6	113.8	112.6	109.1
85 years old and over......	196.8	205.7	191.2	184.7	182.7	178.0	185.8
DEATH RATES FOR MALIGNANT NEOPLASM OF TRACHEA, BRONCHUS, AND LUNG							
All ages, age adjusted [1]	**59.3**	**56.1**	**52.7**	**50.6**	**49.5**	**48.4**	**47.6**
All ages, crude rate	**56.8**	**55.3**	**53.9**	**52.7**	**52.2**	**51.6**	**51.3**
Under 25 years............	(Z)	(Z)	(Z)	(Z)	(Z)	(Z)	(Z)
25 to 34 years............	0.7	0.5	0.3	0.3	0.4	0.4	0.4
35 to 44 years............	6.8	6.1	5.3	4.3	3.8	3.7	3.3
45 to 54 years............	46.8	31.6	29.7	28.4	28.2	27.8	26.9
55 to 64 years............	160.6	122.4	102.4	94.2	90.2	87.5	85.4
65 to 74 years............	288.4	284.2	256.3	244.5	235.5	228.6	223.9
75 to 84 years............	333.3	370.8	375.0	369.5	366.7	359.8	357.2
85 years old and over......	242.5	302.1	328.2	328.0	332.9	328.0	332.4

B Base figure too small to meet statistical standards for reliability of a derived figure. Z Less than 0.05. [1] Age adjusted death rates were prepared using the direct method, in which age specific death rates for a population of interest are applied to a standard population distributed by age. Age adjustment eliminates the differences in observed rates between points in time or among compared population groups that result from age differences in population composition.

Source: U.S. National Center for Health Statistics, "Health, United States 2011, web updates," <http://www.cdc.gov/NCHS/hus.htm>, accessed May 2013.

Table 133. Death Rates From Suicide by Selected Characteristics: 1990 to 2010

[Rates per 100,000 population. Rates for 2005-2009 have been revised using population estimates based on the 2010 Census. Excludes deaths of nonresidents of the United States. Beginning 2000, deaths classified according to the tenth revision of International Classification of Diseases. See Appendix III]

Characteristic	1990	2000	2005	2007	2008	2009	2010
All ages, age adjusted [1]	**12.5**	**10.4**	**10.9**	**11.3**	**11.6**	**11.8**	**12.1**
All ages, crude rate	**12.4**	**10.4**	**11.0**	**11.5**	**11.8**	**12.0**	**12.4**
Under 1 year	(X)	(X)	(X)	(X)	(X)	(X)	(X)
1 to 4 years	(X)	(X)	(X)	(X)	(X)	(X)	(X)
5 to 14 years	0.8	0.7	0.7	0.5	0.5	0.6	0.7
15 to 24 years	13.2	10.2	9.9	9.6	9.9	10.0	10.5
25 to 44 years	15.2	13.4	13.9	14.5	14.6	14.6	15.0
45 to 64 years	15.3	13.5	15.3	16.7	17.5	17.9	18.6
65 to 74 years	17.9	12.5	12.4	12.4	13.6	13.7	13.7
75 to 84 years	24.9	17.6	16.8	16.2	16.1	15.8	15.7
85 years and over	22.2	19.6	18.3	17.0	16.4	16.4	17.6
AGE-ADJUSTED RATES							
Male	21.5	17.7	18.1	18.5	19.0	19.2	19.8
Female	4.8	4.0	4.4	4.6	4.8	4.9	5.0
White male	22.8	19.1	19.8	20.4	21.1	21.4	22.0
Black male	12.8	10.0	9.2	8.7	9.4	8.9	9.1
American Indian, Alaska Native male	20.1	16.0	17.3	15.9	15.4	14.6	15.5
Asian, Pacific Islander male	9.6	8.6	7.3	8.8	7.9	8.7	9.5
Hispanic male [2]	13.7	10.3	9.6	10.3	9.5	9.9	9.9
Non-Hispanic, White male [2]	23.5	20.2	21.4	22.1	23.1	23.4	24.2
White female	5.2	4.3	4.9	5.2	5.4	5.5	5.6
Black female	2.4	1.8	1.8	1.7	1.6	1.8	1.8
American Indian, Alaska Native female	3.6	3.8	4.2	4.3	4.9	5.4	6.1
Asian, Pacific Islander female	4.1	2.8	3.2	3.4	3.5	3.5	3.4
Hispanic female [2]	2.3	1.7	1.8	1.8	1.8	2.0	2.1
Non-Hispanic, White female [2]	5.4	4.7	5.3	5.8	6.0	6.1	6.2

X Not applicable. [1] Age-adjusted death rates were prepared using the direct method, in which age-specific death rates for a population of interest are applied to a standard population distributed by age. Age adjustment eliminates the differences in observed rates between points in time or among compared population groups that result from age differences in population composition. [2] Persons of Hispanic origin may be of any race. Excludes data from states lacking an Hispanic-origin item on their death certificates.

Source: U.S. National Center for Health Statistics, "Health, United States 2011, web updates," <http://www.cdc.gov/NCHS/hus.htm>, accessed May 2013.

Table 134. Death Rates From Human Immunodeficiency Virus (HIV) Disease by Sex, Age, and Race/Ethnicity, 1990 to 2010

[Rates per 100,000 population. Rates for 2005-2009 have been revised using population estimates based on the 2010 Census. Excludes deaths of nonresidents of the United States. Beginning 2000, deaths classified according to tenth revision of International Classification of Diseases. See Appendix III]

Characteristic	1990	1995	2000	2005	2008	2009	2010
All ages, age adjusted [1]	**10.2**	**16.2**	**5.2**	**4.2**	**3.3**	**3.0**	**2.6**
All ages, crude	**10.1**	**16.2**	**5.1**	**4.2**	**3.4**	**3.1**	**2.7**
Under 1 year	2.7	1.5	(B)	(B)	(B)	(B)	(B)
1 to 4 years	0.8	1.3	(B)	(B)	(B)	(B)	(B)
5 to 14 years	0.2	0.5	0.1	(B)	(B)	(B)	(B)
15 to 24 years	1.5	1.7	0.5	0.4	0.4	0.3	0.3
25 to 34 years	19.7	28.3	6.1	3.4	2.4	2.2	1.8
35 to 44 years	27.4	44.2	13.1	10.0	6.7	5.8	4.6
45 to 54 years	15.2	26.0	11.0	10.6	8.4	7.6	6.9
55 to 64 years	6.2	10.9	5.1	5.3	5.6	5.2	5.0
65 to 74 years	2.0	3.6	2.2	2.3	2.5	2.6	2.2
75 to 84 years	0.7	0.7	0.7	0.8	0.9	0.9	0.9
85 years and over	(B)	(B)	(B)	(B)	0.6	0.4	0.4
AGE-ADJUSTED RATES							
Male	18.5	27.3	7.9	6.3	4.8	4.4	3.8
Female	2.2	5.3	2.5	2.3	1.9	1.7	1.4
White male	15.7	20.4	4.6	3.7	2.8	2.5	2.3
Black male	46.3	89.0	35.1	27.7	21.2	19.5	16.5
American Indian, Alaska Native male	3.3	10.5	3.5	3.7	2.8	2.4	2.6
Asian, Pacific Islander male	4.3	6.0	1.2	1.0	1.0	0.7	0.7
Hispanic male [2]	28.8	40.8	10.6	7.7	5.5	5.0	4.6
Non-Hispanic, White male [2]	14.1	17.9	3.8	3.0	2.3	2.0	1.8
White female	1.1	2.5	1.0	0.8	0.7	0.6	0.5
Black female	10.1	24.4	13.2	11.9	9.6	8.8	7.5
American Indian, Alaska Native female	(B)	2.5	1.0	1.3	(B)	(B)	(B)
Asian, Pacific Islander female	(B)	0.6	0.2	(B)	0.3	(B)	(B)
Hispanic female [2]	3.8	8.8	2.9	1.9	1.7	1.4	1.1
Non-Hispanic, White female [2]	0.7	1.7	0.7	0.6	0.5	0.4	0.4

B Base figure too small to meet statistical standards. [1] Age-adjusted death rates were prepared using the direct method, in which age-specific death rates for a population of interest are applied to a standard population distributed by age. Age adjustment eliminates the differences in observed rates between points in time or among compared population groups that result from age differences in population composition. [2] Persons of Hispanic origin may be of any race. Excludes data from states lacking an Hispanic-origin item on their death certificates.

Source: U.S. National Center for Health Statistics, "Health, United States 2011, web updates," <http://www.cdc.gov/NCHS/hus.htm>, accessed May 2013.

Table 135. Suicide Deaths by Age, Sex, and Method: 2008 to 2010

[Data are 2008-2010 annual averages. Deaths based on tenth revision of International Classification of Diseases (ICD)]

Method	Total	Age 5-14 years [1]	Age 15-17 years	Age 18-24 years	Age 25-44 years	Age 45-64 years	Age 65-74 years	Age 75-84 years	Age 85+ years
Total [2]	37,103	254	764	3,659	12,102	14,447	2,896	2,074	899
MEN									
Total [2]	29,272	172	573	3,069	9,503	11,006	2,375	1,792	775
Knife or other sharp object	556	0	1	30	165	286	31	26	17
Drowning	248	0	4	26	84	96	19	13	6
Jumping from a high place	532	1	9	74	212	177	30	15	13
Fire/hot object or substance	105	0	2	11	34	49	7	2	1
Firearm	16,400	54	272	1,548	4,531	6,102	1,811	1,476	605
Poisoning	3,489	5	16	201	1,176	1,744	200	95	51
Hanging, suffocation, strangulation	7,293	108	248	1,089	3,065	2,322	235	149	75
WOMEN									
Total [2]	7,831	82	191	590	2,599	3,441	521	283	124
Knife or other sharp object	113	0	0	4	31	61	10	5	3
Drowning	153	0	1	9	44	66	18	9	6
Jumping from a high place	193	1	2	18	60	79	15	10	8
Fire/hot object or substance	49	0	0	3	16	24	4	2	0
Firearm	2,383	11	42	157	774	1,069	196	105	30
Poisoning	2,990	6	22	112	968	1,541	196	105	40
Hanging, suffocation, strangulation	1,731	62	117	267	630	510	68	43	34

[1] It is generally accepted that children under 5 years of age cannot commit suicide. [2] Includes other methods not shown separately.

Source: Centers for Disease Control and Prevention, National Center for Health Statistics, "Health Data Interactive," <http://www.cdc.gov/nchs/hdi.htm>, accessed August 2013.

136. Firearm Deaths and Death Rates by Sex and Race/Ethnicity: 2007 to 2010

[Rates are on an annual basis per 100,000 population and are based on populations enumerated as of April 1 for Census years and as of July 1 for all other years. Deaths are those attributable to injury by firearms, see source for details]

Sex and Race/Ethnicity	Deaths 2007	Deaths 2008	Deaths 2009	Deaths 2010	Death Rates 2007	Death Rates 2008	Death Rates 2009	Death Rates 2010
Total	31,224	31,593	31,347	31,672	10.4	10.4	10.2	10.3
By Sex:								
Male	27,047	27,336	26,921	27,356	18.3	18.3	17.9	18.0
Female	4,177	4,257	4,426	4,136	2.7	2.8	2.8	2.7
By Race/ethnicity:								
White	22,296	23,065	23,163	23,490	9.2	9.5	9.5	9.6
Male	19,020	19,679	19,623	20,014	15.9	16.4	16.2	16.5
Female	3,276	3,386	3,540	3,476	2.7	2.8	2.9	2.8
Black	8,242	7,847	7,455	7,454	20.4	19.1	17.9	17.7
Male	7,430	7,088	6,700	6,721	38.5	36.2	33.7	33.4
Female	812	759	755	733	3.8	6.4	3.5	3.3
American Indian or Alaska Native	246	279	291	317	6.4	7.0	7.0	7.4
Male	213	233	241	267	11.1	11.7	11.6	12.5
Female	33	46	50	50	1.7	2.3	2.4	2.4
Asian or Pacific Islander	440	402	438	411	2.8	2.5	2.6	2.4
Male	384	336	357	354	5.1	4.4	4.5	4.4
Female	56	66	81	57	0.7	0.8	0.9	0.6
Hispanic [1]	3,492	3,256	3,202	3,008	7.6	6.8	6.5	6.0
Male	3,155	2,912	2,867	2,694	13.4	12.0	11.4	10.5
Female	337	344	335	314	1.5	1.5	1.4	1.3

[1] Persons of Hispanic origin may be of any race. Data for Hispanic persons are not tabulated separately by race.

Source: U.S. National Center for Health Statistics, National Vital Statistics Reports (NVSR), *Deaths: Final Data for 2010*, Vol. 61, No 4., May 2013. See also <http://www.cdc.gov/nchs/deaths.htm>.

Table 137. Marriage and Divorce Rates by State: 1990 to 2011

[Rate per 1,000 population residing in area. Rates for 2001-2009 have been revised using population estimates based on the 2010 Census]

State	Marriage rates [1]						Divorce rates [1,2]					
	1990	2000	2005	2009	2010	2011	1990	2000	2005	2009	2010	2011
United States [3]	**9.8**	**8.2**	**7.6**	**6.8**	**6.8**	**6.8**	**4.7**	**4.0**	**3.6**	**3.5**	**3.6**	**3.6**
Alabama	10.6	10.1	9.2	8.3	8.2	8.4	6.1	5.5	4.9	4.4	4.4	4.3
Alaska	10.2	8.9	8.2	7.8	8.0	7.8	5.5	3.9	4.3	4.4	4.7	4.8
Arizona	10.0	7.5	6.6	5.6	5.9	5.7	6.9	4.6	4.2	3.6	3.5	3.9
Arkansas	15.3	15.4	12.9	10.7	10.8	10.4	6.9	6.4	6.0	5.7	5.7	5.3
California [4]	7.9	5.8	6.4	5.8	5.8	5.8	4.3	(NA)	(NA)	(NA)	(NA)	(NA)
Colorado	9.8	8.3	7.6	6.9	6.9	7.0	5.5	4.7	4.4	4.3	4.3	4.4
Connecticut	7.9	5.7	5.8	5.9	5.6	5.5	3.2	3.3	3.0	3.0	2.9	3.1
Delaware	8.4	6.5	5.9	5.4	5.2	5.2	4.4	3.9	3.8	3.6	3.5	3.6
District of Columbia	8.2	4.9	4.1	4.7	7.6	8.7	4.5	3.2	2.0	2.7	2.8	2.9
Florida	10.9	8.9	8.9	7.5	7.3	7.4	6.3	5.1	4.6	4.2	4.4	4.5
Georgia	10.3	6.8	7.0	6.6	7.3	6.6	5.5	3.3	(NA)	(NA)	(NA)	(NA)
Hawaii	16.4	20.6	22.6	17.2	17.6	17.6	4.6	3.9	(NA)	(NA)	(NA)	(NA)
Idaho	13.9	10.8	10.5	8.9	8.8	8.6	6.5	5.5	5.0	5.0	5.2	4.9
Illinois	8.8	6.9	5.9	5.7	5.7	5.6	3.8	3.2	2.6	2.5	2.6	2.6
Indiana	9.6	7.9	6.9	7.9	6.3	6.8	(NA)	(NA)	(NA)	(NA)	(NA)	(NA)
Iowa	9.0	6.9	6.9	7.0	6.9	6.7	3.9	3.3	2.7	2.4	2.4	2.4
Kansas	9.2	8.3	6.8	6.4	6.4	6.3	5.0	3.6	3.1	3.6	3.7	3.9
Kentucky	13.5	9.8	8.7	7.6	7.4	7.5	5.8	5.1	4.6	4.6	4.5	4.4
Louisiana	9.6	9.1	8.0	7.1	6.9	6.4	(NA)	(NA)	(NA)	(NA)	(NA)	(NA)
Maine	9.7	8.8	8.2	7.1	7.1	7.2	4.3	5.0	4.1	4.1	4.2	4.2
Maryland	9.7	7.5	6.9	5.8	5.7	5.8	3.4	3.3	3.1	2.8	2.8	2.9
Massachusetts	7.9	5.8	6.2	5.6	5.6	5.5	2.8	2.5	2.2	2.2	2.5	2.7
Michigan	8.2	6.7	6.1	5.4	5.5	5.7	4.3	3.9	3.4	3.3	3.5	3.4
Minnesota	7.7	6.8	6.0	5.3	5.3	5.6	3.5	3.2	(NA)	(NA)	(NA)	(NA)
Mississippi	9.4	6.9	5.8	4.8	4.9	4.9	5.5	5.0	4.4	4.1	4.3	4.0
Missouri	9.6	7.8	7.0	6.5	6.5	6.6	5.1	4.5	3.6	3.8	3.9	3.9
Montana	8.6	7.3	7.4	7.3	7.4	7.8	5.1	4.2	4.5	4.0	3.9	4.0
Nebraska	8.0	7.6	7.0	6.6	6.6	6.6	4.0	3.7	3.3	3.4	3.6	3.5
Nevada	99.0	72.2	57.4	40.3	38.3	36.9	11.4	9.9	7.4	6.6	5.9	5.6
New Hampshire	9.5	9.4	7.3	6.5	7.3	7.1	4.7	4.8	3.9	3.7	3.8	3.8
New Jersey	7.6	6.0	5.7	5.0	5.1	4.8	3.0	3.0	2.9	2.7	3.0	2.9
New Mexico	8.8	8.0	6.6	5.0	7.7	8.0	4.9	5.1	4.6	3.9	4.0	3.3
New York	8.6	7.1	6.8	6.5	6.5	6.9	3.2	3.0	2.9	2.6	2.9	2.9
North Carolina	7.8	8.2	7.3	6.6	6.6	6.7	5.1	4.5	4.1	3.8	3.8	3.7
North Dakota	7.5	7.2	6.8	6.4	6.5	6.7	3.6	3.4	2.9	2.8	3.1	2.7
Ohio	9.0	7.8	6.5	5.8	5.8	5.9	4.7	4.2	3.5	3.3	3.4	3.4
Oklahoma	10.6	(NA)	7.3	6.9	7.2	6.9	7.7	(NA)	5.6	4.8	5.2	5.2
Oregon	8.9	7.6	7.3	6.6	6.5	6.6	5.5	4.8	4.2	3.9	4.0	3.8
Pennsylvania	7.1	6.0	5.8	5.3	5.3	5.3	3.3	3.1	2.3	2.7	2.7	2.8
Rhode Island	8.1	7.6	7.0	5.9	5.8	6.0	3.7	2.9	3.0	3.0	3.2	3.2
South Carolina	15.9	10.6	8.3	7.3	7.4	7.2	4.5	3.8	2.9	3.0	3.1	3.2
South Dakota	11.1	9.4	8.4	7.3	7.3	7.5	3.7	3.5	2.8	3.3	3.4	3.3
Tennessee	13.9	15.5	10.9	8.4	8.8	9.0	6.5	5.9	4.6	3.9	4.2	4.3
Texas	10.5	9.4	7.8	7.1	7.1	7.1	5.5	4.0	3.3	3.3	3.3	3.2
Utah	11.2	10.8	9.8	8.4	8.5	8.6	5.1	4.3	4.1	3.7	3.7	3.7
Vermont	10.9	10.0	8.9	8.7	9.3	8.3	4.5	4.1	3.6	3.5	3.8	3.6
Virginia	11.4	8.8	8.2	6.9	6.8	6.8	4.4	4.3	4.0	3.7	3.8	3.8
Washington	9.5	6.9	6.5	6.0	6.0	6.1	5.9	4.6	4.3	3.9	4.2	4.1
West Virginia	7.2	8.7	7.4	6.7	6.7	7.2	5.3	5.1	5.1	5.1	5.1	5.2
Wisconsin	7.9	6.7	6.1	5.3	5.3	5.3	3.6	3.2	2.9	2.9	3.0	2.9
Wyoming	10.7	10.0	9.3	8.0	7.6	7.8	6.6	5.8	5.2	5.2	5.1	4.8

NA Not available. [1] Based on provisional counts of marriages or divorces by State of occurrence. [2] Includes annulments. Includes divorce petitions filed or legal separations for some counties or States. [3] Beginning 2000, divorce rates based solely on the combined counts and populations for reporting States and the District of Columbia. [4] Marriage data includes nonlicensed marriages registered.

Source: U.S. National Center for Health Statistics, National Vital Statistics System, "Marriages and Divorces, Detailed State Tables," <http://www.cdc.gov/nchs/mardiv.htm>, accessed September 2013.

Table 138. People Who Got Married and Divorced in the Past 12 Months by State: 2011

[For 12-month period prior to interview date, which occurred for each month in calendar year. For example, a person interviewed in January 2011 could report they got married between January 2010 and January 2011. Persons 15 years and over. Vital event is counted in state in which respondent lived at the time of survey. Based on 2011 American Community Survey (ACS). The ACS universe includes the household population and the group quarters population. Based on a sample and subject to sampling variability. See Appendix III]

State	People who got married in the past 12 months				People who got divorced in the past 12 months			
	Males	Marriage rate per 1,000 men	Females	Marriage rate per 1,000 women	Males	Divorce rate per 1,000 men	Females	Divorce rate per 1,000 women
United States.............	**2,144,467**	**17.6**	**2,096,359**	**16.3**	**1,143,621**	**9.4**	**1,251,239**	**9.7**
Alabama...................	37,987	20.5	37,530	18.6	22,071	11.9	28,381	14.0
Alaska.....................	7,766	26.6	7,771	28.5	3,398	11.6	4,071	14.9
Arizona....................	48,065	19.0	46,600	18.0	24,130	9.5	30,961	11.9
Arkansas..................	25,519	22.4	24,025	20.0	14,474	12.7	14,026	11.7
California.................	250,693	16.9	238,508	15.7	115,216	7.8	124,512	8.2
Colorado..................	44,725	21.9	41,472	20.3	21,597	10.6	23,319	11.4
Connecticut..............	20,817	14.8	19,534	12.9	13,001	9.2	13,487	8.9
Delaware..................	5,523	15.6	5,692	14.8	1,931	5.5	2,964	7.7
District of Columbia.......	5,581	22.6	4,113	14.6	3,042	12.3	1,911	6.8
Florida....................	115,404	15.1	114,259	14.1	72,892	9.5	80,785	9.9
Georgia...................	72,682	19.4	71,693	17.9	39,877	10.7	42,891	10.7
Hawaii....................	13,490	24.2	12,384	22.0	4,544	8.1	3,734	6.6
Idaho.....................	11,636	19.1	12,846	20.9	6,250	10.3	8,335	13.6
Illinois...................	79,585	15.9	76,853	14.5	44,569	8.9	44,021	8.3
Indiana...................	46,679	18.4	45,266	17.0	28,880	11.4	27,092	10.2
Iowa......................	20,755	17.2	21,144	16.8	13,346	11.1	11,580	9.2
Kansas....................	20,661	18.5	20,002	17.4	10,883	9.8	14,144	12.3
Kentucky..................	28,555	16.7	30,059	16.6	21,621	12.6	19,760	10.9
Louisiana.................	29,803	16.9	29,112	15.5	17,395	9.9	18,130	9.6
Maine.....................	9,215	17.2	9,991	17.5	7,243	13.5	6,993	12.2
Maryland..................	37,730	16.7	36,833	15.0	22,727	10.1	25,581	10.4
Massachusetts............	40,092	15.4	39,343	13.9	15,849	6.1	20,638	7.3
Michigan..................	61,086	15.7	64,480	15.7	38,505	9.9	39,600	9.6
Minnesota................	33,404	15.8	33,522	15.4	15,479	7.3	17,090	7.9
Mississippi...............	22,446	20.0	20,943	17.1	13,157	11.7	12,541	10.2
Missouri..................	40,977	17.5	40,693	16.3	22,614	9.6	27,778	11.1
Montana..................	7,771	19.1	7,868	19.2	4,472	11.0	5,026	12.3
Nebraska.................	14,883	20.8	14,312	19.3	7,393	10.3	7,313	9.9
Nevada...................	18,419	16.9	17,963	16.6	11,556	10.6	12,383	11.4
New Hampshire...........	8,559	16.0	8,366	15.0	4,323	8.1	7,677	13.8
New Jersey...............	49,761	14.5	45,524	12.3	21,590	6.3	26,395	7.1
New Mexico...............	16,850	20.7	14,549	17.4	9,513	11.7	10,162	12.2
New York.................	117,475	15.4	114,694	13.8	52,371	6.9	63,905	7.7
North Carolina............	73,080	19.7	71,957	17.9	37,583	10.1	40,133	10.0
North Dakota.............	6,808	24.3	6,268	22.6	1,877	6.7	2,191	7.9
Ohio......................	74,877	16.6	74,382	15.4	44,322	9.8	46,594	9.7
Oklahoma.................	34,315	23.2	34,612	22.6	21,684	14.7	19,915	13.0
Oregon...................	26,040	16.8	26,521	16.5	14,716	9.5	19,255	12.0
Pennsylvania.............	72,187	14.3	71,159	13.1	37,214	7.4	41,570	7.7
Rhode Island.............	5,334	12.8	5,197	11.4	3,947	9.5	3,810	8.4
South Carolina...........	32,730	18.0	30,640	15.6	16,382	9.0	17,036	8.7
South Dakota.............	5,346	16.5	5,068	15.3	3,912	12.1	3,331	10.1
Tennessee................	45,693	18.3	49,893	18.6	29,228	11.7	34,904	13.0
Texas.....................	200,593	20.5	200,595	19.9	100,353	10.3	119,973	11.9
Utah......................	28,704	27.8	28,270	27.3	10,354	10.0	13,121	12.7
Vermont..................	4,342	17.0	4,605	17.1	2,837	11.1	2,527	9.4
Virginia...................	58,498	18.3	52,865	15.7	32,002	10.0	30,050	8.9
Washington...............	53,778	19.7	50,566	18.2	32,268	11.8	29,470	10.6
West Virginia.............	14,269	19.0	14,159	18.0	6,996	9.3	10,199	13.0
Wisconsin................	38,079	16.7	36,712	15.7	19,312	8.5	17,634	7.5
Wyoming.................	5,200	22.5	4,946	22.1	2,725	11.8	2,340	10.4

Source: U.S. Census Bureau, 2011 American Community Survey, B12501, "Marriage in the Last Year by Sex by Marital Status for the Population 15 Years and Over" and B12503, "Divorces in the Last Year by Sex by Marital Status for the Population 15 Years and Over," <http://factfinder2.census.gov>, accessed March 2013.

Table 139. Percent of First Marriages Reaching Stated Anniversary by Sex and Year of Marriage: 2009

[In percent except number of marriages. For currently married couples aged 15 years and over. Based on the second wave (interview) of the 2008 Survey of Income and Program Participation (SIPP), a longitudinal survey, conducted from January through April 2009]

Sex and year of marriage	Number of marriages (1,000)	Anniversary [1]							
		5th	10th	15th	20th	25th	30th	35th	40th
Men									
1960 to 1964.................	4,150	94.6	83.4	74.7	70.2	66.9	64.5	62.1	60.1
1965 to 1969.................	5,658	91.7	80.0	69.9	65.8	62.7	60.5	57.9	(X)
1970 to 1974.................	7,036	88.0	75.0	65.7	60.2	56.8	53.8	(X)	(X)
1975 to 1979.................	6,901	88.2	73.4	63.7	58.7	54.4	(X)	(X)	(X)
1980 to 1984.................	7,144	90.6	74.3	65.2	60.0	(X)	(X)	(X)	(X)
1985 to 1989.................	7,670	87.7	75.4	66.6	(X)	(X)	(X)	(X)	(X)
1990 to 1994.................	7,569	89.7	77.3	(X)	(X)	(X)	(X)	(X)	(X)
1995 to 1999.................	8,088	89.6	(X)	(X)	(X)	(X)	(X)	(X)	(X)
Women									
1960 to 1964.................	5,495	93.0	82.8	73.5	67.0	60.8	57.2	53.6	49.7
1965 to 1969.................	6,705	90.7	79.3	69.6	64.0	59.1	55.8	52.1	(X)
1970 to 1974.................	7,667	89.2	74.5	66.1	61.3	56.2	52.6	(X)	(X)
1975 to 1979.................	7,619	86.9	72.8	63.2	57.4	53.2	(X)	(X)	(X)
1980 to 1984.................	8,051	87.8	71.1	62.9	56.6	(X)	(X)	(X)	(X)
1985 to 1989.................	8,027	87.9	74.5	66.4	(X)	(X)	(X)	(X)	(X)
1990 to 1994.................	8,164	87.1	74.5	(X)	(X)	(X)	(X)	(X)	(X)
1995 to 1999.................	8,229	89.5	(X)	(X)	(X)	(X)	(X)	(X)	(X)

X Marriage cohort had not sufficient time to reach stated anniversary at time of the survey. [1] People reaching stated anniversary.

Source: U.S. Census Bureau, Current Population Reports, *Number, Timing, and Duration of Marriages and Divorces: 2009*, P70-125, May 2011. See also <http://www.census.gov/hhes/socdemo/marriage/data/sipp/index.html>.

Section 3
Health and Nutrition

This section presents statistics on health expenditures and insurance coverage, including Medicare and Medicaid, medical personnel, hospitals, nursing homes and other care facilities, injuries, diseases, disability status, nutritional intake of the population, and food consumption. Summary statistics showing recent trends in health care and discussions of selected health issues are published annually by the U.S. National Center for Health Statistics (NCHS) in *Health, United States*. Data on national health expenditures, medical costs, and insurance coverage are compiled by the U.S. Centers for Medicare & Medicaid Services (CMS) and appear on the CMS Web site at <http://www.cms.gov/NationalHealthExpendData/> and in the annual *Medicare and Medicaid Statistical Supplement*. Statistics on health insurance are also collected by NCHS and are published in Series 10 of *Vital and Health Statistics*. NCHS also conducts periodic surveys of nutrient levels in the population, including estimates of food and nutrient intake, overweight and obesity, hypercholesterolemia (high blood cholesterol), hypertension (high blood pressure), and clinical signs of malnutrition. Data are published in Series 10 and 11 of *Vital and Health Statistics*. Statistics on hospitals are published annually by the Health Forum, L.L.C., an American Hospital Association (AHA) company, in *AHA Hospital Statistics*. Data on nutrition and on annual per capita consumption of food are issued by the U.S. Department of Agriculture, Economic Research Service, and Center for Nutrition Policy and Promotion. Data are available on the Web sites at <http://www.ers.usda.gov/data-products/food-availability-(per-capita)-data-system.aspx> and <http://www.usda.gov/cnpp/>, respectively.

National health expenditures—CMS compiles estimates of national health expenditures (NHE) to measure spending for health care in the United States. The NHE accounts are structured to show spending by type of expenditure: hospital care, physician and clinical care, dental care, and other professional care; home health care; retail sales of prescription drugs; other medical nondurables; nursing home care and other personal health expenditures; plus other health expenditures such as public health activities, administration, and the net cost of private health insurance; plus medical sector investment, the sum of noncommercial medical research and capital formation in medical sector structures and equipment; and by source of funding (e.g., health insurance, out-of-pocket payments, and other third party payers and programs).

Data used to estimate health expenditures come from existing sources, which are tabulated for other purposes. The type of expenditure estimates rely upon statistics produced by such groups as the AHA, the Census Bureau, and the U.S. Department of Health and Human Services (HHS). Source of funding estimates are constructed using administrative and statistical records from the Medicare and Medicaid programs, the U.S. Department of Defense and VA medical programs, the Social Security Administration, Census Bureau's *Governmental Finances*, state and local governments, other HHS agencies, and other nongovernment sources.

Medicare, Medicaid, and Children's Health Insurance Program (CHIP)—The Medicare program has two components. Hospital Insurance (HI), otherwise known as Medicare Part A, helps pay for hospital, home health following hospital stays, skilled nursing facility, and hospice care for the aged and disabled. Supplementary Medical Insurance (SMI) consists of Medicare Part B and Part D. Part B helps pay for physician, outpatient hospital, home health, and other services for the aged and disabled who have voluntarily enrolled. Part D provides subsidized access to drug insurance coverage on a voluntary basis for all beneficiaries and premium and cost-sharing subsidies for low-income enrollees. Medicare also has a Part C, which serves as an alternative to traditional Part A and Part B coverage; Part C is not covered here. Participants in Parts B and D pay monthly premiums. In addition to covering persons age 65 and older, Medicare covers the disabled of any age after 24 months of entitlement to cash benefits under the social security or railroad retirement programs, and to persons with end stage renal disease. Medicare's HI and SMI have separate trust funds, sources of revenue, and categories of expenditures.

Medicaid is a health insurance program for certain low-income people. These include: certain low-income families with children; people on supplemental security income; certain low-income pregnant women and children; and people who have very high medical bills. There are special rules for those who live in nursing homes and for disabled children living at home. Medicaid is funded and administered through a state/federal partnership. Although there are broad federal requirements for Medicaid, states have a wide degree of flexibility to design their program. The Children's Health Insurance Program Reauthorization Act of 2009 (CHIPRA or Public Law 111-3) reauthorized the Children's Health Insurance Program (CHIP), which was originally signed into law in 1997. The program went into effect on April 1, 2009. CHIP replaces the State Children's Health Insurance Program (SCHIP). It preserves coverage for the millions of children who rely on CHIP, and provides the resources for states to reach millions of additional uninsured children. CHIP was designed as a federal/state partnership, similar to Medicaid, with the goal of expanding health insurance to children whose families earn too much money to be eligible for Medicaid, but not enough money to purchase private insurance.

Health resources—Hospital statistics based on data from AHA's yearly survey are published annually in *AHA Hospital Statistics* and cover all hospitals accepted for registration by the Association. To be accepted for registration, a hospital must meet certain requirements relating to number of beds, construction, equipment, medical and nursing staff, patient care, clinical records, surgical and obstetrical facilities, diagnostic and treatment facilities, laboratory services, etc. Data obtained from NCHS cover all U.S. hospitals that meet certain criteria for inclusion. The criteria are published in *Vital and Health Statistics* reports, Series 13. Statistics on the demographic characteristics of persons employed in the health occupations are compiled by the U.S. Bureau of Labor Statistics and reported in *Employment and Earnings* (monthly) (see Table 642, Section 12,

Labor Force, Employment, and Earnings). Data based on surveys of health personnel and utilization of health facilities providing long-term care, ambulatory care, emergency room care, and hospital care are presented in NCHS Series 13, data from the National Health Interview Survey. Statistics on patient visits to health care providers, as reported in health interviews, appear in NCHS Series 10, data from the National Health Care Survey.

The CMS's annual *Medicare and Medicaid Statistical Supplement* present data for hospitals and nursing homes as well as extended care facilities and home health agencies. These data are based on records of the Medicare program and differ from those of other sources because they are limited to facilities meeting federal eligibility standards for participation in Medicare.

Disability and illness—General health statistics, including morbidity, disability, injuries, preventive care, and findings from physiological testing are collected by NCHS in its National Health Interview Survey and its National Health and Nutrition Examination Surveys and appear in *Vital and Health Statistics*, Series 10 and 11, respectively. Annual incidence data on notifiable diseases are compiled by the Public Health Service (PHS) at its Centers for Disease Control and Prevention in Atlanta, Georgia, and are published as a supplement to its *Morbidity and Mortality Weekly Report* (MMWR). The list of diseases is revised annually and includes those which, by mutual agreement of the states and PHS, are communicable diseases of national importance.

Statistical reliability—For discussion of statistical collection, estimation, and sampling procedures and measures of reliability applicable to data from NCHS and CMS, see Appendix III.

Table 140. National Health Expenditures—Summary: 1960 to 2011

[In billions of dollars (27.4 represents $27,400,000,000). Excludes Puerto Rico and Island Areas]

Year	Total expenditures [1]	Health consumption expenditures, total [2]	Personal health care expenditures									
			Total [3]	Hospital care	Physician and clinical services	Other professional services	Dental services	Home health care	Nursing care facilities [4]	Prescription drugs	Durable medical equipment	Other nondurable medical equipment
1960.....	27.4	24.8	23.4	9.0	5.6	0.4	2.0	0.1	0.8	2.7	0.7	1.6
1961.....	29.2	26.4	24.8	9.8	5.8	0.4	2.1	0.1	0.8	2.7	0.8	1.8
1962.....	31.9	28.4	26.7	10.4	6.3	0.4	2.2	0.1	0.9	3.0	0.9	1.9
1963.....	34.7	30.9	29.1	11.5	7.1	0.5	2.4	0.1	1.0	3.2	0.9	1.9
1964.....	38.5	34.1	32.1	12.5	8.1	0.5	2.6	0.1	1.2	3.3	1.0	2.1
1965.....	42.0	37.2	34.7	13.5	8.6	0.5	2.8	0.1	1.4	3.7	1.1	2.2
1966.....	46.3	41.2	38.4	15.3	9.3	0.6	3.0	0.1	1.7	4.0	1.2	2.4
1967.....	51.8	46.5	43.5	17.8	10.4	0.6	3.4	0.2	2.2	4.2	1.1	2.5
1968.....	58.8	52.8	49.2	20.5	11.3	0.6	3.7	0.2	2.9	4.7	1.3	2.8
1969.....	66.2	59.1	55.5	23.4	12.7	0.7	4.2	0.3	3.4	5.1	1.5	3.0
1970.....	74.9	67.1	63.1	27.2	14.3	0.7	4.7	0.2	4.0	5.5	1.7	3.3
1971.....	83.2	74.4	69.5	30.2	15.9	0.8	5.2	0.2	4.6	5.9	1.8	3.5
1972.....	93.1	83.4	77.2	33.8	17.7	0.9	5.6	0.2	5.2	6.3	2.0	3.7
1973.....	103.4	93.1	86.2	37.9	19.6	1.0	6.4	0.3	6.0	6.8	2.2	4.0
1974.....	117.2	105.9	98.8	44.1	22.2	1.2	7.1	0.4	6.9	7.4	2.5	4.5
1975.....	133.6	121.2	113.3	51.2	25.3	1.3	8.0	0.6	8.0	8.1	2.8	4.9
1976.....	153.0	139.4	129.4	59.4	28.7	1.6	9.0	0.9	9.1	8.7	3.0	5.4
1977.....	174.0	160.0	146.8	67.0	33.1	2.1	10.1	1.1	10.3	9.2	3.2	6.1
1978.....	195.5	180.1	164.3	75.6	35.8	2.4	11.0	1.6	11.8	9.9	3.4	7.1
1979.....	221.7	204.6	187.2	86.2	41.2	2.8	12.0	1.9	13.3	10.7	3.8	8.5
1980.....	255.8	235.7	217.2	100.5	47.7	3.5	13.4	2.4	15.3	12.0	4.1	9.8
1981.....	296.7	273.7	252.0	117.5	55.6	4.3	15.8	2.9	17.3	13.4	4.3	11.3
1982.....	334.7	308.3	283.4	133.6	61.6	4.9	17.1	3.5	19.5	15.0	4.6	12.6
1983.....	369.0	339.7	312.0	144.7	68.6	5.7	18.4	4.2	21.7	17.3	5.3	13.8
1984.....	406.5	375.5	342.1	154.4	77.4	7.4	20.0	5.1	23.8	19.6	6.1	15.0
1985.....	444.6	413.4	376.9	164.6	90.9	8.1	21.8	5.6	26.3	21.8	7.1	16.0
1986.....	476.9	444.4	409.5	175.6	100.7	9.3	23.3	6.4	28.7	24.3	8.1	17.1
1987.....	519.1	483.1	448.5	189.5	112.9	11.4	25.5	6.7	30.7	26.9	9.5	18.3
1988.....	581.7	541.5	499.5	206.5	128.6	13.8	27.5	8.4	34.3	30.6	11.1	19.4
1989.....	647.5	603.5	551.6	226.0	143.3	14.6	29.5	10.2	38.7	34.8	11.9	20.8
1990.....	724.3	675.6	616.8	250.4	158.9	17.4	31.7	12.6	44.9	40.3	13.8	22.4
1991.....	791.5	739.5	677.7	275.8	176.5	18.7	33.5	15.2	49.4	44.4	13.1	23.2
1992.....	857.9	801.0	733.6	298.5	191.3	21.0	37.3	18.7	53.1	47.0	13.5	23.2
1993.....	921.5	860.3	781.2	315.7	202.7	23.2	39.2	22.8	56.0	49.6	14.1	23.7
1994.....	972.7	908.8	823.1	328.4	212.2	24.2	41.7	27.4	58.6	53.1	15.3	24.3
1995.....	1,027.4	961.6	872.9	339.3	222.3	27.0	44.8	32.4	64.5	59.8	15.9	25.1
1996.....	1,081.8	1,014.1	921.8	350.8	231.3	29.2	47.1	35.8	69.6	68.1	17.4	26.0
1997.....	1,142.6	1,070.4	974.6	363.4	242.9	31.7	50.5	37.0	74.4	77.6	19.2	27.6
1998.....	1,208.9	1,129.5	1,029.2	374.9	258.7	33.8	53.8	34.2	79.4	88.4	21.3	28.6
1999.....	1,286.5	1,201.0	1,089.7	393.6	271.9	35.0	57.4	32.9	80.8	104.7	23.0	30.6
2000.....	1,377.2	1,289.6	1,165.4	415.5	290.9	37.0	62.3	32.4	85.1	120.9	25.2	31.6
2001.....	1,493.3	1,402.1	1,265.3	449.4	315.7	40.6	67.8	34.4	90.8	138.7	25.1	32.3
2002.....	1,638.0	1,535.9	1,371.9	486.5	340.9	43.7	73.7	36.6	94.5	158.2	27.1	33.3
2003.....	1,775.4	1,665.5	1,480.2	526.2	368.0	46.7	76.3	39.8	100.3	176.0	28.2	35.1
2004.....	1,901.6	1,784.2	1,589.4	566.0	393.3	50.3	82.1	43.8	105.8	192.2	29.7	35.8
2005.....	2,030.5	1,904.0	1,697.1	609.4	417.2	52.7	87.0	48.7	112.5	204.7	31.2	37.2
2006.....	2,163.3	2,032.4	1,804.4	651.9	438.8	55.0	91.4	52.6	117.3	224.1	32.9	38.7
2007.....	2,298.3	2,154.6	1,914.1	692.5	461.8	59.5	97.3	57.8	126.4	235.9	34.3	41.0
2008.....	2,406.6	2,252.8	2,010.4	729.2	486.4	64.0	102.4	62.3	132.6	242.6	34.9	42.5
2009.....	2,501.2	2,355.1	2,111.6	777.9	503.2	66.8	102.5	67.3	138.5	254.6	34.9	43.5
2010.....	2,600.0	2,450.8	2,190.0	815.9	519.1	69.8	105.3	71.2	143.0	255.7	36.9	45.2
2011.....	2,700.7	2,547.2	2,279.3	850.6	541.4	73.2	108.4	74.3	149.3	263.0	38.9	47.0

[1] Includes Health Consumption Expenditures plus medical research, and medical structures and equipment. [2] Includes Personal Health Expenditures plus government administration, net cost of health insurance, and government public health activities. [3] Includes hospital care, physician and clinical services, dental services, other professional services, other health, residential, and personal services, home health care, nursing care facilities and continuing care retirement communities, prescription drugs, durable medical equipment, and other nondurable medical products. [4] Includes care provided in nursing care facilities (NAICS 6231), continuing care retirement communities (NAICS 623311), state and local government nursing facilities, and nursing facilities operated by the Department of Veterans' Affairs (DVA).

Source: U.S. Centers for Medicare and Medicaid Services, Office of the Actuary, National Health Statistics Group, <http://www.cms.gov/NationalHealthExpendData/>, accessed March 2013.

Table 141. National Health Expenditures by Source of Funds: 1990 to 2011

[In billions of dollars (724.3 represents $724,300,000,000), except percent. Excludes Puerto Rico and Island Areas]

Type of expenditure	1990	2000	2005	2007	2008	2009	2010	2011
National health expenditure, total..........	**724.3**	**1,377.2**	**2,030.5**	**2,298.3**	**2,406.6**	**2,501.2**	**2,600.0**	**2,700.7**
Annual percent change [1].................	11.0	7.1	6.8	6.2	4.7	3.9	4.0	3.9
Percent of gross domestic product..........	12.5	13.8	16.1	16.4	16.8	17.9	17.9	17.9
Out of pocket.................................	138.6	201.7	262.9	286.1	293.0	293.3	299.4	307.7
Health insurance...........................	439.5	920.4	1,417.5	1,613.9	1,705.2	1,801.1	1,879.4	1,960.1
Private health insurance.....................	234.2	459.2	704.0	778.9	809.5	835.0	863.7	896.3
Medicare.................................	110.2	224.8	339.8	433.6	468.2	500.4	522.0	554.3
Medicaid (Title XIX).....................	73.7	200.5	309.5	326.2	344.9	375.4	397.7	407.7
CHIP (Title XIX and Title XXI)...............	(X)	3.0	7.6	9.1	10.2	11.1	11.7	12.0
Department of Defense...................	10.4	13.8	26.8	32.3	34.0	36.7	38.3	39.7
Department of Veterans Affairs..............	10.9	19.1	29.8	33.8	38.4	42.4	46.1	50.1
Other third party payers and programs.......	77.5	124.5	167.6	186.0	182.0	185.1	192.7	200.5
Worksite health care......	2.2	3.5	4.2	4.5	4.5	4.5	4.6	4.8
Other private revenues [2]...............	29.6	57.5	70.3	85.8	80.7	85.5	92.3	96.6
Indian health services.................	1.0	2.0	2.5	2.7	2.8	3.2	3.6	3.6
Workers' compensation...............	17.5	26.2	41.3	40.5	39.6	36.3	34.9	35.0
General assistance.................	5.0	3.9	6.2	6.9	7.1	7.2	7.1	6.7
Maternal/Child health..............	1.6	2.7	2.6	2.8	2.8	2.7	2.6	2.6
Vocational rehabilitation............	0.3	0.4	0.5	0.5	0.5	0.5	0.5	0.5
Other federal programs [3].............	1.6	4.5	6.3	6.7	6.9	7.3	7.7	9.7
Substance Abuse and Mental Health Services Administration.................	1.4	2.6	3.2	3.2	3.2	3.3	3.4	3.4
Other state and local programs [4]..........	16.0	18.8	27.1	28.6	29.7	30.4	31.6	33.1
School health............	1.3	2.5	3.4	3.9	4.1	4.2	4.4	4.5
Public health activity [5].....................	20.0	43.0	56.0	68.7	72.6	75.6	79.3	79.0
Investment.................	**48.7**	**87.5**	**126.5**	**143.7**	**153.8**	**146.1**	**149.1**	**153.5**
Research [6].................	12.7	25.5	40.3	41.9	43.4	45.3	49.0	49.8
Structures & equipment [7]....................	36.0	62.1	86.2	101.7	110.4	100.8	100.1	103.7

X Not applicable. [1] Average annual growth from prior year shown. [2] Most common source of other private funds is philanthropy. Philanthropic support may be direct from individuals or may come through philanthropic fund-raising organizations. Support may also come from foundations or corporations. [3] Includes federal general hospital/medical, and pre-existing conditions insurance plans. [4] Includes Temporary Disability Insurance, state and local subsidies to providers, and non-XIX state and local. [5] Governments are involved in organizing and delivering publicly provided health services such as epidemiological surveillance, inoculations, immunization/vaccination services, disease prevention programs, and the operation of public health laboratories. In the NHEA, spending for these activities is reported in government public health activity. [6] Non-profit or government entities. Research and development expenditures by drug and medical supply and equipment manufacturers are not shown, those expenditures are treated as intermediate purchases under the definitions of national income accounting; that is, the value of that research is deemed to be recouped through product sales. [7] Structures are defined as the value of new construction by the medical sector. Includes establishments engaged in providing health care, but does not include retail establishments that sell non-durable or durable medical goods. Construction includes new buildings; additions, alterations, and major replacements; mechanical and electric installations; and site preparation.

Source: U.S. Centers for Medicare and Medicaid Services, Office of the Actuary, National Health Expenditure Data, <http://www.cms.gov/NationalHealthExpendData/>, accessed March 2013.

Table 142. National Health Expenditures by Source of Funds and Type of Expenditure: 1990 to 2011

[In billions of dollars (724.3 represents $724,300,000,000). Excludes Puerto Rico and Island Areas]

Object of expenditure	1990	2000	2005	2006	2007	2008	2009	2010	2011
Total.......................	**724.3**	**1,377.2**	**2,030.5**	**2,163.3**	**2,298.3**	**2,406.6**	**2,501.2**	**2,600.0**	**2,700.7**
Source of funds:									
Out-of-pocket.................	138.7	201.7	262.9	271.6	286.1	293.0	293.3	299.4	307.7
Health insurance [1]...............	439.5	920.4	1,417.5	1,522.1	1,613.9	1,705.2	1,801.1	1,879.4	1,960.1
Other third party payers and programs [2]..............	77.5	124.5	167.6	176.3	186.0	182.0	185.1	192.7	200.5
Public health activities [3].....................	20.0	43.0	56.0	62.3	68.7	72.6	75.6	79.3	79.0
Investment.................	48.7	87.5	126.5	130.9	143.7	153.8	146.1	149.1	153.5
Type of expenditure:									
Health consumption expenditures.....................	675.6	1,289.6	1,904.0	2,032.4	2,154.6	2,252.8	2,355.1	2,450.8	2,547.2
Personal health care.................	616.8	1,165.4	1,697.1	1,804.4	1,914.1	2,010.4	2,111.6	2,190.0	2,279.3
Hospital care.................	250.4	415.5	609.4	651.9	692.5	729.2	777.9	815.9	850.6
Physician and clinical services.....................	158.9	290.9	417.2	438.8	461.8	486.4	503.2	519.1	541.4
Other professional services [4].....................	17.4	37.0	52.7	55.0	59.5	64.0	66.8	69.8	73.2
Dental services....................	31.7	62.3	87.0	91.4	97.3	102.4	102.5	105.3	108.4
Other health, residential, and personal care [5].......	24.3	64.5	96.5	101.7	107.7	113.6	122.5	128.0	133.1
Home health care.................	12.6	32.4	48.7	52.6	57.8	62.3	67.3	71.2	74.3
Nursing care facilities and continuing care retirement communities..........	44.9	85.1	112.5	117.3	126.4	132.6	138.5	143.0	149.3
Prescription drugs................	40.3	120.9	204.7	224.1	235.9	242.6	254.6	255.7	263.0
Durable medical equipment [6]............	13.8	25.2	31.2	32.9	34.3	34.9	34.9	36.9	38.9
Other nondurable medical products [7]..............	22.4	31.6	37.2	38.7	41.0	42.5	43.5	45.2	47.0
Investment....................	48.7	87.5	126.5	130.9	143.7	153.8	146.1	149.1	153.5
Research [8].................	12.7	25.5	40.3	41.4	41.9	43.4	45.3	49.0	49.8
Structures & equipment [9].................	36.0	62.1	86.2	89.6	101.7	110.4	100.8	100.1	103.7

[1] Includes Private Health Insurance, Medicare, Medicaid, CHIP (Titles XIX and XXI), Department of Defense, and Department of Veterans Affairs. [2] See footnote 2, Table 147. [3] See footnote 5, Table 141. [4] Covers services provided in establishments operated by health practitioners other than physicians and dentists. These professional services include those provided by private-duty nurses, chiropractors, podiatrists, optometrists, and physical, occupational and speech therapists, among others. [5] Includes spending for Medicaid home and community based waivers, residential mental health and substance abuse facilities, ambulance services, school health and worksite health care. Generally these programs provide payments for services in non-traditional settings such as community centers, senior citizens centers, schools, and military field stations. [6] Covers "retail" sales of items such as contact lenses, eyeglasses and other ophthalmic products, surgical and orthopedic products, hearing aids, wheelchairs, and medical equipment rentals. [7] Covers the "retail" sales of non-prescription drugs and medical sundries. [8] See footnote 6, Table 141. [9] See footnote 7, Table 141.

Source: U.S. Centers for Medicare and Medicaid Services, Office of the Actuary, National Health Statistics Group, <http://www.cms.gov/NationalHealthExpendData/>, accessed March 2013.

Table 143. Health Consumption Expenditures—Per Capita Spending by Type of Expenditure: 1990 to 2011

[In dollars, except percent. Based on U.S. Census Bureau estimates of total U.S. resident population plus the net Census undercount. Excludes research, structures and equipment. Excludes Puerto Rico and Island Areas]

Type of expenditure	1990	2000	2005	2006	2007	2008	2009	2010	2011
Total [1]	**2,660**	**4,573**	**6,454**	**6,820**	**7,158**	**7,411**	**7,696**	**7,931**	**8,190**
Annual percent change [2]	10.6	6.6	6.0	5.7	5.0	3.5	3.9	3.1	3.3
Hospital care	986	1,474	2,066	2,188	2,301	2,399	2,542	2,640	2,735
Physician and clinical services	626	1,030	1,413	1,472	1,534	1,601	1,642	1,680	1,740
Other professional services [3]	69	131	178	184	198	211	218	226	235
Dental services	125	221	295	307	323	337	334	341	349
Other health, residential, personal care [4]	96	229	327	341	358	374	400	414	428
Home health care	50	115	165	176	192	205	219	230	239
Nursing care facilities and continuing care retirement communities	177	302	381	393	420	436	452	463	480
Prescription drugs	159	428	693	752	784	798	831	828	845
Durable medical equipment [5]	54	89	106	110	114	115	114	119	125
Other nondurable medical products [6]	88	112	126	130	136	140	142	146	151
Public health activities [7]	79	153	190	209	228	239	247	257	254

[1] Includes other items, not shown separately. [2] Average annual growth from prior year shown. [3] See footnote 4, Table 142. [4] Includes spending for Medicaid home and community based waivers, care provided in residential care facilities, ambulance services, school health and worksite health care. Generally these programs provide payments for services in non-traditional settings such as community centers, senior citizens centers, schools, and military field stations. [5] See footnote 6, Table 142. [6] Covers the "retail" sales of non-prescription drugs and medical sundries. [7] See footnote 5, Table 141.

Source: U.S. Centers for Medicare and Medicaid Services, Office of the Actuary, National Health Statistics Group, <http://www.cms.gov/NationalHealthExpendData/>, accessed March 2013.

Table 144. Health Consumption Expenditures by Type of Expenditure and Source of Funds: 2011

[In billions of dollars (2,547.2 represents $2,547,200,000,000). Excludes Puerto Rico and Island Areas. Excludes research, structures, and equipment]

Type of expenditure	Total	Out–of–pocket	Health insurance				Other health insurance programs [1]	Other third party payers and programs [2]
			Total	Private health insurance	Medicare	Medicaid		
Total	**2,547.2**	**307.7**	**1,960.1**	**896.3**	**554.3**	**407.7**	**101.8**	**200.5**
Personal health care [3]	2,279.3	307.7	1,779.1	786.1	521.6	374.5	97.0	192.5
Hospital care	850.6	28.1	742.4	306.9	231.3	151.0	53.3	80.0
Physician and clinical services	541.4	52.3	440.3	249.1	124.0	44.8	22.5	48.8
Dental services	108.4	45.1	62.8	52.7	0.3	7.3	2.5	0.5
Other health, residential, and personal care [4]	133.1	7.5	84.5	6.4	5.1	69.3	3.8	41.1
Home health care	74.3	5.6	66.5	5.1	32.9	27.6	0.9	2.2
Nursing care facilities and continu–ing care retirement communities	149.3	39.9	100.4	12.4	37.6	46.1	4.3	9.0
Prescription drugs	263.0	45.0	214.3	122.2	63.7	19.0	9.4	3.7
Durable medical equipment [5]	38.9	21.3	17.0	4.6	7.7	4.6	0.1	0.6
Government administration [6]	32.5	(X)	31.1	(X)	8.2	18.9	3.9	1.5
Net cost of health insurance [6]	156.4	(X)	149.9	110.3	24.5	14.2	0.9	6.5
Public health activities [7]	79.0	(X)	(X)	(X)	(X)	(X)	(X)	(X)

X Not applicable. [1] Includes CHIP (Titles XIX and XXI), Department of Defense, and Department of Veterans Affairs. [2] See footnote 2, Table 147. [3] Includes other items, not shown separately. [4] See footnote 5, Table 142. [5] See footnote 6, Table 142. [6] See source material for definitions. [7] See footnote 5, Table 141.

Source: Source: U.S. Centers for Medicare and Medicaid Services, Office of the Actuary, National Health Expenditures Data, "National Health Expenditures by Source of Funds and Type of Expenditures: Calendar Years 2005-2011," <http://www.cms.gov/NationalHealthExpendData/>, accessed March 2013.

Table 145. Personal Health Care Expenditures by Source of Funds: 1990 to 2011

[In billions of dollars (616.8 represents $616,800,000,000), except percent. Excludes Puerto Rico and Island Areas]

Item	1990	2000	2005	2006	2007	2008	2009	2010	2011
Personal health care expenditures	**616.8**	**1,165.4**	**1,697.1**	**1,804.4**	**1,914.1**	**2,010.4**	**2,111.6**	**2,190.0**	**2,279.3**
Out-of-pocket	138.6	201.7	262.9	271.6	286.1	293.0	293.3	299.4	307.7
Health insurance	403.2	844.9	1,282.0	1,372.2	1,456.5	1,546.5	1,641.2	1,705.3	1,779.1
Private health insurance	205.1	406.7	607.2	640.3	674.1	707.4	737.7	757.5	786.1
Medicare	107.3	216.3	326.3	382.3	409.5	443.2	471.9	491.2	521.6
Medicaid	69.7	186.9	287.7	283.4	301.7	318.2	346.8	366.2	374.5
Other health insurance [1]	21.2	37.4	67.2	73.4	78.9	86.4	94.3	100.3	107.2
Other third party payers and programs [2]	74.9	118.8	152.2	160.6	171.6	170.9	177.0	185.3	192.5

[1] Includes Children's Health Insurance Program (Titles XIX and XXI), Department of Defense, and Department of Veterans Affairs. [2] See footnote 2, Table 147.

Source: U.S. Centers for Medicare and Medicaid Services, Office of the Actuary, "National Health Expenditures by Type of Service and Source of Funds: Calendar Years 1960-2011," <http://www.cms.gov/NationalHealthExpendData/>, accessed March 2013.

Table 146. National Health Expenditures by Sponsor: 1990 to 2011

[In billions of dollars (724.3 represents $724,300,000,000). Excludes Puerto Rico and Island Areas]

Type of sponsor	1990	2000	2005	2007	2008	2009	2010	2011
Total.	724.3	1,377.2	2,030.5	2,298.3	2,406.6	2,501.2	2,600.0	2,700.7
Business, households and other private revenues. ...	488.2	888.0	1,227.1	1,364.5	1,407.6	1,407.9	1,437.5	1,485.9
Private business [1]	178.3	346.1	488.5	524.5	531.9	533.0	534.9	557.6
Household [2]	253.0	434.1	596.5	668.2	702.6	707.2	728.7	748.8
Other private revenues.	56.9	107.9	142.1	171.7	173.2	167.7	173.9	179.5
Governments.	236.1	489.2	803.4	933.8	999.0	1,093.3	1,162.4	1,214.9
Federal government [3]	125.3	261.6	452.9	530.9	584.6	684.2	735.2	744.6
State and local government [4]	110.8	227.6	350.5	403.0	414.4	409.1	427.2	470.2

[1] Excludes Medicare Retiree Drug Subsidy (RDS) payments to private plans as of 2006; and small business tax credits and Early Retirement Reinsurance Program (ERRP) Payments as of 2010. Also includes one-half of self employment contribution to Medicare Hospital Insurance Trust Fund. [2] Excludes government-subsidized COBRA payments as of 2009. Includes one-half self-employment contribution to the Medicare Hospital Insurance Trust Fund, and trust fund revenues from taxation of social security benefits. [3] Includes employer contributions to private health insurance premiums and Medicare Hospital Insurance Trust Fund, adjusted Medicare expenditures, and health program expenditures (excluding Medicare), see source for details. [4] Includes employer contributions to private health insurance premiums and Medicare Hospital Insurance Trust Fund, and expenditures for Medicaid and other programs, see source for details.

Source: U.S. Centers for Medicare and Medicaid Services, Office of the Actuary, "National Health Expenditures by Type of Sponsor: Businesses, Households, and Governments, 2011," <http://www.cms.gov/NationalHealthExpendData/>, accessed March 2013.

Table 147. Hospital Care, Physician and Clinical Services, Nursing Care Facilities and Continuing Care Retirement Communities, and Prescription Drug Expenditures by Source of Funds: 1990 to 2011

[In billions of dollars (250.4 represents $250,400,000,000). Excludes Puerto Rico and Island Areas]

Source of payment	1990	2000	2005	2007	2008	2009	2010	2011
Hospital care, total.	**250.4**	**415.5**	**609.4**	**692.5**	**729.2**	**777.9**	**815.9**	**850.6**
Out-of-pocket.	11.2	13.5	19.5	22.3	23.3	25.1	26.4	28.1
Health insurance.	206.8	358.0	532.6	601.7	640.1	681.5	713.2	742.4
Private health insurance.	96.9	141.6	217.5	249.4	265.0	281.1	292.7	306.9
Medicare.	67.4	123.4	176.4	193.8	206.5	216.4	223.0	231.3
Medicaid.	26.7	71.2	104.8	119.5	125.4	137.1	147.5	151.0
Other health insurance [1]	15.8	21.9	33.8	38.9	43.2	46.9	50.0	53.3
Other third party payers and programs [2]	32.5	44.0	57.3	68.5	65.7	71.3	76.3	80.0
Physician and clinical services, total.	**158.9**	**290.9**	**417.2**	**461.8**	**486.4**	**503.2**	**519.1**	**541.4**
Out-of-pocket.	30.1	32.5	42.7	46.9	48.7	47.9	51.0	52.3
Health insurance.	107.8	222.7	330.2	368.2	390.7	409.6	420.8	440.3
Private health insurance.	67.0	138.0	202.4	222.5	233.1	238.0	241.8	249.1
Medicare.	30.5	58.7	85.6	96.0	103.9	111.7	115.3	124.0
Medicaid.	7.0	19.2	29.8	33.3	35.7	40.0	42.7	44.8
Other health insurance [1]	3.3	6.8	12.5	16.4	18.1	19.9	21.0	22.5
Other third party payers and programs [2]	21.1	35.7	44.3	46.7	47.1	45.8	47.3	48.8
Nursing care facilities and continuing care retirement communities, total.	**44.9**	**85.1**	**112.5**	**126.4**	**132.6**	**138.5**	**143.0**	**149.3**
Out-of-pocket.	18.1	27.2	32.5	37.1	38.5	39.4	40.0	39.9
Health insurance.	21.9	52.0	72.8	80.3	85.9	90.7	94.0	100.4
Private health insurance.	2.8	7.5	8.4	10.2	10.8	11.7	12.2	12.4
Medicare.	1.7	10.8	20.5	24.9	27.7	30.1	32.3	37.6
Medicaid.	16.4	31.9	41.1	42.1	43.8	45.0	45.5	46.1
Other health insurance [1]	1.0	1.9	2.8	3.2	3.6	3.9	4.0	4.3
Other third party payers and programs [2]	4.9	5.9	7.2	8.9	8.2	8.5	9.0	9.0
Prescription drugs, total.	**40.3**	**120.9**	**204.7**	**235.9**	**242.6**	**254.6**	**255.7**	**263.0**
Out-of-pocket.	22.9	33.9	51.3	51.8	49.8	49.6	46.2	45.0
Health insurance.	16.2	84.7	149.5	180.2	189.1	201.4	206.0	214.3
Private health insurance.	10.9	60.7	101.8	107.7	111.2	118.3	118.7	122.2
Medicare.	0.2	2.1	3.9	46.0	50.7	54.6	58.9	63.7
Medicaid.	5.1	19.8	36.3	18.1	18.9	19.8	19.6	19.0
Other health insurance [1]	0.1	2.1	7.5	8.4	8.3	8.7	8.8	9.4
Other third party payers and programs [2]	1.2	2.3	3.9	3.8	3.7	3.6	3.4	3.7

[1] Includes Children's Health Insurance Program (Titles XIX and XXI), Department of Defense, and Department of Veterans Affairs. [2] Includes worksite health care, other private revenues, Indian Health Service, workers' compensation, general assistance, maternal and child health, vocational rehabilitation, other federal programs, Substance Abuse and Mental Health Services Administration, other state and local programs, and school health.

Source: U.S. Centers for Medicare and Medicaid Services, Office of the Actuary, National Health Statistics Group, "National Health Expenditures by type of service and source of funds, CY 1960-2011." See also <http://www.cms.gov/NationalHealthExpendData/>.

Table 148. Consumer Price Indexes of Medical Care Prices: 1980 to 2012

[Indexes with base of 1982–1984 = 100. Indexes are annual averages of monthly data based on components of consumer price index for all urban consumers; for explanation, see text, Section 14 and Appendix III]

Year	Medical care, total	Medical care services					Medical care commodities		Annual percent change [3]		
		Total [1]	Professional services			Hospital and related services	Total [2]	Prescription drugs	Medical care, total	Medical care services	Medical care commodities
			Total [1]	Physicians	Dental						
1980.......	74.9	74.8	77.9	76.5	78.9	69.2	75.4	72.5	11.0	11.3	9.3
1985.......	113.5	113.2	113.5	113.3	114.2	116.1	115.2	120.1	6.3	6.1	7.2
1990.......	162.8	162.7	156.1	160.8	155.8	178.0	163.4	181.7	9.0	9.3	8.4
1995.......	220.5	224.2	201.0	208.8	206.8	257.8	204.5	235.0	4.5	5.1	1.9
2000.......	260.8	266.0	237.7	244.7	258.5	317.3	238.1	285.4	4.1	4.3	3.2
2005.......	323.2	336.7	281.7	287.5	324.0	439.9	276.0	349.0	4.2	4.8	2.5
2007.......	351.1	369.3	300.8	303.2	358.4	498.9	290.0	369.2	4.4	5.3	1.4
2008.......	364.1	384.9	311.0	311.3	376.9	534.0	296.0	378.3	3.7	4.2	2.1
2009.......	375.6	397.3	319.4	320.8	388.1	567.9	305.1	391.1	3.2	3.2	3.1
2010.......	388.4	411.2	328.2	331.3	398.8	607.7	314.7	407.8	3.4	3.5	3.1
2011.......	400.3	423.8	335.7	340.3	408.0	641.5	324.1	425.0	3.0	3.1	3.0
2012.......	414.9	440.3	342.0	347.3	417.5	672.1	333.6	440.1	3.7	3.9	2.9

[1] Includes other services not shown separately. [2] Includes other commodities not shown separately. [3] Percent change from the immediate prior year.

Source: U.S. Bureau of Labor Statistics, Consumer Price Index Tables, *CPI Detailed Report,* January 2013. See also <http://www.bls.gov/cpi/>.

Table 149. Average Annual Expenditures Per Consumer Unit for Health Care: 2009 to 2011

[In dollars, except percent. See text, Section 13 and headnote, Table 714. For composition of regions, see map, inside front cover]

Item	Health care, total		Health insurance	Medical services	Drugs and medical supplies [1]	Percent distribution		
	Amount	Percent of total expenditures				Health insurance	Medical services	Drugs and medical supplies [1]
2009..	3,126	6.4	1,785	736	605	57.1	23.5	19.4
2010..	3,157	6.6	1,831	722	604	58.0	22.9	19.1
2011..	**3,313**	**6.7**	**1,922**	**768**	**623**	**58.0**	**23.2**	**18.8**
Age of reference person:								
Under 25 years old...........................	841	2.8	456	254	131	54.2	30.2	15.6
25 to 34 years old.............................	2,094	4.4	1,237	546	311	59.1	26.1	14.9
35 to 44 years old.............................	2,762	4.8	1,581	694	487	57.2	25.1	17.6
45 to 54 years old.............................	3,411	5.9	1,801	942	668	52.8	27.6	19.6
55 to 64 years old.............................	4,048	7.5	2,196	1,013	839	54.2	25.0	20.7
65 to 74 years old.............................	5,038	11.3	3,154	894	990	62.6	17.7	19.7
75 years old and over.......................	4,449	13.6	2,982	656	811	67.0	14.7	18.2
Race of reference person:								
White and other [2]............................	3,542	6.9	2,025	842	675	57.2	23.8	19.1
Asian..	2,919	4.9	1,882	667	369	64.5	22.9	12.6
Black..	1,897	5.2	1,238	300	359	65.3	15.8	18.9
Origin of reference person:								
Hispanic...	1,774	4.2	1,008	453	312	56.8	25.5	17.6
Non-Hispanic...................................	3,531	7.0	2,052	812	666	58.1	23.0	18.9
Region of residence:								
Northeast...	3,368	6.2	2,023	788	557	60.1	23.4	16.5
Midwest...	3,620	7.7	2,029	928	663	56.0	25.6	18.3
South...	3,160	6.9	1,846	677	638	58.4	21.4	20.2
West..	3,216	5.9	1,859	742	615	57.8	23.1	19.1
Size of consumer unit:								
One person.......................................	2,112	6.9	1,232	467	413	58.3	22.1	19.6
Two or more persons.........................	3,815	6.6	2,211	894	709	58.0	23.4	18.6
Two persons..................................	4,197	8.0	2,450	903	844	58.4	21.5	20.1
Three persons...............................	3,744	6.4	2,130	992	621	56.9	26.5	16.6
Four persons.................................	3,455	5.3	2,012	869	574	58.2	25.2	16.6
Five persons or more.....................	3,209	5.1	1,861	749	600	58.0	23.3	18.7
Income before taxes, by quintile:								
Lowest 20 percent...........................	1,489	6.8	875	275	340	58.8	18.5	22.8
Second 20 percent..........................	2,611	8.1	1,613	495	503	61.8	19.0	19.3
Third 20 percent.............................	3,319	7.8	1,951	756	613	58.8	22.8	18.5
Fourth 20 percent...........................	3,994	7.0	2,360	939	694	59.1	23.5	17.4
Highest 20 percent..........................	5,149	5.4	2,811	1,373	966	54.6	26.7	18.8
Education:								
Less than a high school graduate...........	2,257	7.5	1,325	444	488	58.7	19.7	21.6
High school graduate........................	2,986	7.5	1,803	612	571	60.4	20.5	19.1
High school graduate with some college....	3,020	6.7	1,743	703	575	57.7	23.3	19.0
Associate's degree...........................	3,449	6.8	1,874	876	699	54.3	25.4	20.3
Bachelor's degree............................	4,022	6.2	2,334	980	708	58.0	24.4	17.6
Master's, professional, doctoral degree.....	4,490	5.9	2,573	1,157	761	57.3	25.8	16.9

[1] Includes prescription and nonprescription drugs. [2] All other races includes Native Hawaiian or other Pacific Islander, American Indian or Alaska Native, and approximately 1 percent reporting more than one race.

Source: U.S. Bureau of Labor Statistics, "Consumer Expenditure Survey," <http://www.bls.gov/cex/>, accessed April 2013.

Table 150. Children's Health Insurance Program (CHIP)—Enrollment and Expenditures by State: 2010 and 2011

[7,701.1 represents 7,707,100. For year ending September 30. This program provides health benefits coverage to children living in families whose incomes exceed the eligibility limits for Medicaid. Although it is generally targeted to families with incomes at or below 200 percent of the federal poverty level, each state may set its own income eligibility limits, within certain guidelines. For explanation of poverty level, see text, Section 13. States have three options: they may expand their Medicaid programs, develop a separate child health program that functions independently of Medicaid, or do a combination of both. See text, this section, regarding the change from SCHIP to CHIP]

State	Enrollment [1] (1,000)		Expenditures [2] (mil. dol.)		State	Enrollment [1] (1,000)		Expenditures [2] (mil. dol.)	
	2010	2011	2010	2011		2010	2011	2010	2011
U.S. [3]	7,707.1	7,970.9	7,983.3	8,398.9	NV	31.6	29.8	22.7	24.0
AL	100.5	109.3	128.4	144.6	NH	10.6	10.8	11.2	12.8
AK	12.6	12.8	18.7	20.0	NJ	187.2	198.3	562.4	620.5
AZ	39.6	20.0	57.8	33.7	NM	9.7	9.6	230.6	147.7
AR	100.8	103.7	85.8	91.1	NY	539.6	552.1	499.4	533.3
CA	1,731.6	1,763.8	1,186.8	1,377.5	NC	253.9	254.5	346.6	287.2
CO	106.6	105.3	115.6	107.1	ND	6.7	7.1	14.4	15.8
CT	21.0	20.1	23.0	22.3	OH	253.7	280.7	264.0	263.5
DE	12.9	15.3	12.9	14.1	OK	122.9	120.5	113.0	94.9
DC	8.1	8.7	11.3	12.6	OR	93.4	112.2	86.1	117.7
FL	403.3	431.7	308.5	334.2	PA	273.2	272.5	305.6	283.1
GA	248.3	248.5	225.4	246.8	RI	23.3	24.8	28.8	22.6
HI	27.3	30.6	31.4	29.7	SC	73.4	72.1	92.5	95.9
ID	42.2	42.6	34.1	38.4	SD	15.9	16.6	18.9	17.7
IL	329.1	336.9	261.7	237.5	TN	89.3	96.0	127.0	158.4
IN	144.2	158.1	89.8	104.5	TX	928.5	972.7	776.3	852.8
IA	64.0	75.1	71.6	81.1	UT	62.1	59.7	59.5	51.0
KS	56.4	60.4	54.0	55.4	VT	7.0	7.1	5.0	5.4
KY	79.4	84.6	122.9	135.5	VA	173.5	182.1	165.4	173.3
LA	157.0	152.4	175.7	163.8	WA	35.9	43.4	33.0	63.3
ME	33.0	(NA)	33.7	31.0	WV	37.5	37.6	39.2	41.5
MD	118.9	119.9	160.3	142.0	WI	161.5	172.5	97.6	103.2
MA	142.3	144.8	301.5	347.1	WY	8.3	8.6	9.3	10.2
MI	69.8	83.0	114.9	76.2	American Samoa	(NA)	(NA)	1.1	1.2
MN	5.2	4.5	15.8	12.5	Guam	(NA)	(NA)	4.0	4.2
MS	89.9	91.5	152.4	160.7	N. Marianas	(NA)	(NA)	0.8	0.9
MO	91.4	93.7	107.0	108.0	Puerto Rico	(NA)	(NA)	94.6	179.4
MT	25.2	24.4	36.5	47.3	Virgin Islands	(NA)	(NA)	(NA)	2.4
NE	47.9	52.9	36.7	40.6					

NA Not available. [1] Number of children ever enrolled during the year in Children's Health Insurance Program. [2] Expenditures for which states are entitled to federal reimbursement under Title XXI and which reconciles any advance of Title XXI federal funds made on the basis of estimates. Expenditures include both separate CHIP and Medicaid CHIP programs. [3] Total for expenditures includes data for Island Areas, total enrollment does not.

Source: U.S. Centers for Medicare & Medicaid Services, Children's Health Insurance Program (CHIP), "CHIP Quarterly and Annual Enrollment Reports"; and Medicaid Data & Systems, Medicaid Budget and Expenditure System, "CMS-64 Quarterly Expense Report: Financial Management Report for FY 2002 through FY 2011," <http://www.medicaid.gov/Medicaid-CHIP-Program-Information/By-Topics/Childrens-Health-Insurance-Program-CHIP/CHIP-Reports-and-Evaluations.html>, accessed April 2013.

Table 151. Medicare Enrollees: 1990 to 2012

[In millions (34.2 represents 34,200,000). As of July 1. Includes Puerto Rico and Island Areas and enrollees in foreign countries and unknown place of residence. The Medicare program has two components: Medicare Part A Hospital Insurance (HI); and Supplementary Medical Insurance (SMI), consisting of Part B Medical Insurance, and Part D Prescription Drug Coverage. See text in this section for details]

Item	1990	1995	2000	2005	2008	2009	2010	2011	2012
Total	34.2	37.6	39.6	42.5	45.4	46.5	47.7	48.8	50.8
Aged	31.0	33.2	34.3	35.8	37.9	38.8	39.6	40.5	42.2
Disabled	3.3	4.4	5.4	6.7	7.5	7.8	8.0	8.4	8.6
Hospital insurance, Part A	33.7	37.2	39.2	42.1	45.1	46.2	47.3	48.5	50.5
Aged	30.5	32.7	33.8	35.4	37.6	38.4	39.3	40.1	41.9
Disabled	3.3	4.4	5.4	6.7	7.5	7.8	8.0	8.4	8.6
SMI, Part B	32.6	35.7	37.4	39.7	42.0	43.0	44.0	44.9	46.6
Aged	29.7	31.8	32.6	33.8	35.4	36.1	36.8	37.4	38.8
Disabled	2.9	4.0	4.8	6.0	6.7	6.9	7.2	7.5	7.8
SMI, Part D	(X)	(X)	(X)	1.8	25.8	27.0	28.0	29.5	(NA)

X Not applicable. NA Not Available.

Source: U.S. Centers for Medicare and Medicaid Services, Office of Information Products and Data Analysis, *Medicare & Medicaid Statistical Supplement,* 2013, and earlier reports. See also <http://www.cms.gov/Research-Statistics-Data-and-Systems/Statistics-Trends-and-Reports/MedicareMedicaidStatSupp/index.html>.

Table 152. Medicare—Enrollment by State and Other Areas: 2000 to 2011

[In thousands (39,632 represents 39,632,000). Hospital (HI) and/or supplementary medical insurance (SMI) enrollment as of July 1]

State and area	2000	2005	2010	2011	State and area	2000	2005	2010	2011
All areas [1]	39,632	42,500	47,664	48,849	MO	859	912	1,004	1,022
U.S.	38,782	41,536	46,585	47,741	MT	137	148	170	174
AL	686	755	845	864	NE	254	261	279	283
AK	42	52	66	69	NV	246	297	357	372
AZ	676	794	930	962	NH	169	192	223	229
AR	434	472	531	542	NJ	1,212	1,227	1,327	1,352
CA	3,922	4,201	4,757	4,901	NM	234	267	313	322
CO	470	522	625	650	NY	2,695	2,776	2,988	3,041
CT	518	525	568	577	NC	1,131	1,277	1,490	1,533
DE	115	128	149	154	ND	102	104	109	110
DC	75	73	78	80	OH	1,706	1,754	1,901	1,934
FL	2,827	3,046	3,375	3,472	OK	507	541	603	615
GA	928	1,039	1,236	1,281	OR	496	540	621	640
HI	168	182	206	213	PA	2,091	2,132	2,283	2,312
ID	167	192	230	238	RI	170	172	183	186
IL	1,626	1,691	1,839	1,872	SC	570	651	774	799
IN	848	905	1,006	1,027	SD	118	125	137	139
IA	475	490	517	523	TN	830	922	1,058	1,086
KS	386	402	433	439	TX	2,268	2,545	3,001	3,104
KY	618	678	760	777	UT	209	237	283	292
LA	600	610	687	703	VT	89	96	112	115
ME	216	235	265	271	VA	896	993	1,141	1,173
MD	646	695	785	807	WA	736	821	972	1,005
MA	961	971	1,061	1,085	WV	338	355	382	386
MI	1,402	1,483	1,651	1,689	WI	776	826	911	931
MN	655	698	786	804	WY	66	71	80	82
MS	419	454	497	507	Outlying areas [2]	850	964	1,079	1,109

[1] Includes outlying areas. [2] Includes Puerto Rico, Guam, Virgin Islands, residence unknown, and all other outlying areas not shown separately.

Source: U.S. Centers for Medicare and Medicaid Services, *Medicare & Medicaid Statistical Supplement,* annual, <http://www.cms.gov/Research-Statistics-Data-and-Systems/Statistics-Trends-and-Reports/MedicareMedicaidStatSupp/index.html>, accessed April 2013.

Table 153. Medicaid—Selected Characteristics of Persons Covered: 2011

[In thousands, except percent (50,835 represents 50,835,000). Represents number of persons as of March of following year who were enrolled at any time in year shown. Excludes unrelated individuals under age 15. Persons did not have to receive medical care paid for by Medicaid in order to be counted. For explanation of poverty level, see text, Section 13. For information on confidentiality protection, sampling error, nonsampling error, and definitions, see <www.census.gov/apsd/techdoc/cps/cpsmar12.pdf>]

Poverty status	Total [1]	White alone [2]	Black alone [3]	Asian alone [4]	His-panic [5]	Under 18 years	18–44 years	45–64 years	65 years and over
Persons covered, total	50,835	34,302	11,033	2,277	14,437	26,345	13,098	7,508	3,883
Below poverty level	21,741	13,480	6,166	726	6,871	11,949	5,762	2,957	1,074
Above poverty level	29,094	20,822	4,867	1,551	7,566	14,396	7,336	4,551	2,809
Percent of population covered	16.5	14.2	27.8	14.1	27.6	35.5	11.8	9.2	9.4
Below poverty level	47.0	43.7	56.4	36.8	51.9	74.1	32.7	33.3	29.7
Above poverty level	11.1	9.9	16.9	11.0	19.3	24.8	7.8	6.2	7.4

[1] Includes other races, not shown separately. [2] White alone refers to people who reported White and did not report any other race category. [3] Black alone refers to people who reported Black and did not report any other race category. [4] Asian alone refers to people who reported Asian and did not report any other race category. [5] Persons of Hispanic origin may be of any race.

Source: U.S. Census Bureau, *Income, Poverty, and Health Insurance Coverage in the United States: 2011,* Current Population Reports, P60-243; Table HI01, "Health Insurance Coverage Status and Type of Coverage by Selected Characteristics: 2011"; and Table HI03, "Health Insurance Coverage Status and Type of Coverage by Selected Characteristics for Poor People in the Poverty Universe: 2011." See also <http://www.census.gov/hhes/www/hlthins/index.html>.

Table 154. Medicare Insurance Trust Funds: 1990 to 2012

[In billions of dollars (126.3 represents $126,300,000,000), on cash basis, for calendar years. SMI is Supplementary Medical Insurance. Medicare has two components: Hospital Insurance (HI) or Medicare Part A, and Supplementary Medical Insurance (SMI) consisting of Medicare Part B and Part D (prescription drug coverage). See text, this section, for details]

Type of trust fund	1990	1995	2000	2005	2008	2009	2010	2011	2012
TOTAL MEDICARE									
Total income.................................	126.3	175.3	257.1	357.5	480.8	508.3	486.1	530.0	536.9
Total expenditures...........................	111.0	184.2	221.8	336.4	468.2	509.0	522.9	549.1	574.2
Assets, end of year......................	114.4	143.4	221.5	309.8	381.6	380.8	344.0	324.9	287.6
HOSPITAL INSURANCE, PART A									
Net contribution income [1].................	71.9	104.2	155.5	183.3	214.4	208.3	199.5	214.8	228.6
Interest received [2].........................	8.5	10.8	11.7	16.1	16.4	17.1	16.1	14.2	14.5
Benefit payments [3].........................	66.2	116.4	128.5	180.0	232.3	239.3	244.5	252.9	262.9
Trust fund balance, end of year...........	98.9	130.3	177.5	285.8	321.3	304.2	271.9	244.2	220.4
SMI, PART B									
Premiums from enrollees [4]...............	11.3	19.7	20.6	37.5	50.2	56.0	52.0	57.5	58.0
Government contributions [5]...............	33.0	39.0	65.9	118.1	146.8	162.8	153.5	170.2	163.8
Interest received [2].........................	1.6	1.6	3.5	1.4	3.6	3.1	3.3	5.9	5.2
Benefit payments [3].........................	42.5	65.0	88.9	149.9	180.3	202.6	209.7	221.7	236.5
Trust fund balance, end of year...........	15.5	13.1	44.0	24.0	59.4	75.5	71.4	79.7	66.2
SMI, PART D									
Premiums from enrollees [6]...............	(X)	(X)	(X)	–	5.0	6.3	6.5	7.7	8.3
Government contributions [7]...............	(X)	(X)	(X)	1.1	37.3	47.1	51.1	52.6	50.1
Interest received...........................	(X)	(X)	(X)	–	–	–	–	–	–
Benefit payments [8].........................	(X)	(X)	(X)	1.1	49.0	60.5	61.7	66.7	66.5
Trust fund balance, end of year...........	(X)	(X)	(X)	–	0.9	1.1	0.7	1.0	1.0

– Represents or rounds to zero. X Not applicable. [1] Includes income from payroll taxes, taxation of benefits, railroad retirement account transfers, reimbursement for uninsured persons, premiums from voluntary enrollees, and payments for military wage credits. [2] Includes recoveries of amounts reimbursed from the trust fund, receipts from fraud and abuse control program, and other miscellaneous income. [3] Includes monies transferred to the SMI trust fund in 1998-2003 for home health agency costs. In 2008 benefit payments were $223,815 million and include a transfer of $8,484 million to the general fund of the Treasury for HI hospice costs that were misallocated to, and paid from, the Part B account of the SMI trust fund from May 2005 to September 2007. (The general fund, in turn, transferred $8,484 million to the Part B account.) [4] Includes adjustments for benefit checks issued at the end of the year instead of early January. [5] Matching payments from the general fund, plus certain interest-adjustment items. See also footnote 4. [6] Premiums include both amounts withheld from Social Security benefit checks (and other certain Federal benefit payments) and amounts paid directly to Part D plans. [7] Includes all federal government transfers, including amounts for the general subsidy, reinsurance, employer drug subsidy, low-income subsidy, administrative expenses, risk sharing, and State expenses for making low-income eligibility determinations. Includes amounts for the transitional assistance benefits in 2004-2007. [8] Includes payments to plans, subsidies to employer-sponsored retiree prescription drug plans, payments to States for making low-income eligibility determinations, Part D drug premiums collected from beneficiaries and transferred to Medicare Advantage plans and private drug plans, and premium amounts paid directly by enrollees to plans. (The last item is on an estimated basis; see note 6.) Includes amounts for transitional assistance benefits in 2004-2007.

Source: U.S. Centers for Medicare and Medicaid Services, *2013 Annual Report of the Boards of Trustees of the Federal Hospital Insurance and Federal Supplementary Medical Insurance Trust Funds*, May 2013. See also <http://www.cms.gov/Research-Statistics-Data-and-Systems/Statistics-Trends-and-Reports/ReportsTrustFunds/index.html>.

Table 155. Medicare Hospital Insurance and Supplementary Medical Insurance Average Costs per Beneficiary: 1971 to 2012

[In dollars. See headnote, Table 154]

Year	Total	Hospital Insurance	SMI Part B	SMI Part D	Year	Total	Hospital Insurance	SMI Part B	SMI Part D
1971.........	388	282	107	(X)	1992.........	3,840	2,385	1,455	(X)
1972.........	419	304	115	(X)	1993.........	4,218	2,603	1,615	(X)
1973.........	420	307	113	(X)	1994.........	4,495	2,825	1,670	(X)
1974.........	528	384	144	(X)	1995.........	4,953	3,130	1,823	(X)
1975.........	642	462	180	(X)	1996.........	5,312	3,412	1,900	(X)
1976.........	736	528	207	(X)	1997.........	5,612	3,616	1,996	(X)
1977.........	844	605	239	(X)	1998.........	5,540	3,468	2,071	(X)
1978.........	941	662	280	(X)	1999.........	5,486	3,306	2,180	(X)
1979.........	1,080	753	327	(X)	2000.........	5,653	3,272	2,381	(X)
1980.........	1,285	895	390	(X)	2001.........	6,204	3,558	2,646	(X)
1981.........	1,535	1,064	471	(X)	2002.........	6,664	3,743	2,922	(X)
1982.........	1,773	1,227	546	(X)	2003.........	6,942	3,733	3,209	(X)
1983.........	1,959	1,331	628	(X)	2004.........	7,489	4,039	3,450	(X)
1984.........	2,112	1,441	671	(X)	2005.........	8,016	4,262	3,754	0
1985.........	2,322	1,554	768	(X)	2006.........	10,208	4,388	4,111	1,708
1986.........	2,454	1,592	861	(X)	2007.........	10,397	4,548	4,293	1,556
1987.........	2,545	1,553	992	(X)	2008.........	10,945	5,145	4,296	1,504
1988.........	2,697	1,620	1,077	(X)	2009.........	11,692	5,172	4,721	1,798
1989.........	3,011	1,816	1,195	(X)	2010.........	11,715	5,161	4,779	1,775
1990.........	3,267	1,963	1,304	(X)	2011.........	12,019	5,212	4,938	1,868
1991.........	3,502	2,076	1,426	(X)	2012.........	12,103	5,227	5,097	1,779

X Not applicable.

Source: U.S. Centers for Medicare and Medicaid Services, Trustees Report & Trust Funds, "2013 Expanded and Supplementary Tables," <http://www.cms.gov/Research-Statistics-Data-and-Systems/Statistics-Trends-and-Reports/ReportsTrustFunds/index.html>, accessed July 2013.

Table 156. Medicaid—Beneficiaries and Payments: 2000 to 2010

[42,887 represents 42,887,000. For year ending September 30]

Basis of eligibility and type of service	Beneficiaries (1,000) [1]				Payments (mil. dol.)			
	2000	2005	2009	2010	2000	2005	2009	2010
Total	**42,887**	**57,651**	**62,589**	**64,129**	**168,443**	**274,851**	**326,025**	**331,563**
Age 65 and over	3,730	4,395	4,195	4,195	44,560	63,415	64,332	64,436
Blind/Disabled	6,890	8,211	9,036	9,107	72,772	119,305	141,596	143,781
Children	19,018	26,341	28,698	29,709	23,490	41,863	57,675	59,395
Adults	8,671	12,533	14,189	15,065	17,671	32,162	44,250	46,275
Foster care children	761	874	936	894	3,309	5,286	5,920	5,524
Unknown	3,817	5,268	4,837	4,380	6,639	12,539	10,445	10,125
BCCA WOMEN [2]	(NA)	29	49	51	(NA)	281	624	645
All service categories:								
Capitated care [3]	21,292	33,496	41,674	45,483	25,026	46,421	82,981	91,152
Clinic services	7,678	11,918	12,871	12,895	6,138	8,921	10,187	10,112
Dental services	5,922	9,317	11,110	12,503	1,413	3,040	4,701	5,414
Home health services	1,007	1,195	1,087	1,128	3,133	5,362	7,205	7,238
ICF/MR services [4]	119	109	101	98	9,376	11,709	12,876	12,422
Inpatient hospital services	4,913	5,480	5,443	4,463	24,131	35,131	38,481	32,760
Lab and X-ray services	11,439	15,959	16,379	16,565	1,292	2,917	3,238	3,425
Mental health facility services [5]	100	120	115	120	1,769	2,301	2,468	2,514
Nursing facility services	1,706	1,711	1,645	1,500	34,528	44,790	48,625	47,831
Other care [6]	9,022	12,346	12,621	12,489	14,755	26,421	37,798	40,272
Outpatient hospital services	13,170	16,234	16,544	15,335	7,082	10,011	12,153	12,233
Other practitioner services	4,758	5,893	5,480	5,844	664	1,180	937	1,085
PCCM services [7]	5,649	8,723	8,223	8,540	177	232	338	422
Prescribed drugs	20,325	28,390	26,687	28,349	19,898	42,849	25,367	26,125
Physician services	18,965	24,238	23,070	23,846	6,809	11,269	11,435	11,795
Personal support services [8]	4,559	6,807	6,687	6,997	11,629	20,657	26,097	25,110
Sterilizations	137	178	124	131	128	211	147	136
Unknown	74	73	167	137	496	1,428	990	1,514

NA Not available. [1] Beneficiaries data do not add due to number of beneficiaries that are reported in more than one category. [2] Women-Breast and Cervical Cancer Assistance. [3] HMO payments and prepaid health plans. [4] Intermediate care facilities for the mentally retarded. [5] Inpatient mental health facilities for individuals under 21 and for individuals 65 years and older. [6] Includes beneficiaries of, and payments for, other care not shown separately. [7] Primary Care Case Management Services. [8] Includes personal care services, rehabilitative services, physical occupational targeted case management services, speech therapies, hospice services, nurse midwife services, nurse practitioner services, private duty nursing services, and religious nonmedical health care institutions.

Source: U.S. Centers for Medicare and Medicaid Services, "Medicaid Statistical Information System (MSIS) State Summary Datamarts," <https://www.cms.gov/Research-Statistics-Data-and-Systems/Computer-Data-and-Systems/MedicaidDataSourcesGenInfo/MSIS-Mart-Home.html>, accessed July 2013.

Table 157. Medicaid—Summary by State: 2000 and 2010

[42,887 represents 42,887,000. For year ending September 30]

State	Beneficiaries [1] (1,000)		Payments [2] (mil. dol.)		State	Beneficiaries [1] (1,000)		Payments [2] (mil. dol.)	
	2000	2010	2000	2010		2000	2010	2000	2010
U.S.	**42,887**	**64,129**	**168,443**	**331,563**	MO	890	(NA)	3,274	(NA)
AL	619	931	2,393	4,042	MT	104	126	422	762
AK	96	127	473	1,207	NE	229	269	960	1,586
AZ	681	1,805	2,112	9,511	NV	138	334	516	1,300
AR	489	773	1,543	3,799	NH	97	148	651	1,009
CA	7,918	11,212	17,105	34,686	NJ	822	1,229	4,714	8,558
CO	381	682	1,809	3,300	NM	376	557	1,249	2,771
CT	420	664	2,839	5,390	NY	3,420	5,011	26,148	42,724
DE	115	210	529	1,342	NC	1,214	1,876	4,834	9,591
DC	139	211	793	1,806	ND	63	83	358	682
FL	2,373	3,656	7,433	16,131	OH	1,305	2,319	7,115	14,450
GA	1,369	1,875	3,624	6,969	OK	507	853	1,604	3,713
HI	194	288	600	1,353	OR	558	644	1,714	3,187
ID	131	(NA)	594	(NA)	PA	1,492	2,326	6,366	15,894
IL	1,519	2,758	7,807	11,646	RI	179	214	1,070	1,574
IN	706	1,177	2,977	5,753	SC	689	953	2,765	5,090
IA	314	508	1,477	3,005	SD	102	142	402	777
KS	263	364	1,227	2,295	TN	1,568	1,532	3,491	9,061
KY	764	959	2,921	5,304	TX	2,633	4,745	9,277	20,718
LA	761	1,237	2,632	5,491	UT	225	369	960	1,995
ME	194	330	1,310	1,468	VT	139	181	480	1,000
MD	626	940	3,003	6,838	VA	627	969	2,479	5,861
MA	1,060	1,637	5,413	11,069	WA	896	1,330	2,435	6,312
MI	1,352	2,219	4,881	11,380	WV	342	397	1,394	2,690
MN	558	851	3,280	7,136	WI	577	1,230	2,968	5,403
MS	605	801	1,808	3,364	WY	46	76	215	572

NA Not available. [1] Persons who had payments made on their behalf at any time during the fiscal year. [2] Payments are for fiscal year and reflect federal and state contribution payments. Data exclude disproportionate share hospital payments. Disproportionate share hospitals receive higher Medicaid reimbursement than other hospitals because they treat a disproportionate share of Medicaid patients.

Source: U.S. Centers for Medicare and Medicaid Services, "Medicaid Statistical Information System (MSIS) State Summary Datamarts," <http://www.cms.gov/Research-Statistics-Data-and-Systems/Computer-Data-and-Systems/MedicaidDataSourcesGenInfo/MSIS-Mart-Home.html>, accessed July 2013.

Table 158. Medicaid Managed Care Enrollment by State and Other Areas: 1995 to 2011

[In thousands except as noted (33,373 represents 33,373,000). For year ending June 30. The unduplicated Medicaid enrollment figures include individuals in state health care reform programs that expand eligibility beyond traditional Medicaid eligibility standards. The unduplicated managed care enrollment figures includes enrollees receiving comprehensive and limited benefits]

State and other areas	Total enroll-ment	Managed care enrollment		State and other areas	Total enroll-ment	Managed care enrollment		State and other areas	Total enroll-ment	Managed care enrollment	
		Number	Percent of total			Number	Percent of total			Number	Percent of total
1995.......	33,373	9,800	29.4	HI.........	272	269	98.7	NY.........	4,925	3,778	76.7
2000.......	33,690	18,786	55.8	ID.........	231	231	100.0	NC.........	1,488	1,239	83.2
2006.......	45,653	29,830	65.3	IL.........	2,787	1,889	67.8	ND.........	67	42	63.6
2007.......	45,962	29,463	64.1	IN.........	1,056	742	70.3	OH........	2,130	1,606	75.4
2008.......	47,143	33,428	70.1	IA.........	441	402	91.1	OK........	684	592	86.5
2009.......	50,472	36,202	71.7	KS.........	355	310	87.4	OR........	653	641	98.2
2010.......	54,612	39,020	71.5	KY.........	823	736	89.4	PA........	2,135	1,741	81.5
2011				LA........	1,209	790	65.3	RI........	197	135	68.6
Total......	57,107	42,385	74.2	ME......	358	176	49.3	SC........	862	862	100.0
U.S.......	56,007	41,488	74.1	MD.......	986	736	74.6	SD........	120	91	75.8
AL........	931	568	61.1	MA.......	1,566	832	53.1	TN........	1,219	1,219	100.0
AK........	121	–	–	MI.........	1,818	1,607	88.4	TX........	3,943	2,787	70.7
AZ........	1,352	1,199	88.7	MN........	848	557	65.7	UT........	270	269	99.8
AR........	608	477	78.4	MS........	622	542	87.2	VT........	177	104	58.5
CA........	7,581	4,553	60.1	MO.......	896	875	97.7	VA........	915	532	58.2
CO.......	584	552	94.6	MT........	106	81	76.1	WA.......	1,183	1,042	88.1
CT........	579	397	68.6	NE........	237	202	85.1	WV.......	327	167	51.0
DE........	201	162	80.5	NV........	298	249	83.6	WI........	1,173	747	63.7
DC........	202	136	67.4	NH........	135	–	–	WY........	70	–	–
FL........	3,069	1,959	63.8	NJ........	1,099	854	77.7	PR.......	1,089	897	82.3
GA........	1,548	1,414	91.3	NM........	551	401	72.8	VI.........	11	–	–

– Represents zero.

Source: U.S. Centers for Medicare and Medicaid Services, Data and System Group, *2011 Medicaid Managed Care Enrollment Report.* See also <http://www.medicaid.gov/Medicaid-CHIP-Program-Information/By-Topics/Data-and-Systems/Medicaid-Managed-Care/Medicaid-Managed-Care-Enrollment-Report.html>.

Table 159. Medicare Hospital Insurance and Supplemental Medical Insurance Expenditures, Total and as a Percent of GDP: 1970 to 2030

[In millions of dollars (1,038,350 represents $1,038,350,000,000), except percent. Incurred amounts relate to expenditures for services performed in a given year, even if payment for those expenditures occurs in a later year. The Medicare program has two components: Medicare Part A Hospital Insurance (HI); and Supplementary Medical Insurance (SMI), consisting of Part B Medical Insurance, and Part D Prescription Drug Coverage. See text in this section for details]

Year	GDP	Medicare expenditures				Medicare expenditures as percent of GDP			
		Total	HI Part A	SMI Part B	SMI Part D	Total	HI Part A	SMI Part B	SMI Part D
ACTUAL									
1970.............	1,038,350	7,638	5,400	2,237	(X)	0.74	0.52	0.22	(X)
1980.............	2,788,150	36,797	25,249	11,548	(X)	1.32	0.91	0.41	(X)
1990.............	5,800,525	110,410	66,292	44,118	(X)	1.90	1.14	0.76	(X)
2000.............	9,951,475	224,013	130,832	93,180	(X)	2.25	1.31	0.94	(X)
2001.............	10,286,175	246,737	142,778	103,958	(X)	2.40	1.39	1.01	(X)
2002.............	10,642,300	264,674	151,695	112,979	(X)	2.49	1.43	1.06	(X)
2003.............	11,142,225	281,959	157,687	124,272	(X)	2.53	1.42	1.12	(X)
2004.............	11,853,250	309,874	170,144	139,290	440	2.61	1.44	1.18	(X)
2005.............	12,622,950	339,106	184,470	153,539	1,098	2.69	1.46	1.22	0.01
2006.............	13,377,200	410,423	195,301	170,473	44,649	3.07	1.46	1.27	0.33
2007.............	14,028,675	441,483	206,575	183,736	51,173	3.15	1.47	1.31	0.36
2008.............	14,291,550	460,258	222,516	183,579	54,164	3.22	1.56	1.28	0.38
2009.............	13,973,650	500,413	236,430	205,787	58,196	3.58	1.69	1.47	0.42
2010.............	14,498,925	520,529	242,897	214,761	62,871	3.59	1.68	1.48	0.43
2011.............	15,075,675	546,114	253,353	226,335	66,426	3.62	1.68	1.50	0.44
2012.............	15,699,644	572,627	260,325	242,391	69,911	3.65	1.66	1.54	0.45
PROJECTED									
2015.............	18,238,910	638,693	280,363	269,717	88,614	3.50	1.54	1.48	0.49
2020.............	23,746,970	920,520	389,688	392,727	138,104	3.88	1.64	1.65	0.58
2025.............	29,744,270	1,355,407	553,323	589,987	212,097	4.56	1.86	1.98	0.71
2030.............	37,121,131	1,907,491	764,137	833,729	309,625	5.14	2.06	2.25	0.83

X Not applicable.

Source: U.S. Centers for Medicare and Medicaid Services, Trustees Report & Trust Funds, "2013 Expanded and Supplementary Tables," <http://www.cms.gov/Research-Statistics-Data-and-Systems/Statistics-Trends-and-Reports/ReportsTrustFunds/index.html>, accessed July 2013.

Table 160. Health Insurance Coverage Status by Selected Characteristics: 2011

[308,827 represents 308,827,000. Persons as of following year for coverage in the year shown. Government health insurance includes Medicare, Medicaid, and military plans. Based on Current Population Survey, Annual Social and Economic Supplement (ASEC); see text, Section 1 and Appendix III]

Characteristic	Number (1,000)							Percent			
		Covered by private or government health insurance					Not covered by health insur-ance	Covered by private or government health insurance			Not covered by health insur-ance
			Private		Government						
	Total persons	Total [1]	Total	Employer based	Medi-care	Medic-aid		Total [1]	Private	Medic-aid	
2011	**308,827**	**260,214**	**197,323**	**170,102**	**46,922**	**50,835**	**48,613**	**84.3**	**63.9**	**16.5**	**15.7**
Age:											
Under 18 years	74,108	67,143	44,047	40,561	611	26,345	6,964	90.6	59.4	35.5	9.4
Under 6 years	24,299	22,235	13,219	12,420	229	9,926	2,064	91.5	54.4	40.8	8.5
6 to 11 years	24,469	22,248	14,586	13,610	181	8,825	2,221	90.9	59.6	36.1	9.1
12 to 17 years	25,340	22,661	16,242	14,531	201	7,594	2,679	89.4	64.1	30.0	10.6
18 to 24 years	30,140	22,491	18,088	13,945	255	4,832	7,649	74.6	60.0	16.0	25.4
25 to 34 years	41,219	29,690	24,976	22,799	624	4,495	11,529	72.0	60.6	10.9	28.0
35 to 44 years	39,927	31,528	27,678	25,793	998	3,771	8,399	79.0	69.3	9.4	21.0
45 to 54 years	43,955	36,102	31,330	28,759	2,101	4,014	7,853	82.1	71.3	9.1	17.9
55 to 64 years	37,971	32,442	27,106	24,108	3,836	3,494	5,529	85.4	71.4	9.2	14.6
65 years and over	41,507	40,817	24,098	14,137	38,496	3,883	690	98.3	58.1	9.4	1.7
Sex:											
Male	151,175	125,604	96,703	84,404	20,936	23,362	25,571	83.1	64.0	15.5	16.9
Female	157,653	134,610	100,620	85,698	25,985	27,473	23,043	85.4	63.8	17.4	14.6
Race:											
White alone [2]	241,586	205,595	160,923	137,684	39,534	34,302	35,991	85.1	66.6	14.2	14.9
Black alone [2]	39,696	31,974	19,710	17,699	4,997	11,033	7,722	80.5	49.7	27.8	19.5
Asian alone [2]	16,094	13,398	10,715	9,436	1,574	2,277	2,696	83.2	66.6	14.1	16.8
Hispanic origin [3]	52,358	36,582	21,743	19,799	3,563	14,437	15,776	69.9	41.5	27.6	30.1
Household income:											
Less than $25,000	58,732	43,808	15,605	8,828	15,372	22,697	14,923	74.6	26.6	38.6	25.4
$25,000–$49,999	71,864	56,423	36,712	28,717	14,599	15,734	15,442	78.5	51.1	21.9	21.5
$50,000–$74,999	57,124	48,313	40,557	35,942	7,295	6,414	8,811	84.6	71.0	11.2	15.4
$75,000 or more	121,107	111,670	104,449	96,615	9,656	5,990	9,437	92.2	86.2	4.9	7.8
Persons below poverty	46,247	32,573	9,692	5,857	5,617	21,741	13,674	70.4	21.0	47.0	29.6

[1] Includes other private and government insurance, not shown separately. Persons with coverage counted only once in total, even though they may have been covered by more than one type of policy. [2] Refers to people who reported specified race and did not report any other race category. [3] Persons of Hispanic origin may be of any race.

Source: U.S. Census Bureau, *Income, Poverty, and Health Insurance Coverage in the United States: 2011*, Current Population Reports P60-243, September 2012; Table HI01, "Health Insurance Coverage Status and Type of Coverage by Selected Characteristics: 2011" and Table HI03, "Health Insurance Coverage Status and Type of Coverage by Selected Characteristics for Poor People in the Poverty Universe: 2011." See also <http://www.census.gov/hhes/www/hlthins/>.

Table 161. Persons With and Without Health Insurance Coverage by State: 2011

[260,214 represents 260,214,000. Based on the Current Population Survey, Annual Social and Economic Supplement (ASEC), see text, Section 1 and Appendix III]

State	Total persons covered (1,000)	Total persons not covered		Children not covered		State	Total persons covered (1,000)	Total persons not covered		Children not covered	
		Number (1,000)	Percent of total	Number (1,000)	Percent of total			Number (1,000)	Percent of total	Number (1,000)	Percent of total
U.S.	**260,214**	**48,613**	**15.7**	**6,964**	**9.4**	MO	5,020	877	14.9	162	11.5
AL	4,143	622	13.0	86	7.3	MT	806	180	18.3	27	12.3
AK	584	130	18.2	20	10.5	NE	1,600	225	12.3	38	8.3
AZ	5,424	1,137	17.3	219	13.4	NV	2,077	607	22.6	139	21.0
AR	2,401	508	17.5	56	8.1	NH	1,138	163	12.5	21	7.5
CA	30,209	7,425	19.7	1,008	10.8	NJ	7,316	1,336	15.4	190	9.4
CO	4,239	788	15.7	131	10.5	NM	1,640	399	19.6	51	10.0
CT	3,215	303	8.6	43	5.3	NY	16,986	2,355	12.2	284	6.6
DE	812	90	10.0	13	6.3	NC	7,955	1,550	16.3	215	9.3
DC	567	52	8.4	5	4.5	ND	614	61	9.1	7	4.5
FL	15,247	3,765	19.8	516	13.0	OH	9,771	1,549	13.7	230	8.7
GA	7,821	1,862	19.2	278	10.9	OK	3,131	636	16.9	60	6.5
HI	1,235	105	7.8	13	4.2	OR	3,324	532	13.8	64	7.4
ID	1,308	266	16.9	48	11.2	PA	11,341	1,375	10.8	206	7.6
IL	10,837	1,873	14.7	191	6.2	RI	913	125	12.0	13	5.7
IN	5,589	764	12.0	88	5.6	SC	3,736	877	19.0	142	13.2
IA	2,730	303	10.0	36	5.0	SD	706	105	13.0	15	7.5
KS	2,434	380	13.5	68	9.4	TN	5,495	841	13.3	88	5.9
KY	3,689	621	14.4	47	4.7	TX	19,513	6,080	23.8	1,073	15.4
LA	3,568	938	20.8	131	11.6	UT	2,402	412	14.6	95	10.6
ME	1,196	133	10.0	17	6.3	VT	563	53	8.6	5	4.1
MD	5,009	802	13.8	136	10.0	VA	6,910	1,066	13.4	111	5.9
MA	6,304	219	3.4	35	2.5	WA	5,831	986	14.5	143	8.8
MI	8,493	1,209	12.5	123	5.4	WV	1,553	273	14.9	37	9.7
MN	4,798	487	9.2	82	6.4	WI	5,097	589	10.4	77	5.8
MS	2,458	476	16.2	69	9.0	WY	463	100	17.8	14	10.2

Source: U.S. Census Bureau, *Income, Poverty, and Health Insurance Coverage in the United States: 2011*, Current Population Reports, P60-243, September 2012; Table HI06, "Health Insurance Coverage Status by State all People: 2011"; and <http://www.census.gov/hhes/www/cpstc/cps_table_creator.html>, accessed February 2013. See also <http://www.census.gov/hhes/www/hlthins/index.html>.

Table 162. People Without Health Insurance for the Entire Year by Selected Characteristics: 2010 and 2011

[In thousands, except as noted (306,553 represents 306,553,000). Based on the Current Population Survey; Annual Social and Economic Supplement (ASEC); see text, Section 1 and Appendix III]

Characteristic	2010 [1]			2011		
	Total persons	Uninsured Persons		Total persons	Uninsured Persons	
		Number	Percent distribution		Number	Percent distribution
Total [2]	**306,553**	**49,951**	**100.0**	**308,827**	**48,613**	**100.0**
Under 18 years........................	74,296	7,270	14.6	74,108	6,964	14.3
18 to 24 years.........................	29,808	8,141	16.3	30,140	7,649	15.7
25 to 34 years.........................	40,761	11,566	23.2	41,219	11,529	23.7
35 to 44 years.........................	40,153	8,806	17.6	39,927	8,399	17.3
45 to 54 years.........................	44,193	7,976	16.0	43,955	7,853	16.2
55 to 64 years.........................	37,565	5,400	10.8	37,971	5,529	11.4
65 years and over.....................	39,777	791	1.6	41,507	690	1.4
Male...................................	149,967	26,545	53.1	151,175	25,571	52.6
Female.................................	156,586	23,405	46.9	157,653	23,043	47.4
White alone [3]........................	240,281	36,688	73.4	241,586	35,991	74.0
White alone or in combination.......	246,879	37,703	75.5	248,198	37,001	76.1
Black alone [3]........................	39,350	8,202	16.4	39,696	7,722	15.9
Black alone or in combination.......	42,472	8,674	17.4	42,750	8,183	16.8
Asian alone [3]........................	15,619	2,881	5.8	16,094	2,696	5.5
Asian alone or in combination.......	17,249	3,075	6.2	17,821	2,888	5.9
Hispanic [4]...........................	51,074	15,667	31.4	52,358	15,776	32.5
White alone, not Hispanic...........	194,996	22,542	45.1	195,148	21,681	44.6

[1] Implementation of Census 2010-based population controls. [2] Includes other races not shown separately. [3] Refers to people who reported specified race and did not report any other race category. [4] Persons of Hispanic origin may be any race.

Source: U.S. Census Bureau, *Income, Poverty, and Health Insurance Coverage in the United States: 2011*, September 2012; and Health Insurance Detailed Tables HI01, "Health Insurance Coverage Status and Type of Coverage by Selected Characteristics: 2011," <http://www.census.gov/hhes/www/hlthins/index.html>, accessed March 2013.

Table 163. Percent of Workers Participating in Health Care Benefit Programs and Percent of Participants Required to Contribute: 2012

[Based on the March 2012 National Compensation Survey; survey drew responses from 6,618 private industry establishments of all sizes, representing about 103.9 million workers. Excludes farm and private households, the self-employed, Federal government, and establishments with no workers in the survey scope. For more information, see Appendix III, and the Bureau of Labor Statistics (BLS) Website <http://www.bls.gov/ncs/ebs/sp/ebnr0018.txt>]

Characteristic	Percent of workers participating—				Single coverage medical plans		Family coverage medical plans	
	Medical care	Dental care	Vision care	Out-patient prescription drug coverage	Employee contributions required (percent)	Average monthly contribution [1] (dol.)	Employee contributions required (percent)	Average monthly contribution [1] (dol.)
Total............................	**51**	**35**	**19**	**50**	**82**	**107.78**	**91**	**426.71**
Worker characteristics:								
Management, professional, and related..	67	52	27	66	85	105.78	92	418.82
Management, business, and financial...	72	58	30	71	85	105.26	93	431.36
Professional and related.................	64	49	26	63	85	106.08	92	411.61
Service.................................	25	17	9	25	83	106.30	91	528.95
Sales and office........................	50	34	16	49	84	111.66	93	431.43
Sales and related.......................	42	28	12	41	87	117.41	93	438.57
Office and administrative support.......	56	38	19	55	83	108.63	92	427.86
Natural resources, construction, and maintenance..........................	57	36	24	56	69	115.77	82	450.36
Production, transportation, and material moving........................	57	36	21	56	81	103.11	89	362.74
Production.............................	64	42	22	62	84	100.26	91	338.93
Transportation, and material moving...	50	31	20	49	78	106.98	86	394.71
Full-time [2]............................	64	45	24	63	83	106.57	91	424.14
Part-time [2]...........................	13	8	5	13	81	124.96	87	464.05
Union [3]...............................	78	61	47	77	60	102.63	68	337.47
Nonunion..............................	48	33	16	47	86	108.37	94	437.32
Average hourly wage: [4]								
$8.25 to under $10.69..................	19	10	6	19	84	115.77	93	512.17
$8.25 and less..........................	9	4	2	9	84	125.85	90	574.55
$10.69 to under $15.87.................	51	33	16	50	85	105.48	93	426.17
$15.87 to under $24.81.................	65	45	24	64	82	108.51	91	420.61
$24.81 and more.......................	73	57	32	72	81	106.19	88	404.79
$37.89 and more.......................	74	60	33	73	82	104.09	89	389.76

[1] The average is presented for all covered workers and excludes workers without the plan provision. Averages are for plans stating a flat monthly cost. [2] Employees are classified as working either a full-time or part-time schedule based on the definition used by each establishment. [3] Union workers are those whose wages are determined through collective bargaining. [4] The National Compensation Survey—Benefits program presents wage data in percentiles rather than dollar amounts; see "Technical Note" in source.

Source: U.S. Bureau of Labor Statistics, Annual Bulletin on Benefit Coverage, *National Compensation Survey: Employee Benefits in the United States, March 2012*, September 2012. See also <http://www.bls.gov/ncs/ebs/>.

Table 164. Retail Prescription Drug Sales: 1995 to 2010

[2,125 represents 2,125,000,000]

Sales outlet	Unit	1995	2000	2004	2005	2006	2007	2008	2009	2010
Number of prescriptions.............	**Mil.**	**2,125**	**2,865**	**3,274**	**3,279**	**3,419**	**3,530**	**3,559**	**3,633**	**3,676**
Traditional chain............	Mil.	908	1,335	1,494	1,513	1,599	1,652	1,677	1,731	1,760
Independent.................	Mil.	672	698	744	719	738	753	739	730	729
Mass merchant.............	Mil.	238	293	353	359	375	390	400	423	433
Supermarkets..............	Mil.	221	394	470	465	476	478	481	488	490
Mail order....................	Mil.	86	146	214	223	232	257	262	261	264
Percent distribution of brand/generic mix:										
Brand drugs................	Percent	59.8	57.6	54.1	50.6	44.8	40.8	35.5	32.6	28.8
Generic drugs...............	Percent	40.2	42.4	45.9	49.4	55.2	59.2	64.5	67.4	71.2
Retail sales..............	**Bil. dol.**	**72.2**	**145.6**	**216.7**	**226.1**	**243.2**	**249.2**	**249.2**	**261.3**	**266.4**
Traditional chain............	Bil. dol.	27.8	59.1	86.7	90.7	96.0	100.5	101.2	105.3	106.6
Independent.................	Bil. dol.	22.0	33.4	44.2	45.4	46.7	45.3	43.3	43.6	44.7
Mass merchant.............	Bil. dol.	7.7	13.5	16.8	17.5	21.6	23.6	24.2	25.6	26.6
Supermarkets..............	Bil. dol.	7.4	17.4	26.4	26.9	28.1	27.3	25.2	25.9	25.9
Mail order....................	Bil. dol.	7.4	22.1	42.7	45.5	50.9	52.5	55.4	61.3	62.6
Average prices [1]										
All prescriptions.............	Dollars	30.01	45.79	62.64	63.87	66.97	68.77	71.69	75.66	79.39
Brand drugs................	Dollars	40.22	65.29	91.80	97.65	112.24	121.26	137.98	151.06	166.61
Generic drugs...............	Dollars	14.84	19.33	28.23	29.21	30.17	32.60	35.21	39.25	44.14

[1] Excludes mail order.

Source: National Association of Chain Drug Stores, Alexandria, VA, *NACDS Foundation Chain Pharmacy Industry Profile, 2011-12*, ©. See also <http://www.nacds.org>.

Table 165. Annual Revenue for Health Care Industries: 2009 to 2011

[In millions of dollars (1,842,674 represents $1,842,674,000,000). For all firms, and tax-exempt employer firms. Estimates have been adjusted to the results of the 2007 Economic Census. Based on the Service Annual Survey and administrative data; see Appendix III. All firms in NAICS 6211, 6212, 6213, and 6215 are defined as taxable]

Kind of business	2007 NAICS code [1]	Total, all firms [2]			Taxable employer firms		
		2009	2010	2011	2009	2010	2011
Health care and social assistance...............	**62**	**1,842,674**	**1,917,183**	**1,998,260**	**907,384**	**938,503**	**982,197**
Ambulatory health care services [3]......................	621	731,930	756,477	786,448	662,037	683,658	709,719
Offices of physicians...................................	6211	361,897	372,579	385,929	361,897	372,579	385,929
Offices of dentists....................................	6212	99,175	101,619	103,758	99,175	101,619	103,758
Offices of other health practitioners....................	6213	57,333	60,003	62,743	57,333	60,003	62,743
Offices of chiropractors.............................	62131	10,383	10,642	10,999	10,383	10,642	10,999
Offices of optometrists..............................	62132	11,414	11,684	12,009	11,414	11,684	12,009
Offices of mental health practitioners...............	62133	6,222	6,702	7,360	6,222	6,702	7,360
Offices of PT/OT/speech therapy & audiology [4]....	62134	21,263	22,363	23,335	21,263	22,363	23,335
Outpatient care centers................................	6214	84,234	88,821	94,299	41,692	45,344	47,925
Medical & diagnostic laboratories......................	6215	44,944	45,318	47,189	44,944	45,318	47,189
Home health care services............................	6216	55,367	58,116	61,075	38,496	40,204	42,453
Other ambulatory health care services..............	6219	28,980	30,021	31,455	17,740	18,591	19,722
Hospitals [3]..	622	787,121	822,590	862,086	97,458	99,860	109,500
General medical & surgical hospitals..................	6221	735,136	767,738	803,730	79,159	79,912	87,718
Psychiatric & substance abuse hospitals.............	6222	18,500	19,216	18,716	4,331	4,620	4,042
Other specialty hospitals.............................	6223	33,485	35,636	39,640	13,968	15,328	17,740
Nursing and residential care facilities [3].................	623	183,916	192,035	200,107	112,422	118,453	124,805
Nursing care facilities.................................	6231	100,832	105,297	110,314	77,499	81,648	86,432
Residential mental retardation/health facilities.......	6232	30,490	31,948	32,633	9,348	9,885	10,043
Residential mental retardation facilities.............	62321	20,933	21,807	22,377	5,899	6,184	6,246
Community care facilities for the elderly..............	6233	44,502	46,594	48,915	24,242	25,608	26,951
Continuing care retirement communities............	623311	28,437	29,332	30,475	11,516	11,780	12,152
Homes for the elderly...............................	623312	16,065	17,262	18,440	12,726	13,828	14,799
Other residential care facilities........................	6239	8,092	8,196	8,245	1,333	1,312	1,379
Social assistance [3]......................................	624	139,707	146,081	149,619	35,467	36,532	38,173
Individual and family services..........................	6241	68,551	71,847	73,748	13,922	14,832	15,911
Community food and housing, and emergency and other relief services............................	6242	26,709	28,569	29,240	477	468	499
Vocational rehabilitation services......................	6243	12,610	13,220	13,604	1,872	1,980	1,976
Child day care services................................	6244	31,837	32,445	33,027	19,196	19,252	19,787

[1] North American Industry Classification System (NAICS), 2007; see text, Section 15. [2] Includes taxable and tax-exempt employer firms. [3] Includes other kinds of business, not shown separately. [4] Offices of physical, occupational, and speech therapists, and audiologists.

Source: U.S. Census Bureau, "2011 Annual Services Report: Health Care and Social Assistance Sector Services," January 2013. See also <http://www.census.gov/services/index.html>.

Table 166. Revenue for Selected Health Care Industries by Source of Revenue: 2010 and 2011

[In millions of dollars (372,579 represents $372,579,000,000). For aggregate taxable and tax-exempt employer firms. Estimates have been adjusted to the results of the 2007 Economic Census. Based on Service Annual Survey; see Appendix III]

Source of revenue	Offices of physicians (NAICS 6211)		Offices of dentists (NAICS 6212)		Hospitals (NAICS 622)		Nursing and residential care facilities (NAICS 623) [1]	
	2010	2011	2010	2011	2010	2011	2010	2011
Total.................................	**372,579**	**385,929**	**101,619**	**103,758**	**822,590**	**862,086**	**192,035**	**200,107**
Government [2]........................	98,625	102,626	11,079	11,116	314,554	328,542	117,861	123,509
Private insurance...................	168,716	174,834	43,308	44,304	356,925	373,214	12,874	13,597
Patient out-of-pocket from patients and families.........	32,954	34,165	38,751	40,038	32,896	34,755	40,728	42,090
Patient out-of-pocket from Social Security benefits.............	1,486	1,430	623	610	1,062	1,070	2,413	2,520
Other patient care revenue.........	52,787	54,044	6,913	6,756	58,988	64,793	7,765	7,982
Contributions, gifts, grants..........	2,443	2,627	(S)	(S)	17,418	18,313	3,133	3,220
Investment, property income.......	1,086	1,095	(S)	(S)	9,955	9,454	1,867	1,762
All other non-operating revenue...........................	14,481	15,107	(S)	(S)	30,790	31,942	5,392	5,424

S Figure does not meet publication standards. [1] Includes NAICS 6231 Nursing care facilities, NAICS 6232 Residential mental retardation, mental health and substance abuse facilities, NAICS 6233 Community care facilities for the elderly, and NAICS 6239 Other residential care facilities. [2] Includes Medicare, Medicaid, other government, and workers compensation.

Source: U.S. Census Bureau, *2011 Annual Services Report*, January 2013. See also <http://www.census.gov/services/index.html>.

Table 167. Employment in the Health Service Industries: 1990 to 2012

[In thousands (9,296 represents 9,296,000). See headnote, Table 659. Based on the 2012 North American Industry Classification System (NAICS); see text, Section 15. For more information on the NAICS changes, please see <http://www.bls.gov/ces/cesnaics12.htm>]

Industry	2012 NAICS code	1990	2000	2005	2008	2009	2010	2011	2012
Health care and social assistance [1].........	62	**9,296**	**12,718**	**14,536**	**15,798**	**16,103**	**16,375**	**16,634**	**16,972**
Ambulatory health care services [1]................	621	2,842	4,320	5,114	5,647	5,793	5,975	6,136	6,318
Offices of physicians.............................	6211	1,278	1,840	2,094	2,253	2,279	2,313	2,344	2,391
Offices of dentists................................	6212	513	688	774	818	818	828	844	853
Offices of other health practitioners............	6213	276	438	549	627	647	671	697	724
Medical and diagnostic laboratories............	6215	129	162	198	217	219	228	232	234
Home health care services......................	6216	288	633	821	961	1,027	1,085	1,140	1,199
Hospitals [1]..	622	3,513	3,954	4,345	4,627	4,667	4,679	4,722	4,791
General medical and surgical hospitals........	6221	3,305	3,745	4,096	4,337	4,367	4,357	4,363	4,417
Psychiatric and substance abuse hospitals....	6222	113	86	93	102	104	109	120	122
Other hospitals..................................	6223	95	123	156	188	196	213	239	252
Nursing and residential care facilities [1]..........	623	1,856	2,583	2,855	3,016	3,082	3,124	3,168	3,194
Nursing care facilities............................	6231	1,170	1,514	1,577	1,619	1,645	1,657	1,670	1,665

[1] Includes other industries, not shown separately.

Source: U.S. Bureau of Labor Statistics, Current Employment Statistics, "Employment, Hours, and Earnings—National," <http://www.bls.gov/ces/data.htm>, accessed March 2013.

Table 168. Osteopathic Physicians: 2002 to 2012

[As of May 31. Osteopathic physicians are fully qualified physicians licensed to practice medicine and to perform surgery. Osteopathic medicine has a strong emphasis on the interrelationship of the body's nerves, muscles, bones and organs. Doctors of osteopathic medicine, or D.O.s, apply the philosophy of treating the whole person to the prevention, diagnosis and treatment of illness, disease, and injury]

Characteristics	2002	2007	2012	Characteristics	2002	2007	2012
Total number of DOs............	**49,210**	**61,379**	**77,784**	Self-identified practice specialty [1].........	33,452	42,877	59,030
Female............................	11,832	17,667	26,277	Family and general practice..............	14,929	18,976	22,363
Male................................	37,378	43,712	51,478	General internal Medicine................	2,700	4,037	7,618
Age:				Pediatrics/adolescent medicine [2]........	985	1,791	3,373
Less than 35 years old..........	10,528	12,464	18,215	Obstetrics and gynecology...............	1,293	1,637	2,727
35 to 44 years old...............	14,993	17,870	22,243	Pediatric specialties [3].....................	334	392	(NA)
45 to 54 years old...............	13,434	15,812	15,973	Osteopathic specialties [4].................	423	602	946
55 to 64 years old...............	5,305	8,958	12,986	Other specialties [5].......................	12,292	14,665	22,003
65 years old and over...........	4,915	5,838	7,787	Unknown................................	496	777	(NA)
Unknown...........................	35	437	580				

NA Not available [1] DOs are assumed to be in active practice if they are under age 65 and have not informed the AOA that they are retired or inactive. DOs are assumed to be in postdoctoral training (internship, residency or fellowship) if they graduated within the last 3 years or if the AOA received information that they are in a postdoctoral program. [2] "Pediatric and adolescent medicine" includes all specialties where the patient is a child or adolescent and includes both general pediatricians and pediatric specialties. [3] Beginning in 2009, separate data for "Pediatric specialties" are no longer available. [4] Family physicians who stress osteopathic manipulative treatment specialties in their practices, and osteopathic physicians who specialize in osteopathic manipulative medicine. [5] The categories "Family and general practice" and "General internal medicine" do not include family physicians, general practitioners and general internists who also practice secondary specialties. Those osteopathic physicians are counted under "Other Specialties."

Source: American Osteopathic Association, Chicago, IL, AOA Annual Statistics, *2012 Osteopathic Medical Profession Report* ©, and previous reports. See also <http://www.osteopathic.org>.

Table 169. Physicians by Sex and Specialty: 1990 to 2011

[In thousands (615.4 represents 615,400). As of Dec. 31, except 1990 as of Jan. 1, and as noted. Includes Puerto Rico and Island Areas]

Activity	1990 Total	1990 Office-based	2000 Total	2000 Office-based	2010 Total	2010 Office-based	2011 Total	2011 Office-based
Doctors of medicine, total [1]	**615.4**	**361.0**	**813.8**	**490.4**	**985.4**	**565.0**	**1,004.6**	**575.6**
Place of medical education:								
U.S./Canadian medical graduates.........	483.7	286.2	616.8	376.5	731.0	424.8	741.1	431.8
International medical graduates [2].........	131.8	74.8	197.0	113.9	254.4	140.2	263.5	143.8
Sex:								
Male........	511.2	311.7	618.2	382.3	688.5	399.4	694.9	400.1
Female.........	104.2	49.2	195.5	108.1	296.9	165.6	309.7	175.6
Allergy/immunology....................	3.4	2.5	4.0	3.1	4.3	3.4	4.4	3.5
Anesthesiology....................	26.0	17.8	35.7	27.6	43.4	31.8	43.8	32.1
Cardiovascular diseases....................	15.9	10.7	21.0	16.3	22.9	17.5	23.0	17.5
Child psychiatry....................	4.3	2.6	6.2	4.3	7.4	5.4	7.6	5.5
Dermatology....................	7.6	6.0	9.7	8.0	11.3	9.3	11.6	9.5
Diagnostic radiology....................	15.4	9.8	21.1	14.6	26.1	17.5	26.4	17.8
Emergency medicine....................	14.2	8.4	23.1	14.5	33.3	20.7	34.5	21.4
Family practice....................	47.6	37.5	71.6	54.2	87.6	69.9	89.4	71.4
Gastroenterology....................	7.5	5.2	10.6	8.5	13.2	10.5	13.5	10.7
General practice....................	22.8	20.5	15.2	13.0	8.6	7.2	7.5	6.3
General surgery....................	38.4	24.5	36.7	24.5	37.1	24.3	37.4	24.4
Internal medicine....................	98.3	58.0	134.5	89.7	161.3	110.6	166.5	114.1
Neurological surgery....................	4.4	3.1	5.0	3.7	5.8	4.0	5.9	4.0
Neurology....................	9.2	5.6	12.3	8.6	15.9	10.5	16.4	11.0
Obstetrics and gynecology....................	33.7	25.5	40.2	31.7	42.8	34.1	43.2	34.4
Ophthalmology....................	16.1	13.1	18.1	15.6	18.5	15.7	18.7	15.9
Orthopedic surgery....................	19.1	14.2	22.3	17.4	25.2	19.3	25.4	19.4
Otolaryngology....................	8.1	6.4	9.4	7.6	10.3	8.0	10.4	8.0
Pathology....................	16.6	7.5	18.8	10.6	19.0	10.7	19.2	10.9
Pediatrics....................	41.9	27.1	63.9	43.2	76.4	53.1	78.8	55.1
Physical med./rehab....................	4.1	2.2	6.5	4.3	9.0	6.5	9.4	6.8
Plastic surgery....................	4.6	3.8	6.2	5.3	7.4	6.2	7.6	6.2
Psychiatry....................	35.2	20.1	39.5	25.0	39.7	25.7	39.7	25.8
Pulmonary diseases....................	6.1	3.7	8.7	5.9	11.1	7.8	11.4	8.1
Radiology....................	8.5	6.1	8.7	6.7	9.4	7.0	9.4	7.1
Urological surgery....................	9.4	7.4	10.3	8.5	10.7	8.6	10.7	8.6
Unspecified....................	8.1	1.6	8.3	3.8	9.5	.0	10.1	3.7
Not classified....................	12.7	(X)	45.1	(X)	64.2	(X)	60.1	(X)
Other categories [3]....................	55.4	(X)	75.2	(X)	126.4	(X)	135.0	(X)

X Not applicable. [1] Includes other categories not shown. [2] International medical graduates received their medical education in schools outside the United States and Canada. [3] Includes inactive and address unknown.

Source: American Medical Association, *Physician Characteristics and Distribution in the U.S., 2013 Edition* ©, Chicago, IL, and previous reports. For more information, see <http://www.ama-assn.org/>.

Table 170. Active Physicians and Nurses by State: 2011

[Physicians as of December; nurses as of May. Excludes doctors of osteopathy. Includes physicians not classified according to activity status. Data on nurses are from the Bureau of Labor Statistics]

State	Physicians Total	Physicians Rate [1]	Registered Nurses Total	Registered Nurses Rate [1]	State	Physicians Total	Physicians Rate [1]	Registered Nurses Total	Registered Nurses Rate [1]
United States......	**857,397**	**275**	**2,724,570**	**874**	Missouri................	15,260	254	67,630	1,125
Alabama................	10,435	217	45,400	945	Montana................	2,124	213	8,700	872
Alaska................	1,661	230	5,460	755	Nebraska................	4,583	249	19,170	1,040
Arizona................	14,591	225	44,710	690	Nevada................	4,985	183	16,470	605
Arkansas................	6,010	205	23,550	802	New Hampshire........	3,906	296	13,850	1,051
California................	102,145	271	250,230	664	New Jersey............	27,375	310	78,180	886
Colorado................	13,610	266	42,510	831	New Mexico............	4,969	239	15,400	740
Connecticut............	13,632	381	36,320	1,014	New York................	77,475	398	176,180	905
Delaware................	2,261	249	10,510	1,159	North Carolina........	24,745	256	91,300	945
District of Columbia. ..	5,307	859	10,680	1,728	North Dakota..........	1,650	241	8,960	1,310
Florida................	47,720	250	164,800	865	Ohio................	32,135	278	124,790	1,081
Georgia................	21,985	224	65,240	665	Oklahoma............	6,679	176	28,290	746
Hawaii................	4,146	302	10,210	743	Oregon................	11,110	287	30,960	800
Idaho................	2,650	167	11,660	736	Pennsylvania..........	39,662	311	130,740	1,026
Illinois................	37,341	290	123,770	962	Rhode Island..........	4,125	392	12,340	1,174
Indiana................	14,175	218	61,150	938	South Carolina........	10,711	229	42,650	911
Iowa................	5,787	189	33,230	1,085	South Dakota..........	1,828	222	11,120	1,349
Kansas................	6,571	229	28,180	981	Tennessee............	17,086	267	60,570	946
Kentucky................	10,243	234	44,810	1,026	Texas................	56,277	219	184,890	720
Louisiana................	12,525	274	40,840	893	Utah................	6,103	217	19,100	678
Maine................	3,684	277	14,810	1,115	Vermont................	2,316	370	6,370	1,017
Maryland................	24,473	420	49,620	851	Virginia................	22,228	275	62,210	768
Massachusetts........	32,296	490	87,040	1,321	Washington............	18,561	272	54,490	798
Michigan................	26,248	266	89,670	908	West Virginia..........	4,328	233	18,280	985
Minnesota................	16,218	303	56,660	1,060	Wisconsin............	15,020	263	56,430	988
Mississippi................	5,412	182	29,640	995	Wyoming................	1,030	181	4,800	845

[1] Per 100,000 resident population. Based on U.S. Census Bureau estimates as of July 1, 2011.

Source: Physicians: American Medical Association, Chicago, IL, *Physician Characteristics and Distribution in the U.S., 2013 Edition* ©. Nurses: U.S. Bureau of Labor Statistics, Occupational Employment Statistics, Occupational Employment and Wages, "May 2011 Occupational Employment and Wage Estimates," <http://www.bls.gov/oes/>, accessed June 2013.

Table 171. Medical Record Confidentiality Breaches Reported, Incidents and Persons Affected, by Type of Facility and Breach: 2010 to 2012

[For breaches reported between February 2010 and February 2013. Data shown for breaches affecting 500 or more individuals. As required by section 13402(e)(4) of the Health Information Technology for Economic and Clinical Health (HITECH) Act, the Secretary of Health and Human Services must post a list of breaches of unsecured protected health information affecting 500 or more individuals]

Type of Facility and Breach	Incidents	Persons affected	Type of Facility and Breach	Incidents	Persons affected
Total...........................	543	21,516,294	Pharmacy.................................	4	16,535
			Physical therapy.......................	4	15,731
Type of facility or service [1]			Physician practice.....................	49	228,622
			Skilled nursing/rehabilitation /assisted living.......................	7	24,065
Clinic, primary care........................	21	94,807	Social services..........................	13	83,709
Clinic, specialized care...................	43	493,523	State/local government agency......	39	8,491,814
Consultant/contractor......................	4	24,589	University health center..............	37	497,037
Dental practice...............................	20	103,343	Veterans facility.........................	11	20,271
Diagnostic imaging..........................	7	240,487	Other/unknown..........................	11	25,289
Emergency medical service..............	14	204,633			
Employee benefit plan......................	6	39,887	**Type of Breach**		
Insurance provider..........................	42	1,560,791			
Home healthcare.............................	8	201,706	Computer/equipment theft...........	234	8,144,871
Hospital..	125	3,534,720	Hacking/IT incident....................	35	1,758,544
Integrated healthcare network...........	43	5,412,889	Loss/improper disposal...............	90	10,006,414
Laboratory....................................	6	18,089	Unauthorized access/disclosure.....	105	1,183,427
Medical school..............................	5	27,015	Unknown/Other........................	79	423,038
Medical technology/equipment provider..	4	60,679			
Mental health services....................	20	96,063			

[1] Categorization of types of facilities and services has been determined by ProQuest research.

Source: U.S. Department of Health and Human Services, "Health Information Privacy, Breaches Affecting 500 or More Individuals," <http://www.hhs.gov/ocr/privacy/hipaa/administrative/breachnotificationrule/breachtool.html>, accessed March 2013.

Table 172. Adults 18 Years and Over Who Used Complementary and Alternative Medicine (CAM) in the Past 12 Months by Type of Therapy: 2002 and 2007

[2,136 represents 2,136,000. The denominators for statistics shown exclude persons with unknown CAM information. Estimates were age adjusted to the year 2000 U.S. standard population using four age groups: 18 to 24 years, 25 to 44 years, 45 to 64 years, and 65 years and over]

Therapy	2002		2007	
	Number (1,000)	Percent	Number (1,000)	Percent
Alternative medical systems:				
Acupuncture.............................	2,136	1.1	3,141	1.4
Homeopathic treatment...............	3,433	1.7	3,909	1.8
Biologically based therapies:				
Nonvitamin, nonmineral, natural products [1]...	38,183	18.9	38,797	17.7
Diet-based therapies [2, 3]............	7,099	3.5	7,893	3.6
Vegetarian diet........................	3,184	1.6	3,351	1.5
Atkins diet.............................	3,417	1.7	2,673	1.2
South Beach............................	(X)	(X)	2,334	1.1
Megavitamin therapy..................	5,739	2.8	(X)	(X)
Manipulative and body-based therapies:				
Chiropractic care [4]...................	15,226	7.5	(X)	(X)
Chiropractic or osteopathic manipulation [4]...	(X)	(X)	18,740	8.6
Massage..................................	10,052	5.0	18,068	8.3
Movement therapies....................	(X)	(X)	3,146	1.5
Pilates....................................	(X)	(X)	3,015	1.4
Mind-body therapies:				
Meditation................................	15,336	7.6	20,541	9.4
Guided imagery.........................	4,194	2.1	4,866	2.2
Progressive relaxation.................	6,185	3.0	6,454	2.9
Deep breathing exercises.............	23,457	11.6	27,794	12.7
Yoga.......................................	10,386	5.1	13,172	6.1
Tai chi....................................	2,565	1.3	2,267	1.0
Energy healing therapy/Reiki.........	1,080	0.5	1,216	0.5

X Not applicable. [1] While questions were asked about nonvitamin, nonmineral, natural products in both 2002 and 2007, the data are not comparable due primarily to question order and the specific nonvitamin, nonmineral, natural product covered. [2] The totals of the numbers and percents of the categories listed under "Diet-based therapies" are greater than the number and percent of their respective category heading because respondents could choose more than one of the categories. [3] While questions were asked about Diet-based therapies in both 2002 and 2007, the data are not comparable because respondents were asked about the South Beach Diet in 2007, but not in 2002. [4] While questions were asked about chiropractic therapy in both 2002 and 2007, the data are not comparable because respondents were asked about chiropractic care in 2002 and chiropractic or osteopathic manipulation in 2007.

Source: U.S. National Center for Health Statistics, *Complementary and Alternative Medicine Use Among Adults and Children: United States, 2007*, National Health Statistics Reports, Number 12, 2008. See also <http://www.cdc.gov/nchs/products/nhsr.htm> and <http://nccam.nih.gov/news/camstats>.

Table 173. Percent Distribution of Visits to Health Care Professionals by Selected Patient Characteristics: 2005 and 2011

[Covers ambulatory visits to doctor's offices and emergency departments, and home health care visits during a 12-month period. Based on the National Health Interview Survey, a sample survey of the civilian noninstitutionalized population; see Appendix III]

Characteristic	None		1–3 visits		4–9 visits		10 or more visits	
	2005	2011	2005	2011	2005	2011	2005	2011
All persons [1,2]	15.5	15.5	45.9	46.8	25.1	24.7	13.6	13.0
SEX [2]								
Male	20.4	20.0	46.7	47.8	22.2	21.9	10.7	10.3
Female	10.7	11.0	45.1	45.9	27.9	27.6	16.3	15.5
AGE								
Under 18 years	10.2	8.3	56.0	57.3	26.5	27.0	7.4	7.4
Under 6 years	5.1	4.5	47.4	50.1	38.0	36.3	9.5	9.1
6 to 17 years	12.6	10.3	60.1	61.0	20.9	22.1	6.3	6.5
18 to 44 years	22.9	23.7	45.8	45.5	19.2	19.2	12.0	11.6
18 to 24 years	24.2	25.3	44.4	46.1	19.6	18.6	11.8	10.1
25 to 44 years	22.5	23.2	46.3	45.4	19.1	19.4	12.1	12.1
45 to 64 years	14.0	14.6	42.9	44.0	26.8	26.0	16.3	15.3
45 to 54 years	15.8	16.8	44.8	45.2	24.3	24.1	15.0	13.9
55 to 64 years	11.4	12.0	40.2	42.7	30.3	28.3	18.2	17.0
65 years and over	5.6	5.5	30.7	34.0	37.5	35.8	26.2	24.7
65 to 74 years	5.9	6.2	34.4	36.0	35.8	34.9	23.9	22.9
75 years and over	5.2	4.7	26.4	31.5	39.5	37.0	28.8	26.8
RACE [2,3]								
Single race:								
White	15.1	15.2	45.6	46.4	25.4	25.1	13.9	13.2
Black or African American	15.9	15.0	47.4	47.6	23.8	24.3	12.9	13.1
American Indian or Alaska Native	20.4	18.6	36.4	47.5	29.8	22.2	13.4	11.7
Asian	21.5	20.4	49.3	49.8	20.8	22.1	8.4	7.8
Two or more races	15.4	14.0	37.3	45.7	27.6	24.3	19.7	15.9
HISPANIC ORIGIN AND RACE [2,3,4]								
Hispanic or Latino	23.9	23.3	42.1	43.7	22.2	22.6	11.8	10.4
Mexican	26.6	25.6	41.5	42.8	20.8	21.8	11.1	9.9
Not Hispanic or Latino	13.9	13.9	46.5	47.4	25.7	25.2	13.9	13.4
White, non-Hispanic	13.0	13.1	46.4	47.1	26.2	25.9	14.5	13.9
Black, non-Hispanic	15.9	14.8	47.4	47.9	23.8	24.3	12.9	13.0
HEALTH INSURANCE STATUS [5,6]								
Insured	12.4	12.4	49.6	50.3	25.0	24.9	13.0	12.4
Private	12.8	12.7	51.5	53.1	24.5	24.2	11.2	9.9
Medicaid	9.9	10.6	37.8	40.0	26.8	26.4	25.5	23.0
Uninsured	37.5	37.1	42.0	43.5	14.7	13.9	5.8	5.5
Insured continuously all 12 months prior to interview	12.3	12.2	49.8	50.5	25.0	25.0	12.9	12.3
Uninsured for any period up to 12 months prior to interview	18.9	19.0	44.9	47.3	22.5	21.5	13.7	12.2
Uninsured more than 12 months prior to interview	43.5	43.0	40.0	41.7	12.3	11.2	4.2	4.1

[1] Includes other categories not shown separately. [2] Estimates are age adjusted to the year 2000 standard using six age groups: Under 18 years, 18–44 years, 45–54 years, 55–64 years, 65–74 years, and 75 years and over. [3] The race groups include persons of Hispanic and non-Hispanic origin. Estimates by race and Hispanic origin are tabulated using the 1997 standards for federal data on race and ethnicity. Race-specific estimates are for persons who reported only once race group; the category of 2 or more races includes persons who reported more than one race group. [4] Persons of Hispanic or Latino origin may be of any race. [5] For persons under age 65, at time of interview. Estimates for persons under age 65 are age-adjusted to the year 2000 standard population using four age groups: Under 18 years, 18-44 years, 45-54 years, and 55-64 years. [6] Health insurance categories are mutually exclusive. Persons who reported both Medicaid and private coverage are classified as having private coverage. State-sponsored health plans and the Children's Health Insurance Program (CHIP) are included with Medicaid coverage. The insured category also includes military plans, other government-sponsored health plans, and Medicare, not shown separately. Persons not covered by private insurance, Medicaid, CHIP, state-sponsored or other government-sponsored health plans, Medicare, or military plans are considered to have no health insurance coverage. Persons with only Indian Health Service coverage are considered to have no health insurance coverage.

Source: U.S. National Center for Health Statistics, *Health, United States, 2012*, May 2013. See also <http://www.cdc.gov/nchs/hus.htm>.

Table 174. Ambulatory Care Visits to Physicians' Offices and Hospital Outpatient and Emergency Departments: 2010

[1,239.3 represents 1,239,300,000. Based on the annual National Ambulatory Medical Care Survey and National Hospital Ambulatory Medical Care Survey, and subject to sampling error; see source for details]

Characteristic	Number of visits (mil.)				Visits per 100 persons			
	Total	Physician offices	Out-patient dept.	Emer-gency dept.	Total	Physician offices	Out-patient dept.	Emer-gency dept.
Total..........	**1,239.3**	**1,008.8**	**100.7**	**129.8**	**408.2**	**332.2**	**33.2**	**42.8**
Age:								
Under 15 years old..........	212.6	166.0	21.1	25.5	343.3	268.0	34.1	41.2
15 to 24 years old..........	112.6	81.3	10.5	20.8	266.2	192.2	24.9	49.1
25 to 44 years old..........	263.8	206.1	21.4	36.3	327.4	255.8	26.6	45.0
45 to 64 years old..........	352.0	296.4	27.7	27.9	440.6	371.0	34.7	34.9
65 to 74 years old..........	151.1	132.2	10.7	8.2	713.0	623.9	50.4	38.7
75 years old and over..........	147.4	126.8	9.3	11.3	831.1	715.4	52.2	63.5
Sex:								
Male..........	521.1	422.1	40.7	58.3	349.7	283.3	27.3	39.1
Female..........	718.2	586.7	60.0	71.5	464.5	379.4	38.8	46.3
Race/Ethnicity: [2]								
White..........	1,017.7	842.9	77.4	97.4	421.2	348.9	32.0	40.3
Black/African American..........	163.9	116.9	19.2	27.8	424.6	302.8	49.7	72.1
Hispanic or Latino..........	149.5	115.0	15.6	18.9	305.2	234.7	31.9	38.6
Expected sources of payment: [3]								
Private insurance..........	727.7	631.1	44.1	47.9	(X)	(X)	(X)	(X)
Medicare..........	293.4	248.2	22.1	22.9	(X)	(X)	(X)	(X)
Medicaid/CHIP [4]..........	214.6	142.7	32.0	40.7	(X)	(X)	(X)	(X)
Worker's compensation..........	15.6	13.5	0.5	1.6	(X)	(X)	(X)	(X)
No insurance: [5]..........	71.2	43.0	7.0	20.9	(X)	(X)	(X)	(X)
Self pay..........	62.5	37.3	5.4	19.6	(X)	(X)	(X)	(X)
No charge..........	7.4	[1] 5.9	[1] 1.7	1.9	(X)	(X)	(X)	(X)
Other..........	34.8	25.5	4.7	4.8	(X)	(X)	(X)	(X)
Unknown..........	44.4	31.7	3.6	6.1	(X)	(X)	(X)	(X)

X Not applicable. [1] Figure does not meet standards of reliability or precision. [2] The race groups, White, and Black or African American, include persons of Hispanic and not Hispanic origin. Persons of Hispanic origin may be of any race. For physicians visits, race data were missing for 24.9 percent and ethnicity data were missing for 23.2 percent of visits. For hospital outpatient visits, race data were missing for 14.5 percent and ethnicity data were missing for 16.2 percent of visits. For emergency department visits, race data were missing for 9.9 percent and ethnicity data were missing for 13.2 percent of visits. Missing data were imputed, and readers are advised to treat the resulting estimates with caution. More information is available at the Web site below. [3] Estimates include all expected sources of payment reported at the visit. [4] CHIP is Children's Health Insurance Program. [5] "No insurance" is defined as having only "self-pay" or "no charge/charity" as payment sources.

Source: U.S. National Center for Health Statistics, *National Ambulatory Medical Care Survey: 2010 Summary Tables, 2010 Outpatient Department Summary Tables,* and *2010 Emergency Department Summary Tables.* See also <http://www.cdc.gov/nchs/ahcd/web_tables.htm>.

Table 175. Average Cost to Community Hospitals Per Patient: 1990 to 2011

[In dollars, except percent. Covers non-federal short-term general or special hospitals (excluding psychiatric or tuberculosis hospitals and hospital units of institutions). Total cost per patient based on total hospital expenses (payroll, employee benefits, professional fees, supplies, etc.). Data have been adjusted for outpatient visits]

Type of expense and hospital	1990	1995	2000	2005	2006	2007	2008	2009	2010	2011
Average cost per day, total..........	**687**	**968**	**1,149**	**1,522**	**1,612**	**1,690**	**1,782**	**1,853**	**1,910**	**1,960**
Annual percent change [1]..........	7.8	4.0	4.2	5.0	5.9	4.8	5.4	4.0	3.1	2.6
Nongovernmental nonprofit..........	692	994	1,182	1,585	1,686	1,772	1,876	1,957	2,025	2,088
For profit..........	752	947	1,057	1,412	1,472	1,519	1,556	1,574	1,629	1,628
State and local government..........	635	878	1,064	1,329	1,400	1,460	1,552	1,611	1,625	1,667
Average cost per stay, total..........	**4,947**	**6,216**	**6,649**	**8,793**	**8,970**	**9,342**	**9,788**	**10,043**	**10,313**	**10,533**
Nongovernmental nonprofit..........	5,001	6,279	6,717	8,670	9,190	9,574	10,081	10,379	10,652	10,933
For profit..........	4,727	5,425	5,642	7,351	7,422	7,740	7,985	8,037	8,336	8,263
State and local government..........	4,838	6,445	7,106	8,793	9,147	9,446	9,827	10,068	10,283	10,532

[1] Change from immediate prior year.

Source: Health Forum, An American Hospital Association Company, Chicago, IL, *AHA Hospital Statistics 2013 Edition,* and prior years ©. For more information: <http://www.ahadataviewer.com/>.

Table 176. Visits to Hospital Emergency Departments by Diagnosis: 2010

[58,308 represents 58,308,000. See headnote, Table 174]

Leading diagnosis	Number (1,000)	Rate per 1,000 persons [1]	Leading diagnosis	Number (1,000)	Rate per 1,000 persons [1]
MALE			**FEMALE**		
All ages........	**58,308**	**384**	**All ages**........	**71,535**	**456**
Under 15 years old [2]........	**14,152**	**452**	**Under 15 years old** [2]........	**11,351**	**379**
Acute upper respiratory infections [3]........	1,310	42	Acute respiratory infections [3]........	955	32
Otitis media and eustachian tube disorders........	1,182	38	Otitis media and eustachian tube disorders........	698	23
Open wound of head........	850	27	Pyrexia of unknown origin........	664	22
Pyrexia of unknown origin........	701	22	Contusion with intact skin surface........	413	14
Contusion with intact skin surface........	563	18	Acute pharyngitis........	320	11
15 to 64 years old [2]........	**36,175**	**351**	**15 to 64 years old** [2]........	**48,711**	**468**
Chest pain........	1,883	18	Abdominal pain........	3,424	33
Spinal disorders........	1,582	15	Chest pain........	2,137	21
Open wound, excluding head........	1,581	15	Spinal disorders........	1,850	18
Abdominal pain........	1,567	15	Complications of pregnancy, childbirth, and the puerperium........	1,639	16
Contusion with intact skin surfaces........	1,480	14	Contusion with intact skin surface........	1,567	15
65 years old and over [2]........	**7,981**	**460**	**65 years old and over** [2]........	**11,473**	**501**
Heart disease, excluding ischemic........	528	30	Chest pain........	789	34
Chest pain........	427	25	Contusion with intact skin surface........	525	23
Abdominal pain........	266	15	Abdominal pain........	491	21
Pneumonia........	265	15	Heart disease, excluding ischemic........	477	21
Open wound, excluding head........	247	14	Urinary tract infection site not specified....	431	19

[1] Based on U.S. Census Bureau population data for 2010, revised in October 2012. [2] Includes other first-listed diagnosis, not shown separately. [3] Excluding pharyngitis.

Source: U.S. National Center for Health Statistics, *National Hospital Ambulatory Medical Care Survey: 2010 Emergency Department Summary Tables.* See also <http://www.cdc.gov/nchs/ahcd/web_tables.htm>.

Table 177. Procedures for Inpatients Discharged From Short-Stay Hospitals: 1990 to 2010

[23,051 represents 23,051,000. Procedure categories are based on the International Classification of Diseases, 9th Revision, Clinical Modification. See headnote, Table 181]

Sex and type of procedure	Number of procedures (1,000)				Rate per 1,000 population [1]			
	1990	2000	2009	2010	1990	2000	2009	2010
Surgical procedures, total [2]........	**23,051**	**23,244**	**29,215**	**27,804**	**92.4**	**83.6**	**95.5**	**90.3**
Cesarean section........	945	855	1,329	1,325	3.8	3.1	4.3	4.3
Repair of current obstetric laceration........	795	1,136	1,339	1,286	3.2	4.1	4.4	4.2
Cardiac catheterization........	995	1,221	1,071	947	4.0	4.4	3.5	3.1
Reduction of fracture [3]........	609	628	621	651	2.4	2.3	2.0	2.1
Male, total [2]........	**8,538**	**8,689**	**11,758**	**10,979**	**70.6**	**63.9**	**78.2**	**72.4**
Cardiac catheterization........	620	732	622	585	5.1	5.4	4.1	3.9
Coronary artery bypass graft [4]........	286	371	304	292	2.4	2.7	2.0	1.9
Reduction of fracture [3]........	300	285	283	272	2.5	2.1	1.9	1.8
Female, total [2]........	**14,513**	**14,556**	**17,457**	**16,826**	**113.0**	**102.4**	**112.4**	**107.8**
Cesarean section........	945	855	1,329	1,325	7.4	6.0	8.6	8.5
Repair of current obstetric laceration........	795	1,136	1,339	1,286	6.2	8.0	8.6	8.2
Hysterectomy........	591	633	494	497	4.6	4.5	3.2	3.2
Diagnostic and other nonsurgical procedures [5]........	**17,455**	**16,737**	**18,748**	**18,530**	**70.0**	**60.2**	**61.3**	**60.2**
Angiocardiography and arteriography [6]........	1,735	2,005	1,919	1,763	7.0	7.2	6.3	5.7
Respiratory therapy........	1,164	991	1,276	1,264	4.7	3.6	4.2	4.1
Manual assisted delivery........	750	898	1,246	1,198	3.0	3.2	4.1	3.9
Diagnostic ultrasound........	1,608	886	902	898	6.4	3.2	2.9	2.9
Fetal electrocardiogram (EKG) and fetal monitoring....	1,377	750	1,038	985	5.6	2.7	3.4	3.2
Male, total [5]........	**7,378**	**6,965**	**7,439**	**7,437**	**61.0**	**51.2**	**49.5**	**49.0**
Angiocardiography and arteriography [6]........	1,051	1,157	1,061	1,020	8.7	8.5	7.1	6.7
Respiratory therapy........	586	507	627	639	4.9	3.7	4.2	4.2
Computerized Axial Tomographic scan [7]........	736	345	226	(S)	6.1	2.5	1.5	(S)
Female, total [5]........	**10,077**	**9,772**	**11,309**	**11,093**	**78.5**	**68.8**	**72.8**	**71.0**
Manual assisted delivery........	750	898	1,246	1,198	5.9	6.3	8.0	7.7
Fetal electrocardiogram (EKG) and fetal monitoring....	1,377	750	1,038	985	10.8	5.5	6.7	6.3
Respiratory therapy........	578	484	649	625	4.5	3.4	4.2	4.0
Diagnostic ultrasound........	941	501	469	477	7.3	3.5	3.0	3.1

S Figure does not meet publication standards. [1] Based on Census Bureau estimated civilian population as of July 1. Population estimates based on the 1990 census were used to calculate rates for 1990 through 2000. Population estimates based on the 2000 census were used to calculate rates for 2001 through 2010. [2] Includes other types of surgical procedures, not shown separately. [3] Excluding skull, nose, and jaw. [4] It is possible for a discharge to have more than one type of these recorded. [5] Includes other nonsurgical procedures, not shown separately. [6] Using contrast material. [7] Also known as CAT scan.

Source: U.S. National Center for Health Statistics, National Hospital Discharge Survey, unpublished data. See also <http://www.cdc.gov/nchs/nhds.htm>.

Table 178. Hospitals—Summary Characteristics: 1990 to 2011

[In units indicated (for beds, 1,213 represents 1,213,000). Covers hospitals accepted for registration by the American Hospital Association; see text, this section. Short-term hospitals have an average patient stay of less than 30 days; long-term, an average stay of longer duration. Special hospitals include obstetrics and gynecology; eye, ear, nose, and throat; rehabilitation; orthopedic; chronic; and other special hospitals except psychiatric, tuberculosis, alcoholism, and chemical dependency hospitals]

Item	1990	2000	2005	2006	2007	2008	2009	2010	2011
Number:									
All hospitals	**6,649**	**5,810**	**5,756**	**5,747**	**5,708**	**5,815**	**5,795**	**5,754**	**5,724**
With 100 beds or more	3,620	3,102	2,942	2,928	2,901	2,884	2,861	2,832	2,790
Nonfederal [1]	6,312	5,565	5,530	5,526	5,495	5,602	5,584	5,541	5,516
Community hospitals [2]	5,384	4,915	4,936	4,927	4,897	5,010	5,008	4,985	4,973
Nongovernmental nonprofit	3,191	3,003	2,958	2,919	2,913	2,923	2,918	2,904	2,903
For profit	749	749	868	889	873	982	998	1,013	1,025
State and local government	1,444	1,163	1,110	1,119	1,111	1,105	1,092	1,068	1,045
Long term general and special	131	131	115	127	135	128	115	109	110
Psychiatric	757	496	456	462	444	447	444	435	421
Tuberculosis	4	4	3	2	1	1	2	2	2
Federal	337	245	226	221	213	213	211	213	208
Beds (1,000): [3]									
All hospitals	1,213	984	947	947	945	951	944	942	924
Rate per 1,000 population [4]	4.9	3.5	3.2	3.2	3.1	3.1	3.1	3.0	3.0
Beds per hospital	182	169	165	165	166	164	163	164	161
Nonfederal [1]	1,113	931	901	901	899	905	900	897	886
Community hospitals [2]	927	824	802	802	801	808	806	805	797
Rate per 1,000 population [4]	3.7	2.9	2.7	2.7	2.7	2.7	2.6	2.6	2.6
Nongovernmental nonprofit	657	583	561	559	554	557	556	556	548
For profit	102	110	114	115	116	121	122	125	128
State and local government	169	131	128	128	131	131	127	125	121
Long term general and special	25	18	15	16	17	16	16	15	15
Psychiatric	158	87	82	84	79	79	76	76	73
Tuberculosis	(Z)	(Z)	(Z)	(Z)	(Z)	(Z)	(Z)	(Z)	(Z)
Federal	98	53	46	46	46	46	45	45	38
Average daily census (1,000): [5]									
All hospitals	844	650	656	653	645	649	641	627	615
Community hospitals [2]	619	526	540	538	533	536	528	520	513
Nongovernmental nonprofit	455	382	388	384	380	380	375	368	362
For profit	54	61	68	67	66	70	70	71	73
State and local government	111	83	85	86	87	86	83	80	78
Expenses (bil. dol.): [6]									
All hospitals	234.9	395.4	570.5	607.3	638.5	690.0	726.7	750.6	773.5
Nonfederal [1]	219.6	371.5	533.7	569.8	599.7	646.1	676.6	698.2	722.3
Community hospitals [2]	203.7	356.6	515.7	551.8	581.0	626.6	656.2	678.0	702.1
Nongovernmental nonprofit	150.7	267.1	386.0	412.8	435.5	468.1	492.9	510.7	528.3
For profit	18.8	35.0	51.8	54.9	55.8	61.8	64.4	67.2	70.3
State and local government	34.2	54.5	77.9	83.9	89.8	96.7	98.9	100.1	103.4
Long term general and special	2.7	2.8	3.6	4.0	3.9	4.5	4.2	4.2	3.9
Psychiatric	12.9	11.9	13.9	15.0	14.5	14.7	15.1	15.8	15.6
Tuberculosis	0.1	(Z)	(Z)	(Z)	(Z)	(Z)	(Z)	(Z)	(Z)
Federal	15.2	23.9	36.8	37.5	38.8	44.0	50.1	52.4	51.2
Personnel (1,000): [7]									
All hospitals	4,063	4,454	4,790	4,907	5,024	5,116	5,178	5,184	5,196
Nonfederal [1]	3,760	4,157	4,479	4,569	4,699	4,775	4,814	4,825	4,864
Community hospitals [2]	3,420	3,911	4,260	4,343	4,465	4,550	4,585	4,600	4,650
Nongovernmental nonprofit	2,533	2,919	3,154	3,207	3,286	3,340	3,369	3,388	3,427
For profit	273	378	421	423	432	450	464	474	485
State and local government	614	614	681	713	747	760	751	738	738
Long term general and special	55	41	38	43	44	41	37	39	35
Psychiatric	280	200	182	180	187	182	183	182	175
Tuberculosis	1	1	1	1	1	(Z)	(Z)	(Z)	(Z)
Federal	303	297	311	339	325	341	364	359	331
Outpatient visits (mil.)	368.2	592.7	673.7	690.4	693.5	710.0	742.0	750.4	754.5
Emergency visits	92.8	106.9	118.9	122.6	124.7	126.7	131.4	131.5	133.4

Z Less than 500 or $50 million. [1] Includes hospital units of institutions. [2] Short-term (average length of stay less than 30 days) general and special (e.g., obstetrics and gynecology; eye, ear, nose and throat; rehabilitation, etc. except psychiatric, tuberculosis, alcoholism, and chemical dependency). Excludes hospital units of institutions. [3] Number of beds at end of reporting period. [4] Based on Census Bureau estimated resident population as of July 1. 1990 and 2000 based on enumerated resident population as of April 1. Other years are estimates, which reflect revisions based on the 2000 Census of Population. [5] The average number of people served on an inpatient basis on a single day during the reporting period. [6] Excludes new construction. [7] Includes full-time equivalents of part-time personnel.

Source: Health Forum, An American Hospital Association Company, Chicago, IL, *AHA Hospital Statistics 2013 Edition*, and prior years ©. For more information: <http://www.ahadataviewer.com/>.

Table 179. Community Hospitals—States: 2000 and 2011

[In thousands (823.6 represents 823,600), unless otherwise noted. Community hospitals are defined as all nonfederal, short-term general, and other special hospitals. Other special hospitals include obstetrics and gynecology; eye, ear, nose, and throat; rehabilitation; orthopedic; and other individually described specialty services. Community hospitals include academic medical centers or other teaching hospitals if they are nonfederal short-term hospitals. Excluded are hospitals not accessible by the general public, such as prison hospitals or college infirmaries]

State	Number of hospitals		Beds (1,000)		Patients admitted (1,000)		Average daily census [1] (1,000)		Outpatient visits (mil.)		Average cost per day (dol.)	
	2000	2011	2000	2011	2000	2011	2000	2011	2000	2011	2000	2011
United States............	4,915	4,973	823.6	797.4	33,089	34,843	525.7	512.9	521.4	656.1	1,149	1,960
Alabama....................	108	102	16.4	15.4	680	625	9.8	8.9	8.0	8.7	980	1,366
Alaska......................	18	23	1.4	1.6	47	55	0.8	0.9	1.3	1.8	1,495	2,137
Arizona....................	61	70	10.9	13.4	539	701	6.8	8.5	5.3	8.6	1,311	2,194
Arkansas.................	83	84	9.8	9.4	368	364	5.7	5.2	4.4	4.8	908	1,451
California.................	389	345	72.7	70.0	3,315	3,393	47.8	46.8	44.9	52.7	1,438	2,706
Colorado..................	69	82	9.4	10.2	397	433	5.4	5.9	6.7	8.7	1,280	2,273
Connecticut..............	35	35	7.7	7.7	349	403	5.8	5.8	6.7	8.5	1,373	2,401
Delaware..................	5	7	1.8	2.1	83	100	1.4	1.6	1.5	1.9	1,311	2,242
District of Columbia.......	11	11	3.3	3.6	129	132	2.5	2.6	1.3	2.5	1,512	2,386
Florida.....................	202	213	51.2	53.0	2,119	2,508	31.0	33.9	21.8	24.4	1,161	1,809
Georgia...................	151	153	23.9	25.3	863	957	15.0	16.7	11.2	14.8	978	1,353
Hawaii.....................	21	23	3.1	2.6	100	105	2.3	2.0	2.5	2.0	1,088	1,705
Idaho......................	42	40	3.5	3.3	123	129	1.8	1.7	2.2	4.0	1,003	1,928
Illinois.....................	196	188	37.3	32.8	1,531	1,512	22.4	20.3	25.1	31.7	1,278	2,025
Indiana....................	109	125	19.2	17.5	700	737	10.8	10.2	14.1	18.5	1,132	2,025
Iowa.......................	115	118	11.8	10.0	360	340	6.8	5.6	9.2	10.3	740	1,324
Kansas....................	129	132	10.8	10.0	310	302	5.7	5.3	5.3	7.0	837	1,330
Kentucky..................	105	106	14.8	14.2	582	600	9.1	8.4	8.7	10.5	929	1,589
Louisiana.................	123	127	17.5	15.3	654	607	9.8	8.9	10.0	9.5	1,075	1,563
Maine......................	37	37	3.7	3.6	147	145	2.4	2.2	3.2	6.2	1,148	1,941
Maryland..................	49	48	11.2	11.9	587	684	8.2	8.6	6.0	8.8	1,315	2,368
Massachusetts............	80	79	16.6	15.9	740	838	11.7	11.4	16.7	22.3	1,467	2,414
Michigan..................	146	153	26.1	25.4	1,106	1,191	16.9	16.9	24.9	31.0	1,211	1,977
Minnesota.................	135	132	16.7	15.0	571	596	11.2	9.8	7.3	10.8	932	1,825
Mississippi................	95	99	13.6	12.9	425	394	8.0	6.9	3.7	4.8	719	1,166
Missouri...................	119	120	20.1	18.7	773	816	11.7	11.4	14.8	20.2	1,185	1,998
Montana...................	52	48	4.3	3.6	99	95	2.9	2.3	2.6	3.5	579	1,255
Nebraska..................	85	86	8.2	6.6	209	203	4.8	3.6	3.4	5.0	743	1,614
Nevada....................	22	38	3.8	5.5	199	250	2.7	3.7	2.2	2.7	1,285	1,856
New Hampshire............	28	28	2.9	2.8	111	122	1.7	1.7	2.8	5.0	1,201	2,220
New Jersey...............	80	73	25.3	20.4	1,074	1,051	17.3	14.6	16.3	15.8	1,299	2,228
New Mexico...............	35	36	3.5	4.1	174	175	2.0	2.4	3.1	4.6	1,388	2,066
New York..................	215	182	66.4	58.1	2,416	2,491	52.1	46.4	46.4	54.0	1,118	1,954
North Carolina............	113	117	23.1	23.1	971	1,035	16.0	16.0	12.4	18.6	1,061	1,698
North Dakota..............	42	41	3.9	3.1	89	94	2.3	1.9	1.7	2.9	747	1,374
Ohio.......................	163	183	33.8	33.8	1,404	1,505	20.6	20.4	26.9	35.9	1,198	2,170
Oklahoma.................	108	115	11.1	11.3	429	424	6.2	6.2	4.7	6.0	1,031	1,573
Oregon....................	59	59	6.6	6.8	330	343	3.9	4.0	7.3	9.4	1,461	2,967
Pennsylvania..............	207	194	42.3	39.7	1,796	1,766	28.8	26.5	31.8	37.9	1,080	1,960
Rhode Island..............	11	11	2.4	2.5	119	120	1.7	1.7	2.1	2.2	1,313	2,427
South Carolina............	63	66	11.5	12.3	495	509	8.0	7.9	7.8	6.4	1,101	1,881
South Dakota.............	48	53	4.3	4.1	99	102	2.8	2.6	1.7	2.1	476	1,141
Tennessee.................	121	133	20.6	20.0	737	806	11.5	12.4	10.3	11.0	1,078	1,541
Texas......................	403	420	55.9	60.8	2,367	2,535	33.1	35.8	29.4	39.3	1,274	2,001
Utah.......................	42	46	4.3	5.1	194	236	2.4	2.7	4.5	5.9	1,375	2,240
Vermont...................	14	14	1.7	1.2	52	49	1.1	0.9	1.2	3.1	888	1,618
Virginia....................	88	89	16.9	17.8	727	788	11.4	12.0	9.5	14.1	1,057	1,759
Washington...............	84	85	11.1	11.7	505	576	6.6	7.3	9.6	12.5	1,511	2,875
West Virginia..............	57	55	8.0	7.4	288	282	4.8	4.5	5.2	6.8	844	1,316
Wisconsin.................	118	125	15.3	13.1	558	573	9.1	7.9	10.9	15.5	1,055	2,030
Wyoming..................	24	24	1.9	2.0	48	46	1.1	1.0	0.9	1.1	677	1,096

[1] The average number of people served on an inpatient basis on a single day during the reporting period.

Source: Health Forum, An American Hospital Association Company, Chicago, IL, *AHA Hospital Statistics 2013 Edition*, and prior years ©. For more information: <http://www.ahadataviewer.com/>.

Table 180. Hospital Utilization Rates by Type of Hospital: 1990 to 2011

[In units as indicated]

Type of hospital	1990	1995	2000	2005	2008	2009	2010	2011
Community hospitals: [1]								
Admissions per 1,000 population [2]	125	116	117	119	118	116	114	112
Admissions per bed	34	35	40	44	44	44	44	44
Average length of stay (days) [3]	7.2	6.5	5.8	5.6	5.5	5.4	5.4	5.4
Outpatient visits per admission	9.7	13.4	15.8	16.6	17.5	18.1	18.5	18.8
Outpatient visits per 1,000 population [2]	1,207	1,556	1,852	1,976	2,053	2,091	2,108	2,106
Surgical operations (million) [4]	21.9	23.2	26.1	27.5	27.5	27.5	27.3	26.9
Number per admission	0.7	0.7	0.8	0.8	0.8	0.8	0.8	0.8
Nonfederal psychiatric:								
Admissions per 1,000 population [2]	2.9	2.7	2.4	2.5	2.4	2.5	2.5	2.4
Days in hospital per 1,000 population [2]	190	122	93	89	80	80	77	73

[1] Nonfederal, short-term general, and other special hospitals. Other special hospitals include obstetrics and gynecology; eye, ear, nose, and throat; rehabilitation; orthopedic; and other individually described specialty services. Includes academic medical centers or other teaching hospitals if they are nonfederal short-term hospitals. Excluded are hospitals not accessible by the general public, such as prison hospitals or college infirmaries. [2] Based on U.S. Census Bureau estimated resident population as of July 1. Estimates reflect revisions based on the 2000 Census of Population. 1990 and 2000 based on enumerated resident population as of April 1. [3] Number of inpatient days divided by number of admissions. [4] 21.9 represents 21,900,000.

Source: Health Forum, An American Hospital Association Company, Chicago, IL, *AHA Hospital Statistics 2013 Edition*, and prior years ©. For more information: <http://www.ahadataviewer.com/>.

Table 181. Hospital Utilization Rates by Sex: 1990 to 2010

[30,788 represents 30,788,000. Represents estimates of inpatients discharged from noninstitutional, short-stay hospitals, exclusive of federal hospitals. Excludes newborn infants. Based on sample data collected from the National Hospital Discharge Survey, a sample survey of hospital records of patients discharged in year shown; subject to sampling variability]

Item and sex	1990	1995	2000	2005	2006	2007	2008	2009	2010
Patients discharged (1,000)	30,788	30,722	31,706	34,667	34,854	34,369	35,697	36,120	35,079
Patients discharged per 1,000 persons, total [1]	122	116	113	117	117	114	118	118	114
Male	100	94	91	96	95	94	97	98	94
Female	143	136	134	138	138	134	139	138	134
Days of care per 1,000 persons, total [1]	784	620	555	562	558	554	577	575	545
Male	694	551	486	498	495	494	518	518	491
Female	869	686	620	624	619	612	635	630	598
Average stay (days)	6.4	5.4	4.9	4.8	4.8	4.8	4.9	4.9	4.8
Male	6.9	5.8	5.3	5.2	5.2	5.3	5.4	5.3	5.2
Female	6.1	5.0	4.6	4.5	4.5	4.6	4.6	4.6	4.5

[1] Rates are computed using Census Bureau estimates of the civilian population as of July 1. Rates for 1990 and 1995 were based on population estimates adjusted for the net underenumeration in the 1990 census. Rates for 2000 and later were calculated using 2000-based postcensal estimates.

Source: U.S. National Center for Health Statistics, National Hospital Discharge Survey, "Average length of stay and days of care: Number and rate of discharges by sex and age, 2010," <http://www.cdc.gov/nchs/nhds/nhds_products.htm>, accessed March 2013.

Table 182. Hospital Utilization Measures for HIV Patients: 1990 to 2010

[HIV represents human immunodeficiency virus. See headnote, Table 181]

Measure of utilization	Unit	1990	1995	2000	2005	2008	2009	2010
Number of patients discharged	1,000	146	249	173	185	215	155	170
Male	1,000	114	183	115	113	133	106	118
Female	1,000	32	66	58	72	81	49	53
Rate of patient discharges [1]	Rate	5.8	9.4	6.2	6.3	7.1	5.1	5.5
Number of days of care	1,000	2,188	2,326	1,257	1,244	1,342	960	1,040
Male	1,000	1,777	1,649	895	751	875	651	732
Female	1,000	411	677	362	493	468	309	308
Rate of days of care [1]	Rate	86.9	87.6	45.2	42.2	44.3	31.4	33.8
Average length of stay	Days	14.9	9.3	7.3	6.7	6.3	6.2	6.1
Male	Days	15.5	9.0	7.8	6.7	6.6	6.2	6.2
Female	Days	12.9	10.3	6.3	6.8	5.7	6.3	5.8

[1] Per 10,000 population. Based on Census Bureau estimated civilian population as of July 1. Rates for 1990 and 1995 were based on population estimates adjusted for the net undernumeration in the 1990 census. Populations for 2000 and later were 2000-based postcensal estimates.

Source: U.S. National Center for Health Statistics, unpublished data. See also <http://www.cdc.gov/nchs/nhds.htm>.

Table 183. Hospital Discharges and Days of Care: 2009 and 2010

[36,120 represents 36,120,000. See headnote, Table 181. For composition of regions, see map, inside front cover]

Age, race, and region	Discharges Number (1,000) 2009	2010	Discharges Per 1,000 persons [1] 2009	2010	Days of care per 1,000 persons [1] 2009	2010	Average stay (days) 2009	2010
Total [2]	**36,120**	**35,079**	**118**	**114**	**575**	**545**	**4.9**	**4.8**
AGE								
Under 1 year old	661	636	155	153	928	906	6.0	5.9
1 to 4 years old	571	593	34	35	104	118	3.1	3.4
5 to 14 years old	786	744	19	18	85	76	4.4	4.2
15 to 24 years old	2,950	2,829	69	66	240	233	3.5	3.5
25 to 34 years old	4,104	4,009	100	97	348	320	3.5	3.3
35 to 44 years old	3,427	3,193	83	79	343	315	4.1	4.0
45 to 64 years old	9,686	9,483	122	118	618	593	5.1	5.0
65 to 74 years old	5,312	5,189	255	242	1,389	1,313	5.4	5.4
75 years old and over	8,623	8,402	459	440	2,663	2,460	5.8	5.6
RACE								
White	23,109	23,224	95	95	467	459	4.9	4.8
Black	4,954	4,843	126	122	666	609	5.3	5.0
Asian/Pacific Islander	657	629	45	42	242	190	5.4	4.5
American Indian/Eskimo/Aleut	[3] 148	[3] 159	[3] 47	[3] 50	[3] 305	[3] 472	[3] 6.5	[3] 9.5
REGION								
Northeast	8,085	7,458	146	135	822	737	5.6	5.5
Midwest	8,004	7,973	120	119	526	517	4.4	4.3
South	13,273	13,150	118	116	580	564	4.9	4.9
West	6,758	6,497	95	90	420	394	4.4	4.4

[1] Rates were calculated using U.S. Census Bureau 2000-based postcensal estimates of the civilian population as of July 1. [2] Includes other races not shown separately. [3] Figure does not meet standard of reliability or precision.

Source: U.S. National Center for Health Statistics, National Hospital Discharge Survey, unpublished data. See also <http://www.cdc.gov/nchs/nhds.htm>.

Table 184. Hospital Discharges and Days of Care by Selected Diagnosis, by Patient Sex and Age: 2010

[14,200 represents 14,200,000. Represents estimates of inpatients discharged from noninstitutional, short-stay hospitals, exclusive of federal hospitals. Excludes newborn infants. Diagnostic categories are based on the International Classification of Diseases, Ninth Revision, Clinical Modification. See headnote, Table 181]

Sex, age, and selected first-listed diagnosis [1]	Discharges Number (1,000) [2]	Per 1,000 persons [2]	Average stay (days) [2]	Sex, age, and selected first-listed diagnosis [1]	Discharges Number (1,000) [2]	Per 1,000 persons [2]	Average stay (days) [2]
MALE				**FEMALE**			
All ages [3]	**14,200**	**93.6**	**5.2**	**All ages [3]**	**20,879**	**133.7**	**4.5**
Under 18 years old [3]	**1,290**	**33.8**	**4.7**	**Under 18 years old [3]**	**1,186**	**32.6**	**4.1**
Injury	131	3.4	4.0	Childbirth	107	2.9	2.7
Pneumonia	81	2.1	3.8	Injury	89	2.5	3.2
Asthma	84	2.2	2.2	Schizophrenia, mood disorders, delusional disorders, nonorganic psychoses [5]	[4] 121	[4] 3.3	[4] 6.6
18-44 years old [3]	**2,343**	**41.2**	**4.5**	**18-44 years old [3]**	**7,186**	**129.4**	**3.3**
Injury	342	6.0	4.8	Childbirth	3,841	69.2	2.7
Schizophrenia, mood disorders, delusional disorders, nonorganic psychoses [5]	494	8.7	5.5	Schizophrenia, mood disorders, delusional disorders, nonorganic psychoses [5]	412	7.4	5.2
Heart disease	135	2.4	3.2	Injury	289	5.2	4.2
Alcohol and drug [6]	88	1.5	3.8	Uterine fibroids	88	1.6	2.1
45-64 years old [3]	**4,640**	**118.4**	**5.2**	**45-64 years old [3]**	**4,843**	**117.6**	**4.8**
Heart disease	704	18.0	4.1	Heart disease	416	10.1	4.8
Injury	450	11.5	7.1	Cancer, all	236	5.7	6.5
Cancer, all	230	5.9	6.2	Osteoarthritis	272	6.6	3.2
65-74 years old [3]	**2,511**	**252.2**	**5.6**	**65-74 years old [3]**	**2,679**	**233.4**	**5.3**
Heart disease	481	48.4	4.7	Heart disease	351	30.6	4.6
Cancer, all	164	16.5	6.8	Osteoarthritis	204	17.8	3.6
Stroke	123	12.3	4.8	Cancer, all	133	11.6	5.2
Pneumonia	91	9.1	5.9	Pneumonia	89	7.7	5.8
75-84 years old [3]	**2,255**	**403.5**	**5.8**	**75-84 years old [3]**	**2,909**	**379.9**	**5.6**
Heart disease	452	80.9	4.8	Heart disease	475	62.0	4.9
Cancer, all	109	19.5	6.6	Injury	296	38.7	5.8
Pneumonia	104	18.6	4.8	Pneumonia	136	17.7	5.7
Stroke	109	19.6	6.4	Stroke	152	19.9	6.0
85 years old and over [3]	**1,161**	**598.0**	**5.5**	**85 years old and over [3]**	**2,076**	**530.2**	**5.4**
Heart disease	220	113.3	5.1	Heart disease	380	97.1	4.8
Pneumonia	86	44.4	5.0	Injury	264	67.4	5.3
Injury	115	59.0	5.6	Pneumonia	115	29.3	6.1

[1] The first-listed diagnosis is the one specified as the principal diagnosis or the first diagnosis listed on the face sheet or discharge summary of the medical record. It is usually the main cause of the hospitalization. The number of first-listed diagnoses is the same as the number of discharges. [2] Crude estimates. [3] Includes discharges with first-listed diagnoses not shown in table. [4] Figure does not meet standard of reliability or precision. [5] These estimates are for nonfederal short-stay hospitals only and do not include mental illness discharges from other types of facilities such as Veterans Affairs hospitals. [6] Includes abuse, dependence, and withdrawal. These estimates are for non-federal short-stay hospitals only and do not include alcohol and drug discharges from other types of facilities or programs such as the Department of Veterans Affairs or day treatment programs.

Source: U.S. National Center for Health Statistics, National Hospital Discharge Survey, unpublished data. See also <http://www.cdc.gov/nchs/nhds.htm>.

Table 185. Medicare-Certified Hospices, Utilization, and Costs: 1994 to 2011

[Total persons served and covered days in thousands (266 represents 266,000). Total program payments in millions of dollars (1,614 represents $1,614,000,000)]

Year	Total Hospices, Number	Persons Served (1,000)	Covered Days of Care		Program Payments [1]	
			Number (1,000)	Per Person Served	Total (mil. dol.)	Per Person Served (dol.) [2]
1994	1,726	266	16,038	60	1,614	6,071
1995	1,992	309	18,197	59	1,873	6,058
1996	2,161	349	18,884	54	1,991	5,704
1997	2,344	383	19,166	50	2,058	5,374
1998	2,317	421	20,308	48	2,206	5,242
1999	2,326	474	21,657	47	2,525	5,324
2000	2,267	534	25,958	49	2,926	5,476
2001	2,275	595	30,684	52	3,690	6,208
2002	2,323	662	36,195	55	4,539	6,863
2003	2,434	731	45,512	60	5,630	7,724
2004	2,645	800	50,530	64	6,716	8,428
2005	2,872	874	57,437	66	7,902	9,118
2006	3,071	942	64,997	70	9,236	9,837
2007	3,255	1,000	70,552	71	10,343	10,385
2008	3,346	1,055	74,017	71	11,196	10,662
2009	3,405	1,094	77,410	71	12,084	11,089
2010	3,509	1,163	81,655	71	12,950	11,175
2011	3,630	1,224	85,449	70	13,828	11,342

[1] Medicare program payments represent fee-for-service only and exclude amounts paid for managed care services. [2] Excludes persons who received covered services, but for whom no program payments were reported during the reporting year.

Source: Centers for Medicare & Medicaid Services, *Medicare and Medicaid Statistical Supplement, 2012*, Table 8.1. See also <http://www.cms.gov/Research-Statistics-Data-and-Systems/Statistics-Trends-and-Reports/MedicareMedicaidStatSupp/index.html>.

Table 186. Hospital Outpatient Department Visits by Leading Reason for Visit and Primary Diagnosis: 2010

[100,742 represents 100,742,000. Based on the 2010 National Hospital Ambulatory Medical Care Survey (NHAMCS). NHAMCS is an annual nationally representative sample survey of visits to emergency departments, hospital outpatient departments, ambulatory surgical centers (ASCs) of nonfederal short-stay and general hospitals, and freestanding ASCs. Data are subject to sampling and nonsampling errors]

Leading Reason for Visit	Number of visits (1,000)	Percent distribution	Leading Diagnosis for Visit	Number of visits (1,000)	Percent distribution
All visits	**100,742**	**100.0**	**All visits**	**100,742**	**100.0**
Progress visit, not otherwise specified	11,960	11.9	Diabetes mellitus	4,838	4.8
General medical examination	5,275	5.2	Malignant neoplasms	4,447	4.4
Prenatal examination, routine	3,015	3.0	Essential hypertension	3,580	3.6
Diabetes mellitus	2,831	2.8	Routine infant or child health check	3,339	3.3
Medication, other and unspecified kinds	2,436	2.4	Acute upper respiratory infections	2,716	2.7
Cough	2,253	2.2	Normal pregnancy	2,481	2.5
Counseling, not otherwise specified	2,235	2.2	Spinal disorders	2,360	2.3
Postoperative visit	2,233	2.2	Arthropathies and related disorders	2,347	2.3
Stomach and abdominal pain, cramps and spasms	1,655	1.6	Heart disease, excluding ischemic	([1]) 1,986	([1]) 2.0
Symptoms referable to throat	1,585	1.6	Psychoses, excluding major depressive disorder	1,766	1.8
Well-baby examination	1,226	1.2	General medical examination	1,706	1.7
Earache, or ear infection	1,164	1.2	Complications of pregnancy, childbirth, and the puerperium	1,601	1.6
Knee symptoms	1,151	1.1	Specific procedures and aftercare	1,590	1.6
Hypertension	1,146	1.1	Rheumatism, excluding back	1,516	1.5
Other special examination	([1]) 1,126	([1]) 1.1	Otitis media and eustachian tube disorders	1,481	1.5
Back symptoms	1,002	1.0	Asthma	1,337	1.3
Gynecological examination	942	0.9	Follow up examination	1,094	1.1
Skin rash	940	0.9	Potential health hazards related to personal and family history	1,035	1.0
Headache, pain in head	927	0.9	Acute pharyngitis	1,034	1.0
Fever	915	0.9	Attention deficit disorder	1,009	1.0
All other reasons	54,725	54.3	All other diagnoses	57,478	57.1

[1] Figure does not meet standards of reliability or precision.

Source: U.S. National Center for Health Statistics, *National Hospital Ambulatory Medical Care Survey: 2010 Outpatient Department Summary Tables*. See also <http://www.cdc.gov/nchs/ahcd/web_tables.htm>.

Table 187. Physician Office Visits by Sex and Leading Reason for Visit and Primary Diagnosis: 2010

[1,008,802 represents 1,008,802,000. Based on the 2010 National Ambulatory Medical Care Survey (NAMCS). NAMCS is an annual nationally representative sample survey of visits to nonfederal office-based patient care physicians, excluding anesthesiologists, radiologists, and pathologists. The sampling frame for the 2010 NAMCS was composed of all physicians contained in the master files maintained by the American Medical Association and the American Osteopathic Association. Data are subject to sampling and nonsampling errors]

Leading Reason for Visit	Number of visits (1,000)	Male percent distribution [1]	Female percent distribution [2]	Leading Diagnosis for Visit	Number of visits (1,000)	Male percent distribution [1]	Female percent distribution [2]
All visits	**1,008,802**	**100.0**	**100.0**	**All visits**	**1,008,802**	**100.0**	**100.0**
Progress visit, not otherwise specified	93,196	9.3	9.2	Routine infant or child health check	44,634	5.4	3.7
General medical examination	82,986	10.1	6.9	Essential hypertension	38,916	4.4	3.5
Cough	30,981	3.4	2.9	Arthropathies and related disorders	36,130	3.4	3.7
Postoperative visit	26,581	2.7	2.6	Acute upper respiratory infections [3]	32,207	3.3	3.2
Medication, other and				Spinal disorders	31,593	3.5	2.9
unspecified kinds	22,031	2.5	2.0	Diabetes mellitus	30,560	3.8	2.5
Knee symptoms	18,624	2.1	1.7	Malignant neoplasms	29,155	3.4	2.5
Prenatal examination, routine	18,595	(X)	3.2	Rheumatism, excluding back	21,835	1.9	2.4
Gynecological examination	17,713	(X)	3.0	Normal pregnancy	20,879	(X)	3.6
Well baby examination	16,628	1.9	1.4	General medical examination	19,705	2.5	1.5
For other and unspecified test results	16,340	1.8	1.5	Gynecological examination	16,345	(X)	2.8
Stomach and abdominal pain,				Follow up examination	15,603	1.4	1.6
cramps and spasms	15,028	1.2	1.7	Otitis media and			
Counseling, not otherwise specified	14,958	1.5	1.5	eustachian tube disorders	14,650	1.9	1.1
Diabetes mellitus	13,633	1.7	1.1	Specific procedures and aftercare	14,286	1.6	1.3
Symptoms referable to throat	13,251	1.4	1.3	Asthma	14,232	1.5	1.4
Back symptoms	13,226	1.4	1.2	Heart disease, excluding ischemic	12,405	1.3	1.2
Hypertension	12,513	1.4	1.1	Disorders of lipoid metabolism	12,350	1.6	0.9
Earache, or ear infection	12,023	1.4	1.0	Cataract	11,266	1.0	1.2
Skin rash	11,626	1.1	1.2	Allergic rhinitis	11,057	1.2	1.0
Shoulder symptoms	11,488	1.3	1.0	Benign neoplasms	10,663	1.0	1.1
Vision dysfunctions	10,556	0.9	1.1	All other diagnoses [4]	570,331	56.0	56.9
All other reasons	536,826	52.9	53.4				

X Not applicable. [1] Based on 422,131,000 visits made by males. [2] Based on 586,671,000 visits made by females. [3] Excluding pharyngitis. [4] Includes all other diagnoses not listed above, as well as unknown and blank diagnoses.

Source: U.S. National Center for Health Statistics, *National Ambulatory Medical Care Survey: 2010 Summary Tables*. See also <http://www.cdc.gov/nchs/ahcd/web_tables.htm>.

Table 188. Emergency Room Visits by Wait Time and Total Time Spent: 2010

[129,843 represents 129,843,000. Based on the 2010 National Hospital Ambulatory Medical Care Survey (NHAMCS). The NHAMCS is an annual nationally representative sample survey of visits to emergency departments, outpatient departments, ambulatory surgical centers (ASCs) of nonfederal short-stay and general hospitals, and freestanding ASCs. Data are subject to sampling and nonsampling errors]

Visit characteristic	Number of visits (1,000)	Percent	Visit characteristic	Number of visits (1,000)	Percent
Total visits [1]	**129,843**	**100.0**	TIME SPENT IN EMERGENCY DEPARTMENT		
TIME SPENT WAITING TO SEE A MEDICAL PROFESSIONAL [2]			Less than 1 hour	16,203	12.5
Fewer than 15 minutes	32,612	25.1	1 hour, but less than 2 hours	31,314	24.1
15-59 minutes	53,939	41.5	2 hours, but less than 4 hours	44,635	34.4
1 hour, but less than 2 hours	18,842	14.5	4 hours, but less than 6 hours	19,825	15.3
2 hours, but less than 3 hours	6,376	4.9	6 hours, but less than 10 hours	10,379	8.0
3 hours, but less than 4 hours	2,526	1.9	10 hour, but less than 14 hours	1,995	1.5
4 hours, but less than 6 hours	1,679	1.3	14 hours, but less than 24 hours	1,222	0.9
6 hours or more	864	0.7	24 hours or more	614	0.5

[1] Totals include nonresponse and nonapplicable categories. [2] Medical professional may be a medical doctor, doctor of osteopathy, physician assistance, or nurse practitioner.

Source: U.S. National Center for Health Statistics, *National Hospital Ambulatory Medical Care Survey: 2010 Emergency Department Summary Tables*. See also <http://www.cdc.gov/nchs/ahcd/web_tables.htm>.

Table 189. Percent Distribution of Persons Age 18 Years Old and Over by Usual Source of Health Care by Selected Characteristics: 2011

[In percent, except as noted. Data are age-adjusted, unless otherwise noted. Based on a survey question that asked, "Is there a place that you usually go to when you are sick or need advice about your health?" If there was at least one such place, a follow-up question was asked: "What kind of place [is it/do you go to most often]—a clinic, a doctor's office, an emergency room, or some other place?" From the National Health Interview Survey, a sample survey of the civilian noninstitutionalized population; see Appendix III]

Characteristic	Adults age 18 and over (1,000)	Without a usual place for health care	With a usual place for health care	Usual place of health care			
				Physician office or Health Maintenance Organization (HMO)	Clinic or health center	Hospital emergency room or outpatient department	Other place
Total [2]	**231,376**	**15.5**	**84.5**	**73.6**	**22.3**	**3.0**	**1.2**
SEX							
Male............................	112,093	19.4	80.6	72.4	22.3	3.8	1.6
Female..........................	119,283	11.7	88.3	74.5	22.3	2.4	0.8
AGE [3]							
18 to 44 years old..............	110,815	22.6	77.4	69.4	25.7	3.5	1.4
45 to 64 years old..............	80,849	10.0	90.0	76.5	19.8	2.8	0.9
65 to 74 years old..............	21,902	3.9	96.1	80.5	16.5	2.3	0.8
75 and over.....................	17,810	2.5	97.5	82.5	15.0	1.5	1.0
RACE							
Single race [4]	227,770	15.5	84.5	73.6	22.2	3.0	1.1
White...........................	186,233	15.4	84.6	74.8	21.7	2.3	1.2
Black or African American.......	27,666	15.4	84.6	68.0	23.6	7.3	1.1
American Indian or Alaska Native...........	1,980	15.6	84.4	35.4	57.9	[1] 5.1	[1] 1.6
Asian...........................	11,468	17.5	82.5	75.4	20.7	3.0	0.9
Native Hawaiian or Other Pacific Islander. ..	423	[1] 12.3	87.7	70.1	27.8	(B)	—
Two or more races [5]	3,605	15.5	84.5	67.9	27.0	3.9	[1] 1.3
Black or African American, white.............	675	25.0	75.0	68.0	28.9	(B)	—
American Indian or Alaska Native, white.....	1,457	16.6	83.4	63.8	32.9	[1] 2.2	(B)
HISPANIC ORIGIN AND RACE [6]							
Hispanic or Latino...............	32,762	26.0	74.0	59.8	34.6	4.7	0.9
Mexican or Mexican American...............	20,101	28.3	71.7	57.4	38.1	3.7	0.8
Not Hispanic or Latino...........	198,614	13.5	86.5	75.6	20.4	2.8	1.2
White, single race...............	156,482	12.8	87.2	77.3	19.5	2.0	1.2
Black or African American, single race.........	26,552	14.9	85.1	68.4	23.0	7.5	1.1
EDUCATION [7]							
Less than high school diploma................	28,318	23.0	77.0	57.6	35.3	6.6	0.5
High school diploma or GED [8]	52,560	16.8	83.2	72.9	22.4	3.5	1.1
Some college...................	58,568	13.6	86.4	75.1	20.4	3.2	1.3
Bachelor's degree or higher......	60,869	8.6	91.4	82.1	15.6	1.2	1.1
FAMILY INCOME							
Less than $35,000..............	74,445	23.3	76.7	58.9	33.5	6.1	1.5
$35,000 to $49,999.............	31,262	18.7	81.3	70.7	24.4	3.5	1.3
$50,000 to $74,999.............	39,095	13.9	86.1	78.2	19.2	1.6	1.0
$75,000 to $99,999.............	26,539	10.2	89.8	81.3	16.5	1.5	0.8
$100,000 or more...............	45,931	6.0	94.0	83.6	14.1	1.3	1.1
HEALTH INSURANCE COVERAGE [9]							
Under age 65:							
Private.........................	123,512	9.7	90.3	80.9	17.1	1.1	0.9
Medicaid.......................	19,167	9.4	90.6	58.4	36.1	4.8	[1] 0.7
Other..........................	8,580	8.0	92.0	54.3	34.5	9.2	2.0
Uninsured......................	39,635	48.0	52.0	42.0	44.0	11.1	2.9
Age 65 and over:							
Private.........................	20,987	2.1	97.9	84.8	13.8	1.1	[1] 0.3
Medicare and Medicaid...........	2,637	4.2	95.8	70.8	23.6	5.0	(B)
Medicare only..................	12,948	4.3	95.7	82.5	15.3	1.1	[1] 1.0
Other..........................	2,762	[1] 2.4	97.6	62.1	25.0	8.4	4.5
Uninsured......................	290	37.6	62.4	42.3	[1] 36.8	(B)	(B)

– Represents zero. B Figure too small to meet statistical standards for reliability of a derived figure. [1] Figure has a relative standard error greater than 30% and less than or equal to 50%, and does not meet standards of reliability or precision. [2] Includes other races not shown separately and persons with unknown education, family income, and health insurance characteristics. [3] Estimates for age groups are not age adjusted. [4] Persons who indicated only a single race group. [5] Persons who indicated more than one race group. [6] Persons of Hispanic or Latino origin may be of any race or combination of races. [7] Shown only for adults aged 25 and over. [8] GED is General Educational Development high school equivalency diploma. [9] Based on a hierarchy of mutually exclusive categories. Persons with more than one type of health insurance were assigned to the first appropriate category in the hierarchy.

Source: U.S. National Center for Health Statistics, *Summary Health Statistics for U.S. Adults: National Health Interview Survey, 2011*, Vital and Health Statistics, Series 10, Number 256, December 2012. See also <http://www.cdc.gov/nchs/products/series/series10.htm>.

Table 190. Organ Transplants: 1990 to 2012

[As of end of year. Based on reports of procurement programs and transplant centers in the United States, except as noted]

Procedure	Number of procedures								Number of people waiting		
	1990	1995	2000	2005	2009	2010	2011	2012	2010	2011	2012
Transplant: [1]											
Heart.................	2,107	2,363	2,199	2,125	2,211	2,332	2,322	2,378	3,165	3,116	(NA)
Heart-lung..........	52	69	48	35	30	42	27	29	67	(NA)	(NA)
Lung.................	203	872	959	1,406	1,660	1,769	1,822	1,754	1,819	1,681	(NA)
Liver.................	2,690	3,934	5,001	6,444	6,320	6,291	6,342	6,256	16,067	15,988	(NA)
Kidney..............	9,417	11,084	13,623	16,485	16,829	16,899	16,814	16,485	85,117	87,838	(NA)
Kidney-pancreas. ..	458	919	915	903	854	828	795	801	2,281	(NA)	(NA)
Pancreas...........	69	109	439	542	375	349	287	242	1,385	(NA)	(NA)
Intestine............	5	46	82	178	180	151	129	106	265	271	(NA)
Multi-organ.........	71	127	222	522	555	560	579	625	(NA)	(NA)	(NA)

NA Not available. [1] Kidney-pancreas and heart-lung transplants are each counted as one procedure. All other multiorgan transplants, excluding kidney-pancreas and heart-lung, are included in the multiorgan row. The data have been supplied by UNOS under contract with Health and Human Services (HHS). This work was supported in part by Health Resources and Services Administration contract 231-00-0015. The authors alone are responsible for the reporting and interpretation of these data. Data subject to change based on future data submission or correction.

Source: U.S. Department of Health and Human Services, Health Resources and Services Administration, Organ Procurement and Transplantation Network, <http://optn.transplant.hrsa.gov/latestData/viewDataReports.asp>, accessed September 2013.

Table 191. Selected Cosmetic Plastic Surgical and Nonsurgical Procedures: 2005 to 2012

[In thousands (11,428.8 represents 11,428,800). As of December 31. The final data are projected to reflect nationwide statistics and are based on a survey of doctors who have been certified by the American Board of Medical Specialties recognized boards, including but not limited to the American Board of Plastic Surgery. Data for the procedures include but are not limited to those performed by American Society for Aesthetic Plastic Surgery (ASAPS) members. ASAPS members are plastic surgeons certified by the American Board of Plastic Surgery who specialize in cosmetic surgery of the face and the entire body]

Procedure	2005	2007	2008	2009	2010	2011	2012
Total all procedures.................	11,428.8	11,701.0	10,258.6	9,964.4	9,183.2	9,194.5	10,105.2
Total surgical procedures [1]...................	2,131.0	2,079.0	1,766.7	1,491.9	1,624.3	1,638.5	1,688.7
Breast augmentation......................	364.6	399.4	355.7	312.0	318.1	316.8	330.6
Lipoplasty (Liposuction).........................	455.5	456.8	341.1	283.7	289.0	325.3	313.0
Abdominoplasty (tummy tuck)..................	169.3	185.3	147.4	127.9	144.9	149.4	156.5
Blepharoplasty (eyelid surgery).................	231.5	240.8	195.1	149.9	152.1	147.5	153.2
Rhinoplasty (nose reshaping)...................	200.9	151.8	152.4	138.3	133.5	126.1	143.8
Total nonsurgical procedures [1]..............	9,297.7	9,622.0	8,491.9	8,472.6	7,558.9	7,556.0	8,416.5
Botox injection [2]...........................	3,294.8	2,775.2	2,464.1	2,557.1	2,437.2	2,619.7	3,257.9
Hyaluronic acid [3].............................	1,194.2	1,448.7	1,262.8	1,313.0	1,315.1	1,206.2	1,423.7
Laser hair removal...........................	1,566.9	1,412.7	1,281.0	1,280.0	936.3	919.8	883.9
Microdermabrasion [4].........................	1,023.9	829.7	557.1	621.9	450.7	499.4	498.8
Chemical peel..............................	556.2	575.1	591.8	529.3	493.9	384.2	443.8
Total female procedures................	10,443.8	10,602.5	9,394.8	9,058.5	8,586.7	8,398.4	9,136.7
Total surgical procedures [1]..................	1,918.1	1,877.1	1,600.7	1,310.7	1,479.7	1,493.6	1,528.2
Breast augmentation......................	364.6	399.4	355.7	312.0	318.1	316.8	330.6
Lipoplasty (Liposuction).........................	402.9	398.8	309.7	243.2	251.8	283.7	271.4
Abdominoplasty (tummy tuck)..................	164.1	180.5	143.0	123.0	137.9	142.7	149.0
Blepharoplasty (eyelid surgery).................	198.1	208.2	166.4	124.9	131.4	124.6	129.9
Breast reduction............................	160.5	153.1	139.9	113.5	138.2	113.0	112.8
Total nonsurgical procedures [1]..............	8,525.7	8,725.4	7,794.1	7,747.8	7,107.1	6,904.8	7,608.5
Botox injection [2]...........................	2,990.7	2,445.7	2,239.0	2,299.3	2,211.9	2,355.5	2,915.9
Hyaluronic acid [3].............................	1,149.2	1,364.5	1,200.4	1,221.8	1,245.3	1,127.2	1,318.2
Laser hair removal...........................	1,334.7	1,227.0	1,101.3	1,114.0	817.4	812.4	757.5
Microdermabrasion [4].........................	939.5	743.7	517.3	565.0	416.3	468.5	454.1
Chemical peel..............................	533.0	536.0	554.5	492.3	469.6	360.3	418.8
Laser skin resurfacing.........................	432.6	479.8	532.0	463.3	518.3	319.8	401.9
IPL laser treatment [5].........................	(X)	584.5	479.9	404.5	345.5	396.9	308.8
Sclerotherapy (Spider veins)....................	548.0	467.8	417.5	442.0	435.0	348.5	283.2
Total male procedures.................	984.9	1,098.6	863.7	935.2	750.1	796.1	968.5
Total surgical procedures [1]..................	212.9	202.0	166.0	160.9	142.6	144.9	160.5
Lipoplasty (Liposuction).........................	52.5	58.0	31.5	40.5	37.2	41.7	41.6
Rhinoplasty (nose reshaping)....................	45.9	31.7	30.2	32.7	30.1	24.5	30.0
Blepharoplasty (eyelid surgery).................	33.4	32.6	28.7	25.0	20.7	22.9	23.3
Gynecomastia (male breast reduction).........	17.7	20.3	19.1	16.8	18.3	17.6	22.7
Hair transplantation............................	11.2	16.5	18.1	13.1	(NA)	(NA)	(NA)
Facelift......................................	13.0	12.4	13.4	10.5	10.4	(NA)	11.4
Total nonsurgical procedures [1]..............	772.0	896.6	697.8	774.4	607.4	651.2	808.0
Botox injection [2]...........................	304.1	329.5	225.1	257.8	225.2	264.3	342.0
Laser hair removal...........................	232.2	185.7	179.7	166.0	118.9	107.5	126.4
Hyaluronic acid [3].............................	45.0	84.2	62.4	91.2	69.8	79.0	105.5
Microdermabrasion [4].........................	84.4	85.9	39.8	56.9	34.4	31.0	44.8
Laser skin resurfacing.........................	43.1	30.1	38.9	49.0	44.4	25.8	30.6
IPL laser treatment [5].........................	(X)	63.2	46.9	47.7	35.9	42.3	28.7

X Not applicable. NA Not available. [1] Totals include procedures not shown separately. [2] As of 2009, includes Dysport. [3] In 2003, the FDA approved hyaluronan injections for filling soft tissue defects such as facial wrinkles. [4] Procedure for reducing fine lines, "crow's feet," age spots, and acne scars. [5] IPL is intense pulse light, a procedure for facial rejuvenation.

Source: The American Society for Aesthetic Plastic Surgery, *Statistics, 2012* ©, and earlier reports. See also <http://www.surgery.org/media/statistics>.

Table 192. Cancer Survival Rates by Type/Site: 1990–2009

[For invasive cancer, unless otherwise noted. The 5-year relative survival rate, which is derived by adjusting the observed survival rate for expected mortality, represents the proportion of patients alive within 5 years subsequent to their diagnosis of cancer. Survival data for 2003 to 2009 are based on follow-up of patients in 2010. Data are based on information collected as part of the National Cancer Institute's Surveillance, Epidemiology and End Results (SEER) program, a collection of population-based registries in 9 areas.]

| Site | 5-year relative survival rates by year of diagnosis (percent) | | | | | | | | | |
| | White | | | | | Black | | | | |
	1990 to 1992	1993 to 1995	1996 to 1998	1999 to 2001	2003 to 2009	1990 to 1992	1993 to 1995	1996 to 1998	1999 to 2001	2003 to 2009
All sites [1]	61.3	62.4	64.3	67.5	69.2	47.7	52.6	55.0	58.1	60.8
Lung and bronchus	13.9	14.5	14.8	15.6	18.0	10.4	12.8	12.3	12.4	14.2
Breast [2]	86.4	87.6	89.3	91.1	91.7	71.4	72.7	76.1	78.2	79.1
Colon and rectum	61.9	60.5	63.1	66.7	67.0	52.7	51.7	53.8	55.1	57.3
Prostate	94.0	95.9	97.9	99.7	99.8	84.3	91.6	94.7	97.4	98.0
Bladder [3]	80.2	81.0	79.8	81.1	80.5	63.2	59.7	62.1	66.0	63.7
Corpus uteri	85.7	84.8	85.1	85.9	85.5	53.8	58.5	61.3	61.4	63.7
Non-Hodgkin's lymphoma [4]	51.6	53.2	59.5	66.3	72.3	42.0	42.1	54.0	57.2	63.5
Oral cavity and pharynx	57.9	60.0	59.9	62.6	67.3	32.6	37.9	36.0	43.9	45.7
Leukemia [4]	46.2	48.3	49.3	52.7	60.0	35.7	40.9	38.0	44.6	53.2
Melanoma of skin	89.2	89.5	90.8	92.4	93.1	60.4	70.2	73.3	73.1	76.5
Pancreas	4.4	3.9	4.2	5.3	6.5	3.6	3.6	3.4	5.0	5.5
Kidney and renal pelvis	60.6	61.9	62.1	65.9	73.3	56.9	57.4	66.9	63.2	71.9
Stomach	18.8	19.9	20.3	23.1	27.7	22.7	19.3	22.4	24.2	29.0
Ovary	40.3	40.5	43.1	43.0	43.9	35.8	41.5	39.1	36.2	35.9
Cervix uteri	70.8	74.1	73.6	72.8	70.5	57.9	62.9	64.9	65.0	62.7

X Not applicable. [1] Includes other sites, not shown separately. [2] Survival rates for female only. [3] Invasive and in situ. [4] All types combined.

Source: U.S. National Cancer Institute, Surveillance Epidemiology and End Results, "Cancer Statistics Review (CSR), 1975-2010," <http://www.seer.cancer.gov/statistics/>, accessed September 2013.

Table 193. Cancer—Estimated New Cases and Deaths by State: 2013

[Excludes basal and squamous cell skin cancers and in situ carcinomas, except urinary bladder. State estimates may not add to U.S. totals due to rounding]

| State | New cases [1] | | | Deaths | | | State | New cases [1] | | | Deaths | | |
	Total [2]	Female breast	Lung & bron-chus	Total [2]	Female breast	Lung & bron-chus		Total [2]	Female breast	Lung & bron-chus	Total [2]	Female breast	Lung & bron-chus
U.S.	1,660,290	232,340	228,190	580,350	39,620	159,480	MO	33,950	4,680	5,410	12,730	890	3,940
AL	27,080	3,720	4,550	10,430	690	3,290	MT	5,450	740	700	2,000	120	550
AK	3,290	510	470	980	70	270	NE	9,060	1,230	1,220	3,440	210	900
AZ	34,010	4,660	4,250	11,210	790	2,850	NV	13,830	1,760	1,970	4,760	360	1,480
AR	16,330	2,280	2,700	6,650	420	2,170	NH	8,470	1,180	1,150	2,680	170	750
CA	171,330	25,360	18,720	57,290	4,220	12,700	NJ	49,440	6,960	5,960	16,410	1,330	4,060
CO	23,410	3,300	2,550	7,350	510	1,710	NM	10,090	1,360	1,050	3,540	240	770
CT	21,180	3,050	2,780	6,890	460	1,740	NY	108,760	14,950	13,480	34,240	2,390	8,790
DE	5,370	770	760	1,940	120	580	NC	53,200	7,430	8,040	18,620	1,260	5,660
DC	2,920	450	320	1,030	80	240	ND	3,510	450	460	1,280	90	310
FL	118,320	15,710	17,960	42,370	2,660	12,070	OH	66,610	9,060	10,230	25,130	1,720	7,350
GA	49,280	7,310	6,690	16,010	1,200	4,670	OK	20,160	2,690	3,370	7,850	490	2,440
HI	6,650	960	900	2,400	140	580	OR	21,720	3,310	2,860	7,820	490	2,110
ID	7,670	1,010	930	2,660	180	670	PA	79,560	10,490	10,980	28,680	1,950	7,640
IL	66,090	9,350	9,270	24,000	1,610	6,560	RI	6,280	900	870	2,140	130	600
IN	35,550	4,540	5,500	13,250	850	4,110	SC	27,620	3,580	4,390	9,800	660	2,990
IA	17,480	2,310	2,350	6,420	400	1,780	SD	4,570	600	620	1,590	110	440
KS	14,370	2,160	1,930	5,430	360	1,590	TN	36,580	5,070	6,200	14,080	910	4,600
KY	25,100	3,300	4,560	9,970	590	3,510	TX	112,230	14,980	15,000	37,180	2,650	9,670
LA	24,930	3,630	3,740	9,040	650	2,670	UT	10,810	1,550	800	2,790	260	450
ME	9,190	1,150	1,380	3,240	190	950	VT	4,200	550	590	1,300	80	380
MD	30,680	4,760	4,040	10,480	800	2,810	VA	40,870	6,280	5,380	14,720	1,110	4,130
MA	38,250	5,820	4,880	12,840	810	3,530	WA	37,290	5,610	4,700	12,390	800	3,260
MI	57,560	8,140	8,250	20,570	1,360	5,940	WV	11,450	1,460	2,100	4,660	280	1,480
MN	28,410	4,260	3,860	9,610	610	2,500	WI	31,590	4,490	4,310	11,220	700	2,980
MS	15,830	2,080	2,630	6,300	420	2,010	WY	2,700	380	320	950	60	240

[1] Estimates are offered as a rough guide and should be interpreted with caution. [2] Includes other types of cancer, not shown separately.

Source: American Cancer Society, Inc., *Cancer Facts and Figures 2013* ©, Atlanta, GA, 2013. Reprinted by the permission of the American Cancer Society, Inc from <www.cancer.org>. All rights reserved.

Table 194. Selected Notifiable Diseases—Cases Reported: 1980 to 2011

[29.1 represents 29,100. As of June 30, 2012. Figures should be interpreted with caution. Although reporting of some of these diseases is incomplete, the figures are of value in indicating trends of disease incidence. Includes cases imported from outside the United States]

Disease	1980	1990	1995	2000	2005	2008	2009	2010	2011
AIDS [1]	(²)	41,595	71,547	40,758	41,120	39,202	(¹)	(¹)	(¹)
Botulism [3]	89	92	97	138	135	145	118	112	153
Brucellosis (undulant fever)	183	85	98	87	120	80	115	115	79
Coccidoidomycosis	(²)	(²)	(²)	2,867	6,542	7,523	12,926	(²)	22,634
Cryptosporidiosis	(²)	(²)	(²)	3,128	5,659	9,113	7,654	8,944	9,250
Domestic arboviral diseases: [4]									
West Nile: neuroinvasive	(²)	(²)	(²)	(²)	1,309	689	386	629	486
nonneuroinvasive	(²)	(²)	(²)	(²)	1,691	667	334	392	226
Giardiasis	(²)	(²)	(²)	(²)	19,733	18,908	19,399	19,811	16,747
Haemophilus influenza	(²)	(²)	1,180	1,398	2,304	2,886	3,022	3,151	3,539
Hansen disease (Leprosy)	223	198	144	91	87	80	103	98	82
Hepatitis: A (infectious) (1,000) [5]	29.1	31.4	31.6	13.4	4.5	2.6	2.0	1.7	1.4
B (serum) (1,000)	19.0	21.1	10.8	8.0	5.1	4.0	3.4	3.4	2.9
C/Non-A, non-B	(²)	2,600	4,576	3,197	652	877	782	849	1,229
Human immunodeficiency virus diagnoses	(X)	(X)	(X)	(X)	(X)	(X)	36,870	35,741	35,266
Legionellosis	(²)	1,370	1,241	1,127	2,301	3,181	3,522	3,346	4,202
Lyme disease	(²)	(²)	11,700	17,730	23,305	35,198	38,468	30,158	33,097
Malaria	2,062	1,292	1,419	1,560	1,494	1,255	1,451	1,773	1,724
Measles	13,500	27,800	309	86	66	140	71	63	220
Meningococcal infections	2,840	2,451	3,243	2,256	1,245	1,172	980	833	759
Mumps (1,000)	8.6	5.3	0.9	0.3	0.3	0.5	2.0	2.6	0.4
Pertussis [6] (1,000)	1.7	4.6	5.1	7.9	25.6	13.3	16.9	27.6	18.7
Psittacosis	124	113	64	17	16	8	9	4	2
Rabies, animal	6,421	4,826	7,811	6,934	5,915	4,196	5,343	4,331	4,357
Rubella [7]	3,904	1,125	128	176	11	16	3	5	4
Salmonellosis [8] (1,000)	33.7	48.6	46.0	39.6	45.3	51.0	49.2	54.4	51.9
Shigellosis [9] (1,000)	19.0	27.1	32.1	22.9	16.2	22.6	15.9	14.8	13.4
Streptococcus pneumoniae, invasive: [10]									
All ages	(²)	(²)	(²)	4,533	2,996	3,448	3,370	16,569	17,138
Age less than 5 years	(²)	(²)	(²)	(²)	1,495	532	583	2,186	1,459
Tetanus	95	64	41	35	27	19	18	26	36
Toxic-shock syndrome	(²)	322	191	135	90	71	74	82	78
Trichinellosis	131	129	29	16	16	39	13	7	15
Tuberculosis [11] (1,000)	27.7	25.7	22.9	16.4	14.1	12.9	11.5	11.2	10.5
Typhoid fever	510	552	369	377	324	449	397	467	390
Varicella (chickenpox) [12] (1,000)	190.9	173.1	120.6	27.4	32.2	30.4	20.5	15.4	14.5
Sexually transmitted diseases:									
Chlamydia (1,000)	(²)	(²)	478	702	976	1,211	1,244	1,308	1,413
Gonorrhea (1,000)	1,004	690	393	359	340	337	301	309	322
Syphilis (1,000)	69	134	69	32	33	46	45	46	46

X Not applicable. [1] Acquired immunodeficiency syndrome was not a notifiable disease until 1984. Includes all cases reported to the Division of HIV/AIDS Prevention, National Center for HIV/AIDS, Viral Hepatitis, STD, and TB Prevention. In 2008 CDC published a revised HIV case definition which combined definitions for HIV infection and AIDS into a single case definition for HIV infection that includes AIDS. [2] Disease was not notifiable. [3] Includes foodborne, infant, wound, and unspecified cases. [4] The national surveillance case definitions for the arboviral diseases was revised in 2005, and nonneuroinvasive arboviral diseases were added to the list of nationally notifiable infectious diseases. [5] Data on chronic hepatitis B and hepatitis C virus infection (past or present) are not included because they are undergoing data quality review. [6] Whooping cough. [7] German measles. Excludes congenital syndrome. [8] Excludes typhoid fever. [9] Bacillary dysentery. [10] Beginning with 2010, all cases of invasive Streptococcus pneumoniae disease, regardless of age or drug resistance, are reported under a single disease code. [11] Newly reported active cases. [12] Varicella (chickenpox) was removed from the nationally notifiable disease list in 1981. Varicella became nationally notifiable again in 2003.

Source: U.S. Centers for Disease Control and Prevention, "Summary of Notifiable Diseases, United States, 2011," *Morbidity and Mortality Weekly Report,* 60:53, July 5, 2013, and earlier reports. See also <http://www.cdc.gov/mmwr/mmwr_nd/index.html>.

Table 195. HIV Diagnoses, Chlamydia, and Lyme Disease Cases Reported by State: 2011

State	HIV diagnoses [1]	Chlamydia [2]	Lyme disease	State	HIV diagnoses [1]	Chlamydia [2]	Lyme disease	State	HIV diagnoses [1]	Chlamydia [2]	Lyme disease
U.S.	**35,266**	**1,412,791**	**33,097**	KS	126	10,598	17	NC	1,439	54,819	88
AL	592	29,626	24	KY	233	16,629	3	ND	12	2,445	27
AK	25	5,739	11	LA	1,281	31,614	2	OH	987	52,653	53
AZ	494	29,251	15	ME	46	3,094	1,006	OK	262	14,596	2
AR	199	16,052	–	MD	851	27,212	1,351	OR	213	13,643	38
CA	3,679	166,773	92	MA	523	22,764	2,476	PA	1,269	52,884	5,362
CO	362	21,811	–	MI	610	49,568	104	RI	88	4,146	159
CT	305	13,649	3,039	MN	283	16,902	2,124	SC	771	28,932	37
DE	99	4,508	873	MS	552	21,216	5	SD	21	3,409	4
DC	495	6,585	(NA)	MO	481	27,887	8	TN	814	31,105	37
FL	4,890	76,033	115	MT	17	3,406	11	TX	3,225	124,882	74
GA	1,431	54,403	32	NE	46	6,780	11	UT	76	7,086	9
HI	50	6,001	(NA)	NV	320	10,507	5	VT	1	1,483	623
ID	16	4,699	4	NH	40	3,010	1,299	VA	857	36,314	1,023
IL	1,351	64,939	194	NJ	812	26,209	4,262	WA	449	23,280	19
IN	434	27,801	94	NM	111	11,374	6	WV	92	4,295	118
IA	116	10,705	100	NY	3,547	102,763	4,490	WI	259	24,619	3,649
								WY	14	2,092	2

– Represents zero. NA Not available. [1] Total number of HIV diagnoses reported to the Division of HIV/AIDS Prevention, National Center for HIV/AIDS, Viral Hepatitis, STD, and TB Prevention (NCIRD), as of December 31, 2011. In 2008, CDC combined separate surveillance case definitions for HIV infection and AIDS into a single case definition for HIV infection that includes AIDS (and incorporates the HIV infection classification system). [2] As of June 7, 2012.

Source: Centers for Disease Control and Prevention, "Summary of Notifiable Diseases, United States, 2011," *Morbidity and Mortality Weekly Report*, 60:53, July 5, 2013. See also <http://www.cdc.gov/mmwr/mmwr_nd/index.html>.

Table 196. Estimated Numbers of AIDS Diagnoses Among Adults and Adolescents by Sex and Transmission Category: 2008 to 2011

[All data are provisional. Data are included for 50 states, the District of Columbia, Puerto Rico, the U.S. Virgin Islands, Guam, and the U.S. Pacific Islands. Estimated numbers resulted from statistical adjustment that accounted for reporting delays and missing transmission category, but not for incomplete reporting. Acquired immunodeficiency syndrome (AIDS) is a specific group of diseases or conditions which are indicative of severe immunosuppression related to infection with the human immunodeficiency virus (HIV). Data are subject to retrospective changes and may differ from those data in Table 194. For information on HIV death rates, go to Table 134]

Transmission category	2008	2009	2010	2011	Cumulative through 2011 [1]
Persons 13 years old and over, total [2]	**33,382**	**31,897**	**30,017**	**32,544**	**1,180,774**
Males, total	**24,563**	**23,708**	**22,437**	**24,443**	**939,219**
Male-to-male sexual contact	15,583	15,606	15,058	16,812	560,860
Injection drug use	3,215	2,740	2,466	2,447	201,271
Male-to-male sexual contact and injection drug use	1,743	1,524	1,418	1,411	83,455
Heterosexual contact [3]	3,852	3,705	3,371	3,638	81,477
Other [4]	171	135	124	134	12,157
Females, total	**8,818**	**8,188**	**7,579**	**8,102**	**241,553**
Injection drug use	2,087	1,826	1,615	1,642	92,833
Heterosexual contact [3]	6,612	6,238	5,834	6,330	142,153
Other [4]	120	124	130	129	6,567

[1] From the beginning of the epidemic through 2011. [2] Because column totals for estimated numbers were calculated independently of the values for the subpopulations, the values in each column may not sum to the column total. [3] Heterosexual contact with a person known to have, or to be at high risk for, HIV infection. [4] Includes hemophilia, blood transfusion, perinatal exposure, and risk factor not reported or not identified.

Source: U.S. Centers for Disease Control and Prevention, *HIV Surveillance Report: Diagnoses of HIV Infection in the United States and Dependent Areas, 2011,* Vol. 23, February 2013. See also <http://www.cdc.gov/hiv/library/reports/index.html>.

Table 197. Estimated Numbers of Persons Living With an AIDS Diagnosis by Selected Characteristics: 2000 to 2010

[See headnote, Table 196]

Age and characteristic	2000	2005	2008	2009	2010
Total [1, 2]	**323,679**	**432,846**	**470,144**	**485,220**	**499,167**
AGE AS OF END OF YEAR					
Less than 13 years old	2,954	1,506	713	554	463
13 and 14 years old	528	811	631	492	334
15 to 24 years old	5,158	7,806	9,347	9,925	10,427
25 to 34 years old	56,129	45,923	43,961	44,472	45,272
35 to 44 years old	146,206	164,551	143,927	135,510	127,403
45 to 54 years old	85,474	149,284	180,884	191,217	199,523
55 to 64 years old	21,717	50,376	72,387	81,969	91,597
65 years old and over	5,513	12,589	18,292	21,081	24,147
RACE/ETHNICITY					
American Indian/Alaska Native	1,035	1,506	1,566	1,624	1,697
Asian [3]	2,293	3,777	4,690	5,039	5,384
Black/African American	131,826	183,083	195,963	202,823	209,707
Hispanic/Latino [4]	66,271	90,836	103,182	107,243	110,778
Native Hawaiian/Other Pacific Islander	174	331	428	470	499
White	118,189	147,585	155,471	159,261	162,308
Multiple races	3,719	5,566	8,745	8,665	8,700
TRANSMISSION CATEGORY					
Males 13 years old and over, total	251,286	330,239	358,183	369,598	380,164
Male-to-male sexual contact	143,594	196,973	219,782	229,262	238,339
Injection drug use	58,437	65,366	62,550	62,186	61,745
Male-to-male sexual contact and injection drug use	25,635	30,289	31,818	31,961	32,120
Heterosexual contact [5]	20,922	34,563	39,625	41,684	43,401
Other [6]	2,698	3,048	4,409	4,505	4,560
Females 13 years old and over, total	68,423	98,500	111,245	115,066	118,538
Injection drug use	28,644	34,207	34,312	34,430	34,481
Heterosexual contact [5]	38,269	62,252	73,418	76,995	80,289
Other [6]	1,510	2,041	3,516	3,641	3,767
Children less than 13 years old at diagnosis, total [7]	3,971	4,107	713	554	463
Perinatal	3,756	3,889	689	535	444
Other [6]	215	218	24	19	18

[1] Total numbers include persons of unknown race/ethnicity. [2] Because column totals were calculated independently of the values for the subpopulations, the values in each column may not sum to the column total. [3] Includes Asian/Pacific Islander legacy cases. [4] Hispanics/Latinos can be of any race. [5] Heterosexual contact with a person known to have, or to be at high risk for, HIV infection. [6] Includes hemophilia, blood transfusion, perinatal exposure, and risk factor not reported or not identified. [7] Beginning with 2008, data on children living with AIDS are shown for children under age 13 as of end of year. Prior to 2008, data are shown for population who were under age 13 at time of AIDS diagnosis.

Source: U.S. Centers for Disease Control and Prevention, *HIV Surveillance Report: Diagnoses of HIV Infection in the United States and Dependent Areas, 2011,* Vol. 23, February 2013. See also <http://www.cdc.gov/hiv/library/reports/index.html>.

Table 198. Learning Disability and Attention Deficit Hyperactivity Disorder Among Children 3 to 17 Years of Age by Selected Characteristics: 2011

[In thousands, except percent (62,116 represents 62,116,000). Learning disability is based on the question, "Has a representative from a school or a health professional ever told you that (child's name) had a learning disability?" Attention Deficit Hyperactivity Disorder is based on the question, "Has a doctor or health professional ever told you that (child's name) had Attention Hyperactivity Disorder or Attention Deficit Disorder?"]

Selected characteristic	Total	Ever told had—			
		Learning disability		Attention deficit hyperactivity disorder	
		Number [1]	Percent [2]	Number [1]	Percent [2]
Total [3]........................	**62,116**	**4,660**	**7.6**	**5,240**	**8.5**
SEX [4]					
Male........................	31,742	2,928	9.3	3,803	12.1
Female........................	30,423	1,732	5.8	1,436	4.8
AGE					
3 to 4 years old........................	8,858	233	2.6	158	1.8
5 to 11 years old........................	28,845	2,029	7.0	2,174	7.6
12 to 17 years old........................	24,463	2,398	9.8	2,907	11.9
RACE					
Race Alone [4,5]........................	59,640	4,512	7.6	5,071	8.6
White........................	46,565	3,510	7.6	4,102	8.9
Black or African American........................	9,307	783	8.6	792	8.7
American Indian or Alaska Native........................	711	[6] 61	[6] 8.2	[6] 71	[6] 9.9
Asian........................	2,938	147	5.0	[6] 81	2.80
Native Hawaiian or Other Pacific Islander........................	119	(B)	(B)	(B)	(B)
Two or more races [4,7]........................	2,526	148	5.9	168	6.8
Black or African American and White........................	1,054	[6] 77	[6] 7.2	[6] 108	10.3
American Indian or Alaska Native and White........................	393	[6] 18	[6] 5.3	[6] 16	[6] 4.6
HISPANIC ORIGIN AND RACE [4,8]					
Hispanic or Latino........................	14,365	900	6.5	802	5.9
Mexican or Mexican American........................	9,752	622	6.7	438	4.8
Not Hispanic or Latino........................	47,801	3,761	7.9	4,437	9.3
White, single race........................	33,913	2,743	8.0	3,435	10.0
Black or African American, single race........................	8,677	758	8.8	761	8.9

B Base figure too small to meet statistical standards for reliability of a derived figure. [1] Unknowns for the columns are not included in the frequencies, but they are included in the "Total" column. [2] Unknowns for the column variables are not included in the denominators when calculating percentages. [3] Includes other races not shown separately. [4] Percents are age-adjusted to the 2000 projected U.S. standard population using age groups 3–4 years, 5–11 years, and 12–17 years. [5] Refers to persons who indicated only a single race group. [6] Figures do not meet standard of reliability or precision. [7] Refers to all persons who indicated more than one race group. [8] Persons of Hispanic or Latino origin may be of any race.

Source: National Center for Health Statistics, *Summary Health Statistics for U.S. Children: National Health Interview Survey, 2011,* Vital and Health Statistics, Series 10, Number 254, December 2012. See also <http://www.cdc.gov/nchs/products/series/series10.htm>.

Table 199. Children and Youth With Disabilities Served by Type of Disability: 1995 to 2011

[In thousands (5,078.8 represents 5,078,800). As of fall. For children and youth aged 6 to 21 served under the Individuals with Disabilities Education Act (IDEA) Part B. Includes outlying areas]

Disability	1995	2000	2006	2007	2008	2009	2010	2011
Total........................	**5,078.8**	**5,773.9**	**6,081.9**	**6,007.8**	**5,889.8**	**5,882.2**	**5,822.8**	**5,789.9**
Specific learning disabilities...........	2,601.8	2,881.6	2,710.5	2,620.2	2,525.9	2,486.4	2,415.6	2,357.5
Speech or language impairments......	1,026.9	1,093.4	1,160.9	1,154.2	1,122.0	1,107.4	1,090.4	1,071.6
Mental retardation........................	585.6	613.4	523.2	498.2	476.1	461.3	445.3	431.2
Emotional disturbance...................	439.2	474.3	458.9	440.2	418.1	405.5	387.6	371.6
Multiple disabilities......................	94.5	122.9	134.2	132.6	124.1	124.5	123.6	125.2
Hearing impairments...................	68.0	70.8	72.6	72.2	70.8	70.7	69.8	69.3
Orthopedic impairments................	63.2	73.0	61.9	60.5	62.4	58.0	55.7	54.4
Other health impairments..............	134.2	294.0	599.5	631.2	648.4	679.0	704.3	734.3
Visual impairments.....................	25.5	26.0	26.4	26.4	25.8	25.8	25.7	25.7
Autism........................	29.1	79.6	224.6	258.3	292.8	333.2	370.0	407.2
Deaf-blind........................	1.4	1.3	1.5	1.4	1.7	1.4	1.3	1.4
Traumatic brain injury..................	9.6	14.9	23.9	23.9	24.9	24.4	24.6	24.9
Developmental delay [1]...............	(X)	28.6	83.9	88.6	96.9	104.5	109.1	115.6

X Not applicable. [1] States had the option of reporting children aged 3 to 9 under developmental delay beginning 1997.

Source: U.S. Department of Education, Office of Special Education Programs, Data Accountability Center, "Part B Data & Notes: IDEA 618 Data Tables," <http://www.ideadata.org/PartBData.asp>, accessed May 2013.

Table 200. Children Under 18 Years of Age Receiving Special Education or Early Intervention Services: 2011

[In thousands, except percent (74,517 represents 74,517,000). Receiving special education or early intervention services is based on the question, "Do any of the following (family members under 18 years of age) receive special education or early intervention services?"]

Selected Characteristic	Total	Persons under 18 years who were receiving special education early intervention services		
		Number [1]	Percent [2]
Total [3]...	**74,517**	**5,153**	**6.9**
SEX [4]			
Male..	38,103	3,426	9.0
Female...	36,414	1,727	4.8
AGE			
Under 12 years...	50,267	3,135	6.2
12 to 17 years..	24,249	2,018	8.3
RACE			
Race Alone [4,5]..	71,430	4,977	7.0
White..	55,990	3,981	7.1
Black or African American........................	10,991	800	7.3
American Indian or Alaska Native.............	825	57	6.9
Asian..	3,454	125	3.7
Native Hawaiian or Other Pacific Islander.	171	(B)	[6] 8.6
Two or more races [4,7]............................	3,087	176	5.8
HISPANIC ORIGIN AND RACE [4,8]			
Hispanic or Latino....................................	17,516	973	5.6
Mexican or Mexican American..................	11,916	644	5.4
Not Hispanic or Latino..............................	57,000	4,180	7.3
White, single race....................................	40,451	3,163	7.8
Black or African American, single race......	10,252	743	7.2

B Base figure too small to meet statistical standards for reliability of a derived figure. [1] Unknowns for the columns are not included in the frequencies, but they are included in the "Total" column. [2] Unknowns for the column variables are not included in the denominators when calculating percentages. [3] Includes other races not shown separately. [4] Percents are age-adjusted to the 2000 projected U.S. standard population using two age groups 0-11 years, and 12-17 years. [5] Refers to persons who indicated only a single race group. [6] Figures do not meet standard of reliability or precision. [7] Refers to all persons who indicated more than one race group. [8] Persons of Hispanic or Latino origin may be of any race.

Source: National Center for Health Statistics, *Summary Health Statistics for the U.S. Population: National Health Interview Survey, 2011,* Vital and Health Statistics, Series 10, Number 255, December 2012. See also <http://www.cdc.gov/nchs/products/series/series10.htm>.

Table 201. Population With a Disability, by Age Group and by State: 2011

[In thousands (37,022 represents 37,022,000). Based on data from the American Community Survey (ACS). Disability data limited to civilian noninstitutionalized population. People aged 5 to 14 were classified as having a disability if they were reported to have any one of the following five limitations: hearing difficulty, vision difficulty, cognitive difficulty, ambulatory difficulty, or self-care difficulty. People aged 15 and over were classified as having a disability if they reported any one of the five limitations listed above or independent living difficulty. Based on a sample and subject to sampling variability. See text, Section 1 and Appendix III]

State	Total	5 to 17 years	18 to 64 years	65 years and over	State	Total	5 to 17 years	18 to 64 years	65 years and over
U.S.............	**37,022**	**2,780**	**19,583**	**14,659**	MO............	818	60	449	309
AL...............	763	52	433	278	MT............	130	7	68	55
AK...............	73	5	44	24	NE............	189	15	94	80
AZ...............	729	52	375	301	NV............	301	19	166	116
AR...............	483	36	269	178	NH............	151	12	78	61
CA...............	3,730	269	1,880	1,581	NJ............	868	67	413	388
CO...............	514	43	282	189	NM............	275	16	147	112
CT...............	376	28	185	163	NY............	2,083	149	1,063	872
DE...............	107	8	56	43	NC............	1,253	94	688	471
DC...............	67	5	37	25	ND............	70	3	34	33
FL...............	2,414	146	1,132	1,136	OH............	1,511	121	817	573
GA...............	1,155	91	664	399	OK............	574	41	322	211
HI...............	140	9	63	68	OR............	521	39	279	204
ID...............	199	19	101	80	PA............	1,666	126	862	677
IL...............	1,310	95	659	556	RI............	123	7	65	51
IN...............	839	69	459	310	SC............	628	38	352	238
IA...............	342	27	169	146	SD............	93	6	47	40
KS...............	344	28	182	134	TN............	958	65	546	346
KY...............	718	52	421	245	TX............	2,889	255	1,572	1,062
LA...............	677	57	384	235	UT............	245	24	134	87
ME...............	203	17	108	78	VT............	80	6	42	31
MD...............	582	42	306	234	VA............	864	63	459	342
MA...............	735	61	373	301	WA............	836	65	458	314
MI...............	1,351	106	750	495	WV............	345	19	199	127
MN...............	530	46	270	214	WI............	635	58	327	250
MS...............	470	32	265	173	WY............	63	3	36	24

Source: U.S. Census Bureau, 2011 American Community Survey, B18101, "Sex by Age by Disability Status," <http://factfinder2.census.gov>, accessed February 2013.

Table 202. Children Immunized Against Specified Diseases: 1995 to 2011

[In percent. Covers civilian noninstitutionalized population aged 19 months to 35 months. Based on estimates from the National Immunization Survey. The health care providers of the children are contacted to verify and/or complete vaccination information. Results are based on race/ethnic status of the child]

Vaccination	1995, total	2001, total	2011 [1]					
			Total	White [2]	Black [2]	Hispanic [3]	American Indian/ Alaska Native only [2]	Asian [2]
Diphtheria-tetanus-pertussis (DTP) diphtheria-tetanus:								
3+ doses	95.0	94.0	95.5	95.5	94.7	95.6	89.6	97.9
4+ doses	79.0	82.0	84.6	85.0	81.3	84.1	72.7	92.0
Polio: 3+ doses	88.0	90.0	93.9	93.9	93.9	93.8	88.1	96.5
Measles, mumps, rubella vaccine	90.0	91.0	91.6	91.1	90.8	92.4	94.8	93.9
Hib: 3+ doses [4]	92.0	93.0	94.2	94.2	93.0	94.5	91.7	94.6
Hepatitis B: 3+ doses	68.0	90.0	91.1	90.3	92.1	91.5	92.6	95.5
Varicella [5]	(NA)	68.0	90.8	89.6	91.2	92.0	90.1	93.5
PCV: 3+ doses [6]	(X)	(X)	93.6	93.4	93.4	94.3	85.5	92.5
4+ DT:3+ polio:1+ MMR:3+ Hib [7]	74.0	76.0	81.9	82.0	78.9	81.9	72.4	88.2
4+ DTP:3+ polio:1+ MMR:3+ Hib:3+ HepB [8]	55.1	72.8	(NA)	(NA)	(NA)	(NA)	(NA)	(NA)
4+ DTP:3+ polio:1+ MMR:2+ Hib: 3+ HepB:1+ Varicella	(NA)	(NA)	77.0	76.9	74.6	77.1	71.9	83.2

NA Not available. X Not applicable. [1] Children in the 2011 National Immunization Survey were born January 2008-May 2010. [2] Non-Hispanic. [3] Children of Hispanic origin may be of any race. [4] Haemophilus influenzae type B. [5] Data collection for varicella (chicken pox) began in July 1996. [6] PCV = Pneumococcal conjugate vaccine. [7] MMR = Measles, mumps, and rubella. [8] Beginning with 2010, this data no longer available. [9] 4+ DTP/3+ polio/1+ MMR/3+ Hib/3+ HepB/1+ Varicella

Source: U.S. Centers for Disease Control and Prevention, Vaccines & Immunizations, Vaccination Coverage and Surveillance, "National Immunization Survey, Children," <http://www.cdc.gov/vaccines/stats-surv/nis/default.htm#nis>, accessed May 2013.

Table 203. Asthma Incidence Among Children Under 18 Years of Age by Selected Characteristics: 2011

[In thousands, except percent (74,518 represents 74,518,000). Based on the National Health Interview Survey, a sample survey of the civilian noninstitutionalized population; see Appendix III]

Characteristic	Total	Ever told had asthma		Still have asthma	
		Number [1]	Percent [2]	Number [1]	Percent [2]
Total [3]	**74,518**	**10,463**	**14.2**	**7,074**	**9.6**
SEX [4]					
Male	38,103	5,821	15.4	3,876	10.3
Female	36,415	4,642	12.9	3,198	8.8
AGE					
0 to 4 years old	21,210	1,753	8.3	1,452	6.9
5 to 11 years old	28,845	4,139	14.4	2,849	9.9
12 to 17 years old	24,463	4,571	18.7	2,773	11.4
RACE					
Single race [4, 5]	71,363	9,872	13.9	6,626	9.3
White	55,876	6,994	12.6	4,489	8.1
Black or African American	10,990	2,282	20.9	1,804	16.5
American Indian or Alaska Native	873	134	14.8	[6] 69	[6] 7.8
Asian	3,455	419	12.4	240	7.1
Native Hawaiian or Other Pacific Islander	169	(B)	[6] 23.9	[6] 24	[6] 13.0
Two or more races [4, 7]	3,155	592	19.6	447	14.6
HISPANIC ORIGIN AND RACE [4, 8]					
Hispanic or Latino	17,517	2,452	14.5	1,679	9.8
Mexican or Mexican American	11,956	1,455	12.7	929	8.1
Not Hispanic or Latino	57,001	8,012	14.1	5,395	9.5
White, single race	40,459	4,993	12.3	3,157	7.8
Black or African American, single race	10,221	2,119	20.9	1,664	16.4

B Figure too small to meet statistical standards for reliability of a derived figure. [1] Unknowns for the columns are not included in the frequencies, but they are included in the "Total" column. [2] Unknowns for the column variables are not included in the denominators when calculating percentages. [3] Includes other races, not shown separately. [4] Estimates are age-adjusted to the 2000 projected U.S. standard population using age groups 0–4 years, 5–11 years, and 12–17 years. [5] Refers to persons who indicated only a single race group. [6] Figures do not meet standard of reliability or precision. [7] Refers to all persons who indicated more than one race group. [8] Persons of Hispanic or Latino origin may be of any race or combination of races.

Source: National Center for Health Statistics, *Summary Health Statistics for the U.S. Population: National Health Interview Survey, 2011*, Vital and Health Statistics, Series 10, Number 255, December 2012. See also <http://www.cdc.gov/nchs/products/series/series10.htm>.

Table 204. Nursing Homes, Beds, Residents, and Occupancy Rate by State: 2011

[Based on a census of certified nursing facilities]

State	Nursing homes	Beds	Residents	Occupancy rate[1]	State	Nursing homes	Beds	Residents	Occupancy rate[1]
U.S.........	15,702	1,703,486	1,389,241	81.6	MO.........	514	55,114	37,519	68.1
AL............	228	26,692	22,855	85.6	MT.........	85	6,927	4,799	69.3
AK............	15	662	607	91.7	NE.........	222	16,141	12,522	77.6
AZ............	141	16,401	11,472	69.9	NV.........	51	5,984	4,717	78.8
AR............	234	24,600	18,071	73.5	NH.........	78	7,710	6,906	89.6
CA............	1,235	120,833	102,377	84.7	NJ.........	362	51,681	45,486	88.0
CO............	212	20,115	16,099	80.0	NM.........	71	6,789	5,645	83.1
CT............	238	29,045	25,748	88.6	NY.........	634	117,931	108,077	91.6
DE............	47	4,990	4,195	84.1	NC.........	422	44,421	37,486	84.4
DC............	19	2,772	2,610	94.2	ND.........	84	6,370	5,733	90.0
FL............	681	82,567	72,068	87.3	OH.........	962	92,584	78,673	85.0
GA............	359	39,857	34,272	86.0	OK.........	312	29,073	19,491	67.0
HI............	48	4,315	3,800	88.1	OR.........	137	12,232	7,498	61.3
ID............	79	6,131	4,315	70.4	PA.........	710	88,927	80,253	90.2
IL............	781	100,346	74,580	74.3	RI.........	85	8,792	8,053	91.6
IN............	510	58,782	38,994	66.3	SC.........	188	19,605	17,240	87.9
IA............	442	32,548	25,121	77.2	SD.........	111	6,892	6,471	93.9
KS............	341	25,683	18,877	73.5	TN.........	319	37,235	31,437	84.4
KY............	282	25,934	23,242	89.6	TX.........	1,194	133,268	92,133	69.1
LA............	281	35,990	25,586	71.1	UT.........	100	8,377	5,448	65.0
ME............	109	7,121	6,391	89.7	VT.........	40	3,250	2,833	87.2
MD............	231	28,763	24,683	85.8	VA.........	286	32,358	28,308	87.5
MA............	426	49,095	42,801	87.2	WA.........	228	21,811	17,578	80.6
MI............	425	46,903	39,545	84.3	WV.........	125	10,789	9,448	87.6
MN............	384	31,620	28,529	90.2	WI.........	393	35,859	29,801	83.1
MS............	203	18,632	16,447	88.3	WY.........	38	2,969	2,401	80.9

[1] Percentage of beds occupied (number of nursing home residents per 100 nursing home beds).

Source: U.S. National Center for Health Statistics, *Health, United States, 2012,* May 2013. See also <http://www.cdc.gov/nchs/hus.htm>.

Table 205. Injuries Associated With Selected Consumer Products: 2011

[Estimates are based on a national probability sample of hospitals in the U.S. and its territories. Patient information is collected from each participating hospital for every emergency visit involving an injury associated with consumer products. From this sample, the total number of product-related injuries treated in hospital emergency rooms nationwide is estimated]

Product Type	Number	Product Type	Number
Items for infants/children:		Housewares:	
All nursery equipment..............................	101,165	Cans, other containers................................	285,919
Baby strollers...	17,449	Cleaning agents (excludes soaps)...................	40,622
High chairs...	9,959	Drinking glasses.......................................	77,310
Playground equipment (excl. swings)........................	244,641	Knives...	349,424
Swings or swings sets.................................	59,841	Tableware and accessories...........................	90,756
Toys...	252,249		
		Tools & garden equipment:	
Sports & recreational equipment:		Chain saws..	30,212
ATV's, mopeds, minibikes, etc..........................	221,465	Hand garden tools......................................	66,495
Bicycles & accessories................................	549,182	Lawn mowers..	83,291
Exercise equipment....................................	410,024	Power home tools (excl. saws)........................	24,667
Fireworks..	9,599	Power home workshop saws.........................	75,343
Nonpowder guns, bb's, pellets........................	20,993	Workshop manual tools................................	128,881
Skateboards..	108,510		
Snowskiing, snowboarding............................	83,580	Household appliances:	
Toboggans, sleds, snow discs, etc....................	25,131	Cooking ranges, ovens, etc..........................	50,032
Trampolines...	83,292	Heating stoves, space heaters.......................	26,928
Water slides..	6,394	Small kitchen appliances..............................	53,392
		Washers, dryers..	22,308
Home entertainment equipment:			
Computers (equipment and electronic games).............	37,082	Home furnishings & fixtures:	
Television sets & stands..............................	73,271	Bathroom structures & fixtures.......................	423,496
		Bathtubs or showers...................................	295,907
Personal use items:		Beds, mattresses, pillows.............................	711,800
Grooming devices.......................................	44,216	Carpets, rugs..	149,185
Mobility carts, electric.................................	12,888	Chairs, sofas, sofa beds..............................	579,793
Razors, shavers, razor blades.........................	43,898	Hot tubs or home spas................................	5,835
		Tables [1]..	342,120
		Toilets...	101,504

[1] Excludes baby-changing and television tables or stands.

Source: Consumer Product Safety Commission, National Electronic Injury Surveillance System (NEISS), *NEISS Data Highlights - 2011,* and <https://www.cpsc.gov/cgibin/NEISSQuery/home.aspx>, accessed May 2013.

Table 206. Persons 18 Years of Age and Over With Selected Diseases and Conditions by Selected Characteristics: 2011

[In thousands (231,376 represents 231,376,000). Based on National Health Interview Survey, a sample survey of the civilian noninstitutionalized population; see Appendix III]

Selected characteristic	Total persons	Persons with selected diseases and conditions					
		Diabetes[1,2]	Ulcers[1]	Kidney disease[3,4]	Liver disease[3]	Arthritis diagnosis[5]	Chronic joint symptoms[5]
Total[6]	231,376	20,589	15,502	4,381	3,016	53,782	68,749
SEX							
Male	112,093	10,342	7,021	1,897	1,449	22,248	31,542
Female	119,283	10,247	8,481	2,484	1,568	31,534	37,207
AGE							
18 to 44 years	110,815	2,708	4,556	1,007	764	8,833	18,753
45 to 64 years	80,849	9,702	6,541	1,491	1,747	25,182	30,948
65 to 74 years	21,902	4,860	2,492	868	383	10,408	10,151
75 years and over	17,810	3,319	1,914	1,015	123	9,359	8,897
RACE							
Single race[7]	227,770	20,263	15,209	4,294	2,959	52,990	67,555
White	186,233	15,814	12,787	3,398	2,376	45,100	57,275
Black or African American	27,666	3,226	1,672	689	333	5,953	7,619
American Indian or Alaska Native	1,980	267	166	[8]49	[8]60	527	661
Asian	11,468	910	550	141	188	1,306	1,909
Native Hawaiian or other Pacific Islander	423	[8]44	(B)	(B)	(B)	[8]104	[8]91
Two or more races[9]	3,605	326	292	[8]87	[8]57	792	1,194
HISPANIC ORIGIN[10]							
Hispanic or Latino	32,762	3,051	1,611	621	511	4,046	6,696
Mexican or Mexican American	20,101	1,963	889	409	261	2,295	4,090

B Figure too small to meet statistical standards for reliability (relative standard error greater than 50%). [1] Respondents were asked if they had ever been told by a health professional that they had an ulcer or diabetes. A person may be represented in more than one column. [2] Excludes borderline diabetes. [3] Respondents were asked if they had been told in the last 12 months by a health professional that they had weak or failing kidneys or any kind of liver condition. [4] Excludes kidney stones, bladder infections, or incontinence. [5] Respondents were asked if they had ever been told by a health professional that they had some form of arthritis, rheumatoid arthritis, gout, lupus or fibromyalgia. Those that answered "yes" were classified as having an arthritis diagnosis. Respondents with joint symptoms (excluding back and neck) that began more than 3 months prior to interview were classified as having chronic joint symptoms. [6] Total includes other races not shown separately. [7] Refers to persons who indicated only a single race group. [8] Figures do not meet standard of reliability or precision. [9] Refers to all persons who indicated more than one race group. [10] Persons of Hispanic or Latino origin may be of any race or combination of races.

Source: National Center for Health Statistics, *Summary Health Statistics for U.S. Adults: National Health Interview Survey, 2011*, Vital and Health Statistics, Series 10, Number 256, December 2012. See also <http://www.cdc.gov/nchs/products/series/series10.htm>.

Table 207. Persons 18 Years of Age and Over With Selected Circulatory Diseases by Selected Characteristics: 2011

[In thousands (231,376 represents 231,376,000). In separate questions, respondents were asked if they had ever been told by a doctor or other health professional that they had: hypertension (or high blood pressure); coronary heart disease, angina (or angina pectoris); heart attack (or myocardial infarction); any other heart condition or disease not already mentioned; or a stroke. A person may be represented in more than one column. Based on National Health Interview Survey, a sample survey of the civilian noninstitutionalized population; see Appendix III]

Characteristic	Total adults	Selected circulatory diseases			
		Heart disease		Hypertension[3]	Stroke
		All types[1]	Coronary[2]		
Total[4]	231,376	26,485	15,300	58,959	6,171
SEX					
Male	112,093	13,767	9,203	28,683	2,654
Female	119,283	12,718	6,097	30,277	3,517
AGE					
18 to 44 years	110,815	3,952	981	10,058	577
45 to 64 years	80,849	10,323	5,952	26,531	2,296
65 to 74 years	21,902	5,843	3,991	12,149	1,428
75 years and over	17,810	6,366	4,376	10,222	1,870
RACE					
Race alone[5]	227,770	26,029	15,074	58,166	6,081
White	186,233	22,219	12,735	46,775	4,548
Black or African American	27,666	2,789	1,770	8,820	1129
American Indian or Alaska Native	1,980	249	137	505	90
Asian	11,468	748	421	1,975	268
Native Hawaiian or Other Pacific Islander	423	(B)	(B)	[6]91	(B)
Two or more races[7]	3,605	456	226	793	90
HISPANIC ORIGIN[8]					
Hispanic or Latino	32,762	2,138	1352	5,623	644
Mexican or Mexican American	20,101	1,181	725	3,126	357

B Figure too small to meet statistical standards for reliability of a derived figure. [1] Heart disease includes coronary heart disease, angina pectoris, heart attack, or any other heart condition or disease. [2] Coronary heart disease includes coronary heart disease, angina pectoris, or heart attack. [3] Persons had to have been told on two or more different visits that they had hypertension, or high blood pressure, to be classified as hypertensive. [4] Includes other races not shown separately. [5] Refers to persons who indicated only a single race group. [6] Figures do not meet standard of reliability or precision. [7] Refers to all persons who indicated more than one race group. [8] Persons of Hispanic or Latino origin may be of any race or combination of races.

Source: National Center for Health Statistics, *Summary Health Statistics for the U.S. Population: National Health Interview Survey, 2011*, Vital and Health Statistics, Series 10, Number 256, December 2012. See also <http://www.cdc.gov/nchs/nhis.htm>.

Table 208. Selected Respiratory Diseases Among Persons 18 Years of Age and Over by Selected Characteristics: 2011

[In thousands (231,376 represents 231,376,000). Respondents were asked in two separate questions if they had ever been told by a doctor or other health professional that they had emphysema or asthma. Respondents who had been told they had asthma were asked if they still had asthma. Respondents were asked in three separate questions if they had been told by a doctor or other health professional in the past 12 months that they had hay fever, sinusitis, or bronchitis. Based on the National Health Interview Survey, a sample survey of the civilian noninstitutionalized population; see Appendix III]

| Selected characteristic | Total persons | Emphy-sema | Selected respiratory conditions [1] | | Hay fever | Sinusitis | Chronic bronchitis |
| | | | Asthma | | | | |
			Ever	Still			
Total [2]	**231,376**	**4,680**	**29,041**	**18,869**	**16,869**	**29,611**	**10,071**
SEX							
Male.........................	112,093	2,129	12,282	6,923	6,882	10,116	3,316
Female.......................	119,283	2,552	16,759	11,946	9,986	19,495	6,754
AGE							
18 to 44 years.................	110,815	365	15,090	8,850	6,142	10,890	3,170
45 to 64 years.................	80,849	2,146	9,840	7,010	7,985	12,820	4,356
65 to 74 years.................	21,902	1,275	2,458	1,807	1,694	3,594	1,487
75 years and over.............	17,810	895	1,653	1,202	1047	2,307	1,058
RACE							
Race alone [3]	227,770	4,631	28,289	18,338	16,573	29,166	9,937
White.........................	186,233	3,936	22,709	14,750	14,203	24,780	8,233
Black or African American......	27,666	496	4,201	2,698	1,531	3,378	1,358
American Indian or Alaska Native.	1,980	90	390	279	96	223	111
Asian.........................	11,468	[4] 97	917	568	743	727	225
Native Hawaiian or other Pacific Islander....	423	(B)	[4] 72	(B)	–	[4] 58	(B)
Two or more races [5]	3,605	[4] 49	752	531	296	445	133
HISPANIC ORIGIN AND RACE [6]							
Hispanic or Latino.............	32,094	231	3,289	2,224	1,440	2,783	878
Mexican or Mexican American...	19,712	112	1,686	1,173	804	1,545	509
Not Hispanic or Latino.........	197,411	4,083	25,768	16,510	16,497	27,038	9,005
White, single race.............	156,119	3,600	19,926	12,552	13,659	21,752	7,525
Black or African American, single race.......	26,689	279	4,118	2,841	1,744	3,833	1,074

– Represents zero. B Figure too small to meet statistical standards for reliability of a derived figure. [1] A person may be represented in more than one column. [2] Total includes other races not shown separately. [3] Refers to persons who indicated only a single race group. [4] Figure does not meet standard of reliability or precision. [5] Refers to all persons who indicated more than one race group. [6] Persons of Hispanic or Latino origin may be of any race or combination of races.

Source: National Center for Health Statistics, *Summary Health Statistics for the U.S. Population: National Health Interview Survey, 2011*, Vital and Health Statistics, Series 10, Number 256, December 2012. See also <http://www.cdc.gov/nchs/nhis.htm>.

Table 209. Injury and Poisoning Episodes by Age and Sex: 2011

[In thousands (37,876 represents 37,876,000) except as noted. Covers all medically attended injuries and poisonings occurring during the 5–week period prior to the survey interview. Age adjustment is used to adjust for differences in the age distribution of populations being compared. There may be more than one condition per episode. Based on the National Health Interview Survey, a sample survey of the civilian noninstitutionalized population; see Appendix III]

| External cause and nature of injury | Both sexes | | | | | | | Male | Female |
	Total	Rate, age adjusted [1]	Under 12 years	12 to 17 years	18 to 44 years	45 to 64 years	65 years and over		
EPISODES									
Number (1,000).................	37,876	(X)	5,395	4,202	13,025	9,589	5,664	18,622	19,254
Annual rate per 1,000 population, total [2]	123.8	124.1	107.3	173.3	117.5	118.6	287.1	125.0	122.6
Fall............................	13,409	43.67	2,732	1,014	3,216	3,172	3,276	5,158	8,252
Struck by or against a person or an object......................	4,581	15.32	439	774	2,014	925	[4] 431	2,453	2,128
Transportation [3]	4,057	13.59	812	528	1,713	686	[4] 266	2,300	1,757
Overexertion....................	4,647	14.69	[4] 187	483	1,638	1,969	[4] 369	2,578	2,069
Cutting, piercing instruments.....	2,925	9.58	[4] 266	[4] 390	1,150	863	[4] 111	1,756	1,169
Poisoning [5]	[4] 459	[4] 1.41	(B)	(B)	(B)	[4] 268	(B)	(B)	[4] 310

X Not applicable. B Base figure too small to meet statistical standards for reliability of a derived figure. [1] Total annual rate per 1,000 population. Age-adjusted using the 2000 standard population using five age groups: under 12 years, 12-17 years, 18-44 years, 45-64 years, and 65 years and over. [2] Includes other items not shown separately. [3] Includes the categories "Motor vehicle traffic;" "Pedal cycle, other;" "Pedestrian, other;" and "Transport, other." [4] Figure does not meet standard of reliability or precision. [5] Poisoning episodes are assumed to have a single condition resulting from the episode.

Source: National Center for Health Statistics, *Summary Health Statistics for the U.S. Population: National Health Interview Survey, 2011*, Vital and Health Statistics, Series 10, Number 255, December 2012. See also <http://www.cdc.gov/nchs/nhis.htm>.

Table 210. Persons 18 Years of Age and Over With Migraines and Pains in the Neck, Lower Back, Face, or Jaw by Selected Characteristics: 2011

[In thousands (231,376 represents 231,376,000). Based on National Health Interview Survey, a sample survey of the civilian noninstitutionalized population. See Appendix III]

Selected characteristic	Total persons	Migraine and pain [1]			
		Migraine or severe headache [2]	Pain in neck [3]	Pain in lower back [3]	Pain in face or jaw [3]
Total [4]	**231,376**	**37,904**	**35,798**	**66,917**	**11,436**
SEX					
Male	112,093	12,097	14,442	30,611	3,809
Female	119,283	25,807	21,355	36,306	7,627
AGE					
18 to 44 years	110,815	21,495	13,686	27,079	5,346
45 to 64 years	80,849	13,250	15,700	26,874	4,494
65 to 74 years	21,902	2,077	3,866	7,270	929
75 years and over	17,810	1,083	2,545	5,694	667
RACE					
Single race [5]	227,770	37,155	35,095	65,616	11,181
White	186,233	30,518	29,938	55,049	9,531
Black or African American	27,666	4,858	3,603	7,634	1,278
American Indian or Alaska Native	1,980	426	326	612	[6] 127
Asian	11,468	1,292	1,197	2,237	241
Native Hawaiian or other Pacific Islander	423	[6] 61	[6] 31	[6] 85	(B)
Two or more races [7]	3,605	750	703	1,301	255
HISPANIC ORIGIN AND RACE [8]					
Hispanic or Latino	32,762	5,397	4,391	8,507	1,346
Mexican or Mexican American	20,101	3,220	2,530	4,928	939
Not Hispanic or Latino	198,614	32,508	31,407	58,410	10,090
White, single race	156,482	25,606	25,922	47,221	8,285
Black or African American, single race	26,552	4,661	3,447	7,347	1,235

B Base figure too small to meet statistical standards for reliability of a derived figure. [1] A person may be represented in more than one column. [2] Respondents were asked, "During the past 3 months, did you have a severe headache or migraine?" Respondents were instructed to report pain that had lasted a whole day or more and, conversely, not to report fleeting or minor aches or pains. [3] Respondents were asked, "During the past 3 months, did you have a neck pain; or low back pain; or facial ache or pain in the jaw muscles or the joint in front of the ear?" Respondents were instructed to report pain that had lasted a whole day or more and, conversely, not to report fleeting or minor aches or pains. [4] Total includes other races not shown separately. [5] Refers to persons who indicated only a single race group. [6] Figure does not meet standard of reliability or precision. [7] Refers to all persons who indicated more than one race group. [8] Persons of Hispanic or Latino origin may be of any race or combination of races.

Source: National Center for Health Statistics, *Summary Health Statistics for U.S. Adults: National Health Interview Survey, 2011*, Vital and Health Statistics, Series 10, Number 256, December 2012. See also <http://www.cdc.gov/nchs/products/series/series10.htm>.

Table 211. Use of Mammography for Women 40 Years Old and Over by Patient Characteristics: 2000 to 2010

[Percent of women having a mammogram within the past 2 years. Covers civilian noninstitutional population. Based on National Health Interview Survey; see Appendix III]

Characteristic	2000 [1]	2005 [1]	2010 [1]	Characteristic	2000 [1]	2005 [1]	2010 [1]
Total [2]	**70.4**	**66.8**	**67.1**	Years of school completed:			
Age:				No high school diploma or GED	57.7	52.8	53.0
40 to 49 years old	64.3	63.5	62.3	High school diploma or GED	69.7	64.9	64.4
50 years old and over	73.6	68.4	69.2	Some college or more	76.2	72.7	72.1
50 to 64 years old	78.7	71.8	72.6				
65 years old and over	67.9	63.8	64.4				
Race/ethnicity:				Poverty status: [4]			
White, non-Hispanic	72.2	68.4	67.8	Below poverty	54.8	48.5	51.4
Black, non-Hispanic	67.9	65.2	67.4	At or above poverty	72.1	68.8	(NA)
Hispanic origin [3]	61.2	58.8	64.2				

NA Not available. [1] Adjusted data—data have been reweighted using the 2000 Census population controls. [2] Includes other races not shown separately and unknown education level and poverty status. [3] Persons of Hispanic origin may be any race or combination of races. [4] For explanation of poverty level, see text, Section 13.

Source: U.S. National Center for Health Statistics, *Health, United States, 2012*, May 2013. See also <http://www.cdc.gov/nchs/hus.htm>.

Table 212. Current Cigarette Smoking: 1990 to 2011

[In percent. Prior to 1992, a current smoker is a person who has smoked at least 100 cigarettes and who now smokes. Beginning 1992, definition includes persons who smoke only "some days." Excludes unknown smoking status. Race groups white and black include persons of Hispanic and non-Hispanic origin. For definition of age adjustment, see text, Section 2. Based on National Health Interview Survey; for details, see Appendix III]

Sex, age, and race	1990[1]	2000	2005	2011	Sex, age, and race	1990[1]	2000	2005	2011
Total smokers, age-adjusted[2]	**25.3**	**23.1**	**20.8**	**19.0**	Black, total	32.5	26.2	26.5	23.8
Male	28.0	25.2	23.4	21.2	18 to 24 years	21.3	20.9	21.6	18.4
Female	22.9	21.1	18.3	16.8	25 to 34 years	33.8	23.2	29.8	25.0
					35 to 44 years	42.0	30.7	23.3	24.3
White male	27.6	25.4	23.3	21.4	45 to 64 years	36.7	32.2	32.4	28.9
Black male	32.8	25.7	25.9	23.2	65 years and over	21.5	14.2	16.8	13.7
					Female, total	22.8	20.9	18.1	16.5
White female	23.5	22.0	19.1	17.7	18 to 24 years	22.5	24.9	20.7	16.4
Black female	20.8	20.7	17.1	15.2	25 to 34 years	28.2	22.3	21.5	19.5
					35 to 44 years	24.8	26.2	21.3	19.9
Total smokers[3]	**25.5**	**23.2**	**20.9**	**19.0**	45 to 64 years	24.8	21.7	18.8	18.5
Male, total	28.4	25.6	23.9	21.6	65 years and over	11.5	9.3	8.3	7.1
18 to 24 years	26.6	28.1	28.0	21.3	White, total	23.4	21.4	18.7	17.2
25 to 34 years	31.6	28.9	27.7	27.5	18 to 24 years	25.4	28.5	22.6	18.4
35 to 44 years	34.5	30.2	26.0	21.2	25 to 34 years	28.5	24.9	23.1	20.6
45 to 64 years	29.3	26.4	25.2	24.4	35 to 44 years	25.0	26.6	22.2	21.5
65 years and over	14.6	10.2	8.9	8.9	45 to 64 years	25.4	21.4	18.9	19.0
White, total	28.0	25.7	23.6	21.6	65 years and over	11.5	9.1	8.4	7.0
18 to 24 years	27.4	30.4	29.7	22.1	Black, total	21.2	20.8	17.3	15.3
25 to 34 years	31.6	29.7	27.7	28.6	18 to 24 years	[4]10.0	14.2	14.2	9.1
35 to 44 years	33.5	30.6	26.3	21.4	25 to 34 years	29.1	15.5	16.9	17.5
45 to 64 years	28.7	25.8	24.5	24.0	35 to 44 years	25.5	30.2	19.0	17.4
65 years and over	13.7	9.8	7.9	8.6	45 to 64 years	22.6	25.6	21.0	18.3
					65 years and over	11.1	10.2	10.0	9.1

[1] Data prior to 1997 are not strictly comparable with data for later years due to the 1997 questionnaire redesign. [2] Data are age-adjusted to the year 2000 standard using five age groups: 18–24 years, 25–34 years, 35–44 years, 45–64 years, 65 years and over. [3] Crude, not age-adjusted. [4] Figure does not meet standard of reliability or precision.

Source: U.S. National Center for Health Statistics, *Health, United States, 2012,* May 2013. See also <http://www.cdc.gov/nchs/hus.htm>.

Table 213. Substance Abuse Treatment Facilities and Clients: 1995 to 2011

[As of October 2 (1995), as of October 1 (1997–2000), as of March 31 (2003–2006), as of March 30 (2007), and as of March 31 (2008–2011). Based on National Survey of Substance Abuse Treatment Services, a census of all known facilities that provide substance abuse treatment in the United States and associated jurisdictions. Selected missing data for responding facilities were imputed]

Primary focus	Number	Primary focus	Number	Type of care and type of problem	Number of clients
FACILITIES		CLIENTS			
1995	10,746	1995	1,009,127		
2000	13,428	2000	1,000,896	Outpatient	1,095,897
2005	13,371	2005	1,081,049	Regular	617,715
2006	13,771	2006	1,130,881	Intensive	141,964
2007	13,648	2007	1,135,425	Detoxification	13,450
2008	13,688	2008	1,192,490	Residential (non-hospital)	112,827
2009	13,513	2009	1,182,077	Hospital inpatient	15,403
2010	13,339	2010	1,175,462	Detoxification	6,179
2011, total	**13,720**	**2011, total**	**1,224,127**	Treatment	9,224
Substance abuse treatment services	8,094	Substance abuse treatment services	792,248	Drug only	464,406
Mental health services	877	Mental health services	42,099	Alcohol only	221,632
General health care	190	General health care	16,496	Both alcohol & drug	535,258
Both substance abuse and mental health	4,385	Both substance abuse and mental health	364,965	Both substance abuse and mental health disorders	506,162
Other	174	Other	8,319		

Note: Number of clients column header row: **2011, total[1]** **1,224,127**

[1] Includes clients at facilities that did not provide data on type of substance abuse problem treated.

Source: U.S. Substance Abuse and Mental Health Services Administration, Uniform Facility Data Set, 1995–1999; and Center for Behavioral Health Statistics and Quality, Substance Abuse and Mental Health Services Administration, *National Survey of Substance Abuse Treatment Services (N-SSATS): 2011 Data on Substance Abuse Treatment Facilities*, November 2012, and earlier reports. See also <http://www.samhsa.gov/data/DASIS.aspx>.

Table 214. Current Cigarette Smoking by Sex and State: 2011

[In percent. Current cigarette smoking is defined as persons 18 years and older who reported having smoked 100 or more cigarettes during their lifetime and who currently smoke every day or some days. Based on the Behavioral Risk Factor Surveillance System, a telephone survey of health behaviors of the civilian, noninstitutionalized U.S. population, 18 years old and over. New methods, including surveying cellular telephone-only households, and a new weighting method, were implemented for the 2011 BRFSS; data for 2011 cannot accurately be compared to previous survey results; for details, see source]

State	Total	Male	Female	State	Total	Male	Female	State	Total	Male	Female
U.S. [1]	**21.2**	**23.6**	**18.8**	KS	22.0	24.6	19.5	NC	21.8	24.5	19.2
AL	24.3	28.0	21.0	KY	29.0	31.6	26.6	ND	21.9	24.2	19.5
AK	22.9	22.9	23.0	LA	25.7	29.5	22.3	OH	25.1	26.0	24.2
AZ	19.3	21.0	17.5	ME	22.8	25.1	20.6	OK	26.1	28.1	24.3
AR	27.0	28.9	25.2	MD	19.1	21.2	17.2	OR	19.7	21.1	18.4
CA	13.7	17.3	10.1	MA	18.2	19.7	16.9	PA	22.4	23.5	21.5
CO	18.3	21.3	15.2	MI	23.3	27.2	19.7	RI	20.0	21.4	18.8
CT	17.1	19.0	15.4	MN	19.1	21.2	17.0	SC	23.1	25.8	20.7
DE	21.8	25.6	18.3	MS	26.0	30.5	21.8	SD	23.0	24.4	21.7
DC	20.8	25.1	17.1	MO	25.0	26.4	23.6	TN	23.0	24.8	21.3
FL	19.3	21.8	16.9	MT	22.1	23.2	21.0	TX	19.2	23.6	15.0
GA	21.2	24.4	18.2	NE	20.0	22.1	17.9	UT	11.8	14.1	9.6
HI	16.8	19.7	13.9	NV	22.9	25.6	20.2	VT	19.1	21.8	16.5
ID	17.2	19.4	15.0	NH	19.4	20.4	18.5	VA	20.9	21.3	20.5
IL	20.9	24.2	17.8	NJ	16.8	19.1	14.6	WA	17.5	18.8	16.2
IN	25.6	27.6	23.8	NM	21.5	24.9	18.2	WV	28.6	31.5	25.9
IA	20.4	22.2	18.6	NY	18.1	19.5	16.8	WI	20.9	22.7	19.1
								WY	23.0	24.2	21.8

[1] Represents median value among the states and DC. For definition of median, see Guide to Tabular Presentations.

Source: U.S. Centers for Disease Control and Prevention, Behavioral Risk Factor Surveillance System, "Prevalence Data and Data Analysis Tools, Prevalence and Trends Data," <http://www.cdc.gov/brfss/data_tools.htm>, accessed June 2013.

Table 215. Drug Use by Type of Drug and Age Group: 2009 and 2010

[In percent. Data comes from the National Survey on Drug Use and Health (NSDUH). Current users are those who used drugs at least once within month prior to this study. Based on a representative sample of the U.S. population 12 years old and over, including persons living in households, noninstitutional group quarters such as dormitories and homeless shelters, and civilians on military bases. Estimates are based on computer-assisted interviews of about 67,500 respondents. Subject to sampling variability; see source]

Age and type of drug	Ever used 2009	Ever used 2010	Current user 2009	Current user 2010	Age and type of drug	Ever used 2009	Ever used 2010	Current user 2009	Current user 2010
12 YEARS OLD AND OVER					**18 TO 25 YEARS OLD**				
Any illicit drug [1]	47.1	47.1	8.7	8.9	Any illicit drug [1]	58.1	57.0	21.2	21.5
Marijuana and hashish	41.5	41.9	6.6	6.9	Marijuana and hashish	52.2	51.1	18.1	18.5
Cocaine	14.5	14.7	0.7	0.6	Cocaine	14.8	13.3	1.4	1.5
Crack	3.3	3.6	0.2	0.1	Hallucinogens	19.0	18.4	1.8	2.0
Heroin	1.5	1.6	0.1	0.1	Inhalants	10.7	9.9	0.4	0.4
Hallucinogens	14.8	14.8	0.5	0.5	Any psychotherapeutic [2,3]	(NA)	(NA)	(NA)	(NA)
LSD	9.4	9.2	0.1	0.1	Alcohol	85.8	85.7	61.8	61.5
Ecstasy	5.7	6.3	0.3	0.3	"Binge" alcohol use [4]	(NA)	(NA)	41.7	40.6
Inhalants	8.9	8.5	0.2	0.3	Cigarettes	63.7	62.1	35.8	34.2
Any psychotherapeutic [2,3]	20.6	20.4	2.8	2.7	Smokeless tobacco	21.0	20.9	6.1	6.4
Pain relievers	13.9	13.7	2.1	2.0	Cigars	41.7	40.7	11.4	11.2
Tranquilizers	8.6	8.7	0.8	0.9					
Stimulants [3]	8.7	8.5	0.5	0.4	**26 TO 34 YEARS OLD**				
Methamphetamine [3]	5.1	5.1	0.2	0.1	Any illicit drug [1]	59.3	59.7	12.3	13.8
Sedatives	3.4	3.0	0.1	0.1	Marijuana and hashish	53.0	53.9	9.6	10.5
Alcohol	82.8	82.5	51.9	51.8	Cocaine	18.1	19.1	1.0	1.1
"Binge" alcohol use [4]	(NA)	(NA)	23.7	23.1	Hallucinogens	23.9	23.7	0.9	0.7
Cigarettes	64.6	64.2	23.3	23.0	Inhalants	13.7	13.2	0.2	0.2
Smokeless tobacco	17.8	17.7	3.4	3.5	Any psychotherapeutic [2,3]	29.2	28.9	3.8	4.4
Cigars	35.8	34.8	5.3	5.2					
Pipe tobacco	13.9	13.5	0.8	0.8	**35 YEARS OLD AND OVER**				
					Any illicit drug [1]	45.2	45.4	4.9	4.9
12 TO 17 YEARS OLD					Marijuana and hashish	40.4	41.0	3.4	3.4
Any illicit drug [1]	26.8	25.7	10.0	10.1	Cocaine	15.7	16.0	0.5	0.3
Marijuana and hashish	17.0	17.0	7.3	7.4	Hallucinogens	13.5	13.6	0.1	0.0
Cocaine	1.6	1.5	0.3	0.2	Inhalants	7.4	7.2	0.1	0.1
Hallucinogens	4.1	4.1	0.9	0.9	Any psychotherapeutic [2,3]	18.2	18.1	1.7	1.7
Inhalants	9.2	8.2	1.0	1.1					
Any psychotherapeutic [2,3]	(NA)	(NA)	(NA)	(NA)	**26 YEARS OLD AND OVER**				
Alcohol	38.1	35.2	14.7	13.6	Alcohol	88.0	87.9	54.9	54.9
"Binge" alcohol use [4]	(NA)	(NA)	8.8	7.8	"Binge" alcohol use [4]	(NA)	(NA)	22.4	21.9
Cigarettes	22.2	20.3	8.9	8.3	Cigarettes	70.1	70.0	23.0	22.8
Smokeless tobacco	7.6	7.2	2.3	2.3	Smokeless tobacco	18.5	18.5	3.1	3.1
Cigars	12.4	11.0	4.0	3.2	Cigars	37.7	36.8	4.4	4.4

NA Not available. [1] Illicit drugs include marijuana/hashish, cocaine (including crack), heroin, hallucinogens, inhalants, or prescription-type psychotherapeutics used nonmedically. [2] Nonmedical use of prescription-type psychotherapeutics includes the nonmedical use of pain relievers, tranquilizers, stimulants, or sedatives and does not include over-the-counter drugs. [3] Includes data from new methamphetamine items added in 2006 and 2007. Previous estimates have been adjusted to be comparable with new data and differ from those in reports prior to the 2007 data year. [4] Binge alcohol use is defined as drinking five or more drinks on the same occasion (i.e., at the same time or within a couple of hours of each other) on at least 1 day in the past 30 days.

Source: U.S. Substance Abuse and Mental Health Services Administration, Center for Behavioral Health Statistics and Quality, "Results from the 2010 National Survey on Drug Use and Health: Detailed Tables," and earlier reports, <http://www.samhsa.gov/data/NSDUH.aspx>, accessed May 2013.

Table 216. Estimated Use of Selected Drugs by State: 2010 to 2011

[22,553 represents 22,553,000. Data in this table cover a 2-year period. Data is based on the National Survey on Drug Use and Health (NSDUH). Current users are those persons 12 years old and over who used drugs at least once within month prior to this study. Based on national sample of respondents (see also headnote, Table 215). The state estimates were produced by combining the prevalence rate based on the state sample data and the prevalence rate based on a national regression model applied to local-area county and census block group/tract-level estimates from the state (i.e., a survey-weighted hierarchical Bayes estimation approach). The parameters of the regression model are estimated from the entire national sample. For comparison purposes, the data shown here display estimates for all 50 states and the District of Columbia utilizing the modeled estimates for all 51 areas]

State	Estimated current users (1,000)					Current users as percent of population				
	Any illicit drug [1]	Mari-juana	Any illicit drug other than mari-juana [1]	Ciga-rettes	Binge alcohol [2]	Any illicit drug [1]	Mari-juana	Any illicit drug other than mari-juana [1]	Ciga-rettes	Binge alcohol [2]
U.S.	22,553	17,741	8,518	57,569	58,440	8.8	6.9	3.3	22.5	22.9
AL.	299	205	126	1,059	776	7.6	5.2	3.2	26.9	19.7
AK.	77	64	20	156	135	13.6	11.4	3.6	27.7	24.1
AZ.	509	375	197	1,235	1,195	9.5	7.0	3.7	23.2	22.4
AR.	182	122	94	649	454	7.6	5.1	3.9	27.1	19.0
CA.	3,213	2,642	1,083	5,165	6,743	10.5	8.6	3.5	16.8	22.0
CO.	559	458	165	927	1,020	13.4	11.0	3.9	22.2	24.5
CT.	271	216	104	642	785	9.1	7.2	3.5	21.5	26.3
DE.	67	52	30	182	174	9.0	7.0	4.0	24.4	23.3
DC.	71	59	23	122	169	13.6	11.1	4.3	23.2	32.2
FL.	1,320	1,009	490	3,488	3,158	8.3	6.4	3.1	22.0	19.9
GA.	517	394	214	1,656	1,540	6.5	5.0	2.7	20.9	19.4
HI.	95	75	33	218	250	8.8	6.9	3.1	20.1	23.1
ID.	118	90	47	286	273	9.4	7.1	3.7	22.6	21.6
IL.	910	731	326	2,366	2,697	8.6	6.9	3.1	22.2	25.3
IN.	479	347	195	1,349	1,209	9.0	6.5	3.7	25.3	22.7
IA.	161	131	66	602	670	6.4	5.2	2.6	23.9	26.6
KS.	155	126	73	553	540	6.7	5.4	3.1	23.9	23.4
KY.	249	182	107	1,124	748	6.9	5.1	3.0	31.4	20.9
LA.	251	179	127	996	841	6.8	4.8	3.4	27.0	22.8
ME.	109	91	37	284	253	9.6	8.0	3.2	25.0	22.3
MD.	355	266	138	930	1,003	7.4	5.6	2.9	19.4	20.9
MA.	647	558	189	1,069	1,516	11.5	10.0	3.4	19.1	27.0
MI.	889	720	299	2,177	2,100	10.7	8.7	3.6	26.2	25.3
MN.	362	284	139	975	1,155	8.2	6.4	3.2	22.1	26.2
MS.	195	141	79	645	459	8.2	5.9	3.3	27.0	19.2
MO.	362	300	139	1,340	1,128	7.3	6.0	2.8	27.0	22.7
MT.	100	85	26	202	231	12.0	10.3	3.1	24.4	28.0
NE.	99	83	44	346	365	6.7	5.6	2.9	23.3	24.6
NV.	218	168	78	499	539	9.9	7.6	3.5	22.7	24.5
NH.	124	98	46	250	272	11.0	8.7	4.0	22.1	24.1
NJ.	584	469	241	1,675	1,795	8.0	6.4	3.3	22.9	24.5
NM.	177	138	64	353	339	10.6	8.3	3.9	21.1	20.3
NY.	1,525	1,214	530	3,424	3,891	9.3	7.4	3.2	20.9	23.7
NC.	692	573	237	1,918	1,518	8.9	7.3	3.0	24.6	19.5
ND.	31	25	13	126	169	5.5	4.5	2.3	22.7	30.5
OH.	815	620	324	2,549	2,224	8.5	6.5	3.4	26.6	23.2
OK.	274	200	123	879	637	9.0	6.6	4.1	29.0	21.0
OR.	425	356	135	723	725	13.1	11.0	4.2	22.3	22.3
PA.	862	654	346	2,595	2,620	8.1	6.1	3.2	24.3	24.5
RI.	130	107	43	216	250	14.5	11.9	4.8	24.1	27.9
SC.	282	226	117	1,028	870	7.4	5.9	3.1	27.0	22.8
SD.	40	34	18	164	184	6.0	5.0	2.6	24.6	27.5
TN.	402	287	193	1,457	973	7.6	5.4	3.7	27.6	18.4
TX.	1,442	1,103	623	4,329	4,850	7.1	5.5	3.1	21.5	24.0
UT.	108	78	63	299	309	5.0	3.6	2.9	13.7	14.2
VT.	83	71	24	122	137	15.3	13.1	4.4	22.7	25.3
VA.	523	389	219	1,317	1,523	8.0	5.9	3.3	20.1	23.2
WA.	670	556	238	1,278	1,318	11.9	9.9	4.2	22.7	23.4
WV.	125	93	54	474	319	8.0	6.0	3.5	30.4	20.5
WI.	369	274	168	1,041	1,289	7.8	5.8	3.5	21.9	27.2
WY.	33	23	13	109	102	7.1	5.1	2.9	23.9	22.4

[1] Illicit drugs include marijuana/hashish, cocaine (including crack), heroin, hallucinogens, inhalants, or prescription-type psychotherapeutics used nonmedically. [2] Binge alcohol use is defined as drinking five or more drinks on the same occasion (i.e., at the same time or within a couple of hours of each other) on at least 1 day in the past 30 days.

Source: U.S. Substance Abuse and Mental Health Services Administration, "2010-2011 NSDUH State Estimates of Substance Use and Mental Disorders," <http://www.samhsa.gov/data/NSDUH/2k11State/NSDUHsae2011/Index.aspx>, accessed June 2013.

Table 217. Height in Inches of Population Aged 20 and Over by Sex, Age, and Race/Ethnicity: 2007 to 2010

[Data are based on National Health and Nutrition Examination Survey (NHANES), a sample of the civilian noninstitutional population. Data are collected through household interviews and health examinations. Height was measured without shoes. The oversampling of all Hispanic persons is new to the 2007–2010 data collection methodology; see source]

Age and Race/Ethnicity	Males, height in inches						Females, height in inches					
	Mean	Percentile					Mean	Percentile				
		10th	25th	50th	75th	90th		10th	25th	50th	75th	90th
Total [1]												
20 years and over........	69.3	65.4	67.3	69.3	71.2	73.0	63.8	60.3	61.9	63.8	65.7	67.3
20-29 years..............	69.4	65.5	67.4	69.4	71.5	73.1	64.2	60.6	62.2	64.1	66.0	67.6
30-39 years..............	69.5	65.4	67.5	69.5	71.6	73.3	64.3	60.9	62.5	64.3	66.1	67.9
40-49 years..............	69.6	66.0	67.6	69.6	71.5	73.5	64.2	60.8	62.4	64.0	66.0	67.6
50-59 years..............	69.5	65.8	67.7	69.7	71.3	72.8	63.9	60.4	62.0	64.0	65.6	67.0
60-69 years..............	68.8	64.8	66.9	69.0	70.7	72.6	63.6	60.2	62.0	63.8	65.3	66.8
70-79 years..............	68.2	64.6	66.3	68.2	70.0	71.9	62.6	59.3	60.7	62.8	64.3	66.1
80 years and over........	67.2	63.7	65.3	67.3	69.2	70.4	61.4	57.9	59.8	61.5	62.9	64.3
Non-Hispanic white												
20 years and over........	69.8	66.4	68.0	69.8	71.6	73.3	64.2	60.8	62.5	64.2	66.0	67.5
20-39 years..............	70.2	66.9	68.2	70.2	72.1	73.6	64.9	51.7	63.2	64.9	66.5	68.4
40-59 years..............	70.2	67.0	68.5	70.2	71.8	73.6	64.5	61.2	62.8	64.4	66.1	67.6
60 years and over........	68.7	64.9	66.9	68.9	70.6	72.4	63.1	59.8	61.5	63.1	64.8	66.4
Non-Hispanic black												
20 years and over........	69.5	65.9	67.6	69.4	71.2	73.0	64.2	60.9	62.3	64.1	66.0	67.5
20-39 years..............	69.7	66.2	67.9	69.4	71.4	73.3	64.4	61.2	62.6	64.4	66.2	67.6
40-59 years..............	69.6	66.1	67.7	69.6	71.4	73.2	64.4	61.1	62.5	64.2	66.2	67.6
60 years and over........	68.6	64.9	66.7	68.9	70.3	72.1	63.2	59.9	61.4	63.2	64.9	66.3
Hispanic												
20 years and over........	67.1	63.5	65.1	67.0	68.9	70.9	61.9	58.6	60.1	61.8	63.6	65.2
20-39 years..............	67.4	63.6	65.2	67.3	69.4	71.6	62.3	58.9	60.5	62.2	63.9	65.6
40-59 years..............	67.1	63.7	65.1	67.0	68.8	70.5	61.9	58.6	60.1	61.7	63.6	64.9
60 years and over........	65.9	62.8	64.2	66.0	67.4	68.8	60.5	57.5	58.8	60.4	62.1	63.6

[1] Total includes persons of other race/ethnicities not shown separately.

Source: Centers for Disease Control and Prevention, National Health and Nutrition Examination Survey, *Anthropometric Reference Data For Children and Adults: United States, 2007-2010*, Series 11, No. 252, October 2012. See also <http://www.cdc.gov/nchs/>.

Table 218. Weight of Population Aged 20 and Over by Age, Sex, and Race/Ethnicity: 2007 to 2010

[Data are based on National Health and Nutrition Examination Survey (NHANES). Weight was measured without shoes. Pregnant females were excluded from the tabulations on weight. The oversampling of all Hispanic persons is new to the 2007–2010 data collection methodology; see source]

Age and Race/Ethnicity	Males, weight in pounds						Females, weight in pounds					
	Mean	Percentile					Mean	Percentile				
		10th	25th	50th	75th	90th		10th	25th	50th	75th	90th
Total [1]												
20 years and over........	195.5	146.6	165.2	189.8	218.0	252.2	166.2	118.2	134.6	157.2	188.6	225.3
20–29 years..............	183.9	137.9	153.2	176.5	206.6	240.4	161.9	114.8	126.3	149.4	181.2	227.3
30–39 years..............	199.5	149.4	166.2	191.1	222.9	259.7	169.1	118.8	137.2	159.8	194.2	225.4
40–49 years..............	200.6	153.2	173.1	193.7	221.9	256.1	168.0	120.8	134.9	158.4	189.0	228.7
50–59 years..............	201.3	152.2	172.3	195.4	226.9	259.3	170.0	123.3	138.5	161.4	193.8	230.2
60–69 years..............	199.4	149.8	168.5	195.1	223.0	253.8	170.5	126.1	140.4	165.7	192.5	226.3
70–79 years..............	190.6	147.2	165.5	186.8	209.8	241.1	164.9	118.0	136.9	159.4	187.1	218.4
80 years and over........	174.9	135.5	152.2	171.8	194.4	214.5	143.1	109.8	123.1	140.0	158.5	182.7
Non-Hispanic white												
20 years and over........	199.2	151.8	170.3	194.0	221.7	254.9	165.4	118.6	134.9	156.6	187.4	223.7
20–39 years..............	194.7	145.3	162.8	188.1	217.2	250.3	164.7	117.7	132.0	154.0	186.6	225.4
40–59 years..............	204.9	159.0	177.3	198.5	227.4	259.5	167.7	121.3	136.2	158.5	189.7	227.0
60 years and over........	196.3	152.0	168.8	191.8	217.1	248.1	163.0	117.9	135.2	157.5	185.5	217.1
Non-Hispanic black												
20 years and over........	199.4	143.5	163.1	191.3	224.5	264.7	187.9	129.5	151.0	177.5	215.5	255.1
20–39 years..............	198.1	141.6	158.9	188.7	223.5	264.5	186.2	125.6	145.1	176.2	216.6	258.9
40–59 years..............	203.1	146.0	169.5	196.4	227.7	266.3	194.7	133.9	156.4	183.4	221.5	257.3
60 years and over........	193.6	140.8	158.7	188.0	216.0	256.5	177.8	125.9	149.1	171.4	200.3	233.9
Hispanic												
20 years and over........	186.1	143.4	157.5	180.0	205.4	236.4	160.6	117.0	133.4	154.7	181.5	210.7
20–39 years..............	185.1	140.4	154.9	176.1	204.6	241.2	159.4	114.8	129.6	151.4	183.6	212.8
40–59 years..............	189.4	150.3	165.2	184.2	207.7	232.4	164.5	125.6	140.9	158.9	182.3	210.1
60 years and over........	180.8	138.8	154.7	177.1	200.5	223.7	155.8	114.2	133.5	153.0	174.3	198.8

[1] Total includes persons of other race/ethnicities, not shown separately.

Source: Centers for Disease Control and Prevention, National Health and Nutrition Examination Survey, *Anthropometric Reference Data For Children and Adults: United States, 2007-2010*, Series 11, No. 252, October 2012. See also <http://www.cdc.gov/nchs/>.

Table 219. Body Mass Index of Population Aged 20 and Over by Age, Sex, and Race/Ethnicity: 2007 to 2010

[Body Mass Index (BMI) is a measure that adjusts body weight for height, and is calculated as weight in kilograms divided by height in meters squared. For both men and women, BMI indicates weight status as follows: under 18.5 underweight, 18.5-24.9 normal, 25.0-29.9 overweight, and 30.0 and over obese. Data are based on National Health and Nutrition Examination Survey (NHANES), a sample of the civilian noninstitutional population. Data are collected through household interviews and health examinations. Excludes pregnant women. Height and weight were measured without shoes. The oversampling of all Hispanic persons is new to the 2007–2010 data collection methodology; see source)]

| Age and Race/Ethnicity | Males, BMI | | | | | | Females, BMI | | | | | |
| | Mean | Percentile | | | | | Mean | Percentile | | | | |
		10th	25th	50th	75th	90th		10th	25th	50th	75th	90th
Total [1]												
20 years and over.......	**28.6**	**22.2**	**24.7**	**27.8**	**31.5**	35.8	28.7	20.7	23.3	27.3	32.5	38.2
20–29 years.............	26.8	20.7	22.9	25.6	29.9	33.8	27.5	19.9	21.7	25.3	31.5	38.0
30–39 years.............	29.0	22.4	24.9	28.1	32.0	36.2	28.7	20.6	23.4	27.2	32.8	38.1
40–49 years.............	29.0	22.9	25.4	28.2	31.7	36.1	28.6	20.6	23.3	27.3	32.4	38.1
50–59 years.............	29.2	22.9	25.5	28.2	32.0	37.1	29.3	21.3	24.0	28.3	33.5	39.3
60–69 years.............	29.5	22.7	25.3	28.8	32.5	37.0	29.6	21.6	24.8	28.8	33.5	38.5
70–79 years.............	28.8	22.9	25.6	28.3	31.3	35.4	29.5	21.6	24.7	28.6	33.4	38.7
80 years and over.......	27.2	21.8	24.4	27.0	29.6	32.7	26.7	20.7	23.1	26.3	29.7	32.5
Non-Hispanic white												
20 years and over.......	28.7	22.4	24.8	27.9	31.5	35.8	28.2	20.5	23.0	26.9	32.0	37.7
20–39 years.............	27.7	21.1	23.6	26.8	30.9	34.2	27.5	19.9	22.1	25.6	31.3	37.5
40–59 years.............	29.2	23.1	25.5	28.3	31.8	36.8	28.3	20.5	23.2	26.9	32.4	38.0
60 years and over.......	29.2	23.2	25.5	28.6	31.9	35.9	28.7	21.4	24.0	27.8	32.2	37.6
Non-Hispanic black												
20 years and over.......	29.0	21.4	23.7	28.0	32.7	38.1	32.0	22.1	25.9	30.8	36.5	42.8
20–39 years.............	28.7	21.1	23.1	27.3	32.6	38.1	31.4	21.6	25.0	30.3	35.9	42.1
40–59 years.............	29.4	22.1	24.8	28.3	33.1	38.4	33.1	23.0	26.7	31.2	37.7	44.8
60 years and over.......	28.8	21.6	24.1	28.2	31.6	36.9	31.1	22.9	26.6	30.3	34.8	40.0
Hispanic												
20 years and over.......	28.9	23.0	25.5	28.1	31.6	35.6	29.5	21.9	24.9	28.5	33.0	38.0
20–39 years.............	28.5	21.9	24.8	27.5	31.1	35.5	28.8	21.3	23.6	26.9	32.7	38.2
40–59 years.............	29.5	24.2	26.5	28.8	32.1	35.7	30.2	23.0	26.2	29.6	33.2	37.8
60 years and over.......	29.2	23.2	25.9	28.3	31.9	35.6	29.9	22.8	25.7	29.4	33.2	37.7

[1] Total includes persons of other race/ethnicities not shown separately.

Source: Centers for Disease Control and Prevention, National Health and Nutrition Examination Survey, *Anthropometric Reference Data For Children and Adults: United States, 2007-2010*, Series 11, No. 252, October 2012. See also <http://www.cdc.gov/nchs/>.

Table 220. Age-Adjusted Percentage of Persons Engaging in Physical Activity and Fitness by Selected Characteristics: 2011

[In percent. Covers persons 18 years old and over. Based on the National Health Interview Survey, a sample survey of the civilian noninstitutionalized population. Measures of physical activity reflect the federal 2008 physical activity guidelines for Americans. The guidelines include an aerobic component; the full physical activity guidelines include muscle-strengthening and aerobic activities. For information on the physical activity guidelines, see <http://www.cdc.gov/physicalactivity/everyone/guidelines/index.html>. NHIS questions ask about frequency and duration of light-to moderate-intensity and vigorous-intensity leisure-time physical activities, and frequency of leisure-time muscle strengthening activities. Questions are phrased in terms of current behavior and lack a specific reference period. For definition of age adjustment, see text, Section 2.]

Characteristic	Inactive/ insufficiently active [1]	Sufficiently active [2]	Met muscle strengthening and aerobic guidelines [3]	Characteristic	Inactive/ insufficiently active [1]	Sufficiently active [2]	Met muscle strengthening and aerobic guidelines [3]
Total.............................	**51.1**	**48.9**	**21.0**	Native Hawaiian/			
SEX				Pacific Islander................	60.8	39.2	15.5
Male.............................	47.3	52.7	24.9	Two or more races.............	49.1	50.9	24.1
Female...........................	54.5	45.5	17.1				
				HISPANIC ORIGIN AND RACE			
AGE [4]				Hispanic or Latino [5].............	59.8	40.1	15.4
18 to 44 years of age...........	44.1	55.8	26.0	Not Hispanic or Latino..........	49.5	50.5	21.9
45 to 64 years of age...........	55.1	44.9	17.5	White, non-Hispanic...........	47.4	52.5	23.0
65 to 74 years of age...........	58.9	41.0	14.3	Black, non-Hispanic...........	58.8	41.2	18.0
75 years and over...............	72.6	27.4	7.7				
				EDUCATION [7]			
RACE				Less than high school			
Race alone:				diploma..........................	71.4	28.6	7.3
White.........................	49.6	50.3	21.7	High school diploma			
Black or African American.....	58.7	41.4	17.8	or GED [6]........................	62.1	37.8	12.2
American Indian/				Some college.................	52.4	47.7	19.9
Alaska Native.................	57.0	43.1	17.0	Bachelor's degree or higher....	37.6	62.5	30.5
Asian..........................	55.1	44.9	16.7				

[1] "Inactive" is having no leisure-time aerobic activity that lasted at least 10 minutes. "Insufficiently active" is having aerobic activities for 10 minutes or more but less than 150 minutes per week. [2] "Sufficiently active," which meets the aerobic component of the 2008 federal physical activity guidelines, is participating in moderate-intensity leisure-time physical activity 150 minutes or more per week, or in vigorous-intensity leisure-time physical activity 75 minutes or more per week, or an equivalent combination. [3] Persons who are sufficiently active and who engage in muscle strengthening activities at least 2 times a week. [4] Age data are not age-adjusted. [5] Persons of Hispanic or Latino origin may be of any race. [6] General educational development high school equivalency diploma. [7] For persons aged 25 and over.

Source: U.S. National Center for Health Statistics, *Summary of Health Statistics for U.S. Adults: National Health Interview Survey, 2011*, December 2012, Series 10, No. 256. See also <http://www.cdc.gov/nchs/products/series/series10.htm>.

Table 221. High School Students Engaged in Physical Activity by Sex: 2011

[In percent. For students in grades 9 to 12. Based on the Youth Risk Behavior Survey, a school-based survey and subject to sampling error; for details, see source]

Characteristic	Participated in 60+ min. of physical activity on 5 of last 7 days [1]	Participated in 60+ min. of physical activity on all 7 days [2]	Did not participate in 60+ min. of physical activity on any day [3]	Attended physical education class		Played on at least one sports team [6]	Used computers 3 or more hours/ day [7]	Watched three or more hours/ day of TV [8]
				Total [4]	Attended daily [5]			
All students.....	**49.5**	**28.7**	**13.8**	**51.8**	**31.5**	**58.4**	**31.1**	**32.4**
Male................	**59.9**	**38.3**	**10.0**	**56.7**	**35.5**	**64.0**	**35.3**	**33.3**
Grade 9...........	61.0	38.8	8.7	70.8	44.0	65.6	35.5	33.9
Grade 10..........	62.3	42.6	10.0	59.2	36.7	68.2	36.1	35.3
Grade 11..........	58.5	36.2	10.5	49.2	31.6	60.9	36.7	32.3
Grade 12..........	57.3	34.9	10.8	44.7	27.9	60.2	32.4	30.9
Female............	**38.5**	**18.5**	**17.7**	**46.7**	**27.2**	**52.6**	**26.6**	**31.6**
Grade 9...........	44.5	22.2	13.9	65.3	38.6	57.1	29.5	33.8
Grade 10..........	40.3	18.1	17.9	49.8	29.3	56.1	26.7	31.7
Grade 11..........	35.7	18.0	19.0	36.3	18.4	51.3	24.6	30.4
Grade 12..........	32.0	14.9	20.6	32.1	20.4	44.5	25.0	29.9

[1] Were physically active doing any kind of physical activity that increased their heart rate and made them breathe hard some of the time for a total of at least 60 minutes/day for at least 5 or more days out of the 7 days preceding the survey. [2] Participated in 60 or more minutes of any kind of physical activity that increased their heart rate and made them breathe hard some of the time on all 7 days before the survey. [3] Did not participate in 60 or more minutes of any kind of physical activity that increased their heart rate and made them breathe hard some of the time on at least 1 day during the 7 days before the survey. [4] On one or more days in an average week when they were in school. [5] Five days in an average week when they were in school. [6] Run by their school or community groups during the 12 months before the survey. [7] Played video or computer games or used computer for something that was not school work on an average school day. [8] On an average school day.

Source: U.S. Centers for Disease Control and Prevention, *Morbidity and Mortality Weekly Report, Surveillance Summaries*, 61:4, June 8, 2012, "Youth Risk Behavior Surveillance— United States, 2011." See also <http://www.cdc.gov/HealthyYouth/yrbs/index.htm>.

Table 222. Households and Persons Having Problems With Access to Food: 2005 to 2011

[114,437 represents 114,437,000. Food security status of households is measured through a series of questions about experiences and behaviors known to characterize households that are having difficulty meeting basic food needs. All questions refer to the previous 12 months and include a qualifying phrase reminding respondents to report only conditions resulting from inadequate financial resources; restrictions to food intake due to dieting and volunteer fasting are excluded. Food-secure households report 0-2 food-insecure conditions. Food-insecure households report 3 or more conditions. Low and very low food security differ in the extent and character of the adjustments the household makes to its eating patterns and food intake. Households classified as having low food security report multiple indications of food access problems, but typically report few, if any, indications of reduced food intake. Those classified as having very low food security report multiple indications of reduced food intake and disrupted eating patterns due to inadequate resources for food. The omission of homeless persons may be a cause of underreporting. Data are from the Food Security Supplement to the Current Population Survey (CPS); for details about the CPS, see text, Section 1 and Appendix III]

Household food	Number (1,000)					Percent distribution				
	2005	2008	2009	2010	2011	2005	2008	2009	2010	2011
Households, total.....................	**114,437**	**117,565**	**118,174**	**118,756**	**119,484**	**100.0**	**100.0**	**100.0**	**100.0**	**100.0**
Food-secure.............................	101,851	100,416	100,820	101,527	101,631	89.0	85.4	85.3	85.5	85.1
Food-insecure...........................	12,586	17,149	17,354	17,229	17,853	11.0	14.6	14.7	14.5	14.9
With low food security [1]..............	8,158	10,426	10,601	10,872	11,014	7.1	8.9	9.0	9.1	9.2
With very low food security [2]..........	4,428	6,723	6,753	6,357	6,839	3.9	5.7	5.7	5.4	5.7
Adult members.......................	**217,897**	**225,461**	**227,543**	**229,129**	**231,385**	**100.0**	**100.0**	**100.0**	**100.0**	**100.0**
In food-secure households..............	195,172	193,026	194,579	196,505	197,923	89.6	85.6	85.5	85.8	85.5
In food-insecure households............	22,725	32,435	32,964	32,624	33,462	10.4	14.4	14.5	14.2	14.5
With low food security..................	15,146	20,320	20,741	21,357	21,371	7.0	9.0	9.1	9.3	9.2
With very low food security [2]..........	7,579	12,115	12,223	11,267	12,091	3.5	5.4	5.4	4.9	5.2
Child members.......................	**73,604**	**74,106**	**74,207**	**74,905**	**74,508**	**100.0**	**100.0**	**100.0**	**100.0**	**100.0**
In food-secure households..............	61,201	57,433	57,010	58,697	57,850	83.1	77.5	76.8	78.4	77.6
In food-insecure households............	12,403	16,673	17,197	16,208	16,658	16.9	22.5	23.2	21.6	22.4
With very low food security among children [3]......................	606	1,077	988	976	845	0.8	1.5	1.3	1.3	1.1

[1] Prior to 2006, USDA described these households as food insecure without hunger. [2] Food intake of one or more members in these households was reduced and normal eating patterns disrupted at some time during the year because of the household's food insecurity. Prior to 2006, USDA described these households as food insecure with hunger. [3] Percentages omit households with no children. The food security survey measures food security status at the household level. Not all children residing in food-insecure households were directly affected by the households' food insecurity. Similarly, not all children in households classified as having very low food security among children were subject to the reductions in food intake and disruptions in eating patterns that characterize this condition. Young children, in particular, are often protected from effects of the households' food insecurity.

Source: U.S. Department of Agriculture, Economic Research Service, *Household Food Security in the United States in 2011*, Economic Research Report Number 141, September 2012. See also <http://www.ers.usda.gov/publications/err-economic-research-report/err141.aspx>.

Table 223. Children Who Are Obese by Age, Sex, Race, and Hispanic Origin: 1976 to 2010

[In percent. For children aged 6-17. Data are from U.S. National Center for Health Statistics, National Health and Nutrition Examination Surveys, a program of studies that combines interviews and physical examinations to assess the health and nutritional status of adults and children. Children classified as obese have a body mass index (BMI) at or above the 95th percentile of the sex-specific BMI growth charts]

Selected characteristic	1976–1980	1988–1994	1999–2000	2001–2002	2003–2004	2005–2006	2007–2008	2009–2010
Total	**5.7**	**11.2**	**15.0**	**16.5**	**18.0**	**16.5**	**19.2**	**18.0**
RACE AND HISPANIC ORIGIN [1]								
White, non-Hispanic	4.9	10.5	11.3	14.6	17.3	13.8	17.4	14.6
Black, non-Hispanic	8.2	14.0	21.1	20.4	21.7	21.3	22.4	25.7
Hispanic origin [2, 3]	(NA)	(NA)	(NA)	(NA)	(NA)	(NA)	24.4	23.1
Mexican-American [2, 3]	(NA)	15.4	24.1	21.5	19.6	25.6	24.2	23.4
SEX								
Male	5.5	11.8	15.7	18.0	19.1	17.2	21.0	19.7
Female	5.8	10.6	14.3	15.1	16.8	15.9	17.3	16.2
Ages 6-11	6.5	11.3	15.1	16.3	18.8	15.1	19.6	18.0
Male	6.7	11.6	15.7	17.5	19.9	16.2	21.2	20.1
Female	6.4	11.0	14.3	14.9	17.6	14.1	18.0	15.7
Ages 12-17	5.0	11.1	14.9	16.8	17.2	17.8	18.8	18.0
Male	4.5	12.0	15.6	18.4	18.3	18.1	20.8	19.4
Female	5.4	10.2	14.2	15.2	16.0	17.5	16.7	16.5

NA Not available. [1] Includes other races not shown separately. [2] Persons of Hispanic and Mexican origin may be of any race. [3] From 1976 to 2006, the survey sample was designed to provide estimates specifically for persons of Mexican origin. Beginning in 2007, the survey allows for reporting of both total Hispanics and Mexican Americans.

Source: Federal Interagency Forum on Child and Family Statistics, *America's Children: Key National Indicators of Well-Being, 2013*, July 2013. See also <http://www.childstats.gov/americaschildren/index.asp>.

Table 224. Youth Aged 12-17 with a Major Depressive Episode in the Past Year by Selected Characteristics: 2005 to 2011

[In percent. Data are from Substance Abuse and Mental Health Services Administration, National Survey on Drug Use and Health. Data collection is through in-person interviews with sampled persons. Major Depressive Episode is defined as a period of at least 2 weeks when a person experienced a depressed mood or loss of interest or pleasure in daily activities and had at least four additional symptoms (such as problems with sleep, eating, energy, concentration, and feelings of self-worth)]

Item	2005	2006	2007	2008	2009	2010	2011
Total	**8.8**	**7.9**	**8.2**	**8.3**	**8.1**	**8.0**	**8.2**
Age:							
12-13 years	5.2	4.9	4.3	4.9	4.6	4.3	4.1
14-15 years	9.5	7.9	8.4	8.5	8.8	9.0	8.6
16-17 years	11.5	10.7	11.5	11.2	10.4	10.6	11.7
Sex:							
Male	4.5	4.2	4.6	4.3	4.7	4.4	4.5
Female	13.3	11.8	11.9	12.5	11.7	11.9	12.1
Race and Hispanic Origin: [1]							
White	9.1	8.2	8.7	8.8	8.4	8.6	8.6
Black	7.6	6.4	7.8	7.1	7.9	6.8	7.0
American Indian or Alaska Native	6.1	9.3	4.6	10.1	7.5	7.4	11.4
Asian	6.0	7.7	6.6	7.7	7.6	5.5	7.6
Two or more races	10.5	13.0	9.9	12.0	8.0	9.4	10.6
Hispanic	9.1	8.0	7.1	7.5	7.7	7.8	8.1
Poverty status:							
Below 100% poverty	8.1	7.6	7.6	7.7	7.4	7.2	8.1
100-199% poverty	9.6	9.0	8.9	9.1	8.6	9.0	8.9
200% poverty and above	8.7	7.6	8.0	8.2	8.2	7.9	8.1

[1] Respondents could choose more than one race. Those reporting more than one race were classified as "Two or more races." Data on Hispanic origin are collected separately. Persons of Hispanic origin may be of any race. Included in the total but not shown separately are persons of Native Hawaiian or Other Pacific Islander origin.

Source: Federal Interagency Forum on Child and Family Statistics, *America's Children: Key National Indicators of Well-Being, 2013*, July 2013. See also <http://www.childstats.gov/americaschildren/index.asp>.

Table 225. Prevalence of Allergies Among Children by Allergy Type and Age, Race/Ethnicity, and Poverty Status: 2000 to 2011

[In percent; three year annual averages. Based on the Sample Child component of the National Health Interview Survey of the civilian noninstitutionalized population. A parent or responsible adult for the sample child answered questions to estimate the prevalence of allergic conditions. See source for more information]

Age, Race/Ethnicity, and Poverty Status	Hay Fever/Respiratory Allergy				Food Allergy				Skin Allergy			
	2000-2002	2003-2005	2006-2008	2009-2011	2000-2002	2003-2005	2006-2008	2009-2011	2000-2002	2003-2005	2006-2008	2009-2011
By Age:												
0-17.............	17.7	17.3	16.5	17.0	3.6	3.8	4.3	5.1	8.1	9.6	10.1	12.5
0-4 years........	10.4	10.1	10.5	10.8	4.0	4.3	4.8	5.1	8.7	11.0	11.7	14.2
5-17 years.......	20.4	20.0	18.9	19.5	3.4	3.6	4.1	5.1	7.9	9.1	9.4	11.8
5-9 years........	18.2	17.9	17.4	17.4	3.6	3.5	4.0	5.2	8.5	10.0	10.3	13.1
10-17 years......	21.8	21.2	19.7	20.8	3.3	3.6	4.1	5.1	7.6	8.6	8.9	10.9
By Race/Ethnicity:												
White												
0-17 years.......	18.5	17.8	17.1	17.3	3.6	3.8	4.1	4.8	7.7	9.0	9.5	11.4
0-4 years........	10.4	10.4	10.5	10.8	4.1	4.3	5.0	4.8	8.2	10.1	10.6	12.7
5-17 years.......	21.4	20.6	19.6	19.9	3.5	3.5	3.8	4.8	7.5	8.6	9.0	10.9
Black												
0-17 years.......	15.7	15.2	14.1	15.6	3.0	3.7	4.2	6.1	10.3	12.4	12.7	17.3
0-4 years........	10.5	9.5	10.2	11.9	3.0	3.9	3.3	6.0	11.6	13.8	17.0	20.8
5-17 years.......	17.5	17.3	15.5	17.1	3.0	3.6	4.5	6.1	9.9	11.8	11.0	15.8
American Indian/Alaska Native												
0-17 years.......	16.5	16.5	13.9	14.8	4.8	(B)	8.3	4.5	9.3	11.3	8.1	9.3
0-4 years........	(B)	16.3	(B)	(B)	(B)	(B)	(B)	(B)	(B)	16.3	(B)	(B)
5-17 years.......	18.0	16.5	17.0	17.2	(B)	(B)	7.9	5.9	7.2	10.0	(B)	9.3
Asian												
0-17 years.......	12.6	11.3	13.0	14.1	4.4	4.3	4.8	6.1	8.4	7.5	8.9	12.3
0-4 years........	9.7	4.7	10.2	9.4	5.1	5.4	5.7	6.1	8.8	12.5	11.0	12.7
5-17 years.......	13.8	13.5	14.1	15.9	4.1	3.9	4.5	6.2	8.3	5.8	8.1	12.2
Hispanic												
0-17 years.......	12.3	12.8	12.5	13.0	2.5	2.8	3.3	3.6	5.6	7.2	8.1	10.1
0-4 years........	8.0	8.9	9.2	9.5	2.2	2.8	3.3	3.2	5.5	7.9	8.4	11.0
5-17 years.......	14.3	14.5	14.0	14.7	2.6	2.8	3.3	3.8	5.7	6.9	7.9	9.7
By Poverty Status:												
Poor [1]												
0-17 years.......	14.0	14.2	13.6	14.9	3.2	3.3	3.6	4.4	7.1	9.0	10.3	13.1
0-4 years........	9.8	10.1	10.5	11.8	3.4	3.8	4.1	4.2	6.9	8.1	10.9	13.9
5-17 years.......	15.9	16.2	15.3	16.5	3.2	3.1	3.3	4.5	7.2	9.3	10.0	12.7
Near Poor [2]												
0-17 years.......	15.7	16.0	13.8	15.8	3.4	3.8	4.3	5.0	7.6	8.7	9.4	12.2
0-4 years........	10.9	10.2	8.7	10.4	4.1	4.4	3.8	4.3	8.3	10.0	11.5	13.4
5-17 years.......	17.6	18.3	15.9	18.1	3.2	3.5	4.5	5.3	7.3	8.2	8.6	11.7
Not Poor [3]												
0-17 years.......	19.5	18.6	18.6	18.3	3.7	3.9	4.5	5.4	8.6	10.2	10.3	12.4
0-4 years........	10.4	10.0	11.4	10.5	4.1	4.5	5.7	6.0	9.5	12.5	12.2	14.8
5-17 years.......	22.6	21.6	21.1	21.1	3.6	3.8	4.1	5.3	8.3	9.4	9.6	11.5

B Prevalence rates with standard error over 30% or based on fewer than 25 interviews. [1] Data from families below 100% of Federal poverty level. [2] Data from families at 100% to less than 200% of Federal poverty level. [3] Data from families at and over 200% of Federal poverty level.

Source: U.S. National Center for Health Statistics, National Health Interview Surveys, "Health Data Interactive," <http://www.cdc.gov/nchs/hdi.htm>, accessed May 2013. See also <http://www.cdc.gov/nchs/data/databriefs/db121.htm>.

Table 226. Percent Distribution of Hours of Sleep for Adults Age 18 and Over by Selected Characteristics: 2008 to 2010

[227,368 represents 227,368,000. Data are crude estimates for civilian noninstitutionalized population aged 18 and older. Based on 76,669 interviews from the Sample Adult component of the 2008-10 National Health Interview Survey. Survey respondents were asked, "On average, how many hours of sleep do you get in a 24 hour period?" Response options were 1-24 hours]

Characteristic	Adults age 18 and over	Hours of sleep		
		6 or less	7 to 8	9 or more
Unit	Number (1,000)	Percent distribution		
Total [1]	**227,368**	**28.5**	**62.3**	**9.2**
SEX				
Male	109,843	28.4	62.9	8.6
Female	117,525	28.7	61.7	9.7
AGE [2]				
18 to 24 years old	29,130	23.4	62.5	14.0
25 to 44 years old	81,392	30.5	63.2	6.2
45 to 64 years old	78,909	31.3	62.0	6.7
65 to 74 years old	20,585	23.7	63.8	12.5
75 years old and over	17,351	21.0	56.7	22.4
RACE				
Single race [3]				
White	183,907	27.2	63.6	9.2
Black or African American	27,316	36.2	53.6	10.3
American Indian or Alaska Native	1,943	29.7	59.2	11.1
Asian	10,787	29.6	64.5	5.9
Native Hawaiian or Other Pacific Islander	392	39.2	53.2	(S)
Two or more races [4]	3,023	35.3	54.3	10.4
Black or African American, white	532	34.3	52.4	13.3
American Indian or Alaska Native, white	1,411	33.1	53.6	13.3
HISPANIC ORIGIN AND RACE [5]				
Hispanic or Latino	31,330	26.0	64.9	9.1
Mexican or Mexican American	19,496	23.4	66.5	10.1
Not Hispanic or Latino	196,038	28.9	61.9	9.2
White, single race	155,262	27.5	63.3	9.2
Black or African American, single race	26,318	36.3	53.5	10.2
EDUCATION				
Less than high school graduate	33,672	28.2	56.9	14.9
GED diploma [6]	6,405	34.4	53.8	11.8
High school graduate	55,686	28.9	59.8	11.3
Some college, no degree	45,503	31.3	60.3	8.4
Associate of arts degree	23,135	31.5	61.7	6.9
Bachelor of arts, science degree	40,489	25.5	68.7	5.8
Masters, doctorate, medical degree	21,173	23.2	72.2	4.5
POVERTY STATUS [7]				
Below poverty level	28,535	31.0	55.5	13.5
100% to less than 200% poverty level	42,229	30.0	58.0	12.0
200% to less than 400% poverty level	69,616	29.2	61.5	9.3
400% or more of poverty level	86,988	26.5	67.2	6.3
MARITAL STATUS				
Never married	48,209	26.3	62.2	11.6
Married	123,910	27.3	65.0	7.7
Cohabiting	15,650	32.0	59.4	8.7
Divorced or separated	25,654	36.7	55.3	8.0
Widowed	13,586	28.4	54.0	17.6

(S) Does not meet publication standards. [1] Includes persons of other races and unknown race and ethnicity, unknown education, unknown poverty status, and unknown marital status. [2] Estimates for age groups are not age adjusted. [3] Refers to persons who indicated only a single race group. [4] Refers to all persons who indicated more than one race group. [5] Persons of Hispanic or Latino origin may be of any race or combination of races. [6] General Educational Development high school equivalency diploma. [7] Based on family income and family size using the U.S. Census Bureau poverty thresholds for 2007-2009.

Source: U.S. National Center for Health Statistics, *Health Behaviors of Adults: United States, 2008-10,* Vital and Health Statistics, Series 10, Number 257, May 2013. See also <http://www.cdc.gov/nchs/products/series/series10.htm>.

Table 227. Percent of Population with Prescription Drug Use in Past 30 Days by Selected Characteristics: 2005 to 2010

[Based on the National Health and Nutrition Examination Survey, covering a sample of the civilian noninstitutionalized population]

Sex and Age	Total [1]		White [2]		Black or African American [2]		Mexican origin	
	2005-2008	2007-2010	2005-2008	2007-2010	2005-2008	2007-2010	2005-2008	2007-2010
Using at least one prescription drug in past 30 days								
Both sexes, age adjusted [4]...........	47.2	47.5	52.0	52.8	42.1	42.3	32.2	33.9
Male..................................	41.8	42.8	46.1	47.5	37.2	36.7	28.8	31.0
Female................................	52.4	52.0	57.9	57.9	46.0	46.8	35.6	37.0
Both sexes, crude.....................	47.9	48.5	55.0	56.2	39.5	40.2	24.5	26.4
Male..................................	41.7	43.0	48.4	50.3	33.9	33.9	21.4	23.7
Female................................	53.9	53.8	61.5	61.8	44.4	45.7	27.9	29.4
By Age:								
Under 18 years......................	25.3	24.0	29.9	28.1	20.8	21.7	17.0	16.8
18 to 44.............................	37.8	38.7	45.1	47.5	29.4	28.5	17.7	19.4
45 to 64.............................	64.8	66.2	67.7	69.7	62.6	64.2	50.1	49.7
65 and over..........................	90.1	89.7	91.1	90.2	89.1	89.1	76.7	86.2
Male, by age:								
Under age 18........................	25.3	24.5	29.2	27.4	23.4	24.8	17.3	17.6
18 to 44.............................	27.5	29.5	33.3	37.1	20.9	18.8	14.2	16.7
45 to 64.............................	59.3	61.3	62.3	65.2	54.7	54.6	46.0	43.9
65 and over..........................	89.7	88.8	91.6	90.1	85.1	85.3	67.8	80.2
Female, by age:								
Under age 18........................	25.2	23.5	30.7	28.8	18.1	18.6	16.7	16.0
18 to 44.............................	47.9	47.6	56.6	57.6	36.6	36.7	22.0	22.8
45 to 64.............................	70.2	70.8	73.0	74.1	69.1	72.1	54.1	55.7
65 and over..........................	90.5	90.4	90.7	90.2	91.7	91.5	83.9	91.1
Using 3 or more prescription drugs in past 30 days								
Both sexes, age adjusted [4]...........	20.8	20.8	22.3	22.4	20.0	20.7	13.8	15.0
Male..................................	18.3	19.1	19.5	20.6	17.5	17.7	11.6	13.4
Female................................	23.2	22.5	25.1	24.3	21.8	22.9	15.9	16.6
Both sexes, crude.....................	21.4	21.7	25.3	25.8	17.5	18.6	7.8	9.0
Male..................................	17.8	19.0	21.3	22.9	14.4	15.0	6.1	7.6
Female................................	24.8	24.2	29.1	28.6	20.2	21.7	9.7	10.6
By Age:								
Under 18 years......................	4.4	3.8	5.3	4.0	3.6	3.9	2.7	2.6
18 to 44.............................	9.8	9.7	12.1	12.3	7.3	7.7	2.7	[3] 3.0
45 to 64.............................	34.1	34.4	35.6	36.6	34.5	36.9	24.5	24.1
65 and over..........................	65.0	66.6	65.7	66.8	67.0	66.7	52.5	61.6
Male, by age:								
Under age 18........................	5.0	4.4	5.7	4.5	5.3	5.6	3.5	3.1
18 to 44.............................	6.2	7.1	8.0	9.1	[3] 4.9	[3] 5.3	[3] 1.5	2.6
45 to 64.............................	28.6	30.4	29.4	32.7	29.0	29.5	19.7	19.7
65 and over..........................	64.6	66.8	66.3	67.8	61.5	60.6	45.0	56.6
Female, by age:								
Under age 18........................	3.8	3.1	4.8	3.6	[3] 1.9	[3] 2.3	1.8	2.1
18 to 44.............................	13.3	12.2	16.1	15.3	9.4	9.7	4.1	[3] 3.5
45 to 64.............................	39.4	38.1	41.8	40.4	39.1	43.1	29.0	28.5
65 and over..........................	65.3	66.4	65.3	66.1	70.6	70.6	58.6	65.7

[1] Includes persons of all races and Hispanic origins, including those not shown separately. [2] Not Hispanic or Latino. [3] Estimates are considered unreliable. Data have a relative standard error of 20%-30%. [4] Age-adjusted to the 2000 standard population.

Source: U.S. Centers for Disease Control and Prevention, National Center for Health Statistics, *Health, United States, 2012*, May 2013. See also <http://www.cdc.gov/nchs/hus.htm>.

Table 228. Per Capita Consumption of Selected Beverages by Type: 1980 to 2010

[In gallons. See headnote, Table 230. Per capita consumption uses U.S. resident population, July 1, for all beverages except coffee, tea, and fruit juices which use U.S. total population (resident plus Armed Forces overseas), July 1]

Beverages	1980	1990	1995	2000	2005	2007	2008	2009	2010
Nonalcoholic............................	104.0	112.6	107.5	114.8	(NA)	(NA)	(NA)	(NA)	(NA)
Milk (plain and flavored)..............	27.5	25.7	23.9	22.5	21.0	20.6	20.8	20.6	20.1
Whole...............................	17.0	10.5	8.6	8.1	7.0	6.4	6.1	5.9	5.6
Reduced-fat, light, and skim [1]......	10.5	15.2	15.3	14.4	14.1	14.3	14.6	14.6	14.6
Tea.....................................	7.3	6.9	7.9	7.8	8.0	8.4	8.0	9.0	8.9
Coffee..................................	26.7	26.8	20.2	26.3	24.3	24.6	24.2	23.3	23.2
Carbonated soft drinks................	35.1	46.2	47.4	49.3	(NA)	(NA)	(NA)	(NA)	(NA)
Diet.................................	5.1	10.7	10.9	11.6	(NA)	(NA)	(NA)	(NA)	(NA)
Regular.............................	29.9	35.6	36.5	37.7	(NA)	(NA)	(NA)	(NA)	(NA)
Fruit juices............................	7.4	7.0	8.1	8.9	8.1	7.9	6.9	7.4	7.2

NA Not available. [1] Includes buttermilk.

Source: U.S. Department of Agriculture, Economic Research Service, "Food Availability (Per Capita) Data System," <http://www.ers.usda.gov/data-products/food-availability-(per-capita)-data-system.aspx>.

Table 229. Per Capita Utilization of Selected Commercially Produced Fruits and Vegetables: 1980 to 2010

[In pounds, farm weight. Domestic food use of fresh fruits and vegetables reflects the fresh-market share of commodity production plus imports and minus exports. Based on Census Bureau estimated resident population]

Commodity	1980	1990	1995	2000	2005	2007	2008	2009	2010
Fruits and vegetables, total [1]	**603.0**	**648.4**	**688.2**	**710.5**	**684.3**	**667.6**	**649.0**	**644.2**	**651.4**
Fruits, total	265.0	256.8	273.7	286.0	269.7	261.3	256.6	253.4	258.3
Fresh fruits	106.2	116.6	123.1	128.5	125.0	123.3	126.5	124.1	127.9
Noncitrus [2]	80.1	95.2	99.2	105.0	103.4	105.4	105.8	103.4	106.4
Apples	19.2	19.6	18.7	17.5	16.7	16.4	15.9	16.3	15.5
Avocados	2.1	1.4	1.6	2.2	3.5	3.5	3.8	4.2	3.5
Bananas	20.8	24.3	27.1	28.4	25.2	26.0	25.0	22.0	25.6
Blueberries	0.2	0.1	0.3	0.3	0.4	0.6	0.8	1.0	1.1
Cantaloupes	5.8	9.2	9.0	11.1	9.6	9.6	8.9	9.1	8.5
Cherries	0.7	0.4	0.3	0.6	0.9	1.2	1.0	1.6	1.3
Grapes	4.0	7.8	7.4	7.4	8.6	8.0	8.5	7.9	8.2
Honeydew melons	1.4	2.1	1.9	2.3	1.9	1.8	1.7	1.6	1.5
Mangoes	0.2	0.5	1.1	1.8	1.9	2.1	2.1	2.0	2.2
Papayas	0.2	0.2	0.4	0.7	0.9	1.1	1.0	1.2	1.2
Peaches and nectarines	7.1	5.5	5.3	5.3	4.8	4.5	5.1	4.4	4.7
Pears	2.6	3.2	3.4	3.4	2.9	3.1	3.1	3.2	2.9
Pineapples	1.5	2.0	1.9	3.2	4.9	5.0	5.1	5.1	5.7
Plums and prunes	1.5	1.5	0.9	1.2	1.1	1.0	0.9	0.7	0.8
Strawberries	2.0	3.3	4.1	4.9	5.9	6.3	6.5	7.2	7.3
Watermelons	10.7	13.3	15.2	13.8	13.5	14.4	15.6	14.9	15.5
Fresh citrus	26.1	21.4	23.8	23.5	21.6	17.9	20.6	20.7	21.6
Oranges and temples	14.3	12.4	11.8	11.7	11.4	7.5	9.9	9.1	9.7
Tangerines and tangelos	2.2	1.3	2.0	2.9	2.5	2.6	3.1	3.1	3.8
Lemons	1.9	2.6	2.8	2.4	2.9	2.8	2.0	3.1	2.8
Limes	0.4	0.7	1.2	1.4	2.1	2.3	2.5	2.5	2.6
Grapefruit	7.3	4.4	6.0	5.1	2.6	2.8	3.2	2.8	2.8
Processed fruits	158.8	140.3	150.6	157.5	144.7	138.0	130.1	129.3	130.3
Frozen fruits [3]	3.3	4.3	4.3	4.6	5.2	5.3	4.9	4.9	5.0
Dried fruits [4]	11.3	12.1	12.7	10.4	10.0	9.8	9.8	9.2	9.4
Canned fruits [5]	24.4	20.8	17.2	17.5	16.6	16.0	15.6	15.5	14.8
Fruit juices [6]	119.0	102.7	116.2	124.6	112.3	106.3	99.0	99.1	100.5
Vegetables, total	338.0	391.6	414.5	424.6	414.6	406.3	392.4	390.8	393.1
Fresh vegetables [7]	151.6	176.4	188.1	200.7	196.5	194.0	188.9	184.8	187.1
Asparagus	0.3	0.6	0.6	1.0	1.1	1.2	1.2	1.3	1.4
Bell peppers (all uses)	2.9	5.9	7.0	8.2	9.2	9.4	9.6	9.8	9.9
Broccoli	1.4	3.4	4.3	5.9	5.3	5.6	6.0	6.2	5.6
Cabbage	8.0	8.3	8.1	8.9	7.8	8.0	8.1	7.3	7.5
Carrots	6.2	8.3	11.2	9.2	8.7	8.0	8.1	7.4	7.6
Cauliflower	1.1	2.2	1.6	1.7	1.8	1.7	1.6	1.7	1.3
Celery (all uses)	7.4	7.2	6.9	6.3	5.9	6.3	6.2	6.2	6.2
Corn (sweet)	6.5	6.7	7.8	9.0	8.7	9.2	9.1	9.2	9.2
Cucumbers	3.9	4.7	5.6	6.4	6.2	6.4	6.4	6.8	6.8
Garlic (all uses)	0.9	1.3	1.8	2.2	2.4	2.7	2.8	2.4	2.3
Lettuce, head	25.6	27.7	22.2	23.5	20.9	18.4	16.8	16.1	16.1
Lettuce, Romaine and leaf	(NA)	3.8	5.9	8.4	9.7	11.5	10.4	10.0	10.7
Mushrooms	1.2	2.0	2.0	2.6	2.6	2.5	2.4	2.4	2.5
Onions	11.4	15.1	17.8	18.9	20.9	21.6	20.2	19.6	19.9
Potatoes	51.1	46.7	49.2	47.1	41.3	38.7	37.8	36.4	35.6
Pumpkin (all uses)	(NA)	4.5	6.0	4.7	4.9	5.0	4.8	4.1	4.5
Snap beans	1.3	1.1	1.6	2.0	1.8	2.2	2.0	1.7	1.9
Spinach	0.4	0.8	0.7	1.4	2.3	1.6	1.8	2.1	1.8
Squash (all uses)	2.3	3.5	3.8	4.5	4.4	4.1	4.2	4.4	4.3
Sweet potatoes (all uses)	4.4	4.4	4.2	4.2	4.5	5.1	5.0	5.2	6.3
Tomatoes	12.8	15.5	16.8	19.0	20.2	19.2	18.5	19.6	20.9
Processed vegetables	186.5	215.2	226.4	223.8	218.1	212.3	203.5	206.0	206.0
Selected vegetables for freezing [8]	51.5	66.8	78.8	79.3	76.4	75.8	72.6	71.3	70.2
Selected vegetables for canning [9]	102.5	110.3	108.2	103.2	104.8	96.7	94.6	100.4	99.1
Vegetables for dehydrating [10]	10.5	14.6	14.5	17.3	13.9	14.1	13.9	13.7	12.7
Potatoes for chips	16.5	16.4	16.4	15.6	16.0	18.6	15.7	13.7	15.0
Legumes [11]	5.4	7.2	8.4	8.4	6.9	7.1	6.8	6.8	8.9

NA Not available. [1] Excludes wine grapes. [2] Includes other fruits not shown separately. [3] Apples, apricots, blackberries, blueberries, boysenberries, cherries, loganberries, peaches, plums, prunes, raspberries, and strawberries. [4] Apples, apricots, dates, figs, peaches, pears, prunes, and raisins. [5] Apples, apricots, cherries, olives, peaches, pears, pineapples, plums, and prunes. [6] Apple, cranberry, grape, grapefruit, lemon, lime, orange, pineapple, and prunes. [7] Includes other vegetables not shown separately. [8] Asparagus, snap beans, lima beans, broccoli, carrots, cauliflower, sweet corn, green peas, potatoes, spinach, and miscellaneous vegetables. [9] Asparagus, snap beans, beets, cabbage, carrots, chili peppers, sweet corn, cucumbers for pickling, green peas, lima beans, mushrooms, spinach, and tomatoes. [10] Onions and potatoes. [11] Dry peas, lentils, and dry edible beans.

Source: U.S. Department of Agriculture, Economic Research Service, "Food Availability (Per Capita) Data System," <http://www.ers.usda.gov/data-products/food-availability-(per-capita)-data-system.aspx>.

Table 230. Per Capita Consumption of Major Food Commodities: 1980 to 2010

[In pounds, retail weight, except as indicated. Consumption represents the residual after exports, nonfood use and ending stocks are subtracted from the sum of beginning stocks, domestic production, and imports. Based on Census Bureau estimated resident population plus Armed Forces overseas for most commodities. For commodities not shipped overseas in substantial amounts, such as fluid milk and cream, the resident population is used]

Commodity	Unit	1980	1990	2000	2005	2008	2009	2010
Red meat, total (boneless, trimmed weight) [1, 2]	Pounds	126.4	112.2	113.7	110.2	106.6	105.7	102.1
Beef	Pounds	72.1	63.9	64.5	62.5	59.6	58.1	56.7
Veal	Pounds	1.3	0.9	0.5	0.4	0.3	0.3	0.3
Lamb and mutton	Pounds	1.0	1.0	0.8	0.7	0.7	0.7	0.7
Pork	Pounds	52.1	46.4	47.8	46.6	45.9	46.6	44.3
Poultry (boneless, trimmed weight) [2]	Pounds	40.8	56.2	67.9	73.7	72.6	69.4	70.9
Chicken	Pounds	32.7	42.4	54.2	60.5	58.7	56.0	58.0
Turkey	Pounds	8.1	13.8	13.7	13.2	13.9	13.3	12.9
Fish and shellfish (boneless, trimmed weight)	Pounds	12.4	14.9	15.2	16.2	16.0	15.8	15.8
Eggs	Number	271	234	251	256	247	247	246
Shell	Number	236	186	172	173	165	169	167
Processed	Number	35	48	79	83	81	77	79
Dairy products, total [3]	Pounds	543.1	568.0	591.7	597.8	603.1	604.6	610.7
Fluid milk products [4]	Gallons	27.9	26.2	23.2	22.2	22.1	22.1	21.7
Beverage milks	Gallons	27.6	25.7	22.5	21.0	20.7	20.6	20.1
Plain whole milk	Gallons	16.5	10.2	7.7	6.7	5.9	5.7	5.4
Plain reduced-fat milk (2%)	Gallons	6.3	9.1	7.1	6.9	7.3	7.3	7.0
Reduced fat milk (1%) and skim milk	Gallons	3.1	4.9	6.1	5.6	5.7	5.7	5.8
Flavored whole milk	Gallons	0.6	0.3	0.4	0.3	0.2	0.2	0.2
Flavored milks other than whole	Gallons	0.6	0.8	1.0	1.4	1.4	1.4	1.6
Buttermilk	Gallons	0.5	0.4	0.3	0.2	0.2	0.2	0.2
Yogurt (excl. frozen)	1/2 pints	4.6	7.8	12.0	19.1	21.7	23.1	25.0
Fluid cream products [5]	1/2 pints	10.5	14.3	18.3	24.1	23.8	23.6	22.6
Cream [6]	1/2 pints	6.3	8.7	11.6	14.9	15.1	15.0	14.1
Sour cream and dips	1/2 pints	3.4	4.7	6.1	8.3	7.9	7.8	7.7
Condensed and evaporated milks	Pounds	7.0	7.9	5.8	5.9	7.3	7.1	7.0
Whole milk	Pounds	3.8	3.1	2.0	2.2	2.2	2.2	1.8
Skim milk	Pounds	3.3	4.8	3.8	3.7	5.1	5.0	5.2
Cheese [7]	Pounds	17.5	24.6	29.8	32.5	33.1	33.3	33.2
American [8]	Pounds	9.6	11.1	12.7	13.5	13.6	13.9	13.3
Cheddar	Pounds	6.8	9.0	9.7	10.1	10.1	10.4	10.4
Italian [8]	Pounds	4.4	9.0	12.1	13.4	14.0	14.0	14.6
Mozzarella	Pounds	3.0	6.9	9.3	10.2	10.6	10.7	11.3
Other [8]	Pounds	3.3	4.3	5.0	5.7	5.6	5.5	5.1
Swiss	Pounds	1.3	1.4	1.0	1.3	1.1	1.2	1.2
Cream and Neufchatel	Pounds	0.9	1.6	2.4	2.4	2.5	2.5	2.4
Cottage cheese, total	Pounds	4.5	3.4	2.6	2.6	2.3	2.4	2.3
Lowfat	Pounds	0.8	1.2	1.3	1.4	1.3	1.3	1.3
Frozen dairy products	Pounds	23.9	26.1	25.4	23.0	22.6	21.8	21.2
Ice cream	Pounds	16.4	14.8	15.6	14.6	13.7	13.4	13.3
Lowfat ice cream	Pounds	5.8	6.3	6.4	5.8	5.9	6.1	5.8
Sherbet	Pounds	1.2	1.2	1.1	1.1	1.1	1.0	1.0
Frozen yogurt	Pounds	(NA)	2.8	2.0	1.3	1.5	0.9	1.0
Fats and oils:								
Total, fat content only	Pounds	55.6	60.3	81.7	85.5	85.0	77.7	82.1
Butter (product weight)	Pounds	4.5	4.0	4.5	4.6	5.0	5.0	4.9
Margarine (product weight)	Pounds	11.3	10.9	8.2	4.0	4.2	3.7	3.5
Lard (direct use)	Pounds	2.3	0.9	0.8	1.6	1.0	1.5	1.5
Edible beef tallow (direct use)	Pounds	1.1	0.6	4.0	3.8	2.9	0.7	3.3
Shortening	Pounds	16.9	20.6	31.5	29.0	18.0	15.9	15.3
Salad and cooking oils	Pounds	21.2	25.1	33.7	42.7	54.0	51.0	53.6
Other edible fats and oils	Pounds	1.5	1.2	1.5	1.6	1.6	1.7	1.7
Flour and cereal products [9]	Pounds	146.3	180.8	199.2	192.4	196.5	194.6	194.8
Wheat flour	Pounds	116.9	135.6	146.3	134.3	136.5	134.6	134.7
Rice, milled	Pounds	10.9	15.9	18.9	21.0	21.1	21.2	21.2
Corn products	Pounds	12.9	21.4	28.4	31.4	33.0	33.0	33.1
Oat products	Pounds	3.9	6.5	4.3	4.6	4.8	4.7	4.7
Caloric sweeteners, total [10]	Pounds	120.2	132.5	148.9	142.1	135.6	130.5	131.6
Sugar, refined cane and beet	Pounds	83.6	64.4	65.5	63.0	65.0	63.4	65.8
Corn sweeteners [11]	Pounds	35.3	66.8	81.8	77.6	69.1	65.7	64.3
High-fructose corn syrup	Pounds	19.0	49.6	62.6	59.1	53.0	50.1	48.8
Other:								
Cocoa beans	Pounds	3.4	5.4	5.9	6.5	5.6	5.5	5.5
Coffee (green beans)	Pounds	10.3	10.3	10.3	9.5	9.5	9.1	9.0
Peanuts (shelled)	Pounds	5.0	6.1	5.8	6.7	6.4	6.6	6.9
Tree nuts (shelled)	Pounds	1.8	2.5	2.6	2.6	3.5	3.7	4.0

NA Not available. [1] Excludes edible offals. [2] Excludes shipments to Puerto Rico and the other U.S. possessions. [3] Milk-equivalent, milk-fat basis. Includes butter. [4] Fluid milk figures are aggregates of commercial sales and milk produced and consumed on farms. [5] Includes eggnog, not shown separately. [6] Heavy cream, light cream, and half-and-half. [7] Excludes full-skim American, cottage, pot, and baker's cheese. [8] Includes other cheeses, not shown separately. [9] Includes rye flour and barley products, not shown separately. Excludes quantities used in alcoholic beverages. [10] Dry weight. Includes edible syrups (maple, molasses, etc.) and honey, not shown separately. [11] Includes glucose and dextrose, not shown separately.

Source: U.S. Department of Agriculture, Economic Research Service, "Food Availability (Per Capita) Data System," <http://www.ers.usda.gov/data-products/food-availability-(per-capita)-data-system.aspx>.

Table 231. Nutrition—Nutrients in Foods Available for Civilian Consumption Per Capita Per Day: 1970 to 2006

[Computed by the Center for Nutrition Policy and Promotion (CNPP). Based on Economic Research Service (ERS) estimates of per capita quantities of food available for consumption from "Food Consumption, Prices, and, Expenditures," on imputed consumption data for foods no longer reported by ERS, and on CNPP estimates of quantities of produce from home gardens. Food supply estimates do not reflect loss of food or nutrients from further marketing or home processing. Enrichment and fortification levels of iron, zinc, thiamin, riboflavin, niacin, folate, vitamin A, vitamin B6, vitamin B12, and Vitamin C are included]

Nutrient	Unit	1970–79	1980–89	1990–99	2000	2006
Food energy	Kilocalories	3,200	3,400	3,600	3,900	3,900
Carbohydrate	Grams	395	421	478	495	474
Fiber	Grams	20	22	24	24	25
Protein	Grams	96	100	108	111	111
Total fat [1]	Grams	143	151	150	169	178
Saturated	Grams	49	50	48	52	54
Monounsaturated	Grams	57	61	64	75	77
Polyunsaturated	Grams	27	30	31	35	39
Cholesterol	Milligrams	430	420	400	410	420
Vitamin A	Micrograms RAE [2]	1,050	1,050	1,100	1,090	940
Carotene	Micrograms	560	600	710	690	690
Vitamin E	Milligrams a-TE [3]	14	16	17	20	21
Vitamin C	Milligrams	109	115	118	121	106
Thiamin	Milligrams	2	3	3	3	3
Riboflavin	Milligrams	3	3	3	3	3
Niacin	Milligrams	25	29	31	32	32
Vitamin B6	Milligrams	2	2	2	2	2
Folate [4]	Micrograms DFE [5]	341	383	504	902	874
Vitamin B12	Micrograms	9	8	8	8	8
Calcium	Milligrams	930	930	980	980	960
Phosphorus	Milligrams	1,540	1,590	1,690	1,720	1,700
Magnesium	Milligrams	340	360	390	400	400
Iron	Milligrams	17	20	23	23	23
Zinc	Milligrams	13	14	15	15	16
Copper	Milligrams	2	2	2	2	2
Potassium	Milligrams	3,510	3,550	3,720	3,780	3,620
Sodium [6]	Milligrams	1,210	1,210	1,240	1,230	1,150
Selenium	Micrograms	133	143	163	179	181

[1] Includes other types of fat not shown separately. [2] Retinol activity equivalents. [3] Alpha-Tocopherol equivalents. [4] Reflects new terminology from Institute of Medicine's Dietary Reference Intakes reports. [5] Dietary Folate Equivalents (DFE). [6] Does not include amount from processed foods; underestimates actual availability.

Source: U.S. Department of Agriculture, Center for Nutrition Policy and Promotion, *Nutrient Content of the U.S. Food Supply, 1909–2006*, <http://www.cnpp.usda.gov/USFoodSupply.htm>.

Section 4
Education

This section presents data primarily concerning formal education as a whole, at various levels, and for public and private schools. Data shown relate to the school-age population and school enrollment, educational attainment, education personnel, and financial aspects of education. In addition, data are shown for charter schools, homeschooling, post-secondary education, security measures used in schools, technology usage in schools, and academic libraries. The chief sources are the decennial census of population and the Current Population Survey (CPS), both conducted by the U.S. Census Bureau (see text, Section 1, Population); annual, biennial, and other periodic surveys conducted by the National Center for Education Statistics (NCES), a part of the U.S. Department of Education; and surveys conducted by the National Education Association.

The censuses of population have included data on school enrollment since 1840 and on educational attainment since 1940. The CPS has reported on school enrollment annually since 1945 and on educational attainment periodically since 1947.

The NCES is continuing the pattern of statistical studies and surveys conducted by the U.S. Office of Education since 1870. The annual *Digest of Education Statistics* provides summary data on pupils, staff, finances, including government expenditures, and organization at the elementary, secondary, and higher education levels. It is also a primary source for detailed information on federal funds for education, projections of enrollment, graduates, and teachers. The *Condition of Education*, issued annually, presents a summary of information on education of particular interest to policymakers. NCES also conducts special studies periodically.

The census of governments, conducted by the Census Bureau every 5 years (for the years ending in "2" and "7"), provides data on school district finances and state and local government expenditures for education. Reports published by the Bureau of Labor Statistics contain data relating civilian labor force experience to educational attainment (see also Tables 620, 646, and 655 in Section 12, Labor Force, Employment, and Earnings).

Types and sources of data— The statistics in this section are of two general types. One type, exemplified by data from the Census Bureau, is based on direct interviews with individuals to obtain information about their own and their family members' education. Data of this type relate to school enrollment and level of education attained, classified by age, sex, and other characteristics of the population. The school enrollment statistics reflect attendance or enrollment in any regular school within a given period; educational attainment statistics reflect the highest grade completed by an individual, or beginning 1992, the highest diploma or degree received.

Beginning in 2012, CPS estimates reflect population controls based on Census 2010. From 2000-2011, the CPS used Census 2000 population controls. From 1994 to 2000, the CPS used 1990 census population controls plus adjustment for undercount. Also the survey changed from paper to computer-assisted technology. For years 1981 through 1993, 1980 census population controls were used; 1971 through 1980, 1970 census population controls had been used. These changes had little impact on summary measures (e.g., medians) and proportional measures (e.g., enrollment rates); however, use of the controls may have significant impact on absolute numbers.

The second type, generally exemplified by data from the NCES and the National Education Association, is based on reports from administrators of educational institutions and of state and local agencies having jurisdiction over education. Data of this type relate to enrollment, attendance, staff, and finances for the nation, individual states, and local areas.

Unlike the NCES, the Census Bureau does not regularly include specialized vocational, trade, business, or correspondence schools in its surveys. The NCES includes nursery schools and kindergartens that are part of regular grade schools in their enrollment figures. The Census Bureau includes all nursery schools and kindergartens. At the higher education level, the statistics of both agencies are concerned with institutions granting degrees or offering work acceptable for degree-credit, such as junior colleges.

School attendance—All states require that children attend school. While state laws vary as to the ages and circumstances of compulsory attendance, generally they require that formal schooling begin by age 6 and continue to age 16.

Schools—The NCES defines a school as "a division of the school system consisting of students composing one or more grade groups or other identifiable groups, organized as one unit with one or more teachers to give instruction of a defined type, and housed in a school plant of one or more buildings. More than one school may be housed in one school plant, as is the case when the elementary and secondary programs are housed in the same school plant."

Regular schools are those which advance a person toward a diploma or degree. They include public and private nursery schools, kindergartens, graded schools, colleges, universities, and professional schools.

Public schools are schools controlled and supported by local, state, or federal governmental agencies; private schools are those controlled and supported mainly by religious organizations or by private persons or organizations.

The Census Bureau defines *elementary* schools as including grades 1 through 8; *high* schools as including grades 9 through 12; and *colleges* as including junior or community colleges, regular 4-year colleges, and universities and graduate or professional schools. Statistics reported by the NCES and the National Education Association by type of organization, such as elementary level and secondary level, may not be strictly comparable with those from the Census Bureau because the grades included at the two levels vary, depending on the level assigned to the middle or junior high school by the local school systems.

School year—Except as otherwise indicated in the tables, data refer to the school year which, for elementary and secondary schools, generally begins in September of the preceding year and ends in June of the year stated. For the most part, statistics concerning school finances are for a 12-month period, usually July 1 to June 30. Enrollment data generally refer to a specific point in time, such as fall, as indicated in the tables.

Statistical reliability—For a discussion of statistical collection, estimation, and sampling procedures and measures of statistical reliability applicable to the Census Bureau and the NCES data, see Appendix III.

Table 232. School Enrollment: 1980 to 2020

[In thousands (58,305 represents 58,305,000). As of Fall]

Year	All levels			Pre-kindergarten through grade 8		Grades 9 through 12		College [3]	
	Total	Public	Private	Public	Private [1,2]	Public	Private [1]	Public	Private
1980...................	58,305	50,335	7,971	27,647	3,992	13,231	1,339	9,457	2,640
1985...................	57,226	48,901	8,325	27,034	4,195	12,388	1,362	9,479	2,768
1990...................	60,683	52,061	8,622	29,876	4,512	11,341	1,136	10,845	2,974
1991...................	62,087	53,357	8,730	30,506	4,518	11,541	1,163	11,310	3,049
1992...................	62,987	54,208	8,779	31,088	4,528	11,735	1,148	11,385	3,102
1993...................	63,438	54,654	8,784	31,504	4,536	11,961	1,132	11,189	3,116
1994...................	64,385	55,245	9,139	31,896	4,856	12,215	1,138	11,134	3,145
1995...................	65,020	55,933	9,087	32,338	4,756	12,502	1,163	11,092	3,169
1996...................	65,911	56,732	9,180	32,762	4,755	12,849	1,178	11,121	3,247
1997...................	66,574	57,323	9,251	33,071	4,759	13,056	1,185	11,196	3,306
1998...................	67,033	57,676	9,357	33,344	4,776	13,195	1,212	11,138	3,369
1999...................	67,667	58,167	9,500	33,486	4,789	13,371	1,229	11,309	3,482
2000...................	68,685	58,956	9,729	33,686	4,906	13,517	1,264	11,753	3,560
2001...................	69,920	59,905	10,014	33,936	5,023	13,736	1,296	12,233	3,695
2002...................	71,015	60,935	10,080	34,114	4,915	14,069	1,306	12,752	3,860
2003...................	71,551	61,399	10,152	34,201	4,788	14,339	1,311	12,859	4,053
2004...................	72,154	61,776	10,379	34,178	4,756	14,618	1,331	12,980	4,292
2005...................	72,674	62,135	10,539	34,204	4,724	14,909	1,349	13,022	4,466
2006...................	73,066	62,496	10,570	34,235	4,631	15,081	1,360	13,180	4,579
2007...................	73,451	62,783	10,668	34,205	4,546	15,087	1,364	13,491	4,757
2008...................	74,076	63,238	10,838	34,286	4,365	14,980	1,342	13,972	5,131
2009...................	75,290	64,184	11,106	34,418	4,179	14,955	1,309	14,811	5,617
2010, proj. [4]	75,720	64,449	11,271	34,637	4,092	14,668	1,306	15,143	5,873
2011, proj...........	76,321	65,063	11,258	34,892	4,057	14,530	1,266	15,640	5,934
2012, proj...........	76,522	65,309	11,212	35,129	4,034	14,512	1,229	15,668	5,949
2013, proj...........	76,988	65,749	11,238	35,368	4,025	14,545	1,194	15,836	6,019
2014, proj...........	77,708	66,389	11,319	35,579	4,027	14,689	1,160	16,121	6,132
2015, proj...........	78,448	67,037	11,410	35,829	4,042	14,830	1,134	16,378	6,234
2016, proj...........	79,169	67,662	11,507	36,161	4,073	14,877	1,103	16,624	6,331
2017, proj...........	79,879	68,277	11,602	36,491	4,110	14,939	1,077	16,847	6,415
2018, proj...........	80,588	68,881	11,708	36,803	4,146	15,000	1,060	17,078	6,502
2019, proj...........	81,309	69,496	11,813	37,121	4,181	15,083	1,052	17,292	6,579
2020, proj...........	82,014	70,110	11,905	37,444	4,216	15,222	1,056	17,444	6,632

[1] Since the biennial Private School Universe Survey (PSS) is collected in the fall of odd numbered years, even numbered years are estimated based on data from the PSS. [2] Includes private nursery and prekindergarten enrollment in schools that offer kindergarten or higher grades. [3] Data beginning 1996 based on new classification system. See footnote 1, Table 282. [4] Pre-K through 12 are projections; college data are actual.

Source: U.S. National Center for Education Statistics, *Digest of Education Statistics: 2011*, May 2012. See also <http://nces.ed.gov/programs/digest/d11/>; and *Projections of Education Statistics to 2020*, September 2011. See also <http://nces.ed.gov/pubsearch/pubsinfo.asp?pubid=2011026>.

Table 233. School Expenditures by Type of Control and Level of Instruction in Current and Constant (2011 to 2012) Dollars: 1980 to 2012

[In millions of dollars (160,075 represents $160,075,000,000). For school years ending in year shown. Data shown reflect historical revisions. Total expenditures for public elementary and secondary schools include current expenditures, interest on school debt and capital outlay. Based on survey of state education agencies; see source for details]

Year	Current dollars			Constant 2011-12 dollars [1]			
	Total	Elementary and secondary schools	Colleges and universities [2]	Total	Elementary and secondary schools		Colleges and universities [2]
		Total	Total		Total	Public	Total
1980..................	160,075	103,162	56,914	469,227	302,397	281,291	166,830
1985..................	239,351	149,400	89,951	514,981	321,444	294,765	193,536
1990..................	365,825	231,170	134,656	655,633	414,303	381,326	241,330
1995..................	485,169	302,200	182,969	734,053	457,224	422,123	276,829
1996..................	508,523	318,046	190,476	749,009	468,455	432,516	280,555
1997..................	538,854	338,951	[3] 199,903	771,668	485,397	448,450	[3] 286,272
1998..................	570,471	361,615	[3] 208,856	802,632	508,779	470,369	[3] 293,853
1999..................	603,847	384,638	219,209	835,133	531,962	492,131	303,170
2000..................	649,322	412,538	236,784	872,829	554,540	513,273	318,289
2001..................	705,017	444,811	260,206	916,302	578,116	533,926	338,186
2002..................	752,780	472,064	280,715	961,358	602,863	555,994	358,495
2003..................	795,691	492,807	302,884	994,308	615,819	568,459	378,489
2004..................	830,293	513,542	316,751	1,015,334	627,991	579,932	387,343
2005..................	875,988	540,969	335,019	1,039,919	642,205	593,057	397,714
2006..................	925,712	572,135	353,577	1,058,633	654,287	604,655	404,347
2007..................	984,034	608,495	375,539	1,096,962	678,326	626,713	418,636
2008..................	1,054,200	645,710	408,490	1,133,192	694,094	641,315	439,098
2009..................	1,089,670	658,926	430,744	1,155,190	698,546	647,024	456,644
2010..................	1,101,119	654,636	446,483	1,156,141	687,347	637,578	468,794
2011 [4].............	1,153,000	681,000	471,000	1,187,000	701,000	649,000	485,000
2012 [3].............	1,183,000	700,000	483,000	1,183,000	700,000	650,000	483,000

[1] Constant dollars based on the Consumer Price Index, prepared by the Bureau of Labor Statistics, U.S. Department of Labor, adjusted to a school-year basis. [2] Postsecondary data through 1996 are for institutions of higher education; thereafter, data are for degree-granting institutions. See source for details. [3] Estimated. [4] Data for elementary and secondary education are estimated; data for degree-granting institutions are actual.

Source: U.S. National Center for Education Statistics, Digest of Education Statistics, "Advance Release of Selected 2012 Digest Tables," <http://www.nces.ed.gov/programs/digest/>, accessed May 2013.

Table 234. School Enrollment, Faculty, Graduates, and Finances—Projections: 2012 to 2018

[55,091 represents 55,091,000. As of Fall, except as indicated]

Item	Unit	2012	2013	2014	2015	2016	2017	2018
ELEMENTARY AND SECONDARY SCHOOLS								
School enrollment, total	1,000	**55,091**	**55,288**	**55,599**	**55,957**	**56,330**	**56,722**	**57,098**
Pre-kindergarten through grade 8	1,000	39,115	39,334	39,539	39,788	40,114	40,451	40,797
Grades 9 through 12	1,000	15,976	15,954	16,060	16,169	16,217	16,271	16,301
Public	1,000	49,828	50,067	50,407	50,773	51,146	51,524	51,880
Pre-kindergarten through grade 8	1,000	35,076	35,301	35,502	35,735	36,029	36,329	36,639
Grades 9 through 12	1,000	14,752	14,766	14,905	15,038	15,116	15,195	15,241
Private	1,000	5,263	5,221	5,192	5,183	5,185	5,198	5,218
Pre-kindergarten through grade 8	1,000	4,039	4,033	4,037	4,053	4,085	4,122	4,158
Grades 9 through 12	1,000	1,224	1,188	1,155	1,130	1,100	1,076	1,061
Classroom teachers, total FTE [1]	1,000	**3,711**	**3,738**	**3,782**	**3,830**	**3,881**	**3,935**	**3,988**
Public	1,000	3,283	3,312	3,357	3,403	3,451	3,500	3,549
Private	1,000	428	426	425	427	430	434	439
High school graduates, total [2]	1,000	**3,376**	**3,315**	**3,307**	**3,325**	**3,348**	**3,396**	**3,396**
Public	1,000	3,092	3,037	3,043	3,066	3,097	3,149	3,155
Public schools: [2]								
Average daily attendance (ADA)	1,000	46,602	46,825	47,143	47,486	47,834	48,188	48,521
Current dollars: [3]								
Current school expenditure	Bil. dol.	571	591	619	(NA)	(NA)	(NA)	(NA)
Per pupil in fall enrollment	Dollar	11,467	11,810	12,281	(NA)	(NA)	(NA)	(NA)
Constant (2010–2011) dollars: [3,4]								
Current school expenditure	Bil. dol.	549	557	571	586	599	613	626
Per pupil in fall enrollment	Dollar	11,012	11,121	11,335	11,534	11,711	11,888	12,058
HIGHER EDUCATION								
Enrollment, total	1,000	**21,556**	**21,792**	**22,042**	**22,252**	**22,509**	**22,842**	**23,219**
Male	1,000	9,286	9,341	9,370	9,388	9,442	9,533	9,643
Full-time	1,000	5,954	5,985	6,000	6,009	6,044	6,104	6,175
Part-time	1,000	3,332	3,356	3,370	3,379	3,398	3,429	3,468
Female	1,000	12,270	12,451	12,673	12,864	13,067	13,309	13,576
Full-time	1,000	7,375	7,460	7,562	7,643	7,731	7,848	7,988
Part-time	1,000	4,895	4,991	5,111	5,221	5,336	5,461	5,588
Public	1,000	15,530	15,694	15,871	16,020	16,203	16,441	16,712
Four-year institutions	1,000	8,141	8,227	8,315	8,387	8,478	8,596	8,731
Two-year institutions	1,000	7,389	7,467	7,556	7,633	7,725	7,845	7,980
Private	1,000	6,027	6,098	6,171	6,233	6,307	6,401	6,508
Four-year institutions	1,000	5,558	5,624	5,692	5,750	5,818	5,905	6,003
Two-year institutions	1,000	469	474	479	483	488	496	505
Undergraduate	1,000	18,528	18,704	18,894	19,050	19,248	19,515	19,824
Postbaccalaureate	1,000	3,029	3,088	3,148	3,202	3,261	3,327	3,394
Full-time equivalent	1,000	16,300	16,459	16,625	16,759	16,930	17,164	17,435
Public	1,000	11,262	11,368	11,479	11,568	11,685	11,845	12,033
2-year	1,000	4,463	4,505	4,552	4,592	4,642	4,712	4,793
4-year	1,000	6,799	6,863	6,926	6,976	7,043	7,133	7,240
Private	1,000	5,038	5,092	5,146	5,190	5,245	5,318	5,403
2-year	1,000	438	442	447	450	455	462	470
4-year	1,000	4,600	4,650	4,700	4,740	4,790	4,856	4,932
Degrees conferred, total [2]	1,000	**3,680**	**3,734**	**3,783**	**3,828**	**3,874**	**3,924**	**3,980**
Associate's	1,000	937	943	951	959	967	977	989
Bachelor's	1,000	1,812	1,836	1,855	1,870	1,886	1,902	1,922
Master's	1,000	756	778	798	817	836	857	879
Doctoral	1,000	175	177	179	182	185	188	190

NA Not available. [1] Full-time equivalent. [2] For school year ending in June the following year. [3] Limited financial projections are shown due to the uncertain behavior of inflation over the long term. [4] Based on the Consumer Price Index (CPI) for all urban consumers, U.S. Bureau of Labor Statistics. CPI adjusted to a school year basis by NCES.

Source: U.S. National Center for Education Statistics, *Projections of Education Statistics to 2021*, January 2013. See also <http://www.nces.ed.gov/>.

Table 235. School Enrollment by Control and Level: 1980 to 2011

[In thousands (58,305 represents 58,305,000). As of Fall. Data below college level are for regular day schools and exclude subcollegiate departments of colleges, federal schools, and home-schooled children. College data include degree-credit and nondegree-credit enrollment. Based on survey of state education agencies; see source for details. For more projections, see Tables 232 and 234]

Control of school and level	1980	1990	1995	2000	2005	2007	2008	2009	2010, proj.	2011, proj.
Total	**58,305**	**60,683**	**65,020**	**68,685**	**72,674**	**73,451**	**74,076**	**75,290**	**75,720**	**76,321**
Public	50,335	52,061	55,933	58,956	62,135	62,783	63,238	64,184	64,449	65,062
Private	7,971	8,622	9,087	9,729	10,539	10,668	10,838	11,106	11,271	11,258
Pre-kindergarten through 8	**31,639**	**34,388**	**37,094**	**38,592**	**38,928**	**38,751**	**38,651**	**38,597**	**38,729**	**38,949**
Public	27,647	29,876	32,338	33,686	34,204	34,205	34,286	34,418	34,637	34,892
Private	3,992	[1] 4,512	4,756	[1] 4,906	4,724	4,546	[1] 4,365	4,179	4,092	4,057
Grades 9 through 12	**14,570**	**12,476**	**13,665**	**14,781**	**16,258**	**16,451**	**16,322**	**16,265**	**15,975**	**15,797**
Public	13,231	11,341	12,502	13,517	14,909	15,087	14,980	14,955	14,668	14,530
Private	1,339	[1] 1,136	1,163	[1] 1,264	1,349	1,364	[1] 1,342	1,309	1,306	1,266
College [2,3]	**12,097**	**13,819**	**14,262**	**15,312**	**17,487**	**18,248**	**19,103**	**20,428**	**21,016**	**21,575**
Public	9,457	10,845	11,092	11,753	13,022	13,491	13,972	14,811	15,143	15,640
Private	2,640	2,974	3,169	3,560	4,466	4,757	5,131	5,617	5,873	5,934
Not-for-profit	2,528	2,760	2,929	3,109	3,455	3,571	3,662	3,765	3,855	(NA)
For profit	112	214	240	450	1,011	1,186	1,469	1,852	2,018	(NA)

NA Not available. [1] Estimated. [2] Beginning 2000, reflects new classification system. See footnote 1, Table 282. [3] Data for 2010 are actual.

Source: U.S. National Center for Education Statistics, *Digest of Education Statistics: 2011*, May 2012. See also <http://nces.ed.gov/programs/digest/d11/>; and *Projections of Education Statistics to 2020*, September 2011.

Table 236. Federal Funds for Education and Related Programs: 2005 to 2012

[In millions of dollars (146,207.0 represents $146,207,000,000), except percent. For fiscal years ending in September. Figures represent on-budget funds]

Level, agency, and program	2005	2011	2012 [1]
Total, all programs	**146,207.0**	**185,209.8**	**(NA)**
Percent of federal budget outlays	5.9	5.1	(NA)
Elementary/secondary education programs	**68,957.7**	**76,902.3**	**78,980.6**
Department of Education [2]	37,477.6	38,652.2	38,601.6
Grants for the disadvantaged	14,635.6	15,515.4	15,741.7
School improvement programs	7,918.1	6,738.5	6,327.9
Indian education	121.9	127.0	130.8
Special education	10,940.3	12,526.7	12,640.7
Vocational and adult education	1,967.1	1,737.5	1,737.2
Education reform—Goals 2000	-35.0	(X)	(X)
Department of Agriculture [2]	12,577.3	18,843.6	20,849.1
Child nutrition programs	11,901.9	17,290.6	19,504.3
Agricultural Marketing Service—commodities [3]	399.3	1,006.0	952.0
Department of Defense [2]	1,786.3	2,047.8	2,132.0
Overseas dependents schools	1,060.9	1,193.6	1,235.7
Section VI schools [4]	410.2	476.7	504.7
Department of Health and Human Services	8,003.3	8,871.4	9,307.4
Head Start	6,842.3	7,559.2	7,969.2
Social security student benefits	1,161.0	1,312.2	1,338.2
Department of Homeland Security [2]	0.5	1.1	1.2
Department of the Interior [2]	938.5	815.9	786.4
Mineral Leasing Act and other funds	140.0	77.4	84.5
Indian Education	797.5	737.5	701.0
Department of Justice	554.5	911.8	965.8
Inmate programs	554.5	910.8	964.8
Department of Labor	5,654.0	6,121.0	5,662.0
Job Corps	1,521.0	1,660.0	1,789.0
Department of Veterans Affairs	1,815.0	472.0	516.0
Vocational rehab for disabled veterans	1,815.0	472.0	516.0
Other agencies and programs	150.7	165.5	159.1
Higher education programs [2]	**38,587.3**	**64,517.8**	**69,940.2**
Department of Education [2]	31,420.0	49,260.3	54,470.2
Student financial assistance	15,209.5	43,753.2	43,324.9
Federal Family Education Loans	10,777.5	-91.8	1,498.4
Department of Agriculture	62.0	81.7	81.7
Department of Commerce	(NA)	(NA)	(NA)
Department of Defense	1,858.3	2,297.2	2,407.6
Tuition assistance for military personnel	608.1	567.4	590.6
Service academies [5]	300.8	348.8	375.3
Senior ROTC	537.5	851.9	844.5
Professional development education	411.9	529.1	597.3
Department of Health and Human Services [2]	1,433.5	1,358.9	(NA)
Health professions training programs	581.7	498.0	459.0
National Health Service Corps scholarships	45.0	25.0	10.0
National Institutes of Health training grants [6]	756.0	771.8	777.8
Department of Homeland Security	36.4	69.1	69.9
Department of the Interior	249.2	99.7	109.8
Shared revenues, Mineral Leasing Act and other receipts—estimated education share	146.2	20.4	29.9
Indian programs	103.0	79.2	79.9
Department of State	424.0	661.0	621.0
Department of Transportation	73.0	77.0	123.0
Department of Veterans Affairs [2]	2,478.6	9,861.1	9,978.1
Post-Vietnam veterans	1.1	1.3	1.1
All-volunteer-force educational assistance	2,071.0	1,626.7	1,595.0
Other agencies and programs [2]	552.2	751.8	772.9
National Endowment for the Humanities	29.3	40.2	45.0
National Science Foundation	490.0	672.4	689.2
Other education programs [2]	**6,908.5**	**11,020.2**	**9,561.9**
Department of Education [2]	3,538.9	5,255.9	5,464.7
Administration	548.8	1,755.4	1,928.8
Rehabilitative services and handicapped research	2,973.3	3,474.7	3,511.3
Department of Agriculture	468.6	552.0	547.1
Department of Health and Human Services	313.0	337.0	338.0
Department of Homeland Security	278.2	1,892.0	282.5
Department of Justice	26.1	33.6	33.6
Department of State	109.3	121.6	123.5
Other agencies and programs [2]	2,172.2	2,827.9	2,772.5
Agency for International Development	574.0	486.9	651.6
Library of Congress	430.0	521.0	651.0
National Endowment for the Arts	2.5	2.5	2.2
National Endowment for the Humanities	88.0	90.9	91.0
Research programs at universities and related institutions [2]	**31,753.5**	**32,769.4**	**(NA)**
Department of Agriculture	709.7	893.9	(NA)
Department of Defense	2,675.9	2,444.8	(NA)
Department of Commerce	(NA)	(NA)	(NA)
Department of Energy	4,339.9	3,064.5	(NA)
Department of Health and Human Services	16,358.0	18,693.1	(NA)
National Aeronautics and Space Administration	2,763.1	1,771.1	(NA)
National Science Foundation	3,503.2	4,657.9	(NA)

NA Not available. X Not applicable. [1] Estimated except U.S. Department of Education, which are actual budget reports. [2] Includes other programs and agencies, not shown separately. [3] Purchased under Section 32 of the Act of August 1935 for use in child nutrition programs. [4] Program provides for the education of dependents of federal employees residing on federal property where free public education is unavailable in the nearby community. [5] Instructional costs only including academics, audiovisual, academic computer center, faculty training, military training, physical education, and libraries. [6] Includes alcohol, drug abuse, and mental health training programs.

Source: U.S. National Center for Education Statistics, *Digest of Education Statistics*, "Advance Release of Selected 2012 Digest Tables," <http://www.nces.ed.gov/programs/digest/>, accessed April 2013.

Table 237. School Enrollment by Age: 1970 to 2011

[As of October (60,357 represents 60,357,000). Covers civilian noninstitutional population enrolled in nursery school and above. Based on Current Population Survey; see text, Section 1 and Appendix III]

Age	1970	1980	1985	1990	1995	2000	2005	2009	2010	2011
ENROLLMENT (1,000)										
Total, 3 to 34 years old.........	**60,357**	**57,348**	**58,013**	**60,588**	**66,939**	**69,560**	**72,768**	**73,905**	**78,519**	**79,043**
3 and 4 years old..................	1,461	2,280	2,801	3,292	4,042	4,097	4,383	4,475	4,706	4,597
5 and 6 years old..................	7,000	5,853	6,697	7,207	7,901	7,648	7,486	7,783	7,955	8,009
7 to 13 years old..................	28,943	23,751	22,849	25,016	27,003	28,296	27,936	27,609	27,984	28,260
14 and 15 years old...............	7,869	7,282	7,362	6,555	7,651	7,885	8,375	7,789	7,736	7,825
16 and 17 years old...............	6,927	7,129	6,654	6,098	6,997	7,341	8,472	7,939	7,963	7,906
18 and 19 years old...............	3,322	3,788	3,716	4,044	4,274	4,926	5,109	5,935	5,904	6,017
20 and 21 years old...............	1,949	2,515	2,708	2,852	3,025	3,314	4,069	4,163	4,552	4,618
22 to 24 years old................	1,410	1,931	2,068	2,231	2,545	2,731	3,254	3,818	3,602	3,961
25 to 29 years old................	1,011	1,714	1,942	2,013	2,216	2,030	2,340	2,819	3,088	3,139
30 to 34 years old................	466	1,105	1,218	1,281	1,284	1,292	1,344	1,576	1,658	1,571
35 years old and over.............	(NA)	1,290	1,766	2,439	2,830	2,653	3,013	3,383	3,372	3,138
ENROLLMENT RATE										
Total, 3 to 34 years old.........	**56.4**	**49.7**	**48.3**	**50.2**	**53.7**	**55.8**	**56.5**	**56.5**	**56.5**	**56.8**
3 and 4 years old..................	20.5	36.7	38.9	44.4	48.7	52.1	53.6	52.4	53.2	52.4
5 and 6 years old..................	89.5	95.7	96.1	96.5	96.0	95.6	95.4	94.1	94.5	95.1
7 to 13 years old..................	99.2	99.3	99.2	99.6	98.9	98.2	98.6	98.2	98.0	98.3
14 and 15 years old...............	98.1	98.2	98.1	99.0	98.9	98.7	98.0	98.0	98.1	98.6
16 and 17 years old...............	90.0	89.0	91.7	92.5	93.6	92.8	95.1	94.6	96.1	95.7
18 and 19 years old...............	47.7	46.4	51.6	57.3	59.4	61.2	67.6	68.9	69.2	71.1
20 and 21 years old...............	31.9	31.0	35.3	39.7	44.9	44.1	48.7	51.7	52.4	52.7
22 to 24 years old................	14.9	16.3	16.9	21.0	23.2	24.6	27.3	30.4	28.9	31.1
25 to 29 years old................	7.5	9.3	9.2	9.7	11.6	11.4	11.9	13.5	14.6	14.8
30 to 34 years old................	4.2	6.4	6.1	5.8	6.0	6.7	6.9	8.1	8.3	7.7
35 years old and over.............	(NA)	1.4	1.6	2.1	2.2	1.9	2.0	2.1	2.6	2.0

NA Not available.

Source: U.S. Census Bureau, Current Population Reports, PPL-148, P-20, and earlier reports; and "School Enrollment," <http://www.census.gov/hhes/school/index.html>, accessed April 2013.

Table 238. School Enrollment by Race, Hispanic Origin, and Age: 2000 to 2011

[54,257 represents 54,257,000. As of October. See headnote, Table 237]

Age	White [1]			Black [1]			Hispanic [2]		
	2000	2005	2011	2000	2005	2011	2000	2005	2011
ENROLLMENT (1,000)									
Total, 3 to 34 years old............	**54,257**	**55,715**	**57,432**	**11,115**	**10,885**	**11,352**	**9,928**	**12,502**	**15,833**
3 and 4 years old....................	3,091	3,380	3,311	725	655	772	518	773	956
5 and 6 years old....................	5,959	5,707	6,085	1,219	1,144	1,109	1,390	1,532	2,050
7 to 13 years old....................	22,061	21,310	21,402	4,675	4,317	4,164	4,373	5,394	6,511
14 and 15 years old..................	6,176	6,429	5,970	1,260	1,321	1,168	1,093	1,431	1,604
16 and 17 years old..................	5,845	6,520	6,002	1,106	1,281	1,206	959	1,357	1,591
18 and 19 years old..................	3,924	4,006	4,572	716	707	975	617	681	1,136
20 and 21 years old..................	2,688	3,262	3,660	416	430	515	311	447	775
22 to 24 years old...................	2,101	2,411	3,024	393	475	603	309	419	598
25 to 29 years old...................	1,473	1,740	2,310	353	307	527	198	310	429
30 to 34 years old...................	939	950	1,096	252	248	313	160	158	183
35 years old and over................	2,087	2,299	2,213	387	499	684	235	307	298
ENROLLMENT RATE									
Total, 3 to 34 years old............	**55.1**	**55.9**	**56.2**	**59.0**	**58.4**	**58.4**	**51.3**	**50.9**	**55.6**
3 and 4 years old....................	50.2	54.2	51.4	52.1	52.2	55.2	35.9	43.0	41.7
5 and 6 years old....................	95.3	95.3	95.7	94.2	95.9	92.0	94.3	93.8	95.6
7 to 13 years old....................	98.2	98.6	98.4	97.9	98.6	97.9	97.5	97.6	98.4
14 and 15 years old..................	98.4	98.3	98.6	98.0	95.8	98.6	96.2	97.3	98.2
16 and 17 years old..................	92.8	95.4	95.5	96.2	93.1	95.7	87.0	92.6	94.6
18 and 19 years old..................	61.3	68.0	70.3	70.0	62.8	74.1	49.5	54.3	65.2
20 and 21 years old..................	44.9	49.3	53.8	51.6	37.6	41.1	26.1	30.0	45.7
22 to 24 years old...................	23.7	26.0	30.9	28.1	28.0	31.2	18.2	19.5	23.6
25 to 29 years old...................	10.4	11.3	14.0	13.9	11.7	18.1	7.4	7.8	10.5
30 to 34 years old...................	6.0	6.2	6.9	7.8	10.0	11.4	5.6	4.2	4.5
35 years old and over................	1.8	1.8	1.7	2.6	3.1	3.8	2.0	2.0	1.6

[1] Starting 2005, data are for persons who selected this race group only. See footnote 2, Table 241. [2] Persons of Hispanic origin may be of any race.

Source: U.S. Census Bureau, Current Population Reports, PPL-148, P-20, and earlier reports; and "School Enrollment," <http://www.census.gov/hhes/school/index.html>, accessed April 2013.

Table 239. Enrollment in Public and Private Schools: 1970 to 2011

[In millions (52.2 represents 52,200,000), except percent. As of October. For civilian noninstitutional population. Prior to 1995, total enrolled does not include the population aged 35 and over. For enrollment of population aged 35 and over, see Table 237]

Year	Public						Private					
	Total	Nursery	Kinder-garten	Elemen-tary	High school	College	Total	Nursery	Kinder-garten	Elemen-tary	High school	College
1970...........	52.2	0.3	2.6	30.0	13.5	5.7	8.1	0.8	0.5	3.9	1.2	1.7
1975...........	52.8	0.6	2.9	27.2	14.5	7.7	8.2	1.2	0.5	3.3	1.2	2.0
1980...........	(NA)	0.6	2.7	24.4	(NA)	(NA)	(NA)	1.4	0.5	3.1	(NA)	(NA)
1985...........	49.0	0.9	3.2	23.8	12.8	8.4	9.0	1.6	0.6	3.1	1.2	2.5
1990 [1].......	53.8	1.2	3.3	26.6	11.9	10.7	9.2	2.2	0.6	2.7	0.9	2.9
1995...........	58.7	2.0	3.2	28.4	13.7	11.4	11.1	2.4	0.7	3.4	1.2	3.3
1996...........	59.5	1.9	3.4	28.1	14.1	12.0	10.8	2.3	0.7	3.4	1.2	3.2
1997...........	61.6	2.3	3.3	29.3	14.6	12.1	10.5	2.2	0.7	3.1	1.2	3.3
1998...........	60.8	2.3	3.1	29.1	14.3	12.0	11.3	2.3	0.7	3.4	1.2	3.6
1999...........	60.8	2.3	3.2	29.2	14.4	11.7	11.4	2.3	0.7	3.6	1.3	3.5
2000...........	61.2	2.2	3.2	29.4	14.4	12.0	11.0	2.2	0.7	3.5	1.3	3.3
2001...........	62.4	2.2	3.1	29.8	14.8	12.4	10.8	2.1	0.6	3.4	1.2	3.5
2002...........	62.8	2.2	3.0	29.7	15.1	12.8	11.3	2.2	0.6	3.5	1.3	3.7
2003...........	63.8	2.6	3.1	29.2	15.8	13.1	11.1	2.4	0.6	3.4	1.3	3.5
2004...........	64.3	2.5	3.4	29.2	15.5	13.7	11.3	2.3	0.6	3.4	1.3	3.7
2005...........	64.2	2.5	3.3	29.0	15.8	13.4	11.5	2.1	0.6	3.4	1.4	4.0
2006...........	64.1	2.5	3.6	29.0	15.6	13.5	11.1	2.2	0.5	3.1	1.5	3.8
2007...........	65.1	2.6	3.7	29.1	15.8	14.1	10.8	2.1	0.5	3.1	1.3	3.9
2008...........	65.5	2.6	3.6	29.2	15.4	14.7	10.8	2.0	0.5	3.2	1.3	4.0
2009...........	66.9	2.7	3.8	29.4	15.3	15.7	10.4	2.0	0.4	2.9	1.2	4.0
2010...........	67.9	2.8	3.8	29.8	15.3	16.2	10.6	2.1	0.4	2.8	1.2	4.1
2011...........	68.2	2.9	3.7	30.0	15.4	16.1	10.9	2.0	0.5	2.9	1.2	4.3
Percent White:												
1970..........	84.5	59.5	84.4	83.1	85.6	90.7	93.4	91.1	88.2	94.1	96.1	92.8
1980..........	(NA)	68.2	80.7	80.9	(NA)	(NA)	(NA)	89.0	87.0	90.7	(NA)	(NA)
1990..........	79.8	71.7	78.3	78.9	79.2	84.1	87.4	89.6	83.2	88.2	89.4	85.0
2000..........	77.0	69.4	77.3	76.7	78.0	78.0	83.5	84.9	82.8	85.9	84.6	79.8
2005 [2].......	75.7	71.3	78.0	75.2	76.0	76.7	81.4	83.6	79.0	83.0	83.6	78.4
2009 [2].......	75.2	66.8	75.9	75.8	74.8	76.0	79.3	80.0	80.3	80.7	85.5	76.2
2010 [2].......	74.9	71.8	72.9	75.0	75.1	75.4	78.9	81.0	79.4	80.9	84.5	74.7
2011 [2].......	74.7	68.8	75.2	74.8	74.8	75.4	80.2	79.7	81.5	84.1	84.8	76.3

NA Not available. [1] Beginning 1990, based on a revised edit and tabulation package. [2] Beginning 2005, for persons who selected this race group only. See footnote 2, Table 241.

Source: U.S. Census Bureau, "School Enrollment, Historical Time Series Tables," <http://www.census.gov/hhes/school/data/cps/historical/index.html>, accessed July 2013.

Table 240. School Enrollment by Sex and Level: 1970 to 2011

[In millions (60.4 represents 60,400,000). As of October. For the civilian noninstitutional population. Prior to 1980, persons 3 to 34 years old; beginning 1980, 3 years old and over. Elementary includes kindergarten and grades 1–8; high school, grades 9–12; and college, 2-year and 4-year colleges, universities, and graduate and professional schools. Data for college represent degree-credit enrollment. See headnote, Table 237]

Year	All levels [1]			Elementary			High school			College		
	Total	Male	Female	Total	Male	Female	Total	Male	Female	Total	Male	Female
1970...........	60.4	31.4	28.9	37.1	19.0	18.1	14.7	7.4	7.3	7.4	4.4	3.0
1980...........	58.6	29.6	29.1	30.6	15.8	14.9	14.6	7.3	7.3	11.4	5.4	6.0
1990 [2]........	63.0	31.5	31.5	33.2	17.1	16.0	12.8	6.5	6.4	13.6	6.2	7.4
1993...........	65.4	32.9	32.5	34.8	17.9	16.9	13.6	7.0	6.6	13.9	6.3	7.6
1994...........	69.3	34.6	34.6	35.4	18.2	17.2	14.6	7.4	7.2	15.0	6.8	8.2
1995...........	69.8	35.0	34.8	35.7	18.3	17.4	15.0	7.7	7.3	14.7	6.7	8.0
1996...........	70.3	35.1	35.2	35.5	18.3	17.3	15.3	7.9	7.4	15.2	6.8	8.4
1997...........	72.0	35.9	36.2	36.3	18.7	17.6	15.8	8.0	7.7	15.4	6.8	8.6
1998...........	72.1	36.0	36.1	36.4	18.7	17.7	15.6	7.9	7.6	15.5	6.9	8.6
1999...........	72.4	36.3	36.1	36.7	18.8	17.9	15.9	8.2	7.7	15.2	7.0	8.2
2000...........	72.2	35.8	36.4	36.7	18.9	17.9	15.8	8.1	7.7	15.3	6.7	8.6
2001...........	73.1	36.3	36.9	36.9	19.0	17.9	16.1	8.2	7.8	15.9	6.9	9.0
2002...........	74.0	36.8	37.3	36.7	18.9	17.8	16.4	8.3	8.0	16.5	7.2	9.3
2003...........	74.9	37.3	37.6	36.3	18.7	17.6	17.1	8.6	8.4	16.6	7.3	9.3
2004...........	75.5	37.4	38.0	36.5	19.0	17.6	16.8	8.4	8.4	17.4	7.6	9.8
2005...........	75.8	37.4	38.4	36.4	18.6	17.7	17.4	8.9	8.5	17.5	7.5	9.9
2006...........	75.2	37.2	38.0	36.1	18.5	17.6	17.1	8.8	8.4	17.2	7.5	9.7
2007...........	76.0	37.6	38.4	36.3	18.6	17.7	17.1	8.8	8.3	18.0	7.8	10.1
2008...........	76.4	37.8	38.6	36.4	18.7	17.7	16.7	8.5	8.2	18.6	8.3	10.3
2009...........	77.3	38.0	39.3	36.4	18.6	17.7	16.4	8.4	8.1	19.8	8.6	11.1
2010...........	78.5	38.7	39.8	36.8	18.8	18.1	16.6	8.5	8.0	20.3	9.0	11.3
2011...........	79.0	39.2	39.8	37.1	19.0	18.1	16.6	8.6	8.1	20.4	9.1	11.3

[1] Includes nursery schools, not shown separately. [2] For data beginning 1990, based on a revised edit and tabulation package.

Source: U.S. Census Bureau, Current Population Reports, PPL-148, P20, and earlier reports; and "School Enrollment," <http://www.census.gov/hhes/school/data/cps/index.html>, accessed February 2013.

Table 241. Educational Attainment by Race and Hispanic Origin: 1970 to 2012

[In percent. For persons 25 years old and over. 1970 and 1980 data as of April 1 and based on sample data from the censuses of population. Other years as of March and based on the Current Population Survey; see text, Section 1 and Appendix III. See Table 242 for data by sex]

Year	Total [1]	White [2]	Black [2]	Asian and Pacific Islander [2, 6]	Hispanic [3]			
					Total [4]	Mexican	Puerto Rican	Cuban
HIGH SCHOOL GRADUATE OR MORE [5]								
1970..............	52.3	54.5	31.4	62.2	32.1	24.2	23.4	43.9
1980..............	66.5	68.8	51.2	74.8	44.0	37.6	40.1	55.3
1990..............	77.6	79.1	66.2	80.4	50.8	44.1	55.5	63.5
1995..............	81.7	83.0	73.8	(NA)	53.4	46.5	61.3	64.7
2000..............	84.1	84.9	78.5	85.7	57.0	51.0	64.3	73.0
2005..............	85.2	85.8	81.1	87.6	58.5	52.2	72.4	73.3
2009..............	86.7	87.1	84.1	88.2	61.9	55.7	76.6	78.5
2010..............	87.1	87.6	84.2	88.9	62.9	57.4	74.8	81.4
2011..............	87.6	88.1	84.5	88.6	64.3	(NA)	(NA)	(NA)
2012..............	87.6	88.1	85.0	88.9	65.0	(NA)	(NA)	(NA)
COLLEGE GRADUATE OR MORE [5]								
1970..............	10.7	11.3	4.4	20.4	4.5	2.5	2.2	11.1
1980..............	16.2	17.1	8.4	32.9	7.6	4.9	5.6	16.2
1990..............	21.3	22.0	11.3	39.9	9.2	5.4	9.7	20.2
1995..............	23.0	24.0	13.2	(NA)	9.3	6.5	10.7	19.4
2000..............	25.6	26.1	16.5	43.9	10.6	6.9	13.0	23.0
2005..............	27.7	28.1	17.6	50.2	12.0	8.2	13.8	24.6
2009..............	29.5	29.9	19.3	52.3	13.2	9.5	16.5	27.9
2010..............	29.9	30.3	19.8	52.4	13.9	10.6	17.5	26.2
2011..............	30.4	31.0	19.9	50.4	14.1	(NA)	(NA)	(NA)
2012..............	30.9	31.3	21.2	51.0	14.5	(NA)	(NA)	(NA)

NA Not available. [1] Includes other races not shown separately. [2] Beginning 2005, for persons who selected this race group only. The 2003 Current Population Survey (CPS) allowed respondents to choose more than one race. Therefore, beginning with 2003, data represent persons who selected this race group only and exclude persons reporting more than one race. The CPS in prior years only allowed respondents to report one race group. See also comments on race in the text for Section 1. [3] Persons of Hispanic origin may be of any race. [4] Includes persons of other Hispanic origin not shown separately. [5] Through 1990, completed 4 years of high school or more and 4 years of college or more. [6] Starting in 2003, data are for Asians only, excludes Pacific Islanders.

Source: U.S. Census Bureau, U.S. Census of Population, 1970 and 1980, Vol. 1; Current Population Reports, P20-550, and earlier reports; and "Educational Attainment," <http://www.census.gov/hhes/socdemo/education/>, accessed April 2013.

Table 242. Educational Attainment by Race, Hispanic Origin, and Sex: 1970 to 2012

[In percent. See Table 241 for headnote and totals for both sexes]

Year	All races [1]		White [2]		Black [2]		Asian and Pacific Islander [2, 5]		Hispanic [3]	
	Male	Female	Male	Female	Male	Female	Male	Female	Male	Female
HIGH SCHOOL GRADUATE OR MORE [4]										
1970..............	51.9	52.8	54.0	55.0	30.1	32.5	61.3	63.1	37.9	34.2
1980..............	67.3	65.8	69.6	68.1	50.8	51.5	78.8	71.4	45.4	42.7
1990..............	77.7	77.5	79.1	79.0	65.8	66.5	84.0	77.2	50.3	51.3
1995..............	81.7	81.6	83.0	83.0	73.4	74.1	(NA)	(NA)	52.9	53.8
2000..............	84.2	84.0	84.8	85.0	78.7	78.3	88.2	83.4	56.6	57.5
2005..............	84.9	85.5	85.2	86.2	81.0	81.2	90.4	85.2	57.9	59.1
2009..............	86.2	87.1	86.5	87.7	84.0	84.1	90.4	86.2	60.6	63.3
2010..............	86.6	87.6	86.9	88.2	83.6	84.6	91.2	87.0	61.4	64.4
2011..............	87.1	88.0	87.4	88.6	83.8	85.0	90.4	87.0	63.6	65.1
2012..............	87.3	88.0	87.6	88.5	84.3	85.5	90.4	87.6	64.0	66.0
COLLEGE GRADUATE OR MORE [4]										
1970..............	13.5	8.1	14.4	8.4	4.2	4.6	23.5	17.3	7.8	4.3
1980..............	20.1	12.8	21.3	13.3	8.4	8.3	39.8	27.0	9.4	6.0
1990..............	24.4	18.4	25.3	19.0	11.9	10.8	44.9	35.4	9.8	8.7
1995..............	26.0	20.2	27.2	21.0	13.6	12.9	(NA)	(NA)	10.1	8.4
2000..............	27.8	23.6	28.5	23.9	16.3	16.7	47.6	40.7	10.7	10.6
2005..............	28.9	26.5	29.4	26.8	16.0	18.8	54.0	46.8	11.8	12.1
2009..............	30.1	29.1	30.6	29.3	17.8	20.6	55.7	49.3	12.5	14.0
2010..............	30.3	29.6	30.8	29.9	17.7	21.4	55.6	49.5	12.9	14.9
2011..............	30.8	30.1	31.5	30.5	18.0	21.4	53.3	47.7	13.1	15.2
2012..............	31.4	30.6	31.9	30.8	19.2	22.9	53.7	48.8	13.3	15.8

NA Not available. [1] Includes other races not shown separately. [2] Beginning 2005, for persons who selected this race group only. See footnote 2, Table 241. [3] Persons of Hispanic origin may be of any race. [4] Through 1990, completed 4 years of high school or more and 4 years of college or more. [5] Starting in 2003, data are for Asians only, excludes Pacific Islanders.

Source: U.S. Census Bureau, U.S. Census of Population, 1970 and 1980, Vol. 1; Current Population Reports, P20-550, and earlier reports; and "Educational Attainment," <http://www.census.gov/hhes/socdemo/education/index.html>, accessed April 2013.

Table 243. Educational Attainment by Selected Characteristics: 2012

[204,579 represents 204,579,000. For persons 25 years old and over. As of March. Based on the Current Population Survey; see text, Section 1 and Appendix III]

Characteristic	Population (1,000)	Not a high school graduate	High school graduate	Some college, but no degree	Associate's degree [1]	Bachelor's degree	Advanced degree
Total persons............	204,579	12.4	30.4	16.7	9.6	19.8	11.1
Age:							
25 to 34 years old...........	41,219	10.7	26.6	18.6	9.9	24.6	9.5
35 to 44 years old...........	39,927	11.0	26.8	16.7	10.8	22.3	12.5
45 to 54 years old...........	43,955	10.9	31.7	16.4	10.4	19.9	10.7
55 to 64 years old...........	37,971	10.1	31.0	17.1	10.6	18.7	12.5
65 to 74 years old...........	23,383	15.8	34.5	15.3	7.4	15.1	12.0
75 years old or over........	18,123	22.9	36.9	13.9	5.6	12.0	8.6
Sex:							
Male.........................	98,119	12.7	30.8	16.4	8.7	19.8	11.6
Female.......................	106,460	12.0	30.0	17.0	10.5	19.9	10.7
Race:							
White [2].....................	164,562	11.9	30.5	16.5	9.8	20.1	11.2
Black [2].....................	23,899	15.0	34.1	20.3	9.4	13.7	7.5
Asian [2].....................	10,851	11.1	20.7	10.2	7.0	31.4	19.6
Hispanic origin:							
Hispanic.....................	28,445	35.0	30.0	13.7	6.8	10.3	4.2
Non-Hispanic white........	139,001	7.5	30.5	17.1	10.4	22.0	12.5
Marital status:							
Never married...............	37,952	13.1	30.0	18.0	8.8	21.1	9.0
Married, spouse present..	119,570	10.2	29.0	15.7	10.0	21.9	13.2
Married, spouse absent [3]..	3,207	24.1	32.2	13.7	6.4	15.0	8.6
Separated...................	5,149	22.1	33.7	20.0	8.8	10.4	5.0
Widowed.....................	14,015	24.2	38.2	14.8	6.5	10.4	5.9
Divorced.....................	24,687	11.3	32.0	20.5	11.7	15.9	8.6
Civilian labor force status:							
Employed....................	123,667	8.1	27.1	16.7	10.8	23.7	13.7
Unemployed.................	9,834	16.0	33.9	20.3	9.6	14.5	5.7
Not in the labor force.......	71,079	19.3	35.6	16.2	7.6	13.9	7.4

[1] Includes vocational degrees. [2] For persons who selected this race group only. See footnote 2, Table 241. [3] Excludes those separated.

Source: U.S. Census Bureau, "Educational Attainment in the United States: 2012 - Detailed Tables," <http://www.census.gov/hhes/socdemo/education/>, accessed April 2013.

Table 244. Mean Earnings by Highest Degree Earned: 2011

[In dollars. Persons as of March 2012. For persons 18 years old and over with earnings. Based on Current Population Survey; see text, Section 1 and Appendix III. For definition of mean, see Guide to Tabular Presentation]

Characteristic	Total persons [1]	Ninth to twelfth grade, non-graduate	High school graduate only	Some college, no degree	Associate's	Bachelor's	Master's	Professional	Doctorate
All persons [2]..............	44,729	20,936	32,493	32,793	40,907	59,415	76,650	126,233	108,061
Age:									
25 to 34 years old..............	38,089	20,913	28,272	31,427	36,764	47,757	58,736	88,933	66,251
35 to 44 years old..............	51,270	25,262	35,596	40,942	44,704	66,467	79,949	133,262	106,928
45 to 54 years old..............	54,469	27,366	38,493	45,089	47,441	72,370	88,392	141,556	125,956
55 to 64 years old..............	55,019	27,383	38,901	44,093	45,712	66,851	82,495	158,396	128,924
65 years old and over.........	41,569	22,473	30,224	32,413	31,109	48,484	63,077	92,174	94,809
Sex:									
Male..........................	53,273	25,395	38,679	40,349	49,241	71,162	96,220	145,024	121,098
Female.......................	35,205	14,327	24,460	25,155	33,768	47,418	59,739	91,995	86,527
White [3].....................	46,053	21,673	33,719	33,477	41,204	61,253	78,151	129,262	112,000
Male..........................	55,013	26,282	40,247	41,546	49,329	73,630	99,550	146,930	125,061
Female.......................	35,635	14,154	24,793	25,092	33,972	48,064	59,483	93,463	89,543
Black [3].....................	34,755	17,115	27,562	30,050	39,735	45,477	61,447	107,853	84,305
Male..........................	38,633	20,658	31,219	34,348	48,551	49,390	64,984	161,220	97,622
Female.......................	31,455	13,763	23,795	26,293	34,022	42,721	59,693	63,902	67,662
Asian [3].....................	51,500	23,673	28,302	31,214	41,748	57,150	77,795	116,533	101,348
Male..........................	60,397	28,799	32,500	37,556	51,664	65,740	90,468	123,795	109,954
Female.......................	41,727	17,571	23,926	24,098	32,498	48,647	61,217	106,150	85,992
Hispanic [4]..................	30,739	20,915	26,681	29,484	36,039	47,873	67,038	102,298	128,461
Male..........................	34,135	24,202	29,872	34,812	41,350	54,936	79,365	111,376	(B)
Female.......................	26,230	15,110	21,988	23,787	31,044	41,483	57,919	(B)	(B)

B Base figure too small to meet statistical standards for reliability of a derived figure. [1] Includes those with less than ninth grade education not shown separately. [2] Includes other races not shown separately. [3] For persons who selected this race group only. See footnote 2, Table 241. [4] Persons of Hispanic origin may be of any race.

Source: U.S. Census Bureau, *Income, Poverty, and Health Insurance Coverage in the United States: 2011*, Current Population Reports, P60-243, and "Detailed Table -- PINC-04," <http://www.census.gov/hhes/www/income/data/index.html>, accessed June 2013.

Table 245. Educational Attainment by State: 1990 to 2011

[In percent. 1990 and 2000 as of April; 2011 represents annual averages for calendar year. For persons 25 years old and over. Based on the 1990 and 2000 Census of Population and the 2011 American Community Survey, which includes the household population and the population living in institutions, college dormitories, and other group quarters. See text, Section 1 and Appendix III. For margin of error data, see source]

State	1990			2000			2011		
	High school graduate or more	Bachelor's degree or more	Advanced degree or more	High school graduate or more	Bachelor's degree or more	Advanced degree or more	High school graduate or more	Bachelor's degree or more	Advanced degree or more
United States	**75.2**	**20.3**	**7.2**	**80.4**	**24.4**	**8.9**	**85.9**	**28.5**	**10.6**
Alabama	66.9	15.7	5.5	75.3	19.0	6.9	82.7	22.3	8.4
Alaska	86.6	23.0	8.0	88.3	24.7	8.6	91.8	26.4	9.5
Arizona	78.7	20.3	7.0	81.0	23.5	8.4	85.7	26.6	9.5
Arkansas	66.3	13.3	4.5	75.3	16.7	5.7	83.8	20.3	7.2
California	76.2	23.4	8.1	76.8	26.6	9.5	81.1	30.3	11.1
Colorado	84.4	27.0	9.0	86.9	32.7	11.1	90.2	36.7	13.4
Connecticut	79.2	27.2	11.0	84.0	31.4	13.3	89.1	36.2	15.7
Delaware	77.5	21.4	7.7	82.6	25.0	9.4	87.0	28.8	11.7
District of Columbia	73.1	33.3	17.2	77.8	39.1	21.0	87.2	52.5	29.2
Florida	74.4	18.3	6.3	79.9	22.3	8.1	85.9	25.8	9.3
Georgia	70.9	19.3	6.4	78.6	24.3	8.3	84.3	27.6	9.8
Hawaii	80.1	22.9	7.1	84.6	26.2	8.4	90.6	29.1	9.9
Idaho	79.7	17.7	5.3	84.7	21.7	6.8	88.6	25.2	7.8
Illinois	76.2	21.0	7.5	81.4	26.1	9.5	87.2	31.0	11.7
Indiana	75.6	15.6	6.4	82.1	19.4	7.2	87.3	23.0	8.2
Iowa	80.1	16.9	5.2	86.1	21.2	6.5	90.6	25.8	8.1
Kansas	81.3	21.1	7.0	86.0	25.8	8.7	90.0	30.1	10.4
Kentucky	64.6	13.6	5.5	74.1	17.1	6.9	83.1	21.1	8.8
Louisiana	68.3	16.1	5.6	74.8	18.7	6.5	82.5	21.1	7.1
Maine	78.8	18.8	6.1	85.4	22.9	7.9	90.9	28.4	10.5
Maryland	78.4	26.5	10.9	83.8	31.4	13.4	88.9	36.9	16.5
Massachusetts	80.0	27.2	10.6	84.8	33.2	13.7	89.2	39.1	16.8
Michigan	76.8	17.4	6.4	83.4	21.8	8.1	88.8	25.6	9.9
Minnesota	82.4	21.8	6.3	87.9	27.4	8.3	92.0	32.4	10.5
Mississippi	64.3	14.7	5.1	72.9	16.9	5.8	81.1	19.8	7.3
Missouri	73.9	17.8	6.1	81.3	21.6	7.6	87.6	26.1	9.7
Montana	81.0	19.8	5.7	87.2	24.4	7.2	92.3	28.2	8.6
Nebraska	81.8	18.9	5.9	86.6	23.7	7.3	91.0	27.9	9.1
Nevada	78.8	15.3	5.2	80.7	18.2	6.1	84.0	22.5	7.6
New Hampshire	82.2	24.4	7.9	87.4	28.7	10.0	91.4	33.4	12.4
New Jersey	76.7	24.9	8.8	82.1	29.8	11.0	88.1	35.3	13.3
New Mexico	75.1	20.4	8.3	78.9	23.5	9.8	83.2	25.6	11.1
New York	74.8	23.1	9.9	79.1	27.4	11.8	85.0	32.9	14.2
North Carolina	70.0	17.4	5.4	78.1	22.5	7.2	84.7	26.9	9.2
North Dakota	76.7	18.1	4.5	83.9	22.0	5.5	90.7	26.3	7.0
Ohio	75.7	17.0	5.9	83.0	21.1	7.4	88.3	24.7	9.2
Oklahoma	74.6	17.8	6.0	80.6	20.3	6.8	86.3	23.8	7.8
Oregon	81.5	20.6	7.0	85.1	25.1	8.7	89.4	29.3	10.9
Pennsylvania	74.7	17.9	6.6	81.9	22.4	8.4	88.6	27.0	10.4
Rhode Island	72.0	21.3	7.8	78.0	25.6	9.7	84.8	31.1	12.3
South Carolina	68.3	16.6	5.4	76.3	20.4	6.9	84.2	24.1	8.4
South Dakota	77.1	17.2	4.9	84.6	21.5	6.0	90.6	26.3	8.1
Tennessee	67.1	16.0	5.4	75.9	19.6	6.8	84.2	23.6	8.3
Texas	72.1	20.3	6.5	75.7	23.2	7.6	81.1	26.4	8.7
Utah	85.1	22.3	6.8	87.7	26.1	8.3	90.3	29.7	9.7
Vermont	80.8	24.3	8.9	86.4	29.4	11.1	91.8	35.4	14.0
Virginia	75.2	24.5	9.1	81.5	29.5	11.6	87.8	35.1	14.6
Washington	83.8	22.9	7.0	87.1	27.7	9.3	90.1	31.9	11.7
West Virginia	66.0	12.3	4.8	75.2	14.8	5.9	84.2	18.5	6.8
Wisconsin	78.6	17.7	5.6	85.1	22.4	7.2	90.4	26.5	9.0
Wyoming	83.0	18.8	5.7	87.9	21.9	7.0	92.0	24.7	8.3

Source: U.S. Census Bureau, 1990 Census of Population, CPH-L-96; 2000 Census of Population, P37. "Sex by Educational Attainment for the Population 25 Years and Over;" and American Community Survey, GCT1501, "Percent of People 25 Years and Over Who Have Completed High School (Includes Equivalency)," GCT1502, "Percent of People 25 Years and Over Who Have Completed a Bachelor's Degree," and GCT1503, "Percent of People 25 Years and Over Who Have Completed an Advanced Degree," <http://factfinder2.census.gov>, accessed April 2013.

Table 246. Children With Parental Involvement in Home Literacy Activities: 1993 to 2007

[In percent, except number of children (8,579 represents 8,579,000). For children 3 to 5 years old not yet enrolled in kindergarten who participated in activities with a family member. Based on the School Readiness Early Childhood Program Participation Surveys of the National Household Education Surveys Program; see source and Appendix III. See also Table 247]

Characteristic	Children (1,000)		Read to [1]		Told a story [1]		Taught letters, words, or numbers [1]		Visited a library [2]	
	1993	2007	1993	2007	1993	2005	1993	2005	1993	2007
Total..........................	**8,579**	**8,686**	**78**	**83**	**43**	**54**	**58**	**77**	**38**	**36**
Age:										
3 years old....................	3,889	3,755	79	84	46	54	57	75	34	36
4 years old....................	3,713	3,738	78	83	41	53	58	77	41	35
5 years old....................	976	1,193	76	83	36	55	58	80	38	39
Race/ethnicity:										
White, non-Hispanic..............	5,902	4,664	85	91	44	53	58	76	42	41
Black, non-Hispanic.............	1,271	1,312	66	78	39	54	63	81	29	25
Hispanic [3].....................	1,026	1,899	58	68	38	50	54	74	26	27
Other........................	381	812	73	87	50	64	59	82	43	46
Mother's home language: [4]										
English......................	7,805	7,244	81	88	44	55	58	78	39	38
Not English...................	603	1,312	42	57	36	45	52	69	26	24
Mother's highest education: [4]										
Less than high school..........	1,036	808	60	56	37	39	56	70	22	20
High school...................	3,268	2,048	76	74	41	51	56	78	31	29
Vocational ed or some college...........	2,624	2,658	83	86	45	57	60	79	44	33
College degree................	912	1,849	90	95	48	56	56	75	55	43
Graduate/professional training or degree....................	569	1,194	90	95	50	64	60	76	59	53

[1] Three or more times in the past week. [2] At least once in the past month. [3] Persons of Hispanic origin may be of any race. [4] Excludes children with no mother in the household and no female guardian.

Source: U.S. National Center for Education Statistics, Statistical Brief, NCES 2000–026, November 1999; the Early Childhood Program Participation Survey, National Household Education Surveys Program (NHES), 2005, unpublished data; and the NHES School Readiness Survey, 2007, unpublished data, <http://nces.ed.gov/nhes>.

Table 247. Children's School Readiness Skills: 1993 to 2007

[In percent. For children 3 to 5 years old not yet enrolled in kindergarten. Based on the School Readiness Surveys of the National Household Education Survey Program; see source for details. See also Table 246]

Characteristic	Recognizes all letters		Counts to 20 or higher		Writes name		Reads or pretends to read storybooks		Has 3 to 4 skills	
	1993	2007	1993	2007	1993	2007	1993	2005	1993	2005
Total........................	**21**	**32**	**52**	**63**	**50**	**60**	**72**	**70**	**35**	**42**
Age:										
3 years old....................	11	17	37	47	22	34	66	67	15	24
4 years old....................	28	38	62	73	70	76	75	73	49	55
5 years old....................	36	59	78	84	84	88	81	72	65	66
Sex:										
Male........................	19	31	49	61	47	56	68	70	32	40
Female......................	23	33	56	65	53	63	76	71	39	45
Race/ethnicity:										
White, non-Hispanic..............	23	36	56	69	52	64	76	75	39	47
Black, non-Hispanic.............	18	37	53	69	45	58	63	67	31	44
Hispanic [1].....................	10	15	32	41	42	49	59	55	22	26
Other........................	22	39	49	69	52	61	70	79	36	48
Mother's employment status: [2]										
Employed.....................	23	34	57	66	52	63	75	72	39	46
Unemployed....................	17	14	41	42	46	41	67	61	29	32
Not in the labor force...............	18	31	49	60	47	58	68	69	32	39
Family type:										
Two parents....................	22	33	54	64	51	62	74	72	37	44
None or one parent................	18	27	49	57	47	52	65	65	31	36
Poverty status: [3]										
Above threshold....................	24	35	57	67	53	64	74	75	40	47
Below threshold..................	12	21	41	48	41	46	64	54	23	26

[1] Persons of Hispanic origin may be of any race. [2] Excludes children with no mother in the household and no female guardian. [3] Children are considered poor if they lived in households with incomes below the poverty threshold, which is a dollar amount determined by the federal government to meet the household's need, given its size and composition. For more information about the poverty threshold, see text, section 13.

Source: U.S. Department of Education, U.S. National Center for Education Statistics, *Home Literacy Activities and Signs of Children's Emerging Literacy, 1993*, NCES 2000–026, November 1999; the Early Childhood Program Participation Survey, National Household Education Surveys Program (NHES), 2005, unpublished data; and the NHES School Readiness Survey, 2007, unpublished data, <http://nces.ed.gov/nhes>.

Table 248. Children Who Speak a Language Other Than English at Home by Region: 2011

[In thousands (11,838 represents 11,838,000), except percent. For children 5 to 17 years old. For more on languages spoken at home, see Table 57 and Table 58. Based on the American Community Survey; see text Section 1, and Appendix III. For composition of regions, see map inside front cover]

Characteristic	U.S.	Northeast	Midwest	South	West
Children who speak another language at home	11,838	1,961	1,481	3,939	4,456
Percent of children 5 to 17 years old	22.0	21.8	12.7	19.5	34.4
Speak Spanish	8,471	1,057	885	3,117	3,412
Speak English "very well"	6,600	841	683	2,365	2,711
Speak English less than "very well"	1,870	215	202	752	701
Speak other Indo-European languages	1,557	542	297	399	319
Speak English "very well"	1,267	437	228	334	268
Speak English less than "very well"	290	105	69	65	51
Speak Asian and Pacific Island languages	1,325	254	172	306	592
Speak English "very well"	983	184	122	233	444
Speak English less than "very well"	342	70	50	73	148
Speak other languages	485	108	127	117	133
Speak English "very well"	394	87	103	98	106
Speak English less than "very well"	91	22	23	19	27
Have difficulty speaking English [1]	2,593	412	345	909	927
Language spoken at home in linguistically isolated households [2]	2,899	470	341	1,037	1,052
Speak only English	160	37	17	56	50
Speak Spanish	2,101	262	213	834	793
Speak other Indo-European languages	203	75	41	49	38
Speak Asian and Pacific Island languages	351	76	48	78	148
Speak other languages	84	19	23	19	23

[1] Children aged 5 to 17 who speak English less than "very well." [2] A household in which no person aged 14 or over speaks English at least "very well."

Source: U.S. Census Bureau, 2011 American Community Survey, B16003, "Age by Language Spoken at Home for the Population 5 Years and Over" and C16004, "Age by Language Spoken at Home by Ability to Speak English for the Population 5 Years and Over," <http://factfinder2.census.gov>, accessed June 2013.

Table 249. Preprimary School Enrollment—Summary: 1970 to 2011

[10,949 represents 10,949,000. As of October. Civilian noninstitutional population. Includes public and nonpublic nursery school and kindergarten programs. Excludes 5-year-olds enrolled in elementary school. Based on Current Population Survey. See text, Section 1 and Appendix III]

Item	1970	1980	1990	1995	2000	2005	2009	2010	2011
NUMBER OF CHILDREN (1,000)									
Population, 3 to 5 years old	**10,949**	**9,284**	**11,207**	**12,518**	**11,858**	**12,134**	**12,717**	**12,949**	**12,966**
Total enrolled [1]	**4,104**	**4,878**	**6,659**	**7,739**	**7,592**	**7,801**	**8,075**	**8,493**	**8,260**
Nursery	1,094	1,981	3,378	4,331	4,326	4,529	4,648	4,797	4,911
Public	332	628	1,202	1,950	2,146	2,409	2,703	2,749	2,876
Private	762	1,353	2,177	2,381	2,180	2,120	1,945	2,048	2,035
Kindergarten	3,010	2,897	3,281	3,408	3,266	3,272	3,428	3,449	3,349
Public	2,498	2,438	2,767	2,799	2,701	2,804	3,144	3,079	2,947
Private	511	459	513	608	565	468	284	369	403
White [2]	3,443	3,994	5,389	6,144	5,861	6,025	5,943	6,160	6,128
Black [2]	586	725	964	1,236	1,265	1,148	1,338	1,301	1,230
Hispanic [3]	(NA)	370	642	1,040	1,155	1,494	1,721	1,874	1,878
3 years old	454	857	1,205	1,489	1,540	1,715	1,776	1,718	1,651
4 years old	1,007	1,423	2,086	2,553	2,556	2,668	2,698	2,988	2,946
5 years old	2,643	2,598	3,367	3,697	3,496	3,418	3,601	3,787	3,663
ENROLLMENT RATE									
Total enrolled [1]	**37.5**	**52.5**	**59.4**	**61.8**	**64.0**	**64.3**	**63.5**	**63.7**	**63.7**
White [2]	37.8	52.7	59.7	63.0	63.2	65.1	62.8	63.4	63.6
Black [2]	34.9	51.8	57.8	58.9	68.5	62.0	66.3	64.1	62.8
Hispanic [3]	(NA)	43.3	49.0	51.1	52.6	56.1	54.1	56.0	55.8
3 years old	12.9	27.3	32.6	35.9	39.2	41.3	40.7	38.2	38.5
4 years old	27.8	46.3	56.0	61.6	64.9	66.2	64.6	68.6	65.9
5 years old	69.3	84.7	88.8	87.5	87.6	86.4	86.1	88.1	87.2

NA Not available. [1] Includes races not shown separately. [2] Beginning 2005, for persons who selected this race group only. See footnote 2, Table 232. [3] Persons of Hispanic origin may be of any race. The method of identifying Hispanic children was changed in 1980 from allocation based on status of mother to status reported for each child. The number of Hispanic children using the new method is larger.

Source: U.S. Census Bureau, Current Population Reports, PPL-148; earlier PPL and P-20 reports and unpublished data; and "School Enrollment," <http://www.census.gov/hhes/school/index.html>, accessed April 2013.

Table 250. Type of School Attended by Student and Household Characteristics: 1996 and 2007

[In percent, except total in thousands (34,600 represent 34,600,000). For students in grades 1 to 12. Includes homeschooled students enrolled in public or private school 9 or more hours per week. Based on the Parent and Family Involvement Survey of the National Household Education Survey Program; see source and Appendix III for details]

Characteristic	Public				Private			
	Assigned		Chosen		Church related		Not church related	
	1996	2007	1996	2007	1996	2007	1996	2007
Total students (1,000)	**34,600**	**34,700**	**6,200**	**7,400**	**3,700**	**4,100**	**1,000**	**1,200**
Percent distribution	76.0	73.2	13.7	15.5	8.0	8.7	2.3	2.6
Grade level:								
1 to 5	74.1	71.4	14.8	17.0	8.9	8.7	2.2	2.8
6 to 8	79.4	77.0	11.2	11.9	7.4	8.6	2.0	2.5
9 to 12	75.9	72.6	14.1	16.4	7.3	8.6	2.7	2.3
Race/ethnicity:								
White, non-Hispanic	77.1	73.6	11.1	12.5	9.2	10.8	2.7	3.1
Black, non-Hispanic	72.9	68.9	21.5	23.7	4.2	5.5	1.4	1.8
Other, non-Hispanic	69.3	72.7	19.0	17.4	9.5	6.4	2.2	3.5
Hispanic [1]	76.4	75.8	16.1	17.4	6.3	5.6	1.3	1.2
Family type:								
Two-parent household	76.3	72.7	11.7	14.4	9.5	10.0	2.4	2.9
One-parent household	74.6	74.9	18.4	17.7	5.0	5.4	1.9	2.0
Nonparent guardians	80.2	72.8	14.6	22.7	2.3	3.9	2.9	0.6
Parents' education:								
Less than high school	78.8	85.4	17.4	12.4	2.0	1.5	1.8	0.6
High school diploma or equivalent	82.1	79.8	12.3	15.4	5.0	3.5	0.7	1.3
Some college, including vocational/technical	76.4	75.4	14.7	16.3	7.1	7.3	1.8	1.0
Bachelor's degree	70.7	70.7	13.1	15.3	13.0	11.6	3.3	2.4
Graduate/professional degree	66.1	62.2	12.6	15.8	15.3	15.1	6.0	6.8
Region: [2]								
Northeast	74.3	72.3	12.9	13.3	9.2	10.9	3.6	3.4
South	78.7	75.2	12.5	14.0	6.4	8.5	2.4	2.3
Midwest	75.4	73.6	12.4	15.0	10.9	9.9	1.3	1.5
West	74.0	70.6	17.7	20.1	6.3	6.1	2.0	3.3

[1] Persons of Hispanic origin may be of any race. [2] For composition of regions see map inside front cover.

Source: U.S. National Center for Education Statistics, *Condition of Education, 2009*, NCES 2009-081, June 2009, and earlier reports. See also <http://nces.ed.gov/programs/coe/>.

Table 251. Public Charter and Traditional Schools—Selected Characteristics: 2007 to 2008

[47,432 represents 47,432,000. For school year ending in 2008. A public charter school is a public school that, in accordance with an enabling state statute, has been granted a charter exempting it from selected state and local rules and regulations]

Characteristic	All schools		Elementary		Secondary		Combined	
	Tradi-tional	Public charter	Tradi-tional	Public charter	Tradi-tional	Public charter	Tradi-tional	Public charter
Number of schools	87,190	3,560	60,390	2,050	20,720	920	6,080	590
Enrollment (1,000)	47,432	1,047	29,194	619	16,513	229	1,725	200
PERCENT DISTRIBUTION OF STUDENTS								
Race/ethnicity	100.0	100.0	100.0	100.0	100.0	100.0	100.0	100.0
White, non-Hispanic	58.2	41.0	56.2	35.9	60.3	43.5	71.3	54.0
Black, non-Hispanic	15.7	29.0	15.8	36.1	15.8	(S)	12.2	17.6
Hispanic [1]	20.3	23.8	22.1	21.6	18.0	31.5	11.5	22.0
Asian/Pacific Islander	4.4	3.8	4.5	3.8	4.7	3.5	1.3	(S)
American Indian/Alaska Native	1.4	2.3	1.4	2.6	1.2	1.5	3.8	(S)
PERCENT DISTRIBUTION OF SCHOOLS								
Size of enrollment	100.0	100.0	100.0	100.0	100.0	100.0	100.0	100.0
Less than 300 students	28.1	64.2	24.1	59.3	28.9	81.1	65.8	54.9
300 to 599 students	40.6	25.8	49.2	29.2	20.8	14.8	22.8	31.2
600 to 999 students	20.8	7.4	22.5	10.0	19.9	(S)	7.5	6.9
1,000 students or more	10.5	2.7	4.3	(S)	30.4	(S)	4.0	(S)
Percent minority enrollment	100.0	100.0	100.0	100.0	100.0	100.0	100.0	100.0
Less than 10.0	28.7	(S)	27.7	(S)	30.2	(S)	33.8	(S)
10.0 to 24.9	17.9	17.0	18.1	15.7	18.4	(S)	14.5	30.7
25.0 to 49.9	19.7	18.0	19.5	15.1	21.3	20.8	17.4	23.9
50.0 to 74.9	12.6	14.1	13.1	11.8	11.4	20.7	12.2	(S)
75.0 or more	21.0	42.7	21.7	50.4	18.7	39.2	22.1	21.2
Percent of students eligible for free or reduced-price lunch [2]	100.0	100.0	100.0	100.0	100.0	100.0	100.0	100.0
Less than 15.0	4.0	24.5	1.7	16.2	8.5	35.8	11.0	35.3
15.0 to 29.9	27.6	9.9	27.4	9.4	32.7	(S)	11.9	(S)
30.0 to 49.9	27.7	18.8	26.5	16.6	30.9	28.7	28.6	(S)
50.0 to 74.9	21.4	21.4	23.2	25.9	15.6	(S)	22.6	27.5
75.0 or more	19.4	25.5	21.2	31.9	12.2	16.6	25.9	16.9

S Figure does not meet publication standards. [1] Persons of Hispanic origin may be of any race. [2] Excludes data for schools not providing information on eligibility for free or reduced-price lunch.

Source: U.S. National Center for Education Statistics, School and Staffing Survey (SASS), "Public School Questionnaire 2007-08", and "Public Teacher Questionnaire 2007-08", <http://nces.ed.gov/surveys/sass/>, accessed September 2013.

Table 252. Students Who Are Homeschooled by Selected Characteristics: 2007

[51,135 represents 51,135,000. As of spring. For students 5 to 17 with a grade equivalent of K–12. Homeschoolers are students whose parents reported them to be schooled at home instead of a public or private school. Excludes students who were enrolled in school for more than 25 hours a week or were homeschooled due to a temporary illness. Based on the Parent and Family Involvement Survey of the National Household Education Surveys Program; see source and Appendix III for details]

Characteristic	Number of students			Percent distribution		
	Total (1,000)	Home-schooled (1,000)	Percent home-schooled	Total	Home-schooled	Non-Home-schooled
Total	51,135	1,508	2.9	100.0	100.0	100.0
Grade equivalent: [1]						
K–5	23,529	717	3.0	46.0	47.6	46.0
Kindergarten	3,669	114	3.1	7.2	7.6	7.2
Grades 1 to 3	11,965	406	3.4	23.4	26.9	23.3
Grades 4 to 5	7,895	197	2.5	15.4	13.1	15.5
Grades 6 to 8	12,435	359	2.9	24.3	23.8	24.3
Grades 9 to 12	15,161	422	2.8	29.6	28.0	29.7
Sex:						
Male	26,286	633	2.4	51.4	41.9	51.7
Female	24,849	875	3.5	48.6	58.1	48.3
Race/ethnicity:						
White, non-Hispanic	29,815	1,159	3.9	58.3	76.8	57.7
Black, non-Hispanic	7,523	61	0.8	14.7	4.0	15.0
Hispanic [2]	9,589	147	1.5	18.8	9.8	19.0
Other	4,208	141	3.3	8.2	9.3	8.2
Number of children in the household:						
One child	8,463	187	2.2	16.6	12.4	16.7
Two children	20,694	412	2.0	40.5	27.3	40.9
Three or more children	21,979	909	4.1	43.0	60.3	42.5
Number of parents in the household:						
Two parents	37,262	1,348	3.6	72.9	89.4	72.4
One parent	11,734	115	1.0	22.9	7.6	23.4
Nonparental guardians	2,139	45	2.1	4.2	3.0	4.2
Parents' participation in the labor force:						
Two parents—one in labor force	26,075	509	2.0	51.0	33.8	51.5
Two parents—both in labor force	10,776	808	7.5	21.1	53.6	20.1
One parent in labor force	9,989	127	1.3	19.5	8.4	19.9
No parent in labor force	4,296	64	1.5	8.4	4.3	8.5
Household income:						
$25,000 or less	11,544	239	2.1	22.6	15.9	22.8
$25,001 to 50,000	10,592	364	3.4	20.7	24.1	20.6
$50,001 to 75,000	10,289	405	3.9	20.1	26.8	19.9
$75,001 or more	18,710	501	2.7	36.6	33.2	36.7
Parents' highest educational attainment:						
High school diploma or less	14,303	206	1.4	28.0	13.7	28.4
Voc/tech degree or some college	14,584	549	3.8	28.5	36.4	28.3
Bachelor's degree	12,321	502	4.1	24.1	33.3	23.8
Graduate/professional school	9,927	251	2.5	19.4	16.6	19.5

[1] Excludes those ungraded. [2] Persons of Hispanic origin may be of any race.

Source: U.S. National Center for Education Statistics, "Parent and Family Involvement in Education Survey," National Household Education Surveys Program, 2007, unpublished data. See also <http://nces.ed.gov/nhes>.

Table 253. Public Elementary and Secondary Schools by Type and Size of School: 2010 to 2011

[Enrollment in thousands (49,178 represents 49,178,000), except for average enrollment. For school year ending in 2011. Data reported by schools, rather than school districts. Based on the Common Core of Data Survey; see source for details]

Enrollment size of school	Number of schools					Enrollment [1]				
	Total	Elemen-tary [2]	Second-ary [3]	Com-bined [4]	Other [5]	Total	Elemen-tary [2]	Second-ary [3]	Com-bined [4]	Other [5]
Total	98,817	67,086	24,544	6,137	1,050	49,178	31,582	15,693	1,898	6
PERCENT										
Total	100.00	100.00	100.00	100.00	100.00	100.00	100.00	100.00	100.00	100.00
Under 100 students	10.51	5.51	18.27	37.19	81.44	0.91	0.59	1.12	4.36	49.35
100 to 199 students	9.25	7.96	11.49	15.47	15.46	2.67	2.55	2.46	6.45	34.74
200 to 299 students	11.01	11.84	9.08	9.30	2.06	5.36	6.31	3.29	6.68	7.95
300 to 399 students	13.86	16.34	8.02	8.45	–	9.39	12.08	4.07	8.53	–
400 to 499 students	13.94	17.07	6.61	6.86	1.03	12.09	16.14	4.30	8.98	7.95
500 to 599 students	11.51	13.97	5.87	5.41	–	12.18	16.11	4.70	8.60	–
600 to 699 students	8.50	10.12	4.98	3.69	–	10.62	13.78	4.71	6.96	–
700 to 799 students	5.94	6.84	4.02	3.22	–	8.57	10.75	4.40	6.97	–
800 to 999 students	6.51	6.69	6.69	3.73	–	11.14	12.43	8.72	9.70	–
1,000 to 1,499 students	5.32	3.33	11.40	4.16	–	12.31	8.11	20.48	14.61	–
1,500 to 1,999 students	2.02	0.28	7.24	1.36	–	6.74	0.98	18.35	6.72	–
2,000 to 2,999 students	1.36	0.03	5.37	0.76	–	6.21	0.16	18.48	5.29	–
3,000 or more students	0.26	–	0.97	0.42	–	1.80	0.00	4.89	6.14	–
Average enrollment [1]	(X)	(X)	(X)	(X)	(X)	517	475	684	343	57

X Not applicable. – Represents zero. [1] Exclude data for schools not reporting enrollment. [2] Includes schools beginning with grade 6 or below and with no grade higher than 8. [3] Includes schools with no grade lower than 7. [4] Includes schools beginning with grade 6 or below and ending with grade 9 or above. [5] Includes special education, alternative, and other schools not classified by grade span.

Source: U.S. National Center for Education Statistics, *Digest of Education Statistics*, "Advance Release of Selected 2012 Digest Tables," <http://www.nces.ed.gov/programs/digest/>, accessed April 2013.

Table 254. Public Elementary and Secondary Schools—Summary: 1980 to 2011

[48,041 represents 48,041,000. For school year ending in year shown, except as indicated. Data are estimates]

Item	Unit	1980	1990	2000	2005	2009	2010	2011
School districts, total	**Number**	**16,044**	**15,552**	**15,403**	**15,731**	**15,757**	**15,782**	**15,761**
ENROLLMENT								
Population 5-17 years old [1]	1,000	48,041	44,949	53,119	53,606	53,890	53,980	53,772
Percent of resident population	Percent	21.4	18.2	18.9	18.1	17.6	17.5	17.3
Fall enrollment [2]	1,000	41,778	40,527	46,577	48,417	48,982	49,127	49,179
Percent of population 5-17 years old	Percent	87.0	90.2	87.7	90.3	90.9	91.0	91.5
Elementary [3]	1,000	24,397	26,253	29,243	29,632	30,297	30,423	30,487
Secondary [4]	1,000	17,381	14,274	17,334	18,784	18,685	18,704	18,691
Average daily attendance (ADA)	1,000	38,411	37,573	43,313	45,088	46,402	46,720	47,070
High school graduates	1,000	2,762	2,327	2,544	2,803	3,051	3,114	3,163
INSTRUCTIONAL STAFF								
Total [5]	**1,000**	**2,521**	**2,685**	**3,273**	**3,509**	**3,670**	**3,658**	**3,608**
Classroom teachers	1,000	2,211	2,362	2,891	3,072	3,207	3,188	3,137
Average salaries:								
Instructional staff	Dollar	16,715	32,638	43,837	49,135	56,267	56,967	57,282
Classroom teachers	Dollar	15,970	31,367	41,807	47,516	54,354	55,224	55,489
REVENUES								
Revenue receipts	**Mil. dol.**	**97,635**	**208,656**	**369,754**	**477,371**	**560,795**	**570,308**	**583,788**
Federal	Mil. dol.	9,020	13,184	26,346	42,908	55,978	66,643	68,166
State	Mil. dol.	47,929	100,787	183,986	225,142	261,047	256,000	266,318
Local	Mil. dol.	40,686	94,685	159,421	209,321	243,771	247,665	249,305
EXPENDITURES								
Total	**Mil. dol.**	**96,105**	**209,698**	**374,782**	**496,199**	**590,110**	**590,170**	**601,802**
Current expenditures (day schools)	Mil. dol.	85,661	186,583	320,954	422,346	506,791	513,213	524,677
Other current expenditures [6]	Mil. dol.	1,859	3,341	6,618	8,710	9,599	9,854	9,723
Capital outlay	Mil. dol.	6,504	16,012	37,552	48,757	56,175	49,125	47,979
Interest on school debt	Mil. dol.	2,081	3,762	9,659	16,385	17,545	17,979	19,423
Current expenditures per pupil enrolled	Dollar	2,050	4,604	6,891	8,723	10,346	10,447	10,669

[1] Estimated resident population as of July 1 of the previous year, except 1980, 1990, 2000, and 2010 population enumerated as of April 1. Estimates reflect revisions based on the 2010 Census of Population. [2] Fall enrollment of the previous year. [3] Kindergarten through grade 6. [4] Grades 7 through 12. [5] Full-time equivalent. [6] Current expenses for summer schools, adult education, post-high school vocational education, personnel retraining, etc., when operated by local school districts and not part of regular public elementary and secondary day-school program.

Source: National Education Association, Washington, DC. Data from *Rankings of the States 2012 and Estimates of School Statistics 2013*, used with permission of the National Education Association © 2013. All rights reserved.

Table 255. Public Elementary and Secondary School Enrollment by Grade: 1980 to 2010

[In thousands (40,877 represents 40,877,000). As of Fall of year. Based on survey of state education agencies; see source for details]

Grade	1980	1990	1995	2000	2004	2005	2006	2007	2008	2009	2010
Pupils enrolled [1]	**40,877**	**41,217**	**44,840**	**47,204**	**48,795**	**49,113**	**49,316**	**49,293**	**49,266**	**49,361**	**49,484**
Pre-Kindergarten to 8 [1]	27,647	29,878	32,341	33,688	34,178	34,205	34,235	34,205	34,286	34,409	34,625
Pre-K and Kindergarten	2,689	3,610	4,173	4,158	4,534	4,656	4,715	4,691	4,819	4,901	4,961
First	2,894	3,499	3,671	3,636	3,663	3,691	3,751	3,750	3,708	3,729	3,754
Second	2,800	3,327	3,507	3,634	3,560	3,606	3,641	3,704	3,699	3,665	3,701
Third	2,893	3,297	3,445	3,676	3,580	3,586	3,627	3,659	3,708	3,707	3,686
Fourth	3,107	3,248	3,431	3,711	3,612	3,578	3,586	3,624	3,647	3,701	3,711
Fifth	3,130	3,197	3,438	3,707	3,635	3,633	3,602	3,600	3,629	3,652	3,718
Sixth	3,038	3,110	3,395	3,663	3,735	3,670	3,660	3,628	3,614	3,644	3,682
Seventh	3,085	3,067	3,422	3,629	3,818	3,777	3,716	3,701	3,653	3,641	3,676
Eighth	3,086	2,979	3,356	3,538	3,825	3,802	3,766	3,709	3,692	3,651	3,659
Grades 9 to 12 [1]	13,231	11,338	12,500	13,340	14,617	14,909	15,081	15,087	14,980	14,952	14,860
Ninth	3,377	3,169	3,704	3,963	4,281	4,287	4,260	4,200	4,123	4,080	4,008
Tenth	3,368	2,896	3,237	3,491	3,750	3,866	3,882	3,863	3,822	3,809	3,800
Eleventh	3,195	2,612	2,826	3,083	3,369	3,455	3,551	3,558	3,548	3,541	3,538
Twelfth	2,925	2,381	2,487	2,803	3,094	3,180	3,277	3,375	3,400	3,432	3,472

[1] Includes unclassified students not shown separately.

Source: U.S. National Center for Education Statistics, *Digest of Education Statistics*, "Advance Release of Selected 2012 Digest Tables," <http://www.nces.ed.gov/programs/digest/>, accessed April 2013.

Table 256. Selected Statistics for the Largest Public School Districts: 2007 to 2009

[For the 50 largest districts by enrollment size. For 2008-09 school year unless otherwise noted. Data from the Common Core Data Program; see source for details. School district boundaries are not necessarily the same as city or county boundaries]

School district	City	County	Number of students [1]	Number of full-time equivalent (FTE) teachers [2]	Number of 2007-08 com-pleters [3]	Number of schools [4]
New York City Public Schools, NY..................	New York	New York	981,690	71,824	55,290	1,496
Los Angeles Unified, CA............................	Los Angeles	Los Angeles	687,534	35,084	30,580	860
City of Chicago School District, IL.................	Chicago	Cook	421,430	21,512	20,285	630
Dade County School District, FL...................	Miami	Miami-Dade	345,525	22,384	20,791	496
Clark County School District, NV..................	Las Vegas	Clark	312,761	15,348	13,031	350
Broward County School District, FL...............	Fort Lauderdale	Broward	256,351	18,729	15,742	303
Houston Independent School District, TX..........	Houston	Harris	200,225	11,994	7,976	296
Hillsborough County School District, FL..........	Tampa	Hillsborough	192,007	13,986	10,503	285
Hawaii Department of Education, HI..............	Honolulu	Honolulu	179,478	11,294	11,833	290
Orange County School District, FL................	Orlando	Orange	172,257	10,975	10,672	236
Palm Beach County School District, FL............	West Palm Beach	Palm Beach	170,757	13,213	10,879	247
Fairfax County Public Schools, VA................	Falls Church	Fairfax	169,030	9,274	12,150	193
Philadelphia City School District, PA.............	Philadelphia	Philadelphia	159,867	10,258	8,732	274
Dallas Independent School District, TX...........	Dallas	Dallas	157,352	10,937	6,371	232
Gwinnett County, GA.............................	Lawrenceville	Gwinnett	157,219	10,978	8,472	115
Montgomery County Public Schools, MD.........	Rockville	Montgomery	139,282	9,401	10,316	204
Wake County Schools, NC........................	Raleigh	Wake	138,443	9,317	7,717	156
Charlotte-Mecklenburg Schools, NC..............	Charlotte	Mecklenburg	135,064	9,312	6,611	166
San Diego Unified, CA............................	San Diego	San Diego	132,256	6,855	6,778	218
Prince George's County Public Schools, MD......	Upper Marlboro	Prince George's	127,977	8,870	8,644	215
Duval County School District, FL.................	Jacksonville	Duval	122,606	7,973	6,502	175
Memphis City School District, TN.................	Memphis	Shelby	111,954	7,201	6,547	200
Cobb County, GA.................................	Marietta	Cobb	106,747	8,215	7,090	118
Pinellas County School District, FL...............	Largo	Pinellas	106,061	7,878	6,790	173
Baltimore County Public Schools, MD............	Towson	Baltimore	103,180	7,339	7,571	172
Cypress-Fairbanks Independent School District, TX...	Houston	Harris	100,685	6,411	5,294	78
DeKalb County, GA..............................	Decatur	Dekalb	99,775	6,902	5,424	146
Jefferson County, KY.............................	Louisville	Jefferson	98,774	6,144	5,396	174
Detroit City School District, MI..................	Detroit	Wayne	97,577	5,953	(NA)	197
Albuquerque Public Schools, NM.................	Albuquerque	Bernalillo	95,934	6,542	5,239	174
Polk County School District, FL..................	Bartow	Polk	94,657	7,548	5,068	156
Northside Independent School District, TX........	San Antonio	Bexar	89,000	5,782	4,704	101
Fulton County, GA...............................	Atlanta	Fulton	88,299	6,530	5,087	98
Long Beach Unified, CA...........................	Long Beach	Los Angeles	87,509	4,017	5,054	92
Jefferson County, CO.............................	Golden	Jefferson	85,946	4,959	5,968	162
Milwaukee, WI..................................	Milwaukee	Milwaukee	85,381	5,158	(NA)	215
Austin Independent School District, TX...........	Austin	Travis	83,483	5,890	3,903	120
Baltimore City Public Schools, MD................	Baltimore	Baltimore City	82,266	5,839	4,116	194
Jordan District, UT..............................	Sandy	Salt Lake	81,485	3,221	(NA)	99
Lee County School District, FL...................	Fort Myers	Lee	79,434	5,034	4,491	117
Fort Worth Independent School District, TX.......	Fort Worth	Tarrant	79,285	5,167	3,529	147
Fresno Unified, CA...............................	Fresno	Fresno	76,621	3,922	3,870	106
Davidson County School District, TN.............	Nashville	Davidson	74,312	5,307	4,018	139
Denver County, CO..............................	Denver	Denver	74,189	4,356	3,190	143
Prince William County, VA........................	Manassas	Prince William	73,917	3,845	4,560	83
Anne Arundel County Public Schools, MD.........	Annapolis	Anne Arundel	73,653	4,939	5,297	124
Brevard School District, FL.......................	Viera	Brevard	73,098	5,290	5,018	121
Guilford County Schools, NC......................	Greensboro	Guilford	72,951	5,091	4,776	119
Virginia Beach City Public Schools, VA............	Virginia Beach	Virginia Beach	71,554	3,984	5,341	84
Greenville County Schools, SC....................	Greenville	Greenville	70,441	4,542	(NA)	94

NA Not Available. [1] Number of students receiving educational services from the school district. [2] Full-time equivalent is the amount of time required to perform an assignment stated as a proportion of a full-time position. [3] Includes high school diploma recipients and other completers (for example certificates of attendance) but does not include high school equivalents (GEDs). [4] Totals for number of schools may differ from published estimates since they exclude closed, inactive, and future schools.

Source: U.S. Department of Education, National Center for Education Statistics, Common Core of Data (CCD), *Characteristics of the 100 Largest Public Elementary and Secondary School Districts in the United States: 2008-09*, November 2010. See also <http://nces.ed.gov/pubsearch/pubsinfo.asp?pubid=2011301>.

Table 257. Public Elementary and Secondary School Enrollment by State: 1990 to 2010

[In thousands (29,878 represents 29,878,000). As of Fall. Includes unclassified students. Based on survey of state education agencies; see source for details]

State	Prekindergarten through grade 8					Grades 9 through 12				
	1990	2000	2005	2009	2010	1990	2000	2005	2009	2010
United States..............	**29,878**	**33,688**	**34,205**	**34,409**	**34,625**	**11,338**	**13,515**	**14,908**	**14,952**	**14,860**
Alabama.........................	527	539	529	529	534	195	201	212	219	222
Alaska...........................	85	94	91	91	92	29	39	42	41	40
Arizona.........................	479	641	740	760	752	161	237	355	317	320
Arkansas.......................	314	318	336	344	346	123	132	138	136	136
California.......................	3,615	4,408	4,466	4,264	4,294	1,336	1,733	1,971	1,999	1,996
Colorado........................	420	517	550	591	601	154	208	230	241	242
Connecticut....................	347	406	400	390	387	122	156	175	174	173
Delaware.......................	73	81	85	88	90	27	34	36	39	39
District of Columbia...........	61	54	56	52	54	19	15	21	18	18
Florida..........................	1,370	1,760	1,873	1,851	1,858	492	675	802	784	785
Georgia.........................	849	1,060	1,145	1,195	1,202	303	385	453	473	475
Hawaii..........................	123	132	127	127	128	49	52	55	53	52
Idaho...........................	160	170	183	195	194	61	75	79	82	82
Illinois..........................	1,310	1,474	1,480	1,464	1,455	512	575	631	640	637
Indiana.........................	676	703	724	731	729	279	286	311	316	318
Iowa............................	345	334	326	341	348	139	161	157	151	148
Kansas.........................	320	323	321	333	343	117	147	147	141	141
Kentucky.......................	459	471	487	484	480	177	194	192	196	193
Louisiana.......................	586	547	482	510	512	199	197	172	181	184
Maine...........................	155	146	133	129	129	60	61	62	61	60
Maryland........................	527	609	589	582	588	188	244	271	267	264
Massachusetts.................	604	703	675	667	666	230	273	297	291	289
Michigan........................	1,145	1,222	1,191	1,115	1,076	440	498	551	534	511
Minnesota......................	546	578	558	565	570	211	277	281	272	268
Mississippi......................	372	364	358	352	351	131	134	137	141	140
Missouri........................	588	645	635	638	643	228	268	283	280	276
Montana........................	111	105	98	98	98	42	50	48	44	43
Nebraska.......................	198	195	195	207	210	76	91	92	89	88
Nevada.........................	150	251	296	306	307	51	90	116	123	130
New Hampshire.................	126	147	139	133	132	46	61	67	64	63
New Jersey.....................	784	968	971	968	981	306	346	425	428	421
New Mexico.....................	208	225	230	235	239	94	95	97	99	99
New York........................	1,828	2,029	1,909	1,847	1,869	770	853	906	919	866
North Carolina..................	783	945	1,003	1,054	1,058	304	348	413	430	432
North Dakota...................	85	72	66	65	66	33	37	33	30	30
Ohio............................	1,258	1,294	1,261	1,225	1,223	514	541	578	539	531
Oklahoma.......................	425	445	457	477	483	154	178	178	178	176
Oregon..........................	340	379	380	404	393	132	167	173	178	178
Pennsylvania...................	1,172	1,258	1,228	1,200	1,210	496	556	603	586	584
Rhode Island....................	102	114	104	98	98	37	44	50	47	46
South Carolina..................	452	493	498	512	516	170	184	204	211	210
South Dakota...................	95	88	84	86	88	34	41	38	38	38
Tennessee......................	598	668	677	687	702	226	241	277	286	286
Texas...........................	2,511	2,943	3,268	3,520	3,587	872	1,117	1,257	1,330	1,349
Utah............................	325	333	358	413	425	122	148	151	158	161
Vermont.........................	71	70	65	62	68	25	32	32	29	29
Virginia.........................	728	816	841	864	871	270	329	372	381	380
Washington.....................	613	694	699	705	714	227	310	333	330	330
West Virginia....................	224	201	197	200	201	98	85	84	82	81
Wisconsin.......................	566	595	584	593	598	232	285	291	279	274
Wyoming........................	71	60	57	62	63	27	30	27	26	26

Source: U.S. National Center for Education Statistics, *Digest of Education Statistics*, "Advance Release of Selected 2012 Digest Tables," <http://www.nces.ed.gov/programs/digest/>, accessed April 2013.

Table 258. Parent Participation in School-Related Activities by Selected School, Student, and Family Characteristics: 2012

[In percent, except as noted (52,211 represents 52,211,000). For school year ending in 2012. Covers parents with children in kindergarten through grade 12. Homeschooled students are excluded]

Characteristic	Number of students in grades K through 12 (thousands)	Attended a general school or PTO/PTA meeting [1]	Attended regularly scheduled parent-teacher conference	Attended a school or class event	Volunteered or served on school committee	Participated in school fundraising
Total.....	**52,211**	**87**	**76**	**74**	**42**	**58**
School type: [2]						
Public, assigned.....	40,097	86	74	73	38	56
Public, chosen.....	7,448	89	76	75	44	57
Private, religious.....	3,271	96	85	88	69	84
Private, nonreligious.....	788	95	89	91	66	78
Student's sex:						
Male.....	26,964	87	76	72	40	57
Female.....	25,247	88	75	76	44	60
Student's race/ethnicity:						
White, non-Hispanic.....	26,938	89	77	82	50	67
Black, non-Hispanic.....	7,466	85	76	68	31	52
Hispanic [3].....	12,110	86	73	64	32	46
Asian or Pacific Islander, non-Hispanic.....	2,871	84	72	65	37	47
Other, non-Hispanic [4].....	2,827	88	78	76	44	58
Student's grade level: [5]						
K–2nd grade.....	13,610	93	89	79	56	67
3rd–5th grade.....	1,243	92	89	82	51	69
6th–8th grade.....	11,717	87	71	70	32	53
9th–12th grade.....	14,642	79	57	66	28	47
Parents' highest education level:						
Less than high school.....	6,335	77	64	48	19	31
High school graduate or equivalent.....	10,571	82	72	62	28	46
Vocational/technical or some college.....	15,810	88	77	77	41	61
Bachelor's degree.....	11,839	92	80	85	55	71
Graduate or professional school.....	7,656	95	82	89	61	75
Parents' language at home:						
Both/only parent(s) speak(s) English.....	44,525	88	77	78	45	63
One of two parents speaks English.....	1,856	88	69	62	29	38
No parent speaks English.....	5,830	82	65	50	23	32

[1] Parent Teacher Organization (PTO) or Parent Teacher Association (PTA) meeting. [2] School type classifies the school currently attended as either public or private. Public schools are further classified according to whether the school was chosen or assigned. Private schools are also classified as being religious or nonreligious. [3] Persons of Hispanic origin may be of any race. [4] Includes children who were multiracial and not of Hispanic ethnicity, were American Indian or Alaska Native, or were not Hispanic, White, Black, Asian, or Pacific Islander. [5] Students whose parents reported the student's grade equivalent as "ungraded" were excluded from the analyses of grade level.

Source: U.S. Department of Education, National Center for Education Statistics, *Parent and Family Involvement in Education,* from the *National Household Education Surveys Program of 2012,* August 2013. See also <http://nces.ed.gov/nhes/>.

Table 259. School Enrollment Below Postsecondary—Summary by Sex, Race, and Hispanic Origin: 2012

[In thousands (58,496 represents 58,496,000), except percent. As of October. Covers civilian noninstitutional population enrolled in nursery school through high school. Based on Current Population Survey, see text, Section 1 and Appendix III]

Characteristic	Total			Race and Hispanic origin				
				White [2]				
	Number [1]	Male	Female	Total	Non-Hispanic	Black [2]	Asian [2]	Hispanic [3]
All students.....	58,496	29,902	28,593	43,073	31,127	8,879	2,829	13,644
Nursery.....	4,628	2,342	2,286	3,393	2,509	708	208	988
Full day.....	2,261	(NA)	(NA)	1,520	1,118	486	83	443
Part day.....	2,367	(NA)	(NA)	1,873	1,392	222	125	544
Public schools.....	2,732	(NA)	(NA)	1,925	1,227	516	90	781
Full day.....	1,291	(NA)	(NA)	844	528	326	26	346
Part day.....	1,441	(NA)	(NA)	1,082	699	189	64	436
Private schools.....	1,896	(NA)	(NA)	1,468	1,283	193	118	206
Full day.....	970	(NA)	(NA)	677	590	160	57	98
Part day.....	926	(NA)	(NA)	791	693	33	61	109
Kindergarten.....	4,138	2,113	2,025	2,940	2,011	646	224	1,050
Elementary.....	32,683	16,854	15,828	24,187	17,413	4,856	1,540	7,841
High school.....	17,047	8,593	8,454	12,554	9,193	2,669	857	3,765
Population 18 to 24 years old.....	30,377	15,252	15,125	22,712	17,072	4,714	1,537	6,415
Percent dropouts [4].....	7.6	8.5	6.7	7.2	4.8	9.9	3.5	15.1
Percent high school graduates.....	85.1	83.6	86.7	86.1	89.1	79.6	90.0	76.4
Percent enrolled in college.....	41.0	37.6	44.5	41.0	42.1	35.8	59.5	37.5

[1] Includes other races not shown separately. [2] For persons who selected this race group only. See footnote 2, Table 241. [3] Persons of Hispanic origin may be of any race. [4] For persons not in regular school and who have not completed the 12th grade nor received a general equivalency degree.

Source: U.S. Census Bureau, "School Enrollment, Historical Time Series Tables," <http://www.census.gov/hhes/school/data/cps/historical/index.html>, accessed September 2013.

Table 260. Elementary and Secondary Schools—Teachers, Enrollment, and Pupil-Teacher Ratio: 1970 to 2011

[In thousands (2,292 represents 2,292,000), except ratios. As of Fall. Data are for full-time equivalent teachers. Based on surveys of state education agencies and private schools; see source for details]

Year	Teachers			Enrollment			Pupil-teacher ratio		
	Total	Public	Private	Total	Public	Private	Total	Public	Private
1970................	2,292	2,059	233	51,257	45,894	5,363	22.4	22.3	23.0
1975................	2,453	2,198	255	49,819	44,819	5,000	20.3	20.4	19.6
1980................	2,485	2,184	301	46,208	40,877	5,331	18.6	18.7	17.7
1985................	2,549	2,206	343	44,979	39,422	5,557	17.6	17.9	16.2
1986................	2,592	2,244	348	45,205	39,753	5,452	17.4	17.7	15.7
1987................	2,631	2,279	352	45,487	40,008	5,479	17.3	17.6	15.6
1988................	2,668	2,323	345	45,430	40,189	5,242	17.0	17.3	15.2
1989................	2,713	2,357	356	45,741	40,543	5,198	17.0	17.2	15.7
1990................	2,759	2,398	361	46,451	41,217	5,234	17.0	17.2	15.6
1991................	2,797	2,432	365	47,728	42,047	5,681	17.1	17.3	15.6
1992................	2,827	2,459	368	48,500	42,823	5,677	17.2	17.4	15.4
1993................	2,874	2,504	370	49,133	43,465	5,668	17.1	17.4	15.3
1994 [1].............	2,925	2,552	373	49,898	44,111	5,787	17.1	17.3	15.5
1995................	2,974	2,598	376	50,759	44,840	5,918	17.1	17.3	15.7
1996 [1].............	3,051	2,667	384	51,544	45,611	5,933	16.9	17.1	15.5
1997................	3,138	2,746	391	52,071	46,127	5,944	16.6	16.8	15.2
1998 [1].............	3,230	2,830	400	52,525	46,539	5,988	16.3	16.4	15.0
1999................	3,319	2,911	408	52,876	46,857	6,018	15.9	16.1	14.7
2000 [1].............	3,366	2,941	424	53,373	47,204	6,169	15.9	16.0	14.5
2001................	3,440	3,000	441	53,992	47,672	6,320	15.7	15.9	14.3
2002 [1].............	3,476	3,034	442	54,403	48,183	6,220	15.7	15.9	14.1
2003................	3,490	3,049	441	54,639	48,540	6,099	15.7	15.9	13.8
2004 [1].............	3,536	3,091	445	54,882	48,795	6,087	15.5	15.8	13.7
2005................	3,593	3,143	450	55,187	49,113	6,073	15.4	15.6	13.5
2006 [1].............	3,622	3,166	456	55,307	49,316	5,991	15.3	15.6	13.2
2007................	3,634	3,178	456	55,203	49,293	5,910	15.2	15.5	13.0
2008 [1].............	3,670	3,222	448	54,973	49,266	5,707	15.0	15.3	12.8
2009................	3,647	3,210	437	54,862	49,361	5,488	15.0	15.4	12.5
2010 [1].............	3,542	3,099	443	54,876	49,484	5,391	15.5	16.0	12.2
2011 [2].............	3,679	3,246	432	54,956	49,636	5,320	14.9	15.3	12.3

[1] Private school numbers are estimated based on data from the Private School Universe Survey. [2] Projected.

Source: U.S. National Center for Education Statistics, *Digest of Education Statistics*, "Advance Release of Selected 2012 Digest Tables," <http://www.nces.ed.gov/programs/digest/>, accessed April 2013.

Table 261. Public Elementary and Secondary School Teachers—Selected Characteristics: 2007 to 2008

[612 represents 612,000. For school year. Based on the 2007-2008 Schools and Staffing Survey and subject to sampling error; for details, see source Web site at <http://nces.ed.gov/surveys/sass/>. Excludes prekindergarten teachers. See Table 270 for similar data on private school teachers]

Characteristic	Unit	Age					Sex		Race/ethnicity		
		Under 30 years old	30 to 39 years old	40 to 49 years old	50 to 59 years old	Over 60 years old	Male	Female	White [1]	Black [1]	His-panic [2]
Total teachers [3].............	1,000	612	898	808	879	207	821	2,584	2,829	239	240
Highest degree held:											
Bachelor's.................	Percent	70.1	46.8	43.7	38.4	35.0	47.0	47.5	46.8	47.0	56.3
Master's..................	Percent	28.0	46.1	47.3	50.4	51.1	43.9	44.8	45.7	41.4	34.1
Education specialist...........	Percent	1.5	6.0	7.3	8.7	9.6	5.5	6.7	6.0	8.7	7.7
Doctorate..................	Percent	(S)	0.4	0.7	1.5	3.2	1.6	0.7	0.8	2.0	1.1
Full-time teaching experience:											
Less than 3 years............	Percent	44.1	10.3	7.4	3.4	2.9	13.6	13.4	13.0	13.1	18.0
3 to 9 years................	Percent	55.9	53.5	25.1	11.4	8.5	33.2	33.7	32.6	38.0	39.0
10 to 20 years..............	Percent	(S)	36.3	40.9	26.3	20.0	26.6	27.5	27.6	24.9	26.7
20 years or more............	Percent	–	(S)	26.6	59.0	68.6	26.6	25.5	26.8	24.1	16.3
Full-time teachers..............	1,000	572	828	739	803	185	776	2,351	2,579	229	230
Earned income.................	Dollars	41,790	48,380	52,850	58,760	59,610	53,910	50,790	51,530	51,110	51,520
Salary.......................	Dollars	39,760	46,320	50,870	56,760	57,910	50,560	49,230	49,570	48,910	49,260

– Represents or rounds to zero. S Reporting standards not met, the standard error for this estimate is 50% or more of the estimate's value. [1] Non-Hispanic. [2] Persons of Hispanic origin may be of any race. [3] Includes teachers with no degrees and associate's degrees not shown separately.

Source: U.S. Department of Education, National Center for Education Statistics, Schools and Staffing Survey (SASS), "Public School Teacher Data Files 2007–08," accessed September 2013. See also <http://nces.ed.gov/surveys/sass/tables_list.asp>.

Table 262. Public Elementary and Secondary Schools—Number and Average Salary of Classroom Teachers: 1990 to 2011, and by State, 2011

[2,362 represents 2,362,000. Estimates for school year ending in June of year shown. Elementary includes kindergarten]

Year and state	Teachers [1] (1,000)			Avg. salary ($1,000)		
	Total	Elementary	Secondary	All teachers	Elementary	Secondary
1990	2,362	1,390	972	31.4	30.8	32.0
1995	2,565	1,517	1,048	36.7	36.1	37.5
2000	2,891	1,696	1,195	41.8	41.3	42.5
2003	3,020	1,769	1,251	45.7	45.4	46.1
2004	3,042	1,782	1,260	46.5	46.2	47.0
2005	3,072	1,799	1,273	47.5	47.1	47.7
2006	3,125	1,811	1,313	49.1	48.6	49.5
2007	3,172	1,848	1,324	51.1	50.7	51.5
2008	3,201	1,860	1,341	52.8	52.4	53.3
2009	3,228	1,884	1,344	54.3	53.9	54.8
2010	3,215	1,876	1,340	55.2	54.9	55.6
2011, U.S.	**3,137**	**1,841**	**1,297**	**55.5**	**55.1**	**56.1**
AL	46.8	25.5	21.3	47.8	47.2	48.6
AK	8.2	4.4	3.8	62.9	62.1	63.7
AZ	58.3	41.2	17.1	47.6	47.6	47.6
AR	30.5	13.8	16.7	46.0	44.5	47.2
CA	263.6	181.6	82.1	67.9	67.9	67.9
CO	48.5	25.3	23.2	49.2	48.8	49.6
CT	41.5	27.8	13.6	69.2	69.2	69.2
DE	8.7	4.3	4.4	57.9	57.9	57.9
DC	5.8	3.8	2.0	66.6	66.6	66.6
FL	169.7	88.0	81.8	45.7	45.7	45.7
GA	112.1	68.4	43.7	52.8	52.5	53.4
HI	10.9	5.8	5.1	55.1	55.1	55.1
ID	15.7	8.2	7.4	47.4	47.4	47.4
IL	129.3	95.9	33.4	64.5	62.5	71.2
IN	63.3	33.9	29.3	50.8	50.8	50.8
IA	34.6	23.2	11.4	49.8	50.1	49.3
KS	34.3	17.1	17.2	46.6	46.6	46.3
KY	41.3	29.5	11.8	48.9	48.7	49.4
LA	48.9	33.9	15.0	49.0	49.0	49.0
ME	15.6	10.5	5.1	47.2	47.9	46.2

State	Teachers [1] (1,000)			Avg. salary ($1,000)		
	Total	Elementary	Secondary	All teachers	Elementary	Secondary
MD	59.3	35.0	24.4	64.0	63.7	64.2
MA	70.2	46.4	23.8	70.3	70.3	70.3
MI	85.2	47.2	38.0	61.6	61.6	61.6
MN	52.5	26.7	25.8	53.7	53.7	53.7
MS	32.0	18.8	13.2	42.0	41.3	43.0
MO	67.4	34.4	33.0	45.3	45.3	45.3
MT	10.6	7.1	3.4	47.1	47.1	47.1
NE	26.5	16.4	10.1	47.4	47.4	47.4
NV	25.0	14.5	10.5	53.0	53.0	53.0
NH	15.6	10.6	5.0	52.8	52.8	52.8
NJ	110.0	42.7	67.3	66.6	65.8	68.2
NM	21.3	14.7	6.6	46.9	45.6	47.0
NY	223.9	99.4	124.4	72.7	72.7	72.7
NC	94.9	67.3	27.6	46.7	46.7	46.7
ND	8.0	5.6	2.4	44.8	44.9	44.5
OH	108.9	70.2	38.7	56.7	57.6	55.7
OK	41.3	29.0	12.3	44.3	44.0	45.1
OR	27.6	17.9	9.8	56.5	56.2	57.1
PA	125.9	63.0	62.9	60.8	60.8	60.8
RI	11.1	6.9	4.2	60.9	60.9	60.9
SC	47.2	32.8	14.4	47.1	45.5	45.8
SD	9.3	6.6	2.7	39.9	39.3	41.3
TN	65.0	45.3	19.8	45.9	45.9	45.9
TX	334.9	171.4	163.6	48.6	48.2	49.1
UT	26.3	14.8	11.5	47.0	47.0	47.0
VT	8.9	4.6	4.3	50.1	50.1	50.1
VA	101.8	60.9	40.9	47.6	47.4	47.8
WA	53.9	29.8	24.1	52.9	52.7	53.2
WV	19.8	14.3	5.5	44.3	44.0	45.0
WI	58.0	40.8	17.2	54.2	53.8	55.3
WY	7.1	3.7	3.4	56.1	55.8	56.4

[1] Full-time equivalent.

Source: National Education Association, Washington, DC. Data from *Rankings of the States 2012 and Estimates of School Statistics 2013*, used with permission of the National Education Association © 2013. All rights reserved.

Table 263. Teacher Stayers, Movers, and Leavers by Selected Characteristics: 2000 to 2001 and 2008 to 2009

[2,994.7 represents 2,994,700. Data compare the teaching status of teacher between one school year and the prior year. Stayers are teachers who were teaching in the same school in both years. Movers are teachers who were still teaching in the current school year but in a different school. Leavers are teachers who left the teaching profession. Based on the School and Staffing Survey; see source for details]

Characteristic	Public				Private			
	Total [1]	Stayers	Movers	Leavers	Total [1]	Stayers	Movers	Leavers
NUMBER (1,000)								
2000-01..	2,994.7	2,542.2	231.0	221.4	448.6	354.8	37.6	56.2
2008-09..	3,380.3	2,854.9	255.7	269.8	487.3	386.0	24.0	77.3
PERCENT DISTRIBUTION								
Total, 2008-09..	100.0	84.5	7.6	8.0	100.0	79.2	4.9	15.9
Age:								
Less than 30 years old...........................	100.0	76.1	14.7	9.2	100.0	68.9	10.0	21.1
30 to 39 years old..................................	100.0	84.4	7.3	8.4	100.0	76.9	4.9	18.2
40 to 49 years old..................................	100.0	89.6	6.6	3.9	100.0	83.7	5.4	10.9
50 to 59 years old..................................	100.0	85.9	5.7	8.4	100.0	85.2	2.4	12.4
60 years old and over.............................	100.0	82.4	[2] 2.0	15.6	100.0	77.7	[2] 2.7	19.6
Sex:								
Male..	100.0	84.4	7.8	7.9	100.0	80.0	5.7	14.3
Female...	100.0	84.5	7.5	8.0	100.0	78.9	4.7	16.4
Race/ethnicity:								
White, non-Hispanic...............................	100.0	85.0	7.0	8.0	100.0	80.7	4.6	[2] 14.7
Black, non-Hispanic...............................	100.0	80.5	10.4	9.0	100.0	67.2	[2] 8.6	[2] 24.2
Hispanic, single or more than one race.....	100.0	83.8	10.7	[2] 5.6	100.0	69.2	(S)	[2] 23.7
Asian, Native Hawaiian, or Other Pacific Islander, non-Hispanic..............	100.0	80.1	(S)	[2] 8.0	100.0	[2] 58.7	(S)	(S)
American Indian/Alaska Native, non-Hispanic.............	100.0	[2] 82.5	(S)	(S)	100.0	(S)	(S)	(S)
More than one race, non-Hispanic...........	100.0	82.5	(S)	(S)	100.0	100.0	–	–
Years as a teacher:								
3 or fewer...	100.0	76.2	14.1	9.7	100.0	70.5	6.5	22.9
4 to 9..	100.0	83.4	8.6	7.9	100.0	74.8	7.8	17.4
10 to 19..	100.0	90.4	5.2	4.4	100.0	84.3	2.8	12.9
20 or more...	100.0	84.0	5.2	10.8	100.0	85.8	2.7	11.4
Main assignment field:								
Early childhood/general elementary.........	100.0	87.0	7.4	5.6	100.0	79.7	6.5	13.8
Special education..................................	100.0	78.0	9.8	12.3	100.0	62.9	(S)	[2] 27.5
Arts/music..	100.0	88.4	7.5	4.1	100.0	87.9	(S)	9.0
English/language arts.............................	100.0	81.8	7.7	10.5	100.0	80.5	[2] 2.9	16.5
Mathematics...	100.0	85.6	6.7	7.7	100.0	85.3	(S)	[2] 12.7
Natural sciences...................................	100.0	83.9	7.1	[2] 9.0	100.0	80.6	[2] 4.8	[2] 14.6
Social sciences.....................................	100.0	84.2	[2] 8.2	7.6	100.0	83.3	[2] 4.3	[2] 12.4
Other...	100.0	84.2	6.7	9.1	100.0	72.3	4.9	22.8

– Represents or rounds to zero. S Reporting standards not met. [1] Total teachers prior school year. [2] Interpret data with caution. The standard error for this estimate is equal to 30 percent or more of the estimate's value.

Source: U.S. National Center for Education Statistics, Teacher Follow-up Survey (TFS), "Current Teacher Data File" and "Former Teacher Data File, 2008–09," accessed September 2013. See also <http://nces.ed.gov/surveys/sass/index.asp>.

Table 264. Public and Private School Teachers Who Moved to a Different School or Left Teaching by Reason: 2008 to 2009

[In percent. Movers are teachers who were still teaching in the current year but had moved to a different school after the 2007–08 school year. Leavers are teachers who left the teaching profession after the 2007–08 school year. Based on the School and Staffing Survey; see source for details]

Primary reason for moving	Movers		Primary reason for moving	Leavers	
	Public	Private		Public	Private
Contract was not renewed..................	10.7	12.7	Contract was not renewed..................	5.3	13.0
Primary reason for moving, other than contract was not renewed:			Primary reason for leaving, other than contract was not renewed:		
Personal life factors.........................	26.2	16.0	Personal life factors.........................	42.9	27.8
Assignment and credential factors.......	[1] 7.5	(S)	Assignment and credential factors.......	[1] 1.2	[1] 1.6
Salary and other job benefits.............	[1] 4.0	23.2	Salary and other job benefits.............	[1] 4.0	[1] 10.7
Classroom factors...........................	1.8	(S)	Classroom factors...........................	(S)	(S)
School factors................................	16.1	18.9	School factors................................	9.8	12.1
Student performance factors.............	[1] 1.6	(S)	Student performance factors.............	3.5	(S)
Other factors..................................	32.0	24.3	Other career factors.........................	14.8	22.8
			Other factors..................................	17.1	10.3

S Reporting standards not met. [1] Interpret data with caution. The standard error of this estimate is equal to 30 percent or more of the estimate's value.

Source: U.S. National Center for Education Statistics, *Teacher Attrition and Mobility: Results from the 2008-09 Teacher Follow-up Survey*, NCES 2010-353, August 2010. See also <http://nces.ed.gov/surveys/btls/index.asp>.

Table 265. Average Salary and Wages Paid in Public School Systems: 1985 to 2011

[In dollars. For school year ending in year shown. Data reported by a stratified sample of school systems enrolling 300 or more pupils. Data represent unweighted means of average salaries paid school personnel reported by each school system]

Position	1985	1990	1995	2000	2005	2008	2009	2010	2011
ANNUAL SALARY									
Central-office administrators:									
Superintendent (contract salary).......	56,954	75,425	90,198	112,158	128,770	148,387	155,634	159,634	161,992
Deputy/assoc. superintendent..........	52,877	69,623	81,266	97,251	116,186	134,245	136,832	139,463	138,061
Assistant superintendent................	48,003	62,698	75,236	88,913	103,212	116,833	119,755	123,509	122,333
Administrators for—									
Finance and business..................	40,344	52,354	61,323	73,499	83,678	96,490	98,590	100,306	101,347
Instructional services..................	43,452	56,359	66,767	79,023	88,950	99,748	102,322	103,974	103,025
Public relations/information...........	35,287	44,926	53,263	60,655	70,502	80,534	83,235	86,567	84,629
Staff personnel services..............	44,182	56,344	65,819	76,608	86,966	98,190	100,620	102,269	101,578
Technology...........................	(X)	(X)	(X)	(X)	76,308	86,085	87,898	90,530	90,914
Subject area supervisors..............	34,422	45,929	54,534	63,103	68,714	78,309	80,290	80,964	80,534
School building administrators:									
Principals:									
Elementary............................	36,452	48,431	58,589	69,407	76,182	85,907	88,062	89,673	89,591
Junior high/middle....................	39,650	52,163	62,311	73,877	81,514	91,334	93,478	95,003	95,426
Senior high...........................	42,094	55,722	66,596	79,839	86,938	97,486	99,365	102,387	102,191
Assistant principals:									
Elementary............................	30,496	40,916	48,491	56,419	63,140	71,192	71,893	73,181	71,764
Junior high/middle....................	33,793	44,570	52,942	60,842	67,600	76,053	77,476	79,164	78,131
Senior high...........................	35,491	46,486	55,556	64,811	71,401	79,391	81,083	83,074	82,027
Classroom teachers....................	23,587	31,278	37,264	42,213	45,884	51,329	52,900	54,370	54,220
Auxiliary professional personnel:									
Counselors.............................	27,593	35,979	42,486	48,195	52,500	57,618	58,775	60,142	60,188
Librarians..............................	24,981	33,469	40,418	46,732	50,720	56,933	57,974	59,495	59,093
School nurses..........................	19,944	26,090	31,066	35,540	40,520	46,025	46,476	48,032	48,044
Secretarial/clerical personnel:									
Central office:									
Secretaries............................	15,343	20,238	23,935	28,405	32,716	36,657	37,785	38,601	38,606
Accounting/payroll clerks.............	15,421	20,088	24,042	28,498	33,217	37,732	39,031	39,895	39,790
Typists/data entry clerks..............	12,481	16,125	18,674	22,853	26,214	30,072	31,718	32,555	32,636
School building level:									
Secretaries............................	12,504	16,184	19,170	22,630	25,381	28,810	29,480	30,474	30,226
Library clerks..........................	9,911	12,152	14,381	16,509	18,443	21,004	21,190	21,639	21,142
HOURLY WAGE RATE									
Other support personnel:									
Teacher aides:									
Instructional..........................	5.89	7.43	8.77	10.00	11.35	12.86	13.23	13.48	13.55
Noninstructional......................	5.60	7.08	8.29	9.77	11.23	12.70	13.13	13.59	13.58
Custodians............................	6.90	8.54	10.05	11.35	12.61	14.19	14.59	15.04	14.92
Cafeteria workers.....................	5.42	6.77	7.89	9.02	10.33	11.60	11.94	12.18	12.23
Bus drivers............................	7.27	9.21	10.69	12.48	14.18	16.56	16.44	16.62	16.61

X Not applicable.

Source: Editorial Projects in Education and Educational Research Service, Bethesda MD, *National Survey of Salaries and Wages in Public Schools*, ©. See also: <http://www.edweek.org/ew/marketplace/products/ers/publications.html>.

Table 266. Public School Employment by Occupation, Sex, and Race/Ethnicity: 1990 and 2010

[In thousands (3,181 represents 3,181,000). Covers all public elementary-secondary school districts with 100 or more full-time employees]

Occupation	1990					2010				
	Total	Male	Female	White [1]	Black [1]	Total	Male	Female	White [1]	Black [1]
All occupations [2]................	**3,181**	**914**	**2,267**	**2,502**	**463**	**4,592**	**1,155**	**3,437**	**3,420**	**579**
Officials, administrators.............	43	28	15	37	4	65	31	34	53	7
Principals and assistant										
principals...........................	90	56	34	70	13	114	52	62	83	20
Classroom teachers [3]................	1,746	468	1,278	1,469	192	2,492	594	1,898	2,004	225
Elementary schools.................	875	128	747	722	103	1,212	154	1,059	966	101
Secondary schools..................	662	304	358	570	66	967	375	592	793	85
Other professional staff..............	227	58	170	187	30	353	62	291	275	46
Teachers' aides [4]....................	324	54	270	208	69	538	78	459	359	91
Clerical, secretarial staff.............	226	5	221	181	24	317	19	299	221	37
Service workers [5]...................	524	245	279	348	129	712	318	393	426	152

[1] Excludes individuals of Hispanic origin. [2] 2010 data includes other occupations not shown separately. [3] Includes other classroom teachers not shown separately. [4] Includes technicians. [5] Includes craftworkers and laborers.

Source: U.S. Equal Employment Opportunity Commission, "Equal Employment Opportunity, EEO-5 Statistical File- 2010, United States Summary," <http://www.eeoc.gov/eeoc/statistics/employment/jobpat-eeo5/2010/us.html>, accessed July 2013.

Table 267. Public Elementary and Secondary School Finances by Enrollment-Size Group: 2010 to 2011

[In millions of dollars, unless otherwise noted. (599,146 represents $599,146,000,000). Fiscal year ending in 2011. Enrollment as of Fall 2010. Data are based on the Annual Government Finance Survey. For details, see source. See also Appendix III]

Item	All school systems	School systems with enrollment of—						
		50,000 or more	25,000 to 49,999	15,000 to 24,999	7,500 to 14,999	5,000 to 7,499	3,000 to 4,999	Under 3,000
TOTAL								
General revenue............................	599,146	128,089	73,620	55,108	85,039	53,017	70,655	133,617
From federal sources.........................	73,707	18,997	9,883	6,767	9,597	5,250	6,975	16,238
Through state..............................	69,418	18,134	9,421	6,505	8,901	4,959	6,612	14,885
Child nutrition programs....................	12,298	3,025	1,787	1,319	1,723	968	1,207	2,268
Direct.......................................	4,288	862	462	262	696	291	363	1,353
From state sources [1]	265,949	53,375	34,438	27,188	39,511	22,266	29,172	59,999
General formula assistance.................	182,135	33,444	24,812	19,319	28,160	15,549	19,666	41,187
Compensatory programs....................	4,608	1,104	832	579	733	306	330	724
Special education...........................	16,784	4,167	1,787	1,316	2,052	1,280	2,036	4,147
From local sources..........................	259,490	55,718	29,299	21,153	35,932	25,501	34,508	57,380
Taxes.......................................	178,230	28,629	20,406	15,282	26,511	19,070	25,699	42,632
Contributions from parent government..................................	46,985	20,602	4,912	2,905	4,828	3,587	4,931	5,219
From other local governments..............	6,492	681	1,004	455	728	569	756	2,299
Current charges.............................	14,190	2,392	1,606	1,297	2,043	1,251	1,710	3,890
School lunch...............................	6,392	950	730	621	1,021	659	857	1,555
Other..	13,594	3,415	1,370	1,213	1,822	1,023	1,411	3,340
General expenditure..........................	595,079	129,341	73,606	55,113	83,959	52,237	69,124	131,700
Current spending............................	522,094	112,459	63,747	47,784	74,057	46,227	61,159	116,661
By function:								
Instruction.................................	316,328	71,251	38,405	28,757	44,908	28,144	37,022	67,841
Support services...........................	178,667	35,400	21,958	16,326	25,333	15,814	21,149	42,687
Other current spending.....................	27,099	5,808	3,384	2,700	3,817	2,269	2,987	6,133
By object:								
Total salaries and wages..................	308,337	64,900	38,633	29,206	44,565	27,661	36,286	67,087
Total employee benefits....................	109,213	23,610	12,723	10,004	15,782	9,940	13,076	24,078
Capital outlay...............................	52,342	12,440	7,054	5,298	6,894	4,075	5,691	10,889
Interest on debt.............................	17,787	4,102	2,662	1,899	2,680	1,587	1,912	2,946
Payments to other governments..................................	2,857	340	143	132	327	348	363	1,204
Debt outstanding.............................	407,125	99,407	54,839	42,971	56,567	34,570	46,159	72,611
Long-term...................................	398,514	97,442	54,081	42,499	55,726	33,674	45,170	69,922
Short-term..................................	8,610	1,965	758	472	841	896	989	2,689
Long-term debt issued.......................	47,797	10,150	5,785	4,715	6,657	3,862	5,886	10,742
Long-term debt retired.......................	37,871	6,881	4,811	3,450	5,430	3,742	5,054	8,503
PER PUPIL								
Fall enrollment (1,000)........................	48,276	10,228	6,606	4,994	7,269	4,235	5,450	9,495
General revenue..............................	12,411	12,524	11,145	11,036	11,699	12,518	12,965	14,072
From federal sources.........................	1,527	1,857	1,496	1,355	1,320	1,240	1,280	1,710
From state sources [1]	5,509	5,219	5,213	5,445	5,435	5,257	5,353	6,319
General formula assistance.................	3,773	3,270	3,756	3,869	3,874	3,671	3,609	4,338
Special education...........................	348	407	270	263	282	302	374	437
From local sources [1]	5,375	5,448	4,435	4,236	4,943	6,021	6,332	6,043
Taxes.......................................	3,692	2,799	3,089	3,060	3,647	4,503	4,716	4,490
Contributions from parent government..................................	973	2,014	744	582	664	847	905	550
Current charges.............................	294	234	243	260	281	295	314	410
School lunch...............................	132	93	111	124	141	156	157	164
General expenditure [1]	12,072	12,314	10,890	10,828	11,339	12,089	12,435	13,631
Current spending............................	10,560	10,663	9,397	9,360	9,977	10,670	10,974	12,047
By function:								
Instruction.................................	6,425	6,773	5,669	5,675	6,079	6,517	6,673	7,051
Support services...........................	3,701	3,461	3,324	3,269	3,485	3,734	3,881	4,496
By object:								
Total salaries and wages..................	6,387	6,346	5,848	5,849	6,131	6,531	6,659	7,065
Total employee benefits....................	2,262	2,308	1,926	2,003	2,171	2,347	2,399	2,536
Capital outlay...............................	1,084	1,216	1,068	1,061	948	962	1,044	1,147
Interest on debt.............................	368	401	403	380	369	375	351	310
Debt outstanding.............................	8,433	9,719	8,302	8,605	7,782	8,162	8,470	7,647
Long-term...................................	8,255	9,527	8,187	8,511	7,666	7,951	8,289	7,364

[1] Includes other sources not shown separately.

Source: U.S. Census Bureau, *Public Education Finances, 2011*, May 2013. See also <http://www.census.gov/govs/school>.

Table 268. Public Elementary and Secondary Schools by Selected Characteristics: 1999 and 2009

[For school year ending in June of year shown]

Characteristic	1999 Total	1999 Elementary	1999 Secondary	1999 Combined	2009 Total	2009 Elementary	2009 Secondary	2009 Combined
Total number of schools [1]	90,874	63,382	21,790	5,067	98,706	67,082	24,275	5,623
Percent [1]	100.0	69.7	24.0	5.6	100.0	68.0	24.6	5.7
PERCENT								
School type	100.0	100.0	100.0	100.0	100.0	100.0	100.0	100.0
Regular	92.0	98.5	85.4	49.2	90.0	98.3	79.9	49.7
Special education	2.2	0.8	1.2	17.2	2.3	0.8	1.4	16.7
Vocational	1.2	–	2.9	7.2	1.4	–	4.9	1.5
Alternative	4.6	0.7	10.5	26.3	6.3	0.9	13.8	32.2
Charter school [2]	0.6	0.5	0.5	1.7	4.8	3.7	5.2	15.4
Title I school [3]	–	–	–	–	63.1	72.7	44.9	47.3
Magnet school/program [4]	1.3	1.4	1.3	0.5	3.1	3.3	3.0	1.6
Enrollment size:	100.0	100.0	100.0	100.0	100.0	100.0	100.0	100.0
Less than 300	30.8	27.1	34.3	68.1	31.5	26.6	37.9	65.8
300–499	26.3	31.2	14.5	12.1	27.6	33.1	14.5	14.5
500–999	33.3	37.1	26.0	15.0	31.8	36.5	22.0	14.5
1,000 or more	9.6	4.7	25.3	4.8	9.1	3.8	25.7	5.1
Racial/ethnic concentration: [5]								
More than 50 percent White	72.0	71.2	76.4	62.8	62.7	62.0	66.1	57.1
More than 50 percent Black	10.9	11.4	8.8	13.8	11.5	11.4	10.5	16.4
More than 50 percent Hispanic	8.2	8.7	6.8	6.8	13.4	14.1	11.8	10.3
Percentage of students in school eligible for free or reduced-price lunch	100.0	100.0	100.0	100.0	100.0	100.0	100.0	100.0
0–25 percent	22.1	18.8	31.4	25.6	24.7	23.6	28.6	21.9
26–50 percent	20.9	20.6	23.0	16.2	28.9	27.1	35.2	23.6
51–75 percent	14.5	16.3	9.1	17.2	24.7	25.6	21.7	26.1
76–100 percent	9.7	11.8	3.7	9.4	19.1	21.7	11.2	20.4
Missing/school did not participate	32.8	32.4	32.8	31.5	2.7	2.0	3.3	8.0
Region:	100.0	100.0	100.0	100.0	100.0	100.0	100.0	100.0
Northeast	16.2	17.4	13.7	8.6	15.5	16.6	14.0	9.1
Midwest	29.2	28.5	31.5	28.5	26.9	26.3	29.8	23.7
South	33.0	32.8	32.3	40.2	34.4	34.5	31.5	38.4
West	21.6	21.3	22.5	22.7	23.1	22.5	24.7	28.8
Locale:								
City	(NA)	(NA)	(NA)	(NA)	26.0	27.2	22.1	28.3
Suburban	(NA)	(NA)	(NA)	(NA)	27.5	29.8	23.4	19.3
Town	(NA)	(NA)	(NA)	(NA)	14.4	13.5	16.4	14.5
Rural	(NA)	(NA)	(NA)	(NA)	32.0	29.4	38.2	37.9

– Represents or rounds to zero. [1] Schools reporting membership are those which report at least one student enrolled on October 1 of the school year. In any given year, some small schools will not have any students. The Common Core of Data (CCD) allows a student to be reported for only a single school or agency. For example, a vocational school (identified as a "shared time" school) may provide classes for students from a number of districts and show no membership. [2] A charter school is a school that provides free public elementary and/or secondary education to eligible students under a specific charter granted by the state legislature or other appropriate authority and that is designated by such authority to be a charter school. [3] A Title I School is designated under appropriate state and federal regulations as a high-poverty school that is eligible for participation in programs authorized by Title I of P.L. 107-110. The 1998-99 estimates exclude a large number of schools that did not report whether they were Title I. [4] A magnet school or program is a special school or program designed to attract students of different racial/ethnic backgrounds in an effort to reduce, prevent, or eliminate racial isolation and/or provide an academic or social focus on a particular theme. [5] Race categories exclude persons of Hispanic ethnicity.

Source: U.S. Department of Education, National Center for Education Statistics, *The Condition of Education 2011,* May 2011. See also <nces.ed.gov/pubsearch/pubsinfo.asp?pubid=2011033>.

Table 269. Private Schools: 2009 to 2010

[5,488 represents 5,488,000. Based on the Private School Survey, conducted every 2 years; see source for details. For composition of regions, see map inside front cover]

Characteristic	Schools				Students (1,000)				Teachers (1,000) [1]			
	Number	Ele-mentary	Sec-ondary	Com-bined	Total	Ele-mentary	Sec-ondary	Com-bined	Total	Ele-mentary	Sec-ondary	Com-bined
Total	**33,366**	**21,425**	**2,776**	**9,165**	**5,488**	**2,937**	**786**	**1,766**	**437**	**194**	**68**	**175**
School type:												
Catholic	7,115	5,679	1,097	339	2,160	1,455	587	118	143	89	43	10
Parochial	3,111	2,893	145	73	856	762	67	28	53	46	5	2
Diocesan	2,969	2,384	487	98	909	613	261	35	58	37	18	3
Private	1,035	402	465	168	395	80	259	55	31	6	20	6
Other religious	15,616	8,903	776	5,937	2,076	884	107	1,086	172	63	11	98
Conservative Christian	4,614	1,645	147	2,823	737	209	18	511	60	15	2	43
Affiliated	2,882	1,789	259	834	516	246	43	226	45	19	5	21
Unaffiliated	8,120	5,470	370	2,280	823	429	46	349	67	29	5	33
Nonsectarian	10,635	6,842	903	2,889	1,252	599	92	562	123	43	13	67
Regular	5,231	3,899	319	1,014	818	361	64	392	76	24	9	43
Special emphasis	3,821	2,703	322	797	328	223	16	89	29	17	2	10
Special education	1,582	240	263	1,079	107	14	12	81	18	2	2	14
Program emphasis:												
Regular elem/sec	22,565	13,812	2,048	6,705	4,648	2,366	742	1,541	367	161	61	144
Montessori	2,653	2,438	8	207	213	193	1	19	15	13	(Z)	2
Special program emphasis	917	411	102	405	128	50	12	66	15	5	1	9
Special education	1,779	278	276	1,225	118	16	12	90	20	3	2	15
Vocational/technical	2	–	1	1	1	–	(Z)	1	(Z)	–	(Z)	(Z)
Alternative	1,327	363	341	623	95	26	19	50	10	3	2	6
Early childhood	4,122	4,122	(X)	–	285	285	(X)	–	10	10	(X)	–
Size:												
Less than 50	11,065	7,113	842	3,110	296	198	19	79	34	17	4	13
50 to 149	10,469	7,160	541	2,767	950	656	48	245	82	46	6	30
150 to 299	6,695	4,742	446	1,506	1,423	1,004	99	320	107	64	10	33
300 to 499	3,013	1,770	382	861	1,155	676	150	329	87	43	13	30
500 to 749	1,276	536	284	456	769	312	176	281	57	18	13	25
750 or more	848	104	279	464	896	91	294	511	70	5	20	44
Region:												
Northeast	7,643	4,982	923	1,739	1,310	686	270	353	115	47	25	43
Midwest	8,419	6,226	636	1,557	1,296	840	212	243	92	53	16	23
South	10,483	5,618	601	4,263	1,842	807	159	876	153	56	14	83
West	6,821	4,600	616	1,605	1,041	604	144	293	77	38	12	27

– Represents zero. X Not applicable. Z Less than 500. [1] Full-time equivalents.

Source: U.S. National Center for Education Statistics, Private School Universe Survey, 2009-2010; <http://nces.ed.gov/surveys/pss/>.

Table 270. Private Elementary and Secondary School Teachers—Selected Characteristics: 2007 to 2008

[80 represents 80,000. For school year. Based on the 2007–08 Schools and Staffing Survey Private School Teacher Questionnaire, and subject to sampling error; for details, see source at <http://nces.ed.gov/surveys/sass/>. Excludes prekindergarten teachers. See Table 261 for similar data on public school teachers]

Characteristic	Unit	Age					Sex		Race/ethnicity		
		Under 30 years old	30 to 39 years old	40 to 49 years old	50 to 59 years old	60 years old and over	Male	Fe-male	White [1]	Black [1]	His-panic [2]
Total teachers [3]	**1,000**	**80**	**109**	**116**	**128**	**56**	**127**	**362**	**423**	**20**	**29**
Highest degree held:											
Bachelor's	Percent	68.3	52.9	54.4	49.8	43.6	45.7	56.8	53.5	55.3	59.3
Master's	Percent	19.1	33.7	30.1	39.8	39.9	37.6	31.1	34.2	22.2	20.9
Education specialist	Percent	1.2	2.3	2.9	2.7	6.5	4.2	2.4	2.9	1.6	3.7
Doctorate	Percent	–	1.9	3.5	2.0	5.1	5.4	1.3	2.4	(S)	(S)
Full-time teaching experience:											
Less than 3 years	Percent	55.5	24.4	20.4	13.2	7.2	24.1	23.5	22.5	30.2	31.9
3 to 9 years	Percent	44.2	49.7	30.4	17.8	7.5	29.5	31.6	30.6	40.6	29.8
10 to 20 years	Percent	(S)	25.8	34.3	25.8	17.2	22.2	22.8	22.6	16.4	25.9
20 years or more	Percent	–	(S)	14.9	43.2	68.1	24.2	22.2	24.3	12.7	12.3
Full-time teachers	1,000	69	90	89	99	41	99	289	334	17	23
School related income	Dol.	31,800	36,380	36,780	41,310	44,280	42,960	35,940	38,000	32,630	36,120
Annual salary	Dol.	30,090	34,650	35,270	39,850	42,740	40,380	34,700	36,500	30,300	34,070

– Represents or rounds to zero. S Reporting standards not met. The standard error for this estimate is 50 percent or more of the estimate's value. [1] Non-Hispanic. [2] Persons of Hispanic origin may be of any race. [3] Includes teachers with no degrees and associate's degrees, not shown separately.

Source: U.S. Department of Education, National Center for Education Statistics, Schools and Staffing Survey (SASS), "Private School Teacher Data Files, 2007–08", accessed September 2013. See <http://nces.ed.gov/surveys/sass/>.

Table 271. SAT Scores and Characteristics of College-Bound Seniors: 1980 to 2012

[For school year ending in year shown. Data are for the SAT I: Reasoning Tests. SAT I: Reasoning Test replaced the SAT in March 1994. Scores between the two tests have been equated to the same 200–800 scale and are thus comparable. Scores for 1995 and prior years have been recentered and revised]

Type of test and characteristic	Unit	1980	1990	2000	2005	2007 [2]	2008	2009	2010	2011	2012
AVERAGE TEST SCORES [1]											
Critical reading, total.........	Point	502	500	505	508	501	500	499	500	497	496
Male.....................	Point	506	505	507	513	503	502	502	502	500	498
Female...................	Point	498	496	504	505	500	499	497	498	495	493
Math, total...................	Point	492	501	514	520	514	514	514	515	514	514
Male.....................	Point	515	521	533	538	532	532	533	533	531	532
Female...................	Point	473	483	498	504	499	499	498	499	500	499
Writing.....................	Point	(X)	(X)	(X)	(X)	493	493	492	491	489	488
Male.....................	Point	(X)	(X)	(X)	(X)	487	486	485	485	482	481
Female...................	Point	(X)	(X)	(X)	(X)	499	499	498	497	496	494
PARTICIPANTS											
Total [3].....................	1,000	991	1,026	1,260	1,476	1,534	1,563	1,573	1,597	1,647	1,664
Male.....................	Percent	48.3	47.8	46.3	46.5	46.4	46.6	46.7	46.8	46.8	46.7
White [4]...................	Percent	(NA)	73.4	66.4	62.3	60.4	59.3	57.7	56.3	54.6	53.0
Black [4]...................	Percent	(NA)	10.0	11.1	11.6	12.0	12.4	13.0	13.3	13.6	13.5
Obtaining scores [1] of— 600 or above:											
Critical reading............	Percent	(NA)	20.3	21.0	22.5	20.9	20.8	20.3	20.3	20.2	19.5
Math.....................	Percent	(NA)	20.4	24.2	26.5	24.3	24.8	25.5	25.2	25.3	25.6
Writing...................	Percent	(X)	(X)	(X)	(X)	18.2	18.0	18.4	18.2	18.1	17.8
Below 400:											
Critical reading............	Percent	(NA)	17.3	15.9	15.5	16.9	17.4	17.8	17.8	18.3	19.0
Math.....................	Percent	(NA)	15.8	14.7	13.8	15.1	15.4	15.5	15.1	15.2	15.5
Writing...................	Percent	(X)	(X)	(X)	(X)	18.8	19.1	19.8	19.8	20.6	20.9

NA Not available. X Not applicable. [1] Minimum score, 200; maximum score, 800. [2] Starting with 2007, data reflect examinees who tested through June of senior year. [3] 991 represents 991,000. [4] Nonresponse excluded from denominator.

Source: The College Board, *2012 College-Bound Seniors: Total Group Profile Report*, © 1975 to 2012. Reproduced with permission. See also <http://www.collegeboard.com>.

Table 272. ACT Program Scores and Characteristics of College-Bound Students: 1970 to 2013

[For academic year ending in year shown. Except as indicated, test scores and characteristics of college-bound students. Through 1980, data based on 10 percent sample; thereafter, based on all ACT tested graduating seniors]

Type of test and characteristic	Unit	1970	1980	1990 [1]	1995 [1]	2000 [1]	2009 [1]	2010 [1]	2011 [1]	2012 [1]	2013 [1]
TEST SCORES [2]											
Composite.........................	Point	19.9	18.5	20.6	20.8	21.0	21.1	21.0	21.1	21.1	20.9
Male.............................	Point	20.3	19.3	21.0	21.0	21.2	21.3	21.2	21.2	21.2	20.9
Female...........................	Point	19.4	17.9	20.3	20.7	20.9	20.9	20.9	21.0	21.0	20.9
English..........................	Point	18.5	17.9	20.5	20.2	20.5	20.6	20.5	20.6	20.5	20.2
Male.............................	Point	17.6	17.3	20.1	19.8	20.0	20.2	20.1	20.2	20.2	19.8
Female...........................	Point	19.4	18.3	20.9	20.6	20.9	20.9	20.8	20.9	20.9	20.6
Math.............................	Point	20.0	17.4	19.9	20.2	20.7	21.0	21.0	21.1	21.1	20.9
Male.............................	Point	21.1	18.9	20.7	20.9	21.4	21.6	21.6	21.6	21.7	21.4
Female...........................	Point	18.8	16.2	19.3	19.7	20.2	20.4	20.5	20.6	20.6	20.5
Reading [3].......................	Point	19.7	17.2	(NA)	21.3	21.4	21.4	21.3	21.3	21.3	21.1
Male.............................	Point	20.3	18.2	(NA)	21.1	21.2	21.3	21.1	21.1	21.2	20.9
Female...........................	Point	19.0	16.4	(NA)	21.4	21.5	21.4	21.4	21.4	21.4	21.4
Science reasoning [4].............	Point	20.8	21.1	(NA)	21.0	21.0	20.9	20.9	20.9	20.9	20.7
Male.............................	Point	21.6	22.4	(NA)	21.6	21.6	21.4	21.4	21.4	21.4	21.2
Female...........................	Point	20.0	20.0	(NA)	20.5	20.6	20.4	20.5	20.5	20.5	20.4
PARTICIPANTS [5]											
Total [6].........................	1,000	788	822	817	945	1,065	1,480	1,569	1,623	1,666	1,799
Male.............................	Percent	52	45	46	44	43	45	45	46	46	46
White............................	Percent	(NA)	83	73	69	72	64	62	60	59	58
Black............................	Percent	4	8	9	9	10	13	14	14	13	13
Obtaining composite scores of: [7]											
27 or above......................	Percent	14	13	12	13	14	16	16	17	17	16
18 or below......................	Percent	21	33	35	34	32	34	35	34	34	36

NA Not available. [1] Beginning 1990, not comparable with previous years because a new version of the ACT was introduced. Estimated average composite scores for prior years: 1989, 20.6; 1988, 1987, and 1986, 20.8. [2] Minimum score, 1; maximum score, 36. [3] Prior to 1990, social studies; data not comparable with previous years. [4] Prior to 1990, natural sciences; data not comparable with previous years. [5] Beginning 1985, data are for seniors who graduated in year shown and had taken the ACT in their sophomore, junior, or senior years. Data by race are for those responding to the race question. [6] 788 represents 788,000. [7] Prior to 1990, 26 or above and 15 or below.

Source: ACT, Inc., Iowa City, IA, Most recent score reported in the *High School Profile Report*, annual ©. Reproduced with permission.

Table 273. Proficiency Levels on Selected NAEP Tests for Students in Public Schools by State: 2011

[Represents percent of public school students scoring at or above basic and proficient levels. Basic denotes mastery of the knowledge and skills that are fundamental for proficient work at a given grade level. Proficient represents solid academic performance. Students reaching this level demonstrated competency over challenging subject matter. For more detail, see <http://nationsreportcard.gov/>. Based on the National Assessment of Educational Progress (NAEP) tests which are administered to a representative sample of students in public schools, private schools, and Department of Defense schools. Data shown here are for public school students only]

State	Grade 4 Math At or above Basic	Grade 4 Math At or above Proficient	Grade 8 Math At or above Basic	Grade 8 Math At or above Proficient	Grade 4 Reading At or above Basic	Grade 4 Reading At or above Proficient	Grade 8 Reading At or above Basic	Grade 8 Reading At or above Proficient
U.S. average..................	82	40	72	34	66	32	75	32
Alabama.........................	75	27	60	20	67	31	69	26
Alaska............................	78	37	74	35	56	26	73	31
Arizona..........................	77	34	68	31	58	26	71	28
Arkansas.......................	81	37	70	29	63	30	71	28
California.......................	74	34	61	25	56	25	65	24
Colorado........................	84	47	80	43	71	39	81	40
Connecticut....................	82	45	75	38	73	42	83	45
Delaware........................	84	39	74	32	72	36	77	33
District of Columbia..........	60	22	48	17	44	19	51	16
Florida...........................	84	37	68	28	71	35	73	30
Georgia..........................	80	37	68	28	66	32	74	28
Hawaii............................	80	40	68	30	59	27	68	26
Idaho.............................	83	39	77	37	69	33	81	34
Illinois...........................	80	38	73	33	65	33	77	34
Indiana...........................	87	44	77	34	68	33	78	32
Iowa..............................	86	43	77	34	69	33	77	33
Kansas...........................	90	48	80	41	71	36	79	35
Kentucky........................	85	39	72	31	72	35	79	36
Louisiana.......................	73	26	63	22	55	23	66	22
Maine............................	87	45	78	39	70	32	80	39
Maryland........................	86	48	74	40	75	43	80	40
Massachusetts................	93	58	86	51	83	50	84	46
Michigan........................	78	35	71	31	66	31	77	32
Minnesota......................	88	53	83	48	70	35	81	39
Mississippi.....................	72	25	58	19	55	22	65	21
Missouri.........................	83	41	73	32	67	34	79	35
Montana.........................	87	45	83	46	73	36	86	42
Nebraska........................	83	39	74	33	70	36	81	35
Nevada..........................	79	36	67	29	58	25	69	26
New Hampshire................	92	57	82	44	78	43	84	40
New Jersey.....................	89	51	82	47	78	44	84	45
New Mexico.....................	75	30	64	24	53	21	68	22
New York........................	80	36	70	30	68	35	76	35
North Carolina.................	88	44	75	37	68	34	74	31
North Dakota...................	90	46	85	43	74	36	83	34
Ohio..............................	86	45	79	39	71	34	79	37
Oklahoma.......................	83	33	72	27	64	27	73	27
Oregon...........................	77	37	72	33	63	30	76	33
Pennsylvania...................	87	48	74	39	74	41	77	38
Rhode Island...................	84	43	73	34	70	35	76	33
South Carolina.................	79	36	70	32	61	28	72	27
South Dakota..................	86	40	82	42	69	31	83	35
Tennessee......................	75	30	64	24	60	26	70	27
Texas............................	85	39	81	40	64	28	74	27
Utah..............................	85	43	73	35	68	33	79	35
Vermont.........................	89	49	82	46	73	41	82	44
Virginia..........................	87	46	78	40	72	39	78	36
Washington.....................	83	45	77	40	67	34	77	37
West Virginia...................	78	31	65	21	61	27	68	24
Wisconsin.......................	86	47	79	41	68	34	79	35
Wyoming........................	88	44	80	37	71	34	82	38

Source: U.S. National Center for Education Statistics, "National Assessment of Educational Progress (NAEP), 2011 Mathematics and Reading Assessments" <http://nces.ed.gov/nationsreportcard/naepdata/dataset.aspx>, accessed August 2013.

Table 274. Public High School Graduates by State: 1990 to 2011

[In thousands (2,320.3 represents 2,320,300). For school year ending in year shown]

State	1990	2000	2010	2011, proj.	State	1990	2000	2010	2011, proj.
United States	**2,320.3**	**2,553.8**	**3,128.0**	**3,103.5**	Missouri	49.0	52.8	64.0	62.5
Alabama	40.5	37.8	43.2	44.5	Montana	9.4	10.9	10.1	9.7
Alaska	5.4	6.6	8.2	7.7	Nebraska	17.7	20.1	19.4	19.6
Arizona	32.1	38.3	61.1	66.5	Nevada	9.5	14.6	21.0	25.0
Arkansas	26.5	27.3	28.3	28.4	New Hampshire	10.8	11.8	15.0	14.3
California	236.3	309.9	405.0	386.2	New Jersey	69.8	74.4	96.2	95.2
Colorado	33.0	38.9	49.3	51.8	New Mexico	14.9	18.0	18.6	19.1
Connecticut	27.9	31.6	34.5	38.5	New York	143.3	141.7	183.8	185.9
Delaware	5.6	6.1	8.1	8.2	North Carolina	64.8	62.1	88.7	87.4
District of Columbia [1]	3.6	2.7	3.6	3.3	North Dakota	7.7	8.6	7.2	7.1
Florida	88.9	106.7	156.1	163.6	Ohio	114.5	111.7	123.4	108.0
Georgia	56.6	62.6	91.6	92.2	Oklahoma	35.6	37.6	38.5	38.1
Hawaii	10.3	10.4	11.0	11.1	Oregon	25.5	30.2	34.7	35.4
Idaho	12.0	16.2	17.8	17.4	Pennsylvania	110.5	114.0	131.2	132.1
Illinois	108.1	111.8	139.0	132.7	Rhode Island	7.8	8.5	9.9	9.9
Indiana	60.0	57.0	64.6	65.5	South Carolina	32.5	31.6	40.4	39.9
Iowa	31.8	33.9	34.5	33.7	South Dakota	7.7	9.3	8.2	8.6
Kansas	25.4	29.1	31.6	31.3	Tennessee	46.1	41.6	62.4	62.5
Kentucky	38.0	36.8	42.7	41.9	Texas	172.5	212.9	280.9	280.0
Louisiana	36.1	38.4	36.6	34.5	Utah	21.2	32.5	31.5	30.3
Maine	13.8	12.2	14.1	14.0	Vermont	6.1	6.7	7.2	6.8
Maryland	41.6	47.8	59.1	57.9	Virginia	60.6	65.6	81.5	81.6
Massachusetts	55.9	53.0	64.5	63.8	Washington	45.9	57.6	66.0	66.6
Michigan	93.8	97.7	110.7	110.3	West Virginia	21.9	19.4	17.7	17.3
Minnesota	49.1	57.4	59.7	59.7	Wisconsin	52.0	58.5	64.7	63.6
Mississippi	25.2	24.2	25.5	26.9	Wyoming	5.8	6.5	5.7	5.6

[1] Beginning in 1990, graduates from adult programs are excluded.

Source: U.S. National Center for Education Statistics, *Digest of Education Statistics*, "Advance Release of Selected 2012 Digest Tables," <http://www.nces.ed.gov/programs/digest/>, accessed May 2013.

Table 275. High School Dropouts by Race and Hispanic Origin: 1980 to 2011

[In percent. As of October. Dropouts are persons 18 to 24 years old who have not completed high school and are not enrolled, regardless of when they dropped out]

Item	1980	1985	1990 [1]	1995	2000	2005	2007	2008	2009	2010	2011
Total [2]	15.6	13.9	14.4	13.9	12.4	11.3	10.2	9.3	9.4	8.7	8.3
White [3]	14.4	13.5	14.1	13.6	12.2	11.3	10.0	8.8	9.1	8.5	8.2
Male	15.7	14.7	15.4	14.3	13.5	13.2	11.7	9.8	10.5	9.7	9.1
Female	13.2	12.3	12.8	13.0	10.9	9.4	8.3	7.8	7.7	7.3	7.2
Black [3]	23.5	17.6	16.4	14.4	15.3	12.9	10.2	12.0	11.6	10.1	8.8
Male	26.0	18.8	18.6	14.2	17.4	14.8	10.0	10.2	13.9	12.1	9.4
Female	21.5	16.6	14.5	14.6	13.5	11.2	10.3	13.7	9.5	8.2	8.3
Hispanic [4]	40.3	31.5	37.7	34.7	32.3	27.3	25.3	22.3	20.8	18.5	16.3
Male	42.6	35.8	40.3	34.2	36.8	32.1	29.2	24.3	22.5	21.3	17.5
Female	38.1	27.0	35.0	35.4	27.3	21.8	21.1	20.2	19.1	15.4	14.9

[1] Beginning 1990, reflects new editing procedures for cases with missing data on school enrollment. [2] Includes other races, not shown separately. [3] Beginning 2005, for persons who selected this race group only. See footnote 2, Table 241. [4] Persons of Hispanic origin may be of any race.

Source: U.S. Census Bureau, Current Population Reports, PPL-148, P-20, and earlier reports; and "School Enrollment." <http://www.census.gov/hhes/school/index.html>, accessed August 2013.

Table 276. High School Dropouts by Age, Race, and Hispanic Origin: 1980 to 2011

[5,212 represents 5,212,000. As of October. For persons 14 to 24 years old. See headnote, Table 275 for definition of dropouts. Based on Current Population Survey; see text, Section 1 and Appendix III]

Age and race	Number of dropouts (1,000)					Percent of population				
	1980	1990	2000	2010	2011	1980	1990	2000	2010	2011
Total dropouts [1,2]	**5,212**	**3,854**	**3,883**	**2,952**	**2,821**	**12.0**	**10.1**	**9.1**	**6.4**	**6.1**
16 to 17 years	709	418	460	227	233	8.8	6.3	5.8	2.7	2.8
18 to 21 years	2,578	1,921	2,005	1,445	1,300	15.8	13.4	12.9	8.4	7.5
22 to 24 years	1,798	1,458	1,310	1,144	1,181	15.2	13.8	11.8	9.2	9.3
White [2,3]	4,169	3,127	3,065	2,232	2,142	11.3	10.1	9.1	6.3	6.0
16 to 17 years	619	334	366	181	176	9.2	6.4	5.8	2.9	2.8
18 to 21 years	2,032	1,516	1,558	1,048	1,010	14.7	13.1	12.6	8.0	7.6
22 to 24 years	1,416	1,235	1,040	893	876	14.0	14.0	11.7	9.2	8.9
Black [2,3]	934	611	705	498	457	16.0	10.9	10.9	7.2	6.6
16 to 17 years	80	73	84	30	40	6.9	6.9	7.0	2.3	3.2
18 to 21 years	486	345	383	283	200	23.0	16.0	16.0	10.5	7.8
22 to 24 years	346	185	232	167	200	24.0	13.5	14.3	9.4	10.3
Hispanic [2,4]	919	1,122	1,499	1,122	1,070	29.5	26.8	23.5	12.8	11.5
16 to 17 years	92	89	121	40	65	16.6	12.9	11.0	2.7	3.9
18 to 21 years	470	502	733	506	416	40.3	32.9	30.0	15.2	12.1
22 to 24 years	323	523	602	543	559	40.6	42.8	35.5	23.2	22.0

[1] Includes other groups not shown separately. [2] Includes persons 14 to 15 years not shown separately. [3] Beginning 2005, for persons who selected this race only. See footnote 2, Table 241. [4] Persons of Hispanic origin may be of any race.

Source: U.S. Census Bureau, "School Enrollment, Detailed Tables, Table 1," <http://www.census.gov/hhes/school/data/index.html>, accessed June 2013; and earlier Current Population Reports, series PPL and P-20.

Table 277. Enrollment Status by Race, Hispanic Origin, and Sex: 2000 and 2011

[15,553 represents 15,553,000. As of October. For persons 18 to 21 years old. For the civilian noninstitutional population. Based on the Current Population Survey; see text, Section 1 and Appendix III]

Characteristic	Total persons 18 to 21 years old (1,000)		Percent distribution							
			Enrolled in high school		High school graduates				Not high school graduates and not enrolled in high school	
					Total		In college			
	2000	2011	2000	2011	2000	2011	2000	2011	2000	2011
Total [1]	**15,553**	**17,225**	**9.4**	**11.1**	**77.6**	**81.2**	**43.5**	**50.5**	**12.9**	**7.5**
White	12,383	13,299	8.9	10.3	78.5	82.0	44.4	51.5	12.6	7.6
Black	2,389	2,570	12.6	16.4	71.3	75.8	34.7	41.6	16.0	7.8
Hispanic [2]	2,439	3,438	12.5	11.6	57.2	76.1	25.3	43.8	30.0	12.1
Male [1]	7,814	8,839	11.0	12.6	74.7	79.3	38.9	46.1	14.3	8.0
White	6,313	6,823	10.6	11.8	75.7	79.9	39.8	46.9	13.7	8.1
Black	1,096	1,316	14.9	18.1	66.0	73.2	27.4	36.9	19.1	8.7
Hispanic [2]	1,269	1,875	14.4	13.1	51.8	73.4	21.9	38.8	33.7	13.2
Female [1]	7,739	8,386	7.9	9.5	80.6	83.3	48.1	55.2	11.5	7.1
White	6,070	6,475	7.1	8.7	81.3	84.1	49.3	56.3	11.4	7.0
Black	1,293	1,253	10.7	14.7	75.9	78.6	40.9	46.5	13.5	6.8
Hispanic [2]	1,169	1,563	10.6	9.9	63.1	79.4	28.9	49.8	26.1	10.7

[1] Includes other races not shown separately. [2] Persons of Hispanic origin may be of any race.

Source: U.S. Census Bureau, Current Population Reports, PPL-148, P-20, and earlier reports; and "School Enrollment," <http://www.census.gov/hhes/school/index.html>, accessed June 2013.

Table 278. General Educational Development (GED) Credentials Issued: 1980 to 2011

[GEDs issued in thousands (479 represents 479,000). For the 50 states and DC]

Year	GEDs issued	Percent distribution of GED test takers				
		16 to 18 years old [1]	19 to 24 years old [1]	25 to 29 years old	30 to 34 years old	35 years old and over
1980	479	37	27	13	8	15
1985	413	32	26	15	10	16
1990	410	22	39	13	10	15
1995	504	27	36	13	9	15
2000	487	33	37	11	7	13
2005	424	34	37	12	7	11
2006	398	35	36	12	6	11
2007	429	35	35	12	7	11
2008	469	34	35	13	7	11
2009	448	31	36	13	8	12
2010	452	27	37	14	9	14
2011	434	27	37	13	9	14

[1] For 1985 and prior years, 19-year-olds are included with the 16- to 18-year-olds instead of the 19- to 24-year-olds.

Source: U.S. National Center for Education Statistics, *Digest of Education Statistics*, "Advance Release of Selected 2012 Digest Tables," <http://www.nces.ed.gov/programs/digest/>, accessed May 2013.

Table 279. Public Elementary and Secondary School Estimated Finances by State: 2011

[In millions of dollars (599,146 represents $599,146,000,000), except as noted. For the school year ending in June]

State	Revenue receipts				Expenditures				
		Source					Current expenditures		
						Per capita [2] (dol.)	Elementary and secondary schools	Average per enrolled public school pupil [3]	
	Total	Federal	State	Local	Total [1]			Amount (dol.)	Rank
Total............................	**599,146**	**73,707**	**265,949**	**259,490**	**595,079**	**1,924**	**522,094**	**10,616**	**(X)**
Alabama........................	7,375	1,077	3,966	2,332	7,403	1,547	6,699	9,141	37
Alaska..........................	2,358	420	1,416	522	2,444	3,422	2,205	16,689	4
Arizona.........................	8,336	1,246	3,055	4,035	8,610	1,343	7,264	6,791	49
Arkansas.......................	5,157	827	3,701	629	5,631	1,927	4,892	10,146	27
California.......................	68,528	9,990	37,691	20,847	66,788	1,789	57,916	9,329	34
Colorado.......................	8,700	969	3,494	4,236	8,628	1,709	7,348	8,718	42
Connecticut....................	9,575	796	3,172	5,607	9,191	2,570	8,534	15,241	6
Delaware.......................	1,712	192	1,010	510	1,756	1,952	1,551	12,029	15
District of Columbia..........	1,283	156	(X)	1,128	1,297	2,144	971	13,623	10
Florida..........................	26,446	4,710	9,069	12,667	26,992	1,433	23,999	9,081	38
Georgia.........................	18,028	2,267	7,492	8,268	17,175	1,768	15,551	9,273	35
Hawaii..........................	2,500	347	2,089	63	2,259	1,657	2,174	12,103	14
Idaho...........................	2,089	293	1,320	476	1,961	1,248	1,817	6,588	50
Illinois..........................	28,695	2,895	10,031	15,769	26,497	2,063	22,634	10,871	20
Indiana.........................	11,852	1,024	7,338	3,489	10,854	1,672	9,656	9,272	36
Iowa............................	5,877	597	2,538	2,742	5,828	1,911	4,865	10,033	29
Kansas.........................	5,537	612	2,945	1,980	5,654	1,978	4,591	9,565	30
Kentucky.......................	7,103	1,165	3,704	2,234	7,252	1,668	6,330	9,403	32
Louisiana.......................	8,017	1,497	3,269	3,251	8,090	1,780	7,152	10,279	26
Maine...........................	2,374	289	820	1,264	2,445	1,842	2,228	12,144	13
Maryland........................	13,439	1,256	5,508	6,675	12,994	2,246	11,838	13,891	9
Massachusetts.................	15,256	1,197	5,783	8,275	14,788	2,256	13,715	14,357	8
Michigan........................	18,410	2,526	9,846	6,039	18,262	1,849	16,086	10,354	25
Minnesota......................	10,756	843	6,290	3,624	10,445	1,967	8,970	10,705	22
Mississippi.....................	4,508	1,006	2,071	1,430	4,346	1,463	3,906	7,979	47
Missouri........................	9,843	1,345	3,828	4,670	9,749	1,626	8,608	9,393	33
Montana........................	1,618	265	714	640	1,635	1,650	1,515	10,694	23
Nebraska.......................	3,802	572	1,153	2,077	3,657	1,998	3,225	10,812	21
Nevada.........................	4,145	447	2,360	1,339	4,257	1,574	3,689	8,444	44
New Hampshire................	2,845	185	1,061	1,599	2,838	2,155	2,587	13,335	11
New Jersey.....................	25,306	1,284	9,331	14,691	24,965	2,837	23,658	17,435	2
New Mexico.....................	3,591	636	2,355	600	3,688	1,785	3,009	8,956	40
New York.......................	57,536	5,118	23,188	29,230	59,175	3,051	53,712	19,649	1
North Carolina..................	14,410	2,047	7,489	4,874	13,693	1,432	12,106	8,135	46
North Dakota...................	1,263	187	630	445	1,253	1,857	1,107	11,747	18
Ohio............................	22,787	2,534	9,834	10,419	22,851	1,981	19,581	11,188	19
Oklahoma.......................	5,833	969	2,741	2,124	5,623	1,495	5,049	7,652	48
Oregon..........................	6,062	849	2,793	2,421	6,303	1,642	5,557	10,038	28
Pennsylvania...................	27,044	3,372	9,261	14,411	26,155	2,057	22,916	12,994	12
Rhode Island...................	2,199	234	769	1,196	2,183	2,074	2,090	14,662	7
South Carolina.................	7,761	1,042	3,339	3,381	7,940	1,712	6,507	8,979	39
South Dakota..................	1,295	262	375	658	1,340	1,641	1,112	8,833	41
Tennessee.....................	8,646	1,273	3,955	3,417	9,087	1,429	8,214	8,322	45
Texas...........................	50,856	7,818	19,623	23,415	52,528	2,080	41,955	8,504	43
Utah............................	4,136	501	2,058	1,577	4,193	1,511	3,492	5,963	51
Vermont.........................	1,506	107	1,329	70	1,526	2,439	1,449	17,016	3
Virginia..........................	14,418	1,427	5,351	7,640	14,465	1,803	13,043	10,433	24
Washington.....................	11,816	1,368	6,759	3,690	11,889	1,763	9,949	9,534	31
West Virginia...................	3,465	510	1,928	1,027	3,668	1,978	3,382	11,957	16
Wisconsin.......................	11,406	1,003	5,227	5,176	11,187	1,965	10,287	11,794	17
Wyoming........................	1,647	155	879	613	1,642	2,909	1,406	15,839	5

X Not applicable. [1] Includes interest on school debt and payments to state and local governments, not shown separately. [2] Based on U.S. Census Bureau estimated resident population, as of July 1, 2010. [3] Based on 2009-2010 enrollment counts, National Center for Education Statistics, Common Core of Data.

Source: U.S. Census Bureau, *Public Education Finances: 2011,* May 2013. See also <http://www.census.gov/govs/school/>.

Table 280. College Enrollment of Recent High School Completers: 1970 to 2011

[2,758 represents 2,758,000. For persons 16 to 24 years old who graduated from high school in the preceding 12 months. Includes persons receiving GEDs. Based on surveys and subject to sampling error; data will not agree with data in other tables]

Year	Number of high school completers (1,000)						Percent enrolled in college [5]					
	Total [1]	Male	Female	White [2]	Black [2,3]	His-panic [3,4]	Total [1]	Male	Female	White [2]	Black [2,3]	His-panic [3,4]
1970	2,758	1,343	1,415	2,461	(NA)	(NA)	51.7	55.2	48.5	52.0	(NA)	(NA)
1975	3,185	1,513	1,672	2,701	302	132	50.7	52.6	49.0	51.1	41.7	58.0
1980	3,088	1,498	1,589	2,554	350	130	49.3	46.7	51.8	49.8	42.7	52.3
1985	2,668	1,287	1,381	2,104	332	141	57.7	58.6	56.8	60.1	42.2	51.0
1990	2,362	1,173	1,189	1,819	331	121	60.1	58.0	62.2	63.0	46.8	42.7
1995	2,599	1,238	1,361	1,861	349	288	61.9	62.6	61.3	64.3	51.2	53.7
2000	2,756	1,251	1,505	1,938	393	300	63.3	59.9	66.2	65.7	54.9	52.9
2001	2,549	1,277	1,273	1,834	381	241	61.8	60.1	63.5	64.3	55.0	51.7
2002	2,796	1,412	1,384	1,903	382	344	65.2	62.1	68.4	69.1	59.4	53.6
2003	2,677	1,306	1,372	1,832	327	314	63.9	61.2	66.5	66.2	57.5	58.6
2004	2,752	1,327	1,425	1,854	398	286	66.7	61.4	71.5	68.8	62.5	61.8
2005	2,675	1,262	1,414	1,799	345	390	68.6	66.5	70.4	73.2	55.7	54.0
2006	2,692	1,328	1,363	1,805	318	382	66.0	65.8	66.1	68.5	55.5	57.9
2007	2,955	1,511	1,444	2,043	416	355	67.2	66.1	68.3	69.5	55.7	64.0
2008	3,151	1,640	1,511	2,091	416	458	68.6	65.9	71.6	71.7	55.7	63.9
2009	2,937	1,407	1,531	1,863	415	459	70.1	66.0	73.8	71.3	69.5	59.3
2010	3,160	1,679	1,482	1,937	461	507	68.1	62.8	74.0	70.5	62.0	59.7
2011	3,079	1,611	1,468	1,747	464	623	68.2	64.7	72.2	68.3	67.1	66.6

NA Not available. [1] Includes other races not shown separately. [2] Beginning 2003, for persons of this race group only. See footnote 2, Table 241. [3] Due to small sample size, data are subject to relatively large sampling errors. [4] Persons of Hispanic origin may be of any race. [5] As of October.

Source: U.S. National Center for Education Statistics, Digest of Education Statistics, "Advance Release of Selected 2012 Digest Tables," and earlier releases, <http://www.nces.ed.gov/programs/digest/>, accessed May 2013.

Table 281. College Enrollment by Sex and Attendance Status: 2005 to 2012

[In thousands (17,487 represents 17,487,000). As of Fall. Includes enrollment at branch campuses, some additional (primarily 2-year) colleges, and excludes a few institutions that did not award degrees. Includes enrollment at institutions that were eligible to participate in Title IV federal financial aid programs. Includes unclassified students (students taking courses for credit, but are not candidates for degrees)]

Sex and age	2005		2009		2010		2011		2012 proj.	
	Total	Part-time	Total	Part-time	Total	Part-time	Total	Part-time	Total	Part-time
Total	17,487	6,690	20,428	7,705	21,016	7,934	20,994	7,993	21,253	8,107
Male	7,456	2,653	8,770	3,099	9,045	3,208	9,026	3,233	9,107	3,264
14 to 17 years old	68	15	103	25	94	23	95	20	90	31
18 to 19 years old	1,523	184	1,806	226	1,820	245	1,819	287	1,896	308
20 to 21 years old	1,658	260	1,876	329	1,948	362	1,973	382	2,102	460
22 to 24 years old	1,410	428	1,606	430	1,723	508	1,682	510	1,760	491
25 to 29 years old	1,057	551	1,382	717	1,410	695	1,442	706	1,354	714
30 to 34 years old	591	365	709	428	731	430	715	419	691	400
35 years old and over	1,149	850	1,287	944	1,320	944	1,300	908	1,215	859
Female	10,032	4,038	11,658	4,606	11,971	4,726	11,968	4,760	12,146	4,843
14 to 17 years old	119	21	114	11	108	9	108	12	118	13
18 to 19 years old	1,920	233	2,236	303	2,236	316	2,206	325	2,447	390
20 to 21 years old	1,905	327	2,069	345	2,154	377	2,201	400	2,284	487
22 to 24 years old	1,704	564	1,987	629	2,036	666	2,027	694	2,063	643
25 to 29 years old	1,413	745	1,713	858	1,844	953	1,877	985	1,703	866
30 to 34 years old	847	526	1,032	651	1,074	630	1,092	629	987	632
35 years old and over	2,123	1,623	2,507	1,810	2,520	1,775	2,458	1,716	2,544	1,812

Source: U.S. National Center for Education Statistics, Digest of Education Statistics, "Advance Release of Selected 2012 Digest Tables," <http://www.nces.ed.gov/programs/digest/>, accessed June 2013.

Table 282. Higher Education—Institutions and Enrollment: 1980 to 2011

[686 represents 686,000. As of Fall. Covers universities, colleges, professional schools, junior and teachers' colleges, both publicly and privately controlled, regular session. Includes estimates for institutions not reporting. See also Appendix III]

Item	Unit	1980	1990	2000	2005	2008	2009	2010	2011
ALL INSTITUTIONS									
Number of institutions [1]	**Number**	**3,231**	**3,559**	**4,182**	**4,276**	**4,409**	**4,495**	**4,599**	**4,706**
4-year	Number	1,957	2,141	2,450	2,582	2,719	2,774	2,870	2,968
2-year	Number	1,274	1,418	1,732	1,694	1,690	1,721	1,729	1,738
Instructional staff—									
(lecturer or above) [2]	**1,000**	**686**	**817**	**(NA)**	**1,290**	**(NA)**	**1,439**	**(NA)**	**1,524**
Percent full-time	Percent	66	61	(NA)	52	(NA)	51	(NA)	50
Total enrollment [3],[4]	**1,000**	**12,097**	**13,819**	**15,312**	**17,487**	**19,103**	**20,428**	**21,016**	**20,994**
Male	1,000	5,874	6,284	6,722	7,456	8,189	8,770	9,045	9,026
Female	1,000	6,223	7,535	8,591	10,032	10,914	11,658	11,971	11,968
4-year institutions	1,000	7,571	8,579	9,364	10,999	12,131	12,906	13,335	13,494
2-year institutions	1,000	4,526	5,240	5,948	6,488	6,971	7,521	7,681	7,500
Full-time	1,000	7,098	7,821	9,010	10,797	11,748	12,723	13,082	13,001
Part-time	1,000	4,999	5,998	6,303	6,690	7,355	7,705	7,934	7,993
Public	1,000	9,457	10,845	11,753	13,022	13,972	14,811	15,143	15,110
Private	1,000	2,640	2,974	3,560	4,466	5,131	5,617	5,873	5,884
Not-for-profit	1,000	2,528	2,760	3,109	3,455	3,662	3,765	3,855	3,927
For profit	1,000	112	213	450	1,011	1,469	1,852	2,018	1,957
Undergraduate [4]	1,000	10,475	11,959	13,155	14,964	16,366	17,565	18,079	18,063
Men	1,000	5,000	5,380	5,778	6,409	7,067	7,595	7,835	7,817
Women	1,000	5,475	6,579	7,377	8,555	9,299	9,970	10,244	10,246
First-time freshmen	1,000	2,588	2,257	2,428	2,657	3,025	3,210	3,157	3,093
First professional	1,000	278	273	307	337	(NA)	(NA)	(NA)	(NA)
Men	1,000	199	167	164	170	(NA)	(NA)	(NA)	(NA)
Women	1,000	78	107	143	167	(NA)	(NA)	(NA)	(NA)
Graduate [4]	1,000	1,343	1,586	1,850	2,186	(NA)	(NA)	(NA)	(NA)
Men	1,000	675	737	780	877	(NA)	(NA)	(NA)	(NA)
Women	1,000	670	849	1,071	1,309	(NA)	(NA)	(NA)	(NA)
2-YEAR INSTITUTIONS									
Number of institutions [1]	Number	1,274	1,418	1,732	1,694	1,690	1,721	1,729	1,738
Public	Number	945	972	1,076	1,053	1,024	1,000	978	967
Private	Number	329	446	656	641	666	721	751	771
Instructional staff—									
(lecturer or above) [2]	1,000	192	(NA)	(NA)	373	(NA)	401	(NA)	408
Enrollment [3],[4]	1,000	4,526	5,240	5,948	6,488	6,971	7,521	7,681	7,500
Public	1,000	4,329	4,996	5,697	6,184	6,640	7,101	7,218	7,062
Private	1,000	198	244	251	304	331	420	463	438
Male	1,000	2,047	2,233	2,559	2,680	2,936	3,197	3,265	3,172
Female	1,000	2,479	3,007	3,390	3,808	4,035	4,325	4,416	4,328
4-YEAR INSTITUTIONS									
Number of institutions [1]	Number	1,957	2,141	2,450	2,582	2,719	2,774	2,870	2,968
Public	Number	552	595	622	640	652	672	678	682
Private	Number	1,405	1,546	1,828	1,942	2,067	2,102	2,192	2,286
Instructional staff—									
(lecturer or above) [2]	1,000	494	(NA)	(NA)	917	(NA)	1,038	(NA)	1,116
Enrollment [3],[4]	1,000	7,571	8,579	9,364	10,999	12,131	12,906	13,335	13,494
Public	1,000	5,129	5,848	6,055	6,838	7,332	7,709	7,925	8,048
Private	1,000	2,442	2,730	3,308	4,162	4,800	5,197	5,410	5,446
Male	1,000	3,827	4,051	4,163	4,776	5,253	5,573	5,780	5,855
Female	1,000	3,743	4,527	5,201	6,224	6,878	7,333	7,556	7,639

NA Not available. [1] Number of institutions includes count of branch campuses. Due to revised survey procedures, data beginning 1990 are not comparable with previous years. Beginning 2000, data reflect a new classification of institutions; this classification includes some additional, primarily 2-year, colleges and excludes a few institutions that did not award degrees. Includes institutions that were eligible to participate in Title IV federal financial aid programs. Includes schools accredited by the National Association of Trade and Technical Schools. [2] Due to revised survey methods, data beginning 1990 not comparable with previous years. [3] Branch campuses counted according to actual status, e.g., 2-year branch in 2-year category. [4] Includes unclassified students (those taking courses for credit, but not candidates for degrees).

Source: U.S. National Center for Education Statistics, Digest of Education Statistics, "Advance Release of Selected 2012 Digest Tables," and earlier releases, <http://nces.ed.gov/Programs/digest/>, accessed August 2013.

Table 283. College Enrollment by Selected Characteristics: 1990 to 2011

[In thousands (13,818.6 represents 13,818,600). As of Fall. Nonresident alien students are not distributed among racial/ethnic groups]

Characteristic	1990	2000 [1]	2005 [1]	2008 [1]	2009 [1]	2010 [1]	2011 [1]
Total	**13,818.6**	**15,312.3**	**17,487.5**	**19,102.8**	**20,427.7**	**21,016.1**	**20,994.1**
Male	6,283.9	6,721.8	7,455.9	8,188.9	8,769.5	9,044.8	9,026.5
Female	7,534.7	8,590.5	10,031.6	10,913.9	11,658.2	11,971.3	11,967.6
Public	10,844.7	11,752.8	13,021.8	13,972.2	14,810.6	15,142.8	15,110.2
Private	2,973.9	3,559.5	4,465.6	5,130.7	5,617.1	5,873.3	5,883.9
2-year	5,240.1	5,948.4	6,488.1	6,971.4	7,521.4	7,680.9	7,500.0
4-year	8,578.6	9,363.9	10,999.4	12,131.4	12,906.3	13,335.3	13,494.1
Undergraduate	11,959.2	13,155.4	14,964.0	16,365.7	17,565.3	18,078.7	18,063.0
Graduate	1,586.2	1,850.3	2,186.5	(NA)	(NA)	(NA)	(NA)
First professional	273.4	306.6	337.0	(NA)	(NA)	(NA)	(NA)
White [2]	**10,722.5**	**10,462.1**	**11,495.4**	**12,088.8**	**12,730.8**	**12,722.5**	**12,394.2**
Male	4,861.0	4,634.6	5,007.2	5,302.9	5,594.4	5,606.8	5,453.8
Female	5,861.5	5,827.5	6,488.2	6,785.9	7,136.4	7,115.7	6,940.3
Public	8,385.4	7,963.4	8,518.2	8,817.7	9,234.6	9,187.1	8,935.1
Private	2,337.0	2,498.7	2,977.3	3,271.1	3,496.2	3,535.4	3,459.1
2-year	3,954.3	3,804.1	3,998.6	4,101.6	4,373.4	4,324.4	4,087.2
4-year	6,768.1	6,658.0	7,496.9	7,987.1	8,357.4	8,398.2	8,307.0
Undergraduate	9,272.6	8,983.5	9,828.6	10,339.2	10,915.3	10,897.7	10,611.6
Graduate	1,228.4	1,258.5	1,428.7	(NA)	(NA)	(NA)	(NA)
First professional	221.5	220.1	238.1	(NA)	(NA)	(NA)	(NA)
Black [2]	**1,247.0**	**1,730.3**	**2,214.6**	**2,584.5**	**2,919.8**	**3,038.8**	**3,067.9**
Male	484.7	635.3	774.1	911.8	1,037.1	1,089.1	1,103.5
Female	762.3	1,095.0	1,440.4	1,672.7	1,882.7	1,949.7	1,964.5
Public	976.4	1,319.2	1,580.4	1,759.2	1,937.2	1,988.6	2,013.3
Private	270.6	411.1	634.2	825.3	982.7	1,050.1	1,054.6
2-year	524.3	734.9	901.1	1,019.5	1,152.8	1,197.7	1,197.1
4-year	722.8	995.4	1,313.4	1,565.0	1,767.0	1,841.0	1,870.9
Undergraduate	1,147.2	1,548.9	1,955.4	2,269.3	2,577.4	2,676.5	2,698.9
Graduate	83.9	157.9	233.2	(NA)	(NA)	(NA)	(NA)
First professional	15.9	23.5	26.0	(NA)	(NA)	(NA)	(NA)
Hispanic	**782.4**	**1,461.8**	**1,882.0**	**2,272.9**	**2,546.7**	**2,741.4**	**2,890.1**
Male	353.9	627.1	774.6	946.7	1,066.2	1,154.6	1,214.2
Female	428.5	834.7	1,107.3	1,326.1	1,480.4	1,586.9	1,676.0
Public	671.4	1,229.3	1,525.6	1,832.4	2,017.7	2,157.4	2,275.8
Private	111.0	232.5	356.4	440.5	529.0	584.1	614.3
2-year	424.2	843.9	981.5	1,180.7	1,309.0	1,386.4	1,436.6
4-year	358.2	617.9	900.5	1,092.2	1,237.7	1,355.1	1,453.5
Undergraduate	724.6	1,351.0	1,733.6	2,103.5	2,362.5	2,543.6	2,685.1
Graduate	47.2	95.4	130.7	(NA)	(NA)	(NA)	(NA)
First professional	10.7	15.4	17.7	(NA)	(NA)	(NA)	(NA)
American Indian/ Alaska Native	**102.8**	**151.2**	**176.3**	**193.3**	**207.9**	**196.4**	**186.1**
Male	43.1	61.4	68.4	76.9	83.4	78.8	73.7
Female	59.7	89.7	107.9	116.4	124.5	117.6	112.4
Public	90.4	127.3	143.0	153.0	161.8	151.0	142.4
Private	12.4	23.9	33.3	40.3	46.1	45.4	43.6
2-year	54.9	74.7	80.7	85.5	90.3	87.4	81.0
4-year	47.9	76.5	95.6	108.6	117.7	109.0	105.1
Undergraduate	95.5	138.5	160.4	175.6	189.4	179.3	169.9
Graduate	6.2	10.3	13.4	(NA)	(NA)	(NA)	(NA)
First professional	1.1	2.3	2.5	(NA)	(NA)	(NA)	(NA)
Asian/Pacific Islander	**572.4**	**978.2**	**1,134.4**	**1,302.8**	**1,337.7**	**1,282.2**	**1,282.5**
Male	294.9	465.9	522.0	597.4	621.5	600.8	602.4
Female	277.5	512.3	612.4	705.4	716.1	681.3	680.1
Public	461.0	770.5	881.9	982.9	1,018.5	969.5	958.3
Private	111.5	207.7	252.4	319.9	319.1	312.7	324.2
2-year	215.2	401.9	434.4	479.4	495.7	463.8	444.7
4-year	357.2	576.3	700.0	823.4	842.0	818.4	837.8
Undergraduate	500.5	845.5	971.4	1,117.9	1,142.3	1,087.9	1,085.1
Graduate	53.2	95.8	118.4	(NA)	(NA)	(NA)	(NA)
First professional	18.7	36.8	44.6	(NA)	(NA)	(NA)	(NA)
Nonresident alien	**391.5**	**528.7**	**584.5**	**660.6**	**684.9**	**709.6**	**740.5**
Male	246.3	297.3	309.5	353.3	366.7	380.3	399.1
Female	145.2	231.4	275.3	307.3	318.1	329.2	341.4
Public	260.0	343.1	372.8	427.0	440.8	454.3	471.7
Private	131.4	185.6	212.0	233.6	244.0	255.3	268.7
2-year	67.1	89.0	91.8	104.7	100.2	100.6	95.9
4-year	324.3	439.7	493.1	555.9	584.6	608.9	644.6
Undergraduate	218.7	288.0	314.7	360.3	378.4	400.3	422.3
Graduate	167.3	232.3	262.1	(NA)	(NA)	(NA)	(NA)
First professional	5.4	8.4	8.1	(NA)	(NA)	(NA)	(NA)

NA Not available. [1] Data beginning 2000 reflect a new classification of institutions; see footnote 1, Table 282. [2] Non-Hispanic.

Source: U.S. National Center for Education Statistics, Digest of Education Statistics, "Advance Release of Selected 2012 Digest Tables," and earlier releases, <http://nces.ed.gov/Programs/digest/>, accessed August 2013.

Table 284. Degree-Granting Institutions, Number and Enrollment by State and Selected Characteristics: 2011

[20,994 represents 20,994,000. Number of institutions beginning in academic year. Opening Fall enrollment of resident and extension students attending full-time or part-time]

State	Number of institutions[1]	Enrollment (1,000) Total	Male	Female	Public	Private	Full-time	White[2]	Minority Total[3]	Black[2]	Hispanic	Non-resident alien
United States........	4,706	20,994	9,026	11,968	15,110	5,884	13,001	12,394	7,427	3,068	2,890	740
Alabama..............	76	319	134	185	261	58	217	196	114	98	8	6
Alaska...............	9	35	14	21	32	3	16	22	10	1	3	1
Arizona...............	87	797	298	499	366	431	561	448	314	128	137	19
Arkansas..............	51	179	73	106	159	21	115	125	46	35	7	5
California..............	460	2,686	1,219	1,466	2,179	507	1,433	953	1,549	202	890	94
Colorado..............	91	366	161	205	269	97	217	251	97	29	50	8
Connecticut...........	47	202	85	116	126	75	128	132	58	24	24	8
Delaware.............	12	57	23	33	41	16	37	35	18	12	3	3
District of Columbia....	20	90	38	53	5	85	63	43	38	26	6	8
Florida................	240	1,144	476	667	803	340	665	563	531	231	257	31
Georgia...............	139	565	225	341	429	137	379	289	250	197	27	15
Hawaii................	21	79	33	46	60	19	44	16	42	2	7	4
Idaho.................	18	90	40	50	66	24	62	76	11	1	7	2
Illinois................	182	893	388	504	577	316	515	529	318	141	123	32
Indiana...............	107	458	200	257	340	118	306	348	81	49	20	21
Iowa..................	67	372	145	227	178	194	248	267	90	56	22	10
Kansas...............	67	217	96	121	186	30	130	159	41	17	15	13
Kentucky..............	79	294	126	168	233	60	179	243	41	30	6	5
Louisiana.............	73	266	107	159	225	41	180	154	102	83	10	7
Maine.................	32	72	30	42	50	22	46	64	6	2	2	1
Maryland..............	62	380	161	219	314	66	200	193	162	114	22	16
Massachusetts........	124	509	219	289	227	282	350	330	128	43	46	39
Michigan..............	111	686	300	386	555	131	397	491	155	105	23	26
Minnesota.............	116	458	184	273	274	184	259	327	104	62	18	15
Mississippi............	42	179	69	110	161	18	138	97	78	73	3	2
Missouri...............	137	457	194	263	261	196	276	335	100	68	17	15
Montana...............	22	54	25	29	49	5	40	44	7	(Z)	2	1
Nebraska..............	42	143	64	79	107	36	93	115	22	9	8	4
Nevada................	26	121	53	68	105	16	61	65	49	11	23	2
New Hampshire........	29	77	33	44	43	34	53	65	9	3	4	3
New Jersey............	68	444	201	243	359	84	280	238	182	65	78	17
New Mexico............	44	158	67	90	147	11	84	59	92	5	69	4
New York..............	303	1,318	569	749	732	586	919	725	493	186	186	82
North Carolina.........	148	585	237	348	471	114	375	360	202	152	27	16
North Dakota..........	21	56	27	28	49	7	39	46	6	1	1	3
Ohio..................	222	735	316	419	543	192	485	556	144	105	21	25
Oklahoma.............	63	230	100	130	197	33	147	148	64	24	12	9
Oregon...............	62	259	117	142	215	44	160	192	50	8	23	9
Pennsylvania..........	265	788	344	444	428	360	566	573	171	93	41	32
Rhode Island..........	13	85	37	48	43	41	63	61	18	6	8	4
South Carolina........	77	260	104	156	208	52	179	164	88	75	7	4
South Dakota..........	25	56	24	32	44	12	35	47	7	2	1	1
Tennessee.............	111	350	146	205	242	108	248	245	92	74	10	7
Texas.................	260	1,564	677	888	1,367	197	840	676	811	221	498	55
Utah..................	42	264	129	136	179	85	170	213	39	7	21	7
Vermont...............	24	45	20	25	27	18	34	39	4	1	2	1
Virginia...............	131	588	252	336	414	175	356	351	207	135	36	16
Washington............	88	373	167	206	317	56	251	251	90	18	32	16
West Virginia..........	46	162	80	82	96	67	87	126	30	12	7	3
Wisconsin..............	88	377	164	212	297	80	240	303	58	25	17	10
Wyoming..............	11	38	18	20	36	2	21	33	4	(Z)	2	1
U.S. military[4]........	5	16	13	3	16	(X)	16	11	4	1	2	(Z)

X Not applicable. Z Fewer than 500. [1] Branch campuses counted as separate institutions. [2] Non-Hispanic. [3] Includes other races not shown separately. [4] Service schools.

Source: U.S. National Center for Education Statistics, *Digest of Education Statistics*, "Advance Release of Selected 2012 Digest Tables," and earlier releases, <http://www.nces.ed.gov/programs/digest/>, accessed May 2013.

Table 285. College Enrollment by Sex, Age, Race, and Hispanic Origin: 1980 to 2011

[In thousands (11,387 represents 11,387,000). As of October for the civilian noninstitutional population, 14 years old and over. Based on the Current Population Survey; see text, Section 1 and Appendix III]

Characteristic	1980	1990 [1]	1995	2000	2005	2006	2007	2008	2009	2010	2011
Total [2]	11,387	13,621	14,715	15,314	17,472	17,020	17,770	18,632	19,764	20,275	20,397
Male [3]	5,430	6,192	6,703	6,682	7,539	7,427	7,749	8,311	8,642	9,007	9,132
18 to 24 years...................	3,604	3,922	4,089	4,342	4,972	4,874	5,156	5,383	5,640	5,698	5,953
25 to 34 years...................	1,325	1,412	1,561	1,361	1,486	1,571	1,625	1,806	1,843	2,055	1,986
35 years old and over..........	405	772	985	918	1,019	982	968	989	1,069	1,161	1,084
Female [3]	5,957	7,429	8,013	8,631	9,933	9,593	10,021	10,321	11,123	11,268	11,266
18 to 24 years...................	3,625	4,042	4,452	5,109	5,859	5,712	6,004	6,083	6,432	6,515	6,618
25 to 34 years...................	1,378	1,749	1,788	1,846	2,115	2,087	2,212	2,207	2,450	2,569	2,630
35 years old and over..........	802	1,546	1,684	1,589	1,838	1,793	1,804	1,922	2,124	2,049	1,922
White [3, 4]	9,925	11,488	12,021	11,999	13,467	13,112	13,693	14,405	15,027	15,258	15,412
18 to 24 years...................	6,334	6,635	7,011	7,566	8,499	8,298	8,780	9,141	9,327	9,324	9,813
25 to 34 years...................	2,328	2,698	2,686	2,339	2,647	2,725	2,769	2,859	3,163	3,414	3,339
35 years old and over..........	1,051	2,023	2,208	1,978	2,206	2,090	2,144	2,234	2,377	2,365	2,120
Male..............................	4,804	5,235	5,535	5,311	5,844	5,772	5,989	6,570	6,681	6,883	7,054
Female...........................	5,121	6,253	6,486	6,689	7,624	7,340	7,705	7,834	8,346	8,375	8,358
Black [3, 4]	1,163	1,393	1,772	2,164	2,297	2,304	2,473	2,481	2,889	3,083	3,146
18 to 24 years...................	688	894	988	1,216	1,229	1,321	1,395	1,349	1,604	1,692	1,639
25 to 34 years...................	289	258	426	567	520	502	629	646	663	715	818
35 years old and over..........	156	207	334	361	448	480	449	451	587	642	651
Male..............................	476	587	710	815	864	886	1,006	919	1,058	1,185	1,212
Female...........................	686	807	1,062	1,349	1,435	1,418	1,468	1,562	1,831	1,898	1,934
Hispanic origin [3, 5]	443	748	1,207	1,426	1,942	1,914	2,131	2,227	2,434	2,879	2,953
18 to 24 years...................	315	435	745	899	1,216	1,182	1,375	1,338	1,465	1,814	2,079
25 to 34 years...................	118	168	250	309	438	461	487	500	590	652	582
35 years old and over..........	(NA)	130	193	195	257	271	269	338	336	372	256
Male..............................	222	364	568	619	804	789	864	1,042	1,080	1,302	1,438
Female...........................	221	384	639	807	1,139	1,125	1,267	1,185	1,354	1,576	1,515

NA Not available. [1] Beginning 1990, based on a revised edit and tabulation package. [2] Includes other races not shown separately. [3] Includes persons 14 to 17 years old not shown separately. [4] Beginning 2003, for persons who selected this race group only. See footnote 2, Table 241. [5] Persons of Hispanic origin may be of any race.

Source: U.S. Census Bureau, Current Population Reports, PPL-148, P-20, and earlier reports; and "School Enrollment," <http://www.census.gov/hhes/school/index.html>, accessed June 2013.

Table 286. Foreign (Nonimmigrant) Student Enrollment in College: 1980 to 2012

[In thousands (286 represents 286,000). For fall of the previous year]

Region of origin	1980	1990	1995	2000	2002	2003	2004	2005	2006	2007	2008	2009	2010	2011	2012
All regions.........	286	387	453	515	583	586	573	565	565	583	624	672	691	723	764
Africa.................	36	25	21	30	38	40	38	36	36	36	36	37	37	37	35
Nigeria...............	16	4	2	4	4	6	6	6	6	6	6	6	7	7	7
Asia [1, 2, 3]	165	245	292	315	363	367	356	356	346	367	405	444	469	504	547
China.................	1	33	39	54	63	65	62	63	63	68	81	98	128	158	194
Taiwan...............	18	31	36	29	29	28	26	26	28	29	29	28	27	25	23
Hong Kong..........	10	11	13	8	8	8	7	7	8	8	8	8	8	8	8
India..................	9	26	34	42	67	75	80	80	77	84	95	103	105	104	100
Indonesia...........	2	9	12	11	12	10	9	8	8	7	8	8	7	7	7
Iran...................	51	7	3	2	2	2	2	2	2	3	3	4	5	6	7
Japan................	12	30	45	47	47	46	41	42	39	35	34	29	25	21	20
Malaysia.............	4	14	14	9	7	7	6	6	6	5	5	6	6	7	7
Saudi Arabia.........	10	4	4	5	6	4	4	3	3	8	10	13	16	23	34
South Korea.........	5	22	34	41	49	52	52	53	59	62	69	75	72	73	73
Thailand.............	7	7	11	11	12	10	9	9	9	9	9	9	9	8	8
Europe [4]	23	46	65	78	82	78	74	72	85	83	84	88	85	84	85
Latin America [1, 5]	42	48	47	62	68	69	66	68	65	65	64	68	66	64	64
Mexico..............	6	7	9	11	13	13	13	13	14	14	15	15	13	14	14
Venezuela...........	10	3	4	5	6	5	6	5	5	5	4	5	5	5	6
North America........	16	19	23	24	27	27	28	29	29	29	29	30	29	28	27
Canada..............	15	18	23	24	27	27	27	28	28	28	29	30	28	28	27
Oceania...............	4	4	4	5	5	5	5	4	5	4	5	5	5	6	6

[1] Includes countries not shown separately. [2] Includes the Middle East. [3] Beginning 2006, excludes Cyprus and Turkey. [4] Beginning 2006, includes Cyprus and Turkey. [5] Includes Mexico, Central America, Caribbean, and South America.

Source: Institute of International Education, New York, NY, *Open Doors Report on International Educational Exchange* ©, annual (2012). See also <http://www.iie.org/opendoors>.

Table 287. College Enrollment—by Type of College and Sex: 2011

[In thousands (20,397 represents 20,397,000). As of October. Covers civilian noninstitutional population 15 years old and over enrolled in colleges and graduate schools. Based on Current Population Survey. See text, Section 1 and Appendix III]

Characteristic	Total				Male		Female	
	Total enrolled	Two-year college	Four-year college	Graduate school	Total enrolled [1]	Four-year college	Total enrolled [1]	Four-year college
Total enrollment [2]	**20,397**	**5,705**	**10,920**	**3,773**	**9,132**	**5,061**	**11,266**	**5,858**
15 to 19 years old	4,445	1,596	2,838	11	2,058	1,304	2,388	1,534
20 to 24 years old	8,328	2,033	5,336	959	4,003	2,563	4,325	2,774
25 to 34 years old	4,617	1,237	1,783	1,598	1,987	804	2,631	979
35 years old and over	3,007	839	962	1,204	1,084	390	1,923	572
White [3]	15,412	4,251	8,390	2,771	7,054	3,921	8,358	4,469
White non-Hispanic [3]	12,703	3,062	7,130	2,511	5,731	3,347	6,972	3,783
Black [3]	3,146	1,021	1,577	549	1,212	660	1,934	917
Asian [3]	1,204	219	635	351	567	326	637	309
Hispanic [4]	2,953	1,267	1,393	292	1,438	649	1,515	745
Type of school:								
Public	16,134	5,265	8,551	2,318	7,255	4,013	8,879	4,538
Private	4,263	441	2,368	1,454	1,876	1,048	2,387	1,320
Employed full-time	5,244	1,386	2,040	1,818	2,407	964	2,838	1,076
Employed part-time	5,612	1,691	3,251	670	2,348	1,367	3,264	1,883
Not employed	9,541	2,627	5,629	1,285	4,377	2,730	5,164	2,898
Full time students	14,903	3,717	9,022	2,166	6,734	4,166	8,169	4,855
15 to 19 years old	4,064	1,341	2,717	6	1,872	1,230	2,192	1,488
20 to 24 years old	6,850	1,340	4,749	761	3,271	2,260	3,579	2,490
25 to 34 years old	2,713	672	1,086	954	1,172	505	1,541	581
35 years old and over	1,276	363	469	444	418	172	857	297
Part time students	5,494	1,989	1,898	1,607	2,398	896	3,097	1,003
15 to 19 years old	381	255	121	5	185	74	196	46
20 to 24 years old	1,478	693	587	198	732	303	746	284
25 to 34 years old	1,905	565	697	643	814	300	1,090	397
35 years old and over	1,731	477	493	761	666	218	1,065	275

[1] Includes enrollment in two-year colleges and graduate school not shown separately. [2] Includes other races not shown separately. [3] For persons who selected this race group only. See footnote 2, Table 241. [4] Persons of Hispanic origin may be of any race.

Source: U.S. Census Bureau, "School Enrollment," <http://www.census.gov/hhes/school/index.html>, accessed August 2013.

Table 288. Higher Education Enrollment in Languages Other Than English: 1970 to 2009

[1,111.5 represents 1,111,500. As of Fall. For credit enrollment]

Enrollment	1970	1980	1986	1990	1995	1998	2002	2006	2009
Registrations [1] (1,000)	**1,111.5**	**924.8**	**1,003.2**	**1,184.1**	**1,138.8**	**1,193.8**	**1,397.3**	**1,577.8**	**1,682.6**
By selected language (1,000):									
Spanish	389.2	379.4	411.3	533.9	606.3	656.6	746.3	823.0	865.0
French	359.3	248.4	275.3	272.5	205.4	199.1	202.0	206.4	216.4
German	202.6	126.9	121.0	133.3	96.3	89.0	91.1	94.3	96.3
American Sign Language	(NA)	(NA)	(NA)	1.6	4.3	11.4	60.8	78.8	91.8
Italian	34.2	34.8	40.9	49.7	43.8	49.3	63.9	78.4	80.8
Japanese	6.6	11.5	23.5	45.7	44.7	43.1	52.2	66.6	73.4
Chinese	6.2	11.4	16.9	19.5	26.5	28.5	34.2	51.6	61.0
Arabic	1.3	3.5	3.4	3.5	4.4	5.5	10.6	24.0	35.1
Latin	27.6	25.0	25.0	28.2	25.9	26.1	29.8	32.2	32.6
Russian	36.2	24.0	34.0	44.6	24.7	23.8	23.9	24.8	26.9
Hebrew	16.6	19.4	15.6	13.0	13.1	15.8	22.8	23.8	22.1
Ancient Greek	16.7	22.1	17.6	16.4	16.3	16.4	20.4	22.8	20.7
Portuguese	5.1	4.9	5.1	6.2	6.5	6.9	8.4	10.3	11.4
Korean	0.1	0.4	0.9	2.3	3.3	4.5	5.2	7.1	8.5
Index (1965=100)	107.3	89.3	96.8	114.3	109.9	115.2	134.9	152.3	162.4

NA Not available. [1] Includes other languages, not shown separately.

Source: Modern Language Association, Nelly Furman, David Goldberg, and Natalia Lusin. *Enrollments in Languages Other Than English in United States Institutions of Higher Education, Fall 2009*, December 2010 ©. For 1970 to 2006, consult Association of Departments of Foreign Languages (ADFL) Bulletins.

Table 289. Students Reporting Disability Status by Selected Characteristic: 2007 to 2008

[20,928 represents 20,928,000. Disabled students reported that they had one or more of the following conditions: a specific learning disability, a visual handicap, hard of hearing, deafness, a speech disability, an orthopedic handicap, or a health impairment. Based on the 2007–2008 National Postsecondary Student-Aid Study; see source for details. Includes Puerto Rico. See also Appendix III]

Student characteristic	Undergraduate			Graduate and first-professional		
	All students	Disabled students	Nondisabled students	All students	Disabled students	Nondisabled students
Total students (1,000).............................	20,928	2,266	18,662	3,456	261	3,195
PERCENT DISTRIBUTION						
Total...	100.0	10.8	89.2	100.0	7.6	92.4
Age:						
15 to 23 years old.............................	59.7	54.0	60.4	11.4	7.8	11.7
24 to 29 years old.............................	17.3	20.1	17.0	39.9	36.2	40.2
30 years or older..............................	23.0	25.9	22.7	48.7]	56.0	48.1
Sex:						
Male...	43.1	42.7	43.1	40.1	39.2	40.2
Female...	56.9	57.3	56.9	59.9	60.8	59.8
Race/ethnicity of student:						
White, non-Hispanic...........................	61.8	66.3	61.2	66.6	63.6	66.9
Black, non-Hispanic...........................	14.0	12.7	14.1	11.7	19.0	11.1
Hispanic...	14.1	12.3	14.4	8.0	7.4	8.0
Asian/Pacific Islander.........................	6.6	4.8	6.8	11.1	7.3	11.4
American Indian/Alaska Native..............	0.8	0.8	0.9	0.3	0.5	0.3
Other..	2.7	3.2	2.6	2.3	2.3	2.3
Attendance status:						
Full-time, full-year............................	39.3	34.7	39.8	34.1	32.6	34.2
Part-time or part-year........................	60.7	65.3	60.2	65.9	67.4	65.8
Student housing status:						
On-campus......................................	14.2	11.1	14.5	(NA)	(NA)	(NA)
Off-campus......................................	54.0	56.3	53.7	(NA)	(NA)	(NA)
With parents or relatives.....................	31.9	32.6	31.8	(NA)	(NA)	(NA)
Dependency status:						
Dependent......................................	53.0	46.8	53.7	(S)	(S)	(S)
Independent, unmarried......................	15.3	19.5	14.7	50.0	52.7	49.8
Independent, married.........................	6.4	6.9	6.3	16.9	12.9	17.2
Independent with dependents...............	25.4	26.7	25.2	33.1	34.4	33.0

NA Not available. S Figure does not meet publication standards.

Source: U.S. National Center for Education Statistics, *Digest of Education Statistics: 2011,* May 2012. See also <http://nces.ed.gov/programs/digest/d11/>.

Table 290. College Freshmen—Summary Characteristics: 1980 to 2012

[In percent, except as indicated (24.5 represents $24,500). As of Fall for first-time full-time freshmen in 4-year colleges and universities. Based on sample survey and subject to sampling error; see source]

Characteristic	1980	1990	1995	2000	2005	2009	2010	2011	2012
Sex:									
Male..	48.8	46.9	45.6	45.2	45.0	45.9	44.3	45.1	44.1
Female...	51.2	53.1	54.4	54.8	55.0	54.1	55.7	54.9	55.9
Applied to more than three colleges.....................	31.5	42.9	44.4	50.5	55.4	61.9	64.1	67.4	65.0
Average grade in high school:									
A– to A+.......................................	26.6	29.4	36.1	42.9	46.6	48.1	48.4	49.7	49.5
B– to B+.......................................	58.2	57.0	54.2	50.5	48.0	47.5	47.5	46.2	46.4
C to C+..	14.9	13.4	9.6	6.5	5.4	4.4	4.1	4.1	4.0
D...	0.2	0.2	0.1	0.1	0.1	0.1	0.1	0.0	0.0
Political orientation:									
Liberal...	21.0	24.6	22.9	24.8	27.1	29.0	27.3	27.6	26.8
Middle of the road...........................	57.0	51.7	51.3	51.9	45.0	44.4	46.4	47.4	47.5
Conservative..................................	19.0	20.6	21.8	18.9	22.6	21.8	21.7	20.7	21.1
Probable field of study:									
Biological sciences...........................	4.5	4.9	8.3	6.6	7.6	9.7	10.8	10.9	12.9
Business.......................................	21.2	21.1	15.4	16.7	17.4	14.3	13.7	14.9	14.4
Education......................................	8.4	10.3	10.1	11.0	9.9	8.1	7.2	5.9	5.8
Engineering....................................	11.2	9.7	8.1	8.7	8.3	9.7	10.3	12	10.3
Physical science..............................	3.2	2.8	3.1	2.6	3.1	3.4	2.7	3.7	2.5
Social science.................................	8.2	11.0	9.9	10.0	10.7	11.7	8.9	12.1	11.1
Data processing/computer programming..............	1.7	0.7	0.8	1.5	0.5	0.6	0.5	0.6	(NA)
Other [1].....................................	41.6	39.5	44.3	42.9	42.5	42.5	45.9	46.2	43.0
Communications [2].........................	2.4	2.9	1.8	2.7	2.0	1.9	1.8	1.6	3.0
Computer science............................	2.6	1.7	2.2	3.7	1.1	1.0	1.0	1.1	2.0
Personal objectives—very important or essential:									
Being very well off financially...............	62.5	72.3	72.8	73.4	74.5	78.1	77.4	79.6	81.0
Developing a meaningful philosophy of life...........	62.5	45.9	45.4	42.4	45.0	48.0	46.9	46.8	45.6
Keeping up to date with political affairs...............	45.2	46.6	32.3	28.1	36.4	36.0	33.2	32.8	34.5
Median family income ($1,000)........................	24.5	46.6	54.8	64.4	73.2	76.6	76.1	(NA)	(NA)

NA Not available. [1] Includes other fields not shown separately. [2] Beginning in 2012, communications majors are reported in combination with journalism majors.

Source: The Higher Education Research Institute, University of California, Los Angeles, CA, *The American Freshman: National Norms Fall 2012* ©, 2012, and earlier editions. See also <http://www.heri.ucla.edu/tfsPublications.php>.

Table 291. Residence and Migration of College Freshmen by State: 2010

[As of Fall. Includes first-time postsecondary students who had graduated from high school in the previous 12 months and were enrolled at public and private not-for-profit 4-year degree-granting institutions that participated in Title IV federal financial aid programs. Excludes respondents for whom state residence and/or migration are unknown. Also excludes U.S. Service Academies (Air Force Academy, Coast Guard Academy, Merchant Marine Academy, Military Academy, and Naval Academy)]

State	Total freshmen enrollment in institutions located in the state	Ratio of in-state students to freshmen enrollment	Ratio of in-state students to residents enrolled in any state [1]	State	Total freshmen enrollment in institutions located in the state	Ratio of in-state students to freshmen enrollment	Ratio of in-state students to residents enrolled in any state [1]
U.S.......	1,476,522	0.73	0.75	MO.........	30,204	0.70	0.78
AL.........	23,817	0.67	0.86	MT.........	6,037	0.64	0.79
AK.........	2,633	0.90	0.63	NE.........	11,071	0.75	0.82
AZ.........	22,043	0.66	0.80	NV.........	8,413	0.88	0.75
AR.........	16,040	0.73	0.89	NH.........	9,093	0.40	0.45
CA.........	114,035	0.88	0.79	NJ.........	27,560	0.85	0.44
CO.........	23,523	0.74	0.71	NM.........	7,710	0.81	0.80
CT.........	19,340	0.53	0.42	NY.........	106,279	0.71	0.73
DE.........	1,743	0.44	0.29	NC.........	46,834	0.73	0.85
DC.........	8,802	0.06	0.23	ND.........	6,252	0.48	0.78
FL.........	93,625	0.86	0.88	OH.........	70,277	0.80	0.83
GA.........	49,722	0.83	0.81	OK.........	19,147	0.72	0.88
HI.........	3,974	0.64	0.50	OR.........	15,047	0.59	0.70
ID.........	7,144	0.56	0.65	PA.........	86,453	0.64	0.79
IL.........	50,222	0.77	0.61	RI.........	10,928	0.26	0.52
IN.........	45,077	0.72	0.87	SC.........	23,652	0.65	0.85
IA.........	19,109	0.55	0.78	SD.........	5,798	0.64	0.75
KS.........	13,941	0.73	0.77	TN.........	30,650	0.77	0.80
KY.........	23,426	0.74	0.86	TX.........	91,495	0.92	0.82
LA.........	23,435	0.78	0.89	UT.........	19,114	0.68	0.92
ME.........	6,519	0.62	0.57	VT.........	6,593	0.27	0.46
MD.........	18,774	0.65	0.45	VA.........	39,251	0.69	0.73
MA.........	49,910	0.50	0.58	WA.........	23,515	0.76	0.70
MI.........	50,546	0.85	0.85	WV.........	12,902	0.60	0.89
MN.........	27,047	0.73	0.62	WI.........	35,727	0.73	0.78
MS.........	10,671	0.62	0.82	WY.........	1,402	0.57	0.54

[1] Students residing in a particular state when admitted to an institution anywhere, either in their home state or another state.

Source: U.S. Department of Education, National Center for Education Statistics, Integrated Postsecondary Education Data System (IPEDS), Spring 2011 and *Digest of Education Statistics*, annual. See also <http://nces.ed.gov/programs/digest/>.

Table 292. Average Total Price of Attendance of Undergraduate Education: 2007 to 2008

[In dollars. For school year ending in 2008. Excludes students attending more than one institution. Price of attendance includes tuition and fees, books and supplies, room and board, transportation, and personal and other expenses allowed for federal cost of attendance budgets. Based on the 2007–2008 National Postsecondary Student-Aid Study; see source for details. Includes Puerto Rico. See also Appendix III]

Student characteristic	All institutions [1]	Public 2-year	Public 4-year Non-doctorate	Public 4-year Doctorate	Private not-for-profit 4-year Non-doctorate	Private not-for-profit 4-year Doctorate	Private for-profit
Total.....................	**14,006**	**7,033**	**12,657**	**16,615**	**25,194**	**31,628**	**20,636**
Age: [2]							
18 years or younger...............	17,065	12,630	16,664	19,888	32,586	38,311	19,868
19 to 23 years....................	16,059	6,830	10,128	12,513	17,861	22,540	20,376
24 to 29 years....................	11,551	8,035	11,188	13,833	17,823	21,294	20,275
30 to 39 years....................	10,994	3,854	5,739	7,319	8,446	10,419	21,305
40 years or older.................	9,269	8,268	14,912	18,501	31,809	37,581	21,265
Sex:							
Male............................	13,957	7,406	13,778	17,661	30,099	35,206	21,765
Female..........................	14,044	6,856	10,701	13,005	17,458	20,772	20,133
Race:							
One race:							
White...........................	14,446	6,546	9,690	12,452	15,561	17,839	20,888
Black or African American.........	13,235	5,992	9,062	10,623	14,722	14,452	20,141
Asian...........................	15,122	7,121	12,668	16,486	25,512	31,163	22,203
American Indian/Alaska Native.....	12,150	7,013	13,170	16,707	26,717	32,236	25,013
Native Hawaiian or other Pacific Islander............	12,904	6,974	12,824	15,891	21,412	26,817	23,122
Other race.......................	12,788	6,990	10,511	15,513	19,548	27,808	24,076
More than one race................	15,077	7,313	13,285	18,271	29,162	36,973	23,245
Hispanic or Latino [3]...............	12,419	6,920	12,644	16,757	24,765	32,182	19,753
Attendance pattern:							
Full-time, full-year...............	22,368	7,330	10,436	15,078	27,614	(S)	28,638
Full-time, part-year...............	12,227	6,718	12,988	16,878	18,659	40,521	16,653
Part-time, full-year...............	10,655	6,759	10,879	15,650	16,534	(S)	19,259
Part-time, part-year...............	5,231	7,495	13,028	17,256	28,172	34,460	11,810

S Data do not meet publication standards. [1] Includes public less-than-2-year and private not-for-profit less-than-4-year. [2] As of December 31, 2007. [3] Persons of Hispanic origin may be of any race.

Source:Source: U.S. National Center for Education Statistics, *Student Financial Aid Estimates for 2007–08,* NCES 2009-166, April 2009. See also <http://nces.ed.gov/pubsearch/pubsinfo.asp?pubid=2009166>.

Table 293. Average Out-of-Pocket Net Price of Attendance for Undergraduates: 2007 to 2008

[In dollars. For school year ending in 2008. Excludes students attending more than one institution. Net price of attendance is the price that students pay to receive postsecondary education after taking financial aid into account. Based on net tuition and net price for all students. Based on the 2007–2008 National Postsecondary Student-Aid Study; see source for details. Includes Puerto Rico. See also Appendix III]

Student characteristic	All institu- tions [1]	Public 2-year	Public 4-year		Private not-for-profit 4 year		Private for-profit
			Non-doctorate	Doctorate	Non-doctorate	Doctorate	
Total	**8,769**	**5,645**	**7,801**	**10,627**	**12,772**	**18,103**	**11,647**
Age: [2]							
18 years or younger	10,219	6,612	8,927	11,313	15,067	20,967	9,974
19 to 23 years	9,974	5,995	8,488	11,509	14,672	20,217	11,460
24 to 29 years	7,160	5,303	6,559	7,508	9,755	11,380	11,239
30 to 39 years	7,073	5,168	5,916	7,360	8,858	9,832	12,353
40 years or older	6,487	4,998	5,933	7,180	9,365	8,822	12,379
Sex:							
Male	8,985	5,705	8,061	11,042	12,946	19,016	11,942
Female	8,603	5,599	7,586	10,248	12,644	17,313	11,517
Race:							
One race:							
White	9,211	5,674	8,266	11,196	13,550	18,899	11,858
Black or African American	7,286	5,192	6,039	7,318	10,564	12,319	11,109
Asian	10,613	6,386	9,518	12,615	17,147	24,543	12,809
American Indian/Alaska Native	7,715	5,493	6,047	8,115	(S)	(S)	16,623
Native Hawaiian or other Pacific Islander	8,445	5,627	8,840	9,499	7,855	29,807	11,896
Other race	8,286	5,435	(S)	7,968	(S)	(S)	15,868
More than one race	8,867	5,854	7,581	10,100	11,828	17,450	13,817
Hispanic or Latino [3]	7,567	5,638	6,941	8,657	9,761	12,824	11,028
Attendance pattern:							
Full-time, full-year	13,218	9,428	9,654	12,419	15,659	21,293	16,875
Full-time, part-year	7,751	5,442	6,672	8,522	10,386	14,220	8,825
Part-time, full-year	7,410	6,544	7,588	9,030	9,561	12,597	9,174
Part-time, part-year	3,906	3,348	4,193	5,297	5,498	6,791	5,933

S Data do not meet publication standards. [1] Includes public less-than-2-year and private not-for-profit less-than-4-year. [2] As of December 2007. [3] Persons of Hispanic origin may be of any race.

Source: U.S. National Center for Education Statistics, *Student Financial Aid Estimates for 2007–08,* NCES 2009-166, April 2009. See also <http://nces.ed.gov/pubsearch/pubsinfo.asp?pubid=2009166>.

Table 294. Higher Education Price Indexes: 2004 to 2012

[1983=100. For years ending June 30. The Higher Education Price Index (HEPI), calculated for the July-June academic fiscal year, reflects prices paid by colleges and universities for the following eight cost factors: faculty salaries, administrative salaries, clerical and service employees, fringe benefits, miscellaneous services, supplies and materials, and utilities. Minus sign (-) indicates decrease]

Item and year	Total	Personnel compensation					Contracted services, supplies, and equipment		
		Faculty salaries	Admin- istrative salaries	Clerical salaries	Service employ- ees salaries	Fringe benefits	Miscel- laneous services	Supplies and materials	Utilities
INDEXES									
2004	231.7	234.2	263.3	217.1	197.6	312.8	216.4	135.6	176.4
2005	240.8	240.7	274.0	223.4	201.4	327.2	222.7	145.5	200.2
2006	253.1	248.2	287.7	229.5	205.5	343.7	228.8	158.1	255.7
2007	260.3	257.6	299.2	237.7	213.6	360.8	238.3	165.3	220.6
2008	273.2	268.1	314.0	245.0	220.4	380.7	246.5	180.0	252.0
2009	279.3	277.3	330.9	251.6	226.7	394.4	253.1	181.6	213.8
2010	281.8	280.6	337.6	255.2	230.0	402.8	255.8	179.3	193.6
2011	288.4	284.5	343.2	260.2	233.2	417.6	260.3	193.9	201.6
2012	293.2	289.6	352.3	264.8	235.7	425.3	264.6	203.9	191.7
ANNUAL PERCENT CHANGE [1]									
2004	3.7	2.1	3.0	2.8	1.9	7.0	3.3	2.6	11.9
2005	3.9	2.8	4.1	2.9	1.9	4.6	2.9	7.3	13.5
2006	5.1	3.1	5.0	2.7	2.0	5.0	2.7	8.7	27.7
2007	2.8	3.8	4.0	3.6	4.0	5.0	4.2	4.5	-13.7
2008	5.0	4.1	5.0	3.1	3.2	5.5	3.4	8.9	14.2
2009	2.3	3.4	5.4	2.7	2.9	3.6	2.7	0.9	-15.1
2010	0.9	1.2	2.0	1.4	1.4	2.1	1.1	-1.3	-9.5
2011	2.3	1.4	1.7	2.0	1.4	3.7	1.8	8.2	4.1
2012	1.7	1.8	2.7	1.7	1.1	1.8	1.7	5.2	-4.9

[1] Percent change from the immediate prior year.

Source: The Commonfund Institute, Wilton, CT ©, <http://www.commonfund.org>.

Table 295. Federal Student Financial Assistance: 1995 to 2013

[35,477 represents $35,477,000,000. For award years July 1 of year shown to the following June 30. Funds utilized exclude operating costs, etc., and represent funds given to students]

Type of assistance	1995	2000	2005	2010	2011	2012, est.	2013, est.
FUNDS UTILIZED (mil. dol.)							
Total.	**35,477**	**44,007**	**72,634**	**144,182**	**144,772**	**141,261**	**143,279**
Federal Pell Grants.	5,472	7,956	12,693	35,677	33,575	32,798	33,728
Academic Competitiveness Grants [1].	(X)	(X)	(X)	553	(X)	(X)	(X)
SMART Grants [1].	(X)	(X)	(X)	433	(X)	(X)	(X)
TEACH Grants [2].	(X)	(X)	(X)	121	137	111	116
Federal Supplemental Educational Opportunity Grant.	764	907	1,084	1,022	10	982	982
Federal Work-Study.	764	939	1,050	1,198	1,176	1,162	1,162
Federal Perkins Loan.	1,029	1,144	1,593	857	949	857	857
Federal Direct Student Loan (FDSL).	8,296	10,348	12,930	84,704	108,926	105,351	106,434
Federal Family Education Loans (FFEL) [4].	19,152	22,712	43,284	19,618	(X)	(X)	(X)
NUMBER OF AWARDS (1,000)							
Total.	**13,667**	**15,043**	**21,317**	**34,895**	**35,539**	**33,926**	**33,157**
Federal Pell Grants.	3,612	3,899	5,167	9,308	9,444	8,965	9,171
Academic Competitiveness Grants [1].	(X)	(X)	(X)	729	(X)	(X)	(X)
SMART Grants [1].	(X)	(X)	(X)	140	(X)	(X)	(X)
TEACH Grants [2].	(X)	(X)	(X)	39	42	37	39
Federal Supplemental Educational Opportunity Grant.	1,083	1,175	1,419	1,633	1,646	1,584	1,584
Federal Work-Study.	702	713	710	718	704	697	697
Federal Perkins Loan.	688	639	727	461	485	461	461
Federal Direct Student Loan (FDSL).	2,339	2,739	2,971	16,647	23,218	22,182	21,205
Federal Family Education Loans (FFEL) [4].	5,243	5,878	10,323	5,220	(X)	(X)	(X)
AVERAGE AWARD (dol.)							
Total.	**2,596**	**2,925**	**3,407**	**4,132**	**4,074**	**4,164**	**4,321**
Federal Pell Grants.	1,515	2,041	2,456	3,833	3,555	3,658	3,678
Academic Competitiveness Grants [1].	(X)	(X)	(X)	759	(X)	(X)	(X)
SMART Grants [1].	(X)	(X)	(X)	3,095	(X)	(X)	(X)
TEACH Grants [2].	(X)	(X)	(X)	3,137	3,300	2,979	2,979
Federal Supplemental Educational Opportunity Grant.	705	772	764	620	588	620	620
Federal Work-Study.	1,088	1,318	1,478	1,668	1,670	1,668	1,668
Federal Perkins Loan.	1,496	1,790	2,190	1,860	1,957	1,860	1,860
Federal Direct Student Loan (FDSL).	3,547	3,778	4,352	5,088	4,691	4,749	5,019
Federal Family Education Loans (FFEL) [4].	3,653	3,864	4,193	3,758	(X)	(X)	(X)
COHORT DEFAULT RATE [3]							
Federal Perkins Loan.	12.6	9.9	8.1	10.5	11.1	(NA)	(NA)

NA Not available. X Not applicable. [1] National Science and Mathematics Access to Retain Talent (SMART). Funding for Academic Competitiveness Grants and SMART Grants was terminated in 2011. [2] Teacher Education Assistance for College and Higher Education (TEACH) Grant Program. [3] As of June 30. Represents the percent of borrowers entering repayment status in year shown who defaulted in the following year. [4] The FFEL Program was terminated effective 2011.

Source: U.S. Department of Education, Office of Postsecondary Education, unpublished data.

Table 296. Institutions of Higher Education—Average Charges: 1985 to 2012

[In current dollars. Estimated. For the entire academic year ending in year shown. Figures are average charges per full-time equivalent student. Room and board are based on full-time students]

Academic control and year	Tuition and required fees [1]			Board rates [2]			Dormitory charges		
	All institutions	2-yr. colleges	4-yr. institutions	All institutions	2-yr. colleges	4-yr. institutions	All institutions	2-yr. colleges	4-yr. institutions
Public:									
1985.	971	584	1,228	1,241	1,302	1,237	1,196	921	1,217
1990.	1,356	756	1,780	1,635	1,581	1,638	1,513	962	1,557
1995.	2,057	1,192	2,681	1,949	1,712	1,967	1,959	1,232	2,023
2000.	2,504	1,348	3,349	2,364	1,834	2,406	2,440	1,549	2,519
2005.	3,629	1,849	5,027	2,931	2,353	2,981	3,304	2,174	3,418
2008.	4,291	2,061	5,943	3,331	2,409	3,404	3,952	2,506	4,082
2009.	4,512	2,136	6,312	3,554	2,769	3,619	4,190	2,664	4,331
2010.	4,751	2,285	6,695	3,653	2,574	3,754	4,399	2,845	4,565
2011.	5,076	2,439	7,136	3,848	2,685	3,958	4,640	2,960	4,824
2012.	5,500	2,647	7,701	3,947	2,829	4,052	4,844	3,085	5,036
Private:									
1985.	5,315	3,485	5,556	1,462	1,294	1,469	1,426	1,424	1,426
1990.	8,147	5,196	8,396	1,948	1,811	1,953	1,923	1,663	1,935
1995.	11,111	6,914	11,481	2,509	2,023	2,520	2,587	2,233	2,601
2000.	14,100	8,225	14,616	2,877	2,753	2,879	3,236	3,067	3,242
2005.	18,154	12,122	18,604	3,485	3,700	3,483	4,178	4,475	4,173
2008.	20,972	13,126	21,427	3,992	4,074	3,991	4,804	4,484	4,808
2009.	21,570	13,562	22,036	4,209	4,627	4,206	5,025	4,537	5,032
2010.	21,444	14,876	21,908	4,331	4,390	4,331	5,249	5,217	5,249
2011.	22,186	14,467	22,771	4,434	4,475	4,433	5,406	4,928	5,413
2012.	22,817	13,879	23,479	4,591	4,456	4,591	5,639	5,111	5,646

[1] For public institutions, data are for in-state students. [2] Beginning 1990, rates reflect 20 meals per week, rather than meals served 7 days a week.

Source: U.S. National Center for Education Statistics, *Digest of Education Statistics*, "Advance Release of Selected 2012 Digest Tables," <http://www.nces.ed.gov/programs/digest/>, accessed May 2013.

Table 297. State and Local Financial Support for Higher Education by State: 2012

[11,549.0 represents 11,549,000. For fiscal year ending in 2012. Data for the 50 states]

State	FTE enrollment [1] (1,000)	Educational appropriations per FTE enrollment [2] (dollars)	State	FTE enrollment [1] (1,000)	Educational appropriations per FTE enrollment [2] (dollars)
Total	11,549.0	5,906			
AL	205.3	5,195	MT	40.8	4,468
AK	21.8	14,891	NE	83.9	7,385
AZ	275.2	4,929	NV	64.7	6,426
AR	126.0	5,635	NH	39.1	1,835
CA	1,495.9	6,542	NJ	278.9	6,794
CO	192.5	3,069	NM	97.7	7,272
CT	85.7	9,016	NY	586.2	8,105
DE	34.7	5,813	NC	412.3	8,163
FL	638.0	4,834	ND	37.5	7,192
GA	379.0	6,277	OH	455.5	3,965
HI	40.6	10,358	OK	146.5	5,834
ID	59.0	5,434	OR	170.4	3,911
IL	422.3	8,591	PA	369.0	4,368
IN	261.8	4,869	RI	31.7	5,819
IA	132.4	4,784	SC	176.4	4,095
KS	143.0	5,184	SD	33.5	4,347
KY	159.3	6,269	TN	203.6	5,245
LA	181.6	5,243	TX	972.9	6,749
ME	37.9	6,252	UT	126.6	5,116
MD	243.0	6,596	VT	21.8	2,925
MA	170.2	6,332	VA	325.5	4,269
MI	423.2	4,608	WA	253.9	4,874
MN	214.1	4,817	WV	80.2	4,902
MS	142.0	4,887	WI	233.3	5,907
MO	196.4	5,244	WY	26.2	12,337

[1] Full-time equivalent. Includes degree enrollment and enrollment in public postsecondary programs resulting in a certificate or other formal recognition. Includes summer sessions. Excludes medical enrollments. [2] State and local appropriations for general operating expenses of public postsecondary education. Includes American Recovery and Reinvestment Act of 2009 (ARRA) funds, state-funded financial aid to students attending in-state public institutions. Excludes sums for research, agricultural extension, and teaching hospitals and medical schools.

Source: State Higher Education Executive Officers, Boulder, CO, *State Higher Education Finance Report* ©, 2013. See also <http://www.sheeo.org/projects/shef-%E2%80%94-state-higher-education-finance>.

Table 298. Voluntary Financial Support of Higher Education: 1990 to 2012

[9,800 represents $9,800,000,000. For school years ending in years shown. Voluntary support, as defined in Gift Reporting Standards, excludes income from endowment and other invested funds as well as all support received from federal, state, and local governments and their agencies and contract research]

Item	Unit	1990	1995	2000	2005	2009	2010	2011	2012
Estimated support, total	Mil. dol.	9,800	12,750	23,200	25,600	27,850	28,000	30,300	31,000
Individuals	Mil. dol.	4,770	6,540	12,220	12,100	12,125	12,020	13,450	13,525
Alumni	Mil. dol.	2,540	3,600	6,800	7,100	7,130	7,100	7,800	7,700
Business corporations	Mil. dol.	2,170	2,560	4,150	4,400	4,620	4,730	5,020	5,250
Foundations	Mil. dol.	1,920	2,460	5,080	7,000	8,235	8,400	8,675	9,150
Fundraising consortia and other organizations	Mil. dol.	700	940	1,380	1,730	2,545	2,545	2,850	2,800
Religious organizations	Mil. dol.	240	250	370	370	325	305	305	275
Current operations	Mil. dol.	5,440	7,230	11,270	14,200	16,955	17,000	17,800	18,900
Capital purposes	Mil. dol.	4,360	5,520	11,930	11,400	10,895	11,000	12,500	12,100
Support per student	Dollars	724	908	1,608	1,562	1,458	1,507	1,595	1,613
In 2012 dollars	Dollars	(NA)	1,368	2,144	1,836	1,530	1,587	1,628	1,613
Expenditures, higher education	Bil. dol.	134.7	183.0	236.8	326.2	432.0	426.5	446.3	463.7
Expenditures per student	Dollars	9,946	13,028	16,408	19,899	22,614	22,961	23,494	24,121
In 2012 dollars	Dollars	(NA)	19,628	21,877	23,394	23,725	24,176	23,980	24,121
Institutions reporting support	Number	1,056	1,086	945	997	1,027	996	1,009	1,005
Total support reported	Mil. dol.	8,214	10,992	19,419	20,953	23,693	23,487	25,702	25,596
Private 4-year institutions	Mil. dol.	5,072	6,500	11,047	11,011	12,351	12,189	12,517	13,461
Public 4-year institutions	Mil. dol.	3,056	4,382	8,254	9,780	11,141	11,114	11,992	11,933
2-year colleges	Mil. dol.	85	110	117	163	201	185	193	202

NA Not available.

Source: Council for Aid to Education, New York, NY, *Voluntary Support of Education* ©, annual. See also <www.cae.org>.

Table 299. Average Salaries for College Faculty Members: 2011 to 2013

[In thousands of dollars (78.3 represents $78,300). For academic year ending in year shown. Figures are for 9 months teaching for full-time faculty members in 2-year and 4-year institutions with ranks. Fringe benefits averaged in 2013, $24,451 in public institutions and $28,081 in private institutions]

Type of control and academic rank	2011	2012	2013	Type of control and academic rank	2011	2012	2013
Public: All ranks..................	78.3	79.5	80.6	Private: [1] All ranks...............	94.6	96.9	99.8
Professor........................	105.8	107.9	110.1	Professor........................	131.6	135.1	139.6
Associate professor............	76.2	77.2	78.5	Associate professor............	84.6	86.2	88.3
Assistant professor.............	64.7	65.9	67.1	Assistant professor.............	71.0	72.7	74.7
Instructor.......................	45.7	46.3	46.9	Instructor.......................	53.6	55.0	56.5

[1] Excludes church-related colleges and universities.

Source: American Association of University Professors, Washington, DC, *AAUP Annual Report on the Economic Status of the Profession* © 2013. See also: <http://www.aaup.org/>.

Table 300. Employees in Higher Education Institutions by Sex and Occupation: 1995 to 2011

[In thousands (2,662.1 represents 2,662,100). As of Fall. Based on complete census taken every other year; see source]

Year and status	Total	Professional staff										Non–professional staff, total
		Total	Executive, administrative, and managerial		Faculty [1]		Graduate assistants		Other		
			Male	Female	Male	Female	Male	Female	Male	Female	
1995, total..........	**2,662.1**	**1,744.9**	**82.1**	**65.3**	**562.9**	**368.8**	**124.0**	**91.9**	**177.2**	**272.7**	**917.2**
Full–time...........	1,801.4	1,066.5	79.2	61.8	360.2	190.7	–	–	151.5	223.2	734.9
Part–time..........	860.7	678.4	2.9	3.6	202.7	178.1	124.0	91.9	25.6	49.5	182.3
2005, total [2]........	**3,379.1**	**2,459.9**	**95.2**	**101.1**	**714.5**	**576.0**	**167.5**	**149.6**	**262.8**	**393.2**	**919.2**
Full–time...........	2,179.9	1,432.1	92.9	97.2	401.5	274.1	–	–	231.4	335.0	747.8
Part–time..........	1,199.2	1,027.8	2.4	3.9	312.9	301.9	167.5	149.6	31.4	58.2	171.4
2009, total..........	**3,723.4**	**2,782.1**	**106.9**	**123.7**	**761.0**	**678.1**	**180.9**	**161.5**	**305.0**	**465.0**	**941.3**
Full–time...........	2,381.7	1,619.5	103.8	118.5	415.8	313.2	–	–	268.6	399.7	762.2
Part–time..........	1,341.7	1,162.6	3.1	5.2	345.2	365.0	180.9	161.5	36.4	65.3	179.1
2011, total..........	**3,841.0**	**2,924.0**	**109.4**	**129.3**	**798.2**	**734.4**	**188.5**	**167.4**	**315.7**	**490.1**	**917.0**
Full–time...........	2,435.5	1,693.1	106.7	124.9	427.0	334.6	–	–	277.9	421.9	742.4
Part–time..........	1,405.4	1,230.9	2.7	4.4	362.2	399.8	188.5	167.4	37.7	68.1	174.6

– Represents zero. [1] Instruction and research. [2] 2005 data reflect the new classification of institutions. See footnote 1, Table 282.

Source: U.S. National Center for Education Statistics, *Digest of Education Statistics*, July 2012. See also <http://www.nces.ed.gov/programs/digest>.

Table 301. Faculty in Institutions of Higher Education: 1980 to 2011

[In thousands (686 represents 686,000), except percent. As of Fall. Based on complete census taken every other year; see source]

Year	Total	Employment status		Control		Level		Percent		
		Full-time	Part-time	Public	Private	4-Year	2-Year or less	Part-time	Public	2-Year or less
1980 [1]...............	686	450	236	495	191	494	192	34	72	28
1985 [1]...............	715	459	256	503	212	504	211	36	70	30
1991 [2]...............	826	536	291	581	245	591	235	35	70	28
1995.................	932	551	381	657	275	647	285	41	70	31
2001 [3]...............	1,113	618	495	771	342	764	349	44	69	31
2003 [3]...............	1,174	630	544	792	382	814	359	46	67	31
2005 [3]...............	1,290	676	615	841	449	917	373	48	65	29
2007 [3, 4].............	1,371	703	668	877	494	991	381	49	64	28
2009 [3, 4].............	1,439	729	710	914	525	1,038	401	49	63	28
2011 [3, 4].............	1,524	762	762	953	570	1,116	408	50	63	27

[1] Estimated on the basis of enrollment. [2] Data beginning 1991 not comparable to prior years. [3] Beginning in 2001, data reflect the new classification of institutions. See footnote 1, Table 282. [4] Beginning in 2007, data include institutions with fewer than 15 full-time employees; these institutions did not report staff data prior to 2007.

Source: U.S. National Center for Education Statistics, *Digest of Education Statistics*, July 2012. See also <http://www.nces.ed.gov/programs/digest/>.

Table 302. Salary Offers to Candidates for Degrees: 2005 to 2012

[In dollars. Data are average beginning salaries based on offers made by business, industrial, government, nonprofit, and educational employers to graduating students. Data from representative colleges throughout the United States]

Field of study	Bachelor's			Master's [1]			Doctoral		
	2005	2011	2012	2005	2011	2012	2005	2011	2012
Accounting..........................	42,940	49,407	50,400	45,992	46,741	63,800	(NA)	(NA)	(NA)
Business administration/ management [2]..................	39,480	46,372	52,500	[3] 50,513	76,786	64,100	[3] 66,500	[3] 109,005	(NA)
Marketing..........................	36,409	42,923	53,400	[3] 47,000	[3]53,000	(NA)	(NA)	(NA)	(NA)
Engineering:									
Civil................................	43,774	52,058	57,500	48,619	[3]57,812	(NA)	[3] 59,216	[3] 72,682	(NA)
Chemical.........................	53,639	66,058	66,200	62,845	[3]72,000	(NA)	[3] 73,317	86,954	(NA)
Computer.........................	52,242	62,849	71,800	58,631	[3]76,822	(NA)	[3] 69,625	[3] 100,929	(NA)
Electrical.........................	51,773	60,411	60,500	64,781	73,857	73,000	[3] 75,066	90,936	(NA)
Mechanical.......................	50,175	60,142	61,300	60,223	68,065	75,700	69,757	[3] 80,793	(NA)
Nuclear [4]........................	[3] 51,225	61,678	(NA)	[3] 59,059	[3]66,456	(NA)	(NA)	(NA)	(NA)
Petroleum........................	62,236	82,740	(NA)	[3] 65,000	(NA)	(NA)	(NA)	(NA)	(NA)
Engineering technology..........	45,790	55,715	(NA)	(NA)	(NA)	(NA)	(NA)	(NA)	(NA)
Chemistry...........................	38,635	41,001	44,500	(NA)	[3]29,000	(NA)	55,874	[3] 71,378	(NA)
Mathematics.......................	43,304	54,333	49,500	[3] 34,500	[3]46,666	48,500	[3] 55,047	[3] 64,133	(NA)
Physics..............................	[3] 44,700	53,338	33,600	[3] 62,500	[3]45,000	(NA)	[3] 54,897	[3] 67,722	(NA)
Humanities.........................	31,565	37,225	37,300	[3] 35,212	[3]43,587	(NA)	[3] 43,728	[3] 48,857	(NA)
Social sciences [5].................	31,621	36,526	38,100	[3] 40,575	[3]49,143	50,000	[3] 46,838	[3] 57,011	(NA)
Computer science.................	50,664	66,084	62,200	64,840	72,703	80,400	[3] 84,025	[3] 86,244	(NA)

NA Not available. [1] Candidates with 1 year or less of full-time nonmilitary employment. [2] For master's degree, offers are after nontechnical undergraduate degree. [3] Fewer than 50 offers reported. [4] Includes engineering physics. [5] Excludes economics.

Source: National Association of Colleges and Employers, Bethlehem, PA ©. Reprinted with permission from Fall 2005, 2011, and 2012 Salary Survey. All rights reserved. See also <http://www.naceweb.org>.

Table 303. Degrees Earned by Level and Sex: 1960 to 2011

[In thousands (477 represents 477,000), except percent. Based on survey; see Appendix III]

Year ending	All degrees		Associate's		Bachelor's		Master's		Doctoral [1]	
	Total	Percent Male	Male	Female	Male	Female	Male	Female	Male	Female
1960..............	477	64.0	(NA)	(NA)	[2] 254	[2] 138	51	24	9	1
1970..............	1,271	59.2	117	89	451	341	131	83	54	6
1975..............	1,666	56.0	191	169	505	418	166	131	71	14
1980..............	1,732	51.1	184	217	474	456	157	148	70	26
1985..............	1,828	49.3	203	252	483	497	149	144	66	35
1990..............	1,940	46.6	191	264	492	560	158	172	64	40
1995..............	2,218	44.9	218	321	526	634	183	221	67	47
1996..............	2,248	44.2	220	336	522	642	183	229	67	48
1997..............	2,288	43.6	224	347	521	652	185	240	68	50
1998..............	2,298	43.2	218	341	520	664	189	247	67	52
1999..............	2,323	42.7	218	342	519	682	190	256	65	51
2000..............	2,385	42.6	225	340	530	708	196	267	65	54
2001..............	2,416	42.4	232	347	532	712	198	276	64	55
2002..............	2,494	42.2	238	357	550	742	203	285	63	57
2003..............	2,622	42.1	253	380	573	775	215	304	63	59
2004..............	2,755	41.8	260	405	595	804	233	331	64	62
2005..............	2,850	41.6	268	429	613	826	237	343	67	67
2006..............	2,936	41.3	270	443	631	855	242	358	69	69
2007..............	3,007	41.2	275	453	650	875	242	368	71	73
2008..............	3,093	41.2	283	468	668	895	250	380	73	76
2009..............	3,205	41.3	298	489	685	916	264	399	76	79
2010..............	3,351	41.2	323	527	707	943	275	418	77	82
2011..............	3,553	41.3	361	581	734	982	292	439	80	84

NA Not available. [1] Includes Ph.D., Ed.D, and comparable degrees at the doctoral level. Includes most degrees formerly classified as first-professional, such as M.D., D.D.S., and law degrees. [2] Includes some degrees classified as master's or doctor's degrees in later years.

Source: U.S. National Center for Education Statistics, *Digest of Education Statistics*, "Advance Release of Selected 2012 Digest Tables," <http://www.nces.ed.gov/programs/digest/>, accessed May 2013.

Table 304. Degrees Earned by Level and Race/Ethnicity: 1990 to 2011

[For school year ending in year shown. Based on survey; see Appendix III]

Level of degree and race/ethnicity	Total					Percent distribution		
	1990	2000 [1]	2005 [1]	2010 [1]	2011 [1]	1990	2000 [1]	2011 [1]
Associate's degrees, total............	**455,102**	**564,933**	**696,660**	**849,452**	**942,327**	**100.0**	**100.0**	**100.0**
White, non-Hispanic...................	376,816	408,772	475,513	552,863	604,110	82.8	72.4	64.1
Black, non-Hispanic...................	34,326	60,221	86,402	113,905	128,703	7.5	10.7	13.7
Hispanic.............................	21,504	51,573	78,557	112,211	125,616	4.7	9.1	13.3
Asian or Pacific Islander.............	13,066	27,782	33,669	44,021	45,876	2.9	4.9	4.9
American Indian/Alaska Native.......	3,430	6,497	8,435	10,337	10,173	0.8	1.2	1.1
Two or more races....................	(NA)	(NA)	(NA)	(NA)	11,275	(NA)	(NA)	1.2
Nonresident alien....................	5,960	10,088	14,084	16,115	16,574	1.3	1.8	1.8
Bachelor's degrees, total.............	**1,051,344**	**1,237,875**	**1,439,264**	**1,650,014**	**1,715,913**	**100.0**	**100.0**	**100.0**
White, non-Hispanic...................	887,151	929,106	1,049,141	1,167,499	1,182,405	84.4	75.1	68.9
Black, non-Hispanic...................	61,046	108,013	136,122	164,844	173,017	5.8	8.7	10.1
Hispanic.............................	32,829	75,059	101,124	140,316	154,063	3.1	6.1	9.0
Asian or Pacific Islander.............	39,230	77,912	97,209	117,422	121,066	3.7	6.3	7.1
American Indian/Alaska Native.......	4,390	8,719	10,307	12,399	11,933	0.4	0.7	0.7
Two or more races....................	(NA)	(NA)	(NA)	(NA)	20,804	(NA)	(NA)	1.2
Nonresident alien....................	26,698	39,066	45,361	47,534	52,625	2.5	3.2	3.1
Master's degrees, total..............	**324,301**	**457,056**	**574,618**	**693,025**	**730,635**	**100.0**	**100.0**	**100.0**
White, non-Hispanic...................	254,299	320,485	379,350	445,038	462,903	78.4	70.1	63.4
Black, non-Hispanic...................	15,336	35,874	54,482	76,458	80,706	4.7	7.8	11.0
Hispanic.............................	7,892	19,253	31,485	43,535	46,787	2.4	4.2	6.4
Asian or Pacific Islander.............	10,439	23,218	32,783	42,707	43,728	3.2	5.1	6.0
American Indian/Alaska Native.......	1,090	2,246	3,295	3,960	3,948	0.3	0.5	0.5
Two or more races....................	(NA)	(NA)	(NA)	(NA)	6,700	(NA)	(NA)	0.9
Nonresident alien....................	35,245	55,980	73,223	81,332	85,863	10.9	12.2	11.8
Doctoral degrees, total..............	**38,371**	**44,808**	**52,631**	**158,558**	**163,765**	**100.0**	**100.0**	**100.0**
White, non-Hispanic...................	26,221	27,843	30,261	104,426	105,932	68.3	62.1	64.7
Black, non-Hispanic...................	1,149	2,246	3,056	10,417	10,925	3.0	5.0	6.7
Hispanic.............................	780	1,305	1,824	8,085	8,650	2.0	2.9	5.3
Asian or Pacific Islander.............	1,225	2,420	2,911	16,625	17,078	3.2	5.4	10.4
American Indian/Alaska Native.......	98	160	237	952	947	0.3	0.4	0.6
Two or more races....................	(NA)	(NA)	(NA)	(NA)	1,271	(NA)	(NA)	0.8
Nonresident alien....................	8,898	10,834	14,342	18,053	18,962	23.2	24.2	11.6
First-professional degrees, total.....	**70,988**	**80,057**	**87,289**	**94,103**	**95,749**	**100.0**	**100.0**	**100.0**
White, non-Hispanic...................	60,487	59,637	63,429	66,172	66,211	85.2	74.5	69.2
Black, non-Hispanic...................	3,409	5,555	6,313	6,850	6,915	4.8	6.9	7.2
Hispanic.............................	2,425	3,865	4,445	5,430	5,800	3.4	4.8	6.1
Asian or Pacific Islander.............	3,362	8,584	10,501	12,691	12,843	4.7	10.7	13.4
American Indian/Alaska Native.......	257	564	564	665	662	0.4	0.7	0.7
Two or more races....................	(NA)	(NA)	(NA)	(NA)	842	(NA)	(NA)	0.9
Nonresident alien....................	1,048	1,852	2,037	2,295	2,476	1.5	2.3	2.6

NA Not Available. [1] Beginning 2000, data reflect the new classification of institutions. See footnote 1, Table 282.

Source: U.S. National Center for Education Statistics, *Digest of Education Statistics*, "Advance Release of Selected 2012 Digest Tables," <http://www.nces.ed.gov/programs/digest/>, accessed May 2013.

Table 305. Bachelor's Degrees Earned by Field: 1980 to 2011

[The new Classification of Instructional Programs was introduced in 2009-10. Data for previous years has been reclassified where necessary to conform to the new classifications. Based on survey; see Appendix III]

Field of study	1980	1990	2000	2005	2010	2011
Total [1]...	929,417	1,051,344	1,237,875	1,439,264	1,650,014	1,715,913
Agriculture and natural resources...................	22,802	12,900	24,238	23,002	26,336	28,623
Architecture and related services...................	9,132	9,364	8,462	9,237	10,051	9,832
Area, ethnic, cultural, and gender studies..........	2,840	4,447	6,212	7,569	8,621	9,100
Biological and biomedical sciences.................	46,190	37,204	63,005	64,611	86,400	90,003
Business..	186,264	248,568	256,070	311,574	358,293	365,093
Communication, journalism, and related programs [2].................	28,616	51,572	57,058	75,238	81,266	88,132
Computer and information sciences.................	11,154	27,347	37,788	54,111	39,589	43,072
Education...	118,038	105,112	108,034	105,451	101,265	103,992
Engineering and engineering technologies..........	69,387	82,480	73,419	79,743	88,729	93,117
English language and literature/letters.............	32,187	46,803	50,106	54,379	53,231	52,744
Family and consumer sciences/human sciences.....	18,411	13,514	16,321	20,074	21,818	22,444
Foreign languages, literatures, and linguistics......	12,480	13,133	15,886	18,386	21,516	21,706
Health professions and related clinical sciences.....	63,848	58,983	80,863	80,685	129,634	143,430
Homeland security, law enforcement, and firefighting.................	15,015	15,354	24,877	30,723	43,667	47,602
Legal professions and studies.......................	683	1,632	1,969	3,161	3,886	4,429
Liberal arts and sciences, general studies, and humanities..........	23,196	27,985	36,104	43,751	46,953	46,727
Mathematics and statistics..........................	11,378	14,276	11,418	14,351	16,030	17,182
Multi/interdisciplinary studies.......................	11,457	16,557	28,561	30,243	37,648	42,228
Parks, recreation, leisure, and fitness studies.......	5,753	4,582	17,571	22,888	33,318	35,924
Philosophy and religious studies....................	7,069	7,034	8,535	11,584	12,504	12,836
Physical sciences and science technologies.........	23,407	16,056	18,331	18,905	23,379	24,712
Psychology...	42,093	53,952	74,194	85,614	97,216	100,893
Public administration and social services...........	16,644	13,908	20,185	21,769	25,414	26,774
Social sciences and history.........................	103,662	118,083	127,101	156,892	172,780	177,144
Theology and religious vocations....................	6,170	5,185	6,789	9,284	8,718	9,074
Transportation and materials moving................	213	2,387	3,395	4,904	4,998	4,941
Visual and performing arts..........................	40,892	39,934	58,791	80,955	91,802	93,956

[1] Includes other fields of study, not shown separately. [2] Includes technologies.

Source: U.S. National Center for Education Statistics, *Digest of Education Statistics*, "Advance Release of Selected 2012 Digest Tables," <http://www.nces.ed.gov/programs/digest/>, accessed May 2013.

Table 306. Associate's Degrees and Certificates Below the Associate's Degree Level by Field, 2011

[For school year ending in 2011. The new Classification of Instructional Programs was introduced in 2011. Covers certificates below the associate's degree level based on postsecondary curriculums of less than 4 years in degree- and nondegree-granting institutions of higher education and associate's degrees conferred by degree-granting institutions. Based on survey; see Appendix III]

Field of study	Less than 1-year awards		1- to less than 4-year awards		Associate's degree	
	Total	Female	Total	Female	Total	Female
Total [1]	**482,947**	**281,585**	**546,610**	**356,289**	**942,327**	**581,018**
Agriculture and natural resources, total	3,636	1,266	2,511	945	6,425	2,336
Architecture and related services	219	78	125	59	569	259
Area, ethnic, cultural, and gender studies	415	295	72	53	209	149
Biological and biomedical sciences	162	96	86	54	3,245	2,129
Business, management, marketing, and support services	42,599	29,229	23,591	17,211	121,728	79,109
Communications and communications technologies	4,704	1,711	3,412	986	7,260	3,075
Computer and information sciences and support services	17,332	5,400	10,493	2,769	37,677	8,617
Construction trades	12,021	701	17,529	881	5,402	297
Education	5,095	4,456	3,211	2,801	20,459	17,726
Engineering technologies and engineering-related fields	16,563	2,033	20,238	1,857	35,521	4,427
English language and literature/letters	2,315	1,513	198	137	2,019	1,372
Family and consumer sciences	13,806	12,066	3,192	2,939	8,532	8,174
Foreign languages, literatures, and linguistics	967	761	543	463	1,876	1,499
Health professions and related programs	213,619	172,123	249,418	214,002	201,831	171,758
Homeland security, law enforcement, and firefighting	24,233	5,489	7,790	2,655	44,923	20,992
Legal professions and studies	2,368	2,029	3,510	2,949	11,620	9,785
Liberal arts and sciences, general studies, and humanities	2,417	1,572	23,579	14,080	306,670	188,114
Library science	213	183	73	70	160	139
Mathematics and statistics	61	11	14	3	1,644	620
Mechanics and repair technologies/technicians	33,700	1,819	55,482	2,125	19,969	971
Military technologies and applied sciences	32	7	88	15	856	163
Multi/interdisciplinary studies	1,530	756	1,309	750	23,729	14,824
Parks, recreation, leisure, and fitness studies	912	403	829	316	2,366	934
Personal and culinary services	37,152	30,213	93,554	80,855	18,258	9,706
Philosophy and religion	90	49	34	14	283	106
Physical sciences and science technologies	633	260	541	187	5,078	2,120
Precision production trades	16,095	821	13,269	681	3,254	230
Psychology	15	9	54	47	3,866	2,970
Public administration and social service professions	1,167	937	654	511	7,472	6,447
Social sciences and history	565	233	296	122	12,767	8,256
Theology and religious vocations	135	81	1,061	589	758	363
Transportation and material moving	22,587	1,819	980	60	1,697	279
Visual and performing arts	5,229	3,110	8,680	5,068	21,379	12,673

[1] Includes other fields of study, not shown separately.

Source: U.S. National Center for Education Statistics, *Digest of Education Statistics*, "Advance Release of Selected 2012 Digest Tables," <http://www.nces.ed.gov/programs/digest/>, accessed May 2013.

Table 307. Master's and Doctoral Degrees Earned by Field: 1971 to 2011

[For school years ending in years shown. The new Classification of Instructional Programs was introduced in 2009-2010. Data for previous years has been reclassified where necessary to conform to the new classifications. Based on survey; see Appendix III]

Field of study	1971	1981	1991	2001	2010	2011
MASTER'S DEGREES						
Total [1]	**235,564**	**302,637**	**342,863**	**473,502**	**693,025**	**730,635**
Agriculture and natural resources	2,457	4,003	3,295	4,272	5,211	5,773
Architecture and related services	1,705	3,153	3,490	4,302	7,280	7,788
Area, ethnic, cultural, gender, and group studies	1,032	802	1,233	1,555	1,775	1,914
Biological and biomedical sciences	5,625	5,766	4,834	7,017	10,725	11,327
Business	26,490	57,888	78,255	115,602	177,684	187,213
Communication, journalism, and related programs	1,770	2,896	4,123	5,218	7,636	8,303
Communications technologies	86	209	204	427	463	502
Computer and information sciences	1,588	4,218	9,324	16,911	17,953	19,446
Education	87,666	96,713	87,352	127,829	182,139	185,009
Engineering	16,813	16,893	24,454	25,174	35,088	38,719
Engineering technologies	134	323	996	2,013	4,258	4,515
English language and literature/letters	10,441	5,742	6,784	6,763	9,201	9,476
Family and consumer sciences/human sciences	1,452	2,570	1,541	1,838	2,580	2,918
Foreign languages, literatures, and linguistics	5,480	2,934	3,049	3,035	3,755	3,727
Health professions and related programs	5,330	16,176	21,354	43,623	69,084	75,579
Homeland security, law enforcement, and firefighting	194	1,538	1,108	2,514	6,714	7,433
Legal professions and studies	955	1,832	2,057	3,829	5,734	6,300
Liberal arts and sciences, general studies, and humanities	885	2,375	2,213	3,193	3,804	3,971
Library science	7,001	4,859	4,763	4,727	7,448	7,727
Mathematics and statistics	5,191	2,567	3,549	3,209	5,634	5,843
Military technologies and applied sciences	2	43	–	–	–	–
Multi/interdisciplinary studies	924	2,356	2,079	3,413	5,973	6,748
Parks, recreation, leisure, and fitness studies	218	643	483	2,354	5,617	6,553
Philosophy and religious studies	1,326	1,231	1,471	1,386	2,043	1,833
Physical sciences and science technologies	6,336	5,246	5,281	5,134	6,063	6,386
Precision production	–	–	–	2	10	5
Psychology	5,717	10,223	11,349	16,539	23,752	25,051
Public administration and social services	7,785	17,803	17,905	25,268	35,729	38,634
Social sciences and history	16,539	11,945	12,233	13,791	20,222	21,084
Theology and religious vocations	7,747	11,061	10,498	9,876	12,824	13,191
Transportation and materials moving	–	–	406	756	1,074	1,390
Visual and performing arts	6,675	8,629	8,657	11,404	15,552	16,277
DOCTORAL DEGREES						
Total [1]	**64,998**	**98,016**	**105,547**	**119,585**	**158,558**	**163,765**
Agriculture and natural resources	1,086	1,067	1,185	1,127	1,147	1,246
Architecture and related services	36	93	135	153	210	205
Area, ethnic, cultural, gender, and group studies	143	161	159	216	253	278
Biological and biomedical sciences	3,603	3,640	4,152	5,225	7,666	7,693
Business	774	808	1,185	1,180	2,245	2,286
Communication, journalism, and related programs	145	171	259	368	570	577
Communications technologies	–	11	13	2	3	1
Computer and information sciences	128	252	676	768	1,599	1,588
Education	6,041	7,279	6,189	6,284	9,233	9,623
Engineering	3,687	2,598	5,316	5,485	7,704	8,369
Engineering technologies	1	10	14	62	67	56
English language and literature/letters	1,554	1,040	1,056	1,330	1,332	1,344
Family and consumer sciences/human sciences	123	247	229	354	296	320
Foreign languages, literatures, and linguistics	1,084	931	889	1,078	1,091	1,158
Health professions and related programs	15,988	29,595	29,842	39,019	57746	60153
Homeland security, law enforcement, and firefighting	1	21	28	44	106	131
Legal professions and studies	17,441	36,391	38,035	38,190	44,626	44,877
Liberal arts and sciences, general studies, and humanities	32	121	70	102	96	95
Library science	39	71	56	58	64	50
Mathematics and statistics	1,199	728	978	997	1,592	1,586
Multi/interdisciplinary studies	101	236	306	512	631	660
Parks, recreation, leisure, and fitness studies	2	42	28	177	266	257
Philosophy and religious studies	555	411	464	600	667	805
Physical sciences and science technologies	4,324	3,105	4,248	3,968	5,063	5,295
Psychology	2,144	3,576	3,932	5,091	5,540	5,851
Public administration and social services	174	362	430	574	838	851
Social sciences and history	3,660	3,122	3,012	3,930	4,238	4,390
Theology and religious vocations	312	1,273	1,076	1,461	2,070	2,374
Visual and performing arts	621	654	838	1,167	1,599	1,646

– Represents zero. [1] Includes other fields of study, not shown separately.

Source: U.S. National Center for Education Statistics, *Digest of Education Statistics*, "Advance Release of Selected 2012 Digest Tables," <http://www.nces.ed.gov/programs/digest/>, accessed May 2013.

Table 308. First Professional Degrees Earned in Selected Professions: 1970 to 2011

[First professional degrees include degrees which require at least 6 years of college work for completion (including at least 2 years of preprofessional training). Based on survey; see Appendix III]

Type of degree and sex of recipient	1970	1980	1985	1990	1995	2000	2005	2009	2010	2011
Medicine (M.D.):										
Institutions conferring degrees..............	86	112	120	124	119	118	120	120	120	120
Degrees conferred, total.....................	8,314	14,902	16,041	15,075	15,537	15,286	15,461	15,987	16,356	16,863
Percent to women.........................	8.4	23.4	30.4	34.2	38.8	42.7	47.3	48.9	48.2	48.4
Dentistry (D.D.S. or D.M.D.):										
Institutions conferring degrees..............	48	58	59	57	53	54	53	55	55	55
Degrees conferred, total.....................	3,718	5,258	5,339	4,100	3,897	4,250	4,454	4,918	5,062	5,071
Percent to women.........................	0.9	13.3	20.7	30.9	36.4	40.1	43.8	46.4	45.8	45.5
Law (LL.B. or J.D.):										
Institutions conferring degrees..............	145	179	181	182	183	190	198	203	205	206
Degrees conferred, total.....................	14,916	35,647	37,491	36,485	39,349	38,152	43,423	44,045	44,345	44,445
Percent to women.........................	5.4	30.2	38.5	42.2	42.6	45.9	48.7	45.8	47.2	47.1
Theological (B.D., M.Div., M.H.L.):										
Institutions conferring degrees..............	(NA)	(NA)	(NA)	(NA)	192	198	(NA)	(NA)	(NA)	(NA)
Degrees conferred, total.....................	5,298	7,115	7,221	5,851	5,978	6,129	5,533	5,362	5,672	5,832
Percent to women.........................	2.3	13.8	18.5	24.8	25.7	29.2	35.6	33.1	33.8	31.6

NA Not available.

Source: U.S. National Center for Education Statistics, *Digest of Education Statistics*, "Advance Release of Selected 2012 Digest Tables," <http://www.nces.ed.gov/programs/digest/>, accessed May 2013.

Table 309. Mean Student Loan Debt of Households: 1989 to 2010

[In 2011 dollars, unless otherwise noted. Includes education loans that are currently in deferment and loans in scheduled repayment period. Pew Research Center tabulations of Survey of Consumer Finances data. See source for details]

Household Characteristic	1989	1992	1995	1998	2001	2004	2007	2010
All households.......................	**9,634**	**11,086**	**11,714**	**17,942**	**17,562**	**20,022**	**23,349**	**26,682**
Age of household head								
Younger than 35.............................	10,304	10,449	11,841	20,682	15,478	19,586	25,795	26,842
35-44..	8,632	12,743	10,056	13,455	26,239	22,651	20,477	27,634
45-54..	11,010	7,659	14,907	17,269	12,717	19,042	22,440	25,152
55-64..	5,488	16,826	11,746	21,203	19,258	17,321	19,778	29,853
65 and older..................................	9,419	10,854	4,794	5,771	2,579	25,145	21,443	17,578
Highest education of household head								
Less than HS diploma.......................	5,156	4,083	5,739	8,104	5,573	9,257	10,260	9,477
HS graduate..................................	6,344	6,280	6,349	7,687	10,745	14,792	13,573	13,227
Some college.................................	8,140	6,716	12,475	16,109	10,756	13,837	14,839	20,509
College graduate.............................	12,373	15,254	14,359	22,310	24,561	25,405	31,470	36,809
Household annual income								
Lowest fifth..................................	9,126	6,887	9,552	13,444	11,388	18,312	19,018	20,640
Second fifth..................................	5,955	10,328	9,976	16,880	15,861	21,426	17,400	18,659
Middle fifth...................................	12,843	15,474	14,092	19,890	16,610	18,146	20,887	29,953
Fourth fifth...................................	11,083	8,639	9,764	18,157	16,136	19,041	26,283	24,076
80%–89.9%...................................	6,367	10,516	15,804	15,155	19,822	19,678	25,921	31,989
Richest 10%..................................	11,014	17,025	14,756	27,990	33,215	28,855	36,033	44,810
Household wealth								
Lowest fourth................................	11,623	13,773	14,842	23,703	18,405	21,352	23,121	35,096
Second fourth................................	6,071	7,598	8,399	11,813	11,923	15,430	20,548	18,071
Third fourth..................................	7,777	8,587	8,319	15,603	14,849	22,800	23,150	21,108
75%–89.9%...................................	15,155	7,797	15,227	9,353	24,981	24,330	27,312	21,564
Wealthiest 10%...............................	6,223	17,883	11,519	19,256	72,373	12,930	37,616	26,145
Percent of student loan debt to household income....................	**1.2**	**1.9**	**2.1**	**2.8**	**2.3**	**3.2**	**3.9**	**6.3**

Source: Pew Research Center, Social and Demographic Trends, *A Record One-in-Five Households Now Owe Student Loan Debt*, September 2012, <http://pewresearch.org/>.

Table 310. Online Course Enrollment in Degree-Granting Postsecondary Institutions: 2002 to 2011

[Enrollment in thousands (16,612 represents 16,612,000). For school year beginning in Fall of year shown]

	Total Enrollment		Online course enrollment			
	Total Enrollment	Annual Growth Rate	Students Taking at Least One Online Course	Increase Over Previous Year	Annual Growth Rate	As a Percent of Total Enrollment
2002..............	16,612	(X)	1,603	(X)	(X)	9.6
2003..............	19,911	1.8	1,971	368	23.0	11.7
2004..............	17,272	2.1	2,330	358	18.2	13.5
2005..............	17,487	1.2	3,180	850	36.5	18.2
2006..............	17,759	1.6	3,488	308	9.7	19.6
2007..............	18,248	2.8	3,938	450	12.9	21.6
2008..............	19,103	4.7	4,606	668	16.9	24.1
2009..............	20,428	6.9	5,579	973	21.1	27.3
2010..............	21,016	2.9	6,142	563	10.1	29.2
2011..............	20,994	-0.1	6,715	573	9.3	32.0

X Not applicable.

Source: Babson Survey Research Group, *Changing Course: Ten Years of Tracking Online Education in the United States* ©, January 2013.

Table 311. Bachelor's Degree Recipients with Loans and Amount Borrowed in Constant (2009) Dollars by Selected Characteristics: 1994 to 2009

[Data shown for first-time Bachelor's degree recipients. Based on Baccalaureate and Beyond Longitudinal Studies]

Characteristic	Percent with loans			Average Cumulative Amount Borrowed for Undergraduate Education (2009 Dollars)		
	1994	2001	2009	1994	2001	2009
Total Loans.............................	**49.3**	**63.5**	**65.6**	**14,700**	**21,800**	**24,700**
Sex						
Male............................	50.1	62.5	62.9	15,000	21,300	23,900
Female..........................	49.4	64.3	67.6	14,400	22,100	25,200
Race/Ethnicity [1]						
White...........................	47.8	62.2	64.6	14,900	21,700	24,500
Black...........................	65.5	79.8	80.3	13,800	25,200	28,700
Hispanic........................	60.5	66.7	67.0	11,400	19,900	22,800
Asian...........................	43.1	55.5	53.4	16,800	19,100	21,000
Other...........................	63.4	62.8	68.8	14,900	21,500	25,600
Age at receipt of Bachelor's degree						
18-23...........................	43.9	60.0	61.0	15,200	20,800	23,700
24-29...........................	62.9	71.3	76.8	13,800	23,100	24,900
30 and older....................	55.9	65.7	72.5	13,800	23,000	28,300
Time to complete Bachelor's degree						
48 months or less..............	41.4	59.2	59.5	16,000	21,000	24,100
49-60 months...................	49.5	63.0	64.9	14,900	21,100	23,800
61-72 months...................	51.6	68.5	73.4	14,100	21,500	22,900
73-120 months..................	63.4	69.3	76.8	13,600	24,500	26,200
Over 120 months................	56.1	67.0	72.4	13,300	22,100	27,600
Institution Type						
2-Year or less						
Public 2-year..................	53.1	67.8	67.5	13,300	21,500	24,500
Other 2-year or less...........	56.8	64.6	85.0	13,600	24,500	31,600
4-Year						
Public.........................	45.7	59.5	62.1	12,900	20,100	21,900
Private nonprofit..............	53.4	69.0	69.4	18,200	24,100	27,900
For-profit.....................	63.4	77.3	87.7	(X)	27,400	36,000

X Not applicable. [1] Black includes African American; Hispanic includes Latino; Asian includes Pacific Islander and Native Hawaiian; other includes American Indian, Alaska Native, and graduates having origins in two or more races or a race not listed. Race categories exclude persons of Hispanic ethnicity unless specified. In 1994, graduates of two or more races were asked to choose one category, in subsequent studies graduates could identify as multiracial.

Source: National Center for Education Statistics, *Trends in Debt for Bachelor's Degree Recipients a Year After Graduation: 1994, 2001, and 2009*, December 2012. See also <http://nces.ed.gov/>.

Table 312. Academic Libraries by Selected Characteristics: 2010

[As of Fall of year shown. For information on public libraries, see Tables 1180 and 1181]

Institution characteristic	Number of libraries	Circulation (1,000)		Expendi-tures (mil. dol.)	Paid staff [1]			
		General collection	Reserve collection		Total [2]	Librar-ians	Other pro-fessional staff	Student assistants
All U.S. academic libraries............	**3,689**	**136,003**	**40,733**	**6,829**	**88,943**	**26,706**	**7,441**	**22,382**
Control:								
Public...............................	1,559	87,090	28,993	4,020	53,606	15,387	4,319	12,700
Private..............................	2,130	48,913	11,740	2,809	35,337	11,319	3,122	9,682
Level: [3]								
Total 4-year and above...............	2,363	118,003	33,100	6,199	76,683	22,563	6,376	19,830
Doctor's...........................	821	87,255	23,309	4,986	56,436	16,072	4,936	13,601
Master's...........................	833	20,533	6,878	852	13,934	4,355	961	4,221
Bachelor's.........................	709	10,216	2,913	361	6,313	2,135	478	2,008
Less than 4-year.....................	1,326	18,000	7,633	630	12,260	4,144	1,065	2,552
Size (FTE enrollment): [4]								
Less than 1,000......................	1,236	7,208	1,115	295	5,475	2,029	508	1,734
1,000 to 2,999.......................	1,145	18,512	5,594	811	13,329	4,345	1,107	4,050
3,000 to 4,999.......................	470	11,444	3,713	547	8,690	2,813	656	2,238
5,000 to 9,999.......................	428	18,606	7,126	1,055	14,547	4,451	1,089	3,680
10,000 to 19,999.....................	277	29,607	10,904	1,627	19,709	5,666	1,568	4,413
20,000 or more.......................	133	50,624	12,280	2,495	27,194	7,402	2,512	6,268

[1] Full-time equivalent (FTE) staff is calculated by dividing the total number of hours for all part-time positions by the number of hours the library defines as a full-time position. [2] Includes other staff not shown separately. [3] Level refers to the highest level of any degree offered by the institution. Doctoral, master's, and bachelor's level institutions do not sum to total number of 4-year and above institutions because there are 4-year and above institutions that grant "other" degrees and are thus not included in the breakdown. [4] Full-time equivalent (FTE) enrollment is calculated by adding one-third of part-time enrollment to full-time enrollment.

Source: U.S. National Center for Education Statistics, *Academic Libraries: 2010, First Look,* December 2011. See also <http://nces.ed.gov/surveys/libraries/academic.asp>.

Table 313. Public Schools Reporting Incidents of Crime by Incident Type and Selected School Characteristics: 2009 to 2010

[For school year ending in 2010. Includes incidents that happen in school buildings, on school grounds, on school buses, and at places that hold school-sponsored events or activities. Based on sample; see source for details]

School characteristic	Total number of schools	Percent of schools with—				Rate per 1,000 students			
		Violent incidents[1]	Serious violent incidents[2]	Theft[3]	Other incidents[4]	Violent incidents[1]	Serious violent incidents[2]	Theft[3]	Other incidents[4]
All public schools[5]	**82,800**	**73.8**	**16.4**	**44.1**	**68.1**	**25.0**	**1.1**	**5.5**	**9.2**
Level:[6]									
Primary	48,900	64.4	13.0	25.7	57.3	21.3	1.0	1.8	4.5
Middle	15,300	90.5	18.9	65.2	81.9	40.0	1.5	7.4	11.1
High school	12,200	90.9	27.6	82.6	92.2	21.4	1.1	10.1	16.2
Enrollment size:									
Less than 300	18,900	62.8	10.4	30.7	55.3	27.2	[7]1.5	5.2	8.9
300 to 499	25,200	71.3	15.7	36.4	63.3	26.5	1.4	3.9	6.9
500 to 999	29,800	76.4	15.9	46.7	72.5	25.0	0.8	4.2	6.9
1,000 or more	8,900	95.4	32.8	84.9	94.3	23.2	1.2	8.6	14.4
Percent minority enrollment:									
Less than 5 percent	11,700	69.6	12.6	40.8	59.0	23.3	[7]1.2	4.9	7.4
5 to 20 percent	20,900	67.9	9.9	38.3	61.2	17.2	0.6	4.8	7.1
20 to 50 percent	20,000	75.9	18.6	46.2	69.7	23.1	1.2	5.8	8.9
50 percent or more	30,100	78.2	21.1	48.0	75.5	31.4	1.4	5.8	11.1

[1] Violent incidents include rape, sexual battery other than rape, physical attack or fight with or without a weapon, threat of physical attack with or without a weapon, and robbery with or without a weapon. [2] Serious violent incidents include rape, sexual battery other than rape, physical attack or fight with a weapon, threat of physical attack with a weapon, and robbery with or without a weapon. [3] Theft or larceny (taking things worth over $10 without personal confrontation). Includes pocket picking, stealing purse or backpack (if left unattended or no force was used to take from owner), theft from motor vehicles, etc. [4] Other incidents include possession of a firearm or explosive device, possession of knife or sharp object, distribution of illegal drugs, possession or use of alcohol or illegal drugs, and vandalism. [5] Includes combined schools, not shown separately, which include all other combination of grades, including K–12 schools. [6] Primary schools are defined as schools in which the lowest grade is not higher than grade 3 and the highest grade is not higher than grade 8. Middle schools are defined as schools in which the lowest grade is not lower than grade 4 and the highest grade is not higher than grade 9. High schools are defined as schools in which the lowest grade is not lower than grade 9 and the highest grade is not higher than grade 12. [7] Interpret data with caution.

Source: U.S. National Center for Education Statistics, *Indicators of School Crime and Safety: 2012,* June 2013. See also <http://nces.ed.gov/programs/crimeindicators/crimeindicators2012/>.

Table 314. Percent of Public Schools Reporting Selected Types of Disciplinary Problems Occurring at School by Selected School Characteristics: 2009 to 2010

[In percent. For school year. "At school" includes activities that happen in school buildings, on school grounds, on school buses, and at places that hold school-sponsored events or activities. Based on sample; see source for details]

School characteristic	Happens at least once a week						Happens at all	
	Student racial tensions	Student bullying	Student sexual harassment of other students[1]	Student verbal abuse of teachers	Wide-spread disorder in classrooms	Student acts of disrespect for teachers	Undesirable gang activities[2]	Undesirable cult or extremist group activities[3]
All public schools	**2.8**	**23.1**	**3.2**	**4.8**	**2.5**	**8.6**	**16.4**	**1.7**
Level:[4]								
Primary	2.1	19.6	[5]1.8	3.4	[5]1.9	6.1	7.5	[5]1.4
Middle	5.4	38.6	6.1	6.8	4.1	13.7	29.2	1.4
High school	3.3	19.8	3.2	8.6	4.4	14.3	38.4	3.9
Combined	(S)	18.6	[5]7.5	(S)	–	[5]4.4	11.1	(S)
Enrollment size:								
Less than 300	(S)	16.5	[5]4.5	(S)	(S)	[5]3.3	6.5	(S)
300 to 499	[5]2.5	24.0	[5]2.4	5.2	2.4	[5]9.5	11.9	[5](S)
500 to 999	3.0	25.3	2.6	4.3	2.6	8.3	16.4	[5]1.3
1,000 or more	5.5	27.0	4.7	11.2	4.3	18.2	49.8	5.6
Percent minority enrollment:								
Less than 5 percent	(S)	22.0	[5]4.5	(S)	(S)	[5]3.6	1.5	[5]0.4
5 to 20 percent	1.5	21.3	[5]1.8	1.8	[5]0.5	6.1	5.8	[5]1.8
20 to 50 percent	3.2	22.3	2.6	4.5	[5]1.1	[5]9.6	16.9	1.4
50 percent or more	4.3	25.2	[5]4.1	8.5	5.7	11.7	29.1	2.4

S Figure does not meet publication standards. – Represents zero [1] Sexual harassment includes "unsolicited, offensive behavior that inappropriately asserts sexuality over another person. This behavior may be verbal or nonverbal." [2] Gang includes an "ongoing loosely organized association of three or more persons, whether formal or informal, that has a common name, signs, symbols, or colors, whose members engage, either individually or collectively, in violent or other forms of illegal behavior." [3] Cult or extremist group includes "a group that espouses radical beliefs and practices, which may include a religious component, that are widely seen as threatening the basic values and cultural norms of society at large." [4] Primary schools are defined as schools in which the lowest grade is not higher than grade 3 and the highest grade is not higher than grade 8. Middle schools are defined as schools in which the lowest grade level is not lower than grade 4 and the highest grade is not higher than grade 9. High schools are defined as schools in which the lowest grade is not lower than grade 9 and the highest grade is not higher than grade 12. Combined schools include all other combinations of grades, including K–12 schools. [5] Interpret data with caution.

Source: U.S. National Center for Education Statistics, *Indicators of School Crime and Safety: 2012,* June 2013. See also: <http://nces.ed.gov/programs/crimeindicators/crimeindicators2012/>.

Table 315. Students Who Reported Being Threatened or Injured With a Weapon on School Property by Selected Student Characteristics: 1997 to 2011

[In percent. Based on a survey of students in public and private schools, in grades 9 to 12. Data are for previous 12 months. "On school property" was not defined for survey respondents. "Weapon" was defined as a gun, knife, or club for survey respondents]

Characteristic	1997	1999	2001	2003	2005	2007	2009	2011
Total	**7.4**	**7.7**	**8.9**	**9.2**	**7.9**	**7.8**	**7.7**	**7.4**
Sex:								
Male	10.2	9.5	11.5	11.6	9.7	10.2	9.6	9.5
Female	4.0	5.8	6.5	6.5	6.1	5.4	5.5	5.2
Race/ethnicity: [1]								
White	6.2	6.6	8.5	7.8	7.2	6.9	6.4	6.1
Black	9.9	7.6	9.3	10.9	8.1	9.7	9.4	8.9
Hispanic	9.0	9.8	8.9	9.4	9.8	8.7	9.1	9.2
Asian	([2])	7.7	11.3	11.5	4.6	[3] 7.6	5.5	7.0
American Indian/Alaska Native	[3] 2.5	[3] 13.2	[3] 15.2	22.1	9.8	5.9	16.5	8.2
Pacific Islander/Native Hawaiian	([2])	15.6	24.8	16.3	[3] 14.5	[3] 8.1	12.5	11.3
More than one race	([2])	9.3	10.3	18.7	10.7	13.3	9.2	9.9
Grade:								
9th	10.1	10.5	12.7	12.1	10.5	9.2	8.7	8.3
10th	7.9	8.2	9.1	9.2	8.8	8.4	8.4	7.7
11th	5.9	6.1	6.9	7.3	5.5	6.8	7.9	7.3
12th	5.8	5.1	5.3	6.3	5.8	6.3	5.2	5.9

[1] Race categories exclude persons of Hispanic ethnicity. [2] The response categories for race/ethnicity changed in 1999 making comparisons of some categories with earlier years problematic. In 1997, Asian students and Pacific Islander students were not categorized separately and students were not given the option of choosing more than one race. [3] Interpret data with caution.

Source: National Center for Education Statistics, *Indicators of School Crime and Safety: 2012*, June 2013. See also <http://nces.ed.gov/programs/crimeindicators/crimeindicators2012/index.asp>.

Table 316. Public Schools Using Selected Safety and Security Measures by School Characteristics: 2000 to 2010

[In percent. For school year ending in year shown. Based on survey of principals or persons knowledgeable about discipline issues at the school. Refers only to those times during normal school hours or when school activities or events were in session. Based on the School Survey on Crime and Safety and subject to sampling error; for details see source]

Measure	2000	2006	2008	2010
Controlled access during school hours:				
Buildings (locked or monitored doors)	74.6	84.9	89.5	91.7
Grounds (locked or monitored gates)	33.7	41.1	42.6	46.0
Closed the campus for most students during lunch	64.6	66.1	65.0	66.9
Drug testing:				
Any students	4.1	(NA)	(NA)	(NA)
Athletes	(NA)	5.0	6.4	6.0
Students in extracurricular activities other than athletes	(NA)	3.4	4.5	4.6
Any other students	(NA)	3.0	3.0	3.0
Prohibited all tobacco use on school grounds	90.1	90.3	91.4	(NA)
Required to wear badges or picture IDs:				
Students	3.9	6.1	7.6	6.9
Faculty and staff	25.4	47.8	58.3	62.9
Metal detector checks on students:				
Random checks [1]	7.2	4.9	5.3	5.2
Required to pass through daily	0.9	1.1	1.3	1.4
Sweeps and technology:				
Random dog sniffs to check for drugs [1]	20.6	23.0	21.5	22.9
Random sweeps for contraband [1, 2]	11.8	13.1	11.4	12.1
Provided telephones in most classrooms	44.6	66.8	71.6	74.0
Used security cameras to monitor school [1]	19.4	42.8	55.0	61.1
Provided two-way radios	(NA)	70.8	73.1	73.3
Limited access to social networking websites from school computers	(NA)	(NA)	(NA)	93.4
Prohibited use of cell phones and text messaging devices	(NA)	(NA)	(NA)	90.9
Visitor requirements:				
Sign-in or check-in	96.6	97.6	98.7	99.3
Pass through metal detectors	0.9	1.0	(NA)	(NA)
Dress code:				
Required students to wear uniforms	11.8	13.8	17.5	18.9
Enforced a strict dress code	47.4	55.3	54.8	56.9
School supplies and equipment:				
Required clear book bags or banned book bags on school grounds	5.9	6.4	6.0	5.5
Provided school lockers to students	46.5	50.6	48.9	52.1

NA Not available. [1] One or more check, sweep, or camera. [2] For example, drugs or weapons. Does not include dog sniffs.

Source: U.S. National Center for Education Statistics, *Indicators of School Crime and Safety: 2012*, June 2013. See also: <http://nces.ed.gov/programs/crimeindicators/crimeindicators2012/>.

Table 317. Students Who Reported Being Bullied at School or Cyber-Bullied by Student Characteristics: 2011

[In percent. For school year ending in 2011. For students aged 12 through 18. "At school" includes the school building, on school property, on a school bus, or going to and from school. For more information, see Appendix A of source]

Characteristic	Total [1]	Bullied at school					Cyber-bullying anywhere [2]
		Total bullying at school	Made fun of, called names, or insulted	Subject of rumors	Threatened with harm	Pushed, shoved, tripped, spit on	
Total......................	**29.7**	**27.8**	**17.6**	**18.3**	**5.0**	**7.9**	**9.0**
Sex:							
Male........................	26.7	24.5	16.2	13.2	5.0	8.9	6.9
Female......................	32.9	31.4	19.1	23.8	5.1	6.8	11.2
Race/ethnicity: [3]							
White........................	33.5	31.5	20.6	20.3	5.8	8.6	10.6
Black........................	28.5	27.2	16.4	18.6	5.5	9.3	7.0
Hispanic....................	23.8	21.9	12.7	15.1	3.3	6.2	7.6
Asian........................	16.2	14.9	9.0	7.7	(S)	[4] 2.1	[4] 5.5
Other........................	24.3	23.7	15.0	17.0	6.5	7.2	[4] 3.8
Grade:							
6th..........................	37.4	37.0	27.0	23.1	4.9	12.7	6.4
7th..........................	31.9	30.3	22.4	18.3	6.9	12.6	8.1
8th..........................	32.0	30.7	20.7	19.0	5.3	10.8	8.6
9th..........................	27.9	26.5	16.4	16.3	5.4	7.3	8.3
10th.........................	30.8	28.0	16.9	19.6	5.1	6.7	11.6
11th.........................	26.8	23.8	12.7	17.1	4.0	3.9	11.1
12th.........................	23.8	22.0	10.6	16.7	3.5	2.7	7.8

S Reporting standards not met. [1] Bullying types do not sum to total because students could have experienced more than one type of bullying. Total includes other types of bullying not shown separately. [2] Cyber-bullied students includes students who responded that another student had posted hurtful information about them on the Internet; purposefully shared private information about them on the Internet; harassed them via instant messaging, via Short Message Service (SMS) text messaging, or via email; harassed them while gaming; or excluded them online. [3] Race categories exclude persons of Hispanic ethnicity. Other includes American Indian, Alaska Native, Pacific Islander, and more than one race. [4] Interpret data with caution.

Source: U.S. National Center for Education Statistics, *Indicators of School Crime and Safety: 2012,* June 2013. See also <http://nces.ed.gov/surveys/ssocs/>.

Table 318. Violent Deaths, Homicides, and Suicides Occurring at Schools, Total and for Youth Aged 5-18: 1993 to 2011

[For school year ending in year shown. A school-associated violent death is defined as a homicide, suicide, or legal intervention (involving a law enforcement officer) in which the fatal injury occurred on the campus of a functioning elementary or secondary school in the United States, including while the victim was on the way to or from regular sessions at school or while the victim was attending or traveling to or from an official school-sponsored event. Victims include students, staff members, and others who are not students]

Year	School-associated violent deaths				Homicides of Youth Aged 5-18		Suicides of Youth Aged 5-18	
	Total [1]	Homicides	Suicides	Legal inter-ventions	Total	At School	Total	At School
1993...................	57	47	10	0	2,713	34	1,680	6
1994...................	48	38	10	0	2,922	29	1,723	7
1995...................	48	39	8	0	2,705	28	1,767	7
1996...................	53	46	6	1	2,552	32	1,725	6
1997...................	48	45	2	1	2,229	28	1,633	1
1998...................	57	47	9	1	2,106	34	1,626	6
1999...................	47	38	6	2	1,781	33	1,597	4
2000 [2]...............	37	26	11	0	1,566	14	1,415	8
2001 [2]...............	34	26	7	1	1,503	14	1,493	6
2002 [2]...............	36	27	8	1	1,503	16	1,400	5
2003 [2]...............	36	25	11	0	1,548	18	1,331	10
2004 [2]...............	45	37	7	1	1,465	23	1,285	5
2005 [2]...............	52	40	10	2	1,551	22	1,471	8
2006 [2]...............	44	37	6	1	1,689	21	1,408	3
2007 [2]...............	63	48	13	2	1,811	32	1,296	9
2008 [2]...............	48	39	7	2	1,743	21	1,231	5
2009 [2]...............	44	29	15	0	1,595	17	1,344	7
2010 [2]...............	35	27	5	3	1,396	19	1,467	2
2011 [2]...............	31	25	6	0	(NA)	11	1,456	3

NA Not available. [1] Total includes unintentional firearm-related deaths, not shown separately. [2] Data from school year 2000 onward are subject to change until interviews with school and law enforcement officials have been completed. The details learned during interviews can occasionally change the classification of a case.

Source: National Center for Education Statistics, *Indicators of School Crime and Safety: 2012,* June 2013. See also <http://nces.ed.gov/programs/crimeindicators/crimeindicators2012/>.

Law Enforcement, Courts, and Prisons

This section presents data on crimes committed, victims of crimes, arrests, and data related to criminal violations and the criminal justice system. The major sources of these data are the Bureau of Justice Statistics (BJS), the Federal Bureau of Investigation (FBI), and the Administrative Office of the U.S. Courts. BJS issues many reports—see our Guide to Sources for a complete listing. The Federal Bureau of Investigation's major annual reports are *Crime in the United States, Law Enforcement Officers Killed and Assaulted*, and *Hate Crimes*, which present data on reported crimes as gathered from state and local law enforcement agencies.

Legal jurisdiction and law enforcement— Law enforcement is, for the most part, a function of state and local officers and agencies. The U.S. Constitution reserves general police powers to the states. By act of Congress, federal offenses include only offenses against the U.S. government and against or by its employees while engaged in their official duties, and offenses which involve the crossing of state lines or an interference with interstate commerce. Excluding the military, there are 52 separate criminal law jurisdictions in the United States: one in each of the 50 states, one in the District of Columbia, and the federal jurisdiction. Each of these has its own criminal law and procedure and its own law enforcement agencies. While the systems of law enforcement are quite similar among the states, there are often substantial differences in the penalties for like offenses.

Law enforcement can be divided into three parts: Investigation of crimes and arrests of persons suspected of committing them; prosecution of those charged with crime; and the punishment or treatment of persons convicted of crime.

Crime—The U.S. Department of Justice administers two statistical programs to measure the magnitude, nature, and impact of crime in the nation: the Uniform Crime Reporting (UCR) Program and the National Crime Victimization Survey (NCVS). Each of these programs produces valuable information about aspects of the nation's crime problem. Because the UCR and NCVS programs are conducted for different purposes, use different methods, and focus on somewhat different aspects of crime, the information they produce together provides a more comprehensive panorama of the nation's crime problem than either could produce alone.

Uniform Crime Reports (UCR)—The FBI's UCR Program, which began in 1929, collects information on the following crimes reported to law enforcement authorities—Part 1 offenses (detailed data reported): murder and nonnegligent manslaughter, forcible rape, robbery, aggravated assault, burglary, larceny-theft, motor vehicle theft, and arson. For Part 2 offenses, law enforcement agencies report only arrest data for 20 additional crime categories. For UCR definitions of criminal offenses (including those listed), please go to: <http://www.fbi.gov/about-us/cjis/ucr/crime-in-the-u.s/2011/crime-in-the-u.s.-2011/offense-definitions>.

The UCR Program compiles data from monthly law enforcement reports or individual crime incident records transmitted directly to the FBI or to centralized state agencies that then report to the FBI. The Program thoroughly examines each report it receives for reasonableness, accuracy, and deviations that may indicate errors. Large variations in crime levels may indicate modified records procedures, incomplete reporting, or changes in a jurisdiction's boundaries. To identify any unusual fluctuations in an agency's crime counts, the Program compares monthly reports to previous submissions of the agency and with those for similar agencies.

The UCR Program presents crime counts for the nation as a whole, as well as for regions, states, counties, cities, towns, tribal law enforcement, and colleges and universities. This permits studies among neighboring jurisdictions and among those with similar populations and other common characteristics.

The UCR Program annually publishes its findings online in a preliminary release in the spring of the following calendar year, followed by a detailed annual report, *Crime in the United States*, issued in the fall. In addition to crime counts and trends, this report includes data on crimes cleared, persons arrested (age, sex, and race), law enforcement personnel (including the number of sworn officers killed or assaulted), and the characteristics of homicides (including age, sex, and race of victims and offenders; victim-offender relationships; weapons used; and circumstances surrounding the homicides). Other periodic reports are also available from the UCR Program.

National Crime Victimization Survey (NCVS)—A second perspective on crime is provided by this survey of the Bureau of Justice Statistics (BJS). The NCVS is an annual data collection (interviews of persons aged 12 or older), conducted by the U.S. Census Bureau for the BJS. As an ongoing survey of households, the NCVS measures crimes of violence and property both reported and not reported to police. It produces national rates and levels of personal and property victimization. No attempt is made to validate the information against police records or any other source.

The NCVS measures rape/sexual assault, robbery, assault, pocket-picking, purse snatching, burglary, and motor vehicle theft. The NCVS includes crimes reported to the police, as well as those not reported. Murder and kidnaping are not covered. The so-called victimless crimes, such as drunkenness, drug abuse, and prostitution, also are excluded, as are crimes for which it is difficult to identify knowledgeable respondents or to locate data records.

Crimes of which the victim may not be aware also cannot be measured effectively. Buying stolen property may fall into this category, as may some instances of embezzlement. Attempted crimes of many types probably are under recorded for this reason. Events in which the victim has shown a willingness to participate in illegal activity also are excluded.

In any encounter involving a personal crime, more than one criminal act can be committed against an individual. For example, a rape may be associated with a robbery, or a household offense, such as a burglary, can escalate into something more serious in the event of a personal confrontation. In classifying the survey measured crimes, each criminal incident has been counted only once, by the most serious act that took place during the incident, and ranked in accordance with the seriousness classification system used by the FBI. The order of seriousness for crimes against persons is as follows: rape, robbery, assault, and larceny. Personal crimes take precedence over household offenses.

A *victimization*, the basic measure of the occurrence of crime, is a specific criminal act as it affects a single victim. The number of victimizations is determined by the number of victims of such acts. Victimization counts serve as key elements in computing rates of victimization. For crimes against persons, the rates are based on the total number of individuals aged 12 and over or on a portion of that population sharing a particular characteristic or set of traits. As general indicators of the danger of having been victimized during the reference period, the rates are not sufficiently refined to represent true measures of risk for specific individuals or households.

An *incident* is a specific criminal act involving one or more victims; therefore the number of incidents of personal crimes is lower than that of victimizations.

Courts—Statistics on criminal offenses and the outcome of prosecutions are incomplete for the country as a whole, although data are available for many states individually.

Since 1986, through its National Judicial Reporting Program, the BJS has surveyed a nationally representative sample of 300 counties every 2 years and collected detailed information on demographic characteristics of felons, conviction offenses, type of sentences, sentence lengths, and time from arrest to conviction and sentencing.

The bulk of civil and criminal litigation in the country is commenced and determined in the various state courts. Only when the U.S. Constitution and acts of Congress specifically confer jurisdiction upon the federal courts may civil or criminal litigation be heard and decided by them. Generally, the federal courts have jurisdiction over the following types of cases: suits or proceedings by or against the United States; civil actions between private parties arising under the Constitution, laws, or treaties of the United States; civil actions between private litigants who are citizens of different states; civil cases involving admiralty, maritime, or private jurisdiction; and all matters in bankruptcy.

There are several types of courts with varying degrees of legal jurisdiction. These jurisdictions include original, appellate, general, and limited or special. A court of original jurisdiction is one having the authority initially to try a case and pass judgment on the law and the facts; a court of appellate jurisdiction is one with the legal authority to review cases and hear appeals; a court of general jurisdiction is a trial court of unlimited original jurisdiction in civil and/or criminal cases, also called a "major trial court"; a court of limited or special jurisdiction is a trial court with legal authority over only a particular class of cases, such as probate, juvenile, or traffic cases.

The 94 federal courts of original jurisdiction are known as the U.S. district courts. One or more of these courts is established in every state and one each in the District of Columbia, Puerto Rico, the Virgin Islands, the Northern Mariana Islands, and Guam. Appeals from the district courts are taken to intermediate appellate courts of which there are 13, known as U.S. courts of appeals and the United States Court of Appeals for the Federal Circuit. The Supreme Court of the United States is the final and highest appellate court in the federal system of courts.

Juvenile offenders—For statistical purposes, the FBI and most states classify as juvenile offenders persons under the age of 18 years who have committed a crime or crimes.

Delinquency cases are all cases of youths referred to a juvenile court for violation of a law or ordinance or for seriously "antisocial" conduct. Several types of facilities are available for those adjudicated delinquents, ranging from the short-term physically unrestricted environment to the long-term very restrictive atmosphere.

Prisoners and jail inmates—BJS started to collect annual data in 1979 on prisoners in federal and state prisons and reformatories. Adults convicted of criminal activity may be given a prison or jail sentence. A *prison* is a confinement facility having custodial authority over adults sentenced to confinement of more than 1 year. A *jail* is a facility, usually operated by a local law enforcement agency, holding persons detained pending adjudication and/or persons committed after adjudication to 1 year or less.

Data on inmates in local jails were collected by the BJS for the first time in 1970. Since then, BJS has conducted censuses of facilities and inmates every 5 to 6 years. In 1984, BJS initiated an annual survey of jails conducted in noncensus years.

Statistical reliability—For discussion of statistical collection, estimation and sampling procedures, and measures of statistical reliability pertaining to the National Crime Victimization Survey and Uniform Crime Reporting Program, see Appendix III.

Table 319. Crimes and Crime Rates by Type of Offense: 1980 to 2011

[(13,408 represents 13,408,000). Data include offenses reported to law enforcement, offense estimations for nonreporting and partially reporting agencies within each state. Rates are based on Census Bureau estimated resident population as of July 1, except 1980, 1990, 2000, and 2010, which are enumerated as of April 1. See source for details]

Item and year	All crimes	Violent crime					Property crimes			
		Total	Murder [1]	Forcible rape	Robbery	Aggra-vated assault	Total	Burglary	Larceny/ theft	Motor vehicle theft
Number of offenses (1,000):										
1980	13,408	1,345	23.0	83.0	566	673	12,064	3,795	7,137	1,132
1985	12,430	1,328	19.0	87.7	498	723	11,103	3,073	6,926	1,103
1990	14,476	1,820	23.4	102.6	639	1,055	12,655	3,074	7,946	1,636
1995	13,863	1,799	21.6	97.5	581	1,099	12,064	2,594	7,998	1,472
2000	11,608	1,425	15.6	90.2	408	912	10,183	2,051	6,972	1,160
2001 [2]	11,877	1,439	16.0	90.9	424	909	10,437	2,117	7,092	1,228
2002	11,879	1,424	16.2	95.2	421	891	10,455	2,151	7,057	1,247
2003	11,827	1,384	16.5	93.9	414	859	10,443	2,155	7,027	1,261
2004	11,679	1,360	16.1	95.1	401	847	10,319	2,144	6,937	1,238
2005	11,565	1,391	16.7	94.3	417	862	10,175	2,155	6,783	1,236
2006	11,455	1,435	17.3	94.5	449	874	10,020	2,195	6,626	1,198
2007	11,305	1,423	17.1	92.2	447	866	9,882	2,190	6,592	1,100
2008	11,169	1,394	16.5	90.8	444	844	9,774	2,229	6,586	959
2009	10,663	1,326	15.4	89.2	409	813	9,337	2,203	6,338	796
2010	10,364	1,251	14.7	85.6	369	782	9,113	2,168	6,205	740
2011	10,267	1,204	14.6	83.4	354	751	9,063	2,188	6,160	715
Rate per 100,000 population:										
1980	5,950	597	10.2	36.8	251	299	5,353	1,684	3,167	502
1985	5,225	558	8.0	36.8	209	304	4,666	1,292	2,911	464
1990	5,803	730	9.4	41.1	256	423	5,073	1,232	3,185	656
1995	5,276	685	8.2	37.1	221	418	4,591	987	3,043	560
2000	4,125	507	5.5	32.0	145	324	3,618	729	2,477	412
2001 [2]	4,163	505	5.6	31.8	149	319	3,658	742	2,486	431
2002	4,125	494	5.6	33.1	146	310	3,631	747	2,451	433
2003	4,067	476	5.7	32.3	143	295	3,591	741	2,417	434
2004	3,977	463	5.5	32.4	137	289	3,514	730	2,362	422
2005	3,901	469	5.6	31.8	141	291	3,432	727	2,288	417
2006	3,826	479	5.8	31.6	150	292	3,347	733	2,213	400
2007	3,748	472	5.7	30.6	148	287	3,276	726	2,185	365
2008	3,673	459	5.4	29.8	146	278	3,215	733	2,166	315
2009	3,473	432	5.0	29.1	133	265	3,041	718	2,065	259
2010	3,350	405	4.8	27.7	119	253	2,946	701	2,006	239
2011	3,295	386	4.7	26.8	114	241	2,909	702	1,977	230

[1] Includes nonnegligent manslaughter. [2] The murder and nonnegligent homicides that occurred as a result of the events of September 11, 2001 were not included in this table.

Source: U.S. Department of Justice, Federal Bureau of Investigation, "Crime in the United States 2011," <http://www.fbi.gov/about-us/cjis/ucr>, accessed February 2013.

Table 320. Crimes and Crime Rates by Type and Geographic Community: 2011

[In thousands (1,203.6 represents 1,203,600), except rate. Rate per 100,000 population. See headnote, Table 319]

Type of crime	United States		Metropolitan statistical area [1]		Cities outside metropolitan areas		Nonmetropolitan counties	
	Total	Rate	Total	Rate	Total	Rate	Total	Rate
Violent crime	1,203.6	386.3	1,067.7	410.3	78.5	382.1	57.4	186.1
Murder [2]	14.6	4.7	12.8	4.9	0.9	4.4	1.0	3.1
Forcible rape	83.4	26.8	68.7	26.4	8.4	40.7	6.4	20.7
Robbery	354.4	113.7	338.1	129.9	11.5	56	4.8	15.5
Aggravated assault	751.1	241.1	648.1	249.1	57.8	281	45.3	146.8
Property crime	9,063.2	2,908.7	7,818.8	3,004.8	739.3	3,596.6	505.0	1,638.6
Burglary	2,188.0	702.2	1,843.9	708.6	168.9	821.7	175.2	568.4
Larceny-theft	6,159.8	1,976.9	5,317.5	2,043.5	542.3	2,638.5	300.0	973.3
Motor vehicle theft	715.4	229.6	657.5	252.7	28.0	136.4	29.9	96.9

[1] For definition, see Appendix II. [2] Includes nonnegligent manslaughter.

Source: U.S. Department of Justice, Federal Bureau of Investigation, "Crime in the United States 2011," <http://www.fbi.gov/about-us/cjis/ucr>, accessed February 2013.

Table 321. Crime Rates by State, 2010 and 2011, and by Type, 2011

[For year ending December 31. Rates per 100,000 population. Offenses reported to law enforcement. Based on Census Bureau estimated resident population as of July 1]

State	Violent crime 2010 total	Violent crime 2011 Total	Violent crime 2011 Murder	Violent crime 2011 Forcible rape	Violent crime 2011 Robbery	Violent crime 2011 Aggravated assault	Property crime 2010 total	Property crime 2011 Total	Property crime 2011 Burglary	Property crime 2011 Larceny/theft	Property crime 2011 Motor vehicle theft
United States............	404.5	386.3	4.7	26.8	113.7	241.1	2,945.9	2,908.7	702.2	1,976.9	229.6
Alabama [2]..................	383.7	420.1	6.3	28.5	102.2	283.0	3,528.0	3,606.1	1,064.3	2,319.7	222.0
Alaska.....................	635.3	606.5	4.0	58.1	79.7	464.6	2,836.8	2,632.8	391.0	2,056.0	185.8
Arizona...................	413.6	405.9	6.2	34.9	109.9	254.8	3,536.5	3,554.5	847.3	2,401.3	305.9
Arkansas..................	503.5	480.9	5.5	41.3	82.6	351.5	3,553.5	3,754.1	1,173.3	2,383.0	197.8
California.................	439.6	411.1	4.8	20.3	144.0	242.0	2,629.9	2,583.8	610.4	1,583.8	389.6
Colorado..................	323.7	320.2	2.9	44.5	64.6	208.1	2,674.5	2,606.3	503.6	1,886.8	215.9
Connecticut...............	282.0	272.8	3.6	19.2	102.7	147.3	2,188.8	2,167.4	437.9	1,542.1	187.4
Delaware..................	623.3	559.5	4.5	31.9	169.5	353.5	3,453.9	3,410.6	830.2	2,411.8	168.7
District of Columbia [1]......	1,326.8	1,202.1	17.5	28.0	662.3	494.3	4,761.4	4,795.5	623.0	3,451.5	721.0
Florida....................	541.3	515.3	5.2	27.7	134.4	348.0	3,551.4	3,522.0	892.9	2,421.1	207.9
Georgia...................	402.3	373.2	5.6	20.9	123.8	222.9	3,639.2	3,626.5	974.6	2,351.7	300.3
Hawaii....................	264.3	287.2	1.2	31.6	75.8	178.6	3,349.6	3,337.8	728.0	2,305.6	304.3
Idaho.....................	220.5	200.9	2.3	27.4	11.6	159.6	2,000.9	2,068.6	436.6	1,547.9	84.1
Illinois....................	444.9	429.3	5.6	28.8	157.4	237.5	2,718.1	2,688.8	604.1	1,861.1	223.5
Indiana...................	323.3	331.8	4.8	27.0	107.1	193.0	3,070.2	3,161.8	775.7	2,158.8	227.3
Iowa......................	268.5	255.6	1.5	27.2	26.9	199.9	2,253.6	2,330.3	568.2	1,633.6	128.5
Kansas....................	370.8	353.9	3.8	37.8	50.8	261.5	3,116.6	3,080.1	654.4	2,193.2	232.5
Kentucky..................	243.9	238.2	3.5	33.5	84.5	116.7	2,557.3	2,708.8	745.0	1,811.1	152.7
Louisiana.................	555.3	555.3	11.2	27.7	114.5	401.9	3,644.8	3,688.5	1,012.5	2,476.6	199.4
Maine.....................	122.1	123.2	2.0	29.6	27.8	63.8	2,478.6	2,545.5	591.3	1,873.0	81.2
Maryland..................	546.3	494.1	6.8	20.5	177.5	289.3	2,995.5	2,860.2	614.0	1,970.5	275.7
Massachusetts.............	468.9	428.4	2.8	24.7	102.7	298.1	2,356.8	2,258.7	554.6	1,540.3	163.7
Michigan..................	493.0	445.3	6.2	44.0	105.2	289.9	2,748.8	2,612.1	724.9	1,629.0	258.2
Minnesota [3]..............	(NA)	(NA)	1.4	(NA)	63.4	125.4	2,569.0	2,549.4	481.3	1,915.1	153.1
Mississippi................	269.3	269.8	8.0	29.0	83.7	149.1	2,983.0	3,025.5	1,037.7	1,822.5	165.4
Missouri [2].................	457.7	447.4	6.1	24.3	104.3	312.7	3,350.0	3,308.8	745.7	2,308.3	254.8
Montana [2].................	275.8	267.5	2.8	35.8	16.9	212.0	2,564.1	2,319.7	339.6	1,834.0	146.1
Nebraska..................	278.3	253.2	3.6	37.7	54.1	157.7	2,667.9	2,752.9	472.9	2,057.3	222.7
Nevada....................	663.0	562.1	5.2	33.5	157.9	365.6	2,773.5	2,560.5	742.3	1,470.0	348.3
New Hampshire............	167.4	188.0	1.3	32.5	36.0	118.2	2,219.8	2,283.9	436.1	1,773.9	73.9
New Jersey................	307.5	308.4	4.3	11.4	138.4	154.3	2,080.1	2,150.7	490.2	1,463.1	197.4
New Mexico...............	588.0	567.5	7.5	41.2	82.7	436.2	3,425.9	3,531.5	1,028.9	2,242.9	259.7
New York.................	394.4	398.1	4.0	14.1	145.9	234.1	1,957.8	1,912.4	336.0	1,477.2	99.2
North Carolina............	362.7	349.8	5.3	20.7	98.9	224.9	3,443.5	3,526.8	1,099.2	2,251.2	176.4
North Dakota..............	229.5	247.0	3.5	37.9	13.3	192.3	1,780.2	1,936.7	355.7	1,437.7	143.3
Ohio......................	314.7	307.4	4.4	31.5	139.1	132.4	3,266.1	3,354.7	976.3	2,195.9	182.5
Oklahoma.................	481.4	454.8	5.5	37.0	86.6	325.7	3,443.0	3,356.2	958.5	2,106.8	290.9
Oregon....................	251.4	247.6	2.1	31.4	57.4	156.6	3,039.3	3,114.6	528.1	2,352.8	233.7
Pennsylvania..............	366.5	355.0	5.0	26.1	126.6	197.3	2,173.1	2,222.3	454.0	1,636.1	132.2
Rhode Island..............	257.4	247.5	1.3	28.9	71.0	146.3	2,561.4	2,676.8	662.4	1,796.8	217.5
South Carolina............	602.2	571.9	6.8	34.5	92.2	438.4	3,905.4	3,904.2	1,002.8	2,609.4	292.0
South Dakota..............	268.9	254.1	2.5	60.2	20.3	171.1	1,859.9	1,817.7	351.8	1,351.1	114.8
Tennessee................	612.0	608.2	5.8	31.6	126.2	444.5	3,662.7	3,595.6	979.9	2,396.8	219.2
Texas.....................	448.4	408.5	4.4	29.0	110.6	264.5	3,766.8	3,472.3	838.3	2,387.3	246.7
Utah......................	213.5	195.0	1.9	30.3	38.4	124.4	3,182.0	2,973.1	465.8	2,287.8	219.5
Vermont...................	131.0	135.2	1.3	19.0	13.6	101.4	2,262.3	2,309.0	581.5	1,647.7	79.7
Virginia...................	214.2	196.7	3.7	19.0	67.1	106.9	2,335.5	2,249.6	377.9	1,751.6	120.1
Washington................	313.5	294.6	2.4	33.5	82.5	176.1	3,699.1	3,574.6	827.7	2,383.3	363.6
West Virginia..............	301.2	315.9	4.3	20.9	49.0	241.6	2,227.2	2,273.9	603.2	1,549.2	121.5
Wisconsin.................	248.9	236.9	2.4	20.4	78.2	135.9	2,508.6	2,432.7	466.7	1,821.9	144.1
Wyoming..................	197.9	219.3	3.2	25.7	12.5	177.9	2,456.6	2,266.4	327.9	1,846.8	91.7

NA Not available. [1] Includes offenses reported by the Zoological Police and the Metro Transit Police. [2] Because of changes in the state's reporting practices, figures are not comparable to previous years' data. [3] The data collection methodology for the offense of forcible rape used by the Minnesota state Uniform Crime Reporting (UCR) Programs (with the exception of Minneapolis and St. Paul, Minnesota) does not comply with national UCR guidelines. Consequently, their state figures for forcible rape and violent crime (of which forcible rape is a part) are not published in this table.

Source: U.S. Department of Justice, Federal Bureau of Investigation, "Crime in the United States 2011," <http://www.fbi.gov/about-us/cjis/ucr/ucr>, accessed February 2013.

Table 322. Crime Rates by Type—Selected Large Cities: 2011

[For year ending December 31. Rates per 100,000 population. Offenses reported to law enforcement]

Cities ranked by population size, 2011	Violent crime					Property crime			
	Total	Murder	Forcible rape	Robbery	Aggra-vated assault	Total	Burglary	Larceny/ theft	Motor vehicle theft
New York, NY.....................	624	6.3	13.3	241	363	1,710	221	1,374	115
Los Angeles, CA.................	522	7.7	21.6	263	230	2,250	450	1,393	406
Chicago, IL [1]	(NA)	15.9	(NA)	517	459	4,373	977	2,677	719
Houston, TX......................	975	9.2	36.0	376	554	5,054	1,281	3,200	573
Philadelphia, PA.................	1,193	21.2	54.4	539	579	3,894	788	2,620	486
Phoenix, AZ.......................	552	7.9	38.1	227	279	4,398	1,273	2,610	515
Las Vegas, NV....................	741	5.6	44.6	239	452	2,840	868	1,507	465
San Antonio, TX..................	519	6.6	36.3	132	345	5,967	1,131	4,400	435
San Diego, CA....................	388	2.9	22.2	111	252	2,256	443	1,337	475
Dallas, TX.........................	681	10.9	35.0	332	303	5,058	1,531	2,874	653
San Jose, CA.....................	335	4.1	23.6	115	192	2,296	441	1,319	535
Jacksonville, FL..................	621	8.5	41.9	189	381	4,328	1,021	3,084	223
Indianapolis, IN..................	1,101	11.5	52.2	405	632	5,638	1,815	3,192	631
San Francisco, CA...............	660	6.1	16.1	379	258	4,037	541	2,983	512
Austin, TX.........................	430	3.5	26.1	137	263	5,235	873	4,098	265
Charlotte-Mecklenburg, NC.....	606	7.1	27.6	204	367	4,054	1,081	2,707	266
Columbus, OH....................	658	11.0	71.7	412	164	6,227	1,926	3,842	459
Fort Worth, TX....................	604	6.3	46.2	167	384	4,640	1,329	2,988	323
Detroit, MI.........................	2,137	48.2	59.9	696	1,334	6,144	2,242	2,307	1,594
Louisville Metro, KY.............	614	7.2	34.1	247	326	4,803	1,222	3,241	340
El Paso, TX.......................	431	2.4	32.7	70	326	2,461	280	1,961	220
Memphis, TN......................	1,584	17.9	61.0	472	1,032	6,489	2,031	3,932	526
Baltimore, MD....................	1,417	31.3	54.4	551	780	4,758	1,374	2,714	670
Boston, MA........................	845	10.1	43.6	306	485	3,129	560	2,263	306
Seattle, WA.......................	593	3.2	16.2	229	344	5,143	1,101	3,492	550
Washington, DC..................	1,130	17.5	27.8	608	477	4,581	623	3,256	702
Nashville, TN.....................	1,181	8.2	60.9	308	804	4,774	1,231	3,262	282
Denver, CO.......................	607	5.6	64.9	187	350	3,684	797	2,299	587
Milwaukee, WI....................	999	14.2	32.5	496	456	5,038	1,116	3,162	760
Portland, OR......................	515	3.4	43.7	155	312	5,089	729	3,813	547
Oklahoma City, OK...............	871	9.9	47.3	210	604	5,819	1,681	3,446	692
Albuquerque, NM................	762	6.3	47.8	181	527	5,068	1,084	3,473	511
Tucson, AZ........................	652	9.7	38.7	220	383	([2])	944	([2])	521
Fresno, CA........................	582	7.0	10.2	204	361	5,079	1,142	2,983	955
Sacramento, CA..................	711	7.6	28.4	246	428	3,933	877	2,349	707
Long Beach, CA..................	611	5.3	23.9	282	299	2,740	700	1,567	473
Kansas City, MO.................	1,200	23.4	57.4	361	758	5,536	1,484	3,317	735
Mesa, AZ..........................	413	4.0	29.4	112	268	3,395	622	2,562	211
Virginia Beach, VA...............	175	3.4	13.5	93	65	2,737	460	2,176	102
Atlanta, GA.......................	1,433	20.7	34.8	551	827	7,084	1,762	4,059	1,262
Colorado Springs, CO...........	440	6.1	75.3	106	253	3,745	784	2,685	276
Omaha, NE........................	560	10.4	53.3	169	327	4,548	805	3,101	642
Raleigh, NC.......................	422	4.2	31.1	166	220	3,238	730	2,284	223
Miami, FL..........................	1,198	16.8	23.7	494	663	5,661	1,270	3,724	667
Cleveland, OH....................	1,366	18.6	89.1	795	464	6,377	2,696	2,650	1,031
Tulsa, OK..........................	1,000	12.4	67.2	275	645	5,535	1,856	3,064	614
Oakland, CA......................	1,683	26.3	51.1	851	754	5,288	1,308	2,385	1,595
Minneapolis, MN.................	965	8.3	100.1	412	445	4,978	1,324	3,193	460
Wichita, KS........................	767	6.5	61.9	127	571	5,056	1,041	3,521	494
Arlington, TX......................	502	5.9	36.4	145	315	4,612	1,176	3,151	285
Bakersfield, CA...................	531	5.1	11.1	156	359	4,221	1,229	2,311	682
New Orleans, NO................	792	57.6	47.0	305	382	4,039	1,112	2,195	732
Tampa, FL.........................	655	8.2	17.0	173	457	3,054	799	2,069	186
Anaheim, CA......................	377	4.4	30.9	131	210	2,496	414	1,753	329
Aurora, CO........................	438	2.7	55.3	152	227	2,986	648	2,074	263
Santa Ana, CA....................	400	4.0	18.9	180	197	2,002	325	1,286	392
St. Louis, MO.....................	1,857	35.3	58.7	664	1,099	8,010	2,189	4,770	1,051
Corpus Christi, TX...............	638	3.9	62.3	119	453	4,780	856	3,774	150
Pittsburgh, PA....................	802	14.3	21.7	365	401	3,261	870	2,235	156
Riverside, CA.....................	426	4.2	18.5	149	254	3,133	677	2,042	414
Lexington, KY.....................	456	4.7	35.3	167	249	4,174	915	3,034	225
Cincinnati, OH....................	1,032	20.5	61.6	597	353	6,886	2,246	4,211	429
Anchorage, AK...................	804	4.0	95.3	157	548	3,184	364	2,610	210
Stockton, CA......................	1,408	19.7	30.5	448	909	5,239	1,400	3,270	569
St. Paul, MN.......................	655	2.8	58.7	210	384	4,148	1,111	2,395	641
Toledo, OH........................	998	10.4	43.1	401	543	([2])	2,911	([2])	510
Newark, NJ........................	1,166	33.8	20.9	711	401	3,602	862	1,410	1,330
Plano, TX..........................	162	1.9	15.1	54	91	2,549	450	1,953	147
Buffalo, NY........................	1,238	13.7	46.1	556	623	5,450	1,704	3,319	427
Lincoln, NE........................	371	1.5	63.7	68	237	3,909	537	3,231	140
Henderson, NV...................	220	0.8	22.3	76	121	1,838	492	1,181	165
Fort Wayne, IN...................	308	9.4	36.9	122	140	3,544	740	2,654	149
Mobile, AL.........................	643	11.9	19.1	253	359	5,419	1,611	3,530	278
Jersey City, NJ...................	767	7.2	19.7	387	353	2,295	564	1,384	346
St. Petersburg, FL...............	1,021	8.5	36.3	290	686	5,160	1,375	3,444	341

NA Not available. [1] The data collection methodology for the offense of forcible rape used by Chicago, Illinois, and the Minnesota state UCR Program (with the exception of Minneapolis and St. Paul, Minnesota) does not comply with national UCR Program guidelines. Its figures for forcible rape and violent crime (of which forcible rape is a part) are not published in this table. [2] It was determined that the agency did not follow the national UCR program guidelines for reporting an offense. Consequently, this figure is not included in this table.

Source: U.S. Department of Justice, Federal Bureau of Investigation, "Crime in the United States 2011," <http://www.fbi.gov/about-us/cjis/ucr>, accessed February 2013.

Table 323. Murder Victims—Circumstances and Weapons Used or Cause of Death: 2000 to 2011

[For year ending December 31. The FBI's Uniform Crime Reporting (UCR) Program defines murder and nonnegligent manslaughter as the willful (nonnegligent) killing of one human being by another. The classification of this offense is based solely on police investigation as opposed to the determination of a court, medical examiner, coroner, jury, or other judicial body. The UCR Program does not include the following situations in this offense classification: deaths caused by negligence, suicide, or accident; justifiable homicides; and attempts to murder, which are scored as aggravated assaults]

Characteristic	2000	2005	2010	2011	Characteristic	2000	2005	2010	2011
Murders, total	**13,230**	**14,965**	**13,164**	**12,664**	Juvenile gang killings	653	756	675	523
CIRCUMSTANCES					Institutional killings	10	12	17	22
Felonies, total	2,229	2,189	1,974	1,816	Sniper attack	8	2	3	1
Rape	58	45	41	15	Other—not specified	1,901	1,938	1,834	1,647
Robbery	1,077	930	803	734	Unknown	4,070	5,635	4,637	4,812
Burglary	76	91	85	92					
Larceny-theft	23	12	21	11	TYPE OF WEAPON OR				
Motor vehicle theft	25	32	35	23	CAUSE OF DEATH				
Arson	81	39	35	37	Total firearms	8,661	10,158	8,874	8,583
Prostitution and					Handguns	6,778	7,565	6,115	6,220
commercialized vice	6	13	5	3	Rifles	411	445	367	323
Other sex offenses	10	9	14	9	Shotguns	485	522	366	356
Narcotic drug laws	589	597	474	390	Other guns	53	138	93	97
Gambling	12	2	7	8	Firearms, type not stated	934	1,488	1,933	1,587
Other—not specified	272	419	454	494	Knives or cutting instruments	1,782	1,920	1,732	1,694
Suspected felony type	60	45	68	60	Blunt objects [1]	617	608	549	496
Other than felony type	6,871	7,096	6,485	5,976	Personal weapons (hands, fists,				
Romantic triangle	122	118	90	85	feet, pushed, etc.)	927	905	769	728
Child killed by babysitter	30	26	36	39	Poison	8	9	11	5
Brawl due to influence of					Explosives	9	2	4	12
alcohol	188	123	122	111	Fire	134	125	78	75
Brawl due to influence of					Narcotics	20	46	45	29
narcotics	99	97	60	115	Drowning	15	20	10	15
Argument over money or					Strangulation	166	118	122	85
property	206	210	187	155	Asphyxiation	92	96	98	89
Other arguments	3,589	3,718	3,280	3,128	Other weapons				
Gangland killings	65	96	181	150	or weapons not stated	799	958	872	853

[1] Refers to club, hammer, etc.

Source: U.S. Department of Justice, Federal Bureau of Investigation, "Crime in the United States 2011," <http://www.fbi.gov/about-us/cjis/ucr>, accessed February 2013.

Table 324. Murder Victims by Age, Sex, and Race: 2011

[See headnote, Table 323]

Age	Total	Sex			Race			
		Male	Female	Unknown	White	Black	Other	Unknown
Murders, total	**12,664**	**9,829**	**2,813**	**22**	**5,825**	**6,329**	**335**	**175**
Percent of total [1]	100.0	77.6	22.2	0.2	46.0	50.0	2.6	1.4
Under 18 years old [2]	1,187	813	371	3	572	559	36	20
18 years old and over [2]	11,350	8,931	2,410	9	5,204	5,729	294	123
Infant (under 1 year old)	196	115	78	3	108	70	8	10
1 to 4 years old	301	166	135	–	165	125	5	6
5 to 8 years old	84	47	37	–	46	30	6	2
9 to 12 years old	65	32	33	–	39	18	8	–
13 to 16 years old	300	248	52	–	126	164	8	2
17 to 19 years old	1,069	926	143	–	380	664	21	4
20 to 24 years old	2,329	2,010	316	3	781	1,471	52	25
25 to 29 years old	1,892	1,573	317	2	698	1,125	50	19
30 to 34 years old	1,414	1,164	248	2	601	772	29	12
35 to 39 years old	1,046	792	254	–	476	525	30	15
40 to 44 years old	900	665	235	–	478	384	27	11
45 to 49 years old	854	612	241	1	477	343	24	10
50 to 54 years old	673	476	197	–	411	237	16	9
55 to 59 years old	500	364	136	–	311	166	18	5
60 to 64 years old	307	215	92	–	205	89	11	2
65 to 69 years old	184	109	75	–	143	34	3	4
70 to 74 years old	145	89	56	–	101	32	8	4
75 years old and over	278	141	136	1	230	39	6	3
Age unknown	127	85	32	10	49	41	5	32

– Represents zero. [1] Because of rounding, the percentages may not add to 100.0. [2] Does not include unknown ages.

Source: U.S. Department of Justice, Federal Bureau of Investigation, "Crime in the United States 2011," <http://www.fbi.gov/about-us/cjis/ucr>, accessed February 2013.

Table 325. Homicide Trends: 1980 to 2008

[Based on Federal Bureau of Investigation's Uniform Crime Reports Supplementary Homicide Reports. Homicide includes murder and nonnegligent manslaughter, which is the willful killing of one human being by another. Excludes deaths caused by negligence, suicide, or accident; justifiable homicides; and attempts to murder. Justifiable homicides based on the reports of law enforcement agencies are analyzed separately. Deaths from the terrorist attacks of September 11, 2001 are not included. Data based solely on police investigation, as opposed to the determination of a court, medical examiner, coroner, jury, or other judicial body]

| Year | Number of victims | | | | | | Rate [1] | | | | | |
	Total	Male	Female	White	Black	Other	Total	Male	Female	White	Black	Other
1980.............	23,040	17,803	5,237	12,275	9,767	327	10.2	16.1	4.5	6.3	37.7	5.7
1985.............	18,980	14,095	4,885	10,590	7,891	399	7.9	12.2	4.0	5.2	27.6	5.5
1990.............	23,440	18,320	5,121	11,278	11,489	400	9.4	15.1	4.0	5.4	37.6	4.2
1995.............	21,610	16,579	5,030	10,376	10,444	581	8.2	12.7	3.7	4.8	31.6	4.9
1996.............	19,650	15,175	4,475	9,483	9,476	512	7.4	11.5	3.3	4.3	28.3	4.1
1997.............	18,210	14,079	4,132	8,620	8,842	524	6.8	10.5	3.0	3.9	26.0	4.1
1998.............	16,970	12,812	4,158	8,389	7,931	393	6.3	9.5	3.0	3.8	23.0	2.9
1999.............	15,522	11,718	3,804	7,777	7,139	458	5.7	8.6	2.7	3.5	20.5	3.3
2000.............	15,586	11,844	3,742	7,560	7,425	399	5.5	8.6	2.6	3.3	20.3	2.7
2001.............	16,037	12,256	3,782	7,884	7,522	424	5.6	8.8	2.6	3.4	20.2	2.8
2002.............	16,204	12,432	3,772	7,784	7,759	437	5.6	8.8	2.6	3.3	20.6	2.8
2003.............	16,528	12,828	3,700	7,932	7,893	468	5.7	9.0	2.5	3.4	20.7	2.9
2004.............	16,148	12,596	3,552	7,944	7,562	417	5.5	8.7	2.4	3.3	19.6	2.5
2005.............	16,740	13,169	3,571	8,045	8,015	443	5.6	9.0	2.4	3.3	20.5	2.6
2006.............	17,030	13,433	3,597	7,906	8,428	461	5.7	9.1	2.4	3.3	21.3	2.6
2007.............	16,929	13,286	3,643	7,924	8,352	402	5.6	8.9	2.4	3.3	20.9	2.2
2008.............	16,272	12,731	3,541	7,995	7,901	376	5.4	8.5	2.3	3.3	19.6	2.0

[1] Rate is per 100,000 inhabitants.

Source: U.S. Department of Justice, Bureau of Justice Statistics, *Homicide Trends in the United States, 1980–2008*, NCJ 236018, November 2011. See also <http://bjs.ojp.usdoj.gov/index.cfm?ty=tp&tid=311>.

Table 326. Homicide Victims by Race and Sex: 1980 to 2009

[Excludes deaths to nonresidents of United States. Effective with data for 1999, causes of death are classified by The Tenth Revision International Classification of Diseases (ICD-10), replacing the Ninth Revision (ICD-9) used for 1979–98 data. In ICD-9, the category Homicide also includes death as a result of legal intervention. ICD-10 has two separate categories for these two causes of death. Some caution should be used in comparing data. See text, Section 2]

| Year | Homicide victims | | | | | Homicide rate [2] | | | | |
| | Total [1] | White | | Black | | Total [1] | White | | Black | |
		Male	Female	Male	Female		Male	Female	Male	Female
1980.............	24,278	10,381	3,177	8,385	1,898	10.7	10.9	3.2	66.6	13.5
1985.............	19,893	8,122	3,041	6,616	1,666	8.3	8.2	2.9	48.4	11.0
1990.............	24,932	9,147	3,006	9,981	2,163	10.0	9.0	2.8	69.2	13.5
1995.............	22,895	8,336	3,028	8,847	1,936	8.7	7.8	2.7	56.3	11.1
1997.............	19,846	7,343	2,570	7,601	1,652	7.4	6.7	2.3	47.1	9.3
1998.............	18,272	6,707	2,534	6,873	1,547	6.8	6.1	2.2	42.1	8.6
1999.............	16,889	6,162	2,466	6,214	1,434	6.2	5.6	2.2	37.5	7.8
2000.............	16,765	5,925	2,414	6,482	1,385	6.1	5.3	2.1	38.6	7.5
2001.............	20,308	8,254	3,074	6,780	1,446	7.1	7.2	2.6	38.3	7.4
2002.............	17,638	6,282	2,403	6,896	1,391	6.1	5.4	2.0	38.4	7.0
2003.............	17,732	6,337	2,372	7,083	1,309	6.1	5.4	2.0	38.9	6.6
2004.............	17,357	6,302	2,341	6,839	1,296	5.9	5.3	1.9	37.1	6.4
2005.............	18,124	6,457	2,313	7,412	1,257	6.1	5.4	1.9	39.7	6.2
2006.............	18,573	6,514	2,346	7,677	1,355	6.2	5.4	1.9	40.6	6.6
2007.............	18,361	6,541	2,373	7,584	1,286	6.1	5.4	1.9	39.7	6.2
2008.............	17,826	6,556	2,337	7,148	1,187	5.9	5.4	1.9	37.1	5.6
2009.............	16,799	5,983	2,340	6,715	1,159	5.5	4.9	1.9	34.2	5.4

[1] Includes races not shown separately. [2] Rates per 100,000 resident population in specified group. Based on enumerated population figures as of April 1 for 1980, 1990, and 2000; estimated resident population as of July 1 for other years.

Source: U.S. National Center for Health Statistics, *Deaths: Final Data for 2009*, Vol. 60, No.3, Dec. 2011, and earlier reports. See also <http://www.cdc.gov/nchs/products/nvsr.htm>.

Table 327. Criminal Victimizations and Victimization Rates: 1995 to 2009

[(39,926 represents 39,926,000). Based on National Crime Victimization Survey (NCVS); see text, this section and Appendix III]

Type of crime	Number of victimizations (1,000)				Victimization rates [1]			
	1995	2000	2005	2009	1995	2000	2005	2009
All crimes, total	**39,926**	**25,893**	**23,441**	**20,057**	(X)	(X)	(X)	(X)
Population: Aged 12 or older	*215,709*	*226,805*	*244,505*	*254,106*	(X)	(X)	(X)	(X)
Personal crimes [2]	**10,436**	**6,597**	**5,401**	**4,477**	**46.2**	**29.1**	**22.1**	**17.6**
Crimes of violence	10,022	6,323	5,174	4,343	44.5	27.9	21.2	17.1
Completed violence	2,960	2,044	1,659	1,383	12.9	9.0	6.8	5.4
Attempted/threatened violence	7,061	4,279	3,515	2,960	31.6	18.9	14.4	11.6
Rape/sexual assault	363	261	192	126	1.6	1.2	0.8	0.5
Rape/attempted rape	252	147	130	88	1.1	0.6	0.5	0.3
Rape	153	92	69	37	0.7	0.4	0.3	0.1
Attempted rape	99	55	61	50	0.4	0.2	0.2	0.2
Sexual assault	112	114	62	38	0.5	0.5	0.3	0.2
Robbery	1,171	732	625	534	5.3	3.2	2.6	2.1
Completed/property taken	753	520	415	368	3.5	2.3	1.7	1.4
With injury	224	160	143	153	1.0	0.7	0.6	0.6
Without injury	529	360	272	215	2.4	1.6	1.1	0.8
Attempted to take property	418	212	210	166	1.8	0.9	0.9	0.7
With injury	84	66	64	63	0.4	0.3	0.3	0.2
Without injury	335	146	145	103	1.4	0.6	0.6	0.4
Assault	8,487	5,330	4,357	3,684	37.6	23.5	17.8	14.5
Aggravated	2,050	1,293	1,052	823	8.8	5.7	4.3	3.2
With injury	533	346	331	313	2.4	1.5	1.4	1.2
Threatened with weapon	1,517	946	722	510	6.4	4.2	3.0	2.0
Simple	6,437	4,038	3,305	2,860	28.9	17.8	13.5	11.3
With minor injury	1,426	989	795	638	6.0	4.4	3.3	2.5
Without injury	5,012	3,048	2,510	2,222	22.9	13.4	10.3	8.7
Personal theft [3]	414	274	227	133	1.7	1.2	0.9	0.5
Total number of households (1,000)	*101,888*	*108,353*	*117,100*	*122,328*	(X)	(X)	(X)	(X)
Property crimes	**29,490**	**19,297**	**18,040**	**15,581**	**279.5**	**178.1**	**154.0**	**127.4**
Household burglary	5,004	3,444	3,456	3,135	47.4	31.8	29.5	25.6
Completed	4,232	2,909	2,900	2,604	40.0	26.9	24.8	21.3
Attempted forcible entry	773	534	556	531	7.4	4.9	4.7	4.3
Motor vehicle theft	1,717	937	978	736	16.2	8.6	8.4	6.0
Completed	1,163	642	775	570	10.8	5.9	6.6	4.7
Attempted	554	295	203	166	5.5	2.7	1.7	1.4
Theft	22,769	14,916	13,606	11,710	215.9	137.7	116.2	95.7
Completed [4]	21,857	14,300	13,116	11,219	207.6	132.0	112.0	91.7
Attempted	911	616	489	491	8.4	5.7	4.2	4.0

X Not applicable. [1] Per 1,000 persons age 12 or older for "Personal crime;" per 1,000 households for "Property crime." [2] The victimization survey cannot measure murder because of the inability to question the victim. [3] Includes pocket picking, purse snatching, and attempted purse snatching. [4] Includes thefts in which the amount taken was not ascertained.

Source: U.S. Department of Justice, Bureau of Justice Statistics, *Criminal Victimization, 2009*, NCJ 231327, October 2010, annual. See also <http://bjs.ojp.usdoj.gov/index.cfm?ty=pbdetail&iid=2217>.

Table 328. Victimization Rates by Type of Crime and Characteristics of the Victim: 2009

[Rate per 1,000 persons age 12 years or older. Based on the National Crime Victimization Survey. See text, this section and Appendix III]

Characteristic of the victim	Personal crimes	Crimes of violence						Personal theft [1]
		Total	Rape/sexual assault	Robbery	Assault			
					Total	Aggravated	Simple	
Total	**17.6**	**17.1**	**0.5**	**2.1**	**14.5**	**3.2**	**11.3**	**0.5**
Male	18.8	18.4	[2] 0.2	2.7	15.6	4.3	11.3	0.4
Female	16.5	15.8	0.8	1.6	13.5	2.3	11.2	0.6
12 to 15 years old	37.3	36.8	[2] 0.9	3.1	32.8	6.9	25.9	[2] 0.4
16 to 19 years old	32.3	30.3	[2] 0.6	5.2	24.6	5.3	19.3	[2] 1.9
20 to 24 years old	28.8	28.1	[2] 0.8	3.5	23.8	7.5	16.3	[2] 0.7
25 to 34 years old	22.1	21.5	[2] 0.8	2.8	17.9	4.5	13.4	[2] 0.7
35 to 49 years old	16.3	16.1	[2] 0.4	2.0	13.7	2.6	11.1	[2] 0.2
50 to 64 years old	11.0	10.7	[2] 0.3	1.1	9.3	1.9	7.5	[2] 0.4
65 years old and over	3.7	3.2	[2] 0.2	[2] 0.4	2.5	[2] 0.3	2.2	[2] 0.5
White	16.3	15.8	0.4	1.6	13.7	2.7	11.0	0.5
Black	27.8	26.8	1.2	5.6	19.9	6.8	13.0	[2] 1.0
Other [3]	9.8	9.8	(Z)	[2] 0.5	9.3	[2] 1.9	7.4	(Z)
Two or more races	43.3	42.1	(Z)	[2] 5.2	36.9	[2] 9.3	27.5	21.2
Hispanic	18.6	18.1	[2] 0.5	3.4	14.2	3.2	11.0	20.5
Non-Hispanic	17.5	17.0	0.5	1.9	14.6	3.3	11.3	0.5
Household income:								
Less than $7,500	49.0	47.7	[2] 3.9	7.3	36.5	15.5	21.0	[2] 1.2
$7,500 to $14,999	40.4	40.0	[2] 1.8	5.7	32.6	6.0	26.6	[2] 0.4
$15,000 to $24,999	23.3	22.3	[2] 0.9	3.8	17.6	4.0	13.5	[2] 1.0
$25,000 to $34,999	18.7	18.6	[2](Z)	2.0	16.6	3.9	12.8	[2] 0.2
$35,000 to $49,999	16.7	16.6	[2] 0.3	2.0	14.3	4.5	9.8	[2] 0.1
$50,000 to $74,999	13.0	12.6	[2] 0.2	[2] 0.9	11.5	2.0	9.5	[2] 0.4
$75,000 or more	12.4	11.5	[2] 0.2	1.1	10.2	2.1	8.1	0.9

Z Rounds to less than 0.05 victimizations per 1,000 persons. [1] Includes pocket picking, completed purse snatching, and attempted purse snatching. [2] Based on 10 or fewer sample cases. [3] Includes American Indians, Alaska Natives, Asians, Native Hawaiians, and other Pacific Islanders.

Source: U.S. Department of Justice, Bureau of Justice Statistics, *Criminal Victimization, 2009*, NCJ 231327, October 2010. See also <http://bjs.ojp.usdoj.gov/index.cfm?ty=pbdetail&iid=2217>.

Table 329. Violent Crimes by Characteristics of Incident: 2009

[In percent, except as indicated. Based on National Crime Victimization Survey; see text, this section, and Appendix III]

Selected characteristics of incident	Number of incidents	Violent Crime					
		Total	Rape/ sexual assault	Robbery	Assault		
					Total	Aggra-vated [1]	Simple
Total.........	4,343,450	100.0	100.0	100.0	100.0	100.0	100.0
Victim/offender relationship: [2]							
Relatives.........	523,670	12.1	[3] 6.6	13.3	12.1	[3] 3.7	14.5
Well-known.........	1,126,240	25.9	39.4	11.5	27.6	27.8	27.5
Casual acquaintance.........	552,530	12.7	[3] 22.4	[3] 2.3	13.9	14.3	13.8
Stranger.........	1,813,850	41.8	[3] 29.1	56.8	40.0	46.2	38.3
Time of day: [4]							
6 a.m. to 6 p.m..........	2,264,520	54.8	43.9	49.2	56.1	43.0	59.5
6 p.m. to midnight.........	1,183,920	28.7	[3] 26.8	32.3	28.2	39.0	25.3
Midnight to 6 a.m..........	488,190	11.8	[3] 21.8	13.2	11.2	15.7	10.1
Location of crime:							
At or near victim's home or lodging.........	1,649,510	40.0	56.2	43.1	38.9	33.5	40.4
Friend's/relative's/neighbor's home.........	323,110	7.8	[3] 11.2	[3] 5.3	8.1	12.5	6.9
Commercial places.........	397,910	9.7	[3] 1.6	[3] 6.3	10.4	10.9	10.2
Parking lots/garages.........	214,000	5.2	[3] 2.5	8.9	4.7	6.0	4.4
School.........	540,780	13.1	[3] 3.2	[3] 6.9	14.4	6.3	16.5
Streets other than near victim's home......	575,950	13.9	[3] 11.9	26.7	12.1	20.6	9.9
Other [5].........	428,870	10.3	[3] 13.4	2.7	11.8	10.1	11.7
Victim's activity: [6]							
At work or traveling to or from work.........	668,280	16.2	[3] 9.8	10.0	(NA)	15.1	17.9
School.........	576,590	14.0	[3] 8.1	11.3	(NA)	9.7	15.9
Activities at home.........	1,151,300	27.9	37.1	20.6	(NA)	20.6	30.8
Shopping/errands.........	206,430	5.0	[3] 2.5	13.1	(NA)	[3] 3.4	4.0
Leisure activities away from home.........	901,550	21.8	[3] 21.9	23.1	(NA)	34.8	18.1
Traveling.........	292,520	7.1	[3] 6.8	13.6	(NA)	9.0	5.4
Other [7].........	285,080	6.9	[3] 11.8	7.8	(NA)	6.7	6.6
Distance from victim's home: [8]							
Inside home or lodging.........	884,320	21.4	51.2	25.1	19.8	11.9	21.9
Near victim's home.........	749,310	18.1	[3] 10.8	11.0	19.5	18.6	19.7
1 mile or less.........	749,020	18.1	[3] 12.9	28.2	16.8	26.3	14.3
5 miles or less.........	890,500	21.6	[3] 14.7	17.2	22.5	22.6	22.4
50 miles or less.........	709,520	17.2	[3] 10.4	15.7	17.6	15.7	18.2
More than 50 miles.........	127,840	3.1	[3] –	[3] 2.8	3.2	[3] 4.9	2.8
Weapons:							
No weapons present.........	2,999,560	72.6	84.7	47.5	75.9	11.3	93.2
Weapons present.........	904,820	21.9	[3] 10.3	46.9	18.6	88.2	[3] –

– Represents zero. NA Not available. [1] An aggravated assault is any assault in which an offender possesses or uses a weapon or inflicts serious injury. [2] Excludes "don't know" relationships. [3] Based on 10 or fewer sample cases. [4] Excludes "not known and not available" time of day. [5] Includes areas on public transportation or inside station, in apartment yard, park, field, playground, or other areas. [6] Excludes "don't know" and "not available" victim activity. [7] Includes sleeping. [8] Excludes "don't know" and "not available" distance from victim's home.

Source: U.S. Department of Justice, Bureau of Justice Statistics, *Criminal Victimization, 2009*, NCJ 231327, October 2010. See also <http://bjs.ojp.usdoj.gov/index.cfm?ty=pbdetail&iid=2217>.

Table 330. Violent Crime Between Intimate Partners by Sex of Victims: 2000 to 2008

[Violence includes rape and sexual assault, robbery, aggravated assault, simple assault and homicide. Intimate partners are defined as spouses, ex-spouses, current boy/girlfriends, and ex-boy/girlfriends. Based on the National Crime Victimization Survey, for 2000 to 2008, and the Federal Bureau of Investigation's Uniform Crime Reporting Program's Supplementary Homicide Reports for 2000 to 2007; see text, this section and Appendix III]

Year and type of crime	All persons		Female victims		Male victims	
	Number	Rate per 1,000 [1]	Number	Rate per 1,000 [1]	Number	Rate per 1,000 [1]
2000.........	684,970	3.0	584,390	5.0	100,580	0.9
2005.........	519,130	2.1	410,970	3.3	108,160	0.9
2006 [2].........	823,360	3.3	665,600	5.3	157,760	1.3
2007.........	663,780	2.7	587,680	4.6	76,100	0.6
2008, total.........	**652,660**	**2.6**	**551,590**	**4.3**	**101,060**	**0.8**
Rape or sexual assault.........	44,000	0.2	(B)	(B)	(B)	(B)
Robbery.........	(B)	(B)	(B)	(B)	(B)	(B)
Aggravated assault.........	111,530	0.4	70,550	0.5	(B)	(B)
Simple assault.........	458,310	1.8	406,530	3.1	51,770	0.4
Homicide.........	(NA)	(NA)	(NA)	(NA)	(NA)	(NA)

B Base figure too small to meet statistical standards for reliability of derived figure. NA Not available. [1] Rates are the number of victimizations per 1,000 persons. Rates are not available for all categories. Except for homicide, the number of victimizations is per 100,000 persons aged 12 or older. [2] Due to changes in methodology, the 2006 national crime victimization rates are not comparable to previous years and cannot be used for yearly trend comparisons. However, the overall patterns of victimization at the national level can be examined.

Source: U.S. Department of Justice, Bureau of Justice Statistics, *Female Victims of Violence*, NCJ 228356, September 2009; See also <http://bjs.ojp.usdoj.gov/index.cfm?ty=pbdetail&iid=2020>.

Table 331. Stalking and Harassment Victimization in the United States: 2006

[Data has been revised. Survey based on a total population 220,995,170, age 18 or older. The survey defines stalking as a course of conduct directed at a specific person that would cause a reasonable person to feel fear. The survey characterizes individuals as victims of harassment who experience the behaviors associated with stalking but neither reported feeling fear as a result of such conduct nor experienced actions that would cause a reasonable person to feel fear]

Characteristic	Total population	Victims as percent of persons age 18 or older		
		All	Stalking	Harassment
Overall.............................	**220,995,170**	**2.4**	**1.5**	**0.9**
Sex:				
Male.............................	107,014,170	1.6	0.8	0.9
Female.............................	113,981,000	3.1	2.2	1.0
Age:				
18 to 19 years old............	8,053,370	4.5	2.9	1.6
20 to 24 years old............	20,348,250	4.4	2.8	1.6
25 to 34 years old............	39,760,010	2.9	2.0	0.9
35 to 49 years old............	65,878,490	2.7	1.7	1.0
50 to 64 years old............	51,483,100	1.7	1.0	0.7
65 years old and over........	35,471,950	0.8	0.3	0.4
Race and Hispanic ethnicity:				
White.............................	181,858,650	2.4	1.5	0.9
Black.............................	25,672,890	2.4	1.4	1.1
American Indian/				
Alaska Native................	1,483,760	3.8	[1] 2.2	[1] 1.5
Asian/Pacific Islander.........	9,837,830	1.3	0.6	0.6
More than one race............	2,142,040	6.3	4.1	2.3
Hispanic origin				
Hispanic.........................	23,440,950	1.9	1.3	0.6
Non-Hispanic....................	195,655,390	2.5	1.5	0.9
Unknown.........................	1,898,830	2.8	[1] 1.2	[1] 1.6
Marital status:				
Never married...................	54,100,740	3.8	2.4	1.4
Married...........................	124,145,550	1.4	0.8	0.6
Divorced or separated.........	26,704,680	4.8	3.3	1.5
Widowed.........................	14,179,710	1.4	0.7	0.7
Unknown.........................	1,864,500	1.9	[1] 1.5	[1] 0.4
Household income:				
Less than $7,500................	7,702,700	4.8	3.3	1.5
$7,500 to $14,999..............	13,236,960	4.2	2.9	1.3
$15,000 to $24,999............	20,221,710	3.2	2.2	1.0
$25,000 to $34,999............	20,373,140	2.9	1.7	1.1
$35,000 to $49,999............	27,910,030	2.5	1.7	0.8
$50,000 to $74,999............	34,011,190	2.3	1.4	0.9
$75,000 or more................	50,709,700	1.8	1.0	0.8
Unknown.........................	46,829,750	1.6	0.9	0.7

[1] Interpret data with caution; estimate based on 10 or fewer sample cases, or the coefficient of variation is greater than 50%.

Source: U.S. Department of Justice, Bureau of Justice Statistics, National Crime Victimization Survey, Supplemental Victimization Survey, *Stalking Victims in the United States -Revised*, Series NCJ 224527, September 2012. See also <http://bjs.ojp.usdoj.gov/index.cfm?ty=pbdetail&iid=1211>.

Table 332. Property Crime by Selected Household Characteristics: 2011

[123,039 represents 123,039,000. For crimes against households (burglary, theft, and motor vehicle theft), each household affected by a crime is counted as a single victimization. Based on National Crime Victimization Survey; see text, this section and Appendix III]

Characteristic	Number of house-holds (1,000)	Property crimes							
		Number of victimizations (1,000)				Victimization rate per 1,000 households			
		Total	Burglary	Motor vehicle theft	Theft	Total	Burglary	Motor vehicle theft	Theft
Total..................	**123,039**	**17,067**	**3,613**	**628**	**12,826**	**138.7**	**29.4**	**5.1**	**104.2**
Race:									
White.................	99,479	13,170	2,693	403	10,074	132.4	27.1	4.0	101.3
Black.................	16,218	2,562	617	165	1,780	158.0	38.0	10.2	109.8
Other.................	5,991	846	145	44	657	141.3	24.2	7.4	109.7
Two or more races.....	1,351	489	159	[1] 16	314	361.9	117.6	[1] 12.1	232.2
Ethnicity:									
Hispanic...............	14,410	2,499	460	138	1,901	173.4	31.9	9.6	131.9
Non-Hispanic..........	108,331	14,560	3,153	490	10,916	134.4	29.1	4.5	100.8
Household income:									
Less than $7,500......	4,515	1,101	304	[1] 29	768	243.8	67.2	[1] 6.5	170.1
$7,500 to $14,999....	7,105	1,483	420	47	1,016	208.7	59.1	6.6	143.0
$15,000 to $24,999....	10,202	1,749	437	38	1,274	171.5	42.8	3.8	124.9
$25,000 to $34,999....	10,408	1,517	347	60	1,110	145.8	33.4	5.7	106.7
$35,000 to $49,999....	13,492	2,000	355	66	1,579	148.2	26.3	4.9	117.0
$50,000 to $74,999....	14,669	1,963	316	92	1,555	133.8	21.5	6.2	106.0
$75,000 or more.......	23,895	2,812	293	86	2,432	117.7	12.3	3.6	101.8
Unknown..............	38,753	4,443	1,143	210	3,091	114.7	29.5	5.4	79.8
Number of persons in household:									
1.........................	35,650	3,699	1,088	140	2,471	103.8	30.5	3.9	69.3
2 or 3..................	61,645	8,196	1,695	303	6,199	133.0	27.5	4.9	100.6
4 or 5..................	21,915	4,097	672	147	3,279	187.0	30.7	6.7	149.6
6 or more..............	3,829	1,074	158	39	877	280.5	41.3	10.1	229.1

[1] Based on 10 or fewer sample cases.

Source: U.S. Department of Justice, Bureau of Justice Statistics, National Crime Victimization Survey, "Victimization Analysis Tool," <http://www.bjs.gov/index.cfm?ty=nvat>, accessed September 2013.

Table 333. Robbery and Property Crimes by Type and Average Value Lost: 1990 to 2009

[639 represents 639,000. For year ending December 31]

Characteristic of offense	Number of offenses (1,000)				Rate per 100,000 population				Average value lost (dol.)			
	1990	2000	2005	2009	1990	2000	2005	2009	1990	2000	2005	2009
Robbery, total [1]	**639**	**408**	**417**	**342**	**256.3**	**144.9**	**140.7**	**125.1**	**631**	**1,127**	**1,239**	**1,246**
Type of crime:												
Street or highway	359	188	184	146	144.2	66.7	62.1	53.5	511	858	1,020	865
Commercial house	73	57	60	46	29.5	20.1	20.1	16.9	945	1,685	1,662	1,774
Gas station	18	12	12	8	7.1	4.1	4.0	3.0	423	679	1,104	862
Convenience store	39	26	24	18	15.6	9.3	8.0	6.7	344	566	677	717
Residence	62	50	59	58	25.1	17.7	20.0	21.1	828	1,243	1,332	1,674
Bank	9	9	9	7	3.8	3.1	3.0	2.7	2,885	4,379	4,113	4,202
Weapon used:												
Firearm	234	161	175	131	94.1	57.0	59.0	55.3	(NA)	(NA)	(NA)	(NA)
Knife or cutting instrument	76	36	37	24	30.7	12.8	12.5	9.9	(NA)	(NA)	(NA)	(NA)
Other weapon	61	53	39	27	24.5	18.9	13.2	11.3	(NA)	(NA)	(NA)	(NA)
Strong-arm	268	159	166	126	107.7	56.4	56.0	53.3	(NA)	(NA)	(NA)	(NA)
Burglary, total [2]	**3,074**	**2,050**	**2,154**	**1,955**	**1,232.2**	**728.4**	**726.7**	**715.7**	**1,014**	**1,458**	**1,771**	**2,087**
Forcible entry [2]	2,150	1,297	1,310	1,224	864.5	460.7	440.0	448.1	(NA)	(NA)	(NA)	(NA)
Unlawful entry [2]	678	615	701	655	272.8	218.7	237.5	239.7	(NA)	(NA)	(NA)	(NA)
Attempted forcible entry [2]	245	138	133	129	98.7	49.0	45.2	47.4	(NA)	(NA)	(NA)	(NA)
Residence	2,033	1,335	1,417	1,127	817.4	474.3	477.9	412.9	1,037	1,378	1,813	2,709
Nonresidence	1,041	715	738	407	418.5	254.1	248.8	148.8	967	1,610	1,687	2,521
Occurred during the night [2]	1,135	699	708	625	456.4	248.3	238.9	229.0	(NA)	(NA)	(NA)	(NA)
Occurred during the day [2]	1,151	836	890	910	462.8	297.2	328.8	332.8	(NA)	(NA)	(NA)	(NA)
Larceny-theft, total	**7,946**	**6,972**	**6,783**	**5,560**	**3,185.1**	**2,477.3**	**2,286.3**	**2,035.1**	**426**	**727**	**857**	**865**
Pocket picking	81	36	29	24	32.4	12.7	9.8	8.8	384	437	346	489
Purse snatching	82	37	42	27	32.8	13.2	14.2	9.8	228	387	404	440
Shoplifting	1,291	959	940	1,002	519.1	340.7	317.0	366.9	104	185	184	178
From motor vehicles	1,744	1,754	1,752	1,520	701.3	623.3	590.6	556.5	461	692	704	737
Motor vehicle accessories	1,185	677	693	501	476.3	240.6	233.6	183.2	297	451	482	528
Bicycles	443	312	249	187	178.2	110.9	83.9	67.6	188	273	267	345
From buildings	1,118	914	852	620	449.4	324.6	287.3	226.8	673	1,184	1,738	1,233
From coin-operated machines	63	46	41	22	25.4	16.2	13.8	8.1	144	272	232	348
Other	1,940	2,232	2,184	1,660	780.0	793.0	736.1	607.5	615	957	1,137	1,439
Motor vehicles, total [3]	**1,636**	**1,160**	**1,236**	**731**	**655.8**	**412.2**	**417.4**	**258.6**	**5,117**	**6,581**	**6,204**	**6,495**
Automobiles	1,304	877	907	527	524.3	311.5	304.5	193.0	(NA)	(NA)	(NA)	(NA)
Trucks and buses	238	209	219	205	95.5	74.1	76.2	74.9	(NA)	(NA)	(NA)	(NA)

NA Not available. [1] Includes other crimes, not shown separately. [2] Unknown data not included. [3] Includes other types of motor vehicles, not shown separately.

Source: U.S. Department of Justice, Federal Bureau of Investigation, Uniform Crime Reports, Return A and Supplement to Return A Master Files, unpublished.

Table 334. Hate Crimes—Number of Incidents, Offenses, Victims, and Known Offenders by Bias Motivation: 2000 to 2011

[The FBI collected statistics on hate crimes from 14,575 law enforcement agencies representing over an estimated 286 million people in 2011. Not all law enforcement agencies participated in the Hate Crimes Statistics Program. Hate crime offenses cover incidents motivated by race, religion, sexual orientation, ethnicity/national origin, and disability. See source and Appendix III]

Bias motivation	Incidents reported	Offenses	Victims [1]	Known offenders [2]
2000............	8,213	9,619	10,117	7,690
2005............	7,163	8,380	8,804	6,804
2011, total............	**6,222**	**7,254**	**7,713**	**5,731**
Bias motive:				
Race, total............	**2,917**	**3,465**	**3,645**	**2,787**
Anti-White............	504	577	593	594
Anti-Black............	2,076	2,494	2,619	1,935
Anti-American Indian/Alaska native............	61	67	70	60
Anti-Asian/Pacific Islander............	138	165	175	120
Anti-multiracial group............	138	162	188	78
Ethnicity/national origin, total............	**720**	**891**	**939**	**749**
Anti-Hispanic............	405	506	534	452
Anti-other ethnicity/national origin............	315	385	405	297
Religion, total............	**1,233**	**1,318**	**1,480**	**590**
Anti-Jewish............	771	820	936	287
Anti-Catholic............	67	68	84	21
Anti-Protestant............	44	49	51	32
Anti-Islamic............	157	175	185	138
Anti-other religious group............	130	139	155	74
Anti-multi-religious group............	60	63	65	37
Anti-atheism/agnosticism/etc............	4	4	4	1
Sexual orientation, total............	**1,293**	**1,508**	**1,572**	**1,511**
Anti-male homosexual............	760	871	891	978
Anti-female homosexual............	137	168	174	123
Anti-homosexual............	359	429	465	362
Anti-heterosexual............	16	17	19	19
Anti-bisexual............	21	23	23	29
Disability, total............	**53**	**58**	**61**	**87**
Anti-physical............	19	23	26	29
Anti-mental............	34	35	35	58
Multiple bias [3]............	**6**	**14**	**16**	**7**

[1] The term "victim" may refer to a person, business, institution, or a society as a whole. [2] The term "known offender" does not imply that the identity of the suspect is known, but only that an attribute of the suspect has been identified which distinguishes him/her from an unknown offender. [3] In a "multiple-bias incident" two conditions must be met: more than one offense type must occur in the incident and at least two offense types must be motivated by different biases.

Source: U.S. Department of Justice, Federal Bureau of Investigation, "Hate Crime Statistics 2011," <http://www.fbi.gov/about-us/cjis/ucr/hate-crime/2011>, accessed February 2013.

Table 335. Hate Crimes by Bias Motivation and Location of Incident: 2011

[See headnote, Table 334]

Location	Total incidents	Race	Religion	Sexual orientation	Ethnic/nat'l origin	Disability	Multiple-bias incidents [1]
				Bias motivation			
Total............	**6,222**	**2,917**	**1,233**	**1,293**	**720**	**53**	**6**
Air/bus/train terminal............	59	32	4	14	8	1	–
Bank/savings and loan............	13	10	2	–	1	–	–
Bar/nightclub............	153	66	6	64	16	1	–
Church/synagogue/temple/mosque............	276	25	237	7	7	–	–
Commercial office building............	114	55	32	12	15	–	–
Convenience store............	79	35	10	12	22	–	–
Department/discount store............	72	39	15	12	6	–	–
Drug store/Doctor's office/hospital............	62	30	14	7	7	4	–
Field/woods............	52	26	9	10	7	–	–
Government/public building............	89	51	20	10	8	–	–
Grocery/supermarket............	59	36	4	6	12	1	–
Highway/road/alley/street/sidewalk............	1,121	562	96	309	143	9	2
Hotel/motel/etc............	43	28	2	5	7	1	–
Jail/prison/corrections facility............	38	24	1	7	5	1	–
Parking/drop lot/garage............	366	183	30	90	59	4	–
Park/playground............	36	19	4	6	7	–	–
Rental storage facility............	13	7	–	3	3	–	–
Residence/home............	1,993	984	353	413	221	20	2
Restaurant............	115	60	11	21	23	–	–
School/college [2]............	375	175	89	77	30	4	–
School—college/university............	53	28	8	12	5	–	–
School—elementary/secondary............	150	73	35	30	10	1	1
Service/gas station............	48	25	9	3	11	–	–
Shopping mall............	27	14	3	5	4	1	–
Specialty store (TV, fur, etc.)............	48	20	11	9	7	1	–
Other/unknown............	704	279	219	138	64	4	–
Multiple locations............	7	5	–	–	1	–	1

– Represents zero. [1] See footnote 3, Table 334. [2] The location designation School/college has been retained for agencies that have not updated their records management systems to include the new location designations of School—college/university and School—elementary/secondary, which allow for more specificity in reporting.

Source: U.S. Department of Justice, Federal Bureau of Investigation, "Hate Crime Statistics 2011," <http://www.fbi.gov/about-us/cjis/ucr/hate-crime/2011>, accessed February 2013.

Table 336. Financial Crimes: 2005 to 2011

[For the year ending September 30. The FBI focuses its financial crimes investigations on such criminal activities as corporate fraud, securities and commodities fraud, health care fraud, financial institution fraud, mortgage fraud, insurance fraud, mass marketing fraud, and money laundering]

Type of financial fraud	Unit indicator	2005	2006	2007	2008	2009	2010	2011
Corporate fraud:								
Cases pending	Number	423	486	529	545	592	661	726
Indictments	Number	178	176	183	160	161	(NA)	242
Convictions	Number	150	134	181	134	162	(NA)	241
Restitution	Bil. dol.	5.6	1.1	12.6	8.2	6.1	(NA)	2.4
Recoveries	1,000 dol.	68.0	41,400.0	27,400.0	6,590.0	16,100.0	(NA)	(NA)
Fines	Mil. dol.	122.4	14.2	38.6	193.7	5.3	(NA)	16.1
Seizures	Mil. dol.	12.6	82.4	70.1	9.3	40.6	(NA)	(NA)
Securities/Commodities fraud:								
Cases pending	Number	1,139	1,165	1,217	1,210	1,510	1,703	1,846
Indictments	Number	327	320	408	359	412	(NA)	520
Convictions	Number	363	279	321	302	309	(NA)	394
Restitution	Bil. dol.	2.3	2.1	1.5	3.0	2.1	(NA)	8.8
Recoveries	Mil. dol.	76.3	20.6	25.4	43.7	47.3	(NA)	36.0
Fines	Mil. dol.	14.8	80.7	202.8	128.5	7.4	(NA)	113.0
Seizures	Mil. dol.	281.9	41.8	83.0	77.5	85.0	(NA)	751.0
Insurance fraud:								
Cases pending	Number	270	233	209	177	152	156	140
Indictments	Number	72	56	39	73	43	(NA)	19
Convictions	Number	79	66	47	60	42	(NA)	21
Restitution	Mil. dol.	171.7	30.4	27.6	553.7	22.9	(NA)	87.6
Recoveries	1,000 dol.	913.0	14.0	21.0	10,400.0	31,400.0	(NA)	(NA)
Fines	1,000 dol.	112.0	212.0	447.0	31.0	138.0	(NA)	(NA)
Seizures	Mil. dol.	10.7	3.5	15.9	25.3	2.2	(NA)	(NA)
Mass marketing fraud:								
Cases pending	Number	161	147	127	100	92	86	96
Indictments	Number	28	15	13	50	9	(NA)	(NA)
Convictions	Number	43	46	11	23	23	(NA)	(NA)
Restitution	Mil. dol.	503.8	273.2	30.6	4.2	4.4	(NA)	(NA)
Recoveries	1,000 dol.	4.0	468.0	542.0	173.0	–	(NA)	(NA)
Fines	1,000 dol.	362.0	86,900.0	121.0	23.0	2.1	(NA)	(NA)
Seizures	Mil. dol.	8.1	12.7	(Z)	–	(Z)	(NA)	(NA)
Health care fraud:								
Cases pending	Number	2,547	2,423	2,493	2,434	2,494	2,573	2,690
Indictments	Number	589	588	847	851	982	(NA)	1,676
Convictions	Number	550	535	642	707	674	(NA)	736
Restitution	Bil. dol.	1.1	0.4	1.1	1.1	1.3	(NA)	1.2
Recoveries	Mil. dol.	115.0	1,600.0	439.8	102.4	517.1	(NA)	(NA)
Fines	Mil. dol.	42.4	172.8	33.7	25.6	68.9	(NA)	1,000.0
Seizures	Mil. dol.	52.7	28.9	86.1	48.3	55.7	(NA)	96.0
Money laundering:								
Cases pending	Number	507	473	443	404	350	323	303
Indictments	Number	126	264	140	114	63	(NA)	37
Convictions	Number	91	112	115	134	96	(NA)	45
Restitution	Mil. dol.	313.0	17.1	69.4	222.4	81.9	(NA)	18.4
Recoveries	Mil. dol.	9.3	3.2	2.7	20.9	0.6	(NA)	0.8
Fines	Mil. dol.	0.3	0.4	11.4	34.1	1.5	(NA)	1.0
Seizures	Mil. dol.	7.8	6.4	10.9	24.2	4.5	(NA)	(NA)
Mortgage fraud:								
Cases pending	Number	721	881	1,211	1,644	2,794	3,129	2,691
Indictments	Number	93	138	328	574	822	(NA)	1,233
Convictions	Number	60	123	283	354	494	(NA)	1,082
Restitution	Mil. dol.	151.2	308.3	600.6	825.2	2,540.0	(NA)	1,380.0
Recoveries	Mil. dol.	(Z)	1.2	21.8	3.3	7.5	(NA)	7.3
Fines	Mil. dol.	44.0	300.8	1.6	3.1	58.4	(NA)	116.3
Seizures	Mil. dol.	(NA)	(NA)	5.1	6.6	5.0	(NA)	15.7
Suspicious Activity Reports (SARs) [1,2]								
Mortgage fraud related—								
Number of violations:								
Mortgage fraud	Number	21,994	35,617	46,717	63,713	67,190	70,533	93,508
Commercial loan	Number	2,126	2,409	3,240	4,189	4,514	3,347	2,947
False statement	Number	11,611	21,023	28,692	37,622	38,159	(NA)	(NA)
Dollars losses reported on:								
Mortgage fraud SARs	Bil. dol.	1.0	0.9	0.8	1.5	2.8	3.2	3.0
Reported on commercial loan SARs	Bil. dol.	0.7	0.5	1.0	1.9	1.7	(NA)	(NA)
False statement SARs	Bil. dol.	1.0	1.4	0.8	2.5	2.1	(NA)	(NA)

– Represents zero. NA Not available. Z represents a value less than 50 thousand. [1] Reports filed by federally-insured financial institutions. [2] SARs are cataloged according to the year in which they are submitted and the information contained within them may describe activity that occurred in previous month or years.

Source: U.S. Department of Justice, Federal Bureau of Investigation, "Financial Crimes Report to the Public" and "2010 Mortgage Fraud Report, Year in Review," <http://www.fbi.gov/stats-services/publications>, accessed May 2012.

Table 337. Fraud and Identity Theft—Consumer Complaints by State: 2012

[Rate per 100,000 population. As of December 31. Rates based on 2010 Census population estimates. The Consumer Sentinel Network is a secure online database of consumer complaints available only to law enforcement. Based on unverified complaints reported by consumers. Excludes complaints outside of the U.S. and the North Carolina and Oregon Department of Justice, the South Carolina Department of Consumer Affairs, the Tennessee Division of Consumer Affairs, and the Offices of the Attorneys General for California, Colorado, Idaho, Iowa, Michigan, Mississippi, Montana, Ohio, and Washington]

State	Fraud and other complaints [1]		Identity theft victims [1]		State	Fraud and other complaints [1]		Identity theft victims [1]	
	Number	Rate	Number	Rate		Number	Rate	Number	Rate
U.S.....	1,456,988	464.1	353,492	112.6	MO.......	25,725	427.2	4,505	74.8
AL.........	19,470	403.8	5,060	104.9	MT.......	3,729	371.0	501	49.8
AK........	2,878	393.5	378	51.7	NE......	7,067	380.9	1,068	57.6
AZ........	33,434	510.2	7,032	107.3	NV.......	15,446	559.9	3,032	109.9
AR........	10,149	344.1	2,195	74.4	NH.......	6,600	499.7	782	59.2
CA........	187,270	492.3	46,658	122.7	NJ.......	42,565	480.2	8,430	95.1
CO........	28,285	545.2	4,864	93.8	NM......	8,675	416.0	1,858	89.1
CT........	15,906	443.0	2,915	81.2	NY.......	82,289	420.5	21,538	110.1
DE........	5,165	563.2	902	98.4	NC......	41,212	422.6	7,910	81.1
DC........	4,756	752.1	1,069	169.1	ND......	2,826	403.9	288	41.2
FL........	133,973	693.5	69,795	361.3	OH......	50,128	434.2	8,891	77.0
GA........	58,543	590.2	19,232	193.9	OK......	13,173	345.3	2,586	67.8
HI.........	5,973	429.0	658	47.3	OR......	18,399	471.8	2,467	63.3
ID.........	6,693	419.4	905	56.7	PA.......	56,397	441.9	11,324	88.7
IL..........	51,206	397.7	12,993	100.9	RI........	4,549	433.1	963	91.7
IN.........	24,489	374.6	4,412	67.5	SC.......	19,850	420.2	4,282	90.6
IA.........	9,110	296.3	1,608	52.3	SD......	2,427	291.2	330	39.6
KS........	10,644	368.8	2,077	72.0	TN......	28,091	435.1	5,690	88.1
KY........	15,770	360.0	2,463	56.2	TX........	119,510	458.6	28,299	108.6
LA........	18,402	399.9	4,031	87.6	UT.......	9,907	347.0	1,586	55.5
ME........	5,224	393.0	666	50.1	VT........	2,273	363.1	326	52.1
MD.......	33,199	564.2	6,178	105.0	VA.......	42,355	517.4	6,616	80.8
MA........	29,469	443.4	4,879	73.4	WA.......	33,720	488.9	5,373	77.9
MI........	49,501	500.9	12,075	122.2	WV.......	6,204	334.4	1,002	54.0
MN........	21,051	391.3	3,437	63.9	WI.......	21,678	378.6	4,055	70.8
MS........	9,526	319.1	2,990	100.2	WY.......	2,107	365.5	318	55.2

[1] Includes non-U.S. residents and people who did not report residence.

Source: U.S. Federal Trade Commission, *Consumer Sentinel Network Data Book for January–December 2012,* February 2013. See also <http://www.ftc.gov/sentinel/reports.shtml>.

Table 338. Firearm Violence, Homicides and Nonfatal Victimizations: 1993 to 2011

[Detail may not sum to total due to rounding. Data are primarily from the Bureau of Justice Statistics' National Crime Victimization Survey and Centers for Disease Control and Prevention's Injury Statistics Query and Reporting System]

Year	Fatal and Nonfatal Firearm Violence				Percent		Rate of nonfatal firearm victimization [3]
	Total	Firearm homicides	Nonfatal firearm victimizations [1]	Nonfatal firearm incidents [2]	All violence involving firearms	All firearm violence that was homicide	
1993........	1,548,000	18,253	1,529,700	1,222,700	9.2	1.2	7.3
1994........	1,585,700	17,527	1,568,200	1,287,200	9.3	1.1	7.4
1995........	1,208,800	15,551	1,193,200	1,028,900	7.9	1.3	5.5
1996........	1,114,800	14,037	1,100,800	939,500	7.9	1.3	5.1
1997........	1,037,300	13,252	1,024,100	882,900	7.7	1.3	4.7
1998........	847,200	11,798	835,400	673,300	7.0	1.4	3.8
1999........	651,700	10,828	640,900	523,600	6.1	1.7	2.9
2000........	621,000	10,801	610,200	483,700	7.3	1.7	2.7
2001........	574,500	11,348	563,100	507,000	7.7	2.0	2.5
2002........	551,800	11,829	540,000	450,800	7.4	2.1	2.3
2003........	479,300	11,920	467,300	385,000	6.2	2.5	2.0
2004........	468,100	11,624	456,500	405,800	6.9	2.5	1.9
2005........	515,900	12,352	503,500	446,400	7.4	2.4	2.1
2006........	627,200	12,791	614,400	552,000	7.4	2.0	2.5
2007........	567,400	12,632	554,800	448,400	8.3	2.2	2.2
2008........	383,500	12,179	371,300	331,600	6.0	3.2	1.5
2009........	421,600	11,493	410,100	383,400	7.4	2.7	1.6
2010........	426,100	11,078	415,000	378,800	8.6	2.6	1.6
2011 [4]......	478,400	11,101	467,300	414,600	8.2	2.3	1.8

[1] A victimization refers to a single victim that experienced a criminal incident. [2] An incident is a specific criminal act involving one or more victims or victimizations. [3] Per 1,000 persons age 12 or older. [4] Preliminary homicide estimates from Centers for Disease Control, *Deaths: Preliminary Data for 2011,* NVSR Vol. 61, No. 6.

Source: Department of Justice, Bureau of Justice Statistics, *Firearm Violence, 1993-2011,* NCJ 241730, May 2013. See also <http://www.bjs.gov/index.cfm?ty=pbdetail&iid=4616>

Table 339. Nonfatal Firearm and Nonfirearm Violence by Victim-Offender Relationship and Location of Crime: 2007 to 2011

[Data are for victimizations. Detail may not sum to total due to rounding. Data from National Crime Victimization Survey]

Characteristic	Total nonfatal violence		Firearm violence		Nonfirearm violence	
	Number	Percent [1]	Number	Percent [1]	Number	Percent [1]
RELATIONSHIP TO VICTIM						
Total................	**29,611,300**	(X)	**2,218,500**	7.5	**27,392,800**	92.5
Nonstranger................	15,715,900	(X)	738,000	4.7	14,977,900	95.3
Intimate [2]................	4,673,600	(X)	195,700	4.2	4,477,900	95.8
Other relative................	2,157,700	(X)	158,100	7.3	1,999,500	92.7
Friend/acquaintance................	8,884,600	(X)	384,100	4.3	8,500,500	95.7
Stranger................	10,983,100	(X)	1,177,900	10.7	9,805,200	89.3
Unknown [3]................	2,912,300	(X)	302,600	10.4	2,609,600	89.6
LOCATION						
Total................	**29,618,300**	100.0	**2,218,500**	100.0	**27,399,800**	100.0
Victim's home or lodging................	6,491,400	21.9	427,600	19.3	6,063,800	22.1
Near victim's home................	4,804,700	16.2	504,500	22.7	4,300,200	15.7
In, at, or near a friend, neighbor, or relative's home......	2,175,900	7.3	132,600	6.0	2,043,300	7.5
Commercial place................	2,878,600	9.7	195,400	8.8	2,683,200	9.8
Parking lot or garage................	1,688,400	5.7	340,600	15.4	1,347,900	4.9
School [4]................	3,931,100	13.3	[5] 12,600	[5] 0.6	3,918,500	14.3
Open area, on street, or public transportation.............	4,636,900	15.7	508,400	22.9	4,128,500	15.1
Other location................	3,011,200	10.2	96,800	4.4	2,914,400	10.6

(X) Not applicable. [1] Percent of total violence is shown for data by relationship to victim. Percent distribution of specified type of violence is shown for data by location. [2] Includes current or former spouses, boyfriends, or girlfriends. [3] Includes relationships unknown and number of offenders unknown. [4] Includes inside a school building or on school property. [5] Interpret with caution. Estimate based on 10 or fewer sample cases, or coefficient of variation is greater than 50%.

Source: Department of Justice, Bureau of Justice Statistics, *Firearm Violence, 1993-2011*, NCJ 241730, May 2013. See also <http://www.bjs.gov/index.cfm?ty=pbdetail&iid=4616>.

Table 340. Background Checks for Firearm Transfers: 1994 to 2010

[In thousands (12,740 represents 12,740,000), except rates. The Brady Handgun Violence Prevention Act (Brady Act) requires a background check on an applicant for a firearm purchase from a dealer who is a Federal Firearms Licensee]

Inquiries and rejections	Interim period 1994–1998 [1]	Permanent Brady [2]									
		2001	2002	2003	2004	2005	2006	2007	2008	2009	2010
Applications and denials:											
Applications received..............	12,740	7,958	7,806	7,831	8,084	8,278	8,612	8,658	9,900	10,764	10,405
Applications denied..............	312	151	136	126	126	132	135	136	147	150	153
Denied (percent)..................	2.4	1.9	1.7	1.6	1.6	1.6	1.6	1.6	1.5	1.4	1.5
Selective reasons for rejection:											
Felony indictment/conviction......	44	87	65	53	53	57	52	49	77	67	62
Other....................	18	64	71	73	73	75	83	87	70	83	91
Felony denials per 1,000 applications..............	(NA)	10.9	8.3	6.8	6.6	6.9	6.0	5.7	7.2	6.2	6.0

NA Not available. [1] Background checks on applicants were conducted by state and local agencies, mainly on handgun transfers. See "Presale Handgun Checks, the Brady Interim Period, 1994–98" (NCJ 175034). [2] The period beginning November 30, 1998 is the effective date for the Brady Handgun Violence Prevention Act, P.L. 103–159, 1993. The National Instant Criminal Background Check System (NICS) began operations in 1998. Checks on handgun and long gun transfers are conducted by the FBI, and by state and local agencies. Totals combine Firearm Inquiry Statistics (FIST) estimates for state and local agencies with transactions and denials reported by the FBI.

Source: U.S. Department of Justice, Bureau of Justice Statistics, *Background Checks for Firearm Transfers, 2010—Statistical Tables*, Series NCJ 238226, February 2013. See also <http://bjs.ojp.usdoj.gov/index.cfm?ty=pbse&sid=13>.

Table 341. Denials of Firearm Transfer Applications by Reason and Agency Type: 1999 to 2010

[In percent. Reasons for denials are based on The Brady Handgun Violence Prevention Act, pursuant to 18 U.S.C. 922 and state laws. Denial occurs when an applicant is prohibited from receiving a firearm or a permit that can be used to receive a firearm because a disqualifying factor was found during a background check. Application for firearm transfer is information submitted by a person to a state or local checking agency to purchase a firearm or obtain a permit that can be used for a purchase. Information may be submitted directly to a checking agency or forwarded by a prospective seller]

Reason for denial	2009			2010			1999-2010		
	FBI [1]	State	Local	FBI [1]	State	Local [3]	FBI [1]	State	Local [3]
Felony indictment/conviction..............	48.5	39.4	21.7	47.4	30.9	(NA)	63.0	50.7	(NA)
State law prohibition........................	11.2	10.7	6.3	10.6	15.6	(NA)	3.3	8.5	(NA)
Domestic violence.........................	11.5	13.5	15.8	10.4	10.3	(NA)	15.5	13.2	(NA)
Misdemeanor conviction................	7.2	10.2	13.9	6.2	8.2	(NA)	11.1	9.9	(NA)
Restraining order........................	4.3	3.3	1.9	4.3	2.1	(NA)	4.4	3.3	(NA)
Fugitive....................................	16.8	7.1	1.0	19.1	6.6	(NA)	7.7	6.8	(NA)
Illegal alien................................	1.0	0.3	0.7	0.8	0.3	(NA)	1.2	0.4	(NA)
Mental illness or disability................	1.4	6.2	5.3	1.8	5.7	(NA)	0.7	2.8	(NA)
Drug user/addict.........................	9.3	1.6	15.2	9.6	5	(NA)	7.9	1.4	(NA)
Local law prohibition........................	(X)	(NA)	1.5	(X)	(NA)	(NA)	(X)	(NA)	(NA)
Other prohibitions [2]........................	0.3	21.2	32.5	0.3	25.5	(NA)	0.7	16.2	(NA)

– Represents zero. NA not available. X not applicable. [1] During 2008 the FBI began a new classification system and reclassified all denials from 1999 to 2008; therefore, data are not comparable with prior years. [2] Includes juveniles, persons dishonorably discharged from the Armed Services, persons who have renounced their U.S. citizenship, and other unspecified persons. [3] Data was not available for local law prohibition, see source.

Source: U.S. Department of Justice, Bureau of Justice Statistics, *Background Checks For Firearm Transfers, 2010 - Statistical Tables*, Series NCJ 238226, February 2013. See also <http://bjs.ojp.usdoj.gov/index.cfm?ty=pbse&sid=13>.

Law Enforcement, Courts, and Prisons

Table 342. Arrests by Sex and Age: 2011

[(9,537.6 represents 9,537,600) For year ending December 31. Based on Uniform Crime Reporting (UCR) Program. Represents arrests reported (not charged) by 12,023 agencies with a total population of 238,952,977 as estimated by the FBI. Some persons may be arrested more than once during a year; therefore, in some cases, the data in this table could represent multiple arrests of the same person]

Offense charged	Total			Male			Female		
	Total	Under 18 years	18 years and over	Total	Under 18 years	18 years and over	Total	Under 18 years	18 years and over
Total	**9,537.7**	**1,129.5**	**8,408.2**	**7,066.3**	**799.1**	**6,267.2**	**2,471.4**	**330.4**	**2,141.0**
Violent crime	**411.5**	**52.4**	**359.2**	**330.9**	**42.8**	**288.0**	**80.7**	**9.5**	**71.1**
Murder and nonnegligent manslaughter	8.4	0.7	7.7	7.4	0.6	6.8	1.0	0.1	0.9
Forcible rape	14.7	2.1	12.6	14.5	2.0	12.5	0.2	–	0.1
Robbery	82.6	18.4	64.2	72.5	16.7	55.8	10.1	1.7	8.4
Aggravated assault	305.9	31.3	274.7	236.5	23.5	213.0	69.5	7.8	61.7
Property crime	**1,269.5**	**259.3**	**1,010.2**	**798.5**	**165.2**	**633.3**	**471.0**	**94.1**	**376.9**
Burglary	228.4	47.7	180.7	192.7	42.0	150.6	35.7	5.6	30.1
Larceny-theft	981.1	197.2	784.0	556.5	110.9	445.6	424.6	86.2	338.4
Motor vehicle theft	51.0	10.8	40.2	41.9	9.1	32.8	9.1	1.7	7.4
Arson	9.0	3.7	5.3	7.4	3.2	4.2	1.6	0.5	1.1
Other assaults	955.6	145.4	810.2	693.9	93.6	600.3	261.7	51.8	209.9
Forgery and counterfeiting	54.0	1.2	52.8	33.7	0.9	32.9	20.2	0.4	19.9
Fraud	128.2	3.9	124.3	75.7	2.5	73.2	52.5	1.4	51.1
Embezzlement	12.5	0.3	12.2	6.3	0.2	6.1	6.2	0.1	6.1
Stolen property; buying, receiving, possessing	71.9	10.3	61.6	57.4	8.6	48.8	14.5	1.7	12.8
Vandalism	183.2	52.2	131.0	148.2	44.5	103.7	35.0	7.7	27.3
Weapons; carrying, possessing, etc.	118.1	21.7	96.3	108.5	19.5	89.0	9.6	2.2	7.4
Prostitution and commercialized vice	44.2	0.8	43.4	13.8	0.2	13.6	30.4	0.6	29.8
Sex offenses [1]	53.0	9.6	43.5	49.1	8.6	40.5	4.0	1.0	3.0
Drug abuse violations	1,175.1	112.9	1,062.2	942.3	94.1	848.3	232.8	18.8	213.9
Gambling	6.5	0.8	5.8	5.7	0.7	5.0	0.8	–	0.7
Offenses against family and children	88.0	2.7	85.2	66.0	1.7	64.3	22.0	1.1	20.9
Driving under the influence	929.9	7.7	922.2	701.0	5.8	695.3	228.9	2.0	226.9
Liquor laws	383.9	69.8	314.1	270.0	42.1	228.0	113.9	27.7	86.1
Drunkenness	414.9	8.7	406.1	339.5	6.5	333.0	75.3	2.3	73.1
Disorderly conduct	449.7	106.3	343.4	323.9	69.3	254.6	125.8	37.0	88.8
Vagrancy	22.6	1.4	21.2	18.2	1.1	17.1	4.4	0.3	4.1
All other offenses (except traffic)	2,704.9	202.4	2,502.4	2,040.9	149.4	1,891.5	664.0	53.0	611.0
Suspicion	1.2	0.1	1.0	0.9	0.1	0.8	0.3	–	0.2
Curfew and loitering law violations	59.4	59.4	(X)	41.9	41.9	(X)	17.5	17.5	(X)

– Represents or rounds to zero. X Not applicable. [1] Except forcible rape and prostitution.

Source: U.S. Department of Justice, Federal Bureau of Investigation, "Crime in the United States 2011," <http://www.fbi.gov/about-us/cjis/ucr>, accessed February 2013.

Table 343. Arrests by Race: 2011

[Based on Uniform Crime Reporting (UCR) Program. Represents arrests reported (not charged) by 12,023 agencies with a total population of 238,952,977 as estimated by the FBI. See headnote, Table 342]

Offense charged	Total	White	Black	American Indian/Alaskan Native	Asian Pacific Islander
Total	**9,499,725**	**6,578,133**	**2,697,539**	**142,422**	**81,631**
Violent crime	**410,608**	**243,928**	**157,384**	**5,434**	**3,862**
Murder and nonnegligent manslaughter	8,341	4,000	4,149	105	87
Forcible rape	14,611	9,504	4,811	170	126
Robbery	82,436	35,443	45,827	619	547
Aggravated assault	305,220	194,981	102,597	4,540	3,102
Property crime	**1,265,509**	**861,756**	**372,993**	**17,982**	**12,778**
Burglary	227,899	151,934	72,244	2,095	1,626
Larceny-theft	977,743	670,768	281,197	15,122	10,656
Motor vehicle theft	50,902	32,575	17,250	658	419
Arson	8,965	6,479	2,302	107	77
Other assaults	952,421	625,330	304,083	14,875	8,133
Forgery and counterfeiting	53,791	35,239	17,695	295	562
Fraud	127,664	84,919	40,621	1,140	984
Embezzlement	12,454	8,155	4,032	65	202
Stolen property; buying, receiving, possessing	71,727	47,434	23,191	542	560
Vandalism	182,482	132,850	45,055	3,029	1,548
Weapons—carrying, possessing, etc.	117,820	68,453	47,515	859	993
Prostitution and commercialized vice	44,090	23,555	19,227	255	1,053
Sex offenses [1]	52,891	38,422	13,189	729	551
Drug abuse violations	1,171,866	783,564	371,248	8,275	8,779
Gambling	6,507	1,937	4,351	40	179
Offenses against the family and children	87,586	56,973	28,183	1,848	582
Driving under the influence	924,210	788,175	111,480	13,618	10,937
Liquor laws	380,663	312,106	51,446	12,896	4,215
Drunkenness	413,723	339,019	64,268	7,619	2,817
Disorderly conduct	447,201	281,531	153,840	8,771	3,059
Vagrancy	22,375	12,989	8,794	447	145
All other offenses (except traffic)	2,693,823	1,794,893	837,095	42,869	18,966
Suspicion	1,150	634	506	5	5
Curfew and loitering law violations	59,164	36,271	21,343	829	721

[1] Except forcible rape and prostitution.

Source: U.S. Department of Justice, Federal Bureau of Investigation, "Crime in the United States 2011," <http://www.fbi.gov/about-us/cjis/ucr>, accessed February 2013.

Table 344. Juvenile Arrests for Drug Abuse Offenses: 1980 to 2009

[For year ending December 31. Juveniles are persons under 18 years of age. Some persons may be arrested more than once during a year. Therefore, this table could, in some cases, represent multiple arrests of the same person]

Offense	1980	1990	2000	2003	2004	2005	2006	2007	2008	2009
Drug arrests, total...............	**86,685**	**66,300**	**146,594**	**134,746**	**135,056**	**137,809**	**145,153**	**143,270**	**134,661**	**130,317**
Sale and manufacturing..............	13,004	24,575	26,432	21,987	21,136	21,607	22,466	21,493	19,467	18,840
Heroin/cocaine......................	1,318	17,511	11,000	7,848	7,852	7,863	8,261	7,334	6,288	4,975
Marijuana...........................	8,876	4,372	11,792	10,463	9,743	9,845	10,333	10,640	9,678	9,871
Synthetic narcotics.................	465	346	945	1,043	1,119	1,071	1,262	1,162	1,093	1,170
Dangerous nonnarcotic drugs.....	2,345	2,346	2,695	2,633	2,422	2,828	2,610	2,357	2,408	2,824
Possession..........................	73,681	41,725	120,432	112,759	113,920	116,202	122,687	121,777	115,194	111,477
Heroin/cocaine......................	2,614	15,194	12,586	9,932	10,805	11,131	12,024	9,756	7,944	6,208
Marijuana...........................	64,465	20,940	95,962	87,909	87,717	88,909	95,120	97,671	93,042	90,927
Synthetic narcotics.................	1,524	1,155	2,052	2,872	3,279	3,235	3,337	3,142	3,286	3,385
Dangerous nonnarcotic drugs.....	5,078	4,436	9,832	12,046	12,119	12,927	12,206	11,208	10,922	10,957

Source: U.S. Department of Justice, Federal Bureau of Investigation Uniform Crime Reports, Arrests Master File, and unpublished data.

Table 345. Federal Drug Incidents and Seizures by Type of Drug: FY2000 to FY2012

[For fiscal years ending in year shown. Previously, data for amount of drugs seized at the Federal level was obtained from the Federal-wide Drug Seizure System (FDSS). A new system has been created called the National Seizure System (NSS), which broadens the scope of data collected for the amount of drugs seized (in pounds) at the national level. Data for "Seizure in (pounds)" are from NSS. Includes only information that has been reported to El Paso Intelligence Center (EPIC) by Federal, State, Local, Tribal, and International agencies, who reported seizures and may not necessarily reflect total seizures nationwide. There is no mandatory reporting for local and state agencies]

Drug	2000	2005	2007	2008	2009	2010	2011	2012
Number of incidents, total [1]........	**37,201**	**57,127**	**55,064**	**55,593**	**68,541**	**72,612**	**55,046**	**40,271**
Cannabis [2].................................	21,159	32,735	35,697	36,560	46,362	47,034	31,266	23,708
Methamphetamine.......................	5,233	9,310	6,109	5,667	7,014	8,607	8,119	7,207
Cocaine...................................	8,670	11,927	11,061	10,845	12,067	13,543	11,925	6,675
Heroin....................................	2,135	2,941	1,923	2,274	2,803	3,126	3,504	2,532
MDMA [3]...................................	4	214	274	247	295	302	232	149
Seizure in (pounds), total...........	**2,447,710**	**3,210,311**	**4,180,386**	**3,665,022**	**4,846,001**	**5,141,789**	**5,359,037**	**4,287,415**
Cannabis [2].................................	2,339,439	3,062,572	4,025,023	3,539,544	4,705,320	4,990,423	5,173,627	4,133,141
Cocaine...................................	95,231	126,208	133,172	101,364	116,157	115,213	145,078	96,283
Methamphetamine.......................	9,966	14,760	14,067	14,042	14,894	24,571	29,436	47,005
Heroin....................................	2,738	4,297	3,764	4,238	5,122	6,619	8,624	9,904
MDMA [3]...................................	337	2,474	4,361	5,833	4,509	4,964	2,271	1,081

[1] Seizure of drugs, weapons, currency, etc., which can occur without any arrest taking place. [2] Includes hashish. [3] MDMA methylene dioxymethamphetamine, an amphetamine derivative, used illicitly as a hallucinogen and mood-enhancer.

Source: Drug Enforcement Administration, El Paso Intelligence Center, unpublished data from the National Seizure System.

Table 346. Drug Arrest Rates for Drug Abuse Violations, 1990 to 2005, and by Region: 2009

[Rate per 100,000 population. For year ending December 31. Based on Census Bureau estimated resident population as of July 1, except 1990 and 2000, enumerated as of April 1. For composition of regions, see map, inside front cover]

Offense	1990	2000	2005	2009 Total	2009 Region North-east	2009 Region Mid-west	2009 Region South	2009 Region West
Drug arrest rate, total.........................	**435.3**	**587.1**	**600.9**	**416.0**	**382.5**	**295.3**	**425.8**	**538.9**
Sale and/or manufacture..........................	139.0	122.7	109.9	76.9	85.4	57.9	76.9	87.9
Heroin or cocaine [1]...............................	93.7	60.8	47.8	29.5	48.6	15.0	29.1	28.7
Marijuana..	26.4	34.2	29.6	25.2	24.4	26.1	21.7	30.4
Synthetic or manufactured drugs................	2.7	6.4	8.6	7.5	5.5	3.9	13.2	3.3
Other dangerous nonnarcotic drugs.............	16.2	21.3	23.9	14.8	6.9	12.9	13.0	25.5
Possession.......................................	296.3	464.4	490.9	339.1	297.1	237.4	348.9	451.0
Heroin or cocaine [1]...............................	144.4	138.7	131.5	72.8	71.8	31.6	71.9	113.5
Marijuana..	104.9	244.4	228.9	190.0	179.5	157.7	216.5	186.1
Synthetic or manufactured drugs...............	6.6	12.0	21.0	15.6	10.8	11.4	21.3	14.2
Other dangerous nonnarcotic drugs.............	40.4	69.4	109.6	60.7	35.0	36.6	39.2	137.3

[1] Includes other derivatives such as morphine, heroin, and codeine.

Source: U.S. Department of Justice, Federal Bureau of Investigation, Uniform Crime Reports, Arrests Master Files, and unpublished data.

Table 347. State and Local Government Expenditures Per Capita by Criminal Justice Function and State: 2010

[Preliminary data. In dollars. Based on Census Bureau's Annual Government Finance Survey and Annual Survey of Public Employment. Population figures are from the Bureau of the Census, Current Population Reports, Series P-25, No. 1045, July 2011]

State	Total justice system	Police protec- tion	Judicial and legal	Correc- tions	State	Total justice system	Police protec- tion	Judicial and legal	Correc- tions
Total	**683**	**309**	**139**	**235**	Missouri	505	267	88	150
Alabama	480	236	89	155	Montana	648	248	150	250
Alaska	1,236	462	387	386	Nebraska	515	219	99	197
Arizona	746	336	149	260	Nevada	834	422	165	247
Arkansas	420	183	67	170	New Hampshire	517	263	99	155
California	1,007	420	241	347	New Jersey	804	375	184	245
Colorado	691	316	114	261	New Mexico	786	316	164	306
Connecticut	662	293	182	188	New York	982	450	220	312
Delaware	774	317	165	292	North Carolina	532	250	77	205
District of Columbia	1,578	949	199	430	North Dakota	469	199	124	146
Florida	756	395	122	240	Ohio	595	287	151	157
Georgia	564	229	102	234	Oklahoma	502	228	91	183
Hawaii	629	283	194	152	Oregon	679	286	115	279
Idaho	548	235	120	192	Pennsylvania	630	246	132	252
Illinois	627	360	114	153	Rhode Island	643	349	113	181
Indiana	425	194	75	155	South Carolina	455	225	75	155
Iowa	455	206	109	140	South Dakota	492	201	91	199
Kansas	536	257	105	174	Tennessee	526	264	102	160
Kentucky	436	158	113	165	Texas	586	256	101	229
Louisiana	747	317	161	269	Utah	531	228	125	178
Maine	427	188	80	158	Vermont	536	231	107	199
Maryland	796	354	141	301	Virginia	576	247	102	227
Massachusetts	627	298	148	182	Washington	597	227	123	247
Michigan	576	242	104	230	West Virginia	455	180	109	166
Minnesota	606	318	125	162	Wisconsin	671	296	108	267
Mississippi	470	212	76	182	Wyoming	948	394	198	356

Source: U.S. Department of Justice, Bureau of Justice Statistics, "Justice Expenditure and Employment Extracts, 2010 – Preliminary," Series NCJ 242544, July 2013. See also <http://www.bjs.gov/index.cfm?ty=pbse&sid=33>.

Table 348. Employment by State and Local Law Enforcement Agencies by Type of Agency and Employee: 2008

[As of September 30. Based on census of all state and local law enforcement agencies operating nationwide, conducted every 4 years]

Type of agency	Number of agencies	Number of employees					
		Full-time			Part-time		
		Total	Sworn	Civilian	Total	Sworn	Civilian
Total [1]	**17,985**	**1,133,905**	**765,237**	**368,668**	**100,340**	**44,062**	**56,278**
Local police	12,501	593,003	461,054	131,949	58,129	27,810	30,319
Sheriffs' offices	3,063	353,461	182,979	170,482	26,052	11,334	14,718
Primary State	50	93,148	60,772	32,376	947	54	893
Special jurisdiction	1,733	90,262	56,968	33,294	14,681	4,451	10,230
Constable/marshal	638	4,031	3,464	567	531	413	118

[1] Excludes agencies with less than one full-time officer or the equivalent in part-time officers.

Source: U.S. Bureau of Justice Statistics, "Census of State and Local Law Enforcement Agencies, 2008." See also <http://bjs.ojp.usdoj.gov/index.cfm?ty=dcdetail&iid=249>.

Table 349. Law Enforcement Officers Killed and Assaulted: 1990 to 2011

[The statistics presented in this table are based on information collected by the staff of the FBI's Law Enforcement Officers Killed and Assaulted Program from law enforcement agencies throughout the U.S. and U.S. Territories. It contains statistics on line-of-duty felonious deaths, accidental deaths, and assaults of duly sworn local, state, tribal, and federal law enforcement officers]

Item	1990	1995	2000	2005	2007	2008	2009	2010	2011
OFFICERS KILLED									
Total killed............................	132	133	134	122	141	109	96	128	125
Geographical region:									
Northeast..................................	13	16	13	12	13	14	13	11	18
Midwest....................................	20	19	32	23	20	14	14	24	28
South.......................................	68	63	67	58	78	52	42	61	56
West..	23	32	19	24	28	26	25	29	20
Puerto Rico.............................	8	2	3	5	1	2	2	3	3
Island Areas, foreign countries.......	–	1	–	–	1	1	–	–	–
Total feloniously killed..............	65	74	51	55	58	41	48	56	72
Firearms.................................	56	63	47	50	56	35	45	55	63
Handgun..............................	47	44	33	42	39	25	28	38	50
Rifle....................................	8	14	10	3	8	6	15	15	7
Shotgun...............................	1	5	4	5	8	4	2	2	6
Type of firearm not reported........	–	–	–	–	1	–	–	–	–
Blunt instrument.........................	–	–	–	–	–	–	–	–	–
Bomb.......................................	–	8	–	–	–	2	–	–	–
Knife/cutting instrument...............	3	1	1	–	–	–	–	–	1
Personal weapons [1]...................	2	–	–	–	–	–	–	–	2
Vehicle....................................	1	2	3	5	2	4	3	1	6
Other.......................................	3	–	–	1	–	–	–	–	–
Total accidentally killed.............	67	59	83	67	83	68	48	72	53
OFFICERS ASSAULTED									
Population covered (1,000) [2]..........	197,426	191,759	204,599	222,874	234,734	238,731	245,926	248,727	251,004
Number of—									
Reporting agencies....................	9,343	8,503	8,940	10,119	10,973	10,835	11,691	11,826	11,944
Officers employed.....................	410,131	428,379	452,531	489,393	523,944	541,906	560,387	557,884	535,651
Total assaulted......................	72,091	57,762	58,398	57,820	61,257	61,087	58,364	56,491	54,774
Firearm....................................	3,651	2,354	1,749	2,157	2,216	2,292	2,007	1,925	2,208
Knife/cutting instrument...............	1,647	1,356	1,015	1,059	1,028	958	886	918	997
Other dangerous weapon..............	7,423	6,414	8,132	8,379	8,692	8,466	7,966	7,413	7,808
Personal weapons [1]..................	59,370	47,638	47,502	46,225	49,321	49,371	47,505	46,235	43,761

– Represents zero. [1] Includes hands, fists, feet, etc. [2] Represents the number of persons covered by reporting agencies.

Source: U.S. Department of Justice, Federal Bureau of Investigation, "Law Enforcement Officers Killed and Assaulted, 2011," and previous reports, <http://www.fbi.gov/about-us/cjis/ucr/leoka/2011>, accessed August 2013.

Table 350. Forensic Services Requests and Backlog by Type of Request: 2009

[Numbers are rounded to the nearest hundred. Census of 411 Laboratories, with a 97% return rate. Totals exclude requests outsourced to other laboratories. Request is classified as backlogged if it has been submitted to a crime lab, but has not yet been examined and reported to the submitting agency within 30 days. Estimates based on imputations for labs that did not report backlog data, see source for details]

Type of Request	Received		Completed		Backlogged Requests	
	Number	Percent	Number	Percent	Number	Percent
All requests................................	4,120,000	100	3,905,000	100	1,193,800	100
Forensic Biology [1]......................	1,389,000	34	1,312,000	34	905,200	76
Convicted Offender/Arrestee Samples.............	1,045,000	25	36,542	26	498,500	42
Casework..............................	343,000	8	295,000	8	406,700	34
Controlled Substances................	1,356,000	33	1,262,000	32	137,700	12
Latent Prints..............................	271,000	7	275,000	7	49,500	4
Firearms/Toolmarks.....................	147,000	4	131,000	3	48,700	4
Toxicology.................................	613,000	15	591,000	15	28,600	2
Trace Evidence...........................	56,000	1	46,000	1	13,200	(Z)
Impressions...............................	11,000	(Z)	10,000	(Z)	5,700	(Z)
Questioned documents.................	13,000	(Z)	12,000	(Z)	2,400	(Z)
Digital Evidence.........................	31,000	1	31,000	1	1,300	(Z)
Other Forensic Requests...............	42,000	1	42,000	1	1,500	(Z)
Crime Scene..............................	190,000	5	190,000	5	(NA)	(NA)

(Z) Less than 0.5%. [1] Includes biology screening and DNA analysis

Source: Bureau of Justice Statistics, *Census of Publicly Funded Forensic Crime Laboratories, 2009*, NCJ 238252, August 2012. See also <www.bjs.gov>.

Table 351. U.S. Supreme Court—Cases Filed and Disposition: 1980 to 2011

[Statutory term of court begins first Monday in October. Often the Court grants or denies cases after the Court recesses but before the next statutory term]

Action	1980	1990	1995	2000	2005	2008	2009	2010	2011
Total cases on docket	**5,144**	**6,316**	**7,565**	**8,965**	**9,608**	**8,966**	**9,302**	**9,066**	**8,952**
Appellate cases on docket	2,749	2,351	2,456	2,305	2,025	1,941	1,908	1,895	1,876
From prior term	527	365	361	351	354	345	328	337	324
Docketed during present term	2,222	1,986	2,095	1,954	1,671	1,596	1,580	1,558	1,552
Cases acted upon	2,324	2,042	2,130	2,024	1,703	1,654	1,607	1,618	(NA)
Granted review	167	114	92	85	63	78	69	76	59
Denied, dismissed, or withdrawn	1,999	1,802	1,945	1,842	1,554	1,505	1,452	1,461	(NA)
Summarily decided	90	81	62	63	46	29	45	45	(NA)
Cases not acted upon	425	309	326	281	322	287	301	277	303
Pauper cases on docket	2,371	3,951	5,098	6,651	7,575	7,021	7,388	7,167	7,082
Cases acted upon [1]	2,027	3,436	4,514	5,736	6,533	6,214	6,524	6,250	(NA)
Granted review	17	27	13	14	15	9	8	14	7
Denied, dismissed, or withdrawn	1,968	3,369	4,439	5,658	6,459	6,136	6,465	6,195	(NA)
Summarily decided	32	28	55	61	58	65	46	37	(NA)
Cases not acted upon	344	515	584	915	1,042	807	864	917	992
Original cases on docket	24	14	11	9	8	4	6	4	3
Cases disposed of during term	7	3	5	2	4	1	2	2	1
Total cases available for argument	**264**	**201**	**145**	**138**	**122**	**136**	**125**	**131**	**111**
Cases disposed of	162	131	93	89	87	88	86	88	80
Cases argued	154	125	90	86	88	87	82	86	79
Cases dismissed or remanded without argument	8	6	3	3	1	1	4	2	1
Cases remaining	102	70	52	49	31	48	40	43	31
Cases decided by signed opinion	144	121	87	83	82	83	77	83	73
Cases decided by per curiam opinion	8	4	3	4	5	3	4	3	5
Number of signed opinions	123	112	75	77	69	74	73	75	64

NA Not available. [1] Includes cases granted review and carried over to next term, not shown separately.

Source: Office of the Clerk, Supreme Court of the United States, unpublished data. Beginning 2011 *Journal of the Supreme Court of the United States*, July 2012; and "Table A-1 Cases on Docket, Disposed of, and Remaining on Docket, 2007 Through 2011, September 2012," <http://www.uscourts.gov/Statistics.aspx>. See also <http://www.supremecourt.gov/orders/journal.aspx>

Table 352. Judicial Caseloads for the Federal Judiciary: 2000 to 2012

[For 12-month periods ending June 30]

Judicial caseload	2000	2005	2008	2009	2010	2011	2012
U.S. Courts of Appeals [1]:							
Cases filed	54,642	67,999	59,406	59,399	56,097	55,353	57,699
Cases terminated	56,509	59,577	59,152	60,144	59,343	58,146	57,272
Cases pending	40,815	57,349	52,478	50,954	46,816	44,051	44,478
U.S. District Courts Civil:							
Cases filed	263,049	282,758	256,354	257,204	285,215	289,630	286,232
Cases terminated	260,277	280,455	230,930	255,361	295,908	301,773	286,953
Cases pending	247,973	266,938	295,414	298,493	285,071	275,068	274,347
Criminal (includes transfers):							
Cases filed	62,523	69,876	70,024	75,324	78,213	78,764	73,455
Defendants filed	84,147	92,356	91,782	96,718	100,031	102,605	96,915
Cases terminated	57,543	65,239	69,008	74,478	77,633	78,855	76,589
Cases pending	46,796	70,692	75,566	78,186	80,506	80,415	76,679
U.S. Bankruptcy Courts:							
Cases filed	1,276,922	1,637,254	967,831	1,306,315	1,572,597	1,529,560	1,311,602
Cases terminated	1,271,300	1,583,959	929,206	1,109,993	1,441,419	1,486,950	1,354,274
Cases pending	1,396,916	1,748,038	1,325,220	1,527,073	1,659,399	1,704,548	1,661,831
Post-conviction supervision:							
Persons under supervision	99,577	113,008	120,051	123,839	126,642	129,319	132,785
Pretrial services:							
Total cases activated	86,067	98,946	98,862	103,610	110,666	113,120	111,557
Pretrial services cases activated	84,107	97,045	97,315	102,434	109,711	112,181	110,593
Pretrial diversion cases activated	1,960	1,901	1,547	1,176	955	939	964
Total released on supervision	31,607	34,348	32,460	29,937	29,748	30,265	29,971
Pretrial supervision	31,927	32,438	31,089	28,754	28,440	28,903	28,625
Diversion supervision	2,166	1,910	1,371	1,183	1,308	1,362	1,346

[1] Excludes the U.S. Court of Appeals for the Federal Circuit.

Source: Administrative Office of the United States Courts, "Statistical Tables for the Federal Judiciary," <http://www.uscourts.gov/Statistics/StatisticalTablesForTheFederalJudiciary.aspx>, accessed May 2013.

Table 353. U.S. District Courts—Civil Cases Filed: by Basis of Jurisdiction and Nature of Suit: 2006 to 2012

[For years ending June 30]

Type of case	Cases filed						
	2006	2007	2008	2009	2010	2011	2012
Cases total [1]	**244,343**	**272,067**	**256,354**	**257,204**	**285,215**	**289,630**	**286,232**
BASIS OF JURISDICTION							
U.S. cases:							
U.S. plaintiff	9,693	9,218	9,868	9,030	8,427	10,282	9,707
U.S. defendant	35,194	35,299	35,527	33,286	34,306	36,502	37,569
Private cases:							
Federal question	133,656	141,044	134,623	133,697	137,776	141,334	144,387
Diversity of citizenship	65,800	86,506	76,284	81,188	104,703	101,508	94,568
NATURE OF SUIT							
Contract actions [1]	28,139	34,071	34,818	35,229	31,461	32,366	29,771
Recovery of overpayments [2]	2,856	3,053	3,491	3,214	3,079	4,623	4,041
Real property actions [1]	4,761	4,456	5,607	5,413	6,809	10,078	12,609
Foreclosure	2,982	2,441	2,689	2,639	3,836	6,569	8,194
Tort actions	53,809	77,257	59,588	61,936	87,256	79,394	70,204
Personal injury	49,834	73,004	55,777	57,332	82,057	74,921	65,898
Personal injury product liability [1]	32,515	51,557	39,664	43,055	66,958	60,631	51,850
Other personal injury [1]	17,319	21,447	16,113	14,277	15,099	14,290	14,048
Medical malpractice	1,158	1,234	1,242	1,076	1,120	1,089	1,061
Personal property damage	3,975	4,253	3,811	4,604	5,199	4,473	4,306
Actions under statutes [1]	157,536	156,152	156,277	154,572	159,683	167,791	173,648
Bankruptcy suits	3,193	3,182	2,630	2,334	2,615	2,597	4,073
Civil rights [1]	33,417	31,975	31,632	33,188	34,427	37,000	37,676
Employment	14,851	13,608	13,036	13,778	14,343	15,255	15,207
Environmental matters	874	763	900	735	826	881	696
Prisoner petitions	55,775	53,222	55,374	52,237	52,450	53,692	53,606
Forfeiture and penalty	2,318	2,221	2,324	2,322	2,297	2,372	2,297
Labor laws	16,853	18,630	16,685	17,153	18,878	18,025	19,222
Immigration	(NA)	(NA)	1,110	2,166	1,262	1,097	1,032
Protected property rights [3]	11,745	11,132	9,636	8,714	8,519	9,944	10,985
Securities commodities and exchanges	1,654	1,369	1,669	1,720	1,442	1,394	1,422
Social security laws	14,052	12,964	13,329	13,222	13,725	15,697	17,043
Tax suits	1,498	1,485	1,448	1,411	1,171	1,217	1,208
Freedom of information	309	325	294	279	315	354	366
Other actions	98	131	64	54	6	1	–

NA Not available. – represents zero [1] Includes other types not shown separately. [2] Includes enforcement of judgments in student loan cases, and overpayments of veterans' benefits. [3] Includes copyright, patent, and trademark rights.

Source: Administrative Office of the United States Courts, "Statistical Tables for the Federal Judiciary," <http://www.uscourts.gov/Statistics/StatisticalTablesForTheFederalJudiciary.aspx>, accessed May 2013.

Table 354. U.S. Courts of Appeals—Nature of Suit or Offense in Cases Arising From the U.S. District Courts: 2000 to 2012

[For 12-month periods ending June 30. Excludes data for the U.S. Court of Appeals for the Federal Circuit. Includes appeals reopened, remanded, and reinstated (after being terminated due to procedural defaults) as well as original appeals]

Nature of suit and offense	2000	2005	2008	2009	2010	2011	2012
Total cases	**46,682**	**48,907**	**43,671**	**45,490**	**43,880**	**43,113**	**44,317**
Criminal cases	10,570	15,831	13,011	14,259	12,863	12,412	13,580
Civil cases	36,112	33,076	30,660	31,231	31,017	30,701	30,737
U.S cases	8,707	9,055	7,688	8,536	7,772	7,427	7,589
U.S. plaintiff	615	356	386	382	435	364	360
U.S. defendant	8,092	8,699	7,302	8,154	7,337	7,063	7,229
Private cases	27,405	24,021	22,972	22,695	23,245	23,274	23,148
Federal question	24,155	21,000	20,289	20,044	20,599	20,412	20,004
Diversity of citizenship	3,239	3,020	2,678	2,651	2,646	2,860	3,142
General local jurisdiction	11	1	5	–	–	2	2
Criminal cases	10,570	15,831	13,011	14,259	12,863	12,412	13,580
Violent offenses	683	768	637	653	621	658	610
Property offenses	1,520	1,974	1,585	1,526	1,624	1,630	1,749
Drug offenses	4,388	5,962	5,125	6,519	5,066	4,444	5,653
Firearms, explosives offenses	1,029	2,488	1,947	1,997	1,927	1,749	1,749
Sex offenses	190	403	611	657	651	708	755
Justice system offenses	179	216	166	172	142	147	160
Immigration offenses	1,109	2,888	1,663	1,644	1,787	1,736	1,680
General offenses	579	553	484	432	411	369	346
Other	893	579	793	659	634	971	906

– Represents or rounds to zero.

Source: Administrative Office of the United States Courts, "Statistical Tables for the Federal Judiciary," <http://www.uscourts.gov/Statistics/StatisticalTablesForTheFederalJudiciary.aspx>, accessed May 2013.

Table 355. Total Incoming Caseloads in State Trial Courts by Case Category: 2010

[Represents total incoming caseloads (i.e., new filings, plus reopened and reactivated cases when provided) as reported to the Court Statistics Project. Some figures may be incomplete and/or overinclusive. Since state court caseload statistics should only be viewed in the context of each state's court structure, comparisons of the data reported here should not be made without additional information]

State	Total	Civil [1]	Domestic relations [2]	Criminal [3]	Juvenile [4]	Traffic/ violations [5]
United States..................	103,461,125	18,966,580	5,862,112	20,437,849	1,854,603	54,564,385
Alabama.........................	2,190,581	215,386	96,275	261,477	50,084	1,567,359
Alaska...........................	162,069	25,783	14,473	38,847	2,737	80,229
Arizona..........................	2,706,028	372,856	137,203	689,712	19,430	1,475,930
Arkansas........................	1,559,910	118,564	54,570	604,553	24,737	757,486
California........................	10,351,728	1,235,421	454,105	1,835,385	127,387	6,699,430
Colorado........................	1,037,456	378,845	54,294	172,048	19,170	413,099
Connecticut.....................	873,508	225,814	39,245	185,140	25,292	398,017
Delaware........................	534,672	67,523	40,677	179,390	6,832	240,250
District of Columbia............	109,597	61,556	11,961	30,285	4,183	1,612
Florida...........................	5,118,744	1,471,700	487,096	1,273,280	171,796	1,714,872
Georgia..........................	4,248,308	978,162	177,816	820,694	99,943	441,162
Hawaii...........................	552,330	43,550	14,084	86,311	14,770	393,615
Idaho............................	462,936	83,554	25,709	113,646	14,187	225,840
Illinois...........................	3,828,028	671,908	149,548	428,146	30,896	2,547,530
Indiana...........................	1,927,253	488,379	110,054	299,577	53,813	975,430
Iowa.............................	958,972	162,142	44,515	91,388	12,602	648,325
Kansas..........................	985,992	193,402	40,226	58,409	18,932	675,023
Kentucky........................	971,346	266,465	80,811	236,410	40,649	347,011
Louisiana........................	1,917,154	268,497	59,314	352,225	42,801	1,194,317
Maine............................	285,305	47,225	21,836	61,998	4,364	149,882
Maryland.........................	2,153,056	1,042,848	101,011	292,585	31,964	659,557
Massachusetts..................	1,070,341	405,668	138,461	255,482	33,667	233,482
Michigan.........................	3,929,411	735,548	124,807	930,324	51,053	2,087,679
Minnesota.......................	1,648,579	211,898	49,410	114,757	47,774	1,224,740
Mississippi......................	150,062	83,530	65,518	(NA)	1,014	(NA)
Missouri.........................	2,478,892	317,613	129,845	171,806	14,696	1,844,932
Montana.........................	353,600	66,599	15,038	50,530	2,170	219,263
Nebraska........................	457,759	132,878	23,794	125,429	11,172	159,420
Nevada..........................	1,021,707	166,192	60,455	164,766	15,025	615,269
New Hampshire.................	160,470	53,719	19,443	51,331	1,265	50,325
New Jersey......................	7,502,953	1,023,204	277,256	733,201	62,759	5,406,533
New Mexico......................	449,040	101,231	43,251	116,142	6,837	181,579
New York........................	4,398,340	1,714,862	657,566	750,866	119,315	1,155,731
North Carolina..................	3,273,431	458,803	143,545	1,886,857	36,633	747,593
North Dakota....................	193,953	35,633	12,683	39,437	8,686	97,514
Ohio.............................	3,770,981	786,558	248,240	829,243	133,223	1,773,717
Oklahoma.......................	527,648	197,523	43,636	107,400	10,541	168,548
Oregon..........................	566,824	193,458	46,425	89,738	15,229	221,974
Pennsylvania [6]................	3,726,142	549,848	359,253	546,143	51,200	2,219,698
Rhode Island....................	203,992	57,743	13,341	41,012	8,477	83,419
South Carolina..................	1,896,484	355,230	62,338	815,597	15,730	647,589
South Dakota....................	237,337	60,091	16,345	25,967	9,966	124,968
Tennessee......................	485,140	70,681	87,070	176,463	136,904	(NA)
Texas............................	12,324,024	846,839	389,651	2,377,732	39,842	8,669,960
Utah.............................	854,213	145,423	22,412	121,952	43,670	520,756
Vermont.........................	178,812	22,755	21,316	17,727	1,915	113,078
Virginia..........................	4,051,996	907,267	355,671	1,100,969	82,051	1,606,038
Washington......................	2,698,860	247,572	70,768	338,545	39,997	2,001,978
West Virginia....................	403,932	79,756	54,851	132,166	9,307	127,852
Wisconsin.......................	1,014,235	293,153	50,573	121,115	20,212	529,182
Wyoming........................	198,980	44,152	8,738	29,007	1,498	115,585
Puerto Rico......................	298,014	181,573	35,589	64,639	6,206	10,007

NA Not available. [1] Includes tort, contract, real property, small claims, probate, mental health, and civil appeals cases. [2] Includes divorce/dissolution, paternity, custody, support, visitation, adoption, and civil protection/restraining order cases. [3] Includes felony, misdemeanor, and appeals from limited jurisdiction courts. [4] Includes delinquency, dependency, and status offense petitions. [5] Includes non-criminal traffic violations (infractions), parking violations, and ordinance violations. [6] Data for Pennsylvania are preliminary.

Source: National Center for State Courts, Court Statistics Project, "State Court Caseload Statistics," <http://www.courtstatistics.org/Other-Pages/StateCourtCaseloadStatistics.aspx>, accessed May 2013 ©.

Table 356. U.S. District Courts—National Petit and Grand Juror Service: 2008 to 2012

[For years ending September 30. Includes data on jury selection days only. Data on juror service after the selection day are not included]

Juror service	2008	2009	2010	2011	2012
PETIT JUROR SERVICE					
Jurors present for jury selection or orientation	297,820	282,668	262,376	249,266	237,411
Percent selected	23.0	22.2	22.7	23.0	23.1
Percent challenged	39.8	37.9	38.5	39.4	39.5
Percent not selected or challenged	37.3	39.9	38.7	37.7	37.3
Voir Dire [1]	24.2	24.9	24.9	25.0	24.7
Non-Voir Dire [2]	13.2	15.0	13.9	12.7	12.7
Total juries selected	6,039	5,378	5,332	5,565	4,899
GRAND JUROR SERVICE					
Juries serving	749	766	784	799	783
Sessions convened	9,357	9,257	9,277	9,083	8,923
Jurors in session	186,586	186,194	186,020	182,106	179,076
Average per session	19.9	20.1	20.1	20.0	20.1
Hours in session	44,731	44,676	44,845	43,083	41,477
Average hours per session	4.8	4.8	4.8	4.7	4.6

[1] Jurors who completed pre-screening questionnaires or were in the courtroom during the conducting of voir dire. [2] Other jurors not selected or challenged who were not called to the courtroom or otherwise did not participate in the actual voir dire.

Source: Administrative Office of the United States Courts, "Judicial Business of the United States Courts 2012," <http://www.uscourts.gov/Statistics/JudicialBusiness.aspx>, accessed May 2013.

Table 357. Federal Prosecutions of Public Corruption: 1990 to 2011

[As of December 31. Prosecution of persons who have corrupted public office in violation of Federal Criminal Statutes]

Prosecution status	1990			2000			2005			2011		
	Charged	Convicted	Awaiting trial	Charged	Convicted	Awaiting trial	Charged	Convicted	Awaiting trial	Charged	Convicted	Awaiting trial
Total [1]	**1,176**	**1,084**	**300**	**1,000**	**938**	**327**	**1,163**	**1,027**	**453**	**1,082**	**1,107**	**469**
Federal officials	615	583	103	441	422	92	445	390	118	412	392	110
State officials	96	79	28	92	91	37	96	94	51	93	143	41
Local officials	257	225	98	211	183	89	309	232	148	282	276	127
Others involved	208	197	71	256	242	109	313	311	136	295	296	191

[1] Includes individuals who are neither public officials nor employees, but were involved with public officials or employees in violating the law, not shown separately.

Source: U.S. Department of Justice, Criminal Division, *Report to Congress on the Activities and Operations of the Public Integrity Section for 2011*, 2012. See also <http://www.justice.gov/criminal/pin/>.

Table 358. Felony Convictions in State Courts: 2000 to 2006

[In 2006, an estimated 1,205,273 persons were convicted of a felony (federal and state courts). Of that number, 1,132,290 were convicted in state courts, the vast majority (94 percent) of whom pleaded guilty. At the time of sentencing, about 3 out of 4 felons sentenced (77 percent) were sentenced for a single felony]

Most serious conviction	Felony convictions in state courts							
	2000		2002		2004		2006	
	Number	Percent	Number	Percent	Number	Percent	Number	Percent
All offenses	**924,700**	**100.0**	**1,051,000**	**100.0**	**1,078,920**	**100.0**	**1,132,290**	**100.0**
Violent offenses	173,200	18.7	197,030	18.8	194,570	18.0	206,140	18.2
Murder [1]	8,600	0.9	8,990	0.9	8,400	0.8	8,670	0.8
Rape/Sexual assault	31,500	3.4	35,500	3.4	33,190	3.1	33,200	2.9
Robbery	36,800	4.0	38,430	3.7	38,850	3.6	41,740	3.7
Aggravated assault	79,400	8.6	95,600	9.1	94,380	8.7	100,560	8.9
Other violent [2]	17,000	1.8	18,510	1.8	19,750	1.8	21,980	1.9
Property offenses	262,000	28.3	325,200	30.9	310,680	28.8	321,570	28.4
Burglary	79,300	8.6	100,640	9.6	93,870	8.7	99,910	8.8
Larceny [3]	100,000	10.8	124,320	11.8	119,340	11.1	125,390	11.1
Fraud/forgery [4]	82,700	8.9	100,240	9.5	97,470	9.0	96,260	8.5
Drug offenses	319,700	34.6	340,330	32.4	362,850	33.6	377,860	33.4
Possession	116,300	12.6	127,530	12.1	161,090	14.9	165,360	14.6
Trafficking	203,400	22.0	212,810	20.2	201,760	18.7	212,490	18.8
Weapon offenses	28,200	3.1	32,470	3.1	33,010	3.1	38,010	3.4
Other offenses [5]	141,600	15.3	155,970	14.8	177,810	16.5	188,730	16.7

[1] A small number of cases were classified as nonnegligent manslaughter when it was unclear if the conviction offense was murder or nonnegligent manslaughter. [2] Includes offenses such as negligent manslaughter and kidnapping. [3] When vehicle theft could not be distinguished from other theft, the case was coded as "other theft." This results in a conservative estimate of vehicle thefts. [4] Includes embezzlement. [5] Composed of nonviolent offenses such as receiving stolen property and vandalism.

Source: U.S. Department of Justice, Bureau of Justice Statistics, *Felony Sentences in State Courts, 2006– Statistical Tables*, Series NCJ 226846, November 2010. See also <http://www.bjs.gov/index.cfm?ty=pbse&sid=28>.

Table 359. Delinquency Cases Disposed by Juvenile Courts by Type of Offense: 1990 to 2010

[In thousands (1,341 represents 1,341,000), except rate. A delinquency offense is an act committed by a juvenile for which an adult could be prosecuted in a criminal court. Disposition of a case involves taking a definite action such as waiving the case to criminal court, dismissing the case, placing the youth on probation, placing the youth in a facility for delinquents, or actions such as fines, restitution, and community service]

Type of offense	1990	1995	2000	2001	2002	2003	2004	2005	2006	2007	2008	2009	2010
All delinquency offenses	**1,341**	**1,827**	**1,709**	**1,686**	**1,679**	**1,684**	**1,685**	**1,679**	**1,631**	**1,632**	**1,615**	**1,484**	**1,368**
Case rate [1]	52.3	63.7	55.6	54.0	53.1	52.9	52.6	52.3	50.8	51.1	50.9	47.1	43.4
Person offenses [2]	257	410	402	408	407	415	422	434	416	411	400	366	347
Criminal homicide	2	3	1	1	2	1	1	1	1	1	1	1	1
Forcible rape	4	5	4	5	4	5	5	5	4	4	4	4	4
Robbery	27	42	22	22	21	22	22	26	30	31	32	29	26
Aggravated assault	53	74	52	51	48	49	50	52	50	49	47	42	40
Property offenses [2]	781	920	706	665	662	652	635	613	589	600	610	565	502
Burglary	147	150	119	114	112	111	105	102	104	105	107	98	90
Larceny-theft	348	436	326	303	303	296	293	275	248	260	280	273	244
Motor vehicle theft	70	55	38	38	38	38	34	32	29	27	23	19	16
Arson	7	10	9	9	9	8	9	8	8	8	8	7	5
Drug law violations	70	163	188	192	186	185	187	186	182	183	177	166	164
Public order offenses [2]	233	333	414	420	424	432	441	447	444	438	427	388	355
Obstruction of justice	89	135	208	208	203	206	200	198	196	194	193	182	166
Disorderly conduct	56	89	103	108	118	121	131	132	129	130	125	111	101
Weapons offenses	30	47	34	34	33	34	39	43	44	40	39	33	30
Liquor law violations	17	13	17	16	16	16	18	18	20	21	20	17	16
Nonviolent sex offenses	11	10	14	14	15	14	14	13	12	11	11	11	11

[1] Number of cases disposed per 1,000 juveniles (ages 10 to upper age of juvenile court jurisdiction). The upper age of juvenile court jurisdiction is defined by statute in each state. [2] Total includes other offenses not shown.

Source: National Center for Juvenile Justice, Pittsburgh, PA, *Juvenile Court Statistics*, April 2013. Case rates adapted from: "Delinquency Case Rates by Offense, Sex, and Race (1985-2010)," <http://www.ojjdp.gov/ojstatbb/court/data.html>. Case estimates adapted from "Easy Access to Juvenile Court Statistics, Detailed Offenses," <http://ojjdp.gov/ojstatbb/ezajcs/>.

Table 360. Delinquency Cases Disposed by Juvenile Courts by Type of Offense, Sex, and Race: 1995 to 2010

[See headnote, Table 359]

Sex, race, and offense	Number of cases disposed				Case rate [1]			
	1995	2000	2005	2010	1995	2000	2005	2010
Male, total	**1,416,200**	**1,276,300**	**1,220,200**	**986,700**	**96.1**	**80.8**	**74.1**	**61.1**
Person	308,100	289,300	305,200	240,600	20.9	18.3	18.5	14.9
Property	712,100	525,700	444,400	354,600	48.3	33.3	27.0	22.0
Drugs	139,200	156,900	149,500	134,700	9.4	9.9	9.1	8.3
Public order	256,800	304,300	321,200	256,700	17.4	19.3	19.5	15.9
Female, total	**410,400**	**433,000**	**459,000**	**381,500**	**29.4**	**28.9**	**29.3**	**24.8**
Person	102,300	112,500	129,000	106,200	7.3	7.5	8.2	6.9
Property	207,900	180,100	168,300	147,800	14.9	12.0	10.8	9.6
Drugs	23,500	30,900	36,000	29,400	1.7	2.1	2.3	1.9
Public order	76,600	109,600	125,700	98,100	5.5	7.3	8.0	6.4
White, total	**1,230,600**	**1,166,900**	**1,074,100**	**876,400**	**53.9**	**48.3**	**43.4**	**36.4**
Person	246,400	252,800	247,300	198,900	10.8	10.5	10.0	8.3
Property	659,600	498,000	414,500	329,500	28.9	20.6	16.7	13.7
Drugs	106,700	137,300	135,600	125,400	4.7	5.7	5.5	5.2
Public order	217,900	278,900	276,800	222,600	9.5	11.5	11.2	9.2
Black, total	**546,600**	**492,500**	**556,100**	**451,100**	**125.5**	**101.7**	**104.2**	**87.6**
Person	153,900	138,800	176,100	139,100	35.3	28.7	33.0	27.0
Property	232,000	182,800	177,700	156,000	53.3	37.8	33.3	30.3
Drugs	53,300	46,100	45,000	34,000	12.2	9.5	8.4	6.6
Public order	107,400	124,700	157,300	121,900	24.7	25.8	29.5	23.7
American Indian, total	**26,200**	**26,300**	**24,900**	**21,100**	**69.5**	**57.1**	**46.7**	**36.6**
Person	5,100	5,400	5,700	4,800	13.6	11.7	10.6	8.3
Property	15,100	12,800	10,100	8,200	40.1	27.9	18.9	14.2
Drugs	1,500	2,500	2,900	2,700	3.9	5.5	5.4	4.6
Public order	4,500	5,500	6,300	5,400	11.8	12.0	11.7	9.4
Asian, total	**23,200**	**23,600**	**24,000**	**19,500**	**20.8**	**18.3**	**16.1**	**11.6**
Person	5,000	4,800	5,000	4,000	4.5	3.7	3.4	2.3
Property	13,300	12,200	10,500	8,700	11.9	9.4	7.0	5.1
Drugs	1,200	1,900	2,100	2,100	1.1	1.5	1.4	1.2
Public order	3,700	4,800	6,500	4,800	3.3	3.7	4.3	2.9

[1] Cases per 1,000 juveniles (ages 10 to upper age of juvenile court jurisdiction). The upper age of juvenile court jurisdiction is defined by statute in each state.

Source: National Center for Juvenile Justice, Pittsburgh, PA, *Juvenile Court Statistics*, April 2013. Case rates adapted from "Delinquency Case Rates by Offense, Sex, and Race (1985-2010)," <http://www.ojjdp.gov/ojstatbb/court/data.html>. Case estimates adapted from "Easy Access to Juvenile Court Statistics, Detailed Offenses," <http://ojjdp.gov/ojstatbb/ezajcs/>.

Table 361. Child Victims of Abuse and Neglect, Total and First-Time Victims, by State: FY2010 and FY2011

[Data are unique counts, which count a child once, regardless of the number of reports concerning that child. Based on available State submissions to National Child Abuse and Neglect Data System (NCANDS) of alleged child abuse and neglect, see headnote Table 362. States reporting 95 percent or more first-time victims are excluded due to potential issues with data quality. See source for details]

State	Fiscal Year 2010				Fiscal Year 2011			
	Child Population	Victims	First-Time Victims Number	First-Time Victims Rate	Child Population	Victims	First-Time Victims Number	First-Time Victims Rate
Total..............	68,664,161	646,902	479,348	7.0	68,621,767	639,416	467,820	6.8
Alabama.............	1,130,523	9,367	7,883	7.0	1,127,143	8,601	7,186	6.4
Alaska..............	188,169	2,825	1,980	10.5	188,441	2,898	2,113	11.2
Arizona.............	1,630,756	6,023	5,271	3.2	1,625,114	8,708	7,604	4.7
Arkansas............	711,084	11,729	9,660	13.6	710,474	11,105	9,022	12.7
California...........	9,297,344	76,758	65,070	7.0	9,271,919	80,100	68,112	7.3
Colorado............	1,225,617	11,166	8,562	7.0	1,230,088	10,604	8,143	6.6
Connecticut.........	815,431	9,954	7,109	8.7	803,314	10,012	7,213	9.0
Delaware............	205,616	2,125	1,746	8.5	204,668	2,466	2,018	9.9
District of Columbia.....	(NA)	(NA)	(NA)	(NA)	(NA)	(NA)	(NA)	(NA)
Florida.............	3,996,070	50,239	26,994	6.8	3,994,431	51,920	26,982	6.8
Georgia.............	(NA)	(NA)	(NA)	(NA)	(NA)	(NA)	(NA)	(NA)
Hawaii..............	304,573	1,744	1,342	4.4	304,604	1,346	1,028	3.4
Idaho...............	428,721	1,609	1,306	3.0	428,116	1,470	1,190	2.8
Illinois.............	3,123,630	26,442	19,636	6.3	3,098,125	25,832	19,151	6.2
Indiana.............	1,605,298	21,362	18,694	11.6	1,597,603	17,930	15,068	9.4
Iowa................	726,778	12,005	8,322	11.5	724,370	11,028	7,481	10.3
Kansas..............	726,079	1,504	1,337	1.8	723,922	1,729	1,559	2.2
Kentucky............	1,023,118	17,029	11,869	11.6	1,020,955	16,994	12,032	11.8
Louisiana...........	1,116,293	8,344	6,228	5.6	1,118,196	9,545	7,101	6.4
Maine...............	273,457	3,269	1,488	5.4	269,218	3,118	1,444	5.4
Maryland............	1,352,083	13,059	10,168	7.5	1,346,635	13,740	10,052	7.5
Massachusetts.........	1,417,262	24,428	13,270	9.4	1,405,015	20,262	11,359	8.1
Michigan............	2,333,718	32,412	23,171	9.9	2,295,812	33,366	23,460	10.2
Minnesota...........	1,282,527	4,462	3,648	2.8	1,277,526	4,342	3,629	2.8
Mississippi..........	754,068	7,403	6,625	8.8	750,239	6,712	5,945	7.9
Missouri............	1,423,109	5,313	4,503	3.2	1,412,121	5,826	5,002	3.5
Montana.............	222,979	1,383	1,013	4.5	222,354	1,066	820	3.7
Nebraska............	458,894	4,572	3,483	7.6	460,065	4,307	3,285	7.1
Nevada..............	664,456	4,654	3,079	4.6	663,775	5,355	3,608	5.4
New Hampshire........	286,377	851	196	0.7	279,984	876	270	1.0
New Jersey..........	2,062,462	8,981	7,459	3.6	2,042,810	8,238	6,739	3.3
New Mexico..........	518,998	5,440	4,151	8.0	519,419	5,601	4,209	8.1
New York............	4,317,426	77,011	48,767	11.3	4,286,008	72,625	44,714	10.4
North Carolina........	2,279,498	21,895	16,755	7.4	2,287,593	22,940	17,926	7.8
North Dakota.........	(NA)	(NA)	(NA)	(NA)	151,156	1,295	1,202	8.0
Ohio................	2,723,536	31,295	26,746	9.8	2,693,092	30,601	21,511	8.0
Oklahoma............	929,314	7,207	5,639	6.1	936,159	7,836	6,078	6.5
Oregon..............	(NA)	(NA)	(NA)	(NA)	(NA)	(NA)	(NA)	(NA)
Pennsylvania.........	2,789,150	3,555	3,326	1.2	2,761,159	3,287	3,074	1.1
Puerto Rico..........	(NA)	(NA)	(NA)	(NA)	(NA)	(NA)	(NA)	(NA)
Rhode Island.........	223,542	3,268	2,287	10.2	219,536	3,131	2,198	10.0
South Carolina........	1,079,569	11,802	9,241	8.6	1,080,555	11,324	8,589	7.9
South Dakota.........	202,892	1,360	1,023	5.0	203,156	1,353	986	4.9
Tennessee............	1,494,958	8,760	7,104	4.8	1,492,136	9,243	7,852	5.3
Texas...............	6,879,384	64,937	52,205	7.6	6,960,738	63,474	51,235	7.4
Utah................	871,474	12,854	8,547	9.8	880,309	10,586	6,856	7.8
Vermont.............	128,735	658	533	4.1	126,018	630	526	4.2
Virginia.............	(NA)	(NA)	(NA)	(NA)	(NA)	(NA)	(NA)	(NA)
Washington..........	1,580,986	6,593	4,720	3.0	1,581,757	6,541	4,640	2.9
West Virginia........	386,435	3,961	2,762	7.1	384,794	4,000	2,960	7.7
Wisconsin...........	1,336,617	4,569	3,826	2.9	1,326,208	4,750	4,058	3.1
Wyoming.............	135,155	725	604	4.5	134,937	703	590	4.4

NA Not available

Source: U.S. Department of Health and Human Services, Administration for Children and Families, Statistics and Research, *Child Maltreatment 2011*, December 2012. See also <http://www.acf.hhs.gov/programs/cb/research-data-technology/statistics-research/child-maltreatment>.

Table 362. Child Abuse and Neglect Victims by Selected Characteristics: FY2005 to FY2011

[Data are unique counts, which count a child once, regardless of the number of reports concerning that child. Based on available State submissions to National Child Abuse and Neglect Data System (NCANDS) of alleged child abuse and neglect. NCANDS collects case level data on children who received child protective services response in the form of an investigative or alternative response. Each state has its own definition of child abuse and neglect based on standards set by federal law. Child abuse is defined as any recent act or failure to act on the part of a parent or caretaker which results in death, serious physical or emotional harm, sexual abuse or exploitation; or an act or failure to act which presents an imminent risk or serious harm]

Item	FY2005	FY2006	FY2007	FY2008	FY2009	FY2010	FY2011
TYPES OF MALTREATMENT [1]							
Victims, total [2, 3]	792,685	809,494	690,849	704,732	693,507	688,251	676,569
Neglect	505,737	522,914	489,275	504,717	502,417	499,691	531,413
Physical abuse	139,783	137,678	118,137	121,735	120,510	118,502	118,825
Sexual abuse	79,486	75,638	68,024	68,156	64,358	62,057	61,472
Psychological or Emotional	57,420	56,500	49,848	49,947	50,466	53,426	60,839
Medical neglect	16,728	18,572	15,597	16,067	16,373	15,711	15,074
Other and unknown	119,728	132,880	58,035	61,083	64,394	68,590	71,217
SEX OF VICTIM							
Male	381,364	390,269	332,445	340,300	334,404	333,864	329,004
Female	408,784	416,591	356,226	361,787	354,677	352,174	345,587
AGE OF VICTIM							
1 year and younger	139,541	147,146	132,122	138,231	136,502	136,910	133,942
2 to 5 years old	197,372	201,295	171,332	175,573	177,126	180,271	181140
6 to 9 years old	171,686	176,500	150,593	152,196	147,812	145,354	142,412
10 to 13 years old	154,171	150,719	123,127	123,805	120,577	119,555	117,876
14 to 17 years old	125,830	129,686	108,228	111,493	108,633	103,764	98,607
18 years old and over	436	500	398	627	638	490	(NA)
Unknown [4]	2,941	2,787	4,231	1,938	1,327	979	2,592

NA Not available. [1] Not all states use this taxonomy, nor do states define the categories in the same way. [2] Total victims is the sum of the states contributing data to the Child File. The number of states not contributing data varies by year. [3] This is a count of the number of distinct victims of the specified types of maltreatment. A child may be a victim of more than one type of maltreatment, so the sum of types is greater than the count of victims. [4] Beginning in 2011, includes unborn, unknown, and victims aged 18–21. Unknown age is defined as victims whose ages were unable to be determined or older than 17 years, a few States include victims ages 18–21 as child victims.

Source: U.S. Department of Health and Human Services, Administration for Children and Families, Statistics and Research, *Child Maltreatment 2011*, December 2012, and unpublished data. See also <http://www.acf.hhs.gov/programs/cb/research-data-technology/statistics-research/child-maltreatment>.

Table 363. Prisoners Under Jurisdiction of Federal or State Correctional Authorities—Summary by State: 1990 to 2011

[For years ending December 31. Jurisdiction refers to the legal authority over a prisoner, regardless of where held]

State	1990	2000	2005	2010	2011	State	1990	2000	2005	2010	2011
U.S. [1]	773,919	1,391,261	1,527,929	1,613,803	1,598,780	MS	8,375	20,241	20,515	21,067	21,386
Federal	65,526	145,416	187,618	209,771	216,362	MO	14,943	27,543	30,823	30,623	30,833
State	708,393	1,245,845	1,340,311	1,404,032	1,382,418	MT	1,425	3,105	3,532	3,716	3,678
AL	15,665	26,332	27,888	31,764	32,270	NE	2,403	3,895	4,455	4,587	4,616
AK [2]	2,622	4,173	4,812	5,391	5,412	NV	5,322	10,063	11,782	12,653	12,778
AZ [3]	14,261	26,510	33,565	40,209	40,020	NH	1,342	2,257	2,530	2,761	2,614
AR	7,322	11,915	13,541	16,204	16,108	NJ	21,128	29,784	27,359	25,007	23,834
CA	97,309	163,001	170,676	165,062	149,569	NM	3,187	5,342	6,571	6,763	6,998
CO	7,671	16,833	21,456	22,815	21,978	NY	54,895	70,199	62,743	56,656	55,436
CT [2]	10,500	18,355	19,442	19,321	18,324	NC	18,411	31,266	36,365	40,382	39,440
DE [2, 3]	3,471	6,921	6,966	6,615	6,739	ND	483	1,076	1,385	1,487	1,423
DC [4, 5]	9,947	7,456	(NA)	(NA)	(NA)	OH	31,822	45,833	45,854	51,712	50,964
FL	44,387	71,319	89,768	104,306	103,055	OK	12,285	23,181	26,676	26,252	25,977
GA [3]	22,411	44,232	48,749	56,432	55,944	OR	6,492	10,580	13,411	14,876	14,510
HI [2, 6]	2,533	5,053	6,146	5,912	6,037	PA	22,290	36,847	42,380	51,264	51,578
ID	1,961	5,535	6,818	7,431	7,739	RI [2, 6]	2,392	3,286	3,654	3,357	3,337
IL	27,516	45,281	44,919	48,418	48,427	SC	17,319	21,778	23,160	23,578	22,914
IN	12,736	20,125	24,455	28,028	28,906	SD	1,341	2,616	3,463	3,434	3,535
IA [3]	3,967	7,955	8,737	9,455	9,116	TN	10,388	22,166	26,369	27,451	28,479
KS	5,775	8,344	9,068	9,051	9,327	TX	50,042	166,719	169,003	173,649	172,224
KY	9,023	14,919	19,662	20,544	21,545	UT	2,496	5,637	6,382	6,807	6,879
LA	18,599	35,207	36,083	39,445	39,710	VT [2]	1,049	1,697	2,078	2,079	2,053
ME	1,523	1,679	2,023	2,154	2,145	VA	17,593	30,168	35,344	37,638	38,130
MD	17,848	23,538	22,737	22,645	22,558	WA	7,995	14,915	17,382	18,235	17,847
MA	8,345	10,722	10,701	11,313	11,623	WV	1,565	3,856	5,312	6,681	6,826
MI	34,267	47,718	49,546	44,165	42,940	WI	7,465	20,754	22,697	22,729	22,654
MN	3,176	6,238	9,281	9,796	9,800	WY	1,110	1,680	2,047	2,112	2,183

NA Not available. [1] Includes inmates held in nonsecure privately operated community corrections facilities and juveniles held in contract facilities. [2] Data include both total jail and prison population. Prisons and jails form one integrated system. [3] Numbers are for custody rather than jurisdiction counts. [4] The transfer of responsibility for sentenced felons from the District of Columbia to the federal system was completed by the year end 2001. [5] The District of Columbia inmates sentenced to more than 1 year are now under the responsibility of the Bureau of Prisons. [6] Counts include dual jurisdiction cases where the inmate is currently housed in another jurisdiction's facilities.

Source: Source: U.S. Department of Justice, Bureau of Justice Statistics, *Prisoners in 2011*, Series NCJ 239808, December 2012 and earlier reports. See also <http://bjs.ojp.usdoj.gov/index.cfm?ty=pbse&sid=40>.

Table 364. Jail Inmates by Sex, Race, and Hispanic Origin: 1990 to 2012

[As of the last week day in June. Data for 2000 and 2010-2012 are based on the Annual Survey of Jails]

Characteristic	1990	1995	2000	2005	2010	2011	2012
Total inmates [1, 2]	**405,320**	**507,044**	**621,149**	**747,529**	**748,728**	**735,601**	**744,524**
Incarceration rate per 100,000							
U.S. residents	163	193	220	252	242	236	237
Rated capacity [3, 4]	389,171	545,763	677,787	786,954	866,782	879,722	886,947
Adult	403,019	499,300	613,534	740,770	741,168	729,700	739,100
Male	365,821	448,000	543,120	646,807	649,284	636,900	640,900
Female	37,198	51,300	70,414	93,963	91,884	92,800	98,100
Juveniles [5]	2,301	7,800	7,615	6,759	7,560	5,900	5,400
White, non-Hispanic	169,600	203,300	260,500	331,000	331,600	329,400	341,100
Black, non-Hispanic	172,300	220,600	256,300	290,500	283,200	276,400	274,600
Hispanic/Latino [6]	58,100	74,400	94,100	111,900	118,100	113,900	112,700
Other [7]	5,400	8,800	10,200	13,000	15,000	14,700	14,700
Two or more races	(NA)	(NA)	(NA)	1,000	800	1,200	1,500

NA Not available. [1] Total does not include offenders who were supervised outside of jail facilities. [2] Prior to 2005, race and Hispanic origin data do not include two or more races. [3] Beginning 1995, rated capacity subject to sampling error. [4] Rated capacity is the number of beds or inmates assigned by a rating official to facilities within each jurisdiction. [5] Juveniles are persons held under the age of 18. Includes juveniles who were tried or awaiting trial as adults. [6] Persons of Hispanic origin may be of any race. [7] Excludes persons of Hispanic or Latino origin. Includes American Indians, Alaska Natives, Asians, and Pacific Islanders.

Source: U.S. Department of Justice, Bureau of Justice Statistics, *Jail Inmates at Midyear 2012 - Statistical Tables*, Series NCJ 241264, May 2013. See also <http://bjs.ojp.usdoj.gov/index.cfm?ty=pbse&sid=38>.

Table 365. Prisoners Under Federal or State Jurisdiction by Sex: 1980 to 2011

[As of December 31. Represents prisoners sentenced to more than one year under jurisdiction of federal or state authorities rather than those in the custody of such authorities. Federal prisoners includes inmates held in nonsecure privately operated community corrections facilities and juveniles held in contract facilities.]

Year	Total [1]	Rate [2]	State	Male	Female	Year	Total [1]	Rate [2]	State	Male	Female
1980	315,974	139	295,363	303,643	12,331	2003	1,408,361	483	1,256,442	1,315,790	92,571
1985	480,568	202	447,873	459,223	21,345	2004	1,433,728	487	1,274,591	1,337,730	95,998
1990	739,980	297	689,577	699,416	40,564	2005	1,462,866	492	1,296,693	1,364,178	98,688
1995	1,085,022	411	1,001,359	1,021,059	63,963	2006	1,504,598	501	1,331,065	1,401,261	103,337
1998	1,245,402	461	1,141,720	1,167,802	77,600	2007	1,532,851	506	1,353,647	1,427,088	105,763
1999	1,304,074	476	1,189,799	1,221,611	82,463	2008	1,547,742	506	1,365,409	1,441,384	106,358
2000	1,334,174	[3] 470	1,209,130	1,249,130	85,044	2009	1,553,574	504	1,365,688	1,448,239	105,335
2001	1,345,217	470	1,208,708	1,260,033	85,184	2010	1,552,669	500	1,362,028	1,447,766	104,903
2002	1,380,516	477	1,237,476	1,291,450	89,066	2011	1,537,415	492	1,340,365	1,433,741	103,674

[1] Includes prisoners under the legal authority of state or federal correctional officials. [2] Rate per 100,000 estimated population. Based on U.S. Census Bureau estimated resident population. [3] Decrease in incarceration rate from 1999 to 2000 due to use of new Census numbers.

Source: U.S. Department of Justice, Bureau of Justice Statistics, *Prisoners in 2011*, Series NCJ 239808, December 2012. See also <http://bjs.ojp.usdoj.gov/index.cfm?ty=pbse&sid=40>.

Table 366. Prisoners Under Sentence of Death by Characteristic: 1980 to 2011

[As of December 31. Excludes prisoners under sentence of death who remained within local correctional systems pending exhaustion of appellate process or who had not been committed to prison]

Characteristic	1980	1990	2000	2003	2004	2005	2006	2007	2008	2009	2010	2011
Total [1, 2]	**688**	**2,346**	**3,601**	**3,377**	**3,320**	**3,245**	**3,233**	**3,215**	**3,210**	**3,173**	**3,139**	**3,082**
White	418	1,368	1,989	1,882	1,856	1,802	1,806	1,806	1,795	1,780	1,703	1,703
Black and other	270	978	1,612	1,495	1,464	1,443	1,427	1,409	1,415	1,393	1,436	1,379
Under 20 years old	11	8	11	1	1	–	–	1	–	–	(NA)	–
20 to 24 years old	173	168	237	133	95	61	51	42	44	39	(NA)	28
25 to 34 years old	334	1,110	1,103	965	896	816	735	680	610	564	(NA)	471
35 to 54 years old	186	1,006	2,019	1,969	1,977	2,012	2,043	2,060	2,076	2,062	(NA)	1,982
55 years old and over	10	64	223	306	345	365	399	437	477	508	(NA)	601
Years of school completed:												
7 years or less	68	178	214	213	207	192	186	183	176	176	(NA)	(NA)
8 years	74	186	233	227	221	206	195	189	185	180	(NA)	347
9 to 11 years	204	775	1,157	1,073	1,053	1,030	1,015	989	977	950	(NA)	899
12 years	162	729	1,184	1,108	1,091	1,105	1,098	1,089	1,094	1,097	(NA)	1,067
More than 12 years	43	209	315	270	262	256	248	248	247	238	(NA)	235
Unknown	163	279	490	483	480	465	486	522	528	532	(NA)	534
Marital status:												
Never married	268	998	1,749	1,641	1,622	1,586	1,577	1,558	1,552	1,531	(NA)	1,488
Married	229	632	739	684	658	649	626	635	630	613	(NA)	608
Divorced [3]	217	726	1,105	1,049	1,034	1,019	1,025	1,027	1,025	1,029	(NA)	986
Time elapsed since sentencing:												
Less than 12 months	185	231	208	137	117	122	105	110	106	103	(NA)	(NA)
12 to 47 months	389	753	786	495	421	399	382	352	339	329	(NA)	(NA)
48 to 71 months	102	438	507	451	388	299	262	262	244	237	(NA)	(NA)
72 months and over	38	934	2,092	2,291	2,388	2,434	2,479	2,496	2,518	2,504	(NA)	(NA)
Legal status at arrest:												
Not under sentence	384	1,345	2,202	2,048	2,026	1,979	1,952	1,963	1,961	1,931	(NA)	(NA)
Parole or probation [4]	115	578	921	845	809	792	778	760	753	739	(NA)	(NA)
Prison or escaped	45	128	126	137	145	144	142	143	146	156	(NA)	(NA)
Unknown	170	305	344	344	334	339	356	354	347	347	(NA)	(NA)

– Represents zero. NA Not available [1] Revisions to the total number of prisoners were not carried to the characteristics except for race. [2] Includes races not shown separately. [3] Includes persons married but separated, widows, widowers, and unknown. [4] Includes prisoners on mandatory conditional release, work release, other leave, AWOL, or bail. Covers 28 prisoners in 1990; 17 in 2001, 2002, and 2003; 15 in 2004; 14 in 2005, 2006, 2007, and 2009; and 12 in 2008.

Source: U.S. Department of Justice, Bureau of Justice Statistics, *Capital Punishment, 2011*, Series NCJ 242185, July 2013, and earlier reports. See also: <http://www.bjs.gov/index.cfm?ty=pbse&sid=1>.

Table 367. Prisoners Executed Under Civil Authority by Sex and Race: 1930 to 2012

[Excludes executions by military authorities]

Year or period	Total[1]	Male	Female	White[2]	Black[2]	Executed for murder Total[1]	White	Black
All years, 1930–2011	**5,136**	**5,092**	**44**	**2,476**	**2,509**	**4,613**	**2,479**	**2,072**
1960 to 1967	191	190	1	98	93	155	87	68
1968 to 1976	–	–	–	–	–	–	–	–
1977 to 2011	1,277	1,265	12	722	440	1,279	815	442
1985	18	18	0	9	0	18	11	7
1990	23	23	0	16	0	23	16	7
1995	56	56	0	31	1	56	33	22
2000	85	83	2	43	1	85	49	35
2003	65	65	0	41	1	65	44	20
2004	59	59	0	36	1	59	39	19
2005	60	59	1	38	0	60	41	19
2006	53	53	0	25	0	53	32	21
2007	42	42	0	22	0	42	28	14
2008	37	37	0	17	0	37	20	17
2009	52	52	0	24	0	52	31	21
2010	46	45	1	28	0	46	34	12
2011	43	43	0	22	0	43	22	16
2012	43	43	0	(NA)	(NA)	43	(NA)	(NA)

– Represents zero. NA Not available. [1] Includes races other than White or Black. [2] Excludes persons of Hispanic or Latino origin.

Source: Through 1978, U.S. Law Enforcement Assistance Administration; thereafter, U.S. Department of Justice, Bureau of Justice Statistics, *Capital Punishment, 2011*, NCJ 242185, July 2013. See also <http://bjs.ojp.usdoj.gov/index.cfm?ty=pbse&sid=1>.

Table 368. Prisoners Executed Under Civil Authority by State: 1977 to 2012

[Alaska, District of Columbia, Hawaii, Illinois, Iowa, Maine, Massachusetts, Michigan, Minnesota, New Jersey, North Dakota, Rhode Island, Vermont, West Virginia, and Wisconsin are jurisdictions without a death penalty. New Mexico abolished the death penalty for offenses committed after July 1, 2009; two men under previously imposed death sentences are still subject to execution]

State	1977 to 2011	2000	2010	2011	2012	State	1977 to 2011	2000	2010	2011	2012	State	1977 to 2011	2000	2010	2011	2012
U.S.[1]	**1,277**	**85**	**46**	**43**	**43**	IL	12	–	–	–	–	OH	46	–	8	5	3
						IN	20	–	–	–	–	OK	96	11	3	2	6
AL	55	4	5	6	–	KY	3	–	–	–	–	OR	2	–	–	–	–
AZ	28	3	1	4	6	LA	28	1	1	–	–	PA	3	–	–	–	–
AR	27	2	–	–	–	MD	5	–	–	–	–	SC	43	1	–	1	–
CA	13	1	–	–	–	MS	15	–	3	2	6	SD	1	–	–	–	2
CO	1	–	–	–	–	MO	68	5	–	1	–	TN	6	1	–	–	–
CT	1	–	–	–	–	MT	3	–	–	–	–	TX	477	40	17	13	15
DE	15	1	–	1	1	NE	3	–	–	–	–	UT	7	–	1	–	–
FL	71	6	1	2	3	NV	12	–	–	–	–	VA	109	8	3	1	–
GA	52	–	2	4	–	NM	1	–	–	–	–	WA	5	–	1	–	–
ID	2	–	–	1	1	NC	43	1	–	–	–	WY	1	–	–	–	–

– Represents zero. [1] Includes persons executed within the Federal system.

Source: Through 1978, U.S. Law Enforcement Assistance Administration; thereafter, U.S. Department of Justice, Bureau of Justice Statistics, *Capital Punishment 2011*, NCJ 242185, July 2013, and earlier reports. See also <http://bjs.ojp.usdoj.gov/index.cfm?ty=pbse&sid=1>.

Table 369. Adults Under Community Supervision, Probation, and Parole by State: 2011

[As of December 31, 2011, unless otherwise noted. Rates per 100,000, computed using the estimated U.S. adult resident population in each jurisdiction on January 1, 2012. Counts may not be actual as reporting agencies may provide estimates on some or all detailed data, see source for details. Based on Bureau of Justice Statistics' Annual Survey of Probation and Parole]

Area	Community Supervision		Probation		Parole	
	Number [1]	Rate (100,000)	Number	Rate (100,000)	Number	Rate (100,000)
U.S. Total..................	4,814,200	2,015	3,971,319	1,662	[2] 853,852	357
Federal.........................	131,800	55	22,668	9	109,124	46
States.........................	4,682,400	1,960	3,948,651	1,653	744,728	312
Alabama......................	69,500	1,884	60,914	1,651	8,601	233
Alaska........................	8,800	1,636	7,044	1,310	1,777	330
Arizona.......................	83,800	1,714	76,109	1,557	7,708	158
Arkansas.....................	52,100	2,328	29,355	1,312	22,704	1,015
California.....................	380,800	1,331	269,754	943	[2] 111063	388
Colorado [3].................	86,900	2,220	76,173	1,946	10,775	275
Connecticut..................	51,800	1,857	49,195	1,764	2,561	92
Delaware.....................	16,700	2,364	16,195	2,293	553	78
District of Columbia........	14,600	2,821	9,013	1,741	6,098	1,178
Florida [3]....................	248,900	1,640	244,686	1,612	4,203	28
Georgia......................	[4] 478,700	6,498	[4] 457,141	6,205	25,463	346
Hawaii........................	24,100	2,241	22,316	2,075	1,791	167
Idaho.........................	44,500	3,825	39,977	3,436	4,512	388
Illinois [3]....................	150,900	1,539	125,442	1,279	[5] 25,465	260
Indiana.......................	139,600	2,826	129,399	2,619	10,154	206
Iowa..........................	34,100	1,451	29,828	1,270	4,446	189
Kansas.......................	22,400	1,039	17,352	805	5,052	234
Kentucky.....................	61,200	1,821	47,247	1,406	14,223	423
Louisiana....................	69,500	2,002	41,916	1,207	27,640	796
Maine.........................	7,200	678	7,166	675	21	2
Maryland.....................	109,600	2,433	96,359	2,139	13,237	294
Massachusetts..............	70,900	1,361	68,615	1,318	2,303	44
Michigan [3].................	207,800	2,733	185,167	2,435	22,598	297
Minnesota....................	113,600	2,779	107,786	2,637	5,840	143
Mississippi...................	36,600	1,637	29,466	1,318	7,127	319
Missouri......................	77,900	1,688	56,760	1,230	21,138	458
Montana......................	10,800	1,385	9,859	1,265	958	123
Nebraska.....................	17,100	1,230	15,905	1,144	1,149	83
Nevada.......................	17,000	823	11,637	563	5,332	258
New Hampshire.............	6,300	605	4,121	396	2,204	212
New Jersey...................	133,300	1,959	118,131	1,736	15,178	223
New Mexico [3]..............	22,800	1,453	19,638	1,251	3,135	200
New York.....................	159,200	1,044	111,908	734	47,243	310
North Carolina..............	103,800	1,401	100,479	1,356	3,744	51
North Dakota................	5,000	930	4,516	840	436	81
Ohio [3]......................	265,800	2,994	253,497	2,855	12,344	139
Oklahoma....................	27,000	941	24,503	854	2,459	86
Oregon.......................	61,300	2,027	38,701	1,280	22,646	749
Pennsylvania................	272,400	2,717	177,851	1,774	94,581	944
Rhode Island................	25,100	3,010	24,513	2,939	543	65
South Carolina..............	39,500	1,093	33,674	931	6,408	177
South Dakota................	9,600	1,536	6,819	1,091	2,764	442
Tennessee...................	75,100	1,522	62,568	1,268	12,533	254
Texas.........................	513,000	2,718	408,472	2,164	106,518	564
Utah..........................	14,800	758	11,909	610	2,940	151
Vermont......................	7,100	1,415	6,072	1,210	1,069	213
Virginia.......................	56,700	903	55,685	887	2,244	36
Washington [3].............	96,200	1,822	87,825	1,663	8,422	159
West Virginia................	10,600	719	8,599	583	2,043	139
Wisconsin....................	64,300	1,460	45,965	1,044	20,143	457
Wyoming.....................	6,100	1,402	5,429	1,248	639	147

[1] Rounded to nearest hundred. [2] Includes 12,339 persons in California under post-release custody supervision. [3] Includes estimates for nonreporting agencies, see source for details. [4] Counts include private agency cases and may overstate the number of persons under supervision. [5] Based on a count provided as of June 30, 2011.

Source: U.S. Department of Justice, Bureau of Justice Statistics, *Probation and Parole in the United States, 2011*, NCJ 239686, November 2012. See also <http://www.bjs.gov/index.cfm?ty=tp&tid=15>.

Table 370. Rate of Adults Under Community Supervision, Probation, and Parole: 2000 to 2011

[Rate per 100,000 population. Based on Bureau of Justice Statistics' Annual Survey of Probation and Parole. Probation is a court-ordered period of correctional supervision in the community, generally as an alternative to incarceration. In some cases, probation can be a combined sentence of incarceration followed by a period of community supervision. Parole is a period of conditional supervised release in the community following a prison term. It includes parolees released through discretionary or mandatory supervised release from prison, those released through other types of post-custody conditional supervision, and those sentenced to a term of supervised release. The community supervision population includes adults on probation, parole, or any other post-prison supervision]

Year	Rate			U.S. residents on—		
	Community supervision [1]	Probation	Parole	Community supervision [1]	Probation	Parole
2000.............	2,162	1,818	344	1 in 46	1 in 55	1 in 291
2001.............	2,184	1,842	342	1 in 46	1 in 54	1 in 292
2002.............	2,198	1,849	349	1 in 45	1 in 54	1 in 287
2003.............	2,219	1,865	354	1 in 45	1 in 55	1 in 282
2004.............	2,226	1,875	351	1 in 45	1 in 53	1 in 285
2005.............	2,215	1,864	351	1 in 45	1 in 54	1 in 285
2006.............	2,228	1,875	353	1 in 45	1 in 53	1 in 283
2007.............	2,239	1,878	361	1 in 45	1 in 53	1 in 277
2008 [2,3].......	2,203	1,846	358	1 in 45	1 in 54	1 in 279
2009 [2].........	2,147	1,796	353	1 in 47	1 in 56	1 in 284
2010 [2].........	2,067	1,715	355	1 in 48	1 in 58	1 in 281
2011 [2].........	2,015	1,662	357	1 in 50	1 in 60	1 in 280

[1] Includes adults on probation and adults on parole. [2] Detail does not sum to total because the community supervision rate was adjusted to exclude parolees who were also on probation. [3] The apparent decrease observed in the community supervison and probation rates between 2007 and 2008 was due to a change in scope for two jurisdictions and does not reflect actual declines in the populations.

Source: U.S. Department of Justice, Bureau of Justice Statistics, *Probation and Parole in the United States, 2011*, NCJ 239686, November 2012. See also <http://www.bjs.gov/index.cfm?ty=tp&tid=15>.

Table 371. Fire Losses—Total and Per Capita: 1980 to 2011

[5,579 represents $5,579,000,000. Includes allowances for FAIR Plan and uninsured losses]

Year	Total (mil. dol.)	Per capita [1] (dol.)	Year	Total (mil. dol.)	Per capita [1] (dol.)	Year	Total (mil. dol.)	Per capita [1] (dol.)
1980.............	5,579	24.56	1996.........	12,544	47.29	2004........	17,344	59.23
1985.............	7,753	32.70	1997.........	12,940	48.32	2005........	20,427	69.12
1990.............	9,495	38.07	1998.........	11,510	45.59	2006........	20,340	68.17
1991.............	11,302	44.82	1999.........	12,428	45.58	2007........	24,399	81.00
1992.............	13,588	53.28	2000.........	13,457	47.69	2008........	24,734	81.34
1993.............	11,331	43.96	2001 [2]......	17,118	60.07	2009........	22,911	74.68
1994.............	12,778	49.08	2002.........	17,586	61.14	2010........	20,486	66.22
1995.............	11,887	45.23	2003.........	21,129	72.83	2011........	23,479	75.35

[1] Based on U.S. Census Bureau estimated resident population as of July 1. Enumerated population as of April 1 for 1980, 1990, and 2000. [2] Does not include insured fire losses related to terrorism.

Source: Insurance Information Institute, New York, NY. *The Insurance Fact Book, 2013* ©, and previous reports. See also <http://www.iii.org>.

Table 372. Fires and Property Loss for Incendiary and Suspicious Fires and Civilian Fire Deaths and Injuries by Selected Property Type: 2005 to 2011

[In thousands (511 represents 511,000), except as indicated. Based on sample survey of fire departments]

Characteristic	2005	2006	2007	2008	2009	2010	2011
NUMBER (1,000)							
Structure fires, total................	**511**	**524**	**531**	**515**	**481**	**482**	**485**
Structure fires that were intentionally set.........	32	31	32	31	27	28	27
PROPERTY LOSS (mil. dol.) [1]							
Structure fires, total................	**9,193**	**9,636**	**10,638**	**12,361**	**10,842**	**9,716**	**9,693**
Structure fires that were intentionally set.........	664	775	773	866	684	585	601
CIVILIAN FIRE DEATHS							
Deaths, total [2]....................	**3,675**	**3,245**	**3,430**	**3,320**	**3,010**	**3,120**	**3,005**
Residential property...................	3055	2620	2895	2780	2590	2665	2550
One- and two-family dwellings..................	2,575	2,155	2,350	2,365	2,100	2,200	2,105
Apartments.........................	460	425	515	390	465	440	415
Vehicles............................	520	490	385	365	280	310	300
CIVILIAN FIRE INJURIES							
Injuries, total [2]...................	**17,925**	**16,400**	**17,675**	**16,705**	**17,050**	**17,720**	**17,500**
Residential property...................	13,825	12,925	14,000	13,560	13,050	13,800	14,360
One- and two-family dwellings..................	10,300	8,800	9,650	9,185	9,300	9,400	9,485
Apartments.........................	3,000	3,700	3,950	3,975	3,350	3,950	4,425
Vehicles............................	1,650	1,200	1,675	1,065	1,610	1,590	1,190

[1] Direct property loss only. [2] Includes other not shown separately.

Source: National Fire Protection Association, Quincy, MA, *Fire Loss in the United States During 2011* ©, September 2012, and earlier reports. See also <http://www.nfpa.org/research>.

Table 373. The U.S. Fire Service: Departments, Personnel, and Responses, by Type: 1990 to 2011

[In thousands, where noted. 1,025.7 represents 1,025,700. A fire department is a public or private organization that provides fire prevention, fire suppression, and associated emergency and non-emergency services to a jurisdiction such as a county, municipality, or organized fire district]

Items	1990	1995	2000	2005	2007	2008	2009	2010	2011
Fire departments (Number)									
Total	**30,391**	**31,197**	**30,339**	**30,300**	**30,185**	**30,170**	**30,165**	**30,125**	**30,145**
All career	1,949	1,831	2,178	2,087	2,263	2,315	2,457	2,495	2,550
Mostly career	1,338	1,660	1,667	1,766	1,765	1,790	1,752	1,860	1,865
Mostly volunteer	4,000	4,581	4,523	4,902	4,989	4,830	5,099	5,290	5,530
All volunteer	23,104	23,125	21,971	21,575	21,168	21,235	20,857	20,480	20,200
Fire Department personnel (1,000)	1,025.7	1,098.9	1,064.2	1,136.7	1,148.5	1,148.9	1,148.1	1,103.3	1,100.5
Career [1]	253.0	260.9	286.8	313.3	323.4	321.7	336.0	335.2	344.0
Volunteer [2]	772.7	838.0	777.4	823.7	825.5	827.2	812.1	768.2	756.5
Type of Response (1,000)	13,708	16,392	20,520	23,252	25,335	25,253	26,535	28,205	30,098
Fires	2,019	1,966	1,708	1,602	1,558	1,452	1,349	1,332	1,389
Medical Aid	7,650	9,381	12,251	14,375	15,784	15,768	17,104	18,522	19,803
False Alarms [3]	1,476	1,673	2,127	2,134	2,209	2,242	2,177	2,187	2,383
Mutual Aid/Assistance	487	616	864	1,091	1,110	1,215	1,296	1,190	1,252
Hazardous material	210	255	319	375	396	395	397	402	379
Other Hazardous [4]	423	470	544	667	687	698	625	660	720
All other [5]	1,443	2,033	2,708	3,009	3,593	3,486	3,587	3,913	4,172

[1] Includes full-time uniform firefighters regardless of assignment (i.e., suppression, administrative, prevention/inspection, etc.). Does not include firefighters who work for the state or federal government or in private fire brigades. [2] Volunteer firefighters include any active part-time (call or volunteer) firefighters. [3] Malicious mischievous, system malfunction, unintentional call, and other false alarms (bomb scares, etc.). [4] Arcing wires, bomb removal, power line down, biological hazard, etc. [5] Smoke scares, lock-outs, animal rescue, unauthorized burning, severe weather, etc.

Source: National Fire Protection Association, Quincy, MA, *U.S. Fire Department Profile Through 2011* ©, and *Fire Loss in the United States During 2011* ©, and earlier reports. See also <http://www.nfpa.org/research>.

Table 374. Fires—Number and Loss by Type and Property Use: 2008 to 2011

[1,451 represents 1,451,000; property loss of 15,478 represents $15,478,000,000. Based on annual sample survey of fire departments. No adjustments were made for unreported fires and losses]

Type and property use	Number (1,000)				Direct property loss (mil. dol.) [1]			
	2008	2009	2010	2011	2008	2009	2010	2011
Fires, total	**1,451**	**1,349**	**1,331**	**1,390**	**15,478**	**12,531**	**11,593**	**11,659**
Structure	515	481	482	485	12,361	10,842	9,716	9,693
Outside of structure [2]	71	69	73	79	129	254	413	541
Brush and rubbish	523	477	477	519	–	–	–	–
Vehicle	236	219	216	219	1,494	1,361	1,376	1,350
Other	106	103	85	89	[3] 1,494	74	88	75
Structure by property use:								
Public assembly	14	14	12	13	518	757	421	446
Educational	6	6	6	5	66	83	76	44
Institutional	7	6	6	7	22	32	37	52
Stores and offices	20	16	18	19	684	713	730	625
Residential	403	377	384	386	8,550	7,796	7,079	7,054
1–2 family homes [4]	291	273	279	275	6,892	6,391	5,895	5,746
Apartments	96	90	91	96	1,351	1,225	1,033	1,168
Other residential [5]	16	14	15	16	307	180	151	140
Storage	30	30	28	27	661	796	756	721
Industry, utility, defense [6]	10	10	9	10	[7] 1,401	572	515	620
Special structures	25	22	20	19	459	98	102	131

– Represents zero. [1] Direct property damage figures do not include indirect losses, like business interruption and adjustments for inflation. [2] Includes outside storage, crops, timber, etc. [3] Includes California Wildfires 2008 with an estimated $1.4 billion in property loss. [4] Includes mobile homes. [5] Includes hotels and motels, college dormitories, boarding houses, etc. [6] Data underreported as some incidents were handled by private fire brigades or fixed suppression systems which do not report. [7] Includes three industrial property incidents that resulted in $775 million in property loss.

Source: National Fire Protection Association, *Fire Loss in the United States During 2011* ©, September 2012, and earlier reports. See also <http://www.nfpa.org/research>.

Table 375. Firefighter On-Duty Fatalities by Firefighter Type and Nature and Cause of Fatal Injury: 2005 to 2011

[On-duty refers to involvement in operations at the scene of an emergency, whether it is a fire or nonfire incident; responding to or returning from an incident; performing other officially assigned duties including training; and being on call]

Item	2005	2006	2007	2008	2009	2010	2011
Total Fatalities...................................	**115**	**107**	**119**	**120**	**91**	**87**	**83**
By incident type							
Wildland related fatalities............................	19	22	11	26	16	11	10
Incidents with multiple fatalities......................	4	6	7	5	6	4	3
Firefighter classification							
Career...	34	29	50	34	36	28	27
Volunteer [1]..	81	77	68	66	47	56	51
Wildland...	10	16	5	18	7	3	5
Other/unknown.......................................	–	1	1	2	1	–	–
Cause of fatal injury							
Vehicle collision.....................................	25	19	27	28	16	11	5
Stress/overexertion..................................	62	54	55	52	50	55	50
Caught/trapped......................................	9	13	7	6	3	5	10
Fall...	5	–	4	6	6	4	6
Other [2]...	14	20	25	26	15	12	12
Unknown...	–	1	1	2	1	–	–
Nature of fatal injury							
Trauma...	32	24	33	42	26	20	14
Heart attack..	55	50	52	46	39	50	48
Burns...	3	8	7	4	2	–	7
Asphyxiation..	8	12	18	9	5	7	5
Other [2]...	17	12	8	17	18	10	9
Unknown...	–	1	1	2	1	–	–

– Represents zero. [1] Prior to 2008, includes wildland classification in its total. [2] Includes other categories not shown.

Source: U.S. Department of Homeland Security, Federal Emergency Management Agency, U.S. Fire Administration, *Firefighter Fatalities in the United States in 2011*, July 2012, and earlier reports. See also <http://apps.usfa.fema.gov/firefighter-fatalities/fatalityData/statistics>.

Geography and Environment

This section presents a variety of information on the physical environment of the United States, starting with basic area measurement data and ending with climatic data for selected weather stations around the country. The subjects covered between those points are mostly concerned with environmental trends but include related subjects such as land use, water consumption, air pollutant emissions, toxic releases, oil spills, hazardous waste sites, municipal waste and recycling, threatened and endangered wildlife, and the environmental industry.

The information in this section is selected from a wide range of federal agencies that compile the data for various administrative or regulatory purposes, such as the Environmental Protection Agency (EPA), U.S. Geological Survey (USGS), National Oceanic and Atmospheric Administration (NOAA), Natural Resources Conservation Service (NRCS), and National Atlas® of the United States. Data on 11 coastline counties most frequently hit by hurricanes may be found in Table 380.

Area—2010 Area measurements are the latest available. These measurements were calculated by computer based on the information contained in a single, consistent geographic database, the Topologically Integrated Geographic Encoding & Referencing system (TIGER®) database. The 2010 area measurements may be found in Table 376.

Geography—The USGS conducts investigations, surveys, and research in the fields of geography, geology, topography, geographic information systems, mineralogy, hydrology, and geothermal energy resources as well as natural hazards. The USGS provides United States cartographic data through the Earth Sciences Information Center and water resources data through the *Water Resources of the United States* at <http://water.usgs.gov/pubs/>. In a joint project with the U.S. Census Bureau, during the 1980s, the USGS provided the basic information on geographic features for input into a national geographic and cartographic database prepared by the Census Bureau, called TIGER® database. Since then, using a variety of sources, the Census Bureau has updated these features and their related attributes (names, descriptions, etc.) and inserted current information on the boundaries, names, and codes of legal and statistical geographic entities. The 2010 area measures, land and water, including their classifications, reflect base feature updates made in the Master Address File (MAF)/TIGER database through August 2010. The boundaries of the states and equivalent areas are as of January 1, 2010. Maps prepared by the Census Bureau using the TIGER® database show the names and boundaries of entities and are available on a current basis.

An inventory of the nation's land resources by type of use/cover was conducted by the NRCS every 5 years beginning in 1977 through 2007. The most recent survey results, which were published for the year 2007, covered all nonfederal land for the contiguous 48 states.

Environment—The principal federal agency responsible for pollution abatement and control activities is the EPA. It is responsible for establishing and monitoring national air quality standards, water quality activities, solid and hazardous waste disposal, and control of toxic substances. Many of these series now appear in the Envirofacts portion of the EPA Web site at <http://www.epa.gov/enviro/>.

The Clean Air Act, which was last amended in 1990, requires the EPA to set National Ambient Air Quality Standards (NAAQS) (40 CFR part 50) for pollutants considered harmful to public health and the environment. The Clean Air Act established two types of national air quality standards. **Primary standards** set limits to protect public health, including the health of "sensitive" populations such as asthmatics, children, and the elderly. **Secondary standards** set limits to protect public welfare, including protection against decreased visibility, damage to animals, crops vegetation, and buildings. See <http://www.epa.gov/air/criteria.html>. The EPA Office of Air Quality Planning and Standards (OAQPS) has set National Ambient Air Quality Standards for six principal pollutants, which are called "criteria" pollutants. These pollutants are: Carbon Monoxide, Lead, Nitrogen Dioxide, Particulate Matter (PM2.5 and 10), Ozone, and Sulfur Dioxide. NAAQS are periodically reviewed and revised to include any additional or new health or welfare data. Table 390 gives some of the health-related standards for the six air pollutants having NAAQS. Data gathered from state networks are periodically submitted to EPA's National Aerometric Information Retrieval System (AIRS) for summarization in annual reports on the nationwide status and trends in air quality. For details, see "Air Trends" on the EPA Web site at <http://www.epa.gov/airtrends/>.

The Toxics Release Inventory (TRI), published by the EPA, is a valuable source of information on approximately 682 chemicals that are being used, manufactured, treated, transported, or released into the environment. Sections 313 of the Emergency Planning and Community Right-to-Know Act (EPCRA) and 6607 of the Pollution Prevention Act (PPA), mandate that a publicly-accessible toxic chemical database be developed and maintained by EPA. This database, known as the TRI, contains information concerning waste management activities and the release of toxic chemicals by facilities that manufacture, process, or otherwise use said materials. Data on the release of these chemicals are collected from about 21,000 facilities and facilities added in 1998 that have the equivalent of 10 or more full time employees and meet the established thresholds for manufacturing, processing, or "other use" of listed chemicals. Facilities must report their releases and other waste management quantities. Since 1994 federal facilities have been required to report their data regardless of industry classification. In May 1997, EPA added seven new industry sectors that reported to the TRI for the first time in July 1999 for the 1998 reporting year. More current information on this program can be found at <http://www.epa.gov/tri>.

Climate—NOAA, through the National Weather Service and the National Environmental Satellite, Data, and Information Service, is responsible for climate data. NOAA maintains about 11,600 weather stations, of which over 3,000 produce autographic precipitation records, about 600 take hourly readings of a series of weather elements, and the remainder record data once a day. These data are reported monthly in the Climatological Data and Storm Data, published monthly and annually in the Local Climatological Data (published by location for major cities). Data can be found in tables 405 and 408–413.

Table 376. Land and Water Area of States and Other Entities: 2010

[One square mile = 2.59 square kilometers. The area measurements were derived from the Census Bureau's Master Address File/Topologically Integrated Geographic Encoding and Referencing (MAF/TIGER®) database. The boundaries of the states and equivalent areas are as of January 1, 2010. The land and water areas, including their classifications, reflect base feature updates made in the MAF/TIGER® database through August, 2010. For more details, see <http://www.census.gov/geo/www/tiger/tgrshp2010/tgrshp2010.html>]

State and other areas [2]	Total area Sq. mi.	Total area Sq. km.	Land area [1] Sq. mi.	Land area [1] Sq. km.	Water area [1] Total Sq. mi.	Water area [1] Total Sq. km.	Inland (sq. mi.)	Coastal (sq. mi.)	Great Lakes (sq. mi.)	Territorial (sq. mi.)
Total [3]	3,805,927	9,857,306	3,535,932	9,158,022	269,995	699,284	85,763	42,371	60,094	81,767
United States [4]	3,796,742	9,833,517	3,531,905	9,147,593	264,837	685,924	85,647	42,337	60,094	76,759
Alabama	52,420	135,767	50,645	131,171	1,775	4,597	1,058	517	(X)	199
Alaska	665,384	1,723,337	570,641	1,477,953	94,743	245,383	19,304	26,119	(X)	49,320
Arizona	113,990	295,234	113,594	294,207	396	1,026	396	—	(X)	—
Arkansas	53,179	137,732	52,035	134,771	1,143	2,961	1,143	—	(X)	—
California	163,695	423,967	155,779	403,466	7,916	20,501	2,833	245	(X)	4,837
Colorado	104,094	269,601	103,642	268,431	452	1,170	452	—	(X)	—
Connecticut	5,543	14,357	4,842	12,542	701	1,816	171	530	(X)	—
Delaware	2,489	6,446	1,949	5,047	540	1,399	91	355	(X)	94
District of Columbia	68	177	61	158	7	19	7	—	(X)	—
Florida	65,758	170,312	53,625	138,887	12,133	31,424	5,027	1,349	(X)	5,757
Georgia	59,425	153,910	57,513	148,959	1,912	4,951	1,412	46	(X)	453
Hawaii	10,932	28,313	6,423	16,635	4,509	11,678	42	9	(X)	4,458
Idaho	83,569	216,443	82,643	214,045	926	2,398	926	—	(X)	—
Illinois	57,914	149,995	55,519	143,793	2,395	6,202	820	—	1,575	—
Indiana	36,420	94,326	35,826	92,789	593	1,537	361	—	233	—
Iowa	56,273	145,746	55,857	144,669	416	1,077	416	—	(X)	—
Kansas	82,278	213,100	81,759	211,754	520	1,346	520	—	(X)	—
Kentucky	40,408	104,656	39,486	102,269	921	2,387	921	—	(X)	—
Louisiana	52,378	135,659	43,204	111,898	9,174	23,761	4,562	2,880	(X)	1,732
Maine	35,380	91,633	30,843	79,883	4,537	11,750	2,314	591	(X)	1,633
Maryland	12,406	32,131	9,707	25,142	2,699	6,990	768	1,820	(X)	111
Massachusetts	10,554	27,336	7,800	20,202	2,754	7,134	486	1,177	(X)	1,092
Michigan	96,714	250,487	56,539	146,435	40,175	104,052	2,001	—	38,174	—
Minnesota	86,936	225,163	79,627	206,232	7,309	18,930	4,763	—	2,546	—
Mississippi	48,432	125,438	46,923	121,531	1,509	3,907	769	616	(X)	123
Missouri	69,707	180,540	68,742	178,040	965	2,501	965	—	(X)	—
Montana	147,040	380,831	145,546	376,962	1,494	3,869	1,494	—	(X)	—
Nebraska	77,348	200,330	76,824	198,974	524	1,356	524	—	(X)	—
Nevada	110,572	286,380	109,781	284,332	791	2,048	791	—	(X)	—
New Hampshire	9,349	24,214	8,953	23,187	397	1,027	328	—	(X)	69
New Jersey	8,723	22,591	7,354	19,047	1,368	3,544	436	427	(X)	506
New Mexico	121,590	314,917	121,298	314,161	292	757	292	—	(X)	—
New York	54,555	141,297	47,126	122,057	7,429	19,240	1,989	975	3,986	479
North Carolina	53,819	139,391	48,618	125,920	5,201	13,471	4,052	—	(X)	1,149
North Dakota	70,698	183,108	69,001	178,711	1,698	4,397	1,698	—	(X)	—
Ohio	44,826	116,098	40,861	105,829	3,965	10,269	474	—	3,491	—
Oklahoma	69,899	181,037	68,595	177,660	1,304	3,377	1,304	—	(X)	—
Oregon	98,379	254,799	95,988	248,608	2,391	6,191	1,068	72	(X)	1,251
Pennsylvania	46,054	119,280	44,743	115,883	1,312	3,397	563	—	748	—
Rhode Island	1,545	4,001	1,034	2,678	511	1,324	182	64	(X)	266
South Carolina	32,020	82,933	30,061	77,857	1,960	5,076	1,064	110	(X)	786
South Dakota	77,116	199,729	75,811	196,350	1,305	3,379	1,305	—	(X)	—
Tennessee	42,144	109,153	41,235	106,798	909	2,355	909	—	(X)	—
Texas	268,596	695,662	261,232	676,587	7,365	19,075	5,616	401	(X)	1,347
Utah	84,897	219,882	82,170	212,818	2,727	7,064	2,727	—	(X)	—
Vermont	9,616	24,906	9,217	23,871	400	1,035	400	—	(X)	—
Virginia	42,775	110,787	39,490	102,279	3,285	8,508	1,282	1,565	(X)	438
Washington	71,298	184,661	66,456	172,119	4,842	12,542	1,715	2,468	(X)	660
West Virginia	24,230	62,756	24,038	62,259	192	497	192	—	(X)	—
Wisconsin	65,496	169,635	54,158	140,268	11,339	29,367	1,997	—	9,342	—
Wyoming	97,813	253,335	97,093	251,470	720	1,864	720	—	(X)	—
Puerto Rico	5,325	13,791	3,424	8,868	1,901	4,924	76	13	(X)	1,812
Island Areas:	3,860	9,998	603	1,562	3,257	8,436	40	22	(X)	3,196
American Samoa	581	1,505	76	198	505	1,307	8	—	(X)	497
Guam	571	1,478	210	543	361	935	8	1	(X)	352
No. Mariana Islands	1,976	5,117	182	472	1,793	4,644	6	5	(X)	1,782
U.S. Virgin Islands	733	1,898	134	348	599	1,550	18	16	(X)	565

— Represents or rounds to zero. X Not applicable. [1] Water area calculations in this table include only perennial water. All other water (intermittent, glacier, and marsh/swamp) is included in this table as part of land area calculations. [2] This table does not include area calculations for the U.S. Minor Outlying Islands. [3] Includes all 50 states, the District of Columbia, Puerto Rico, and the Island Areas. [4] Includes all 50 states and the District of Columbia.

Source: U.S. Census Bureau, unpublished data from the MAF/TIGER® database. See <http://www.census.gov/geo/www/tiger/>.

Table 377. Great Lakes Profile

[The Great Lakes contain the largest supply of freshwater in the world, holding about 18% of the world's total freshwater and about 90% of the United States' total freshwater. The Lakes are a series of five interconnecting large lakes, one small lake, four connecting channels, and the St. Lawrence Seaway. Combined, the lakes cover an area of over 94,000 square miles (245,000 square kilometers) and contain over 5,400 cubic miles (23,000 cubic kilometers) of water]

Characteristics	Unit	Lake Superior	Lake Michigan	Lake Huron	Lake Erie	Lake Ontario
Length.....................................	Miles	350	307	206	241	193
Breadth..................................	Miles	160	118	183	57	53
Depth						
Average..............................	Feet	489	279	159	62	283
Maximum.............................	Feet	1,333	923	750	210	802
Volume...................................	Cubic miles	2,935	1,180	849	116	393
Water surface area [1]................	Square miles	31,700	22,300	23,000	9,910	7,340
Surface area in U.S..................	Square miles	20,598	22,300	9,111	4,977	3,560
Retention/replacement time [2]........	Years	191	99	22	3	6

[1] Includes surface area in both U.S. and Canada. [2] The amount of time it takes for lakes to get rid of pollutants.

Source: Department of Commerce, National Oceanic and Atmospheric Administration, Great Lakes Environmental Research Laboratory, "About Our Great Lakes, Lake by Lake Profiles," June 2004, <http://www.glerl.noaa.gov/pr/ourlakes/intro.html\>.

Table 378. Great Lakes Length of Shoreline in Separate Basin

[In statute miles]

	Total	Canada	U.S.	MI	MN	WI	IL	IN	OH	PA	NY
Total...............	**10,368**	**5,127**	**5,241**	**3,288**	**189**	**820**	**63**	**45**	**312**	**51**	**473**
Lake Superior......	2,980	1,549	1,431	917	189	325	–	–	–	–	–
St. Marys River.....	297	206	91	91	–	–	–	–	–	–	–
Lake Michigan......	1,661	–	1,661	1,058	–	495	63	45	–	–	–
Lake Huron.........	3,350	2,416	934	934	–	–	–	–	–	–	–
St. Clair River......	128	47	81	81	–	–	–	–	–	–	–
Lake St. Clair.......	160	71	89	89	–	–	–	–	–	–	–
Detroit River.......	107	43	64	64	–	–	–	–	–	–	–
Lake Erie...........	860	366	494	54	–	–	–	–	312	51	77
Niagara River.......	99	34	65	–	–	–	–	–	–	–	65
Lake Ontario........	726	395	331	–	–	–	–	–	–	–	331

– Represents zero.

Source: State of Michigan, Department of Environment Quality, "Great Lakes, Shorelines of the Great Lakes," and U.S. Lake Survey, File no. 3-3284 corrected to 1952. <http://www.michigan.gov/deq/0,4561,7-135-3313_3677-15959--,00.html>.

Table 379. Largest Lakes in the United States

[The list of lakes include manmade lakes and those that are only partially within the United States]

Lake	Location	Area in sq. mi.	Lake	Location	Area in sq. mi.
Lake Superior...................	MI-MN-WI-Ontario	31,700	Lake Pontchartrain......	Louisiana	631
Lake Huron.....................	MI-Ontario	23,000	Lake Sakakawea [1].......	North Dakota	520
Lake Michigan..................	IL-IN-MI-WI	22,300	Lake Champlain.........	NY-VT-Quebec	490
Lake Erie......................	MI-NY-OH-PA-Ontario	9,910	Becharof Lake............	Alaska	453
Lake Ontario...................	NY-Ontario	7,340	Lake St. Clair.............	MI-Ontario	430
Great Salt Lake.................	Utah	2,117	Red Lake................	Minnesota	427
Lake of the Woods.............	MN-Manitoba-Ontario	1,485	Selawik Lake............	Alaska	404
Iliamna Lake....................	Alaska	1,014	Fort Peck Lake [1]........	Montana	393
Lake Oahe [1]....................	ND-SD	685	Salton Sea...............	California	347
Lake Okeechobee..............	Florida	662	Rainy Lake...............	MN-Ontario	345

[1] Manmade lakes.

Source: U.S. Geological Survey, 2003, and National Oceanic and Atmospheric Administration, "Great Lakes, 2002" and The National Atlas of the United States of America, Lakes, <http://nationalatlas.gov/articles/mapping/a_general.html>.

Table 380. Coastline Counties Most Frequently Hit by Hurricanes: 1960 to 2008

[Hurricane is a type of tropical cyclone, an intense tropical weather system of strong thunderstorms with a well-defined surface circulation and maximum sustained winds of 74 miles per hour or higher]

County and State	Coastline region	Number of hurricanes	Percent change in population		Percent change in housing units	
			1960 to 2008	2000 to 2008	1960 to 2008	2000 to 2008
Monore Conty, FL.....................	Gulf of Mexico	15	50.8	-9.2	221.8	4.3
Lafourche Parish, LA.................	Gulf of Mexico	14	67.2	2.9	151.5	8.9
Carteret County, NC.................	Atlantic	14	104.3	6.4	366.4	12.4
Dare County, NC.....................	Atlantic	13	465.9	12.1	709.6	22.8
Hyde County, NC.....................	Atlantic	13	-10.1	-11.1	83.7	5.8
Jefferson Parish, LA..................	Gulf of Mexico	12	108.9	-4.2	201.4	-3.5
Palm Beach County, FL.............	Atlantic	12	454.7	11.9	616.9	15.2
Miami-Dade County, FL.............	Atlantic	11	156.5	6.4	180.6	14.9
St. Bernard Parish, LA..............	Gulf of Mexico	11	17.2	-43.9	-2.6	-67.9
Cameron Parish, LA.................	Gulf of Mexico	11	4.8	-27.6	87.7	-8.1
Terrebonne Parish, LA..............	Gulf of Mexico	11	78.7	3.9	179.4	11.0

Source: National Oceanic and Atmospheric Administration (NOAA), Coastal Services Center, Historical Hurricane Tracks: 1851 to to 2008; U.S. Census Bureau, Current Population Reports, P25-1139, Population Estimates and Projections, "Coastline Population Trends in the United States: 1960 to 2008," May 2010. See also <http://www.census.gov/prod/www/abs/p25.html>

Table 381. U.S.–Canada and U.S.–Mexico Border Lengths

[In statute miles. Each statute mile equals one mile. For 2012, there were over 62 million personal vehicle passengers entering the United States from Canada, and over 115 million personal vehicle passengers entering the United States from Mexico]

State	Length of international border	State	Length of international border
United States–Canada total...............	**5,525**	Ohio.................................	146
Alaska....................................	1,538	Pennsylvania.......................	42
Idaho.....................................	45	Vermont..............................	90
Maine.....................................	611	Washington..........................	427
Michigan..................................	721		
Minnesota................................	547	**United States–Mexico total**...............	**1,933**
Montana..................................	545	Arizona...............................	373
New Hampshire.........................	58	California.............................	140
New York.................................	445	New Mexico..........................	180
North Dakota............................	310	Texas.................................	1,241

Source: U.S.–Canada lengths: International Boundary Commission, 2003; U.S. Mexico lengths: U.S. Geological Survey; and The National Atlas of the United States, 1976, "Borders," <http://nationalatlas.gov/articles/mapping/a_general.html>.

Table 382. Coastline and Shoreline of the United States by State

[In statute miles. Each statute mile equals one mile. The term coastline is United States coastline measurements were made from small-scale maps, and the coastline was generalized. The coastlines of large sounds and used to describe the general outline of the seacoast. For the table below, bays were included. Measurements were made in 1948. Shoreline is the term used to describe a more detailed measure of the seacoast. The tidal shoreline figures in the table below were obtained in 1939–1940 from the largest-scale charts and maps then available. Shoreline of the outer coast, offshore islands, sounds, and bays was included, as well as the tidal portion of rivers and creeks. Only states with coastline or shoreline are included in the following table]

State	General coastline	Tidal shoreline	State	General coastline	Tidal shoreline
United States................	**12,383**	**88,633**	Mississippi..................	44	359
Alabama.......................	53	607	New Hampshire.............	13	131
Alaska.........................	6,640	33,904	New Jersey..................	130	1,792
California......................	840	3,427	New York.....................	127	1,850
Connecticut...................	–	618	North Carolina..............	301	3,375
Delaware......................	28	381	Oregon.......................	296	1,410
Florida.........................	1,350	8,426	Pennsylvania................	–	89
Georgia........................	100	2,344	Rhode Island................	40	384
Hawaii.........................	750	1,052	South Carolina..............	187	2,876
Louisiana......................	397	7,721	Texas.........................	367	3,359
Maine..........................	228	3,478	Virginia........................	112	3,315
Maryland.......................	31	3,190	Washington..................	157	3,026
Massachusetts...............	192	1,519			

– Represents zero.

Source: National Oceanic Atmospheric Administration, 1975 and The National Atlas of the United States, "Coastline and Shoreline," <http://nationalatlas.gov/articles/mapping/a_general.html>.

Table 383. Flows of Largest U.S. Rivers—Length, Discharge, and Drainage Area

[A flow of 1,000 cubic ft per second is equal to 646 million gallons per day, 724,000 acre-feet per year, or 28.3 cubic meters per second. One acre-foot is the volume of water that would cover 1 acre to a depth of 1 foot]

River	Location of mouth	Source stream (name and location)	Length (miles) [1]	Average discharge at mouth (1,000 cubic feet per second) [8]	Drainage area (1,000 sq. miles)
Missouri.................	Missouri	Red Rock Creek, MT	[3] 2,540	76.2	[2] 529
Mississippi..............	Louisiana	Mississippi River, MN	2,340	[4] 593	[2,5] 1,150
Yukon....................	Alaska	McNeil River, Canada	1,980	225	[2] 328
St. Lawrence............	Canada	North River, MN	1,900	348	[2] 396
Rio Grande..............	Mexico-Texas	Rio Grande, CO	1,900	([7])	336
Arkansas.................	Arkansas	East Fork Arkansas River, CO	1,460	41	161
Colorado.................	Mexico	Colorado River, CO	1,450	([7])	246
Atchafalaya [6]...........	Louisiana	Tierra Blanca Creek, NM	1,420	58	95.1
Ohio......................	Illinois-Kentucky	Allegheny River, PA	1,310	281	203
Red [6]....................	Louisiana	Tierra Blanca Creek, NM	1,290	56	93.2
Brazos...................	Texas	Blackwater Draw, NM	1,280	([7])	45.6
Columbia................	Oregon-Washington	Columbia River, Canada	1,240	265	[2] 258
Snake....................	Washington	Snake River, WY	1,040	56.9	108
Platte....................	Nebraska	Grizzly Creek, CO	990	([7])	84.9
Pecos....................	Texas	Pecos River, NM	926	([7])	44.3
Canadian................	Oklahoma	Canadian River, CO	906	([7])	46.9
Tennessee...............	Kentucky	Courthouse Creek, NC	886	68	40.9

[1] From source to mouth. [2] Drainage area includes both the United States and Canada. [3] The length from the source of the Missouri River to the Mississippi River and thence to the Gulf of Mexico is about 3,710 miles. [4] Includes about 167,000 cubic feet per second diverted from the Mississippi into the Atchafalaya River but excludes the flow of the Red River. [5] Excludes the drainage areas of the Red and Atchafalaya Rivers. [6] In east-central Louisiana, the Red River flows into the Atchafalaya River, a distributary of the Mississippi River. Data on average discharge, length, and drainage area include the Red River, but exclude all water diverted into the Atchafalaya from the Mississippi River. [7] Less than 15,000 cubic feet per second.

Source: U.S. Geological Survey, *Largest Rivers in the United States*, September 2005, <http://pubs.usgs.gov/of/1987/ofr87-242/>.

Table 384. Extreme and Mean Elevations by State and Other Areas

[One foot = .305 meter. There are 2,130 square miles of the United States below sea level (Death Valley is the lowest point). There are 20,230 square miles above 10,000 feet (Mount McKinley is the highest point in the United States). Minus sign (-) indicates below sea level]

State and other areas	Highest point Name	Elevation Feet	Elevation Meters	Lowest point Name	Elevation Feet	Elevation Meters	Approximate mean elevation Feet	Approximate mean elevation Meters
U.S.	Mt. McKinley (AK)	20,320	6,198	Death Valley (CA)	-282	-86	2,500	763
AL.	Cheaha Mountain	2,407	734	Gulf of Mexico	(1)	(1)	500	153
AK.	Mount McKinley	20,320	6,198	Pacific Ocean	(1)	(1)	1,900	580
AZ.	Humphreys Peak	12,633	3,853	Colorado River	70	21	4,100	1,251
AR.	Magazine Mountain	2,753	840	Ouachita River	55	17	650	198
CA.	Mount Whitney	14,494	4,419	Death Valley	-282	-86	2,900	885
CO.	Mt. Elbert	14,433	4,402	Arikaree River	3,315	1,011	6,800	2,074
CT.	Mt. Frissell on south slope	2,380	726	Long Island Sound	(1)	(1)	500	153
DE [2]	Ebright Road [2]	448	137	Atlantic Ocean	(1)	(1)	60	18
DC.	Tenleytown at Reno Reservoir	410	125	Potomac River	1	(Z)	150	46
FL.	Britton Hill	345	105	Atlantic Ocean	(1)	(1)	100	31
GA.	Brasstown Bald	4,784	1,459	Atlantic Ocean	(1)	(1)	600	183
HI.	Pu'u Wekiu, Mauna Kea	13,796	4,208	Pacific Ocean	(1)	(1)	3,030	924
ID.	Borah Peak	12,662	3,862	Snake River	710	217	5,000	1,525
IL.	Charles Mound	1,235	377	Mississippi River	279	85	600	183
IN.	Hoosier Hill	1,257	383	Ohio River	320	98	700	214
IA.	Hawkeye Point	1,670	509	Mississippi River	480	146	1,100	336
KS.	Mount Sunflower	4,039	1,232	Verdigris River	679	207	2,000	610
KY.	Black Mountain	4,145	1,264	Mississippi River	257	78	750	229
LA.	Driskill Mountain	535	163	New Orleans	-8	-2	100	31
ME.	Mount Katahdin	5,268	1,607	Atlantic Ocean	(1)	(1)	600	183
MD.	Hoye Crest	3,360	1,025	Atlantic Ocean	(1)	(1)	350	107
MA.	Mount Greylock	3,491	1,065	Atlantic Ocean	(1)	(1)	500	153
MI.	Mount Arvon	1,979	604	Lake Erie	571	174	900	275
MN.	Eagle Mountain	2,301	702	Lake Superior	601	183	1,200	366
MS.	Woodall Mountain	806	246	Gulf of Mexico	(1)	(1)	300	92
MO.	Taum Sauk Mountain	1,772	540	St. Francis River	230	70	800	244
MT.	Granite Peak	12,799	3,904	Kootenai River	1,800	549	3,400	1,037
NE.	Panorama Point	5,424	1,654	Missouri River	840	256	2,600	793
NV.	Boundary Peak	13,140	4,007	Colorado River	479	146	5,500	1,678
NH.	Mount Washington	6,288	1,918	Atlantic Ocean	(1)	(1)	1,000	305
NJ.	High Point	1,803	550	Atlantic Ocean	(1)	(1)	250	76
NM.	Wheeler Peak	13,161	4,014	Red Bluff Reservoir	2,842	867	5,700	1,739
NY.	Mount Marcy	5,344	1,630	Atlantic Ocean	(1)	(1)	1,000	305
NC.	Mount Mitchell	6,684	2,039	Atlantic Ocean	(1)	(1)	700	214
ND.	White Butte	3,506	1,069	Red River of the North	750	229	1,900	580
OH.	Campbell Hill	1,550	473	Ohio River	455	139	850	259
OK.	Black Mesa	4,973	1,517	Little River	289	88	1,300	397
OR.	Mount Hood	11,239	3,428	Pacific Ocean	(1)	(1)	3,300	1,007
PA.	Mount Davis	3,213	980	Delaware River	(1)	(1)	1,100	336
RI.	Jerimoth Hill	812	248	Atlantic Ocean	(1)	(1)	200	61
SC.	Sassafras Mountain	3,560	1,086	Atlantic Ocean	(1)	(1)	350	107
SD.	Harney Peak	7,242	2,209	Big Stone Lake	966	295	2,200	671
TN.	Clingmans Dome	6,643	2,026	Mississippi River	178	54	900	275
TX.	Guadalupe Peak	8,749	2,668	Gulf of Mexico	(1)	(1)	1,700	519
UT.	Kings Peak	13,528	4,126	Beaverdam Wash	2,000	610	6,100	1,861
VT.	Mount Mansfield	4,393	1,340	Lake Champlain	95	29	1,000	305
VA.	Mount Rogers	5,729	1,747	Atlantic Ocean	(1)	(1)	950	290
WA.	Mount Rainier	14,411	4,395	Pacific Ocean	(1)	(1)	1,700	519
WV.	Spruce Knob	4,863	1,483	Potomac River	240	73	1,500	458
WI.	Timms Hill	1,951	595	Lake Michigan	579	177	1,050	320
WY.	Gannett Peak	13,804	4,210	Belle Fourche River	3,099	945	6,700	2,044
Other areas:								
Puerto Rico	Cerro de Punta	4,390	1,339	Atlantic Ocean	(1)	(1)	1,800	549
American Samoa	Lata Mountain	3,160	964	Pacific Ocean	(1)	(1)	1,300	397
Guam	Mount Lamlam	1,332	406	Pacific Ocean	(1)	(1)	330	101
U.S. Virgin Islands	Crown Mountain	1,556	475	Atlantic Ocean	(1)	(1)	750	229

Z Less than .5 meter. [1] Sea level. [2] At DE–PA state line.

Source: For highest and lowest points, see U.S. Geological Survey, "Elevations and Distances in the United States," <http://egsc.usgs.gov/isb/pubs/booklets/elvadist/elvadist.html\>, released April 2005. For mean elevations, see *Elevations and Distances in the United States*, 1983 edition.

Table 385. Land Cover/Use by Type: 1982 to 2007

[In millions of acres (1,937.7 represents 1,937,700,000), except percent. Excludes Alaska, Hawaii, and District of Columbia. For inventory-specific glossary of key terms, see <http://www.nrcs.usda.gov/technical/NRI/glossaries.html>]

Year	Total surface area	Nonfederal rural land						Devel- oped land	Water areas	Federal land
		Rural land total [1]	Crop- land	Pasture- land	Range- land	Forest land	Other rural land			
Land										
1982	1,937.7	1,419.0	420.0	131.0	417.9	403.4	47.2	71.0	48.7	399.1
1992	1,937.7	1,402.8	381.4	125.0	408.9	405.2	48.1	83.9	49.4	401.5
1997	1,937.7	1,391.5	376.1	119.8	407.5	406.6	48.7	94.6	49.9	401.7
2002	1,937.7	1,381.3	367.1	117.8	408.2	407.3	48.9	104.0	50.4	401.9
2007	1,937.7	1,373.7	357.0	118.6	409.1	406.4	49.6	111.3	50.8	401.9
Percent of total land										
1982	100.0	73.2	21.7	6.8	21.6	20.8	2.4	3.7	2.5	20.6
1992	100.0	72.4	19.7	6.5	21.1	20.9	2.5	4.3	2.5	20.7
1997	100.0	71.8	19.4	6.2	21.0	21.0	2.5	4.9	2.6	20.7
2002	100.0	71.3	18.9	6.1	21.1	21.0	2.5	5.4	2.6	20.7
2007	100.0	70.9	18.4	6.1	21.1	21.0	2.6	5.7	2.6	20.7

[1] Includes Conservation Reserve Program (CRP) land not shown separately. CRP is a federal program established under the Food Security Act of 1985 to assist private landowners to convert highly erodible cropland to vegetative cover for 10 years.

Source: U.S. Department of Agriculture, Natural Resources and Conservation Service, *Summary Report: 2007 National Resources Inventory*, December 2009. See also <http://www.nrcs.usda.gov/technical/NRI>.

Table 386. Wetlands on Nonfederal Land and Water Areas by Land Cover/Use and Farm Production Region: 2007

[In thousands of acres (107,648 represents 107,648,000). Represents palustrine and estuarine wetlands; see source]

Farm production region [1]	Total	Cropland [2]	Forest land	Range- land	Other rural land	Developed land	Water area
Wetlands, total	**107,648**	**16,470**	**63,400**	**7,989**	**14,725**	**1,547**	**3,517**
Lake states	22,461	2,867	15,494	–	3,700	170	230
Southeast	22,263	869	16,353	956	3,072	427	587
Delta states	14,865	2,859	8,329	258	2,818	162	439
Northeast	14,156	1,192	11,054	–	1,431	253	227
Northern plains	7,668	3,076	191	2,868	1,075	76	382
Appalachian	7,459	405	6,090	–	531	115	317
Southern plains	5,567	1,068	2,412	936	401	175	575
Mountain	4,801	1,471	241	2,223	706	24	136
Corn belt	4,716	1,398	2,397	5	347	108	461
Pacific	3,693	1,265	838	744	646	36	164

– Represents or rounds to zero. [1] Ten regions established by USDA, Economic Research Service, that group states according to differences in soils, slope of land, climate, distance to market, and storage and marketing facilities. [2] Includes pastureland and Conservation Reserve Program (CRP) lands.

Source: U.S. Department of Agriculture, Natural Resources Conservation Service, *Summary Report: 2007 Annual National Resources Inventory*, December 2009. See also <http://www.nrcs.usda.gov/technical/NRI/>.

Table 387. Land Cover/Use by State: 2007

[In thousands of acres (1,937,664 represents 1,937,664,000), except percent. Excludes Alaska, District of Columbia, Hawaii, and Island Areas]

State	Total surface area [1]	Selected nonfederal rural land, percent of total			State	Total surface area [1]	Selected nonfederal rural land, percent of total		
		Crop- land	Range- land	Forest land			Crop- land	Range- land	Forest land
United States	**1,937,664**	**18.4**	**21.1**	**21.0**	Montana	94,110	14.8	39.3	5.8
					Nebraska	49,510	39.4	46.7	1.7
Alabama	33,424	6.6	0.2	64.4	Nevada	70,763	0.7	11.9	0.4
Arizona	72,964	1.0	44.5	5.6	New Hampshire	5,941	1.8	–	65.3
Arkansas	34,037	21.7	0.1	44.4	New Jersey	5,216	9.4	–	32.2
California	101,510	9.3	17.3	14.2	New Mexico	77,823	1.9	51.8	7.0
Colorado	66,625	11.4	37.9	4.9	New York	31,361	15.9	–	55.9
Connecticut	3,195	5.4	–	50.7	North Carolina	33,709	15.5	–	46.1
Delaware	1,534	27.4	–	22.1	North Dakota	45,251	52.9	24.4	1.0
Florida	37,534	7.7	7.0	35.1	Ohio	26,445	41.8	–	26.8
Georgia	37,741	10.6	–	58.2	Oklahoma	44,738	19.6	31.7	16.7
Idaho	53,488	9.8	12.2	7.5	Oregon	62,161	5.8	15.1	20.5
Illinois	36,059	66.3	–	10.9	Pennsylvania	28,995	17.0	–	53.8
Indiana	23,158	57.1	–	16.5	Rhode Island	813	2.2	–	45.1
Iowa	36,017	70.7	–	6.5	South Carolina	19,939	11.2	–	56.0
Kansas	52,661	48.7	30.0	3.2	South Dakota	49,358	34.0	45.0	1.1
Kentucky	25,863	20.0	–	40.9	Tennessee	26,974	15.4	–	43.9
Louisiana	31,377	16.3	0.7	42.4	Texas	171,052	14.0	57.3	6.2
Maine	20,966	1.8	–	84.1	Utah	54,339	2.6	20.1	3.5
Maryland	7,870	18.0	–	29.4	Vermont	6,154	8.8	–	66.8
Massachusetts	5,339	4.5	–	48.5	Virginia	27,087	10.2	–	48.2
Michigan	37,349	21.0	–	44.4	Washington	44,035	14.7	13.5	28.6
Minnesota	54,010	38.3	–	30.6	West Virginia	15,508	4.9	–	67.8
Mississippi	30,527	15.4	–	55.1	Wisconsin	35,920	27.9	–	40.6
Missouri	44,614	29.8	0.2	27.9	Wyoming	62,603	3.4	44.7	1.5

– Represents zero. [1] Total surface area includes both Federal and non-Federal land.

Source: U.S. Department of Agriculture, Natural Resources and Conservation Service, *Summary Report, 2007 Annual National Resources Inventory*, December 2009. See also <http://www.nrcs.usda.gov/technical/NRI/>.

Table 388. U.S. Wetland Resources and Deepwater Habitats by Type: 2004 and 2009

[In thousands of acres (153,121.4 represents 153,121,400). Wetlands and deepwater habitats are defined separately because the term wetland does not include permanent water bodies. Deepwater habitats are permanently flooded land lying below the deepwater boundary of wetlands. Deepwater habitats include environments where surface water is permanent and often deep, so that water, rather than air, is the principal medium within which the dominant organisms live, whether or not they are attached to the substrate. As in wetlands, the dominant plants are hydrophytes; however, the substrates are considered nonsoil because the water is too deep to support emergent vegetation. In general terms, wetlands are lands where saturation with water is the dominant factor determining the nature of soil development and the types of plant and animal communities living in the soil and on its surface. The single feature that most wetlands share is soil or substrate that is at least periodically saturated with or covered by water. Wetlands are lands transitional between terrestrial and aquatic systems where the water table is usually at or near the surface or the land is covered by shallow water. For more information on wetlands, see the "Classification of Wetlands and Deepwater Habitats of the United States" at <http://www.npwrc.usgs.gov/resource/wetlands/classwet/index.htm>]

Wetland or deepwater category	Estimated area, 2004	Estimated area, 2009	Change, 2004 to 2009
All wetlands and deepwater habitats, total	**153,121.4**	**153,206.4**	**85.0**
All deepwater habitats, total	42,999.4	43,146.6	147.2
Lacustrine [1]	16,786.0	16,859.6	73.6
Riverine [2]	7,517.9	7,510.5	-7.4
Estuarine Subtidal [3]	18,695.4	18,776.5	81.1
All wetlands, total	110,122.1	110,059.8	-62.3
Intertidal wetlands [4]	5,869.3	5,785.2	-84.1
Marine intertidal	219.2	227.8	8.5
Estuarine intertidal nonvegetated	999.4	1,017.7	18.3
Estuarine intertidal vegetated	4,650.7	4,539.7	-110.9
Freshwater wetlands	104,252.7	104,274.6	21.9
Freshwater nonvegetated	6,502.1	6,709.3	207.2
Freshwater vegetated	97,750.6	97,565.3	-185.3
Freshwater emergent [5]	27,162.7	27,430.5	267.8
Freshwater forested [6]	52,256.5	51,623.3	-633.1
Freshwater shrub [7]	18,331.4	18,511.5	180.1

[1] The lacustrine system includes deepwater habitats with all of the following characteristics: (1) situated in a topographic depression or a dammed river channel; (2) lacking trees, shrubs, persistent emergents, emergent mosses or lichens with greater than 30 percent coverage; and (3) total area exceeds 20 acres (8 hectares). [2] The riverine system includes deepwater habitats contained within a channel, with the exception of habitats with water containing ocean derived salts in excess of 0.5 parts per thousand. [3] The estuarine system consists of deepwater tidal habitats and adjacent tidal wetlands that are usually semi-enclosed by land but have open, partly obstructed, or sporadic access to the open ocean, and in which ocean water is at least occasionally diluted by freshwater runoff from the land. Subtidal is where the substrate is continuously submerged by marine or estuarine waters. [4] Intertidal is where the substrate is exposed and flooded by tides. Intertidal includes the splash zone of coastal waters. [5] Emergent wetlands are characterized by erect, rooted, herbaceous hydrophytes, excluding mosses and lichens. This vegetation is present for most of the growing season in most years. These wetlands are usually dominated by perennial plants. [6] Forested wetlands are characterized by woody vegetation that is 20 feet tall or taller. [7] Shrub wetlands include areas dominated by woody vegetation less than 20 feet tall. The species include true shrubs, young trees, and trees or shrubs that are small or stunted because of environmental conditions.

Source: U.S. Fish and Wildlife Service, *Status and Trends of Wetlands in the Conterminous United States, 2004 to 2009*, September 2011. See also <http://www.fws.gov/wetlands/Status-And-Trends-2009/index.html>.

Table 389. U.S. Water Withdrawals Per Day by End Use: 1950 to 2005

[180 represents 180,000,000,000. Includes the District of Columbia, Puerto Rico and U.S. Virgin Islands. Withdrawal signifies water physically withdrawn from a source. Includes fresh and saline water; excludes water used for hydroelectric power. For information on changes for the 2005 report, see source report *Estimated Use of Water in the United States in 2005*, Table 14]

Year	Total with- drawals	Public supply	Rural domestic and livestock		Irri- gation	Thermo electric power	Other			
			Self supplied domestic	Live- stock			Self supplied industrial	Mining	Com- mercial	Aqua- culture
1950 [1]	180	14	2.1	1.5	89	40	37	(5)	(5)	(5)
1955 [2]	240	17	2.1	1.5	110	72	39	(5)	(5)	(5)
1960 [3]	270	21	2.0	1.6	110	100	38	(5)	(5)	(5)
1965 [4]	310	24	2.3	1.7	120	130	46	(5)	(5)	(5)
1970 [4]	370	27	2.6	1.9	130	170	47	(5)	(5)	(5)
1975 [3]	420	29	2.8	2.1	140	200	45	(5)	(5)	(5)
1980 [3]	430	33	3.4	2.2	150	210	45	(5)	(5)	(5)
1985 [3]	397	36.4	3.32	2.23	135	187	25.9	3.44	1.23	2.24
1990 [3]	404	38.8	3.39	2.25	134	194	22.6	4.93	2.39	2.25
1995 [3]	399	40.2	3.39	2.28	130	190	22.4	3.72	2.89	3.22
2000 [3]	413	43.2	3.58	2.38	139	195	19.7	4.50	(NA)	5.77
2005 [3]	410	44.2	3.83	2.14	128	201	18.2	4.02	(NA)	8.78

NA Not available. [1] Population covered: 48 states, District of Columbia, and Hawaii. [2] Population covered: 48 states. [3] Population covered: 50 states, District of Columbia, Puerto Rico, and the Virgin Islands. [4] Population covered: 50 states, District of Columbia, and Puerto Rico. [5] Included in "Self-Supplied Industrial."

Source: 1940–1960, U.S. Bureau of Domestic Business Development, based principally on committee prints, *Water Resources Activities in the United States*, for the Senate Committee on National Water Resources, U.S. Senate, thereafter, U.S. Geological Survey, *Estimated Use of Water in the United States in 2005*, circular 1344, October 2009. See also <http://pubs.usgs.gov/circ/1344/>.

Table 390. National Ambient Air Pollutant Concentrations by Type of Pollutant: 2006 to 2012

[Data represent composite averages across monitoring stations meeting minimum data completeness requirements for the trend period. Carbon monoxide is based on the second-highest, nonoverlapping, 8-hour average; ozone, the fourth-highest maximum 8-hour value; particulates (PM-10) on the second highest daily 24-hour average; fine particulates (PM2.5) daily average on the 98th percentile daily 24-hour average; fine particulates (PM2.5) annual average on the weighted annual mean of daily 24-hour averages; and lead on the 'maximum rolling three-month average. Based on data from the Air Quality System. µmg/m ^{3} = micrograms of pollutant per cubic meter of air; ppm = parts per million; ppb = parts per billion]

Pollutant	Unit	Monitoring stations, number	Air quality standard [1]	2006	2007	2008	2009	2010	2011	2012
Carbon monoxide.............	ppm	225	[2] 9	2.2	2.0	1.8	1.8	1.6	1.6	1.5
Ozone.............	ppm	897	[3] 0.075	0.077	0.078	0.074	0.069	0.072	0.072	0.074
Sulfur dioxide.................	ppb	260	[4] 75	62	59	53	46	42	35	34
Particulates (PM-10).........	µmg/m ^{3}	511	[5] 150	79.9	68.1	67.0	57.8	60.1	63.8	63.8
Fine particulates (PM2.5) annual average.............	µmg/m ^{3}	570	[6] 12	11.8	12.1	10.9	9.8	10.0	9.8	9.3
Fine particulates (PM2.5) daily average................	µmg/m ^{3}	741	[7] 35	29	32	27	24	25	24	22
Nitrogen dioxide...............	ppb	191	[8] 100	49	48	47	43	44	43	41
Lead......................	µmg/m ^{3}	50	[9] 0.15	0.15	0.18	0.22	0.12	0.11	0.15	0.13

[1] Refers to the primary National Ambient Air Quality Standard. [2] Based on 8-hour standard of 9 ppm. [3] Based on 8-hour standard of 0.075 ppm. On March 12, 2008, EPA revised the level of the primary and secondary 8-hour ozone standards to 0.075 ppm. [4] Based on annual standard of 0.03 ppm. [5] Based on 24-hour (daily) standard of 150 µg/m ^{3}. The particulates (PM-10) standard replaced the previous standard for total suspended particulates in 1987. In 2006, EPA revoked the annual PM-10 standard. [6] Based on annual standard of 12 µg/m ^{3}. The PM-2.5 national monitoring network was deployed in 1999. National trend data prior to that time is not available. [7] Based on daily standard of 35 µg/m ^{3}. The PM-2.5 national monitoring network was deployed in 1999. National trend data prior to that time is not available. [8] Based on annual standard of 0.053 ppm. [9] Based on 3-month rolling average of 0.15 µg/m ^{3}.

Source: U.S. Environmental Protection Agency, "Air Trends," <http://www.epa.gov/airtrends/index.html>, accessed September 2013.

Table 391. Selected National Air Pollutant Emissions: 1970 to 2012

[In thousands of tons (4,319 represents 4,319,000), except as indicated. The methodology used to estimate emission data for 1970-1984 and for 1985 through the current year is different. Beginning with 1985, the methodology for more recent years is described in the document available at <http://www.epa.gov/ttn/chief/net/2011inventory.html>]

Year	Ammonia	Carbon monoxide	Nitrogen oxide	PM-10 [1]	PM-10 [2]	PM-2.5 [1]	PM-2.5 [2]	Sulfur dioxide	V.O.C. [3]
1970.............	(NA)	204,043	26,883	13,023	13,023	(NA)	(NA)	31,218	34,659
1980.............	(NA)	185,407	27,079	7,013	7,013	(NA)	(NA)	25,925	31,106
1990.............	4,319	154,186	25,529	27,752	27,752	7,559	7,559	23,076	24,108
2000.............	4,908	114,467	22,598	23,747	22,961	7,288	6,502	16,347	17,512
2005.............	4,082	92,415	19,046	21,144	14,377	5,452	2,490	14,826	18,340
2009.............	4,349	77,422	15,230	21,533	18,238	5,983	3,332	8,242	17,493
2010.............	4,335	73,674	14,310	21,501	18,199	5,945	3,286	7,557	17,024
2011.............	4,317	68,587	12,866	21,460	18,150	5,895	3,227	6,872	16,392
2012.............	4,298	62,770	11,160	21,420	18,100	5,841	3,164	5,620	15,680

NA Not available. [1] PM=Particular Matter; PM-10 is equal to or less than ten microns in diameter; PM-2.5 to or less than 2.5 microns effective diameter. [2] Without condensibles. [3] Volatile organic compound.

Source: U.S. Environmental Protection Agency, "National Emissions Inventory Air Pollution Emissions Trends Data, 1970-2012," <http://www.epa.gov/ttn/chief/trends/index.html>, accessed June 2013.

Table 392. Selected Air Pollutant Emissions by Pollutant and Source: 2012

[In thousands of tons, (4,298 represents 4,298,000). See headnote, Table 391]

Source	Ammonia	Carbon monoxide	Nitrogen oxide	PM-10 [1]	PM-2.5 [1]	Sulfur dioxide	V.O.C. [2]
Total emissions....................................	**4,298**	**62,770**	**11,160**	**21,420**	**5,841**	**5,620**	**15,680**
Fuel combustion, stationary sources.................	104	4,366	3,695	977	829	4,667	556
Electric utilities...	28	724	1,720	400	304	3,308	43
Industrial...	13	894	1,391	189	145	1,069	107
Other fuel combustion................................	63	2,748	585	388	380	291	406
Industrial processes...................................	151	3,114	1,088	1,504	679	792	6,905
Chemical and allied product manufacturing........	19	183	55	26	20	185	88
Metals processing....................................	2	840	79	81	63	177	37
Petroleum and related industries....................	1	262	425	30	23	149	1,742
Other...	56	426	416	1,074	340	253	362
Solvent utilization.....................................	–	7	6	4	4	1	3,298
Storage and transport.................................	5	18	10	51	24	6	1,193
Waste disposal and recycling.........................	67	1,378	97	238	205	21	185
Highway vehicles.......................................	78	22,766	3,858	270	154	10	1,953
Off highway [3].......................................	4	11,409	2,256	188	170	11	1,572
Miscellaneous [4].......................................	3,961	21,115	262	18,480	4,010	139	4,694

– Rounds to zero. [1] See footnote 1, Table 391. [2] Volatile organic compound. [3] Includes emissions from farm tractors and other farm machinery, construction equipment, industrial machinery, recreational marine vessels, and small general utility engines such as lawn mowers. [4] Includes emissions such as from forest fires and other kinds of burning, various agricultural activities, fugitive dust from paved and unpaved roads, and other construction and mining activities, and natural sources.

Source: U.S. Environmental Protection Agency, "National Emissions Inventory Air Pollution Emissions Trends Data, 1970-2012," <http://www.epa.gov/ttn/chief/trends/index.html#tables>, accessed June 2013.

Table 393. Emissions of Greenhouse Gases by Type and Source: 1990 to 2011

[In teragrams of carbon dioxide equivalent (Tg CO2 Eq.). (6,183.3 teragrams represents 6,183,300,000 million metric tons). Tg CO2 Eq. weights each gas by its global warming potential (GWP) value. GWP is a quantified measure of the globally averaged relative radiative forcing impacts of a particular greenhouse gas. The reference gas used is CO2; therefore, GWP-weighted emissions are measured in Tg CO2 Eq. See source for details]

Type and Source	1990	2005	2008	2009	2010	2011
Total Emissions	**6,183.3**	**7,195.3**	**7,048.8**	**6,586.6**	**6,810.3**	**6,702.3**
BY SOURCE						
Energy	5,267.3	6,251.6	6,096.2	5,699.2	5,889.1	5,745.7
Industrial [1]	316.1	330.8	318.7	265.3	303.4	326.5
Sulfur hexafluoride (SF6)	32.6	15.0	11.4	9.8	10.1	9.4
Hydrofluorocarbons (HFCs)	36.9	115.0	117.5	112.0	121.3	129.0
Perfluorocarbons (PFCs)	20.6	6.2	6.6	4.4	5.9	7.0
Solvent and other product use	4.4	4.4	4.4	4.4	4.4	4.4
Agriculture	413.9	446.2	463.6	459.2	462.3	461.5
Land use, land-use change, and forestry	13.7	25.4	27.2	20.4	19.7	36.6
Waste	167.8	136.9	138.6	138.1	131.4	127.7
Net CO2 flux from land use, land-use	*-794.5*	*-997.8*	*-902.6*	*-882.6*	*-888.8*	*-905*
Net emissions (sources and sinks) [2]	5,388.7	6,197.4	6,146.2	5,704.0	5,921.5	5,797.3
BY TYPE						
Carbon dioxide (CO2), total	**5,108.8**	**6,109.3**	**5,944.8**	**5,517.9**	**5,736.4**	**5,612.8**
Energy	4,912.0	5,934.1	5,774.9	5,390.6	5,585.6	5,452.5
Fossil fuel combustion	4,748.5	5,748.7	5,590.6	5,222.4	5,408.1	5,277.2
Electricity	1,820.8	2,402.1	2,360.9	2,146.4	2,259.2	2,158.5
Transportation	1,494.0	1,891.7	1,816.0	1,749.2	1,763.9	1,745.0
Industrial	848.6	823.4	802.0	722.6	780.2	773.2
Residential	338.3	357.9	347.0	337.0	334.6	328.8
Commercial	219.0	223.5	223.8	223.4	220.6	222.1
Biomass (wood) [3]	214.4	205.7	197.0	182.8	191.8	191.8
Industrial	188.7	166.3	160.3	119.0	141.4	151.3
Land use	8.1	8.9	9.6	8.3	9.4	9.0
Methane (CH4), total	**639.9**	**593.6**	**616.8**	**604.3**	**599.5**	**591.2**
Energy	298.6	259.7	274.4	264.8	259.9	252.3
Agriculture	171.5	191.5	200.3	198.6	199.9	196.3
Waste management	164.0	130.5	129.8	131.9	131.4	124.7
Industrial	3.3	3.9	3.6	3.3	3.6	3.7
Land use	2.5	8.0	8.7	5.7	4.7	14.2
Nitrous oxide (N2O), total	**340.0**	**351.8**	**345.2**	**334.4**	**339.4**	**352.3**
Agriculture	242.3	254.7	263.3	260.6	262.4	265.2
Energy	56.8	57.9	46.9	43.8	43.6	40.8
Industrial	34.0	24.4	19.4	16.8	21.1	26.1
Land use	3.1	8.4	8.9	6.4	5.6	13.4
Waste management	3.8	6.4	6.7	6.8	6.7	6.8

[1] Total includes items not shown separately. [2] The net CO2 flux total includes both emissions and sequestration, and constitutes a sink in the United States. Sinks are only included in net emissions total. [3] Emissions from wood biomass and ethanol consumption are not included specifically in summing energy sector totals. Net carbon fluxes from changes in biogenic carbon reservoirs are accounted for in the estimates for land use, land-use change, and forestry.

Source: U.S. Environmental Protection Agency, *Inventory of U.S. Greenhouse Gas Emissions and Sinks, 1990-2011*, April 2013. See also <http://www.epa.gov/climatechange/ghgemissions/usinventoryreport.html>

Table 394. Carbon Dioxide Emissions from Fossil Fuel Combustion by Fuel Type and Sector: 1990 to 2011

[In teragrams of carbon dioxide equivalent (Tg CO2 Eq.). (4,748.5 teragrams represents 4,748,500,000 million metric tons)]

Fuel and Sector	1990	2005	2007	2008	2009	2010	2011
Total [1]	**4,748.5**	**5,748.7**	**5,767.7**	**5,590.6**	**5,222.4**	**5,408.1**	**5,277.2**
Coal	**1,718.4**	**2,112.3**	**2,105.1**	**2,072.6**	**1,834.3**	**1,933.5**	**1,821.9**
Residential	3.0	0.8	0.7	0.7	0.7	0.6	0.5
Commercial	12.0	9.3	6.7	6.5	6.0	5.7	5.1
Industrial	155.3	115.3	107.0	102.6	83.3	96.2	90.1
Electricity generation	1,547.6	1,983.8	1,987.3	1,959.4	1,740.9	1,827.6	1,722.7
Natural Gas	**1,000.3**	**1,166.7**	**1,226.3**	**1,237.9**	**1,216.6**	**1,276.0**	**1,290.3**
Residential	238.0	262.2	256.3	265.5	258.8	258.6	254.6
Commercial	142.1	162.9	163.5	171.1	168.9	167.7	170.4
Industrial	408.9	388.5	398.6	401.0	377.3	411.1	416.3
Transportation	36.0	33.1	35.2	36.7	37.9	38.1	38.8
Electricity Generation	175.3	318.8	371.3	361.9	372.2	399.0	408.8
Petroleum	**2,029.4**	**2,469.3**	**2,435.8**	**2,279.8**	**2,171.1**	**2,198.2**	**2,164.6**
Residential	97.4	94.9	84.6	80.7	77.6	75.4	73.6
Commercial	64.9	51.3	48.7	46.1	48.5	47.2	46.7
Industrial	284.4	319.6	338.7	298.4	261.9	273.0	266.8
Transportation	1,457.9	1,858.7	1,869.5	1,779.3	1,711.3	1,725.8	1,706.2
Electricity Generation	97.5	99.2	53.9	39.2	33.0	32.2	26.6

[1] Includes data not shown separately.

Source: U.S. Environmental Protection Agency, *Inventory of U.S. Greenhouse Gas Emissions and Sinks, 1990-2011*, April 2013. See also <http://www.epa.gov/climatechange/ghgemissions/usinventoryreport.html>.

Table 395. Municipal Solid Waste Generation, Materials Recovery, Combustion With Energy Recovery, and Discards: 1980 to 2011

[In millions of tons (151.6 represents 151,600,000), except as indicated. Covers post-consumer residential and commercial solid wastes which comprise the major portion of typical municipal collections. Excludes mining, agricultural and industrial processing, demolition and construction wastes, sewage sludge and junked autos and obsolete equipment wastes. Based on material-flows estimating procedure and wet weight as generated]

Item and material	1980	1990	2000	2005	2009	2010	2011
Waste generated	**151.6**	**208.3**	**243.5**	**253.7**	**244.3**	**250.5**	**250.4**
Per person per day (lb.)	3.7	4.6	4.7	4.7	4.4	4.4	4.4
Total materials recovery	**14.5**	**33.2**	**69.5**	**79.8**	**82.4**	**85.1**	**86.9**
Per person per day (lb.)	0.4	0.7	1.4	1.5	1.5	1.5	1.5
Recovery for recycling	14.5	29.0	53.0	59.2	61.6	65.0	66.2
Per person per day (lb.)	0.4	0.6	1.0	1.1	1.1	1.2	1.2
Recovery for composting [1]	(Z)	4.2	16.5	20.6	20.8	20.2	20.7
Per person per day (lb.)	(Z)	0.1	0.3	0.4	0.4	0.4	0.4
Combustion with energy recovery	2.7	29.7	33.7	31.6	29.0	29.3	29.3
Per person per day (lb.)	0.1	0.7	0.7	0.6	0.5	0.5	0.5
Discards to landfill, other disposal	134.4	145.3	140.3	142.3	132.9	136.1	134.3
Per person per day (lb.)	3.2	3.2	2.7	2.6	2.4	2.4	2.36
PERCENT DISTRIBUTION OF GENERATION							
Percent of total generation	**71.8**	**70.3**	**73.4**	**72.9**	**70.4**	**70.9**	**70.5**
Paper and paperboard	36.4	34.9	36.0	33.4	28.0	28.5	28.0
Glass	10.0	6.3	5.2	4.9	4.8	4.6	4.6
Metals	10.2	7.9	7.8	8.0	8.7	8.9	8.8
Plastics	4.5	8.2	10.5	11.6	12.3	12.5	12.7
Rubber and leather	2.8	2.8	2.7	2.9	3.0	3.0	3.0
Textiles	1.7	2.8	3.9	4.5	5.3	5.2	5.2
Wood	4.6	5.9	5.6	5.8	6.4	6.3	6.4
Other	1.7	1.5	1.6	1.7	1.9	1.9	1.9
Total other waste	**28.2**	**29.7**	**26.6**	**27.1**	**29.6**	**29.1**	**29.5**
Food waste	8.6	11.5	12.6	13.0	14.4	14.3	14.5
Yard trimmings	18.1	16.8	12.5	12.6	13.6	13.3	13.5
Miscellaneous inorganic wastes	1.5	1.4	1.4	1.5	1.6	1.5	1.5

Z Less than 5,000 tons or 0.05 percent. [1] Composting of yard trimmings, food scraps, and other municipal solid waste organic material. Does not include backyard composting.

Source: Franklin Associates, a Division of ERG, Prairie Village, KS, © *Municipal Solid Waste in the United States: 2011 Facts and Figures*. Prepared for the U.S. Environmental Protection Agency. See also <http://www.epa.gov/epawaste/nonhaz/municipal/index.htm>.

Table 396. Generation and Recovery of Selected Materials in Municipal Solid Waste: 1980 to 2011

[In millions of tons (151.6 represents 151,600,000), except as indicated. Covers post-consumer residential and commercial solid wastes which comprise the major portion of typical municipal collections. Excludes mining, agricultural and industrial processing, demolition and construction wastes, sewage sludge, and junked autos and obsolete equipment wastes. Based on material-flows estimating procedure and wet weight as generated]

Item and material	1980	1990	2000	2005	2009	2010	2011
Waste generated, total [1]	**151.6**	**205.2**	**243.5**	**252.4**	**244.3**	**250.5**	**250.4**
Paper and paperboard	55.2	72.7	87.7	84.8	68.4	71.3	70.0
Glass	15.1	13.1	12.8	12.5	11.8	11.5	11.5
Metals: Ferrous	12.6	12.6	14.2	15.0	15.9	16.8	16.5
Aluminum	1.7	2.8	3.2	3.3	3.4	3.5	3.5
Other nonferrous	1.2	1.1	1.6	1.9	1.9	2.0	2.0
Plastics	6.8	17.1	25.6	29.3	30.1	31.3	31.8
Food waste	13.0	20.8	30.7	32.0	35.3	35.7	36.3
Yard trimmings	27.5	35.0	30.5	32.1	33.2	33.4	33.7
Materials recovered, total [1]	**14.5**	**33.2**	**69.5**	**79.9**	**82.4**	**85.1**	**86.9**
Paper and paperboard	11.7	20.2	37.6	42.0	42.5	44.6	45.9
Glass	0.8	2.6	2.9	2.6	3.0	3.1	3.2
Metals: Ferrous	0.4	2.2	4.7	5.0	5.3	5.8	5.5
Aluminum	0.3	1.0	0.9	0.7	0.7	0.7	0.7
Other nonferrous	0.5	0.7	1.1	1.3	1.3	1.4	1.3
Plastics	0.2	0.4	1.5	1.8	2.1	2.5	2.7
Food waste	(Z)	(Z)	0.7	0.7	0.9	1.0	1.4
Yard trimmings	(Z)	4.2	15.8	19.9	19.9	19.2	19.3
Percent of generation recovered, total [1]	**9.6**	**16.2**	**29.7**	**31.6**	**35.8**	**36.6**	**37.5**
Paper and paperboard	21.3	27.8	42.8	49.5	62.1	62.5	65.6
Glass	5.0	20.1	22.6	20.7	25.5	27.1	27.6
Metals: Ferrous	2.9	17.6	33.1	33.1	33.5	34.2	33.0
Aluminum	17.9	35.9	27.0	20.7	20.1	19.4	20.7
Other nonferrous	46.6	66.4	66.3	68.8	68.4	69.5	68.4
Plastics	0.3	2.2	5.8	6.0	7.1	8.0	8.3
Food waste	(Z)	(Z)	2.2	2.2	2.4	2.7	3.9
Yard trimmings	(Z)	12.0	51.7	61.9	59.9	57.5	57.3

Z Less than 5,000 tons or 0.05 percent. [1] Includes products not shown separately.

Source: Franklin Associates, a Division of ERG, Prairie Village, KS, © *Municipal Solid Waste in the United States: 2011 Facts and Figures*. Prepared for the U.S. Environmental Protection Agency. See also <http://www.epa.gov/epawaste/nonhaz/municipal/index.htm>.

Table 397. Municipal Solid Waste—Generation, Recovery, and Discards by Selected Type of Product: 2011

[70,020 represents 70,020,000. See headnote, Table 396]

Type of product	Generation (1,000 tons)	Recovery Products recovered (1,000 tons)	Recovery Percent of generation	Discards (1,000 tons)
Paper and paperboard products [1]	**70,020**	**45,900**	**65.6**	**24,120**
Nondurable goods	31,940	17,240	54.0	14,700
Newspapers/Mechanical Papers	9,150	6,630	72.5	2,520
Other paper nondurable goods	22,790	10,610	46.6	12,180
Containers and packaging	38,020	28,660	75.4	9,360
Corrugated boxes	29,440	26,800	91.0	2,640
Other paper and paperboard packaging	8,580	1,860	21.7	6,720
Glass products [1]	**11,470**	**3,170**	**27.6**	**8,300**
Containers and packaging	9,280	3,170	34.2	6,110
Beer and soft drink bottles	5,520	2,270	41.1	3,250
Wine and liquor bottles	1,770	600	33.9	1,170
Food and other bottles and jars	1,990	300	15.1	1,690
Metal products [1]	**21,950**	**7,510**	**34.2**	**14,440**
Metals in durable goods	17,730	5,220	29.4	12,510
Ferrous	14,340	3,880	27.1	10,460
Aluminum	1,430	(Z)	(Z)	1,430
Other nonferrous	1,960	1,340	68.4	620
Plastics [1]	**31,840**	**2,650**	**8.3**	**29,190**
Plastics in durable goods	11,420	740	6.5	10,680
Plastics in nondurable goods	6,520	110	1.7	6,410
Plastics in containers and packaging	13,900	1,800	12.9	12,100
Rubber and leather [1]	**7,490**	**1,310**	**17.5**	**6,180**
Rubber in tires	2,940	1,310	44.6	1,630

Z Less than 5,000 tons or 0.05 percent. [1] Includes products not shown separately.

Source: Franklin Associates, a Division of ERG, Prairie Village, KS, © *Municipal Solid Waste in the United States: 2011 Facts and Figures.* Prepared for the U.S. Environmental Protection Agency. See also <http://www.epa.gov/epawaste/nonhaz/municipal/index.htm>.

Table 398. Environmental Industry—Revenues and Employment by Industry Segment: 2000 to 2011

[211.2 represents $211,200,000,000. Covers approximately 30,000 private and public companies engaged in revenue-generating environmental activities]

Industry segment	Revenue (bil. dol.) 2000	2005	2010	2011	Employment 2000	2005	2010	2011
Industry total	**211.2**	**251.6**	**303.1**	**319.6**	**1,305,800**	**1,454,000**	**1,630,700**	**1,667,700**
SERVICES								
Analytical services [1]	1.8	1.8	1.9	1.9	20,200	20,000	19,800	20,000
Wastewater treatment works [2]	28.7	35.6	45.2	47.4	118,800	141,100	168,900	173,100
Solid waste management [3]	39.4	47.8	53.4	54.6	221,400	256,500	278,000	283,200
Hazardous waste management [4]	8.2	8.7	9.0	9.2	44,800	45,000	43,600	44,200
Remediation/industrial services	10.1	11.0	12.8	13.2	100,200	96,600	108,400	109,600
Consulting and engineering	17.4	22.4	26.6	27.6	184,000	220,800	255,800	257,700
EQUIPMENT								
Water equipment and chemicals	19.8	24.8	26.9	27.7	130,500	153,000	160,100	162,700
Instrument manufacturing	3.8	4.7	5.4	5.7	30,200	34,600	37,300	38,400
Air pollution control equipment [5]	19.0	18.8	14.9	15.1	129,600	123,400	96,400	96,500
Waste management equipment [6]	10.0	10.1	10.8	11.1	75,500	72,900	73,800	74,900
Process and prevention technology	1.2	1.5	1.9	1.9	29,000	28,100	28,900	28,800
RESOURCES								
Water utilities [7]	29.9	35.1	42.7	44.3	130,000	145,200	169,000	173,300
Resource recovery [8]	16.0	21.1	28.5	32.5	61,900	79,300	102,600	107,500
Clean energy systems and power [9]	5.9	8.3	23.1	27.4	29,700	37,500	88,100	97,800

[1] Covers environmental laboratory testing and services. [2] Mostly revenues collected by municipal entities for sewage or wastewater plants. [3] Covers such activities as collection, transportation, transfer stations, disposal, landfill ownership and management for solid waste and recyclables. [4] Transportation and disposal of hazardous, medical, and nuclear waste. [5] Includes stationary and mobile sources. [6] Includes vehicles, containers, liners, processing, and remediation equipment. [7] Revenues generated from the sale of water, majority in public sector. [8] Revenues generated from the sale of recovered metals, paper, plastic, etc. [9] Revenues generated from the sale of equipment and systems and electricity.

Source: Environmental Business International, Inc., San Diego, CA, publisher of *Environmental Business Journal;* © 2013 EBI Inc. See also <http://www.ebionline.org>.

Table 399. Toxic Chemical Releases and Transfers by Media: 2007 to 2012

[In millions of pounds (4,123.8 represents 4,123,800,000), except as indicated. Based on reports filed to the Toxic Release Inventory (TRI) Program, as required by Section 313 of the Emergency Planning and Community Right-to-Know Act (EPCRA). The Pollution Prevention Act (PPA) of 1990 mandates collection of data on toxic chemicals that are treated on-site, recycled, and combusted for energy recovery. Owners and operators of facilities within specific 2007 North American Industry Classification System industries that have 10 or more full-time employees, and that manufacture, process, or otherwise use any listed toxic chemical in quantities greater than the established threshold in the course of a calendar year are covered and required to report. Includes carcinogens, Persistent, Bioaccumulative, Toxic (PBT) chemicals, and dioxin and dioxin-like compounds. Does not include off-site disposal or other releases transferred to other TRI program facilities that reported the amounts as on-site disposal or other releases]

Media	2007	2008	2009	2010	2011	2012, prelim.
Total facilities reporting	**23,351**	**22,713**	**21,673**	**21,436**	**21,302**	**20,979**
Total on- and off-site disposal or other releases	**4,123.8**	**3,875.6**	**3,393.1**	**3,796.7**	**4,087.1**	**3,605.5**
On-site releases	3,574.3	3,389.1	3,036.1	3,385.5	3,673.4	3,166.2
Air emissions [1]	1,336.2	1,153.8	926.3	864.2	801.6	736.6
Surface water discharges	239.0	246.5	204.9	222.8	213.1	206.7
Underground injection class I	188.8	173.9	155.0	201.8	195.7	198.1
Underground injection class II-V	0.3	0.2	0.2	0.2	0.2	0.2
RCRA subtitle C landfills [2]	154.3	127.5	83.9	68.1	69.4	91.7
Other landfills	270.5	282.2	240.4	283.7	273.3	267.4
Land treatment/application farming	22.0	23.9	16.3	14.5	14.1	16.1
Surface impoundments	769.3	740.1	800.0	798.7	885.9	725.2
Other land disposal	593.9	640.8	609.2	931.5	1,220.2	924.3
Off-site releases	549.5	486.5	356.9	411.3	413.7	439.3
Total transfers offsite for further waste management	**3,882.3**	**3,528.3**	**2,852.2**	**3,262.4**	**3,613.7**	**3,759.8**
Transfers to recycling	2,134.8	1,987.9	1,640.2	1,904.7	2,279.5	2,383.9
Transfers to energy recovery	525.8	451.4	367.2	426.7	355.2	380.6
Transfers to treatment	296.3	258.4	230.8	253.7	292.8	277.5
Transfers to POTWs (non metals) [3]	254.2	256.2	218.3	231.0	239.2	242.8
Transfers to POTWs metal and metal compounds [3]	1.8	1.1	0.8	0.8	0.8	0.9
Other off-site transfers	0.7	0.2	0.0	0.2	0.5	0.4
Transfers off-site for disposal or other releases	668.7	573.3	394.9	445.2	445.7	473.7
Total production-related waste managed	**24,018.1**	**22,962.3**	**20,325.6**	**21,767.6**	**22,548.4**	**21,778.5**
Recycled on-site	6,890.7	6,833.2	6,056.5	6,038.3	6,389.5	5,970.1
Recycled off-site	2,142.3	1,985.9	1,625.6	1,904.5	2,276.0	2,078.1
Energy recovery on-site	2,232.8	2,229.2	1,864.3	1,982.4	2,105.2	2,284.6
Energy recovery off-site	523.9	450.2	369.3	426.8	355.4	379.7
Treated on-site	7,444.1	7,015.6	6,535.7	7,113.1	6,784.5	6,956.6
Treated off-site	519.1	483.5	426.1	460.5	507.3	498.5
Quantity disposed or otherwise release of on- and off-site	4,265.1	3,964.8	3,448.0	3,842.0	4,130.5	3,610.9
Non-production-related waste managed	14.2	33.8	10.9	13.4	14.7	50.6

[1] Air emissions include both fugitive and point source. [2] RCRA=Resource Conservation and Recovery Act. [3] POTW (Publicly Owned Treatment Work) is a wastewater treatment facility that is owned by a state or municipality.

Source: Environmental Protection Agency, Toxic Release Inventory (TRI) Program, *2012 TRI National Analysis*. See also <http://www2.epa.gov/toxics-release-inventory-tri-program/2012-tri-preliminary-dataset>, accessed September 2013.

Table 400. Toxic Chemical Releases by Industry: 2011

[In millions of pounds (4,086.5 represents 4,086,500,000). See headnote, Table 399]

Industry	2007 NAICS [1] code	Total on- and off-site releases	On-site releases Total	On-site releases Air emissions	On-site releases Other surface impound-ments	Off-site releases/ transfers to [2] disposal
Total [3]	(X)	**4,086.5**	**3,674.8**	**798.9**	**882.0**	**411.7**
Coal mining	2121	9.8	9.8	0.8	0.9	(Z)
Metal mining	2122	1,894.7	1,892.0	3.1	746.2	2.7
Electric utilities	2211	611.2	544.8	257.8	101.7	66.4
Food/beverages/tobacco	311/312	135.0	126.6	42.1	0.2	8.4
Textiles	313/314	2.8	2.3	1.7	0.1	0.5
Apparel	315	(Z)	(Z)	(Z)	(Z)	(Z)
Leather	316	0.9	0.2	0.2	(Z)	0.7
Wood products	321	8.7	8.3	8.1	(Z)	0.4
Paper	322	175.7	168.5	131.0	4.0	7.3
Printing and publishing	323/51	8.5	8.2	8.2	(Z)	0.3
Petroleum	324	65.8	61.3	37.4	(Z)	4.5
Chemicals	325	480.2	427.3	160.1	18.0	52.9
Plastics and rubber	326	34.5	28.2	28.0	(Z)	6.3
Stone/clay/glass	327	21.6	18.3	15.3	(Z)	3.3
Cement	32731	5.9	5.6	4.7	(Z)	0.3
Primary metals	331	362.9	180.3	39.1	6.9	182.6
Fabricated metals	332	41.2	21.5	19.9	(Z)	19.7
Machinery	333	5.4	3.1	3.0	(Z)	2.4
Computers/electronic products	334	4.3	3.0	1.4	(Z)	1.2
Electrical equipment	335	6.9	1.4	1.3	(Z)	5.5
Transportation equipment	336	33.2	24.4	24.1	(Z)	8.8
Furniture	337	3.7	3.6	3.6	(Z)	(Z)
Miscellaneous Manufacturing	339	3.6	2.6	2.6	(Z)	1.0
Chemical wholesalers	4246	1.3	1.0	1.0	(Z)	0.3
Petroleum bulk terminals	4247	2.5	1.8	1.8	(Z)	0.7
Hazardous waste	562	128.1	94.6	0.3	1.5	33.5
No codes [3]	(X)	38.1	36.0	2.0	2.5	2.0

– Represents zero. X Not applicable. Z less than 50,000 lbs. [1] North American Industry Classification System, see text, Section 12. [2] Includes off-site disposal to underground injection for Class I wells, Class II to V wells, other surface impoundments, land releases, and other releases, not shown separately. [3] Includes industries with no specific industry identified.

Source: Environmental Protection Agency, *2011 TRI National Analysis*, January 2013. See also <http://www.epa.gov/tri/tridata/tri11/national_analysis/index.htm>.

Table 401. Toxic Chemical Releases by State and Outlying Area: 2011

[In millions of pounds (4,086.5 represents 4,086,500,000). Based on reports filed as required by Section 313 of the EPCRA. See headnote, Table 399]

State and outlying areas	Total on-and off-site releases	On-site releases or other disposal			Off-site releases/ trans-fers to disposal	State and outlying areas	Total on-and off-site releases	On-site releases or other disposal			Off-site releases/ trans-fers to disposal
		Total [2]	Air emis-sions	Other surface im-pound-ments				Total [2]	Air emis-sions	Other surface im-pound-ments	
Total [1]	4,086.5	3,674.8	798.9	882.0	411.7	MO	73.4	71.0	10.3	43.5	2.4
U.S. total	4,079.8	3,668.8	793.3	882.0	411.0	MT	33.8	32.4	1.5	4.5	1.4
AL	84.1	70.7	32.4	13.6	13.4	NE	27.0	24.1	5.0	(Z)	2.9
AK	1,048.8	1,048.1	0.6	388.5	0.6	NV	529.3	526.3	1.4	160.7	3.0
AZ	97.7	97.1	2.8	16.5	0.6	NH	2.1	2.0	2.0	–	0.1
AR	35.2	28.2	13.6	1.3	7.0	NJ	14.1	11.2	2.3	(Z)	3.0
CA	38.3	32.3	7.8	(Z)	6.0	NM	14.4	14.3	0.9	1.2	0.1
CO	26.3	21.7	2.4	5.0	4.7	NY	18.9	13.8	7.7	(Z)	5.1
CT	2.1	1.2	0.9	–	0.9	NC	59.0	51.1	28.3	3.8	7.9
DE	6.2	3.9	2.4	(Z)	2.2	ND	21.0	14.4	3.3	4.6	6.7
DC	(Z)	(Z)	(Z)	(Z)	(Z)	OH	150.5	114.2	58.8	8.8	36.2
FL	73.7	70.5	28.7	0.3	3.3	OK	39.6	38.2	19.5	0.6	1.4
GA	71.7	68.6	42.2	12.0	3.1	OR	23.3	22.5	6.4	(Z)	0.8
HI	2.6	2.4	1.8	–	0.2	PA	100.9	54.5	33.9	1.6	46.4
ID	54.5	53.6	4.2	14.8	0.8	RI	0.4	0.1	0.1	–	0.3
IL	105.4	56.5	28.6	10.1	48.9	SC	51.2	41.7	30.8	3.2	9.5
IN	149.2	98.1	44.2	6.6	51.2	SD	5.9	5.7	1.3	(Z)	0.2
IA	40.0	31.3	18.9	0.8	8.7	TN	87.7	76.2	31.5	20.3	11.5
KS	23.2	20.6	9.8	0.4	2.6	TX	209.0	191.3	60.9	5.3	17.7
KY	83.6	73.0	47.7	9.9	10.6	UT	197.0	195.4	11.5	110.8	1.6
LA	130.8	122.2	48.1	4.4	8.6	VT	0.4	0.2	(Z)	–	0.2
ME	10.8	8.5	4.2	–	2.3	VA	46.1	42.5	22.7	1.0	3.6
MD	11.3	8.4	6.0	(Z)	2.8	WA	19.1	15.3	8.7	2.6	3.8
MA	3.2	1.9	1.9	(Z)	1.3	WV	38.8	31.7	20.2	1.6	7.1
MI	81.6	50.4	30.0	3.9	31.1	WI	36.1	19.7	13.8	(Z)	16.4
MN	25.2	19.8	8.5	6.9	5.4	WY	19.1	17.7	2.7	2.8	1.3
MS	56.3	52.4	20.4	10.2	3.9	PR	4.7	3.9	3.9	–	0.7

– Represents zero. Z Less than 50,000 lbs. [1] Total includes all states and outlying areas. [2] Includes other types of release, not shown separately.

Source: Environmental Protection Agency, Toxic Release Inventory (TRI) Program, *2011 TRI National Analysis*, January 2013. See also <http://www.epa.gov/tri/tridata/tri11/national_analysis/index.htm>.

Table 402. Hazardous Waste Sites on the National Priority List by State and Outlying Area: 2012

[As of January 2013. Includes both proposed and final sites listed on the National Priorities List for the Superfund program as authorized by the Comprehensive Environmental Response, Compensation, and Liability Act (CERCLA) of 1980 and the Superfund Amendments and Reauthorization Act (SARA) of 1986. For information on CERCLA and SARA, see <http://www.epa.gov/superfund/policy/cercla.htm>]

State and outlying areas	Total sites	Rank	Per-cent distri-bution	Federal	Non-fed-earal	State and outlying areas	Total sites	Rank	Per-cent distri-bution	Federal	Non-fed-earal
Total	1,312	(X)	(X)	156	1,156	Missouri	33	14	2.6	3	30
United States	1,293	(X)	(X)	154	1,139	Montana	16	22	1.2	–	16
Alabama	14	26	1.1	3	11	Nebraska	13	33	1.0	1	12
Alaska	6	44	0.5	5	1	Nevada	1	49	0.1	–	1
Arizona	9	38	0.7	–	9	New Hampshire	20	20	1.5	1	19
Arkansas	9	39	0.7	2	7	New Jersey	111	1	8.6	6	105
California	98	2	7.6	24	74	New Mexico	14	29	1.1	1	13
Colorado	18	21	1.4	3	15	New York	87	4	6.7	4	83
Connecticut	14	27	1.1	1	13	North Carolina	37	11	2.9	2	35
Delaware	13	31	1.0	1	12	North Dakota	–	50	–	–	–
District of Columbia	1	(X)	0.1	1	–	Ohio	37	12	2.9	3	34
Florida	55	6	4.3	6	49	Oklahoma	8	43	0.6	1	7
Georgia	15	23	1.2	2	13	Oregon	14	30	1.1	2	12
Hawaii	3	46	0.2	2	1	Pennsylvania	96	3	7.4	6	90
Idaho	6	45	0.5	2	4	Rhode Island	12	34	0.9	2	10
Illinois	45	9	3.5	4	41	South Carolina	27	17	2.1	2	25
Indiana	33	13	2.6	–	33	South Dakota	2	47	0.2	1	1
Iowa	11	35	0.9	1	10	Tennessee	15	24	1.2	3	12
Kansas	11	36	0.9	1	10	Texas	50	7	3.9	4	46
Kentucky	14	28	1.1	1	13	Utah	15	25	1.2	4	11
Louisiana	9	40	0.7	1	8	Vermont	11	37	0.9	–	11
Maine	13	32	1.0	3	10	Virginia	31	15	2.4	11	20
Maryland	20	19	1.5	10	10	Washington	49	8	3.8	13	36
Massachusetts	30	16	2.3	6	24	West Virginia	9	41	0.7	2	7
Michigan	65	5	5.0	–	65	Wisconsin	38	10	2.9	–	38
Minnesota	25	18	1.9	2	23	Wyoming	2	48	0.2	1	1
Mississippi	8	42	0.6	–	8	Puerto Rico	16	(X)	(X)	1	15

– Represents zero. X Not applicable.

Source: U.S. Environmental Protection Agency, "National Priorities List," <http://www.epa.gov/superfund/sites/npl/>, accessed January 2013.

Table 403. Hazardous Waste Generated, Shipped, and Received by State and Other Areas: 2011

[In thousands of tons (35,334.1 represents 35,334,100). Covers hazardous waste regulated under the Resource Conservation and Recovery Act (RCRA) of 1976 as amended. The data have been revised. See source for exclusions of data from the 2011 National Biennial RCRA Hazardous Waste Report]

State and other areas	Hazardous waste quantity (1,000) tons			State and other areas	Hazardous waste quantity (1,000) tons		
	Generated	Shipped	Received		Generated	Shipped	Received
Total..................	**34,334.1**	**5,951.4**	**6,180.0**	Missouri......................	251.0	80.9	152.4
				Montana.....................	5.9	6.0	–
United States..............	**34,295.4**	**5,914.8**	**6,178.8**	Nebraska....................	35.4	43.7	37.4
				Nevada......................	9.8	11.9	78.7
Alabama......................	578.3	193.0	246.2	New Hampshire.............	3.9	3.9	–
Alaska........................	2.5	2.0	–	New Jersey..................	290.5	328.2	242.4
Arizona.......................	202.9	26.5	17.9	New Mexico.................	1,042.4	10.4	4.7
Arkansas.....................	922.7	206.6	240.6	New York.....................	186.5	165.8	83.4
California.....................	534.7	428.7	183.1	North Carolina..............	83.1	91.0	12.3
Colorado.....................	31.8	34.6	43.8	North Dakota................	455.9	1.2	0.3
Connecticut..................	25.0	24.1	8.8	Ohio..........................	1,617.8	565.6	621.1
Delaware.....................	43.3	43.0	0.1	Oklahoma....................	44.3	29.9	94.3
District of Columbia.........	1.1	1.1	–	Oregon.......................	93.2	77.6	55.2
Florida........................	198.4	33.5	10.8	Pennsylvania................	308.7	262.7	428.4
Georgia.......................	211.1	42.3	3.9	Rhode Island................	8.6	16.2	10.0
Hawaii........................	425.6	1.3	0.2	South Carolina..............	140.5	171.2	154.6
Idaho.........................	3.7	6.4	112.2	South Dakota................	1.3	1.4	0.1
Illinois........................	675.5	205.0	379.9	Tennessee...................	89.4	52.8	28.9
Indiana.......................	888.1	389.4	463.1	Texas........................	15,683.4	607.3	653.6
Iowa..........................	51.0	50.7	0.6	Utah..........................	49.7	79.4	145.6
Kansas.......................	1,238.3	135.5	262.2	Vermont......................	2.0	2.6	1.5
Kentucky.....................	142.2	182.0	106.4	Virginia.......................	74.8	71.6	0.5
Louisiana.....................	4,399.5	516.5	486.3	Washington..................	334.0	75.7	51.9
Maine.........................	2.4	2.3	0.1	West Virginia................	62.3	39.5	6.4
Maryland.....................	44.3	54.6	56.5	Wisconsin....................	289.4	173.0	52.8
Massachusetts...............	35.6	42.0	8.9	Wyoming.....................	4.1	4.1	–
Michigan......................	282.9	177.9	443.7	Guam........................	0.1	0.1	–
Minnesota....................	357.4	69.2	169.1	Navajo Nation...............	–	–	–
Mississippi...................	1,828.9	73.0	17.9	Puerto Rico..................	37.3	35.2	1.2
				Virgin Islands...............	1.3	1.3	–

– Represents or rounds to zero.

Source: U.S. Environmental Protection Agency, *The National Biennial RCRA Hazardous Waste Report (Based on 2011 data)*, 2012. See also <http://www.epa.gov/epawaste/inforesources/data/biennialreport/index.htm>.

Table 404. Oil Spills in U.S. Water—Number and Volume: 2000 to 2011

[These summary statistics are based on reported discharges of oil and petroleum based products into U.S. navigable waters, including territorial waters (extending 3 to 12 miles from the coastline), tributaries, the contiguous zone, onto shoreline, or into other waters that threaten the marine environment]

Spill characteristic	Number of spills				Spill volume (gallons)			
	2000	2005	2010	2011	2000	2005	2010	2011
Total.....................	**8,354**	**3,881**	**3,008**	**3,065**	**1,431,370**	**9,926,581**	**206,712,792**	**210,270**
Size of spill (gallons):								
1 to 100...................	8,058	3,657	2,874	2,924	39,355	31,872	21,846	21,858
101 to 1,000.............	219	167	115	117	78,779	63,123	39,839	41,631
1,001 to 3,000...........	37	25	8	12	67,529	43,289	16,645	18,818
3,001 to 5,000...........	12	9	2	6	45,512	36,803	7,587	26,085
5,001 to 10,000..........	16	7	4	3	112,415	59,167	32,275	19,790
10,001 to 50,000........	6	7	1	3	108,400	142,024	18,000	82,088
50,001 to 100,000.......	4	1	–	–	266,380	84,000	–	–
100,001 to 1,000,000....	2	4	3	–	713,000	1,368,236	996,400	–
1,000,000 and over......	–	4	1	–	–	8,098,067	205,580,200	–
Source:								
Tankship..................	111	37	23	26	608,176	2,976	421,583	1,702
Tankbarge.................	229	126	73	67	133,540	2,006,774	965	15,852
All other vessels.........	5,220	1,672	1,412	1,438	291,927	115,058	472,386	90,109
Facilities..................	1,054	1,020	869	1,004	311,604	7,633,248	221,642	89,467
Pipelines..................	25	24	34	38	17,021	136,465	4,627	1,687
All other nonvessels.....	566	102	105	117	45,136	1,934	206,582,872	3,605
Unknown...................	1,149	900	492	375	23,966	30,126	8,718	7,849

– Represents zero.

Source: U.S. Coast Guard, *Pollution Incidents In and Around U.S. Waters, A Spill/Release Compendium: 1969–2011*, December 2012. See also <http://homeport.uscg.mil>.

Table 405. Tornadoes, Floods, Tropical Storms, and Lightning: 2000 to 2012

[(424 represents 424,000,000)]

Weather type	2000	2004	2005	2006	2007	2008	2009	2010	2011	2012
Tornadoes: [1]										
Number..............................	1,072	1,820	1,262	1,117	1,102	1,685	1,305	1,543	1,894	1,119
Lives lost..........................	41	35	38	67	81	126	21	45	553	70
Injuries............................	882	396	537	990	659	1,714	351	699	5,483	822
Property loss (mil. dol.)..............	424	537	422	752	1,401	1,846	566	1,107	9,463	1,649
Floods and flash floods:										
Lives lost..........................	38	82	43	76	87	82	56	103	113	29
Injuries............................	47	128	38	23	59	46	27	310	40	25
Property loss (mil. dol.)..............	1,255	1,696	1,538	3,768	1,740	3,406	1,050	3,927	7,978	494
North Atlantic tropical cyclones and hurricanes: [2]...........	15	16	27	9	17	17	11	21	20	19
Hurricanes.........................	8	9	15	5	6	8	3	12	7	10
Lives lost..........................	–	34	1,016	–	1	12	2	–	9	4
Property loss (mil.dol.)..............	8	18,902	93,064	2	39	7,619	1	15	344	172
Lightning:										
Deaths............................	51	32	38	48	45	27	34	29	26	28
Injuries............................	364	280	309	246	138	216	201	182	187	139

– Represents zero. [1] Source: U.S. National Weather Service, <http://www.spc.noaa.gov/climo/torn/monthlytornstats.html>. A violent, rotating column of air descending from a cumulonimbus cloud in the form of a tubular- or funnel-shaped cloud, usually characterized by movements along a narrow path and wind speeds from 100 to over 300 miles per hour. Also known as a "twister" or "waterspout." [2] Tropical cyclones include depressions, storms and hurricanes. For data on individual hurricanes, see National Hurricane Center (NHC) at <http://www.nhc.noaa.gov/>.

Source: Except as noted, U.S. National Oceanic and Atmospheric Administration (NOAA), National Weather Service (NWS), Office of Climate, Water, and Weather Services, "Natural Hazard Statistics," <http://www.nws.noaa.gov/om/hazstats.shtml>, accessed September 2013.

Table 406. Number of Earthquakes in the United States: 2000 to 2012

[The United States Geological Survey (USGS) detects but does not generally locate mine blasts (explosions) throughout the United States on any given business day. For more information, see "Routine United States Mining Seismicity" at <http://earthquake.usgs.gov/earthquakes/eqarchives/mineblast/>. For information on "Top Earthquake States," see <http://earthquake.usgs.gov/earthquakes/states/top_states.php>]

Magnitude	2000	2004	2005	2006	2007	2008	2009	2010	2011	2012	Top earthquake states	1974–2003 [1]
Total...............	2,342	3,550	3,685	2,783	2,791	3,618	4,262	8,496	5,237	3,836	Total	21,080
8.0 to 9.9..........	–	–	–	–	–	–	–	–	–	–	AK [2]	1,2053
7.0 to 7.9..........	–	–	1	–	1	–	–	1	1	–	CA	4,895
6.0 to 6.9..........	6	2	4	7	9	9	4	8	3	5	HI	1,533
5.0 to 5.9..........	63	25	47	51	72	85	58	89	51	27	NE	778
4.0 to 4.9..........	281	284	345	346	366	432	288	631	347	271	WA	424
3.0 to 3.9..........	917	1,362	1,475	1,213	1,137	1,486	1,492	3,584	1,838	1,236	ID	404
2.0 to 2.9..........	660	1,336	1,738	1,145	1,173	1,573	2,379	4,132	2,941	2,251	WY	217
1.0 to 1.9..........	–	1	2	7	11	13	26	39	47	43	MT	186
0.1 to 0.9..........	–	–	–	1	–	–	1	–	1	–	UT	139
No magnitude......	415	540	73	13	22	20	14	12	8	3	OR	73

– Represents zero. [1] The total number represents earthquakes of a magnitude range of 3.5 and greater. [2] The number of earthquakes is underreported. Events in the magnitude range of 3.5 to 4.0 in the Aleutian Islands are not recorded on enough seismograph stations to be located.

Source: U.S. Geological Survey, *Earthquake Facts and Statistics*, <http://earthquake.usgs.gov/earthquakes/eqarchives>, accessed September 2013.

Table 407. Wildland Fires, Number, and Acres: 1970 to 2012

[Acres in thousands (3,279 represents 3,279,000), as indicated. As of December 31. There are three distinct types of wildland fires: wildfire, wildland fire use, and prescribed fire. Wildland fire is any nonstructural fire that occurs in the wildland]

Year	Total [1]		Year	Total [1]		State	Top states ranked by wildland acres burned for 2012			
							Wildland [1]		Prescribed [2]	
	Fires (number)	Acres (1,000)		Fires (number)	Acres (1,000)		Fires	Acres	Fires	Acres
1970...........	121,736	3,279	2001........	84,079	3,571	Total	67,774	9,326,238	16,626	1,971,834
1975...........	134,872	1,791	2002........	73,457	7,185	ID	1,149	1,667,654	317	31,064
1980...........	234,892	5,261	2003........	63,629	3,961	OR	963	1,256,049	605	60,838
1985...........	82,591	2,896	2004 [3].......	65,461	8,098	MT	2,213	1,220,655	376	28,594
1990...........	66,481	4,622	2005........	66,753	8,689	CA	7,950	869,599	632	56,830
1995...........	82,234	1,841	2006........	96,385	9,874	NV	944	613,126	41	6,310
1996...........	96,363	6,066	2007........	85,705	9,328	UT	1,534	415,267	82	16,432
1997...........	66,196	2,857	2008........	78,979	5,292	NM	1,029	372,497	59	30,014
1998...........	81,043	1,330	2009........	78,792	5,922	WY	838	357,117	45	7,786
1999...........	92,487	5,626	2010........	71,971	3,423	NE	149	316,015	26	9,064
2000...........	92,250	7,393	2011........	74,126	8,711	AK	416	286,887	24	13,226

[1] Data are for wildland fires only. The data do not include wildland fire use and prescribed fires. [2] Prescribed fire is any fire which is ignited by management action under certain predetermined conditions to meet specific objectives related to hazardous fuels or habitat improvement. [3] 2004 fires and acres do not include state lands for North Carolina.

Source: National Interagency Coordination Center, *Wildland Fire Summary and Statistics Annual Report, 2012*, and earlier reports. See also <http://www.predictiveservices.nifc.gov/intelligence/intelligence.htm>.

Table 408. Highest and Lowest Temperatures by State Through 2012

[Data have been evaluated by the National Oceanic and Atmospheric Administration National Climatic Data Center, and/or by the State Climate Extremes Committee and determined to be valid. The data may come from sources other than official NOAA-supervised weather stations, but are archived, officially recognized observations]

State	Highest temperatures			Lowest temperatures		
	Station	Temperature (°F)	Date	Station	Temperature (°F)	Date
AL............	Centerville	112	Sep. 5, 1925	New Market	-27	Jan. 30, 1966
AK............	Fort Yukon	100	June 27, 1915	Prospect Creek Camp	-80	Jan. 23, 1971
AZ............	Lake Havasu City	128	June 29, 1994	Hawley Lake	-40	Jan. 7, 1971
AR............	Ozark	120	Aug. 10, 1936	Gravette	-29	Feb. 13, 1905
CA............	Greenland Ranch	134	July 10, 1913	Boca	-45	Jan. 20, 1937
CO............	Sedgwick	114	[1] July 11, 1954	Maybell	-61	Feb. 1, 1985
CT............	Danbury	106	[1] July 15, 1995	Coventry	-32	[1] Jan. 22, 1961
DE............	Millsboro	110	July 21, 1930	Millsboro	-17	Jan. 17, 1893
FL............	Monticello	109	June 29, 1931	Tallahassee	-2	Feb. 13, 1899
GA............	Greenville 2 NNW	112	[1] Aug. 20, 1983	CCC Camp F-16	-17	Jan. 27, 1940
HI............	Pahala	100	Apr. 27, 1931	Mauna Kea Obs. 111.2	12	May 17, 1979
ID............	Orofino	118	July 28, 1934	Island Park Dam	-60	Jan. 18, 1943
IL............	East St. Louis	117	July 14, 1954	Congerville	-36	Jan. 5, 1999
IN............	Collegeville	116	July 14, 1936	New Whiteland	-36	Jan. 19, 1994
IA............	Keokuk	118	July 20, 1934	Elkader	-47	[1] Feb. 3, 1996
KS............	Alton	121	July 24, 1936	Lebanon	-40	Feb. 13, 1905
KY............	Greensburg	114	July 28, 1930	Shelbyville	-37	Jan. 19, 1994
LA............	Plain Dealing	114	Aug. 10, 1936	Minden	-16	Feb. 13, 1899
ME............	North Bridgton	105	[1] July 10, 1911	Big Black River	-48	Jan. 16, 2009
MD............	Cumberland & Frederick	109	[1] July 10, 1936	Oakland	-40	Jan. 13, 1912
MA............	New Bedford & Chester	107	[1] Aug. 2, 1975	Chester	-35	[1] Jan. 12, 1981
MI............	Mio Hydro Plant & Stanwood	112	July 13, 1936	Vanderbilt	-51	Feb. 9, 1934
MN............	Beardsley	115	July 29, 1917	Tower	-60	Feb. 2, 1996
MS............	Holly Springs	115	July 29, 1930	Corinth	-19	Jan. 30, 1966
MO............	Warsaw & Union	118	[1] July 14, 1954	Warsaw	-40	Feb. 13, 1905
MT............	Medicine Lake	117	[1] July 5, 1937	Rogers Pass	-70	Jan. 20, 1954
NE............	Minden	118	[1] July 24, 1936	Oshkosh	-47	[1] Dec. 22, 1989
NV............	Laughlin	125	June 29, 1994	San Jacinto	-50	Jan. 8, 1937
NH............	Nashua	106	July 4, 1911	Mt. Washington	-47	Jan. 22, 1885
NJ............	Runyon	110	July 10, 1936	River Vale	-34	Jan. 5, 1904
NM............	Waste Isolat Pilot Plt	122	June 27, 1994	Gavilan	-50	Feb. 1, 1951
NY............	Troy	108	July 22, 1926	Old Forge	-52	Feb. 18, 1979
NC............	Fayetteville	110	Aug. 21, 1983	Mt. Mitchell	-34	Jan. 21, 1985
ND............	Steele	121	July 6, 1936	Parshall	-60	Feb. 15, 1936
OH............	Gallipolis (near)	113	July 21, 1934	Milligan	-39	Feb. 10, 1899
OK............	Altus Irig Res	120	[1] Aug. 12, 1936	Nowata	-31	Feb. 10, 2011
OR............	Pendleton.	119	[1] Aug. 10, 1898	Seneca	-54	[1] Feb. 10, 1933
PA............	Phoenixville	111	July 10, 1936	Smethport	-42	Jan. 5, 1904
RI............	Providence	104	Aug. 2, 1975	Wood River Junction	-25	Jan. 11, 1942
SC............	Columbis Univ. of SC	113	June 29, 2012	Caesars Head	-19	Jan. 21, 1985
SD............	Fort Pierre	120	[1] July 15, 2006	McIntosh	-58	Feb. 17, 1936
TN............	Perryville	113	Aug. 9, 1930	Mountain City	-32	Dec. 30, 1917
TX............	Monahans	120	[1] June 28, 1994	Seminole	-23	Feb. 8, 1933
UT............	Saint George	117	July 5, 1985	East Portal	-69	Jan. 5, 1913
VT............	Vernon	107	July 7, 1912	Bloomfield	-50	Dec. 30, 1933
VA............	Balcony Falls	110	[1] July 15, 1954	Mtn. Lake Bio. Stn.	-30	Jan. 22, 1985
WA............	Ice Harbor Dam	118	[1] Aug. 5, 1961	Mazama & Winthrop	-48	[1] Dec. 30, 1968
WV............	Martinsburg	112	[1] July 10, 1936	Lewisburg	-37	Dec. 30, 1917
WI............	Wisconsin Dells	114	July 13, 1936	Couderay	-55	[1] Feb. 4, 1996
WY............	Diversion Dam	115	[1] July 15, 1988	Riverside R.S.	-66	Feb. 9, 1933

[1] Also on earlier dates at the same or other places.

Source: U.S. National Oceanic and Atmospheric Administration, National Climatic Data Center, State Climate Extremes Committee, "Maximum and Minimum Temperature Records," <http://www.ncdc.noaa.gov/extremes/scec/records>, accessed May 2013.

Table 409. Major U.S. Weather Disasters: 2012

[30.0 represents $30,000,000,000. Covers only weather-related disasters costing $1 billion or more]

Event	Description	Time period	Estimated cost [1] (bil.dol.)	Deaths (number)
U.S. Drought/Heat wave	The most extensive drought in the U.S. since the 1930s. Moderate to extreme drought conditions affected more than half the country for a majority of 2012. The following states were affected: CA, NV, ID, MT, WY, UT, CO, AZ, NM, TX, ND, SD, NE, KS, OK, AR, MO, IA, MN, IL, IN, GA. Costly drought impacts occurred across the central agriculture states resulting in widespread harvest failure for corn, sorghum and soybean crops, among others. The associated summer heat wave also caused 123 direct deaths, but an estimate of the excess mortality due to heat stress is still unknown.	2012	30.0	123
Western Wildfires	Wildfires burned over 9.2 million acres across the U.S. in 2012. This is the 3rd highest annual total since the year 2000. The most damaging wildfires occurred in CO, ID, WY, MT, CA, NV, OR, and WA. Colorado experienced the most costly wildfires (e.g., Waldo Canyon fire) where several hundred residences were destroyed.	Summer-Fall 2012	1.0	8
Sandy	Extensive damage across several northeastern states (MD, DE, NJ, NY, CT, MA, RI) due to high wind and coastal storm surge, particularly NY and NJ. Damage from wind, rain and heavy snow also extended more broadly to NC, VA, WV, OH, PA, and NH, as Sandy merged with a developing Nor'easter. Sandy's impact on major population centers caused widespread interruption to critical water and electrical services and also caused 159 deaths (72 direct, 87 indirect). Sandy also caused the New York Stock Exchange to close for two consecutive business days, which last happened in 1888 due to a major winter storm.	October 2012	65.0	159
Hurricane Isaac	Category 1 hurricane made landfall over Louisiana. Isaac's slow motion and large size led to a large storm surge and flooding rains. This created damage across LA, MS, AL, and FL, including 9 deaths (5 direct, 4 indirect).	August 2012	2.3	9
Plains/East/Northeast Severe Weather	Sustained outbreak of thunderstorms and high winds from a strong derecho event over IL, IN, KY, OH, WV, SC, NC, VA, MD, DC, and NJ.	June 29-July 2, 2012	2.9	28
Rockies/Southwest Severe Weather	Severe storms and damaging hail over CO, NM, and TX, with 25 confirmed tornadoes. Colorado experienced over $1.0 billion in damage due to hail.	June 6-12, 2012	2.6	–
Southern Plains/Midwest/Northeast Severe Weather	Severe storms over TX, OK, KS, MN, PA, and NY, with 27 confirmed tornadoes. Significant damage also from severe hail and straight-line winds.	May 25-30, 2012	2.3	1
Midwest/Ohio Valley Severe Weather	Severe weather over TX, OK, KS, MO, IL, IN, and KY, with 38 confirmed tornadoes. Considerable damage resulting from hail.	April 28-May 1, 2012	3.3	1
Midwest Tornadoes	Outbreak of tornadoes and severe weather over OK, KS, NE, and IA, with 98 confirmed tornadoes including many tornadoes that remained on the ground for an extended time - traveling tens of miles.	April 13-14, 2012	1.1	6
Texas Tornadoes	Outbreak of tornadoes across the greater Dallas-Ft. Worth metropolitan area. Several moderate strength tornadoes (EF-2 and EF-3) affected towns in this area with a total of 22 confirmed tornadoes.	April 2-3, 2012	1.0	–
Southeast/Ohio Valley Tornadoes	Outbreak of tornadoes and severe weather over AL, GA, IN, OH, KY, and TN, with 75 confirmed tornadoes.	March 2-3, 2012	3.1	42

– Represents zero. [1] Represents actual dollar costs at the time of event and is not adjusted for inflation.

Source: U.S. National Oceanic and Atmospheric Administration, National Climatic Data Center, "Billion Dollar U.S. Weather Disasters, 1980–2012," <http://www.ncdc.noaa.gov/billions/events>, accessed September 2013.

Table 410. Highest Temperature of Record—Selected Cities

[In degrees Fahrenheit. Airport data, except as noted. For period of record through 2012]

State	Station	Length of record (years)	Jan.	Feb.	Mar.	Apr.	May	June	July	Aug.	Sept.	Oct.	Nov.	Dec.	Annual [1]
AL....	Mobile	71	84	82	90	94	100	103	104	105	99	93	87	81	105
AK....	Juneau	68	57	57	61	74	82	86	90	84	73	61	56	54	90
AZ....	Phoenix	75	88	92	100	105	113	122	121	117	118	107	96	88	122
AK....	Little Rock	71	83	85	91	95	98	107	112	114	106	97	86	80	114
CA....	Los Angeles	77	91	92	95	102	97	104	97	98	110	106	101	94	110
CA....	Sacramento	62	74	76	88	95	105	115	114	110	108	104	87	73	115
CA....	San Diego	72	88	90	93	98	96	101	99	98	111	107	100	88	111
CA....	San Francisco	85	72	78	85	92	97	106	105	100	103	99	85	75	106
CO..	Denver	70	73	77	84	90	96	105	105	104	97	89	80	75	105
CT....	Hartford	58	72	73	89	96	99	100	103	102	99	91	81	76	103
DE....	Wilmington	65	75	78	86	94	96	100	103	101	100	91	85	75	103
DC..	Washington	71	79	82	89	95	99	104	105	105	101	94	86	79	105
FL....	Jacksonville	71	85	88	91	95	100	103	105	102	100	96	88	84	105
FL....	Miami	70	88	89	93	96	96	98	98	98	97	95	91	89	98
GA..	Atlanta	64	79	80	89	93	95	106	105	104	98	95	84	79	105
HI.....	Honolulu	43	88	88	88	91	93	92	94	93	95	94	93	89	95
ID.....	Boise	73	63	71	81	92	99	109	111	110	102	94	78	65	111
IL.....	Chicago	54	65	72	88	91	97	104	104	101	99	91	78	71	104
IL.....	Peoria	73	70	72	86	92	94	105	104	103	100	93	81	71	105
IN.....	Indianapolis	73	71	76	85	89	93	104	105	102	100	91	81	74	104
IA.....	Des Moines	73	67	73	91	93	98	103	106	108	101	95	81	69	108
KS....	Wichita	60	75	87	89	96	100	110	113	111	108	97	86	83	113
KY....	Louisville	65	77	77	86	91	95	105	106	105	104	93	84	76	106
LA....	New Orleans	66	83	85	89	92	96	101	101	102	101	94	87	84	102
ME..	Portland	72	67	64	88	92	94	98	100	103	95	88	74	71	103
MD..	Baltimore	62	75	79	89	94	98	103	106	105	100	94	83	77	106
MA..	Boston	61	69	70	89	94	95	100	103	102	100	90	79	76	103
MI....	Detroit	54	64	70	86	89	95	104	102	100	98	91	77	69	104
MI....	Sault Ste. Marie	72	45	49	83	85	89	93	97	98	95	81	68	62	98
MN..	Duluth	71	52	55	78	88	90	94	97	97	95	86	71	55	97
MN..	Minneapolis-St. Paul	74	58	61	83	95	97	103	105	102	98	90	77	68	105
MS..	Jackson	49	83	85	89	94	99	105	106	107	104	95	88	84	107
MO..	Kansas City	40	71	78	86	93	95	105	107	109	106	95	82	74	109
MO..	St. Louis	55	76	85	89	93	95	108	108	107	104	94	85	76	107
MT..	Great Falls	75	67	70	78	89	93	101	105	106	98	91	76	69	106
NE....	Omaha	76	69	78	91	97	99	105	114	110	104	96	83	72	114
NV....	Reno	71	71	75	83	90	97	103	108	105	101	93	77	70	108
NH..	Concord	71	69	67	89	95	97	98	102	101	98	90	80	73	102
NJ....	Atlantic City	69	78	75	87	94	99	106	105	103	99	90	84	77	106
NM..	Albuquerque	73	69	76	85	89	98	107	105	101	100	91	77	72	107
NY....	Albany	66	71	68	89	92	94	99	100	99	100	89	82	71	100
NY....	Buffalo	69	72	71	82	94	91	96	97	99	98	87	80	74	99
NY....	New York [2]	144	72	75	86	96	99	101	106	104	102	94	84	75	106
NC..	Charlotte	73	79	82	90	93	100	104	104	104	104	98	85	80	104
NC..	Raleigh	68	80	84	92	95	97	105	105	105	104	98	88	81	105
ND..	Bismarck	73	63	69	81	93	98	111	112	109	105	95	79	65	112
OH..	Cincinnati	51	69	75	84	89	93	102	104	102	100	91	81	75	103
OH..	Cleveland	71	73	74	83	88	92	104	103	102	101	90	82	77	104
OH..	Columbus	73	74	75	85	89	94	102	101	101	100	91	80	76	102
OK..	Oklahoma City	59	80	92	93	100	104	105	110	113	108	96	87	86	110
OR..	Portland	72	66	71	80	90	100	102	107	107	105	92	73	65	107
PA....	Philadelphia	71	74	74	87	95	97	100	104	101	100	96	81	73	104
PA....	Pittsburgh	60	72	76	82	89	91	98	103	100	97	87	82	74	103
RI.....	Providence	59	69	72	85	98	96	97	102	104	100	86	78	77	104
SC....	Columbia	65	84	84	91	94	101	109	107	107	101	101	90	83	107
SD....	Sioux Falls	67	66	70	87	94	100	110	108	108	104	94	81	63	110
TN....	Memphis	71	79	81	86	94	99	104	108	107	103	95	86	81	108
TN....	Nashville	73	78	84	86	91	97	109	107	106	105	94	84	79	107
TX....	Dallas-Fort Worth	59	88	95	96	101	103	113	110	110	111	102	89	89	113
TX....	El Paso	73	80	83	90	98	105	114	112	108	104	96	87	80	114
TX....	Houston	43	84	91	91	95	99	105	104	109	109	96	89	85	109
UT....	Salt Lake City	84	63	69	80	89	99	104	107	106	100	89	75	69	107
VT....	Burlington	69	66	62	84	91	93	100	100	101	98	85	75	67	101
VA....	Norfolk	64	80	82	88	97	100	101	105	104	99	95	86	80	105
VA....	Richmond	83	81	83	93	96	100	104	105	104	103	99	86	81	105
WA..	Seattle-Tacoma	68	64	70	78	85	93	96	103	99	98	89	74	64	103
WA..	Spokane	65	59	63	71	90	96	101	103	108	98	86	67	56	108
WV....	Charleston	65	79	79	89	94	94	103	104	104	102	93	85	80	104
WI....	Milwaukee	72	63	68	84	91	93	101	103	103	98	89	77	68	103
WY..	Cheyenne	77	66	71	74	83	91	100	100	98	95	84	75	69	100
PR....	San Juan	58	92	96	96	97	96	97	95	97	97	98	96	94	98

[1] Represents the highest observed temperature in any month. [2] City office data.

Source: U.S. National Oceanic and Atmospheric Administration, *Comparative Climatic Data*, 2012. See also <http://www.ncdc.noaa.gov/statistical-weather-and-climate-information>.

Table 411. Lowest Temperature of Record—Selected Cities

[In degrees Fahrenheit. Airport data, except as noted. For period of record through 2012]

State	Station	Length of record (years)	Jan.	Feb.	Mar.	Apr.	May	June	July	Aug.	Sept.	Oct.	Nov.	Dec.	Annual[1]
AL.....	Mobile	71	3	11	21	32	43	49	60	59	42	30	22	8	3
AK....	Juneau	68	-22	-22	-15	6	25	31	36	27	23	11	-5	-21	-22
AZ.....	Phoenix	75	17	22	25	32	40	50	61	60	47	34	25	22	17
AR....	Little Rock	71	-4	-5	11	28	40	46	54	52	37	29	17	-1	-5
CA....	Los Angeles	77	23	32	34	39	43	48	49	51	47	41	34	32	23
CA....	Sacramento	62	21	23	26	31	36	41	48	49	42	36	26	18	18
CA....	San Diego	72	29	36	39	41	48	51	55	57	51	43	38	34	29
CA....	San Francisco	85	24	25	30	31	36	41	43	42	38	34	25	20	20
CO....	Denver	70	-25	-30	-11	-2	21	30	43	41	17	3	-8	-25	-30
CT....	Hartford	58	-26	-21	-6	9	28	35	44	36	30	17	1	-14	-26
DE....	Wilmington	65	-14	-6	2	18	30	41	48	43	36	24	14	-7	-14
DC....	Washington	71	-5	4	11	24	34	47	54	49	39	29	16	1	-5
FL.....	Jacksonville	71	7	19	23	31	45	47	61	59	48	33	21	11	7
FL.....	Miami	70	30	32	32	46	53	60	69	68	68	51	39	30	30
GA....	Atlanta	64	-8	5	10	26	37	46	53	55	36	28	3	0	-8
HI.....	Honolulu	43	53	53	55	57	60	65	66	65	66	61	57	54	53
ID.....	Boise	73	-17	-15	6	19	22	31	35	34	23	11	-3	-25	-25
IL......	Chicago	54	-27	-19	-8	7	24	36	40	41	28	17	1	-25	-27
IL......	Peoria	73	-25	-19	-10	14	25	39	47	41	26	19	-2	-23	-25
IN.....	Indianapolis	73	-27	-21	-7	16	28	37	44	41	28	17	-2	-23	-27
IA.....	Des Moines	73	-24	-26	-22	9	30	38	47	40	26	14	-4	-22	-26
KS....	Wichita	60	-12	-21	-2	15	31	43	51	48	31	18	1	-16	-21
KY....	Louisville	65	-22	-19	-1	22	31	42	50	46	33	23	-1	-15	-22
LA.....	New Orleans	66	14	16	25	32	41	50	60	60	42	35	24	11	11
ME....	Portland	72	-26	-39	-21	8	23	33	40	33	23	15	3	-21	-39
MD....	Baltimore	62	-7	-3	6	20	32	40	50	45	35	25	13	0	-7
MA....	Boston	61	-12	-4	5	16	34	45	50	47	38	28	15	-7	-12
MI.....	Detroit	54	-21	-15	-4	10	25	36	41	38	29	17	9	-10	-21
MI.....	Sault Ste. Marie	72	-36	-35	-24	-2	18	26	36	29	25	16	-10	-31	-36
MN....	Duluth	71	-39	-39	-29	-5	17	27	35	32	22	8	-23	-34	-39
MN....	Minneapolis-St. Paul	74	-34	-32	-32	2	18	34	43	39	26	13	-17	-29	-34
MS....	Jackson	49	2	10	15	27	38	47	51	54	35	26	17	4	2
MO....	Kansas City	40	-17	-19	-10	12	30	42	51	43	31	17	1	-23	-23
MO....	St. Louis	55	-18	-12	-5	22	31	43	51	47	36	23	1	-16	-18
MT....	Great Falls	75	-37	-35	-29	-8	12	31	36	30	16	-11	-25	-43	-43
NE....	Omaha	76	-23	-21	-16	5	27	38	44	43	25	13	-9	-23	-23
NV....	Reno	71	-16	-16	-2	13	18	21	33	24	20	8	1	-16	-16
NH....	Concord	71	-33	-37	-16	8	21	30	35	29	21	10	-5	-22	-37
NJ.....	Atlantic City	69	-10	-11	3	12	25	37	42	40	32	20	10	-7	-11
NM....	Albuquerque	73	-17	-7	8	19	16	40	52	50	37	21	-7	-7	-17
NY....	Albany	66	-28	-21	-21	10	26	36	40	34	24	16	5	-22	-28
NY....	Buffalo	69	-16	-20	-7	12	26	35	43	38	32	20	9	-10	-20
NY....	New York[2]	144	-6	-15	3	12	32	44	52	50	39	28	5	-13	-15
NC....	Charlotte	73	-5	5	4	21	32	45	53	50	39	24	11	2	-5
NC....	Raleigh	68	-9	0	11	23	31	38	48	46	37	19	11	4	-9
ND....	Bismarck	73	-44	-43	-31	-12	15	30	35	33	11	-10	-30	-43	-44
OH....	Cincinnati	51	-25	-11	-11	15	27	39	47	43	31	16	1	-20	-25
OH....	Cleveland	71	-20	-15	-5	10	25	31	41	38	32	19	3	-15	-20
OH....	Columbus	73	-22	-13	-6	14	25	35	43	39	31	20	5	-17	-22
OK....	Oklahoma City	59	-4	-5	3	20	36	47	53	51	36	16	11	-8	-8
OR....	Portland	72	-2	-3	19	29	29	39	43	44	34	26	13	6	-3
PA.....	Philadelphia	71	-7	-4	7	19	28	44	51	44	35	25	15	1	-7
PA.....	Pittsburgh	60	-22	-12	-1	14	26	34	42	39	31	16	-1	-12	-22
RI.....	Providence	59	-13	-7	1	14	29	41	48	40	33	20	6	-10	-13
SC....	Columbia	65	-1	5	4	26	34	44	54	53	40	23	12	4	-1
SD....	Sioux Falls	67	-36	-31	-23	5	17	33	38	34	22	9	-17	-28	-36
TN....	Memphis	71	-4	-11	12	28	38	48	52	48	36	25	9	-13	-13
TN....	Nashville	73	-17	-13	2	23	34	42	51	47	36	26	-1	-10	-17
TX.....	Dallas-Fort Worth	59	4	7	15	29	41	51	59	56	43	29	20	-1	-1
TX.....	El Paso	73	-8	1	14	23	31	46	57	56	41	25	1	5	-8
TX.....	Houston	43	12	3	22	31	44	52	62	60	48	29	19	7	3
UT....	Salt Lake City	84	-22	-30	2	14	25	35	40	37	27	16	-14	-21	-30
VT.....	Burlington	69	-30	-30	-20	2	24	33	39	35	25	15	-2	-26	-30
VA.....	Norfolk	64	-3	-8	18	28	36	45	54	49	45	27	20	7	-3
VA.....	Richmond	83	-12	-10	10	23	31	40	51	46	35	21	10	-1	-12
WA....	Seattle-Tacoma	68	0	1	11	29	28	38	43	44	35	28	6	6	0
WA....	Spokane	65	-22	-24	-7	17	24	33	37	35	22	7	-21	-25	-25
WV....	Charleston	65	-16	-12	0	19	26	33	46	41	34	17	6	-12	-16
WI....	Milwaukee	72	-26	-26	-10	12	21	33	40	44	28	18	-5	-20	-26
WY....	Cheyenne	77	-29	-34	-21	-8	16	25	38	36	8	-1	-16	-28	-34
PR....	San Juan	58	61	62	60	64	66	69	69	70	69	46	66	59	46

[1] Represents the lowest observed temperature in any month. [2] City office data.

Source: U.S. National Oceanic and Atmospheric Administration, *Comparative Climatic Data*, 2012. See also <http://www.ncdc.noaa.gov/statistical-weather-and-climate-information>.

Table 412. Snow, Hail, Ice Pellets, and Sleet—Selected Cities

[In inches. Airport data, except as noted. For period of record through 2012. T denotes trace. Stations may show snowfall (hail) during the warm months]

State	Station	Length of record (years)	Jan.	Feb.	Mar.	Apr.	May	June	July	Aug.	Sept.	Oct.	Nov.	Dec.	Annual
AL....	Mobile	70	0.1	0.1	0.1	T	T	–	T	–	–	–	T	0.1	0.4
AK....	Juneau	68	26.7	18.6	15.3	3.5	T	T	–	–	T	1.1	12.8	21.2	99.0
AZ....	Phoenix	62	T	–	T	T	T	–	–	–	–	T	–	T	T
AR....	Little Rock	61	2.5	1.7	0.5	T	T	T	–	–	–	T	0.2	0.8	5.5
CA....	Los Angeles	62	T	T	T	–	–	–	–	–	–	–	–	T	T
CA....	Sacramento	50	T	T	T	–	T	–	–	–	–	–	–	T	T
CA....	San Diego	60	T	–	T	T	–	–	–	–	–	–	T	T	T
CA....	San Francisco	69	–	T	T	–	–	–	–	–	–	–	–	–	T
CO...	Denver	68	7.9	7.6	12.1	8.3	1.6	–	T	T	1.6	4.1	8.5	7.9	59.6
CT....	Hartford	55	13.8	12.3	9.7	1.5	–	T	–	–	–	0.3	2.1	11.0	51.0
DE. ..	Wilmington	62	6.7	7.1	3.3	0.2	T	T	T	–	–	0.1	0.9	3.5	22.1
DC. ..	Washington	69	5.1	5.6	2.3	2.3	T	T	T	T	–	–	0.8	3.2	19.5
FL....	Jacksonville	60	T	–	–	T	T	–	–	–	–	–	–	–	T
FL....	Miami	59	–	–	–	–	T	–	–	–	–	–	–	–	T
GA....	Atlanta	73	1.0	0.5	0.5	T	–	–	T	–	–	T	T	0.2	2.2
HI....	Honolulu	52	–	–	–	–	–	–	–	–	–	–	–	–	–
ID....	Boise	73	6.3	3.7	1.7	0.6	0.1	T	T	T	T	0.1	2.4	5.8	20.7
IL....	Chicago	53	11.4	8.7	6.2	1.6	0.1	T	T	T	T	0.4	2.1	8.7	39.5
IL....	Peoria	69	6.7	5.6	4.2	0.8	T	T	T	–	T	0.1	2.1	6.5	26.1
IN....	Indianapolis	81	7.1	5.8	3.5	0.5	T	T	T	–	T	0.2	1.9	5.7	24.6
IA....	Des Moines	69	8.5	7.7	5.9	1.9	T	T	T	–	T	0.3	3.1	7.0	34.5
KS....	Wichita	59	4.0	4.3	2.8	0.2	T	T	T	T	T	–	1.4	3.5	16.2
KY....	Louisville	65	5.2	4.3	3.2	0.1	T	T	T	T	T	0.1	1.0	2.6	16.6
LA....	New Orleans	51	T	0.1	T	T	T	–	–	–	–	–	T	0.1	0.2
ME. ..	Portland	72	19.2	16.3	13.0	3.1	0.2	–	T	–	T	0.3	3.3	15.0	70.5
MD. ..	Baltimore	62	6.0	7.5	3.6	0.1	T	T	T	–	–	T	1.0	3.6	22.0
MA. ..	Boston	75	13.1	11.8	7.8	0.9	–	T	T	T	–	–	1.3	8.4	43.7
MI....	Detroit	54	11.4	10.1	6.9	2.0	T	–	–	–	T	0.2	2.5	10.1	43.3
MI....	Sault Ste. Marie	65	28.9	18.5	14.3	5.9	0.5	T	T	T	0.1	2.5	15.4	30.7	116.7
MN....	Duluth	69	17.4	12.1	13.9	6.8	0.8	T	T	T	0.1	1.7	12.4	16.1	81.5
MN....	Minneapolis-St. Paul	70	10.3	8.3	10.5	2.8	0.1	T	T	T	T	0.5	7.4	10.3	50.4
MS....	Jackson	38	0.5	0.2	0.2	T	–	–	–	T	–	–	T	0.1	1.0
MO...	Kansas City	78	5.4	4.8	3.5	0.8	T	T	T	T	T	0.1	1.3	4.5	20.5
MO...	St. Louis	76	5.4	4.5	3.8	0.5	T	T	T	–	–	T	1.4	4.2	19.8
MT....	Great Falls	75	9.4	8.8	10.4	8.0	1.9	0.4	T	0.1	1.5	3.5	7.7	8.5	60.3
NE. ..	Omaha	77	7.6	7.0	6.1	1.1	0.1	T	T	T	T	0.3	2.6	6.0	30.8
NV. ..	Reno	63	5.7	5.5	4.1	1.2	0.8	–	–	–	–	0.3	2.5	4.8	25.1
NH. ..	Concord	71	18.4	14.4	11.5	2.8	0.1	T	–	–	T	0.4	3.8	14.2	65.9
NJ....	Atlantic City	63	5.2	6.0	2.6	0.3	T	T	T	–	–	T	0.4	2.9	17.5
NM. ..	Albuquerque	73	2.5	2.1	1.8	0.6	T	T	T	T	T	0.1	1.2	3.0	11.3
NY. ..	Albany	66	16.9	13.8	11.2	2.8	0.1	T	T	–	T	0.3	3.8	14.7	64.0
NY. ..	Buffalo	69	24.5	17.9	12.3	3.2	0.2	T	T	T	T	0.7	10.7	24.1	94.2
NY. ..	New York [1]	144	7.9	8.8	5.1	0.9	T	–	T	–	–	–	0.9	5.7	29.4
NC. ..	Charlotte	73	2.2	1.8	1.2	T	T	T	–	–	–	T	0.1	0.5	5.8
NC. ..	Raleigh	68	2.8	2.6	1.3	T	T	T	–	–	–	–	0.1	0.9	7.7
ND. ..	Bismarck	73	7.8	7.0	8.5	4.0	0.9	T	T	T	T	0.2	1.9	6.8	44.9
OH. ..	Cincinnati	65	7.2	5.8	4.2	0.5	–	T	T	T	T	–	0.3	2.0	4.1	24.2
OH. ..	Cleveland	71	14.9	13.0	10.8	2.9	0.1	T	T	T	T	0.6	4.8	12.4	59.8
OH. ..	Columbus	65	9.0	6.6	4.6	1.0	T	T	T	–	T	0.1	2.2	5.4	28.9
OK. ..	Oklahoma City	73	3.2	2.6	1.5	T	T	T	T	T	T	T	0.6	2.1	10.0
OR. ..	Portland	55	3.2	1.1	0.4	T	–	–	T	–	T	–	0.4	1.4	6.5
PA....	Philadelphia	70	6.2	7.6	3.5	0.3	T	T	T	–	–	–	0.7	3.8	22.3
PA....	Pittsburgh	60	12.4	10.3	8.0	1.8	0.1	T	T	T	T	0.4	3.4	8.4	44.6
RI....	Providence	59	10.0	9.5	7.1	0.7	0.2	–	–	–	–	0.1	1.3	7.6	36.7
SC....	Columbia	64	0.6	0.9	0.2	T	T	–	–	–	–	–	T	0.3	2.0
SD. ..	Sioux Falls	67	7.0	8.0	9.0	3.3	T	T	T	T	T	0.9	5.8	7.6	41.6
TN....	Memphis	55	2.3	1.5	0.9	T	T	T	–	–	–	T	0.1	0.6	5.4
TN....	Nashville	66	3.5	3.0	1.5	–	T	–	–	T	–	–	0.4	1.4	9.9
TX....	Dallas-Fort Worth	54	1.1	1.3	0.2	T	T	–	–	–	–	T	0.1	0.3	3.0
TX....	El Paso	63	1.3	0.8	0.4	0.3	T	T	–	–	T	–	1.0	1.7	5.5
TX....	Houston	78	0.2	0.2	T	T	T	T	–	–	–	–	T	–	0.4
UT....	Salt Lake City	84	13.1	9.9	8.9	4.9	0.6	T	T	T	0.1	1.3	7.1	12.2	58.2
VT....	Burlington	69	19.8	17.2	13.7	4.0	0.2	–	T	T	T	0.2	6.5	19.1	80.9
VA....	Norfolk	62	3.1	2.9	1.0	–	T	T	T	–	–	–	–	1.3	8.3
VA....	Richmond	73	5.0	3.8	2.5	0.1	T	–	T	–	–	T	0.4	2.2	14.0
WA...	Seattle-Tacoma	56	5.0	1.6	1.3	0.1	T	–	–	–	T	–	1.1	2.4	11.4
WA...	Spokane	65	15.1	7.3	4.1	0.8	0.1	T	–	T	T	0.4	6.5	14.7	49.0
WV...	Charleston	58	10.8	8.7	5.1	0.9	–	T	T	T	–	0.4	2.4	5.5	33.9
WI....	Milwaukee	72	13.9	10.1	8.4	2.0	0.1	T	T	T	T	0.2	3.0	10.9	48.7
WY...	Cheyenne	77	6.0	6.7	11.8	9.4	3.5	0.2	T	T	1.1	4.2	7.2	6.9	56.9
PR. ..	San Juan	57	–	–	–	–	–	–	–	–	T	–	–	–	T

– Represents zero. [1] City office data.

Source: U.S. National Oceanic and Atmospheric Administration, *Comparative Climatic Data*, 2012. See also <http://www.ncdc.noaa.gov/statistical-weather-and-climate-information>.

Table 413. Cloudiness, Average Wind Speed, Heating and Cooling Degree Days, and Average Relative Humidity—Selected Cities

[Airport data, except as noted. For period of record through 2012, except Heating and Cooling Degree Days, these are for the 1981 - 2010 period. M=morning. A=afternoon]

State	Station	Cloudiness-average percentage of days [1] — Length of record (yr.)	Annual	Average wind speed (miles per hour, m.p.h.) — Length of record (yr.)	Annual	Jan.	July	Heating degree days	Cooling degree days	Length of record (yr.)	Annual M	Annual A	Jan. M	Jan. A	July M	July A
AL.....	Mobile	47	72.1	64	8.7	10.0	6.9	1,655	2,536	50	81	68	89	69	86	67
AK.....	Juneau	47	87.9	67	8.1	7.9	7.5	8,351	–	46	79	75	79	68	81	71
AZ.....	Phoenix	57	42.3	67	6.2	5.3	7.1	935	4,607	52	62	31	42	20	48	22
AR....	Little Rock	35	67.5	70	7.7	8.4	6.7	3,052	2,206	48	78	67	84	64	81	65
CA....	Los Angeles	60	59.8	64	7.5	6.7	7.9	1,419	551	53	70	60	85	68	79	66
CA....	Sacramento	49	48.5	62	7.7	6.7	8.9	2,619	1,178	26	90	69	77	29	83	46
CA....	San Diego	55	60.0	72	7.0	6.0	7.5	1,225	720	52	71	57	82	67	77	63
CA....	San Francisco	68	56.2	85	10.6	7.2	13.6	2,653	164	53	86	68	86	60	84	63
CO....	Denver	61	68.5	56	8.7	8.7	8.3	6,058	769	44	62	50	66	34	66	41
CT.....	Hartford	41	77.5	58	8.4	8.9	7.3	5,839	805	53	72	56	77	51	76	52
DE.....	Wilmington	47	73.4	64	9.0	9.8	7.8	4,819	1,145	65	75	59	78	54	78	55
DC....	Washington	48	73.8	64	9.4	10.0	8.3	4,031	1,549	52	70	55	75	52	74	53
FL.....	Jacksonville	47	74.2	63	7.8	8.1	7.0	1,349	2,665	76	87	56	88	58	88	56
FL.....	Miami	46	79.7	63	9.2	9.4	7.9	128	4,575	48	83	58	81	63	82	61
GA....	Atlanta	61	69.9	74	9.1	10.4	7.7	2,768	1,883	52	78	58	86	58	81	55
HI.....	Honolulu	47	75.3	63	11.2	9.4	13.1	–	4,628	43	79	61	66	51	71	56
ID.....	Boise	56	67.1	73	8.7	7.9	8.4	5,514	942	73	80	70	53	20	68	43
IL......	Chicago	37	77.0	54	10.3	11.6	8.4	6,340	843	54	77	71	80	63	79	66
IL......	Peoria	52	73.9	69	9.7	10.7	7.8	5,831	1,039	53	79	72	85	67	82	68
IN.....	Indianapolis	64	76.0	64	9.6	10.9	7.5	5,348	1,058	53	81	70	85	58	83	61
IA.....	Des Moines	46	71.3	63	10.7	11.4	8.9	6,622	777	51	76	71	81	65	79	64
KS.....	Wichita	39	64.9	59	12.2	11.9	11.2	4,626	1,580	59	78	67	77	57	79	62
KY.....	Louisville	47	74.6	65	8.3	9.5	6.8	4,268	1,444	52	77	64	83	56	80	58
LA....	New Orleans	47	72.3	64	8.2	9.3	6.1	1,280	3,005	64	83	70	89	71	86	68
ME....	Portland	54	72.3	72	8.7	9.0	7.6	7,107	359	72	75	60	79	59	78	59
MD....	Baltimore	45	71.2	62	8.6	9.1	7.5	4,764	1,164	59	72	56	78	52	77	53
MA....	Boston	60	73.2	55	12.3	13.6	11.0	5,681	747	48	68	57	72	56	72	58
MI.....	Detroit	37	79.5	54	10.1	11.6	8.5	6,168	823	54	80	69	80	53	81	59
MI.....	Sault Ste. Marie	54	81.9	71	9.1	9.4	7.8	8,663	196	71	80	73	87	61	84	66
MN....	Duluth	47	79.0	63	11.0	11.5	9.4	9,444	204	51	77	73	84	66	80	69
MN....	Minneapolis-St. Paul	57	74.0	74	10.5	10.5	9.4	7,580	753	53	75	70	78	62	77	65
MS....	Jackson	30	69.6	49	6.8	8.0	5.2	2,218	2,336	49	84	70	91	69	88	67
MO....	Kansas City	23	67.1	40	10.6	11.0	9.1	4,686	1,671	40	76	69	82	68	79	68
MO....	St. Louis	47	72.4	63	9.6	10.6	8.0	4,535	1,646	52	78	69	81	63	80	65
MT....	Great Falls	57	78.4	71	12.5	14.7	10.0	7,726	298	51	66	60	67	30	68	46
NE....	Omaha	49	69.6	76	10.5	10.9	8.8	6,167	1,113	48	78	70	83	67	80	67
NV....	Reno	53	56.7	70	6.6	5.6	7.2	4,924	839	49	78	50	56	17	67	31
NH....	Concord	54	75.3	70	6.7	7.2	5.7	7,235	452	47	76	58	82	51	80	53
NJ....	Atlantic City	37	74.2	54	9.7	10.6	8.3	4,905	1,055	48	77	57	81	56	80	56
NM....	Albuquerque	56	54.2	73	8.9	8.0	8.9	4,179	1,322	52	66	38	58	27	58	29
NY....	Albany	57	81.1	74	8.9	9.8	7.5	6,680	598	47	77	63	79	55	79	57
NY....	Buffalo	52	85.2	73	11.8	13.8	10.2	6,617	544	52	79	72	77	55	79	62
NY....	New York [2]	42	70.8	74	9.1	10.3	7.5	4,750	1,105	78	67	58	74	55	72	56
NC....	Charlotte	49	70.2	63	7.4	7.8	6.6	3,388	1,518	52	77	54	84	55	81	53
NC....	Raleigh	47	69.7	63	7.5	8.1	6.7	3,247	1,730	48	78	53	86	56	83	53
ND....	Bismarck	56	74.5	73	10.2	10.0	9.2	8,558	520	53	76	72	82	58	80	65
OH....	Cincinnati	44	77.8	65	9.0	10.4	7.2	4,958	1,067	50	80	68	84	57	82	59
OH....	Cleveland	54	81.9	71	10.5	12.2	8.6	5,762	817	52	78	70	80	56	79	62
OH....	Columbus	46	80.3	63	8.3	9.8	6.5	5,250	1,035	53	77	67	82	55	80	58
OK....	Oklahoma City	44	61.9	64	12.2	12.5	10.8	3,365	2,099	47	75	64	77	59	78	63
OR....	Portland	47	81.3	64	7.9	9.8	7.6	4,278	424	72	85	75	81	44	85	59
PA....	Philadelphia	55	74.5	72	9.5	10.3	8.2	4,613	1,301	53	72	58	77	52	75	54
PA.....	Pittsburgh	43	83.8	60	8.9	10.3	7.3	5,710	736	52	77	65	82	53	79	57
RI.....	Providence	42	73.2	59	10.3	10.8	9.4	5,618	744	49	71	56	75	55	75	55
SC....	Columbia	48	68.5	64	6.8	7.2	6.3	2,552	2,170	46	81	52	86	52	85	50
SD....	Sioux Falls	50	71.2	64	11.0	10.9	9.8	7,706	690	49	78	72	82	64	81	68
TN.....	Memphis	43	67.7	64	8.8	10.0	7.5	2,964	2,258	73	76	65	82	62	79	62
TN.....	Nashville	54	72.0	71	7.9	9.0	6.5	3,688	1,646	47	77	68	85	66	81	65
TX.....	Dallas-Fort Worth	42	63.0	59	10.7	11.0	9.7	2,284	2,756	49	76	65	75	57	78	63
TX.....	El Paso	53	47.1	70	8.8	8.3	8.3	2,474	2,331	52	63	33	60	29	55	27
TX.....	Houston	26	75.3	43	7.6	8.1	6.6	1,291	2,940	43	83	71	90	69	88	70
UT....	Salt Lake City	69	65.8	83	8.8	7.5	9.5	5,607	1,160	52	79	70	50	21	67	44
VT....	Burlington	52	84.1	69	8.9	9.6	8.0	7,434	491	47	73	64	77	53	77	58
VA....	Norfolk	47	71.0	64	10.4	11.3	8.9	3,377	1,629	64	74	58	80	58	78	57
VA....	Richmond	50	72.7	64	7.7	8.1	6.9	3,773	1,549	78	79	56	83	55	82	53
WA....	Seattle-Tacoma	51	84.2	64	8.8	9.5	8.1	4,697	189	53	82	75	81	49	84	62
WA....	Spokane	48	76.4	65	8.9	8.7	8.6	6,593	450	53	86	79	64	26	78	52
WV....	Charleston	47	82.2	65	5.8	6.9	4.8	4,478	1,097	65	78	62	89	59	83	56
WI.....	Milwaukee	55	75.3	72	11.5	12.6	9.7	6,894	641	52	75	70	80	66	79	68
WY....	Cheyenne	60	71.0	55	12.8	15.0	10.4	7,111	348	53	57	50	68	37	65	45
PR....	San Juan	40	80.0	57	8.3	8.3	9.6	–	5,855	57	81	65	78	67	79	66

– Represents zero. [1] Percent of days that are either partly cloudy or cloudy. [2] Airport data for sunshine.

Source: U.S. National Oceanic and Atmospheric Administration, *Comparative Climatic Data*, 2012. See also <http://www.ncdc.noaa.gov/statistical-weather-and-climate-information>.

Table 414. Significant Flood Event Losses Covered by the National Flood Insurance Program: 1978 to 2012

[In nominal dollars. Covers period 1978 through January 31, 2013]

Event	Date	Number of Paid Losses	Amount Paid ($)	Average Paid Loss ($)
Hurricane Katrina	Aug. 2005	167,722	16,273,634,517	97,027
Hurricane Ike	Sept. 2008	46,418	2,664,781,987	57,408
Hurricane Sandy	Oct. 2012	63,723	2,649,099,182	41,572
Hurricane Ivan	Sept. 2004	27,658	1,590,436,206	57,504
Hurricane Irene	Aug. 2011	43,856	1,303,527,799	29,723
Tropical Storm Allison	June 2001	30,663	1,103,877,235	36,000
Louisiana Flood	May 1995	31,343	585,071,593	18,667
Hurricane Isabel	Sept. 2003	19,869	493,452,308	24,835
Tropical Storm Isaac	Aug. 2012	11,287	487,738,772	43,212
Hurricane Rita	Sept. 2005	9,506	472,382,374	49,693
Hurricane Floyd	Sept. 1999	20,437	462,252,753	22,618
Tropical Storm Lee	Sept. 2011	9,758	444,770,502	45,580
Hurricane Opal	Oct. 1995	10,343	405,527,543	39,208
Hurricane Hugo	Sept. 1989	12,840	376,433,739	29,317
Hurricane Wilma	Oct. 2005	9,614	365,030,822	37,969
Nor'Easter	Dec. 1992	25,142	346,150,356	13,768
Midwest Flood	June 1993	10,472	272,819,515	26,052
PA, NJ, NY Floods	June 2006	6,423	228,743,070	35,613
Torrential Rain – TN	Apr. 2010	4,098	227,684,455	55,560
Nor'Easter	Apr. 2007	8,636	225,657,504	26,130

Source: U.S. Department of Homeland Security, Federal Emergency Management Agency, National Flood Insurance Program Statistics, "Significant Floods (1978 - Current Month)," <http://www.fema.gov/policy-claim-statistics-flood-insurance/policy-claim-statistics-flood-insurance/policy-claim-13>, accessed April 2013.

Table 415. Threatened and Endangered Wildlife and Plant Species: 2013

[As of May 2013. Endangered species: One in danger of becoming extinct throughout all or a significant part of its natural range. Threatened species: One likely to become endangered in the foreseeable future]

Item	Mammals	Birds	Reptiles	Amphibians	Fishes	Snails	Clams	Crustaceans	Insects	Arachnids	Plants
Total listings	360	317	124	35	165	41	85	22	71	12	821
Endangered species, total	325	286	83	24	94	28	74	19	61	12	668
United States	69	78	14	16	83	27	72	19	57	12	667
Foreign	256	208	69	8	11	1	2	–	4	–	1
Threatened species, total	35	31	41	11	71	13	11	3	10	–	153
United States	15	15	22	10	70	13	11	3	10	–	151
Foreign	20	16	19	1	1	–	–	–	–	–	2

– Represents zero.

Source: U.S. Fish and Wildlife Service, Environmental Conservation Online System, "Summary of Listed Species Listed Populations and Recovery Plans," <http://ecos.fws.gov/tess_public/pub/boxScore.jsp>, accessed May 2013.

Elections

This section relates primarily to presidential, congressional, and gubernatorial elections. Also presented are summary tables on congressional legislation; state legislatures; Hispanic and female officeholders; population of voting age; voter participation; and campaign finances.

Official statistics on federal elections, collected by the Clerk of the House, are published biennially in Statistics of the Presidential and Congressional Election and Statistics of the Congressional Election. Federal elections data also appear in the U.S. Congress, *Congressional Directory*, and in official state documents. Data on reported registration and voting for social and economic groups are obtained by the U.S. Census Bureau as part of the Current Population Survey (CPS) and are published in Current Population Reports, Series P20 (see text, Section 1).

Almost all federal, state, and local governmental units in the United States conduct elections for political offices and other purposes. The conduct of elections is regulated by state laws or, in some cities and counties, by local charter. An exception is that the U.S. Constitution prescribes the basis of representation in Congress and the manner of electing the president and grants to Congress the right to regulate the times, places, and manner of electing federal officers. Amendments to the Constitution have prescribed national criteria for voting eligibility. The 15th Amendment, adopted in 1870, gave all citizens the right to vote regardless of race, color, or previous condition of servitude. The 19th Amendment, adopted in 1920, further extended the right to vote to all citizens regardless of sex. The payment of poll taxes as a prerequisite to voting in federal elections was banned by the 24th Amendment in 1964. In 1971, as a result of the 26th Amendment, eligibility to vote in national elections was extended to all citizens, 18 years old and over.

Presidential election— The Constitution specifies how the president and vice president are selected. Each state elects, by popular vote, a group of electors equal in number to its total of members of Congress. The 23rd Amendment, adopted in 1961, grants the District of Columbia three presidential electors, a number equal to that of the least populous state. Subsequent to the election, the electors meet in their respective states to vote for president and vice president. Usually, each elector votes for the candidate receiving the most popular votes in his or her state. A majority vote of all electors is necessary to elect the president and vice president. If no candidate receives a majority, the House of Representatives, with each state having one vote, is empowered to elect the president and vice president, again, with a majority of votes required.

The 22nd Amendment to the Constitution, adopted in 1951, limits presidential tenure to two elective terms of 4 years each or to one elective term for any person who, upon succession to the presidency, has held the office or acted as President for more than 2 years.

Congressional election— The Constitution provides that representatives be apportioned among the states according to their population, that a census of population be taken every 10 years as a basis for apportionment, and that each state have at least one representative. At the time of each apportionment, Congress decides what the total number of representatives will be. Since 1912, the total has been 435, except during 1960 to 1962 when it increased to 437, adding one representative each for Alaska and Hawaii. The total reverted to 435 after reapportionment following the 1960 census. Members are elected for 2-year terms, all terms covering the same period. The District of Columbia, American Samoa, Guam, and the Virgin Islands each elect one nonvoting delegate, and Puerto Rico elects a nonvoting resident commissioner.

The Senate is composed of 100 members, two from each state, who are elected to serve for a term of 6 years. One-third of the Senate is elected every 2 years. Senators were originally chosen by the state legislatures. The 17th Amendment to the Constitution, adopted in 1913, prescribed that senators be elected by popular vote.

Voter eligibility and participation—The Census Bureau publishes estimates of the population of voting age and the percent casting votes in each state for presidential and congressional election years. These voting-age estimates include a number of persons who meet the age requirement but are not eligible to vote, (e.g. aliens and some institutionalized persons). In addition, since 1964, voter participation and voter characteristics data have been collected during November of election years as part of the CPS. These survey data include noncitizens in the voting- age population estimates, but exclude members of the Armed Forces and the institutional population.

Statistical reliability— For a discussion of statistical collection and estimation, sampling procedures, and measures of statistical reliability applicable to Census Bureau data, see Appendix III.

Table 416. Participation in Elections for President and U.S. Representatives: 1934 to 2012

[77,997 represents 77,997,000. As of November, except as noted. Estimated resident population 21 years old and over, 1934-70, except as noted, and 18 years old and over thereafter; includes Armed Forces stationed in the U.S. Prior to 1958, excludes Alaska and prior to 1960, excludes Hawaii. District of Columbia is included in votes cast for President beginning 1964]

Year	Resident population (includes aliens) of voting age [1] (1,000)	Votes cast			
		For President (1,000)	Percent of voting-age population	For U.S. Representatives (1,000)	Percent of voting-age population
1934...............	77,997	(X)	(X)	32,804	42.1
1936...............	80,174	45,647	56.9	(NA)	(NA)
1938...............	82,354	(X)	(X)	(NA)	(NA)
1940...............	84,728	49,815	58.8	(NA)	(NA)
1942...............	86,465	(X)	(X)	28,074	32.5
1944...............	85,654	48,026	56.1	45,110	52.7
1946...............	92,659	(X)	(X)	34,410	37.1
1948...............	95,573	48,834	51.1	46,220	48.4
1950...............	98,134	(X)	(X)	40,430	41.2
1952...............	99,929	61,552	61.6	57,571	57.6
1954...............	102,075	(X)	(X)	42,583	41.7
1956...............	104,515	62,027	59.3	58,886	56.3
1958...............	106,447	(X)	(X)	45,719	43.0
1960...............	109,672	68,836	62.8	64,124	58.5
1962...............	112,952	(X)	(X)	51,242	45.4
1964...............	114,090	70,098	61.4	65,879	57.7
1966...............	116,638	(X)	(X)	52,902	45.4
1968...............	120,285	73,027	60.7	66,109	55.0
1970...............	124,498	(X)	(X)	54,259	43.6
1972...............	140,777	77,625	55.1	71,188	50.6
1974...............	146,338	(X)	(X)	52,313	35.7
1976...............	152,308	81,603	53.6	74,259	48.8
1978...............	158,369	(X)	(X)	54,584	34.5
1980...............	163,945	86,497	52.8	77,874	47.5
1982...............	169,643	(X)	(X)	63,881	37.7
1984...............	173,995	92,655	53.3	82,422	47.4
1986...............	177,922	(X)	(X)	59,758	33.6
1988...............	181,956	91,587	50.3	81,682	44.9
1990...............	185,812	(X)	(X)	62,355	33.6
1992...............	189,493	104,600	55.2	97,198	51.3
1994...............	193,010	(X)	(X)	70,494	36.5
1996...............	196,789	96,390	49.0	90,233	45.9
1998...............	201,270	(X)	(X)	66,605	33.1
2000...............	[2] 209,786	105,594	61.6	98,800	47.1
2002...............	[2] 214,689	(X)	(X)	74,707	34.8
2004...............	[2] 219,508	122,349	55.7	113,192	51.6
2006...............	[2] 224,622	(X)	(X)	80,976	36.0
2008...............	[2] 229,989	131,407	57.1	122,586	53.3
2010...............	[2] 235,206	(X)	(X)	86,785	36.9
2012...............	[2] 240,186	129,140	53.8	122,346	50.9

NA Not available. X Not applicable. [1] Population 18 and over in Georgia, 1944-70, and in Kentucky, 1956–70; and 20 and over in Alaska and Hawaii, 1960–70. Source: Through 1990, U.S. Census Bureau, "Table 4. Participation in Elections for President and U.S. Representatives: 1930 to 1992," May 1994, <http://www.census.gov/population/socdemo/voting/p25-1117/tab03-04.pdf>. For 1992–1998, "Estimates and Projections of the Voting-Age Population, 1992 to 2000, and Percent Casting Votes for President, by State: November 1992 and 1996," July 2000, <http://www.census.gov/population/socdemo/voting/proj00/tab03.txt>. For 2000-2009, "Annual Estimates of the Resident Population for Selected Age Groups by Sex for the United States, States, Counties, and Puerto Rico Commonwealth and Municipios: April 1, 2000 to July 1, 2009," <http://www.census.gov/popest/data/index.html>, accessed July 2013. Starting 2010, "Annual Estimates of the Resident Population for Selected Age Groups by Sex for the United States, States, Counties, and Puerto Rico Commonwealth and Municipios: April 1, 2010 to July 1, 2012," <http://factfinder2.census.gov>, accessed July 2013. [2] As of July 1.

Source: Except as noted, U.S. House of Representatives, Office of the Clerk, *Statistics of the Presidential and Congressional Election*, February 2013. See also <http://clerk.house.gov/member_info/election.aspx>.

Table 417. Resident Population of Voting-Age, Total Votes Cast, and Percent Casting Votes—States: 2010 to 2012

[234,566 represents 234,566,000. As of November. Estimated population, 18 years old and over. Includes Armed Forces stationed in each state, aliens, and institutional population]

State	Voting-age population (1,000) [1]		Total votes cast			Percent casting votes for–		
			Presidential Electors	U.S. Representative		Presidential Electors	U.S. Representatives	
	2010	2012	2012	2010	2012	2012	2010	2012
U.S..............	234,566	240,186	129,140	86,785	122,346	53.8	37.0	50.9
AL..............	3,647	3,698	2,074	1,368	1,934	56.1	37.5	52.3
AK..............	523	544	300	254	290	55.2	48.6	53.2
AZ..............	4,763	4,932	2,299	1,698	2,173	46.6	35.7	44.1
AR..............	2,204	2,238	1,069	774	1,038	47.8	35.1	46.4
CA..............	27,959	28,801	13,039	9,648	12,204	45.3	34.5	42.4
CO..............	3,804	3,956	2,570	1,763	2,450	64.9	46.4	61.9
CT..............	2,757	2,797	1,558	1,138	1,467	55.7	41.3	52.4
DE..............	692	712	414	306	388	58.1	44.2	54.5
DC..............	501	523	294	(X)	(X)	56.2	(X)	(X)
FL..............	14,801	15,315	8,474	5,117	7,514	55.3	34.6	49.1
GA..............	7,196	7,430	3,898	2,469	3,553	52.5	34.3	47.8
HI..............	1,056	1,089	437	360	437	40.1	34.1	40.1
ID..............	1,139	1,169	652	447	635	55.8	39.3	54.3
IL..............	9,701	9,811	5,242	3,696	5,058	53.4	38.1	51.6
IN..............	4,876	4,946	2,625	1,748	2,554	53.1	35.8	51.6
IA..............	2,319	2,351	1,582	1,107	1,537	67.3	47.7	65.4
KS..............	2,126	2,162	1,160	836	1,058	53.7	39.3	48.9
KY..............	3,316	3,362	1,797	1,354	1,745	53.5	40.8	51.9
LA..............	3,415	3,484	1,994	1,036	1,706	57.2	30.3	49.0
ME..............	1,054	1,063	725	564	725	68.2	53.6	68.2
MD..............	4,421	4,541	2,707	1,825	2,586	59.6	41.3	56.9
MA..............	5,129	5,245	3,184	2,224	3,184	60.7	43.4	60.7
MI..............	7,540	7,616	4,731	3,195	4,575	62.1	42.4	60.1
MN..............	4,020	4,103	2,937	2,091	2,813	71.6	52.0	68.6
MS..............	2,212	2,240	1,286	789	1,208	57.4	35.7	53.9
MO..............	4,563	4,619	2,757	1,921	2,676	59.7	42.1	57.9
MT..............	766	783	484	360	480	61.8	47.1	61.3
NE..............	1,367	1,392	794	486	773	57.1	35.5	55.5
NV..............	2,036	2,095	1,015	703	974	48.4	34.5	46.5
NH..............	1,029	1,046	711	450	682	68.0	43.7	65.2
NJ..............	6,727	6,838	3,638	2,122	3,282	53.2	31.5	48.0
NM..............	1,541	1,571	784	597	766	49.9	38.7	48.8
NY..............	15,053	15,307	7,117	4,744	7,116	46.5	31.5	46.5
NC..............	7,254	7,466	4,505	2,663	4,384	60.3	36.7	58.7
ND..............	523	545	323	236	316	59.3	45.2	58.0
OH..............	8,806	8,881	5,581	3,825	5,142	62.8	43.4	57.9
OK..............	2,822	2,877	1,335	793	1,326	46.4	28.1	46.1
OR..............	2,965	3,039	1,789	1,429	1,708	58.9	48.2	56.2
PA..............	9,910	10,024	5,742	3,956	5,556	57.3	39.9	55.4
RI..............	829	834	446	335	428	53.5	40.5	51.3
SC..............	3,545	3,644	1,964	1,340	1,803	53.9	37.8	49.5
SD..............	611	629	364	319	361	57.8	52.2	57.4
TN..............	4,850	4,962	2,459	1,559	2,284	49.5	32.1	46.0
TX..............	18,280	19,074	7,994	4,746	7,664	41.9	26.0	40.2
UT..............	1,893	1,967	1,017	640	999	51.7	33.8	50.8
VT..............	497	502	299	239	290	59.6	48.0	57.7
VA..............	6,147	6,329	3,854	2,190	3,740	60.9	35.6	59.1
WA..............	5,143	5,312	3,126	2,479	3,006	58.8	48.2	56.6
WV..............	1,466	1,471	670	514	641	45.6	35.1	43.6
WI..............	4,347	4,409	3,071	2,140	2,866	69.7	49.2	65.0
WY..............	428	441	251	191	251	56.9	44.6	56.9

X Not applicable. [1] For 2010, as of April 1; for 2012, as of July 1. Source: U.S. Census Bureau, "Annual Estimates of the Resident Population for Selected Age Groups by Sex for the United States, States, Counties, and Puerto Rico Commonwealth and Municipios: April 1, 2010 to July 1, 2012," <http://factfinder2.census.gov>, accessed July 2013.

Source: Except as noted, U.S. House of Representatives, Office of the Clerk, *Statistics of the Presidential and Congressional Election, 2012,* February 2013, and earlier reports. See also <http://history.house.gov/Institution/Election-Statistics/Election-Statistics/>.

Table 418. Voting-Age Population—Reported Registration and Voting by Selected Characteristics: 2000 to 2012

[202.6 represents 202,600,000. As of November. Covers civilian noninstitutional population 18 years old and over. Includes aliens. Figures are based on Current Population Survey (see text, Section 1 and Appendix III) and differ from those in Table 416 based on population estimates and official vote counts]

Characteristic	Voting-age population (mil.)							Percent reporting they registered							Percent reporting they voted						
								Presidential election years				Congressional election years			Presidential election years				Congressional election years		
	2000	2002	2004	2006	2008	2010	2012	2000	2004	2008	2012	2002	2006	2010	2000	2004	2008	2012	2002	2006	2010
Total [1]	**202.6**	**210.4**	**215.7**	**220.6**	**225.5**	**229.7**	**235.2**	**63.9**	**65.9**	**64.9**	**65.1**	**60.9**	**61.6**	**59.8**	**54.7**	**58.3**	**58.2**	**56.5**	**42.3**	**43.6**	**41.8**
18 to 20 years old	11.9	11.7	11.5	11.6	11.7	12.2	12.3	40.5	50.7	49.3	44.2	32.6	37.0	34.4	28.4	41.0	41.0	35.1	15.1	17.1	16.4
21 to 24 years old	14.9	15.6	16.4	16.2	16.6	16.7	17.6	49.3	52.1	56.2	53.1	42.5	44.9	47.2	35.4	42.5	46.6	40.0	18.7	21.9	22.0
25 to 34 years old	37.3	38.5	39.0	39.4	40.2	41.2	41.1	54.7	55.6	56.5	57.0	50.2	50.3	49.8	43.7	46.9	48.5	46.1	27.1	28.3	26.9
35 to 44 years old	44.5	43.7	43.1	42.6	41.5	39.9	39.6	63.8	64.2	61.4	61.7	60.0	59.3	57.3	55.0	56.9	55.2	52.9	40.2	40.1	37.7
45 to 64 years old	61.4	66.9	71.0	75.0	78.1	80.7	82.1	71.2	72.7	70.4	70.4	69.4	69.6	66.3	64.1	66.6	65.0	63.4	53.1	54.3	51.1
65 years old and over	32.8	33.9	34.7	35.8	37.5	39.0	42.5	76.1	76.9	75.0	76.9	75.8	75.4	72.5	67.6	68.9	68.1	69.7	61.0	60.5	58.9
Male	97.1	100.9	103.8	106.5	109.0	111.1	113.2	62.2	64.0	62.6	63.1	58.9	59.5	57.9	53.1	56.3	55.7	54.4	41.4	42.4	40.9
Female	105.5	109.5	111.9	114.1	116.5	118.6	122.0	65.6	67.6	67.0	67.0	62.8	63.5	61.5	56.2	60.1	60.4	58.5	43.0	44.7	42.7
White [2]	168.7	174.1	176.6	179.9	183.8	185.8	187.1	65.6	67.9	66.6	66.7	63.1	64.0	61.6	56.4	60.3	59.6	57.6	44.1	45.8	43.4
Black [2]	24.1	24.4	24.9	25.7	26.5	27.4	28.7	63.6	64.4	65.5	68.5	58.8	57.4	58.8	53.5	56.3	60.8	62.0	39.7	38.6	40.7
Asian [2,3]	8.0	9.6	9.3	9.9	10.5	11.0	12.5	30.7	34.9	37.3	37.2	30.7	32.9	34.1	25.4	29.8	32.1	31.3	19.4	21.8	21.3
Hispanic [4]	21.6	25.2	27.1	29.0	30.9	32.5	35.2	34.9	34.3	37.6	38.9	32.6	32.1	33.8	27.5	28.0	31.6	31.8	18.9	19.3	20.5
Region: [5]																					
Northeast	38.9	41.1	41.0	41.2	41.5	42.3	42.9	63.7	65.3	63.7	65.2	60.8	60.3	59.7	55.2	58.6	57.4	56.6	41.4	42.8	41.6
Midwest	46.4	48.8	48.4	49.1	49.4	50.1	50.6	70.2	72.8	70.6	71.4	66.5	68.3	65.0	60.9	65.0	63.4	62.3	47.1	50.7	45.1
South	71.8	74.2	77.2	80.0	82.4	84.2	87.1	64.5	65.5	65.5	65.3	61.6	62.0	59.4	53.5	56.4	57.7	55.7	41.6	40.3	39.3
West	45.5	46.3	49.1	50.4	52.2	53.2	54.6	56.9	60.1	59.4	58.9	54.0	55.4	55.5	49.9	54.4	54.6	52.3	39.0	42.4	42.7
School years completed:																					
8 years or less	12.9	12.3	12.6	12.1	11.1	11.1	10.5	36.1	32.5	30.1	28.7	32.4	29.5	27.0	26.8	23.6	23.4	21.6	19.4	17.1	15.8
High school:																					
Less than high school graduate	20.1	20.9	20.7	20.2	19.1	18.8	18.7	45.9	45.8	43.2	42.6	41.6	39.6	37.8	33.6	34.6	33.7	32.2	23.3	22.8	20.8
High school graduate or GED [6]	66.3	68.9	68.5	70.0	70.4	71.0	70.6	60.1	61.5	59.5	59.0	57.1	57.5	54.0	49.4	52.4	50.9	48.7	37.1	37.6	35.2
College:																					
Some college or Associate's degree	55.3	57.3	58.9	60.2	63.8	65.3	67.7	70.0	73.7	72.0	71.2	66.7	68.3	65.5	60.3	66.1	65.0	61.5	45.8	47.3	44.4
Bachelor's or advanced degree	48.0	51.0	54.9	58.2	61.1	63.5	67.8	77.3	78.1	76.8	77.2	74.4	73.9	72.5	72.0	74.2	73.3	71.7	58.5	59.5	57.1
Employed	133.4	134.9	138.8	143.8	143.2	138.3	142.6	64.7	67.1	66.4	67.1	61.7	62.7	61.5	55.5	60.0	60.1	58.6	42.1	43.9	42.5
Unemployed	4.9	7.7	7.3	6.2	9.5	13.9	11.1	46.1	56.3	57.2	56.9	48.1	48.5	52.3	35.1	46.4	48.8	46.1	27.2	28.0	31.6
Not in labor force	64.2	67.8	69.6	70.5	72.8	77.5	81.6	63.8	64.4	62.9	62.8	60.9	60.7	58.0	54.5	56.2	55.5	54.3	44.2	44.3	42.3

[1] Includes other races, not shown separately. [2] Beginning with the 2003 Current Population Survey (CPS), respondents could choose more than one race. As of 2004, data represent persons who selected this race group only and exclude persons reporting more than one race. The CPS in prior years only allowed respondents to report one race group. See also comment on race in the text for Section 1. [3] Prior to 2004, this category was "Asian and Pacific Islanders," therefore rates are not comparable with prior years. [4] Persons of Hispanic origin may be of any race. [5] For composition of regions, see map, inside cover. [6] The General Educational Development (GED) Test measures how well a non-high school graduate has mastered the skills and general knowledge that are acquired in a 4-year high school education. Successfully passing the exam is a credential generally considered to be equivalent to a high school diploma.

Source: U.S. Census Bureau, *Voting and Registration in the Election of November 2012*; Current Population Reports, P20-568, 2012, and earlier reports; and unpublished data. See also <http://www.census.gov/hhes/www/socdemo/voting/index.html>.

Table 419. Persons Reported Registered and Voted by State: 2012

[235,248 represents 235,248,000. As of November. See headnote, Table 418]

State	Voting-age population (1,000)	Percent of voting-age population Registered	Voted	State	Voting-age population (1,000)	Percent of voting-age population Registered	Voted
U.S.............	235,248	65.1	56.5	MO.............	4,521	74.8	62.3
AL................	3,594	71.1	59.9	MT................	768	72.0	64.5
AK................	516	69.9	56.0	NE................	1,371	65.7	58.2
AZ................	4,863	57.8	49.6	NV................	2,039	57.7	51.4
AR................	2,198	62.6	51.1	NH................	1,028	73.1	66.9
CA................	28,357	54.2	47.5	NJ................	6,730	64.3	54.5
CO................	3,817	69.0	65.4	NM................	1,553	63.0	56.5
CT................	2,726	64.6	57.5	NY................	15,066	59.0	50.9
DE................	693	67.8	62.2	NC................	7,265	72.9	63.7
DC................	517	74.4	67.7	ND................	528	72.5	62.2
FL................	15,034	60.5	53.9	OH................	8,750	69.4	61.7
GA................	7,179	66.4	58.1	OK................	2,808	64.3	51.0
HI................	1,013	54.1	47.4	OR................	2,998	69.6	63.3
ID................	1,129	65.9	60.2	PA................	9,847	69.0	59.1
IL................	9,651	66.6	56.2	RI................	817	67.5	57.4
IN................	4,852	67.4	57.7	SC................	3,516	70.5	62.2
IA................	2,320	75.2	66.7	SD................	616	73.7	60.1
KS................	2,120	69.2	58.9	TN................	4,849	66.2	53.7
KY................	3,291	70.0	57.6	TX................	18,642	57.7	46.4
LA................	3,321	75.2	64.7	UT................	1,917	59.4	53.3
ME................	1,042	75.5	67.2	VT................	496	72.0	62.1
MD................	4,449	64.9	58.7	VA................	6,094	69.1	62.0
MA................	5,170	72.7	65.4	WA................	5,230	67.6	60.7
MI................	7,496	75.0	64.5	WV................	1,452	67.6	47.5
MN................	4,055	76.1	70.5	WI................	4,352	76.3	71.9
MS................	2,166	82.8	73.3	WY................	427	62.8	57.8

Source: Source: U.S. Census Bureau, *Voting and Registration in the Election of November 2012,* May 2013. See also <http://www.census.gov/hhes/www/socdemo/voting/index.html>.

Table 420. Reported Voting and Registration Among Native and Naturalized Citizens by Race and Hispanic Origin: 2012

[In thousands, except percent. 215,081 represents 215,081,000. As of November]

Nativity status, race, and Hispanic origin	Total citizen population (1,000)	U.S. Citizen Reported registered Number (1,000)	Percent	Not registered Number (1,000)	Percent	Reported voted Number (1,000)	Percent	Did not vote Number (1,000)	Percent
Total:									
All races [1]........................	215,081	153,157	71.2	33,134	15.4	132,948	61.8	54,531	25.4
White alone [2]........................	173,466	124,697	71.9	26,607	15.3	107,846	62.2	44,372	25.6
Black alone [2]........................	26,915	19,680	73.1	3,076	11.4	17,813	66.2	5,051	18.8
Asian alone [2]........................	8,254	4,649	56.3	1,906	23.1	3,904	47.3	2,751	33.3
Hispanic [3]...........................	23,329	13,697	58.7	6,026	25.8	11,188	48.0	8,765	37.6
Native citizen:									
All races [1].......................	197,756	142,404	72.0	29,130	14.7	123,654	62.5	48,866	24.7
White alone [2]........................	163,801	118,628	72.4	24,333	14.9	102,621	62.6	41,157	25.1
White alone, non-Hispanic.........	148,498	109,853	74.0	20,362	13.7	95,622	64.4	35,249	23.7
Black alone [2]........................	24,864	18,280	73.5	2,767	11.1	16,525	66.5	4,613	18.6
Asian alone [2]........................	3,079	1,614	52.4	611	19.9	1,351	43.9	887	28.8
Hispanic [3]........................	17,623	10,200	57.9	4,525	25.7	8,130	46.1	6,779	38.5
White alone or in combination [4].....	166,828	120,694	72.3	25,016	15.0	104,323	62.5	42,244	25.3
Black alone or in combination [4].....	26,044	19,140	73.5	2,983	11.5	17,253	66.2	4,968	19.1
Asian alone or in combination [4].....	3,798	2,099	55.3	762	20.1	1,743	45.9	1,138	30.0
Naturalized citizen:									
All races [1].......................	17,325	10,753	62.1	4,004	23.1	9,294	53.6	5,665	32.7
White alone [2]........................	9,665	6,069	62.8	2,274	23.5	5,226	54.1	3,215	33.3
White alone, non-Hispanic.........	4,364	2,853	65.4	859	19.7	2,419	55.4	1,345	30.8
Black alone [2]........................	2,051	1,400	68.3	309	15.1	1,288	62.8	438	21.4
Asian alone [2]........................	5,174	3,035	58.6	1,294	25.0	2,553	49.3	1,863	36.0
Hispanic [3]........................	5,706	3,497	61.3	1,502	26.3	3,058	53.6	1,986	34.8
White alone or in combination [4].....	9,784	6,128	62.6	2,307	23.6	5,280	54.0	3,254	33.3
Black alone or in combination [4].....	2,109	1,418	67.2	335	15.9	1,305	61.9	464	22.0
Asian alone or in combination [4].....	5,235	3,074	58.7	1,305	24.9	2,588	49.4	1,880	35.9

[1] Includes other races, not shown separately. [2] Beginning with the 2003 Current Population Survey (CPS), respondents could choose more than one race. Data shown represent persons who selected this race group only and exclude persons reporting more than one race. [3] Persons of Hispanic origin may be of any race. [4] In combination with one or more races.

Source: U.S. Census Bureau, *Voting and Registration in the Election of November 2012,* May 2013. See also <http://www.census.gov/hhes/www/socdemo/voting/index.html>.

Table 421. Vote Cast for President by Major Political Party: 1954 to 2012

[In thousands (62,027 represents 62,027,000), except percent and electoral vote. Prior to 1960, excludes Alaska and Hawaii; prior to 1964, excludes DC. Vote cast for major party candidates includes the votes of minor parties cast for those candidates]

Year	Candidates for President		Total popular vote [1] (1,000)	Vote cast for President					
	Democratic	Republican		Democratic			Republican		
				Popular vote		Electoral vote	Popular vote		Electoral vote
				Number (1,000)	Percent		Number (1,000)	Percent	
1956..........	Stevenson	Eisenhower	62,027	26,739	43.1	73	35,581	57.4	457
1960..........	Kennedy	Nixon	68,836	34,227	49.7	303	34,108	49.5	219
1964..........	Johnson	Goldwater	70,098	42,825	61.1	486	27,147	38.7	52
1968..........	Humphrey	Nixon	73,027	30,989	42.4	191	31,710	43.4	301
1972..........	McGovern	Nixon	77,625	28,902	37.2	17	46,740	60.2	520
1976..........	Carter	Ford	81,603	40,826	50.0	297	39,148	48.0	240
1980..........	Carter	Reagan	86,497	35,481	41.0	49	43,643	50.5	489
1984..........	Mondale	Reagan	92,655	37,450	40.4	13	54,167	58.5	525
1988..........	Dukakis	Bush	91,587	41,717	45.5	111	48,643	53.1	426
1992..........	Clinton	Bush	104,600	44,858	42.9	370	38,799	37.1	168
1996..........	Clinton	Dole	96,390	47,402	49.2	379	39,198	40.7	159
2000..........	Gore	Bush	105,594	50,996	48.3	266	50,465	47.8	271
2004..........	Kerry	Bush	122,349	58,895	48.1	251	61,873	50.6	286
2008..........	Obama	McCain	131,407	69,498	52.9	365	59,948	45.6	173
2012..........	Obama	Romney	129,140	65,752	50.9	332	60,670	47.0	206

[1] Include votes for minor party candidates, independents, unpledged electors, and scattered write-in votes.

Source: U.S. House of Representatives, Office of the Clerk, *Statistics of the Presidential and Congressional Election*, February 2013, and earlier reports. See also <http://clerk.house.gov/member_info/election.html>.

Table 422. Vote Cast for Leading Minority Party Candidates for President: 1956 to 2012

[In thousands (91 represents 91,000). See headnote, Table 421. Data do not include write-ins, scatterings, or votes for candidates who ran on party tickets not shown, unless otherwise noted]

Year	Candidate	Party	Popular vote (1,000)	Candidate	Party	Popular vote (1,000)
1956 [1]........	T. Coleman Andrews	States' Rights	91	Eric Hass	Socialist Labor	41
1960..........	Eric Hass	Socialist Labor	46	Rutherford Decker	Prohibition	46
1964..........	Eric Hass	Socialist Labor	43	Clifton DeBerry	Socialist Workers	22
1968..........	George Wallace	American Independent	9,446	Henning Blomen	Socialist Labor	52
1972 [1]........	John Schmitz	American	993	Benjamin Spock	People's	9
1976..........	Eugene McCarthy	Independent	680	Roger McBride	Libertarian	172
1980..........	John Anderson	Independent	5,251	Ed Clark	Libertarian	920
1984..........	David Bergland	Libertarian	227	Lyndon H. LaRouche	Independent	79
1988..........	Ron Paul	Libertarian	410	Lenora B. Fulani	New Alliance	129
1992..........	H. Ross Perot	Independent	19,722	Andre Marrou	Libertarian	281
1996..........	H. Ross Perot	Reform	7,137	Ralph Nader	Green	527
2000..........	Ralph Nader	Green	2,530	Pat Buchanan	Reform	324
2004..........	Ralph Nader	Independent	156	Michael Badnarik	Libertarian	369
2008..........	Ralph Nader	Independent	739	Bob Barr	Libertarian	515
2012..........	Gary Johnson	Libertarian	1,216	Jill Stien	Green	401

[1] Data include write-ins, scatterings, and/or votes for candidates who ran on party tickets not shown.

Source: U.S. House of Representatives, Office of the Clerk, *Statistics of the Presidential and Congressional Election*, February 2013, and earlier reports. See also <http://clerk.house.gov/member_info/election.aspx>.

Table 423. Democratic and Republican Percentages of Two-Party Presidential Vote by Selected Characteristics of Voters: 2004 and 2008

[In percent. Covers citizens of voting age living in private housing units in the contiguous United States. Percentages for Democratic Presidential vote are computed by subtracting the percentage Republican vote from 100 percent; third-party or independent votes are not included as valid data. Data are from the National Election Studies and are based on a sample and subject to sampling variability; for details, see source]

Characteristic	2004		2008		Characteristic	2004		2008	
	Demo-cratic	Republi-can	Demo-cratic	Republi-can		Demo-cratic	Republi-can	Demo-cratic	Republi-can
Total [1]...............	**50**	**50**	**55**	**45**	Race:				
Year of birth:					White.....................	42	58	44	56
1975 or later.............	66	34	65	35	Black.....................	90	10	99	1
1959 to 1974.............	45	55	56	44	Education:				
1943 to 1958.............	44	56	54	46	Less than high school. ..	69	31	72	28
1927 to 1942.............	51	49	41	59	High school diploma/				
1911 to 1926.............	52	48	52	48	equivalent..............	46	54	57	43
1895 to 1910.............	–	–	–	–	Some college,				
Sex:					no degree..............	47	53	53	47
Male....................	46	54	52	48	College..................	50	50	51	49
Female..................	53	47	57	43	Union household.........	64	36	60	40
					Nonunion household......	46	54	54	46

– Represents zero. [1] Includes other characteristics, not shown separately.

Source: American National Election Studies, <http://www.electionstudies.org/> ©.

Table 424. Electoral Vote Cast for President by Major Political Party—States: 1972 to 2012

[D = Democratic, R = Republican. For composition of regions, see map, inside front cover]

State	1972 [1]	1976 [2]	1980	1984	1988 [3]	1992	1996	2000 [4]	2004 [5]	2008 [6]	2012
Democratic........	**17**	**297**	**49**	**13**	**111**	**370**	**379**	**266**	**251**	**365**	**332**
Republican........	**520**	**240**	**489**	**525**	**426**	**168**	**159**	**271**	**286**	**173**	**206**
Northeast:											
Democratic..........	14	86	4	–	53	106	106	102	101	101	96
Republican..........	108	36	118	113	60	–	–	4	–	–	–
Midwest:											
Democratic..........	–	58	10	10	29	100	100	68	57	97	80
Republican..........	145	87	135	127	108	29	29	61	66	27	38
South:											
Democratic..........	3	149	31	3	8	68	80	15	16	71	58
Republican..........	165	20	138	174	168	116	104	168	173	118	138
West:											
Democratic..........	–	4	4	–	21	96	93	81	77	96	98
Republican..........	102	97	98	111	90	23	26	38	47	28	30
AL..................	R-9	D-9	R-9	R-9	R-9	R-9	R-9	R-9	R-9	R-9	R-9
AK..................	R-3	R-3	R-3	R-3	R-3	R-3	R-3	R-3	R-3	R-3	R-3
AZ..................	R-6	R-6	R-6	R-7	R-7	R-8	D-8	R-8	R-10	R-10	R-11
AR..................	R-6	D-6	R-6	R-6	R-6	D-6	D-6	R-6	R-6	R-6	R-6
CA..................	R-45	R-45	R-45	R-47	R-47	D-54	D-54	D-54	D-55	D-55	D-55
CO..................	R-7	R-7	R-7	R-8	R-8	D-8	R-8	R-8	R-9	D-9	D-9
CT..................	R-8	R-8	R-8	R-8	R-8	D-8	D-8	D-8	D-7	D-7	D-7
DE..................	R-3	D-3	R-3	R-3	R-3	D-3	D-3	D-3	D-3	D-3	D-3
DC..................	D-3	D-3	D-3	D-3	D-3	D-3	D-3	[4] D-2	D-3	D-3	D-3
FL..................	R-17	D-17	R-17	R-21	R-21	R-25	D-25	R-25	R-27	D-27	D-29
GA..................	R-12	D-12	D-12	R-12	R-12	D-13	R-13	R-13	R-15	R-15	R-16
HI..................	R-4	D-4	D-4	R-4	D-4	D-4	D-4	D-4	D-4	D-4	D-4
ID..................	R-4	R-4	R-4	R-4	R-4	R-4	R-4	R-4	R-4	R-4	R-4
IL..................	R-26	R-26	R-26	R-24	R-24	D-22	D-22	D-22	D-21	D-21	D-20
IN..................	R-13	R-13	R-13	R-12	R-12	R-12	R-12	R-12	R-11	D-11	R-11
IA..................	R-8	R-8	R-8	R-8	D-8	D-7	D-7	D-7	R-7	D-7	D-6
KS..................	R-7	R-7	R-7	R-7	R-7	R-6	R-6	R-6	R-6	R-6	R-6
KY..................	R-9	D-9	R-9	R-9	R-9	D-8	D-8	R-8	R-8	R-8	R-8
LA..................	R-10	D-10	R-10	R-10	R-10	D-9	D-9	R-9	R-9	R-9	R-8
ME..................	R-4	R-4	R-4	R-4	R-4	D-4	D-4	D-4	D-4	D-4	D-4
MD..................	R-10	D-10	D-10	R-10	R-10	D-10	D-10	D-10	D-10	D-10	D-10
MA..................	D-14	D-14	D-14	R-13	D-13	D-12	D-12	D-12	D-12	D-12	D-11
MI..................	R-21	R-21	R-21	R-20	R-20	D-18	D-18	D-18	D-17	D-17	D-16
MN..................	R-10	D-10	D-10	D-10	D-10	D-10	D-10	D-10	[5] D-9	D-10	D-10
MS..................	R-7	D-7	R-7	R-7	R-7	R-7	R-7	R-7	R-6	R-6	R-6
MO..................	R-12	D-12	R-12	R-11	R-11	D-11	D-11	R-11	R-11	R-11	R-10
MT..................	R-4	R-4	R-4	R-4	R-4	D-3	R-3	R-3	R-3	R-3	R-3
NE..................	R-5	R-5	R-5	R-5	R-5	R-5	R-5	R-5	R-5	[6] R-4	R-5
NV..................	R-3	R-3	R-3	R-4	R-4	D-4	D-4	R-4	R-5	D-5	D-6
NH..................	R-4	R-4	R-4	R-4	R-4	D-4	D-4	R-4	D-4	D-4	D-4
NJ..................	R-17	R-17	R-17	R-16	R-16	D-15	D-15	D-15	D-15	D-15	D-14
NM..................	R-4	R-4	R-4	R-5	R-5	D-5	D-5	D-5	R-5	D-5	D-5
NY..................	R-41	D-41	R-41	R-36	D-36	D-33	D-33	D-33	D-31	D-31	D-29
NC..................	R-13	D-13	R-13	R-13	R-13	R-14	R-14	R-14	R-15	D-15	R-15
ND..................	R-3	R-3	R-3	R-3	R-3	R-3	R-3	R-3	R-3	R-3	R-3
OH..................	R-25	D-25	R-25	R-23	R-23	D-21	D-21	R-21	R-20	D-20	D-18
OK..................	R-8	R-8	R-8	R-8	R-8	R-8	R-8	R-8	R-7	R-7	R-7
OR..................	R-6	R-6	R-6	R-7	D-7	D-7	D-7	D-7	D-7	D-7	D-7
PA..................	R-27	D-27	R-27	R-25	R-25	D-23	D-23	D-23	D-21	D-21	D-20
RI..................	R-4	D-4	D-4	R-4	D-4	D-4	D-4	D-4	D-4	D-4	D-4
SC..................	R-8	D-8	R-8	R-8	R-8	R-8	R-8	R-8	R-8	R-8	R-9
SD..................	R-4	R-4	R-4	R-3	R-3	R-3	R-3	R-3	R-3	R-3	R-3
TN..................	R-10	D-10	R-10	R-11	R-11	D-11	D-11	R-11	R-11	R-11	R-11
TX..................	R-26	D-26	R-26	R-29	R-29	R-32	R-32	R-32	R-34	R-34	R-38
UT..................	R-4	R-4	R-4	R-5	R-5	R-5	R-5	R-5	R-5	R-5	R-6
VT..................	R-3	R-3	R-3	R-3	R-3	D-3	D-3	D-3	D-3	D-3	D-3
VA..................	[1] R-11	R-12	R-12	R-12	R-12	R-13	R-13	R-13	R-13	D-13	D-13
WA..................	R-9	[2] R-8	R-9	R-10	D-10	D-11	D-11	D-11	D-11	D-11	D-12
WV..................	R-6	D-6	D-6	R-6	[3] D-5	D-5	D-5	R-5	R-5	R-5	R-5
WI..................	R-11	D-11	R-11	R-11	D-11	D-11	D-11	D-11	D-10	D-10	D-10
WY..................	R-3	R-3	R-3	R-3	R-3	R-3	R-3	R-3	R-3	R-3	R-3

– Represents zero. [1] Excludes one electoral vote cast for Libertarian John Hospers in Virginia. [2] Excludes one electoral vote cast for Ronald Reagan in Washington. [3] Excludes one electoral vote cast for Lloyd Bentsen for President in West Virginia. [4] Excludes one electoral vote left blank by a Democratic elector in the District of Columbia. [5] Excludes one electoral vote cast for Democratic vice presidential nominee John Edwards in Minnesota. [6] Excludes one electoral vote for Barack Obama in Nebraska.

Source: U.S. House of Representatives, Office of the Clerk, *Statistics of the Presidential and Congressional Election*, February 2013. See also <http://clerk.house.gov/member_info/election.html>.

Table 425. Popular Vote Cast for President by Political Party—States: 2008 and 2012

[In thousands (131,407 represents 131,407,000), except percent]

State	2008					2012				
	Total [1]	Demo-cratic party	Republi-can party	Percent of total vote		Total [1]	Demo-cratic party	Republi-can party	Percent of total vote	
				Demo-cratic party	Republi-can party				Demo-cratic party	Republi-can party
United States.........	**131,407**	**69,498**	**59,948**	**52.9**	**45.6**	**129,140**	**65,752**	**60,670**	**50.9**	**47.0**
Alabama.................	2,100	813	1,267	38.7	60.3	2,074	796	1,256	38.4	60.5
Alaska...................	326	124	194	37.9	59.4	300	123	165	40.8	54.8
Arizona.................	2,293	1,035	1,230	45.1	53.6	2,299	1,025	1,234	44.6	53.7
Arkansas...............	1,087	422	638	38.9	58.7	1,069	394	648	36.9	60.6
California..............	13,562	8,274	5,012	61.0	37.0	13,039	7,854	4,840	60.2	37.1
Colorado...............	2,401	1,289	1,074	53.7	44.7	2,570	1,323	1,185	51.5	46.1
Connecticut...........	1,647	998	629	60.6	38.2	1,558	905	635	58.1	40.7
Delaware..............	412	255	152	61.9	36.9	414	243	165	58.6	40.0
District of Columbia.....	266	246	17	92.5	6.5	294	267	21	90.9	7.3
Florida.................	8,391	4,282	4,046	51.0	48.2	8,474	4,238	4,163	50.0	49.1
Georgia................	3,924	1,844	2,049	47.0	52.2	3,898	1,774	2,079	45.5	53.3
Hawaii.................	456	326	121	71.5	26.4	437	307	121	70.1	27.7
Idaho..................	655	236	403	36.1	61.5	652	213	421	32.6	64.5
Illinois.................	5,522	3,419	2,031	61.9	36.8	5,242	3,020	2,135	57.6	40.7
Indiana................	2,751	1,374	1,346	49.9	48.9	2,625	1,153	1,421	43.9	54.1
Iowa...................	1,537	829	682	53.9	44.4	1,582	823	731	52.0	46.2
Kansas................	1,236	515	700	41.7	56.6	1,160	441	693	38.0	59.7
Kentucky..............	1,827	752	1,048	41.2	57.4	1,797	679	1,087	37.8	60.5
Louisiana..............	1,961	783	1,148	39.9	58.6	1,994	809	1,152	40.6	57.8
Maine..................	731	422	295	57.7	40.4	725	401	292	55.4	40.3
Maryland..............	2,632	1,629	960	61.9	36.5	2,707	1,678	972	62.0	35.9
Massachusetts..........	3,103	1,904	1,109	61.4	35.7	3,184	1,921	1,188	60.3	37.3
Michigan..............	5,002	2,873	2,049	57.4	41.0	4,731	2,565	2,115	54.2	44.7
Minnesota.............	2,910	1,573	1,275	54.1	43.8	2,937	1,546	1,320	52.7	45.0
Mississippi.............	1,290	555	725	43.0	56.2	1,286	563	711	43.8	55.3
Missouri...............	2,925	1,442	1,446	49.3	49.4	2,757	1,224	1,482	44.4	53.8
Montana...............	490	232	243	47.3	49.5	484	202	268	41.7	55.4
Nebraska..............	801	333	453	41.6	56.5	794	302	475	38.0	59.8
Nevada................	968	534	413	55.1	42.7	1,015	531	464	52.4	45.7
New Hampshire.........	711	385	317	54.1	44.5	711	370	330	52.0	46.4
New Jersey.............	3,868	2,215	1,613	57.3	41.7	3,638	2,123	1,478	58.3	40.6
New Mexico............	830	472	347	56.9	41.8	784	415	336	53.0	42.8
New York..............	7,722	4,805	2,753	62.2	35.6	7,117	4,324	2,223	60.8	31.2
North Carolina.........	4,298	2,143	2,128	49.8	49.5	4,505	2,178	2,270	48.4	50.4
North Dakota...........	317	141	169	44.6	53.3	323	125	188	38.7	58.3
Ohio...................	5,708	2,940	2,678	51.5	46.9	5,581	2,828	2,661	50.7	47.7
Oklahoma..............	1,463	502	960	34.4	65.6	1,335	444	891	33.2	66.8
Oregon................	1,828	1,037	738	56.7	40.4	1,789	970	754	54.2	42.1
Pennsylvania..........	6,013	3,276	2,656	54.5	44.2	5,742	2,990	2,680	52.1	46.7
Rhode Island..........	472	297	165	62.9	35.1	446	280	157	62.7	35.2
South Carolina.........	1,921	862	1,035	44.9	53.9	1,964	866	1,072	44.1	54.6
South Dakota...........	382	171	203	44.7	53.2	364	145	211	39.9	57.9
Tennessee.............	2,600	1,087	1,479	41.8	56.9	2,459	961	1,462	39.1	59.5
Texas.................	8,078	3,529	4,479	43.7	55.5	7,994	3,308	4,570	41.4	57.2
Utah...................	952	328	596	34.4	62.6	1,017	252	741	24.7	72.8
Vermont...............	325	219	99	67.5	30.4	299	199	93	66.6	31.0
Virginia................	3,723	1,960	1,725	52.6	46.3	3,854	1,972	1,823	51.2	47.3
Washington............	3,037	1,751	1,229	57.7	40.5	3,126	1,755	1,291	56.2	41.3
West Virginia...........	713	304	397	42.6	55.7	670	238	418	35.5	62.3
Wisconsin..............	2,983	1,677	1,262	56.2	42.3	3,071	1,621	1,411	52.8	45.9
Wyoming...............	255	83	165	32.5	64.7	251	69	171	27.6	68.2

[1] Includes other parties.

Source: U.S. House of Representatives, Office of the Clerk, *Statistics of the Presidential and Congressional Election*, February 2013. See also <http://clerk.house.gov/member_info/election.html>.

Table 426. Vote Cast for U.S. Senators, 2010 and 2012, and Incumbent Senators, 2013—States

[1,485 represents 1,485,000. D = Democrat, R = Republican, I = Independent]

State	2010		2012		Incumbent senators and year term expires [1]	
	Total [2] (1,000)	Percent for leading party	Total [2] (1,000)	Percent for leading party	Name, party, and year	Name, party, and year
Alabama	1,485	R-65.2	(X)	(X)	Jeff Sessions (R) 2015	Richard C. Shelby (R) 2017
Alaska	256	R-35.6	(X)	(X)	Lisa Murkowski (R) 2017	Mark Begich (D) 2015
Arizona	1,708	R-58.9	2,243	R-49.2	Jeff Flake (R) 2019	John McCain (R) 2017
Arkansas	780	R-57.9	(X)	(X)	John Boozman (R) 2017	Mark L. Pryor (D) 2015
California	10,000	D-52.2	12,579	D-62.5	Barbara Boxer (D) 2017	Dianne Feinstein (D) 2019
Colorado	1,772	D-48.1	(X)	(X)	Mark Udall (D) 2015	Michael F. Bennett (D) 2017
Connecticut	1,153	D-52.5	1,512	D-52.5	Richard Blumenthal (D) 2017	Chris Murphy (D) 2019
Delaware	307	D-56.6	400	D-66.4	Christopher Coons (D) 2015	Thomas R. Carper (D) 2019
Florida	5,411	R-48.9	8,190	D-55.2	Marco Rubio (R) 2017	Bill Nelson (D) 2019
Georgia	2,555	R-58.3	(X)	(X)	Saxby Chambliss (R) 2015	Johnny Isakson (R) 2017
Hawaii	371	D-74.8	437	D-61.6	Brian Schatz (D) 2017	Mazie Hirono (D) 2019
Idaho	450	R-71.2	(X)	(X)	James E. Risch (R) 2015	Mike Crapo (R) 2017
Illinois	3,704	R-48.0	(X)	(X)	Richard J. Durbin (D) 2015	Mark Kirk (R) 2017
Indiana	1,744	R-54.6	2,560	D-50.0	Daniel Coats (R) 2017	Joe Donnelly (D) 2019
Iowa	1,116	R-64.4	(X)	(X)	Chuck Grassley (R) 2017	Tom Harkin (D) 2015
Kansas	838	R-70.1	(X)	(X)	Jerry Moran (R) 2017	Pat Roberts (R) 2015
Kentucky	1,356	R-55.7	(X)	(X)	Rand Paul (R) 2017	Mitch McConnell (R) 2015
Louisiana [3]	1,265	R-56.6	(X)	(X)	Mary L. Landrieu (D) 2015	David Vitter (R) 2017
Maine	(X)	(X)	725	I-52.6	Susan M. Collins (R) 2015	Angus King (I) 2019
Maryland	1,834	D-62.2	2,633	D-56.0	Barbara A. Mikulski (D) 2017	Benjamin L. Cardin (D) 2019
Massachusetts	(X)	(X)	3,184	D-53.3	Elizabeth Warren (D) 2019	William M. Cowan [4] (D) 2015
Michigan	(X)	(X)	4,653	D-58.8	Carl Levin (D) 2015	Debbie Stabenow (D) 2019
Minnesota	(X)	(X)	2,843	D-65.2	Al Franken (D) 2015	Amy Klobuchar (D) 2019
Mississippi	(X)	(X)	1,242	R-57.2	Thad Cochran (R) 2015	Roger F. Wicker (R) 2019
Missouri	1,944	R-54.2	2,726	D-54.8	Roy Blunt (R) 2017	Claire McCaskill (D) 2019
Montana	(X)	(X)	486	D-48.6	Max Baucus (D) 2015	John Tester (D) 2019
Nebraska	(X)	(X)	789	R-57.8	Mike Johanns (R) 2015	Deb Fischer (R) 2019
Nevada	721	D-50.3	998	R-45.9	Dean Heller (R) 2019	Harry Reid (D) 2017
New Hampshire	455	R-60.1	(X)	(X)	Kelly Ayotte (R) 2017	Jeanne Shaheen (D) 2015
New Jersey	(X)	(X)	3,377	D-58.9	Robert Menendez (D) 2019	Vacant [5]
New Mexico	(X)	(X)	776	D-51.0	Martin Heinrich (D) 2019	Tom Udall (D) 2015
New York	4,764	D-64.0	7,117	D-62.1	Kirsten E. Gillibrand (D) 2019	Charles E. Schumer (D) 2017
North Carolina	2,660	R-54.8	(X)	(X)	Richard Burr (R) 2017	Kay R. Hagan (D) 2015
North Dakota	239	R-76.2	321	D-50.2	Heidi Heitkamp (D) 2019	John Hoeven (R) 2017
Ohio	3,815	R-56.8	5,449	D-50.7	Sherrod Brown (D) 2019	Rob Portman (R) 2017
Oklahoma	1,017	R-70.6	(X)	(X)	Tom Coburn (R) 2017	James M. Inhofe (R) 2015
Oregon	1,443	D-57.2	(X)	(X)	Jeff Merkley (D) 2015	Ron Wyden (D) 2017
Pennsylvania	3,978	R-51.0	5,627	D-53.7	Robert P. Casey Jr. (D) 2019	Patrick J. Toomey (R) 2017
Rhode Island	(X)	(X)	418	D-64.8	Sheldon Whitehouse (D) 2019	Jack Reed (D) 2015
South Carolina	1,319	R-61.5	(X)	(X)	Tim Scott [6] (R) 2017	Lindsey Graham (R) 2015
South Dakota	228	R-100	(X)	(X)	Tim Johnson (D) 2015	John Thune (R) 2017
Tennessee	(X)	(X)	2,321	R-64.9	Lamar Alexander (R) 2015	Bob Corker (R) 2019
Texas	(X)	(X)	7,865	R-56.5	John Cornyn (R) 2015	Ted Cruz (R) 2019
Utah	585	R-61.6	1,007	R-65.3	Mike Lee (R) 2017	Orrin G. Hatch (R) 2019
Vermont	235	D-64.3	293	I-71.0	Bernard Sanders (I) 2019	Patrick J. Leahy (D) 2017
Virginia	(X)	(X)	3,802	D-52.9	Tim Kaine (D) 2019	Mark R. Warner (D) 2015
Washington	2,511	D-52.4	3,069	D-60.5	Maria Cantwell (D) 2019	Patty Murray (D) 2017
West Virginia	(X)	(X)	660	D-60.6	Joe Manchin III (D) 2019	John D. Rockefeller IV (D) 2015
Wisconsin	2,171	R-51.9	3,009	D-51.4	Ronald H. Johnson (R) 2017	Tammy Baldwin (D) 2019
Wyoming	(X)	(X)	251	R-73.9	Michael B. Enzi (R) 2015	John Barrasso (R) 2019

X Not applicable. [1] As of June 05, 2013, see <http://www.senate.gov/pagelayout/reference/three_column_table/Senators.htm>. [2] Includes vote cast for minor parties. [3] Louisiana holds an open-primary election with candidates from all parties running on the same ballot. Any candidate who receives a majority is elected. [4] Appointed February 1, 2013 to fill the vacancy due to the resignation of John F. Kerry, February 1, 2013. [5] Vacancy due to the death of Frank R. Lautenberg, June 3, 2013. [6] Appointed January 2, 2013 to fill the vacancy caused by the resignation of James DeMint.

Source: U.S. House of Representatives, Office of the Clerk, *Statistics of the Presidential and Congressional Election*, February 2013. See also <http://clerk.house.gov/member_info/election.html>.

Table 427. Apportionment of Membership in House of Representatives by State: 1800 to 2010

[Total membership includes Representatives assigned to newly admitted States after the apportionment acts. Population figures used for apportionment purposes are those determined for States by each decennial census. No reapportionment based on 1920 population census. For method of calculating apportionment and a short history of apportionment, see House Report 91-1314, 91st Congress, 2d session, The Decennial Population Census and Congressional Apportionment]

State	Membership based on census of—																				
	1800	1820	1830	1840	1850	1860	1870	1880	1890	1900	1910	1920	1930	1940	1950	1960	1970	1980	1990	2000	2010
U.S.	**142**	**213**	**242**	**232**	**237**	**243**	**293**	**332**	**357**	**391**	**435**	**435**	**435**	**435**	**437**	**435**	**435**	**435**	**435**	**435**	**43**
AL	(X)	3	5	7	7	6	8	8	9	9	10	10	9	9	9	8	7	7	7	7	
AK	(X)	(X)	(X)	(X)	(X)	(X)	(X)	(X)	(X)	(X)	(X)	(X)	(X)	(X)	[1]1	1	1	1	1	1	
AZ	(X)	(X)	(X)	(X)	(X)	(X)	(X)	(X)	(X)	(X)	[2]2	1	1	2	2	3	4	5	6	8	
AR	(X)	(X)	[1]1	1	2	3	4	5	6	7	7	7	7	7	6	4	4	4	4	4	
CA	(X)	(X)	(X)	[1]2	2	3	4	6	7	8	11	11	20	23	30	38	43	45	52	53	5
CO	(X)	(X)	(X)	(X)	(X)	(X)	[1]1	1	2	3	4	4	4	4	4	4	5	6	6	7	
CT	7	6	6	4	4	4	4	4	4	5	5	5	6	6	6	6	6	6	6	5	
DE	1	1	1	1	1	1	1	1	1	1	1	1	1	1	1	1	1	1	1	1	
FL	(X)	(X)	(X)	[1]1	1	1	2	2	2	3	4	4	5	6	8	12	15	19	23	25	2
GA	4	7	9	8	8	7	9	10	11	11	12	12	10	10	10	10	10	10	11	13	1
HI	(X)	(X)	(X)	(X)	(X)	(X)	(X)	(X)	(X)	(X)	(X)	(X)	(X)	(X)	[1]1	2	2	2	2	2	
ID	(X)	(X)	(X)	(X)	(X)	(X)	(X)	(X)	[1]1	1	2	2	2	2	2	2	2	2	2	2	
IL	(X)	1	3	7	9	14	19	20	22	25	27	27	27	26	25	24	24	22	20	19	1
IN	(X)	3	7	10	11	11	13	13	13	13	13	13	12	11	11	11	11	10	10	9	
IA	(X)	(X)	(X)	[1]2	2	6	9	11	11	11	11	11	9	8	8	7	6	6	5	5	
KS	(X)	(X)	(X)	(X)	(X)	1	3	7	8	8	8	8	7	6	6	5	5	5	4	4	
KY	6	12	13	10	10	9	10	11	11	11	11	11	9	9	8	7	7	7	6	6	
LA	(X)	3	3	4	4	5	6	6	6	7	8	8	8	8	8	8	8	8	7	7	
ME	(X)	7	8	7	6	5	5	4	4	4	4	4	3	3	3	2	2	2	2	2	
MD	9	9	8	6	6	5	6	6	6	6	6	6	6	6	7	8	8	8	8	8	
MA	17	13	12	10	11	10	11	12	13	14	16	16	15	14	14	12	12	11	10	10	
MI	(X)	(X)	[1]1	3	4	6	9	11	12	12	13	13	17	17	18	19	19	18	16	15	1
MN	(X)	(X)	(X)	(X)	[1]2	2	3	5	7	9	10	10	9	9	9	8	8	8	8	8	
MS	(X)	1	2	4	5	5	6	7	7	8	8	8	7	7	6	5	5	5	5	4	
MO	(X)	1	2	5	7	9	13	14	15	16	16	16	13	13	11	10	10	9	9	9	
MT	(X)	(X)	(X)	(X)	(X)	(X)	(X)	[1]1	1	1	2	2	2	2	2	2	2	2	1	1	
NE	(X)	(X)	(X)	(X)	(X)	(X)	[1]1	1	3	6	6	6	5	4	4	3	3	3	3	3	
NV	(X)	(X)	(X)	(X)	(X)	(X)	[1]1	1	1	1	1	1	1	1	1	1	1	2	2	3	
NH	5	6	5	4	3	3	3	2	2	2	2	2	2	2	2	2	2	2	2	2	
NJ	6	6	6	5	5	5	7	7	8	10	12	12	14	14	14	15	15	14	13	13	1
NM	(X)	(X)	(X)	(X)	(X)	(X)	(X)	(X)	(X)	(X)	[2]1	1	1	2	2	2	2	3	3	3	
NY	17	34	40	34	33	31	33	34	34	37	43	43	45	45	43	41	39	34	31	29	2
NC	12	13	13	9	8	7	8	9	9	10	10	10	11	12	12	11	11	11	12	13	1
ND	(X)	(X)	(X)	(X)	(X)	(X)	(X)	[1]1	1	2	3	3	2	2	2	2	1	1	1	1	
OH	[1]1	14	19	21	21	19	20	21	21	21	22	22	24	23	23	24	23	21	19	18	1
OK	(X)	(X)	(X)	(X)	(X)	(X)	(X)	(X)	(X)	[1]5	8	8	9	8	6	6	6	6	6	5	
OR	(X)	(X)	(X)	(X)	[1]1	1	1	1	2	2	3	3	3	4	4	4	4	5	5	5	
PA	18	26	28	24	25	24	27	28	30	32	36	36	34	33	30	27	25	23	21	19	1
RI	2	2	2	2	2	2	2	2	2	2	3	3	2	2	2	2	2	2	2	2	
SC	8	9	9	7	6	4	5	7	7	7	7	7	6	6	6	6	6	6	6	6	
SD	(X)	(X)	(X)	(X)	(X)	(X)	(X)	[1]2	2	2	3	3	2	2	2	2	2	1	1	1	
TN	3	9	13	11	10	8	10	10	10	10	10	10	9	10	9	9	8	9	9	9	
TX	(X)	(X)	(X)	[1]2	2	4	6	11	13	16	18	18	21	21	22	23	24	27	30	32	3
UT	(X)	(X)	(X)	(X)	(X)	(X)	(X)	(X)	[1]1	1	2	2	2	2	2	2	2	3	3	3	
VT	4	5	5	4	3	3	3	2	2	2	2	2	1	1	1	1	1	1	1	1	
VA	22	22	21	15	13	11	9	10	10	10	10	10	9	9	10	10	10	10	11	11	1
WA	(X)	(X)	(X)	(X)	(X)	(X)	(X)	[1]1	2	3	5	5	6	6	7	7	7	8	9	9	1
WV	(X)	(X)	(X)	(X)	(X)	(X)	3	4	4	5	6	6	6	6	6	5	4	4	3	3	
WI	(X)	(X)	(X)	[1]2	3	6	8	9	10	11	11	11	10	10	10	10	9	9	9	8	
WY	(X)	(X)	(X)	(X)	(X)	(X)	(X)	[1]1	1	1	1	1	1	1	1	1	1	1	1	1	

X Not applicable. [1] Assigned after apportionment. [2] Included in apportionment in anticipation of statehood.

Source: U.S. Census Bureau, Congressional Apportionment, Census 2010, <http://www.census.gov/population/apportionment/>.

Table 428. Vote Cast for U.S. Representatives by Major Political Party— States: 2008 to 2012

[In thousands (122,586 represents 122,586,000), except percent. R = Republican, D = Democrat, and I = Independent. In each state, totals represent the sum of votes cast in each Congressional District or votes cast for Representative-at-Large in states where only one member is elected. In all years there are numerous districts within the state where either the Republican or Democratic party had no candidate. In some states the Republican and Democratic vote includes votes cast for the party candidate by endorsing parties]

State	2008 Total [1]	2008 Democratic	2008 Republican	2008 Percent for leading party	2010 Total [1]	2010 Democratic	2010 Republican	2010 Percent for leading party	2012 Total [1]	2012 Democratic	2012 Republican	2012 Percent for leading party
U.S.	122,586	64,888	51,953	D-52.9	86,785	38,854	44,594	R-51.4	122,346	59,215	57,623	D-48.4
AL	1,855	718	1,121	R-60.4	1,368	419	914	R-66.9	1,934	693	1,234	R-63.8
AK	317	143	159	R-50.1	254	78	175	R-69.0	290	83	185	R-63.9
AZ	2,156	1,055	1,022	D-49.0	1,698	712	901	R-53.0	2,173	947	1,132	R-52.1
AR	787	415	215	D-52.8	774	318	435	R-56.2	1,038	305	638	R-61.4
CA	12,322	7,381	4,516	D-59.9	9,648	5,149	4,195	D-53.4	12,204	7,393	4,530	D-60.6
CO	2,284	1,260	991	D-55.2	1,763	801	884	R-50.1	2,450	1,080	1,144	R-46.7
CT	1,527	909	505	D-59.5	1,138	635	458	D-55.8	1,467	884	491	D-60.3
DE [2]	385	146	235	R-61.1	306	174	125	D-56.8	388	250	130	D-64.4
FL [2]	7,421	3,435	3,792	R-51.1	5,117	1,854	3,004	R-58.7	7,514	3,392	3,827	R-50.9
GA	3,655	1,858	1,797	D-50.8	2,469	940	1,528	R-61.9	3,553	1,449	2,104	R-59.2
HI	456	320	83	D-70.2	360	226	129	D-62.9	437	285	138	D-65.2
ID	638	260	377	R-59.2	447	151	264	R-59.0	635	208	407	R-64.0
IL	5,248	3,176	1,961	D-60.5	3,696	1,876	1,720	D-50.8	5,058	2,744	2,208	D-54.2
IN	2,677	1,389	1,241	D-51.9	1,748	679	973	R-55.7	2,554	1,143	1,352	R-52.9
IA	1,482	759	698	D-51.3	1,107	480	597	R-54.0	1,537	772	727	D-50.3
KS	1,208	470	690	R-57.1	836	275	528	R-63.2	1,058	196	741	R-70.1
KY	1,750	761	955	R-54.6	1,354	506	844	R-62.3	1,745	685	1,028	R-58.9
LA [2]	1,046	398	594	R-56.8	1,036	311	675	R-65.2	1,706	359	1,143	R-67.0
ME	710	432	278	D-60.8	564	316	248	D-56.0	725	428	266	D-59.0
MD	2,498	1,677	763	D-67.2	1,825	1,104	674	D-60.5	2,586	1,627	858	D-62.9
MA	3,103	2,246	318	D-72.4	2,224	1,336	808	D-60.1	3,184	2,081	698	D-65.3
MI	4,811	2,517	2,114	D-52.3	3,195	1,415	1,672	R-52.3	4,575	2,328	2,087	D-50.9
MN	2,803	1,612	1,069	D-57.5	2,091	1,002	971	D-47.9	2,813	1,561	1,210	D-55.5
MS	1,265	732	527	D-57.9	789	351	424	R-53.7	1,208	411	704	R-58.2
MO	2,821	1,413	1,313	D-50.1	1,921	708	1,103	R-57.4	2,676	1,120	1,464	R-54.7
MT	481	156	308	R-64.1	360	122	218	R-60.4	480	205	255	R-53.3
NE	775	265	511	R-65.8	486	138	328	R-67.5	773	276	496	R-64.2
NV	908	457	384	D-50.4	703	318	357	R-50.9	974	453	457	R-47.0
NH	675	365	295	D-54.1	450	201	230	R-51.2	682	341	312	D-50.0
NJ	3,438	1,912	1,462	D-55.6	2,122	1,025	1,055	R-49.7	3,282	1,794	1,430	D-54.7
NM	815	457	321	D-56.1	597	308	289	D-51.6	766	422	343	D-55.1
NY	7,722	4,006	1,800	D-51.9	4,744	2,515	1,613	D-53.0	7,116	3,898	1,733	D-54.8
NC	4,215	2,294	1,902	D-54.4	2,663	1,205	1,441	R-54.1	4,384	2,218	2,137	D-50.6
ND	314	195	119	D-62.0	236	107	130	R-54.9	316	132	174	R-54.9
OH	5,374	2,752	2,491	D-51.2	3,825	1,611	2,053	R-53.7	5,142	2,412	2,620	R-51.0
OK [2]	1,337	504	803	R-60.0	793	222	520	R-65.5	1,326	410	857	R-64.6
OR	1,683	1,036	436	D-61.6	1,429	733	657	D-51.3	1,708	853	547	D-49.9
PA	5,788	3,209	2,521	D-55.4	3,956	1,882	2,034	R-51.4	5,556	2,794	2,710	D-50.3
RI	438	304	119	D-69.3	335	186	127	D-55.4	428	233	162	D-54.4
SC	1,874	920	940	R-50.1	1,340	537	754	R-56.3	1,803	714	1,026	R-56.9
SD	379	256	123	D-67.6	319	147	154	R-48.1	361	154	208	R-57.4
TN	2,302	1,196	978	D-51.9	1,559	542	955	R-61.3	2,284	797	1,370	R-60.0
TX	7,529	2,979	4,204	R-55.8	4,746	1,450	3,058	R-64.4	7,664	2,950	4,429	R-57.8
UT	937	394	504	R-53.8	640	218	391	R-61.0	999	324	648	R-64.9
VT	298	248	(X)	D-83.2	239	154	76	D-64.6	290	209	68	D-71.9
VA	3,495	1,853	1,591	D-53.0	2,190	911	1,186	R-54.2	3,740	1,806	1,877	R-50.2
WA	2,914	1,725	1,189	D-59.2	2,479	1,297	1,135	D-52.3	3,006	1,637	1,370	D-54.4
WV	646	432	213	D-66.9	514	228	283	R-55.0	641	257	384	R-59.9
WI	2,775	1,384	1,275	D-49.9	2,140	939	1,166	R-54.5	2,866	1,445	1,402	D-50.4
WY	250	107	131	R-52.6	191	46	132	R-69.0	251	58	166	R-66.4

X Not applicable. [1] Includes votes cast for minor parties. [2] State law does not require tabulation of votes for unopposed candidates.

Source: U.S. House of Representatives, Office of the Clerk, *Statistics of the Presidential and Congressional Election*, February 2013. See also <http://clerk.house.gov/member_info/election.html>.

Table 429. Vote Cast for U.S. Representatives by Major Political Party—Congressional Districts: 2012

[As of February 2013. Does not include special elections, see <http://clerk.house.gov/member_info/vacancies.html>. In some states the Democratic and Republican vote includes votes cast for the party candidate by endorsing parties]

State and district	Democratic candidate Name	Percent of total	Republican candidate Name	Percent of total	State and district	Democratic candidate Name	Percent of total	Republican candidate Name	Percent of total
AL......	(X)	(X)	(X)	(X)	2d......	Polis	55.69	Lundberg	38.58
1st.....	(¹)	(¹)	Bonner	97.86	3d......	Pace	41.07	Tipton	53.36
2d.....	Ford	36.31	Roby	63.60	4th....	Shaffer	36.75	Gardner	58.42
3d.....	Harris	35.83	Rogers	64.00	5th....	(¹)	(¹)	Lamborn	64.98
4th....	Boman	25.90	Aderholt	73.97	6th....	Miklosi	45.77	Coffman	47.81
5th....	Holley	34.94	Brooks	64.95	7th....	Perlmutter	53.51	Coors	40.79
6th....	Bailey	28.65	Bachus	71.17	**CT**......	(X)	(X)	(X)	(X)
7th....	Sewell	75.85	Chamberlain	24.09	1st......	Larson	64.92	Decker	27.71
AK......	Cissna	28.61	Young	63.94	2d......	Courtney	63.16	Formica	29.37
AZ......	(X)	(X)	(X)	(X)	3d......	DeLauro	67.68	Winsley	25.31
1st.....	Kirkpatrick	48.80	Paton	45.15	4th....	Himes	57.02	Obsitnik	40.04
2d.....	Barber	50.41	McSally	49.57	5th....	Esty	48.33	Roraback	45.28
3d.....	Grijalva	58.37	Saucedo-Mercer	37.15	**DE**......	Carney	64.41	Kovach	33.44
4th....	Robinson	28.37	Gosar	66.83	**FL**......	(X)	(X)	(X)	(X)
5th....	Morgan	32.81	Salmon	67.19	1st......	Bryan	27.13	Miller	69.60
6th....	Jette	33.31	Schweikert	61.30	2d......	Lawson	47.24	Southerland	52.70
7th....	Pastor	81.74	(¹)	(¹)	3d......	Gaillot	32.46	Yoho	64.73
8th....	Scharer	35.06	Franks	63.35	4th....	(¹)	(¹)	Crenshaw	76.07
9th....	Sinema	48.73	Parker	44.63	5th....	Brown	70.77	Kolb	26.27
AR......	(X)	(X)	(X)	(X)	6th....	Beaven	42.78	Desantis	57.22
1st.....	Ellington	39.13	Crawford	56.23	7th....	Kendall	41.29	Mica	58.71
2d.....	Rule	39.48	Griffin	55.19	8th....	Roberts	37.51	Posey	58.88
3d.....	(¹)	(¹)	Womack	75.90	9th....	Grayson	62.52	Long	37.48
4th....	Jeffress	36.69	Cotton	59.53	10th....	Demings	48.25	Webster	51.73
CA......	(X)	(X)	(X)	(X)	11th....	Werder	35.52	Nugent	64.48
1st.....	Reed	42.62	LaMalfa	57.38	12th....	Snow	32.94	Bilirakis	63.48
2d.....	Huffman	71.24	Roberts	28.76	13th....	Ehrlich	42.43	Young	57.57
3d.....	Garamendi	54.23	Vann	45.77	14th....	Castor	70.25	Otero	29.75
4th....	Uppal	38.89	McClintock	61.11	15th....	(¹)	(¹)	Ross	(²)
5th....	Thompson	74.47	Loftin	25.53	16th....	Fitzgerald	46.39	Buchanan	53.61
6th....	Matsui	75.05	McCray	24.95	17th....	Bronson	41.37	Rooney	58.63
7th....	Bera	51.68	Lungren	48.32	18th....	Murphy	50.28	West	49.70
8th....	Imus	42.61	Cook	57.39	19th....	Roach	35.84	Radel	61.99
9th....	McNerney	55.55	Gill	44.45	20th....	Hastings	87.90	(¹)	(¹)
10th....	Hernandez	47.29	Denham	52.71	21st....	Deutch	77.80	(¹)	(¹)
11th....	Miller	69.73	Fuller	30.27	22d.....	Frankel	54.63	Hasner	45.37
12th....	Pelosi	85.08	Dennis	14.92	23d.....	Wasserman	63.25	Harrington	35.62
13th....	Lee	86.78	(¹)	(¹)	24th....	Wilson	(²)	(¹)	(¹)
14th....	Speier	78.92	Bacigalupi	21.08	25th....	(¹)	(¹)	Diaz-Balart	75.65
15th....	Swalwell	52.11	(¹)	(¹)	26th....	Garcia	53.64	Rivera	43.02
16th....	Costa	57.41	Whelan	42.59	27th....	Yevancey	36.94	Ros-Lehtinen	60.17
17th....	Honda	73.54	Li	26.46	**GA**......	(X)	(X)	(X)	(X)
18th....	Eshoo	70.49	Chapman	29.51	1st......	Messinger	37.02	Kingston	62.98
19th....	Lofgren	73.24	Murray	26.76	2d......	Bishop	63.78	House	36.22
20th....	Farr	74.07	Taylor	25.93	3d......	(¹)	(¹)	Westmoreland	100.00
21st....	Hernandez	42.24	Valadao	57.76	4th....	Johnson	73.57	Vaughn	26.43
22d.....	Lee	38.12	Nunes	61.88	5th....	Lewis	84.39	Stopeck	15.61
23d.....	(¹)	(¹)	McCarthy	73.22	6th....	Kazanow	35.49	Price	64.51
24th....	Capps	55.10	Maldonado	44.90	7th....	Reilly	37.84	Woodall	62.16
25th....	Rogers	45.22	McKeon	54.78	8th....	(¹)	(¹)	Scott	100.00
26th....	Brownley	52.69	Strickland	47.31	9th....	Cooley	23.82	Collins	76.18
27th....	Chu	63.98	Orswell	36.02	10th....	(¹)	(¹)	Broun	100.00
28th....	Schiff	76.49	Jennerjahn	23.51	11th....	Thompson	31.45	Gingrey	68.55
29th....	Cardenas	74.05	(¹)	(¹)	12th....	Barrow	53.70	Anderson	46.30
30th....	Sherman	60.30	(¹)	(¹)	13th....	Scott	71.74	Malik	28.26
31st....	(¹)	(¹)	Miller	55.18	14th....	Grant	27.03	Graves	72.97
32d.....	Napolitano	65.70	Miller	34.30	**HI**......	(X)	(X)	(X)	(X)
33d.....	Waxman	53.96	(¹)	(¹)	1st......	Hanabusa	53.47	Djou	44.44
34th....	Becerra	85.62	Smith	14.38	2d......	Gabbard	76.84	Crowley	18.56
35th....	Negrete-McLeod	55.86	(¹)	(¹)	**ID**......	(X)	(X)	(X)	(X)
36th....	Ruiz	52.94	Mack	47.06	1st......	Farris	30.77	Labrador	62.96
37th....	Bass	86.42	Osborne	13.58	2d......	LeFavour	34.80	Simpson	65.12
38th....	Sanchez	67.54	Campos	32.46	**IL**......	(X)	(X)	(X)	(X)
39th....	Chen	42.21	Royce	57.79	1st......	Rush	73.82	Peloquin	26.18
40th....	Roybal-Allard	58.89	(¹)	(¹)	2d......	Jackson	63.25	Woodworth	23.22
41st....	Takano	58.97	Tavaglione	41.03	3d......	Lipinski	68.48	Grabowski	31.52
42d.....	Williamson	39.41	Calvert	60.59	4th....	Gutierrez	83.00	Concepcion	17.00
43d.....	Waters	71.24	(¹)	(¹)	5th....	Quigley	65.73	Schmitt	28.59
44th....	Hahn	60.22	(¹)	(¹)	6th....	Coolidge	40.78	Roskam	59.22
45th....	Kang	41.54	Campbell	58.46	7th....	Davis	84.64	Zak	10.99
46th....	Sanchez	63.87	Hayden	36.13	8th....	Duckworth	54.74	Walsh	45.26
47th....	Lowenthal	56.56	DeLong	43.44	9th....	Schakowsky	66.33	Wolfe	33.67
48th....	Varasteh	39.02	Rohrabacher	60.98	10th....	Schneider	50.63	Dold	49.37
49th....	Tetalman	41.84	Issa	58.16	11th....	Foster	58.57	Biggert	41.43
50th....	Secor	32.31	Hunter	67.69	12th....	Enyart	51.65	Plummer	42.74
51st....	Vargas	71.48	Crimmins	28.52	13th....	Gill	46.21	Davis	46.55
52d.....	Peters	51.18	Bilbray	48.82	14th....	Anderson	41.18	Hultgren	58.82
53d.....	Davis	61.43	Popaditch	38.57	15th....	Michael	31.39	Shimkus	68.61
CO......	(X)	(X)	(X)	(X)	16th....	Rohl	38.19	Kinzinger	61.81
1st......	DeGette	68.23	Stroud	26.77	17th....	Bustos	53.28	Schilling	46.72

See footnotes at end of table.

Table 429. Vote Cast for U.S. Representatives by Major Political Party—
Congressional Districts: 2012-Continued.
See headnote on page 274.

State and district	Democratic candidate Name	Percent of total	Republican candidate Name	Percent of total
18th....	Waterworth	25.84	Schock	74.16
IN.......	(X)	(X)	(X)	(X)
1st.....	Visclosky	67.28	Phelps	32.72
2d.....	Mullen	47.58	Walorski	49.01
3d.....	Boyd	32.96	Stutzman	67.04
4th....	Nelson	34.16	Rokita	61.96
5th....	Reske	37.60	Brooks	58.37
6th....	Bookout	35.12	Messer	59.08
7th....	Carson	62.85	May	37.15
8th....	Crooks	43.07	Bucshon	53.36
9th....	Yoder	44.55	Young	55.45
IA......	(X)	(X)	(X)	(X)
1st.....	Braley	56.91	Lange	41.57
2d.....	Loebsack	55.57	Archer	42.48
3d.....	Boswell	43.59	Latham	52.22
4th....	Vilsack	44.85	King	52.94
KS......	(X)	(X)	(X)	(X)
1st.....	(1)	(1)	Huelskamp	100.00
2d.....	Schlingensiepen	38.72	Jenkins	57.01
3d.....	(1)	(1)	Yoder	68.45
4th....	Tillman	31.58	Pompeo	62.22
KY......	(X)	(X)	(X)	(X)
1st.....	Hatchett	30.37	Whitfield	69.63
2d.....	Williams	31.72	Guthrie	64.30
3d.....	Yarmuth	63.96	Wicker	34.54
4th....	Adkins	34.98	Massie	62.13
5th....	Stepp	22.10	Rogers	77.90
6th....	Chandler	46.68	Barr	50.57
LA......	(X)	(X)	(X)	(X)
1st.....	Mendoza	21.25	Scalise	66.63
2d.....	Richmond	55.16	Bailey	13.50
3d.....	Richard	21.54	Boustany	44.68
4th....	(1)	(1)	Fleming	75.30
5th....	(1)	(1)	Alexander	77.83
6th....	(1)	(1)	Cassidy	79.41
ME......	(X)	(X)	(X)	(X)
1st.....	Pingree	62.08	Courtney	33.74
2d.....	Michaud	55.67	Raye	39.99
MD......	(X)	(X)	(X)	(X)
1st.....	Rosen	27.48	Harris	63.42
2d.....	Ruppersberger	65.58	Jacobs	31.11
3d.....	Sarbanes	66.83	Knowles	29.56
4th....	Edwards	77.17	Loudon	20.72
5th....	Hoyer	69.40	O'Donnell	27.71
6th....	Delaney	58.77	Bartlett	37.90
7th....	Cummings	76.52	Mirabile	20.82
8th....	Van Hollen	63.37	Timmerman	32.93
MA......	(X)	(X)	(X)	(X)
1st.....	Neal	77.83	(1)	(1)
2d.....	McGovern	75.64	(1)	(1)
3d.....	Tsongas	63.30	Golnik	32.64
4th....	Kennedy	59.31	Bielat	34.82
5th....	Markey	70.70	Tierney	22.77
6th....	Tierney	46.41	Tisei	45.30
7th....	Capuano	73.93	(1)	(1)
8th....	Lynch	71.03	Selvaggi	22.13
9th....	Keating	55.15	Sheldon	30.21
MI......	(X)	(X)	(X)	(X)
1st.....	McDowell	47.60	Benishek	48.14
2d.....	German	34.24	Huizenga	61.16
3d.....	Pestka	44.17	Amash	52.62
4th....	Wirth	33.55	Camp	63.07
5th....	Kildee	64.98	Slezak	31.48
6th....	O'Brien	42.61	Upton	54.59
7th....	Haskell	43.02	Walberg	53.34
8th....	Enderle	37.29	Rogers	58.60
9th....	Levin	61.91	Volaric	34.02
10th...	Stadler	29.74	Miller	68.80
11th...	Taj	44.36	Bentivolio	50.76
12th...	Dingell	67.94	Kallgren	28.97
13th...	Conyers	82.79	Sawicki	13.64
14th...	Peters	82.26	Hauler	15.63
MN......	(X)	(X)	(X)	(X)
1st.....	Walz	57.52	Quist	42.33
2d.....	Obermueller	45.85	Kline	54.01
3d.....	Barnes	41.79	Paulsen	58.10
4th....	McCollum	62.27	Hernandez	31.51
5th....	Ellison	74.47	Fields	25.22
6th....	Graves	49.26	Bachman	50.47
7th....	Peterson	60.38	Byberg	34.85
8th....	Nolan	54.28	Cravaack	45.39
MS......	(X)	(X)	(X)	(X)

State and district	Democratic candidate Name	Percent of total	Republican candidate Name	Percent of total
1st......	Morris	36.90	Nunnelee	60.41
2d......	Thompson	67.13	Marcy	30.96
3d......	(1)	(1)	Harper	80.02
4th....	Moore	28.85	Palazzo	64.11
MO......	(X)	(X)	(X)	(X)
1st.....	Clay	78.67	Hamlin	17.86
2d.....	Koenen	37.08	Wagner	60.08
3d.....	Mayer	32.86	Luetkemeyer	63.49
4th....	Hensley	35.49	Hartzler	60.31
5th....	Cleaver	60.52	Turk	36.91
6th....	Yarber	32.52	Graves	65.00
7th....	Evans	30.90	Long	63.87
8th....	Rushin	24.55	Emerson	71.93
MT......	Gillan	42.72	Daines	53.25
NE......	(X)	(X)	(X)	(X)
1st.....	Reiman	31.71	Fortenberry	68.29
2d.....	Ewing	49.20	Terry	50.80
3d.....	Sullivan	25.83	Smith	74.17
NV......	(X)	(X)	(X)	(X)
1st.....	Titus	63.57	Edwards	31.53
2d.....	Koepnick	36.25	Amodei	57.63
3d.....	Oceguera	42.87	Heck	50.36
4th....	Horsford	50.11	Tarkanian	42.11
NH......	(X)	(X)	(X)	(X)
1st.....	Shea-Porter	49.75	Guinta	45.99
2d.....	Kuster	50.17	Bass	45.34
NJ......	(X)	(X)	(X)	(X)
1st.....	Andrews	68.22	Horton	29.97
2d.....	Shober	40.29	LoBiondo	57.66
3d.....	Adler	44.85	Runyan	53.72
4th....	Froelich	35.26	Smith	63.72
5th....	Gussen	42.74	Garrett	55.03
6th....	Pallone	63.34	Little	35.20
7th....	Chivukula	40.04	Lance	57.16
8th....	Sires	77.99	Karczewski	18.93
9th....	Pascrell	73.97	Boteach	25.03
10th...	Payne	87.56	Kelemen	10.55
11th...	Arvanites	39.98	Frelinghuysen	58.81
12th...	Holt	69.22	Beck	29.49
NM......	(X)	(X)	(X)	(X)
1st.....	Grisham	59.06	Arnold-Jones	40.77
2d.....	Erhard	40.87	Pearce	59.06
3d.....	Lujan	63.12	Byrd	36.88
NY......	(X)	(X)	(X)	(X)
1st.....	Bishop	45.56	Altschuler	36.21
2d.....	Falcone	34.35	King	42.70
3d.....	Israel	47.67	Labate	32.15
4th....	McCarthy	50.95	Becker	28.38
5th....	Meeks	74.76	Jennings	7.96
6th....	Meng	57.51	Halloran	24.60
7th....	Velazquez	74.07	(1)	(1)
8th....	Jeffries	75.62	Bellone	6.70
9th....	Clarke	74.56	Cavanagh	8.75
10th...	Nadler	65.97	Chan	15.00
11th...	Murphy	40.85	Grimm	42.39
12th...	Maloney	68.91	Wight	15.64
13th...	Rangel	73.11	Schley	5.20
14th...	Crowley	67.91	Gibbons	11.22
15th...	Serrano	84.10	Della Valle	1.95
16th...	Engel	64.33	McLaughlin	19.95
17th...	Lowey	54.35	Carvin	30.90
18th...	Maloney	44.83	Hayworth	38.38
19th...	Schreibman	39.33	Gibson	40.10
20th...	Tonko	57.00	Dieterich	24.90
21st...	Owens	43.85	Doheny	38.84
22d.....	Lamb	36.43	Hanna	51.77
23d.....	Shinagawa	40.95	Reed	42.05
24th...	Maffei	44.11	Buerkle	34.78
25th...	Slaughter	52.29	Brooks	33.86
26th...	Higgins	64.02	Madigan	18.81
27th...	Hochul	42.46	Collins	41.62
NC......	(X)	(X)	(X)	(X)
1st.....	Butterfield	75.32	DiLauro	22.86
2d.....	Wilkins	41.42	Ellmers	55.90
3d.....	Anderson	36.89	Jones	63.11
4th....	Price	74.47	D'Annunzio	25.53
5th....	Motsinger	42.46	Foxx	57.54
6th....	Foriest	39.08	Coble	60.92
7th....	McIntyre	50.10	Rouzer	49.90
8th....	Kissell	45.37	Hudson	53.16
9th....	Roberts	45.65	Pittenger	51.78
10th...	Keever	43.01	McHenry	56.99

See footnotes at end of table.

Table 429. Vote Cast for U.S. Representatives by Major Political Party— Congressional Districts: 2012-Continued.

See headnote on page 274.

State and district	Democratic candidate Name	Percent of total	Republican candidate Name	Percent of total	State and district	Democratic candidate Name	Percent of total	Republican candidate Name	Percent of total
11th....	Rogers	42.58	Meadows	57.42	3d.....	(1)	(1)	Johnson	100.00
12th....	Watt	79.63	Brosch	20.37	4th....	Hathcox	24.05	Hall	72.97
13th....	Malone	43.20	Holding	56.80	5th....	Mrosko	33.22	Hensarling	64.40
ND......	Gulleson	41.70	Cramer	54.89	6th....	Sanders	39.23	Barton	58.02
OH......	(X)	(X)	(X)	(X)	7th....	Cargas	36.43	Culberson	60.81
1st.....	Sinnard	37.60	Chabot	57.73	8th....	Burns	20.33	Brady	77.29
2d.....	Smith	41.37	Wenstrup	58.63	9th....	Green	78.49	Mueller	19.69
3d.....	Beatty	68.29	Long	26.35	10th....	Cadien	36.25	McCaul	60.52
4th....	Slone	36.49	Jordan	58.35	11th....	Riley	18.57	Conaway	78.64
5th....	Zimmann	39.16	Latta	57.27	12th....	Robinson	26.68	Granger	70.91
6th....	Wilson	46.75	Johnson	53.25	13th....	(1)	(1)	Thornberry	90.98
7th....	Healy-Abrams	43.60	Gibbs	56.40	14th....	Lampson	44.62	Weber	53.47
8th....	(1)	(1)	Boehner	99.22	15th....	Hinojosa	60.89	Brueggemann	36.86
9th....	Kaptur	73.04	Wurzelbacher	23.03	16th....	O'Rourke	65.42	Carrasco	32.93
10th....	Swartz-Neuhardt	37.49	Turner	59.54	17th....	(1)	(1)	Flores	79.93
11th....	Fudge	100.00	(1)	(1)	18th....	Lee	75.01	Seibert	22.58
12th....	Reese	36.53	Tiberi	63.47	19th....	(1)	(1)	Neugebauer	84.99
13th....	Ryan	72.77	Agana	27.23	20th....	Castro	63.93	Rosa	33.50
14th....	Blanchard	38.73	Joyce	54.03	21st....	Duval	35.40	Smith	60.55
15th....	Lang	38.44	Stivers	61.56	22d.....	Rogers	31.96	Olson	64.03
16th....	Sutton	47.95	Renacci	52.05	23d.....	Gallego	50.31	Canseco	45.56
OK......	(X)	(X)	(X)	(X)	24th....	Rusk	36.00	Marchant	61.02
1st.....	Olson	32.04	Bridenstine	63.47	25th....	Henderson	37.44	Williams	58.44
2d.....	Wallace	38.34	Mullin	57.34	26th....	Sanchez	28.69	Burgess	68.27
3d.....	Murray	19.95	Lucas	75.28	27th....	Meza Harrison	39.22	Farenthold	56.75
4th....	Bebo	27.60	Cole	67.89	28th....	Cuellar	67.89	Hayward	29.77
5th....	Guild	37.26	Lankford	58.70	29th....	Green	90.00	(1)	(1)
OR......	(X)	(X)	(X)	(X)	30th....	Johnson	78.82	Washington	19.00
1st.....	Bonamici	59.60	Morgan	33.04	31st....	Wyman	34.98	Carter	61.28
2d.....	Segers	29.12	Walden	68.63	32d.....	McGovern	39.46	Sessions	58.28
3d.....	Blumenauer	74.46	Green	19.76	33d.....	Veasey	72.51	Bradley	25.77
4th....	DeFazio	59.11	Robinson	39.03	34th....	Vela	61.89	Bradshaw	36.23
5th....	Schrader	54.04	Thompson	42.45	35th....	Doggett	63.95	Narvaiz	32.02
PA......	(X)	(X)	(X)	(X)	36th....	Martin	26.58	Stockman	70.74
1st.....	Brady	84.95	Featherman	15.05	UT......	(X)	(X)	(X)	(X)
2d	Fattah	89.28	Mansfield	9.37	1st.....	McAleer	24.69	Bishop	71.47
3d.....	Eaton	40.97	Kelly	54.82	2d.....	Seegmiller	33.47	Stewart	62.17
4th....	Perkinson	34.42	Perry	59.74	3d.....	Simonsen	23.39	Chaffetz	76.61
5th....	Dumas	37.08	Thompson	62.92	4th....	Matheson	48.84	Love	48.53
6th....	Trivedi	42.86	Gerlach	57.14	VT......	Welch	71.95	Donka	23.30
7th....	Badey	40.60	Meehan	59.40	VA......	(X)	(X)	(X)	(X)
8th....	Boockvar	43.40	Fitzpatrick	56.60	1st.....	Cook	41.21	Wittman	56.29
9th....	Ramsburg	38.33	Shuster	61.67	2d.....	Hirschbiel	46.10	Rigell	53.76
10th....	Scollo	34.42	Marino	65.58	3d.....	Scott	81.27	Longo	18.48
11th....	Stilp	41.46	Barletta	58.54	4th....	Ward	42.91	Forbes	56.93
12th....	Critz	48.26	Rothfus	51.74	5th....	Douglass	42.86	Hurt	55.44
13th....	Schwartz	69.09	Rooney	30.91	6th....	Schmookler	34.56	Goodlatte	65.23
14th....	Doyle	76.89	Lessmann	23.11	7th....	Powell	41.37	Cantor	58.39
15th....	Daugherty	43.25	Dent	56.75	8th....	Moran	64.59	Murray	30.57
16th....	Strader	39.04	Pitts	54.85	9th....	Flaccavento	38.59	Griffith	61.29
17th....	Cartwright	60.31	Cummings	39.69	10th....	Cabral	38.76	Wolf	58.41
18th....	Maggi	36.04	Murphy	63.96	11th....	Connolly	60.98	Perkins	35.49
RI.......	(X)	(X)	(X)	(X)	WA......	(X)	(X)	(X)	(X)
1st.....	Cicilline	52.95	Doherty	40.82	1st.....	DelBene	53.94	Koster	46.06
2d.....	Langevin	55.72	Riley	35.12	2d.....	Larsen	61.14	Matthews	38.86
SC......	(X)	(X)	(X)	(X)	3d.....	Haugen	39.62	Beutler	60.38
1st.....	Rose	33.84	Scott	62.03	4th....	Baechler	33.78	Hastings	66.22
2d.....	(1)	(1)	Wilson	96.27	5th....	Cowan	38.08	McMorris	61.92
3d.....	Doyle	33.26	Duncan	66.54	6th....	Kilmer	59.00	Driscoll	41.00
4th....	Morrow	31.51	Gowdy	64.90	7th....	McDermott	79.65	Bemis	20.35
5th....	Knott	40.97	Mulvaney	55.51	8th....	Porterfield	40.35	Reichert	59.65
6th....	Clyburn	93.62	(1)	(1)	9th....	Smith	71.62	Postma	28.38
7th....	Tinubu	41.56	Rice	55.51	10th....	Heck	58.56	Muri	41.44
SD......	Varilek	42.55	Noem	57.45	WV......	(X)	(X)	(X)	(X)
TN......	(X)	(X)	(X)	(X)	1st.....	Thorn	37.52	McKinley	62.48
1st.....	Woodruff	19.89	Roe	76.04	2d.....	Swint	30.23	Capito	69.77
2d.....	Goodale	20.61	Duncan	74.44	3d.....	Rahall	53.98	Snuffer	46.02
3d.....	Headrick	35.46	Fleischmann	61.43	WI......	(X)	(X)	(X)	(X)
4th....	Stewart	44.24	DesJarlais	55.76	1st.....	Zerban	43.39	Ryan	54.90
5th....	Cooper	65.23	Staats	32.78	2d.....	Pocan	67.90	Lee	31.90
6th....	(1)	(1)	Black	76.43	3d.....	Kind	64.08	Boland	35.82
7th....	Amouzouvik	23.97	Blackburn	71.02	4th....	Moore	72.21	Sebring	24.80
8th....	Dixon	28.45	Fincher	68.33	5th....	Heaster	32.05	Sensenbrenner	67.72
9th....	Cohen	75.07	Flinn	23.80	6th....	Kallas	37.78	Petri	62.12
TX......	(X)	(X)	(X)	(X)	7th....	Kreitlow	43.80	Duffy	56.08
1st.....	McKellar	26.93	Gohmert	71.43	8th....	Wall	43.97	Ribble	55.95
2d.....	Dougherty	32.68	Poe	64.82	WY......	Henrichsen	22.96	Lummis	66.39

X Not applicable. [1] No candidate. [2] According to state law, it is not required to tabulate votes for unopposed candidates.

Source: U.S. House of Representatives, Office of the Clerk, *Statistics of the Presidential and Congressional Election of November 6, 2012*, February 2013. See also <http://clerk.house.gov/member_info/election.html>.

Table 430. Composition of Congress by Political Party Affiliation—States: 2007 to 2013

[Figures are for the beginning of the first session, except as noted. Dem. = Democratic; Rep. = Republican]

State	Representatives								Senators							
	110th Cong., 2007		111th Cong.,[1] 2009		112th Cong., 2011		113th Cong.,[4] 2013		110th Cong.,[2] 2007		111th Cong.,[2,3] 2009		112th Cong.,[2] 2011		113th Cong.,[5] 2013	
	Dem.	Rep.	Dem.	Rep.	Dem.	Rep.	Dem.	Rep.	Dem.	Rep.	Dem.	Rep.	Dem.	Rep.	Dem.	Rep.
U.S.	**233**	**202**	**256**	**178**	**193**	**242**	**201**	**232**	**49**	**49**	**55**	**41**	**51**	**47**	**53**	**45**
AL	2	5	3	4	1	6	1	6	–	2	–	2	–	2	–	2
AK	–	1	–	1	–	1	–	1	–	2	1	1	1	1	1	1
AZ	4	4	5	3	3	5	5	4	–	2	–	2	–	2	–	2
AR	3	1	3	1	1	3	–	4	2	–	2	–	1	1	1	1
CA	34	19	34	19	34	19	38	15	2	–	2	–	2	–	2	–
CO	4	3	5	2	3	4	3	4	1	1	2	–	2	–	2	–
CT	4	1	5	–	5	–	5	–	1	–	1	–	1	–	1	–
DE	–	1	–	1	1	–	1	–	2	–	2	–	2	–	2	–
FL	9	16	10	15	6	19	10	17	1	1	1	1	1	1	1	1
GA	6	7	6	7	5	8	5	9	–	2	–	2	–	2	–	2
HI	2	–	2	–	2	–	2	–	2	–	2	–	2	–	2	–
ID	–	2	1	1	–	2	0	2	–	2	–	2	–	2	–	2
IL	10	9	11	7	8	11	12	6	2	–	1	–	1	1	1	1
IN	5	4	5	4	3	6	2	7	1	1	1	1	–	2	1	1
IA	3	2	3	2	3	2	2	2	1	1	1	1	1	1	1	1
KS	2	2	1	3	–	4	–	4	–	2	–	2	–	2	–	2
KY	2	4	2	4	2	4	1	5	–	2	–	2	–	2	–	2
LA	2	5	1	6	1	6	1	5	1	1	1	1	1	1	1	1
ME	2	–	2	–	2	–	2	–	–	2	–	2	–	2	–	1
MD	6	2	7	1	6	2	7	1	2	–	2	–	2	–	2	–
MA	10	–	10	–	10	–	9	–	2	–	2	–	1	1	2	–
MI	6	9	8	7	6	9	5	9	2	–	2	–	2	–	2	–
MN	5	3	5	3	4	4	5	3	1	1	1	–	2	–	2	–
MS	2	2	3	1	1	3	1	3	–	2	–	2	–	2	–	2
MO	4	5	4	5	3	6	2	5	1	1	1	1	1	1	1	1
MT	–	1	–	1	–	1	–	1	2	–	2	–	2	–	2	–
NE	–	3	–	3	–	3	–	3	1	1	1	1	1	1	–	2
NV	1	2	2	1	1	2	2	2	1	1	1	1	1	1	1	1
NH	2	–	2	–	–	2	2	–	–	2	1	1	1	1	1	1
NJ	7	6	8	5	7	6	6	6	2	–	2	–	2	–	2	–
NM	1	2	3	–	2	1	2	1	1	1	2	–	2	–	2	–
NY	23	6	26	3	21	8	21	6	2	–	2	–	2	–	2	–
NC	7	6	8	5	7	6	4	9	–	2	1	1	1	1	1	1
ND	1	–	1	–	–	1	–	1	2	–	2	–	1	1	1	1
OH	7	11	10	8	5	13	4	12	1	1	1	1	1	1	1	1
OK	1	4	1	4	1	4	–	5	–	2	–	2	–	2	–	2
OR	4	1	4	1	4	1	4	1	1	1	2	–	2	–	2	–
PA	11	8	12	7	7	12	5	13	1	1	1	1	1	1	1	1
RI	2	–	2	–	2	–	2	–	2	–	2	–	2	–	2	–
SC	2	4	2	4	1	5	1	5	–	2	–	2	–	2	–	2
SD	1	–	1	–	–	1	–	1	1	1	1	1	1	1	1	1
TN	5	4	5	4	2	7	2	7	–	2	–	2	–	2	–	2
TX	13	19	12	20	9	23	12	24	–	2	–	2	–	2	–	2
UT	1	2	1	2	1	2	1	3	–	2	–	2	–	2	–	2
VT	1	–	1	–	1	–	1	–	1	–	1	–	1	–	1	–
VA	3	8	6	5	3	8	3	8	1	1	2	–	2	–	2	–
WA	6	3	6	3	5	4	6	4	2	–	2	–	2	–	2	–
WV	2	1	2	1	1	2	1	2	2	–	2	–	2	–	2	–
WI	5	3	5	3	3	5	3	5	2	–	2	–	1	1	1	1
WY	–	1	–	1	–	1	–	1	–	2	–	2	–	2	–	2

– Represents zero. [1] One vacancy due to the resignation of Rahm Emanuel, January 6, 2009. [2] Vermont and Connecticut both had one Independent senator. [3] Two vacancies—one in Illinois due to the resignation of Barack Obama, November 16, 2008, and one in Minnesota due to election dispute between Norm Coleman and Al Franken. [4] Two vacancies--one in Missouri due to the resignation of Jo Ann Emerson, January 22, 2013 and one in South Carolina due to the resignation of Tim Scott, January 2, 2013. [5] Vermont and Maine both had one Independent senator.

Source: U.S. House of Representatives, Office of the Clerk, *Official List of Members*, April 2013, and earlier editions. See also <http://clerk.house.gov/member_info/>.

Table 431. Composition of Congress by Political Party: 1977 to 2013

[D = Democratic, R = Republican. As of beginning of first session of each Congress. Data reflect immediate result of elections. Vacancies and third party candidates are noted]

Year	Party and president	Congress	House Majority party	House Minority party	House Other	Senate Majority party	Senate Minority party	Senate Other
1977 [1]	D (Carter)	95th	D-292	R-143	–	D-61	R-38	1
1979 [1]	D (Carter)	96th	D-277	R-158	–	D-58	R-41	1
1981 [2]	R (Reagan)	97th	D-242	R-192	1	R-53	D-46	1
1983	R (Reagan)	98th	D-269	R-166	–	R-54	D-46	–
1985	R (Reagan)	99th	D-253	R-182	–	R-53	D-47	–
1987	R (Reagan)	100th	D-258	R-177	–	D-55	R-45	–
1989	R (Bush)	101st	D-260	R-175	–	D-55	R-45	–
1991 [3]	R (Bush)	102d	D-267	R-167	1	D-56	R-44	–
1993 [3]	D (Clinton)	103d	D-258	R-176	1	D-57	R-43	–
1995 [3]	D (Clinton)	104th	R-230	D-204	1	R-52	D-48	–
1997 [4]	D (Clinton)	105th	R-226	D-207	2	R-55	D-45	–
1999 [3]	D (Clinton)	106th	R-223	D-211	1	R-55	D-45	–
2001 [4]	R (Bush)	107th	R-221	D-212	2	D-50	R-50	–
2003 [2,5]	R (Bush)	108th	R-229	D-204	1	R-51	D-48	1
2005 [2]	R (Bush)	109th	R-232	D-202	1	R-55	D-44	1
2007 [6]	R (Bush)	110th	D-233	R-202	–	D-49	R-49	2
2009 [5,6,7]	D (Obama)	111th	D-256	R-178	–	D-55	R-41	2
2011 [6]	D (Obama)	112th	R-242	D-193	–	D-51	R-47	2
2013 [5,6]	D (Obama)	113th	R-234	D-200	–	D-53	R-45	2

– Represents zero. [1] Senate had one Independent. [2] House and Senate each had one Independent. [3] House had one Independent-Socialist. [4] House had one Independent-Socialist and one Independent. [5] House had one vacancy. [6] Senate had two Independents. [7] Senate had two vacancies.

Source: U.S. House of Representatives, Office of the Clerk, *Official List of Members, 2013*, annual. See also <http://clerk.house.gov/member_info/>.

Table 432. Members of Congress—Selected Characteristics: 1995 to 2011

[As of beginning of first session of each Congress, except as noted. Figures for Representatives exclude vacancies]

Members of Congress and year	Male	Female	Black	API [4]	Hispanic	Age [1] (in years) Under 40	40 to 49	50 to 59	60 to 69	70 and over	Seniority [2,3] Less than 2 yrs.	2 to 9 yrs.	10 to 19 yrs.	20 to 29 yrs.	30 yrs. or more
REPRESENTATIVES															
104th Cong., 1995...	388	47	[5] 40	7	17	53	155	135	79	13	92	188	110	36	9
107th Cong., 2001...	376	59	[5] 39	7	19	14	97	167	117	35	44	155	158	63	14
108th Cong., 2003...	376	59	[5] 39	5	22	19	86	174	121	32	54	178	140	48	13
109th Cong., 2005...	369	65	[5] 42	4	23	22	96	175	113	28	37	173	158	48	18
110th Cong., 2007...	362	73	[5] 42	4	23	20	91	172	118	34	62	159	160	37	17
111th Cong., 2009...	361	74	[5] 41	8	(NA)	24	84	156	126	44	66	166	142	42	18
112th Cong., 2011...	364	71	[5] 42	9	29	(NA)	(NA)	(NA)	(NA)	(NA)	100	140	131	42	22
SENATORS															
104th Cong., 1995...	92	8	1	2	0	1	14	41	27	17	12	38	30	15	5
107th Cong., 2001...	87	13	0	2	0	0	8	39	33	18	11	34	30	14	9
108th Cong., 2003...	86	14	0	2	0	1	12	29	34	24	9	42	29	13	7
109th Cong., 2005...	86	14	1	2	2	0	17	29	33	21	9	41	29	14	7
110th Cong., 2007...	84	16	1	2	3	0	11	31	34	24	12	42	24	13	9
111th Cong., 2009...	83	17	1	1	(NA)	0	7	31	38	22	9	34	28	17	10
112th Cong., 2011...	83	17	0	1	2	(NA)	(NA)	(NA)	(NA)	(NA)	20	35	24	13	8

NA Not available. [1] Some members do not provide date of birth. [2] Represents consecutive years of service. [3] Some members do not provide years of service. [4] Asian and Pacific Islander. [5] Includes District of Columbia and Virgin Islands delegate.

Source: Congressional Research Service, *Membership of 112th Congress: A Profile,* April 2011; and compiled by ProQuest from data published in *Congressional Directory,* biennial. See also <http://www.gpoaccess.gov/cdirectory/browse.html>.

Table 433. U.S. Congress—Measures Introduced and Enacted and Time in Session: 1995 to 2012

[Excludes simple and concurrent resolutions]

Item	104th Cong., 1995–96	105th Cong., 1997–98	106th Cong., 1999–00	107th Cong., 2001–02	108th Cong., 2003–04	109th Cong., 2005–06	110th Cong., 2007–08	111th Cong., 2009–10	112th Cong., 2011-12
Measures introduced.............	6,808	7,732	9,158	9,130	8,625	10,703	11,228	10,778	10,612
Bills................................	6,545	7,532	8,968	8,953	8,468	10,560	11,081	10,629	10,439
Joint resolutions...................	263	200	190	177	157	143	147	149	173
Measures enacted.................	337	404	604	337	504	590	460	385	239
Public [1].........................	333	394	580	331	498	589	460	383	238
Private [2]........................	4	10	24	6	6	1	0	2	1
HOUSE OF REPRESENTATIVES									
Number of days.....................	290	251	272	265	243	241	283	286	327
Number of hours....................	2,445	2,001	2,179	1,694	1,894	1,917	2,138	2,126	1,718
Number of hours per day..........	8.4	8.0	8.0	6.4	7.8	8.0	7.6	7.4	5.3
SENATE									
Number of days.....................	343	296	303	322	300	297	374	349	323
Number of hours....................	2,876	2,188	2,200	2,279	2,486	2,250	2,364	2,495	2,032
Number of hours per day..........	8.4	7.4	7.3	7.1	8.3	7.6	6.3	7.1	6.3

[1] Laws on public matters that apply to all persons. [2] Laws designed to provide legal relief to specified persons or entities adversely affected by laws of general applicability.

Source: U.S. Congress, *Résumé of Congressional Activity*, January 2013, and earlier reports. See also <http://www.senate.gov/pagelayout/reference/two_column_table/Resumes.htm>.

Table 434. Congressional Bills Vetoed: 1961 to 2013

Period	President	Total vetoes	Regular vetoes	Pocket vetoes	Vetoes sustained	Bills passed over veto
1961–1963.................	John F. Kennedy	21	12	9	21	–
1963–1969.................	Lyndon B. Johnson	30	16	14	30	–
1969–1974.................	Richard M. Nixon	43	26	17	36	7
1974–1977.................	Gerald R. Ford	66	48	18	54	12
1977–1981.................	Jimmy Carter	31	13	18	29	2
1981–1989.................	Ronald W. Reagan	78	39	39	69	9
1989–1993.................	George Bush	44	29	15	43	1
1993–2001.................	William J. Clinton	37	36	1	35	2
2001–2009.................	George W. Bush	12	12	–	8	4
2009–2013 [1].............	Barack Obama	2	2	–	2	–

– Represents zero. [1] For the period January 20, 2009 through April 22, 2013.

Source: Congressional Research Service, *Regular Vetoes and Pocket Vetoes: An Overview,* April 2013. See also <http://www.senate.gov/reference/reference_index_subjects/Vetoes_vrd.htm>.

Table 435. Number of Governors by Political Party Affiliation: 1975 to 2013

[Reflects figures after inaugurations for each year]

Year	Demo-cratic	Republi-can	Inde-pendent/other	Year	Demo-cratic	Republi-can	Inde-pendent/other	Year	Demo-cratic	Republi-can	Inde-pendent/other
1975..............	36	13	1	2002.....	22	27	1	2008.....	28	22	–
1980..............	31	19	–	2003.....	23	27	–	2009.....	28	22	–
1985..............	34	16	–	2004.....	22	28	–	2010.....	26	24	–
1990..............	29	21	–	2005.....	22	28	–	2011.....	20	29	1
1995..............	19	30	1	2006.....	22	28	–	2012.....	20	29	1
2000..............	18	30	2	2007.....	28	22	–	2013.....	20	30	–

– Represents zero.

Source: ProQuest research.

Table 436. Vote Cast for and Governor Elected by State: 2009 to 2011

[D = Democratic, R = Republican, I = Independent]

State	Current governor [1]	Year of election	Total vote [2]	Republican	Democratic	Percent leading party
Alabama	Robert Bentley	2010	1,485,324	860,272	625,052	R-57.9
Alaska	Sean Parnell	2010	256,192	151,318	96,519	R-59.1
Arizona	Jan Brewer	2010	1,728,081	938,934	733,935	R-54.3
Arkansas	Mike Beebe	2010	781,333	262,784	503,336	D-64.4
California	Jerry Brown	2010	10,095,185	4,127,391	5,428,149	D-53.8
Colorado	John Hickenlooper	2010	1,787,730	199,034	912,005	D-51.0
Connecticut	Dan Malloy	2010	1,145,799	560,874	567,278	D-49.5
Delaware	Jack Markell	2012	398,029	113,793	275,993	D-69.3
Florida	Rick Scott	2010	5,359,735	2,619,335	2,557,785	R-48.9
Georgia	Nathan Deal	2010	2,576,161	1,365,832	1,107,011	R-53.0
Hawaii	Neil Abercrombie	2010	382,583	157,311	222,724	D-58.2
Idaho	C.L. "Butch" Otter	2010	452,535	267,483	148,680	R-59.1
Illinois	Patrick Quinn	2010	3,729,989	1,713,385	1,745,219	D-46.8
Indiana	Mike Pence	2012	2,577,329	1,275,424	1,200,016	R-49.5
Iowa	Terry Branstad	2010	1,122,013	592,494	484,798	R-52.8
Kansas	Sam Brownback	2010	838,790	530,760	270,166	R-63.3
Kentucky	Steven L. Beshear	2011	833,139	294,034	464,245	D-55.7
Louisiana	Bobby Jindal	2011	1,023,163	673,239	288,161	R-65.8
Maine	Paul LePage	2010	572,766	218,065	109,387	R-38.1
Maryland	Martin O'Malley	2010	1,857,880	776,319	1,044,961	D-56.2
Massachusetts	Deval L. Patrick	2010	2,297,039	964,866	1,112,283	D-48.4
Michigan	Rick Snyder	2010	3,226,088	1,874,834	1,287,320	R-58.1
Minnesota	Mark Dayton	2010	2,107,021	910,462	919,232	D-43.6
Mississippi	Phil Bryant	2011	893,468	544,851	348,617	R-61.0
Missouri	Jay Nixon	2012	2,727,883	1,160,265	1,494,056	D-54.8
Montana	Steve Bullock	2012	486,734	158,268	318,670	D-65.5
Nebraska	Dave Heineman	2010	487,988	360,645	127,343	R-73.9
Nevada	Brian Sandoval	2010	716,529	382,350	298,171	R-53.4
New Hampshire	Maggie Hassan	2012	693,877	295,026	378,934	D-54.6
New Jersey	Chris Christie	2009	2,423,684	1,174,445	1,087,731	R-48.5
New Mexico	Susana Martinez	2010	602,827	321,219	280,614	R-53.3
New York	Andrew Cuomo	2010	4,654,352	1,548,184	2,911,721	D-62.6
North Carolina	Pat McCrory	2012	4,474,892	2,447,988	1,931,750	R-54.7
North Dakota	Jack Dalrymple	2012	317,814	200,525	109,048	R-63.1
Ohio	John Kasich	2010	3,852,469	1,889,186	1,812,059	R-49.0
Oklahoma	Mary Fallin	2010	1,034,767	625,506	409,261	R-60.4
Oregon	John Kitzhaber	2010	1,453,548	694,287	716,525	D-49.3
Pennsylvania	Tom Corbett	2010	3,987,551	2,172,763	1,814,788	R-54.5
Rhode Island	Lincoln Chafee	2010	342,290	114,911	78,896	I-43.4
South Carolina	Nikki Haley	2010	1,344,198	690,525	630,534	R-51.4
South Dakota	Dennis Daugaard	2010	317,083	195,046	122,037	R-61.5
Tennessee	Bill Haslam	2010	1,601,549	1,041,545	529,851	R-65.0
Texas	Rick Perry	2010	4,979,870	2,737,481	2,106,395	R-55.0
Utah	Gary Hebert	2012	643,307	412,151	205,246	R-64.1
Vermont	Peter Shumlin	2012	295,412	110,940	170,749	D-57.8
Virginia	Robert McDonnell	2009	1,982,424	1,163,523	818,901	R-58.7
Washington	Jay Inslee	2012	3,002,862	1,404,124	1,598,738	D-53.2
West Virginia	Earl Ray Tomblin	2012	656,034	299,682	331,116	D-50.5
Wisconsin	Scott Walker	2010	2,158,974	1,128,941	1,004,303	R-52.3
Wyoming	Matt Mead	2010	188,463	123,780	43,240	R-65.7

[1] As of January 2012. [2] Includes minor party and scattered votes.

Source: The Council of State Governments, Lexington, KY, *The Book of the States 2013*, and earlier reports ©. See <http://www.csg.org/>.

Table 437. Political Party Control of State Legislatures by Party: 1985 to 2012

[As of beginning of year. Nebraska has a nonpartisan legislature]

Year	Legislatures under—			Year	Legislatures under—			Year	Legislatures under—		
	Demo-cratic control	Split control or tie	Repub-lican control		Demo-cratic control	Split control or tie	Repub-lican control		Demo-cratic control	Split control or tie	Repub-lican control
1985	27	11	11	1998	20	12	17	2006	19	10	20
1990	29	11	9	2000	16	15	18	2007	22	12	15
1993	25	16	8	2001	16	15	18	2008	23	14	12
1994	24	17	8	2002	17	15	17	2009	27	8	14
1995	18	12	19	2003	16	12	21	2010	27	8	14
1996	16	15	18	2004	17	11	21	2011	15	8	26
1997	20	11	18	2005	19	10	20	2012	15	8	26

Source: National Conference of State Legislatures, Denver, CO, *State Legislatures*. See <ncsl.org>.

[2013 data are as of March; 2012 data are as of February. Figures reflect immediate results of elections, including holdover members in state houses which do not have all of their members running for reelection. Dem. = Democrat, Rep. = Republican, Vac. = Vacancies. In general, Lower House refers to body consisting of state representatives and Upper House of state senators]

State	Lower House 2012				Lower House 2013				Upper House 2012				Upper House 2013			
	Dem.	Rep.	Other	Vac.	Dem.	Rep.	Other	Vac.	Dem.	Rep.	Other	Vac.	Dem.	Rep.	Other	Vac.
U.S.	2,430	2,939	18	24	2,548	2,825	21	17	875	1,039	5	3	884	1,027	6	6
AL[1]	40	65	–	–	37	65	1	2	12	22	1	–	11	22	1	1
AK[2]	16	24	–	–	14	26	–	–	10	10	–	–	7	13	–	–
AZ[3]	20	40	–	–	24	36	–	–	9	21	–	–	13	17	–	–
AR[2]	54	46	–	–	49	51	–	–	20	15	–	–	14	21	–	–
CA[2]	52	28	–	–	55	25	–	–	25	15	–	–	26	11	–	3
CO[2]	32	33	–	–	37	28	–	–	20	15	–	–	20	15	–	–
CT[3]	99	52	–	–	99	52	–	–	22	14	–	–	22	14	–	–
DE[2]	26	15	–	–	27	14	–	–	14	7	–	–	13	8	–	–
FL[2]	39	81	–	–	44	76	–	–	12	28	–	–	14	26	–	–
GA[3]	63	115	1	1	60	119	1	–	20	36	–	–	18	38	–	–
HI[2]	42	8	–	1	44	7	–	–	24	1	–	–	24	1	–	–
ID[3]	13	57	–	–	13	57	–	–	7	28	–	–	7	28	–	–
IL[4]	64	54	–	–	71	47	–	–	35	24	–	–	40	19	–	–
IN[2]	40	60	–	–	31	69	–	–	13	37	–	–	13	37	–	–
IA[2]	40	60	–	–	47	53	–	–	26	24	–	–	26	24	–	–
KS[2]	33	92	–	–	33	92	–	–	8	32	–	–	8	32	–	–
KY[2]	59	40	–	1	55	45	–	–	15	22	1	–	14	23	1	–
LA[1]	45	58	2	–	45	58	2	–	15	24	–	–	15	24	–	–
ME[3]	72	77	1	1	58	89	4	–	14	20	1	–	19	15	1	–
MD[1]	98	43	–	–	98	43	–	–	35	12	–	–	35	12	–	–
MA[3]	125	33	–	2	129	29	–	2	36	4	–	–	36	4	–	–
MI[2]	46	62	–	2	51	59	–	–	12	26	–	–	11	26	–	1
MN[2]	62	72	–	–	73	61	–	–	30	37	–	–	39	28	–	–
MS[1]	58	64	–	–	56	65	–	1	21	31	–	–	20	31	–	1
MO[2]	56	106	–	1	52	109	–	2	8	26	–	–	10	24	–	–
MT[2]	32	68	–	–	39	61	–	–	22	28	–	–	21	29	–	–
NE[5]	(5)	(5)	(5)	(5)	(5)	(5)	(5)	(5)	(5)	(5)	(5)	(5)	(5)	(5)	(5)	(5)
NV[2]	26	16	–	–	27	15	–	–	11	10	–	–	11	10	–	–
NH[3]	104	292	–	4	217	178	–	5	5	19	–	–	11	13	–	–
NJ[2]	47	32	–	1	48	31	–	1	24	16	–	–	24	16	–	–
NM[2]	36	33	1	–	38	32	–	–	28	14	–	–	25	17	–	–
NY[3]	96	49	1	4	106	42	1	1	29	32	–	1	33	30	–	–
NC[3]	52	68	–	–	43	77	–	–	19	31	–	–	17	33	–	–
ND[1]	25	69	–	–	23	71	–	–	12	35	–	–	14	33	–	–
OH[2]	40	59	–	–	39	60	–	–	10	23	–	–	10	23	–	–
OK[2]	33	68	–	–	29	72	–	–	15	31	–	2	12	36	–	–
OR[2]	30	30	–	–	34	26	–	–	16	14	–	–	16	14	–	–
PA[2]	87	110	–	6	90	111	–	2	20	30	–	–	23	27	–	–
RI[3]	65	10	–	–	69	6	–	–	29	8	1	–	32	5	1	–
SC[2]	48	76	–	–	46	77	–	1	19	27	–	–	18	28	–	–
SD[3]	19	50	1	–	17	53	–	–	5	30	–	–	7	28	–	–
TN[2]	34	64	1	–	28	70	1	–	13	20	–	–	7	26	–	–
TX[2]	49	101	–	–	56	94	–	–	12	19	–	–	12	19	–	–
UT[2]	17	58	–	–	14	61	–	–	7	22	–	–	5	24	–	–
VT[3]	94	48	8	–	96	45	9	–	21	8	1	–	21	7	2	–
VA[2]	32	67	1	–	32	67	1	–	20	20	–	–	20	20	–	–
WA[2]	56	42	–	–	55	43	–	–	27	22	–	–	26	23	–	–
WV[2]	65	35	–	–	53	47	–	–	28	6	–	–	25	9	–	–
WI[2]	39	59	1	–	39	59	1	–	16	17	–	–	15	18	–	–
WY[2]	10	50	–	–	8	52	–	–	4	26	–	–	4	26	–	–

– Represents zero. [1] Members of both houses serve 4-year terms. [2] Upper House members serve 4-year terms and Lower House members serve 2-year terms. [3] Members of both houses serve 2-year terms. [4] Illinois—4- and 2-year term depending on district. [5] Nebraska—4-year term and only state to have a nonpartisan legislature.

Source: The Council of State Governments, Lexington, KY, *The Book of the States 2013*, and earlier reports ©. See <http://www.csg.org/>.

Table 439. Women Holding State Public Offices by Office and State: 2013

[As of January. For data on women in U.S. Congress, see Table 432]

State	Total	Statewide elective executive office [1]	State legislature Total	State legislature Percent	State	Total	Statewide elective executive office [1]	State legislature Total	State legislature Percent
U.S.	**1,862**	**73**	**1,783**	**24**	MO	44	1	43	22
					MT	44	3	41	27
AL	24	4	20	14	NE	11	1	10	20
AK	17	–	17	28	NV	21	3	18	29
AZ	36	4	32	36	NH	141	1	140	33
AR	24	1	23	17	NJ	36	1	35	29
CA	33	2	31	25	NM	36	5	31	28
CO	41	–	41	41	NY	46	–	46	22
CT	58	3	55	29	NC	43	6	37	22
DE	17	1	16	26	ND	27	3	24	17
FL	41	1	40	25	OH	32	1	31	24
GA	54	–	54	23	OK	24	4	20	13
HI	24	–	24	33	OR	28	2	26	29
ID	28	1	27	26	PA	46	1	45	18
IL	60	3	57	32	RI	33	2	31	27
IN	34	3	31	21	SC	23	1	22	13
IA	36	1	35	23	SD	25	1	24	23
KS	40	1	39	24	TN	23	–	23	17
KY	26	1	25	18	TX	40	2	38	21
LA	17	–	17	12	UT	17	–	17	16
ME	53	–	53	29	VT	74	1	73	41
MD	57	–	57	30	VA	25	–	25	18
MA	53	2	51	26	WA	47	2	45	31
MI	29	1	28	19	WV	23	1	22	16
MN	70	3	67	33	WI	34	1	33	25
MS	30	2	28	16	WY	17	2	15	17

– Represents zero. [1] Excludes women elected to the judiciary, women appointed to state cabinet-level positions, women elected to executive posts by the legislature, and elected members of university Board of Trustees or Board of Education.

Source: Center for the American Woman and Politics, Eagleton Institute of Politics, Rutgers University, New Brunswick, NJ, "Women in Elective Office," <http://www.cawp.rutgers.edu/index.php>, accessed July 2013 ©.

Table 440. Hispanic Public Elected Officials by Office, 1985 to 2013, and State, 2013

[As of January of year shown. For states not shown, no Hispanic public officials had been identified]

State	Total	State executives and legislators [1]	County and municipal officials	Judicial and law enforcement	Education and school boards	State	Total	State executives and legislators [1]	County and municipal officials	Judicial and law enforcement	Education and school boards
1985	3,147	129	1,316	517	1,185	LA	6	1	1	3	1
1990	4,004	144	1,819	583	1,458	ME	1	1	0	0	0
2000	5,019	217	1,852	447	2,503	MD	8	3	5	0	0
2005	4,853	266	2,149	678	1,760	MA	34	6	14	0	14
2006	4,932	244	2,151	693	1,835	MI	17	3	2	5	7
2007	4,954	270	2,152	685	1,847	MN	8	3	1	4	0
2008	5,240	283	2,266	738	1,952	MO	3	2	1	0	0
2009	5,670	252	2,264	842	2,037	MT	4	0	2	1	1
2010	5,739	251	2,270	874	2,072	NV	20	9	3	6	2
2011	5,850	260	2,282	864	2,173	NH	3	3	0	0	0
2012	5,928	266	2,293	881	2,225	NJ	128	9	73	1	43
2013	**6,011**	**289**	**2,285**	**878**	**2,287**	NM	701	52	322	129	157
AK	1	0	1	0	0	NY	159	20	63	38	35
AZ	339	17	129	45	139	NC	1	1	0	0	0
AR	2	0	0	0	2	OH	12	2	7	1	2
CA	1,365	26	407	84	717	OK	1	1	0	0	0
CO	161	13	88	18	34	OR	13	3	2	5	3
CT	45	11	21	0	13	PA	14	2	5	3	4
DE	5	2	2	1	0	RI	12	4	7	0	1
FL	175	17	93	53	7	TN	4	1	2	1	0
GA	6	2	3	1	0	TX	2,524	40	917	450	1,054
HI	2	2	0	0	0	UT	9	4	3	1	1
ID	3	1	0	1	0	VT	1	1	0	0	0
IL	117	13	60	17	19	VA	6	1	2	1	2
IN	24	3	11	3	7	WA	43	1	21	1	19
IA	3	0	2	0	1	WI	8	1	3	4	0
KS	14	6	6	1	1	WY	9	2	6	0	1

[1] Includes U.S. Senators and Representatives, not shown separately.

Source: National Association of Latino Elected and Appointed Officials (NALEO) Educational Fund, Washington, DC, *National Directory of Latino Elected Officials* ©, and earlier reports. See also <http://www.naleo.org/>.

Table 441. Political Action Committees—Number by Committee Type: 1980 to 2012

[As of December 31]

Committee type	1980	1990	2000	2005	2008	2009	2010	2011	2012
Total	2,551	4,172	3,907	4,210	4,611	4,578	4,859	4,657	6,331
Corporate	1,206	1,795	1,545	1,622	1,598	1,628	1,683	1,652	1,664
Labor	297	346	317	290	272	280	283	280	290
Trade/membership/health [1]	576	774	860	925	995	968	1,004	985	960
Nonconnected	374	1,062	1,026	1,233	1,594	1,567	1,747	1,601	2,193
Cooperative	42	59	41	37	49	40	39	35	40
Corporation without stock	56	136	118	103	103	95	103	104	107

[1] As of July 2011, health organizations are no longer an organization type but are included in either the trade or membership categories.

Source: U.S. Federal Election Commission, "PAC Count—1974 to Present," <http://www.fec.gov/press/summaries/2011/2011paccount.shtml>, accessed June 2013.

Table 442. Political Action Committees—Financial Activity Summary by Committee Type: 2007 to 2012

[In millions of dollars (1,208.1 represents $1,208,100,000). Covers financial activity during 2-year calendar period indicated]

Committee type	Receipts			Disbursements [1]			Contributions to candidates		
	2007–08	2009–10	2011–12	2007–08	2009–10	2011–12	2007–08	2009–10	2011-12
Total	1,208.1	1,305.1	2,259.1	1,180.3	1,274.6	2,198.4	412.8	431.5	446.3
Corporate	313.2	314.1	361.1	299.7	302.8	343.0	158.3	165.5	181.1
Labor	245.4	261.1	282.6	252.3	256.9	279.4	62.7	64.2	57.5
Trade	125.3	127.7	136.4	117.0	125.6	132.3	(NA)	(NA)	79.1
Membership	185.8	145.8	134.0	177.9	143.2	132.2	(NA)	(NA)	42.2
Cooperative	10.3	6.3	7.3	9.9	6.3	6.7	6.9	5.0	5.3
Corporation without stock	13.2	16.3	17.3	12.7	15.9	16.2	5.5	7.5	7.5
Nonconnected	314.9	433.8	1,320.4	310.7	424.1	1,288.5	66.6	74.1	73.5

NA Not Available. [1] Comprises contributions to candidates, independent expenditures, and other disbursements.

Source: U.S. Federal Election Commission, 2010 Full Election Cycle Summary Data, "2009-2010 PAC Financial Activity," <http://www.fec.gov/press/2010_Full_summary_Data.shtml>, accessed August 2013.

Table 443. Presidential Campaign Finances—Federal Funds for General Election: 2000 to 2012

[In millions of dollars (147.7 represents $147,700,000). Based on FEC certifications, audit reports, and Dept. of Treasury reports]

2000		2004		2008		2012	
Candidate	Amount	Candidate	Amount	Candidate	Amount	Candidate	Amount
Total	147.7	Total	150.1	Total	84.2	Total	1.28
Bush	67.6	Bush	74.6	Obama	–	Obama	–
Gore	67.6	Kerry	74.6	McCain	84.1	Romney	–
Buchanan	12.6	Nader	0.9	Nader	0.1	Johnson	0.6

– Represents zero.

Source: U.S. Federal Election Commission, "Presidential Campaign Receipts," <http://www.fec.gov/press/summaries/2012/ElectionCycle/24m_PresCand.shtml>, accessed September 2013.

Table 444. Presidential Campaign Finances—Primary Campaign Receipts and Disbursements: 2003 to 2012

[In millions of dollars (673.9 represents $673,900,000). Covers campaign finance activity during 2-year calendar period indicated. Covers candidates who received federal matching funds or who had significant financial activity]

Item	Total [1]			Democratic			Republican		
	2003–04	2007–08 [2, 3]	2011-12	2003–04	2007–08 [2]	2011-12	2003–04	2007–08 [3]	2011-12
Receipts, total [4]	673.9	1,550.3	1,379.8	401.8	1,073.8	738.5	269.6	472.4	630.4
Individual contributions	611.4	1,325.6	997.0	351.0	932.6	549.6	258.9	390.0	441.0
Federal matching funds	28.0	21.0	1.3	27.2	17.5	–	–	2.6	–
Disbursements	661.1	1,498.0	1,359.8	389.7	1,043.9	737.1	268.9	450.2	633.4

– Represents zero. [1] Includes other parties, not shown separately. [2] Obama activity includes both Primary and General election funds because he used a single committee for both elections. Dodd received $1,961,742 in matching funds; however his committee reported the receipt of $1,447,568. Gravel received an additional $115,966 in matching funds in early 2009. [3] Tancredo received an additional $83,775 in matching funds in early 2009. [4] Includes other types of receipts, not shown separately.

Source: U.S. Federal Election Commission, "Presidential Campaign Finance Summaries", <http://www.fec.gov/press/bkgnd/pres_cf/pres_cf_Even.shtml>, accessed September 2013, and "Presidential Candidate 24-Month Data Summaries", <http://www.fec.gov/press/summaries/2012/ElectionCycle/24m_PresCand.shtml>, accessed September 2013.

Table 445. Congressional Campaign Finances—Receipts and Disbursements: 2003 to 2012

[702.8 represents $702,800,000. Covers all campaign finance activity during 2-year calendar period indicated for primary, general, run-off, and special elections. Data have been adjusted to eliminate transfers between all committees within a campaign. For further information on legal limits of contributions, see Federal Election Campaign Act of 1971, as amended]

Item	House of Representatives					Senate				
	Amount (mil. dol.)									
	2003–04	2005–06	2007–08	2009–10	2011–12	2003–04	2005–06	2007–08	2009–10	2011–12
Total receipts [1]	**702.8**	**878.7**	**983.3**	**1,103.2**	**1,136.5**	**502.9**	**565.5**	**433.7**	**757.2**	**742.3**
Individual contributions	393.4	479.7	529.5	640.6	637.0	332.2	383.9	268.7	468.0	466.1
Other committees	229.9	295.3	315.0	326.2	351.0	67.2	70.8	78.8	87.6	80.9
Candidate contributions & loans	55.6	71.3	103.1	109.6	108.2	81.1	84.7	30.5	149.6	167.3
Democrats	307.3	416.8	536.8	510.3	486.8	250.1	312.2	237.2	314.7	307.9
Incumbents	200.9	217.3	326.9	393.0	249.1	104.0	176.0	83.8	139.5	172.1
Challengers	55.3	126.7	120.2	64.4	174.8	21.6	91.8	115.5	38.8	71.4
Open seats [2]	51.1	72.8	89.6	52.9	62.9	124.4	44.5	37.9	136.5	64.4
Republicans	386.9	455.0	435.1	587.5	632.7	251.9	245.3	196.0	427.4	416.1
Incumbents	239.2	324.8	246.6	231.7	436.2	67.3	120.4	150.3	109.5	77.8
Challengers	58.8	50.6	103.4	266.0	125.7	45.4	75.5	26.1	148.9	143.1
Open seats [2]	88.9	79.6	85.1	89.8	70.7	139.3	49.4	19.6	169.1	195.3
Others	8.5	6.9	11.4	5.4	17.0	0.9	8.0	0.5	15.0	18.3
Incumbents	7.5	2.5	5.7	1.7	2.2	(Z)	(Z)	(Z)	(Z)	6.3
Challengers	1.0	2.7	3.0	3.2	13.5	0.8	1.7	0.4	0.5	8.7
Open seats [2]	0.1	1.7	2.7	0.5	1.3	0.1	6.3	0.1	14.5	3.3
Total disbursements	**655.7**	**859.1**	**941.0**	**1,096.3**	**1,099.3**	**501.7**	**563.8**	**442.9**	**737.3**	**747.9**
Democrats	288.7	395.0	495.5	534.7	479.1	253.8	307.2	230.6	319.3	315.7
Republicans	358.7	458.0	434.6	556.6	604.3	247.1	248.9	211.9	403.2	417.7
Others	8.3	6.1	10.9	5.1	15.9	0.8	7.8	0.5	14.9	14.5

Z Less than $50,000. [1] Includes other types of receipts, not shown separately. [2] Elections in which an incumbent did not seek reelection.

Source: U.S. Federal Election Commission, "Campaign Finance Statistics", <http://www.fec.gov/press/campaign_finance_statistics.shtml>, accessed September 2013.

Table 446. Contributions to Congressional Campaigns by Political Action Committees (PAC) by Type of Committee: 2001 to 2012

[In millions of dollars (206.9 represents $206,900,000). Covers amounts given to candidates in primary, general, run-off, and special elections during the 2-year calendar period indicated. For number of political action committees, see Table 441]

Type of committee	Total [1]	Democrats	Republicans	Incumbents	Challengers	Open seats [2]
HOUSE OF REPRESENTATIVES						
2001–02	206.9	102.6	104.2	161.0	13.8	32.1
2003–04	225.4	98.6	126.6	187.3	15.6	22.5
2005–06	279.2	124.9	154.2	229.3	26.2	23.6
2007–08	308.1	185.6	122.4	253.5	35.8	18.8
2009–10	313.6	184.4	129.2	262.8	30.0	20.7
2011–12, total [3]	**341.3**	**148.1**	**192.1**	**285.4**	**36.1**	**19.8**
Corporate	134.5	45.1	88.9	125.4	5.0	4.1
Trade association [4]	96.9	34.2	62.4	84.8	7.2	4.9
Labor	49.4	44.1	5.2	32.2	11.8	5.4
Nonconnected [5]	50.6	21.0	29.4	34.1	11.5	4.9
SENATE						
2001–02	59.2	25.4	33.8	37.0	14.2	8.1
2003–04	63.7	28.4	35.3	39.3	5.6	18.8
2005–06	66.1	28.6	37.5	47.7	10.0	8.3
2007–08	79.8	33.9	45.9	57.7	13.0	9.1
2009–10	88.8	39.9	49.0	48.9	10.4	29.5
2011–12, total [3]	**103.2**	**53.5**	**48.9**	**70.7**	**12.8**	**19.7**
Corporate	45.8	20.9	24.7	34.9	4.4	6.5
Trade association [4]	24.2	11.5	12.5	16.8	2.7	4.6
Labor	8.1	7.3	0.5	4.8	1.2	2.1
Nonconnected [5]	22.3	12.3	9.8	12.3	4.2	5.8

[1] Includes other parties, not shown separately. [2] Elections in which an incumbent did not seek reelection. [3] Includes other types of political action committees, not shown separately. [4] Includes membership organizations and health organizations. [5] Represents "ideological" groups as well as other issue groups not necessarily ideological in nature.

Source: U.S. Federal Election Commission, "Campaign Finance Statistics", <http://www.fec.gov/press/campaign_finance_statistics.shtml>, accessed September 2013.

Section 8
State and Local Government Finances and Employment

This section presents data on revenues, expenditures, debt, and employment of state and local governments. Nationwide statistics relating to state and local governments, their numbers, finances, and employment are compiled primarily by the U.S. Census Bureau through a program of censuses and surveys. Every fifth year (for years ending in "2" and "7"), the Census Bureau conducts a census of governments involving collection of data for all governmental units in the United States. In addition, the Census Bureau conducts annual surveys which cover all the state governments and a sample of local governments.

Annually, the Census Bureau releases information on the Internet which presents financial data for the federal government, nationwide totals for state and local governments, and state-local data by states. Also released annually is a series on state, city, county, and school finances and on state and local public employment. There is also a series of quarterly data releases covering tax revenue and finances of major public employee retirement systems.

Basic information for Census Bureau statistics on governments is obtained by mail canvass from state and local officials; however, financial data for each state government and for many of the large local governments are compiled from their official records and reports by Census Bureau personnel. In over two-thirds of the states, all or part of local government financial data are obtained through central collection arrangements with state governments. Financial data on the federal government are primarily based on the *Budget* published by the Office of Management and Budget.

Governmental units—The governmental structure of the United States includes, in addition to the federal government and the states, thousands of local governments—counties, municipalities, townships, school districts, and many "special districts." In 2007, 89,476 local governments were identified by the census of governments (see table 447 through table 448). As defined by the census, governmental units include all agencies or bodies having an organized existence, governmental character, and substantial autonomy. While most of these governments can impose taxes, many of the special districts—such as independent public housing authorities and numerous local irrigation, power, and other types of districts—are financed from rentals, charges for services, benefit assessments, grants from other governments, and other nontax sources. The count of governments excludes semi-autonomous agencies through which states, cities, and counties sometimes provide for certain functions—for example, "dependent" school systems, state institutions of higher education, and certain other "authorities" and special agencies which are under the administrative or fiscal control of an established governmental unit.

Finances—The financial statistics relate to government fiscal years ending June 30 or at some date within the 12 previous months. The following governments are exceptions and are included as though they were part of the June 30 group; ending September 30, the state governments of Alabama and Michigan, the District of Columbia, and Alabama school districts; and ending August 31, the state government of Texas. New York State ends its fiscal year on March 31. The federal government ended the fiscal year June 30 until 1976 when its fiscal year, by an act of Congress, was revised to extend from Oct. 1 to Sept. 30. A 3-month quarter (July 1 to Sept. 30, 1976) bridged the transition.

Nationwide government finance statistics have been classified and presented in terms of uniform concepts and categories, rather than according to the highly diverse terminology, organization, and fund structure utilized by individual governments.

Statistics on governmental finances distinguish among general government, utilities, liquor stores, and insurance trusts. *General government* comprises all activities except utilities, liquor stores, and insurance trusts. Utilities include government water supply, electric light and power, gas supply, and transit systems. Liquor stores are operated by 17 states and by local governments in 6 states. Insurance trusts relate to employee retirement, unemployment compensation, and other social insurance systems administered by the federal, state, and local governments.

Data for cities or counties relate only to municipal or county and their dependent agencies and do not include amounts for other local governments in the same geographic location. Therefore, expenditure figures for "education" do not include spending by the separate school districts which administer public schools within most municipal or county areas. Variations in the assignment of governmental responsibility for public assistance, health, hospitals, public housing, and other functions to a lesser degree also have an important effect upon reported amounts of city or county expenditure, revenue, and debt.

Employment and payrolls—These data are based mainly on mail canvassing of state and local governments. Payroll includes all salaries, wages, and individual fee payments for the month specified, and employment relates to all persons on governmental payrolls during a pay period of the month covered—including paid officials, temporary help, and (unless otherwise specified) part-time as well as full-time personnel. Effective with the 1997 Census of Governments, the reference period for measuring government employment was changed from October of the calendar year to March of the calendar year. As a result, there was no annual survey of government employment covering the October 1996 period. The prior reference month of October was used from 1958 to 1995. Figures shown for individual governments cover major dependent agencies such as institutions of higher education, as well as the basic central departments and agencies of the government.

Statistical reliability—For a discussion of statistical collection and estimation, sampling procedures, and measures of statistical reliability applicable to Census Bureau data, see Appendix III.

Table 447. Number of Governmental Units by Type: 1962 to 2007

Type of government	1962	1967	1972	1977	1982	1987	1992	1997	2002	2007
Total units....................	91,237	81,299	78,269	79,913	81,831	83,237	85,006	87,504	87,576	89,527
U.S. government.............	1	1	1	1	1	1	1	1	1	1
State governments...........	50	50	50	50	50	50	50	50	50	50
Local governments...........	91,186	81,248	78,218	79,862	81,780	83,186	84,955	87,453	87,525	89,476
County....................	3,043	3,049	3,044	3,042	3,041	3,042	3,043	3,043	3,034	3,033
Municipal.................	18,000	18,048	18,517	18,862	19,076	19,200	19,279	19,372	19,429	19,492
Township and town..........	17,142	17,105	16,991	16,822	16,734	16,691	16,656	16,629	16,504	16,519
School district.............	34,678	21,782	15,781	15,174	14,851	14,721	14,422	13,726	13,506	13,051
Special district..............	18,323	21,264	23,885	25,962	28,078	29,532	31,555	34,683	35,052	37,381

Source: U.S. Census Bureau, *Census of Governments*, Volume 1, Number 1, Government Organization, Series GC07(1)-1), quinquennial. See also <http://www.census.gov/govs/cog/>.

Table 448. Number of Local Governments by Type—States: 2007

[Governments in existence in January. Limited to governments actually in existence. Excludes, therefore, a few counties and numerous townships and incorporated places existing as areas for which statistics can be presented as to population and other subjects, but lacking any separate organized county, township, or municipal government. See Appendix III]

State	All govern-mental units [1]	County	Municipal	Township [1]	School district	Special district [2] Total [3]	Natural resources	Fire protection	Housing [4]
United States...........	**89,476**	**3,033**	**19,492**	**16,519**	**13,051**	**37,381**	**7,227**	**5,873**	**3,463**
Alabama......................	1,185	67	458	–	131	529	69	11	150
Alaska.......................	177	14	148	–	–	15	–	–	14
Arizona......................	645	15	90	–	239	301	78	150	–
Arkansas.....................	1,548	75	502	–	247	724	250	81	119
California....................	4,344	57	478	–	1,044	2,765	473	353	70
Colorado.....................	2,416	62	270	–	180	1,904	180	252	89
Connecticut..................	649	–	30	149	17	453	1	72	114
Delaware.....................	338	3	57	–	19	259	238	–	3
District of Columbia........	2	–	1	–	–	1	–	–	–
Florida.......................	1,623	66	411	–	95	1,051	125	61	94
Georgia......................	1,439	154	535	–	180	570	38	2	191
Hawaii.......................	19	3	1	–	–	15	14	–	–
Idaho........................	1,240	44	200	–	116	880	174	150	10
Illinois.......................	6,994	102	1,299	1,432	912	3,249	1,026	841	113
Indiana.......................	3,231	91	567	1,008	293	1,272	139	1	65
Iowa.........................	1,954	99	947	–	380	528	247	66	23
Kansas.......................	3,931	104	627	1,353	316	1,531	258	1	197
Kentucky.....................	1,346	118	419	–	175	634	126	156	13
Louisiana....................	526	60	303	–	68	95	8	3	–
Maine........................	850	16	22	466	98	248	15	–	34
Maryland.....................	256	23	157	–	–	76	38	–	20
Massachusetts..............	861	5	45	306	82	423	16	16	252
Michigan.....................	2,893	83	533	1,242	579	456	79	25	–
Minnesota...................	3,526	87	854	1,788	341	456	144	–	162
Mississippi..................	1,000	82	296	–	164	458	249	33	55
Missouri.....................	3,723	114	952	312	536	1,809	329	357	124
Montana......................	1,273	54	129	–	332	758	132	220	13
Nebraska....................	2,659	93	530	454	288	1,294	83	417	168
Nevada.......................	198	16	19	–	17	146	33	18	5
New Hampshire.............	545	10	13	221	164	137	10	16	21
New Jersey.................	1,383	21	324	242	549	247	15	196	–
New Mexico.................	863	33	101	–	96	633	576	–	6
New York....................	3,403	57	618	929	680	1,119	3	891	–
North Carolina..............	963	100	548	–	–	315	145	–	94
North Dakota...............	2,699	53	357	1,320	198	771	78	281	35
Ohio.........................	3,702	88	938	1,308	668	700	106	85	77
Oklahoma....................	1,880	77	594	–	567	642	100	30	137
Oregon.......................	1,546	36	242	–	234	1,034	204	271	21
Pennsylvania................	4,871	66	1,016	1,546	515	1,728	5	–	90
Rhode Island................	134	–	8	31	4	91	4	37	25
South Carolina..............	698	46	268	–	85	299	48	83	43
South Dakota................	1,983	66	309	916	166	526	103	84	49
Tennessee...................	928	92	347	–	14	475	109	1	96
Texas........................	4,835	254	1,209	–	1,081	2,291	442	139	387
Utah.........................	599	29	242	–	40	288	82	18	17
Vermont......................	733	14	45	237	293	144	14	16	10
Virginia......................	511	95	229	–	1	186	47	–	–
Washington..................	1,845	39	281	–	296	1,229	178	375	43
West Virginia................	663	55	232	–	55	321	14	–	37
Wisconsin...................	3,120	72	592	1,259	441	756	251	–	177
Wyoming.....................	726	23	99	–	55	549	131	64	–

– Represents zero. [1] Includes town governments in the six New England States and in Minnesota, New York, and Wisconsin. [2] Single function districts. [3] Includes other special districts not shown separately. [4] Includes community development.

Source: U.S. Census Bureau, *Census of Governments*, Volume 1, Number 1, Government Organization, Series GC07(1)–1), quinquennial. See also <http://www.census.gov/cog/>.

Table 449. State and Local Government Current Receipts and Expenditures in the National Income and Product Accounts: 1990 to 2012

[In billions of dollars (729.6 represents $729,600,000,000). For explanation of national income, see text, Section 13. Minus sign (-) indicates net loss]

Item	1990	1995	2000	2005	2008	2009	2010	2011	2012
Current receipts	**729.6**	**979.8**	**1,303.1**	**1,708.8**	**1,909.1**	**1,919.2**	**1,998.5**	**2,029.9**	**2,039.4**
Current tax receipts	519.1	672.1	893.2	1,166.5	1,328.9	1,268.1	1,305.6	1,366.3	1,405.2
Personal current taxes	122.6	158.1	236.7	276.4	333.5	287.8	297.6	327.0	348.8
Income taxes	109.6	141.7	217.4	251.5	307.0	259.5	267.1	296.1	317.3
Other	13.0	16.4	19.4	24.9	26.5	28.3	30.5	30.9	31.6
Taxes on production and imports	374.1	482.4	621.3	835.1	947.9	934.8	960.4	988.5	1,004.9
Sales taxes	184.3	242.7	316.8	402.5	444.8	423.9	446.0	463.7	474.9
Property taxes	161.5	202.6	254.7	351.3	413.8	435.1	435.0	436.9	440.0
Other	28.3	37.0	49.8	81.4	89.4	75.8	79.4	87.9	90.0
Taxes on corporate income	22.5	31.7	35.2	54.9	47.4	45.6	47.7	50.7	51.4
Contributions for government social insurance	10.0	13.6	10.8	24.6	18.7	18.6	18.1	18.3	17.5
Income receipts on assets	68.5	69.1	93.9	88.6	105.7	87.8	82.6	80.0	78.5
Interest receipts	64.1	63.6	86.3	76.8	91.0	74.4	69.1	66.3	64.2
Dividends	0.2	1.0	1.4	2.0	2.6	2.1	2.3	2.3	2.4
Rents and royalties	4.2	4.5	6.3	9.8	12.1	11.2	11.2	11.4	11.9
Current transfer receipts	126.4	214.4	299.7	436.4	477.8	566.1	612.0	581.8	552.6
Federal grants-in-aid	104.4	174.5	233.1	343.4	371.0	458.1	505.3	472.5	443.2
From business (net)	7.1	13.5	28.6	36.5	43.6	44.0	43.4	44.2	41.9
From persons	14.9	26.5	38.0	56.5	63.3	64.0	63.2	65.2	67.5
Current surplus of government enterprises	5.6	10.6	5.4	-7.3	-22.0	-21.4	-19.8	-16.5	-14.3
Current expenditures	**736.0**	**1,011.4**	**1,293.2**	**1,775.4**	**2,074.1**	**2,191.2**	**2,235.8**	**2,243.0**	**2,292.1**
Consumption expenditures	546.2	716.8	969.1	1,256.6	1,488.7	1,508.4	1,518.3	1,517.4	1,536.4
Government social benefit payments to persons	127.7	217.6	271.4	406.6	455.4	492.6	523.8	532.0	544.3
Interest payments	61.8	76.6	52.1	111.8	127.0	188.8	192.1	192.9	211.0
Subsidies	0.4	0.3	0.5	0.4	3.0	1.4	1.6	0.5	0.5
Net state and local government saving	**-6.5**	**-31.5**	**9.9**	**-66.6**	**-165.1**	**-271.9**	**-237.3**	**-213.1**	**-252.7**
Social insurance funds	2.0	4.0	2.0	7.2	1.7	2.2	3.2	4.2	3.9
Other	-8.4	-35.6	7.9	-73.8	-166.8	-274.1	-240.5	-217.3	-256.6

Source: U.S. Bureau of Economic Analysis, National Income and Product Accounts Tables, "Table 3.3 State and Local Government Current Receipts and Expenditures," <http://www.bea.gov/itable/>, accessed August 2013.

Table 450. Federal Grants-in-Aid to State and Local Governments: 1990 to 2013

[135,325 represents $135,325,000,000, except as indicated. For fiscal year ending Sept. 30. Minus sign (-) indicates decrease]

Year	Current dollars							Constant (2005) dollars	
			Grants to individuals		Grants as percent of—				
	Total grants (mil. dol.)	Annual percent change [1]	Grants to individuals, total (mil. dol.)	Percent of total grants	State and local government expenditures from own sources [2]	Federal outlays	Gross domestic product	Total grants (bil. dol.)	Annual percent change [1]
1990	135,325	11.0	77,264	57.1	25.2	10.8	2.4	198.1	6.2
1995	224,991	6.8	144,427	64.2	31.5	14.8	3.1	283.5	3.9
1999	267,886	8.8	172,384	64.3	31.2	15.7	2.9	314.7	7.1
2000	285,874	6.7	182,592	63.9	27.4	16.0	2.9	326.7	3.8
2001	318,542	11.4	203,920	64.0	28.4	17.1	3.1	354.8	8.6
2002	352,895	10.8	227,373	64.4	29.5	17.5	3.3	387.3	9.2
2003	388,542	10.1	246,570	63.5	30.5	18.0	3.5	416.1	7.4
2004	407,512	4.9	262,177	64.3	30.9	17.8	3.5	424.2	1.9
2005	428,018	5.0	273,898	64.0	30.8	17.3	3.4	428.0	0.9
2006	434,099	1.4	272,585	62.8	29.7	16.3	3.3	417.3	-2.5
2007	443,797	2.2	284,362	64.1	28.4	16.3	3.2	412.5	-1.2
2008	461,317	3.9	300,820	65.2	27.4	15.5	3.2	411.2	-0.3
2009	537,991	16.6	356,692	66.3	33.1	15.3	3.9	477.3	16.1
2010	608,390	13.1	384,480	63.2	37.5	17.6	4.2	532.5	11.6
2011	606,766	-0.3	387,806	63.9	(NA)	16.8	4.1	519.7	-2.4
2012	544,569	-10.3	360,058	66.1	(NA)	15.4	3.5	455.7	-12.3
2013, est	560,987	3.0	382,154	68.1	(NA)	15.2	3.5	459.9	0.9

NA Not available. [1] Average annual percent change from prior year shown; For 1990, change from 1989. For explanation, see Guide to Tabular Presentation. [2] Expenditures from own sources as defined in the national income and product accounts.

Source: U.S. Office of Management and Budget, *Fiscal Year 2014 Budget of the U.S. Government: Historical Tables*, April 2013. See also <http://www.whitehouse.gov/omb/budget>.

Table 451. Total Outlays for Grants to State and Local Governments—Selected Agencies and Programs: 1990 to 2013

[In millions of dollars (135,325 represents $135,325,000,000). For fiscal year ending Sept. 30. Includes trust funds]

Agency and Program	1990	2000	2005	2009	2010	2011	2012	2013, est.
Total outlays for grants	135,325	285,874	428,018	537,991	608,390	606,766	544,569	560,987
Energy	461	433	636	999	2,656	5,128	4,223	1,329
Natural resources and environment	3,745	4,595	5,858	6,285	9,132	8,259	7,777	7,065
Environmental Protection Agency [1]	2,874	3,490	3,734	3,580	6,883	5,979	5,572	4,782
Agriculture	1,285	724	933	937	843	938	635	876
Transportation	19,174	32,222	43,370	55,438	60,981	60,986	60,749	62,879
Grants for airports [1]	1,220	1,624	3,530	3,759	3,156	3,095	3,012	3,810
Federal-aid highways [2]	13,854	24,711	30,915	36,049	30,385	35,754	39,634	40,253
Urban mass transportation [1]	3,728	5,262	8,114	11,182	12,939	11,783	12,098	13,994
Community and regional development	4,965	8,665	20,167	17,394	18,908	20,002	20,258	17,117
Rural Community Advancement Program	139	479	814	–	–	–	–	–
Community Development Fund	2,818	4,955	4,985	6,408	7,043	7,037	6,794	6,402
Homeland Security	1,184	2,439	13,541	9,094	8,483	9,523	10,206	6,678
State and local programs	–	–	2,116	2,555	3,337	3,319	3,857	3,360
Firefighter assistance grants	–	–	1,185	–	–	–	–	–
Operations, planning, and support	11	192	132	–	–	–	–	–
Predisaster mitigation grants	–	13	39	11	–	–	–	–
Disaster relief	1,173	2,234	10,069	6,525	5,141	6,201	6,346	3,132
Education, training, employment, social services	21,780	36,672	57,247	73,986	97,586	89,147	68,126	67,138
Accelerating Achievement & Ensuring Equity [3,4]	4,437	8,511	14,539	15,797	19,515	19,486	17,047	17,375
School improvement programs [4]	1,080	2,394	6,569	5,247	5,184	5,309	4,823	4,543
Special education	1,485	4,696	10,661	12,536	17,075	16,832	13,335	12,864
Social Services Block Grant	2,749	1,827	1,822	1,854	2,035	1,787	1,715	1,964
Children and family services programs	2,618	5,843	8,490	8,793	10,473	10,141	9,492	9,437
Training and employment services	3,042	2,957	3,372	3,768	4,592	3,666	3,040	2,939
Health	43,890	124,843	197,848	268,320	290,168	292,847	268,277	286,444
Substance abuse and mental health services [4]	1,241	1,931	3,203	2,888	2,846	2,964	2,741	3,233
Grants to states for Medicaid [4]	41,103	117,921	181,720	250,924	272,771	274,964	250,534	266,565
State children's health insurance fund [4]	–	1,220	5,129	7,547	7,887	8,629	9,065	9,897
Income security	36,768	68,653	90,885	103,169	115,156	113,625	102,574	104,598
SNAP (formerly Food Stamp Program) [4]	2,130	3,508	4,385	5,624	5,739	5,973	6,832	6,949
Child nutrition programs [4]	4,871	9,060	11,726	15,083	16,259	17,112	18,287	20,844
Temporary Assistance for Needy Families [4]	–	15,464	17,357	17,861	17,513	17,116	16,136	16,848
Veterans benefits and services [4]	134	434	552	809	836	996	1,081	1,113
Administration of justice	574	5,263	4,784	4,810	5,086	4,876	4,690	5,377

– Represents zero. [1] Grants include trust funds. [2] Trust funds. [3] Formerly Education for the Disadvantaged. [4] Includes grants for payments to individuals.

Source: U.S. Office of Management and Budget, *Fiscal Year 2014 Budget of the U.S. Government: Historical Tables*, April 2013. See also <http://www.whitehouse.gov/omb/budget>.

Table 452. Federal Aid to State and Local Governments by State: 2005 to 2010

[In millions of dollars (403,660 represents $403,660,000,000). For fiscal year ending September 30]

State	2005	2008	2009	2010	State	2005	2008	2009	2010
U.S. [1]	403,660	469,773	552,108	630,170	MO	7,407	8,273	10,293	12,717
AL	6,306	6,994	7,610	8,609	MT	2,021	2,109	2,566	2,810
AK	2,671	2,604	3,624	3,326	NE	2,256	2,439	2,826	3,122
AZ	7,965	9,940	12,997	13,370	NV	2,213	2,450	3,143	3,610
AR	4,179	4,733	5,598	6,418	NH	1,483	1,692	1,986	2,355
CA	46,029	53,818	61,971	66,565	NJ	10,479	11,580	13,515	16,309
CO	4,538	5,321	6,333	7,651	NM	4,097	5,381	6,635	6,811
CT	4,539	5,279	6,759	7,673	NY	43,438	44,454	52,183	61,341
DE	1,142	1,363	1,679	3,325	NC	11,568	12,906	15,308	15,522
DC	3,450	11,946	9,659	9,942	ND	1,394	1,402	1,806	2,169
FL	19,046	20,659	22,686	27,731	OH	13,726	15,230	19,115	23,072
GA	8,914	10,675	12,953	15,879	OK	4,935	5,922	7,828	8,022
HI	1,731	2,120	2,560	2,520	OR	4,808	5,498	6,807	7,849
ID	1,814	2,688	2,458	3,057	PA	18,103	18,832	21,796	26,291
IL	14,616	16,267	20,941	23,194	RI	1,937	2,037	2,310	2,944
IN	6,483	8,272	10,194	10,400	SC	5,326	6,035	6,863	8,296
IA	3,594	4,014	5,033	5,871	SD	1,336	1,473	2,068	2,145
KS	2,872	3,514	3,965	4,980	TN	9,083	9,201	10,210	12,514
KY	5,779	6,867	8,245	9,756	TX	25,622	30,580	35,330	43,732
LA	7,148	12,457	11,534	13,437	UT	2,633	3,160	3,942	4,212
ME	2,623	2,695	3,399	3,581	VT	1,213	1,441	1,671	2,044
MD	6,800	7,473	9,405	10,832	VA	6,330	7,724	8,970	10,647
MA	9,989	11,402	15,200	15,121	WA	7,681	8,668	10,631	11,945
MI	12,113	13,587	16,580	19,646	WV	3,482	3,557	4,031	4,830
MN	5,878	7,533	9,304	10,872	WI	6,563	7,000	9,556	10,710
MS	5,168	7,484	7,642	8,611	WY	2,243	2,334	2,214	2,356

[1] Total includes U.S. Island Areas.

Source: U.S. Census Bureau, *Federal Aid to States For Fiscal Year 2010*, September 2011, and earlier reports. See also <http://www.census.gov/govs/>.

Table 453.
Table 453. Federal Aid Total and from Dept. of Agriculture and Dept. of Education to State and Local Governments—Selected Programs by State: 2010

[In millions of dollars (630,170 represents $630,170,000,000). For fiscal year ending September 30. Negative amounts (-) are refunds (from the recipients) of advances from a prior year, or represent reductions in the amount of funds originally obligated to the recipients for the particular program or program category during the fiscal year. For similar data from other Federal agencies, see Tables 454 to 455]

State and Island Areas	Federal aid total [1]	Department of Agriculture					Department of Education				
			Food and Nutrition Service						Office of Elementary and Secondary Education		
		Total	Child nutrition programs	Supplemental Nutrition Assistance Program (SNAP) [2]	Special mental food program (WIC)	Other	Total	Special education programs	No Child Left Behind Act	Title 1 programs	Other
United States, total	630,170	32,793	16,281	5,619	6,457	4,435	73,209	16,695	5,014	18,110	33,390
Alabama	8,609	525	290	45	108	82	904	274	79	343	208
Alaska	3,326	159	46	12	25	76	401	57	29	50	266
Arizona	13,370	665	359	59	141	106	1,480	261	86	374	759
Arkansas	6,418	383	211	37	68	68	757	176	51	186	344
California	66,565	4,165	1,990	632	1,117	426	6,165	1,792	516	2,236	1,620
Colorado	7,651	363	172	48	76	66	1,067	217	66	195	589
Connecticut	7,673	224	119	34	43	29	840	229	46	165	400
Delaware	3,325	93	48	14	13	17	220	44	24	48	105
District of Columbia	9,942	76	38	14	15	9	225	19	26	40	139
Florida	27,731	1,591	947	133	354	158	4,011	953	236	905	1,917
Georgia	15,879	1,179	686	90	254	150	2,663	480	140	602	1,441
Hawaii	2,520	125	51	14	32	28	319	50	26	53	190
Idaho	3,057	180	77	11	29	64	469	86	25	65	294
Illinois	23,194	1,099	620	126	237	117	3,066	769	212	830	1,256
Indiana	10,400	570	335	54	108	73	1,201	374	79	311	438
Iowa	5,871	301	143	29	48	81	796	217	43	121	415
Kansas	4,980	302	156	19	45	82	688	182	34	129	343
Kentucky	9,756	516	260	64	96	96	1,238	261	82	303	591
Louisiana	13,437	637	346	78	122	91	1,410	293	134	392	591
Maine	3,581	125	55	18	18	34	337	87	33	76	141
Maryland	10,832	414	211	54	98	52	1,346	300	70	264	712
Massachusetts	15,121	439	247	56	88	48	547	14	8	3	522
Michigan	19,646	894	436	157	175	126	2,641	603	185	705	1,148
Minnesota	10,872	544	235	90	99	120	1,484	315	74	196	899
Mississippi	8,611	481	261	40	90	91	913	171	73	244	425
Missouri	12,717	555	301	66	87	100	1,535	364	81	294	796
Montana	2,810	133	47	16	15	54	315	59	32	61	162
Nebraska	3,122	195	102	18	31	44	444	108	34	76	226
Nevada	3,610	185	91	19	44	30	572	104	32	113	323
New Hampshire	2,355	71	34	8	12	17	366	69	26	46	225
New Jersey	16,309	635	327	119	127	61	2,277	537	106	354	1,280
New Mexico	6,811	326	162	32	40	93	783	141	49	169	424
New York	61,341	1,942	1,000	359	419	166	5,552	1,019	433	1,518	2,582
North Carolina	15,522	914	520	89	191	114	1,473	486	126	489	372
North Dakota	2,169	88	36	11	12	28	285	44	26	48	167
Ohio	23,072	960	513	158	179	110	2,880	710	190	725	1,255
Oklahoma	8,022	531	262	62	96	111	984	205	78	174	528
Oregon	7,849	519	172	110	72	165	848	218	65	194	370
Pennsylvania	26,291	1,081	483	192	197	208	3,173	659	189	732	1,592
Rhode Island	2,944	85	44	9	20	12	269	67	26	71	106
South Carolina	8,296	457	276	24	89	68	1,078	256	85	249	488
South Dakota	2,145	118	47	15	18	38	113	1	2	–	110
Tennessee	12,514	617	343	69	119	85	1,424	353	92	353	627
Texas	43,732	2,924	1,907	210	532	276	6,965	1,503	450	1,810	3,202
Utah	4,212	249	129	31	43	45	573	149	38	81	304
Vermont	2,044	93	25	28	14	26	213	43	26	48	97
Virginia	10,647	517	239	100	92	86	1,050	386	88	279	297
Washington	11,945	559	265	69	125	100	1,469	356	88	250	775
West Virginia	4,830	207	99	19	37	51	496	124	41	130	202
Wisconsin	10,710	471	232	67	87	84	1,208	323	82	270	534
Wyoming	2,356	59	25	8	9	17	157	36	27	39	55
Island Areas:											
American Samoa	198	32	18	5	7	1	31	8	1	–	23
Micronesia	117	–	–	–	–	–	–	–	–	–	–
Guam	319	23	9	2	9	3	36	16	1	–	20
Marshall Islands	98	–	–	–	–	–	–	–	–	–	–
Northern Marianas	140	27	9	12	5	1	21	6	–	–	14
Palau	24	–	–	–	–	–	3	1	–	–	2
Puerto Rico	6,886	2,218	202	1,749	225	42	1,424	121	124	702	477
Virgin Islands	412	45	21	12	7	4	2	–	–	–	2
Undistributed	1,231	-95	–	–	–	-95	–	–	–	–	–

– Represents or rounds to zero. [1] Total includes programs, not shown separately. [2] For Puerto Rico, amount shown is for nutritional assistance grant program, all other amounts are grant payments for food stamp administration.

Source: U.S. Census Bureau, *Federal Aid to States For Fiscal Year 2010*, September 2011. See also <http://www.census.gov/govs/>.

Table 454. Federal Aid from FEMA, HUD, and Dept. of Labor to State and Local Governments—Selected Programs by State: 2010

[In millions of dollars (4,972 represents $4,972,000,000). For fiscal year ending September 30. Negative amounts (-) are refunds (from the recipients) of advances from a prior year, or represent reductions in the amount of funds originally obligated to the recipients for the particular program or program category during the fiscal year. For similar data from other Federal agencies, see Tables 453 and 455]

State and Island Areas	FEMA [1] total	Department of Housing and Urban Development						Department of Labor			
		Total	Community development block grants	Public housing programs			Other	Total	State unemployment insurance and employment service	Workforce investment	Other
				Low rent housing assistance	Housing certificate program	Capital program					
United States, total	**4,972**	**55,272**	**7,361**	**30,699**	**1,292**	**5,686**	**10,234**	**11,362**	**4,727**	**4,370**	**2,265**
Alabama	50	764	99	410	6	141	109	126	57	42	27
Alaska	10	260	15	58	2	6	178	65	38	18	9
Arizona	5	627	74	240	4	20	290	178	69	66	43
Arkansas	78	311	39	185	5	42	40	107	45	37	26
California	169	6,901	1,268	4,272	91	182	1,087	1,478	672	660	146
Colorado	12	573	52	366	10	34	112	139	67	49	23
Connecticut	11	900	55	595	64	73	113	147	82	39	26
Delaware	2	141	13	71	15	12	29	29	14	11	5
District of Columbia	7	2,890	202	816	9	784	1,079	225	15	17	194
Florida	362	2,210	212	1,263	21	141	573	426	173	199	54
Georgia	51	1,474	128	808	9	157	373	257	116	116	26
Hawaii	4	239	22	160	2	18	37	48	22	12	14
Idaho	1	111	19	59	3	3	26	71	40	12	19
Illinois	51	2,580	202	1,597	90	330	361	528	221	218	89
Indiana	20	757	120	430	9	61	138	249	93	103	52
Iowa	169	340	107	156	3	18	56	108	46	33	29
Kansas	343	256	35	134	4	25	58	74	35	25	15
Kentucky	161	594	46	365	6	83	93	175	55	82	39
Louisiana	1,335	1,338	644	484	7	90	112	127	45	65	18
Maine	10	262	29	147	24	15	48	63	28	20	16
Maryland	30	1,361	80	752	35	169	324	264	93	44	127
Massachusetts	42	2,250	144	1,610	114	134	248	222	106	85	31
Michigan	31	1,250	150	642	116	93	249	633	221	306	106
Minnesota	35	766	67	385	74	95	146	197	78	80	39
Mississippi	349	1,080	699	263	6	45	68	128	39	74	15
Missouri	123	737	105	410	10	74	137	204	71	91	42
Montana	8	152	19	58	–	7	67	48	20	10	18
Nebraska	17	181	25	97	2	23	35	40	24	6	10
Nevada	3	308	31	172	1	15	89	105	57	36	11
New Hampshire	12	231	23	139	7	14	48	39	25	9	6
New Jersey	30	1,814	125	1,226	99	172	192	304	185	87	32
New Mexico	7	240	32	114	3	18	73	62	23	15	23
New York	129	6,641	691	4,383	72	645	850	634	269	283	82
North Carolina	26	999	82	621	12	125	159	323	128	128	67
North Dakota	124	103	9	50	–	6	39	29	15	7	6
Ohio	9	1,928	187	1,187	23	181	350	462	175	211	77
Oklahoma	77	488	45	231	4	34	175	95	44	33	18
Oregon	24	481	41	293	2	29	117	219	102	72	45
Pennsylvania	22	2,207	251	1,168	110	321	357	459	231	139	89
Rhode Island	7	373	24	259	5	33	52	53	25	19	9
South Carolina	8	512	54	302	7	54	95	181	62	100	18
South Dakota	20	154	18	50	10	7	70	31	14	7	9
Tennessee	22	801	57	472	14	121	137	199	68	108	22
Texas	610	2,715	515	1,519	20	245	416	620	237	262	121
Utah	11	195	29	103	2	7	53	72	40	14	18
Vermont	2	119	11	69	7	8	24	33	12	10	10
Virginia	201	1,115	71	605	64	166	208	317	84	52	181
Washington	70	957	85	552	2	84	234	313	161	88	65
West Virginia	11	245	47	144	4	20	29	61	27	18	16
Wisconsin	22	652	119	284	51	47	151	232	106	64	63
Wyoming	2	57	6	26	–	3	22	29	15	8	5
Island Areas:											
American Samoa	9	–	–	–	–	–	–	2	–	–	1
Micronesia	1	–	–	–	–	–	–	–	–	–	–
Guam	-1	52	7	39	–	3	3	7	–	4	3
Marshall Islands	–	–	–	–	–	–	–	–	–	–	–
Northern Marianas	1	6	–	5	–	–	1	2	–	2	1
Palau	–	–	–	–	–	–	–	–	–	–	–
Puerto Rico	22	961	125	506	28	199	103	109	34	66	8
Virgin Islands	6	69	3	46	1	16	3	10	4	4	2
Undistributed	–	-458	1	-698	–	241	-1	–	–	–	–

– Represents or rounds to zero. [1] FEMA = Federal Emergency Management Agency. FEMA is part of the U.S. Department of Homeland Security.

Source: U.S. Census Bureau, *Federal Aid to States For Fiscal Year 2010*, September 2011. See also <http://www.census.gov/govs/>.

Table 455. Federal Aid from Dept. of Health and Human Services, Dept. of Transportation, and Other Aid to State and Local Governments—Selected Programs by State: 2010

[In millions of dollars (348,197 represents $348,197,000,000). For fiscal year ending September 30. Negative amounts (-) are refunds (from the recipients) of advances from a prior year, or represent reductions in the amount of funds originally obligated to the recipients for the particular program or program category during the fiscal year. For similar data from other Federal agencies, see Tables 453 to 454]

State and Island Areas	Department of Health and Human Services						Department of Transportation				Other, federal aid [1]
	Administration for Children and Families				Centers for Medicare and Medicaid Services	Other	Total	Highway trust fund	Federal Transit Administration	Other	
	Total	Children & family services (Head Start)	Foster care and adoption assistance	Temporary Assistance for Needy Families							
United States, total	348,197	10,388	6,958	19,868	278,041	32,942	63,882	30,273	13,041	20,568	40,482
Alabama	4,853	176	42	150	3,980	505	834	675	57	102	553
Alaska	1,221	50	26	49	911	184	711	352	80	280	499
Arizona	8,582	206	164	255	7,403	553	810	512	184	113	1,023
Arkansas	3,897	109	57	87	3,338	306	573	341	43	189	311
California	39,605	1,257	1,697	4,251	29,247	3,153	4,809	1,881	1,553	1,376	3,273
Colorado	3,807	260	81	226	2,723	517	997	416	240	340	692
Connecticut	4,354	88	96	288	3,464	419	889	584	157	148	308
Delaware	1,018	22	5	50	834	108	1,633	1,547	26	60	188
District of Columbia	2,054	71	62	112	1,493	315	3,083	154	480	2,449	1,382
Florida	15,358	414	265	669	12,297	1,713	2,360	1,269	357	735	1,412
Georgia	7,728	266	132	394	6,075	861	1,723	1,135	200	388	803
Hawaii	1,312	41	34	148	933	156	239	138	35	66	233
Idaho	1,430	53	16	22	1,179	160	446	286	23	137	348
Illinois	12,488	402	248	729	9,835	1,274	2,070	859	618	593	1,311
Indiana	5,615	149	149	200	4,570	547	1,353	722	150	481	637
Iowa	3,121	92	63	172	2,469	325	672	349	70	253	363
Kansas	2,364	87	46	145	1,823	263	644	398	36	209	308
Kentucky	5,613	182	101	220	4,666	444	876	497	86	293	583
Louisiana	6,691	229	80	235	5,538	610	1,086	604	89	394	812
Maine	2,219	49	35	95	1,840	199	271	151	21	99	294
Maryland	5,933	129	105	351	4,574	774	863	418	257	187	622
Massachusetts	9,650	189	103	553	7,860	944	1,157	623	302	233	814
Michigan	11,470	366	223	992	8,701	1,188	1,724	809	205	710	1,004
Minnesota	6,023	152	72	315	4,842	641	1,169	511	247	411	655
Mississippi	4,503	231	20	130	3,715	407	697	377	27	292	459
Missouri	7,315	204	89	255	6,152	615	1,584	939	193	451	664
Montana	1,103	56	21	49	807	171	562	342	26	194	489
Nebraska	1,601	72	31	50	1,232	216	321	131	31	160	322
Nevada	1,416	43	54	66	1,020	232	565	290	106	169	457
New Hampshire	1,092	28	21	50	835	158	264	161	18	85	280
New Jersey	8,704	186	138	606	6,840	935	1,751	622	713	415	795
New Mexico	3,795	101	45	176	3,187	287	565	305	42	218	1,032
New York	39,344	656	566	2,741	32,737	2,644	4,876	1,632	2,684	560	2,224
North Carolina	10,135	326	129	348	8,369	964	973	376	128	469	680
North Dakota	723	46	17	28	523	109	411	192	17	202	406
Ohio	14,034	397	375	877	11,299	1,087	1,707	968	276	464	1,092
Oklahoma	4,113	167	72	185	3,218	471	1,067	653	57	357	667
Oregon	4,124	143	138	247	3,193	403	1,041	513	256	272	593
Pennsylvania	15,516	374	363	762	12,688	1,328	2,498	1,235	599	664	1,336
Rhode Island	1,597	44	27	93	1,280	153	312	175	44	93	248
South Carolina	4,848	122	50	111	4,119	446	779	456	50	273	433
South Dakota	845	61	11	23	626	124	389	214	17	158	475
Tennessee	7,415	193	82	251	6,346	542	1,177	660	118	399	859
Texas	24,184	783	353	665	20,095	2,288	3,435	1,611	661	1,162	2,279
Utah	1,930	73	30	75	1,490	261	695	248	267	180	487
Vermont	1,107	30	20	55	890	111	288	163	24	100	189
Virginia	5,287	170	87	171	4,221	639	1,292	854	249	189	868
Washington	6,192	214	148	553	4,474	804	1,390	479	427	484	994
West Virginia	2,819	86	53	193	2,224	262	606	396	41	169	387
Wisconsin	6,121	160	112	316	4,942	592	1,228	660	108	459	776
Wyoming	499	30	4	24	365	75	405	239	11	155	1,148
Island Areas:											
American Samoa	31	5	–	–	13	12	40	9	–	30	54
Micronesia	7	–	–	–	–	7	–	–	–	–	109
Guam	57	7	–	4	18	28	56	33	1	22	89
Marshall Islands	5	–	–	–	–	5	25	–	–	25	68
Northern Marianas	22	4	–	–	10	8	17	–	1	16	43
Palau	7	2	–	–	–	6	–	–	–	–	13
Puerto Rico	1,233	319	2	50	501	361	221	91	78	52	698
Virgin Islands	64	15	–	4	18	28	17	7	1	9	199
Undistributed	3	–	–	–	–	3	1,639	16	250	1,374	141

– Represents or rounds to zero. [1] Represents aid for other programs, not shown in Tables 453 to 455.

Source: U.S. Census Bureau, *Federal Aid to States For Fiscal Year 2010,* September 2011. See also <http://www.census.gov/govs/>.

State and Local Government Finances and Employment

Table 456. State and Local Governments—Summary of Finances: 1990 to 2011

[In millions of dollars (1,032,115 represents $1,032,115,000,000). For fiscal year ending in year shown; see text, this section. Local government amounts are estimates subject to sampling variation; see Appendix III and source. Minus sign (-) indicates deficit]

Item	1990	2000	2005	2009	2010	2011
Revenue [1]	**1,032,115**	**1,942,328**	**2,528,546**	**2,099,813**	**3,168,242**	**3,433,536**
From federal government	136,802	291,950	438,558	536,823	623,081	645,962
Public welfare	59,961	148,549	(NA)	(NA)	(NA)	(NA)
Highways	14,368	24,414	(NA)	(NA)	(NA)	(NA)
Education	23,233	45,873	(NA)	(NA)	(NA)	(NA)
Health and hospitals	5,904	15,611	(NA)	(NA)	(NA)	(NA)
Housing and community development	9,655	17,690	(NA)	(NA)	(NA)	(NA)
Other and unallocable	23,683	39,812	(NA)	(NA)	(NA)	(NA)
From state and local sources	**895,313**	**1,650,379**	**2,089,988**	**1,562,990**	**2,545,161**	**2,787,574**
General, net intergovernmental	712,700	1,249,373	1,587,476	1,888,043	1,879,468	1,966,815
Taxes	501,619	872,351	1,098,513	1,277,648	1,270,896	1,338,437
Property	155,613	249,178	335,779	430,935	440,577	443,259
Sales and gross receipts	177,885	309,290	384,266	433,252	432,470	460,824
Individual income	105,640	211,661	242,273	270,862	260,315	284,938
Corporation net income	23,566	36,059	43,256	46,281	43,865	48,547
Other	38,915	66,164	92,939	96,318	93,670	100,868
Charges and miscellaneous	211,081	377,022	488,963	610,395	608,572	628,379
Utility and liquor stores	58,642	89,546	119,608	154,246	152,891	157,199
Water supply system	17,674	30,515	37,378	46,785	48,810	51,332
Electric power system	29,268	42,436	59,157	76,961	74,691	76,655
Gas supply system	5,216	8,049	6,937	9,770	8,583	7,958
Transit system	3,043	3,954	10,146	13,029	13,006	13,271
Liquor stores	3,441	4,592	5,990	7,701	7,801	7,984
Insurance trust revenue [2]	123,970	311,460	382,904	-479,300	512,802	663,560
Employee retirement	94,268	273,881	316,576	-545,318	414,936	553,135
Unemployment compensation	18,441	23,366	35,367	42,115	75,191	87,578
Direct expenditure	**972,695**	**1,742,914**	**2,363,696**	**2,985,739**	**3,111,968**	**3,158,332**
By function:						
Direct general expenditure [2]	831,573	1,502,768	2,007,490	2,184,380	2,538,214	2,583,101
Education [2]	288,148	521,612	688,314	851,149	858,259	861,131
Elementary and secondary	202,009	365,181	473,843	577,206	572,534	564,862
Higher education	73,418	134,352	182,003	234,752	242,763	252,270
Highways	61,057	101,336	126,350	154,047	155,688	153,005
Public welfare	107,287	233,350	360,730	431,884	456,804	492,007
Health	24,223	51,366	66,637	83,088	81,559	82,369
Hospitals	50,412	75,976	103,555	137,680	142,668	148,136
Police protection	30,577	56,798	74,131	94,336	94,981	96,332
Fire protection	13,186	23,102	30,830	41,614	42,426	42,252
Natural resources	12,330	20,235	23,519	30,746	29,284	29,071
Sanitation and sewerage	28,453	45,261	57,940	75,911	76,532	78,746
Housing and community development	15,479	26,590	40,014	49,173	53,460	56,121
Parks and recreation	14,326	25,038	31,925	41,333	40,189	38,694
Financial administration	16,217	29,300	36,695	40,646	40,519	39,689
Interest on general debt [3]	49,739	69,814	81,122	105,053	105,765	108,658
Utility and liquor stores [3]	77,801	114,916	160,470	215,700	214,391	213,830
Water supply system	22,101	35,789	45,695	59,849	61,985	62,438
Electric power system	30,997	39,719	58,612	80,776	77,059	78,411
Gas supply system	2,989	3,724	7,075	9,879	8,354	7,624
Transit system	18,788	31,883	44,203	58,827	60,566	58,748
Liquor stores	2,926	3,801	4,885	6,369	6,427	6,608
Insurance trust expenditure [2]	63,321	125,230	195,735	275,054	359,362	361,402
Employee retirement	38,355	95,679	145,796	190,497	205,138	221,090
Unemployment compensation	16,499	18,648	29,849	66,159	135,367	121,870
By character and object:						
Current operation	700,131	1,288,746	1,760,283	2,184,380	2,228,862	2,287,231
Capital outlay	123,102	217,063	278,063	362,853	356,105	335,861
Construction	89,144	161,694	218,691	284,822	284,261	268,613
Equipment, land, and existing structures	33,958	55,369	59,372	78,030	71,844	67,247
Assistance and subsidies	27,227	31,375	37,755	44,646	47,632	50,268
Interest on debt (general and utility)	58,914	80,499	91,859	118,807	120,007	123,572
Insurance benefits and repayments	63,321	125,230	195,735	275,054	359,362	361,402
Expenditure for salaries and wages [4]	340,654	548,796	694,583	831,703	844,700	848,105
Debt outstanding, year end	**858,006**	**1,451,815**	**2,085,026**	**2,723,101**	**2,842,322**	**2,907,756**
Long-term	838,700	1,427,524	2,054,268	2,686,233	2,797,112	2,873,017
Short-term	19,306	24,291	30,758	36,868	45,209	34,739
Long-term debt:						
Issued	108,468	184,831	323,739	371,774	397,977	360,066
Retired	64,831	121,897	224,639	256,948	274,942	274,117

NA Not available. [1] Aggregates exclude duplicative transactions between state and local governments; see source. [2] Includes amounts not shown separately. [3] Interest on utility debt included in "utility and liquor stores expenditure." For total interest on debt, see "Interest on debt (general and utility)." [4] Included in items above.

Source: U.S. Census Bureau, Federal, State, and Local Governments, Government Finance Statistics, "Annual Surveys of State and Local Government Finances," <http://www.census.gov/govs/local/>, accessed July 2013.

Table 457. State and Local Governments—Revenue and Expenditures by Function: 2010 and 2011

[In millions of dollars (3,168,242 represents $3,168,242,000,000). For fiscal year ending in year shown; see text, this section. Local government amounts are estimates subject to sampling variation; see Appendix III and source]

Item	2010 Total	2010 State	2010 Local	2011 Total	2011 State	2011 Local
Revenue [1]	**3,168,242**	**2,035,163**	**1,628,612**	**3,433,536**	**2,265,213**	**1,669,421**
Intergovernmental revenue [1]	623,081	574,684	543,930	645,962	592,998	554,062
Total revenue from own sources [1]	2,545,161	1,460,479	1,084,682	2,787,574	1,672,215	1,115,359
General revenue from own sources	1,879,468	989,506	889,962	1,966,815	1,061,316	905,499
Taxes [2]	1,270,896	703,444	567,451	1,338,437	760,259	578,177
Property	440,577	14,545	426,032	443,259	14,173	429,086
Individual income	260,315	235,994	24,320	284,938	259,309	25,629
Corporation income	43,865	37,761	6,104	48,547	41,383	7,164
Sales and gross receipts	432,470	343,401	89,069	460,824	367,746	93,079
General sales	285,363	223,040	62,324	301,370	235,939	65,431
Selective sales [2]	147,106	120,361	26,745	159,454	131,806	27,648
Motor fuel	37,938	36,642	1,296	41,227	39,883	1,344
Alcoholic beverages	6,027	5,505	523	6,240	5,729	512
Tobacco products	17,267	16,832	436	17,654	17,250	403
Public utilities	28,465	14,761	13,704	28,730	14,673	14,056
Motor vehicle and operators' licenses	22,343	20,721	1,623	23,205	21,543	1,662
Charges and miscellaneous [2]	608,572	286,061	322,510	628,379	301,057	327,322
Current charges [2]	409,490	169,858	239,633	428,852	181,101	247,751
Education [2]	121,694	94,530	27,164	129,896	102,080	27,816
School lunch sales	6,614	34	6,580	6,371	28	6,343
Higher education	106,054	93,081	12,974	114,539	100,758	13,782
Natural resources	4,650	2,788	1,862	4,773	3,097	1,676
Hospitals	110,768	42,938	67,830	116,738	45,392	71,346
Sewerage	43,490	612	42,878	46,302	601	45,701
Solid waste management	15,705	420	15,285	16,143	420	15,724
Parks and recreation	9,368	1,516	7,852	9,385	1,477	7,908
Housing and community development	5,873	622	5,252	5,978	614	5,364
Airports	18,011	1,327	16,684	18,839	1,375	17,464
Sea and inland port facilities	3,879	1,038	2,841	4,173	1,180	2,993
Highways	12,086	6,885	5,201	12,675	7,086	5,589
Interest earnings	60,772	34,578	26,193	57,578	34,287	23,291
Special assessments	7,348	171	7,178	7,025	36	6,990
Sale of property	2,953	692	2,261	2,846	766	2,080
Utility and liquor store revenue	152,891	21,617	131,275	157,199	21,281	135,918
Insurance trust revenue	512,802	449,357	63,446	663,560	589,618	73,942
Expenditures [1]	**3,116,307**	**1,943,588**	**1,667,915**	**3,162,628**	**2,004,325**	**1,664,494**
Intergovernmental expenditure [1]	4,339	485,544	13,991	4,296	496,756	13,730
Direct expenditure [1]	3,111,968	1,458,044	1,653,923	3,158,332	1,507,569	1,650,763
General expenditure [2]	2,538,214	1,108,052	1,430,162	2,583,101	1,158,126	1,424,975
Education [1]	858,259	253,758	604,501	861,131	261,866	599,265
Elementary and secondary education	572,534	7,832	564,702	564,862	6,674	558,188
Higher education	242,763	202,964	39,799	252,270	211,193	41,077
Public welfare	456,804	404,331	52,473	492,007	439,319	52,689
Hospitals	142,668	58,708	83,960	148,136	61,195	86,941
Health	81,559	40,044	41,514	82,369	41,243	41,126
Highways	155,688	93,028	62,660	153,005	92,086	60,918
Police protection	94,981	12,376	82,605	96,332	12,857	83,475
Fire protection	42,426	–	42,426	42,252	–	42,252
Corrections	73,000	46,095	26,905	73,151	46,711	26,440
Natural resources	29,284	19,336	9,949	29,071	19,272	9,799
Sewerage	52,743	1,118	51,626	54,867	1,299	53,567
Solid waste management	23,789	2,281	21,507	23,880	2,531	21,348
Housing and community development	53,460	10,715	42,745	56,121	11,350	44,771
Governmental administration	127,214	52,146	75,069	124,511	51,494	73,017
Parks and recreation	40,189	4,912	35,278	38,694	4,829	33,864
Interest on general debt	105,765	45,260	60,506	108,658	46,834	61,824
Utility	207,964	23,977	183,988	207,222	23,549	183,673
Liquor store expenditure	6,427	5,244	1,183	6,608	5,407	1,201
Insurance trust expenditure	359,362	320,772	38,590	361,402	320,488	40,914
By character and object:						
Current operation	2,228,862	934,349	1,294,512	2,287,231	982,437	1,304,793
Capital outlay	356,105	118,011	238,094	335,861	115,828	220,033
Construction	284,261	100,962	183,298	268,613	98,325	170,288
Equipment, land, and existing structures	71,844	17,048	54,796	67,247	17,503	49,745
Assistance and subsidies	47,632	37,562	10,070	50,268	39,880	10,388
Interest on debt (general and utility)	120,007	47,351	72,656	123,572	48,936	74,635
Insurance benefits and repayments	359,362	320,772	38,590	361,402	320,488	40,914
Expenditure for salaries and wages [3]	844,700	244,952	599,748	848,105	252,054	596,051

– Represents or rounds to zero. [1] Aggregates exclude duplicative transactions between levels of government; see source. [2] Includes other items, not shown separately. [3] Included in items shown above.

Source: U.S. Census Bureau, Federal, State, and Local Governments, Government Finance Statistics, "Annual Surveys of State and Local Government Finances," <http://www.census.gov/govs/local/>, accessed July 2013.

Table 458. State and Local Governments—Capital Outlays: 1990 to 2011

[In millions of dollars (123,102 represents $123,102,000,000), except percent. For fiscal year ending in year shown; see text, this section. Local government amounts are subject to sampling variation; see Appendix III and source]

Level and function	1990	2000	2005	2007	2008	2009	2010	2011
State & local governments: Total	**123,102**	**217,063**	**278,063**	**325,267**	**349,710**	**362,853**	**356,105**	**335,861**
Percent of direct expenditure	12.7	12.5	11.8	12.2	12.3	12.2	11.4	10.6
By function:								
Education [1]	25,997	60,968	77,780	91,541	98,284	101,379	92,825	86,356
Elementary and secondary	18,057	45,150	54,563	65,532	70,285	69,259	60,294	52,990
Higher education	7,441	15,257	22,735	25,366	27,379	31,548	30,853	31,811
Highways	33,867	56,439	70,689	83,332	88,589	86,809	90,152	85,856
Health and hospitals [2]	3,848	5,502	6,100	7,647	9,114	9,424	8,545	8,313
Natural resources	2,545	4,347	4,541	6,341	6,752	6,593	5,182	5,350
Sewerage	8,356	10,093	14,081	17,698	18,902	21,246	21,818	23,299
Parks and recreation	3,877	6,916	8,136	10,059	11,683	11,487	10,711	9,206
Utilities	16,601	24,847	34,790	39,029	41,221	49,534	50,527	47,488
State governments: Total	**45,524**	**76,233**	**95,155**	**110,044**	**112,695**	**116,990**	**118,011**	**115,828**
Percent of direct expenditure	11.5	10.1	8.9	9.4	8.9	8.7	8.1	7.7
By function:								
Education [1]	7,253	14,077	20,585	23,752	25,132	28,358	28,643	29,037
Elementary and secondary	388	521	447	1,734	1,592	1,593	1,066	747
Higher education	6,366	12,995	19,656	21,375	22,921	26,193	25,899	26,734
Highways	24,850	41,651	52,607	61,218	62,009	61,945	64,755	62,626
Health and hospitals [2]	1,531	2,228	2,363	2,790	3,350	3,048	2,654	2,738
Natural resources	1,593	2,758	2,667	3,324	3,026	3,208	2,337	2,411
Sewerage	333	403	486	740	601	516	488	671
Parks and recreation	601	1,044	915	1,176	1,192	1,076	910	889
Utilities	2,605	4,232	4,319	4,859	4,809	6,151	5,318	5,025
Local governments: Total	**77,578**	**140,830**	**182,908**	**215,223**	**237,014**	**245,863**	**238,094**	**220,033**
Percent of direct expenditure	13.5	14.3	14.1	14.5	15.0	14.9	14.4	13.3
By function:								
Education [1]	18,744	46,890	57,195	67,790	73,152	73,021	64,182	57,319
Elementary and secondary	17,669	44,629	54,116	63,799	68,694	67,666	59,228	52,243
Higher education	1,076	2,261	3,079	3,991	4,458	5,354	4,954	5,077
Highways	9,017	14,789	18,083	22,115	26,580	24,864	25,398	23,231
Health and hospitals [2]	2,316	3,274	3,737	4,857	5,765	6,376	5,892	5,575
Natural resources	952	1,589	1,873	3,018	3,726	3,385	2,846	2,939
Sewerage	8,023	9,690	13,595	16,958	18,301	20,730	21,330	22,629
Parks and recreation	3,276	5,872	7,221	8,883	10,491	10,411	9,802	8,317
Utilities	13,996	20,615	30,471	34,170	36,413	43,383	45,209	42,462

[1] Includes other education, not shown separately. [2] After 2003, only includes hospital outlays.

Source: U.S. Census Bureau, Federal, State, and Local Governments, Government Finance Statistics, "Annual Surveys of State and Local Government Finances," <http://www.census.gov/govs/local/>, accessed August 2013.

Table 459. State and Local Governments—Indebtedness: 1990 to 2011

[In billions of dollars (858.0 represents $858,000,000,000). For fiscal year ending in year shown; see text, this section. Local government amounts are estimates subject to sampling variation; see Appendix III and source]

| Item | Debt outstanding | | | | | | Long-term | | |
| | Total | Cash and security holdings | Long-term | | | Short-term | Net long-term [1] | Debt issued | Debt retired |
			Total	Public debt for private purposes	All other				
1990: Total.......	858.0	1,490.8	838.7	294.1	544.6	19.3	474.4	108.5	64.8
State...........	318.3	963.3	315.5	154.4	161.1	2.8	125.5	43.5	22.9
Local...........	539.8	527.5	523.2	139.7	383.5	16.5	348.9	65.0	42.0
1995: Total......	1,115.4	2,058.5	1,088.3	300.6	787.7	27.0	697.3	129.3	95.1
State...........	427.2	1,393.9	421.1	176.8	244.4	6.1	205.3	52.6	37.5
Local...........	688.1	664.6	667.2	123.9	543.3	20.9	491.9	76.8	57.6
2000: Total......	1,451.8	3,503.7	1,427.5	372.6	1,054.9	24.3	959.6	184.8	121.9
State...........	547.9	2,518.9	541.5	227.3	314.2	6.4	266.9	75.0	44.4
Local...........	903.9	984.8	886.0	145.3	740.7	17.9	692.7	109.8	77.5
2001: Total......	1,554.0	3,592.1	1,531.9	395.1	1,136.8	22.1	1,038.6	199.6	130.6
State...........	576.5	2,537.7	572.8	238.2	334.7	3.7	287.4	81.3	50.7
Local...........	977.5	1,054.3	959.1	157.0	802.1	18.5	751.2	118.3	79.9
2002: Total......	1,681.4	3,650.7	1,638.1	417.7	1,220.5	43.2	1,121.0	262.7	161.9
State...........	636.8	2,555.4	618.2	258.5	359.6	18.6	311.8	104.2	64.9
Local...........	1,044.6	1,095.3	1,020.0	159.2	860.8	24.6	809.2	158.5	97.0
2003: Total......	1,812.7	3,696.1	1,772.2	431.4	1,340.8	40.5	1,242.7	345.8	215.2
State...........	697.9	2,594.2	681.8	267.3	414.5	16.1	366.2	148.8	85.9
Local...........	1,114.7	1,101.9	1,090.4	164.1	926.3	24.3	876.5	196.9	129.3
2004: Total......	1,976.6	4,137.8	1,938.3	459.3	1,479.0	38.3	(NA)	359.8	242.1
State...........	779.5	2,944.9	766.0	279.1	486.9	13.6	(NA)	170.8	107.4
Local...........	1,197.0	1,192.9	1,172.3	180.2	992.1	24.7	(NA)	189.0	134.7
2005: Total......	2,085.0	4,439.2	2,054.3	483.3	1,571.0	30.8	(NA)	323.7	224.6
State...........	810.9	3,153.8	805.3	297.4	507.9	5.6	(NA)	131.6	93.6
Local...........	1,274.2	1,285.4	1,249.0	185.9	1,063.0	25.2	(NA)	192.2	131.1
2006: Total......	2,204.0	4,818.1	2,170.8	509.6	1,661.3	33.2	(NA)	341.9	229.5
State...........	870.0	3,443.2	859.4	318.0	541.5	10.6	(NA)	148.2	95.9
Local...........	1,334.0	1,374.8	1,311.4	191.6	1,119.8	22.6	(NA)	193.7	133.6
2007: Total......	2,404.7	5,457.7	2,373.3	553.3	1,820.0	31.4	(NA)	381.8	228.4
State...........	936.0	3,918.8	929.4	353.9	575.6	6.6	(NA)	161.6	93.4
Local...........	1,468.7	1,538.9	1,443.9	199.5	1,244.4	24.8	(NA)	220.3	135.0
2008: Total......	2,564.4	5,310.8	2,518.7	602.9	1,915.8	45.7	(NA)	373.6	243.5
State...........	1,006.4	3,755.7	992.2	379.0	613.2	14.2	(NA)	151.7	93.4
Local...........	1,558.0	1,555.2	1,526.5	223.9	1,302.6	31.6	(NA)	221.9	150.1
2009: Total......	2,723.1	4,505.3	2,686.2	627.5	2,058.7	36.9	(NA)	371.8	256.9
State...........	1,048.9	3,081.0	1,041.6	395.1	646.5	7.3	(NA)	154.2	109.0
Local...........	1,674.2	1,424.3	1,644.7	232.4	1,412.3	29.5	(NA)	217.6	148.0
2010: Total......	2,842.3	4,822.0	2,797.1	626.9	2,170.2	45.2	(NA)	398.0	274.9
State...........	1,115.7	3,322.6	1,101.0	397.1	703.9	14.7	(NA)	183.7	125.1
Local...........	1,726.6	1,499.5	1,696.1	229.8	1,466.4	30.5	(NA)	214.2	149.8
2011: Total......	2,907.8	5,220.2	2,873.0	615.9	2,257.1	34.7	(NA)	360.1	274.1
State...........	1,132.8	3,664.9	1,127.5	388.3	739.2	5.3	(NA)	136.6	111.9
Local...........	1,774.9	1,555.3	1,745.5	227.6	1,517.9	29.4	(NA)	223.4	162.3

NA Not available. [1] Net long-term debt outstanding is the amount of long-term debt held by a government for which no funds have been set aside for its repayment.

Source: U.S. Census Bureau, Federal, State, and Local Governments, Government Finance Statistics, "Annual Surveys of State and Local Government Finances," <http://www.census.gov/govs/local/>, accessed July 2013.

State and Local Government Finances and Employment

Table 460. State and Local Governments—Expenditures for Public Works: 2000 to 2011

[In millions of dollars (230,569 represents $230,569,000,000), except percent. Public works include expenditures for current operations and capital outlays on highways, airports, sea and inland port facilities, sewerage, solid waste management, water supply, and mass transit systems. Represents direct expenditures excluding intergovernmental grants]

Item	Total	Highways	Air trans-portation	Sea and inland port facilities	Sewerage	Solid waste manage-ment	Water supply	Mass transit
2000, Total.............................	**230,569**	**101,336**	**13,160**	**3,141**	**28,052**	**17,208**	**35,789**	**31,883**
State..................................	74,974	61,942	1,106	863	955	2,347	354	7,407
Local..................................	155,595	39,394	12,054	2,277	27,098	14,861	35,435	24,476
Capital expenditures (percent).....	41.9	55.7	51.0	51.5	36.0	8.9	29.5	30.5
2005, Total.............................	**296,054**	**126,350**	**17,970**	**3,896**	**36,478**	**21,462**	**45,695**	**44,203**
State..................................	94,569	78,316	1,405	1,156	1,118	3,177	319	9,077
Local..................................	201,484	48,034	16,565	2,740	35,360	18,285	45,375	35,125
Capital expenditures (percent).....	(NA)	55.9	(NA)	(NA)	38.6	9.3	(NA)	(NA)
2011, Total.............................	**380,825**	**153,005**	**22,719**	**5,168**	**54,867**	**23,880**	**62,438**	**58,748**
State..................................	111,003	92,086	1,794	1,396	1,299	2,531	349	11,547
Local..................................	269,822	60,918	20,925	3,773	53,567	21,348	62,089	47,202
Capital expenditures (percent).....	(NA)	56.1	(NA)	(NA)	42.5	7.9	(NA)	(NA)

NA Not available.

Source: U.S. Census Bureau, Federal, State, and Local Governments, Government Finance Statistics, "Annual Surveys of State and Local Government Finances," <http://www.census.gov/govs/local/>, accessed July 2013, and unpublished data.

Table 461. New Security Issues, State and Local Governments: 1990 to 2012

[In billions of dollars (122.9 represents 122,900,000,000)]

Type of issue, issuer, or use	1990	1995	2000	2005	2007	2008	2009	2010	2011	2012
All issues, new and refunding [1]..........	**122.9**	**145.7**	**180.4**	**409.6**	**426.2**	**394.5**	**437.1**	**460.8**	**320.2**	**390.4**
By type of issue:										
General obligation............................	39.5	57.0	64.5	145.8	130.5	115.5	142.0	137.5	96.0	126.6
Revenue.......................................	83.3	88.7	115.9	263.8	295.7	279.0	295.1	323.2	224.2	263.8
By type of issuer:										
State..	15.0	14.7	19.9	31.6	35.0	35.1	63.5	55.2	(NA)	(NA)
Special district or statutory authority [2].....	75.9	93.5	121.2	298.6	315.3	286.2	270.8	294.9	(NA)	(NA)
Municipality, county, or township...........	32.0	37.5	39.3	79.4	75.9	73.2	80.5	86.6	(NA)	(NA)
Issues for new capital......................	**97.9**	**102.4**	**154.3**	**223.8**	**275.3**	**217.4**	**279.0**	**278.5**	**172.6**	**159.5**
By use of proceeds:										
Education......................................	17.1	24.0	38.7	71.0	70.9	56.4	60.3	60.4	37.4	34.1
Transportation................................	11.8	11.9	19.7	25.4	27.9	25.0	23.7	32.3	18.9	20.5
Utilities and conservation....................	10.0	9.6	11.9	9.9	11.4	14.5	14.9	22.3	16.7	11.5
Industrial aid.................................	6.6	6.6	7.1	18.6	38.1	24.9	27.5	35.7	16.5	21.3
Other purposes...............................	31.7	30.8	47.3	60.6	82.9	66.1	105.1	92.4	50.1	48.3

NA Not Available [1] Par amounts of long-term issues based on date of sale. [2] Includes school districts.

Source: Board of Governors of the Federal Reserve System, "New Security Issues, State and Local Governments," <http://www.federalreserve.gov/econresdata/releases/statisticsdata.htm>, accessed August 2013.

Table 462. State and Local Governments—Total Revenue and Expenditures by State: 2000 to 2011

[In millions of dollars (1,942,328 represents $1,942,328,000,000). For fiscal year ending in year shown; see text, this section. These data cannot be used to compute the deficit or surplus for any single government, as these are estimates for all state and local governments within a state area. For further information, see the *2006 Government Finance and Employment Classification Manual* at <http://http://www.census.gov/govs/pubs/>]

State	Revenue				Expenditures			
	2000	2005	2010	2011	2000	2005	2010	2011
United States	**1,942,328**	**2,528,546**	**3,168,242**	**3,433,536**	**1,746,943**	**2,368,316**	**3,116,307**	**3,162,628**
Alabama	25,726	33,377	41,043	40,658	25,319	31,752	41,881	42,161
Alaska	10,525	11,404	15,749	18,444	8,628	10,027	14,516	14,687
Arizona	27,778	41,057	54,194	58,723	27,293	39,458	53,335	52,534
Arkansas	13,833	18,866	24,527	27,841	12,245	16,682	22,785	23,769
California	270,380	381,059	450,011	519,382	236,645	342,546	434,793	457,591
Colorado	29,603	38,915	50,271	53,015	26,173	35,063	50,079	51,577
Connecticut	25,828	30,490	39,275	42,151	24,011	29,631	39,160	40,676
Delaware	6,224	7,637	9,770	11,201	5,153	7,595	9,719	9,898
District of Columbia	6,383	10,046	11,643	12,878	6,527	8,947	13,682	13,641
Florida	92,402	135,491	167,658	181,174	84,301	130,860	163,731	164,062
Georgia	49,310	60,297	76,990	85,077	43,517	60,730	78,416	78,094
Hawaii	8,488	11,000	14,501	15,959	8,254	10,534	14,262	14,389
Idaho	7,590	10,004	12,332	14,097	6,404	8,915	11,972	12,066
Illinois	80,695	99,670	124,763	133,626	74,727	97,723	130,406	130,777
Indiana	32,716	44,302	54,300	56,856	31,250	42,164	52,661	52,682
Iowa	17,220	23,204	31,058	34,541	17,275	21,486	29,442	30,325
Kansas	16,235	19,990	26,371	28,562	14,419	18,948	26,550	26,534
Kentucky	25,200	28,069	36,584	40,788	21,473	27,308	38,656	39,063
Louisiana	27,109	35,858	46,920	49,139	25,018	32,578	48,561	48,757
Maine	8,554	11,383	12,557	13,986	7,652	10,207	12,398	12,616
Maryland	33,949	45,076	57,521	62,843	30,598	41,373	57,361	57,612
Massachusetts	46,103	62,019	75,904	82,042	44,362	57,862	76,078	75,734
Michigan	70,112	81,138	94,282	93,406	61,506	76,063	90,839	89,818
Minnesota	38,785	45,465	57,094	63,624	35,424	42,936	55,911	55,684
Mississippi	16,672	21,113	28,542	31,412	15,379	20,041	27,072	27,308
Missouri	31,635	41,340	51,339	57,095	27,953	37,186	50,244	49,877
Montana	5,643	7,438	9,660	10,235	4,983	6,412	9,254	9,294
Nebraska	11,650	15,905	19,760	21,653	10,831	14,332	19,395	19,527
Nevada	11,885	18,953	22,750	25,914	11,230	17,405	23,802	23,269
New Hampshire	6,948	8,911	11,550	12,219	6,222	8,679	11,396	11,637
New Jersey	62,331	79,126	99,618	105,225	54,590	78,522	102,706	101,256
New Mexico	13,073	16,656	21,844	24,273	11,195	15,427	22,332	22,415
New York	188,907	234,689	312,652	323,769	171,858	226,867	295,036	300,324
North Carolina	50,542	64,813	86,035	93,302	46,135	60,080	79,701	80,849
North Dakota	4,495	5,239	7,819	9,645	4,041	4,794	6,658	7,137
Ohio	80,074	102,498	122,859	131,659	68,418	91,972	113,734	116,247
Oklahoma	18,760	24,552	32,789	35,378	15,962	22,044	31,591	30,717
Oregon	28,644	32,406	41,055	47,047	24,086	29,084	39,521	39,932
Pennsylvania	80,546	103,692	124,473	134,310	75,624	101,484	130,731	132,879
Rhode Island	7,427	9,731	11,692	12,742	6,432	9,226	11,274	11,466
South Carolina	23,467	33,278	42,536	45,779	23,436	33,012	42,856	42,784
South Dakota	4,277	5,857	6,954	8,463	3,760	4,973	6,832	7,014
Tennessee	33,625	44,888	54,075	60,327	32,010	42,800	53,174	55,155
Texas	120,666	162,806	209,197	224,475	109,634	151,960	218,555	221,030
Utah	14,954	19,183	23,785	25,188	13,044	17,247	24,476	24,928
Vermont	4,019	5,393	7,016	7,581	3,766	5,172	6,764	6,922
Virginia	44,175	56,658	70,972	76,355	38,092	51,529	67,535	69,226
Washington	46,372	57,510	71,051	77,840	41,794	55,800	74,575	74,905
West Virginia	10,760	14,587	16,907	18,739	9,990	12,110	15,667	16,400
Wisconsin	43,003	48,235	65,863	62,693	34,559	43,146	55,487	56,696
Wyoming	7,030	7,269	10,134	10,208	3,743	5,619	8,742	8,688

Source: U.S. Census Bureau, Federal, State, and Local Governments, Government Finance Statistics, "Annual Surveys of State and Local Government Finances," <http://www.census.gov/govs/local/>, accessed July 2013.

Table 463. State and Local Governments—Revenue by State: 2011

[In millions of dollars (3,433,536 represents $3,433,536,000,000). For fiscal year ending in year shown; see text, this section]

Column groups: Columns 3–4 = Intergovernmental from federal government (Total; from federal government). Columns 5–19 = General revenue (from own sources). Columns 6–11 = Select taxes. Columns 13–16 = Current charges. Columns 17–19 = Miscellaneous revenue.

State	Total revenue	Intergov. Total	Intergov. from federal government	General revenue from own sources	Taxes Total[1]	Property	Sales and gross receipt	Individual income	Corporation income	Other taxes	Total (charges + misc.)	Current charges Total[1]	Education	Hospitals	Sewerage	Misc. Total[1]	Interest earnings	Special assessments	Utility and liquor stores	Insurance trust revenue
U.S.	3,433,536	2,612,777	645,962	1,966,815	1,338,437	443,259	460,824	284,938	48,547	77,663	628,379	428,852	129,896	116,738	46,302	199,527	57,578	7,025	157,199	663,560
AL	40,658	34,574	9,590	24,983	13,879	2,588	6,655	2,905	301	1,209	11,105	8,801	3,184	4,076	453	2,304	495	26	3,077	3,008
AK	18,444	15,820	3,361	12,459	7,292	1,492	669	—	721	4,337	5,167	1,348	228	299	87	3,819	929	11	345	2,280
AZ	58,723	44,014	13,026	30,988	21,655	7,104	10,160	2,864	560	620	9,332	6,181	2,597	822	805	3,152	799	79	4,549	10,160
AR	27,841	21,544	6,723	14,820	9,950	1,813	4,990	2,270	377	356	4,871	3,349	1,309	1,115	276	1,522	341	24	908	5,390
CA	519,382	344,101	75,877	268,224	185,218	53,506	59,179	50,508	9,614	9,279	83,006	60,339	10,168	17,008	6,486	22,667	6,253	1,466	25,316	149,965
CO	53,015	41,504	7,446	34,058	21,792	8,320	7,145	4,541	384	932	12,267	8,499	3,157	1,917	836	3,768	1,331	146	2,736	8,775
CT	42,151	34,941	7,201	27,740	22,763	9,230	5,523	6,469	673	673	4,977	3,134	1,480	449	346	1,843	633	92	799	6,412
DE	11,201	8,864	1,899	6,965	4,072	666	506	1,229	347	1,274	2,893	1,499	737	14	150	1,394	204	—	448	1,888
DC	12,878	10,774	4,117	6,657	5,369	1,757	1,409	1,311	382	477	1,289	633	31	114	247	655	59	5	971	1,133
FL	181,174	138,875	32,024	106,851	65,259	25,935	32,380	—	1,870	3,821	41,592	28,979	5,194	6,839	2,883	12,613	2,611	1,884	9,570	32,729
GA	85,077	64,104	16,553	47,551	31,133	10,349	11,610	7,659	670	548	16,418	12,173	3,521	4,383	1,091	4,246	969	61	4,837	16,137
HI	15,959	12,913	3,181	9,732	6,573	1,325	3,532	1,247	68	139	3,159	2,174	498	527	395	985	234	28	318	2,728
ID	14,097	10,760	2,988	7,773	4,711	1,368	1,642	1,169	170	221	3,061	2,317	551	839	178	744	206	39	324	3,012
IL	133,626	102,086	22,527	79,558	59,552	24,172	17,725	11,225	3,024	1,752	20,006	12,279	4,865	1,461	1,122	7,727	2,079	496	3,986	27,554
IN	56,856	47,298	11,538	35,760	23,152	6,313	8,989	6,203	717	545	12,607	8,789	3,852	2,745	1,044	3,818	1,346	23	2,049	7,509
IA	34,541	27,567	7,524	20,042	12,649	4,369	4,205	2,944	250	360	7,393	5,644	1,948	2,441	432	1,749	369	14	1,194	5,781
KS	28,562	23,538	5,159	18,380	11,757	3,916	4,366	2,693	247	331	6,623	4,600	1,422	1,963	357	2,022	745	111	1,291	3,732
KY	40,788	31,641	9,415	22,226	14,556	3,003	5,467	4,502	626	713	7,669	5,341	1,869	1,579	509	2,328	1,061	20	1,556	7,591
LA	49,139	40,570	13,650	26,920	16,612	3,537	9,203	2,404	197	1,163	10,308	6,869	1,397	3,290	386	3,438	1,226	11	1,242	7,327
ME	13,986	11,479	3,399	8,080	6,054	2,401	1,689	1,421	209	236	2,026	1,372	500	78	186	654	236	5	145	2,362
MD	62,843	51,115	12,453	38,662	29,037	8,425	7,362	10,601	776	1,429	9,625	6,297	2,885	164	967	3,328	804	43	1,195	10,533
MA	82,042	64,897	15,518	49,379	35,841	13,287	7,343	11,597	1,932	1,304	13,538	8,611	2,874	1,148	1,906	4,927	1,989	28	3,317	13,827
MI	93,406	78,211	21,859	56,352	36,102	13,569	13,190	6,799	720	933	20,250	14,450	6,186	3,275	1,720	5,800	1,447	205	3,391	11,804
MN	63,624	48,792	10,577	38,216	26,823	8,180	8,518	7,482	1,004	1,051	11,393	7,439	2,883	1,572	734	3,954	1,153	435	2,218	12,615
MS	31,412	24,771	9,323	15,449	9,269	2,546	4,322	1,398	348	526	6,179	5,115	1,329	2,908	214	1,064	263	4	1,106	5,536
MO	57,095	42,311	12,526	29,785	19,642	5,878	7,344	4,837	387	924	10,144	6,878	2,664	2,052	684	3,265	1,144	32	2,256	12,528
MT	10,235	7,941	2,669	5,272	3,435	1,339	542	813	124	472	1,838	1,146	532	89	82	691	268	73	185	2,108
NE	21,653	15,392	3,747	11,645	7,801	2,874	2,408	1,722	155	450	3,845	2,588	942	820	166	1,257	316	38	3,784	2,476
NV	25,914	17,879	3,368	14,511	10,214	3,011	5,600	—	—	1,452	4,297	2,890	583	527	430	1,407	329	74	971	7,064
NH	12,219	9,798	2,128	7,670	5,311	3,317	904	83	583	297	2,359	1,410	705	12	124	948	434	—	665	1,755
NJ	105,225	84,839	15,247	69,592	53,150	25,514	12,065	10,617	2,216	2,150	16,442	10,661	4,121	1,233	1,648	5,780	1,568	7	2,233	18,153
NM	24,273	18,798	6,744	12,054	7,250	1,366	3,591	1,097	230	828	4,804	2,365	774	861	162	2,439	670	10	558	4,917
NY	323,769	250,700	59,817	190,883	144,734	45,420	36,888	44,525	10,167	6,319	46,149	27,678	5,281	7,647	2,438	18,471	5,208	91	14,286	58,783
NC	93,302	71,012	17,989	53,023	33,711	8,640	12,275	9,869	1,092	1,226	19,312	14,561	3,825	6,944	1,274	4,751	1,459	18	4,845	17,444
ND	9,645	8,351	1,903	6,448	4,709	730	1,314	433	161	1,979	1,738	1,081	476	7	49	657	271	92	139	1,155
OH	131,659	93,688	26,041	67,647	45,124	13,159	14,529	13,094	340	3,214	22,523	15,498	6,598	3,691	1,950	7,025	1,808	267	3,469	34,502
OK	35,378	27,757	8,200	19,557	12,011	2,224	5,179	2,385	354	1,222	7,546	4,863	2,123	1,166	348	2,683	645	15	1,900	5,721
OR	47,047	31,774	8,749	23,025	14,111	5,054	1,462	5,494	517	993	8,915	6,348	2,146	1,619	876	2,566	527	43	1,674	13,598
PA	134,310	106,629	27,103	79,526	55,771	16,610	17,958	13,933	2,279	4,157	23,755	16,217	6,016	2,366	2,734	7,538	2,605	70	4,413	23,268
RI	12,742	10,131	2,889	7,242	5,080	2,273	1,485	1,016	148	99	2,162	1,153	545	20	184	1,008	379	6	212	2,399
SC	45,779	35,335	8,726	26,609	13,744	4,804	4,688	2,908	216	931	12,865	9,680	2,590	5,231	660	3,186	929	23	3,376	7,068
SD	8,463	6,203	2,055	4,148	2,699	981	1,467	—	15	173	1,448	776	373	49	77	672	288	27	320	1,941
TN	60,327	42,648	13,014	29,635	19,078	5,101	10,963	190	1,069	1,336	10,557	7,277	2,058	2,580	761	3,280	840	198	9,163	8,516
TX	224,475	181,956	46,737	135,218	90,778	39,596	41,017	—	—	8,240	44,440	29,858	9,641	8,892	3,262	14,582	4,754	173	11,942	30,577
UT	25,188	20,116	5,046	15,069	9,057	2,551	3,498	2,298	248	340	6,012	4,296	1,603	1,216	342	1,716	528	51	2,161	2,911

See footnotes at end of table.

Table 463. State and Local Governments—Revenue by State: 2011-Continued.

See headnote on page 298.

State	Total revenue	General revenue			Select taxes						Current charges and miscellaneous revenue								Utility and liquor stores	Insurance trust revenue
		Total	Intergovernmental from federal government	General revenue from own sources	Total [1]	Property	Sales and gross receipt	Individual income	Corporation income	Other taxes	Total	Current charges				Miscellaneous revenue				
												Total [1]	Education	Hospitals	Sewerage	Total [1]	Interest earnings	Special assessments		
VT...	7,581	6,465	2,117	4,348	3,140	1,376	922	556	105	117	1,208	818	580	–	67	390	135	4	274	842
VA...	76,355	60,687	11,511	49,176	32,153	11,104	8,250	9,531	798	1,876	17,023	11,918	4,285	3,156	1,175	5,105	1,561	144	2,441	13,227
WA...	77,840	55,990	12,385	43,605	28,410	8,675	17,540	–	–	1,692	15,195	11,593	3,005	3,157	1,882	3,602	913	202	6,516	15,334
WV...	18,739	15,789	4,945	10,844	6,975	1,429	2,610	1,666	307	959	3,869	2,363	936	331	255	1,506	385	20	310	2,640
WI...	62,693	47,256	11,024	36,232	25,605	9,827	7,218	6,429	851	822	10,627	7,309	2,618	1,184	809	3,318	1,185	83	1,944	13,493
WY...	10,208	8,580	2,354	6,226	3,673	1,231	1,208	–	–	1,146	2,553	1,392	212	862	56	1,160	647	7	275	1,353

– Represents or rounds to zero. [1] Includes items not shown separately.

Source: U.S. Census Bureau, Federal, State, and Local Governments, Government Finance Statistics, "Annual Surveys of State and Local Government Finances," <http://www.census.gov/govs/local/>, accessed July 2013.

State and Local Government Finances and Employment 299

Table 464. State and Local Governments—Expenditures and Debt by State: 2011

[In millions of dollars (3,162,628 represents $3,162,628,000,000). For fiscal year ending in year shown; see text, this section]

State	Total expenditures	General expenditures Total[1]	Direct general expenditures Total[1]	Education	Public welfare	Health	Hospitals	Highways	Police protection	Corrections	Natural resources	Parks and recreation	Housing and community development	Sewerage	Solid waste	Governmental administration	Interest on general debt	Other direct general expenditures	Utility and liquor store expenditures	Insurance trust expenditures	Total debt outstanding
U.S....	3,162,628	2,587,397	2,583,101	861,131	492,007	82,369	148,136	153,005	96,332	73,151	29,071	38,694	56,121	54,867	23,880	124,511	108,658	241,169	213,830	361,402	2,907,756
AL...	42,161	35,385	35,385	13,371	5,940	938	4,483	2,200	1,141	746	261	603	603	266	266	1,527	969	2,167	3,089	3,687	29,315
AK...	14,687	12,790	12,790	3,377	1,857	288	362	1,692	327	287	396	130	384	107	110	860	392	2,222	624	1,273	10,198
AZ...	52,534	42,685	42,685	13,385	9,205	1,969	968	2,501	2,099	1,464	459	691	635	913	428	2,204	2,127	3,639	4,861	4,988	50,926
AR...	23,769	20,785	20,785	8,446	4,501	326	1,021	1,381	543	541	314	259	257	359	207	997	487	1,144	943	2,041	13,544
CA...	457,591	356,555	353,675	102,228	67,670	12,091	21,087	14,726	15,085	13,619	5,422	5,775	10,190	7,130	3,808	20,658	16,775	37,411	39,213	61,823	418,833
CO...	51,577	41,288	41,286	13,204	4,945	1,527	2,264	2,396	1,650	1,212	474	1,322	720	1,119	99	2,475	2,294	5,586	3,971	6,317	52,186
CT...	40,676	33,367	33,367	11,789	6,157	803	1,459	1,548	1,073	688	143	242	877	552	364	1,769	1,853	4,049	1,542	5,767	41,490
DE...	9,898	8,587	8,586	3,134	1,755	402	52	537	290	267	102	65	166	241	114	581	342	536	509	801	8,278
DC...	13,641	10,385	10,385	2,342	2,834	395	226	244	591	257	43	241	659	404	68	501	482	1,068	2,525	731	11,277
FL...	164,062	137,974	137,974	38,691	23,543	4,920	8,367	8,200	7,350	4,295	3,507	2,873	3,330	3,330	2,598	6,968	4,904	15,099	11,894	14,193	151,904
GA...	78,094	64,038	64,038	24,832	10,119	2,043	5,222	2,904	2,274	2,255	545	889	1,363	1,212	567	3,323	1,509	4,980	6,157	7,899	54,367
HI...	14,389	12,206	12,206	3,345	2,147	641	667	565	386	191	101	274	231	329	314	649	545	1,821	676	1,507	13,377
ID...	12,066	10,488	10,488	3,131	2,210	218	821	1,002	381	291	242	151	147	179	141	590	265	717	341	1,237	6,231
IL...	130,777	104,306	104,306	34,669	18,488	3,009	2,576	7,088	4,623	2,213	456	2,504	2,329	2,771	488	4,870	6,116	12,105	7,239	19,233	145,485
IN...	52,682	45,869	45,838	16,270	8,496	879	3,270	2,702	1,296	1,003	335	540	1,210	1,034	310	1,940	1,929	4,627	2,378	4,436	49,405
IA...	30,325	26,457	26,457	9,636	4,330	522	2,663	2,096	644	468	563	320	302	562	202	1,039	598	2,012	1,294	2,574	18,328
KS...	26,534	22,967	22,967	8,466	3,566	570	2,104	1,755	733	504	271	318	291	351	161	1,061	1,148	1,768	1,319	2,244	27,125
KY...	39,063	32,330	32,329	11,466	7,235	1,085	1,611	2,232	701	733	380	294	448	677	242	1,530	1,843	1,853	1,986	4,747	42,168
LA...	48,757	42,827	42,827	12,119	6,418	809	4,563	3,014	1,506	1,308	850	747	1,651	731	326	2,207	1,819	4,760	1,496	4,433	38,622
ME...	12,616	11,359	11,354	3,459	2,926	476	140	932	264	197	170	90	320	193	128	491	363	1,206	167	1,089	8,983
MD...	57,612	49,843	49,843	18,258	9,502	1,628	482	2,945	2,163	1,720	582	824	1,305	875	634	2,573	1,773	4,578	2,412	5,358	44,603
MA...	75,734	61,761	61,545	18,761	14,505	1,222	2,049	2,565	2,116	1,051	333	381	2,152	1,479	393	2,570	3,696	8,270	3,246	10,728	92,558
MI...	89,818	73,723	73,705	28,697	13,293	3,903	3,510	3,470	2,377	2,244	477	681	1,348	1,987	412	2,816	2,972	5,517	3,913	12,182	73,842
MN...	55,684	47,241	47,241	15,389	11,390	1,175	1,880	3,538	1,652	873	843	1,066	949	705	327	2,258	1,797	2,899	2,421	6,022	46,761
MS...	27,308	23,831	23,831	7,251	5,181	491	3,232	1,684	661	553	299	251	350	395	172	1,009	528	1,776	1,079	2,398	14,186
MO...	49,877	41,565	41,479	13,747	7,741	1,745	2,878	3,198	1,670	862	379	762	742	810	139	1,449	1,656	3,702	2,969	5,342	46,105
MT...	9,294	8,113	8,112	2,596	1,411	269	138	889	258	240	291	93	147	120	70	575	210	806	235	946	5,977
NE...	19,527	14,571	14,524	5,701	2,178	463	890	1,148	412	366	446	271	176	189	90	601	369	1,224	3,977	979	12,942
NV...	23,269	18,696	18,695	5,577	2,346	364	971	1,404	1,146	694	336	666	251	474	28	1,286	925	2,225	1,450	3,122	27,708
NH...	11,637	10,238	10,238	3,773	2,093	121	50	751	352	184	71	112	231	112	128	520	497	1,243	589	811	11,238
NJ...	101,256	81,578	81,559	30,551	14,429	1,589	2,483	4,318	3,344	2,072	578	848	1,559	1,562	1,070	3,361	3,439	10,413	3,457	16,221	102,260
NM...	22,415	19,440	19,440	6,778	4,429	578	1,088	1,186	637	624	298	322	216	166	202	1,089	532	1,295	722	2,254	16,649
NY...	300,324	235,984	235,262	71,545	50,390	6,753	15,084	11,029	9,017	5,890	668	2,839	5,534	4,500	2,687	10,266	11,070	27,988	28,630	35,711	334,622
NC...	80,849	67,309	67,309	23,735	11,388	2,869	7,248	3,829	2,456	1,921	741	874	1,111	1,187	748	2,569	2,041	4,591	4,807	8,733	51,187
ND...	7,137	6,426	6,426	2,232	962	128	71	946	153	121	283	124	92	59	49	237	175	796	212	499	4,426
OH...	116,247	94,294	94,278	33,310	20,288	3,943	4,137	5,037	3,198	1,925	408	1,194	2,458	2,892	434	5,238	3,083	6,733	3,975	17,978	77,533
OK...	30,717	25,817	25,759	9,393	5,434	873	1,163	2,403	897	653	218	480	359	372	185	1,098	691	1,539	2,036	2,864	19,202
OR...	39,932	31,798	31,798	10,514	5,673	1,053	1,991	2,013	1,078	1,050	533	572	622	964	126	1,646	1,171	2,791	2,017	6,118	34,754
PA...	132,879	108,817	108,685	35,400	25,676	4,476	3,114	8,995	3,133	3,239	725	1,337	2,332	3,225	811	5,769	4,490	5,961	6,297	17,766	123,484
RI...	11,466	9,251	9,230	3,049	2,333	184	59	347	356	197	45	42	225	148	82	501	550	1,112	419	1,796	11,940
SC...	42,784	35,580	35,580	12,067	6,812	1,103	5,033	1,533	1,059	656	214	404	569	603	333	1,456	207	2,082	3,230	3,974	41,054
SD...	7,014	6,165	6,165	2,086	973	169	116	907	162	160	180	154	112	102	48	329	207	461	396	452	5,735
TN...	55,155	42,064	42,056	12,760	10,060	1,418	2,910	2,389	1,713	1,018	329	494	1,176	636	343	1,904	1,258	3,650	9,274	3,817	38,303
TX...	221,030	185,644	185,644	74,047	30,826	4,578	12,340	10,939	6,582	5,833	1,800	2,423	2,448	3,347	1,364	6,812	9,323	12,982	16,523	18,863	258,241
UT...	24,928	20,370	20,370	7,773	2,863	516	1,000	1,837	659	494	214	467	365	521	162	1,420	545	1,534	2,761	1,797	20,133

See footnotes at end of table.

Table 464. State and Local Governments—Expenditures and Debt by State: 2011-Continued.

See headnote on page 300.

State	Total expendi-tures	General expenditures Total [1]	Direct general expenditures																Utility and liquor store expend-itures	Insur-ance trust expend-itures	Total debt out-standing
			Total [1]	Educa-tion	Public welfare	Health	Hospi-tals	High-ways	Police protec-tion	Correc-tions	Natural resour-ces	Parks and recre-ation	Hous-ing and com-munity devel-opment	Sewer-age	Solid waste	Govern-mental adminis-tration	Inter-est on general debt	Other direct general expendi-tures			
VT...	6,922	6,174	6,174	2,378	1,464	185	20	586	173	126	85	50	142	88	40	233	156	446	322	426	4,729
VA...	69,226	60,913	60,912	22,270	10,188	1,555	3,509	3,672	2,041	2,208	251	939	978	1,337	683	3,122	2,505	5,653	2,806	5,507	63,816
WA...	74,905	57,782	57,777	18,786	8,852	2,625	4,322	4,046	1,571	1,569	1,045	996	1,546	2,068	638	2,272	2,518	4,922	8,350	8,773	74,091
WV...	16,400	14,466	14,466	5,596	3,238	319	383	1,307	357	324	187	176	150	280	79	824	339	907	410	1,525	10,992
WI...	56,696	47,714	47,714	17,350	10,035	1,809	1,188	3,679	1,770	1,544	831	595	339	1,015	349	1,758	1,833	3,618	2,259	6,724	44,272
WY...	8,688	7,579	7,557	2,496	764	350	871	697	214	202	348	130	27	81	85	511	95	687	414	695	2,370

[1] Includes items not shown separately.

Source: U.S. Census Bureau, Federal, State, and Local Governments, Government Finance Statistics, "Annual Surveys of State and Local Government Finances," <http://www.census.gov/govs/local/>, accessed July 2013.

Table 465. State Resources, Expenditures, and Balances: 2011 and 2012

[In millions of dollars (1,662,545 represents $1,662,545,000,000). For fiscal year ending in year shown; see text; this section. General funds exclude special funds earmarked for particular purposes, such as highway trust funds and federal funds; they support most on-going broad-based state services, and are available for appropriation to support any governmental activity. Minus sign (-) indicates deficit]

State	Total, 2011 actual	Expenditures by fund source 2012 estimated			State general fund Resources [3,4]		Expenditures [4]		Balance [5]	
		Total [2]	General fund	Federal fund	2011	2012 [1]	2011	2012 [1]	2011	2012 [1]
United States......	1,662,545	1,664,751	662,780	519,437	678,414	695,675	645,174	666,856	21,680	20,424
Alabama..............	21,021	20,849	7,076	8,307	6,927	7,445	7,359	7,598	51	35
Alaska................	13,923	11,884	7,394	3,135	7,696	9,917	5,450	7,013	1,969	818
Arizona..............	28,121	27,595	8,421	11,287	8,375	8,817	8,372	8,421	3	396
Arkansas............	20,484	20,686	4,578	6,296	4,479	4,606	4,479	4,606	0	0
California.............	215,745	213,344	87,027	78,235	89,910	83,944	91,549	87,027	-3,079	-2,882
Colorado.............	30,917	28,079	7,240	7,621	7,381	8,032	6,936	7,168	446	864
Connecticut.........	25,944	26,875	18,781	2,562	18,157	18,562	17,920	18,705	237	-144
Delaware.............	8,412	8,942	3,592	1,777	4,069	4,157	3,271	3,592	798	565
Florida...............	65,462	69,368	23,170	25,111	24,533	24,749	23,787	23,749	746	1,000
Georgia..............	40,458	39,433	16,511	11,099	18,195	18,559	17,064	17,428	1,131	1,131
Hawaii................	11,221	11,513	5,509	1,953	5,095	5,787	4,969	5,511	126	275
Idaho.................	6,602	6,944	2,548	2,708	2,519	2,644	2,450	2,545	69	100
Illinois...............	49,099	51,352	29,163	9,937	37,019	34,092	29,175	29,272	469	40
Indiana..............	26,392	26,304	13,579	9,272	14,161	15,382	13,050	13,590	1,124	1,803
Iowa..................	18,051	19,123	6,010	6,514	5,899	6,693	5,344	6,004	555	688
Kansas...............	14,685	14,734	6,129	3,891	5,855	6,593	5,667	6,126	188	466
Kentucky.............	25,433	25,649	9,334	8,687	9,136	9,683	8,789	9,435	290	90
Louisiana............	31,200	32,755	8,374	11,871	7,768	8,401	7,782	8,249	-14	152
Maine................	8,274	8,106	3,087	2,649	2,990	3,191	2,873	3,130	19	42
Maryland.............	33,851	35,800	15,041	9,438	14,228	15,487	13,238	14,935	990	551
Massachusetts.......	53,302	52,187	24,486	11,238	33,978	34,447	32,078	32,458	1,901	1,990
Michigan.............	48,580	48,628	8,855	19,550	8,770	9,111	8,217	8,383	554	728
Minnesota...........	31,401	32,680	18,073	9,009	16,623	17,900	15,335	16,802	1,289	1,098
Mississippi..........	22,226	23,965	4,309	12,813	4,579	4,812	4,528	4,803	50	9
Missouri..............	23,103	23,364	7,938	7,539	8,011	8,143	7,631	7,938	379	205
Montana.............	6,164	5,919	1,764	2,131	2,092	2,222	1,747	1,775	342	453
Nebraska............	9,807	9,877	3,446	2,988	3,824	3,944	3,322	3,446	502	499
Nevada..............	8,506	7,949	3,105	2,351	3,722	3,357	3,398	3,114	324	205
New Hampshire......	5,340	5,108	1,280	1,648	1,460	1,404	1,311	1,241	27	23
New Jersey..........	47,142	49,681	29,929	12,344	29,038	30,560	28,168	29,991	870	569
New Mexico........	15,431	15,198	5,432	5,660	5,808	6,392	5,307	5,687	501	705
New York............	132,765	133,504	56,489	40,311	56,749	58,276	55,373	56,489	1,376	1,787
North Carolina.......	51,126	52,987	18,893	17,781	19,394	20,116	18,503	19,576	582	394
North Dakota........	5,018	6,191	2,223	1,980	2,710	3,517	1,651	2,223	997	1,294
Ohio.................	60,300	57,905	31,011	13,144	28,274	28,030	26,248	26,395	431	371
Oklahoma............	21,337	21,102	5,018	8,326	5,759	6,232	5,417	5,797	93	107
Oregon..............	33,442	30,082	6,897	7,448	6,115	6,899	6,043	6,897	72	2
Pennsylvania.........	69,130	68,227	27,161	25,382	29,213	27,690	28,321	27,186	1,073	659
Rhode Island........	7,842	8,228	3,139	2,838	3,025	3,246	2,956	3,117	69	116
South Carolina.......	22,188	21,904	5,456	9,324	5,879	6,581	5,167	5,517	712	956
South Dakota........	3,870	3,698	1,215	1,488	1,148	1,282	1,148	1,207	0	48
Tennessee...........	30,097	31,077	12,067	13,125	11,181	11,969	9,996	11,458	595	427
Texas................	95,461	92,300	44,164	30,847	39,853	44,486	38,717	43,911	1,136	574
Utah.................	12,688	13,227	4,743	3,638	4,785	4,859	4,710	4,830	60	0
Vermont..............	4,860	4,849	756	1,741	1,228	1,250	1,162	1,250	0	0
Virginia..............	42,332	43,372	16,986	9,212	16,299	17,027	15,457	16,351	841	675
Washington..........	33,621	32,238	15,114	6,710	14,731	14,910	14,823	15,325	-92	-415
West Virginia........	21,198	22,517	4,053	4,402	4,616	4,902	3,772	4,140	793	611
Wisconsin...........	42,844	41,324	13,381	10,572	13,580	13,795	13,565	13,868	86	342
Wyoming............	6,129	6,128	2,833	1,547	1,580	1,580	1,580	1,580	0	0

[1] Estimated. [2] Includes bonds and other state funds, not shown separately. [3] Includes funds budgeted, adjustments, and balances from previous year. [4] May or may not include budget stabilization fund transfers, depending on state accounting practices. [5] Resources less expenditures, minus adjustments.

Source: National Association of State Budget Officers, Washington, DC, *State Expenditure Report* ©, 2012; and *Fiscal Survey of the States, Fall 2012* ©, 2012. See also <http://www.nasbo.org>.

Table 466. Estimated State and Local Taxes Paid by a Family of Three for Largest City in Selected States: 2011

[Data based on average family of three (two wage earners and one school age child) owning their own home and living in a city where taxes apply. Comprises state and local sales, income, auto, and real estate taxes. For definition of median, see Guide to Tabular Presentation]

City	Total taxes paid by gross family income level (dollars)					Total taxes paid as percent of income				
	$25,000	$50,000	$75,000	$100,000	$150,000	$25,000	$50,000	$75,000	$100,000	$150,000
Albuquerque, NM.......	2,808	4,567	6,634	8,349	12,266	11.2	9.1	8.8	8.3	8.2
Anchorage, AK..........	2,236	3,321	4,006	4,336	5,095	8.9	6.6	5.3	4.3	3.4
Atlanta, GA..............	3,696	4,784	7,236	9,016	13,645	14.8	9.6	9.6	9.0	9.1
Baltimore, MD..........	2,703	6,027	8,840	11,398	17,134	10.8	12.1	11.8	11.4	11.4
Boston, MA.............	3,414	6,125	7,932	9,535	13,401	13.7	12.2	10.6	9.5	8.9
Charlotte, NC..........	3,340	4,886	7,539	9,737	14,697	13.4	9.8	10.1	9.7	9.8
Chicago, IL.............	3,898	6,412	8,825	10,627	14,814	15.6	12.8	11.8	10.6	9.9
Columbus, OH..........	3,369	7,212	9,891	12,451	18,241	13.5	14.4	13.2	12.5	12.2
Denver, CO.............	2,955	3,627	5,558	6,968	10,873	11.8	7.3	7.4	7.0	7.2
Detroit, MI.............	3,270	5,922	8,704	10,817	15,522	13.1	11.8	11.6	10.8	10.3
Honolulu, HI.............	4,124	3,574	5,617	7,502	11,660	16.5	7.1	7.5	7.5	7.8
Houston, TX.............	2,709	3,272	4,333	4,911	6,571	10.8	6.5	5.8	4.9	4.4
Indianapolis, IN........	3,496	4,849	7,094	8,899	13,104	14.0	9.7	9.5	8.9	8.7
Jacksonville, FL........	2,956	3,296	4,134	4,760	6,429	11.8	6.6	5.5	4.8	4.3
Kansas City, MO........	3,281	5,031	7,643	9,540	14,913	13.1	10.1	10.2	9.5	9.9
Las Vegas, NV..........	3,027	3,849	4,734	5,099	6,305	12.1	7.7	6.3	5.1	4.2
Los Angeles, CA.......	3,425	6,634	8,453	10,023	15,764	13.7	13.3	11.3	10.0	10.5
Memphis, TN............	2,941	3,314	4,206	4,802	6,450	11.8	6.6	5.6	4.8	4.3
Milwaukee, WI..........	2,763	5,933	8,367	10,698	15,434	11.1	11.9	11.2	10.7	10.3
New Orleans, LA.......	3,319	2,865	5,491	6,802	10,030	13.3	5.7	7.3	6.8	6.7
New York City, NY......	3,273	5,880	8,813	11,587	18,811	13.1	11.8	11.8	11.6	12.5
Oklahoma City, OK.....	2,611	3,926	5,944	7,687	11,770	10.4	7.9	7.9	7.7	7.8
Omaha, NE..............	2,609	4,693	6,772	8,997	14,149	10.4	9.4	9.0	9.0	9.4
Philadelphia, PA........	4,513	8,327	11,381	14,178	19,951	18.1	16.7	15.2	14.2	13.3
Phoenix, AZ.............	3,654	4,215	5,812	7,181	10,860	14.6	8.4	7.7	7.2	7.2
Portland, OR............	2,765	5,688	8,223	10,650	16,432	11.1	11.4	11.0	10.6	11.0
Seattle, WA.............	3,118	5,120	6,033	6,374	7,652	12.5	10.2	8.0	6.4	5.1
Virginia Beach, VA.....	3,270	4,491	6,772	8,465	12,350	13.1	9.0	9.0	8.5	8.2
Washington, DC........	2,847	4,637	6,684	8,389	13,157	11.4	9.3	8.9	8.4	8.8
Wichita, KS.............	2,654	4,449	6,056	8,238	13,067	10.6	8.9	8.1	8.2	8.7
Average [1].............	**3,065**	**4,971**	**7,041**	**8,719**	**12,831**	**12.3**	**9.9**	**9.4**	**8.7**	**8.6**
Median [1]...............	**2,956**	**4,693**	**7,009**	**8,974**	**13,325**	**11.8**	**9.4**	**9.3**	**9.0**	**8.9**

[1] Based on selected cities and District of Columbia. For complete list of cities, see Table 467.

Source: Government of the District of Columbia, Office of the Chief Financial Officer, *Tax Rates and Tax Burdens in the District of Columbia – A Nationwide Comparison*, September 2012, and earlier reports. See also <http://cfo.dc.gov/>.

Table 467. Residential Property Tax Rates for Largest City in Each State: 2011

[The real property tax is a function of housing values, real estate tax rates, assessment levels, homeowner exemptions and credits. Effective rate is the amount each jurisdiction considers based upon assessment level used. Assessment level is ratio of assessed value to assumed market value. Nominal rates represent the "announced" rates levied by the jurisdiction]

City	Effective tax rate per $100		Assessment level (percent)	Nominal rate per $100	City	Effective tax rate per $100		Assessment level (percent)	Nominal rate per $100
	Rank	Rate				Rank	Rate		
Columbus, OH..........	1	3.56	35.7	9.99	Atlanta, GA..............	28	1.61	40.0	4.03
Providence, RI..........	2	3.19	100.0	3.19	New Orleans, LA.......	29	1.58	10.0	15.75
Indianapolis, IN.........	3	3.05	100.0	3.05	Albuquerque, NM.......	30	1.56	33.3	4.68
Philadelphia, PA........	4	2.91	32.0	9.08	Kansas City, MO........	31	1.54	19.0	8.10
Detroit, MI..............	5	2.83	42.0	6.73	Minneapolis, MN........	32	1.42	97.1	1.46
Bridgeport, CT..........	6	2.77	70.0	3.96	Little Rock, AR.........	33	1.41	20.0	7.05
Milwaukee, WI..........	7	2.69	100.0	2.69	Wichita, KS..............	34	1.41	11.5	12.23
Louisville, KY...........	8	2.55	100.0	2.55	Boston, MA.............	35	1.30	100.0	1.30
Houston, TX.............	9	2.53	100.0	2.53	Portland, OR............	36	1.29	63.1	2.05
Des Moines, IA.........	10	2.33	50.8	4.60	Oklahoma City, OK.....	37	1.29	11.0	11.76
Baltimore, MD..........	11	2.27	100.0	2.27	Charlotte, NC..........	38	1.20	96.0	1.25
Newark , NJ.............	12	2.23	67.1	3.33	Las Vegas, NV..........	39	1.15	35.0	3.28
Omaha, NE..............	13	2.09	96.0	2.18	Los Angeles, CA........	40	1.13	100.0	1.13
Burlington, VT..........	14	2.03	100.0	2.03	Phoenix, AZ.............	41	1.11	10.0	11.07
Salt Lake City, UT......	15	2.01	100.0	2.01	Seattle, WA.............	42	0.97	89.9	1.08
Columbia, SC...........	16	1.97	4.0	49.31	Virginia Beach, VA.....	43	0.95	100.0	0.95
Sioux Falls, SD.........	17	1.97	85.0	2.32	Washington, DC........	44	0.85	100.0	0.85
Memphis, TN...........	18	1.88	26.1	7.21	Charleston, WV.........	45	0.84	60.0	1.40
Portland, ME............	19	1.88	100.0	1.88	Birmingham , AL.......	46	0.80	10.0	8.02
Boise, ID................	20	1.83	100.0	1.83	New York City, NY......	47	0.75	4.3	17.28
Wilmington, DE.........	21	1.80	47.2	3.81	Cheyenne, WV..........	48	0.67	9.5	7.10
Jacksonville, FL........	22	1.80	100.0	1.80	Denver, CO.............	49	0.60	8.0	7.50
Billings, MT.............	23	1.80	28.2	6.37	Chicago, IL..............	50	0.50	10.0	5.02
Manchester, NH........	24	1.78	100.0	1.78	Honolulu, HI.............	51	0.35	100.0	0.35
Anchorage, AK..........	25	1.72	100.0	1.72					
					Unweighted				
Jackson, MS............	26	1.71	10.0	17.14	**average**................	(X)	1.71	59.5	6.45
Fargo, ND...............	27	1.70	4.4	38.68	**Median**.................	(X)	1.71	63.1	3.28

X Not applicable.

Source: Government of the District of Columbia, Office of the Chief Financial Officer, *Tax Rates and Tax Burdens in the District of Columbia—A Nationwide Comparison*, September 2012, and earlier reports. See also <http://cfo.dc.gov/>.

Table 468. Gross Revenue From Parimutuel and Amusement Taxes and Lotteries by State: 2009 to 2011

[In millions of dollars (58,933.1 represents $58,933,100,000). For fiscal years; see text, this section]

State	2009, total gross revenue	2010, total gross revenue	2011 Total gross revenue	2011 Amusement taxes [1]	2011 Parimutuel taxes	2011 Lottery revenue Total [2]	2011 Apportionment of funds Prizes	2011 Apportionment of funds Administration	2011 Apportionment of funds Proceeds available from ticket sales
United States..........	**58,933.1**	**59,680.0**	**61,481.0**	**6,609.6**	**136.9**	**54,734.4**	**33,759.3**	**2,673.5**	**18,301.7**
Alabama..................	2.5	2.2	2.1	.1	2.0	–	–	–	–
Alaska....................	9.2	8.9	8.3	8.3	(X)	–	–	–	–
Arizona..................	452.8	515.3	545.1	.5	.3	544.3	360.5	39.0	144.8
Arkansas.................	12.4	375.6	456.9	15.0	4.1	437.8	307.5	37.9	92.5
California................	2,777.9	2,842.4	3,452.1	(X)	13.5	3,438.6	1,904.8	193.5	1,340.3
Colorado.................	553.2	562.1	575.8	95.9	.6	479.3	326.6	40.9	111.8
Connecticut..............	1,388.4	1,368.2	1,376.1	409.2	7.2	959.7	620.1	41.2	298.3
Delaware.................	429.8	454.0	451.3	(X)	.1	451.1	75.8	49.1	326.2
Florida...................	3,851.8	3,888.0	3,928.5	137.6	9.4	3,781.6	2,460.2	134.3	1,187.0
Georgia..................	3,158.2	3,153.1	3,109.3	(X)	(X)	3,109.3	2,120.8	140.4	848.1
Hawaii...................	(X)	(X)	(X)	(X)	(X)	–	–	–	–
Idaho....................	130.6	136.7	136.2	(X)	.8	135.4	90.2	8.7	36.5
Illinois...................	2,659.5	2,713.0	2,762.7	491.2	6.7	2,264.7	1,368.5	232.8	663.4
Indiana..................	1,567.1	1,567.0	1,603.8	864.3	4.3	735.2	494.5	48.2	192.5
Iowa.....................	521.7	523.5	552.1	276.7	3.9	271.5	159.0	40.3	72.3
Kansas...................	211.8	222.2	219.0	.4	.0	218.6	132.3	20.2	66.1
Kentucky.................	719.4	676.3	676.9	.2	4.6	672.1	422.4	35.2	214.5
Louisiana................	1,078.9	1,024.2	1,039.2	671.9	5.1	362.2	202.9	24.4	135.0
Maine....................	226.2	233.6	232.7	28.0	2.3	202.3	135.6	15.7	51.0
Maryland.................	1,597.7	1,618.4	1,628.3	26.5	1.2	1,600.7	1,029.0	104.0	467.7
Massachusetts...........	4,168.5	4,161.2	4,172.0	3.4	1.5	4,167.1	3,199.4	88.6	879.1
Michigan.................	2,506.3	2,281.5	2,253.6	108.1	6.2	2,139.2	1,368.2	70.7	700.2
Minnesota................	467.5	471.7	510.6	35.8	.6	474.2	327.5	24.0	122.7
Mississippi...............	172.4	155.1	147.0	147.0	(X)	–	–	–	–
Missouri..................	1,279.4	1,302.9	1,379.4	397.8	(X)	981.5	639.0	42.2	300.3
Montana..................	103.9	97.0	93.2	49.8	.0	43.3	24.8	7.6	10.9
Nebraska.................	122.0	129.3	128.9	5.0	.2	123.7	76.9	16.5	30.3
Nevada...................	905.7	864.3	885.8	885.8	(X)	–	–	–	–
New Hampshire..........	229.1	223.1	217.8	.2	1.4	216.2	139.3	14.6	62.4
New Jersey...............	2,739.5	2,756.3	2,755.7	266.3	(X)	2,489.5	1,505.2	53.1	931.1
New Mexico..............	197.4	196.2	202.4	72.2	.4	129.8	76.7	11.6	41.4
New York................	6,849.5	6,966.0	7,008.5	.7	21.5	6,986.3	3,967.7	323.1	2,695.5
North Carolina...........	1,217.4	1,337.3	1,375.1	16.7	X	1,358.4	861.5	59.8	437.1
North Dakota............	31.4	31.9	30.8	8.2	.7	21.9	11.9	3.9	6.0
Ohio.....................	2,277.2	2,345.1	2,447.2	(X)	7.6	2,439.7	1,603.1	89.2	747.4
Oklahoma................	208.8	228.1	229.6	17.1	1.1	211.4	106.6	12.4	92.4
Oregon...................	889.6	833.0	839.8	.0	1.2	838.6	208.7	75.2	554.8
Pennsylvania.............	3,884.9	4,007.9	4,336.2	1,415.7	14.8	2,905.6	1,958.4	69.2	878.0
Rhode Island.............	496.8	496.4	506.9	(X)	1.3	505.6	142.3	6.9	356.3
South Carolina...........	967.4	951.3	1,010.7	37.7	(X)	973.0	667.6	37.3	268.1
South Dakota............	157.1	160.0	149.7	9.0	.2	140.5	27.2	6.7	106.6
Tennessee................	1,016.4	1,063.7	1,108.9	(X)	(X)	1,108.9	611.2	52.0	445.7
Texas....................	3,579.9	3,590.1	3,645.5	38.8	7.7	3,599.0	2,387.2	205.5	1,006.3
Utah.....................	(X)	(X)	(X)	(X)	(X)	–	–	–	–
Vermont..................	90.3	91.8	89.9	(X)	(X)	89.9	50.6	7.9	31.4
Virginia..................	1,288.8	1,354.8	1,398.9	.1	(X)	1,398.8	881.0	72.1	445.7
Washington..............	459.9	462.1	480.3	(X)	1.8	478.5	295.2	44.4	139.0
West Virginia............	802.3	755.2	817.2	68.2	2.3	746.7	120.7	39.3	586.7
Wisconsin................	474.4	481.6	502.9	.3	(X)	502.7	290.5	33.8	178.4
Wyoming.................	.2	.2	.1	(X)	.1	–	–	–	–

– Represents or rounds to zero. X Not applicable. [1] Represents nonlicense taxes. [2] Excludes commissions.

Source : U.S. Census Bureau, "State Government Finances: Lottery Table," <http://www.census.gov/govs/state/>, and "State Government Tax Collections," <http://www.census.gov/govs/statetax/>; accessed September 2013.

Table 469. Lottery Sales—Type of Game and Proceeds: 1990 to 2012

[In millions of dollars (20,137 represents $20,137,000,000). For fiscal years]

Game	1990	1995	2000	2005	2009	2010	2011	2012
Total ticket sales.....................	**20,137**	**32,147**	**37,201**	**52,055**	**59,630**	**60,846**	**62,546**	**68,175**
Instant [1]..............................	5,204	11,511	15,387	26,006	30,328	30,665	32,101	35,281
Three-digit [2].........................	4,572	5,738	5,780	5,858	5,970	5,861	5,854	5,817
Four-digit [2]..........................	1,302	1,918	2,273	2,869	3,315	3,424	3,435	3,553
Lotto [3]...............................	8,563	10,594	9,339	9,828	10,053	10,879	10,566	11,905
Other [4]..............................	497	2,388	4,423	7,493	9,964	10,017	10,590	11,620
State proceeds (net income) [5]........	7,703	11,100	11,871	15,792	17,596	17,957	18,484	18,656

[1] Player scratches a latex section on ticket which reveals instantly whether ticket is a winner. [2] Players choose and bet on three or four digits, depending on game, with various payoffs for different straight order or mixed combination bets. [3] Players typically select six digits out of a large field of numbers. Varying prizes are offered for matching three through six numbers drawn by lottery. [4] Includes break-open tickets, spiel, keno, video lottery, etc. [5] Sales minus prizes and expenses equal net government income.

Source: TLF Publications, Inc. © 2013. All Rights Reserved.

Table 470. State Governments—Summary of Finances: 1990 to 2010

[In millions of dollars (632,172 represents $632,172,000,000). For fiscal year ending in year shown; see text, this section]

Item	1990	2000	2005	2006	2007	2008	2009	2010
Total revenue	**632,172**	**1,260,829**	**1,642,469**	**1,774,649**	**1,995,162**	**1,613,002**	**1,133,015**	**2,036,240**
General revenue	517,429	984,783	1,286,901	1,391,134	1,451,715	1,511,123	1,493,719	1,562,240
Taxes [1]	300,489	539,655	650,629	715,973	757,467	779,717	713,475	703,444
Sales and gross receipts	147,069	252,147	312,602	337,949	352,706	358,825	342,621	343,401
General	99,702	174,461	212,921	229,630	238,304	240,165	226,782	223,040
Motor fuels	19,379	29,968	34,567	35,710	36,543	37,632	36,471	36,642
Alcoholic beverages	3,191	4,104	4,706	4,925	5,166	5,290	5,348	5,505
Tobacco products	5,541	8,391	12,917	14,537	15,299	16,068	16,690	16,832
Other	19,256	35,222	47,491	53,147	57,393	59,669	57,377	61
Licenses	18,842	32,598	42,584	44,949	46,697	49,067	49,146	50,330
Motor vehicles	9,848	15,099	18,221	18,997	19,470	19,558	19,627	20,721
Corporations in general	3,099	6,460	7,148	7,497	8,570	10,437	10,195	9,924
Other	5,895	11,039	17,216	18,456	18,657	19,072	19,482	20
Individual income	96,076	194,573	221,597	245,646	265,863	277,996	245,881	235,994
Corporation net income	21,751	32,522	38,691	47,469	52,915	49,860	39,278	36,740
Property	5,848	10,996	11,342	12,284	12,618	12,686	12,964	14,545
Other	10,902	16,819	23,813	27,676	26,668	31,283	23,584	21,414
Charges and miscellaneous	90,612	170,747	228,497	255,520	267,215	286,975	285,572	285,671
Intergovernmental revenue	126,329	274,382	407,792	419,641	427,030	442,361	494,672	575,564
From Federal Government	118,353	259,114	386,314	398,200	406,934	419,760	475,065	555,297
Public welfare	59,397	147,150	(NA)	(NA)	(NA)	(NA)	(NA)	(NA)
Education	21,271	42,086	(NA)	(NA)	(NA)	(NA)	(NA)	(NA)
Highways	13,931	23,790	(NA)	(NA)	(NA)	(NA)	(NA)	(NA)
Health and hospitals	5,475	14,223	(NA)	(NA)	(NA)	(NA)	(NA)	(NA)
Other	18,279	31,865	(NA)	(NA)	(NA)	(NA)	(NA)	(NA)
From local governments	7,976	15,268	21,478	21,440	20,096	22,600	19,607	20,267
Utility revenue	3,305	4,513	14,628	15,817	16,736	16,522	16,471	15,122
Liquor store revenue	2,907	3,895	5,118	5,475	5,799	6,128	6,377	6,495
Insurance trust revenue [2]	108,530	267,639	335,822	362,223	520,912	79,228	-383,552	452,384
Employee retirement	78,898	230,166	269,617	295,603	457,650	20,890	-449,271	353,374
Unemployment compensation	18,370	23,260	35,243	36,864	34,063	34,360	41,976	75,038
Borrowing	40,948	75,968	(NA)	(NA)	(NA)	(NA)	(NA)	(NA)
Total expenditure	**572,318**	**1,084,097**	**1,472,542**	**1,554,533**	**1,634,809**	**1,734,251**	**1,831,969**	**1,943,963**
General expenditure [3]	508,284	964,723	1,278,434	1,349,968	1,422,831	1,504,121	1,559,234	1,593,628
Education	184,935	346,465	454,348	483,477	514,124	546,875	567,674	571,147
Public welfare	104,971	238,890	368,765	376,675	392,796	411,158	439,187	463,853
Health	20,029	42,066	48,634	50,703	57,212	60,850	62,554	58,318
Hospitals	22,637	32,578	43,623	45,960	48,983	53,749	58,041	64,465
Highways	44,249	74,415	92,816	100,842	103,201	107,368	107,191	111,071
Police protection	5,166	9,788	11,395	12,221	12,856	13,594	13,677	13,828
Correction	17,266	35,129	40,562	42,794	46,485	49,881	50,382	48,550
Natural resources	9,909	15,967	18,822	20,036	22,038	22,524	22,605	21,515
Housing and community development	2,856	4,726	(NA)	(NA)	(NA)	(NA)	(NA)	(NA)
Other and unallocable	96,267	164,698	199,467	217,260	225,135	238,122	237,922	240,881
Utility expenditure	7,131	10,723	21,827	24,922	24,530	24,946	26,416	23,977
Liquor store expenditure	2,452	3,195	4,082	4,338	4,664	4,945	5,175	5,244
Insurance trust expenditure [2]	54,452	105,456	168,200	175,304	182,784	200,239	241,183	321,204
Employee retirement	29,562	75,971	118,333	127,501	136,201	146,714	156,709	166,956
Unemployment compensation	16,423	18,583	29,776	28,009	28,854	35,471	65,974	134,908
By character and object:								
Intergovernmental expenditure	175,028	327,070	405,925	432,265	460,184	479,010	491,304	486,025
Direct expenditure	397,291	757,027	1,066,617	1,122,268	1,174,625	1,255,241	1,340,704	1,457,938
Current operation	258,046	523,114	738,886	774,003	807,565	863,426	900,202	934,147
Capital outlay	45,524	76,233	95,155	103,253	110,044	112,252	116,990	117,538
Construction	34,803	59,681	78,049	85,713	90,788	92,346	97,930	100,798
Land and existing structures	3,471	4,681	17,106	17,540	19,256	19,906	(NA)	(NA)
Equipment	7,250	11,871	(NA)	(NA)	(NA)	(NA)	(NA)	(NA)
Assistance and subsidies	16,902	22,136	28,403	29,565	30,652	32,603	35,534	37,660
Interest on debt	22,367	30,089	35,974	40,143	43,580	46,721	47,323	47,388
Insurance benefits [4]	54,452	105,456	168,200	175,304	182,784	200,239	241,080	321,204
Debt redemption	19,895	41,730	(NA)	(NA)	(NA)	(NA)	(NA)	(NA)
Debt outstanding, year end	**318,254**	**547,876**	**810,852**	**870,032**	**936,008**	**1,005,311**	**1,048,929**	**1,113,208**
Long term [5]	315,490	541,497	805,300	859,430	929,431	991,130	1,041,599	1,098,499
Full-faith and credit	74,972	138,525	(NA)	(NA)	(NA)	(NA)	(NA)	(NA)
Nonguaranteed	240,518	402,972	(NA)	(NA)	(NA)	(NA)	(NA)	(NA)
Short-term	2,764	6,379	5,551	10,602	6,577	14,181	7,330	14,709
Net long term [6]	125,524	266,870	(NA)	(NA)	(NA)	(NA)	(NA)	(NA)
Full-faith and credit only	63,481	128,384	(NA)	(NA)	(NA)	(NA)	(NA)	(NA)

NA Not available. [1] Tax data are from U.S. Census Bureau, Annual Surveys of State Government Tax Collections. [2] Includes other items not shown separately. [3] Data on general expenditures are from U.S. Census Bureau, Annual Surveys of State Government Finances. [4] Includes repayments. [5] As of fiscal year 2005, the Census Bureau no longer collects government debt information by the character of long-term debt. For further information, see the 2006 Government Finance and Employment Classification Manual at <http://www.census.gov/govs/pubs/>. [6] Less cash and investment assets specifically held for redemption of long-term debt.

Source: U.S. Census Bureau, "Survey of State Government Finances," <http://www.census.gov/govs>, accessed June 2013.

Table 471. State Government Tax Collections by State: 2012

[In millions of dollars (794,570 represents $794,570,000,000)]

State	All taxes	Total property taxes	Sales & gross receipts: Total	General sales & gross receipts: Total	Selective sales tax: Total[1]	Alcoholic beverage sales	Insurance premiums	Motor fuels sales	Public utilities	Tobacco products	Other	License taxes: Total[1]	License: Corporation	License: Motor vehicle operators	License: Occupancy & business n.e.c.[2]	Income taxes: Total	Individual income	Corporation net income	Other taxes: Total[1]	Death and gift	Severance
U.S.	794,570	12,994	374,763	242,697	132,066	6,019	16,660	39,915	14,478	17,086	37,909	54,011	10,944	2,625	13,304	322,101	280,360	41,741	30,701	4,485	18,753
AL	9,053	325	4,626	2,275	2,352	173	278	541	737	126	496	518	131	22	124	3,431	3,017	413	153	—	116
AK	7,049	215	248	—	248	40	62	41	4	67	34	135	—	—	39	663	—	663	5,787	—	5,787
AZ	12,973	754	8,066	6,211	1,855	68	426	897	21	319	123	370	11	30	129	3,742	3,094	648	41	—	41
AR	8,288	1,009	3,983	2,809	1,173	49	157	467	—	247	254	359	25	18	125	2,806	2,402	404	131	—	83
CA	112,372	2,080	38,624	28,536	10,088	346	2,416	5,545	766	896	119	8,658	53	307	4,293	62,973	55,024	7,949	37	—	37
CO	10,251	—	4,091	2,302	1,788	39	198	631	12	203	706	617	16	31	39	5,368	4,876	492	175	—	175
CT	15,420	—	6,677	3,759	2,918	61	206	487	251	418	1,496	441	28	44	144	7,997	7,371	625	305	175	—
DE	3,360	—	491	—	491	18	92	113	60	121	88	1,230	625	5	375	1,574	1,312	262	65	12	—
FL	32,997	—	27,264	19,404	7,863	527	705	2,274	3,163	381	814	2,205	276	350	204	2,003	—	2,003	1,521	—	50
GA	16,577	69	7,254	5,304	1,950	175	309	881	—	227	358	506	44	47	74	8,733	8,142	591	16	—	—
HI	5,516	—	3,582	2,698	884	49	122	93	151	122	347	259	2	—	31	1,621	1,541	80	55	14	—
ID	3,374	65	1,665	1,225	440	8	70	237	3	48	74	299	2	11	70	1,402	1,213	189	8	—	8
IL	36,438	—	14,296	8,034	6,261	279	369	1,290	1,750	606	1,966	2,602	321	105	391	19,187	15,692	3,495	288	235	—
IN	15,705	—	9,173	6,622	2,551	44	203	784	216	465	838	629	12	221	32	5,724	4,766	959	178	176	2
IA	7,832	—	3,533	2,423	1,110	15	101	440	—	225	328	752	35	8	112	3,455	3,030	426	92	80	—
KS	7,418	74	3,686	2,826	860	118	166	435	—	104	36	315	21	22	52	3,209	2,892	318	134	1	133
KY	10	530	5,035	3,052	1,982	118	133	790	65	277	599	431	100	16	88	4,087	3,512	575	391	41	346
LA	8,994	51	4,889	2,816	2,073	57	357	575	13	133	938	402	105	12	110	2,765	2,475	290	887	—	886
ME	3,777	38	1,749	1,064	684	17	109	242	29	140	148	252	9	11	105	1,674	1,442	232	64	45	—
MD	17,064	756	7,174	4,077	3,097	31	428	733	127	411	1,366	757	96	26	145	7,997	7,117	880	381	197	—
MA	22,806	4	7,319	5,079	2,240	78	342	668	24	574	554	900	26	99	259	13,935	11,933	2,002	647	293	—
MI	23,969	1,798	13,119	9,566	3,553	149	298	974	26	951	1,155	1,416	22	56	150	7,437	6,828	609	199	—	64
MN	20,561	808	9,139	4,942	4,197	79	361	849	—	422	2,486	1,187	7	45	374	9,054	7,988	1,066	373	166	46
MS	6,953	24	4,397	3,072	1,324	42	189	417	2	157	516	518	146	40	92	1,897	1,501	396	118	—	116
MO	10,801	29	4,764	3,103	1,661	34	270	708	—	105	543	563	63	18	134	5,433	5,132	302	11	—	—
MT	2,459	257	545	—	545	34	71	212	50	87	91	316	3	9	100	1,033	900	132	309	—	306
NE	4,358	—	2,085	1,457	629	28	46	300	56	34	165	183	26	5	12	2,073	1,838	234	17	1	5
NV	6,775	235	5,232	3,434	1,798	42	238	291	23	103	1,102	584	67	22	225	—	—	—	725	—	303
NH	2,206	381	875	—	875	10	74	144	84	215	349	264	47	13	88	603	82	521	84	—	—
NJ	27,456	6	12,010	8,100	3,910	135	532	540	958	792	552	1,425	214	53	472	13,058	11,128	1,929	958	642	—
NM	5,088	60	2,651	1,991	661	41	118	235	27	75	166	177	22	4	26	1,432	1,150	281	768	—	768
NY	71,546	—	22,869	11,900	10,969	239	1,339	1,605	943	1,632	5,208	1,927	52	132	186	43,340	38,772	4,568	3,410	1,079	—
NC	22,713	—	9,539	5,574	3,966	323	480	1,862	382	295	624	1,476	523	123	219	11,604	10,384	1,220	94	58	—
ND	5,620	2	1,595	1,123	472	8	43	205	40	28	147	188	5	5	63	648	433	216	3,187	—	3,187
OH	25,924	—	13,120	8,273	4,847	98	478	1,684	1,052	843	692	3,580	1,682	81	861	9,147	9,030	117	77	67	10
OK	8,826	16	3,724	2,416	1,308	104	229	445	39	293	199	1,020	51	15	96	3,220	2,774	446	862	—	849
OR	8,700	38	1,399	—	1,399	17	101	533	94	256	398	903	19	29	302	6,259	5,826	433	123	102	14
PA	32,950	2	17,152	9,167	7,985	324	791	2,074	1,337	1,119	2,341	2,646	656	62	890	11,939	10,102	1,837	1,174	805	—
RI	2,805	9	1,475	839	635	13	86	118	102	131	186	106	5	2	40	1,187	1,064	122	36	28	—
SC	8,036	—	4,198	2,926	1,272	154	144	532	46	26	371	450	101	44	129	3,350	3,097	253	30	—	—
SD	1,521	—	1,197	838	359	15	67	136	4	60	76	251	4	4	125	60	—	60	14	—	14
TN	11,982	—	8,962	6,512	2,450	133	639	838	9	279	551	1,282	626	46	297	1,408	182	1,226	330	149	2
TX	48,597	—	37,432	24,501	12,931	938	1,508	3,178	620	1,470	5,217	7,509	4,544	131	620	—	—	—	3,656	—	3,656
UT	5,810	—	2,722	1,857	865	46	104	372	26	124	193	256	1	15	48	2,725	2,466	259	107	—	107
VT	2,757	949	968	342	626	22	59	108	13	80	343	101	2	8	18	695	598	97	44	13	—

See footnotes at end of table.

Table 471. State Government Tax Collections by State: 2012-Continued.

See headnote on page 306.

State	All taxes	Total property taxes	Selective sales and gross receipts — Total general sales and gross receipts (Total)	Total general sales and gross receipts (gross receipts)	Selective sales tax (Total [1])	Alcoholic beverage sales	Insurance premiums	Motor fuels sales	Public utilities	Tobacco products	Other	License taxes (Total [1])	Selected license taxes — Corporation	Motor vehicle operators	Occupancy and business oper- ators n.e.c.[2]	Income taxes (Total [1])	Individual income	Corporation net income	Other taxes (Total [1])	Selected other taxes — Death and gift	Severance
VA......	18,138	34	5,853	3,487	2,366	191	391	866	151	192	575	777	57	60	184	11,055	10,216	839	418	–	2
WA......	17,625	1,897	14,171	10,614	3,557	349	430	1,178	460	471	669	995	30	70	253	–	–	–	561	105	36
WV......	5,356	6	2,630	1,277	1,352	87	145	387	156	110	468	138	4	104	13	1,948	1,756	192	634	–	626
WI......	14,748	156	6,395	3,872	2,523	50	152	894	385	598	445	995	19	41	323	7,150	6,261	890	53	–	5
WY......	2,551	317	1,120	994	126	2	26	66	4	26	1	140	13	2	24	–	–	–	974	–	969

– Represents zero or rounds to zero. [1] Includes other items not shown separately. [2] n.e.c. means not elsewhere classified.

Source: U.S. Census Bureau, State Government Tax Collections Summary Report: 2012, April 2013. See also <http://www.census.gov/govs/statetax>.

Table 472. State Governments—Expenditures and Debt by State: 2010

[In millions of dollars (1,943,963 represents $1,943,963,000,000) except as indicated. For fiscal year ending in year shown; see text, this section]

State	Total expend-itures	General expenditures — Total	General expenditures — Inter-govern-mental	Direct expenditures — Total	Educa-tion	Public welfare	Health	Hospi-tals	High-ways	Police protec-tion	Correc-tions	Parks and recre-ation	Hous-ing and com-munity devel-opment	Sewer-age	Solid waste man-age-ment	Gov-ern-men-tal admin-istra-tion	Inter-est on gen-eral debt	Other	Expenditures — Utility and liquor store	Expenditures — Insur-ance trust	Cash and security holdings	Total debt out-stand-ing
U.S.	1,943,963	1,593,628	486,025	1,457,938	254,063	404,331	40,065	58,708	93,097	12,376	46,095	4,939	10,715	1,118	2,281	51,632	45,297	433,221	29,220	321,255	3,322,560	1,115,706
AL	27,700	24,016	6,604	21,096	5,521	5,957	574	1,532	1,306	154	519	32	16	—	1	586	373	4,526	242	3,442	34,218	8,785
AK	11,009	9,735	1,655	9,354	1,300	1,764	127	51	1,443	90	271	19	179	—	1	607	296	3,208	108	1,157	60,119	6,417
AZ	33,016	27,982	9,180	23,836	3,740	8,199	1,852	62	1,444	228	1,008	68	122	—	2	639	596	5,866	32	5,001	41,843	13,960
AR	18,009	15,801	5,058	12,951	2,714	4,291	253	809	772	81	369	64	35	—	9	566	149	2,839	—	2,204	23,180	4,247
CA	257,117	210,372	90,530	166,587	27,596	35,957	1,206	6,996	8,612	1,607	7,720	361	1,210	174	1,277	8,266	6,339	59,266	3,850	43,040	480,186	148,929
CO	27,661	21,818	7,178	20,483	4,670	3,467	1,109	574	1,012	127	823	89	98	2	1	832	817	6,861	28	5,816	58,034	16,710
CT	27,485	21,572	4,877	22,608	2,991	5,488	612	1,424	1,075	209	671	13	182	2	144	1,101	1,458	7,240	526	5,359	39,251	30,365
DE	7,827	6,917	1,236	6,591	1,323	1,648	381	56	513	103	262	40	88	—	59	434	288	1,394	125	784	12,860	5,515
FL	81,832	68,685	18,478	63,353	8,784	20,794	3,675	881	4,968	441	2,504	144	75	—	155	2,254	1,377	17,301	98	13,049	164,686	41,324
GA	44,482	36,710	10,748	33,735	7,425	9,474	840	849	2,041	288	1,396	185	303	11	48	722	699	9,454	44	7,728	68,883	13,789
HI	11,286	9,743	157	11,129	3,254	1,960	540	640	469	32	207	91	108	—	—	409	309	3,109	3	1,463	13,951	7,701
ID	8,514	7,119	2,023	6,491	1,087	1,785	179	52	692	50	215	34	96	—	—	316	174	1,812	91	1,304	16,364	3,872
IL	75,270	59,248	15,383	59,886	7,601	17,152	2,256	1,182	5,282	399	1,299	84	244	2	32	1,268	3,117	19,948	—	16,022	112,440	61,361
IN	35,474	30,503	9,705	25,769	6,436	7,977	507	166	1,872	223	630	50	399	1	6	506	1,000	5,994	—	4,971	53,584	23,635
IA	19,109	16,306	4,528	14,581	2,837	4,489	137	1,079	1,355	83	288	22	105	—	2	520	250	3,413	147	2,656	30,931	7,398
KS	16,584	14,176	4,177	12,407	2,243	3,342	195	1,076	1,014	99	295	31	144	—	4	514	341	3,110	—	2,408	15,920	6,509
KY	29,098	24,193	5,079	24,019	5,220	7,051	562	1,172	1,783	165	492	101	199	—	31	811	598	5,834	51	4,854	36,425	14,393
LA	33,615	29,561	6,658	26,957	4,416	6,319	639	2,287	1,996	271	605	269	1,368	—	—	989	1,058	6,741	4	4,049	52,527	17,450
ME	9,024	7,930	1,347	7,678	980	2,891	474	56	562	76	137	15	144	2	—	300	255	1,785	6	1,091	15,977	6,034
MD	37,521	32,110	8,593	28,928	4,812	8,772	1,175	489	2,048	399	1,379	132	309	115	25	1,262	1,033	6,979	885	4,526	52,115	24,475
MA	51,803	41,791	9,107	42,695	5,171	13,476	1,033	487	1,751	532	1,056	153	496	314	9	1,653	3,418	13,146	260	9,752	88,116	73,940
MI	63,908	51,510	19,410	44,498	9,503	11,760	983	2,477	1,519	263	1,648	90	673	—	8	734	1,192	13,647	635	11,772	75,389	32,146
MN	37,943	31,603	10,428	27,515	5,410	10,201	452	238	1,458	278	439	204	81	—	28	866	552	7,308	119	6,182	51,850	11,570
MS	20,023	17,500	5,272	14,750	2,371	4,896	370	1,066	1,060	97	337	72	56	—	—	378	235	3,813	207	2,315	27,828	6,492
MO	30,782	25,805	6,228	24,554	3,621	7,244	1,368	1,472	2,015	211	676	38	189	3	13	521	820	6,366	—	4,977	62,767	20,421
MT	7,052	6,005	1,334	5,718	933	1,267	152	47	716	42	185	17	95	3	1	381	170	1,707	76	971	15,519	4,400
NE	9,561	8,711	2,192	7,369	1,786	2,242	361	258	652	69	238	37	2	5	11	216	97	1,394	—	769	12,634	2,443
NV	12,935	9,478	3,704	9,231	1,554	1,825	210	232	610	89	293	19	25	—	7	267	200	3,900	86	3,371	23,762	4,436
NH	7,706	6,351	1,261	6,444	955	1,848	88	53	519	59	114	24	110	2	17	267	403	1,985	437	918	11,588	8,347
NJ	67,776	49,106	11,878	55,898	8,380	12,845	1,295	2,082	2,692	441	1,491	403	255	3	36	1,838	2,080	22,056	2,745	15,925	104,168	60,968
NM	17,996	15,989	4,309	13,687	2,437	4,391	535	919	838	131	414	70	106	—	2	641	340	2,864	14	2,092	41,487	8,740
NY	174,308	137,973	54,318	119,989	11,883	37,955	3,024	5,762	4,631	873	3,172	541	865	—	124	5,615	4,051	41,494	12,175	24,606	299,110	129,530
NC	52,190	43,014	13,430	38,760	8,209	9,672	1,512	1,530	2,829	462	1,434	221	259	3	13	1,121	602	10,895	55	9,121	83,941	18,853
ND	5,134	4,688	1,246	3,888	968	815	109	64	507	26	72	20	28	—	—	147	114	1,018	—	446	13,848	2,198
OH	76,690	57,301	18,374	58,316	10,353	15,294	1,301	2,573	2,469	272	1,437	118	329	365	30	1,287	1,484	21,005	470	18,890	172,499	30,004
OK	22,640	19,233	4,546	18,094	4,248	5,364	570	232	1,559	174	571	86	33	—	1	566	435	4,255	546	2,861	32,346	9,963
OR	26,978	20,560	5,865	21,113	3,300	4,828	330	1,477	1,334	170	639	67	114	1	7	841	445	7,560	243	6,175	61,257	13,510
PA	87,285	69,431	18,871	68,414	9,406	20,431	715	2,887	6,738	822	1,820	208	165	7	29	3,207	1,737	20,243	1,450	16,404	114,304	44,738
RI	8,211	6,352	1,124	7,087	894	2,250	190	58	294	77	175	5	46	34	33	322	429	2,279	159	1,700	15,362	9,498
SC	29,037	22,920	5,370	23,667	4,594	6,132	995	1,435	1,166	156	459	88	201	—	—	883	471	7,087	1,940	4,177	33,469	15,771
SD	4,429	3,988	737	3,692	708	971	128	64	492	31	109	40	45	—	—	230	126	748	—	441	11,404	3,483
TN	29,675	26,327	6,665	23,011	4,145	9,223	1,061	471	1,495	203	616	88	270	—	6	768	243	4,419	—	3,349	36,920	5,835
TX	119,872	102,373	27,461	92,410	21,893	28,293	2,448	4,042	5,541	813	3,551	148	210	3	59	1,910	1,170	22,330	—	17,499	248,614	42,034

See footnotes at end of table.

Table 472. State Governments—Expenditures and Debt by State: 2010—Continued.

See headnote on page 308.

State	Total expenditures	General expenditures Total	Inter-govern-mental	Direct expenditures Total	Educa-tion	Public welfare	Health	Hospi-tals	High-ways	Police protec-tion	Correc-tions	Parks and recre-ation	Hous-ing and com-munity devel-opment	Sewer-age	Solid waste man-age-ment	Gov-ern-men-tal admin-istra-tion	Inter-est on gen-eral debt	Other	Utility and liquor store	Insur-ance trust	Cash and security holdings	Total debt out-stand-ing
UT...	16,267	14,183	3,028	13,240	3,383	2,654	345	931	1,495	128	302	42	102	–	–	790	255	2,811	174	1,910	25,385	6,478
VT...	5,746	5,172	1,518	4,228	873	1,405	157	20	338	70	124	13	81	10	12	131	154	841	75	499	6,586	3,493
VA...	43,457	37,994	10,959	32,498	7,652	8,002	613	3,219	2,360	284	1,130	103	176	28	3	1,071	1,070	6,787	455	4,848	69,947	25,047
WA...	46,238	36,469	9,798	36,440	6,990	8,521	1,378	1,893	2,350	227	1,064	71	226	–	11	707	1,167	11,834	547	9,222	72,524	27,522
WV...	12,343	10,767	2,383	9,960	2,050	3,000	231	122	1,144	73	270	62	20	10	8	393	267	2,309	70	1,505	17,684	7,144
WI...	38,590	31,678	10,253	28,337	4,896	8,016	528	1,160	1,718	128	1,023	26	20	–	10	678	976	9,158	7	6,905	88,918	22,319
WY...	5,757	4,957	1,761	3,996	546	734	290	5	546	53	136	23	12	–	6	301	63	1,280	71	729	19,829	1,514

– Represents or rounds to zero.

Source: U.S. Census Bureau, "State and Local Government Finances by Level of Government and by State: 2009-10" at <http://www.census.gov/govs/local/>, and "State Government Finances: 2010" at <http://www.census.gov/govs/state/historical_data_2010.html>, both accessed May 2013.

State and Local Government Finances and Employment

Table 473. Local Governments—Revenue by State: 2011

[In millions of dollars (1,669,421 represents $1,669,421,000,000). For fiscal year ending in year shown; see text, this section. Minus sign (−) indicates decrease]

State	Total revenue	General revenue, total	Inter-governmental revenue	Gen. rev. from own sources — Total [1]	Taxes — Total	Property	Sales and gross receipt	Individual income	Corporation income	Other taxes	Current charges and miscellaneous general revenue	Current charges — Total [1]	Education	Hospitals	Sewerage	Misc. gen. rev. — Total [1]	Interest earnings	Special assessment	Utility revenue	Liquor store revenue	Insurance trust revenue
U.S.	1,669,421	1,459,561	554,062	905,499	578,177	429,086	93,079	25,629	7,164	23,220	327,322	247,751	27,816	71,346	45,701	79,571	23,291	6,990	134,673	1,245	73,942
AL	20,706	17,649	7,061	10,588	5,243	2,269	2,080	109	−	785	5,345	4,349	333	2,745	453	996	204	26	2,810	−	246
AK	5,246	4,877	2,043	2,834	1,754	1,308	413	−	−	33	1,079	762	28	295	87	318	187	11	327	−	42
AZ	28,807	23,660	8,778	14,882	9,390	6,346	2,656	−	−	388	5,492	3,903	621	822	805	1,588	547	79	4,520	−	627
AR	9,832	8,889	5,186	3,703	1,997	852	1,113	−	−	32	1,706	1,029	147	147	276	677	190	24	4,908	−	36
CA	278,013	225,608	100,311	125,297	68,523	50,299	14,031	−	−	4,192	56,774	43,637	2,910	10,466	6,486	13,136	3,879	1,466	22,820	−	29,586
CO	29,737	26,610	7,407	19,202	12,354	8,320	3,348	−	−	657	6,878	5,166	465	1,489	836	1,712	462	146	2,736	−	391
CT	17,624	15,833	5,017	10,816	9,354	9,230	−	52	−	124	1,462	1,037	119	−	346	425	58	92	768	−	1,023
DE	3,221	2,681	1,378	1,303	811	666	13	−	5	75	492	365	16	−	150	127	26	5	432	−	108
DC	12,878	10,774	4,117	6,657	5,369	1,757	1,409	1,311	382	510	1,289	633	31	114	247	655	59	−	971	−	1,133
FL	95,465	84,042	24,677	59,364	32,701	25,935	5,224	−	−	1,542	26,664	19,945	2,489	6,224	2,883	6,719	1,743	1,884	9,550	−	1,874
GA	44,066	38,220	12,570	25,650	15,129	10,272	4,501	−	−	356	10,520	8,250	532	4,157	1,091	2,270	776	61	4,827	−	1,019
HI	3,271	2,953	506	2,447	1,715	1,325	197	−	−	194	732	574	−	−	395	158	92	19	318	−	−
ID	5,666	5,462	2,229	3,233	1,450	1,368	25	−	−	56	1,783	1,515	120	768	178	268	50	39	203	−	2
IL	71,336	61,106	21,336	39,770	28,946	24,114	4,112	−	−	720	10,825	7,548	1,605	833	1,122	3,277	551	496	3,986	−	6,244
IN	27,354	25,241	10,073	15,168	8,243	6,313	158	1,619	−	153	6,925	5,080	344	2,745	1,044	1,845	273	23	2,049	−	64
IA	15,241	14,258	5,269	8,989	5,413	4,369	879	92	−	72	3,576	3,014	622	1,372	432	562	127	14	980	−	−
KS	13,973	12,543	4,211	8,332	4,959	3,844	1,033	3	−	79	3,373	2,231	460	815	357	1,142	555	111	1,291	−	138
KY	14,564	12,900	5,217	7,683	4,358	2,489	572	1,084	109	104	3,325	2,254	125	548	509	1,071	766	20	1,556	−	108
LA	21,950	20,417	7,903	12,514	7,747	3,485	4,072	−	−	190	4,767	3,570	68	2,007	386	1,197	471	11	1,235	−	298
ME	4,776	4,631	1,559	3,072	2,378	2,355	7	−	−	16	694	581	45	74	186	113	30	5	145	−	−
MD	28,585	25,575	8,597	16,978	13,014	7,632	708	3,956	−	717	3,964	3,048	822	−	856	916	158	43	786	256	1,969
MA	34,068	28,663	10,042	18,621	13,754	13,281	237	−	−	236	4,867	4,034	318	1,147	1,520	832	88	28	3,108	−	2,297
MI	47,632	42,150	20,600	21,550	12,573	11,672	270	408	−	222	8,977	7,055	1,419	862	1,720	1,923	347	205	2,579	−	2,903
MN	28,653	26,053	11,469	14,583	7,870	7,405	282	−	−	182	6,714	4,656	485	1,414	734	2,057	664	435	1,984	234	382
MS	12,713	11,871	5,338	6,532	2,719	2,522	105	−	−	93	3,813	3,351	490	2,209	214	462	125	4	842	−	−
MO	25,150	21,890	7,172	14,718	9,532	5,851	2,717	303	64	597	5,186	4,100	741	1,420	684	1,086	371	32	2,256	−	1,003
MT	3,513	3,401	1,483	1,918	1,131	1,096	9	−	−	27	787	541	77	83	82	247	57	73	112	−	−
NE	12,468	8,341	2,684	5,658	3,647	2,874	375	−	−	398	2,010	1,551	263	595	166	460	109	38	3,784	−	342
NV	12,893	12,011	5,117	6,894	3,882	2,691	910	−	−	281	3,012	2,156	46	508	430	856	214	71	882	−	−
NH	5,399	5,248	1,692	3,555	2,970	2,923	−	−	−	47	585	424	52	−	122	161	23	1	125	−	26
NJ	46,412	45,147	12,440	32,708	25,967	25,510	143	−	−	314	6,741	4,848	1,297	343	1,627	1,893	378	7	1,247	−	17
NM	8,543	7,985	4,422	3,563	2,365	1,300	1,006	−	−	59	1,199	878	110	143	162	320	42	10	558	−	−
NY	176,179	159,815	57,573	102,242	76,789	45,420	14,520	8,316	6,152	2,381	25,453	18,472	1,726	4,297	2,438	6,981	1,964	91	6,296	728	10,068
NC	42,852	37,904	14,685	23,219	11,310	8,640	2,340	−	−	330	11,909	9,873	828	5,811	1,274	2,036	624	18	4,117	−	103
ND	2,850	2,678	1,177	1,502	887	728	145	−	−	15	615	339	51	−	49	276	38	92	139	−	33
OH	55,420	52,481	22,541	29,940	20,106	13,159	1,938	4,274	−	632	9,834	7,242	1,210	1,342	1,948	2,593	721	267	2,660	−	278
OK	13,295	11,710	4,478	7,231	4,234	2,224	1,935	−	103	76	2,997	2,303	278	887	348	694	137	15	1,327	−	259
OR	17,946	16,647	6,837	9,811	5,992	5,033	365	−	49	545	3,819	2,992	665	302	876	827	229	43	1,235	−	63
PA	63,998	58,524	24,654	33,869	23,419	16,563	1,174	4,101	300	1,280	10,451	7,594	1,058	54	2,734	2,856	1,228	70	2,841	−	2,633
RI	4,427	4,047	1,230	2,816	2,326	2,271	20	−	−	35	491	360	30	−	108	131	24	6	181	−	199
SC	19,353	17,851	5,343	12,507	6,056	4,796	623	−	−	638	6,451	5,210	244	3,572	660	1,241	548	23	1,495	−	7
SD	3,261	2,893	991	1,902	1,320	981	313	−	−	25	583	439	98	49	77	144	40	27	293	27	48
TN	32,413	21,895	7,636	14,259	7,870	5,101	2,387	−	−	382	6,389	4,989	233	2,557	761	1,400	531	198	9,163	−	1,355

See footnotes at end of table.

Table 473. Local Governments—Revenue by State: 2011-Continued.

See headnote on page 310.

State	Total revenue	General revenue, total	Inter-govern-mental revenue	General revenue from own sources								Current charges				Miscellaneous general revenue			Utility revenue	Liquor store revenue	Insurance trust revenue
				Total	Taxes						Current charges and miscellaneous general revenue	Total [1]	Educa-tion	Hospi-tals	Sewer-age	Total [1]	Interest earn-ings	Special assess-ment			
					Total	Prop-erty	Sales and gross receipt	Indi-vidual income	Corpo-ration income	Other taxes											
TX..	121,552	106,188	35,259	70,929	47,632	39,596	7,219	–	–	817	23,297	17,416	2,592	4,640	3,262	5,881	2,160	173	11,942	–	3,422
UT.	11,027	9,105	3,505	5,600	3,581	2,551	891	–	–	139	2,018	1,341	82	38	342	677	172	50	1,910	–	11
VT..	2,578	2,340	1,585	755	452	420	18	–	–	14	303	211	25	–	67	92	14	4	227	–	11
VA..	36,460	32,380	11,885	20,494	14,744	11,065	2,399	–	–	1,280	5,750	4,221	358	288	1,175	1,529	552	144	1,865	–	2,215
WA.	38,165	31,743	12,187	19,556	10,999	6,817	3,436	–	–	746	8,557	7,092	352	2,043	1,882	1,465	319	202	5,929	–	494
WV..	5,466	5,200	2,322	2,878	1,764	1,423	123	–	–	219	1,114	879	35	–	253	234	50	20	223	–	43
WI..	27,805	25,042	10,407	14,635	10,258	9,680	409	–	–	170	4,377	3,491	662	–	809	886	281	61	1,944	–	819
WY..	4,622	4,431	1,861	2,570	1,211	946	221	–	–	44	1,359	1,202	86	861	56	157	40	7	191	–	–

– Represents or rounds to zero. [1] Includes items not shown separately.

Source: U.S. Census Bureau, Federal, State, and Local Governments, Government Finance Statistics, "Annual Surveys of State and Local Government Finances," <http://www.census.gov/govs/local/>, accessed August 2013.

State and Local Government Finances and Employment

Table 474. Local Governments—Expenditures and Debt by State: 2011

[In millions of dollars (1,664,494 represents $1,664,494,C00,000). For fiscal year ending in year shown; see text, this section]

State	Total expenditures [1]	Total [1]	Direct expenditures — Direct General expenditures — Total	Education	Public welfare	Hospitals	Health	Highways	Police protection	Corrections	Parks and recreation	Housing and community development	Sewerage	Solid Waste Management	Governmental administration	Interest on general debt	Other	Utility expenditures	Insurance trust expenditures	Debt outstanding
U.S.	1,664,494	1,650,763	1,424,975	599,265	52,689	86,941	41,126	60,918	83,475	26,440	33,864	44,771	53,567	21,348	73,017	61,824	185,730	183,673	40,914	1,774,941
AL	20,931	20,901	17,896	7,603	78	3,074	370	801	985	214	374	588	372	264	952	619	1,601	2,845	161	20,248
AK	5,090	5,090	4,557	1,967	7	306	102	284	233	3	110	216	107	110	281	108	722	504	29	3,780
AZ	28,491	28,327	23,230	9,319	315	915	246	1,126	1,870	599	638	508	913	426	1,604	1,466	3,286	4,829	268	36,763
AR	10,068	10,059	9,077	5,362	7	165	48	485	446	130	200	178	359	196	421	335	744	943	40	9,795
CA	264,386	263,687	217,872	73,268	16,511	13,215	10,764	7,821	13,487	5,091	5,398	9,844	6,954	2,261	12,300	9,473	31,487	36,109	9,707	269,162
CO	29,540	29,495	25,346	8,323	908	1,604	380	1,328	1,520	340	1,208	595	1,116	98	1,567	1,422	4,936	3,941	209	35,851
CT	17,072	17,067	15,603	8,533	115	—	140	546	871	—	222	694	552	204	591	370	2,767	926	538	10,966
DE	3,255	3,253	2,822	1,734	1	—	33	81	179	—	31	84	241	25	151	75	186	383	49	2,470
DC	13,641	13,641	10,385	2,342	2,834	226	395	244	591	257	241	659	404	98	501	482	1,110	2,525	731	11,277
FL	99,517	99,154	85,715	29,413	1,353	7,418	1,180	3,338	6,911	1,830	2,756	2,937	3,330	2,449	4,663	3,472	14,665	11,756	1,684	108,432
GA	43,987	43,943	37,228	16,916	208	4,397	1,111	1,378	1,989	829	694	987	1,200	531	2,530	821	3,636	6,113	603	40,965
HI	3,121	3,121	2,450	266	61	3	59	207	355	1	164	93	329	314	239	183	446	671	—	5,464
ID	5,370	5,369	5,120	2,094	35	777	63	291	331	80	123	49	179	141	317	89	550	247	2	2,303
IL	71,833	71,833	60,512	27,280	680	1,393	919	2,770	4,222	699	2,426	1,932	2,748	463	3,617	2,859	8,503	7,239	4,082	80,684
IN	26,667	26,656	24,201	9,739	118	3,092	356	823	1,090	384	491	497	1,033	305	1,410	929	3,935	2,378	77	27,261
IA	15,638	15,539	14,390	6,636	103	1,576	388	962	553	138	301	156	561	200	507	354	1,955	1,147	3	10,754
KS	14,055	14,051	12,649	6,030	36	876	286	722	641	210	284	158	348	161	615	876	1,405	1,319	84	20,232
KY	14,774	14,762	12,722	6,146	54	485	475	484	532	234	185	187	677	213	682	1,151	1,220	1,986	53	27,416
LA	21,951	21,940	20,272	7,787	112	2,358	211	885	1,185	720	439	717	731	326	1,248	776	2,777	1,489	179	20,175
ME	4,815	4,813	4,650	2,431	38	85	30	308	195	65	68	138	193	128	207	113	649	163	—	3,079
MD	28,163	28,064	25,661	13,392	229	50	474	907	1,709	355	729	974	767	610	1,270	707	3,539	1,293	883	19,353
MA	32,681	31,795	27,191	13,031	86	1,534	127	864	1,423	1	234	1,661	1,222	383	922	565	5,138	3,018	1,586	18,242
MI	46,803	46,570	41,382	19,168	1,223	989	2,880	2,141	2,122	619	598	507	1,987	405	2,095	1,834	4,815	3,252	1,936	42,867
MN	28,397	28,298	25,673	9,985	1,553	1,592	734	2,070	1,356	436	844	864	705	305	1,367	1,205	2,658	2,054	320	33,864
MS	12,405	12,404	11,538	4,991	36	2,159	108	643	564	243	169	247	395	172	622	260	928	866	—	7,418
MO	25,096	25,092	21,654	10,125	159	1,385	347	1,350	1,451	173	724	504	810	136	924	834	2,727	2,969	468	25,423
MT	3,542	3,541	3,383	1,667	59	90	118	197	216	52	63	61	117	69	192	54	429	158	—	1,710
NE	12,434	12,430	8,213	3,942	135	629	72	554	338	124	232	174	185	79	391	277	1,083	3,977	240	10,596
NV	13,997	13,969	12,609	4,012	346	735	145	719	1,051	424	647	199	474	21	1,010	732	2,092	1,360	—	23,507
NH	5,249	5,190	5,053	2,768	208	—	34	234	296	71	81	103	107	109	264	104	673	126	11	2,788
NJ	45,696	45,290	43,994	22,471	1,151	384	383	1,331	2,845	663	566	1,094	1,559	1,031	1,684	1,372	7,461	1,284	12	38,255
NM	8,910	8,876	8,171	4,389	100	168	83	424	512	218	257	104	166	200	452	192	906	705	—	8,530
NY	183,669	175,291	148,882	58,706	10,868	8,970	3,973	6,165	8,198	2,972	2,370	4,923	4,500	2,573	4,752	6,954	22,957	15,501	10,908	199,693
NC	41,540	41,394	36,608	15,083	1,532	5,626	1,461	634	1,996	500	692	765	1,182	736	1,440	1,471	3,489	4,061	28	32,631
ND	2,928	2,922	2,695	1,234	69	4	31	367	123	33	102	58	59	49	79	74	414	212	16	2,365
OH	55,974	55,442	51,777	22,739	3,031	1,477	2,517	2,338	2,921	472	1,103	2,076	2,291	403	3,506	1,587	5,316	3,478	187	46,559
OK	12,760	12,759	11,225	5,493	100	880	157	736	686	137	390	333	371	184	557	258	1,020	1,467	68	8,947
OR	18,375	18,370	16,461	7,185	245	362	693	784	918	447	491	507	963	120	859	716	2,117	1,784	126	20,684
PA	61,902	61,901	55,172	25,792	4,048	38	2,710	1,900	2,292	1,381	1,068	2,185	3,211	780	2,851	2,689	4,228	4,807	1,922	78,216
RI	4,248	4,248	3,896	2,148	8	—	13	111	285	15	36	180	115	50	180	122	633	180	172	2,766
SC	19,048	19,017	17,506	7,379	71	3,555	177	455	887	211	333	334	603	333	917	985	1,265	1,508	4	25,713
SD	3,290	3,290	2,878	1,395	14	54	30	345	132	49	111	53	102	48	163	78	305	370	16	2,190
TN	31,414	31,411	21,596	8,611	179	2,495	388	842	1,496	415	406	817	636	338	1,154	1,002	2,818	9,274	542	32,404
TX	125,845	124,756	106,710	51,782	470	8,154	2,142	4,622	5,705	2,209	2,283	1,975	3,340	1,309	4,876	7,898	9,946	16,523	1,523	219,710
UT	11,386	11,352	8,768	4,084	78	45	216	404	518	196	424	285	521	162	633	270	931	2,577	7	12,928

See footnotes at end of table.

Table 474. Local Governments—Expenditures and Debt by State: 2011-Continued.

See headnote on page 312.

State	Total expenditures [1]	Total [1]	Direct expenditures — Direct General expenditures															Utility expenditures	Insurance trust expenditures	Debt outstanding
			Total	Education	Public welfare	Hospitals	Health	Highways	Police protection	Corrections	Parks and recreation	Housing and community development	Sewerage	Solid Waste Management	Governmental administration	Interest on general debt	Other			
VT...	2,622	2,621	2,336	1,471	1	29	10	220	89	5	32	61	79	33	96	30	213	276	9	1,244
VA...	35,200	35,165	32,051	14,434	1,559	255	883	879	1,734	1,015	830	799	1,308	680	2,007	1,399	4,267	2,339	775	37,337
WA...	38,312	38,247	30,235	11,421	191	2,271	1,209	1,674	1,339	567	922	1,259	2,068	628	1,577	1,249	3,861	7,814	197	45,938
WV...	5,937	5,934	5,554	3,315	6	263	61	96	281	54	116	127	280	71	415	96	373	336	44	3,585
WI...	27,807	27,775	25,102	12,245	1,411	–	1,325	1,847	1,643	496	554	314	1,015	341	1,076	805	2,029	2,254	420	21,393
WY...	4,662	4,646	4,305	1,885	25	867	68	183	164	65	101	10	81	80	283	29	465	341	–	1,005

– Represents or rounds to zero. [1] Includes other items not shown separately.

Source: U.S. Census Bureau, Federal, State, and Local Governments, Government Finance Statistics, "Annual Surveys of State and Local Government Finances," <http://www.census.gov/govs/local/>, accessed September 2013.

State and Local Government Finances and Employment

Table 475. City Governments—Revenue for Largest Cities: 2006

[In millions of dollars (83,520 represents $83,520,000,000). For fiscal years ending in year shown; see text, this section. Cities ranked by estimated resident population as of July 1. Data reflect inclusion of fiscal activity of dependent school systems where applicable. Regarding intercity comparisons, see text, this section. See Appendix III]

Cities ranked by 2006 population	Total revenue	Gen. rev. Total[1]	Intergov. Total	From federal govt.	From state/local govt.	From local govt.	Own sources Total[1]	Taxes Total[1]	Property	Sales & gross receipts Total[1]	General sales	Public utilities	Current charges Total[1]	Parks and recreation	Sewerage	Misc. Total[1]	Interest earnings	Utility revenue[2]	Insurance trust revenue
New York, NY[3]	83,520	70,823	25,957	3,722	22,045	191	44,866	35,104	12,754	5,953	4,439	516	6,380	63	1,151	3,382	1,153	3,472	9,224
Los Angeles, CA	14,199	7,863	952	282	670	—	6,911	3,233	1,090	1,362	552	673	2,413	105	599	1,264	461	3,143	3,193
Chicago, IL	8,812	7,257	1,325	449	876	—	5,933	2,179	429	1,454	275	555	2,872	—	144	881	248	347	1,207
Houston, TX	4,449	3,119	550	195	328	27	2,569	1,492	781	664	423	187	808	26	330	269	153	341	989
Phoenix, AZ	3,377	2,903	1,115	581	488	46	1,788	1,023	261	692	537	84	581	26	232	184	137	288	186
Philadelphia, PA[3]	7,345	5,809	2,478	653	1,712	113	3,332	2,450	394	225	125	—	698	1	240	184	105	1,007	529
San Antonio, TX	3,283	1,469	191	54	120	17	1,278	612	292	287	200	27	431	24	280	234	107	1,573	242
San Diego, CA	3,266	2,100	411	175	216	20	1,690	744	313	323	173	45	694	63	396	252	110	332	833
Dallas, TX	3,027	2,277	164	123	36	6	2,112	857	488	329	198	89	861	35	240	394	144	207	543
San Jose, CA	1,924	1,498	217	50	141	27	1,281	660	285	238	106	112	440	15	185	181	100	20	406
Honolulu, HI[3]	1,483	1,337	197	117	79	—	1,140	807	591	114	—	62	284	23	241	50	29	146	—
Detroit, MI	3,184	2,132	694	97	543	54	1,439	867	309	218	—	61	452	4	351	119	47	314	739
Jacksonville, FL[3]	3,292	1,829	323	72	251	—	1,506	745	365	371	213	106	383	16	158	379	207	1,187	276
Indianapolis, IN[3]	3,749	3,014	646	86	550	10	2,367	1,638	1,486	47	—	1	506	26	74	224	94	687	48
San Francisco, CA[3]	7,955	5,647	2,155	87	1,664	404	3,492	2,047	923	598	327	91	1,045	25	165	400	178	426	1,882
Columbus, OH	1,227	1,058	198	82	103	13	860	560	40	20	—	7	228	11	172	72	26	169	—
Austin, TX	2,272	1,037	108	54	30	24	929	457	255	186	124	30	378	23	166	94	26	1,032	203
Louisville/Jefferson, KY[3]	1,090	975	170	73	89	8	805	515	124	55	—	4	117	11	—	173	93	115	—
Memphis, TN[3]	3,777	1,882	1,149	63	557	529	733	449	301	135	99	5	150	11	102	134	86	1,587	308
Ft. Worth, TX[3]	1,132	712	56	—	56	—	656	417	236	144	102	32	153	5	120	85	32	184	237
Baltimore, MD[3]	3,339	2,922	1,504	262	1,205	38	1,418	1,023	558	87	—	56	261	10	149	134	48	109	308
Charlotte City, NC	1,613	1,507	351	76	114	161	1,157	366	286	39	2	—	398	3	199	392	50	80	26
El Paso, TX	822	627	91	74	17	—	535	339	178	141	107	32	134	—	71	62	20	81	115
Boston, MA	3,626	3,103	1,368	100	1,264	3	1,735	1,333	1,255	40	—	—	194	42	122	209	48	112	411
Seattle, WA	2,481	1,424	144	41	100	3	1,279	784	284	307	146	124	387	26	288	108	23	882	176
Washington, DC	9,248	8,674	2,589	2,589	—	—	6,085	4,545	1,214	1,257	817	214	574	—	178	966	205	96	478
Milwaukee, WI	1,392	931	442	69	306	67	489	250	237	—	—	—	191	—	109	48	17	59	402
Denver, CO[3]	2,472	2,121	237	17	219	2	1,884	849	226	534	460	26	810	45	70	225	72	166	185
Las Vegas, NV	883	882	401	22	272	107	481	233	121	60	—	54	185	11	78	63	15	—	—
Nashville-Davidson, TN[3]	3,237	1,955	446	8	438	—	1,509	1,101	720	327	271	15	236	9	82	172	99	1,008	275
Oklahoma City, OK	1,069	950	96	56	39	2	854	451	45	358	319	31	268	12	84	135	33	78	41
Portland, OR	1,053	961	181	54	71	56	780	419	254	65	—	49	294	24	205	67	33	91	1
Tucson, AZ	953	756	265	79	170	15	492	305	54	243	196	28	149	21	38	37	6	126	72
Albuquerque, NM	1,146	1,047	321	28	259	33	727	414	102	248	219	19	239	15	98	74	43	98	—
Atlanta, GA	1,696	1,517	323	118	114	90	1,194	354	186	110	—	38	650	31	148	190	155	146	34

— Represents or rounds to zero. [1] Includes revenue sources not shown separately. [2] Includes water, electric, and transit. [3] Represents, in effect, city-county consolidated government.

Source: U.S. Census Bureau, Federal, State, and Local Governments, Survey of State & Local Government Finances, 2006, July 2009. See also <http://www.census.gov/govs/>.

Table 476. City Governments—Expenditures and Debt for Largest Cities: 2006

[In millions of dollars (82,454 represents $82,454,000,000). For fiscal year ending in year shown; see headnote, Table 475]

Cities ranked by 2006 population	Total expenditures [1]	Total direct expenditures	General expenditures														Utility expenditures [3]	Insurance trust expenditures	Debt outstanding
			Total [1]	Education	Housing and community development	Public welfare	Health and hospitals	Police protection	Fire protection	Corrections	Highways	Parks and recreation	Sewerage	Solid waste management	Governmental administration [2]	Interest on general debt			
New York, NY [4]	82,454	77,456	66,237	17,472	3,710	9,811	8,976	3,971	1,519	1,314	1,526	559	2,161	1,100	1,178	3,205	8,699	7,517	85,234
Los Angeles, CA	12,315	12,315	7,252	–	275	–	202	1,659	589	–	561	332	498	238	842	410	3,675	1,388	15,723
Chicago, IL	7,622	7,544	6,033	1	257	135	178	1,175	390	–	454	77	101	183	153	756	316	1,272	15,862
Houston, TX	3,982	3,953	3,295	–	255	–	98	571	381	20	139	129	384	67	139	357	307	381	11,403
Phoenix, AZ	3,362	3,349	2,592	18	100	–	–	367	187	13	127	577	198	99	114	251	672	97	7,373
Philadelphia, PA [4]	6,745	6,660	5,077	23	234	555	1,292	510	172	350	71	94	189	98	332	114	1,054	614	5,825
San Antonio, TX	3,625	3,625	1,546	45	35	43	35	242	161	–	112	157	248	57	52	81	2,010	70	6,055
San Diego, CA	2,431	2,418	1,803	–	339	–	44	336	160	9	82	142	290	52	88	70	413	215	2,795
Dallas, TX	2,713	2,704	2,194	–	41	7	27	268	143	8	121	124	196	67	80	229	276	242	8,557
San Jose, CA	1,894	1,866	1,703	–	186	–	15	227	116	–	95	138	144	79	192	204	36	156	4,368
Honolulu, HI [4]	1,473	1,473	1,228	–	46	–	26	180	82	–	107	100	159	137	98	100	246	–	3,155
Detroit, MI	3,349	3,248	2,168	35	98	16	66	447	192	–	146	79	402	107	157	147	627	554	7,515
Jacksonville, FL [4]	3,474	3,343	1,847	–	33	47	84	206	96	62	200	77	198	86	97	217	1,447	180	11,022
Indianapolis, IN	3,412	3,398	2,592	–	268	91	619	188	70	75	110	149	301	40	173	193	741	79	4,125
San Francisco, CA [4]	6,908	6,908	5,305	102	148	605	1,246	317	211	170	143	200	155	–	714	406	1,008	595	8,738
Columbus, OH	1,152	1,144	1,012	–	8	–	32	212	144	10	94	60	193	34	72	93	140	–	1,703
Austin, TX	2,304	2,304	1,159	–	35	10	124	176	88	–	83	96	137	43	58	80	1,036	110	2,520
Louisville-Jefferson, KY [4]	925	924	868	999	39	17	75	130	47	41	15	38	–	18	31	102	57	–	2,747
Memphis, TN	3,508	3,479	1,815	–	36	–	11	180	132	–	65	56	33	43	45	62	1,502	191	1,231
Ft. Worth, TX	1,047	1,047	766	–	21	–	15	161	81	–	85	58	76	35	31	26	197	83	2,287
Baltimore, MD [4]	3,289	3,212	2,930	1,029	86	2	147	348	134	–	192	391	147	69	128	58	101	259	2,665
Charlotte City, NC	1,448	1,436	1,019	–	42	–	5	151	77	–	96	52	253	40	21	44	413	16	1,005
El Paso, TX	725	725	476	–	22	–	16	81	52	–	35	25	44	13	27	25	187	61	1,459
Boston, MA	3,341	3,038	2,813	950	82	150	184	279	160	106	51	34	215	58	55	57	171	357	3,465
Seattle, WA	2,424	2,311	1,400	–	45	36	14	190	135	13	113	195	175	114	67	52	932	93	
Washington, DC	8,543	8,291	8,256	1,478	560	1,846	669	493	176	206	96	332	237	266	434	320	169	118	7,824
Milwaukee, WI	1,302	1,274	1,026	–	123	–	32	218	99	–	132	4	66	76	37	37	72	203	1,199
Denver, CO [4]	2,415	2,357	2,110	–	103	98	55	165	87	75	86	216	79	–	132	289	199	106	5,845
Las Vegas, NV	747	600	745	–	18	–	3	124	105	39	90	80	40	5	117	16	1	–	352
Nashville-Davidson, TN [4]	3,270	3,269	2,046	679	–	28	168	158	101	52	38	72	109	21	105	148	1,084	140	3,837
Oklahoma City, OK	1,115	1,115	960	–	9	–	–	125	111	–	91	83	146	31	137	30	138	17	1,049
Portland, OR	1,210	1,210	1,059	–	54	–	–	137	79	–	162	89	192	3	52	85	71	80	2,524
Tucson, AZ	874	874	694	–	43	–	–	134	56	–	70	71	–	36	71	46	146	35	1,090
Albuquerque, NM	843	843	760	–	32	19	9	122	66	49	55	107	29	45	31	37	83	–	777
Atlanta, GA	2,025	1,979	1,552	–	5	–	–	152	66	36	43	103	185	45	61	87	407	65	6,425

– Represents or rounds to zero. [1] Includes expenditure categories, not shown separately. [2] Excludes public buildings. [3] Includes water, electric, and transit. [4] Represents, in effect, city-county consolidated government.

Source: U.S. Census Bureau, Federal, State, and Local Governments, Survey of State & Local Government Finances, 2006, July 2009. See also <http://www.census.gov/govs/>.

Table 477. County Governments—Revenue for Largest Counties: 2006

[In millions of dollars (21,586 represents $21,586,000,000). For fiscal year ending in year shown; see text, this section. See Appendix III]

Counties ranked by 2006 population	Total revenue [1]	General revenue		Intergovernmental							General revenue from own sources										
		Total	From federal government		From state government			From local government	Total	Taxes		Sales and gross receipts		Current charges				Miscellaneous general revenue	
			Total	Total [1]	Housing and community development	Total [1]	Public welfare	Health and hospitals			Total [1]	Property	Total	General sales	Total [1]	Parks and recreation	Sanitation [2]	Hospitals	Total [1]	Interest earnings
Los Angeles, CA	21,586	17,015	9,177	386	4	8,556	4,815	1,311	235	7,838	3,285	3,009	127	42	3,802	95	83	2,220	751	235
Cook, IL	3,378	2,851	606	41	–	564	287	–	1	2,245	1,536	810	702	358	577	47	–	333	132	49
Harris, TX	3,165	3,165	647	91	23	471	174	216	85	2,518	1,318	1,232	56	–	815	3	–	256	385	245
Maricopa, AZ	2,015	2,015	952	55	9	869	167	27	28	1,062	781	604	144	144	80	4	114	–	202	128
Orange, CA	4,439	3,464	1,926	51	8	1,800	650	172	75	1,538	626	536	46	43	622	42	24		289	181
San Diego, CA	5,117	4,027	2,880	167	120	2,447	986	473	266	1,147	686	585	27	18	259	3	508	1,084	201	110
Dade, FL	6,528	6,263	1,353	896	254	413		55	44	4,910	1,871	1,283	480	119	2,477	36		545	562	289
Dallas, TX	1,662	1,623	254	9		233	150	19	12	1,369	649	597	12		608		71	184	111	29
Riverside, CA	3,399	3,399	1,898	61	13	1,683	904	208	154	1,502	666	534	43	35	581	7	73	331	255	99
San Bernardino, CA	3,919	3,290	2,043	134	18	1,826	918	240	83	1,247	383	326	25	17	680	7	75	10	183	62
Wayne, MI	1,991	1,848	1,117	122	8	862	14	522	134	731	448	423	16		229	7	333		54	19
King, WA	2,239	2,108	520	135	16	266		178	119	1,588	1,005	446	534	431	499	4	172		84	51
Broward, FL	2,326	2,270	466	119	10	203		6	144	1,804	927	780	124	113	676	16	96	475	201	111
Clark, NV	4,446	3,980	1,051	87	16	792	38	23	173	2,928	1,333	577	484	140	1,082	66	3	688	513	83
Santa Clara, CA	3,497	3,497	1,717	37	3	1,603	971	180	78	1,779	800	605	143		872	4		146	107	37
Tarrant, TX	1,150	1,150	273	51	24	219	7	189	4	877	515	478	15		203			389	158	124
Bexar, TX	1,113	1,113	203	6	7	188	101	44	9	909	396	363	27		421		24		93	70
Suffolk, NY	2,744	2,592	580	29	3	538	275	153	13	2,012	1,701	556	1,119	1,114	174	10		341	137	50
Alameda, CA	3,198	2,696	1,468	31		1,399	737	311	38	1,228	480	399	26	15	609		83		139	66
Sacramento, CA	3,235	2,559	1,563	46	21	1,457	811	202	60	997	428	275	89	63	373	13	2	247	195	65
Nassau, NY	3,347	3,347	769	73	19	696	397	136		2,578	1,903	906	965	953	431	23	5	341	244	39
Cuyahoga, OH	2,170	2,170	964	20	9	940	503	260	4	1,206	565	336	184	169	383	13	199		258	198
Palm Beach, FL	1,873	1,823	239	102		136			1	1,584	967	685	154		421				196	37
Allegheny, PA	1,486	1,419	1,026	63	47	961	282	467	2	393	302	262	38	23	64	4	18	4	27	6
Oakland, MI	1,162	1,051	574	201	6	218	6	61	155	477	350	326	9		85	9	78		42	15
Hillsborough, FL	1,836	1,663	259	75	32	183	45	169	1	1,404	901	605	274	199	395	2	70	284	108	44
Hennepin, MN	1,843	1,843	854	50	8	785	353	128	19	989	478	459			388		3		123	30
Franklin, OH	1,158	1,156	459	14	4	419	193		26	696	459	334	104	85	97	4			140	124
Orange, FL	1,753	1,704	285	85		199	5	113		1,420	941	506	225		322	47	146		156	95
Contra Costa, CA	2,506	2,071	899	113	102	705	391	76	81	1,173	406	342	24	10	670	45	24	404	96	33
Fairfax, VA	5,137	4,343	1,024	122	68	874	146	5	28	3,319	2,673	2,117	326	155	426	1	232		220	127
St Louis, MO	727	683	71	17	11	54	1			612	512	152	347	312	78	7	4		21	6
Salt Lake, UT	532	532	76	15		51		14	9	456	346	203	112	79	70		12		40	5
Fulton, GA	1,162	1,000	102	29	23	70	32		2	898	733	522	178	164	71		46		94	37
Westchester, NY	2,468	2,459	508	14		484	245	116	10	1,951	1,041	607	426	407	838	31	30	563	73	46

– Represents or rounds to zero. [1] Includes revenue sources, not shown separately. [2] Includes fee for sewerage and solid waste management.

Source: U.S. Census Bureau, Federal, State, and Local Governments, *Survey of State & Local Government Finances, 2006*, July 2009. See also <http://www.census.gov/govs/>.

Table 478. County Governments—Expenditures and Debt for Largest Counties: 2006

[In millions of dollars (18,720 represents $18,720,000,000). For fiscal year ending in year shown; see text, this section and Appendix III]

Counties ranked by 2006 population	Total expenditures [1]	Total direct expenditures	General expenditures Total [1]	Education [1]	Housing and community development	Public welfare	Health	Hospitals	Police protection	Correction	Highways	Parks and recreation	Natural resources	Sewage and solid waste management	Governmental administration	General public building	Interest on general debt	Utility expenditures [2]	Employee retirement expenditures	Debt outstanding
Los Angeles, CA	18,720	18,439	16,859	890	5	4,515	1,925	2,454	1,213	1,128	273	248	424	66	1,572	114	63	1,798	2,713	3
Cook, IL	3,048	3,036	2,665	—	10	8	41	916	85	350	119	118	—	—	620	149	—	383	3,246	3
Harris, TX	3,207	3,207	3,207	—	12	43	208	888	364	70	266	24	142	—	329	450	—	—	8,538	8
Maricopa, AZ	1,813	1,517	1,813	34	13	376	81	—	69	354	138	8	90	6	391	108	—	—	1,880	2
Orange, CA	3,482	3,428	3,217	244	14	764	328	—	282	263	54	—	67	100	433	174	—	265	2,856	3
San Diego, CA	4,205	3,843	3,879	425	102	989	518	1,380	207	297	175	20	20	29	523	125	—	326	1,845	2
Dade, FL	6,931	6,921	6,344	—	295	298	71	1,010	425	229	153	278	47	502	273	620	587	—	10,985	10
Dallas, TX	1,547	1,547	1,533	4	32	7	42	271	32	99	43	3	—	1	131	22	—	13	423	1
Riverside, CA	3,156	2,994	3,156	367	78	660	325	376	265	177	162	10	66	66	277	74	—	—	1,298	2
San Bernardino, CA	3,335	3,187	3,131	379	—	799	219	49	242	203	74	18	56	71	247	116	—	204	1,912	1
Wayne, MI	1,828	1,771	1,717	—	8	153	474	1	35	250	124	67	46	67	330	50	—	111	643	1
King, WA	2,226	2,180	1,785	—	30	2	344	—	121	127	112	53	9	413	246	163	441	—	3,167	3
Broward, FL	2,215	2,160	2,068	—	15	46	99	495	353	190	43	127	19	149	183	165	147	—	3,225	3
Clark, NV	4,013	3,953	3,487	214	22	187	60	905	467	136	483	319	11	42	268	218	526	—	5,865	5
Santa Clara, CA	3,350	3,274	3,350	—	9	624	365	446	105	258	102	31	4	3	336	58	—	—	910	1
Tarrant, TX	1,034	1,034	1,034	—	23	7	95	578	34	98	35	2	—	—	136	114	—	—	1,981	2
Bexar, TX	1,029	1,004	1,029	—	—	43	52	—	42	73	11	43	1	—	89	67	—	—	933	1
Suffolk, NY	2,750	2,454	2,568	161	7	504	337	—	431	124	42	1	32	79	116	65	182	—	1,797	2
Alameda, CA	2,563	2,559	2,303	39	6	557	319	394	87	271	27	34	36	—	281	41	44	216	1,327	3
Sacramento, CA	2,804	2,741	2,603	154	10	741	430	—	224	233	133	61	4	94	240	81	18	183	2,167	3
Nassau, NY	3,633	3,243	3,631	181	23	573	298	380	688	215	127	—	2	111	189	153	2	—	3,532	3
Cuyahoga, OH	2,131	2,112	2,131	—	20	438	327	576	26	94	54	92	7	13	260	201	—	—	3,338	2
Palm Beach, FL	1,777	1,690	1,686	—	57	72	50	—	216	102	112	62	37	169	193	63	91	—	1,818	1
Allegheny, PA	1,477	1,385	1,416	32	63	351	461	8	32	76	29	9	—	—	106	24	—	60	613	1
Oakland, MI	988	964	926	10	9	7	266	—	52	102	123	78	30	98	131	13	27	36	339	—
Hillsborough, FL	1,911	1,781	1,718	—	32	89	134	480	165	132	109	3	55	75	222	56	193	—	2,174	2
Hennepin, MN	1,856	1,847	1,849	—	23	458	288	—	85	83	108	20	—	52	112	25	7	—	544	2
Franklin, OH	1,164	1,126	1,160	—	7	289	320	—	30	58	47	36	6	6	162	118	3	—	2,178	3
Orange, FL	1,689	1,652	1,675	—	30	79	42	437	142	153	159	20	28	232	128	128	14	198	3,074	3
Contra Costa, CA	2,253	2,198	2,054	127	106	379	189	—	89	116	100	144	9	23	155	58	1	—	1,106	4
Fairfax, VA	4,831	4,759	4,328	2,195	162	227	178	—	196	37	37	30	5	259	174	177	197	306	3,701	4
St Louis, MO	725	495	696	—	10	24	47	—	77	20	83	30	—	4	66	16	4	25	410	1
Salt Lake, UT	519	519	519	—	1	46	26	—	32	63	25	78	5	14	92	6	—	—	197	1
Fulton, GA	1,111	909	952	—	8	62	35	78	65	83	26	4	1	62	259	14	100	59	749	1
Westchester, NY	2,629	2,311	2,586	95	8	455	277	591	41	134	43	56	1	146	107	53	44	—	1,594	1

— Represents or rounds to zero. [1] Includes expenditure categories, not shown separately. [2] Includes water, gas, electric, and transit.

Source: U.S. Census Bureau, Federal, State, and Local Governments, *State & Local Government Finances, 2006*, July 2009. See also <http://www.census.gov/govs/>.

State and Local Government Finances and Employment

Table 479. State Governments—Revenue by State: 2011

[In millions of dollars (2,265,213 represents $2,265,213,000,000). For fiscal year ending in year shown. See text, this section. Includes local shares of state imposed taxes. Minus sign (–) indicates decrease]

State		General revenue							Utilities and liquor store revenue	Insurance trust revenue
	Total revenue [1,2]		Intergovernmental revenue		General revenue from own sources					
		Total	Total [1]	From federal govern-ment	Total	Total taxes	Current charges	Miscel-laneous general revenue		
United States........	**2,265,213**	**1,654,313**	**592,998**	**573,404**	**1,061,316**	**760,259**	**181,101**	**119,956**	**21,281**	**589,618**
Alabama................	26,305	23,277	8,882	8,497	14,395	8,636	4,452	1,307	267	2,761
Alaska.................	14,921	12,666	3,041	3,035	9,625	5,538	586	3,501	18	2,238
Arizona................	38,029	28,466	12,360	12,059	16,105	12,265	2,277	1,563	30	9,533
Arkansas..............	22,785	17,431	6,313	6,305	11,118	7,953	2,320	845	–	5,354
California..............	334,311	211,436	68,509	64,582	142,927	116,695	16,702	9,530	2,496	120,379
Colorado..............	29,489	21,105	6,249	6,172	14,856	9,468	3,333	2,056	–	8,384
Connecticut...........	28,905	23,485	6,561	6,552	16,924	13,409	2,097	1,418	31	5,389
Delaware..............	9,350	7,553	1,891	1,826	5,663	3,262	1,134	1,267	16	1,780
Florida................	106,166	75,291	27,804	27,355	47,487	32,559	9,034	5,894	20	30,855
Georgia...............	52,295	37,168	15,266	14,988	21,901	16,003	3,923	1,975	10	15,117
Hawaii................	12,932	10,204	2,918	2,911	7,285	4,858	1,600	828	–	2,728
Idaho.................	10,476	7,344	2,805	2,795	4,539	3,262	802	476	122	3,011
Illinois................	80,685	59,375	19,587	19,219	39,788	30,606	4,732	4,450	–	21,310
Indiana...............	38,895	31,450	10,858	10,792	20,592	14,909	3,709	1,973	–	7,445
Iowa..................	24,089	18,097	7,044	6,822	11,053	7,236	2,630	1,187	214	5,777
Kansas................	18,582	14,988	4,941	4,871	10,047	6,798	2,369	880	–	3,594
Kentucky..............	31,052	23,568	9,025	8,862	14,543	10,199	3,087	1,257	–	7,483
Louisiana.............	33,975	26,939	12,533	12,438	14,406	8,865	3,300	2,241	6	7,029
Maine.................	10,611	8,249	3,241	3,228	5,008	3,676	792	540	–	2,361,950
Maryland..............	41,737	33,020	11,336	10,977	21,684	16,024	3,249	2,412	153	8,565
Massachusetts........	56,634	44,896	14,137	13,843	30,759	22,087	4,577	4,095	209	11,530
Michigan..............	64,430	54,717	19,914	19,712	34,803	23,530	7,395	3,878	812	8,901
Minnesota.............	45,684	33,452	9,819	9,656	23,632	18,953	2,782	1,897	–	12,233
Mississippi............	23,442	17,643	8,727	8,607	8,916	6,550	1,764	602	263	5,536
Missouri..............	38,607	27,083	12,015	11,703	15,068	10,110	2,778	2,180	–	11,524
Montana...............	7,951	5,769	2,415	2,407	3,354	2,304	606	445	73	2,108
Nebraska..............	11,523	9,389	3,402	3,353	5,988	4,153	1,037	797	–	2,134
Nevada................	17,597	10,444	2,827	2,656	7,617	6,332	735	550	89	7,064
New Hampshire........	8,542	6,273	2,159	1,943	4,115	2,341	986	788	540	1,729
New Jersey............	70,798	51,676	14,793	14,155	36,884	27,183	5,814	3,887	986	18,136
New Mexico...........	19,771	14,854	6,364	6,175	8,490	4,885	1,486	2,119	–	4,917
New York..............	205,546	148,841	60,200	53,714	88,641	67,945	9,206	11,490	7,991	48,715
North Carolina.........	63,194	45,853	16,049	15,711	29,804	22,401	4,689	2,715	27	17,341
North Dakota..........	7,806	6,683	1,737	1,701	4,946	3,822	742	381	–	1,123
Ohio..................	96,873	61,840	24,133	23,570	37,707	25,018	8,256	4,433	809	34,224
Oklahoma.............	26,235	20,199	7,874	7,756	12,326	7,776	2,560	1,989	573	5,462
Oregon................	34,797	20,823	7,609	7,589	13,215	8,119	3,356	1,740	438,829	13,535
Pennsylvania..........	91,705	69,499	23,843	23,614	45,657	32,352	8,623	4,682	1,571	20,635
Rhode Island..........	9,388	7,157	2,732	2,688	4,425	2,755	794	877	31	2,200
South Carolina........	31,733	22,792	8,690	8,235	14,102	7,687	4,470	1,944	1,881	7,061
South Dakota..........	6,017	4,124	1,879	1,850	2,245	1,380	337	529	–	1,893
Tennessee............	34,653	27,493	12,117	12,049	15,376	11,208	2,288	1,880	–	7,161
Texas.................	134,302	107,148	42,859	42,219	64,289	43,146	12,442	8,701	–	27,155
Utah..................	16,985	13,835	4,365	4,359	9,470	5,476	2,956	1,038	250	2,900
Vermont...............	6,506	5,628	2,035	2,026	3,593	2,688	607	298	47	831
Virginia...............	50,782	39,194	10,513	9,997	28,682	17,409	7,697	3,576	576	11,012
Washington............	50,420	34,993	10,944	10,637	24,049	17,411	4,501	2,137	587	14,840
West Virginia..........	15,398	12,714	4,749	4,668	7,966	5,211	1,484	1,271	86	2,597
Wisconsin.............	44,807	32,133	10,536	10,319	21,597	15,347	3,817	2,432	–	12,675
Wyoming..............	7,494	6,050	2,401	2,204	3,656	2,462	191	1,003	85	1,353

– Represents or rounds to zero. [1] Includes amounts for categories not shown separately. [2] Duplicate intergovernmental transactions are excluded.

Source: U.S. Census Bureau, Federal, State, and Local Governments, Government Finance Statistics, "Annual Surveys of State and Local Government Finances," <http://www.census.gov/govs/local/>, accessed August 2013.

Table 480. Governmental Employment and Payrolls: 1982 to 2011

[Employees in thousands (15,841 represents 15,841,000), payroll in millions of dollars (23,173 represents $23,173,000,000). Data are for the month of October through 1992. Beginning with the 1997 survey, data are for the month of March. Covers both full-time and part-time employees. Local government data are estimates subject to sampling variation; see Appendix III and source]

Type of government	1982	1987	1992	1997	2000	2005	2008	2009	2010	2011
EMPLOYEES (1,000)										
Total	**15,841**	**17,212**	**18,745**	**19,540**	**20,876**	**21,725**	**22,462**	**22,668**	**22,607**	**22,267**
Federal (civilian) [1]	2,848	3,091	3,047	2,807	2,899	2,720	2,769	2,824	3,008	2,854
State and local	12,993	14,121	15,698	16,733	17,976	19,004	19,693	19,844	19,599	19,413
Percent of total	82	82	84	86	86	87	88	88	87	87
State	3,744	4,116	4,595	4,733	4,877	5,078	5,270	5,346	5,326	5,314
Local	9,249	10,005	11,103	12,000	13,099	13,926	14,423	14,498	14,274	14,099
Counties	1,824	1,963	2,253	2,425	(NA)	(NA)	(NA)	(NA)	(NA)	(NA)
Municipalities	2,397	2,493	2,665	2,755	(NA)	(NA)	(NA)	(NA)	(NA)	(NA)
School districts	4,194	4,627	5,134	5,675	(NA)	(NA)	(NA)	(NA)	(NA)	(NA)
Townships	356	393	424	455	(NA)	(NA)	(NA)	(NA)	(NA)	(NA)
Special districts	478	529	627	691	(NA)	(NA)	(NA)	(NA)	(NA)	(NA)
PAYROLLS (mil. dol.)										
Total	**23,173**	**32,669**	**43,120**	**49,156**	**58,166**	**71,599**	**83,268**	**85,281**	**86,643**	**86,496**
Federal (civilian) [1]	5,959	7,924	9,937	9,744	11,485	13,475	15,472	15,106	16,238	16,119
State and local	17,214	24,745	33,183	39,412	46,681	58,123	67,796	70,175	70,404	70,378
Percent of total	74	76	77	80	80	81	81	82	81	81
State	5,022	7,263	9,828	11,413	13,279	16,062	18,726	19,425	19,579	19,972
Local	12,192	17,482	23,355	27,999	33,402	42,062	49,070	50,750	50,825	50,406
Counties	2,287	3,270	4,698	5,750	(NA)	(NA)	(NA)	(NA)	(NA)	(NA)
Municipalities	3,428	4,770	6,207	7,146	(NA)	(NA)	(NA)	(NA)	(NA)	(NA)
School districts	5,442	7,961	10,394	12,579	(NA)	(NA)	(NA)	(NA)	(NA)	(NA)
Townships	370	522	685	869	(NA)	(NA)	(NA)	(NA)	(NA)	(NA)
Special districts	665	959	1,370	1,654	(NA)	(NA)	(NA)	(NA)	(NA)	(NA)

NA Not available. [1] Includes employees outside the United States.

Source: U.S. Census Bureau, Governments Division, "Government Employment & Payroll," <http://www.census.gov/govs/apes/>, accessed July 2013.

Table 481. All Governments—Employment and Payroll by Function: 2011

[Employees in thousands (22,156 represents 22,156,000), payroll in millions of dollars (86,602 represents $86,602,000,000). See headnote, Table 480]

Function	Employees, total	Federal (civilian) [1]	State and local Total	State and local State	State and local Local	Payrolls Total	Federal (civilian) [1]	State and local Total	State and local State	State and local Local
Total	**22,156**	**2,854**	**19,302**	**5,314**	**13,988**	**86,602**	**16,119**	**70,483**	**19,972**	**50,512**
National defense [2]	806	806	(X)	(X)	(X)	3,020	3,020	(X)	(X)	(X)
Postal Service	632	632	(X)	(X)	(X)	3,628	3,628	(X)	(X)	(X)
Space research and technology	19	19	(X)	(X)	(X)	177	177	(X)	(X)	(X)
Elem. and secondary education	7,800	(X)	7,800	61	7,739	26,221	(X)	26,221	223	25,998
Higher education	3,169	(X)	3,169	2,550	619	9,855	(X)	9,855	8,215	1,640
Other education	104	11	93	93	–	450	75	375	375	–
Health	644	163	481	203	278	3,081	1,203	1,878	832	1,046
Hospitals	1,259	209	1,050	426	624	5,992	1,431	4,560	1,863	2,697
Public welfare	529	9	519	236	283	1,999	76	1,923	880	1,043
Social insurance administration	162	71	91	91	–	790	426	365	363	2
Police protection	1,200	189	1,011	106	905	6,256	1,179	5,077	569	4,508
Fire protection	410	(X)	410	(X)	410	1,982	(X)	1,982	(X)	1,982
Correction	772	38	733	466	267	3,243	223	3,020	1,921	1,099
Streets & highways	525	3	522	230	292	2,115	23	2,092	986	1,106
Air transportation	96	48	48	3	45	664	438	226	16	210
Water transport/terminals	19	5	13	5	9	81	13	68	24	44
Solid waste management	112	(X)	112	2	110	400	(X)	400	11	389
Sewerage	130	(X)	130	2	128	570	(X)	570	10	560
Parks & recreation	420	27	393	41	352	1,007	146	862	117	745
Natural resources	381	188	193	152	41	1,861	1,127	734	580	154
Housing & community development	130	15	114	–	114	577	112	465	–	465
Water supply	180	(X)	180	1	179	779	(X)	779	4	775
Electric power	80	(X)	80	4	76	518	(X)	518	27	491
Gas supply	11	(X)	11	–	11	46	(X)	46	–	46
Transit	240	(X)	240	34	206	1,205	(X)	1,205	190	1,015
Libraries	188	4	184	1	184	445	23	421	2	419
State liquor stores	12	(X)	12	12	(X)	30	(X)	30	30	(X)
Financial administration	542	128	414	166	247	2,469	774	1,695	718	977
Other government administration	403	25	378	58	319	1,326	158	1,168	244	924
Judicial and legal	503	64	439	177	262	2,470	437	2,032	903	1,129
Other & unallocable	680	199	481	194	287	3,343	1,428	1,915	868	1,047

– Represents or rounds to zero. X Not applicable. [1] Includes employees outside the United States. [2] Includes international relations.

Source: U.S. Census Bureau, Governments Division, *Annual Survey of Public Employment and Payroll Summary Report: 2011*, August 2013, and earlier reports. See also <http://www.census.gov//govs/apes/>.

Table 482. State and Local Government—Employer Costs Per Hour Worked: 2013

[In dollars. As of March. Based on a sample; see source for details]

Occupation and industry	Total compensation	Wages and salaries	Benefit cost					
			Total	Paid leave	Supplemental pay	Insurance	Retirement and savings	Legally required benefits
Total workers...	**42.12**	**27.27**	**14.85**	**3.09**	**0.33**	**5.10**	**3.78**	**2.55**
Occupational group:								
Management, professional, and related............	51.19	34.46	16.73	3.43	0.24	5.65	4.47	2.93
Professional and related............................	50.28	34.07	16.21	3.11	0.24	5.61	4.43	2.82
Teachers [1]..	57.53	40.26	17.26	2.82	0.14	6.06	5.14	3.10
Primary, secondary, and special education school teachers....................................	57.90	40.14	17.76	2.51	0.16	6.77	5.36	2.96
Sales and office.......................................	28.96	17.48	11.47	2.52	0.19	4.52	2.39	1.85
Office and administrative support................	29.15	17.55	11.60	2.56	0.19	4.59	2.41	1.85
Service..	31.17	18.37	12.80	2.72	0.56	4.19	3.25	2.09
Industry group:								
Education and health services.....................	44.10	29.60	14.50	2.77	0.21	5.27	3.75	2.49
Educational services...............................	44.77	30.24	14.53	2.62	0.15	5.36	3.91	2.48
Elementary and secondary schools............	44.30	29.97	14.33	2.26	0.16	5.56	3.95	2.40
Junior colleges, colleges, and universities......	46.71	31.49	15.23	3.87	0.13	4.59	3.87	2.76
Health care and social assistance................	39.82	25.54	14.28	3.69	0.58	4.70	2.73	2.58
Hospitals..	44.44	28.76	15.68	4.21	0.74	5.05	2.95	2.71
Public administration................................	40.14	24.10	16.04	3.78	0.55	4.97	4.07	2.67

[1] Includes postsecondary teachers; primary, secondary, and special education teachers; and other teachers and instructors.

Source: U.S. Bureau of Labor Statistics, National Compensation Survey, *Employer Costs for Employee Compensation–March 2013*, June 2013. See also <http://www.bls.gov/schedule/archives/ecec_nr.htm>.

Table 483. State and Local Government—Full-Time Employment and Salary by Sex and Race and Ethnic Group: 1980 to 2011

[2,350 represents 2,350,000. As of June 30. Excludes school systems and educational institutions. Based on reports from state governments (42 in 1980; 47 in 1983; 42 in 1980; 47 in 1983; 49 in 1981 and 1984 through 1987; and 50 in 1989 through 1991) and a sample of county, municipal, township, and special district jurisdictions employing 15 or more nonelected, nonappointed full-time employees. Beginning 1993, only for state and local governments with 100 or more employees. For definition of median, see Guide to Tabular Presentation]

Year and occupation	Employment (1,000)						Median annual salary ($1,000)					
				Minority						Minority		
	Male	Female	White [1]	Total [2]	Black [1]	Hispanic [3]	Male	Female	White [1]	Total [2]	Black [1]	Hispanic [3]
1980......................	2,350	1,637	3,146	842	619	163	15.2	11.4	13.8	11.8	11.5	12.3
1984......................	2,700	1,880	3,458	1,121	799	233	21.4	16.2	19.6	17.4	16.5	18.4
1985......................	2,789	1,952	3,563	1,179	835	248	22.3	17.3	20.6	18.4	17.5	19.2
1986......................	2,797	1,982	3,549	1,230	865	259	23.4	18.1	21.5	19.6	18.7	20.2
1987......................	2,818	2,031	3,600	1,249	872	268	24.2	18.9	22.4	20.9	19.3	21.1
1989......................	3,030	2,227	3,863	1,394	961	308	26.1	20.6	24.1	22.1	20.7	22.7
1990......................	3,071	2,302	3,918	1,456	994	327	27.3	21.8	25.2	23.3	22.0	23.8
1991......................	3,110	2,349	3,965	1,494	1,011	340	28.4	22.7	26.4	23.8	22.7	24.5
1993......................	2,820	2,204	3,588	1,436	948	341	30.6	24.3	28.5	25.9	24.2	26.8
1995......................	2,960	2,355	3,781	1,534	993	379	33.5	27.0	31.4	26.3	26.8	28.6
1997......................	2,898	2,307	3,676	1,529	973	392	34.6	27.9	32.2	30.2	27.4	29.5
1999......................	2,939	2,393	3,723	1,609	1,012	417	37.0	29.9	34.8	31.1	29.6	31.2
2001......................	3,080	2,554	3,888	1,746	1,077	471	39.8	32.1	37.5	34.0	31.5	33.8
2003......................	3,134	2,610	3,919	1,826	1,097	508	42.2	34.7	40.0	35.9	33.6	36.6
2005......................	3,185	2,644	3,973	1,856	1,100	532	44.1	36.4	41.5	37.7	35.3	38.9
2007......................	3,383	2,823	4,156	(NA)	(NA)	(NA)	(NA)	(NA)	(NA)	(NA)	(NA)	(NA)
2009......................	3,239	2,742	3,976	2,004	1,145	601	50.3	41.5	47.6	(NA)	40.3	44.8
2011, total.............	**2,924**	**2,477**	**3,561**	**1,839**	**1,015**	**570**	**51.8**	**43.1**	**49.1**	**(NA)**	**41.7**	**47.0**
Officials/ administrators.........	205	140	271	74	41	20	72.1	70.5	71.5	(NA)	71.2	71.8
Professionals............	617	868	1,019	466	244	115	63.9	54.8	58.8	(NA)	52.5	58.3
Technicians..............	244	185	289	140	70	46	50.7	41.9	47.5	(NA)	40.8	47.2
Protective service......	907	214	773	348	189	130	53.2	42.8	51.9	(NA)	44.1	58.1
Paraprofessionals.......	98	259	195	162	104	41	37.9	34.8	36.9	(NA)	33.1	36.5
Administrative support..	113	674	485	302	158	109	38.6	36.4	36.2	(NA)	36.3	38.0
Skilled craft..............	364	19	272	112	59	40	46.4	40.4	36.1	(NA)	42.6	47.8
Service/maintenance. ..	376	117	257	236	149	69	38.5	30.5	30.1	(NA)	34.9	37.4

NA Not available [1] Non-Hispanic. [2] Includes other minority groups, not shown separately. [3] Persons of Hispanic origin may be of any race.

Source: U.S. Equal Employment Opportunity Commission, 1980–1991, "Job Patterns for Minorities and Women in State and Local Government," annual; beginning 1993, biennial, <www.eeoc.gov>, accessed February 2013.

Table 484. State and Local Government Full-Time Equivalent Employment by Selected Function and State: 2011

[In thousands (1,846.9 represents 1,846,900). For March. Local government amounts are estimates subject to sampling variation; see Appendix III and source]

State	Total[1]		Education — Elementary and secondary		Higher education		Public welfare		Health		Hospitals		Highways		Police protection		Fire protection		Corrections		Parks and recreation	
	State	Local	State	Local	State	Local	State	Local	State	Local	State	Local	State	Local	State	Local	State	Local	State	Local	State	Local
U.S.	1,847	7,021	48.7	6,675	1,713	346.0	232.2	266.4	196.4	249.2	399.2	566.2	225.0	279.8	104.5	843.6	(X)	339.2	462.5	260.5	34.0	220.6
AL	41.5	102.4	—	102.4	38.4	—	4.4	1.4	6.2	5.7	12.2	25.0	4.7	6.3	1.6	12.3	(X)	5.9	5.5	3.4	.5	3.5
AK	9.0	17.4	3.2	17.3	5.4	.1	1.9	.2	.7	.3	.2	.8	3.1	.7	.7	1.2	(X)	.7	1.9	.1	.1	.6
AZ	33.3	122.0	—	108.6	30.1	13.3	4.8	1.5	2.4	4.0	.7	2.6	2.7	4.0	1.9	18.1	(X)	8.1	10.1	5.8	.3	4.8
AR	26.5	74.6	—	74.4	25.1	.2	4.0	.1	4.0	.1	6.8	1.5	3.4	3.5	1.2	8.0	(X)	3.2	5.4	2.5	.8	1.5
CA	162.6	702.2	—	631.3	158.2	70.9	3.5	65.9	12.9	45.9	43.4	65.9	20.3	19.9	11.6	91.3	(X)	33.1	60.0	34.2	3.4	32.3
CO	38.9	103.6	—	102.3	37.6	1.3	2.1	6.4	1.3	4.1	5.3	10.1	3.0	4.7	1.5	14.2	(X)	5.9	7.5	3.2	.3	6.7
CT	20.7	87.0	—	87.0	18.2	—	5.7	1.6	4.0	1.2	6.5	—	2.9	3.3	1.9	8.4	(X)	4.7	7.1	—	.3	1.9
DE	8.5	17.2	—	17.2	8.1	—	2.1	—	2.1	.3	1.6	—	1.5	.5	1.0	1.5	(X)	—	2.9	—	.3	.3
DC	(X)	8.8	(X)	7.7	(X)	1.0	(X)	2.0	(X)	.7	(X)	1.4	(X)	.9	(X)	4.5	(X)	1.9	(X)	1.3	(X)	.7
FL	59.0	382.6	—	351.5	55.9	31.2	10.1	5.3	20.2	5.1	3.8	51.2	7.4	12.8	4.3	59.8	(X)	30.4	30.4	16.0	1.3	16.8
GA	58.5	239.7	—	239.7	55.3	—	8.5	1.5	4.8	9.1	7.2	18.3	5.1	7.7	1.9	25.4	(X)	12.7	17.4	10.2	1.6	5.4
HI	37.5	—	27.4	—	10.0	1.9	.4	.2	2.0	.3	4.6	—	.8	1.0	—	3.9	(X)	1.9	2.3	—	.2	2.1
ID	8.7	34.1	—	32.2	8.3	—	1.6	6.1	2.0	.8	—	3.7	1.6	1.6	.5	3.9	(X)	1.2	1.7	1.7	.2	.8
IL	64.1	290.7	—	266.4	62.0	24.4	9.1	.9	2.4	6.7	11.1	11.9	6.8	12.7	3.5	53.9	(X)	17.4	11.7	10.6	.5	16.4
IN	59.2	137.8	—	137.8	58.1	7.0	4.6	1.2	1.7	2.8	2.2	25.3	3.8	5.0	1.9	13.6	(X)	7.6	6.3	6.1	.1	3.2
IA	23.9	75.2	—	68.2	22.7	—	2.8	.5	.5	2.1	7.9	11.3	2.3	5.3	1.0	6.2	(X)	1.9	3.1	1.6	.1	1.9
KS	20.6	100.1	—	90.9	19.9	9.2	2.2	.4	1.2	3.3	2.5	8.4	3.2	4.6	1.1	7.8	(X)	3.9	3.4	3.1	.6	2.2
KY	39.7	114.7	—	114.6	37.8	—	5.8	.8	3.2	6.1	5.2	5.1	4.5	2.8	2.3	7.5	(X)	4.1	4.2	3.7	1.1	1.7
LA	34.0	97.4	1.3	97.4	29.5	—	5.3	.4	3.1	1.8	13.2	19.6	4.6	4.9	1.8	16.4	(X)	5.0	6.6	7.4	1.0	4.2
ME	7.6	41.2	.38	41.2	7.4	.2	3.4	.5	1.0	.2	.5	.8	2.1	1.5	.5	2.4	(X)	1.7	1.2	.8	.4	.6
MD	30.1	142.6	—	130.1	28.1	12.5	6.4	3.3	6.2	4.7	3.9	—	4.5	5.6	2.3	17.3	(X)	6.8	12.3	3.8	.4	6.8
MA	32.4	145.6	.1	145.6	31.2	—	6.9	2.7	6.5	3.1	5.8	2.5	2.4	5.8	6.0	17.8	(X)	12.7	5.9	5.7	1.0	2.1
MI	76.4	194.0	—	178.3	75.8	15.7	10.4	3.0	1.7	10.3	18.9	9.6	2.6	8.5	2.4	18.9	(X)	7.0	14.5	5.1	.3	4.0
MN	40.9	117.8	—	117.8	37.0	—	2.8	10.3	2.5	3.0	4.7	7.2	4.7	7.4	1.0	11.0	(X)	2.7	4.2	2.2	.6	4.6
MS	21.0	78.4	—	73.3	19.5	5.1	2.9	.5	3.1	.2	12.3	19.9	3.3	4.6	1.2	8.6	(X)	3.4	3.2	3.4	.4	1.1
MO	30.3	138.8	—	130.6	28.6	8.1	7.3	3.1	2.9	3.6	10.5	13.9	6.1	6.2	2.5	16.3	(X)	7.4	12.3	3.8	.5	4.4
MT	7.7	23.1	—	22.7	7.3	.4	1.7	.5	.9	1.0	.6	.6	2.1	1.2	.5	2.2	(X)	.7	1.3	.7	.1	.4
NE	13.1	53.0	—	49.6	12.5	3.3	2.4	1.0	.7	1.6	3.8	4.8	2.1	2.9	.8	4.2	(X)	1.4	2.9	1.5	.3	.9
NV	10.0	47.4	—	47.4	9.9	—	1.7	2.6	1.4	1.0	1.4	4.0	1.8	1.1	1.0	7.6	(X)	3.0	3.5	2.8	.2	3.4
NH	7.2	36.1	—	36.1	6.9	—	1.6	.6	.9	2.6	.7	—	1.9	1.7	.5	3.5	(X)	1.1	1.1	1.1	.2	.5
NJ	52.2	214.9	15.9	203.1	33.5	11.3	8.9	10.1	4.4	4.1	17.6	2.3	5.9	10.0	4.1	31.6	(X)	7.2	9.2	6.6	2.0	5.5
NM	19.9	50.3	—	46.8	19.0	3.5	1.7	.8	2.4	.6	7.5	1.1	2.1	1.9	.5	5.4	(X)	2.3	3.8	2.5	.7	1.8
NY	56.2	496.0	—	473.3	52.2	22.7	4.7	46.3	9.1	17.5	43.8	47.8	11.5	26.3	6.1	78.5	(X)	24.0	31.8	24.2	2.3	11.8
NC	68.4	228.2	—	205.6	65.5	22.6	1.3	15.5	2.8	16.5	20.0	41.5	11.0	4.0	3.4	24.5	(X)	8.9	21.2	5.3	1.8	6.0
ND	9.3	16.9	—	16.9	8.9	—	.5	.1	1.4	.8	.9	—	1.1	1.1	.2	1.3	(X)	1.3	.8	—	.6	.3
OH	71.2	253.5	—	249.2	68.9	4.3	2.8	20.2	3.5	16.7	15.8	10.8	6.9	12.4	2.5	28.9	(X)	15.4	15.3	8.0	.6	8.3
OK	32.1	93.4	—	93.0	30.3	.4	6.3	.1	5.3	1.6	1.9	10.2	3.0	5.4	1.9	8.8	(X)	4.1	4.9	1.7	.8	1.4
OR	24.2	77.2	—	68.8	23.5	8.5	7.6	1.1	1.6	4.3	6.5	2.4	3.9	3.3	1.3	7.8	(X)	3.8	5.1	3.6	.5	3.2
PA	65.1	271.5	.625	267.2	60.9	4.4	11.8	18.0	1.9	5.8	11.6	—	14.7	10.8	6.6	27.1	(X)	5.1	18.5	12.9	2.5	3.8
RI	6.8	19.5	—	19.5	5.7	—	1.3	.1	1.0	.1	1.8	—	.8	1.0	.3	3.1	(X)	2.4	1.5	.6	.1	.6
SC	32.4	98.9	—	98.9	29.4	—	4.9	.5	5.8	2.2	6.9	22.5	4.6	2.6	1.9	12.3	(X)	4.7	7.5	3.4	.7	2.9
SD	5.8	19.9	—	19.4	5.5	.6	1.1	.2	.7	.3	1.0	.3	1.0	1.7	.3	1.7	(X)	.5	.9	.7	.6	.6
TN	36.9	136.4	—	136.4	34.7	—	7.8	2.3	9.5	4.2	25.4	19.8	4.0	6.2	6.6	17.4	(X)	8.1	7.0	5.8	1.1	3.3
TX	136.9	751.1	—	704.1	132.1	47.0	23.0	3.4	29.9	24.7	7.0	52.2	13.4	20.4	6.6	70.6	(X)	25.2	43.4	25.4	1.2	14.6
UT	27.6	56.0	—	56.0	26.5	—	2.9	.8	1.8	4.0	7.0	.4	1.6	2.1	.8	5.8	(X)	2.5	3.1	2.1	.3	3.2
VT	6.0	19.9	—	19.9	5.5	.1	1.3	.3	.5	.3	.3	—	1.0	1.2	.5	.9	(X)	.4	1.1	.2	.3	.2
VA	58.3	198.4	—	196.5	55.5	1.9	2.8	8.6	5.5	5.9	14.6	2.5	7.0	3.6	2.9	18.2	(X)	10.9	13.9	10.7	1.1	7.4

See footnotes at end of table.

Table 484. State and Local Government Full-Time Equivalent Employment by Selected Function and State: 2011-Continued.

See headnote on page 321.

State	Total [1]		Education				Public welfare		Health		Hospitals		Highways		Police protection		Fire protection		Corrections		Parks and recreation	
			Elementary and secondary		Higher education																	
	State	Local	State	Local	State	Local	State	Local	State	Local	State	Local	State	Local	State	Local	State	Local	State	Local	State	Local
WA....	56.7	100.4	—	100.4	54.6	—	9.4	1.7	4.9	3.6	10.5	15.7	7.3	6.9	2.2	12.7	(X)	9.6	9.1	4.8	.6	5.0
WV....	14.8	43.6	—	43.6	13.5	5	3.4	25	.8	1.2	1.8	2.6	5.2	.8	1.0	2.8	(X)	1.0	3.4	.1	.6	.8
WI....	39.3	127.8	—	115.7	38.3	12.1	1.9	11.7	1.5	5.6	3.1	1.2	1.4	8.8	.9	14.8	(X)	4.7	9.8	4.0	.1	3.0
WY....	4.0	21.4	—	20.1	3.7	1.3	.8	.1	.8	.5	.7	6.8	1.8	.8	.3	1.7	(X)	.5	1.4	.7	.2	1.0

— Represents or rounds to zero. X Not applicable. [1] Includes other categories, not shown separately.

Source: U.S. Census Bureau, 2011 Annual Survey of Public Employment and Payroll, August 2013. See also <http://www.census.gov/govs/apes/>.

Table 485. State and Local Government Employment and Average Monthly Earnings by State: 2000 to 2011

[4,083 represents 4,083,000. As of March. Full-time equivalent employment is a derived statistic that provides an estimate of a government's total full-time employment by converting part-time employees to a full-time amount]

State	Full-time equivalent employment (1,000)						Average monthly earnings [2] (dol.)					
	State			Local [1]			State			Local [1]		
	2000	2010	2011	2000	2010	2011	2000	2010	2011	2000	2010	2011
United States...	**4,083**	**4,378**	**4,359**	**10,995**	**12,171**	**11,974**	**3,374**	**4,620**	**4,735**	**3,169**	**4,310**	**4,356**
Alabama..........	80	90	90	182	198	195	2,841	4,099	4,172	2,431	3,240	3,267
Alaska............	23	27	27	25	28	28	3,842	5,176	5,312	3,818	4,935	5,006
Arizona...........	65	67	69	182	225	210	3,055	4,365	4,434	2,942	4,163	4,159
Arkansas.........	49	63	63	96	106	113	2,842	3,795	3,940	2,175	3,208	3,081
California.........	355	411	407	1,322	1,381	1,349	4,451	5,740	6,161	4,062	5,787	5,891
Colorado.........	66	71	72	164	199	198	3,779	5,033	5,044	3,076	4,230	4,282
Connecticut......	66	63	62	111	123	122	3,909	5,632	5,866	3,856	5,063	5,201
Delaware.........	24	26	26	21	23	23	3,222	4,113	4,241	3,163	4,484	4,577
District of Columbia.......	(X)	(X)	(X)	45	44	43	(X)	(X)	(X)	3,923	5,900	6,069
Florida............	185	184	184	580	727	706	3,149	3,861	3,883	2,865	3,986	3,997
Georgia...........	120	124	124	334	392	385	2,899	3,795	3,907	2,677	3,439	3,461
Hawaii............	55	58	58	14	15	16	2,926	3,943	4,024	3,352	5,040	4,927
Idaho.............	23	22	22	51	55	56	3,022	4,280	4,510	2,478	3,341	3,286
Illinois............	128	131	131	493	513	511	3,441	5,324	5,432	3,307	4,716	4,955
Indiana...........	83	90	90	232	254	239	2,990	4,023	4,158	2,711	3,547	3,654
Iowa..............	55	51	50	121	124	123	3,656	5,326	5,609	2,727	3,831	3,928
Kansas...........	43	44	44	128	156	152	3,071	4,178	4,228	2,491	3,361	3,394
Kentucky.........	74	81	81	149	161	165	3,051	3,940	3,867	2,339	3,101	3,120
Louisiana.........	95	89	84	185	187	185	2,807	4,282	4,313	2,278	3,397	3,414
Maine.............	21	21	21	51	51	56	2,983	4,063	4,156	2,609	3,545	3,551
Maryland.........	91	88	87	182	215	222	3,312	4,650	4,703	3,535	5,190	5,060
Massachusetts. ..	96	95	92	232	233	230	3,683	4,973	5,110	3,403	4,800	4,956
Michigan..........	142	146	145	351	329	310	3,934	5,208	5,304	3,518	4,618	4,649
Minnesota........	73	80	80	206	201	198	3,892	5,338	5,437	3,255	4,447	4,532
Mississippi........	56	57	58	133	136	133	2,752	3,537	3,690	2,121	2,985	2,972
Missouri..........	91	89	87	208	234	230	2,678	3,518	3,549	2,678	3,502	3,538
Montana..........	18	20	21	34	38	36	2,931	4,016	4,126	2,546	3,476	3,603
Nebraska.........	30	33	32	78	88	88	2,514	4,013	4,125	2,779	3,785	3,955
Nevada...........	22	28	28	61	86	86	3,444	4,891	4,856	3,817	5,149	5,128
New Hampshire...	19	19	19	46	53	53	3,079	4,584	4,650	2,830	3,813	3,881
New Jersey.......	133	152	147	316	356	340	4,075	5,767	5,930	3,967	5,449	5,498
New Mexico.......	48	48	47	70	80	79	2,811	3,978	3,961	2,494	3,440	3,451
New York.........	251	251	244	924	975	934	3,859	5,484	5,679	3,961	5,315	5,445
North Carolina....	123	146	154	328	402	401	3,012	3,886	3,963	2,708	3,690	3,553
North Dakota......	16	18	19	23	26	26	2,826	4,103	4,255	2,778	3,550	3,626
Ohio..............	136	140	139	459	466	455	3,369	4,995	5,049	3,118	4,101	4,154
Oklahoma.........	64	71	68	134	146	146	2,821	3,864	3,913	2,280	3,119	3,096
Oregon...........	53	65	66	124	133	132	3,269	4,452	4,622	3,332	4,348	4,458
Pennsylvania.....	150	168	169	388	429	428	3,436	4,564	4,687	3,296	4,290	4,383
Rhode Island.....	20	19	19	36	31	31	3,772	5,298	5,483	3,550	4,953	5,091
South Carolina....	79	77	77	155	171	175	2,741	3,810	3,799	2,474	3,557	3,433
South Dakota.....	13	14	14	28	31	31	2,777	3,938	3,971	2,359	3,149	3,166
Tennessee.......	81	83	86	218	247	241	2,786	3,822	3,718	2,631	3,358	3,308
Texas.............	269	318	318	909	1,134	1,130	3,095	4,280	4,392	2,643	3,604	3,658
Utah..............	49	51	54	73	90	94	2,880	4,409	4,438	2,836	3,706	3,701
Vermont..........	14	14	14	23	26	25	3,153	4,645	4,609	2,534	3,589	3,701
Virginia...........	119	125	125	269	319	315	3,229	4,384	4,373	2,928	3,905	3,875
Washington.......	112	123	121	193	226	220	3,551	4,913	5,086	3,835	5,416	5,571
West Virginia......	32	39	40	61	62	63	2,694	3,554	3,618	2,517	3,219	3,207
Wisconsin........	64	72	71	220	211	209	3,710	4,901	5,003	3,210	4,239	4,331
Wyoming.........	11	14	13	29	37	39	2,589	4,240	4,248	2,660	4,068	4,082

X Not applicable. [1] Estimates subject to sampling variation; see Appendix III and source. [2] For full-time employees.

Source: U.S. Census Bureau; *2011 Annual Survey of Public Employment and Payroll*, August 2013. See also <http://www.census.gov/govs/apes/>.

Table 486. City Government Employment and Payroll—Largest Cities: 2000 to 2011

[In thousands (458.1 represents 458,100), except as noted. As of March. Full-time equivalent employment is a derived statistic that provides an estimate of a government's total full-time employment by converting part-time employees to a full-time amount.]

Cities ranked by 2011 population [1]	Total employment (1,000)			Full-time equivalent employment total (1,000)			Payroll (mil. dol.)			Average monthly earnings for full-time employees (dol.)		
	2000	2010	2011	2000	2010	2011	2000	2010	2011	2000	2010	2011
New York, NY	458.1	444.0	443.0	429.3	413.0	399.9	1,708.8	2,407.5	2,360.6	4,150	5,918	6,000
Los Angeles, CA	49.4	55.1	59.1	48.4	51.0	51.3	230.1	385.2	384.1	4,793	7,850	7,793
Chicago, IL	41.3	35.8	49.1	40.7	35.8	48.1	171.3	216.5	324.6	4,239	6,052	6,746
Houston, TX	25.2	22.8	22.5	24.9	22.6	22.1	75.2	99.0	95.1	3,037	4,389	4,316
Philadelphia, PA	31.1	30.8	30.8	30.0	29.9	29.6	109.2	144.7	144.0	3,637	4,867	4,879
Phoenix, AZ	13.0	14.9	14.9	12.7	14.4	13.9	50.3	80.7	78.4	4,024	5,718	5,724
San Antonio, TX	16.9	16.5	16.2	15.7	15.4	15.3	48.0	64.9	66.3	3,160	4,293	4,403
San Diego, CA	12.3	10.8	10.7	11.4	10.2	9.5	46.9	63.0	61.1	4,201	6,288	6,563
Dallas, TX	15.6	15.5	15.1	15.2	15.1	14.5	50.4	72.8	67.9	3,332	4,884	4,731
San Jose, CA	7.6	7.6	7.4	6.9	6.7	5.9	36.3	52.5	46.7	5,569	8,401	8,315
Jacksonville, FL	10.1	9.7	10.0	9.7	9.4	9.4	35.6	41.8	43.2	3,815	4,487	4,633
Indianapolis, IN	12.4	14.2	13.9	12.0	13.7	12.4	36.7	54.8	49.1	3,115	4,050	4,000
Austin, TX	10.6	12.6	12.9	10.1	12.3	12.4	31.2	59.5	61.7	3,128	4,863	4,986
San Francisco, CA	27.7	30.7	32.2	27.7	27.3	28.7	141.6	207.2	213.7	5,112	7,666	7,559
Columbus, OH	9.1	8.2	8.4	8.8	7.9	7.9	30.1	40.6	42.0	3,478	5,210	5,357
Ft Worth, TX	6.1	6.3	7.1	5.7	6.2	6.4	18.9	28.7	32.0	3,394	4,618	5,124
Charlotte, NC	5.2	7.4	7.9	5.1	6.9	7.1	17.1	31.2	32.8	3,408	4,570	4,733
Detroit, MI	40.7	13.1	12.0	36.1	12.9	11.6	132.1	58.4	54.3	3,693	4,570	4,708
El Paso, TX	5.9	5.9	6.3	5.8	5.6	6.0	15.6	21.2	23.7	2,701	3,836	4,013
Memphis, TN	28.2	24.5	24.6	26.9	23.5	22.6	80.3	87.1	80.0	3,024	3,746	3,569
Boston, MA	23.3	19.9	20.6	22.0	19.3	19.2	80.2	104.0	109.8	3,734	5,452	5,818
Seattle, WA	11.4	13.9	12.4	10.3	12.5	10.7	48.3	72.4	69.9	4,726	5,948	6,791
Denver, CO	14.5	13.0	13.6	13.7	12.3	12.2	47.3	65.2	66.9	3,534	5,388	5,542
Baltimore, MD	30.8	27.9	28.2	29.2	26.7	26.5	95.3	121.8	119.1	3,361	4,597	4,560
Washington, DC	37.7	35.2	34.4	36.5	34.0	32.4	139.4	197.8	192.8	3,863	5,893	6,055
Nashville, TN	20.6	23.9	24.8	19.6	21.7	21.6	62.3	91.4	83.3	3,235	4,311	3,925
Louisville, KY	4.6	8.9	9.1	4.3	8.6	8.4	11.8	33.9	33.3	2,844	4,028	4,026
Milwaukee, WI	7.9	6.9	6.9	7.7	6.7	6.5	28.5	33.3	33.3	3,706	5,020	5,144
Portland, OR	6.2	6.8	7.0	5.4	5.8	5.7	23.4	35.1	35.0	4,416	6,253	6,349
Oklahoma City, OK	5.1	4.7	4.7	4.8	4.4	4.3	16.0	21.0	22.0	3,457	4,858	5,219
Las Vegas, NV	2.6	3.2	3.1	2.5	2.9	2.6	11.2	19.3	17.9	4,681	7,162	7,343
Albuquerque, NM	7.1	7.0	7.4	6.6	6.5	6.5	18.3	22.9	33.2	2,868	3,654	5,303
Tucson, AZ	7.1	5.6	5.5	5.8	5.3	4.9	16.0	23.5	22.7	2,787	4,545	4,722
Fresno, CA	3.2	4.1	4.0	3.1	4.0	3.7	12.7	20.2	20.0	4,073	5,260	5,612
Sacramento, CA	4.4	5.7	5.0	4.0	5.0	4.2	17.0	28.1	26.3	4,400	6,061	6,569
Long Beach, CA	6.1	6.6	6.9	5.7	6.1	6.0	25.7	35.0	34.2	4,855	5,982	5,985
Kansas City, MO	6.8	6.4	6.6	6.6	6.3	6.6	21.3	27.3	29.8	3,246	4,324	4,481
Mesa, AZ	3.5	3.6	3.8	3.3	3.5	3.7	13.4	19.2	20.5	4,072	5,532	5,674
Virginia Beach, VA	19.7	19.2	22.5	17.4	17.7	18.3	43.4	61.1	63.5	2,679	3,775	3,758
Atlanta, GA	8.8	8.1	8.1	8.6	8.1	8.1	25.6	31.5	31.0	2,974	3,872	3,828
Colorado Springs, CO	7.4	8.3	8.0	6.9	7.6	6.9	25.3	39.8	36.6	3,747	5,307	5,401
Raleigh, NC	3.2	5.1	4.6	2.9	4.2	3.9	8.9	16.3	15.7	3,114	4,166	4,209
Omaha, NE	3.4	3.1	3.4	2.9	2.9	2.8	10.6	14.8	14.6	3,874	5,491	5,437
Miami, FL	3.8	4.3	4.3	3.6	4.1	3.9	15.1	21.2	20.0	4,276	5,378	5,185
Tulsa, OK	4.5	4.0	4.0	4.5	3.9	3.9	13.7	16.8	18.1	3,126	4,376	4,719
Oakland, CA	4.2	4.1	5.5	4.2	3.6	4.2	24.8	28.4	31.3	5,861	8,702	8,225
Cleveland, OH	10.1	8.4	8.4	9.4	7.9	7.8	27.8	35.2	35.4	2,989	4,462	4,577
Minneapolis, MN	6.3	5.5	5.7	5.8	5.1	5.1	21.3	25.7	25.9	3,866	5,159	5,192
Wichita, KS	3.6	3.1	3.3	3.1	3.1	3.2	9.3	13.0	11.6	3,072	4,198	3,697
Arlington, TX	3.0	2.9	3.0	2.4	2.6	2.5	7.1	12.1	12.2	3,090	4,878	5,021
New Orleans, LA	(NA)	6.9	6.8	(NA)	6.8	6.6	(NA)	25.9	25.7	(NA)	3,815	3,920
Bakersfield, CA	1.3	1.5	1.5	1.2	1.5	1.4	5.3	8.2	8.2	4,468.7	5,691	5,903
Tampa, FL	4.3	4.5	4.5	4.2	4.4	4.2	14.1	23.2	22.5	3,370	5,376	5,395
Anaheim, CA	3.2	3.2	3.6	2.5	2.6	2.5	11.5	17.4	16.5	5,267	7,982	7,613
Honolulu, HI	9.8	9.5	10.2	9.1	8.8	9.3	30.9	45.8	46.2	3,435	5,266	5,048
Aurora, CO	2.5	2.6	2.6	2.5	2.6	2.6	9.0	13.8	14.0	3,682	5,374	5,431
Santa Ana, CA	2.5	1.7	2.0	2.2	1.5	1.6	10.1	12.1	12.2	5,606	8,623	8,256
St Louis, MO	8.0	6.9	6.5	7.6	6.8	6.3	24.1	26.8	25.0	3,176	3,973	3,964
Riverside, CA	2.1	2.4	2.6	1.9	2.2	2.2	8.0	13.8	14.3	4,625	6,536	6,853
Corpus Christi, TX	3.5	2.8	2.9	3.3	2.8	2.7	8.6	10.5	10.6	2,675	3,848	3,933
Pittsburgh, PA	4.4	3.3	3.5	4.3	3.3	3.3	15.3	13.8	15.3	3,593	4,210	4,782
Lexington, KY	4.0	4.1	4.2	3.6	3.8	3.8	10.2	16.6	16.8	2,910	4,575	4,569
Stockton, CA	2.3	1.8	2.0	1.9	1.6	1.6	7.1	9.4	9.9	4,054	6,160	6,661
Cincinnati, OH	6.5	5.9	6.3	6.4	5.6	5.6	21.3	27.9	26.4	3,504	5,122	4,860
Anchorage, AK	10.1	11.1	11.3	9.0	9.9	9.8	34.6	50.6	52.2	3,973	5,142	5,372
St Paul, MN	4.2	3.2	3.6	3.2	3.0	3.0	13.3	16.4	16.5	4,189	5,751	5,842
Toledo, OH	2.8	2.6	2.2	2.8	2.6	2.2	10.0	11.7	10.2	3,628	4,551	4,681
Newark, NJ	5.5	4.7	4.2	5.2	4.5	3.8	22.3	26.6	22.1	4,371	6,061	5,939
Greensboro, NC	(NA)	3.4	3.5	(NA)	3.1	3.1	(NA)	11.6	11.4	(NA)	3,837	3,789
Plano, TX	2.0	2.5	2.8	1.8	2.2	2.3	6.4	10.2	10.4	3,702	4,927	4,649
Lincoln, NE	2.7	2.9	3.1	2.5	2.6	2.6	8.2	12.4	13.1	3,382	4,982	5,211
Buffalo, NY	11.4	11.3	10.7	10.5	10.0	9.2	43.4	45.9	45.1	4,457	4,569	4,920
Henderson, NV	(NA)	2.7	3.1	(NA)	2.2	2.2	(NA)	13.7	13.5	(NA)	7,007	7,046
Ft Wayne, IN	(NA)	2.1	2.1	(NA)	2.0	2.0	(NA)	8.6	8.6	(NA)	4,319	4,480
Jersey City, NJ	(NA)	3.6	3.7	(NA)	3.4	3.3	(NA)	20.2	19.6	(NA)	6,122	6,102
Chula Vista, CA	(NA)	1.4	1.3	(NA)	1.3	1.1	(NA)	7.9	7.2	(NA)	6,314	6,635

NA Not applicable. [1] Based on estimated resident population as of July 1.

Source: U.S. Census Bureau, *2011 Annual Survey of Public Employment and Payroll*, August 2013. See also <http://www.census.gov/govs/apes/>.

Table 487. County Government Employment and Payroll—Largest Counties: 1999 to 2011

[In thousands (93.3 represents 93,300). As of March. Full-time equivalent employment is a derived statistic that provides an estimate of a government's total full-time employment by converting part-time employees to a full-time amount.]

Counties ranked by 2011 population [1]	Total employment (1,000)			Total full-time equivalent employment (1,000)		Payroll (mil. dol.)			Average monthly earnings for full-time employees (dol.)	
	1999	2010	2011	1999	2011	1999	2010	2011	1999	2011
Los Angeles, CA.........	93.3	107.5	108.6	89.7	105.3	368.6	610.3	607.9	4,165	5,807
Cook, IL....................	27.4	22.8	25.0	27.4	24.9	91.2	120.7	139.1	3,333	5,593
Harris, TX.................	19.4	27.8	26.1	19.1	25.6	56.8	119.8	116.0	2,981	4,572
Maricopa, AZ.............	14.6	13.7	13.0	14.5	12.7	36.9	54.2	54.1	2,562	4,247
San Diego, CA...........	19.1	20.9	20.3	18.1	18.9	62.8	101.1	100.7	3,513	5,302
Orange, CA...............	22.8	17.7	18.2	21.4	17.7	71.1	102.9	107.1	3,358	6,085
Dade, FL..................	36.6	51.1	45.5	35.6	44.4	123.3	285.0	280.5	3,546	6,443
Dallas, TX................	12.5	18.1	17.9	11.9	16.7	34.2	76.6	77.8	2,881	4,643
Riverside, CA............	14.7	21.0	21.3	14.3	20.4	51.9	110.8	117.1	3,688	5,764
San Bernardino, CA.....	18.1	21.2	20.7	16.8	19.4	58.2	101.7	100.2	3,553	5,305
Clark, NV.................	15.6	22.4	21.4	14.2	19.6	54.8	121.5	120.4	3,982	6,307
King, WA.................	16.1	14.1	13.8	14.2	13.0	52.9	82.3	81.7	3,867	6,379
Tarrant, TX..............	6.6	11.0	12.8	6.4	12.0	17.1	46.0	50.0	2,717	4,138
Santa Clara, CA.........	15.2	19.0	18.9	14.6	18.0	62.3	129.6	127.4	3,658	7,232
Wayne, MI................	6.7	4.7	4.5	6.6	4.5	24.0	21.5	20.6	4,342	4,682
Broward, FL..............	10.7	12.1	11.5	10.5	11.2	33.5	61.4	54.3	3,220	4,883
Bexar, TX................	9.2	11.0	11.0	8.9	10.6	22.4	41.3	42.5	2,545	3,957
Alameda, CA.............	11.5	12.1	13.5	10.6	13.0	45.4	77.2	94.6	4,263	7,347
Suffolk, NY..............	12.7	15.0	14.7	11.8	12.8	49.1	74.7	75.0	4,300	5,994
Sacramento, CA.........	12.7	13.1	12.9	11.7	12.1	46.7	72.5	73.6	3,963	6,117
Nassau, NY...............	18.5	18.0	16.5	17.4	14.8	73.5	88.5	84.0	4,518	5,762
Palm Beach, FL..........	8.4	11.3	11.2	8.2	10.7	26.0	60.7	60.4	3,193	5,784
Cuyahoga, OH...........	15.7	14.6	14.8	15.7	14.4	46.2	62.1	65.1	2,939	4,463
Hillsborough, FL.........	14.5	10.5	10.3	12.4	9.9	30.2	45.7	44.5	2,640	4,543
Allegheny, PA............	7.3	7.1	7.3	7.2	7.2	18.0	26.3	27.1	2,530	3,833
Oakland, MI..............	4.7	4.3	4.2	4.4	3.9	15.2	18.8	18.1	3,537	4,792
Franklin, OH.............	7.1	6.7	6.7	6.8	6.4	18.1	25.3	25.5	2,727	4,017
Orange, FL...............	9.4	11.3	11.1	8.8	10.3	26.1	43.8	42.6	3,705	4,152
Hennepin, MN............	12.9	7.7	7.7	10.9	7.5	40.0	40.3	40.7	2,986	5,568
Fairfax, VA...............	34.3	47.6	41.5	31.5	39.1	107.5	200.7	199.3	3,514	5,143
Contra Costa, CA........	9.9	8.6	8.6	9.1	7.9	41.0	49.8	49.4	4,620	6,328
Travis, TX................	3.6	5.3	5.3	3.5	5.3	10.4	22.0	22.4	3,176	4,254
Salt Lake, UT............	5.6	7.1	7.5	4.2	5.7	12.2	18.2	21.2	2,949	4,167
St. Louis, MO............	4.1	4.1	4.0	4.0	3.9	12.0	15.9	15.7	3,052	4,022
Montgomery, MD........	36.8	43.3	42.6	28.5	35.6	116.3	232.5	220.3	2,717	6,551
Pima, AZ.................	7.9	7.7	7.3	7.1	6.8	18.8	28.3	27.0	4,401	4,057
Westchester, NY.........	10.4	11.6	10.9	9.8	9.6	40.0	66.5	65.8	4,067	6,884
Milwaukee, WI...........	8.2	7.3	7.2	7.8	6.8	25.9	30.1	30.8	3,374	4,583
Fulton, GA...............	7.9	6.0	6.0	7.6	5.8	23.5	23.1	23.1	3,190	4,074
Mecklenburg, NC........	23.1	28.3	26.8	20.4	25.3	54.0	104.4	91.3	2,825	3,637
Fresno, CA...............	7.5	9.0	8.8	7.2	8.3	22.3	37.6	37.6	3,203	4,562
Shelby, TN...............	13.6	13.9	13.8	12.9	13.2	36.2	48.5	50.2	2,722	3,815
Wake, NC................	16.9	25.5	25.7	14.9	22.6	39.5	88.1	89.1	3,538	3,935
Du Page, IL..............	3.6	3.0	2.8	3.4	2.7	10.3	12.5	11.6	3,097	4,303
Erie, NY..................	12.3	11.2	7.1	10.6	5.9	35.5	44.2	25.5	2,915	4,417
Pinellas, FL..............	5.7	6.2	5.5	5.6	5.4	16.2	26.9	24.3	2,686	4,522
Bergen, NJ...............	5.7	6.0	5.9	4.1	4.9	13.2	26.8	27.1	3,273	5,883
Prince Georges, MD.....	30.0	35.7	35.2	27.2	29.1	84.6	155.6	154.3	3,195	5,447
Kern, CA.................	9.0	11.3	10.0	8.7	9.6	29.4	55.6	53.3	3,426	5,685
Macomb, MI..............	3.0	3.1	2.5	2.8	2.3	8.7	11.7	9.6	3,245	4,372
Ventura, CA..............	8.3	9.3	9.4	8.1	8.9	30.2	57.0	57.9	3,754	6,651
Gwinnett, GA.............	3.7	5.3	5.2	3.5	5.0	10.7	20.4	21.3	3,528	4,348
El Paso, TX..............	3.7	5.1	5.3	3.6	5.2	9.0	20.4	21.3	3,090	4,235
Middlesex, NJ............	5.5	4.6	4.9	4.9	4.1	16.9	19.5	21.8	3,172	5,506
Collin, TX................	1.0	2.0	2.0	1.0	2.0	2.7	7.6	7.8	2,573	3,959
Baltimore, MD............	25.7	30.6	30.8	22.6	26.4	66.5	122.2	121.6	2,604	4,931
Pierce, WA...............	3.4	3.5	3.4	3.2	3.3	13.7	20.2	20.4	2,690	6,162
Montgomery, PA.........	3.7	3.6	3.6	3.5	3.5	9.0	13.0	13.1	4,367	3,849
Hamilton, OH.............	6.0	5.1	5.0	5.8	4.9	15.0	19.0	18.9	2,617	3,897
Hidalgo, TX..............	1.6	2.9	3.0	1.6	3.0	3.3	9.1	9.2	3,573	3,127
Essex, NJ................	6.5	5.2	5.9	5.8	5.3	20.2	24.3	27.8	2,040	5,450
Multnomah, OR..........	5.7	4.9	5.0	4.6	4.6	12.6	22.4	23.4	3,157	5,125
Monroe, NY..............	6.9	7.1	7.1	6.0	6.0	18.9	25.6	25.5	2,990	4,336
Oklahoma, OK...........	2.4	2.4	2.3	2.3	2.2	4.2	6.5	6.5	1,834	3,045
San Mateo, CA..........	6.1	7.3	7.1	5.8	6.6	23.9	41.7	40.9	4,346	7,191
Snohomish, WA..........	2.4	2.7	2.7	2.4	2.7	8.6	14.9	14.5	3,643	5,472
Lake, IL..................	2.9	3.3	3.2	2.7	2.9	8.5	14.2	14.1	3,000	4,967
Dekalb, GA..............	6.2	7.5	7.0	6.1	6.8	18.1	27.9	25.8	2,933	3,798
Cobb, GA................	4.0	5.0	5.0	3.8	4.5	10.7	18.7	18.8	3,364	4,271
San Joaquin, CA.........	7.1	8.3	7.4	6.5	6.6	20.7	37.6	36.8	3,052	5,779
Denton, TX...............	(NA)	1.9	1.9	(NA)	1.9	(NA)	7.0	7.1	2,403	3,772
Will, IL....................	1.9	2.4	2.4	1.8	2.3	5.5	9.7	10.0	3,180	4,381
Jackson, MO.............	1.9	2.0	1.9	1.8	1.9	4.4	6.7	6.4	2,810	3,494

NA Not available. [1] Based on estimated resident population as of July 1.

Source: U.S. Census Bureau, 2011 Annual Survey of Public Employment and Payroll, August 2013. See also <http://www.census.gov/govs/apes/>.

Federal Government Finances and Employment

This section presents statistics relating to the financial structure and the civilian employment of the federal government. The fiscal data cover taxes, other receipts, outlays, and debt. The principal sources of fiscal data are the *Budget of the United States Government* and related documents, published annually by the Office of Management and Budget (OMB), and the U.S. Department of the Treasury's *Combined Statement of Receipts, Outlays, and Balances of the United States Government*. Detailed data on tax returns and collections are published annually by the Internal Revenue Service. The personnel data relate to staffing and payrolls. They are published by the Office of Personnel Management and the Bureau of Labor Statistics. Data on federally owned land and real property are collected by the General Services Administration and presented in its annual *Federal Real Property Report*.

Budget concept—Under the unified budget concept, all federal monies are included in one comprehensive budget. These monies comprise both federal funds and trust funds. Federal funds are derived mainly from taxes and borrowing and are not restricted by law to any specific government purpose. Trust funds, such as the Unemployment Trust Fund, collect certain taxes and other receipts for use in carrying out specific purposes or programs in accordance with the terms of the trust agreement or statute. Fund balances include both cash balances with the Treasury and investments in U.S. securities. Part of the balance is obligated, part unobligated. Prior to 1985, the budget totals, under provisions of law, excluded some federal activities—including the Federal Financing Bank, the Postal Service, the Synthetic Fuels Corporation, and the lending activities of the Rural Electrification Administration. The Balanced Budget and Emergency Deficit Control Act of 1985 (P.L.99-177) repealed the off-budget status of these entities and placed Social Security (Federal Old-Age and Survivors Insurance and the Federal Disability Insurance Trust Funds) off-budget. Though Social Security is now off-budget and, by law, excluded from coverage of the congressional budget resolutions, it continues to be a federal program. Receipts arising from the government's sovereign powers are reported as governmental receipts and all other receipts, i.e., from business or market-oriented activities, are offset against outlays. Outlays are reported on a checks-issued (net) basis (i.e., outlays are recorded at the time the checks to pay bills are issued).

Debt concept—For most of U.S. history, the total debt consisted of debt borrowed by the Treasury (i.e., public debt). The present debt series includes both public debt and agency debt. The *gross federal debt* includes money borrowed by the Treasury and by various federal agencies; it is the broadest generally used measure of the federal debt. *Total public debt* is covered by a statutory debt limitation and includes only borrowing by the Treasury.

Treasury receipts and outlays—All receipts of the government, with a few exceptions, are deposited to the credit of the U.S. Treasury regardless of ultimate disposition. Under the Constitution, no money may be withdrawn from the Treasury unless appropriated by the Congress.

The day-to-day cash operations of the federal government clearing through the accounts of the U.S. Treasury are reported in the *Daily Treasury Statement*. Extensive detail on the public debt is published in the *Monthly Statement of the Public Debt of the United States*.

Budget receipts such as taxes, customs duties, and miscellaneous receipts, which are collected by government agencies, and outlays represented by checks issued and cash payments made by disbursing officers as well as government agencies are reported in the *Monthly Treasury Statement of Receipts and Outlays of the United States Government* and in the Treasury's *Combined Statement of Receipts, Outlays, and Balances of the United States Government*. These deposits in and payments from accounts maintained by government agencies are on the same basis as the unified budget.

The quarterly *Treasury Bulletin* contains data on fiscal operations and related Treasury activities, including financial statements of government corporations and other business-type activities.

Income tax returns and tax collections—Tax data are compiled by the Internal Revenue Service of the Treasury Department. The annual *Internal Revenue Service Data Book* gives a detailed account of tax collections by kind of tax. The agency's annual *Statistics of Income* reports present detailed data from individual income tax returns and corporation income tax returns. The quarterly *Statistics of Income Bulletin* presents data on such diverse subjects as tax-exempt organizations, unincorporated businesses, fiduciary income tax and estate tax returns, sales of capital assets by individuals, international income and taxes reported by corporations and individuals, and estate tax wealth.

Employment and payrolls—The Office of Personnel Management collects employment and payroll data from all departments and agencies of the federal government, except the Central Intelligence Agency, the National Security Agency, and the Defense Intelligence Agency. Employment figures represent the number of persons who occupied civilian positions at the end of the report month shown and who are paid for services rendered to the federal government, regardless of the nature of appointment or method of payment. Federal payrolls include all payments for personal services rendered during the report month and payments for accumulated annual leave of employees who separate from the service. Since most federal employees are paid on a biweekly basis, the calendar month earnings are partially estimated on the basis of the number of work days in each month where payroll periods overlap.

Federal employment and payroll figures are published by the Office of Personnel Management in its *Federal Civilian Workforce Statistics—Employment and Trends* and FedScope database system. It also publishes employment data on minority groups, white- and blue-collar workers, employment by geographic area, and salary and wage distribution of federal employees. General schedule is primarily white-collar; wage system primarily blue-collar. Data on federal employment are also issued by the Bureau of Labor Statistics in its *Monthly Labor Review* and *Employment and Earnings Online* and by the U.S. Census Bureau in its annual report series *Federal, State, and Local Governments: Public Employment and Payroll Data.*

Table 488. Federal Budget—Receipts and Outlays: 1960 to 2013

[92.5 represents $92,500,000,000. For fiscal years ending in year shown; See text, Section 8. See also headnote, Table 490]

Fiscal year	In current dollars (bil. dol.)			In constant (2005) dollars (bil. dol.)			As percentage of GDP [1]		
	Receipts	Outlays	Surplus or deficit (-)	Receipts	Outlays	Surplus or deficit (-)	Receipts	Outlays	Surplus or deficit (-)
1960.............	92.5	92.2	0.3	630.5	628.4	2.0	17.8	17.8	0.1
1970.............	192.8	195.6	-2.8	967.9	982.2	-14.3	19.0	19.3	-0.3
1980.............	517.1	590.9	-73.8	1,197.3	1,368.2	-170.9	19.0	21.7	-2.7
1990.............	1,032.0	1,253.0	-221.0	1,508.3	1,831.3	-323.1	18.0	21.9	-3.9
1995.............	1,351.8	1,515.7	-164.0	1,690.8	1,895.9	-205.1	18.4	20.6	-2.2
1996.............	1,453.1	1,560.5	-107.4	1,774.8	1,906.1	-131.2	18.8	20.2	-1.4
1997.............	1,579.2	1,601.1	-21.9	1,889.0	1,915.2	-26.2	19.2	19.5	-0.3
1998.............	1,721.7	1,652.5	69.3	2,040.2	1,958.1	82.1	19.9	19.1	0.8
1999.............	1,827.5	1,701.8	125.6	2,135.4	1,988.6	146.8	19.8	18.5	1.4
2000.............	2,025.2	1,789.0	236.2	2,309.2	2,039.9	269.4	20.6	18.2	2.4
2001.............	1,991.1	1,862.8	128.2	2,214.3	2,071.7	142.6	19.5	18.2	1.3
2002.............	1,853.1	2,010.9	-157.8	2,027.9	2,200.6	-172.6	17.6	19.1	-1.5
2003.............	1,782.3	2,159.9	-377.6	1,900.5	2,303.2	-402.6	16.2	19.7	-3.4
2004.............	1,880.1	2,292.8	-412.7	1,949.3	2,377.2	-427.9	16.1	19.6	-3.5
2005.............	2,153.6	2,472.0	-318.3	2,153.6	2,472.0	-318.3	17.3	19.9	-2.6
2006.............	2,406.9	2,655.0	-248.2	2,324.6	2,564.3	-239.7	18.2	20.1	-1.9
2007.............	2,568.0	2,728.7	-160.7	2,413.1	2,564.1	-151.0	18.5	19.7	-1.2
2008.............	2,524.0	2,982.5	-458.6	2,288.1	2,703.8	-415.7	17.6	20.8	-3.2
2009.............	2,105.0	3,517.7	-1,412.7	1,901.0	3,176.8	-1,275.8	15.1	25.2	-10.1
2010.............	2,162.7	3,457.1	-1,294.4	1,929.1	3,083.6	-1,154.6	15.1	24.1	-9.0
2011.............	2,303.5	3,603.1	-1,299.6	2,013.7	3,149.8	-1,136.1	15.4	24.1	-8.7
2012.............	2,450.2	3,537.1	-1,087.0	2,093.4	3,022.2	-928.7	15.8	22.8	-7.0
2013, est............	2,712.0	3,684.9	-972.9	2,271.4	3,086.2	-814.8	16.7	22.7	-6.0

[1] Gross domestic product; see text, Section 13.

Source: U.S. Office of Management and Budget, *Fiscal Year 2014 Budget of the U.S. Government: Historical Tables*, April 2013. See also <http://www.whitehouse.gov/omb/budget>.

Table 489. Federal Budget Debt: 1960 to 2013

[290.5 represents $290,500,000,000. As of the end of the fiscal year. See text, Section 8]

Fiscal year	Total (bil. dol.)					As percentages of GDP [1]				
	Gross federal debt	Federal government accounts	Held by the public			Gross federal debt	Federal government accounts	Held by the public		
			Total	Federal Reserve System	Other			Total	Federal Reserve System	Other
1960.............	290.5	53.7	236.8	26.5	210.3	56.0	10.3	45.6	5.1	40.5
1970.............	380.9	97.7	283.2	57.7	225.5	37.6	9.6	28.0	5.7	22.3
1980.............	909.0	197.1	711.9	120.8	591.1	33.4	7.2	26.1	4.4	21.7
1985.............	1,817.4	310.2	1,507.3	169.8	1,337.5	43.8	7.5	36.4	4.1	32.3
1989.............	2,867.8	677.1	2,190.7	220.1	1,970.6	53.1	12.5	40.6	4.1	36.5
1990.............	3,206.3	794.7	2,411.6	234.4	2,177.1	55.9	13.9	42.1	4.1	38.0
1991.............	3,598.2	909.2	2,689.0	258.6	2,430.4	60.7	15.3	45.3	4.4	41.0
1992.............	4,001.8	1,002.1	2,999.7	296.4	2,703.3	64.1	16.1	48.1	4.7	43.3
1993.............	4,351.0	1,102.6	3,248.4	325.7	2,922.7	66.1	16.7	49.3	4.9	44.4
1994.............	4,643.3	1,210.2	3,433.1	355.2	3,077.9	66.6	17.3	49.2	5.1	44.1
1995.............	4,920.6	1,316.2	3,604.4	374.1	3,230.3	67.0	17.9	49.1	5.1	44.0
1996.............	5,181.5	1,447.4	3,734.1	390.9	3,343.1	67.1	18.8	48.4	5.1	43.3
1997.............	5,369.2	1,596.9	3,772.3	424.5	3,347.8	65.4	19.4	45.9	5.2	40.8
1998.............	5,478.2	1,757.1	3,721.1	458.2	3,262.9	63.2	20.3	43.0	5.3	37.7
1999.............	5,605.5	1,973.2	3,632.4	496.6	3,135.7	60.9	21.4	39.4	5.4	34.1
2000.............	5,628.7	2,218.9	3,409.8	511.4	2,898.4	57.3	22.6	34.7	5.2	29.5
2001.............	5,769.9	2,450.3	3,319.6	534.1	2,785.5	56.4	24.0	32.5	5.2	27.2
2002.............	6,198.4	2,658.0	3,540.4	604.2	2,936.2	58.8	25.2	33.6	5.7	27.8
2003.............	6,760.0	2,846.6	3,913.4	656.1	3,257.3	61.6	25.9	35.6	6.0	29.7
2004.............	7,354.7	3,059.1	4,295.5	700.3	3,595.2	63.0	26.2	36.8	6.0	30.8
2005.............	7,905.3	3,313.1	4,592.2	736.4	3,855.9	63.6	26.7	36.9	5.9	31.0
2006.............	8,451.4	3,622.4	4,829.0	768.9	4,060.0	64.0	27.4	36.6	5.8	30.7
2007.............	8,950.7	3,915.6	5,035.1	779.6	4,255.5	64.6	28.2	36.3	5.6	30.7
2008.............	9,986.1	4,183.0	5,803.1	491.1	5,311.9	69.7	29.2	40.5	3.4	37.1
2009.............	11,875.9	4,331.1	7,544.7	769.2	6,775.5	85.1	31.0	54.0	5.5	48.5
2010.............	13,528.8	4,509.9	9,018.9	811.7	8,207.2	94.3	31.4	62.9	5.7	57.2
2011.............	14,764.2	4,636.0	10,128.2	1,664.7	8,463.5	98.9	31.1	67.8	11.2	56.7
2012.............	16,050.9	4,769.8	11,281.1	1,645.3	9,635.8	103.2	30.7	72.6	10.6	62.0
2013, est..........	17,249.2	4,845.7	12,403.6	(NA)	(NA)	106.5	29.9	76.6	(NA)	(NA)

NA Not available. [1] Gross domestic product; see text, Section 13.

Source: U.S. Office of Management and Budget, *Fiscal Year 2014 Budget of the U.S. Government, Historical Tables*, April 2013. See also <http://www.whitehouse.gov/omb/budget>.

Table 490. Federal Budget Outlays by Type: 1990 to 2013

[1,253.0 represents $1,253,000,000,000. For fiscal years ending September 30. Given the inherent imprecision in adjusting outlays for inflation, the data shown in constant dollars present a reasonable perspective—not precision. The deflators and the categories that are deflated are as comparable over time as feasible. Minus sign (-) indicates offset]

Type	Unit	1990	2000	2005	2010	2011	2012	2013, est.
Current dollar outlays	Bil. dol.	**1,253.0**	**1,789.0**	**2,472.0**	**3,457.1**	**3,603.1**	**3,537.1**	**3,684.9**
National defense [1]	Bil. dol.	299.3	294.4	495.3	693.5	705.6	677.9	660.0
Nondefense, total	Bil. dol.	953.7	1,494.6	1,976.6	2,763.6	2,897.5	2,859.3	3,024.9
Payments for individuals	Bil. dol.	585.7	1,054.6	1,490.3	2,285.7	2,344.4	2,296.5	2,439.2
Direct payments [2]	Bil. dol.	507.0	867.8	1,212.3	1,893.4	1,949.1	1,932.8	2,054.3
Grants to State and local governments	Bil. dol.	78.7	186.8	278.1	392.3	395.4	363.7	384.9
All other grants	Bil. dol.	56.4	99.1	149.9	216.1	211.4	180.8	176.1
Net interest [2]	Bil. dol.	184.3	222.9	184.0	196.2	230.0	220.4	222.8
All other [2]	Bil. dol.	163.9	160.5	217.6	147.7	200.2	265.1	282.0
Undistributed offsetting receipts [2]	Bil. dol.	-36.6	-42.6	-65.2	-82.1	-88.5	-103.5	-95.1
Constant (2005) dollar outlays	Bil. dol.	**1,831.3**	**2,039.9**	**2,472.0**	**3,083.6**	**3,149.8**	**3,022.2**	**3,086.2**
National defense [1]	Bil. dol.	461.1	361.3	495.3	614.1	615.2	580.6	553.6
Nondefense, total	Bil. dol.	1,370.0	1,678.6	1,976.6	2,469.5	2,534.6	2,441.5	2,532.6
Payments for individuals	Bil. dol.	815.0	1,171.9	1,490.3	2,048.3	2,056.4	1,963.7	2,044.8
Direct payments [2]	Bil. dol.	705.4	964.2	1,212.3	1,697.4	1,710.2	1,652.9	1,722.4
Grants to state and local governments	Bil. dol.	109.6	207.8	278.1	351.0	346.2	310.7	322.5
All other grants	Bil. dol.	87.9	118.5	149.9	182.0	173.9	145.1	137.6
Net interest [2]	Bil. dol.	255.5	250.6	184.0	176.0	202.1	190.2	188.3
All other [2]	Bil. dol.	278.8	190.3	217.6	135.2	179.0	230.7	241.4
Undistributed offsetting receipts [2]	Bil. dol.	-67.1	-52.9	-65.2	-71.9	-76.8	-88.3	-79.5
Outlays as percent of GDP [3]	**Percent**	**21.9**	**18.2**	**19.9**	**24.1**	**24.1**	**22.8**	**22.7**
National defense [1]	Percent	5.2	3.0	4.0	4.8	4.7	4.4	4.1
Nondefense, total	Percent	16.6	15.2	15.9	19.3	19.4	18.4	18.7
Payments for individuals	Percent	10.2	10.7	12.0	15.9	15.7	14.8	15.1
Direct payments [2]	Percent	8.8	8.8	9.8	13.2	13.1	12.4	12.7
Grants to state and local governments	Percent	1.4	1.9	2.2	2.7	2.6	2.3	2.4
All other grants	Percent	1.0	1.0	1.2	1.5	1.4	1.2	1.1
Net interest [2]	Percent	3.2	2.3	1.5	1.4	1.5	1.4	1.4
All other [2]	Percent	2.9	1.6	1.8	1.0	1.3	1.7	1.7
Undistributed offsetting receipts [2]	Percent	-0.6	-0.4	-0.5	-0.6	-0.6	-0.7	-0.6

[1] Includes a small amount of grants to state and local governments and direct payments for individuals. [2] Includes some off-budget amounts; most of the off-budget amounts are direct payments for individuals (social security benefits). [3] Gross domestic product; see text, Section 13.

Source: U.S. Office of Management and Budget, *Fiscal Year 2014 Budget of the U.S. Government, Historical Tables*, April 2013. See also <http://www.whitehouse.gov/omb/budget>.

Table 491. Federal Budget Outlays by Agency: 1990 to 2013

[In billions of dollars (1,253.0 represents $1,253,000,000,000). For fiscal years ending September 30]

Department or other unit	1990	2000	2005	2010	2011	2012	2013, est.
Outlays, total [1]	**1,253.0**	**1,789.0**	**2,472.0**	**3,457.1**	**3,603.1**	**3,537.1**	**3,684.9**
Legislative branch	2.2	2.9	4.0	5.8	4.6	4.4	5.0
Judicial branch	1.6	4.1	5.5	7.2	7.3	7.2	7.6
Agriculture	45.9	75.1	85.3	129.5	139.4	139.7	156.0
Commerce	3.7	7.8	6.1	13.2	9.9	10.3	9.9
Defense—Military	289.7	281.0	474.4	666.7	678.1	650.9	633.3
Education	23.0	33.5	72.9	93.7	65.5	57.2	48.1
Energy	12.1	15.0	21.3	30.8	31.4	32.5	28.9
Health and Human Services	175.5	382.3	581.4	854.1	891.2	848.1	907.7
Homeland Security	7.2	13.2	38.7	44.5	45.7	47.4	60.8
Housing and Urban Development	20.2	30.8	42.5	60.1	57.0	49.6	60.5
Interior	5.8	8.0	9.3	13.2	13.5	12.9	10.4
Justice	5.9	16.8	22.4	29.6	30.5	31.2	35.3
Labor	26.1	31.9	46.9	173.1	132.0	104.6	95.2
State	4.8	6.7	12.7	23.8	24.4	26.9	31.0
Transportation	25.6	41.6	56.6	77.8	77.3	75.1	80.1
Treasury	253.9	390.5	410.2	444.3	538.7	464.7	490.7
Veterans Affairs	29.0	47.0	69.8	108.3	126.9	124.1	139.2
Army Corps of Engineers	3.3	4.2	4.7	9.9	10.1	7.8	5.5
Other Defense—Civil Programs	21.7	32.8	43.5	54.0	54.8	77.3	59.7
Environmental Protection Agency	5.1	7.2	7.9	11.0	10.8	12.8	9.2
Executive Office of the President	0.2	0.3	7.7	0.6	0.5	0.4	0.4
International Assistance Programs	10.1	12.1	15.0	20.0	20.6	20.0	24.5
National Aeronautics and Space Administration	12.4	13.4	15.6	18.9	17.6	17.2	17.8
National Science Foundation	1.8	3.4	5.4	6.7	7.1	7.3	8.4
Office of Personnel Management	31.9	48.7	59.5	69.9	74.1	79.5	89.8
Social Security Administration (on-budget)	17.3	45.1	54.6	70.8	155.3	188.2	110.5
Social Security Administration (off-budget)	245.0	396.2	506.8	683.4	628.9	632.9	762.2
Undistributed offsetting receipts [2]	-98.9	-173.0	-226.2	-267.9	-276.5	-230.7	-251.7

[1] Includes other agencies, not shown separately. [2] See footnote 2, Table 490.

Source: U.S. Office of Management and Budget, *Fiscal Year 2014 Budget of the U.S. Government, Historical Tables*, April 2013. See also <http://www.whitehouse.gov/omb/budget>.

Table 492. Federal Budget Outlays by Detailed Function: 1990 to 2013

[In billions of dollars (1,253.0 represents $1,253,000,000,000). For fiscal years ending September 30. Minus sign (-) indicates decrease]

Superfunction and function	1990	2000	2005	2008	2009	2010	2011	2012	2013, est.
Total outlays	**1,253.0**	**1,789.0**	**2,472.0**	**2,982.5**	**3,517.7**	**3,457.1**	**3,603.1**	**3,537.1**	**3,684.9**
National defense [1]	299.3	294.4	495.3	616.1	661.0	693.5	705.6	677.9	660.0
Department of Defense—Military	289.7	281.0	474.1	594.6	636.7	666.7	678.1	650.9	633.3
Military personnel	75.6	76.0	127.5	138.9	147.3	155.7	161.6	152.3	161.4
Operation and maintenance	88.3	105.8	188.1	244.8	259.3	276.0	291.0	282.3	268.5
Procurement	81.0	51.7	82.3	117.4	129.2	133.6	128.0	124.7	116.9
Research, development, test, and evaluation	37.5	37.6	65.7	75.1	79.0	77.0	74.9	70.4	69.6
Military construction	5.1	5.1	5.3	11.6	17.6	21.2	19.9	14.6	15.2
Atomic energy defense activities	9.0	12.1	18.0	17.1	17.6	19.3	20.4	19.2	19.1
International affairs [1]	13.8	17.2	34.6	28.9	37.5	45.2	45.7	47.2	56.9
International development and humanitarian assistance	5.5	6.5	17.7	14.1	22.1	19.0	21.3	21.9	25.5
International security assistance	8.7	6.4	7.9	9.5	6.2	11.4	12.0	11.5	15.1
Conduct of foreign affairs	3.0	4.7	9.1	10.4	12.2	13.6	12.5	13.6	16.1
General science, space, and technology	14.4	18.6	23.6	26.8	28.4	30.1	29.5	29.1	30.7
General science and basic research	2.8	6.2	8.8	9.6	10.0	11.7	12.4	12.5	13.4
Space flight, research, and supporting activities	11.6	12.4	14.8	17.2	18.4	18.4	17.0	16.6	17.3
Energy	3.3	-0.8	0.4	0.6	4.7	11.6	12.2	14.9	15.1
Energy supply	2.0	-1.8	-0.9	-0.4	2.0	5.8	8.1	9.0	11.8
Natural resources and environment [1]	17.1	25.0	28.0	31.8	35.6	43.7	45.5	41.6	37.7
Water resources	4.4	5.1	5.7	6.1	8.1	11.7	11.6	9.2	6.8
Conservation and land management	4.0	6.8	6.2	8.7	9.8	10.8	12.0	11.1	11.6
Recreational resources	1.4	2.5	3.0	3.2	3.6	3.9	4.2	3.8	3.7
Pollution control and abatement	5.2	7.4	8.1	8.1	8.3	10.8	10.9	10.8	9.4
Agriculture	11.8	36.5	26.6	18.4	22.2	21.4	20.7	17.8	27.0
Farm income stabilization	9.7	33.4	22.0	13.8	17.6	16.6	16.0	13.2	21.7
Agricultural research and services	2.1	3.0	4.5	4.6	4.6	4.8	4.6	4.6	5.3
Commerce and housing credit [1]	67.6	3.2	7.6	27.9	291.5	-82.3	-12.6	40.8	17.7
Mortgage credit	3.8	-3.3	-0.9	0.0	99.8	35.8	14.2	-8.1	-6.1
Postal service	2.1	2.1	-1.2	-3.1	-1.0	-0.7	0.9	2.7	-0.3
Deposit insurance	57.9	-3.1	-1.4	18.8	22.6	-32.0	-8.7	6.7	18.6
Transportation [1]	29.5	46.9	67.9	77.6	84.3	92.0	93.0	93.0	94.5
Ground transportation	19.0	31.7	42.3	50.0	54.1	60.8	60.9	61.3	62.5
Air transportation	7.2	10.6	18.8	19.4	20.8	21.4	21.4	21.7	21.6
Water transportation	3.2	4.4	6.4	8.1	9.1	9.4	10.4	9.7	9.6
Community and regional development [1]	8.5	10.6	26.3	24.0	27.7	23.9	23.9	25.1	38.0
Community development	3.5	5.5	5.9	10.2	7.7	9.9	9.6	8.8	8.9
Disaster relief and insurance	2.1	2.6	17.7	11.2	16.7	10.7	10.2	11.9	26.8
Education, training, employment, and social services [1]	37.2	53.8	97.6	91.3	79.7	128.6	101.2	90.8	84.6
Elementary, secondary, and vocational education	9.9	20.6	38.3	38.9	53.2	73.3	66.5	47.5	45.8
Higher education	11.1	10.1	31.4	23.6	-3.3	20.9	1.1	12.1	6.1
Research and general education aids	1.6	2.5	3.1	3.2	3.5	3.6	3.7	3.7	3.8
Training and employment	5.6	6.8	6.9	7.2	7.7	9.9	9.1	7.8	8.3
Social services	8.1	12.6	16.3	16.8	17.0	19.2	18.9	17.9	18.6
Health	57.7	154.5	250.5	280.6	334.3	369.1	372.5	346.7	371.7
Health care services	47.6	136.2	219.6	247.7	300.0	330.7	332.2	308.2	333.9
Health research and training	8.6	16.0	28.1	29.9	30.6	34.2	36.2	34.5	33.1
Consumer and occupational health and safety	1.5	2.3	2.9	3.0	3.8	4.1	4.1	4.1	4.6
Medicare	98.1	197.1	298.6	390.8	430.1	451.6	485.7	471.8	510.5
Income security [1]	148.7	253.7	345.8	431.3	533.2	622.2	597.4	541.3	564.0
General retirement and disability insurance (excluding social security)	5.1	5.2	7.0	8.9	8.2	6.6	6.7	7.8	8.0
Federal employee retirement and disability	52.0	77.2	93.4	109.0	118.1	119.9	124.5	122.4	133.6
Unemployment compensation	18.9	23.0	35.4	45.3	122.5	160.1	120.6	93.8	82.6
Housing assistance	15.9	28.9	37.9	40.6	50.9	58.7	55.4	47.9	57.6
Food and nutrition assistance	24.0	32.5	50.8	60.7	79.1	95.1	103.2	106.9	112.2
Social security	248.6	409.4	523.3	617.0	683.0	706.7	730.8	773.3	818.4
Veterans benefits and services [1]	29.0	47.0	70.1	84.7	95.4	108.4	127.2	124.6	139.6
Income security for veterans	15.3	24.9	35.8	41.3	46.0	49.2	58.7	55.9	67.4
Veterans education, training, and rehabilitation	0.2	1.3	2.8	2.7	3.5	8.1	10.7	10.4	13.1
Hospital and medical care for veterans	12.1	19.5	28.8	37.0	41.9	45.7	50.1	50.6	52.5
Veterans housing	0.5	0.4	0.9	-0.4	-0.6	0.5	1.3	1.4	1.3
Administration of justice	10.2	28.5	40.0	48.1	52.6	54.4	56.1	56.3	60.6
Federal law enforcement activities	4.8	12.1	19.9	25.6	28.6	28.7	29.8	29.0	30.0
Federal litigative and judicial activities	3.6	7.8	9.6	11.8	12.1	13.1	13.6	14.7	17.9
Federal correctional activities	1.3	3.7	5.9	6.9	7.3	7.7	8.1	8.3	7.0
Criminal justice assistance	0.5	4.9	4.6	3.9	4.6	4.8	4.6	4.3	5.7
General government	10.5	13.0	17.0	20.3	22.0	23.0	27.5	28.0	30.5
Net interest [1]	184.3	222.9	184.0	252.8	186.9	196.2	230.0	220.4	222.8
Interest on Treasury debt securities (gross)	264.7	361.9	352.3	451.1	383.1	413.9	454.0	359.2	420.6
Interest received by on-budget trust funds	-46.3	-69.3	-69.2	-77.8	-63.6	-67.3	-72.0	-14.8	-51.0
Interest received by off-budget trust funds	-16.0	-59.8	-91.8	-113.7	-118.0	-118.5	-116.0	-112.4	-105.6
Allowances	–	–	–	–	–	–	–	–	-0.2
Undistributed offsetting receipts [2]	-36.6	-42.6	-65.2	-86.2	-92.6	-82.1	-86.5	-98.9	-95.1

– Represents or rounds to zero. [1] Includes functions not shown separately. [2] See footnote 2, Table 490.

Source: U.S. Office of Management and Budget, *Fiscal Year 2014 Budget of the U.S. Government: Historical Tables*, April 2013. See also <http://www.whitehouse.gov/omb/budget>.

Federal Government Finances and Employment

Table 493. Outlays for Payments for Individuals by Category and Major Program: 1990 to 2013

[In billions of dollars (585.7 represents 585,700,000,000). For fiscal years ending September 30]

Category and program	1990	2000	2005	2009	2010	2011	2012	2013, est.
Total, payments for individuals..........................	**585.7**	**1,054.7**	**1,491.1**	**2,094.2**	**2,286.8**	**2,345.7**	**2,297.7**	**2,440.5**
Social security and railroad retirement......................	250.5	410.5	523.4	681.0	706.5	730.6	773.8	819.2
Social security:								
Old age and survivors insurance...........................	221.9	351.4	434.0	561.4	576.6	595.6	631.4	670.9
Disability insurance..	24.4	54.4	84.2	115.5	123.5	128.6	135.7	140.9
Railroad retirement (excl. social security)...............	4.1	4.6	5.3	4.1	6.5	6.4	6.7	7.5
Federal employees retirement and insurance..............	64.1	100.3	126.9	161.7	166.5	181.3	175.8	198.2
Military retirement..	21.5	32.8	39.0	50.0	50.6	54.9	48.8	53.7
Civil service retirement....................................	31.0	45.1	54.7	67.5	69.4	70.4	73.9	79.9
Veterans service-connected compensation..............	10.7	20.8	30.9	40.4	43.4	52.8	50.1	60.8
Other..	0.8	1.7	2.4	3.8	3.1	3.3	3.1	3.9
Unemployment assistance....................................	17.4	21.1	33.1	119.8	158.3	118.6	92.3	79.8
Medical care...	164.3	362.7	562.5	813.8	865.5	913.0	879.5	942.0
Medicare:								
Hospital insurance...	65.9	127.9	182.8	240.0	250.2	260.9	261.6	274.2
Supplementary medical insurance......................	41.5	87.2	151.0	257.6	268.9	297.4	288.2	316.6
State children's health insurance........................	–	1.2	5.1	7.5	7.9	8.6	9.1	10.0
Medicaid..	41.1	117.9	181.7	250.9	272.8	275.0	250.5	266.6
Indian health...	1.1	2.4	3.1	3.6	4.4	4.2	4.5	4.7
Hospital and medical care for veterans...............	12.0	19.3	23.1	35.3	38.2	41.3	41.7	44.8
Health resources and services..........................	1.4	3.9	5.9	6.5	7.1	7.5	7.8	7.5
Substance abuse and mental health services............	1.2	2.5	3.2	3.4	3.3	3.4	3.0	3.6
Health care tax credit.....................................	–	–	0.1	0.1	0.2	(NA)	(NA)	(NA)
Uniformed Services retiree health care fund..............	–	–	6.3	8.4	8.4	8.6	8.7	9.9
Other..	(Z)	0.3	0.3	0.6	4.3	2.7	0.9	1.0
Assistance to students...	11.2	10.9	32.1	30.6	55.5	58.6	59.8	61.6
Veterans education benefits..............................	0.8	1.6	3.2	4.3	8.7	11.1	10.7	13.4
Student assistance, Department of Education and other...	10.4	9.2	28.9	26.3	46.8	47.5	49.1	48.2
Housing assistance..	15.9	24.1	31.8	43.6	50.0	45.9	40.0	49.7
Food and nutrition assistance................................	23.9	32.4	50.7	78.9	95.0	103.1	106.7	111.5
Food stamp program (including Puerto Rico)..............	15.9	18.3	32.6	55.6	70.5	77.6	80.4	82.6
Child nutrition and special milk programs................	5.0	9.2	11.9	15.3	16.4	17.3	18.3	20.9
Supplemental feeding programs (WIC [1] and CSFP [2])...........................	2.1	4.0	5.0	6.5	6.5	6.8	6.8	6.7
Commodity donations and other.........................	0.8	0.9	1.2	1.6	1.6	1.3	1.2	1.3
Public assistance and related programs....................	34.9	88.5	123.4	156.2	183.2	188.6	163.8	171.8
Supplemental security income program..................	11.5	29.7	35.4	41.5	44.0	49.7	44.2	50.5
Family support payments to states and TANF [3]........	12.2	18.4	21.3	22.2	21.9	21.3	20.1	20.8
Low income home energy assistance.....................	1.3	1.5	2.1	4.5	4.6	4.4	3.8	3.7
Earned income tax credit..................................	4.4	26.1	34.6	42.4	54.7	55.7	54.9	55.1
Legal services...	0.3	0.3	0.3	–	–	(NA)	(NA)	(NA)
Payments to states for daycare assistance..............	–	3.3	4.9	5.3	5.9	6.1	5.0	5.2
Veterans non-service-connected pensions..............	3.6	3.0	3.7	4.2	4.4	4.7	4.5	5.2
Payments to states for foster care/adoption assistance..	1.6	5.5	6.4	6.9	7.0	6.9	6.8	6.7
Payment where child credit exceeds tax liability..	–	0.8	14.6	24.3	22.7	22.7	22.1	23.1
Other public assistance...................................	0.3	0.3	0.4	4.1	17.1	16.7	2.1	1.3
All other payments for individuals............................	3.5	4.3	7.1	8.7	6.3	6.2	6.0	6.6
Coal miners and black lung benefits......................	1.5	1.0	0.7	3.0	0.5	0.5	0.4	0.4
Veterans insurance and burial benefits..................	1.4	1.4	1.4	1.4	1.3	1.3	1.2	1.3
D.C. employee retirement.................................	–	0.4	2.2	–	–	(NA)	(NA)	(NA)
Aging services programs.................................	–	0.9	1.4	1.5	1.5	1.6	1.5	1.5
Energy employees compensation fund....................	–	–	0.6	1.0	1.1	1.2	1.2	1.2
September 11th victim compensation.....................	–	–	(Z)	–	–	–	–	0.3
Refugee assistance and other............................	0.6	1.0	3.0	1.8	1.9	1.6	1.7	1.8

NA Not Available – Represents zero. Z Less than $50,000,000. [1] WIC means Women, Infants, and Children. [2] CSFP means Commodity Supplemental Food Program. [3] TANF means Temporary Assistance for Needy Families.

Source: U.S. Office of Management and Budget, *Fiscal Year 2014 Budget of the U.S. Government: Historical Tables*, April 2013. See also <http://www.whitehouse.gov/omb/budget>.

Table 494. Federal Budget Receipts by Source: 1990 to 2013

[In billions of dollars (1,032.0 represents $1,032,000,000,000). For fiscal years ending September 30. Receipts reflect collections. Covers both federal funds and trust funds; see text, this section. Minus sign (-) indicates decrease]

Source	1990	2000	2005	2009	2010	2011	2012	2013, est.
Total federal receipts	**1,032.0**	**2,025.2**	**2,153.6**	**2,105.0**	**2,162.7**	**2,303.5**	**2,450.2**	**2,712.0**
Individual income taxes	466.9	1,004.5	927.2	915.3	898.5	1,091.5	1,132.2	1,234.0
Corporation income taxes	93.5	207.3	278.3	138.2	191.4	181.1	242.3	287.7
Social insurance and retirement receipts	380.0	652.9	794.1	890.9	864.8	818.8	845.3	951.1
Excise taxes	35.3	68.9	73.1	62.5	66.9	72.4	79.1	85.3
Other	56.2	91.7	80.9	98.1	141.0	139.7	151.3	153.9
Social insurance and retirement receipts	**380.0**	**652.9**	**794.1**	**890.9**	**864.8**	**818.8**	**845.3**	**951.1**
Employment and general retirement, total	353.9	620.5	747.7	848.9	815.9	758.5	774.9	886.8
Old–age and survivors insurance (off–budget)	255.0	411.7	493.6	559.1	540.0	483.7	486.8	575.7
Disability insurance (off–budget)	26.6	68.9	83.8	94.9	91.7	82.1	82.7	97.8
Hospital insurance	68.6	135.5	166.1	190.7	180.1	188.5	201.1	208.4
Railroad retirement/pension fund	2.3	2.7	2.3	2.3	2.3	2.4	2.5	2.8
Unemployment insurance funds	21.6	27.6	42.0	37.9	44.8	56.2	66.6	60.6
Other retirement	4.5	4.8	4.5	4.1	4.1	4.0	3.7	3.7
Federal employees retirement—employee share	4.4	4.7	4.4	4.1	4.1	4.0	3.7	3.7
Excise taxes, total	**35.3**	**68.9**	**73.1**	**62.5**	**66.9**	**72.4**	**79.1**	**85.3**
Federal funds [1]	15.6	22.7	22.5	13.9	18.3	18.9	20.4	27.3
Alcohol	5.7	8.1	8.1	9.9	9.2	9.3	9.8	9.7
Tobacco	4.1	7.2	7.9	12.8	17.2	16.7	16.4	15.9
Telephone	3.0	5.7	6.0	1.1	1.0	0.9	0.8	0.6
Ozone–depleting chemicals/products	0.4	0.1	–	–	–	–	–	–
Transportation fuels	–	0.8	-0.8	-10.3	-11.0	-8.6	-5.8	-3.0
Indoor tanning services	–	–	–	–	–	0.1	0.1	0.1
Trust funds [1]	19.8	46.2	50.5	48.6	48.7	53.5	58.7	58.1
Highway	13.9	35.0	37.9	35.0	35.0	36.9	40.2	38.7
Airport and airway	3.7	9.7	10.3	10.6	10.6	11.5	12.5	11.9
Black lung disability	0.7	0.5	0.6	0.6	0.6	0.6	0.6	0.6
Inland waterway	0.1	0.1	0.1	0.1	0.1	0.1	0.1	0.1
Oil spill liability	0.1	0.2	–	0.4	0.5	0.5	0.5	0.5
Aquatic resources	0.2	0.3	0.4	0.6	0.6	0.6	0.6	0.5
Tobacco assessments	–	–	0.9	1.0	0.9	0.9	0.9	1.0
Vaccine injury compensation	0.2	0.1	0.1	0.2	0.2	0.3	0.3	0.3

– Represents zero. [1] Includes other funds, not shown separately.

Source: U.S. Office of Management and Budget, *Fiscal Year 2014 Budget of the U.S. Government: Historical Tables*, April 2013. See also <http://www.whitehouse.gov/omb/budget>.

Table 495. Federal Trust Fund Income, Outlays, and Balances: 2012 to 2014

[In billions of dollars (12.8 represents $12,800,000,000). For fiscal years ending September 30. Income reflects receipts deposited. Outlays are on a checks-issued basis less refunds collected. Balances reflect funds that not been spent. See text, this section, for discussion of the budget concept and trust funds. Minus sign (-) indicates negative balance]

Description	Income			Outlays			Balances [1]		
	2012	2013, est.	2014, est.	2012	2013, est.	2014, est.	2012	2013, est.	2014, est.
Airport and airway trust fund	12.8	12.3	13.3	11.5	12.3	13.4	11.6	11.6	11.5
Federal civilian employees' retirement funds	96.8	93.2	93.3	74.1	80.0	85.5	826.6	839.7	847.6
Federal employees' health benefits fund	44.7	46.0	48.0	42.6	45.3	47.8	21.2	21.8	22.0
Foreign military sales trust fund	26.3	31.4	33.0	25.9	32.2	33.3	18.9	18.1	17.8
Medicare:									
Hospital insurance (HI) trust fund	248.9	249.8	269.3	265.3	278.4	283.9	229.3	200.7	186.1
Supplemental medical insurance trust fund	292.9	318.3	343.8	293.9	320.2	345.0	71.7	69.9	68.6
Military retirement fund	55.9	100.3	103.8	48.8	53.7	55.4	375.7	422.3	470.7
Railroad retirement trust funds	13.4	10.6	10.8	11.7	12.1	12.5	20.3	18.8	17.2
Social security: Old-age, survivors and disability insurance trust funds	849.4	863.3	896.9	784.9	830.2	877.7	2,718.1	2,751.1	2,770.3
Transportation trust fund	42.8	45.2	54.5	49.5	51.3	54.2	15.6	9.5	9.8
Unemployment trust funds	110.4	93.1	67.2	96.2	84.1	58.8	-12.6	-3.6	4.7
Veterans' life insurance trust funds	0.8	0.7	0.6	1.5	1.4	1.4	8.9	8.1	7.4
Other trust funds	17.3	19.7	20.4	16.6	14.7	9.0	83.2	88.1	99.5

[1] Balances available on a cash basis (rather than an authorization basis) at the end of the year. Balances are primarily invested in federal debt securities.

Source: U.S. Office of Management and Budget, *Fiscal Year 2014 Budget of the U.S. Government: Analytical Perspectives*, April 2013. See also <http://www.whitehouse.gov/omb/budget>.

Table 496. Tax Expenditure Estimates Relating to Individual and Corporate Income Taxes by Selected Function: 2012 to 2015

[In millions of dollars (14,140 represents $14,140,000,000). For fiscal years ending September 30. Tax expenditures are defined as revenue losses attributable to provisions of the federal tax laws which allow a special exclusion, exemption, or deduction from gross income or which provide a special credit, a preferential rate of tax, or a deferral of liability. Minus sign (-) indicates decrease]

Function and provision	2012	2013	2014	2015
National defense:				
Exclusion of benefits and allowances to armed forces personnel.............................	14,140	14,640	15,150	14,170
International affairs:				
Exclusion of income earned abroad by U.S. citizens...	5,400	5,800	6,140	6,430
Exclusion of certain allowances for Federal employees abroad.............................	1,070	1,120	1,180	1,240
Inventory property sales source rules exception...	3,310	3,610	3,940	4,300
Deferral of income from controlled foreign corporations (normal tax method).................	42,000	41,810	41,770	43,020
Deferred taxes for financial firms on certain income earned overseas.......................	2,510	–	–	–
General science, space, and technology:				
Expensing of research and experimentation expenditures (normal tax method)............	3,740	4,810	5,040	5,530
Credit for increasing research activities..	4,390	2,320	2,130	1,970
Energy:				
Alternative fuel production credit...	20	10	–	–
Energy production credit..	1,500	1,730	1,770	1,730
Energy investment credit...	1,040	1,270	1,360	1,670
Commerce and housing:				
Financial institutions and insurance:				
Exclusion of interest on life insurance savings...	17,580	18,350	21,010	23,130
Housing:				
Deductibility of mortgage interest on owner–occupied homes.................................	81,890	93,090	101,470	112,730
Deductibility of state and local property tax on owner–occupied homes.....................	15,460	20,310	25,160	26,110
Capital gains exclusion on home sales..	30,900	38,130	45,870	48,790
Exclusion of net imputed rental income...	68,230	74,080	75,520	80,880
Exception from passive loss rules for $25,000 of rental loss..................................	10,200	12,250	14,420	16,070
Credit for low–income housing investments..	7,670	7,410	8,310	8,280
Commerce:				
Capital gains (except agriculture, timber, iron ore, and coal).................................	65,360	61,840	46,690	56,700
Step–up basis of capital gains at death...	15,490	21,170	27,100	28,460
Accelerated depreciation of machinery and equipment (normal tax method)................	69,500	14,750	17,850	40,260
Graduated corporation income tax rate (normal tax method)..................................	4,270	4,300	4,210	4,180
Deduction for U.S. production activities...	11,570	12,860	13,630	14,370
Transportation:				
Exclusion of reimbursed employee parking expenses...	2,640	2,880	3,010	3,140
Education, training, employment, and social services:				
Education:				
HOPE tax credit..	–	430	4,310	4,270
Lifetime Learning tax credit..	2,000	2,290	4,450	4,420
Exclusion of interest on bonds for private nonprofit educational facilities...................	2,150	2,440	2,870	3,160
Parental personal exemption for students age 19 years or over..............................	2,800	2,700	2,810	2,550
Deductibility of charitable contributions (education)...	3,960	4,590	5,080	5,450
Training, employment, and social services:				
Child credit..	24,790	18,430	8,650	8,380
Credit for child and dependent care expenses..	3,410	1,550	1,290	1,250
Deductibility of charitable contributions, other than education and health..................	33,770	39,610	44,060	47,330
Health:				
Exclusion of employer contributions for medical insurance premiums and medical care..	184,320	202,530	212,820	224,610
Self–employed medical insurance premiums...	5,210	6,140	6,740	7,160
Deductibility of medical expenses..	7,230	8,990	10,270	10,820
Exclusion of interest on hospital construction bonds...	3,040	3,430	4,040	4,440
Deductibility of charitable contributions (health)...	3,820	4,470	4,980	5,350
Income security:				
Exclusion of workers' compensation benefits..	10,080	9,120	11,440	11,570
Net exclusion of pension contributions and earnings:				
Employer plans...	38,740	47,410	53,060	57,400
Defined contribution employer plans...	51,830	68,820	79,720	90,870
Individual Retirement Accounts (IRAs)..	16,180	21,240	19,260	19,370
Keogh (self-employed) plans..	15,930	19,380	23,260	25,490
Exclusion of other employee benefits:				
Premiums on group term life insurance...	1,870	1,910	1,940	1,970
Earned income tax credit...	1,610	4,040	5,640	5,920
Social security:				
Exclusion of social security benefits:				
Social security benefits for retired workers..	22,170	27,920	32,910	34,330
Social security benefits for disabled...	7,510	8,960	9,970	10,280
Social security benefits for dependents and survivors...	3,740	3,970	4,130	4,230
Veterans' benefits and services:				
Exclusion of veterans' death benefits and disability compensation..........................	4,240	5,210	6,880	7,480
General purpose fiscal assistance:				
Exclusion of interest on public purpose state and local bonds.................................	25,950	29,270	34,420	37,920
Deductibility of nonbusiness state and local tax, other than owner-occupied homes.........	29,480	43,940	51,560	54,520
Interest:				
Deferral of interest on U.S. savings bonds...	980	1,020	1,080	1,090
Addendum: Aid to state and local governments:				
Deductibility of:				
Property taxes on owner–occupied homes..	15,460	20,310	25,160	26,110
Nonbusiness state and local taxes other than on owner–occupied homes..................	29,480	43,940	51,560	54,520
Exclusion of interest on state and local bonds for:				
Public purposes..	25,950	29,270	34,420	37,920
Private nonprofit educational facilities...	2,150	2,440	2,870	3,160
Hospital construction..	3,040	3,430	4,040	4,440

– Represents zero.

Source: U.S. Office of Management and Budget, *Fiscal Year 2014 Budget of the U.S. Government: Supplemental Materials*, April 2013. See also <http://www.whitehouse.gov/omb/budget/>.

Table 497. Federal Funds—Summary Distribution by State: 2010

[In millions of dollars (3,276,422 represents $3,276,422,000,000), except as indicated. For fiscal year ending September 30. Data for grants, salaries and wages, and direct payments to individuals are on an expenditure basis; procurement data are on an obligation basis]

State	Federal funds		Agency		Object category			
	Total	Per capita [1] (dollars)	Defense	Non-defense	Direct payments	Procure-ment	Grants	Salaries and wages
United States [2]	**3,276,422**	**10,460**	**556,959**	**2,719,463**	**818,570**	**516,714**	**683,361**	**342,933**
Alabama	56,496	11,820	13,029	43,466	13,151	10,482	9,273	5,613
Alaska	12,615	17,762	5,211	7,404	1,040	2,464	3,465	4,055
Arizona	64,427	10,079	14,263	50,164	13,738	12,813	14,361	4,980
Arkansas	28,904	9,912	2,968	25,936	7,529	1,751	6,843	2,418
California	333,809	8,960	55,750	278,059	87,976	57,537	78,869	24,585
Colorado	49,687	9,880	12,211	37,476	9,169	10,367	8,793	8,519
Connecticut	55,978	15,662	11,980	43,998	23,672	11,957	8,299	1,903
Delaware	8,076	8,994	817	7,259	1,895	363	2,055	708
District of Columbia	61,920	102,904	8,699	53,221	3,982	21,250	10,872	23,030
Florida	186,704	9,930	22,647	164,056	63,317	17,981	28,066	12,964
Georgia	92,387	9,537	22,794	69,594	19,744	12,461	16,751	17,372
Hawaii	20,855	15,331	10,003	10,852	2,819	2,745	3,026	7,898
Idaho	14,252	9,092	1,079	13,173	2,835	2,633	2,980	1,245
Illinois	109,967	8,571	10,442	99,525	32,513	11,601	24,060	7,949
Indiana	58,603	9,038	7,147	51,456	17,098	5,498	11,965	4,360
Iowa	28,379	9,316	2,581	25,797	8,246	2,373	6,394	1,902
Kansas	29,046	10,180	6,921	22,124	6,845	3,060	4,736	5,818
Kentucky	57,271	13,198	13,252	44,018	16,241	7,486	9,502	9,205
Louisiana	53,214	11,738	9,297	43,917	13,101	7,291	15,088	4,703
Maine	14,644	11,024	2,152	12,492	3,094	1,736	3,787	1,134
Maryland	96,261	16,673	18,677	77,584	21,137	26,522	14,441	15,041
Massachusetts	82,454	12,593	14,562	67,892	21,196	15,987	22,352	4,506
Michigan	90,921	9,199	6,057	84,865	26,675	6,467	20,577	4,798
Minnesota	44,376	8,367	3,114	41,261	13,256	2,950	10,528	3,368
Mississippi	31,419	10,588	4,070	27,349	8,081	2,666	7,871	3,017
Missouri	70,348	11,746	15,133	55,215	16,801	13,002	14,003	7,321
Montana	10,758	10,874	946	9,812	2,401	819	2,939	1,195
Nebraska	16,532	9,052	2,112	14,420	4,478	1,307	3,507	1,783
Nevada	19,771	7,321	2,896	16,875	4,475	2,407	3,702	1,942
New Hampshire	11,335	8,610	1,603	9,732	2,405	1,435	2,311	880
New Jersey	80,990	9,212	10,351	70,639	24,895	10,236	15,457	5,578
New Mexico	27,959	13,578	3,236	24,723	4,343	7,499	6,720	2,768
New York	202,266	10,438	15,244	187,023	57,533	13,883	63,104	13,936
North Carolina	90,737	9,516	17,607	73,130	19,587	6,091	20,099	15,349
North Dakota	8,696	12,930	1,039	7,657	2,485	685	2,237	1,083
Ohio	106,449	9,227	9,954	96,495	31,106	8,829	24,399	6,975
Oklahoma	38,475	10,256	7,008	31,466	9,098	3,375	7,855	5,575
Oregon	33,974	8,868	2,160	31,814	8,586	2,047	8,694	2,569
Pennsylvania	145,934	11,489	16,254	129,680	44,909	19,352	29,411	8,803
Rhode Island	11,759	11,172	1,488	10,271	3,276	1,001	3,152	997
South Carolina	46,578	10,070	8,853	37,726	9,653	8,171	8,210	4,618
South Dakota	9,507	11,676	1,180	8,327	2,688	913	2,250	1,031
Tennessee	68,866	10,852	5,647	63,219	19,677	10,141	14,094	3,837
Texas	225,725	8,977	54,249	171,476	50,157	40,594	44,624	29,926
Utah	23,545	8,519	4,782	18,764	5,580	3,758	4,987	3,195
Vermont	7,405	11,834	1,101	6,304	1,362	932	2,380	724
Virginia	136,083	17,008	58,115	77,968	16,101	58,338	12,228	21,112
Washington	70,437	10,475	14,964	55,474	13,650	10,041	14,725	11,539
West Virginia	21,511	11,609	1,129	20,382	5,081	1,783	4,970	1,936
Wisconsin	54,866	9,648	9,980	44,886	13,310	9,805	11,992	2,926
Wyoming	6,211	11,019	621	5,590	1,034	569	2,254	709

[1] Based on U.S. Census Bureau estimated resident population as of April 1. [2] Includes Island Areas, not shown separately.

Source: U.S. Census Bureau, *Consolidated Federal Funds Report for Fiscal Year 2010,* September 2011. See also <http://www.census.gov/govs/cffr/>.

Table 498. U.S. Savings Bonds: 1990 to 2011

[In billions of dollars (122.5 represents $122,500,000,000), except percent. For fiscal years ending September 30]

Item	Unit	1990	1995	2000	2004	2005	2006	2007	2008	2009	2010	2011
Amounts outstanding, total [1]	Bil. dol	122.5	181.5	177.7	194.1	189.9	189.2	181.5	177.8	175.6	172.3	169.0
Sales	Bil. dol	7.8	7.2	5.6	10.3	6.5	8.5	3.6	3.6	3.0	2.6	1.8
Accrued discounts	Bil. dol	8.0	9.5	6.9	6.9	6.7	7.5	7.2	7.1	6.9	5.2	5.6
Redemptions [2]	Bil. dol	7.5	11.8	14.5	14.6	13.8	16.0	17.4	13.6	11.7	11.5	11.0
Percent of total outstanding	Percent	6.1	6.5	8.2	7.5	7.3	8.5	9.6	7.6	6.7	6.7	6.5

[1] Interest-bearing debt only for amounts at end of year. [2] Matured and unmatured bonds.

Source: U.S. Department of the Treasury, Bureau of Public Debt, "Savings Bonds and Notes Tables", <http://www.treasurydirect.gov/govt/reports/pd/pd.htm>, accessed September 2013.

Table 499. Internal Revenue Gross Collections by Type of Tax: 2005 to 2012

[2,269 represents $2,269,000,000,000, except percent. For fiscal years ending September 30. See text, this section, for information on taxes]

Type of tax	Gross collections (bil. dol.)						Percent of total					
	2005	2008	2009	2010	2011	2012	2005	2008	2009	2010	2011	2012
United States, total............	**2,269**	**2,745**	**2,345**	**2,345**	**2,415**	**2,524**	**100.0**	**100.0**	**100.0**	**100.0**	**100.0**	**100.0**
Individual income taxes...........	1,108	1,400	1,175	1,164	1,331	1,371	48.8	51.0	50.2	49.7	55.1	54.3
Withheld by employers..........	787	971	881	900	1,010	1,038	34.7	35.4	37.6	38.4	41.8	41.1
Tax payments [1].................	321	430	295	264	321	333	14.1	15.7	12.6	11.3	13.3	13.2
Estate and trust income tax.......	(NA)	26	15	12	15	16	(NA)	0.9	0.6	0.5	0.6	0.7
Employment taxes.................	771	883	858	824	768	784	34.0	32.2	36.6	35.1	31.8	31.1
Old-age and disability insurance........................	760	871	847	813	756	772	33.5	31.7	36.1	34.7	31.3	30.6
Unemployment insurance........	7	7	7	7	7	7	0.3	0.3	0.3	0.3	0.3	0.3
Railroad retirement...............	5	5	5	5	5	5	0.2	0.2	0.2	0.2	0.2	0.2
Business income taxes [2].........	307	354	225	278	243	281	13.5	12.9	9.6	11.9	10.1	11.1
Estate and gift taxes..............	26	30	25	20	9	14	1.1	1.1	1.1	0.8	0.4	0.6
Excise taxes......................	57	52	47	47	49	56	2.5	1.9	2.0	2.0	2.0	2.2

NA Not available. [1] Includes estimated income tax collections and payments made with tax filings. Also includes estate and trust income tax for 2005–2007. [2] Includes corporate income tax and tax-exempt organization unrelated business income tax.

Source: U.S. Internal Revenue Service, *IRS Data Book* (Publication 55B), 2012, and earlier editions. See also <http://www.irs.gov/uac/Tax-Stats-2>.

Table 500. Individual Income Tax Returns Filed—Audits Coverage: 1995 to 2012

[114,683 represents 114,683,000, except percent. See the annual *IRS Data Book* (Publication 55B) for a detailed explanation. An IRS audit is a review/examination of an organization's or individual's tax return]

Year	Returns filed [1] (1,000)	Returns examined		Total recommended additional tax [3] ($1,000)	Average recommended additional tax per return (dol.) [3]
		Total [2] (1,000)	Percent coverage		
1995................	114,683	1,919	1.7	7,756,954	4,041
1999................	122,547	1,100	0.9	4,458,474	4,052
2000................	124,887	618	0.5	3,388,905	5,486
2001................	127,097	732	0.6	3,301,860	4,512
2002................	129,445	744	0.6	3,636,486	4,889
2003................	130,341	849	0.7	4,559,902	5,369
2004................	130,134	997	0.8	6,201,693	6,220
2005................	130,577	1,199	0.9	13,355,087	11,138
2006................	132,276	1,284	1.0	13,045,221	10,160
2007................	134,543	1,385	1.0	15,705,155	11,343
2008................	137,850	1,392	1.0	12,462,770	8,956
2009 [4]............	138,950	1,426	1.0	14,940,892	10,478
2010................	142,823	1,581	1.1	15,066,486	9,527
2011................	140,837	1,565	1.1	14,652,239	9,364
2012................	143,400	1,482	1.0	15,310,908	10,331

[1] Returns generally filed in previous calendar year. [2] Includes taxpayer examinations by correspondence. [3] For 1995 to 1997, amount includes associated penalties. [4] Excludes returns filed by individuals only to receive an economic stimulus payment and who had no other reason to file.

Source: U.S. Internal Revenue Service, *IRS Data Book* (Publication 55B), 2012, and earlier editions. See also <http://www.irs.gov/uac/Tax-Stats-2>.

Table 501. Federal Individual Income Tax Returns—Adjusted Gross Income, Taxable Income, and Total Income Tax: 2008 to 2010

[142,451 represents 142,451,000. For tax years. Based on a sample of returns, see source and Appendix III]

Year	2008		2009		2010		Percent change in amount, 2009-10
	Number of returns (1,000)	Amount (mil. dol.)	Number of returns (1,000)	Amount (mil. dol.)	Number of returns (1,000)	Amount (mil. dol.)	
Adjusted gross income (less deficit).....	**142,451**	**8,262,860**	**140,494**	**7,626,431**	**142,892**	**8,089,142**	**6.1**
Exemptions [1]....................	282,929	980,977	284,240	1,029,070	287,679	1,049,272	2.0
Taxable income...................	107,995	5,652,925	104,161	5,088,388	107,304	5,502,001	8.1
Total income tax..................	90,660	1,031,581	81,890	865,949	84,476	951,674	9.9
Alternative minimum tax..........	3,935	25,649	3,828	22,580	4,020	27,461	21.6

[1] The number of returns columns represent the number of exemptions.

Source: U.S. Internal Revenue Service, *Statistics of Income Bulletin*, Vol. 32, No. 2, Fall 2012, and earlier reports. See also <http://www.irs.gov/uac/Tax-Stats-2>.

Table 502. Federal Individual Income Tax Returns—Adjusted Gross Income (AGI) by Selected Source of Income and Income Class: 2010

[In millions of dollars (8,089,142 represents $8,089,142,000,000), except as indicated. For the tax year. Minus sign (-) indicates net loss was greater than net income. Based on sample; see Appendix III]

Item	Total [1]	Under $10,000	$10,000 to $19,999	$20,000 to $29,999	$30,000 to $39,999	$40,000 to $49,999	$50,000 to $99,999	$100,000 and over
Number of all returns (1,000)	142,892	24,796	24,529	19,135	14,613	10,992	30,533	18,294
Adjusted gross income [2]	8,089,142	-69,695	364,682	473,852	508,013	492,085	2,171,323	4,148,881
Salaries and wages	5,837,350	114,222	258,539	370,137	409,400	393,259	1,674,821	2,616,973
Interest received	214,775	15,018	7,662	7,713	7,094	6,963	34,852	135,473
Dividends in AGI	183,539	7,024	4,610	4,067	4,013	4,538	25,731	133,556
Business, profession, net profit less loss	267,266	4,248	33,223	17,206	13,935	12,355	49,407	136,892
Sales of property, net gain less loss [3]	345,733	-8,310	-803	-290	35	245	8,652	346,204
Pensions and annuities in AGI	558,541	12,144	34,443	39,038	41,270	42,725	197,349	191,571
Rents and royalties, net income less loss [4]	31,569	-7,512	27	-91	-661	-508	1,002	39,313

[1] Includes a small number of returns with no adjusted gross income. [2] Includes other sources, not shown separately. [3] Includes sales of capital assets and other property. [4] Excludes rental passive losses disallowed in the computation of AGI.

Source: U.S. Internal Revenue Service, *Statistics of Income--2010 Individual income Tax Returns*, Publication 1304. See also <http://www.irs.gov/uac/Tax-Stats-2>.

Table 503. Federal Individual Income Tax Returns—Total and Selected Sources of Adjusted Gross Income: 2009 and 2010

[140,494 represents 140,494,000. For tax years. Based on a sample of returns, see source and Appendix III. Minus sign (-) indicates decrease]

Item	2009 Number of returns (1,000)	2009 Amount (mil. dol.)	2010 Number of returns (1,000)	2010 Amount (mil. dol.)	Change in amount, 2009-10 Net change (mil. dol.)	Percent change
Adjusted gross income (less deficit) [1]	**140,494**	**7,626,431**	**142,892**	**8,089,142**	**462,711**	**6.1**
Salaries and wages	116,669	5,707,088	117,820	5,837,350	130,262	2.3
Taxable interest	57,811	168,001	55,130	139,611	-28,390	-16.9
Ordinary dividends	29,288	163,459	28,008	183,539	20,080	12.3
Qualified dividends	25,413	123,570	25,049	136,483	12,913	10.5
Business or profession net income (less loss)	22,112	244,983	22,506	267,266	22,283	9.1
Net capital gain	20,291	231,548	21,315	364,410	132,862	57.4
Capital gain distributions [2]	4,191	2,411	6,567	6,270	3,859	160.1
Sales of property other than capital assets, net gain (less loss)	1,788	-18,027	1,977	-18,076	-49	-0.3
Sales of property other than capital assets, net gain	675	11,898	795	15,719	3,821	32.1
Taxable social security benefits	15,320	174,650	16,180	190,746	16,096	9.2
Total rental and royalty net income (less net loss) [3]	10,636	22,473	10,727	31,569	9,096	40.5
Partnership and S corporation net income (less loss)	8,013	345,097	8,010	394,473	49,376	14.3
Estate and trust net income (less loss)	652	17,382	639	19,692	2,310	13.3
Farm net income (less loss)	1,924	-14,095	1,909	-11,732	2,363	16.8
Farm net income	523	11,616	583	12,252	636	5.5
Unemployment compensation	11,299	83,538	14,937	120,250	36,712	43.9
Taxable pensions and annuities	26,020	523,296	26,597	558,541	35,245	6.7
Taxable Individual Retirement Account (IRA) distributions	9,659	135,203	12,517	194,333	59,130	43.7
Other net income (less loss) [4]	(NA)	31,316	(NA)	34,629	3,313	10.6
Gambling earnings	1,768	23,776	1,842	25,188	1,412	5.9

NA Not available. [1] Includes other sources of income, not shown separately. [2] Includes both Schedule D and Form 1040 or 1040A capital gain distributions. [3] Includes farm rental net income (less loss). [4] Other net income (less loss) represents data reported on Form 1040, line 21, except net operating losses, foreign-earned income exclusions, cancellation of debt, taxable health savings account distributions, and gambling earnings.

Source: U.S. Internal Revenue Service, *Statistics of Income Bulletin*, Vol. 32, No. 2, Fall 2012. See also <http://www.irs.gov/uac/Tax-Stats-2>.

Table 504. Federal Individual Income Tax Returns—Net Capital Gains and Capital Gain Distributions From Mutual Funds: 1991 to 2010

[15,009 represents 15,009,000. For tax years. Based on a sample of returns, see source and Appendix III. Minus sign (-) indicates decrease]

Tax year	Net capital gain (less loss)				Capital gain distributions [2]			
	Number of returns (1,000)	Current dollars (mil. dol.)	Constant (1982–1984) dollars [1]		Number of returns (1,000)	Current dollars (mil. dol.)	Constant (1982–1984) dollars [1]	
			Amount (mil. dol.)	Percent change			Amount (mil. dol.)	Percent change
1991...................	15,009	102,776	75,460	-13.7	5,796	4,665	3,425	14.6
1992...................	16,491	118,230	84,269	11.7	5,917	7,426	5,293	54.5
1993...................	18,409	144,172	99,773	18.4	9,998	11,995	8,301	56.8
1994...................	18,823	142,288	96,011	-3.8	9,803	11,322	7,640	-8.0
1995...................	19,963	170,415	111,821	16.5	10,744	14,391	9,443	23.6
1996...................	22,065	251,817	160,495	43.5	12,778	24,722	15,757	66.9
1997...................	24,240	356,083	221,859	38.2	14,969	45,132	28,120	78.5
1998...................	25,690	446,084	273,671	23.4	16,070	46,147	28,311	0.7
1999...................	27,701	542,758	325,785	19.0	17,012	59,473	35,698	26.1
2000...................	29,521	630,542	366,169	12.4	17,546	79,079	45,923	28.6
2001...................	25,956	326,527	184,375	-49.6	12,216	13,609	7,685	-83.3
2002...................	24,189	238,789	132,734	-28.0	7,567	5,343	2,970	-61.4
2003...................	22,985	294,354	159,975	20.5	7,265	4,695	2,552	-14.1
2004...................	25,267	473,662	250,747	56.7	10,733	15,336	8,119	218.1
2005...................	26,196	668,015	342,046	36.4	13,393	35,581	18,219	124.4
2006...................	26,668	779,462	386,638	13.0	14,511	59,417	29,473	61.8
2007...................	27,156	907,656	437,758	13.2	15,714	86,397	41,669	41.4
2008...................	23,731	469,273	217,959	-50.2	11,544	21,954	10,197	-75.5
2009...................	20,291	231,548	107,929	-50.5	4,191	2,411	1,124	-89.0
2010...................	21,315	364,410	167,118	54.8	6,567	6,270	2,875	155.9

[1] Constant dollars were calculated using the U.S. Bureau of Labor Statistics consumer price index for urban consumers (CPI-U, 1982–84 = 100). See Table 753. [2] Capital gain distributions are included in net capital gain (less loss). For 1991–1996, and 1999 and later years, capital gain distributions from mutual funds are the sum of the amounts reported on the Form 1040 and Schedule D. For 1997 and 1998, capital gain distributions were reported entirely on the Schedule D.

Source: U.S. Internal Revenue Service, *Statistics of Income Bulletin*, Vol. 32, No. 2, Fall 2012. See also <http://www.irs.gov/uac/Tax-Stats-2>.

Table 505. Alternative Minimum Tax: 1987 to 2010

[140 represents 140,000. For tax years. Based on a sample of returns, see source and Appendix III]

Tax year	Highest statutory alternative minimum tax rate (percent)	Alternative minimum tax		Tax year	Highest statutory alternative minimum tax rate (percent)	Alternative minimum tax	
		Number of returns (1,000)	Amount (mil. dol.)			Number of returns (1,000)	Amount (mil. dol.)
1987.................	21	140	1,675	1999...........	[1] 28	1,018	6,478
1988.................	21	114	1,028	2000...........	[1] 28	1,304	9,601
1989.................	21	117	831	2001...........	[1] 28	1,120	6,757
1990.................	21	132	830	2002...........	[1] 28	1,911	6,854
1991.................	24	244	1,213	2003...........	[1] 28	2,358	9,470
1992.................	24	287	1,357	2004...........	[1] 28	3,096	13,029
1993.................	28	335	2,053	2005...........	[1] 28	4,005	17,421
1994.................	28	369	2,212	2006...........	[1] 28	3,967	21,565
1995.................	28	414	2,291	2007...........	[1] 28	4,109	24,110
1996.................	28	478	2,813	2008...........	[1] 28	3,935	25,649
1997.................	[1] 28	618	4,005	2009...........	[1] 28	3,828	22,580
1998.................	[1] 28	853	5,015	2010...........	[1] 28	4,020	27,461

[1] Top rate on most long-term capital gains was 20 percent; beginning 2003, the rate was 15 percent.

Source: U.S. Internal Revenue Service, *Statistics of Income Bulletin*, Winter issues. See also <http://www.irs.gov/uac/Tax-Stats-2>.

Table 506. Federal Individual Income Tax Returns—Sources of Net Losses Included in Adjusted Gross Income: 2008 to 2010

[5,677 represents 5,677,000. For tax years. Based on a sample of returns, see source and Appendix III]

Item	2008 Number of returns (1,000)	2008 Amount (mil. dol.)	2009 Number of returns (1,000)	2009 Amount (mil. dol.)	2010 Number of returns (1,000)	2010 Amount (mil. dol.)
Total net losses...	(NA)	477,538	(NA)	493,543	(NA)	486,798
Business or profession net loss.........................	5,677	60,646	5,572	63,905	5,497	55,510
Net capital loss [1].......................................	12,357	28,568	13,532	31,912	12,806	29,820
Net loss, sales of property other than capital assets..	949	20,764	1,113	29,926	1,182	33,795
Total rental and royalty net loss [2].................	4,936	57,145	5,002	55,406	4,967	53,069
Partnership and S corporation net loss................	2,959	175,489	3,006	152,676	2,872	131,065
Estate and trust net loss................................	48	3,748	52	3,106	49	2,526
Farm net loss...	1,399	26,596	1,401	25,711	1,327	23,985
Net operating loss [3]....................................	920	97,019	1,120	124,079	1,147	144,553
Other net loss [4]...	244	7,564	250	6,822	289	12,477

NA Not available. [1] Includes only the portion of capital losses allowable in the calculation of adjusted gross income. Only $3,000 of net capital loss per return ($1,500 for married filing separately) are allowed to be included in negative total income. Any excess is carried forward to future years. [2] Includes farm rental net loss. [3] Net operating loss is a carryover of the loss from a business when taxable income from a prior year was less than zero. [4] Other net loss represents losses reported on Form 1040, line 21, except net operating loss and the foreign-earned income exclusion.

Source: U.S. Internal Revenue Service, *Statistics of Income Bulletin, Vol. 32, No. 2,* Fall 2012, and earlier reports. See also <http://www.irs.gov/uac/SOI-Tax-Stats-Fall-Bulletin-2012>.

Table 507. Federal Individual Income Tax Returns—Number, Income Tax, and Average Tax by Size of Adjusted Gross Income: 2000 and 2010

[129,374 represents 129,374,000. Based on sample of returns; see Appendix III. Minus sign (-) indicates net loss was greater than net income]

Size of adjusted gross income	Number of returns (1,000) 2000	2010	Adjusted gross income (AGI) (bil. dol.) 2000	2010	Income tax total [1] (bil. dol.) 2000	2010	Taxes as percent of AGI (for taxable returns only) 2000	2010	Average tax (for taxable returns only) (dol.) 2000	2010
Total..........................	129,374	142,892	6,365	8,089	981	952	16	13	10,129	11,266
Less than $1,000 [2]...........	2,966	4,269	-58	-188	–	–	(X)	(X)	648	59
$1,000 to $2,999..............	5,385	4,026	11	8	–	–	7	6	134	123
$3,000 to $4,999..............	5,599	4,224	22	17	–	–	4	5	179	192
$5,000 to $6,999..............	5,183	4,619	31	28	1	–	5	2	297	96
$7,000 to $8,999..............	4,972	4,928	40	40	1	–	4	3	331	240
$9,000 to $10,999.............	5,089	5,241	51	52	1	–	5	4	470	356
$11,000 to $12,999............	4,859	5,212	58	63	2	–	6	3	704	362
$13,000 to $14,999............	4,810	5,085	67	71	3	–	6	2	883	264
$15,000 to $16,999............	4,785	4,860	76	78	3	1	7	2	1,052	381
$17,000 to $18,999............	4,633	4,668	83	84	4	1	7	3	1,279	538
$19,000 to $21,999............	6,502	6,420	133	131	7	2	8	4	1,565	816
$22,000 to $24,999............	5,735	5,961	135	140	8	3	8	5	1,815	1,111
$25,000 to $29,999............	8,369	8,950	229	245	16	7	8	5	2,248	1,497
$30,000 to $39,999............	13,548	14,613	471	508	40	21	9	6	3,094	2,139
$40,000 to $49,999............	10,412	10,992	466	492	46	27	10	7	4,462	3,055
$50,000 to $74,999............	17,076	18,727	1,045	1,151	116	81	11	8	6,824	4,828
$75,000 to $99,999............	8,597	11,805	738	1,020	100	86	14	9	11,631	7,561
$100,000 to $199,999.........	8,083	13,998	1,066	1,870	184	224	17	12	22,783	16,180
$200,000 to $499,999.........	2,136	3,472	614	985	146	193	24	20	68,628	55,781
$500,000 to $999,999.........	396	544	269	368	76	89	28	24	192,092	163,605
$1,000,000 or more...........	240	280	817	925	226	215	28	23	945,172	771,285

– Represents or rounds to zero. X Not applicable. [1] Consists of income tax after credits (including alternative minimum tax). [2] In addition to low-income taxpayers, this size class (and others) includes taxpayers with "tax preferences," not reflected in adjusted gross income or taxable income, which are subject to the "alternative minimum tax" (included in total income tax).

Source: U.S. Internal Revenue Service, "Statistics of Income Bulletin, Historical Tables," <http://www.irs.gov/uac/Tax-Stats-2>, accessed September 2013.

Table 508. Federal Individual Income Tax Returns—Selected Itemized Deductions and the Standard Deduction: 2009 and 2010

[45,696 represents 45,696,000. For tax years. Based on a sample of returns, see source and Appendix III. Minus sign (-) indicates decrease]

Item	2009 Number of returns [1] (1,000)	2009 Amount (mil. dol.)	2010 Number of returns [1] (1,000)	2010 Amount (mil. dol.)	Percent change, 2009–10 Number of returns [1] (1,000)	Percent change, 2009–10 Amount (percent)
Total itemized deductions before limitation...............	**45,696**	**1,216,313**	**46,645**	**1,216,989**	**2.1**	**0.1**
Medical and dental expenses after 7.5 percent Adjusted Gross Income (AGI) limitation.......................	10,090	79,866	10,431	85,337	3.4	6.8
Taxes paid [2]..	45,424	432,032	46,316	445,097	2.0	3.0
State and local income taxes.................................	33,755	236,096	33,473	246,234	-0.8	4.3
State and local general sales taxes.........................	10,262	15,563	11,396	16,463	11.0	5.8
Interest paid [3]..	37,004	442,051	37,481	414,713	1.3	-6.2
Home mortgage interest.......................................	36,542	420,813	36,958	393,958	1.1	-6.4
Charitable contributions [4]..	37,243	158,017	38,143	170,236	2.4	7.7
Other than cash contributions................................	21,867	31,816	22,485	44,322	2.8	39.3
Casualty and theft losses.....................................	134	2,330	105	2,234	-22.0	-4.1
Miscellaneous deductions after 2-percent AGI limitation...	11,868	80,903	11,558	78,925	-2.6	-2.4
Total unlimited miscellaneous deductions....................	1,411	21,114	1,402	20,448	-0.7	-3.2
Itemized deductions in excess of limitation..................	5,706	12,504	133	322	-97.7	-97.4
Total itemized deductions after limitation [5]..................	45,696	1,203,808	46,645	1,216,667	2.1	1.1
Total standard deduction.......................................	92,269	747,780	93,678	738,539	1.5	-1.2
Total deductions (after itemized deduction limitation)...	137,965	1,951,588	140,323	1,955,206	1.7	0.2

[1] Returns with no adjusted gross income are excluded from the deduction counts. For this reason, the sum of the number of returns with total itemized deductions and the number of returns with total standard deduction is less than the total number of returns for all filers. [2] Includes real estate taxes, personal property taxes, and other taxes, not shown separately. [3] Includes investment interest, deductible mortgage "points," and qualified mortgage interest premiums, not shown separately. [4] For more information, see Table 609. [5] The itemized deduction limitation was eliminated in 2010. The number of returns and the amount for 2010 represent prior year returns only.

Source: U.S. Internal Revenue Service, *Statistics of Income Bulletin*, Vol. 32, No. 2, Fall 2012. See also <http://www.irs.gov/uac/Tax-Stats-2>.

Table 509. Federal Individual Income Tax Returns—Statutory Adjustments: 2009 and 2010

[34,764 represents 34,764,000. For tax years. Based on a sample of returns, see source and Appendix III. Minus sign (-) indicates decrease]

Item	2009 Number of returns (1,000)	2009 Amount (mil. dol.)	2010 Number of returns (1,000)	2010 Amount (mil. dol.)	Percent change in amount, 2009–10
Total statutory adjustments..	**34,764**	**112,967**	**35,261**	**119,299**	**5.6**
Payments to an Individual Retirement Account (IRA).................	2,588	11,215	2,583	11,443	2.0
Educator expenses deduction..	3,841	970	3,614	915	-5.7
Certain business expenses of reservists, performing artists, etc.....	143	558	132	473	-15.3
Moving expenses adjustment...	856	2,100	1,002	2,674	27.4
Student loan interest deduction...	9,719	8,340	10,119	9,093	9.0
Tuition and fees deduction..	2,423	5,453	1,997	4,365	-20
Health savings account deduction......................................	946	2,589	1,005	2,913	12.5
Self-employment tax deduction...	17,436	23,834	17,668	24,174	1.4
Self-employment health insurance deduction........................	3,626	21,820	3,831	23,336	6.9
Payments to a self-employed retirement (Keogh) plan...............	923	18,857	910	18,906	0.3
Forfeited interest penalty..	1,205	339	1,102	356	5.1
Alimony paid...	570	9,844	597	10,416	5.8
Domestic production activities deduction..............................	491	5,698	616	8,675	52.2
Other adjustments [1]...	(NA)	1,350	(NA)	1,558	15.5

NA Not available. [1] Includes foreign housing adjustment, Archer medical savings accounts deduction, and other adjustments for 2009 and 2010.

Source: U.S. Internal Revenue Service, *Statistics of Income Bulletin*, Vol. 32, No. 2, Fall 2012. See also <http://www.irs.gov/uac/Tax-Stats-2>.

Table 510. Federal Individual Income Tax Returns—Itemized Deductions and Statutory Adjustments by Size of Adjusted Gross Income: 2010

[46,645 represents 46,645,000. Based on a sample of returns; see Appendix III]

Item	Unit	Adjusted gross income class							
		Total	Under $10,000	$10,000 to $19,999	$20,000 to $29,999	$30,000 to $39,999	$40,000 to $49,999	$50,000 to $99,999	$100,000 and over
Returns with itemized deductions:									
Number of returns [1]	1,000	46,645	1,013	2,044	2,807	3,564	3,965	17,258	15,994
Amount [1, 2]	Mil. dol	1,216,667	16,140	31,039	42,960	55,787	64,644	337,216	668,880
Medical and dental expenses: [3]									
Returns	1,000	10,431	689	1,309	1,326	1,268	1,140	3,536	1,163
Amount	Mil. dol	85,337	6,222	11,269	9,932	9,380	8,080	26,527	13,927
Taxes paid:									
Returns	1,000	46,316	947	1,997	2,747	3,510	3,931	17,208	15,976
Amount	Mil. dol	445,097	3,168	6,053	9,383	12,899	16,729	105,299	291,565
State and local taxes: [4]									
Returns	1,000	44,869	807	1,836	2,567	3,355	3,804	16,768	15,731
Amount	Mil. dol	262,698	617	1,389	2,799	4,680	6,964	51,727	194,521
Real estate taxes:									
Returns	1,000	40,983	746	1,573	2,154	2,852	3,281	15,392	14,985
Amount	Mil. dol	172,201	2,457	4,327	6,128	7,719	9,120	50,246	92,204
Interest paid:									
Returns	1,000	37,481	607	1,201	1,871	2,624	3,043	14,336	13,799
Amount	Mil. dol	414,713	5,192	9,107	14,566	20,730	24,860	134,939	205,319
Home mortgage interest:									
Returns	1,000	36,958	586	1,171	1,841	2,601	3,010	14,210	13,539
Amount	Mil. dol	393,958	5,033	8,834	14,123	20,000	23,931	130,470	191,568
Charitable contributions:									
Returns	1,000	38,143	576	1,362	1,945	2,571	2,975	14,189	14,524
Amount	Mil. dol	170,236	693	2,550	4,119	5,779	6,873	39,927	110,295
Unreimbursed employee business expenses:									
Returns	1,000	14,632	73	297	701	1,113	1,330	6,198	4,919
Amount	Mil. dol	72,143	411	1,183	3,661	5,772	7,106	28,777	25,233
Returns with statutory adjustments:									
Number of returns	1,000	35,261	4,552	4,919	3,470	3,090	2,867	9,293	7,070
Amount of adjustments [2]	Mil. dol	119,299	6,834	6,503	6,280	6,117	6,189	24,726	62,650
Payments to IRAs: [5]									
Returns	1,000	2,583	64	136	229	263	305	941	645
Amount	Mil. dol	11,443	180	428	759	960	1,236	4,072	3,808
Deduction for self-employment tax:									
Returns	1,000	17,668	3,401	3,460	1,687	1,276	1,032	3,510	3,302
Amount	Mil. dol	24,174	1,559	2,659	1,631	1,436	1,240	4,917	10,733
Self-employment health insurance:									
Returns	1,000	3,831	433	367	320	282	264	884	1,281
Amount	Mil. dol	23,336	1,772	1,411	1,324	1,289	1,260	4,920	11,359
Payments to Keogh plans:									
Returns	1,000	910	9	17	22	23	29	156	654
Amount	Mil. dol	18,906	123	122	95	136	142	1,623	16,666

[1] After limitations. [2] Includes other deductions and adjustments, not shown separately. [3] Before limitation. [4] State and local taxes include income taxes and sales taxes. [5] Individual Retirement Accounts.

Source: U.S. Internal Revenue Service, *Statistics of Income Bulletin*, Vol. 32, No. 2, Fall 2012. See also <http://www.irs.gov/uac/Tax-Stats-2>.

Table 511. Federal Individual Income Tax Returns—Selected Tax Credits: 2008 to 2010

[55,229 represents 55,229,000. For tax years. Based on a sample of returns, see source and Appendix III]

Item	2008		2009		2010	
	Number of returns (1,000)	Amount (mil. dol.)	Number of returns (1,000)	Amount (mil. dol.)	Number of returns (1,000)	Amount (mil. dol.)
Total tax credits [1]	**55,229**	**75,352**	**87,501**	**110,076**	**90,735**	**113,579**
Child care credit	6,587	3,527	6,286	3,317	6,338	3,398
Earned income credit [2]	3,382	971	1,489	489	1,409	451
Foreign tax credit	6,708	16,572	6,310	13,060	6,662	15,223
General business credit	304	1,649	293	1,601	462	2,168
Minimum tax credit	416	945	320	759	260	663
Child tax credit [3]	25,174	30,538	23,563	28,417	23,580	28,504
Education credits	7,741	7,633	10,599	10,837	11,867	12,272
Retirement savings contribution credit	5,961	977	6,253	1,040	6,130	1,030
Residential energy credits [2]	226	217	6,712	5,823	7,156	6,173
Making work pay credit [2]	(NA)	(NA)	68,570	34,429	71,827	37,090

NA Not available. [1] Includes credits not shown separately. [2] Represents portion of credit used to offset income tax before credits. [3] Excludes refundable portion.

Source: U.S. Internal Revenue Service, *Statistics of Income Bulletin*, Vol. 32, No. 2, Fall 2012 and earlier reports. See also <http://www.irs.gov/uac/Tax-Stats-2>.

Table 512. Federal Individual Income Tax Returns by State: 2011

[146,456 represents 146,456,000. For tax year. Data may not agree with data in other tables due to differing survey methodology used to derive state data]

State	Total number of returns (1,000)	Adjusted gross income (mil. dol.)			Itemized deductions (mil. dol.)				Income tax (mil. dol.)
		Total [1]	Salaries and wages	Net capital gain [2]	Total [1]	State and local income tax	Real estate taxes	Mortgage interest paid	
U.S................	146,456	8,378,794	6,072,881	369,295	1,254,760	267,619	172,618	360,579	1,058,666
AL.....................	2,092	100,318	73,826	2,349	12,971	2,073	637	3,812	10,985
AK.....................	371	21,706	15,642	475	1,887	26	328	833	2,816
AZ.....................	2,790	141,315	104,346	4,707	21,575	2,837	1,913	7,649	16,462
AR.....................	1,234	57,281	41,501	1,712	6,862	1,666	417	1,681	6,066
CA.....................	17,062	1,066,050	774,235	53,883	205,964	53,600	23,727	66,194	141,283
CO.....................	2,421	150,646	107,032	9,125	22,179	4,114	2,011	8,346	19,237
CT.....................	1,747	146,102	101,255	8,977	24,206	7,192	4,691	6,024	22,900
DE.....................	434	24,590	17,888	607	3,504	825	313	1,318	2,868
DC.....................	330	25,218	17,897	1,732	4,232	1,326	341	1,141	3,914
FL.....................	9,696	485,461	321,109	32,094	59,609	2,324	8,243	18,375	63,243
GA.....................	4,672	223,941	171,840	6,343	36,824	7,278	3,553	10,998	25,671
HI.....................	662	34,372	24,758	1,048	5,247	1,180	301	2,160	3,655
ID.....................	671	30,728	22,459	1,118	5,413	1,016	395	1,562	3,128
IL.....................	6,122	371,414	269,820	16,278	55,241	11,010	11,583	15,251	48,748
IN.....................	3,018	147,574	110,659	3,664	17,597	3,924	1,469	4,861	16,173
IA.....................	1,421	75,360	54,049	2,234	9,356	2,283	1,226	2,284	8,244
KS.....................	1,325	73,272	51,928	2,811	9,544	2,290	1,152	2,285	8,581
KY.....................	1,877	88,207	65,697	2,275	11,387	3,189	996	3,151	9,211
LA.....................	2,023	99,162	73,373	2,794	10,470	1,757	623	2,857	11,461
ME.....................	633	30,652	22,315	917	4,292	1,139	670	1,245	3,195
MD.....................	2,838	194,975	146,202	5,582	37,964	10,576	4,588	11,900	24,844
MA.....................	3,258	241,985	171,553	14,599	36,783	9,770	6,063	10,642	35,294
MI.....................	4,677	234,472	169,681	4,441	30,800	5,949	4,528	8,989	27,008
MN.....................	2,602	157,793	116,634	5,292	24,663	6,616	3,083	7,515	19,335
MS.....................	1,287	52,670	39,947	1,001	6,524	988	428	1,577	5,058
MO.....................	2,729	138,422	100,808	4,435	19,135	3,995	1,961	5,099	15,735
MT.....................	481	22,419	15,186	1,072	3,214	692	324	938	2,424
NE.....................	868	46,459	33,592	1,723	6,017	1,375	871	1,411	5,202
NV.....................	1,298	67,018	47,380	4,425	9,700	336	848	3,276	8,285
NH.....................	678	42,424	31,267	1,857	5,791	457	1,449	1,907	5,338
NJ.....................	4,326	316,449	235,603	10,147	59,915	13,810	13,989	14,545	45,519
NM.....................	914	41,850	29,950	1,220	5,033	851	466	1,747	4,491
NY.....................	9,388	646,262	449,092	46,542	115,168	41,211	18,851	21,365	95,094
NC.....................	4,295	215,963	160,852	6,157	35,704	8,380	3,318	9,993	23,569
ND.....................	344	20,833	13,492	1,146	1,732	256	195	384	2,729
OH.....................	5,509	277,608	203,569	7,104	35,394	9,569	5,386	9,633	31,567
OK.....................	1,617	84,813	59,719	3,481	10,212	1,940	799	2,315	9,984
OR.....................	1,758	91,954	64,706	3,530	16,796	4,521	2,094	5,287	9,999
PA.....................	6,183	348,613	252,904	11,516	44,663	9,823	7,778	12,570	43,183
RI.....................	513	29,193	21,003	1,245	4,942	1,038	838	1,353	3,523
SC.....................	2,091	96,748	70,871	2,390	14,773	3,100	1,027	4,278	10,029
SD.....................	411	21,290	13,724	1,343	1,815	56	232	486	2,483
TN.....................	2,903	140,012	105,232	4,347	15,648	405	1,455	4,859	16,059
TX.....................	11,417	665,901	484,548	35,170	69,752	1,222	12,700	19,027	88,969
UT.....................	1,160	61,131	46,900	2,345	10,884	1,962	853	3,510	6,194
VT.....................	321	16,394	11,667	823	2,159	474	443	617	1,825
VA.....................	3,802	252,171	188,266	9,004	44,180	9,018	4,679	14,546	32,546
WA.....................	3,217	200,198	145,558	9,153	26,234	601	4,114	11,037	25,744
WV.....................	792	37,424	27,354	1,246	3,188	957	191	904	3,974
WI.....................	2,773	148,184	108,916	4,820	22,501	5,934	4,077	5,764	16,726
WY.....................	295	18,086	11,606	1,610	1,809	79	138	548	2,325
Other [3].............	1,110	55,706	53,472	5,385	3,303	609	262	529	5,773

[1] Includes other items, not shown separately. [2] Less loss. [3] Includes returns filed from Army Post Office and Fleet Post Office addresses by members of the armed forces stationed overseas; returns by other U.S. citizens abroad; and returns filed by residents of Puerto Rico with income from sources outside of Puerto Rico or with income earned as U.S. government employees.

Source: U.S. Internal Revenue Service, Statistics of Income Bulletin, "Historical Data Tables," <http://www.irs.gov/uac/SOI-Tax-Stats-Historical-Data-Tables>, accessed July 2013.

Table 513. Federal Individual Income Tax—Tax Liability and Effective and Marginal Tax Rates for Selected Income Groups: 2000 to 2010

[Refers to income after exclusions but before deductions for itemized or standard deductions and for personal exemptions. Tax liability is after reductions for tax credits. As a result of the tax credits, tax liability can be negative, which means that the taxpayer receives a payment from the government. The effective rate represents tax liability, which may be negative as a result of the tax credits, divided by stated income. The marginal tax rate is the percentage of the first additional dollar of income which would be paid in income tax. Tax credits which increase with income can result in negative marginal tax rates. Computations assume itemized deductions (in excess of floors) of 18 percent of adjusted gross income or the standard deduction, whichever is greater. All income is assumed to be from wages and salaries. Does not include Social Security and Medicare taxes imposed on most wages and salaries. Minus sign (-) indicates negative tax liability]

Adjusted gross income	2000	2005	2007	2008 [1]	2009	2010
TAX LIABILITY (dol.)						
Single person, no dependents:						
$5,000	[2]-353	[2]-383	[2]-383	[1,2]-683	[2,5]-693	[2,5]-693
$10,000	[2]391	[2]46	[2]-73	[1,2]-415	[2,5]-598	[2,5]-600
$20,000	1,920	1,405	1,296	[1]656	[5]780	[5]779
$30,000	3,270	2,845	2,789	2,156	[5]2,280	[5]2,279
$40,000	4,988	4,075	4,019	3,394	[5]3,555	[5]3,554
$50,000	7,284	6,115	5,824	5,119	[5]5,125	[5]5,119
$75,000	13,024	11,240	10,949	10,244	[5]10,250	[5]10,244
$100,000	19,233	16,571	16,119	15,969	[5]15,775	[5]15,769
Married couple, two dependents, with one spouse working:						
$5,000	-2,000	[2]-2,000	[2]-2,000	[1,2]-3,200	-2,610	[2,4,5]-2,610
$10,000	-3,888	[2]-4,000	[2]-4,000	[1,2,4]-5,425	-5,670	[2,4,5]-5,670
$20,000	-2,349	[2,4]-4,986	[2,5]-5,404	[1,2,4]-7,484	-7,828	[2,4,5]-7,836
$30,000	475	[2,3,4]-2,810	[2,4,5]-3,490	[1,2,3,4]-5,143	-5,621	[2,3,4,5]-5,637
$40,000	2,218	[3,4]-150	[4,5]-428	[1,2,3,4]-2,637	-2,515	[2,3,4,5]-2,531
$50,000	3,470	[3]1,350	[4]1,073	[1,3]-838	-35	[3,5]-37
$75,000	7,384	[3]4,575	[4]4,403	[1,3]2,523	3,400	[3,5]3,398
$100,000	13,124	[3]8,630	[4]7,948	[1,3]5,888	6,475	[3,5]6,473
EFFECTIVE RATE (percent)						
Single person, no dependents:						
$5,000	-7.1	[2]-7.7	[2]-7.7	[1,2]-13.7	[2,5]-13.9	[2,5]-13.9
$10,000	3.9	[2]0.5	[2]-0.7	[1,2]-4.2	[2,5]-6.0	[2,5]-6.0
$20,000	9.6	7.0	6.5	[1]3.3	[5]3.9	[5]3.9
$30,000	10.9	9.5	9.3	[1]7.2	[5]7.6	[5]7.6
$40,000	12.5	10.2	10.1	[1]8.5	[5]8.9	[5]8.9
$50,000	14.6	12.2	11.6	[1]10.2	[5]10.3	[5]10.2
$75,000	17.4	15.0	14.6	[1]13.7	[5]13.7	[5]13.7
$100,000	19.2	16.6	16.1	16.0	15.8	15.8
Married couple, two dependents, with one spouse working:						
$5,000	[2]-40.0	[2]-40.0	[2]-40.0	[1,2]-64.0	[2,4,5]-52.2	[2,4,5]-52.2
$10,000	[2]-38.9	[2]-40.0	[2]-40.0	[1,2,4]-54.3	[2,4,5]-56.7	[2,4,5]-56.7
$20,000	[2,3]-11.7	[2,4]-24.9	[2,5]-27.0	[1,2,4]-37.4	[2,4,5]-39.1	[2,4,5]-39.2
$30,000	[2,3]1.6	[2,3,4]-9.4	[2,4,5]-11.6	[1,2,3,4]-17.1	[2,3,4,5]-18.7	[2,3,4,5]-18.8
$40,000	[3]5.5	[3,4]-0.4	[4,5]-1.1	[1,2,3,4]-6.6	[2,3,4,5]-6.3	[2,3,4,5]-6.3
$50,000	[3]6.9	[3]2.7	[4]2.1	[1,3]-1.7	[3,5]-0.1	[3,5]-0.1
$75,000	[3]9.8	[3]6.1	[4]5.9	[1,3]3.4	[3,5]4.5	[3,5]4.5
$100,000	[3]13.1	[3]8.6	[4]7.9	[1,3]5.9	[3,5]6.5	[3,5]6.5
MARGINAL TAX RATE (percent)						
Single person, no dependents:						
$5,000	–	[2]-7.7	[2]-7.7	[2]-7.7	[2,5]-13.9	[2,5]-13.9
$10,000	[2]22.7	[2]17.7	[2]17.7	[2]17.7	[2]17.7	[2]17.7
$20,000	15.0	15.0	15.0	15.0	15.0	15.0
$30,000	15.0	15.0	15.0	15.0	15.0	15.0
$40,000	28.0	15.0	15.0	15.0	15.0	15.0
$50,000	28.0	25.0	25.0	25.0	25.0	25.0
$75,000	28.0	25.0	25.0	25.0	[5]27.0	[5]27.0
$100,000	31.0	28.0	28.0	25.0	25.0	25.0
Married couple, two dependents, with one spouse working:						
$5,000	[2]-40.0	[2]-40.0	[2]-40.0	[2]-40.0	[2,4,5]-61.2	[2,4,5]-61.2
$10,000	–	[2]-40.0	[2]-40.0	[2,4]-55.0	[2,4,5]-61.2	[2,4,5]-61.2
$20,000	[2,3]21.1	[2,4]6.1	[2,5]6.1	[2,4]6.1	–	–
$30,000	[2]36.1	[2,3,4]31.1	[2,4,5]31.1	[2,3,4]31.1	[2]31.1	[2]31.1
$40,000	15.0	[3,4]15.0	[4,5]15.0	[2,3,4]31.1	[2]31.1	[2]31.1
$50,000	15.0	15.0	15.0	15.0	15.0	15.0
$75,000	28.0	15.0	15.0	15.0	15.0	15.0
$100,000	28.0	25.0	25.0	25.0	15.0	15.0

– Represents zero. [1] Includes effect of the Recovery Rebate paid in 2008 under the Economic Stimulus Act of 2008 (P.L. 110–185). [2] Includes effect from the refundable earned income tax credit. [3] Includes effect from the child tax credit. [4] Includes effect from the additional (refundable) child tax credit. [5] Includes effect from the (refundable) Making Work Pay tax credit.

Source: U.S. Department of the Treasury, Office of Tax Analysis, unpublished data.

Table 514. Federal Individual Income Tax—Current Income Equivalent to 2000 Constant Income for Selected Income Groups: 2000 to 2010

[Constant 2000 incomes are calculated by using the U.S. Bureau of Labor Statistics Consumer Price Index for Urban Consumers (CPI–U); see Table 753, Section 14. See also headnote, Table 513. Minus sign (-) indicates negative tax liability]

Adjusted gross income (constant 2000 dollars)	2000	2005	2007	2008 [1]	2009	2010
REAL INCOME EQUIVALENT (dol.)						
$5,000	5,000	5,670	6,020	6,250	6,230	6,330
$10,000	10,000	11,340	12,040	12,500	12,460	12,660
$20,000	20,000	22,680	24,080	25,010	24,920	25,330
$30,000	30,000	34,020	36,120	37,510	37,380	37,990
$40,000	40,000	45,370	48,160	50,010	49,830	50,650
$50,000	50,000	56,710	60,200	62,520	62,290	63,310
$75,000	75,000	85,060	90,310	93,770	93,440	94,970
$100,000	100,000	113,410	120,410	125,030	124,590	126,630
TAX LIABILITY (dol.)						
Single person, no dependents:						
$5000	[2] -353	[2] -399	[2] -428	[1,2] -738	[2,5] -843	[2,5] -850
$10,000	[2] 391	[2] 283	[2] 287	[1,2] -29	[2,5] -164	[2,5] -130
$20,000	1,920	1,807	1,908	[1] 1,408	[5] 1,518	[5] 1,578
$30,000	3,270	3,339	3,542	[1] 3,087	[5] 3,233	[5] 3,307
$40,000	4,988	5,166	5,447	[1] 5,121	[5] 5,090	[5] 5,252
$50,000	7,284	7,491	7,915	[1] 7,685	[5] 7,644	[5] 7,847
$75,000	13,024	13,302	14,087	[1] 14,692	[5] 14,399	[5] 14,737
$100,000	19,233	19,649	20,805	[1] 21,705	[5] 21,304	21,761
Married couple, 2 dependents with one spouse working:						
$5,000	[2] -2,000	[2] -2,268	[2] -2,408	[1,2] -3,700	[2,4,5] -3,363	[2,4,5] -3,424
$10,000	[2] -3,888	[2,4] -4,451	[2] -4,760	[1,2,4] -6,624	[2,4,5] -7,176	[2,4,5] -7,270
$20,000	[2,3] -2,349	[2,4] -4,823	[2,4] -5,157	[1,2,3,4] -6,693	[2,4,5] -7,091	[2,4,5] -7,021
$30,000	[2,3] 475	[2,3,4] -1,561	[2,3,4] -1,589	[1,2,3,4] -3,410	[2,3,4,5] -3,329	[2,4,5] -3,156
$40,000	[3] 2,218	[3] 656	[3,4] 797	[1,3] -836	[3,5] -60	3,560
$50,000	[3] 3,470	[3] 2,325	[3] 2,582	[1,3] 987	[3,5] 1,809	[3,5] 1,959
$75,000	[3] 7,384	[3] 5,812	[3] 6,286	[1,3] 4,831	[3,5] 5,668	[3,5] 5,854
$100,000	[3] 13,124	[3] 11,579	[3] 12,682	[1,3] 11,819	[3,5] 12,216	[3,5] 12,722
EFFECTIVE TAX RATE (percent)						
Single person, no dependents:						
$5,000	[2] -7.1	[2] -7.0	[2] -7.1	[1,2] -11.8	[2,5] -13.5	[2,5] -13.4
$10,000	[2] 3.9	[2] 2.5	[2] 2.4	[1,2] -0.2	[2,5] -1.3	[2,5] -1.0
$20,000	9.6	8.0	7.9	[1] 5.6	[5] 6.1	[5] 6.2
$30,000	10.9	9.8	9.8	[1] 8.2	[5] 8.6	[5] 8.7
$40,000	12.5	11.4	11.3	[1] 10.2	[5] 10.2	[5] 10.4
$50,000	14.6	13.2	13.1	[1] 12.3	[5] 12.3	[5] 12.4
$75,000	17.4	15.6	15.6	[1] 15.7	[5] 15.4	[5] 15.5
$100,000	19.2	17.3	17.3	[1] 17.4	17.1	17.2
Married couple, 2 dependents with one spouse working:						
$5,000	[2] -40.0	[2] -40.0	[2] -40.0	[1,2] -59.2	[2,4,5] -54.0	[2,4,5] -54.1
$10,000	[2] -38.9	[2,4] -39.3	[2] -39.5	[1,2,4] -53.0	[2,4,5] -57.6	[2,4,5] -57.4
$20,000	[2,3] -11.7	[2,4] -21.3	[2,4] -21.4	[1,2,3,4] -26.8	[2,4,5] -28.5	[2,4,5] -27.7
$30,000	[2,3] 1.6	[2,3,4] -4.6	[2,3,4] -4.4	[1,2,3,4] -9.1	[2,3,4,5] -8.9	[2,4,5] -8.3
$40,000	[3] 5.5	[3] 1.4	[3,4] 1.7	[1,3] -1.7	[3,5] -0.1	[3,5] 0.1
$50,000	[3] 6.9	[3] 4.1	[3] 4.3	[1,3] 1.6	[3,5] 2.9	[3,5] 3.1
$75,000	[3] 9.8	[3] 6.8	[3] 7.0	[1,3] 5.2	[3,5] 6.1	[3,5] 6.2
$100,000	[3] 13.1	[3] 10.2	[3] 10.5	[1,3] 9.5	[3,5] 9.8	[3,5] 10.0
MARGINAL TAX RATE (percent)						
Single person, no dependents:						
$5,000	−	−	−	−	[5] -6.2	[5] -6.2
$10,000	[2] 22.7	[2] 17.7	[2] 17.7	[2] 7.7	[2] 17.7	[2] 17.7
$20,000	15.0	15.0	15.0	15.0	15.0	15.0
$30,000	15.0	15.0	15.0	15.0	15.0	15.0
$40,000	28.0	25.0	25.0	25.0	25.0	25.0
$50,000	28.0	25.0	25.0	25.0	25.0	25.0
$75,000	28.0	25.0	25.0	25.0	[5] 27.0	[5] 27.0
$100,000	31.0	28.0	28.0	28.0	28.0	28.0
Married couple, 2 dependents with one spouse working:						
$5,000	[2] -40.0	[2] -40.0	[2] -40.0	[2] -40.0	[2,4,5] -61.2	[2,4,5] -61.2
$10,000		[4] -15.0	[4] -15.0		[2,4,5] -61.2	[2,4,5] -21.2
$20,000	[2,3] 21.1	[2,4] 6.1	[2,3,4] 6.1	[2,3,4] 31.1	[2] 21.1	[2] 21.1
$30,000	[2] 36.1	[2,3,4] 31.1	[2,3,4] 31.1	[2,3,4] 31.1	[2] 31.1	[2] 31.1
$40,000	15.0	15.0	15.0	15.0	15.0	15.0
$50,000	15.0	15.0	15.0	15.0	15.0	15.0
$75,000	28.0	15.0	15.0	15.0	15.0	15.0
$100,000	28.0	[3] 30.1	[3] 30.1	[3] 30.1	[3] 30.1	[3] 30.1

− Represents zero. [1] Includes effect of the Recovery Rebate paid in 2008 under the Economic Stimulus Act of 2008 (P.L. 110–185). [2] Includes effect from the refundable earned income tax credit. [3] Includes effect from the child tax credit. [4] Includes effect from the additional (refundable) child tax credit. [5] Includes effect from the (refundable) Making Work Pay tax credit.

Source: U.S. Department of the Treasury, Office of Tax Analysis, unpublished data.

Table 515. Federal Civilian Employment and Annual Payroll by Branch: 1970 to 2012

[2,997 represents 2,997,000. For fiscal year ending in year shown. See text, Section 8. Includes employees in U.S. territories and foreign countries. Data represent employees in active-duty status, including intermittent employees. Annual employment figures are averages of monthly figures. Excludes Central Intelligence Agency, National Security Agency and as of November 1984, Defense Intelligence Agency; and as of October 1996, National Imagery and Mapping Agency]

| Year | Employment | | | | | | Payroll (mil. dol.) | | | | |
| | Total (1,000) | Percent of U.S. employed [1] | Executive (1,000) | | Legis-lative (1,000) | Judicial (1,000) | Total | Executive | | Legis-lative | Judicial |
			Total	Defense				Total	Defense		
1970...........	[2] 2,997	3.81	2,961	1,263	29	7	27,322	26,894	11,264	338	89
1975...........	2,877	3.35	2,830	1,044	37	10	39,126	38,423	13,418	549	154
1980...........	[2] 2,987	3.01	2,933	971	40	14	58,012	56,841	18,795	883	288
1985...........	3,001	2.80	2,944	1,080	39	18	80,599	78,992	28,330	1,098	509
1990...........	[2] 3,233	2.72	3,173	1,060	38	23	99,138	97,022	31,990	1,329	787
1995...........	2,943	2.36	2,880	852	34	28	118,304	115,328	31,753	1,598	1,379
2000...........	[2] 2,879	2.10	2,816	681	31	32	130,832	127,472	29,607	1,619	1,741
2005...........	2,701	1.91	2,636	671	31	34	152,222	148,275	29,331	2,048	1,900
2006...........	2,700	1.87	2,637	676	29	34	160,570	156,543	29,580	2,109	1,918
2007...........	2,699	1.85	2,636	673	30	33	161,394	157,010	29,025	2,119	2,265
2008...........	2,758	1.90	2,694	694	30	34	167,166	162,675	29,749	2,162	2,328
2009...........	2,838	2.03	2,774	737	31	34	174,804	170,349	30,995	2,203	2,252
2010...........	2,841	2.04	2,777	773	31	34	152,321	147,554	32,377	2,515	2,251
2011...........	2,820	2.02	2,756	774	30	34	166,508	161,897	33,075	2,359	2,255
2012...........	2,761	1.94	2,697	730	30	34	182,030	177,332	32,670	2,442	2,256

[1] Civilian employment only. See Table 613, Section 12. [2] Includes temporary census workers.

Source: U.S. Office of Personnel Management, "Federal Civilian Workforce Statistics—Employment and Trends," <http://www.opm.gov/policy-data-oversight/data-analysis-documentation/federal-employment-reports/#url=Employment-Trends>, accessed September 2013.

Table 516. Full-Time Federal Civilian Employment—Employees and Average Pay by Pay System: 2009 to 2012

[(2,038 represents 2,038,000). As of September 30. Includes employees in U.S., U.S. territories, foreign countries, and unspecified locations. Excludes employees of Congress and federal courts, maritime seamen of U.S. Department of Commerce, and small number for whom rates were not reported. See text, this section, for explanation of general schedule and wage system]

| Pay system | Employees (1,000) | | | | Average annual pay (dol.) | | | |
	2009	2010	2011	2012	2009	2010	2011	2012
Total, excluding postal...............	**2,038**	**2,113**	**2,130**	**2,110**	**71,887**	**74,302**	**75,296**	**76,357**
General schedule and equivalently graded......	1,278	1,499	1,524	1,534	68,574	72,120	73,272	74,557
Prevailing rate pay plans (blue collar)...........	206	208	205	200	49,998	51,216	51,496	51,803
Other white collar pay plans.....................	553	407	401	375	87,709	94,157	95,210	96,847
Postal pay system [1].............................	623	584	557	528	49,951	53,304	(NA)	(NA)

NA Not Available. [1] Source: Career employees--U.S. Postal Service, *Annual Report of the Postmaster General 2012,* 2012, and earlier reports. Average pay--U.S. Postal Service, *Comprehensive Statement of Postal Operations 2010,* December 2010, and earlier reports. See also <http://about.usps.com/news/welcome.htm>.

Source: Except as noted, U.S. Office of Personnel Management, "FedScope," <http://www.fedscope.opm.gov/>, accessed August 2013.

Table 517. Federal Government Civilian Employment by State: 2000 to 2012

[As of September 30. In thousands (1,697.8 represents 1,697,800). For agencies excluded from total, see <http://www.fedscope.opm.gov/datadefn/aboutehri_sdm.asp>]

State	2000	2011	2012	State	2000	2011	2012	State	2000	2011	2012
U.S. [1] ...	**1,697.8**	**2,076.6**	**2,057.7**								
AL.........	34.4	43.2	41.7	KY........	18.3	26.0	25.8	ND........	5.6	6.6	6.4
AK.........	12.5	13.7	13.2	LA........	20.9	21.7	21.3	OH........	44.6	53.5	52.2
AZ.........	30.9	43.2	42.7	ME........	8.6	11.1	11.1	OK........	33.6	39.8	39.3
AR.........	12.4	14.5	14.4	MD........	110.1	137.0	135.9	OR........	20.0	21.9	21.6
CA.........	146.8	172.9	170.7	MA........	25.8	29.4	28.9	PA........	62.1	69.0	67.7
CO.........	34.7	41.7	41.3	MI........	22.8	30.4	30.5	RI........	6.1	7.3	7.4
CT.........	7.4	8.9	8.9	MN........	14.5	18.4	18.2	SC........	16.9	22.3	22.5
DE.........	2.7	3.5	3.3	MS........	17.8	19.4	19.3	SD........	7.6	8.8	8.9
DC.........	146.6	166.3	165.0	MO........	31.9	37.3	36.8	TN........	25.3	28.7	28.6
FL.........	62.6	90.2	90.2	MT........	9.8	11.9	11.8	TX........	103.7	142.8	142.6
GA.........	64.8	80.6	79.0	NE........	8.4	10.9	11.1	UT........	25.9	30.6	29.5
HI.........	20.3	25.6	25.7	NV........	7.9	11.9	12.7	VT........	3.2	4.7	4.7
ID.........	9.3	10.1	10.3	NH........	3.5	4.6	4.6	VA........	117.2	147.8	148.9
IL.........	42.7	50.7	49.3	NJ........	26.5	26.8	26.2	WA........	45.8	58.7	58.4
IN.........	21.1	24.8	24.5	NM........	22.6	27.3	26.4	WV........	12.6	16.3	16.3
IA.........	7.9	9.3	9.1	NY........	60.8	67.9	67.2	WI........	12.4	16.2	16.2
KS.........	15.4	18.1	17.6	NC........	32.7	45.2	45.1	WY........	5.5	6.7	6.6

[1] Total includes data that has been suppressed for security purposes, see source for details.

Source: U.S. Office of Personnel Management, "FedScope," <http://www.fedscope.opm.gov/>, accessed August 2013.

Federal Government Finances and Employment   345

Table 518. Federal Civilian Employment by Branch and Agency: 1990 to 2012

[For years ending September 30. Annual averages of monthly figures. Excludes Central Intelligence Agency, National Security Agency, Defense Intelligence Agency, and as of October 1996, National Imagery and Mapping Agency]

Agency	1990	2000	2005	2010	2011	2012
Total, all agencies [4]	**3,128,267**	**2,708,101**	**2,700,965**	**2,841,143**	**2,820,460**	**2,760,569**
Legislative branch	37,495	31,157	30,816	30,643	30,465	29,837
Judicial branch	23,605	32,186	34,064	33,756	33,762	33,771
Executive branch	3,067,167	2,644,758	2,636,085	2,776,744	2,756,233	2,696,961
Executive Office of the President	1,731	1,658	1,693	1,965	1,922	1,880
Executive departments	2,065,542	1,592,200	1,685,211	1,937,291	1,950,293	1,912,997
State	25,288	27,983	33,948	39,016	40,611	41,438
Treasury	158,655	143,508	107,950	110,099	107,612	112,461
Defense	1,034,152	676,268	671,364	772,601	774,022	729,559
Justice	83,932	125,970	105,458	117,916	117,369	117,016
Interior	77,679	73,818	75,973	70,231	77,019	76,827
Agriculture	122,594	104,466	107,852	106,867	103,881	99,503
Commerce [1]	69,920	47,652	39,836	56,856	44,827	44,317
Labor	17,727	16,040	15,383	17,592	17,266	17,752
Health & Human Services [2]	123,959	62,605	60,736	69,839	71,669	74,017
Housing & Urban Development	13,596	10,319	9,941	9,585	9,092	8,655
Transportation [3]	67,364	63,598	55,559	57,972	57,739	57,036
Energy	17,731	15,692	15,010	16,145	16,153	15,632
Education	4,771	4,734	4,321	4,452	4,501	4,250
Veterans Affairs	248,174	219,547	235,210	304,665	314,545	323,208
Homeland Security [3]	(X)	(X)	146,670	183,455	193,987	191,326
Independent agencies [4]	999,894	1,050,900	949,181	837,488	804,018	782,084
Board of Governors Federal Reserve System	1,525	2,372	1,860	1,873	1,873	1,873
Environmental Protection Agency	17,123	18,036	17,824	18,740	18,705	18,055
Equal Employment Opportunity Commission	2,880	2,780	2,360	2,543	2,480	2,337
Federal Communications Commission	1,778	1,965	1,885	1,838	1,788	1,759
Federal Deposit Insurance Corporation	17,641	6,958	4,635	6,436	8,396	8,314
Federal Trade Commission	988	1,019	1,007	1,131	1,131	1,131
General Services Administration	20,277	14,334	12,769	12,820	12,736	12,383
National Archives & Records Administration	3,120	2,702	3,029	3,523	3,527	3,330
National Aeronautics & Space Administration	24,872	18,819	18,752	18,664	18,614	18,134
National Labor Relations Board	2,263	2,054	1,869	1,715	1,734	1,684
National Science Foundation	1,318	1,247	1,305	1,474	1,459	1,465
Nuclear Regulatory Commission	3,353	2,858	3,242	4,240	4,096	3,884
Office of Personnel Management	6,636	3,780	4,939	5,892	6,205	5,558
Peace Corps	1,178	1,065	1,072	1,082	906	1,081
Railroad Retirement Board	1,772	1,176	1,008	981	957	957
Securities & Exchange Commission	2,302	2,955	3,907	3,917	3,846	3,907
Small Business Administration	5,128	4,150	4,343	4,037	4,037	4,037
Smithsonian Institution	5,092	5,065	4,901	4,984	5,002	5,005
Social Security Administration [2]	(X)	64,474	66,144	69,975	67,145	65,114
Tennessee Valley Authority	28,392	13,145	12,703	12,457	12,872	12,762
U.S. Information Agency	8,555	2,436	2,175	1,953	1,922	1,845
U.S. Agency for International Development	4,698	2,552	2,493	2,515	2,515	2,515
U.S. Postal Service	816,886	860,726	764,165	643,420	609,921	592,750

X Not applicable. [1] Includes enumerators for the 1990 and 2000 censuses. [2] The Social Security Administration was separated from the Department of Health and Human Services to become an independent agency effective April 1995. [3] See text, Section 10, National Security and Veteran Affairs, concerning the development of the Department of Homeland Security. [4] Includes agencies not shown separately.

Source: U.S. Office of Personnel Management, "Federal Civilian Workforce Statistics--Employment and Trends," <http://www.opm.gov/feddata/html/empt.asp>, accessed August 2013.

Table 519. Federal Employees—Summary Characteristics: 1990 to 2012

[In percent, except as indicated. As of September 30. For civilian employees of executive branch agencies participating in Office of Personnel Management's Central Personnel Data File (CPDF)]

Characteristics	1990	1995	2000	2005	2008	2009	2010	2011 [2]	2012
Average age (years) [1]	42.3	44.3	46.3	46.9	46.8	46.8	46.8	(NA)	47.0
Average length of service (years)	13.4	15.5	17.1	16.4	15.5	15.1	14.3	(NA)	13.7
Retirement eligible: [2]									
Civil Service Retirement System	8	10	17	33	46	51	57	(NA)	67
Federal Employees Retirement System	3	5	11	13	13	(NA)	(NA)	(NA)	(NA)
Bachelor's degree or higher	35	39	41	43	44	45	46	(NA)	48
Sex: Male	57	56	55	56	56	56	56	(NA)	56
Female	43	44	45	44	44	44	44	(NA)	44
Race and national origin:									
Total minorities	27.4	28.9	30.4	31.7	33.0	33.0	33.3	(NA)	34.0
Black	16.7	16.8	17.1	17.0	17.5	17.5	17.5	(NA)	17.7
Hispanic	5.4	5.9	6.6	7.4	7.7	7.7	7.7	(NA)	8.0
Asian/Pacific Islander	3.5	4.2	4.5	5.1	5.2	5.6	5.6	(NA)	5.8
American Indian/Alaska Native	1.8	2.0	2.2	2.1	2.1	2.1	2.1	(NA)	2.1
Disabled	7.0	7.0	7.0	7.0	6.8	6.9	7.0	(NA)	7.9
Veterans preference	30.0	26.0	24.0	22.0	22.4	22.7	23.1	(NA)	24.5
Vietnam era veterans	17.0	17.0	14.0	11.0	8.0	7.1	8.0	(NA)	5.0
Retired military	4.9	4.2	3.9	5.4	6.2	6.6	7.0	(NA)	7.7
Retired officers	0.5	0.5	0.5	1.0	1.3	1.4	1.6	(NA)	1.7

NA Not available. [1] For full-time permanent employees. [2] Represents full-time permanent employees under the Civil Service Retirement System (excluding hires since January 1984), and the Federal Employees Retirement System (since January 1984). [3] Data for 2011 was not made available.

Source: U.S. Office of Personnel Management, Office of Workforce Information, *The Fact Book, Federal Civilian Workforce Statistics*, annual. Beginning 2008, Central Personnel Data File, "Profile of Federal Civilian Non-Seasonal Full-Time Employees," <http://www.opm.gov/policy-data-oversight/data-analysis-documentation/federal-employment-reports/reports-publications/profile-of-federal-civilian-non-postal-employees/>, accessed September 2013.

Table 520. Federal Executive Branch (Non-postal) Employment by Race and Hispanic Origin: 1990 to 2012

[As of September 30. Covers total employment for executive branch agencies]

Pay system	1990	1995	2000	2005	2006	2008	2010
All personnel [1]	**2,150,359**	**1,960,577**	**1,755,689**	**1,856,966**	**1,848,339**	**1,916,726**	**2,108,639**
White, non-Hispanic	1,562,846	1,394,690	1,224,836	1,267,922	1,254,308	1,297,772	1,406,609
General schedule and related	1,218,188	1,101,108	961,261	973,767	948,740	858,050	1,029,711
Grades 1 to 4	132,028	79,195	55,067	46,671	43,450	44,324	50,000
Grades 5 to 8	337,453	288,755	239,128	227,387	219,168	211,004	233,096
Grades 9 to 12	510,261	465,908	404,649	408,111	399,400	351,302	428,980
Grades 13 to 15	238,446	267,250	262,417	291,598	286,722	251,420	317,635
Total executive/senior pay levels	9,337	13,307	14,332	16,409	16,118	21,793	22,947
Wage pay system	244,220	186,184	146,075	135,383	133,942	134,933	136,493
Other pay systems	91,101	94,091	103,168	142,363	155,508	282,996	217,458
Black	356,867	327,302	298,701	315,644	317,697	337,742	368,814
General schedule and related	272,657	258,586	241,135	246,691	246,248	236,525	283,175
Grades 1 to 4	65,077	41,381	26,895	19,774	18,326	18,286	19,238
Grades 5 to 8	114,993	112,962	99,937	94,655	93,717	90,410	98,964
Grades 9 to 12	74,985	79,795	82,809	90,809	91,869	86,054	110,023
Grades 13 to 15	17,602	24,448	31,494	41,453	42,336	41,775	54,950
Total executive/senior pay levels	479	942	1,180	1,270	1,218	1,565	1,857
Wage pay system	72,755	55,637	42,590	37,666	37,378	38,540	37,260
Other pay systems	10,976	12,137	13,796	30,017	32,853	61,973	46,522
Hispanic	115,170	115,964	115,247	138,507	138,596	136,167	163,975
General schedule and related	83,218	86,762	89,911	104,927	105,236	95,016	123,913
Grades 1 to 4	15,738	11,081	8,526	7,768	6,854	5,459	6,890
Grades 5 to 8	28,727	31,152	31,703	33,653	33,834	31,261	35,813
Grades 9 to 12	31,615	34,056	36,813	46,268	46,951	42,542	57,491
Grades 13 to 15	7,138	10,473	12,869	17,238	17,597	15,754	23,719
Total executive/senior pay levels	154	382	547	682	699	1,109	1,191
Wage pay system	26,947	22,128	16,926	15,945	15,822	15,639	15,643
Other pay systems	4,851	6,692	7,863	16,953	16,839	28,646	23,228
American Indian, Alaska Native, Asian, and Pacific Islander	115,476	122,621	116,905	134,893	136,593	145,045	169,241
General schedule and related	81,499	86,768	86,074	97,866	97,870	93,197	119,895
Grades 1 to 4	15,286	11,854	9,340	8,357	7,877	7,608	8,710
Grades 5 to 8	24,960	26,580	25,691	27,417	26,986	26,046	30,794
Grades 9 to 12	31,346	33,810	33,167	38,276	38,492	35,259	47,656
Grades 13 to 15	9,907	14,524	17,876	23,816	24,515	24,284	32,735
Total executive/senior pay levels	148	331	504	804	873	2,851	3,176
Wage pay system	24,927	21,553	17,613	16,938	16,728	17,022	17,753
Other pay systems	8,902	13,969	12,714	19,285	21,122	33,834	28,417

[1] Beginning 2006, includes persons classified as multiracial, not shown separately.

Source: U.S. Office of Personnel Management, *Demographic Profile of the Federal Workforce as of September 2010,* April 2011, and earlier reports. See also <http://www.opm.gov/policy-data-oversight/data-analysis-documentation/federal-employment-reports/demographics/2010-demographic-profile/>.

Table 521. Area of Federally Owned Buildings in the United States by State: 2010

[2,914.0 represents 2,914,000,000. As of September 30. For executive branch agencies. For data on federal land by state, see Table 376]

State	Total building area [1] (mil. sq. ft.)	Owned building area (mil. sq. ft.)	Leased building area (mil. sq. ft.)	State	Total building area [1] (mil. sq. ft.)	Owned building area (mil. sq. ft.)	Leased building area (mil. sq. ft.)
U.S. [2]	**2,914.0**	**2,487.5**	**308.4**	MO	53.2	42.4	8.5
AL	55.8	48.1	4.5	MT	18.4	15.5	2.2
AK	48.3	44.3	3.3	NE	15.1	12.3	1.6
AZ	55.5	50.5	3.9	NV	32.6	29.7	2.1
AR	24.2	19.3	1.6	NH	4.1	2.6	0.6
CA	295.4	269.4	21.2	NJ	46.5	39.1	5.1
CO	58.2	50.3	7.3	NM	61.6	55.4	4.8
CT	14.1	11.4	1.0	NY	95.6	81.0	9.7
DE	6.2	5.1	0.4	NC	85.4	77.5	5.3
DC	91.2	65.7	24.9	ND	23.1	20.5	1.0
FL	110.9	95.5	11.8	OH	68.6	60.7	5.0
GA	116.7	104.0	10.8	OK	65.3	51.5	11.5
HI	50.6	49.0	0.8	OR	25.2	19.9	2.6
ID	22.3	18.8	2.8	PA	81.7	68.6	9.8
IL	71.8	62.0	6.0	RI	13.9	13.0	0.5
IN	37.2	31.5	3.2	SC	53.5	48.9	2.3
IA	17.1	12.1	1.9	SD	18.2	14.8	2.0
KS	37.1	32.7	2.8	TN	66.3	58.2	5.0
KY	52.5	44.7	5.6	TX	202.0	175.9	22.3
LA	45.6	32.9	6.0	UT	37.4	32.1	3.3
ME	13.3	11.6	0.9	VT	4.4	2.6	1.2
MD	126.0	101.6	22.2	VA	174.4	142.3	30.5
MA	36.0	30.4	3.1	WA	86.6	77.8	7.1
MI	31.3	22.5	4.6	WV	20.7	16.0	2.9
MN	21.5	14.7	2.0	WI	24.2	18.9	2.6
MS	43.8	33.5	2.6	WY	15.2	13.4	0.8

[1] Includes otherwised managed square feet, not shown separately. [2] Includes location not reported, not shown separately.

Source: U.S. General Services Administration, Federal Real Property Council, *Fiscal Year 2010 Federal Real Property Report,* 2011. See also <http://www.gsa.gov/portal/content/102880>.

National Security and Veterans Affairs

This section displays data for national security (national defense and homeland security) and benefits for veterans. Data are presented on national defense and its human and financial costs; active and reserve military personnel; federally sponsored programs and benefits for veterans; and funding, budget and selected agencies for homeland security. The principal sources of these data are the annual *Selected Manpower Statistics* and the *Atlas/Data Abstract for the United States* (both discontinued), U.S. Department of Defense; *Annual Report of Secretary of Veterans Affairs*, U.S. Department of Veterans Affairs (VA); *Budget in Brief*, U.S. Department of Homeland Security; and *The Budget of the United States Government*, Office of Management and Budget. For data on international expenditures and personnel, see Table 1431, Section 30.

Department of Defense (DoD)—The U.S. Department of Defense is responsible for providing the military forces of the United States. It includes the Office of the Secretary of Defense, the Joint Chiefs of Staff, the Army, the Navy, the Air Force, and the defense agencies. The President serves as Commander-in-Chief of the Armed Forces; from him, the authority flows to the Secretary of Defense and through the Joint Chiefs of Staff to the commanders of unified and specified commands (e.g., U.S. Strategic Command).

Reserve components—The Reserve Components of the Armed Forces consist of the Army National Guard of the United States, Army Reserve, Naval Reserve, Marine Corps Reserve, Air National Guard, Air Force Reserve, and Coast Guard Reserve. They provide trained personnel and units available for active duty in the Armed Forces during times of war or national emergency, and at such other times as national security may require. The National Guard has dual federal/state responsibilities and uses jointly provided equipment, facilities, and budget support. The President is empowered to mobilize the National Guard and to use such of the Armed Forces as he considers necessary to enforce federal authority in any state. There is in each Armed Force a ready reserve, a standby reserve, and a retired reserve. The Ready Reserve includes the Selected Reserve, which provides trained and ready units and individuals to augment the active forces during times of war or national emergency, or at other times when required; and the Individual Ready Reserve, which is a manpower pool that can be called to active duty during times of war or national emergency and would normally be used as individual fillers for active, guard, and reserve units, and as a source of combat replacements. Most of the Ready Reserve serves in an active status.

Department of Veterans Affairs (VA)—A veteran is someone 18 years and older (there are a few 17-year-old veterans) who is not currently on active duty, but who once served on active duty in the United States Army, Navy, Air Force, Marine Corps, or Coast Guard, or who served in the Merchant Marine during World War II. There are many groups whose active service makes them veterans including: those who incurred a service-connected disability during active duty for training in the Reserves or National Guard, even though that service would not otherwise have counted for veteran status and members of a national guard or reserve component who have been ordered to active duty by order of the President or those who have a full-time military job. The latter are called AGRs (Active Guard and Reserve). No one who has received a dishonorable discharge is a veteran.

The VA administers laws authorizing benefits for eligible former and present members of the Armed Forces and for the beneficiaries of deceased members. Veterans' benefits available under various acts of Congress include compensation for service-connected disability or death; pensions for non-service-connected disability or death; vocational rehabilitation, education and training; home loan insurance; life insurance; health care; special housing and automobiles or other conveyances for certain disabled veterans; burial and plot allowances; and educational assistance to families of deceased or totally disabled veterans, servicemen missing in action, or prisoners of war. Since these benefits are legislated by Congress, the dates they were enacted and the dates they apply to veterans may be different from the actual dates the conflicts occurred. VA estimates of veterans cover all persons discharged from active U.S. military service under conditions other than dishonorable.

Department of Homeland Security (DHS)—The creation of DHS, which began operations in March 2003, represents a fusion of 22 federal agencies (legacy agencies, Coast Guard and Secret Service remained intact) to coordinate and centralize the leadership of many homeland security activities under a single department. The largest organizations under DHS include: Customs and Border Protection (CBP), Immigration and Customs Enforcement (ICE), Transportation Security Administration (TSA), Federal Emergency Management Agency (FEMA), and the Coast Guard.

Coast Guard—With more than 218 years of service to the Nation, the Coast Guard is a military, multi-mission, maritime organization that promotes safety and safeguards U.S. economic and security interests throughout the maritime environment. As one of the five Armed Services of the United States, it is the only military organization within the DHS. Unlike its sister services in the Department of Defense (DoD), the Coast Guard is also a law enforcement and regulatory agency with broad domestic authorities.

Federal Emergency Management Agency (FEMA)—FEMA manages and coordinates the federal response to and recovery from major domestic disasters and emergencies of all types in accordance with the Robert T. Stafford Disaster Relief and Emergency Assistance Act. The agency ensures the effectiveness of emergency response providers at all levels of government in responding to terrorist attacks, major disasters, and other emergencies. Through the Disaster Relief Fund, FEMA provides individual and public assistance to help families and communities impacted by declared disasters rebuild and recover. FEMA is also the principal component for preparing state and local governments to prevent or respond to threats or incidents of terrorism and other catastrophic events, through their state and local programs.

The Customs and Border Protection (CBP) is responsible for managing, securing, and controlling U.S. borders. This includes carrying out traditional border-related responsibilities, such as stemming the tide of illegal drugs and illegal aliens; securing and facilitating legitimate global trade and travel; and protecting the food supply and agriculture industry from pests and disease. CBP is composed of the Border Patrol and Inspections (both moved from INS) along with Customs (absorbed from the U.S. Department of Treasury) and Animal and Plant Health Inspections Services (absorbed from the U.S. Department of Agriculture).

The Immigration and Customs Enforcement (ICE) mission is to protect America and uphold public safety by targeting the people, money, and materials crossing the nation's borders that support terrorist and criminal activities. ICE is the largest investigation arm of DHS. ICE is composed of five law enforcement divisions: Investigations, Intelligence, Federal Protective Service, International Affairs, and Detention and Removal Operations. ICE investigates a wide range of national security, financial, and smuggling violations including drug smuggling, human trafficking, illegal arms exports, financial crimes, commercial fraud, human smuggling, document fraud, money laundering, child pornography/exploitation, and immigration fraud.

The Transportation Security Administration (TSA) was created as part of the Aviation and Transportation Security Act on November 19, 2001. TSA was originally part of the U.S. Department of Transportation, but was moved to DHS. TSA's mission is to provide security to our nation's transportation systems with a primary focus on aviation security.

Table 522. National Defense Outlays and Veterans' Benefits: 1960 to 2014

[In billions of dollars (53.6 represents $53,600,000,000), except percent. For fiscal year ending in year shown, see text, Section 8. Includes outlays of Department of Defense, Department of Veterans Affairs, and other agencies for activities primarily related to national defense and veterans programs. For explanation of average annual percent change, see Guide to Tabular Presentation. Minus sign (-) indicates decrease]

Year	National defense and veterans' outlays				Annual percent change [1]			Defense outlays, percent of—	
	Total outlays	Defense outlays		Veterans' outlays	Total outlays	Defense outlays	Veterans' outlays	Federal outlays	Gross domestic product [2]
		Current dollars	Constant (FY2005) dollars						
1960	53.6	48.1	369.4	5.4	2.50	2.40	3.10	52.2	9.3
1970	90.4	81.7	463.8	8.7	0.26	-0.98	13.60	41.8	8.1
1980	155.2	134.0	330.1	21.2	13.88	15.17	6.30	22.7	4.9
1985	279.0	252.7	433.1	26.3	10.28	11.14	2.64	26.7	6.1
1990	328.4	299.3	461.1	29.0	-1.56	-1.39	-3.23	23.9	5.2
1995	309.9	272.1	375.5	37.9	-2.91	-3.40	0.81	17.9	3.7
1998	309.9	268.2	346.1	41.7	0.05	-0.85	6.26	16.2	3.1
1999	317.9	274.8	347.6	43.2	2.58	2.45	3.39	16.1	3.0
2000	341.4	294.4	361.3	47.0	7.37	7.13	8.88	16.5	3.0
2001	349.7	304.7	363.0	45.0	2.45	3.52	-4.29	16.4	3.0
2002	399.4	348.5	401.7	50.9	14.21	14.35	13.24	17.3	3.3
2003	461.7	404.7	444.6	57.0	15.61	16.15	11.89	18.7	3.7
2004	515.6	455.8	480.3	59.7	11.66	12.62	4.85	19.9	3.9
2005	565.4	495.3	495.3	70.1	9.67	8.66	17.36	20.0	4.0
2006	591.6	521.8	499.3	69.8	4.64	5.35	-0.44	19.7	3.9
2007	624.1	551.3	509.2	72.8	5.48	5.64	4.31	20.2	4.0
2008	700.7	616.1	547.7	84.7	12.28	11.76	16.25	20.7	4.3
2009	756.5	661.0	588.2	95.4	7.96	7.30	12.73	18.8	4.7
2010	802.0	693.6	614.1	108.4	6.01	4.92	13.58	20.1	4.8
2011	832.7	705.6	615.3	127.2	3.85	1.74	17.35	19.6	4.7
2012	802.5	677.9	580.6	124.6	-3.64	-3.93	-2.04	19.2	4.3
2013, est	799.6	660.0	553.6	139.6	-0.35	-2.63	12.02	17.9	4.0
2014, est	775.0	626.8	518.8	148.2	-3.08	-5.04	6.20	16.6	3.6

[1] Change from immediate prior year; for 1960, change from 1955. [2] Represents fiscal year GDP; for definition, see text, Section 13.

Source: U.S. Office of Management and Budget, *Fiscal Year 2014 Budget of the U.S. Government: Historical Tables*, April 2013. See also <http://www.whitehouse.gov/omb/budget/>.

Table 523. National Defense Budget Authority and Outlays for Defense Functions: 1990 to 2014

[In billions of dollars (303.3 represents $303,300,000,000). For year ending September 30. Data includes defense budget authority and outlays by other departments. Minus sign (-) indicates decrease]

Function	1990	1995	2000	2005	2008	2009	2010	2011	2012	2013 est.	2014 est.
Total budget authority	**303.3**	**266.4**	**304.0**	**505.8**	**696.2**	**697.6**	**721.2**	**717.0**	**681.4**	**647.4**	**648.9**
Department of Defense—Military	293.0	255.7	290.3	483.8	674.7	667.5	695.6	691.5	655.4	620.3	621.6
Military personnel	78.9	71.6	73.8	121.3	139.0	149.3	157.1	158.4	158.4	160.8	144.0
Operation and maintenance	88.4	93.7	108.7	179.2	256.2	271.6	293.6	305.2	286.8	263.3	210.2
Procurement	81.4	43.6	55.0	96.6	165.0	135.4	135.8	131.9	118.3	115.1	99.3
Research, development, test, and evaluation	36.5	34.5	38.7	68.8	79.6	80.0	80.2	76.7	72.0	73.0	67.5
Military construction	5.1	5.4	5.1	7.3	22.1	26.8	22.6	16.0	11.4	11.4	9.5
Family housing	3.1	3.4	3.5	4.1	2.9	3.9	2.3	1.8	1.7	1.7	1.5
Other	-0.4	3.4	5.5	6.6	9.9	0.6	4.0	1.4	6.9	-4.9	89.4
Atomic energy defense activities	9.7	10.1	12.4	17.9	16.6	23.0	18.2	18.5	18.3	19.3	19.3
Defense-related activities	0.7	1.0	1.3	4.0	4.9	7.1	7.3	7.0	7.7	7.8	8.0
Total outlays	**299.3**	**272.1**	**294.4**	**495.3**	**616.1**	**661.0**	**693.5**	**705.6**	**677.9**	**660.0**	**626.8**
Department of Defense—Military	289.8	259.4	281.1	474.1	594.6	636.7	666.7	678.1	650.9	633.3	597.6
Military personnel	75.6	70.8	76.0	127.5	138.9	147.3	155.7	161.6	152.3	161.4	146.0
Operation and maintenance	88.3	91.0	105.8	188.1	244.8	259.3	276.0	291.0	282.3	268.5	218.7
Procurement	81.0	55.0	51.7	82.3	117.4	129.2	133.6	128.0	124.7	116.9	99.5
Research, development, test, and evaluation	37.5	34.6	37.6	65.7	75.1	79.0	77.0	74.9	70.4	69.6	66.1
Military construction	5.1	6.8	5.1	5.3	11.6	17.6	21.2	19.9	14.6	15.2	12.2
Family housing	3.5	3.6	3.4	3.7	3.6	2.7	3.2	3.4	2.3	2.5	1.9
Other	-1.2	-2.4	1.5	1.5	3.2	1.5	0.1	-0.8	4.3	-0.9	53.2
Atomic energy activities	9.0	11.8	12.1	18.0	17.1	17.6	19.3	20.4	19.2	19.1	20.7
Defense-related activities	0.6	0.9	1.2	3.2	4.3	6.7	7.5	7.1	7.8	7.7	8.5

Source: U.S. Office of Management and Budget, *Fiscal Year 2014 Budget of the U.S. Government: Historical Tables*, April 2013. See also <http://www.whitehouse.gov/omb/budget/>.

Table 524. Military Expenditures: 2000 to 2009

[In millions of dollars (229,072 represents $229,072,000,000). For year ending September 30. For definitions, see headnote, Tables 525 and 527]

Item	2000	2005	2006	2007	2008	2009
Expenditures, total	**229,072**	**381,290**	**408,249**	**455,769**	**501,032**	**527,824**
Payroll outlays	103,447	141,018	146,858	154,326	146,781	195,170
Active duty military pay	36,872	50,482	55,829	61,918	52,159	84,460
Civilian pay	29,935	43,798	45,105	43,587	46,170	49,736
Reserve and National Guard pay	4,646	11,087	10,123	12,325	11,068	22,759
Retired military pay	31,994	35,651	35,801	36,496	37,384	38,216
Total contracts [1]	123,295	236,986	257,456	297,363	349,557	327,462
Army	32,615	74,432	79,962	98,171	139,437	109,995
Navy & Marine Corps	38,963	62,775	70,351	82,321	92,679	91,868
Air Force	35,369	51,671	58,552	66,240	59,262	63,946
Other defense activities	16,348	48,108	48,592	50,630	58,178	61,653
Grants	2,330	3,285	3,934	4,080	4,694	5,192

[1] Represents contract awards over $25,000.

Source: U.S. Department of Defense, Statistical Information Analysis Division, *Atlas/Data Abstract for the United States and Selected Areas*, 2010, <http://siadapp.dmdc.osd.mil/personnel/Pubs.htm>, discontinued.

Table 525. Department of Defense Payroll and Contract Awards by State: 2009

[In millions of dollars (195,170 represents $195,170,000,000). For year ending September 30. Payroll outlays include the gross earnings of civilian, active duty military, reserve and national guard, and retired military personnel for services rendered to the government and for cash allowances for benefits. Excludes employer's share of employee benefits, accrued military retirement benefits and most permanent change of station costs. Contracts refer to awards made in year specified; expenditures relating to awards may extend over several years. Includes awards for supplies, services, and construction with a net value of contracts of over $25,000 for work in each state and DC. Figures reflect impact of prime contracting on state distribution of defense work. The state in which a prime contractor is located is often not the state where the subcontracted work is done. Undistributed civilian and military payrolls, and prime contract awards for performance in classified locations are excluded]

State	Payroll — Total	Payroll — Active duty military	Contract awards	Grants	State	Payroll — Total	Payroll — Active duty military	Contract awards	Grants
U.S.	**195,170**	**84,460**	**327,462**	**5,192**	MO	3,787	1,311	10,454	40
AL	4,724	1,255	9,502	66	MT	541	188	289	24
AK	2,660	2,078	2,180	49	NE	1,152	435	931	59
AZ	3,138	1,263	12,065	106	NV	1,415	600	1,819	35
AR	1,622	435	986	66	NH	411	73	1,568	36
CA	14,568	5,183	41,698	477	NJ	2,671	543	8,227	122
CO	5,125	2,966	5,544	56	NM	1,626	571	1,604	40
CT	720	198	11,818	100	NY	4,819	2,701	8,545	199
DE	537	216	315	24	NC	10,558	7,012	3,995	125
DC	3,599	1,907	4,741	66	ND	631	336	437	32
FL	9,418	2,816	13,189	195	OH	3,834	640	6,249	172
GA	11,495	6,668	7,039	74	OK	4,100	1,679	2,880	124
HI	6,344	4,529	2,377	79	OR	1,051	141	1,546	99
ID	709	262	166	59	PA	4,210	574	12,363	216
IL	3,129	738	5,937	172	RI	743	120	662	26
IN	2,338	351	6,795	55	SC	3,683	1,530	5,299	39
IA	747	140	1,285	57	SD	514	198	445	68
KS	3,668	2,465	3,158	42	TN	2,235	282	3,083	44
KY	5,681	4,339	6,534	70	TX	19,299	11,128	22,484	300
LA	2,688	1,417	6,408	54	UT	2,116	432	2,206	39
ME	847	113	1,407	128	VT	262	64	550	17
MD	6,538	2,013	12,912	477	VA	18,071	6,214	38,372	131
MA	1,491	320	13,347	244	WA	8,224	4,407	5,174	127
MI	1,827	264	5,332	130	WV	617	107	396	50
MN	1,208	206	1,530	69	WI	1,152	222	7,674	72
MS	2,224	629	3,447	18	WY	405	177	140	21

Source: U.S. Department of Defense, Statistical Information Analysis Division, *Atlas/Data Abstract for the United States and Selected Areas*, 2010, <http://siadapp.dmdc.osd.mil/personnel/Pubs.htm>, discontinued.

Table 526. Expenditures and Personnel for Selected Major Locations: 2009

[In thousands of dollars (8,406,173 represents $8,406,173,000), except for personnel. For year ending September 30. See headnote, Table 527]

Major locations	Expenditures — Total	Expenditures — Payroll outlays	Expenditures — Contracts/grants	Major locations	Military and civilian personnel — Total	Military and civilian personnel — Active duty military	Military and civilian personnel — Civilian
Washington, DC	8,406,173	3,599,245	4,806,928	Fort Hood, TX	60,309	54,309	6,000
Fort Hood, TX	6,478,403	6,075,895	402,508	Camp Pendleton, CA	49,114	46,242	2,872
San Diego, CA	6,413,361	1,884,891	4,528,470	Camp Lejeune, NC	44,286	40,789	3,497
Oshkosh, WI	5,780,785	20,929	5,759,856	Fayetteville, NC	36,223	36,198	25
Huntsville, AL	5,744,462	366,537	5,377,925	Fort Lewis, WA	35,250	32,220	3,030
Arlington, VA	5,279,716	2,946,069	2,333,647	Fort Campbell, KY	33,971	32,799	1,172
Tucson, AZ	4,879,568	326,019	4,553,549	Fort Carson, CO	26,759	23,796	2,963
Fayetteville, NC	4,658,633	4,623,376	35,257	Arlington, VA	26,335	9,305	17,030
St. Louis, MO	4,623,210	203,614	4,419,596	Fort Benning, GA	26,101	22,123	3,978
Louisville, KY	4,436,075	167,250	4,268,825	Fort Bragg, NC	23,843	15,580	8,263

Source: U.S. Department of Defense, Statistical Information Analysis Division, *Atlas/Data Abstract for the United States and Selected Areas*, 2010, <http://siadapp.dmdc.osd.mil/personnel/Pubs.htm>, discontinued.

Table 527. Military and Civilian Personnel in Installations: 2009

[As of September 30. Civilian personnel includes United States citizens and foreign national direct-hire civilians subject to Office of Management and Budget (OMB) ceiling controls and civilian personnel involved in civil functions in the United States. Excludes indirect-hire civilians and those direct-hire civilians not subject to OMB ceiling controls. Military personnel include active duty personnel based ashore or afloat, excluding personnel temporarily shore-based in a transient status]

State	Active duty military personnel				Reserve and National Guard, total[1]	Civilian personnel			
	Total[1]	Army	Navy/ Marine Corps	Air Force		Total[1]	Army	Navy/ Marine Corps	Air Force
United States.........	1,088,465	537,407	264,375	286,683	819,318	709,265	274,140	186,135	160,339
Alabama...............	11,896	8,121	403	3,372	22,099	24,794	19,768	84	2,472
Alaska.................	23,178	14,087	113	8,978	4,747	5,356	3,049	20	1,938
Arizona................	21,343	5,531	4,118	11,694	13,728	9,591	4,471	637	3,408
Arkansas..............	6,717	1,219	109	5,389	13,051	4,168	3,073	6	973
California..............	117,806	11,097	88,370	18,339	57,792	61,365	9,278	34,798	10,720
Colorado..............	35,404	25,471	715	9,218	12,491	11,585	4,187	65	5,675
Connecticut...........	1,914	624	1,172	118	6,369	2,625	618	1,120	257
Delaware..............	3,870	246	15	3,609	4,881	1,622	292	5	1,248
District of Columbia....	13,424	7,831	3,040	2,553	6,378	16,088	4,708	9,617	853
Florida.................	42,642	5,363	13,782	23,497	34,653	28,429	4,070	11,871	10,297
Georgia................	73,988	59,892	3,724	10,372	29,358	37,012	14,169	4,757	15,222
Hawaii.................	40,874	22,435	13,642	4,797	9,276	18,400	5,532	9,605	2,188
Idaho..................	4,967	526	41	4,400	5,892	1,716	893	51	711
Illinois.................	10,111	2,212	2,805	5,094	25,084	15,770	9,016	1,842	3,688
Indiana................	3,108	2,612	209	287	21,073	10,932	2,403	3,243	952
Iowa...................	1,296	997	118	181	12,390	1,733	1,157	8	525
Kansas................	25,482	21,994	117	3,371	11,479	7,800	6,296	6	1,103
Kentucky..............	43,138	42,532	279	327	13,126	8,962	7,655	164	248
Louisiana..............	17,398	10,223	1,553	5,622	18,011	6,647	4,045	793	1,476
Maine..................	730	334	265	131	4,153	6,946	402	5,580	287
Maryland..............	29,160	8,239	12,652	8,269	16,000	34,966	14,460	15,826	2,384
Massachusetts........	3,205	1,157	574	1,474	15,335	6,918	2,632	192	3,171
Michigan..............	2,858	1,708	743	407	17,618	8,972	6,456	46	892
Minnesota.............	1,897	1,291	378	228	19,256	2,752	1,766	23	798
Mississippi............	9,895	1,443	1,394	7,058	17,332	9,124	3,878	2,428	2,515
Missouri...............	17,925	12,053	2,028	3,844	23,769	9,982	7,569	490	1,246
Montana...............	3,623	397	12	3,214	4,748	1,596	686	1	862
Nebraska..............	6,845	653	450	5,742	7,498	3,785	1,468	15	2,197
Nevada................	10,034	545	584	8,905	6,087	2,319	561	285	1,316
New Hampshire........	675	307	198	170	4,251	1,047	568	34	304
New Jersey............	6,673	1,538	277	4,858	17,312	15,217	10,798	2,122	1,575
New Mexico............	11,038	1,094	166	9,778	5,199	7,029	3,041	46	3,460
New York..............	29,553	26,568	1,676	1,309	30,362	12,318	7,561	151	2,528
North Carolina.........	116,073	53,231	54,942	7,900	22,542	20,426	8,975	7,669	1,472
North Dakota..........	7,209	416	14	6,779	4,669	1,910	617	3	1,214
Ohio...................	8,261	1,939	684	5,638	28,523	25,001	1,884	91	13,671
Oklahoma.............	21,673	12,216	926	8,531	15,640	22,115	5,739	91	14,794
Oregon................	1,615	815	336	464	10,470	3,561	2,893	26	615
Pennsylvania..........	5,215	3,270	1,443	502	32,297	27,107	10,606	6,469	1,290
Rhode Island..........	1,490	420	905	165	4,438	4,372	289	3,777	209
South Carolina........	32,518	11,074	12,613	8,831	19,102	10,406	3,875	3,868	1,912
South Dakota..........	3,910	406	1	3,503	4,982	1,388	565	3	775
Tennessee.............	3,511	1,610	1,422	479	20,606	7,967	4,767	1,202	1,227
Texas.................	131,548	88,346	4,606	38,596	56,367	48,057	27,585	1,404	15,271
Utah..................	6,237	1,614	170	4,453	11,999	14,818	2,470	45	11,244
Vermont...............	565	347	32	186	3,952	729	403	3	290
Virginia...............	63,160	24,386	25,171	13,603	25,109	89,713	23,532	39,844	4,983
Washington............	46,161	34,557	4,907	6,697	19,470	27,980	9,471	15,577	1,980
West Virginia..........	1,199	677	317	205	9,303	2,146	1,431	97	605
Wisconsin.............	2,046	1,522	163	361	15,833	2,810	2,138	34	522
Wyoming..............	3,407	221	1	3,185	3,218	1,193	374	1	776

[1] Includes Other Defense Activities (ODA), not shown separately.

Source: U.S. Department of Defense, Statistical Information Analysis Division, *Atlas/Data Abstract for the United States and Selected Areas*, 2010, <http://siadapp.dmdc.osd.mil/personnel/Pubs.htm>, discontinued.

Table 528. Military Personnel on Active Duty by Location: 1980 to 2012

[In thousands (2,051 represents 2,051,000). As of September 30. Prior to 2012, data from DOD Statistical Information Analysis Division (SIAD). Beginning 2012, data from Defense Manpower Data Center (DMDC)]

Location	1980	1990	1995	2000	2005	2008	2009	2010	2011	2012
Total..........................	2,051	2,046	1,518	1,384	1,389	1,402	1,419	1,431	1,425	1,388
Shore-based[1]....................	1,840	1,794	1,351	1,237	1,262	1,294	1,313	1,328	1,325	(NA)
Afloat[2]...........................	211	252	167	147	127	108	105	103	101	(NA)
United States[3]...................	1,562	1,437	1,280	1,127	1,098	1,113	1,156	1,134	1,220	1,214
Foreign countries................	489	609	238	258	291	289	263	297	205	174

[1] Includes Navy personnel temporarily on shore. [2] Includes Marine Corps. [3] Includes Puerto Rico and Island Areas.

Source: U.S. Department of Defense, DoD Personnel and Procurement Statistics, "Active Duty Military Personnel By Service By Region/Country," <http://siadapp.dmdc.osd.mil/index.html>, accessed April 2013.

Table 529. Department of Defense Personnel: 1960 to 2012

[In thousands (2,475 represents 2,475,000). As of end of fiscal year; see text, Section 8. Includes National Guard, Reserve, and retired regular personnel on extended or continuous active duty. Excludes Coast Guard. Other officer candidates are included under enlisted personnel]

Year	Total [1,2]	Army					Navy [2]					Marine Corps					Air Force				
			Male		Female			Male		Female			Male		Female			Male		Female	
		Total [1]	Officers	Enlisted	Officers	Enlisted	Total [1]	Officers	Enlisted	Officers	Enlisted	Total [1]	Officers	Enlisted	Officers	Enlisted	Total [1]	Officers	Enlisted	Officers	Enlisted
1960...	2,475	873	97	762	4.3	8.3	617	67	540	2.7	5.4	171	16	153	0.1	1.5	815	126	677	3.7	5.7
1965...	2,654	969	108	846	3.8	8.5	670	75	583	2.6	5.3	190	17	172	0.1	1.4	825	128	685	4.1	4.7
1970...	3,065	1,323	162	1,142	5.2	11.5	691	78	600	2.9	5.8	260	25	233	0.3	2.1	791	125	648	4.7	9.0
1975...	2,128	784	98	640	4.6	37.7	535	62	449	3.7	17.5	196	19	174	0.3	2.8	613	100	478	5.0	25.2
1980...	2,051	777	91	612	7.6	61.7	527	58	430	4.9	30.1	189	18	164	0.5	6.2	558	90	404	8.5	51.9
1985...	2,151	781	99	599	10.8	68.4	571	64	449	6.9	45.7	198	19	169	0.7	9.0	602	96	431	11.9	58.1
1986...	2,169	781	99	597	11.3	69.7	581	65	457	7.3	47.2	200	19	170	0.6	9.2	608	97	434	12.4	61.2
1987...	2,174	781	96	596	11.6	71.6	587	65	462	7.2	47.7	200	19	170	0.6	9.1	607	94	432	12.6	63.2
1988...	2,138	772	95	588	11.8	72.0	593	65	466	7.3	49.7	197	19	168	0.7	9.0	576	92	405	12.9	61.5
1989...	2,130	770	95	584	12.2	74.3	593	65	464	7.5	52.1	197	19	168	0.7	9.0	571	91	399	13.4	63.7
1990...	2,044	732	92	553	12.4	71.2	579	64	451	7.8	52.1	197	19	168	0.7	8.7	535	87	370	13.3	60.8
1991...	1,986	711	91	535	12.5	67.8	570	63	444	8.0	51.4	194	19	166	0.7	8.3	510	84	350	13.3	59.1
1992...	1,807	610	83	449	11.7	61.7	542	61	417	8.3	51.0	185	18	157	0.6	7.9	470	77	320	12.7	56.1
1993...	1,705	572	77	420	11.1	60.2	510	58	390	8.3	49.3	178	17	153	0.6	7.2	444	72	302	12.3	54.5
1994...	1,610	541	74	394	10.9	59.0	469	54	355	8.0	47.9	174	17	149	0.6	7.0	426	69	287	12.3	54.0
1995...	1,518	509	72	365	10.8	57.3	435	51	324	7.9	47.9	175	17	150	0.7	7.4	400	66	266	12.1	52.1
1996...	1,472	491	70	347	10.6	59.0	417	50	308	7.8	46.9	175	17	149	0.8	7.8	389	64	256	12.0	52.8
1997...	1,439	492	69	346	10.4	62.4	396	48	290	7.8	44.8	174	17	148	0.8	8.5	377	62	246	12.0	53.8
1998...	1,407	484	68	340	10.4	61.4	382	47	280	7.8	42.9	173	17	146	0.9	8.9	368	60	237	12.0	54.2
1999...	1,386	479	67	337	10.5	61.5	373	46	271	7.7	43.9	173	17	145	0.9	9.3	361	58	232	11.8	54.6
2000...	1,384	482	66	339	10.8	62.9	373	46	272	7.8	43.8	173	17	146	0.9	9.5	356	57	227	11.8	55.0
2001...	1,385	481	65	337	11.0	63.4	378	46	273	8.0	46.6	173	17	145	1.0	9.6	354	57	224	12.0	55.6
2002...	1,414	487	66	341	11.5	63.2	385	47	279	8.2	47.3	174	17	146	1.0	9.5	368	59	233	12.9	58.6
2003...	1,434	499	68	352	12.0	63.5	382	47	276	8.2	47.3	178	18	149	1.1	9.6	375	61	237	13.5	60.0
2004...	1,427	500	69	358	12.3	61.0	373	46	273	8.1	46.1	178	18	149	1.1	9.7	377	61	242	13.6	60.2
2005...	1,389	493	69	353	12.4	57.9	363	45	266	7.8	44.5	180	18	151	1.0	9.8	354	60	225	13.4	55.6
2006...	1,385	505	69	365	12.5	58.5	350	44	255	7.6	43.2	180	18	151	1.1	10.0	349	58	223	12.8	55.8
2007...	1,380	522	71	379	13.0	58.8	338	44	244	7.6	42.2	186	18	156	1.1	10.5	333	54	214	11.8	53.4
2008...	1,402	544	74	392	13.5	59.7	332	44	235	7.7	41.4	199	19	167	1.2	11.1	327	53	207	11.9	51.4
2009...	1,419	553	76	399	14.3	59.4	329	44	231	7.9	42.2	203	19	170	1.2	11.7	333	53	211	12.1	52.0
2010...	1,431	566	79	407	15.1	60.3	328	44	228	8.2	43.4	202	18	169	3.0	12.2	334	54	212	12.4	50.9
2011...	1,425	565	82	403	15.7	60.2	325	44	224	8.5	44.0	201	21	167	1.3	12.4	333	53	213	12.3	50.3
2012...	1,400	550	82	390	16.0	57.4	318	44	217	8.6	44.3	198	20	164	1.3	12.6	333	53	214	12.5	49.8

[1] Includes cadets, midshipmen, and others, not shown separately. [2] Beginning 1980, excludes Navy Reserve personnel on active duty for Training and Administration of Reserves (TARS).

Source: U.S. Department of Defense, Statistical Information Analysis Division, *Selected Manpower Statistics*, discontinued; and "Active Duty Military Personnel by Rank/Grade," September 2012, <http://siadapp.dmdc.osd.mil/>.

Table 530. Military Personnel on Active Duty by Rank or Grade: 1990 to 2012

[In thousands (2,043.7 represents 2,043,700). As of September 30]

Rank/grade	1990	2000	2005	2009	2010	2011	2012
Total..........................	2,043.7	1,384.3	1,389.4	1,418.5	1,431.0	1,425.1	1,399.6
Total Officers..................	296.6	217.2	226.6	228.3	234.0	237.4	238.1
General-Admiral................	(Z)	(Z)	(Z)	(Z)	(Z)	(Z)	(Z)
Lieutenant General-Vice Admiral....	0.1	0.1	0.1	0.2	0.2	0.2	0.2
Major General-Rear Admiral (U).....	0.4	0.3	0.3	0.3	0.3	0.3	0.3
Brigadier General-Rear Admiral (L).....	0.5	0.4	0.4	0.5	0.5	0.5	0.4
Colonel-Captain................	14.0	11.3	11.4	12.0	12.2	12.1	11.9
Lieutenant Colonel-Commander........	32.3	27.5	28.1	28.4	28.8	28.8	28.7
Major-LT Commander............	53.2	43.2	44.4	43.9	45.3	46.2	46.5
Captain-Lieutenant.............	106.6	68.1	72.5	72.5	75.0	76.5	74.8
1st Lieutenant-Lieutenant (JG)......	37.9	24.7	27.5	24.9	25.5	27.0	30.8
2nd Lieutenant-Ensign...........	31.9	26.4	25.9	26.9	27.1	26.1	25.0
Chief Warrant Officer W-5..........	(Z)	0.1	0.5	0.7	0.7	0.8	0.8
Chief Warrant Officer W-4..........	3.0	2.0	2.2	3.1	3.2	3.3	3.2
Chief Warrant Officer W-3..........	5.0	3.8	4.6	4.7	4.8	4.7	5.1
Chief Warrant Officer W-2..........	8.4	6.7	6.2	7.1	7.5	8.1	8.1
Warrant Officer W-1.............	3.2	2.1	2.5	3.2	2.9	2.6	2.4
Total Enlisted.................	1,733.8	1,154.6	1,149.9	1,176.7	1,183.2	1,174.2	1,148.5
E-9.............................	15.3	10.2	10.5	10.4	10.2	10.3	10.3
E-8.............................	38.0	26.0	27.1	27.4	27.3	27.3	27.1
E-7.............................	134.1	97.7	97.8	98.5	97.1	96.2	96.6
E-6.............................	239.1	164.9	172.4	170.5	170.9	168.7	165.7
E-5.............................	361.5	229.5	248.5	248.5	250.0	244.0	237.2
E-4.............................	427.8	251.0	261.7	280.2	279.3	290.0	293.1
E-3.............................	280.1	196.3	201.7	205.9	228.2	223.6	206.6
E-2.............................	140.3	99.0	70.8	84.8	75.2	69.7	64.9
E-1.............................	97.6	80.0	59.5	50.4	45.1	44.3	47.1
Cadets and Midshipmen...........	13.3	12.5	12.9	13.6	13.8	13.5	13.1

Z Fewer than 50.

Source: U.S. Department of Defense, Statistical Information Analysis Division, *Military Personnel Statistics*, annual; and "Active Duty Military Personnel by Rank/Grade," September 2012, <http://siadapp.dmdc.osd.mil/>.

Table 531. Military Retirement System: 2012

[Payment in thousands of dollars (4,105,740 represents $4,105,740,000). As of September 30. The data published in the source report are produced from files maintained by the Defense Manpower Data Center. This report compiles data primarily from the "Retiree Pay and Survivor Pay" files. Any grouping of members by address reflects mailing, not necessarily residence address. Only those members in plans administered by the Department of Defense (DoD) are included in this table. The data are preliminary because of reporting delays about members who retired or died within one month of the September 30 reporting date. These data were not processed in time to be included in this report. For more information, see Introduction and Overview, source]

State	Retired military personnel [1]			Monthly payment ($)	State	Retired military personnel [1]			Monthly payment ($)
	Total	Disabled [2]	Non-disabled			Total	Disabled [2]	Non-disabled	
Total [3]....	2,066,861	196,643	1,870,218	4,105,740	MO...........	37,392	4,121	33,271	64,767
U.S...........	2,025,367	192,937	1,832,430	4,029,489	MT...........	8,999	882	8,117	16,450
AL...........	58,478	4,905	53,573	114,784	NE...........	14,375	1,130	13,245	29,256
AK...........	10,135	832	9,303	19,807	NV...........	27,636	1,954	25,682	55,777
AZ...........	54,762	4,864	49,898	111,767	NH...........	9,511	872	8,639	18,857
AR...........	25,785	2,623	23,162	45,392	NJ...........	19,863	2,641	17,222	31,568
CA...........	162,851	15,828	147,023	328,321	NM...........	21,357	1,747	19,610	44,715
CO...........	50,242	4,648	45,594	115,277	NY...........	39,087	6,259	32,828	56,536
CT...........	10,540	1,320	9,220	18,219	NC...........	89,064	8,296	80,768	180,081
DE...........	8,581	604	7,977	15,584	ND...........	5,094	379	4,715	8,436
DC...........	2,571	386	2,185	5,712	OH...........	45,579	5,943	39,636	79,770
FL...........	188,507	15,957	172,550	400,951	OK...........	35,489	3,237	32,252	64,545
GA...........	92,087	8,448	83,639	179,601	OR...........	20,945	2,582	18,363	37,396
HI...........	16,942	1,196	15,746	36,507	PA...........	50,531	6,064	44,467	86,003
ID...........	13,250	1,218	12,032	24,809	RI...........	5,481	541	4,940	10,644
IL...........	36,583	4,679	31,904	66,545	SC...........	57,118	4,659	52,459	110,333
IN...........	25,017	3,368	21,649	39,759	SD...........	7,774	626	7,148	14,089
IA...........	12,390	1,393	10,997	19,176	TN...........	52,908	5,055	47,853	97,754
KS...........	21,253	1,948	19,305	41,688	TX...........	194,338	18,622	175,716	406,346
KY...........	27,804	3,211	24,593	49,754	UT...........	15,937	1,257	14,680	30,116
LA...........	25,957	2,884	23,073	47,297	VT...........	3,778	373	3,405	6,078
ME...........	12,098	1,182	10,916	20,972	VA...........	151,594	8,558	143,036	403,848
MD...........	53,776	4,171	49,605	118,315	WA...........	71,471	5,584	65,887	146,351
MA...........	18,945	2,529	16,416	30,614	WV...........	11,056	1,426	9,630	17,893
MI...........	28,969	4,441	24,528	44,419	WI...........	20,727	2,552	18,175	31,991
MN...........	18,368	2,138	16,230	28,001	WY...........	5,208	453	4,755	9,565
MS...........	27,164	2,351	24,813	47,053					

[1] Represents military personnel (officers and enlisted) receiving and not receiving pay from DoD. [2] A disabled military member is entitled to disability retired pay if the disability is not the result of the member's intentional misconduct or willful neglect, was not incurred during a period of unauthorized absence, and either: (1) the member has at least 20 years of service; or (2) at the time of determination, the disability is at least 30 percent (under a standard schedule of rating disabilities by the Veterans Administration) and one of four additional conditions are met. For details on these conditions and additional information, see Overview, source. [3] Includes states, U.S. territories, and retirees living in foreign countries.

Source: U.S. Department of Defense, Office of the Actuary, *Statistical Report on the Military Retirement System, Fiscal Year 2012*, May 2013. See also <http://www.defenselink.mil/actuary/>.

Table 532. Military Reserve Personnel: 1995 to 2010

[As of September 30. The Ready Reserve includes the Selected Reserve, which is scheduled to augment active forces during times of war or national emergency, and the Individual Ready Reserve, which during times of war or national emergency would be used to fill out active duty, National Guard, and Reserve units, and which would also be a source for casualty replacements. Ready Reservists serve in an active status (except for the Inactive National Guard—a very small pool within the Army National Guard). The Standby Reserve cannot be called to active duty, other than for training, unless authorized by Congress under "full mobilization," and a determination is made that there are not enough qualified members in the Ready Reserve in the required categories who are readily available. The Retired Reserve represents a lower potential for involuntary mobilization]

Reserve status and branch of service	1995	2000	2005	2007	2008	2009	2010
Total reserves [1]	**1,674,164**	**1,276,843**	**1,136,200**	**1,109,805**	**1,099,915**	**1,094,071**	**1,102,863**
Ready Reserve	**1,648,388**	**1,251,452**	**1,113,427**	**1,088,587**	**1,080,617**	**1,079,627**	**1,078,621**
Army [2]	999,462	725,771	636,355	621,422	626,892	645,394	651,098
Navy	267,356	184,080	140,821	128,421	123,159	109,271	102,349
Marine Corps	103,668	99,855	99,820	100,787	95,748	95,199	97,087
Air Force [3]	263,011	229,009	223,551	226,806	224,545	220,364	218,350
Coast Guard	14,891	12,737	12,880	11,151	10,273	9,399	9,737
Standby Reserve	**25,776**	**25,391**	**22,773**	**21,218**	**19,298**	**25,808**	**24,242**
Army	1,128	701	1,668	[4] 5,294	2,136	2,072	1,673
Navy	12,707	7,213	4,038	3,046	3,310	[4] 10,036	9,742
Marine Corps	216	895	1,129	1,372	1,691	1,205	1,278
Air Force	11,453	16,429	15,897	10,154	10,384	10,530	10,213
Coast Guard	272	153	41	1,352	1,777	1,965	1,336
Retired Reserve	**505,905**	**573,305**	**627,424**	**648,346**	**658,251**	**707,060**	**716,228**
Army	259,553	296,004	321,312	330,121	334,258	378,603	383,220
Navy	97,532	109,531	117,093	120,859	122,000	123,292	124,870
Marine Corps	11,319	12,937	14,693	15,264	15,558	15,948	16,277
Air Force	137,501	154,833	174,326	182,102	186,435	189,217	191,861

[1] Less Retired Reserves. [2] Includes Army National Guard. [3] Includes Air National Guard. [4] The Army for FY2007 and the Navy for FY2009 modified their Individual Ready Reserve (IRR) category and reclassified personnel awaiting retirement or discharge into the Standby Reserve. This action was done in order to give them a better perspective on actual IRR members cleared for mobilization, if required.

Source: U.S. Department of Defense, *Fiscal Year 2010 Official Guard and Reserve Manpower Strengths and Statistics*, discontinued. See also <http://siadapp.dmdc.osd.mil/index.html>.

Table 533. Ready Reserve Personnel by Race, Hispanic Origin, and Sex: 1990 to 2010

[In thousands (1,658.7 represents 1,658,700). As of September 30. For definition of Ready Reserve, see headnote, Table 532]

Year	Total [1]	Race						His-panic [2]	Sex			
		White	Black	Asian	Ameri-can Indian	Pacific Islander	Other/ Unknown		Officer		Enlisted	
									Male	Female	Male	Female
1990	1,658.7	1,304.6	272.3	14.9	7.8	(NA)	59.1	83.1	226.8	40.5	1,204.7	186.7
1995	1,648.4	1,267.7	274.5	22.0	8.8	(NA)	75.4	96.2	209.9	44.7	1,196.8	196.9
1999	1,288.8	980.0	202.6	22.6	7.6	(NA)	76.0	88.9	166.2	38.4	911.2	173.1
2000	1,251.5	942.2	199.6	26.7	8.4	(NA)	74.6	91.8	159.4	36.9	879.9	175.3
2001	1,224.1	912.7	198.4	27.9	8.5	(NA)	76.7	94.3	158.0	36.6	852.2	177.3
2002	1,199.3	891.3	193.2	27.9	8.8	(NA)	78.2	96.0	152.1	35.6	835.2	176.4
2003	1,167.1	865.7	187.5	25.4	8.5	(NA)	80.1	98.0	145.1	34.0	813.7	174.3
2004	1,145.0	845.3	181.3	26.2	9.1	3.6	79.6	100.2	141.9	33.6	799.7	169.8
2005	1,113.4	825.4	169.9	26.9	9.5	4.1	77.6	99.8	139.2	33.3	778.0	162.9
2006	1,101.6	822.4	163.5	27.7	10.1	4.5	73.4	101.1	136.7	33.1	769.4	162.3
2007	1,088.6	818.1	156.6	28.1	10.8	4.8	70.3	102.7	130.0	31.8	766.5	160.2
2008	1,080.7	815.2	153.4	29.0	10.9	5.3	66.9	102.6	128.0	31.2	760.8	160.6
2009	1,070.2	810.6	149.4	30.1	10.8	5.8	63.7	99.9	126.4	30.8	754.3	158.7
2010	1,068.9	809.8	148.2	31.0	10.9	6.1	62.8	99.6	125.9	30.7	754.2	158.1

[1] Includes other races, not shown separately. [2] Persons of Hispanic origin may be of any race.

Source: U.S. Department of Defense, *Fiscal Year 2010 Official Guard and Reserve Manpower Strengths and Statistics*, discontinued. See also <http://siadapp.dmdc.osd.mil/index.html>.

Table 534. National Guard by Sex and Race: 1995 to 2010

[In thousands (375 represents 375,000). As of September 30]

Year	Army National Guard					Air National Guard				
	Total	Male [1]	Female	White	Black	Total	Male [1]	Female	White	Black
1995	375	344	31	299	59	110	94	16	96	9
2000	353	313	40	278	55	106	88	18	90	10
2004	343	299	44	271	50	107	88	19	89	10
2005	333	290	43	264	46	106	87	19	89	9
2006	346	300	47	276	47	106	87	19	88	9
2007	353	304	49	283	47	106	87	19	88	9
2008	360	309	51	288	49	108	88	20	89	9
2009	358	308	50	288	47	109	89	20	90	9
2010	362	310	52	291	48	108	88	20	89	9

[1] Male population includes unknown sex.

Source: U.S. Department of Defense, Statistical Information Analysis Division, *Atlas/Data Abstract for the United States and Selected Areas*, 2010, <http://siadapp.dmdc.osd.mil/personnel/Pubs.htm>, discontinued; *Selected Manpower Statistics*, 2010.

Table 535. U.S. Active Duty Military Deaths by Manner of Death: 1980 to 2011

[As of Nov. 2, 2011]

Manner of death	1980–2011	1980	1990	1995	2000	2004	2005	2006	2007	2008	2009	2010	2011
Deaths, total	50,085	2,392	1,507	1,040	832	1,874	1,929	1,882	1,953	1,440	1,515	1,485	1,251
Accident	25,382	1,556	880	538	429	605	646	561	561	506	467	424	309
Hostile action	5,166	–	–	–	–	735	739	769	847	352	346	456	352
Homicide	2,353	174	74	67	37	46	54	47	52	47	77	39	24
Illness	8,761	419	277	174	180	256	280	257	237	244	277	238	182
Pending	249	–	–	–	–	–	1	8	22	6	19	22	170
Self-inflicted	7,097	231	232	250	153	197	182	213	211	259	302	289	186
Terrorist attack	422	1	1	7	17	–	–	–	–	1	–	–	2
Undetermined	655	11	43	4	16	8	27	27	23	25	27	17	26
Deaths per 100,000 of personnel strength	(X)	110.8	66.7	62.6	54.4	107.9	115.9	116.8	121.4	85.6	92.3	88.1	77.9
Accident	(X)	72.0	39.0	32.4	28.0	35.3	38.8	34.8	34.9	30.1	28.5	25.2	19.2
Hostile action	(X)	–	–	–	–	42.9	44.4	47.7	52.7	20.9	21.1	27.1	21.9
Homicide	(X)	8.1	3.3	4.0	2.4	2.7	3.2	2.9	3.2	2.8	4.7	2.3	1.5
Illness	(X)	19.4	12.3	10.5	11.8	15.0	16.8	15.9	14.7	14.5	16.9	14.1	11.3
Pending	(X)	–	–	–	–	–	0.1	0.5	1.4	0.4	1.2	1.3	10.6
Self-inflicted	(X)	10.7	10.3	15.0	10.0	11.5	10.9	13.2	13.1	15.4	18.4	17.1	11.6
Terrorist attack	(X)	–	–	0.4	1.1	–	–	–	–	0.1	–	–	0.1
Undetermined	(X)	0.5	1.9	0.2	1.0	0.5	1.6	1.7	1.4	1.5	1.6	1.0	1.6

– Represents zero. X Not applicable.

Source: Department of Defense Personnel and Procurement, "DoD Personnel and Military Casualty Statistics, Military Casualty Information," <https://www.dmdc.osd.mil/dcas/pages/main.xhtml>.

Table 536. U.S. Military Personnel on Active Duty in Selected Foreign Countries: 1995 to 2012

[As of September 30. Prior to 2012, data from Statistical Information Analysis Division (SIAD). Beginning 2012, data from Defense Manpower Data Center (DMDC)]

Country	1995	2000	2005	2008	2009	2010	2011	2012
Total in foreign countries [1]	238,064	257,817	290,997	288,550	262,793	297,286	205,118	173,929
Ashore	208,836	212,858	268,214	269,260	242,291	277,151	186,476	(NA)
Afloat	29,228	44,959	22,783	19,290	20,502	20,135	18,642	(NA)
Australia	314	175	196	140	139	130	198	346
Bahrain	618	949	1,641	1,545	1,507	1,349	2,142	2,713
Belgium	1,689	1,554	1,366	1,266	1,267	1,252	1,205	1,174
Bosnia and Herzegovina	1	5,708	263	14	11	8	9	9
Canada	214	156	150	134	128	127	130	147
Colombia	44	224	52	114	77	62	63	73
Cuba (Guantanamo)	5,129	688	950	969	926	913	929	996
Diego Garcia [2]	897	625	683	244	253	238	292	529
Djibouti	7	2	622	1,780	1,207	1,379	335	168
Egypt	1,123	499	410	284	265	275	251	280
Germany	73,280	69,203	66,418	55,140	52,658	53,951	53,766	47,761
Greece	489	678	428	366	361	338	382	351
Greenland	131	125	146	134	144	133	142	139
Honduras	193	351	438	429	416	403	354	408
Italy	12,007	11,190	11,841	9,601	9,707	9,646	10,801	10,922
Japan	39,134	40,159	35,571	33,286	35,965	34,385	39,222	50,937
Korea, South	36,016	36,565	30,983	25,062	(NA)	(NA)	(NA)	(NA)
Kuwait	771	4,602	([3])	([3])	([3])	([3])	([3])	([3])
Netherlands	687	659	583	547	510	442	405	374
Portugal	1,066	1,005	970	783	716	703	723	743
Qatar	2	52	463	433	463	555	621	806
Saudi Arabia	1,077	7,053	258	284	269	239	274	284
Senegal	13	10	42	7	9	9	13	15
Singapore	166	411	169	129	125	132	163	154
Spain	2,799	2,007	1,660	1,220	1,365	1,240	1,479	1,727
Turkey	3,111	2,006	1,780	1,575	1,616	1,530	1,491	1,505
United Kingdom	12,131	11,207	10,752	9,426	9,199	9,229	9,382	9,317
DEPLOYMENTS								
Operation Enduring Freedom (OEF) [4]	(X)	(X)	19,500	32,300	66,400	105,900	109,200	78,055
Operation New Dawn (OND) [5]	(X)	(X)	192,600	190,400	164,100	96,200	92,200	194

X Not applicable. NA Not available. [1] Includes items not shown separately. [2] British Indian Ocean Territory. [3] Military personnel data for Kuwait are included with the Operation New Dawn (OND) data. [4] Total (in/around Afghanistan as of September 30) includes Reserve/National Guard. [5] Total (in/around Iraq as of September 30) includes Reserve/National Guard.

Source: U.S. Department of Defense, DoD Personnel and Procurement Statistics, "Active Duty Military Personnel By Service By Region/Country," <http://siadapp.dmdc.osd.mil/index.html>, accessed April 2013.

Table 537. Suicides and Attempted Suicides of Military Personnel by Selected Characteristics: 2009 to 2011

[Data are shown for suicides reported in Department of Defense Suicide Event Report (DoDSER). DoDSER standardizes suicide surveillance efforts across the military services to support the DoD's suicide prevention mission. Confirmed suicides are those that have been confirmed by the Armed Forces Medical Examiner System (AFMES)]

Characteristics	Suicides			Suicide Attempts Reported [1]		
	2009	2010	2011	2009 [2]	2010	2011
TOTAL						
Suicide attempts reported.....................................	(X)	(X)	(X)	502	863	935
Confirmed suicides...	299	281	287	(X)	(X)	(X)
Suicides confirmed and pending confirmation...............	309	295	301	(X)	(X)	(X)
DEMOGRAPHICS						
By Sex:						
Male..	300	281	285	373	653	687
Female...	9	14	16	129	210	248
By Race/ethnicity:						
White...	247	235	231	319	587	600
Black or African American...................................	33	36	37	78	133	172
Asian or Pacific Islander....................................	15	16	17	14	23	36
American Indian or Alaskan Native........................	10	6	6	(NA)	11	13
Other/Unknown..	4	2	10	65	109	114
By Hispanic Origin:						
Hispanic or Latino..	(NA)	(NA)	18	21	(NA)	99
Non-Hispanic or Latino.......................................	(NA)	(NA)	283	(NA)	(NA)	836
By Age:						
Under 25...	141	140	114	298	514	535
25-29...	73	76	91	119	190	220
30-39...	69	63	68	69	122	141
30-34...	43	30	32	(NA)	(NA)	(NA)
35-39...	26	33	36	(NA)	(NA)	(NA)
40 and older..	26	16	28	16	37	39
40-44...	15	14	22	(NA)	(NA)	(NA)
45 and older..	11	2	6	(NA)	(NA)	(NA)
By Education						
Some high school, did not graduate.......................	2	2	5	7	7	2
GED..	44	26	32	89	63	44
High school graduate...	208	206	194	171	398	409
Some college or technical school..........................	16	15	16	142	210	273
Degree/certificate less than four years...................	9	18	18	19	43	55
Four-year college degree....................................	17	18	22	18	39	31
Master's degree or greater..................................	10	3	6	3	16	13
Unknown...	3	7	8	53	87	108
By Marital Status						
Never Married..	105	125	107	215	364	390
Married...	159	147	167	220	364	406
Legally Separated...	–	1	–	15	41	28
Divorced...	37	20	23	41	73	80
Widowed...	1	–	4	2	1	1
Unknown...	7	2	–	9	20	30
SERVICE DETAILS						
By Rank:						
E1-E4...	167	161	148	373	616	664
E5-E9...	112	118	128	109	209	240
Officer..	23	15	25	12	32	25
Warrant Officer...	4	–	–	1	4	2
Cadet/Midshipman...	(NA)	1	–	2	1	4
Unknown or Not Applicable..................................	3	–	–	5	(NA)	–
By Service Component:						
Regular...	284	269	267	458	817	893
Reserve..	8	9	12	16	24	18
National Guard...	17	17	22	25	20	19
Other...	(NA)	(NA)	(NA)	3	2	5
By Selected Location:						
United States...	234	232	235	396	707	830
Iraq...	31	12	10	43	26	3
Afghanistan...	7	17	18	8	20	20
Asia...	(NA)	11	4	[3] 17	45	36
Europe...	8	2	9	26	50	36
Canada or Mexico...	2	–	–	3	3	2
Other...	6	6	5	24	9	3
Unknown...	1	–	6	2	3	4

– Represents zero. X Not Applicable. NA Not Available. [1] Data are for DoDSERS submitted for suicides, which may include more than one report per individual. [2] 2009 attempt data is for Army only. [3] Data are for Korea only.

Source: Department of Defense, National Center for Telehealth and Technology, *Department of Defense Suicide Event Report, Calendar Year 2011 Annual Report*, November 2012, and earlier reports. See also <http://t2health.org/programs/dodser>.

Table 538. Sexual Assault in the Military—Incident Reports and Victims by Type of Report and Selected Characteristics: 2010 to 2012

[Reports of sexual assault (rape, aggravated sexual assault, sexual assault, aggravated sexual contact, abusive sexual contact, wrongful sexual contact, non-consensual sodomy, and attempts to commit these offenses) by or against Service Members. Restricted Reporting allows victim confidential access to medical care and advocacy services. When a victim makes an Unrestricted Report, the report is also referred to a Military Criminal Investigation Organization for investigation and command is notified]

Item	Unrestricted			Restricted		
	2010	2011	2012	2010	2011	2012
REPORTS [1]						
Total................................	**2,410**	**2,439**	**2,558**	**882**	**877**	**981**
Service member on Service member.....................	1,358	1,366	1,590	352	342	555
Service member on Non-Service member................	691	648	573	(NA)	(NA)	195
Non-Service member on Service member................	104	139	124	115	195	37
Unidentified subject on Service member..................	257	286	271	415	340	194
Victims in Completed Investigations [2]						
Total................................	**1,741**	**1,783**	**2,940**	(X)	(X)	(X)
Service member victims........................	1,303	1,349	2,256	(X)	(X)	(X)
Service member victims in same Service..............	1,253	1,278	2,174	(X)	(X)	(X)
Service member victims in other Service..............	50	71	82	(X)	(X)	(X)
Non-Service member victims.........................	438	434	684	(X)	(X)	(X)
VICTIMS [3]						
By Sex:						
Male...............................	180	212	345	114	122	133
Female.............................	1,561	1,571	2,595	739	732	826
Unknown............................	–	–	–	29	23	22
By Age:						
16-19 years old.................	324	312	516	191	173	202
20-24 years old.................	864	916	1,505	392	406	434
25-34 years old.................	402	404	729	188	186	214
35-49 years old.................	96	102	131	49	44	48
50-64 years old.................	8	13	13	–	–	3
65 years and older.................	–	–	1	–	–	–
Unknown............................	47	36	45	62	68	80
SERVICE MEMBER VICTIMS						
By Service Branch:						
Army................................	681	759	1,122	327	342	214
Navy................................	302	218	593	169	176	250
Marines.............................	134	136	239	51	52	102
Air Force...........................	183	236	297	287	290	359
Coast Guard........................	3	–	5	4	3	1
US Civilian.........................	423	410	(NA)	(NA)	(NA)	(NA)
Foreign national/Foreign military........	15	24	(NA)	(NA)	(NA)	(NA)
Unknown............................	–	–	–	44	14	24
By Service Component:						
Active Duty.........................	1,206	1,202	2,028	733	759	829
Reserve (activated).................	41	60	109	24	16	25
National Guard (Activated Title 10).......	44	69	78	49	33	21
Cadet/Midshipmen..................	12	18	40	23	42	48
US Civilian.........................	423	410	(NA)	6	–	(NA)
Foreign national/Foreign military........	15	24	(NA)	(NA)	(NA)	(NA)
Unknown............................	–	–	1	47	27	27

– Represents zero. X Not applicable. NA Not available. [1] Reports of sexual assault during the fiscal year. [2] Victims in investigations completed during the fiscal year. [3] For 2010 and 2011 service member victims only. Beginning in 2012, data shown for all victims.

Source: Department of Defense, *Annual Report on Sexual Assault in the Military, Fiscal Year 2012, Vol. 1*, April 2013, and earlier reports. See also <http://www.sapr.mil/index.php/annual-reports>.

Table 539. U.S. Military Sales and Assistance to Foreign Governments: 1995 to 2011

[In millions of dollars (8,495 represents $8,495,000,000). For year ending September 30. Department of Defense (DoD) sales deliveries cover deliveries against sales orders authorized under Arms Export Control Act, as well as earlier and applicable legislation. For details regarding individual programs, see source]

Item	1995	2000	2005	2006	2007	2008	2009	2010	2011
Military sales agreements...............	8,495	10,685	8,818	17,522	17,698	28,235	29,629	22,561	26,404
Military construction sales agreements............................	24	284	305	171	439	179	956	912	455
Military sales deliveries [1]................	12,100	10,867	11,139	11,512	12,482	11,796	16,326	13,521	14,087
Military construction sales deliveries...	(NA)	183	349	323	197	267	204	459	536
Military financing program..............	3,712	4,333	4,956	4,450	4,519	4,506	4,580	5,016	5,320
Commercial exports licensed under Arms Export Control Act [2]............	(NA)	478	30,146	31,605	8,874	33,510	(NA)	(NA)	(NA)
Military assistance program delivery [3]............................	20	5	71	11	(NA)	(NA)	(NA)	(NA)	14
IMET program/deliveries [4]..............	26	50	86	85	83	83	90	108	106

NA Not available. [1] Includes military construction sales deliveries. [2] The total dollar value of deliveries made for purchases of munitions-controlled items by foreign governments directly from U.S. manufacturers. [3] Includes Military Assistance Service Funded (MASF) program data and Section 506(a) drawdown authority. [4] International Military Education and Training. Includes military assistance services and emergency drawdowns.

Source: U.S. Department of Defense, Defense Security Cooperation Agency, DSCA Data & Statistics, *Historical Facts Book, As of September 30, 2011*. See also <http://www.dsca.osd.mil/data_stats.htm>.

Table 540. U.S. Military Sales Deliveries by Selected Country: 1995 to 2011

[In millions of dollars (12,100 represents $12,100,000,000). For year ending September 30. Represents Department of Defense military sales]

Country	1995	2000	2005	2006	2007	2008	2009	2010	2011
Total [1]..................................	**12,100**	**10,886**	**11,139**	**11,512**	**12,482**	**11,796**	**16,326**	**13,521**	**14,087**
Afghanistan................................	(NA)	–	169	173	18	7	2	10	13
Argentina..................................	(NA)	10	4	6	8	23	10	26	12
Australia...................................	303	332	350	350	780	908	374	917	755
Bahrain....................................	40	55	63	55	84	42	101	115	51
Belgium....................................	8	61	49	53	49	44	39	26	27
Brazil......................................	(NA)	61	11	28	62	54	46	32	38
Canada....................................	127	84	150	183	240	468	525	383	401
Colombia..................................	(NA)	14	41	86	199	124	110	433	152
Denmark...................................	54	43	40	49	63	57	43	43	67
Ecuador...................................	(NA)	1	4	6	7	3	1	3	1
Egypt......................................	1,479	1,092	1,421	1,194	1,216	856	878	883	978
El Salvador................................	(NA)	13	3	2	2	6	10	6	5
Finland....................................	(NA)	690	38	74	28	86	83	127	97
France.....................................	64	217	69	42	45	57	58	112	211
Georgia....................................	(NA)	3	12	11	25	72	18	10	32
Germany...................................	257	131	207	149	205	173	161	294	161
Greece.....................................	220	389	466	179	204	197	1,252	541	159
India.......................................	(NA)	–	100	49	92	40	15	31	57
Iraq..	(NA)	–	–	2	177	683	693	376	613
Israel......................................	327	585	1,524	1,284	1,314	1,407	727	892	745
Italy.......................................	54	52	127	288	153	76	92	179	101
Japan......................................	693	448	410	766	647	609	859	812	453
Jordan.....................................	47	52	140	102	170	263	170	170	209
Kenya......................................	(NA)	1	7	2	2	1	6	2	16
Korea, South..............................	442	1,399	590	598	728	791	477	600	721
Kuwait.....................................	471	321	278	542	458	245	252	242	485
Malaysia...................................	(NA)	411	49	22	19	17	23	45	31
Mexico.....................................	(NA)	9	4	8	6	4	4	59	38
Morocco...................................	(NA)	5	17	41	8	4	10	30	1,077
Netherlands...............................	153	278	178	231	238	252	249	202	187
Nigeria....................................	(NA)	–	7	3	4	–	3	5	13
Norway....................................	25	64	106	92	163	88	289	127	147
Pakistan...................................	(NA)	–	61	121	196	265	117	1,212	550
Poland.....................................	(NA)	13	84	393	1,483	731	157	75	190
Portugal...................................	88	20	84	57	39	45	94	29	36
Saudi Arabia..............................	3,567	1,968	981	978	1,014	895	1,714	1,587	1,426
Singapore.................................	59	131	229	355	173	167	181	304	252
Spain......................................	193	141	126	104	143	169	176	156	101
Taiwan [2].................................	1,332	784	1,400	1,067	771	617	646	706	802
Thailand...................................	356	114	92	82	46	40	47	42	92
Turkey.....................................	368	216	185	244	182	306	306	253	994
United Arab Emirates.....................	345	42	149	192	69	83	119	584	682
United Kingdom...........................	419	347	381	294	424	297	754	284	356
Venezuela.................................	(NA)	13	8	8	1	1	–	–	356

NA Not available. – Represents or rounds to zero. [1] Includes countries not shown. [2] With the establishment of diplomatic relations with China on January 1, 1979, the U.S. government recognized the People's Republic of China as the sole legal government of China and acknowledged the Chinese position that there is only one China and that Taiwan is part of China.

Source: U.S. Department of Defense, Defense Security Cooperation Agency, DSCA Data and Statistics, *Historical Facts Book, As of September 30, 2011*. See also <http://www.dsca.osd.mil/data_stats.htm>.

Table 541. Arms Transfer Agreements with Developing Nations by Supplier: 2004 to 2011

[In millions of current U.S. dollars (26,983 is 26,983,000,000). Developing nations category excludes the United States, Europe, Canada, Japan, Australia, and New Zealand. All data are for the calendar year given except for U.S. MAP (Military Assistance Program), IMET (International Military Education and Training), and Excess Defense Article data, which are included for the particular fiscal year. All amounts given include the values of all categories of weapons, spare parts, construction, all associated services, military assistance, excess defense articles, and training programs. Statistics for foreign countries are based upon estimated selling prices. All foreign data are rounded to the nearest $100 million]

Supplier	2004	2005	2006	2007	2008	2009	2010	2011	2004-2011
Total...........................	26,983	30,193	39,035	41,218	52,923	50,582	32,279	71,503	344,716
United States.................	6,783	5,493	8,435	11,518	28,023	14,582	14,079	56,303	145,216
Russia..........................	8,500	8,000	15,300	9,600	6,400	13,000	7,600	4,100	72,500
France..........................	1,100	5,400	500	1,400	3,600	9,200	1,800	2,700	25,700
United Kingdom...............	4,100	2,800	4,000	9,500	200	1,100	1,200	300	23,200
China...........................	1,000	2,700	2,000	2,500	2,100	2,300	1,600	2,100	16,300
Germany.......................	200	700	2,400	1,700	4,700	500	0	0	10,200
Italy.............................	300	500	600	1,000	1,600	1,300	1,800	1,100	8,200
All other European.............	2,400	3,600	2,700	2,100	4,400	4,700	2,700	2,400	25,000
All others.......................	2,600	1,000	3,100	1,900	1,900	3,900	1,500	2,500	18,400

Source: Congressional Research Service, *Conventional Arms Transfers to Developing Nations, 2004-2011*, August 2012.

Table 542. Veterans by Selected Period of Service and State: 2012

[In thousands (22,328 represents 22,328,000). As of September 30. "VetPop2011" is the Department of Veterans Affairs (VA) latest official estimate and projection of the veteran population. It is based on tabulations prepared for the VA Office of the Actuary; recent American Community Survey, Internal Revenue Service, and Social Security Administration data; administrative data and projections of service member separations from active duty provided by the Department of Defense, Defense Manpower Data Center and the Office of the Actuary; and VA data on veterans benefits]

State	Total [1,2]	Gulf War era [3]	Vietnam era [4]	State	Total [1,2]	Gulf War era [3]	Vietnam era [4]
United States............	22,328	6,240	7,489	Montana......................	102	30	35
Alabama.....................	418	130	141	Nebraska....................	141	42	48
Alaska.......................	75	35	22	Nevada......................	228	67	81
Arizona......................	532	150	176	New Hampshire...........	113	24	42
Arkansas....................	252	68	88	New Jersey.................	442	84	146
California....................	1,845	522	608	New Mexico................	172	49	59
Colorado....................	396	128	139	New York....................	918	193	297
Connecticut................	215	41	72	North Carolina............	772	235	258
Delaware....................	32	10	9	North Dakota..............	56	21	18
District of Columbia.......	79	20	28	Ohio..........................	900	197	316
Florida.......................	1,543	415	498	Oklahoma...................	343	103	121
Georgia......................	776	272	254	Oregon......................	328	72	126
Hawaii.......................	117	48	34	Pennsylvania..............	981	203	334
Idaho........................	138	45	44	Rhode Island..............	71	14	24
Illinois.......................	764	186	253	South Carolina............	422	134	142
Indiana.......................	499	126	166	South Dakota..............	76	25	26
Iowa..........................	238	56	85	Tennessee..................	526	141	187
Kansas.......................	227	68	78	Texas........................	1,676	572	561
Kentucky....................	342	90	118	Utah..........................	152	50	46
Louisiana....................	319	94	106	Vermont.....................	50	10	18
Maine........................	130	30	46	Virginia......................	837	386	240
Maryland....................	450	154	136	Washington.................	608	196	209
Massachusetts.............	389	77	128	West Virginia..............	175	44	61
Michigan....................	680	131	253	Wisconsin...................	418	92	148
Minnesota..................	369	85	130	Wyoming....................	56	21	18
Mississippi.................	227	70	72	Puerto Rico................	103	25	33
Missouri.....................	506	127	178	Island Areas & Foreign. ...	103	29	32

[1] Veterans serving in more than one period of service are counted only once in the total. [2] Current civilians discharged from active duty, other than for training only without service-connected disability. [3] Service from August 2, 1990 to the present. [4] Service from August 5, 1964 to May 7, 1975.

Source: U.S. Department of Veterans Affairs, National Center for Veterans Analysis and Statistics, "Veteran Population 2011," <http://www.va.gov/vetdata/veteran_population.asp>, accessed May 2013.

Table 543. Veterans Benefits—Expenditures by Program and Compensation for Service-Connected Disabilities: 1990 to 2012

[In millions of dollars (28,998 represents $28,998,000,000). For years ending September 30]

Program	1990	1995	2000	2005	2009	2010	2011	2012
Total expenditures.....................................	28,998	37,775	47,086	69,667	97,144	108,635	122,859	120,405
Medical programs..	11,582	16,255	19,637	29,433	40,079	42,372	43,085	45,521
Construction..	661	641	466	483	1,191	1,618	1,813	1,538
General operating expenses............................	811	954	1,016	1,294	4,962	6,101	6,655	6,445
Compensation and pension..............................	14,674	17,765	22,012	34,694	44,608	47,785	57,596	53,243
Vocational rehabilitation and education................	452	1,317	1,610	2,937	4,270	8,260	10,630	10,425
All other [1]...	818	844	2,345	826	2,034	2,499	3,079	3,233
Compensation for service-connected disabilities.......................................	9,284	11,644	15,511	24,515	34,103	36,486	39,374	44,359

[1] Includes insurance, indemnities, and miscellaneous funds and expenditures and offsets from public receipts. (Excludes expenditures from personal funds of patients.)

Source: U.S. Department of Veterans Affairs, "Summary of Expenditures By State," <http://www.va.gov/vetdata/Expenditures.asp>, accessed June 2013; and *Annual Benefits Report*, June 2013, and earlier reports.

Table 544. Veterans by Sex, Race, and Hispanic Origin: 2011

[Data are based on the American Community Survey (ACS). The survey universe includes the household population and the population living in institutions, college dormitories, and other group quarters. Based on a sample and subject to sampling variability; see text, this section and Appendix III]

Characteristic	Total number	18 to 64 years	65 years and over
Total..	**21,458,427**	**12,242,199**	**9,216,228**
Male..	19,892,449	10,926,854	8,965,595
Female..	1,565,978	1,315,345	250,633
White alone..	18,092,364	9,678,924	8,413,440
Male..	16,965,045	8,778,833	8,186,212
Female..	1,127,319	900,091	227,228
Black or African American alone..	2,344,042	1,802,275	541,767
Male..	2,023,479	1,495,820	527,659
Female..	320,563	306,455	14,108
American Indian/Alaska Native alone..	153,223	112,936	40,287
Male..	137,532	98,462	39,070
Female..	15,691	14,474	1,217
Asian alone..	264,695	174,524	90,171
Male..	238,063	150,568	87,495
Female..	26,632	23,956	2,676
Native Hawaiian and Other Pacific Islander alone..	27,469	22,174	5,295
Male..	24,493	19,377	5,116
Female..	2,976	2,797	179
Some other race alone..	245,966	198,161	47,805
Male..	220,351	173,987	46,364
Female..	25,615	24,174	1,441
Two or more races..	330,668	253,205	77,463
Male..	283,486	209,807	73,679
Female..	47,182	43,398	3,784
Hispanic or Latino origin [1]..	1,194,198	901,148	293,050
Male..	1,077,003	792,240	284,763
Female..	117,195	108,908	8,287

[1] Persons of Hispanic or Latino origin may be of any race.

Source: U.S. Census Bureau, American Community Survey, Tables B21001, B21001A, B21001B, B21001C, B21001D, B21001E, B21001F, B21001G and B21001I, <http://factfinder2.census.gov>, accessed March 2013.

Table 545. Veterans Living by Period of Service, Age, and Sex: 2011

[In thousands (22,234 represents 22,234,000). As of September 30. Includes those veterans living outside the United States]

Age	Total veterans	Wartime veterans					Peacetime veterans
		Total [1]	Gulf War era [2]	Vietnam era [3]	Korean conflict [4]	World War II	
Total........................	**22,234**	**16,546**	**5,946**	**7,391**	**2,275**	**1,711**	**5,688**
Under 20 years old........................	8	8	8	–	–	–	–
20 to 24 years old........................	302	302	302	–	–	–	–
25 to 29 years old........................	745	745	745	–	–	–	–
30 to 34 years old........................	907	907	907	–	–	–	–
35 to 39 years old........................	963	951	951	–	–	–	12
40 to 44 years old........................	1,419	1,117	1,117	–	–	–	303
45 to 49 years old........................	1,724	746	746	–	–	–	978
50 to 54 years old........................	1,905	581	520	66	–	–	1,324
55 to 59 years old........................	1,957	1,381	339	1,160	–	–	576
60 to 64 years old........................	2,943	2,806	206	2,737	–	–	137
65 to 69 years old........................	2,776	2,423	77	2,408	–	–	353
70 to 74 years old........................	1,901	711	19	665	51	–	1,190
75 to 79 years old........................	1,773	1,088	7	203	982	–	685
80 to 84 years old........................	1,481	1,374	2	109	1,081	352	107
85 years & over........................	1,430	1,406	–	43	160	1,359	24
Female, total........................	**1,854**	**1,312**	**952**	**248**	**58**	**86**	**542**

– Represents or rounds to zero. [1] Veterans who served in more than one wartime period are counted only once in the total. [2] Service from August 2, 1990 to the present. [3] Service from August 5, 1964 to May 7, 1975. [4] Service during period June 27, 1950 to January 31, 1955.

Source: Department of Veterans Affairs, National Center for Veterans Analysis and Statistics, "Veteran Population 2007," <http://www1.va.gov/vetdata/Veteran_Population.asp>, accessed April 2012.

Table 546. Veterans Compensation and Pension Benefits—Number on Rolls by Period of Service and Status: 1990 to 2011

[In thousands (3,584 represents 3,584,000). As of September 30. Living refers to veterans receiving compensation for disability incurred or aggravated while on active duty and war veterans receiving pension and benefits for nonservice-connected disabilities. Deceased refers to deceased veterans whose dependents were receiving pensions and compensation benefits]

Period of service and veteran status	1990	1995	2000	2005	2008	2009	2010	2011
Total	**3,584**	**3,330**	**3,236**	**3,503**	**3,801**	**3,919**	**4,070**	**4,226**
Living veterans	2,746	2,669	2,672	2,973	3,268	3,384	3,524	3,668
Service-connected	2,184	2,236	2,308	2,637	2,952	3,070	3,210	3,355
Nonservice-connected	562	433	364	336	316	314	314	314
Deceased veterans	838	662	564	530	533	535	546	557
Service-connected	320	307	307	323	338	341	347	355
Nonservice-connected	518	355	257	207	196	194	199	202
World War I	198	89	34	13	8	7	6	5
Living	18	3	(Z)	(Z)	(Z)	(Z)	(Z)	(Z)
World War II	1,723	1,307	968	718	598	559	529	498
Living	1,294	961	676	466	362	329	298	271
Korean conflict [1]	390	368	323	295	282	276	275	275
Living	305	290	255	231	218	213	209	207
Vietnam era [2]	774	868	969	1,218	1,347	1,393	1,447	1,524
Living	685	766	848	1,068	1,175	1,214	1,261	1,326
Gulf War era [3]	(X)	138	334	630	923	1,028	1,140	1,239
Living	(X)	134	326	617	904	1,007	1,117	1,215
Peacetime	495	559	607	627	644	655	673	685
Living	444	514	567	591	609	621	638	650

X Not applicable. Z Fewer than 500. [1] Service during period June 27, 1950 to January 31, 1955. [2] Service from August 5, 1964 to May 7, 1975. [3] Service from August 2, 1990 to the present.

Source: U.S. Department of Veterans Affairs, 1990 to 1995, *Annual Report of the Secretary of Veterans Affairs*; 1996 to 2010, *Annual Accountability Report* and unpublished data; and beginning 2011, *Annual Benefits Report*, 2012. See also <http://www.vba.va.gov/REPORTS/abr/index.asp>.

Table 547. Federal Funding Obligations for Selected Homeless Veterans Programs: 1988 to 2012

[In thousands of dollars, except as indicated (12,932 represents 12,932,000). For year ending September 30]

Year	Department of Veterans Affairs					Department of Labor
	Health care for homeless veterans [1]	Domiciliary care for homeless veterans	Compensated work therapy/ therapeutic residence	Grant and per diem program	HUD-VA Supported Housing (Supportive Services) [2]	Homeless Veterans Reintegration Program
1988	12,932	15,000	(NA)	(NA)	(NA)	1,915
1989	13,252	10,367	(NA)	(NA)	(NA)	1,877
1990	15,000	15,000	(NA)	(NA)	(NA)	1,920
1991	15,461	15,750	([3])	(NA)	(NA)	2,018
1992	16,500	16,500	([3])	(NA)	2,300	1,366
1993	22,150	22,300	400	(NA)	2,000	5,055
1994	24,513	27,140	3,051	8,000	3,235	5,055
1995	[4] 38,585	38,948	3,387	([4])	4,270	[5] 107
1996	[4] 38,433	41,117	3,886	([4])	4,829	–
1997	[4] 38,063	37,214	3,628	([4])	4,958	–
1998	36,407	38,489	8,612	5,886	5,084	3,000
1999	32,421	39,955	4,092	20,000	5,223	3,000
2000	38,381	34,434	8,068	19,640	5,137	9,636
2001	58,602	34,576	8,144	31,100	5,219	17,500
2002	54,135	45,443	8,028	22,431	4,729	18,250
2003	45,188	49,213	8,371	43,388	4,603	18,131
2004	42,905	51,829	10,240	62,965	3,375	18,888
2005	40,357	57,555	10,004	62,180	3,243	20,832
2006	56,998	63,592	19,529	63,621	5,297	21,780
2007	71,925	77,633	21,514	81,187	7,487	21,809
2008	77,656	96,098	21,497	114,696	4,854	23,620
2009	80,219	115,373	22,206	128,073	26,601	26,330
2010	109,727	175,979	61,205	175,057	71,137	36,330
2011	200,808	221,938	73,420	148,097	119,603	36,257
2012 est	134,738	201,304	57,743	194,477	201,500	38,185

– Represents zero. NA Not available. [1] Through 1991 the program was called the Homeless Chronically Ill Veterans program. [2] Covers funding allocated for supportive services, but not the cost of providing housing. [3] For 1991 and 1992, funds from Homeless Chronically Mentally Ill Veterans program as well as substance abuse treatment funds were used for the program. [4] For 1995 through 1997, funds were obligated with funds for the Health Care for Veterans program. Department of Veterans Affairs budget documents do not provide a separate breakdown for grant and per diem obligations. [5] Congress appropriated $5.011 million for the program in 1995. A subsequent rescission reduced the amount.

Source: Congressional Research Service, *Veterans and Homelessness*, February 2013.

National Security and Veterans Affairs **363**

Table 548. Homeland Security Funding by Agency: 2005 to 2013

[In millions of dollars. (52,657 represents 52,657,000,000). A total of 31 agencies comprise federal homeland security funding. Department of Homeland Security (DHS) is the designated department to coordinate and centralize the leadership of many homeland security activities under a single department. In addition to DHS, the Departments of Defense (DoD), Energy (DoE), Justice (DoJ), Health and Human Services (HHS), and the U.S. State Department account for most of the total government-wide homeland security funding]

Agency	2005	2009	2010	2011	2012	2013
Total budget authority, excluding BioShield [1,2]	**52,657**	**70,445**	**70,009**	**66,983**	**68,586**	**69,196**
Department of Agriculture	596	513	614	580	435	445
Department of Commerce	167	259	284	262	338	543
Department of Defense	16,108	19,414	19,054	16,994	17,780	17,481
Department of Education	24	32	29	30	31	31
Department of Energy	1,562	1,939	2,016	1,994	1,938	1,926
Department of Health and Human Services	4,229	4,627	7,196	4,182	4,118	4,080
Department of Homeland Security [3]	23,980	36,037	32,609	34,901	35,088	35,718
Department of Housing and Urban Development	2	5	5	3	2	2
Department of the Interior	65	50	52	58	58	57
Department of Justice	2,691	3,650	4,094	3,966	4,039	4,054
Department of Labor	56	49	40	43	46	37
Department of State	824	1,809	1,793	1,949	2,674	2,796
Department of Transportation	219	221	228	243	245	235
Department of the Treasury	101	133	125	126	122	124
Department of Veterans Affairs	249	310	427	413	381	368
Army Corps of Engineers	89	40	36	36	15	15
Environmental Protection Agency	106	157	154	108	102	102
Executive Office of the President	30	19	12	9	10	9
General Services Administration	65	125	214	19	38	18
National Aeronautics and Space Administration	221	214	218	228	225	212
National Science Foundation	342	377	390	386	444	444
Office of Personnel Management	3	2	2	2	1	1
Social Security Administration	155	182	190	213	212	242
District of Columbia	15	39	15	15	15	25
Federal Communications Commission	2	2	1	3	3	2
Intelligence Community Management Account	72	33	14	13	9	9
National Archives and Records Administration	17	20	20	22	23	23
Nuclear Regulatory Commission	59	73	65	73	79	79
Securities and Exchange Commission	5	15	6	6	8	8
Smithsonian Institution	75	92	99	98	97	101
United States Holocaust Memorial Museum	8	9	10	10	11	11

NA Not available. [1] The federal spending estimates are for the Executive branch's homeland security activities. These estimates do not include the activities of the Legislative or Judicial branches. [2] The Department of Homeland Security Appropriations Act, 2004, provided $5.6 billion for Project BioShield, to remain available through 2013. Including this uneven funding stream can distort year-over-year comparisons. [3] Not all activities carried out by DHS constitute homeland security funding (e.g. response to natural disasters and Coast Guard search and rescue activities). DHS estimates in this table do not represent the entire DHS budget. See Table 549.

Source: U.S. Office of Management and Budget, *Fiscal Year 2014 Budget of the U.S. Government: Analytical Perspectives*, April 2013. See also <http://www.whitehouse.gov/omb/budget/>.

Table 549. Department of Homeland Security Total Budget Authority and Personnel by Organization: 2012 and 2013

[In thousands of dollars (60,167,956 represents $60,167,956,000). For the fiscal year ending September 30. Not all activities carried out by the Department of Homeland Security (DHS) constitute homeland security funding (e.g., Coast Guard search and rescue activities)]

Organization or Activity	Budget authority		Full-time employees	
	2012 [1]	2013 [2]	2012 [1]	2013 [2]
Total	**60,167,956**	**60,816,756**	**221,264**	**225,285**
Departmental management and operations [3]	804,136	802,768	1,976	2,079
Analysis and operations	338,068	339,957	851	851
Office of the Inspector General	141,000	141,863	676	681
U.S. Customs & Border Protection	11,781,438	11,863,849	60,456	60,469
U.S. Immigration & Customs Enforcement	5,982,977	5,878,209	20,271	20,271
Transportation Security Administration	7,855,938	7,910,532	54,497	55,826
U.S. Coast Guard	10,422,410	10,497,057	50,299	50,711
U.S. Secret Service	1,914,445	1,920,706	6,834	6,834
National Protection and Program Directorate	2,525,688	2,804,087	1,571	1,846
Office of Health Affairs	165,049	168,356	83	101
Federal Emergency Management Agency (FEMA)	11,638,525	11,867,560	9,431	13,072
FEMA Grants [4]	2,285,403	2,308,826	([5])	([5])
U.S. Citizenship & Immigration Services	3,078,465	3,077,782	10,769	10,820
Federal Law Enforcement Training Center	271,413	272,703	1,062	1,103
Science & Technology Directorate (S&T)	673,000	671,807	459	491
Domestic Nuclear Detection Office	290,000	290,695	101	130

[1] Revised enacted. [2] Continuing resolution. [3] Departmental management and operations is comprised of the Office of the Secretary & Executive Management, the Under Secretary for Management, the Office of the Chief Financial Officer, the Office of the Chief Information Officer, and DHS Headquarters Consolidation. [4] Includes the following FEMA appropriations: State and Local Programs and Emergency Management Performance Grants, and Assistance to Firefighters Grants. [5] Employee data are included among FEMA full-time employees.

Source: U.S. Department of Homeland Security, *Budget-in-Brief, Fiscal Year 2014*, February 2013. See also <http://www.dhs.gov/dhs-budget>.

Table 550. Homeland Security Grants by State/Territory: 2012 and 2013

[In thousands of dollars (784,376 represents 784,376,000). For years ending September 30. Grants consist of the following programs: State Homeland Security Program (SHSP) and Urban Areas Security Initiative (UASI). Data for Operation Stonegarden (OPSG) funding not included]

State	2012	2013	State	2012	2013	State/territory	2012	2013
Total.......	**784,376**	**913,390**	KY.............	2,801	3,459	OK.............	2,801	3,459
U.S............	**779,013**	**906,767**	LA.............	4,051	3,459	OR.............	4,959	3,459
AL..............	2,801	3,459	ME.............	2,801	3,459	PA.............	21,534	29,286
AK..............	2,801	3,459	MD.............	8,554	10,826	RI.............	2,801	3,459
AZ..............	7,329	9,472	MA.............	14,935	22,453	SC.............	2,801	3,459
AR..............	2,801	3,459	MI.............	10,131	11,289	SD.............	2,801	3,459
CA..............	146,090	168,239	MN.............	6,072	8,959	TN.............	2,801	3,459
CO..............	5,329	6,459	MS.............	2,801	3,459	TX.............	55,300	57,210
CT..............	2,801	3,459	MO.............	6,960	6,459	UT.............	2,801	3,459
DE..............	2,801	3,459	MT.............	2,801	3,459	VT.............	2,801	3,459
DC..............	54,823	55,420	NE.............	2,801	3,459	VA.............	5,372	6,447
FL..............	18,283	18,074	NV.............	4,628	3,459	WA.............	9,071	11,146
GA..............	10,216	11,419	NH.............	2,801	3,459	WV.............	2,801	3,459
HI..............	2,801	3,459	NJ.............	27,893	28,927	WI.............	2,801	3,459
ID..............	2,801	3,459	NM.............	2,801	3,459	WY.............	2,801	3,459
IL..............	59,556	81,951	NY.............	207,189	241,023	AS [1].........	640	791
IN..............	4,051	3,459	NC.............	5,473	7,773	GU [1].........	640	791
IA..............	2,801	3,459	ND.............	2,801	3,459	NM [1].........	640	791
KS..............	2,801	3,459	OH.............	5,578	6,694	PR [1].........	2,801	3,459
						VI [1].........	640	791

[1] AS—American Samoa, GU—Guam, NM—Northern Mariana Islands, PR—Puerto Rico, VI—Virgin Islands.

Source: Department of Homeland Security, *FY2013 Homeland Security Grant Program Fact Sheet*, August 2013, and earlier reports. See also <http://www.fema.gov/preparedness-non-disaster-grants>.

Table 551. Urban Areas Security Initiative (UASI) Grant Program: 2012

[In thousands of dollars (490,376 represents $490,376,000). For year ending September 30. The UASI Program provides financial assistance to address the unique multi-disciplinary planning, operations, equipment, training, and exercise needs of high-threat, high-density urban areas. The 31 highest risk urban areas were eligible for funding. For a listing of all grant programs and their descriptions, see <http://www.fema.gov/preparedness-non-disaster-grants>]

State	Urban area	Amount	State	Urban area	Amount
Total.............	(X)	490,376			
AZ...............	Phoenix	4,018	MA...............	Boston	10,861
CA...............	Anaheim/Santa Ana	4,455	MI...............	Detroit	5,233
CA...............	Bay Area	26,423	MN...............	Twin Cities	3,271
CA...............	Los Angeles/Long Beach	61,030	MO...............	Kansas City	1,250
CA...............	Riverside	1,522	MO...............	St. Louis	2,908
CA...............	San Diego Area	9,157	NV...............	Las Vegas	1,827
CO...............	Denver	2,528	NJ...............	Jersey City/Newark	21,663
DC...............	National Capital	51,839	NY...............	New York City	151,579
FL...............	Miami/Fort Lauderdale	5,401	NC...............	Charlotte	1,495
FL...............	Orlando	1,447	OR...............	Portland	2,157
FL...............	Tampa	2,595	PA...............	Philadelphia	14,269
GA...............	Atlanta	5,284	TX...............	Dallas/Fort Worth/Arlington	14,293
IL...............	Chicago	47,703	TX...............	Houston	23,937
IN...............	Indianapolis	1,250	TX...............	San Antonio	1,250
LA...............	New Orleans	1,250	WA...............	Seattle	4,365
MD...............	Baltimore	4,116			

X Not applicable.

Source: Department of Homeland Security, FEMA, "FY 2012 Homeland Security Grant Program (HSGP)," <http://www.fema.gov/fy-2012-homeland-security-grant-program>, accessed May 2013.

Table 552. Preparedness Grant Programs: 2009 to 2012

[In dollars. For years ending September 30]

Program	2009	2010	2011	2012
Total [1]...	968,585,000	2,967,879,947	2,191,248,008	1,381,476,000
Homeland Security Grant Program [1]..............................	(X)	1,786,359,956	1,289,296,132	830,976,000
State Homeland Security Program.............................	(X)	842,000,000	526,874,100	294,000,000
Urban Areas Security Initiative..................................	(X)	832,520,000	662,622,100	490,376,000
Operation Stonegarden.......................................	(X)	60,000,000	54,890,000	46,600,000
Emergency Management Performance Grants Program........	(X)	329,799,991	329,040,400	339,500,000
Transit Security Grant Program [1]................................	348,600,000	253,437,597	200,079,000	87,500,000
Port Security Grant Program....................................	388,600,000	288,000,000	235,029,000	97,500,000

X Not applicable. [1] Includes programs not listed separately.

Source: U.S. Department of Homeland Security, Federal Emergency Management Agency, *FY2012 Preparedness Grant Programs Overview*, February 2012. See also <http://www.fema.gov/preparedness-non-disaster-grants>.

Table 553. Deportable Aliens Located by Program and Border Patrol Sector: 2000 to 2011

[As of the end of September. Deportable aliens located refer to Border Patrol apprehensions and ICE administrative arrests]

Program and sector	2000	2005	2008	2009	2010	2011
Total	**1,814,729**	**1,291,065**	**1,043,863**	**869,857**	**752,329**	**641,633**
Investigations	138,291	102,034	31,212	21,280	18,312	16,296
Enforcement and Removal Operations [1]	(X)	–	288,811	292,545	270,635	285,085
Border Patrol	1,676,438	1,189,031	723,840	556,032	463,382	340,252
All Southwest sectors	**1,643,679**	**1,171,462**	**705,022**	**540,851**	**447,731**	**327,577**
San Diego, CA	151,681	126,915	162,392	118,712	68,565	42,447
El Centro, CA	238,126	55,790	40,962	33,520	32,562	30,191
Yuma, AZ	108,747	138,430	8,363	6,952	7,116	5,833
Tucson, AZ	616,346	439,105	317,709	241,667	212,202	123,285
El Paso, TX	115,696	122,691	30,310	14,998	12,251	10,345
Marfa, TX	13,689	10,536	5,390	6,357	5,288	4,036
Del Rio, TX	157,178	68,504	20,761	17,082	14,694	16,144
Laredo, TX	108,973	75,330	43,659	40,571	35,287	36,053
Rio Grande Valley, TX	133,243	134,161	75,476	60,992	59,766	59,243
All other sectors	**32,759**	**17,569**	**18,818**	**15,181**	**15,651**	**12,675**
Blaine, WA	2,581	1,000	951	844	673	591
Buffalo, NY	1,570	406	3,338	2,672	2,422	2,114
Detroit, MI	2,057	1,793	961	1,157	1,669	1,531
Grand Forks, ND	562	754	542	472	543	468
Havre, MT	1,568	948	427	283	290	270
Houlton, ME	489	233	81	60	56	41
Livermore, CA [2]	6,205	(X)	(X)	(X)	(X)	(X)
Miami, FL	6,237	7,243	6,020	4,429	4,651	4,401
New Orleans, LA	6,478	1,358	4,303	3,527	3,171	1,509
Ramey, PR	1,731	1,619	572	418	398	642
Spokane, WA	1,324	279	340	277	356	293
Swanton, VT	1,957	1,936	1,283	1,042	1,422	815

X Not applicable. – Represents zero. [1] Includes arrests of fugitive and nonfugitive aliens under the Office of Detention and Removal Operations (DRO), National Fugitive Operations Program. In 2006 and 2007 includes only arrests of fugitive and nonfugitive aliens under the National Fugitive Operations Program of ICE Enforcement and Removal Operations (ERO); beginning in 2008, includes all administrative arrests conducted by ICE ERO. [2] Livermore sector closed August 31, 2004.

Source: U.S. Department of Homeland Security, Office of Immigration Statistics, *2011 Yearbook of Immigration Statistics*, September 2012. See also <http://www.dhs.gov/yearbook-immigration-statistics>.

Table 554. U.S. Border Patrol Apprehensions by Border, Gender, Age, and Country of Nationality: 2007 to 2010

[As of the end of September]

Characteristic	2007 Number	2007 Percent	2008 Number	2008 Percent	2009 Number	2009 Percent	2010 Number	2010 Percent
Border total	**876,803**	**100.0**	**723,840**	**100.0**	**556,032**	**100.0**	**463,382**	**100.0**
Southwest	858,737	97.9	705,022	97.4	540,851	97.3	447,731	96.6
Coastal	11,687	1.3	10,895	1.5	8,374	1.5	8,220	1.8
Northern	6,379	0.7	7,923	1.1	6,807	1.2	7,431	1.6
GENDER								
Male	730,217	83.3	606,761	83.8	469,994	84.5	397,198	85.7
Female	146,574	16.7	117,061	16.2	86,023	15.5	66,173	14.3
Unknown	12	–	18	–	15	–	11	–
AGE								
17 years and under	77,778	8.9	59,578	8.2	40,461	7.3	31,291	6.8
18 to 24 years	325,901	37.2	257,409	35.6	182,740	32.9	148,969	32.1
25 to 34 years	301,002	34.3	255,261	35.3	205,173	36.9	173,763	37.5
35 to 44 years	127,285	14.5	112,941	15.6	95,922	17.3	82,236	17.7
45 to 54 years	36,661	4.2	32,003	4.4	26,668	4.8	22,981	5.0
55 years and over	7,384	0.8	6,235	0.9	5,029	0.9	4,125	0.9
Unknown	792	0.1	413	0.1	39	–	17	–
COUNTRY OF NATIONALITY								
Mexico	808,773	92.2	661,773	91.4	503,379	90.5	404,365	87.3
Honduras [1]	22,914	2.6	19,351	2.7	14,630	2.6	13,580	2.9
Guatemala	17,337	2.0	16,395	2.3	15,575	2.8	18,406	4.0
El Salvador [1]	14,114	1.6	12,684	1.8	11,693	2.1	13,723	3.0
Cuba	4,295	0.5	3,351	0.5	910	0.2	712	0.2
Ecuador	958	0.1	1,579	0.2	1,313	0.2	1,777	0.4
Nicaragua	1,646	0.2	1,467	0.2	975	0.2	909	0.2
Brazil [1]	1,214	0.1	977	0.1	798	0.1	812	0.2
China, People's Republic	837	0.1	836	0.1	1,499	0.3	1,157	0.2
Dominican Republic	562	0.1	819	0.1	865	0.2	1,330	0.3
Canada	554	0.1	610	0.1	490	0.1	690	0.1
Other	3,599	0.4	3,998	0.6	3,905	0.7	5,921	1.3

– Represents zero. [1] Between 2005 and 2008, the percentage of persons apprehended who were from Honduras, El Salvador, and Brazil declined substantially. These decreases reflect the end of "catch and release," the practice of apprehending illegal aliens from countries other than Mexico and releasing them on their own recognizance pending a removal hearing.

Source: Department of Homeland Security, Office of Immigration Statistics, *Apprehensions by the U.S. Border Patrol: 2005-2010*, July 2011. See also <http://www.dhs.gov/publications>.

Table 555. Deportable Aliens Located: 1925 to 2011

[See headnote, Table 553. Deportable aliens located refer to Border Patrol apprehensions and ICE administrative arrests. Prior to 1952, data refer to Border Patrol Apprehensions. Detention and Removal Operations data are included beginning in FY2006. Beginning in 2008, includes all administrative arrests conducted by the U.S. Immigration and Customs Enforcement, Office of Enforcement and Removal Operations]

Year	Number	Year	Number	Year	Number	Year	Number
1925...........	22,199	1976 [1]........	1,097,739	1988..........	1,008,145	2000..........	1,814,729
1930..........	20,880	1977..........	1,042,215	1989..........	954,243	2001..........	1,387,486
1935..........	11,016	1978..........	1,057,977	1990..........	1,169,939	2002..........	1,062,270
1940..........	10,492	1979..........	1,076,418	1991..........	1,197,875	2003..........	1,046,422
1945..........	69,164	1980..........	910,361	1992..........	1,258,481	2004..........	1,264,232
1950..........	468,339	1981..........	975,780	1993..........	1,327,261	2005..........	1,291,065
1955..........	254,096	1982..........	970,246	1994..........	1,094,719	2006..........	1,206,417
1960..........	70,684	1983..........	1,251,357	1995..........	1,394,554	2007..........	960,772
1965..........	110,371	1984..........	1,246,981	1996..........	1,649,986	2008..........	1,043,863
1970..........	345,353	1985..........	1,348,749	1997..........	1,536,520	2009..........	869,857
1974..........	788,145	1986..........	1,767,400	1998..........	1,679,439	2010..........	752,329
1975..........	766,600	1987..........	1,190,488	1999..........	1,714,035	2011..........	641,633

[1] Includes the 15 months from July 1, 1975 to September 30, 1976, because the end date of fiscal years was changed from June 30 to September 30.

Source: U.S. Department of Homeland Security, Office of Immigration Statistics, *2011 Yearbook of Immigration Statistics*, September 2012. See also <http://www.dhs.gov/yearbook-immigration-statistics>.

Table 556. Aliens Returned or Removed by Leading Crime Category and Country of Nationality: 2006 to 2011

[For definitions of immigration enforcement terms, see *Immigration Enforcement Actions* annual report. "Crime categories" and "Countries of nationality" are ranked by data for most recent year]

Crime category and country of nationality	2006	2007	2008	2009	2010	2011
Total aliens returned or removed:............	**1,324,355**	**1,210,772**	**1,177,058**	**977,893**	**860,713**	**715,495**
Returns [1].............................	1,043,381	891,390	811,263	584,436	475,613	323,542
Removals [2]............................	280,974	319,382	359,795	393,457	385,100	391,953
Noncriminal..........................	182,484	216,988	254,529	261,620	215,444	203,571
Criminal [3]...........................	98,490	102,394	105,266	131,837	169,656	188,382
Leading crime category:						
Dangerous drugs.................	33,485	33,449	34,882	38,940	42,890	43,262
Immigration......................	23,176	21,538	17,542	20,491	31,828	37,458
Assault.........................	9,574	11,048	7,485	9,675	12,175	12,755
Larceny.........................	2,757	2,878	3,282	4,331	5,459	5,705
Fraudulent Activities.............	(NA)	(NA)	2,059	2,997	3,889	4,218
Burglary........................	3,506	3,466	3,292	3,893	4,213	3,795
Robbery........................	2,915	2,908	3,101	3,359	3,646	3,745
Family offenses..................	2,571	2,786	2,929	2,886	3,268	3,572
Sexual assault...................	2,262	2,410	2,343	2,685	3,330	2,961
Stolen vehicles..................	1,934	1,875	(NA)	(NA)	(NA)	(NA)
Sex offenses....................	1,868	1,874	(NA)	(NA)	(NA)	(NA)
Other..........................	13,371	15,692	18,170	21,703	27,896	27,889
Leading country of nationality of criminals removed:						
Mexico.........................	73,171	76,967	77,531	99,616	128,396	144,745
Guatemala......................	3,850	3,917	5,138	6,547	9,432	11,700
Honduras.......................	5,752	5,236	5,476	6,998	10,420	10,801
El Salvador.....................	3,850	4,949	5,558	6,344	8,368	8,486
Dominican Republic..............	2,206	2,044	2,046	2,207	2,241	2,127
Jamaica........................	1,234	1,139	1,214	1,246	1,169	1,219
Colombia.......................	1,307	1,191	1,081	1,124	1,241	1,037
Ecuador........................	470	392	532	602	692	700
Nicaragua......................	592	508	533	620	804	694
Brazil..........................	563	352	368	388	487	541
Canada.........................	423	411	347	418	457	412

NA Not available. [1] Returns are the confirmed movement of an inadmissible or deportable alien out of the United States not based on an order of removal. Most of the voluntary departures are of Mexican nationals who have been apprehended by the U.S. Border Patrol and are returned to Mexico. [2] Removals are the compulsory and confirmed movement of an inadmissible or deportable alien out of the United States based on an order of removal. An alien who is removed has administrative or criminal consequences placed on subsequent reentry owing to the fact of the removal. [3] Refers to persons removed based on a criminal charge or those with a criminal conviction.

Source: U.S. Department of Homeland Security, Office of Immigration Statistics, *2011 Yearbook of Immigration Statistics*, September 2012 and *Immigration Enforcement Actions: 2011*, September 2012. See also <http://www.dhs.gov/yearbook-immigration-statistics>.

Table 557. Coast Guard Migrant Interdictions by Nationality of Alien: 2000 to 2012

[For the year ending September 30]

Year	Total	Haiti	Dominican Republic	China	Cuba	Mexico	Ecuador	Other
2000......................	4,210	1,113	499	261	1,000	49	1,244	44
2005......................	9,455	1,850	3,612	32	2,712	55	1,149	45
2008......................	4,825	1,583	688	1	2,216	47	220	70
2009......................	3,467	1,782	727	35	799	77	6	41
2010......................	2,088	1,377	140	–	422	61	–	88
2011......................	2,474	1,137	222	11	985	68	1	50
2012......................	2,955	977	456	23	1275	79	7	138

– Represents zero.

Source: U.S. Department of Homeland Security, United States Coast Guard, "Alien Migrant Interdiction," <http://www.uscg.mil/hq/cg5/cg531/AMIO/amio.asp>, accessed April 2013.

Table 558. Customs and Border Protection (CBP)—Processed and Cleared Passengers, Planes, Vehicles, and Containers: 2000 to 2007

[In thousands (80,519 represents 80,519,000). For year ending September 30]

Characteristic	2000	2001	2002	2003	2004	2005	2006	2007
Air								
Passengers	80,519	79,676	71,608	72,959	80,866	86,123	87,906	91,574
Commercial planes [1]	829	839	769	790	824	866	881	916
Private planes	146	126	129	132	140	135	139	139
Land								
Passengers [2, 3]	397,312	381,477	333,652	329,998	326,693	317,765	289,048	299,004
Autos [2]	127,095	129,603	118,307	120,376	121,419	121,654	119,372	112,428
Rail containers	2,157	2,257	2,430	2,472	2,588	2,655	2,735	2,737
Truck containers [4]	10,397	11,001	11,129	11,163	11,252	11,308	11,489	11,459
Sea								
Passengers [5]	10,990	11,291	12,224	15,127	22,234	26,228	26,223	27,059
Vessels [6]	211	215	212	204	142	113	168	170
Vessel containers [7]	5,813	5,944	7,248	9,092	9,796	11,341	11,622	11,703

[1] A commercial aircraft is any aircraft transporting passengers and/or cargo for some payment or other consideration, including money or services rendered. [2] See Table 1297 for more details. [3] Includes pedestrians. [4] Truck containers—number of trucks entering the U.S. [5] Does not include passengers on ferries. [6] Includes every description of water craft or other contrivance used or capable of being used as a means of transportation on water, does not include aircraft. [7] Number of vessel containers.

Source: U.S. Department of Homeland Security, Customs and Border Protection, "About CBP, Statistics and Accomplishments, National Workload Statistics, 2000–2007," February 2008, <http://www.cbp.gov/xp/cgov/about/accomplish/previous_year/national_workload_stats.xml>.

Table 559. Prohibited Items Intercepted at U.S. Airport Screening Checkpoints: 2004 to 2008

[Passengers boarding aircraft in thousands (703,692 represents 703,692,000). For the calendar year. Transportation Security Administration (TSA) assumed responsibility for airport security on February 17, 2002, and by November 19, 2002, TSA assumed control over all passenger screenings from private contractors]

Year	2004	2005	2006	2007	2008
Passengers boarding aircraft, total [1]	**703,692**	**738,628**	**744,728**	**769,622**	**743,313**
Domestic	641,470	670,417	671,799	693,372	665,734
International	62,222	68,211	72,929	76,250	77,580
Total prohibited items (number)	**7,104,095**	**15,886,404**	**13,709,684**	**6,516,026**	**(NA)**
Knife [2]	2,055,404	1,822,892	1,607,125	1,056,691	([9])
Other cutting items [3]	3,409,888	3,276,941	163,419	101,387	([9])
Club [4]	28,998	20,531	12,296	9,443	([9])
Box cutter	22,430	21,319	15,999	11,908	([9])
Firearm [5]	254	850	820	1,416	902
Incendiary [6]	697,606	374,487	94,097	73,670	116,200
Lighters [7]	178	9,420,991	11,616,688	5,124,344	([9])
Other [8]	889,337	949,243	200,060	137,167	([9])

NA Not available. [1] Data come from Airlines for America (formerly the Air Transport Association). Data are for U.S. passenger and cargo airlines only. [2] Knife includes any length and type except round-bladed, butter, and plastic cutlery. [3] Other cutting instruments refer to scissors, screwdrivers, swords, sabers, and ice picks, etc. [4] Club refers to baseball bats, night sticks, billy clubs, bludgeons, etc. [5] Firearm refers to items like pistols, revolvers, rifles, automatic weapons, shotguns, parts of guns and firearms. [6] Incendiaries refer to categories of ammunition and gunpowder, flammables/irritants, and explosives. [7] As of April 14, 2005, passengers are prohibited from carrying all lighters on their person or in carry-on luggage or onboard an airplane. [8] Other refers to categories of ammunition and gunpower, dangerous objects, fireworks, replica weapons, and tools. [9] The data for this prohibited item category are no longer collected as of August 8, 2008.

Source: U.S. Department of Homeland Security, Transportation Security Administration, unpublished data, June 2009, <http://www.tsa.gov>; Airlines for America, Washington, DC; "Annual Traffic and Operations: U.S. Airlines" ©, <http://www.airlines.org/pages/home.aspx/>.

Table 560. Value of Seizures for Intellectual Property Rights (IPR) Violations by Commodity and Trading Partner: 2011 and 2012

[In thousands of dollars (1,110,433 represents $1,110,433,000), except as indicated. Customs and Border Protection is dedicated to protecting against the importation of goods which infringe/violate Intellectual Property Rights (IPR) by devoting substantial resources toward identifying and seizing shipments of infringing articles]

Commodity	2011	2012	Trading partner	2011	2012
Number of IPR seizures	**24,792**	**22,848**	China	109,996	906,207
Total domestic value of IPR seizures [1]	1,110,433	1,262,202	Hong Kong	32,156	156,337
Consumer electronics [2]	111,110	104,391	India	4,535	7,021
Footwear	96,977	103,366	Pakistan	3,955	(NA)
Pharmaceuticals	141,751	82,998	Taiwan	2,288	4,501
Media [3]	35,011	38,405	Switzerland	1,407	(NA)
Wearing apparel	142,331	133,000	Malaysia	1,286	(NA)
Jewelry, watches, and parts	172,657	186,990	Korea, South	714	(NA)
Computers/technology components	22,836	34,711	Jordan	(NA)	(NA)
Toys/electronic games	21,889	13,603	Canada	(NA)	(NA)
Handbags/wallets/backpacks	211,072	511,248	Vietnam	(NA)	(NA)
All other commodities	154,792	53,482	All other countries	954,096	178,751

NA Not available. [1] Domestic value is the cost of the seized goods, plus the costs of shipping and importing the goods into the U.S. and an amount for profit. [2] Consumer electronics include cell phones and accessories, radios, power strips, electrical tools and appliances. [3] Includes motion pictures on tape, laser disc, and DVD; interactive and computer software on CD-ROM and floppy discs; and music on CD or tape.

Source: U.S. Department of Homeland Security, Customs and Border Protection, *Intellectual Property Rights FY2012 Seizure Statistics*, January 2013, and earlier reports. See also <http://www.cbp.gov/xp/cgov/trade/priority_trade/ipr/seizure/>.

Section 11
Social Insurance and Human Services

This section presents data related to government expenditures for social insurance and human services; government programs for Old-Age, Survivors, and Disability Insurance (OASDI), commonly known as Social Security; government employee retirement; private retirement plans; government unemployment and temporary disability insurance; federal supplemental security income payments and aid to the needy; child and other welfare services; and federal food programs. Also included here are selected data on workers' compensation and vocational rehabilitation, child support, child care, charity contributions, and philanthropic trusts and foundations.

The principal source for these data is the Social Security Administration's *Annual Statistical Supplement to the Social Security Bulletin* which presents current data on many of the programs.

Social insurance under the Social Security Act—Programs established by the Social Security Act provide protection against wage loss resulting from retirement, prolonged disability, death, or unemployment, and protection against the cost of medical care during old age and disability. The federal OASDI program provides monthly benefits to retired or disabled insured workers and their dependents and to survivors of insured workers. To be eligible, a worker must have had a specified period of employment in which OASDI taxes were paid. The age of eligibility for full retirement benefits had been 65 years old for many years. However, for persons born in 1938 or later that age gradually increases until it reaches age 67 for those born after 1959. Reduced benefits may be obtained as early as age 62. The worker's spouse is under the same limitations. Survivor benefits are payable to dependents of deceased insured workers. Disability benefits are payable to an insured worker under full retirement age with a prolonged disability and to the disabled worker's dependents on the same basis as dependents of retired workers. Disability benefits are provided at age 50 to the disabled widow or widower of a deceased worker who was fully insured at the time of death. Disabled children, aged 18 or older, of retired, disabled, or deceased workers are also eligible for benefits. A lump sum benefit is generally payable on the death of an insured worker to a spouse or minor children. For information on the Medicare program, see Section 3, Health and Nutrition.

Retirement, survivors, and disability insurance benefits are funded by a payroll tax on annual earnings (up to a maximum share of earnings set by law) of workers, employers, and the self-employed. The maximum taxable earnings are adjusted annually to reflect increasing wage levels (see Table 567). Tax receipts and benefit payments are administered through federal trust funds. Special benefits for uninsured persons; hospital benefits for persons aged 65 and over with specified amounts of social security coverage less than that required for cash benefit eligibility; and that part of the cost of supplementary medical insurance not financed by contributions from participants are all financed from federal general revenues.

Unemployment insurance is presently administered by the U.S. Employment and Training Administration and each state's employment security agency. By agreement with the U.S. Secretary of Labor, state agencies also administer unemployment compensation for eligible ex-military personnel and federal employees. Under state unemployment insurance laws, benefits related to an individual's past earnings are paid to unemployed eligible workers. State laws vary concerning the length of time benefits are paid and their amount. In most states, benefits are payable for 26 weeks and, during periods of high unemployment, extended benefits are payable under a federal-state program to those who have exhausted their regular state benefits. Some states also supplement the basic benefit with allowances for dependents.

Unemployment insurance is funded by a federal unemployment tax levied on the taxable payrolls of most employers. Taxable payroll under the federal act and three state or territory laws is the first $7,000 in wages paid each worker during a year. Fifty states or territories have taxable payrolls above $7,000. Employers are allowed a percentage credit of taxable payroll for contributions paid to states under state unemployment insurance laws. The remaining percent of the federal tax finances administrative costs, the federal share of extended benefits, and advances to states. About 97 percent of wage and salary workers are covered by unemployment insurance.

Retirement programs for government employees—The Civil Service Retirement System (CSRS) and the Federal Employees' Retirement System (FERS) are the two major programs providing old-age, disability, and survivor annuities for federal civilian employees. In general, employees hired after December 31, 1983, are covered under FERS and the Social Security program (OASDI), and employees on staff prior to that date are members of CSRS and are covered under Medicare. CSRS employees were offered the option of transferring to FERS during 1987 and 1998. There are separate retirement systems for the uniformed services (supplementing OASDI) and for certain special groups of federal employees. State and local government employees are covered for the most part by state and local retirement systems similar to the federal programs. In many jurisdictions these benefits supplement OASDI coverage.

Workers' compensation—All states provide protection against work-connected injuries and deaths, although some states exclude certain workers (e.g., domestic workers). Federal laws cover federal employees, private employees in the District of Columbia, and longshoremen and harbor workers. In addition, the Department of Labor administers "black lung" benefit programs for coal miners disabled by pneumoconiosis and for specified dependents and survivors. Specified occupational diseases are compensable to some extent. In most states, benefits are related to the worker's salary. The benefits may or may not be augmented by dependents' allowances or automatically adjusted to prevailing wage levels.

Income support—Income support programs are designed to provide benefits for persons with limited income and resources. The Supplemental Security Income (SSI) program and Temporary Assistance for Needy Families (TANF) program are the major programs providing monthly payments. In addition, a number of programs provide money payments or in-kind benefits for special needs or purposes. Several programs offer food and nutritional services. Also, various federal-state programs provide energy assistance, public housing, and subsidized housing to individuals and families with low incomes. General assistance may also be available at the state or local level.

The SSI program, administered by the Social Security Administration, provides income support to persons aged 65 or older and to blind or disabled adults and children. Eligibility requirements and federal payment standards are nationally uniform. Most states supplement the basic SSI payment for all or selected categories of persons.

The Personal Responsibility and Work Opportunity Reconciliation Act of 1996 contained provisions that replaced the Aid to Families With Dependent Children (AFDC), Job Opportunities and Basic Skills (JOBS), and Emergency Assistance programs with the TANF block grant program. This law contains strong work requirements, comprehensive child support enforcement, support for families moving from welfare to work, and other features. The TANF program became effective as soon as each state submitted a complete implementation plan, but no later than July 1, 1997. The older AFDC program provided cash assistance based on need, income, resources, and family size.

Federal food stamp program—Under the Supplemental Nutrition Assistance Program (SNAP), formerly known as the food stamp program, single persons and those living in households meeting nationwide standards for income and assets may receive benefit payments redeemable for food at most retail food stores through electronic benefit transfer. The monthly amount of benefits or allotments a unit receives is determined by household size and income. Households without income receive the determined monthly cost of a nutritionally adequate diet for their household size. This amount is updated to account for food price increases. Households with income receive the difference between the amount of a nutritionally adequate diet and 30 percent of their income, after certain allowable deductions.

To qualify for the program, a household must have less than $2,000 in disposable assets ($3,250 if one member is aged 60 or older), gross income below 130 percent of the official poverty guidelines for the household size, and net income below 100 percent of the poverty guidelines. Households with a person aged 60 or older or a disabled person receiving SSI, social security, state general assistance, or veterans' disability benefits may have gross income exceeding 130 percent of the poverty guidelines. All households in which all members receive TANF or SSI are categorically eligible for SNAP without meeting these income or resource criteria. Households are certified for varying lengths of time, depending on their income sources and individual circumstances.

Health and welfare services—Programs providing health and welfare services are aided through federal grants to states for child welfare services, vocational rehabilitation, activities for the aged, maternal and child health services, maternity and infant care

projects, comprehensive health services, and a variety of public health activities. For information about the Medicaid program, see Section 3, Health and Nutrition.

Noncash benefits—The U.S. Census Bureau annually collects data on the characteristics of recipients of noncash (in-kind) benefits to supplement the collection of annual money income data in the Current Population Survey (see text, Section 1, Population, and Section 13, Income, Expenditures, Poverty, and Wealth). Noncash benefits are those benefits received in a form other than money which serve to enhance or improve the economic well-being of the recipient. As for money income, the data for noncash benefits are for the calendar year prior to the date of the interview. The major categories of noncash benefits covered are public transfers (e.g., food stamps, school lunch, public housing, and Medicaid) and employer or union-provided benefits to employees.

Statistical reliability—For discussion of statistical collection, estimation, and sampling procedures and measures of statistical reliability applicable to Social Security Administration and Census Bureau data, see Appendix III.

Table 561. Selected Benefit Payments to Individuals by Function: 1970 to 2010

[In billions of dollars (108 represents $108,000,000,000). The employee benefit system is composed of voluntary and mandatory programs which are employment-based and financed primarily from employment-based contributions]

Source and sector	1970	1980	1990	1995	2000	2002	2003	2004	2005	2006	2007	2008	2009	2010
All benefits	**108**	**422**	**1,027**	**1,493**	**1,909**	**2,251**	**2,393**	**2,559**	**2,721**	**2,912**	**3,107**	**3,289**	**3,613**	**3,820**
Retirement income benefits	51	202	482	660	864	977	1,023	1,092	1,158	1,265	1,359	1,386	1,478	1,537
Social security—old-age, survivors, and disability insurance	31	119	244	328	401	447	464	486	513	544	576	606	665	690
Private employer pension and profit sharing	7	35	136	191	271	311	323	355	376	433	476	454	465	479
Public employer retirement plans	12	48	102	141	192	219	237	252	269	287	308	326	348	368
Federal civilian employee retirement [1]	3	16	32	39	50	53	55	58	62	67	72	74	78	81
State and local government retirement	4	15	41	65	100	121	133	142	151	162	174	186	200	216
Military retirement [2]	3	13	22	28	33	36	41	43	46	49	52	56	59	60
Railroad retirement	2	5	7	8	8	9	9	9	9	10	10	10	11	11
Health benefits	22	99	300	456	596	705	767	834	901	986	1,044	1,109	1,173	1,231
Medicare hospital insurance and supplementary medical insurance	7	36	108	181	219	259	277	305	332	399	428	462	494	518
Group health insurance	15	62	191	274	376	444	488	528	567	585	614	645	676	709
Military health insurance [3]	–	–	2	1	1	2	2	2	2	3	3	3	3	4
Other employee benefits	17	51	88	103	113	156	162	148	147	148	155	180	271	286
Unemployment insurance [4]	4	16	18	22	21	54	53	36	32	30	33	51	131	139
Workers' compensation [5]	3	13	38	43	48	53	56	57	56	55	57	59	59	60
Group life insurance	3	7	12	16	17	18	18	18	19	20	20	20	24	25
Miscellaneous disability [6]	1	3	4	3	4	4	4	5	5	5	6	6	6	6
Veterans' benefits [7]	7	13	16	19	23	28	30	32	35	37	40	44	50	56
Public assistance [8]	18	70	157	275	336	413	441	485	515	513	549	614	691	765

– Represents or rounds to zero. [1] Consists of civil service, foreign service, Public Health Service officers, Tennessee Valley Authority, and several small retirement programs. [2] Includes the U.S. Coast Guard. [3] Consists of payments for medical services for dependents of active duty military personnel at nonmilitary facilities. [4] Consists of state, railroad employee, and federal employee unemployment benefits; special unemployment benefits; and supplemental unemployment benefits. [5] Includes payments from private, federal, and state and local workers' compensation funds. [6] Includes federal black-lung payments and payments from state and local temporary disability insurance. [7] Consists of pension and disability, readjustment, and other veterans' benefits. [8] Consists of federal benefits (food stamp benefits, Supplemental Security Income, direct relief, earned income tax credit, payments to nonprofit institutions, aid to students, and payments for medical services for retired military personnel and their dependents at nonmilitary facilities) and state benefits (medical care, Aid to Families with Dependent Children, Supplemental Security Income, general assistance, energy assistance, emergency assistance, and medical insurance premium payments on behalf of indigents). Financed from state and federal general revenues.

Source: Employee Benefit Research Institute, Washington, DC, *EBRI Databook on Employee Benefits*, and unpublished data ©. EBRI tabulations based on U.S. Department of Commerce, Bureau of Economic Analysis. See also <http://www.ebri.org/>.

Table 562. Government Transfer Payments to Individuals—Summary: 1990 to 2011

[In billions of dollars (566.1 represents $566,100,000,000)]

Year	Transfer payments, total	Retirement and disability insurance benefits	Medical payments	Income maintenance benefits	Unemployment insurance benefits	Veterans benefits	Education and training assistance payments [1]	Other [2]
1990	566.1	263.9	188.8	63.5	18.2	17.7	12.3	1.7
1995	849.8	350.0	338.6	100.4	21.8	20.5	17.2	1.2
2000	1,027.8	424.5	427.2	106.3	21.0	25.0	21.9	2.0
2001	1,126.7	449.8	480.8	109.4	32.1	26.6	25.4	2.6
2002	1,232.1	474.4	523.8	120.7	53.7	29.5	27.9	2.1
2003	1,299.0	493.5	555.8	133.2	53.6	31.8	28.5	2.7
2004	1,381.2	517.1	610.3	144.2	37.1	34.0	31.2	7.3
2005	1,465.1	545.4	653.2	159.6	32.3	36.4	33.8	4.5
2006	1,565.6	576.9	717.0	163.4	30.9	38.9	35.9	2.7
2007	1,669.8	609.1	771.4	172.3	33.4	41.7	39.5	2.6
2008	1,823.5	639.7	821.2	216.7	51.8	45.0	45.1	4.0
2009	2,077.7	699.5	886.7	224.1	132.0	51.5	56.6	27.4
2010	2,212.8	726.5	935.6	266.6	139.7	57.9	68.1	18.3
2011	2,250.0	749.9	974.7	278.0	108.6	63.3	71.3	4.2

[1] See footnote 9, Table 563. [2] See footnote 10, Table 563.

Source: U.S. Bureau of Economic Analysis, Interactive Regional Data, GDP & Personal Income, "Personal Current Transfer Receipts," <http://www.bea.gov/iTable/index_regional.cfm>, accessed March 2013.

Table 563. Government Transfer Payments to Individuals by Type: 1990 to 2011

[In millions of dollars (566,100 represents $566,100,000,000)]

Item	1990	2000	2005	2008	2009	2010	2011
Total	566,100	1,027,827	1,465,125	1,823,460	2,077,739	2,212,771	2,249,960
Retirement & disability insurance benefit payments	263,888	424,461	545,361	639,718	699,532	726,507	749,880
Old-age, survivors, & disability insurance	244,135	401,393	512,728	605,542	664,470	690,174	713,276
Railroad retirement and disability	7,221	8,267	9,191	10,068	10,630	10,779	10,961
Workers' compensation payments (federal & state)	8,618	10,898	15,866	15,831	16,006	16,721	16,904
Other government disability insurance & retirement [1]	3,914	3,903	7,576	8,277	8,426	8,833	8,739
Medical payments	188,808	427,194	653,193	821,180	886,692	935,646	974,728
Medicare	107,638	219,117	331,924	461,634	494,534	515,258	545,096
Public assistance medical care [2]	78,176	205,021	315,032	352,028	383,785	411,031	418,330
Military medical insurance [3]	2,994	3,056	6,237	7,518	8,373	9,357	11,302
Income maintenance benefit payments	63,481	106,285	159,624	216,660	224,077	266,642	278,037
Supplemental Security Income (SSI)	16,670	31,675	38,285	44,102	47,666	49,244	50,423
Family assistance [4]	19,187	18,440	18,216	19,255	21,393	22,550	21,052
Supplemental Nutrition Assistance Program	14,741	14,565	29,492	37,034	54,763	66,517	72,741
Other income maintenance [5]	12,883	41,605	73,631	116,269	100,255	128,331	133,821
Unemployment insurance benefit payments	18,208	20,989	32,276	51,800	131,988	139,713	108,555
State unemployment insurance compensation	17,644	20,223	31,001	50,096	129,699	137,018	105,933
Unemployment compensation for federal civilian employees	215	226	224	255	439	535	671
Unemployment compensation for railroad employees	89	81	72	84	179	116	85
Unemployment compensation for veterans	144	181	446	467	841	1,151	1,245
Other unemployment compensation [6]	116	278	533	898	830	893	621
Veterans benefit payments	17,687	25,004	36,371	45,008	51,470	57,926	63,263
Veterans pension and disability	15,550	21,966	32,505	40,715	45,545	48,476	52,194
Veterans readjustment [7]	257	1,322	2,256	2,749	4,405	7,976	9,622
Veterans life insurance benefits	1,868	1,706	1,596	1,523	1,493	1,442	1,411
Other assistance to veterans [8]	12	10	14	21	27	32	36
Federal education & training assistance payments [9]	12,286	21,851	33,796	45,057	56,604	68,061	71,291
Other payments to individuals [10]	1,742	2,043	4,504	4,037	27,376	18,276	4,206

[1] Mostly temporary disability, pension benefit guaranty, black lung, and Panama Canal construction annuity payments. [2] Medicaid and other medical vendor payments. [3] Payments made under TriCare Management Program (formerly called CHAMPUS) for medical care of dependents of active duty and retired military personnel and their dependents at nonmilitary medical facilities. [4] Through 1995, consists of Emergency Assistance and Aid to Families with Dependent Children. Beginning with 1998, consists of benefits from Temporary Assistance for Needy Families provided under Personal Responsibility and Work Opportunity Reconciliation Act of 1996. For 1996 through 1997, covers payments under all three of these programs. [5] Mostly general assistance; food expenditures under Special Supplemental Nutrition Program for Women, Infants, and Children (WIC); Other Needs Assistance; refugee assistance; foster home care and adoption assistance; 2008 Economic Stimulus Act Rebates; Earned Income Tax Credits (EITC); Child Tax Credits; ARRA funded tax credits; other tax credits; and energy assistance. [6] Trade readjustment allowance, Redwood Park benefit, public service employment benefit, and transitional benefit. [7] Mostly veterans' readjustment benefit payments, educational assistance to spouses and children of disabled or deceased veterans, and payments to paraplegics and for autos and conveyances for disabled veterans. [8] Mostly state and local government payments to veterans. [9] Mostly federal fellowship payments (National Science Foundation fellowships and traineeships, subsistence payments to state maritime academy cadets, and other federal fellowships), interest subsidy on higher education loans, Pell Grants, Job Corps payments, education exchange payments, and state education assistance payments. [10] Mostly Bureau of Indian Affairs payments; Alaska Permanent Fund dividend payments; compensation of survivors of public safety officers; compensation of victims of crime; disaster relief payments; compensation for Japanese internment; American Recovery and Reinvestment Act of 2009 funded Federal Additional Compensation for unemployment, COBRA premium reduction, and Economic Recovery lump sum payment; and other special payments to individuals.

Source: U.S. Bureau of Economic Analysis, Interactive Regional Data, GDP & Personal Income, "Personal Current Transfer Receipts," <http://www.bea.gov/iTable/index_regional.cfm>, accessed March 2013.

Table 564. Government Transfer Payments to Individuals by State: 2000 to 2011

[In millions of dollars (1,027,827 represents $1,027,827,000,000)]

State	2000, total	2010, total	2011							
			Total	Retire-ment and disability insurance benefits	Medical payments	Income mainte-nance benefits	Unem-ployment insurance benefits	Veterans benefits	Educa-tion and training assistance pay-ments [1]	Other [2]
U.S.	1,027,827	2,212,771	2,249,960	749,880	974,728	278,037	108,555	63,263	71,291	4,206
AL	16,803	36,381	37,103	13,496	14,534	5,376	935	1,452	1,269	41
AK	2,950	4,821	5,011	1,035	2,041	613	268	244	78	731
AZ	15,948	45,485	46,089	15,373	19,578	5,095	1,335	1,505	2,972	230
AR	10,168	22,639	23,222	8,238	9,794	2,785	709	903	765	28
CA	114,879	253,093	253,437	74,826	112,081	34,586	17,694	5,588	8,290	372
CO	11,144	27,417	28,419	10,044	11,236	2,878	1,831	1,341	1,039	50
CT	14,222	27,727	28,170	9,262	13,280	2,540	1,966	422	662	37
DE	2,908	6,833	7,170	2,549	3,294	665	264	178	211	9
DC	2,695	5,259	5,608	943	3,168	902	304	91	193	8
FL	64,580	144,506	148,828	52,278	64,484	17,695	4,467	4,830	4,904	169
GA	24,190	58,464	60,823	20,175	23,157	9,871	2,557	2,412	2,567	83
HI	3,887	8,744	9,124	3,108	3,643	1,304	489	408	161	12
ID	3,868	9,671	9,743	3,813	3,625	1,157	443	356	330	20
IL	42,291	88,528	84,617	29,168	34,361	11,030	5,490	1,497	2,946	125
IN	20,472	44,403	44,735	17,240	17,705	4,889	2,030	997	1,813	61
IA	10,242	20,830	21,498	8,051	8,710	2,082	852	491	1,285	27
KS	9,091	18,120	18,680	7,032	7,663	2,105	839	528	483	30
KY	16,058	34,040	34,760	11,983	14,335	4,488	1,377	1,109	1,429	39
LA	16,744	33,053	33,697	10,181	15,681	5,145	658	954	1,040	38
ME	5,351	10,811	11,408	3,827	5,262	1,224	363	486	231	15
MD	17,140	37,006	38,182	12,469	17,572	4,253	1,702	1,124	1,016	47
MA	26,575	53,836	54,494	15,685	26,592	6,425	3,733	987	1,008	64
MI	36,987	79,383	79,526	28,834	32,247	10,459	3,875	1,484	2,508	119
MN	16,106	36,749	37,469	12,553	16,755	3,768	1,846	1,104	1,384	59
MS	10,916	23,267	24,047	7,601	10,886	3,673	508	622	720	37
MO	21,121	43,566	44,717	15,921	19,929	4,719	1,500	1,279	1,316	53
MT	3,197	6,710	6,697	2,764	2,492	651	248	323	196	24
NE	5,753	11,144	11,490	4,385	4,760	1,152	307	532	340	15
NV	5,580	15,760	15,952	5,734	5,815	1,885	1,475	608	398	38
NH	4,003	8,587	8,642	3,606	3,450	861	223	284	207	12
NJ	33,512	67,516	67,945	23,104	29,244	6,476	6,316	999	1,715	92
NM	6,035	15,227	15,532	4,677	6,671	2,224	640	698	480	141
NY	96,578	175,688	178,541	48,653	93,403	22,178	7,544	2,208	4,366	189
NC	28,335	67,108	69,101	23,909	27,985	8,636	4,113	2,592	1,760	107
ND	2,339	4,227	4,360	1,702	1,827	414	95	161	123	38
OH	43,906	88,005	90,974	32,311	38,965	11,120	3,350	1,841	3,274	113
OK	12,064	26,425	27,048	9,590	11,225	3,274	619	1,480	817	44
OR	12,330	27,905	28,630	10,551	10,782	3,324	2,011	1,090	811	61
PA	55,370	106,161	107,620	37,144	48,884	10,190	6,567	1,970	2,712	153
RI	4,702	9,164	9,283	2,950	4,205	1,065	609	190	251	11
SC	14,601	34,710	35,242	12,860	13,592	4,572	1,232	1,426	1,513	46
SD	2,499	5,057	5,187	1,977	2,129	563	61	226	155	75
TN	21,977	48,161	49,421	16,925	21,027	6,805	1,633	1,532	1,445	55
TX	60,244	149,556	154,756	46,450	69,084	22,904	5,671	5,962	4,494	189
UT	5,025	12,419	12,815	4,704	4,711	1,762	522	380	699	36
VT	2,308	5,123	5,233	1,737	2,412	602	165	135	176	7
VA	20,239	46,505	48,566	17,979	19,272	5,601	1,259	2,614	1,782	59
WA	21,190	47,427	47,655	17,718	17,420	5,853	3,225	1,822	1,524	94
WV	8,909	16,253	16,624	6,352	6,918	1,850	411	625	452	16
WI	18,185	39,876	38,588	14,938	15,507	4,079	2,079	1,040	866	79
WY	1,613	3,427	3,481	1,475	1,335	270	144	131	118	9

[1] Mostly federal fellowship payments (National Science Foundation fellowships and traineeships, subsistence payments to state maritime academy cadets, and other federal fellowships), interest subsidy on higher education loans, Pell Grants, Job Corps payments, education exchange payments, and state education assistance payments. [2] Mostly Bureau of Indian Affairs payments; Alaska Permanent Fund dividend payments; compensation of survivors of public safety officers; compensation of victims of crime; disaster relief payments; compensation for Japanese internment; the American Recovery and Reinvestment Act of 2009 funded Federal Additional Compensation for unemployment, COBRA premium reduction, and the Economic Recovery lump sum payment; and other special payments to individuals.

Source: U.S. Bureau of Economic Analysis, Regional GDP & Personal Income, "Personal current transfer receipts (SA35)," <http://www.bea.gov/iTable/index_regional.cfm>, accessed March 2013.

Table 565. Number of Persons With Income by Specified Source of Income: 2011

[In thousands (214,559 represents 214,559,000). Persons 15 years old and over as of March of following year. Based on Current Population Survey (CPS); see text, Sections 1 and 13, and Appendix III]

Source of income	Total persons with income	Under 65 years	65 years and over	White [1]	Black [2]	Hispanic origin [3]
Total	214,559	174,365	40,195	173,075	24,932	28,943
Earnings	154,460	145,812	8,648	124,535	17,425	23,238
Wages and salary	145,678	138,305	7,373	117,024	16,824	22,019
Nonfarm self-employment	11,578	10,290	1,288	9,812	884	1,461
Farm self-employment	1,853	1,561	291	1,629	110	106
Unemployment compensation	10,230	9,694	536	7,933	1,502	1,508
State or local only	9,798	9,293	505	7,601	1,434	1,436
Combinations	432	401	31	332	68	72
Workers' compensation	1,524	1,361	163	1,203	197	227
State payments	481	445	36	380	57	79
Employment insurance	660	594	66	520	84	103
Own insurance	21	21	–	14	5	2
Other	411	344	67	335	54	48
Social Security	46,934	11,765	35,169	39,972	4,736	3,315
SSI (Supplemental Security Income)	6,118	4,821	1,297	3,911	1,590	989
Public assistance, total	2,348	2,243	105	1,513	627	628
TANF/welfare (AFDC) only [4]	1,586	1,541	45	986	474	447
Other assistance only	709	650	60	495	138	163
Both	52	52	–	32	15	18
Veterans' benefits	3,200	1,901	1,299	2,613	434	166
Disability only	2,037	1,299	738	1,679	263	96
Survivors only	243	92	151	192	38	12
Pension only	603	267	336	497	84	35
Education only	105	105	–	80	16	5
Other only	77	45	32	58	13	6
Combinations	135	92	43	107	20	12
Means-tested	583	340	243	483	79	37
Nonmeans-tested	2,617	1,561	1,056	2,130	355	129
Survivors benefits [5]	2,776	917	1,859	2,495	183	105
Company or union	1,296	270	1,027	1,179	82	39
Federal government	239	68	171	203	22	14
Military retirement	167	15	152	149	12	3
Disability benefits [5]	1,730	1,432	297	1,328	270	231
Workers' compensation	80	63	17	66	10	9
Company or union	380	295	85	312	43	35
Federal government	113	93	20	94	15	17
Military retirement	47	39	8	34	10	10
State or local government	339	278	61	244	53	50
Pension income [5]	17,848	5,388	12,460	15,588	1,608	706
Company or union retirement	11,729	3,219	8,510	10,352	984	453
Federal government retirement	1,906	587	1,319	1,578	240	94
Military retirement	1,259	628	631	1,049	148	58
State or local government retirement	5,091	1,861	3,229	4,458	422	261
Property income [6]	93,664	72,318	21,346	81,257	5,839	5,995
Interest	87,332	67,470	19,862	75,869	5,385	5,480
Dividends	29,535	21,951	7,584	26,474	1,147	997
Rents, royalties, estates or trusts	11,029	7,926	3,103	9,592	639	620
Educational assistance [5]	9,735	9,686	49	7,055	1,679	1,351
Pell grant only	3,399	3,390	9	2,229	815	642
Other government only	1,415	1,401	13	1,044	240	207
Scholarships only	2,603	2,600	4	2,035	265	276
Child support	4,756	4,728	27	3,546	910	725
Alimony	422	334	87	366	24	16
Financial assistance from outside the household	2,468	2,256	212	1,746	390	279
Other income, not elsewhere classified	917	766	151	710	94	54
Combinations of income types:						
Government transfer payments	71,706	34,828	36,878	57,980	9,377	7,135
Public assistance or SSI or both	8,175	6,804	1,371	5,240	2,141	1,572

– Represents or rounds to zero. [1] Beginning with the 2003, CPS respondents could choose one or more races. "White" refers to people who reported White and did not report any other race category. [2] "Black" refers to people who reported Black and did not report any other race category. [3] Persons of Hispanic origin may be of any race. [4] TANF— Temporary Assistance for Needy Families Program; AFDC—Aid to Families With Dependent Children Program. [5] Includes other sources not shown separately. [6] Includes estates and trusts reported as survivor benefits.

Source: U.S. Census Bureau, Table PINC-09 "Source of Income in 2011—Number With Income and Mean Income of Specified Type in 2010 of People 15 Years Old and Over, by Age, Race, Hispanic Origin and Sex," <http://www.census.gov/hhes/www/income/index.html>, accessed February 2013.

Table 566. Persons Living in Households Receiving Selected Noncash Benefits: 2011

[308,456 represents 308,456,000, except percent. Persons, as of March 2011, who lived with someone (a nonrelative or a relative) who received aid. Not every person tallied here received the aid themselves. Persons living in households receiving more than one type of aid are counted only once. Excludes members of the Armed Forces except those living off post or with their families on post. Population controls are based on the Census 2010. Based on Current Population Survey (CPS); see text, Section 1 and Appendix III. SNAP = Supplemental Nutrition Assistance Program]

Age, sex, and race	Total (1,000)	In household that received means-tested assistance [1]		In household that received means-tested cash assistance		In household that received food stamps (SNAP)		In household in which one or more persons were covered by Medicaid		Lived in public or authorized housing	
		(1,000)	Percent	(1,000)	Percent	(1,000)	Percent	(1,000)	Percent	(1,000)	Percent
Total....................	308,456	99,691	32.3	21,725	7.0	40,235	13.0	78,819	25.6	11,675	3.8
Under 18 years...........	73,737	35,236	47.8	5,999	8.1	15,680	21.3	28,747	39.0	4,076	5.5
18 to 24 years............	30,140	10,999	36.5	2,268	7.5	4,599	15.3	8,526	28.3	1,349	4.5
25 to 34 years............	41,219	13,813	33.5	2,582	6.3	6,004	14.6	11,242	27.3	1,490	3.6
35 to 44 years............	39,927	12,556	31.4	2,351	5.9	4,368	10.9	9,761	24.4	1,067	2.7
45 to 54 years............	43,955	11,032	25.1	3,023	6.9	4,058	9.2	8,453	19.2	1,095	2.5
55 to 59 years............	20,470	4,459	21.8	1,565	7.6	1,697	8.3	3,476	17.0	517	2.5
60 to 64 years............	17,501	3,610	20.6	1,359	7.8	1,265	7.2	2,778	15.9	470	2.7
65 years and over........	41,507	7,987	19.2	2,578	6.2	2,565	6.2	5,837	14.1	1,612	3.9
65 to 74 years.........	23,383	4,370	18.7	1,441	6.2	1,456	6.2	3,264	14.0	777	3.3
75 years and over......	18,123	3,617	20.0	1,138	6.3	1,109	6.1	2,573	14.2	834	4.6
Male......................	150,990	46,722	30.9	9,949	6.6	18,092	12.0	36,804	24.4	4,649	3.1
Female....................	157,466	52,969	33.6	11,777	7.5	22,143	14.1	42,015	26.7	7,026	4.5
White alone [2].............	241,334	68,940	28.6	13,975	5.8	26,013	10.8	54,528	22.6	5,715	2.4
Black alone [2].............	39,609	20,597	52.0	5,333	13.5	10,704	27.0	15,874	40.1	4,701	11.9
Asian alone [2]............	16,086	4,671	29.0	1,099	6.8	1,102	6.9	3,969	24.7	521	3.2
Hispanic [3]................	52,279	29,095	55.7	4,926	9.4	11,210	21.4	23,281	44.5	2,609	5.0
White alone, Non-Hispanic [2].........	194,960	43,209	22.2	9,751	5.0	16,214	8.3	34,124	17.5	3,602	1.8

[1] Means-tested assistance includes means-tested cash assistance, food stamps, Medicaid, and public or authorized housing. [2] Refers to people who reported specific race and did not report any other race category. [3] People of Hispanic origin may be of any race.

Source: U.S. Census Bureau, *Income, Poverty, and Health Insurance Coverage in the United States: 2011* (P60-243), September 2012. See also <http://www.census.gov/hhes/www/poverty/index.html>.

Table 567. Social Security—Covered Employment, Earnings, and Contribution Rates: 1990 to 2012

[164.4 represents 164,400,000. Includes the Island areas of the U.S.. Represents all reported employment. Data are estimated. OASDI = Old-age, survivors, and disability insurance; SMI = Supplementary medical insurance. All data are subject to revision by source]

Item	Unit	1990	1995	2000	2005	2008	2009	2010	2011	2012
Workers with insured status [1]......	**Million**	**164.4**	**173.2**	**185.1**	**194.8**	**201.4**	**202.8**	**203.8**	**205.7**	**207.6**
Male..................................	Million	86.7	90.3	95.3	99.5	102.4	102.9	103.2	104.1	104.9
Female...............................	Million	77.6	82.9	89.7	95.3	99.0	99.9	100.6	101.7	102.7
Under 20 years old..................	Million	4.8	4.0	4.9	3.6	3.6	3.1	2.4	2.4	2.4
Age 20 to 24.......................	Million	16.6	15.0	15.9	16.4	16.5	16.3	16.0	15.9	15.7
Age 25 to 29.......................	Million	20.6	18.6	17.5	18.3	19.3	19.3	19.3	19.3	19.2
Age 30 to 34.......................	Million	21.3	21.0	19.2	18.1	17.9	18.3	18.7	19.1	19.4
Age 35 to 39.......................	Million	19.3	21.4	21.2	19.5	19.1	18.7	18.3	17.9	17.9
Age 40 to 44.......................	Million	17.0	19.3	21.4	21.3	19.9	19.6	19.6	19.6	19.5
Age 45 to 49.......................	Million	12.8	16.9	19.1	21.3	21.6	21.5	21.2	20.7	20.2
Age 50 to 54.......................	Million	10.1	12.6	16.5	18.8	20.3	20.6	20.9	21.1	21.2
Age 55 to 59.......................	Million	8.8	9.8	12.2	16.0	17.2	17.7	18.3	18.8	19.3
Age 60 to 64.......................	Million	8.5	8.4	9.3	11.7	13.8	14.5	15.3	15.8	16.0
Age 65 to 69.......................	Million	8.0	7.9	7.8	8.8	10.3	10.7	11.1	11.7	12.4
Age 70 to 74.......................	Million	6.5	7.1	7.0	7.0	7.6	7.8	8.0	8.4	8.9
Age 75 and older...................	Million	10.1	11.4	12.8	13.8	14.4	14.6	14.8	15.1	15.3
Workers reported with—										
Taxable earnings [2]..................	Million	133	141	155	159	163	158	157	159	161
Maximum earnings [2]................	Million	8	8	10	10	10	9	9	9	9
Earnings in covered employment [2]...	Bil. dol.	2,716	3,408	4,843	5,699	6,496	6,185	6,324	6,573	6,841
Reported taxable [2]..................	Bil. dol.	2,359	2,920	4,009	4,764	5,433	5,272	5,310	5,487	5,717
Percent of total.....................	Percent	86.8	85.7	82.8	83.6	83.6	85.2	84.0	83.5	83.6
Average per worker:										
Total earnings [2]..................	Dollars	20,410	24,190	31,315	35,879	39,969	39,218	40,216	41,439	42,517
Taxable earnings [2]................	Dollars	17,725	20,722	25,920	29,992	33,426	33,427	33,768	34,593	35,532
Annual maximum taxable earnings [3]........................	Dollars	51,300	61,200	76,200	90,000	102,000	106,800	106,800	106,800	110,100
Contribution rates for OASDI: [4]										
Each employer and employee......	Percent	7.65	7.65	7.65	7.65	7.65	7.65	7.65	7.65	7.65
Self-employed [5]....................	Percent	15.30	15.30	15.30	15.30	15.30	15.30	15.30	15.30	15.30
SMI, monthly premium [6]..............	Dollars	28.60	46.10	45.50	78.20	96.40	96.40	110.50	115.40	99.90

[1] Estimated number fully insured for retirement and/or survivor benefits as of end of year. [2] Includes self-employment. Averages per worker computed with unrounded earnings and worker amounts, and may not agree with rounded table amounts. [3] Beginning in 1994, the upper limit on earnings subject to HI taxes was removed. [4] OASDI tax rates for employees and self-employed workers were reduced by 2 percent for 2011 and 2012. This reduction is being made up by transfers from the General Fund of the Treasury to the OASI and DI trust funds. [5] Half of self-employment tax is deductible for income tax purposes and for computing self-employment income subject to social security tax. [6] As of January 1.

Sources: U.S. Social Security Administration, *Annual Statistical Supplement to the Social Security Bulletin,* February 2013, and unpublished data. See also <http://www.ssa.gov/policy/docs/statcomps/supplement/2013/>.

Table 568. Social Security (OASDI)—Benefits by Type of Beneficiary: 1990 to 2012

[39,832 represents 39,832,000. A person eligible to receive more than one type of benefit is generally classified or counted only once as a retired-worker beneficiary. OASDI = Old-age, survivors, and disability insurance. See also headnote, Table 569, and Appendix III]

Type of beneficiary	1990	1995	2000	2005	2007	2008	2009	2010	2011	2012
Number of benefits [1] (1,000)	**39,832**	**43,387**	**45,415**	**48,434**	**49,865**	**50,898**	**52,523**	**54,032**	**55,404**	**56,758**
Retired workers [2] (1,000)	24,838	26,673	28,499	30,461	31,528	32,274	33,514	34,593	35,600	36,720
Disabled workers [3] (1,000)	3,011	4,185	5,042	6,519	7,099	7,427	7,788	8,204	8,576	8,827
Wives and husbands [2,4] (1,000)	3,367	3,290	2,963	2,680	2,585	2,525	2,502	2,477	2,456	2,443
Children (1,000)	3,187	3,734	3,803	4,025	4,051	4,132	4,231	4,313	4,375	4,419
Under age 18	2,497	2,956	2,976	3,130	3,120	3,118	3,158	3,209	3,245	3,258
Disabled children [5]	600	686	729	768.54	794.68	871	921	949	977	1,007
Students [6]	89	92	98	126.77	136.49	142	152	155	153	154
Of retired workers	422	442	459	488.43	494.3	525	561	580	594	612
Of deceased workers	1,776	1,884	1,878	1,903	1,892	1,915	1,921	1,913	1,907	1,907
Of disabled workers	989	1,409	1,466	1,633	1,665	1,692	1,748	1,820	1,874	1,900
Widowed mothers [7] (1,000)	304	275	203	178.4	164.67	160	160	158	157.52	154
Widows and widowers [2,8] (1,000)	5,111	5,226	4,901	4,569	4,436	4,380	4,327	4,286	4,239	4,193
Parents [2] (1,000)	6	4	3	1.992	1.809	2	2	2	1.5	1
Special benefits [9] (1,000)	7	1	(Z)	(Z)	(Z)	(Z)	(Z)	(Z)	(Z)	(NA)
AVERAGE MONTHLY BENEFIT, CURRENT DOLLARS										
Retired workers [2]	603	720	844	1,002	1,079	1,153	1,164	1,176	1,229	1,262
Retired worker and wife [2]	1,027	1,221	1,420	1,660	1,776	1,894	1,913	1,930	2,019	2,078
Disabled workers [3]	587	682	786	938	1,004	1,063	1,064	1,068	1,111	1,130
Wives and husbands [2,4]	298	354	416	485	516	551	556	561	587	605
Children of retired workers	259	322	395	493	538	568	570	577	603	617
Children of deceased workers	406	469	550	656	704	745	747	752	783	799
Children of disabled workers	164	183	228	279	299	318	318	318	330	336
Widowed mothers [7]	409	478	595	725	782	835	842	849	884	900
Widows and widowers, nondisabled [2]	556	680	810	967	1,040	1,112	1,124	1,134	1,185	1,215
Parents [2]	482	591	704	851	918	979	988	998	1,045	1,073
Special benefits [9]	167	192	217	247	261	276	276	276	286	(NA)
AVERAGE MONTHLY BENEFIT, CONSTANT (2011) DOLLARS [10]										
Retired workers [2]	1,035	1,077	1,114	1,169	1,179	1,259	1,238	1,231	1,250	1,262
Retired worker and wife [2]	1,762	1,826	1,874	1,937	1,942	2,069	2,034	2,022	2,054	2,078
Disabled workers [3]	1,007	1,020	1,038	1,094	1,098	1,161	1,132	1,118	1,130	1,130
Wives and husbands [2,4]	511	530	549	565	564	602	591	588	597	605
Children of deceased workers	697	702	726	766	770	814	795	787	797	799
Widowed mothers [7]	702	715	785	845	855	912	895	889	899	900
Widows and widowers, nondisabled [2]	954	1,017	1,069	1,128	1,138	1,215	1,195	1,188	1,205	1,215
Number of benefits awarded (1,000)	**3,717**	**3,882**	**4,290**	**4,672**	**4,711**	**5,135**	**5,728**	**5,697**	**5,567**	**5,655**
Retired workers [2]	1,665	1,609	1,961	2,000	2,036	2,279	2,740	2,634	2,578	2,735
Disabled workers [3]	468	646	622	830	805	877	971	1,027	999	960
Wives and husbands [2,4]	379	322	385	379	364	395	429	409	399	420
Children	695	809	777	908	902	961	1,008	1,045	1,017	959
Widowed mothers [7]	58	52	40	38	34	33	33	32	30	29
Widows and widowers [2,8]	452	445	505	517	570	590	547	550	545	552
Parents [2]	(Z)	(Z)	(Z)	(Z)	(Z)	(Z)	(Z)	(Z)	(Z)	(Z)
Special benefits [9]	(Z)	(Z)	(Z)	(Z)	(Z)	(Z)	(Z)	(Z)	(Z)	(NA)
BENEFIT PAYMENTS DURING YEAR (bil. dol.)										
Total [11]	**247.8**	**332.6**	**407.6**	**520.8**	**585.0**	**615.4**	**675.5**	**701.6**	**725.1**	**774.8**
Monthly benefits [12]	247.6	332.4	407.4	520.6	584.8	615.2	675.3	701.4	724.9	774.6
Retired workers [2]	156.8	205.3	253.5	321.7	364.3	384.0	424.0	443.4	461.2	497.5
Disabled workers [3]	22.1	36.6	49.8	78.4	91.3	98.1	109.5	115.1	119.6	127.2
Wives and husbands [2,4]	14.5	17.9	19.4	20.5	22.1	22.6	24.2	24.6	24.8	26.0
Children	12.0	16.1	19.3	24.5	27.0	28.2	30.2	30.7	31.2	0.0
Under age 18	9.0	11.9	14.1	17.9	19.5	20.1	21.2	21.4	21.2	22.2
Disabled children [5]	2.5	3.6	4.6	5.8	6.5	6.9	7.8	8.0	8.7	8.9
Students [6]	0.5	0.6	0.7	0.8	1.0	1.1	1.2	1.3	1.3	1.3
Of retired workers	1.3	1.7	2.1	2.9	3.3	3.5	3.9	4.1	4.3	4.6
Of deceased workers	8.6	10.7	12.5	15.1	16.5	17.0	18.1	18.0	18.1	18.8
Of disabled workers	2.2	3.7	4.7	6.5	7.3	7.7	8.2	8.5	8.8	9.1
Widowed mothers [7]	1.4	1.6	1.4	1.5	1.6	1.6	1.6	1.6	1.6	1.7
Widows and widowers [2,8]	40.7	54.8	63.9	73.4	78.5	80.7	85.6	86.0	86.5	89.9
Parents [2]	(Z)	(Z)	(Z)	(Z)	(Z)	(Z)	(Z)	(Z)	(Z)	(Z)
Special benefits [9]	(Z)	(Z)	(Z)	(Z)	(Z)	(Z)	(Z)	(Z)	(Z)	(NA)
Lump sum	0.2	0.2	0.2	0.2	0.2	0.2	0.2	0.2	0.2	0.2

NA Not available. Z Fewer than 500 or less than $50 million. [1] Number of benefit payments in current-payment status, i.e., actually being made at a specified time with no deductions or with deductions amounting to less than a month's benefit. [2] 62 years and over. [3] Disabled workers under age 65. [4] Includes wife beneficiaries with entitled children in their care and entitled divorced wives. [5] 18 years old and over. Disability began before age 22. [6] Full-time students aged 18 and 19. [7] Includes surviving divorced mothers with entitled children in their care and widowed fathers with entitled children in their care. [8] Includes widows aged 60–61, surviving divorced wives aged 60 and over, disabled widows and widowers aged 50 and over; and widowers aged 60–61. [9] Benefits for persons aged 72 and over not insured under regular or transitional provisions of Social Security Act. [10] Constant dollar figures are based on the consumer price index (CPI-U) for December as published by the U.S. Bureau of Labor Statistics. [11] Represents total disbursements of benefit checks by the U.S. Department of the Treasury during the years specified. [12] Distribution by type estimated.

Source: U.S. Social Security Administration, *Annual Statistical Supplement to the Social Security Bulletin, 2013*. See also <http://www.ssa.gov/policy/index.html>.

Table 569. Social Security—Beneficiaries, Annual Payments, and Average Monthly Benefit, 1990 to 2011, and by State and Other Areas, 2012

[Number of beneficiaries in current-payment status (39,832 represents 39,832,000) and annual and average monthly benefit as of December. Data for 1990-2005 are based on 10-percent sample of administrative records. All other years are 100 percent data. See also headnote, Table 568, and Appendix III]

Year, state, and other area	Number of beneficiaries (1,000)				Annual payments [2] (mil. dol.)				Average monthly benefit (dol.)		
	Total	Retired workers and dependents [1]	Survivors	Disabled workers and dependents	Total	Retired workers and dependents [1]	Survivors	Disabled workers and dependents	Retired workers [3]	Disabled workers	Widows and widowers [4]
1990...............	39,832	28,369	7,197	4,266	247,796	172,042	50,951	24,803	603	587	557
2000...............	45,417	31,761	6,981	6,675	407,431	274,645	77,848	54,938	844.6	787	810.2
2005...............	48,446	33,488	6,650	8,307	520,561	345,094	90,073	85,394	1,002	937.9	966.7
2009...............	52,523	36,419	6,410	9,694	675,288	451,579	105,380	118,329	1,164	1,064	1,124
2010...............	54,032	37,489	6,358	10,184	701,436	471,505	105,740	124,191	1,176	1,068	1,134
2011...............	55,404	38,486	6,305	10,613	724,943	489,698	106,310	128,935	1,229	1,111	1,185
2012, total [5, 6]......	**56,758**	**39,613**	**6,256**	**10,889**	**774,626**	**527,402**	**110,346**	**136,878**	**1,262**	**1,130**	**1,215**
United States...........	55,286	38,632	6,033	10,625	761,774	520,002	107,727	134,045	(NA)	(NA)	(NA)
Alabama...............	1,061	639	130	291	14,051	8,349	2,137	3,565	1,234	1,111	1,098
Alaska...............	85	59	10	16	1,096	739	157	200	1,200	1,113	1,124
Arizona...............	1,141	840	112	190	15,900	11,408	2,005	2,487	1,287	1,174	1,220
Arkansas...............	658	406	75	177	8,450	5,153	1,200	2,097	1,195	1,076	1,071
California...............	5,280	3,882	544	854	71,487	50,513	9,771	11,203	1,246	1,158	1,192
Colorado...............	749	548	76	125	10,180	7,199	1,378	1,603	1,250	1,141	1,207
Connecticut............	640	480	61	99	9,651	7,125	1,211	1,315	1,385	1,173	1,330
Delaware...............	182	132	18	33	2,665	1,884	334	447	1,347	1,199	1,279
District of Columbia......	77	53	8	16	965	652	125	188	1,152	999	1,021
Florida...............	4,005	2,972	381	651	54,711	39,529	6,863	8,319	1,254	1,140	1,201
Georgia...............	1,582	1,058	182	342	21,198	13,911	3,022	4,265	1,244	1,134	1,130
Hawaii...............	240	190	22	29	3,276	2,519	382	375	1,250	1,159	1,155
Idaho...............	288	207	29	53	3,827	2,674	518	635	1,229	1,102	1,205
Illinois...............	2,103	1,504	243	356	29,862	20,709	4,551	4,602	1,296	1,155	1,251
Indiana...............	1,245	849	142	253	17,789	11,972	2,642	3,175	1,323	1,138	1,255
Iowa...............	601	442	67	92	8,300	5,932	1,248	1,120	1,260	1,077	1,225
Kansas...............	508	359	56	92	7,128	4,966	1,038	1,124	1,295	1,102	1,248
Kentucky...............	930	549	119	262	12,084	6,944	1,933	3,207	1,203	1,102	1,079
Louisiana...............	826	495	135	197	10,582	6,055	2,172	2,355	1,179	1,100	1,086
Maine...............	314	211	30	74	3,990	2,617	520	853	1,170	1,050	1,131
Maryland...............	895	647	96	151	12,755	8,996	1,758	2,001	1,307	1,166	1,226
Massachusetts...........	1,185	822	112	251	16,426	11,224	2,101	3,101	1,281	1,122	1,230
Michigan...............	2,062	1,400	228	433	30,128	20,134	4,361	5,633	1,356	1,185	1,277
Minnesota...............	927	684	91	153	12,998	9,392	1,701	1,905	1,292	1,122	1,238
Mississippi...............	622	374	81	167	7,898	4,688	1,231	1,979	1,185	1,078	1,038
Missouri...............	1,213	810	135	268	16,379	10,752	2,344	3,283	1,244	1,102	1,176
Montana...............	203	148	22	34	2,659	1,870	380	409	1,195	1,073	1,175
Nebraska...............	317	231	35	51	4,336	3,079	640	617	1,249	1,070	1,213
Nevada...............	442	328	41	74	6,075	4,356	729	990	1,254	1,194	1,216
New Hampshire...........	271	188	23	61	3,829	2,646	432	751	1,320	1,152	1,264
New Jersey...............	1,526	1,129	151	246	23,227	16,812	2,996	3,419	1,397	1,241	1,305
New Mexico...............	382	261	43	78	4,860	3,245	687	928	1,184	1,080	1,094
New York...............	3,394	2,414	337	643	48,536	33,858	6,298	8,380	1,323	1,168	1,232
North Carolina...........	1,860	1,273	186	400	25,246	17,061	3,110	5,075	1,257	1,127	1,125
North Dakota............	122	89	16	17	1,603	1,110	289	204	1,182	1,051	1,146
Ohio...............	2,204	1,501	281	422	30,317	20,037	5,146	5,134	1,260	1,095	1,210
Oklahoma...............	730	485	89	156	9,691	6,283	1,510	1,898	1,221	1,092	1,143
Oregon...............	757	560	72	126	10,468	7,497	1,350	1,621	1,265	1,131	1,238
Pennsylvania...........	2,660	1,863	299	498	37,793	25,886	5,646	6,261	1,304	1,134	1,240
Rhode Island............	211	147	19	45	2,909	2,015	339	555	1,275	1,096	1,223
South Carolina...........	986	665	105	216	13,429	8,909	1,737	2,783	1,262	1,146	1,114
South Dakota............	159	118	18	23	2,062	1,480	310	272	1,182	1,052	1,127
Tennessee...............	1,322	862	152	308	17,702	11,410	2,525	3,767	1,248	1,101	1,121
Texas...............	3,658	2,474	469	715	48,334	31,679	7,950	8,705	1,231	1,111	1,137
Utah...............	347	249	38	60	4,736	3,337	679	720	1,277	1,125	1,248
Vermont...............	136	95	13	28	1,831	1,279	227	325	1,263	1,059	1,192
Virginia...............	1,354	949	145	260	18,682	12,812	2,550	3,320	1,277	1,138	1,165
Washington...............	1,164	844	111	209	16,516	11,707	2,110	2,699	1,315	1,142	1,265
West Virginia............	456	272	64	120	6,185	3,524	1,103	1,558	1,245	1,154	1,137
Wisconsin...............	1,110	804	111	195	15,640	11,126	2,092	2,422	1,297	1,124	1,253
Wyoming...............	96	71	10	15	1,332	948	189	195	1,266	1,118	1,228
American Samoa.......	6	3	2	2	52	21	14	17	822	863	682
Guam...............	15	10	3	2	139	86	31	22	845	983	781
Northern Mariana....... Islands	3	2	1	(Z)	18	11	5	2	683	748	557
Puerto Rico............	838	486	111	241	7971	4146	1267	2558	844	1003	733
U.S. Virgin Islands.....	21	16	2	2	244	186	31	27	1,112	1,124	954
Abroad.................	586	463	105	18	4,434	2,956	1,270	208	667	1,048	738

NA Not available. Z Less than 500. [1] Data for 1990-2006 include special benefits for persons aged 72 years and over not insured under regular or transitional provisions of Social Security Act. [2] Unnegotiated checks not deducted. 1990 data include lump-sum payments to survivors of deceased workers. [3] Excludes persons with special benefits. [4] Nondisabled only. [5] Includes those with state or area unknown. [6] 2012 data are preliminary.

Source: U.S. Social Security Administration, *Annual Statistical Supplement to the Social Security Bulletin, 2013*. See also <http://www.ssa.gov/policy/index.html>.

Table 570. Social Security Trust Funds: 1995 to 2012

[In billions of dollars (304.6 represents $304,600,000,000)]

Type of trust fund	1995	2000	2005	2007	2008	2009	2010	2011	2012
Old-age and survivors insurance (OASI):									
Net payroll tax contributions	304.6	421.4	506.9	560.9	574.6	570.4	544.8	482.4	503.9
Taxation of benefits	5.5	11.6	13.8	17.2	15.6	19.9	22.1	22.2	26.7
Interest received [1]	32.8	57.5	84.0	97.0	105.3	107.9	108.2	106.5	102.8
Benefit payments [2]	291.6	352.7	435.4	489.1	509.3	557.2	577.4	596.2	637.9
Assets, end of year	458.5	931.0	1,663.0	2,023.6	2,202.9	2,336.8	2,429.0	2,524.1	2,609.7
Disability insurance (DI):									
Net payroll tax contributions	54.4	71.1	86.1	95.2	97.6	96.9	92.5	81.9	85.6
Taxation of benefits	0.3	0.7	1.1	1.4	1.3	2.0	1.9	1.6	0.6
Interest received [1]	2.2	6.9	10.3	13.2	11.0	10.5	9.3	7.9	6.4
Benefit payments [2]	40.9	55.0	85.4	95.9	106.0	118.3	124.2	128.9	136.9
Assets, end of year	37.6	118.5	195.6	214.9	215.8	203.6	179.9	153.9	122.7

[1] In 1990, includes interest on advance tax transfers. Includes interest on reimbursement for unnegotiated checks. [2] Includes payments for vocational rehabilitation services furnished to disabled persons receiving benefits because of their disabilities. Amounts reflect deductions for unnegotiated benefit checks.

Source: U.S. Social Security Administration, *The 2013 Annual Report of the Board of Trustees of the Federal Old-Age and Survivors Insurance and Federal Disability Insurance Trust Funds*, and earlier reports. See also <http://www.ssa.gov/OACT/TR/index.html>.

Table 571. Percent of Workers Participating in Retirement Benefits by Worker Characteristics: 2007 to 2012

[Based on National Compensation Survey. The March 2012 NCS obtained data from 6,618 private industry establishments of all sizes, representing over 100 million workers; see Appendix III. For a definition of defined benefit and defined contribution, see headnote, Table 575. See also Table 684]

Characteristic	Total [1]				Defined benefit				Defined contribution			
	2007	2010	2011	2012	2007	2010	2011	2012	2007	2010	2011	2012
Total	**51**	**50**	**49**	**48**	**20**	**19**	**18**	**17**	**43**	**41**	**41**	**41**
Management, professional, and related	69	68	68	68	28	25	25	24	60	60	60	61
Service	25	23	22	21	7	7	7	6	20	18	18	16
Sales and office	54	53	52	51	17	16	15	14	47	46	46	45
Natural resources, construction, and maintenance	51	51	49	51	25	26	24	23	40	40	39	42
Production, transportation, and material moving	54	51	51	50	25	24	23	21	41	38	38	38
Full-time	60	59	59	59	23	22	22	20	50	50	50	51
Part-time	23	21	20	19	9	8	8	7	18	15	14	14
Union	81	82	83	85	67	67	67	66	41	44	42	45
Nonunion	47	46	45	45	15	13	13	12	43	41	41	41

[1] Total is less than the sum of the individual retirement items because many employees participated in both types of plans.

Source: U.S. Bureau of Labor Statistics, *National Compensation Survey: Employee Benefits in the United States, March 2012*, July 2012. See also <http://www.bls.gov/ncs/ebs/benefits>.

Table 572. Federal Civil Service Retirement: 1990 to 2010

[As of September 30 or for fiscal year ending September 30 (2,945 represents 2,945,000). Covers both Civil Service Retirement System and Federal Employees Retirement System]

Item	Unit	1990	1995	2000	2005	2006	2007	2008	2009	2010
Employees covered [1]	1,000	2,945	2,668	2,764	2,674	2,611	2,618	2,613	2,672	2,756
Annuitants, total	**1,000**	**2,143**	**2,311**	**2,376**	**2,433**	**2,449**	**2,463**	**2,471**	**2,481**	**2,479**
Age and service	1,000	1,288	1,441	1,501	1,568	1,602	1,625	1,643	1,662	1,674
Disability	1,000	297	263	242	229	226	222	218	216	210
Survivors	1,000	558	607	633	636	621	616	610	603	595
Receipts, total [2]	**Mil. dol**	**52,689**	**65,684**	**75,967**	**83,691**	**87,164**	**89,860**	**90,892**	**93,061**	**95,662**
Employee contributions	Mil. dol	4,501	4,498	4,637	4,353	4,304	4,205	4,111	4,083	4,015
Federal government contributions	Mil. dol	27,368	33,130	37,722	43,093	46,427	48,397	49,547	51,789	55,019
Disbursements, total [3]	**Mil. dol**	**31,416**	**38,435**	**45,194**	**54,790**	**57,983**	**78,146**	**63,687**	**67,669**	**69,452**
Age and service annuitants [4]	Mil. dol	26,495	32,070	37,546	46,029	48,895	68,776	54,202	57,782	59,594
Survivors	Mil. dol	4,366	5,864	7,210	8,338	8,642	8,905	9,011	9,463	9,532
Average monthly benefit:										
Age and service	Dollars	1,369	1,643	1,885	2,240	2,363	2,473	2,550	2,710	2,723
Disability	Dollars	1,008	1,164	1,240	1,327	1,366	1,394	1,409	1,469	1,453
Survivors	Dollars	653	819	952	1,106	1,157	1,200	1,232	1,309	1,315
Cash and security holdings	Bil. dol	238.0	366.2	508.1	660.8	690.0	701.7	728.9	754.3	780.4

[1] Excludes employees in leave-without-pay status. [2] Includes interest on investments. [3] Includes refunds, death claims, and administration. [4] Includes disability annuitants.

Source: U.S. Office of Personnel Management, *Civil Service Retirement and Disability Trust Fund Annual Report*. See also <http://www.opm.gov/feddata/>.

Table 573. Public Employee Retirement Systems—Participants and Finances: 1980 to 2009

[For participants, 4,629 represents 4,629,000. For finances, 258 represents $258,000,000,000. For fiscal year of retirement system, except data for the Thrift Savings Plan are for calendar year. For a definition of defined benefit, see headnote, Table 575]

Retirement plan	Unit	1980	1990	2000	2005	2006	2007	2008	2009, proj.
TOTAL PARTICIPANTS [1]									
Federal retirement systems:									
Defined benefit:									
Civil Service Retirement System	1,000	4,629	4,167	3,256	2,958	2,878	2,789	2,650	2,575
Federal Employees Retirement System [2]	1,000	(X)	1,180	1,935	2,196	2,290	2,371	2,572	2,748
Military Service Retirement System [3]	1,000	3,380	3,763	3,397	3,536	3,560	3,585	3,657	3,676
Thrift Savings Plan [4]	1,000	(X)	1,625	2,500	3,600	3,700	3,900	4,000	4,300
State and local retirement systems [5,6]	1,000	(NA)	16,858	23,126	24,997	25,781	26,071	26,841	27,470
ACTIVE PARTICIPANTS									
Federal retirement systems:									
Defined benefit:									
Civil Service Retirement System	1,000	2,700	1,826	978	722	650	580	477	426
Federal Employees Retirement System [2]	1,000	(X)	1,136	1,668	1,952	2,014	2,066	2,195	2,330
Military Service Retirement System [3]	1,000	2,050	2,130	1,437	1,445	1,443	1,438	1,461	1,480
Thrift Savings Plan [4]	1,000	(X)	1,419	1,900	2,800	2,600	2,600	2,700	2,800
State and local retirement systems [5,6]	1,000	(NA)	11,345	13,917	14,116	14,529	14,422	14,701	14,830
ASSETS									
Total	Bil. dol.	258	1,047	2,951	3,695	4,022	4,533	4,380	3,758
Federal retirement systems	Bil. dol.	73	326	783	1,037	1,110	1,156	1,190	1,292
Defined benefit	Bil. dol.	73	318	685	864	903	924	987	1,048
Civil Service Retirement System	Bil. dol.	73	220	395	438	442	426	423	422
Federal Employees Retirement System [2]	Bil. dol.	(X)	18	127	228	253	280	311	348
Military Service Retirement System [3]	Bil. dol.	([7])	80	163	198	208	218	253	278
Thrift Savings Plan [4]	Bil. dol.	(X)	8	98	173	207	232	203	244
State and local retirement systems [5]	Bil. dol.	185	721	2,168	2,658	2,912	3,377	3,190	2,466
CONTRIBUTIONS									
Total	Bil. dol.	83	103	143	196	206	224	260	274
Federal retirement systems	Bil. dol.	19	61	78	105	109	117	141	148
Defined benefit	Bil. dol.	19	59	69	86	89	96	119	125
Civil Service Retirement System	Bil. dol.	19	28	33	33	35	36	35	36
Federal Employees Retirement System [2]	Bil. dol.	(X)	4	9	15	15	17	19	20
Military Service Retirement System [3]	Bil. dol.	([7])	27	27	38	39	43	65	69
Thrift Savings Plan [4]	Bil. dol.	(X)	2	9	19	20	21	22	23
State and local retirement systems [5]	Bil. dol.	64	42	65	91	97	107	119	126
BENEFITS									
Total	Bil. dol.	39	89	172	240	258	274	295	311
Federal retirement systems	Bil. dol.	27	53	81	99	106	112	120	124
Defined benefit	Bil. dol.	27	53	78	94	99	104	112	117
Civil Service Retirement System	Bil. dol.	15	31	44	52	55	57	59	63
Federal Employees Retirement System [2]	Bil. dol.	(X)	(Z)	1	3	3	4	4	5
Military Service Retirement System [3]	Bil. dol.	12	22	33	39	41	43	49	49
Thrift Savings Plan [4]	Bil. dol.	(X)	(Z)	3	5	7	8	8	7
State and local retirement systems [5]	Bil. dol.	12	36	91	141	152	162	175	187

NA Not available. X Not applicable. Z Less than $500 million. [1] Includes active, separated, vested, and retired employees and survivors. [2] The Federal Employees Retirement System was established June 6, 1986. [3] Includes nondisability and disability retirees, surviving families, and all active personnel with the exception of active reserves. [4] The Thrift Savings Plan (a defined contribution plan) was established April 1, 1987. [5] Excludes state and local plans that are fully supported by employee contributions. [6] Not adjusted for double counting of individuals participating in more than one plan. [7] The Military Retirement System was unfunded until October 1, 1984.

Source: Employee Benefit Research Institute, Washington, DC, *EBRI Databook on Employee Benefits*, and unpublished data ©. See also <http://www.ebri.org>.

Table 574. State and Local Government Retirement Systems—Beneficiaries and Finances: Fiscal Years 1990 to 2011

[In billions of dollars (111.3 represents $111,300,000,000), except as indicated. For fiscal years closed during the 12 months ending June 30. Minus sign (−) indicates negative earnings on investment. Based on the Annual Survey of Public Pensions]

Year and level of government	Number of beneficiaries (1,000)	Receipts					Benefits and withdrawals			Cash and security holdings
		Total	Employee contributions	Government contributions		Earnings on investments	Total	Benefits	Withdrawals	
				State	Local					
1990: All systems	4,026	111.3	13.9	14.0	18.6	64.9	38.4	36.0	2.4	721
State-administered	3,232	89.2	11.6	14.0	11.5	52.0	29.6	27.6	2.0	575
Locally administered	794	22.2	2.2	(Z)	7.0	12.9	8.8	8.4	0.4	145
2000: All systems	6,292	297.0	25.0	17.5	22.6	231.9	95.7	91.3	4.4	2,169
State-administered	4,786	247.4	20.7	17.2	16.7	192.8	76.0	72.2	3.8	1,798
Locally administered	1,506	49.7	4.3	0.4	5.9	39.1	19.8	19.1	0.7	371
2010: All systems	8,246	471.6	39.1	36.1	50.3	346.1	213.8	201.0	4.2	2,675
State-administered	6,994	387.2	33.0	35.6	29.2	289.5	173.5	163.5	3.5	2,221
Locally administered	1,253	84.4	6.1	0.5	21.1	56.6	40.3	37.5	0.7	453
2011: All systems	8,607	616.1	40.3	39.7	56.5	479.6	232.0	216.3	4.7	3,027
State-administered	7,322	518.4	34.2	39.1	32.6	412.6	189.1	176.7	3.9	2,543
Locally administered	1,285	97.7	6.1	0.6	23.9	67.1	42.8	39.6	0.8	484

Z Less than $50 million.

Source: U.S. Census Bureau, through 1995, *Finances of Employee-Retirement Systems of State and Local Governments*, Series GF, No. 2, annual; and beginning 2000, "Federal, State, and Local Governments, State and Local Government Public Employee Retirement Systems," <http://www.census.gov/govs/retire>, accessed June 2013.

Social Insurance and Human Services **379**

Table 575. Private Pension Plans—Summary by Type of Plan: 1990 to 2010

[In units as indicated. "Pension plan" is defined by the Employee Retirement Income Security Act (ERISA) as "any plan, fund, or program which was heretofore or is hereafter established or maintained by an employer or an employee organization, or by both, to the extent that such plan (a) provides retirement income to employees, or (b) results in a deferral of income by employees for periods extending to the termination of covered employment or beyond, regardless of the method of calculating the contributions made to the plan, the method of calculating the benefits under the plan, or the method of distributing benefits from the plan." A defined benefit plan provides a definite benefit formula for calculating benefit amounts—such as a flat amount per year of service or a percentage of salary times years of service. A defined contribution plan is a pension plan in which the contributions are made to an individual account for each employee. The retirement benefit is dependent upon the account balance at retirement. The balance depends upon amounts contributed, investment outcomes, and, in the case of profit sharing plans, amounts which may be allocated to the account due to forfeitures by terminating employees. Employee Stock Ownership Plans (ESOP) and 401(k) plans are included among defined contribution plans. Data are based on Form 5500 series reports filed with the U.S. Department of Labor and exclude (1) selected pension plans qualified under sections 403(b), 457(b) and 457(f) of the Internal Revenue Code, (2) most SARSEP, SEP and SIMPLE IRA plans, (3) unfunded excess benefit plans, (4) selected church plans, (5) top hat plans, (6) individual retirement accounts (IRAs), and (7) governmental plans]

Item	Unit	Total				Defined contribution plan				Defined benefit plan			
		1990	2000	2005	2010	1990	2000	2005	2010	1990	2000	2005	2010
Number of plans [1]	1,000	712.3	735.7	679.1	701.0	599.2	686.9	631.5	654.5	113.1	48.8	47.6	46.5
Total participants [2]	Million	76.9	103.3	117.4	129.7	38.6	61.7	75.5	88.3	38.8	41.6	41.9	41.4
Active participants [3]	Million	61.5	73.1	82.7	90.6	35.6	50.9	62.4	73.4	26.2	22.2	20.3	17.2
Assets [4]	Bil. dol	1,674	4,203	5,062	6,282	834	2,216	2,808	3,833	962	1,986	2,254	2,448
Contributions [5]	Bil. dol	98.8	231.9	341.4	445.3	80.9	198.5	248.8	314.3	24.7	33.4	92.7	131.1
Benefits [6]	Bil. dol	129.4	341.0	354.5	456.9	64.0	213.5	218.0	287.3	66.4	127.5	136.6	169.6

[1] Excludes all plans covering only one participant. [2] Includes active, retired, and separated vested participants not yet in pay status. Also includes double counting of workers in more than one plan. [3] Includes any workers currently in employment covered by a plan and who are earning or retaining credited service under a plan. Also includes any nonvested former employees who have not yet incurred breaks in service. [4] Asset amounts shown exclude funds held by life insurance companies under allocated group insurance contracts for payment of retirement benefits. These excluded funds make up roughly 10 to 15 percent of total private fund assets. [5] Includes both employer and employee contributions. [6] Includes benefits paid directly from trust and premium payments made from plans to insurance carriers. Excludes benefits paid directly by insurance carriers.

Source: U.S. Department of Labor, Employee Benefits Security Administration, *Private Pension Plan Bulletins Abstract of Form 550 Annual Reports;* and "Private Pension Plan Bulletin Historical Tables and Graphs," <http://www.dol.gov/ebsa/publications/form5500dataresearch.html#planbulletins>, accessed May 2013. See also <http://www.dol.gov/ebsa/>.

Table 576. Defined Benefit Retirement Plans—Selected Features: 2010

[In percent. Covers full-time employees in private industry. Based on National Compensation Survey, a sample survey of 9,018 private industry establishments of all sizes, representing nearly 99 million workers; see Appendix III. For definition of defined benefit, see headnote, Table 575. See also Table 684]

Feature	All workers	Goods producing	Service producing	1 to 99 workers	100 workers or more	Union	Nonunion
Benefit formula:							
Percent of terminal earnings	32	27	34	38	30	22	38
Percent of career earnings	11	(NA)	13	(NA)	(NA)	10	12
Dollar amount formula	18	40	(NA)	(NA)	20	45	(NA)
Percent of contribution formula	3	(NA)	(NA)	(NA)	(NA)	7	(NA)
Cash balance	31	19	34	30	31	11	41
Pension equity	5	(NA)	6	(NA)	6	(NA)	(NA)

NA Not available.

Source: U.S. Bureau of Labor Statistics, *National Compensation Survey: Employee Benefits in Private Industry in the United States*, <http://www.bls.gov/ncs/ebs/detailedprovisions/2010/basic_retirement.htm>. See also <http://www.bls.gov/ncs/ebs/home.htm>.

Table 577. Percent of U.S. Households Owning Individual Retirement Accounts (IRAs): 2000 to 2012

[Incidence of IRA ownership is based on an annual tracking survey of approximately 4,000 randomly selected, representative U.S. households; see source for details]

Year and characteristic	Any type of IRA [1]	Traditional IRA	Roth IRA	Employer-sponsored IRA [2]	Year and characteristic	Any type of IRA [1]	Traditional IRA	Roth IRA	Employer-sponsored IRA [2]
2000	35.7	28.7	9.2	6.8	2010	41.4	32.8	16.6	8.0
2003	36.7	29.6	12.5	7.5	2011	38.8	31.2	15.7	7.5
2004	36.5	29.6	11.6	8.0	**2012, total** [3]	**40.4**	**32.5**	**16.8**	**7.6**
2005	37.9	30.0	12.8	7.4	Under 35 years	28.0	19.0	16.0	7.0
2006	38.3	31.7	13.4	7.7	35 to 44 years	44.0	32.0	21.0	8.0
2007	39.8	32.5	14.9	7.9	45 to 54 years	46.0	36.0	17.0	10.0
2008	40.5	32.1	15.9	8.6	55 to 64 years	47.0	42.0	20.0	10.0
2009	39.3	31.2	14.5	8.2	65 years and over	39.0	35.0	11.0	4.0

[1] Excludes ownership of Coverdell Education Savings Accounts, which were referred to as Education IRAs before July 2001. [2] Employer-sponsored IRAs include SEP IRAs, SARSEP IRAs, and SIMPLE IRAs. [3] Age is based on the age of the sole or co-decision maker for household saving and investing.

Source: Investment Company Institute, Washington, DC, ICI Research Perspective, "Appendix: Additional Data on IRA Ownership in 2012," Vol 18, No. 8A, December 2012 ©. See also <http://www.ici.org>.

Table 578. Characteristics of U.S. Households Owning Individual Retirement Accounts (IRAs): 2012

[Incidence of IRA ownership is based on an annual tracking survey of approximately 4,000 randomly selected, representative U.S. households; see source for details]

Characteristic	Unit	Households owning IRAs				House-holds not own-ing IRAs
		Total [1]	Tradi-tional IRA	Roth IRA	Employer-spon-sored [1]	
MEDIAN PER HOUSEHOLD						
Age of household sole or co-decision maker for investing..........	Years	52	54	45	50	49
Household income [2].................................	Dollars	75,000	75,000	90,000	75,000	35,000
Household financial assets [3]...............................	Dollars	200,000	200,000	200,000	160,000	25,000
Household financial assets in all types of IRAs......................	Dollars	45,000	60,000	48,000	65,000	(X)
Share of household financial assets in type of IRA indicated.......	Percent	34	29	12	18	(X)
PERCENT OF HOUSEHOLDS						
Household has defined contribution account or defined benefit plan coverage (total) [4].............................	Percent	83	82	85	84	47
Defined contribution retirement plan account........................	Percent	73	72	79	76	38
Defined benefit plan coverage.......................................	Percent	46	47	47	38	22
Types of IRAs owned: [4]						
Traditional IRA...	Percent	80	100	67	64	(X)
Roth IRA...	Percent	42	35	100	35	(X)
Employer-sponsored IRA [1]....................................	Percent	19	15	16	100	(X)

X Not applicable. [1] Employer-sponsored IRAs include SIMPLE IRAs, SEP IRAs, and SARSEP IRAs. [2] Total reported is household income before taxes in 2010. [3] Household financial assets include assets in employer-sponsored retirement plans but exclude the household's primary residence. [4] Multiple responses are included.

Source: Investment Company Institute, Washington, DC, ICI Research Perspective, "Appendix: Additional Data on IRA Ownership in 2012," Vol 18, No. 8A, December 2012 ©. See also <http://www.ici.org>.

Table 579. Percent Distribution of Assets in Individual Retirement Accounts (IRAs) by Type of IRA: 2011 and 2012

[Incidence of individual retirement account (IRA) ownership is based on an annual tracking survey of approximately 4,000 randomly selected, representative U.S. households; see source for details]

Assets by type of IRA	Unit	2011			2012		
		Total assets in IRAs	Type of IRA owned		Total assets in IRAs	Type of IRA owned	
			Traditional IRAs	Roth IRAs		Traditional IRAs	Roth IRAs
PERCENT DISTRIBUTION OF ASSETS IN IRAs							
Less than $10,000.............................	Percent	18	18	33	15	18	30
$10,000 to $24,999............................	Percent	20	20	27	18	18	27
$25,000 to $49,999............................	Percent	14	14	15	17	15	17
$50,000 to $99,999............................	Percent	15	16	13	18	19	15
$100,000 to $249,999..........................	Percent	18	19	10	18	17	8
$250,000 or more.............................	Percent	15	13	2	14	13	3
TOTAL ASSETS IN IRAs							
Mean..	Dollars	122,100	118,000	44,100	116,000	110,000	43,600
Median..	Dollars	42,500	42,500	20,000	45,000	42,500	20,000

Source: Investment Company Institute, Washington, DC, ICI Research Perspective, "Appendix: Additional Data on IRA Ownership in 2012," Vol. 18, No. 8A, December 2012 ©. See also <http://www.ici.org>.

Table 580. Defined Contribution 401(k) Plans—Participants, Assets, Contributions, and Benefits by Type of Plan: 2010

[Participants in thousands (72,165 represents 72,165,000); values in millions of dollars (3,142,141 represents $3,142,141,000,000)]

Type of plan [1]	Total plans [2]	Total participants (1,000) [3]	Total assets (mil. dol.)	Total contributions (mil. dol.) [4]	Total benefits (mil. dol.) [5]
Total...................................	518,675	72,165	3,142,141	267,584	245,474
Profit sharing and thrift-savings.....................	515,900	70,811	3,044,662	262,946	239,838
Stock bonus..	233	623	73,729	2,660	4,075
Target benefit...	46	1	32	3	3
Money purchase.......................................	726	300	13,367	927	864
Annuity—403(b)(1).....................................	706	186	5,495	500	337
Custodial account—403(b)(7)........................	368	108	1,770	256	136
Other defined contribution...........................	695	137	3,087	292	221

[1] About 1 percent of defined contribution plans report more than one plan type. [2] Excludes plans covering only one participant. [3] Includes active, retired, and separated vested participants not yet in pay status. [4] Includes both employer and employee contributions. [5] Amounts shown include benefits paid directly from trust funds and premium payments made by plans to insurance carriers.

Source: U.S. Department of Labor, Employee Benefits Security Administration, *Private Pension Plan Bulletin: Abstract of 2010 Form 5500 Annual Reports,* November 2012. See also <http://www.dol.gov/ebsa/publications/main.html>.

Table 581. State Unemployment Insurance—Summary: 1990 to 2011

[In units as indicated. Includes unemployment compensation for state and local government employees where covered by state law]

Item	Unit	1990	1995	2000	2005	2007	2008	2009	2010	2011
Insured unemployment, average weekly.........	1,000	2,522	2,572	2,110	2,661	2,572	3,306	5,724	4,487	3,681
Percent of covered employment [1].............	Percent	2.4	2.3	1.7	2.1	1.9	2.5	4.5	3.6	2.9
Percent of civilian unemployed..................	Percent	35.8	34.7	37.1	35.1	36.3	37.0	40.1	30.3	26.8
Unemployment benefits, average weekly........	Dollars	162	187	221	267	288	297	309	299	296
Percent of weekly wage..........................	Percent	36.0	35.5	32.9	34.6	34.1	34.4	35.8	33.7	32.4
Weeks compensated.............................	Million	116.0	118.3	96.0	121.2	116.3	149.5	266.0	203.1	165.5
Beneficiaries, first payments....................	1,000	8,629	8,035	7,033	7,917	7,642	10,053	14,173	10,727	9,475
Average duration of benefits [2]..................	Weeks	13.4	14.7	13.7	15.3	15.2	14.9	18.8	18.9	17.5
Claimants exhausting benefits...................	1,000	2,323	2,662	2,144	2,856	2,671	3,424	7,530	6,365	4,837
Percent of first payment [3]....................	Percent	29.4	34.3	31.8	35.9	35.6	41.5	55.3	53.4	48.8
Contributions collected [4].........................	Bil. dol.	15.2	22.0	19.9	34.8	31.7	30.0	28.2	35.9	44.1
Benefits paid...................................	Bil. dol.	17.3	20.1	19.4	29.3	30.5	40.7	75.9	53.8	43.2
Unemployment trust fund reserves [5].............	Bil. dol.	38.4	35.4	54.1	29.0	38.3	30.0	11.1	9.5	11.3
Average employer tax rate [6]......................	Percent	1.95	2.44	1.75	2.86	2.44	2.25	2.29	3.00	3.40

[1] Insured unemployment as percent of average covered employment. [2] Weeks compensated during the year divided by the number of first payments. May include more than one period of continuous unemployment. [3] Based on first payments for 12-month period ending June 30. [4] Contributions collected through unemployment taxes paid by employers and by employees in states that tax workers. [5] Reserves as of December 31 are the funds on deposit in a State's account - as reported by the U.S. Treasury. Trust fund balances are the major portion of reserves. The reserves for all States have been adjusted to contain amounts loaned or advanced from the Federal Unemployment Account. These advances, which can be used only for the payment of unemployment benefits, must be repaid. [6] As percent of taxable wages.

Source: U.S. Department of Labor, Employment and Training Administration, "Unemployment Insurance Financial Data Handbook," <http://www.ows.doleta.gov/unemploy/hb394.asp>, accessed April 2013.

Table 582. State Unemployment Insurance by State and Other Areas: 2011

[Beneficiaries, first payments in thousands (9,475 represents 9,475,000); benefits paid in millions (43,241 represents 43,241,000,000). See headnote, Table 581. For state data on insured unemployment, see Table 657]

State and other areas	Beneficiaries, first payments (1,000)	Benefits paid (mil. dol.)	Avg. weekly unemployment benefits (dol.)	State and other areas	Beneficiaries, first payments (1,000)	Benefits paid (mil. dol.)	Avg. weekly unemployment benefits (dol.)
Total...............	9,475	43,241	296	MT..................	31	131	262
AL....................	126	353	205	NE..................	46	160	256
AK....................	37	154	242	NV..................	107	564	307
AZ....................	155	535	211	NH..................	33	127	275
AR....................	93	341	279	NJ..................	360	2,369	392
CA....................	1,344	6,429	293	NM..................	50	268	293
CO....................	129	673	335	NY..................	628	3,083	302
CT....................	162	793	327	NC..................	309	1,316	291
DE....................	26	120	241	ND..................	16	66	320
DC....................	28	148	296	OH..................	270	1,278	292
FL....................	376	1,509	231	OK..................	65	273	268
GA....................	269	873	269	OR..................	174	806	288
HI....................	36	245	413	PA..................	530	2,969	335
ID....................	64	204	250	RI..................	45	284	378
IL....................	418	2,231	309	SC..................	128	423	237
IN....................	197	764	295	SD..................	11	39	253
IA....................	108	448	316	TN..................	176	573	235
KS....................	85	312	322	TX..................	494	2,220	316
KY....................	122	519	287	UT..................	63	257	313
LA....................	102	361	196	VT..................	25	106	297
ME....................	44	175	274	VA..................	136	605	284
MD....................	139	749	323	WA..................	236	1,187	374
MA....................	255	1,573	388	WV..................	49	188	250
MI....................	361	1,466	290	WI..................	284	1,014	270
MN....................	172	798	346	WY..................	18	86	329
MS....................	71	204	190	PR..................	101	226	117
MO....................	168	632	238	VI..................	3	14	308

Source: U.S. Department of Labor, Employment and Training Administration, "Unemployment Insurance Financial Data Handbook," <http://www.ows.doleta.gov/unemploy/hb394.asp>, accessed April 2013.

Table 583. Persons With Work Disability by Selected Characteristics: 2011

[In thousands, except percent (22,327 represents 22,327,000). As of March. Covers civilian noninstitutional population. Persons are classified as having a work disability if they: (1) have a health problem or disability which prevents them from working or which limits the kind or amount of work they can do; (2) ever retired or left job for health reasons; (3) are not in labor force due to disability; (4) did not work in previous year due to illness or disability; (5) are under age 65 and are covered by Medicare or Supplemental Security Income; or (6) who received Veterans Administration disability income in previous year. Based on Current Population Survey; see text, Section 1 and Appendix III]

Age	Total [1]	Male	Female	White alone [2]	Black alone [2]	Hispanic [3]
Persons with work disability	**22,327**	**10,796**	**11,531**	**16,386**	**4,462**	**2,838**
16 to 24 years old	1,873	1,025	848	1,319	407	398
25 to 34 years old	2,617	1,260	1,358	1,829	596	387
35 to 44 years old	3,373	1,613	1,760	2,390	716	512
45 to 54 years old	6,001	2,846	3,155	4,325	1,287	689
55 to 64 years old	8,463	4,052	4,411	6,524	1,456	852
Percent work-disabled of for each age group—						
16 to 24 years old	4.8	5.2	4.4	4.5	6.8	5.0
25 to 34 years old	6.4	6.2	6.6	5.9	11.0	4.6
35 to 44 years old	8.4	8.2	8.6	7.7	13.8	7.0
45 to 54 years old	13.6	13.2	13.9	12.2	23.4	12.3
55 to 64 years old	22.5	22.4	22.7	21.0	35.9	25.4

[1] Includes other races, not shown separately. [2] Refers to people who reported specified race and did not report any other race category. [3] Hispanic persons may be of any race.

Source: U.S. Census Bureau, Current Population Survey, "CPS Table Creator," <http://www.census.gov/cps/data/cpstablecreator.html>, accessed April 2013. See also <http://www.census.gov/people/disability/>.

Table 584. Workers' Compensation Payments: 1990 to 2011

[In billions of dollars, except as indicated (53.1 represents $53,100,000,000). See headnote, Table 586]

Item	1990	1995	2000	2005	2006	2007	2008	2009	2010	2011
Workers covered (mil.)	105.5	112.8	127.1	128.2	130.3	131.7	130.6	124.9	124.5	125.8
Premium amounts paid [1]	**53.1**	**57.1**	**60.1**	**89.3**	**86.7**	**86.2**	**79.9**	**73.8**	**71.9**	**77.1**
Private carriers [1]	35.1	31.6	35.7	50.7	51.3	52.1	47.3	43.0	42.2	45.7
State funds	8.0	10.5	8.8	18.2	15.6	13.9	12.2	10.6	9.8	10.1
Federal programs [2]	2.2	2.6	3.6	4.1	4.1	4.2	4.3	4.1	4.2	4.4
Self-insurers	7.9	12.5	11.9	16.4	15.7	16.0	16.1	16.1	15.7	16.9
Annual benefits paid [1]	**38.2**	**42.1**	**47.7**	**57.1**	**54.9**	**56.4**	**58.4**	**58.5**	**58.2**	**60.2**
By private carriers [1]	22.2	20.1	26.9	29.0	27.9	29.4	30.8	31.1	31.2	32.2
From state funds [3]	5.9	7.7	7.4	11.1	10.6	10.2	10.3	9.9	9.8	9.8
Federal employees [3]	2.9	3.1	3.0	3.3	3.3	3.3	3.4	3.5	3.7	3.8
Employers' self-insurance [4]	7.2	11.2	10.5	13.7	13.1	13.5	13.9	14.0	13.6	14.4
Type of benefit:										
Medical/hospitalization	15.2	16.7	20.9	26.4	26.2	27.1	28.7	28.2	28.6	29.9
Compensation payments	23.1	25.4	26.8	30.7	28.7	29.3	29.7	30.3	29.6	30.3
Percent of covered payroll: [1]										
Workers' compensation costs	2.18	1.83	1.34	1.71	1.56	1.47	1.34	1.30	1.24	1.27
Benefits	1.57	1.35	1.06	1.09	0.99	0.96	0.98	1.03	1.00	1.00

[1] Premium and benefit amounts include estimated payments under insurance policy deductible provisions. Deductible benefits are allocated to private carriers and state funds. [2] Years 1990–1995 include federal employer compensation program and that portion of federal black lung benefits program financed from employer contributions. Years 2000–2009 include federal employer compensation program only due to changes in reporting methods. [3] Net cash and medical benefits paid by competitive and exclusive state funds and by federal workers' compensation programs. [4] Cash and medical benefits paid by self-insurers, plus value of medical benefits paid by employers carrying workers' compensation policies that exclude standard medical coverage.

Source: National Academy of Social Insurance, Washington, DC, *Workers' Compensation: Benefits, Coverage, and Costs, 2011*, and earlier reports ©. See also <http://www.nasi.org>.

Table 585. Supplemental Security Income—Recipients and Payments: 1990 to 2011

[Recipients in thousands (4,817 represents 4,817,000); payments in millions of dollars (16,133 represents $16,133,000,000); except as noted. Recipients and monthly payment as of December. Total payments for calendar year. Includes persons with a federal SSI payment and/or federally administered state supplementation. See also Appendix III]

Program	Unit	1990	1995	2000	2005	2007	2008	2009	2010	2011
Recipients, total	**1,000**	**4,817**	**6,514**	**6,602**	**7,114**	**7,360**	**7,521**	**7,677**	**7,912**	**8,113**
Aged	1,000	1,454	1,446	1,289	1,214	1,205	1,203	1,186	1,184	1,182
Blind	1,000	84	84	79	75	72	70	69	69	69
Disabled	1,000	3,279	4,984	5,234	5,825	6,083	6,247	6,421	6,659	6,862
Payments, total [1]	**Mil. dol.**	**16,133**	**27,037**	**30,672**	**37,236**	**41,205**	**43,040**	**46,592**	**48,195**	**49,520**
Aged	Mil. dol.	3,559	4,239	4,540	4,965	5,301	5,379	5,569	5,454	5,431
Blind	Mil. dol.	329	367	386	414	419	416	427	423	422
Disabled	Mil. dol.	12,245	22,431	25,746	31,857	35,485	37,246	40,597	42,317	43,667
Average monthly payment, total	**Dollars**	**276**	**335**	**379**	**439**	**468**	**478**	**499**	**501**	**502**
Aged	Dollars	208	250	300	360	384	393	399	400	398
Blind	Dollars	319	355	413	475	500	508	520	522	520
Disabled	Dollars	303	358	398	455	485	494	517	518	519

[1] Totals for Aged, Blind, and Disabled are derived. The derivation creates slight discrepancies between the sum of the group totals and total payments.

Source: U.S. Social Security Administration, *Annual Statistical Supplement to the Social Security Bulletin, 2012*, released February 2013. See also <http://www.ssa.gov/policy/docs/statcomps/>.

Table 586. Workers' Compensation Payments by State: 2000 to 2011

[In millions of dollars (47,699 represents $47,699,000,000). Calendar-year data. Payments represent compensation and medical benefits and include insurance losses paid by private insurance carriers; disbursements of state funds; and self-insurance payments. See source for data estimation methodology]

State	2000	2005	2009	2010	2011	State	2000	2005	2009	2010	2011
Total................	47,699	57,067	58,490	58,168	60,210	Montana................	155	227	261	267	253
Alabama................	529	620	626	629	616	Nebraska................	230	306	300	314	321
Alaska................	139	183	221	221	239	Nevada................	347	457	431	430	381
Arizona................	498	571	657	702	712	New Hampshire........	177	229	247	252	227
Arkansas................	214	227	215	203	189	New Jersey............	1,378	1,702	1,991	2,058	2,169
California................	9,449	10,868	9,651	9,664	10,477	New Mexico............	144	259	246	276	276
Colorado................	810	932	837	803	761	New York............	2,761	3,378	4,137	4,606	5,097
Connecticut............	638	720	843	795	866	North Carolina........	865	1,382	1,414	1,351	1,420
Delaware................	118	215	206	212	220	North Dakota............	70	82	111	115	126
District of Columbia......	78	92	105	105	111	Ohio................	2,099	2,447	2,353	2,269	2,233
Florida................	2,577	3,474	2,899	2,545	2,711	Oklahoma................	485	638	786	844	839
Georgia................	965	1,409	1,527	1,452	1,390	Oregon................	425	555	618	632	569
Hawaii................	231	251	244	242	247	Pennsylvania............	2,379	2,741	2,901	2,909	2,894
Idaho................	114	243	243	237	245	Rhode Island............	127	137	161	160	168
Illinois................	1,944	2,419	3,056	2,990	3,074	South Carolina............	515	925	892	891	874
Indiana................	545	569	597	599	625	South Dakota............	63	86	94	100	91
Iowa................	343	487	552	558	627	Tennessee................	774	862	781	784	784
Kansas................	323	390	416	405	436	Texas................	2,160	1,597	1,592	1,500	1,604
Kentucky................	584	703	684	662	656	Utah................	172	257	274	243	257
Louisiana................	547	705	831	832	870	Vermont................	101	122	144	137	137
Maine................	245	281	261	251	252	Virginia................	597	852	859	778	875
Maryland................	641	784	896	954	1,007	Washington............	1,527	1,848	2,312	2,309	2,317
Massachusetts............	801	922	951	1,013	963	West Virginia............	661	765	519	509	506
Michigan................	1,474	1,474	1,510	1,272	1,301	Wisconsin................	765	1,170	1,116	1,072	1,100
Minnesota................	798	949	1,072	1,035	1,011	Wyoming................	89	117	137	163	162
Mississippi	293	290	322	338	334						
Missouri................	780	892	850	806	814	**Federal total** [1]........	2,957	3,258	3,543	3,672	3,777

[1] Federal benefits include: those paid under the Federal Employees' Compensation Act for civilian employees; the portion of the black lung benefit program that is financed by employers; and a portion of benefits under the Longshore and Harbor Workers' Compensation Act (LHWCA) that are not reflected in state data, namely, benefits paid by self-insured employers and by special funds under the LHWCA. See Appendix H of source for more information about federal programs.

Source: National Academy of Social Insurance, Washington, DC, *Workers' Compensation: Benefits, Coverage, and Costs, 2011*, and earlier reports ©. See also <http://www.nasi.org>.

Table 587. Supplemental Security Income (SSI)—Recipients and Payments by State and Other Area: 2000 to 2011

[Recipients as of December (6,602 represents 6,602,000); payments for calendar year ($30,672 represents $30,672,000,000). Data cover federal SSI payments and/or federally administered state supplementation. For explanation of methodology, see Appendix III]

State and other area	Recipients (1,000)		Payments for the year (mil. dol.)			State and other area	Recipients (1,000)		Payments for the year (mil. dol.)		
	2000	2011	2000	2005	2011		2000	2011	2000	2005	2011
Total [1]............	**6,602**	**8,113**	**30,672**	**37,236**	**49,520**	MO................	112	137	471	573	800
U.S.................	**6,601**	**8,112**	**30,669**	**37,232**	**49,514**	MT................	14	18	57	70	102
AL....................	159	175	659	776	1,009	NE................	21	27	85	103	150
AK....................	9	13	37	53	73	NV................	25	44	108	163	259
AZ....................	81	113	355	482	670	NH................	12	19	49	67	110
AR....................	85	110	333	407	623	NJ................	146	173	672	763	1,024
CA....................	1,088	1,286	6,386	8,146	8,951	NM................	47	62	193	248	346
CO....................	54	69	228	264	402	NY................	617	690	3,197	3,561	4,497
CT....................	49	60	216	260	356	NC................	191	225	732	894	1,270
DE....................	12	16	50	66	94	ND................	8	8	30	33	44
DC....................	20	26	93	113	169	OH................	240	295	1,114	1,295	1,855
FL....................	377	506	1,621	2,031	2,911	OK................	72	96	302	381	554
GA....................	197	239	785	944	1,384	OR................	52	78	228	298	459
HI....................	21	25	104	119	160	PA................	284	367	1,367	1,659	2,287
ID....................	18	28	76	106	160	RI................	28	32	130	161	192
IL....................	249	276	1,174	1,337	1,676	SC................	107	115	429	488	654
IN....................	88	122	382	488	746	SD................	13	14	48	55	77
IA....................	40	49	158	193	273	TN................	164	179	664	752	1,054
KS....................	36	47	151	187	279	TX................	409	640	1,575	2,191	3,486
KY....................	174	193	741	862	1,119	UT................	20	29	87	110	170
LA....................	166	179	715	771	1,022	VT................	13	16	51	63	90
ME....................	30	36	116	146	203	VA................	132	151	535	632	857
MD....................	88	111	400	481	689	WA................	101	143	484	616	905
MA....................	168	198	807	902	1,246	WV................	71	81	318	376	477
MI....................	210	265	988	1,157	1,657	WI................	85	111	357	437	642
MN....................	64	89	272	355	535	WY................	6	7	23	26	36
MS....................	129	126	512	572	710	N. Marianas......	1	1	3	4	6

[1] Includes Northern Mariana Islands.

Source: U.S. Social Security Administration, *Annual Statistical Supplement to the Social Security Bulletin, 2012*, February 2013. See also <http://www.ssa.gov/policy/docs/statcomps/>.

Table 588. Percent of Workers Participating in Defined Benefit Retirement Plans by Plan Type and Accrual Status: 2012

[In percent. As of March. All workers participating in defined benefit plans = 100 percent. Based on the March 2012 National Compensation Survey; survey drew responses from 6,618 private industry establishments of all sizes, representing about 103.9 million workers. Excludes farm and private households, the self-employed, Federal government, and establishments with no workers in the survey scope. For more information, see Appendix III, and source, <http://www.bls.gov/ncs/ebs/glossary20112012.htm> and <http://www.bls.gov/ncs/ebs/sp/ebnr0018.txt>]

Characteristics	Type of Plan		Frozen plans, by accrual status		
	Open plans [1]	Frozen plans [2]	All participants accrue benefits	Some participants accrue benefits	No participants accrue benefits
All workers	**75**	**25**	**62**	**7**	**31**
Occupation					
Management, professional, and related	70	30	66	6	28
Management, business, and financial	71	29	63	5	32
Professional and related	70	30	69	7	25
Service	84	16	58	(S)	(S)
Protective service	55	45	73	(S)	(S)
Sales and office	72	28	51	7	42
Sales and related	65	35	52	12	37
Office and administrative support	74	26	51	5	44
Natural resources, construction, and maintenance	89	11	77	(S)	(S)
Construction, extraction, farming, fishing, and forestry	94	6	84	(S)	(S)
Installation, maintenance, and repair	84	16	75	5	20
Production, transportation, and material moving	78	22	64	(S)	(S)
Production	69	31	70	(S)	(S)
Transportation and material moving	85	15	53	(S)	(S)
Work status					
Full time	74	26	62	8	31
Part time	85	15	62	5	33
Union status					
Union	87	13	73	(S)	(S)
Nonunion	68	32	59	7	34
Average wage percentile: [3]					
Lowest 25 percent	79	21	56	(S)	(S)
Lowest 10 percent	85	15	65	(S)	(S)
Second 25 percent	76	24	53	8	39
Third 25 percent	78	22	54	9	38
Highest 25 percent	73	27	69	7	24
Highest 10 percent	69	31	70	6	24
Industry					
Goods-producing industries	71	29	69	(S)	(S)
Construction	97	3	(NA)	(NA)	(NA)
Manufacturing	65	35	70	(S)	(S)
Service-providing industries	77	23	59	6	35
Trade, transportation, and utilities	79	21	72	(S)	(S)
Information	60	40	61	(S)	(S)
Financial activities	70	30	32	7	61
Professional and business services	81	19	70	(S)	(S)
Education and health services	80	20	70	(S)	(S)

NA Not available. S Data does not meet publication standards. [1] Plans open to new participants. [2] Plans closed to new workers, or plans that ceased accruals for some or all plan participants. [3] Categories are based on the average wage for each occupation surveyed, which may include workers with earnings both above and below the threshold. Average wages are based on estimates published in the "National Compensation Survey: Occupational Earnings in the United States, 2010." See source for details.

Source: U.S. Bureau of Labor Statistics, *National Compensation Survey: Employee Benefits in the United States, March 2012*, September 2012. See also <http://www.bls.gov/ncs/ebs/>.

Table 589. Temporary Assistance for Needy Families (TANF)—Families and Recipients: 1980 to 2012

[In thousands (3,712 represents 3,712,000). Average monthly families and recipients for calendar year. Prior to TANF, the cash assistance program to families was called Aid to Families with Dependent Children (1980–1996). Under the Personal Responsibility and Work Opportunity Reconciliation Act of 1996, the program became TANF. See text, this section. Includes Puerto Rico, Guam, and Virgin Islands]

Year	Families	Recipients	Year	Families	Recipients	Year	Families	Recipients
1980	3,712	10,774	1997	3,740	10,376	2005	1,894	4,469
1985	3,701	10,855	1998	3,050	8,347	2006	1,777	4,148
1990	4,057	11,695	1999	2,554	6,824	2007	1,674	3,897
1992	4,829	13,773	2000	2,215	5,778	2008	1,633	3,795
1993	5,012	14,205	2001	2,104	5,359	2009	1,769	4,154
1994	5,033	14,161	2002	2,048	5,069	2010	1,858	4,403
1995	4,791	13,418	2003	2,024	4,929	2011	1,846	4,363
1996	4,434	12,321	2004	1,979	4,748	2012	1,723	4,017

Source: U.S. Department of Health and Human Services, Administration for Children and Families, Temporary Assistance for Needy Families, "Caseload Data," <http://www.acf.hhs.gov/programs/ofa/data-reports>, accessed April 2013. See also <http://www.acf.hhs.gov/programs/ofa/>.

Table 590. Temporary Assistance for Needy Families (TANF)—Recipients by State and Other Areas: 2000 to 2012

[In thousands (2,215 represents 2,215,000). Average monthly families and recipients for calendar year. See headnote, Table 589]

State or other area	Families 2000	Families 2011	Families 2012	Recipients 2000	Recipients 2011	Recipients 2012	State or other area	Families 2000	Families 2011	Families 2012	Recipients 2000	Recipients 2011	Recipients 2012
Total [1]	2,215	1,846	1,723	5,778	4,363	4,017	MT	5	3	3	13	9	8
U.S.	2,181	1,828	1,707	5,678	4,316	3,974	NE	9	6	6	24	15	13
AL	19	23	21	45	56	51	NV	6	11	11	16	28	27
AK	7	4	4	21	10	10	NH	6	5	4	14	10	8
AZ	33	18	18	84	40	40	NJ	50	35	34	125	84	82
AR	12	8	7	29	18	17	NM	23	20	17	69	51	44
CA	489	599	573	1,262	1,463	1,385	NY	250	123	122	695	279	277
CO	11	13	14	28	32	37	NC	45	23	21	98	44	41
CT	27	16	15	64	32	30	ND	3	2	2	7	4	4
DE	6	5	5	12	15	15	OH	95	96	77	235	215	160
DC	17	8	6	45	23	15	OK	14	9	8	35	20	19
FL	65	53	53	142	94	94	OR	17	30	27	38	79	68
GA	52	20	19	125	37	36	PA	88	65	77	241	163	190
HI	14	9	10	46	27	28	RI	16	7	6	44	16	16
ID	1	2	2	2	3	3	SC	18	17	14	42	40	31
IL	78	30	31	234	88	87	SD	3	3	3	7	7	7
IN	37	25	15	101	58	32	TN	57	61	55	147	153	136
IA	20	17	16	53	44	40	TX	129	49	44	347	111	101
KS	13	14	10	32	37	26	UT	8	6	5	21	14	11
KY	38	31	30	87	63	61	VT	6	3	3	16	6	7
LA	27	10	9	71	24	20	VA	31	33	31	69	73	68
ME	11	11	9	28	26	20	WA	56	59	51	148	139	120
MD	29	25	24	71	61	57	WV	13	10	9	33	23	21
MA	43	50	50	100	99	98	WI	17	26	25	38	63	60
MI	72	62	42	198	158	100	WY	1	–	–	1	1	1
MN	39	23	22	114	49	48	PR	30	16	14	88	43	38
MS	15	12	11	34	25	23	GU	3	1	1	10	3	3
MO	47	36	34	125	86	82	VI	1	–	–	3	1	1

– Represents or rounds to zero. [1] Includes Puerto Rico, Guam, and the Virgin Islands.

Source: U.S. Department of Health and Human Services, Administration for Children and Families, Temporary Assistance for Needy Families, "Caseload Data," <http://www.acf.hhs.gov/programs/ofa/data-reports>, accessed April 2013. See also <http://www.acf.hhs.gov/programs/ofa/>.

Table 591. Temporary Assistance for Needy Families (TANF)—Expenditures by State: 2000 to 2011

[In millions of dollars (24,781 represents $24,781,000,000). Represents federal and state funds expended in fiscal year]

State	2000, Total	2005, Total	2011 Total [1]	2011 Expenditures on assistance	State	2000, Total	2005, Total	2011 Total [1]	2011 Expenditures on assistance
U.S............	24,781	25,580	30,624	11,131	MO............	321	299	323	91
AL.............	96	123	185	61	MT............	44	44	44	20
AK.............	93	74	66	47	NE............	79	78	112	28
AZ.............	261	299	359	88	NV............	69	70	119	47
AR.............	139	67	187	16	NH............	73	63	78	44
CA.............	6,481	5,882	6,675	4,221	NJ............	321	994	1,184	300
CO.............	205	214	318	83	NM............	149	127	192	81
CT.............	436	459	483	98	NY............	3,512	3,970	4,954	1,847
DE.............	55	61	79	35	NC............	440	448	629	75
DC.............	157	156	250	77	ND............	33	34	35	20
FL.............	781	868	834	196	OH............	995	990	1,187	440
GA.............	386	520	562	86	OK............	130	174	173	68
HI.............	162	128	317	78	OR............	169	269	343	201
ID.............	43	40	26	5	PA............	1,327	1,190	943	202
IL.............	879	998	1,311	111	RI............	172	168	140	36
IN.............	342	307	292	72	SC............	245	230	237	39
IA.............	163	162	196	84	SD............	21	30	31	23
KS.............	151	154	213	96	TN............	293	233	361	156
KY.............	203	216	247	161	TX............	727	851	810	159
LA.............	118	186	277	85	UT............	100	108	116	40
ME.............	108	127	130	99	VT............	62	68	73	24
MD.............	336	349	455	88	VA............	418	290	288	123
MA.............	690	689	1,022	337	WA............	535	525	1,063	306
MI.............	1,264	1,175	1,377	194	WV............	134	124	172	74
MN.............	381	392	434	95	WI............	382	446	577	128
MS.............	62	79	110	32	WY............	34	32	37	15

[1] Includes other items not shown separately.

Source: U.S. Department of Health and Human Services, Administration for Children and Families, Temporary Assistance for Needy Families, "Financial Data," <http://www.acf.hhs.gov/programs/ofa/data-reports>, accessed April 2013. See also <http://www.acf.hhs.gov/programs/ofa/>.

Table 592. Federal Food Programs: 1990 to 2012

[20.0 represents 20,000,000, except as noted. For fiscal years ending September 30. Program data include Puerto Rico, Virgin Islands, Guam, American Samoa, Northern Marianas, and the former Trust Territory when a federal food program was operated in these areas. Participation data are average monthly figures except as noted. Participants are not reported for programs. Cost data are direct federal benefits to recipients; they exclude federal administrative payments and applicable state and local contributions. Federal costs for commodities and cash in-lieu of commodities are shown separately from direct cash benefits for those programs receiving both]

Program	Unit	1990	2000	2005	2008	2009	2010	2011	2012
Supplemental nutrition assistance program (SNAP): [1]									
Participants........................	Million	20.0	17.2	25.6	28.2	33.5	40.3	44.7	46.6
Federal cost.......................	Mil. dol.	14,143	14,983	28,568	34,608	50,360	64,702	71,811	74,619
Monthly average coupon value per recipient.......	Dollars	58.78	72.62	92.89	102.19	125.31	133.79	133.85	133.41
Nutrition assistance program for Puerto Rico: [2]									
Federal cost.......................	Mil. dol.	937	1,268	1,495	1,623	2,001	2,001	2,001	2,001
National school lunch program (NSLP):									
Free lunches served...............	Million	1,662	2,205	2,477	2,610	2,723	2,950	3,065	3,107
Reduced-price lunches served........	Million	273	409	479	521	519	496	443	448
Children participating [3]............	Million	24.1	27.3	29.6	31.0	31.3	31.8	31.8	31.6
Federal cost.......................	Mil. dol.	3,214	5,493	7,055	8,265	8,875	9,752	10,106	10,410
School breakfast (SB):									
Children participating [3]............	Million	4.1	7.6	9.4	10.6	11.1	11.7	12.2	12.9
Federal cost.......................	Mil. dol.	596	1,393	1,927	2,366	2,583	2,859	3,035	3,276
Special supplemental food program (WIC): [4]									
Participants........................	Million	4.5	7.2	8.0	8.7	9.1	9.2	9.0	8.9
Federal cost for food...............	Mil. dol.	1,637	2,853	3,603	4,534	4,641	4,563	5,018	4,809
Child and adult care (CAC): [5]									
Participants [6].....................	Million	1.5	2.7	3.1	3.3	3.3	3.4	3.4	3.6
Federal cost.......................	Mil. dol.	719	1,500	1,904	2,169	2,289	2,398	2,472	2,589
Federal cost of commodities donated to— [7]									
Child nutrition (NSLP, CACFP, and SFS) [8]......	Mil. dol.	644	704	1,045	1,139	1,214	1,222	1,298	1,272
TEFAP [9]...........................	Mil. dol.	282	182	314	226	553	566	462	378

[1] The program name was changed from Food Stamp to Supplemental Nutrition Assistance (SNAP) in October 2008. [2] Puerto Rico receives a grant in lieu of SNAP benefits. [3] Average participation per day (excluding summer months of June through August). Includes children in public and private elementary and secondary schools and in residential child care institutes. [4] WIC serves pregnant and postpartum women, infants, and children up to age 5. [5] CACFP provides year-round subsidies to feed preschool children in child care centers and family day care homes. Certain care centers serving disabled or elderly adults also receive meal subsidies. [6] Average quarterly daily attendance at participating institutions. [7] Includes the federal cost of commodity entitlements, cash-in-lieu of commodities, and bonus foods. [8] May include NSLP, CACFP, and Summer Food Service. [9] The Emergency Food Assistance Program distributes foods through nonprofit local emergency feeding organizations. Includes Bonus and Entitlement foods. Administrative cost is excluded.

Source: U.S. Department of Agriculture, "Food and Nutrition Service, Data and Statistics," <http://www.fns.usda.gov/data-and-statistics>, accessed April 2013.

Social Insurance and Human Services 387

Table 593. Federal Supplemental Nutrition Assistance Program (SNAP) by State: 2000 to 2012

[17,194 represents 17,194,000. Participation data are average monthly number participating in year ending September 30]

State	Persons (1,000)			Benefits (mil.dol.)			State	Persons (1,000)			Benefits (mil.dol.)		
	2000	2005	2012	2000	2005	2012		2000	2005	2012	2000	2005	2012
Total [1]......	**17,194**	**25,628**	**46,609**	**14,983**	**28,568**	**74,619**	MO..........	423	677	948	358	736	1,462
U.S..........	**17,156**	**25,588**	**46,541**	**14,927**	**28,493**	**74,453**	MT..........	59	81	126	51	89	193
AL.............	396	559	910	344	616	1,390	NE..........	82	117	176	61	120	259
AK.............	38	56	91	46	80	186	NV..........	61	122	355	57	129	525
AZ.............	259	550	1,124	240	634	1,707	NH..........	36	52	117	28	51	166
AR.............	247	374	502	206	401	733	NJ..........	345	392	826	304	437	1,321
CA.............	1,831	1,992	3,964	1,639	2,315	7,090	NM..........	169	241	438	140	251	674
CO.............	156	246	492	127	313	809	NY..........	1,439	1,755	3,077	1,361	2,136	5,444
CT.............	165	204	403	138	223	697	NC..........	488	800	1,669	403	856	2,430
DE.............	32	62	148	31	65	227	ND..........	32	42	59	25	45	91
DC.............	81	89	141	77	103	233	OH..........	610	1,007	1,808	520	1,155	3,007
FL.............	882	1,382	3,353	771	1,598	5,592	OK..........	253	424	615	208	440	947
GA.............	559	921	1,913	489	1,048	3,119	OR..........	234	429	815	198	456	1,254
HI.............	118	94	177	166	156	453	PA..........	777	1,043	1,799	656	1,105	2,773
ID.............	58	93	233	46	103	361	RI..........	74	76	173	59	79	289
IL.............	817	1,158	1,870	777	1,400	3,129	SC..........	295	521	870	249	566	1,371
IN.............	300	556	909	268	627	1,444	SD..........	43	56	104	37	61	165
IA.............	123	207	408	100	220	593	TN..........	496	850	1,317	415	942	2,089
KS.............	117	178	305	83	180	457	TX..........	1,333	2,442	4,038	1,215	2,659	6,007
KY.............	403	570	849	337	611	1,299	UT..........	82	133	277	68	141	405
LA.............	500	808	949	448	979	1,550	VT..........	41	45	97	32	45	141
ME.............	102	153	253	81	162	377	VA..........	336	488	914	263	500	1,404
MD.............	219	289	716	199	320	1,104	WA..........	295	508	1,108	241	539	1,685
MA.............	232	368	862	182	363	1,370	WV..........	227	262	347	185	258	500
MI.............	603	1,048	1,828	457	1,099	2,980	WI..........	193	346	835	129	317	1,168
MN.............	196	260	539	165	275	750	WY..........	22	25	34	19	27	52
MS.............	276	435	660	226	463	980							

[1] Includes Guam and the Virgin Islands. Several outlying areas receive nutrition assistance grants in lieu of SNAP (Puerto Rico, American Samoa, and the Northern Marianas).

Source: U.S. Department of Agriculture, Food and Nutrition Service, Program Data, Supplemental Nutrition Assistance Program, <http://www.fns.usda.gov/pd/snapmain.htm>, accessed April 2013.

Table 594. Selected Characteristics of Supplemental Nutrition Assistance Program (SNAP) Households and Participants: 1990 to 2011

[7,811 represents 7,811,000. For fiscal years ending September 30. Data for 1990 exclude Guam and the Virgin Islands. Based on a sample of households from the SNAP Quality Control System]

Year	Households				Participants		
	Total [1] (1,000)	Percent of total			Total (1,000)	Percent of total	
		With children	With elderly [2]	With disabled [3]		Children	Elderly [2]
1990......................	7,811	60.3	18.1	8.9	20,440	49.6	7.7
1995......................	10,883	59.7	16.0	18.9	26,955	51.5	7.1
2000......................	7,335	53.9	21.0	27.5	17,091	51.3	10.0
2005......................	10,852	53.7	17.1	23.0	24,794	49.9	8.2
2008......................	12,464	50.6	18.5	22.6	27,607	48.4	9.1
2009......................	14,981	49.9	16.6	21.2	32,889	47.5	8.3
2010......................	18,369	48.7	15.5	19.8	39,759	46.6	7.9
2011......................	20,803	47.1	16.5	20.2	44,148	45.1	8.5

[1] Total does not include those who are ineligible or those receiving disaster benefits. [2] Persons 60 years old and over. [3] The substantial increase in 1995 and decrease in 2005 are due in part to the changes in definition of a disabled household. Prior to 1995, disabled households were defined as households with SSI income but no members over age 59. In 1995, that definition changed to households with at least one member under 65 who received SSI, or at least one member aged 18–61 who received Social Security, veterans' benefits, or other government benefits as a result of a disability. In 2003, the definition of a disabled household changed to households with either SSI income, or a medical expense deduction and without an elderly person, and households containing a nonelderly adult working fewer than 30 hours per week and receiving Social Security, veterans' benefits, or workers' compensation.

Source: U.S. Department of Agriculture, Food and Nutrition Service, *Characteristics of SNAP Households: Fiscal Year 2011*, November 2012. See also <http://www.fns.usda.gov/ora/MENU/Published/snap/SNAPParthh.htm>.

Table 595. Supplemental Nutrition Assistance Program (SNAP) Households and Participants—Summary: 2011

[20,803 represents 20,803,000. For fiscal year ending September 30. Based on a sample of households from the Supplemental Nutrition Assistance Program Quality Control (QC) System. Figures are lower than official participation counts because they do not include ineligible participants or those receiving disaster food stamp assistance]

Household type and income source	Households Number (1,000)	Households Percent	Age, sex, race, and ethnicity	Participants Number (1,000)	Participants Percent
Total	**20,803**	**100.0**	**Total**	**44,148**	**100.0**
With children	9,794	47.1	Children	19,927	45.1
Single-parent households	5,477	26.3	Under 5 years old	6,780	15.4
Married-couple households	1,873	9.0	5 to 17 years old	13,147	29.8
Other [1]	2,444	11.7	Nonelderly adults	20,452	46.3
With elderly	3,426	16.5	18 to 35 years old	10,617	24.0
Living alone	2,730	13.1	36 to 59 years old	9,835	22.3
Not living alone	696	3.3	Elderly (60 years old and over)	3,770	8.5
Disabled nonelderly	4,199	20.2			
Living alone	2,382	11.5	Male	19,212	43.5
Not living alone	1,816	8.7	Female	24,936	56.5
Earned income	6,351	30.5	White, non-Hispanic	15,255	34.6
Wages and salaries	5,581	26.8	Black, non-Hispanic	10,160	23.0
			Hispanic	6,814	15.4
Unearned income	12,487	60.0	Asian	1,138	2.6
TANF [2]	1,591	7.6	Native American	1,587	3.6
Supplemental security income	4,195	20.2	Other [3]	9,194	20.8
Social security	4,660	22.4			
No income	4,151	20.0			

[1] Other households with children include other multiple-adult households and children-only households. [2] Temporary Assistance for Needy Families (TANF) program. [3] This category includes respondents who recorded more than one race, and those with no racial/ethnic data.

Source: U.S. Department of Agriculture, Food and Nutrition Service, *Characteristics of SNAP Households: Fiscal Year 2011*, November 2012. See also <http://www.fns.usda.gov/ora/MENU/Published/snap/snapparthh.htm>.

Table 596. Child Support—Award and Recipient Status of Custodial Parents: 2009

[In thousands except as noted (13,672 represents 13,672,000). Custodial parents 15 years and older with own children under 21 years of age as of spring 2010. Covers civilian noninstitutionalized population. Based on Current Population Survey; see text, Section 1 and Appendix III. For definition of mean, see Guide to Tabular Presentation]

Award and recipient status	All custodial parents — Total Number	All custodial parents — Total Percent distribution	All custodial parents — Mothers	All custodial parents — Fathers	Custodial parents below poverty level — Total Number	Custodial parents below poverty level — Total Percent distribution	Custodial parents below poverty level — Mothers	Custodial parents below poverty level — Fathers
Total	**13,672**	**(X)**	**11,237**	**2,435**	**3,876**	**(X)**	**3,420**	**457**
With child support agreement or award [1]	6,914	(X)	6,174	740	1,823	(X)	1,676	146
Supposed to receive payments in 2009	5,897	100.0	5,278	619	1,524	100.0	1,398	125
Actually received payments in 2009	4,174	70.8	3,723	451	1,011	66.3	920	91
Received full amount	2,428	41.2	2,217	211	550	36.1	498	52
Received partial payments	1,745	29.6	1,506	240	461	30.2	421	39
Did not receive payments in 2009	1,724	29.2	1,555	168	513	33.7	478	34
Child support not awarded	6,759	(X)	5,063	1,695	2,054	(X)	1,743	310
MEAN INCOME AND CHILD SUPPORT								
Received child support payments in 2009:								
Mean total money income (dol.)	31,991	(X)	30,018	48,288	8,642	(X)	8,858	6,453
Mean child support received (dol.)	5,135	(X)	5,248	4,202	3,909	(X)	3,822	4,792
Received the full amount due:								
Mean total money income (dol.)	33,337	(X)	32,042	46,948	8,486	(X)	8,835	(NA)
Mean child support received (dol.)	6,928	(X)	6,917	7,036	5,314	(X)	5,073	(NA)
Received partial payments:								
Mean total money income (dol.)	30,119	(X)	27,036	49,466	8,828	(X)	8,885	(NA)
Mean child support received (dol.)	2,642	(X)	2,790	1,712	2,231	(X)	2,342	(NA)
Received no payments in 2009:								
Mean total money income (dol.)	30,210	(X)	29,056	40,869	9,317	(X)	9,139	11,791
Without child support agreement or award:								
Mean total money income (dol.)	28,957	(X)	23,894	44,079	7,537	(X)	7,515	7,661

X Not applicable. NA Not available. [1] As of April of following year (e.g., 2009 data is as of April 2010).

Source: U.S. Census Bureau, *Custodial Mothers and Fathers and Their Child Support: 2009*. See also <http://www.census.gov/people/childsupport/>.

Table 597. Child Support Enforcement Program—Caseload and Finances: 2007 to 2011

[For fiscal years ending September 30. In units as indicated (15,755 represents 15,755,000). Includes Puerto Rico, Guam, and the Virgin Islands. The Office of Child Support (OCSE) locates absent parents, establishes paternity of children, and establishes and enforces support orders. The OCSE does not assist families directly but rather helps child support agencies in the states and tribes to develop, manage and operate their programs. Case types include IV-A cases in which children are eligible for Temporary Assistance for Needy Families (TANF); and IV-E cases in which children are entitled to foster care maintenance; case types reflect Social Security Act Titles IV-A and IV-E. Child support collected for families not receiving TANF goes to the family to help it remain self-sufficient. Most child support collected on behalf of TANF and foster care families goes to Federal and State governments to offset program payments. Some States pass-through a portion of their collections to help families become self-sufficient. Based on data reported by state agencies. Minus sign (-)indicates net outlay]

Item	Unit	2007	2008	2009	2010	2011, prel.
Total cases...	**1,000**	**15,755**	**15,676**	**15,798**	**15,859**	**15,832**
Number of children.................................	1,000	17,121	17,032	17,414	17,509	17,340
Paternities established, total [1]............................	1,000	640	629	643	620	615
Support orders established, total......................	1,000	1,178	1,193	1,267	1,297	1,248
FINANCES						
Total distributed collections.....................	**Mil. dol.**	**24,855**	**26,561**	**26,386**	**26,556**	**27,297**
Total Payments to Families or Foster Care..............	Mil. dol.	22,794	24,173	24,288	24,471	25,117
Total Medical Support................................	Mil. dol.	154	247	260	305	365
Total Passed Through.................................	Mil. dol.	NA	19	117	135	139
Total Fees Withheld by State.......	Mil. dol.	NA	23	35	37	33
Total Assistance Reimbursement [2]......................	Mil. dol.	1,906	2,098	1,686	1,607	1,642
State Share.....................................	Mil. dol.	852	928	741	704	719
Federal Share..................................	Mil. dol.	1,054	1,170	945	903	923
Current Assistance Collections [3].........................	Mil. dol.	946	978	978	1,015	1,010
Former Assistance Collections [4].........................	Mil. dol.	9,470	9,940	9,294	8,971	8,930
Medicaid Never Assistance Collections [5].................	Mil. dol.	3,116	3,723	4,177	4,729	5,535
Never Assistance Collections [6].........................	Mil. dol.	11,322	11,920	11,936	11,840	11,822
Total Administrative Expenditures......................	Mil. dol.	5,594	5,870	5,850	5,776	5,661
Federal Share..................................	Mil. dol.	3,692	3,671	3,887	3,811	3,477
State Share.....................................	Mil. dol.	1,902	2,200	1,963	1,964	2,184
Cost Effectiveness Ratio.............................	Mil. dol.	4.73	4.80	4.78	4.88	5.12

[1] Does not include in-hospital paternities. [2] Total assistance reimbursement equals collections that will be divided between State and Federal governments to reimburse their respective shares of either Title IV-A (TANF) payments or Title IV-E (foster care) maintenance payments. [3] Current assistance collections are made on behalf of families currently receiving Title IV-A (TANF) or Title IV-E (foster care) assistance. [4] Former assistance collections are made on behalf of families formerly receiving Title IV-A (TANF) or Title IV-E (foster care) assistance. [5] Medicaid Never Assistance Collections are those received and distributed on behalf of children who are receiving Child Support Enforcement services under Title IV-D of the Social Security Act, and who are either currently receiving or who have formerly received Medicaid payments under Title XIX of the Social Security Act, but who were not currently receiving and who have never formerly received assistance under either Title IV-A (TANF or AFDC) or Title IV-E (Foster Care) of the Social Security Act. [6] Never Assistance Collections are those made on behalf of families never receiving public assistance under TANF or Foster Care.

Source: U.S. Department of Health and Human Services, Administration for Children & Families, Office of Child Support Enforcement, *Annual Report to Congress, FY2011 Preliminary Report*. See also <http://www.acf.hhs.gov/programs/css/resource/fy2011-preliminary-report>.

Table 598. Head Start—Summary: 2007 to 2012

[Funding data in millions of dollars (6,888.6 represents $6,888,600,000); all other data in thousands (908.4 represents 908,400). For fiscal years. Federal funding and funded enrollment data revised as of June 2013. Data on cumulative enrollment, staff, and volunteers are submitted by Head Start grantees and delegates, and are as of August 31]

Item	2007	2008	2009	2010	2011	2012
Federal funding (million dollars)........	6,888.6	6,878.0	7,112.8	7,234.8	7,559.6	7,968.5
Funded enrollment slots [1]...............	908.4	907.0	904.2	904.1	964.4	956.5
Cumulative enrollment [2]............	**1,070.1**	**1,071.5**	**1,056.8**	**1,117.7**	**1,141.9**	**1,146.5**
Children age 2 and under..............	107.5	112.4	108.1	146.3	174.0	176.4
Children age 3............................	385.0	387.6	378.5	386.7	389.4	388.2
Children age 4............................	535.2	533.6	531.9	548.0	542.1	547.1
Children age 5 and older................	32.0	27.7	28.7	23.2	19.8	18.5
Hispanic/Latino..........................	371.7	382.2	376.1	405.4	420.3	423.8
Non-Hispanic/non-Latino................	698.3	689.3	680.7	712.3	721.6	722.0
American Indian/Alaska Native.........	42.5	43.0	42.8	41.7	44.7	44.2
Asian..	18.6	19.6	18.1	19.0	19.4	20.2
Black/African American.................	321.3	315.2	314.4	326.5	325.0	331.0
Native Hawaiian/Pacific Islander.......	8.2	8.6	6.5	6.9	7.3	7.2
White..	425.0	419.1	417.7	450.3	468.6	473.5
Biracial/multiracial......................	53.0	69.9	81.6	83.9	90.5	97.9
Other/unspecified........................	201.5	196.2	175.7	189.4	186.4	172.5
Total staff................................	214.4	212.5	212.2	228.3	233.4	230.6
Total volunteers...........................	1,372.7	1,319.7	1,277.7	1,335.9	1,324.0	1,315.7
Parent volunteers.......................	910.8	893.3	852.1	881.1	873.2	867.4

[1] Funded enrollment refers to the number of children and pregnant women supported by federal Head Start funds in a program at any one time during the program year. Data are derived from the annual Administration for Children and Families budget and congressional documents, and do not reflect changes made during the program year. [2] Cumulative enrollment refers to actual number of children and pregnant women served throughout the program year, including enrollees who left during the program year and enrollees who filled those empty slots. More children and families may receive Head Start services cumulatively throughout the program year than indicated by funded enrollment numbers.

Source: U.S. Department of Health and Human Services, Administration for Children and Families, Early Childhood Learning & Knowledge Center, "Head Start Program Facts Sheets," <http://eclkc.ohs.acf.hhs.gov/hslc/mr/factsheets>, and "Office of Head Start Enterprise System," <https://hses.ohs.acf.hhs.gov/pir/welcome>; accessed September 2013.

Table 599. Selected Characteristics of Support Provided on Behalf of Children Under 21 Years Old Living in Another Household by Gender of Provider: 2010

[Numbers in thousands (4,547 represents 5,547,000), except as noted. Data are for whole year. Based on Survey of Income and Program Participation (SIPP), 2008 Panel, Wave 6, May–August 2010. Estimates are based on responses from a sample of the population, and may differ from the actual values because of sampling variability and other factors. Apparent differences between the estimates of two or more groups may not be statistically different]

| Characteristics | Providers on Behalf of Children Under Age 21 | | | | | | | | |
| | Total | | | Male providers | | | Female providers | | |
	Total providers	Percent of providers	Median support provided (dollars)	Total	Percent of providers	Median support provided (dollars)	Total	Percent of providers	Median support provided (dollars)
Total [1]	**4,547**	**100.0**	**3,600**	**3,881**	**100.0**	**3,900**	**666**	**100.0**	**2,400**
NUMBER OF CHILDREN SUPPORTED									
1 child	2,658	58.5	3,000	2,197	56.6	3,200	461	69.2	2,200
2 children	1,416	31.1	5,460	1,290	33.2	5,700	127	19.1	4,416
3 or more children	473	10.4	5,200	395	10.2	5,200	78	11.7	2,892
BASIS FOR SUPPORT									
Child support agreement or court order	3,375	74.2	3,880	3,056	78.7	4,160	319	47.9	2,400
Voluntary and ratified by the court	747	16.4	4,000	702	18.1	4,300	45	6.8	(B)
Court-ordered agreement	2,377	52.3	3,720	2,125	54.8	4,140	252	37.8	2,400
Other written agreement	68	1.5	(B)	60	1.5	(B)	7	1.1	(B)
Non-written agreement	183	4.0	3,600	168	4.3	3,100	15	2.3	(B)
Not result of agreement or court order	1,173	25.8	3,000	826	21.3	3,500	347	52.1	2,500
PAYMENT METHOD									
Wage withholding	1,075	23.6	4,320	991	25.5	4,680	85	12.8	2,500
Directly to other parent	1,011	22.2	4,800	911	23.5	4,800	100	15.0	3,000
Directly to court	454	10.0	2,496	414	10.7	2,600	39	5.9	(B)
Directly to child support agency	702	15.4	3,120	630	16.2	3,600	72	10.8	(B)
Other method	133	2.9	2,400	110	2.8	2,400	23	3.5	(B)
HEALTH INSURANCE PROVISIONS									
Non-custodial parent provides	1,325	29.1	5,000	1,222	31.5	5,184	103	15.5	2,400
Custodial parent provides	839	18.5	4,200	764	19.7	4,200	75	11.3	2,544
Non-custodial parent pays bills	186	4.1	4,800	169	4.4	4,800	17	2.6	(B)
Included in child support payments	138	3.0	3,000	134	3.5	3,000	3	0.5	(B)
Other provision	280	6.2	3,600	253	6.5	3,600	28	4.2	(B)
No provision	845	18.6	2,712	740	19.1	3,000	104	15.6	1,800
CUSTODY ARRANGEMENTS									
Joint legal and physical custody	660	14.5	3,600	587	15.1	4,200	74	11.1	(B)
Joint legal with mother physical custody	1,053	23.2	5,160	1,031	26.6	5,160	22	3.3	(B)
Joint legal with father physical custody	130	2.9	2,544	17	0.4	(B)	113	17.0	2,400
Mother legal and physical custody	971	21.4	3,120	967	24.9	3,120	3	0.5	(B)
Father legal and physical custody	64	1.4	(B)	19	0.5	(B)	45	6.8	(B)
Split custody	230	5.1	4,613	224	5.8	4,800	6	0.9	(B)
Other custody arrangements	268	5.9	2,400	211	5.4	2,400	57	8.6	(B)

B Base figure too small to meet statistical standards for reliability of a derived figure. [1] Excludes 208,000 providers who also provided support for other adult nonhousehold members.

Source: U.S. Census Bureau, People and Households, Child Support, "Support Providers: 2010," <http://www.census.gov/people/childsupport/>, accessed July 2013.

Table 600. Children in Foster Care and Awaiting Adoption: 2000 to 2011

[Data cover the period from October 1 of prior year through September 30 of year shown]

| Characteristic | In foster care | | Entered foster care | | Exited foster care | | Waiting to be adopted | | Adopted from foster care | |
	2000	2011 [1]	2000	2011 [1]	2000	2011 [1]	2000	2011 [1]	2000	2011 [1]
Total	**552,000**	**400,540**	**293,000**	**252,320**	**272,000**	**245,260**	**131,000**	**104,236**	**51,000**	**50,516**
AGE										
Under 1 year	22,839	24,439	37,996	39,697	11,025	10,780	3,957	3,761	939	1,059
1 to 5 years	134,378	127,260	72,365	78,157	70,667	83,333	44,126	41,479	23,135	27,440
6 to 10 years	136,003	80,544	63,346	48,137	63,228	49,841	44,980	26,631	17,831	13,342
11 to 15 years	160,077	90,874	86,555	57,010	65,550	44,380	33,143	24,347	7,946	6,954
16 to 20 years	98,701	77,019	32,737	28,432	61,531	56,508	4,793	8,018	1,149	1,714
RACE										
White	207,970	164,406	136,214	111,563	121,322	106,982	44,898	41,655	19,462	22,864
Black	217,615	109,775	84,460	58,276	84,065	62,454	57,345	29,164	19,566	11,719
Asian	4,370	2,296	3,565	1,744	3,307	1,769	664	439	290	233
Hispanic [2]	81,823	83,810	42,769	51,969	39,909	50,061	17,050	22,929	7,430	10,757
Two or more	8,043	21,837	5,362	13,491	4,026	13,318	2,277	6,513	951	3,634
SEX										
Male	289,187	209,532	(NA)	(NA)	(NA)	(NA)	68,620	55,245	25,472	25,763
Female	262,813	190,932	(NA)	(NA)	(NA)	(NA)	62,380	48,991	25,528	24,753
LENGTH OF STAY										
Mean months	32.3	23.9	(X)	(X)	22.7	21.1	43.5	35.8	(X)	(X)
Median months	19.8	13.5	(X)	(X)	12.0	13.2	35.1	26.5	(X)	(X)

NA Not available. X Not applicable. [1] Preliminary data; estimates as of July 2012. [2] Persons of Hispanic origin may be of any race.

Source: U.S. Department of Health and Human Services, Administration for Children and Families, *Adoption and Foster Care Analysis and Reporting System Reports*, annual. See also <http://www.acf.hhs.gov/programs/cb/research-data-technology/statistics-research/afcars>.

Table 601. Child Care Expenditures of Families with Employed Mothers Making Payments by Selected Characteristics: 2011

[In units indicated (6,720 represents 6,720,000). Based on Survey of Income and Program Participation (SIPP), 2008 Panel, Wave 8, January-April 2011. Estimates are based on responses from a sample of the population, and may differ from the actual values because of sampling variability and other factors. Apparent differences between the estimates of two or more groups may not be statistically different]

Characteristic	Number (1,000)	Income		Expenditures		
		Average monthly family income (dollars)	Average monthly mother's income (dollars)	Average weekly child care expenditures (dollars)	Percent of family's monthly income spent on child care [1]	Ratio of child care expenditures to mother's income [2]
Families with children under age 15...	**6,720**	**8,673**	**3,729**	**143**	**7.2**	**16.6**
MARITAL STATUS OF MOTHER						
Married............................	4,787	10,622	4,017	157	6.4	16.9
Widowed, separated, divorced.............	791	4,264	3,701	106	10.8	12.4
Never married........................	1,142	3,556	2,538	112	13.6	19.1
RACE AND HISPANIC ORIGIN OF MOTHER						
White alone............................	5,287	9,159	3,810	145	6.8	16.4
Non-Hispanic.........................	4,483	9,859	4,044	150	6.6	16.1
Black alone...........................	883	4,824	2,873	115	10.4	17.4
Asian alone..........................	333	12,361	5,029	207	7.3	17.9
Hispanic (of any race).................	864	5,152	2,472	113	9.5	19.9
AGE OF MOTHER						
15 to 24 years.........................	382	3,574	1,507	110	13.4	31.7
25 to 34 years.........................	2,742	6,484	3,190	150	10.0	20.4
35 or more years......................	3,596	10,883	4,376	141	5.6	14.0
EDUCATION OF MOTHER						
Less than high school.................	310	3,483	1,740	111	13.8	27.7
High school graduate.................	861	4,666	2,319	112	10.4	21.0
Some college.........................	2,359	5,730	2,711	111	8.4	17.7
Bachelor's degree or higher...........	3,190	12,433	5,054	178	6.2	15.3
WORK STATUS OF MOTHER						
Employed full-time....................	5,192	8,135	4,134	148	7.9	15.5
Employed part-time...................	1,122	6,791	2,243	120	7.7	23.2
Self-employed........................	406	20,744	2,653	143	3.0	23.3
MONTHLY FAMILY INCOME						
Less than $1,500......................	410	1,023	1,002	91	38.7	39.5
$1,500 to $2,999......................	923	2,194	1,750	95	18.7	23.4
$3,000 to $4,499......................	945	3,717	2,372	116	13.6	21.3
$4,500 and over.......................	4,440	11,782	4,681	164	6.0	15.1
FAMILY POVERTY LEVEL						
Below poverty level...................	521	1,297	1,046	91	30.3	37.6
At or above poverty level.............	6,199	9,293	3,954	147	6.9	16.2
100-199 percent of poverty...........	1,122	2,695	1,764	112	18.0	27.5
200 or more percent of poverty........	5,076	10,751	4,438	155	6.3	15.2

[1] Percent is a ratio of average monthly child care payments (prorated from weekly averages) to average family monthly income. [2] Ratio is of average monthly child care payments (prorated from weekly averages) to mother's average monthly income, shown as a percentage.

Source: U.S. Census Bureau, "Who's Minding the Kids? Child Care Arrangements: 2011 - Detailed Tables," <http://www.census.gov/hhes/childcare/data/sipp/index.html>, accessed July 2013.

Table 602. Social Assistance Services—Revenue for Employer Firms: 2000 to 2011

[In millions of dollars (77,032 represents $77,032,000,000). Estimates have been adjusted to the results of the 2007 Economic Census. Based on the Service Annual Survey and administrative data; see Appendix III]

Kind of business	2007 NAICS code [1]	2000, Total	2005, Total	2011		
				Total	Taxable firms	Tax-exempt firms
Social assistance, total........................	**624**	**77,032**	**112,644**	**149,619**	**38,173**	**111,446**
Individual and family services.....................	6241	37,311	53,703	73,748	15,911	57,837
Child and youth services.........................	62411	7,517	10,471	12,018	1,083	10,935
Services for elderly and disabled persons....................	62412	12,804	20,223	31,834	10,574	21,260
Other individual and family services..............	62419	16,990	23,009	29,896	4,254	25,642
Community, emergency and other relief services..............	6242	12,281	21,462	29,240	499	28,741
Community food services.........................	62421	2,835	4,352	7,561	135	7,426
Community housing services.....................	62422	4,888	7,811	12,542	270	12,272
Emergency and other relief services.............	62423	4,558	9,299	9,137	94	9,043
Vocational rehabilitation services..................	6243	9,458	12,785	13,604	1,976	11,628
Child day care services...........................	6244	17,982	24,694	33,027	19,787	13,240

[1] Based on the North American Industry Classification System, 2007; see text, Section 15.

Source: U.S. Census Bureau, "2011 Annual Services Report," January 2013; and "Service Annual Survey Historical Data Revisions," February 2013; <http://www.census.gov/services/index.html>, accessed April 2013.

Table 603. Social Assistance Services—Nonemployer Establishments and Receipts: 2005 to 2011

[Receipts in millions of dollars (10,265 represents $10,265,000,000). Includes only firms subject to federal income tax. Nonemployers are businesses with no paid employees. Nonemployer firm receipts may include commission or earnings. Data are based on North American Classification of Industry System (NAICS) 2007; see text, Section 15]

Kind of business	NAICS code	Establishments			Receipts		
		2005	2010	2011	2005	2010	2011
Social assistance, total.....................	**624**	**807,729**	**912,247**	**913,457**	**10,265**	**12,753**	**13,035**
Individual and family services.............................	6241	112,909	141,971	147,316	1,920	2,599	2,764
Community/emergency and other relief services..........	6242	5,533	6,080	6,360	81	96	102
Vocational rehabilitation services............................	6243	11,022	11,984	12,345	245	287	304
Child day care services.....................................	6244	678,265	752,212	747,436	8,018	9,772	9,865

Source: U.S. Census Bureau, "Nonemployer Statistics," <http://www.census.gov/econ/nonemployer/index.html>, accessed June 2013.

Table 604. Primary Child Care Arrangements for Children Under Age 5, by Selected Characteristics: Spring 2011

[In percent, except as indicated (10,859 represents 10,859,000). For children with employed mothers. The primary child care arrangement is defined as the arrangement used the most hours per week. The numbers for all arrangements may exceed the total number of children because of ties among arrangements in the greatest number of hours per week. Based on Survey of Income and Program Participation (SIPP), 2008 Panel, Wave 8, January-April 2011. Estimates are based on responses from a sample of the population, and may differ from the actual values because of sampling variability and other factors. Apparent differences between the estimates of two or more groups may not be statistcically different]

Characteristic	Children Number (1,000)	Type of arrangement [1] (percent)			No child care arrangement
		In relative care	In non-relative care	In day care center	
Total..	**10,859**	**51.7**	**40.0**	**19.8**	**11.0**
MARITAL STATUS OF MOTHER					
Married..	7,692	51.0	40.0	19.6	11.7
Widowed, separated, divorced........................	816	47.5	39.0	20.1	11.5
Never married....................................	2,352	55.2	40.3	20.6	8.6
RACE AND HISPANIC ORIGIN OF MOTHER					
White alone......................................	8,391	51.7	39.8	19.3	11.9
Non-Hispanic....................................	6,945	48.9	42.7	21.3	12.5
Black alone......................................	1,539	52.2	38.5	21.2	8.6
Asian alone......................................	497	52.1	41.4	19.0	9.3
Hispanic (of any race).............................	1,604	65.6	25.6	9.7	8.3
AGE OF MOTHER					
15-24 years......................................	1,413	64.5	30.2	18.2	9.4
25-34 years......................................	5,830	51.5	41.0	20.7	10.8
35+ years..	3,616	47.0	42.1	19.2	12.0
EDUCATION OF MOTHER					
Less than high school..............................	751	58.1	22.1	6.5	19.3
High school graduate...............................	2,091	59.7	31.9	16.1	10.8
Some college.....................................	3,690	57.3	36.3	17.2	9.3
Bachelor's degree or higher.........................	4,327	42.0	50.1	26.3	11.1
WORK STATUS OF MOTHER					
Employed full-time.................................	7,264	48.0	45.4	24.1	9.7
Employed part-time................................	2,808	62.2	28.6	12.5	11.6
Self-employed....................................	787	48.2	30.4	6.9	20.3
FAMILY INCOME (monthly)					
Less than $1,500..................................	1,150	58.4	31.8	12.5	12.2
$1,500 - $2,999...................................	1,788	56.4	35.4	19.2	11.0
$3,000 - $4,499...................................	1,668	59.8	36.0	17.5	8.7
$4,500 and over..................................	6,068	46.7	44.4	22.5	11.2
AGE OF CHILD					
Less than 1 year..................................	1,870	58.0	20.3	14.4	13.4
1-2 years..	4,682	54.2	23.3	23.4	10.5
3-4 years..	4,307	46.3	48.3	18.3	10.5

[1] Columns do not add to 100.0 because some children participated in more than one type of arrangement.

Source: U.S. Census Bureau, Survey of Income and Program Participation (SIPP), 2008 Panel, Wave 8, *Who's Minding the Kids? Child Care Arrangements: Spring 2011*, and "Detailed Tables," <http://www.census.gov/hhes/childcare/index.html>, accessed June 2013.

Table 605. Private Philanthropy Funds by Source and Allocation: 1990 to 2012

[In billions of dollars (98.5 represents $98,500,000,000). Estimates for sources of funds based on U.S. Internal Revenue Service reports of individual charitable deductions and household surveys of giving conducted by Independent Sector and the Center on Philanthropy at Indiana University. For corporate giving, data are corporate charitable deductions from the U.S. Internal Revenue Service and the contributions made by corporate foundations as reported by the Foundation Center. Data about foundation donations are based upon surveys of foundations and data provided by the Foundation Center. Estimates of the allocation of funds were derived from surveys of nonprofits conducted by various sources]

Source and allocation	1990	1995	2000	2004	2005	2006	2007	2008	2009	2010	2011	2012
Total funds	**98.5**	**123.1**	**229.7**	**260.3**	**292.4**	**296.1**	**311.1**	**299.6**	**274.4**	**293.0**	**305.5**	**316.2**
Individuals	79.0	94.8	174.1	202.0	220.8	224.8	233.1	213.8	200.4	213.3	220.3	228.9
Foundations [1]	7.2	10.6	24.6	28.4	32.4	34.9	40.0	42.2	41.1	41.0	43.8	45.7
Corporations	5.5	7.4	10.7	11.4	15.2	14.5	14.2	12.4	13.8	15.8	16.2	18.2
Charitable bequests	6.8	10.4	20.3	18.5	24.0	21.9	23.8	31.2	19.1	23.0	25.2	23.4
Allocation:												
Religion	49.8	58.1	77.0	87.5	90.9	94.6	97.8	98.2	99.6	97.5	101.8	101.5
Health	7.8	17.9	15.3	19.1	20.3	24.2	25.3	24.1	26.1	26.6	26.8	28.1
Education	11.8	16.5	28.8	31.7	35.0	40.1	42.7	35.9	35.0	37.3	38.6	41.3
Human service	6.7	10.7	20.8	26.1	30.4	30.7	31.5	35.4	36.0	38.3	38.9	40.4
Arts, culture, and humanities	3.7	5.3	10.6	11.2	12.4	13.9	14.9	12.3	12.6	13.0	13.4	14.4
Public/societal benefit	6.6	8.8	15.0	17.7	20.8	23.2	20.0	18.0	17.3	19.4	20.5	21.6
Environment/wildlife	1.3	2.2	4.9	5.8	6.5	7.4	8.1	7.7	7.3	7.6	7.8	8.3
International	2.1	2.6	6.3	11.5	12.7	13.5	15.8	20.6	16.4	17.1	18.7	19.1
Gifts to foundations [1]	3.8	8.5	24.7	20.3	24.5	27.1	37.7	30.1	32.4	27.5	32.1	30.6
Unallocated [2]	5.0	-7.4	26.4	27.7	36.0	17.5	14.1	13.7	-12.4	5.3	2.7	6.8

[1] Data are from the Foundation Center. [2] Money deducted as a charitable contribution by donors but not allocated to sources. May include gifts to governmental entities, in-kind giving, or gifts to new charities.

Source: Giving USA Foundation, Chicago, IL, *Giving USA: The Annual Report on Philanthropy for the year 2012 (2013)* ©, researched and written at the Indiana University Lilly Family School of Philanthropy. See also <http://givingusareports.org/>.

Table 606. Foundations—Number and Finances by Foundation Type: 1990 to 2011

[Figures are for latest year reported by foundations. In millions of dollars (142,480 represents $142,480,000,000), except number of foundations. Covers nongovernmental nonprofit organizations with funds and programs managed by their own trustees or directors, whose goals were to maintain or aid social, educational, religious, or other activities deemed to serve the common good. Excludes organizations that make general appeals to the public for funds, act as trade associations for industrial or other special groups, or do not currently award grants]

Year	Number	Assets (million dollars)	Gifts received (million dollars)	Total giving [1] (million dollars)
1990	32,401	142,480	5,000	8,680
2000	56,582	486,085	27,614	24,563
2005	71,095	550,552	31,465	36,403
2009	76,545	590,188	40,862	45,778
2010	76,610	643,974	37,961	45,858
Total, 2011	**81,777**	**662,336**	**42,159**	**48,999**
Independent	73,764	540,154	25,697	33,910
Corporate	2,689	22,195	4,362	5,168
Community	750	57,938	5,434	4,311
Operating	4,574	42,049	6,665	5,610
Family [2]	40,444	294,071	20,275	21,325

[1] Includes grants, scholarships, and employee matching gifts; excludes set-asides, loans, program-related investments (PRIs), and program expenses. [2] These funders are included in independent foundation data. Excludes 3,490 family foundations that did not report giving in the latest fiscal year. These foundations held $2.1 billion in assets in 2011, and reported gifts received totaling $507.1 million.

Source: The Foundation Center, New York, NY, *Foundation Yearbook 2011* ©; and "FC Stats - Grantmaker," <http://foundationcenter.org/findfunders/statistics/gm_growth.html>, accessed September 2013.

Table 607. Domestic Private Foundations—Financial Information: 1995 to 2009

[Financial data in billions of dollars (195.6 represents $195,600,000,000). Minus sign (-) indicates loss]

Item	1995	2000	2001	2002	2003	2004	2005	2006	2007	2008	2009
Number of tax returns	47,917	66,738	70,787	73,255	76,348	76,897	79,535	81,850	84,613	90,850	92,624
Nonoperating foundations [1]	43,966	61,501	63,650	67,101	70,004	70,613	72,800	74,364	77,457	83,024	84,660
Operating foundations [2]	3,951	5,238	7,137	6,154	6,344	6,284	6,734	7,486	7,156	7,826	7,964
Total assets, book value [3]	195.6	409.5	413.6	383.5	418.5	455.5	481.8	569.3	591.2	531.4	550.9
Total assets, fair market value [3]	242.9	471.6	455.4	413.0	475.0	509.9	545.9	645.8	652.4	526.5	588.5
Investments in securities	190.7	361.4	329.4	294.4	344.3	361.2	373.1	403.7	400.3	287.6	324.7
Total revenue	30.8	72.8	45.3	27.8	48.4	58.7	76.4	94.1	107.3	49.7	52.2
Total expenses	17.2	37.4	36.7	34.4	35.1	36.6	42.8	48.8	58.8	60.3	56.2
Contributions, gifts, and grants paid	12.3	27.6	27.4	26.3	26.7	27.6	31.9	34.9	42.6	42.8	40.9
Excess of revenue over expenses (net)	13.6	35.3	8.6	-6.6	13.3	22.1	33.5	45.3	48.6	-10.6	-4.0
Net investment income [4]	20.4	48.8	25.7	17.6	25.2	34.0	44.3	54.2	62.8	23.1	17.6

[1] Generally provide charitable support through grants and other financial means to charitable organizations; the majority of foundations are nonoperating. [2] Generally conduct their own charitable activities, e.g., museums. [3] For Tax Years 2007, 2008, and 2009, data shown for book and fair market assets were reduced by $38.7 billion, $29.6 billion, and $33,4 billion, respectively, to avoid overstating joint assets of Bill and Melinda Gates Foundation and Bill and Melinda Gates Foundation Trust. [4] Represents income not considered related to a foundation's charitable purpose, e.g., interest, dividends, and capital gains. Foundations could be subject to an excise tax on such income.

Source: Internal Revenue Service, *Statistics of Income Bulletin*, "SOI Tax Stats—Domestic Private Foundation and Charitable Trust Statistics," <http://www.irs.gov/uac/Tax-Stats-2>, accessed April 2013.

Table 608. Nonprofit Charitable Organizations—Financial Information: 2000 and 2009

[In billions of dollars (1,562.5 represents $1,562,500,000,000), except as indicated. Categories based on The National Taxonomy of Exempt Entities (NTEE), a classification system that uses 26 major field areas that are aggregated into 10 categories. Includes data reported by organizations described in Internal Revenue Code, Section 501(3), excluding private foundations and most religious organizations. Organizations with receipts under $25,000 were not required to file]

Year and major category	Number of tax returns (1,000)	Total assets	Net assets	Revenue			Total expenses	Excess of revenue over expenses (net)
				Total	Program service revenue [1]	Contributions, gifts, and grants		
2000.................................	230.2	1,562.5	1,023.2	866.2	579.1	199.1	796.4	69.8
2009, total....................	**320.8**	**2,697.1**	**1,564.2**	**1,481.1**	**1,085.9**	**327.4**	**1,433.9**	**47.2**
Arts, culture, and humanities...........	34.0	101.0	79.5	29.1	9.7	16.4	28.1	1.0
Education...........................	56.8	880.1	586.4	277.8	172.4	81.9	269.6	8.2
Environment, animals..................	14.5	42.1	35.1	13.6	3.5	9.3	12.7	0.9
Health.............................	37.3	1,079.6	523.0	856.6	769.2	61.1	825.9	30.7
Human services......................	121.9	301.2	140.3	199.3	107.7	83.2	194.8	4.5
International, foreign affairs............	5.7	33.3	22.1	27.6	1.9	24.8	27.2	0.4
Mutual, membership benefit.............	0.8	15.8	7.0	2.3	1.3	0.3	2.4	0.0
Public, societal benefit..................	29.1	217.8	150.0	64.9	18.4	43.2	63.8	1.1
Religion related.......................	20.5	26.3	20.9	9.9	1.8	7.2	9.5	0.4

[1] Represents fees collected by organizations in support of their tax-exempt purposes, and income such as tuition and fees at educational institutions, hospital patient charges, and admission and activity fees collected by museums and other nonprofit organizations or institutions.

Source: Internal Revenue Service, *Statistics of Income Bulletin*, "Nonprofit Charitable Organizations, 2009," Fall 2012. See also <http://www.irs.gov/uac/SOI-Tax-Stats-Charities-and-Other-Tax-Exempt-Organizations-Statistics>.

Table 609. Individual Charitable Contributions by State: 2010

[In millions of dollars (170,230 represents $170,230,000,000), except as indicated. For tax year. Data will not agree with data in other tables due to differing survey methodology used to derive state data]

State	Charitable contribution		State	Charitable contribution		State	Charitable contribution		State	Charitable contribution	
	Number of returns (1,000)	Amount (mil. dol.)		Number of returns (1,000)	Amount (mil. dol.)		Number of returns (1,000)	Amount (mil. dol.)		Number of returns (1,000)	Amount (mil. dol.)
U.S. [1, 2]..	**38,392**	**170,230**	ID.........	175	799	MO.......	656	2,840	PA.......	1,552	5,814
AL........	516	2,832	IL.........	1,701	6,923	MT.......	114	495	RI........	154	436
AK........	68	317	IN........	647	2,747	NE.......	219	1,032	SC.......	530	2,516
AZ........	760	2,726	IA........	367	1,347	NV.......	304	1,210	SD.......	62	399
AR........	241	1,336	KS.......	333	1,657	NH.......	182	516	TN.......	556	3,531
CA........	4,946	21,297	KY.......	443	1,838	NJ........	1,569	5,085	TX.......	2,165	12,953
CO........	736	3,051	LA........	365	1,887	NM.......	179	706	UT.......	385	2,826
CT........	632	2,981	ME.......	147	433	NY.......	2,819	14,838	VT.......	70	225
DE........	126	467	MD.......	1,135	4,784	NC.......	1,223	5,286	VA.......	1,241	5,319
DC........	106	667	MA.......	1,056	4,267	ND.......	51	242	WA.......	890	3,618
FL........	1,932	9,280	MI.......	1,219	4,700	OH.......	1,330	4,789	WV.......	106	468
GA.......	1,315	6,302	MN.......	859	3,083	OK.......	340	2,033	WI.......	803	2,512
HI........	168	554	MS.......	249	1,402	OR.......	550	1,909	WY.......	47	514

[1] The sum for the states does not add to the total because other components are not shown in this table. [2] U.S. totals do not agree with Table 508 in Section 9 because this table also includes (1) "substitutes for returns," whereby the IRS constructs returns for certain nonfilers on the basis of available information and imposes an income tax on the resulting estimate of the tax base and (2) returns of nonresident or departing aliens. In addition, in this table, income tax includes the alternative minimum tax, but differs from total income tax in Table 508 in that it is after subtraction of all tax credits except a portion of the earned income credit.

Source: Internal Revenue Service, Statistics of Income, Individual Income and Tax Data, "Tax Year 2010: Historical Table 2," <http://www.irs.gov/uac/SOI-Tax-Stats---Historic-Table-2>, accessed April 2013. See also <http://www.irs.gov/uac/Tax-Stats-2>.

Table 610. Volunteers by Selected Characteristics: 2012

[In percent, except as noted (64,513 represents 64,513,000). Data on volunteers relate to persons who performed unpaid volunteer activities for an organization at any point from September 1, 2011 through September 2012. Data represent the percent of the population involved in the activity]

Type of main organization [1]	Total, both sexes	Sex		Educational attainment [2]			
		Male	Female	Less than a high school diploma	High school graduate, no college [3]	Less than a bachelor's degree [4]	College graduates
Total volunteers (1,000)............	**64,513**	**27,238**	**37,274**	**2,177**	**10,527**	**15,832**	**27,202**
Percent of population................	26.5	23.2	29.5	8.8	17.3	28.7	42.2
Median annual hours [5]...............	50	50	51	52	50	50	52
Civic and political [6]..................	5.5	6.8	4.6	3.6	5.1	5.5	6.0
Educational or youth service...........	25.5	23.8	26.7	23.2	21.4	25.2	26.8
Environmental or animal care.........	2.6	2.5	2.7	0.6	2.9	2.3	2.8
Hospital or other health...............	7.8	6.2	9.0	3.5	7.0	7.8	7.9
Public safety........................	1.2	1.9	0.6	1.4	1.7	1.4	0.7
Religious...........................	33.1	32.9	33.2	48.6	40.0	34.5	30.5
Social or community service...........	14.2	14.8	13.8	12.0	13.5	13.9	14.3
Sport and hobby [7]...................	3.8	4.5	3.3	2.8	3.3	3.3	4.7

[1] Main organization is defined as the organization for which the volunteer worked the most hours during the year. [2] Data refer to persons 25 years and over. [3] Includes high school diploma or equivalent. [4] Includes the categories "some college, no degree" and "associate degree." [5] At all organizations. For those reporting annual hours. [6] Includes professional and/or international activities. [7] Includes cultural and/or arts activities.

Source: U.S. Bureau of Labor Statistics,"Volunteering in the United States--2012," News Release USDL-13-0285, February 2013. See also <http://www.bls.gov/bls/newsrels.htm>.

Social Insurance and Human Services 395

Table 611. Homeless Population by Type and Shelter Status: 2005 to 2012

[Data are point-in-time counts made on a single night in January by Continuums of Care (CoCs) in all States, Territories, Puerto Rico, and DC. Data are not independently verified by the Department of Housing and Urban Development (HUD). CoCs are required to provide an unduplicated count of homeless persons according to HUD standards. See HUD's two guides to Counting Sheltered and Unsheltered Homeless People: <http://www.hudhre.info/documents/counting_unsheltered.pdf>]

Homeless population by type	2005 [1]	2006 [1]	2007	2008	2009	2010	2011	2012
Total	**763,010**	**759,101**	**671,888**	**664,414**	**643,067**	**649,917**	**636,017**	**633,782**
Sheltered	418,165	427,971	391,401	386,361	403,308	403,543	392,316	390,155
Unsheltered	344,845	331,130	280,487	278,053	239,759	246,374	243,701	243,627
Individuals	444,027	452,580	423,377	415,202	404,957	407,966	399,836	394,379
Sheltered	216,448	224,293	213,073	204,855	215,995	212,218	205,834	199,159
Unsheltered	227,579	228,287	210,304	210,347	188,962	195,748	194,002	195,220
Persons in families with children	318,983	306,521	248,511	249,212	238,110	241,951	236,181	239,403
Sheltered	201,717	203,678	178,328	181,506	187,313	191,325	186,482	190,996
Unsheltered	117,266	102,843	70,183	67,706	50,797	50,626	49,699	48,407
Chronically homeless [2]	175,914	155,623	123,798	124,135	110,917	109,812	107,148	99,894
Sheltered	71,921	53,365	41,768	45,418	45,592	43,374	38,971	32,647
Unsheltered	103,993	102,258	82,030	78,717	65,325	66,438	68,177	67,247
Severely mentally ill	132,314	135,668	124,833	119,249	107,056	110,488	115,364	111,993
Sheltered	80,681	75,217	75,471	69,264	70,298	71,989	70,884	65,443
Unsheltered	51,633	60,451	49,362	49,985	36,758	38,499	44,480	46,550
Chronic substance abuse	180,640	190,094	169,917	158,506	145,760	145,155	144,246	131,363
Sheltered	108,836	106,077	106,658	96,268	95,858	95,049	87,630	75,581
Unsheltered	71,804	84,017	63,259	62,238	49,902	50,106	56,616	55,782
Veterans	71,269	71,900	61,720	62,989	59,390	(NA)	67,495	62,619
Sheltered	44,455	42,115	39,634	38,485	36,224	(NA)	40,033	35,143
Unsheltered	26,814	29,785	22,086	24,504	23,166	(NA)	27,462	27,476
Persons with HIV/AIDS	22,062	19,802	16,291	15,875	14,654	14,783	13,221	11,722
Sheltered	16,707	13,608	11,324	11,066	10,909	10,590	9,698	8,300
Unsheltered	5,355	6,194	4,967	4,809	3,745	4,193	3,523	3,422
Domestic violence victims	77,365	80,002	71,594	70,092	68,732	67,860	73,080	74,290
Sheltered	54,995	53,771	50,697	49,618	48,896	49,709	53,055	54,142
Unsheltered	22,370	26,231	20,897	20,474	19,836	18,151	20,025	20,148
Youth under age 18, unaccompanied	57,436	29,812	12,986	12,028	9,394	8,153	6,826	6,632
Sheltered	39,400	20,557	8,792	8,224	5,712	4,349	2,981	2,746
Unsheltered	18,036	9,255	4,194	3,804	3,682	3,804	3,845	3,886

NA Not Available. [1] Prior to 2007, a standardized methodology to determine unduplicated counts of homeless persons within CoCs had not yet been implemented and the reliability of different street count methodologies can vary. [2] An individual with a disability, and continuously homeless for a year or more, or with at least four episodes of homelessness in the last 3 years.

Source: U.S. Department of Housing and Urban Development, *Continuum of Care Homeless Assistance Programs: Homeless Populations and Subpopulations*, November 2012, and earlier reports. See also <http://www.hudhre.info/index.cfm>.

Table 612. Number of Emergency and Transitional Beds in Homeless Assistance Systems Nationwide: 2012

[Data include beds located in Puerto Rico, Guam, and the Virgin Islands. Data were reported by 427 Continuums of Care, and were collected for a point-in-time during the last week in January 2012. Data were not independently verified by HUD. For more information on data collection and methodology, see *Vol. 1, 2012 Annual Homeless Assessment Report*]

Homeless programs	Year-round units/beds [1]				Total year-round beds	Other beds	
	Family units	Family beds	Adult-only beds [2]	Child-only beds		Seasonal beds [3]	Overflow/ voucher [4]
Emergency shelters	34,031	111,351	115,643	2,212	229,206	19,708	28,098
Transitional housing	34,952	109,861	86,201	1,130	197,192	(NA)	(NA)
Total inventory	**68,983**	**221,212**	**203,973**	**3,342**	**428,527**	**19,708**	**28,098**
Permanent supportive housing	38,832	108,416	166,262	108	274,786	(NA)	(NA)

NA Not available. [1] Year-round beds are available for use throughout the year and are considered part of the stable inventory of beds for homeless persons. [2] Total count for adult-only beds include 2,129 beds in safe haven housing. [3] Seasonal beds are typically available during particularly high-demand seasons of the year (e.g. winter months in the North or summer months in the South) to accommodate increased need for emergency shelters to prevent illness or death due to the weather. [4] Overflow beds are typically used during unanticipated emergencies (e.g., precipitous temperature drops or a natural disaster that displaces residents). Voucher beds are made available in a hotel or motel, and often function like overflow beds.

Source: U.S. Department of Housing and Urban Development, *2012 Continuum of Care Homeless Assistance Programs: Housing Inventory Count Report*, December 2012. See also <http://www.hudhre.info/>.

Labor Force, Employment, and Earnings

This section presents statistics on the labor force; its distribution by occupation and industry affiliation; and the supply of, demand for, and conditions of labor. The chief source of these data is the Current Population Survey (CPS) conducted by the U.S. Census Bureau for the Bureau of Labor Statistics (BLS). Comprehensive historical and current data are available from the BLS Internet site at <http://www.bls.gov/cps/>. These data are published on a current basis in the BLS monthly publication *Employment and Earnings Online*. Detailed data on the labor force are also available from the Census Bureau's decennial census of population.

Types of data—Most statistics in this section are obtained by two methods: household interviews or questionnaires and reports of establishment payroll records. Each method provides data that the other cannot suitably supply. Population characteristics, for example, are readily obtainable only from the household survey, while detailed industrial classifications can be readily derived only from establishment records.

CPS data are obtained from a monthly sample survey of the population. The CPS is used to gather data for the calendar week, generally the week including the 12th of the month, and provides current comprehensive data on the labor force (see text, Section 1, Population). The CPS provides information on the work status of the population without duplication since each person is classified as employed, unemployed, or not in the labor force. Employed persons holding more than one job are counted only once, according to the job at which they worked the most hours during the survey week.

Monthly, quarterly, and annual data from the CPS are published by the BLS in *Employment and Earnings Online*. Data presented include national totals of the number of persons in the civilian labor force by sex, disability status, race, Hispanic origin, and age; the number employed; hours of work; industry and occupational groups; usual weekly earnings; and the number unemployed, reasons for, and duration of unemployment. Annual data shown in this section are averages of monthly figures for each calendar year, unless otherwise specified. Historical national CPS data are available at <http://www.bls.gov/cps/>.

The CPS also produces annual estimates of employment and unemployment for each state, 50 large metropolitan statistical areas, and selected cities. These estimates are published annually in *Geographic Profile of Employment and Unemployment* available at <http://www.bls.gov/gps/>.

Data based on establishment records are compiled by the BLS and cooperating state agencies as part of an ongoing Current Employment Statistics program. The BLS collects survey data monthly from a probability-based sample of nonfarm, business establishments through internet electronic data interchange, touchtone data entry, and computer-assisted telephone interviews, Internet, other electronic media, fax, transcript, or mail. CES data are adjusted annually to data from government unemployment insurance administrative records, which are supplemented by data from other government agencies. The estimates exclude self-employed persons, private household workers, unpaid family workers, agricultural workers, and members of the Armed Forces.

The establishment survey counts workers each time they appear on a payroll during the reference period (the payroll period that includes the 12th of the month). Thus, unlike the CPS, a person with two jobs is counted twice. The establishment survey is designed to provide estimates of nonfarm wage and salary employment, average weekly hours, and average hourly and weekly earnings by detailed industry for the nation, states, and selected metropolitan areas. Establishment survey data also are published in *Employment and Earnings Online*. Historical national data are available at <http://www.bls.gov/ces/>. Historical data for states and metropolitan areas at <http://www.bls.gov/sae/>. CES estimates are currently classified by the 2012 North American Industry Classification System (NAICS). All published series for the nation have a NAICS–based history extending back to at least 1990. Employment series for total nonfarm and other high-level aggregates start in 1939.

For more information on data concepts, sample design, and estimating methods for the CES Survey, see the BLS Handbook of Methods, Chater 2 <http://bls.gov/opub/hom/homch2.htm>.

The completion of the sample redesign and the conversion to NAICS for state and metropolitan area establishment survey data were implemented in March 2003 with the release of January 2003 estimates. For information regarding revisions see <http://www.bls.gov/ces/cesrevinfo.htm>.

Labor force—According to the CPS definitions, the civilian labor force comprises all civilians in the noninstitutionalized population 16 years and over classified as "employed" or "unemployed" according to the following criteria: Employed civilians comprise (a) all civilians, who, during the reference week, did any work for pay or profit (minimum of an hour's work) or worked 15 hours or more as unpaid workers in a family enterprise and (b) all civilians who were not working but who had jobs or businesses from which they were temporarily absent for noneconomic reasons (illness, weather conditions, vacation, labor-management dispute, etc.) whether they were paid for the time off or were seeking other jobs. Unemployed persons comprise all civilians who had no employment during the reference week, who made specific efforts to find a job within the previous 4 weeks (such as applying directly to an employer or to a public employment service or checking with friends) and who were available for work during that week, except for temporary illness. Persons on layoff from a job and expecting recall also are classified as unemployed. All other civilian persons, 16 years old and over, are classified as "not in the labor force."

Various breaks in the CPS data series have occurred over time due to the introduction of population adjustments and other changes. For details on these breaks in series and the effect that they had on the

CPS data, see the BLS Web site at <www.bls.gov.cps/documentation.htm#concepts.>.

Beginning in January of each year, the CPS data reflect the introduction of revised population controls. For additional information on the effects of revised population controls on estimates from the CPS, see <www.bls.gov.cps/documentation.htm#pop>.

Hours and earnings—Average hourly earnings, based on establishment data, are gross earnings (i.e., earnings before payroll deductions) and include overtime premiums; they exclude irregular bonuses and value of payments in kind. Hours are those for which pay was received. Annual wages and salaries from the CPS consist of total monies received for work performed by an employee during the income year. It includes wages, salaries, commissions, tips, piece-rate payments, and cash bonuses earned before deductions were made for taxes, bonds, union dues, etc. Persons who worked 35 hours or more are classified as working full-time.

Industry and occupational groups—Industry data derived from the CPS for 1983-91 utilize the 1980 census industrial classification developed from the 1972 SIC. CPS data from 1971 to 1982 were based on the 1970 census classification system, which was developed from the 1967 SIC. Most of the industry categories were not affected by the change in classification.

The occupational classification system used in the 1980 census and in the CPS for 1983-91, evolved from the 1980 Standard Occupational Classification (SOC) system, first introduced in 1977. Occupational categories used in the 1980 census classification system are so radically different from the 1970 census system used in the CPS through 1982 that their implementation represented a break in historical data series.

Beginning in January 1992, the occupational and industrial classification systems used in the 1990 census were introduced into the CPS. (These systems were largely based on the 1980 SOC and the 1987 SIC systems, respectively.)

Beginning in 2003, the 2002 occupational and industrial classification systems were introduced into the CPS. These systems were derived from the 2000 SOC and the 2002 NAICS. The composition of detailed occupational and industrial classifications in the new classification systems was substantially changed from the previous systems in use, as was the structure for aggregating them into broad groups. Consequently, the use of the new classification systems created breaks in existing data series at all levels of aggregation. CPS data using the new classification systems are available beginning 2000. Additional information on the occupational and industrial classifications systems used in the CPS, including changes over time, appear on the BLS Web site at <www.bls.gov/cps/documentation.htm#oi>. Establishments responding to the establishment survey are classified according to the 2007 NAICS. Previously they were classified according to the SIC manual. See text, Section 15, Business Enterprise, for information about the SIC manual and NAICS.

Productivity—BLS publishes data on output per hour (labor productivity), output per combined unit of labor and capital input (multifactor productivity), and, for industry groups and industries, output per combined unit of capital, labor, energy, materials, and purchased service inputs. Labor productivity and related indexes are published for the business sector as a whole and its major subsectors: nonfarm business, manufacturing, and nonfinancial corporations, and for over 200 detailed industries. Productivity indexes that take into account capital, labor, energy, materials, and service inputs are published for 18 major manufacturing industry groups, 86 detailed manufacturing industries, utility services, and air and railroad transportation. The major sector data are published in the BLS quarterly news release *Productivity and Costs* and in the annual *Multifactor Productivity Trends* release. Industry productivity measures are updated and published annually in the news releases *Productivity and Costs by Industry* and *Multifactor Productivity Trends by Industry*. The latest data are available at the Labor Productivity and Costs Web site at <http://www.bls.gov/lpc/> and the Multifactor Productivity Web site at <http://www.bls.gov/mfp>. Detailed information on methods, limitations, and data sources appears in the BLS *Handbook of Methods*, BLS Bulletin 2490 (1997), Chapters 10 and 11 at <http://www.bls.gov/opub/ hom/home.htm> and <http://www.bls.gov/lpc/ lpcmethods.htm>

Unions—As defined here, unions include traditional labor unions and employee associations similar to labor unions. Data on union membership status provided by BLS are for employed wage and salary workers and relate to their principal job. Earnings by union membership status are usual weekly earnings of full-time wage and salary workers. The information is collected through the Current Population Survey.

Work stoppages—Work stoppages include all strikes and lockouts known to BLS that last for at least 1 full day or shift and involve 1,000 or more workers. All stoppages, whether or not authorized by a union, legal or illegal, are counted. Excluded are work slowdowns and instances where employees report to work late or leave early to attend meetings or rallies.

Seasonal adjustment—Many economic statistics reflect a regularly recurring seasonal movement that can be estimated on the basis of past experience. By eliminating that part of the change which can be ascribed to usual seasonal variation (e.g., climate or school openings and closings), it is possible to observe the cyclical and other nonseasonal movements in the series. However, in evaluating deviations from the seasonal pattern—that is, changes in a seasonally adjusted series—it is important to note that seasonal adjustment is merely an approximation based on past experience. Seasonally adjusted estimates have a broader margin of possible error than the original data on which they are based, since they are subject not only to sampling and other errors, but also are affected by the uncertainties of the adjustment process itself. Consistent with BLS practices, annual estimates will be published only for not seasonally-adjusted data.

Statistical reliability—For discussion of statistical collection, estimation, sampling procedures, and measures of statistical reliability applicable to Census Bureau and BLS data, see Appendix III.

Table 613. Civilian Population—Employment Status: 1970 to 2012

[In thousands (137,085 represents 137,085,000), except as indicated. Annual averages of monthly figures. Civilian noninstitutionalized population 16 years old and over. Data not strictly comparable with data for earlier years, see BLS Handbook of Methods, <http://www.bls.gov/opub/hom/>. Based on Current Population Survey; see text, Section 1 and Appendix III]

Year	Civilian noninstitutional population	Civilian labor force				Unemployed		Not in labor force	
		Total	Percent of population	Employed	Employ-ment/population ratio [1]	Number	Percent of labor force	Number	Percent of population
1970	137,085	82,771	60.4	78,678	57.4	4,093	4.9	54,315	39.6
1980	167,745	106,940	63.8	99,303	59.2	7,637	7.1	60,806	36.2
1990	189,164	125,840	66.5	118,793	62.8	7,047	5.6	63,324	33.5
1995	198,584	132,304	66.6	124,900	62.9	7,404	5.6	66,280	33.4
1999	207,753	139,368	67.1	133,488	64.3	5,880	4.2	68,385	32.9
2000	212,577	142,583	67.1	136,891	64.4	5,692	4.0	69,994	32.9
2001	215,092	143,734	66.8	136,933	63.7	6,801	4.7	71,359	33.2
2002	217,570	144,863	66.6	136,485	62.7	8,378	5.8	72,707	33.4
2003	221,168	146,510	66.2	137,736	62.3	8,774	6.0	74,658	33.8
2004	223,357	147,401	66.0	139,252	62.3	8,149	5.5	75,956	34.0
2005	226,082	149,320	66.0	141,730	62.7	7,591	5.1	76,762	34.0
2006	228,815	151,428	66.2	144,427	63.1	7,001	4.6	77,387	33.8
2007	231,867	153,124	66.0	146,047	63.0	7,078	4.6	78,743	34.0
2008	233,788	154,287	66.0	145,362	62.2	8,924	5.8	79,501	34.0
2009	235,801	154,142	65.4	139,877	59.3	14,265	9.3	81,659	34.6
2010	237,830	153,889	64.7	139,064	58.5	14,825	9.6	83,941	35.3
2011	239,618	153,617	64.1	139,869	58.4	13,747	8.9	86,001	35.9
2012	243,284	154,975	63.7	142,469	58.6	12,506	8.1	88,310	36.3

[1] Civilian employed as a percent of the civilian noninstitutional population.

Source: U.S. Bureau of Labor Statistics, "Employment and Earnings Online," <www.bls.gov/opub/ee/home.htm>, accessed February 2013.

Table 614. Civilian Labor Force and Participation Rates With Projections: 1980 to 2020

[106.9 represents 106,900,000. Civilian noninstitutionalized population 16 years old and over. Annual averages of monthly figures. Rates are based on annual average civilian noninstitutional population of each specified group and represent proportion of each specified group in the civilian labor force. Based on Current Population Survey; see text, Section 1 and Appendix III]

Race, Hispanic origin, sex, and age	Civilian labor force (mil.)						Participation rate (percent) [1]					
	1980	1990	2000	2005	2010	2020, proj.	1980	1990	2000	2005	2010	2020, proj.
Total [2]	106.9	125.8	142.6	149.3	153.9	164.4	63.8	66.5	67.1	66.0	64.7	62.5
White [3]	93.6	107.4	118.5	122.3	125.1	130.5	64.1	66.9	67.3	66.3	65.1	62.8
Male	54.5	59.6	64.5	66.7	67.7	70.4	78.2	77.1	75.5	74.1	72.0	69.0
Female	39.1	47.8	54.1	55.6	57.4	60.1	51.2	57.4	59.5	58.9	58.5	56.9
Black [3]	10.9	13.7	16.4	17.0	17.9	19.7	61.0	64.0	65.8	64.2	62.2	60.3
Male	5.6	6.8	7.7	8.0	8.4	9.4	70.3	71.0	69.2	67.3	65.0	63.1
Female	5.3	6.9	8.7	9.0	9.4	10.3	53.1	58.3	63.1	61.6	59.9	57.9
Asian [3, 4]	(NA)	(NA)	6.3	6.5	7.2	9.4	(NA)	(NA)	67.2	66.1	64.7	63.1
Male	(NA)	(NA)	3.4	3.5	3.9	5.0	(NA)	(NA)	76.1	74.8	73.2	71.0
Female	(NA)	(NA)	2.9	3.0	3.4	4.5	(NA)	(NA)	59.2	58.2	57.0	56.1
Hispanic [5]	6.1	10.7	16.7	19.8	22.7	30.5	64.0	67.4	69.7	68.0	67.5	66.2
Male	3.8	6.5	9.9	12.0	13.5	17.9	81.4	81.4	81.5	80.1	77.8	75.9
Female	2.3	4.2	6.8	7.8	9.2	12.6	47.4	53.1	57.5	55.3	56.5	56.1
Male	61.5	69.0	76.3	80.0	82.0	87.1	77.4	76.4	74.8	73.3	71.2	68.2
16 to 19 years	5.0	4.1	4.3	3.6	3.0	2.4	60.5	55.7	52.8	43.2	34.9	27.9
20 to 24 years	8.6	7.9	7.5	8.1	7.9	7.3	85.9	84.4	82.6	79.1	74.5	69.4
25 to 34 years	17.0	19.9	17.8	17.8	18.4	19.7	95.2	94.1	93.4	91.7	89.7	86.9
35 to 44 years	11.8	17.5	20.1	19.5	18.1	19.3	95.5	94.3	92.7	92.1	91.5	91.3
45 to 54 years	9.9	11.1	16.3	18.1	18.9	17.4	91.2	90.7	88.6	87.7	86.8	86.0
55 to 64 years	7.2	6.6	7.8	10.0	12.1	14.7	72.1	67.8	67.3	69.3	70.0	71.1
65 years and over	1.9	2.0	2.5	3.0	3.7	6.4	19.0	16.3	17.7	19.8	22.1	26.7
Female	45.5	56.8	66.3	69.3	71.9	77.2	51.5	57.5	59.9	59.3	58.6	57.1
16 to 19 years	4.4	3.7	4.0	3.6	2.9	2.1	52.9	51.6	51.2	44.2	35.0	25.2
20 to 24 years	7.3	6.8	6.7	7.1	7.2	6.5	68.9	71.3	73.1	70.1	68.3	62.3
25 to 34 years	12.3	16.1	14.9	14.5	15.3	16.8	65.5	73.5	76.1	73.9	74.7	74.2
35 to 44 years	8.6	14.7	17.5	16.5	15.2	15.8	65.5	76.4	77.2	75.8	75.2	74.0
45 to 54 years	7.0	9.1	14.8	16.3	17.1	15.6	59.9	71.2	76.8	76.0	75.7	75.7
55 to 64 years	4.7	4.9	6.6	8.9	11.2	14.6	41.3	45.2	51.9	57.0	60.2	66.6
65 years and over	1.2	1.5	1.8	2.3	3.0	5.7	8.1	8.6	9.4	11.5	13.8	19.2

NA Not available. [1] Civilian labor force as a percent of the civilian noninstitutional population. [2] Includes other races, not shown separately. [3] The 2005 Current Population Survey allowed respondents to choose more than one race. Beginning 2005, data represent persons who selected this race group only and exclude persons reporting more than one race. Prior to 2005 the CPS only allowed respondents to report one race group. See also comments on race in the text for Section 1. [4] Prior to 2005, includes Pacific Islanders. [5] Persons of Hispanic origin may be of any race.

Source: Bureau of Labor Statistics, "Employment and Earnings Online," January 2012; "Monthly Labor Review," November 2011; and "Employment Projections Program," <http://www.bls.gov/emp/ep_data_labor_force.htm>.

Table 615. Civilian Population—Employment Status by Sex, Race, and Ethnicity: 1980 to 2012

[In thousands (79,398 represents 79,398,000), except as indicated. Annual averages of monthly figures. Data not strictly comparable with data for earlier years, see BLS Handbook of Methods, <http://www.bls.gov/opub/hom/>; see Table 613 for U.S. totals and coverage]

Year, sex, race, and Hispanic origin	Civilian noninstitutionalized population	Civilian labor force				Unemployed		Not in labor force	
		Total	Percent of population	Employed	Employ-ment/population ratio [1]	Number	Percent of labor force	Number	Percent of population
Male:									
1980...............	79,398	61,453	77.4	57,186	72.0	4,267	6.9	17,945	22.6
1990...............	90,377	69,011	76.4	65,104	72.0	3,906	5.7	21,367	23.6
2000...............	101,964	76,280	74.8	73,305	71.9	2,975	3.9	25,684	25.2
2005...............	109,151	80,033	73.3	75,973	69.6	4,059	5.1	29,119	26.7
2010...............	115,174	81,985	71.2	73,359	63.7	8,626	10.5	33,189	28.8
2011...............	116,317	81,975	70.5	74,290	63.9	7,684	9.4	34,343	29.5
2012...............	117,343	82,327	70.2	75,555	64.4	6,771	8.2	35,017	29.8
Female:									
1980...............	88,348	45,487	51.5	42,117	47.7	3,370	7.4	42,861	48.5
1990...............	98,787	56,829	57.5	53,689	54.3	3,140	5.5	41,957	42.5
2000...............	110,613	66,303	59.9	63,586	57.5	2,717	4.1	44,310	40.1
2005...............	116,931	69,288	59.3	65,757	56.2	3,531	5.1	47,643	40.7
2010...............	122,656	71,904	58.6	65,705	53.6	6,199	8.6	50,752	41.4
2011...............	123,300	71,642	58.1	65,579	53.2	6,063	8.5	51,658	41.9
2012...............	125,941	72,648	57.7	66,914	53.1	5,734	7.9	53,293	42.3
White: [2]									
1980...............	146,122	93,600	64.1	87,715	60.0	5,884	6.3	52,523	35.9
1990...............	160,625	107,447	66.9	102,261	63.7	5,186	4.8	53,178	33.1
2000...............	176,220	118,545	67.3	114,424	64.9	4,121	3.5	57,675	32.7
2005...............	184,446	122,299	66.3	116,949	63.4	5,350	4.4	62,148	33.7
2010...............	192,075	125,084	65.1	114,168	59.4	10,916	8.7	66,991	34.9
2011...............	193,077	124,579	64.5	114,690	59.4	9,889	7.9	68,498	35.5
2012...............	193,204	123,684	64.0	114,769	59.4	8,915	7.2	69,520	36.0
Black: [2]									
1980...............	17,824	10,865	61.0	9,313	52.2	1,553	14.3	6,959	39.0
1990...............	21,477	13,740	64.0	12,175	56.7	1,565	11.4	7,737	36.0
2000...............	24,902	16,397	65.8	15,156	60.9	1,241	7.6	8,505	34.2
2005...............	26,517	17,013	64.2	15,313	57.7	1,700	10.0	9,504	35.8
2010...............	28,708	17,862	62.2	15,010	52.3	2,852	16.0	10,846	37.8
2011...............	29,114	17,881	61.4	15,051	51.7	2,831	15.8	11,233	38.6
2012...............	29,907	18,400	61.5	15,856	53.0	2,544	13.8	11,508	38.5
Asian: [2, 3]									
2000...............	9,330	6,270	67.2	6,043	64.8	227	3.6	3,060	32.8
2005...............	9,842	6,503	66.1	6,244	63.4	259	4.0	3,339	33.9
2010...............	11,199	7,248	64.7	6,705	59.9	543	7.5	3,951	35.3
2011...............	11,439	7,386	64.6	6,867	60.0	518	7.0	4,054	35.4
2012...............	12,815	8,188	63.9	7,705	60.1	483	5.9	4,627	36.1
Hispanic: [4]									
1980...............	9,598	6,146	64.0	5,527	57.6	620	10.1	3,451	36.0
1990...............	15,904	10,720	67.4	9,845	61.9	876	8.2	5,184	32.6
2000...............	23,938	16,689	69.7	15,735	65.7	954	5.7	7,249	30.3
2005...............	29,133	19,824	68.0	18,632	64.0	1,191	6.0	9,310	32.0
2010...............	33,713	22,748	67.5	19,906	59.0	2,843	12.5	10,964	32.5
2011...............	34,438	22,898	66.5	20,269	58.9	2,629	11.5	11,540	33.5
2012...............	36,759	24,391	66.4	21,878	59.5	2,514	10.3	12,368	33.6
Mexican:									
1990...............	9,752	6,707	68.8	6,146	63.0	561	8.4	3,045	31.2
2000...............	15,333	10,783	70.3	10,144	66.2	639	5.9	4,550	29.7
2005...............	18,523	12,671	68.4	11,887	64.2	784	6.2	5,851	31.6
2010...............	21,267	14,403	67.7	12,622	59.4	1,781	12.4	6,864	32.3
2011...............	21,519	14,360	66.7	12,697	59.0	1,663	11.6	7,159	33.3
2012...............	22,716	15,128	66.6	13,552	59.7	1,577	10.4	7,588	33.4
Puerto Rican:									
1990...............	1,718	960	55.9	870	50.6	91	9.5	758	44.1
2000...............	2,193	1,411	64.3	1,318	60.1	92	6.6	783	35.7
2005...............	2,654	1,619	61.0	1,492	56.2	126	7.8	1,035	39.0
2010...............	3,110	1,906	61.3	1,612	51.8	293	15.4	1,204	38.7
2011...............	3,201	1,893	59.2	1,627	50.8	266	14.1	1,307	40.8
2012...............	3,462	2,090	60.4	1,830	52.9	260	12.4	1,372	39.6
Cuban:									
1990...............	918	603	65.7	559	60.9	44	7.2	315	34.3
2000...............	1,174	740	63.1	707	60.3	33	4.5	434	37.0
2005...............	1,259	755	60.0	730	58.0	25	3.3	503	40.0
2010...............	1,549	970	62.6	850	54.9	120	12.4	579	37.4
2011...............	1,533	976	63.6	867	56.5	109	11.2	558	36.4
2012...............	1,702	1,102	64.7	994	58.4	108	9.8	601	35.3

[1] Civilian employed as a percent of the civilian noninstitutional population. [2] Beginning in 2002, the Current Population Survey (CPS) allowed respondents to choose more than one race. For 2002 and beyond, data represent persons who selected this race group only and exclude persons reporting more than one race. The CPS in prior years only allowed respondents to report one race group. See also comments on race in the text for Section 1. [3] Prior to 2002, includes Pacific Islanders. [4] Persons of Hispanic origin may be of any race. Includes persons of other Hispanic or Latino ethnicity, not shown separately.

Source: U.S. Bureau of Labor Statistics, Labor Force Statistics from the Current Population Survey, <http://www.bls.gov/cps/tables.htm>, accessed March 2013.

Table 616. Foreign-Born and Native-Born Populations—Employment Status by Selected Characteristics: 2012

[243,284 represents 243,284,000. For civilian noninstitutional population 16 years old and over, except as indicated. The foreign born are persons who reside in the United States but who were born outside the country or in one of its outlying areas to parents who were not U.S. citizens. The foreign born include legally admitted immigrants, refugees, temporary residents such as students and temporary workers and undocumented immigrants. Annual averages of monthly figures. Based on Current Population Survey; see text, Section 1 and Appendix III]

Characteristic	Civilian noninstitutionalized population (1,000)	Civilian labor force					Not in the labor force
		Total (1,000)	Participation rate [1]	Employed (1,000)	Unemployed		
					Number (1,000)	Unemployment rate	
Total..........................	**243,284**	**154,975**	**63.7**	**142,469**	**12,506**	**8.1**	**88,309**
Male...............................	117,343	82,327	70.2	75,555	6,771	8.2	35,016
Female............................	125,941	72,648	57.7	66,914	5,734	7.9	53,293
FOREIGN BORN							
Total [2].....................	**37,727**	**25,026**	**66.3**	**23,006**	**2,021**	**8.1**	**12,701**
Male...............................	18,365	14,424	78.5	13,342	1,082	7.5	3,941
Female............................	19,362	10,602	54.8	9,663	939	8.9	8,760
Age:							
16 to 24 years old...............	3,724	1,905	51.2	1,632	273	14.3	1,819
25 to 34 years old...............	7,674	5,840	76.1	5,373	468	8.0	1,834
35 to 44 years old...............	8,710	6,997	80.3	6,518	479	6.8	1,713
45 to 54 years old...............	7,509	6,071	80.9	5,622	449	7.4	1,438
55 to 64 years old...............	5,021	3,332	66.4	3,051	282	8.5	1,689
65 years old and over...........	5,089	880	17.3	810	70	8.0	4,209
Race and Hispanic ethnicity:							
White non-Hispanic..............	7,595	4,564	60.1	4,242	322	7.1	3,031
Black non-Hispanic...............	3,068	2,166	70.6	1,925	241	11.1	902
Asian non-Hispanic..............	9,146	5,919	64.7	5,582	337	5.7	3,227
Hispanic [3]......................	17,507	12,087	69.0	10,988	1,099	9.1	5,420
Educational attainment:							
Total, 25 years old and over......	34,002	23,121	68.0	21,374	1,747	7.6	10,881
Less than a high school diploma....	9,497	5,688	59.9	5,126	562	9.9	3,809
High school graduates, no college [4]......	8,713	5,783	66.4	5,314	469	8.1	2,930
Some college or associate's degree...........	5,670	4,028	71.0	3,713	315	7.8	1,642
Bachelor's degree and higher [5].................	10,122	7,621	75.3	7,221	401	5.3	2,501
NATIVE BORN							
Total [2].....................	**205,558**	**129,948**	**63.2**	**119,464**	**10,485**	**8.1**	**75,610**
Male...............................	98,979	67,903	68.6	62,213	5,690	8.4	31,076
Female............................	106,579	62,046	58.2	57,251	4,795	7.7	44,533
Age:							
16 to 24 years old...............	35,059	19,379	55.3	16,202	3,177	16.4	15,680
25 to 34 years old...............	33,301	27,625	83.0	25,328	2,297	8.3	5,676
35 to 44 years old...............	30,932	25,737	83.2	24,058	1,679	6.5	5,195
45 to 54 years old...............	36,188	28,983	80.1	27,252	1,731	6.0	7,205
55 to 64 years old...............	33,297	21,377	64.2	20,189	1,189	5.6	11,920
65 years old and over...........	36,780	6,847	18.6	6,435	412	6.0	29,933
Race and Hispanic ethnicity:							
White non-Hispanic..............	152,742	97,328	63.7	90,949	6,379	6.6	55,414
Black non-Hispanic...............	25,137	15,089	60.0	12,925	2,164	14.3	10,048
Asian non-Hispanic..............	3,277	2,014	61.5	1,880	134	6.7	1,263
Hispanic [3]......................	19,252	12,304	63.9	10,890	1,414	11.5	6,948
Educational attainment:							
Total, 25 years and over..........	170,499	110,569	64.9	103,261	7,308	6.6	59,930
Less than a high school diploma....	15,384	5,640	36.7	4,797	843	14.9	9,744
High school graduates, no college [4]......	53,099	30,988	58.4	28,404	2,584	8.3	22,111
Some college or associate's degree...........	48,624	33,332	68.5	30,992	2339	7.0	15,292
Bachelor's degree and higher [5].................	53,392	40,609	76.1	39,067	1,542	3.8	12,783

[1] Civilian labor force as a percent of the civilian noninstitutionalized population. [2] Includes other races, not shown separately. [3] Persons of Hispanic origin may be of any race. [4] Includes persons with a high school diploma or equivalent. [5] Includes persons with bachelor's, master's, professional, and doctoral degrees.

Source: U.S. Bureau of Labor Statistics, *Foreign-Born Workers: Labor Force Characteristics in 2012*, News Release, USDL-13-0991, May 2013. See also <http://www.bls.gov/news.release/forbrn.toc.htm>.

Table 617. Employment Status of Veterans by Period of Service and Sex: 2012

[In thousands (234,393 represents 234,393,000). For civilian noninstitutional population 18 years old and over. Veterans are defined as men and women who have previously served on active duty in the U.S. Armed Forces and who were civilians at the time they were surveyed. See text, Section 10. Annual averages of monthly figures. Based on Current Population Survey; see text, Section 1 and Appendix III]

Veteran status, period of service, and sex	Civilian non-institutionalized population	Civilian labor force						Not in labor force
		Total	Percent of population	Employed		Unemployed		
				Total	Percent of population	Total	Percent of labor force	
Total, 18 years and over....................	234,393	153,022	65.3	141,050	60.2	11,972	7.8	81,371
Veterans...	**21,183**	**11,006**	**52.0**	**10,233**	**48.3**	**773**	**7.0**	**10,177**
Gulf War era, total.............................	5,615	4,618	82.3	4,263	75.9	355	7.7	997
Gulf War era I [1].............................	3,049	2,548	83.6	2,398	78.6	150	5.9	501
Gulf War era II [2]............................	2,566	2,071	80.7	1,866	72.7	205	9.9	496
WWII, Korean War, and Vietnam era [3]......	9,872	3,165	32.1	2,964	30.0	201	6.4	6,707
Other service periods [4]........................	5,696	3,222	56.6	3,006	52.8	217	6.7	2,473
Nonveterans [5].................................	213,211	142,017	66.6	130,817	61.4	11,200	7.9	71,194
Male, 18 years and over....................	112,793	81,377	72.1	74,896	66.4	6,481	8.0	31,417
Veterans...	**19,368**	**9,884**	**51.0**	**9,204**	**47.5**	**680**	**6.9**	**9,484**
Gulf War era, total.............................	4,703	3,958	84.2	3,669	78.0	289	7.3	745
Gulf War era I [1].............................	2,567	2,184	85.1	2,063	80.4	121	5.6	383
Gulf War era II [2]............................	2,136	1,774	83.1	1,606	75.2	168	9.5	362
WWII, Korean War, and Vietnam era [3]......	9,554	3,063	32.1	2,866	30.0	197	6.4	6,491
Other service periods [4]........................	5,112	2,863	56.0	2,669	52.2	194	6.8	2,248
Nonveterans [5].................................	93,425	71,493	76.5	65,692	70.3	5,801	8.1	21,933
Female, 18 years and over.................	121,600	71,645	58.9	66,154	54.4	5,492	7.7	49,955
Veterans...	**1,815**	**1,122**	**61.8**	**1,029**	**56.7**	**93**	**8.3**	**693**
Gulf War era, total.............................	912	660	72.4	594	65.1	66	10.0	252
Gulf War era I [1].............................	482	364	75.5	335	69.5	29	8.0	118
Gulf War era II [2]............................	431	297	68.9	259	60.2	37	12.5	134
WWII, Korean War, and Vietnam era [3]......	318	102	32.1	98	30.7	4	4.1	216
Other service periods [4]........................	584	359	61.5	337	57.7	22	6.2	225
Nonveterans [5].................................	119,785	70,524	58.9	65,125	54.4	5,399	7.7	49,261

[1] Gulf War era I: August 1990–August 2001. [2] Gulf War era II: September 2001–present. [3] World War II: December 1941–December 1946. Korean War: July 1950–January 1955. Vietnam era: August 1964–April 1975. [4] Other service periods; all other time periods. [5] Nonveterans are men and women who never served on active duty in the U.S. Armed Forces.

Source: Bureau of Labor Statistics, "Employment Situation of Veterans - 2012," News Release, USDL-13-0477, March 2013. See also <http://www.bls.gov/news.release/vet.nr0.htm>.

Table 618. Labor Force Status of Persons With and Without a Disability: 2012

[28,251 represents 28,251,000. For civilian noninstitutionalized population 16 years old and over, except as indicated. Persons with a disability are those who have a physical, mental, or emotional condition that causes serious difficulty with their daily activities. Annual averages of monthly figures. Based on Current Population Survey; see text, Section 1 and Appendix III]

Characteristic	Civilian non-institutionalized population (1,000)	Civilian labor force					Not in the labor force
		Total (1,000)	Participation rate [1]	Employed (1,000)	Unemployed		
					Number (1,000)	Unemployment rate	
WITH DISABILITY							
Total.............................	**28,251**	**5,816**	**20.6**	**5,037**	**779**	**13.4**	**22,435**
Male.............................	12,929	3,190	24.7	2,770	420	13.2	9,739
Female............................	15,322	2,626	17.1	2,267	359	13.7	12,696
Both Sexes 65 and over...........	12,912	961	7.4	890	71	7.4	11,951
WITHOUT DISABILITY							
Total.............................	**215,034**	**149,159**	**69.4**	**137,433**	**11,727**	**7.9**	**65,875**
Male.............................	104,415	79,137	75.8	72,785	6,352	8.0	25,278
Female............................	110,619	70,022	63.3	64,647	5,375	7.7	40,597
Both Sexes 65 and over...........	28,957	6,766	23.4	6,355	411	6.1	22,191

[1] Civilian labor force as a percent of the civilian noninstitutionalized population.

Source: U.S. Bureau of Labor Statistics, Current Population Survey, "Persons with A Disability: Labor Force Characteristics 2012," <http://www.bls.gov/news.release/disabl.nr0.htm>, accessed June 2013.

Table 619. Civilian Labor Force—Percent Distribution by Sex and Age: 1980 to 2012

[106,940 represents 106,940,000. Civilian noninstitutionalized population 16 years old and over. Annual averages of monthly figures. Data not strictly comparable with data for earlier years, see BLS Handbook of Methods, <http://www.bls.gov/opub/hom/>. Based on Current Population Survey; see text, Section 1 and Appendix III]

Year and sex	Civilian labor force (1,000)	Percent distribution						
		16 to 19 years	20 to 24 years	25 to 34 years	35 to 44 years	45 to 54 years	55 to 64 years	65 years and over
Total: 1980...............	106,940	8.8	14.9	27.3	19.1	15.8	11.2	2.9
1990.......................	125,840	6.2	11.7	28.6	25.5	16.1	9.2	2.7
2000.......................	142,583	5.8	10.0	23.0	26.3	21.8	10.1	3.0
2011.......................	153,617	3.7	9.9	22.0	21.3	23.0	15.5	4.6
2012.......................	154,975	3.8	10.0	21.6	21.1	22.6	15.9	5.0
Male: 1980...............	61,453	8.1	14.0	27.6	19.3	16.1	11.8	3.1
1990.......................	69,011	5.9	11.4	28.8	25.3	16.1	9.6	2.9
2000.......................	76,280	5.6	9.9	23.4	26.3	21.3	10.2	3.3
2011.......................	81,975	3.5	9.9	22.5	21.6	22.5	15.1	4.9
2012.......................	82,327	3.6	9.9	22.0	21.4	22.3	15.6	5.3
Female: 1980............	45,487	9.6	16.1	26.9	19.0	15.4	10.4	2.6
1990.......................	56,829	6.5	12.0	28.3	25.8	16.1	8.7	2.6
2000.......................	66,303	6.0	10.2	22.5	26.4	22.3	9.9	2.7
2011.......................	71,642	4.0	10.0	21.3	20.9	23.6	15.9	4.4
2012.......................	72,648	4.0	10.1	21.2	20.8	23.0	16.3	4.7

Source: U.S. Bureau of Labor Statistics, "Employment and Earnings Online," <www.bls.gov/opub/ee/home.htm>, accessed March 2013.

Table 620. Civilian Labor Force and Participation Rates by Educational Attainment, Sex, Race, and Hispanic Origin: 2000 to 2012

[120,061 represents 120,061,000. Civilian noninstitutional population 25 years old and over. Annual averages of monthly figures. Data not strictly comparable with data for earlier years, see BLS Handbook of Methods, <http://www.bls.gov/opub/hom/>. See Table 655 for unemployment data. Rates are based on annual average civilian noninstitutional population of each specified group and represent proportion of each specified group in the civilian labor force]

Year, sex, and race	Civilian labor force					Participation rate (percent) [1]				
	Total (1,000)	Percent distribution				Total	Less than a high school diploma	High school graduate, no college	Less than a bach-elor's degree	College graduate
		Less than a high school diploma	High school graduate, no college	Less than a bach-elor's degree	College graduate					
Total: [2]										
2000...............	120,061	10.4	31.4	27.7	30.5	67.3	43.5	64.4	73.9	79.4
2005...............	127,030	10.0	30.1	27.5	32.4	67.1	45.5	63.2	72.5	77.9
2011...............	132,620	8.7	28.2	27.8	35.3	65.8	46.2	60.3	69.4	76.4
2012...............	133,690	8.5	27.5	27.9	36.1	65.4	45.5	59.5	68.8	75.9
Male:										
2000...............	64,490	11.8	31.1	25.9	31.2	76.1	56.0	75.1	80.9	84.4
2005...............	68,389	11.7	30.9	25.4	32.1	75.4	58.6	73.6	79.3	82.9
2011...............	70,979	10.4	29.8	25.7	34.1	73.3	58.9	69.9	75.0	81.3
2012...............	71,277	10.0	29.4	26.0	34.6	72.9	57.9	69.6	74.9	80.5
Female:										
2000...............	55,572	8.8	31.8	29.7	29.7	59.4	32.3	55.5	68.0	74.0
2005...............	58,641	8.0	29.2	30.0	32.8	59.4	32.9	53.8	66.8	72.9
2010...............	61,825	7.0	26.9	30.1	36.0	59.5	33.5	52.4	65.4	72.4
2012...............	62,413	6.7	25.3	30.2	37.8	58.5	33.4	49.9	63.7	71.7
White: [3]										
2000...............	99,964	10.1	31.4	27.5	31.0	67.0	44.1	63.6	73.1	79.0
2005...............	104,240	9.8	29.9	27.6	32.7	66.9	46.4	62.5	72.0	77.5
2011...............	107,745	8.8	27.9	27.6	35.7	65.8	47.8	59.8	68.9	76.2
2012...............	107,101	8.5	27.4	27.8	36.3	65.2	47.2	58.9	68.2	75.6
Black: [3]										
2000...............	13,582	12.4	36.0	31.2	20.5	68.2	39.3	69.9	79.3	84.4
2005...............	14,252	11.2	36.4	30.2	22.2	67.2	39.8	67.9	75.6	82.0
2011...............	15,129	8.9	33.6	32.8	24.7	64.8	37.9	62.2	72.1	78.6
2012...............	15,480	8.2	32.8	32.7	26.2	64.7	36.5	61.9	71.3	79.0
Asian: [3, 4]										
2000...............	5,402	9.1	20.7	20.2	50.1	70.9	46.0	65.6	76.4	79.1
2005...............	5,805	8.0	17.7	17.3	57.0	69.4	45.3	61.8	71.6	77.5
2011...............	6,726	6.9	18.8	17.4	57.0	68.3	42.2	61.1	70.6	76.2
2012...............	7,418	7.0	17.4	17.7	58.0	68.3	44.3	60.4	70.2	75.5
Hispanic: [5]										
2000...............	12,975	36.7	29.3	20.6	13.4	71.5	61.9	75.0	80.8	83.5
2005...............	16,135	35.5	29.4	20.9	14.2	70.8	61.4	74.3	78.8	81.7
2011...............	18,916	31.0	30.7	22.3	16.0	70.5	61.0	72.7	77.1	80.6
2012...............	20,056	29.5	30.8	22.9	16.9	70.1	60.5	71.4	76.7	80.4

[1] See footnote 1, Table 614. [2] Includes other races, not shown separately. [3] Beginning in 2003, data represent persons who selected this race group only and exclude persons reporting more than one race. See footnote 4, Table 614. [4] 2000 data include Pacific Islanders. [5] Persons of Hispanic origin may be of any race.

Source: U.S. Bureau of Labor Statistics, "Employment and Earnings Online," <www.bls.gov/opub/ee/home.htm>, accessed March 2013.

Table 621. Civilian Labor Force by Employment Status and Sex, by State: 2011

[In thousands (153,617 represents 153,617,000), except ratio and rate. Civilian noninstitutionalized population 16 years old and over. Annual averages of monthly figures. Data for states may not sum to national totals due to rounding]

State	Total		Employed		Employ-ment/population ratio [1]	Unemployed					Participation rate [3]	
						Total		Rate [2]				
	Number	Female	Total	Female		Number	Female	Total	Male	Female	Male	Female
United States	**153,617**	**71,642**	**139,869**	**65,579**	**58.4**	**13,747**	**6,063**	**8.9**	**9.4**	**8.5**	**70.5**	**58.1**
Alabama	2,224	1,054	2,006	962	53.8	218	92	9.8	10.8	8.7	66.2	53.6
Alaska	370	167	342	157	64.6	28	10	7.6	8.8	6.1	75.1	64.6
Arizona	3,021	1,370	2,732	1,242	55.5	288	128	9.5	9.7	9.3	67.6	55.1
Arkansas	1,364	644	1,247	589	55.3	117	55	8.6	8.6	8.6	66.3	55.2
California	18,377	8,229	16,239	7,294	56.1	2,138	935	11.6	11.9	11.4	71.1	56.0
Colorado	2,738	1,252	2,507	1,155	63.9	231	97	8.4	9.0	7.8	76.3	63.5
Connecticut	1,916	909	1,745	828	61.8	170	81	8.9	8.9	8.9	74.0	62.2
Delaware	446	218	412	202	58.0	33	15	7.5	7.9	7.1	67.3	58.5
District of Columbia	348	174	312	156	60.7	36	19	10.4	10.1	10.7	73.3	63.0
Florida	9,293	4,390	8,366	3,986	55.0	927	404	10.0	10.7	9.2	66.6	55.9
Georgia	4,743	2,259	4,263	2,030	57.8	480	229	10.1	10.1	10.2	70.4	58.6
Hawaii	668	318	619	300	58.9	49	19	7.3	8.7	5.8	67.8	59.3
Idaho	769	345	702	317	59.4	67	28	8.7	9.2	8.1	72.4	57.9
Illinois	6,559	3,033	5,925	2,765	59.6	634	268	9.7	10.4	8.8	72.9	59.3
Indiana	3,201	1,493	2,913	1,353	58.2	288	140	9.0	8.7	9.4	70.1	58.1
Iowa	1,667	790	1,570	747	66.0	97	43	5.8	6.1	5.4	75.1	65.3
Kansas	1,500	700	1,399	656	64.6	101	44	6.7	7.2	6.2	75.3	63.4
Kentucky	2,055	972	1,859	890	55.1	196	82	9.5	10.5	8.5	66.7	55.6
Louisiana	2,054	959	1,893	876	54.5	161	83	7.8	7.1	8.7	66.5	52.4
Maine	700	339	643	316	59.6	56	24	8.0	9.0	7.0	69.1	60.8
Maryland	3,090	1,500	2,873	1,397	63.2	217	103	7.0	7.2	6.8	73.6	62.9
Massachusetts	3,458	1,678	3,207	1,574	60.8	251	104	7.3	8.2	6.2	70.1	61.3
Michigan	4,658	2,190	4,181	1,998	53.9	477	192	10.2	11.6	8.8	65.6	54.9
Minnesota	2,954	1,403	2,764	1,319	66.6	191	83	6.5	6.9	5.9	75.6	66.8
Mississippi	1,348	654	1,206	593	53.8	142	62	10.5	11.6	9.4	65.8	55.0
Missouri	3,070	1,473	2,812	1,361	60.5	258	112	8.4	9.2	7.6	71.4	61.0
Montana	503	241	466	227	59.3	37	14	7.3	8.7	5.7	67.1	60.8
Nebraska	1,009	481	963	460	68.7	46	21	4.5	4.8	4.3	76.6	67.4
Nevada	1,376	617	1,197	547	57.1	180	70	13.1	14.4	11.4	71.9	59.4
New Hampshire	737	350	697	333	65.8	40	17	5.4	6.0	4.8	74.4	64.9
New Jersey	4,590	2,130	4,159	1,935	60.1	430	194	9.4	9.6	9.1	73.3	59.8
New Mexico	927	423	858	396	54.2	69	27	7.4	8.2	6.5	65.4	52.0
New York	9,476	4,509	8,707	4,157	56.3	769	352	8.1	8.4	7.8	67.0	56.1
North Carolina	4,631	2,163	4,145	1,947	56.0	486	216	10.5	10.9	10.0	70.0	55.8
North Dakota	391	183	377	177	70.8	14	6	3.6	3.8	3.4	77.9	68.9
Ohio	5,765	2,733	5,265	2,517	58.5	500	216	8.7	9.4	7.9	69.9	58.6
Oklahoma	1,768	808	1,657	755	57.7	110	52	6.2	6.0	6.5	69.3	54.4
Oregon	2,005	959	1,818	876	59.3	188	83	9.4	10.0	8.7	69.6	61.3
Pennsylvania	6,395	2,998	5,895	2,780	58.2	499	218	7.8	8.3	7.3	69.7	57.1
Rhode Island	559	274	497	246	59.0	62	28	11.1	12.0	10.1	70.3	62.7
South Carolina	2,167	1,041	1,941	938	53.7	227	103	10.5	11.0	9.9	65.8	54.7
South Dakota	443	211	421	201	67.4	22	10	4.9	5.0	4.7	74.9	66.8
Tennessee	3,142	1,479	2,854	1,350	57.3	288	129	9.2	9.6	8.7	69.9	57.0
Texas	12,449	5,566	11,476	5,124	60.5	973	442	7.8	7.7	7.9	74.0	57.6
Utah	1,337	582	1,244	545	62.4	93	37	7.0	7.4	6.4	76.0	58.1
Vermont	362	174	340	165	66.7	21	9	5.8	6.4	5.3	74.9	66.9
Virginia	4,229	1,999	3,954	1,867	63.4	276	132	6.5	6.4	6.6	74.6	61.6
Washington	3,452	1,622	3,127	1,483	58.8	325	139	9.4	10.2	8.6	70.0	60.1
West Virginia	807	373	742	348	49.9	65	26	8.1	9.1	6.9	59.9	48.9
Wisconsin	3,089	1485	2,848	1,386	63.8	240	99	7.8	8.8	6.7	73.0	65.5
Wyoming	308	138	290	129	66.2	18	9	5.9	5.5	6.5	77.1	63.5

[1] Civilian employment as a percent of civilian noninstitutionalized population. [2] Percent unemployed of the civilian labor force. [3] Percent of civilian noninstitutionalized population of each specified group in the civilian labor force.

Source: U.S. Bureau of Labor Statistics, *Geographic Profile of Employment and Unemployment, 2011*, Bulletin 2774, September 2012. See also <http://www.bls.gov/gps/>.

Table 622. Civilian Labor Force Status by Selected Metropolitan Areas: 2012

[154,975 represents 154,975,000. Civilian noninstitutional population 16 years old and over. Annual averages of monthly figures. Data are derived from the Local Area Unemployment Statistics program, a Federal-State cooperative effort in which monthly estimates of total employment and unemployment are prepared for approximately 7,300 areas. For definitions of metropolitan areas, see Appendix II.]

Metropolitan area ranked by population, 2010	Civilian labor force (1,000)	Unemployment rate [1]	Metropolitan area ranked by population, 2010	Civilian labor force (1,000)	Unemployment rate [1]
U.S. total, 2012............	**154,975**	**8.1**	San Antonio-New Braunfels, TX................	1,026	6.5
New York-Northern New Jersey-Long Island, NY-NJ-PA.	9,556	8.8	Orlando-Kissimmee-Sanford, FL.............	1,148	8.4
Los Angeles-Long Beach-Santa Ana, CA........	6,498	10.1	Cincinnati-Middletown, OH-KY-IN.............	1,089	7.1
Chicago-Joliet-Naperville, IL-IN-WI...............	4,889	8.9	Cleveland-Elyria-Mentor, OH.................	1,055	7.1
Dallas-Fort Worth-Arlington, TX....................	3,340	6.7	Kansas City, MO-KS.......................	1,044	6.6
Philadelphia-Camden-Wilmington, PA-NJ-DE-MD.	3,019	8.6	Las Vegas-Paradise, NV....................	992	11.2
Houston-Sugar Land-Baytown, TX...............	3,038	6.8	Columbus, OH........................	970	6.1
Washington-Arlington-Alexandria, DC-VA-MD-WV.	3,182	5.6	Indianapolis-Carmel, IN.................	905	7.8
Miami-Fort Lauderdale-Pompano Beach, FL.....	2,950	8.5	San Jose-Sunnyvale-Santa Clara, CA............	938	8.6
Atlanta-Sandy Springs-Marietta, GA.........	2,736	8.8	Austin-Round Rock-San Marcos, TX.............	964	5.8
Boston-Cambridge-Quincy, MA-NH NECTA [2]....	2,551	6.1	Virginia Beach-Norfolk-Newport News, VA-NC...	826	6.6
San Francisco-Oakland-Fremont, CA..............	2,324	8.1	Nashville-Davidson-Murfreesboro-Franklin, TN...	851	6.6
Detroit-Warren-Livonia, MI.....................	2,007	10.5	Providence-Fall River-Warwick, RI-MA NECTA [2]..	696	10.3
Riverside-San Bernardino-Ontario, CA...........	1,805	12.1	Milwaukee-Waukesha-West Allis, WI............	795	7.4
Phoenix-Mesa-Glendale, AZ.................	2,037	7.3	Jacksonville, FL......................	696	8.3
Seattle-Tacoma-Bellevue, WA..............	1,891	7.4	Memphis, TN-MS-AR.................	616	9.0
Minneapolis-St. Paul-Bloomington, MN-WI........	1,857	5.5	Oklahoma City, OK.................	595	4.8
San Diego-Carlsbad-San Marcos, CA.............	1,599	8.9	Louisville-Jefferson County, KY-IN.............	633	8.3
St. Louis, MO-IL...............	1,418	7.6	Hartford-West Hartford-East Hartford, CT NECTA [2]	594	8.4
Tampa-St. Petersburg-Clearwater, FL.............	1,325	8.8	Richmond, VA......................	665	6.4
Baltimore-Towson, MD.....................	1,474	7.2	New Orleans-Metairie-Kenner, LA...........	545	6.5
Denver-Aurora-Broomfield, CO.................	1,417	7.9	Buffalo-Niagara Falls, NY...............	573	8.5
Pittsburgh, PA.........................	1,255	7.2	Raleigh-Cary, NC....................	601	7.7
Portland-Vancouver-Hillsboro, OR-WA............	1,187	8.2	Birmingham-Hoover, AL.................	531	6.4
Charlotte-Gastonia-Rock Hill, NC-SC..........	919	9.5	Salt Lake City, UT..................	602	5.5
Sacramento--Arden-Arcade--Roseville, CA.......	1,048	10.4	Rochester, NY.....................	524	8.1

[1] Percent unemployed of the civilian labor force. [2] New England City and Town Areas. See Appendix II.

Source: U.S. Bureau of Labor Statistics, "Local Area Unemployment Statistics," <http://www.bls.gov/lau/>, accessed June 2013.

Table 623. School Enrollment and Labor Force Status: 2012

[In thousands (38,800 represents 38,800,000), except percent. As of October. Based on Current Population Survey; see text, Section 1 and Appendix III]

Characteristic	Population	Civilian labor force	Employed	Unemployed Total	Unemployed Rate [1]	Not in labor force
Total, 16 to 24 years [2]..................	**38,800**	**21,466**	**18,167**	**3,299**	**15.4**	**17,334**
Enrolled in school [2].................................	22,718	8,717	7,520	1,196	13.7	14,002
Enrolled in high school.........................	10,033	2,262	1,742	520	23.0	7,771
Male...............................	5,209	1,093	822	271	24.8	4,116
Female............................	4,824	1,169	920	249	21.3	3,656
Enrolled in college............................	12,685	6,454	5,778	676	10.5	6,231
Enrolled in 2 year college....................	3,956	2,234	1,912	322	14.4	1,722
Enrolled in 4 year college....................	8,729	4,220	3,866	354	8.4	4,509
Race/ethnicity:						
White: [3]						
Enrolled in high school......................	7,327	1,777	1,424	353	19.8	5,550
Enrolled in college........................	9,472	4,938	4,513	425	8.6	4,535
Black or African American: [3]						
Enrolled in high school...................	1,652	338	206	132	39.1	1,314
Enrolled in college.....................	1,716	837	682	155	18.5	879
Asian: [3]						
Enrolled in high school...................	502	39	35	4	([5])	463
Enrolled in college.....................	937	377	341	36	9.6	561
Hispanic: [4]						
Enrolled in high school...................	2,179	338	228	110	32.7	1,841
Enrolled in college.....................	2,459	1,240	1,114	126	10.2	1,218
Not enrolled [2].................................	16,082	12,749	10,647	2,102	16.5	3,333
White [3].................................	12,145	9,914	8,515	1,398	14.1	2,231
Black [3].................................	2,606	1,866	1,320	546	29.2	739
Asian [3].................................	536	379	327	53	13.9	157
Hispanic [4].................................	3,563	2,659	2,187	472	17.8	904

[1] Percent unemployed of civilian labor force in each category. [2] Includes other races, not shown separately. [3] Data for persons in this race group only. See footnote 4, Table 614. [4] Persons of Hispanic origin may be of any race. [5] Data not shown where base is less than 75,000.

Source: U.S. Bureau of Labor Statistics, *College Enrollment and Work Activity of 2012 High School Graduates*, News Release, USDL 13-0670, April 2013. See also <http://www.bls.gov/news.release/hsgec.toc.htm>.

Table 624. Labor Force Participation Rates by Marital Status, Sex, and Age: 1970 to 2012

[In percent. For the civilian noninstitutional population 16 years old and over. Annual averages of monthly figures. Participation rate is the civilian labor force as a percent of the civilian noninstitutional population. Based on Current Population Survey; see text, Section 1 and Appendix III]

Marital status and year	Male participation rate							Female participation rate						
	Total	16–19 years	20–24 years	25–34 years	35–44 years	45–64 years	65 years and over	Total	16–19 years	20–24 years	25–34 years	35–44 years	45–64 years	65 years and over
Single: [1]														
1970............	65.5	54.6	73.8	87.9	86.2	75.7	25.2	56.8	44.7	73.0	81.4	78.6	73.0	19.7
1980............	72.6	59.9	81.3	89.2	82.2	66.9	16.8	64.4	53.6	75.2	83.3	76.9	65.6	13.9
1990............	74.8	55.1	81.6	89.9	84.5	67.3	15.7	66.7	51.7	74.5	80.9	80.8	66.2	12.1
2000............	73.6	52.5	80.5	89.4	82.9	69.7	17.3	68.9	51.1	76.1	83.9	80.9	69.9	10.8
2005............	70.1	42.9	77.0	87.9	82.9	68.6	18.8	66.0	44.2	72.6	81.4	80.7	70.9	15.5
2006............	70.7	43.4	77.8	87.7	83.5	69.9	19.3	65.7	43.7	71.8	81.4	79.8	70.5	15.0
2007............	70.1	40.8	76.9	88.5	84.0	70.3	22.6	65.3	41.4	72.6	82.1	78.0	70.4	18.4
2008............	69.9	39.8	77.1	87.9	84.3	69.5	24.7	65.3	40.3	71.9	82.6	79.6	70.4	20.5
2009............	68.3	37.1	74.6	86.5	83.7	68.5	26.1	64.2	37.5	71.4	81.6	79.5	69.3	19.7
2010............	67.3	34.6	73.1	85.8	83.7	67.6	25.0	63.3	34.9	69.8	81.3	78.2	69.4	20.1
2011............	67.0	33.4	73.3	85.4	82.6	67.4	23.8	62.8	34.3	69.1	79.9	77.8	67.8	21.7
2012............	66.8	33.7	72.9	85.8	81.7	67.1	23.6	62.8	34.5	68.5	79.8	78.1	68.2	20.5
Married: [2]														
1970............	86.1	92.3	94.7	98.0	98.1	91.2	29.9	40.5	37.8	47.9	38.8	46.8	44.0	7.3
1980............	80.9	91.3	96.9	97.5	97.2	84.3	20.5	49.8	49.3	61.4	58.8	61.8	46.9	7.3
1990............	78.6	92.1	95.6	96.9	96.7	82.6	17.5	58.4	49.5	66.1	69.6	74.0	56.5	8.5
2000............	77.3	79.5	94.1	96.7	95.8	83.0	19.2	61.1	53.2	63.8	70.3	74.8	65.4	10.1
2005............	77.2	71.4	93.4	95.3	95.2	83.6	21.4	60.7	44.1	61.1	68.4	73.0	67.0	12.5
2006............	77.1	79.2	93.3	95.5	95.2	83.6	21.8	61.0	39.6	59.8	69.0	73.3	67.8	12.4
2007............	76.9	86.9	92.9	95.7	95.3	83.6	21.8	61.0	43.3	61.7	68.6	73.1	67.7	13.6
2008............	76.8	83.4	92.0	95.3	95.2	84.0	22.8	61.4	38.0	62.3	69.5	73.8	68.3	14.1
2009............	76.3	75.8	91.2	94.7	94.8	83.8	23.3	61.4	44.7	61.8	69.4	73.7	68.6	14.9
2010............	75.8	78.2	89.3	94.3	94.5	83.6	23.5	61.0	40.2	60.9	68.8	72.8	68.8	15.2
2011............	74.9	75.9	90.2	93.9	94.3	82.8	24.5	60.2	44.7	60.6	68.2	72.5	68.0	15.3
2012............	74.6	83.7	91.3	94.2	94.3	83.0	25.6	59.5	42.1	60.5	68.5	72.3	67.3	15.9
Other: [3]														
1970............	60.7	(B)	90.4	93.7	91.1	78.5	19.3	40.3	48.6	60.3	64.6	68.8	61.9	10.0
1980............	67.5	(B)	92.6	94.1	91.9	73.3	13.7	43.6	50.0	68.4	76.5	77.1	60.2	8.2
1990............	68.9	(B)	93.1	93.0	90.7	74.9	12.0	47.2	53.9	65.4	77.0	82.1	65.0	8.4
2000............	66.8	60.5	88.1	93.2	89.9	73.9	12.9	49.0	46.0	74.0	83.1	82.9	69.8	8.7
2005............	64.9	54.9	86.4	90.4	89.4	72.7	15.1	49.4	46.8	67.4	78.1	80.9	69.4	10.5
2006............	65.6	47.8	86.0	91.5	88.9	73.8	16.3	49.6	45.3	71.5	78.2	80.9	69.3	10.9
2007............	65.6	43.4	82.5	92.1	89.4	73.7	16.1	49.5	44.6	63.8	78.4	81.4	69.3	11.4
2008............	65.0	43.2	84.9	90.7	89.4	73.2	16.8	49.2	39.7	64.9	77.4	81.4	69.1	12.1
2009............	63.7	42.6	78.6	88.5	88.5	71.8	17.0	49.3	39.0	68.3	78.2	80.5	68.8	12.1
2010............	63.0	37.6	78.8	89.0	88.5	71.8	17.2	48.8	35.2	66.3	77.7	80.7	68.8	12.1
2011............	62.4	39.7	76.2	88.3	87.2	71.1	17.8	48.8	39.9	65.6	77.1	79.2	68.3	12.3
2012............	61.7	35.1	78.3	88.5	87.4	70.9	17.6	48.3	34.9	68.4	77.4	79.8	67.6	12.6

B Percentage not shown where base is less than 50,000. [1] Never married. [2] Spouse present. [3] Widowed, divorced, and married (spouse absent).

Source: Bureau of Labor Statistics, Bulletin 2217 and unpublished Basic Tabulations, Table 12. See also <http://www.bls.gov/cps/home.htm>.

Table 625. Marital Status of Women in the Civilian Labor Force: 1970 to 2012

[31,543 represents 31,543,000. For civilian noninstitutional population 16 years and over. Annual averages of monthly figures. Based on the Current Population Survey; see text, Section 1 and Appendix III]

Year	Female civilian labor force (1,000)				Female participation rate (percent) [3]			
	Total	Never married	Married [1]	Other [2]	Total	Never married	Married [1]	Other [2]
1970................	31,543	7,265	18,475	5,804	43.3	56.8	40.5	40.3
1980................	45,487	11,865	24,980	8,643	51.5	64.4	49.8	43.6
1990................	56,829	14,612	30,901	11,315	57.5	66.7	58.4	47.2
2000................	66,303	17,849	35,146	13,308	59.9	68.9	61.1	49.0
2003................	68,272	18,397	36,046	13,828	59.5	66.2	61.0	49.6
2004................	68,421	18,616	35,845	13,961	59.2	65.9	60.5	49.6
2005................	69,288	19,183	35,941	14,163	59.3	66.0	60.7	49.4
2006................	70,173	19,474	36,314	14,385	59.4	65.7	61.0	49.6
2007................	70,988	19,745	36,881	14,362	59.3	65.3	61.0	49.5
2008................	71,767	20,231	37,194	14,342	59.5	65.3	61.4	49.2
2009................	72,019	20,224	37,264	14,531	59.2	64.2	61.4	49.3
2010................	71,904	20,592	36,742	14,570	58.6	63.3	61.0	48.8
2011................	71,642	20,878	36,141	14,623	58.1	62.8	60.2	48.8
2012................	72,648	21,506	36,436	14,706	57.7	62.8	59.5	48.3

[1] Husband present. [2] Widowed, divorced, or separated. [3] Civilian labor force as a percent of the civilian noninstitutional population.

Source: Bureau of Labor Statistics, unpublished Basic Tabulations, Table 12. See also <http://www.bls.gov/cps/home.htm>.

Table 626. Employment Status of Women by Marital Status and Presence and Age of Children: 1970 to 2012

[As of March (7.0 represents 7,000,000). Data from Current Population Survey, Annual Social and Economic Supplement (ASEC), which includes civilian noninstitutionalized population, age 16 years old and over. For more information; see text, Section 1 and Appendix III]

Item	Total			With any children under 18								
				Total			Children 6 to 17 years only			Children under 6 years		
	Single [1]	Mar-ried [2]	Other [3]	Single [1]	Mar-ried [2]	Other [3]	Single [1]	Mar-ried [2]	Other [3]	Single [1]	Mar-ried [2]	Other [3]
IN LABOR FORCE (mil.)												
1970	7.0	18.4	5.9	(NA)	10.2	1.9	(NA)	6.3	1.3	(NA)	3.9	0.6
1980	11.2	24.9	8.8	0.6	13.7	3.6	0.2	8.4	2.6	0.3	5.2	1.0
1990	14.0	31.0	11.2	1.5	16.5	4.2	0.6	9.3	3.0	0.9	7.2	1.2
2000	17.8	35.0	13.2	3.1	18.2	4.5	1.2	10.8	3.4	1.8	7.3	1.1
2010	20.0	37.2	14.7	3.6	17.6	4.5	1.6	10.4	3.3	2.1	7.2	1.2
2011	20.6	36.4	14.6	3.8	17.1	4.5	1.6	10.0	3.3	2.2	7.1	1.2
2012	21.4	36.4	14.8	4.1	16.7	4.5	1.7	9.9	3.4	2.4	6.9	1.2
PARTICIPATION RATE [4]												
1970	53.0	40.8	39.1	(NA)	39.7	60.7	(NA)	49.2	66.9	(NA)	30.3	52.2
1980	61.5	50.1	44.0	52.0	54.1	69.4	67.6	61.7	74.6	44.1	45.1	60.3
1990	66.4	58.2	46.8	55.2	66.3	74.2	69.7	73.6	79.7	48.7	58.9	63.6
2000	68.6	62.0	50.2	73.9	70.6	82.7	79.7	77.2	84.9	70.5	62.8	76.6
2010	62.3	61.7	49.2	70.1	69.7	79.2	77.0	75.9	81.8	65.6	62.5	73.1
2011	62.3	60.5	48.9	70.0	69.1	79.7	76.4	74.9	81.9	65.8	62.3	74.2
2012	62.5	59.6	48.8	71.5	68.5	80.2	77.0	73.7	82.8	68.1	62.3	73.5
EMPLOYMENT (mil.)												
1970	6.5	17.5	5.6	(NA)	9.6	1.8	(NA)	6.0	1.2	(NA)	3.6	0.6
1980	10.1	23.6	8.2	0.4	12.8	3.3	0.2	8.1	2.4	0.2	4.8	0.9
1990	12.9	29.9	10.5	1.2	15.8	3.8	0.5	8.9	2.7	0.7	6.9	1.1
2000	16.4	34.0	12.7	2.7	17.6	4.3	1.1	10.6	3.2	1.6	7.1	1.1
2010	17.5	35.0	13.3	3.0	16.5	4.0	1.3	9.8	2.9	1.6	6.7	1.1
2011	18.1	34.3	13.2	3.1	16.1	4.0	1.4	9.4	3.0	1.7	6.6	1.0
2012	18.9	34.4	13.5	3.4	15.9	4.1	1.5	9.4	3.0	2.0	6.5	1.0
UNEMPLOYMENT RATE [5]												
1970	7.1	4.8	4.8	(NA)	6.0	7.2	(NA)	4.8	5.9	(NA)	7.9	9.8
1980	10.3	5.3	6.4	23.2	5.9	9.2	15.6	4.4	7.9	29.2	8.3	12.8
1990	8.2	3.5	5.7	18.4	4.2	8.5	14.5	3.8	7.7	20.8	4.8	10.2
2000	7.3	2.7	4.3	11.0	2.9	5.1	8.7	2.6	4.8	12.6	3.5	5.9
2010	12.3	6.0	9.7	18.1	6.3	11.1	14.4	6.0	10.3	20.9	6.7	13.4
2011	12.0	5.6	9.5	18.9	5.9	11.9	13.5	5.6	10.5	22.9	6.4	15.7
2012	11.8	5.3	8.7	16.7	5.1	10.4	13.9	4.8	9.1	18.7	5.6	14.2

NA Not available. [1] Never married. [2] Husband present. [3] Widowed, divorced, or separated (including married, spouse absent). [4] Percent of women in each specific category in the labor force. [5] Unemployed as a percent of civilian labor force in specified group.

Source: Bureau of Labor Statistics, Bulletin 2307 and unpublished data. See also <http://www.bls.gov/cps/home.htm>

Table 627. Labor Force Participation Rates for Wives, Husband Present, by Age of Own Youngest Child: 1990 to 2012

[In percent. As of March. Base on Current Population Survey, Annual Social and Economic Supplement (ASEC), which includes civilian noninstitutionalized population, 16 years old and over, and military personnel who live in households with at least one other civilian adult. Armed Forces includes only those Armed Forces members living on or off post with their families; all other members of the Armed Forces are excluded. Data refer to persons in primary families. For more information; see text, Section 1 and Appendix III]

Presence and age of child	1990	2000	2005	2011	2012				
					Total	White [1]	Black [1]	Asian [1,2]	His-panic [3]
Wives, total	**58.3**	**62.2**	**60.4**	**60.9**	**59.8**	**59.2**	**65.4**	**59.8**	**56.9**
No children under 18 years	51.1	54.8	54.1	54.9	53.8	53.3	57.2	57.7	54.7
With children under 18 years	66.5	70.9	68.3	69.6	68.8	68.6	75.9	61.9	58.3
Under 6 years, total	59.1	63.1	60.3	62.9	62.6	62.4	72.4	55.3	51.7
Under 3 years	55.9	59.4	57.3	60.6	59.6	59.4	71.1	51.9	46.3
under 1 year	53.9	58.4	55.8	58.2	58.0	58.0	65.4	55.1	43.2
1 year	(NA)	(NA)	(NA)	62.2	58.3	58.2	70.4	45.7	43.7
2 years	60.9	61.9	60.8	61.4	62.7	62.2	76.6	56.2	52.2
3 to 5 years	64.1	68.6	64.8	66.1	66.6	66.4	74.0	59.9	58.2
3 years	63.0	66.0	62.7	64.1	67.3	67.1	77.8	61.5	60.8
4 years	65.0	69.6	64.9	67.1	66.0	64.6	77.2	61.3	57.6
5 years	64.4	70.7	67.5	67.4	66.4	67.6	66.6	56.0	56.0
6 to 13 years	73.1	76.0	73.2	73.7	72.1	71.8	77.3	67.5	62.8
14 to 17 years	75.0	80.8	79.6	78.6	77.7	77.9	81.8	69.8	69.0

NA Not available. [1] Beginning 2005, for persons in this race group only. See footnote 4, Table 614. [2] Excludes Pacific Islanders. [3] Persons of Hispanic origin may be of any race.

Source: Bureau of Labor Statistics, Bulletin 2307 and unpublished data. See also <http://www.bls.gov/cps/home.htm>

Table 628. Married Couples by Labor Force Status of Spouses: 1990 to 2012

[As of March. (52,317 represents 52,317,000). Based on the Annual Social and Economic Supplement (ASEC) to the Current Population Survey, for details see source and Appendix III]

Year	Number (1,000)					Percent distribution				
	All married couples	In labor force			Husband and wife not in labor force	All married couples	In labor force			Husband and wife not in labor force
		Husband and wife	Husband only	Wife only			Husband and wife	Husband only	Wife only	
TOTAL										
1990....................	52,317	28,056	13,013	2,453	8,794	100.0	53.6	24.9	4.7	16.8
2000....................	55,311	31,095	11,815	3,301	9,098	100.0	56.2	21.4	6.0	16.4
2005....................	57,975	31,398	13,385	3,641	9,551	100.0	54.2	23.1	6.3	16.5
2006....................	58,179	31,783	12,990	3,754	9,652	100.0	54.6	22.3	6.5	16.6
2007....................	60,676	33,337	13,351	4,031	9,958	100.0	54.9	22.0	6.6	16.4
2008....................	60,129	32,988	13,141	4,118	9,882	100.0	54.8	21.8	6.8	16.4
2009....................	60,844	33,249	13,207	4,314	10,074	100.0	54.6	21.7	7.1	16.6
2010....................	60,384	32,731	13,074	4,526	10,053	100.0	53.6	21.7	7.5	16.6
2011....................	60,840	32,231	13,455	4,516	10,636	100.0	53.0	22.1	7.4	17.5
2012....................	61,047	31,803	13,820	4,595	10,830	100.0	52.1	22.6	7.5	17.7
WITH CHILDREN UNDER 18										
1990....................	24,537	15,768	7,667	558	544	100.0	64.3	31.2	2.3	2.2
2000....................	25,248	17,116	6,950	795	387	100.0	67.8	27.5	3.1	1.5
2005....................	25,919	16,789	7,806	925	400	100.0	64.8	30.1	3.6	1.5
2006....................	25,982	16,909	7,754	900	420	100.0	65.1	29.9	3.5	1.6
2007....................	26,802	17,670	7,743	920	469	100.0	65.9	28.9	3.4	1.7
2008....................	25,778	16,977	7,398	932	471	100.0	65.9	28.7	3.6	1.8
2009....................	25,799	17,054	7,284	963	501	100.0	66.1	28.2	3.7	1.9
2010....................	25,317	16,710	7,220	962	425	100.0	66.0	28.5	3.8	1.7
2011....................	24,936	16,189	7,270	1,007	469	100.0	64.9	29.2	4.0	1.9
2012....................	24,445	15,752	7,226	1,009	457	100.0	64.4	29.6	4.1	1.9
WITH CHILDREN UNDER 6										
1990....................	12,051	6,932	4,692	192	235	100.0	57.5	38.9	1.6	2.0
2000....................	11,393	6,984	4,077	211	121	100.0	61.3	35.8	1.9	1.1
2005....................	11,802	6,813	4,553	299	137	100.0	57.7	38.6	2.5	1.2
2006....................	11,984	6,939	4,572	324	149	100.0	57.9	38.2	2.7	1.2
2007....................	12,468	7,337	4,633	331	167	100.0	58.8	37.2	2.7	1.3
2008....................	11,848	6,976	4,382	321	168	100.0	58.9	37.1	2.7	1.4
2009....................	11,760	6,917	4,330	329	185	100.0	58.8	36.8	2.8	1.6
2010....................	11,599	6,924	4,181	335	159	100.0	59.7	36.0	2.9	1.4
2011....................	11,416	6,720	4,152	368	177	100.0	58.9	36.4	3.2	1.6
2012....................	11,055	6,509	3,986	383	176	100.0	58.9	36.1	3.5	1.6

Source: U.S. Census Bureau, Families and Living Arrangements, Detailed Table MC-1, "Married Couples by Labor Force Status of Spouses: 1986 to Present," November 2012, <http://www.census.gov/hhes/families/mc1.xls>.

Table 629. Employed Civilians and Weekly Hours: 1980 to 2012

[In thousands (99,303 represents 99,303,000), except as indicated. Annual averages of monthly figures. Civilian noninstitutionalized population 16 years old and over. Based on Current Population Survey; see text, Section 1 and Appendix III]

Item	1980	1990	2000	2005	2010	2011	2012
Total employed.................	**99,303**	**118,793**	**136,891**	**141,730**	**139,064**	**139,869**	**142,469**
Age:							
16 to 19 years old...................	7,710	6,581	7,189	5,978	4,378	4,327	4,426
20 to 24 years old...................	14,087	13,401	13,229	13,792	12,699	13,036	13,408
25 to 34 years old...................	27,204	33,935	31,549	30,680	30,229	30,537	30,701
35 to 44 years old...................	19,523	30,817	36,433	34,630	30,663	30,270	30,576
45 to 54 years old...................	16,234	19,525	30,310	33,207	33,191	32,867	32,874
55 to 64 years old...................	11,586	11,189	14,002	18,349	21,636	22,186	23,239
65 years old and over.................	2,960	3,346	4,179	5,094	6,268	6,647	7,245
Class of worker:							
Nonagricultural industries...............	95,938	115,570	134,427	139,532	136,858	137,615	140,283
Wage and salary worker [1]............	88,525	106,598	125,114	129,931	127,914	128,934	131,452
Self-employed......................	7,000	8,719	9,205	9,509	8,860	8,603	8,749
Unpaid family workers..............	413	253	108	93	84	78	81
Agriculture and related industries..............	3,364	3,223	2,464	2,197	2,206	2,254	2,186
Wage and salary worker [1]...........	1,425	1,740	1,421	1,212	1,353	1,380	1,377
Self-employed......................	1,642	1,378	1,010	955	821	846	780
Unpaid family workers..............	297	105	33	30	33	28	29
Weekly hours:							
Nonagricultural industries:							
Wage and salary workers [1]............	38.1	39.2	39.6	39.1	38.3	38.4	38.6
Self-employed......................	41.2	40.8	39.7	38.4	35.6	35.6	36.0
Unpaid family workers..............	34.7	34.0	32.5	32.2	33.3	33.0	33.2
Agriculture and related industries:							
Wage and salary workers [1]............	41.6	41.2	43.2	43.6	41.6	(NA)	(NA)
Self-employed......................	49.3	46.8	45.3	44.0	42.0	(NA)	(NA)
Unpaid family workers..............	38.6	38.5	38.3	41.1	42.1	(NA)	(NA)

[1] Includes the incorporated self-employed.

Source: Bureau of Labor Statistics, "Labor Force Statistics from the Current Population Survey," <http://www.bls.gov/cps>, accessed August 2013.

Table 630. Persons at Work by Hours Worked: 2012

[In thousands (137,337 represents 137,337,000), except as indicated. Annual averages of monthly figures. Persons "at work" are a subgroup of employed persons "at work," excluding those absent from their jobs during reference period for reasons such as vacation, illness, or industrial dispute. Civilian noninstitutionalized population 16 years old and over. Based on Current Population Survey; see text, Section 1, and Appendix III.]

Hours of work	Persons at work (1,000)			Percent distribution		
	Total	Agriculture and related industries	Non-agricultural industries	Total	Agriculture and related industries	Non-agricultural industries
Total...	**137,337**	**2,102**	**135,235**	**100.0**	**100.0**	**100.0**
1 to 34 hours..............................	34,425	573	33,852	25.1	27.3	25.0
1 to 4 hours.............................	1,481	49	1,432	1.1	2.3	1.1
5 to 14 hours...........................	5,369	133	5,236	3.9	6.3	3.9
15 to 29 hours.........................	17,128	265	16,863	12.5	12.6	12.5
30 to 34 hours.........................	10,448	126	10,322	7.6	6.0	7.6
35 hours and over......................	102,912	1,529	101,383	74.9	72.7	75.0
35 to 39 hours.........................	9,747	95	9,651	7.1	4.5	7.1
40 hours................................	58,778	608	58,169	42.8	28.9	43.0
41 hours and over.....................	34,388	825	33,562	25.0	39.3	24.8
41 to 48 hours........................	11,859	135	11,724	8.6	6.4	8.7
49 to 59 hours........................	13,251	240	13,012	9.6	11.4	9.6
60 hours and over....................	9,277	451	8,826	6.8	21.4	6.5
Average weekly hours: Persons at work...........	38.5	42.3	38.4	(X)	(X)	(X)
Persons usually working full-time [1]...............	42.5	48.5	42.4	(X)	(X)	(X)

X Not applicable. [1] Full-time workers are those who usually worked 35 hours or more (at all jobs).

Source: U.S. Bureau of Labor Statistics, "Persons at Work in Agriculture and Nonagricultural Industries by Hours of Work," <http://www.bls.gov/cps/cpsaat19.htm>, accessed June 2013.

Table 631. Class of Worker by Sex and Selected Characteristics: 2012

[In percent, except as indicated (9,529 represents 9,529,000). Civilian noninstitutionalized population 16 years old and over. Annual averages of monthly figures. Based on Current Population Survey; see text, Section 1 and Appendix III]

Characteristic	Unincorporated self-employed			Incorporated self-employed			Wage and salary workers [1]		
	Total	Male	Female	Total	Male	Female	Total	Male	Female
Total (1,000).....................	**9,529**	**5,828**	**3,701**	**5,253**	**3,779**	**1,473**	**127,576**	**65,898**	**61,680**
PERCENT DISTRIBUTION........	100.0	100.0	100.0	100.0	100.0	100.0	100.0	100.0	100.0
Age:									
16 to 19 years old................	0.8	0.9	0.6	0.2	0.2	0.2	3.4	3.2	3.6
20 to 24 years old................	2.7	2.6	2.8	0.9	0.9	0.7	10.3	10.2	10.3
25 to 34 years old................	13.6	13.0	14.5	10.0	10.0	9.8	22.6	23.5	21.7
35 to 44 years old................	20.3	20.1	20.7	22.5	21.9	24.0	21.5	22.0	21.0
45 to 54 years old................	26.4	25.9	27.1	30.0	29.2	31.9	22.5	22.2	23.0
55 to 64 years old................	23.2	23.6	22.7	25.0	25.4	24.0	15.4	14.8	16.2
65 years old and over.............	13.0	13.9	11.6	11.5	12.4	9.4	4.2	4.2	4.2
Race/ethnicity:									
White [2].............................	85.8	86.4	85.0	87.7	88.9	84.8	79.9	81.3	78.4
Black [2].............................	6.5	6.4	6.7	4.9	4.6	5.6	11.7	10.2	13.3
Asian [2].............................	4.9	4.5	5.5	5.6	4.7	7.7	4.6	5.5	5.3
Hispanic [3].........................	14.2	15.7	11.9	7.0	7.1	6.9	15.8	17.4	14.1
Country of birth:									
U.S. born...........................	81.2	80.9	81.7	84.7	85.1	83.6	84.0	82.3	85.8
Foreign-born.......................	18.8	19.1	18.3	15.3	14.9	16.4	16.0	17.7	14.2

[1] Excludes the incorporated self-employed. [2] For persons in this race group only. [3] Persons of Hispanic origin may be of any race.

Source: Bureau of Labor Statistics, Current Population Survey, unpublished data. See also <http://bls.gov/cps>.

Table 632. Self-Employed Workers by Industry and Occupation: 2000 to 2012

[In thousands (10,214 represents 10,214,000). Civilian noninstitutionalized population 16 years old and over. Annual averages of monthly figures. Data represent the unincorporated self-employed; the incorporated self-employed are considered wage and salary workers. Based on the occupational and industrial classification derived from those used in the 2000 census. See text, this section. Based on the Current Population Survey; see text, Section 1 and Appendix III]

Item	2000	2005	2009	2010	2011	2012
Total self-employed	**10,214**	**10,464**	**9,831**	**9,681**	**9,449**	**9,529**
Industry:						
Agriculture and related industries	1,010	955	836	821	846	780
Mining	12	11	18	20	20	20
Construction	1,728	1,830	1,701	1,699	1,585	1,518
Manufacturing	334	327	324	304	273	308
Wholesale and retail trade	1,221	1,251	963	962	949	872
Transportation and utilities	348	442	402	360	352	355
Information	139	126	145	139	131	141
Financial activities	735	785	667	641	615	651
Professional and business services	1,927	1,957	1,996	1,999	2,011	2,109
Education and health services	1,107	1,071	1,102	1,100	1,077	1,101
Leisure and hospitality	660	674	636	610	636	659
Other services	993	1,036	1,039	1,028	956	1,016
Occupation:						
Management, professional, and related occupations	4,169	4,085	4,079	3,928	(NA)	(NA)
Service occupations	1,775	1,774	1,879	1,885	(NA)	(NA)
Sales and office occupations	1,982	1,986	1,663	1,586	(NA)	(NA)
Natural resources, construction, and maintenance occupations	1,591	1,864	1,535	1,635	(NA)	(NA)
Production, transportation, and material moving occupations	698	756	674	647	(NA)	(NA)

NA Not available.

Source: Bureau of Labor Statistics, "Labor Force Statistics from the Current Population Survey," <http://www.bls.gov/cps/tables.htm>, accessed July 2013.

Table 633. Type of Work Flexibility Provided to Employees: 2012

[In percent. The National Study of Employers does not ask employers to report on whether they have "written policies," but rather whether their organization "allows employees to" or "provides the following benefits or programs." The wording is used for two reasons. First, employers may have written policies, but not "allow" employees to use them. Second, smaller employers are less likely to have written policies than larger ones. For methodology, see source]

Type of work flexibility provided (to employee)	Employer allows all or most employees	Employer size	
		50 to 99 employees	1,000 or more employees
FLEX TIME AND PLACE			
Periodically change starting and quitting times within some range of hours	27	32	16
Change starting and quitting times on a daily basis	9	10	3
Compress workweek by working longer hours on fewer days for at least part of the year	7	9	5
Work some regular paid hours at home occasionally	6	10	3
Work some regular paid hours at home on regular basis	2	3	–
CHOICES IN MANAGING TIME			
Have control over when to take breaks	62	70	42
Have choices about and control over which shifts to work	7	8	11
Have control over paid and unpaid overtime hours	20	20	16
REDUCED TIME			
Move from full time to part time and back again while remaining in same position or level	6	7	7
Work part year (work reduced time on annual basis)	2	2	2
CAREGIVING LEAVE			
Return to work gradually after childbirth or adoption	44	48	29
TIME OFF			
Family or personal time off without loss of pay	55	62	38
Do volunteer work during regular work hours	20	21	203
FLEX CAREERS			
Phase into retirement by working reduced hours over time prior to full retirement	17	21	10
Take sabbaticals (paid or unpaid for six months or more)	9	11	6
Take extended career breaks for caregiving or other personal or family reasons	30	33	20
Receive special consideration when returning to the organization after an extended career break	11	12	7

– Represents zero

Source: Families and Work Institute, "2012 National Study of Employers" ©, <http://familiesandwork.org/site/research/reports/main.html>.

Table 634. Employed Workers With Alternative and Traditional Work Arrangements: 2005

[In thousands (138,952 represents 138,952,000). As of February. For employed workers 16 years old and over. Based on the Current Population Survey; see text, Section 1 and Appendix III]

Characteristic	Total employed [1]	Workers with alternative arrangements				Workers with traditional arrangements
		Independent contractors	On-call workers	Temporary help agency workers	Workers provided by contract firms	
Total employed......................	138,952	10,342	2,454	1,217	813	123,843
16 to 19 years old...................	5,510	89	133	33	7	5,194
20 to 24 years old...................	13,114	356	355	202	87	12,055
25 to 34 years old...................	30,103	1,520	535	362	205	27,427
35 to 44 years old...................	34,481	2,754	571	253	196	30,646
45 to 54 years old...................	32,947	2,799	417	200	186	29,324
55 to 64 years old...................	17,980	1,943	267	135	114	15,496
65 years old and over...............	4,817	881	175	33	18	3,701
Male..................................	73,946	6,696	1,241	574	561	64,673
16 to 19 years old...................	2,579	32	82	24	7	2,389
20 to 24 years old...................	6,928	194	200	107	61	6,331
25 to 34 years old...................	16,624	1,006	299	185	138	14,950
35 to 44 years old...................	18,523	1,824	252	120	140	16,130
45 to 54 years old...................	17,193	1,764	209	71	143	15,003
55 to 64 years old...................	9,485	1,287	108	52	70	7,954
65 years old and over...............	2,615	589	91	16	3	1,917
Female................................	65,006	3,647	1,212	643	252	59,170
16 to 19 years old...................	2,931	57	52	9	–	2,805
20 to 24 years old...................	6,186	162	155	95	27	5,724
25 to 34 years old...................	13,480	514	236	177	67	12,477
35 to 44 years old...................	15,958	930	319	133	57	14,516
45 to 54 years old...................	15,754	1,035	208	129	43	14,322
55 to 64 years old...................	8,495	656	158	83	44	7,542
65 years old and over...............	2,202	292	84	17	15	1,785
Full-time workers......................	113,798	7,732	1,370	979	695	102,889
Part-time workers......................	25,154	2,611	1,084	238	119	20,954

– Represents zero. [1] Includes day laborers (an alternative arrangement) and a small number of workers who were both "on call" and "provided by contract firms," not shown separately.

Source: U.S. Bureau of Labor Statistics, *Contingent and Alternative Employment Arrangements, February 2005*, News Release, USDL 05–1443, July 2005. See also <http://www.bls.gov/bls/newsrels.htm#OEUS>.

Table 635. Persons With a Job, But Not at Work: 1980 to 2012

[In thousands (5,881 represents 5,881,000), except percent. For civilian noninstitutionalized population 16 years old and over. Annual averages of monthly figures. Based on Current Population Survey; see text, Section 1 and Appendix III]

Reason for not working	1980	1990	2000	2005	2006	2007	2008	2009	2010	2011	2012
All industries, number.........	5,881	6,160	5,681	5,511	5,746	5,719	5,539	5,434	5,060	4,990	5,132
Percent of employed...........	5.9	5.2	4.2	3.9	4.0	3.9	3.8	3.9	3.6	3.6	3.6
Reason for not working:											
Vacation......................	3,320	3,529	3,109	2,892	3,101	3,056	2,916	2,806	2,487	2,500	2,633
Illness...........................	1,426	1,341	1,156	1,088	1,096	1,064	1,026	993	942	921	906
Bad weather...................	155	90	89	145	117	140	141	126	172	169	107
Industrial dispute..............	105	24	14	6	7	10	7	6	8	9	6
All other........................	876	1,177	1,313	1,381	1,425	1,449	1,449	1,503	1,451	1,392	1,481

Source: Bureau of Labor Statistics, Current Population Survey, unpublished data. See also <http://www.bls.gov/cps/>.

Table 636. Multiple Jobholders: 2012

[Annual average of monthly figures (6,943 represents 6,943,000). Civilian noninstitutionalized population 16 years old and over. Multiple jobholders are employed persons who either 1) had jobs as wage or salary workers with two employers or more; 2) were self-employed and also held a wage and salary job; or 3) were unpaid family workers and also held a wage and salary job. Based on the Current Population Survey; see text, Section 1 and Appendix III]

Characteristic	Total		Male		Female	
	Number (1,000)	Percent of employed	Number (1,000)	Percent of employed	Number (1,000)	Percent of employed
Total [1]....................	**6,943**	**4.9**	**3,448**	**4.6**	**3,495**	**5.2**
Age:						
16 to 19 years old...............	178	4.0	73	3.4	105	4.6
20 to 24 years old...............	725	5.4	298	4.3	427	6.6
25 to 54 years old...............	4,639	4.9	2,360	4.7	2,280	5.2
55 to 64 years old...............	1,136	4.9	550	4.6	586	5.2
65 years old and over............	264	3.6	168	4.1	96	3.0
Race and Ethnicity:						
White.........................	5,756	5.0	2,879	4.6	2,877	5.5
Black.........................	709	4.5	337	4.6	371	4.3
Asian.........................	249	3.2	116	2.8	133	3.7
Hispanic [2]...................	668	3.1	373	3.0	295	3.2
Marital status:						
Married, spouse present...........	3,683	4.7	2,108	4.8	1,575	4.6
Widowed, divorced, or separated......	1,229	5.3	422	4.3	806	6.0
Single, never married.............	2,031	5.0	917	4.2	1,114	5.9
Full- or part-time status:						
Primary job full-time, secondary job part-time..............	3,590	(X)	2,003	(X)	1,587	(X)
Both jobs part-time...............	1,906	(X)	640	(X)	1,265	(X)
Both jobs full-time...............	252	(X)	157	(X)	95	(X)
Hours vary on primary or secondary job..................	1,146	(X)	621	(X)	525	(X)

X Not applicable. [1] Includes a small number of persons who work part-time on their primary job and full-time on their secondary job(s), not shown separately. Includes other races, not shown separately. [2] Persons of Hispanic origin may be of any race.

Source: U.S. Bureau of Labor Statistics, "Multiple Jobholders by Selected Characteristics," February 2013, <http://www.bls.gov/cps/tables.htm>.

Table 637. Average Number of Jobs Held From Ages 18 to 46: 1978 to 2010

[For persons ages 45 to 53 in 2010-11 (and who were ages 14 to 22 when first interviewed in 1979). A job is an uninterrupted period of work with a particular employer. Educational attainment as of 2010-11. Based on the National Longitudinal Survey of Youth 1979; see source for details]

Sex, Race, Ethnicity and Educational Attainment	Total [1]	Number of jobs held by age				
		18 to 24 years	25 to 29 years	30 to 34 years	35 to 39 years	40 to 46 years
Total [2].......................	**11.3**	**5.5**	**3.0**	**2.4**	**2.1**	**2.1**
Less than a high school diploma...........	11.9	5.0	3.0	2.5	2.1	2.0
High school graduates, no college...........	10.5	5.0	2.8	2.4	2.0	2.0
Some college or associate's degree..........	11.8	5.7	3.1	2.5	2.2	2.2
Bachelor's degree or more.............	11.8	6.2	3.1	2.4	2.1	2.1
Male...........................	11.5	5.7	3.1	2.6	2.1	2.1
Less than a high school diploma...........	13.1	5.9	3.6	2.8	2.2	2.2
High school graduate, no college...........	10.9	5.3	3.1	2.5	2.0	2.1
Some college or associate's degree..........	11.8	6.0	3.2	2.6	2.1	2.1
Bachelor's degree or more.............	11.4	5.9	2.9	2.5	2.2	2.1
Female..........................	11.1	5.3	2.8	2.3	2.0	2.1
Less than a high school diploma...........	10.1	3.8	2.3	2.2	2.0	1.8
High school graduate, no college...........	10.2	4.7	2.5	2.2	2.0	2.0
Some college or associate's degree..........	11.8	5.5	3.0	2.4	2.2	2.3
Bachelor's degree or more.............	12.2	6.4	3.2	2.3	1.9	2.1
White, non-Hispanic.................	11.4	5.7	3.0	2.4	2.1	2.1
Less than a high school diploma...........	12.5	5.5	3.2	2.7	2.2	2.1
High school graduate, no college...........	10.5	5.2	2.8	2.4	2.0	2.0
Some college or associate's degree..........	11.9	5.9	3.0	2.4	2.1	2.1
Bachelor's degree or more.............	11.8	6.3	3.1	2.4	2.0	2.1
Black, non-Hispanic.................	10.9	4.6	2.9	2.5	2.1	2.2
Less than a high school diploma...........	10.3	3.8	2.6	2.1	1.9	1.8
High school graduate, no college...........	10.8	4.3	2.8	2.5	2.1	2.1
Some college or associate's degree..........	11.5	5.2	3.1	2.6	2.4	2.4
Bachelor's degree or more.............	11.1	5.4	3.1	2.7	2.1	2.4
Hispanic [3].......................	11.2	4.9	2.8	2.3	2.1	2.1
Less than a high school diploma...........	11.2	4.5	2.8	2.2	2.0	2.2
High school graduate, no college...........	10.7	5.0	2.7	2.4	2.0	2.2
Some college or associate's degree..........	11.6	5.1	3.1	2.3	2.2	2.4
Bachelor's degree or more.............	12.2	5.4	2.9	2.6	2.1	2.0

[1] Jobs held in more than one age category were counted in each category, but only once in the total. [2] Includes other races, not shown separately. [3] Persons of Hispanic origin may be of any race.

Source: U.S. Bureau of Labor Statistics, "Number of Jobs Held, Labor Market Activity, and Earnings Growth Among the Youngest Baby Boomers: Results from a Longitudinal Survey," USDL 10-1489, July 2012. See also <http://www.bls.gov/news.release/nlsoy.nr0.htm>.

Table 638. Distribution of Workers by Tenure With Current Employer by Selected Characteristics: 2012

[125,516 represents 125,516,000. As of January from the 2012 Displaced Worker Supplement. For employed wage and salary workers 16 years old and over. Data exclude the incorporated and unincorporated self-employed. Based on the Current Population Survey; see source and Appendix III]

Characteristic	Number employed (1,000)	Percent distribution by tenure with current employer								Median years [1]
		12 months or less	13 to 23 months	2 years	3 to 4 years	5 to 9 years	10 to 14 years	15 to 19 years	20 years or more	
Total [2]	125,516	21.1	6.3	4.9	16.6	21.8	12.5	6.1	10.6	4.6
AGE AND SEX										
16 to 19 years old	3,925	72.9	11.9	6.9	7.8	0.4	–	–	–	(NA)
20 years old and over	121,591	19.5	6.1	4.8	16.9	22.4	12.9	6.3	11.0	(NA)
20 to 24 years old	12,712	48.9	12.8	10.6	20.4	7.1	0.2	–	–	1.3
25 to 34 years old	28,381	25.5	8.4	6.9	24.5	27.2	6.8	0.7	–	3.2
35 to 44 years old	27,477	16.1	5.4	4.3	16.8	27.0	17.8	8.8	3.8	5.3
45 to 54 years old	28,535	12.5	4.5	2.9	13.0	22.0	16.8	9.5	18.7	7.8
55 to 64 years old	19,339	9.4	2.8	2.3	10.8	20.2	16.4	9.8	28.3	10.3
65 years old and over	5,148	7.8	2.0	2.1	11.8	20.7	16.6	9.2	29.7	10.3
Male	64,552	21.0	6.3	5.0	16.2	21.3	12.2	6.4	11.5	4.7
16 to 19 years old	1,839	71.2	13.3	7.8	7.4	0.4	–	–	–	(NA)
20 years old and over	62,713	19.6	6.1	4.9	16.5	21.9	12.6	6.5	11.9	(NA)
20 to 24 years old	6,559	48.8	12.5	10.4	20.6	7.4	0.2	–	–	1.4
25 to 34 years old	15,104	24.7	8.5	7.3	23.8	27.8	7.0	0.9	–	3.2
35 to 44 years old	14,570	16.3	5.4	4.0	16.1	26.8	17.3	9.8	4.4	5.4
45 to 54 years old	14,361	12.6	4.5	2.8	12.5	19.6	16.6	10.0	21.4	8.5
55 to 64 years old	9,470	10.0	2.5	2.7	10.1	18.8	15.6	9.2	31.2	10.7
65 years old and over	2,648	7.8	1.3	1.9	11.8	21.7	16.9	8.9	29.7	10.2
Female	60,964	21.3	6.3	4.8	17.1	22.2	12.7	5.9	9.7	4.6
16 to 19 years old	2,085	74.4	10.7	6.2	8.2	0.5	–	–	–	(NA)
20 years old and over	58,879	19.4	6.2	4.7	17.4	23.0	13.2	6.1	10.1	(NA)
20 to 24 years old	6,153	49.0	13.1	10.7	20.3	6.7	0.2	–	–	1.3
25 to 34 years old	13,276	26.5	8.4	6.4	25.3	26.5	6.5	0.5	–	3.1
35 to 44 years old	12,907	15.9	5.4	4.6	17.5	27.4	18.4	7.7	3.1	5.2
45 to 54 years old	14,174	12.4	4.5	3.1	13.6	24.4	17.0	9.0	16.0	7.3
55 to 64 years old	9,868	8.8	3.2	1.9	11.6	21.4	17.2	10.5	25.5	10.0
65 years old and over	2,499	7.7	2.8	2.4	11.9	19.7	16.3	9.6	29.7	10.5
RACE AND HISPANIC ORIGIN										
White [3]	100,679	20.7	6.4	4.8	16.1	21.7	12.6	6.6	11.3	(NA)
Male	52,641	20.5	6.5	4.7	15.7	21.1	12.4	6.8	12.3	(NA)
Female	48,039	20.9	6.3	4.8	16.4	22.2	12.9	6.3	10.2	(NA)
Black [3]	14,204	22.2	5.6	5.2	18.5	22.1	12.4	4.5	9.5	(NA)
Male	6,526	22.9	5.1	5.5	18.9	21.9	10.8	4.8	10.0	(NA)
Female	7,678	21.6	6.0	5.0	18.2	22.2	13.8	4.2	9.1	(NA)
Asian [3]	6,933	21.1	6.6	5.3	20.5	23.8	11.3	4.8	6.6	(NA)
Male	3,502	21.2	5.8	6.6	19.0	23.8	12.8	4.3	6.5	(NA)
Female	3,432	21.0	7.3	4.0	22.1	23.9	9.8	5.2	6.7	(NA)
Hispanic [4]	19,763	23.6	5.9	6.6	20.1	23.7	10.9	4.2	5.1	(NA)
Male	11,262	24.5	6.0	6.8	20.8	22.4	10.0	4.3	5.2	(NA)
Female	8,501	22.3	5.6	6.4	19.2	25.4	12.0	4.2	4.9	(NA)

– Represents zero. NA Not available. [1] For definition of median, see Guide to Tabular Presentation. [2] Includes other races, not shown separately. [3] For persons in this race group only. See footnote 4, Table 614. [4] Persons of Hispanic origin may be of any race.

Source: Bureau of Labor Statistics, "Employee Tenure in 2012," USDL 12-1887, September 2012, <http://www.bls.gov/news.release/tenure.toc.htm>.

Table 639. Part-Time Workers by Reason: 2012

[In thousands (34,425 represents 34,425,000), except hours. For persons working 1 to 34 hours per week. For civilian noninstitutionalized population 16 years old and over. Annual average of monthly figures. Based on the Current Population Survey; see text, Section 1 and Appendix III]

Reason	All industries			Nonagricultural industries		
		Usually work—			Usually work—	
	Total	Full-time	Part-time	Total	Full-time	Part-time
Total working fewer than 35 hours	**34,425**	**9,324**	**25,101**	**33,852**	**9,175**	**24,677**
Economic reasons	8,122	1,828	6,294	8,003	1,771	6,231
Slack work or business conditions	5,255	1,587	3,668	5,178	1,547	3,631
Could find only part time work	2,541	(S)	2,541	2,522	(S)	2,522
Seasonal work	212	126	85	193	114	79
Job started or ended during the week	114	114	(S)	110	110	(S)
Noneconomic reasons	26,303	7,497	18,806	25,849	7,404	18,446
Child-care problems	853	67	786	848	67	781
Other family or personal obligations	4,631	661	3,970	4,560	652	3,908
Health or medical limitations	790	(S)	790	770	(S)	770
In school or training	5,765	88	5,678	5,702	86	5,616
Retired or social security limit on earnings	2,313	(S)	2,313	2,195	(S)	2,195
Vacation or personal day	3,586	3,586	(S)	3,551	3,551	(S)
Holiday, legal, or religious	530	530	(S)	525	525	(S)
Weather-related curtailment	263	263	(S)	251	251	(S)
Other	7,571	2,302	5,269	7,447	2,271	5,176
Average hours per week:						
Economic reasons	22.7	23.9	22.4	22.7	24.0	22.4
Noneconomic reasons	21.2	24.7	19.9	21.3	24.7	19.9

S No data or data do not meet publication standards.

Source: U.S. Bureau of Labor Statistics, "Persons at work 1 to 34 hours in all and in nonagricultural industries by reason for working less than 35 hours and usual full- or part-time status," February 2013, <http://www.bls.gov/cps/tables.htm>.

Table 640. Displaced Workers by Selected Characteristics: 2012

[In percent, except total (6,121 represents 6,121,000). As of January, from the Displaced Worker: 2009-2011 News Release. For persons 20 years old and over with tenure of 3 years or more who lost or left a job between January 2009 and December 2011 because of plant closings or moves, slack work, or the abolishment of their positions. Based on Current Population Survey; see source and Appendix III]

Characteristic	Total (1,000)	Employment status in January 2012			Reason for job loss, 2009-2011		
		Employed	Unemployed	Not in the labor force	Plant or company closed down or moved	Slack/ insufficient work	Position or shift abolished
Total [1]	**6,121**	**56.0**	**26.7**	**17.4**	**30.8**	**39.5**	**29.7**
20 to 24 years old	128	61.7	22.4	15.9	40.5	39.3	20.3
25 to 54 years old	4,268	61.5	26.2	12.3	31.8	40.2	28.0
55 to 64 years old	1,338	47.4	28.1	24.5	27.8	37.0	35.2
65 years old and over	386	23.5	27.5	49.0	26.7	40.8	32.5
Males	3,440	60.9	23.4	15.7	31.1	43.2	25.7
20 to 24 years old	78	70.6	15.0	14.4	40.2	36.7	23.1
25 to 54 years old	2,438	66.7	22.7	10.6	32.6	43.4	24.0
55 to 64 years old	727	50.8	25.6	23.7	27.6	43.0	29.4
65 years old and over	197	23.5	27.3	49.2	21.7	44.2	34.2
Females	2,681	47.9	30.8	19.5	30.4	34.8	34.8
20 to 24 years old	50	([2])	([2])	([2])	([2])	([2])	([2])
25 to 54 years old	1,831	54.6	30.9	14.5	30.8	35.9	33.3
55 to 64 years old	611	43.3	31.1	25.6	28.1	29.9	42.0
65 years old and over	189	23.5	27.7	48.8	31.9	37.3	30.8
White [3]	5,027	57.4	26.1	16.5	30.2	38.9	30.9
Male	2,920	61.9	23.1	14.9	30.5	42.5	27.0
Female	2,107	51.2	30.2	18.7	29.8	34.0	36.2
Black [3]	662	46.1	31.2	22.7	33.5	41.0	25.5
Male	284	52.7	24.8	22.4	35.5	44.9	19.6
Female	378	41.2	35.9	22.9	32.0	38.0	30.0
Asian [3]	230	60.3	26.7	13.1	30.5	46.9	22.7
Male	121	61.5	27.6	10.9	24.3	56.8	18.9
Female	109	58.9	25.6	15.5	37.3	35.9	26.8
Hispanic [4]	901	54.9	27.7	17.4	35.9	50.1	14.0
Male	594	60.3	25.7	14.0	37.3	52.4	10.3
Female	307	44.3	31.6	24.1	33.3	45.6	21.1

[1] Includes other races, not shown separately. [2] Data not shown where base is less than 75,000. [3] For persons in this race group only. See footnote 3, Table 614. [4] Persons of Hispanic origin may be of any race.

Source: Bureau of Labor Statistics, "Worker Displacement, 2009-2011," USDL 12-1719, August 2012. See also <http://www.bls.gov/news.release/disp.toc.htm>.

Table 641. Persons Not in the Labor Force: 2012

[In thousands (83,310 represents 83,310,000). For civilian noninstitutional population 16 years old and over. Annual average of monthly figures. Based on the Current Population Survey; see text, Section 1, and Appendix III]

Status and reason	Total	Age			Sex	
		16 to 24 years old	25 to 54 years old	55 years old and over	Male	Female
Total not in the labor force	**88,310**	**17,499**	**23,061**	**47,750**	**35,017**	**53,293**
Do not want a job now [1]	81,752	15,383	20,248	46,120	31,989	49,763
Want a job now	6,558	2,115	2,813	1,630	3,028	3,530
In the previous year—						
Did not search for a job	3,390	1,064	1,328	998	1,490	1,900
Did search for a job [2]	3,168	1,052	1,484	632	1,537	1,630
Not available for work now	651	282	288	82	253	399
Available for work now, not looking for work [3]	2,516	770	1,196	550	1,285	1,232
Reason for not currently looking for work:						
Discouraged over job prospects [4]	909	217	451	241	541	368
Family responsibilities	229	33	147	49	61	168
In school or training	339	257	73	9	175	164
Ill health or disability	168	18	83	66	80	87
Other [5]	871	245	442	185	427	444

[1] Includes some persons who are not asked if they want a job. [2] Persons who had a job in the prior 12 months must have searched since the end of that job. [3] Persons who have searched for work in the previous year and are available to work now also are referred to as "marginally attached to the labor force." [4] Includes such things as believes no work available, could not find work, lacks necessary schooling or training, employer thinks too young or old, and other types of discrimination. [5] Includes such things as child care and transportation problems.

Source: U.S. Bureau of Labor Statistics, "Persons not in the labor force by desire and availability for work, age, and sex," February 2013, <http://www.bls.gov/cps/tables.htm>.

Table 642. Employed Civilians by Occupation, Sex, Race, and Hispanic Origin: 2012

[142,469 represents 142,469,000. Civilian noninstitutionalized population 16 years old and over. Annual average of monthly figures. Based on Current Population Survey; see text, Section 1 and Appendix III. Occupational classifications are those used in the 2010 Census]

Occupation	Total employed (1,000)	Percent of total			
		Female	Black [1]	Asian [1]	Hispanic [2]
Total, 16 years and over...............................	**142,469**	**47.0**	**11.1**	**5.4**	**15.4**
Management, professional and related occupations........................	**54,043**	**51.5**	**8.7**	**6.9**	**8.4**
Management, business, and financial operations occupations...............	22,678	43.6	7.8	5.8	8.6
Management occupations [3]..................................	16,042	38.6	6.9	5.1	8.8
Chief executives...	1,513	27.4	3.7	4.2	4.7
General and operations managers..............................	1,064	29.1	6.2	4.7	9.3
Marketing and sales managers..................................	967	45.2	4.2	6.0	6.1
Administrative services managers..............................	144	44.1	6.4	4.4	9.5
Computer and information systems managers....................	605	26.8	5.6	14.5	5.8
Financial managers..	1,228	53.5	8.6	5.7	10.3
Human resources managers....................................	224	72.7	11.3	2.4	9.5
Industrial production managers................................	261	17.6	3.4	5.1	11.4
Purchasing managers..	218	50.9	8.4	4.6	10.4
Transportation, storage, and distribution managers.............	287	15.6	11.1	3.3	11.3
Farmers, ranchers, and other agricultural managers............	944	24.5	0.8	1.2	4.0
Construction managers...	983	6.4	3.7	2.2	9.4
Education administrators.......................................	811	64.4	13.8	2.2	7.9
Engineering managers..	120	10.9	2.8	7.7	2.9
Food service managers...	1085	47.2	8.8	9.5	16.5
Lodging managers..	154	45.0	8.0	13.9	11.5
Medical and health services managers..........................	585	69.7	10.9	5.1	8.1
Property, real estate, and community association managers......	644	50.7	8.5	3.4	11.4
Social and community service managers........................	315	70.5	14.6	3.7	8.5
Business and financial operations occupations [3]................	6,636	55.8	9.8	7.4	8.0
Wholesale and retail buyers, except farm products.............	198	55.2	7.1	7.7	10.9
Purchasing agents, except wholesale, retail, and farm products..	261	55.1	6.1	4.4	9.8
Claims adjusters, appraisers, examiners, and investigators......	323	63.4	17.5	3.1	10.3
Compliance officers, except agriculture, construction, health and safety, and transportation............................	199	50.6	9.1	3.3	8.2
Cost estimators..	114	11.7	1.5	2.0	6.8
Human resources workers......................................	603	71.8	15.4	4.4	11.8
Management analysts...	773	39.8	6.8	8.8	4.4
Accountants and auditors......................................	1,765	60.9	9.7	12.0	6.8
Appraisers and assessors of real estate........................	93	40.6	9.8	2.7	1.0
Financial analysts..	89	36.8	3.7	9.0	6.3
Personal financial advisors.....................................	378	31.2	4.8	6.2	4.5
Insurance underwriters...	103	70.4	10.7	0.7	10.2
Loan counselors and officers...................................	333	59.2	13.2	6.0	9.3
Tax preparers..	107	59.6	10.4	7.1	15.9
Professional and related occupations...........................	31,365	57.2	9.3	7.8	8.2
Computer and mathematical occupations [3].....................	3,816	25.6	7.4	17.5	6.1
Computer programmers..	480	22.5	5.9	17.3	5.3
Software developers, applications and systems software........	1,084	19.7	4.0	29.4	5.2
Computer support specialists..................................	476	27.1	12.0	7.7	9.7
Database administrators..	101	36.6	4.1	10.0	9.8
Network and computer systems administrators..................	226	25.0	10.0	11.0	10.7
Operations research analysts..................................	130	54.9	8.3	9.3	6.5
Architecture and engineering occupations [3]....................	2,846	13.7	5.6	10.8	7.4
Architects, except naval.......................................	195	23.5	1.3	6.2	8.2
Aerospace engineers..	119	9.0	1.8	13.4	4.6
Civil engineers...	358	13.7	5.4	9.0	3.7
Computer hardware engineers.................................	91	15.1	8.5	20.8	6.5
Electrical and electronics engineers............................	335	9.0	3.5	16.6	6.7
Industrial engineers, including health and safety................	197	18.8	6.2	9.6	10.5
Mechanical engineers..	288	4.5	6.3	12.3	4.9
Drafters...	149	16.6	3.0	7.7	9.9
Engineering technicians, except drafters.......................	395	16.3	10.8	5.0	12.3
Life, physical, and social science occupations [3]...............	1,316	45.3	6.5	9.9	6.7
Biological scientists...	101	50.1	3.7	11.7	7.2
Medical scientists...	136	52.8	5.3	22.4	5.8
Chemists and materials scientists..............................	105	44.2	4.0	9.2	9.4
Environmental scientists and geoscientists.....................	105	25.7	7.0	1.3	1.7
Psychologists...	178	72.7	6.0	3.9	6.3
Community and social services occupations [3]..................	2,265	63.8	18.8	3.2	11.1
Counselors..	661	69.3	19.4	2.9	10.7
Social workers..	734	80.6	23.0	3.1	12.6
Miscellaneous community and social service specialists.........	94	75.7	16.9	2.4	18.4
Clergy..	408	20.5	11.2	4.2	6.1
Legal occupations...	1,786	50.4	7.1	3.9	7.4
Lawyers...	1,061	31.1	4.4	4.3	4.0
Judges, magistrates, and other judicial workers.................	67	39.0	12.8	0.7	4.5
Paralegals and legal assistants................................	418	85.9	10.7	4.6	17.0
Miscellaneous legal support workers...........................	223	79.0	11.9	1.4	7.0
Education, training, and library occupations [3].................	8,543	73.6	9.5	4.3	9.7
Postsecondary teachers.......................................	1,350	48.2	7.9	11.3	6.2
Preschool and kindergarten teachers..........................	678	98.1	11.8	4.2	12.0
Elementary and middle school teachers........................	2,838	81.4	9.8	2.1	10.3
Secondary school teachers....................................	1,127	57.3	6.0	3.1	7.6
Special education teachers....................................	366	86.2	6.9	1.1	9.4
Other teachers and instructors................................	860	65.6	10.7	5.9	9.5
Librarians...	181	86.8	7.9	2.5	2.8
Teacher assistants..	898	91.1	14.5	2.7	15.7

See footnotes at end of table.

Table 642. Employed Civilians by Occupation, Sex, Race, and Hispanic Origin: 2012-Continued.

See headnote on page 415.

Occupation	Total employed (1,000)	Percent of total			
		Female	Black [1]	Asian [1]	Hispanic [2]
Arts, design, entertainment, sports, and media occupations [3]	2,814	48.3	6.0	5.2	8.9
Artists and related workers	212	51.6	4.0	9.3	6.6
Designers	756	55.3	3.9	5.9	8.9
Producers and directors	121	40.8	8.2	3.3	4.9
Athletes, coaches, umpires, and related workers	267	36.5	6.4	1.4	9.0
Musicians, singers, and related workers	203	35.5	10.9	2.8	6.7
News analysts, reporters and correspondents	82	45.7	9.2	6.1	5.9
Public relations specialists	155	58.2	7.3	5.8	8.0
Editors	159	50.7	4.8	3.2	6.5
Writers and authors	208	55.6	5.4	4.2	2.9
Miscellaneous media and communication workers	98	79.2	5.6	15.0	35.0
Broadcast and sound engineering technicians and radio operators	108	8.4	4.1	1.6	12.6
Photographers	178	52.2	6.2	4.3	10.7
Healthcare practitioner and technical occupations [3]	7,977	75.0	10.6	8.4	7.3
Dentists	167	24.2	1.7	10.6	2.5
Dietitians and nutritionists	116	93.3	13.7	5.1	7.2
Pharmacists	286	53.7	6.8	18.5	5.1
Physicians and surgeons	911	34.3	7.2	18.1	5.2
Physician assistants	108	69.4	8.2	9.0	8.8
Registered nurses	2,875	90.6	11.5	7.3	6.2
Occupational therapists	118	94.0	2.5	4.0	5.8
Physical therapists	211	70.7	4.4	9.1	9.4
Speech-language pathologists	146	95.2	3.1	1.7	8.3
Clinical laboratory technologists and technicians	319	72.8	13.5	14.0	10.7
Dental hygienists	163	99.3	3.3	5.6	8.1
Diagnostic-related technologists and technicians	308	74.5	9.0	4.1	7.8
Emergency medical technicians and paramedics	172	31.2	5.0	1.6	8.1
Health practitioner support technologists and technicians	544	83.6	15.8	5.9	12.2
Licensed practical and licensed vocational nurses	531	94.2	23.3	5.1	9.4
Medical records and health information technicians	90	89.3	17.1	4.3	15.6
Service occupations	**25,459**	**56.3**	**15.9**	**5.6**	**22.6**
Healthcare support occupations [3]	3,496	87.6	26.5	4.5	15.3
Nursing, psychiatric, and home health aides	2,119	87.9	34.5	4.6	14.2
Massage therapists	158	81.5	5.4	7.7	12.0
Dental assistants	274	97.9	9.6	3.6	21.2
Medical assistants and other healthcare support occupations	429	93.8	15.0	3.8	22.9
Protective service occupations [3]	3,096	20.9	17.2	2.7	13.7
First-line supervisors of police and detectives	112	15.2	9.2	4.4	10.6
Fire-fighters	295	3.4	7.7	1.1	9.9
Bailiffs, correctional officers, and jailers	371	28.0	22.7	1.1	18.3
Detectives and criminal investigators	160	24.8	9.8	3.5	10.4
Police and sheriff's patrol officers	657	12.6	12.8	3.1	13.8
Private detectives and investigators	103	44.0	8.0	2.2	11.1
Security guards and gaming surveillance officers	903	18.5	26.6	4.1	15.8
Lifeguards and other protective service workers	162	52.6	7.8	1.2	9.2
Food preparation and serving related occupations	8,018	54.5	12.1	6.2	23.8
Chefs and head cooks	403	21.5	11.9	14.2	18.6
First-line supervisors of food preparation and serving workers	552	59.3	13.9	4.0	17.2
Cooks	1,970	37.7	16.6	6.0	31.7
Food-preparation workers	868	58.0	12.1	5.7	27.5
Bartenders	412	59.9	5.2	3.5	13.2
Combined food preparation and serving workers, including fast food	343	64.9	14.1	3.1	18.0
Counter attendants, cafeteria, food concession, and coffee shop	233	70.8	10.9	4.8	16.6
Waiters and waitresses	2,124	71.2	7.9	7.1	19.6
Food servers, nonrestaurant	217	64.9	22.2	6.4	20.1
Dining room and cafeteria attendants and bartender helpers	359	43.4	10.0	5.5	31.7
Dishwashers	271	18.7	12.9	5.5	40.5
Hosts and hostesses, restaurant, lounge, and coffee shop	260	81.5	10.2	5.4	14.8
Building and grounds cleaning and maintenance occupations	5,591	38.6	15.0	3.3	36.1
First-line supervisors of housekeeping and janitorial workers	277	47.1	16.9	3.3	21.7
First-line supervisors of landscaping, lawn service, and groundskeeping workers	281	7.6	6.6	1.1	19.8
Janitors and building cleaners	2,205	29.7	18.4	3.6	30.9
Maids and housekeeping cleaners	1,457	88.1	17.2	4.8	43.3
Pest control workers	73	4.7	7.7	0.1	20.4
Grounds maintenance workers	1,298	5.1	8.7	1.7	44.4
Personal care and service occupations [3]	5,258	77.7	14.7	9.5	16.4
First-line supervisors of gaming workers	146	43.0	5.2	9.2	10.1
First-line supervisors of personal service workers	246	70.3	10.7	19.8	9.3
Nonfarm animal caretakers	179	74.2	4.3	1.8	12.2
Gaming services workers	106	51.0	9.4	24.3	13.5
Barbers	109	21.9	38.2	2.5	24.1
Hairdressers, hairstylists, and cosmetologists	785	92.8	13.2	6.5	15.0
Miscellaneous personal appearance workers	300	81.5	5.3	59.6	9.5
Baggage porters, bellhops, and concierges	68	25.0	20.8	13.1	18.0
Child care workers	1,314	94.1	15.3	3.3	20.3
Personal and home care aides	1071	84.7	21.8	7.9	21.2
Recreation and fitness workers	406	66.5	10.0	4.5	9.7
Sales and office occupations	**33,152**	**61.8**	**11.8**	**4.7**	**14.0**
Sales and related occupations [3]	15,457	48.7	10.5	5.3	13.5

See footnotes at end of table.

Table 642. Employed Civilians by Occupation, Sex, Race, and Hispanic Origin: 2012-Continued.

See headnote on page 415.

Occupation	Total employed (1,000)	Percent of total			
		Female	Black [1]	Asian [1]	Hispanic [2]
First-line supervisors of retail sales workers..................	3,237	43.4	8.6	5.9	11.3
First-line supervisors of non retail sales workers..............	1,151	24.7	7.2	5.0	10.4
Cashiers..	3,275	71.8	17.2	7.3	19.9
Counter and rental clerks.................................	139	53.4	8.9	5.2	19.6
Parts salespersons.......................................	106	13.3	8.3	4.1	12.3
Retail salespersons......................................	3,341	50.2	12.5	4.4	15.3
Advertising sales agents..................................	230	47.4	9.9	2.3	7.6
Insurance sales agents....................................	540	44.1	8.1	1.8	10.3
Securities, commodities, and financial services sales agents....	280	27.9	3.4	8.3	8.9
Travel agents..	73	79.0	2.5	9.3	4.8
Sales representatives, services, all other....................	457	31.0	7.9	3.7	10.1
Sales representatives, wholesale and manufacturing............	1,277	27.0	3.7	3.7	9.4
Real estate brokers and sales agents........................	761	57.1	4.0	4.7	8.7
Telemarketers...	97	50.3	23.0	1.1	14.7
Door-to-door sales workers, news and street vendors, and related workers.....................................	198	62.2	10.2	3.8	13.5
Office and administrative support occupations [3]..............	17,695	73.3	12.9	4.2	14.5
First-line supervisors of office and administrative support workers............................	1,416	68.5	11.3	3.5	11.9
Bill and account collectors................................	206	69.1	15.3	3.6	17.6
Billing and posting clerks and machine operators..............	475	90.1	11.8	4.0	16.2
Bookkeeping, accounting, and auditing clerks.................	1,268	89.1	7.6	5.0	9.0
Payroll and timekeeping clerks............................	155	92.6	9.5	4.6	15.1
Tellers..	380	87.3	11.6	5.7	18.6
Court, municipal, and license clerks........................	85	77.2	23.0	1.2	13.4
Customer service representatives...........................	1,956	67.8	16.2	4.2	18.0
File clerks...	292	81.3	14.1	4.6	16.4
Hotel, motel, and resort desk clerks........................	110	64.6	18.4	6.3	18.6
Interviewers, except eligibility and loan....................	135	83.7	20.0	6.0	12.1
Library assistants, clerical................................	97	84.0	7.0	3.2	5.8
Loan interviewers and clerks..............................	144	81.2	10.9	4.0	10.4
Order clerks...	104	58.2	5.8	4.1	21.3
Receptionists and information clerks........................	1,237	91.5	12.1	4.3	17.9
Reservation and transportation ticket agents and travel clerks....	117	58.6	21.8	10.9	21.5
Couriers and messengers..................................	213	15.5	13.0	2.4	16.9
Dispatchers...	277	61.5	13.5	2.3	16.7
Postal service clerks......................................	148	50.0	21.3	9.5	12.0
Postal service mail carriers................................	318	37.7	16.5	6.7	8.8
Postal service mail sorters, processors, and processing machine operators...........................	66	47.6	28.6	12.7	9.8
Production, planning, and expediting clerks..................	272	55.0	11.0	3.2	12.5
Shipping, receiving, and traffic clerks......................	527	27.8	15.6	3.6	23.7
Stock clerks and order fillers..............................	1,453	35.5	16.7	4.5	18.1
Weighers, measurers, checkers, and samplers, recordkeeping.....	74	49.1	19.9	2.8	21.9
Secretaries and administrative assistants....................	2,904	95.3	8.6	3.2	10.3
Computer operators......................................	102	50.7	12.2	6.5	10.7
Data entry keyers..	337	77.0	14.0	5.1	13.8
Word processors and typists...............................	119	88.7	12.4	2.8	12.9
Insurance claims and policy processing clerks................	230	81.9	12.7	3.6	13.7
Mail clerks and mail machine operators, except postal service.....	81	41.2	18.1	10.6	10.1
Office clerks, general.....................................	1103	83.4	12.4	5.0	16.9
Natural resources, construction, and maintenance occupations........	**12,821**	**4.3**	**7.0**	**2.1**	**25.5**
Farming, fishing, and forestry occupations [3]..................	994	22.7	5.3	1.8	44.2
Construction and extraction occupations [3]....................	7,005	2.5	6.2	1.6	28.9
First-line supervisors of construction trades and extraction workers.....................................	634	2.8	4.5	1.3	14.0
Brickmasons, blockmasons, and stonemasons.................	122	0.1	5.8	0.3	43.2
Carpenters..	1,223	1.6	4.2	1.9	29.0
Carpet, floor, and tile installers and finishers................	150	2.2	8.8	0.4	37.8
Cement masons, concrete finishers, and terrazzo workers......	68	2.7	5.8	3.1	53.3
Construction laborers.....................................	1,387	2.9	8.4	2.0	41.2
Operating engineers and other construction equipment operators........	348	1.3	6.0	0.2	17.1
Drywall installers, ceiling tile installers, and tapers..........	129	0.3	2.7	0.0	62.0
Electricians...	692	1.8	6.0	2.3	14.8
Painters, construction and maintenance.....................	485	5.5	5.5	2.0	42.6
Pipelayers, plumbers, pipefitters, and steamfitters...........	534	1.3	6.6	1.5	20.9
Roofers...	196	1.5	7.0	0.5	45.1
Sheet metal workers......................................	123	4.6	3.2	1.7	12.1
Construction and building inspectors........................	118	7.8	5.5	2.1	7.7
Highway maintenance workers.............................	108	1.5	11.0	0.1	12.4
Installation, maintenance, and repair occupations [3]............	4,821	3.2	8.4	3.0	16.6
First-line supervisors of mechanics, installers, and repairers..	292	5.9	11.3	1.0	10.4
Computer, automated teller, and office machine repairers......	296	10.7	10.8	7.2	9.9
Radio and telecommunications equipment installers and repairers........	158	5.8	11.2	3.2	13.8
Aircraft mechanics and service technicians..................	153	1.6	7.5	5.4	14.3
Automotive body and related repairers......................	140	1.8	5.7	2.3	25.3
Automotive service technicians and mechanics...............	867	1.2	9.6	4.7	21.3
Bus and truck mechanics and diesel engine specialists.........	316	0.5	8.6	1.3	13.4
Heavy vehicle and mobile equipment service technicians and mechanics...	194	1.0	5.4	2.0	17.3
Heating, air conditioning, and refrigeration mechanics and installers..	340	1.6	7.1	3.2	16.2
Industrial and refractory machinery mechanics...............	454	1.9	4.5	2.9	13.3

See footnotes at end of table.

Table 642. Employed Civilians by Occupation, Sex, Race, and Hispanic Origin: 2012-Continued.

See headnote on page 415.

Occupation	Total employed (1,000)	Percent of total			
		Female	Black [1]	Asian [1]	Hispanic [2]
Maintenance and repair workers, general..................................	442	2.2	8.4	3.2	19.4
Electrical power-line installers and repairers................................	110	2.4	7.8	0.3	7.9
Telecommunications line installers and repairers........................	177	4.8	11.2	1.9	15.7
Production, transportation, and material moving occupations..........	**16,994**	**21.8**	**13.8**	**4.2**	**21.7**
Production occupations [3]...	8,455	27.7	11.6	5.8	21.7
First-line supervisors of production and operating workers..	808	19.5	9.4	5.8	13.9
Electrical, electronics, and electromechanical assemblers................	166	52.8	13.4	16.3	24.0
Bakers...	199	53.9	15.6	5.1	28.4
Butchers and other meat, poultry, and fish processing workers...........	311	23.0	13.5	7.9	41.6
Food batchmakers..	84	59.6	12.2	5.7	33.5
Cutting, punching, and press machine setters, operators, and tenders, metal and plastic.......................................	87	18.9	8.4	3.3	22.9
Machinists...	397	3.8	4.5	4.9	11.7
Welding, soldering, and brazing workers..................................	593	4.8	8.7	2.6	23.0
Printing machine operators..	201	17.2	10.1	3.4	15.6
Laundry and dry-cleaning workers.......................................	185	53.3	20.8	10.3	37.1
Sewing machine operators...	166	74.2	5.6	11.4	43.8
Tailors, dressmakers, and sewers.......................................	86	77.1	5.9	19.5	24.9
Stationary engineers and boiler operators................................	121	5.5	10.4	4.3	13.8
Water and wastewater treatment plant and system operators..............	72	4.5	8.4	1.7	19.6
Crushing, grinding, polishing, mixing, and blending workers...............	100	15.0	14.5	6.8	18.4
Inspectors, testers, sorters, samplers, and weighers......................	689	33.4	11.5	6.7	13.6
Medical, dental, and ophthalmic laboratory technicians...................	95	50.7	1.6	8.9	15.9
Packaging and filling machine operators and tenders.....................	261	52.3	14.1	8.8	38.0
Painting workers..	150	15.1	5.7	4.3	34.9
Transportation and material-moving occupations [3].......................	8,540	15.9	15.9	2.7	21.7
Supervisors, transportation and material-moving workers..................	200	23.0	13.5	4.4	18.4
Aircraft pilots and flight engineers.......................................	129	4.1	2.7	2.5	5.0
Bus drivers...	558	45.5	25.3	2.3	12.9
Driver/sales workers and truck drivers....................................	3,201	5.4	14.0	1.6	19.3
Taxi drivers and chauffeurs...	336	13.2	24.8	13.8	16.0
Parking lot attendants..	81	11.6	23.5	5.3	35.5
Automotive and water craft attendants...................................	94	9.2	12.9	5.2	12.5
Industrial truck and tractor operators.....................................	537	7.4	18.4	1.6	31.3
Cleaners of vehicles and equipment......................................	315	15.2	16.8	2.7	35.9
Laborers and freight, stock, and material movers, hand...................	1,849	18.7	15.9	2.5	23.0
Packers and packagers, hand...	431	53.1	14.0	3.5	42.0
Refuse and recyclable material collectors................................	106	6.6	24.9	1.4	29.4

– Represents or rounds to zero. [1] The Current Population Survey (CPS) allows respondents to choose more than one race. Data represent persons who selected this race group only and exclude persons reporting more than one race. The CPS in prior years only allowed respondents to report one race group. See also comments on race in the text for Section 1. [2] Persons of Hispanic origin may be of any race. [3] Includes other occupations, not shown separately.

Source: Bureau of Labor Statistics, "Employed persons by detailed occupation, sex, race, and Hispanic or Latino ethnicity," February 2013, <http://www.bls.gov/cps/home.htm>.

Table 643. Green Goods and Services Employment by Industry Sector and Type: 2011

[Covers employment in 325 of the 1,083 detailed industries in the 2012 North American Industry Classification System (NAICS) identified by BLS as potentially providing goods and services that directly benefit the environment or conserve natural resources. Data compiled through the Green Goods and Services (GGS) survey under the Quarterly Census of Employment and Wages (QCEW) program. Data may not add to total or sub-total due to rounding. Industries may not add to total because of unclassified employment in the QCEW, not shown separately]

Industry	2012 NAICS code [1]	Private		Federal government		State government		Local government	
		Number	Per-cent [2]	Number	Per-cent [2]	Number	Per-cent [2]	Number	Per-cent [2]
Total, all industries		**2,515,200**	**2.3**	**213,340**	**7.5**	**248,539**	**5.5**	**424,201**	**3.1**
Natural resources and mining....................	11,21	64,689	3.4	(S)	(S)	1,725	79.2	(S)	(S)
Utilities..	22	71,129	12.9	7,218	52	(S)	(S)	93,644	38.9
Construction...................................	23	487,709	8.9	(S)	(S)	(S)	(S)	1242	1.2
Manufacturing..................................	31-33	507,168	4.3	(S)	(S)	(S)	(S)	(S)	(S)
Wholesale & Retail Trade.......................	42,44-45	223,079	1.1	(S)	(S)	(S)	(S)	(S)	(S)
Transportation and warehousing.................	48-49	238,755	5.9	(S)	(S)	27,583	52.3	209,063	77.9
Information....................................	51	29,412	1.1	(S)	(S)	516	7.4	3,644	2.8
Financial activities.............................	52,53	475	–	(S)	(S)	(S)	(S)	(S)	(S)
Professional, scientific, and technical services....................................	54	381,981	5	39,714	55.1	(S)	(S)	1131	6.1
Management of companies and enterprises....	55	69,310	3.6	(X)	(X)	(X)	(X)	(X)	(X)
Administrative and waste services..............	56	335,417	4.3	(S)	(S)	(S)	(S)	32,577	46.4
Education and health services..................	61,62	26,123	0.1	(S)	(S)	42,423	1.7	10,020	0.1
Leisure and hospitality..........................	71,72	23,696	0.2	21,489	36.5	9,024	38.8	20,596	5.3
Other services, except public administration. ..	81	56,257	1.3	(S)	(S)	228	7.3	2,873	6.5
Public administration...........................	92	(X)	(X)	139,884	8.8	164,952	9	49,229	1.3

S Data does not meet disclosure standards. X Not applicable. – Represents zero [1] North American Industry Classification System, 2012; see text, Section 15. [2] Percent of GGS employment compared to total employment.

Source: Department of Labor, Bureau of Labor Statistics, *Employment in Green Goods and Services, 2011*, March 2013. See also <http://www.bls.gov/ggs/>.

Table 644. Employed Civilians by Occupation—States: 2011

[In thousands (139,869 represents 139,869,000). Excludes persons with no previous work experience. Based on the Current Population Survey see text, Section 1 and Appendix III]

| State | Total | Management, professional, and related occupations | | Service occupations | Sales and office occupations | | Natural resources, construction, and maintenance occupations | | | Production, transportation, and material-moving occupations | |
		Management, business, and financial operations	Professional and related occupations		Sales and related occupations	Office and administrative occupations	Farming, fishing, and forestry occupations	Construction and extraction occupations	Installation, maintenance, and repair occupations	Production occupations	Transportation and material-moving occupations
Total.......	139,869	21,589	30,957	24,787	15,330	17,736	1,001	7,125	4,883	8,142	8,318
AL............	2,006	236	437	303	221	263	(S)	108	92	197	137
AK............	342	49	70	62	30	49	(S)	24	18	(S)	25
AZ............	2,732	432	620	495	345	358	(S)	146	86	105	131
AR............	1,247	157	241	223	131	174	(S)	73	50	98	82
CA............	16,239	2,557	3,618	2,866	1,816	2,064	243	784	501	869	922
CO............	2,507	465	607	419	274	294	(S)	139	75	98	123
CT............	1,745	299	456	291	186	213	4	78	60	90	68
DE............	412	65	88	77	43	55	4	22	13	19	26
DC............	312	78	114	52	17	30	(S)	6	3	3	9
FL............	8,366	1,336	1,802	1,636	1,096	1,111	36	369	316	250	415
GA............	4,263	694	862	702	527	536	(S)	228	175	209	308
HI............	619	88	115	132	73	95	(S)	37	19	19	36
ID............	702	98	137	120	79	97	23	39	24	41	44
IL............	5,925	924	1,257	1,044	670	758	(S)	225	198	397	437
IN............	2,913	414	536	515	299	347	26	140	143	296	198
IA............	1,570	244	307	250	164	204	(S)	80	64	131	110
KS............	1,399	225	334	234	127	173	(S)	75	47	92	83
KY............	1,859	250	393	308	192	234	20	102	55	159	146
LA............	1,893	236	399	341	191	263	(S)	128	70	125	131
ME............	643	96	143	118	68	82	9	34	22	38	34
MD............	2,873	532	804	492	271	342	(S)	143	80	69	128
MA............	3,207	566	914	546	327	358	(S)	159	71	140	123
MI............	4,181	598	935	763	444	521	35	155	134	351	245
MN............	2,764	464	632	460	305	335	32	117	88	181	149
MS............	1,206	134	243	211	130	161	(S)	73	56	106	86
MO............	2,812	454	580	453	315	366	(S)	154	111	193	170
MT............	466	75	92	94	51	59	8	26	16	18	27
NE............	963	165	198	154	99	124	(S)	52	28	77	51
NV............	1,197	164	183	324	155	153	(S)	54	37	46	78
NH............	697	117	179	107	76	86	(S)	31	26	40	31
NJ............	4,159	729	922	712	454	569	(S)	192	134	167	271
NM............	858	141	212	159	80	104	(S)	61	31	30	33
NY............	8,707	1,313	2,178	1,721	939	1,086	(S)	409	231	339	483
NC............	4,145	623	934	708	439	462	(S)	247	180	286	244
ND............	377	66	75	69	37	50	(S)	24	15	16	20
OH............	5,265	699	1,093	958	550	675	27	262	184	470	347
OK............	1,657	244	345	272	162	223	(S)	116	92	94	98
OR............	1,818	310	418	316	201	227	33	73	52	93	95
PA............	5,895	905	1,253	1,011	632	769	43	300	198	377	407
RI............	497	75	127	95	49	61	(S)	20	15	28	25
SC............	1,941	269	408	349	226	222	16	80	81	169	120
SD............	421	73	81	68	40	58	9	23	15	29	27
TN............	2,854	393	580	473	334	406	(S)	147	111	208	194
TX............	11,476	1,635	2,343	2,066	1,272	1,466	68	793	456	661	716
UT............	1,244	189	256	176	149	183	(S)	84	47	86	71
VT............	340	52	83	61	31	41	4	20	12	20	17
VA............	3,954	715	941	684	409	459	(S)	195	137	184	206
WA............	3,127	512	762	559	300	374	42	125	114	160	178
WV............	742	84	159	143	74	102	(S)	60	30	36	52
WI............	2,848	431	607	497	296	360	28	104	84	253	188
WY............	290	40	53	51	23	36	(S)	32	15	14	22

S Data are not shown when the labor force does not meet publication standard of reliability for the particular area, as determined by the sample size.

Source: U.S. Bureau of Labor Statistics, *Geographic Profile of Employment and Unemployment, 2011*, Bulletin 2774, September 2012. See also <http://www.bls.gov/gps/>.

Table 645. Employment Projections by Occupation: 2010 to 2020

[In thousands (861.0 represents 861,000), except percent and rank. Estimates based on the Current Employment Statistics Program; the Occupational Employment Statistics Survey; and the Current Population Survey. See source for methodological assumptions. Occupations based on the 2000 Standard Occupational Classification system]

Occupation	Employment (1,000)		Change, 2010–2020		Quartile rank by 2010 median annual earnings [1]	Typical Education Needed for Entry
	2010	2020	Number (1,000)	Percent		
FASTEST GROWING						
Personal care aides.........................	861.0	1,468.0	607.0	70.5	VL	Less than high school
Home health aides...........................	1,017.7	1,723.9	706.3	69.4	VL	Less than high school
Biomedical engineers......................	15.7	25.4	9.7	61.7	VH	Bachelor's degree
Helpers-brickmasons, blockmasons, stonemasons, and tile and marble setters..............	29.4	47.0	17.6	60.1	L	Less than high school
Helpers-carpenters..........................	46.5	72.4	25.9	55.7	L	Less than high school
Veterinary technologists and technicians....................	80.2	121.9	41.7	52.0	L	Associate's degree
Reinforcing iron and rebar workers......................	19.1	28.4	9.3	48.6	H	High school diploma or equivalent
Physical therapist assistants........................	67.4	98.2	30.8	45.7	H	Associate's degree
Helpers-pipelayers, plumbers, pipefitters, and steamfitters...............	57.9	84.2	26.3	45.4	L	High school diploma or equivalent
Meeting, convention, and event planners...............	71.6	102.9	31.3	43.7	H	Bachelor's degree
Diagnostic medical sonographers...................	53.7	77.1	23.4	43.5	VH	Associate's degree
Occupational therapy assistants........................	28.5	40.8	12.3	43.3	H	Associate's degree
Physical therapist aides...................	47.0	67.3	20.3	43.1	L	High school diploma or equivalent
Glaziers....................................	41.9	59.6	17.7	42.4	H	High school diploma or equivalent
Interpreters and translators.................	58.4	83.1	24.6	42.2	H	Bachelor's degree
Medical secretaries.........................	508.7	718.9	210.2	41.3	L	High school diploma or equivalent
Market research analysts and marketing specialists..............................	282.7	399.3	116.6	41.2	VH	Bachelor's degree
Marriage and family therapists.................	36.0	50.8	14.8	41.2	H	Master's degree
Brickmasons and blockmasons..............	89.2	125.3	36.1	40.5	H	High school diploma or equivalent
Physical therapists..........................	198.6	276.0	77.4	39.0	VH	Doctoral or professional degree
Dental hygienists...........................	181.8	250.3	68.5	37.7	VH	Associate's degree
Bicycle repairers............................	9.9	13.6	3.7	37.6	L	High school diploma or equivalent
Audiologists................................	13.0	17.8	4.8	36.8	VH	Doctoral or professional degree
Health educators............................	63.4	86.6	23.2	36.5	H	Bachelor's degree
Stonemasons................................	15.6	21.4	5.7	36.5	H	High school diploma or equivalent
Cost estimators.............................	185.4	252.9	67.5	36.4	VH	Bachelor's degree
Medical scientists, except epidemiologists..............	100.0	136.5	36.4	36.4	VH	Doctoral or professional degree
Mental health counselors...................	120.3	163.9	43.6	36.3	H	Master's degree
Pile-driver operators........................	4.1	5.6	1.5	36.0	H	High school diploma or equivalent
Veterinarians...............................	61.4	83.4	22.0	35.9	VH	Doctoral or professional degree
LARGEST JOB GROWTH						
Registered nurses...........................	2,737.4	3,449.3	711.9	26.0	VH	Associate's degree
Retail salespersons.........................	4,261.6	4,968.4	706.8	16.6	VL	Less than high school
Home health aides...........................	1,017.7	1,723.9	706.3	69.4	VL	Less than high school
Personal care aides.........................	861.0	1,468.0	607.0	70.5	VL	Less than high school
Office clerks, general.......................	2,950.7	3,440.2	489.5	16.6	L	High school diploma or equivalent
Combined food preparation and serving workers, including fast food....................	2,682.1	3,080.1	398.0	14.8	VL	Less than high school
Customer service representatives.................	2,187.3	2,525.6	338.4	15.5	L	High school diploma or equivalent
Heavy and tractor-trailer truck drivers....................	1,604.8	1,934.9	330.1	20.6	H	High school diploma or equivalent
Laborers and freight, stock, and material movers, hand..................	2,068.2	2,387.3	319.1	15.4	L	Less than high school
Postsecondary teachers.....................	1,756.0	2,061.7	305.7	17.4	H	Doctoral or professional degree
Nursing aides, orderlies, and attendants.................	1,505.3	1,807.2	302.0	20.1	L	Postsecondary nondegree award
Childcare workers...........................	1,282.3	1,544.3	262.0	20.4	VL	High school diploma or equivalent
Bookkeeping, accounting, and auditing clerks..........	1,898.3	2,157.4	259.0	13.6	H	High school diploma or equivalent
Cashiers...................................	3,362.6	3,612.8	250.2	7.4	VL	Less than high school
Elementary school teachers, except special education..........................	1,476.5	1,725.3	248.8	16.8	VH	Bachelor's degree
Receptionists and information clerks...................	1,048.5	1,297.0	248.5	23.7	L	High school diploma or equivalent
Janitors and cleaners, except maids and housekeeping cleaners...................	2,310.4	2,556.8	246.4	10.7	L	Less than high school
Landscapers and groundskeepers.......................	1,151.5	1,392.3	240.8	20.9	L	Less than high school
Sales representatives, wholesale and manufacturing, except technical and scientific products..............	1,430.0	1,653.4	223.4	15.6	VH	High school diploma or equivalent
Construction laborers.......................	998.8	1,211.2	212.4	21.3	L	Less than high school
Medical secretaries.........................	508.7	718.9	210.2	41.3	L	High school diploma or equivalent
First-line supervisors of office and administrative support workers..............	1,424.4	1,627.8	203.4	14.3	H	High school diploma or equivalent
Carpenters.................................	1,001.7	1,197.6	196.0	19.6	H	High school diploma or equivalent
Waiters and waitresses......................	2,260.3	2,456.2	195.9	8.7	VL	Less than high school
Security guards.............................	1,035.7	1,230.7	195.0	18.8	L	High school diploma or equivalent
Teacher assistants..........................	1,288.3	1,479.3	191.1	14.8	L	High school diploma or equivalent
Accountants and auditors....................	1,216.9	1,407.6	190.7	15.7	VH	Bachelor's degree
Licensed practical and licensed vocational nurses..........................	752.3	920.8	168.5	22.4	H	Postsecondary nondegree award
Physicians and surgeons....................	691.0	859.3	168.3	24.4	VH	Doctoral or professional degree
Medical assistants..........................	527.6	690.4	162.9	30.9	L	High school diploma or equivalent

[1] Quartile ranks based on the Occupational Employment Statistics annual wages. VH = very high ($51,540 and over), H = high ($32,390 to $51,530), L = low ($21,590 to $32,380), and VL = very low (under $21,590). The rankings were based on quartiles using one-fourth of total employment to define each quartile. Wages are for wage and salary workers.

Source: U.S. Bureau of Labor Statistics "Occupational employment projections to 2020," *Monthly Labor Review*, Volume 135, Number 12, January 2012. See also <http://www.bls.gov/opub/mlr/archive.htm>.

Table 646. Occupations of the Employed by Selected Characteristic: 2012

[In thousands (124,635 represents 124,635,000). Annual averages of monthly figures. Civilian noninstitutional population 25 years old and over. Based on Current Population Survey; see text, Section 1 and Appendix III. See headnote, Table 632, regarding occupations]

Race and educational attainment	Total employed	Managerial, professional, and related	Service	Sales and office	Natural resources, construction, and maintenance	Production, transportation, and material-moving
Total [1]	**124,635**	**51,013**	**19,730**	**27,462**	**11,458**	**14,972**
Less than a high school diploma	9,923	680	3,216	1,263	2,235	2,529
High school graduates, no college	33,718	5,646	7,375	8,629	4,913	7,156
Less than a bachelor's degree	34,705	11,260	6,251	10,029	3,327	3,838
College graduates	46,288	33,427	2,888	7,540	984	1,450
White [2]	100,543	41,897	14,437	22,399	10,049	11,761
Less than a high school diploma	8,100	571	2,403	1,032	2,012	2,083
High school graduates, no college	27,112	4,788	5,219	7,157	4,344	5,605
Less than a bachelor's degree	27,854	9,351	4,626	8,059	2,864	2,954
College graduates	37,476	27,188	2,189	6,151	829	1,120
Black [2]	13,717	4,428	3,335	3,043	821	2,090
Less than a high school diploma	1,016	57	459	132	131	238
High school graduates, no college	4,397	538	1,480	950	350	1,078
Less than a bachelor's degree	4,503	1,231	1,064	1,321	268	618
College graduates	3,801	2,602	333	639	71	156
Asian [2]	7,032	3,546	1,228	1,342	254	663
Less than a high school diploma	481	31	227	68	35	119
High school graduates, no college	1,212	153	428	299	81	252
Less than a bachelor's degree	1,225	347	293	361	80	145
College graduates	4,115	3,015	281	613	59	147
Hispanic [3]	18,309	4,117	4,632	3,437	2,896	3,226
Less than a high school diploma	5,269	227	1,839	461	1,396	1,347
High school graduates, no college	5,613	670	1,534	1,232	944	1,233
Less than a bachelor's degree	4,216	1,185	931	1,200	411	489
College graduates	3,210	2,036	328	544	145	157

[1] Includes other races, not shown separately. [2] For persons in this race group only. See footnote 4, Table 614. [3] Persons of Hispanic origin may be any race.

Source: Bureau of Labor Statistics, Current Population Survey, unpublished data. See also <http://www.bls.gov/cps/>.

Table 647. Employment by Industry: 2000 to 2012

[In thousands (136,891 represents 136,891,000), except percent. Civilian noninstitutional population 16 years old and over. Annual average of monthly figures. Based on Current Population Survey; see text, Section 1, Population, and Appendix III]

Industry	2000	2005	2011	2012	2012, percent			
					Female	Black [1]	Asian [1]	Hispanic [2]
Total employed	**136,891**	**141,730**	**139,869**	**142,469**	**47.0**	**11.1**	**5.4**	**15.4**
Agriculture and related industries	2,464	2,197	2,254	2,186	25.6	2.8	1.5	22.5
Mining	475	624	817	957	13.2	4.7	1.4	17.5
Construction	9,931	11,197	9,039	8,964	9.0	5.6	1.9	24.4
Manufacturing	19,644	16,253	14,336	14,686	29.0	8.7	6.2	15.3
Durable goods	12,519	10,333	9,007	9,244	25.0	7.6	6.6	12.7
Nondurable goods	7,125	5,919	5,329	5,443	35.7	10.6	5.5	19.7
Wholesale trade	4,216	4,579	3,798	3,694	28.6	7.1	5.0	16.8
Retail trade	15,763	16,825	15,927	16,182	48.3	11.4	5.1	15.2
Transportation and utilities	7,380	7,360	7,200	7,271	23.2	15.9	3.9	16.2
Transportation and warehousing	6,096	6,184	5,957	6,082	23.2	17.2	4.2	17.3
Utilities	1,284	1,176	1,243	1,190	23.3	9.4	2.1	10.8
Information	4,059	3,402	3,150	2,971	38.2	11.1	6.2	10.2
Financial activities	9,374	10,203	9,386	9,590	53.3	9.6	5.8	11.7
Finance and insurance	6,641	7,035	6,613	6,786	56.1	9.7	6.4	10.5
Real estate and rental and leasing	2,734	3,168	2,773	2,804	46.5	9.4	4.1	14.4
Professional and business services	13,649	14,294	15,819	16,539	41.1	9.6	6.9	15.2
Professional and technical services	8,266	8,584	9,461	9,913	43.2	6.4	9.4	7.5
Management, administrative, and waste services	5,383	5,709	6,358	6,626	38.0	14.3	3.2	26.7
Education and health services	26,188	29,174	31,867	32,350	74.5	14.3	5.3	11.4
Educational services	11,255	12,264	12,965	12,945	68.6	11.0	4.2	10.5
Health care and social assistance	14,933	16,910	18,902	19,405	78.4	16.5	6.0	12.0
Hospitals	5,202	5,719	6,315	6,113	76.5	16.0	7.1	9.5
Health services, except hospitals	7,009	8,332	9,367	10,009	77.4	16.1	5.7	11.8
Social assistance	2,722	2,860	3,221	3,283	84.9	18.8	4.5	17.0
Leisure and hospitality	11,186	12,071	12,697	13,193	50.8	11.3	6.6	21.9
Arts, entertainment, and recreation	2,539	2,765	2,922	3,022	45.5	8.8	5.0	12.6
Accommodation and food services	8,647	9,306	9,775	10,171	52.4	12.0	7.1	24.7
Other services	6,450	7,020	6,724	7,168	52.0	9.8	7.7	18.0
Other services, except private households	5,731	6,208	6,002	6,430	47.8	10.0	8.1	15.7
Private households	718	812	722	738	88.9	8.4	4.5	37.2
Public administration	6,113	6,530	6,853	6,717	45.4	15.7	4.1	11.1

[1] Persons in this race group only. See footnote 4, Table 614. [3] Persons of Hispanic origin may be of any race.

Source: U.S. Bureau of Labor Statistics, "Employed persons by detailed industry, sex, race, and Hispanic or Latino ethnicity," February 2013, <http://www.bls.gov/cps/tables.htm>.

Table 648. Employment Projections by Industry: 2010 to 2020

[5,525.6 represents 5,525,600. Estimates based on the Current Employment Statistics program. See source for methodological assumptions. Minus sign (-) indicates decline]

Industry	2007 NAICS code [1]	Employment 2010 (1,000)	Employment 2020 (1,000)	Change, 2010–2020 (1,000)	Average annual rate of change 2010–2020
LARGEST GROWTH					
Construction..	23	5,525.6	7,365.1	1,839.5	2.9
Retail trade...	44, 45	14,413.7	16,182.2	1,768.5	1.2
Offices of health practitioners..........................	6211, 6212, 6213	3,818.2	5,209.6	1,391.4	3.2
Hospitals...	622	4,685.3	5,563.6	878.3	1.7
Home health care services.............................	6216	1,080.6	1,952.4	871.8	6.1
Food services and drinking places.....................	722	9,351.8	10,212.2	860.4	0.9
Individual and family services..........................	6241	1,215.0	2,066.4	851.4	5.5
Nursing and residential care facilities.................	623	3,129.0	3,951.0	822.0	2.4
Wholesale trade..	42	5,456.1	6,200.2	744.1	1.3
General local government educational services compensation..................	(X)	8,010.4	8,751.4	741.0	0.9
Computer systems design and related services............................	5415	1,441.5	2,112.8	671.3	3.9
Employment services....................................	5613	2,716.7	3,348.0	631.3	2.1
Management, scientific, and technical consulting services....................	5416	991.4	1,567.0	575.6	4.7
Junior colleges, colleges, universities, and professional schools.............	6112, 6113	1,694.0	2,171.1	477.1	2.5
Outpatient, laboratory, and other ambulatory care services.................	6214-5, 6219	1,077.1	1,471.2	394.1	3.2
Architectural, engineering, and related services.........................	5413	1,276.6	1,635.1	358.5	2.5
Services to buildings and dwellings......................	5617	1,742.5	2,044.8	302.3	1.6
Truck transportation......................................	484	1,244.0	1,544.0	300.0	2.2
General state government educational services compensation.............	(X)	2,377.1	2,661.7	284.6	1.1
Child day care services..................................	6244	851.8	1,101.3	249.5	2.6
FASTEST GROWTH					
Home health care services.............................	6216	1,080.6	1,952.4	871.8	6.1
Individual and family services..........................	6241	1,215.0	2,066.4	851.4	5.5
Management, scientific, and technical consulting services...................	5416	991.4	1,567.0	575.6	4.7
Veneer, plywood, and engineered wood product manufacturing.............	3212	64.7	94.9	30.2	3.9
Computer systems design and related services..................	5415	1,441.5	2,112.8	671.3	3.9
Cement and concrete product manufacturing................	3273	171.8	236.1	64.3	3.2
Outpatient, laboratory, and other ambulatory care services..................	6214-5, 6219	1,077.1	1,471.2	394.1	3.2
Offices of health practitioners..........................	6211-3	3,818.2	5,209.6	1,391.4	3.2
Software publishers......................................	5112	259.8	351.6	91.8	3.1
Construction...	23	5,525.6	7,365.1	1,839.5	2.9
Commercial and industrial machinery and equipment rental and leasing....	5324	113.5	151.2	37.7	2.9
Other professional, scientific, and technical services.........................	5419	573.1	760.2	187.1	2.9
Facilities support services..............................	5612	134.0	177.6	43.6	2.9
Community and vocational rehabilitation services.........................	6242, 6243	557.5	738.4	180.9	2.9
Lessors of nonfinancial intangible assets (except copyrighted works).......	533	25.2	33.4	8.2	2.9
Other educational services..............................	6114–7	604.2	787.1	182.9	2.7
Automotive repair and maintenance.....................	8111	799.7	1,037.2	237.5	2.6
Grantmaking and giving services and social advocacy organizations........	8132, 8133	394.5	510.7	116.2	2.6
Sawmills and wood preservation........................	3211	81.3	105.1	23.8	2.6
Child day care services..................................	6244	851.8	1,101.3	249.5	2.6
MOST RAPIDLY DECLINING					
Apparel knitting mills.....................................	3151	157.7	66.1	−91.6	−8.3
Leather and hide tanning and finishing, and other leather and allied product manufacturing..................	3161, 3169	27.8	12.7	−15.1	−7.6
Postal Service..	491	656.4	474.6	−181.8	−3.2
Communications equipment manufacturing................	3342	118.0	85.7	−32.3	−3.1
Computer and peripheral equipment manufacturing..................	3341	161.6	117.5	−44.1	−3.1
Pipeline transportation...................................	486	42.4	32.6	−9.8	−2.6
Metal ore mining...	2122	36.4	28.1	−8.3	−2.5
Pesticide, fertilizer, and other agricultural chemical manufacturing..........	3253	35.3	27.5	−7.8	−2.5
Federal enterprises except the Postal Service and electric utilities..........	(X)	76.6	60.2	−16.4	−2.4
Other miscellaneous manufacturing.....................	3399	266.0	210.3	−55.7	−2.3
Other chemical product and preparation manufacturing.....................	3259	82.9	68.6	−14.3	−1.9
Metalworking machinery manufacturing.................	3335	153.2	130.5	−22.7	−1.6
Glass and glass product manufacturing.................	3272	80.7	68.8	−11.9	−1.6
Basic chemical manufacturing...........................	3251	142.4	121.6	−20.8	−1.6
Electrical equipment manufacturing.....................	3353	136.3	116.9	−19.4	−1.5
Pulp, paper, and paperboard mills......................	3221	112.7	97.4	−15.3	−1.4
Fiber, yarn, and thread mills............................	3131	237.8	206.1	−31.7	−1.4
Iron and steel mills and ferroalloy manufacturing.................	3311	85.4	74.3	−11.1	−1.4
Petroleum and coal products manufacturing.............	324	114.0	100.0	−14.0	−1.3
Newspaper, periodical, book, and directory publishers......................	5111	501.3	439.7	−61.6	−1.3

X Not applicable. [1] Based on the North American Industry Classification System, 2007; see text, Section 15.

Source: U.S. Bureau of Labor Statistics, "Industry employment and output projections to 2020," *Monthly Labor Review*, Vol. 135, No. 1, January 2012, <http://www.bls.gov/opub/mlr/2012/01/art4exc.htm>.

Table 649. Export-Supported Jobs for Largest Metropolitan Areas: 2010

[1,562.9 represents $1,562,900,000,000. Direct export-production jobs are jobs supported by exports in the industries producing the exported good or service; these are in the metropolitan area where the export is produced. Total export-supported jobs include direct export-production jobs as well as jobs supported by exports in the suppliers to the exporting industry, and in the case of goods exports, in the transportation and wholesale trade industries; some portion of these jobs are outside the metro area producing the export and in other parts of the United States]

Metropolitan areas ranked by 2010 export value	Exports		Direct Export-Production Jobs (1,000)	Total Export-Supported Jobs (1,000)
	Value (bil. dol.)	Percent of Metro GDP		
United States...	**1,562.9**	**10.7**	**5,542.3**	**10,719.9**
Los Angeles-Long Beach-Santa Ana, CA............................	79.8	10.9	312.7	540.7
New York-Northern New Jersey-Long Island, NY-NJ-PA..............	78.0	6.6	329.0	539.3
Chicago-Joliet-Naperville, IL-IN-WI..............................	53.9	10.9	197.6	376.1
Houston-Sugar Land-Baytown, TX..................................	47.9	14.0	141.3	307.0
Dallas-Fort Worth-Arlington, TX.................................	41.1	12.7	147.2	279.7
San Francisco-Oakland-Fremont, CA...............................	31.8	11.2	110.0	194.3
Seattle-Tacoma-Bellevue, WA.....................................	29.0	13.7	104.4	188.4
Detroit-Warren-Livonia, MI......................................	26.6	14.9	79.1	186.3
Philadelphia-Camden-Wilmington, PA-NJ-DE-MD.....................	26.6	8.5	97.0	174.1
Boston-Cambridge-Quincy, MA-NH..................................	26.4	8.9	118.9	196.0
San Jose-Sunnyvale-Santa Clara, CA.............................	22.8	18.0	72.9	144.8
Portland-Vancouver-Hillsboro, OR-WA.............................	21.3	18.2	70.3	142.4
Atlanta-Sandy Springs-Marietta, GA.............................	20.0	8.0	88.3	151.7
Minneapolis-St. Paul-Bloomington, MN-WI.........................	17.6	9.8	63.2	117.2
Phoenix-Mesa-Glendale, AZ.......................................	16.6	9.1	66.7	117.1
Washington-Arlington-Alexandria, DC-VA-MD-WV....................	16.4	4.2	100.2	146.2
San Diego-Carlsbad-San Marcos, CA..............................	16.0	9.3	65.5	113.4
Indianapolis-Carmel, IN..	15.9	17.2	35.7	81.0
Miami-Fort Lauderdale-Pompano Beach, FL.........................	14.7	6.2	75.1	115.4
St. Louis, MO-IL...	14.4	11.5	49.0	94.9
Cleveland-Elyria-Mentor, OH....................................	12.1	12.4	35.6	76.8
Cincinnati-Middletown, OH-KY-IN................................	11.6	12.2	35.2	74.4
Pittsburgh, PA...	11.1	9.5	38.2	74.6
Riverside-San Bernardino-Ontario, CA...........................	10.9	8.3	39.4	73.6
Denver-Aurora-Broomfield, CO...................................	10.2	7.2	44.5	72.8
Charlotte-Gastonia-Rock Hill, NC-SC............................	9.8	10.7	33.1	68.4
Baltimore-Towson, MD...	9.7	6.7	40.0	67.6
Milwaukee-Waukesha-West Allis, WI..............................	9.3	12.3	29.6	61.0
Hartford-West Hartford-East Hartford, CT.......................	8.9	9.3	31.7	59.8
New Orleans-Metairie-Kenner, LA................................	8.7	14.3	21.6	46.0
Austin-Round Rock-San Marcos, TX...............................	8.5	10.5	31.3	58.0
Kansas City, MO-KS...	8.1	8.6	30.2	57.5
Rochester, NY..	8.1	13.6	23.0	47.8
Tampa-St. Petersburg-Clearwater, FL............................	8.0	6.8	34.2	57.5
Columbus, OH...	7.9	8.9	29.5	55.5
Las Vegas-Paradise, NV...	7.4	8.4	43.7	64.4
Orlando-Kissimmee-Sanford, FL..................................	7.3	7.0	37.8	58.0
Baton Rouge, LA..	7.3	18.3	16.6	46.0
Bridgeport-Stamford-Norwalk, CT................................	7.0	10.6	23.5	45.0
Nashville-Davidson-Murfreesboro-Franklin, TN...................	7.0	9.6	24.6	48.2
Virginia Beach-Norfolk-Newport News, VA-NC.....................	6.8	8.0	21.9	40.2
San Antonio-New Braunfels, TX..................................	6.7	7.9	26.7	46.8
Salt Lake City, UT...	6.6	10.8	27.0	52.4
Greensboro-High Point, NC......................................	6.5	17.3	17.9	40.7
Providence-New Bedford-Fall River, RI-MA.......................	6.4	9.1	25.3	46.5
Buffalo-Niagara Falls, NY......................................	6.4	9.9	23.0	45.2
Louisville-Jefferson County, KY-IN.............................	6.4	11.5	19.2	43.8
Oxnard-Thousand Oaks-Ventura, CA...............................	6.2	15.7	16.6	34.2
Sacramento-Arden-Arcade-Roseville, CA..........................	6.0	5.9	26.8	44.3
Tulsa, OK..	5.5	13.8	18.9	36.4

Source: Brookings Institution, *Export Nation 2012: How U.S. Metropolitan Areas Are Driving National Growth*, March 2012 ©. See also <http://www.brookings.edu/research/reports/2012/03/08-exports>.

Table 650. Unemployed Persons by Sex and Reason: 1990 to 2012

[In thousands (3,906 represents 3,906,000). For civilian noninstitutionalized population 16 years old and over. Annual averages of monthly figures. Data not strictly comparable with data for earlier years. Based on Current Population Survey; see text, Section 1 and Appendix III]

Sex and reason	1990	2000	2003	2004	2005	2006	2007	2008	2009	2010	2011	2012
Male, total............	**3,906**	**2,975**	**4,906**	**4,456**	**4,059**	**3,753**	**3,882**	**5,033**	**8,453**	**8,626**	**7,684**	**6,771**
Job losers [1]...............	2,257	1,516	3,024	2,603	2,188	2,021	2,175	3,055	5,967	5,919	4,968	4,103
Job leavers................	528	387	422	437	445	406	408	458	438	457	494	487
Reentrants................	806	854	1,141	1,070	1,067	1,015	956	1,128	1,504	1,608	1545	1,481
New entrants.............	315	217	320	346	359	312	343	393	545	641	678	699
Female, total..........	**3,140**	**2,717**	**3,868**	**3,694**	**3,531**	**3,247**	**3,196**	**3,891**	**5,811**	**6,199**	**6,063**	**5,734**
Job losers [1]...............	1,130	1,001	1,814	1,595	1,479	1,300	1,340	1,735	3,193	3,331	3,139	2,774
Job leavers................	513	393	397	421	427	421	385	438	444	432	463	480
Reentrants................	1,124	1,107	1,336	1,338	1,319	1,223	1,186	1,345	1,683	1,858	1,857	1,864
New entrants.............	373	217	321	340	306	304	285	374	491	579	605	617

[1] Beginning 2000, persons who completed temporary jobs are identified separately and are included as job losers.

Source: Bureau of Labor Statistics, "Unemployed jobseekers by sex, reason for unemployment, and active jobsearch methods used," February 2013, <http://www.bls.gov/cps/tables.htm>.

Table 651. Unemployed Jobseekers' Job Search Activities: 2012

[12,506 represents 12,506,000. For the civilian noninstitutionalized population 16 years old and over. Annual averages of monthly data. Based on the Current Population Survey; see text, Section 1 and Appendix III]

Characteristic	Population (1,000)		Jobseekers' job search methods (percent)							
	Total unemployed	Total jobseekers [1]	Employer directly	Sent out a resume or filled out applications	Placed or answered ads	Friends or relatives	Public employment agency	Private employment agency	Other activities	Average number of methods used
Total, 16 years and over [2]....	**12,506**	**11,322**	**51.3**	**56.3**	**18.4**	**28.5**	**19.3**	**8.6**	**15.4**	**2.0**
16 to 19 years old.............	1,397	1,338	48.6	61.6	13.5	21.0	8.3	3.3	9.5	1.7
20 to 24 years old.............	2,054	1,921	51.4	58.3	16.8	24.0	16.3	6.5	14.4	1.9
25 to 34 years old.............	2,764	2,512	52.3	58.7	19.0	28.3	21.3	9.1	15.4	2.0
35 to 44 years old.............	2,158	1,908	52.0	55.9	19.4	31.1	23.0	10.8	16.4	2.1
45 to 54 years old.............	2,181	1,937	52.5	53.6	20.8	32.7	23.2	11.0	17.2	2.1
55 to 64 years old.............	1,470	1,293	50.9	50.9	19.4	32.5	21.6	10.0	18.0	2.0
65 years old and over........	482	413	44.5	44.8	17.8	31.1	15.1	5.9	18.9	1.8
Male........................	6,771	6,016	52.5	53.6	18.1	30.6	20.1	8.9	15.6	2.0
16 to 19 years old.............	787	758	48.7	60.7	14.1	23.0	8.6	3.6	9.4	1.7
20 to 24 years old.............	1,163	1,067	52.5	55.4	16.6	25.8	17.1	6.9	13.6	1.9
25 to 34 years old.............	1,476	1,304	53.7	56.1	18.6	30.2	21.8	9.3	15.8	2.1
35 to 44 years old.............	1,124	961	54.4	52.9	20.3	34.9	25.3	11.3	17.2	2.2
45 to 54 years old.............	1,142	990	53.7	49.4	20.1	34.8	25.1	11.7	18.8	2.1
55 to 64 years old.............	811	705	52.4	48.4	18.5	34.4	21.6	10.2	17.2	2.0
65 years old and over........	268	230	45.7	44.7	17.3	32.1	15.1	6.5	18.8	1.8
Female......................	5,734	5,306	49.8	59.2	18.6	26.2	18.5	8.2	15.3	2.0
16 to 19 years old.............	609	580	48.4	62.8	12.7	18.3	7.9	3.0	9.6	1.6
20 to 24 years old.............	891	854	50.0	62.0	17.0	21.8	15.3	6.0	15.5	1.9
25 to 34 years old.............	1,288	1,208	50.8	61.5	19.4	26.3	20.8	8.8	15.0	2.0
35 to 44 years old.............	1,034	947	49.5	58.9	18.6	27.2	20.7	10.3	15.7	2.0
45 to 54 years old.............	1,039	947	51.3	58.1	21.5	30.5	21.3	10.3	15.6	2.1
55 to 64 years old.............	659	588	49.2	54.0	20.4	30.2	21.6	9.9	18.9	2.1
65 years old and over........	214	183	43.0	44.9	18.5	29.8	15.1	5.2	19.0	1.8
White [3]............................	8,915	7,939	51.7	55.9	19.0	28.4	18.3	8.2	16.2	2.0
Male......................	4,931	4,298	52.9	53.5	18.7	30.5	19.2	8.7	16.5	2.0
Female....................	3,985	3,640	50.2	58.8	19.3	25.9	17.2	7.6	15.8	2.0
Black [3]............................	2,544	2,406	50.5	56.3	16.6	28.3	23.2	9.2	12.8	2.0
Male......................	1,292	1,211	51.4	53.3	16.8	30.0	23.5	9.2	12.2	2.0
Female....................	1,252	1,195	49.6	59.4	16.3	26.6	22.9	9.2	13.5	2.0
Asian [3]............................	483	455	51.5	55.6	20.5	34.9	17.4	11.8	18.2	2.1
Male......................	249	234	53.3	52.8	19.3	36.3	19.2	12.1	18.3	2.1
Female....................	234	221	49.5	58.6	21.9	33.4	15.4	11.4	18.0	2.1
Hispanic [4].........................	2,514	2,241	54.0	49.9	14.8	33.3	19.8	8.9	13.2	1.9
Male......................	1,383	1,195	56.1	47.7	14.8	35.8	21.3	8.7	13.5	2.0
Female....................	1,130	1,046	51.5	52.5	14.7	30.5	18.2	9.2	12.8	1.9

[1] Excludes persons on temporary layoff. [2] Includes other races not shown separately. [3] Data for this race group only. See footnote 4, Table 614. [4] Persons of Hispanic or Latino origin may be of any race.

Source: Bureau of Labor Statistics, "Unemployed jobseekers by sex, age, race, Hispanic or Latino ethnicity, and active jobsearch methods used," February 2013, <http://www.bls.gov/cps/tables.htm>.

Table 652. Unemployed Workers—Summary: 1990 to 2012

[In thousands (7,047 represents 7,047,000), except as indicated. For civilian noninstitutionalized population 16 years old and over. Annual averages of monthly figures. Data not strictly comparable with data for earlier years. Based on the Current Population Survey; see text, Section 1 and Appendix III]

Item	1990	2000	2005	2008	2009	2010	2011	2012
UNEMPLOYED								
Total [1]	**7,047**	**5,692**	**7,591**	**8,924**	**14,265**	**14,825**	**13,747**	**12,506**
16 to 19 years old	1,212	1,081	1,186	1,285	1,552	1,528	1,400	1,397
20 to 24 years old	1,299	1,022	1,335	1,545	2,207	2,329	2,234	2,054
25 to 34 years old	1,995	1,207	1,661	1,949	3,284	3,386	3,187	2,764
35 to 44 years old	1,328	1,133	1,400	1,604	2,722	2,703	2,389	2,158
45 to 54 years old	723	762	1,195	1,473	2,592	2,769	2,493	2,181
55 to 64 years old	386	355	630	803	1,487	1,660	1,579	1,470
65 years and over	105	132	184	264	421	449	465	482
Male	3,906	2,975	4,059	5,033	8,453	8,626	7,684	6,771
16 to 19 years old	667	599	667	736	898	863	786	787
20 to 24 years old	715	547	775	920	1,329	1,398	1,275	1,163
25 to 34 years old	1,092	602	844	1,119	1,988	1,993	1,795	1,476
35 to 44 years old	711	557	715	875	1,600	1,534	1,316	1,124
45 to 54 years old	413	398	624	804	1,558	1,614	1,370	1,142
55 to 64 years old	249	189	331	425	840	962	882	811
65 years and over	59	83	102	153	241	262	261	268
Female	3,140	2,717	3,531	3,891	5,811	6,199	6,063	5,734
16 to 19 years old	544	483	519	549	654	665	613	609
20 to 24 years old	584	475	560	625	878	931	960	891
25 to 34 years old	902	604	817	830	1,296	1,392	1,392	1,288
35 to 44 years old	617	577	685	730	1,121	1,169	1,073	1,034
45 to 54 years old	310	364	571	669	1,034	1,156	1,123	1,039
55 to 64 years old	137	165	299	377	647	698	697	659
65 years and over	46	50	82	111	180	187	204	214
White [2]	5,186	4,121	5,350	6,509	10,648	10,916	9,889	8,915
Black [2]	1,565	1,241	1,700	1,788	2,606	2,852	2,831	2,544
Asian [2,3]	(NA)	227	259	285	522	543	518	483
Hispanic [4]	876	954	1,191	1,678	2,706	2,843	2,629	2,514
UNEMPLOYMENT RATE [5] (percent)								
Total [1]	**5.6**	**4.0**	**5.1**	**5.8**	**9.3**	**9.6**	**8.9**	**8.1**
16 to 19 years old	15.5	13.1	16.6	18.7	24.3	25.9	24.4	24.0
20 to 24 years old	8.8	7.2	8.8	10.2	14.7	15.5	14.6	13.3
25 to 34 years old	5.6	3.7	5.1	5.8	9.9	10.1	9.5	8.3
35 to 44 years old	4.1	3.0	3.9	4.6	7.9	8.1	7.3	6.6
45 to 54 years old	3.6	2.5	3.5	4.1	7.2	7.7	7.1	6.2
55 to 64 years old	3.3	2.5	3.3	3.7	6.6	7.1	6.6	5.9
65 years and over	3.0	3.1	3.5	4.2	6.4	6.7	6.5	6.2
Male	5.7	3.9	5.1	6.1	10.3	10.5	9.4	8.2
16 to 19 years old	16.3	14.0	18.6	21.2	27.8	28.8	27.2	26.8
20 to 24 years old	9.1	7.3	9.6	11.4	17.0	17.8	15.7	14.3
25 to 34 years old	5.5	3.4	4.7	6.1	10.9	10.9	9.7	8.2
35 to 44 years old	4.1	2.8	3.7	4.6	8.6	8.5	7.4	6.4
45 to 54 years old	3.7	2.4	3.5	4.2	8.2	8.6	7.4	6.2
55 to 64 years old	3.8	2.4	3.3	3.8	7.2	8.0	7.1	6.3
65 years and over	3.0	3.3	3.4	4.5	6.7	7.1	6.5	6.2
Female	5.5	4.1	5.1	5.4	8.1	8.6	8.5	7.9
16 to 19 years old	14.7	12.1	14.5	16.2	20.7	22.8	21.7	21.1
20 to 24 years old	8.5	7.1	7.9	8.8	12.3	13.0	13.4	12.1
25 to 34 years old	5.6	4.1	5.6	5.5	8.6	9.1	9.1	8.4
35 to 44 years old	4.2	3.3	4.1	4.5	7.1	7.7	7.2	6.8
45 to 54 years old	3.4	2.5	3.5	3.9	6.0	6.8	6.7	6.2
55 to 64 years old	2.8	2.5	3.3	3.7	6.0	6.2	6.1	5.6
65 years and over	3.1	2.7	3.5	3.9	6.1	6.2	6.5	6.3
White [2]	4.8	3.5	4.4	5.2	8.5	8.7	7.9	7.2
Black [2]	11.4	7.6	10.0	10.1	14.8	16.0	15.8	13.8
Asian [2,3]	(NA)	3.6	4.0	4.0	7.3	7.5	7.0	5.9
Hispanic [4]	8.2	5.7	6.0	7.6	12.1	12.5	11.5	10.3
Percent without work for—								
Fewer than 5 weeks	46.3	44.9	35.1	32.8	22.2	18.7	19.5	21.1
5 to 14 weeks	32.0	31.9	30.4	31.4	26.8	22.0	21.8	22.9
15 weeks and over	21.6	23.2	34.5	35.7	51.0	59.3	58.8	55.9
15 to 26 weeks	11.7	11.8	14.9	16.0	19.5	16.0	15.0	14.9
27 weeks and over	10.0	11.4	19.6	19.7	31.5	43.3	43.8	41.1
Unemployment duration, average (weeks)	12.0	12.6	18.4	17.9	24.4	33.0	39.3	39.4

NA Not available. [1] Includes other races not shown separately. [2] See footnote 4, Table 614. [3] Prior to 2004, includes Pacific Islanders. [4] Persons of Hispanic or Latino origin may be of any race. [5] Unemployed as percent of civilian labor force in specified group.

Source: Bureau of Labor Statistics, "Labor Force Statistics from the Current Population Survey," <http://www.bls.gov/cps>, accessed August 2013.

Table 653. Unemployment Rates by Industry and by Sex: 2000 to 2012

[In percent. Civilian noninstitutionalized population 16 years old and over. Annual averages of monthly figures. Rate represents unemployment as a percent of labor force in each specified group. Based on Current Population Survey; see text, Section 1 and Appendix III. See also headnote, Table 632, regarding industries]

Industry	Total				Male		Female	
	2000	2005	2011	2012	2011	2012	2011	2012
All employed [1]	**4.0**	**5.1**	**8.9**	**8.1**	**9.4**	**8.2**	**8.5**	**7.9**
Wage and salary workers:								
Agriculture and related industries	9.0	8.3	12.5	12.4	11.5	11.3	15.6	16.0
Mining, quarrying, and oil and gas extraction	4.4	3.1	6.1	6.0	6.1	6.2	6.8	4.6
Construction	6.2	7.4	16.4	13.9	17.0	14.1	11.3	11.1
Manufacturing	3.5	4.9	9.0	7.3	8.4	6.7	10.2	8.7
Wholesale trade	3.3	4.0	6.9	6.0	6.3	5.1	8.4	8.0
Retail trade	4.6	5.7	9.4	8.6	8.8	8.0	10.1	9.2
Transportation and utilities	3.4	4.1	8.2	6.9	8.0	6.6	8.8	8.1
Transportation and warehousing	3.8	4.5	8.8	7.4	8.7	7.1	9.1	8.4
Utilities	1.9	1.9	4.9	4.3	4.0	3.4	7.4	6.7
Information	3.2	5.0	7.3	7.6	7.0	6.6	7.8	9.4
Telecommunications	2.3	5.2	7.3	7.2	6.7	5.4	8.4	10.9
Financial activities	2.4	2.9	6.4	5.1	6.6	4.6	6.2	5.4
Finance and insurance	2.2	2.7	5.9	4.5	5.9	4.0	5.9	4.9
Real estate and rental and leasing	3.1	3.3	7.7	6.6	8.0	6.1	7.3	7.3
Professional and business services	4.8	6.2	9.7	8.9	9.2	8.5	10.4	9.3
Professional and technical services	2.5	3.5	5.8	5.4	4.8	4.5	7.1	6.6
Management, administrative, and waste services	8.1	10.2	15.0	13.7	14.7	13.7	15.5	13.8
Education and health services	2.5	3.4	5.6	5.5	5.3	5.3	5.7	5.6
Educational services	2.4	3.7	6.4	6.5	6.4	5.9	6.5	6.8
Health care and social assistance	2.5	3.3	5.4	5.3	4.9	5.1	5.6	5.4
Leisure and hospitality	6.6	7.8	11.6	10.4	11.3	9.7	11.8	11.0
Arts, entertainment, and recreation	5.9	6.9	11.5	9.7	12.1	10.0	10.7	9.3
Accommodation and food services	6.8	8.0	11.6	10.6	11.1	9.6	12.1	11.4
Other services [2]	3.9	4.8	8.8	7.2	9.3	7.3	8.3	7.0
Government workers	2.1	2.6	4.7	4.3	4.6	4.2	4.7	4.4

[1] Includes the self-employed, unpaid family workers, and persons with no previous work experience, not shown separately. [2] Includes private household workers.

Source: Bureau of Labor Statistics, "Unemployed persons by industry, class of worker, and sex," February 2013, <http://www.bls.gov/cps/tables.htm>.

Table 654. Unemployment by Occupation: 2000 to 2012

[5,692 represents 5,692,000. Civilian noninstitutionalized population 16 years old and over. Annual averages of monthly data. Rate represents unemployment as a percent of the labor force for each specified group. Based on Current Population Survey; see text, Section 1 and Appendix III. See also headnote, Table 632, regarding occupations]

Occupation	Number (1,000)			Unemployment rate				
						2012		
	2000	2011	2012	2000	2011	Total	Male	Female
Total [1]	**5,692**	**13,747**	**12,506**	**4.0**	**8.9**	**8.1**	**8.2**	**7.9**
Management, professional, and related occupations	827	2,458	2,318	1.8	4.5	4.1	3.8	4.4
Management, business, and financial operations	320	1,067	935	1.6	4.7	4.0	3.7	4.3
Management	214	700	615	1.5	4.4	3.7	3.3	4.3
Business and financial operations	106	366	320	2.0	5.5	4.6	4.8	4.5
Professional and related occupations	507	1,392	1,383	1.9	4.3	4.2	3.9	4.4
Computer and mathematical	74	155	144	2.2	4.1	3.6	3.3	4.7
Architecture and engineering	51	149	123	1.7	5.1	4.2	3.7	6.8
Life, physical, and social science	18	51	55	1.4	3.8	4.0	4.4	3.5
Community and social services	40	122	113	2.0	4.9	4.7	5.3	4.4
Legal	18	68	50	1.2	3.7	2.7	1.5	3.9
Education, training, and library	136	410	426	1.8	4.5	4.8	4.1	5.0
Arts, design, entertainment, sports, and media	97	225	225	3.5	7.5	7.4	7.6	7.2
Healthcare practitioner and technical	73	212	246	1.2	2.7	3.0	2.3	3.2
Service occupations	1,132	2,727	2,540	5.2	9.9	9.1	9.0	9.1
Healthcare support	101	284	276	4.0	7.8	7.3	7.7	7.3
Protective service	70	206	205	2.7	6.0	6.2	5.4	9.1
Food preparation and serving-related	469	1,037	925	6.6	11.8	10.3	10.3	10.4
Building and grounds cleaning and maintenance	301	725	692	5.8	11.7	11.0	10.5	11.7
Personal care and service	190	474	443	4.4	8.7	7.8	8.1	7.7
Sales and office occupations	1,446	3,135	2,775	3.8	8.7	7.7	7.3	8.0
Sales and related	673	1,481	1,318	4.1	8.8	7.9	6.3	9.4
Office and administrative support	773	1,653	1,457	3.6	8.5	7.6	8.8	7.1
Natural resources, construction, and maintenance	758	2,000	1,668	5.3	13.3	11.5	11.2	17.9
Farming, fishing, and forestry	133	181	167	10.2	15.3	14.4	12.0	21.6
Construction and extraction	507	1,414	1,181	6.2	16.6	14.4	14.3	17.7
Installation, maintenance, and repair	119	406	320	2.4	7.7	6.2	6.0	12.3
Production, transportation, and material moving occupations	1,081	2,099	1,845	5.1	11.3	9.8	9.3	11.5
Production	575	1,025	865	4.8	11.2	9.3	8.5	11.3
Transportation and material moving	505	1,073	980	5.6	11.4	10.3	10.0	12.0

[1] Includes persons with no previous work experience and those whose last job was in the Armed Forces.

Source: Bureau of Labor Statistics, "Unemployed persons by occupation and sex," February 2013, <http://www.bls.gov/cps/tables.htm>.

Table 655. Unemployed and Unemployment Rates by Educational Attainment, Sex, Race, and Hispanic Origin: 2000 to 2012

[3,589 represents 3,589,000. Annual averages of monthly figures. Civilian noninstitutionalized population 25 years old and over. See Table 620 for civilian labor force and participation rate data. Data not strictly comparable with data for earlier years. Based on Current Population Survey; see text, Section 1 and Appendix III]

Year, sex, and race	Unemployed (1,000)					Unemployment rate [1]				
	Total	Less than a high school diploma	High school graduate, no college	Some college or associate's degree	Bachelor's degree or more	Total	Less than a high school diploma	High school graduate, no college	Some college or associate's degree	Bachelor's degree or more
Total: [2]										
2000...............	3,589	791	1,298	890	610	3.0	6.3	3.4	2.7	1.7
2011...............	10,114	1,632	3,521	2,937	2,024	7.6	14.1	9.4	8.0	4.3
2012...............	9,055	1,405	3,053	2,655	1,942	6.8	12.4	8.3	7.1	4.0
Male:										
2000...............	1,829	411	682	427	309	2.8	5.4	3.4	2.6	1.5
2011...............	5,622	1,009	2,110	1,458	1,045	7.9	13.6	10.0	8.0	4.3
2012...............	4,821	824	1,772	1,285	940	6.8	11.6	8.5	6.9	3.8
Female:										
2000...............	1,760	380	616	463	301	3.2	7.8	3.5	2.8	1.8
2011...............	4,490	623	1,411	1,478	978	7.3	14.8	8.7	7.9	4.3
2012...............	4,234	581	1,281	1,370	1,002	6.8	13.9	8.1	7.3	4.3
White: [3]										
2000...............	2,644	564	924	667	489	2.6	5.6	2.9	2.4	1.6
2011...............	7,318	1,195	2,524	2,083	1,516	6.8	12.7	8.4	7.0	3.9
2012...............	6,557	1,047	2,185	1,874	1,451	6.1	11.4	7.5	6.3	3.7
Black: [3]										
2000...............	731	179	315	169	68	5.4	10.7	6.4	4.0	2.5
2011...............	2,033	330	790	649	264	13.4	24.6	15.5	13.1	7.1
2012...............	1,761	260	683	563	255	11.4	20.4	13.4	11.1	6.3
Asian: [3, 4]										
2000...............	146	28	34	35	49	2.7	5.7	3.0	3.2	1.8
2011...............	425	44	96	86	199	6.3	9.5	7.6	7.4	5.2
2012...............	386	35	79	88	184	5.2	6.8	6.1	6.7	4.3
Hispanic: [5]										
2000...............	569	297	150	85	38	4.4	6.2	3.9	3.2	2.2
2011...............	1,857	703	597	384	173	9.8	12.0	10.3	9.1	5.7
2012...............	1,745	650	554	368	173	8.7	11.0	9.0	8.0	5.1

[1] Unemployed as percent of the civilian labor force. [2] Includes other races, not shown separately. [3] Beginning 2005 data are for persons in this race group only. See footnote 4, Table 614. [4] 2000 data include Pacific Islanders. [5] Persons of Hispanic origin may be of any race.

Source: Bureau of Labor Statistics, "Employment status of the civilian noninstitutional population 25 years and over by educational attainment, sex, race, and Hispanic or Latino ethnicity," February 2013, <http://www.bls.gov/cps/tables.htm>.

Table 656. Unemployed Persons by Reason for Unemployment: 2012

[12,506 represents 12,506,000. Annual averages of monthly data. Based on Current Population Survey; see text, Section 1 and Appendix III]

Age, sex, and reason	Total unemployed (1,000)	Percent distribution by duration				
		Less than 5 weeks	5 to 14 weeks	15 weeks and over		
				Total	15 to 26 weeks	27 weeks or longer
Total 16 years old and over................	**12,506**	**21.1**	**22.9**	**55.9**	**14.9**	**41.1**
16 to 19 years old..........................	1,397	33.4	30.8	35.8	15.5	20.3
Total 20 years old and over................	**11,109**	**(NA)**	**(NA)**	**(NA)**	**(NA)**	**(NA)**
Males, 20 years old and over...............	**5,984**	**19.9**	**21.5**	**58.6**	**14.3**	**44.3**
Job losers and persons who completed temporary jobs..............................	3,996	21.3	21.9	56.7	14.5	42.3
On temporary layoff......................	726	48.0	30.7	21.2	13.1	8.1
Not on temporary layoff..................	3,270	15.4	20.0	64.6	14.8	49.8
Permanent job losers...................	2,515	13.0	18.6	68.5	15.1	53.4
Persons who completed temporary jobs........	754	23.5	24.7	51.8	13.7	38.1
Job leavers..............................	464	22.6	25.0	52.4	15.2	37.2
Reentrants..............................	1,250	15.9	19.5	64.6	13.6	51.0
New entrants............................	274	12.7	18.3	69.1	13.7	55.4
Females, 20 years old and over.............	**5,125**	**19.3**	**22.4**	**58.3**	**15.3**	**43.0**
Job losers and persons who completed temporary jobs..............................	2,705	20.5	21.8	57.7	14.8	42.8
On temporary layoff......................	399	51.5	31.9	16.5	10.5	6.1
Not on temporary layoff..................	2,307	15.1	20.1	64.8	15.6	49.2
Permanent job losers...................	1,863	12.9	19.2	67.9	15.4	52.5
Persons who completed temporary jobs........	444	24.4	23.6	51.9	16.5	35.4
Job leavers..............................	460	22.7	26.9	50.4	17.7	32.6
Reentrants..............................	1,676	16.8	22.2	60.9	15.5	45.4
New entrants............................	284	16.3	21.9	61.8	15.2	46.5

Source: Bureau of Labor Statistics, "Unemployed persons by reason for unemployment, sex, age, and duration of unemployment," February 2013, <http://www.bls.gov/cps/tables.htm>.

Table 657. Total Unemployed and Insured Unemployed by State: 2000 to 2012

[5,692 represents 5,692,000. Civilian noninstitutionalized population 16 years old and over. Annual averages of monthly figures. State total unemployment estimates come from the Local Area Unemployment Statistics program, while U.S. totals come from the Current Population Survey; see text, Section 1 and Appendix III. U.S. totals derived by independent population controls; therefore state data may not add to U.S. totals. Unemployment data are based on population controls from Census 2010]

| State | Total unemployed | | | | | | | | Insured unemployed [2,4] | | | |
| | Number (1,000) | | | | Percent [1] | | | | Number (1,000) | | Percent [3] | |
	2000	2005	2010	2012	2000	2005	2010	2012	2000	2012	2000	2012
United States.......	5,692	7,591	14,825	12,506	4.0	5.1	9.6	8.1	2,110.3	3,297.4	1.7	2.5
Alabama................	87	81	202	157	4.1	3.8	9.3	7.3	29.0	36.4	1.6	2.1
Alaska..................	20	24	29	26	6.2	6.9	8.0	7.0	12.3	12.5	4.8	4.0
Arizona................	100	134	324	252	4.0	4.7	10.4	8.3	20.5	51.5	0.9	2.2
Arkansas..............	53	69	106	99	4.2	5.1	7.9	7.3	23.9	32.8	2.2	2.9
California..............	833	953	2,267	1,935	4.9	5.4	12.4	10.5	338.5	502.0	2.3	3.4
Colorado...............	65	133	245	220	2.7	5.1	9.0	8.0	15.0	44.7	0.7	2.0
Connecticut...........	39	88	178	157	2.3	4.9	9.3	8.4	28.3	55.7	1.7	3.5
Delaware..............	14	17	35	32	3.3	4.0	8.0	7.1	5.9	9.9	1.5	2.5
District of Columbia. ...	18	21	35	32	5.7	6.5	10.0	8.9	5.7	5.4	1.3	1.1
Florida.................	300	330	1,035	807	3.8	3.8	11.3	8.6	70.8	132.6	1.0	1.8
Georgia................	148	241	482	434	3.5	5.2	10.2	9.0	34.5	80.2	0.9	2.1
Hawaii..................	24	17	44	38	4.0	2.8	6.8	5.8	8.4	12.7	1.6	2.2
Idaho...................	31	27	66	55	4.6	3.7	8.7	7.1	12.1	17.5	2.2	2.9
Illinois.................	291	371	691	585	4.5	5.8	10.4	8.9	103.8	158.3	1.8	2.9
Indiana................	92	172	319	264	2.9	5.4	10.1	8.4	31.8	53.9	1.1	1.9
Iowa...................	45	70	105	86	2.8	4.3	6.3	5.2	19.4	28.6	1.4	2.0
Kansas................	53	75	106	85	3.8	5.1	7.1	5.7	15.6	27.1	1.2	2.1
Kentucky...............	83	121	211	171	4.2	6.0	10.2	8.2	25.4	36.2	1.5	2.1
Louisiana..............	101	139	154	134	5.0	6.7	7.4	6.4	24.0	34.4	1.3	1.9
Maine..................	22	34	57	52	3.3	4.9	8.2	7.3	8.9	14.5	1.5	2.6
Maryland..............	100	122	241	213	3.6	4.1	7.8	6.8	28.9	60.5	1.3	2.6
Massachusetts.........	92	164	288	234	2.7	4.8	8.3	6.7	60.1	97.1	1.9	3.0
Michigan...............	190	346	602	426	3.7	6.8	12.7	9.1	81.6	109.1	1.8	2.8
Minnesota.............	87	120	218	168	3.1	4.2	7.4	5.6	31.4	58.4	1.2	2.2
Mississippi............	74	103	139	122	5.7	7.8	10.5	9.2	19.7	26.9	1.8	2.5
Missouri...............	98	162	283	207	3.3	5.4	9.3	6.9	41.8	52.1	1.6	2.0
Montana...............	22	17	33	31	4.8	3.6	6.8	6.0	7.8	12.0	2.1	2.9
Nebraska..............	27	38	46	40	2.8	3.9	4.7	3.9	7.3	13.6	0.8	1.5
Nevada................	48	55	192	152	4.5	4.5	13.8	11.1	19.5	35.2	1.9	3.2
New Hampshire........	19	26	45	41	2.7	3.6	6.1	5.5	3.1	11.0	0.5	1.8
New Jersey............	157	197	437	436	3.7	4.5	9.6	9.5	84.8	140.4	2.2	3.8
New Mexico............	42	47	74	65	5.0	5.2	7.9	6.9	9.5	18.7	1.4	2.5
New York..............	416	474	828	815	4.5	5.0	8.6	8.5	146.2	258.3	1.8	3.1
North Carolina.........	155	229	501	448	3.7	5.3	10.8	9.5	54.3	107.0	1.4	2.8
North Dakota...........	10	12	14	12	2.9	3.4	3.8	3.1	3.9	3.5	1.3	0.9
Ohio...................	234	344	587	413	4.0	5.9	10.0	7.2	71.6	96.3	1.3	1.9
Oklahoma..............	52	77	122	94	3.1	4.5	6.9	5.2	12.2	23.2	0.9	1.6
Oregon................	93	115	212	171	5.1	6.2	10.7	8.7	41.2	57.0	2.6	3.5
Pennsylvania..........	255	312	538	513	4.2	5.0	8.4	7.9	132.4	211.7	2.4	3.9
Rhode Island..........	23	28	67	58	4.2	5.1	11.7	10.4	12.2	14.7	2.7	3.3
South Carolina........	71	140	241	197	3.6	6.8	11.2	9.1	27.1	40.6	1.5	2.3
South Dakota..........	11	16	23	20	2.7	3.7	5.1	4.4	2.0	2.9	0.6	0.7
Tennessee.............	115	164	302	249	4.0	5.6	9.8	8.0	42.2	42.6	1.6	1.6
Texas..................	452	599	1,008	855	4.4	5.4	8.2	6.8	107.9	162.9	1.2	1.5
Utah...................	38	53	110	77	3.4	4.1	8.1	5.7	10.5	16.5	1.0	1.4
Vermont...............	9	12	23	18	2.7	3.5	6.4	5.0	4.8	6.8	1.6	2.3
Virginia................	82	138	294	247	2.3	3.5	7.1	5.9	22.2	46.2	0.7	1.3
Washington............	151	180	349	284	5.0	5.5	9.9	8.2	70.6	78.2	2.7	2.8
West Virginia...........	44	39	68	59	5.5	4.9	8.4	7.3	14.1	18.0	2.1	2.6
Wisconsin..............	101	146	261	211	3.4	4.8	8.5	6.9	53.1	88.2	2.0	3.3
Wyoming...............	10	10	21	16	3.8	3.7	7.0	5.4	2.9	4.4	1.3	1.6

[1] Total unemployment as percent of civilian labor force. [2] Number of jobless workers who are receiving state unemployment benefits.
Source: U.S. Employment and Training Administration, "Unemployment Insurance, Financial Data Handbook 394," <http://www.oui.doleta.gov/unemploy/hb394.asp>, accessed August 2013. [3] Those currently collecting unemployment insurance as a percent of the total number of eligible workers. [4] U.S. totals include Puerto Rico and the Virgin Islands.

Source: Except as noted, U.S. Bureau of Labor Statistics, Local Area Unemployment Statistics, <http://www.bls.gov/lau/> accessed August 2013.

Table 658. Nonfarm Establishments—Employees, Hours, and Earnings by Industry: 1990 to 2012

[Annual averages of monthly data. 109,487 represents 109,487,000. Based on data from establishment reports. Includes all full- and part-time employees who worked during, or received pay for, any part of the pay period reported. Excludes proprietors, the self-employed, farm workers, unpaid family workers, private household workers, and Armed Forces. Establishment data shown here conform to industry definitions in the 2007 North American Industry Classification System (NAICS) and are adjusted to March 2010 employment benchmarks. Based on the Current Employment Statistics Program; see source and Appendix III]

Item and year	Total nonfarm	Total [1]	Construction	Manu-facturing	Whole-sale trade	Retail trade	Transportation and ware-housing	Utilities	Informa-tion	Finance and insur-ance	Real estate and rental and leasing	Profes-sional, scientific, and technical services	Admin-istrative and waste services	Educa-tional services	Health care and social assis-tance	Arts enter-tainment and recre-ation	Accommo-dations and food services	Govern-ment
		Private industry																
EMPLOYEES (1,000)																		
1990	109,487	91,072	5,263	17,695	5,268	13,182	3,476	740	2,688	4,976	1,637	4,538	4,643	1,688	9,296	1,132	8,156	18,415
2000	131,881	111,091	6,787	17,263	5,933	15,280	4,410	601	3,630	5,773	2,011	6,702	8,168	2,390	12,718	1,788	10,074	20,790
2005	133,747	111,943	7,336	14,227	5,764	15,280	4,361	554	3,061	6,063	2,134	7,025	8,170	2,836	14,536	1,892	10,923	21,804
2007	137,645	115,427	7,630	13,879	6,015	15,520	4,541	553	3,032	6,179	2,169	7,660	8,416	2,941	15,380	1,969	11,457	22,218
2008	136,852	114,342	7,162	13,406	5,943	15,283	4,508	559	2,984	6,076	2,130	7,799	8,032	3,040	15,798	1,970	11,466	22,509
2009	130,876	108,321	6,016	11,847	5,587	14,522	4,236	560	2,804	5,844	1,994	7,509	7,203	3,090	16,103	1,916	11,162	22,555
2010	129,917	107,427	5,518	11,528	5,452	14,440	4,191	553	2,707	5,761	1,934	7,441	7,414	3,155	16,375	1,913	11,135	22,490
2011	131,497	109,411	5,533	11,726	5,543	14,668	4,302	553	2,674	5,769	1,927	7,666	7,732	3,250	16,634	1,919	11,434	22,086
2012	133,739	111,822	5,641	11,919	5,673	14,875	4,415	554	2,678	5,834	1,952	7,893	8,029	3,347	16,972	1,965	11,780	21,917
WEEKLY EARNINGS [2] (dol.)																		
1990	(NA)	349.72	513.43	436.13	444.48	235.56	471.82	670.80	479.50	(NA)	(NA)	504.83	273.60	(NA)	319.80	219.02	147.92	(NA)
2000	(NA)	481.36	685.78	591.01	631.24	333.41	562.56	955.09	700.92	(NA)	(NA)	745.94	387.59	(NA)	449.27	273.79	207.44	(NA)
2005	(NA)	544.44	750.37	673.30	685.00	377.58	618.55	1,095.91	805.11	(NA)	(NA)	862.76	431.92	(NA)	560.43	330.31	226.48	(NA)
2007	(NA)	590.24	816.23	711.53	748.94	385.00	654.95	1,182.65	874.45	(NA)	(NA)	956.19	485.15	(NA)	606.74		251.52	(NA)
2008	(NA)	608.11	842.61	724.46	769.62	386.21	670.22	1,230.65	908.78	(NA)	(NA)	995.89	500.14	(NA)	630.06	354.54	259.93	(NA)
2009	(NA)	617.50	851.76	726.12	784.49	388.57	677.56	1,239.34	931.08	(NA)	(NA)	1,036.37	517.27	(NA)	643.19	359.71	261.87	(NA)
2010	(NA)	637.18	891.83	765.18	816.50	400.07	710.85	1,262.89	939.85	(NA)	(NA)	1,073.92	535.79	(NA)	661.03	363.91	266.78	(NA)
2011	(NA)	654.73	921.84	784.29	845.44	412.09	737.00	1,296.92	964.85	(NA)	(NA)	1,091.88	551.61	(NA)	685.85	363.90	269.12	(NA)
2012	(NA)	666.99	942.75	794.81	860.74	421.85	742.23	1,298.19	971.22	(NA)	(NA)	1,108.50	550.61	(NA)	697.90	378.57	276.16	(NA)
WEEKLY HOURS [2]																		
1990	(NA)	34.3	38.3	40.5	38.4	30.6	37.7	41.6	35.8	(NA)	(NA)	36.1	32.3	(NA)	31.8	26.1	25.9	(NA)
2000	(NA)	34.3	39.2	41.3	38.8	30.7	37.4	42.0	36.8	(NA)	(NA)	36.2	33.1	(NA)	32.1	25.6	26.2	(NA)
2005	(NA)	33.8	38.6	40.7	37.7	30.6	37.0	41.1	36.5	(NA)	(NA)	35.7	32.8	(NA)	32.9	25.7	25.7	(NA)
2007	(NA)	33.9	39.0	41.2	38.2	30.2	37.0	42.4	36.5	(NA)	(NA)	36.0	33.5	(NA)	32.8	24.7	25.6	(NA)
2008	(NA)	33.6	39.0	40.8	38.2	30.0	36.4	42.7	36.7	(NA)	(NA)	35.8	33.6	(NA)	32.8	24.1	25.4	(NA)
2009	(NA)	33.1	37.6	39.8	37.6	29.9	36.0	42.0	36.6	(NA)	(NA)	35.7	33.4	(NA)	32.4	23.8	25.0	(NA)
2010	(NA)	33.4	38.4	41.1	37.9	30.2	37.1	42.0	36.3	(NA)	(NA)	35.9	33.9	(NA)	32.3	23.8	25.0	(NA)
2011	(NA)	33.6	39.0	41.4	38.5	30.5	37.8	42.1	36.2	(NA)	(NA)	36.0	34.0	(NA)	32.5		24.9	(NA)
2012	(NA)	33.7	39.3	41.7	38.7	30.5	38.0	41.1	36.0	(NA)	(NA)	36.0	34.2	(NA)	32.6	23.7	25.2	(NA)
HOURLY EARNINGS [2] (dol.)																		
1990	(NA)	10.20	13.42	10.78	11.58	7.71	12.50	16.14	13.40	(NA)	(NA)	13.99	8.48	(NA)	10.05	8.41	5.70	(NA)
2000	(NA)	14.02	17.48	14.32	16.28	10.87	15.05	22.75	19.07	(NA)	(NA)	20.61	11.69	(NA)	13.98	10.68	7.92	(NA)
2005	(NA)	16.13	19.46	16.56	18.16	12.36	16.70	26.68	22.06	(NA)	(NA)	24.14	13.16	(NA)	17.05	12.85	8.80	(NA)
2007	(NA)	17.44	20.95	17.26	19.59	12.75	17.72	27.88	23.96	(NA)	(NA)	26.58	14.47	(NA)	18.48	14.10	9.82	(NA)
2008	(NA)	18.08	21.87	17.75	20.13	12.87	18.41	28.83	24.78	(NA)	(NA)	27.82	14.87	(NA)	19.23	14.73	10.23	(NA)
2009	(NA)	18.63	22.66	18.24	20.84	13.01	18.81	29.48	25.45	(NA)	(NA)	29.03	15.51	(NA)	19.83	15.08	10.49	(NA)
2010	(NA)	19.07	23.22	18.61	21.54	13.25	19.16	30.04	25.87	(NA)	(NA)	29.94	15.80	(NA)	20.44	15.27	10.68	(NA)
2011	(NA)	19.46	23.65	18.93	21.97	13.51	19.49	30.82	26.62	(NA)	(NA)	30.30	16.21	(NA)	21.11	15.67		(NA)
2012	(NA)	19.77	23.98	19.08	22.24	13.81	19.54	31.61	27.01	(NA)	(NA)	30.76	16.09	(NA)	21.41	15.97	10.96	(NA)

NA Not available. [1] Includes other industries not shown separately. [2] Average hours and earnings of production workers for mining and logging, manufacturing, and construction; average hours and earnings of nonsupervisory workers for the service-providing industries.

Source: Bureau of Labor Statistics, Current Employment Statistics, "Employment, Hours, and Earnings—National," <http://www.bls.gov/ces/home.htm>, accessed September 2013.

Table 659. Employees in Nonfarm Establishments—States: 2012

[In thousands (133,724 represents 133,724,000). Includes all full- and part-time employees who worked during, or received pay for, any part of the pay period reported. Excludes proprietors, the self-employed, farm workers, unpaid family workers, private household workers, and Armed Forces. Compiled from data supplied by cooperating state agencies. Based on North American Industry Classification System, 2007; see text, section 15]

State	Total [1]	Construction	Manufacturing	Trade, transportation and utilities	Information	Financial activities [2]	Professional and business services [3]	Education and health services [4]	Leisure and hospitality [5]	Other services [6]	Government
U.S.	133,724	5,599	11,926	25,459	2,691	7,753	17,888	20,298	13,762	5,340	22,172
AL	1,882.6	79.1	243.0	365.3	22.5	92.5	218.4	218.5	173.7	80.5	376.5
AK	334.1	16.6	13.5	63.8	6.2	13.3	28.6	46.4	33.0	11.6	84.0
AZ	2,460.3	115.7	155.2	478.5	38.2	176.5	354.4	366.2	266.7	85.6	410.7
AR	1,177.4	47.4	155.9	242.8	14.5	49.1	123.0	171.8	102.8	43.5	215.9
CA	14,394.5	587.5	1,252.8	2,725.1	430.4	774.6	2,235.1	1,879.2	1,599.1	505.7	2,375.1
CO	2,310.0	115.1	132.1	409.0	69.7	146.1	355.1	282.3	280.3	95.5	394.6
CT	1,639.0	51.1	165.0	295.3	31.1	132.3	203.1	317.7	142.6	61.5	238.7
DE	418.5	18.4	25.8	75.6	5.5	42.3	56.3	68.1	43.4	19.6	63.5
DC	731.8	13.5	1.0	27.8	17.3	28.1	153.3	114.8	65.4	68.1	242.5
FL	7,400.1	341.5	316.8	1,537.1	133.4	497.5	1,067.5	1,109.9	997.7	314.4	1,078.6
GA	3,952.8	141.0	354.6	833.2	100.5	227.2	562.4	495.8	394.8	153.1	681.8
HI	605.3	29.5	13.3	114.6	8.3	27.0	76.4	76.7	107.0	26.4	126.3
ID	622.0	31.3	56.8	126.1	9.3	30.3	76.2	88.7	61.1	21.5	116.7
IL	5,744.4	187.9	582.9	1,155.7	100.1	366.1	861.5	864.0	534.8	249.3	831.9
IN	2,902.1	124.4	482.0	561.6	35.5	130.3	298.4	438.0	286.2	110.2	428.5
IA	1,508.4	64.4	210.5	306.8	27.1	101.6	129.5	220.5	134.0	57.7	254.2
KS	1,357.8	55.1	163.1	257.2	28.3	74.6	153.2	186.1	119.7	51.6	259.0
KY	1,824.4	67.3	223.3	370.6	26.3	86.7	191.2	257.2	174.6	69.5	337.1
LA	1,925.6	126.5	142.1	378.1	24.9	94.0	202.5	282.0	207.5	63.3	350.1
ME	597.6	25.6	50.8	117.4	7.9	31.4	58.0	121.2	61.7	19.9	101.3
MD	2,574.5	145.2	108.6	450.6	39.9	143.0	410.2	415.2	244.5	112.2	505.2
MA	3,273.6	114.6	251.8	550.7	86.8	206.2	491.0	688.1	324.3	121.9	437.3
MI	4,024.2	127.3	536.9	728.5	53.1	196.2	576.6	632.1	387.1	168.3	610.3
MN	2,727.6	94.8	305.4	503.3	53.7	177.1	336.3	478.1	244.3	116.1	411.8
MS	1,103.4	48.3	137.0	215.9	12.5	44.2	96.9	133.3	121.9	37.9	246.2
MO	2,669.4	104.0	248.3	513.8	58.2	164.1	337.9	412.5	275.1	114.0	437.4
MT	440.5	22.9	17.5	88.3	6.9	21.4	41.1	67.5	58.3	17.4	89.9
NE	960.3	42.9	95.1	199.3	17.2	70.9	105.9	140.2	83.7	36.8	168.3
NV	1,142.7	51.8	39.2	218.2	12.5	54.2	144.1	106.7	318.3	33.2	148.9
NH	633.2	22.2	65.9	135.7	12.0	34.9	68.2	114.6	64.5	22.8	91.4
NJ	3,895.5	130.4	245.7	822.4	77.7	249.0	617.0	621.2	345.7	165.0	620.2
NM	804.1	40.7	29.6	135.1	13.6	33.0	97.4	121.9	86.0	28.7	194.2
NY	8,799.9	311.9	458.2	1,509.2	260.6	682.7	1,168.3	1,763.2	800.9	379.3	1,460.4
NC	3,988.1	171.9	439.8	744.2	69.3	203.1	533.3	549.0	416.3	141.9	713.9
ND	429.8	29.6	25.4	96.9	6.9	21.9	32.7	58.1	38.3	16.0	79.5
OH	5,171.0	179.8	656.2	971.4	74.4	279.3	671.0	866.2	498.8	204.7	756.9
OK	1,607.6	69.1	134.7	289.4	22.5	79.9	177.1	224.2	147.5	58.6	347.1
OR	1,638.2	69.5	171.5	316.4	32.5	90.2	195.0	237.8	169.5	57.3	291.5
PA	5,729.7	225.8	567.1	1,102.0	90.2	310.2	730.0	1,168.5	521.1	256.0	721.8
RI	465.0	15.8	39.7	74.3	9.6	31.5	56.2	103.7	51.4	22.5	60.1
SC	1,858.2	77.8	219.8	354.3	25.7	98.8	234.3	210.4	217.6	69.2	346.6
SD	414.0	21.0	41.3	83.0	6.2	28.7	29.0	67.2	44.3	15.8	77.5
TN	2,714.3	109.2	313.5	575.0	43.0	137.6	336.5	394.1	277.2	104.3	423.8
TX	10,879.8	585.2	863.1	2,174.2	197.0	659.5	1,405.8	1,461.5	1,087.3	381.2	1,794.9
UT	1,249.2	69.0	116.9	242.0	31.4	69.4	167.2	163.4	118.6	35.2	223.6
VT	303.2	14.2	31.9	55.6	4.7	12.0	26.1	60.6	33.3	10.2	53.9
VA	3,727.0	175.9	232.1	631.7	71.8	188.2	678.1	477.9	357.5	190.4	712.4
WA	2,871.3	138.5	280.4	536.1	104.7	142.9	348.5	385.7	276.7	110.8	541.1
WV	765.2	35.6	49.0	135.4	9.5	28.0	64.8	125.5	74.5	55.0	154.0
WI	2,784.6	93.0	454.9	511.1	46.2	162.6	289.7	418.0	257.4	137.5	410.7
WY	289.7	21.7	9.4	53.4	3.9	10.8	17.9	26.5	33.6	10.8	74.0

[1] Includes mining and logging, not shown separately. [2] Finance and insurance; real estate and rental and leasing. [3] Professional, scientific, and technical services; management of companies and enterprises; and administrative and support and waste management and remediation services. [4] Education services; health care and social assistance. [5] Arts, entertainment, and recreation; accommodations and food services. [6] Includes repair and maintenance; personal and laundry services; and membership associations and organizations.

Source: Bureau of Labor Statistics, State and Metro Area Employment, Hours, and Earnings, "Employees on nonfarm payrolls in States and selected areas by major industry," <http://www.bls.gov/sae/tables.htm>, accessed August 2013.

Table 660. Nonfarm Industries—Employees and Earnings: 1990 to 2012

[Annual averages of monthly figures (109,487 represents 109,487,000). Covers all full- and part-time employees who worked during, or received pay for, any part of the pay period including the 12th of the month. See also headnote, Table 658]

Industry	2007 NAICS code [1]	All employees (1,000)					Average hourly earnings [2] (dol.)		
		1990	2000	2005	2010	2012	2000	2010	2012
Total nonfarm	(X)	**109,487**	**131,881**	**133,747**	**129,917**	**133,739**	**(NA)**	**(NA)**	**(NA)**
Goods-producing [3]	(X)	23,723	24,649	22,190	17,751	18,410	15.27	20.28	20.95
Service-providing [4]	(X)	85,764	107,232	111,557	112,166	115,329	(NA)	(NA)	(NA)
Total private	(X)	**91,072**	**111,091**	**111,943**	**107,427**	**111,822**	**14.02**	**19.07**	**19.77**
Mining and logging	(X)	**765**	**599**	**628**	**705**	**851**	**16.55**	**23.82**	**25.79**
Logging	1133	85	79	65	50	50	13.70	18.85	20.09
Mining	21	**680**	**520**	**562**	**655**	**800**	**16.94**	**24.24**	**26.14**
Oil and gas extraction	211	190	125	126	159	187	19.43	27.36	28.51
Mining, except oil and gas	212	302	225	213	205	223	18.07	24.63	26.02
Support activities for mining	213	188	171	224	292	391	14.55	22.95	25.43
Construction	23	**5,263**	**6,787**	**7,336**	**5,518**	**5,641**	**17.48**	**23.22**	**23.98**
Construction of buildings	236	1,413	1,633	1,712	1,230	1,236	16.74	22.73	23.12
Residential building	2361	673	823	960	572	574	15.18	19.80	19.92
Nonresidential building	2362	741	809	752	658	662	18.18	25.13	25.67
Heavy and civil engineering construction [5]	237	813	937	951	825	871	16.80	23.76	24.52
Highway, street, and bridge construction	2373	289	340	351	287	292	18.17	23.76	24.58
Specialty trade contractors	238	3,037	4,217	4,673	3,463	3,534	17.91	23.22	24.10
Building foundation and exterior contractors	2381	703	919	1,083	680	687	16.93	21.20	22.14
Building equipment contractors	2382	1,282	1,897	1,918	1,634	1,679	19.52	24.89	25.88
Building finishing contractors	2383	665	857	992	634	633	16.44	22.06	22.66
Manufacturing	31-33	**17,695**	**17,263**	**14,227**	**11,528**	**11,919**	**14.32**	**18.61**	**19.08**
Durable goods	(X)	10,737	10,877	8,956	7,064	7,462	14.92	19.80	20.19
Wood products	321	543	615	561	342	338	11.63	14.85	14.98
Nonmetallic mineral products	327	528	554	505	371	364	14.53	17.48	18.15
Cement and concrete products	3273	195	234	240	170	162	14.64	17.84	18.78
Primary metals	331	689	622	466	362	402	16.64	20.13	20.72
Iron and steel mills and ferroalloy production	3311	187	135	96	87	94	(NA)	(NA)	(NA)
Foundries	3315	214	217	164	112	112	14.72	18.22	18.16
Fabricated metal products	332	1,610	1,753	1,522	1,282	1,411	13.77	17.94	18.26
Architectural and structural metals	3323	357	428	398	321	341	13.43	17.47	18.01
Machine shops and threaded products	3327	309	365	345	313	362	14.53	18.68	19.00
Machinery	333	1,410	1,457	1,166	996	1,098	15.21	18.96	20.17
Agricultural, construction, and mining machinery	3331	229	222	208	208	245	14.21	18.95	20.20
Heating, ventilation and air conditioning, and commercial refrigeration equipment	3334	165	194	154	125	128	13.10	16.16	17.03
Metalworking machinery	3335	267	274	202	155	177	16.66	20.00	20.75
Computer and electronic products	334	1,903	1,820	1,316	1,095	1,094	14.73	22.78	23.34
Computer and peripheral equipment	3341	367	302	205	158	159	(NA)	(NA)	(NA)
Communications equipment	3342	223	239	141	117	110	14.39	23.88	25.34
Semiconductors and electronic components	3344	574	676	452	369	384	13.46	20.35	20.65
Electronic instruments	3345	635	488	441	406	400	15.80	24.82	25.55
Electrical equipment and appliances	335	633	591	434	360	370	13.23	16.87	18.03
Household appliances	3352	114	106	85	60	55	(NA)	(NA)	(NA)
Electrical equipment	3353	244	210	152	136	143	13.28	16.51	18.43
Transportation equipment	336	2,135	2,057	1,772	1,333	1,456	18.89	25.23	24.59
Motor vehicles	3361	271	291	248	153	168	24.45	29.04	28.08
Motor vehicle parts	3363	653	840	678	419	480	17.95	20.66	20.01
Aerospace products and parts	3364	841	517	455	478	497	20.52	33.65	33.02
Ship and boat building	3366	174	154	154	125	129	(NA)	(NA)	(NA)
Furniture and related products	337	602	680	566	357	350	11.73	15.06	15.46
Household and institutional furniture	3371	398	441	381	223	217	11.39	14.75	15.10
Miscellaneous manufacturing	339	686	728	647	567	580	11.93	16.56	17.06
Medical equipment and supplies	3391	283	305	300	303	311	12.70	17.56	18.01
Nondurable goods	(X)	6,958	6,386	5,271	4,464	4,456	13.31	16.80	17.30
Food manufacturing	311	1,507	1,553	1,478	1,451	1,469	11.77	14.41	15.02
Fruit and vegetable preserving and specialty	3114	218	197	174	173	170	11.90	14.56	15.10
Dairy products	3115	145	136	132	130	136	14.85	18.92	20.47
Animal slaughtering and processing	3116	427	507	504	489	485	10.27	12.69	13.27
Bakeries and tortilla manufacturing	3118	292	306	280	277	285	11.45	14.44	14.54
Textile mills	313	492	378	218	119	118	11.23	13.56	13.51
Textile product mills	314	236	230	176	119	117	10.31	11.79	12.77
Apparel	315	903	484	251	157	148	8.61	11.43	12.89
Cut and sew apparel	3152	750	380	193	124	122	(NA)	(NA)	(NA)
Leather and allied products	316	133	69	40	28	29	(NA)	(NA)	(NA)
Paper and paper products	322	647	605	484	395	379	15.91	20.04	20.43
Pulp, paper, and paperboard mills	3221	238	191	142	112	108	20.62	25.12	25.81
Converted paper products	3222	409	413	343	282	271	13.58	17.81	18.04
Printing and related support activities	323	809	807	646	488	462	14.09	16.91	17.28
Petroleum and coal products	324	153	123	112	114	113	22.80	31.31	32.13
Chemicals	325	1,036	980	872	787	784	17.09	21.07	21.45
Basic chemicals	3251	249	188	150	142	143	21.06	24.93	25.44
Resin, rubber, and artificial fibers	3252	158	136	108	89	92	17.09	21.11	20.42
Pharmaceuticals and medicines	3254	207	274	288	277	271	17.27	21.95	23.33
Plastics and rubber products	326	825	951	802	625	645	12.70	15.71	16.05
Plastics products	3261	618	737	634	502	516	12.04	15.47	15.80
Rubber products	3262	207	214	168	123	129	14.83	16.64	16.97
Trade, transportation, and utilities	(X)	**22,666**	**26,225**	**25,959**	**24,636**	**25,516**	**13.31**	**16.82**	**17.42**
Wholesale trade	42	**5,268**	**5,933**	**5,764**	**5,452**	**5,673**	**16.28**	**21.54**	**22.24**
Durable goods	423	2,834	3,251	2,999	2,714	2,830	16.71	20.95	21.57

See footnotes at end of table.

Table 660. Nonfarm Industries—Employees and Earnings: 1990 to 2012-Continued.

See headnote on page 431.

Industry	2007 NAICS code [1]	All employees (1,000)					Average hourly earnings [2] (dol.)		
		1990	2000	2005	2010	2012	2000	2010	2012
Motor vehicles and parts..........................	4231	309	356	344	309	319	14.27	17.61	17.95
Lumber and construction supplies............	4233	181	227	254	188	185	13.61	18.45	19.12
Commercial equipment..........................	4234	597	722	639	604	619	20.29	25.03	25.21
Electric goods....................................	4236	357	425	342	309	316	19.43	23.12	23.62
Hardware and plumbing.........................	4237	216	247	245	218	224	15.07	19.82	21.49
Machinery and supplies.........................	4238	690	725	659	608	646	16.47	21.03	21.87
Nondurable goods..................................	424	1,900	2,065	2,022	1,928	1,972	14.33	19.62	19.91
Paper and paper products.......................	4241	162	177	152	124	121	15.65	22.48	21.97
Druggists' goods..................................	4242	136	192	213	190	191	18.98	23.39	24.82
Apparel and piece goods........................	4243	152	163	148	137	143	14.58	21.34	20.59
Grocery and related products...................	4244	623	689	699	704	722	13.57	19.07	19.20
Alcoholic beverages.............................	4248	115	128	147	163	173	15.72	20.01	20.53
Electronic markets and agents and brokers...	425	535	618	743	811	871	20.79	28.32	29.91
Retail trade..	**44,45**	**13,182**	**15,280**	**15,280**	**14,440**	**14,875**	**10.87**	**13.25**	**13.81**
Motor vehicle and parts dealers...............	441	1,494	1,847	1,919	1,629	1,732	14.94	17.06	17.84
Automobile dealers............................	4411	983	1,217	1,261	1,012	1,091	16.95	18.22	19.10
Auto parts, accessories, and tire stores......	4413	418	499	491	489	511	11.04	14.54	15.12
Furniture and home furnishings stores........	442	432	544	576	438	442	12.33	15.25	15.19
Furniture stores.................................	4421	244	289	298	217	213	13.37	16.17	16.35
Home furnishings stores........................	4422	188	254	278	221	228	11.06	14.03	13.77
Electronics and appliance stores...............	443	451	647	585	522	512	13.16	16.83	21.45
Building material and garden supply stores...	444	891	1,142	1,276	1,132	1,170	11.25	14.11	14.16
Building material and supplies dealers......	4441	753	982	1,134	1,005	1,031	11.30	14.13	14.17
Food and beverage stores........................	445	2,779	2,993	2,818	2,808	2,859	9.76	12.03	12.24
Grocery stores..................................	4451	2,406	2,582	2,446	2,461	2,500	9.71	12.12	12.31
Specialty food stores...........................	4452	232	270	236	211	219	9.97	11.13	11.36
Beer, wine, and liquor stores..................	4453	141	141	136	136	140	10.40	11.89	12.33
Health and personal care stores...............	446	792	928	954	981	1,003	11.68	16.99	17.20
Gasoline stations.................................	447	910	936	871	819	841	8.05	10.25	10.33
Clothing & clothing accessories stores........	448	1,313	1,322	1,415	1,353	1,408	9.96	11.59	11.83
Clothing stores.................................	4481	930	954	1,066	1,040	1,081	9.88	10.91	11.41
Shoe stores.....................................	4482	216	193	180	182	189	8.96	11.80	11.53
Jewelry, luggage, and leather goods stores..	4483	167	175	169	131	138	11.48	15.56	14.67
Sporting goods, hobby, book, and music stores......................................	451	464	603	598	579	579	9.38	11.69	11.73
Sporting goods and musical instrument stores..	4511	352	437	447	459	486	9.55	11.82	11.92
Book, periodical, and music stores...........	4512	111	166	151	120	93	8.91	11.10	10.68
General merchandise stores.....................	452	2,500	2,820	2,934	2,998	3,088	9.22	10.98	11.40
Department stores..............................	4521	1,494	1,755	1,595	1,502	1,501	(NA)	(NA)	(NA)
Miscellaneous store retailers....................	453	738	1,007	900	762	798	10.20	12.50	13.63
Florists...	4531	121	130	101	69	66	8.95	11.05	11.16
Office supplies, stationery, and gift stores....	4532	358	471	391	303	305	10.46	13.06	14.60
Used merchandise stores.......................	4533	56	107	113	125	147	8.07	10.72	10.94
Nonstore retailers................................	454	419	492	435	421	443	13.22	17.73	18.28
Electronic shopping and mail-order houses..	4541	157	257	240	247	276	13.38	18.22	19.26
Transportation and warehousing.............	**48,49**	**3,476**	**4,410**	**4,361**	**4,191**	**4,415**	**15.05**	**19.16**	**19.54**
Air transportation.................................	481	529	614	501	458	458	13.57	24.56	25.09
Scheduled air transportation..................	4811	503	570	456	417	417	(NA)	(NA)	(NA)
Rail transportation...............................	482	272	232	228	216	230	(NA)	(NA)	(NA)
Water transportation.............................	483	57	56	61	62	63	(NA)	(NA)	(NA)
Truck transportation.............................	484	1,122	1,406	1,398	1,250	1,351	15.86	18.62	19.75
General freight trucking.......................	4841	807	1,013	981	868	928	16.37	18.51	19.88
Specialized freight trucking...................	4842	315	393	417	383	423	14.51	18.88	19.45
Transit and ground passenger transportation...................................	485	274	372	389	430	448	11.88	14.98	15.33
Urban, interurban, rural, and charter bus transportation..............................	4851, 2,5	72	97	91	94	96	(NA)	(NA)	(NA)
Taxi and limousine service....................	4853	57	72	66	68	75	(NA)	(NA)	(NA)
School and employee bus transportation. . .	4854	114	152	169	186	186	11.42	14.90	15.28
Pipeline transportation...........................	486	60	46	38	42	44	19.86	29.54	33.34
Scenic and sightseeing transportation.........	487	16	28	29	27	27	(NA)	(NA)	(NA)
Support activities for transportation...........	488	364	537	552	543	578	14.57	21.09	21.49
Support activities for air transportation.......	4881	96	141	148	154	161	13.42	17.04	18.23
Support activities for water transportation....	4883	91	97	94	91	93	19.57	35.16	36.33
Support activities for road transportation.....	4884	35	66	79	80	87	13.98	15.68	15.83
Freight transportation arrangement...........	4885	111	178	177	169	183	13.46	21.24	21.47
Couriers and messengers........................	492	375	605	571	528	533	13.51	17.67	15.27
Couriers and express delivery services......	4921	340	546	522	480	480	(NA)	(NA)	(NA)
Warehousing and storage........................	493	407	514	595	633	682	14.46	15.50	15.91
Utilities..	**22**	**740**	**601**	**554**	**553**	**554**	**22.75**	**30.04**	**31.61**
Power generation and supply...................	2211	550	434	401	398	397	23.13	31.25	32.83
Natural gas distribution..........................	2212	155	121	107	108	110	23.41	28.36	30.75
Water, sewage and other systems...........	2213	35	46	45	47	48	16.93	23.73	22.80
Information..	**51**	**2,688**	**3,630**	**3,061**	**2,707**	**2,678**	**19.07**	**25.87**	**27.01**
Publishing industries, except Internet.........	511	871	1,035	904	759	738	(NA)	(NA)	(NA)
Newspaper, book, and directory publishers. ..	5111	773	774	666	498	452	(NA)	(NA)	(NA)
Software publishers..............................	5112	98	261	238	261	286	28.48	36.41	40.67
Motion picture and sound recording industries......................................	512	255	383	378	370	372	21.25	22.11	23.00
Broadcasting, except Internet...................	515	284	344	328	290	285	16.74	24.01	25.35
Radio and television broadcasting.............	5151	232	253	239	210	211	(NA)	(NA)	(NA)
Cable and other subscription programming. ..	5152	52	91	89	80	74	(NA)	(NA)	(NA)

See footnotes at end of table.

Industry	2007 NAICS code [1]	All employees (1,000)					Average hourly earnings [2] (dol.)		
		1990	2000	2005	2010	2012	2000	2010	2012
Telecommunications....................	517	1,009	1,397	1,071	903	858	18.59	26.24	25.31
Wired telecommunications carriers............	5171	760	922	690	603	581	18.62	25.99	25.54
Wireless telecommunications carriers (except satellite).....................	5172	36	186	191	170	159	14.40	25.35	23.55
Data processing, hosting and related services.............................	518	211	316	263	243	250	16.97	27.03	27.44
Financial activities...................	**(X)**	**6,614**	**7,783**	**8,197**	**7,695**	**7,786**	**15.04**	**21.55**	**22.83**
Finance and insurance............	**52**	**4,976**	**5,773**	**6,063**	**5,761**	**5,834**	**(NA)**	**(NA)**	**(NA)**
Monetary authorities—central bank..........	521	24	23	21	20	17	(NA)	(NA)	(NA)
Credit intermediation and related activities....	522	2,425	2,548	2,869	2,550	2,579	13.14	18.25	19.44
Depository credit intermediation [5]..........	5221	1,909	1,681	1,769	1,729	1,738	11.97	17.55	18.37
Commercial banking.....................	52211	1,362	1,251	1,296	1,306	1,318	11.83	17.56	18.36
Nondepository credit intermediation........	5222	398	644	770	562	570	15.30	20.14	22.26
Activities related to credit intermediation.....	5223	119	222	330	259	271	15.39	18.29	19.85
Securities, commodity contracts, investments...........................	523	458	805	786	801	814	20.20	31.80	34.58
Securities and commodity contracts brokerage and exchanges......................	5231,2	338	566	499	468	458	20.07	31.79	32.46
Other financial investment activities..........	5239	120	239	287	333	356	20.48	31.81	37.49
Insurance carriers and related activities......	524	2,016	2,317	2,303	2,304	2,337	17.47	24.63	25.79
Insurance carriers.....................	5241	1,338	1,529	1,430	1,429	1,425	18.03	26.00	26.87
Insurance agencies, brokerages, and related services.....................	5242	678	788	874	875	912	16.28	22.20	23.90
Funds, trusts, and other financial vehicles.....	525	54	81	84	87	87	17.68	21.33	25.50
Insurance and employee benefit funds.......	5251	33	46	46	49	47	(NA)	(NA)	(NA)
Other investment pools and funds............	5259	20	35	37	38	39	(NA)	(NA)	(NA)
Real estate and rental and leasing............	**53**	**1,637**	**2,011**	**2,134**	**1,934**	**1,952**	**(NA)**	**(NA)**	**(NA)**
Real estate............................	**531**	**1,109**	**1,316**	**1,461**	**1,396**	**1,417**	**12.26**	**17.37**	**17.77**
Lessors of real estate......................	5311	566	610	603	565	565	11.19	16.52	16.81
Offices of real estate agents and brokers....	5312	217	281	356	286	274	12.57	17.10	18.68
Activities related to real estate..............	5313	327	424	502	544	578	13.60	18.37	18.28
Rental and leasing services..............	532	514	667	646	514	511	11.69	15.96	17.21
Automotive equipment rental and leasing....	5321	163	208	199	161	173	(NA)	(NA)	(NA)
Consumer goods rental.....................	5322	220	292	275	198	166	(NA)	(NA)	(NA)
Machinery and equipment rental and leasing.............................	5324	84	103	111	114	132	14.95	19.83	21.74
Lessors of nonfinancial intangible assets......	533	14	28	27	25	24	(NA)	(NA)	(NA)
Professional and business services..........	**(X)**	**10,848**	**16,666**	**16,954**	**16,728**	**17,930**	**(NA)**	**(NA)**	**(NA)**
Professional and technical services [5]........	**54**	**4,538**	**6,702**	**7,025**	**7,441**	**7,893**	**20.61**	**29.94**	**30.76**
Legal services............................	5411	944	1,066	1,168	1,114	1,122	21.38	31.04	31.11
Accounting and bookkeeping services........	5412	664	866	849	887	913	14.42	21.02	22.46
Architectural and engineering services........	5413	942	1,238	1,311	1,275	1,323	20.49	30.22	29.98
Specialized design services................	5414	82	132	131	113	116	15.32	22.36	24.35
Computer systems design and related services.............................	5415	410	1,254	1,195	1,449	1,620	27.13	37.16	37.32
Management and technical consulting services.............................	5416	305	673	824	999	1,121	20.83	28.52	30.33
Scientific research and development services.............................	5417	494	515	577	621	638	21.39	35.67	36.47
Advertising and related services................	5418	382	497	446	408	430	16.99	24.61	27.13
Management of companies and enterprises..	**55**	**1,667**	**1,796**	**1,759**	**1,872**	**2,008**	**15.28**	**23.79**	**24.72**
Administrative and waste services..........	**56**	**4,643**	**8,168**	**8,170**	**7,414**	**8,029**	**11.69**	**15.80**	**16.09**
Administrative and support services [5]...........	561	4,413	7,855	7,833	7,057	7,657	11.53	15.59	15.88
Office administrative services.................	5611	211	264	345	407	426	14.68	23.56	25.30
Facilities support services....................	5612	58	97	120	133	126	16.73	20.97	20.61
Employment services [5].....................	5613	1,512	3,849	3,607	2,723	3,148	11.89	16.19	16.14
Temporary help services.................	56132	1,156	2,636	2,549	2,094	2,508	11.79	14.23	15.26
Business support services....................	5614	505	787	766	809	828	11.08	14.49	14.94
Travel arrangement and reservation services..............................	5615	250	299	224	186	193	12.72	17.10	18.35
Investigation and security services............	5616	507	689	737	781	818	9.78	14.14	14.60
Services to buildings and dwellings............	5617	1,175	1,571	1,738	1,745	1,830	10.02	12.97	13.26
Waste management and remediation services [5]............................	562	229	313	338	357	373	15.29	19.32	20.11
Waste collection..........................	5621	82	100	124	141	150	12.97	17.50	17.35
Waste treatment and disposal..............	5622	77	119	103	96	97	15.02	20.29	24.03
Education and health services.................	**(X)**	**10,984**	**15,109**	**17,372**	**19,531**	**20,319**	**13.95**	**20.12**	**21.09**
Educational services....................	**61**	**1,688**	**2,390**	**2,836**	**3,155**	**3,347**	**(NA)**	**(NA)**	**(NA)**
Elementary and secondary schools............	6111	461	716	837	849	912	(NA)	(NA)	(NA)
Junior colleges...........................	6112	44	79	100	99	86	(NA)	(NA)	(NA)
Colleges and universities....................	6113	939	1,196	1,393	1,591	1,678	(NA)	(NA)	(NA)
Business, computer, and management training.............................	6114	60	86	77	78	71	(NA)	(NA)	(NA)
Technical and trade schools.................	6115	72	91	102	126	136	(NA)	(NA)	(NA)
Other schools and instruction................	6116	96	184	250	309	344	(NA)	(NA)	(NA)
Educational support services.................	6117	17	39	78	103	120	(NA)	(NA)	(NA)
Health care and social assistance.............	**62**	**9,296**	**12,718**	**14,536**	**16,375**	**16,972**	**13.98**	**20.44**	**21.41**
Health care............................	621,2,3	8,211	10,858	12,314	13,777	14,302	14.63	21.71	22.74
Ambulatory health care services..............	621	2,842	4,320	5,114	5,975	6,318	14.99	21.67	23.04
Offices of physicians.........................	6211	1,278	1,840	2,094	2,313	2,391	15.65	24.03	26.72

See footnotes at end of table.

Table 660. Nonfarm Industries—Employees and Earnings: 1990 to 2012-Continued.

See headnote on page 431.

Industry	2007 NAICS code [1]	All employees (1,000)					Average hourly earnings [2] (dol.)		
		1990	2000	2005	2010	2012	2000	2010	2012
Offices of dentists	6212	513	688	774	828	853	15.96	22.65	22.62
Offices of other health practitioners	6213	276	438	549	671	724	14.24	20.48	21.93
Outpatient care centers	6214	261	386	473	600	652	15.29	22.65	23.14
Medical and diagnostic laboratories	6215	129	162	198	228	234	15.74	23.48	22.83
Home health care services	6216	288	633	821	1,085	1,199	12.86	16.64	17.44
Hospitals	622	3,513	3,954	4,345	4,679	4,791	16.71	26.11	27.35
General medical and surgical hospitals	6221	3,305	3,745	4,096	4,357	4,417	16.75	26.33	27.66
Psychiatric and substance abuse hospitals	6222	113	86	93	109	122	(NA)	(NA)	(NA)
Nursing and residential care facilities	623	1,856	2,583	2,855	3,124	3,194	10.67	14.21	14.22
Nursing care facilities	6231	1,170	1,514	1,577	1,657	1,665	11.08	15.26	15.17
Residential mental health facilities	6232	269	437	497	565	581	9.96	13.06	12.80
Community care facilities for the elderly	6233	330	478	615	741	790	9.83	12.89	13.25
Social assistance	624	1,085	1,860	2,222	2,599	2,669	9.78	12.88	13.30
Individual and family services	6241	389	678	921	1,220	1,311	10.57	13.48	14.13
Emergency and other relief services	6242	67	117	129	143	145	10.95	14.41	16.07
Vocational rehabilitation services	6243	242	370	383	388	358	9.57	12.47	12.92
Child day care services	6244	388	696	790	848	856	8.88	11.99	11.83
Leisure and hospitality	(X)	**9,288**	**11,862**	**12,816**	**13,049**	**13,746**	**8.32**	**11.31**	**11.62**
Arts, entertainment, and recreation	**71**	**1,132**	**1,788**	**1,892**	**1,913**	**1,965**	**10.68**	**15.27**	**15.97**
Performing arts and spectator sports	711	273	382	376	406	404	13.11	21.01	23.54
Museums, historical sites, zoos, and parks	712	68	110	121	128	136	12.20	15.60	16.21
Amusements, gambling, and recreation	713	791	1,296	1,395	1,379	1,426	9.86	13.38	13.70
Accommodation and food services	**72**	**8,156**	**10,074**	**10,923**	**11,135**	**11,780**	**7.92**	**10.68**	**10.96**
Accommodation	721	1,616	1,884	1,819	1,760	1,817	9.48	13.02	12.69
Traveler accommodation and other longer-term accommodation	7211	1,582	1,837	1,765	1,703	1,761	9.49	13.07	12.72
Food services and drinking places	722	6,540	8,189	9,104	9,376	9,963	7.49	10.15	10.59
Full-service restaurants	7221	3,070	3,845	4,316	4,482	4,747	7.78	10.93	11.51
Limited-service eating places	7222	2,429	3,042	3,350	3,418	3,657	6.80	8.86	9.00
Special food services	7223	392	491	538	543	580	9.45	11.83	13.31
Drinking places, alcoholic beverages	7224	312	391	361	341	354	7.24	10.15	10.92
Other services	**81**	**4,261**	**5,168**	**5,395**	**5,331**	**5,437**	**12.73**	**17.06**	**17.59**
Repair and maintenance	811	1,009	1,242	1,236	1,139	1,191	13.28	16.82	17.23
Automotive repair and maintenance	8111	659	888	886	801	830	12.45	15.55	15.99
Electronic equipment repair and maintenance	8112	100	107	103	98	99	16.31	19.41	21.61
Commercial machinery repair and maintenance	8113	161	161	170	172	193	15.53	21.03	20.04
Personal and laundry services	812	1,120	1,243	1,277	1,265	1,313	10.18	13.42	13.42
Personal care services	8121	430	490	577	601	628	10.18	13.97	14.25
Death care services	8122	123	136	137	131	133	13.04	17.46	17.67
Dry-cleaning and laundry services	8123	371	388	347	302	298	9.17	11.80	11.45
Dry-cleaning and laundry services, except coin-operated	81232	215	211	180	146	142	8.14	10.56	10.34
Other personal services	8129	196	229	216	232	254	10.52	12.43	12.17
Pet care services, except veterinary	81291	23	31	44	63	75	12.12	12.83	12.86
Parking lots and garages	81293	68	93	103	111	119	8.81	11.18	10.86
Membership associations & organizations	813	2,132	2,683	2,882	2,926	2,933	13.66	18.76	19.59
Grantmaking and giving services	8132	113	116	137	178	168	14.65	23.51	24.61
Social advocacy organizations	8133	126	143	174	202	207	12.08	17.36	17.47
Civic and social organizations	8134	377	404	409	392	395	9.85	12.16	13.37
Professional and similar organizations	8139	379	473	492	477	471	15.98	22.67	23.16
Government	(X)	**18,415**	**20,790**	**21,804**	**22,490**	**21,917**	**(NA)**	**(NA)**	**(NA)**
Federal	(X)	3,196	2,865	2,732	2,977	2,814	(NA)	(NA)	(NA)
State	(X)	4,305	4,786	5,032	5,137	5,052	(NA)	(NA)	(NA)
Local	(X)	10,914	13,139	14,041	14,376	14,051	(NA)	(NA)	(NA)

NA Not available. X Not applicable. [1] Based on the North American Industry Classification System, 2007. See text, Section 15. [2] Production employees in the goods-producing industries and nonsupervisory employees in service-providing industries. See footnotes 3 and 4. [3] Mining and logging, construction, and manufacturing. [4] Trade, transportation and utilities, information, financial activities, professional and business services, education and health services, leisure and hospitality, other services, and government. [5] Includes other industries, not shown separately.

Source: Bureau of Labor Statistics, Current Employment Statistics, "Employment, Hours, and Earnings—National," <http://www.bls.gov/ces/data.htm>, accessed September 2013.

Table 661. Women Employees on Nonfarm Payrolls by Major Industry: 1990 to 2012

[51,587 represents 51,587,000. Annual averages of monthly data. For coverage, see headnote, Table 658]

Industry	Women employees (1,000)				Percent of total employees			
	1990	2000	2010	2012	1990	2000	2010	2012
Total nonfarm [1]	**51,587**	**63,282**	**64,719**	**66,020**	**47.1**	**48.0**	**49.8**	**49.4**
Total private	41,732	51,511	51,890	53,526	45.8	46.4	48.3	47.9
Construction	656	846	723	724	12.5	12.5	13.1	12.8
Manufacturing	5,702	5,359	3,268	3,254	32.2	31.0	28.3	27.3
Trade, transportation, and utilities	9,363	10,859	10,007	10,285	41.3	41.4	40.6	40.3
Wholesale trade	1,611	1,827	1,641	1,704	30.6	30.8	30.1	30.0
Retail trade	6,696	7,680	7,226	7,417	50.8	50.3	50.0	49.9
Transportation and warehousing	879	1,202	1,002	1,027	25.3	27.3	23.9	23.3
Utilities	177	151	139	138	24.0	25.1	25.1	24.8
Information	1,324	1,697	1,104	1,076	49.3	46.7	40.8	40.2
Financial activities	4,055	4,697	4,530	4,520	61.3	60.3	58.9	58.1
Professional and business services	5,105	7,680	7,454	7,930	47.1	46.1	44.6	44.2
Professional and technical services	2,209	3,146	3,522	3,676	48.7	46.9	47.3	46.6
Management of companies and enterprises	849	924	939	988	50.9	51.4	50.1	49.2
Administrative and waste services	2,048	3,610	2,993	3,267	44.1	44.2	40.4	40.7
Education and health services	8,422	11,586	15,067	15,588	76.7	76.7	77.1	76.7
Educational services	958	1,417	1,929	2,045	56.8	59.3	61.2	61.1
Health care and social assistance	7,464	10,168	13,137	13,543	80.3	79.9	80.2	79.8
Leisure and hospitality	4,829	6,082	6,819	7,178	52.0	51.3	52.3	52.2
Arts, entertainment, and recreation	516	815	886	915	45.6	45.6	46.3	46.6
Accommodation and food services	4,312	5,267	5,933	6,263	52.9	52.3	53.3	53.2
Other services	2,164	2,614	2,820	2,857	50.8	50.6	52.9	52.5
Government	9,855	11,771	12,829	12,494	53.5	56.6	57.0	57.0
Federal	1,378	1,231	1,326	1,247	43.1	43.0	44.5	44.3
State government	2,137	2,464	2,639	2,646	49.6	51.5	51.4	52.4
Local government	6,340	8,076	8,864	8,601	58.1	61.5	61.7	61.2

NA Not available [1] Includes other industries, not shown separately.

Source: Bureau of Labor Statistics, Current Employment Statistics, "Employment, Hours, and Earnings—National," <http://www.bls.gov/ces/data.htm>, accessed September 2013.

Table 662. Private Nonfarm Extended Mass Layoff Activity by Industry and Reason for Layoff: 2000 to 2011

[Covers layoffs of at least 31 days duration that involve 50 or more individuals from a single employer. Based on administrative records of unemployment filings and establishment classifications, supplemented with employer confirmation of layoffs, plant closings, and additional employer provided data. See source for more information]

Industry	2007 NAICS code [1]	Extended mass layoff events	Employee Separations	Initial unemployment claimants [2]
2000	(X)	4,591	915,962	846,267
2005	(X)	4,881	884,661	834,533
2007	(X)	5,363	965,935	978,712
2008	(X)	8,259	1,516,978	1,670,042
2009	(X)	11,824	2,108,202	2,442,000
2010	(X)	7,247	1,257,134	1,415,766
Total, 2011	**(X)**	**6,597**	**1,113,170**	**1,293,590**
Mining, quarrying, and gas extraction	21	44	5,891	5,712
Utilities	22	10	1,593	1,811
Construction	23	1,377	169,620	209,468
Manufacturing	31–33	1,196	198,458	219,043
Wholesale trade	42	121	15,528	15,130
Retail trade	44,45	409	87,517	99,323
Transportation and warehousing	48,49	367	72,367	75,378
Information	51	286	75,641	124,696
Finance and Insurance	52	182	29,490	38,427
Real estate and rental and leasing	53	58	8,270	9,770
Professional and technical services	54	326	60,601	75,850
Management of companies and enterprises	55	27	3,245	3,918
Administrative and waste services	56	848	164,252	202,752
Educational services	61	80	9,973	11,906
Health care and social assistance	62	397	47,763	48,461
Arts, entertainment, and recreation	71	238	42,407	36,407
Accommodation and food services	72	503	105,586	98123
Other services	81	126	14,784	17,169
Unclassified	(X)	2	184	246
Reason for layoff:				
Business demand	(X)	2,344	366,629	528,931
Disaster/safety	(X)	31	5,046	5,128
Financial issues	(X)	415	76,335	77,597
Organizational changes	(X)	313	56,533	53,686
Production specific	(X)	94	16,180	18,513
Seasonal	(X)	2,285	393,087	409,428
Other/miscellaneous	(X)	1,115	199,360	200,307

X Not applicable. [1] Based on North American Industry Classification System, 2007. See text, Section 15. [2] A person who files any notice of unemployment to initiate a request either for a determination of entitlement to and eligibility for compensation, or for a subsequent period of unemployment within a benefit year or period of eligibility.

Source: U.S. Bureau of Labor Statistics, *Extended Mass Layoffs in 2011*, December 2012. See also <http://www.bls.gov/mls/home.htm>.

Table 663. Private Sector Gross Job Gains and Job Losses: 2002 to 2012

[In thousands (13,579 represents 13,579,000). For year ending in March. Based on the Quarterly Census of Employment and Wages (QCEW). Excludes self-employed and certain nonprofit organizations. Minus sign (-) indicates a decrease in employment and comes from either closing establishments or contracting establishments. For more information, see source]

Year and industry	Gross job gains Total	Expanding establishments	Opening establishments	Gross job losses Total	Contracting establishments	Closing establishments	Net change[1]
2002	13,579	8,635	4,944	16,308	11,041	5,267	-2,729
2003	13,191	8,599	4,592	13,923	9,290	4,633	-732
2004	13,307	8,953	4,354	12,428	8,237	4,191	879
2005	13,759	9,403	4,356	11,767	7,672	4,095	1,992
2006	14,019	9,625	4,394	11,438	7,711	3,727	2,581
2007	13,441	9,238	4,203	11,941	8,246	3,695	1,500
2008	12,704	8,714	3,990	12,609	8,772	3,837	95
2009	10,048	6,664	3,384	15,912	11,703	4,209	-5,864
2010	9,985	6,834	3,151	12,683	9,137	3,546	-2,698
2011	11,543	8,288	3,255	9,637	6,618	3,019	1,906
2012, Total private	**12,170**	**8,704**	**3,466**	**9,625**	**6,466**	**3,159**	**2,545**
Goods producing	2,353	1,861	492	1,854	1,317	537	499
Natural resources and mining	317	246	71	180	123	57	137
Construction	1,085	783	302	946	635	311	139
Manufacturing	951	832	119	728	559	169	223
Service providing	9,819	6,845	2,974	7,771	5,148	2,623	2,048
Wholesale trade	603	455	148	466	300	166	137
Retail trade	1,350	944	406	1,106	758	348	244
Transportation and warehousing	415	306	109	318	213	105	97
Utilities	23	18	5	24	20	4	-1
Information	253	194	59	262	188	74	-9
Financial activities	754	551	203	690	450	240	64
Professional and business services	2,524	1,877	647	1,984	1,334	650	540
Education and health services	1,548	1,181	367	1,180	827	353	368
Leisure and hospitality	1,703	999	704	1,292	795	497	411
Other services	463	309	154	404	257	147	59

[1] Net change is the difference between total gross job gains and total gross job losses.

Source: Bureau of Labor Statistics, Business Employment Dynamics, "Annual Business Employment Dynamics Data," <http://www.bls.gov/bdm/bdmann.htm#TOTAL>, accessed March 2013.

Table 664. Private Sector Gross Job Gains and Job Losses by State: 2012

[In thousands (12,170 represents 12,170,000). For year ending in March. Based on the Quarterly Census of Employment and Wages (QCEW). Excludes self-employed and certain nonprofit organizations. For more information, see source]

State	Gross job gains Total	Expanding establishments	Opening establishments	Gross job losses Total	Contracting establishments	Closing establishments	Net change[1]
U.S.	12,170	8,704	3,466	9,625	6,466	3,159	2,545
AL	160	114	46	142	102	40	18
AK	26	19	7	20	15	5	6
AZ	238	169	70	187	119	68	52
AR	100	66	34	82	59	23	18
CA	1,512	1,081	430	1,192	746	445	320
CO	216	153	62	166	109	57	50
CT	127	97	30	103	78	25	24
DE	37	26	11	35	23	12	2
DC	54	37	18	41	27	13	14
FL	834	519	315	677	405	271	157
GA	376	252	124	329	209	120	46
HI	47	35	12	42	29	13	5
ID	56	38	18	50	33	17	6
IL	456	341	116	366	252	114	90
IN	251	191	60	187	128	59	64
IA	118	86	32	90	66	25	28
KS	119	82	37	95	64	31	23
KY	154	116	38	124	87	36	31
LA	193	136	56	163	115	48	29
ME	44	32	12	40	27	13	5
MD	229	160	69	191	132	59	38
MA	261	190	71	206	141	65	55
MI	363	269	94	255	167	88	107
MN	237	172	65	184	120	65	53
MS	94	67	27	86	63	23	8
MO	229	159	71	196	130	66	34
MT	39	28	11	30	20	10	9
NE	68	51	17	55	40	14	14
NV	106	76	30	89	60	29	17
NH	52	37	15	45	31	14	8
NJ	360	250	110	300	205	96	59
NM	66	44	22	59	40	18	7
NY	779	550	229	619	396	223	160
NC	366	259	107	298	201	97	67
ND	56	39	17	23	17	6	33
OH	438	329	108	325	232	94	112
OK	146	106	40	115	75	40	31
OR	144	103	40	116	80	36	27
PA	461	343	119	369	263	107	92
RI	39	28	11	33	23	10	6
SC	159	114	45	128	92	36	31
SD	32	24	8	23	17	6	9
TN	246	184	62	181	129	52	65
TX	1,070	792	278	751	532	218	320
UT	125	88	37	89	59	30	36
VT	24	19	6	20	13	6	5
VA	314	221	93	272	187	85	42
WA	254	192	62	200	140	60	54
WV	65	46	19	50	36	15	15
WI	202	154	49	166	117	49	37
WY	26	19	7	20	13	7	6

[1] Net change is the difference between total gross job gains and total gross job losses.

Source: Bureau of Labor Statistics, Business Employment Dynamics, "Annual Business Employment Dynamics Data," <http://www.bls.gov/bdm/bdmann.htm>, accessed March 2013.

Table 665. Hires and Separations Affecting Establishment Payrolls: 2009 to 2012

[46,357 represents 46,357,000. Hires represent any additions to payrolls, including new and rehired employees, full- and part-time workers, short-term and seasonal workers, etc. Separations represent terminations of employment, including quits, layoffs, and discharges, etc. Based on a monthly survey of private nonfarm establishments and governmental entities]

Industry	Annual hires (1,000)				Annual separations (1,000)			
	2009	2010	2011	2012	2009	2010	2011	2012
Total	**46,357**	**48,607**	**49,675**	**51,991**	**51,532**	**47,646**	**47,626**	**49,676**
Total private industry	43,031	44,788	46,552	48,493	48,105	43,532	44,173	46,152
Mining and logging	188	288	335	380	297	217	237	354
Construction	3,681	3,994	4,098	3,900	4,767	4,204	3,906	3,808
Manufacturing	2,755	3,135	3,035	2,967	4,165	3,033	2,820	2,808
Durable goods	1,411	1,797	1,771	1,794	2,512	1,678	1,538	1,659
Nondurable goods	1,343	1,337	1,263	1,174	1,654	1,356	1,283	1,146
Trade, transportation, and utilities	9,437	9,687	9,946	10,447	10,529	9,385	9,436	9,924
Wholesale trade	1,448	1,410	1,485	1,539	1,777	1,407	1,365	1,429
Retail trade	6,323	6,686	6,772	6,995	6,866	6,469	6,476	6,757
Transportation, warehousing, and utilities	1,665	1,591	1,690	1,912	1,883	1,507	1,598	1,739
Information	670	652	732	743	843	711	727	749
Financial activities	1,988	2,018	1,852	2,143	2,321	2,072	1,815	2,043
Finance and insurance	1,190	1,332	1,180	1,402	1,398	1,359	1,147	1,322
Real estate and rental and leasing	797	686	669	739	925	716	669	721
Professional and business services	8,249	9,321	10,181	10,582	9,018	8,809	9,616	10,004
Education and health services	5,951	5,772	5,681	5,997	5,640	5,454	5,269	5,578
Educational services	861	891	941	886	831	808	810	841
Health care and social assistance	5,093	4,881	4,741	5,112	4,809	4,644	4,459	4,740
Leisure and hospitality	7,780	7,823	8,414	8,999	8,091	7,572	8,117	8,616
Arts, entertainment, and recreation	1,203	1,319	1,445	1,533	1,267	1,273	1,472	1,450
Accommodation and food services	6,574	6,506	6,970	7,465	6,825	6,299	6,643	7,163
Other services	2,336	2,100	2,279	2,336	2,432	2,072	2,228	2,268
Government workers	3,326	3,820	3,123	3,503	3,426	4,112	3,453	3,525
Federal	460	1,053	332	353	412	994	370	389
State and local	2,867	2,767	2,790	3,148	3,015	3,117	3,083	3,135

Source: Bureau of Labor Statistics, *Job Openings and Labor Turnover*, News Release, USDL 13-0422, March 2013. See also <http://www.bls.gov/jlt/news.htm>.

Table 666. Type of Separations Affecting Establishment Payrolls: 2012

[25,132 represents 25,132,000. Covers all private nonfarm establishments. Separations are the total number of terminations of employment occurring at any time during the reference month, and are reported by type of separation—quits, layoffs and discharges, and other separations. Annual rate estimates are computed by dividing annual levels by the Current Employment Statistics (CES) annual average employment level, see Table 660, and multiplying that quotient by 100]

Industry	Number (1,000)			Rate (percent) [1]		
	Annual quits level [2]	Annual layoffs and discharge levels [3]	Annual other separations [4]	Annual quits level [2]	Annual layoffs and discharge levels [3]	Annual other separations [4]
Total	**25,132**	**20,546**	**3,997**	**18.8**	**15.4**	**3.0**
Private industry	23,589	19,336	3,229	21.1	17.3	2.9
Mining and logging	196	134	26	23.0	15.7	3.1
Construction	946	2,745	119	16.8	48.7	2.1
Manufacturing	1,284	1,263	262	10.8	10.6	2.2
Durable goods	706	793	160	9.5	10.6	2.1
Nondurable goods	579	469	101	13.0	10.5	2.3
Trade, transportation, and utilities	5,530	3,493	902	21.7	13.7	3.5
Wholesale trade	688	621	120	12.1	10.9	2.1
Retail trade	3,984	2,200	572	26.8	14.8	3.8
Transportation, warehousing, and utilities	855	674	209	17.2	13.6	4.2
Information	431	262	57	16.1	9.8	2.1
Financial activities	1,065	607	371	13.7	7.8	4.8
Finance and insurance	694	329	297	11.9	5.6	5.1
Real estate and rental and leasing	371	280	73	19.0	14.3	3.7
Professional and business services	4,622	4,814	569	25.8	26.9	3.2
Education and health services	3,203	1,900	473	15.8	9.4	2.3
Educational services	395	383	61	11.8	11.4	1.8
Health care and social assistance	2,808	1,517	410	16.5	8.9	2.4
Leisure and hospitality	5,196	3,070	350	37.8	22.3	2.5
Arts, entertainment, and recreation	521	904	27	26.5	46.0	1.4
Accommodation and food services	4,678	2,165	322	39.7	18.4	2.7
Other services	1,114	1,046	111	20.5	19.2	2.0
Government workers	1,543	1,210	768	7.0	5.5	3.5
Federal	131	128	131	4.7	4.5	4.7
State and local	1,413	1,082	639	7.4	5.7	3.3

[1] As a percent of total employment. [2] Quits are voluntary separations by employees (except for retirements, which are reported as other separations). [3] Layoffs and discharges are involuntary separations initiated by the employer and include layoffs with no intent to rehire; formal layoffs lasting or expected to last more than seven days; discharges resulting from mergers, downsizing, or closings, firings or other discharges for cause; terminations of permanent or short term employees; and terminations of seasonal employees. [4] Other separations include retirements, transfers to other locations, deaths, and separations due to disability.

Source: Bureau of Labor Statistics, *Job Openings and Labor Turnover*, News Release, USDL 13-0422, March 2013. See also <http://www.bls.gov/jlt>.

Table 667. Productivity and Related Measures for Selected NAICS Industries: 1987 to 2011 and 2010 to 2011

[For a discussion of productivity measures and methodology, see text, this section and BLS Handbook of Methods, <http://www.bls.gov/opub/hom/homch11.htm>. Minus sign (-) indicates decrease]

Industry	2007 NAICS code [1]	Average annual percent change [2]							
		1987–2011 [3, 4]				2010–2011			
		Output per hour	Output	Hours	Unit labor costs	Output per hour	Output	Hours	Unit labor costs
Mining...	21	-0.4	0.1	0.5	5.1	-11.3	4.2	17.5	11.9
Oil and gas extraction..............................	2111	0.5	-0.2	-0.7	5.7	-11.0	4.7	17.6	5.4
Mining, except oil and gas........................	212	1.5	0.4	-1.1	1.9	-5.1	2.7	8.2	7.3
Support activities for mining.....................	213	1.3	4.1	2.7	4.1	-3.0	19.9	23.6	6.2
Utilities:									
Power generation and supply.....................	2211	1.9	0.7	-1.2	2.2	-5.6	-4.5	1.1	8.8
Natural gas distribution...........................	2212	2.7	1.2	-1.5	2.1	4.3	0.7	-3.4	3.2
Manufacturing:									
Food...	311	1.0	1.2	0.2	1.7	-0.1	-0.4	-0.3	1.3
Animal slaughtering and processing...........	3116	1.0	2.0	1.0	1.3	3.2	1.6	-1.6	-1.7
Bakeries and tortilla manufacturing............	3118	0.5	0.2	-0.3	1.8	0.7	-0.4	-1.1	0.6
Beverages and tobacco products................	312	0.6	-0.3	-0.9	1.6	-5.7	1.2	7.4	1.7
Textile mills..	313	3.4	-2.7	-5.8	-0.5	-1.9	-2.1	-0.1	2.7
Textile product mills...............................	314	1.0	-1.9	-2.9	2.1	6.6	1.2	-5.1	-1.2
Apparel...	315	-1.0	-7.8	-6.9	2.0	1.0	-2.8	-3.7	-0.5
Leather and allied products.......................	316	2.0	-4.3	-6.2	1.4	-0.3	0.5	0.8	2.0
Wood products......................................	321	1.3	-0.9	-2.2	2.0	0.8	1.0	0.2	-0.3
Paper and paper products........................	322	1.9	-0.2	-2.0	1.3	2.7	0.1	-2.5	0.3
Converted paper products......................	3222	1.4	0.0	-1.4	1.7	3.3	0.0	-3.2	0.1
Printing and related support activities..........	3231	1.4	-0.7	-2.1	1.2	4.7	-0.9	-5.3	-0.8
Petroleum and coal products.....................	3241	2.7	1.2	-1.4	2.5	1.9	1.3	-0.5	3.0
Chemicals..	325	1.5	0.7	-0.9	2.2	0.3	-0.2	-0.6	2.9
Pharmaceuticals and medicines................	3254	0.2	2.1	1.9	3.4	2.7	2.0	-0.6	-1.5
Plastics and rubber products.....................	326	1.9	1.2	-0.8	1.1	-0.9	1.8	2.7	1.0
Plastics products.................................	3261	1.8	1.3	-0.4	1.3	-1.5	0.6	2.1	1.9
Nonmetallic mineral products....................	327	1.1	-0.3	-1.4	1.6	2.6	1.7	-1.0	-0.5
Primary metals......................................	331	2.3	0.2	-2.1	0.7	-2.0	7.5	9.7	1.4
Fabricated metal products........................	332	1.4	0.8	-0.6	1.6	1.9	7.9	5.9	-1.4
Architectural and structural metals.............	3323	0.6	0.5	-0.1	2.3	-2.8	3.0	5.9	-0.5
Machine shops and threaded products.........	3327	2.0	2.7	0.7	1.1	3.5	13.6	9.7	-1.9
Other fabricated metal products................	3329	1.4	0.3	-1.1	1.4	6.3	7.9	1.5	-2.4
Machinery..	333	2.5	1.5	-1.0	0.4	4.8	12.8	7.6	-4.1
Agriculture, construction, and mining machinery..	3331	2.8	3.2	0.4	-0.2	6.9	17.5	9.9	-3.4
Other general purpose machinery..............	3339	2.7	1.6	-1.1	1.0	3.1	10.0	6.7	-2.1
Computer and electronic products..............	334	10.7	8.0	-2.5	-6.6	4.4	4.0	-0.4	0.0
Semiconductors and electronic components....	3344	16.1	14.2	-1.6	-11.4	8.5	14.8	5.8	-9.4
Electronic instruments..........................	3345	4.1	1.8	-2.1	0.2	6.4	3.2	-3.0	0.2
Electrical equipment and appliances............	335	2.5	-0.1	-2.5	1.0	4.8	5.8	1.0	-2.6
Transportation equipment........................	336	3.1	1.3	-1.7	-0.4	1.2	5.6	4.4	-0.1
Motor vehicles...................................	3361	4.0	1.3	-2.6	-1.2	7.4	11.6	3.9	-2.1
Motor vehicle parts..............................	3363	3.3	1.9	-1.3	-1.6	1.3	7.2	5.9	-1.0
Aerospace products and parts...................	3364	1.8	-0.3	-2.1	1.3	-4.2	-1.4	2.9	6.0
Furniture and related products...................	337	1.5	-0.7	-2.2	1.5	-0.2	2.8	3.0	-3.7
Household and institutional furniture............	3371	1.3	-1.3	-2.5	1.7	-5.1	-2.5	2.7	0.1
Miscellaneous manufacturing....................	339	2.9	2.4	-0.5	1.4	-1.3	1.0	2.3	1.7
Medical equipment and supplies................	3391	3.3	4.3	0.9	1.0	-2.4	-1.6	0.8	3.9
Other miscellaneous manufacturing............	3399	2.3	0.7	-1.6	1.6	0.6	4.6	4.0	-1.1
Wholesale trade......................................	42	3.1	3.4	0.3	0.7	1.9	4.8	2.9	0.5
Durable goods.......................................	423	5.0	4.9	0.0	-0.9	6.3	9.1	2.6	-2.6
Nondurable goods..................................	424	1.4	1.5	0.1	2.8	-1.1	0.5	1.6	1.8
Electronic markets and agents and brokers.......	4251	1.4	3.9	2.4	0.8	-0.6	6.5	7.1	2.1
Retail trade...	44–45	2.8	3.2	0.4	0.0	2.2	3.7	1.5	-0.8
Motor vehicle and parts dealers.................	441	1.9	2.3	0.4	0.8	2.1	7.0	4.8	-0.2
Automobile dealers..............................	4411	2.0	2.3	0.4	0.8	1.0	8.2	7.1	0.4
Other motor vehicle dealers....................	4412	2.4	2.8	0.4	1.1	-0.2	0.7	0.8	2.2
Auto parts, accessories, and tire stores........	4413	1.4	2.0	0.6	1.2	0.1	1.3	1.2	1.6
Furniture and home furnishings stores............	442	3.8	3.3	-0.5	-0.9	5.9	3.2	-2.5	-3.1
Furniture stores..................................	4421	3.1	2.8	-0.3	-0.8	5.1	2.9	-2.1	-2.6
Home furnishings stores.........................	4422	4.7	3.9	-0.7	-1.1	6.8	3.5	-3.1	-3.6
Electronics and appliance stores................	4431	12.5	13.8	1.1	-8.4	2.8	8.9	6.0	-3.3
Building material and garden supply stores.......	444	2.6	3.2	0.6	0.0	3.3	3.1	-0.1	-1.5
Building material and supplies dealers..........	4441	2.3	3.1	0.9	0.2	3.0	2.0	-1.0	-1.1
Lawn and garden equipment and supplies stores...	4442	4.3	3.7	-0.6	-1.3	3.5	10.0	6.3	-3.0
Food and beverage stores........................	445	0.4	0.2	-0.2	2.7	1.0	1.3	0.3	-0.9
Grocery stores...................................	4451	0.3	0.2	-0.1	2.9	0.6	1.3	0.7	-0.8
Specialty food stores............................	4452	0.0	-0.6	-0.7	2.1	0.8	-3.3	-4.1	-0.2
Beer, wine, and liquor stores...................	4453	2.3	0.9	-1.4	1.0	2.4	4.1	1.6	3.6
Health and personal care stores................	4461	2.2	3.4	1.2	1.4	0.0	1.5	1.5	1.6
Gasoline stations..................................	4471	1.7	1.0	-0.8	1.3	-3.7	-3.1	0.7	4.8
Clothing and clothing accessories stores.........	448	4.4	4.0	-0.4	-1.2	-0.3	3.7	4.1	-0.8
Clothing stores...................................	4481	4.7	4.6	-0.1	-1.7	-0.7	4.1	4.8	-3.1
Shoe stores.......................................	4482	3.4	2.2	-1.1	-0.6	4.3	3.5	-0.8	-1.8
Jewelry, luggage, and leather goods stores.....	4483	3.6	2.8	-0.8	0.4	-3.1	2.1	5.3	8.5
Sporting goods, hobby, book, and music stores..	451	4.1	4.0	-0.1	-0.8	6.5	5.5	-1.0	-3.4
Sporting goods and musical instrument stores..	4511	4.7	5.1	0.4	-1.4	4.7	7.4	2.5	-4.4
Book, periodical, and music stores..............	4512	2.9	1.4	-1.4	0.7	13.4	-0.7	-12.5	0.1
General merchandise stores......................	452	3.0	4.9	1.8	-1.1	-1.5	2.1	3.6	1.1
Department stores................................	4521	0.3	1.6	1.3	0.8	-5.4	-0.9	4.8	3.4

See footnotes at end of table.

Table 667. Productivity and Related Measures for Selected NAICS Industries: 1987 to 2011 and 2010 to 2011-Continued.

See headnote on page 438.

Industry	2007 NAICS code [1]	Average annual percent change [2]							
		1987–2011 [3,4]				2010–2011			
		Output per hour	Output	Hours	Unit labor costs	Output per hour	Output	Hours	Unit labor costs
Other general merchandise stores...............	4529	6.0	8.5	2.3	-3.0	0.8	3.4	2.6	0.4
Miscellaneous store retailers.......................	453	4.0	3.5	-0.4	-1.4	10.7	5.9	-4.4	-7.3
Florists................................	4531	3.8	0.0	-3.7	-0.4	20.6	7.6	-10.8	-22.2
Office supplies, stationery, and gift stores.......	4532	6.2	5.0	-1.1	-3.0	9.3	3.9	-4.9	-9.3
Used merchandise stores........................	4533	4.8	6.0	1.1	-2.2	14.2	14.5	0.2	-9.8
Other miscellaneous store retailers.............	4539	1.6	2.5	0.8	-0.2	10.5	5.3	-4.7	-2.3
Nonstore retailers................................	454	8.8	9.0	0.1	-5.0	16.9	13.2	-3.2	-6.9
Electronic shopping and mail-order houses.....	4541	11.2	15.0	3.4	-6.5	14.6	15.9	1.1	-5.0
Vending machine operators......................	4542	1.1	-1.9	-2.9	2.4	18.7	10.7	-6.8	-5.8
Direct selling establishments...................	4543	3.3	1.4	-1.8	-0.6	13.8	4.3	-8.4	-6.1
Transportation and warehousing:									
Air transportation................................	481	3.1	2.7	-0.4	0.1	0.3	1.9	1.6	1.7
Line-haul railroads.............................	482111	3.9	2.0	-1.8	-0.5	-2.7	3.8	6.8	6.4
Truck transportation.............................	484	0.6	1.7	1.1	0.8	1.1	5.1	4.0	2.3
General freight trucking.......................	4841	1.4	2.3	0.9	0.7	2.3	5.3	2.9	1.1
Used household and office goods moving.......	48421	-1.2	-1.1	0.1	3.0	-12.1	-3.5	9.8	9.5
Postal service................................	4911	0.9	-0.3	-1.2	3.8	1.1	-2.7	-3.8	2.3
Couriers and messengers........................	492	-0.8	1.2	2.0	3.3	0.6	-0.5	-1.1	5.6
Warehousing and storage........................	4931	2.9	5.8	2.8	-0.5	3.3	8.1	4.6	-3.7
General warehousing and storage...............	49311	5.2	8.0	2.7	-2.2	6.0	10.1	3.9	-5.8
Refrigerated warehousing and storage.........	49312	-0.2	3.1	3.3	1.1	-11.8	-1.8	11.3	7.5
Information:									
Publishing.......................................	511	3.8	3.5	-0.3	1.5	1.0	2.4	1.4	3.7
Newspaper, book, and directory publishers.....	5111	0.0	-1.8	-1.8	4.1	-1.7	-2.5	-0.8	4.2
Software publishers.............................	5112	13.0	19.7	6.0	-6.8	1.0	6.4	5.3	3.7
Motion picture and video exhibition...............	51213	1.4	1.6	0.2	1.6	-0.1	-2.3	-2.2	0.9
Broadcasting, except Internet....................	515	2.1	2.6	0.5	1.8	3.5	2.9	-0.6	0.7
Radio and television broadcasting...............	5151	1.0	0.7	-0.4	2.3	0.5	0.8	0.3	2.1
Cable and other subscription programming.....	5152	3.9	7.5	3.5	2.8	7.5	4.8	-2.5	0.3
Wired telecommunications carriers.............	5171	4.3	3.3	-1.0	-1.2	6.3	0.9	-5.2	-3.7
Wireless telecommunications carriers.............	5172	10.4	20.7	9.3	-7.1	10.0	10.5	0.5	-4.5
Finance and insurance:									
Commercial banking.............................	52211	3.6	3.6	-0.1	1.9	-2.8	-1.0	1.8	6.3
Real estate and rental and leasing:									
Passenger car rental................................	532111	2.6	2.7	0.1	2.0	15.2	12.9	-2.0	-9.1
Truck, trailer, and RV rental and leasing..........	53212	2.9	2.0	-0.9	0.9	5.9	4.1	-1.7	-0.2
Video tape and disc rental........................	53223	6.4	1.7	-4.4	-2.4	43.3	-16.0	-41.4	-17.1
Professional and technical services:									
Tax preparation services...........................	541213	0.6	2.7	2.1	1.6	1.2	-0.4	-1.6	8.1
Architectural services...........................	54131	1.2	2.0	0.8	2.1	5.3	3.9	-1.4	-1.2
Engineering services...........................	54133	0.9	2.7	1.7	3.4	-1.7	1.9	3.6	1.7
Advertising agencies...........................	54181	2.2	2.5	0.3	2.1	-0.8	5.0	5.9	4.5
Photography studios, portrait.....................	541921	0.8	1.8	1.0	1.9	11.7	1.4	-9.2	-1.9
Administrative and waste services:									
Employment placement agencies....................	561311	6.4	7.2	0.8	-1.6	9.0	15.7	6.1	-6.7
Travel agencies................................	56151	5.9	4.2	-1.6	-1.1	3.5	6.5	2.9	2.9
Janitorial services................................	56172	2.0	3.7	1.6	1.5	2.5	4.0	1.5	-0.5
Health care and social assistance:									
Medical and diagnostic laboratories...............	6215	2.9	6.2	3.2	-0.2	-2.2	3.9	6.3	-0.5
Arts, entertainment, and recreation:									
Amusement and theme parks....................	71311	-0.5	2.3	2.8	3.6	-0.9	4.6	5.5	0.3
Bowling centers................................	71395	0.2	-1.6	-1.8	2.7	-0.6	4.3	4.9	-3.1
Accommodation and food services................	72	0.8	2.1	1.2	2.8	0.8	3.6	2.7	1.3
Accommodation....................................	721	1.7	2.3	0.6	2.2	4.9	3.6	-1.3	1.5
Traveler accommodation........................	7211	1.7	2.4	0.6	2.1	4.8	3.5	-1.2	1.5
Food services and drinking places................	722	0.6	2.0	1.4	3.0	-0.1	3.6	3.6	1.2
Full-service restaurants........................	7221	0.6	2.1	1.4	3.7	1.3	5.0	3.7	—
Limited-service eating places.....................	7222	0.6	2.1	1.6	2.7	-2.1	2.8	5.0	0.9
Special food services...........................	7223	1.4	2.4	0.9	1.2	3.3	2.5	-0.8	6.0
Drinking places, alcoholic beverages.............	7224	-0.3	-0.7	-0.4	3.1	2.1	-0.3	-2.4	3.7
Other services:									
Automotive repair and maintenance...............	8111	1.0	1.2	0.1	2.2	7.7	3.4	-4.0	-4.1
Reupholstery and furniture repair..................	81142	-0.6	-3.2	-2.6	3.6	5.5	-0.3	-5.5	3.0
Hair, nail, and skin care services..................	81211	2.2	3.0	0.8	1.7	5.4	2.1	-3.2	-4.7
Funeral homes and funeral services...............	81221	-0.7	-0.5	0.2	4.3	-4.5	0.3	5.0	2.4
Drycleaning and laundry services.................	8123	1.6	0.5	-1.2	2.0	9.4	3.6	-5.3	-2.8
Photofinishing....................................	81292	2.8	-4.3	-6.9	1.9	16.6	10.4	-5.3	3.2

— Represents or rounds to zero. [1] North American Industry Classification System, 2007 (NAICS); see text, Section 15. [2] Average annual percent changes based on compound rate formula. Rates of change are calculated using index numbers to three decimal places. [3] For NAICS industries 484, 4841, 48411, 4931, 49311, and 49312, annual percent changes are for 1992-2011. [4] For NAICS industries 561311 and 6215, average annual percent changes are for 1994-2011.

Source: Bureau of Labor Statistics. Labor Productivity and Costs, "Productivity and Costs by Industry," <http://www.bls.gov/lpc/data.htm>, accessed September 2013.

Table 668. Productivity and Related Measures: 1970 to 2012

[See text, this section. Minus sign (-) indicates decrease]

Item	1970	1980	1990	2000	2005	2009	2010	2011	2012
INDEXES (2009=100)									
Output per hour, business sector................	44.2	52.9	63.5	79.4	93.9	100.0	103.3	103.6	105.1
Nonfarm business.............................	45.7	54.3	64.1	79.7	94.0	100.0	103.3	103.8	105.3
Manufacturing...............................	(NA)	(NA)	51.7	77.1	95.9	100.0	106.3	107.3	109.2
Output, [1] business sector.....................	29.3	41.5	58.8	86.8	100.4	100.0	103.1	105.6	109.4
Nonfarm business.............................	29.4	41.8	58.9	86.9	100.5	100.0	103.2	105.7	109.7
Manufacturing...............................	(NA)	(NA)	77.8	114.7	115.9	100.0	106.3	109.5	114.1
Hours, [2] business sector......................	66.3	78.5	92.6	109.4	106.9	100.0	99.9	101.9	104.1
Nonfarm business.............................	64.3	76.9	91.9	109.1	106.9	100.0	99.9	101.9	104.1
Manufacturing...............................	(NA)	(NA)	150.4	148.7	120.8	100.0	99.9	102.1	104.4
Compensation per hour, [3] business sector......	12.9	29.1	49.6	73.8	88.8	100.0	102.0	104.4	107.2
Nonfarm business.............................	13.0	29.4	49.9	74.0	88.8	100.0	102.1	104.6	107.4
Manufacturing...............................	(NA)	(NA)	50.1	73.3	88.4	100.0	102.4	103.8	105.7
Real hourly compensation, [3] business sector....	64.9	72.1	79.0	91.9	97.6	100.0	100.3	99.6	100.1
Nonfarm business.............................	65.6	72.8	79.3	92.1	97.6	100.0	100.4	99.7	100.3
Manufacturing...............................	(NA)	(NA)	79.7	91.3	97.1	100.0	100.7	98.9	98.7
Unit labor costs, [4] business sector............	29.1	54.9	78.2	93.0	94.6	100.0	98.8	100.8	102.0
Nonfarm business.............................	28.5	54.1	77.8	92.9	94.5	100.0	98.8	100.8	102.0
Manufacturing...............................	(NA)	(NA)	96.8	95.0	92.1	100.0	96.3	96.7	96.8
ANNUAL PERCENT CHANGE [5]									
Output per hour, business sector................	2.0	-0.1	2.2	3.4	2.1	3.3	3.3	0.4	1.4
Nonfarm business.............................	1.5	-0.1	1.9	3.3	2.0	3.2	3.3	0.5	1.5
Manufacturing...............................	(NA)	(NA)	2.2	4.4	4.8	0.1	6.3	1.0	1.8
Output, [1] business sector.....................	(Z)	-0.9	1.6	4.5	3.8	-4.1	3.1	2.4	3.6
Nonfarm business.............................	–	-0.9	1.5	4.4	3.7	-4.3	3.2	2.5	3.7
Manufacturing...............................	(NA)	(NA)	-0.3	3.0	3.6	-12.9	6.3	3.1	4.1
Hours, [2] business sector......................	-2.0	-0.9	-0.6	1.0	1.6	-7.1	-0.1	2.0	2.2
Nonfarm business.............................	-1.6	-0.8	-0.4	1.0	1.7	-7.2	-0.1	2.0	2.2
Manufacturing...............................	(NA)	(NA)	-2.5	-1.3	-1.2	-13.0	-0.1	2.1	2.3
Compensation per hour, [3] business sector......	7.5	10.7	6.5	7.3	3.6	1.1	2.0	2.4	2.6
Nonfarm business.............................	7.0	10.7	6.2	7.4	3.6	1.1	2.1	2.5	2.6
Manufacturing...............................	(NA)	(NA)	5.0	7.6	3.8	3.5	2.4	1.3	1.9
Real hourly compensation, [3] business sector....	1.7	-0.3	1.4	3.8	0.3	1.4	0.3	-0.7	0.5
Nonfarm business.............................	1.2	-0.3	1.2	3.9	0.3	1.5	0.4	-0.7	0.5
Manufacturing...............................	(NA)	(NA)	0.0	4.1	0.4	3.8	0.7	-1.8	-0.2
Unit labor costs, [4] business sector............	5.4	10.8	4.2	3.8	1.5	-2.2	-1.2	2.0	1.2
Nonfarm business.............................	5.4	10.8	4.2	4.0	1.6	-2.0	-1.2	2.0	1.2
Manufacturing...............................	(NA)	(NA)	2.7	3.0	-1.0	3.4	-3.7	0.4	0.1

– Represents or rounds to zero. NA Not available. [1] Refers to gross sectoral product, a chain–type, current–weighted index. [2] Hours at work of all persons engaged in the business and nonfarm business sectors (employees, proprietors, and unpaid family workers), and employees' and proprietors' hours in manufacturing. [3] Wages and salaries of employees plus employers' contributions for social insurance and private benefit plans. Also includes an estimate of same for self–employed. Real compensation deflated by the Consumer Price Index research series, see text, Section 14. [4] Hourly compensation divided by output per hour. [5] All changes are from the immediate prior year.

Source: Bureau of Labor Statistics, Labor Productivity and Costs, "Major Sector Productivity and Costs," <http://www.bls.gov/lpc/home.htm>, accessed September 2013.

Table 669. Average Hours Worked Per Day by Employed Persons: 2012

[150,877 represents 150,877,000. Civilian noninstitutionalized population 15 years old and over, except as indicated. Includes work at main and any other job(s). Excludes travel related to work. Based on the American Time Use Survey. Diary day is day prior to interview. See source for details]

Characteristic	Total employed (1,000)	Employed persons who worked on their diary day [1]								
		Number (1,000)	Percent of employed	Hours of work	Worked at workplace			Worked at home [2]		
					Number (1,000)	Percent of employed [3]	Hours of work	Number (1,000)	Percent of employed [3]	Hours of work
Total......................	150,877	102,817	68.1	7.65	86,857	84.5	7.92	23,878	23.2	3.01
Work status: [4]										
Full-time workers [5].......	114,136	83,117	72.8	8.22	72,115	86.8	8.35	18,502	22.3	3.19
Part-time workers [5].......	36,741	19,701	53.6	5.24	14,742	74.8	5.81	5,376	27.3	2.38
Male [4]..........................	79,458	55,361	69.7	8.07	47,369	85.6	8.27	12,828	23.2	3.07
Full-time workers [5].......	66,470	48,759	73.4	8.46	42,695	87.6	8.56	10,828	22.2	3.12
Part-time workers [5].......	12,988	6,602	50.8	5.16	4,673	70.8	5.63	2,000	30.3	2.83
Female [4].........................	71,419	47,456	66.4	7.16	39,488	83.2	7.50	11,050	23.3	2.93
Full-time workers [5].......	47,666	34,358	72.1	7.87	29,419	85.6	8.05	7,674	22.3	3.30
Part-time workers [5].......	23,754	13,099	55.1	5.29	10,069	76.9	5.89	3,377	25.8	2.11
Jobholding status:										
Single jobholders.........	138,106	92,250	66.8	7.65	78,770	85.4	7.92	20,242	21.9	3.02
Multiple jobholders........	12,771	10,567	82.7	7.60	8,087	76.5	7.91	3,636	34.4	2.96
Educational attainment: [6]										
Less than high school....	9,879	6,563	66.4	7.76	6,141	93.6	7.90	357	5.4	3.18
High school diploma [7]....	36,749	24,589	66.9	7.97	22,285	90.6	8.04	3,118	12.7	3.56
Some college..............	33,843	22,569	66.7	7.86	19,032	84.3	8.18	4,769	21.1	3.17
Bachelor's degree or higher..................	49,670	36,252	73.0	7.57	28,069	77.4	7.98	13,914	38.4	2.87

[1] Individuals may have worked at more than one location. [2] "Working at home" includes any time persons did work at home and is not restricted to persons whose usual workplace is their home. [3] Percent of employed who worked on their diary day. [4] Includes workers whose hours vary. [5] Full-time workers usually worked 35 or more hours per week at all jobs combined; part-time workers fewer than 35 hours per week. [6] For those 25 years old and over. [7] Includes persons with a high school diploma or equivalent.

Source: U.S. Bureau of Labor Statistics, American Time Use Survey—2012 Results, News Release, USDL 13-1178, June 2013. See also <http://www.bls.gov/tus/home.htm#news>.

Table 670. Annual Total Compensation and Wages and Salary Accruals Per Full-Time Equivalent Employee by Industry: 2000 to 2012

[In dollars. Wage and salary accruals include executives' compensation, bonuses, tips, and payments-in-kind; total compensation includes in addition to wages and salaries, employer contributions for social insurance, employer contributions to private and welfare funds, director's fees, jury and witness fees, etc. Based on the 2002 North American Industry Classification System (NAICS); see text, Section 15]

Industry	Total annual compensation				Annual salary and wages			
	2000	2005	2011	2012	2000	2005	2011	2012
Compensation of employees..................	**47,619**	**56,775**	**68,241**	**69,709**	**39,238**	**45,602**	**54,724**	**56,071**
Domestic industries....................................	47,520	56,555	67,845	69,247	39,166	45,441	54,420	55,712
Private industries....................................	46,136	53,933	64,287	65,917	38,862	44,629	53,487	54,996
Agriculture, forestry, fishing, and hunting........	25,875	33,431	37,212	37,690	22,146	27,709	30,608	30,695
Mining...	70,434	85,696	112,450	115,896	58,134	73,208	97,309	98,757
Utilities...	84,821	103,526	131,958	130,572	64,772	77,380	93,529	96,810
Construction...	46,190	52,695	64,735	66,708	38,551	43,731	53,763	55,441
Manufacturing.......................................	54,167	64,197	77,686	79,386	43,957	50,908	61,740	63,057
Wholesale trade....................................	59,068	67,570	81,707	83,788	50,896	57,860	69,977	71,997
Retail trade...	31,224	35,459	39,365	39,813	26,589	29,168	32,622	33,223
Transportation and warehousing..............	48,462	55,206	64,375	65,406	39,055	43,810	51,275	52,183
Information...	72,135	84,429	103,068	107,977	62,571	69,124	84,949	89,478
Finance and insurance...........................	76,234	91,847	109,085	111,667	64,574	77,102	91,951	94,873
Real estate and rental and leasing..............	43,235	50,597	59,227	62,452	37,150	43,513	51,152	53,672
Professional, scientific, and technical services..	71,592	81,372	99,148	103,189	62,472	69,640	85,399	89,453
Management of companies and enterprises [1]...	90,766	106,186	131,486	138,677	74,253	88,008	110,373	117,369
Administrative and waste management services..	28,921	36,937	45,396	46,664	25,035	31,331	38,022	39,322
Educational services..............................	34,164	41,492	51,360	52,964	29,244	34,608	42,387	42,972
Health care and social assistance.............	42,009	51,858	60,730	61,813	35,249	42,294	49,964	50,913
Arts, entertainment, and recreation.............	37,384	42,791	51,439	52,837	32,482	36,728	44,021	45,180
Accommodation and food services.............	20,819	24,904	28,650	29,481	18,045	21,044	24,687	25,211
Other services, except government.............	30,412	35,778	42,962	43,842	25,990	30,444	37,059	37,671
Government..	55,070	70,443	85,799	86,493	40,824	49,742	59,125	59,423
Federal...	61,449	87,003	108,416	108,867	46,749	63,261	76,421	76,316
State and local......................................	53,288	66,068	79,611	80,427	39,169	46,171	54,392	54,843

[1] Consists of offices of bank and other holding companies and of corporate, subsidiary, and regional managing offices.

Source: U.S. Bureau of Economic Analysis, National Income and Product Accounts Tables, "Table 6.2D. Compensation of Employees by Industry"; "Table 6.5D. Full-Time Equivalent Employees by Industry"; and "Table 6.6D. Wage and Salary Accruals Per Full-Time Equivalent Employee by Industry"; <http://www.bea.gov/itable/>, accessed August 2013.

Table 671. Average Hours Spent Per Day on Primary Activities by Married Mothers and Fathers by Employment Status: 2007 to 2011

[Data are shown for households with own children under 18. Primary activity refers to an individual's main activity. Other activities done simultaneously are not included]

Activity	Both spouses work full time		Mother employed part time and father employed full time		Mother not employed and father employed full time	
	Mothers	Fathers	Mothers	Fathers	Mothers	Fathers
Total, all activities..	24.00	24.00	24.00	24.00	24.00	24.00
Personal care activities...............................	8.96	8.59	9.15	8.52	9.43	8.74
Sleeping...	8.12	7.98	8.41	7.96	8.80	8.15
Household activities....................................	1.95	1.34	2.62	1.21	3.51	1.07
Housework...	0.82	0.26	1.13	0.21	1.57	0.20
Food preparation and cleanup....................	0.79	0.37	1.00	0.30	1.45	0.28
Lawn and garden care..............................	0.07	0.23	0.11	0.24	0.14	0.18
Purchasing goods and services....................	0.55	0.34	0.63	0.34	0.72	0.37
Grocery shopping....................................	0.13	0.06	0.15	0.06	0.19	0.08
Consumer goods purchases, except grocery shopping........	0.34	0.22	0.38	0.22	0.42	0.23
Caring for and helping household members....................	1.29	0.88	1.92	0.93	2.62	0.84
Caring for and helping household children....................	1.28	0.86	1.89	0.91	2.60	0.82
Physical care.......................................	0.57	0.28	0.76	0.33	1.03	0.25
Education-related activities........................	0.11	0.09	0.17	0.05	0.26	0.04
Reading to/with children...........................	0.05	0.03	0.07	0.03	0.09	0.03
Playing/doing hobbies with children.............	0.22	0.24	0.38	0.30	0.63	0.33
Working and work-related activities [1]...................	5.27	6.07	2.78	6.07	0.08	6.20
Working [1]...	5.24	6.03	2.72	6.02	0.02	6.15
Leisure and sports......................................	2.91	3.68	3.45	3.62	4.09	3.55
Socializing and communicating....................	0.60	0.54	0.78	0.58	0.87	0.55
Watching television..................................	1.53	2.15	1.65	1.89	2.13	2.06
Participating in sports, exercise, and recreation................	0.18	0.32	0.24	0.35	0.24	0.27
Travel..	1.35	1.41	1.37	1.48	1.15	1.40
Travel related to caring for/helping household children........	0.23	0.16	0.28	0.12	0.30	0.09
Other activities, not elsewhere classified.........................	1.73	1.70	2.08	1.83	2.40	1.82

[1] Estimates include a small amount of work time done by persons who do not meet the American Time Use Survey definition of employed.

Source: Bureau of Labor Statistics, "American Time Use Survey," <http://www.bls.gov/tus/#tables>, accessed June 2013.

Table 672. Average Hourly and Weekly Earnings by Private Industry Group: 1990 to 2012

[In dollars. Average earnings include overtime. Data are for production employees in mining and logging, manufacturing, and construction, and nonsupervisory employees in the service providing industries. See headnote, Table 658]

Private industry group	Current dollars					Constant (1982–84) dollars [1]				
	1990	2000	2010	2011	2012	1990	2000	2010	2011	2012
AVERAGE HOURLY EARNINGS										
Total private	**10.20**	**14.02**	**19.07**	**19.46**	**19.77**	**7.91**	**8.30**	**8.91**	**8.78**	**8.74**
Mining and logging	13.40	16.55	23.82	24.50	25.79	10.39	9.80	11.13	11.06	11.40
Construction	13.42	17.48	23.22	23.65	23.98	10.40	10.35	10.85	10.67	10.60
Manufacturing	10.78	14.32	18.61	18.93	19.08	8.36	8.48	8.70	8.54	8.43
Trade, transportation, and utilities [2]	9.83	13.31	16.82	17.15	17.42	7.62	7.88	7.86	7.74	7.70
Information	13.40	19.07	25.87	26.62	27.01	10.39	11.29	12.09	12.01	11.94
Financial activities [2]	9.98	15.04	21.55	21.93	22.83	7.74	8.90	10.07	9.90	10.09
Professional and business services [2]	11.14	15.52	22.78	23.12	23.28	8.64	9.19	10.65	10.43	10.29
Education and health services [2]	10.00	13.95	20.12	20.77	21.09	7.75	8.26	9.40	9.37	9.32
Leisure and hospitality [2]	6.02	8.32	11.31	11.45	11.62	4.67	4.93	5.29	5.17	5.14
Other services	9.08	12.73	17.06	17.32	17.59	7.04	7.54	7.97	7.82	7.78
AVERAGE WEEKLY EARNINGS										
Total private	**350**	**481**	**637**	**655**	**667**	**271**	**285**	**298**	**295**	**295**
Mining and logging	602	735	1,063	1,145	1,202	467	435	497	517	531
Construction	513	686	892	922	943	398	406	417	416	417
Manufacturing	436	591	765	784	795	338	350	358	354	351
Trade, transportation, and utilities	332	450	560	578	589	257	266	262	261	260
Information	480	701	940	965	971	372	415	439	435	429
Financial activities [2]	355	540	780	799	841	275	320	365	360	372
Professional and business services [2]	381	535	799	813	822	295	317	373	367	363
Education and health services [2]	319	449	647	670	683	248	266	302	302	302
Leisure and hospitality [2]	156	217	281	284	290	121	129	131	128	128
Other services	298	413	524	533	539	231	245	245	240	238

[1] Earnings in current dollars divided by the Consumer Price Index (CPI-W) on a 1982–84 base; see text, Section 14. [2] For composition of industries, see Table 653.

Source: Bureau of Labor Statistics, Current Employment Statistics, "Employment, Hours, and Earnings - National," <http://www.bls.gov/ces/data.htm>, accessed September 2013.

Table 673. Mean Hourly Earnings and Weekly Hours by Selected Characteristics: 2010

[Based on the National Compensation Survey (NCS). Covers civilian workers in private industry establishments and state and local governments in the 50 states and D.C. Excludes private households, federal government and agriculture. The NCS obtained data from 35,408 establishments representing over 121 million workers. See source and Appendix III]

Item	Mean hourly earnings (dollars) [1]			Mean weekly hours [2]		
	Total	Private industry	State and local government	Total	Private industry	State and local government
Total	**21.29**	**20.47**	**26.08**	**35.1**	**34.9**	**36.2**
WORKER CHARACTERISTIC						
Management, professional and related	34.49	34.99	33.02	36.7	37.0	35.9
Management, business, and financial	38.81	39.42	35.32	39.3	39.7	37.4
Professional and related	32.55	32.57	32.50	35.6	35.7	35.6
Service	12.14	10.62	19.32	30.7	29.7	36.4
Sales and office	16.44	16.35	17.39	34.7	34.5	36.4
Sales and related	17.11	17.11	16.65	32.3	32.3	33.9
Office and administrative support	16.09	15.90	17.42	36.1	36.0	36.5
Natural resources, construction, and maintenance	21.21	21.24	20.97	39.0	39.0	38.8
Construction and extraction	21.18	21.31	20.13	39.0	39.0	38.7
Installation, maintenance, and repair	21.40	21.34	21.98	39.2	39.2	39.2
Production, transportation, and material moving	16.00	15.88	19.52	37.1	37.2	34.4
Production	16.26	16.18	21.69	38.9	38.8	39.5
Transportation and material moving	15.73	15.55	18.86	35.4	35.6	33.1
Full-time [3]	22.77	22.02	26.75	39.5	39.6	38.9
Part-time [3]	12.10	11.78	16.39	20.7	21.0	18.3
Union [4]	26.04	23.13	29.72	36.6	36.3	37.0
Nonunion	20.46	20.19	23.12	34.8	34.8	35.6
Time [5]	21.06	20.16	26.07	34.9	34.7	36.2
Incentive [5]	26.04	26.03	(S)	38.4	38.4	(S)
ESTABLISHMENT CHARACTERISTIC						
Goods producing [6]	(S)	22.04	(S)	(NA)	39.4	(NA)
Service providing [6]	(S)	20.09	(S)	(NA)	34.0	(NA)
1 to 49 workers	17.86	17.80	19.61	33.5	33.6	33.0
50 to 99 workers	19.24	19.10	21.40	34.3	34.2	35.8
100 to 499 workers	20.88	20.42	24.31	35.9	35.8	36.0
500 workers or more	27.02	26.65	27.68	36.9	37.0	36.7

NA Not available. S Figure does not meet publication standards. [1] Earnings are straight time hourly wages or salary, including incentive pay, cost-of-living adjustments, and hazard pay. Excludes premium pay for overtime, vacations and holidays, nonproduction bonuses and tips. [2] Mean weekly hours are the hours an employee is scheduled to work in a week exclusive of overtime [3] Based on definition used by each establishment. [4] Workers whose wages are determined through collective bargaining. [5] Time worker wages are based solely on an hourly rate or salary. Incentive workers wages are based at least in part on productivity payments such as piece rates or commissions. [6] For private industry only. See footnotes 3 and 4, Table 660, for composition of goods and service producing industries.

Source: U.S. Bureau of Labor Statistics, *National Compensation Survey: Occupational Earnings in the United States, 2010*, Bulletin 2753, May 2011. See also <http://www.bls.gov/ncs/ncswage2010.htm>.

Table 674. Employment and Wages: 2000 to 2011

[(7,879 represents 7,879,000). See headnote, Table 675]

Employment and wages	Unit	2000	2006	2007	2008	2009	2010	2011
Establishments:								
Total	**1,000**	**7,879**	**8,784**	**8,972**	**9,082**	**9,003**	**8,993**	**9,073**
Excluding federal	1,000	7,829	8,731	8,908	9,018	8,938	8,926	9,006
Private	1,000	7,622	8,505	8,681	8,789	8,709	8,696	8,776
State government	1,000	65	67	67	68	67	67	66
Local governments	1,000	141	159	160	161	161	164	164
Federal government	1,000	50	53	64	64	66	67	67
Average annual employment:								
Total	**1,000**	**129,877**	**133,834**	**135,366**	**134,806**	**128,608**	**127,820**	**129,411**
Excluding federal	1,000	127,006	131,105	132,640	132,044	125,781	124,840	126,548
Private	1,000	110,015	112,719	114,012	113,189	106,947	106,201	108,185
State government	1,000	4,370	4,566	4,611	4,643	4,640	4,606	4,554
Local governments	1,000	12,620	13,820	14,016	14,212	14,194	14,032	13,809
Federal government	1,000	2,871	2,729	2,726	2,762	2,827	2,981	2,863
Annual wages:								
Total	**Bil. dol.**	**4,588**	**5,693**	**6,018**	**6,142**	**5,859**	**5,976**	**6,217**
Excluding federal	Bil. dol.	4,455	5,523	5,841	5,959	5,668	5,769	6,008
Private	Bil. dol.	3,888	4,781	5,058	5,135	4,829	4,934	5,173
State government	Bil. dol.	159	200	212	223	226	226	229
Local governments	Bil. dol.	409	541	572	601	612	610	607
Federal government	Bil. dol.	133	170	177	183	192	206	209
Average annual wage per employee:								
Total	**Dol.**	**35,323**	**42,535**	**44,458**	**45,563**	**45,559**	**46,751**	**48,043**
Excluding federal	Dol.	35,077	42,124	44,038	45,129	45,060	46,215	47,478
Private	Dol.	35,337	42,414	44,362	45,371	45,155	46,455	47,815
State government	Dol.	36,296	43,875	45,903	47,980	48,742	48,960	50,252
Local governments	Dol.	32,387	39,179	40,790	42,274	43,140	43,493	43,926
Federal government	Dol.	46,228	62,274	64,871	66,293	67,756	69,198	73,001
Average weekly wage per employee:								
Total	**Dol.**	**679**	**818**	**855**	**876**	**876**	**899**	**924**
Excluding federal	Dol.	675	810	847	868	867	889	913
Private	Dol.	680	816	853	873	868	893	920
State government	Dol.	698	844	883	923	937	942	966
Local governments	Dol.	623	753	784	813	830	836	845
Federal government	Dol.	889	1,198	1,248	1,275	1,303	1,331	1,404

Source: Bureau of Labor Statistics, Quarterly Census of Employment and Wages, "Employment and Wages Online Annual Averages, 2011," and earlier editions, <http://www.bls.gov/cew/#publications>, accessed August 2013.

Table 675. Average Annual Wage, by State: 2010 and 2011

[In dollars, except percent change. Based on federal-state cooperative program, The Quarterly Census of Employment and Wages (QCEW), also referenced as ES-202. Includes workers covered by state unemployment insurance laws and for federal civilian workers covered by unemployment compensation for federal employees, approximately 97 percent of employees on nonfarm payrolls in 2011. Excludes most agricultural workers on small farms, all Armed Forces, elected officials in most states, railroad employees, most domestic workers, most student workers at school, value of meals and lodging, and tips and other gratuities.]

State	Average wage per employee 2010	Average wage per employee 2011	Percent change, 2010–2011	State	Average wage per employee 2010	Average wage per employee 2011	Percent change, 2010–2011
United States	**46,751**	**48,043**	**2.76**	Missouri	40,679	41,461	1.92
Alabama	40,289	41,186	2.23	Montana	34,596	35,791	3.46
Alaska	48,230	49,383	2.39	Nebraska	37,324	38,269	2.53
Arizona	43,299	44,581	2.96	Nevada	42,512	43,102	1.39
Arkansas	36,254	37,280	2.83	New Hampshire	45,957	47,281	2.88
California	53,285	55,013	3.24	New Jersey	56,382	57,546	2.06
Colorado	47,868	49,082	2.54	New Mexico	39,264	40,032	1.95
Connecticut	59,465	61,145	2.83	New York	60,291	61,792	2.49
Delaware	48,669	50,499	3.76	North Carolina	41,119	42,121	2.44
District of Columbia	80,200	81,529	1.66	North Dakota	38,128	41,778	9.57
Florida	41,581	42,313	1.76	Ohio	41,788	42,972	2.83
Georgia	43,899	45,090	2.71	Oklahoma	38,237	40,108	4.89
Hawaii	41,709	42,473	1.83	Oregon	41,675	43,090	3.39
Idaho	34,900	35,626	2.08	Pennsylvania	45,733	47,035	2.85
Illinois	49,497	50,840	2.71	Rhode Island	44,645	45,705	2.37
Indiana	39,256	40,248	2.53	South Carolina	37,553	38,427	2.33
Iowa	38,146	39,204	2.77	South Dakota	34,331	35,413	3.15
Kansas	38,936	39,989	2.71	Tennessee	41,572	42,454	2.12
Kentucky	38,720	39,646	2.39	Texas	46,952	48,735	3.80
Louisiana	41,461	42,375	2.20	Utah	39,389	40,279	2.26
Maine	37,338	38,020	1.83	Vermont	39,434	40,293	2.18
Maryland	51,739	53,008	2.45	Virginia	49,651	50,657	2.03
Massachusetts	57,770	59,671	3.29	Washington	48,516	50,256	3.59
Michigan	44,439	45,828	3.12	West Virginia	37,675	39,092	3.76
Minnesota	46,787	47,858	2.29	Wisconsin	39,966	41,003	2.60
Mississippi	34,343	34,976	1.84	Wyoming	41,963	43,394	3.41

Source: Bureau of Labor Statistics, Quarterly Census of Employment and Wages, "Employment and Wages Online Annual Averages, 2011," and earlier editions, <http://www.bls.gov/cew/#publications>, accessed August 2013.

Table 676. Full-Time Wage and Salary Workers—Number and Earnings: 2000 to 2012

[In current dollars of usual weekly earnings. Data represent annual averages (101,210 represents 101,210,000). Full time workers are those who usually worked 35 hours or more at all jobs combined. Based on the Current Population Survey; see text, Section 1 and Appendix III. For definition of median, see Guide to Tabular Presentation]

Characteristic	Number of workers (1,000)			Median weekly earnings (dollars)		
	2000	2005	2012	2000	2005	2012
All workers [1]	**101,210**	**103,560**	**102,749**	**576**	**651**	**768**
Male	57,107	58,406	57,286	641	722	854
Female	44,103	45,154	45,462	493	585	691
White [2]	83,228	84,110	81,779	590	672	792
Black [2]	12,410	12,388	12,230	474	520	621
Asian [3]	4,598	4,651	5,790	615	753	920
Hispanic [4]	12,761	14,673	16,302	399	471	568
OCCUPATION						
Management, professional and related occupations	34,831	36,908	40,984	810	937	1,108
Management, business, and financial operations	14,240	14,977	16,991	877	997	1,171
Professional and related occupations	20,590	21,931	23,993	770	902	1,053
Computer and mathematical occupations	3,051	2,924	3,416	938	1,132	1,349
Architecture and engineering occupations	2,781	2,509	2,588	949	1,105	1,337
Life, physical, and social science occupations	989	1,164	1,098	811	965	1,134
Community and social services occupations	1,641	1,797	1,891	629	725	838
Legal occupations	1,039	1,162	1,315	919	1,052	1,328
Education, training, and library occupations	5,467	6,066	6,454	704	798	915
Arts, design, entertainment, sports, and media	1,488	1,488	1,440	724	819	969
Healthcare practitioner and technical occupations	4,134	4,821	5,791	727	878	1,028
Service occupations	12,595	14,123	14,839	365	413	485
Healthcare support occupations	1,731	2,085	2,350	358	410	482
Protective service occupations	2,281	2,549	2,655	591	678	791
Food preparation and serving-related occupations	3,483	4,007	4,164	317	356	410
Building and grounds cleaning and maintenance	3,354	3,425	3,430	351	394	465
Personal care and service occupations	1,746	2,057	2,241	351	409	468
Sales and office occupations	25,606	25,193	23,115	492	575	655
Sales and related occupations	9,650	10,031	9,433	525	622	689
Office and administrative support occupations	15,956	15,161	13,683	480	550	643
Natural resources, construction, and maintenance occupations	10,958	12,086	9,968	582	623	740
Farming, fishing, and forestry occupations	842	755	777	310	372	435
Construction and extraction occupations	5,852	6,826	5,102	580	604	740
Installation, maintenance, and repair occupations	4,263	4,504	4,088	628	705	808
Production, transportation, and material-moving occupations	17,221	15,251	13,842	475	540	624
Production occupations	10,378	8,403	7,427	471	538	627
Transportation and material-moving occupations	6,843	6,848	6,415	481	543	621

[1] Includes other races, not shown separately. [2] Beginning 2005, for persons in this race group only. See footnote 4, Table 614. [3] 2000 data includes Pacific Islanders. [4] Persons of Hispanic origin may be of any race.

Source: Bureau of Labor Statistics, "Median weekly earnings of full-time wage and salary workers by selected characteristics" and "Median weekly earnings of full-time wage and salary workers by detailed occupation and sex," February 2013, <http://www.bls.gov/cps/home.htm>.

Table 677. Median Usual Weekly Earnings of Full-Time Wage and Salary Workers by Sex and Education: 1980 to 2012

[In current dollars, except as indicated. For wage and salary workers 25 years and over. Based on Current Population Survey; see text, Section 1 and Appendix III. Wages and salaries are collected before taxes and other deductions and include overtime pay, commissions, or tips usually received at principal job. Earnings reported on basis other than weekly are converted to a weekly equivalent. Excludes all incorporated and unincorporated self employed]

Year and sex	Total	Less than a high school diploma	High school, no college [1]	Some college or associate's degree	Bachelor's degree and higher [2]
CURRENT DOLLARS					
Male:					
1980	339	267	327	358	427
1990 [3]	512	349	459	542	741
2000 [3]	693	406	591	691	1,020
2012 [3]	910	508	735	857	1,371
Female:					
1980	213	164	201	231	290
1990 [3]	369	240	315	395	535
2000 [3]	516	304	420	505	756
2012 [3]	727	386	561	659	1,001
WOMEN'S EARNINGS AS PERCENT OF MEN'S					
1980	62.8	61.4	61.5	64.5	67.9
1990 [3]	72.1	68.8	68.6	72.9	72.2
2000 [3]	74.5	74.9	71.1	73.1	74.1
2012 [3]	79.9	76.0	76.3	76.9	73.0

[1] Includes persons with a high school diploma or equivalent. [2] Includes persons with a bachelor's, master's, professional, or doctoral degree. [3] Data not strictly comparable to data for earlier years. See text this section and <http://www.bls.gov/cps/eetech_methods.pdf>.

Source: U.S. Bureau of Labor Statistics, Current Population Survey, "Labor Force Statistics," <http://www.bls.gov/cps/data.htm>, accessed January 2013.

Table 678. Workers With Earnings by Occupation of Longest Held Job and Sex: 2011

[As of March. 73,094 represents 73,094,000. For definition of median, see Guide to Tabular Presentation. Beginning with 2009 income data, the Census Bureau expanded the income intervals used to calculate medians to $250,000 or more. Medians falling in the upper open-ended interval are plugged with "$250,000." Before 2009, the upper open-ended interval was $100,000 and a plug of "$100,000" was used. Based on Annual Social and Economic Supplement (ASEC) of Current Population Survey; includes civilian noninstitutional population, 15 years old and over, and military personnel who live in households with at least one other civilian adult. See text, Section 1, and Appendix III]

Major occupation group of longest job held in 2011	All workers				Full-time, year-round			
	Female		Male		Female		Male	
	Number (1,000)	Median earnings (dol.)	Number (1,000)	Median earnings (dol.)	Number (1,000)	Median earnings (dol.)	Number (1,000)	Median earnings (dol.)
Total...........................	73,094	26,550	81,366	37,341	43,683	37,118	57,993	48,202
Management, business, and financial occupations....................	10,041	47,374	12,959	67,152	7,872	51,959	10,997	75,147
Professional and related occupations.........................	18,994	40,865	13,692	60,898	12,225	50,194	10,679	70,157
Service occupations....................	16,212	15,442	12,338	21,040	7,332	23,367	7,246	30,955
Sales and office occupations..............	22,847	23,795	13,707	32,104	13,331	33,254	9,481	42,366
Natural resources, construction, and maintenance.....................	659	19,019	13,531	31,896	321	30,182	8,950	40,480
Production, transportation, and material-moving occupations..............	4,252	20,441	14,382	31,448	2,530	25,851	9,962	39,266
Armed Forces.............................	89	45,393	757	45,439	72	(B)	677	46,818

(B) Base less than 75,000

Source: U.S. Census Bureau, *Income, Poverty and Health Insurance in the United States: 2011*, Current Population Reports, P60-243: and "Detailed Tables—Table PINC-06," <http://www.census.gov/hhes/www/income/data/index.html>, accessed May 2013.

Table 679. Employment Cost Index (ECI) by Total Compensation and Occupation and Industry: 2009 to 2012

[As of December (2005 = 100). The ECI is a measure of the rate of change in compensation (wages, salaries, and employer costs for employee benefits). Data are not seasonally adjusted. Based on North American Industry Classification System (NAICS) for classifying by industry. Based on the 2000 Standard Occupational Classification (SOC) for classifying by occupation]

Occupational group and industry	Indexes (December 2005 = 100)				Percent change for 12 months ending December			
	2009	2010	2011	2012	2009	2010	2011	2012
Civilian workers [1]........................	**111.0**	**113.2**	**115.5**	**117.7**	**1.4**	**2.0**	**2.0**	**1.9**
State and local government........................	**114.2**	**116.2**	**117.7**	**119.9**	**2.3**	**1.8**	**1.3**	**1.9**
Workers, by occupational group:								
Management, professional and related occupations...	113.8	115.5	116.9	119.2	2.0	1.5	1.2	2.0
Sales and office occupations....................	114.4	116.6	118.4	120.9	2.8	1.9	1.5	2.1
Service occupations.........................	115.3	118.0	119.5	121.7	2.6	2.3	1.3	1.8
Workers, by industry division:								
Service-providing industries: [2]								
Education and health services.....................	113.9	115.6	117.0	119.1	2.2	1.5	1.2	1.8
Schools............................	113.7	115.3	116.5	118.7	2.2	1.4	1.0	1.9
Health care and social assistance....................	115.4	117.9	120.1	122.2	1.9	2.2	1.9	1.7
Hospitals...........................	114.3	117.0	119.2	121.2	2.7	2.4	1.9	1.7
Public administration [3]........................	114.6	116.8	118.2	120.7	2.3	1.9	1.2	2.1
Private industry workers [4]........................	**110.2**	**112.5**	**115.0**	**117.1**	**1.2**	**2.1**	**2.2**	**1.8**
Workers, by occupational group:								
Management, professional, and related occupations...	110.7	113.0	115.4	117.7	0.7	2.1	2.1	2.0
Sales and office occupations.....................	109.2	111.6	114.2	116.3	1.2	2.2	2.3	1.8
Natural resources, construction, and maintenance occupations.....................	111.2	113.3	115.8	117.8	1.5	1.9	2.2	1.7
Production, transportation, and material moving occupations.....................	108.9	111.5	114.2	116.0	1.9	2.4	2.4	1.6
Service occupations.....................	111.8	113.5	115.4	117.4	1.8	1.5	1.7	1.7
Workers, by industry division:								
Goods-producing industries [5].....................	108.6	111.1	113.8	115.6	1.0	2.3	2.4	1.6
Construction.....................	111.7	112.7	114.5	116.3	0.7	0.9	1.6	1.6
Manufacturing.....................	107.0	110.0	113.1	114.9	1.0	2.8	2.8	1.6
Service-providing industries [2].....................	110.8	113.0	115.3	117.6	1.3	2.0	2.0	2.0
Trade, transportation, and utilities.....................	108.8	111.4	114.1	116.4	1.2	2.4	2.4	2.0
Information.....................	108.3	110.0	112.5	116.9	0.8	1.6	2.3	3.9
Financial activities.....................	108.6	111.4	114.2	115.9	1.4	2.6	2.5	1.5
Professional and business services....................	112.4	114.6	117.1	119.3	0.7	2.0	2.2	1.9
Education and health services.....................	112.8	114.7	116.5	118.9	2.0	1.7	1.6	2.1
Leisure and hospitality.....................	112.7	114.1	115.2	116.5	1.2	1.2	1.0	1.1
Bargaining status:								
Union.....................	111.1	114.8	117.9	120.5	2.9	3.3	2.7	2.2
Nonunion.....................	110.1	112.1	114.5	116.6	0.9	1.8	2.1	1.8

[1] Includes private industry and state and local government workers and excludes farm, household, and federal government workers. [2] Includes all other service industries not shown separately. For a description of NAICS industries, see text, this section. [3] Consists of executive, legislative, judicial, administrative, and regulatory activities. [4] Excludes farm and household workers. [5] Includes the following NAICS industries: construction and manufacturing.

Source: Bureau of Labor Statistics, Employment Cost Trends, "Employment Cost Index," <http://www.bls.gov/ncs/ect/home.htm#data>, accessed September 2013.

Table 680. Federal and State Minimum Wage Rates: 1940 to 2013

[In current dollars. Where an employee is subject to both the state and federal minimum wage laws, the employee is entitled to the higher minimum wage rate]

Year	Federal minimum wage rates per hour	State	2013 minimum wage rates per hour	State	2013 minimum wage rates per hour	State	2013 minimum wage rates per hour
1940	0.30	AL	(1)	KY	7.25	ND	7.25
1945	0.40	AK	7.75	LA	(1)	OH	7.85 [8]
1950	0.75	AZ	7.80	ME	7.50	OK	7.25/2.00 [9]
1955	0.75	AR	6.25 [2]	MD	7.25	OR	8.95
1960	1.00	CA	8.00	MA	8.00	PA	7.25
1965	1.25	CO	7.78	MI	7.40 [4]	RI	7.75
1970	1.60	CT	8.25	MN	6.15/5.25 [5]	SC	(1)
1975	2.10	DE	7.25	MS	(1)	SD	7.25
1980	3.10	DC	8.25	MO	7.35	TN	(1)
1985	3.35	FL	7.79	MT	7.80/4.00 [6]	TX	7.25
1990	3.80	GA	5.15 [3]	NE	7.25 [2]	UT	7.25
1995	4.25	HI	7.25	NV	7.25/8.25 [7]	VT	8.60 [4]
2000	5.15	ID	7.25	NH	7.25	VA	7.25 [2]
2005	5.15	IL	8.25 [2]	NJ	7.25	WA	9.19
2008	6.55	IN	7.25 [4]	NM	7.50	WV	7.25 [3]
2009	7.25	IA	7.25	NY	7.25	WI	7.25
2013	7.25	KS	7.25	NC	7.25	WY	5.15

[1] No state minimum wage law. [2] Employers of 4 or more, Illinois excluding family members. [3] Employers of 6 or more. [4] Employers of 2 or more. [5] Large employer (receipts of $500,000 or more) and small employer (with annual receipts of less than $500,000). [6] Except businesses with gross annual sales of $110,000 or less. [7] $8.25 with no health insurance benefits provided by employer. $7.25 with health insurance provided by employer and received by employee. [8] $7.25 for those employers grossing $283,000 or less. [9] Employees of 10 or more full time employees at any one location and employers with gross sales over $100,000 regardless of number of full-time employees. All other employers $2.00.

Source: Department of Labor, Wage and Hour Division, "Minimum Wage Laws in the States—January 1, 2013," <http://www.dol.gov/esa/minwage/america.htm>, accessed September 2013.

Table 681. Workers Paid Hourly Rates by Selected Characteristics: 2012

[Data are annual averages (75,276 represents 75,276,000). For employed wage and salary workers, excluding the incorporated self-employed. Based on the Current Population Survey; see text, Section 1 and Appendix III]

Characteristic	Number of workers paid hourly rates (1,000)			Percent of workers paid hourly rates		
		At or below federal minimum wage			At or below federal minimum wage	
	Total	Total	Below prevailing federal minimum wage	At prevailing federal minimum wage	Total	Below prevailing federal minimum wage	At prevailing federal minimum wage
Total, 16 years and over [1]	75,276	3,550	1,566	1,984	4.7	2.1	2.6
16 to 24 years	14,909	1,797	862	935	12.1	5.8	6.3
25 years and over	60,367	1,753	704	1,049	2.9	1.2	1.7
Male, 16 years old and over	37,113	1,263	567	696	3.4	1.5	1.9
16 to 24 years	7,454	673	333	340	9.0	4.5	4.6
25 years and over	29,659	591	235	356	2.0	0.8	1.2
Female, 16 years old and over	38,163	2,287	999	1,288	6.0	2.6	3.4
16 to 24 years	7,455	1,124	529	595	15.1	7.1	8.0
25 years and over	30,708	1,163	470	693	3.8	1.5	2.3
White [2]	59,180	2,760	1,185	1,575	4.7	2.0	2.7
Men	29,691	984	444	540	3.3	1.5	1.8
Women	29,490	1,776	741	1035	6.0	2.5	3.5
Black [2]	10,049	533	277	256	5.3	2.8	2.5
Men	4,522	183	85	98	4.0	1.9	2.2
Women	5,527	350	193	157	6.3	3.5	2.8
Asian [2]	3,403	117	48	69	3.4	1.4	2.0
Men	1,568	39	16	23	2.5	1.0	1.5
Women	1,835	78	32	46	4.3	1.7	2.5
Hispanic [3]	14,404	718	337	381	5.0	2.3	2.6
Men	8,114	295	127	168	3.6	1.6	2.1
Women	6,290	423	210	213	6.7	3.3	3.4
Full-time workers	54,745	1,261	501	760	2.3	0.9	1.4
Men	30,052	491	197	294	1.6	0.7	1.0
Women	24,693	770	304	466	3.1	1.2	1.9
Part-time workers [4]	20,411	2,286	1,063	1,223	11.2	5.2	6.0
Men	6,998	772	370	402	11.0	5.3	5.7
Women	13,413	1,513	693	820	11.3	5.2	6.1
Private sector industries	65,927	3,377	1,484	1,893	5.1	2.3	2.9
Public sector industries	9,349	173	82	91	1.9	0.9	1.0

[1] Includes races not shown separately. Also includes a small number of multiple jobholders whose full- or part-time status cannot be determined for their principal job. [2] For persons in this race group only. See footnote 4, Table 614. [3] Persons of Hispanic or Latino origin may be of any race. [4] Working fewer than 35 hours per week.

Source: Bureau of Labor Statistics, Labor Force Statistics from the Current Population Survey, "Characteristics of Minimum Wage Workers: 2012," <http://www.bls.gov/cps/minwage2012.htm>, accessed September 2013.

Table 682. Employer Costs for Employee Compensation Per Hour Worked: 2012

[In dollars. As of December. Based on the National Compensation Survey (NCS). See Appendix III]

Compensation component	Total civilian workers	State and local government workers	Private Industry workers						
			Total	Goods producing [1]	Service providing [2]	Union workers	Non-union workers	1–99 workers	100 workers or more
Total compensation	**30.84**	**41.94**	**28.89**	**34.14**	**27.83**	**39.92**	**27.80**	**23.78**	**34.85**
Wages and salaries	21.35	27.24	20.32	22.85	19.81	23.85	19.97	17.60	23.49
Total benefits	9.49	14.70	8.57	11.29	8.02	16.07	7.83	6.18	11.36
Paid leave	2.15	3.09	1.98	2.23	1.93	2.82	1.90	1.37	2.70
Vacation	1.05	1.16	1.03	1.18	1.00	1.46	0.98	0.70	1.41
Holiday	0.65	0.91	0.61	0.78	0.57	0.81	0.59	0.44	0.80
Sick	0.33	0.80	0.25	0.20	0.26	0.40	0.23	0.16	0.35
Supplemental pay	0.74	0.34	0.82	1.35	0.71	1.29	0.77	0.50	1.19
Overtime [3]	0.23	0.18	0.24	0.55	0.18	0.74	0.20	0.17	0.33
Insurance	2.76	5.02	2.36	3.22	2.19	5.51	2.05	1.60	3.25
Health insurance	2.62	4.86	2.23	3.03	2.06	5.19	1.94	1.52	3.05
Retirement and savings	1.44	3.71	1.04	1.51	0.94	3.11	0.83	0.58	1.57
Defined benefit	0.88	3.37	0.44	0.79	0.37	2.32	0.26	0.21	0.71
Defined contributions	0.56	0.34	0.60	0.72	0.57	0.79	0.58	0.37	0.86
Legally required	2.40	2.54	2.37	2.98	2.25	3.34	2.28	2.13	2.66
Social Security and Medicare	1.73	1.91	1.69	1.94	1.65	2.08	1.66	1.45	1.98
Social Security [4]	1.38	1.48	1.36	1.56	1.32	1.68	1.33	1.17	1.58
Medicare	0.35	0.44	0.33	0.38	0.33	0.40	0.33	0.28	0.39
Federal unemployment	0.03	([5])	0.03	0.03	0.03	0.03	0.03	0.04	0.03
State unemployment	0.22	0.12	0.23	0.31	0.22	0.32	0.22	0.23	0.24
Workers' compensation	0.43	0.51	0.41	0.71	0.35	0.90	0.36	0.40	0.42

[1] Based on the North American Industry Classification System, 2002 (NAICS). See text, this section. Includes mining, construction, and manufacturing. The agriculture, forestry, farming, and hunting sector is excluded. [2] Based on the 2002 NAICS. Includes utilities; wholesale and retail trade; transportation and warehousing; information; finance and insurance; real estate and rental and leasing; professional and technical services; management of companies and enterprises, administrative and waste services; education services; health care and social assistance; arts, entertainment, and recreation; accommodations and food services; and other services, except public administration. [3] Includes premium pay for work in addition to regular work schedule, such as, overtime, weekends, and holidays. [4] Comprises the Old-Age, Survivors, and Disability Insurance Program (OASDI). [5] Cost per hour worked is $0.01 or less.

Source: U.S. Bureau of Labor Statistics, *Employer Costs for Employee Compensation—December 2012*, News Release, USDL-13-0421, March 2013. See also <http://www.bls.gov/ncs/ect/home.htm>.

Table 683. Percent of Workers in Private Industry With Access to Retirement and Health Care Benefits by Selected Characteristics: 2012

[In percent (All workers = 100 percent). As of March. Based on National Compensation Survey (NCS). See headnote, Table 684, and Appendix III]

Characteristic	Retirement benefits			Healthcare benefits			
	All plans [1]	Defined benefit [2]	Defined contribution [2]	Medical care	Dental care	Vision care	Outpatient prescription drug coverage
Total	**65**	**19**	**59**	**70**	**45**	**25**	**69**
WORKER CHARACTERISTICS							
Management, professional, and related occupations	79	26	76	87	63	35	86
Service occupations	40	7	37	41	24	14	40
Sales and office occupations	69	18	64	72	45	21	71
Natural resources, construction, and maintenance occupations	65	23	58	77	45	30	75
Production, transportation, and material moving occupations	66	23	56	75	47	26	74
Full-time [3]	74	22	69	86	56	30	85
Part-time [3]	38	9	33	24	13	8	23
Union [4]	92	69	57	94	73	56	93
Nonunion [4]	62	14	60	67	42	21	66
AVERAGE HOURLY WAGE [5]							
Less than $8.25	38	6	35	34	16	9	34
$8.25 to under $10.69	29	4	26	19	8	5	18
$10.69 to under $15.87	65	14	61	74	44	21	73
$15.87 to under $24.81	75	23	67	86	56	30	84
$24.81 to under $37.89	85	35	79	92	69	40	91
$37.89 or greater	86	36	82	93	73	42	92
ESTABLISHMENT CHARACTERISTICS							
1 to 99 workers	50	8	47	57	30	16	56
100 or more workers	82	31	74	85	63	35	84
Goods producing [6]	74	27	69	86	55	32	84
Service producing [6]	63	17	57	67	43	23	66

[1] Employees may have access to both defined benefit and defined contribution plans. Total excludes duplication. [2] A defined benefit plan is a retirement plan that uses a specific, predetermined formula to calculate the amount of an employee's guaranteed future benefit. A defined contribution plan is a type of retirement plan in which the employer makes specified contributions to individual employee accounts, but the amount of the retirement benefit is not specified. [3] Employees are classified as working either a full-time or part-time schedule based on the definition used by each establishment. [4] See footnote 6, Table 684. [5] The National Compensation Survey—Benefits program presents wage data in percentiles rather than dollar amounts; for calculation detail, see "Technical Note" in source. [6] See Table 660 for composition of goods- and service-producing industries.

Source: Bureau of Labor Statistics, *Employee Benefits in the United States, March 2012*, Bulletin 2773, September 2012. See also <http://www.bls.gov/ncs/ebs/home.htm>.

Table 684. Percent of Workers In Private Industry With Access to Selected Employee Benefits: 2012

[As of March. Based on National Compensation Survey (NCS). The NCS benefits survey obtained data from 6,618 private industry establishments of all sizes, representing over 100 million workers. Excludes agricultural establishments, private households, and the self-employed. An employee has access to a benefit plan if the plan is made available by the employer, regardless of whether the employee participates in the plan. See Appendix III]

Characteristic	Leave benefits						Quality of life benefits			Nonproduction bonuses	
	Paid holidays	Paid sick leave	Paid vacation	Paid jury duty leave	Family leave [1] Paid	Family leave [1] Unpaid	Employer assistance for child care [2]	Flexible workplace [3]	Subsidized commuting [4]	All non-production bonuses [5]	End of year bonus
Total	**77**	**61**	**77**	**63**	**11**	**85**	**9**	**6**	**6**	**42**	**10**
WORKER CHARACTERISTIC											
Management, professional, and related occupations	89	84	87	82	18	90	18	14	11	51	13
Service occupations	53	40	56	40	6	79	8	1	3	27	6
Sales and office occupations	81	65	—	66	12	88	8	6	6	44	12
Natural resources, construction, and maintenance occupations	82	53	82	54	8	81	4	2	3	41	11
Production, transportation, and material moving occupations	84	52	83	63	6	85	4	2	2	41	9
Full-time [6]	90	75	91	73	13	88	11	7	7	48	12
Part-time [6]	40	23	35	32	4	76	6	1	2	24	5
Union [7]	91	73	91	84	10	91	13	2	5	37	6
Nonunion [7]	76	60	75	61	11	85	9	6	6	42	11
AVERAGE HOURLY WAGE [8]											
Less than $8.25	50	29	49	34	4	77	4	1	1	26	5
$8.25 to under $10.69	33	18	37	24	3	74	5	(S)	1	22	6
$10.69 to under $15.87	84	64	83	65	9	86	7	3	4	41	9
$15.87 to under $24.81	90	75	90	74	13	88	10	6	7	47	13
$24.81 to under $37.89	91	84	90	83	19	91	17	14	11	55	14
$37.89 or greater	90	86	90	85	20	91	19	18	14	58	15
ESTABLISHMENT CHARACTERISTICS											
Goods producing [9]	90	56	90	67	9	87	7	5	2	50	13
Service producing [9]	75	62	74	62	11	85	10	6	6	40	10
GEOGRAPHIC AREA [10]											
New England	75	67	76	74	12	87	11	5	9	35	8
Middle Atlantic	79	65	76	73	10	82	10	6	8	44	12
East North Central	79	58	78	64	11	86	12	7	5	44	12
West North Central	75	59	75	59	11	88	8	5	4	40	8
South Atlantic	77	60	78	63	12	83	9	6	5	42	8
East South Central	79	57	78	66	8	89	6	7	5	42	8
West South Central	81	64	79	65	13	85	6	6	2	47	13
Mountain	75	58	77	51	8	86	10	6	6	44	6
Pacific	73	63	72	52	11	86	9	5	8	34	9

S Indicates no workers in this category or data did not meet publication criteria. [1] Some workers may have access to both types of plans. [2] A workplace program that provides for either the full or partial cost of caring for an employee's children in a nursery, day care center, or a baby sitter in facilities either on or off the employer's premises. [3] Permits employees to set their own schedules within a general set of parameters. Employees generally are required to work a minimum number of core hours each day. [4] Employers subsidize employees' cost of commuting to and from work via public transportation, company-sponsored van pool, discounted subway fares, for example. [5] All nonproduction bonuses include cash profit sharing bonuses, employee recognition bonuses, holiday bonuses, end of year bonuses, payment in lieu of benefits bonuses, referral bonuses, and other bonuses. [6] Employees are classified as working either a full-time or part-time schedule based on the definition used by each establishment. [7] Union workers are those whose wages are determined through collective bargaining. [8] The National Compensation Survey—Benefits program presents wage data in percentiles rather than dollar amounts; see "Technical Note" in source. [9] See Table 660, for composition of goods- and service-producing industries. [10] Composition of divisions: New England = Connecticut, Maine, Massachusetts, New Hampshire, Rhode Island, and Vermont; Middle Atlantic = New Jersey, New York, and Pennsylvania; East North Central = Illinois, Indiana, Michigan, Ohio, and Wisconsin; West North Central = Iowa, Kansas, Minnesota, Missouri, Nebraska, North Dakota, and South Dakota; South Atlantic = Delaware, District of Columbia, Florida, Georgia, Maryland, North Carolina, South Carolina, Virginia, and West Virginia; East South Central = Alabama, Kentucky, Mississippi, and Tennessee; West South Central = Arkansas, Louisiana, Oklahoma, and Texas; Mountain = Arizona, Colorado, Idaho, Montana, Nevada, New Mexico, Utah, and Wyoming; and Pacific = Alaska, California, Hawaii, Oregon, and Washington.

Source: Bureau of Labor Statistics, *Employee Benefits in the United States, March 2012*, Bulletin 2773, September 2012. See also <http://www.bls.gov/ncs/ebs/home.htm>.

Table 685. Industries With the Highest Total Case Incidence Rates for Nonfatal Injuries and Illnesses: 2011

[Rates per 100 full-time employees. Private industry unless otherwise noted. Incidence rates refer to any Occupational Safety & Health Administration (OSHA)-recordable occupational injury or illness, whether or not it resulted in days away from work, job transfer, or restriction. Incidence rates were calculated as: number of injuries and illnesses divided by total hours worked by all employees during the year multiplied by 200,000 as base for 100 full-time equivalent workers (working 40 hours per week, 50 weeks per year)]

Industry	2007 NAICS code [1]	Incidence rate	Industry	2007 NAICS code [1]	Incidence rate
All Industries, including State and local government [2]	(X)	3.8			
			Nursing and residential care facilities [3]	623	10.2
Fire protection [3]	92216	13.5	Soft drink manufacturing	312111	9.8
Nursing and residential care facilities [4]	623	13.1	Ambulance services	62191	9.7
Steel foundries (except investment)	331513	12.7	Aluminum foundries (except die-casting)	331524	9.5
Ice manufacturing	312113	11.9	Beet sugar manufacturing	311313	9.4
Skiing facilities	71392	11.5	Light truck and utility vehicle manufacturing	336112	9.4
Police protection [3]	92212	11.3	Truck trailer manufacturing	336212	9.4
Travel trailer and camper manufacturing	336214	11.2	Metal tank (heavy gauge) manufacturing	33242	9.3
Manufactured home (mobile home) manufacturing	321991	10.9	Hospitals (State Government)	622	9.2
Iron foundries	331511	10.9	Heavy and civil engineering construction [3]	237	8.8
			Beef cattle ranching and farming, including feedlots	11211	8.7
Copper foundries (except die-casting)	331525	10.3	Plate work manufacturing	332313	8.6
Pet and pet supplies stores	45391	10.3	Consumer electronics and appliances rental	53221	8.6
Seafood canning	311711	10.2			

X Not applicable [1] Based on the North American Industry Classification System, 2007 (NAICS). See text, this section. [2] Excludes farms with fewer than 11 employees. [3] Local Government. [4] State Government.

Source: Bureau of Labor Statistics, Industry Injury and Illness Data, "Supplemental News Release Tables," <http://www.bls.gov/iif/oshsum.htm>, accessed September 2013.

Table 686. Nonfatal Occupational Injuries and Illnesses by Industry: 2011

[3,599.9 represents 3,599,900. Rates per 100 full-time employees. Except as noted, data refer to any Occupational Safety and Health Administration (OSHA) recordable occupational injury or illness, whether or not it resulted in days away from work, job transfer, or restriction. Incidence rates were calculated as: number of injuries and illnesses divided by total hours worked by all employees during the year multiplied by 200,000 as base for 100 full-time equivalent workers (working 40 hours, per week, 50 weeks per year)]

Industry	2007 NAICS code [1]	Annual average employment [2]	Number of cases (1,000)	Incidence rate of cases
Total [3]	(X)	**126,140.9**	**3,599.9**	**3.6**
Private industry	(X)	**107,654.2**	**2,831.1**	**3.3**
Agriculture, forestry, fishing, hunting	11	974.9	45.6	5.2
Mining [4]	21	669.7	16.6	2.2
Construction	23	5,576.7	184.7	3.8
Manufacturing	31–33	11,627.7	455.6	3.9
Wholesale trade	42	5,580.0	166.7	3.1
Retail trade	44–45	14,773.9	413.2	3.8
Transportation and warehousing [5]	48–49	4,017.8	185.0	4.8
Utilities	22	552.9	17.2	3.1
Information	51	2,692.6	35.7	1.5
Finance and insurance	52	5,543.4	37.0	0.7
Real estate and rental and leasing	53	1,962.2	47.6	2.9
Professional, scientific, and technical services	54	7,711.7	66.4	1.0
Management of companies and enterprises	55	1,919.9	22.9	1.3
Administrative and support and waste management and remediation services	56	7,667.6	116.1	2.6
Educational services	61	2,580.1	35.8	2.0
Health care and social assistance	62	16,485.3	592.6	4.7
Arts, entertainment, and recreation	71	2,065.6	51.7	4.3
Accommodation and food services	72	11,449.2	269.2	3.7
Other services, except public administration	81	3,803.0	71.4	2.5
State and local government [3]	(X)	**18,486.7**	**768.8**	**5.4**
State government	(X)	4,807.9	170.2	4.3
Local government	(X)	13,678.9	598.6	5.8

X Not applicable. [1] North American Industry Classification System, 2007; see text, this section. [2] Employment figure primarily derived from Quarterly Census of Employment and Wages (QCEW). [3] Excludes farms with fewer than 11 employees. [4] Data for Mining (Sector 21 in the North American Industry Classification System—United States, 2007) include establishments not governed by the Mine Safety and Health Administration rules and reporting, such as those in Oil and Gas Extraction and related support activities. Data for mining operators in coal, metal, and nonmetal mining are provided to BLS by the Mine Safety and Health Administration, U.S. Department of Labor. Independent mining contractors are excluded from the coal, metal, and nonmetal mining industries. These data do not reflect the changes the Occupational Safety and Health Administration made to its recordkeeping requirements effective January 1, 2002; therefore, estimates for these industries are not comparable to estimates in other industries. [5] Data for employers in railroad transportation are provided to BLS by the Federal Railroad Administration, U.S. Department of Transportation.

Source: Bureau of Labor Statistics, News Release, *Workplace Injuries and Illnesses—2011*, News Release, USDL-12-2121, October 2012. See also <http://www.bls.gov/iif/home.htm>.

Table 687. Workers Killed on the Job by Industry and Occupation: 2011

[Excludes homicides and suicides]

Industry group	Deaths Number	Deaths Rate [1]	Occupations with highest fatal work injury rates	Deaths Number	Deaths Rate [1]
Total...............................	**4,693**	**3.5**	Fishers and fishing workers........................	42	127.3
			Logging workers.................................	65	104.0
Agriculture [2]...........................	566	24.9	Natural resources, other extraction workers....	31	76.5
Mining [3]...............................	155	15.9	Aircraft pilots and flight engineers..............	71	56.1
Construction............................	738	9.1	Refuse & recyclables collectors..................	30	36.4
Manufacturing..........................	327	2.2	Roofers...	60	34.1
Wholesale trade........................	190	4.9	Structural iron and steel workers................	18	30.3
Retail trade.............................	268	1.9	Recyclable material merchant wholesalers.....	34	28.4
Transportation and warehousing...........	749	15.3	Helpers, construction trades.....................	15	26.8
Utilities.................................	39	4.2	Farmers and ranchers...........................	268	26.1
Information.............................	56	1.9	Truck drivers and driver/sales workers..........	774	24.5
Financial activities [4]....................	98	1.1	Electrical power line installers and repairers. ..	26	19.5
Professional & business services [4]........	433	2.9	Police and sheriff's parole officers..............	130	18.6
Educational & health services.............	154	0.8	Drinking places (alcoholic beverages)...........	31	18.0
Leisure & hospitality [4]..................	231	2.2	Agricultural workers, misc.......................	133	17.2
Other services [5].......................	183	3.0	Grounds maintenance workers..................	183	16.9
Government............................	505	2.2	Construction laborers...........................	191	15.7

[1] The rate represents the number of fatal occupational injuries per 100,000 full-time equivalent workers. [2] Includes forestry, fishing, and hunting. [3] Includes oil and gas extraction. [4] For composition of industry, see Table 660. [5] Excludes public service administration.

Source: Bureau of Labor Statistics, Census of Fatal Occupational Injuries, "Fatal Injury Rates," <http://stats.bls.gov/iif/oshcfoi1.htm#rates>, accessed September 2013.

Table 688. Fatal Work Injuries by Event or Exposure: 2011

[For the 50 states and the District of Columbia. Based on the Census of Fatal Occupational Injuries. For details, see source]

Event or exposure	Number of fatalities	Percent distribu- tion	Event or exposure	Number of fatalities	Percent distribu- tion
Total...........................	**4,693**	**100**	Contacts with objects and equipment [1]........	710	15
Transportation incidents [1].....................	1,937	41	Struck by object or equipment [1]..............	476	10
Highway incident [1]......................	1,103	24	Struck by falling object or equipment.......	219	5
Collision between vehicles, mobile equipment...........................	525	11	Struck by flying object.....................	24	1
Noncollision incidents..................	262	6	Caught in or compressed by equipment or objects...........................	145	3
Nonhighway incident (farm, industrial premises)...........................	222	5	Caught in or crushed in collapsing materials..........................	84	2
Aircraft accidents......................	145	3			
Pedestrians struck by a vehicle, mobile equipment...........................	316	7	Falls..	681	15
Water vehicle accidents....................	72	2	Exposure to harmful substances or environments [1].....................	419	9
Railway accidents.......................	50	1	Contact with electric current..............	174	4
Assaults and violent acts [1]	791	17	Exposure to caustic, noxious or allergenic substances............................	144	3
Homicides [1]...........................	468	10			
Shooting...........................	365	8	Oxygen deficiency........................	35	1
Stabbing...........................	42	1			
Self-inflicted injury......................	250	5	Fires and explosions.........................	144	3

Z Less than 0.5 percent. [1] Includes other causes, not shown separately.

Source: U.S. Bureau of Labor Statistics, "Census of Fatal Occupational Injuries —Current and Revised Data," April 2013, <http://www.bls.gov/iif/oshcfoi1.htm>.

Table 689. Nonfatal Occupational Injury and Illness Cases in Private Industry by Type of Injury or Illness and Days Away from Work: 2011

[(908.3 represents 908,300). Covers work-related injuries and illnesses involving one or more days of missed work]

Type of work-related injury or illness	Number of injury or illness cases (1,000)								Median number of days away from work
	All cases	1 day	2 days	3-5 days	6-10 days	11-20 days	21-30 days	31 days or more	
Total [1].................	**908.3**	**126.3**	**98.1**	**161.7**	**107.5**	**102.2**	**59.4**	**253.2**	**8**
Traumatic injuries and disorders..............	871.5	121.5	95.3	156.2	103.9	97.8	56.2	240.6	8
Fractures.........................	74.7	4.6	4.5	7.2	7.5	8.8	6.0	36.2	29
Sprains, strains, tears..................	340.9	36.6	34.5	64.2	44.0	41.0	23.0	97.7	9
Concussions.......................	7.3	1.3	1.0	1.8	0.7	0.6	0.3	1.6	4
Soreness, pain, hurt-nonspecified injury....	109.2	15.0	11.0	19.9	12.8	10.8	6.6	33.0	9
Carpal tunnel syndrome..................	8.3	0.3	0.5	0.7	0.6	1.1	1.1	4.0	30
Hernia............................	10.9	0.2	0.3	0.8	1.1	2.2	1.7	4.6	26
Vision disorders.....................	1.5	0.6	0.2	0.4	0.1	0.1	0.1	0.1	2
Disease and disorders of body systems......	23.3	2	1.53	2.7	2.28	3.28	2.25	9.26	20
Infectious and parasitic diseases..............	1.2	0.3	0.2	0.3	0.2	0.1	0.0	0.0	3
Mental disorders or syndromes...............	3.1	0.3	0.1	0.4	0.2	0.4	0.2	1.7	32

[1] Total includes unclassified and ill-defined conditions.

Source: Bureau of Labor Statistics, Survey of Occupational Injuries and Illnesses, 2011 Supplemental Tables, "Detailed nature by number of days away from work," <http://stats.bls.gov/iif/oshcdnew2011.htm>, accessed September 2013.

Table 690. Workplace Violence Rates for Government and Private Sector Employees by Selected Characteristics: 2002 to 2011

[Rates per 1,000 population. Data shown for nonfatal workplace violence, which includes rape or sexual assault, robbery, aggravated assault, and simple assault against employed persons age 16 or older that occurred while at work or on duty. Based on Bureau of Justice Statistics' National Crime Victimization Survey]

Victim Characteristic	All Employees		Non-law Enforcement and Security Employees	
	Government	Private-sector	Government	Private-sector
Total	**22.3**	**6.2**	**10.8**	**5.6**
SEX				
Male	35.3	6.7	11.2	5.6
Female	12.0	5.6	10.5	5.6
RACE [2]				
White	25.0	6.7	12.0	6.0
Black or African American	10.6	6.4	5.7	5.4
American Indian or Alaska Native	[1] 42.5	19.1	[1] 28.3	18.1
Asian or Pacific Islander	[1] 8.7	4.9	[1] 4.3	5.0
Two or more races	69.7	14.1	[1] 14.5	14.3
Origin/Ethnicity				
Hispanic	18.3	3.1	9.4	2.8
AGE				
16–17	[1] –	5.6	[1] –	5.6
18–24	18.5	8.6	6.1	7.6
25–34	35.8	8.0	12.1	6.9
35–49	22.8	5.8	11.4	5.3
50–64	16.3	4.4	11.6	4.2
65 or older	3.7	1.0	3.6	0.9
MARITAL STATUS				
Never married	20.7	8.7	9.9	7.7
Married	20.8	4.2	9.8	3.8
Widowed	16.9	7.3	6.2	7.4
Divorced or separated	33.5	9.0	18.2	8.1
ANNUAL HOUSEHOLD INCOME				
Less than $25,000	13.3	7.4	10.3	6.3
$25,000 to $49,999	21.4	6.7	10.2	5.7
$50,000 to $74,999	33.6	7.6	15.5	7.2
$75,000 or more	21.5	5.5	11.2	5.1
Unknown	16.8	4.9	6.1	4.3

– Represents less than .05 percent. [1] Estimate is based on 10 or fewer sample cases or coefficient of variation is greater than 50%. [2] Excludes persons of Hispanic or Latino origin.

Source: Department of Justice, Bureau of Justice Statistics, *Workplace Violence Against Government Employees, 1994-2011*, NCJ 241349, April 2013. See also <http://www.bjs.gov/index.cfm?ty=pbdetail&iid=4615>.

Table 691. Work Stoppages: 1960 to 2012

[896 represents 896,000. Excludes work stoppages involving fewer than 1,000 workers and lasting less than 1 day. The term "major work stoppage" includes both worker-initiated strikes and employer-initiated lockouts that involve 1,000 workers or more. Information is based on reports of labor disputes appearing in daily newspapers, trade journals, and other public sources. The parties to the disputes are contacted by telephone, when necessary, to clarify details of the stoppages]

Year	Number of work stop-pages [1]	Workers involved [2] (1,000)	Days idle total		Year	Number of work stop-pages [1]	Workers involved [2] (1,000)	Days idle total	
			Number [3] (1,000)	Percent estimated working time [4]				Number [3] (1,000)	Percent estimated working time [4]
1960	222	896	13,260	0.09	1994	45	322	5,021	0.02
1970	381	2,468	52,761	0.29	1995	31	192	5,771	0.02
1975	235	965	17,563	0.09	1996	37	273	4,889	0.02
1978	219	1,006	23,774	0.11	1997	29	339	4,497	0.01
1979	235	1,021	20,409	0.09	1998	34	387	5,116	0.02
1980	187	795	20,844	0.09	1999	17	73	1,996	0.01
1981	145	729	16,908	0.07	2000	39	394	20,419	0.06
1982	96	656	9,061	0.04	2001	29	99	1,151	(Z)
1983	81	909	17,461	0.08	2002	19	46	660	(Z)
1984	62	376	8,499	0.04	2003	14	129	4,091	0.01
1985	54	324	7,079	0.03	2004	17	171	3,344	0.01
1986	69	533	11,861	0.05	2005	22	100	1,736	0.01
1987	46	174	4,481	0.02	2006	20	70	2,688	0.01
1988	40	118	4,381	0.02	2007	21	189	1,265	(Z)
1989	51	452	16,996	0.07	2008	15	72	1,954	0.01
1990	44	185	5,926	0.02	2009	5	13	124	(Z)
1991	40	392	4,584	0.02	2010	11	45	302	(Z)
1992	35	364	3,989	0.01	2011	19	113	1,020	(Z)
1993	35	182	3,981	0.01	2012	19	148	1131	(Z)

Z Less than 0.005 percent. [1] Beginning in year indicated. [2] Workers counted more than once if involved in more than one stoppage during the year. [3] Resulting from all stoppages in effect in a year, including those that began in an earlier year. [4] Agricultural and government employees are included in the total working time; private household and forestry and fishery employees are excluded.

Source: U.S. Bureau of Labor Statistics, *Major Work Stoppages in 2012*, News Release, USDL 13-0193, February 2013. See also <http://www.bls.gov/wsp>.

Table 692. Labor Union Membership by Sector: 1985 to 2012

[Annual averages of monthly figures (16,996 represents 16,996,000). For wage and salary workers in agriculture and non-agriculture. Data represent union members by place of residence. Based on the Current Population Survey and subject to sampling error. For methodological details, see source]

Sector	1985	1990	1995	2000	2005	2009	2010	2011	2012
TOTAL (1,000)									
Wage and salary workers:									
Union members.......................	16,996	16,740	16,360	16,258	15,685	15,327	14,715	14,755	14,349
Covered by unions...................	19,358	19,058	18,346	17,944	17,223	16,904	16,290	16,281	15,906
Public sector workers:									
Union members.......................	5,743	6,485	6,927	7,111	7,430	7,897	7,623	7,550	7,319
Covered by unions...................	6,921	7,691	7,987	7,976	8,262	8,678	8,406	8,309	8,062
Private sector workers:									
Union members.......................	11,253	10,255	9,432	9,148	8,255	7,431	7,092	7,205	7,030
Covered by unions...................	12,438	11,366	10,360	9,969	8,962	8,226	7,884	7,972	7,844
PERCENT									
Wage and salary workers:									
Union members.......................	18.0	16.1	14.9	13.5	12.5	12.3	11.9	11.8	11.2
Covered by unions...................	20.5	18.3	16.7	14.9	13.7	13.6	13.1	13.0	12.5
Public sector workers:									
Union members.......................	35.7	36.5	37.7	37.5	36.5	37.4	36.2	37.0	35.9
Covered by unions...................	43.1	43.3	43.5	42.0	40.5	41.1	40.0	40.7	39.6
Private sector workers:									
Union members.......................	14.3	11.9	10.3	9.0	7.8	7.2	6.9	6.9	6.6
Covered by unions................	15.9	13.2	11.3	9.8	8.5	8.0	7.7	7.6	7.3

Source: Bloomberg BNA Union Membership and Earnings Data Book: Compilations from the Current Population Survey (2013 edition), authored by Barry Hirsch of Georgia State University and David Macpherson of Trinity University. Internet sites: <http://www.bna.com/data-book> and <http://unionstats.gsu.edu>. © 2013 by The Bureau of National Affairs, Inc., Research and Customs Solutions (800-372-1033), <http://www.bna.com>.

Table 693. Union Members by Selected Characteristics: 2012

[Annual averages of monthly data. Total workers in thousands (127,577 represents 127,577,000). Covers employed wage and salary workers 16 years old and over. Excludes self-employed workers whose businesses are incorporated and not incorporated although they technically qualify as wage and salary workers. Based on Current Population Survey, see text, Section 1 and Appendix III]

Characteristic	Employed wage and salary workers			Median usual weekly earnings [3] (dollars)			
		Percent					
	Total (1,000)	Union members [1]	Repre-sented by union [2]	Total	Union members [1]	Repre-sented by union [2]	Not repre-sented by union
Total [4].................................	**127,577**	**11.3**	**12.5**	**768**	**943**	**933**	**742**
AGE							
16 to 24 years old......................	17,417	4.2	5.0	444	545	551	434
25 to 34 years old......................	28,875	9.5	10.7	707	871	863	686
35 to 44 years old......................	27,442	12.5	13.6	858	983	974	831
45 to 54 years old......................	28,765	14.0	15.4	878	997	985	850
55 to 64 years old......................	19,694	14.9	16.4	897	1,005	997	870
65 years and over......................	5,385	9.1	10.3	757	839	832	748
SEX							
Men...	65,898	12.0	13.1	854	997	990	821
Women....................................	61,679	10.5	11.9	691	877	865	663
RACE							
White [5].................................	101,851	11.1	12.3	792	973	960	762
Men..	53,542	11.9	12.9	879	1,025	1,017	845
Women....................................	48,309	10.2	11.6	710	902	890	681
Black [5]...................................	14,975	13.4	14.8	621	784	774	599
Men..	6,753	14.8	16.0	665	819	811	624
Women....................................	8,222	12.3	13.9	599	755	747	582
Asian [5]...................................	6,953	9.6	10.9	920	977	986	907
Men..	3,650	8.9	10.1	1,055	1,010	1,022	1,062
Women....................................	3,303	10.4	11.8	770	946	951	747
HISPANIC OR LATINO ETHNICITY							
Hispanic [6]...............................	20,144	9.8	10.9	568	840	823	530
Men..	11,415	10.1	11.1	592	881	868	563
Women....................................	8,730	9.6	10.7	521	767	750	503
INDUSTRY [7]							
Private sector............................	107,191	6.6	7.3	742	887	877	731
Mining....................................	923	7.2	7.7	1,112	1,119	1,112	1,113
Construction............................	6,205	13.2	13.7	768	1,086	1,069	722
Manufacturing..........................	13,941	9.6	10.5	797	872	863	786
Wholesale and retail trade...........	18,174	4.7	5.3	630	650	637	629
Transportation and utilities...........	5,359	20.6	21.9	828	998	989	789
Information..............................	2,575	9.7	10.6	978	1,103	1,087	966
Financial activities....................	8,196	1.9	2.5	889	795	779	893
Professional and business services.................................	12,726	2.4	3.0	910	826	843	912
Education and health services......	20,394	8.1	9.3	748	879	876	736
Leisure and hospitality...............	11,775	2.7	3.2	481	611	604	475
Other services.........................	5,750	2.5	3.0	622	807	763	618
Public sector............................	20,385	35.9	39.6	898	990	980	829

[1] Members of a labor union or an employee association similar to a labor union. [2] Members of a labor union or an employee association similar to a union as well as workers who report no union affiliation but whose jobs are covered by a union or an employee association contract. [3] For full-time employed wage and salary workers. [4] Includes races not shown separately. Also includes a small number of multiple jobholders whose full- and part-time status cannot be determined for their principal job. [5] For persons in this race group only. See footnote 4, Table 614. [6] Persons of Hispanic origin may be of any race. [7] For composition of industries, see Table 660.

Source: U.S. Bureau of Labor Statistics, *Union Members in 2012*, News Release, USDL-13-0105, January 2013.

Table 694. Labor Union Membership by State: 1985 and 2012

[Annual averages of monthly figures (16,996.1 represents 16,996,100). For wage and salary workers in agriculture and non-agriculture. Data represent union members by place of residence. Based on the Current Population Survey and subject to sampling error. For methodological details, see source]

State	Union members (1,000)		Workers covered by unions (1,000)		Percent of workers					
					Union members		Covered by unions		Private sector union members	
	1985	2012	1985	2012	1985	2012	1985	2012	1985	2012
United States......	**16,996.1**	**14,349.4**	**19,358.1**	**15,905.9**	**18.0**	**11.2**	**20.5**	**12.5**	**14.3**	**6.6**
Alabama [1]...........	226.6	166.7	254.9	190.4	15.7	9.2	17.6	10.5	13.5	5.7
Alaska...............	47.7	66.8	53.4	71.4	25.0	22.4	28.0	23.9	17.0	10.3
Arizona [1]...........	115.6	125.6	145.7	159.2	9.5	5.2	12.0	6.5	7.9	3.2
Arkansas [1].........	91.6	36.7	108.4	42.6	11.2	3.2	13.3	3.7	9.5	1.4
California.............	2,123.1	2,485.0	2,485.8	2,662.1	20.4	17.2	23.9	18.4	15.8	8.9
Colorado.............	165.2	169.3	191.1	190.2	11.8	7.8	13.7	8.8	8.9	4.9
Connecticut..........	306.5	216.1	325.9	232.1	20.9	14.0	22.2	15.1	14.4	6.6
Delaware.............	45.6	39.4	50.9	44.5	16.6	10.4	18.5	11.8	12.8	5.6
District of Columbia..	45.2	26.6	58.2	31.7	16.5	8.6	21.2	10.3	13.9	5.6
Florida [1]..............	395.2	438.8	515.7	553.5	9.1	5.8	11.9	7.3	5.3	2.4
Georgia [1]...........	239.5	170.7	273.1	210.0	10.0	4.4	11.4	5.4	9.1	3.1
Hawaii...............	109.6	116.6	121.2	124.8	27.8	21.7	30.8	23.2	19.7	14.6
Idaho [1].............	41.7	29.2	48.4	35.7	11.7	4.8	13.6	5.8	9.8	3.2
Illinois...............	1,031.7	800.4	1,124.9	851.1	22.2	14.6	24.3	15.5	19.2	9.3
Indiana [3].............	476.7	245.4	524.4	268.3	21.3	9.1	23.4	9.9	20.8	7.2
Iowa [1]................	181.7	144.4	212.8	171.4	17.0	10.4	20.0	12.3	14.5	5.5
Kansas [1]............	129.0	85.4	157.3	104.6	12.8	6.9	15.6	8.4	11.4	4.0
Kentucky.............	219.2	173.7	250.8	198.1	16.5	10.0	18.8	11.3	16.4	7.1
Louisiana [1]..........	147.9	107.7	172.8	130.0	9.6	6.2	11.2	7.5	7.9	3.7
Maine................	77.5	64.2	90.0	77.6	17.1	11.5	19.8	13.9	11.2	5.4
Maryland.............	329.9	278.8	412.9	324.5	16.7	10.6	20.9	12.3	13.0	5.5
Massachusetts.......	495.4	416.3	548.4	470.2	18.5	14.3	20.4	16.2	13.0	7.4
Michigan [3]...........	1,004.5	628.8	1,071.0	647.9	28.4	16.6	30.3	17.1	23.5	11.3
Minnesota............	407.5	350.5	452.7	367.5	22.6	14.2	25.1	14.9	16.7	7.7
Mississippi [1].........	81.3	47.9	94.5	63.8	9.3	4.3	10.8	5.7	8.4	3.0
Missouri..............	378.3	224.1	418.9	253.1	18.7	8.9	20.7	10.1	19.1	7.2
Montana..............	57.3	54.5	66.9	64.7	19.4	13.9	22.7	16.5	14.9	5.8
Nebraska [1]..........	78.8	51.4	99.0	70.0	12.7	6.0	16.0	8.1	10.3	3.4
Nevada [1]............	89.7	162.3	102.1	181.0	21.6	14.8	24.6	16.5	19.5	11.1
New Hampshire......	48.8	65.3	54.8	74.4	10.7	10.5	12.0	12.0	6.9	4.2
New Jersey..........	821.0	611.2	937.2	636.4	24.9	16.1	28.4	16.8	19.0	8.5
New Mexico..........	49.4	50.3	62.4	68.1	10.0	6.5	12.7	8.7	8.9	2.8
New York............	2,102.3	1,836.4	2,298.3	1,970.0	30.2	23.2	33.0	24.8	21.3	13.3
North Carolina [1]......	167.0	111.5	209.5	161.4	6.4	2.9	8.0	4.2	4.7	1.8
North Dakota [1].......	27.9	20.0	34.2	26.9	11.4	6.1	14.0	8.2	6.4	3.4
Ohio.................	999.0	604.3	1,090.9	664.7	23.6	12.6	25.7	13.9	20.7	8.4
Oklahoma [2]..........	128.4	114.5	151.0	139.3	10.5	7.5	12.3	9.1	8.2	4.3
Oregon..............	231.6	240.7	260.8	250.5	22.7	15.8	25.6	16.4	16.7	8.6
Pennsylvania........	1,055.4	732.2	1,174.7	785.3	22.8	13.4	25.4	14.4	19.1	7.8
Rhode Island........	90.2	81.1	97.7	83.9	21.1	17.8	22.9	18.4	12.7	10.1
South Carolina [1].....	58.8	58.4	72.5	81.7	4.5	3.3	5.6	4.6	3.8	1.3
South Dakota [1].......	27.9	19.5	34.5	23.6	11.2	5.6	13.8	6.7	7.5	3.1
Tennessee [1]..........	236.8	124.3	281.8	151.7	13.1	4.8	15.6	5.9	10.9	2.9
Texas [1]..............	474.8	598.1	626.2	719.3	7.4	5.7	9.7	6.8	5.6	3.4
Utah [1]................	69.9	60.8	91.9	77.7	11.4	5.2	14.9	6.6	8.0	2.9
Vermont..............	28.5	31.0	35.4	37.6	12.8	10.7	15.9	13.1	7.1	4.1
Virginia [1].............	236.0	159.5	296.7	197.2	9.7	4.4	12.2	5.5	8.6	3.0
Washington..........	405.8	512.9	469.2	540.9	25.0	18.5	28.9	19.5	18.6	11.1
West Virginia........	134.7	83.9	148.3	91.2	22.7	12.0	25.0	13.1	22.2	8.4
Wisconsin............	435.9	292.8	463.9	311.8	22.3	11.2	23.8	12.0	17.8	6.9
Wyoming [1]...........	26.8	17.0	34.2	20.5	13.8	6.7	17.6	8.1	11.2	4.7

[1] Right to work state. [2] Passed right to work law in 2001. [3] Passed right to work law in 2012. [3] Passed right to work law in 2012.

Source: Bloomberg BNA Union Membership and Earnings Data Book: Compilations from the Current Population Survey (2013 edition), authored by Barry Hirsch of Georgia State University and David Macpherson of Trinity University. Internet sites: <http://www.bna.com/data-book> and <http://unionstats.gsu.edu>. © 2013 by The Bureau of National Affairs, Inc., Research and Customs Solutions (800-372-1033), <http://www.bna.com>.

Income, Expenditures, Poverty, and Wealth

This section presents data on gross domestic product (GDP), gross national product (GNP), national and personal income, saving and investment, money income, poverty, and national and personal wealth. The data on income and expenditures measure two aspects of the U.S. economy. One aspect relates to the National Income and Product Accounts (NIPA), a summation reflecting the entire complex of the nation's economic income and output and the interaction of its major components; the other relates to personal and household income and wealth, and consumer expenditures.

The primary source for data on GDP, GNP, national and personal income, gross saving and investment, and fixed assets and consumer durables is the *Survey of Current Business*, published monthly by the Bureau of Economic Analysis (BEA). These data are also available in tables accessible through an interactive tool on the BEA's Web site, <http://www.bea.gov/itable/index.cfm>. A comprehensive revision to the NIPA was released beginning in July 2013. Discussions of the revision are available at the BEA's Web site. Comprehensive revisions are conducted approximately every 5 years.

Sources of income distribution data are the decennial censuses of population, the Current Population Survey (CPS), and the American Community Survey, all products of the U.S. Census Bureau (see text, Section 1). Annual data on income of families, individuals, and households are presented in *Current Population Reports, Income, Poverty, and Health Insurance Coverage in the United States,* in print. Many data series are also found on the Census Web site at <http://www.census.gov/hhes/www/income/>. Data on the household sector's saving and assets are published by the Board of Governors of the Federal Reserve System in the quarterly statistical release *Financial Accounts of the United States.* The Federal Reserve Board also periodically conducts the *Survey of Consumer Finances,* which presents financial information on family assets and net worth. The most recent survey is available at <http://www.federalreserve.gov/econresdata/scf/scfindex.htm>. Detailed information on personal wealth is published periodically by the Internal Revenue Service (IRS) in *the SOI (Statistics of Income) Bulletin.*

National income and product—GDP is the total output of goods and services produced by labor and property located in the United States, valued at market prices. GDP can be viewed in terms of the expenditure categories that comprise its major components: personal consumption expenditures, gross private domestic investment, net exports of goods and services, and government consumption expenditures and gross investment. The goods and services included are largely those bought for final use (excluding illegal transactions) in the market economy. A number of inclusions, however, represent imputed values, the most important of which is the rental value of owner–occupied housing. GDP, in this broad context, measures the output attributable to the factors of production located in the United States. GDP by state is the gross market value of the goods and services attributable to labor and property located in a state. It is the state counterpart of the nation's GDP.

The featured measure of real GDP is an index based on chain-type annual weights. Changes in this measure of real output and prices are calculated as the average of changes based on weights for the current and preceding years. (Components of real output are weighted by price, and components of prices are weighted by output.) These annual changes are "chained" (multiplied) together to form a time series that allows for the effects of changes in relative prices and changes in the composition of output over time. Quarterly and monthly changes are based on quarterly and monthly weights, respectively.

The output indexes are expressed as 2005 = 100 or 2009 = 100, and for recent years, in 2005 or 2009 dollars. Price indexes are based to 1982-84 = 100. For more information on chained-dollar indexes, see the article on this subject in the November 2003 issue of the *Survey of Current Business.*

Chained (2009) dollar estimates of most components of GDP are not published for periods prior to 1990, because during periods far from the base period, the levels of the components may provide misleading information about their contributions to an aggregate. Values are published in index form (2009 = 100) for 1929 to the present to allow users to calculate the percent changes for all components, which are accurate for all periods. In addition, BEA publishes estimates of contributions of major components to the percent change in GDP for all periods.

Gross national product measures the output attributable to all labor and property supplied by United States residents. GNP differs from "national income" mainly in that GNP includes allowances for depreciation—that is, consumption of fixed capital.

National income includes all net incomes, net of consumption of fixed capital (CFC), earned in production. National income is the sum of compensation of employees, proprietors' income with inventory valuation adjustment (IVA) and capital consumption adjustment (CCAdj), rental income of persons with CCAdj, corporate profits with IVA and CCAdj, net interest and miscellaneous payments, taxes on production and imports, business current transfer payments (net), and current surplus of government enterprises, less subsidies.

Capital consumption adjustment for corporations and for nonfarm sole proprietorships and partnerships is the difference between capital consumption based on income tax returns and capital consumption measured using empirical evidence on prices of used equipment and structures in resale markets, which have shown that depreciation for most types of assets approximates a geometric pattern. The tax return data are valued at historical costs and reflect changes over time in service lives and depreciation patterns as permitted by tax regulations. Inventory valuation adjustment represents the difference between the book value of inventories used up in production and the cost of replacing them.

Personal income is the current income received by persons from all sources minus their personal contributions for government social insurance. Classified as "persons" are individuals (including owners of unincorporated firms), nonprofit institutions that primarily serve individuals, private trust funds, and private noninsured welfare funds. Personal income includes personal current transfer receipts (payments not resulting from current production) from government and business such as social security benefits, public assistance, etc., but excludes transfers among persons. Also included are certain nonmonetary types of income; chiefly, estimated net rental value to owner-occupants of their homes and the value of services furnished without payment by financial intermediaries. Capital gains (and losses) are excluded.

Disposable personal income is personal income less personal current taxes. It is the income available to persons for spending or saving. Personal current taxes are tax payments (net of refunds) by persons (except personal contributions for government social insurance) that are not chargeable to business expense. Personal taxes include income taxes, personal property taxes, motor vehicle licenses, and other miscellaneous taxes.

Gross domestic product by industry—The BEA also prepares estimates of value added by industry. *Value added* is a measure of the contribution of each private industry and of government to the nation's GDP. It is defined as an industry's gross output (which consists of sales or receipts and other operating income, commodity taxes, and inventory change) minus its intermediate inputs (which consist of energy, raw materials, semi-finished goods, and services that are purchased from domestic industries or from foreign sources). These estimates of value added are produced for 61 private industries and for 4 government classifications—federal general government and government enterprises, and state and local general government and government enterprises.

The estimates by industry are available in current dollars and are derived from the estimates of gross domestic income, which consists of three components—the compensation of employees, gross operating surplus, and taxes on production and imports, less subsidies. Real, or inflation-adjusted, estimates are also prepared.

Regional Economic Accounts—These accounts consist of estimates of state and local area personal income and of gross domestic product by state and are consistent with estimates of personal income and gross domestic product in the Bureau's national economic accounts. BEA's estimates of state and local area personal income provide a framework for analyzing individual state and local economies, and they show how the economies compare with each other. The *personal income* of a state and/or local area is the income received by, or on behalf of, the residents of that state or area. Estimates of labor and proprietors' earnings by place of work indicate the economic activity of business and government within that area, and estimates of personal income by place of residence indicate the income within the area that is available for spending. BEA prepares estimates for states, counties, metropolitan areas, and BEA economic areas.

Gross domestic product by state estimates measure the value added to the nation's production by the labor and property in each state. GDP by state is often considered the state counterpart of the nation's GDP. The GDP by state estimates provide the basis for

analyzing the regional impacts of national economic trends. GDP by state is measured as the sum of the distributions by industry and state of the components of gross domestic income; that is, the sum of the costs incurred and incomes earned in the production of GDP by state. The GDP estimates are presented in current dollars and in real (chained dollars) for 63 industries.

Consumer Expenditure Survey—The Consumer Expenditure Survey program began in 1980. The principal objective of the survey is to collect current consumer expenditure data, which provide a continuous flow of data on the buying habits of American consumers. The data are necessary for future revisions of the Consumer Price Index.

The survey conducted by the Census Bureau for the Bureau of Labor Statistics consists of two components: (1) an interview panel survey in which the expenditures of consumer units are obtained in five interviews conducted every 3 months, and (2) a diary or recordkeeping survey completed by participating households for two consecutive 1-week periods.

Each component of the survey queries an independent sample of consumer units. Data are collected in 91 areas of the country that are representative of the U.S. civilian noninstitutional population. The survey includes students in student housing. For the diary survey, the Census Bureau selects 12,500 addresses each year for participation; usable diaries are collected from approximately 7,100 households. The placement of diaries is spread out equally over the 52 weeks of the year. The interview survey contacts 15,000 addresses each quarter; usable interviews are obtained from approximately 7,100 households each quarter. Data from the two surveys are combined; integration is necessary to permit analysis of total family expenditures because neither the diary nor quarterly interview survey was designed to collect a complete account of consumer spending.

Distribution of money income to families and individuals—Money income statistics are based on data collected in various field surveys of income conducted since 1936. Since 1947, the Census Bureau has collected the data on an annual basis and published them in *Current Population Reports*, P60 Series. In each of the surveys, field representatives interview samples of the population with respect to income received during the previous year. *Money income* as defined by the Census Bureau differs from the BEA concept of "personal income." Data on consumer income collected in the CPS by the Census Bureau cover money income received (exclusive of certain money receipts such as capital gains) before payments for personal income taxes, social security, union dues, Medicare deductions, etc. Therefore, money income does not reflect the fact that some families receive part of their income in the form of noncash benefits (see Section 11) such as food stamps, health benefits, and subsidized housing; that some farm families receive noncash benefits in the form of rent-free housing and goods produced and consumed on the farm; or that noncash benefits are also received by some nonfarm residents, which often take the form of the use of business transportation and facilities, full or partial payments by business for retirement programs, medical and educational expenses, etc. These elements should be considered when comparing income levels. None of the aggregate income concepts (GDP, national income, or personal income) is exactly comparable with money income, although personal income is the closest. For a definition of families and households, see text, Section 1.

Poverty—Families and unrelated individuals are classified as being above or below poverty following the Office of Management and Budget's Statistical Policy Directive 14. The Census Bureau uses a set of thresholds that vary by family size and composition.

The official poverty thresholds do not vary geographically, but they are updated for inflation using the consumer price index (CPI-U). The offical poverty definition uses money income before taxes and does not include capital gains or noncash benefits (such as public housing, Medicaid, and food stamps).

The original thresholds were based on the U.S. Department of Agriculture's 1961 Economy Food Plan and reflected the different consumption requirements of families. The poverty thresholds are updated every year to reflect changes in the Consumer Price Index. The following technical changes to the thresholds were made in 1981: (1) distinctions based on sex of householder were eliminated, (2) separate thresholds for farm families were dropped, and (3) the matrix was expanded to families of nine or more persons from the old cutoff of seven or more persons. These changes were incorporated in the calculation of poverty data beginning with 1981. Besides the Census Bureau Web site at <http://www.census.gov/hhes/www/poverty/about/overview/measure.html>, information on poverty guidelines and research may be found at the U.S. Department of Human Services Web site at <http://aspe.hhs.gov/poverty/index.cfm>.

In the recent past, the Census Bureau has published a number of technical papers and reports that presented experimental poverty estimates based on income definitions that counted the value of selected government noncash benefits. The Census Bureau has also published reports on after-tax income.

Statistical reliability—For a discussion of statistical collection and estimation, sampling procedures, and measures of statistical reliability pertaining to Census Bureau data, see Appendix III.

Table 695. Gross Domestic Product in Current and Chained (2009) Dollars: 1970 to 2012

[In billions of dollars (1,076 represents $1,076,000,000,000). For explanation of gross domestic product and chained dollars, see text, this section. Minus sign (–) indicates decline in inventories or net imports]

Item	1970	1980	1990	1995	2000	2001	2002	2003	2004	2005	2006	2007	2008	2009	2010	2011	2012
CURRENT DOLLARS																	
Gross domestic product	**1,076**	**2,863**	**5,980**	**7,664**	**10,290**	**10,625**	**10,980**	**11,512**	**12,277**	**13,095**	**13,858**	**14,480**	**14,720**	**14,418**	**14,958**	**15,534**	**16,245**
Personal consumption expenditures	648	1,755	3,826	4,984	6,802	7,107	7,385	7,764	8,258	8,790	9,298	9,744	10,006	9,843	10,202	10,712	11,150
Durable goods	90	226	497	636	913	942	985	1,018	1,080	1,127	1,156	1,185	1,102	1,023	1,071	1,130	1,203
Nondurable goods	229	573	994	1,180	1,540	1,584	1,613	1,704	1,820	1,953	2,080	2,177	2,273	2,175	2,292	2,473	2,567
Services	329	955	2,334	3,169	4,349	4,582	4,787	5,043	5,358	5,710	6,062	6,383	6,630	6,645	6,839	7,109	7,380
Gross private domestic investment	170	530	994	1,318	2,034	1,929	1,925	2,028	2,277	2,527	2,681	2,644	2,425	1,878	2,101	2,232	2,475
Fixed investment	168	536	979	1,286	1,979	1,967	1,907	2,009	2,213	2,468	2,614	2,609	2,457	2,026	2,039	2,196	2,409
Change in private inventories	2	-6	15	31	55	-38	19	19	64	60	67	35	-32	-148	62	36	66
Net exports of goods and services	4	-13	-78	-90	-380	-369	-425	-501	-615	-716	-762	-710	-713	-392	-519	-569	-547
Exports	60	281	552	813	1,094	1,029	1,005	1,043	1,183	1,310	1,479	1,666	1,843	1,584	1,844	2,101	2,196
Imports	56	294	630	903	1,474	1,398	1,430	1,544	1,798	2,026	2,241	2,376	2,556	1,976	2,362	2,670	2,743
Government consumption expenditures and gross investment	254	591	1,238	1,452	1,834	1,959	2,095	2,221	2,357	2,494	2,642	2,802	3,003	3,089	3,174	3,159	3,167
Federal	133	272	560	575	632	669	741	825	892	946	1,002	1,050	1,156	1,218	1,304	1,304	1,296
National defense	101	181	403	376	392	413	457	520	570	608	642	679	754	788	833	836	817
Nondefense	32	91	157	199	241	257	284	305	322	338	360	371	402	429	471	468	479
State and local	121	319	678	877	1,202	1,290	1,354	1,396	1,465	1,547	1,640	1,752	1,848	1,871	1,870	1,855	1,871
CHAINED (2009) DOLLARS [1]																	
Gross domestic product	**4,718**	**6,443**	**8,945**	**10,164**	**12,565**	**12,684**	**12,910**	**13,270**	**13,774**	**14,236**	**14,615**	**14,877**	**14,834**	**14,418**	**14,779**	**15,052**	**15,471**
Personal consumption expenditures	2,903	3,992	5,673	6,528	8,182	8,388	8,600	8,866	9,206	9,528	9,815	10,036	9,999	9,843	10,036	10,291	10,518
Durable goods	(NA)	(NA)	(NA)	(NA)	758	798	857	918	993	1,047	1,092	1,142	1,083	1,023	1,086	1,157	1,220
Nondurable goods	(NA)	(NA)	(NA)	(NA)	1,864	1,896	1,931	1,999	2,064	2,132	2,202	2,239	2,215	2,175	2,224	2,266	2,297
Services	(NA)	(NA)	(NA)	(NA)	5,612	5,736	5,840	5,966	6,154	6,349	6,520	6,650	6,701	6,645	6,727	6,871	6,983
Gross private domestic investment	585	881	1,241	1,551	2,376	2,231	2,218	2,309	2,511	2,673	2,730	2,644	2,396	1,878	2,056	2,225	2,436
Fixed investment	(NA)	(NA)	(NA)	(NA)	2,316	2,280	2,201	2,290	2,444	2,611	2,663	2,610	2,433	2,026	2,056	2,185	2,365
Change in private inventories	(NA)	(NA)	(NA)	(NA)	66	-46	23	23	71	64	72	36	-34	-148	58	34	58
Net exports of goods and services	(NA)	(NA)	(NA)	(NA)	-483	-504	-585	-642	-732	-777	-786	-704	-547	-392	-463	-446	-431
Exports	187	374	641	906	1,272	1,201	1,178	1,197	1,309	1,388	1,512	1,647	1,742	1,584	1,766	1,891	1,957
Imports	254	370	723	1,015	1,755	1,705	1,763	1,839	2,041	2,166	2,299	2,351	2,289	1,976	2,228	2,336	2,388
Government consumption expenditures and gross investment	1,458	1,613	2,224	2,258	2,498	2,592	2,706	2,764	2,808	2,826	2,869	2,914	2,995	3,089	3,091	2,992	2,963
Federal	(NA)	(NA)	(NA)	(NA)	818	850	911	973	1,017	1,035	1,061	1,079	1,152	1,218	1,271	1,238	1,220
National defense	(NA)	(NA)	(NA)	(NA)	512	530	567	615	653	666	679	696	748	788	814	795	769
Nondefense	(NA)	(NA)	(NA)	(NA)	305	320	343	358	365	369	382	383	404	429	457	443	451
State and local	(NA)	(NA)	(NA)	(NA)	1,689	1,752	1,802	1,795	1,793	1,792	1,809	1,836	1,842	1,871	1,821	1,755	1,743
Residual	-161	-45	-110	-64	-84	-91	-70	-45	-19	-2	-4	-10	-13	0.1	-21	-9	-13

NA Not available. [1] Chained (2009) dollar series are calculated as the product of the chain-type quantity index and the 2009 current-dollar value of the corresponding series, divided by 100. Because the formula for the chain-type quantity indexes uses weights of more than one period, the corresponding chained-dollar estimates are usually not additive. The residual line is the difference between the first line and the sum of the most detailed lines.

Source: U.S. Bureau of Economic Analysis, National Income and Product Accounts Tables, "Table 1.1.5. Gross Domestic Product," and "Table 1.1.6. Real Gross Domestic Product, Chained Dollars," <http://www.bea.gov/iTable/>, accessed August 2013.

Table 696. Real Gross Domestic Product, Chained (2009) Dollars—Annual Percent Change: 1990 to 2012

[Change from immediate previous year; for example, 1990, change from 1989. Minus sign (–) indicates decrease]

Component	1990	2000	2005	2006	2007	2008	2009	2010	2011 [*]	2012
Gross domestic product (GDP)	**1.9**	**4.1**	**3.4**	**2.7**	**1.8**	**-0.3**	**-2.8**	**2.5**	**1.8**	**2.8**
Personal consumption expenditures	2.1	5.1	3.5	3.0	2.2	-0.4	-1.6	2.0	2.5	2.2
Durable goods	-0.4	8.6	5.4	4.3	4.6	-5.1	-5.5	6.1	6.6	7.7
Nondurable goods	1.2	3.2	3.3	3.3	1.7	-1.1	-1.8	2.2	1.9	1.4
Services	3.0	5.0	3.2	2.7	2.0	0.8	-0.8	1.2	2.1	1.6
Gross private domestic investment	-2.6	6.5	6.4	2.1	-3.1	-9.4	-21.6	12.9	4.9	9.5
Fixed investment	-1.4	6.9	6.8	2.0	-2.0	-6.8	-16.7	1.5	6.2	8.3
Nonresidential	1.1	9.1	7.0	7.1	5.9	-0.7	-15.6	2.5	7.6	7.3
Structures	1.5	7.8	1.7	7.2	12.7	6.1	-18.9	-16.4	2.1	12.7
Equipment	-2.1	9.7	9.6	8.6	3.2	-6.9	-22.9	15.9	12.7	7.6
Intellectual property products	8.4	8.9	6.5	4.5	4.8	3.0	-1.4	1.9	4.4	3.4
Residential	-8.5	0.7	6.6	-7.6	-18.8	-24.0	-21.2	-2.5	0.5	12.9
Exports	8.8	8.4	6.0	8.9	8.9	5.7	-9.1	11.5	7.1	3.5
Goods	8.4	10.1	7.4	9.4	7.5	6.1	-12.0	14.3	7.1	3.8
Services	9.9	3.9	3.0	7.7	12.3	4.8	-2.1	5.6	7.0	3.0
Imports	3.6	12.8	6.1	6.1	2.3	-2.6	-13.7	12.8	4.9	2.2
Goods	2.9	13.1	6.7	5.9	1.8	-3.7	-15.8	15.2	5.2	2.1
Services	6.5	11.0	3.1	7.4	4.7	3.1	-3.1	2.8	3.1	2.7
Government consumption expenditures and gross investment	3.2	1.9	0.6	1.5	1.6	2.8	3.2	0.1	-3.2	-1.0
Federal	2.1	0.3	1.7	2.5	1.7	6.8	5.7	4.4	-2.6	-1.4
National defense	0.3	-0.9	2.0	2.0	2.5	7.5	5.4	3.2	-2.3	-3.2
Nondefense	7.3	2.3	1.3	3.5	0.3	5.5	6.2	6.4	-3.0	1.8
State and local	4.1	2.8	0.0	0.9	1.5	0.3	1.6	-2.7	-3.6	-0.7

Source: U.S. Bureau of Economic Analysis, National Income and Product Accounts Tables, "Table 1.1.1. Percent Change From Preceding Period in Real Gross Domestic Product," and "Table 1.1.6. Real Gross Domestic Product, Chained Dollars," <http://www.bea.gov/iTable/>, accessed August 2013.

Table 697. Gross Domestic Product in Current and Chained (2009) Dollars by Type of Product and Sector: 1990 to 2012

[In billions of dollars (5,980 represents $5,980,000,000,000). For explanation of chained dollars, see text, this section]

Type of product and sector	1990	2000	2005	2007	2008	2009	2010	2011	2012
CURRENT DOLLARS									
Gross domestic product	**5,980**	**10,290**	**13,095**	**14,480**	**14,720**	**14,418**	**14,958**	**15,534**	**16,245**
Product:									
Goods	2,115	3,438	3,891	4,294	4,217	4,060	4,395	4,653	4,952
Durable goods	1,172	2,083	2,317	2,542	2,467	2,217	2,446	2,614	2,764
Nondurable goods	942	1,355	1,574	1,752	1,750	1,843	1,949	2,039	2,188
Services [1]	3,316	5,866	7,765	8,718	9,134	9,217	9,516	9,828	10,140
Structures	549	985.6	1,439	1,468	1,369	1,141	1,048	1,054	1,153
Sector:									
Business [2]	4,552	7,897	9,922	10,984	11,022	10,597	11,055	11,560	12,195
Nonfarm [3]	4,475	7,820	9,817	10,871	10,895	10,487	10,925	11,394	12,029
Farm	78	76	105	114	126	110	130	166	167
Households and institutions	643	1,203	1,600	1,750	1,855	1,914	1,928	1,972	2,025
General government [4]	785	1,191	1,574	1,747	1,844	1,908	1,976	2,002	2,024
Federal	304	358.7	488	536	570	604	644	663	666
State and local	480	831.8	1,087	1,210	1,273	1,304	1,332	1,339	1,357
CHAINED (2009) DOLLARS									
Gross domestic product	**8,945**	**12,565**	**14,236**	**14,877**	**14,834**	**14,418**	**14,779**	**15,052**	**15,471**
Product:									
Goods	2,198	3,432	3,955	4,334	4,302	4,060	4,408	4,598	4,833
Durable goods	(NA)	1,904	2,262	2,509	2,470	2,217	2,466	2,628	2,768
Nondurable goods	(NA)	1,532	1,691	1,821	1,830	1,843	1,942	1,972	2,068
Services [1]	5,777	7,680	8,658	9,062	9,183	9,217	9,321	9,424	9,536
Structures	1,090	1,457	1,627	1,477	1,347	1,141	1,052	1,034	1,110
Sector:									
Business [2]	6,232	9,197	10,635	11,155	11,050	10,597	10,929	11,192	11,598
Nonfarm [3]	6,178	9,117	10,536	11,075	10,957	10,487	10,818	11,089	11,499
Farm	56	84	102	86	95	110	112	106	105
Households and institutions	1,248	1,699	1,805	1,883	1,910	1,914	1,931	1,949	1,961
General government [4]	1,573	1,681	1,794	1,835	1,873	1,908	1,920	1,912	1,912
Federal	576	501	541	553	574	604	624	631	630
State and local	993	1,181	1,254	1,282	1,299	1,304	1,295	1,282	1,282

NA Not available. [1] Includes government consumption expenditures, which are for services (such as education and national defense) produced by government. In current dollars, these services are valued at their cost of production. [2] Equals gross domestic product excluding gross value added of households and institutions and of general government. [3] Equals gross domestic business value added excluding gross farm value added. [4] Equals compensation of general government employees plus general government consumption of fixed capital.

Source: U.S. Bureau of Economic Analysis, "National Income and Product Accounts Tables," <http://www.bea.gov/iTable/>, accessed August 2013.

Table 698. Gross Domestic Product in Current and Chained (2005) Dollars by Industry: 2000 to 2012

[In billions of dollars (9,952 represents $9,952,000,000,000). Data are based on the 2002 North American Industry Classification System (NAICS); see text, Section 15. Value added GDP is the contribution of each industry's labor and capital to its gross output and to the overall gross domestic product (GDP) of the United States. Value added is equal to an industry's gross output (sales or receipts and other operating income, commodity taxes, and inventory change) minus its intermediate inputs (consumption of goods and services purchased from other industries or imported). Current-dollar value added is calculated as the sum of distributions by an industry to its labor and capital which are derived from the components of gross domestic income]

Industry	Current dollars				Chained (2005) dollars [1]			
	2000	2005	2011	2012	2000	2005	2011	2012
Gross domestic product	**9,952**	**12,623**	**15,076**	**15,685**	**11,216**	**12,623**	**13,299**	**13,593**
Private industries	8,736	11,037	13,082	13,658	9,786	11,037	11,557	11,887
Agriculture, forestry, fishing, and hunting	96	127	174	169	104	127	122	118
Farms	74	102	139	(NA)	84	102	92	(NA)
Forestry, fishing, and related activities	22	25	35	(NA)	21	25	30	(NA)
Mining	109	192	290	285	233	192	235	243
Oil and gas extraction	68	129	174	(NA)	155	129	164	(NA)
Mining, except oil and gas	28	36	58	(NA)	46	36	29	(NA)
Mining support activities	14	27	57	(NA)	29	27	42	(NA)
Utilities	174	206	298	304	223	206	230	232
Construction	467	613	530	559	655	613	450	464
Manufacturing	1,416	1,569	1,732	1,867	1,390	1,569	1,586	1,684
Durable goods	839	878	910	1,000	742	878	968	1,057
Wood products	28	33	23	(NA)	33	33	33	(NA)
Nonmetallic mineral products	42	45	33	(NA)	45	45	30	(NA)
Primary metals	46	54	50	(NA)	62	54	40	(NA)
Fabricated metal products	121	121	122	(NA)	130	121	105	(NA)
Machinery	111	110	132	(NA)	111	110	120	(NA)
Computer and electronic products	172	184	227	(NA)	78	184	362	(NA)
Electrical equipment, appliances, and components	44	40	47	(NA)	43	40	40	(NA)
Motor vehicles, bodies & trailers, & parts	117	113	77	(NA)	94	113	85	(NA)
Other transportation equipment	66	76	94	(NA)	79	76	86	(NA)
Furniture and related products	34	34	26	(NA)	35	34	23	(NA)
Miscellaneous manufacturing	58	70	80	(NA)	60	70	76	(NA)
Nondurable goods	577	691	821	867	649	691	630	648
Food & beverage & tobacco	165	172	215	(NA)	176	172	193	(NA)
Textile mills and textile product mills	28	24	18	(NA)	27	24	16	(NA)
Apparel and leather and allied products	21	16	12	(NA)	20	16	12	(NA)
Paper products	62	54	53	(NA)	58	54	40	(NA)
Printing and related support activities	40	38	32	(NA)	37	38	33	(NA)
Petroleum and coal products	44	139	169	(NA)	74	139	96	(NA)
Chemical products	152	183	254	(NA)	170	183	184	(NA)
Plastics and rubber products	65	66	69	(NA)	66	66	56	(NA)
Wholesale trade	618	726	845	898	606	726	719	753
Retail trade	686	838	906	949	753	838	850	883
Transportation and warehousing	301	370	448	469	319	370	394	399
Air transportation	53	56	70	(NA)	43	56	57	(NA)
Rail transportation	23	27	37	(NA)	27	27	25	(NA)
Water transportation	8	9	15	(NA)	8	9	25	(NA)
Truck transportation	97	120	126	(NA)	106	120	120	(NA)
Transit & ground passenger transport	18	21	28	(NA)	21	21	22	(NA)
Pipeline transportation	9	10	21	(NA)	9	10	14	(NA)
Other transportation & support	68	92	107	(NA)	76	92	90	(NA)
Warehousing and storage	26	35	46	(NA)	29	35	44	(NA)
Information	418	587	647	691	398	587	673	712
Publishing industries (includes software)	100	150	144	(NA)	102	150	144	(NA)
Motion picture and sound recording	37	55	60	(NA)	43	55	55	(NA)
Broadcasting and telecommunications	257	311	364	(NA)	228	311	389	(NA)
Information and data processing services	24	71	78	(NA)	24	71	86	(NA)
Finance and insurance	762	1,019	1,159	1,242	841	1,019	1,031	1,068
Real estate and rental and leasing	1,236	1,579	1,899	1,926	1,422	1,579	1,735	1,755
Professional, scientific, and technical services	662	870	1,152	1,192	745	870	1,007	1,019
Legal services	139	191	209	(NA)	176	191	156	(NA)
Computer systems design, related services	114	131	198	(NA)	102	131	207	(NA)
Miscellaneous services	410	548	744	(NA)	468	548	654	(NA)
Management of companies & enterprises	171	218	284	296	215	218	210	218
Admin/support waste management/remediation services	283	371	449	465	311	371	409	419
Educational services	86	120	174	180	116	120	129	129
Health care and social assistance	592	833	1,137	1,165	711	833	973	977
Ambulatory health care services	288	406	560	(NA)	327	406	488	(NA)
Hospitals, nursing, residential care	253	355	480	(NA)	323	355	402	(NA)
Social assistance	52	73	97	(NA)	62	73	83	(NA)
Arts, entertainment, and recreation	99	119	148	153	115	119	132	136
Performing arts, spectator sports, museums, and related activities	48	66	83	(NA)	59	66	72	(NA)
Amusements, gambling, & recreation	50	53	65	(NA)	55	53	60	(NA)
Accommodation and food services	283	367	443	472	328	367	381	394
Accommodation	89	110	119	(NA)	100	110	114	(NA)
Food services and drinking places	194	256	324	(NA)	227	256	267	(NA)
Other services, except government	278	313	370	377	347	313	298	298
Government	1,215	1,586	1,994	2,026	1,509	1,586	1,647	1,641
Federal	378	502	658	668	482	502	548	545
State and local	837	1,084	1,336	1,358	1,027	1,084	1,099	1,097

NA Not available. [1] Chained (2005) dollar series are calculated as the product of the chain-type quantity index and the 2005 current-dollar value of the corresponding series, divided by 100. Because the formula for the chain-type quantity indexes uses weights of more than one period, the corresponding chained-dollar estimates are usually not additive.

Source: U.S. Bureau of Economic Analysis, Industry Economic Accounts Data, "GDP by Industry, Value Added by Industry," <http://www.bea.gov/industry/index.htm>, accessed August 2013.

Table 699. Gross Domestic Product by State in Current and Chained (2005) Dollars: 2000 to 2012

[In billions of dollars (9,884.2 represents $9,884,200,000,000). For definition of gross domestic product by state or chained dollars, see text, this section]

State	Current dollars					Chained (2005) dollars				
	2000	2005	2010	2011	2012	2000	2005	2010	2011	2012
United States [1]	**9,884.2**	**12,539.1**	**14,388.8**	**14,959.8**	**15,566.1**	**11,225.4**	**12,539.1**	**12,897.1**	**13,108.3**	**13,430.6**
Alabama	116.0	151.0	172.8	178.5	183.5	132.7	151.0	153.8	155.4	157.3
Alaska	25.9	37.8	47.9	51.2	51.9	34.2	37.8	43.5	44.2	44.7
Arizona	161.8	222.6	247.3	256.0	266.9	178.8	222.6	221.0	224.8	230.6
Arkansas	68.3	88.5	103.2	106.6	109.6	77.5	88.5	92.1	92.7	93.9
California	1,319.5	1,688.9	1,845.2	1,909.0	2,003.5	1,472.3	1,688.9	1,672.5	1,692.3	1,751.0
Colorado	172.0	217.3	254.6	264.7	274.0	195.3	217.3	231.0	234.9	239.9
Connecticut	163.5	196.3	221.8	225.4	229.3	184.8	196.3	197.6	197.5	197.2
Delaware	40.6	54.4	62.8	64.4	66.0	46.5	54.4	55.5	56.0	56.1
District of Columbia	58.3	82.5	103.7	107.2	109.8	69.9	82.5	90.0	91.4	92.1
Florida	481.2	681.2	728.0	746.4	777.2	549.3	681.2	650.3	656.3	672.3
Georgia	294.0	363.2	402.0	417.4	433.6	329.3	363.2	358.8	366.3	374.0
Hawaii	41.5	56.9	67.3	70.0	72.4	48.8	56.9	59.7	60.9	61.9
Idaho	36.1	48.7	55.6	57.1	58.2	39.4	48.7	50.7	50.8	51.0
Illinois	474.5	568.1	642.8	670.2	695.2	537.4	568.1	571.2	583.1	594.2
Indiana	198.2	239.3	270.7	284.3	298.6	222.3	239.3	241.9	247.2	255.4
Iowa	93.3	120.0	138.4	146.1	152.4	105.3	120.0	124.0	126.8	129.8
Kansas	85.7	104.9	126.6	134.8	139.0	97.9	104.9	113.3	116.9	118.5
Kentucky	113.2	138.8	161.1	168.0	173.5	128.5	138.8	142.0	144.8	146.8
Louisiana	131.3	196.9	227.4	237.4	243.3	168.0	196.9	200.9	195.6	198.5
Maine	36.4	45.5	51.3	52.5	53.7	41.7	45.5	45.6	45.8	46.0
Maryland	182.9	247.2	296.0	305.2	317.7	209.7	247.2	264.3	268.4	274.9
Massachusetts	273.0	323.3	376.9	388.6	403.8	301.6	323.3	340.2	346.0	353.7
Michigan	337.5	375.8	367.1	385.1	400.5	372.1	375.8	329.8	341.2	348.9
Minnesota	188.8	237.8	268.6	280.0	294.7	211.5	237.8	240.4	244.3	253.0
Mississippi	65.6	81.4	95.8	97.5	101.5	76.1	81.4	85.4	84.4	86.4
Missouri	181.0	216.3	243.9	249.5	258.8	204.9	216.3	216.7	217.4	221.7
Montana	21.6	30.1	36.5	38.9	40.4	25.8	30.1	31.9	32.7	33.4
Nebraska	57.3	72.5	90.9	96.2	99.6	65.3	72.5	80.6	82.2	83.4
Nevada	75.9	114.5	124.8	129.4	133.6	88.0	114.5	109.6	111.6	113.2
New Hampshire	44.2	53.7	61.1	63.3	64.7	48.8	53.7	55.2	56.4	56.7
New Jersey	350.1	430.2	483.0	493.2	508.0	394.4	430.2	431.4	432.4	438.2
New Mexico	50.3	67.8	77.7	79.6	80.6	58.5	67.8	70.8	70.5	70.7
New York	769.3	959.9	1,136.4	1,169.4	1,205.9	862.5	959.9	1,013.3	1,025.0	1,038.5
North Carolina	281.5	354.7	426.9	436.1	456.0	316.6	354.7	380.7	382.7	392.9
North Dakota	18.3	24.7	35.4	40.0	46.0	21.3	24.7	31.6	34.1	38.7
Ohio	380.9	444.1	465.7	490.3	509.4	429.0	444.1	414.0	425.9	435.1
Oklahoma	91.3	120.5	147.6	156.1	161.0	110.4	120.5	132.9	135.5	138.3
Oregon	113.2	143.4	181.5	189.0	198.7	121.1	143.4	174.2	180.3	187.4
Pennsylvania	395.6	482.2	558.8	581.3	600.9	452.4	482.2	493.5	502.8	511.3
Rhode Island	33.6	44.2	48.6	49.4	51.0	38.5	44.2	43.2	43.2	43.8
South Carolina	115.4	141.9	162.3	168.7	176.2	130.9	141.9	143.4	146.7	150.6
South Dakota	24.0	31.5	38.3	41.7	42.5	26.9	31.5	34.4	35.9	36.0
Tennessee	177.5	224.3	253.6	263.6	277.0	198.1	224.3	227.4	232.9	240.5
Texas	731.1	968.6	1,226.7	1,321.0	1,397.4	870.1	968.6	1,116.3	1,156.0	1,211.7
Utah	69.5	90.6	118.2	124.5	130.5	79.7	90.6	105.2	108.1	111.8
Vermont	18.0	22.7	25.8	26.5	27.3	20.0	22.7	23.3	23.6	23.9
Virginia	261.8	356.4	422.8	433.6	445.9	298.3	356.4	377.5	381.5	385.8
Washington	227.7	279.3	342.7	357.1	375.7	259.2	279.3	307.7	313.8	325.2
West Virginia	41.4	51.9	62.7	66.1	69.4	49.6	51.9	53.6	54.6	56.4
Wisconsin	177.4	218.7	245.4	253.3	261.5	198.9	218.7	219.1	221.9	225.1
Wyoming	17.1	26.3	36.5	38.2	38.4	23.2	26.3	32.0	31.2	31.3

[1] For chained (2005) dollar estimates, states will not add to U.S. total.

Source: U.S. Bureau of Economic Analysis, Regional Economic Accounts, "Gross Domestic Product by State," <http://www.bea.gov/regional /index.htm>, accessed August 2013.

Table 700. Gross Domestic Product by Selected Industries and State: 2012

[In billions of dollars (15,566.1 represents $15,566,100,000,000). For definition of gross domestic product by state, see text, this section. Industries based on 2002 North American Industry Classification System, see text, Section 15]

State	Total [1]	Manu- facturing	Whole- sale trade	Retail trade	Infor- mation	Finance and insur- ance	Real estate, rental, and leasing	Profes- sional and technical services	Health care and social assis- tance	Govern- ment [2]
United States	**15,566.1**	**1,866.7**	**897.9**	**949.1**	**690.6**	**1,242.3**	**1,926.3**	**1,192.3**	**1,164.8**	**1,908.5**
Alabama	183.5	30.0	10.0	13.3	4.0	11.3	17.9	11.5	13.4	30.3
Alaska	51.9	1.7	1.1	2.1	1.2	1.7	4.3	2.3	3.2	9.8
Arizona	266.9	21.9	14.6	19.9	7.1	24.0	37.4	16.1	22.1	34.2
Arkansas	109.6	15.6	7.8	8.1	2.6	5.2	11.5	4.0	8.8	15.4
California	2,003.5	213.3	112.6	125.0	144.1	114.6	309.1	188.7	130.3	223.6
Colorado	274.0	20.0	14.4	16.0	22.5	17.0	34.6	26.7	17.0	34.9
Connecticut	229.3	24.1	12.8	12.1	9.6	36.9	33.5	16.5	18.8	21.0
Delaware	66.0	4.4	2.2	2.6	1.2	24.6	7.0	4.6	4.1	6.1
District of Columbia	109.8	0.3	1.0	1.2	5.3	4.8	9.5	23.6	5.0	37.6
Florida	777.2	37.0	51.1	60.2	31.0	54.3	123.5	55.7	67.5	95.7
Georgia	433.6	48.6	32.5	26.9	27.7	29.5	48.3	31.7	28.6	59.7
Hawaii	72.4	1.3	2.1	4.8	1.6	2.8	12.8	3.3	4.5	17.6
Idaho	58.2	7.6	3.2	4.5	1.2	3.0	6.8	3.9	4.6	8.0
Illinois	695.2	92.4	48.5	40.4	23.2	67.2	85.6	59.9	48.8	69.8
Indiana	298.6	84.2	15.0	17.5	6.2	18.4	27.7	12.2	23.4	28.8
Iowa	152.4	25.4	8.9	9.0	4.1	19.3	15.1	5.1	10.3	17.1
Kansas	139.0	20.5	8.5	9.2	6.2	9.5	12.3	7.2	10.4	20.6
Kentucky	173.5	29.7	11.0	11.0	4.6	9.4	15.7	7.1	14.7	28.3
Louisiana	243.3	55.1	10.6	14.3	4.3	8.3	22.0	11.4	14.9	25.7
Maine	53.7	5.5	2.7	4.5	1.0	4.1	7.4	2.9	6.2	7.4
Maryland	317.7	18.7	14.0	17.6	12.0	18.4	50.8	35.4	24.7	58.6
Massachusetts	403.8	41.6	20.2	18.3	19.8	37.0	57.0	49.4	39.7	38.1
Michigan	400.5	66.2	25.0	27.3	10.2	25.8	44.9	31.4	35.8	45.8
Minnesota	294.7	40.4	19.9	16.3	10.1	28.8	36.5	18.5	26.0	28.6
Mississippi	101.5	15.3	4.6	8.1	2.1	4.9	9.5	3.5	7.6	18.4
Missouri	258.8	32.3	15.9	16.9	13.6	17.1	26.7	16.7	23.3	32.2
Montana	40.4	2.9	2.1	2.7	0.9	2.1	4.8	2.1	3.7	6.3
Nebraska	99.6	12.5	5.2	5.7	2.9	8.7	9.0	4.8	7.2	13.0
Nevada	133.6	5.5	4.8	9.2	2.4	15.4	16.7	6.8	7.2	13.8
New Hampshire	64.7	7.7	4.1	5.1	2.4	5.9	8.9	4.6	6.0	6.7
New Jersey	508.0	38.2	39.9	30.9	22.5	40.9	85.1	47.7	39.2	55.7
New Mexico	80.6	5.8	2.7	5.2	2.3	2.8	10.0	6.5	6.2	15.6
New York	1,205.9	63.1	62.8	63.5	86.6	194.4	164.9	111.5	90.7	126.2
North Carolina	456.0	88.3	23.3	24.7	13.6	50.5	45.9	24.4	29.5	65.6
North Dakota	46.0	3.0	3.8	2.7	1.1	2.9	4.8	1.5	3.3	5.2
Ohio	509.4	87.2	31.8	33.1	13.9	39.6	51.4	30.3	46.6	56.6
Oklahoma	161.0	17.5	8.3	10.5	4.1	8.0	16.5	7.2	11.6	27.1
Oregon	198.7	55.2	11.5	9.4	5.5	8.6	23.1	9.8	14.8	22.5
Pennsylvania	600.9	70.6	36.0	34.4	24.3	46.0	72.0	47.7	60.7	57.7
Rhode Island	51.0	3.9	2.6	2.8	2.3	5.6	7.6	2.8	5.2	6.7
South Carolina	176.2	28.7	9.7	12.8	4.3	9.0	19.8	9.5	11.5	30.0
South Dakota	42.5	4.0	2.5	3.0	1.0	6.7	3.4	1.2	3.7	5.2
Tennessee	277.0	41.4	17.6	20.4	8.1	18.4	28.0	16.2	28.4	32.1
Texas	1,397.4	211.0	93.9	81.6	48.0	91.8	121.9	95.6	83.0	148.5
Utah	130.5	19.2	6.3	9.0	4.7	14.3	14.3	8.1	7.1	16.5
Vermont	27.3	3.2	1.3	2.2	0.7	1.5	3.7	1.8	2.8	3.8
Virginia	445.9	40.1	17.0	23.4	18.3	29.1	57.1	61.1	26.9	81.9
Washington	375.7	46.5	20.8	27.1	34.0	17.5	48.9	26.1	24.8	53.7
West Virginia	69.4	6.2	3.1	5.1	1.6	2.4	6.3	2.8	6.4	12.2
Wisconsin	261.5	50.0	15.5	15.4	8.1	21.5	31.0	12.0	23.5	27.2
Wyoming	38.4	2.3	1.4	2.1	0.5	0.9	3.7	1.1	1.5	5.4

[1] Includes industries not shown separately. [2] Includes federal civilian and military and state and local government.

Source: U.S. Bureau of Economic Analysis, Regional Economic Accounts, "Gross Domestic Product by State," <http://www.bea.gov/regional/index.htm>, accessed August 2013.

Table 701. Relation of GDP, GNP, Net National Product, National Income, Personal Income, Disposable Personal Income, and Personal Saving: 1990 to 2012

[In billions of dollars (5,980 represents $5,980,000,000,000). For definitions, see text, this section. Minus sign (–) indicates deficit or net disbursement]

Item	1990	2000	2005	2008	2009	2010	2011	2012
Gross domestic product (GDP)..................	**5,980**	**10,290**	**13,095**	**14,720**	**14,418**	**14,958**	**15,534**	**16,245**
Plus: Income receipts from the rest of the world..	189	383	576	857	644	720	803	819
Less: Income payments to the rest of the world...	154	346	482	684	497	514	542	566
Equals: Gross national product (GNP).........	**6,014**	**10,327**	**13,189**	**14,893**	**14,565**	**15,164**	**15,795**	**16,497**
Less: Consumption of fixed capital.................	887	1,514	1,982	2,363	2,368	2,382	2,453	2,543
Equals: Net national product....................	**5,127**	**8,813**	**11,207**	**12,530**	**12,197**	**12,783**	**13,342**	**13,955**
Less: Statistical discrepancy.........................	91	-95	-34	99	72	43	-54	-17
Equals: National income...........................	**5,036**	**8,907**	**11,241**	**12,431**	**12,125**	**12,740**	**13,396**	**13,972**
Less: Corporate profits [1]...........................	417	781	1,478	1,285	1,393	1,741	1,878	2,010
Taxes on production and imports less subsidies..	398	663	874	989	968	1,001	1,037	1,066
Contributions for government social insurance..	410	706	873	988	964	984	918	951
Net interest and miscellaneous payments on assets...	450	565	497	693	563	489	457	440
Business current transfer payments (net).......	39	85	94	116	127	129	130	107
Current surplus of government enterprises......	3	11	-6	-21	-21	-23	-24	-28
Plus: Personal income receipts on assets.........	991	1,454	1,667	2,167	1,812	1,740	1,885	1,959
Personal current transfer receipts...............	595	1,083	1,512	1,884	2,140	2,277	2,307	2,358
Equals: Personal income..........................	**4,905**	**8,633**	**10,610**	**12,431**	**12,082**	**12,435**	**13,191**	**13,744**
Less: Personal current taxes.........................	593	1,232	1,209	1,435	1,145	1,192	1,404	1,498
Equals: Disposable personal income...........	**4,312**	**7,401**	**9,402**	**10,995**	**10,937**	**11,244**	**11,787**	**12,246**
Less: Personal outlays.............................	3,976	7,103	9,159	10,444	10,267	10,610	11,119	11,558
Equals: Personal saving........................	**335**	**298**	**243**	**551**	**671**	**634**	**668**	**687**

[1] Corporate profits with inventory valuation and capital consumption adjustments.

Source: U.S. Bureau of Economic Analysis, National Income and Product Accounts Tables, "Table 1.7.5. Relation of Gross Domestic Product, Gross National Product, Net National Product, National Income, and Personal Income," and "Table 2.1. Personal Income and Its Disposition," <http://www.bea.gov/itable/>, accessed August 2013.

Table 702. Gross Saving and Investment: 1990 to 2012

[In billions of dollars (1,118 represents $1,118,000,000,000), except as noted]

Item	1990	2000	2005	2008	2009	2010	2011	2012
Gross saving.......................................	**1,118**	**2,109**	**2,337**	**2,282**	**2,072**	**2,255**	**2,461**	**2,672**
Net saving...	231	595	356	-82	-297	-127	9	129
Net private saving....................................	438	429	728	719	1,225	1,440	1,470	1,492
Domestic business....................................	103	131	485	167	554	806	802	804
Undistributed corporate profits.................	90	97	660	265	630	900	772	985
Inventory valuation adjustment, corporate......	-13	-17	-32	-37	7	-41	-56	-10
Capital consumption adjustment, corporate.....	26	51	-144	-60	-82	-53	86	-171
Households and institutions.........................	335	298	243	551	671	634	668	687
Personal saving....................................	335	298	243	551	671	634	668	687
Net government saving...............................	-207	166	-372	-800	-1,522	-1,567	-1,461	-1,362
Federal...	-201	156	-305	-635	-1,250	-1,330	-1,248	-1,110
State and local..	-7	10	-67	-165	-272	-237	-213	-253
Consumption of fixed capital........................	887	1,514	1,982	2,363	2,368	2,382	2,453	2,543
Private..	689	1,237	1,635	1,937	1,926	1,924	1,974	2,049
Domestic business...................................	564	1,007	1,273	1,522	1,522	1,523	1,572	1,639
Households and institutions.......................	125	230	362	415	403	401	403	410
Government..	198	278	347	427	443	458	478	494
Federal...	131	162	189	226	235	245	257	262
State and local..	67	116	157	200	208	213	222	231
Gross domestic investment, capital acct. transactions, and net lending.................	**1,209**	**2,015**	**2,304**	**2,381**	**2,144**	**2,298**	**2,408**	**2,655**
Gross domestic investment..........................	1,284	2,424	3,041	3,059	2,525	2,753	2,865	3,094
Gross private domestic investment................	994	2,034	2,527	2,425	1,878	2,101	2,232	2,475
Gross government investment......................	290	390	514	635	647	652	633	619
Capital account transactions (net) [1]............	7	–	-13	-5	1	1	2	-7
Net lending or net borrowing........................	-82	-410	-724	-673	-382	-455	-459	-432
Statistical discrepancy...............................	91	-95	-34	99	72	43	-54	-17
Addenda:								
Gross private saving..................................	1,127	1,666	2,363	2,656	3,151	3,364	3,445	3,541
Gross government saving.............................	-10	444	-25	-374	-1,079	-1,109	-983	-869
Federal...	-70	317	-116	-409	-1,015	-1,084	-992	-847
State and local..	60	126	91	35	-64	-25	9	-21
Net domestic investment............................	397	910	1,059	696	157	371	412	551
Gross saving as a percentage of gross national income..	18.9	20.2	17.7	15.4	14.3	14.9	15.5	16.2
Net saving as a percentage of gross national income..	3.9	5.7	2.7	-0.6	-2.0	-0.8	0.1	0.8
Disaster losses [2].....................................	–	–	110	19	–	–	–	46

– Represents or rounds to zero. [1] Consists of capital transfers and the acquisition and disposal of nonproduced nonfinancial assets. Prior to 1982, reflects only capital grants paid to the U.S. territories and the Commonwealths of Puerto Rico and Northern Mariana Islands. [2] Consists of damages to fixed assets.

Source: U.S. Bureau of Economic Analysis, National Income and Product Accounts Tables, "Table 5.1 Saving and Investment by Sector," <http://www.bea.gov/iTable/index_nipa.cfm>, accessed August 2013.

Table 703. Financial Accounts of the United States—Composition of Individuals' Savings: 1990 to 2012

[In billions of dollars (532.6 represents $532,600,000,000). Combined statement for households, farm business, and nonfarm noncorporate business. Minus sign (-) indicates decrease]

Composition of savings	1990	2000	2005	2008	2009	2010	2011	2012
Net acquisition of financial assets	**532.6**	**379.6**	**1,306.6**	**586.2**	**195.6**	**689.3**	**966.8**	**1,010.7**
Foreign deposits	1.4	7.6	2.4	-23.7	-6.4	1.6	-1.9	-2.5
Checkable deposits and currency	-9.2	-95.1	-37.3	248.7	49.0	37.6	323.1	147.2
Time and savings deposits	47.9	345.4	507.8	188.7	172.2	155.6	353.9	412.3
Money market fund shares	39.2	176.5	46.8	236.2	-270.3	-180.4	11.5	1.3
Securities	200.9	-624.5	-18.2	-237.1	378.0	155.6	-189.2	179.1
Open market paper	5.8	12.4	14.7	-101.3	28.7	-2.9	-2.6	-0.5
U.S. savings bonds	8.5	-1.7	0.7	-2.4	-2.8	-3.3	-2.7	-2.8
Treasury bills and other Treasury securities	88.8	-206.1	-96.6	246.3	496.8	420.7	-253.7	373.9
Agency and GSE-backed securities [1]	35.3	29.4	171.4	276.6	-633.6	-44.7	12.6	-246.5
Municipal securities	34.7	6.0	78.2	47.5	107.3	44.8	-65.5	-151.2
Corporate and foreign bonds	47.1	93.5	47.9	-81.1	58.7	-323.5	53.1	25.6
Corporate equities [2]	-50.8	-637.5	-414.4	-576.8	-21.2	-170.8	-122.8	-321.3
Mutual fund shares	31.5	79.5	179.9	-45.8	344.1	235.3	192.5	501.8
Life insurance reserves	26.5	50.2	16.1	61.7	23.7	9.0	86.9	-26.3
Pension fund reserves	191.8	263.0	395.6	53.6	30.2	335.2	263.6	239.4
Miscellaneous and other assets	34.1	256.5	393.2	57.9	-180.9	175.1	119.0	60.2
Gross investment in nonfinancial assets	**797.3**	**1,517.3**	**2,094.7**	**1,826.4**	**1,587.9**	**1,599.8**	**1,680.0**	**1,800.4**
Minus: Consumption of fixed capital	571.2	907.7	1,197.7	1,412.4	1,421.1	1,420.6	1,454.9	1,477.4
Equals: Net investment in nonfinancial assets	**226.1**	**609.6**	**897.0**	**414.0**	**166.8**	**179.3**	**225.2**	**322.9**
Net increase in liabilities	**237.2**	**918.7**	**1,705.5**	**284.8**	**-265.1**	**-295.9**	**-176.9**	**179.4**
Home mortgages	207.1	423.9	1,116.3	-108.9	-191.1	-347.2	-252.0	-240.5
Other mortgages	-4.4	106.7	117.7	230.9	22.0	-43.9	-26.3	-17.1
Consumer credit	15.1	176.5	100.4	19.6	-111.5	-17.9	93.4	154.6
Policy loans	4.1	2.8	0.8	5.9	0.7	3.4	2.4	1.4
Security credit	-3.7	7.2	-31.6	-160.7	38.1	75.2	-39.3	64.9
Other liabilities	19.1	201.6	401.9	298.0	-23.3	34.4	44.8	216.3
Personal saving, FOF concept (FOF [3])	537.2	106.1	463.1	703.5	575.0	1,115.8	1,347.9	1,126.1
Personal saving, NIPA concept (FOF [3])	457.4	-131.8	212.9	569.4	516.8	1,024.4	1,214.9	934.4
Personal saving, NIPA concept (NIPA [4])	276.7	213.1	143.2	592.3	508.2	566.7	489.4	490.5

[1] GSE = government-sponsored enterprises. [2] Only directly held and those in closed-end and exchange-traded funds. Other equities are included in mutual funds and life insurance and pension reserves. [3] Flow of Funds measure. [4] National Income and Product Accounts measure.

Source: Board of Governors of the Federal Reserve System, "Federal Reserve Statistical Release, Z.1, Financial Accounts of the United States," June 2013. See also <http://www.federalreserve.gov/apps/fof/FOFTables.aspx>.

Table 704. Government Consumption Expenditures and Gross Investment by Level of Government and Type: 2000 to 2012

[In billions of dollars (1,834.4 represents $1,834,400,000,000). Government consumption expenditures are services (such as education and national defense) produced by government that are valued at their cost of production. Excludes government sales to other sectors and government own-account investment (construction, software, and research and development). Gross government investment consists of general government and government enterprise expenditures for fixed assets; inventory investment is included in government consumption expenditures. For explanation of national income and chained dollars, see text, Section 13]

Item	Current Dollars				Chained (2009) dollars			
	2000	2005	2011	2012	2000	2005	2011	2012
Government consumption expenditures and gross investment, total	**1,834.4**	**2,493.7**	**3,158.7**	**3,167.0**	**2,498.2**	**2,826.2**	**2,992.3**	**2,963.1**
Consumption expenditures	1,444.2	1,980.0	2,526.1	2,548.0	1,998.4	2,239.5	2,379.4	2,374.4
Gross investment	390.3	513.6	632.6	619.0	500.6	586.6	612.6	588.0
Structures	189.7	246.8	295.8	285.3	305.3	314.0	285.3	265.3
Equipment	87.4	113.0	146.3	146.7	79.8	111.4	144.8	144.5
Intellectual property products	113.2	153.9	190.5	186.9	127.2	164.1	182.4	178.3
Federal	**632.4**	**946.3**	**1,304.1**	**1,295.7**	**817.7**	**1,034.8**	**1,237.9**	**1,220.3**
Consumption expenditures	475.1	723.4	1,008.7	1,011.7	645.9	799.7	952.7	947.3
Gross investment	157.4	222.9	295.4	284.0	173.7	235.4	285.1	272.8
Structures	13.8	15.2	30.0	22.7	20.8	18.2	29.4	21.5
Equipment	48.6	75.9	105.5	105.6	47.3	76.6	103.3	103.2
Intellectual property products	95.0	131.7	159.9	155.8	108.0	140.8	152.4	148.0
National defense	**391.7**	**608.3**	**835.8**	**817.1**	**512.3**	**665.5**	**794.6**	**769.1**
Consumption expenditures	308.3	475.9	662.8	652.0	423.3	525.7	627.1	610.4
Gross investment	83.4	132.3	173.0	165.1	91.4	140.0	167.3	158.5
Structures	5.4	7.2	13.4	8.4	8.2	8.5	13.1	8.0
Equipment	37.8	60.7	87.0	86.2	38.3	62.7	84.9	83.9
Intellectual property products	40.2	64.5	72.7	70.5	45.7	68.9	69.3	66.6
Nondefense	**240.7**	**338.1**	**468.2**	**478.6**	**305.4**	**369.4**	**443.3**	**451.2**
Consumption expenditures	166.8	247.5	345.8	359.7	222.7	274.0	325.6	336.9
Gross investment	74.0	90.5	122.4	118.9	82.2	95.4	117.8	114.2
Structures	8.4	8.1	16.7	14.2	12.6	9.7	16.3	13.5
Equipment	10.8	15.2	18.5	19.5	8.8	13.9	18.4	19.3
Intellectual property products	54.8	67.3	87.2	85.3	62.3	71.9	83.1	81.5
State and local	**1,202.0**	**1,547.4**	**1,854.7**	**1,871.3**	**1,689.1**	**1,792.3**	**1,754.5**	**1,742.8**
Consumption expenditures	969.1	1,256.6	1,517.4	1,536.4	1,355.5	1,440.0	1,426.8	1,427.1
Gross investment	232.9	290.8	337.2	334.9	334.0	352.3	327.3	315.1
Structures	176.0	231.5	265.8	262.7	284.7	296.2	255.9	243.7
Equipment	38.8	37.1	40.9	41.1	32.6	34.8	41.5	41.3
Intellectual property products	18.1	22.1	30.6	31.2	19.2	23.3	30.0	30.3

Source: U.S. Bureau of Economic Analysis, National Income and Product Accounts, "Table 3.9.5 Government Consumption Expenditures and Gross Investment" and "Table 3.9.6 Real Government Consumption Expenditures and Gross Investment, Chained Dollars," <http://www.bea.gov/iTable/>, accessed August 2013.

Table 705. Personal Consumption Expenditures by Function: 2000 to 2012

[In billions of dollars (6,801.6 represents $6,801,600,000,000). In current and chained (2009) dollars. For definition of chained dollars, see text, this section. Minus sign (-) indicates decrease]

Function	Current dollars				Chained (2009) dollars			
	2000	2005	2011	2012	2000	2005	2011	2012
Personal consumption expenditures [1]	**6,801.6**	**8,790.3**	**10,711.8**	**11,149.6**	**8,182.1**	**9,527.8**	**10,291.3**	**10,517.6**
Food and nonalcoholic beverages purchased for off-premises consumption	463.1	575.3	715.4	740.9	591.3	655.3	682.5	689.4
Alcoholic beverages purchased for off-premises consumption	77.1	92.6	117.2	121.8	92.9	102.0	116.1	119.7
Clothing, footwear, and related services	297.5	326.6	354.0	370.8	275.7	325.0	349.9	354.0
Clothing	250.6	271.5	288.7	302.2	227.4	267.8	285.5	288.0
Footwear [2]	46.9	55.1	65.3	68.6	48.2	57.0	64.4	66.0
Housing [1]	1,010.5	1,332.5	1,660.0	1,719.9	1,320.5	1,493.6	1,637.0	1,658.4
Rental of tenant-occupied nonfarm housing [3]	227.9	268.3	402.3	430.4	306.4	306.8	395.2	411.7
Imputed rental of owner-occupied nonfarm housing [4]	768.9	1,044.3	1,233.8	1,263.7	993.0	1,164.3	1,219.8	1,224.6
Household utilities and fuels	204.0	273.5	330.3	320.7	310.9	320.2	310.5	301.6
Water supply and sanitation	50.4	61.3	82.1	85.9	76.7	75.9	73.4	72.8
Electricity, gas, and other fuels	153.5	212.2	248.2	234.7	234.1	244.2	237.0	228.5
Furnishings, household equipment, and routine household maintenance [1]	343.4	431.2	434.5	458.3	336.2	435.1	450.6	474.2
Furniture, furnishings, and floor coverings [5]	114.5	149.4	142.3	152.1	100.9	142.1	151.9	163.4
Household appliances [6]	37.6	49.5	47.7	48.8	39.9	53.8	49.9	48.8
Tools and equipment for house and garden	17.1	21.0	18.4	19.6	17.2	21.2	18.7	19.6
Medical products, appliances, and equipment	191.2	291.7	412.0	432.0	247.1	322.4	388.1	395.7
Pharmaceutical and other medical products [7]	159.0	248.5	353.2	370.0	210.7	276.7	329.5	334.5
Outpatient services	436.6	626.2	797.2	827.5	540.9	691.3	769.2	788.9
Physician services [8]	229.2	333.9	418.4	433.9	270.0	363.0	402.2	412.3
Dental services	63.6	87.9	106.8	109.4	95.4	105.3	101.6	101.7
Paramedical services	143.8	204.4	272.1	284.2	177.8	223.4	265.5	275.0
Hospital and nursing home services	481.8	696.1	970.6	1,020.2	680.3	799.1	924.1	949.5
Transportation	795.4	960.8	1,056.5	1,110.2	930.1	1,003.6	886.8	910.3
Motor vehicles	321.4	359.3	309.1	339.9	293.2	339.5	283.0	306.8
New motor vehicles	210.7	248.9	207.8	236.8	198.4	243.5	198.0	221.9
Net purchases of used motor vehicles	110.7	110.5	101.4	103.1	94.9	97.7	86.6	87.5
Motor vehicle operation [1]	399.7	523.8	662.2	682.8	566.9	577.1	528.6	530.8
Motor vehicle parts and accessories	41.8	50.6	59.6	61.8	53.3	59.6	56.4	57.1
Motor vehicle fuels, lubricants, and fluids	168.6	261.1	379.5	390.4	265.8	273.0	255.4	253.7
Motor vehicle maintenance and repair	127.4	155.1	161.9	166.4	174.8	182.4	155.6	157.2
Public transportation	74.3	77.6	85.2	87.5	83.6	87.3	75.8	75.1
Telephone and facsimile equipment	5.5	9.2	13.4	13.3	2.6	7.1	14.4	15.1
Postal and delivery services	9.9	10.4	10.8	10.4	14.0	12.3	9.8	9.1
Telecommunication services	126.4	137.7	156.0	160.6	126.4	144.8	160.0	164.4
Internet access	16.4	29.7	71.3	80.7	13.1	23.7	71.5	80.8
Recreation [1]	633.7	804.6	922.1	966.2	569.1	770.9	963.3	1,019.1
Video and audio equipment	79.9	101.4	101.9	104.4	34.0	61.4	131.5	152.0
Information processing equipment	44.1	67.0	92.0	96.1	(NA)	(NA)	(NA)	(NA)
Services related to video/audio goods and computers	57.2	70.6	90.1	94.8	73.5	77.6	87.5	88.3
Sports and recreational goods and related service	146.0	184.1	181.5	192.8	129.6	178.7	191.3	206.7
Magazines, newspapers, books, and stationery	81.0	85.0	95.1	100.9	90.8	91.1	95.1	99.0
Pets, pet products, and related services	39.7	57.2	79.5	85.1	56.9	71.0	76.8	80.5
Education [1]	134.3	180.5	260.3	274.5	236.8	227.0	237.3	239.3
Higher education	76.8	110.9	170.6	182.4	140.4	141.6	154.4	157.4
Food services	353.8	458.1	567.6	604.2	470.2	529.5	546.5	565.2
Accommodations [9]	55.0	72.5	91.1	97.5	65.1	76.3	87.5	91.6
Financial services	360.0	417.4	490.3	496.1	385.6	408.5	463.6	446.9
Insurance [1]	206.3	272.2	310.7	325.0	275.9	298.8	292.5	299.3
Life insurance	65.0	79.0	100.6	103.7	85.0	85.0	97.3	98.6
Net health insurance	94.4	129.4	143.3	154.5	131.0	147.3	132.8	140.3
Personal care [10]	132.2	175.4	213.9	223.2	157.0	193.1	211.6	217.5
Personal items [11]	63.7	78.8	98.4	106.3	66.2	89.4	92.1	98.9
Social services and religious activities [12]	81.1	110.2	143.7	147.3	104.0	122.3	138.0	139.5
Professional and other services [1]	113.0	148.4	165.9	169.4	162.7	171.8	156.2	155.9
Legal services	65.4	83.8	92.9	93.7	94.7	96.4	86.9	85.8
Accounting and other business services	17.2	25.0	27.7	28.8	24.8	29.4	26.3	26.1
Funeral and burial services	15.8	22.2	24.8	26.0	23.1	26.7	23.7	24.4
Tobacco	68.5	76.7	108.3	108.8	118.5	111.0	94.4	92.8
Net foreign travel and expenditures abroad by:								
U.S. residents [1]	-17.2	-8.5	-37.9	-47.3	-6.3	-6.6	-35.3	-41.0
Foreign travel by U.S. residents	81.8	94.9	105.8	110.0	115.5	107.2	96.3	98.4
Less: Expenditures in the United States by nonresidents	102.2	108.0	150.5	163.6	129.0	119.8	138.4	146.1
Final consumption expenditures of nonprofit institutions serving households NPISHs) [13]	158.0	210.3	277.9	290.5	162.6	209.9	278.9	293.6

NA Not available. [1] Includes other expenditures not shown separately. [2] Shoes and other footwear, and of repair and hire of footwear. [3] Rent for space (see footnote 4) and rent for appliances, furnishings, and furniture. [4] Rent for space and for heating and plumbing facilities, water heaters, lighting fixtures, kitchen cabinets, linoleum, storm windows and doors, window screens, and screen doors, excludes rent for appliances and furniture and purchases of fuel and electricity. [5] Includes clocks, lamps, lighting fixtures, other household decorative items, and repair of furniture, furnishings, and floor coverings. [6] Major household appliances, small electric household appliances, and repair of household appliances. [7] Excludes drug preparations and related products dispensed by physicians, hospitals, and other medical services. [8] Offices of physicians, HMO medical centers, and freestanding ambulatory surgical and emergency centers. [9] Transient hotels, motels, other traveler accommodations, clubs, and housing at schools. [10] Cosmetics and toiletries, electric appliances for personal care, hairdressing salons, and misc. personal care services. [11] Jewelry, watches, luggage, and similar personal items. [12] Household purchases of goods and services from business, government, and nonprofit institutions providing social services and religious activities. Purchases from nonprofit establishments exclude unrelated sales, secondary sales, and sales to businesses, government, and the rest of the world, but include membership dues and fees. [13] Net expenses of NPISHs, defined as their gross operating expenses less primary sales to households.

Source: U.S. Bureau of Economic Analysis, National Income and Product Accounts, "Table 2.4.5 Personal Consumption Expenditures by Function," and "Table 2.4.6 Real Personal Consumption Expenditures by Function, Chained Dollars," <http://www.bea.gov/iTable/>, accessed August 2013.

Table 706. Personal Income and Its Disposition: 1990 to 2012

[In billions of dollars (4,905 represents $4,905,000,000,000), except as indicated. For definition of personal income and chained dollars, see text, this section]

Item	1990	2000	2005	2008	2009	2010	2011	2012
Personal income	**4,905**	**8,633**	**10,610**	**12,431**	**12,082**	**12,435**	**13,191**	**13,744**
Compensation of employees, received	3,343	5,857	7,088	8,079	7,788	7,967	8,279	8,612
Wage and salary disbursements	2,741	4,826	5,693	6,533	6,252	6,378	6,639	6,927
Supplements to wages and salaries	602	1,031	1,395	1,546	1,536	1,590	1,640	1,685
Proprietors' income [1]	354	758	979	1,027	973	1,033	1,155	1,225
Farm	32	32	46	47	36	46	73	75
Nonfarm	322	726	933	980	938	987	1,083	1,150
Rental income of persons [2]	31	188	238	262	334	403	484	541
Personal income receipts on assets	991	1,454	1,667	2,167	1,812	1,740	1,885	1,959
Personal interest income	822	1,070	1,088	1,362	1,264	1,195	1,204	1,212
Personal dividend income	169	383	578	805	548	545	681	747
Personal current transfer receipts	595	1,083	1,512	1,884	2,140	2,277	2,307	2,358
Government social benefits to persons	573	1,041	1,486	1,847	2,102	2,234	2,260	2,317
Social security [3]	244	401	513	606	665	690	713	762
Unemployment insurance	18	21	32	51	131	139	108	84
Veterans' benefits	18	25	36	45	52	58	63	70
Other current transfer receipts, from business (net)	22	42	26	37	39	43	47	41
Less: Contributions for government social insurance	410	706	873	988	964	984	918	951
Less: Personal current taxes	593	1,232	1,209	1,435	1,145	1,192	1,404	1,498
Equals: Disposable personal income	**4,312**	**7,401**	**9,402**	**10,995**	**10,937**	**11,244**	**11,787**	**12,246**
Less: Personal outlays	3,976	7,103	9,159	10,444	10,267	10,610	11,119	11,558
Personal consumption expenditures	3,826	6,802	8,790	10,006	9,843	10,202	10,712	11,150
Personal interest payments [4]	120	218	249	290	274	251	248	248
Personal current transfer payments	31	83	120	149	150	157	159	160
Equals: Personal saving	**335**	**298**	**243**	**551**	**671**	**634**	**668**	**687**
Personal saving as a percentage of disposable personal income	7.8	4.0	2.6	5.0	6.1	5.6	5.7	5.6
Addenda:								
Disposable personal income:								
Total, billions of chained (2009) dollars [5]	6,394	8,903	10,191	10,988	10,937	11,061	11,325	11,552
Per capita:								
Current dollars	17,235	26,206	31,763	36,104	35,598	36,296	37,776	38,965
Chained (2009) dollars	25,556	31,525	34,428	36,082	35,598	35,706	36,293	36,756

[1] With inventory valuation adjustments and capital consumption adjustment. [2] Includes capital consumption adjustment. [3] Social security benefits include old-age, survivors, and disability insurance benefits that are distributed from the federal Old-Age and Survivors Insurance Trust Fund and the Disability Insurance Trust Fund. [4] Consists of nonmortgage interest paid by households. [5] The current-dollar measure is deflated by the implicit price deflator for personal consumption expenditures.

Source: U.S. Bureau of Economic Analysis, National Income and Product Accounts, "Table 2.1 Personal Income and Its Disposition," <http://www.bea.gov/iTable/>, accessed August 2013.

Table 707. Selected Per Capita Income and Product Measures in Current and Chained (2009) Dollars: 1960 to 2012

[In dollars. Based on U.S. Census Bureau estimated population including Armed Forces abroad, and institutionalized population; based on monthly averages. For explanation of chained dollars, see text, this section]

Year	Current dollars					Chained (2009) dollars				
	Gross domestic product	Gross national product	Personal income	Disposable personal income	Personal consumption expenditures	Gross domestic product	Gross national product	Personal income	Disposable personal income	Personal consumption expenditures
1960	3,006	3,023	2,338	2,083	1,834	17,182	17,318		11,877	10,461
1970	5,246	5,277	4,216	3,713	3,158	23,003	23,183		16,643	14,155
1975	7,820	7,880	6,329	5,645	4,782	24,907	25,143		18,614	15,766
1980	12,570	12,720	10,174	8,861	7,705	28,295	28,676		20,159	17,528
1985	18,225	18,331	14,741	12,991	11,416	31,805	32,034		22,961	20,176
1990	23,901	24,040	19,604	17,235	15,291	35,756	35,986		25,556	22,675
1995	28,749	28,856	23,544	20,753	18,696	38,125	38,285		27,180	24,486
1996	30,032	30,150	24,700	21,615	19,532	39,114	39,283		27,719	25,048
1997	31,538	31,626	25,920	22,527	20,372	40,383	40,512		28,398	25,682
1998	32,913	32,979	27,476	23,759	21,376	41,692	41,791		29,724	26,742
1999	34,603	34,701	28,582	24,617	22,615	43,216	43,350		30,351	27,882
2000	36,437	36,568	30,569	26,206	24,085	44,495	44,669		31,525	28,974
2001	37,252	37,434	31,509	27,179	24,917	44,472	44,702		32,077	29,407
2002	38,132	38,300	31,774	28,127	25,647	44,832	45,044		32,754	29,867
2003	39,612	39,846	32,645	29,201	26,716	45,660	45,943		33,345	30,507
2004	41,864	42,171	34,267	30,700	28,158	46,968	47,326		34,224	31,391
2005	44,242	44,558	35,846	31,763	29,698	48,094	48,450		34,428	32,189
2006	46,376	46,605	38,116	33,591	31,114	48,910	49,163		35,461	32,846
2007	47,996	48,416	39,761	34,829	32,299	49,311	49,751		35,870	33,264
2008	48,336	48,903	40,817	36,104	32,854	48,708	49,284		36,082	32,834
2009	46,927	47,406	39,325	35,598	32,037	46,927	47,406		35,598	32,037
2010	48,287	48,952	40,143	36,296	32,933	47,710	48,314		35,706	32,397
2011	49,782	50,618	42,275	37,776	34,329	48,239	48,990		36,293	32,981
2012	51,689	52,493	43,731	38,965	35,477	49,226	49,934		36,756	33,466

Source: U.S. Bureau of Economic Analysis, National Income and Product Accounts, "Table 7.1 Selected Per Capita Product and Income Series in Current and Chained Dollars," <http://www.bea.gov/iTable/>, accessed September 2013.

Table 708. Personal Income in Current and Chained (2009) Dollars by State: 2000 to 2012

[In billions of dollars (8,554.9 represents $8,554,900,000,000). Represents a measure of income received from all sources during the calendar year by residents of each state. Data exclude federal employees overseas and U.S. residents employed by private U.S. firms on temporary foreign assignment. Totals may differ from those in Tables 701, 706, and 707]

State	Current dollars					Chained (2009) dollars [1]				
	2000	2005	2010	2011	2012	2000	2005	2010	2011	2012
United States	**8,554.9**	**10,476.7**	**12,308.5**	**12,949.9**	**13,401.9**	**10,291.2**	**11,355.6**	**12,108.2**	**12,441.5**	**12,642.2**
Alabama	107.2	135.6	161.3	167.5	171.8	128.9	147.0	158.7	160.9	162.0
Alaska	19.2	24.6	31.2	33.0	34.2	23.0	26.7	30.7	31.7	32.3
Arizona	135.7	188.2	216.6	227.3	235.8	163.2	203.9	213.1	218.4	222.4
Arkansas	60.5	77.5	94.6	99.1	102.4	72.7	84.0	93.0	95.2	96.6
California	1,135.3	1,387.7	1,564.2	1,645.1	1,711.1	1,365.8	1,504.1	1,538.8	1,580.6	1,614.1
Colorado	147.1	179.7	212.5	225.4	234.1	176.9	194.8	209.1	216.6	220.9
Connecticut	143.0	168.8	198.2	207.3	211.5	172.0	183.0	195.0	199.2	199.5
Delaware	24.4	31.1	35.5	37.6	38.5	29.3	33.7	34.9	36.1	36.3
District of Columbia	23.1	32.0	43.1	45.6	47.2	27.8	34.6	42.4	43.8	44.6
Florida	466.6	633.2	722.4	755.4	779.3	561.4	686.3	710.6	725.7	735.2
Georgia	234.8	292.5	335.4	353.1	365.7	282.5	317.1	329.9	339.3	345.0
Hawaii	35.2	45.3	55.8	59.0	61.3	42.4	49.1	54.9	56.7	57.8
Idaho	32.1	42.2	49.6	52.1	53.9	38.6	45.7	48.8	50.1	50.8
Illinois	405.9	472.1	539.7	562.7	577.0	488.3	511.7	530.9	540.6	544.3
Indiana	167.3	195.5	220.9	232.6	241.2	201.2	211.9	217.3	223.5	227.6
Iowa	79.9	95.5	115.5	126.0	129.5	96.1	103.5	113.7	121.1	122.2
Kansas	76.7	90.9	110.2	117.4	120.7	92.2	98.5	108.4	112.8	113.9
Kentucky	100.4	119.2	141.3	148.5	153.5	120.7	129.1	139.0	142.7	144.8
Louisiana	105.3	135.3	168.7	176.4	181.4	126.7	146.7	166.0	169.4	171.1
Maine	34.1	42.0	48.6	50.9	52.5	41.0	45.5	47.8	48.9	49.5
Maryland	184.2	237.1	281.3	295.2	305.8	221.6	257.0	276.7	283.6	288.5
Massachusetts	243.1	282.4	335.3	352.2	363.5	292.5	306.1	329.8	338.4	342.9
Michigan	292.6	325.7	339.0	358.2	370.6	352.0	353.1	333.5	344.1	349.6
Minnesota	160.8	194.0	225.9	238.2	248.7	193.5	210.3	222.2	228.8	234.6
Mississippi	61.4	77.7	91.6	95.3	98.7	73.9	84.3	90.1	91.6	93.1
Missouri	156.4	186.8	218.3	228.2	235.2	188.1	202.4	214.7	219.3	221.8
Montana	21.2	28.2	34.1	36.0	37.6	25.5	30.5	33.5	34.5	35.4
Nebraska	49.0	60.1	72.2	78.2	80.1	58.9	65.1	71.0	75.1	75.5
Nevada	62.5	91.8	96.8	100.7	103.1	75.2	99.5	95.2	96.7	97.2
New Hampshire	42.3	50.0	57.9	60.5	62.2	50.9	54.2	57.0	58.1	58.6
New Jersey	326.0	379.7	443.7	462.5	475.4	392.1	411.5	436.5	444.3	448.4
New Mexico	41.4	55.3	68.1	71.1	73.2	49.8	60.0	66.9	68.3	69.0
New York	657.9	786.5	952.7	995.2	1,019.5	791.4	852.5	937.2	956.1	961.7
North Carolina	225.5	277.7	330.8	347.9	361.3	271.3	301.0	325.4	334.2	340.8
North Dakota	16.4	20.5	28.6	32.3	36.3	19.8	22.3	28.2	31.0	34.2
Ohio	326.1	371.9	414.6	436.8	453.6	392.3	403.1	407.8	419.7	427.8
Oklahoma	85.0	107.6	133.6	142.9	148.8	102.2	116.7	131.4	137.3	140.4
Oregon	98.5	117.6	137.8	145.3	151.2	118.5	127.5	135.6	139.6	142.7
Pennsylvania	369.9	432.2	514.4	538.9	556.7	445.0	468.5	506.0	517.8	525.1
Rhode Island	31.0	38.6	44.2	46.1	47.3	37.3	41.8	43.5	44.3	44.6
South Carolina	100.9	124.4	149.3	156.2	161.9	121.4	134.8	146.9	150.1	152.7
South Dakota	20.0	25.8	32.3	36.4	36.4	24.0	28.0	31.8	35.0	34.3
Tennessee	152.2	187.7	223.2	234.2	243.3	183.1	203.4	219.5	225.0	229.5
Texas	597.0	756.7	965.2	1,030.7	1,080.7	718.2	820.2	949.5	990.3	1,019.5
Utah	55.0	71.5	89.2	94.4	98.8	66.2	77.5	87.7	90.7	93.2
Vermont	17.2	20.7	24.9	26.0	26.9	20.7	22.4	24.5	25.0	25.4
Virginia	224.8	294.7	354.1	373.3	385.4	270.4	319.5	348.4	358.7	363.6
Washington	191.6	230.1	283.4	299.7	313.2	230.4	249.4	278.8	287.9	295.5
West Virginia	40.1	48.1	59.0	62.0	64.0	48.2	52.2	58.0	59.5	60.3
Wisconsin	156.6	186.5	216.3	226.0	232.1	188.4	202.2	212.8	217.2	219.0
Wyoming	14.5	20.0	25.6	27.2	28.1	17.4	21.6	25.2	26.1	26.5

[1] Chained dollar estimates are computed by ProQuest using the national implicit price deflator for personal consumption expenditures from the Bureau of Economic Analysis' National Income and Product Accounts Tables. Any regional differences in the rate of inflation are not reflected in these constant dollar estimates.

Source: Except as noted, U.S. Bureau of Economic Analysis, Regional Economic Accounts, Annual State Personal Income and Employment, "Table SA1-3 Personal Income Summary," <http://www.bea.gov/iTable/>, accessed September 2013.

Table 709. Personal Income Per Capita in Current and Chained (2009) Dollars by State: 1990 to 2012

[In dollars, except as indicated. See headnote, Table 708]

State	Current dollars				Chained (2009) dollars [1]				Income rank	
	1990	2000	2010	2012	1990	2000	2010	2012	2010	2012
United States	**19,354**	**30,319**	**39,791**	**42,693**	**28,699**	**36,473**	**39,144**	**40,273**	**(X)**	**(X)**
Alabama	15,618	24,067	33,710	35,625	23,159	28,952	33,162	33,606	43	43
Alaska	22,594	30,508	43,749	46,778	33,503	36,700	43,037	44,126	10	11
Arizona	16,806	26,293	33,773	35,979	24,920	31,630	33,223	33,940	42	42
Arkansas	14,402	22,574	32,373	34,723	21,356	27,156	31,846	32,755	46	46
California	21,380	33,404	41,893	44,980	31,703	40,184	41,211	42,430	17	16
Colorado	19,377	33,986	42,107	45,135	28,733	40,884	41,422	42,577	13	14
Connecticut	26,198	41,920	55,427	58,908	38,847	50,428	54,525	55,569	2	2
Delaware	21,209	31,009	39,425	41,940	31,449	37,303	38,784	39,563	23	24
District of Columbia	26,015	40,462	71,220	74,710	38,576	48,674	70,061	70,475	1	1
Florida	19,437	29,079	38,345	40,344	28,822	34,981	37,721	38,057	25	28
Georgia	17,563	28,541	34,531	36,869	26,043	34,334	33,969	34,779	38	41
Hawaii	21,818	29,024	40,952	44,024	32,352	34,915	40,286	41,529	18	18
Idaho	15,603	24,685	31,556	33,749	23,136	29,695	31,043	31,836	50	50
Illinois	20,835	32,645	42,025	44,815	30,895	39,271	41,341	42,275	14	17
Indiana	17,454	27,459	34,028	36,902	25,881	33,032	33,474	34,810	41	40
Iowa	17,350	27,285	37,882	42,126	25,727	32,823	37,266	39,738	28	23
Kansas	18,034	28,468	38,545	41,835	26,741	34,246	37,918	39,464	24	25
Kentucky	15,360	24,785	32,504	35,041	22,776	29,815	31,975	33,055	45	45
Louisiana	15,171	23,554	37,116	39,413	22,496	28,335	36,512	37,179	29	30
Maine	17,211	26,699	36,629	39,481	25,521	32,118	36,033	37,243	30	29
Maryland	22,681	34,678	48,621	51,971	33,632	41,716	47,830	49,025	6	6
Massachusetts	22,797	38,222	51,143	54,687	33,804	45,980	50,311	51,587	3	3
Michigan	18,719	29,400	34,326	37,497	27,757	35,367	33,767	35,372	40	36
Minnesota	19,710	32,599	42,528	46,227	29,226	39,215	41,836	43,607	11	12
Mississippi	13,117	21,555	30,841	33,073	19,450	25,930	30,339	31,198	51	51
Missouri	17,582	27,885	36,406	39,049	26,071	33,545	35,814	36,836	31	32
Montana	15,346	23,457	34,405	37,370	22,755	28,218	33,845	35,252	39	37
Nebraska	17,948	28,590	39,445	43,143	26,614	34,393	38,803	40,697	22	21
Nevada	20,042	30,977	35,777	37,361	29,719	37,264	35,195	35,243	34	38
New Hampshire	20,236	34,102	43,968	47,058	30,006	41,023	43,253	44,391	9	10
New Jersey	24,354	38,667	50,428	53,628	36,113	46,515	49,607	50,588	4	4
New Mexico	14,823	22,746	32,940	35,079	21,980	27,363	32,404	33,091	44	44
New York	23,710	34,623	49,119	52,095	35,158	41,650	48,320	49,142	5	5
North Carolina	17,194	27,906	34,604	37,049	25,496	33,570	34,041	34,949	37	39
North Dakota	15,866	25,592	42,462	51,893	23,526	30,786	41,771	48,952	12	7
Ohio	18,638	28,695	35,931	39,289	27,637	34,519	35,346	37,062	32	31
Oklahoma	16,077	24,602	35,535	39,006	23,839	29,595	34,957	36,795	35	33
Oregon	17,895	28,728	35,906	38,786	26,535	34,559	35,322	36,587	33	34
Pennsylvania	19,433	30,113	40,444	43,616	28,816	36,225	39,786	41,144	19	20
Rhode Island	19,821	29,498	42,001	44,990	29,391	35,485	41,318	42,440	16	15
South Carolina	15,844	25,076	32,193	34,266	23,494	30,166	31,669	32,324	47	49
South Dakota	16,075	26,421	39,558	43,659	23,836	31,784	38,914	41,184	21	19
Tennessee	16,574	26,689	35,103	37,678	24,576	32,106	34,532	35,542	36	35
Texas	17,260	28,506	38,222	41,471	25,593	34,292	37,600	39,120	26	26
Utah	14,847	24,515	32,121	34,601	22,015	29,491	31,598	32,640	48	47
Vermont	17,643	28,196	39,736	42,994	26,161	33,919	39,089	40,557	20	22
Virginia	20,312	31,634	44,134	47,082	30,119	38,055	43,416	44,413	8	9
Washington	19,637	32,410	42,024	45,413	29,118	38,988	41,340	42,839	15	13
West Virginia	14,436	22,173	31,806	34,477	21,406	26,673	31,288	32,523	49	48
Wisconsin	17,986	29,141	38,010	40,537	26,670	35,056	37,392	38,239	27	27
Wyoming	17,910	29,261	45,353	48,670	26,557	35,200	44,615	45,911	7	8

X Not applicable. [1] Chained dollar estimates are computed by ProQuest using the national implicit price deflator for personal consumption expenditures from the Bureau of Economic Analysis' National Income and Product Accounts Tables. Any regional differences in the rate of inflation are not reflected in these constant dollar estimates.

Source: Except as noted, U.S. Bureau of Economic Analysis, Regional Economic Accounts, State Annual Personal Income & Employment, "Table SA-3 Personal Income Summary," <http://www.bea.gov/iTable/>, accessed September 2013.

Table 710. Disposable Personal Income Per Capita in Current and Chained (2009) Dollars by State: 1990 to 2012

[In dollars, except percent. Disposable personal income is the income available to persons for spending or saving; it is calculated as personal income less personal tax and nontax payments. See headnote, Table 708]

State	Current dollars				Chained (2009) dollars [1]				Index, compared to U.S. average [2]	
	1990	2000	2010	2012	1990	2000	2010	2012	2010	2012
United States...........	16,985	25,956	35,932	38,000	25,186	31,224	35,347	35,846	100.0	100.0
Alabama.................	13,943	21,355	31,087	32,467	20,675	25,689	30,581	30,627	86.5	85.4
Alaska...................	19,937	27,081	40,167	42,306	29,563	32,577	39,513	39,908	111.8	111.3
Arizona.................	14,932	22,966	31,187	32,797	22,141	27,627	30,680	30,938	86.8	86.3
Arkansas................	12,928	20,031	29,843	31,675	19,170	24,097	29,357	29,880	83.1	83.4
California...............	18,614	27,669	37,218	39,416	27,601	33,285	36,612	37,182	103.6	103.7
Colorado................	17,003	28,865	37,957	40,069	25,212	34,724	37,339	37,798	105.6	105.4
Connecticut.............	22,815	33,837	47,753	49,562	33,831	40,705	46,976	46,753	132.9	130.4
Delaware................	18,262	26,428	35,378	36,983	27,079	31,792	34,802	34,887	98.5	97.3
District of Columbia......	22,400	33,441	63,532	65,677	33,215	40,228	62,498	61,954	176.8	172.8
Florida.................	17,398	25,392	35,392	36,760	25,798	30,546	34,816	34,676	98.5	96.7
Georgia.................	15,424	24,614	31,462	33,168	22,871	29,610	30,950	31,288	87.6	87.3
Hawaii..................	18,901	25,454	37,586	39,956	28,027	30,620	36,974	37,691	104.6	105.1
Idaho...................	13,868	21,577	29,148	30,913	20,564	25,956	28,674	29,161	81.1	81.4
Illinois.................	18,180	27,885	37,872	39,242	26,958	33,545	37,256	37,018	105.4	103.3
Indiana.................	15,331	23,983	30,994	33,217	22,733	28,851	30,490	31,334	86.3	87.4
Iowa....................	15,330	24,129	34,640	38,257	22,732	29,026	34,076	36,088	96.4	100.7
Kansas..................	15,921	24,833	34,964	37,539	23,608	29,873	34,395	35,411	97.3	98.8
Kentucky................	13,544	21,725	29,659	31,676	20,083	26,134	29,176	29,880	82.5	83.4
Louisiana...............	13,687	21,059	34,341	36,042	20,295	25,333	33,782	33,999	95.6	94.8
Maine...................	15,222	23,230	33,492	35,834	22,572	27,945	32,947	33,803	93.2	94.3
Maryland................	19,420	29,229	43,097	45,324	28,796	35,161	42,396	42,755	119.9	119.3
Massachusetts...........	19,549	30,795	44,751	46,947	28,988	37,045	44,023	44,286	124.5	123.5
Michigan................	16,368	25,293	31,333	33,672	24,271	30,427	30,823	31,763	87.2	88.6
Minnesota...............	17,123	27,781	38,051	40,670	25,390	33,420	37,432	38,365	105.9	107.0
Mississippi..............	11,938	19,491	28,669	30,449	17,702	23,447	28,203	28,723	79.8	80.1
Missouri................	15,492	24,330	33,268	35,229	22,972	29,268	32,727	33,232	92.6	92.7
Montana................	13,693	20,770	31,488	33,734	20,304	24,986	30,976	31,822	87.6	88.8
Nebraska................	15,996	25,063	36,042	38,883	23,719	30,150	35,456	36,679	100.3	102.3
Nevada.................	17,562	26,875	32,842	33,866	26,041	32,330	32,308	31,946	91.4	89.1
New Hampshire..........	18,016	29,286	40,244	42,502	26,715	35,230	39,589	40,093	112.0	111.8
New Jersey..............	21,163	32,334	44,705	46,856	31,381	38,897	43,978	44,200	124.4	123.3
New Mexico.............	13,313	20,196	30,551	32,314	19,741	24,295	30,054	30,482	85.0	85.0
New York................	20,371	28,618	42,539	44,355	30,207	34,426	41,847	41,841	118.4	116.7
North Carolina..........	15,145	24,246	31,509	33,333	22,457	29,167	30,996	31,444	87.7	87.7
North Dakota............	14,380	23,092	38,873	46,460	21,323	27,779	38,241	43,826	108.2	122.3
Ohio....................	16,341	24,758	32,572	35,153	24,231	29,783	32,042	33,160	90.6	92.5
Oklahoma...............	14,170	21,721	32,720	35,461	21,012	26,130	32,188	33,451	91.1	93.3
Oregon.................	15,709	24,544	32,300	34,466	23,294	29,526	31,774	32,512	89.9	90.7
Pennsylvania............	17,091	26,002	36,386	38,739	25,343	31,279	35,794	36,543	101.3	101.9
Rhode Island............	17,453	25,351	38,152	40,361	25,880	30,496	37,531	38,073	106.2	106.2
South Carolina...........	14,044	22,161	29,717	31,346	20,825	26,659	29,233	29,569	82.7	82.5
South Dakota............	14,725	23,876	36,958	40,427	21,835	28,722	36,357	38,135	102.9	106.4
Tennessee..............	15,004	24,009	32,899	34,898	22,248	28,882	32,364	32,920	91.6	91.8
Texas...................	15,463	25,168	35,301	37,723	22,929	30,276	34,727	35,585	98.2	99.3
Utah....................	13,131	21,453	29,436	31,329	19,471	25,807	28,957	29,553	81.9	82.4
Vermont................	15,527	24,535	36,454	38,981	23,024	29,515	35,861	36,771	101.5	102.6
Virginia.................	17,735	26,775	39,382	41,369	26,298	32,209	38,741	39,024	109.6	108.9
Washington.............	17,449	27,954	38,731	41,259	25,874	33,628	38,101	38,920	107.8	108.6
West Virginia............	12,908	19,815	29,223	31,270	19,140	23,837	28,748	29,497	81.3	82.3
Wisconsin...............	15,716	25,079	34,364	36,230	23,304	30,169	33,805	34,176	95.6	95.3
Wyoming................	16,056	25,312	41,408	43,788	23,808	30,449	40,734	41,306	115.2	115.2

[1] Constant dollar estimates are computed by ProQuest using the national implicit price deflator for personal consumption expenditures from the Bureau of Economic Analysis' National Income and Product Accounts Tables. Any regional differences in the rate of inflation are not reflected in these constant dollar estimates. [2] Indexes calculated using disposable personal income per capita in current dollars.

Source: Except as noted, U.S. Bureau of Economic Analysis, Regional Economic Accounts, State Annual Personal Income & Employment, "Table SA51-53 Disposable Personal Income Summary," <http://www.bea.gov/regional/index.htm>, accessed September 2013.

Table 711. Personal Income by Selected Large Metropolitan Area: 2005 to 2011

[9,152,380 represents $9,152,380,000,000. MSA = Metropolitan Statistical Area. Local area personal income estimates for these areas are based on the definitions in the Office of Management and Budget Bulletin No. 10-02 issued December 1, 2009. Per capita personal income was computed using Census Bureau midyear population estimates. Estimates for 2005-2011 reflect county population estimates available as of April 2012. See Appendix II. Minus sign (–) indicates decrease]

Metropolitan statistical areas ranked by 2011 population	Personal income			Personal income per capita			Annual percent change, 2010–2011	Index (U.S.= 100), 2011
	2005 (mil. dol.)	2010 (mil. dol.)	2011 (mil. dol.)	2005 (dol.)	2010 (dol.)	2011 (dol.)		
United States, metro portion...............	9,152,380	10,718,343	11,271,658	37,177	41,404	43,169	4.3	100.0
New York-Northern New Jersey-Long Island, NY-NJ-PA MSA...........	863,632	1,032,838	1,079,532	46,510	54,591	56,770	4.0	131.5
Los Angeles-Long Beach-Santa Ana, CA MSA...........	496,595	550,283	575,045	39,021	42,842	44,423	3.7	102.9
Chicago-Joliet-Naperville, IL-IN-WI MSA.......	375,515	419,999	436,998	40,481	44,338	45,977	3.7	106.5
Dallas-Fort Worth-Arlington, TX MSA...........	220,482	268,492	285,260	38,494	41,948	43,708	4.2	101.2
Houston-Sugar Land-Baytown, TX MSA.......	209,655	268,695	289,790	39,868	44,959	47,612	5.9	110.3
Philadelphia-Camden-Wilmington, PA-NJ-DE-MD MSA...........	236,491	279,708	291,970	40,571	46,840	48,723	4.0	112.9
Washington-Arlington-Alexandria, DC-VA-MD-WV MSA...........	262,193	321,521	338,498	50,187	57,321	59,345	3.5	137.5
Miami-Fort Lauderdale-Pompano Beach, FL MSA...........	210,605	233,377	244,224	38,921	41,838	43,072	3.0	99.8
Atlanta-Sandy Springs-Marietta, GA MSA...........	179,145	201,632	212,830	37,683	38,142	39,713	4.1	92.0
Boston-Cambridge-Quincy, MA-NH MSA......	212,251	252,553	265,794	48,042	55,392	57,893	4.5	134.1
San Francisco-Oakland-Fremont, CA MSA....	227,850	254,377	269,588	55,065	58,567	61,395	4.8	142.2
Riverside-San Bernardino-Ontario, CA MSA...........	108,598	123,561	128,982	28,020	29,107	29,961	2.9	69.4
Detroit-Warren-Livonia, MI MSA...........	164,087	161,676	171,473	37,031	37,680	40,009	6.2	92.7
Phoenix-Mesa-Glendale, AZ MSA...........	131,597	149,094	157,026	34,863	35,422	36,833	4.0	85.3
Seattle-Tacoma-Bellevue, WA MSA...........	138,212	167,885	178,307	43,215	48,692	50,944	4.6	118.0
Minneapolis-St. Paul-Bloomington, MN-WI MSA...........	133,840	152,789	161,468	42,740	46,498	48,657	4.6	112.7
San Diego-Carlsbad-San Marcos, CA MSA...........	122,030	139,578	146,956	41,530	44,951	46,800	4.1	108.4
Tampa-St. Petersburg-Clearwater, FL MSA....	91,393	106,083	110,901	34,467	38,048	39,261	3.2	90.9
St. Louis, MO-IL MSA...........	101,082	115,355	120,763	36,697	40,983	42,864	4.6	99.3
Baltimore-Towson, MD MSA...........	111,453	132,286	139,528	42,150	48,732	51,126	4.9	118.4
Denver-Aurora-Broomfield, CO MSA...........	101,788	119,986	127,324	43,634	46,969	48,980	4.3	113.5
Pittsburgh, PA MSA...........	84,956	100,489	106,146	35,779	42,617	44,982	5.6	104.2
Portland-Vancouver-Hillsboro, OR-WA MSA...	74,750	87,940	93,449	36,158	39,384	41,302	4.9	95.7
San Antonio-New Braunfels, TX MSA...........	58,670	75,810	80,732	30,939	35,197	36,781	4.5	85.2
Sacramento-Arden-Arcade-Roseville, CA MSA...........	75,029	85,088	88,670	36,872	39,492	40,745	3.2	94.4
Orlando-Kissimmee-Sanford, FL MSA...........	64,007	73,619	77,159	32,727	34,408	35,535	3.3	82.3
Cincinnati-Middletown, OH-KY-IN MSA.......	75,148	83,388	87,485	36,294	39,105	40,918	4.6	94.8
Cleveland-Elyria-Mentor, OH MSA...........	76,110	83,241	87,622	36,042	40,106	42,365	5.6	98.1
Kansas City, MO-KS MSA...........	70,738	84,533	88,392	36,558	41,443	43,062	3.9	99.8
Las Vegas-Paradise, NV MSA...........	64,181	67,738	70,289	37,109	34,668	35,680	2.9	82.7
San Jose-Sunnyvale-Santa Clara, CA MSA...........	89,629	104,472	113,844	51,810	56,723	61,028	7.6	141.4
Columbus, OH MSA...........	60,968	70,531	74,688	35,307	38,320	40,188	4.9	93.1
Charlotte-Gastonia-Rock Hill, NC-SC MSA...........	57,216	67,899	72,220	37,678	38,492	40,223	4.5	93.2
Austin-Round Rock-San Marcos, TX MSA.....	51,047	67,321	72,152	35,124	38,953	40,455	3.9	93.7
Indianapolis-Carmel, IN MSA...........	60,018	68,429	72,161	36,550	38,862	40,572	4.4	94.0
Virginia Beach-Norfolk-Newport News, VA-NC MSA...........	56,595	67,182	70,516	34,413	40,121	41,976	4.6	97.2
Nashville-Davidson-Murfreesboro-Franklin, TN MSA...........	52,294	64,674	68,129	36,382	40,551	42,129	3.9	97.6
Providence-New Bedford-Fall River, RI-MA MSA...........	57,418	66,193	69,116	35,589	41,343	43,192	4.5	100.1
Milwaukee-Waukesha-West Allis, WI MSA.....	58,251	66,928	69,691	38,263	42,986	44,610	3.8	103.3
Jacksonville, FL MSA...........	45,618	52,940	55,375	36,521	39,253	40,709	3.7	94.3
Memphis, TN-MS-AR MSA...........	44,057	49,138	51,198	34,865	37,280	38,622	3.6	89.5
Louisville-Jefferson County, KY-IN MSA.......	41,228	48,093	50,546	33,820	37,400	39,037	4.4	90.4
Oklahoma City, OK MSA...........	38,462	47,508	51,124	33,120	37,761	40,002	5.9	92.7
Richmond, VA MSA...........	44,587	51,643	54,641	37,749	40,974	43,046	5.1	99.7
Hartford-West Hartford-East Hartford, CT MSA...........	51,428	61,302	64,401	43,292	50,559	53,081	5.0	123.0
New Orleans-Metairie-Kenner, LA MSA........	43,498	49,946	51,935	31,866	42,559	43,603	2.5	101.0
Raleigh-Cary, NC MSA...........	35,209	44,557	47,275	37,269	39,178	40,631	3.7	94.1
Salt Lake City, UT MSA...........	35,347	42,882	45,373	34,273	38,007	39,595	4.2	91.7
Buffalo-Niagara Falls, NY MSA...........	36,232	43,571	45,499	31,546	38,379	40,121	4.5	92.9
Birmingham-Hoover, AL MSA...........	39,199	44,156	46,215	36,084	39,108	40,816	4.4	94.5
Rochester, NY MSA...........	35,256	42,157	43,987	33,728	39,970	41,683	4.3	96.6
Tucson, AZ MSA...........	28,574	33,278	34,596	31,048	33,884	34,961	3.2	81.0
Honolulu, HI MSA...........	34,264	42,397	44,927	37,317	44,365	46,624	5.1	108.0
Tulsa, OK MSA...........	30,734	37,162	39,996	34,812	39,529	42,236	6.9	97.8
Fresno, CA MSA...........	24,078	28,539	29,741	27,598	30,583	31,542	3.1	73.1
Bridgeport-Stamford-Norwalk, CT MSA.......	61,073	69,692	72,687	68,036	75,890	78,504	3.4	181.9
Albuquerque, NM MSA...........	25,338	30,293	31,459	31,299	34,039	35,007	2.8	81.1
Omaha-Council Bluffs, NE-IA MSA...........	31,077	36,987	39,005	38,164	42,606	44,470	4.4	103.0
Albany-Schenectady-Troy, NY MSA...........	30,672	37,601	39,168	35,890	43,172	44,944	4.1	104.1
New Haven-Milford, CT MSA...........	33,857	40,636	42,606	39,965	47,118	49,478	5.0	114.6

Source: U.S. Bureau of Economic Analysis, Regional Economic Accounts, Local Areas Personal Income and Employment, "Table CA1-3 Personal Income Summary," <http://www.bea.gov/regional/index.htm>, accessed September 2013.

Table 712. Household Income—Distribution by Income Level and State: 2011

[In thousands (114,992 represents 114,992,000), except as indicated. The American Community Survey universe includes the household population and the population living in institutions, college dormitories, and other group quarters. Based on a sample and subject to sampling variability; see text, Section 1 and Appendix III. For definition of median, see Guide to Tabular Presentation]

State	Number of households (1,000)								Median income (dollars)
	Total	Under $25,000	$25,000 to $49,999	$50,000 to $74,999	$75,000 to $99,999	$100,000 to $149,999	$150,000 to $199,999	$200,000 or more	
United States.......	**114,992**	**28,820**	**28,088**	**20,698**	**13,503**	**13,865**	**5,111**	**4,908**	**50,502**
Alabama...............	1,845	584	483	316	193	174	51	43	41,415
Alaska................	257	39	53	51	40	45	19	11	67,825
Arizona...............	2,356	622	623	434	264	257	84	72	46,709
Arkansas..............	1,128	377	310	192	109	92	27	20	38,758
California.............	12,469	2,765	2,759	2,112	1,488	1,768	772	804	57,287
Colorado..............	1,975	425	466	370	245	268	108	93	55,387
Connecticut...........	1,352	261	264	225	179	211	99	112	65,753
Delaware..............	333	64	78	62	47	50	17	15	58,814
District of Columbia. ..	269	62	47	42	29	40	18	30	63,124
Florida................	7,106	1,970	1,944	1,284	747	690	236	236	44,299
Georgia...............	3,495	974	890	635	374	375	129	117	46,007
Hawaii................	449	80	99	85	63	75	27	21	61,821
Idaho.................	580	157	171	111	63	55	13	10	43,341
Illinois................	4,737	1,119	1,099	873	585	605	230	226	53,234
Indiana...............	2,467	648	665	487	294	251	64	58	46,438
Iowa..................	1,217	289	325	247	154	133	39	30	49,427
Kansas................	1,102	262	298	212	136	125	36	32	48,964
Kentucky..............	1,672	532	446	291	171	154	40	37	41,141
Louisiana..............	1,702	546	422	271	188	176	55	45	41,734
Maine.................	552	153	143	101	70	56	16	13	46,033
Maryland..............	2,135	359	397	381	285	376	170	168	70,004
Massachusetts.........	2,532	543	492	413	320	401	182	182	62,859
Michigan..............	3,772	1,036	979	689	434	402	128	104	45,981
Minnesota.............	2,096	433	485	417	286	295	96	84	56,954
Mississippi............	1,081	379	296	179	103	80	24	20	36,919
Missouri...............	2,341	633	637	433	266	234	75	62	45,247
Montana...............	404	112	116	78	46	36	9	8	44,222
Nebraska..............	724	173	187	144	93	81	24	22	50,296
Nevada................	982	231	268	188	115	114	36	31	48,927
New Hampshire.......	516	94	115	94	73	85	31	25	62,647
New Jersey............	3,168	585	615	519	407	530	249	263	67,458
New Mexico...........	767	238	201	128	79	75	25	21	41,963
New York.............	7,188	1,763	1,530	1,208	856	963	413	454	55,246
North Carolina........	3,683	1,047	993	661	387	368	121	106	43,916
North Dakota..........	283	69	69	55	38	35	8	9	51,704
Ohio..................	4,539	1,247	1,187	852	513	472	149	119	45,749
Oklahoma.............	1,443	415	397	263	157	139	36	35	43,225
Oregon...............	1,517	400	400	289	179	157	50	43	46,816
Pennsylvania..........	4,937	1,236	1,222	929	590	578	198	185	50,228
Rhode Island..........	412	102	91	72	51	59	22	16	53,636
South Carolina........	1,769	531	473	321	182	172	50	40	42,367
South Dakota..........	323	82	83	67	42	32	9	8	48,321
Tennessee.............	2,467	746	675	430	262	223	68	63	41,693
Texas.................	8,850	2,257	2,209	1,574	1,001	1,054	379	375	49,392
Utah..................	884	175	219	195	121	112	33	29	55,869
Vermont...............	257	57	65	51	36	30	10	8	52,776
Virginia...............	2,991	576	640	532	390	441	201	209	61,882
Washington............	2,633	542	618	506	351	365	132	117	56,835
West Virginia..........	735	249	198	124	73	62	17	12	38,482
Wisconsin.............	2,275	540	589	460	295	259	75	58	50,395
Wyoming..............	223	43	57	44	33	32	8	6	56,322

Source: U.S. Census Bureau, 2011 American Community Survey, B19001, "Household Income in the Past 12 Months" and B19013, "Median Household Income in the Past 12 Months (In 2011 Inflation-Adjusted Dollars)," <http://factfinder2.census.gov>, accessed February 2013.

Table 713. Family Income—Distribution by Income Level and State: 2011

[In thousands (76,084 represents 76,084,000), except as indicated. The American Community Survey universe includes the household population and the population living in institutions, college dormitories, and other group quarters. Based on a sample and subject to sampling variability; see text, Section 1 and Appendix III. For definition of median, see Guide to Tabular Presentation]

State	Number of families (1,000)								Median income (dollars)
	Total	Less than $25,000	$25,000 to $49,999	$50,000 to $74,999	$75,000 to $99,999	$100,000 to $149,999	$150,000 to $199,999	$200,000 and over	
United States.......	76,084	13,242	17,450	14,712	10,561	11,511	4,374	4,234	61,455
Alabama...............	1,252	283	317	244	166	156	46	38	51,991
Alaska.................	173	18	31	36	27	35	16	9	75,786
Arizona................	1,544	300	388	305	205	211	71	63	55,328
Arkansas.............	757	177	210	152	93	83	24	18	48,713
California..............	8,519	1,480	1,814	1,467	1,094	1,373	622	669	65,476
Colorado..............	1,256	173	263	246	181	220	93	81	69,110
Connecticut..........	893	105	153	142	132	174	87	100	83,106
Delaware..............	227	28	50	43	38	40	15	13	69,663
District of Columbia. ..	114	24	18	15	10	16	10	21	75,603
Florida.................	4,560	892	1,207	911	584	568	198	199	53,958
Georgia...............	2,376	492	588	460	299	320	114	102	55,001
Hawaii.................	312	36	61	60	50	63	23	18	74,234
Idaho..................	399	71	117	86	55	48	12	9	52,814
Illinois.................	3,099	496	658	598	450	504	199	195	65,579
Indiana................	1,641	288	412	367	244	221	57	51	57,148
Iowa...................	785	105	188	185	128	117	35	27	62,821
Kansas................	722	102	180	153	116	109	33	29	61,947
Kentucky..............	1,120	249	290	228	147	136	37	33	51,917
Louisiana.............	1,118	260	269	197	155	151	48	39	53,601
Maine..................	348	59	89	72	56	48	13	11	58,375
Maryland..............	1,416	152	236	238	205	292	145	148	83,823
Massachusetts........	1,598	207	279	262	225	313	154	158	80,425
Michigan..............	2,473	457	595	506	354	354	114	94	58,068
Minnesota............	1,356	166	269	283	226	253	84	75	71,321
Mississippi............	741	191	206	145	88	71	22	18	46,304
Missouri...............	1,535	276	388	322	221	204	67	56	56,616
Montana..............	253	43	68	59	38	30	8	7	56,217
Nebraska.............	470	66	107	106	77	72	22	20	63,491
Nevada...............	637	106	170	130	88	88	30	24	56,544
New Hampshire.......	350	35	69	67	58	71	28	22	76,609
New Jersey............	2,191	257	375	358	309	437	217	238	82,255
New Mexico...........	502	118	126	94	64	63	22	17	51,744
New York..............	4,608	813	918	808	613	752	335	368	66,852
North Carolina........	2,456	495	634	488	315	320	109	94	54,082
North Dakota..........	175	24	37	38	30	31	8	8	66,924
Ohio...................	2,916	519	711	620	418	410	133	104	58,565
Oklahoma.............	958	185	255	201	132	124	31	29	53,742
Oregon................	957	177	234	201	140	127	42	37	58,356
Pennsylvania..........	3,194	481	734	667	474	499	175	164	63,283
Rhode Island..........	256	41	51	47	38	47	18	14	69,604
South Carolina........	1,202	261	310	241	155	155	44	35	52,240
South Dakota.........	211	33	48	51	35	29	8	7	62,059
Tennessee............	1,626	347	426	328	217	191	62	55	52,273
Texas..................	6,171	1,210	1,465	1,142	798	894	332	331	58,016
Utah...................	662	93	153	155	104	102	30	26	62,809
Vermont...............	162	22	35	35	27	25	9	7	66,190
Virginia................	2,011	258	391	363	292	355	169	183	74,500
Washington...........	1,700	233	359	338	261	298	112	99	68,628
West Virginia..........	478	107	134	95	61	55	15	11	49,693
Wisconsin.............	1,463	210	336	327	242	228	67	53	63,732
Wyoming..............	143	19	29	32	25	27	7	5	68,629

Source: U.S. Census Bureau, 2011 American Community Survey, B19101, "Family Income in the Past 12 Months" and B19113, "Median Family Income in the Past 12 Months (In 2011 Inflation-Adjusted Dollars)," <http://factfinder2.census.gov>, accessed February 2013.

Table 714. Average Annual Expenditures of All Consumer Units by Selected Major Types of Expenditure: 1990 to 2011

[In dollars, except as indicated; consumer units in thousands (96,968 represents 96,968,000). Based on Consumer Expenditure Survey. Data are averages for the noninstitutional population. Expenditures are direct out-of-pocket expenditures. Consumers units may be all members in a housing unit (families), a person living alone or sharing a household with others and financially independent, or 2 or more unrelated persons living together who share expenses]

Type of expenditure	1990	1995	2000	2005	2008	2009	2010	2011
Number of consumer units (1,000).............	96,968	103,123	109,367	117,356	120,770	120,847	121,107	122,287
Expenditures, avg. (dol.) [1]..................	**28,381**	**32,264**	**38,045**	**46,409**	**50,486**	**49,067**	**48,109**	**49,705**
Food...	4,296	4,505	5,158	5,931	6,443	6,372	6,129	6,458
Food at home [1].................................	2,485	2,803	3,021	3,297	3,744	3,753	3,624	3,838
Meats, poultry, fish, and eggs..............	668	752	795	764	846	841	784	832
Dairy products..................................	295	297	325	378	430	406	380	407
Fruits and vegetables..........................	408	457	521	552	657	656	679	715
Other food at home............................	746	856	927	1,158	1,305	1,343	1,278	1,353
Food away from home..........................	1,811	1,702	2,137	2,634	2,698	2,619	2,505	2,620
Alcoholic beverages.............................	293	277	372	426	444	435	412	456
Housing [1].......................................	8,703	10,458	12,319	15,167	17,109	16,895	16,557	16,803
Shelter...	4,836	5,928	7,114	8,805	10,183	10,075	9,812	9,825
Utilities, fuels, and public services............	1,890	2,191	2,489	3,183	3,649	3,645	3,660	3,727
Apparel and services............................	1,618	1,704	1,856	1,886	1,801	1,725	1,700	1,740
Transportation [1]................................	5,120	6,014	7,417	8,344	8,604	7,658	7,677	8,293
Vehicle purchases..............................	2,129	2,638	3,418	3,544	2,755	2,657	2,588	2,669
Gasoline and motor oil..........................	1,047	1,006	1,291	2,013	2,715	1,986	2,132	2,655
Other vehicle expenses.........................	1,642	2,015	2,281	2,339	2,621	2,536	2,464	2,454
Health care..	1,480	1,732	2,066	2,664	2,976	3,126	3,157	3,313
Entertainment.....................................	1,422	1,612	1,863	2,388	2,835	2,693	2,504	2,572
Reading..	153	162	146	126	116	110	100	115
Tobacco products, smoking supplies...........	274	269	319	319	317	380	362	351
Personal insurance and pensions...............	2,592	2,964	3,365	5,204	5,605	5,471	5,373	5,424
Life and other personal insurance.............	345	373	399	381	317	309	318	317
Pensions and Social Security.................	2,248	2,591	2,966	4,823	5,288	5,162	5,054	5,106

[1] Includes expenditures not shown separately.

Source: U.S. Bureau of Labor Statistics, Consumer Expenditure Survey program, "Annual Calendar Year Tables," <http://www.bls.gov/cex/tables.htm>, accessed March 2013. See also <http://www.bls.gov/cex/home.htm>.

Table 715. Average Annual Expenditures of All Consumer Units by Metropolitan Statistical Area: 2010 to 2011

[In dollars. Covers 2-year period, 2010-2011. MSA = Metropolitan Statistical Area. See text, Section 1 and Appendix II. See headnote, Table 714]

Metropolitan area	Total expenditures [1]	Food	Housing			Transportation			Health care
			Total [1]	Shelter	Utility fuels [2]	Total [1]	Vehicle purchases	Gasoline and motor oil	
Atlanta, Georgia MSA.........................	49,692	5,798	18,448	10,681	4,348	7,998	2,761	2,645	2,724
Baltimore, Maryland MSA....................	55,363	6,920	20,695	12,946	4,424	6,606	[3] 1,962	2,401	3,283
Boston, Massachusetts MSA................	64,802	8,080	21,053	12,862	4,121	9,127	3,382	2,489	4,107
Chicago, Illinois MSA.........................	57,579	7,158	20,520	13,063	3,981	8,342	2,624	2,445	4,085
Cleveland, Ohio MSA.........................	45,768	5,665	14,653	8,554	3,434	7,815	2,598	2,086	2,849
Dallas-Fort Worth, Texas MSA.............	54,628	6,994	18,241	10,248	4,461	9,314	3,175	2,918	3,464
Detroit, Michigan MSA........................	50,467	6,329	16,267	9,341	4,036	8,790	2,705	2,606	3,178
Houston, Texas MSA.........................	54,659	6,857	18,287	9,925	4,472	9,146	2,542	3,050	3,224
Los Angeles, California MSA................	54,321	7,148	20,435	13,773	3,150	8,784	2,464	2,615	2,475
Miami, Florida MSA...........................	38,354	4,933	15,911	10,391	3,496	6,039	[3] 1,149	2,268	1,872
Minneapolis-St. Paul, Minnesota MSA.....	54,457	6,767	17,586	10,252	3,315	8,808	2,908	2,538	4,008
New York City MSA...........................	58,172	7,371	23,154	15,479	4,273	7,843	1,891	2,006	3,089
Philadelphia, Pennsylvania MSA............	50,985	5,997	19,810	12,008	4,442	7,337	2,289	2,147	3,086
Phoenix, Arizona MSA........................	49,662	6,433	16,641	9,235	3,832	8,372	3,046	2,409	2,566
San Diego, California MSA...................	53,031	5,861	21,639	15,210	3,251	7,900	2,106	2,673	2,668
San Francisco, California MSA.............	71,613	8,260	26,990	19,182	3,318	9,348	2,351	2,340	3,759
Seattle, Washington MSA....................	61,773	6,951	21,557	13,612	3,630	9,485	3,390	2,411	3,681
Washington, District of Columbia MSA.....	72,448	8,342	25,590	16,628	4,254	10,889	3,176	2,479	4,306

[1] Includes expenditures not shown separately. [2] Includes public services. [3] Data are likely to have large sampling errors.

Source: U.S. Bureau of Labor Statistics, Consumer Expenditure Survey program, "Metropolitan Statistical Area Tables," <http://www.bls.gov/cex/tables.htm>, accessed March 2013.

Table 716. Average Annual Expenditures of All Consumer Units by Race, Hispanic Origin, and Age of Householder: 2011

[In dollars. See headnote, Table 714]

Type	All con- sumer units [1]	White and all other races	Asian	Black or African American	His- panic [2]	Age of householder Under 25 years	Age of householder 65 years old and over
Expenditures, total............................	**49,705**	**51,113**	**60,136**	**36,644**	**42,086**	**29,912**	**39,173**
Food..	6,458	6,623	8,163	4,743	6,373	4,354	5,158
Food at home...................................	3,838	3,931	4,439	2,989	3,849	2,382	3,309
Cereals and bakery products.............	531	545	618	405	493	336	469
Cereals and cereal products...........	175	175	265	143	181	114	142
Bakery products............................	356	369	353	263	312	222	328
Meats, poultry, fish, and eggs [3].......	832	821	1,094	822	968	527	671
Beef..	223	229	201	189	268	137	186
Pork..	162	156	210	183	191	96	138
Poultry..	154	149	186	185	196	122	108
Fish and seafood...........................	121	109	327	134	138	69	103
Dairy products..................................	407	434	337	246	388	244	359
Fresh milk and cream.....................	150	157	161	98	163	97	126
Other dairy products......................	257	277	175	148	226	148	233
Fruits and vegetables [3]....................	715	725	1,059	527	778	424	663
Fresh fruits....................................	247	253	392	157	293	132	237
Fresh vegetables...........................	224	226	415	145	241	130	206
Processed fruits.............................	116	117	111	109	120	80	105
Other food at home [3].......................	1,353	1,407	1,332	988	1,221	850	1,147
Sugar and other sweets..................	144	151	157	98	117	78	136
Nonalcoholic beverages..................	361	374	324	280	370	236	284
Food away from home.......................	2,620	2,692	3,724	1,754	2,524	1,973	1,849
Alcoholic beverages.............................	456	501	311	199	281	418	338
Housing..	16,803	17,019	20,834	13,985	15,648	10,282	13,706
Shelter..	9,825	9,859	14,269	8,111	9,766	6,732	7,178
Owned dwellings...............................	6,148	6,416	8,209	3,651	4,713	1,277	4,953
Mortgage interest and charges........	3,184	3,279	4,348	2,151	2,814	740	1,419
Property taxes..............................	1,845	1,946	2,523	930	1,202	306	2,025
Maintenance, repair, insurance, other expenses.......	1,120	1,190	1,338	570	697	231	1,509
Rented dwellings...............................	3,029	2,756	4,843	4,268	4,806	5,111	1,480
Other lodging..................................	648	687	1,217	192	248	345	745
Utilities, fuels, and public services.....	3,727	3,753	3,279	3,701	3,462	1,918	3,485
Natural gas....................................	420	417	436	429	350	172	430
Electricity.....................................	1,423	1,431	1,035	1,497	1,283	757	1,362
Fuel oil and other fuels..................	157	175	62	67	42	[4] 19	247
Telephone.....................................	1,226	1,224	1,229	1,242	1,288	777	921
Water and other public services......	501	505	517	465	499	193	525
Household operations........................	1,122	1,145	1,593	810	755	505	1,093
Personal services...........................	398	392	808	307	319	174	300
Other household expenses..............	724	754	785	503	436	331	793
Housekeeping supplies [3]..................	615	653	393	426	536	268	636
Laundry and cleaning supplies........	145	145	108	155	195	82	140
Postage and stationery...................	130	141	74	76	86	46	148
Household furnishings and equipment [3]............	1,514	1,609	1,300	938	1,129	858	1,314
Household textiles..........................	109	119	69	52	73	37	129
Furniture.......................................	358	364	381	306	310	260	229
Major appliances...........................	194	202	153	152	128	82	175
Miscellaneous household equipment..	744	804	603	378	550	397	668
Apparel and services [3]........................	1,740	1,721	2,324	1,669	1,989	1,448	1,129
Men and boys....................................	404	406	603	324	518	335	210
Women and girls................................	721	725	911	629	672	498	545
Footwear..	321	301	342	454	452	298	189
Other apparel products and services.....	226	225	359	185	256	189	173
Transportation....................................	8,293	8,542	10,281	5,944	7,520	5,474	5,751
Vehicle purchases (net outlay) [3]........	2,669	2,787	3,450	1,608	2,208	2,068	1,588
Cars and trucks, new......................	1,265	1,306	2,342	634	691	610	975
Cars and trucks, used.....................	1,339	1,407	1,100	959	1,511	1,431	587
Gasoline and motor oil.......................	2,655	2,737	2,283	2,221	2,721	1,840	1,755
Other vehicle expenses......................	2,454	2,514	3,075	1,833	2,174	1,265	1,994
Vehicle finance charges..................	233	242	168	194	215	128	100
Maintenance and repair..................	805	841	717	587	638	456	650
Vehicle insurance...........................	983	984	1,608	767	934	[4] 505	894
Vehicle rental, leases, licenses, other charges...........	433	447	582	285	386	176	350
Public transportation.........................	516	503	1,473	283	417	300	414
Health care [5].....................................	3,313	3,542	2,919	1,897	1,774	841	4,769
Entertainment [6]..................................	2,572	2,753	2,301	1,432	1,738	1,345	2,009
Personal care products and services....	634	650	602	533	611	324	567
Reading..	115	126	111	48	46	45	157
Education..	1,051	1,075	2,267	479	624	2,253	247
Tobacco products and smoking supplies..	351	374	152	260	164	256	212
Miscellaneous......................................	775	817	696	521	476	285	753
Cash contributions...............................	1,721	1,793	1,405	1,341	812	367	2,392
Personal insurance and pensions..........	5,424	5,579	7,771	3,593	4,030	2,220	1,985
Life and other personal insurance......	317	326	337	250	115	67	280
Pensions and social security.............	5,106	5,252	7,434	3,344	3,915	2,154	1,706
Personal taxes.................................	**2,012**	**2,142**	**3,894**	**500**	**465**	**19**	**907**

[1] Includes other races not shown separately. [2] People of Hispanic origin may be of any race. [3] Includes other types, not shown separately. [4] Data are likely to have large sampling errors. [5] For additional health care expenditures, see Table 149. [6] For additional recreation expenditures, see Section 26.

Source: U.S. Bureau of Labor Statistics, Consumer Expenditure Survey, "2011 Current Expenditure Tables," <http://stats.bls.gov/cex/>, accessed February 2013.

Table 717. Average Annual Expenditures of All Consumer Units by Region and Size of Unit: 2011

[In dollars. For composition of regions, see map, inside front cover. See headnote, Table 714]

Type	Region				Size of consumer unit				
	North-east	Mid-west	South	West	One person	Two persons	Three persons	Four persons	Five or more
Expenditures, total....................	**54,547**	**47,192**	**45,699**	**54,745**	**30,613**	**52,385**	**58,388**	**65,597**	**62,429**
Food..........................	6,799	6,236	5,980	7,188	3,638	6,431	7,466	8,983	9,747
Food at home.......................	4,099	3,841	3,505	4,169	2,072	3,691	4,410	5,411	6,400
Cereals and bakery products..............	610	545	478	538	285	502	596	782	893
Cereals and cereal products.............	205	171	154	189	91	163	194	260	312
Bakery products.....................	405	375	324	348	194	339	403	522	581
Meats, poultry, fish, and eggs [1]..........	882	791	811	868	397	776	984	1,224	1,510
Beef..........................	215	219	218	241	92	212	254	329	439
Pork..........................	152	161	174	151	79	153	194	228	291
Poultry..........................	168	132	154	167	72	137	181	238	295
Fish and seafood..................	146	91	111	146	66	121	146	162	187
Dairy products......................	444	409	356	458	221	393	464	567	682
Fresh milk and cream..............	149	143	142	169	79	135	173	215	279
Other dairy products..............	295	267	213	289	142	258	291	352	403
Fruits and vegetables [1]...............	811	696	612	825	402	703	804	980	1,159
Fresh fruits......................	278	243	201	302	145	246	266	347	380
Fresh vegetables..................	261	203	189	273	123	233	255	302	334
Processed fruits..................	131	119	98	128	67	106	129	160	206
Other food at home [1]..............	1,351	1,401	1,248	1,481	767	1,318	1,563	1,858	2,156
Sugar and other sweets..............	149	153	123	167	82	138	155	196	256
Nonalcoholic beverages..............	374	359	347	374	202	351	434	491	564
Food away from home..................	2,700	2,395	2,474	3,019	1,567	2,740	3,056	3,571	3,347
Alcoholic beverages......................	491	387	386	614	370	569	448	449	358
Housing..........................	19,557	14,926	14,968	19,373	11,456	17,119	19,371	21,886	20,694
Shelter..........................	12,033	8,409	8,110	12,193	7,176	9,851	11,026	12,750	11,769
Owned dwellings..................	7,642	5,691	5,110	7,060	3,438	6,483	7,194	8,949	7,709
Mortgage interest and charges..........	3,305	2,632	2,741	4,341	1,480	2,960	4,125	5,285	4,629
Property taxes..................	3,000	1,936	1,340	1,634	1,127	2,108	2,041	2,424	2,054
Maintenance, repair, insurance, other expenses..................	1,338	1,124	1,029	1,085	831	1,415	1,028	1,240	1,026
Rented dwellings..................	3,567	2,153	2,505	4,297	3,443	2,367	3,154	3,117	3,565
Other lodging..................	823	565	494	835	295	1,000	678	684	495
Utilities, fuels, and public services..........	4,096	3,486	3,898	3,385	2,380	3,843	4,313	4,767	5,011
Natural gas..................	596	600	243	387	284	424	468	533	577
Electricity..................	1,338	1,225	1,763	1,135	927	1,467	1,643	1,783	1,914
Fuel oil and other fuels..................	487	121	70	64	113	189	151	200	138
Telephone..................	1,291	1,136	1,276	1,182	745	1,236	1,496	1,609	1,677
Water and other public services..........	384	406	545	617	311	527	554	641	705
Household operations..................	1,267	934	967	1,439	692	979	1,559	1,780	1,287
Personal services..................	499	334	282	568	166	143	757	950	595
Other household expenses..............	768	601	686	870	526	836	803	830	693
Housekeeping supplies [1]..............	641	645	567	642	348	702	675	751	811
Laundry and cleaning supplies..........	134	156	142	149	76	156	165	188	218
Postage and stationery..............	122	124	114	169	83	159	139	139	143
Household furnishings and equipment [1]....	1,520	1,451	1,427	1,714	859	1,744	1,797	1,838	1,816
Household textiles..................	102	99	95	149	71	120	134	126	127
Furniture..........................	356	370	360	345	213	386	376	496	485
Major appliances..................	184	183	199	204	91	239	245	246	206
Miscellaneous household equipment......	745	689	691	883	417	856	926	847	903
Apparel and services [1]..................	1,905	1,624	1,615	1,926	1,021	1,634	2,016	2,404	2,842
Men and boys..................	445	354	392	438	250	346	458	530	776
Women and girls..................	776	738	648	780	459	695	814	967	1,086
Footwear..........................	331	292	308	363	161	301	361	503	545
Other apparel products and services.......	279	179	195	277	137	261	260	277	254
Transportation..........................	8,435	8,114	8,264	8,399	4,367	8,637	10,321	11,682	11,042
Vehicle purchases (net outlay) [1]..........	2,675	2,805	2,736	2,420	1,235	2,638	3,479	4,251	3,618
Cars and trucks, new..............	1,417	1,255	1,290	1,113	582	1,404	1,626	1,804	1,565
Cars and trucks, used..............	1,161	1,464	1,403	1,257	629	1,167	1,775	2,322	1,979
Gasoline and motor oil..................	2,510	2,632	2,794	2,569	1,399	2,708	3,255	3,675	3,875
Other vehicle expenses..................	2,519	2,223	2,400	2,713	1,418	2,678	3,020	3,061	3,067
Vehicle finance charges..................	198	220	267	216	99	225	327	359	337
Maintenance and repair..................	823	759	719	975	500	888	942	994	968
Vehicle insurance..................	870	848	1,098	1,023	574	1,070	1,223	1,117	1,329
Vehicle rental, leases, licenses, other charges..................	628	395	316	499	245	495	528	590	434
Public transportation..................	730	453	334	698	316	614	567	696	481
Health care [2]..........................	3,368	3,620	3,160	3,216	2,112	4,197	3,744	3,455	3,209
Entertainment [3]..........................	2,632	2,505	2,350	2,950	1,522	2,915	2,876	3,416	2,957
Personal care products and services........	627	582	606	739	388	698	737	806	763
Reading..........................	130	123	88	140	90	147	117	112	92
Education..........................	1,620	1,095	680	1,145	782	746	1,400	1,764	1,310
Tobacco products/smoking supplies..........	356	364	391	268	255	352	422	399	447
Miscellaneous..........................	858	764	661	903	577	887	900	753	835
Cash contributions..................	1,809	1,675	1,613	1,869	1,446	2,225	1,547	1,468	1,559
Personal insurance and pensions..........	5,961	5,178	4,936	6,016	2,588	5,827	7,023	8,019	6,576
Life and other personal insurance..........	406	296	307	282	179	366	431	387	302
Pensions and social security..............	5,554	4,882	4,629	5,734	2,409	5,461	6,592	7,632	6,274
Personal taxes..........................	**2,398**	**1,502**	**1,575**	**2,901**	**1,378**	**2,591**	**2,750**	**2,261**	**632**

[1] Includes other types not shown separately. [2] For additional health care expenditures, see Table 149. [3] For additional recreation expenditures, see Section 26.

Source: U.S. Bureau of Labor Statistics, Consumer Expenditure Survey, "2011 Current Expenditure Tables," <http://stats.bls.gov/cex/>, accessed February 2013.

Table 718. Average Annual Expenditures of All Consumer Units by Income Level: 2011

[In dollars. See headnote, Table 714]

Income level	Total expendi-tures [1]	Food	Housing			Transportation			Health care	Pen-sions and social security
			Total [1]	Shelter	Utilities, fuels [2]	Total [1]	Vehicle pur-chases	Gaso-line and motor oil		
All consumer units........	**49,705**	**6,458**	**16,803**	**9,825**	**3,727**	**8,293**	**2,669**	**2,655**	**3,313**	**5,106**
Consumer units with incomes:										
Less than $70,000............	34,391	4,854	12,568	7,253	3,141	5,772	1,642	2,090	2,632	2,064
$70,000 to $79,999...........	57,977	7,679	19,178	10,887	4,273	9,804	3,095	3,345	4,130	6,099
$80,000 to $99,999...........	65,390	8,139	20,926	12,247	4,537	12,185	4,455	3,612	4,106	7,876
$100,000 and over............	97,728	11,233	30,212	18,158	5,395	15,538	5,595	4,121	5,258	15,100
$100,000 to $119,999.......	76,496	9,569	23,660	13,546	4,903	13,962	4,966	3,921	4,590	10,099
$120,000 to $149,999.......	87,239	10,674	27,420	16,546	5,126	14,274	4,878	4,150	5,038	13,158
$150,000 and over...........	123,056	13,055	37,700	23,175	6,001	17,756	6,639	4,267	5,976	20,681

[1] Includes expenditures not shown separately. [2] Includes public service.

Source: U.S. Bureau of Labor Statistics, Consumer Expenditure Survey, "2011 Current Expenditure Tables," <http://stats.bls.gov/cex/>, accessed February 2013.

Table 719. Annual Expenditure Per Child by Husband-Wife Families by Family Income and Expenditure Type: 2011

[In dollars. Data are for a child in a two-child family. Excludes expenses for college. Expenditures based on before-tax income data from the 2005–2006 Consumer Expenditure Survey updated to 2011 dollars using the Consumer Price Index. For more on the methodology, see source]

Family income and age of child	Total	Expenditure type						
		Housing	Food	Transpor-tation	Clothing	Health care	Child care and educa-tion [1]	Miscella-neous [2]
INCOME: LESS THAN $59,410								
Less than 2 years old........................	9,050	2,990	1,160	1,170	640	630	2,040	420
3 to 5 years old.............................	9,100	2,990	1,260	1,230	500	590	1,910	620
6 to 8 years old.............................	8,760	2,990	1,710	1,350	570	660	850	630
9 to 11 years old............................	9,520	2,990	1,970	1,350	580	710	1,290	630
12 to 14 years old...........................	9,960	2,990	2,130	1,480	690	1,090	880	700
15 to 17 years old...........................	9,970	2,990	2,120	1,630	730	1,010	910	580
INCOME: $59,410 TO $102,870								
Less than 2 years old........................	12,370	3,920	1,400	1,690	760	850	2,860	980
3 to 5 years old.............................	12,390	3,920	1,490	1,740	610	800	2,740	1,090
6 to 8 years old.............................	12,290	3,920	2,100	1,860	680	940	1,680	1,110
9 to 11 years old............................	13,110	3,920	2,400	1,870	710	1,000	2,110	1,100
12 to 14 years old...........................	13,820	3,920	2,580	1,990	840	1,410	1,910	1,170
15 to 17 years old...........................	14,320	3,920	2,570	2,150	900	1,330	2,400	1,050
INCOME: MORE THAN $102,870								
Less than 2 years old........................	20,460	7,100	1,900	2,550	1,050	980	5,090	1,790
3 to 5 years old.............................	20,480	7,100	2,000	2,610	880	930	4,970	1,990
6 to 8 years old.............................	20,420	7,100	2,630	2,730	970	1,080	3,910	2,000
9 to 11 years old............................	21,320	7,100	2,980	2,730	1,010	1,150	4,350	2,000
12 to 14 years old...........................	22,700	7,100	3,190	2,860	1,170	1,610	4,700	2,070
15 to 17 years old...........................	24,510	7,100	3,180	3,020	1,280	1,520	6,460	1,950

[1] Includes only families with child care and education expenses. [2] Expenses include personal care items, entertainment, and reading materials.

Source: U.S. Department of Agriculture, Center for Nutrition Policy and Promotion, *Expenditures on Children by Families, 2011*, June 2012. See also <http://www.cnpp.usda.gov/Publications.htm>.

Table 720. Money Income of Households—Percent Distribution by Income Level, Race, and Hispanic Origin, in Constant (2011) Dollars: 1990 to 2011

[94,312 represents 94,312,000. Households as of March of following year. Constant dollars based on CPI-U-RS deflator. Based on Current Population Survey, Annual Social and Economic Supplement (ASEC); see text, this section and Section 1, and Appendix III. For definition of median, see Guide to Tabular Presentation]

Year	Number of house-holds (1,000)	Percent distribution							Median income (dollars)
		Under $15,000	$15,000 to $24,999	$25,000 to $34,999	$35,000 to $49,999	$50,000 to $74,999	$75,000 to $99,999	$100,000 and over	
ALL HOUSEHOLDS [1]									
1990.	94,312	13.1	11.2	10.8	14.9	20.3	12.8	16.9	49,950
2000 [2]	108,209	11.1	10.6	10.2	14.1	18.3	13.0	22.7	54,841
2010 [3, 4]	119,927	13.4	11.8	10.6	13.7	17.6	11.5	21.4	50,831
2011 [3, 4]	121,084	13.5	11.5	10.9	13.9	17.6	11.5	21.0	50,054
WHITE									
1990.	80,968	11.2	10.8	10.6	15.1	20.8	13.4	18.0	52,099
2000 [2]	90,030	9.9	10.2	9.9	14.1	18.4	13.5	23.9	57,356
2010 [3, 4, 5]	96,306	11.5	11.5	10.4	13.8	18.0	12.1	22.7	53,340
2011 [3, 4, 5]	96,964	11.6	11.1	10.8	14.1	18.0	12.0	22.3	52,214
BLACK									
1990.	10,671	27.7	14.7	12.2	13.9	16.1	8.2	7.3	31,155
2000 [2]	13,174	19.7	13.8	12.9	14.8	17.7	9.4	11.7	38,747
2010 [3, 4, 6]	15,265	25.2	14.6	12.4	14.4	15.1	8.2	10.2	33,137
2011 [3, 4, 6]	15,583	25.6	15.0	12.2	13.5	15.3	8.0	10.4	32,229
ASIAN AND PACIFIC ISLANDER									
1990.	1,958	9.8	8.4	8.9	11.5	19.9	13.9	27.5	64,142
2000 [2]	3,963	8.7	7.1	7.5	11.2	17.1	14.9	33.6	72,821
2010 [3, 4, 7]	5,212	10.6	9.4	7.1	10.8	17.9	11.3	32.9	66,286
2011 [3, 4, 7]	5,374	10.6	8.8	8.3	11.3	17.4	12.8	30.8	65,129
HISPANIC									
1990.	6,220	18.3	15.8	13.0	16.6	19.1	8.6	8.5	37,251
2000 [2]	10,034	13.3	14.2	12.5	17.3	19.2	11.1	12.6	43,319
2010 [3, 4, 8]	14,435	17.1	14.7	13.5	15.5	17.4	9.8	12.1	38,818
2011 [3, 4, 8]	14,939	16.5	14.7	14.0	16.8	17.0	9.2	11.7	38,624

[1] Includes other races not shown separately. [2] Data reflect implementation of Census 2000-based population controls and a 28,000 household sample expansion to 78,000 households. [3] Implementation of Census 2010-based population controls. Median income is calculated using $2,500 income intervals. Beginning with 2009 data, Census Bureau expanded upper income intervals used to calculate medians to $250,000 or more. Medians falling in the upper open-ended interval are plugged with "$250,000." Before 2009, the upper open-ended interval was $100,000 and a plug of "$100,000" was used. [4] Beginning with the 2003 Current Population Survey (CPS), the questionnaire allowed respondents to choose more than one race. For 2002 and later, data represent persons who selected this race group only and exclude persons reporting more than one race. The CPS in prior years allowed respondents to report only one race group. See also comments on race in the text for Section 1. [5] Data represent White alone, which refers to people who reported White and did not report any other race category. [6] Data represent Black alone, which refers to people who reported Black and did not report any other race category. [7] Data represent Asian alone, which refers to people who reported Asian and did not report any other race category. [8] People of Hispanic origin may be of any race.

Source: U.S. Census Bureau, *Income, Poverty, and Health Insurance Coverage in the United States: 2011*, Current Population Reports, P60-243; and "Historical Tables—Table H17," <http://www.census.gov/hhes/www/income/data/historical/index.html>, accessed February 2013.

Table 721. Money Income of Households—Median Income by Race and Hispanic Origin, in Current and Constant (2011) Dollars: 1980 to 2011

[In dollars. See headnote, Table 720]

Year	Median income in current dollars					Median income in constant (2011) dollars				
	All house-holds [1]	White [2]	Black [3]	Asian, Pacific Islander [4]	His-panic [5]	All house-holds [1]	White [2]	Black [3]	Asian, Pacific Islander [4]	His-panic [5]
1980.	17,710	18,684	10,764	(NA)	13,651	46,024	48,555	27,973	(NA)	35,475
1990.	29,943	31,231	18,676	38,450	22,330	49,950	52,099	31,155	64,142	37,251
1995 [6]	34,076	35,766	22,393	40,614	22,860	49,935	52,411	32,815	59,516	33,499
2000 [7, 8]	41,990	43,916	29,667	55,757	33,168	54,841	57,356	38,747	72,821	43,319
2005.	46,326	48,554	30,858	61,094	35,967	53,371	55,938	35,551	70,385	41,437
2008.	50,303	52,312	34,218	65,637	37,913	52,546	54,645	35,744	68,564	39,604
2009 [9]	49,777	51,861	32,584	65,469	38,039	52,195	54,380	34,167	68,649	39,887
2010 [10]	49,276	51,709	32,124	64,259	37,631	50,831	53,340	33,137	66,286	38,818
2011.	50,054	52,214	32,229	65,129	38,624	50,054	52,214	32,229	65,129	38,624

NA Not available. [1] Includes other races, not shown separately. [2] Beginning with 2002, data represents White alone, which refers to people who reported White and did not report any other race category. [3] Beginning with 2002, data represents Black alone, which refers to people who reported Black and did not report any other race category. [4] Beginning with 2002, data represents Asian alone, which refers to people who reported Asian and did not report any other race category. [5] People of Hispanic origin may be of any race. [6] Data reflect full implementation of the 1990 Census-based sample design and metropolitan definitions, 7,000 household sample reduction, and revised race edits. [7] Implementation of Census 2000-based population controls. [8] Implementation of a 28,000 household sample expansion. [9] Median income is calculated using $2,500 income intervals. Beginning with 2009 income data, the Census Bureau expanded the upper income intervals used to calculate medians to $250,000 or more. Before 2009, the upper open-ended interval was $100,000 and a plug of "$100,000" was used. [10] Implementation of Census 2010-based population controls.

Source: U.S. Census Bureau, *Income, Poverty and Health Insurance Coverage in the United States: 2011*, Current Population Reports, P60-243; and "Historical Tables—Table H-5," <http://www.census.gov/hhes/www/income/data/historical/index.html>, accessed February 2013.

Table 722. Money Income of Households—Distribution by Income Level and Selected Characteristics: 2011

[121,084 represents 121,084,000. Households as of March of the following year. Based on Current Population Survey, Annual Social and Economic Supplement (ASEC); see text, this section and Section 1, and Appendix III. For definition of median, see Guide to Tabular Presentation. Median income is calculated using $2,500 income intervals. Beginning with 2009 income data, the Census Bureau expanded the upper income intervals used to calculate medians to $250,000 or more. Medians falling in the upper open-ended interval are plugged with "$250,000." Before 2009, the upper open-ended interval was $100,000 and a plug of "$100,000" was used]

Characteristic	Number of households (1,000)								Median house-hold income (dollars)
	Total house-holds	Under $15,000	$15,000 to $24,999	$25,000 to $34,999	$35,000 to $49,999	$50,000 to $74,999	$75,000 to $99,999	$100,000 and over	
Total....................	**121,084**	**16,360**	**13,977**	**13,258**	**16,876**	**21,293**	**13,898**	**25,421**	**50,054**
Age of householder:									
15 to 24 years..............	6,180	1,564	1,038	918	1,042	959	311	348	30,460
25 to 34 years..............	19,846	2,390	2,079	2,238	3,019	4,074	2,536	3,511	50,774
35 to 44 years..............	21,241	1,903	1,764	1,965	2,833	4,101	2,931	5,744	61,916
45 to 54 years..............	24,195	2,634	1,848	1,995	2,995	4,326	3,237	7,160	63,861
55 to 64 years..............	22,779	3,010	2,128	2,077	3,045	3,982	2,822	5,714	55,937
65 years and over..........	26,843	4,859	5,120	4,066	3,942	3,852	2,061	2,943	33,118
Region: [1]									
Northeast..................	21,774	2,951	2,279	2,143	2,767	3,693	2,588	5,355	53,864
Midwest....................	26,865	3,601	3,194	3,039	3,841	4,830	3,172	5,189	48,722
South......................	45,604	6,584	5,615	5,227	6,503	8,069	5,022	8,584	46,899
West.......................	26,840	3,225	2,890	2,851	3,764	4,702	3,116	6,292	52,376
Size of household:									
One person................	33,188	9,605	6,461	4,728	4,682	4,325	1,614	1,774	25,902
Two people................	40,983	3,344	4,082	4,605	6,293	8,089	5,380	9,192	55,555
Three people..............	19,241	1,621	1,544	1,720	2,591	3,724	2,713	5,328	63,370
Four people...............	16,049	963	1,067	1,196	1,792	3,014	2,503	5,513	74,913
Five people...............	7,271	519	487	611	925	1,288	1,049	2,392	70,652
Six people................	2,734	192	225	227	360	536	413	781	66,930
Seven or more people.......	1,617	117	112	172	233	317	227	440	63,946
Type of household:									
Family household..........	80,506	6,120	6,881	7,797	11,103	15,362	11,273	21,969	62,273
Married-couple............	58,949	2,250	3,685	4,755	7,523	11,556	9,429	19,751	74,130
Male householder, spouse absent..........	5,888	553	711	760	936	1,302	720	906	49,567
Female householder, spouse absent..........	15,669	3,317	2,485	2,281	2,644	2,504	1,124	1,312	33,637
Nonfamily household.........	40,578	10,241	7,096	5,461	5,773	5,931	2,625	3,452	30,221
Male householder.........	19,195	3,877	2,946	2,647	2,842	3,161	1,518	2,203	35,482
Female householder........	21,383	6,364	4,149	2,814	2,931	2,770	1,107	1,248	25,492
Educational attainment of householder: [2]									
Total...................	**114,904**	**14,796**	**12,940**	**12,340**	**15,833**	**20,335**	**13,587**	**25,073**	**51,244**
Less than 9th grade...........	5,076	1,669	1,160	761	654	494	188	151	21,823
9th to 12th grade (no diploma).................	8,431	2,499	1,759	1,267	1,126	978	445	357	24,695
High school graduate........	32,822	5,283	4,860	4,429	5,376	6,034	3,199	3,641	39,420
Some college, no degree.......	20,451	2,475	2,381	2,569	3,264	3,853	2,483	3,427	47,484
Associate's degree...........	11,387	1,079	1,061	1,190	1,656	2,360	1,615	2,427	55,928
Bachelor's degree or more.....	36,737	1,792	1,718	2,124	3,759	6,616	5,658	15,070	83,985
Bachelor's degree............	23,197	1,266	1,200	1,556	2,604	4,362	3,633	8,578	78,251
Master's degree.............	9,792	401	402	423	913	1,714	1,558	4,381	90,947
Professional degree..........	1,835	45	62	84	94	250	219	1,082	120,580
Doctoral degree..............	1,912	80	54	62	148	290	248	1,029	107,046
Number of earners:									
No earners.................	28,569	11,226	6,338	4,021	3,193	2,199	867	724	19,315
One earner..................	45,578	4,628	6,302	6,924	8,571	9,023	4,264	5,866	42,173
Two earners and more........	46,938	506	1,337	2,314	5,111	10,071	8,767	18,831	85,648
Two earners.................	37,943	479	1,244	2,102	4,490	8,553	7,014	14,061	81,263
Three earners..............	6,905	26	86	191	557	1,261	1,385	3,399	98,869
Four earners or more........	2,089	0	7	21	65	257	368	1,371	121,918
Work experience of householder:									
Total....................	**121,084**	**16,360**	**13,977**	**13,258**	**16,876**	**21,293**	**13,898**	**25,421**	**50,054**
Worked....................	79,416	4,335	6,381	7,616	11,362	16,298	11,303	22,122	64,210
Worked at full-time jobs......	65,847	2,134	4,464	5,937	9,341	14,057	10,024	19,891	68,763
50 weeks or more...........	55,837	842	3,176	4,758	7,716	12,159	8,906	18,280	72,585
27 to 49 weeks............	5,937	447	652	691	973	1,249	764	1,161	53,227
26 weeks or less...........	4,073	845	636	487	651	649	354	450	36,099
Worked at part-time jobs. ...	13,569	2,201	1,917	1,679	2,021	2,241	1,279	2,231	41,878
50 weeks or more...........	7,557	843	1,076	947	1,207	1,303	786	1,395	45,863
27 to 49 weeks.............	2,691	457	389	317	365	471	274	417	42,954
26 weeks or less...........	3,321	901	452	415	449	467	219	419	32,046
Did not work................	41,668	12,025	7,597	5,643	5,514	4,996	2,596	3,299	26,902
Housing Tenure:									
Owner occupied..............	79,175	6,527	7,078	7,332	10,336	14,933	10,950	22,018	62,526
Renter occupied.............	40,233	9,317	6,626	5,693	6,317	6,148	2,844	3,288	31,769
Occupier paid no cash rent. ...	1,676	517	274	233	222	212	104	114	26,668

[1] For composition of regions, see map, inside front cover. [2] People 25 years old and over.

Source: U.S. Census Bureau, *Income, Poverty and Health Insurance Coverage in the United States: 2011*, Current Population Reports, P60-243; and "Detailed Tables—Table HINC-01," <http://www.census.gov/hhes/www/income/data/index.html>, accessed February 2012.

Table 723. Money Income of Households—Number and Distribution by Race and Hispanic Origin: 2011

[121,084 represents 121,084,000. Households as of March of the following year. Based on Current Population Survey, Annual Social and Economic Supplement (ASEC); see text, this section and Section 1, and Appendix III. The 2011 CPS allowed respondents to choose more than one race. Data represent persons who selected this race group only and excludes persons reporting more than one race. See also comments on race in the text for Section 1]

Income interval	Number of households (1,000)					Percent distribution				
	All races	White alone	Black alone	Asian alone	His-panic [1]	All races	White alone	Black alone	Asian alone	His-panic [1]
All households............	**121,084**	**96,964**	**15,583**	**5,374**	**14,939**	**100.0**	**100.0**	**100.0**	**100.0**	**100.0**
Under $10,000.................	9,233	6,056	2,484	370	1,473	7.6	6.2	15.9	6.9	9.9
$10,000 to $14,999............	7,127	5,200	1,498	201	992	5.9	5.4	9.6	3.7	6.6
$15,000 to $19,999............	6,882	5,241	1,197	226	1,066	5.7	5.4	7.7	4.2	7.1
$20,000 to $24,999............	7,095	5,497	1,139	249	1,126	5.9	5.7	7.3	4.6	7.5
$25,000 to $29,999............	6,591	5,226	947	205	1,044	5.4	5.4	6.1	3.8	7.0
$30,000 to $34,999............	6,667	5,275	949	239	1,047	5.5	5.4	6.1	4.4	7.0
$35,000 to $39,999............	6,136	4,922	813	231	932	5.1	5.1	5.2	4.3	6.2
$40,000 to $44,999............	5,795	4,724	730	180	850	4.8	4.9	4.7	3.3	5.7
$45,000 to $49,999............	4,945	4,050	567	193	731	4.1	4.2	3.6	3.6	4.9
$50,000 to $59,999............	9,420	7,641	1,145	378	1,188	7.8	7.9	7.3	7.0	8.0
$60,000 to $74,999............	11,874	9,823	1,242	556	1,355	9.8	10.1	8.0	10.3	9.1
$75,000 to $84,999............	6,488	5,397	601	326	617	5.4	5.6	3.9	6.1	4.1
$85,000 to $99,999............	7,411	6,243	645	360	762	6.1	6.4	4.1	6.7	5.1
$100,000 to $149,999........	14,441	12,167	1,061	935	1,126	11.9	12.5	6.8	17.4	7.5
$150,000 to $199,999........	5,875	5,091	329	357	386	4.9	5.3	2.1	6.6	2.6
$200,000 to $249,999........	2,297	1,958	136	152	111	1.9	2.0	0.9	2.8	0.7
$250,000 and above...........	2,808	2,453	100	213	134	2.3	2.5	0.6	4.0	0.9

[1] Persons of Hispanic origin may be of any race.

Source: U.S. Census Bureau, *Income, Poverty and Health Insurance Coverage in the United States: 2011*, Current Population Reports, P60-243; and "Detailed Tables—Table HINC-06," <http://www.census.gov/hhes/www/income/index.html>, accessed February 2013.

Table 724. Share of Aggregate Income Received by Each Fifth and Top 5 Percent of Households: 1980 to 2011

[83,368 represents 82,368,000. Households as of March of the following year. Income in constant 2011 CPI-U-RS-adjusted dollars. The shares method ranks households from highest to lowest on the basis of income and then divides them into groups of equal population size, typically quintiles. The aggregate income of each group is then divided by the overall aggregate income to derive shares. Based on the Current Population Survey, Annual Social and Economic Supplement (ASEC); see text, this section and Section 1, and Appendix III. For data collection changes over time, see <http://www.census.gov/hhes/www/income/data/historical/ftnotes.html>]

Year	Number of house-holds (1,000)	Income at selected positions in constant (2011) dollars					Percent distribution of aggregate income					
		Upper limit of each fifth				Top 5 percent	Lowest 5th	Second 5th	Third 5th	Fourth 5th	Highest 5th	Top 5 percent
		Lowest	Second	Third	Fourth							
1980..........	82,368	19,433	36,445	55,873	81,808	131,655	4.2	10.2	16.8	24.7	44.1	16.5
1990..........	94,312	20,852	39,473	60,388	92,092	158,057	3.8	9.6	15.9	24.0	46.6	18.5
1995 [1].......	99,627	21,102	39,440	61,550	95,432	165,590	3.7	9.1	15.2	23.3	48.7	21.0
2000 [2, 3]......	108,209	23,404	43,100	68,142	106,790	189,665	3.6	8.9	14.8	23.0	49.8	22.1
2003..........	112,000	21,992	41,578	66,590	106,228	188,470	3.4	8.7	14.8	23.4	49.8	21.4
2004 [4]......	113,343	22,011	41,287	65,762	104,784	187,121	3.4	8.7	14.7	23.2	50.1	21.8
2005..........	114,384	22,095	41,475	66,429	105,651	191,245	3.4	8.6	14.6	23.0	50.4	22.2
2006..........	116,011	22,349	42,137	66,930	108,239	194,111	3.4	8.6	14.5	22.9	50.5	22.3
2007..........	116,783	22,010	42,413	67,253	108,473	191,997	3.4	8.7	14.8	23.4	49.7	21.2
2008..........	117,181	21,636	40,739	65,522	104,710	188,027	3.4	8.6	14.7	23.3	50.0	21.5
2009..........	117,538	21,446	40,422	64,803	104,857	188,744	3.4	8.6	14.6	23.2	50.3	21.7
2010 [5].........	119,927	20,631	39,199	63,440	103,184	186,178	3.3	8.5	14.6	23.4	50.3	21.3
2011..........	121,084	20,262	38,520	62,434	101,582	186,000	3.2	8.4	14.3	23.0	51.1	22.3

[1] Data reflect full implementation of the 1990 Census-based sample design and metropolitan definitions, 7,000 household sample reduction, and revised race edits. [2] Implementation of Census 2000-based population controls. [3] Implementation of a 28,000 household sample expansion. [4] Data have been revised to reflect a correction to the weights in the 2005 ASEC. [5] Implementation of Census 2010-based population controls.

Source: U.S. Census Bureau, *Income, Poverty and Health Insurance Coverage in the United States: 2011*, Current Population Reports, P60-243; and "Historical Tables—Tables H1 and H2," <http://www.census.gov/hhes/www/income/data/historical/index.html>, accessed February 2013.

Table 725. Money Income of Families—Number and Distribution by Race and Hispanic Origin: 2011

[80,529 represents 80,529,000. Families as of March of the following year. Based on Current Population Survey, Annual Social and Economic Supplement (ASEC); see text, this section, Section 1, and Appendix III. Since 2003, the CPS allows respondents to choose more than one race. Data represent persons who selected this race group only and excludes persons reporting more than one race. See also comments on race in the text for Section 1]

Income interval	Number of families (1,000)					Percent distribution				
	All races	White alone	Black alone	Asian alone	His-panic [1]	All races	White alone	Black alone	Asian alone	His-panic [1]
All families [1]	**80,529**	**64,625**	**9,656**	**4,153**	**11,589**	**100.0**	**100.0**	**100.0**	**100.0**	**100.0**
Under $10,000	4,276	2,767	1,152	148	1,053	5.3	4.3	11.9	3.6	9.1
$10,000 to $14,999	2,630	1,788	623	113	603	3.3	2.8	6.4	2.7	5.2
$15,000 to $19,999	3,247	2,297	659	154	793	4.0	3.6	6.8	3.7	6.8
$20,000 to $24,999	3,917	2,974	645	176	929	4.9	4.6	6.7	4.2	8.0
$25,000 to $29,999	3,871	3,001	595	145	848	4.8	4.6	6.2	3.5	7.3
$30,000 to $34,999	4,022	3,175	557	161	788	5.0	4.9	5.8	3.9	6.8
$35,000 to $39,999	3,975	3,158	541	168	771	4.9	4.9	5.6	4.0	6.7
$40,000 to $44,999	3,712	3,014	458	135	630	4.6	4.7	4.7	3.2	5.4
$45,000 to $49,999	3,347	2,701	371	171	564	4.2	4.2	3.8	4.1	4.9
$50,000 to $59,999	6,536	5,265	786	311	957	8.1	8.1	8.1	7.5	8.3
$60,000 to $74,999	8,548	6,998	925	443	1,052	10.6	10.8	9.6	10.7	9.1
$75,000 to $84,999	5,077	4,254	455	249	509	6.3	6.6	4.7	6.0	4.4
$85,000 to $99,999	5,917	4,957	528	300	625	7.3	7.7	5.5	7.2	5.4
$100,000 to $149,999	12,091	10,200	884	820	924	15.0	15.8	9.2	19.7	8.0
$150,000 to $199,999	4,938	4,263	282	317	324	6.1	6.6	2.9	7.6	2.8
$200,000 to $249,999	1,968	1,668	121	143	104	2.4	2.6	1.3	3.4	0.9
$250,000 and above	2,456	2,148	75	199	114	3.1	3.3	0.8	4.8	1.0

[1] Persons of Hispanic origin may be any race.

Source: U.S. Census Bureau, *Income, Poverty and Health Insurance Coverage in the United States: 2011*, Current Population Reports, P60-243; and "Detailed Tables—Table FINC-07," <http://www.census.gov/hhes/www/income/>, accessed February 2013.

Table 726. Money Income of Families—Percent Distribution by Income Level in Constant (2011) Dollars: 1990 to 2011

[66,322 represents 66,322,000. Families as of March of following year. Constant dollars based on CPI-U-RS deflator. Based on Current Population Survey, Annual Social and Economic Supplement (ASEC); see text, this section, Section 1, and Appendix III. For data collection changes over time, see <http://www.census.gov/hhes/www/income/data/historical/history.html>. For definition of median, see Guide to Tabular Presentation]

Year	Number of families (1,000)	Percent distribution							Median income (dollars)
		Under $15,000	$15,000 to $24,999	$25,000 to $34,999	$35,000 to $49,999	$50,000 to $74,999	$75,000 to $99,999	$100,000 and over	
ALL FAMILIES [1]									
1990	66,322	8.1	8.8	9.7	14.6	22.3	15.2	21.3	58,975
2000 [2]	73,778	6.4	8.0	8.9	13.8	19.4	15.3	28.2	66,259
2010 [3]	79,559	8.7	8.9	9.6	13.4	18.7	13.7	27.1	62,136
2011	80,529	8.6	8.9	9.8	13.7	18.7	13.7	26.6	60,974
WHITE									
1990	56,803	6.1	8.1	9.4	14.8	23.0	15.9	22.6	61,581
2000 [2]	61,330	5.2	7.3	8.4	13.7	19.6	15.9	29.9	69,259
2010 [3, 4, 5]	63,976	7.2	8.1	9.2	13.4	19.1	14.3	28.8	64,898
2011	64,625	7.0	8.2	9.6	13.7	19.0	14.3	28.3	64,081
BLACK									
1990	7,471	22.3	14.6	12.3	14.1	17.8	9.7	9.1	35,737
2000 [2]	8,731	14.4	13.4	12.7	15.4	18.8	11.0	14.4	43,983
2010 [3, 4, 6]	9,571	18.8	13.7	12.6	14.8	16.8	10.1	13.2	39,811
2011	9,656	18.4	13.5	11.9	14.2	17.7	10.2	14.1	40,495
ASIAN AND PACIFIC ISLANDER									
1990	1,536	7.2	7.0	8.7	11.0	19.0	15.5	31.6	70,474
2000 [2]	2,982	5.4	6.1	6.5	10.3	17.6	15.5	38.6	81,781
2010 [3, 4, 7]	3,879	6.5	7.8	6.3	11.0	17.3	12.8	38.4	77,590
2011	4,153	6.3	7.9	7.4	11.4	18.2	13.2	35.5	72,996
HISPANIC ORIGIN [8]									
1990	4,981	15.6	15.6	13.7	16.4	19.9	9.3	9.5	39,087
2000 [2]	8,017	11.4	13.8	12.7	17.9	19.6	11.4	13.2	44,983
2010 [3]	11,284	15.4	14.7	13.6	15.5	18.2	10.0	12.7	40,540
2011	11,589	14.3	14.9	14.1	17.0	17.3	9.8	12.7	40,061

[1] Includes other races not shown separately. [2] Data reflect implementation of Census 2000-based population controls and a 28,000 household sample expansion to 78,000 households. [3] Median income is calculated using $2,500 income intervals. Beginning with 2009 income data, the Census Bureau expanded the upper income intervals used to calculate medians to $250,000 or more. Medians falling in the upper open-ended interval are plugged with "$250,000." Before 2009, the upper open-ended interval was $100,000 and a plug of "$100,000" was used. 2010 data contain implementation of Census 2010-based population controls. [4] Beginning with the 2003 Current Population Survey (CPS), the questionnaire allowed respondents to choose more than one race. For 2002 and later, data represent persons who selected this race group only and exclude persons reporting more than one race. The CPS in prior years allowed respondents to report only one race group. See also comments on race in the text for Section 1. [5] Data represent White alone, which refers to people who reported White and did not report any other race category. [6] Data represent Black alone, which refers to people who reported Black and did not report any other race category. [7] Data represent Asian alone, which refers to people who reported Asian and did not report any other race category. [8] People of Hispanic origin may be of any race.

Source: U.S. Census Bureau, *Income, Poverty and Health Insurance Coverage in the United States: 2011*, Current Population Reports, P60-243; and "Historical Tables—Table F-23," <http://www.census.gov/hhes/www/income/data/historical/index.html>, accessed February 2013.

Table 727. Money Income of Families—Median Income by Race and Hispanic Origin in Current and Constant (2011) Dollars: 1990 to 2011

[In dollars. See headnote, Table 710]

Year	Median income in current dollars					Median income in constant (2011) dollars				
	All families [1]	White [2]	Black [2]	Asian, Pacific Islander [2]	His-panic [3]	All families [1]	White [2]	Black [2]	Asian, Pacific Islander [2]	His-panic [3]
1990.........	35,353	36,915	21,423	42,246	23,431	58,975	61,581	35,737	70,474	39,087
1995 [4].........	40,611	42,646	25,970	46,356	24,570	59,511	62,493	38,056	67,930	36,005
2000 [5,6].........	50,732	53,029	33,676	62,617	34,442	66,259	69,259	43,983	81,781	44,983
2005.........	56,194	59,317	35,464	68,957	37,867	64,740	68,338	40,857	79,444	43,626
2007.........	61,355	64,427	40,143	77,133	40,566	66,554	69,886	43,544	83,668	44,003
2008.........	61,521	65,000	39,879	73,578	40,466	64,264	67,898	41,657	76,859	42,270
2009 [7].........	60,088	62,545	38,409	75,027	39,730	63,007	65,583	40,275	78,671	41,660
2010 [8].........	60,236	62,914	38,594	75,217	39,300	62,136	64,898	39,811	77,590	40,540
2011.........	60,974	64,081	40,495	72,996	40,061	60,974	64,081	40,495	72,996	40,061

[1] Includes other races not shown separately. [2] Beginning with 2002, data represent White alone, Black alone, or Asian alone which refers to people who reported each race only and did not report any other race. [3] People of Hispanic origin may be any race. [4] Data reflect full implementation of the 1990 Census-based sample design and metropolitan definitions, 7,000 household sample reduction, and revised race edits. [5] Implementation of Census 2000-based population controls. [5] Implementation of 28,000 household sample expansion. [7] Median income calculated using $2,500 income intervals. Beginning 2009, Census Bureau expanded upper income intervals used to calculate medians to $250,000 or more. Medians falling in the upper open-ended interval are plugged with "$250,000." Before 2009, the upper open-ended interval was $100,000 and a plug of "$100,000" was used. See also comments on race in the text for Section 1. [8] Implementation of Census 2010-based population controls.

Source: U.S. Census Bureau, *Income, Poverty and Health Insurance Coverage in the United States: 2011*, Current Population Reports, P60-243; and "Historical Tables—Table F-05," <http://www.census.gov/hhes/www/income/data/historical/index.html>, accessed February 2013.

Table 728. Money Income of Families—Distribution by Family Characteristics and Income Level: 2011

[80,529 represents 80,529,000. See headnote, Table 726. Median income is calculated using $2,500 income intervals. Beginning with 2009 income data, the Census Bureau expanded the upper income intervals used to calculate medians to $250,000 or more. Medians falling in the upper open-ended interval are plugged with "$250,000." Before 2009, the upper open-ended interval was $100,000 and a plug of "$100,000" was used. For composition of regions, see map inside front cover]

Characteristic	Number of families (1,000)								Median income (dollars)
	Total	Under $15,000	$15,000 to $24,999	$25,000 to $34,999	$35,000 to $49,999	$50,000 to $74,999	$75,000 to $99,999	$100,000 and over	
All families.................	**80,529**	**6,907**	**7,163**	**7,893**	**11,034**	**15,085**	**10,994**	**21,454**	**60,974**
Age of householder:									
15 to 24 years old...............	3,335	910	524	465	526	502	187	220	30,286
25 to 34 years old...............	13,520	1,886	1,470	1,379	1,924	2,634	1,752	2,474	50,643
35 to 44 years old...............	16,785	1,351	1,320	1,450	2,098	3,116	2,438	5,011	66,259
45 to 54 years old...............	17,552	1,083	1,101	1,247	1,960	3,175	2,635	6,351	76,551
55 to 64 years old...............	14,906	964	993	1,091	1,833	2,782	2,285	4,957	72,757
65 years old and over........	14,431	713	1,755	2,261	2,693	2,875	1,695	2,440	48,538
Region:									
Northeast....................	14,083	1,056	1,074	1,226	1,793	2,509	1,975	4,451	68,084
Midwest......................	17,494	1,507	1,417	1,697	2,367	3,382	2,580	4,543	61,824
South........................	30,849	2,869	3,026	3,195	4,423	5,947	4,110	7,280	56,869
West.........................	18,102	1,475	1,647	1,775	2,451	3,246	2,328	5,180	62,458
Type of family:									
Married-couple families..........	58,963	2,294	3,710	4,774	7,548	11,567	9,424	19,647	73,790
Male householder, no spouse present.......................	5,888	728	816	766	1,006	1,217	611	743	43,069
Female householder, no spouse present.......................	15,678	3,885	2,637	2,353	2,480	2,300	959	1,064	30,259
Unrelated subfamilies............	671	243	117	109	100	69	18	15	22,194
Educational attainment of householder:									
Persons 25 years old and over, total....................	77,194	5,996	6,639	7,428	10,508	14,582	10,807	21,233	62,381
Less than 9th grade...............	3,330	690	771	603	531	438	162	135	27,815
9th to 12th grade (no diploma)....	5,373	1,057	1,046	882	887	835	379	286	31,332
High school graduate (includes equivalency)....................	21,879	2,118	2,466	2,809	3,838	4,709	2,724	3,215	48,460
Some college, no degree.........	13,637	1,081	1,151	1,445	2,198	2,858	2,000	2,903	57,005
Associate's degree...............	7,817	430	534	684	1,045	1,707	1,325	2,092	66,252
Bachelor's degree or more........	25,159	621	672	1,005	2,008	4,035	4,216	12,602	100,096
Bachelor's degree...............	15,856	435	487	744	1,418	2,788	2,810	7,173	92,087
Master's degree.................	6,665	148	138	180	438	968	1,110	3,684	107,116
Professional degree..............	1,300	11	24	50	58	130	125	901	146,311
Doctoral degree.................	1,338	26	23	31	94	149	171	844	122,208
Number of earners:									
No earners......................	13,207	3,766	2,469	2,172	2,047	1,532	687	533	26,478
One earner......................	27,408	2,789	3,678	3,906	4,913	5,252	2,717	4,153	44,185
Two earners or more.............	39,914	352	1,016	1,816	4,074	8,300	7,589	16,768	88,342

Source: U.S. Census Bureau, Current Population Reports, *Income, Poverty and Health Insurance Coverage in the United States: 2011*, September 2012; and "Detailed Tables—Table FINC-01," <http://www.census.gov/hhes/www/income/index.html>, accessed March 2013.

Table 729. Median Income of Families by Type of Family in Current and Constant (2011) Dollars: 1990 to 2011

[In dollars. See headnote, Table 726. For definition of median, see Guide to Tabular Presentation]

Year	Current dollars						Constant (2011) dollars					
	All families	Married-couple families			Male house-holder, no spouse present	Female house-holder, no spouse present	All families	Married-couple families			Male house-holder, no spouse present	Female house-holder, no spouse present
		Total	Wife in paid labor force	Wife not in paid labor force				Total	Wife in paid labor force	Wife not in paid labor force		
1990............	35,353	39,895	46,777	30,265	29,046	16,932	58,975	66,552	78,033	50,488	48,454	28,246
1995 [1]..........	40,611	47,062	55,823	32,375	30,358	19,691	59,511	68,964	81,803	47,442	44,486	28,855
2000 [2, 3]........	50,732	59,099	69,235	39,982	37,727	25,716	66,259	77,186	90,424	52,218	49,273	33,586
2007............	61,355	72,589	86,435	47,329	44,358	30,296	66,554	78,739	93,759	51,339	48,116	32,863
2008............	61,521	72,743	86,621	48,502	43,571	30,129	64,264	75,987	90,484	50,665	45,514	31,473
2009 [4]..........	60,088	71,627	85,948	47,649	41,501	29,770	63,007	75,106	90,123	49,963	43,517	31,216
2010 [5]..........	60,236	72,241	87,397	48,733	43,206	29,155	62,136	74,520	90,154	50,270	44,569	30,075
2011............	60,974	73,790	89,017	50,414	43,069	30,259	60,974	73,790	89,017	50,414	43,069	30,259

[1] Data reflect full implementation of the 1990 Census-based sample design and metropolitan definitions, 7,000 household sample reduction, and revised race edits. [2] Implementation of Census 2000-based population controls. [3] Implementation of a 28,000 household sample expansion. [4] Median income is calculated using $2,500 income intervals. Beginning with 2009 income data, the Census Bureau expanded the upper income intervals used to calculate medians to $250,000 or more. Before 2009, the upper open-ended interval was $100,000. [5] Implementation of Census 2010-based population controls.

Source: U.S. Census Bureau, *Income, Poverty and Health Insurance Coverage in the United States: 2011*, Current Population Reports, P60-243, September 2012, and "Historical Tables—Table F-7," <http://www.census.gov/hhes/www/income/income.html>, accessed March 2013.

Table 730. Married-Couple Families—Number and Median Income by Work Experience of Husbands and Wives and Presence of Related Children: 2011

[58,963 represents 58,963,000. See headnote, Table 726. For definition of median, see Guide to Tabular Presentation]

Work experience of husband or wife	Number (1,000)					Median income (dollars)				
	All married-couple families	With no related children	One or more related children under 18 years old			All married-couple families	With no related children	One or more related children under 18 years old		
			Total	One child	Two children or more			Total	One child	Two children or more
All married-couple families........	**58,963**	**33,882**	**25,081**	**9,806**	**15,275**	**73,790**	**70,053**	**78,699**	**79,834**	**77,540**
Husband worked......................	44,279	21,331	22,948	8,765	14,183	86,027	90,082	82,229	83,863	81,457
Wife worked........................	31,241	15,262	15,979	6,565	9,414	95,234	97,493	92,267	92,032	92,435
Wife did not work....................	13,038	6,070	6,968	2,199	4,769	62,195	68,075	56,388	60,069	55,298
Husband year-round, full-time worker................................	35,531	16,179	19,351	7,350	12,001	92,141	97,170	88,323	89,769	87,400
Wife worked........................	25,369	11,925	13,445	5,498	7,946	101,206	104,236	97,965	97,693	98,134
Wife did not work....................	10,161	4,255	5,906	1,851	4,055	67,500	74,252	62,333	63,457	61,928
Husband did not work.................	14,684	12,551	2,134	1,042	1,092	40,358	40,978	36,309	39,440	32,379
Wife worked........................	4,731	3,456	1,275	592	683	55,636	59,083	46,275	50,719	42,316
Wife did not work....................	9,954	9,095	859	450	409	35,209	36,065	21,570	24,222	18,521

Source: U.S. Census Bureau, *Income, Poverty and Health Insurance Coverage in the United States: 2011*, Current Population Reports, P60-243, September 2012, and "Detailed Tables—Table FINC-04," <http://www.census.gov/hhes/www/income/data/index.html>, accessed February 2013.

Table 731. Median Income of People in Constant (2011) Dollars by Sex, Race, and Hispanic Origin: 1990 to 2011

[In dollars. People as of March of following year. People 15 years old and over. Constant dollars based on CPI-U-RS deflator. Based on the Current Population Survey, Annual Social and Economic Supplement (ASEC); see text, this section and Section 1 and Appendix III. For data collection changes over time, see <http://www.census.gov/hhes/www/income/data/historical/history.html>]

Race and Hispanic Origin	Male					Female				
	1990	2000 [1]	2005 [2]	2010 [3]	2011	1990	2000 [1]	2005 [2]	2010 [3]	2011
All races [4]...................	**33,852**	**37,017**	**36,031**	**33,221**	**32,986**	**16,799**	**20,979**	**21,401**	**21,430**	**21,102**
White [5]........................	35,315	38,916	37,073	35,458	35,344	17,211	21,000	21,508	21,555	21,379
Black [6]........................	21,466	27,875	26,098	24,031	23,475	13,893	20,741	20,312	20,266	19,755
Asian [7]........................	32,353	40,269	39,418	36,953	36,334	18,493	22,668	24,932	24,306	22,039
Hispanic [8].....................	22,470	25,465	25,448	23,127	23,731	12,565	15,996	17,323	16,806	16,829
White non-Hispanic..........	36,630	41,151	40,720	38,326	38,148	17,651	21,765	22,409	22,400	22,226

[1] Implementation of Census 2000-based population controls and sample expanded by 28,000 households. [2] Beginning with the 2003 Current Population Survey (CPS), the questionnaire allowed respondents to choose more than one race. For 2005 and later, data represent persons who selected this race group only and excludes persons reporting more than one race. The CPS in prior years allowed respondents to report only one race group. See also comments on race in the text for Section 1. [3] Median income calculated using $2,500 income intervals. Beginning 2009, Census Bureau expanded upper income intervals used to calculate medians to $250,000 or more. Before 2009, the upper open ended interval was $100,000. Beginning in 2010, data reflect implementation of Census 2010-based population controls. [4] Includes other races not shown separately. [5] Beginning with 2005, data represent White alone, which refers to people who reported White and did not report any other race category. [6] Beginning with 2005, data represent Black alone, which refers to people who reported Black and did not report any other race category. [7] Beginning with 2005, data represent Asian alone, which refers to people who reported Asian and did not report any other race category. [8] People of Hispanic origin may be any race.

Source: U.S. Census Bureau, *Income, Poverty and Health Insurance Coverage in the United States: 2011*, Current Population Reports, P60-243, September 2012, and "Historical Tables—Table P-2," <http://www.census.gov/hhes/www/income/data/historical/people/index.html>, accessed March 2013.

Table 732. Money Income of People—Selected Characteristics by Income Level: 2011

[People as of March of following year (119,946 represents 119,946,000). Covers people 15 years old and over. For definition of median, see Guide to Tabular Presentation. Median income is calculated using $2,500 income intervals. Beginning with 2009 income data, the Census Bureau expanded the upper income intervals used to calculate medians to $250,000 or more. Medians falling in the upper open-ended interval are plugged with "$250,000." Before 2009, the upper open-ended interval was $100,000 and a plug of "$100,000" was used. For composition of regions, see map, inside front cover. Based on the Current Population Survey, Annual Social and Economic Supplement (ASEC), see Appendix III]

Characteristic	All persons (1,000)	People with income Total (1,000)	Under $5,000	$5,000 to $9,999	$10,000 to $14,999	$15,000 to $24,999	$25,000 to $34,999	$35,000 to $49,999	$50,000 to $74,999	$75,000 and over	Median income (current dollars)
MALE											
Total	119,946	106,228	7,090	7,441	9,020	17,059	14,073	16,249	16,426	18,869	32,986
15 to 24 years old	21,826	13,086	3,798	2,490	1,801	2,531	1,286	767	284	130	10,518
25 to 34 years old	20,464	18,883	952	1,182	1,331	3,191	3,148	3,620	3,219	2,240	32,581
35 to 44 years old	19,677	18,612	589	754	1,045	2,338	2,366	3,304	3,722	4,493	43,967
45 to 54 years old	21,490	20,320	646	951	1,272	2,413	2,242	3,422	3,788	5,587	45,950
55 to 64 years old	18,157	17,408	744	1,034	1,274	2,215	2,084	2,638	3,235	4,185	41,550
65 years old and over	18,332	17,918	362	1,030	2,296	4,371	2,947	2,499	2,179	2,234	27,707
Region:											
Northeast	21,666	19,302	1,364	1,269	1,480	2,936	2,385	2,872	3,041	3,954	35,752
Midwest	25,567	23,056	1,527	1,625	1,914	3,589	3,047	3,783	3,858	3,713	34,034
South	44,168	38,968	2,483	2,734	3,505	6,408	5,395	6,027	5,911	6,506	32,116
West	28,545	24,902	1,716	1,813	2,121	4,126	3,246	3,567	3,616	4,697	32,211
Educational attainment of householder: [1]											
Total	98,119	93,141	3,292	4,951	7,219	14,528	12,787	15,483	16,142	18,739	37,653
Less than 9th grade	5,117	4,633	190	705	999	1,308	730	465	175	61	17,505
9th to 12th grade [2]	7,388	6,650	415	822	1,189	1,559	1,186	808	422	249	20,437
High school graduate [3]	30,216	28,295	1,044	1,745	2,622	5,809	4,944	5,388	4,344	2,399	30,616
Some college, no degree	16,072	15,301	655	705	1,008	2,461	2,381	2,966	2,912	2,215	36,552
Associate's degree	8,560	8,286	250	325	461	1,108	1,108	1,667	1,856	1,510	41,916
Bachelor's degree or more	30,766	29,976	739	650	940	2,282	2,438	4,189	6,433	12,305	62,282
Bachelor's degree	19,415	18,859	482	464	716	1,588	1,772	3,036	4,222	6,579	56,404
Master's degree	7,397	7,238	185	131	144	488	459	851	1,523	3,458	71,537
Professional degree	1,938	1,903	25	23	54	101	113	138	275	1,173	98,883
Doctoral degree	2,016	1,976	47	32	26	105	94	164	413	1,095	82,376
Tenure:											
Owner-occupied	83,066	74,568	4,718	4,117	5,405	10,425	9,068	11,623	12,956	16,257	39,064
Renter-occupied	35,394	30,390	2,267	3,187	3,483	6,346	4,784	4,459	3,335	2,529	24,805
Occupier paid no cash rent	1,485	1,269	105	137	132	287	220	168	134	84	23,712
FEMALE											
Total	127,751	108,332	12,472	14,270	14,043	20,083	14,249	14,130	11,263	7,822	21,102
15 to 24 years old	21,291	12,927	4,152	2,740	1,909	2,336	966	568	199	57	9,107
25 to 34 years old	20,755	17,635	1,971	1,698	1,662	3,201	3,054	3,020	2,030	1,000	25,723
35 to 44 years old	20,251	17,672	1,830	1,335	1,595	2,967	2,585	2,938	2,595	1,827	29,095
45 to 54 years old	22,465	19,954	1,847	1,802	1,748	3,384	2,876	3,197	2,841	2,258	28,460
55 to 64 years old	19,814	17,867	1,656	1,950	2,006	3,042	2,317	2,599	2,402	1,894	25,923
65 years old and over	23,174	22,276	1,016	4,744	5,123	5,152	2,451	1,810	1,195	785	15,362
Region:											
Northeast	23,448	20,326	2,355	2,610	2,577	3,530	2,559	2,552	2,318	1,824	21,871
Midwest	27,406	24,148	2,738	3,110	3,185	4,666	3,296	3,261	2,450	1,443	20,860
South	47,623	39,710	4,363	5,455	5,298	7,536	5,263	5,365	3,957	2,475	20,830
West	29,275	24,148	3,016	3,094	2,983	4,351	3,131	2,954	2,539	2,080	21,209
Educational attainment of householder: [1]											
Total	106,460	95,404	8,320	11,530	12,133	17,747	13,282	13,563	11,064	7,765	23,395
Less than 9th grade	5,167	3,839	439	1,209	991	812	258	80	35	14	11,113
9th to 12th grade [2]	7,604	6,235	703	1,676	1,423	1,529	558	220	94	32	12,193
High school graduate [3]	31,898	28,051	2,419	4,509	4,729	6,799	4,265	3,258	1,477	594	17,887
Some college, no degree	18,091	16,427	1,524	1,794	2,079	3,411	2,954	2,500	1,499	666	22,499
Associate's degree	11,176	10,353	813	855	1,045	1,988	1,667	1,850	1,484	652	27,180
Bachelor's degree or more	32,524	30,498	2,423	1,486	1,865	3,208	3,580	5,655	6,475	5,808	41,338
Bachelor's degree	21,146	19,629	1,740	1,078	1,303	2,354	2,703	3,756	3,796	2,899	36,812
Master's degree	9,062	8,650	541	336	476	729	727	1,632	2,195	2,012	48,738
Professional degree	1,155	1,098	87	48	39	68	65	126	232	433	61,206
Doctoral degree	1,162	1,121	56	24	46	56	84	140	252	462	63,913
Tenure:											
Owner-occupied	87,185	75,621	8,437	8,948	9,248	13,047	9,809	10,492	9,015	6,626	23,072
Renter-occupied	39,118	31,506	3,863	5,072	4,592	6,785	4,315	3,531	2,189	1,160	17,469
Occupier paid no cash rent	1,448	1,204	172	250	204	251	124	107	59	37	14,369

[1] Persons 25 years and over. [2] No diploma attained. [3] Includes high school equivalency.

Source: U.S. Census Bureau, *Income, Poverty and Health Insurance Coverage in the United States: 2011*, Current Population Reports, P60-243, September 2012, and "Detailed Tables—Table PINC-01," <http://www.census.gov/hhes/www/income/data/index.html>, accessed March 2013.

Table 733. Average Earnings of Year-Round, Full-Time Workers by Educational Attainment: 2011

[In dollars. For people 18 years old and over, as of March 2012. See headnote, Table 731]

Sex and age	All workers	Less than 9th grade	High school		College		
			9th to 12th grade (no diploma)	High school graduate [1]	Some college, no degree	Associate degree	Bachelor's degree or more
Male, total...............	**64,958**	**28,771**	**35,524**	**46,038**	**53,628**	**57,479**	**95,038**
18 to 24 years old..........	28,657	20,560	23,360	26,851	26,647	28,753	42,935
25 to 34 years old..........	49,815	24,506	29,997	37,906	45,507	47,340	67,500
35 to 44 years old..........	67,991	28,092	35,796	47,607	56,302	62,159	96,813
45 to 54 years old..........	74,787	31,793	40,075	52,588	62,556	65,129	110,543
55 to 64 years old..........	77,102	35,265	44,123	51,288	63,845	63,717	109,308
65 years old and over......	73,693	29,381	37,513	62,400	54,293	51,011	99,861
Female, total.............	**46,882**	**21,150**	**22,662**	**32,249**	**36,723**	**42,514**	**65,557**
18 to 24 years old..........	24,192	(B)	16,217	20,298	21,760	25,032	35,291
25 to 34 years old..........	41,768	20,434	22,267	28,311	32,269	39,133	52,609
35 to 44 years old..........	50,307	19,731	23,881	32,701	38,091	43,881	70,104
45 to 54 years old..........	50,178	22,961	23,115	34,735	42,415	44,501	72,343
55 to 64 years old..........	52,032	20,948	23,048	35,815	40,697	47,603	75,118
65 years old and over......	45,137	(B)	24,239	32,779	38,925	42,104	67,828

B Base figure too small to meet statistical standards for reliability of derived figure. [1] Includes equivalency.

Source: U.S. Census Bureau, Current Population Reports, *Income, Poverty and Health Insurance Coverage in the United States: 2011*, September 2012; and "Detailed Tables—Table PINC-04," <http://www.census.gov/hhes/www/income/index.html>, accessed March 2013.

Table 734. Per Capita Money Income in Current and Constant (2011) Dollars by Race and Hispanic Origin: 1990 to 2011

[In dollars. Constant dollars based on CPI-U-RS deflator. People as of March of following year. Based on the Current Population Survey, Annual Social and Economic Supplement (ASEC); see text, this section, Section 1, and Appendix III. For data collection changes over time, see <http://www.census.gov/hhes/www/income/data/historical/history.html>]

Year	Current dollars					Constant (2011) dollars				
	All races [1]	White [2]	Black [2]	Asian and Pacific Islander [2]	His-panic [3]	All races [1]	White [2]	Black [2]	Asian and Pacific Islander [2]	His-panic [3]
1990...............	14,387	15,265	9,017	(NA)	8,424	24,000	25,465	15,042	(NA)	14,053
1995 [4].............	17,227	18,304	10,982	16,567	9,300	25,244	26,823	16,093	24,277	13,628
2000 [5, 6]...........	22,346	23,582	14,796	23,350	12,651	29,185	30,799	19,324	30,496	16,523
2005 [7, 8]...........	25,036	26,496	16,874	27,331	14,483	28,843	30,525	19,440	31,487	16,686
2008.............	26,964	20,502	18,406	30,292	15,674	28,166	29,773	19,227	31,643	16,373
2009 [9].............	26,530	28,034	18,135	30,653	15,063	27,819	29,396	19,016	32,142	15,795
2010 [10]............	26,558	28,356	18,019	28,673	15,044	27,396	29,250	18,587	29,577	15,519
2011.............	27,554	29,401	18,988	29,235	15,479	27,554	29,401	18,988	29,235	15,479

NA Not available. [1] Includes other races, not shown separately. [2] Beginning with 2002, data represents White alone, Black alone, or Asian alone which refers to people who reported either White, Black, or Asian and did not report any other race category. [3] People of Hispanic origin may be any race. [4] Data reflect full implementation of the 1990 Census-based sample design and metropolitan definitions, 7,000 household sample reduction, and revised race edits. [5] Implementation of Census 2000-based population controls. [6] Implementation of a 28,000 household sample expansion. [7] See footnote 4, Table 726. See also comments on race, text, Section 1. [8] Data have been revised to reflect a correction to the weights in the 2005 ASEC. [9] Median income is calculated using $2,500 income intervals. Beginning with 2009 income data, the Census Bureau expanded the upper income intervals used to calculate medians to $250,000 or more. Before 2009, the upper open-ended interval was $100,000. [10] Implementation of Census 2010-based population controls.

Source: U.S. Census Bureau, *Income, Poverty and Health Insurance Coverage in the United States: 2011*, Current Population Reports, P60-243, September 2012, and "Historical Tables—Table P-1," <http://www.census.gov/hhes/www/income/data/historical/index.html>, accessed March 2013.

Table 735. Money Income of People—Number by Income Level and by Sex, Race, and Hispanic Origin: 2011

[In thousands (119,946 represents 119,946,000). People age 15 years and over as of March of the following year. Based on Current Population Survey, Annual Social and Economic Supplement (ASEC); see text, this section, Section 1, and Appendix III]

Income interval	Male					Female				
	All races [1]	White alone [4]	Black alone [4]	Asian alone [4]	His-panic [2]	All races [1]	White alone [4]	Black alone [4]	Asian alone [4]	His-panic [2]
All households...............	**119,946**	**96,422**	**13,842**	**6,107**	**18,867**	**127,751**	**100,331**	**16,662**	**6,931**	**18,633**
Under $10,000 [3]................	28,249	20,042	5,201	1,706	5,846	46,161	35,128	6,345	2,945	9,322
$10,000 to $19,999.............	17,557	13,961	2,308	720	3,747	24,908	19,736	3,456	1,010	3,556
$20,000 to $29,999.............	15,577	12,655	1,767	675	3,081	16,559	13,125	2,193	799	2,207
$30,000 to $39,999.............	13,029	10,775	1,334	565	2,156	12,693	10,062	1,725	573	1,450
$40,000 to $49,999.............	10,239	8,616	994	377	1,378	8,345	6,782	952	401	772
$50,000 to $59,999.............	7,969	6,813	641	375	840	5,821	4,681	729	261	463
$60,000 to $74,999.............	8,456	7,218	650	434	747	5,442	4,499	548	307	432
$75,000 to $84,999.............	4,184	3,554	288	261	310	2,238	1,756	253	177	148
$85,000 to $99,999.............	3,562	3,040	203	243	211	1,777	1,471	153	123	97
$100,000 to $149,999...........	6,447	5,580	301	470	369	2,560	2,049	243	225	127
$150,000 to $199,999...........	2,410	2,155	82	135	88	686	574	38	60	31
$200,000 to $249,999...........	845	743	26	58	27	236	194	12	22	10
$250,000 and above.............	1,422	1,271	47	88	67	324	274	15	30	19

[1] Includes races not shown separately. [2] Persons of Hispanic origin may be of any race. [3] Includes persons without income. [4] Refers to people who reported specified race and did not report any other race category

Source: U.S. Census Bureau, *Income, Poverty and Health Insurance Coverage in the United States: 2011*, Current Population Reports, P60-243, September 2012, and "Detailed Tables—Table PINC-11," <http://www.census.gov/hhes/www/income/data/index.html>, accessed March 2013.

Table 736. Household, Family, and Per Capita Income, and Individuals and Families Below Poverty Level, by City: 2011

[The American Community Survey universe includes the household population and the population living in institutions, college dormitories, and other group quarters. Based on a sample and subject to sampling variability; see text, Section 1 and Appendix III. For definition of median, see Guide to Tabular Presentation. CDP is the abbreviation for Census designated place]

City	Median household income (dol.)	Median family income (dol.)	Per capita income (dol.)	Number below poverty level [1]		Percent below poverty level [1]	
				Individuals	Families	Individuals	Families
Albuquerque, NM	43,606	54,825	25,580	106,397	20,411	19.4	15.4
Anaheim, CA	56,858	60,161	22,049	54,212	9,482	16.1	12.8
Anchorage municipality, AK	72,813	85,483	34,768	21,980	3,301	7.6	4.7
Arlington, TX	50,655	57,394	22,907	73,786	14,286	20.0	16.1
Atlanta, GA	43,903	53,094	33,117	106,312	15,172	26.2	20.3
Aurora, CO	49,593	55,352	23,139	52,893	9,487	16.0	12.2
Austin, TX	49,987	63,672	30,324	162,490	25,399	20.3	14.6
Bakersfield, CA	51,667	59,725	22,115	74,988	14,817	21.4	18.2
Baltimore, MD	38,721	47,247	22,754	149,605	23,768	25.1	19.5
Boston, MA	49,081	55,857	31,934	136,214	21,006	23.2	17.8
Buffalo, NY	29,158	34,935	19,108	78,210	16,037	30.9	26.8
Charlotte, NC	50,177	59,786	30,526	136,669	26,550	18.5	14.6
Chicago, IL	43,628	49,442	26,300	629,464	109,157	23.7	19.7
Cincinnati, OH	31,301	40,516	23,792	84,558	15,039	29.5	24.9
Cleveland, OH	25,371	33,071	16,779	131,430	24,529	34.3	29.3
Colorado Springs, CO	50,945	64,217	28,047	64,395	11,867	15.4	11.2
Columbus, OH	40,463	50,464	22,447	180,449	30,031	23.2	18.0
Corpus Christi, TX	44,893	51,228	23,340	57,461	11,361	19.1	15.1
Dallas, TX	40,585	43,412	25,757	305,701	55,648	25.3	21.5
Denver, CO	47,371	63,290	31,869	111,979	16,833	18.4	13.4
Detroit, MI	25,193	30,524	13,965	284,421	51,492	40.9	35.5
El Paso, TX	40,702	45,067	19,519	144,596	30,071	22.0	19.1
Fort Wayne, IN	42,277	52,451	22,166	52,742	10,648	20.8	17.1
Fort Worth, TX	47,399	53,900	22,868	162,776	30,990	21.8	17.5
Fresno, CA	40,533	42,311	18,252	142,014	25,920	28.8	23.8
Honolulu, HI [2]	53,614	67,301	27,927	41,187	6,631	12.5	9.3
Houston, TX	42,877	47,463	26,179	504,248	96,290	23.8	20.3
Indianapolis, IN [3]	39,015	48,009	22,408	172,840	32,100	21.4	16.9
Jacksonville, FL	44,802	56,290	24,510	148,599	28,270	18.3	14.4
Kansas City, MO	43,810	55,887	26,091	89,106	16,596	19.5	15.2
Las Vegas, NV	46,995	54,664	24,196	113,079	19,609	19.4	14.5
Lexington-Fayette, KY	47,207	67,119	28,778	51,471	7,857	17.8	11.1
Long Beach, CA	51,214	56,371	25,945	97,438	16,623	21.2	17.1
Los Angeles, CA	46,148	50,588	26,148	846,162	144,269	22.6	18.4
Memphis, TN	34,960	40,781	20,463	173,418	31,976	27.2	22.6
Mesa, AZ	44,527	56,218	22,653	74,709	14,037	16.9	13.2
Miami, FL	28,536	32,217	19,747	124,570	22,599	31.0	26.9
Milwaukee, WI	33,122	37,395	18,201	171,550	32,271	29.4	25.4
Minneapolis, MN	46,682	65,159	30,256	88,325	11,960	23.7	16.4
Nashville-Davidson, TN [3]	42,639	53,495	26,136	115,563	19,663	19.7	14.9
New Orleans, LA	35,041	43,217	25,053	100,709	18,121	28.9	23.4
New York, NY	49,461	54,330	30,200	1,695,088	325,904	20.9	18.0
Newark, NJ	31,731	35,270	15,654	83,669	15,902	31.6	28.4
Oakland, CA	50,500	57,474	31,536	81,952	14,864	21.0	17.2
Oklahoma City, OK	42,995	54,215	23,506	114,838	21,386	19.8	15.2
Omaha, NE	45,536	59,584	26,735	69,226	11,744	17.1	12.5
Philadelphia, PA	34,207	42,668	20,642	423,305	69,225	28.4	22.6
Phoenix, AZ	43,960	51,139	22,389	332,662	60,760	22.9	18.4
Pittsburgh, PA	35,947	49,632	24,527	67,867	11,213	23.8	17.3
Plano, TX	80,184	96,584	38,530	19,040	3,932	7.0	5.3
Portland, OR	47,033	63,405	29,405	115,621	17,348	19.9	14.1
Raleigh, NC	52,040	61,619	28,357	65,913	11,060	16.6	11.9
Riverside, CA	51,331	57,230	20,561	61,446	9,620	20.5	15.3
Sacramento, CA	47,908	53,170	23,585	106,780	18,030	23.0	18.5
San Antonio, TX	42,613	50,283	21,356	266,716	49,536	19.9	15.8
San Diego, CA	60,797	73,106	30,482	206,651	30,652	16.0	11.2
San Francisco, CA	69,894	83,540	44,905	110,210	13,302	13.8	8.5
San Jose, CA	76,593	85,050	32,301	116,949	18,419	12.2	8.3
Santa Ana, CA	51,264	51,151	15,341	69,649	10,858	21.5	18.2
Seattle, WA	61,037	91,299	39,886	89,063	10,013	14.8	7.8
St. Louis, MO	32,570	43,299	21,180	83,142	14,331	27.0	22.7
St. Paul, MN	42,069	57,396	24,641	67,263	10,709	23.9	17.6
St. Petersburg, FL	40,881	55,251	25,647	42,784	6,864	17.8	12.7
Stockton, CA	44,310	47,560	18,421	75,180	13,949	25.8	21.6
Tampa, FL	40,073	47,391	27,403	74,942	13,317	22.4	17.4
Toledo, OH	31,090	38,073	17,245	84,154	16,414	30.1	24.1
Tucson, AZ	35,362	43,973	19,682	134,548	22,803	26.6	20.2
Tulsa, OK	40,123	50,744	26,635	77,322	14,545	19.9	15.4
Virginia Beach, VA	64,614	74,341	30,609	37,168	8,006	8.6	7.2
Washington, DC	63,124	75,603	44,578	109,363	17,608	18.7	15.4
Wichita, KS	44,184	57,877	23,231	67,923	12,150	17.9	13.1

[1] See headnote, Table 737. [2] Data shown for census designated place (CDP). [3] Represents the portion of a consolidated city that is not within one or more separately incorporated places.

Source: U.S. Census Bureau, 2011 American Community Survey, 2011 ACS 1-year estimates: DP03, B01003, B17001, and B17019, <http://factfinder2.census.gov>, accessed March 2013. See also <http://www.census.gov/acs/www/>.

Table 737. Individuals and Families Below Poverty Level—Number and Rate by State: 2001 and 2011

[In thousands (33,420 represents 33,420,000), except as indicated. Represents number and percent below poverty in the past 12 months. Prior to 2006, the American Community Survey universe was limited to the household population and excluded the population living in institutions, college dormitories, and other group quarters. Poverty status was determined for all people except institutionalized people, people in military group quarters, people in college dormitories, and unrelated individuals under 15 years old. These groups were excluded from the numerator and denominator when calculating poverty rates. Based on a sample and subject to sampling variability; see Appendix III]

State	Number below poverty (1,000)				Percent below poverty			
	Individuals		Families		Individuals		Families	
	2001	2011	2001	2011	2001	2011	2001	2011
United States	**33,420**	**48,452**	**6,631**	**8,939**	**12.1**	**15.9**	**9.2**	**11.7**
Alabama	716	892	157	186	16.5	19.0	13.0	14.9
Alaska	44	74	8	12	7.2	10.5	5.4	6.9
Arizona	710	1,204	140	218	13.7	19.0	10.7	14.1
Arkansas	402	556	85	113	15.4	19.5	11.8	14.9
California	4,298	6,119	763	1,056	12.8	16.6	9.7	12.4
Colorado	411	674	77	115	9.6	13.5	6.8	9.1
Connecticut	242	378	47	71	7.3	10.9	5.3	7.9
Delaware	75	105	14	18	9.8	11.9	7.1	8.0
District of Columbia	97	109	17	18	18.1	18.7	16.2	15.4
Florida	1,995	3,173	391	564	12.5	17.0	9.3	12.4
Georgia	947	1,828	195	349	11.7	19.1	9.2	14.7
Hawaii	124	161	23	27	10.4	12.0	7.9	8.6
Idaho	154	255	33	46	12.0	16.5	9.4	11.6
Illinois	1,351	1,880	244	340	11.2	15.0	8.0	11.0
Indiana	579	1,011	116	193	9.8	16.0	7.3	11.7
Iowa	274	379	54	64	9.7	12.8	7.0	8.1
Kansas	295	383	55	67	11.3	13.8	7.9	9.2
Kentucky	607	811	135	164	15.4	19.1	12.3	14.7
Louisiana	820	908	173	180	19.1	20.4	15.2	16.1
Maine	132	182	28	32	10.6	14.1	7.9	9.3
Maryland	424	572	81	100	8.1	10.1	6.0	7.1
Massachusetts	536	739	102	132	8.7	11.6	6.5	8.3
Michigan	1,024	1,693	206	310	10.6	17.5	7.9	12.5
Minnesota	376	622	76	103	7.8	11.9	5.7	7.6
Mississippi	513	651	109	129	18.6	22.6	14.9	17.4
Missouri	637	920	128	176	11.7	15.8	8.5	11.5
Montana	128	144	28	25	14.6	14.8	11.6	9.7
Nebraska	170	235	31	43	10.3	13.1	7.1	9.1
Nevada	200	427	37	76	9.7	15.9	7.2	11.9
New Hampshire	73	113	13	20	6.0	8.8	4.1	5.6
New Jersey	653	897	138	172	7.9	10.4	6.4	7.8
New Mexico	315	440	66	83	17.7	21.5	14.3	16.6
New York	2,452	3,027	487	568	13.4	16.0	10.5	12.3
North Carolina	1,110	1,681	231	325	14.1	17.9	10.5	13.2
North Dakota	74	81	13	14	12.1	12.2	8.1	7.9
Ohio	1,211	1,846	251	350	11.0	16.4	8.5	12.0
Oklahoma	518	633	109	122	15.5	17.2	12.2	12.8
Oregon	452	662	88	114	13.4	17.5	9.7	11.9
Pennsylvania	1,270	1,696	254	307	10.7	13.8	8.0	9.6
Rhode Island	122	149	23	27	12.0	14.7	9.0	10.6
South Carolina	524	857	104	172	13.4	18.9	9.9	14.3
South Dakota	84	111	16	20	11.6	13.9	8.3	9.6
Tennessee	797	1,142	174	223	14.3	18.3	11.2	13.7
Texas	3,093	4,629	636	886	15.0	18.5	12.1	14.4
Utah	190	375	34	69	8.6	13.5	6.2	10.4
Vermont	61	69	12	11	10.4	11.5	7.5	6.9
Virginia	647	906	134	165	9.3	11.5	7.2	8.2
Washington	627	929	120	161	10.8	13.9	8.0	9.4
West Virginia	300	335	70	65	17.2	18.6	14.3	13.7
Wisconsin	510	726	93	129	9.8	13.1	6.8	8.8
Wyoming	54	63	11	11	11.4	11.3	8.3	7.9

Source: U.S. Census Bureau, 2011 American Community Survey; B17001, "Poverty Status in the Past 12 Months by Sex and Age" and B17010, "Poverty Status in the Past 12 Months of Families by Family Type by Presence of Related Children under 18 Years by Age of Related Children," <http://factfinder2.census.gov>, accessed March 2013. See also <http://www.census.gov/acs/www/>.

Table 738. Poverty Thresholds by Size of Family Unit: 1980 to 2011

[In dollars per year. For information on the official poverty thresholds, see text, this section. For more on poverty, see <http://www.census.gov/hhes/www/poverty/about/overview/measure.html>]

Size of family unit	1980	1990	1995	2000 [1]	2005	2008	2009	2010 [3]	2011
One person (unrelated individual) [2]	4,190	6,652	7,763	8,791	9,973	10,991	10,956	11,137	11,484
Under 65 years old	4,290	6,800	7,929	8,959	10,160	11,201	11,161	11,344	11,702
65 years old and over	3,949	6,268	7,309	8,259	9,367	10,326	10,289	10,458	10,788
Two persons	5,363	8,509	9,933	11,235	12,755	14,051	13,991	14,216	14,657
Householder under 65 years old	5,537	8,794	10,259	11,589	13,145	14,417	14,366	14,676	15,139
Householder 65 years old and over	4,983	7,905	9,219	10,418	11,815	13,014	12,968	13,194	13,609
Three persons	6,565	10,419	12,158	13,740	15,577	17,163	17,098	17,373	17,916
Four persons	8,414	13,359	15,569	17,604	19,971	22,025	21,954	22,315	23,021
Five persons	9,966	15,792	18,408	20,815	23,613	26,049	25,991	26,442	27,251
Six persons	11,269	17,839	20,804	23,533	26,683	29,456	29,405	29,904	30,847
Seven persons	12,761	20,241	23,552	26,750	30,249	33,529	33,372	34,019	35,085
Eight persons	14,199	22,582	26,237	29,701	33,610	37,220	37,252	37,953	39,064
Nine or more persons	16,896	26,848	31,280	35,150	40,288	44,346	44,366	45,224	46,572

[1] Implementation of Census 2000-based population controls and sample expanded by 28,000 households. [2] A person living alone or with non-relatives. [3] Implementation of Census 2010-based population controls.

Source: U.S. Census Bureau, *Income, Poverty, and Health Insurance Coverage in the United States: 2011*, Current Population Reports, P60-243, September 2012, and "Historical Tables—Table 1," <http://www.census.gov/hhes/www/poverty/data/index.html>, accessed March 2013.

Table 739. People Below Poverty Level by Race and Hispanic Origin, and Below 125 Percent of Poverty Level: 1980 to 2011

[29,272 represents 29,272,000. People as of March of the following year. Based on Current Population Survey, Annual Social and Economic Supplement (ASEC); see text, this section, Section 1, and Appendix III. For data collection changes over time, see <http://www.census.gov/hhes/www/income/data/historical/history.html>]

Year	Number of persons below poverty (1,000)					Percent of persons below poverty					Below 125 percent of poverty level [1]	
	All races [2]	White [3]	Black [4]	Asian and Pacific Islander [5]	His-panic [6]	All races [2]	White [3]	Black [4]	Asian and Pacific Islander [5]	His-panic [6]	Number (1,000)	Percent of total pop-ulation
1980	29,272	19,699	8,579	(NA)	3,491	13.0	10.2	32.5	(NA)	25.7	40,658	18.1
1985	33,064	22,860	8,926	(NA)	5,236	14.0	11.4	31.3	(NA)	29.0	44,166	18.7
1990	33,585	22,326	9,837	858	6,006	13.5	10.7	31.9	12.2	28.1	44,837	18.0
1991	35,708	23,747	10,242	996	6,339	14.2	11.3	32.7	13.8	28.7	47,527	18.9
1992 [7]	38,014	25,259	10,827	985	7,592	14.8	11.9	33.4	12.7	29.6	50,592	19.7
1993 [8]	39,265	26,226	10,877	1,134	8,126	15.1	12.2	33.1	15.3	30.6	51,801	20.0
1994	38,059	25,379	10,196	974	8,416	14.5	11.7	30.6	14.6	30.7	50,401	19.3
1995	36,425	24,423	9,872	1,411	8,574	13.8	11.2	29.3	14.6	30.3	48,761	18.5
1996	36,529	24,650	9,694	1,454	8,697	13.7	11.2	28.4	14.5	29.4	49,310	18.5
1997	35,574	24,396	9,116	1,468	8,308	13.3	11.0	26.5	14.0	27.1	47,853	17.8
1998	34,476	23,454	9,091	1,360	8,070	12.7	10.5	26.1	12.5	25.6	46,036	17.0
1999 [9]	32,791	22,169	8,441	1,285	7,876	11.9	9.8	23.6	10.7	22.7	45,030	16.3
2000 [10]	31,581	21,645	7,982	1,258	7,747	11.3	9.5	22.5	9.9	21.5	43,612	15.6
2001	32,907	22,739	8,136	1,275	7,997	11.7	9.9	22.7	10.2	21.4	45,320	16.1
2002 [11]	34,570	23,466	8,602	1,161	8,555	12.1	10.2	24.1	10.1	21.8	47,084	16.5
2003	35,861	24,272	8,781	1,401	9,051	12.5	10.5	24.4	11.8	22.5	48,687	16.9
2004 [12]	37,040	25,327	9,014	1,201	9,122	12.7	10.8	24.7	9.8	21.9	49,693	17.1
2005	36,950	24,872	9,168	1,402	9,368	12.6	10.6	24.9	11.1	21.8	49,327	16.8
2006	36,460	24,416	9,048	1,353	9,243	12.3	10.3	24.3	10.3	20.6	49,688	16.8
2007	37,276	25,120	9,237	1,349	9,890	12.5	10.5	24.5	10.2	21.5	50,876	17.0
2008	39,829	26,990	9,379	1,576	10,987	13.2	11.2	24.7	11.8	23.2	53,805	17.9
2009	43,569	29,830	9,944	1,746	12,350	14.3	12.3	25.8	12.5	25.3	56,840	18.7
2010 [13]	46,343	31,083	10,746	1,899	13,522	15.1	13.0	27.4	12.2	26.5	60,669	19.8
2011	46,247	30,849	10,929	1,973	13,244	15.0	12.8	27.6	12.3	25.3	60,949	19.8

NA Not available. [1] Includes those in poverty, plus those who have income above poverty but less than 1.25 times their poverty threshold. [2] Includes other races, not shown separately. [3] Beginning 2002, data represent White alone, which refers to people who reported White and did not report any other race category. [4] Beginning 2002, data represent Black alone, which refers to people who reported Black and did not report any other race category. [5] Beginning 2002, data represent Asian alone, which refers to people who reported Asian and did not report any other race category. [6] People of Hispanic origin may be any race. [7] Implementation of 1990 Census population controls. [8] The March 1994 income supplement was revised to allow for the coding of different income amounts on selected questionnaire items. Limits either increased or decreased in the following categories: earnings increased to $999,999; Social Security increased to $49,999; Supplemental Security Income and public assistance increased to $24,999; veterans' benefits increased to $99,999; child support and alimony decreased to $49,999. [9] Implementation of Census-2000-based population controls. [10] Implementation of sample expansion by 28,000 households. [11] Beginning with the 2003 Current Population Survey (CPS), the questionnaire allowed respondents to choose more than one race. For 2002 and later, data represent persons who selected this race group only and exclude persons reporting more than one race. The CPS in prior years allowed respondents to report only one race group. See also comments on race in the text for Section 1. [12] Data have been revised to reflect a correction to the weights in the 2005 ASEC. [13] Implementation of Census 2010-based population controls.

Source: U.S. Census Bureau, *Income, Poverty, and Health Insurance Coverage in the United States: 2011*, Current Population Reports, P60-243, September 2012, and "Historical Tables—Tables 2 and 6," <http://www.census.gov/hhes/www/poverty/data/index.html>, accessed March 2013.

Table 740. Children Below Poverty Level by Race and Hispanic Origin: 1980 to 2011

[11,114 represents 11,114,000. Persons as of March of the following year. Covers only related children in families under 18 years old. Based on Current Population Survey, Annual Social and Economic Supplement (ASEC); see text, this section, Section 1, and Appendix III. For data collection changes over time, see <http://www.census.gov/hhes/www/income/data/historical/history.html>]

Year	Number of children below poverty level (1,000)					Percent of children below poverty level				
	All races [1]	White [2]	Black [3]	Asian and Pacific Islander [4]	His-panic [5]	All races [1]	White [2]	Black [3]	Asian and Pacific Islander [4]	His-panic [5]
1980............	11,114	6,817	3,906	(NA)	1,718	17.9	13.4	42.1	(NA)	33.0
1985............	12,483	7,838	4,057	(NA)	2,512	20.1	15.6	43.1	(NA)	39.6
1990............	12,715	7,696	4,412	356	2,750	19.9	15.1	44.2	17.0	37.7
1993 [6,7]........	14,961	9,123	5,030	358	3,666	22.0	17.0	45.9	17.6	39.9
1994............	14,610	8,826	4,787	308	3,956	21.2	16.3	43.3	17.9	41.1
1995............	13,999	8,474	4,644	532	3,938	20.2	15.5	41.5	18.6	39.3
1996............	13,764	8,488	4,411	553	4,090	19.8	15.5	39.5	19.1	39.9
1997............	13,422	8,441	4,116	608	3,865	19.2	15.4	36.8	19.9	36.4
1998............	12,845	7,935	4,073	542	3,670	18.3	14.4	36.4	17.5	33.6
1999 [8]........	11,678	7,194	3,698	367	3,561	16.6	13.1	32.8	11.5	29.9
2000 [9]........	11,005	6,834	3,495	407	3,342	15.6	12.4	30.9	12.5	27.6
2001............	11,175	7,086	3,423	353	3,433	15.8	12.8	30.0	11.1	27.4
2002 [10]......	11,646	7,203	3,570	302	3,653	16.3	13.1	32.1	11.4	28.2
2003............	12,340	7,624	3,750	331	3,982	17.2	13.9	33.6	12.1	29.5
2004 [11]......	12,473	7,876	3,702	265	3,985	17.3	14.3	33.4	9.4	28.6
2005............	12,335	7,652	3,743	312	3,977	17.1	13.9	34.2	11.0	27.7
2006............	12,299	7,522	3,690	351	3,959	16.9	13.6	33.0	12.0	26.6
2007............	12,802	8,002	3,838	345	4,348	17.6	14.4	34.3	11.8	28.3
2008............	13,507	8,441	3,781	430	4,888	18.5	15.3	34.4	14.2	30.3
2009............	14,774	9,440	3,919	444	5,419	20.1	17.0	35.3	13.6	32.5
2010 [12]......	15,598	9,590	4,271	477	5,815	21.5	17.9	39.0	14.0	34.3
2011............	15,539	9,643	4,247	466	5,820	21.4	18.1	38.6	13.0	33.7

NA Not available. [1] Includes other races, not shown separately. [2] Beginning 2002, data represent White alone, which refers to people who reported White and did not report any other race category. [3] Beginning 2002, data represent Black alone, which refers to people who reported Black and did not report any other race category. [4] Beginning 2002, data represent Asian alone, which refers to people who reported Asian and did not report any other race category. [5] People of Hispanic origin may be of any race. [6] Implementation of 1990 Census population controls began in 1992. [7] The March 1994 income supplement was revised to allow for the coding of different income amounts on selected questionnaire items. Limits either increased or decreased in the following categories: earnings increased to $999,999; Social Security increased to $49,999; Supplemental Security Income and public assistance increased to $24,999; veterans' benefits increased to $99,999; child support and alimony decreased to $49,999. [8] Implementation of Census 2000-based population controls. [9] Implementation of sample expansion to 28,000 households. [10] Beginning with the 2003 Current Population Survey (CPS), the questionnaire allowed respondents to choose more than one race. For 2002 and later, data represent persons who selected this race group only and excludes persons reporting more than one race. The CPS in prior years allowed respondents to report only one race group. See also comments on race in the text for Section 1. [11] Data have been revised to reflect a correction to the weights in the 2005 ASEC. [12] Implementation of Census 2010-based population controls.

Source: U.S. Census Bureau, *Income, Poverty, and Health Insurance Coverage in the United States: 2011,* Current Population Reports, P60-243, September 2012, and "Historical Tables—Table 3," <http://www.census.gov/hhes/www/poverty/data/index.html>, accessed March 2013.

Table 741. People Below Poverty Level by Selected Characteristics: 2011

[46,247 represents 46,247,000. People as of March of the following year. Based on Current Population Survey (CPS); see text, this section, Sections 1 and 13, and Appendix III. The CPS currently allows respondents to choose more than one race. For 2011, data represent persons who selected each race group only and exclude persons reporting more than one race. Prior to 2003, the CPS allowed respondents to select only one race group. See also comments on race in the text for Section 1. For composition of regions, see map, inside front cover]

Sex, age, region, nativity	Number below poverty level (1,000)					Percent below poverty level				
	All races [1]	White alone	Black alone	Asian alone	His-panic [2]	All races [1]	White alone	Black alone	Asian alone	His-panic [2]
Total..................	**46,247**	**30,849**	**10,929**	**1,973**	**13,244**	**15.0**	**12.8**	**27.6**	**12.3**	**25.3**
Male......................	20,501	13,702	4,706	923	6,078	13.6	11.5	25.5	12.1	23.0
Female...................	25,746	17,147	6,223	1,050	7,166	16.3	14.0	29.4	12.4	27.7
Under 18 years old............	16,134	10,103	4,320	494	6,008	21.9	18.6	38.8	13.5	34.1
18 to 24 years old............	6,209	4,069	1,422	371	1,507	20.6	18.0	31.1	23.5	24.2
25 to 34 years old............	6,537	4,477	1,451	317	1,960	15.9	14.2	26.6	11.8	23.0
35 to 44 years old............	4,873	3,386	1,011	251	1,580	12.2	11.0	19.7	9.4	21.0
45 to 54 years old............	4,795	3,185	1,209	213	941	10.9	9.1	22.1	9.5	16.2
55 to 59 years old............	2,181	1,457	564	63	358	10.7	8.7	23.9	6.7	17.6
60 to 64 years old............	1,898	1,433	322	82	320	10.8	9.8	17.7	10.6	21.1
65 years old and over.........	3,620	2,739	630	182	569	8.7	7.7	17.3	11.7	18.7
65 to 74 years old.........	1,739	1,284	322	91	340	7.4	6.5	14.5	9.7	18.4
75 years old and over........	1,882	1,455	308	91	230	10.4	9.2	21.7	14.9	19.3
Northeast......................	7,208	4,648	1,807	523	1,938	13.1	10.7	25.9	15.2	26.1
Midwest.......................	9,221	6,213	2,206	223	1,257	14.0	11.2	32.3	11.8	27.3
South.........................	18,380	11,339	5,922	369	4,593	16.0	13.3	26.7	9.9	24.7
West..........................	11,437	8,648	994	858	5,456	15.8	15.1	27.7	12.2	25.2
Native.........................	38,661	25,637	10,003	715	8,680	14.4	11.9	28.0	11.6	25.8
Foreign born...................	7,586	5,212	926	1,258	4,564	19.0	20.8	23.5	12.7	24.4
Naturalized citizen..........	2,233	1,385	370	439	940	12.5	13.5	19.8	8.1	15.6
Not a citizen.................	5,353	3,827	556	818	3,625	24.3	25.8	26.9	18.2	28.7

[1] Includes other races, not shown separately. [2] Persons of Hispanic origin may be of any race.

Source: U.S. Census Bureau, *Income, Poverty, and Health Insurance Coverage in the United States: 2011,* Current Population Reports, P60-243, September 2012, and "Detailed Tables—Tables POV01, POV29, and POV41," <http://www.census.gov/hhes/www/poverty/index.html>, accessed March 2013.

Table 742. Work Experience of People During Year by Poverty Status, by Sex and Age: 2011

[101,700 represents 101,700,000. Covers only persons 16 years old and over. Based on Current Population Survey, Annual Social and Economic Supplement (ASEC); see text, this section, Section 1, and Appendix III]

Sex and age	Worked full-time year-round			Did not work full-time year-round			Did not work		
		Below poverty level			Below poverty level			Below poverty level	
	Number (1,000)	Number (1,000)	Percent	Number (1,000)	Number (1,000)	Percent	Number (1,000)	Number (1,000)	Percent
BOTH SEXES									
Total...................	101,700	2,770	2.7	52,630	7,818	14.9	89,208	21,042	23.6
16 to 17 years old.......	110	7	6.7	1,388	89	6.4	7,321	1,420	19.4
18 to 64 years old.......	97,443	2,732	2.8	46,720	7,614	16.3	49,049	16,147	32.9
18 to 24 years old......	6,399	393	6.1	12,576	2,221	17.7	11,165	3,595	32.2
25 to 34 years old......	22,616	840	3.7	10,243	2,232	21.8	8,360	3,465	41.4
35 to 54 years old......	50,578	1,280	2.5	16,600	2,471	14.9	16,704	5,917	35.4
55 to 64 years old......	17,850	219	1.2	7,301	690	9.5	12,820	3,170	24.7
65 years old and over....	4,146	31	0.7	4,522	115	2.5	32,838	3,474	10.6
MALE									
Total...................	58,004	1,458	2.5	23,268	3,295	14.2	36,550	8,362	22.9
16 to 17 years old.......	59	7	(B)	670	41	6.1	3,813	699	18.3
18 to 64 years old.......	55,383	1,442	2.6	20,244	3,224	15.9	19,319	6,569	34.0
18 to 24 years old......	3,656	167	4.6	6,009	918	15.3	5,495	1,637	29.8
25 to 34 years old......	13,029	437	3.4	4,601	884	19.2	2,834	1,195	42.2
35 to 54 years old......	28,820	713	2.5	6,638	1,114	16.8	5,709	2,357	41.3
55 to 64 years old......	9,879	125	1.3	2,996	309	10.3	5,281	1,379	26.1
65 years old and over....	2,561	10	0.4	2,353	30	1.3	13,418	1,095	8.2
FEMALE									
Total...................	43,696	1,312	3.0	29,362	4,523	15.4	52,658	12,680	24.1
16 to 17 years old.......	50	1	(B)	718	48	6.7	3,508	721	20.6
18 to 64 years old.......	42,060	1,290	3.1	26,476	4,389	16.6	29,730	9,578	32.2
18 to 24 years old......	2,743	226	8.2	6,567	1,303	19.8	5,670	1,958	34.5
25 to 34 years old......	9,587	403	4.2	5,642	1,349	23.9	5,527	2,269	41.1
35 to 54 years old......	21,759	567	2.6	9,963	1,356	13.6	10,995	3,560	32.4
55 to 64 years old......	7,971	94	1.2	4,304	381	8.9	7,539	1,791	23.8
65 years old and over....	1,585	21	1.3	2,169	85	3.9	19,420	2,380	12.3

B Base figure too small to meet statistical standards for reliability of a derived figure.

Source: U.S. Census Bureau, *Income, Poverty, and Health Insurance Coverage in the United States: 2011*, Current Population Reports, P60-243, and "Detailed Tables—Table POV22," <http://www.census.gov/hhes/www/poverty/index.html>, accessed March 2013.

Table 743. Families Below Poverty Level and Below 125 Percent of Poverty by Race and Hispanic Origin: 1980 to 2011

[6,217 represents 6,217,000. Families as of March of the following year. Based on Current Population Survey, Annual Social and Economic Supplement (ASEC); see text, this section and Section 1, and Appendix III. For data collection changes over time, see <http://www.census.gov/hhes/www/income/data/historical/history.html>]

Year	Number of families below poverty (1,000)					Percent of families below poverty					Below 125 percent [1] of poverty level	
	All races [2]	White [3]	Black [4]	Asian and Pacific Islander [5]	Hispanic [6]	All races [2]	White [3]	Black [4]	Asian and Pacific Islander [5]	Hispanic [6]	Number (1,000)	Percent
1980.........	6,217	4,195	1,826	(NA)	751	10.3	8.0	28.9	(NA)	23.2	8,764	14.5
1985.........	7,223	4,983	1,983	(NA)	1,074	11.4	9.1	28.7	(NA)	25.5	9,753	15.3
1990.........	7,098	4,622	2,193	169	1,244	10.7	8.1	29.3	11.0	25.0	9,564	14.4
1995.........	7,532	4,994	2,127	264	1,695	10.8	8.5	26.4	12.4	27.0	10,223	14.7
2000 [7]......	6,400	4,333	1,686	233	1,540	8.7	7.1	19.3	7.8	19.2	9,032	12.2
2003 [8]......	7,607	5,058	1,986	311	1,925	10.0	8.1	22.3	10.2	20.8	10,360	13.6
2004 [9]......	7,835	5,293	2,035	232	1,953	10.2	8.4	22.8	7.4	20.5	10,499	13.7
2005.........	7,657	5,068	1,997	289	1,948	9.9	8.0	22.1	9.0	19.7	10,442	13.5
2006.........	7,668	5,118	2,007	260	1,922	9.8	8.0	21.6	7.8	18.9	10,531	13.4
2007.........	7,623	5,046	2,045	261	2,045	9.8	7.9	22.1	7.9	19.7	10,551	13.5
2008.........	8,147	5,414	2,055	341	2,239	10.3	8.4	22.0	9.8	21.3	11,164	14.2
2009.........	8,792	5,994	2,125	337	2,369	11.1	9.3	22.7	9.4	22.7	11,620	14.7
2010 [10]......	9,400	6,305	2,311	362	2,739	11.8	9.9	24.1	9.3	24.3	12,448	15.6
2011.........	9,497	6,334	2,334	401	2,651	11.8	9.8	24.2	9.7	22.9	12,500	15.5

NA Not available. [1] See footnote 1, Table 739. [2] Includes other races, not shown separately. [3] Beginning 2002, data represent White alone, which refers to people who reported White and did not report any other race category. [4] Beginning 2002, data represent Black alone, which refers to people who reported Black and did not report any other race category. [5] Beginning 2002, data represent Asian alone, which refers to people who reported Asian and did not report any other race category. [6] People of Hispanic origin may be of any race. [7] Implementation of a 28,000 household sample expansion. [8] Beginning with the 2003 Current Population Survey (CPS), the questionnaire allowed respondents to choose more than one race. For 2002 and later, data represent persons who selected this race group only and excludes persons reporting more than one race. The CPS in prior years allowed respondents to report only one race group. See also comments on race in the text for Section 1, Population. [9] Data have been revised to reflect a correction to the weights in the 2005 Annual Social and Economic Supplement (ASEC). [10] Implementation of Census 2010-based population controls.

Source: U.S. Census Bureau, *Income, Poverty, and Health Insurance Coverage in the United States: 2011*, Current Population Reports, P60-243, and "Historical and Detailed Tables—Tables 4 and POV04," <http://www.census.gov/hhes/www/poverty/index.html>, accessed March 2013.

Table 744. Families Below Poverty Level by Selected Characteristics: 2011

[In thousands (9,497 represents 9,497,000) except as noted. Families as of March of the following year. Based on Current Population Survey (CPS), Annual Social and Economic Supplement (ASEC); see text, this section and Section 1, and Appendix III. As of 2003, the CPS allowed respondents to choose more than one race. Data below represent persons who selected each race group only and exclude persons reporting more than one race. See also comments on race in the text for Section 1. For composition of regions, see map, inside front cover]

Characteristic	Number below poverty level (1,000)					Percent below poverty level				
	All races [1]	White alone	Black alone	Asian alone	His-panic [2]	All races [1]	White alone	Black alone	Asian alone	His-panic [2]
Total families	**9,497**	**6,334**	**2,334**	**401**	**2,651**	**11.8**	**9.8**	**24.2**	**9.7**	**22.9**
Age of householder:										
18 to 24 years old	1,061	678	293	34	273	33.7	29.8	50.1	23.7	32.3
25 to 34 years old	2,774	1,789	743	86	855	20.5	17.5	37.9	11.1	29.6
35 to 44 years old	2,162	1,474	497	99	747	12.9	11.4	21.8	9.1	24.0
45 to 54 years old	1,530	990	398	81	384	8.7	7.0	19.6	8.6	16.0
55 to 64 years old	1,178	835	248	46	233	7.9	6.8	15.7	6.7	17.2
65 years old and over	731	539	136	45	135	5.1	4.3	11.5	9.1	14.7
Region:										
Northeast	1,421	915	373	99	414	10.1	8.0	22.9	11.5	24.8
Midwest	1,968	1,341	485	46	236	11.3	8.9	28.9	9.5	25.1
South	3,886	2,424	1,260	76	929	12.6	10.3	22.8	7.8	21.6
West	2,222	1,655	216	180	1,072	12.3	11.4	26.3	9.8	22.9
Type of family:										
Married couple	3,652	2,863	408	256	1,145	6.2	5.7	9.4	7.8	15.9
Male householder, no spouse present	950	614	234	44	234	16.1	14.1	24.4	13.6	18.4
Female householder, no spouse present	4,894	2,857	1,693	101	1,272	31.2	28.0	39.0	19.1	41.2

[1] Includes other races, not shown separately. [2] Hispanic persons may be of any race.

Source: U.S. Census Bureau, *Income, Poverty, and Health Insurance Coverage in the United States: 2011*, Current Population Reports, P60-243, and "Detailed Tables—Tables POV04 and POV44," <http://www.census.gov/hhes/www/poverty/index.html>, accessed March 2013.

Table 745. Top Wealth Holders With Gross Assets of $2.0 Million or More— Debts, Mortgages, and Net Worth: 2007

[2,290 represents 2,290,000. Net worth is defined as assets minus liabilities. Figures are estimates based on a sample of federal estate tax returns (Form 706). Based on the estate multiplier technique; for more information on this methodology, see source]

Sex and net worth	Total assets		Debts and mortgages		Net worth	
	Number of top wealth holders (1,000)	Amount (mil. dol.)	Number of top wealth holders (1,000)	Amount (mil. dol.)	Number of top wealth holders (1,000)	Amount (mil. dol.)
Both sexes, total	**2,290**	**13,221,799**	**1,792**	**1,124,478**	**2,290**	**12,097,321**
Size of net worth:						
Under $2.0 million [1]	449	860,731	403	390,799	449	469,932
$2.0 million under $3.5 million	1,008	2,810,250	744	196,440	1,008	2,613,810
$3.5 million under $5.0 million	364	1,607,665	275	96,621	364	1,511,044
$5.0 million under $10.0 million	286	2,091,670	222	141,875	286	1,949,794
$10.0 million under $20.0 million	116	1,687,934	95	97,133	116	1,590,801
$20.0 million or more	66	4,163,549	54	201,609	66	3,961,939
Males, total	**1,320**	**8,062,977**	**1,038**	**872,850**	**1,320**	**7,190,127**
Size of net worth:						
Under $2.0 million [1]	324	613,092	284	325,369	324	287,723
$2.0 million under $3.5 million	526	1,502,230	385	134,813	526	1,367,417
$3.5 million under $5.0 million	190	846,527	146	62,021	190	784,506
$5.0 million under $10.0 million	169	1,257,007	131	107,010	169	1,149,997
$10.0 million under $20.0 million	71	1,029,068	58	67,473	71	961,595
$20.0 million or more	41	2,815,052	35	176,164	41	2,638,888
Females, total	**970**	**5,158,822**	**754**	**251,629**	**970**	**4,907,194**
Size of net worth:						
Under $2.0 million [1]	125	247,639	119	65,430	125	182,209
$2.0 million under $3.5 million	482	1,308,020	359	61,627	482	1,246,393
$3.5 million under $5.0 million	175	761,139	129	34,600	175	726,538
$5.0 million under $10.0 million	117	834,663	91	34,866	117	799,797
$10.0 million under $20.0 million	46	658,866	37	29,660	46	629,206
$20.0 million or more	26	1,348,496	20	25,445	26	1,323,051

[1] Includes individuals with zero net worth.

Source: U.S. Internal Revenue Service, Statistics of Income Division, "SOI Data Tables," January 2012. See also <http://www.irs.gov/uac/SOI-Tax-Stats-Personal-Wealth-Statistics>.

Table 746. Top Wealth Holders With Gross Assets of $2.0 Million or More by Type of Property, Sex, and Size of Net Worth: 2007

[2,290 represents 2,290,000. Net worth is defined as assets minus liabilities. Figures are estimates based on a sample of federal estate tax returns (Form 706). Based on the estate multiplier technique; for more information on this methodology, see source]

Sex and net worth	Number of top wealth holders (1,000)	Assets (mil. dol.)				
		Total [1]	Personal residences	Other real estate	Closely held stock	Publicly traded stock
Both sexes, total.	2,290	13,221,799	1,247,026	1,659,926	1,577,715	2,553,437
Size of net worth:						
Under $2.0 million [2].	449	860,731	181,133	208,138	56,760	63,121
$2.0 million under $3.5 million.	1,008	2,810,250	413,215	435,218	140,964	467,856
$3.5 million under $5.0 million.	364	1,607,665	193,726	236,360	115,070	311,686
$5.0 million under $10.0 million.	286	2,091,670	195,830	310,222	242,341	384,644
$10.0 million under $20.0 million.	116	1,687,934	134,600	195,331	203,913	361,193
$20.0 million or more.	66	4,163,549	128,522	274,657	818,667	964,936
Males, total.	1,320	8,062,977	656,699	978,024	1,142,747	1,445,410
Size of net worth:						
Under $2.0 million [2].	324	613,092	117,898	144,801	46,276	42,054
$2.0 million under $3.5 million.	526	1,502,230	192,820	232,863	95,870	215,697
$3.5 million under $5.0 million.	190	846,527	91,968	121,207	77,869	143,539
$5.0 million under $10.0 million.	169	1,257,007	114,668	175,414	193,956	205,132
$10.0 million under $20.0 million.	71	1,029,068	68,834	119,681	155,875	197,680
$20.0 million or more.	41	2,815,052	70,510	184,059	572,901	641,308
Females, total.	970	5,158,822	590,327	681,902	434,968	1,108,027
Size of net worth:						
Under $2.0 million [2].	125	247,639	63,235	63,337	10,484	21,068
$2.0 million under $3.5 million.	482	1,308,020	220,395	202,355	45,094	252,159
$3.5 million under $5.0 million.	175	761,139	101,757	115,153	37,201	168,148
$5.0 million under $10.0 million.	117	834,663	81,162	134,808	48,385	179,512
$10.0 million under $20.0 million.	46	658,866	65,765	75,650	48,038	163,513
$20.0 million or more.	26	1,348,496	58,012	90,599	245,766	323,628

[1] Includes other types of assets, not shown separately. [2] Includes individuals with zero net worth.

Source: U.S. Internal Revenue Service, Statistics of Income Division, Statistics of Income Division, "Tax Statistics, Personal Wealth Statistics," January 2012. See also <http://www.irs.gov/uac/SOI-Tax-Stats-Personal-Wealth-Statistics>.

Table 747. Top Wealth Holders With Net Worth of $2.0 Million or More— Number and Net Worth by State: 2007

[1,841 represents 1,841,000. Estimates based on a sample of federal estate tax returns (Form 706). Estimates of wealth by state can be subject to significant year-to-year fluctuations, especially for individuals at the extreme tail of the net worth distribution and for states with relatively small decedent populations. Based on the estate multiplier technique; for more information on this methodology, see source]

State	Number of top wealth holders (1,000)	Net worth (mil. dol.)	State	Number of top wealth holders (1,000)	Net worth (mil. dol.)
Total [1].	1,841	11,627,389	Montana.	7	34,794
Alabama.	17	94,464	Nebraska.	6	36,643
Alaska.	3	11,579	Nevada.	16	226,904
Arizona.	34	196,438	New Hampshire.	13	68,492
Arkansas.	8	91,058	New Jersey.	71	332,456
California.	329	1,941,513	New Mexico.	10	40,482
Colorado.	32	243,210	New York.	159	1,201,654
Connecticut.	36	286,124	North Carolina.	45	240,370
Delaware.	5	23,788	North Dakota.	4	13,673
District of Columbia.	3	30,140	Ohio.	50	237,826
Florida.	155	1,105,649	Oklahoma.	17	76,728
Georgia.	41	213,487	Oregon.	24	90,338
Hawaii.	7	75,601	Pennsylvania.	57	323,679
Idaho.	8	52,888	Rhode Island.	6	29,640
Illinois.	83	493,809	South Carolina.	25	189,396
Indiana.	25	115,056	South Dakota.	7	78,126
Iowa.	14	56,740	Tennessee.	26	116,288
Kansas.	11	58,061	Texas.	100	662,518
Kentucky.	15	76,777	Utah.	9	49,879
Louisiana.	16	129,584	Vermont.	6	23,205
Maine.	8	39,673	Virginia.	49	269,648
Maryland.	43	331,467	Washington.	41	359,004
Massachusetts.	51	394,752	West Virginia.	5	27,085
Michigan.	39	217,591	Wisconsin.	32	165,770
Minnesota.	24	158,224	Wyoming.	6	45,258
Mississippi.	9	37,101			
Missouri.	26	145,218	Other areas [1].	8	67,541

[1] Includes U.S. territories and possessions.

Source: U.S. Internal Revenue Service, Statistics of Income Division, "Tax Statistics, Personal Wealth Statistics," January 2012. See also <http://www.irs.gov/uac/SOI-Tax-Stats-Top-Wealthholders-by-State-of-Residence>.

Table 748. Nonfinancial Assets Held by Families by Type of Asset: 2010

[187.2 represents $187,200. Families include one-person units and, as used in this table, are more comparable to the U.S. Census Bureau's household concept. Based on Survey of Consumer Finance; see Appendix III and <http://www.federalreserve.gov/pubs/oss/oss2/papers/measurement.pdf>. For definition of median, see Guide to Tabular Presentation. For data on financial assets, see Table 1194]

Family characteristic	Any financial or non-financial asset	Any non-financial asset	Vehicles	Primary residence	Other residential property	Equity in nonresidential property	Business equity	Other asset
PERCENT OF FAMILIES HOLDING ASSET								
All families, total...................	97.4	91.3	86.7	67.3	14.3	7.7	13.3	7.0
Age of family head:								
Under 35 years old.................	95.5	82.8	79.4	37.5	4.5	2.3	8.4	6.1
35 to 44 years old.................	97.4	92.7	88.9	63.8	9.7	3.9	11.2	4.2
45 to 54 years old.................	98.3	94.7	91.0	75.2	17.0	7.5	16.8	6.6
55 to 64 years old.................	98.3	94.4	90.3	78.1	22.1	12.6	19.6	9.6
65 to 74 years old.................	97.1	92.6	86.5	82.6	22.8	11.0	15.9	11.1
75 years old and over..............	98.7	93.0	83.4	81.9	14.6	13.4	6.0	6.0
Race or ethnicity of respondent:								
White non-Hispanic.................	99.1	94.9	90.9	75.3	16.5	9.4	15.6	8.8
Non-White or Hispanic.............	94.1	84.0	78.1	50.6	9.9	4.2	8.3	3.3
Tenure:								
Owner occupied....................	100.0	100.0	93.9	100.0	19.1	10.5	17.0	8.4
Renter occupied or other...........	92.2	73.6	71.9	(B)	4.6	1.9	5.5	4.2
MEDIAN VALUE [1] ($1,000)								
All families, total...................	187.2	154.6	15.3	170.0	120.0	65.0	78.7	15.0
Age of family head:								
Under 35 years old.................	35.7	34.2	12.4	140.0	72.0	24.0	30.0	5.0
35 to 44 years old.................	156.3	142.8	16.5	170.0	75.0	50.0	50.0	10.0
45 to 54 years old.................	248.4	191.4	18.4	200.0	103.5	50.0	80.0	15.0
55 to 64 years old.................	286.6	206.6	17.8	185.0	165.0	102.0	100.0	20.0
65 to 74 years old.................	281.7	199.8	16.0	165.0	125.0	60.0	100.0	28.1
75 years old and over..............	237.7	168.2	10.6	150.0	125.0	65.0	220.9	26.0
Race or ethnicity of respondent:								
White non-Hispanic.................	238.9	183.5	16.7	175.0	140.0	75.0	97.2	15.0
Non-White or Hispanic.............	76.8	86.0	12.3	139.0	70.0	50.0	43.0	10.0
Tenure:								
Owner occupied....................	296.2	217.0	18.8	170.0	120.0	70.0	95.0	20.0
Renter occupied or other...........	12.6	9.7	8.5	(B)	120.0	22.5	25.0	5.3

B Base too small to meet statistical standards for reliability of derived figure. [1] Median value of asset for families holding such assets.

Source: Source: Board of Governors of the Federal Reserve System, "2010 Survey of Consumer Finances," July 2010, <http://www.federalreserve.gov/econresdata/scf/scf_2010.htm>.

Table 749. Family Net Worth—Median and Mean Net Worth in Constant (2010) Dollars by Selected Family Characteristics: 2001 to 2010

[Net worth in thousands of constant (2010) dollars (106.1 represents $106,100). Constant dollar figures are based on Consumer Price Index for all urban consumers published by U.S. Bureau of Labor Statistics. Families include one-person units and as used in this table are comparable to the U.S. Census Bureau's household concept. Based on Survey of Consumer Finance; see Appendix III. For definition of mean and median, see Guide to Tabular Presentation]

Family characteristic	2001 Median	2001 Mean	2004 Median	2004 Mean	2007 Median	2007 Mean	2010 Median	2010 Mean
All families............................	106.1	487.0	107.2	517.1	126.4	584.6	77.3	498.8
Age of family head:								
Under 35 years old......................	14.3	111.2	16.3	84.6	12.4	111.1	9.3	65.3
35 to 44 years old......................	95.1	318.6	79.9	345.2	92.4	341.9	42.1	217.4
45 to 54 years old......................	164.9	595.9	167.1	625.8	193.7	694.6	117.9	573.0
55 to 64 years old......................	227.2	898.6	290.0	976.4	266.2	986.7	179.4	880.5
65 to 74 years old......................	217.8	831.4	218.8	795.1	250.8	1,064.1	206.7	848.4
75 years old and over...................	190.3	574.8	187.7	607.7	223.7	668.8	216.8	677.9
Race or ethnicity of respondent:								
White non-Hispanic.....................	150.4	599.0	162.2	648.3	179.4	727.4	130.5	654.5
Non-White or Hispanic..................	22.0	144.1	28.5	176.2	29.7	240.3	20.4	175.9
Tenure:								
Owner occupied.........................	211.5	687.2	212.6	720.9	246.0	817.6	174.5	713.4
Renter occupied or other..............	5.9	67.7	4.6	62.3	5.4	74.7	5.1	57.2

Source: Board of Governors of the Federal Reserve System, "2010 Survey of Consumer Finances," Tables 1 and 4, July 2012, <http://www.federalreserve.gov/econresdata/scf/scf_2010.htm>.

Table 750. Household and Nonprofit Organization Sector Balance Sheet: 1990 to 2012

[In billions of dollars (24,418 represents $24,418,000,000,000). As of December 31. Sector includes domestic hedge funds, private equity funds, and personal trusts. For details of financial assets and liabilities, see Table 1193 and Table 1195]

Item	1990	1995	2000	2005	2009	2010	2011	2012
Assets	**24,418**	**33,256**	**50,634**	**73,358**	**70,073**	**73,859**	**74,743**	**80,784**
Nonfinancial assets [1]	9,723	11,472	16,864	28,452	23,769	23,473	23,433	25,189
Real estate	7,607	8,844	13,525	24,130	18,893	18,584	18,383	19,969
Households [2, 3]	6,801	8,055	12,193	22,023	17,156	16,624	16,233	17,691
Consumer durable goods [4]	2,039	2,531	3,196	4,098	4,582	4,584	4,732	4,885
Financial assets [1]	14,695	21,783	33,771	44,906	46,304	50,386	51,310	55,595
Deposits [1]	3,366	3,399	4,438	6,217	8,022	8,004	8,649	9,139
Time and savings deposits	2,512	2,317	3,047	4,929	6,265	6,384	6,734	7,097
Money market fund shares	389	472	937	943	1,313	1,130	1,110	1,110
Credit market instruments [1]	1,741	2,380	2,566	4,226	5,648	5,928	5,402	5,469
Treasury securities	504	828	579	440	906	1,265	816	1,198
Municipal securities	648	533	532	1,601	1,829	1,873	1,808	1,656
Corporate and foreign bonds	238	617	663	1,353	2,315	2,252	2,273	2,402
Corporate equities [2]	1,961	4,434	8,140	8,179	7,518	8,844	8,866	10,178
Mutual fund shares [5]	512	1,253	2,708	3,636	4,131	4,618	4,453	5,372
Security credit	62	128	412	575	669	694	752	776
Life insurance reserves	392	566	819	1,083	1,109	1,137	1,204	1,186
Pension fund reserves	3,310	5,725	9,171	11,512	11,959	13,210	13,434	14,444
Equity in noncorporate business [6]	3,097	3,570	5,138	8,868	6,460	7,120	7,673	8,141
Liabilities [1]	**3,694**	**5,043**	**7,353**	**12,158**	**13,875**	**13,637**	**13,415**	**13,438**
Credit market instruments [1]	3,572	4,846	6,964	11,716	13,397	13,060	12,864	12,819
Home mortgages [7]	2,489	3,319	4,814	8,907	10,374	9,895	9,666	9,432
Consumer credit	824	1,168	1,741	2,321	2,420	2,522	2,616	2,768
Net worth	**20,724**	**28,212**	**43,282**	**61,200**	**56,198**	**60,222**	**61,328**	**67,346**
Replacement cost value of structures:								
Residential [1]	4,618	6,091	8,469	13,475	14,132	14,215	14,363	14,633
Households	4,512	5,975	8,326	13,276	13,919	14,003	14,153	14,422
Nonresidential (nonprofits)	479	600	819	1,196	1,439	1,451	1,502	1,510
Disposable personal income	4,254	5,457	7,327	9,277	10,722	11,127	11,549	11,951
Net worth as percent of disposable income	487	517	591	660	524	541	531	564
Owners' equity in household real estate	4,312	4,736	7,379	13,116	6,782	6,729	6,567	8,259
Owners' equity as percentage of household real estate	63.4	58.8	60.5	59.6	39.5	40.5	40.5	46.7

[1] Includes types of assets and/or liabilities not shown separately. [2] At market value. [3] Includes all types of owner-occupied housing including farm houses and mobile homes, second homes that are not rented, vacant homes for sale, and vacant land. [4] At replacement (current) cost. [5] Value based on the market values of equities held and the book value of other assets held by mutual funds. [6] Net worth of nonfinancial noncorporate business and owners' equity in unincorporated security brokers and dealers. [7] Includes loans made under home equity lines of credit and home equity loans secured by junior liens.

Source: Board of Governors of the Federal Reserve System, "Financial Accounts of the United States, Z.1 Release," Balance Sheet Table B.100, <http://www.federalreserve.gov/apps/fof/FOFTables.aspx>, accessed July 2013.

Table 751. Net Stock of Fixed Assets and Consumer Durable Goods in Current and Chained (2005) Dollars: 1990 to 2011

[In billions of dollars (18,307 represents $18,307,000,000,000). Data revised Aug 15, 2012]

Item	1990	1995	2000	2005	2008	2009	2010	2011
CURRENT DOLLARS								
Net stock, total	**18,307**	**22,846**	**30,129**	**42,610**	**49,625**	**48,759**	**49,562**	**51,117**
Fixed assets	16,268	20,315	26,932	38,512	45,059	44,177	44,978	46,385
Private	12,671	15,811	21,230	30,593	34,869	33,983	34,388	35,193
Nonresidential	6,564	7,990	10,563	14,063	17,185	16,608	16,946	17,632
Equipment and software	2,507	3,100	4,134	4,937	5,766	5,688	5,757	5,944
Structures	4,057	4,890	6,429	9,127	11,419	10,921	11,189	11,688
Residential	6,107	7,821	10,668	16,530	17,685	17,375	17,442	17,561
Government	3,598	4,504	5,702	7,919	10,189	10,195	10,589	11,192
Nonresidential	3,449	4,316	5,473	7,587	9,856	9,869	10,260	10,859
Equipment and software	551	675	704	802	956	991	1,044	1,089
Structures	2,898	3,641	4,769	6,785	8,900	8,878	9,216	9,770
Residential	149	188	229	332	333	326	330	333
Federal	1,077	1,292	1,432	1,744	2,036	2,024	2,095	2,176
Defense	734	868	904	1,081	1,255	1,261	1,309	1,354
State and local	2,521	3,213	4,271	6,175	8,153	8,170	8,494	9,016
Consumer durable goods	2,039	2,531	3,196	4,098	4,567	4,582	4,584	4,732
Motor vehicles and parts	650	811	1,042	1,302	1,261	1,284	1,272	1,310
Furnishings and durable household equipment	649	787	977	1,242	1,415	1,397	1,371	1,414
Other [1]	741	934	1,177	1,554	1,892	1,901	1,941	2,008
CHAINED (2005) DOLLARS								
Net stock, total	**(NA)**	**30,357**	**35,726**	**41,144**	**44,186**	**44,538**	**44,902**	**45,337**
Fixed assets	(NA)	28,414	32,883	37,021	39,476	39,772	40,046	40,356
Private	(NA)	22,082	25,959	29,364	31,374	31,511	31,634	31,837
Nonresidential	(NA)	10,216	12,327	13,584	14,615	14,670	14,727	14,862
Equipment and software	(NA)	3,044	4,205	4,906	5,424	5,369	5,384	5,476
Structures	(NA)	7,361	8,149	8,678	9,203	9,304	9,345	9,393
Residential	(NA)	11,898	13,626	15,780	16,751	16,833	16,901	16,963
Government	(NA)	6,334	6,926	7,657	8,102	8,249	8,387	8,488
Nonresidential	(NA)	6,058	6,628	7,339	7,778	7,921	8,053	8,151
Equipment and software	(NA)	714	734	796	891	925	957	980
Structures	(NA)	5,328	5,891	6,543	6,892	7,005	7,107	7,184
Residential	(NA)	281	298	318	324	327	332	336
Consumer durable goods	(NA)	2,174	2,942	4,123	4,743	4,804	4,903	5,045

NA Not available. [1] Includes recreational goods and vehicles.

Source: U.S. Bureau of Economic Analysis, National Data, "Fixed Assets Accounts Tables," <http://www.bea.gov/iTable/>, accessed September 2013.

Income, Expenditures, Poverty, and Wealth   **493**

Section 14
Prices

The Prices section contains producer and consumer prices indexes and actual prices for selected commodities. The primary sources of the data are monthly publications of the U.S. Department of Labor, Bureau of Labor Statistics (BLS), which include *Consumer Price Index Detailed Report*, *Producer Price Index Detailed Report*, and *U.S. Import and Export Price Indexes*. The Bureau of Economic Analysis is the source for gross domestic product measures. Cost of living data for many urban and metropolitan areas are provided by The Council for Community and Economic Research, a private organization in Arlington, VA. Table 756 on housing price indexes, contains data from the Federal Housing Finance Agency, Housing Price Index. Other commodity, housing, and energy prices may be found in the Energy and Utilities; Forestry, Fishing and Mining; and Construction and Housing sections.

Most price data is measured by an index. An index is a tool that simplifies the measurement of movements in a numerical series. An index allows you to properly compare two or more values in different time periods or places by comparing both to a base year. An index of 110, for example, means there has been a 10-percent increase in price since the reference period; similarly, an index of 90 means a 10-percent decrease. Movements of the index from one date to another can be expressed as changes in index points (simply, the difference between index levels), but it is more useful to express the movements as percent changes. This is because index points are affected by the level of the index in relation to its reference period, while percent changes are not.

Consumer price indexes (CPI)—The CPI is a measure of the average change in prices over time in a "market basket" of goods and services purchased either by urban wage earners and clerical workers or by all urban consumers. The all urban consumer group represents 87 percent of the total U.S. population and is based on the expenditures of residents of urban or metropolitan areas, including professionals, the self-employed, the poor, the unemployed, and retired people, as well as urban wage earners and clerical workers. Not included in the CPI are the spending patterns of people living in rural nonmetropolitan areas, farm families, people in the Armed Forces, and those in institutions, such as prisons and mental hospitals. Consumer inflation for all urban consumers is measured by two indexes, the Consumer Price Index for All Urban Consumers (CPI-U) and the Chained Consumer Price Index for All Urban Consumers (C-CPI-U). The broadest and most comprehensive CPI is called the All Items Consumer Price Index for All Urban Consumers (CPI-U) for the U.S. City Average. CPIs in this section generally have a base of 1982–84 = 100.

The CPI is a product of a series of interrelated samples. Data from the 1990 Census of Population determines the urban areas from which data on prices are collected and the housing units within each area that are eligible for use in the shelter component of the CPI. The Census of Population also provides data on the number of consumers represented by each area selected as a CPI price collection area. A sample (of about 14,500 families each year) serves as the basis

for a Point-of-Purchase Survey that identified the places where households purchased various types of goods and services. The CPI market basket is developed from detailed expenditure information provided by families and individuals on what they actually bought. In calculating the index, each item is assigned a weight to account for its relative importance in consumers' budgets. Price changes for the various items in each location are then averaged and local data are combined to obtain a U.S. city average. For the current CPI, this information was collected from the Consumer Expenditure Surveys for 2009 and 2010. In each of those years, about 7,000 families from around the country provided information each quarter on their spending habits in the interview survey. To collect information on frequently purchased items, such as food and personal care products, another 7,000 families in each of these years kept diaries listing everything they bought during a 2-week period. Over the 2 year period, expenditure information came from approximately 28,000 weekly diaries and 60,000 quarterly interviews used to determine the importance, or weight, of the more than 200 item categories in the CPI index structure.

The CPI represents all goods and services purchased for consumption by the reference population. BLS has classified all expenditure items into more than 200 categories, arranged into eight major groups which are food and beverages, housing, apparel, transportation, medical care, recreation, education and communication, and other goods. The CPI does not include investment items, such as stocks, bonds, real estate, and life insurance, as these items relate to savings and not to day-to-day consumption expenses.

Producer price index (PPI)— Dating from 1890, the PPI is the oldest continuous statistical series published by BLS. The PPI is a family of indexes that measures the average change over time in the selling prices received by domestic producers of goods and services. Imports are excluded. The target set of goods and services included in the PPI is the entire marketed output of U.S. producers. The set includes both goods and services purchased by other producers as inputs to their operations or as capital investment, as well as goods and services purchased by consumers either directly from the service producer or indirectly from a retailer. Over 10,000 PPIs for individual products and groups of products are released each month.

Prices used in constructing the index are collected from sellers and generally apply to the first significant large-volume commercial transaction for each commodity. The weights used in the index represent the total net selling value of commodities produced or processed in this country. Most producer price indexes have a reference base year of 1982 = 100. The reference year of the PPI shipment weights has been taken primarily from the 2002 Census of Manufactures. For further detail regarding the PPI, see the *BLS Handbook of Methods*, Chapter 14, <http://www.bls.gov/opub/hom/homch14.htm>.

BEA price indexes—BEA chain-weighted price indexes are weighted averages of the detailed price indexes used in the deflation of the goods and services that make up the gross domestic product (GDP) and its major components. Growth rates are constructed for years and quarters using quantity weights for the current and preceding year or quarter; these growth rates are used to move the index for the preceding period forward a year or quarter at a time. All chain-weighted price indexes are expressed in terms of the reference year value 2009 = 100.

Personal consumption expenditures (PCE) price and quantity indexes are based on market transactions for which there are corresponding price measures. The price index provides a measure of the prices paid by persons for domestic purchases of goods and services. PCEs are defined as market value of spending by individuals and not-for-profit institutions on all goods and services. Personal consumption expenditures also include the value of certain imputed goods and services—such as the rental value of owner-occupied homes and compensation paid in kind—such as employer-paid health and life insurance premiums. More information on this index may be found at <http://www.bea.gov/national/index.htm>.

Measures of inflation—Inflation is a period of rising price levels for goods and factors of production. Inflation results in a decline in the purchasing power of the dollar. It is suggested that changes in price levels be compared from the same month of the prior year and not as a change from the prior month. The BLS offers several indexes that measure different aspects of inflation, three of which are included in this section. The CPI measures inflation as experienced by consumers in their day-to-day living expenses. The PPI measures prices at the producer level only. The International Price Program measures change in the prices of imports and exports of nonmilitary goods between the United States and other countries.

Whereas the CPI and PPI measure a benchmark approach to price levels, the BEA's Personal Consumption Expenditures uses a chain-weight approach which links weighted averages from adjoining years.

Other measures of inflation include the futures price and spot market price indexes from the Commodity Research Bureau and the employment cost, hourly compensation, and unit labor cost indexes from the BLS. Found in Section 12, Labor Force, Employment, and Earnings, these BLS indexes are used as a measure of the change in cost of the labor factor of production and changes in long-term interest rates that are often used to measure changes in the cost of the capital factor of production.

International price indexes—The BLS International Price Program produces export and import price indexes for nonmilitary goods traded between the United States and the rest of the world.

The export price index provides a measure of price change for all products sold by U.S. residents to foreign buyers. The import price index provides a measure of price change for goods purchased from other countries by U.S. residents. The reference period for the indexes is 2000 = 100, unless otherwise indicated. The product universe for both the import and export indexes includes raw materials, agricultural products, semifinished manufactures, and finished manufactures, including both capital and consumer goods. Price data for these items are collected primarily by mail questionnaire. In nearly all cases, the data are collected directly from the exporter or importer.

To the extent possible, the data gathered refer to prices at the U.S. border for exports and at either the foreign border or the U.S. border for imports. For nearly all products, the prices refer to transactions completed during the first week of the month. Survey respondents are asked to indicate all discounts, allowances, and rebates applicable to the reported prices, so that the price used in the calculation of the indexes is the actual price for which the product was bought or sold.

Table 752. Purchasing Power of the Dollar: 1950 to 2012

[Indexes: PPI, 1982 = $1.00; CPI, 1982-84 = $1.00. Producer prices prior to 1961, and consumer prices prior to 1964, exclude Alaska and Hawaii. Producer prices based on finished goods index. Obtained by dividing the average price index for the 1982 = 100, PPI; 1982-84 = 100, CPI base periods (100.0) by the price index for a given period and expressing the result in dollars and cents. Annual figures are based on average of monthly data]

Year	Annual average as measured by—		Year	Annual average as measured by—	
	Producer prices	Consumer prices		Producer prices	Consumer prices
1950	3.546	4.149	1983	0.984	1.004
1954	3.289	3.717	1984	0.964	0.962
1955	3.279	3.731	1985	0.955	0.929
1956	3.195	3.676	1986	0.969	0.912
1957	3.077	3.559	1987	0.949	0.880
1958	3.012	3.460	1988	0.926	0.845
1959	3.021	3.436	1989	0.880	0.806
1960	2.994	3.378	1990	0.839	0.765
1961	2.994	3.344	1991	0.822	0.734
1962	2.985	3.311	1992	0.812	0.713
1963	2.994	3.268	1993	0.802	0.692
1964	2.985	3.226	1994	0.797	0.675
1965	2.933	3.175	1995	0.782	0.656
1966	2.841	3.086	1996	0.762	0.637
1967	2.809	2.994	1997	0.759	0.623
1968	2.732	2.874	1998	0.765	0.613
1969	2.632	2.725	1999	0.752	0.600
1970	2.545	2.577	2000	0.725	0.581
1971	2.469	2.469	2001	0.711	0.565
1972	2.392	2.392	2002	0.720	0.556
1973	2.193	2.252	2003	0.698	0.543
1974	1.901	2.028	2004	0.673	0.529
1975	1.718	1.859	2005	0.642	0.512
1976	1.645	1.757	2006	0.623	0.496
1977	1.546	1.650	2007	0.600	0.482
1978	1.433	1.534	2008	0.565	0.464
1979	1.289	1.377	2009	0.580	0.466
1980	1.136	1.214	2010	0.556	0.459
1981	1.041	1.100	2011	0.525	0.445
1982	1.000	1.036	2012	0.515	0.436

Source: Bureau of Labor Statistics, "CPI Databases," <http://www.bls.gov/cpi/#data>, accessed May 2013; and "PPI Databases," <http://www.bls.gov/ppi/#data>, accessed May 2013.

Table 753. Consumer Price Indexes (CPI-U) by Major Groups: 1990 to 2012

[1982-84 = 100, except as indicated. Represents annual averages of monthly figures. Reflects buying patterns of all urban consumers. Minus sign (-) indicates decrease. See text, this section]

Year	All items	Com-mod-ities	Ser-vices	Food	Energy	All items less food and energy	Food and bever-ages	Hous-ing	Apparel	Trans-porta-tion	Medical care	Educa-tion and com-munica-tion [1]
1990	130.7	122.8	139.2	132.4	102.1	135.5	132.1	128.5	124.1	120.5	162.8	(NA)
1995	152.4	136.4	168.7	148.4	105.2	161.2	148.9	148.5	132.0	139.1	220.5	92.2
2000	172.2	149.2	195.3	167.8	124.6	181.3	168.4	169.6	129.6	153.3	260.8	102.5
2001	177.1	150.7	203.4	173.1	129.3	186.1	173.6	176.4	127.3	154.3	272.8	105.2
2002	179.9	149.7	209.8	176.2	121.7	190.5	176.8	180.3	124.0	152.9	285.6	107.9
2003	184.0	151.2	216.5	180.0	136.5	193.2	180.5	184.8	120.9	157.6	297.1	109.8
2004	188.9	154.7	222.8	186.2	151.4	196.6	186.6	189.5	120.4	163.1	310.1	111.6
2005	195.3	160.2	230.1	190.7	177.1	200.9	191.2	195.7	119.5	173.9	323.2	113.7
2006	201.6	164.0	238.9	195.2	196.9	205.9	195.7	203.2	119.5	180.9	336.2	116.8
2007	207.3	167.5	246.8	202.9	207.7	210.7	203.3	209.6	119.0	184.7	351.1	119.6
2008	215.3	174.8	255.5	214.1	236.7	215.6	214.2	216.3	118.9	195.5	364.1	123.6
2009	214.5	169.7	259.2	218.0	193.1	219.2	218.2	217.1	120.1	179.3	375.6	127.4
2010	218.1	174.6	261.3	219.6	211.4	221.3	220.0	216.3	119.5	193.4	388.4	129.9
2011	224.9	183.9	265.8	227.8	243.9	225.0	227.9	219.1	122.1	212.4	400.3	131.5
2012	229.6	187.6	271.4	233.8	246.1	229.8	233.7	222.7	126.3	217.3	414.9	133.8
PERCENT CHANGE [2]												
1990	5.4	5.2	5.5	5.8	8.3	5.0	5.8	4.5	4.6	5.6	9.0	(NA)
1995	2.8	1.9	3.4	2.8	0.6	3.0	2.8	2.6	-1.0	3.6	4.5	3.8
2000	3.4	3.3	3.4	2.3	16.9	2.4	2.3	3.5	-1.3	6.2	4.1	1.3
2001	2.8	1.0	4.1	3.2	3.8	2.6	3.1	4.0	-1.8	0.7	4.6	2.6
2002	1.6	-0.7	3.1	1.8	-5.9	2.4	1.8	2.2	-2.6	-0.9	4.7	2.6
2003	2.3	1.0	3.2	2.2	12.2	1.4	2.1	2.5	-2.5	3.1	4.0	1.8
2004	2.7	2.3	2.9	3.4	10.9	1.8	3.4	2.5	-0.4	3.5	4.4	1.6
2005	3.4	3.6	3.3	2.4	17.0	2.2	2.5	3.3	-0.7	6.6	4.2	1.9
2006	3.2	2.4	3.8	2.4	11.2	2.5	2.4	3.8	–	4.0	4.0	2.7
2007	2.8	2.1	3.3	4.0	5.5	2.3	3.9	3.1	-0.4	2.1	4.4	2.4
2008	3.8	4.3	3.5	5.5	13.9	2.3	5.4	3.2	-0.1	5.9	3.7	3.4
2009	-0.4	-2.9	1.4	1.8	-18.4	1.7	1.9	0.4	1.0	-8.3	3.2	3.0
2010	1.6	2.9	0.8	0.8	9.5	1.0	0.8	-0.4	-0.5	7.9	3.4	2.0
2011	3.2	5.3	1.7	3.7	15.4	1.7	3.6	1.3	2.2	9.8	3.0	1.2
2012	2.1	2.0	2.1	2.6	0.9	2.1	2.5	1.6	3.4	2.3	3.7	1.8

– Represents zero. NA Not available. [1] Dec. 1997 = 100. [2] Change from immediate prior year. 1990 change from 1989.

Source: U.S. Bureau of Labor Statistics, "CPI Databases," <http://www.bls.gov/cpi/#data>, accessed May 2013.

Table 754. Annual Percent Changes From Prior Year in Consumer Price Indexes (CPI-U)—Selected Areas: 2012

[Percent changes computed from annual averages of monthly figures published by source. Local area CPI indexes are by-products of the national CPI program. Each local index has a smaller sample size than the national index and is therefore subject to substantially more sampling and other measurement error. As a result, local area indexes show greater volatility than the national index, although their long-term trends are similar. Minus sign (-) indicates decrease. See also text, this section and Appendix I]]

Area	All items	Food and beverage	Food	Housing	Apparel	Transportation	Medical care	Fuel and other utilities
U.S. city average	**2.1**	**2.5**	**2.6**	**1.6**	**3.4**	**2.3**	**3.7**	**-0.6**
Anchorage, AK	2.2	2.4	2.9	2.7	4.3	2.0	4.3	0.5
Atlanta, GA	1.8	2.7	2.7	0.7	0.9	2.7	9.6	-0.8
Boston-Brockton-Nashua, MA-NH-ME-CT	1.6	2.3	2.4	1.6	4.9	0.9	1.6	-1.8
Chicago-Gary-Kenosha, IL-IN-WI	1.5	2.3	2.4	0.9	2.5	2.3	3.3	-3.9
Cincinnati-Hamilton, OH-KY-IN	2.5	2.6	2.7	0.9	3.7	3.1	9.3	-6.6
Cleveland-Akron, OH	1.7	3.1	3.2	0.7	3.9	1.2	3.2	-4.0
Dallas-Fort Worth, TX	2.1	2.7	2.7	2.1	-1.1	2.5	3.7	-1.2
Denver-Boulder-Greeley, CO	1.9	3.1	3.2	1.4	1.1	1.2	5.1	-5.1
Detroit-Ann Arbor-Flint, MI	2.0	1.5	1.4	1.9	0.9	2.7	2.8	3.0
Honolulu, HI	2.4	4.4	4.3	1.9	2.6	0.9	3.2	7.5
Houston-Galveston-Brazoria, TX	1.9	2.6	2.6	1.0	3.2	2.2	5.2	-7.4
Kansas City, MO-KS	2.3	3.3	3.4	1.6	7.6	2.0	3.8	0.1
Los Angeles-Riverside-Orange County, CA	2.0	1.9	2.0	1.7	1.8	3.0	3.8	1.6
Miami-Fort Lauderdale, FL	1.9	2.0	2.1	1.4	3.0	4.1	4.2	-0.5
Milwaukee-Racine, WI	2.3	2.9	3.0	0.5	6.6	0.5	7.4	-1.8
Minneapolis-St. Paul, MN-WI	2.0	3.3	3.8	1.3	5.7	1.4	5.0	-3.4
New York-Northern New Jersey-Long Island, NY-NJ-CT-PA	1.8	2.8	2.9	1.2	1.7	2.5	5.0	-1.3
Philadelphia-Wilmington-Atlantic City, PA-NJ-DE-MD	2.2	2.2	2.2	1.7	5.7	2.6	1.8	-1.5
Phoenix-Mesa, AZ	3.5	1.9	1.8	2.3	7.2	3.0	2.9	0.5
Pittsburgh, PA	2.3	3.2	3.0	3.8	4.1	2.3	5.3	2.0
Portland-Salem, OR-WA	1.6	2.3	2.4	2.4	7.3	0.5	4.4	-4.7
San Diego, CA	2.7	1.0	1.0	1.1	2.3	2.2	3.0	2.8
San Francisco-Oakland-San Jose, CA	2.5	2.5	2.5	3.3	3.9	3.4	1.6	4.7
Seattle-Tacoma-Bremerton, WA	2.4	2.0	2.0	2.8	4.9	2.1	(NA)	2.8
St. Louis, MO-IL	2.4	4.0	4.3	2.4	7.2	1.9	1.4	-0.1
Tampa-St. Petersburg-Clearwater, FL	2.4	2.2	2.1	1.7	6.7	2.8	5.1	1.8
Washington-Baltimore, DC-MD-VA-WV	2.2	2.1	2.1	2.4	1.4	1.8	4.2	-1.7

NA Not available.

Source: U.S. Bureau of Labor Statistics, CPI Databases, "All Urban Consumers (Current Series)," <http://www.bls.gov/cpi/data.htm>, accessed June 2013.

Table 755. Consumer Price Indexes for All Urban Consumers (CPI-U) for Selected Items and Groups: 2000 to 2012

[1982-84 = 100, except as noted. Annual averages of monthly figures. Minus sign (-) indicates decrease. See headnote, Table 753]

Item	2000	2005	2007	2008	2009	2010	2011	2012
All items...	**172.2**	**195.3**	**207.3**	**215.3**	**214.5**	**218.1**	**224.9**	**229.6**
Food and beverages...................................	**168.4**	**191.2**	**203.3**	**214.2**	**218.2**	**220.0**	**227.9**	**233.7**
Food...	167.8	190.7	202.9	214.1	218.0	219.6	227.8	233.8
Food at home.......................................	167.9	189.8	201.2	214.1	215.1	215.8	226.2	231.8
Cereals and bakery products.......................	188.3	209.0	222.1	244.9	252.6	250.4	260.3	267.7
Cereals and cereal products.....................	175.9	186.7	194.7	214.4	221.8	217.6	227.2	232.9
Rice, pasta, and cornmeal......................	150.7	165.3	181.4	218.8	229.9	224.4	234.1	239.4
Rice [1,2]...................................	99.3	108.8	120.1	152.8	161.0	156.9	163.9	167.3
Bakery products................................	194.1	220.5	236.6	261.0	268.9	268.0	278.0	286.6
Bread [2]......................................	107.4	126.2	140.1	160.6	162.6	159.8	168.7	173.4
Cakes, cupcakes, and cookies..................	187.9	209.8	221.7	239.9	250.7	251.7	256.0	266.2
Other bakery products.........................	191.5	211.4	220.5	236.5	245.9	247.1	253.1	260.4
Meats, poultry, fish and eggs......................	154.5	184.7	195.6	204.7	203.8	207.7	223.2	231.0
Meats, poultry, and fish.........................	155.5	186.7	195.4	203.6	204.6	208.6	223.9	231.9
Meats...	150.7	187.5	195.0	201.8	200.5	206.2	224.4	232.0
Beef and veal...............................	148.1	200.4	211.1	220.6	218.3	224.5	247.4	263.1
Uncooked ground beef.....................	125.2	175.1	184.3	196.4	198.5	203.6	226.7	242.7
Uncooked beef steaks [2].................	109.1	145.1	151.8	155.3	150.1	153.3	166.5	177.0
Pork.......................................	156.5	177.7	180.9	185.0	181.4	190.0	206.1	206.6
Other meats................................	152.0	177.5	184.8	190.6	194.9	194.8	207.3	210.9
Poultry.......................................	159.8	185.3	191.4	200.9	204.2	204.0	209.9	221.4
Chicken [2].................................	102.5	120.6	124.4	130.7	132.6	131.8	134.3	140.8
Fish and seafood.............................	190.4	200.1	219.1	232.1	240.6	243.2	260.5	266.7
Dairy products..................................	160.7	182.4	194.8	210.4	197.0	199.2	212.7	217.3
Milk [2]..	107.8	127.0	140.1	148.5	129.0	133.6	145.8	147.4
Cheese and related products...................	162.8	183.3	191.5	214.5	203.5	204.8	217.5	222.4
Ice cream and related products................	164.4	177.6	183.4	192.8	196.6	195.0	209.1	215.5
Fruits and vegetables............................	204.6	241.4	262.6	278.9	272.9	273.5	284.7	282.8
Fresh fruits and vegetables....................	238.8	285.3	312.1	328.3	312.7	314.8	328.9	322.3
Fresh fruits.................................	258.3	297.4	329.5	345.4	324.4	322.3	333.1	336.6
Fresh vegetables...........................	219.4	271.7	293.5	309.8	299.3	305.5	322.5	306.1
Processed fruits and vegetables [2]...........	105.6	119.3	127.2	139.3	148.6	146.6	150.9	156.7
Nonalcoholic beverages and beverage materials...	137.8	144.4	153.4	160.0	163.0	161.6	166.8	168.6
Juices and nonalcoholic drinks [2].............	105.6	110.6	117.9	123.1	126.3	124.5	126.7	128.2
Carbonated drinks...........................	123.4	131.9	140.1	147.0	154.1	154.7	158.8	161.0
Nonfrozen noncarbonated juices and drinks [2]....	104.2	106.5	112.9	117.5	118.0	114.8	116.0	116.9
Beverage materials including coffee and tea [2].....	97.9	102.4	108.2	112.8	113.3	114.0	122.5	123.7
Other food at home..............................	155.6	167.0	173.3	184.2	191.2	191.1	197.4	204.8
Sugar and sweets.............................	154.0	165.2	176.8	186.6	196.9	201.2	207.8	214.7
Candy and chewing gum [2]..................	103.8	109.5	116.1	123.2	130.2	132.5	136.0	140.9
Fats and oils.................................	147.4	167.7	172.9	196.8	201.2	200.6	219.2	232.6
Other foods..................................	172.2	182.5	188.2	198.1	205.5	204.6	209.3	216.6
Frozen and freeze dried prepared food.........	148.5	153.2	156.7	163.5	168.1	165.3	167.8	169.8
Snacks.....................................	166.3	178.5	184.9	199.8	213.2	216.6	224.3	238.8
Spices, seasonings, condiments, sauces........	175.6	188.0	195.5	204.6	214.7	214.4	219.9	225.9
Other miscellaneous food [2]..................	107.5	111.3	115.1	119.9	122.4	121.7	124.0	128.3
Food away from home..............................	169.0	193.4	206.7	215.8	223.3	226.1	231.4	238.0
Full service meals and snacks [2]................	106.8	121.9	130.2	135.4	139.2	141.1	144.4	148.1
Limited service meals and snacks [2].............	106.3	122.4	130.6	136.9	142.6	143.9	147.1	151.7
At employee sites and schools [2]................	104.4	118.6	126.7	131.8	137.3	141.0	145.7	150.2
From vending machines and mobile vendors [2].......	102.4	112.6	118.3	124.1	129.7	133.1	135.8	140.2
Other food away from home [2]....................	109.0	131.3	144.1	150.6	155.9	159.3	162.8	166.5
Alcoholic beverages...............................	174.7	195.9	207.0	214.5	220.8	223.3	226.7	230.8
Alcoholic beverages at home.......................	158.1	172.3	179.1	184.9	190.3	191.0	191.8	193.4
Beer, ale, and other malt beverages at home.........	156.8	176.4	184.1	190.3	197.4	201.0	203.9	207.6
Distilled spirits at home.......................	162.3	177.4	181.0	185.0	189.2	188.8	189.0	188.9
Wine at home..................................	151.6	156.2	162.9	168.7	172.1	169.7	168.5	168.2
Alcoholic beverages away from home..............	207.1	244.5	266.0	277.4	285.6	291.9	300.9	310.5
Housing...	**169.6**	**195.7**	**209.6**	**216.3**	**217.1**	**216.3**	**219.1**	**222.7**
Shelter..	193.4	224.4	240.6	246.7	249.4	248.4	251.6	257.1
Rent of primary residence.........................	183.9	217.3	234.7	243.3	248.8	249.4	253.6	260.4
Lodging away from home [2]........................	117.5	130.3	142.8	143.7	134.2	133.7	137.4	140.5
Other lodging away from home including hotels and motels..	252.4	274.2	299.9	301.0	279.2	280.4	287.4	292.6
Owners' equivalent rent of primary residence [3]........	198.7	230.2	246.2	252.4	256.6	256.6	259.6	264.8
Tenants' and household insurance [2]...............	103.7	117.6	117.0	118.8	121.5	125.7	127.4	131.3
Fuels and utilities...............................	137.9	179.0	200.6	220.0	210.7	214.2	220.4	219.0
Household energy................................	122.8	161.6	181.7	200.8	188.1	189.3	193.6	189.3
Fuel oil and other fuels........................	129.7	208.6	251.5	334.4	239.8	275.1	337.1	335.9
Fuel oil....................................	130.3	216.4	262.6	365.0	240.2	282.9	367.8	376.1
Propane, kerosene and firewood [4]..........	155.5	240.6	286.0	344.2	293.1	320.6	348.1	328.4
Energy services...............................	128.0	166.5	186.3	202.2	193.6	192.9	194.4	189.7
Electricity..................................	128.5	150.8	175.8	187.1	192.7	193.1	196.7	196.6
Utility (piped) gas service..................	132.0	215.4	217.7	247.8	193.7	189.7	184.3	166.6
Water and sewer and trash collection services [2]......	106.5	130.3	143.7	152.1	161.1	170.9	179.6	189.3
Water and sewerage maintenance.....................	227.5	283.4	312.6	331.3	354.4	380.7	402.9	428.6
Garbage and trash collection [5]...................	269.8	314.0	345.6	364.7	376.4	384.4	395.1	404.7
Household furnishings and operations.................	**128.2**	**126.1**	**126.9**	**127.8**	**128.7**	**125.5**	**124.9**	**125.7**
Furniture and bedding............................	(NA)	(NA)	(NA)	(NA)	(NA)	98.4	97.7	98.0
Bedroom furniture...............................	134.4	125.9	125.8	124.5	124.8	119.7	118.6	120.2
Living room, kitchen, and dining room furniture [2].......	102.4	92.7	91.6	90.5	90.7	88.9	88.9	90.8
Appliances [2]...................................	96.3	86.9	89.8	89.9	91.1	86.9	85.9	88.1
Other household equipment and furnishings [2].......	98.0	85.5	76.9	75.6	74.0	70.8	68.5	65.7
Clocks, lamps, and decorator items.............	111.7	88.0	73.6	69.9	67.2	62.9	59.5	56.1
Nonelectric cookware and tableware [2]..........	98.4	91.3	93.1	95.9	97.1	96.6	97.9	97.7
Tools, hardware, outdoor equipment and supplies [2]....	97.0	94.4	94.6	93.5	94.2	91.6	91.6	92.0

See footnotes at end of table.

Table 755. Consumer Price Indexes for All Urban Consumers (CPI-U) for Selected Items and Groups: 2000 to 2012-Continued.

See headnote on page 499.

Item	2000	2005	2007	2008	2009	2010	2011	2012
Tools, hardware, and supplies [2]	97.3	98.1	99.7	99.0	99.2	96.5	98.1	99.6
Outdoor equipment and supplies [2]	96.8	92.4	92.0	90.7	91.4	88.9	88.3	88.2
Housekeeping supplies	153.4	159.9	169.4	176.5	183.1	183.3	185.4	189.8
Household cleaning products [2]	105.1	107.9	112.3	115.9	121.4	120.6	121.4	123.0
Household paper products [2]	113.8	125.4	135.6	146.8	156.1	158.0	161.7	167.8
Miscellaneous household products [2]	104.3	106.4	113.6	116.3	116.8	116.9	117.9	120.8
Household operations [2]	110.5	130.3	140.6	147.5	150.3	150.3	151.8	155.2
Domestic services [2]	109.7	128.3	138.1	142.8	144.1	144.4	145.4	147.4
Gardening and lawncare services [2]	111.4	127.9	140.5	151.2	156.5	155.3	156.9	159.7
Apparel	**129.6**	**119.5**	**119.0**	**118.9**	**120.1**	**119.5**	**122.1**	**126.3**
Men's and boy's apparel	129.7	116.1	112.4	113.0	113.6	111.9	114.7	119.5
Men's apparel	133.1	121.4	118.2	118.4	118.6	117.5	119.8	124.3
Men's shirts and sweaters [2]	98.3	84.2	82.5	80.4	81.0	78.6	79.6	82.2
Boys' apparel	116.2	97.0	91.7	93.5	95.2	91.5	95.9	101.5
Women's and girl's apparel	121.5	110.8	110.3	107.5	108.1	107.1	109.2	113.0
Women's apparel	121.9	111.8	112.1	109.3	109.9	109.5	111.3	115.0
Women's suits and separates [2]	98.2	87.3	88.9	85.7	84.9	83.9	84.2	86.6
Women's underwear, nightwear, sportswear, and accessories [2]	101.8	95.4	91.8	90.4	93.1	96.0	98.6	101.7
Girls' apparel	119.7	105.3	101.1	98.5	99.0	95.4	98.5	103.2
Footwear	123.8	122.6	122.4	124.2	126.9	128.0	128.5	131.8
Men's footwear	129.5	121.3	120.9	122.9	126.4	127.6	129.2	133.4
Women's footwear	119.6	121.9	122.5	122.6	123.4	125.3	123.7	127.2
Jewelry and watches [4]	137.0	127.6	137.1	146.5	149.2	152.4	165.2	167.3
Jewelry [4]	141.2	131.3	142.4	153.8	157.0	161.2	176.6	178.2
Transportation	**153.3**	**173.9**	**184.7**	**195.5**	**179.3**	**193.4**	**212.4**	**217.3**
Private transportation	149.1	170.2	180.8	191.0	174.8	188.7	207.6	212.8
New and used motor vehicles [2]	100.8	95.6	94.3	93.3	93.5	97.1	99.8	100.6
New vehicles	142.8	137.9	136.3	134.2	135.6	138.0	141.9	144.2
Used cars and trucks	155.8	139.4	135.7	134.0	127.0	143.1	149.0	150.3
Leased cars and trucks [6]	(NA)	92.7	92.6	95.1	102.4	97.0	94.4	89.5
Motor fuel	129.3	195.7	239.1	279.7	202.0	239.2	302.6	312.7
Gasoline (all types)	128.6	194.7	238.0	277.5	201.6	238.6	301.7	311.5
Motor vehicle parts and equipment	101.5	111.9	121.6	128.7	134.1	137.0	143.9	148.6
Motor vehicle maintenance and repair	177.3	206.9	223.0	233.9	243.3	248.0	253.1	257.6
Motor vehicle insurance	256.7	329.9	333.1	341.5	357.0	375.2	388.7	402.5
Motor vehicle fees [2]	107.3	134.7	141.2	145.8	155.7	165.5	167.3	172.1
Public transportation	209.6	217.3	230.0	250.5	236.3	251.4	269.4	271.4
Airline fare	239.4	236.6	251.7	282.0	258.0	278.2	304.0	305.0
Medical care	**260.8**	**323.2**	**351.1**	**364.1**	**375.6**	**388.4**	**400.3**	**414.9**
Medical care commodities	238.1	276.0	290.0	296.0	305.1	314.7	324.1	333.6
Prescription drugs	285.4	349.0	369.2	378.3	391.1	407.8	425.0	440.1
Nonprescription drugs [4]	(NA)	(NA)	(NA)	(NA)	(NA)	100.0	98.6	99.3
Medical care services	266.0	336.7	369.3	384.9	397.3	411.2	423.8	440.3
Professional medical services	237.7	281.7	300.8	311.0	319.4	328.2	335.7	342.0
Physicians' services	244.7	287.5	303.2	311.3	320.8	331.3	340.3	347.3
Dental services	258.5	324.0	358.4	376.9	388.1	398.8	408.0	417.5
Eyeglasses and eye care [4]	149.7	163.2	171.6	174.1	175.5	176.7	178.3	179.9
Services by other medical professionals [4]	161.9	186.8	197.4	205.5	209.8	214.4	217.4	219.6
Hospital and related services	317.3	439.9	498.9	534.0	567.9	607.7	641.5	672.1
Hospital services [7]	115.9	161.6	183.6	197.2	210.7	227.2	241.2	253.6
Health insurance [9]	(NA)	(NA)	113.5	114.2	110.5	106.6	105.5	118.3
Recreation [2]	**103.3**	**109.4**	**111.4**	**113.3**	**114.3**	**113.3**	**113.4**	**114.7**
Video and audio [2]	101.0	104.2	102.9	102.6	101.3	99.1	98.4	99.4
Cable and satellite television and radio service [5]	266.8	331.9	351.5	359.9	367.6	372.4	379.0	395.6
Pets, pet products and services [2]	106.1	123.6	133.8	144.5	153.4	154.4	158.7	162.4
Sporting goods	119.0	115.5	116.4	118.4	119.9	118.8	118.5	118.7
Other recreational goods [2]	87.8	69.5	64.3	62.1	60.2	57.8	55.9	54.0
Other recreation services [2]	111.7	130.5	139.4	142.9	144.6	145.1	145.3	148.4
Club membership dues and fees for participant sports [2]	108.9	117.4	123.7	125.8	125.7	123.5	122.1	125.5
Admissions	230.5	282.3	303.8	312.3	317.8	322.8	325.0	332.1
Education and communication [2]	**102.5**	**113.7**	**119.6**	**123.6**	**127.4**	**129.9**	**131.5**	**133.8**
Education [2]	112.5	152.7	171.4	181.3	190.9	199.3	207.8	216.3
Tuition, other school fees, and childcare	324.0	440.9	494.1	522.1	549.0	573.2	597.2	621.0
College tuition and fees	331.9	475.1	538.7	572.3	606.7	638.2	670.3	702.8
Communication [2]	93.6	84.7	83.4	84.2	85.0	84.7	83.3	83.1
Information and information processing [2]	92.8	82.6	80.7	81.4	81.9	81.5	80.0	79.5
Telephone services [2]	98.5	94.9	98.2	100.5	102.4	102.4	101.2	101.7
Wireless telephone services [2]	76.0	65.0	64.4	64.2	64.3	62.4	60.1	59.7
Land-line telephone services [10]	(NA)	(NA)	(NA)	(NA)	(NA)	101.6	103.3	105.6
Information technology, hardware, and services [8]	25.9	13.6	10.6	10.1	9.7	9.4	9.0	8.7
Other goods and services	**271.1**	**313.4**	**333.3**	**345.4**	**368.6**	**381.3**	**387.2**	**394.4**
Tobacco and smoking products	394.9	502.8	554.2	588.7	730.3	807.3	834.8	853.5
Cigarettes [2]	159.9	203.5	224.8	239.0	297.4	329.0	340.0	347.5
Personal care	165.6	185.6	195.6	201.3	204.6	206.6	208.6	212.1
Personal care products	153.7	154.4	158.3	159.3	162.6	161.1	160.5	162.2
Hair, dental, shaving, and miscellaneous personal care products [2]	103.3	101.8	103.6	104.3	105.4	104.3	102.4	103.1
Cosmetics, perfume, bath, nail preparations and implements	166.8	171.3	177.0	178.0	183.6	182.2	184.3	186.7
Personal care services	178.1	203.9	216.6	223.7	227.6	229.6	230.8	234.2
Haircuts and other personal care services [2]	108.7	124.4	132.1	136.5	138.9	140.1	140.8	142.9
Miscellaneous personal services	252.3	303.0	325.0	338.9	344.5	354.1	362.9	372.7
Legal services [4]	189.3	241.8	260.3	270.7	278.1	288.1	297.4	303.5

See footnotes at end of table.

Table 755. Consumer Price Indexes for All Urban Consumers (CPI-U) for Selected Items and Groups: 2000 to 2012-Continued.

See headnote on page 499.

Item	2000	2005	2007	2008	2009	2010	2011	2012
Funeral expenses [4]	187.8	228.8	252.6	265.4	275.7	282.0	288.3	293.8
SPECIAL AGGREGATE INDEXES								
Commodities	**149.2**	**160.2**	**167.5**	**174.8**	**169.7**	**174.6**	**183.9**	**187.6**
Commodities less food and beverages	137.7	142.5	147.5	153.0	144.4	150.4	159.9	162.7
Nondurables less food and beverages	147.4	168.4	182.5	196.2	179.0	189.9	208.4	213.8
Nondurables less food, beverages, and apparel	162.5	202.6	226.2	248.8	219.6	238.1	267.0	273.2
Durables	125.4	115.3	112.5	110.9	109.9	111.3	112.6	112.8
Services	195.3	230.1	246.8	255.5	259.2	261.3	265.8	271.4
Rent of shelter [3]	201.3	233.7	250.8	257.2	259.9	258.8	262.2	267.8
Transportation services	196.1	225.7	233.7	244.1	251.0	259.8	268.0	272.9
Other services	229.9	268.4	285.6	295.8	304.0	309.6	314.4	322.3
All items less food	173.0	196.0	208.1	215.5	214.0	217.8	224.5	229.0
All items less shelter	165.7	186.1	196.6	205.5	203.3	208.6	217.0	221.4
All items less medical care	167.3	188.7	200.1	207.8	206.6	209.7	216.3	220.6
Commodities less food	139.2	144.5	149.7	155.3	147.1	153.0	162.4	165.3
Nondurables less food	149.1	170.1	184.0	197.3	181.5	191.9	209.6	215.0
Nondurables less food and apparel	162.9	201.2	223.4	244.4	218.7	235.6	262.1	268.2
Nondurables	158.2	180.2	193.5	205.9	198.5	205.3	219.0	224.6
Apparel less footwear	126.2	114.4	113.8	113.4	114.2	113.3	116.2	120.4
Services less rent of shelter [3]	202.9	243.2	260.8	273.0	278.1	284.4	290.6	296.6
Services less medical care services	188.9	221.2	236.8	245.0	248.1	249.6	253.6	258.5
Energy	124.6	177.1	207.7	236.7	193.1	211.4	243.9	246.1
All items less energy	178.6	198.7	208.9	214.8	218.4	220.5	224.8	229.7
All items less food and energy	181.3	200.9	210.7	215.6	219.2	221.3	225.0	229.8
Commodities less food and energy commodities	144.9	140.3	140.1	140.2	142.0	143.6	145.5	147.3
Energy commodities	129.5	197.4	241.0	284.4	205.3	242.6	306.4	316.0
Services less energy services	202.1	236.6	253.1	261.0	265.9	268.3	273.1	279.7
Domestically produced farm food	170.1	195.0	206.5	220.1	220.4	221.6	232.5	238.7
Utilities and public transportation	152.6	176.6	191.3	202.8	200.3	203.1	206.5	207.5

NA Not available. [1] Special indexes based on a substantially smaller sample. [2] December 1997=100. [3] December 1982=100. [4] December 1986=100. [5] December 1983=100. [6] December 2001=100. [7] December 1996=100. [8] December 1988=100. [9] December 2005=100. [10] December 2009=100.

Source: Bureau of Labor Statistics, CPI Databases, "All Urban Consumers (Current Series)," <http://www.bls.gov/cpi/data.htm>, accessed September 2013.

Table 756. Single-Family Housing Price Indexes by State: 2000 to 2012

[Index 1991, 1st quarter = 100. Purchase only indexes. Data are seasonally adjusted. The index reflects average price changes in repeat sales or refinancings on the same properties. Since the data are for the fourth quarter, the index represents the annual percentage change in home values in the fourth quarter of the year shown relative to the fourth quarter of the previous year. The information is obtained by reviewing repeat mortgage transactions on single-family properties whose mortgages have been purchased or securitized by either Fannie Mae or Freddie Mac; for more information on methodology, see Appendix III. Minus sign (-) indicates decrease]

State	2000	2005	2011	2012	Percent Change 2011-12	State	2000	2005	2011	2012	Percent Change 2011-12
U.S.	**144.1**	**217.1**	**180.5**	**190.3**	**5.4**	MO	150.4	197.9	177.4	185.7	4.7
AL	142.7	182.8	174.0	181.1	4.0	MT	179.9	277.3	287.8	307.7	6.9
AK	136.7	207.5	227.1	229.2	1.0	NE	162.8	195.0	193.0	202.7	5.0
AZ	155.7	303.9	166.6	201.8	21.2	NV	128.5	271.2	109.6	130.4	19.0
AR	141.5	185.8	180.0	184.4	2.4	NH	146.7	238.6	192.9	189.5	-1.7
CA	123.6	283.1	152.3	170.7	12.1	NJ	133.7	254.6	209.2	208.1	-0.5
CO	217.3	271.7	258.6	284.9	10.2	NM	145.8	215.4	202.6	203.9	0.6
CT	118.1	195.6	166.3	164.5	-1.0	NY	128.9	214.6	202.2	204.5	1.2
DE	121.5	208.8	177.5	178.4	0.5	NC	146.5	183.1	177.6	179.2	0.9
DC	135.9	327.2	350.3	382.5	9.2	ND	138.0	191.0	233.6	259.1	10.9
FL	139.8	298.9	170.6	187.2	9.7	OH	148.5	175.3	150.8	154.8	2.6
GA	151.6	191.2	149.6	160.3	7.2	OK	144.1	177.9	193.9	199.2	2.7
HI	92.8	204.7	168.9	193.7	14.7	OR	184.4	298.1	248.7	264.1	6.2
ID	154.7	229.7	183.6	208.2	13.4	PA	121.4	190.2	183.4	188.1	2.6
IL	145.9	204.1	167.7	168.9	0.7	RI	120.5	237.4	177.2	179.9	1.5
IN	142.4	165.7	159.0	161.6	1.6	SC	144.9	185.5	176.9	175.1	-1.0
IA	157.7	191.4	194.7	200.3	2.9	SD	160.9	210.1	224.4	232.2	3.5
KS	153.9	187.9	186.9	191.8	2.7	TN	147.4	186.0	182.4	188.7	3.4
KY	150.6	184.4	184.1	189.5	2.9	TX	143.2	172.6	189.7	202.7	6.8
LA	156.9	212.8	225.4	233.5	3.6	UT	194.3	256.6	238.0	265.4	11.5
ME	133.4	221.0	203.5	203.6	0.1	VT	127.1	208.0	210.2	206.6	-1.7
MD	122.4	255.0	204.0	210.9	3.4	VA	131.3	234.6	206.8	215.6	4.2
MA	157.6	254.4	213.6	217.9	2.0	WA	154.9	243.5	205.3	224.8	9.5
MI	173.9	202.0	143.1	154.1	7.7	WV	138.1	180.5	185.0	199.7	8.0
MN	172.9	254.2	200.4	211.7	5.7	WI	166.9	223.8	200.8	200.2	-0.3
MS	142.3	177.7	177.2	175.8	-0.8	WY	169.3	258.9	277.5	300.3	8.2

Source: Federal Housing Finance Agency, "Housing Price Indexes, Quarterly Index Data, Purchase-Only Indexes," <http://www.fhfa.gov/Default.aspx?Page=87>, accessed June 2013.

Table 757. Cost of Living Index-Selected Urban Areas, Annual Average: 2012

[Data are for a selected urban area within the larger metropolitan area shown. Measures relative price levels for consumer goods and services in participating areas for a mid-management standard of living. The nationwide average equals 100 and each index is read as a percent of the national average. The index does not measure inflation, but compares prices at a single point in time. Excludes taxes. Metropolitan areas as defined by the Office of Management and Budget. For definitions, urban areas, and components of MSAs, see source. Beginning February 2008, data are based on an annual average survey compiled from data submitted in the first 3 quarters of the year. To calculate the annual average index, actual and estimated prices are collected to calculate an annual average price for each item used to represent the various spending categories. The share of consumer spending devoted to the category determines that category's importance, or weight, in the Index. Weights are based on the Bureau of Labor Statistics' most recent Consumer Expenditure Survey]

Urban Area	Composite Index (100.0%)	Grocery items (13.56%)	Housing (27.02%)	Utilities (10.3%)	Trans- portation (12.35%)	Health care (4.6%)	Misc. goods and services (32.17%)
Akron, OH.	102.6	108.3	110.7	97.0	105.5	98.2	94.6
Albany, GA.	91.7	106.8	79.0	88.9	96.3	89.7	95.3
Albany, NY.	109.9	104.9	119.1	93.8	109.4	100.2	110.9
Allentown, PA.	102.0	100.9	102.6	111.0	98.1	96.4	101.5
Amarillo, TX.	93.3	91.4	94.1	80.0	95.6	94.6	96.5
Ames, IA.	97.9	94.6	96.6	88.4	103.2	103.0	100.6
Anchorage, AK.	129.6	129.1	153.0	100.4	108.0	136.6	126.9
Anderson, SC.	89.3	102.3	75.4	97.9	90.7	92.8	91.9
Ann Arbor, MI.	102.0	95.1	111.1	107.5	100.4	99.3	96.4
Anniston-Calhoun County, AL.	93.3	98.3	81.3	107.1	92.3	91.8	97.3
Ardmore, OK.	85.9	91.7	78.8	78.7	95.1	90.3	87.5
Asheville, NC.	101.2	105.3	96.0	103.1	101.3	107.8	102.4
Ashland, OH.	87.6	98.8	73.8	86.7	102.1	101.5	87.2
Athens-Henderson County, TX.	91.3	95.5	71.1	98.2	90.3	94.4	104.2
Atlanta, GA.	96.9	106.4	84.3	93.2	105.0	101.1	101.1
Auburn-Opelika, AL.	96.2	102.7	80.2	103.3	92.3	88.5	107.1
Augusta-Aiken, GA-SC.	90.6	93.3	79.1	97.0	97.4	82.7	95.6
Austin, TX.	95.6	89.7	87.8	93.2	99.6	104.5	102.8
Bakersfield, CA.	101.2	101.5	92.2	110.0	107.1	102.8	103.4
Baltimore, MD.	116.3	112.6	155.6	103.6	103.6	101.4	95.9
Baton Rouge, LA.	91.9	99.3	89.6	81.3	92.8	105.4	91.8
Beaufort, SC.	99.2	104.4	90.4	113.5	99.1	94.3	100.5
Beaumont, TX.	93.5	88.4	94.6	86.7	94.5	89.7	97.0
Bergen-Passaic, NJ.	135.0	101.5	197.1	136.1	104.9	105.1	112.4
Bethesda-Gaithersburg-Frederick, MD.	129.7	114.6	196.0	115.1	105.7	100.0	98.6
Birmingham, AL.	88.5	93.3	74.8	104.0	88.7	82.1	93.9
Blacksburg, VA.	94.4	92.5	91.4	88.7	99.5	93.5	97.8
Bloomington, IN.	93.9	98.3	80.0	90.9	106.8	103.0	98.4
Boise, ID.	96.2	98.4	84.4	94.2	101.3	103.6	102.7
Boston, MA.	139.9	118.9	173.6	147.3	107.3	126.4	132.7
Bozeman, MT.	102.9	109.7	105.1	93.6	94.3	102.2	104.7
Bradenton, FL.	99.5	103.2	100.1	96.0	100.4	92.9	99.3
Brazoria County, TX.	90.0	85.3	80.1	91.9	93.1	98.1	97.4
Brownsville, TX.	91.3	87.8	79.4	97.9	97.7	93.6	97.7
Bryan-College Station, TX.	91.3	86.3	92.4	97.5	94.8	91.2	89.1
Buffalo, NY.	98.5	93.0	108.7	107.3	101.9	87.7	89.7
Bullhead City, AZ.	91.9	100.5	84.5	84.3	99.0	94.0	93.9
Burlington, IA.	90.9	96.5	86.3	98.7	87.4	83.8	92.3
Burlington, NC.	95.0	100.5	84.8	81.2	95.2	97.4	105.4
Burlington-Chittenden Co., VT.	119.8	108.9	143.6	128.9	109.2	104.8	107.8
Camden, SC.	94.2	101.2	85.0	104.5	87.1	85.3	99.8
Cape Coral-Fort Myers, FL.	95.6	100.7	86.1	90.9	107.7	96.9	98.0
Carbondale, IL.	94.8	97.3	83.7	99.2	101.0	98.5	98.8
Carlsbad, NM.	90.8	95.1	85.4	88.3	92.3	96.4	92.9
Cedar City, UT.	87.9	98.1	70.0	87.5	95.8	87.6	95.8
Cedar Rapids, IA.	92.1	94.9	78.3	95.0	94.2	95.1	100.2
Champaign-Urbana, IL.	98.8	98.0	93.7	114.1	100.7	110.5	96.1
Chapel Hill, NC.	106.4	102.1	113.7	83.7	98.3	103.2	113.0
Charleston, WV.	94.7	91.7	95.0	100.2	97.6	91.9	93.3
Charleston-N Charleston, SC.	98.4	106.0	85.4	113.2	95.8	105.2	101.4
Charlotte, NC.	94.7	103.2	81.4	100.1	96.9	97.4	99.4
Charlottesville, VA.	105.6	100.0	120.2	93.0	97.8	99.4	103.7
Chattanooga, TN.	94.1	100.1	89.8	93.7	98.0	93.2	94.0
Chicago, IL.	117.2	112.6	137.3	108.0	121.8	101.9	105.5
Cincinnati, OH.	91.9	100.2	78.6	88.8	102.6	103.5	94.7
Cleveland, OH.	101.6	108.4	97.2	98.8	99.2	107.0	103.5
Cleveland, TN.	92.7	98.4	85.5	100.6	93.0	92.4	93.9
Colorado Springs, CO.	96.4	95.3	94.5	96.3	97.9	101.3	97.1
Columbia, MO.	94.4	96.2	81.8	100.8	93.7	99.4	101.6
Columbia, SC.	95.1	103.4	75.7	117.6	106.9	99.0	95.6
Columbus, OH.	89.7	93.4	79.9	95.1	98.1	98.3	90.0
Conroe, TX.	91.9	90.0	80.5	97.5	96.1	97.1	98.2
Conway, AR.	87.9	91.8	78.5	89.0	106.2	83.4	87.6
Cookeville, TN.	89.8	94.3	75.6	78.2	92.8	93.2	102.1
Coppell, TX.	100.5	97.3	92.2	118.7	100.0	116.6	101.0
Corpus Christi, TX.	92.0	83.2	84.5	115.0	95.9	88.0	93.6
Covington, KY.	89.4	91.7	75.0	99.7	98.7	98.4	92.3
Dallas, TX.	98.9	100.1	76.2	118.0	106.6	104.0	107.7
Dalton, GA.	91.1	96.7	75.1	98.6	99.8	94.6	95.9
Danville City, VA.	91.4	92.4	85.3	94.8	96.5	99.5	91.9
Danville, IL.	93.1	92.2	72.5	113.9	113.1	95.6	96.0
Dare County, NC.	109.2	107.1	125.6	94.4	103.1	118.6	101.9
Davenport-Moline-Rock Is., IA-IL.	98.8	96.1	104.2	82.0	110.1	101.4	96.1
Dayton, OH.	93.3	93.8	74.8	107.2	103.2	85.5	101.4
Daytona Beach, FL.	96.2	106.0	86.3	94.5	101.8	99.0	98.3
Decatur, IL.	89.1	90.6	81.5	90.0	95.2	89.9	92.3
Decatur-Hartselle, AL.	90.9	97.3	74.4	103.9	94.2	89.6	96.8

See footnotes at end of table.

Table 757. Cost of Living Index-Selected Urban Areas, Annual Average: 2012-Continued.

See headnote on page 502.

Urban Area	Composite Index (100.0%)	Grocery items (13.56%)	Housing (27.02%)	Utilities (10.3%)	Trans-portation (12.35%)	Health care (4.6%)	Misc. goods and services (32.17%)
Denton, TX...............................	92.3	91.7	80.2	84.7	105.1	98.6	99.5
Denver, CO...............................	104.5	95.5	115.2	90.0	99.2	108.4	105.4
Des Moines, IA...........................	90.2	92.6	87.6	87.5	97.0	85.7	90.4
Detroit, MI................................	97.0	94.1	91.6	104.3	101.8	101.3	98.1
Dodge City, KS...........................	94.3	89.3	83.4	99.7	96.4	94.2	103.2
Dothan, AL................................	90.0	102.2	78.4	90.7	94.0	84.1	93.5
Dover, DE.................................	104.7	111.1	90.7	120.3	98.5	99.8	111.8
Dubuque, IA..............................	93.7	94.2	87.1	87.3	99.2	105.8	97.3
Durham, NC..............................	92.7	99.6	79.1	90.1	100.2	98.0	98.5
Eau Claire, WI...........................	91.0	97.0	77.0	84.2	99.5	110.5	96.3
Edmond, OK..............................	95.2	88.1	90.2	94.7	99.5	92.3	101.3
El Paso, TX...............................	92.6	100.3	86.0	86.9	98.0	87.5	95.5
Elkhart-Goshen, IN......................	91.5	96.2	84.2	86.3	97.6	92.4	94.9
Enid, OK..................................	95.1	100.6	89.8	95.8	96.8	94.9	96.4
Erie, PA...................................	101.9	103.8	104.3	103.1	100.6	93.4	100.5
Evansville, IN............................	95.2	92.6	85.3	100.5	97.3	91.2	102.7
Everett, WA..............................	111.9	106.0	128.0	91.0	111.4	128.8	105.4
Fairbanks, AK............................	139.4	132.5	139.4	240.5	113.7	143.7	119.1
Fargo-Moorhead, ND-MN................	94.8	107.6	84.6	87.4	96.6	102.5	98.4
Fayetteville, AR..........................	86.0	88.8	79.1	86.8	84.7	90.3	90.4
Fayetteville, NC.........................	96.2	107.5	80.7	101.8	93.6	101.5	102.8
Findlay, OH..............................	95.0	102.2	81.2	85.6	97.7	88.4	106.4
Fitchburg-Leominster, MA..............	104.4	99.1	97.7	112.7	108.5	126.7	104.8
Flagstaff, AZ.............................	111.6	111.7	140.3	91.4	105.2	99.8	98.2
Florence, AL.............................	92.1	97.9	80.2	101.5	95.2	82.8	96.8
Fort Lauderdale, FL......................	112.8	110.8	125.8	101.7	111.3	107.3	107.6
Fort Wayne-Allen County, IN...........	91.6	92.0	89.3	79.5	100.1	95.8	93.3
Fort Worth, TX...........................	91.4	90.6	79.0	98.6	97.1	97.4	96.7
Fresno, CA...............................	106.6	106.4	105.7	118.6	111.7	103.5	101.9
Gainesville, FL...........................	98.5	103.2	106.4	97.3	100.8	96.5	89.6
Galesburg, IL............................	90.7	99.9	70.8	102.7	96.2	96.0	96.9
Gastonia, NC............................	91.8	98.0	74.1	101.2	99.8	86.5	98.7
Glenwood Springs, CO..................	108.2	103.0	117.1	96.4	108.0	116.1	105.8
Grand Junction, CO......................	101.9	101.8	108.4	90.9	101.3	107.0	99.6
Grand Rapids, MI........................	93.3	96.1	75.3	99.6	104.6	89.8	101.5
Green Bay, WI............................	96.8	94.0	86.6	104.6	99.5	108.4	101.3
Greenville, NC...........................	95.5	108.2	78.7	96.7	96.0	113.4	101.1
Greenville, SC...........................	93.1	101.5	73.7	97.9	98.0	102.4	101.0
Gunnison, CO............................	105.3	106.6	122.0	90.8	99.9	95.6	98.7
Hammond, LA............................	90.9	97.6	79.4	86.1	93.2	97.7	97.5
Hampton Roads-SE Virginia, VA........	101.0	98.9	104.6	102.2	95.7	101.3	100.5
Harlingen, TX............................	81.8	83.7	75.5	97.3	84.5	92.5	78.7
Harrisburg, PA...........................	100.2	97.4	91.9	117.6	104.2	90.1	102.7
Harrisonburg, VA........................	98.9	97.2	101.9	101.3	90.8	99.3	99.3
Hartford, CT..............................	124.0	119.9	141.1	115.2	114.6	117.7	118.6
Hastings, NE.............................	93.6	100.7	85.9	103.2	90.1	86.2	96.4
Hattiesburg, MS..........................	97.2	103.6	85.4	101.8	98.5	98.3	102.3
Hilton Head Island, SC..................	111.2	109.7	108.6	102.9	102.3	119.3	118.8
Honolulu, HI..............................	167.0	158.1	249.2	167.6	127.8	116.7	123.8
Hot Springs, AR..........................	94.4	104.2	82.0	95.8	93.4	96.8	100.4
Houston, TX..............................	94.9	85.4	95.7	89.5	95.2	98.5	99.2
Huntsville, AL............................	93.2	93.8	78.8	103.3	96.2	96.5	100.1
Hutchinson, KS...........................	91.2	88.4	88.8	87.5	93.8	96.7	93.9
Idaho Falls, ID...........................	88.0	98.2	70.8	90.5	93.8	93.7	94.3
Indiana County, PA......................	96.3	100.4	87.8	105.8	99.9	92.6	97.8
Indianapolis, IN..........................	94.4	94.5	84.2	90.7	97.3	115.1	99.9
Indianapolis-Morgan County, IN........	89.8	95.7	72.8	97.4	91.3	101.3	96.9
Ithaca, NY...............................	104.6	104.6	105.1	109.1	109.2	117.7	99.0
Jackson, MS..............................	93.4	90.0	87.2	106.4	93.4	86.4	96.7
Jackson-Madison County, TN...........	93.2	92.4	74.5	91.4	103.5	88.6	106.6
Jacksonville, FL..........................	96.8	100.0	84.8	104.3	108.5	87.3	100.0
Jacksonville, NC.........................	98.1	105.1	83.9	105.1	95.7	105.2	104.9
Janesville, WI............................	96.4	96.5	81.6	115.0	99.7	103.6	100.6
Jefferson City, MO.......................	92.9	96.4	80.0	97.4	93.3	95.9	100.2
Johnstown, PA............................	97.3	100.3	82.3	113.3	102.1	98.1	101.6
Joliet-Will County, IL....................	100.9	97.6	99.9	113.5	107.7	104.7	96.1
Jonesboro, AR............................	88.8	91.6	81.1	82.2	89.4	86.9	96.2
Joplin, MO...............................	89.8	92.8	76.8	118.9	97.0	95.1	86.5
Juneau, AK...............................	139.8	133.2	171.2	167.9	113.9	146.7	116.2
Kalamazoo, MI...........................	88.8	91.4	73.1	104.0	98.1	93.4	91.6
Kalispell, MT.............................	97.4	107.2	88.2	93.8	100.1	108.7	99.6
Kankakee, IL.............................	98.0	96.4	96.2	102.0	106.6	97.1	95.7
Kansas City, MO-KS......................	99.5	100.6	93.2	105.7	100.5	96.8	102.5
Kennewick-Richland-Pasco, WA........	95.3	96.9	97.1	89.0	99.5	102.8	92.4
Kinston, NC..............................	96.2	102.7	79.8	106.5	107.1	103.0	98.8
Klamath Falls, OR........................	97.0	95.3	87.8	101.7	109.5	115.3	96.5
Knoxville, TN............................	89.3	90.2	85.8	88.9	86.5	91.9	92.7
Kodiak, AK...............................	129.0	148.8	126.3	164.2	125.2	134.8	112.2
Lafayette, IN.............................	92.5	97.8	80.5	100.7	105.4	96.8	92.2
Lafayette, LA.............................	98.2	94.5	111.2	82.5	102.8	85.9	93.8
Lake Charles, LA.........................	95.6	96.0	102.7	84.9	97.6	93.0	92.4
Lake Havasu City, AZ....................	104.3	104.3	120.1	96.8	101.2	104.5	94.7
Laramie, WY.............................	101.7	104.6	109.7	96.1	90.4	100.8	100.0

See footnotes at end of table.

Table 757. Cost of Living Index-Selected Urban Areas, Annual Average: 2012-Continued.

See headnote on page 502.

Urban Area	Composite Index (100.0%)	Grocery items (13.56%)	Housing (27.02%)	Utilities (10.3%)	Transportation (12.35%)	Health care (4.6%)	Misc. goods and services (32.17%)
Las Cruces, NM	97.7	100.7	99.0	89.4	95.1	92.4	99.8
Las Vegas, NV	98.2	101.5	90.1	90.5	104.1	106.5	102.7
Lawton, OK	97.3	96.2	89.5	93.1	111.5	104.9	99.1
Lexington, KY	90.2	91.4	78.1	84.5	99.8	100.8	96.6
Lexington-Buena Vista-Rockbridge, VA	93.2	94.4	93.8	95.5	99.8	89.4	89.5
Lima, OH	96.2	97.6	75.4	99.5	100.7	105.6	108.9
Lincoln, NE	92.9	93.7	81.9	100.5	99.4	96.4	96.3
Little Rock-North Little Rock, AR	100.4	98.3	96.5	108.8	97.9	91.8	104.0
Los Alamos, NM	102.9	96.2	113.2	89.7	103.1	96.0	102.1
Los Angeles-Long Beach, CA	130.8	107.7	197.1	104.6	112.0	107.8	103.8
Louisville, KY	90.8	91.1	81.2	92.9	97.3	90.1	95.7
Lubbock, TX	89.1	94.6	80.5	69.7	97.3	97.6	95.9
Lufkin, TX	92.9	95.7	85.5	87.1	96.4	116.0	95.2
Lynchburg, VA	92.4	94.0	82.1	106.8	90.0	100.1	95.5
Madison, WI	109.3	101.3	111.6	108.0	105.7	121.7	110.8
Manchester, NH	119.7	100.2	126.6	125.6	104.1	114.4	126.9
Manhattan, KS	92.9	93.0	95.3	85.7	94.1	91.7	92.9
Mankato, MN	95.6	101.9	80.5	98.8	104.1	108.1	99.5
Marietta, GA	98.5	98.8	91.5	95.5	103.8	98.3	103.3
Marion-McDowell County, NC	93.8	103.8	88.3	102.8	91.1	100.3	91.4
Marshfield, WI	100.7	100.7	93.5	103.8	98.4	105.1	106.1
Martinsville-Henry County, VA	89.1	97.3	81.0	82.8	84.2	99.9	94.8
Mason City, IA	92.6	94.0	89.1	100.3	93.1	96.2	91.9
McAllen, TX	85.4	85.6	74.1	93.7	88.6	88.7	90.3
Memphis, TN	86.0	93.3	71.8	83.9	90.9	97.9	91.8
Miami-Dade County, FL	109.0	109.2	117.3	101.0	112.1	108.4	103.4
Middlesex-Monmouth, NJ	124.6	108.0	158.5	128.2	103.3	112.6	111.8
Milwaukee-Waukesha, WI	100.9	98.4	105.3	105.0	98.9	115.8	95.5
Minneapolis, MN	108.8	104.4	118.4	101.5	101.3	102.7	108.6
Minot, ND	105.1	100.0	120.3	72.9	102.0	106.4	106.0
Mobile, AL	93.3	100.1	83.3	103.6	93.3	87.6	96.2
Monroe, LA	95.6	94.7	91.9	85.5	95.8	100.0	101.6
Montgomery, AL	95.9	101.6	88.6	105.4	99.0	89.6	96.2
Morristown, TN	90.8	94.9	76.5	92.7	95.0	94.7	98.2
Moses Lake, WA	94.0	100.4	83.4	73.9	101.9	118.5	100.0
Murfreesboro-Smyrna, TN	90.2	96.6	78.5	90.2	90.1	97.8	96.2
Muskogee, OK	86.9	94.9	70.9	95.5	84.5	107.1	92.2
Myrtle Beach, SC	94.8	105.9	74.3	116.8	93.6	102.5	99.7
Nacogdoches, TX	92.9	93.8	83.6	101.2	93.9	101.4	96.3
Nashville-Franklin, TN	88.9	95.7	74.1	87.1	93.9	85.9	97.7
Nassau County, NY	132.4	119.4	181.0	121.9	106.9	110.1	113.5
New Haven, CT	127.9	115.8	147.6	115.2	119.3	120.6	124.8
New York (Brooklyn), NY	178.6	127.8	342.6	124.7	106.1	111.4	116.9
New York (Manhattan), NY	225.4	149.7	454.5	128.9	123.6	129.6	148.5
New York (Queens), NY	148.3	124.8	226.8	128.2	113.5	111.0	117.5
Newark-Elizabeth, NJ	129.7	112.6	170.7	137.2	106.0	103.1	113.0
Norman, OK	85.6	91.0	78.0	86.8	98.0	81.2	85.2
Oakland, CA	135.0	122.5	203.5	96.0	104.3	109.7	110.6
Odessa, TX	93.9	89.6	97.9	86.8	94.1	94.3	94.6
Ogden, UT	94.3	97.3	84.1	91.1	101.6	89.2	100.6
Oklahoma City, OK	90.8	88.7	86.9	89.5	97.2	100.7	91.5
Olympia, WA	105.9	104.4	107.4	88.1	111.5	116.6	107.2
Omaha, NE	89.6	94.4	80.9	89.9	99.6	99.0	89.6
Orange County, CA	140.6	108.5	235.1	105.2	114.0	108.4	101.1
Orlando, FL	97.7	100.8	80.6	109.7	100.6	93.3	106.3
Paducah, KY	91.3	93.1	85.7	93.4	90.8	92.9	94.5
Palm Springs, CA	119.8	109.0	151.6	106.6	111.2	101.1	107.8
Paris, TX	91.4	92.3	85.2	95.2	102.0	95.3	90.3
Peoria, IL	100.9	96.4	97.2	96.8	108.3	98.9	104.6
Philadelphia, PA	122.9	122.2	140.6	131.6	105.6	102.6	114.9
Phoenix, AZ	96.8	101.0	94.7	95.4	105.6	94.6	94.2
Pierre, SD	102.1	105.9	114.8	99.3	94.8	100.2	93.9
Pittsburgh, PA	94.5	101.1	79.4	99.8	106.6	94.1	98.3
Plano, TX	100.6	99.5	92.5	116.3	101.5	98.7	102.8
Ponca City, OK	90.1	94.1	78.6	94.3	84.6	90.6	99.0
Portland, ME	110.8	105.0	129.0	102.5	101.7	113.5	103.8
Portland, OR	115.7	105.3	132.8	104.0	118.4	114.6	108.7
Prescott-Prescott Valley, AZ	98.6	103.3	100.2	89.4	97.4	99.2	98.6
Providence, RI	123.4	111.0	131.7	127.3	105.3	116.5	128.5
Provo-Orem, UT	96.2	100.1	83.7	88.1	108.7	94.4	103.1
Pryor Creek, OK	89.0	92.1	76.9	91.8	92.5	92.4	95.2
Pueblo, CO	87.1	95.4	73.3	93.7	100.9	87.1	87.7
Punta Gorda-Charlotte Co., FL	93.8	99.7	74.5	99.6	103.1	112.3	99.3
Raleigh, NC	90.8	101.0	71.6	104.8	95.9	93.6	95.7
Reno-Sparks, NV	92.3	101.5	85.9	76.4	109.3	99.2	91.3
Richmond, IN	90.9	94.4	77.8	88.1	102.3	96.1	96.3
Richmond, VA	102.1	103.5	91.4	105.9	101.1	114.7	107.9
Rio Rancho, NM	98.2	98.1	88.3	97.3	99.1	97.7	106.7
Riverside City, CA	113.0	108.0	139.9	104.6	111.8	101.1	97.4
Roanoke, VA	91.5	92.5	88.6	95.0	93.7	87.5	92.0
Rochester, MN	101.4	96.0	96.9	114.7	102.3	109.6	101.6
Rochester, NY	102.8	96.7	100.1	98.3	109.4	101.8	106.8
Rockford, IL	92.6	96.2	78.6	102.1	99.5	103.4	95.6

See footnotes at end of table.

ProQuest Statistical Abstract of the United States: 2014

Table 757. Cost of Living Index-Selected Urban Areas, Annual Average: 2012-Continued.

See headnote on page 502.

Urban Area	Composite Index (100.0%)	Grocery items (13.56%)	Housing (27.02%)	Utilities (10.3%)	Trans-portation (12.35%)	Health care (4.6%)	Misc. goods and services (32.17%)
Round Rock, TX..........................	92.5	84.4	86.6	101.5	97.4	97.8	95.3
Sacramento, CA........................	117.7	110.8	144.7	115.4	110.5	106.1	103.2
Salina, KS..............................	90.1	93.3	78.7	86.7	94.5	91.7	97.6
Salt Lake City, UT......................	95.2	96.6	89.0	82.4	101.1	97.8	101.4
San Angelo, TX........................	89.8	86.5	78.4	106.1	95.4	90.1	93.3
San Antonio, TX........................	88.5	81.9	82.2	84.2	98.7	97.3	92.7
San Diego, CA.........................	131.9	110.4	201.1	97.0	109.7	111.9	105.3
San Francisco, CA.....................	163.4	121.5	295.0	95.5	110.3	114.7	119.5
San Jose, CA..........................	153.4	121.4	263.9	126.6	111.4	118.2	103.9
San Marcos, TX........................	87.6	85.4	81.8	83.8	95.9	89.3	91.3
Sarasota, FL...........................	99.5	104.9	92.3	100.1	103.7	109.3	100.0
Savannah, GA..........................	91.0	97.3	73.6	107.0	97.0	90.0	95.6
Scottsdale, AZ.........................	115.4	103.2	149.9	92.5	110.0	101.9	102.9
Seattle, WA............................	115.2	108.2	135.3	91.5	108.6	118.8	111.0
Seguin, TX.............................	91.2	85.3	88.2	104.0	93.0	88.0	91.8
Sherman-Denison, TX...................	88.2	90.6	77.0	93.6	91.4	91.7	93.3
Shreveport-Bossier City, LA............	98.2	94.8	95.3	96.6	94.2	93.6	104.9
Sierra Vista, AZ........................	102.5	97.8	102.9	103.4	106.6	99.5	102.7
Slidell-St. Tammany Parish, LA.........	94.6	96.8	89.5	88.7	98.5	94.2	98.4
South Bend, IN.........................	91.0	95.7	78.9	77.4	95.2	96.9	101.2
Spartanburg, SC.......................	94.6	103.5	78.9	91.0	98.8	99.6	102.9
Spokane, WA...........................	96.2	96.7	88.0	99.6	100.8	103.6	99.1
Springfield, IL.........................	87.7	90.8	71.8	84.8	103.1	100.9	93.0
Springfield, MO........................	89.9	97.3	78.1	92.6	96.2	96.2	92.5
St. Cloud, MN..........................	96.2	107.0	78.1	98.9	98.3	111.2	102.9
St. George, UT.........................	92.1	98.1	82.2	87.1	95.3	92.7	98.2
St. Louis, MO-IL........................	91.6	96.8	74.2	107.4	98.2	96.0	95.7
St. Paul, MN...........................	108.0	102.6	115.9	100.0	101.8	103.2	109.4
Stamford, CT...........................	146.1	116.8	208.1	132.4	118.5	120.3	125.2
Staunton-Augusta County, VA...........	94.6	95.3	92.7	98.6	94.5	98.0	94.1
Stillwater, OK..........................	90.6	94.9	85.9	99.5	89.6	88.9	90.6
Sumter, SC............................	90.5	103.1	80.1	98.0	89.6	89.3	91.9
Tacoma, WA............................	107.8	104.1	102.1	98.1	109.3	109.4	116.4
Tampa, FL..............................	93.0	98.7	78.2	95.6	104.1	98.7	97.0
Temple, TX.............................	88.5	83.8	78.3	99.6	89.5	95.6	94.1
Texarkana, TX-AR......................	93.2	94.0	84.0	89.9	92.6	95.0	101.5
Thomasville-Lexington, NC..............	90.6	104.6	78.7	84.3	88.5	109.4	95.0
Topeka, KS.............................	92.5	95.0	87.2	81.5	96.5	93.0	97.8
Tucson, AZ.............................	95.5	98.7	83.9	89.2	103.6	105.8	101.2
Tulsa, OK..............................	89.2	91.6	66.8	97.1	98.4	94.6	100.1
Tupelo, MS.............................	89.0	90.9	72.9	107.4	93.2	88.5	94.1
Tuscaloosa, AL.........................	98.2	108.5	78.4	108.9	102.6	92.6	106.0
Twin Falls, ID..........................	92.0	89.6	83.1	99.5	98.9	92.7	95.5
Tyler, TX...............................	94.0	91.2	90.1	94.6	99.3	90.8	96.8
Valdosta, GA...........................	96.7	104.2	89.0	105.6	98.4	106.1	95.0
Vancouver, WA.........................	103.6	99.8	97.1	96.9	111.1	112.3	108.8
Vero Beach-Indian River, FL............	101.7	109.8	91.6	109.4	98.4	103.4	105.3
Waco, TX...............................	91.6	83.7	89.0	84.4	101.5	93.1	95.3
Washington-Arlington-Alexandria, DC-VA.........	144.7	113.4	256.6	105.5	106.5	101.1	97.3
Waterloo-Cedar Falls, IA................	92.8	93.0	93.0	85.2	97.4	103.4	91.7
Wausau, WI............................	96.6	101.6	83.0	107.1	99.6	105.0	100.2
Weatherford, TX........................	93.7	102.2	79.0	95.5	98.5	94.4	99.9
Wichita Falls, TX.......................	86.4	90.0	86.2	82.8	83.1	94.1	86.5
Wichita, KS............................	91.4	89.3	79.0	98.7	99.6	93.5	96.9
Williamsport-Lycoming Co., PA..........	98.6	98.4	98.0	121.5	95.1	99.2	92.9
Wilmington, DE.........................	111.6	109.5	110.5	125.1	105.8	101.6	112.8
Wilmington, NC.........................	99.1	107.7	84.5	112.2	100.3	96.0	103.6
Winchester, VA-WV.....................	101.5	102.7	93.7	102.5	95.7	106.9	108.6
Winston-Salem, NC.....................	88.5	100.4	71.0	93.2	85.6	103.0	95.8
Wooster, OH...........................	92.9	96.2	82.5	111.3	95.8	89.7	93.7
Yakima, WA............................	92.5	100.2	86.8	77.8	101.2	106.5	93.5
York County, PA........................	100.2	101.5	96.0	102.5	99.9	98.4	103.0
Youngstown-Warren, OH................	88.2	87.1	80.2	105.7	86.3	84.5	91.0
Yuma, AZ..............................	105.2	109.3	100.2	124.9	99.9	98.2	104.5

Source: C2ER, Arlington, VA, Cost of Living Index, Annual Average 2012 ©. See also <http://www.c2er.org>.

Table 758. Average Prices of Selected Fuels and Electricity: 1990 to 2012

[In dollars per unit, except electricity, in cents per kWh. Represents price to end-users, except as noted]

Item	Unit	1990	2000	2005	2006	2007	2008	2009	2010	2011	2012
Crude oil, composite [1]	Barrel	22.22	28.26	50.24	60.24	67.94	94.74	59.29	76.69	101.87	100.94
Motor gasoline: [2]											
Unleaded regular	Gallon	1.16	1.51	2.30	2.59	2.80	3.27	2.35	2.79	3.53	3.64
Unleaded premium	Gallon	1.35	1.69	2.49	2.81	3.03	3.52	2.61	3.05	3.79	3.92
No. 2 heating oil	Gallon	0.73	0.93	1.71	1.98	2.24	2.99	1.96	2.46	3.19	3.36
No. 2 diesel fuel	Gallon	0.73	0.94	1.79	2.10	2.27	3.15	1.83	2.31	3.12	3.20
Propane, consumer grade	Gallon	0.75	0.60	1.09	1.36	1.49	1.89	1.22	1.48	1.71	1.14
Residual fuel oil	Gallon	0.44	0.60	1.05	1.22	1.37	1.96	1.34	1.71	2.40	2.59
Natural gas, residential	1,000 cu/ft	5.80	7.76	12.70	13.73	13.08	13.89	12.14	11.39	11.03	10.68
Electricity, residential	kWh	7.83	8.24	9.45	10.40	10.65	11.26	11.51	11.54	11.72	11.88

[1] Refiner acquisition cost. [2] Average, all service.

Source: U.S. Energy Information Administration, *Monthly Energy Review*, April 2013. See also <http://www.eia.gov/totalenergy/data/monthly/index.cfm>.

Table 759. Retail Gasoline Prices—Selected Areas: 2000 to 2012

[In dollars per gallon. Prices are annual averages]

Area	Regular				Midgrade				Premium			
	2000	2005	2010	2012	2000	2005	2010	2012	2000	2005	2010	2012
Boston, MA	(NA)	2.26	2.74	3.64	(NA)	2.36	2.87	3.82	(NA)	2.46	2.98	3.94
Chicago, IL	1.57	2.32	2.94	3.85	1.67	2.42	3.05	3.99	1.78	2.52	3.16	4.11
Cleveland, OH	(NA)	2.22	2.75	3.58	(NA)	2.32	2.86	3.70	(NA)	2.43	2.96	3.81
Denver, CO	1.54	2.24	2.65	3.48	1.67	2.35	2.77	3.60	1.78	2.45	2.89	3.71
Houston, TX	1.45	2.17	2.59	3.42	1.56	2.27	2.74	3.60	1.65	2.37	2.87	3.74
Los Angeles, CA	1.62	2.49	3.11	4.09	1.72	2.59	3.21	4.19	1.81	2.68	3.31	4.29
Miami, FL	(NA)	2.39	2.86	3.71	(NA)	2.49	3.01	3.91	(NA)	2.59	3.11	4.02
New York, NY	1.63	2.30	2.81	3.72	1.73	2.42	2.96	3.91	1.80	2.51	3.07	4.03
San Francisco, CA	1.88	2.48	3.12	4.04	1.98	2.59	3.23	4.15	2.09	2.69	3.34	4.25
Seattle, WA	(NA)	2.36	3.00	3.85	(NA)	2.47	3.12	3.98	(NA)	2.58	3.23	4.09

NA Not available.

Source: U.S. Energy Information Administration, "Weekly Retail Gasoline and Diesel Prices," <http://www.eia.gov/dnav/pet/pet_pri_gnd_a_epm0_pte_dpgal_w.htm>, accessed May 2013.

Table 760. Weekly Food Cost of a Nutritious Diet by Type of Family and Individual: 2010 and 2012

[In dollars. As of December. Assumes that food for all meals and snacks is purchased at the store and prepared at home. All four Food Plans are based on 2001-02 data and updated to current dollars by using the Consumer Price Index for specific food items. See source for details]

Family type	Thrifty plan		Low-cost plan		Moderate plan		Liberal plan	
	2010	2012	2010	2012	2010	2012	2010	2012
FAMILIES								
Family of two:								
19 to 50 years	81.10	87.30	103.40	111.50	128.40	138.70	160.80	173.30
51 to 70 years	76.90	82.50	99.20	106.70	122.60	132.30	148.00	159.20
Family of four:								
Couple, 19 to 50 years and children—								
2 to 3 and 4 to 5 years	118.10	127.00	150.20	161.50	185.50	199.70	229.90	247.40
6 to 8 and 9 to 11 years	135.60	145.70	176.60	190.70	221.00	237.70	268.50	288.60
INDIVIDUALS [1]								
Child:								
1 year	20.10	21.30	26.80	28.50	30.60	32.30	37.10	39.50
2 to 3 years	21.70	23.30	27.50	29.40	33.30	35.70	40.50	43.40
4 to 5 years	22.70	24.30	28.70	30.70	35.50	37.90	43.30	46.40
6 to 8 years	28.80	31.10	39.20	42.60	48.20	51.70	56.90	61.10
9 to 11 years	33.00	35.20	43.40	46.70	56.10	59.90	65.50	69.90
Male:								
12 to 13 years	35.10	37.80	49.50	53.40	61.70	67.00	72.70	78.30
14 to 18 years	36.20	38.90	50.80	54.50	63.80	68.90	73.40	79.10
19 to 50 years	39.00	42.00	50.30	54.20	62.90	68.00	77.10	83.30
51 to 70 years	35.60	38.30	47.60	51.10	58.60	63.20	71.10	76.30
71 years and over	35.80	38.60	47.00	50.80	58.50	62.70	71.90	77.30
Female:								
12 to 13 years	35.30	37.90	42.90	46.20	51.90	55.20	63.00	67.70
14 to 18 years	34.80	37.30	43.10	46.40	52.00	56.10	63.90	69.10
19 to 50 years	34.70	37.40	43.70	47.10	53.80	58.20	69.00	74.30
51 to 70 years	34.30	36.80	42.50	45.90	52.90	57.00	63.50	68.40
71 years and over	33.80	36.00	42.10	45.70	52.50	56.60	63.40	68.00

[1] The costs given are for individuals in 4-person families. For individuals in other size families, the following adjustments are suggested: 1-person, add 20 percent; 2-person, add 10 percent; 3-person, add 5 percent; 5- or 6-person, subtract 5 percent; and 7-or-more person, subtract 10 percent.

Source: U.S. Department of Agriculture, Center for Nutrition Policy and Promotion, *Official USDA Food Plans: Cost of Food at Home at Four Levels, U.S. Average, December 2012*, January 2013, and earlier reports. See also <http://www.cnpp.usda.gov/USDAFoodCost-Home.htm>.

Table 761. Food—Retail Prices of Selected Items: 2000 to 2012

[In dollars per pound, except as indicated. As of December. See Appendix III]

Food	2000	2010	2012	Food	2000	2010	2012
Cereals and bakery products:				Fresh fruits and vegetables:			
Flour, white, all purpose...............	0.28	0.44	0.50	Apples, Red Delicious....................	0.82	1.20	1.42
Rice, white, lg. grain, raw................	(NA)	0.73	0.71	Bananas..................................	0.49	0.59	0.61
Spaghetti and macaroni.................	0.88	1.19	1.31	Oranges, navel...........................	0.62	1.02	1.04
Bread, white, pan......................	0.99	1.39	1.44	Grapefruit................................	0.58	0.99	1.07
Bread, whole wheat.....................	1.36	1.88	1.93	Grapes, Thompson seedless...........	2.36	2.87	3.09
Beef:				Lemons...................................	1.11	1.60	1.53
Ground beef, 100% beef...............	1.63	2.38	3.08	Pears, Anjou.............................	(NA)	1.42	(NA)
Ground chuck, 100% beef..............	1.98	2.93	3.46	Potatoes, white..........................	0.35	0.58	0.62
Ground beef, lean and extra lean.......	2.33	3.49	4.21	Lettuce, iceberg.........................	0.85	0.99	0.87
Round steak, USDA Choice.............	3.28	4.30	4.70	Tomatoes, field grown...................	1.57	1.59	1.59
Sirloin steak, boneless..................	4.81	6.07	6.78				
Pork:				Processed fruits and vegetables:			
Bacon, sliced...........................	3.03	4.16	4.64	Orange juice, frozen concentrate,			
Chops, center cut, bone-in..............	3.46	3.58	3.57	12 oz. can, per 16 oz....................	1.88	2.46	2.60
Ham, boneless, excluding				Sugar and sweets:			
canned...............................	2.75	3.47	3.74	Sugar, white, all sizes...................	0.41	0.64	0.68
Poultry, fish, and eggs:				Sugar, white, 33–80 oz. pkg.............	0.40	0.62	0.68
Chicken, fresh, whole...................	1.08	1.28	1.48	Fats and oils:			
Chicken legs, bone-in...................	1.26	1.48	1.65	Margarine, stick.........................	(NA)	1.12	(NA)
Turkey, frozen, whole...................	0.99	1.38	1.43	Margarine, tubs, soft....................	0.84	1.62	2.08
Eggs, Grade A, large, (dozen)..........	0.96	1.79	2.01	Peanut butter, creamy, all sizes........	1.96	1.99	2.90
Dairy products:							
Milk, fresh, whole, fortified				Nonalcoholic beverages:			
(per gal.)............................	2.79	3.32	3.58	Coffee, 100% ground roast,			
Butter, salted, grade AA, stick..........	2.80	3.42	(NA)	all sizes...............................	3.2	4.1	5.9
American processed cheese............	3.69	3.80	4.24				
Cheddar cheese, natural...............	3.76	4.93	5.87	Other prepared foods:			
Ice cream, prepack., bulk, reg.				Potato chips, per 16 oz..................	3.4	4.7	4.7
(1/2 gal.)............................	3.66	4.58	5.10				

NA Not available.

Source: U.S. Bureau of Labor Statistics, *CPI Detailed Report*, December 2012, and earlier reports. See also <http://www.bls.gov/cpi/cpi_dr.htm>.

Table 762. Indexes of Spot Primary Market Prices: 1990 to 2012

[1967 = 100. Represents unweighted geometric average of price quotations of 23 commodities. Computed daily and therefore much more sensitive to changes in market conditions than a monthly producer price index]

Items and number	1990	1995	2000	2004	2005	2006	2007	2008	2009	2010	2011	2012
All commodities (23).....	**258.1**	**289.1**	**224.0**	**293.0**	**303.3**	**362.4**	**413.4**	**313.0**	**424.2**	**520.3**	**481.8**	**482.1**
Foodstuffs (10)..............	206.4	236.4	184.7	256.0	241.7	276.0	335.9	294.2	344.7	440.3	435.5	423.9
Raw industrials (13).........	301.2	332.2	255.8	321.5	354.7	437.3	477.0	326.5	489.4	583.8	516.5	526.8
Livestock and products (5)..	292.7	307.4	265.5	365.0	326.6	378.6	402.6	310.8	407.6	528.0	575.4	599.7
Metals (5)...................	283.2	300.6	214.0	357.7	440.9	693.9	811.9	390.9	809.1	1,006.2	837.8	918.7
Textiles and fibers (4).......	257.6	274.3	245.7	237.9	252.5	254.4	267.5	241.3	294.0	342.1	290.2	276.8
Fats and oils (4).............	188.7	226.7	163.6	262.6	223.4	273.9	363.4	268.0	339.7	478.3	497.7	471.5

Source: Commodity Research Bureau, Chicago, IL, *CRB Commodity Index Report*, weekly ©. See also <http://www.crbtrader.com>.

Table 763. Commodity Research Bureau Futures Price Index: 1990 to 2012

[1967 = 100. Index computed daily. Represents unweighted geometric average of commodity futures prices (through 6 months forward) of 17 major commodity futures markets. Represents end of year index]

Commodity	1990	1995	2000	2004	2005	2006	2007	2008	2009	2010	2011	2012
All commodities............	**222.6**	**243.2**	**227.8**	**283.9**	**347.9**	**394.9**	**476.1**	**363.1**	**484.4**	**629.5**	**563.0**	**554.6**
Softs [1]...........................	276.0	354.4	254.4	343.5	420.5	475.9	467.5	487.2	(NA)	(NA)	(NA)	(NA)
Industrials.......................	245.5	272.5	211.0	232.1	302.5	368.8	418.3	475.4	(NA)	(NA)	(NA)	(NA)
Grains and Oilseeds [2].........	171.2	218.6	174.9	177.0	193.8	279.1	427.0	545.5	(NA)	(NA)	(NA)	(NA)
Energy...........................	246.0	180.0	355.8	457.3	705.3	591.6	825.1	1263.2	(NA)	(NA)	(NA)	(NA)
Oilseeds [3].......................	223.6	277.5	[3]	[3]	[3]	[3]	[3]	[3]	[3]	[3]	[3]	[3]
Livestock and Meats..........	226.2	192.4	253.6	303.6	300.3	294.6	297.7	337.0	(NA)	(NA)	(NA)	(NA)
Metals (precious).............	257.8	276.0	265.7	396.6	478.1	611.9	773.6	894.6	(NA)	(NA)	(NA)	(NA)

NA Not available. [1] Prior to 1997, reported as imported. Softs include commodities that are grown and not mined such as coffee, cocoa, lumber, cotton, and sugar. [2] Prior to 1997, reported as grains. [3] Incorporated into grains and oilseeds beginning 1997.

Source: Commodity Research Bureau (CRB), Chicago, IL, *CRB Commodity Index Report*, weekly ©. See also <http://www.crbtrader.com>.

Table 764. Producer Price Indexes by Stage of Processing: 1990 to 2012

[1982 = 100. Minus sign (-) indicates decrease. For information on producer prices, see Bureau of Labor Statistics, <http://stats.bls.gov/opub/hom/homch14_itc.htm>. See also Appendix III]

Year	Crude materials — Total	Crude materials — Foodstuffs and feedstuffs	Crude materials — Fuel	Crude materials — Crude nonfood materials, except fuel	Intermediate materials and supplies, components	Finished goods — Total	Finished goods — Consumer goods	Finished goods — Capital equipment	Consumer foods — Crude	Consumer foods — Processed	Finished consumer goods, excluding food
1990	108.9	113.1	84.8	107.3	114.5	119.2	118.2	122.9	123.0	124.2	115.3
1991	101.2	105.5	82.9	97.5	114.4	121.7	120.5	126.7	119.3	124.4	118.7
1992	100.4	105.1	84.0	94.2	114.7	123.2	121.7	129.1	107.6	124.4	120.8
1993	102.4	108.4	87.1	94.1	116.2	124.7	123.0	131.4	114.4	126.5	121.7
1994	101.8	106.5	82.4	97.0	118.5	125.5	123.3	134.1	111.3	127.9	121.6
1995	102.7	105.8	72.1	105.8	124.9	127.9	125.6	136.7	118.8	129.8	124.0
1996	113.8	121.5	92.6	105.7	125.7	131.3	129.5	138.3	129.2	133.8	127.6
1997	111.1	112.2	101.3	103.5	125.6	131.8	130.2	138.2	126.6	135.1	128.2
1998	96.8	103.9	86.7	84.5	123.0	130.7	128.9	137.6	127.2	134.8	126.4
1999	98.2	98.7	91.2	91.1	123.2	133.0	132.0	137.6	125.5	135.9	130.5
2000	120.6	100.2	136.9	118.0	129.2	138.0	138.2	138.8	123.5	138.3	138.4
2001	121.0	106.1	151.4	101.5	129.7	140.7	141.5	139.7	127.7	142.4	141.4
2002	108.1	99.5	117.3	101.0	127.8	138.9	139.4	139.1	128.5	141.0	138.8
2003	135.3	113.5	185.7	116.9	133.7	143.3	145.3	139.5	130.0	147.2	144.7
2004	159.0	127.0	211.4	149.2	142.6	148.5	151.7	141.4	138.2	153.9	150.9
2005	182.2	122.7	279.7	176.7	154.0	155.7	160.4	144.6	140.2	156.9	161.9
2006	184.8	119.3	241.5	210.0	164.0	160.4	166.0	146.9	151.3	157.1	169.2
2007	207.1	146.7	236.8	238.7	170.7	166.6	173.5	149.5	170.2	166.7	175.6
2008	251.8	163.4	298.3	308.5	188.3	177.1	186.3	153.8	175.5	178.6	189.1
2009	175.2	134.5	166.3	211.1	172.5	172.5	179.1	156.7	157.8	177.3	179.4
2010	212.2	152.4	188.0	280.8	183.4	179.8	189.1	157.3	172.6	183.3	190.4
2011	249.4	188.4	181.5	342.0	199.8	190.5	203.3	159.7	182.3	195.0	205.5
2012	241.3	196.3	143.9	332.4	200.7	194.2	207.3	162.8	167.9	202.0	209.1
PERCENT CHANGE [1]											
1990	5.6	1.7	-0.6	12.0	2.2	4.9	5.4	3.5	2.8	4.9	5.9
1991	-7.1	-6.7	-2.2	-9.1	-0.1	2.1	1.9	3.1	-3.0	0.0	2.9
1992	-0.8	-0.4	1.3	-3.4	0.3	1.2	1.0	1.9	-9.8	0.0	1.8
1993	2.0	3.1	3.7	-0.1	1.3	1.2	1.1	1.8	6.3	1.7	0.7
1994	-0.6	-1.8	-5.4	3.1	2.0	0.6	0.2	2.1	-2.7	1.1	-0.1
1995	0.9	-0.7	-12.5	9.1	5.4	1.9	1.9	1.9	6.7	1.5	2.0
1996	10.8	14.8	28.4	-0.1	0.6	2.7	3.1	1.2	8.8	3.1	2.9
1997	-2.4	-7.7	9.4	-2.1	-0.1	0.4	0.5	-0.1	-2.0	1.0	0.5
1998	-12.9	-7.4	-14.4	-18.4	-2.1	-0.8	-1.0	-0.4	0.5	-0.2	-1.4
1999	1.4	-5.0	5.2	7.8	0.2	1.8	2.4	0.0	-1.3	0.8	3.2
2000	22.8	1.5	50.1	29.5	4.9	3.8	4.7	0.9	-1.6	1.8	6.1
2001	0.3	5.9	10.6	-14.0	0.4	2.0	2.4	0.6	3.4	3.0	2.2
2002	-10.7	-6.2	-22.5	-0.5	-1.5	-1.3	-1.5	-0.4	0.6	-1.0	-1.8
2003	25.2	14.1	58.3	15.7	4.6	3.2	4.2	0.3	1.2	4.4	4.3
2004	17.5	11.9	13.8	27.6	6.7	3.6	4.4	1.4	6.3	4.6	4.3
2005	14.6	-3.4	32.3	18.4	8.0	4.8	5.7	2.3	1.4	1.9	7.3
2006	1.4	-2.8	-13.7	18.8	6.5	3.0	3.5	1.6	7.9	0.1	4.5
2007	12.1	23.0	-1.9	13.7	4.1	3.9	4.5	1.8	12.5	6.1	3.8
2008	21.6	11.4	26.0	29.2	10.3	6.3	7.4	2.9	3.1	7.1	7.7
2009	-30.4	-17.7	-44.3	-31.6	-8.4	-2.6	-3.9	1.9	-10.1	-0.7	-5.1
2010	21.1	13.3	13.0	33.0	6.3	4.2	5.6	0.4	9.4	3.4	6.1
2011	17.5	23.6	-3.5	21.8	8.9	6.0	7.5	1.5	5.6	6.4	7.9
2012	-3.2	4.2	-20.7	-2.8	0.5	1.9	2.0	1.9	-7.9	3.6	1.8

[1] Change from immediate prior year. 1990, change from 1989.

Source: U.S. Bureau of Labor Statistics, PPI Databases, "Commodity Data Including Stage-of-Processing Indexes," <http://www.bls.gov/ppi/#data>, accessed July 2013.

Table 765. Producer Price Indexes by Stage of Processing and Commodity: 1990 to 2012

[1982=100, except as indicated. See Appendix III]

Stage of processing	1990	1995	2000	2005	2009	2010	2011	2012
Finished goods.....................................	**119.2**	**127.9**	**138.0**	**155.7**	**172.5**	**179.8**	**190.5**	**194.2**
Finished consumer goods....................	**118.2**	**125.6**	**138.2**	**160.4**	**179.1**	**189.1**	**203.3**	**207.3**
Finished consumer foods....................	**124.4**	**129.0**	**137.2**	**155.7**	**175.5**	**182.4**	**193.9**	**199.0**
Fresh fruits and melons............................	118.1	85.8	91.4	102.8	110.4	123.8	117.7	119.0
Fresh and dry vegetables..........................	118.1	144.4	126.7	142.6	162.2	178.5	195.1	156.5
Eggs for fresh use (December 1991=100)..........	(NA)	86.3	84.9	79.6	123.3	123.4	138.4	138.7
Bakery products..................................	141.0	164.3	182.3	201.1	245.8	244.8	253.6	261.1
Milled rice......................................	102.5	113.1	101.2	120.1	205.8	183.6	200.2	201.6
Pasta products (June 1985=100)..................	114.1	125.0	121.6	127.9	180.3	170.7	185.8	205.0
Beef and veal....................................	116.0	100.9	113.7	147.4	142.4	157.1	180.7	198.8
Pork...	119.8	101.5	113.4	131.9	115.7	142.6	160.4	153.8
Processed young chickens.........................	111.0	113.5	110.4	136.2	147.7	149.0	143.5	166.6
Processed turkeys................................	107.6	104.9	98.7	105.1	119.9	132.1	148.7	146.4
Finfish and shellfish............................	147.2	170.8	198.1	222.6	250.9	272.4	287.6	287.5
Dairy products..................................	117.2	119.7	133.7	154.5	157.1	174.0	195.9	192.8
Processed fruits and vegetables...................	124.7	122.4	128.6	140.4	176.2	176.6	183.2	192.2
Confectionery end products.......................	140.0	160.7	170.6	205.1	230.6	236.4	249.3	259.4
Soft drinks......................................	122.3	133.1	144.1	159.1	181.8	183.9	186.9	192.7
Roasted coffee...................................	113.0	146.5	133.5	151.1	179.2	190.2	223.9	216.6
Shortening and cooking oils.......................	123.2	142.5	132.4	176.7	225.6	233.6	301.1	294.2
Finished consumer goods excluding foods......	**115.3**	**124.0**	**138.4**	**161.9**	**179.4**	**190.4**	**205.5**	**209.1**
Alcoholic beverages..............................	117.2	128.5	140.6	158.5	172.0	175.1	180.8	186.9
Apparel...	117.5	124.2	127.4	125.6	129.3	129.5	133.7	136.8
Women's / girls / infants' cut & sew apparel (December 2003 = 100)..............	(NA)	(NA)	(NA)	100.3	102.1	101.6	103.0	104.0
Men's and boy's cut and sew apparel (December 2003 = 100).....................	(NA)	(NA)	(NA)	98.7	101.2	101.5	106.6	113.3
Textile house furnishings.........................	109.5	119.5	122.0	122.9	129.1	131.7	138.8	142.8
Footwear..	125.6	139.2	144.9	148.1	159.9	162.4	168.0	176.5
Residential electric power (December 1990=100)...	(NA)	111.8	110.8	126.4	150.5	154.7	158.9	159.8
Residential gas (December 1990=100).............	(NA)	104.4	135.5	216.8	205.1	201.7	199.1	179.8
Gasoline...	78.7	63.7	94.6	168.6	178.4	225.3	295.7	303.1
Fuel oil No. 2....................................	73.3	56.6	93.5	178.4	162.7	207.5	279.3	284.9
Pharmaceutical preparations (June 2001=100)......	(NA)	(NA)	(NA)	117.9	146.3	155.1	161.8	171.5
Soaps and synthetic detergents....................	117.7	122.9	128.2	134.6	161.4	161.2	166.0	175.1
Cosmetics and other toilet preparations...........	121.6	129.0	137.4	143.0	148.1	149.9	152.1	153.8
Tires, tubes, and tread...........................	96.8	100.2	93.0	108.1	131.0	138.1	154.0	159.1
Sales and subscriptions of newspapers.............	144.1	185.6	210.0	241.5	267.4	277.6	286.9	299.0
Sale of books....................................	153.4	185.0	218.2	264.0	306.9	317.1	324.7	335.9
Household furniture..............................	125.1	141.8	152.7	166.5	186.9	187.4	191.6	196.6
Floor coverings..................................	119.0	123.7	129.6	146.4	167.5	169.3	176.1	180.4
Household appliances.............................	110.8	112.4	107.3	103.3	111.1	110.5	111.8	117.1
Home electronic equipment........................	82.7	78.9	71.8	62.6	53.6	52.9	52.4	52.4
Lawn and garden equipment, except tractors.......	123.0	130.4	132.0	134.5	142.3	141.7	140.5	142.6
Passenger cars..................................	118.3	134.1	132.8	131.8	130.9	129.0	129.9	131.2
Toys, games, and children's vehicles..............	118.1	124.3	121.9	127.0	143.1	140.7	143.9	149.7
Sporting and athletic goods........................	112.6	122.0	126.1	124.6	132.2	133.9	133.0	134.4
Tobacco products................................	221.4	231.3	397.2	457.8	539.3	570.5	604.9	633.8
Mobile homes....................................	117.5	145.6	161.3	200.8	222.3	228.5	236.4	245.4
Jewelry, platinum, and karat gold..................	122.8	127.8	127.2	138.6	169.7	187.8	219.7	238.9
Capital Equipment............................	**122.9**	**136.7**	**138.8**	**144.6**	**156.7**	**157.3**	**159.7**	**162.8**
Agricultural machinery and equipment..............	121.7	142.9	153.7	174.7	199.9	203.5	209.6	214.0
Construction machinery and equipment.............	121.6	136.7	148.6	168.3	191.0	191.4	197.4	205.4
Pumps, compressors, and equipment..............	119.2	139.4	154.1	178.5	212.6	215.1	223.4	230.0
Industrial material handling equipment............	115.0	125.3	134.7	150.6	181.6	183.1	187.7	194.4
Electronic computers (December 2004=100).........	(NA)	850.1	261.6	85.5	34.0	30.3	26.8	24.8
Textile machinery................................	128.8	146.7	156.2	160.5	166.3	165.9	166.9	168.9
Printing trades machinery.........................	124.9	133.6	142.1	144.3	157.1	155.4	156.5	158.5
Transformers and power regulators................	120.9	128.9	135.8	150.3	210.6	223.1	229.8	227.0
X-ray and electromedical equipment...............	109.8	111.8	101.5	95.7	90.1	89.4	88.3	88.3
Oil field and gas field machinery...................	102.4	114.1	128.2	155.9	202.7	200.7	205.0	210.7
Mining machinery and equipment..................	121.0	135.6	146.1	175.9	217.3	221.5	233.7	245.3
Office and store machines and equipment..........	109.5	111.5	112.7	115.1	123.5	121.0	122.2	121.2
Commercial furniture.............................	133.4	148.2	158.4	172.7	196.1	196.3	201.2	205.3
Light motor trucks...............................	130.0	159.0	157.6	148.4	151.8	153.3	154.6	160.1
Heavy motor trucks..............................	120.3	144.1	148.0	162.4	190.3	195.7	200.0	205.8
Truck trailers....................................	110.8	131.7	139.4	157.1	177.7	181.5	190.0	195.8
Civilian aircraft (December 1985=100)..............	115.3	141.8	159.6	202.2	235.4	238.0	244.3	252.0
Ships (December 1985=100).......................	110.1	132.8	146.9	176.6	210.0	215.1	220.2	220.5
Railroad equipment..............................	118.6	134.8	135.7	160.4	181.9	184.4	187.0	191.8
Intermediate materials, supplies, and components...................................	**114.5**	**124.9**	**129.2**	**154.0**	**172.5**	**183.4**	**199.8**	**200.7**
Intermediate foods and feeds.....................	113.3	114.8	111.7	133.8	166.0	171.7	192.3	201.5
Flour..	103.6	123.0	103.8	133.6	182.9	182.4	224.5	229.0
Refined sugar....................................	122.7	119.3	110.6	124.9	157.8	185.7	206.9	205.4
Soft drink beverage bases (December 1985=100)...	126.2	148.3	167.1	180.4	223.5	223.3	227.0	233.4
Intermediate materials less foods and feeds....	**114.5**	**125.5**	**130.1**	**155.1**	**173.0**	**184.4**	**200.4**	**200.6**
Synthetic fibers.................................	106.7	109.4	107.2	112.3	113.3	111.6	117.7	122.4
Processed yarns and threads......................	112.6	112.8	107.9	111.7	119.9	130.0	157.6	142.8
Leather...	177.5	191.4	182.2	219.6	221.1	233.0	261.8	258.8
Liquefied petroleum gas..........................	77.4	65.1	127.1	244.7	224.7	301.8	374.1	291.0
Commercial electric power........................	115.3	131.7	131.5	149.8	178.6	182.5	183.9	184.0
Industrial electric power..........................	119.6	130.8	131.5	156.2	190.6	193.1	203.5	209.6

See footnotes at end of table.

Stage of processing	1990	1995	2000	2005	2009	2010	2011	2012
Commercial natural gas (December 1990=100).....	(NA)	96.5	134.7	232.5	211.9	208.0	200.1	177.7
Industrial natural gas (December 1990=100)........	(NA)	90.9	139.0	249.4	210.2	202.0	195.5	167.8
Natural gas to electric utilities (December 1990=100).................................	(NA)	87.7	120.7	204.0	164.0	174.8	166.1	153.5
Jet fuels...................................	76.0	55.0	88.5	169.6	169.3	225.5	307.3	312.1
Number 2 Diesel fuel........................	74.1	57.0	93.3	189.1	180.6	232.9	316.2	326.1
Residual fuel.............................	57.7	52.6	84.7	148.9	156.6	212.5	277.5	284.8
Industrial chemicals........................	113.2	128.4	129.1	188.5	234.1	269.2	324.7	306.9
Prepared paint............................	124.8	142.1	160.8	187.9	236.4	237.1	248.1	270.3
Paint materials...........................	136.3	139.4	148.5	190.4	218.7	223.6	261.1	295.0
Medicinal and botanical chemicals..............	102.2	128.3	146.2	136.0	169.1	175.2	175.7	178.0
Fats and oils, inedible......................	88.1	126.9	70.1	146.9	210.3	244.3	344.9	336.9
Mixed fertilizers..........................	103.3	111.1	112.4	138.9	192.8	177.2	197.3	202.1
Nitrogenates.............................	92.3	129.4	118.2	196.6	240.8	248.5	343.4	363.5
Phosphates..............................	96.5	109.1	96.9	128.1	195.4	222.7	296.7	270.8
Other agricultural chemicals.................	119.9	144.3	146.1	151.1	185.7	175.6	175.7	182.6
Plastic resins and materials.................	124.1	143.5	141.6	193.0	190.8	210.1	229.7	235.2
Synthetic rubber..........................	111.9	126.3	119.1	151.3	185.9	215.5	269.9	262.2
Plastic construction products.................	117.2	133.8	135.8	158.8	186.2	190.9	199.0	207.1
Softwood lumber..........................	123.8	178.5	178.6	203.6	141.4	160.8	160.5	171.7
Hardwood lumber.........................	131.0	167.0	185.9	196.6	171.2	187.3	185.8	183.7
Millwork................................	130.4	163.8	176.4	197.2	205.4	207.0	210.1	216.5
Plywood................................	114.2	165.3	157.6	186.8	163.7	176.7	171.3	189.1
Woodpile...............................	151.3	183.2	145.3	138.0	150.2	186.0	194.8	185.9
Paper..................................	128.8	159.0	149.8	159.6	179.6	182.1	191.2	191.6
Paperboard..............................	135.7	183.1	176.7	175.5	207.2	224.9	230.5	228.0
Paper boxes and containers..................	129.9	163.8	172.6	183.7	211.9	219.4	225.6	226.9
Building paper and board....................	112.2	144.9	138.8	184.9	156.5	168.4	163.6	187.1
Foundry and forge shop products..............	117.2	129.3	136.5	156.2	185.2	191.2	201.7	207.9
Steel mill products........................	112.1	120.1	108.4	159.7	165.2	191.7	216.2	208.0
Primary nonferrous metals...................	133.4	146.8	113.6	158.2	177.6	210.3	238.9	215.8
Aluminum mill shapes......................	127.9	160.4	149.0	161.1	154.1	171.9	188.9	178.6
Copper and brass mill shapes.................	174.6	195.2	162.3	235.8	345.5	421.3	471.1	431.7
Nonferrous wire and cable...................	142.6	151.5	143.7	169.4	222.4	258.1	282.3	267.6
Metal containers..........................	114.0	117.2	106.8	123.9	155.4	156.4	151.8	151.8
Hardware...............................	125.9	141.1	151.2	168.0	194.0	194.0	199.3	202.7
Plumbing fixtures and brass fittings............	144.3	166.0	180.4	197.6	228.9	231.4	237.0	241.5
Heating equipment........................	131.6	147.5	155.6	179.9	219.1	221.5	227.6	235.3
Mechanical power transmission equipment........	125.3	146.9	163.9	189.5	231.0	232.0	240.9	247.9
Air conditioning and refrigeration equipment.......	122.1	130.2	135.3	146.2	164.7	163.8	168.3	171.1
Motors, generators, motor generator sets.........	132.9	143.9	146.2	157.8	187.0	190.6	202.1	206.5
Switchgear and switchboard equipment..........	124.4	140.3	153.0	170.2	201.0	205.5	210.3	213.2
Electronic components and accessories...........	118.4	113.6	97.1	87.0	75.4	73.5	71.0	69.3
Internal combustion engines..................	120.2	135.6	143.8	147.7	162.3	161.7	164.5	165.7
Cement.................................	103.7	128.1	150.1	176.4	206.8	193.5	187.8	190.6
Concrete products.........................	113.5	129.4	147.8	177.2	214.0	210.6	210.8	215.0
Asphalt felts and coatings...................	97.1	100.0	104.1	130.8	220.6	222.7	233.5	232.0
Glass containers..........................	120.4	130.5	127.4	146.4	178.7	181.2	184.3	187.6
Motor vehicle parts........................	111.2	116.0	113.6	113.1	120.7	121.8	123.9	125.2
Aircraft engines and engine parts (December 1985=100).....................	113.5	132.8	141.0	165.9	193.1	197.4	204.0	211.5
Photographic supplies......................	127.6	126.8	125.2	120.1	127.8	124.4	130.4	146.9
Medical/surgical/personal aid devices...........	127.3	141.3	146.0	159.2	167.5	169.0	171.6	173.0
Crude materials for further processing........	**108.9**	**102.7**	**120.6**	**182.2**	**175.2**	**212.2**	**249.4**	**241.3**
Crude foodstuffs and feedstuffs..............	**113.1**	**105.8**	**100.2**	**122.7**	**134.5**	**152.4**	**188.4**	**196.3**
Wheat..................................	87.6	118.6	80.3	102.7	149.3	157.2	216.2	210.5
Corn...................................	100.9	109.0	76.4	75.9	146.9	160.8	267.3	278.8
Slaughter cattle..........................	122.5	99.5	104.1	131.5	122.0	139.8	170.7	185.3
Slaughter hogs...........................	94.1	70.2	72.7	82.7	68.9	92.6	110.6	105.1
Slaughter broilers/fryers....................	119.5	129.1	127.6	181.0	202.6	221.3	210.0	235.4
Slaughter turkeys.........................	116.9	120.3	120.7	131.1	146.7	173.0	200.6	208.0
Raw milk...............................	100.8	93.6	92.0	113.5	95.9	121.9	150.6	138.4
Soybeans...............................	100.8	102.2	83.4	102.6	175.9	177.1	219.6	248.6
Cane sugar, raw (December 2003=100)...........	(NA)	(NA)	(NA)	115.2	129.7	165.8	(NA)	167.1
Crude nonfood materials....................	101.5	96.8	130.4	223.4	197.5	249.3	284.0	263.1
Raw cotton..............................	118.2	156.2	95.2	78.9	82.6	117.9	145.5	132.4
Hides and skins (June 2001=100)...............	217.9	215.5	174.0	189.9	124.0	224.9	272.7	272.2
Coal...................................	97.5	95.0	87.9	116.8	182.5	189.5	207.1	211.4
Natural gas..............................	80.4	66.6	155.5	335.4	160.0	185.8	171.4	117.9
Crude petroleum..........................	71.0	51.1	85.2	150.1	161.7	218.6	275.5	273.6
Logs and timber..........................	142.8	220.4	196.4	197.4	187.8	213.4	228.2	232.0
Wastepaper..............................	138.9	371.1	282.5	230.9	237.0	421.5	482.5	370.7
Iron ore................................	83.3	91.8	94.8	116.9	145.0	147.1	165.4	180.8
Iron and steel scrap.......................	166.0	202.7	142.1	289.8	338.1	541.1	646.8	566.0
Nonferrous metal ores (December 1983=100).......	98.3	101.6	68.0	150.0	215.4	298.6	373.2	359.7
Copper base scrap.........................	181.3	193.5	123.7	258.6	375.4	548.2	638.2	605.7
Aluminum base scrap.......................	172.6	209.4	177.0	210.1	166.8	241.6	268.2	236.9
Construction sand, gravel, and crushed stone.......	125.4	142.3	163.1	195.8	259.1	262.2	266.5	272.8
Industrial sand...........................	117.6	132.5	146.0	174.4	238.1	239.8	247.0	275.9

NA Not available.

Source: U.S. Bureau of Labor Statistics, Producer Price Indexes, "PPI Databases," <http://www.bls.gov/ppi/#data>, accessed September 2013.

Table 766. Chain-Type Price Indexes for Personal Consumption Expenditures by Type of Expenditure: 1990 to 2012

[2009 = 100. For explanation of "chain-type," see text, Section 13. See also Table 705]

Type of Expenditure	1990	1995	2000	2005	2010	2011	2012
Personal consumption expenditures	**67.4**	**76.4**	**83.1**	**92.3**	**101.7**	**104.1**	**106.0**
Household consumption expenditures [1]	66.8	76.2	82.8	92.1	101.7	104.2	106.2
Food and beverages purchased for off-premises consumption	65.2	71.4	79.0	88.2	100.3	104.3	106.7
Food and nonalcoholic beverages purchased for off-premises consumption	65.1	70.7	78.3	87.8	100.3	104.8	107.5
Alcoholic beverages purchased for off-premises consumption	65.7	75.6	83.1	90.7	100.4	100.9	101.8
Food produced and consumed on farms	101.9	88.9	85.4	104.6	113.1	134.6	136.8
Clothing, footwear, and related services	114.4	113.1	107.9	100.5	99.5	101.2	104.8
Clothing	117.4	115.2	110.2	101.4	99.2	101.1	104.9
Garments	122.9	119.4	113.2	102.4	98.9	100.9	104.8
Women's and girls' clothing	128.5	122.3	112.4	102.5	99.1	101.0	104.5
Men's and boys' clothing	115.7	115.8	114.2	102.2	98.5	100.9	105.2
Children's and infants' clothing	116.2	113.7	114.0	101.9	99.7	99.2	104.6
Footwear [2]	100.6	103.2	97.3	96.6	100.9	101.3	104.0
Housing, utilities, and fuels	56.6	64.8	74.5	88.5	100.5	102.2	104.2
Housing	57.3	66.1	76.5	89.2	100.1	101.4	103.7
Rental of tenant-occupied nonfarm housing [3]	56.2	64.2	74.4	87.5	100.1	101.8	104.5
Imputed rental of owner-occupied nonfarm housing [4]	57.9	66.8	77.4	89.7	100.0	101.1	103.2
Household utilities and fuels	52.9	58.9	65.6	85.4	102.5	106.4	106.3
Water supply and sanitation	43.5	57.3	65.8	80.7	106.3	111.8	118.0
Electricity, gas, and other fuels	55.7	59.5	65.6	86.9	101.3	104.7	102.7
Electricity	61.0	67.3	66.7	78.3	100.2	102.0	102.0
Natural gas	50.3	53.1	69.0	111.0	98.0	95.4	86.0
Fuel oil and other fuels	40.9	36.1	54.1	88.6	117.0	148.7	150.6
Furnishings, household equipment, and routine household maintenance	94.5	99.8	102.1	99.1	97.2	96.4	96.7
Furniture, furnishings, and floor coverings [5]	106.5	113.5	113.4	105.2	95.5	93.7	93.1
Household textiles	159.6	158.5	144.1	119.7	94.7	92.2	88.9
Household appliances [6]	97.1	97.0	94.3	91.9	96.4	95.6	100.0
Glassware, tableware, and household utensils [7]	116.0	119.5	116.1	103.7	97.4	95.5	91.7
Health	52.1	67.5	75.7	89.1	102.6	104.7	106.8
Medical products, appliances, and equipment	56.6	67.9	77.4	90.5	103.0	106.1	109.2
Pharmaceutical and other medical products [8]	54.1	65.4	75.5	89.8	103.6	107.2	110.6
Pharmaceutical products	53.9	65.2	75.3	89.7	103.7	107.3	110.8
Other medical products	75.9	89.4	94.7	96.0	97.9	98.2	99.4
Therapeutic appliances and equipment	70.8	82.6	89.2	94.4	99.4	100.0	101.0
Outpatient services	56.9	72.1	80.7	90.6	102.2	103.6	104.9
Physician services	60.4	78.3	84.9	92.0	102.4	104.0	105.2
Dental services	40.4	53.3	66.6	83.5	102.7	105.1	107.6
Paramedical services	60.2	71.9	80.9	91.5	101.6	102.5	103.3
Hospital and nursing home services	47.1	63.4	70.8	87.1	102.8	105.0	107.4
Hospitals	47.7	65.4	71.0	87.3	102.9	105.2	107.8
Nursing homes	45.0	55.5	70.1	86.4	102.0	104.4	105.9
Transportation	69.8	78.1	85.5	95.7	108.2	119.1	122.0
Motor vehicles	87.8	106.9	109.6	105.8	106.5	109.2	110.8
New motor vehicles	89.4	104.2	106.2	102.2	102.1	104.9	106.7
Net purchases of used motor vehicles	83.5	112.5	116.7	113.0	114.5	117.0	117.8
Motor vehicle operation	57.4	60.8	70.5	90.8	109.5	125.3	128.6
Motor vehicle parts and accessories	80.0	79.7	78.4	84.9	101.9	105.6	108.3
Motor vehicle fuels, lubricants, and fluids	49.7	49.4	63.4	95.8	118.2	148.6	153.9
Public transportation	77.2	81.5	88.8	88.9	105.8	112.3	116.6
Ground transportation	55.4	62.4	70.5	85.9	104.3	109.4	112.8
Air transportation	91.0	92.5	99.6	90.2	107.2	115.7	121.2
Water transportation	127.9	148.6	142.4	113.0	101.1	100.2	97.4
Communication	106.2	112.0	106.2	100.9	99.7	98.4	98.5
Recreation	115.0	120.4	111.4	104.4	97.5	95.7	94.8
Video and audio equipment, computers, and related services	338.9	286.5	184.0	132.7	92.9	87.3	82.7
Video and audio equipment	348.2	305.7	235.1	165.1	86.4	77.5	68.7
Sports and recreational goods and related services	116.0	122.4	112.7	103.0	97.1	94.8	93.3
Sports and recreational vehicles	81.4	90.1	94.2	96.3	100.4	102.8	104.4
Other sporting and recreational goods	131.2	136.5	120.5	105.8	96.1	92.7	90.4
Magazines, newspapers, books, and stationery	66.7	81.6	89.2	93.3	100.3	100.0	101.9
Education	31.9	44.6	56.7	79.5	104.7	109.7	114.7
Higher education	28.8	43.7	54.7	78.3	105.2	110.5	115.8
Net foreign travel and expenditures abroad by U.S. residents							
Foreign travel by U.S. residents	56.9	67.5	70.8	88.6	105.5	109.8	111.8
Less: Expenditures in the United States by nonresidents	60.9	69.1	79.2	90.1	103.5	108.7	112.0

[1] Consists of household purchases of goods and services from business, government, nonprofit institutions, and the rest of the world. [2] Consists of shoes and other footwear, and of repair and hire of footwear. [3] Consists of rent for space (see footnote 4) and rent for appliances, furnishings, and furniture. [4] Consists of rent for space and for heating and plumbing facilities, water heaters, lighting fixtures, kitchen cabinets, linoleum, storm windows and doors, window screens, and screen doors, but excludes rent for appliances and furniture and purchases of fuel and electricity. [5] Includes clocks, lamps, lighting fixtures, and other household decorative items; also includes repair of furniture, furnishings, and floor coverings. [6] Consists of major household appliances, small electric household appliances, and repair of household appliances. [7] Consists of dishes, flatware, and non-electric cookware and tableware. [8] Excludes drug preparations and related products dispensed by physicians, hospitals, and other medical services.

Source: U.S. Bureau of Economic Analysis, National Income and Product Accounts Tables, "Table 2.5.4. Price Indexes for Personal Consumption Expenditures by Function," <http://www.bea.gov/itable/>, accessed August 2013.

Table 767. Chain-Type Price Indexes for Gross Domestic Product: 1990 to 2012

[2009 = 100. For explanation of "chain-type," see text, Section 13]

Component	1990	2000	2005	2008	2009	2010	2011	2012
Gross domestic product..........................	**66.8**	**81.9**	**92.0**	**99.2**	**100.0**	**101.2**	**103.2**	**105.0**
Personal consumption expenditures...........	**67.4**	**83.1**	**92.3**	**100.1**	**100.0**	**101.7**	**104.1**	**106.0**
Durable goods..	126.3	120.3	107.7	101.8	100.0	98.6	97.6	96.5
Nondurable goods...................................	70.5	82.7	91.6	102.7	100.0	103.1	109.1	111.8
Services..	58.5	77.5	89.9	98.9	100.0	101.7	103.5	105.7
Gross private domestic investment............	**80.1**	**85.6**	**94.5**	**101.0**	**100.0**	**99.1**	**100.4**	**101.6**
Fixed investment.......................................	79.3	85.5	94.5	101.0	100.0	99.2	100.5	101.9
Nonresidential..	90.4	90.7	93.8	100.3	100.0	99.1	100.5	102.0
Structures..	44.2	59.6	82.1	102.3	100.0	98.8	101.7	103.7
Equipment and software........................	124.6	105.4	98.6	98.7	100.0	98.0	98.9	100.2
Intellectual property products................	86.5	96.1	96.0	100.8	100.0	100.5	101.8	103.2
Residential...	57.1	76.1	98.1	103.6	100.0	99.6	100.4	101.2
Net exports of goods and services:								
Exports..	86.1	86.0	94.4	105.8	100.0	104.4	111.1	112.2
Goods..	94.9	88.4	95.5	107.2	100.0	105.0	113.0	113.5
Services...	67.7	80.7	92.0	102.8	100.0	103.1	107.0	109.3
Imports..	87.1	84.0	93.6	111.7	100.0	106.0	114.3	114.9
Goods..	93.1	86.0	94.6	113.9	100.0	106.7	116.2	116.9
Services...	63.7	75.4	89.6	102.2	100.0	102.8	105.7	105.9
Government consumption expenditures and gross investment..........	**55.7**	**73.4**	**88.2**	**100.3**	**100.0**	**102.7**	**105.6**	**106.9**
Federal..	60.8	77.3	91.4	100.3	100.0	102.6	105.3	106.2
National defense.....................................	60.9	76.5	91.4	100.8	100.0	102.4	105.2	106.3
Nondefense...	60.3	78.8	91.5	99.3	100.0	103.1	105.6	106.1
State and local...	52.8	71.2	86.3	100.3	100.0	102.7	105.7	107.4

Source: U.S. Bureau of Economic Analysis, National Income and Product Accounts Tables, "Table 1.1.4. Price Indexes for Gross Domestic Product," <http://www.bea.gov/itable/>, accessed August 2013.

Table 768. Import and Export Price Indexes by End-Use Category: 1990 to 2013

[As of June. Import indexes are weighted by the 2000 Tariff Schedule of the United States Annotated, a scheme for describing and reporting product composition and value of U.S. imports. Import prices are based on U.S. dollar prices paid by importer. Export indexes are weighted by 2000 export values according to the Schedule B classification system of the U.S. Census Bureau. Prices used in these indexes were collected from a sample of U.S. manufacturers of exports and are factory transaction prices, except as noted. Minus sign (-) indicates decrease]

	Index (2000 = 100)						Percent change [1]					
	Imports			Exports			Imports			Exports		
Year	Total	Petroleum imports	Non-petroleum imports	Total	Agricultural exports	Non-agricultural exports	Total	Petroleum imports	Non-petroleum imports	Total	Agricultural exports	Non-agricultural exports
1990..........	90.8	55.4	96.4	95.1	107.7	93.5	-0.8	-13.4	0.5	-0.1	-4.0	0.5
1991..........	93.4	63.2	98.3	96.1	104.3	95.3	2.9	14.1	2.0	1.1	-3.2	1.9
1992..........	94.8	66.0	99.5	96.5	104.0	95.8	1.5	4.4	1.2	0.4	-0.3	0.5
1993..........	95.0	60.4	100.5	96.9	100.3	96.7	0.2	-8.5	1.0	0.4	-3.6	0.9
1994..........	96.3	57.6	102.6	98.5	109.3	97.5	1.4	-4.6	2.1	1.7	9.0	0.8
1995..........	101.4	62.9	107.6	104.5	117.0	103.3	5.3	9.2	4.9	6.1	7.0	5.9
1996..........	100.7	66.4	106.2	105.4	140.8	101.7	-0.7	5.6	-1.3	0.9	20.3	-1.5
1997..........	98.8	62.5	104.3	103.2	120.5	101.5	-1.9	-5.9	-1.8	-2.1	-14.4	-0.2
1998..........	93.1	44.3	100.5	99.9	110.8	98.8	-5.8	-29.1	-3.6	-3.2	-8.0	-2.7
1999..........	92.9	54.5	98.8	98.2	101.1	97.9	-0.2	23.0	-1.7	-1.7	-8.8	-0.9
2000..........	100.2	101.9	99.9	100.1	100.5	100.0	7.9	87.0	1.1	1.9	-0.6	2.1
2001..........	97.6	89.4	98.9	99.4	100.9	99.3	-2.6	-12.3	-1.0	-0.7	0.4	-0.7
2002..........	94.1	85.3	96.2	98.0	100.7	97.8	-3.6	-4.6	-2.7	-1.4	-0.2	-1.5
2003..........	96.2	96.4	97.3	99.5	110.0	98.7	2.2	13.0	1.1	1.5	9.2	0.9
2004..........	101.7	129.7	99.7	103.4	127.4	101.5	5.7	34.5	2.5	3.9	15.8	2.8
2005..........	109.2	181.5	102.0	106.7	123.9	105.4	7.4	39.9	2.3	3.2	-2.7	3.8
2006..........	117.3	242.6	104.2	111.2	124.1	110.3	7.4	33.7	2.2	4.2	0.2	4.6
2007..........	120.0	245.6	107.1	116.0	146.7	113.8	2.3	1.2	2.8	4.3	18.2	3.2
2008..........	145.5	450.3	114.9	126.1	195.2	121.2	21.3	83.3	7.3	8.7	33.1	6.5
2009..........	120.0	241.5	107.4	117.8	169.7	114.1	-17.5	-46.4	-6.5	-6.6	-13.1	-5.9
2010..........	125.2	267.4	110.7	122.2	165.3	119.1	4.3	10.7	3.1	3.7	-2.6	4.4
2011..........	142.2	397.8	116.4	134.5	217.2	128.6	13.6	48.8	5.1	10.1	31.4	8.0
2012..........	138.7	357.2	116.3	131.7	204.5	126.5	-2.5	-10.2	-0.1	-2.1	-5.8	-1.6
2013..........	138.8	364.5	115.7	132.8	224.1	126.2	0.1	2.0	-0.5	0.8	9.6	-0.2

[1] Percent change from immediate prior year.

Source: U.S. Bureau of Labor Statistics, U.S. Import and Export Price Indexes, "History Tables: Complete Historical Index Information," <http://www.bls.gov/mxp/>, accessed September 2013.

Table 769. Export Price Indexes—Selected Commodities: 2000 to 2013

[2000 = 100. As of June. Indexes are weighted by 2000 export values according to the Schedule B classification system of the U.S. Census Bureau. Prices used in these indexes were collected from a sample of U.S. manufacturers of exports and are factory transaction prices, except as noted]

Commodity	2000 [1]	2005	2008	2009	2010	2011	2012	2013
All commodities	**100.1**	**106.7**	**126.1**	**117.8**	**122.2**	**134.5**	**131.7**	**132.7**
Animal products	102.2	130.9	174.5	159.7	172.2	194.2	202.8	211.5
Fish	99.1	114.2	149.1	140.7	152.3	187.4	207.9	182.4
Vegetable products	100.0	130.3	239.3	205.4	177.5	256.3	241.3	271.5
Fruit and nuts	94.8	126.5	123.0	101.2	131.0	131.5	139.4	154.3
Cereals	100.0	118.1	293.6	222.1	171.4	319.1	264.3	307.0
Wheat and meslin	99.4	130.0	276.7	228.5	151.6	290.0	229.9	272.2
Corn (maize)	101.0	111.8	286.4	212.1	174.3	348.0	281.0	324.4
Oilseeds	102.8	136.2	259.3	238.1	196.2	268.0	267.6	299.5
Prepared foodstuffs, beverages, and tobacco	100.0	110.3	136.3	141.0	139.3	151.9	157.8	167.6
Mineral products	97.8	182.3	360.5	203.9	247.9	336.3	295.2	292.4
Fuels	97.4	172.8	361.9	198.3	239.2	333.4	290.7	289.4
Chemicals and related products	100.3	115.3	145.4	135.7	144.5	153.9	154.1	154.2
Plastics and rubber products	101.5	118.4	142.2	129.8	136.8	151.4	148.1	150.2
Hides, skins, and leather products	95.7	113.0	117.3	79.1	121.2	137.4	130.1	146.5
Wood products	100.0	104.3	112.3	102.5	111.1	109.4	110.3	113.4
Woodpulp and paper products	101.6	101.9	117.5	107.3	117.6	127.2	117.8	121.1
Textiles	100.2	100.8	108.0	101.9	115.7	148.7	124.9	130.0
Stone and glass products	100.7	103.5	111.1	115.9	115.9	115.9	117.7	118.2
Gems and precious metals	98.1	106.5	183.1	171.2	211.0	278.0	277.6	254.8
Base metals	100.5	131.8	181.2	143.5	160.4	187.1	172.9	165.6
Iron and steel	101.7	164.0	243.3	150.0	194.3	244.5	209.3	185.9
Articles of iron and steel	100.2	124.8	156.6	163.6	158.1	170.5	172.5	169.2
Copper	98.7	143.1	261.2	172.0	217.0	278.2	242.4	236.9
Aluminum	98.4	113.2	150.6	100.5	117.8	139.1	124.9	122.8
Machinery	99.9	94.9	95.3	95.3	95.5	96.4	97.2	97.1
Nonelectrical machinery	100.0	100.5	103.7	105.1	106.8	108.7	110.6	111.3
Electrical machinery	99.8	88.6	86.2	84.7	83.2	83.0	82.7	81.8
Transportation equipment	100.0	108.8	116.6	120.5	121.4	123.6	126.7	128.0
Motor vehicles	100.0	103.2	106.7	107.7	108.5	109.7	113.0	113.7
Instruments	100.0	101.3	107.1	107.8	106.2	105.3	106.0	107.1
Miscellaneous manufactured articles	100.4	100.6	108.6	106.9	108.1	110.0	110.4	110.3

[1] June 2000 may not equal 100 because indexes were reweighted to an "average" trade value in 2000.

Source: U.S. Bureau of Labor Statistics, *U.S. Import and Export Price Indexes*, June 2013, and earlier reports. See also <http://www.bls.gov/mxp/>.

Table 770. Import Price Indexes—Selected Commodities: 2000 to 2013

[2000 = 100. As of June. Indexes are weighted by the 2000 Tariff Schedule of the United States Annotated, a scheme for describing and reporting product composition and value of U.S. imports. Import prices are based on U.S. dollar prices paid by importer]

Commodity	2000 [1]	2005	2007	2008	2009	2010	2011	2012	2013
All commodities	**100.2**	**109.2**	**120.0**	**145.5**	**120.0**	**125.2**	**142.2**	**138.7**	**139.0**
Animal products	99.9	112.7	127.4	141.6	129.0	143.0	167.6	164.8	177.8
Meat	100.5	138.7	146.8	165.4	150.8	183.2	209.7	214.1	218.4
Fish	100.2	88.3	100.2	106.3	99.8	107.1	126.8	118.6	133.0
Vegetable products	97.1	116.9	129.3	159.5	161.2	169.5	210.6	221.0	204.1
Vegetables	93.9	136.8	175.3	202.6	293.1	326.2	299.8	322.1	347.5
Fruit and nuts	96.9	89.7	90.9	112.8	103.8	106.8	124.6	117.7	110.2
Prepared foodstuffs, beverages and tobacco	100.0	114.0	124.3	140.0	134.4	141.2	156.8	157.4	156.6
Mineral products	101.3	178.1	234.0	418.5	224.5	248.5	360.0	320.2	334.9
Fuels	101.3	177.5	233.7	421.6	221.3	244.9	356.1	316.4	331.5
Chemicals and related products	99.8	111.3	123.8	139.2	131.3	139.3	146.9	150.8	150.3
Organic chemicals	100.6	109.6	120.5	132.9	124.6	133.8	136.7	138.0	135.3
Pharmaceutical products	99.8	111.0	107.6	114.1	113.3	117.9	111.9	117.4	125.0
Plastics and rubber products	99.9	113.5	121.7	133.2	129.7	136.7	151.7	152.7	152.3
Hides, skins, and leather products	100.2	104.0	107.0	112.4	113.7	114.5	120.9	126.4	125.3
Wood products	100.5	124.2	113.5	118.5	110.2	134.3	129.6	140.7	150.3
Woodpulp and paper products	100.0	102.3	108.0	115.3	108.1	112.5	115.8	114.0	113.6
Textiles	99.7	100.4	102.1	103.5	102.6	103.1	112.9	115.3	114.2
Footwear	99.6	100.3	101.3	104.7	107.2	106.1	111.8	117.7	120.4
Stone and glass products	99.5	105.4	110.4	115.4	125.3	123.8	128.8	132.1	131.8
Gems and precious metals	99.3	98.3	132.8	157.1	140.6	161.5	198.0	199.1	186.0
Gold	98.3	150.7	238.2	317.4	331.7	430.5	539.4	566.3	504.8
Platinum	(NA)	125.7	257.2	368.6	196.6	292.6	336.5	260.2	273.1
Base metals	101.5	132.1	176.7	206.9	151.1	180.2	200.2	188.7	181.2
Iron and steel	104.1	170.6	206.2	308.8	174.8	238.8	263.5	241.7	215.3
Articles of iron and steel	100.6	122.7	129.0	159.7	139.6	149.9	160.1	160.8	156.0
Copper	97.2	142.7	307.5	326.2	234.8	313.8	392.5	349.4	335.8
Aluminum	97.9	113.2	146.8	155.8	105.7	132.8	156.9	137.7	137.6
Machinery	100.2	89.7	87.8	88.9	86.9	86.5	85.8	85.7	85.1
Nonelectrical machinery	99.8	90.1	88.2	89.3	87.9	87.9	88.6	89.8	89.8
Electrical machinery	100.5	89.4	87.5	88.5	85.8	85.2	83.1	81.8	80.6
Transportation equipment	100.0	104.4	105.9	109.5	109.7	109.7	114.7	115.8	116.1
Motor vehicles	100.1	103.8	105.1	108.7	108.6	108.8	113.9	114.8	114.9
Instruments	99.8	100.1	99.4	101.5	102.0	100.8	105.0	104.3	103.8
Miscellaneous manufactured articles	99.7	99.4	101.1	106.4	107.7	106.5	110.1	112.8	112.8
Furniture	99.5	103.4	104.6	111.9	112.2	109.4	113.5	116.5	116.6

NA Not available. [1] June 2000 may not equal 100 because indexes were reweighted to an "average" trade value in 2000.

Source: U.S. Bureau of Labor Statistics, *U.S. Import and Export Price Indexes*, June 2013, and earlier reports. See also <http://stats.bls.gov/mxp/>.

Section 15
Business Enterprise

This section relates to the place and behavior of the business firm and to business initiative in the American economy. It includes data on the number, type, and size of businesses; financial data of domestic and multinational U.S. corporations; business investments, expenditures, and profits; and sales and inventories.

The principal sources of these data are the *Survey of Current Business*, published by the Bureau of Economic Analysis (BEA); the Web site of the Board of Governors of the Federal Reserve System at <http://www.federalreserve.gov/econresdata/default.htm>; the annual *Statistics of Income (SOI)* reports of the Internal Revenue Service (IRS); and the U.S. Census Bureau's Economic Census, *County Business Patterns, Quarterly Financial Report for Manufacturing, Mining, and Trade Corporations (QFR), Survey of Business Owners*, and *Annual Capital Expenditures Survey*. See also BEA Interactive Tables <http://www.bea.gov/itable/index.cfm>.

Business firms—A firm is generally defined as a business organization or entity consisting of one or more domestic establishment locations under common ownership or control. The terms firm, business, company, and enterprise are used interchangeably throughout this section. A firm doing business in more than one industry is classified by industry according to the major activity of the firm as a whole.

The IRS concept of a business firm relates primarily to the legal entity used for tax reporting purposes. A sole proprietorship is an unincorporated business owned by one person and may include large enterprises with many employees and hired managers and part-time operators. A partnership is an unincorporated business owned by two or more persons, each of whom has a financial interest in the business. A corporation is a business that is legally incorporated under state laws. While many corporations file consolidated tax returns, most corporate tax returns represent individual corporations, some of which are affiliated through common ownership or control with other corporations filing separate returns.

Economic census—The economic census is the major source of facts about the structure and functioning of the nation's economy. It provides essential information for government, business, industry, and the general public. It furnishes an important part of the framework for such composite measures as the gross domestic product estimates, input/output measures, production and price indexes, and other statistical series that measure short–term changes in economic conditions. The Census Bureau takes the economic census every 5 years, covering years ending in "2" and "7."

The economic census is collected on an establishment basis. A company operating at more than one location is required to file a separate report for each store, factory, shop, or other location. Each establishment is assigned a separate industry classification based on its primary activity and not that of its parent company. Establishments responding to the establishment survey are classified into industries on the basis of

their principal product or activity (determined by annual sales volume). The statistics issued by industry in the 2007 Economic Census are classified primarily on the 2007 North American Industry Classification System (NAICS), and, to a lesser extent, on the 2002 NAICS used in the previous census (see below).

More detailed information about the scope, coverage, methodology, classification system, data items, and publications for each of the economic censuses and related surveys is published in the 2007 *Economic Census User Guide* at <http://www.census.gov/econ/census07/www/user_guide.html>.

Data from the 2007 Economic Census are released through the Census Bureau's American FactFinder® service on the Census Bureau Web site. For more information, see <http://www.census.gov/econ/census07/>.

Survey of Business Owners—The Survey of Business Owners (SBO) provides statistics that describe the composition of U.S. businesses by gender, ethnicity, race and veteran status. Data from SBO are published in a series of releases: *American Indian- and Alaska Native-Owned Firms, Asian-Owned Firms, Black-Owned Firms, Hispanic-Owned Firms, Native Hawaiian- and Other Pacific Islander-Owned Firms, Women-Owned Firms, Veteran-Owned Firms, Characteristics of Business Owners* and *Company Summary*. Data are presented by industry classifications, geographic area, and size of firm (employment and receipts). Each owner had the option of selecting more than one race and therefore is included in each race selected. For more information, see <http://www.census.gov/econ/sbo/>.

North American Industry Classification System (NAICS)—NAICS is the standard used by federal statistical agencies in classifying business establishments for the purpose of collecting, analyzing, and publishing statistical data related to the U.S. business economy. NAICS was developed under the auspices of the Office of Management and Budget (OMB), and adopted in 1997 to replace the Standard Industrial Classification (SIC) system. The official *2007 U.S. NAICS Manual* includes definitions for each industry, background information, tables showing changes between 2002 and 2007, and a comprehensive index. For more information, see <http://www.census.gov/eos/www/naics/>.

Changes between 2002 NAICS and 2007 NAICS are relatively minor, but do affect totals for sectors 52 (finance and insurance), 53 (real estate, rental, and leasing), 54 (professional, scientific, and technical services), and 56 (administrative, support, waste management, and remediation services). Nearly all industries are comparable from 2002 to 2007 NAICS classifications. Several industries in the Information sector have been consolidated.

Quarterly Financial Report—The Quarterly Financial Report (QFR) program publishes quarterly aggregate statistics on the financial conditions of U.S. corporations. The QFR requests companies to report estimates from their statements of income and retained earnings, and balance sheets. The statistical data are classified and aggregated by type of industry and asset size. The QFR sample includes corporations that have a plurality of business activity in manufacturing industries with domestic assets of $250,000 and above, and mining, wholesale, retail, and selected service industries with assets of $50 million and above. The data are available quarterly in the *Quarterly Financial Report for Manufacturing, Mining, and Trade Corporations* at <http://www.census.gov/econ/qfr/index.html>.

Multinational companies—BEA collects financial and operating data on U.S. multinational companies. These data provide a picture of the overall activities of foreign affiliates and U.S. parent companies, using a variety of indicators of their financial structure and operations. The data on foreign affiliates cover the entire operations of the affiliate, irrespective of the percentage of U.S. ownership. These data cover items such as sales, value added, employment and compensation of employees, capital expenditures, exports and imports, and research and development expenditures. Separate tabulations are available for all affiliates and for affiliates that are majority-owned by their U.S. parent(s). More information is available at <http://www.bea.gov/international/index.htm#omc>.

Statistical reliability—For a discussion of statistical collection, estimation, and sampling procedures and measures of reliability applicable to data from the Census Bureau and the Internal Revenue Service, see Appendix III.

Table 771. Number of Tax Returns, Receipts, and Net Income by Type of Business: 1990 to 2010

[14,783 represents 14,783,000. Covers active enterprises only. Figures are estimates based on sample of unaudited tax returns; see Appendix III]

Item	Number of returns (1,000)			Business receipts [1] (bil. dol.)			Net income (less loss) [2] (bil. dol.)		
	Nonfarm proprietor-ships	Partner-ships	Corpora-tions	Nonfarm proprietor-ships	Partner-ships	Corpora-tions	Nonfarm proprietor-ships	Partner-ships	Corpora-tions
1990............	14,783	1,554	3,717	731	483	9,860	141	17	383
1991............	15,181	1,515	3,803	713	483	9,966	142	21	361
1992............	15,495	1,485	3,869	737	515	10,360	154	43	414
1993............	15,848	1,468	3,965	757	561	10,866	156	67	510
1994............	16,154	1,494	4,342	791	656	11,884	167	82	595
1995............	16,424	1,581	4,474	807	761	12,786	169	107	736
1996............	16,955	1,654	4,631	843	916	13,659	177	145	839
1997............	17,176	1,759	4,710	870	1,142	14,461	187	168	957
1998............	17,409	1,855	4,849	918	1,357	15,010	202	187	895
1999............	17,576	1,937	4,936	969	1,616	16,314	208	228	985
2000............	17,905	2,058	5,045	1,021	2,062	17,637	215	269	987
2001............	18,338	2,132	5,136	1,017	2,278	17,504	217	276	649
2002............	18,926	2,242	5,267	1,030	2,414	17,297	221	271	597
2003............	19,710	2,375	5,401	1,050	2,546	18,264	230	301	822
2004............	20,591	2,547	5,558	1,140	2,819	19,976	248	385	1,170
2005............	21,468	2,764	5,671	1,223	3,280	21,800	270	546	2,027
2006............	22,075	2,947	5,841	1,278	3,571	23,310	278	667	2,024
2007............	23,123	3,096	5,869	1,324	3,847	24,217	281	683	1,950
2008............	22,614	3,146	5,847	1,317	4,344	24,718	265	458	1,061
2009............	22,660	3,169	5,825	1,178	3,562	21,585	245	410	(NA)
2010............	23,004	3,248	5,814	1,196	3,946	23,058	268	594	(NA)

NA Not available. [1] Excludes investment income except for partnerships and corporations in finance, insurance, and real estate before 1998. Beginning 1998, finance and insurance, real estate, and management of companies included investment income for partnerships and corporations. Excludes investment income for S corporations; for definition, see footnote 1, Table 780. [2] Net income (less loss) is defined differently by form of organization, basically as follows: (a) Proprietorships: Total taxable receipts less total business deductions, including cost of sales and operations, depletion, and certain capital expensing, excluding charitable contributions and owners' salaries; (b) Partnerships: Total taxable receipts (including investment income except capital gains) less deductions, including cost of sales and operations and certain payments to partners, excluding charitable contributions, oil and gas depletion, and certain capital expensing; (c) Corporations: Includes "Total net income (less deficit)" from S Corporations and is more comprehensive than what Statistics of Income generally publishes; net income is before income tax.

Source: U.S. Internal Revenue Service, "Tax Statistics",<http://www.irs.gov/uac/Tax-Stats-2>, accessed September 2013.

Table 772. Number of Tax Returns by Size of Receipts: 2000 to 2010

[In thousands (5,045 represents 5,045,000). Covers active enterprises only. Figures are estimates based on sample of unaudited tax returns; see Appendix III]

Size-class of receipts	2000	2002	2003	2004	2005	2006	2007	2008	2009	2010
Corporations, total...............	**5,045**	**5,267**	**5,401**	**5,558**	**5,671**	**5,841**	**5,869**	**5,847**	**5,825**	**5,814**
Under $25,000 [1]...................	1,220	1,283	1,280	1,317	1,300	1,363	1,391	1,444	1,501	1,484
$25,000 to $49,999................	305	314	346	334	340	341	356	368	399	385
$50,000 to $99,999................	477	514	522	545	544	554	570	556	576	592
$100,000 to $499,999.............	1,515	1,583	1,650	1,703	1,755	1,780	1,766	1,734	1,714	1,731
$500,000 to $999,999.............	582	611	623	635	644	668	657	663	641	618
$1,000,000 or more................	946	962	981	1,023	1,088	1,135	1,129	1,084	994	1,005
Partnerships, total...............	**2,058**	**2,242**	**2,375**	**2,547**	**2,764**	**2,947**	**3,096**	**3,146**	**3,169**	**3,248**
Under $25,000 [1]...................	1,105	1,204	1,284	1,373	1,465	1,568	1,650	1,705	1,746	1,788
$25,000 to $49,999................	183	185	192	193	218	240	233	230	241	238
$50,000 to $99,999................	187	195	206	226	233	245	275	266	279	289
$100,000 to $499,999.............	353	394	410	436	489	498	530	537	511	531
$500,000 to $999,999.............	92	105	111	121	131	149	149	147	148	151
$1,000,000 or more................	137	159	172	198	227	248	261	260	244	252
Nonfarm proprietorships, total...............	**17,905**	**18,926**	**19,710**	**20,591**	**21,468**	**22,075**	**23,123**	**22,614**	**22,660**	**23,004**
Under $25,000 [1]...................	11,997	12,716	13,308	13,916	14,456	14,867	15,752	15,532	15,951	16,258
$25,000 to $49,999................	2,247	2,358	2,450	2,536	2,587	2,721	2,796	2,729	2,722	2,652
$50,000 to $99,999................	1,645	1,752	1,805	1,792	1,981	1,983	2,027	1,936	1,825	1,892
$100,000 to $499,999.............	1,733	1,803	1,851	2,020	2,091	2,139	2,173	2,051	1,834	1,869
$500,000 to $999,999.............	190	203	200	218	235	236	242	229	211	219
$1,000,000 or more................	92	93	96	109	117	128	132	137	116	114

[1] Includes firms with no receipts.

Source: U.S. Internal Revenue Service, "Statistics of Income Bulletin, Historical Table 12," <http://www.irs.gov/uac/SOI-Tax-Stats-Historical-Table-12>, accessed September 2013.

Table 773. Number of Tax Returns, Receipts, and Net Income by Type of Business and Industry: 2010

[Tax returns in thousands (23,004 represents 23,004,000); receipts and income in billions of dollars (1,196 represents $1,196,000,000,000). Covers active enterprises only. Figures are estimates based on sample of unaudited tax returns; see Appendix III. Based on the North American Industry Classification System (NAICS), 2007; see text, this section. Minus sign (-) indicates net loss]

Industry	2007 NAICS code	Number of returns (1,000)			Business receipts [1] (bil. dol.)			Net income (less loss) [2] (bil. dol.)		
		Non-farm propri-etor-ships	Part-ner-ships	Corpo-rations	Non-farm propri-etor-ships	Part-ner-ships	Corpo-rations	Non-farm propri-etor-ships	Part-ner-ships	Corpo-rations
Total................................	(X)	23,004	3,248	5,814	1,196	3,946	23,058	268	594	1,356
Agriculture, forestry, fishing, and hunting [3]........................	11	305	121	137	20	25	147	1	2	4
Mining..............................	21	125	42	40	12	126	375	2	45	35
Utilities............................	22	6	7	7	(Z)	177	585	(Z)	-1	1
Construction.......................	23	2,660	168	718	162	192	1,066	28	-1	17
Special trade contractors...........	238	2,126	69	449	116	54	467	23	2	14
Manufacturing.....................	31–33	336	60	251	24	875	6,857	3	62	447
Wholesale and retail trade [4]..........	(X)	2,620	220	961	233	964	7,137	15	20	189
Wholesale trade...................	42	344	60	373	52	583	3,804	5	15	102
Retail trade [5]......................	44–45	2,276	160	587	182	381	3,333	11	5	87
Motor vehicle and parts dealers....	441	145	17	86	38	108	668	2	2	10
Food and beverage stores..........	445	108	23	75	27	82	495	1	1	8
Gasoline stations.................	447	16	10	44	23	72	292	(Z)	(Z)	1
Transportation and warehousing......	48–49	1,066	51	198	76	142	714	9	3	20
Information [5]........................	51	363	47	123	11	259	922	3	32	68
Broadcasting (except Internet).......	515	93	6	7	4	38	94	1	5	5
Telecommunications...............	517	([6])	5	18	([6])	174	408	([6])	24	22
Finance and insurance...............	52	642	284	242	75	165	1,914	16	287	353
Real estate and rental and leasing....	53	1,221	1,557	643	54	122	216	14	8	31
Professional, scientific, and technical services [5]....................	54	3,228	228	880	165	365	1,045	71	83	51
Legal services....................	5411	356	30	118	39	137	98	17	50	9
Accounting, tax preparation, bookkeeping, and payroll services...	5412	382	21	86	13	55	60	5	13	5
Management, scientific, and technical consulting services..................	5416	946	63	227	45	65	197	25	9	15
Management of companies and enterprises.....................	55	(NA)	25	50	(NA)	15	185	(NA)	27	57
Administrative and support and waste management and remediation services..................	56	2,408	82	274	61	78	464	19	4	19
Educational services....................	61	669	13	60	9	4	64	3	(Z)	7
Health care and social assistance.....	62	2,192	73	433	120	208	660	49	29	37
Arts, entertainment, and recreation. ..	71	1,403	62	121	31	50	91	8	-2	2
Accommodation and food services....	72	431	116	297	47	154	423	2	-5	11
Accommodation...................	721	49	30	32	5	60	80	(Z)	-6	-3
Food services and drinking places...	722	382	86	265	42	94	343	1	1	15
Other services [5]....................	81	2,779	87	378	87	26	193	23	(Z)	6
Auto repair and maintenance.......	8111	366	28	110	24	10	66	3	(Z)	2
Personal and laundry services.......	812	1,769	47	162	44	11	76	15	(Z)	3
Religious, grantmaking, civic, professional, and similar organizations.................	813	242	2	45	4	(Z)	10	2	(Z)	(Z)
Unclassified............................	(X)	550	5	1	6	(Z)	(Z)	3	(Z)	(Z)

NA Not available. X Not applicable. Z Less than $500 million. [1] Includes investment income for partnerships and corporations in finance and insurance, real estate, and management of companies' industries. Excludes investment income for S corporations; for definition, see footnote 1, Table 780. [2] Net income (less loss) is defined differently by form of organization, basically as follows: (a) Proprietorships: Total taxable receipts less total business deductions, including cost of sales and operations, depletion, and certain capital expensing, excluding charitable contributions and owners' salaries; (b) Partnerships: Total taxable receipts (including investment income except capital gains) less deductions, including cost of sales and operations and certain payments to partners, excluding charitable contributions, oil and gas depletion, and certain capital expensing; (c) Corporations: Total taxable receipts (including investment income, capital gains, and income from foreign subsidiaries deemed received for tax purposes, except for S corporations) less business deductions, including cost of sales and operations, depletion, certain capital expensing, and officers' compensation excluding S corporation charitable contributions and investment expenses; net income is before income tax. [3] For corporations, represents agricultural services only. [4] For corporations, includes trade business not identified as wholesale or retail. [5] Includes other industries, not shown separately. [6] Broadcasting includes telecommunications.

Source: U.S. Internal Revenue Service, "SOI Tax Stats - Business Tax Statistics," <http://www.irs.gov/uac/SOI-Tax-Stats-Business-Tax-Statistics>, accessed July 2013.

Table 774. Nonfarm Sole Proprietorships—Selected Income and Deduction Items: 1990 to 2010

[In billions of dollars (731 represents $731,000,000,000), except as indicated. All figures are estimates based on samples. Tax law changes have affected the comparability of the data over time; see Statistics of Income reports for a description. See Appendix III]

Item	1990	1995	2000	2005	2006	2007	2008	2009	2010
Number of returns (1,000)	14,783	16,424	17,905	21,468	22,075	23,123	22,614	22,660	23,004
Returns with net income (1,000)	11,222	12,213	13,308	15,750	16,207	16,929	16,434	16,528	17,007
Business receipts	731	807	1,021	1,223	1,278	1,324	1,317	1,178	1,196
Income from sales and operations	719	797	1,008	1,205	1,259	1,304	1,296	1,159	1,176
Business deductions [1]	589	638	806	953	1,001	1,044	1,054	935	929
Cost of sales and operations [1]	291	307	387	397	410	423	435	366	367
Purchases	210	219	269	253	260	264	281	239	240
Labor costs	23	24	29	32	32	35	31	28	27
Materials and supplies	30	34	43	56	60	62	57	45	45
Advertising	(NA)	(NA)	10	14	15	16	15	14	13
Car and truck expenses	22	33	46	71	75	82	85	75	73
Commissions	9	10	12	15	16	15	13	12	12
Contract labor	(NA)	(NA)	(NA)	28	35	37	35	32	34
Depreciation	24	27	32	39	39	40	41	35	35
Insurance	13	13	14	19	19	19	18	17	16
Interest paid [2]	13	10	12	12	14	15	15	13	11
Office expenses	(NA)	(NA)	10	13	13	13	13	12	12
Rent paid [3]	23	28	33	39	41	43	44	41	42
Repairs	9	10	12	15	16	16	15	14	15
Salaries and wages (net)	47	54	63	75	77	79	79	75	74
Supplies	(NA)	(NA)	22	29	32	32	32	30	30
Taxes paid	10	13	14	17	18	18	18	17	18
Utilities	14	17	19	23	24	25	25	24	24
Net income (less loss) [4]	141	169	215	270	278	281	265	245	268
Net income [4]	162	192	245	315	327	335	325	309	323
Constant (2005) Dollars [5]									
Business receipts	1,012	990	1,152	1,223	1,238	1,246	1,213	1,075	1,077
Business deductions	816	783	910	953	970	983	970	853	837
Net income (less loss)	196	208	242	270	269	264	244	223	241
Net income	224	235	277	315	317	315	299	282	291

NA Not available. [1] Includes other amounts not shown separately. [2] Interest paid includes "mortgage interest" and "other interest paid on business indebtedness." [3] Rent paid includes "Rent on machinery and equipment" and "Rent on other business property." [4] After adjustment for the passive loss carryover from prior years. Therefore, "business receipts" minus "total deductions" do not equal "net income." [5] Based on the overall implicit price deflator for gross domestic product.

Source: U.S. Internal Revenue Service, Statistics of Income Tax Stats - Nonfarm Sole Proprietorship Statistics, <http://www.irs.gov/uac/SOI-Tax-Stats-Nonfarm-Sole-Proprietorship-Statistics>, accessed May 2013.

Table 775. Partnerships—Selected Income and Balance Sheet Items: 1990 to 2010

[In billions of dollars (1,735 represents $1,735,000,000,000), except as indicated. Covers active partnerships only. All figures are estimates based on samples. See Appendix III]

Item	1990	1995	2000	2005	2006	2007	2008	2009	2010
Number of returns (1,000)	1,554	1,581	2,058	2,764	2,947	3,096	3,146	3,169	3,248
Returns with net income (1,000)	854	955	1,261	1,580	1,623	1,659	1,609	1,608	1,635
Number of partners (1,000)	17,095	15,606	13,660	16,212	16,728	18,516	19,300	21,142	22,428
Assets [1,2]	1,735	2,719	6,694	13,734	17,146	20,386	19,260	18,798	19,820
Depreciable assets (net)	681	767	1,487	2,176	2,490	2,865	3,254	3,181	3,263
Inventories, end of year	57	88	150	315	446	339	431	277	277
Land	215	221	359	607	731	820	885	892	913
Liabilities [1,2]	1,415	1,886	3,696	7,483	9,350	10,440	10,167	9,085	8,994
Accounts payable	67	91	230	400	505	430	513	444	492
Short-term debt [3]	88	124	252	373	456	565	582	432	481
Long-term debt [4]	498	544	1,132	1,772	2,227	2,556	2,767	2,737	2,693
Nonrecourse loans	470	466	639	914	1,103	1,210	1,283	1,282	1,225
Partners' capital accounts [2]	320	832	2,999	6,251	7,796	9,946	9,092	9,713	10,826
Receipts [1]	566	890	2,405	3,863	4,301	4,727	5,169	4,265	4,721
Business receipts [5]	483	761	2,062	3,280	3,571	3,847	4,344	3,562	3,946
Interest received	21	31	82	134	193	260	245	178	183
Deductions [1]	550	784	2,136	3,317	3,634	4,043	4,711	3,749	4,026
Cost of goods sold/operations	243	395	1,226	1,976	2,109	2,310	2,717	2,055	2,336
Salaries and wages	56	80	201	293	332	373	403	390	405
Taxes paid	9	13	31	47	53	56	63	62	63
Interest paid	30	43	93	103	137	174	143	94	86
Depreciation	60	23	59	71	79	86	130	125	130
Net income (less loss)	17	107	269	546	667	683	458	410	594
Net income	116	179	410	724	871	976	929	796	904

[1] Includes items not shown separately. [2] Assets, liabilities, and partners' capital accounts are understated because not all partnerships file complete balance sheets. [3] Mortgages, notes, and bonds payable in less than 1 year. [4] Mortgages, notes, and bonds payable in 1 year or more. [5] Excludes investment income.

Source: U.S. Internal Revenue Service, "SOI Tax Stats: SOI Bulletins," <http://www.irs.gov/uac/SOI-Tax-Stats-SOI-Bulletins>, accessed May 2013.

Table 776. Partnerships—Selected Items by Industry: 2010

[In billions of dollars (19,820 represents $19,820,000,000,000), except as indicated. Covers active partnerships only. Figures are estimates based on samples. Based on the North American Industry Classification System (NAICS), 2007; see text, this section. Minus sign (-) indicates net loss]

Industry and year	2007 NAICS code	Number of partnerships (1,000)			Total assets [1]	Business receipts	Total deduc-tions	Net income less loss	Net income	Net loss
		Total	With net income	With net loss						
Total [2]	(X)	**3,248**	**1,635**	**1,613**	**19,820**	**3,946**	**4,026**	**593.7**	**904.4**	**310.7**
Agriculture, forestry, fishing, and hunting	11	121	63	58	167	25	35	1.5	9.2	7.7
Mining	21	42	25	17	373	126	99	44.6	55.6	11.0
Utilities	22	7	1	5	257	177	181	-0.7	7.0	7.6
Construction	23	168	85	83	218	192	197	-0.8	13.9	14.7
Manufacturing	31–33	60	22	38	665	875	850	61.9	75.1	13.2
Wholesale trade	42	60	29	31	202	583	576	14.6	19.7	5.1
Retail trade	44–45	160	65	95	134	381	385	5.5	10.6	5.1
Transportation and warehousing	48–49	51	21	30	310	142	147	3.4	11.4	8.0
Information	51	47	21	26	662	259	254	31.9	46.9	14.9
Finance and insurance	52	284	188	96	10,983	165	273	287.0	333.5	46.5
Real estate and rental and leasing	53	1,557	762	795	4,586	122	168	7.6	136.8	129.2
Professional, scientific, and technical services	54	228	127	101	186	365	304	82.8	90.1	7.3
Management of companies and enterprises	55	25	16	9	534	15	31	26.7	36.0	9.3
Administrative and support and waste management and remediation services	56	82	49	33	65	78	80	4.3	7.2	2.9
Educational services	61	13	6	7	3	4	4	0.2	0.5	0.3
Health care and social assistance	62	73	51	22	133	208	191	29.5	34.7	5.2
Arts, entertainment, and recreation	71	62	19	42	95	50	60	-1.8	5.7	7.5
Accommodation and food services	72	116	49	67	226	154	164	-5.0	8.2	13.2
Other services	81	87	36	51	22	26	27	0.3	2.2	1.8

X Not applicable. [1] Total assets are understated because not all partnerships file complete balance sheets. [2] Includes businesses not allocable to individual industries.

Source: U.S. Internal Revenue Service, "SOI Tax Stats -- Partnership Statistics," <http://www.irs.gov/uac/SOI-Tax-Stats-Partnership-Statistics-by-Sector-or-Industry>, accessed May 2013.

Table 777. Nonfinancial Noncorporate Business-Sector Balance Sheet: 1990 to 2012

[In billions of dollars (4,546 represents $4,546,000,000,000), except as noted. Represents year-end (4th quarter) outstandings]

Item	1990	2000	2005	2007	2008	2009	2010	2011	2012
Assets	**4,546**	**7,922**	**13,037**	**14,666**	**13,516**	**12,157**	**12,760**	**13,364**	**13,911**
Nonfinancial assets	4,154	6,450	10,440	11,071	9,823	8,565	9,061	9,624	10,122
Real estate [1]	3,662	5,791	9,630	10,159	8,883	7,650	8,105	8,611	9,183
Residential	2,100	3,483	6,247	5,858	4,928	4,525	4,665	4,862	5,241
Nonresidential	1,562	2,308	3,384	4,301	3,956	3,126	3,441	3,749	3,942
Equipment and software [2]	347	474	594	667	702	695	702	731	657
Residential [3]	28	35	43	47	49	46	44	46	48
Nonresidential	319	438	551	620	653	649	658	685	610
Inventories [2]	145	185	216	245	238	220	253	282	282
Financial assets	391	1,473	2,597	3,596	3,693	3,592	3,699	3,741	3,789
Checkable deposits and currency	83	181	374	516	519	540	522	528	535
Time and savings deposits	51	248	324	359	358	353	356	360	364
Money market fund shares	7	49	69	74	75	74	77	78	79
Treasury securities	13	40	56	59	52	46	48	49	49
Municipal securities	–	2	4	5	5	5	6	6	6
Mortgages	31	23	36	42	39	38	42	43	43
Trade receivables	98	342	431	526	523	496	533	539	546
Miscellaneous assets	109	587	1,302	2,014	2,122	2,040	2,115	2,139	2,167
Insurance receivables	60	77	99	107	111	112	113	119	121
Equity investment in GSEs [4]	2	3	4	5	6	6	7	7	7
Other	47	506	1,198	1,902	2,004	1,921	1,996	2,013	2,039
Liabilities	**1,453**	**2,796**	**4,180**	**5,349**	**5,795**	**5,710**	**5,654**	**5,704**	**5,787**
Credit market instruments	1,191	1,912	2,898	3,775	4,093	3,973	3,940	3,952	4,024
Depository institution loans n.e.c. [5]	167	402	670	927	1,046	944	924	980	1,070
Other loans and advances	99	129	135	165	177	172	174	175	184
Mortgages	925	1,381	2,093	2,683	2,870	2,857	2,842	2,797	2,769
Trade payables	66	267	335	375	381	388	417	421	425
Taxes payable	32	65	87	99	106	100	99	100	102
Miscellaneous liabilities	164	552	861	1,100	1,214	1,248	1,198	1,231	1,237
Net worth	**3,093**	**5,126**	**8,857**	**9,317**	**7,721**	**6,448**	**7,107**	**7,660**	**8,123**
Debt/net worth (percent)	38.5	37.3	32.7	40.5	53.0	61.6	55.4	51.6	49.5

– Represents or rounds to zero. [1] At market value. [2] At replacement (current) cost. [3] Durable goods in rental properties. [4] GSEs = government-sponsored enterprises. Equity in the Farm Credit System. [5] Not elsewhere classified.

Source: Board of Governors of the Federal Reserve System, "Federal Reserve Statistical Release, Z.1, Financial Accounts of the United States," June 2013, <http://www.federalreserve.gov/releases/z1/>.

Table 778. Nonfinancial Corporate Business-Sector Balance Sheet: 1990 to 2012

[In billions of dollars (9,794 represents $9,794,000,000,000). Represents year-end (4th quarter) outstandings]

Item	1990	2000	2005	2007	2008	2009	2010	2011	2012
Assets....................	**9,794**	**19,660**	**25,269**	**30,533**	**28,876**	**26,197**	**28,071**	**29,683**	**31,387**
Nonfinancial assets....................	6,204	9,898	13,361	16,771	15,938	12,857	14,050	15,147	15,936
Real estate [1]....................	3,432	5,440	8,171	10,926	9,961	7,063	8,041	8,867	9,405
Equipment and software [2]....................	1,862	3,119	3,602	4,012	4,191	4,125	4,182	4,314	4,474
Inventories [2]....................	910	1,339	1,588	1,833	1,787	1,670	1,827	1,967	2,057
Financial assets [3]....................	3,589	9,762	11,909	13,762	12,938	13,340	14,021	14,535	15,451
Checkable deposits and currency....................	167	226	268	143	14	157	232	269	312
Time and savings deposits....................	75	272	450	441	382	489	549	563	591
Money market fund shares....................	20	214	352	548	727	656	498	462	458
Commercial paper....................	14	58	111	69	57	56	68	68	62
Treasury securities....................	38	18	52	38	30	43	48	43	58
Consumer credit....................	67	81	60	57	56	54	46	48	49
Trade receivables....................	967	1,939	2,108	2,254	2,085	2,054	2,156	2,238	2,348
Mutual fund shares [1]....................	10	118	134	178	106	162	187	166	182
Liabilities [3]....................	**4,740**	**9,632**	**11,182**	**12,916**	**13,225**	**12,898**	**13,221**	**13,433**	**13,968**
Credit market instruments....................	2,577	4,769	5,784	7,199	7,564	7,330	7,486	8,013	8,705
Commercial paper....................	117	278	90	124	131	58	83	116	130
Municipal securities [4]....................	115	154	227	349	415	452	485	494	509
Corporate bonds [5]....................	1,008	2,379	3,187	3,729	3,954	4,366	4,805	5,216	5,795
Depository institution loans n.e.c. [6]....................	588	900	591	716	780	546	481	550	610
Other loans and advances....................	463	701	903	1,316	1,384	1,139	980	1,039	1,071
Mortgages....................	286	357	785	965	899	768	652	598	589
Trade payables....................	627	1,542	1,701	1,898	1,673	1,588	1,743	1,761	1,886
Taxes payable....................	38	78	86	36	39	36	43	52	56
Net worth (market value)....................	**5,054**	**10,028**	**14,087**	**17,617**	**15,651**	**13,299**	**14,850**	**16,250**	**17,419**
Debt/net worth (percent)....................	51.0	47.6	41.1	40.9	48.3	55.1	50.4	49.3	50.0

[1] At market value. [2] At replacement (current) cost. [3] Includes items not shown separately. [4] Industrial revenue bonds. Issued by state and local governments to finance private investment and secured in interest and principal by the industrial user of the funds. [5] Through 1992, corporate bonds include net issues by Netherlands Antillean financial subsidiaries. [6] Not elsewhere classified.

Source: Board of Governors of the Federal Reserve System, "Federal Reserve Statistical Release, Z.1, Financial Accounts of the United States," June 2013, <http://www.federalreserve.gov/releases/z1/>.

Table 779. Corporate Funds—Sources and Uses: 1990 to 2012

[In billions of dollars (243 represents $243,000,000,000). Beginning 4th quarter 2011, includes farm and nonfarm nonfinancial corporate businesses. Minus sign (-) indicates a deficit]

Item	1990	2000	2005	2007	2008	2009	2010	2011	2012
Profits before tax....................	243	432	957	1,042	831	713	990	1,007	1,247
– Taxes on corporate income....................	98	170	272	294	227	178	223	247	308
– Net dividends....................	118	251	171	485	474	352	386	425	467
+ Capital consumption allowance [1]....................	367	640	614	682	832	806	823	955	784
= U.S. internal funds, book....................	394	651	1,128	945	961	989	1,205	1,290	1,256
+ Foreign earnings retained abroad....................	45	103	-18	170	184	194	226	239	239
+ Inventory valuation adjustment (IVA)....................	-13	-17	-31	-47	-44	3	-39	-63	-11
– Net capital transfers....................	0	0	-16	(-Z)	-4	38	21	-6	-13
= Internal funds + IVA....................	426	737	1,095	1,068	1,104	1,148	1,371	1,472	1,498
Gross investment....................	376	916	937	941	169	1,328	1,103	1,121	1,341
Capital expenditures [2]....................	435	950	957	1,147	1,112	766	975	1,056	1,193
Fixed investment [3]....................	424	898	911	1,120	1,136	907	917	1,019	1,129
Inventory change + IVA....................	12	53	47	28	-40	-145	61	39	67
Net lending (+) or net borrowing (-)....................	-59	-34	-20	-206	-943	562	128	65	148
Net acquisition of financial assets [2]....................	125	1,205	946	1,075	-604	307	614	519	845
Foreign deposits....................	(Z)	-7	10	1	-26	7	9	-6	-22
Checkable deposits and currency....................	6	35	61	-8	-129	142	75	37	44
Time and savings deposits....................	-6	35	50	-56	-59	107	60	14	28
Credit market instruments [2]....................	-26	26	42	-76	-35	10	3	-5	22
Commercial paper....................	(-Z)	10	16	-53	-12	-1	12	(Z)	-6
Treasury securities....................	-14	-1	18	-7	-8	13	5	-5	15
Municipal securities....................	-8	7	(Z)	1	-3	1	-3	-1	13
Trade receivables....................	29	282	278	160	-169	-31	106	82	110
Miscellaneous assets [2]....................	114	818	444	938	-347	108	504	444	669
U.S. direct investment abroad [4]....................	36	138	25	307	263	257	325	397	333
Net increase in liabilities [2]....................	184	1,238	966	1,281	339	-255	486	454	696
Net funds raised in markets....................	68	257	31	68	34	-215	-83	53	246
Net new equity issues....................	-63	-118	-342	-787	-336	-65	-278	-472	-401
Credit market instruments....................	131	376	373	855	370	-151	195	525	647
Commercial paper....................	10	48	-8	11	8	-73	25	33	14
Municipal securities [5]....................	(-Z)	1	42	68	66	37	33	9	15
Corporate bonds [4]....................	47	169	63	323	225	412	439	411	580
Depository institution loans n.e.c [6]....................	-11	55	-27	96	64	-234	-83	69	73
Other loans and advances [7]....................	62	78	110	288	68	-161	-90	60	-23
Mortgages....................	23	24	192	69	-61	-131	-128	-56	-12
Trade payables....................	28	313	199	85	-225	-85	156	19	118
Miscellaneous liabilities [2]....................	88	661	737	1,177	527	49	407	374	329
Foreign direct investment in U.S.....................	59	249	99	212	190	105	157	207	162

Z Less than $500 million. [1] Consumption of fixed capital plus capital consumption adjustment. [2] Includes other items not shown separately. [3] Nonresidential fixed investment plus residential fixed investment. [4] Through 1992 fourth quarter, corporate bonds include net issues by Netherlands Antillean financial subsidiaries, and U.S. direct investment abroad excludes net inflows from those bond issues. [5] Industrial revenue bonds. Issued by state and local governments to finance private investment and secured in interest and principal by industrial user of the funds. [6] Not elsewhere classified. [7] Loans from rest of the world, U.S. government, and nonbank financial institutions.

Source: Board of Governors of the Federal Reserve System, "Federal Reserve Statistical Release, Z.1, Financial Accounts of the United States," June 2013, <http://www.federalreserve.gov/releases/z1/>.

Table 780. Corporations—Selected Financial Items: 1990 to 2010

[In billions of dollars (18,190 represents $18,190,000,000,000), except as noted. Covers active corporations only. All corporations are required to file returns except those specifically exempt. See source for changes in law affecting comparability of historical data. Based on samples; see Appendix III]

Item	1990	1995	2000	2005	2006	2007	2008	2009	2010
Number of returns (1,000)	3,717	4,474	5,045	5,671	5,841	5,869	5,847	5,825	5,814
Number with net income (1,000)	1,911	2,455	2,819	3,324	3,367	3,368	3,184	3,149	3,265
S Corporation returns [1](1,000)	1,575	2,153	2,860	3,684	3,873	3,990	4,050	4,095	4,128
Assets [2]	18,190	26,014	47,027	66,445	73,081	81,486	76,799	75,965	79,905
Cash	771	962	1,820	2,823	2,902	3,625	4,384	4,853	3,893
Notes and accounts receivable	4,198	5,307	8,754	11,962	13,611	15,315	13,855	12,544	12,718
Inventories	894	1,045	1,272	1,505	1,613	1,656	1,619	1,474	1,544
Investments in government obligations	921	1,363	1,236	1,613	1,714	1,785	2,193	2,501	2,730
Mortgage and real estate	1,538	1,713	2,822	4,777	5,232	5,177	5,450	4,847	7,914
Other investments	4,137	7,429	17,874	25,162	27,903	30,939	27,169	27,574	29,389
Depreciable assets	4,318	5,571	7,292	8,416	8,817	9,222	9,467	9,613	9,875
Depletable assets	129	154	191	310	382	497	587	629	661
Land	210	242	303	407	457	493	509	517	548
Liabilities [2]	18,190	26,014	47,027	66,445	73,081	81,486	76,799	75,965	79,905
Accounts payable	1,094	1,750	3,758	6,029	7,779	7,724	6,822	5,694	5,768
Short-term debt [3]	1,803	2,034	4,020	4,192	4,709	4,735	4,726	4,542	3,752
Long-term debt [4]	2,665	3,335	6,184	8,332	9,399	10,786	11,062	10,718	14,680
Net worth [5]	4,739	8,132	17,349	23,525	25,996	28,812	25,469	24,567	28,938
Capital stock	1,585	2,194	3,966	2,482	2,513	2,775	3,184	3,019	3,064
Paid-in or capital surplus	2,814	5,446	12,265	17,828	19,142	21,792	23,574	24,110	24,283
Retained earnings [6]	1,410	2,191	3,627	4,331	5,764	5,970	613	2,024	3,534
Receipts [2, 7]	11,410	14,539	20,606	25,505	27,402	28,763	28,590	24,773	26,199
Business receipts [7, 8]	9,860	12,786	17,637	21,800	23,310	24,217	24,718	21,585	23,058
Interest [9]	977	1,039	1,628	1,773	2,307	2,640	2,179	1,540	1,366
Rents and royalties	133	145	254	290	299	314	317	296	307
Deductions [2, 7]	11,033	13,821	19,692	23,613	25,502	26,974	27,687	23,944	24,944
Cost of sales and operations [8]	6,611	8,206	11,135	13,816	14,800	15,513	16,080	13,286	14,502
Compensation of officers	205	304	401	445	474	479	467	428	435
Rent paid on business property	185	232	380	439	462	477	491	476	467
Taxes paid	251	326	390	473	497	509	469	473	493
Interest paid	825	744	1,272	1,287	1,787	2,085	1,659	1,070	888
Depreciation	333	437	614	531	564	599	759	712	728
Advertising	126	163	234	253	277	277	267	241	256
Net income (less loss) [7, 10]	371	714	928	1,949	1,933	1,837	984	919	1,356
Net income	553	881	1,337	2,235	2,240	2,253	1,807	1,615	1,836
Deficit	182	166	409	286	306	416	823	696	480
Income subject to tax	366	565	760	1,201	1,291	1,248	978	895	1,022
Income tax before credits [11]	119	194	266	419	453	437	342	313	358
Tax credits	32	42	62	107	100	106	114	108	135
Foreign tax credit	25	30	49	82	78	87	100	94	118
Income tax after credits [12]	96	156	204	312	353	331	229	205	223

[1] Represents certain small corporations with a limit on the number of shareholders, mostly individuals, electing to be taxed at the shareholder level. [2] Includes items not shown separately. [3] Payable in less than 1 year. [4] Payable in 1 year or more. [5] Net worth is the sum of "capital stock," "additional paid-in capital," "retained earnings, appropriated," "retained earnings, unappropriated," "adjustments to shareholders' equity," minus "cost of treasury stock." [6] Appropriated and unappropriated and "adjustments to shareholders' equity." [7] Receipts, deductions, and net income of S corporations are limited to those from trade or business. Those from investments are excluded. [8] Includes gross sales and cost of sales of securities, commodities, and real estate by exchanges, brokers, or dealers selling on their own accounts. Excludes investment income. [9] Includes tax-exempt interest in state and local government obligations. [10] Excludes regulated investment companies. [11] Consists of regular (and alternative tax) only. [12] Includes minimum tax, alternative minimum tax, adjustments for prior year credits, and other income-related taxes.

Source: U.S. Internal Revenue Service, "SOI Tax Stats - Corporation Complete Report," <http://www.irs.gov/uac/SOI-Tax-Stats-Corporation-Complete-Report>, accessed August 2013.

Table 781. Corporations by Receipt-Size Class and Industry: 2010

[Number of returns in thousands (5,814 represents 5,814,000); receipts and net income in billions of dollars (23,058 represents $23,058,000,000,000). Covers active enterprises only. Figures are estimates based on a sample of unaudited tax returns; see Appendix III. Numbers in parentheses represent North American Industry Classification System 2007 codes; see text, this section]

Industry	Total	Under $1 mil.[1]	$1 to $4.9 mil.	$5 to $9.9 mil.	$10 to $49.9 mil.	$50 mil. or more
Total:[2]						
Number of returns	5,814	4,809	738	121	114	32
Business receipts [3]	23,058	924	1,570	813	2,208	17,544
Net income (less loss)	1,356	40	53	28	97	1,139
Agriculture, forestry, fishing, and hunting (11):						
Returns	137	117	16	2	1	(Z)
Business receipts	147	19	33	12	28	54
Mining (21):						
Returns	40	32	5	1	1	(Z)
Business receipts	375	5	13	7	17	333
Utilities (22):						
Returns	7	6	(Z)	(Z)	(Z)	(Z)
Business receipts	585	1	1	1	3	579
Construction (23):						
Returns	718	590	98	15	13	2
Business receipts	1,066	124	213	105	253	372
Manufacturing (31–33):						
Returns	251	159	53	14	18	7
Business receipts	6,857	41	125	100	369	6,223
Wholesale and retail trade (42, 44–45):						
Returns	961	662	201	44	42	12
Business receipts	7,137	169	457	308	888	5,316
Transportation and warehousing (48–49):						
Returns	198	159	28	5	5	1
Business receipts	714	30	60	33	95	496
Information (51):						
Returns	123	107	11	2	2	1
Business receipts	922	17	25	12	50	817
Finance and insurance (52):						
Returns	242	208	21	5	6	3
Business receipts [3]	1,914	33	31	16	45	1,789
Real estate and rental and leasing (53):						
Returns	643	621	18	2	1	(Z)
Business receipts	216	48	38	12	24	95
Professional, scientific, and technical services (54):						
Returns	880	774	84	12	8	2
Business receipts	1,045	127	178	79	158	504
Management of companies and enterprises (55):						
Returns	50	43	3	1	2	1
Business receipts [3]	185	(Z)	1	2	8	173
Administrative and support and waste management and remediation services (56):						
Returns	274	232	33	4	3	1
Business receipts	464	44	69	28	73	250
Educational services (61):						
Returns	60	55	4	1	(Z)	(Z)
Business receipts	64	7	8	4	6	38
Health care and social assistance (62):						
Returns	433	341	78	7	7	1
Business receipts	660	101	157	46	119	237
Arts, entertainment, and recreation (71):						
Returns	121	110	9	2	(Z)	(Z)
Business receipts	91	17	19	11	9	36
Accommodation and food services (72):						
Returns	297	245	46	4	2	(Z)
Business receipts	423	74	90	24	40	196
Other services (81):						
Returns	378	346	28	2	1	(Z)
Business receipts	193	69	53	13	22	36

Z Less than 500 returns or $500 million in receipts. [1] Includes businesses without receipts. [2] Includes businesses not allocable to individual industries. [3] Size of total receipts was used instead of size of business receipts to classify data for "Finance and insurance" and "Management of companies and enterprises."

Source: U.S. Internal Revenue Service, "SOI Tax Stats - Corporation Complete Report," <http://www.irs.gov/uac/SOI-Tax-Stats-Corporation-Complete-Report>, accessed August 2013.

Table 782. Corporations by Asset-Size Class and Industry: 2010

[In billions of dollars (168 represents $168,000,000,000), except number of returns. Covers active corporations only. Excludes corporations not allocable by industry. Numbers in parentheses represent North American Industry Classification System 2007 codes; see text, this section]

Industry	Total	Under $10 mil. [1]	$10 to $24.9 mil.	$25 to $49.9 mil.	$50 to $99.9 mil.	$100 to $249.9 mil.	$250 mil. and over
Agriculture, forestry, fishing, and hunting (11):							
Returns........	136,968	135,697	808	243	123	59	(D)
Total receipts........	168	102	14	7	10	11	(D)
Mining (21):							
Returns........	39,826	38,077	748	357	219	166	259
Total receipts........	425	34	10	8	9	13	351
Utilities (22):							
Returns........	6,654	6,156	142	72	50	54	179
Total receipts........	620	5	1	3	2	9	599
Construction (23):							
Returns........	718,378	711,722	4,496	1,168	545	270	177
Total receipts........	1,084	624	113	64	59	54	171
Manufacturing (31–33):							
Returns........	251,069	235,803	7,320	3,019	1,781	1,351	1,795
Total receipts........	7,381	475	199	167	178	271	6,091
Wholesale and retail trade (42, 44–45):							
Returns........	961,024	942,446	11,624	3,384	1,691	956	923
Total receipts........	7,285	1,814	567	350	303	338	3,914
Transportation and warehousing (48–49):							
Returns........	197,818	195,685	1,196	369	214	156	198
Total receipts........	737	207	36	23	22	27	421
Information (51):							
Returns........	122,747	120,089	1,180	477	325	269	407
Total receipts........	1,058	85	21	14	18	28	892
Finance and insurance (52):							
Returns........	242,108	222,594	3,763	2,591	2,519	3,397	7,244
Total receipts........	3,217	154	21	25	31	63	2,924
Real estate and rental and leasing (53):							
Returns........	642,718	634,485	4,899	1,432	772	549	581
Total receipts........	332	134	15	10	10	15	149
Professional, scientific, and technical services (54):							
Returns........	879,564	874,591	2,739	956	549	387	342
Total receipts........	1,083	545	67	47	40	56	328
Management of companies and enterprises (55):							
Returns........	50,330	42,834	1,423	1,131	1,220	1,801	1,921
Total receipts........	823	12	2	4	5	19	781
Administrative and support and waste management and remediation services (56):							
Returns........	274,160	272,766	674	284	162	113	160
Total receipts........	477	218	25	17	16	27	174
Educational services (61):							
Returns........	59,620	59,291	166	57	38	(D)	(D)
Total receipts........	65	22	3	3	3	(D)	(D)
Health care and social assistance (62):							
Returns........	433,398	432,120	636	263	146	116	116
Total receipts........	691	439	25	18	17	25	167
Arts, entertainment, and recreation (71):							
Returns........	121,488	120,725	387	181	81	56	57
Total receipts........	98	51	4	3	4	7	28
Accommodation and food services (72):							
Returns........	297,140	295,674	863	248	135	89	131
Total receipts........	455	218	16	9	12	20	181
Other services (81):							
Returns........	377,648	377,022	403	112	45	(D)	(D)
Total receipts........	200	156	7	5	5	(D)	(D)

D Data withheld to avoid disclosure. [1] Includes returns with zero assets.

Source: U.S. Internal Revenue Service, *2010 Statistics of Income, Corporation Income Tax Returns*, 2011. See also <http://www.irs.gov/uac/SOI-Tax-Stats-Corporation-Complete-Report>.

Table 783. Economic Census Summary (NAICS 2002 Basis): 2002 and 2007

[24 represents 24,000. Covers establishments with payroll. Data are based on the 2002 and 2007 economic censuses which are subject to nonsampling error. Data for the construction sector are also subject to sampling errors. For details on survey methodology and nonsampling and sampling errors, see Appendix III]

Kind of business	2002 NAICS code [1]	Establish-ments (1,000)		Sales, receipts, or shipments (bil. dol.)		Annual payroll (bil. dol.)		Paid employees [2] (1,000)	
		2002	2007	2002	2007	2002	2007	2002	2007
Mining..	21	24	23	183	414	21	41	478	739
Oil & gas extraction.........................	211	8	6	113	255	5	10	100	150
Mining (except oil & gas).................	212	7	6	48	86	9	12	197	211
Mining support activities..................	213	9	10	22	73	7	20	181	377
Utilities...	22	17	17	399	584	42	52	663	637
Construction.....................................	23	710	729	1,209	1,732	254	331	7,193	7,316
Manufacturing...................................	31–33	351	333	3,916	5,319	576	614	14,700	13,396
Wholesale trade...............................	42	436	435	4,635	6,516	260	336	5,878	6,227
Merchant wholesalers, durable goods..........	423	260	255	2,171	2,898	157	207	3,357	3,619
Merchant wholesalers, nondurable goods......	424	143	135	1,980	2,991	93	116	2,273	2,320
Wholesale electronic markets and agents and brokers.................	425	32	45	483	627	10	13	249	289
Retail trade......................................	44–45	1,115	1,128	3,056	3,918	302	363	14,648	15,515
Motor vehicle & parts dealers..........	441	125	127	802	891	65	73	1,845	1,914
Furniture & home furnishings stores..............	442	65	65	92	108	13	15	535	557
Electronics & appliance stores....................	443	47	51	82	109	9	11	391	486
Bldg. material & garden equipment & supplies dealers...............	444	(NA)	91	(NA)	318	(NA)	38	(NA)	1,331
Food & beverage stores.............................	445	149	146	457	539	49	55	2,839	2,827
Health & personal care stores....................	446	82	88	178	234	20	28	1,024	1,068
Gasoline stations..............................	447	121	119	249	450	14	15	927	891
Clothing & clothing accessories stores.........	448	150	156	168	216	21	27	1,427	1,644
Sporting goods, hobby, book, & music stores....	451	62	57	73	81	9	9	611	619
General merchandise stores.....................	452	41	46	445	577	43	54	2,525	2,763
Miscellaneous store retailers...................	453	129	122	91	104	13	14	792	792
Nonstore retailers..........................	454	55	59	173	290	17	23	571	621
Transportation & warehousing [3]..................	48-49	200	220	382	640	116	173	3,651	4,454
Information......................................	51	138	142	892	1,072	195	229	3,736	3,497
Publishing industries (except Internet).........	511	32	31	242	282	66	81	1,090	1,093
Motion picture & sound recording industries....	512	22	24	78	95	13	18	303	336
Broadcasting (except Internet)...................	515	10	10	74	100	14	18	291	295
Internet publishing and broadcasting...........	516	2	3	6	15	2	5	40	57
Telecommunications............................	517	49	49	412	480	72	73	1,440	1,216
Internet service providers, Web search portals, and data processing............	518	19	21	75	94	26	33	514	448
Other information services................	519	3	4	5	6	2	2	58	53
Finance & insurance [4].............................	52	440	507	2,804	3,711	378	505	6,579	6,649
Real estate & rental & leasing [4]...............	53	323	380	336	443	60	82	1,949	2,147
Professional, scientific, & technical services.....	54	771	855	887	1,258	376	505	7,244	7,908
Management of companies & enterprises........	55	49	51	107	104	179	250	2,605	2,664
Admin/support waste management/remediation services..	56	351	388	433	624	206	298	8,742	10,213
Administrative & support services..............	561	332	366	381	549	194	281	8,410	9,827
Waste management & remediation services....	562	19	22	51	75	12	17	332	386
Educational services........................	61	49	61	31	45	10	14	430	540
Health care and social assistance................	62	705	785	1,207	1,668	496	663	15,052	16,792
Ambulatory health care services..............	621	489	548	489	668	203	275	4,925	5,703
Hospitals.......................................	622	6	7	500	703	197	265	5,174	5,529
Nursing & residential care facilities..............	623	69	76	127	169	59	75	2,831	3,071
Social assistance..............................	624	140	154	91	128	36	48	2,123	2,489
Arts, entertainment, & recreation.................	71	110	125	142	189	45	58	1,849	2,061
Performing arts, spectator sports, & related industries..........................	711	38	44	58	78	21	28	423	438
Museums, historical sites, & like institutions....	712	7	7	9	13	3	4	123	130
Amusement, gambling, & recreation industries.......................................	713	66	74	75	98	21	27	1,303	1,494
Accommodation & food services..................	72	566	634	449	614	128	171	10,121	11,601
Accommodation.................................	721	61	63	128	180	35	46	1,813	1,971
Food services & drinking places...............	722	505	572	321	433	93	124	8,308	9,630
Other services (except public administration)....	81	538	540	307	405	83	99	3,475	3,479
Repair & maintenance.........................	811	231	222	118	138	35	40	1,285	1,261
Personal and laundry services...................	812	201	210	72	82	23	27	1,297	1,338
Religious/grantmaking/prof/like organizations...	813	106	108	117	185	25	32	893	880

NA Not available. [1] Based on North American Industry Classification System, 2002; see text, this section. [2] For pay period including March 12. [3] For detailed industries, see Table 1087. [4] For detailed industries, see Table 1187.

Source: U.S. Census Bureau, "2007 Economic Census, Comparative Statistics for the United States and the States (2002 NAICS Basis): 2007 and 2002," <http://factfinder2.census.gov/faces/nav/jsf/pages/index.xhtml>, accessed September 2013.

Table 784. Nonemployer Establishments and Receipts by Industry: 2000 to 2011

[16,530 represents 16,530,000. Includes only firms subject to federal income tax. Nonemployers are businesses with no paid employees. Data originate chiefly from administrative records of the Internal Revenue Service; see Appendix III. Data for 2000 based on the North American Industry Classification System (NAICS), 1997. Data for 2010 and 2011 based on NAICS 2007. See text, this section]

Kind of business	NAICS code	Establishments (1,000)			Receipts (mil. dol.)		
		2000	2010	2011	2000	2010	2011
All industries...	(X)	**16,530**	**22,111**	**22,491**	**709,379**	**950,814**	**989,629**
Agriculture, forestry, fishing and hunting.................	11	223	237	238	9,196	10,115	10,259
Mining, quarrying, and oil and gas extraction............	21	86	106	110	5,227	6,923	7,623
Utilities..	22	14	17	17	504	698	737
Construction..	23	2,014	2,424	2,388	107,538	120,151	122,633
Manufacturing..	31–33	285	318	330	13,022	14,572	15,472
Wholesale trade......................................	42	388	393	403	31,684	34,082	36,221
Retail trade...	44–45	1,743	1,822	1,848	73,810	75,720	79,731
Transportation & warehousing...........................	48–49	747	1,021	1,038	37,824	60,746	66,390
Information...	51	238	311	318	7,620	10,739	11,323
Finance & insurance..................................	52	692	717	714	49,058	50,626	50,312
Real estate & rental & leasing.........................	53	1,696	2,343	2,346	133,398	209,549	215,428
Professional, scientific, & technical services.............	54	2,420	3,121	3,164	90,272	130,613	136,702
Admin/support waste mgt/remediation services..........	56	1,032	1,937	1,985	23,754	39,111	40,887
Educational services..................................	61	283	567	578	3,736	7,703	8,049
Health care & social assistance........................	62	1,317	1,935	1,968	36,550	57,686	59,111
Arts, entertainment, & recreation.......................	71	782	1,154	1,188	17,713	26,756	28,194
Accommodation & food services.........................	72	218	329	341	13,418	14,355	14,863
Other services (except public administration)............	81	2,350	3,358	3,517	55,056	80,669	85,693

X Not applicable.

Source: U.S. Census Bureau, Nonemployer Statistics, "Geographic Area Series: Nonemployer Statistics for the US, States, Metropolitan Areas, and Counties," <http://factfinder2.census.gov>, accessed June 2013.

Table 785. Establishments, Employees, and Payroll by Employment-Size Class: 1990 to 2011

[In units as noted (6,176 represents 6,176,000). Excludes most government employees, railroad employees, and self-employed persons. Employees are for the week including March 12. Covers establishments with payroll. An establishment is a single physical location where business is conducted or where services or industrial operations are performed. For statement on methodology, see Appendix III]

Employment-size class	Unit	1990	2000	2005	2007	2008	2009	2010	2011
Establishments, total..............	1,000	**6,176**	**7,070**	**7,500**	**7,705**	**7,601**	**7,433**	**7,397**	**7,354**
Under 20 employees.................	1,000	5,354	6,069	6,468	6,633	6,528	6,413	6,408	6,352
20 to 99 employees..................	1,000	684	826	856	892	890	852	824	835
100 to 499 employees...............	1,000	122	157	157	161	164	151	148	149
500 to 999 employees...............	1,000	10	12	12	12	12	11	11	11
1,000 or more employees...........	1,000	6	7	7	7	7	7	7	7
Employees, total..................	1,000	**93,476**	**114,065**	**116,317**	**120,604**	**120,904**	**114,510**	**111,970**	**113,426**
Under 20 employees.................	1,000	24,373	27,569	28,874	30,057	29,839	29,099	28,958	28,677
20 to 99 employees..................	1,000	27,414	33,147	34,302	35,615	35,508	33,895	32,730	33,275
100 to 499 employees...............	1,000	22,926	29,736	29,591	30,453	30,850	28,249	27,718	28,128
500 to 999 employees...............	1,000	6,551	8,291	8,053	8,284	8,236	7,770	7,331	7,608
1,000 or more employees...........	1,000	12,212	15,322	15,497	16,196	16,471	15,496	15,233	15,738
Annual payroll, total..............	Bil. dol.	**2,104**	**3,879**	**4,483**	**5,027**	**5,131**	**4,856**	**4,941**	**5,165**
Under 20 employees.................	Bil. dol.	485	818	970	1,067	1,078	1,037	1,057	1,081
20 to 99 employees..................	Bil. dol.	547	1,006	1,177	1,313	1,334	1,267	1,281	1,331
100 to 499 employees...............	Bil. dol.	518	1,031	1,176	1,310	1,348	1,253	1,280	1,341
500 to 999 employees...............	Bil. dol.	174	336	376	428	432	414	410	437
1,000 or more employees...........	Bil. dol.	381	690	784	910	939	885	913	976

Source: U.S. Census Bureau, "County Business Patterns," <http://www.census.gov/econ/cbp/index.html>, accessed May 2013.

Table 786. Establishments, Employees, and Payroll by Employment-Size Class and Industry: 2000 to 2011

[Establishments and employees in thousands (7,070.0 represents 7,070,000); payroll in billions of dollars. See headnote, Table 785. Data for 2000 based on the North American Industry Classification System (NAICS), 1997; 2010 and 2011 data based on NAICS 2007. Svcs = services. See text, this section]

Industry	NAICS code	2000, total	2010, total	2011					
				Total	Under 20 employ-ees	20 to 99 employ-ees	100 to 499 employ-ees	500 to 999 or employ-ees	1,000 more employ-ees
Establishments, total [1]	(X)	**7,070.0**	**7,396.6**	**7,354.0**	**6,351.8**	**835.3**	**149.1**	**11.1**	**6.8**
Forestry, fishing & hunting, & ag support svcs.	113–115	26.1	21.7	21.3	20.0	1.2	0.2	(Z)	(Z)
Mining, quarrying, and oil and gas extraction.	21	23.7	27.1	28.0	22.5	4.4	1.0	0.1	(Z)
Utilities.	22	17.3	17.6	17.6	12.2	4.1	1.1	0.1	0.1
Construction.	23	709.6	682.7	657.7	607.2	45.0	5.2	0.3	0.1
Manufacturing.	31–33	354.5	300.0	295.6	208.5	63.9	20.6	1.9	0.8
Wholesale trade.	42	446.2	414.6	411.9	354.1	50.0	7.2	0.4	0.2
Retail trade.	44–45	1,113.6	1,068.0	1,062.9	917.3	119.1	26.2	0.3	(Z)
Transportation and warehousing.	48–49	190.0	208.5	211.9	177.5	27.3	6.2	0.6	0.3
Information.	51	133.6	135.4	134.5	108.6	20.3	4.7	0.5	0.2
Finance and insurance.	52	423.7	473.5	467.5	427.4	32.6	6.1	0.9	0.5
Real estate and rental and leasing.	53	300.2	347.3	341.7	327.5	12.6	1.4	0.1	(Z)
Professional, scientific, and technical services.	54	722.7	851.5	850.9	788.6	52.4	8.7	0.7	0.4
Management of companies and enterprises.	55	47.4	50.9	49.5	32.4	11.7	4.4	0.6	0.4
Admin/support waste mgt/remediation svcs.	56	351.5	381.8	380.7	321.6	43.1	13.6	1.5	0.9
Educational services.	61	68.0	90.1	91.5	70.1	16.9	3.6	0.5	0.4
Health care and social assistance.	62	658.6	812.9	818.7	688.8	102.2	23.9	1.8	2.0
Arts, entertainment, and recreation.	71	103.8	123.2	123.3	103.9	16.0	3.1	0.2	0.1
Accommodation and food services.	72	542.4	644.0	649.0	470.4	169.5	8.5	0.4	0.2
Other services [2].	81	723.3	725.5	722.4	675.9	42.9	3.4	0.2	0.1
Unclassified establishments.	99	99.0	20.5	17.2	17.2	(Z)	–	–	–
Employees, total [1]	(X)	**114,065**	**111,970**	**113,426**	**28,677**	**33,275**	**28,128**	**7,608**	**15,738**
Forestry, fishing & hunting, & ag support svcs.	113–115	184	156	157	69	45	30	4	8
Mining, quarrying, and oil and gas extraction.	21	456	582	651	104	179	211	73	84
Utilities.	22	655	638	640	66	180	217	99	78
Construction.	23	6,573	5,389	5,191	2,119	1,728	933	177	234
Manufacturing.	31–33	16,474	10,863	10,984	1,171	2,804	4,094	1,253	1,663
Wholesale trade.	42	6,112	5,599	5,626	1,683	1,960	1,344	295	345
Retail trade.	44–45	14,841	14,497	14,699	4,980	4,719	4,754	180	67
Transportation and warehousing.	48–49	3,790	4,012	4,106	725	1,132	1,194	426	629
Information.	51	3,546	3,124	3,121	489	844	932	374	482
Finance and insurance.	52	5,963	5,929	5,887	1,839	1,254	1,243	603	949
Real estate and rental and leasing.	53	1,942	1,946	1,918	1,058	475	252	62	71
Professional, scientific, and technical services.	54	6,816	7,822	7,930	2,635	2,045	1,671	508	1,071
Management of companies and enterprises.	55	2,874	2,833	2,922	181	525	938	437	841
Admin/support waste mgt/remediation svcs.	56	9,138	8,977	9,390	1,231	1,865	2,724	998	2,572
Educational services.	61	2,532	3,274	3,386	341	720	683	316	1,325
Health care and social assistance.	62	14,109	17,788	18,059	3,663	4,112	4,431	1,282	4,572
Arts, entertainment, and recreation.	71	1,741	2,004	2,003	383	677	569	150	225
Accommodation and food services.	72	9,881	11,312	11,556	3,088	6,457	1,335	266	411
Other services [2].	81	5,293	5,204	5,182	2,834	1,556	572	106	114
Unclassified establishments.	99	144	(NA)	(NA)	(NA)	1	–	–	–
Annual payroll, total [1]	(X)	**3,879**	**4,941**	**5,165**	**1,081**	**1,331**	**1,341**	**437**	**976**
Forestry, fishing & hunting, & ag support svcs.	113–115	5	5	5	3	2	1	(Z)	(Z)
Mining, quarrying, and oil and gas extraction.	21	22	46	55	7	14	20	6	9
Utilities.	22	41	55	58	5	15	20	10	8
Construction.	23	240	261	265	88	94	58	11	14
Manufacturing.	31–33	644	550	575	47	130	210	72	117
Wholesale trade.	42	270	339	357	90	115	89	24	39
Retail trade.	44–45	303	359	371	118	122	121	6	3
Transportation and warehousing.	48–49	126	167	176	29	47	50	18	32
Information.	51	209	224	234	30	54	74	30	45
Finance and insurance.	52	347	472	494	104	111	120	50	108
Real estate and rental and leasing.	53	59	80	84	41	23	13	4	3
Professional, scientific, and technical services.	54	362	543	568	147	154	142	44	81
Management of companies and enterprises.	55	211	282	299	19	48	93	46	93
Admin/support waste mgt/remediation svcs.	56	210	304	326	48	67	84	28	99
Educational services.	61	62	110	115	9	21	24	9	52
Health care and social assistance.	62	431	753	780	161	158	153	59	248
Arts, entertainment, and recreation.	71	43	62	64	16	15	21	6	6
Accommodation and food services.	72	126	186	194	49	97	28	7	13
Other services [2].	81	110	140	144	71	44	21	4	4
Unclassified establishments.	99	4	(Z)	(Z)	(Z)	(Z)	–	–	–

– Represents zero. NA Not available. X Not applicable. Z Less than 50 establishments or $500 million. [1] Totals for 2000 include auxiliaries. Beginning 2007, cases previously classified under NAICS code 95 (auxiliaries) are coded in the operating NAICS sector of the establishment. [2] Except public administration.

Source: U.S. Census Bureau, "County Business Patterns," American FactFinder, <http://factfinder2.census.gov>, accessed May 2013.

Table 787. Employer Firms, Employment, and Annual Payroll by Employment Size of Firm and Industry: 2010

[5,735 represents 5,735,000. A firm is an aggregation of all establishments owned by a parent company (within a geographic location and/or industry) with some annual payroll. A firm may be a single location or it can include multiple locations. Employment is measured in March and payroll is annual leading to some firms with zero employment. Numbers in parentheses represent North American Industry Classification System codes, 2007; see text, this section]

Industry and data type	Unit	All industries—employment size of firm							
		Total	0 to 4	5 to 9	10 to 19	20 to 99	100 to 499	Less than 500	500 or more
Total [1]:									
Firms................	1,000	5,735	3,575	968	617	475	82	5,717	17
Employment............	1,000	111,970	5,926	6,359	8,288	18,554	15,869	54,997	56,973
Annual payroll................	Bil. dol	4,941	227	212	283	719	666	2,107	2,834
Construction (23):									
Firms................	1,000	670	465	97	62	40	5	669	1
Employment............	1,000	5,389	711	637	824	1,486	888	4,546	843
Annual payroll................	Bil. dol	261	26	24	34	76	47	207	54
Manufacturing (31–33):									
Firms................	1,000	259	110	47	40	46	12	255	3
Employment............	1,000	10,863	205	315	549	1,864	1,986	4,919	5,943
Annual payroll................	Bil. dol	550	8	11	21	81	92	213	337
Wholesale trade (42):									
Firms................	1,000	314	182	52	37	33	7	311	3
Employment............	1,000	5,599	308	342	495	1,218	972	3,335	2,263
Annual payroll................	Bil. dol	339	15	16	24	65	54	174	165
Retail trade (44–45):									
Firms................	1,000	664	402	132	74	47	7	662	2
Employment............	1,000	14,497	752	865	978	1,731	1,075	5,400	9,096
Annual payroll................	Bil. dol	359	18	20	24	54	34	151	209
Transportation & warehousing (48–49):									
Firms................	1,000	162	105	23	16	14	3	160	2
Employment............	1,000	4,012	157	149	212	504	459	1,482	2,530
Annual payroll................	Bil. dol	167	5	5	7	19	18	55	112
Information (51):									
Firms................	1,000	70	42	10	7	7	2	69	1
Employment............	1,000	3,124	62	66	100	289	309	827	2,297
Annual payroll................	Bil. dol	224	4	3	5	17	21	50	174
Finance & insurance (52):									
Firms................	1,000	238	171	33	15	14	4	236	2
Employment............	1,000	5,929	300	207	196	560	697	1,959	3,969
Annual payroll................	Bil. dol	472	14	11	13	42	52	133	340
Professional, scientific and technical services (54):									
Firms................	1,000	766	566	97	57	37	7	763	3
Employment............	1,000	7,822	842	631	762	1,384	1,044	4,664	3,158
Annual payroll................	Bil. dol	543	44	32	42	95	76	289	254
Management of companies and enterprises (55):									
Firms................	1,000	27	3	1	1	6	9	20	7
Employment............	1,000	2,833	4	4	8	72	283	370	2,463
Annual payroll................	Bil. dol	282	1	(Z)	1	5	21	27	255
Admin/support waste mgt/ remediation services (56):									
Firms................	1,000	323	210	46	30	26	8	320	3
Employment............	1,000	8,977	316	302	404	1,044	1,322	3,389	5,589
Annual payroll................	Bil. dol	304	12	10	13	35	39	109	195
Educational services (61):									
Firms................	1,000	80	39	12	10	13	3	78	1
Employment............	1,000	3,274	62	80	140	561	573	1,416	1,858
Annual payroll................	Bil. dol	110	2	2	3	16	19	42	69
Health care and social assistance (62):									
Firms................	1,000	631	323	143	83	61	17	627	4
Employment............	1,000	17,788	600	947	1,105	2,443	3,255	8,350	9,437
Annual payroll................	Bil. dol	753	31	39	46	96	107	318	435
Accommodation and food services (72):									
Firms................	1,000	482	204	95	90	83	8	480	2
Employment............	1,000	11,312	343	636	1,220	3,054	1,524	6,776	4,536
Annual payroll................	Bil. dol	186	8	8	16	46	24	101	84
Other services (except public administration) (81):									
Firms................	1,000	664	424	129	66	38	4	662	1
Employment............	1,000	5,204	795	838	878	1,357	592	4,459	746
Annual payroll................	Bil. dol	140	19	20	21	36	20	115	25

Z Less than $500 million. [1] Includes other industries, not shown separately.

Source: U.S. Small Business Administration, Office of Advocacy, Firm Size Data, "Statistics of U.S. Businesses," <http://www.sba.gov/advocacy/849/12162>, accessed May 2013.

Table 788. Employer Firms, Employment, and Payroll by Employment Size of Firm and State: 2000 and 2010

[5,653 represents 5,653,000. A firm is an aggregation of all establishments owned by a parent company (within a state) with some annual payroll. A firm may be a single location or it can include multiple locations. Employment is measured in March and payroll is annual leading to some firms with zero employment]

| State | Employer firms (1,000) | | | | | Employment, 2010 (1,000) | | | Annual payroll, 2010 (bil. dol.) | | |
| | 2000 | | 2010 | | | | | | | | |
	Total	Less than 20 employees	Total	Less than 20 employees	Less than 500 employees	Total	Less than 20 employees	Less than 500 employees	Total	Less than 20 employees	Less than 500 employees
U.S.	5,653	5,035	5,735	5,160	5,717	111,970	20,574	54,997	4,941.0	721.8	2,106.5
AL.	80	68	76	64	73	1,568	284	768	57.4	8.6	25.6
AK.	16	14	16	14	16	255	57	135	12.8	2.5	5.9
AZ.	93	79	102	88	99	2,065	338	926	84.0	11.3	32.6
AR.	52	45	51	44	49	965	184	483	33.7	5.2	14.3
CA.	665	581	690	616	685	12,536	2,396	6,323	635.6	97.4	273.2
CO.	116	102	126	111	123	1,955	395	961	89.2	14.1	37.7
CT.	79	67	73	62	71	1,437	262	714	79.9	11.2	33.9
DE.	20	17	20	16	18	359	63	169	17.2	2.4	6.8
DC.	16	12	17	12	16	463	56	217	31.0	3.6	13.2
FL.	354	319	401	367	397	6,627	1,226	2,840	253.0	41.5	101.2
GA.	160	138	170	149	166	3,315	568	1,484	137.5	18.9	53.1
HI.	24	21	25	22	24	479	93	259	17.5	3.0	8.8
ID.	32	28	37	32	35	488	124	282	16.2	3.3	8.1
IL.	254	218	254	221	249	4,980	849	2,389	235.7	32.4	99.7
IN.	116	98	111	95	108	2,400	410	1,157	90.4	12.2	38.4
IA.	66	56	63	54	62	1,253	229	643	44.9	6.5	20.6
KS.	62	52	59	50	57	1,127	209	595	42.7	6.2	19.7
KY.	72	61	70	59	67	1,457	258	697	52.2	7.3	21.9
LA.	82	70	81	69	79	1,600	307	871	62.3	9.9	30.6
ME.	34	30	34	30	33	481	112	282	17.3	3.4	9.2
MD.	106	90	108	93	106	2,076	381	1,072	97.8	14.8	46.1
MA.	148	128	137	119	134	2,929	486	1,357	158.4	20.9	64.8
MI.	194	167	174	153	171	3,288	627	1,700	138.8	21.3	62.9
MN.	116	99	118	102	115	2,358	401	1,181	105.5	13.3	42.7
MS.	48	42	46	39	44	882	170	437	28.6	4.6	12.9
MO.	118	101	118	102	115	2,293	405	1,110	88.6	12.1	36.9
MT.	28	25	31	28	31	338	106	232	10.7	2.8	6.6
NE.	41	36	42	36	41	769	147	391	28.0	4.2	12.5
NV.	40	33	47	40	45	1,003	153	418	37.9	5.7	15.2
NH.	32	27	31	26	30	563	111	285	24.2	4.1	11.2
NJ.	202	178	194	171	191	3,367	655	1,689	178.7	26.6	75.1
NM.	36	30	36	30	34	600	127	331	21.3	3.8	10.6
NY.	425	379	445	401	441	7,266	1,444	3,738	418.4	59.6	177.6
NC.	164	142	169	147	166	3,235	594	1,545	125.2	18.2	50.8
ND.	17	15	18	15	17	295	65	182	10.5	1.9	5.8
OH.	213	181	190	163	186	4,352	720	2,075	174.5	22.9	72.0
OK.	70	61	72	62	70	1,241	256	673	46.1	7.8	22.1
OR.	85	74	88	77	86	1,351	310	750	54.4	9.2	25.4
PA.	238	205	231	200	227	4,976	862	2,419	211.6	28.7	89.2
RI.	25	22	25	21	24	399	83	221	16.8	2.9	8.3
SC.	78	67	79	68	77	1,503	284	728	52.5	8.1	22.3
SD.	21	18	22	19	21	329	79	204	10.8	2.1	6.0
TN.	102	87	98	83	95	2,264	367	1,018	87.5	11.5	35.9
TX.	369	321	394	343	389	8,785	1,456	4,076	386.7	52.5	155.4
UT.	46	39	58	50	56	1,021	183	492	38.0	5.6	16.5
VT.	19	17	19	16	18	264	64	158	9.3	2.0	5.4
VA.	140	120	149	129	146	2,998	530	1,437	139.1	18.9	58.8
WA.	138	121	144	128	142	2,327	506	1,250	111.4	17.0	48.4
WV.	34	29	30	25	28	560	114	298	19.3	3.0	8.8
WI.	116	98	110	94	108	2,321	410	1,202	90.9	12.5	40.6
WY.	16	14	18	15	17	205	61	133	8.4	2.0	4.7

Source: U.S. Small Business Administration, Office of Advocacy, Research and Statistics, Firm Size Data, "Statistics of U.S. Businesses," <http://www.sba.gov/advocacy/849/12162>, accessed May 2013.

Table 789. Employer Firms, Establishments, Employment, and Annual Payroll by Firm Size: 1990 to 2010

[In thousands except as noted (5,074 represents 5,074,000). Firms are an aggregation of all establishments owned by a parent company with some annual payroll. Establishments are locations with active payroll in any quarter. This table illustrates the changing importance of enterprise sizes over time, not job growth, as enterprises can grow or decline and change enterprise size cells over time]

Item	Total	All industries—employment size of firm						
		0 to 4 [1]	5 to 9	10 to 19	20 to 99	100 to 499	Less than 500	500 or more
Firms:								
1990...............	5,074	3,021	952	563	454	70	5,060	14
2000...............	5,653	3,397	1,021	617	516	84	5,635	17
2005...............	5,984	3,678	1,050	630	521	87	5,966	17
2006...............	6,022	3,670	1,061	647	536	91	6,004	18
2007...............	6,050	3,705	1,060	645	532	89	6,031	18
2008...............	5,930	3,618	1,044	633	526	90	5,912	18
2009...............	5,767	3,559	1,001	611	496	83	5,750	18
2010...............	5,735	3,575	968	617	475	82	5,717	17
Establishments:								
1990...............	6,176	3,032	971	600	590	255	5,448	728
2000...............	7,070	3,406	1,035	652	674	312	6,080	990
2005...............	7,500	3,684	1,063	662	679	332	6,421	1,079
2006...............	7,601	3,677	1,073	679	698	346	6,473	1,129
2007...............	7,705	3,711	1,074	682	723	356	6,546	1,159
2008...............	7,601	3,625	1,057	667	705	360	6,414	1,187
2009...............	7,433	3,565	1,015	646	673	354	6,253	1,180
2010...............	7,397	3,583	982	653	648	354	6,220	1,176
Employment:								
1990...............	93,469	5,117	6,252	7,543	17,710	13,545	50,167	43,302
2000...............	114,065	5,593	6,709	8,286	20,277	16,260	57,124	56,941
2005...............	116,317	5,937	6,898	8,454	20,444	16,911	58,645	57,672
2006...............	119,917	5,960	6,974	8,676	21,077	17,537	60,224	59,693
2007...............	120,604	6,139	6,975	8,656	20,923	17,174	59,867	60,737
2008...............	120,904	6,086	6,878	8,497	20,685	17,548	59,694	61,210
2009...............	114,510	5,966	6,581	8,191	19,390	16,153	56,282	58,228
2010...............	111,970	5,926	6,359	8,288	18,554	15,869	54,997	56,973
Annual payroll (bil. dol.):								
1990...............	2,104	117	114	144	352	279	1,007	1,097
2000...............	3,879	186	174	231	608	528	1,727	2,152
2005...............	4,483	220	206	269	700	617	2,013	2,470
2006...............	4,792	230	214	282	742	661	2,129	2,664
2007...............	5,027	235	222	292	769	687	2,205	2,822
2008...............	5,131	232	223	294	775	706	2,229	2,901
2009...............	4,856	220	213	278	719	655	2,085	2,771
2010...............	4,941	227	212	283	719	666	2,107	2,834

[1] Employment is measured in March, thus some firms (start-ups after March, closures before March, and seasonal firms) will have zero employment and some annual payroll.

Source: U.S. Small Business Administration, Office of Advocacy, Research and Statistics, Firm Size Data, "Statistics of U.S. Businesses," <http://www.sba.gov/advocacy/847>, accessed May 2013.

Table 790. Number of Active Establishments by Firm Age and Firm Size: 2011

[In thousands (2,674 represents 2,674,000). A firm may have one establishment (a single unit establishment) or many establishments (a multi-unit firm). Firms are defined at the enterprise level such that all establishments under the operational control of the enterprise are considered part of the firm. Data cover nonfarm private establishments with paid employees; major exclusions are self—employed individuals, employees of private households, railroad employees, agricultural production employees, and most government employees. Establishments are used in the tabulation of Business Dynamics Statistics (BDS) statistics. Although the BDS program is based on the same basic source data as the Census Bureau's County Business Patterns and Statistics of U.S. Business programs, differences in how the source data are processed lead to differences in published statistics. For more information about concepts and methodology, see <http://www.census.gov/ces/dataproducts/bds/overview.html>]

Firm age [1]	Firm size							Share of employment	Share of job creation	Share of job destruction
	1 to 4 employ-ees	5 to 9 employ-ees	10 to 19 employ-ees	20 to 99 employ-ees	100 to 499 employ-ees	Less than 500 employ-ees	500 or more employ-ees			
Total......................	2,674	934	548	494	207	4,858	342	1.00	1.00	1.00
Startups...................	355	33	13	10	2	414	(Z)	0.04	0.24	0.00
1 to 5 years..............	838	254	131	93	23	1,339	8	0.17	0.19	0.29
6 to 10 years..............	518	196	113	92	23	942	19	0.15	0.13	0.18
11 to 20 years.............	580	250	154	138	51	1,172	69	0.25	0.18	0.24
21 years and over.........	383	202	137	161	109	992	247	0.39	0.26	0.28
Share of employment.....	0.09	0.10	0.11	0.24	0.16	0.70	0.30	(X)	(X)	(X)
Share of job creation......	0.16	0.11	0.11	0.21	0.14	0.73	0.27	(X)	(X)	(X)

X Not applicable. Z Less than 500. [1] Establishment age is computed by taking the difference between the current year of operation and the birth year. Firm age is computed from the age of the establishments belonging to that particular firm.

Source: U.S. Census Bureau, Center for Economic Studies, "Business Dynamics Statistics," <http://www.census.gov/ces/dataproducts/bds/data_firm.html>, accessed August 2013.

Table 791. Firm Births and Deaths by Employment Size of Enterprise: 1990 to 2010

[In thousands (541.1 represents 541,100). Data represent activity from March of the beginning year to March of the ending year. Establishments with no employment in the first quarter of the beginning year were excluded. This table provides the number of births and deaths of initial establishments (based on Census ID) as an approximation of firm births and deaths]

Item	Births (initial locations)				Deaths (initial locations)			
	Total	Less than 20 employees	Less than 500 employees	500 employees or more	Total	Less than 20 employees	Less than 500 employees	500 employees or more
Firms:								
1990 to 1991..................	541.1	515.9	540.9	0.3	546.5	517.0	546.1	0.4
2000 to 2001..................	585.1	558.0	584.8	0.3	553.3	524.0	552.8	0.5
2004 to 2005 [1]..............	644.1	616.0	643.9	0.3	565.7	539.1	565.5	0.3
2005 to 2006..................	670.1	640.7	669.8	0.2	599.3	573.3	599.1	0.3
2006 to 2007..................	668.4	639.1	668.2	0.2	592.4	564.3	592.1	0.3
2007 to 2008..................	597.1	570.3	596.8	0.2	641.4	613.8	641.2	0.2
2008 to 2009 [2]..............	518.5	497.5	518.4	0.1	680.7	655.9	680.5	0.2
2009 to 2010 [2]..............	533.9	514.4	533.8	0.1	593.3	572.9	593.2	0.2
Employment:								
1990 to 1991..................	3,105	1,713	2,907	198	3,208	1,723	3,044	164
2000 to 2001..................	3,418	1,821	3,109	310	3,262	1,701	3,050	212
2004 to 2005 [1]..............	3,609	1,931	3,279	330	3,307	1,685	2,981	326
2005 to 2006..................	3,682	1,999	3,412	270	3,220	1,711	2,964	256
2006 to 2007..................	3,554	1,945	3,325	229	3,482	1,734	3,126	356
2007 to 2008..................	3,376	1,784	3,058	318	3,413	1,846	3,174	240
2008 to 2009 [2]..............	2,697	1,545	2,523	173	3,459	1,928	3,195	264
2009 to 2010 [2]..............	2,697	1,613	2,550	147	2,857	1,664	2,602	256

[1] A change in methodology ("based on Census ID" rather than "plant number") has affected the allocation of firms by employment size. [2] Methodology from 2008 forward is defining firm births/deaths as establishment births/deaths for single location firms.

Source: U.S. Small Business Administration, Office of Advocacy, Research and Statistics, Firm Size Data, "Statistics of U.S. Businesses," <http://www.sba.gov/advocacy/849/12162>, accessed May 2013.

Table 792. Establishments and Employment Changes from Births, Deaths, Expansions, and Contractions by Employment Size of Enterprise: 2009 to 2010

[In thousands (6,706 represents 6,706,000), except percent. See headnote, Table 791. An establishment is a single physical location at which business is conducted or where services or industrial operations are performed. An enterprise is a business organization consisting of one or more domestic establishments under common ownership or control. Minus sign (-) indicates decrease]

Employment size of firm	Establishments			Employment		Percent change in employment due to—			
	Total	Births [1]	Deaths [2]	Total	Change in employment	Births [1]	Deaths [2]	Births and expansions [3]	Deaths and contractions [4]
Total.....................	**6,706**	**647**	**719**	**114,491**	**-2,535**	**4.3**	**-4.6**	**12.1**	**-14.3**
1 to 4........................	2,875	418	478	5,962	582	12.6	-13.9	31.0	-21.3
5 to 9........................	1,014	60	67	6,577	-89	5.8	-6.5	16.6	-18.0
10 to 19......................	646	38	35	8,188	-216	6.1	-5.3	14.3	-16.9
20 to 99......................	672	24	29	19,385	-740	3.8	-4.1	10.8	-14.6
100 to 499...................	350	24	16	16,151	-366	4.5	-3.1	11.3	-13.5
Less than 500.............	5,557	564	625	56,263	-828	5.5	-5.3	14.3	-15.7
500 or more..............	1,149	83	94	58,228	-1,707	3.2	-3.8	10.0	-12.9

[1] Births are establishments that have zero employment in the first quarter of the initial year and positive employment in the first quarter of the subsequent year. [2] Deaths are establishments that have positive employment in the first quarter of the initial year and zero employment in the first quarter of the subsequent year. [3] Expansions are establishments that have positive first quarter employment in both the initial and subsequent years and increase employment during the time period between the first quarter of the initial year and the first quarter of the subsequent year. [4] Contractions are establishments that have positive first quarter employment in both the initial and subsequent years and decrease employment during the time period between the first quarter of the initial year and the first quarter of the subsequent year.

Source: U.S. Census Bureau, "Statistics of U.S. Businesses," <http://www.census.gov/econ/susb/>, accessed May 2013.

Table 793. Small Business Administration Loans to Minority-Owned Small Businesses: 2000 to 2012

[3,675 represents $3,675,000,000. For year ending September 30. A small business must be independently owned and operated, must not be dominant in its particular industry, and must meet standards set by the Small Business Administration as to its annual receipts or number of employees]

Minority group	Number of loans					Amount (mil. dol.)				
	2000	2005	2010	2011	2012	2000	2005	2010	2011	2012
Total minority loans [1]...................	**12,041**	**30,226**	**11,866**	**13,156**	**11,843**	**3,675**	**6,294**	**4,000**	**5,989**	**5,353**
African American...........................	2,183	7,302	1,764	1,565	1,210	415	756	335	403	283
Asian American.............................	5,827	13,353	6,137	7,120	6,499	2,390	4,072	2,760	4,388	3,949
Hispanic American.........................	3,491	8,748	3,524	3,987	3,712	767	1,341	816	1,065	1,040
Native American............................	540	823	430	477	422	102	125	88	132	81

[1] Data for 2010 and 2011 include other minority loans not shown separately.

Source: U.S. Small Business Administration, "SBA Lending Statistics for Major Programs (as of September 30, 2012)," <http://www.sba.gov/content/sba-lending-statistics-major-programs-9302012>, accessed August 2013.

Table 794. U.S. Firms—Ownership by Gender, Ethnicity, Race, and Veteran Status: 2007

[27,093 represents 27,093,000. Based on the 2007 Survey of Business Owners; see text, this section and Appendix III]

Group	All firms [1] Firms (1,000)	All firms [1] Sales and receipts (bil. dol.)	Firms with paid employees Firms (1,000)	Firms with paid employees Sales and receipts (bil. dol.)	Firms with paid employees Employees (1,000)	Firms with paid employees Annual payroll (bil. dol.)
All firms..............................	27,093	30,032	5,736	29,059	117,310	4,823
Female..............................	7,792	1,197	910	1,014	7,520	215
Male..............................	13,901	8,478	3,230	7,909	41,051	1,510
Equally male/female..............................	4,602	1,275	1,050	1,092	8,055	215
Hispanic [2]..............................	2,260	351	249	280	1,908	54
Equally Hispanic [2]/non-Hispanic..............................	243	56	47	47	378	11
Non-Hispanic..............................	23,792	10,543	4,895	9,688	54,341	1,875
Minority..............................	5,759	1,025	767	860	5,816	164
Equally minority/nonminority..............................	435	108	86	92	696	22
Nonminority..............................	20,101	9,816	4,338	9,063	50,114	1,754
Veteran..............................	2,448	1,220	491	1,126	5,793	210
Equally veteran/nonveteran..............................	1,220	414	271	365	2,448	75
Nonveteran..............................	22,628	9,316	4,428	8,525	48,386	1,656
White..............................	22,595	10,241	4,640	9,407	52,518	1,824
Black or African American..............................	1,922	136	107	97	910	23
American Indian and Alaska Native..............................	237	34	24	27	185	6
Asian..............................	1,550	506	397	454	2,808	79
Native Hawaiian and Other Pacific Islander..............................	38	6	4	5	38	1
Some other race..............................	81	17	13	14	84	2
Publicly held and other firms [3]..............................	798	19,082	546	19,044	60,684	2,882
Classifiable firms [4]..............................	26,295	10,949	5,190	10,015	56,627	1,941

[1] Both firms with paid employees and firms with no paid employees. [2] An Hispanic firm may be of any race and therefore may be included in more than one race group. [3] Publicly held and other firms not classifiable by gender, ethnicity, race, and veteran status. [4] All firms classifiable by gender, ethnicity, race, and veteran status.

Source: U.S. Census Bureau, 2007 Economic Census, *Survey of Business Owners*, <http://www.census.gov/econ/sbo/>, accessed July 2012.

Table 795. Women-Owned Firms by Kind of Business: 2007

[7,792 represents 7,792,000. See headnote, Table 794]

Kind of business	2007 NAICS code [1]	All firms [2] Firms (1,000)	All firms [2] Sales and receipts (mil. dol.)	Firms with paid employees Firms (1,000)	Firms with paid employees Sales and receipts (mil. dol.)	Firms with paid employees Employees (1,000)	Firms with paid employees Annual payroll (mil. dol.)
Total [3]..............................	(X)	7,792	1,196,608	910	1,014,366	7,520	214,673
Forestry, fishing and hunting, and agricultural support services..............................	113–115	27	2,033	2	1,309	10	264
Mining..............................	21	18	11,545	2	10,694	23	1,012
Utilities..............................	22	4	1,773	(Z)	1,707	2	80
Construction..............................	23	269	96,889	54	87,884	492	21,127
Manufacturing..............................	31–33	113	113,527	34	111,281	568	20,481
Wholesale trade..............................	42	133	245,269	39	240,320	378	15,680
Retail trade..............................	44–45	919	190,162	126	171,031	836	17,835
Transportation and warehousing [4]..............................	48–49	143	32,849	19	27,867	216	7,050
Information..............................	51	97	25,839	9	23,772	118	6,153
Finance and insurance [5]..............................	52	200	32,062	35	24,683	160	6,911
Real estate and rental and leasing..............................	53	658	58,622	57	29,127	183	5,734
Professional, scientific, and technical services..............................	54	1,097	107,075	143	77,436	632	28,217
Management of companies and enterprises..............................	55	2	2,630	2	2,630	51	3,481
Administrative and support and waste management and remediation services..............................	56	786	65,609	64	53,875	1,151	26,691
Educational services..............................	61	276	9,798	16	6,795	127	2,556
Health care and social assistance..............................	62	1,232	92,334	127	69,214	1,130	28,887
Arts, entertainment, and recreation..............................	71	376	16,452	19	9,717	114	3,045
Accommodation and food services..............................	72	192	47,184	86	43,907	957	12,223
Other services (except public administration) [6]..............................	81	1,252	44,777	77	20,939	367	7,195
Industries not classified..............................	99	3	179	3	179	4	50

X Not applicable. Z Less than 500. [1] Based on the 2007 North American Industry Classification System (NAICS); see text, this section. [2] Both firms with paid employees and firms with no paid employees. [3] Firms with more than one establishment are counted in each industry in which they operate, but only once in the total. [4] Excludes scheduled passenger air transportation (NAICS 481111), rail transportation (NAICS 482), and the postal service (NAICS 491). [5] Excludes funds, trusts, and other financial vehicles (NAICS 525). [6] Excludes religious, grantmaking, civic, professional, and similar organizations (NAICS 813) and private households (NAICS 814).

Source: U.S. Census Bureau, 2007 Economic Census, *Survey of Business Owners*, <http://www.census.gov/econ/sbo/>, accessed July 2012.

Table 796. Minority-Owned Firms by Kind of Business: 2007

[1,024,802 represents $1,024,802,000,000. See headnote, Table 794. A minority-owned firm is one in which Blacks or African Americans, American Indians and Alaska Natives, Asians, Native Hawaiians and Other Pacific Islanders, and/or Hispanics own 51 percent or more of the interest or stock of the business]

Kind of business	2007 NAICS code [1]	All firms [2]		Firms with paid employees			
		Firms	Sales and receipts (mil. dol.)	Firms	Sales and receipts (mil. dol.)	Employees	Annual payroll (mil. dol.)
Total [3]	(X)	5,759,209	1,024,802	766,533	860,492	5,816,114	164,065
Forestry, fishing and hunting, and agricultural support services	113–115	24,420	1,966	1,053	988	13,836	257
Mining	21	4,757	2,026	585	1,761	8,629	389
Utilities	22	3,684	413	163	341	832	29
Construction	23	551,209	96,203	62,747	74,195	425,949	15,699
Manufacturing	31–33	81,949	65,651	24,813	63,367	342,183	11,278
Wholesale trade	42	126,845	215,611	46,919	208,760	333,551	13,221
Retail trade	44–45	525,859	191,647	117,905	174,798	627,792	13,135
Transportation and warehousing [4]	48–49	432,204	42,717	23,247	20,572	153,207	4,583
Information	51	63,789	14,700	6,004	13,093	56,066	3,246
Finance and insurance [5]	52	137,969	26,164	21,912	20,157	100,519	4,314
Real estate and rental and leasing	53	345,806	28,293	24,962	12,760	88,492	2,694
Professional, scientific, and technical services	54	575,857	80,515	78,385	64,747	452,297	24,903
Management of companies and enterprises	55	963	2,182	963	2,182	33,552	2,381
Administrative and support and waste management and remediation services	56	606,667	42,679	41,089	32,849	619,762	14,508
Educational services	61	111,860	4,562	6,761	3,339	51,883	1,208
Health care and social assistance	62	754,919	83,869	104,295	69,722	797,444	27,027
Arts, entertainment, and recreation	71	196,639	8,853	6,671	5,116	46,619	1,676
Accommodation and food services	72	241,031	78,325	134,775	73,913	1,408,938	18,522
Other services (except public administration) [6]	81	972,980	38,229	63,480	17,635	252,740	4,955
Industries not classified	99	1,534	198	1,534	198	1,820	39

X Not applicable. [1] Based on the 2007 North American Industry Classification System (NAICS); see text, this section. [2] Both firms with paid employees and firms with no paid employees. [3] Firms with more than one establishment are counted in each industry in which they operate, but only once in the total. [4] Excludes scheduled passenger air transportation (NAICS 481111), rail transportation (NAICS 482), and the postal service (NAICS 491). [5] Excludes funds, trusts, and other financial vehicles (NAICS 525). [6] Excludes religious, grantmaking, civic, professional, and similar organizations (NAICS 813) and private households (NAICS 814).

Source: U.S. Census Bureau, 2007 Economic Census, *Survey of Business Owners*, <http://www.census.gov/econ/sbo/>, accessed July 2012.

Table 797. Hispanic-Owned Firms by Kind of Business: 2007

[350,661 represents $350,661,000,000. See headnote, Table 794]

Kind of business	2007 NAICS code [1]	All firms [2]		Firms with paid employees			
		Firms	Sales and receipts (mil. dol.)	Firms	Sales and receipts (mil. dol.)	Employees	Annual payroll (mil. dol.)
Total [3]	(X)	2,260,269	350,661	248,852	279,921	1,908,161	54,296
Forestry, fishing and hunting, and agricultural support services	113-115	10,201	936	576	595	11,161	179
Mining	21	2,328	1,021	309	899	5,400	242
Utilities	22	1,866	81	41	41	187	9
Construction	23	340,770	56,770	38,319	41,512	260,420	8,919
Manufacturing	31-33	36,619	22,317	10,547	21,159	135,019	4,395
Wholesale trade	42	43,971	63,998	13,112	61,589	98,064	3,777
Retail trade	44-45	186,417	60,974	29,714	54,777	186,781	4,415
Transportation and warehousing [4]	48-49	200,567	21,268	11,903	9,697	70,873	2,069
Information	51	21,435	3,275	2,134	2,684	14,213	710
Finance and insurance [5]	52	51,715	10,888	8,850	8,821	40,381	1,580
Real estate and rental and leasing	53	130,365	10,196	9,240	4,564	31,489	948
Professional, scientific, and technical services	54	185,420	22,394	24,736	17,137	129,693	6,305
Management of companies and enterprises	55	282	911	282	911	15,801	1,156
Administrative and support and waste management and remediation services	56	313,313	19,833	20,874	14,311	262,892	6,168
Educational services	61	33,144	1,378	1,596	1,011	13,992	372
Health care and social assistance	62	234,824	19,260	23,171	15,174	181,742	6,027
Arts, entertainment, and recreation	71	63,918	2,767	2,315	1,394	13,559	507
Accommodation and food services	72	65,602	18,472	31,164	17,277	354,305	4,697
Other services (except public administration) [6]	81	337,637	13,826	20,093	6,273	81,709	1,803
Industries not classified	99	425	95	425	95	480	17

X Not applicable. [1] Based on the 2007 North American Industry Classification System (NAICS); see text, this section. [2] Both firms with paid employees and firms with no paid employees. [3] Firms with more than one establishment are counted in each industry in which they operate, but only once in the total. [4] Excludes scheduled passenger air transportation (NAICS 481111), rail transportation (NAICS 482), and the postal service (NAICS 491). [5] Excludes funds, trusts, and other financial vehicles (NAICS 525). [6] Excludes religious, grantmaking, civic, professional, and similar organizations (NAICS 813) and private households (NAICS 814).

Source: U.S. Census Bureau, 2007 Economic Census, *Survey of Business Owners*, <http://www.census.gov/econ/sbo/>, accessed July 2012.

Table 798. Black-Owned Firms by Kind of Business: 2007

[135,740 represents $135,740,000,000. See headnote, Table 794]

Kind of business	2007 NAICS code [1]	All firms [2]		Firms with paid employees			
		Firms	Sales and receipts (mil. dol.)	Firms	Sales and receipts (mil. dol.)	Employees	Annual payroll (mil dol.)
Total [3]	(X)	**1,921,864**	**135,740**	**106,566**	**97,145**	**909,552**	**23,335**
Forestry, fishing and hunting, and agricultural support services	113–115	4,347	335	230	137	1,254	27
Mining	21	(S)	(S)	(S)	(S)	(S)	(S)
Utilities	22	1,316	68	18	48	92	4
Construction	23	125,818	13,188	9,605	9,808	56,088	1,977
Manufacturing	31–33	16,041	6,848	1,854	6,501	28,399	1,014
Wholesale trade	42	19,384	15,153	2,300	14,497	17,976	743
Retail trade	44–45	148,181	20,512	11,142	17,486	57,335	1,432
Transportation and warehousing [4]	48–49	168,386	11,158	5,827	3,961	40,111	1,040
Information	51	23,442	2,532	1,204	2,120	11,094	731
Finance and insurance [5]	52	42,100	3,148	4,737	2,032	15,982	605
Real estate and rental and leasing	53	92,655	3,957	3,323	1,301	10,972	296
Professional, scientific, and technical services	54	163,761	12,600	12,916	9,129	79,597	3,671
Management of companies and enterprises	55	196	351	196	351	3,318	191
Administrative and support and waste management and remediation services	56	216,763	9,937	9,630	7,175	167,507	3,490
Educational services	61	47,727	1,121	1,457	675	11,895	253
Health care and social assistance	62	365,140	16,752	24,372	11,447	226,145	4,965
Arts, entertainment, and recreation	71	86,357	3,401	2,156	2,022	11,385	567
Accommodation and food services	72	40,959	6,790	7,347	6,105	139,491	1,695
Other services (except public administration) [6]	81	358,443	7,619	8,023	2,105	29,548	590
Industries not classified	99	487	37	487	37	486	6

X Not applicable. S Withheld because estimate did not meet publication standards. [1] Based on the 2007 North American Industry Classification System (NAICS); see text, this section. [2] Both firms with paid employees and firms with no paid employees. [3] Firms with more than one establishment are counted in each industry in which they operate, but only once in the total. [4] Excludes scheduled passenger air transportation (NAICS 481111), rail transportation (NAICS 482), and the postal service (NAICS 491). [5] Excludes funds, trusts, and other financial vehicles (NAICS 525). [6] Excludes religious, grantmaking, civic, professional, and similar organizations (NAICS 813) and private households (NAICS 814).

Source: U.S. Census Bureau, 2007 Economic Census, *Survey of Business Owners*, <http://www.census.gov/econ/sbo/>, accessed July 2012.

Table 799. Asian–Owned Firms by Kind of Business: 2007

[506,048 represents $506,048,000,000. See headnote, Table 794]

Kind of business	2007 NAICS code [1]	All firms [2]		Firms with paid employees			
		Firms	Sales and receipts (mil. dol.)	Firms	Sales and receipts (mil. dol.)	Employees	Annual payroll (mil. dol.)
Total [3]	(X)	**1,549,559**	**506,048**	**397,426**	**453,574**	**2,807,771**	**79,230**
Forestry, fishing and hunting, and agricultural support services	113–115	5,125	429	122	165	798	27
Mining	21	3	(D)	1	(D)	([4])	(D)
Utilities	22	474	119	63	108	375	11
Construction	23	70,722	18,664	10,542	16,005	77,302	3,353
Manufacturing	31–33	26,375	33,723	11,856	33,022	166,307	5,399
Wholesale trade	42	60,458	130,742	30,525	127,076	208,221	8,272
Retail trade	44–45	190,830	106,981	77,357	99,408	375,276	7,021
Transportation and warehousing [5]	48–49	74,117	10,105	5,284	6,487	37,094	1,314
Information	51	17,428	8,561	2,501	8,023	28,752	1,755
Finance and insurance [6]	52	42,099	11,343	7,579	8,648	39,133	1,907
Real estate and rental and leasing	53	116,035	13,196	11,467	6,345	41,566	1,280
Professional, scientific, and technical services	54	213,705	42,339	38,190	35,918	225,756	13,842
Management of companies and enterprises	55	441	847	441	847	13,182	941
Administrative and support and waste management and remediation services	56	75,485	11,239	9,932	9,758	157,040	4,086
Educational services	61	29,515	1,943	3,545	1,545	24,201	541
Health care and social assistance	62	164,224	44,662	54,839	39,999	362,344	14,672
Arts, entertainment, and recreation	71	40,220	2,202	1,964	1,367	19,445	434
Accommodation and food services	72	133,729	52,073	96,015	49,556	891,886	11,844
Other services (except public administration) [7]	81	287,831	16,350	35,310	8,816	137,171	2,450
Industries not classified	99	613	62	613	62	730	14

X Not applicable. D Withheld to avoid disclosing data for individual companies; data are included in higher level totals. [1] Based on the 2007 North American Industry Classification System (NAICS); see text, this section. [2] Both firms with paid employees and firms with no paid employees. [3] Firms with more than one establishment are counted in each industry in which they operate, but only once in the total. [4] 20 to 99 employees. [5] Excludes scheduled passenger air transportation (NAICS 481111), rail transportation (NAICS 482), and the postal service (NAICS 491). [6] Excludes funds, trusts, and other financial vehicles (NAICS 525). [7] Excludes religious, grantmaking, civic, professional, and similar organizations (NAICS 813) and private households (NAICS 814).

Source: U.S. Census Bureau, 2007 Economic Census, *Survey of Business Owners*, <http://www.census.gov/econ/sbo/>, accessed July 2012.

Table 800. Native Hawaiian- and Other Pacific Islander-Owned Firms by Kind of Business: 2007

[6,319 represents $6,319,000,000. See headnote, Table 794]

Kind of business	2007 NAICS code [1]	All firms [2]		Firms with paid employees			
		Firms	Sales and receipts (mil. dol.)	Firms	Sales and receipts (mil. dol.)	Employees	Annual payroll (mil.dol.)
Total [3].............................	(X)	37,687	6,319	4,151	5,250	37,801	1,217
Forestry, fishing and hunting, and agricultural support services................................	113–115	(S)	(S)	(S)	(S)	(S)	(S)
Mining...	21	31	(D)	1	(D)	([4])	(D)
Utilities..	22	186	8	31	(D)	([4])	(D)
Construction.....................................	23	4,991	1,555	847	1,354	5,993	284
Manufacturing...................................	31–33	623	295	99	280	1,714	53
Wholesale trade................................	42	631	488	156	432	923	44
Retail trade......................................	44–45	3,880	1,258	464	1,116	3,278	100
Transportation and warehousing [5]........	48–49	2,274	261	133	162	896	32
Information.......................................	51	414	120	31	108	610	31
Finance and insurance [6].....................	52	1,030	101	179	79	491	16
Real estate and rental and leasing........	53	2,528	227	189	110	613	22
Professional, scientific, and technical services........	54	3,619	606	464	499	3,930	226
Management of companies and enterprises...........	55	13	(D)	13	(D)	([7])	(D)
Administrative and support and waste management and remediation services............................	56	3,542	385	293	339	7,948	166
Educational services..........................	61	614	40	29	34	524	11
Health care and social assistance........	62	3,723	290	460	225	2,332	89
Arts, entertainment, and recreation.......	71	2,625	113	(S)	(S)	(S)	(S)
Accommodation and food services........	72	1,316	380	558	369	6,030	92
Other services (except public administration) [8]........	81	5,264	168	182	57	759	18
Industries not classified......................	99	(S)	(S)	(S)	(S)	(S)	(S)

X Not applicable. D Withheld to avoid disclosing data for individual companies; data are included in higher level totals. S Withheld because estimate did not meet publication standards. [1] Based on the 2007 North American Industry Classification System (NAICS); see text, this section. [2] Both firms with paid employees and firms with no paid employees. [3] Firms with more than one establishment are counted in each industry in which they operate, but only once in the total. [4] 0 to 19 employees. [5] Excludes scheduled passenger air transportation (NAICS 481111), rail transportation (NAICS 482), and the postal service (NAICS 491). [6] Excludes funds, trusts, and other financial vehicles (NAICS 525). [7] 100 to 249 employees. [8] Excludes religious, grantmaking, civic, professional, and similar organizations (NAICS 813) and private households (NAICS 814).

Source: U.S. Census Bureau, 2007 Economic Census, *Survey of Business Owners*, <http://www.census.gov/econ/sbo/>, accessed July 2012.

Table 801. American Indian- and Alaska Native-Owned Firms by Kind of Business: 2007

[34,354 represents $34,354,000,000. See headnote, Table 794]

Kind of business	2007 NAICS code [1]	All firms [2]		Firms with paid employees			
		Firms	Sales and receipts (mil. dol.)	Firms	Sales and receipts (mil. dol.)	Employees	Annual payroll (mil.dol.)
Total [3].............................	(X)	236,691	34,354	23,662	27,494	185,037	5,930
Forestry, fishing and hunting, and agricultural support services................................	113–115	5,026	279	153	84	493	23
Mining...	21	814	293	159	228	1,111	43
Utilities..	22	248	(D)	13	(D)	([4])	(D)
Construction.....................................	23	37,693	8,450	5,178	7,026	37,722	1,529
Manufacturing...................................	31–33	4,985	2,664	1,011	2,558	13,947	512
Wholesale trade................................	42	4,810	4,288	955	4,124	7,275	296
Retail trade......................................	44–45	19,776	5,396	2,546	4,777	18,312	409
Transportation and warehousing [5]........	48–49	12,916	1,519	871	805	6,116	195
Information.......................................	51	3,002	383	261	309	2,720	88
Finance and insurance [6].....................	52	4,573	675	1,013	484	5,485	203
Real estate and rental and leasing........	53	12,410	887	894	377	3,402	106
Professional, scientific, and technical services........	54	23,886	2,583	2,869	1,805	14,252	699
Management of companies and enterprises...........	55	31	34	31	34	789	60
Administrative and support and waste management and remediation services............................	56	22,714	1,935	1,405	1,465	25,928	675
Educational services..........................	61	5,193	133	140	82	1,454	34
Health care and social assistance........	62	25,112	1,663	2,324	1,214	16,912	467
Arts, entertainment, and recreation.......	71	13,506	604	265	327	1,103	175
Accommodation and food services........	72	5,385	1,172	2,012	1,091	21,283	251
Other services (except public administration) [7].......	81	34,545	1,250	1,498	562	6,538	159
Industries not classified......................	99	132	8	132	8	120	3

D Withheld to avoid disclosing data for individual companies; data are included in higher level totals. X Not applicable. [1] Based on the 2007 North American Industry Classification System (NAICS); see text, this section. [2] Both firms with paid employees and firms with no paid employees. [3] Firms with more than one establishment are counted in each industry in which they operate, but only once in the total. [4] 20 to 99 employees. [5] Excludes scheduled passenger air transportation (NAICS 481111), rail transportation (NAICS 482), and the postal service (NAICS 491). [6] Excludes funds, trusts, and other financial vehicles (NAICS 525). [7] Excludes religious, grantmaking, civic, professional, and similar organizations (NAICS 813) and private households (NAICS 814).

Source: U.S. Census Bureau, 2007 Economic Census, *Survey of Business Owners*, <http://www.census.gov/econ/sbo/>, accessed July 2012.

Table 802. Bankruptcy Petitions Filed and Pending by Type and Chapter: 1990 to 2012

[For years ending June 30. Covers only bankruptcy cases filed under the Bankruptcy Reform Act of 1978. Bankruptcy: legal recognition that a company or individual is insolvent and must restructure or liquidate. Petitions "filed" means the commencement of a proceeding through the presentation of a petition to the clerk of the court; "pending" is a proceeding in which the administration has not been completed]

Item	1990	1995	2000	2005	2008	2009	2010	2011	2012
Total filed	725,484	858,104	1,276,922	1,637,254	967,831	1,306,315	1,572,597	1,529,560	1,311,602
Chapter 7 [3]	505,337	581,390	885,447	1,196,212	615,748	907,603	1,133,320	1,083,671	914,015
Chapter 9 [6]	7	12	8	6	6	6	12	7	17
Chapter 11 [4]	19,591	13,221	9,947	6,703	7,293	13,951	14,272	12,714	10,921
Chapter 12 [7]	1,351	904	732	290	314	422	660	717	582
Chapter 13 [5]	199,186	262,551	380,770	433,945	344,421	384,187	424,242	432,333	385,949
Section 304 [8]	12	26	18	98	(X)	(X)	(X)	(X)	(X)
Chapter 15 [9]	(X)	(X)	(X)	(X)	51	146	91	118	118
Business [1]	64,688	51,288	36,910	32,406	33,822	55,021	59,608	52,134	44,435
Nonbusiness [2]	660,796	806,816	1,240,012	1,604,848	934,009	1,251,294	1,512,989	1,477,426	1,267,167
Chapter 7 [3]	468,171	552,244	864,183	1,174,681	592,376	870,266	1,091,322	1,047,131	883,119
Chapter 11 [4]	2,116	1,755	722	847	780	1,088	1,827	1,884	1,636
Chapter 13 [5]	190,509	252,817	375,107	429,315	340,852	379,939	419,836	428,410	382,409
Total pending	961,919	1,090,446	1,400,416	1,750,562	1,325,220	1,527,073	1,659,399	1,702,005	1,661,831

X Not applicable. [1] Business bankruptcies include those filed under Chapters 7, 9, 11, 12, 13, or 15. [2] Includes other petitions, not shown separately. [3] Chapter 7, liquidation of nonexempt assets of businesses or individuals. [4] Chapter 11, individual or business reorganization. [5] Chapter 13, adjustment of debts of an individual with regular income. [6] Chapter 9, adjustment of debts of a municipality. [7] Chapter 12, adjustment of debts of a family farmer with regular income, effective November 26, 1986. [8] Chapter 11, U.S.C., Section 304, cases ancillary to foreign proceedings. [9] Chapter 15 was added and Section 304 was terminated by changes in the Bankruptcy Laws effective October 17, 2005.

Source: Administrative Office of the U.S. Courts, *Bankruptcy Statistics*, <http://www.uscourts.gov/Statistics/BankruptcyStatistics.aspx>, accessed May 2013.

Table 803. Bankruptcy Cases Filed by State: 2000 to 2012

[In thousands (1,276.9 represents 1,276,900). For years ending June 30. Covers only bankruptcy cases filed under the Bankruptcy Reform Act of 1978. Bankruptcy: legal recognition that a company or individual is insolvent and must restructure or liquidate. Petitions "filed" means the commencement of a proceeding through the presentation of a petition to the clerk of the court]

State	2000	2010	2011	2012	State	2000	2010	2011	2012
Total [1]	1,276.9	1,572.6	1,529.6	1,311.6	Missouri	26.3	32.9	31.6	27.7
Alabama	31.4	34.9	32.3	29.2	Montana	3.3	3.1	2.8	2.3
Alaska	1.4	1.1	1.1	0.9	Nebraska	5.6	7.9	7.4	6.0
Arizona	21.7	40.7	41.4	32.1	Nevada	14.3	31.0	28.0	21.0
Arkansas	16.3	16.9	15.9	13.6	New Hampshire	3.9	5.7	5.4	4.4
California	160.6	242.0	260.6	213.5	New Jersey	38.7	39.7	41.1	34.8
Colorado	15.6	31.9	32.1	28.6	New Mexico	7.1	6.6	6.3	5.1
Connecticut	11.4	11.3	10.8	8.9	New York	61.7	58.2	53.2	45.7
Delaware	4.9	4.5	4.2	4.1	North Carolina	25.8	27.7	25.4	22.7
District of Columbia	2.6	1.3	1.1	1.0	North Dakota	2.0	1.6	1.5	1.1
Florida	74.0	107.4	105.0	87.7	Ohio	53.6	72.9	65.3	53.8
Georgia	57.9	77.8	77.7	69.3	Oklahoma	19.3	15.1	14.0	12.7
Hawaii	5.0	3.7	3.8	2.9	Oregon	18.1	20.1	19.0	16.7
Idaho	7.3	8.3	8.2	7.0	Pennsylvania	43.8	38.8	37.5	31.1
Illinois	62.3	80.8	78.8	70.7	Rhode Island	4.8	5.4	5.4	4.5
Indiana	37.5	49.3	43.4	37.3	South Carolina	11.7	9.7	8.9	8.0
Iowa	8.2	10.4	8.9	7.2	South Dakota	2.1	2.0	2.0	1.7
Kansas	11.4	11.4	10.7	9.6	Tennessee	47.1	52.5	49.1	45.6
Kentucky	20.8	26.0	23.5	21.1	Texas	62.9	57.8	56.1	50.3
Louisiana	23.1	19.5	18.5	16.9	Utah	14.4	17.0	19.2	17.1
Maine	4.1	4.1	4.0	3.3	Vermont	1.6	1.7	1.4	1.1
Maryland	31.1	29.1	28.5	24.3	Virginia	37.1	37.8	35.6	31.8
Massachusetts	16.7	22.9	22.2	18.8	Washington	31.2	33.5	33.8	30.0
Michigan	36.4	71.0	63.4	53.5	West Virginia	8.2	6.6	5.5	4.3
Minnesota	15.4	22.6	21.1	18.2	Wisconsin	18.0	30.0	29.1	26.5
Mississippi	17.9	14.8	14.0	13.2	Wyoming	2.0	1.5	1.5	1.3

[1] Includes Island Areas, not shown separately.

Source: Administrative Office of the United States Courts, Bankruptcy Statistics, <http://www.uscourts.gov/Statistics/BankruptcyStatistics.aspx>, accessed May 2013.

Table 804. Patents and Trademarks: 1990 to 2012

[In thousands (99.2 represents 99,200). Calendar year data. Covers U.S. patents issued to citizens of the United States and residents of foreign countries. For data on foreign countries, see Table 1417]

Type	1990	1995	2000	2005	2008	2009	2010	2011	2012
Patents issued	**99.2**	**113.8**	**176.0**	**157.7**	**185.2**	**191.9**	**244.3**	**247.7**	**276.8**
Inventions	90.4	101.4	157.5	143.8	157.8	167.3	219.6	224.5	253.2
Individuals	17.3	17.4	22.4	14.7	12.6	12.6	16.6	15.6	17.2
Corporations:									
United States	36.1	44.0	70.9	65.2	70.0	74.8	97.8	99.5	111.8
Foreign [1]	36.0	39.1	63.3	63.2	74.5	79.3	104.3	108.5	123.2
U.S. government	1.0	1.0	0.9	0.7	0.7	0.7	0.9	0.9	1.0
Designs	8.0	11.7	17.4	13.0	25.6	23.1	22.8	21.4	22.0
Botanical plants	0.3	0.4	0.5	0.7	1.2	1.0	1.0	0.8	0.9
Reissues	0.4	0.3	0.5	0.2	0.6	0.5	0.9	1.0	0.8
U.S. residents	52.8	64.4	96.9	82.6	92.0	95.0	121.2	121.2	134.2
Foreign country residents	46.2	49.4	79.1	75.2	93.2	96.9	123.2	126.5	142.6
Percent of total	46.7	43.4	44.9	47.6	50.3	50.5	50.4	51.1	51.5
Trademarks:									
Applications filed	127.3	181.0	361.8	334.7	390.8	351.9	370.2	405.7	418.0
Issued	60.8	92.5	115.2	154.8	233.9	222.1	210.6	(NA)	(NA)
Trademarks	53.6	85.6	106.4	121.6	194.4	177.4	165.2	(NA)	(NA)
Trademark renewals	7.2	6.9	8.8	33.3	39.5	44.7	45.4	(NA)	(NA)

NA Not available. [1] Includes patents to foreign governments.

Source: U.S. Patent and Trademark Office, "Statistical Reports Available For Viewing, Calendar Year Patent Statistics," <http://www.uspto.gov/web/offices/ac/ido/oeip/taf/reports.htm>; "Data Visualization Center, Trademarks Dashboard," <http://www.uspto.gov/dashboards/trademarks/main.dashxml>; and unpublished sources.

Table 805. Patents by State and Island Areas: 2012

[Includes only U.S. patents granted to residents of the United States and territories]

State	Total	Inventions	Designs	Botanical plants	Reissues	State	Total	Inventions	Designs	Botanical plants	Reissues
Total	**134,187**	**121,026**	**12,445**	**315**	**401**	Missouri	1,165	1,015	149	0	1
						Montana	133	119	13	0	1
Alabama	478	413	63	0	2	Nebraska	336	292	43	0	1
Alaska	46	28	18	0	0	Nevada	882	752	128	0	2
Arizona	2,370	2,210	152	1	7	New Hampshire	791	734	50	0	7
Arkansas	238	178	57	3	0	New Jersey	4,656	4,224	413	1	18
California	34,659	32,107	2,369	84	99	New Mexico	444	417	27	0	0
Colorado	2,744	2,442	298	1	3	New York	8,557	7,640	890	4	23
Connecticut	2,297	2,108	180	2	7	North Carolina	3,252	2,977	261	4	10
Delaware	485	445	40	0	0	North Dakota	98	96	2	0	0
District of Columbia	148	131	17	0	0	Ohio	4,110	3,387	708	4	11
Florida	4,453	3,686	707	48	12	Oklahoma	521	471	44	1	5
Georgia	2,501	2,128	344	21	8	Oregon	2,462	2,059	334	59	10
Hawaii	131	108	21	1	1	Pennsylvania	3,894	3,483	397	4	10
Idaho	979	930	46	0	3	Rhode Island	415	329	85	0	1
Illinois	5,078	4,345	704	11	18	South Carolina	978	850	123	0	5
Indiana	1,963	1,741	218	0	4	South Dakota	129	113	16	0	0
Iowa	914	854	59	0	1	Tennessee	1,065	930	130	1	4
Kansas	1,100	1,004	96	0	0	Texas	8,929	8,367	531	0	31
Kentucky	620	543	76	0	1	Utah	1,327	1,167	151	0	9
Louisiana	445	364	47	33	1	Vermont	506	487	19	0	0
Maine	222	211	11	0	0	Virginia	1,813	1,691	111	1	10
Maryland	1,715	1,609	101	1	4	Washington	5,985	5,390	567	5	23
Massachusetts	6,119	5,734	362	4	19	West Virginia	142	135	6	1	0
Michigan	4,997	4,598	377	12	10	Wisconsin	2,289	1,785	492	4	8
Minnesota	4,278	3,902	364	3	9	Wyoming	125	120	5	0	0
Mississippi	161	140	18	1	2	Island areas	42	37	5	0	0

Source: U.S. Patent and Trademark Office, "Statistical Reports Available For Viewing, Calendar Year Patent Statistics," <http://www.uspto.gov/web/offices/ac/ido/oeip/taf/reports.htm>, accessed May 2013.

Table 806. Copyright Registration by Subject Matter: 2000 to 2012

[In thousands (497.6 represents 497,600). For years ending September 30. Comprises claims to copyrights registered for both U.S. and foreign works. Semiconductor chips and renewals are not considered copyright registration claims]

Subject matter	2000	2010	2011	2012	Subject matter	2000	2010	2011	2012
Total copyright claims	**497.6**	**636.0**	**669.5**	**508.7**	Performing arts [2]	138.9	124.5	146.8	114.8
Monographs [1]	169.7	245.8	265.8	198.5	Works of the visual arts [3]	85.8	97.2	91.2	72.8
Serials	69.0	90.5	58.0	48.2	Semiconductor chip products	0.7	0.3	0.3	2.6
Sound recordings	34.2	77.9	107.7	74.3	Renewals	16.8	0.1	0.2	0.2

[1] Includes computer software and machine readable works. [2] Includes musical works, dramatic works, choreography, pantomimes, motion pictures, and filmstrips. [3] Two-dimensional works of fine and graphic art, including prints and art reproductions; sculptural works; technical drawings and models; photographs; commercial prints and labels; and works of applied arts, cartographic works, and multimedia works.

Source: The Library of Congress, *Annual Report of the Librarian of Congress, For the Fiscal Year Ending September 30, 2012*, 2013. See also <http://www.loc.gov/about/reports/annualreports/index.html>.

Table 807. Net Stock of Private Fixed Assets by Industry: 2000 to 2011

[In billions of dollars (21,230 represents $21,230,000,000,000). Estimates as of Dec. 31. Net stock estimates are presented in terms of current cost and cover equipment, software, and structures. Fixed assets are assets that are used repeatedly, or continuously, in processes of production for an extended period of time. (pt) = part]

Industry	NAICS code [1]	2000	2005	2010	2011
Private fixed assets...................................	(X)	**21,230**	**30,593**	**34,388**	**35,193**
Agriculture, forestry, fishing, and hunting..................	11	338	431	492	515
Farms [2]..	111, 112	310	396	447	465
Forestry, fishing, and related activities...................	113-115	27	35	45	50
Mining..	21	535	1,018	1,423	1,579
Oil and gas extraction................................	211	405	860	1,211	1,352
Mining, except oil and gas...........................	212	89	100	119	125
Support activities for mining.........................	213	42	57	94	102
Utilities...	22	1,038	1,379	1,857	1,960
Construction...	23	172	232	267	274
Manufacturing...	31-33	1,763	1,988	2,224	2,280
Durable goods...	(X)	996	1,109	1,211	1,239
Wood products......................................	321	31	35	36	36
Nonmetallic mineral products........................	327	56	67	75	75
Primary metals......................................	331	125	131	151	157
Fabricated metal products...........................	332	113	127	145	149
Machinery...	333	134	140	153	157
Computer and electronic products....................	334	247	274	290	292
Electrical equipment, appliances, and components......	335	45	47	50	51
Motor vehicles, bodies and trailers, and parts.........	3361-3363	109	134	143	149
Other transportation equipment.......................	3364, 3365, 3369	75	79	87	89
Furniture and related products.......................	337	16	19	20	20
Miscellaneous manufacturing........................	339	45	56	63	65
Nondurable goods.....................................	(X)	767	879	1,013	1,042
Food and beverage and tobacco products............	311, 312	186	223	264	275
Textile mills and textile product mills................	313, 314	44	41	39	38
Apparel and leather and allied products..............	315, 316	17	17	16	16
Paper products......................................	322	100	102	105	106
Printing and related support activities................	323	40	46	46	45
Petroleum and coal products.........................	324	93	118	168	176
Chemical products...................................	325	221	256	294	302
Plastics and rubber products.........................	326	67	76	81	84
Wholesale trade.......................................	42	338	429	502	523
Retail trade...	44-45	654	960	1,139	1,177
Transportation and warehousing [3].....................	48-49	819	961	1,099	1,132
Air transportation...................................	481	184	209	214	215
Railroad transportation..............................	482	284	316	363	373
Water transportation.................................	483	37	38	41	41
Truck transportation.................................	484	72	98	107	113
Transit and ground passenger transportation..........	485	37	40	43	44
Pipeline transportation..............................	486	73	112	168	181
Warehousing and storage............................	493	22	30	40	41
Information..	51	888	1,119	1,397	1,450
Publishing industries (includes software).............	511, 516 (pt)	60	89	113	116
Motion picture and sound recording industries.........	512	33	43	46	46
Broadcasting and telecommunications................	515, 517	766	929	1,148	1,184
Information and data processing services.............	516 (pt), 518, 519	28	57	90	104
Finance and insurance.................................	52	843	1,164	1,330	1,365
Federal Reserve banks...............................	521	9	9	10	10
Credit intermediation and related activities...........	522	480	638	673	692
Securities, commodity contracts, and investments.....	523	88	117	152	155
Insurance carriers and related activities..............	524	169	221	245	249
Funds, trusts, and other financial vehicles............	525	97	178	250	258
Real estate and rental and leasing.....................	53	11,513	17,610	18,614	18,759
Real estate..	531	11,289	17,318	18,300	18,435
Rental and leasing services and lessors of intangible assets [4]..	532, 533	224	292	314	324
Professional, scientific, and technical services [3].......	54	211	318	418	439
Legal services......................................	5411	23	35	39	40
Computer systems design and related services........	5415	45	48	61	64
Management of companies and enterprises [5]...........	55	268	340	401	411
Admin/support waste mgt..............................	56	153	207	247	258
Administrative and support services..................	561	87	127	153	159
Waste management and remediation services.........	562	66	80	94	98
Educational services...................................	61	213	327	457	483
Health care and social assistance......................	62	681	979	1,192	1,236
Ambulatory health care services.....................	621	201	266	314	326
Hospitals..	622	423	617	760	788
Nursing and residential care facilities................	623	32	55	69	72
Social assistance....................................	624	25	40	48	50
Arts, entertainment, and recreation....................	71	128	199	247	253
Performing arts, spectator sports, museums, and related activities........	711, 712	48	76	96	99
Amusements, gambling, and recreation industries......	713	80	124	150	153
Accommodation and food services.....................	72	342	457	552	557
Accommodation......................................	721	188	263	334	335
Food services and drinking places....................	722	154	193	218	222
Other services, except government......................	81	336	477	531	543

X Not applicable. [1] Based on North American Industry Classification System, 2002; see text this section. [2] NAICS crop and animal production. [3] Includes other activities, not shown separately. [4] Intangible assets include patents, trademarks, and franchise agreements, but not copyrights. [5] Consists of bank and other holding companies.

Source: U.S. Bureau of Economic Analysis, "Table 3.1ES. Current-Cost Net Stock of Private Fixed Assets by Industry," <http://www.bea.gov/itable/>, accessed May 2013.

Table 808. Private Domestic Investment in Current and Chained (2005) Dollars: 2000 to 2011

[In billions of dollars (1,772 represents $1,772,000,000,000). Covers equipment, software, and structures. Minus sign (-) indicates decrease. For explanation of chained dollars; see text, Section 13]

Item	2000	2005	2006	2007	2008	2009	2010	2011
CURRENT DOLLARS								
Gross private domestic investment.............	**1,772**	**2,172**	**2,327**	**2,295**	**2,088**	**1,549**	**1,737**	**1,855**
Less: Consumption of fixed capital................	987	1,291	1,391	1,476	1,543	1,543	1,540	1,587
Equals: Net private domestic investment.........	785	882	936	819	545	7	197	268
Fixed investment........................	1,718	2,122	2,267	2,266	2,129	1,704	1,679	1,818
Less: Consumption of fixed capital.............	987	1,291	1,391	1,476	1,543	1,543	1,540	1,587
Equals: Net fixed investment.....................	731	832	876	790	586	161	139	231
Nonresidential.............................	1,269	1,347	1,505	1,638	1,656	1,349	1,338	1,480
Residential.................................	449	775	762	629	472	354	341	339
Change in private inventories......................	55	50	60	29	-41	-154	58	37
CHAINED (2005) DOLLARS								
Gross private domestic investment.............	**1,963**	**2,172**	**2,232**	**2,160**	**1,940**	**1,458**	**1,658**	**1,744**
Less: Consumption of fixed capital................	1,063	1,291	1,341	1,396	1,437	1,455	1,459	1,479
Equals: Net private domestic investment.........	900	882	891	764	503	3	199	265
Fixed investment........................	1,907	2,122	2,173	2,131	1,979	1,602	1,599	1,705
Nonresidential.............................	1,311	1,347	1,456	1,550	1,538	1,260	1,269	1,378
Residential.................................	580	775	718	584	444	345	332	328
Change in private inventories......................	60	50	59	28	-36	-139	51	31

Source: U.S. Bureau of Economic Analysis, "Table 5.2.5. Gross and Net Domestic Investment by Major Type" and "Table 5.2.6. Real Gross and Net Domestic Investment by Major Type, Chained Dollars," <http://www.bea.gov/itable/>, accessed May 2013.

Table 809. Information and Communications Technology (ICT) Equipment and Computer Software Expenditures: 2010 and 2011

[In millions of dollars (92,551 represents $92,551,000,000). Covers only companies with employees. The Information and Communication Technology Survey collects noncapitalized and capitalized data on information and communication technology equipment, including computer software. This survey is sent to a sample of approximately 46,500 private nonfarm employer businesses operating in the United States]

Type of expenditure and industry	NAICS code [1]	Noncapitalized expenditures [2]		Capitalized expenditures [3]	
		2010	2011	2010	2011
Total expenditures for ICT equipment and computer software...............	(X)	**92,551**	**100,154**	**169,647**	**189,717**
Total equipment expenditures................	(X)	33,286	34,918	(NA)	(NA)
Purchases............................	(X)	17,186	19,201	105,735	117,494
Computer and peripheral equipment..........	(X)	11,087	13,153	53,214	57,167
Information and communication technology equipment...............	(X)	5,797	5,733	47,343	54,998
Electromedical and electrotherapeutic apparatus....................	(X)	302	315	5,178	5,330
Operating leases and rental payments............	(X)	16,100	15,716	(NA)	(NA)
Computer and peripheral equipment..........	(X)	10,286	10,226	(NA)	(NA)
Information and communication technology equipment...............	(X)	4,413	4,237	(NA)	(NA)
Electromedical and electrotherapeutic apparatus....................	(X)	1,400	1,253	(NA)	(NA)
Total computer software expenditures............	(X)	59,265	65,236	(NA)	(NA)
Purchases and payroll for developing software....	(X)	27,885	29,909	63,912	72,223
Software licensing and service/maintenance agreements...............	(X)	31,380	35,327	(NA)	(NA)
Forestry, fishing, and agricultural services........	113–115	59	51	94	108
Mining...	21	1,204	1,349	1,044	1,749
Utilities..	22	1,694	1,993	4,300	4,328
Construction...	23	796	952	1,287	1,088
Manufacturing.......................................	31–33	15,716	16,563	15,125	18,158
Durable goods industries.........................	321, 327, 33	10,173	11,207	8,774	11,296
Nondurable goods industries.....................	31, 322-326	5,543	5,356	6,350	6,862
Wholesale trade....................................	42	2,895	3,182	6,014	7,399
Retail trade...	44–45	5,407	4,848	11,243	12,524
Transportation and warehousing....................	48–49	1,800	1,996	3,102	3,513
Information..	51	13,370	14,661	57,917	65,841
Finance and insurance..............................	52	22,026	22,836	26,123	26,760
Real estate and rental and leasing.................	53	1,206	1,240	1,750	1,517
Professional, scientific, and technical services.....	54	10,620	12,311	12,079	12,773
Management of companies and enterprises........	55	1,154	1,101	1,994	2,559
Admin/support and waste management/remediation services..........	56	2,333	2,774	4,183	5,092
Educational services................................	61	1,897	2,088	2,503	2,671
Health care and social assistance..................	62	7,839	8,510	15,121	17,406
Arts, entertainment, and recreation................	71	502	677	1,041	1,135
Accommodation and food services.................	72	826	1,029	1,414	1,923
Other services (except public administration).......	81	1,427	1,411	2,403	2,220
Equipment expenditures serving multiple industry codes................	(X)	816	581	807	950

NA Not available. X Not applicable. [1] Based on North American Industry Classification System, 2007; see text, this section. [2] Expenses for ICT equipment including computer software not charged to asset accounts for which depreciation or amortization accounts are ordinarily maintained. [3] Expenses for ICT equipment including computer software chargeable to asset accounts for which depreciation or amortization accounts are ordinarily maintained.

Source: U.S. Census Bureau, "2011 Information and Communication Technology Survey," March 2013, <http://www.census.gov/econ/ict/>.

Table 810. Capital Expenditures: 2000 to 2011

[In billions of dollars (1,161 represents $1,161,000,000,000). Based on a sample survey and subject to sampling error; see source for details]

Item	All companies				Companies with employees				Companies without employees			
	2000	2005	2010	2011	2000	2005	2010	2011	2000	2005	2010	2011
Capital expenditures, total.........	**1,161**	**1,145**	**1,106**	**1,226**	**1,090**	**1,063**	**1,036**	**1,152**	**71**	**82**	**70**	**73**
Structures................................	364	402	430	455	338	369	396	424	26	33	33	31
New.......................................	329	366	395	425	309	341	368	397	20	25	28	28
Used......................................	35	36	34	30	29	28	29	26	6	8	6	3
Equipment and software................	797	743	676	771	752	694	640	728	45	49	36	42
New.......................................	751	701	638	730	718	665	612	698	32	37	27	32
Used......................................	46	42	38	41	34	29	28	31	12	13	10	10
Capital leases [1].....................	20	18	16	20	19	18	15	20	(Z)	(Z)	1	(Z)

Z Less than $500 million. [1] Included in structures and equipment data shown above.

Source: U.S. Census Bureau, "2011 Annual Capital Expenditures Survey," February 2013 and earlier reports, <http://www.census.gov/econ/aces/index.html>.

Table 811. Capital Expenditures by Industry: 2010 and 2011

[In billions of dollars (1,036 represents $1,036,000,000,000). Covers only companies with employees. Data based on the North American Industry Classification System (NAICS), 2007; see text this section. Based on a sample survey and subject to sampling error; see source for details]

Industry	NAICS code	2010	2011	Industry	NAICS code	2010	2011
Total expenditures	(X)	**1,036**	**1,152**				
Forestry, fishing, and agricultural services................................	113–115	3	3	Professional, scientific, and technical services...........................	54	28	28
Mining.....................................	21	116	150	Management of companies and enterprises.............................	55	5	5
Utilities....................................	22	94	98	Admin/support waste mgt/remediation services...........................	56	17	18
Construction..............................	23	18	22				
Manufacturing............................	31–33	161	193	Educational services..................	61	23	21
Durable goods..........................	321, 327, 33	87	111	Health care and social assistance......	62	78	83
Nondurable goods.....................	31, 322–326	74	83	Arts, entertainment, and recreation.....	71	12	11
Wholesale trade.........................	42	31	35	Accommodation and food services.....	72	20	25
Retail trade...............................	44–45	65	67	Other services (except public			
Transportation and warehousing......	48–49	59	72	administration).......................	81	21	16
Information................................	51	97	100	Structure and equipment expenditures			
Finance and insurance..................	52	103	110	serving multiple industry categories. ...	(X)	2	3
Real estate and rental and leasing......	53	81	91				

X Not applicable.

Source: U.S. Census Bureau, "2011 Annual Capital Expenditures Survey," February 2013 and earlier reports, <http://www.census.gov/econ/aces/index.html>.

Table 812. Business Cycle Expansions and Contractions—Months of Duration: 1945 to 2009

[A trough is the low point of a business cycle; a peak is the high point. Contraction, or recession, is the period from peak to subsequent trough; expansion is the period from trough to subsequent peak. Business cycle reference dates are determined by the National Bureau of Economic Research, Inc]

Business cycle reference date				Contraction (Peak to trough)	Expansion (Previous trough to peak)	Length of cycle	
Peak		Trough				Trough from previous trough	Peak from previous peak
Month	Year	Month	Year				
February......................	1945	October	1945	8	[1]80	[1]88	[2]93
November...................	1948	October	1949	11	37	48	45
July..........................	1953	May	1954	10	45	55	56
August.......................	1957	April	1958	8	39	47	49
April..........................	1960	February	1961	10	24	34	32
December...................	1969	November	1970	11	106	117	116
November..................	1973	March	1975	16	36	52	47
January......................	1980	July	1980	6	58	64	74
July..........................	1981	November	1982	16	12	28	18
July..........................	1990	March	1991	8	92	100	108
March........................	2001	November	2001	8	120	128	128
December...................	2007	June	2009	18	73	91	81
Average, all cycles: 1945 to 2009 (11 cycles)...				11.1	59.4	69.5	68.5

[1] Previous trough: June 1938. [2] Previous peak: May 1937.

Source: National Bureau of Economic Research, Inc., Cambridge, MA, "US Business Cycle Expansions and Contractions," <http://www.nber.org/cycles.html>, accessed September 2013 (copyright).

Table 813. The Conference Board Leading, Coincident, and Lagging Economic Indexes®: 2000 to 2012

[299.4 represents 299,400]

Item	Unit	2000	2005	2008	2009	2010	2011	2012
The Conference Board Leading Economic Index® (LEI) for the U.S., composite...	2004 = 100	94.1	105.4	93.1	80.5	86.9	91.3	93.1
Average weekly hours, manufacturing...	Hours	41.2	40.6	40.8	39.9	41.1	41.4	41.7
Average weekly initial claims for unemployment insurance...	1,000	299.4	330.6	420.6	573.7	458.9	408.8	375.4
Manufacturers' new orders, consumer goods and materials (1982 dollars)...	Million dollars	152,066	150,483	136,344	112,044	122,957	126,576	129,590
ISM New Orders Index[1]...	Percent	51.9	57.6	42.0	51.9	59.2	56.4	52.9
Manufacturers' new orders, nondefense capital goods excl. aircraft (1982 dollars)...	Million dollars	45,990	40,668	42,339	31,328	36,563	39,715	38,789
Building permits, new private housing units[1]...	1,000	1,598	2,160	896	582	604	624	801
Stock prices, 500 common stocks[1]...	1941-43 = 10	1,426.8	1,207.1	1,220.9	946.7	1,139.3	1,268.9	1,379.6
Leading Credit Index™ (std. dev.)...	Standard Deviation above or below the mean	1.30	-0.78	5.40	0.63	-0.78	-0.46	-0.73
Interest rate spread, 10-year Treasury bonds less federal funds...	Percent	-0.21	1.08	1.74	3.10	3.04	2.68	1.66
Avg. consumer expectations for business conditions (std. dev.)[1]...	Standard Deviation above or below the mean	1.26	0.00	-2.15	-1.19	-0.63	-1.03	-0.55
The Conference Board Coincident Economic Index® (CEI) for the U.S., composite...	2004 = 100	98.2	102.4	105.8	98.6	99.7	102.1	104.2
Employees on nonagricultural payrolls...	1,000	131,891	133,738	136,849	130,859	129,911	131,500	133,737
Personal income less transfer payments (chain 2005 dollars)...	Billion dollars	8,324	8,981	9,708	8,929	9,036	9,340	9,526
Industrial production...	2007 = 100	92.3	95.5	96.5	85.4	90.1	93.7	97.4
Manufacturing and trade sales (chain 2005 dollars)...	Million dollars	920,306	1,014,342	1,012,203	921,165	961,234	995,218	1,024,807
The Conference Board Lagging Economic Index® (LAG) for the U.S., composite...	2004 = 100	97.9	103.4	112.8	111.4	107.9	110.8	114.9
Average duration of unemployment...	Weeks	12.7	18.4	17.8	24.3	33.1	39.4	39.5
Inventories to sales ratio, manufacturing and trade (chain 2005 dollars)...	Ratio	1.36	1.31	1.39	1.42	1.34	1.33	1.34
Change in labor cost per unit of output, manufacturing (six-month change, annual rate)...	Percent	2.5	-2.0	9.2	0.3	-3.0	0.2	1.9
Average prime rate...	Percent	9.2	6.2	5.1	3.3	3.3	3.3	3.3
Commercial and industrial loans outstanding (chain 2005 dollars)...	Million dollars	983,019	682,747	902,610	810,432	677,724	728,886	830,362
Consumer installment credit to personal income ratio...	Percent	18.9	21.4	20.6	21.1	19.6	19.9	20.2
Change in consumer price index for services (six-month change, annual rate)...	Percent	3.8	3.5	3.6	0.8	0.9	2.0	2.1

[1] Data are from private sources and provided through the courtesy of the compilers and are subject to their copyrights: stock prices, Standard & Poor's Corporation; index of consumer expectations, University of Michigan's Survey Research Center; ISM New Orders Index, Institute for Supply Management.

Source: The Conference Board, New York, NY 10022-6601, *Business Cycle Indicators*, monthly. Reproduced with permission from The Conference Board, Inc. © 2013, The Conference Board, Inc. For more information, see <http://www.conference-board.org/data/>.

Table 814. Manufacturing and Trade—Sales and Inventories: 1992 to 2012

[In billions of dollars (540 represents $540,000,000,000), except ratios. Based on North American Industry Classification System (NAICS), 2007; see text, this section]

Year	Sales, average monthly [1]				Inventories [2]				Inventory-sales ratio [3]			
	Total	Manufac-turing	Retail trade	Mer-chant whole-salers	Total	Manufac-turing	Retail trade	Mer-chant whole-salers	Total	Manufac-turing	Retail trade	Mer-chant whole-salers
1992......	540	242	151	147	836	378	260	197	1.53	1.57	1.67	1.31
1993......	567	252	161	154	863	380	278	205	1.50	1.50	1.68	1.30
1994......	610	270	175	165	926	400	305	222	1.46	1.44	1.66	1.29
1995......	655	290	185	180	985	425	322	238	1.48	1.44	1.72	1.29
1996......	687	300	197	190	1,005	430	333	241	1.45	1.44	1.67	1.27
1997......	723	320	206	198	1,046	444	344	258	1.42	1.37	1.64	1.26
1998......	742	325	215	202	1,078	449	357	272	1.43	1.39	1.62	1.32
1999......	786	336	234	217	1,138	463	384	290	1.40	1.35	1.59	1.30
2000......	834	351	249	235	1,196	481	406	309	1.41	1.35	1.59	1.29
2001......	818	331	255	232	1,119	428	394	298	1.42	1.38	1.58	1.32
2002......	823	326	261	236	1,139	423	415	301	1.36	1.29	1.55	1.26
2003......	855	335	272	248	1,148	408	431	308	1.34	1.25	1.56	1.22
2004......	926	359	289	277	1,241	441	461	340	1.30	1.19	1.56	1.18
2005......	1,005	395	308	302	1,314	473	472	369	1.27	1.17	1.51	1.17
2006......	1,068	418	323	327	1,410	522	487	400	1.28	1.20	1.50	1.18
2007......	1,127	443	333	350	1,490	561	502	427	1.29	1.22	1.49	1.18
2008......	1,156	456	329	372	1,466	541	480	444	1.32	1.26	1.52	1.21
2009......	981	368	303	311	1,327	502	433	392	1.39	1.39	1.47	1.31
2010......	1,077	409	320	348	1,444	551	460	433	1.28	1.28	1.40	1.17
2011......	1,195	458	345	392	1,558	608	478	473	1.27	1.29	1.36	1.17
2012......	1,250	478	363	410	1,637	622	516	499	1.29	1.29	1.38	1.19

[1] Averages of monthly not-seasonally-adjusted figures. [2] Seasonally adjusted end-of-year data. [3] Averages of seasonally adjusted monthly ratios.

Source: U.S. Council of Economic Advisors, *Economic Indicators*, monthly. See also <http://www.gpo.gov/fdsys/browse/collection.action?collectionCode=ECONI>.

Table 815. Industrial Production Indexes by Industry: 1990 to 2012

[2007 = 100. Except as noted, based on the North American Industry Classification System (NAICS); 2007; see text, this section]

Industry	NAICS code [1]	1990	2000	2005	2008	2009	2010	2011	2012
Total index.................................	([2])	**62.2**	**92.2**	**95.5**	**96.6**	**85.7**	**90.6**	**93.6**	**97.0**
Manufacturing (SIC) [3]........................	([4])	**58.7**	**91.3**	**95.0**	**95.3**	**82.4**	**87.4**	**90.3**	**93.9**
Manufacturing (NAICS)........................	31–33	56.8	89.8	94.4	95.4	82.4	87.9	91.1	95.0
Durable goods................................	([5])	42.7	84.8	91.2	96.6	78.6	87.3	93.2	99.9
Wood products...............................	321	80.7	99.3	105.9	85.4	65.3	67.6	68.4	71.3
Nonmetallic mineral products...............	327	76.2	94.9	99.4	88.4	66.6	68.6	70.2	71.0
Primary metals...............................	331	87.1	100.3	95.2	100.0	74.0	91.1	97.4	99.4
Fabricated metal products..................	332	70.0	96.6	90.9	96.4	74.2	79.0	85.3	91.4
Machinery....................................	333	71.9	97.7	91.6	97.3	75.7	84.6	95.6	102.2
Computers and electronic products..................................	334	7.2	53.6	76.9	108.1	97.0	111.6	122.5	130.2
Electrical equipment, appliances, and components.............................	335	82.0	113.9	95.3	96.3	75.6	78.6	83.4	86.3
Motor vehicles and parts...................	3361–3	54.4	97.4	102.3	80.0	58.6	77.8	84.8	99.6
Aerospace and other misc transportation equipment....................	3364–9	94.4	76.0	80.2	101.9	92.8	94.0	94.3	102.0
Furniture and related products.............	337	75.6	103.6	105.5	90.3	65.5	64.7	66.5	69.6
Miscellaneous products.....................	339	60.1	86.8	99.5	101.6	94.2	97.5	98.4	103.8
Nondurable goods...........................	([6])	82.4	95.9	98.3	94.1	86.9	88.7	88.9	89.9
Food, beverage, and tobacco products...................................	311,2	84.7	95.3	99.8	97.2	96.5	96.7	96.8	99.6
Textile and product mills...................	313,4	128.5	144.2	124.5	87.9	69.7	74.4	74.0	75.3
Apparel and leather.........................	315,6	266.5	235.2	126.1	80.6	59.4	60.0	58.9	57.4
Paper..	322	100.1	107.7	100.7	95.8	85.4	87.2	87.3	85.2
Printing and related support...............	323	97.8	107.8	98.6	93.8	78.8	78.8	78.0	76.9
Petroleum and coal products...............	324	77.1	85.2	95.6	95.6	94.3	93.5	94.7	95.7
Chemical....................................	325	67.5	81.9	92.9	92.5	83.5	86.3	86.3	86.4
Plastics and rubber products...............	326	66.8	102.3	102.2	90.6	75.8	82.6	84.0	86.7
Other manufacturing (non-NAICS) [7]..........	1133, 5111	111.2	121.9	107.3	93.5	80.7	76.4	74.8	72.1
Mining..	**21**	**106.3**	**102.8**	**97.0**	**101.2**	**95.7**	**100.7**	**106.8**	**113.5**
Utilities.......................................	**2211,2**	**71.9**	**89.9**	**97.3**	**99.9**	**97.5**	**101.0**	**100.8**	**98.6**
Electric power generation, transmission, and distribution.................	2211	69.4	87.9	97.0	99.4	96.9	100.7	100.4	98.7
Natural gas distribution......................	2212	87.1	100.3	98.9	102.3	100.4	102.2	102.3	97.1

[1] Based on North American Industry Classification System, 2007; see text, this section. [2] Includes NAICS codes 31–33, 1133, 5111, 21, 2211, and 2212. [3] Standard Industrial Classification (SIC); see text, this section. [4] Includes NAICS codes 31–33, 1133, and 5111. [5] Includes NAICS codes 321, 327, 331–339. [6] Includes NAICS codes 311–316, 322–326. [7] Those industries—logging and newspaper, periodical, book, and directory publishing—that have traditionally been considered to be manufacturing.

Source: Board of Governors of the Federal Reserve System, *Industrial Production and Capacity Utilization*, Statistical Release G.17, "Data Download Program," <http://www.federalreserve.gov/datadownload/default.htm>, accessed May 2013.

Table 816. Index of Industrial Capacity and Utilization Rate: 1990 to 2012

[2007 output = 100. Annual figures are averages of monthly data. The capacity index is an indicator of the maximum sustainable output a plant can maintain under realistic circumstances; capacity here is expressed as a proportion of 2007 actual output. Capacity utilization rate is a measure of output as a proportion of capacity; this is the output index divided by the capacity index]

| Year | Index of capacity | | Utilization rate | | | | |
| | | | | Stage of process | | | |
	Total industry	Manufacturing [1]	Total industry	Crude [2]	Primary and semifinished [3]	Finished [4]	Manufacturing [1]
1990...........	75.4	71.9	82.5	87.7	82.7	80.7	81.6
1995...........	85.5	82.8	84.0	88.8	86.4	79.8	83.2
2000...........	113.3	114.6	81.4	88.6	84.0	76.7	79.3
2003...........	119.0	120.3	76.0	84.8	78.1	71.5	73.5
2004...........	118.6	119.9	77.9	86.4	79.9	73.2	75.9
2005...........	119.6	121.7	79.8	86.4	81.5	75.3	77.9
2006...........	121.7	124.2	80.2	87.8	81.0	76.1	78.3
2007...........	124.3	127.3	80.5	88.4	80.7	77.0	78.7
2008...........	124.7	128.0	77.5	86.9	76.8	74.0	74.3
2009...........	124.9	125.4	68.7	77.8	66.2	68.4	65.4
2010...........	122.5	122.6	74.0	83.7	72.2	72.1	71.4
2011...........	122.4	122.1	76.5	85.8	74.5	74.5	74.4
2012...........	125.1	123.9	77.6	86.5	75.4	76.3	76.3

[1] Based on North American Industry Classification Systems (NAICS); see text, this section. [2] Crude processing covers a relatively small portion of total industrial capacity and consists of logging (NAICS 1133), much of mining (excluding stone, sand, and gravel mining, and oil and gas drilling, which are NAICS 21231, 21221–2, and 213111) and some basic manufacturing industries, including basic chemicals (NAICS 3251); fertilizers, pesticides, and other agricultural chemicals (NAICS 32531,2); pulp, paper, and paperboard mills (NAICS 3221); and alumina, aluminum, and other nonferrous production and processing mills (NAICS 3313,4). [3] Primary and semifinished processing loosely corresponds to the previously published aggregate, primary processing. Includes utilities and portions of several 2-digit SIC industries included in the former advanced processing group. These include printing and related support activities (NAICS 3231); paints and adhesives (NAICS 3255); and newspaper, periodical, book, and directory publishers (NAICS 5111). [4] Finished processing generally corresponds to the previously published aggregate, advanced processing. Includes oil and gas well drilling and carpet and rug mills.

Source: Board of Governors of the Federal Reserve System, *Industrial Production and Capacity Utilization*, Statistical Release G.17, monthly, <http://www.federalreserve.gov/releases/g17/>.

Table 817. Corporate Profits, Taxes, and Dividends: 2000 to 2012

[In billions of dollars (819 represents $819,000,000,000). Covers corporations organized for profit and other entities treated as corporations. Represents profits to U.S. residents, without deduction of depletion charges and exclusive of capital gains and losses; intercorporate dividends from profits of domestic corporations are eliminated; and net receipts of dividends, reinvested earnings of incorporated foreign affiliates, and earnings of unincorporated foreign affiliates are added]

Item	2000	2005	2008	2009	2010	2011	2012
Corporate profits with IVA and CCA [1].................................	819	1,456	1,248	1,342	1,702	1,827	1,951
Taxes on corporate income...	265	412	309	269	373	379	449
Profits after tax with IVA and CCA [1]....................................	554	1,044	939	1,073	1,329	1,448	1,501
Net dividends...	378	557	787	554	601	697	780
Undistributed profits with IVA and CCA [1].............................	176	486	153	519	728	751	721
Cash flow:							
Net cash flow with IVA and CCA [1].....................................	861	1,337	1,245	1,633	1,775	1,851	1,834
Undistributed profits with IVA and CCA [1].............................	176	486	153	519	728	751	721
Consumption of fixed capital...	685	863	1,029	1,030	1,027	1,062	1,108
Less: Capital transfers paid (net)..	0	12	-64	-84	-20	-38	-5
Less: Inventory valuation adjustment (IVA)............................	-17	-31	-45	3	-39	-63	-11
Equals: Net cash flow with CCA...	878	1,368	1,290	1,630	1,814	1,913	1,845

[1] Inventory valuation adjustment and capital consumption adjustment.

Source: U.S. Bureau of Economic Analysis, National Income and Product Accounts Tables, "Table 1.12. National Income by Type of Income," <http://www.bea.gov/itable/>, accessed May 2013.

Table 818. Corporate Profits With Inventory Valuation and Capital Consumption Adjustments—Financial and Nonfinancial Industries: 2000 to 2012

[In billions of dollars (819 represents $819,000,000,000). Based on the North American Industry Classification System, 2002; see text, this section. Minus sign (–) indicates loss. See headnote, Table 817]

Industry group	2000	2005	2009	2010	2011	2012
Corporate profits with IVA/CCA [1]...........................	**819**	**1,456**	**1,342**	**1,702**	**1,827**	**1,951**
Domestic industries...	674	1,217	990	1,301	1,388	1,521
Rest of the world..	146	239	353	402	439	430
Corporate profits with IVA [1].................................	**756**	**1,610**	**1,444**	**1,778**	**1,792**	**2,151**
Domestic industries...	610	1,370	1,091	1,376	1,353	1,721
Financial [2]...	190	444	375	424	408	485
Nonfinancial...	420	926	716	952	944	1,237
Utilities...	26	30	23	28	18	39
Manufacturing...	144	247	131	234	245	372
Wholesale trade...	59	92	87	98	96	139
Retail trade..	61	123	108	123	109	140
Transportation and warehousing.................................	15	29	25	48	46	54
Information...	-16	81	73	86	86	112
Other nonfinancial [3]...	132	324	270	335	346	380
Rest of the world..	146	239	353	402	439	430

[1] Inventory valuation adjustment and capital consumption adjustment. [2] Consists of finance and insurance and bank and other holding companies. [3] Consists of agriculture, forestry, fishing, and hunting; mining; construction; real estate and rental and leasing; professional, scientific, and technical services; administrative and waste management services; educational services; health care and social assistance; arts, entertainment, and recreation; accommodation and food services; and other services, except government.

Source: U.S. Bureau of Economic Analysis, National Income and Product Accounts Tables, "Table 6.16D. Corporate Profits by Industry," <http://www.bea.gov/itable/>, accessed May 2013.

Table 819. Corporate Profits Before Taxes by Industry: 2000 to 2011

[In billions of dollars (772 represents $772,000,000,000). Profits are without inventory valuation and capital consumption adjustments. Minus sign (–) indicates loss. See headnote, Table 817]

Industry	2002 NAICS code [1]	2000	2005	2009	2010	2011
Corporate profits before tax	**(X)**	**772**	**1,640**	**1,440**	**1,816**	**1,854**
Domestic industries	(X)	627	1,401	1,088	1,415	1,415
Agriculture, forestry, fishing, and hunting	11	1	5	4	8	7
Mining	21	15	43	19	29	34
Utilities	221	26	31	23	28	18
Construction	23	42	85	32	38	45
Manufacturing	31-33	154	260	125	249	272
Wholesale trade	42	62	101	87	112	116
Retail trade	44–45	63	128	111	130	120
Transportation and warehousing	48–49	15	30	25	48	46
Information	51	-16	81	73	86	86
Finance and insurance	52	102	282	227	242	237
Real estate and rental and leasing	53	10	29	8	17	12
Professional, scientific, and technical services	54	2	42	64	75	80
Management of companies and enterprises [2]	551111, 551112	88	161	148	183	171
Administrative and waste management services	56	9	24	23	30	30
Educational services	61	2	5	10	11	9
Health care and social assistance	62	26	54	74	85	86
Arts, entertainment, and recreation	71	2	7	7	9	10
Accommodation and food services	72	15	22	14	19	19
Other services, except public administration	81	9	12	13	17	17
Rest of the world [3]	(X)	146	239	353	402	439

X Not applicable. [1] Based on North American Industry Classification System, 2002; see text, this section. [2] Consists of bank and other holding companies. [3] Consists of receipts by all U.S. residents, including both corporations and persons, of dividends from foreign corporations, and, for U.S. corporations, their share of reinvested earnings of their incorporated foreign affiliates, and earnings of unincorporated foreign affiliates, net of corresponding payments.

Source: U.S. Bureau of Economic Analysis, National Income and Product Accounts Tables, "Table 6.17D. Corporate Profits Before Tax by Industry," <http://www.bea.gov/itable/>, accessed May 2013.

Table 820. Manufacturing, Mining, and Trade Corporations—Profits and Stockholders' Equity by Industry: 2011 and 2012

[Averages of quarterly figures at annual rates. Manufacturing data exclude estimates for corporations with less than $250,000 in assets at time of sample selection. Mining, wholesale and retail trade data excludes estimates for corporations with less than $50 million in assets at time of sample selection. Based on sample; see source for discussion of methodology. Based on North American Industry Classification System (NAICS), 2012; see text, this section. Minus sign (-) indicates loss]

Industry	2012 NAICS code	Ratio of profits after taxes to stockholders' equity (percent)		Profits after taxes per dollar of sales (cents)		Ratio of stockholders' equity to debt	
		2011	2012	2011	2012	2011	2012
Manufacturing	**31–33**	**17.0**	**15.7**	**9.2**	**8.5**	**1.9**	**1.8**
Nondurable manufacturing	(X)	17.6	17.2	8.7	8.6	1.6	1.5
Food	311	11.5	12.7	3.9	4.3	1.1	1.1
Beverage and tobacco products	312	23.3	22.0	20.4	19.3	1.5	1.4
Textile mills and textile product mills	313, 314	6.6	9.7	2.8	4.0	2.1	2.1
Apparel and leather products	315, 316	19.7	19.8	8.1	8.4	2.2	2.3
Paper	322	12.7	11.6	4.7	4.3	1.0	0.9
Printing and related support activities	323	12.5	19.3	2.6	3.9	0.6	0.5
Petroleum and coal products	324	21.1	19.3	7.7	7.2	2.9	3.3
Chemicals	325	16.4	16.3	14.0	14.0	1.4	1.3
Plastics and rubber products	326	15.8	17.4	4.8	5.5	1.1	1.2
Durable manufacturing	(X)	16.3	14.3	9.7	8.5	2.3	2.2
Wood products	321	1.5	11.2	0.5	3.5	1.1	1.1
Nonmetallic mineral products	327	2.7	3.5	1.7	2.4	1.5	1.6
Primary metals	331	13.2	11.5	5.9	5.5	1.9	1.9
Fabricated metal products	332	18.9	21.4	7.2	7.9	1.6	1.2
Machinery	333	15.5	16.5	8.4	8.8	2.2	2.0
Computer and electronic products	334	16.7	13.7	16.8	15.2	3.2	3.2
Electrical equipment, appliances, & components	335	11.4	11.3	12.4	11.7	3.7	3.2
Transportation equipment	336	27.5	19.2	8.2	5.5	1.7	1.7
Furniture and related products	337	9.1	14.5	3.1	4.0	1.2	1.3
Miscellaneous manufacturing	339	13.3	11.6	11.7	9.5	2.1	1.8
All mining	**21**	**11.2**	**3.8**	**18.9**	**6.6**	**2.1**	**1.8**
All wholesale trade	**42**	**11.4**	**11.4**	**1.6**	**1.6**	**1.3**	**1.3**
Durable goods	423	11.0	9.4	2.3	1.8	1.6	1.6
Nondurable goods	424, 425	12.1	14.6	1.1	1.4	1.1	1.1
All retail trade	**44–45**	**15.4**	**15.8**	**3.0**	**3.0**	**1.6**	**1.5**
Food and beverage stores	445	11.4	13.8	1.3	1.5	1.2	1.2
Clothing and general merchandise stores	448, 452	16.6	19.6	3.8	4.3	1.6	1.6
All other retail trade	(X)	15.2	13.2	3.0	2.7	1.7	1.6

X Not applicable.

Source: U.S. Census Bureau, *Quarterly Financial Report for Manufacturing, Mining, and Trade Corporations*, <http://www.census.gov/econ/qfr/index.html>.

Table 821. Value Added, Employment, and Capital Expenditures of U.S. Multinational Companies: 1989 to 2010

[Data for 2010 are preliminary. Value added and capital expenditures in billions of dollars (1,401 represents $1,401,000,000,000); employees in thousands. For the years shown prior to 2007, the data items needed to calculate value added and capital expenditures for individual U.S. parents and foreign affiliates were collected for nonbank businesses only. The value added and capital expenditures statistics for bank parents and affiliates for those years are estimates. See headnote, Table 822. MNC = Multinational company. MOFA = Majority-owned foreign affiliate]

Item	1989	1994	1999	2004	2007	2008	2009	2010
VALUE ADDED								
MNCs worldwide:								
Parents and MOFAs..................	1,401	1,773	2,645	3,221	3,866	3,741	3,741	4,127
Parents.............................	1,077	1,362	2,064	2,366	2,705	2,501	2,596	2,886
MOFAs..............................	324	411	580	854	1,161	1,240	1,145	1,241
EMPLOYEES								
MNCs worldwide:								
Parents and all affiliates..............	26,370	26,571	33,398	32,892	34,991	34,892	35,962	36,076
Parents and MOFAs..................	24,826	25,142	31,913	31,466	33,203	32,737	33,727	33,890
Parents.............................	19,617	19,330	23,985	22,446	22,832	22,273	22,933	22,820
Affiliates, total.......................	6,753	7,241	9,412	10,445	12,160	12,619	13,029	13,256
MOFAs..............................	5,209	5,812	7,928	9,020	10,372	10,463	10,794	11,070
Other...............................	1,544	1,429	1,484	1,426	1,788	2,155	2,235	2,186
CAPITAL EXPENDITURES								
MNCs worldwide:								
Parents and all affiliates..............	279	331	563	500	(NA)	(NA)	(NA)	(NA)
Parents and MOFAs..................	263	306	531	476	670	685	599	605
Parents.............................	204	235	417	351	495	502	432	438
Affiliates, total.......................	75	96	146	149	(NA)	(NA)	(NA)	(NA)
MOFAs..............................	59	72	115	125	174	184	167	166
Other...............................	16	25	31	24	(NA)	(NA)	(NA)	(NA)

NA Not available.

Source: U.S. Bureau of Economic Analysis, *Survey of Current Business*, November 2012. See also <http://www.bea.gov/scb/date_guide.asp>.

Table 822. U.S. Multinational Companies—Selected Characteristics: 2010

[In billions of dollars (29,508 represents $29,508,000,000,000), except as indicated. Consists of U.S. parent companies and their foreign affiliates. U.S. parent comprises the domestic operations of a multinational and is a U.S. person that owns or controls, directly or indirectly, 10 percent or more of the voting securities of an incorporated foreign business enterprise, or an equivalent interest in an unincorporated foreign business enterprise. A U.S. person can be an incorporated business enterprise. A majority-owned foreign affiliate (MOFA) is a foreign business enterprise in which a U.S. parent company owns or controls more than 50 percent of the voting securities]

Industry	2007 NAICS code [1]	U.S. parents [2]				MOFAs [3]		
		Total assets	Capital expenditures	Value added	Employment (1,000)	Capital expenditures	Value added	Employment (1,000)
All industries.........................	(X)	29,508	438	2,886	22,820	166	1,241	11,070
Mining..............................	21	466	35	75	204	57	193	202
Manufacturing [4]......................	31-33	6,111	152	1,132	6,919	55	528	4,630
Petroleum and coal products..........	324	940	47	133	300	3	70	39
Chemicals..........................	325	1,236	17	194	798	13	110	620
Computers and electronic products. . .	334	646	14	157	885	7	60	714
Transportation equipment.............	336	1,301	33	233	1,646	9	56	878
Wholesale trade........................	42	951	29	145	1,097	7	156	779
Retail trade...........................	44, 45	545	23	250	4,308	7	57	1,248
Information [4]...........................	51	1,503	60	327	1,625	7	51	406
Broadcasting (except Internet) and telecommunications.............	515, 517	979	49	198	898	5	14	99
Finance and insurance..................	52	17,643	37	340	2,481	7	77	599
Professional, scientific, and technical services.......................	54	474	9	195	1,231	4	78	853
Other industries.......................	(X)	1,814	93	422	4,955	22	101	2,354

X Not applicable. [1] Based on North American Industry Classification System, 2007; see text, this section. [2] Data are by industry of U.S. parent. [3] Data are by industry of foreign affiliate. [4] Includes other industries, not shown separately.

Source: U.S. Bureau of Economic Analysis, "U.S. Direct Investment Abroad: Financial and Operating Data for U.S. Multinational Companies," <http://www.bea.gov/international/di1usdop.htm>, accessed May 2013.

Table 823. U.S. Multinational Companies—Value Added: 2000 and 2010

[In billions of dollars (2,748 represents $2,748,000,000,000). Data for 2000 consist of non-bank multinational companies and are based on the North American Industry Classification System (NAICS), 2002; data for 2010 consist of all multinationals including banking companies and are based on the North American Industry Classification System (NAICS), 2007. See headnote, Table 822. Data are by industry of U.S. parent]

Industry	NAICS code	U.S. multinationals 2000	U.S. multinationals 2010 [1]	U.S. parents 2000	U.S. parents 2010 [1]	Majority-owned foreign affiliates 2000	Majority-owned foreign affiliates 2010 [1]
All industries	(X)	**2,748**	**4,127**	**2,141**	**2,886**	**607**	**1,241**
Mining	21	39	118	28	75	11	43
Manufacturing [2]	31–33	1,410	1,884	995	1,132	415	752
Petroleum and coal products	324	232	381	112	133	120	247
Chemicals	325	212	334	141	194	71	140
Computers and electronic products	334	188	237	142	157	46	80
Transportation equipment	336	271	318	209	233	62	85
Wholesale trade	42	133	176	99	145	34	32
Retail trade	44, 45	166	296	149	250	18	45
Information [2]	51	325	384	302	327	22	58
Broadcasting (except Internet) and telecommunications	515, 517	(NA)	215	(NA)	198	(NA)	17
Finance and insurance	52	181	471	157	340	24	130
Professional, scientific, and technical services	54	141	271	101	195	41	76
Other industries	(X)	352	527	311	422	41	105

NA Not available. X Not applicable. [1] Data for 2010 include bank companies. [2] Includes other industries, not shown separately.

Source: U.S. Bureau of Economic Analysis, "Direct Investment and Multinational Corporations," <http://www.bea.gov/iTable/index_MNC.cfm>, accessed May 2013.

Table 824. U.S. Majority-Owned Foreign Affiliates—Value Added by Industry of Affiliate and Country: 2010

[Preliminary. In millions of dollars (1,241,272 represents $1,241,272,000,000). See headnote, Table 822. Numbers in parentheses represent North American Industry Classification System 2007 codes; see text, this section]

Country	All industries [1]	Mining (21)	Manufacturing (31-33) Total [1]	Manufacturing (31-33) Chemicals (325)	Wholesale trade (42)	Finance and insurance (52)	Professional, scientific, and technical services (54)
All countries [2]	**1,241,272**	**192,877**	**528,409**	**110,386**	**155,816**	**77,289**	**78,218**
United Kingdom	152,577	10,343	54,830	6,702	16,852	19,985	15,053
Canada	128,694	15,027	52,971	8,666	11,732	4,031	8,684
Germany	84,418	1,251	53,525	7,148	10,835	1,203	4,777
Ireland	62,526	7	40,084	16,742	1,603	1,829	958
France	49,269	297	27,096	6,083	7,563	1,426	3,241
Australia	48,787	9,818	14,497	1,897	6,758	5,953	4,422
Japan	48,630	8	22,460	5,035	8,878	2,861	7,176
Brazil	45,071	3,032	27,943	6,927	3,918	2,028	1,644
China	36,942	3,020	21,803	6,329	4,191	334	2,139
Mexico	36,717	1,859	19,648	3,234	2,236	3,175	1,037

[1] Includes other industries, not shown separately. [2] Includes other countries, not shown separately.

Source: U.S. Bureau of Economic Analysis, "U.S. Direct Investment Abroad, All Majority-owned Foreign Affiliates (data for 2009 and forward), Value Added (Gross Product)," <http://www.bea.gov/iTable/index_MNC.cfm>, accessed May 2013.

Science and Technology

This section presents statistics on scientific, engineering, and technological resources, with emphasis on patterns of research and development (R&D) funding and on scientific, engineering, and technical personnel; education; and employment.

The National Science Foundation (NSF) gathers data chiefly through recurring surveys and report the data via detailed statistical tables; info briefs; and annual, biennial, and special reports; see <http://www.nsf.gov/statistics>. Areas of coverage include R&D expenditures; Federal R&D funding; scientific employment; graduate enrollment and support in academic science and engineering; characteristics of doctoral scientists and engineers and of recent graduates in the United States. Report titles include: *Science and Engineering Indicators; National Patterns of R&D Resources; Federal Funds for Research and Development; Federal R&D Funding by Budget Function; Federal S&E Support to Universities, Colleges, and Selected Nonprofit Institutions;* and *Research and Development in Industry.* Statistical surveys in these areas pose problems of concept and definition and the data should therefore be regarded as broad estimates rather than precise, quantitative statements. See sources for methodological and technical details.

The National Science Board's biennial *Science and Engineering Indicators* at <http://www.nsf.gov/statistics/seind/> contains data and analysis of international and domestic science and technology, including measures of inputs and outputs.

Research and development outlays—NSF defines research as "systematic study directed toward fuller scientific knowledge of the subject studied" and development as "the systematic use of scientific knowledge directed toward the production of useful materials, devices, systems, or methods, including design and development of prototypes and processes."

National coverage of R&D expenditures is developed primarily from periodic surveys in four principal economic sectors: (1) *Government*, made up primarily of federal executive agencies; (2) *Industry*, consisting of manufacturing and nonmanufacturing firms and the federally funded research and development centers (FFRDCs) they administer; (3) *Universities and colleges*, composed of universities, colleges, and their affiliated institutions, agricultural experiment stations, and associated schools of agriculture and of medicine, and FFRDCs administered by educational institutions; and (4) *Other nonprofit institutions*, consisting of such organizations as private philanthropic foundations, nonprofit research institutes, voluntary health agencies, and FFRDCs administered by nonprofit organizations.

The R&D funds reported consist of current operating costs, including planning and administration costs, except as otherwise noted. They exclude funds for routine testing, mapping and surveying, collection of general purpose data, dissemination of scientific information, and training of scientific personnel.

Scientists, engineers, and technicians—Scientists and engineers are defined as persons engaged in scientific and engineering work at a level requiring a knowledge of sciences equivalent at least to that acquired through completion of a 4-year college course. Technicians are defined as persons engaged in technical work at a level requiring knowledge acquired through a technical institute, junior college, or other type of training less extensive than 4-year college training. Craftsmen and skilled workers are excluded.

Table 825. Research and Development (R&D) Expenditures by Source of Funding: 1960 to 2010

[In millions of dollars (13,711 represents $13,711,000,000), except for percents]

Year	Total	Sources of funds					Percent of total				
		Federal government	Industry	Universities\colleges[1]	Non-profit	Non-federal government[2]	Federal government	Industry	Universities\colleges[1]	Non-profit	Non-federal government[2]
1960......	13,711	8,915	4,516	67	123	90	65.0	32.9	0.5	0.9	0.7
1970......	26,271	14,984	10,449	259	343	237	57.0	39.8	1.0	1.3	0.9
1980......	63,224	29,986	30,929	920	871	519	47.4	48.9	1.5	1.4	0.8
1981......	72,292	33,739	35,948	1,058	967	581	46.7	49.7	1.5	1.3	0.8
1982......	80,748	37,133	40,692	1,207	1,095	621	46.0	50.4	1.5	1.4	0.8
1983......	89,950	41,451	45,264	1,357	1,220	658	46.1	50.3	1.5	1.4	0.7
1984......	102,244	46,470	52,187	1,514	1,351	721	45.5	51.0	1.5	1.3	0.7
1985......	114,671	52,641	57,962	1,743	1,491	834	45.9	50.5	1.5	1.3	0.7
1986......	120,249	54,622	60,991	2,019	1,647	969	45.4	50.7	1.7	1.4	0.8
1987......	126,360	58,609	62,576	2,262	1,849	1,065	46.4	49.5	1.8	1.5	0.8
1988......	133,881	60,131	67,977	2,527	2,081	1,165	44.9	50.8	1.9	1.6	0.9
1989......	141,891	60,466	74,966	2,852	2,333	1,274	42.6	52.8	2.0	1.6	0.9
1990......	151,993	61,610	83,208	3,187	2,589	1,399	40.5	54.7	2.1	1.7	0.9
1991......	160,876	60,783	92,300	3,458	2,852	1,483	37.8	57.4	2.1	1.8	0.9
1992......	165,350	60,915	96,229	3,569	3,113	1,525	36.8	58.2	2.2	1.9	0.9
1993......	165,730	60,528	96,549	3,709	3,388	1,557	36.5	58.3	2.2	2.0	0.9
1994......	169,207	60,777	99,204	3,938	3,665	1,623	35.9	58.6	2.3	2.2	1.0
1995......	183,625	62,969	110,871	4,110	3,925	1,751	34.3	60.4	2.2	2.1	1.0
1996......	197,346	63,394	123,417	4,436	4,239	1,861	32.1	62.5	2.2	2.1	0.9
1997......	212,152	64,574	136,228	4,838	4,590	1,922	30.4	64.2	2.3	2.2	0.9
1998......	226,457	66,383	147,825	5,163	5,114	1,972	29.3	65.3	2.3	2.3	0.9
1999......	245,318	67,366	164,606	5,619	5,628	2,098	27.5	67.1	2.3	2.3	0.9
2000......	268,905	67,862	186,037	6,231	6,528	2,246	25.2	69.2	2.3	2.4	0.8
2001......	279,716	74,966	188,336	6,826	7,192	2,395	26.8	67.3	2.4	2.6	0.9
2002......	279,387	80,315	180,643	7,617	8,203	2,610	28.7	64.7	2.7	2.9	0.9
2003......	293,060	86,705	186,113	8,226	9,160	2,856	29.6	63.5	2.8	3.1	1.0
2004......	304,547	92,360	191,307	8,562	9,310	3,008	30.3	62.8	2.8	3.1	1.0
2005......	327,185	97,041	207,725	9,265	10,095	3,060	29.7	63.5	2.8	3.1	0.9
2006......	352,567	101,558	227,110	10,076	10,641	3,182	28.8	64.4	2.9	3.0	0.9
2007......	379,454	106,631	246,741	10,833	11,810	3,438	28.1	65.0	2.9	3.1	0.9
2008......	405,630	118,443	258,691	11,640	13,151	3,706	29.2	63.8	2.9	3.2	0.9
2009......	403,803	126,572	247,274	11,884	14,264	3,808	31.3	61.2	2.9	3.5	0.9
2010......	406,708	126,962	249,182	11,990	14,793	3,782	31.2	61.3	2.9	3.6	0.9

[1] Figures for University and College (U&C) R&D prior to 2003 cover only science and engineering (S&E) fields; in 2003 and later years, R&D in non-S&E fields is also included. Also, adjustments have been made to U&C R&D for 1998 and later years to eliminate double counting of funds passed through from one academic institution to another. [2] Nonfederal R&D expenditures to university and college performers.

Source: U.S. National Science Foundation, *National Patterns of R&D Resources, 2010-11*, NSF 13-318, April 2013. See also <http://www.nsf.gov/statistics/>.

Table 826. National Research and Development (R&D) Expenditures as a Percent of Gross Domestic Product by Country: 1990 to 2011

Year	United States	Japan[1]	Germany[2]	France	United Kingdom	Italy	Canada	South Korea	OECD Total[3]	Russia[4]	China[5]
1990...	[6] 2.65	[9] 2.91	[10] 2.61	2.32	2.09	[11] 1.25	1.51	(NA)	[13] 2.24	2.03	(NA)
1995...	[6] 2.50	[9] 2.87	[10] 2.19	2.28	1.89	0.97	1.70	[12] 2.3	[7] 2.05	0.85	[14] 0.57
2000...	[6] 2.71	3.00	2.47	[7] 2.15	1.82	1.04	1.91	[12] 2.30	[13] 2.20	1.05	[7] 0.90
2002...	[6] 2.62	3.12	2.50	2.24	1.80	1.12	2.04	[12] 2.40	[13] 2.21	1.25	1.07
2003...	[6] 2.61	3.14	2.54	2.18	1.75	1.10	2.04	[12] 2.49	[13] 2.21	1.29	1.13
2004...	[6] 2.55	3.13	2.50	[7] 2.16	1.69	1.09	2.07	[12] 2.68	[13] 2.18	1.15	1.23
2005...	[6] 2.59	3.31	2.51	2.11	1.72	1.09	2.04	[12] 2.79	[13] 2.22	1.07	1.32
2006...	[7] 2.65	3.41	2.54	2.11	1.74	1.13	2.00	[12] 3.01	[13] 2.26	1.07	1.39
2007...	[6] 2.72	3.46	2.53	2.08	1.78	1.17	1.96	[7] 3.21	[13] 2.29	1.12	1.40
2008...	[6] 2.86	[7] 3.47	2.69	2.12	[10] 1.78	1.21	1.92	3.36	[13] 2.36	1.04	1.47
2009...	[6] 2.91	3.36	2.82	2.27	[10] 1.84	1.26	1.94	3.56	[13] 2.41	1.25	1.70
2010...	[6] 2.83	3.25	2.80	[7] 2.24	[10] 1.80	1.26	1.85	3.74	[13] 2.37	1.13	1.76
2011...	[6,8] 2.77	3.39	[10] 2.88	2.24	[8] 1.77	[8] 1.25	[8] 1.74	4.03	[8,13] 2.37	1.09	1.84

NA Not Available. [1] Data on Japanese research and development after 1995 may not be consistent with data in earlier years because of changes in methodology. [2] Data for 1990 are for West Germany only. [3] Organization for Economic Cooperation and Development. [4] As of May 2007 Russia is an OECD accession candidate country. [5] As of 2007 China is an OECD enhanced engagement country. [6] Excludes most or all capital expenditure. [7] Break in series with previous year for which data is available. [8] Provisional. [9] Overestimated or based on overestimated data. [10] National estimate or projection. [11] Including extramural R&D expenditure. [12] Excluded R&D in the social sciences and humanities. [13] Secretariat estimate or projection based on national sources. [14] Underestimated or based on underestimated data.

Source: Organisation for Economic Cooperation and Development, "Main Science and Technology Indicators," 2013 ©. See also <http://www.oecd.org/>.

Table 827. Research and Development (R&D) Expenditures By Performing Sector and Source of Funds: 1990 to 2011

[In millions of dollars (151,993 represents $151,993,000,000). For calendar year. FFRDCs are federally funded research and development centers]

Year	Total[1]	Federal government	Industry Total	Industry Funded by— Federal government	Industry Funded by— Industry[2]	Industry FFRDCs	Universities and colleges Total	U&C Funded by— Federal government	U&C Funded by— Non-federal government[3]	U&C Funded by— Industry	U&C Funded by— Universities & colleges	U&C Funded by— Non-profits	University & college FFRDCs[4]	Other nonprofit institutions Total	ONP Funded by— Federal government	ONP Funded by— Industry	ONP Funded by— Non-profits
RESEARCH AND DEVELOPMENT TOTAL																	
1990	151,993	15,671	107,404	25,802	81,602	2,323	16,939	9,939	1,399	1,166	3,187	1,249	4,894	4,126	2,346	440	1,340
2000	268,905	19,247	199,961	17,117	182,844	2,001	30,693	17,719	2,246	2,174	6,231	2,324	5,742	9,734	4,510	1,020	4,204
2005	327,185	26,322	226,159	21,909	204,250	2,601	47,006	29,019	3,060	2,368	9,265	3,294	7,817	14,452	6,545	1,107	6,800
2006	352,567	28,240	247,669	24,304	223,365	3,122	48,951	29,600	3,182	2,563	10,076	3,530	7,306	14,336	6,044	1,182	7,111
2007	379,454	29,859	269,267	26,585	242,682	5,165	51,149	30,160	3,438	2,803	10,833	3,915	5,567	15,132	5,980	1,257	7,896
2008	405,630	29,839	290,681	36,360	254,321	6,346	53,917	31,178	3,706	3,069	11,640	4,324	4,766	16,363	6,236	1,301	8,827
2009	403,803	30,560	282,393	39,573	242,820	6,646	56,939	33,433	3,808	3,196	11,884	4,617	5,052	18,002	7,097	1,258	9,647
2010[5]	406,708	31,217	278,977	34,199	244,778	7,214	60,235	36,561	3,782	3,139	11,990	4,764	5,315	18,294	7,000	1,265	10,029
2011[5]	414,035	31,505	283,784	39,274	244,510	7,037	63,102	38,710	3,832	3,173	12,488	4,899	5,294	17,756	6,274	1,264	10,218
BASIC RESEARCH																	
1990	23,029	2,319	4,629	869	3,760	499	11,126	6,889	847	705	1,929	756	2,470	1,922	947	245	730
2000	42,752	3,765	7,040	925	6,115	547	22,910	13,960	1,549	1,499	4,298	1,603	2,874	5,000	2,099	566	2,334
2005	61,321	4,770	8,667	1,108	7,559	136	35,454	22,788	2,155	1,667	6,525	2,319	3,820	7,293	2,903	614	3,776
2006	62,996	4,716	8,384	1,444	6,940	652	37,205	23,312	2,285	1,840	7,233	2,535	3,344	7,454	2,849	656	3,948
2007	68,061	4,621	11,268	2,780	8,488	2,258	38,929	23,673	2,499	2,037	7,874	2,845	1,724	7,911	2,829	698	4,384
2008	72,149	4,957	12,368	1,475	10,893	2,423	40,582	24,149	2,679	2,218	8,412	3,124	1,672	8,697	3,073	722	4,901
2009	75,824	5,441	14,784	1,340	13,444	2,628	39,982	24,098	2,573	2,161	8,036	3,115	1,902	9,553	3,498	698	5,357
2010[5]	77,187	5,091	16,371	1,406	14,965	2,848	39,415	24,499	2,383	1,978	7,554	3,001	2,196	9,688	3,417	702	5,568
2011[5]	78,466	4,875	16,563	1,615	14,949	2,761	40,952	25,662	2,402	1,989	7,828	3,071	2,212	9,483	3,108	702	5,673
APPLIED RESEARCH																	
1990	34,897	3,652	24,399	5,967	18,432	386	4,406	2,140	453	377	1,031	404	689	1,284	780	120	384
2000	56,681	6,105	39,176	2,682	36,494	269	6,494	3,194	571	553	1,585	591	1,291	3,155	1,831	258	1,066
2005	70,001	7,557	45,284	5,289	39,995	1,414	9,395	5,032	743	575	2,247	799	1,637	4,435	2,432	280	1,723
2006	76,735	7,435	51,173	6,140	45,033	1,314	9,794	5,318	736	593	2,331	816	1,827	4,694	2,592	300	1,802
2007	83,559	7,222	57,570	8,945	48,625	1,168	10,249	5,548	770	628	2,426	877	1,354	4,902	2,583	318	2,001
2008	74,819	7,316	46,864	5,397	41,467	1,975	11,316	6,144	843	698	2,647	983	855	5,167	2,600	330	2,237
2009	72,881	7,874	41,055	7,797	33,258	2,010	13,434	7,699	929	779	2,898	1,128	1,282	5,813	3,049	319	2,445
2010[5]	79,543	7,985	44,906	4,705	40,201	2,249	15,562	9,439	978	812	3,101	1,232	1,277	5,922	3,060	321	2,542
2011[5]	80,735	7,747	45,560	5,403	40,157	2,223	16,614	10,256	999	827	3,255	1,277	1,314	5,676	2,766	320	2,590
DEVELOPMENT																	
1990	94,067	9,700	78,376	18,966	59,410	1,438	1,407	910	99	83	226	89	1,735	920	619	75	226
2000	169,472	9,377	153,745	13,510	140,235	1,185	1,289	565	125	121	348	130	1,577	1,579	580	195	804
2005	195,864	13,994	172,208	15,512	156,696	1,052	2,157	1,199	163	126	493	175	2,360	2,723	1,211	212	1,301
2006	212,836	16,089	188,112	16,720	171,392	1,156	1,952	970	162	130	512	179	2,136	2,189	603	226	1,360
2007	227,834	18,016	200,429	14,860	185,569	1,738	1,971	939	169	138	533	192	2,488	2,319	568	240	1,511
2008	258,663	17,566	231,449	29,488	201,961	1,948	2,020	885	185	153	581	216	2,239	2,500	562	249	1,689
2009	255,099	17,245	226,554	30,436	196,118	2,008	3,523	1,636	306	256	951	374	1,868	2,636	550	241	1,846
2010[5]	249,979	18,141	217,700	28,088	189,612	2,118	5,259	2,623	421	349	1,335	530	1,842	2,684	523	242	1,919
2011[5]	254,835	18,884	221,661	32,256	189,404	2,053	5,536	2,792	431	357	1,405	551	1,768	2,597	400	242	1,955

[1] Total includes nonprofit FFRDCs, not shown separately. [2] Includes all nonfederal sources of industry R&D expenditures. [3] Includes all nonfederal sources. [4] Includes all R&D expenditures of FFRDCs administered by academic institutions and funded by the federal government. [5] Estimated.

Source: National Science Foundation, National Center for Science and Engineering Statistics, *National Patterns of R&D Resources: 2010-11 Data Update*, NSF 13-318, April 2013. See also <http://www.nsf.gov/statistics/natlpatterns/>.

Table 828. Federal Obligations for Research in Current and Constant (2005) Dollars by Field of Science: 2005 to 2012

[In millions of dollars (53,738 represents $53,738,000,000). For years ending September 30. Excludes R&D plant]

Field of science	Current dollars				Constant (2005) dollars [1]			
	2005	2010	2011, prel.	2012, prel.	2005	2010	2011, prel.	2012, prel.
Research, total............	**53,738**	**63,728**	**58,167**	**60,712**	**53,738**	**57,416**	**51,312**	**52,616**
Basic.........................	27,140	31,795	29,061	30,665	27,140	28,646	25,636	26,576
Applied........................	26,598	31,933	29,106	30,048	26,598	28,770	25,676	26,041
Life sciences..................	28,128	33,909	30,203	30,804	28,128	30,551	26,643	26,696
Psychology....................	1,892	2,156	1,905	1,960	1,892	1,942	1,681	1,699
Physical sciences..............	5,494	5,871	5,534	5,902	5,494	5,289	4,882	5,115
Environmental sciences.........	3,503	3,339	3,125	3,313	3,503	3,008	2,756	2,871
Mathematics and computer sciences.......	2,983	3,412	3,276	3,590	2,983	3,074	2,889	3,112
Engineering...................	8,553	11,081	10,139	10,856	8,553	9,984	8,945	9,408
Social sciences................ [2]	1,097	1,197	1,222	1,258	1,097	1,079	1,078	1,090
Other sciences, n.e.c. [2]...........	2,089	2,763	2,764	3,029	2,089	2,490	2,438	2,625

[1] Based on gross domestic product implicit price deflator. [2] Not elsewhere classified.

Source: U.S. National Science Foundation, *Federal Funds for Research and Development, Fiscal Years 2010-12*, NSF 13-326, July 2013, and earlier reports. See also <http://www.nsf.gov/statistics/fedfunds/>.

Table 829. Federal Budget Authority for Research and Development (R&D) in Current and Constant (2005) Dollars by Selected Budget Functions: 2009 to 2012

[In millions of dollars (156,009 represents $156,009,000,000). For year ending September 30. Excludes R&D plant. Represents budget authority. Functions shown are those for which $1 billion or more was authorized since 2001]

Function	Current dollars				Constant (2005) dollars [1]			
	2009 [2]	2010	2011	2012 [3]	2009 [2]	2010	2011	2012 [3]
Total [4]......................	**156,009**	**146,596**	**142,457**	**138,146**	**142,436**	**132,077**	**125,669**	**119,724**
National defense...............	85,166	86,517	82,972	78,471	77,757	77,948	73,194	68,007
Health........................	40,389	31,488	30,903	31,024	36,875	28,369	27,261	26,887
Space research and technology..........	6,891	8,232	8,398	8,642	6,291	7,417	7,408	7,490
Energy........................	3,318	2,455	2,233	2,367	3,029	2,212	1,970	2,051
General science...............	11,840	9,547	9,483	9,372	10,810	8,601	8,365	8,122
Natural resources and environment......	2,245	2,237	2,171	2,137	2,050	2,015	1,915	1,852
Transportation.................	1,440	1,496	1,395	1,421	1,315	1,348	1,231	1,232
Agriculture....................	1,935	2,043	1,916	1,875	1,767	1,841	1,690	1,625

[1] Based on gross domestic product implicit price deflator. [2] Includes ARRA (American Recovery and Reinvestment Act) funds. [3] Preliminary. [4] Includes other functions, not shown separately.

Source: U.S. National Science Foundation, *Federal R&D Funding by Budget Function*, NSF 13-308, January 2013. See also <http://www.nsf.gov/statistics/fedbudget/>.

Table 830. Federal Research and Development (R&D) by Federal Agency: Fiscal Year 2012 and 2013

[In millions of dollars (142,524 represents $142,524,000,000). For fiscal years ending September 30. R&D refers to actual research and development activities as well as R&D facilities. R&D facilities (also known as R&D plants) includes construction, repair, or alteration of physical plant used in the conduct of R&D. Based on Office of Management and Budget data]

Federal agency	2012	2013	Federal agency	2012	2013
Total research and development..............	**142,524**	**133,212**			
Defense R&D................	78,717	72,132	Department of Veterans Affairs...............	1,160	1,131
Nondefense R&D.............	63,807	61,080	Department of Homeland Security...........	481	773
			Department of Transportation.................	919	857
Department of Defense............	74,460	68,036	Department of Interior..................	820	765
Science and technology...........	13,330	12,712	U.S. Geological Survey..................	673	643
All other Department of Defense R&D...........	61,130	55,325	Environmental Protection Agency...........	568	532
Health and Human Services.......	31,377	29,765	Department of Education.....................	397	376
National Institute of Health..........	30,012	28,458	Smithsonian................................	243	232
All other Health and Human Services			International Assistance Programs..........	188	179
R&D................................	1,365	1,307	Department of Housing and Urban		
Department of Energy............	10,811	10,332	Development..............................	58	55
Atomic Energy Defense............	4,257	4,096	Department of State.........................	81	77
Office of Science.................	4,463	4,239	Nuclear Regulatory Commission.............	83	79
Energy R&D.......................	2,091	1,997	Department of Justice.......................	92	91
NASA............................	11,315	10,566	Social Security Administration................	8	8
National Science Foundation.......	5,705	5,478	U.S. Postal Service.........................	17	16
Department of Agriculture..........	2,331	2,177	Tennessee Valley Authority..................	17	17
Department of Commerce..........	1,254	1,359	Army Corps of Engineers....................	11	10
National Oceanic and Atmospheric					
Administration..................	574	650	Telecommunications Development		
National Institute of Standards and			Agency..................................	4	(NA)
Technology......................	557	588	Department of Labor.........................	4	4

NA Not available.

Source: American Association for the Advancement of Science (AAAS), *AAAS Report XXXVIII: Research and Development FY2014* ©, 2013. See also <http://www.aaas.org/spp/rd/>.

Table 831. Funds for Domestic Business Research and Development (R&D) Performed by Manufacturing and Nonmanufacturing Companies by Industry: 2008 to 2010

[Based on the Business R&D Innovation Survey. For information about the survey, see http://www.nsf.gov/statistics/srvyindustry/about/brdis/]

Industry	NAICS [1] code	Total R&D funds as a percent of net sales			Company R&D funds as a percent of net sales		
		2008	2009	2010	2008	2009	2010
All industries, total...........	(X)	**3.7**	**3.8**	**3.2**	**3.0**	**3.0**	**2.5**
All manufacturing industries, total.........	(X)	**4.4**	**4.5**	**4.1**	**3.5**	**3.7**	**3.3**
Paper, printing, and support activities..........	322, 323	1.4	(NA)	(NA)	1.3	(NA)	(NA)
Chemicals..........	325	6.5	6.6	5.7	6.1	6.1	5.3
Pharmaceuticals and medicines..........	3254	13.0	13.2	12.7	12.2	12.3	11.7
Plastic and rubber products..........	326	1.1	(NA)	(NA)	1.1	(NA)	(NA)
Nonmetallic mineral products..........	327	2.0	(NA)	(NA)	1.9	(NA)	(NA)
Fabricated metal products..........	332	1.6	(NA)	(NA)	1.6	(NA)	(NA)
Machinery..........	333	3.6	4.0	3.9	3.5	3.9	3.7
Computer and electronic products..........	334	11.6	11.4	9.6	10.1	9.2	8.2
Electrical equipment, appliances, and components...........	335	2.9	3.4	3.0	2.7	3.2	2.8
Transportation equipment..........	336	5.7	5.9	4.7	2.6	3.0	2.3
Aerospace products and parts..........	3364	9.9	10.4	9.7	2.8	3.7	3.3
All nonmanufacturing industries, total.........	(X)	**2.8**	**2.8**	**2.1**	**2.2**	**2.1**	**1.6**
Information..........	51	4.9	4.6	4.6	4.8	4.4	4.5
Software publishing..........	5112	10.8	10.1	9.7	10.6	9.8	9.8
Internet service and data processing providers..........	518	6.3	(NA)	(NA)	6.2	(NA)	(NA)
Finance and insurance..........	52	0.3	0.3	0.2	0.3	0.3	0.2
Professional, scientific, and technical services..........	54	8.4	9.9	6.9	4.5	5.7	3.2
Architectural, engineering, and related services..........	5413	8.2	(NA)	(NA)	3.3	(NA)	(NA)
Computer systems design and related services..........	5415	5.9	6.8	6.2	4.2	5.8	5.3
Scientific research and development services..........	5417	13.2	18.1	14.2	6.4	8.4	2.7

NA Not Available X Not applicable. [1] North American Industry Classification System (NAICS); see text, Section 15.

Source: U.S. National Science Foundation, National Center for Science and Engineering Statistics, *Business R&D Performed in the United States Cost $291 Billion in 2008 and $282 Billion in 2009*, InfoBrief NSF 12-309, March 2012; and *Business R&D Performance Remained Virtually Unchanged in 2010*, InfoBrief NSF 13-324, June 2013. See also <http://www.nsf.gov/statistics/industry/>.

Table 832. Funds for Domestic Performance of Business Research and Development (R&D) in Current and Constant (2005) Dollars by Source of Funds and Selected Industries: 2005 to 2010

[In millions of dollars (204,250 represents $204,250,000,000). For calendar years. Covers basic research, applied research, and development. Based on the Business R&D and Innovation Survey, sponsored by National Science Foundation; for information about the surveys and methodology, see <http://www.nsf.gov/statistics/srvyindustry/>]

Industry	NAICS [1] code	2005	2008	2009	2010
CURRENT DOLLARS					
Company and other funds..........	(X)	204,250	254,321	242,819	244,778
Federal funds..........	(X)	21,909	36,360	39,573	34,199
Total funds..........	**(X)**	**226,159**	**290,681**	**282,393**	**278,977**
Chemicals and allied products..........	325	42,995	58,249	53,328	58,038
Pharmaceuticals and medicines..........	3254	34,839	48,113	44,936	49,415
Machinery..........	333	8,531	10,104	9,138	9,955
Computer and electronic products..........	334	(D)	60,463	60,464	59,875
Navigational, measuring, electromedical, and control instruments..........	3345	15,204	15,460	(NA)	(NA)
Electrical equipment, appliances, and components..........	335	2,424	3,143	3,334	3,321
Motor vehicles, trailers, and parts..........	3361-3363	(D)	13,140	(D)	(NA)
Aerospace products and parts..........	3364	15,055	36,941	34,554	29,854
Information..........	51	23,836	37,964	33,806	36,853
Software publishers..........	5112	16,926	28,221	26,395	26,982
Professional, scientific, and technical services..........	54	32,021	37,594	44,946	33,690
Computer systems design and related services..........	5415	13,592	12,146	12,560	11,050
Scientific R&D services..........	5417	12,299	17,913	17,270	12,140
CONSTANT (2005) DOLLARS [2]					
Company and other funds..........	(X)	204,250	234,220	221,694	220,535
Federal funds..........	(X)	21,909	33,486	36,130	30,812
Total funds..........	**(X)**	**226,159**	**267,706**	**257,825**	**251,346**
Chemicals..........	325	42,995	53,645	48,688	52,290
Pharmaceuticals and medicines..........	3254	34,839	44,327	41,027	44,521
Machinery..........	333	8,531	9,305	8,343	8,969
Computer and electronic products..........	334	(D)	55,684	55,204	53,945
Navigational, measuring, electromedical, and control instruments..........	3345	15,204	14,238	(NA)	(NA)
Electrical equipment, appliances, and components..........	335	2,424	2,895	3,044	2,992
Motor vehicles, trailers, and parts..........	3361-3363	(D)	12,101	(D)	(NA)
Aerospace products and parts..........	3364	15,055	34,021	31,548	26,897
Information..........	51	23,836	34,963	30,865	33,203
Software publishers..........	5112	16,926	25,990	24,099	24,310
Professional, scientific, and technical services..........	54	32,021	34,623	41,036	30,353
Computer systems design and related services..........	5415	13,592	11,186	11,467	9,956
Scientific R&D services..........	5417	12,299	16,497	15,768	10,938

X Not applicable. NA Not Available. D Figure withheld to avoid disclosure of information pertaining to a specific organization or individual. [1] North American Industry Classification System; see text, Section 15. [2] Based on gross domestic product implicit price deflator. Update from May 30, 2013.

Source: U.S. National Science Foundation, National Center for Science and Engineering Statistics, *Research and Development in Industry*, annual; *Business R&D Performed in the United States Cost $291 Billion in 2008 and $282 Billion in 2009*, InfoBrief NSF 12-309, March 2012; and *Business R&D Performance Remained Virtually Unchanged in 2010*, InfoBrief NSF 13-324, June 2013. See also <http://www.nsf.gov/statistics/industry/>.

Table 833. Academic and Industrial Research and Development (R&D) Performed by State: 2010

[In millions of dollars (60,235 represents 60,235,000,000). Industry R&D data refer to calendar years; other R&D data refer to fiscal years but are used here as approximations to calendar year data. For definition of Research and Development see text this section]

State	Academic R&D[2] (mil. dol.)	Academic R&D per $1,000 of state GDP	Industry-performed R&D (mil. dol.)	Industry R&D per $1,000 of state GDP	State	Academic R&D[2] (mil. dol.)	Academic R&D per $1,000 of state GDP	Industry-performed R&D (mil. dol.)	Industry R&D per $1,000 of state GDP
U.S.[1]	60,235	4.15	278,977	19.20	MO	1,087	4.47	8,106	33.31
AL	847	4.98	1,449	8.51	MT	208	5.69	145	3.97
AK	181	3.79	74	1.55	NE	368	4.09	527	5.85
AZ	945	3.78	4,054	16.23	NV	174	1.38	709	5.62
AR	268	2.62	276	2.70	NH	311	5.05	1,818	29.50
CA	7,833	4.17	64,914	34.57	NJ	1,076	2.24	15,925	33.15
CO	1,180	4.66	3,899	15.40	NM	423	5.49	546	7.08
CT	889	4.02	6,498	29.36	NY	4,951	4.39	10,954	9.70
DE	169	2.64	2,144	33.49	NC	2,465	5.81	5,749	13.54
DC	470	4.54	235	2.27	ND	204	5.72	236	6.62
FL	1,995	2.71	5,127	6.97	OH	2,052	4.39	6,857	14.69
GA	1,627	4.03	3,644	9.04	OK	401	2.72	478	3.24
HI	318	4.85	257	3.92	OR	696	3.76	4,396	23.74
ID	126	2.25	1,120	19.99	PA	3,128	5.60	9,246	16.54
IL	2,224	3.44	12,221	18.89	RI	429	8.78	531	10.87
IN	1,186	4.44	4,985	18.65	SC	660	4.12	1,316	8.21
IA	707	5.02	1,950	13.84	SD	131	3.43	120	3.14
KS	483	3.83	1,492	11.83	TN	938	3.66	1,244	4.86
KY	575	3.61	889	5.58	TX	4,416	3.61	14,384	11.76
LA	714	3.07	428	1.84	UT	562	4.71	2,066	17.33
ME	138	2.72	251	4.95	VT	133	5.26	313	12.39
MD	3,139	10.70	4,384	14.94	VA	1,199	2.86	4,655	11.10
MA	2,750	7.28	14,020	37.11	WA	1,358	4.00	13,545	39.86
MI	2,031	5.51	12,144	32.97	WV	195	3.15	240	3.88
MN	832	3.07	6,246	23.07	WI	1,336	5.44	3,927	15.98
MS	444	4.65	243	2.55	WY	55	1.53	39	1.09

[1] U.S. totals will not equal state totals because the US totals include data for outlying areas (Puerto Rico, Guam, and Virgin Islands), R&D expenditures that can not be allocated to specific states, and double counting of U&C data (see footnote 2). [2] State level university R&D data have not been adjusted to eliminate double counting of funds passed through from one academic institution to another. See source for more information.

Source: National Science Foundation, National Patterns of R&D Resources: 2010-11 Data Update, NSF-13-318, April 2013. See also <http://www.nsf.gov/statistics/natpatterns/>.

Table 834. Research and Development (R&D) Expenditures in Science and Engineering at Universities and Colleges in Current and Constant (2005) Dollars: 2000 to 2011

[In millions of dollars (30,084 represents $30,084,000,000). Totals may not add due to rounding. Reference period is the fiscal year of the surveyed institutions. Data are based the Higher Education R&D (HERD) Survey, which in 2010 succeeded the Survey of Research and Development Expenditures at Colleges and Universities; see source for details]

Characteristic	Current dollars				Constant (2005) dollars [1]			
	2000	2005	2010	2011	2000	2005	2010	2011
Total..........................	**30,084**	**45,774**	**58,311**	**61,891**	**33,908**	**45,774**	**52,536**	**54,597**
Basic research [2]...................	22,547	34,353	(NA)	(NA)	25,413	34,353	(NA)	(NA)
Applied R&D [2]....................	7,537	11,421	(NA)	(NA)	8,495	11,421	(NA)	(NA)
Source of funds:								
Federal government................	17,548	29,187	36,509	39,658	19,778	29,187	32,893	34,984
State and local government...........	2,200	2,940	3,605	3,563	2,480	2,940	3,248	3,143
Institutions' own funds..................	5,925	8,265	10,627	11,048	6,678	8,265	9,574	9,746
Industry...........................	2,156	2,291	3,124	3,078	2,430	2,291	2,815	2,715
Other..............................	2,255	3,092	4,446	4,544	2,542	3,092	4,006	4,009
Field:								
Physical sciences...................	2,713	3,703	4,619	4,779	3,058	3,703	4,162	4,216
Environmental sciences...............	1,766	2,554	2,992	3,167	1,990	2,554	2,696	2,794
Mathematical sciences.................	342	494	592	636	385	494	533	561
Computer sciences.....................	877	1,404	1,637	1,735	988	1,404	1,475	1,531
Life sciences.........................	17,471	27,604	34,924	37,232	19,692	27,604	31,465	32,844
Psychology...........................	517	825	1,075	1,119	582	825	969	987
Social sciences.......................	1,300	1,685	1,991	2,045	1,465	1,685	1,794	1,804
Other sciences........................	543	761	1,154	1,132	612	761	1,040	999
Engineering...........................	4,557	6,743	9,327	10,045	5,136	6,743	8,403	8,861

NA Not available. [1] Based on gross domestic product implicit price deflator (updated June 2013). [2] Basic research and applied R&D statistics were re-estimated for FY1998 and forward. These data are not directly comparable to those from earlier years.

Source: U.S. National Science Foundation, *Higher Education Research and Development: Fiscal Year 2011*, NSF 13-325, July 2013, and earlier reports. See also <http://www.nsf.gov/statistics/herd/>.

Table 835. Federal Research and Development (R&D) Obligations to Selected Universities and Colleges: 2008 and 2009

[In millions of dollars (25,481.9 represents $25,481,900,000). For fiscal years ending September 30. For the top 40 institutions receiving federal R&D funds in 2009. Awards to the administrative offices of university systems are excluded from totals for individual institutions because that allocation of funds is unknown, but those awards are included in "total all institutions"]

Major institution ranked by total 2009 federal R&D obligations	2008	2009 [2]	Major institution ranked by total 2009 federal R&D obligations	2008	2009 [2]
Total, all institutions [1]............	**25,481.9**	**32,420.7**	Vanderbilt University........................	319.6	405.7
Johns Hopkins University...............	1,034.2	1,465.6	University of Colorado.....................	318.4	404.5
University of Michigan..................	542.1	727.6	University Southern California.............	261.2	346.5
University of Washington...............	568.5	714.2	Northwestern University....................	241.5	331.9
University of Pennsylvania..............	486.4	636.2	University of California—Davis.............	258.2	329.5
Columbia University—City of New York..........	400.4	632.6	University of Chicago.......................	274.8	326.0
University of California—San Diego.............	475.4	588.7	Emory University...........................	266.2	319.2
University of California—Los Angeles...........	490.1	584.3	University of Rochester.....................	248.9	308.6
University of California—San Francisco.........	498.0	544.1	Case Western Reserve University.........	268.0	298.8
University of Wisconsin—Madison...............	394.2	538.1	University of California—Berkeley.........	247.2	289.5
University of Pittsburgh................	409.6	525.1	Ohio State University.......................	230.6	281.7
Harvard University.....................	411.3	525.0	Mt. Sinai School of Medicine...............	188.1	281.1
Duke University........................	412.8	513.4	Baylor College of Medicine.................	246.3	278.3
University of North Carolina at Chapel Hill........	385.7	486.4	University of Alabama—Birmingham.......	212.4	277.0
Washington University..................	403.6	472.5	University of Arizona.......................	217.0	273.5
Stanford University....................	396.6	467.7	Boston University...........................	227.3	273.4
University of Minnesota................	353.7	466.9	University of Maryland at Baltimore........	167.3	263.8
Yale University........................	393.4	460.4	Georgia Institute of Technology............	177.7	253.8
Cornell University.....................	338.6	445.5	The Scripps Research Institute.............	208.5	253.8
Massachusetts Institute of Technology...........	388.2	416.3	University of Virginia.......................	174.7	236.8
Pennsylvania State University..........	314.3	409.7			

[1] Includes other institutions, not shown separately. [2] Includes American Recovery and Reinvestment Act of 2009 obligations.

Source: U.S. National Science Foundation, *Federal S&E Support to Universities and Colleges and Nonprofit Institutions*, NSF13-303, December 2012. See also <http://www.nsf.gov/statistics/fedsupport/>.

Table 836. Graduate Science/Engineering Students in Doctorate-Granting Colleges by Characteristic and Field: 2000 to 2011

[In thousands (443.5 represents 443,500). As of Fall. Includes outlying areas]

Field of science or engineering	Total			Characteristic								
				Female			Foreign			Part-time		
	2000	2010	2011	2000	2010	2011	2000	2010	2011	2000	2010	2011
Total, all surveyed fields	**443.5**	**575.8**	**570.5**	**201.8**	**265.0**	**259.9**	**123.3**	**165.9**	**169.3**	**123.6**	**142.5**	**139.9**
Science/engineering	374.8	508.1	511.8	150.3	215.3	216.9	118.0	158.3	162.0	99.3	121.7	122.8
Engineering, total	98.8	141.8	139.9	19.7	32.9	32.4	46.3	64.2	65.1	28.2	35.4	34.8
Sciences, total [1]	275.9	366.3	371.8	130.7	182.4	184.5	71.7	94.1	97.0	71.1	86.4	87.9
Physical sciences	29.6	37.9	38.7	8.8	12.4	12.7	11.5	15.0	15.2	3.5	3.6	3.6
Environmental	13.0	14.8	14.9	5.3	6.7	6.7	2.6	2.9	3.1	2.8	2.9	2.9
Math sciences	14.4	21.3	22.0	5.2	7.4	7.6	5.9	8.4	8.9	3.0	4.4	4.4
Computer sciences	40.3	45.9	46.1	11.7	11.2	11.2	19.7	22.6	23.2	16.7	15.8	15.7
Agricultural sciences	11.3	14.6	15.1	4.8	7.2	7.5	2.4	3.2	3.4	2.4	4.1	4.2
Biological sciences	53.1	69.5	69.7	27.8	39.3	39.3	11.6	16.9	17.0	7.6	9.5	9.9
Psychology [2]	40.3	45.2	45.6	29.0	33.8	34.0	2.1	2.9	2.9	10.8	11.7	12.1
Social sciences	73.9	95.9	97.2	38.1	51.0	51.6	15.8	18.8	19.7	24.3	28.1	28.5
Health fields, total [2]	68.8	67.7	58.8	51.5	49.7	43.0	5.4	7.6	7.2	24.3	20.8	17.1

[1] Total in 2010 includes newly eligible fields (communication, family and consumer science/human science, and multidisciplinary/interdisciplinary studies) and neuroscience, previously reported under health field "neurology," not shown separately. [2] Counts in psychology and health declined in 2010, potentially due to more rigorous follow-up with institutions regarding the exclusion of practitioner-oriented graduate degree programs. These decreases may not reflect changes in actual enrollments.

Source: U.S. National Science Foundation, *Survey of Graduate Science Engineering Students and Postdoctorates, Fall 2009*, December 2011, and earlier reports; and unpublished data. See also <http://www.nsf.gov/statistics/gradpostdoc>.

Table 837. Temporary Visa Holders Awarded Doctorates in Science and Engineering by Country of Citizenship: 2000 to 2011

[Based on the Survey of Earned Doctorates; for information, see <http://www.nsf.gov/statistics/srvydoctorates/>]

Country of citizenship	2000	2003	2004	2005	2006	2007	2008	2009	2010	2011
All temporary visa holders	**7,664**	**8,393**	**9,164**	**10,426**	**11,587**	**12,369**	**12,625**	**12,216**	**11,309**	**11,825**
Canada	243	280	337	312	315	341	354	373	325	298
Mexico	190	198	164	193	169	166	160	169	165	156
Brazil	121	99	124	140	128	111	123	121	126	121
United Kingdom	64	77	73	68	77	82	83	76	68	66
France	64	68	82	98	106	120	120	112	96	100
Germany	169	154	153	145	128	126	137	166	153	156
China [1]	2,034	2,263	2,718	3,281	4,056	4,211	4,071	3,678	3,367	3,574
Japan	166	170	166	183	187	201	196	187	163	170
Korea	695	915	1,003	1,118	1,167	1,093	1,110	1,155	1,053	1,049
Taiwan	611	407	359	401	403	433	414	510	462	541
Thailand	149	307	263	248	194	218	274	193	171	205
India	726	688	788	1,033	1,415	1,839	2,061	2,030	1,902	1,939
Iran	40	45	45	112	124	127	129	137	142	191
Turkey	248	348	319	321	321	410	466	446	412	427
Science	5,213	5,475	5,852	6,664	7,289	7,768	8,135	8,000	7,451	7,664
Engineering	2,451	2,918	3,312	3,762	4,298	4,601	4,490	4,216	3,858	4,161

[1] Includes Hong Kong.

Source: U.S. National Science Foundation, National Center for Science and Engineering Statistics, Survey of Earned Doctorates, special tabulation (2013).

Table 838. Science and Engineering (S&E) Degrees Awarded by Degree Level and Sex of Recipient: 1990 to 2010

[For a description of science and engineering degree categories, see source, Appendix B, <http://www.nsf.gov/statistics/nsf13327/>]

Academic year ending	Bachelor's degree				Master's degree				Doctoral degree			
	Total S&E	Men	Women	Percent women	Total S&E	Men	Women	Percent women	Total S&E	Men	Women	Percent women [1]
1990	329,094	189,082	140,012	42.5	77,788	51,230	26,558	34.1	22,867	16,498	6,369	27.9
2000	398,602	197,650	200,952	50.4	96,230	54,560	41,670	43.3	25,912	16,518	9,394	36.3
2005	470,214	233,924	236,290	50.3	120,870	67,244	53,626	44.4	27,945	17,405	10,540	37.7
2006	478,858	238,029	240,829	50.3	120,999	66,249	54,750	45.2	29,844	18,370	11,474	38.4
2007	485,772	241,697	244,075	50.2	120,278	65,353	54,925	45.7	31,768	19,508	12,260	38.6
2008	496,168	246,719	249,449	50.3	126,404	68,810	57,594	45.6	32,804	19,845	12,959	39.5
2009	505,435	250,742	254,693	50.4	134,517	73,489	61,028	45.4	33,438	19,842	13,596	40.7
2010	525,374	261,091	264,283	50.3	139,926	76,266	63,660	45.5	33,132	19,584	13,548	40.9

[1] Percentage of women doctoral degree recipients are calculated based on the total of men plus women, not on the total number of degrees.

Source: U.S. National Science Foundation, *Science and Engineering Degrees: 1966–2010*, NSF-13-327, June 2013. See also <http://www.nsf.gov/statistics/degrees/>.

Table 839. Science and Engineering (S&E) Degrees as Share of Higher Education Degrees Conferred by State: 2009

[S&E degrees include physical, computer, agricultural, biological, earth, atmospheric, ocean, and social sciences; psychology; mathematics; and engineering]

State	S&E degrees conferred [1]	All higher education degrees [1]	S&E higher education degrees (percent)	State	S&E degrees conferred [1]	All higher education degrees [1]	S&E higher education degrees (percent)	State	S&E degrees conferred [1]	All higher education degrees [1]	S&E higher education degrees (percent)
U.S.........	667,790	2,322,054	28.8	KY.........	6,481	28,070	23.1	ND.......	1,610	7,128	22.6
AL...........	8,899	35,725	24.9	LA.........	7,199	28,256	25.5	OH.......	21,129	83,813	25.2
AK...........	802	2,267	35.4	ME.........	2,749	8,717	31.5	OK.......	6,384	25,995	24.6
AZ...........	13,432	72,140	18.6	MD.........	16,514	44,369	37.2	OR.......	7,975	24,858	32.1
AR...........	3,390	16,089	21.1	MA.........	26,712	83,467	32.0	PA.......	34,537	119,761	28.8
CA...........	84,579	230,605	36.7	MI.........	22,804	78,332	29.1	RI.......	3,783	13,002	29.1
CO...........	14,280	43,834	32.6	MN.........	13,887	52,323	26.5	SC.......	7,279	26,666	27.3
CT...........	9,615	29,078	33.1	MS.........	3,937	17,023	23.1	SD.......	1,990	6,377	31.2
DE...........	2,241	8,118	27.6	MO.........	13,464	59,466	22.6	TN.......	9,601	40,553	23.7
DC...........	8,469	22,525	37.6	MT.........	2,298	6,559	35.0	TX.......	38,196	142,321	26.8
FL...........	29,004	112,165	25.9	NE.........	4,193	17,411	24.1	UT.......	8,339	27,003	30.9
GA...........	15,775	57,165	27.6	NV.........	2,585	9,884	26.2	VT.......	3,144	8,031	39.1
HI...........	2,656	8,001	33.2	NH.........	3,684	12,375	29.8	VA.......	20,822	60,840	34.2
ID...........	2,797	10,816	25.9	NJ.........	16,535	49,544	33.4	WA.......	13,215	40,136	32.9
IL...........	28,725	111,875	25.7	NM.........	3,255	11,366	28.6	WV.......	3,772	15,787	23.9
IN...........	13,251	54,032	24.5	NY.........	54,412	193,777	28.1	WI.......	12,881	43,694	29.5
IA...........	9,079	33,315	27.3	NC.........	18,671	60,854	30.7	WY.......	839	2,262	37.1
KS...........	5,920	24,284	24.4								

[1] Includes bachelor's, master's, and doctorate degrees.

Source: National Science Foundation, *Science and Engineering Indicators, 2012*, January 2012. See also <http://www.nsf.gov/statistics/seind/>.

Table 840. Doctorates Conferred in Science and Engineering by Field, Sex, and Race/Ethnicity: 2011

[In percent, except as indicated. Based on the Survey of Earned Doctorates. For description of methodology, see source. This table has been revised to align the major field definitions with those of the source; therefore, some data is not comparable to data presented in previous issues of the Statistical Abstract]

Characteristic	All fields [1]	Life Sciences			Physical Sciences			Social Sciences			Engineering
		Total [1]	Biological Sciences	Health Sciences	Total [1]	Chemistry	Physics [2]	Total [1]	Psychology	Economics [3]	Engineering
Total conferred (number)............	**49,010**	**11,467**	**8,135**	**2,123**	**8,678**	**2,439**	**2,065**	**8,120**	**3,594**	**1,124**	**8,004**
Male............................	53.5	45.2	47.6	31.2	71.4	62.1	80.5	40.5	27.9	65.6	77.7
Female..........................	46.4	54.7	52.4	68.8	28.6	37.8	19.5	59.5	72.1	34.4	22.2
RACE/ETHNICITY [4]											
Total conferred (number)............	**31,789**	**7,855**	**5,606**	**1,550**	**4,730**	**1,412**	**1,130**	**5,981**	**3,078**	**429**	**3,325**
American Indian/Alaska Native......................	0.4	0.3	0.2	0.7	0.3	0.4	0.2	0.6	0.5	0.2	0.2
Asian [5].........................	9.0	10.8	11.7	9.6	10.7	9.6	8.3	6.7	5.8	14.7	16.9
Black.............................	6.1	5.7	4.5	10.8	3.0	4.3	1.6	6.6	6.0	4.0	4.0
Hispanic [6].....................	6.3	6.0	6.3	4.3	4.5	6.4	4.2	8.4	9.3	5.6	5.8
White............................	74.1	73.4	73.2	71.2	77.3	75.8	79.5	73.5	73.8	73.0	69.1
Two or more races.............	2.3	2.3	2.4	1.9	2.4	1.9	3.7	2.5	2.6	1.4	2.2
Other/unknown [7]..............	1.7	1.5	1.6	1.6	1.9	1.6	2.5	1.8	1.8	1.2	1.8

[1] Includes other fields, not shown separately. [2] Includes astronomy. [3] Includes econometrics. [4] Excludes those with temporary visas. [5] Excludes Native Hawaiians or Other Pacific Islanders who are not Hispanic. [6] Includes persons reporting Hispanic ethnicity, whether singly or in combination with one or more races. [7] Includes Native Hawaiians and other Pacific Islanders who are not Hispanic, recipients who are not Hispanic and did not indicate race, and recipients with unknown race and ethnicity.

Source: U.S. National Science Foundation, National Center for Science and Engineering Statistics, "Science and Engineering Doctorates: 2011. Data Tables," <http://www.nsf.gov/statistics/sed/2011/data_table.cfm>, accessed April 2013.

Table 841. Doctorates Awarded by Field of Study and Year of Doctorate: 2000 to 2011

[Based on the Survey of Earned Doctorates; for information, see source]

Field of Study	2000	2005	2007	2008	2009	2010	2011
Total, all fields...............	41,372	43,385	48,131	48,775	49,552	48,034	49,010
Science and engineering, total................	25,677	27,691	31,503	32,505	33,105	32,775	34,146
Engineering, total...............	5,323	6,427	7,749	7,864	7,643	7,549	8,004
Aeronautical/astronautical...............	214	219	267	266	297	252	261
Chemical...............	619	774	817	873	807	822	826
Civil...............	480	622	703	713	707	643	636
Electrical...............	1,330	1,547	1,967	1,888	1,693	1,778	1,891
Industrial/manufacturing...............	176	221	279	280	251	215	263
Materials/metallurgical...............	404	493	646	636	625	670	662
Mechanical...............	807	892	1,071	1,082	1,095	984	1,084
Other...............	1,293	1,659	1,999	2,126	2,168	2,185	2,381
Science, total...............	20,354	21,264	23,754	24,641	25,462	25,226	26,142
Biological/agricultural sciences...............	7,033	7,528	8,559	8,995	9,308	9,148	9,344
Agricultural sciences...............	1,180	1,161	1,321	1,198	1,283	1,100	1,209
Biological sciences...............	5,853	6,367	7,238	7,797	8,025	8,048	8,135
Earth, atmospheric, and ocean sciences, total...............	694	714	875	865	877	862	856
Atmospheric...............	143	145	167	188	167	170	178
Earth/ocean sciences...............	551	569	708	677	710	692	678
Mathematical/computer sciences, total...............	1,911	2,334	3,043	3,187	3,163	3,254	3,318
Computer sciences...............	861	1,129	1,655	1,787	1,610	1,664	1,711
Mathematics...............	1,050	1,205	1,388	1,400	1,553	1,590	1,607
Physical sciences, total...............	3,378	3,643	4,081	4,081	4,284	4,194	4,504
Astronomy...............	185	186	223	249	262	266	288
Chemistry...............	1,989	2,126	2,318	2,246	2,392	2,304	2,439
Physics...............	1,204	1,331	1,540	1,586	1,630	1,624	1,777
Psychology...............	3,615	3,322	3,274	3,356	3,472	3,421	3,594
Social sciences, total...............	3,723	3,723	3,922	4,157	4,358	4,347	4,526
Economics...............	933	1,031	974	1,055	1,088	1,039	1,096
Political science...............	669	618	588	628	682	728	686
Sociology...............	617	536	576	601	662	639	656
Other social sciences...............	1,504	1,538	1,784	1,873	1,926	1,941	2,088
Non-science and engineering, total...............	15,695	15,694	16,628	16,270	16,447	15,259	14,864
Education...............	6,442	6,227	6,448	6,561	6,528	5,288	4,691
Health...............	1,591	1,784	2,143	2,091	2,096	2,112	2,123
Humanities...............	5,404	5,141	5,092	4,719	4,891	4,971	5,214
Professional/other/unknown...............	2,258	2,542	2,945	2,899	2,932	2,888	2,836

Source: U.S. National Science Foundation, Statistics, Education, Science and Engineering Doctorate Awards, *Doctorate Recipients from U.S. Universities*, annual. See also <http://www.nsf.gov/statistics/doctorates/>.

Table 842. Scientists and Engineers by Selected Demographic Characteristics: 2010

[In thousands (26,882 represents 26,882,000). Scientists and engineers refer to all persons who have received a bachelor's degree or higher in science and engineering (S&E), or S&E related field, plus persons holding a non-S&E degree or higher, employed in S&E or S&E related field. Detail may not add to total due to rounding]

Characteristic	Both sexes	Female	Male	Characteristic	Both sexes	Female	Male
All scientists and engineers.....	26,882	12,464	14,419	Highest degree attained:			
				Bachelor's.....................	15,436	7,286	8,150
Age:				Master's.....................	7,878	3,901	3,976
29 or younger.....................	3,423	1,839	1,584	Doctorate.....................	1,297	430	867
30-39 years.....................	6,295	3,181	3,113	Professional.....................	2,272	847	1,425
40-49 years.....................	6,196	2,840	3,356				
50-59 years.....................	5,945	2,773	3,172	Citizenship status:			
60-69 years.....................	3,964	1,506	2,458	U.S. citizen, native...........	21,912	10,329	11,582
70-75.....................	1,059	324	735	U.S. citizen, naturalized......	2,943	1,323	1,620
				Non-U.S. citizen, permanent			
Race/ethnicity:				resident.....................	1,268	513	755
Hispanic or Latino...............	1,766	899	867	Non-U.S. citizen, temporary			
American Indian/Alaska				resident.....................	760	299	461
Native [1].....................	75	37	38				
Asian [1].....................	3,099	1,337	1,762	Marital status:			
Black/African American [1]........	1,625	920	705	Married.....................	18,637	7,983	10,654
White [1].....................	19,880	9,053	10,827	Living in marriage-like			
Native Hawaiian/Other Pacific				relationship...................	1,230	667	564
Islander [1].....................	78	37	42	Widowed.....................	395	276	118
Two or more races [1]..............	360	181	179	Separated.....................	318	155	163
				Divorced.....................	1,961	1,161	801
Children in the home?				Never married.................	4,341	2,222	2,119
Yes.....................	14,534	6,623	7,911				
No.....................	12,348	5,841	6,507				

[1] Non-Hispanic.

Source: National Science Foundation, National Center for Science and Engineering Statistics, "Scientists and Engineers Statistical Data System (SESTAT)," <http://www.nsf.gov/statistics/sestat/>, Special Tabulation, April 2013.

Table 843. Civilian Employment of Scientists, Engineers, and Related Occupations by Occupation and Industry: 2010

[In thousands (307.9 represents 307,900). Standard Occupational Classification system categorizes workers in 1 of 801 detailed occupations. Industry classifications correspond to 2007 North American Industry Classification (NAICS) industrial groups. For definition of scientists and engineers, see text this section]

Occupation	Total employ-ment, all workers	Wage and salary workers						Self employ-ed [2]
		Mining (NAICS 21) [1]	Con-struction (NAICS 23)	Manu-facturing (NAICS 31–33)	Informa-tion (NAICS 51)	Profes-sional, scientific and technical services (NAICS 54)	Govern-ment (NAICS 99)	
Computer and information systems managers..........................	307.9	0.4	0.6	27.2	34.4	78.1	21.2	8.3
Engineering managers........................	176.8	0.4	4.2	67.3	4.4	56.8	17.5	0.1
Natural science managers....................	49.3	0.2	(NA)	7.8	(NA)	15.5	16.1	1.2
Computer and mathematical scientists.........	3,542.8	5.4	8.9	270.4	411.5	1,122.1	259.0	155.0
Computer specialists......................	3,246.0	5.3	8.9	263.9	405.3	1,096.8	237.5	153.0
Mathematical science occupations...........	116.8	(NA)	(NA)	6.6	6.2	25.3	21.6	2.0
Surveyors, cartographers, and photogrammetrists.............................	65.0	0.8	3.2	0.5	0.4	39.0	9.8	9.0
Engineers [3].................................	1,519.0	32.9	39.3	514.6	37.7	453.2	203.5	38.4
Aerospace engineers.........................	81.0	(NA)	(NA)	38.8	(NA)	26.4	10.5	0.9
Civil engineers..............................	262.8	0.9	24.4	2.5	0.5	132.8	75.3	10.0
Computer and hardware engineers............	70.0	(NA)	(NA)	26.0	3.7	26.2	5.1	0.9
Electrical and electronics engineers...........	294.0	0.8	4.1	97.7	30.5	75.0	28.8	6.3
Industrial engineers [4].......................	227.6	1.8	5.7	146.5	1.0	32.4	6.2	0.2
Mechanical engineers........................	243.2	1.3	3.0	118.0	0.2	69.9	15.4	5.6
Drafters, engineering, and mapping technicians [5]...............................	714.0	6.2	20.6	204.7	12.5	256.1	106.5	13.4
Engineering technicians......................	451.9	5.2	4.6	153.2	10.5	112.9	90.2	2.1
Surveying and mapping technicians...........	56.9	0.1	(NA)	0.1	0.5	35.7	11.6	2.7
Life, physical, and social science occupations.................................	1,228.8	18.9	0.7	116.8	1.6	306.3	331.8	91.4
Life scientists..............................	285.9	(NA)	(NA)	33.9	0.1	74.7	73.5	11.1
Physical scientists..........................	282.0	0.7	0.2	37.4	1.1	98.8	79.5	11.0
Social scientists and related occupations.................................	306.1	0.1	(NA)	0.5	0.3	39.8	85.7	68.2
Life, physical, and social science technicians.................................	354.8	9.4	0.4	45.0	0.1	93.0	93.1	1.1

NA Not available. [1] Includes oil and gas extraction. [2] Includes secondary jobs and unpaid private household employment. [3] Includes kinds of engineers not shown separately. [4] Includes health and safety engineers. [5] Includes other drafters, technicians, and mapping technicians.

Source: U.S. Bureau of Labor Statistics, National Employment Matrix "Employment Projections," <http://www.bls.gov/emp/tables.htm>, February 2012.

Table 844. Workers in Science and Engineering (S&E) and Science, Technology, Engineering and Mathematics (STEM) Occupations in Largest Metropolitan Statistical Areas: May 2010

[Includes only metropolitan statistical areas with multiple metropolitan divisions. Data are from BLS's Occupational Employment Statistics Survey. Differences among employment estimates may not be statistically significant, see source for details]

Metropolitan statistical area	Workers employed			Percent of workforce	
	All occupations	S&E occupations	STEM occupations	S&E occupations	STEM occupations
U.S. total.................	127,097,160	5,549,980	7,427,350	4.4	5.8
New York-Northern New Jersey-Long Island, NY-NJ-PA................................	8,101,890	(D)	443,200	(D)	5.5
Washington-Arlington-Alexandria, DC-VA-MD-WV....	2,840,740	298,180	360,580	10.5	12.7
Los Angeles-Long Beach-Santa Ana, CA..............	5,191,880	237,430	308,090	4.6	5.9
Boston-Cambridge-Quincy, MA-NH....................	2,413,780	190,260	244,740	7.9	10.1
Chicago-Naperville-Joliet, IL-IN-WI.....................	4,169,840	155,760	214,310	3.7	5.1
Dallas-Fort Worth-Arlington, TX.......................	2,832,560	151,090	198,860	5.3	7.0
Seattle-Tacoma-Bellevue, WA.........................	1,601,010	138,350	174,920	8.6	10.9
San Francisco-Oakland-Fremont, CA...................	1,900,110	138,280	177,380	7.3	9.3
Philadelphia-Camden-Wilmington, PA-NJ-DE-MD.....	2,619,360	129,910	168,720	5.0	6.4
Detroit-Warren-Livonia, MI............................	1,686,920	102,210	135,190	6.1	8.0
Miami-Fort Lauderdale-Pompano Beach, FL..........	2,143,470	63,060	83,940	2.9	3.9

D Figure suppressed for reasons of confidentiality and/or reliability.

Source: National Science Foundation, *Science and Engineering Indicators, 2012*, January 2012. See also <http://www.nsf.gov/statistics/seind/>.

Table 845. Employment and Median Salary in Science and Engineering (S&E) Occupations by Sex: 2008

[Rounded to the nearest 1,000. Percents based on unrounded numbers. Data are for full-time workers who typically work 35 or more hours weekly in their principal job. Data are from National Science Foundation's Scientists and Engineers Statistical Data System (SESTAT)]

Occupation	Total		Female			Male		
	Number	Median salary (dollars)	Number	Percent	Median Salary (dollars)	Number	Percent	Median Salary (dollars)
All occupations	8,869,000	70,000	3,018,000	34.0	52,000	5,851,000	66.0	80,000
S&E	3,554,000	80,000	837,000	23.5	70,000	2,718,000	76.5	85,000
Engineers	1,293,000	87,000	162,000	12.5	75,000	1,131,000	87.5	89,000
Computer and mathematical scientists	1,345,000	85,000	302,000	22.4	78,000	1,044,000	77.6	87,000
Biological, agricultural, and other life scientists	365,000	59,000	156,000	42.7	50,000	210,000	57.3	65,000
Physical scientists	269,000	70,000	74,000	27.3	60,000	196,000	72.7	76,000
Social scientists	281,000	68,000	143,000	50.9	63,000	138,000	49.1	73,000
S&E related occupations	1,139,000	65,000	454,000	39.9	51,000	685,000	60.1	80,000
Health-related occupations	353,000	50,000	217,000	61.5	48,000	136,000	38.5	60,000
Non-S&E related occupations	4,176,000	58,000	1,727,000	41.4	46,000	2,499,000	58.6	70,000

Source: National Science Foundation, National Center for Science and Engineering Statistics, *Science and Engineering Indicators 2012*, January 2012. See also <http://www.nsf.gov/statistics/seind/>.

Table 846. Federal Discretionary Outlays for General Science, Space, and Other Technology: 1970 to 2012, and Projections for 2013 and 2014

[In billions of dollars (4.5 represents $4,500,000,000). For fiscal years ending in year shown; see text, Section 8]

Year	Current dollars			Constant (2005) dollars		
	Total	General science and research	Space/other technologies	Total	General science and research	Space/other technologies
1970	4.5	0.9	3.6	23.4	4.9	18.5
1980	5.8	1.4	4.5	14.6	3.5	11.2
1985	8.6	2.0	6.6	16.7	3.9	12.8
1990	14.4	2.8	11.6	24.5	4.8	19.7
1995 [1]	16.7	4.1	12.6	22.0	5.4	16.6
2000	18.6	6.2	12.4	22.1	7.3	14.7
2002	20.7	7.2	13.5	23.1	8.1	15.1
2003	20.8	7.9	12.9	22.6	8.6	14.0
2004	23.0	8.3	14.6	23.9	8.7	15.2
2005	23.6	8.8	14.8	23.6	8.8	14.8
2006	23.5	9.0	14.5	22.7	8.7	14.0
2007	24.4	9.1	15.3	22.9	8.6	14.3
2008	26.7	9.5	17.2	24.4	8.7	15.7
2009	28.3	9.9	18.4	25.4	8.9	16.5
2010	30.0	11.6	18.4	27.5	10.6	16.8
2011	29.4	12.3	17.0	26.3	11.0	15.2
2012	28.9	12.3	16.6	25.2	10.7	14.5
2013, proj	30.6	13.3	17.3	26.2	11.3	14.8
2014, proj	30.0	12.6	17.4	25.3	10.7	14.7

[1] Due to the effects of the Credit Reform Act of 1990 on the measurement and classification of federal credit activities, the discretionary outlays for years prior to 1995 are not strictly comparable to those for 1995 and after. However, the discretionary outlays shown for 1995 are no more than $1 billion higher than they would have been if measured on the same (pre-credit reform) basis as the 1990 outlays.

Source: U.S. Office of Management and Budget, *Fiscal Year 2014 Budget of the U.S. Government: Historical Tables*, April 2013. See also <http://www.whitehouse.gov/omb/budget>.

Table 847. Worldwide Space Launch Events: 2000 to 2012

[2,729 represents $2,729,000,000]

Country	Non-commercial launches				Commercial launches				Launch revenues for commercial launch events (mil. dol.)			
	2000	2010	2011	2012	2000	2010	2011	2012	2000	2010	2011	2012
Total	50	51	66	58	35	23	18	20	2,729	2,453	1,927	2,413
United States	21	11	18	11	7	4	–	2	370	307	–	108
Russia	23	18	21	17	13	13	10	7	671	826	707	595
Europe	–	–	3	4	12	6	4	6	1,433	1,320	880	1,320
China	5	15	17	17	–	–	2	2	(X)	(X)	140	90
India	–	3	3	2	–	–	–	–	(X)	(X)	(X)	(X)
Japan	1	2	3	2	–	–	–	–	(X)	(X)	(X)	(X)
Israel	–	1	–	–	–	–	–	–	(X)	(X)	(X)	(X)
Iran	–	–	1	3	–	–	–	–	(X)	(X)	(X)	(X)
Korea, North	–	–	–	2	–	–	–	–	(X)	(X)	(X)	(X)
Korea, South	–	1	–	–	–	–	–	–	(X)	(X)	(X)	(X)
Multinational	–	–	–	–	3	–	2	3	255	(X)	200	300

– Represents zero. X Not applicable.

Source: Federal Aviation Administration, *Commercial Space Transportation: 2012 Year in Review*, January 2013, and earlier editions. See also <http://www.faa.gov/about/office_org/headquarters_offices/ast/reports_studies/year_review>.

This section presents statistics on farms and farm operators; farm income, expenditures, and debt; farm output, productivity, and marketings; foreign trade in agricultural products; specific crops; and livestock, poultry, and their products.

The principal sources are the data collected by the National Agricultural Statistics Service (NASS), the Economic Research Service (ERS), and the Foreign Agricultural Service (FAS) of the U.S. Department of Agriculture (USDA) and published in reports or databases. The information from the 2007 Census of Agriculture is available in printed form in the Volume 1, Geographic Area Series; in electronic format on CD-ROM; and on the Internet at <http://www.agcensus.usda.gov/Publications/2007/Full_Report/>. The ERS publishes data on farm assets, debt, and income on the Internet at <http://www.ers.usda.gov/briefing/farmincome/>. The ERS also provides data on commodity supply and disappearance via commodity outlook reports, yearbooks, and databases, available on the ERS site at <http://www.ers.usda.gov/data-products.aspx>. Sources of current data on agricultural exports and imports include the Global Agricultural Trade System database provided by the FAS at <http://www.fas.usda.gov/gats> and the "Foreign Agricultural Trade of the United States (FATUS)" data, published by the ERS, available on the the ERS Internet site at <http://www.ers.usda.gov/data-products/foreign-agricultural-trade-of-the-united-states-(fatus).aspx>.

The field offices of the NASS collect data on crops, livestock and products, agricultural prices, farm employment, and other related subjects mainly through sample surveys. Information is obtained on crops and livestock items pertaining to agricultural production and marketing. State estimates and supporting information are sent to the Agricultural Statistics Board of NASS, which reviews the estimates and issues reports containing state and national data. Among these reports are annual summaries such as *Crop Production, Crop Values, Agricultural Prices,* and *Meat Animals Production, Disposition and Income.* The NASS also provides data through the QuickStats database at <http://quickstats.nass.usda.gov>.

Farms and farmland—The definitions of a farm have varied through time. Since 1850, when minimum criteria defining a farm for census purposes first were established, the farm definition has changed nine times. The current definition, first used for the 1974 census, is any place from which $1,000 or more of agricultural products were produced and sold, or normally would have been sold, during the census year.

Acreage designated as "land in farms" consists primarily of agricultural land used for crops, pasture, or grazing. It also includes woodland and wasteland not actually under cultivation or used for pasture or grazing, provided it was part of the farm operator's total operation. Land in farms includes acres set aside under annual commodity acreage programs as well as acres idled by federal conservation programs for places meeting the farm definition. Land in farms is an operating unit concept and includes land owned and operated as well as land rented from others. All

grazing land, except land used under government permits on a per-head basis, was included as "land in farms" provided it was part of a farm or ranch.

An evaluation of coverage has been conducted for each census of agriculture since 1945 to provide estimates of the completeness of census farm counts. Beginning with the 1997 Census of Agriculture, census farm counts and totals were statistically adjusted for coverage and reported at the county level. The size of the adjustments varies considerably by state. In general, farms not on the census mail list tended to be small in acreage, production, and sales of farm products. The response rate for the 2007 Census of Agriculture was 85.2 percent as compared with a response rate of 88.0 for the 2002 Census of Agriculture and 86.2 percent for the 1997 Census of Agriculture.

For more explanation about census mail list compilation, collection methods, coverage measurement, and adjustments, see Appendix A, *2007 Census of Agriculture,* Volume 1 reports <http://www.agcensus.usda.gov/Publications/2007/Full_Report/index.asp>.

Farm income—The final agricultural sector output comprises cash receipts from farm marketings of crops and livestock, federal government payments made directly to farmers for farm-related activities, rental value of farm homes, value of farm products consumed in farm homes, and other farm-related income such as machine hire and custom work. Farm marketings represent quantities of agricultural products sold by farmers multiplied by prices received per unit of production at the local market. Information on prices received for farm products is generally obtained by the NASS Agricultural Statistics Board from surveys of firms (such as grain elevators, packers, and processors) purchasing agricultural commodities directly from producers. In some cases, the price information is obtained directly from the producers.

Crops—Estimates of crop acreage and production by the NASS are based on current sample survey data obtained from individual producers and objective yield counts, reports of carlot shipments, market records, personal field observations by field statisticians, and reports from other sources.

Prices received by farmers are marketing year average prices and do not include allowances for outstanding loans, government purchases, deficiency payments or disaster payments. These averages are based on monthly prices weighted by monthly sales during specific periods. All state marketing year average prices are based on individual state marketing years, while U.S. marketing year average prices are based on standard U.S. marketing years for each crop. For a description of how U.S. prices are computed as well as a listing of the crop marketing years, see *Crop Values Annual Summary.*

Value of production is computed by multiplying state prices by each state's production. The U.S. value of production is the sum of state values for all states. Value of production figures should not be confused with cash receipts from farm marketings which relate to sales during a calendar year, irrespective of the year of production.

Livestock—Annual inventory numbers of livestock and estimates of livestock, dairy, and poultry production prepared by the Department of Agriculture are based on information from farmers and ranchers obtained by probability survey sampling methods.

Statistical reliability—For a discussion of statistical collection and estimation, sampling procedures, and measures of statistical reliability pertaining to Department of Agriculture data, see Appendix III.

Table 848. Selected Characteristics of Farms by North American Industry Classification System (NAICS): 2007

[297,220,491 represents $297,220,491,000. See text this section and Appendix III]

Industry	2007 NAICS code [1]	Farms	Land in farms (acres)	Harvested cropland (acres)	Market value of agricultural products sold (1,000)		
					Total	Crops	Livestock [2]
Total....................................	(X)	**2,204,792**	**922,095,840**	**309,607,601**	**297,220,491**	**143,657,928**	**153,562,563**
Crop production................................	111	1,051,889	416,961,540	244,213,836	141,921,405	135,806,093	6,115,312
Oilseed and grain farming....................	1111	338,237	266,831,616	194,191,397	74,559,692	69,851,934	4,707,758
Soybean farming............................	11111	62,923	22,094,100	17,599,156	5,637,504	5,532,934	104,570
Oilseed (except soybean) farming........	11112	515	458,591	306,033	62,238	61,081	1,157
Dry pea and bean farming..................	11113	526	382,071	269,759	79,297	78,454	844
Wheat farming..............................	11114	35,232	55,992,672	29,062,744	6,157,944	5,821,678	336,267
Corn farming................................	11115	161,874	103,071,231	86,627,715	39,675,674	38,524,804	1,150,870
Rice farming................................	11116	3,853	4,233,156	3,396,230	1,936,574	1,915,447	21,127
Other grain farming........................	11119	73,314	80,599,795	56,929,760	21,010,459	17,917,536	3,092,923
Vegetable and melon farming.................	11121	40,589	9,272,945	6,018,702	14,975,322	14,850,087	125,235
Potato farming.............................	111211	2,182	2,577,795	1,992,430	2,885,906	2,854,320	31,586
Other vegetable (except potato) and melon farming.........................	111219	38,407	6,695,150	4,026,272	12,089,416	11,995,767	93,649
Fruit and tree nut farming....................	1113	98,281	12,141,683	5,339,755	18,351,629	18,225,583	126,046
Orange groves.............................	11131	8,771	1,535,483	800,921	2,423,976	2,382,844	41,131
Citrus (except orange) groves.............	11132	3,429	402,617	205,522	783,426	778,099	5,326
Noncitrus fruit and tree nut farming........	11133	86,081	10,203,583	4,333,312	15,144,228	15,064,639	79,589
Apple orchards.............................	111331	11,550	2,078,125	488,273	2,259,839	2,251,555	8,284
Grape vineyards...........................	111332	17,036	2,067,987	1,061,070	3,890,152	3,883,341	6,811
Strawberry farming........................	111333	1,503	149,972	55,461	1,185,736	1,182,263	3,473
Berry (except strawberry) farming..........	111334	8,535	870,154	220,530	1,211,820	1,209,450	2,370
Tree nut farming...........................	111335	22,821	3,239,199	1,652,915	3,655,251	3,626,067	29,184
Fruit and tree nut combination farming..................................	111336	995	292,842	106,488	301,611	286,946	14,666
Other noncitrus fruit farming...............	111339	23,641	1,505,304	748,575	2,639,819	2,625,018	14,801
Greenhouse, nursery, and floriculture production................................	1114	54,889	3,974,530	1,698,564	16,967,123	16,930,975	36,147
Food crops grown under cover..............	11141	2,044	85,809	18,712	1,552,287	1,550,756	1,531
Nursery and floriculture production.........	11142	52,845	3,888,721	1,679,852	15,414,835	15,380,219	34,616
Nursery and tree production..............	111421	34,532	3,287,008	1,505,323	8,901,860	8,875,417	26,443
Floriculture production....................	111422	18,313	601,713	174,529	6,512,975	6,504,801	8,173
Other crop farming...........................	1119	519,893	124,740,766	36,965,418	17,067,639	15,947,514	1,120,126
Tobacco farming...........................	11191	9,626	2,518,697	1,219,827	1,147,173	1,077,481	69,692
Cotton farming.............................	11192	9,968	13,081,671	9,778,279	4,357,082	4,300,124	56,958
Sugarcane farming.........................	11193	614	1,299,318	969,321	885,028	881,698	3,330
Hay farming................................	11194	254,042	49,923,443	18,606,436	6,488,172	5,807,594	680,578
All other crop farming......................	11199	245,643	57,917,637	6,391,555	4,190,184	3,880,617	309,568
Animal production............................	112	1,152,903	505,134,300	65,393,765	155,299,086	7,851,835	147,447,251
Cattle ranching and farming.................	1121	744,858	413,261,549	55,185,767	92,538,429	5,109,567	87,428,862
Beef cattle ranching and farming including feedlots..........................	11211	687,540	391,990,769	41,893,929	57,784,399	3,895,789	53,888,610
Beef cattle ranching and farming..........	112111	656,475	376,170,540	36,675,357	27,535,096	2,626,582	24,908,514
Cattle feedlots..........................	112112	31,065	15,820,229	5,218,572	30,249,303	1,269,207	28,980,096
Dairy cattle and milk production............	11212	57,318	21,270,780	13,291,838	34,754,031	1,213,778	33,540,252
Hog and pig farming.........................	1122	30,546	6,949,176	4,747,504	18,127,114	1,614,030	16,513,083
Poultry and egg production..................	1123	64,570	7,040,000	2,140,320	37,797,542	547,736	37,249,806
Chicken egg production....................	11231	35,651	2,259,774	477,371	7,546,997	104,546	7,442,452
Broilers and other meat-type chicken production..............................	11232	17,888	3,370,828	1,209,528	22,400,358	306,268	22,094,090
Turkey production..........................	11233	3,405	836,551	396,096	4,643,075	127,009	4,516,067
Poultry hatcheries.........................	11234	775	69,558	9,985	2,777,612	1,790	2,775,822
Other poultry production...................	11239	6,851	503,289	47,340	429,499	8,124	421,375
Sheep and goat farming.....................	1124	67,254	11,963,667	429,300	554,107	21,374	532,732
Sheep farming.............................	11241	30,974	8,971,952	324,835	435,107	18,396	416,711
Goat farming..............................	11242	36,280	2,991,715	104,465	119,000	2,979	116,021
Animal aquaculture..........................	1125	4,777	2,451,244	70,954	1,407,750	18,384	1,389,366
Other animal production.....................	1129	240,898	63,468,664	2,819,920	4,874,144	540,743	4,333,401
Apiculture.................................	11291	7,979	503,609	92,280	263,268	19,827	243,440
Horse and other equine production.........	11292	168,694	22,370,495	675,383	2,088,845	17,332	2,071,512
Fur-bearing animal and rabbit production..............................	11293	2,252	89,224	16,894	154,325	2,744	151,581
All other animal production.................	11299	61,973	40,505,336	2,035,363	2,367,706	500,839	1,866,867

X Not applicable [1] North American Industry Classification System (NAICS) 2007; see text, Section 15. [2] Includes poultry, and their products sold.

Source: U.S. Department of Agriculture, National Agricultural Statistics Service, *2007 Census of Agriculture*, Vol. 1, February 2009. See also <http://www.agcensus.usda.gov/Publications/index.php>.

Table 849. Farms—Number and Acreage: 2000 to 2012

[As of June (2,167 represents 2,167,000). Based on 1974 census definition; for definition of farms and farmland, see text, this section. Data for 2007 have been adjusted for underenumeration]

Year	Unit	2000	2005	2006	2007	2008	2009	2010	2011	2012
Number of farms.........	1,000	2,167	2,099	2,089	2,205	2,200	2,200	2,192	2,182	2,170
Land in farms.............	Mil. acres	945	928	926	921	920	920	919	917	914
Average per farm........	Acres	436	442	443	418	418	418	419	420	421

Source: U.S. Department of Agriculture, National Agricultural Statistics Service, *Farm Numbers and Land in Farms, Final Estimates, 1998–2002; Farms and Land in Farms, Final Estimates, 2003-2007*; and *Farms, Land in Farms, and Livestock Operations 2012 Summary*, February 2013. See also <http://www.nass.usda.gov/Publications/index.asp>.

Table 850. Farms—Number and Acreage by State: 2000 to 2012

[As of June 1 (2,167 represents 2,167,000). See headnote, Table 849]

State	Farms (1,000) 2000	Farms (1,000) 2012	Land in farms (mil. acres) 2000	Land in farms (mil. acres) 2012	Acreage per farm 2000	Acreage per farm 2012	State	Farms (1,000) 2000	Farms (1,000) 2012	Land in farms (mil. acres) 2000	Land in farms (mil. acres) 2012	Acreage per farm 2000	Acreage per farm 2012
United States.....	**2,167**	**2,170**	**945**	**914**	**436**	**421**							
Alabama.............	47	47	9	9	191	190	Montana............	28	29	59	59	2,133	2,056
Alaska...............	1	1	1	1	1,569	1,294	Nebraska...........	52	47	46	46	887	974
Arizona.............	11	16	27	26	2,514	1,684	Nevada.............	3	3	6	6	2,065	1,980
Arkansas...........	48	48	15	14	304	282	New Hampshire....	3	4	(Z)	(Z)	133	113
California...........	83	81	28	25	337	316	New Jersey.........	10	10	1	1	86	72
Colorado...........	30	36	32	31	1,053	862	New Mexico........	18	24	45	44	2,494	1,845
Connecticut........	4	5	(Z)	(Z)	86	82	New York..........	38	36	8	7	205	194
Delaware...........	3	3	1	(Z)	215	196	North Carolina......	56	50	9	9	166	170
Florida.............	44	48	10	9	236	195	North Dakota.......	31	32	39	40	1,279	1,253
Georgia.............	49	47	11	10	222	221	Ohio..............	79	73	15	14	187	185
Hawaii.............	6	8	1	1	251	148	Oklahoma...........	85	86	34	35	400	407
Idaho.............	25	25	12	11	486	465	Oregon............	40	38	17	17	433	433
Illinois.............	77	74	28	27	357	358	Pennsylvania.......	59	62	8	8	130	124
Indiana.............	63	60	15	15	240	245	Rhode Island.......	1	1	(Z)	(Z)	75	57
Iowa.............	94	92	33	31	346	333	South Carolina......	24	27	5	5	203	180
Kansas.............	65	66	48	46	736	702	South Dakota.......	32	31	44	44	1,358	1,408
Kentucky.............	90	86	14	14	152	164	Tennessee.........	88	76	12	11	134	142
Louisiana.............	29	29	8	8	277	274	Texas.............	228	245	131	128	573	523
Maine.............	7	8	1	1	190	167	Utah.............	16	16	12	11	748	677
Maryland.............	12	13	2	2	172	160	Vermont...........	7	7	1	1	192	174
Massachusetts.....	6	8	1	1	89	68	Virginia...........	49	46	9	8	180	174
Michigan.............	53	55	10	10	192	181	Washington........	37	39	16	15	420	377
Minnesota.........	81	79	28	27	344	338	West Virginia......	21	22	4	4	173	164
Mississippi.........	42	42	11	11	266	264	Wisconsin..........	78	77	16	15	206	195
Missouri.............	109	106	30	29	277	274	Wyoming...........	9	11	35	30	3,750	2,796

Z Less than 500,000 acres.

Source: U.S. Department of Agriculture, National Agricultural Statistics Service, *Farm Numbers and Land in Farms, Final Estimates, 1998–2002* and *Farms, Land in Farms, and Livestock Operations, 2012 Summary*, February 2013. See also <http://www.nass.usda.gov/Publications/index.asp>.

Table 851. Farms by Size and Type of Organization: 1978 to 2007

[2,258 represents 2,258,000. For comments on adjustment, see text, this section]

Size and type of organization	Unit	Not adjusted for coverage 1978	1982	1987	1992	1997	Adjusted for coverage 1997[1]	2002[1]	2007[1]
Farms...............	1,000	2,258	2,241	2,088	1,925	1,912	2,216	2,129	2,205
Land in farms.............	Mil. acres	1,015	987	964	946	932	955	938	922
Average size of farm...............	Acres	449	440	462	491	487	431	441	418
Farms by size:									
1 to 9 acres...............	1,000	151	188	183	166	154	205	179	233
10 to 49 acres...............	1,000	392	449	412	388	411	531	564	620
50 to 179 acres...............	1,000	759	712	645	584	593	694	659	661
180 to 499 acres...............	1,000	582	527	478	428	403	428	389	368
500 to 999 acres...............	1,000	213	204	200	186	176	179	162	150
1,000 to 1,999 acres...............	1,000	98	97	102	102	101	103	99	93
2,000 acres or more...............	1,000	63	65	67	71	75	74	78	80
Farms by type of organization:									
Family or individual...............	1,000	1,966	1,946	1,809	1,653	1,643	1,923	1,910	1,906
Partnership...............	1,000	233	223	200	187	169	186	130	174
Corporation...............	1,000	50	60	67	73	84	90	74	96
Other[2]...............	1,000	9	12	12	12	15	17	16	28

[1] Data have been adjusted for coverage; see text, this section. [2] Cooperative, estate or trust, institutional, etc.

Source: U.S. Department of Agriculture, National Agricultural Statistics Service, *2007 Census of Agriculture*, Vol. 1, February 2009. See also <http://www.agcensus.usda.gov/Publications/index.php>.

Table 852. Farms—Number and Acreage by Size of Farm: 2002 and 2007

[2,129 represents 2,129,000. Data have been adjusted for coverage; see text, this section]

Size of farm	Number of farms (1,000)		Land in farms (mil. acres)		Cropland harvested (mil. acres)		Percent distribution, 2007		
	2002	2007	2002	2007	2002	2007	Number of farms	All land in farms	Cropland harvested
Total..........................	2,129	2,205	938.3	922.1	302.7	309.6	100.0	100.0	100.0
Under 10 acres...............	179	233	0.8	1.1	0.2	0.3	10.6	0.1	0.1
10 to 49 acres.................	564	620	14.7	15.9	4.1	4.3	28.1	1.7	1.4
50 to 69 acres.................	152	154	8.8	8.9	2.5	2.5	7.0	1.0	0.8
70 to 99 acres.................	191	192	15.7	15.8	4.7	4.5	8.7	1.7	1.5
100 to 139 acres..............	175	175	20.2	20.3	6.1	5.8	7.9	2.2	1.9
140 to 179 acres..............	142	139	22.3	22.0	7.3	6.6	6.3	2.4	2.1
180 to 219 acres..............	91	88	18.0	17.3	6.2	5.6	4.0	1.9	1.8
220 to 259 acres..............	72	68	17.1	16.3	6.5	5.7	3.1	1.8	1.9
260 to 499 acres..............	226	213	80.6	75.9	34.1	30.4	9.6	8.2	9.8
500 to 999 acres..............	162	150	112.4	104.1	56.7	51.6	6.8	11.3	16.7
1,000 to 1,999 acres..........	99	93	135.7	127.6	72.8	69.8	4.2	13.8	22.6
2,000 acres or more...........	78	80	491.9	496.9	101.6	122.5	3.6	53.9	39.6

Source: U.S. Department of Agriculture, National Agricultural Statistics Service, *2007 Census of Agriculture*, Vol. 1, February 2009. See also <http://www.agcensus.usda.gov/Publications/index.php>.

Table 853. Farms—Number, Acreage, and Value by Tenure of Principal Operator and Type of Organization: 2002 and 2007

[2,129 represents 2,129,000. Full owners own all the land they operate. Part owners own a part and rent from others the rest of the land they operate. A principal operator is the person primarily responsible for the on-site, day-to-day operation of the farm or ranch business. Data have been adjusted for coverage; see text, this section]

Item and year	Unit	Total [1]	Tenure of operator			Type of organization		
			Full owner	Part owner	Tenant	Family or individual	Partner-ship	Corpora-tion
NUMBER OF FARMS								
2002.................................	1,000	2,129	1,428	551	150	1,910	130	74
2007.................................	1,000	2,205	1,522	542	141	1,906	174	96
Under 50 acres...................	1,000	853	739	70	44	774	45	26
50 to 179 acres...................	1,000	661	492	130	38	588	45	18
180 to 499 acres..................	1,000	368	198	143	27	312	34	16
500 to 999 acres..................	1,000	150	51	84	14	118	18	12
1,000 acres or more..............	1,000	173	41	114	17	114	32	24
LAND IN FARMS								
2002.................................	Mil. acres	938	357	495	87	622	146	108
2007.................................	Mil. acres	922	344	496	82	574	161	125
Value of land and buildings, 2007 [2]...............	Bil. dol.	1,744	726	868	150	1,203	277	227
Value of farm products sold, 2007...................	Bil. dol.	297	117	148	32	148	62	84

[1] Includes other types, not shown separately. [2] Based on a sample of farms.

Source: U.S. Department of Agriculture, National Agricultural Statistics Service, *2007 Census of Agriculture*, Vol. 1, February 2009. See also <http://www.agcensus.usda.gov/Publications/2007/Full_Report/index.asp>.

Table 854. Corporate Farms—Characteristics by Type: 2007

[125.3 represents 125,300,000. Data have been adjusted for coverage; see text, this section and Appendix III]

Item	Unit	All corpora-tions	Family held corporations			Other corporations		
			Total	1 to 10 stock-holders	11 or more stock-holders	Total	1 to 10 stock-holders	11 or more stock-holders
Farms...	Number	96,074	85,837	83,796	2,041	10,237	9,330	907
Percent distribution......................	Percent	100	89	87	2	11	10	1
Land in farms..............................	Mil. acres	125.3	114.3	106.4	7.8	11.1	7.7	3.3
Average per farm.........................	Acres	1,304	1,331	1,270	3,834	1,080	829	3,657
Value of—								
Land and buildings [1].....................	Bil. dol.	226.6	200.6	189.5	11.0	26.0	20.2	5.8
Average per farm.......................	$1,000	2,358	2,336	2,262	5,399	2,542	2,170	6,371
Farm products sold......................	Bil. dol.	84.1	65.8	58.9	6.9	18.3	12.2	6.2
Average per farm.......................	$1,000	876	766	703	3,378	1,791	1,305	6,787

[1] Based on a sample of farms.

Source: U.S. Department of Agriculture, National Agricultural Statistics Service, *2007 Census of Agriculture*, Vol. 1, February 2009. See also <http://www.agcensus.usda.gov/Publications/index.php>.

Table 855. Family Farm Household Income and Wealth, 2007 to 2011, and by Farm Type, 2011

[In dollars, except for number of farms. Based on Agricultural Resource Management Survey (ARMS) Phase III. A family farm is defined as one in which the majority of the ownership of the farm business is held by related individuals. Nearly all farms (97 percent in 2011) are family farms. The farm operator is the person who runs the farm, making the day-to-day management decisions. The operator could be an owner, hired manager, cash tenant, share tenant, and/or a partner. If land is rented or worked on shares, the tenant or renter is the operator. For multiple-operator farms, a principal operator is identified as the individual making most of the day-to-day decisions about the operation. About 40 percent of farms have more than one operator, but three-quarters of these are operated by a husband-wife team. Therefore, both operators are considered part of the principal operator household. Minus sign (-) indicates loss]

Item	2007	2008	2009	2010	2011 Total	2011 ERS farm typology Rural residence farms [1]	2011 ERS farm typology Intermediate farms [2]	2011 ERS farm typology Commercial farms [3]
Number of family farms..................	2,143,398	2,129,869	2,131,007	2,143,063	2,114,668	1,254,256	640,991	219,422
INCOME PER FAMILY FARM HOUSEHOLD								
Net earnings from farming activities..................................	11,364	9,764	6,866	11,788	14,623	-4,644	4,321	154,859
Off-farm income of the household.........	77,432	70,032	70,302	72,671	72,665	88,455	49,405	50,356
Earned income........................	58,933	50,761	50,852	52,161	51,376	66,260	27,564	35,861
Off-farm wages and salaries...........	48,947	42,606	43,852	(NA)	(NA)	(NA)	(NA)	(NA)
Off-farm business income..............	9,986	8,155	7,000	(NA)	(NA)	(NA)	(NA)	(NA)
Unearned income......................	18,499	19,271	19,450	20,510	21,289	22,196	21,841	14,494
Total household income, mean [4].........	88,796	79,796	77,169	84,459	87,289	83,811	53,725	205,215
WEALTH PER FAMILY FARM HOUSEHOLD								
Assets, mean [4]............................	1,006,020	988,156	1,031,000	1,082,120	1,131,522	799,467	1,040,573	3,295,304
Farm assets.............................	739,905	749,190	761,894	799,316	856,589	502,865	818,806	2,988,918
Non-farm assets.........................	266,115	238,966	269,106	282,804	274,933	296,601	221,767	306,385
Debt, mean [4].............................	106,874	112,705	115,981	123,640	120,213	83,888	80,184	444,793
Farm debt...............................	56,859	61,131	66,149	67,404	69,387	27,252	46,664	376,616
Non-farm debt...........................	50,015	51,574	49,832	56,235	50,827	56,636	33,520	68,177
Net worth, mean [4].........................	899,146	875,451	915,019	958,480	1,011,309	715,579	960,389	2,850,511
Farm net worth..........................	683,046	688,059	695,745	731,911	787,203	475,613	772,143	2,612,302
Non-farm net worth......................	216,101	187,392	219,274	226,568	224,106	239,966	188,246	238,209

NA Not available. [1] Farms in which the principal operator is retired or has a major occupation other than farming. [2] Farms with farming as the operator's major occupation, but with less than $250,000 in gross sales. [3] Farms with more than $250,000 in gross sales. [4] For definition of mean see Guide to Tabular Presentation.

Source: U.S. Department of Agriculture, Economic Research Service, *Agricultural Income and Finance Situation and Outlook*, December 2011; and "Farm Household Income and Characteristics," <http://www.ers.usda.gov/data-products/farm-household-income-and-characteristics.aspx>, accessed August 2013.

Table 856. Farm Type, Acreage, and Production: 2000 to 2011

[2,166 represents 2,166,000. Based on Agricultural Resource Management Survey (ARMS) Phase III]

Type of farm	Unit	2000	2004	2005	2006	2007	2008	2009	2010	2011
Total farms										
Number of farms.....................	1,000	2,166	2,108	2,095	2,083	2,197	2,192	2,192	2,193	2,173
Total value of production............	Mil dol.	177,286	225,698	215,295	226,045	289,530	299,066	278,051	286,792	334,920
Total acres operated.................	Mil.	995	990	916	893	878	894	913	912	902
Acres operated per farm.............	Acres	459	470	437	429	400	408	417	416	415
Commercial farms [1]										
Number of farms.....................	1,000	178	205	216	219	257	272	271	264	278
Total value of production............	Mil dol.	121,202	170,130	166,566	178,104	241,728	249,759	230,717	240,751	284,281
Total acres operated.................	Mil.	392	429	418	382	424	429	443	482	487
Acres operated per farm.............	Acres	2,205	2,096	1,939	1,747	1,650	1,580	1,635	1,829	1,754
Intermediate farms [2]										
Number of farms.....................	1,000	668	624	550	566	546	583	577	618	641
Total value of production............	Mil dol.	41,813	38,438	33,872	32,533	30,933	32,718	30,830	30,325	34,121
Total acres operated.................	Mil.	392	342	307	318	237	253	270	242	233
Acres operated per farm.............	Acres	587	547	558	561	434	434	469	392	363
Rural residence farms [3]										
Number of farms.....................	1,000	1,320	1,279	1,329	1,298	1,394	1,338	1,344	1,311	1,254
Total value of production............	Mil dol.	14,272	17,130	14,856	15,408	16,869	16,589	16,521	15,716	16,518
Total acres operated.................	Mil.	211	219	191	193	217	212	200	187	182
Acres operated per farm.............	Acres	160	172	144	149	156	158	149	143	145

[1] Includes farms with sales of $250,000 or more. [2] Small family farms whose operators report farming as their major occupation. [3] Includes retirement and residential farms.

Source: U.S. Department of Agriculture, Economic Research Service, ARMS Phase III—"Structural Characteristics Report," <http://www.ers.usda.gov/data-products/arms-farm-financial-and-crop-production-practices.aspx>, accessed June 2013.

Table 857. Organic Agriculture—Number of Farms, Acreage, and Value of Sales: 2007

[2,577 represents 2,577,000. Data have been adjusted for coverage; see text, this section and Appendix III]

Size and usage	Number of farms	Acreage (1,000)	Sales value of organically produced commodities and commodity	Number of farms	Value (mil. dol.)
Total acres used for organic production........	20,437	2,577	Organic product sales, total..................	18,211	1,709
1 to 9 organic acres...............................	9,251	29	$1 to $4,999..............................	8,285	13
10 to 49 organic acres............................	4,994	115	$5,000 to $9,999.........................	1,935	13
50 to 179 organic acres...........................	3,498	348	$10,000 to $24,999.......................	2,318	37
180 to 499 organic acres..........................	1,808	528	$25,000 to $49,999.......................	1,515	54
500 organic acres or more.......................	886	1,557	$50,000 or more..........................	4,158	1,593
Acres from which organic crops harvested......	16,778	1,288	Crops [1]...................................	14,968	1,122
Acres of organic pastureland.....................	7,268	975	Livestock and poultry......................	2,496	110
Acres being converted to organic production.....................	11,901	616	Livestock and poultry products.............	3,191	477

[1] Includes nursery and greenhouse crops.

Source: U.S. Department of Agriculture, National Agricultural Statistics Service, *2007 Census of Agriculture*, Vol. 1, February 2009. See also <http://www.agcensus.usda.gov/Publications/index.php>.

Table 858. Adoption of Genetically Engineered Crops: 2000 to 2012

[As percent of all crops planted. As of June. Based on June Agricultural Survey conducted by National Agricultural Statistical Services (NASS). Excludes conventionally bred herbicide resistant varieties. Insect resistant varieties include only those containing bacillus thuringiensis (Bt). The Bt varieties include those that contain more than one gene that can resist different types of insects. Stacked gene varieties include only those varieties containing biotech traits for both herbicide and insect resistance]

Genetically engineered crop	2000	2003	2004	2005	2006	2007	2008	2009	2010	2011	2012
Corn................................	25	40	47	52	61	73	80	85	86	88	88
Insect resistant..................	18	25	27	26	25	21	17	17	16	16	15
Herbicide resistant..............	6	11	14	17	21	24	23	22	23	23	21
Stacked gene...................	1	4	6	9	15	28	40	46	47	49	52
Cotton..............................	61	73	76	79	83	87	86	88	93	90	94
Insect resistant..................	15	14	16	18	18	17	18	17	15	17	14
Herbicide resistant..............	26	32	30	27	26	28	23	23	20	15	17
Stacked gene...................	20	27	30	34	39	42	45	48	58	58	63
Soybean............................	54	81	85	87	89	91	92	91	93	94	93
Insect resistant..................	(X)	(X)	(X)	(X)	(X)	(X)	(X)	(X)	(X)	(X)	(X)
Herbicide resistant..............	54	81	85	87	89	91	92	91	93	94	93
Stacked gene...................	(X)	(X)	(X)	(X)	(X)	(X)	(X)	(X)	(X)	(X)	(X)

X Not applicable.

Source: U.S. Department of Agriculture, Economic Research Service, "Adoption of Genetically Engineered Crops in the U.S.," <http://www.ers.usda.gov/data-products/adoption-of-genetically-engineered-crops-in-the-us.aspx>, accessed August 2013.

Table 859. Farm Production Expenses: 2002 and 2007

[2,129 represents 2,129,000. Data have been adjusted for coverage; see text, this section and Appendix III]

Production expenses	2002			2007		
	Farms (1,000)	Expenses (mil. dol.)	Percent of total	Farms (1,000)	Expenses (mil. dol.)	Percent of total
Total.................................	**2,129**	**173,199**	**100.0**	**2,205**	**241,114**	**100.0**
Fertilizer...............................	1,190	9,751	5.6	1,148	18,107	7.5
Chemicals.............................	947	7,609	4.4	919	10,075	4.2
Seeds, plants, vines, and trees...........	875	7,599	4.4	776	11,741	4.9
Livestock and poultry [1].................	554	27,421	15.8	491	38,004	15.8
Feed...................................	1,241	31,695	18.3	1,136	49,095	20.4
Gasoline and fuel........................	2,024	6,675	3.9	2,149	12,912	5.4
Utilities.................................	1,241	4,874	2.8	1,103	5,918	2.5
Supplies, repairs, and maintenance........	1,899	13,387	7.7	1,992	15,897	6.6
Farm labor [2]...........................	783	22,020	12.7	665	26,392	11.0
Customwork and custom hauling...........	450	3,314	1.9	362	4,091	1.7
Cash rent for land, buildings and grazing fees..............	498	9,046	5.2	490	13,275	5.5
Rent and lease for machinery, equipment, and farm share..	151	1,468	0.8	109	1,385	0.6
Interest expense........................	758	9,572	5.5	667	10,881	4.5
Property taxes..........................	1,963	5,351	3.1	1,996	6,223	2.6
Other production expenses...............	1,254	13,418	7.7	1,116	17,119	7.1

[1] Purchased or leased. 2002 does not include breeding livestock leased. [2] Includes hired and contract labor.

Source: U.S. Department of Agriculture, National Agricultural Statistics Service, *2007 Census of Agriculture*, Vol. 1, February 2009. See also <http://www.agcensus.usda.gov/Publications/index.php>.

Table 860. Farms—Number, Acreage, and Value of Sales by Size of Sales: 2002 and 2007

[2,129 represents 2,129,000. Data have been adjusted for coverage; see text, this section and Appendix III]

Market value of agricultural products sold	Farms (1,000)	Acreage Total (mil.)	Acreage Average per farm	Value of sales Total (mil. dol.)	Value of sales Average per farm (dol.)	Percent distribution Farms	Percent distribution Acreage	Percent distribution Value of sales
2002								
Total	**2,129**	**938.3**	**441**	**200,646**	**94,244**	**100.0**	**100.0**	**100.0**
Less than $2,500	827	107.0	129	485	586	38.8	11.4	0.2
$2,500 to $4,999	213	23.1	108	763	3,582	10.0	2.5	0.4
$5,000 to $9,999	223	34.8	156	1,577	7,072	10.5	3.7	0.8
$10,000 to $24,999	256	69.5	271	4,068	15,891	12.0	7.4	2.0
$25,000 to $49,999	158	77.9	494	5,594	35,405	7.4	8.3	2.8
$50,000 to $99,999	140	110.1	784	10,024	71,600	6.6	11.7	5.0
$100,000 to $249,999	159	189.4	1,191	25,401	159,755	7.5	20.2	12.7
$250,000 to $499,999	82	140.8	1,723	28,530	347,927	3.9	15.0	14.2
$500,000 to $999,999	42	94.0	2,241	28,944	689,143	2.0	10.0	14.4
$1,000,000 or more	29	91.7	3,198	95,259	3,284,793	1.4	9.8	47.5
2007								
Total	**2,205**	**922.1**	**418**	**297,220**	**134,807**	**100.0**	**100.0**	**100.0**
Less than $2,500	900	121.5	135	435	483	40.8	13.2	0.1
$2,500 to $4,999	200	17.5	87	718	3,585	9.1	1.9	0.2
$5,000 to $9,999	219	27.6	126	1,553	7,104	9.9	3.0	0.5
$10,000 to $24,999	248	65.8	265	3,960	15,949	11.3	7.1	1.3
$25,000 to $49,999	155	59.8	386	5,480	35,419	7.0	6.5	1.8
$50,000 to $99,999	125	78.2	623	8,961	71,429	5.7	8.5	3.0
$100,000 to $249,999	148	147.6	1,000	24,213	164,156	6.7	16.0	8.1
$250,000 to $499,999	93	140.7	1,507	33,410	357,811	4.2	15.3	11.2
$500,000 to $999,999	61	119.4	1,965	42,691	702,417	2.8	13.0	14.4
$1,000,000 or more	56	144.0	2,593	175,800	3,167,050	2.5	15.6	59.1

Source: U.S. Department of Agriculture, National Agricultural Statistics Service, *2007 Census of Agriculture*, Vol. 1, February 2009. See also <http://www.agcensus.usda.gov/Publications/index.php>.

Table 861. Farms—Number, Value of Sales, and Government Payments by Economic Class of Farm: 2002 and 2007

[2,129 represents 2,129,000. Economic class of farm is a combination of market value of agricultural products sold and federal farm program payments. Data have been adjusted for coverage; see text, this section and Appendix III]

Economic class	Number of farms (1,000) 2002, total	Number of farms (1,000) 2007 Total	Number of farms (1,000) 2007 Receiving government payments	Market value of agricultural products sold and government payments (mil. dol.) 2002, total	Market value of agricultural products sold and government payments (mil. dol.) 2007 Total	Market value of agricultural products sold and government payments (mil. dol.) 2007 Agricultural products sold	Market value of agricultural products sold and government payments (mil. dol.) 2007 Government payments
Total	**2,129**	**2,205**	**838**	**207,192**	**305,204**	**297,220**	**7,984**
Less than $1,000	431	500	42	72	96	77	19
$1,000 to $2,499	307	271	85	508	448	332	116
$2,500 to $4,999	243	246	80	870	884	685	199
$5,000 to $9,999	247	255	87	1,746	1,811	1,488	323
$10,000 to $24,999	272	274	110	4,320	4,364	3,810	554
$25,000 to $49,999	164	164	87	5,804	5,795	5,286	508
$50,000 to $99,999	143	129	83	10,202	9,219	8,644	575
$100,000 to $249,999	163	149	110	26,119	24,401	23,256	1,145
$250,000 to $499,999	86	96	75	30,084	34,367	32,980	1,387
$500,000 to $999,999	44	64	46	30,598	44,578	43,156	1,422
$1,000,000 to $2,499,999	21	42	27	31,701	62,751	61,508	1,243
$2,500,000 to $4,999,999	5	10	6	16,056	33,190	32,839	352
$5 million or more	3	6	2	49,112	83,300	83,159	141

Source: U.S. Department of Agriculture, National Agricultural Statistics Service, *2007 Census of Agriculture*, Vol. 1, February 2009. See also <http://www.agcensus.usda.gov/Publications/index.php>.

Table 862. Farms—Number, Acreage, and Value by State: 2002 and 2007

[2,129 represents 2,129,000. Data have been adjusted for coverage; see text, this section and Appendix III]

State	Number of farms (1,000)		Land in farms (mil. acres)		Average size of farm (acres)		Total value of land and buildings [1] (bil. dol.)		Market value of agricultural products sold and government payments, 2007 (mil.dol.)	Total number of operators, 2007 (1,000)
	2002	2007	2002	2007	2002	2007	2002	2007		
U.S.	2,129	2,205	938.3	922.1	441	418	1,144.9	1,744.3	305,204	3,337
AL	45	49	8.9	9.0	197	185	15.1	20.7	4,540	71
AK	1	1	0.9	0.9	1,479	1,285	0.3	0.3	59	1
AZ	7	16	26.6	26.1	3,645	1,670	10.6	19.5	3,290	26
AR	47	49	14.5	13.9	305	281	21.2	32.5	7,778	75
CA	80	81	27.6	25.4	346	313	96.1	162.5	34,125	131
CO	31	37	31.1	31.6	991	853	23.8	33.1	6,217	61
CT	4	5	0.4	0.4	85	83	3.5	5.1	556	8
DE	2	3	0.5	0.5	226	200	2.3	5.3	1,092	4
FL	44	47	10.4	9.2	236	195	29.3	52.1	7,831	73
GA	49	48	10.7	10.2	218	212	22.6	31.6	7,337	69
HI	5	8	1.3	1.1	241	149	4.6	8.6	516	11
ID	25	25	11.8	11.5	470	454	15.3	22.7	5,788	40
IL	73	77	27.3	26.8	374	348	66.7	101.5	13,816	111
IN	60	61	15.1	14.8	250	242	38.4	52.9	8,532	92
IA	91	93	31.7	30.7	350	331	64.2	104.2	21,124	136
KS	64	66	47.2	46.3	733	707	32.6	42.2	14,840	97
KY	87	85	13.8	14.0	160	164	25.5	37.5	4,928	124
LA	27	30	7.8	8.1	286	269	12.2	16.7	2,787	44
ME	7	8	1.4	1.3	190	166	2.3	3.0	626	13
MD	12	13	2.1	2.1	170	160	8.5	14.4	1,868	20
MA	6	8	0.5	0.5	85	67	4.6	6.4	494	12
MI	53	56	10.1	10.0	190	179	27.1	34.2	5,872	85
MN	81	81	27.5	26.9	340	332	41.8	69.2	13,626	120
MS	42	42	11.1	11.5	263	273	15.6	21.4	5,108	61
MO	107	108	29.9	29.0	280	269	45.3	63.2	7,832	164
MT	28	30	59.6	61.4	2,139	2,079	23.3	47.6	3,025	47
NE	49	48	45.9	45.5	930	953	35.7	52.7	15,893	72
NV	3	3	6.3	5.9	2,118	1,873	2.8	3.6	517	5
NH	3	4	0.4	0.5	132	113	1.4	2.3	202	7
NJ	10	10	0.8	0.7	81	71	7.4	11.3	994	16
NM	15	21	44.8	43.2	2,954	2,066	10.6	14.6	2,218	32
NY	37	36	7.7	7.2	206	197	12.9	16.3	4,481	58
NC	54	53	9.1	8.5	168	160	28.0	34.7	10,461	77
ND	31	32	39.3	39.7	1,283	1,241	15.8	30.6	6,444	45
OH	78	76	14.6	14.0	187	184	39.6	49.2	7,302	114
OK	83	87	33.7	35.1	404	405	23.8	40.6	6,016	131
OR	40	39	17.1	16.4	427	425	20.4	31.0	4,463	65
PA	58	63	7.7	7.8	133	124	26.3	37.3	5,885	95
RI	1	1	0.1	0.1	71	56	0.6	1.1	67	2
SC	25	26	4.8	4.9	197	189	10.1	14.0	2,420	37
SD	32	31	43.8	43.7	1,380	1,401	19.6	39.1	6,841	47
TN	88	79	11.7	11.0	133	138	28.5	37.1	2,713	117
TX	229	247	129.9	130.4	567	527	100.5	165.6	21,722	373
UT	15	17	11.7	11.1	768	664	9.0	13.9	1,438	26
VT	7	7	1.2	1.2	189	177	2.5	3.6	680	11
VA	48	47	8.6	8.1	181	171	23.3	34.1	2,961	71
WA	36	39	15.3	15.0	426	381	22.4	29.8	6,931	64
WV	21	24	3.6	3.7	172	157	4.8	8.8	595	35
WI	77	78	15.7	15.2	204	194	35.8	49.0	9,163	123
WY	9	11	34.4	30.2	3,651	2,726	10.2	15.5	1,186	19

[1] Based on reports for a sample of farms.

Source: U.S. Department of Agriculture, National Agricultural Statistics Service, *2007 Census of Agriculture*, Vol. 1, February 2009. See also <http://www.agcensus.usda.gov/Publications/index.php>.

Table 863. Balance Sheet of the Farming Sector: 1990 to 2012

[In billions of dollars, except as indicated (841 represents $841,000,000,000). As of December 31]

Item	1990	2000	2004	2005	2006	2007	2008	2009	2010	2011	2012
Assets	841	1,203	1,506	1,716	1,911	2,077	2,140	2,140	2,358	2,530	2,811
Real estate	619	946	1,183	1,398	1,565	1,704	1,740	1,749	1,887	2,078	2,311
Livestock and poultry [1]	71	77	79	80	81	81	79	78	77	76	74
Machinery, motor vehicles [2]	86	90	149	144	155	195	189	191	207	223	251
Crops [3]	23	28	35	33	30	31	39	39	43	36	30
Purchased inputs	3	5	11	12	13	17	21	20	22	23	22
Financial assets	38	57	48	49	68	49	73	63	122	93	123
Debt [4]	131	164	197	208	214	241	261	268	279	294	300
Real estate debt	68	85	103	113	112	132	148	146	154	167	173
Farm Credit System	23	30	37	48	50	58	63	69	72	75	80
Farm Service Agency	7	3	2	2	2	3	2	3	3	3	4
FARMER MAC [5]	(NA)	(NA)	(NA)	(NA)	(NA)	3	2	2	4	4	4
Commercial banks	15	30	35	37	37	41	46	44	51	53	59
Life insurance companies	9	11	11	11	12	11	14	13	12	13	13
Individuals and others [6]	14	11	18	14	10	16	20	14	10	18	13
Non-real estate debt	63	79	93	95	102	109	113	122	125	127	127
Farm Credit System	10	17	22	24	27	31	36	39	39	41	42
Farm Service Agency	10	4	3	3	3	3	3	3	4	4	3
Commercial banks	31	45	47	49	48	54	56	57	56	59	60
Individuals and others [6]	12	13	22	19	24	20	18	23	26	23	21
Equity	709	1,039	1,309	1,508	1,697	1,837	1,879	1,872	2,080	2,235	2,511
FINANCIAL RATIOS (percent)											
Farm debt/equity ratio	18.5	15.8	15.0	13.8	12.6	13.1	13.9	14.3	13.4	13.2	12.0
Farm debt/asset ratio	15.6	13.6	13.1	12.1	11.2	11.6	12.2	12.5	11.8	11.6	10.7

NA Not available. [1] Excludes horses and mules. [2] Includes only farm share value for trucks and autos. [3] All non-CCC crops held on farms plus the value above loan rate for crops held under Commodity Credit Corporation (CCC). [4] Includes CCC storage and drying facility loans but excludes debt on operator dwellings and for nonfarm purposes. [5] The Federal Agricultural Mortgage Corporation (known as FARMER MAC) operates as federally sponsored enterprise providing a secondary market for agricultural real estate mortgage loans, rural housing mortgage loans, and rural utility cooperative loans. [6] Savings and loan associations not included beginning in 2012.

Source: U.S. Department of Agriculture, Economic Research Service, "U.S. and State Farm Income and Wealth Statistics," <http://www.ers.usda.gov/data-products/farm-income-and-wealth-statistics.aspx>, accessed August 2013.

Table 864. Farm Sector Output and Value Added: 1990 to 2012

[In billions of dollars (179.9 represents $179,900,000,000). For definition of value added, see text, Section 13. Minus sign (–) indicates decrease]

Item	1990	2000	2004	2005	2006	2007	2008	2009	2010	2011	2012
CURRENT DOLLARS											
Farm output	**179.9**	**204.3**	**261.8**	**253.0**	**255.8**	**302.5**	**336.1**	**301.2**	**328.2**	**383.9**	**396.2**
Cash receipts from farm marketings	171.9	197.6	240.2	241.4	245.5	290.0	318.9	289.8	322.2	374.3	392.0
Farm products consumed on farms	0.6	0.3	0.3	0.4	0.5	0.4	0.4	0.4	0.4	0.4	0.6
Other farm income	4.9	8.4	12.3	11.3	13.1	12.6	14.7	12.7	12.5	15.0	14.9
Change in farm finished goods inventories	2.4	-2.0	9.0	-0.1	-3.3	-0.5	2.1	-1.7	-6.8	-5.9	-11.3
Less: Intermediate goods and services consumed	102.6	128.3	142.9	148.5	156.4	189.0	209.8	191.4	198.5	217.9	229.3
Equals: Gross farm value added	**77.3**	**76.0**	**118.9**	**104.5**	**99.4**	**113.5**	**126.3**	**109.8**	**129.7**	**166.0**	**166.9**
Less: Consumption of fixed capital	17.9	22.8	25.8	27.8	29.5	31.0	32.9	34.2	35.0	37.1	38.9
Equals: Net farm value added	**59.3**	**53.2**	**93.1**	**76.7**	**69.8**	**82.6**	**93.5**	**75.6**	**94.7**	**128.9**	**128.0**
Compensation of employees	13.4	19.7	22.2	22.0	21.9	25.0	25.7	25.6	24.2	23.1	23.1
Taxes on production and imports	3.8	4.6	5.3	5.3	5.9	6.7	6.7	6.7	6.9	7.0	9.9
Less: Subsidies to operators	7.6	20.0	11.1	20.9	13.5	10.6	10.3	10.4	10.5	8.8	9.0
Net operating surplus	49.8	48.8	76.7	70.2	55.5	61.4	71.4	53.7	74.2	107.5	104.0
CHAINED (2009) DOLLARS [1]											
Farm output, total	**(NA)**	**276.2**	**287.1**	**290.5**	**292.5**	**292.1**	**290.4**	**301.2**	**304.5**	**290.0**	**286.2**
Cash receipts from farm marketings	(NA)	268.0	262.7	275.8	279.5	278.3	275.1	289.8	298.4	281.6	281.4
Farm products consumed on farms	(NA)	0.4	0.3	0.4	0.5	0.4	0.4	0.4	0.4	0.3	0.4
Other farm income	(NA)	12.5	15.6	15.2	16.7	13.7	13.2	12.7	12.3	12.4	11.9
Change in farm finished goods inventories	(NA)	-2.9	9.1	-0.1	-3.8	-0.7	1.6	-1.7	-6.5	-4.1	-7.2
Less: Intermediate goods and services consumed	(NA)	197.6	192.1	188.0	189.1	209.6	196.5	191.4	193.0	184.2	181.5
Equals: Gross farm value added	**(NA)**	**83.9**	**96.1**	**101.6**	**102.4**	**86.2**	**94.7**	**109.8**	**111.5**	**105.8**	**104.6**
Less: Consumption of fixed capital	(NA)	28.7	30.2	31.2	32.0	32.6	33.4	34.2	35.1	36.4	37.5
Equals: Net farm value added	**(NA)**	**56.1**	**66.1**	**70.5**	**70.6**	**54.8**	**61.8**	**75.6**	**76.4**	**70.5**	**68.8**

NA Not available. [1] For more information; see text, Section 13.

Source: U.S. Bureau of Economic Analysis, National Income and Product Accounts Tables, "Table 7.3.5 Farm Sector Output, Gross Value Added, and Net Value Added,' and "Table 7.3.6 Real Farm Sector Output, Real Gross Value Added, and Real Net Value Added, Chained Dollars," <http://www.bea.gov/itable/>, accessed August 2013.

Table 865. Value Added to Economy by Agricultural Sector: 1990 to 2012

[In billions of dollars (188.5 represents $188,500,000,000). Data are consistent with the net farm income accounts and include income and expenses related to the farm operator dwellings. Value of agricultural sector production is the gross value of the commodities and services produced within a year. Net value-added is the sector's contribution to the national economy and is the sum of the income from production earned by all factors-of-production. Net farm income is the farm operators' share of income from the sector's production activities. The concept presented is consistent with that employed by the Organization for Economic Cooperation and Development. Minus sign (–) indicates decrease]

Item	1990	2000	2004	2005	2006	2007	2008	2009	2010	2011	2012
Value of agricultural production	**188.5**	**218.4**	**281.9**	**274.1**	**275.4**	**327.7**	**365.4**	**331.2**	**353.1**	**420.1**	**444.3**
Value of crop production	83.2	95.0	125.1	114.4	118.7	151.1	183.0	168.6	172.8	206.9	216.9
Food grains	7.5	6.5	8.9	8.6	9.1	13.6	18.7	14.8	14.1	16.8	18.2
Feed crops	18.7	20.5	27.4	24.6	29.4	42.3	58.5	50.5	54.8	72.1	79.1
Cotton	5.5	2.9	4.8	6.4	5.5	6.5	5.2	4.0	7.6	7.4	8.6
Oil crops	12.3	13.5	17.9	18.4	18.5	24.6	28.6	35.6	36.5	35.6	44.3
Fruits and tree nuts	9.4	12.3	15.1	17.1	17.3	18.7	19.0	19.3	21.7	24.4	26.1
Vegetables	11.3	15.8	16.6	17.3	18.1	19.3	19.9	20.4	20.2	20.7	20.6
Tobacco and all other crops	15.6	21.0	23.7	23.5	24.2	25.2	24.9	24.3	24.6	25.0	26.6
Home consumption	0.1	0.2	0.1	0.1	0.1	0.1	0.1	0.1	0.1	0.1	0.1
Value of inventory adjustment [1]	2.8	2.2	10.6	-1.7	-3.6	0.9	8.2	-0.3	-6.9	4.8	-6.7
Value of livestock production	90.0	99.1	124.3	126.5	119.3	138.4	140.4	119.8	140.8	164.6	170.4
Meat animals	51.1	53.0	62.3	64.8	63.7	65.1	65.0	59.0	69.5	84.7	90.1
Dairy products	20.2	20.6	27.4	26.7	23.4	35.5	34.8	24.3	31.4	39.5	37.0
Poultry and eggs	15.3	21.9	29.5	28.8	26.6	33.1	36.8	32.5	35.5	36.2	39.0
Miscellaneous livestock	2.5	4.1	4.4	4.6	4.8	4.9	5.0	4.5	5.1	5.5	5.4
Home consumption	0.5	0.1	0.2	0.3	0.3	0.3	0.3	0.3	0.3	0.3	0.3
Value of inventory adjustment [1]	0.4	-0.6	0.6	1.3	0.5	-0.4	-1.6	-0.7	-0.9	-1.6	-1.4
Services and forestry	15.3	24.4	32.5	33.2	36.4	38.1	42.0	42.7	39.5	48.6	56.9
Machine hire and custom work	1.8	2.2	3.4	2.8	2.6	2.7	3.0	4.0	3.5	3.8	3.8
Forest products sold	1.8	0.8	1.0	0.9	1.0	0.7	0.7	0.7	0.6	0.6	0.7
Other farm income	4.5	8.7	11.3	10.7	13.2	14.2	17.7	17.3	14.1	21.6	29.1
Gross imputed rental value of farm dwellings	7.2	12.7	16.8	18.8	19.5	20.6	20.5	20.7	21.2	22.4	23.3
Less: Purchased inputs	92.2	121.8	137.4	144.1	153.7	184.3	202.3	189.4	192.3	217.6	236.5
Farm origin	39.5	47.9	57.5	57.1	61.1	73.4	79.8	77.3	81.4	94.2	102.9
Feed purchased	20.4	24.5	29.7	28.0	31.4	41.9	46.9	45.0	45.4	54.6	59.1
Livestock and poultry purchased	14.6	15.9	18.2	18.7	18.6	18.8	17.7	16.7	19.6	21.7	23.4
Seed purchased	4.5	7.5	9.6	10.4	11.0	12.6	15.1	15.5	16.3	17.8	20.3
Manufactured inputs	22.0	28.7	31.6	35.4	37.5	46.3	55.0	49.0	49.6	57.5	63.2
Fertilizers and lime	8.2	10.0	11.4	12.8	13.3	17.7	22.5	20.1	21.0	25.1	28.5
Pesticides	5.4	8.5	8.6	8.8	9.0	10.5	11.7	11.5	10.7	11.8	13.7
Petroleum fuel and oils	5.8	7.2	8.2	10.3	11.3	13.8	16.2	12.7	13.2	15.6	15.7
Electricity	2.6	3.0	3.4	3.5	3.8	4.3	4.5	4.6	4.6	4.9	5.3
Other purchased inputs	30.7	45.2	48.3	51.6	55.2	64.6	67.5	63.2	61.3	65.9	70.4
Repair and maintenance of capital items	8.6	10.9	11.9	11.9	12.5	14.3	14.8	14.7	14.8	15.5	16.6
Machine hire and custom work	3.0	4.1	3.6	3.5	3.5	3.8	4.1	3.9	4.3	4.0	4.8
Marketing, storage, and transportation expenses	4.2	7.5	7.2	8.9	9.1	10.3	10.1	10.3	10.3	10.2	10.1
Contract labor	1.6	2.7	3.1	3.1	3.0	4.4	4.7	3.9	3.9	4.5	4.3
Miscellaneous expenses	13.4	19.9	22.4	24.3	27.1	31.7	33.7	30.4	28.0	31.8	34.6
Plus: Net government transactions [2]	3.1	15.8	5.4	15.8	6.2	0.9	0.9	1.1	0.9	-1.6	-1.6
Direct Government payments [3]	9.3	23.2	13.0	24.4	15.8	11.9	12.2	12.2	12.4	10.4	10.6
Motor vehicle registration and licensing fees	0.4	0.5	0.5	0.6	0.6	0.6	0.6	0.6	0.6	0.7	0.7
Property taxes	5.8	6.9	7.0	8.0	9.0	10.3	10.7	10.4	10.8	11.3	11.5
Equals: Gross value added	**99.3**	**112.5**	**149.9**	**145.8**	**126.9**	**144.3**	**164.0**	**142.9**	**161.7**	**200.9**	**206.2**
Less: Capital consumption	18.1	20.1	23.1	24.9	26.2	27.0	28.7	30.1	30.7	32.1	34.2
Equals: Net value added	**81.2**	**92.4**	**126.8**	**120.9**	**100.7**	**117.3**	**135.4**	**112.8**	**131.0**	**168.8**	**172.1**
Less: Employee compensation	12.4	17.9	20.2	20.5	21.2	24.5	25.3	25.0	23.5	22.3	26.6
Less: Net rent received by nonoperator landlords	9.0	9.2	8.5	9.0	7.6	7.6	9.6	9.8	12.6	12.5	15.5
Less: Real estate and nonreal estate interest	13.5	14.6	10.7	12.6	14.4	15.1	16.8	17.6	16.9	16.0	16.1
Equals: Net farm income	**46.3**	**50.7**	**87.4**	**78.8**	**57.4**	**70.0**	**83.7**	**60.4**	**78.0**	**118.0**	**113.8**

[1] A positive value of inventory change represents current-year production not sold by December 31. A negative value is an offset to production from prior years included in current-year sales. [2] Direct government payments minus motor vehicle registration and licensing fees and property taxes. [3] Government payments reflect payments made directly to all recipients in the farm sector, including landlords. The nonoperator landlords share is offset by its inclusion in rental expenses paid to these landlords and thus is not reflected in net farm income or net cash income.

Source: U.S. Department of Agriculture, Economic Research Service, "U.S. and State Farm Income and Wealth Statistics," <http://www.ers.usda.gov/data-products/farm-income-and-wealth-statistics.aspx>, accessed August 2013.

Table 866. Value of Agricultural Production, Income, and Government Payments by State: 2011 and 2012

[In millions of dollars (420,074 represents $420,074,000,000). Farm income data are after inventory adjustment and include income and expenses related to the farm operator's dwelling. Minus sign (–) indicates decrease]

State	Value of agricultural production 2011	2012	Net farm income 2011	2012	Government payments, 2012	State	Value of agricultural production 2011	2012	Net farm income 2011	2012	Government payments, 2012
U.S.	420,074	444,251	117,956	113,813	10,635						
AL	5,662	6,407	641	1,385	118	MT	4,277	4,734	971	1,295	239
AK	39	41	8	11	12	NE	23,878	25,582	7,419	5,952	480
AZ	5,100	4,480	1,555	903	50	NV	817	817	222	223	13
AR	9,159	10,307	1,409	1,979	365	NH	244	239	26	1	15
CA	47,265	47,918	15,998	16,001	288	NJ	1,333	1,395	408	340	12
CO	8,240	8,426	1,736	1,753	216	NM	4,263	4,260	1,327	1,358	98
CT	650	678	124	75	9	NY	5,704	5,765	1,708	1,296	104
DE	1,224	1,377	232	272	15	NC	11,888	13,495	2,898	4,320	430
FL	9,074	9,084	2,336	2,522	69	ND	8,310	11,709	2,228	4,279	409
GA	9,800	11,528	2,412	4,214	257	OH	10,923	11,211	3,788	2,568	280
HI	823	833	237	330	11	OK	7,548	8,506	1,563	1,404	296
ID	8,126	8,435	2,481	2,745	127	OR	5,573	5,518	1,012	960	118
IL	21,391	19,950	6,232	4,174	631	PA	7,564	8,102	1,927	1,833	119
IN	12,948	13,015	3,816	3,291	323	RI	80	83	10	5	4
IA	32,980	33,404	10,885	9,255	855	SC	3,099	3,467	453	735	110
KS	17,405	18,654	5,130	3,015	519	SD	10,926	11,266	4,628	3,643	331
KY	6,106	6,555	1,466	1,541	303	TN	4,490	4,727	807	813	176
LA	3,856	4,549	1,207	1,779	219	TX	26,120	27,633	5,216	5,145	838
ME	775	825	202	192	22	UT	2,041	2,036	346	364	39
MD	2,538	2,928	563	727	56	VT	818	794	235	160	22
MA	657	694	125	99	17	VA	4,235	4,698	753	932	140
MI	9,230	9,327	3,459	2,237	175	WA	9,816	10,363	3,095	2,160	204
MN	20,000	23,771	5,956	8,172	535	WV	805	891	41	64	25
MS	6,276	7,017	1,196	1,940	219	WI	13,032	13,474	3,814	3,201	282
MO	11,096	11,454	3,268	1,795	396	WY	1,868	1,827	387	356	43

Source: U.S. Department of Agriculture, Economic Research Service, "U.S. and State Farm Income and Wealth Statistics," <http://www.ers.usda.gov/data-products/farm-income-and-wealth-statistics.aspx>, accessed August 2013.

Table 867. Farm Income—Cash Receipts From Farm Marketings: 2000 to 2012

[In millions of dollars (192,098 represents $192,098,000,000). Represents gross receipts from commercial market sales as well as net Commodity Credit Corporation loans. The source estimates and publishes individual cash receipt values only for major commodities and major producing states. The U.S. receipts for individual commodities, computed as the sum of the reported states, may understate the value of sales for some commodities, with the balance included in the appropriate category labeled "other" or "miscellaneous." The degree of underestimation in some of the minor commodities can be substantial]

Commodities	2000	2010	2011	2012	Commodities	2000	2010	2011	2012
Total [1]	192,098	320,988	367,940	395,069	Broccoli	622	727	639	687
Livestock and products	99,597	141,448	165,909	171,584	Carrots	390	647	740	643
Meat animals	53,012	69,459	84,711	90,143	Corn, sweet	709	989	1,064	1,195
Cattle and calves	40,783	51,493	62,956	67,950	Lettuce	1,996	2,228	2,454	1,883
Hogs	11,758	17,967	21,755	22,193	Head	1,341	1,058	1,142	806
Sheep and lambs [2]	470	(NA)	(NA)	(NA)	Onions	713	1,176	906	957
Dairy products	20,587	31,367	39,514	37,004	Peppers, green, fresh	531	649	699	628
Poultry/eggs [1]	21,854	35,493	36,218	39,022	Tomatoes	1,845	2,285	1,987	1,867
Broilers	13,989	23,692	22,988	24,765	Fresh	1,195	1,358	1,050	870
Chicken eggs	4,289	6,535	7,316	7,823	Cantaloupes	372	320	351	326
Turkeys	2,771	4,374	4,961	5,441	Watermelons	240	500	519	521
Miscellaneous livestock [1,2]	4,144	5,129	5,467	5,416	Fruits/nuts [1]	12,284	21,712	24,417	26,134
Horses/mules	1,218	759	846	835	Grapefruit	377	277	270	269
Aquaculture [1,3]	798	1,335	1,372	1,314	Lemons	267	390	380	430
Catfish	501	403	423	341	Oranges	1,775	1,988	2,309	2,191
Crops	92,501	179,539	202,031	223,485	Apples	1,466	2,290	2,502	3,017
Food grains [1]	6,525	14,104	16,815	18,178	Cherries	327	756	904	894
Rice	837	3,022	2,900	2,815	Grapes	3,100	3,634	4,291	4,909
Wheat	5,672	11,051	13,878	15,333	Wine	1,909	2,257	2,301	(NA)
Feed crops [1]	20,546	54,813	72,063	79,109	Raisins	487	731	863	(NA)
Corn	15,162	47,191	62,912	69,211	Peaches	470	619	588	631
Hay	3,855	5,271	7,001	7,262	Pears	288	368	382	399
Sorghum grain	864	1,464	1,230	1,405	Strawberries	1,045	2,107	2,197	2,207
Cotton	2,950	7,561	7,425	8,585	Blueberries	223	644	880	851
Tobacco	2,316	1,246	1,056	1,497	Raspberries	79	259	279	290
Oil crops [1]	13,478	36,510	35,597	44,283	Almonds	666	2,903	4,008	4,347
Peanuts	897	928	1,154	2,281	Pistachios	245	1,159	879	1,113
Soybeans	12,047	34,466	33,269	40,734	All other crops [1]	18,645	23,368	23,918	25,110
Vegetables [1]	15,758	20,225	20,739	20,589	Sugar beets	1,113	2,142	2,008	2,446
Beans, dry	436	779	981	1,068	Cane for sugar	881	1,162	1,225	1,484
Potatoes	2,369	3,281	3,645	3,793	Greenhouse/nursery	13,710	15,299	15,180	15,555
Beans, snap	393	451	467	515	Mushrooms	860	942	1,015	1,088

NA Not available. [1] Includes commodities not shown separately. [2] Beginning in 2010, income for sheep and lambs is incorporated in miscellaneous livestock totals, and not with meat animals. [3] See also Table 923.

Source: U.S. Department of Agriculture, Economic Research Service, "U.S. and State Farm Income and Wealth Statistics," <http://www.ers.usda.gov/data-products/farm-income-and-wealth-statistics.aspx>, accessed August 2013.

Table 868. Cash Receipts for Selected Commodities—Leading States: 2012

[In millions of dollars (67,950 represents $67,950,000,000). See headnote Table 867]

State	Value	State	Value	State	Value	State	Value
Cattle and calves.......	**67,950**	**Corn**..............	**69,211**	**Soybeans**............	**40,734**	**Dairy products**......	**37,004**
Texas......................	10,543	Iowa.................	12,674	Iowa.................	5,923	California..............	6,900
Nebraska..................	10,361	Illinois................	10,592	Illinois................	5,397	Wisconsin.............	5,229
Kansas....................	7,882	Nebraska.............	8,520	Minnesota.............	3,720	New York..............	2,554
Iowa......................	3,842	Minnesota.............	6,972	Indiana................	3,218	Idaho.................	2,422
Colorado..................	3,664	Indiana...............	4,747	Nebraska.............	3,028	Pennsylvania..........	2,087

Source: U.S. Department of Agriculture, Economic Research Service, "U.S. and State Farm Income and Wealth Statistics," <http://www.ers.usda.gov/data-products/farm-income-and-wealth-statistics.aspx>, accessed August 2013.

Table 869. Farm Marketings, 2011 and 2012, and Principal Commodities, 2012, by State

[In millions of dollars (367,940 represents $367,940,000,000)]

State	2011 Total	2011 Crops	2011 Livestock and products	2012 Total	2012 Crops	2012 Livestock and products	2012 State rank for total farm marketings and three principal commodities in order of marketing receipts
U.S............	**367,940**	**202,031**	**165,909**	**395,069**	**223,485**	**171,584**	**Corn, cattle and calves, soybeans**
AL.............	4,814	1,148	3,666	5,349	1,420	3,929	25-Broilers, cattle and calves, chicken eggs,
AK.............	31	24	7	31	25	6	50-Hay, potatoes, cattle and calves
AZ.............	4,315	2,497	1,818	3,910	2,137	1,772	31-Cattle and calves, lettuce, hay
AR.............	8,144	3,767	4,377	9,422	4,774	4,647	15-Broilers, soybeans, rice
CA.............	43,331	30,971	12,360	44,738	32,583	12,155	1-Grapes, almonds, greenhouse/nursery
CO.............	6,992	2,835	4,158	7,638	2,898	4,740	20-Cattle and calves, corn, wheat,
CT.............	542	363	179	544	362	181	46-Greenhouse/nursery, chicken eggs, aquaculture
DE.............	1,065	316	749	1,181	377	803	39-Broilers, corn, soybeans
FL.............	8,339	6,844	1,495	8,253	6,592	1,661	19-Greenhouse/nursery, oranges, cane for sugar
GA.............	8,185	3,414	4,771	9,779	4,474	5,305	14-Broilers, cotton lint, peanuts
HI.............	723	632	91	729	631	98	41-Cane for sugar, greenhouse/nursery, cattle and calves
ID.............	7,368	3,387	3,981	7,587	3,590	3,997	21-Cattle and calves, potatoes, wheat
IL.............	18,902	16,273	2,629	19,650	17,034	2,616	6-Corn, soybeans, hogs
IN.............	11,735	8,436	3,299	12,053	8,575	3,478	9-Corn, soybeans, hogs
IA.............	28,847	16,487	12,360	31,985	18,862	13,124	2-Corn, hogs, soybeans
KS.............	15,027	6,113	8,913	16,223	7,097	9,126	7-Cattle and calves, wheat, corn
KY.............	4,931	2,183	2,747	5,284	2,422	2,862	27-Broilers, corn, soybeans
LA.............	3,485	2,426	1,059	4,128	2,963	1,165	29-Soybeans, cane for sugar, corn
ME.............	705	361	344	703	363	340	43-Potatoes, aquaculture, blueberries
MD.............	2,106	973	1,133	2,330	1,143	1,187	36-Broilers, greenhouse/nursery, corn
MA.............	512	400	112	510	398	112	47-Greenhouse/nursery, cranberries, apples
MI.............	8,045	5,022	3,023	8,294	5,330	2,964	18-Corn, soybeans, greenhouse/nursery
MN.............	17,756	10,742	7,015	20,581	13,161	7,420	5-Corn, soybeans, hogs
MS.............	5,158	2,286	2,871	6,236	3,176	3,060	24-Broilers, soybeans, corn
MO.............	9,647	5,456	4,191	9,940	5,517	4,423	13-Soybeans, corn, cattle and calves
MT.............	3,669	2,246	1,423	3,745	2,261	1,484	33-Wheat, cattle and calves, hay
NE.............	22,203	12,145	10,058	24,466	12,695	11,771	3-Cattle and calves, corn, soybeans
NV.............	691	285	406	718	287	431	42-Cattle and calves, hay, potatoes
NH.............	189	93	96	184	90	94	48-Greenhouse/nursery, cattle and calves, apples
NJ.............	1,121	995	127	1,139	1,036	103	40-Greenhouse/nursery, blueberries, miscellaneous vegetables
NM.............	4,133	836	3,297	4,020	828	3,192	30-Cattle and calves, hay, pecans
NY.............	5,255	2,044	3,210	5,288	2,195	3,093	26-Corn, greenhouse/nursery, cattle and calves
NC.............	10,313	3,485	6,829	11,707	4,356	7,350	10-Broilers, hogs, turkeys
ND.............	7,249	6,121	1,128	8,684	7,556	1,129	17-Wheat, soybeans, corn
OH.............	8,689	5,575	3,115	10,067	6,794	3,273	11-Soybeans, corn, hogs
OK.............	6,918	1,132	5,786	7,038	1,528	5,510	22-Cattle and calves, hogs, wheat
OR.............	4,658	3,275	1,383	4,817	3,398	1,420	28-Greenhouse/nursery, cattle and calves, wheat
PA.............	6,497	2,158	4,340	6,868	2,559	4,310	23-Corn, cattle and calves, chicken eggs
RI.............	63	51	11	62	52	11	49-Greenhouse/nursery, aquaculture, sweet corn
SC.............	2,604	1,155	1,449	2,928	1,370	1,558	35-Broilers, turkeys, greenhouse/nursery
SD.............	9,194	5,735	3,460	10,013	6,439	3,575	12-Corn, cattle and calves, soybeans
TN.............	3,389	1,991	1,398	3,850	2,300	1,550	32-Cattle and calves, soybeans, corn
TX.............	22,344	6,519	15,825	22,726	7,660	15,066	4-Cattle and calves, cotton lint, broilers
UT.............	1,635	503	1,132	1,689	525	1,163	37-Cattle and calves, hay, hogs
VT.............	757	120	637	699	107	592	44-Cattle and calves, maple products, greenhouse/nursery
VA.............	3,332	1,214	2,118	3,576	1,448	2,129	34-Broilers, cattle and calves, turkeys
WA.............	8,756	6,371	2,386	9,294	6,982	2,312	16-Apples, wheat, cattle and calves
WV.............	564	106	458	652	126	526	45-Broilers, cattle and calves, turkeys
WI.............	11,523	4,120	7,403	12,110	4,560	7,550	8-Corn, cattle and calves, soybeans
WY.............	1,484	397	1,087	1,651	428	1,222	38-Cattle and calves, hay, hogs

Source: U.S. Department of Agriculture, Economic Research Service, "U.S. and State Farm Income and Wealth Statistics," <http://www.ers.usda.gov/data-products/farm-income-and-wealth-statistics.aspx>, accessed August 2013.

Table 870. Indexes of Prices Received and Paid by Farmers: 2000 to 2012

[1990–1992 = 100, except as noted]

Item	2000	2010	2011	2012	Item	2000	2010	2011	2012
Prices received, all products...	**96**	**141**	**178**	**191**	Feed.........................	102	180	226	260
Crops...........................	96	153	204	222	Livestock and poultry........	110	133	155	169
Food grains..................	85	177	239	246	Seed.........................	124	310	332	359
Feed grains and hay..........	86	165	253	284	Fertilizer.....................	110	252	328	333
Cotton........................	82	117	145	131	Agricultural chemicals........	120	144	145	153
Tobacco.......................	107	103	83	104	Fuels.........................	129	284	362	360
Oil-bearing crops..............	85	172	224	247	Supplies and repairs..........	120	160	166	171
Fruits and nuts................	98	148	169	189	Autos and trucks.............	119	113	116	118
Commercial vegetables [1]......	121	162	169	146	Farm machinery..............	139	230	244	257
Potatoes and dry beans.......	93	140	171	164	Building materials............	121	166	171	176
All other crops.................	110	126	131	133	Farm services...............	118	161	164	167
Livestock and products..........	97	130	152	157	Rent........................	110	190	205	212
Meat animals.................	94	123	151	160	Interest.....................	113	133	145	147
Dairy products................	94	125	154	142	Taxes.......................	123	213	222	227
Poultry and eggs..............	106	152	150	163	Wage rates..................	140	189	192	199
Prices paid, total [2].............	**119**	**183**	**203**	**215**					
Production....................	115	188	215	228	Parity ratio (1910–14 = 100) [3]...	39	37	42	43

[1] Excludes potatoes and dry beans. [2] Includes production items, interest, taxes, wage rates, and a family living component. The family living component is the Consumer Price Index for all urban consumers from the Bureau of Labor Statistics. See text, Section 14 and Table 752. [3] Ratio of prices received by farmers to prices paid.

Source: U.S. Department of Agriculture, National Agricultural Statistics Service, *Agricultural Prices: Annual Summary*, and beginning 2009, "Quick Stats," <http://quickstats.nass.usda.gov/>, accessed August 2013.

Table 871. Farm and Marketing Bill Share of the U.S. Food Dollar (Nominal) by Selected Characteristics: 1995 to 2011

[In percent. The food dollar series measures annual expenditures by U.S. consumers on domestically produced food; a food dollar represents the average $1 expenditure. Farm share is measured as the average payment from each food dollar expenditure that farmers receive for their raw food dollar commodities. The food marketing bill is measured as the average value added to the raw food dollar from each consumer food dollar expenditure. Based on input-output data from the Bureau of Labor Statistics and Bureau of Economic Analysis]

Item	1995	2000	2005	2006	2007	2008	2009	2010	2011 [8]
SHARE OF FOOD DOLLAR									
Food dollar, total									
Farm share............................	18.1	15.9	15.3	14.2	15.8	15.8	14.4	14.1	15.5
Marketing bill share...................	81.9	84.1	84.7	85.8	84.2	84.2	85.6	85.9	84.5
Food at home dollar									
Farm share............................	23.9	22.3	22.5	22.2	24.0	24.3	22.5	22.0	23.6
Marketing bill share...................	76.1	77.7	77.5	77.8	76.0	75.7	77.5	78.0	76.4
Food away from home dollar									
Farm share............................	9.7	6.2	5.0	4.1	4.8	4.7	3.9	4.0	4.5
Marketing bill share...................	90.3	93.8	95.0	95.9	95.2	95.3	96.1	96.0	95.5
Food and beverage dollar [1]									
Farm share............................	15.6	13.5	13.0	12.6	13.7	14.0	12.8	12.6	(NA)
Marketing bill share...................	84.4	86.5	87.0	87.4	86.3	86.0	87.2	87.4	(NA)
Home food and beverage dollar [1]									
Farm share............................	19.6	18.2	18.3	17.9	19.4	19.7	18.2	17.8	19.2
Marketing bill share...................	80.4	81.8	81.7	82.1	80.6	80.3	81.8	82.2	80.8
Away food and beverage dollar [1]									
Farm share............................	9.0	5.5	4.5	4.1	4.6	4.6	3.9	4.0	(NA)
Marketing bill share...................	91.0	94.5	95.5	95.9	95.4	95.4	96.1	96.0	(NA)
MARKETING BILL COST COMPONENTS									
Primary factors:									
Salary and benefits [2]..................	(NA)	54.6	52.9	53.2	51.3	50.8	50.7	49.7	50.0
Output taxes [3].......................	(NA)	6.7	7.3	7.9	8.1	8.4	8.5	8.4	5.4
Property income [4]....................	(NA)	32.6	32.8	31.9	33.2	33.0	34.9	35.5	37.1
Imports [5]...........................	5.3	6.0	7.0	7.0	7.4	7.8	6.0	6.5	7.5
Industry groups: [6]									
Farm and agribusiness [7]...............	14.4	12.4	11.3	10.7	11.8	11.6	10.0	10.1	10.8
Food processing.......................	22.5	21.7	20.4	18.9	19.0	18.6	20.7	21.7	22.0
Packaging............................	5.2	4.7	4.3	4.1	4.1	4.0	3.9	3.9	4.0
Transportation........................	4.5	4.1	3.8	3.8	3.5	3.5	3.3	3.4	3.5
Retail Trade..........................	14.4	14.2	14.3	13.7	13.8	13.6	12.9	12.8	12.2
Food services........................	27.5	29.4	31.5	34.9	33.3	33.7	34.7	34.0	31.2
Energy...............................	4.3	4.8	6.2	5.8	6.2	6.8	5.1	4.8	5.5
Finance and insurance.................	3.5	4.3	4.1	4.0	4.2	4.4	5.4	5.2	6.1
Advertising...........................	2.4	2.7	2.3	2.3	2.3	2.0	2.0	2.2	2.4
Legal and accounting..................	1.3	1.6	1.8	1.8	1.7	1.8	2.0	1.9	2.1

NA Not available. [1] Includes alcoholic beverages and soft drinks. [2] Pre-tax employee wages plus employer and employee costs for employee benefits. [3] Value of excise, sales, property, and severance taxes (less subsidies), customs duties, and other non-tax government fees levied on establishments. [4] Allocated compensation to various owners for services on behalf of a domestic establishment that directs sales to the U.S. food supply. Includes machinery, equipment, structures, natural resources, product inventory, and other tangible or intangible assets. [5] Food and non-food commodities imported from international sources and used by U.S. food supply chain industries producing for the U.S. market. [6] For each industry group the amount shown excludes value-added contributions to the food dollar that trace back to other supply chain industry groups. For example, the value of energy used by the transportation and packaging industries is deducted from those groups and included with the energy group. [7] Farm and agribusiness value-added contributions from non-farm supply chain industry groups, such as energy, transportation, and financial services, are deducted from the farm share and therefore the industry group series value for farms and agribusiness is smaller than the farm share value of the marketing bill series. [8] Preliminary.

Source: U.S. Department of Agriculture, Economic Research Service, "Food Dollar Series," <http://www.ers.usda.gov/data-products/food-dollar-series/food-dollar-application.aspx>, accessed June 2013.

Table 872. Agricultural Exports and Imports—Value: 1990 to 2012

[In billions of dollars, except percent (16.6 represents $16,600,000,000). Includes Puerto Rico, U.S. territories, and shipments under foreign aid programs. Excludes fish, forest products, distilled liquors, manufactured tobacco, and products made from cotton; but includes raw tobacco, raw cotton, rubber, beer and wine, and processed agricultural products]

Calendar Year	Trade balance	Exports, domestic products	Percent of all exports	Imports for consumption	Percent of all imports	Year	Trade balance	Exports, domestic products	Percent of all exports	Imports for consumption	Percent of all imports
1990.........	16.6	39.5	11	22.9	5	2006......	5.6	70.9	8	65.3	4
1995.........	26.0	56.3	10	30.3	4	2007......	18.1	90.0	9	71.9	4
2000.........	12.3	51.3	7	39.0	4	2008......	34.3	114.8	10	80.5	4
2002.........	11.2	53.1	8	41.9	4	2009......	43.1	114.8	12	71.7	5
2003.........	12.0	59.4	9	47.4	4	2010......	34.0	115.8	10	81.9	4
2004.........	7.4	61.4	8	54.0	4	2011......	37.4	136.4	9	98.9	4
2005.........	3.9	63.2	8	59.3	4	2012......	38.5	141.3	10	102.9	5

Source: U.S. Department of Agriculture, Economic Research Service, "Foreign Agricultural Trade of the United States (FATUS)," <http://www.ers.usda.gov/data/fatus/>, accessed July 2013.

Table 873. Agricultural Imports—Value by Selected Commodity: 1990 to 2012

[In millions of dollars (22,918 represents $22,918,000,000). For calendar year. Includes Puerto Rico, U.S. territories, and shipments under foreign aid programs. Excludes fish, forest products, distilled liquors, manufactured tobacco, and products made from cotton; but includes raw tobacco, raw cotton, rubber, beer and wine, and processed agricultural products]

Commodity [1]	Value (mil. dol.)							Percent distribution		
	1990	2000	2005	2009	2010	2011	2012	1990	2000	2012
Total [2]...........................	**22,918**	**38,974**	**59,291**	**71,681**	**81,858**	**98,949**	**102,871**	**100.0**	**100.0**	**100.0**
Cattle, live.....................	978	1,152	1,039	1,299	1,575	1,449	1,761	4.3	3.0	1.7
Beef and veal...................	1,872	2,399	3,651	2,725	2,828	3,161	3,670	8.2	6.2	3.6
Pork............................	938	997	1,281	978	1,185	1,288	1,284	4.1	2.6	1.2
Dairy products.................	891	1,671	2,686	2,528	2,619	2,938	3,181	3.9	4.3	3.1
Grains and feeds..............	1,188	3,075	4,527	7,435	7,787	8,934	10,111	5.2	7.9	9.8
Fruits and preparations........	2,170	3,851	5,842	8,210	9,167	9,950	10,594	9.5	9.9	10.3
Vegetables and preparations [3]...	1,979	3,958	6,410	8,044	9,318	10,289	10,472	8.6	10.2	10.2
Sugar and related products.......	1,213	1,555	2,494	3,075	4,047	5,145	4,786	5.3	4.0	4.7
Wine...........................	917	2,207	3,762	4,020	4,279	4,857	5,108	4.0	5.7	5.0
Malt beverages.................	923	2,179	3,096	3,339	3,506	3,565	3,699	4.0	5.6	3.6
Oilseeds and products...........	874	1,773	2,998	4,799	5,390	8,252	8,104	3.8	4.5	7.9
Coffee and products............	1,915	2,700	2,976	4,070	4,943	8,097	7,025	8.4	6.9	6.8
Cocoa and products............	1,072	1,404	2,751	3,476	4,295	4,680	4,096	4.7	3.6	4.0
Rubber, crude natural..........	707	842	1,552	1,274	2,820	4,773	3,382	3.1	2.2	3.3

[1] Commodity and commodity grouping definitions used are the Foreign Agricultural Trade of the United States (FATUS) commodity code groupings. See source for more details. [2] Includes other commodities, not shown separately. [3] Includes pulses.

Source: U.S. Department of Agriculture, Foreign Agricultural Service, "Global Agricultural Trade System," <http://www.fas.usda.gov/gats>, accessed June 2013.

Table 874. Agricultural Imports—Value by Selected Countries of Origin: 1990 to 2012

[In millions of dollars (22,918 represents $22,918,000,000). Totals include transshipments through Canada, but transshipments are not distributed by country after 1998. See headnote Table 872]

Country	Value (mil. dol.)							Percent distribution		
	1990	2000	2005	2009	2010	2011	2012	1990	2000	2012
Total.........................	**22,918**	**38,974**	**59,291**	**71,681**	**81,858**	**98,949**	**102,871**	**100.0**	**100.0**	**100.0**
Canada.........................	3,171	8,661	12,270	14,710	16,244	18,917	20,228	13.8	22.2	19.7
European Union [1]..............	5,016	8,303	13,410	13,378	14,353	16,068	16,720	21.9	21.3	16.3
Mexico.........................	2,614	5,077	8,331	11,373	13,578	15,837	16,397	11.4	13.0	15.9
China..........................	273	812	1,872	2,877	3,367	3,992	4,533	1.2	2.1	4.4
Brazil..........................	1,563	1,144	1,952	2,433	2,892	4,056	3,406	6.8	2.9	3.3
Indonesia......................	683	998	1,702	1,787	2,886	4,288	3,349	3.0	2.6	3.3
Australia [2]....................	1,174	1,592	2,421	2,316	2,307	2,361	2,677	5.1	4.1	2.6
Chile...........................	481	1,026	1,521	2,145	2,293	2,370	2,457	2.1	2.6	2.4
Thailand.......................	470	779	1,094	1,567	2,034	2,626	2,414	2.0	2.0	2.3
Colombia.......................	790	1,123	1,437	1,772	1,977	2,466	2,154	3.4	2.9	2.1
Malaysia.......................	308	353	666	1,295	1,729	2,424	1,914	1.3	0.9	1.9
New Zealand [2]................	855	1,132	1,712	1,608	1,665	1,971	2,240	3.7	2.9	2.2
India...........................	285	826	923	1,236	1,592	2,676	5,355	1.2	2.1	5.2
Guatemala.....................	497	710	920	1,297	1,386	1,888	2,008	2.2	1.8	2.0
Costa Rica.....................	400	812	916	1,102	1,295	1,449	1,533	1.7	2.1	1.5
Argentina......................	389	672	831	1,091	1,159	1,628	1,698	1.7	1.7	1.7
Peru...........................	90	196	448	807	974	1,320	1,241	0.4	0.5	1.2
Vietnam........................	(NA)	200	422	727	970	1,284	1,364	(NA)	0.5	1.3
Philippines.....................	418	468	568	724	884	1,375	1,143	1.8	1.2	1.1
Ecuador........................	482	451	596	928	869	1,070	938	2.1	1.2	0.9
Rest of world...................	2,958	3,636	5,281	6,508	7,404	8,883	9,102	12.9	9.3	8.8

NA Not available. [1] For consistency, data for all years are shown on the basis of 27 countries in the European Union; see footnote 3, Table 1403. [2] Data is a summarization of component countries.

Source: U.S. Department of Agriculture, Foreign Agricultural Service, "Global Agricultural Trade System Online (GATS)," <http://www.fas.usda.gov/gats>, accessed June 2013.

Table 875. Agricultural Exports and Imports—Volume by Principal Commodities: 1990 to 2012

[In thousands (7,703 represents 7,703,000). 1,000 hectoliters equals 264.18 gallons. Includes Puerto Rico, U.S. territories, and shipments under foreign aid programs. Excludes fish, forest products, distilled liquors, manufactured tobacco, and products made from cotton; but includes raw tobacco, raw cotton, rubber, beer and wine, and processed agricultural products]

Commodity [1]	Unit	1990	2000	2005	2009	2010	2011	2012
EXPORTS								
Fruit juices and wine	Hectoliters	7,703	14,356	13,982	13,675	14,982	17,128	14,849
Beef, pork, lamb, and poultry meats [2]	Metric tons	1,451	4,935	4,343	6,151	6,368	7,090	7,120
Wheat, unmilled	Metric tons	27,384	27,568	27,040	21,920	27,613	32,801	25,710
Wheat products	Metric tons	863	844	313	404	446	420	410
Rice, paddy, milled	Metric tons	2,534	3,241	4,388	3,426	4,481	3,696	3,802
Feed grains	Metric tons	61,066	54,946	50,865	51,388	54,622	49,315	33,287
Feed grain products	Metric tons	1,430	2,062	3,442	1,228	1,081	1,040	992
Feeds and fodders [3]	Metric tons	10,974	13,065	11,422	14,594	19,046	18,121	17,614
Fresh fruits and nuts	Metric tons	2,648	3,450	3,675	4,101	4,311	4,586	4,732
Fruit products	Metric tons	390	471	394	506	570	616	599
Vegetables, fresh	Metric tons	1,297	2,029	2,077	1,972	2,141	2,240	2,285
Vegetables, frozen and canned	Metric tons	529	1,112	1,086	1,397	1,409	1,656	1,739
Oilcake and meal	Metric tons	5,079	6,462	6,905	9,251	10,003	8,245	10,074
Oilseeds	Metric tons	15,820	28,017	26,462	41,210	43,172	35,142	44,232
Vegetable oils	Metric tons	1,226	2,043	1,937	3,036	3,544	2,876	3,075
Tobacco, unmanufactured	Metric tons	223	180	154	173	179	184	160
Cotton, excluding linters	Metric tons	1,696	1,485	3,405	2,540	2,959	2,761	2,760
IMPORTS								
Fruit juices	Hectoliters	33,116	31,154	41,488	44,234	42,734	42,091	38,169
Wine	Hectoliters	2,510	4,584	7,262	9,460	9,592	10,385	11,948
Malt beverages	Hectoliters	10,382	23,464	29,947	30,278	31,607	32,015	32,485
Coffee, including products	Metric tons	1,214	1,370	1,307	1,348	1,390	1,495	1,490
Rubber and allied gums, crude	Metric tons	840	1,232	1,169	704	945	1,049	969
Beef, pork, lamb, and poultry meats [2]	Metric tons	1,169	1,579	1,778	1,430	1,351	1,249	1,316
Grains [4]	Metric tons	2,071	4,622	3,726	5,587	5,166	4,944	6,850
Biscuits, pasta, and noodles	Metric tons	300	711	1,001	1,019	1,097	1,154	1,207
Feeds and fodders [3]	Metric tons	959	1,224	963	1,330	1,423	1,839	2,020
Fruits, nuts, and preparations [5]	Metric tons	5,401	8,354	9,570	10,302	10,919	11,235	11,918
Vegetables, fresh or frozen	Metric tons	1,898	3,763	5,183	6,118	6,861	7,154	7,288
Tobacco, unmanufactured	Metric tons	173	216	233	199	164	164	209
Oilseeds and oilnuts	Metric tons	509	1,056	818	1,249	1,223	1,362	1,221
Vegetable oils and waxes	Metric tons	1,204	1,846	2,386	3,523	3,730	4,350	4,182
Oilcake and meal	Metric tons	316	1,254	1,541	1,539	1,504	2,489	3,079

[1] Commodity and commodity grouping definitions used are the Foreign Agricultural Trade of the United States (FATUS) commodity code groupings. See source for more details. [2] Includes variety meats. [3] Excluding oil meal. [4] Includes wheat, corn, oats, barley, and rice. [5] Includes bananas and plantains.

Source: U.S. Department of Agriculture, Foreign Agricultural Service, "Global Agricultural Trade System," <http://www.fas.usda.gov/gats/>, accessed June 2013.

Table 876. U.S. Exports and General Imports of Fertilizer and Agricultural Chemicals by Type: 2000 to 2012

[In thousands of metric tons (21,480 represents 21,480,000). Metric ton = 1.102 short tons or .984 long tons. Includes Puerto Rico, U.S. territories, and shipments under foreign aid programs. Commodity and commodity grouping definitions used are Foreign Agricultural Trade of the United States (FATUS) groupings. See source for details]

Commodity	2000	2005	2006	2007	2008	2009	2010	2011	2012
IMPORTS [1]									
Fertilizers, total	**21,480**	**30,397**	**27,267**	**45,935**	**35,823**	**19,923**	**43,657**	**34,858**	**32,795**
Nitrogen	10,552	17,901	15,987	32,236	16,786	12,655	17,171	17,722	18,054
Potassium	9,324	10,215	8,956	10,792	10,798	4,628	10,230	10,664	8,464
Phosphate	1,592	2,243	2,303	2,881	8,203	2,598	16,200	6,435	6,185
Mixed/organic fertilizer	13	37	20	26	36	41	56	38	93
Agricultural chemicals, total	**58**	**80**	**75**	**74**	**96**	**96**	**90**	**97**	**116**
Herbicides	12	23	24	16	21	22	15	18	22
Fungicides	17	21	19	20	26	28	25	25	26
Insecticides	10	7	9	2	1	1	1	1	1
Other pesticides	19	29	23	36	47	44	49	54	68
EXPORTS									
Fertilizers, total	**21**	**32**	**26**	**41**	**10,780**	**11,324**	**10,310**	**10,860**	**10,673**
Nitrogen	19	26	23	37	1,624	1,793	1,741	1,719	2,180
Potassium	–	–	–	–	178	384	333	147	223
Phosphate	2	6	4	4	8,552	8,689	7,820	8,608	7,761
Mixed/organic fertilizer	–	–	–	–	426	458	416	385	509
Agricultural chemicals, total	**154**	**127**	**135**	**125**	**140**	**123**	**146**	**151**	**160**
Herbicides	60	56	65	57	74	69	83	84	92
Fungicides	14	18	16	14	16	14	15	17	17
Insecticides	62	23	27	31	26	21	27	27	29
Other pesticides	19	29	27	23	24	18	22	23	23

– Represents or rounds to zero. [1] Total shipments arriving in the U.S., including both merchandise that enters consumption channels immediately and merchandise entered into bonded warehouses or Foreign Trade Zones under Customs custody.

Source: U.S. Department of Agriculture, Foreign Agricultural Service, "Global Agricultural Trade System," <http://www.fas.usda.gov/gats>, accessed July 2013.

Table 877. Selected Farm Products—U.S. and World Production and Exports: 2000 to 2012

[In millions of metric tons, except as indicated (60.6 represents 60,600,000). Metric ton = 1.102 short tons or .984 long tons]

| Commodity | Unit | Amount | | | | | | United States as percent of world | | |
| | | United States | | | World | | | | | |
		2000	2010	2012	2000	2010	2012	2000	2010	2012
PRODUCTION [1]										
Wheat...........	Million	60.6	60.1	61.8	583.2	652.3	655.3	10.4	9.2	9.4
Corn for grain..............	Million	251.9	316.2	273.8	591.6	831.7	855.0	42.6	38.0	32.0
Soybeans.................	Million	75.1	90.6	82.1	175.8	263.9	268.0	42.7	34.3	30.6
Rice, milled................	Million	5.9	7.6	6.3	399.3	449.3	469.8	1.5	1.7	1.3
Cotton [2]...................	Million bales [3]	17.2	18.1	17.3	89.1	116.3	121.2	19.3	15.6	14.3
EXPORTS [4]										
Wheat [5]...................	Million	28.9	35.1	27.5	101.3	133.1	138.3	28.5	26.4	19.9
Corn...................	Million	49.3	46.6	17.8	76.7	91.4	89.9	64.3	51.0	19.8
Soybeans.................	Million	27.1	40.8	36.2	53.8	91.6	96.4	50.4	44.6	37.6
Rice, milled basis...........	Million	2.6	3.5	3.5	24.1	34.9	37.5	10.7	10.1	9.2
Cotton [2]...................	Million bales [3]	6.7	14.4	13.3	26.2	35.5	46.5	25.7	40.5	28.6

[1] Production years vary by commodity. In most cases, includes harvests from July 1 of the year shown through June 30 of the following year. [2] For production and trade years ending in year shown. [3] Bales of 480 lb. net weight. [4] Trade years may vary by commodity. Wheat, corn, and soybean data are for trade year beginning in year shown. Rice data are for calendar year. [5] Includes wheat flour on a grain equivalent.

Source: U.S. Department of Agriculture, Foreign Agricultural Service, "Production, Supply and Distribution Online," <http://www.fas.usda.gov/psdonline/>, accessed July 2013.

Table 878. Percent of U.S. Agricultural Commodity Output Exported: 1990 to 2010

[In percent. All export shares are estimated from export and production volumes]

Commodity group	1990	1995	2000	2005	2007	2008	2009	2010
Total agriculture [1]........................	**19.0**	**23.4**	**20.0**	**19.3**	**21.7**	**19.9**	**20.1**	**22.1**
Livestock [2]............................	4.5	8.2	7.0	6.2	8.2	9.9	8.2	8.6
Red meat...........................	3.2	6.0	8.1	7.4	9.4	13.2	12.2	13.3
Poultry................................	4.3	11.6	12.4	11.8	13.0	14.7	14.8	14.4
Dairy.................................	1.3	2.8	1.1	1.2	2.4	3.9	1.8	2.2
Crops [3].............................	21.3	26.1	22.2	21.5	24.0	21.7	22.1	24.5
Food grains...........................	37.5	51.9	44.6	45.8	57.9	38.8	38.1	54.1
Feed grains...........................	22.5	30.5	20.8	20.1	20.0	15.8	15.9	15.5
Oilseeds.............................	25.8	34.6	33.0	27.8	40.1	40.0	42.2	41.7
Fruit and nuts........................	17.0	16.1	17.6	17.2	20.5	21.9	19.7	21.8
Vegetables...........................	7.6	9.9	10.8	11.9	11.6	14.5	15.5	16.7
Sweeteners...........................	5.3	4.4	3.9	5.3	7.8	7.2	7.2	10.8
Wine and beer........................	3.3	5.1	6.7	8.1	10.4	11.3	8.6	(NA)

NA Not available [1] All export shares are computed from physical weights or weight equivalents. [2] Includes animal fats; excludes live farm animals and fish/shellfish. [3] Exports include vegetable oils and oilseed meal. Excludes nursery crops.

Source: U.S. Department of Agriculture, Economic Research Service, Global Agricultural Trade System, "Production, Supply, and Distribution" database, <http://www.fas.usda.gov/gats>, and unpublished data.

Table 879. Top 10 U.S. Export Markets for Selected Commodities: 2012

[In thousands of metric tons (31,361 represents 31,361,000). Commodity and commodity grouping definitions used are the Foreign Agricultural Trade of the United States (FATUS) commodity code groupings. See source for details]

Corn		Wheat [1]		Soybeans		Poultry meat	
Country	Amount	Country	Amount	Country	Amount	Country	Amount
World, total..........	**31,361**	**World, total**...........	**25,710**	**World, total**............	**43,470**	**World, total**...........	**3,735**
Japan....................	9,998	Mexico..................	3,625	China...................	26,345	Mexico..................	768
Mexico..................	8,465	Japan...................	3,375	Mexico.................	3,295	Russia..................	271
China....................	4,366	Nigeria.................	2,851	Japan...................	1,942	Canada.................	205
Korea, South............	2,003	Korea, South...........	2,243	Indonesia...............	1,780	Angola.................	186
Venezuela..............	1,390	Philippines.............	1,860	Germany................	1,579	Cuba...................	153
Taiwan..................	1,004	Taiwan.................	997	Taiwan.................	1,345	China..................	143
Canada.................	596	Egypt..................	819	Egypt..................	1,316	Taiwan.................	127
Cuba....................	489	Venezuela..............	743	Turkey.................	810	Hong Kong.............	116
Guatemala.............	446	Indonesia..............	730	Thailand................	686	Kazakhstan.............	90
Costa Rica.............	394	China..................	594	Korea, South...........	672	Philippines.............	89
Rest of world..........	2,211	Rest of world..........	7,872	Rest of world...........	3,699	Rest of world...........	1,587

[1] Unmilled.

Source: U.S. Department of Agriculture, Foreign Agricultural Service, "Global Agricultural Trade System Online (GATS)," <http://www.fas.usda.gov/gats/>, accessed June 2013.

Table 880. Agricultural Exports—Value by Principal Commodities: 1990 to 2012

[In millions of dollars (39,495 represents $39,495,000,000). Includes Puerto Rico, U.S. territories, and shipments under foreign aid programs. Excludes fish, forest products, distilled liquors, manufactured tobacco, and products made from cotton; but includes raw tobacco, raw cotton, rubber, beer and wine, and processed agricultural products]

Commodity [1]	Value (mil. dol.)							Percent distribution		
	1990	2000	2005	2009	2010	2011	2012	1990	2000	2012
Total agricultural exports	**39,495**	**51,265**	**63,182**	**98,454**	**115,820**	**136,374**	**141,342**	**100.0**	**100.0**	**100.0**
Animals and animal products [2]	6,636	11,600	12,227	18,047	22,346	27,841	29,016	16.8	22.6	20.5
Meat and meat products	2,558	5,276	4,299	7,722	9,338	12,080	12,397	6.5	10.3	8.8
Poultry and poultry products	910	2,235	3,139	4,775	4,808	5,631	6,257	2.3	4.4	4.4
Grains and feeds [2]	14,386	13,620	16,364	25,293	29,254	38,689	31,962	36.4	26.6	22.6
Wheat and products	4,035	3,578	4,520	5,681	7,060	11,471	8,479	10.2	7.0	6.0
Corn	6,037	4,469	4,789	8,746	9,808	13,672	9,324	15.3	8.7	6.6
Fruits and preparations	2,007	2,743	3,468	4,661	5,263	6,046	6,536	5.1	5.4	4.6
Nuts and preparations	978	1,322	2,992	4,075	4,799	5,693	6,881	2.5	2.6	4.9
Vegetables and preparations [3]	1,836	3,112	3,571	5,008	5,376	5,823	6,214	4.6	6.1	4.4
Oilseeds and products [2]	5,725	8,584	10,229	24,081	27,219	26,051	35,111	14.5	16.7	24.8
Soybeans	1,001	1,252	1,478	3,482	3,501	3,191	4,822	2.5	2.4	3.4
Vegetable oils and waxes	832	1,259	1,656	3,092	3,903	4,017	4,168	2.1	2.5	2.9
Tobacco, unmanufactured	1,441	1,204	990	1,159	1,167	1,149	1,098	3.6	2.3	0.8
Cotton, excluding linters	2,783	1,873	3,921	3,316	5,739	8,387	6,246	7.0	3.7	4.4
Other	3,703	7,207	9,420	12,814	14,657	16,695	18,278	9.4	14.1	12.9

[1] Commodity and commodity grouping definitions used are the Foreign Agricultural Trade of the United States (FATUS) commodity code groupings. See source for more details. [2] Includes commodities not shown separately. [3] Includes pulses.

Source: U.S. Department of Agriculture, Foreign Agricultural Service, "Global Agricultural Trade System," <http://www.fas.usda.gov/gats>, accessed June 2013.

Table 881. Agricultural Exports—Value by Selected Countries of Destination: 1990 to 2012

[39,495 represents $39,495,000,000. Includes Puerto Rico, U.S. territories, and shipments under foreign aid programs. Excludes fish, forest products, distilled liquors, manufactured tobacco, and products made from cotton; but includes raw tobacco, raw cotton, rubber, beer and wine, and processed agricultural products]

Country	Value (mil. dol.)							Percent distribution		
	1990	2000	2005	2009	2010	2011	2012	1990	2000	2012
Total agricultural exports [1]	**39,495**	**51,265**	**63,182**	**98,454**	**115,820**	**136,374**	**141,342**	**100.0**	**100.0**	**100.0**
Canada	4,214	7,643	10,619	15,726	16,899	19,037	20,570	10.7	14.9	14.6
Mexico	2,560	6,410	9,429	12,932	14,598	18,348	18,906	6.5	12.5	13.4
Caribbean	1,015	1,408	1,913	3,082	3,178	3,417	3,538	2.6	2.7	2.5
Central America	483	1,121	1,589	2,553	2,905	3,731	3,503	1.2	2.2	2.5
South America	1,063	1,704	1,943	3,459	4,247	5,273	5,436	2.7	3.3	3.8
Asia, excluding Middle East [2]	15,857	19,877	22,543	40,614	49,736	58,274	63,201	40.1	38.8	44.7
Japan	8,142	9,292	7,931	11,072	11,797	14,070	13,497	20.6	18.1	9.5
Korea, South	2,650	2,546	2,233	3,917	5,307	6,971	6,037	6.7	5.0	4.3
Taiwan	1,663	1,996	2,301	2,988	3,189	3,612	3,219	4.2	3.9	2.3
China [3]	818	1,716	5,233	13,109	17,519	18,865	25,964	2.1	3.3	18.4
Indonesia	275	668	958	1,796	2,245	2,814	2,492	0.7	1.3	1.8
Europe/Eurasia [2]	8,140	7,654	8,361	9,377	11,367	12,579	12,498	20.6	14.9	8.8
European Union [4]	7,474	6,515	7,052	7,445	8,906	9,665	10,057	18.9	12.7	7.1
Russia	(X)	580	972	1,429	1,133	1,239	1,655	(X)	1.1	1.2
Middle East	1,728	2,323	2,844	4,745	5,998	7,660	5,987	4.4	4.5	4.2
Africa [2]	486	737	1,491	1,930	2,311	2,971	2,648	1.2	1.4	1.9
Egypt	687	1,050	819	1,354	2,095	2,507	1,855	1.7	2.0	1.3
Oceania	343	490	742	1,282	1,389	1,601	1,771	0.9	1.0	1.3

X Not applicable. [1] Totals include transshipments through Canada, but transshipments are not distributed by country after 2000. [2] Includes areas not shown separately. [3] China includes Macao. However Hong Kong remains separate economically until 2050 and is not included. [4] For consistency, data for all years are shown on the basis of 27 countries in the European Union; see footnote 3, Table 1403.

Source: U.S. Department of Agriculture, Foreign Agricultural Service, "Global Agricultural Trade System (GATS)," <http://www.fas.usda.gov/gats>, accessed June 2013.

Table 882. Cropland Used for Crops and Acreages of Crops Harvested: 1990 to 2012

[In millions of acres, except as indicated (341 represents 341,000,000)]

Item	1990	1995	2000	2005	2007	2008	2009	2010	2011	2012 [4]
Cropland used for crops	**341**	**332**	**345**	**336**	**335**	**337**	**333**	**335**	**328**	**341**
Index (1977 = 100)	90	88	91	89	89	89	88	89	87	90
Cropland harvested [1]	310	302	314	314	312	315	310	315	302	316
Crop failure	6	8	11	7	8	9	8	5	13	10
Cultivated summer fallow	25	22	20	16	15	14	15	14	14	14
Cropland idled by all federal programs [2]	62	55	31	35	37	35	34	31	31	30
Acres of crops harvested [3]	**322**	**314**	**325**	**321**	**322**	**327**	**319**	**322**	**311**	**326**

[1] Land supporting one or more harvested crops. [2] Beginning in 2000, includes only the Conservation Reserve Program; all other federal acreage reduction programs were eliminated by the Federal Agricultural Improvement Act of 1996. [3] Area in principal crops harvested plus acreages in fruits, vegetables for sale, tree nuts, and other minor crops. Acres are counted twice for land that is doublecropped. [4] Preliminary.

Source: U.S. Department of Agriculture, Economic Research Service, "Major Land Uses," <http://www.ers.usda.gov/data-products/major-land-uses.aspx>, accessed August 2013; *Agricultural Resources and Environmental Indicators*, 2006, and earlier reports; and U.S. Department of Agriculture, Farm Service Agency, "CRP Enrollment and Rental Payments by State, 1986-2012," <http://www.fsa.usda.gov/FSA/webapp?area=home&subject=copr&topic=rns-css>, accessed August 2013.

Table 883. Crops—Supply and Use: 2000 to 2012

[72.4 represents 72,400,000. Marketing year beginning January 1 for potatoes, May 1 for hay, June 1 for wheat, August 1 for cotton, September 1 for soybeans and corn. Acreage, production, and yield of all crops periodically revised on basis of census data]

Item	Unit	2000	2005	2008	2009	2010	2011	2012
CORN								
Acreage harvested	Million	72.4	75.1	78.6	79.5	81.4	84.0	87.4
Yield per acre	Bushel	136.9	147.9	153.9	164.7	152.8	147.2	123.4
Production	Mil. bu.	9,915	11,112	12,092	13,092	12,447	12,360	10,780
Imports	Mil. bu.	6.82	8.81	13.53	8.34	27.67	29.37	165.00
Total supply [1]	Mil. bu.	11,639	13,235	13,729	14,774	14,182	13,517	11,934
Ethanol	Mil. bu.	628	1,603	3,709	4,591	5,019	5,011	4,650
Exports	Mil. bu.	1,941	2,134	1,849	1,980	1,830	1,543	715
Total use [2]	Mil. bu.	9,740	11,268	12,056	13,066	13,055	12,528	11,215
Ending stocks	Mil. bu.	1,899	1,967	1,673	1,708	1,128	989	719
Price per unit [3]	Dol./bu.	1.85	2.00	4.06	3.55	5.18	6.22	7.20
Value of production	Mil. dol.	18,499	22,198	49,313	46,734	64,643	76,940	77,352
SOYBEANS								
Acreage harvested	Million	72.4	71.3	74.7	76.4	76.6	73.8	[9] 76.1
Yield per acre	Bushel	38.1	43.1	39.7	44.0	43.5	41.9	[9] 39.6
Production	Mil. bu.	2,758	3,068	2,967	3,359	3,329	3,094	[9] 3,015
Imports	Mil. bu.	4	3	13	15	14	16	[9] 20
Total supply [1]	Mil. bu.	3,052	3,327	3,185	3,512	3,495	3,325	[9] 3,204
Crushings	Mil. bu.	1,640	1,739	1,662	1,752	1,648	1,703	[9] 1,615
Exports	Mil. bu.	996	940	1,279	1,499	1,501	1,362	[9] 1,345
Total use [2]	Mil. bu.	2,804	2,878	3,047	3,361	3,280	3,155	[9] 3,079
Ending stocks	Mil. bu.	248	449	138	151	215	169	[9] 125
Price per unit [3]	Dol./bu.	4.54	5.66	9.97	9.59	11.30	12.50	14.30
Value of production	Mil. dol.	12,520	17,367	29,458	32,145	37,547	38,498	43,194
WHEAT								
Acreage harvested	Million	53.1	50.1	55.7	49.9	47.6	45.7	49.0
Yield per acre	Bushel	42.0	42.0	44.9	44.5	46.3	43.7	46.3
Production	Mil. bu.	2,228	2,103	2,499	2,218	2,207	1,999	2,269
Imports	Mil. bu.	89.8	81.4	127.0	118.6	96.9	112.1	122.8
Total supply [1, 4]	Mil. bu.	3,268	2,725	2,932	2,993	3,279	2,974	3,134
Exports	Mil. bu.	1,062	1,003	1,015	879	1,291	1,051	1,007
Total use [2]	Mil. bu.	2,392	2,154	2,275	2,018	2,417	2,231	2,416
Ending stocks	Mil. bu.	876	571	657	976	862	743	718
Price per unit [3]	Dol./bu.	2.62	3.42	6.78	4.87	5.70	7.24	7.90
Value of production	Mil. dol.	5,782	7,171	16,626	10,654	12,827	14,323	17,943
COTTON								
Acreage harvested	Million	13.1	13.8	7.6	7.5	10.7	9.5	10.4
Yield per acre	Pounds	632	831	813	777	812	790	802
Production	Mil. bales [5]	17.2	23.9	12.8	12.2	18.1	15.6	17.4
Imports	Mil. bales [5]	–	–	–	–	–	–	–
Total supply [1]	Mil. bales [5]	21.1	29.4	22.9	18.5	21.1	18.2	20.8
Exports	Mil. bales [5]	6.7	17.7	13.3	12.0	14.4	11.7	11.6
Total use [2]	Mil. bales [5]	15.6	23.5	16.8	15.6	18.3	15.0	15.0
Ending stocks	Mil. bales [5]	6.0	6.1	6.3	3.0	2.6	3.4	5.8
Price per unit [3]	Cents/lb.	51.6	47.7	49.1	64.8	84.6	93.5	73.1
Value of production	Mil. dol.	4,260	5,695	3,021	3,788	7,348	6,986	5,970
HAY								
Acreage harvested	Million	60.4	61.6	60.2	59.8	59.9	55.7	56.3
Yield per acre	Sh. tons	2.54	2.44	2.43	2.47	2.43	2.36	2.13
Production	Mil. sh. tons	154	150	146	148	146	131	120
Price per unit [6, 7]	Dol./ton	84.60	98.20	152.00	108.00	114.00	178.00	191.00
Value of production	Mil. dol.	11,557	12,534	18,639	14,716	14,656	18,251	18,558
POTATOES								
Acreage harvested	Million	1.3	1.1	1.0	1.0	1.0	1.1	1.1
Yield per acre	Cwt. [8]	381	390	396	414	401	399	412
Production	Mil. cwt. [8]	514	424	415	433	404	430	467
Price per unit [3]	Dol./cwt. [8]	5.08	7.06	9.09	8.25	9.20	9.41	8.39
Value of production	Mil. dol.	2,590	2,992	3,770	3,558	3,722	4,041	3,915

– Represents zero or rounds to less than half the unit of measurement shown. [1] Comprises production, imports, and beginning stocks. [2] Includes feed, residual, and other domestic uses not shown separately. [3] Marketing year average price. U.S. prices are computed by weighting U.S. monthly prices by estimated monthly marketings and do not include an allowance for outstanding loans and government purchases and payments. [4] Includes flour and selected other products expressed in grain-equivalent bushels. [5] Bales of 480 pounds, net weight. [6] Prices are for hay sold baled. [7] Season average prices received by farmers. U.S. prices are computed by weighting state prices by estimated sales. [8] Cwt = hundredweight (100 pounds). [9] Forecast.

Source: Production and prices—U.S. Department of Agriculture, National Agricultural Statistics Service, *Crop Values Annual Summary*, February 2013 and earlier reports; <http://www.nass.usda.gov/Publications/index.asp>. Supply and disappearance--U.S. Department of Agriculture, Economic Research Service, "Feed Grains Database," "Oil Crops Yearbook," "Wheat Data," "Cotton and Wool Outlook Yearbook," and "Vegetables and Pulses Yearbook Tables," <http://www.ers.usda.gov/data-products.aspx>, accessed September 2013.

Table 884. Corn—Acreage, Production, and Value by Leading States: 2010 to 2012

[81,446 represents 81,446,000. One bushel of corn (bu.) = 56 pounds. State value of production is computed by multiplying the state price by its production; value for the United States is the sum of state values]

State	Acreage harvested (1,000 acres)			Yield per acre (bu.)			Production (mil. bu.)			Price per unit ($/bu.)			Value of production (mil. dol.)		
	2010	2011	2012	2010	2011	2012	2010	2011	2012	2010	2011	2012	2010	2011	2012
U.S. [1]....	81,446	83,989	87,375	153	147	123	12,447	12,360	10,780	5.18	6.22	7.20	64,643	76,940	77,352
IA.........	13,050	13,700	13,700	165	172	137	2,153	2,356	1,877	5.23	6.20	7.20	11,261	14,610	13,514
IL.........	12,400	12,400	12,250	157	157	105	1,947	1,947	1,286	5.24	6.25	7.25	10,201	12,168	9,325
NE........	8,850	9,600	9,100	166	160	142	1,469	1,536	1,292	5.09	6.11	7.05	7,478	9,385	9,110
MN.......	7,300	7,700	8,330	177	156	165	1,292	1,201	1,374	5.01	6.09	7.00	6,473	7,315	9,621
IN.........	5,720	5,750	6,030	157	146	99	898	840	597	5.38	6.31	7.45	4,831	5,297	4,447
SD........	4,220	4,950	5,300	135	132	101	570	653	535	5.09	6.03	7.05	2,900	3,940	3,774
KS........	4,650	4,200	3,950	125	107	96	581	449	379	4.95	6.28	7.25	2,877	2,822	2,749
OH........	3,270	3,220	3,650	163	158	123	533	509	449	5.45	6.44	7.45	2,905	3,276	3,345
ND........	1,880	2,060	3,460	132	105	122	248	216	422	5.01	5.81	6.85	1,243	1,257	2,892
MO........	3,000	3,070	3,300	123	114	75	369	350	248	5.35	6.40	7.50	1,974	2,240	1,856
WI........	3,100	3,320	3,300	162	156	121	502	518	399	5.27	6.02	6.90	2,647	3,118	2,755
MI........	2,100	2,190	2,390	150	153	133	315	335	318	5.56	6.14	7.10	1,751	2,057	2,257
TX........	2,080	1,470	1,550	145	93	130	302	137	202	4.67	6.61	7.25	1,408	904	1,461
KY........	1,230	1,300	1,530	124	139	68	153	181	104	5.15	6.30	7.20	785	1,138	749
CO........	1,210	1,300	1,010	151	133	133	183	173	134	4.98	6.15	7.05	910	1,063	947
PA........	910	960	1,000	128	111	132	116	107	132	6.12	7.05	7.60	713	751	1,003
TN........	640	735	960	117	131	85	75	96	82	4.74	6.56	7.35	355	632	600
NC........	840	815	820	91	84	117	76	68	96	5.18	7.04	7.65	396	482	734
MS........	670	740	795	136	128	165	91	95	131	4.37	6.23	6.95	398	590	912
AR........	300	520	695	150	142	178	57	74	124	4.55	6.27	6.95	259	463	860

[1] Includes other states, not shown separately.

Source: U.S. Department of Agriculture, National Agricultural Statistics Service, *Crop Production Annual Summary*, January 2013, and *Crop Values Annual Summary*, February 2013. See also <http://www.nass.usda.gov/index.asp>.

Table 885. Soybeans—Acreage, Production, and Value by Leading States: 2010 to 2012

[76,610 represents 76,610,000. One bushel of soybeans (bu.) = 60 pounds. State value of production is computed by multiplying the state price by its production; value for the United States is the sum of state values]

State	Acreage harvested (1,000 acres)			Yield per acre (bu.)			Production (mil. bu.)			Price per unit ($/bu.)			Value of production (mil. dol.)		
	2010	2011	2012	2010	2011	2012	2010	2011	2012	2010	2011	2012	2010	2011	2012
U.S. [1]...	76,610	73,776	76,104	44	42	40	3,329	3,094	3,015	11.30	12.50	14.30	37,547	38,498	43,194
IA.......	9,730	9,230	9,300	51	52	45	496	475	414	11.20	12.60	14.30	5,558	5,989	5,918
IL.......	9,050	8,910	8,920	52	48	43	466	423	384	11.80	12.80	14.60	5,500	5,417	5,600
MN......	7,310	7,040	6,990	45	39	43	329	275	301	10.90	12.40	14.20	3,586	3,405	4,268
MO.....	5,070	5,210	5,260	42	37	30	210	190	155	11.70	12.50	14.50	2,462	2,377	2,250
IN.......	5,330	5,290	5,140	49	46	44	259	241	224	11.50	12.70	14.60	2,973	3,057	3,264
NE......	5,100	4,840	4,990	53	54	42	268	261	207	11.00	12.00	14.00	2,945	3,136	2,899
ND......	4,070	3,960	4,730	34	29	34	138	115	161	10.90	11.90	14.20	1,508	1,367	2,284
SD......	4,140	4,070	4,710	38	37	30	157	151	141	10.90	12.20	14.10	1,715	1,837	1,992
OH......	4,590	4,540	4,580	48	48	45	220	218	206	11.50	13.00	14.50	2,534	2,833	2,988
KS......	4,250	3,760	3,810	33	27	22	138	102	84	11.50	12.10	14.30	1,588	1,228	1,199
AR......	3,150	3,280	3,160	35	39	43	110	126	136	10.90	12.30	14.40	1,202	1,553	1,957
MI.......	2,040	1,940	1,990	44	44	43	89	85	86	11.10	12.10	14.00	985	1,033	1,198
MS......	1,980	1,800	1,950	39	39	45	76	70	88	10.40	12.00	14.40	793	842	1,264
WI......	1,630	1,610	1,700	51	47	42	82	75	71	10.80	12.40	13.90	889	928	981

[1] Includes other states, not shown separately.

Source: U.S. Department of Agriculture, National Agricultural Statistics Service, *Crop Production Annual Summary*, January 2013, and *Crop Values Annual Summary*, February 2013. See also <http://www.nass.usda.gov/index.asp>.

Table 886. Wheat—Acreage, Production, and Value by Leading States: 2010 to 2012

[47,619 represents 47,619,000. One bushel of wheat (bu.) = 60 pounds. State value of production is computed by multiplying the price per unit by total production, for each state; value for the United States is the sum of production values for all states]

State	Acreage harvested (1,000 acres)			Yield per acre (bu.)			Production (mil. bu.)			Price per unit ($/bu.)			Value of production (mil. dol.)		
	2010	2011	2012	2010	2011	2012	2010	2011	2012	2010	2011	2012	2010	2011	2012
U.S. [1]......	47,619	45,705	48,991	46	44	46	2,207	1,999	2,269	5.70	7.24	7.90	12,809	14,312	17,909
KS..........	8,000	7,900	9,100	45	35	42	360	277	382	5.14	7.03	7.55	1,850	1,944	2,886
ND.........	8,400	6,590	7,760	43	30	44	362	200	339	6.61	8.24	8.45	2,390	1,647	2,866
MT.........	5,210	4,975	5,585	41	35	35	215	175	195	6.29	7.68	8.45	1,355	1,344	1,646
OK.........	3,900	3,200	4,300	31	22	36	121	70	155	5.06	7.05	7.60	612	496	1,176
TX..........	3,750	1,900	3,000	34	26	32	128	49	96	5.25	7.34	6.80	669	363	653
SD..........	2,725	2,817	2,235	45	37	46	123	105	102	6.43	7.56	8.20	794	792	840
CO..........	2,377	2,044	2,182	46	40	34	108	82	75	5.54	6.60	8.05	600	540	603
WA.........	2,285	2,345	2,175	65	72	67	148	168	146	6.24	6.78	8.30	923	1,138	1,215

[1] Includes other states, not shown separately.

Source: U.S. Department of Agriculture, National Agricultural Statistics Service, *Crop Production Annual Summary*, January 2013, and *Crop Values Annual Summary*, February 2013. See also <http://www.nass.usda.gov/index.asp>.

Table 887. Commercial Vegetable and Other Specified Crops—Area, Production, and Value, 2010 to 2012

[282 represents 282,000. Except as noted, relates to commercial production for fresh market and processing combined. Includes market garden areas but excludes minor producing acreage in minor producing states. Excludes production for home use in farm and nonfarm gardens. Value is for season or crop year and should not be confused with calendar-year income. Hundredweight (cwt.) is the unit used for fresh market yield and production and is equal to one hundred pounds]

Crop	Area harvested (1,000 acres) [1]			Production (1,000 cwt.) [2]			Value of production (mil. dol.) [3]		
	2010	2011	2012	2010	2011	2012	2010	2011	2012
Beans, snap.................	282	259	263	20,383	18,985	20,071	451	467	515
Fresh market...............	89	95	93	5,062	5,367	5,402	304	306	323
Processed..................	193	164	170	15,321	13,618	14,669	148	161	192
Beans, dry edible.............	1,843	1,168	1,690	31,801	19,890	31,925	899	851	1,270
Broccoli...................	130	123	126	19,289	18,149	20,472	727	639	687
Cabbage [4].................	67	61	61	23,238	21,159	21,271	396	364	389
Cantaloupes [4].............	75	71	64	19,228	18,870	16,952	319	350	325
Carrots.....................	79	84	83	29,580	28,634	29,676	647	740	643
Cauliflower..................	38	36	36	7,087	6,649	6,690	295	306	240
Celery......................	28	28	29	19,923	19,362	19,760	371	382	366
Corn, sweet.................	585	570	602	83,512	81,230	90,306	989	1,064	1,195
Fresh market...............	250	243	244	29,628	28,684	31,380	759	759	822
Processed..................	335	327	359	53,884	52,546	58,926	230	305	373
Cucumbers..................	132	124	132	19,412	17,036	19,865	378	373	421
Garlic......................	23	25	26	3,752	4,204	4,319	267	287	227
Lettuce, head [4]............	132	131	127	50,120	49,665	45,576	1,058	1,142	806
Lettuce, leaf [4]............	51	47	51	13,004	11,939	12,384	500	413	444
Lettuce, Romaine [4]........	79	82	86	27,389	28,142	27,481	656	886	622
Onions.....................	149	148	148	73,599	74,097	72,256	1,050	742	944
Peas, green [5].............	173	159	191	6,913	5,898	7,905	99	118	169
Peppers, bell...............	53	52	56	16,156	17,928	16,803	649	699	628
Spinach....................	43	43	44	5,767	9,025	7,806	268	266	241
Squash.....................	44	45	44	6,728	7,248	7,497	209	256	249
Tomatoes...................	392	362	371	283,487	276,154	291,165	2,279	1,980	1,875
Fresh market...............	103	94	95	27,961	28,231	27,590	1,352	1,043	864
Processed..................	289	268	276	255,526	247,923	263,575	927	937	1,011
Watermelons [4]............	134	121	128	41,736	37,215	39,036	500	519	521

[1] Area of crops for harvest for fresh market, including any partially harvested or not harvested because of low prices or other factors, plus area harvested for processing. [2] Excludes some quantities not marketed. [3] Fresh market vegetables valued at f.o.b. shipping point. Processing vegetables are equivalent returns at packinghouse door. [4] Fresh market only. [5] Processed only.

Source: U.S. Department of Agriculture, National Agricultural Statistics Service, "Quick Stats," <http://quickstats.nass.usda.gov/>, accessed August 2013.

Table 888. Fruits and Nuts—Utilized Production and Value, 2010 to 2012, and Leading Producing States: 2012

[4,607 represents 4,607,000]

Fruits and nuts	Unit	Utilized production [1]			Value of production (mil. dol.)			Leading states in order of production, 2012
		2010	2011	2012	2010	2011	2012	
FRUITS								
Apples [2]..........................	1,000 tons	4,607	4,659	4,498	2,314	2,823	3,089	WA, NY, PA
Avocados........................	1,000 tons	174	263	(NA)	479	406	(NA)	(NA)
Blackberries, cultivated (OR)........	1,000 tons	22	26	27	33	43	45	OR
Blueberries.......................	1,000 tons	247	259	277	644	880	851	ME, MI, OR
Cranberries......................	1,000 tons	340	386	402	299	346	386	WI, MA, NJ
Dates (CA)......................	1,000 tons	29	33	31	37	44	42	CA
Figs (fresh) (CA).................	1,000 tons	41	39	39	22	20	(NA)	CA
Grapefruit........................	1,000 tons	1,264	1,153	1,184	283	279	243	FL, TX, CA
Grapes (13 states)................	1,000 tons	7,469	7,440	7,337	3,635	4,294	4,911	CA, WA, NY
Kiwifruit (CA).....................	1,000 tons	33	37	27	25	28	(NA)	CA
Lemons..........................	1,000 tons	920	850	912	387	449	405	CA, AZ
Nectarines.......................	1,000 tons	233	225	189	129	131	145	(NA)
Olives (CA)......................	1,000 tons	206	71	160	137	52	130	CA
Oranges.........................	1,000 tons	8,905	8,982	8,349	2,230	2,622	2,064	FL, CA, TX
Papayas (Hawaii).................	1,000 tons	15	14	(NA)	11	10	(NA)	HI
Peaches.........................	1,000 tons	1,131	1,043	965	619	588	631	CA, SC, GA
Pears...........................	1,000 tons	813	965	858	387	367	437	WA, OR, CA
Plums (CA)......................	1,000 tons	141	160	115	78	64	80	CA
Plums and prunes (fresh) [3].......	1,000 tons	11	13	12	5	5	7	OR, WA, ID
Prunes (dried basis) (CA)...........	1,000 tons	390	444	395	176	179	156	CA
Raspberries......................	1,000 tons	75	94	84	259	279	290	CA,
Strawberries.....................	1,000 tons	1,427	1,452	1,508	2,262	2,395	2,405	CA, FL, OR
Tangelos (FL)....................	1,000 tons	52	52	45	10	14	13	FL
Tangerines.......................	1,000 tons	657	644	684	331	349	426	CA, FL, AZ
NUTS								
Almonds, shelled basis (CA)........	1,000 tons	1,414	170	1,730	2,903	4,008	4,347	CA
Hazelnuts, in the shell (OR).........	1,000 tons	28	39	35	67	90	63	OR
Macadamia nuts (HI)..............	1,000 tons	20	25	22	30	38	35	HI
Pecans, in the shell (11 states)......	1,000 tons	147	135	151	675	656	477	GA, NM, TX
Pistachios (CA)...................	1,000 tons	261	222	276	1,159	879	1,113	CA
Walnuts, in the shell (CA)...........	1,000 tons	504	461	470	1,028	1,337	(NA)	CA

NA Not available. [1] Excludes quantities not harvested or not marketed. Utilized production is the amount sold plus the quantities used at home or held in storage. [2] Production in commercial orchards with 100 or more bearing-age trees. [3] Idaho, Michigan, Oregon and Washington.

Source: U.S. Department of Agriculture, National Agricultural Statistics Service, *Citrus Fruits 2013 Summary*, September 2013; and *Noncitrus Fruits and Nuts 2012 Preliminary Summary*, January 2013. See also <http://www.nass.usda.gov/Publications/index.asp>.

Table 889. Nuts—Supply and Use: 2000 to 2011

[In thousands of pounds (shelled) (331,466 represents 331,466,000). For marketing season beginning July 1 for almonds, hazelnuts, and pecans; August 1 for walnuts; and September 1 for pistachios]

Year	Beginning stocks	Marketable production [1]	Imports	Supply, total	Consumption	Exports	Ending stocks
Total nuts: [2]							
2000	331,466	1,127,940	293,172	1,752,577	733,921	780,988	237,669
2005	262,883	1,502,439	431,881	2,197,203	803,929	1,125,570	267,705
2009	543,740	2,113,256	467,303	3,124,299	1,156,735	1,545,432	422,132
2010	422,132	2,482,240	473,293	3,377,664	1,180,621	1,784,906	412,137
2011, total [2, 3]	**412,137**	**2,874,697**	**439,177**	**3,726,010**	**1,238,394**	**2,015,400**	**472,216**
Almonds	253,959	1,989,507	15,933	2,259,399	566,682	1,357,484	335,233
Pecans	42,817	(NA)	74,690	242,108	123,613	70,293	48,202
Pistachios	76,532	301,748	914	379,193	109,425	225,233	44,535
Hazelnuts	2,969	30,347	9,719	43,035	20,728	20,815	1,492
Walnuts	35,859	406,234	4,902	446,995	143,844	260,396	42,755

NA Not available. [1] Utilized production minus inedibles and noncommercial usage. [2] Includes macadamia nuts, Brazil nuts, cashew nuts, pine nuts, chestnuts, and mixed nuts not shown separately. [3] Data are preliminary.

Source: U.S. Department of Agriculture, Economic Research Service, *2012 Fruit and Tree Nuts Yearbook*. See also <http://www.ers.usda.gov/topics/crops/fruit-tree-nuts.aspx>.

Table 890. Honey—Number of Bee Colonies, Yield, and Production: 1990 to 2012

[Includes only beekeepers with five or more colonies. Colonies were not included if honey was not harvested]

Year	Honey-producing colonies [1] (1,000)	Yield per colony (pounds)	Production (1,000 pounds)	Average price per pound (cents)	Value of production (1,000 dollars)
1990	3,220	61.7	198,674	54	106,688
1995	2,655	79.5	211,073	69	144,585
2000	2,622	84.0	220,286	60	132,865
2005	2,409	72.5	174,614	92	160,994
2009	2,498	58.6	146,416	147	215,671
2010	2,692	65.6	176,462	162	285,692
2011	2,491	59.6	148,357	177	261,850
2012	2,624	56.1	147,092	195	286,976

[1] Honey producing colonies are the maximum number of colonies from which honey was taken during the year. It is possible to take honey from colonies which did not survive the entire year.

Source: U.S. Department of Agriculture, National Agricultural Statistics Service, *Honey*, March 2013, and earlier editions. See also <http://www.nass.usda.gov/Surveys/Guide_to_NASS_Surveys/Bee_and_Honey/index.asp>.

Table 891. Farmers Markets Characteristics: 2005

[In percent. Based on 2006 National Farmers Market Survey. A farmers market is defined as a retail outlet in which two or more vendors sell agricultural products directly to customers through a common marketing channel. Markets included were in business in the 2005 season and conducted 51 percent of their retail sales directly with consumers]

Characteristic	Total, U.S.	Region [1]						
		North-east	Mid-Atlantic	South-east	North Central	South-west	Rocky Mountain	Far West
Number of vendors:								
Less than 10	23.9	42.4	37.4	24.1	17.8	32.3	15.9	9.4
10 to 19	25.3	27.9	28.4	22.8	29.4	29.0	19.3	12.5
20 to 39	29.0	23.6	22.6	29.7	32.3	17.7	28.4	35.6
40 or more	21.8	6.1	11.6	23.4	20.5	21.0	36.4	42.5
Vendor sales:								
$1 to $5,000	71.4	70.0	61.2	68.1	81.4	71.6	80.4	56.1
$5,001 to $25,000	22.1	26.2	22.8	25.2	15.5	23.0	18.3	31.5
$25,000 to $100,000	5.9	3.8	15.4	4.3	2.9	5.3	1.3	11.8
$100,001 and above	0.6	–	0.7	2.4	0.2	0.2	–	0.6
Months of operation:								
Year-round	12.1	3.5	13.7	19.6	4.1	17.5	4.3	35.4
Seasonal	87.9	96.5	86.3	80.4	95.9	82.5	95.7	64.6
Less than 4 months	20.0	26.3	15.5	16.9	19.2	22.2	39.6	11.4
4 to 6 months	59.5	68.0	57.4	42.6	72.0	47.6	52.7	42.9
7 to 9 months	7.6	2.3	12.9	18.2	4.6	9.5	3.3	8.6
More than 9 months	12.9	3.4	14.2	22.3	4.2	20.6	4.4	37.1
Source of goods sold:								
Grew products sold (their own products)	(NA)	65.0	72.3	69.8	76.8	78.0	60.3	68.6
Organic products	47.0	67.3	37.2	35.5	39.8	30.4	56.8	74.5
Locally grown	87.9	89.3	84.8	90.5	91.2	80.6	88.1	82.1
Pasture raised/free range	38.4	33.6	40.2	21.6	42.5	32.3	34.3	46.3
Natural	46.9	39.3	41.1	45.9	50.9	32.3	55.2	50.4
Hormone or antibiotic free	29.3	20.5	27.7	20.3	34.4	19.4	28.4	36.6
Chemical free/pesticide free	47.6	36.9	39.3	45.9	46.9	41.9	56.7	65.0
Other	12.3	13.9	13.4	12.2	7.3	19.4	16.4	17.1

– Represents zero. NA Not available. [1] Composition of regions—Northeast: Connecticut, Maine, Massachusetts, New Hampshire, New York, Rhode Island, and Vermont. Mid-Atlantic: Delaware, District of Columbia, Maryland, New Jersey, Pennsylvania, Virginia, and West Virginia. Southeast: Alabama, Florida, Georgia, Kentucky, Mississippi, North Carolina, South Carolina, and Tennessee. North Central: Illinois, Indiana, Iowa, Kansas, Minnesota, Missouri, Nebraska, North Dakota, Ohio, South Dakota, and Wisconsin. Southwest: Arkansas, Louisiana, Oklahoma, and Texas. Rocky Mountain: Arizona, Colorado, Idaho, New Mexico, Montana, Utah, and Wyoming. Far West: Alaska, California, Hawaii, Nevada, Oregon, and Washington.

Source: U.S. Department of Agriculture, Agricultural Marketing Service, *National Farmers Market Manager Survey 2006*, May 2009. See also <http://www.ams.usda.gov/AMSv1.0/FARMERSMARKETS>.

Table 892. Horticultural Specialty Crop Operations, Value of Sales, and Total Land Area Used to Grow Horticultural Crops: 2009

[Horticultural specialty operation is defined as any place that produced and sold $10,000 or more of horticultural specialty products]

Item	Operations	Value of sales (1,000)	Total land area [1]			
			Greenhouses (1,000 square feet)	Shade structures (1,000 square feet)	Natural shade (acres)	Area in open (acres)
Horticultural specialty crops, total [2]	**21,585**	**11,687,323**	**859,063**	**406,072**	**8,160**	**572,269**
Annual bedding/garden plants	7,989	2,305,913	258,823	13,858	140	6,815
Herbaceous perennial plants	6,416	843,788	27,101	4,330	314	3,981
Potted flowering plants for indoor or patio use	4,043	871,474	62,208	23,893	41	1,693
Foliage plants for indoor or patio use	2,728	509,873	39,583	76,645	144	2,314
Cut flowers	1,703	403,254	53,495	14,248	76	12,068
Cut cultivated greens	634	84,148	5,443	152,512	2,835	2,998
Nursery stock sold	8,441	3,850,363	217,482	87,228	4,184	323,539
Propagative material [3]	1,178	601,657	29,733	3,208	53	8,169
Sod, sprigs, or plugs	1,403	876,847	419	36	(D)	85,842
Dried bulbs, corms, rhizomes, and tubers	223	48,512	183	(D)	(D)	3,736
Food crops grown under protection	1,476	553,270	61,324	1,562	19	5,863
Transplants for commercial vegetable production [4]	502	330,647	32,095	467	4	7,250
Vegetable seeds	340	89,031	163	(D)	–	38,819
Flower seeds	141	30,825	289	308	2	5,695
Aquatic plants	375	26,000	1,373	134	1	1,320
Cut Christmas trees	2,699	249,821	1,010	95	84	45,091
Other	212	11,901	68,340	27,519	227	17,075

D Withheld to avoid disclosure. – Represents zero. [1] Total land area represents the land utilized on the operation as the area used for horticultural production. Includes volume of stacked benches and stacked pots and the area used to produce multiple crop types. [2] Excludes acres in production for Christmas trees or sod, sprigs, or plugs. [3] Includes cuttings, plug seedlings, liners, tissue cultured plantlets, and prefinished plants. [4] Includes strawberries.

Source: U.S. Department of Agriculture, National Agricultural Statistics Service, *2009 Census of Horticultural Specialties*, Vol. 3, AC-07-SS-3. See also <http://www.agcensus.usda.gov/Publications/Census_of_Horticulture_Specialties/>.

Table 893. Meat Supply and Use: 2000 to 2011 and Preliminary 2012

[In millions of pounds (carcass weight equivalent) (82,372 represents 82,372,000,000). Carcass weight equivalent is the weight of the animal minus entrails, head, hide, and internal organs; includes fat and bone. Covers federal and state inspected, and farm slaughtered]

Year and type of meat	Production	Imports	Supply [1]	Exports	Consumption [2]	Ending stocks
RED MEAT AND POULTRY						
2000	82,372	4,144	88,460	9,343	77,073	2,044
2005	86,783	4,856	93,787	9,274	82,328	2,185
2009	90,632	3,758	96,841	13,497	81,350	1,994
2010	91,769	3,458	97,221	13,965	81,142	2,114
2011	92,387	3,151	97,652	15,760	79,927	1,965
2012 [3]	92,601	3,310	97,876	16,021	79,649	2,207
ALL RED MEATS						
2000	46,299	4,127	51,313	3,760	46,556	996
2005	45,849	4,803	51,805	3,373	47,367	1,066
2009	49,412	3,631	54,350	6,045	47,191	1,114
2010	49,180	3,322	53,616	6,539	45,932	1,145
2011	49,346	3,021	53,513	7,993	11,358	1,162
2012 [3]	49,552	3,173	53,887	7,850	44,779	1,259
Beef:						
2000	26,888	3,032	30,332	2,468	27,338	525
2005	24,787	3,599	29,022	697	27,754	571
2009	26,068	2,626	29,336	1,935	26,836	565
2010	26,412	2,297	29,274	2,299	26,390	585
2011	26,281	2,057	28,923	2,785	25,538	600
2012 [3]	25,996	2,219	28,815	2,455	25,752	608
Pork:						
2000	18,952	965	20,378	1,287	18,639	453
2005	20,705	1,024	22,239	2,666	19,093	480
2009	23,020	834	24,489	4,094	19,870	525
2010	22,456	859	23,840	4,224	19,075	541
2011	22,775	803	24,120	5,189	18,388	542
2012 [3]	23,270	801	24,613	5,384	18,604	625
Veal:						
2000	225	(NA)	230	(NA)	225	5
2005	165	(NA)	169	(NA)	164	5
2009	147	(NA)	156	(NA)	147	9
2010	145	(NA)	154	(NA)	150	4
2011	136	(NA)	140	(NA)	137	3
2012 [3]	126	(NA)	129	(NA)	124	5
Lamb and mutton:						
2000	234	130	372	5	354	13
2005	191	180	375	9	356	10
2009	177	171	369	16	338	15
2010	168	166	349	16	318	15
2011	153	162	330	19	294	17
2012 [3]	161	153	331	11	299	21
POULTRY, TOTAL						
2000	36,073	16	37,147	5,583	30,516	1,048
2005	40,935	54	41,981	5,902	34,961	1,119
2009	41,220	127	42,491	7,452	34,159	880
2010	42,589	136	43,605	7,426	35,209	969
2011	43,040	130	44,139	7,767	35,569	803
2012 [3]	43,049	137	43,989	8,171	34,870	948
Broilers:						
2000	30,209	13	31,017	4,918	25,302	798
2005	34,986	42	35,730	5,203	29,617	910
2009	35,131	99	35,974	6,818	28,540	616
2010	36,515	107	37,238	6,765	29,700	773
2011	36,804	107	37,684	6,971	30,123	590
2012 [3]	36,643	112	37,345	7,281	29,413	651
Mature chicken:						
2000	531	2	541	220	312	9
2005	516	3	522	130	390	2
2009	500	8	511	100	408	2
2010	503	4	510	79	427	4
2011	521	2	527	93	432	2
2012 [3]	517	2	521	90	430	1
Turkeys:						
2000	5,333	1	5,589	445	4,902	241
2005	5,432	9	5,730	570	4,954	206
2009	5,589	20	6,006	534	5,210	262
2010	5,570	25	5,857	582	5,083	192
2011	5,715	21	5,928	703	5,014	211
2012 [3]	5,889	23	6,123	800	5,027	296

NA Not available. [1] Total supply equals production plus imports plus ending stocks of previous year. [2] Includes shipments to territories. [3] Preliminary data.

Source: U.S. Department of Agriculture, Economic Research Service, "Livestock and Meat Domestic Data," <http://www.ers.usda.gov/data-products/livestock-meat-domestic-data.aspx>, accessed June 2013.

Table 894. Livestock Inventory and Production: 1990 to 2012

[95.8 represents 95,800,000. Production in live weight; includes animals-for-slaughter market, younger animals shipped to other states for feeding or breeding purposes, farm slaughter and custom slaughter consumed on farms where produced, minus livestock shipped into states for feeding or breeding with an adjustment for changes in inventory]

Type of livestock	Unit	1990	1995	2000	2005	2007	2008	2009	2010	2011	2012
ALL CATTLE [1]											
Inventory: [2] Number on farms	Mil.	95.8	102.8	98.2	95.0	96.6	96.0	94.5	93.9	92.7	90.8
Total value	Bil. dol.	59.0	63.2	67.1	87.0	89.1	95.1	82.4	78.2	87.8	100.8
Value per head	Dol.	616	615	683	916	922	990	872	832	947	1,111
Production: Quantity	Bil. lb.	39.2	42.5	43.0	41.2	41.4	41.6	41.2	41.6	41.6	41.2
Beef, price per 100 pounds	Dol.	74.60	61.80	68.60	89.70	89.90	89.10	80.30	92.20	113.00	122.00
Calves, price per 100 pounds	Dol.	95.60	73.10	104.00	135.00	119.00	110.00	105.00	117.00	142.00	168.00
Value of production	Bil. dol.	29.3	24.7	28.5	36.3	36.0	35.6	32.0	37.0	45.2	49.2
HOGS AND PIGS											
Inventory: [3] Number on farms	Mil.	53.8	59.7	59.3	61.0	62.5	68.2	67.2	64.9	64.9	66.4
Total value	Bil. dol.	4.3	3.2	4.3	6.3	5.6	5.0	6.0	5.4	6.9	8.2
Value per head	Dol.	79	53	72	103	90	73	89	83	106	123
Production: Quantity	Bil. lb.	21.3	24.4	25.7	27.4	29.6	31.4	31.4	30.4	31.1	32.2
Price per 100 pounds	Dol.	53.70	40.50	42.30	50.20	46.60	47.00	41.60	54.10	65.30	64.20
Value of production	Bil. dol.	11.3	9.8	10.8	13.6	13.5	14.5	12.6	16.1	20.2	20.4
SHEEP AND LAMBS											
Inventory: [2] Number on farms	Mil.	11.4	9.0	7.0	6.1	6.1	6.0	5.7	5.6	5.5	5.4
Total value	Mil. dol.	901	671	670	798	818	823	765	761	931	1,185
Value per head	Dol.	79	93	95	130	134	138	133	135	170	221
Production: Quantity	Mil. lb.	781	602	512	472	440	417	422	405	(NA)	(NA)
Value of production	Mil. dol.	374	414	365	451	363	351	365	443	(NA)	(NA)

NA Not available. [1] Includes milk cows. [2] As of January 1. [3] As of December 1 of preceding year.

Source: U.S. Department of Agriculture, National Agricultural Statistics Service, "Quick Stats," <http://quickstats.nass.usda.gov/>, accessed May 2013. Also, *Meat Animals--Production, Disposition, and Income Final Estimates 1998-2002*, May 2004; and *Meat Animals--Production, Disposition, and Income Final Estimates 2003-2007*, May 2009. See also <http://www.nass.usda.gov/Publications/index.asp>.

Table 895. Livestock Operations by Size of Herd: 2000 to 2012

[In thousands (1,076 represents 1,076,000). An operation is any place having one or more head on hand at any time during the year]

Size of herd	2000	2010	2011	2012	Size of herd	2000	2010	2011	2012
CATTLE [1]					MILK COWS [2]				
Total operations	**1,076**	**935**	**922**	**915**	**Total operations**	**105**	**63**	**60**	**58**
1 to 49 head	671	635	627	624	1 to 49 head	53	31	30	29
50 to 99 head	186	129	127	125	50 to 99 head	31	16	15	15
100 to 499 head	192	142	139	137	100 head or more	21	16	16	15
500 to 999 head	19	19	19	18					
1,000 head or more	10	11	11	11	HOGS AND PIGS				
					Total operations	**87**	**69**	**69**	**68**
					1 to 99 head	50	49	49	49
BEEF COWS [2]					100 to 499 head	17	5	5	5
Total operations	**831**	**742**	**734**	**729**	500 to 999 head	8	3	2	2
1 to 49 head	655	588	583	581	1,000 to 1,999 head	6	4	3	3
50 to 99 head	100	82	81	79	2,000 to 4,999 head	5	5	6	6
100 to 499 head	71	66	64	63	5,000 head or more	2	3	3	3
500 head or more	6	6	6	6					

[1] Includes calves. [2] Included in operations with cattle.

Source: U.S. Department of Agriculture, National Agricultural Statistics Service, *Livestock Operations Final Estimates 2003–2007*, March 2009; and *Farms, Land in Farms, and Livestock Operations 2012 Summary*, February 2013. See also <http://www.nass.usda.gov/Publications/index.asp>.

Table 896. Hogs and Pigs—Number, Production, and Slaughter by States: 2010 to 2012

[64,925 represents 64,925,000. Production in live weight. See headnote Table 894]

State	Number on farms [1] (1,000)			Quantity produced (mil. lb.)			Value of production (mil. dol.)			Commercial slaughter [2] (mil. lb.)	
	2010	2011	2012	2010	2011	2012	2010	2011	2012	2011	2012
U.S. [3]	**64,925**	**66,361**	**66,413**	**30,437**	**31,066**	**32,244**	**16,095**	**20,176**	**20,389**	**30,422**	**31,092**
IA	19,100	20,000	20,600	9,244	9,816	10,372	4,521	5,944	6,192	8,177	8,292
NC	9,000	8,900	9,000	3,767	3,663	3,921	2,178	2,493	2,550	2,997	3,098
MN	7,700	7,800	7,650	3,699	3,703	4,028	1,856	2,314	2,429	2,782	2,880
IL	4,400	4,650	4,600	1,926	1,911	2,004	1,121	1,351	1,387	2,701	2,988
IN	3,650	3,850	3,800	1,754	1,762	1,779	901	1,098	1,097	2,281	2,289
NE	3,150	3,150	3,000	1,367	1,318	1,280	811	906	868	2,105	2,155
MO	2,900	2,750	2,750	1,288	1,322	1,340	711	934	921	2,270	2,295

[1] As of December 1. [2] Includes slaughter in federally inspected and other slaughter plants; excludes animals slaughtered on farms. [3] Includes other states, not shown separately.

Source: U.S. Department of Agriculture, National Agricultural Statistics Service, *Meat Animals Production, Disposition and Income 2012 Summary*, April 2013, and *Livestock Slaughter 2012 Summary*, April 2013. See also <http://www.nass.usda.gov/Publications/index.asp>.

Table 897. Cattle and Calves—Number, Production, and Value by State: 2010 to 2013

[92,682 represents 92,682,000. Includes milk cows. See headnote, Table 894]

State	Number on farms [1] (1,000)			Production (mil. lb.)			Value of production (mil. dol.)			Commercial slaughter [2] (mil. lb.)	
	2011	2012	2013	2010	2011	2012	2010	2011	2012	2011	2012
U.S. [3]	92,682	90,769	89,300	41,569	41,608	41,208	36,969	45,186	49,214	43,402	42,818
TX	13,300	11,900	11,300	6,789	7,177	6,337	6,097	8,101	7,785	8,323	8,090
NE	6,200	6,450	6,300	4,553	4,584	5,102	4,137	4,978	6,089	9,056	9,164
KS	6,300	6,100	5,850	4,090	4,010	3,780	3,444	4,233	4,368	8,257	8,114
CA	5,200	5,350	5,300	1,974	2,094	2,195	1,338	2,014	2,288	2,228	2,224
OK	5,100	4,500	4,200	2,216	2,268	2,074	2,178	2,647	2,641	26	24
IA	3,900	3,900	3,850	1,809	1,757	1,880	1,672	1,967	2,293	(D)	(D)
SD	3,700	3,650	3,850	1,481	1,467	1,519	1,559	1,757	1,986	(D)	(D)
MO	3,950	3,900	3,650	1,256	1,282	1,192	1,249	1,587	1,633	78	62
WI	3,450	3,400	3,450	1,159	1,150	1,137	864	1,160	1,271	2,268	2,087
CO	2,650	2,750	2,600	1,725	1,677	1,765	1,770	1,932	2,222	3,278	3,347
MT	2,500	2,500	2,600	1,112	1,020	1,067	1,042	1,108	1,239	23	24

D Data withheld to limit disclosure. [1] As of January 1. [2] Data cover cattle only. Includes slaughter in federally inspected and other slaughter plants; excludes animals slaughtered on farms. [3] Includes other states, not shown separately.

Source: U.S. Department of Agriculture, National Agricultural Statistics Service, *Meat Animals—Production, Disposition and Income 2012 Summary*, April 2013, and *Livestock Slaughter 2012 Summary*, April 2013. See also <http://www.nass.usda.gov/Publications/index.asp>.

Table 898. Milk Cows—Number, Production, and Value by State: 2010 to 2012

[9,119 represents 9,119,000]

State	Number on farms [1] (1,000)			Milk produced on farms [2] (mil. lb.)			Milk produced per milk cow (pounds) [2]			Value of production [3] (mil. dol.)		
	2010	2011	2012	2010	2011	2012	2010	2011	2012	2010	2011	2012
U.S. [4]	9,119	9,194	9,233	192,848	196,164	200,324	21,148	21,336	21,697	31,531	39,714	37,188
CA	1,754	1,769	1,782	40,385	41,462	41,801	23,025	23,438	23,457	5,933	7,687	6,906
WI	1,262	1,265	1,270	26,035	26,058	27,224	20,630	20,599	21,436	4,192	5,290	5,281
NY	611	610	610	12,713	12,838	13,196	20,807	21,046	21,633	2,212	2,747	2,560
ID	564	578	580	12,779	13,256	13,558	22,658	22,934	23,376	1,904	2,439	2,427
PA	541	541	536	10,737	10,547	10,493	19,847	19,495	19,576	1,965	2,331	2,099
MN	470	468	465	9,102	8,890	9,071	19,366	18,996	19,508	1,465	1,822	1,778
TX	413	431	436	8,828	9,582	9,596	21,375	22,232	22,009	1,510	1,993	1,794
MI	358	366	375	8,333	8,478	8,889	23,277	23,164	23,704	1,417	1,780	1,680

[1] Average number during year. Represents cows and heifers that have calved, kept for milk; excluding heifers not yet fresh. [2] Excludes milk sucked by calves. [3] Valued at average returns per 100 pounds of milk in combined marketings of milk and cream. Includes value of milk fed to calves. [4] Includes other states, not shown separately.

Source: U.S. Department of Agriculture, National Agricultural Statistics Service, *Milk Production, Disposition, and Income 2012 Summary*, April 2013 and earlier editions. See also <http://www.nass.usda.gov/Publications/index.asp>.

Table 899. Milk Production and Manufactured Dairy Products: 1990 to 2012

[193 represents 193,000]

Item	Unit	1990	2000	2005	2007	2008	2009	2010	2011	2012
Number of farms with milk cows	1,000	**193**	**105**	**78**	**70**	**67**	**65**	**63**	**60**	**58**
Cows and heifers that have calved, kept for milk	Mil. head	10.0	9.2	9.1	9.2	9.3	9.2	9.1	9.2	9.2
Milk produced on farms	Bil. lb.	148	167	177	186	190	189	193	196	200
Production per cow	1,000 lb.	14.8	18.2	19.6	20.2	20.4	20.6	21.1	21.3	21.7
Milk marketed by producers [1]	Bil. lb.	146	166	176	185	189	188	192	195	199
Value of milk produced	Bil. dol.	20.4	20.7	26.9	35.7	35.1	24.5	31.5	39.7	37.2
Cash receipts from marketing of milk and cream [1]	Bil. dol.	20.1	20.6	26.7	35.5	34.8	24.3	31.4	39.5	37.0
Number of dairy manufacturing plants	Number	**1,723**	**1,164**	**1,088**	**1,123**	**1,125**	**1,203**	**1,250**	**1,278**	**1,288**
Manufactured dairy products:										
Butter (including whey butter)	Mil. lb.	1,302	1,256	1,347	1,533	1,644	1,572	1,564	1,810	1,860
Cheese, total [2]	Mil. lb.	6,059	8,258	9,149	9,777	9,913	10,074	10,433	10,595	10,890
American (excl. full-skim American)	Mil. lb.	2,894	3,642	3,808	3,877	4,109	4,203	4,289	4,267	4,358
Cream and Neufchatel	Mil. lb.	431	687	715	773	764	767	745	715	808
All Italian varieties	Mil. lb.	2,207	3,289	3,803	4,199	4,121	4,181	4,416	4,585	4,634
Cottage cheese—creamed and lowfat	Mil. lb.	832	735	784	774	714	731	719	704	709
Nonfat dry milk [3]	Mil. lb.	902	1,457	1,210	1,298	1,519	1,512	1,563	1,499	1,764
Dry whey [4]	Mil. lb.	1,143	1,188	1,041	1,134	1,082	1,001	1,013	1,010	999
Yogurt, plain and fruit-flavored	Mil. lb.	(NA)	1,837	3,058	3,476	3,570	3,839	4,181	4,271	4,416
Ice cream, regular	Mil. gal.	824	980	960	956	931	918	929	888	899
Ice cream, lowfat [5]	Mil. gal.	352	373	360	383	384	400	415	415	467

NA Not available. [1] Comprises sales to plants and dealers, and retail sales by farmers direct to consumers. [2] Includes varieties not shown separately. [3] Includes dry skim milk for animal feed through 2000. [4] Includes animal but excludes modified whey production. [5] Includes freezer-made milkshake in most states.

Source: U.S. Department of Agriculture, National Agricultural Statistics Service, *Milk Disposition and Income Final Estimates 2003-2007*, May 2009; *Dairy Products 2012 Summary*, April 2013; *Milk Production, Disposition, and Income 2012 Summary*, April 2013; and *Farms, Land in Farms, And Livestock Operations, 2012 Summary*, February 2013. See also <http://www.nass.usda.gov/Publications/index.asp>.

Table 900. Milk Production and Commercial Use in All Products: 2000 to 2011 and Preliminary 2012

[In billions of pounds milkfat basis (167.4 represents 167,400,000,000) except as noted. This table has been revised due to a change in the data source; therefore, data might not be comparable to data presented in previous editions of the *Statistical Abstract of the United States*]

Year	Produc-tion	Farm use	Commercial Farm market-ings	Commercial Begin-ning stocks	Imports	Com-mercial supply, total	Commercial USDA net removals	Commercial Ending stocks	Disap-pear-ance	Milk price per 100 pounds [1] (dollars)
2000......	167.4	1.3	166.1	6.1	4.4	176.7	0.8	6.9	169.0	12.40
2005......	176.9	1.1	175.9	7.2	5.1	188.1	–	8.0	180.2	15.19
2008......	190.0	1.1	188.9	10.4	3.9	203.2	–	10.0	193.1	18.45
2009......	189.3	1.0	187.3	10.0	4.1	201.4	0.7	11.3	189.4	12.93
2010......	192.8	1.0	191.9	11.3	3.1	206.3	0.1	10.9	195.3	16.26
2011......	196.2	1.0	195.2	10.9	3.2	209.4	–	11.0	198.4	20.14
2012 [2].....	200.3	1.0	199.4	11.0	3.7	214.0	–	12.2	201.8	18.51

– Represents zero. [1] Wholesale price received by farmers for all milk delivered to plants and dealers. [2] Preliminary.

Source: U.S. Department of Agriculture, Economic Research Service, "Dairy Data," <http://www.ers.usda.gov/data-products/dairy-data. aspx>, accessed June 2013.

Table 901. Broiler, Turkey, and Egg Production: 1990 to 2012

[353 represents 353,000,000. For years ending November 30, except as noted]

Item	Unit	1990	1995	2000	2005	2007	2008	2009	2010	2011	2012
Chickens: [1]											
Number [2]................	Million	353	388	437	456	459	447	452	455	448	456
Value per head [2]........	Dollars	2.29	2.41	2.44	2.52	2.95	3.39	3.34	3.59	3.80	4.06
Value, total [2]............	Mil. dol.	808	935	1,064	1,150	1,352	1,517	1,508	1,633	1,703	1,847
Number sold............	Million	208	180	218	194	168	176	176	173	182	178
Price per pound........	Cents	9.6	6.5	5.7	6.5	5.6	6.6	(NA)	(NA)	(NA)	(NA)
Value of sales..........	Mil. dol.	94	60	64	65	51	62	65	73	81	79
PRODUCTION											
Broilers: [3]											
Number.................	Million	5,864	7,326	8,284	8,872	8,907	9,009	8,550	8,624	8,608	8,438
Weight..................	Bil. lb.	25.6	34.2	41.6	47.9	49.3	50.4	47.8	49.2	50.1	49.5
Price per pound........	Cents	32.6	34.4	33.6	43.6	43.6	(NA)	(NA)	(NA)	(NA)	(NA)
Production value........	Mil. dol.	8,366	11,762	13,989	20,878	21,514	23,203	21,823	23,692	22,988	24,765
Turkeys:											
Number.................	Million	282	292	270	250	267	273	247	24	249	254
Weight..................	Bil. lb.	6.0	6.8	7.0	7.0	7.6	7.9	7.1	7.1	7.3	7.5
Price per pound........	Cents	39.6	41.0	40.6	44.5	52.3	56.5	(NA)	(NA)	(NA)	(NA)
Production value........	Mil. dol.	2,393	2,769	2,828	3,108	3,952	4,477	3,573	4,374	4,961	5,441
Eggs:											
Average number of layers..................	Thousand	270,946	294,350	329,067	345,027	346,498	339,131	337,848	340,335	338,475	339,698
Eggs per layer..........	Number	25	254	257	262	263	266	268	269	271	274
Total production........	Billion	68.1	74.8	84.7	90.3	91.1	90.0	90.5	91.5	91.9	92.9
Price per dozen.........	Cents	70.8	62.5	61.7	54.0	88.5	109.0	(NA)	(NA)	(NA)	(NA)
Production value........	Mil. dol.	4,021	3,893	4,359	4,067	6,719	8,216	6,166	6,535	7,316	7,823

NA Not available. [1] Excludes commercial broilers. [2] As of December 1. [3] Young chickens of the heavy breeds and other meat-type birds, to be marketed at 2–5 lbs. live weight and from which no pullets are kept for egg production. Not included in sales of chickens.

Source: U.S. Department of Agriculture, National Agricultural Statistics Service, *Poultry Production and Value Final Estimates 1998–2002*, April 2004; *Turkeys Final Estimates 1998–2002*, April 2004; *Poultry Production and Value Final Estimates 2003–2007*, May 2009; *Chickens and Eggs Final Estimates 1998–2002*, April 2004; *Chickens and Eggs Final Estimates 2003–2007*, March 2009; *Poultry—Production and Value*, annual; and *Chickens and Eggs*, annual. See also <http://www.nass.usda.gov/Publications/index.asp>.

Table 902. Broiler Chickens and Turkey Production by State: 2010 to 2012

[In millions of pounds, live weight production (49,153 represents 49,153,000,000)]

State	Broiler Chickens 2010	2011	2012	Turkeys 2010	2011	2012	State	Broiler Chickens 2010	2011	2012	Turkeys 2010	2011	2012
U.S. [1].....	49,153	50,082	49,530	7,111	7,274	7,547	MS......	4,766	4,626	4,508	(NA)	(NA)	(NA)
AL..........	5,787	5,820	5,620	(NA)	(NA)	(NA)	MO......	(NA)	1,369	1,304	583	565	576
AR..........	5,938	5,856	5,765	552	607	577	NC......	5,419	5,587	5,678	969	1,030	1,177
CA..........	(NA)	(NA)	(NA)	409	422	431	OH......	377	376	379	193	201	219
DE..........	1,625	1,525	1,505	(NA)	(NA)	(NA)	OK......	1,503	1,589	1,419	(NA)	(NA)	(NA)
FL..........	314	383	357	(NA)	(NA)	(NA)	PA......	839	871	865	175	176	167
GA..........	6,883	7,426	7,626	(NA)	(NA)	(NA)	SC......	1,557	1,542	1,537	428	481	498
IL...........	(NA)	(NA)	(NA)	(NA)	(NA)	(NA)	SD......	(NA)	(NA)	(NA)	191	186	194
IN..........	(NA)	(NA)	(NA)	574	578	606	TN......	987	990	872	(NA)	(NA)	(NA)
IA..........	(NA)	(NA)	(NA)	(NA)	(NA)	(NA)	TX......	3,645	3,657	3,495	(NA)	(NA)	(NA)
KY..........	1,673	1,705	1,733	(NA)	(NA)	(NA)	UT......	(NA)	(NA)	(NA)	117	105	103
MD........	1,433	1,649	1,611	(NA)	(NA)	(NA)	VA......	1,292	1,292	1,299	449	460	449
MI..........	(NA)	(NA)	(NA)	(NA)	(NA)	(NA)	WV......	346	342	376	88	92	96
MN..........	231	241	264	1,175	1,163	1,164	WI......	198	195	217	(NA)	(NA)	(NA)

NA Not available. [1] Includes other states, not shown separately.

Source: U.S. Department of Agriculture, National Agricultural Statistics Service, *Poultry—Production and Value*, April 2013, and earlier reports. See also <http://www.nass.usda.gov/Publications/index.asp>.

Table 903. Vegetables and Dry Edible Beans—Supply and Utilization: 2000 to 2012

[40,556 represents 40,556,000,000. Data for calendar year except where noted. Cwt = hundredweight (100 pounds). Vegetable data excludes melons]

Item	Unit	2000	2005	2008	2009	2010	2011	2012 [1]
VEGETABLES, FRESH MARKET								
Production	Mil. lbs.	40,556	40,332	38,877	38,267	38,044	37,978	38,590
Imports	Mil. lbs.	5,492	7,773	9,005	9,307	10,924	11,087	11,478
Total supply	Mil. lbs.	47,393	49,597	49,354	49,048	50,537	50,546	51,646
Exports	Mil. lbs.	3,710	3,712	3,473	3,236	3,383	3,434	3,579
Ending stocks	Mil. lbs.	1,266	1,280	1,475	1,570	1,481	1,578	1,338
Domestic consumption	Mil. lbs.	41,461	43,864	43,661	43,516	44,838	44,721	45,984
Per capita consumption	Lbs.	146.8	148.1	143.2	141.5	144.7	143.4	146.3
VEGETABLES, PROCESSED MARKET [2]								
Production	Mil. lbs.	35,369	33,264	36,369	40,451	36,633	35,308	37,867
Imports	Mil. lbs.	3,581	5,562	6,249	6,179	6,354	6,507	6,635
Total supply	Mil. lbs.	62,174	62,652	67,231	71,484	71,335	69,790	71,428
Exports	Mil. lbs.	4,479	4,874	7,411	6,236	6,590	8,053	8,027
Ending stocks	Mil. lbs.	23,291	20,838	24,854	28,348	27,976	26,926	27,776
Domestic consumption	Mil. lbs.	34,404	36,940	34,966	36,899	36,769	34,812	35,626
Per capita consumption	Lbs.	121.8	124.7	114.7	120.0	118.7	111.6	113.4
POTATOES, FRESH MARKET								
Utilized production [3]	Mil. lbs.	13,185	12,076	10,995	11,059	11,342	10,534	11,369
Imports	Mil. lbs.	806	788	1,178	936	916	1,084	778
Total supply	Mil. lbs.	13,990	12,863	12,173	11,995	12,258	11,618	12,147
Exports	Mil. lbs.	677	639	642	729	856	990	985
Domestic consumption	Mil. lbs.	13,314	12,224	11,531	11,267	11,402	10,628	11,162
Per capita consumption	Lbs.	47.2	41.3	37.8	36.7	36.8	34.1	35.5
DRY EDIBLE BEANS								
Production	1,000 cwt	26,543	26,576	25,558	25,427	31,801	19,890	31,925
Imports	1,000 cwt	1,289	2,249	3,271	2,969	2,888	3,202	3,059
Exports	1,000 cwt	7,822	5,598	9,025	9,315	9,191	8,912	11,664
Domestic consumption	Mil. lbs.	2,143	1,795	1,956	1,855	2,171	1,718	2,041
Per capita consumption	Lbs.	7.6	6.1	6.4	6.0	7.0	5.5	6.5

[1] Preliminary. [2] Includes vegetables for canning and freezing. Excludes potatoes and mushrooms. [3] Crop year utilization for the past season and the current season distributed on a calendar year basis using National Agricultural Statistics Service potato marketing distributions.

Source: U.S. Department of Agriculture, Economic Research Service, *Vegetable and Pulses Yearbook*, June 2013. See also <http://www.ers.usda.gov/data-products/vegetables-and-pulses-data.aspx>.

Section 18
Forestry, Fishing, and Mining

This section presents data on the area, ownership, production, trade, reserves, and disposition of natural resources. Natural resources is defined here as including forestry, fisheries, and mining and mineral products.

Forestry—Presents data on the area, ownership, and timber resource of commercial timberland; forestry statistics covering the National Forests and Forest Service cooperative programs; product data for lumber, pulpwood, woodpulp, paper and paperboard, and similar data.

The principal sources of data relating to forests and forest products are *Forest Resources of the United States, 2007; Timber Demand and Technology Assessment; U.S. Timber Production, Trade, Consumption, and Price Statistics, 1965 to 2005; Land Areas of the National Forest System*, issued annually by the Forest Service of the U.S. Department of Agriculture; *Agricultural Statistics* issued by the Department of Agriculture; and reports of the Annual Survey of Manufactures issued by the U.S. Census Bureau, see <http://www.census.gov/manufacturing/asm/>. Further sources used in this section and issued by the U.S. Census Bureau include the annual *County Business Patterns* reports, and the 2007 Economic Census. Additional information is published in the annual *Wood Pulp and Fiber Statistics* and *The Annual Statistics of Paper, Paperboard, and Wood Pulp* of the American Forest and Paper Association, Washington, DC.

The completeness and reliability of statistics on forests and forest products vary considerably. The data for forest land area and stand volumes are much more reliable for areas that have been recently surveyed than for those for which only estimates are available. In general, more data are available for lumber and other manufactured products such as particle board and softwood panels, etc., than for the primary forest products such as poles and piling and fuelwood.

Fisheries—The principal source of data relating to fisheries is *Fisheries of the United States*, issued annually by the National Marine Fisheries Service (NMFS), National Oceanic and Atmospheric Administration (NOAA). The NMFS collects and disseminates data on commercial landings of fish and shellfish. Annual reports include quantity and value of commercial landings of fish and shellfish disposition of landings and number and kinds of fishing vessels and fishing gear. Reports for the fish-processing industry include annual output for the wholesaling and fish processing establishments, annual and seasonal employment. The principal source for these data is the annual *Fisheries of the United States*. Additional

government sources include Agricultural Statistics, issued by the Department of Agriculture; and Trout Production, Catfish Production, and Catfish Processing, issued by the National Agricultural Statistics service of the U.S. Department of Agriculture.

Mining and mineral products—Presents data relating to mineral industries and their products, general summary measures of production and employment, and more detailed data on production, prices, imports and exports, consumption, and distribution for specific industries and products. Data on mining and mineral products may also be found in Sections 19, 21, 28, and 30 of this *Abstract*; data on mining employment may be found in Section 12.

Mining comprises the extraction of minerals occurring naturally (coal, ores, crude petroleum, natural gas) and quarrying, well operation, milling, refining and processing, and other preparation customarily done at the mine or well site or as a part of extraction activity. (Mineral preparation plants are usually operated together with mines or quarries.) Exploration for minerals is included as is the development of mineral properties.

The principal governmental sources of these data are the *Minerals Yearbook* and *Mineral Commodity Summaries*, published by the U.S. Geological Survey, U.S. Department of the Interior, and various monthly and annual publications of the Energy Information Administration, U.S. Department of Energy. See text, Section 19, for a list of Department of Energy publications. In addition, the Census Bureau conducts a census of mineral industries every 5 years.

Mineral statistics, with principal emphasis on commodity detail, have been collected by the U.S. Geological Survey and the former Bureau of Mines since 1880. Current data in U.S. Geological Survey publications include quantity and value of nonfuel minerals produced, sold, or used by producers, or shipped; quantity of minerals stocked; crude materials treated and prepared minerals recovered; and consumption of mineral raw materials.

The Economic Census, conducted by the Census Bureau at various intervals since 1840, collects data on mineral industries. Beginning with the 1967 census, legislation provides for a census to be conducted every 5 years for years ending in "2" and "7." The most recent results, published for 2007, are based on the North American Industry Classification System (NAICS). The censuses provide, for the various types of mineral establishments, information on operating costs, capital expenditures, labor, equipment, and energy requirements in relation to their value of shipments and other receipts.

Table 904. Natural Resource–Related Industries—Establishments, Sales, Payroll, and Employees by Industry: 2002 and 2007

[183 represents $183,000,000,000. Includes only establishments of firms with payroll. Data are based on the 2002 and 2007 economic censuses, which are subject to nonsampling error. For details on methodology and nonsampling and sampling errors, see Appendix III]

Industry	2002 NAICS code [1]	Establishments (number)		Value of shipments (bil. dol.)		Annual payroll (bil. dol.)		Paid employees [2] (1,000)	
		2002	2007	2002	2007	2002	2007	2002	2007
Mining....................................	21	24,087	21,169	183	369	21	37	475	703
Oil & gas extraction..................	211	7,730	6,293	113	231	5	10	99	162
Mining (except oil & gas)...........	212	7,253	6,465	48	81	9	11	196	220
Mining support activities............	213	9,104	8,411	22	57	7	16	180	322
Manufacturing [3]......................	31–33	350,728	293,919	3,915	5,339	568	612	15	13
Wood product mfg.....................	321	17,192	14,862	89	102	16	17	540	520
Paper mfg..............................	322	5,520	4,803	154	176	21	21	491	417
Petroleum & coal products manufacturing...	324	2,268	2,284	216	606	6	8	104	105

[1] 2002 data based on North American Industry Classification System (NAICS), 2002. 2007 data based on 2007 NAICS. [2] For pay period including March 12. [3] Includes other industries, not shown separately.

Source: U.S. Census Bureau, "2007 Economic Census, "Comparative Statistics", <http://www.census.gov/econ/census07/>, accessed September 2013.

Table 905. Natural Resource–Related Industries—Establishments, Employees, and Annual Payroll by Industry: 2000 and 2011

[In units as indicated (1,791.3 represents 1,791,300; 66.58 represents $66,580,000,000). Excludes most government employees, railroad employees, self-employed persons, etc. See "General Explanation" in source for definitions and statement on reliability of data. An establishment is a single physical location where business is conducted or where services or industrial operations are performed. See Appendix III]

Industry	2007 NAICS Code [1]	Establishments (number)		Number of employees [2] (1,000)		Annual payroll (bil. dol.)	
		2000	2011	2000	2011	2000	2011
Natural resource–related industries, total..............	(X)	**72,932**	**67,715**	**1,791.3**	**1,515.1**	**66.58**	**92.78**
Forestry, fishing, hunting, and agriculture support..........	11	26,076	21,340	183.6	156.5	4.68	5.48
Forestry and logging...........................	113	13,347	8,616	83.1	53.0	2.26	2.01
Timber tract operations.....................	1131	469	387	3.3	2.0	0.13	0.10
Forest nurseries and gathering forest products...........	1132	258	175	1.7	1.6	0.07	0.05
Logging...........................	1133	12,620	8,054	78.1	49.5	2.06	1.86
Fishing, hunting and trapping.............................	114	2,671	2,401	10.0	7.5	0.34	0.36
Fishing...........................	1141	2,308	2,102	7.5	6.0	0.27	0.32
Hunting and trapping...........................	1142	363	299	2.5	1.5	0.08	0.05
Agriculture and forestry support activities.................	115	10,058	10,323	90.4	95.9	2.08	3.11
Crop production support activities...................	1151	5,061	4,516	57.6	66.0	1.35	2.16
Animal production support activities...................	1152	3,450	4,188	18.2	19.4	0.38	0.57
Forestry support activities.................	1153	1,547	1,619	14.7	10.6	0.35	0.37
Mining, quarrying and oil, and gas extraction...............	21	23,738	28,022	456.1	651.2	22.09	55.25
Oil and gas extraction...........................	211	7,740	8,095	83.0	119.0	5.39	14.48
Mining (except oil and gas)...........................	212	7,231	6,652	204.3	200.3	9.34	14.12
Coal mining...........................	2121	1,253	1,072	70.7	86.2	3.54	6.64
Metal ore mining...........................	2122	522	355	34.8	34.9	1.72	2.97
Nonmetallic mineral mining and quarrying...............	2123	5,456	5,225	98.8	79.2	4.08	4.51
Mining support activities...........................	213	8,767	13,275	168.8	332.0	7.35	26.65
Timber–related manufacturing.............................	(X)	23,118	18,353	1,151.6	707.4	39.80	32.04
Wood product manufacturing...........................	321	17,328	13,859	597.7	344.3	16.51	12.12
Sawmills and wood preservation........................	3211	4,695	3,405	131.4	79.4	3.78	2.93
Veneer, plywood and engineered wood product manufacturing...........................	3212	1,904	1,497	120.6	61.8	3.75	2.45
Other wood product manufacturing.....................	3219	10,729	8,957	345.8	203.2	8.95	6.73
Paper manufacturing...........................	322	5,790	4,494	553.9	363.0	23.29	19.92
Pulp, paper and paperboard mills.......................	3221	597	470	177.1	111.0	9.48	7.76
Converted paper product manufacturing..................	3222	5,193	4,024	376.8	252.0	13.82	12.16

X Not applicable. [1] 2000 data based on North American Industry Classification System (NAICS), 1997. 2011 data based on 2007 NAICS. [2] Covers full- and part-time employees who are on the payroll in the pay period including March 12.

Source: U.S. Census Bureau, "County Business Patterns," <http://www.census.gov/econ/cbp/index.html>, accessed June 2013.

Table 906. Gross Domestic Product of Natural Resource-Related Industries in Current and Real (2005) Dollars by Industry: 2000 to 2012

[In billions of dollars (9,951.5 represents $9,951,500,000,000). Data are based on the 2002 North American Industry Classification System (NAICS); see text, Section 15. Data include nonfactor charges (capital consumption allowances, indirect business taxes, etc.) as well as factor charges against gross product; corporate profits and capital consumption allowances have been shifted from a company to an establishment basis]

Industry	Current dollars				Chained (2005) dollars			
	2000	2005	2011	2012	2000	2005	2011	2012
All industries, total [1]..........................	9,951.5	12,623.0	15,075.7	15,684.8	11,216.4	12,623.0	13,299.1	13,593.2
Industries covered.................................	294.5	406.3	539.5	(NA)	427.4	406.3	430.0	(NA)
Percent of all industries..........................	3.0	3.2	3.6	(NA)	3.8	3.2	3.2	(NA)
Agriculture, forestry, fishing, and hunting......	95.6	127.1	173.5	168.6	103.7	127.1	122.1	117.6
Farms...	73.6	102	138.7	(NA)	83.5	102	91.9	(NA)
Forestry, fishing, and related activities.......	22	25.1	34.9	(NA)	20.5	25.1	29.9	(NA)
Mining..	108.9	192.3	289.9	285.2	232.7	192.3	234.6	243.3
Oil and gas extraction.........................	67.5	128.7	174.2	(NA)	155	128.7	164.1	(NA)
Mining, except oil and gas.....................	27.8	36.3	58.4	(NA)	45.5	36.3	28.8	(NA)
Support activities for mining..................	13.7	27.3	57.3	(NA)	29.4	27.3	41.5	(NA)
Timber-related manufacturing..................	90.0	86.9	76.1	(NA)	91.0	86.9	73.3	(NA)
Wood products.................................	28.3	33	22.9	(NA)	32.8	33	32.9	(NA)
Paper products.................................	61.7	53.9	53.2	(NA)	58.2	53.9	40.4	(NA)

NA Not available. [1] Includes industries not shown separately.

Source: U.S. Bureau of Economic Analysis, Industry Economic Data, GDP-by-Industry, "Value Added by Industry" and "Real Value Added by Industry," <http://www.bea.gov/itable/>, accessed August 2013.

Table 907. Timber–Based Manufacturing Industries—Establishments, Shipments, Payroll, and Employees: 2007

[101,711,917 represents $101,711,917,000. Includes only establishments or firms with payroll. Data for industries with NAICS codes less than 6-digits were derived by summing values with the corresponding 6-digit NAICS codes. See Appendix III]

Industry	2007 NAICS code [1]	Establish-ments (number)	Value of shipments ($1,000)	Annual payroll ($1,000)	Paid employees [2]
Wood product manufacturing.......................	321	16,868	101,711,917	17,426,832	523,899
Sawmills and wood preservation....................	3211	4,102	27,911,240	3,642,165	103,413
Sawmills.......................................	321113	3,589	22,075,666	3,144,796	90,044
Wood preservation.............................	321114	513	5,835,574	497,369	13,369
Veneer, plywood, and engineered wood product manufacturing...................................	3212	1,958	22,258,829	3,829,184	106,848
Other wood product manufacturing.............................	3219	10,810	51,777,100	9,993,940	314,393
Millwork.......................................	32191	4,713	28,300,862	5,201,356	153,739
Wood container and pallet manufacturing...................	32192	2,909	7,235,876	1,519,970	58,467
All other wood product manufacturing......................	32199	3,151	16,339,726	3,274,866	102,353
Paper manufacturing..............................	322	4,988	176,687,641	20,858,769	418,241
Pulp, paper, and paperboard mills.............................	3221	486	80,550,214	7,925,398	125,483
Pulp mills......................................	32211	39	5,027,395	504,602	7,268
Paper mills....................................	32212	262	49,732,085	4,919,950	80,838
Paperboard mills..............................	32213	187	25,354,745	2,451,849	36,641
Converted paper product manufacturing.......................	3222	4,502	96,137,427	12,933,371	292,758
Paperboard container manufacturing.................	32221	2,402	50,900,190	7,387,042	165,839
Paper bag and coated and treated paper manufacturing...................................	32222	891	21,737,348	2,798,096	60,373
Stationery product manufacturing.............................	32223	549	8,242,007	1,197,456	31,628
Other converted paper product manufacturing...............	32229	654	15,024,475	1,545,024	34,780

[1] North American Industry Classification System, 2007. [2] For pay period including March 12.

Source: U.S. Census Bureau, 2007 Economic Census, "Economy–Wide Key Statistics," <http://www.census.gov/econ/census07/>, accessed September 2013.

Table 908. Timber-Based Manufacturing Industries—Employees, Payroll, and Shipments: 2011

[In thousands (10,649 represents 10,649,000). Based on the Annual Survey of Manufactures, see Appendix III]

Selected industry	2007 NAICS code [1]	All employees			Production workers, total (1,000)	Value added by manufactures		Value of shipments (mil. dol.)
		Number (1,000)	Payroll			Total (mil. dol.)	Per production worker (dol.)	
			Total (mil. dol.)	Per employee (dol.)				
Manufacturing, all industries [2]	31–33	10,649	559,518	52,540	7,440	2,295,220	308,491	5,498,599
Timber-based manufacturing, total	321–322	671	31,168	46,429	532	110,655	207,914	246,436
Percent of total manufacturing	(X)	6.30	5.57	(X)	7.15	4.82	(X)	4.48
Wood product manufacturing	321	325	11,863	36,517	263	28,711	109,273	70,558
Sawmills and wood preservation	3211	73	2,912	39,881	62	7,812	126,952	21,613
Veneer, plywood, and engineered wood product	3212	57	2,270	39,983	45	5,255	115,876	13,902
Other wood product	3219	195	6,681	34,249	156	15,644	100,372	35,043
Millwork	32191	91	3,357	36,758	73	8,092	111,343	18,025
Wood container and pallet	32192	46	1,390	30,046	38	2,946	77,114	6,545
All other wood products	32199	57	1,934	33,645	45	4,605	102,400	10,474
Paper manufacturing	322	346	19,305	55,723	269	81,944	304,095	175,877
Pulp, paper, and paperboard mills	3221	108	7,572	70,415	85	41,981	491,138	82,275
Pulp mills	32211	7	520	75,487	5	2,401	462,411	5,263
Paper mills	32212	66	4,484	68,202	53	25,559	484,601	48,627
Paperboard mills	32213	35	2,568	73,582	27	13,941	509,349	28,384
Converted paper product	3222	239	11,733	49,110	184	39,963	217,201	93,603
Paperboard container	32221	136	6,838	50,298	106	21,170	200,633	51,950
Paper bag and coated and treated paper	32222	50	2,493	50,187	37	8,694	234,842	19,997
Stationery product	32223	21	844	40,885	16	2,420	151,906	6,416
Other converted paper products	32229	33	1,558	47,719	26	7,678	300,892	15,240

X Not applicable. [1] North American Industry Classification System, 2007; see text, Section 15. [2] Includes other industries, not shown separately.

Source: U.S. Census Bureau, "Annual Survey of Manufactures, 2011," November 2012, <http://www.census.gov/manufacturing/asm/index.html>, accessed May 2013.

Table 909. Forest Land and Timberland by Type of Owner and Region: 2007

[In thousands of acres (751,228 represents 751,228,000). As of January 1. Forest land is land at least 10 percent stocked by forest trees of any size, including land that formerly had such tree cover and that will be naturally or artificially regenerated. The minimum area for classification of forest land is 1 acre or strips of timber with a crown width of at least 120 feet wide. Timberland is forest land that is producing or is capable of producing crops of industrial wood and that is not withdrawn from timber utilization by statute or administrative regulation]

Region	Forest land, total	Timberland					
		Total	Federal			State, county, and municipal	Private [1]
			Total	National forest	Other		
Total	751,228	514,213	112,733	98,721	14,015	44,994	356,485
North	172,039	164,018	11,897	10,126	1,771	25,252	126,868
Northeast	84,796	79,803	2,971	2,401	570	9,308	67,523
North Central	87,243	84,215	8,926	7,725	1,201	15,944	59,345
South	214,644	204,030	17,164	12,225	4,940	7,880	178,986
Southeast	87,889	85,665	7,559	4,970	2,590	4,689	73,417
South Central	126,756	118,365	9,605	7,255	2,350	3,191	105,569
Rocky Mountains	150,661	70,968	48,612	45,386	3,228	3,185	19,169
Great Plains	5,757	5,287	1,294	1,056	239	198	3,795
Intermountain	144,905	65,681	47,318	44,330	2,989	2,987	15,374
Pacific Coast	213,883	75,197	35,060	30,984	4,076	8,677	31,462
Alaska	126,869	11,865	4,750	3,772	978	4,344	2,771
Pacific Northwest	52,449	43,489	20,403	17,937	2,466	3,704	19,383
Pacific Southwest [2]	34,565	19,843	9,907	9,275	632	629	9,308

[1] Includes Indian lands. [2] Includes Hawaii.

Source: U.S. Forest Service, "RPA Assessment Tables," <http://www.fs.fed.us/research/rpa/>, accessed 2007.

Table 910. National Forest System Lands by State: 2012

[In thousands of acres (232,896 represents 232,896,000). As of September 30, 2012. Data do not include Delaware, District of Columbia, Iowa, Maryland, Massachusetts, New Jersey, or Rhode Island]

State	Total lands	National Forest System lands [1]	Other lands [2]	State	Total lands	National Forest System lands [1]	Other lands [2]
U.S.	**232,896**	**192,977**	**39,919**	NE.	560	352	208
				NV.	6,276	5,766	510
AL.	1,289	671	617	NH.	828	736	92
AK.	24,359	21,951	2,408	NM.	10,457	9,412	1,045
AZ.	11,891	11,265	627	NY.	16	16	–
AR.	3,553	2,599	954	NC.	3,165	1,256	1,909
CA.	24,444	20,828	3,616	ND.	1,107	1,107	–
CO.	16,035	14,537	1,498	OH.	834	241	593
CT.	–	–	–	OK.	755	401	354
FL.	1,435	1,178	257	OR.	17,580	15,692	1,888
GA.	1,858	868	990	PA.	743	513	230
HI.	–	–	–	SC.	1,376	631	748
ID.	21,658	20,465	1,193	SD.	2,452	2,018	435
IL.	923	298	625	TN.	1,276	721	555
IN.	644	203	441	TX.	1,994	755	1,239
KS.	116	108	8	UT.	9,213	8,209	1,004
KY.	2,208	814	1,394	VT.	823	401	421
LA.	1,025	604	420	VA.	3,223	1,664	1,559
ME.	93	54	40	WA.	10,115	9,292	824
MI.	4,894	2,876	2,018	WV.	1,896	1,045	851
MN.	5,467	2,841	2,626	WI.	2,023	1,534	489
MS.	2,318	1,174	1,144	WY.	9,706	9,241	465
MO.	3,060	1,494	1,567	PR.	56	28	28
MT.	19,145	17,116	2,029	VI.	–	–	–

– Represents or rounds to zero. [1] National Forest System is a nationally significant system of federally owned units of forest, range, and related land consisting of national forests, purchase units, national grasslands, land utilization project areas, experimental forest areas, experimental range areas, designated experimental areas, and other land areas; water areas; and interests in lands that are administered by USDA Forest Service or designated for administration through the Forest Service. [2] Other lands are lands within the unit boundaries in private, state, county, and municipal ownership and the federal lands over which the Forest Service has no jurisdiction. Also includes lands offered to the United States and approved for acquisition and subsequent Forest Service administration, but to which title has not yet been accepted by the United States.

Source: U.S. Forest Service, *Land Areas of the National Forest System as of September 30, 2012*, January 2013. See also <http://www.fs.fed.us/land/staff/lar/LAR2012/lar2012index.html>.

Table 911. Timber Volume, Growth, and Removal on Timberland by Species, Group, and Region: 2007

[932,096 represents 932,096,000,000]

Region	Net volume [1]						Timber growth [4] (mil. cu. ft.)			Timber removals [5] (mil. cu. ft.)		
	Growing stock [2] (mil. cu. ft.)			Sawtimber [3] (bil. board ft.)								
	All species	Soft-woods	Hard-woods	All spe-cies	Soft-woods	Hard-woods	All spe-cies	Soft-woods	Hard-woods	All spe-cies	Soft-woods	Hard-woods
Total	**932,096**	**529,203**	**402,893**	**1,013**	**558**	**455**	**26,744**	**15,241**	**11,503**	**15,533**	**9,859**	**5,675**
North	248,007	55,866	192,141	268	60	209	6,576	1,489	5,087	2,820	677	2,143
Northeast	137,585	34,252	103,333	146	37	109	3,249	836	2,412	1,169	353	815
North Central	110,422	21,614	88,808	122	23	99	3,327	652	2,675	1,651	324	1,328
South	288,522	118,471	170,051	325	123	202	13,272	7,632	5,640	9,696	6,317	3,379
Southeast	126,747	56,722	70,025	143	58	84	6,115	3,876	2,239	4,306	2,961	1,345
South Central	161,775	61,749	100,026	182	64	118	7,157	3,756	3,401	5,391	3,357	2,034
Rocky Mountains	137,263	124,809	12,454	159	144	15	1,761	1,577	184	543	521	22
Great Plains	4,539	1,641	2,898	7	2	5	72	27	45	41	25	16
Intermountain	132,724	123,168	9,556	153	142	11	1,689	1,550	139	502	496	6
Pacific Coast	258,304	230,057	28,247	261	232	29	5,135	4,543	593	2,474	2,344	131
Alaska	31,998	29,125	2,873	34	31	3	248	130	118	66	59	7
Pacific Northwest	158,896	146,006	12,890	159	146	13	3,340	3,039	301	1,939	1,818	121
Pacific Southwest [6]	67,410	54,926	12,484	68	55	13	1,548	1,374	174	469	466	3

[1] As of January 1. [2] Live trees of commercial species meeting specified standards of quality or vigor. Cull trees are excluded. Includes only trees 5.0-inches in diameter or larger at 4 1/2 feet above ground. [3] Live trees of commercial species containing at least one 12-foot sawlog or two noncontiguous 8-foot logs, and meeting regional specifications for freedom from defect. Softwood trees must be at least 9.0 inches in diameter and hardwood trees must be at least 11.0-inches in diameter at 4 1/2 feet above ground. [4] The net increase in the volume of trees during a specified year. Components include the increment in net volume of trees at the beginning of the specific year surviving to its end, plus the net volume of trees reaching the minimum size class during the year, minus the volume of trees that died during the year, and minus the net volume of trees that became cull trees during the year. [5] The net volume of trees removed from the inventory during a specified year by harvesting, cultural operations such as timber stand improvement, or land clearing. [6] Includes Hawaii.

Source: U.S. Forest Service, "RPA Assessment Tables,"<http://www.fs.fed.us/research/rpa/>, accessed 2007.

Table 912. Timber Removals—Roundwood Product Output by Source and Species Group: 2006

[In million cubic feet (14,990 represents 14,990,000,000)]

Source and species group	Total	Sawlogs	Pulpwood	Veneer logs	Other products [1]	Fuelwood [2]
Total..........................	**14,990**	**7,179**	**4,394**	**1,211**	**798**	**1,408**
Softwoods...........................	9,948	5,289	2,634	1,068	479	477
Hardwoods..........................	5,042	1,890	1,760	143	319	931
Growing stock [3].....................	13,002	6,781	3,872	1,156	703	490
Softwoods...........................	8,897	5,030	2,345	1,020	417	86
Hardwoods..........................	4,105	1,752	1,527	136	286	404
Other sources [4].....................	1,988	398	522	55	95	918
Softwoods...........................	1,051	260	289	48	63	391
Hardwoods..........................	937	138	233	7	33	526

[1] Includes such items as cooperage, pilings, poles, posts, shakes, shingles, board mills, charcoal, and export logs. [2] Downed and dead wood volume left on the ground after trees have been cut on timberland. [3] Includes live trees of commercial species meeting specified standards of quality or vigor. Cull trees are excluded. Includes only trees 5.0-inches in diameter or larger at 4 1/2 feet above the ground. [4] Includes salvable dead trees, rough and rotten trees, trees of noncommercial species, trees less than 5.0-inches in diameter at 4 1/2 feet above the ground, tops, and roundwood harvested from nonforest land (for example, fence rows).

Source: U.S. Forest Service, "RPA Assessment Tables,"<http://www.fs.fed.us/research/rpa/>, accessed 2007.

Table 913. Timber Products—Production, Foreign Trade, and Consumption by Type of Product: 1990 to 2010

[In millions of cubic feet, roundwood equivalent (15,577 represents 15,577,000,000)]

Type of Product	1990	1995	2000	2003	2004	2005	2006	2007	2008	2009	2010
Industrial roundwood:											
Domestic production..........	15,577	15,537	15,436	14,571	15,139	15,465	14,836	13,932	12,493	11,264	11,933
Softwoods...................	10,968	10,191	10,201	10,290	10,710	11,002	10,413	9,566	8,389	7,213	7,302
Hardwoods..................	4,609	5,347	5,235	4,282	4,428	4,463	4,423	4,366	4,104	4,052	4,631
Imports.......................	3,091	3,907	4,529	5,096	5,805	5,802	5,292	4,147	3,065	1,986	1,722
Exports.......................	2,307	2,282	1,996	1,535	1,604	1,646	1,596	1,481	1,517	1,248	1,291
Consumption.................	16,361	17,161	17,969	18,132	19,339	19,622	18,841	16,598	14,041	12,002	13,279
Softwoods...................	11,779	11,961	12,659	13,398	14,357	14,652	13,732	12,009	9,845	7,941	8,451
Hardwoods..................	4,582	5,200	5,310	4,734	4,983	4,970	4,799	4,589	4,197	4,062	4,728
Lumber:											
Domestic production.........	7,317	6,815	7,199	7,131	7,510	7,889	7,552	6,964	5,928	5,020	4,800
Imports.......................	1,909	2,522	2,845	3,193	3,704	3,737	3,415	2,743	1,922	1,336	1,440
Exports.......................	589	460	428	347	348	389	390	359	345	272	224
Consumption.................	8,637	8,877	9,616	9,977	10,866	11,237	10,577	9,347	7,506	6,084	5,906
Plywood and veneer:											
Domestic production.........	1,423	1,303	1,187	1,054	1,086	1,068	1,003	912	743	617	177
Imports.......................	97	107	155	240	354	373	339	265	185	177	104
Exports.......................	109	89	42	35	43	37	35	40	45	37	58
Consumption.................	1,410	1,321	1,300	1,259	1,397	1,403	1,308	1,136	882	757	780
Pulp products:											
Domestic production.........	5,313	6,079	5,881	5,557	5,692	5,679	5,470	5,176	4,926	4,818	4,841
Imports.......................	1,038	1,248	1,459	1,579	1,669	1,570	1,440	1,071	918	434	566
Exports.......................	646	905	842	643	680	708	681	526	556	423	492
Consumption.................	5,704	6,422	6,498	6,493	6,680	6,541	6,229	5,721	5,288	4,829	4,915
Logs:											
Imports.......................	4	13	68	80	73	114	94	67	35	29	32
Exports.......................	674	451	331	356	366	345	339	350	313	321	407
Pulpwood chips, exports.......	288	377	353	155	168	166	151	205	257	195	195
Fuelwood consumption.........	3,019	2,937	2,561	1,515	1,540	1,550	1,555	1,605	1,510	1,400	1,134

Source: U.S. Forest Service. *U.S. Timber Production, Trade, Consumption, and Price Statistics, 1965-2005,* September 2007 and unpublished data. See also <http://www.treesearch.fs.fed.us/pubs/28972>.

Table 914. Selected Timber Products—Imports and Exports: 1990 to 2010

[In million board feet (13,063 represents 13,063,000,000), except as indicated]

Product	Unit	1990	1995	2000	2005	2006	2007	2008	2009	2010
IMPORTS [1]										
Lumber, total [2]	Mil. bd. ft.	13,063	17,524	19,906	25,738	23,037	18,906	13,042	9,172	6,101
From Canada	Percent	91	97	92	85	86	89	72	54	93
Logs, total	Mil. bd. ft. [3]	23	80	435	710	585	418	253	179	198
From Canada	Percent	84	70	96	85	85	91	(NA)	(NA)	(NA)
Paper and board [4]	1,000 tons	12,195	14,292	17,555	20,438	20,293	18,634	16,872	12,133	11,546
Woodpulp	1,000 tons	4,893	5,969	7,227	6,762	6,939	6,793	6,272	5,044	6,136
Plywood	Mil. sq. ft. [5]	1,687	1,951	2,917	6,325	6,324	4,969	3,722	2,778	3,350
EXPORTS										
Lumber, total [2]	Mil. bd. ft.	4,623	2,958	2,700	2,348	2,359	2,193	2,148	1,690	2,133
To: Canada	Percent	14	22	26	28	28	27	27	27	26
Japan	Percent	28	33	12	3	4	4	5	4	–
Europe	Percent	15	17	19	15	16	16	5	7	–
Logs, total	Mil. bd. ft. [3]	4,213	2,820	2,068	2,157	2,120	2,189	2,240	2,005	2,541
To: Canada	Percent	9	25	41	54	52	34	33	32	27
Japan	Percent	62	61	45	27	26	26	28	28	16
China	Percent	9	1	–	4	5	7	9	12	30
Paper and board [4]	1,000 tons	5,163	7,621	10,003	13,434	13,349	14,582	12,907	12,569	13,185
Woodpulp	1,000 tons	5,905	8,261	6,409	6,413	6,606	6,831	7,790	7,519	8,265
Plywood	Mil. sq. ft. [5]	1,766	1,517	754	568	749	501	621	473	418

– Represents zero. NA Not available. [1] Customs value of imports; see text, Section 28. [2] Includes railroad ties. [3] Log scale. [4] Includes paper and board products. Excludes hardboard. [5] 3/8 inch basis.

Source: U.S. Forest Service. *U.S. Timber Production, Trade, Consumption, and Price Statistics, 1965-2005,* September 2007 and unpublished data. See also <http://www.treesearch.fs.fed.us/pubs/28972>.

Table 915. Lumber Consumption by Species Group and End Use: 1995 to 2010

[In billion board feet (59.3 represents 59,300,000,000), except per capita in board feet. Per capita consumption based on estimated resident population as of July 1]

Item	1995	2000	2002	2003	2004	2005	2006	2007	2008	2009	2010
Consumption, total	**59.3**	**66.1**	**67.5**	**67.0**	**73.1**	**75.6**	**71.3**	**62.7**	**49.7**	**40.3**	**39.6**
Per capita	225	240	235	230	249	255	238	208	163	131	129
SPECIES GROUP											
Softwoods	47.6	54.0	56.4	56.5	62.0	64.4	60.4	52.6	40.7	31.2	33.1
Hardwoods	11.7	12.2	11.1	10.5	11.1	11.2	10.9	10.2	9.0	9.1	6.5
END USE											
New housing	18.1	21.1	22.5	24.0	25.4	27.7	23.8	17.5	11.2	(NA)	(NA)
Residential upkeep and improvements	15.0	15.3	16.4	16.2	17.6	18.3	18.6	17.8	16.1	(NA)	(NA)
New nonresidential construction [1]	4.7	5.5	4.8	4.4	4.5	4.7	5.2	4.9	5.2	(NA)	(NA)
Shipping	6.9	7.6	7.1	7.0	7.7	8.1	8.6	7.9	6.8	(NA)	(NA)
Other [2]	7.2	8.7	9.9	9.8	13.2	11.3	9.8	10.0	6.0	(NA)	(NA)

NA Not available. [1] In addition to new construction, includes railroad ties laid as replacements in existing track and lumber used by railroads for railcar repair. [2] Includes upkeep and improvement of nonresidential buildings and structures; made-at-home projects, such as furniture, boats, and picnic tables; made-on-the-job items such as advertising and display structures; and miscellaneous products and uses.

Source: U.S. Forest Service. *U.S. Timber Production, Trade, Consumption, and Price Statistics, 1965-2005,* September 2007 and unpublished data. See also <http://www.treesearch.fs.fed.us/pubs/28972>.

Table 916. Selected Species—Stumpage Prices in Current and Constant (1996) Dollars: 2000 to 2010

[In dollars per 1,000 board feet. Stumpage prices are based on sales of sawtimber from national forests]

Species	Current dollars				Constant (1996) dollars [1]			
	2000	2005	2009	2010	2000	2005	2009	2010
Softwoods:								
Douglas fir [2]	433	321	(NA)	(NA)	397	260	(NA)	(NA)
Southern pine [3]	258	193	105	105	237	157	71	70
Sugar pine [4]	187	114	63	100	172	93	46	50
Ponderosa pine [4,5]	155	103	38	30	142	84	25	22
Western hemlock [6]	46	70	(NA)	(NA)	42	57	(NA)	(NA)
Hardwoods:								
All eastern hardwoods [7]	341	415	(NA)	(NA)	313	337	(NA)	(NA)
Oak, white, red, and black [7]	258	329	(NA)	(NA)	237	267	(NA)	(NA)
Maple, sugar [8]	314	648	(NA)	(NA)	288	526	(NA)	(NA)

NA Not available. [1] Deflated by the producer price index, all commodities. [2] Western Washington and western Oregon. [3] Southern region. [4] Pacific Southwest region (formerly California region). [5] Includes Jeffrey pine. [6] Pacific Northwest region. [7] Eastern and Southern regions. [8] Eastern region.

Source: U.S. Forest Service, "RPA Assessment Tables," <http://www.fs.fed.us/research/rpa/>, accessed 2007.

Table 917. Selected Timber Products—Producer Price Indexes: 1990 to 2012

[1982 = 100. For information about producer prices, see text, Section 14]

Product	1990	1995	2000	2005	2008	2009	2010	2011	2012
Lumber and wood products [1]	**129.7**	**178.1**	**178.2**	**196.5**	**191.3**	**182.8**	**192.7**	**194.7**	**201.6**
Lumber	124.6	173.4	178.8	198.6	163.5	149.4	167.3	166.6	172.5
Softwood lumber	123.8	178.5	178.6	203.6	156.3	141.4	160.8	160.5	171.7
Hardwood lumber	131.0	167.0	185.9	196.6	184.5	171.2	187.3	185.8	183.7
Millwork [1]	130.4	163.8	176.4	197.2	204.8	205.4	207.0	210.1	216.5
General millwork	132.0	165.4	178.0	196.1	207.7	210.3	211.2	214.2	220.0
Prefabricated structural members	122.3	163.5	175.1	206.9	189.0	181.1	185.6	189.4	198.5
Plywood	114.2	165.3	157.6	186.8	174.7	163.7	176.7	171.3	189.1
Softwood plywood	119.6	188.1	173.3	223.5	193.1	171.9	197.1	185.8	218.6
Hardwood plywood and related products	102.7	122.2	130.2	138.1	(NA)	(NA)	(NA)	(NA)	106.0
Other wood products [1]	114.7	143.7	130.5	139.2	144.7	141.8	142.5	144.1	146.6
Boxes	119.1	145.0	155.2	164.9	174.6	176.5	183.0	191.1	194.5
Pulp, paper, and allied products [1]	**141.2**	**172.2**	**183.7**	**202.6**	**226.8**	**225.6**	**236.9**	**245.1**	**244.2**
Pulp, paper, and prod., excl. bldg. paper [1]	132.9	163.4	161.4	169.8	199.1	194.1	206.8	216.0	213.6
Woodpulp	151.3	183.2	145.3	138.0	171.4	150.2	186.0	194.8	185.9
Wastepaper	138.9	371.1	282.5	230.9	372.5	237.0	421.5	482.5	370.7
Paper [1]	128.8	159.0	149.8	159.6	184.3	179.6	182.1	191.2	191.6
Writing and printing papers	129.1	158.4	146.6	156.1	181.6	180.5	179.5	185.8	184.9
Newsprint	119.6	161.8	127.5	138.5	148.0	126.4	125.6	137.2	(NA)
Paperboard	135.7	183.1	176.7	175.5	217.9	207.2	224.9	230.5	228.0
Converted paper and paperboard products [1]	135.2	157.0	162.7	176.1	199.2	202.9	209.0	216.6	218.6
Office supplies and accessories	121.4	134.9	133.8	143.1	158.3	158.9	159.9	164.7	167.7
Building paper & building board mill prods	112.2	144.9	138.8	184.9	163.9	156.5	168.4	163.6	187.1

NA Not available. [1] Includes other products not shown separately.

Source: U.S. Bureau of Labor Statistics, "Producer Price Indexes," <http://www.bls.gov/ppi/>, accessed June 2013.

Table 918. Pulpwood Consumption, Woodpulp Production, and Paper and Board Production and Consumption: 1995 to 2010

[Revised to match data from American Forest and Paper Association and American Pulpwood Association]

Item	Unit	1995	2000	2004	2005	2006	2007	2008	2009	2010
Pulpwood consumption [1]	1,000 cords [2]	97,052	95,904	87,110	88,595	86,284	84,076	77,442	70,401	72,321
Woodpulp production [3]	1,000 tons	67,103	62,758	54,301	60,267	60,568	56,636	52,899	44,990	52,607
Paper and board: [4]										
Production	1,000 tons	89,509	94,491	83,612	91,031	91,800	91,570	87,619	71,219	82,469
Consumption or new supply [5]	1,000 tons	96,126	103,147	95,068	101,864	102,948	99,825	93,640	79,141	84,968
Per capita	Pounds	731	731	627	687	688	661	613	515	548

[1] Includes changes in stocks. [2] One cord equals 128 cubic feet. [3] Excludes defibrated and exploded woodpulp used for hard pressed board. [4] Excludes hardboard. [5] Production plus imports, minus exports (excludes products); changes in inventories not taken into account.

Source: U.S. Forest Service. *U.S. Timber Production, Trade, Consumption, and Price Statistics, 1965-2005,* September 2007 and unpublished data. See also <http://www.treesearch.fs.fed.us/pubs/28972>.

Table 919. Paper and Paperboard—Production and New Supply: 1990 to 2012

[In millions of short tons (80.55 represents 80,550,000). 1 short ton = 2,000 lbs]

Item	1990	1995	2000	2005	2008	2009	2010	2011	2012
Production, total	**80.55**	**91.21**	**96.05**	**92.61**	**88.45**	**79.06**	**83.70**	**82.73**	**81.83**
Paper, total	39.36	42.90	45.52	41.40	38.96	33.81	35.51	34.34	33.14
Paperboard, total	39.42	46.55	48.97	49.71	48.45	44.49	47.46	47.66	47.90
Unbleached kraft	20.36	22.73	21.80	22.58	22.17	20.55	21.36	21.62	21.84
Semichemical	5.64	5.67	5.95	6.41	5.82	5.21	5.44	5.43	5.41
Bleached kraft	4.26	5.16	5.30	5.58	5.69	5.29	5.62	5.52	5.48
Recycled	9.03	12.84	15.79	15.06	14.69	13.44	15.05	15.09	15.17
Wet machine board and construction grades	1.82	1.82	1.56	1.50	1.04	0.76	0.73	0.72	0.78
New supply, all grades, excluding products	**87.68**	**98.08**	**105.02**	**101.81**	**91.99**	**80.36**	**84.16**	**82.48**	**81.03**
Paper, total	49.49	52.77	57.13	53.69	46.71	39.37	40.34	38.50	37.03
Newsprint	13.41	12.76	12.92	10.12	7.25	5.26	5.00	4.57	4.41
Printing/writing papers	25.46	29.55	32.99	31.99	28.06	23.03	23.73	22.46	21.08
Packaging and industrial converting papers	4.72	4.24	4.27	4.05	4.05	3.66	4.18	4.00	4.07
Tissue	5.90	6.22	6.95	7.54	7.36	7.43	7.43	7.48	7.47
Paperboard, total	36.30	43.39	46.02	46.51	44.25	40.19	43.06	43.22	43.25

Source: American Forest and Paper Association, Washington, DC, *Annual Statistics of Paper, Paperboard and Wood Pulp* ©.

Table 920. Fishery Products—Domestic Catch, Imports, and Disposition: 1990 to 2011

[Live weight, in millions of pounds (16,349 represents 16,349,000,000). Data for 2011 are preliminary]

Item	1990	1995	2000	2005	2007	2008	2009	2010	2011
Total supply...............	**16,349**	**16,484**	**17,340**	**20,612**	**20,561**	**19,199**	**18,899**	**19,748**	**21,106**
For human food..................	12,662	13,584	14,738	18,147	18,253	17,037	16,637	17,560	18,732
For industrial use...............	3,687	2,900	2,599	2,382	2,308	2,163	2,262	2,188	2,374
Domestic catch..................	**9,404**	**9,788**	**9,069**	**9,707**	**9,309**	**8,325**	**8,031**	**8,231**	**9,858**
For human food..................	7,041	7,667	6,912	7,997	7,490	6,633	6,198	6,526	7,909
For industrial use...............	2,363	2,121	2,157	1,710	1,819	1,692	1,833	1,705	1,949
Imports [1]......................	**6,945**	**6,696**	**8,271**	**10,905**	**11,252**	**10,874**	**10,868**	**11,517**	**11,248**
For human food..................	5,621	5,917	7,828	10,158	10,763	10,404	10,439	11,034	10,823
For industrial use [2]............	1,324	779	443	747	489	471	430	483	425
Exports [1]......................	**4,627**	**5,166**	**5,758**	**8,420**	**7,057**	**6,353**	**5,738**	**6,129**	**7,695**
For human food..................	3,832	4,175	4,587	6,385	5,761	5,253	4,760	5,170	6,602
For industrial use [2]............	795	991	1,171	2,035	1,296	1,100	978	959	1,093
Disposition of domestic catch..............	**9,404**	**9,788**	**9,069**	**9,707**	**9,309**	**8,325**	**8,031**	**8,231**	**9,858**
Fresh and frozen [3]...............	6,501	7,099	6,657	7,776	7,450	6,538	6,204	6,515	7,817
Canned [3].........................	751	769	530	563	514	336	392	373	371
Cured...............................	126	90	119	160	121	138	103	102	52
Reduced to meal, oil, etc..........	2,026	1,830	1,763	1,208	1,224	1,313	1,332	1,241	1,618

[1] Excludes imports of edible fishery products consumed in Puerto Rico; includes landings of tuna caught by foreign vessels in American Samoa. [2] Processed into meal, oil, solubles, and shell products, or used as bait and animal food. [3] Includes for human food, and bait and animal food.

Source: U.S. National Oceanic and Atmospheric Administration, National Marine Fisheries Service, *Fisheries of the United States 2011*, August 2012, and earlier editions. See also <http://www.st.nmfs.noaa.gov/commercial-fisheries/index>.

Table 921. Fisheries—Quantity and Value of Domestic Catch: 1980 to 2011

[In millions of pounds (6,482 represents 6,482,000,000), except as noted. Data for 2011 are preliminary]

Year	Quantity (mil. lbs. [1])			Value (mil. dol.)	Average price per lb. (cents)	Year	Quantity (mil. lbs. [1])			Value (mil . dol.)	Average price per lb. (cents)
	Total	For human food	For industrial products [2]				Total	For human food	For industrial products [2]		
1980......	6,482	3,654	2,828	2,237	34.5	2004....	9,683	7,794	1,889	3,756	38.8
1985......	6,258	3,294	2,964	2,326	37.2	2005....	9,707	7,997	1,710	3,942	40.6
1990......	9,404	7,041	2,363	3,522	37.5	2006....	9,483	7,842	1,641	4,024	42.4
1995......	9,788	7,667	2,121	3,770	38.5	2007....	9,309	7,490	1,819	4,192	45.0
1999......	9,339	6,832	2,507	3,467	37.1	2008....	8,325	6,633	1,692	4,383	52.6
2000......	9,069	6,912	2,157	3,550	39.1	2009....	8,031	6,198	1,833	3,891	48.4
2002......	9,397	7,205	2,192	3,092	32.9	2010....	8,231	6,526	1,705	4,520	54.9
2003......	9,507	7,521	1,986	3,347	35.2	2011....	9,858	7,909	1,949	5,289	53.7

[1] Live weight. [2] Meal, oil, solubles, shell products, bait, and animal food.

Source: U.S. National Oceanic and Atmospheric Administration, National Marine Fisheries Service, *Fisheries of the United States 2011*, August 2012, and earlier editions. See also <http://www.st.nmfs.noaa.gov/commercial-fisheries/index>.

Table 922. Domestic Fish and Shellfish Catch and Value by Major Species Caught: 2000 to 2011

[In thousands (9,068,985 represents 9,068,985,000). Data for 2011 are preliminary]

Species	Quantity (1,000 lbs.)				Value ($1,000)			
	2000	2005	2010	2011	2000	2005	2010	2011
Total [1].......................	**9,068,985**	**9,707,275**	**8,230,587**	**9,858,445**	**3,549,481**	**3,942,376**	**4,519,510**	**5,288,959**
Fish, total [1]...................	**7,689,661**	**8,462,473**	**6,918,013**	**8,466,790**	**1,594,815**	**1,836,448**	**2,155,593**	**2,567,261**
Cod: Atlantic....................	25,060	13,920	17,714	17,602	26,384	20,828	28,119	32,612
Pacific.....................	530,505	548,746	539,635	664,293	142,330	150,738	146,941	203,574
Flounder........................	412,723	419,430	624,358	707,360	109,910	135,176	146,243	159,858
Halibut..........................	75,190	76,263	56,497	42,840	143,826	177,593	206,553	213,007
Herring, Atlantic................	160,269	215,565	144,513	173,809	9,972	20,467	21,275	24,810
Herring, Pacific.................	74,835	87,295	108,868	102,532	12,043	13,799	23,308	12,906
Menhaden.......................	1,760,498	1,243,723	1,471,803	1,875,035	112,403	62,465	107,193	143,651
Pollock, Alaska..................	2,606,802	3,411,307	1,947,580	2,810,796	160,525	306,972	282,399	362,594
Salmon..........................	628,638	899,457	787,740	780,088	270,213	330,699	554,816	618,316
Tuna............................	50,779	44,316	48,047	49,835	95,176	85,922	108,453	136,200
Whiting (Atlantic, silver)........	26,855	16,561	17,564	17,131	11,370	8,284	10,862	10,984
Whiting (Pacific, hake).........	452,718	569,381	355,272	496,372	18,809	29,145	27,316	52,633
Shellfish, total [1]..............	**1,379,324**	**1,244,802**	**1,276,366**	**1,353,096**	**1,954,666**	**2,105,928**	**2,341,902**	**2,699,249**
Clams...........................	118,482	105,640	88,891	86,449	153,973	173,655	200,657	186,644
Crabs...........................	299,006	299,137	349,604	369,152	405,006	415,057	572,797	650,237
Lobsters: American.............	83,180	88,032	115,433	126,318	301,300	416,597	396,757	423,531
Oysters.........................	41,146	33,963	28,080	28,504	90,667	110,679	117,590	131,656
Scallops, sea....................	32,747	56,702	57,454	59,117	164,609	433,512	455,088	584,905
Shrimp..........................	332,486	260,884	258,972	312,658	690,453	406,344	413,980	517,697
Squid, Pacific...................	259,508	126,107	286,403	267,985	27,077	31,601	70,706	66,563

[1] Includes other species not shown separately.

Source: U.S. National Oceanic and Atmospheric Administration, National Marine Fisheries Service, *Fisheries of the United States 2011*, August 2012, and earlier editions. See also <http://www.st.nmfs.noaa.gov/commercial-fisheries/index>.

Table 923. U.S. Private Aquaculture—Trout and Catfish Production and Value: 1990 to 2012

[67.8 represents 67,800,000. Data are for calendar year and foodsize fish (those over 12 inches long)]

Item	Unit	1990	1995	2000	2005	2009	2010	2011	2012
TROUT FOODSIZE									
Number sold...................	Mil.	67.8	60.2	58.4	55.6	40.8	38.7	38.2	40.4
Total weight...................	Mil. lb.	56.8	55.6	59.0	59.9	48.7	45.3	44.8	47.7
Total value of sales............	Mil. dol.	64.6	60.8	63.3	63.5	67.2	63.2	68.3	72.7
Avg. price received by processors............	Dol./lb.	1.14	1.09	1.07	1.06	1.38	1.40	1.52	1.52
Percent sold to processors...........	Percent	58	68	70	66	63	63	50	52
CATFISH FOODSIZE									
Number sold...................	Mil.	272.9	321.8	420.1	395.6	266.3	263.4	201.9	206.6
Total weight...................	Mil. lb.	392.4	481.5	633.8	605.5	476.0	478.9	348.0	340.2
Total value of sales............	Mil. dol.	305.1	378.1	468.8	427.8	352.0	375.1	390.7	318.8
Avg. price received by processors....	Dol./lb.	0.78	0.79	0.74	0.71	0.74	0.78	1.12	0.94
Fish sold to processors..............	Mil. lb.	360.4	446.9	593.6	600.7	466.1	471.7	334.1	300.2
Avg. price paid by processors.........	Cents/lb.	75.8	78.6	75.1	72.5	77.1	80.2	117.7	97.6
Processor sales..................	Mil. lb.	183.1	227.0	297.2	300.0	229.2	231.6	167.2	161.4
Avg. price received by processors............	Dol./lb.	2.24	2.40	2.36	2.29	2.53	2.51	3.43	3.08
Inventory (Jan. 1).....................	Mil. lb.	9.4	10.9	13.6	13.7	14.5	12.3	12.9	(NA)

NA Not available.

Source: U.S. Department of Agriculture, National Agricultural Statistics Service, *Trout Production*, February 2013, and *Catfish Production*, January 2013; see also <http://www.nass.usda.gov/Publications/index.asp>. U.S. Department of Agriculture, Economic Research Service, *Catfish: Grower and Processor Sales and Prices*, May 2013; see also <http://www.ers.usda.gov/data-products/aquaculture-data.aspx>.

Table 924. Supply of Selected Shellfish and Fish Products: 1990 to 2011

[In millions of pounds (734 represents 734,000,000). Totals available for U.S. consumption are supply minus exports plus imports. Round weight is the complete or full weight as caught. Data for 2011 is preliminary]

Species	Unit	1990	1995	2000	2005	2007	2008	2009	2010	2011
Shrimp........................	Heads-off weight	734	832	1,173	1,559	1,743	1,722	1,746	1,739	1,792
Tuna, canned..................	Canned weight	856	875	980	895	812	848	762	834	793
Snow crab.....................	Round weight	37	42	122	171	208	197	224	197	177
Clams.........................	Meat weight	152	144	133	120	127	121	116	105	107
Salmon, canned...............	Canned weight	148	147	95	123	51	26	67	73	50
American lobster..............	Round weight	95	94	125	144	128	144	159	186	185
Spiny lobster..................	Round weight	89	89	99	83	78	83	57	60	59
Scallops......................	Meat weight	74	62	78	86	92	88	90	85	85
Sardines, canned..............	Canned weight	61	44	(NA)	(NA)	(NA)	(NA)	(NA)	(NA)	(NA)
Oysters.......................	Meat weight	56	63	71	65	70	54	59	57	63
King crab.....................	Round weight	19	21	41	78	134	71	62	44	35
Crab meat, canned............	Canned weight	9	12	29	59	66	68	59	66	63

NA Not available.

Source: U.S. National Oceanic and Atmospheric Administration, National Marine Fisheries Service, *Fisheries of the United States 2011*, August 2012, and earlier editions. See also <http://www.st.nmfs.noaa.gov/commercial-fisheries/index>.

Table 925. Canned, Fresh, and Frozen Fishery Products—Production and Value: 1990 to 2011

[Production in millions of pounds (1,178 represents 1,178,000,000); value in millions of dollars (1,562 represents $1,562,000,000). Fresh fishery products exclude Alaska and Hawaii. Canned fishery products data are for natural pack only. Data for 2011 are preliminary]

Product	Production (mil. lbs.)					Value (mil. dol.)				
	1990	2000	2005	2010	2011	1990	2000	2005	2010	2011
Canned, total.................	**1,178**	**1,747**	**1,082**	**956**	**945**	**1,562**	**1,626**	**1,211**	**1,414**	**1,474**
Tuna..........................	581	671	446	395	385	902	856	628	724	769
Salmon........................	196	171	219	146	148	366	288	301	356	377
Clam products.................	110	127	123	110	105	76	120	127	98	99
Sardines, Maine................	13	(Z)	(NA)	[1] (D)	[1] (D)	17	(Z)	(NA)	[1] (D)	[1] (D)
Shrimp........................	1	2	1	[1] (D)	[1] (D)	3	11	3	[1] (D)	[1] (D)
Crab [2].......................	1	(Z)	(Z)	1	1	4	(Z)	(Z)	8	1
Oysters [3]....................	1	(Z)	(Z)	[1] (D)	[1] (D)	1	1	(Z)	[1] (D)	[1] (D)
Other.........................	275	776	293	304	307	193	350	152	237	229
Fish fillets and steaks [4]........	**441**	**368**	**615**	**585**	**760**	**843**	**823**	**1,136**	**1,486**	**1,704**
Cod...........................	65	56	47	49	66	132	167	116	131	173
Flounder......................	54	27	20	32	18	154	71	65	53	55
Haddock.......................	7	6	24	23	26	24	24	89	89	101
Ocean perch, Atlantic..........	1	(Z)	1	1	1	1	1	4	3	5
Rockfish......................	33	11	3	2	2	53	25	8	6	6
Pollock, Atlantic..............	12	2	3	2	2	21	4	6	7	7
Pollock, Alaska................	164	160	383	290	461	174	178	404	368	568
Other.........................	105	106	134	186	182	284	353	444	829	789

D Figure withheld to avoid disclosure pertaining to a specific organization or individual. NA Not available. Z Less than 500,000 pounds or $500,000. [1] Included with "other." [2] Includes crab meat specialties. [3] Includes oyster specialties. [4] Fresh and frozen.

Source: U.S. National Oceanic and Atmospheric Administration, National Marine Fisheries Service, *Fisheries of the United States 2011*, August 2012, and earlier reports. See also <http://www.st.nmfs.noaa.gov/commercial-fisheries/index>.

Table 926. Mineral Industries—Employment, Hours, and Earnings: 1990 to 2012

[In thousands (680 represents 680,000), except as noted. Based on the Current Employment Statistics Program, see Appendix III]

Industry and item	Unit	1990	1995	2000	2005	2009	2010	2011	2012
All mining: [1]									
All employees...................	1,000	680	558	520	562	643	655	739	800
Production workers................	1,000	469	391	383	419	466	483	552	601
Avg. weekly hours................	Number	46.1	46.8	45.5	46.4	43.5	44.8	47.1	47.0
Avg. weekly earnings.............	Dollars	630	711	771	884	1,037	1,086	1,170	1,229
Oil and gas extraction:									
All employees...................	1,000	190	152	125	126	160	159	172	187
Production workers................	1,000	84	73	67	72	85	89	97	106
Avg. weekly hours................	Number	44.4	43.6	41.3	44.3	40.6	39.0	43.2	46.6
Avg. weekly earnings.............	Dollars	591	677	802	856	1,119	1,066	1,179	1,329
Coal mining:									
All employees...................	1,000	136	97	72	74	82	81	87	87
Production workers................	1,000	110	78	59	61	71	70	78	76
Avg. weekly hours................	Number	44.7	45.7	45.6	48.5	47.8	48.4	49.3	47.2
Avg. weekly earnings.............	Dollars	822	929	945	1,071	1,249	1,366	1,403	1,348
Metal ore mining:									
All employees...................	1,000	53	48	38	29	35	37	42	45
Production workers................	1,000	43	39	29	22	28	28	(NA)	(NA)
Avg. weekly hours................	Number	42.5	43.4	43.4	44.2	42.3	42.5	(NA)	(NA)
Avg. weekly earnings.............	Dollars	646	788	871	1,001	1,095	1,158	(NA)	(NA)
Nonmetallic minerals mining, and quarrying:									
All employees...................	1,000	113	108	115	110	92	87	89	91
Production workers................	1,000	85	81	87	84	71	65	(NA)	(NA)
Avg. weekly hours................	Number	45.0	46.3	46.1	45.9	41.9	43.8	(NA)	(NA)
Avg. weekly earnings.............	Dollars	532	632	722	830	808	848	(NA)	(NA)

NA Not available. [1] Includes other industries not shown separately.

Source: U.S. Bureau of Labor Statistics, Current Employment Statistics, "Employment, Hours, and Earnings—National," <http://www.bls.gov/ces/home.htm\>, accessed July 2013.

Table 927. Mine Safety: 2000 to 2012

[Reported injury rates per 200,000 employee hours]

Item	All Mines			Coal			Metal and non-metal		
	2000	2011	2012	2000	2011	2012	2000	2011	2012
Number of mines....................	14,413	14,176	14,093	2,124	1,973	1,871	12,289	12,203	12,222
Number of miners...................	348,548	381,209	387,878	108,098	143,437	137,650	240,450	237,772	250,228
Fatalities..........................	85	37	36	38	21	20	47	16	16
Fatal injury rate...................	0.03	0.01	0.01	0.04	0.02	0.02	0.02	0.01	0.01
All injury rate.....................	5.13	2.73	2.56	6.64	3.38	3.16	4.45	2.28	2.19
Total mining area inspection hours/mine........................	57	62	61	178	258	250	28	23	22
Citations and orders...............	120,269	156,802	139,770	58,394	93,330	79,250	61,875	63,472	60,520
S&S [1] citations and orders (percent).....	36	30	29	42	33	31	31	26	27
Amount assessed [2] (mil. dol.)...........	24.7	160.8	120.5	12.0	119.8	87.8	12.7	41.0	32.7
Coal production (mil. tons)...............	1,078	1,095	1,018	1,078	1,095	1,018	(X)	(X)	(X)

X Not applicable. [1] A violation that "significantly and substantially" contributes to the cause and effect of a coal or other mine safety or health hazard. [2] Government penalties or fines.

Source: U.S. Mine Safety and Health Administration, Office of Program Education and Outreach Services, *Mine Safety and Health At a Glance,* June 2013, and earlier reports. See also <http://www.msha.gov/MSHAINFO/FactSheets/MSHAFCT10.HTM>.

Table 928. Mining and Primary Metal Production Indexes: 1990 to 2012

[Index 2007 = 100]

Industry group	NAICS [1] code	1990	1995	2000	2005	2008	2009	2010	2011	2012
Mining [2]....................	**21**	**106.3**	**103.9**	**102.8**	**97.0**	**101.2**	**95.7**	**100.7**	**106.8**	**113.6**
Oil and gas extraction [2]...............	211	113.6	110.2	106.9	97.7	101.2	106.3	109.7	115.6	126.7
Crude oil and natural gas............	211111	115.8	111.1	106.8	97.8	101.3	106.3	109.4	115.2	126.4
Coal mining....................	2121	95.2	93.7	96.1	99.3	102.0	93.5	93.9	95.1	88.0
Metal ore mining.................	2122	110.1	120.4	117.3	100.5	103.0	90.4	96.4	98.4	97.4
Iron ore......................	21221	107.8	119.6	119.9	103.3	102.1	50.2	94.6	103.6	100.6
Gold ore and silver ore.............	21222	124.4	133.1	148.3	107.2	97.9	93.8	97.2	97.9	96.4
Copper, nickel, lead, and zinc.......	21223	119.1	136.5	119.8	96.7	108.3	98.7	93.9	93.9	96.3
Oil and gas drilling..................	213111	60.1	52.6	67.2	83.7	104.4	61.4	82.3	99.2	103.9
Primary metal manufacturing [2]......	**331**	**87.1**	**95.6**	**100.3**	**95.2**	**100.0**	**74.0**	**91.1**	**97.4**	**99.4**
Iron and steel...................	3311, 3312	83.9	93.3	97.3	94.3	106.4	68.5	89.4	97.5	101.1
Aluminum......................	3313	102.0	97.9	103.6	106.9	92.6	75.9	91.9	98.4	101.8
Nonferrous metals [2].................	3314	88.8	98.9	91.7	84.2	102.6	93.9	112.1	114.2	111.4

[1] Based on the 2007 North American Industry Classification System (NAICS). [2] Includes other industries not shown separately.

Source: Board of Governors of the Federal Reserve System,"Industrial Production and Capacity Utilization, Statistical Release G.17," <http://www.federalreserve.gov/datadownload/default.htm>, accessed July 2013.

Table 929. Mineral Production: 1990 to 2011

[In units as indicated (1,029.1 represents 1,029,100,000). Data represent production as measured by mine shipments, mine sales, or marketable production; see Appendix IV]

Minerals and metals	Unit	1990	2000	2009	2010	2011
FUEL MINERALS						
Coal, total [1]	Mil. sh. tons	1,029.1	1,073.6	1,074.9	1,084.4	1,094.3
Bituminous	Mil. sh. tons	693.2	574.3	504.1	489.5	500.5
Subbituminous	Mil. sh. tons	244.3	409.2	496.4	514.8	510.5
Lignite	Mil. sh. tons	88.1	85.6	72.5	78.2	81.0
Anthracite [1]	Mil. sh. tons	3.5	4.6	1.9	1.8	2.3
Natural gas (marketed production)	Tril. cu. ft.	18.59	20.20	21.68	22.38	24.04
Petroleum (crude)	Mil. bbl. [2]	2,685	2,131	1,954	2,000	2,063
Uranium (recoverable content)	Mil. lb.	8.9	4.0	3.7	4.2	4.0
NONFUEL MINERALS						
Asbestos (sales)	1,000 metric tons	(D)	5	–	–	–
Barite, primary, sold/used by producers	1,000 metric tons	430	392	383	662	710
Boron minerals, sold or used by producers	1,000 metric tons	1,090	1,070	(D)	(D)	(D)
Bromine, sold or used by producers	1,000 metric tons	177	228	(D)	(D)	(D)
Cement (excludes Puerto Rico):	Mil. metric tons	(NA)	(NA)	64	66	68
Portland	Mil. metric tons	67	84	62	61	66
Masonry	Mil. metric tons	3	4	2	2	2
Clays	1,000 metric tons	42,900	40,800	24,500	25,400	25,300
Diatomite	1,000 metric tons	631	677	575	595	813
Feldspar	1,000 metric tons	630	790	550	550	650
Fluorspar, finished shipments	1,000 metric tons	64	–	(NA)	(NA)	(NA)
Garnet (industrial)	1,000 metric tons	47	60	46	53	56
Gypsum, crude	Mil. metric tons	15	20	10	9	9
Helium [3]	Mil. cu. meters	65	98	78	75	71
Lime, sold or used by producers	Mil. metric tons	16	20	16	18	19
Mica, scrap/flake, sold or used by producers	1,000 metric tons	109	101	51	53	50
Peat, sales by producers	1,000 metric tons	721	847	644	605	595
Perlite, processed, sold or used	1,000 metric tons	576	672	348	414	420
Phosphate rock, marketable	Mil. metric tons	46	39	26	26	28
Potash (K2O equivalent), marketable	1,000 metric tons	1,710	1,300	720	930	1,000
Pumice & pumicite, sold and used	1,000 metric tons	443	1,050	410	390	489
Salt	Mil. metric tons	37	46	43	44	45
Sand & gravel:	Mil. metric tons	855	1,148	859	827	846
Construction [4]	Mil. metric tons	829	1,120	831	795	802
Industrial	Mil. metric tons	26	28	28	32	44
Soda ash (sodium carbonate)	1,000 metric tons	9,100	10,200	9,310	10,600	10,700
Sodium sulfate (natural and synthetic) [5]	1,000 metric tons	349	(NA)	260	297	(NA)
Stone:	Mil. metric tons	2,230	2,810	2,780	2,830	2,870
Crushed and broken	Mil. metric tons	1,110	1,560	1,160	1,160	1,160
Dimension [6]	1,000 metric tons	1,120	1,250	1,620	1,670	1,710
Sulfur: total shipments	1,000 metric tons	11,500	10,700	8,860	9,140	8,910
Sulfur: Frasch mines (shipments)	1,000 metric tons	3,680	900	(NA)	(NA)	(NA)
Talc and pyrophyllite, crude [7]	1,000 metric tons	1,270	851	511	604	616
Vermiculite concentrate	1,000 metric tons	209	150	100	100	100
METALS						
Antimony ore and concentrate	Metric tons	(D)	(D)	–	–	–
Aluminum	1,000 metric tons	4,048	3,668	1,727	1,726	1,986
Bauxite (dried)	1,000 metric tons	(D)	(NA)	(NA)	(NA)	(NA)
Copper (recoverable content)	1,000 metric tons	1,590	1,450	1,180	1,110	1,110
Gold (recoverable content)	Metric tons	294	353	223	231	234
Iron ore, usable (gross weight)	Mil. metric tons	57	61	27	50	55
Lead (recoverable content)	1,000 metric tons	484	449	406	369	342
Magnesium metal	1,000 metric tons	139	(D)	(D)	(D)	(D)
Mercury, byproduct [8]	Metric tons	(NA)	(NA)	(NA)	(NA)	(NA)
Molybdenum, mine	1,000 metric tons	62	41	48	59	64
Nickel ore, refinery byproduct	1,000 metric tons	330	(D)	(D)	(D)	(D)
Palladium metal	Kilograms	5,930	10,300	12,700	11,600	12,400
Platinum metal	Kilograms	1,810	3,110	3,830	3,450	3,700
Silicon (Si content) [13]	1,000 metric tons	418	367	139	176	(D)
Silver (recoverable content)	Metric tons	2,120	1,860	1,250	1,280	1,120
Titanium concentrate, (TiO2 content) [14]	1,000 metric tons	(D)	300	200	200	300
Tungsten ore and concentrate [15]	Metric tons	(D)	–	(D)	(D)	(D)
Vanadium (recoverable content)	Metric tons	2,310	–	230	1060	590
Zinc, ore and concentrate	1,000 metric tons	508	796	736	748	769

– Represents or rounds to zero. D Withheld to avoid disclosing individual company data. NA Not available. [1] Data for coal for 2011 are estimated and preliminary. [2] 42-gal. bbl. [3] Extracted from natural gas. Both grade A and crude helium. [4] Data for 2011 are estimates. [5] Beginning 2011, data for total sodium sulfate production is no longer available. [6] Includes Puerto Rico. [7] After 1990, includes only talc. [8] Mercury has not been produced as a principal mineral commodity in the U.S. since 1992. Mercury is recovered as a byproduct from processing gold-silver ore. [9] For 2006-2011, ferrosilicon only; silicon metal withheld to avoid disclosing proprietary data.

Source: Nonfuels, through 1994, U.S. Bureau of Mines, thereafter; U.S. Geological Survey, *Minerals Yearbook 2011,* March 2013, and *Mineral Commodity Summaries 2013,* January 2013, and earlier reports. Fuels, U.S. Energy Information Administration, *Annual Energy Review 2011,* September 2012, and earlier reports; and "Natural Gas Gross Withdrawals and Production," <http://www.eia.gov/naturalgas/data.cfm#production>, "Uranium & Nuclear Fuel Summary Production Statistics," <http://www.eia.gov/nuclear/data.cfm#biomass>, and "Crude Oil Production," <http://www.eia.gov/petroleum/data.cfm#crude>; accessed September 2013.

Table 930. Nonfuel Mineral Commodities—Summary: 2011

[1,986 represents 1,986,000. Average price in dollars per metric tons except as noted. < = less than]

Mineral	Unit	Mineral disposition				Average price per unit (dollars)	Employment (number)
		Production	Exports	Net import reliance [1,2] (percent)	Consumption, apparent		
Aluminum............................	1,000 metric tons	1,986	3,420	3	3,550	[4] 1.16	30,300
Antimony (contained)......................	Metric tons	–	4,170	86	22,700	[4] 6.50	20
Asbestos............................	Metric tons	–	169	100	1,180	[6] 931	(NA)
Barite............................	1,000 metric tons	710	98	76	2,930	[6] 86	350
Bauxite and alumina (metal equivalent).....	1,000 metric tons	(NA)	1,695	100	2,750	[6,7] 39	(NA)
Beryllium (contained)......................	Metric tons	235	21	29	333	[4] 203	(NA)
Bismuth (contained)......................	Metric tons	–	1,030	90	796	[4] 11.47	(NA)
Boron (B2O3 content)......................	1,000 metric tons	(D)	[8] 235	(3)	(D)	[6,9] 361	1,180
Bromine (contained)......................	Metric tons	(D)	7,150	<25	(D)	(NA)	950
Cadmium (contained)......................	Metric tons	[5] (D)	[12] 63	(3)	(D)	[10,13] 2.76	(NA)
Cement............................	1,000 metric tons	[14] 67,895	1,414	7	72,200	[6] 89.50	11,500
Chromium............................	1,000 metric tons	[11] 147	232	67	451	[16] 355	(NA)
Clays............................	1,000 metric tons	[17] 25,300	4,600	(3)	21,300	(NA)	5,010
Cobalt (contained)......................	Metric tons	[15] 2,210	3,390	76	9,230	[4] 17.99	(NA)
Copper (mine, recoverable)............	1,000 metric tons	1,110	252	[5] 34	1,730	[4] 4.05	10,600
Diamond, stones (industrial)..............	Million carats	57	–	4	59	[18] 19.67	(NA)
Diatomite............................	1,000 metric tons	813	106	(3)	709	[6] 269	660
Feldspar............................	1,000 metric tons	650	17	(3)	635	[6] 62	380
Fluorspar............................	1,000 metric tons	(NA)	24	100	672	(NA)	(NA)
Garnet (industrial)......................	Metric tons	56,400	14,500	64	158,000	[6] 50-2,000	160
Gemstones............................	Million dollars	[36] 42.9	18,200	99	5,360	(NA)	1,100
Germanium (contained)......................	Kilograms	3,000	5,900	90	(NA)	[10] 1,450	100
Gold (contained)......................	Metric tons	234	514	(3)	(NA)	[19] 1,572	11,200
Graphite (crude)......................	Metric tons	–	6	100	66	[6,20] 1,180	(NA)
Gypsum (crude)......................	1,000 metric tons	8,900	316	13	23,700	[6] 7.0	4,500
Iodine............................	Metric tons	(D)	900	100	(D)	[10,21] 38.13	30
Iron ore (usable)......................	Million metric tons	[22] 54.7	11	(3)	49	[6] 99.45	5,270
Iron and steel scrap (metal)............	Million metric tons	82	24	[37] 63	[6,23] 392	30,000	
Iron and steel slag (metal)............	1,000 metric tons	[24] 15.4	(Z)	9	15	[6] 16.50	2,000
Lead (contained)......................	1,000 metric tons	342	270	4	1,540	[4] 1.22	3,440
Lime............................	1,000 metric tons	19,100	231	1	19,400	[6,25] 107.90	5,100
Lithium............................	Metric tons	(D)	1,310	>80	(D)	(NA)	68
Magnesium compounds..................	1,000 metric tons	306	20	49	602	(NA)	300
Magnesium metal......................	1,000 metric tons	(D)	12	33	110	[4] 2.13	400
Manganese (gross weight)..............	1,000 metric tons	–	1	100	699	[26] 7.88	(NA)
Mercury [38]............................	Metric tons	[15] (NA)	132	(3)	(NA)	[27] 1,850	(NA)
Mica, scrap and flake..................	1,000 metric tons	130	6	30	72	[6] 122	(NA)
Molybdenum (contained)............	Metric tons	63,700	35,400	(3)	48,300	[10] 34.13	940
Nickel (contained) [28]............	Metric tons	(D)	77,200	47	124,000	[29] 22,890	(NA)
Niobium (columbium)..................	Metric tons	–	363	100	9,156	[6] 41,000	(NA)
Nitrogen (fixed)-ammonia..............	1,000 metric tons	9,350	26	37	14,900	[6] 531	1,050
Peat............................	1,000 metric tons	568	49	61	1,500	[6] 22.73	600
Perlite............................	1,000 metric tons	420	36	27	577	[6] 56	95
Phosphate rock......................	1,000 metric tons	28,100	(NA)	13	(NA)	[6] 96.64	2,270
Platinum-group metals..................	Kilograms	[31] 16,100	45,820	[32] 89	[32] (NA)	[19,33] 1,724.51	1,570
Potash (K2O equivalent)............	1,000 metric tons	1,000	202	83	5,800	[6,34] 745	1,200
Pumice and pumicite..................	1,000 metric tons	489	14	2	498	[6] 22.89	140
Salt............................	1,000 metric tons	45,000	846	22	58,500	[6,35] 174	4,100
Silicon, metal......................	1,000 metric tons	(D)	[39] 79	<40	(D)	[4] 1.58	(NA)
Silver (contained)......................	Metric tons	1,120	904	64	7,910	[19] 35.26	950
Soda ash (sodium carbonate)............	1,000 metric tons	10,700	5,470	(3)	5,220	[40] 260	2,400
Sodium sulfate......................	1,000 metric tons	(NA)	199	(3)	(NA)	[41] 134	225
Stone (crushed)......................	Million metric tons	1,160	1	1	1,200	[6] 9.68	79,000
Sulfur (all forms)......................	1,000 metric tons	8,930	1,419	23	11,600	[6,42] 159.83	2,600
Talc............................	1,000 metric tons	616	233	6	653	[6] 155	290
Thallium (contained)......................	Kilograms	–	545	100	(NA)	[10] 6,000	(NA)
Tin (contained)......................	Metric tons	[15] 11,000	5,450	73	39,900	[4] 12.16	(NA)
Titanium dioxide......................	1,000 metric tons	1,290	789	(3)	706	(NA)	3,400
Tungsten (contained)......................	Metric tons	[15] 11,000	7,129	40	18,100	[44] 248	(NA)
Vermiculite............................	1,000 metric tons	100	2	30	150	[6] 160	80
Zinc (contained)......................	1,000 metric tons	769	660	74	939	[4,45] 1.06	2,484
Zirconium (ZrO2)......................	Metric tons	(D)	15,800	(NA)	(D)	[6,46] 2,650	

– Represents or rounds to zero. D Withheld to avoid disclosing company proprietary data. NA Not available. [1] Data are rounded to no more than three significant digits; except prices. [2] Calculated as a percent of apparent consumption. [3] Net exporter. [4] Dollars per pound. [5] Refinery production. [6] Dollars per metric ton. [7] Bauxite, average value U.S. imports (f.a.s.). [8] Boric acid, gross weight. [9] Average value of mineral imports at port of exportation. [10] Dollars per kilogram. [11] Recycling production, based on reported stainless steel scrap receipts. [12] Metal only. [13] Average New York dealer price for 99.95% purity in 5-short-ton lots. Source: Platts Metals Week. [14] Excludes Puerto Rico. [15] Secondary production. [16] Unit value of imported chromite ore. Dollars per metric ton gross weight. [17] Excludes attapulgite. [18] Value of imports, dollars per carat. [19] Dollars per troy ounce. [20] Price of flake imports. [21] C.i.f. value, crude, per kilogram. [22] Shipments of usable ore. [23] Delivered, No. 1 Heavy Melting composite price. [24] Sales include imports and reprocessed slag from past years and decades, and only some from current production. [25] Quicklime only. [26] 46%-48% Mn metallurgical ore, per unit contained Mn, c.i.f. U.S. ports. [27] Dollars per 76-pound flask. [28] Primary and secondary materials. [29] London Metal Exchange cash price; dollars per metric ton. [30] F.o.b. Gulf Coast. [31] Platinum and palladium. [32] Platinum. [33] Dealer price of platinum. [34] Price of K2O, muriate. [35] Vacuum and open pan, bulk, pellets and packaged, f.o.b. mine and plant. [36] Natural gemstone production, $11 million; laboratory-created (synthetic) gemstone production, $31.9 million. [37] Iron and steel scrap reported consumption. [38] Mercury has not been produced as principal mineral commodity In U.S. since 1992. Mercury secondary production (recycled) not reported. [39] Silicon metal. Ferrosilicon statistics include: production (D), exports (20,000t), net import reliance (greater than 50%), and price 50% Si ($1.11 per pound). [40] Quoted year-end price, dense, bulk, f.o.b. Green River, WY, dollars per short ton. [41] Quoted price, bulk, f.o.b. works, East, dollars per short ton. [42] Elemental sulfur, f.o.b. plant. [43] Year-end. Unit value based on landed-duty-paid U.S. imports for consumption of pigment with 80% or more TiO2. [44] Dollars per metric ton unit WO3 (7.93 kilograms of contained tungsten per metric ton unit). [45] Platts Metals Week North American price for Special High Grade zinc. [46] Price for domestic zircon.

Source: U.S. Geological Survey, *Mineral Commodity Summaries, 2013*, January 2013. See also <http://minerals.er.usgs.gov/minerals/pubs/mcs/>.

Table 931. Selected Mineral Products—Average Prices: 1990 to 2012

[Excludes Alaska and Hawaii, except as noted]

Year	Nonfuels									Fuels		
	Copper, cathode [1] (cents per lb.)	Plati-num [2] (dol./troy oz.)	Gold (dol./troy oz. [3])	Silver (dol./troy oz. [3])	Lead [4] (cents per lb.)	Nickel [5] (cents per pound)	Tin (New York) [5] (cents per lb.)	Zinc [6] (cents per lb.)	Sulfur, crude [7] (dol./metric ton)	Bitumi-nous coal [8] (dol./short ton)	Crude petrol-eum [8] (dol./bbl.)	Natural gas [8] (dol./1,000 cu. ft.)
1990........	123	467	385	4.82	46	402	386	75	80	27.43	20.03	1.71
1995........	138	425	386	5.15	42	373	416	56	44	25.56	14.62	1.55
1999........	76	379	280	5.25	44	273	366	53	38	23.92	15.56	2.19
2000........	88	549	280	5.00	44	392	370	56	25	24.15	26.72	3.69
2001........	77	533	272	4.39	44	270	315	44	10	25.36	21.84	4.12
2002........	76	543	311	4.62	44	307	292	39	12	26.57	22.51	2.95
2003........	85	694	365	4.91	44	437	340	41	29	26.57	27.56	4.98
2004........	134	849	411	6.69	55	627	547	52	33	30.56	36.77	5.46
2005........	174	900	446	7.34	61	669	483	67	31	36.80	50.28	7.33
2006........	315	1,144	606	11.61	77	1,100	565	159	33	39.32	59.69	6.39
2007........	328	1,308	699	13.43	124	1,688	899	154	36	40.80	66.52	6.25
2008........	319	1,578	874	15.00	120	957	1,129	89	264	51.39	94.04	7.96
2009........	241	1,208	975	14.69	87	665	837	78	2	55.44	56.35	3.67
2010........	348	1,616	1,227	20.20	109	989	1,240	102	70	60.88	74.71	4.48
2011........	406	1,725	1,572	35.26	122	1,038	1,575	106	160	[9] 57.64	95.73	3.95
2012 [9]......	370	1,580	1,700	30.00	114	799	1,645	93	160	(NA)	94.52	2.66

NA Not Available. [1] U.S. producer price. [2] Average annual dealer prices. [3] 99.95 percent purity. [4] Nationwide delivered basis. [5] Composite price. [6] Platt's Metals Week price for North American Special High Grade zinc. Average prices for 1990 are for U.S. High Grade Zinc. [7] F.o.b. (Free on Board) works. [8] Average value at the point of production or domestic first purchase price. [9] Estimated.

Source: Nonfuels, through 1994, U.S. Bureau of Mines; thereafter, U.S. Geological Survey, *Mineral Commodities Summaries 2013*, January 2013, and earlier reports; see also <http://minerals.usgs.gov/minerals/pubs/mcs/>. Fuels, U.S. Energy Information Administration, *Monthly Energy Review*, July 2013, and earlier reports; see also <http://www.eia.gov/totalenergy/data/monthly/>.

Table 932. Value of Domestic Nonfuel Mineral Production by State: 2000 to 2012

[In millions of dollars (39,400 represents $39,400,000,000)]

State	2000	2010	2011	2012 [1]	State	2000	2010	2011	2012 [1]
United States [2]......	**39,400**	**66,400**	**74,700**	**76,500**					
Alabama.................	930	969	960	1,010	Montana............	596	1,140	1,440	1,420
Alaska.................	1,140	3,400	3,810	3,500	Nebraska............	[3] 84	234	238	335
Arizona................	2,510	6,790	8,390	8,050	Nevada.............	2,980	7,700	10,000	11,200
Arkansas...............	484	709	789	800	New Hampshire......	57	[3] 94	[3] 100	[3] 157
California..............	3,270	2,890	3,210	3,580	New Jersey.........	[3] 291	[3] 258	[3] 275	[3] 292
Colorado..............	592	1,850	1,930	1,930	New Mexico.......	786	1,020	1,250	1,490
Connecticut............	[3] 112	[3] 148	[3] 156	[3] 173	New York..........	1,020	1,310	1,340	1,270
Delaware..............	[3] 14	[3] 12	[3] 11	[3] 13	North Carolina......	744	880	843	911
Florida................	1,820	2,680	3,430	3,640	North Dakota.......	35	[3] 70	[3] 125	[3] 97
Georgia...............	1,620	1,430	1,450	1,440	Ohio...............	999	1,170	[3] 962	[3] 1,220
Hawaii................	392	106	101	107	Oklahoma.........	473	702	608	651
Idaho.................	358	1,180	1,320	728	Oregon............	299	312	305	316
Illinois................	913	924	1,070	1,170	Pennsylvania.......	[3] 1,250	[3] 1,670	1,600	[3] 1,790
Indiana...............	695	782	762	838	Rhode Island.......	[3] 20	[3] 33	[3] 42	[3] 41
Iowa..................	503	583	653	731	South Carolina......	[3] 551	[3] 468	[3] 483	[3] 498
Kansas................	629	1,090	1,120	1,220	South Dakota.......	233	258	312	364
Kentucky..............	501	762	791	786	Tennessee..........	737	831	878	1,030
Louisiana..............	325	549	[3] 465	492	Texas.............	1,950	2,780	3,030	3,390
Maine.................	96	110	118	133	Utah..............	1,430	4,380	4,300	3,490
Maryland..............	[3] 358	[3] 305	[3] 293	[3] 289	Vermont............	[3] 67	[3] 121	[3] 118	[3] 117
Massachusetts.........	[3] 200	[3] 233	[3] 225	[3] 209	Virginia............	710	1,040	1,190	1,250
Michigan..............	1,640	2,190	2,410	2,240	Washington.........	607	712	742	689
Minnesota.............	1,460	[3] 4,180	[3] 4,490	[3] 4,500	West Virginia........	172	272	324	341
Mississippi............	149	198	195	196	Wisconsin..........	[3] 372	509	[3] 683	[3] 660
Missouri...............	1,370	2,010	2,200	2,640	Wyoming...........	978	1,860	2,140	2,220

[1] Preliminary. [2] Includes undistributed not shown separately. [3] Partial data only; excludes values withheld to avoid disclosing individual company data.

Source: U.S. Geological Survey, *Minerals Yearbook, 2011*, July 2013, and earlier reports; and *Mineral Commodities Summaries 2013*, January 2013, and earlier reports. See also <http://minerals.er.usgs.gov/minerals/pubs/mcs/>.

Table 933. Principal Fuels, Nonmetals, and Metals—World Production and the U.S. Share: 2000 to 2011

[In units as indicated (4,894 represents 4,894,000,000), except as indicated; see Appendix IV]

Mineral	Unit	World production 2000	2005	2010	2011	U.S. share 2011
FUELS						
Coal.............................	Mil. sh. tons	4,894	6,554	7,934	8,440	13.0
Petroleum (crude) [1].........	Bil. bbl.	25.0	26.9	27.0	27.1	7.6
Natural gas (dry, marketable).......................	Tril. cu. ft.	87.1	98.4	112.0	116.0	19.7
Natural gas plant liquids......	Bil. bbl.	2.3	2.8	3.1	3.1	25.7
NONMETALS						
Asbestos.........................	1,000 metric tons	2,110	2,210	2,040	2,030	–
Barite.............................	1,000 metric tons	6,470	7,870	8,130	8,370	8.5
Cement, hydraulic.............	Mil. metric tons	1,660	2,350	3,270	3,610	1.9
Feldspar..........................	1,000 metric tons	9,580	16,800	21,300	21,200	3.1
Fluorspar........................	1,000 metric tons	4,470	5,360	7,180	7,520	–
Gypsum..........................	Mil. metric tons	106	147	147	148	5.7
Mica (incl. scrap).............	1,000 metric tons	328	354	1,080	1,090	4.6
Nitrogen (N content).........	Mil. metric tons	108	122	131	135	6.9
Phosphate rock (gross wt.)..	Mil. metric tons	132	152	181	198	14.2
Potash (K2O equivalent)....	Mil. metric tons	27	34	34	36	2.8
Sulfur, elemental basis.......	Mil. metric tons	59	69	69	71	12.7
METALS, mine basis						
Bauxite...........................	Mil. metric tons	136	178	239	262	(NA)
Copper...........................	1,000 metric tons	13,300	15,000	16,100	16,100	6.9
Gold..............................	Metric tons	2,570	2,470	2,570	2,660	8.8
Iron ore (gross wt.)...........	Mil. metric tons	1,079	1,550	2,590	2,940	1.9
Lead [2].........................	1,000 metric tons	3,170	3,470	4,150	4,690	7.1
Mercury..........................	Metric tons	1,350	1,520	2,250	2,010	(NA)
Molybdenum....................	1,000 metric tons	133	186	244	264	24.1
Nickel [2].......................	1,000 metric tons	1,290	1,460	1,710	1,960	–
Silver.............................	1,000 metric tons	18	21	24	23	4.8
Tantalum concentrates (Ta content).................	Metric tons	1,040	1,380	640	770	(NA)
Titanium mineral concentrates (titanium content) [3]............	1,000 metric tons	(NA)	5,200	6,959	7,239	(NA)
Tungsten [2]...................	1,000 metric tons	44	59	68	73	(NA)
Vanadium [2]...................	1,000 metric tons	56	56	74	74	(NA)
Zinc [2].........................	1,000 metric tons	8,788	10,000	12,200	12,800	6.0
METALS, smelter basis						
Aluminum........................	1,000 metric tons	24,400	31,900	41,200	44,400	4.5
Cadmium.........................	1,000 metric tons	20	20	23	22	(NA)
Copper...........................	1,000 metric tons	11,000	13,500	15,500	15,700	3.4
Iron, pig.........................	Mil. metric tons	573	802	1,040	1,090	2.8
Lead [3].........................	1,000 metric tons	6,580	7,660	9,610	10,200	12.3
Magnesium [4, 5].............	1,000 metric tons	428	622	755	771	(NA)
Raw Steel.......................	Mil. metric tons	850	1,140	1,440	1,520	5.7
Tin [6]...........................	1,000 metric tons	278	296	337	339	3.2
Zinc..............................	1,000 metric tons	9,137	10,300	12,800	13,100	1.9

– Represents zero. NA Not available. [1] Crude oil including lease condensate. [2] Content of ore and concentrate. [3] Refinery production. [4] Primary production; no smelter processing necessary. [5] Starting 2005, excludes U.S. production. [6] Production from primary sources only.

Source: U.S. Energy Information Administration, "International Energy Statistics," <http://www.eia.gov/cfapps/ipdbproject/iedindex3.cfm>, accessed September 2013; and U.S. Geological Survey, *Minerals Yearbook 2011*, July 2013, and earlier reports.

Table 934. Supply, Disposition, and Ending Stocks of Crude Oil and Petroleum Products: 2012

[In millions of barrels (2,374.0 represents 2,374,000,000). Minus sign (-) indicates decrease]

Commodity	Supply				Disposition				Ending stocks
	Field production [1]	Refinery and blender net production	Imports	Adjustments [2]	Stock change	Refinery and blender net inputs	Exports	Products supplied [3]	
Crude oil.........................	2,374.0	(X)	3,107.8	65.5	33.4	5,492.0	21.9	–	1,060.3
Natural gas liquids and LRG [4]...	878.2	229.4	73.2	(X)	24.7	185.4	113.6	850.5	153.5
Pentanes plus..................	115.6	(X)	10.7	(X)	-5.0	63.2	41.6	19.9	12.6
Liquefied petroleum gases.....	762.6	229.4	62.6	(X)	29.7	122.2	71.9	830.7	140.9
Ethane/ethylene..............	355.3	6.6	0.1	(X)	12.5	(NA)	(NA)	349.5	35.4
Propane/propylene............	259.4	201.6	50.6	(X)	13.4	(NA)	62.5	435.7	68.0
Normal butane/butylene......	65.7	20.2	7.5	(X)	2.2	51.5	9.4	30.2	28.7
Isobutane/isobutylene........	82.2	1.0	4.4	(X)	1.7	70.7	(NA)	15.3	8.8
Finished motor gasoline........	(X)	3,267.0	16.1	38.4	-5.4	(X)	149.7	3,177.7	55.2
Kerosene-type jet fuel..........	(X)	538.3	20.0	(X)	-1.9	(X)	48.5	511.7	39.6
Distillate fuel oil [5]............	(X)	1,665.3	46.2	12.2	-14.4	(X)	368.6	1,369.4	134.8

– Represents or rounds to zero. NA Not available. X Not applicable. [1] Represents crude oil production on leases, natural gas liquids production at natural gas processing plants, new supply of other hydrocarbons/oxygenates and motor gasoline blending components, fuel ethanol, and distillate fuel oil. See Appendix B of source for more details. [2] Includes an adjustment for crude oil, previously referred to as "Unaccounted For Crude Oil." Also included is an adjustment for motor gasoline blending components, fuel ethanol, and distillate fuel oil. [3] Products supplied is equal to field production, plus refinery and blender net production, plus import, plus adjustments, minus stock change, minus refinery and blender net inputs, minus export. [4] Liquefied Refinery Gases (LRGs) are liquefied petroleum gases fractionated from refinery or still gases through compression and/or refrigeration. They are retained in the liquid state. Excludes still gas. [5] Distillate stocks located in the "Northeast Heating Oil Reserve" are not included.

Source: U.S. Energy Information Administration, "Petroleum Supply and Disposition," <http://www.eia.gov/petroleum/>, accessed September 2013.

Table 935. Petroleum Industry—Wells Drilled, Production, Foreign Trade, Reserves, and Refineries: 1990 to 2011

[602 represents 602,000. Includes all costs incurred for drilling and equipping wells to point of completion as productive wells or abandonment after drilling becomes unproductive. Based on sample of operators of different size drilling establishments]

Item	Unit	1990	1995	2000	2005	2008	2009	2010	2011 [1]
Crude oil producing wells, (Dec. 31)	1,000	602	574	534	498	526	526	520	536
Daily output per well [2]	Bbl.	12.2	11.4	10.9	10.4	9.4	10.2	10.5	10.6
Completed wells drilled, total	1,000	32.33	21.14	29.29	44.02	54.35	33.05	37.50	(NA)
Crude oil	1,000	12.84	8.25	8.09	10.78	16.65	11.26	16.25	(NA)
Natural gas	1,000	11.25	8.08	17.05	28.59	32.27	18.23	16.97	(NA)
Dry holes	1,000	8.25	4.81	4.15	4.65	5.43	3.55	4.28	(NA)
Average depth per well	Feet	4,827	5,542	4,932	5,459	6,154	7,247	7,183	(NA)
Average cost per well	$1,000	384	513	755	1,721	(NA)	(NA)	(NA)	(NA)
Average cost per foot	Dollars	76.07	87.22	142.16	306.50	(NA)	(NA)	(NA)	(NA)
Crude oil production, total [3]	Mil. bbl.	2,685	2,394	2,131	1,890	1,812	1,957	1,999	2,067
Value at wells [3, 4]	Bil. dol.	53.77	35.00	56.93	95.03	170.38	110.25	149.32	197.83
Average price per barrel	Dollars	20.03	14.62	26.72	50.28	94.04	56.35	74.71	95.73
Lower 48 states [5]	Mil. bbl.	2,037	1,853	1,776	1,575	1,562	1,721	1,779	1,858
Alaska	Mil. bbl.	647	542	355	315	250	236	220	209
Onshore	Mil. bbl.	2,290	1,838	1,482	1,265	1,263	1,322	1,367	1,525
Offshore	Mil. bbl.	395	556	649	625	548	634	632	542
Imports: Crude oil [3, 6]	Mil. bbl.	2,151	2,639	3,320	3,696	3,581	3,290	3,363	3,256
Refined petroleum products	Mil. bbl.	775	586	874	1,310	1,146	977	942	890
Exports: Crude oil [3]	Mil. bbl.	39.7	34.5	18.4	11.6	10.5	16.0	15.2	17.2
Proved reserves	Bil. bbl.	26.3	22.4	22.0	21.8	19.1	20.7	23.3	(NA)
Operable refineries	Number	205	175	158	148	150	150	148	148
Daily Capacity (Jan. 1)	1,000 bbl.	15,572	15,434	16,512	17,125	17,594	17,672	17,584	17,736
Refinery input, total	Mil. bbl.	5,325	5,555	5,964	6,136	6,278	6,170	6,345	6,409
Crude oil [3]	Mil. bbl.	4,894	5,100	5,514	5,555	5,361	5,233	5,374	5,414
Natural gas plant liquids	Mil. bbl.	171	172	139	161	178	177	161	178
Other liquids [7]	Mil. bbl.	260	283	311	420	739	760	810	817
Refinery output, total [8]	Mil. bbl.	5,574	5,838	6,311	6,497	6,641	6,527	6,735	6,805
Motor gasoline [9]	Mil. bbl.	2,540	2,722	2,910	3,036	3,129	3,207	3,306	3,298
Jet fuel [10]	Mil. bbl.	543	517	588	564	546	510	517	529
Distillate fuel oil	Mil. bbl.	1,067	1,152	1,310	1,443	1,572	1,478	1,542	1,638
Residual fuel oil	Mil. bbl.	347	288	255	229	227	218	213	196
Liquefied petroleum gases	Mil. bbl.	182	239	258	209	230	227	240	226
Utilization rate	Percent	87.1	92.0	92.6	90.6	85.3	82.9	86.4	86.2

NA Not available. [1] Preliminary. [2] Based on number of wells producing at end of year. [3] Includes lease condensate. [4] Values based on domestic first purchase price. [5] Excluding Alaska and Hawaii. [6] Includes imports for the Strategic Petroleum Reserve. [7] Unfinished oils (net), other hydrocarbons, hydrogen, aviation and motor gasoline blending components (net). Beginning 1995, also includes oxygenates (net). [8] Includes other products not shown separately. [9] Finished motor gasoline. Beginning 1995, also includes ethanol blended into motor gasoline. [10] Prior to 2005, kerosene-type jet fuel is included with kerosene in "Other products." Beginning 2005, naphtha-type jet fuel is also included in "Other products."

Source: U.S. Energy Information Administration, *Annual Energy Review 2011*, September 2012. See also <http://www.eia.gov/totalenergy/>.

Table 936. Net U.S. Imports of Selected Minerals and Metals as Percent of Apparent Consumption: 1980 to 2012

[In percent. Based on net imports which equal the difference between imports and exports plus or minus government stockpile and industry stock changes]

Minerals and metals	1980	1990	1995	2000	2005	2009	2010	2011	2012 [1]
Bauxite [2]	(NA)	98	99	100	100	100	100	100	100
Fluorspar	87	91	92	100	100	100	100	100	100
Manganese	98	100	100	100	100	100	100	100	100
Niobium	100	100	100	100	100	100	100	100	100
Strontium	100	100	100	100	100	100	100	100	100
Tantalum	90	86	80	80	100	100	100	100	100
Mica (sheet)	100	100	100	100	100	100	100	100	100
Vanadium	35	(D)	84	100	100	78	81	92	96
Platinum	(NA)	(NA)	(NA)	78	93	95	91	89	91
Potash	65	68	75	80	80	73	83	83	81
Barite	44	71	65	84	84	78	75	76	80
Cobalt	93	84	79	78	83	76	81	76	78
Titanium	(NA)	(NA)	70	79	71	68	65	77	77
Tin	79	71	84	88	78	74	74	73	75
Zinc	60	64	71	72	67	77	73	74	72
Chromium	67	80	75	77	68	12	62	67	70
Silver	7	(NA)	(NA)	43	72	58	65	64	57
Palladium	(NA)	(NA)	(NA)	84	84	62	49	64	54
Nickel	76	64	60	54	48	22	41	47	49
Tungsten	53	81	90	66	68	68	63	40	42
Copper	16	15	27	37	42	21	32	34	35

D Withheld to avoid disclosure. NA Not available. [1] Preliminary. [2] Includes alumina.

Source: Through 1990, U.S. Bureau of Mines; thereafter, U.S. Geological Survey, *Mineral Commodity Summaries 2013*, January 2013, and earlier reports. See also <http://minerals.usgs.gov/minerals/pubs/mcs/>.

Table 937. Crude Petroleum and Natural Gas—Production and Value by Major Producing States: 2010 to 2012

[2,000 represents 2,000,000,000 barrels]

State	Crude petroleum Quantity (mil. bbl.) 2010	2011	2012	Value (mil. dol.) [4] 2010	2011	2012	Natural gas marketed production [1] Quantity (bil. cu. ft.) 2010	2011	2012	Value (mil. dol.) [5] 2010	2011	2012
Total [2]	2,000	2,063	2,376	149,400	197,485	224,581	22,382	24,036	25,319	100,271	94,944	67,350
AL	7	8	10	536	888	997	223	196	(NA)	994	(NA)	(NA)
AK [3]	220	205	192	15,879	20,235	18,987	374	356	351	1,186	(NA)	(NA)
AR	6	6	7	407	515	584	927	1,072	(NA)	3,558	(NA)	(NA)
CA	201	194	196	15,005	19,853	20,437	287	250	(NA)	1,397	(NA)	(NA)
CO	33	39	49	2,370	3,453	4,231	1,578	1,638	(NA)	6,250	(NA)	(NA)
FL	2	2	2	(NA)	(NA)	(NA)	12	15	(NA)	(NA)	(NA)	(NA)
IL	9	9	10	664	819	869	2	2	(NA)	28	(NA)	(NA)
IN	2	2	2	134	175	208	7	9	(NA)	28	(NA)	(NA)
KS	40	42	44	2,931	3,674	3,837	325	309	(NA)	1,374	(NA)	(NA)
KY	3	2	3	178	200	278	135	124	(NA)	605	(NA)	(NA)
LA	67	69	71	5,271	7,326	7,487	2,210	3,029	3,003	9,349	(NA)	(NA)
MI	7	7	7	509	645	659	131	138	(NA)	497	(NA)	(NA)
MS	24	24	24	1,840	2,432	2,435	74	81	(NA)	307	(NA)	(NA)
MT	25	24	26	1,779	2,140	2,198	88	75	(NA)	319	(NA)	(NA)
NE	2	3	3	162	217	257	2	2	(NA)	9	(NA)	(NA)
NM	65	71	85	4,946	6,481	7,445	1,292	1,237	1,266	6,874	(NA)	(NA)
NY	–	–	–	(NA)	(NA)	(NA)	36	31	(NA)	167	(NA)	(NA)
ND	113	153	242	7,942	13,576	20,383	82	97	(NA)	321	(NA)	(NA)
OH	5	5	5	350	441	453	78	79	(NA)	362	(NA)	(NA)
OK	68	77	89	5,092	6,973	8,034	1,827	1,889	2,021	8,607	(NA)	(NA)
PA	3	3	4	225	295	384	573	1,311	(NA)	(NA)	(NA)	(NA)
TX	427	532	730	32,580	48,895	67,492	6,715	7,113	7,240	31,562	(NA)	(NA)
UT	25	26	30	1,680	2,168	2,505	432	458	(NA)	1,828	(NA)	(NA)
WV	2	2	2	130	186	191	265	394	(NA)	(NA)	(NA)	(NA)
WY	53	55	58	3,626	4,566	4,647	2,306	2,159	2,055	9,914	(NA)	(NA)
Federal offshore	588	500	481	(NA)	(NA)	(NA)	(NA)	(NA)	(NA)	(NA)	(NA)	(NA)
Lower 48 states	1,780	1,858	2,184	133,586	177,170	205,503	22,008	23,680	24,968	99,084	(NA)	(NA)

– Represents zero. NA Not available. [1] Excludes nonhydrocarbon gases. [2] Includes other states, not shown separately. State production includes state offshore production, as well as extractions from the Gulf not distributed to states. U.S. level totals shown in Table 935 and Table 942 may contain revisions not carried to state level. [3] Alaska crude oil production value using price data for North Slope only. [4] Crude petroleum production value calculated using production quantity and domestic crude oil first purchase price. [5] Natural gas production value calculated using marketed production quantity and wellhead price.

Source: U.S. Energy Information Administration, "Petroleum & Other Liquids Data," <http://www.eia.gov/petroleum/data.cfm>, and "Natural Gas Data,"<http://www.eia.gov/naturalgas/data.cfm>; accessed July 2013.

Table 938. Crude Oil and Natural Gas—Reserves by State: 2008 to 2011

[19,121 mil. bbl. represents 19,121,000,000 bbl. As of December 31. Proved reserves are estimated quantities of the mineral, which geological and engineering data demonstrate with reasonable certainty, to be recoverable in future years from known reservoirs under existing economic and operating conditions. Based on a sample of operators of oil and gas wells]

Area	2008 Crude oil proved reserves (mil. bbl.)	2008 Natural gas (bil. cu. ft.)	2009 Crude oil proved reserves (mil. bbl.)	2009 Natural gas (bil. cu. ft.)	2010 Crude oil proved reserves (mil. bbl.)	2010 Natural gas (bil. cu. ft.)	2011 Crude oil proved reserves (mil. bbl.)	2011 Natural gas (bil. cu. ft.)
United States [1]	19,121	244,656	20,682	272,509	23,267	304,625	26,544	334,067
Alabama	38	3,290	37	2,871	42	2,629	46	2,475
Alaska	3,507	7,699	3,566	9,101	3,722	8,838	3,816	9,424
Arkansas	30	5,626	28	10,869	40	14,178	38	16,370
California	2,705	2,406	2,835	2,773	2,938	2,647	3,005	2,934
Colorado	288	23,302	279	23,058	386	24,119	423	24,821
Florida	3	1	9	7	18	56	22	6
Illinois	54	(NA)	66	(NA)	64	(NA)	54	(NA)
Indiana	15	(NA)	8	(NA)	8	(NA)	7	(NA)
Kansas	243	3,557	259	3,279	295	3,673	343	3,486
Kentucky	17	2,714	20	2,782	15	2,613	17	2,006
Louisiana	388	11,573	370	20,688	424	29,277	417	30,358
Michigan	48	3,174	33	2,763	40	2,919	44	2,505
Mississippi	249	1,030	244	917	247	853	238	860
Montana	321	1,000	343	976	369	944	384	778
Nebraska	8	(NA)	9	(NA)	10	(NA)	14	(NA)
New Mexico	654	16,285	700	15,598	823	15,412	866	15,005
New York	(NA)	389	(NA)	196	(NA)	281	(NA)	253
North Dakota	573	541	1,046	1,079	1,814	1,667	2,649	2,381
Ohio	38	985	38	896	42	832	41	758
Oklahoma	581	20,845	622	22,769	710	26,345	879	27,830
Pennsylvania	14	3,577	10	6,985	22	13,960	24	26,529
Texas	4,555	77,546	5,006	80,424	5,674	88,997	7,014	98,165
Utah	286	6,643	398	7,257	449	6,981	504	7,857
Virginia	(NA)	2,378	(NA)	3,091	(NA)	3,215	(NA)	2,832
West Virginia	23	5,136	19	5,946	17	7,000	21	10,345
Wyoming	556	31,143	583	35,283	567	35,074	660	35,290
Federal offshore	3,903	13,546	4,129	12,552	4,496	11,765	4,976	10,420
Lower 48 states	15,614	236,957	17,116	263,408	19,545	295,787	22,728	324,643

NA Not available. [1] Includes other states, not shown separately.

Source: U.S. Energy Information Administration, "Petroleum & Other Liquids Data," <http://www.eia.gov/petroleum/data.cfm>; and "Natural Gas Data," <http://www.eia.gov/naturalgas/data.cfm>; accessed August 2013.

Table 939. Federal Offshore Leasing, Exploration, Production, and Revenue: 1990 to 2012

[In millions (56.79 represents 56,790,000), except as indicated. Data presented by fiscal year. See source for explanation of terms and for reliability statement]

Item	Unit	1990	1995	2000	2005	2009	2010	2011	2012
Tracts offered..........................	Number	10,459	10,995	7,992	11,447	9,893	6,958	3,913	11,307
Tracts leased...........................	Number	825	835	553	989	483	446	181	570
Acres offered...........................	Millions	56.79	59.70	42.89	61.08	52.98	36.96	21.01	60.06
Acres leased............................	Millions	4.30	4.34	2.92	5.24	2.66	2.37	1.04	2.99
New wells being drilled:									
Active..................................	Number	120	237	236	135	54	48	(NA)	(NA)
Suspended...........................	Number	266	155	139	59	67	76	(NA)	(NA)
Cumulative wells (since 1953):									
Wells completed...................	Number	13,167	13,423	13,733	13,398	11,384	10,404	(NA)	(NA)
Wells plugged and abandoned.......	Number	14,677	21,478	26,893	31,884	35,544	36,695	(NA)	(NA)
Revenue, total [1]......................	Bil. dol.	3.4	2.7	5.2	6.3	5.8	5.3	6.5	6.86
Bonuses.............................	Bil. dol.	0.8	0.4	0.4	0.6	1.2	1.0	0.4	0.66
Oil and gas royalties...............	Bil. dol.	2.6	2.1	4.1	5.5	4.4	3.6	6.0	5.46
Rentals..............................	Bil. dol.	0.09	0.09	0.21	0.22	0.23	0.25	0.22	0.23
Sales value [2].........................	Bil. dol.	17.0	13.8	27.4	37.2	32.6	25.1	39.0	40.28
Oil..................................	Bil. dol.	7.0	6.3	11.5	15.4	23.5	21.3	36.7	37.83
Natural gas.........................	Bil. dol.	9.5	7.5	15.9	21.8	9.2	3.7	2.2	2.45
Sales volume: [3]									
Oil..................................	Mil. bbl.	324	409	566	332	425	261	385	347
Natural gas.........................	Bil. cu. ft.	5,093	4,692	4,723	3,504	3,539	1,043	1,870	1,612

NA Not available [1] Includes condensate royalties. Excludes gas plant product royalties. [2] Sales value is value at time of sale, not current value. [3] Excludes sales volumes for gas plant products and sulfur.

Source: U.S. Department of the Interior, Bureau of Ocean Energy Management, Regulation and Enforcement, *Federal Lease Offerings and Acreage Leased Since 1954*, 2012; see also <http://www.boem.gov/Oil-and-Gas-Energy-Program/Leasing/Regional-Leasing/Table_1.aspx>. And Office of Natural Resources Revenue, "Annual Reported Royalty Revenue," <http://statistics.onrr.gov/ReportTool.aspx>, accessed July 2013.

Table 940. Natural Gas Plant Liquids—Production and Value: 1990 to 2012

[Barrels of 42 gallons (569 represents 569,000,000)]

Item	Unit	1990	1995	2000	2005	2008	2009	2010	2011	2012
Field production [1]................	Mil. bbl.	569	643	699	627	653	697	757	809	878
Pentanes plus......................	Mil. bbl.	113	122	112	97	97	99	101	106	116
Liquefied petroleum gases...........	Mil. bbl.	456	521	587	529	556	598	656	703	763
Natural gas processed...............	Tril. cu. ft.	15	17	17	15	15	16	16	17	(NA)

NA Not available. [1] Includes other finished petroleum products, not shown separately.

Source: U.S. Energy Information Administration, "Natural Gas Navigator," <http://www.eia.gov/naturalgas/index.cfm>, accessed August 2013.

Table 941. Natural Gas Liquid Extraction Industry—Establishments, Employees, and Payroll by State: 2011

[1,028,577 represents 1,028,577,000. Excludes government employees, railroad employees, self-employed persons, etc. See "General Explanation" in source for definitions and statement on reliability of data. An establishment is a single physical location where business is conducted or where services or industrial operations are performed. See Appendix III]

State	Natural gas liquid extraction (NAICS 211112) [1]			State	Natural gas liquid extraction (NAICS 211112) [1]		
	Establish-ments	Number of employees [2]	Annual payroll ($1,000)		Establish-ments	Number of employees [2]	Annual payroll ($1,000)
United States......	338	10,005	1,028,577	Mississippi............	3	(4)	(D)
Alabama.............	2	(4)	(D)	Montana............	4	(4)	(D)
Alaska..............	1	(4)	(D)	New Mexico.........	18	605	55,779
Arizona.............	1	(3)	(D)	North Carolina........	1	(3)	(D)
Arkansas............	2	(3)	(D)	North Dakota.........	1	(5)	(D)
California...........	5	132	14,190	Ohio................	3	(3)	359
Colorado............	19	1,314	181,508	Oklahoma............	37	776	85,319
Florida..............	1	(3)	(D)	Pennsylvania.........	16	(7)	(D)
Illinois..............	4	(5)	(D)	Tennessee...........	1	(3)	(D)
Indiana.............	2	(4)	(D)	Texas...............	107	3,053	285,086
Kansas..............	9	(5)	(D)	Utah................	2	(4)	(D)
Kentucky...........	7	(5)	(D)	Virginia.............	4	110	8,187
Louisiana...........	43	831	72,387	West Virginia........	9	363	38,924
Michigan............	10	(4)	6,412	Wyoming............	24	1,104	100,465
Minnesota...........	2	(3)	(D)				

D Withheld to avoid disclosing data for individual companies; data are included in higher level totals. NA Not available. [1] North American Industry Classification System, 2007. [2] Covers full- and part-time employees who are on the payroll in the pay period including March 12. [3] 0 to 19 employees. [4] 20 to 99 employees. [5] 100 to 249 employees. [6] 250 to 499 employees. [7] 500 to 999 employees.

Source: U.S. Census Bureau, County Business Patterns, "Geography Area Series: County Business Patterns," <http://factfinder2.census.gov>, accessed August 2013.

Table 942. Natural Gas—Supply, Consumption, Reserves, and Marketed Production: 1990 to 2012

[270 represents 270,000. Data are for dry natural gas, plus a small amount of supplemental gaseous fuels. Minus sign (-) indicates debit]

Item	Unit	1990	1995	2000	2005	2008	2009	2010	2011	2012 [8]
Producing wells (year-end).........	1,000	270	299	342	426	477	493	488	515	(NA)
Production value at wells............	Bil. of dol.	31.8	30.3	74.3	138.8	168.3	79.3	100.3	(NA)	(NA)
Avg. per 1,000 cu. ft...............	Dollars	1.71	1.55	3.68	7.33	7.97	3.67	4.48	3.95	2.66
Proved reserves [1]....................	Tril. cu. ft.	169	165	177	204	245	273	305	334	(NA)
Marketed production [2]...........	**Bil. cu. ft.**	**18,594**	**19,506**	**20,198**	**18,927**	**21,112**	**21,648**	**22,382**	**240,364**	**25,319**
Minus: Extraction losses [3]..........	Bil. cu. ft.	784	908	1,016	876	953	1,024	1,066	1,134	1,257
Equals: Dry production...............	Bil. cu. ft.	17,810	18,599	19,182	18,051	20,159	20,624	21,316	22,902	24,063
Plus: Supplemental gas supplies. ..	Bil. cu. ft.	123	110	90	64	61	65	65	60	62
Equals: Dry production with supplemental gas.............	Bil. cu. ft.	17,932	18,709	19,272	18,114	20,219	20,689	21,380	22,962	24,125
Plus: Withdrawals from storage [5]...	Bil. cu. ft.	1,934	2,974	3,498	3,057	3,374	2,966	3,274	3,074	2,815
Plus: Imports...........................	Bil. cu. ft.	1,532	2,841	3,782	4,341	3,984	3,751	3,741	3,469	3,138
Plus: Balancing item [4]...............	Bil. cu. ft.	307	396	-306	236	2	-103	115	-185	-132
Equals: Total supply.................	Bil. cu. ft.	21,706	24,920	26,246	25,748	27,580	27,303	28,511	29,320	29,946
Minus: Exports.......................	Bil. cu. ft.	86	154	244	729	963	1,072	1,137	1,507	1,619
Minus: Additions to storage [5].......	Bil. cu. ft.	2,433	2,566	2,684	3,002	3,340	3,315	3,291	3,422	2,824
Equals: Consumption, total.......	**Bil. cu. ft.**	**19,174**	**22,207**	**23,333**	**22,014**	**23,277**	**22,910**	**24,087**	**24,385**	**25,502**
Lease and plant fuel...............	Bil. cu. ft.	1,236	1,220	1,151	1,112	1,220	1,275	1,286	1,323	1,393
Pipeline fuel [6].......................	Bil. cu. ft.	660	700	642	584	648	670	674	684	715
Residential...........................	Bil. cu. ft.	4,391	4,850	4,996	4,827	4,892	4,779	4,782	4,714	4,180
Commercial [7].......................	Bil. cu. ft.	2,623	3,031	3,182	2,999	3,153	3,119	3,103	3,154	2,907
Industrial.............................	Bil. cu. ft.	(NA)	(NA)	8,142	6,601	6,670	6,167	6,826	6,905	7,138
Vehicle fuel..........................	Bil. cu. ft.	(Z)	5	13	23	26	27	29	32	33
Electric power sector..............	Bil. cu. ft.	3,245	4,237	5,206	5,869	6,668	6,873	7,387	7,574	9,137
World production (dry)..............	Tril. cu. ft.	73.8	78.1	87.1	98.4	107.7	105.2	112.0	116.0	(NA)
U.S. production (dry)..............	Tril. cu. ft.	17.8	18.6	19.2	18.1	20.2	20.6	21.3	22.9	24.1
Percent U.S. of world.............	Percent	24.1	23.8	22.0	18.3	18.7	19.6	19.0	19.7	(NA)

NA Not available. Z Less than 500 million cubic feet. [1] Estimated, end of year. [2] Marketed production includes gross withdrawals from reservoirs less quantities used for reservoir repressuring and quantities vented or flared. Excludes nonhydrocarbon gases subsequently removed. [3] Volumetric reduction in natural gas resulting from the removal of natural gas plant liquids, which are transferred to petroleum supply. [4] Quantities lost and imbalances in data due to differences among data sources. Since 1980, excludes intransit shipments that cross U.S.-Canada border (i.e., natural gas delivered to its destination via the other country). [5] Underground storage. [6] Natural gas consumed in the operation of pipelines and delivery to consumers. [7] Includes deliveries to municipalities and public authorities for institutional heating and other purposes. [8] Data for 2012 are preliminary.

Source: U.S. Energy Information Administration, "Natural Gas Data," <http://www.eia.gov/naturalgas/data.cfm>, and "International Energy Statistics," <http://www.eia.gov/countries/data.cfm>, accessed September 2013.

Table 943. Unconventional Dry Natural Gas Production and Proved Reserves: 2010 to 2011

[In billions of cubic feet (1,886 represents 1,886,000,000,000). For states not shown, no production or reserves were reported]

State	Production				Proved reserves [1]			
	Coalbed methane [2]		Shale gas [3]		Coalbed methane [2]		Shale gas [3]	
	2010	2011	2010	2011	2010	2011	2010	2011
U.S...................	**1,886**	**1,763**	**5,336**	**7,994**	**17,508**	**16,817**	**97,449**	**131,616**
Alabama...............	102	98	–	(NA)	1,298	1,210	–	(NA)
Alaska.................	–	–	–	–	–	–	–	–
Arkansas..............	3	4	794	940	28	21	12,526	14,808
California..............	–	–	(NA)	101	–	–	(NA)	855
Colorado..............	533	516	1	3	6,485	6,580	4	10
Florida.................	–	–	(NA)	(NA)	–	–	(NA)	(NA)
Kansas................	41	37	(NA)	(NA)	258	228	(NA)	(NA)
Kentucky..............	–	–	4	4	–	–	10	41
Louisiana.............	–	–	1,232	2,084	–	–	20,070	21,950
Michigan..............	–	–	120	106	–	–	2,306	1,947
Mississippi............	–	–	(NA)	(NA)	–	–	(NA)	(NA)
Montana..............	10	6	13	13	64	25	186	192
New Mexico...........	402	374	6	9	3,532	3,358	123	144
New York..............	–	–	(NA)	(NA)	–	–	(NA)	(NA)
North Dakota.........	–	–	64	95	–	–	1,185	1,649
Ohio....................	–	–	–	(NA)	–	–	–	(NA)
Oklahoma.............	45	39	403	476	325	374	9,670	10,733
Pennsylvania..........	3	4	396	1,068	129	124	10,708	23,581
Texas..................	–	–	2,218	2,900	–	–	38,048	49,588
Utah....................	66	60	(NA)	(NA)	718	679	(NA)	(NA)
Virginia................	97	100	(NA)	(NA)	1,752	1,623	(NA)	(NA)
West Virginia..........	17	18	80	192	220	139	2,491	6,043
Wyoming..............	566	506	–	–	2,683	2,539	1	–

– Represents or rounds to zero. NA Not Available. [1] Proved reserves of natural gas as of December 31 of the report year are the estimated quantities which analysis of geological and engineering data demonstrate with reasonable certainty to be recoverable in future years from known reservoirs under existing economic and operating conditions. [2] Methane is generated during coal formation and is contained in the coal microstructure. Typical recovery entails pumping water out of the coal to allow the gas to escape. Methane is the principal component of natural gas. Coal bed methane can be added to natural gas pipelines without any special treatment. [3] Natural gas produced from low permeability shale formations.

Source: U.S. Energy Information Administration, "Natural Gas Data," <http://www.eia.gov/naturalgas/data.cfm>, accessed August 2013.

Table 944. Coal Supply, Disposition, and Prices: 2000 to 2012

[In millions of short tons (1,073.6 represents 1,073,600,000). 1 short ton = 2,000 lbs]

Item	2000	2005	2008	2009	2010	2011	2012
United States, total supply	**1,073.6**	**1,131.5**	**1,171.8**	**1,074.9**	**1,084.4**	**1,095.6**	**1,016.4**
Consumption by sector:							
Total	1,084.1	1,126.0	1,120.5	997.5	1,048.5	1002.9	890.5
Electric power	985.8	1,037.5	1,040.6	933.6	975.1	932.5	824.8
Coke plants	28.9	23.4	22.1	15.3	21.1	21.4	20.8
Other industrial plants	65.2	60.3	54.4	45.3	49.3	46.2	42.9
Combined heat and power (CHP)	28.0	25.9	21.9	19.8	24.6	22.3	20.7
Noncombined heat and power	37.2	34.5	32.5	25.5	24.7	23.9	22.2
Commercial	3.7	4.3	3.5	3.2	3.1	2.8	2.0
Residential [4]	0.5	0.4	(NA)	(NA)	(NA)	(NA)	(NA)
Year-end coal stocks:							
Total [1]	140.0	144.3	205.1	244.8	231.7	232.0	239.9
Electric power	102.0	101.1	161.6	189.5	174.9	173.0	184.9
Coke plants	1.5	2.6	2.3	2.0	1.9	2.6	2.5
Other industrial plants	4.6	5.6	6.0	5.1	4.5	4.5	4.5
Producers/distributors	31.9	35.0	34.7	47.7	49.8	51.9	[3] 47.4
U.S. coal trade:							
Net exports [2]	46.0	19.5	47.3	36.5	62.3	(NA)	(NA)
Exports	58.5	49.9	81.5	59.1	81.7	107.3	125.7
Steam coal	25.7	21.3	39.0	21.8	25.6	37.7	55.9
Metallurgical coal	32.8	28.7	42.5	37.3	56.1	69.5	69.9
Imports	12.5	30.5	34.2	22.6	19.4	13.1	9.2
Average delivered price (dollars per short ton):							
Electric utilities	24.28	31.22	41.32	44.47	44.27	46.29	(NA)
Independent power producers	(NA)	30.39	38.98	39.94	41.49	(NA)	(NA)
Coke plants	44.38	83.79	118.09	143.01	153.59	184.44	(NA)
Other industrial plants	31.46	47.63	63.44	64.87	64.38	70.66	(NA)
Average free alongside ship (f.a.s.):							
Exports	34.90	67.10	97.68	101.44	120.41	(NA)	(NA)
Steam coal	29.67	47.64	57.35	73.63	65.54	(NA)	(NA)
Metallurgical coal	38.99	81.56	134.62	117.73	145.44	(NA)	(NA)
Imports	30.10	46.71	59.83	63.91	71.77	(NA)	(NA)

NA Not available. [1] Includes other stocks, not shown separately. [2] Exports minus imports. [3] Estimated. [4] Beginning in 2008, residential coal consumption data are not collected by Energy Information Administration.

Source: U.S. Energy Information Administration, "Coal Data," <http://www.eia.gov/coal/data.cfm>, and "Monthly Energy Review, Coal," <http://www.eia.gov/totalenergy/data/monthly/#coal>, accessed September 2013.

Table 945. Coal and Coke—Summary: 1990 to 2011

[In millions of short tons (1,029 represents 1,029,000,000), except as indicated. Includes coal consumed at mines. Recoverability varies between 40 and 90 percent for individual deposits; 50 percent or more of overall U.S. coal reserve base is believed to be recoverable]

Item	Unit	1990	1995	2000	2005	2008	2009	2010	2011
COAL									
Production, total [1,2]	Mil. sh. tons	**1,029**	**1,033**	**1,074**	**1,131**	**1,172**	**1,075**	**1,084**	**1,096**
Value [3]	Bil. dol.	22.39	19.45	18.02	26.69	36.62	35.73	38.61	40.39
Anthracite production [2]	Mil. sh. tons	3.5	4.7	4.6	1.7	1.7	1.7	1.7	2.2
Bituminous coal and lignite [4]	Mil. sh. tons	1,026	1,028	1,069	1,130	1,170	1,071	1,083	1,093
Underground	Mil. sh. tons	425	396	374	369	357	332	337	346
Surface [2]	Mil. sh. tons	605	637	700	762	815	743	745	748
Exports	Mil. sh. tons	106	89	58	50	82	59	82	107
Imports	Mil. sh. tons	3	9	13	30	34	23	19	13
Consumption [5]	Mil. sh. tons	904	962	1,084	1,126	1,121	997	1,049	1,003
Electric power sector [6]	Mil. sh. tons	783	850	986	1,037	1,041	934	975	932
Industrial	Mil. sh. tons	115	106	94	84	77	61	70	68
Number of mines	Number	3,243	2,104	1,453	1,415	1,458	1,407	1,285	1,325
Daily employment	1,000	131	90	72	79	87	88	86	92
Production, by state:									
Alabama	Mil. sh. tons	29	25	19	21	21	19	20	19
Illinois	Mil. sh. tons	60	48	33	32	33	34	33	38
Indiana	Mil. sh. tons	36	26	28	34	36	36	35	37
Kentucky	Mil. sh. tons	173	154	131	120	120	107	105	109
Montana	Mil. sh. tons	38	39	38	40	45	39	45	42
Ohio	Mil. sh. tons	35	26	22	25	26	28	27	28
Pennsylvania	Mil. sh. tons	71	62	75	67	65	58	59	59
Virginia	Mil. sh. tons	47	34	33	28	25	21	22	23
West Virginia	Mil. sh. tons	169	163	158	154	158	137	135	135
Wyoming	Mil. sh. tons	184	264	339	404	468	431	443	439
Other states	Mil. sh. tons	187	192	197	206	176	165	161	167
World production	Mil. sh. tons	5,292	4,975	4,893	6,527	7,397	7,642	7,934	8,440
Percent U.S. of world	Percent	19.4	20.8	21.9	17.3	15.8	14.1	13.7	13.0
COKE									
Production	Mil. sh. tons	27.6	20.0	20.8	16.7	15.6	11.1	15.0	15.4
Imports	Mil. sh. tons	0.8	3.8	3.8	3.5	3.6	0.0	1.2	1.4
Exports	Mil. sh. tons	0.6	1.4	1.1	1.7	2.0	1.3	1.5	1.0
Consumption [7]	Mil. sh. tons	27.8	25.8	23.2	18.2	17.0	10.3	14.8	15.8

[1] Includes bituminous coal, subbituminous coal, lignite, and anthracite. [2] Beginning 2005, includes a small amount of refuse recovery. [3] Coal values are based on free-on-board rail/barge prices, which are the free-on-board prices of coal at the point of first sale, excluding freight or shipping and insurance costs. [4] Includes subbituminous. [5] Includes some categories not shown separately. [6] Electricity-only and combined-heat-and-power (CHP) plants whose primary business is to sell electricity and/or heat to the public. [7] Consumption is calculated as the sum of production and imports minus exports and stock change.

Source: U.S. Energy Information Administration, *Annual Energy Review 2011,* September 2012, and *Annual Coal Report 2011,* November 2012; and "International Energy Statistics," <http://www.eia.gov/countries/data.cfm>, accessed July 2013. See also <http://www.eia.gov/totalenergy> and <http://www.eia.gov/coal/annual/>.

Table 946. Demonstrated Coal Reserves by Major Producing State: 2010 and 2011

[In millions of short tons (485,511 represents 485,511,000,000), except as number of mines. As of January 1. The demonstrated reserve base represents the sum of coal in both measured and indicated resource categories of reliability. Measured resources of coal are estimates that have a high degree of geologic assurance from sample analyses and measurements from closely spaced and geological well-known sample sites. Indicated resources are estimates based partly from sample and analyses and measurements and partly from reasonable geologic projections]

| State | 2010 | | | | 2011 | | | |
| | | | Method of mining | | | | Method of mining | |
	Number of mines	Total reserves	Under- ground	Surface	Number of mines	Total reserves	Under- ground	Surface
United States [1]	**1,285**	**485,511**	**331,202**	**153,309**	**1,325**	**482,898**	**330,504**	**152,393**
Alabama	50	4,039	890	3,149	52	4,007	869	3,139
Alaska	1	6,100	5,423	677	1	6,097	5,423	674
Arkansas	2	416	272	144	2	416	272	144
Colorado	10	15,935	11,175	4,759	10	15,885	11,126	4,759
Illinois	22	104,160	87,644	16,516	24	104,088	87,578	16,510
Indiana	29	9,217	8,620	597	28	9,158	8,587	570
Iowa	(NA)	2,189	1,732	457	(NA)	2,189	1,732	457
Kansas	1	971	(NA)	971	1	971	(NA)	971
Kentucky	392	29,055	16,377	12,678	400	28,870	16,246	12,624
Kentucky, Eastern	367	9,841	759	9,082	375	9,731	692	9,039
Kentucky, Western	25	19,214	15,618	3,596	25	19,139	15,554	3,584
Maryland	22	620	567	53	22	615	565	50
Missouri	2	5,987	1,479	4,508	2	5,986	1,479	4,507
Montana	6	118,958	70,946	48,012	6	118,901	70,936	47,965
New Mexico	4	11,954	6,091	5,863	4	11,923	6,083	5,840
North Dakota	4	8867	–	8,867	4	8,832	(NA)	8,832
Ohio	42	23,080	17,380	5,700	46	23,031	17,342	5,689
Oklahoma	10	1,544	1,227	317	6	1,542	1,226	316
Pennsylvania	240	26,889	22,707	4,182	242	26,780	22,612	4,167
Anthracite	59	7,188	3,842	3,347	60	7,186	3,841	3,344
Bituminous	181	19,701	18,865	835	182	19,594	18,771	823
Tennessee	19	757	502	255	21	754	501	253
Texas	12	12,132	(NA)	12,132	13	12,074	(NA)	12,074
Utah	8	5,164	4,897	268	8	5,125	4,857	268
Virginia	106	1,481	976	505	110	1,441	945	496
Washington	(NA)	1,340	1,332	8	(NA)	1,340	1,332	8
West Virginia	252	31,723	28,338	3,385	273	31,492	28,171	3,321
Wyoming	19	61,007	42,472	18,535	18	60,456	42,466	17,991

– Represents zero. NA Not available. [1] Includes other states not shown separately.

Source: U.S. Energy Information Administration, *Annual Coal Report, 2011*, November 2013. See also <http://www.eia.gov/coal/annual/>.

Table 947. Uranium Concentrate Industry—Summary: 1990 to 2012

[In units as indicated. See also Section 19, Table 969]

Item	Unit	1990	1995	2000	2007	2008	2009	2010	2011	2012
Exploration and development, surface drilling	Mil. ft.	1.7	1.3	1.0	5.2	5.1	3.7	4.9	6.3	7.2
Expenditures	Mil. dol.	(NA)	2.6	5.6	67.5	81.9	35.4	44.6	53.6	66.6
Number of mines operated	Number	39	12	10	12	17	20	9	11	12
Underground	Number	27	–	1	6	10	14	4	5	6
Openpit	Number	2	–	–	–	–	–	–	–	–
In situ leaching	Number	7	5	4	5	6	4	4	5	5
Other sources [1]	Number	3	7	5	1	1	2	1	1	1
Mine production	1,000 pounds	5,876	3,528	3,123	4,541	3,879	4,145	4,237	4,114	4,335
Underground	1,000 pounds	(D)	–	(D)	(D)	(D)	(D)	(D)	(D)	(D)
Openpit	1,000 pounds	1,881	–	–	–	–	–	–	–	–
In situ leaching	1,000 pounds	(D)	3,372	2,995	(D)	(D)	(D)	(D)	(D)	(D)
Other sources [1]	1,000 pounds	3,995	156	128	(D)	(D)	(D)	(D)	(D)	(D)
Uranium concentrate production	1,000 pounds	8,886	6,043	3,958	4,534	3,092	3,708	4,228	3,991	4,146
Concentrate shipments from mills and plants	1,000 pounds	12,957	5,500	3,187	4,050	4,130	3,620	5,137	4,000	3,911
Employment	Person-years	1,335	1,107	627	1,231	1,563	1,096	1,073	1,191	1,196

– Represents zero. D Data withheld to avoid disclosing figures for individual companies. NA Not available. [1] Includes mine water, mill site cleanup and mill tailings, and well field restoration as sources of uranium.

Source: U.S. Energy Information Administration, through 2002, *Uranium Industry,* annual. Thereafter, *Domestic Uranium Production Report,* June 2013, and earlier reports. See also <http://www.eia.gov/uranium/production/annual/>.

Table 948. Crude Petroleum and Natural Gas Extraction Industry—Establishments, Employees, and Payroll by State: 2011

[13,456,021 represents 13,456,021,000. Excludes government employees, railroad employees, self-employed persons, etc. See "General Explanation" in source for definitions and statement on reliability of data. An establishment is a single physical location where business is conducted or where services or industrial operations are performed. See Appendix III]

State	Crude petroleum and natural gas extraction (NAICS 211111) [1]			State	Crude petroleum and natural gas extraction (NAICS 211111) [1]		
	Establish-ments	Number of employees [2]	Annual payroll ($1,000)		Establish-ments	Number of employees [2]	Annual payroll ($1,000)
United States........	**7,757**	**108,954**	**13,456,021**	Missouri.............	9	([4])	(D)
Alabama...............	32	509	45,365	Montana............	95	864	92,478
Alaska..................	20	([7])	(D)	Nebraska...........	21	68	2,713
Arizona................	16	67	4,492	Nevada..............	19	67	4,819
Arkansas..............	111	2,026	168,044	New Hampshire.....	1	([3])	(D)
California..............	207	6,060	864,536	New Jersey.........	1	([3])	(D)
Colorado..............	388	5,378	849,077	New Mexico........	162	2,978	263,914
Connecticut............	2	([6])	(D)	New York...........	41	393	35,988
Delaware.............	4	5	1,676	North Carolina......	6	([4])	(D)
District of Colombia....	2	([3])	(D)	North Dakota........	58	1,758	166,006
Florida.................	30	([6])	(D)	Ohio.................	191	([7])	(D)
Georgia...............	3	([4])	(D)	Oklahoma..........	1,216	16,066	1,894,003
Idaho..................	3	([3])	(D)	Oregon.............	3	([3])	261
Illinois.................	156	889	43,821	Pennsylvania.......	213	3,883	395,663
Indiana................	43	([5])	8,147	Rhode Island........	2	([3])	(D)
Iowa...................	1	([3])	(D)	South Carolina......	3	([3])	(D)
Kansas................	408	2,358	155,624	South Dakota......	6	([4])	(D)
Kentucky..............	89	743	55,630	Tennessee..........	11	114	7,884
Louisiana..............	385	8,263	828,267	Texas................	3,184	43,875	6,148,282
Maryland..............	2	([3])	(D)	Utah................	55	1,422	147,282
Massachusetts.......	7	10	781	Virginia.............	13	([5])	(D)
Michigan..............	83	825	67,198	Washington..........	2	([3])	(D)
Minnesota.............	5	([3])	832	West Virginia........	201	2,352	175,380
Mississippi............	78	844	94,362	Wyoming............	169	2,776	283,353

D Withheld to avoid disclosing data for individual companies; data are included in higher level totals. [1] North American Industry Classification System, 2007. [2] Covers full- and part-time employees who are on the payroll in the pay period including March 12. [3] 0 to 19 employees. [4] 20 to 99 employees. [5] 100 to 249 employees. [6] 250 to 499 employees. [7] 1,000 to 2,499 employees.

Source: U.S. Census Bureau, County Business Patterns, "Geography Area Series: County Business Patterns," <http://factfinder2.census.gov>, accessed August 2013.

Section 19
Energy and Utilities

This section presents statistics on fuel resources, energy production and consumption, electric energy, hydroelectric power, nuclear power, solar and wind energy, biomass, and the electric and gas utility industries. The principal sources are the U.S. Department of Energy's Energy Information Administration (EIA), the Edison Electric Institute, Washington, DC, and the American Gas Association, Arlington, VA. The Department of Energy was created in October 1977 and assumed and centralized the responsibilities of all or part of several agencies including the Federal Power Commission (FPC), the U.S. Bureau of Mines, the Federal Energy Administration, and the U.S. Energy Research and Development Administration. For additional data on transportation, see Section 23; on fuels, see Section 18; and on energy-related housing characteristics, see Section 20.

The EIA, in its *Annual Energy Review*, provides statistics and trend data on energy supply, demand, and prices. Information is included on petroleum and natural gas, coal, electricity, hydroelectric power, nuclear power, solar, wind, wood, and geothermal energy. Due to budget constraints, in 2013, the EIA suspended publication of the *Annual Energy Review*. In order to continue publishing similar data, the EIA plans to expand data covered in their *Monthly Energy Review*, which presents current supply, disposition, and price data and monthly publications on petroleum, coal, natural gas, and electric power. Additional EIA reports include the *Electric Power Annual*; *Natural Gas Annual*; *Petroleum Supply Annual*; *U.S. Crude Oil, Natural Gas, and Natural Gas Liquids Reserves Annual Report*; *Electric Sales, Revenue, and Price*; *State Energy Consumption, Price, and Expenditure Data*; *Annual Energy Outlook*; and *International Energy Statistics*. These various reports contain state, national, and international data on the production of electricity, net summer capability of generating plants, fuels used in energy production, energy sales and consumption, and hydroelectric power.

Data on residential energy consumption, expenditures, and conservation activities are available from EIA's Residential Energy Consumption Survey (RECS) and are published every 4 years. The Commercial Buildings Energy Consumption Survey (CBECS), conducted on a quadrennial basis, collects information on the stock of U.S. commercial buildings, their energy-related characteristics, and their energy consumption and expenditures. Data on manufacturing energy consumption, use, and expenditures are also collected every 4 years from EIA's Manufacturing Energy Consumption Survey (MECS). Due to the long gaps between the RECS, CBECS, and MECS, tables are rotated in and out of Section 19 in an effort to keep the data as current as possible. The results from these surveys are published at <http://www.eia.gov/consumption/>.

The Edison Electric Institute's monthly bulletin and annual *Statistical Year Book of the Electric Power Industry* contain data on the distribution of electric energy by public utilities. The American Gas Association, in its monthly and quarterly bulletins and its yearbook, *Gas Facts*, presents data on gas utilities and financial and operating statistics.

Btu conversion factors—Various energy sources are converted from original units to the thermal equivalent using British thermal units (Btu). A Btu is the amount of energy required to raise the temperature of 1 pound of water 1 degree Fahrenheit (F) at or near 39.2 degrees F. Factors are calculated annually from the latest final annual data available; some are revised as a result.

Electric power industry—In recent years, EIA has restructured the industry categories it once used to gather and report electricity statistics. The electric power industry, previously divided into electric utilities and non-utilities, now consists of the Electric Power Sector, the Commercial Sector, and the Industrial Sector.

The Electric Power Sector is composed of electricity-only and combined-heat-and-power plants (CHPs) whose primary business is to sell electricity, or electricity and heat, to the public.

Electricity-only plants are composed of traditional electric utilities, and nontraditional participants, including energy service providers, power marketers, independent power producers (IPPs), and the portion of CHPs that produce only electricity.

A utility is defined as a corporation, person, agency, authority, or other legal entity or instrumentality aligned with distribution facilities for delivery of electric energy for use primarily by the public. Electric utilities include investor-owned electric utilities, municipal and state utilities, federal electric utilities, and rural electric cooperatives.

An independent power producer is an entity defined as a corporation, person, agency, authority, or other legal entity or instrumentality that owns or operates facilities whose primary business is to produce electricity for use by the public. They are not generally aligned with distribution facilities and are not considered electric utilities.

Combined-heat-and-power producers are plants designed to produce both heat and electricity from a single heat source. These types of electricity producers can be independent power producers or industrial or commercial establishments. As some independent power producers are CHPs, their information is included in the data for the combined-heat-and-power sector.

The Commercial Sector consists of commercial CHPs and commercial electricity-only plants. Industrial CHPs and industrial electricity-only plants make up the Industrial Sector. For more information, please refer to the *Electric Power Annual 2011* Web site at <http://www.eia.gov/electricity/annual/>.

Table 949. Utilities—Establishments, Revenue, Payroll, and Employees by Kind of Business: 2007

[584,193 represents $584,193,000,000. Includes only establishments or firms with payroll. Data based on the 2007 Economic Census. See headnote, Table 782 and Appendix III]

Kind of business	2007 NAICS code [1]	Establish-ments (number)	Revenue Total (mil. dol.)	Revenue Per paid employee (dol.)	Annual payroll Total (mil. dol.)	Annual payroll Per paid employee (dol.)	Paid employees for pay period including March 12 (number)
Utilities................................	22	16,578	584,193	916,744	51,654	81,057	637,247
Electric power generation, transmission, & distribution..................	2211	9,554	445,693	871,368	43,618	85,277	511,487
Electric power generation.................	22111	1,934	120,968	985,134	11,297	92,001	122,793
Hydroelectric power generation...........	221111	295	2,185	534,773	290	71,092	4,086
Fossil fuel electric power generation......	221112	1,248	85,362	1,140,283	6,413	85,667	74,860
Nuclear electric power generation........	221113	79	28,996	763,603	4,083	107,525	37,972
Other electric power generation..........	221119	312	4,425	753,252	511	86,927	5,875
Electric power transmission, control & distribution.................................	22112	7,620	324,726	835,428	32,321	83,153	388,694
Electric bulk power transmission & control..................................	221121	74	4,268	697,997	543	88,795	6,114
Electric power distribution.................	221122	7,546	320,458	837,625	31,778	83,063	382,580
Natural gas distribution........................	2212	2,377	128,555	1,542,000	6,038	72,420	83,369
Water, sewage, & other systems............	2213	4,647	9,944	234,582	1,998	47,125	42,391
Water supply & irrigation systems..........	22131	3,889	7,623	225,070	1,596	47,115	33,871
Sewage treatment facilities..................	22132	689	1,309	187,718	297	42,634	6,974
Steam & air-conditioning supply............	22133	69	1,012	654,375	105	67,603	1,546

[1] North American Industry Classification System, 2007; see text, Section 15.

Source: U.S. Census Bureau, "2007 Economic Census," <http://www.census.gov/econ/census07/>, accessed September 2010.

Table 950. Utilities—Employees, Annual Payroll, and Establishments by Industry: 2011

[57,909 represents $57,909,000,000. Excludes most government employees, railroad employees, and self-employed persons, etc. An establishment is a single physical location where business is conducted or where services or industrial operations are performed. See Appendix III]

Industry	2007 NAICS code [1]	Number of employ-ees [2]	Annual payroll (mil. dol.)	Average payroll per employ-ee (dol.)	Establishments by employment size-class Total	Under 20 employ-ees	20 to 99 employ-ees	100 to 499 employ-ees	500 employ-ees and over
Utilities, total............................	22	639,795	57,909	90,512	17,634	12,244	4,095	1,103	192
Electric power generation, transmission and distribution............	2211	511,990	48,630	94,982	10,266	6,108	3,112	867	179
Electric power generation................	22111	135,653	13,818	101,859	2,486	1,577	614	236	59
Hydroelectric power generation........	221111	3,625	294	81,101	362	320	40	2	–
Fossil fuel electric power generation............................	221112	72,192	6,957	96,361	1,309	642	445	215	7
Nuclear electric power generation............................	221113	50,778	5,674	111,750	142	64	17	10	51
Other electric power generation............................	221119	9,058	893	98,537	673	551	112	9	1
Electric power transmission, control & distribution..................	22112	376,337	34,812	92,503	7,780	4,531	2,498	631	120
Electric bulk power transmission & control............................	221121	10,559	1,143	108,225	207	132	52	19	4
Electric power distribution..............	221122	365,778	33,669	92,049	7,573	4,399	2,446	612	116
Natural gas distribution....................	2212	85,874	6,959	81,035	2,558	1,737	615	193	13
Water, sewage, & other systems........	2213	41,931	2,320	55,337	4,810	4,399	368	43	–
Water supply & irrigation systems..................................	22131	32,979	1,816	55,058	4,017	3,722	260	35	–
Sewage treatment facilities..............	22132	6,619	317	47,820	677	600	71	6	–
Steam & air-conditioning supply........	22133	2,333	188	80,610	116	77	37	2	–

– Represents zero. [1] North American Industry Classification System, 2007; see text, Section 15. [2] Covers full- and part-time employees who are on the payroll in the pay period including March 12.

Source: U.S. Census Bureau, County Business Patterns, "Geography Area Series: County Business Patterns by Employment Size Class," <http://factfinder2.census.gov>, accessed August 2013.

Table 951. Energy Supply and Disposition by Type of Fuel: 1973 to 2012

[In quadrillion British thermal units (Btu) (63.56 represents 63,560,000,000,000,000). For definition of Btu, see source and text, this section]

Year	Production										Net imports, total [7]	Consumption					
	Total [1]	Crude oil [2]	Dry natural gas	Coal [3]	Nuclear electric power	Renewable energy [4]						Total [1,8]	Petro-leum [9]	Dry natural gas [10]	Coal	Nuclear electric power	Renew-able energy, [4] total
						Total [1]	Hydro-electric power [5]	Bio-mass [6]	Solar/photo-voltaic	Wind							
1973.....	63.56	19.49	22.19	13.99	0.91	4.41	2.86	1.53	(NA)	(NA)	12.58	75.68	34.84	22.51	12.97	0.91	4.41
1975.....	61.32	17.73	19.64	14.99	1.90	4.69	3.15	1.50	(NA)	(NA)	11.71	71.96	32.73	19.95	12.66	1.90	4.69
1980.....	67.18	18.25	19.91	18.60	2.74	5.43	2.90	2.48	(NA)	(NA)	12.10	78.07	34.20	20.24	15.42	2.74	5.43
1985.....	67.70	18.99	16.98	19.33	4.08	6.08	2.97	3.02	(Z)	(Z)	7.58	76.39	30.92	17.70	17.48	4.08	6.08
1990.....	70.70	15.57	18.33	22.49	6.10	6.04	3.05	2.74	0.06	0.03	14.06	84.49	33.55	19.60	19.17	6.10	6.04
1995.....	71.17	13.89	19.08	22.13	7.08	6.56	3.21	3.10	0.07	0.03	17.75	91.03	34.44	22.67	20.09	7.08	6.56
1996.....	72.49	13.72	19.34	22.79	7.09	7.01	3.59	3.16	0.07	0.03	19.07	94.02	35.68	23.08	21.00	7.09	7.01
1997.....	72.47	13.66	19.39	23.31	6.60	7.02	3.64	3.11	0.07	0.03	20.70	94.60	36.16	23.22	21.45	6.60	7.02
1998.....	72.88	13.24	19.61	24.05	7.07	6.49	3.30	2.93	0.07	0.03	22.28	95.02	36.82	22.83	21.66	7.07	6.49
1999.....	71.74	12.45	19.34	23.30	7.61	6.52	3.27	2.97	0.07	0.05	23.54	96.65	37.84	22.91	21.62	7.61	6.52
2000.....	71.33	12.36	19.66	22.74	7.86	6.10	2.81	3.01	0.07	0.06	24.97	98.81	38.26	23.82	22.58	7.86	6.11
2001.....	71.73	12.28	20.17	23.55	8.03	5.16	2.24	2.62	0.06	0.07	26.39	96.17	38.19	22.77	21.91	8.03	5.16
2002.....	70.71	12.16	19.38	22.73	8.15	5.73	2.69	2.71	0.06	0.11	25.74	97.65	38.22	23.51	21.90	8.15	5.73
2003.....	69.93	11.95	19.63	22.09	7.96	5.95	2.79	2.81	0.06	0.11	27.01	97.94	38.81	22.83	22.32	7.96	5.95
2004.....	70.22	11.54	19.07	22.85	8.22	6.07	2.69	3.00	0.06	0.14	29.11	100.16	40.29	22.92	22.47	8.22	6.08
2005.....	69.44	10.98	18.56	23.19	8.16	6.23	2.70	3.10	0.06	0.18	30.15	100.28	40.39	22.57	22.80	8.16	6.24
2006.....	70.75	10.77	19.02	23.79	8.22	6.60	2.87	3.22	0.07	0.26	29.81	99.63	39.96	22.24	22.45	8.22	6.65
2007.....	71.42	10.75	19.79	23.49	8.46	6.53	2.45	3.48	0.08	0.34	29.22	101.31	39.77	23.66	22.75	8.46	6.54
2008.....	73.24	10.61	20.70	23.85	8.43	7.22	2.51	3.88	0.09	0.55	25.93	99.29	37.28	23.84	22.39	8.43	7.20
2009.....	72.68	11.33	21.14	21.62	8.36	7.65	2.67	3.97	0.10	0.72	22.74	94.60	35.40	23.42	19.69	8.36	7.64
2010.....	74.79	11.60	21.81	22.04	8.43	8.13	2.54	4.33	0.13	0.92	21.64	97.97	36.01	24.57	20.79	8.43	8.08
2011.....	78.00	11.97	23.41	22.22	8.27	9.17	3.10	4.52	0.17	1.17	18.40	97.47	35.47	24.86	19.66	8.27	9.07
2012.....	79.15	13.81	24.59	20.60	8.05	8.87	2.69	4.36	0.24	1.36	15.16	95.10	34.69	26.00	17.37	8.05	8.83

NA Not available. Z Less than 5 trillion. [1] Includes other types of fuel, not shown separately. [2] Includes lease condensate. [3] Beginning 1989, includes waste coal supplied. Beginning 2001, also includes a small amount of refuse recovery. [4] Electricity net generation from conventional hydroelectric power, geothermal, solar, and wind; consumption of electricity from wood, waste, and alcohol fuels; geothermal heat pump and direct use energy; and solar thermal direct use energy. [5] Conventional hydroelectricity net generation. [6] Organic nonfossil material of biological origin constituting a renewable energy source. [7] Imports minus exports. [8] Includes coal coke net imports and electricity net imports, not shown separately. [9] Petroleum products supplied, including natural gas plant liquids and crude oil burned as fuel. Does not include biofuels that have been blended with petroleum. [10] Excludes supplemental gaseous fuels.

Source: U.S. Energy Information Administration, *Monthly Energy Review*, May 2013. See also <http://www.eia.gov/totalenergy/data/monthly/>.

Table 952. Energy Supply and Disposition by Type of Fuel— Estimates, 2010 and 2011, and Projections, 2015 to 2035

[Quadrillion Btu (75.31 represents 75,310,000,000,000,000) per year. Btu = British thermal unit. For definition of Btu, see source and text, this section. Projections are "reference" or mid-level forecasts. See report for methodology and assumptions used in generating projections]

Type of Fuel	2010	2011	Projections				
			2015	2020	2025	2030	2035
Production, total.............................	**75.31**	**79.02**	**83.46**	**89.16**	**91.29**	**92.18**	**94.59**
Crude oil and lease condensate.......................	11.59	12.16	15.58	15.95	14.50	13.47	13.40
Natural gas plant liquids.............................	2.78	2.88	3.74	4.14	4.20	3.85	3.87
Natural gas, dry....................................	21.82	23.51	24.56	27.19	29.22	30.44	32.04
Coal [1]..	22.04	22.21	21.12	21.74	22.54	23.25	23.60
Nuclear power.......................................	8.43	8.26	8.57	9.25	9.54	9.49	9.14
Renewable energy [2].................................	7.89	8.80	9.12	10.05	10.45	10.79	11.64
Other [3]...	0.76	1.20	0.76	0.83	0.85	0.88	0.90
Imports, total...............................	**29.75**	**28.66**	**25.30**	**23.26**	**23.57**	**24.41**	**24.57**
Crude oil [4].......................................	20.14	19.46	16.08	15.02	15.57	16.33	16.43
Petroleum products [5]................................	5.26	5.24	5.63	5.55	5.47	5.33	5.13
Natural gas...	3.83	3.54	3.38	2.58	2.36	2.63	2.53
Other imports [6]....................................	0.52	0.43	0.21	0.11	0.17	0.13	0.48
Exports, total...............................	**8.11**	**10.35**	**10.94**	**11.17**	**12.25**	**13.47**	**14.42**
Petroleum [7].......................................	4.86	6.08	6.04	5.37	5.14	5.25	5.55
Natural gas...	1.15	1.52	1.89	2.67	3.92	4.71	5.07
Coal..	2.10	2.75	3.00	3.13	3.18	3.51	3.80
Consumption, total...........................	**98.35**	**97.70**	**97.72**	**101.04**	**102.34**	**102.81**	**104.41**
Petroleum products [8]...............................	37.76	37.02	37.04	37.54	36.87	36.08	35.82
Natural gas...	24.32	24.91	25.86	26.77	27.28	27.95	29.06
Coal..	20.81	19.66	18.18	18.59	19.35	19.70	20.09
Nuclear power.......................................	8.43	8.26	8.57	9.25	9.54	9.49	9.14
Renewable energy [9].................................	6.72	7.49	7.75	8.58	9.00	9.31	10.04
Other [10]..	0.31	0.35	0.32	0.31	0.30	0.28	0.26
Net imports of petroleum......................	**20.53**	**18.62**	**15.67**	**15.20**	**15.89**	**16.40**	**16.00**
Prices (2011 dollars per unit):							
Crude oil spot prices (dol. per barrel)							
Brent Spot Price.................................	81.31	111.26	95.91	105.57	117.36	130.47	145.41
West Texas Intermediate Spot Price...............	81.08	94.86	88.21	103.57	115.36	128.47	143.41
Natural Gas at Henry Hub (dol. per mil. BTU)........	4.46	3.98	3.12	4.13	4.87	5.40	6.32
Coal minemouth price (dol. per ton) [11]............	36.37	41.16	45.68	49.26	52.02	55.64	58.57
Average Electric Price (cents per kWh)...............	10.03	9.91	9.18	9.38	9.48	9.69	10.08

[1] Includes waste coal. [2] Includes grid-connected electricity from conventional hydroelectric; wood and wood waste; landfill gas; municipal solid waste; other biomass; wind; photovoltaic and solar thermal sources; nonelectric energy from renewable sources, such as active and passive solar systems, and wood. Excludes electricity imports using renewable sources and nonmarketed renewable energy. [3] Includes nonbiogenic municipal solid waste, liquid hydrogen, methanol, and some domestic inputs to refineries. [4] Includes imports of crude oil for the Strategic Petroleum Reserve. [5] Includes imports of finished petroleum products, imports of unfinished oils, alcohols, ethers, blending components, and renewable fuels such as ethanol. [6] Includes coal, coal coke (net), and electricity (net). [7] Includes crude oil and petroleum products. [8] Includes petroleum-derived fuels and non-petroleum-derived fuels, such as ethanol, biodiesel, and coal-based synthetic liquids. Petroleum coke, which is a solid, is included. Also included are natural gas plant liquids, crude oil consumed as a fuel, and liquid hydrogen. [9] Includes grid-connected electricity from wood and wood waste, non-electric energy from wood, and biofuels heat and coproducts used in the production of liquid fuels, but excludes the energy content of the liquid fuels. Also includes non-biogenic municipal solid waste and net electricity imports. [10] Includes non-biogenic municipal solid waste and net electricity imports. [11] Includes reported prices for both open market and captive mines.

Source: U.S. Energy Information Administration, *Annual Energy Outlook 2013*, April 2013. See also <http://www.eia.gov/forecasts/aeo/index.cfm>.

Table 953. Fossil Fuel Production Prices by Type of Fuel: 1980 to 2011

[In dollars per million British thermal units (Btu). For definition of Btu and mineral fuel conversions, see source and text, this section. All fuel prices taken as close to the point of production as possible]

Fuel	1980	1990	1995	2000	2005	2006	2007	2008	2009	2010	2011 [1]
CURRENT DOLLARS											
Composite [2]..................	2.04	1.84	1.47	2.60	4.74	4.73	4.95	6.52	3.97	4.96	5.50
Crude oil [3]..................	3.72	3.45	2.52	4.61	8.67	10.29	11.47	16.21	9.72	12.88	16.51
Natural gas [4]................	1.45	1.55	1.40	3.32	6.64	5.79	5.67	7.25	3.33	4.08	3.60
Coal [5]......................	1.10	1.00	0.88	0.80	1.16	1.24	1.29	1.55	1.67	1.77	1.83
CONSTANT (2005) DOLLARS											
Composite [2]..................	4.27	2.55	1.80	2.93	4.74	4.58	4.66	6.01	3.62	4.47	4.85
Crude oil [3]..................	7.79	4.78	3.09	5.19	8.67	9.97	10.80	14.93	8.85	11.61	14.56
Natural gas [4]................	3.03	2.14	1.72	3.75	6.64	5.61	5.34	6.67	3.04	3.68	3.18
Coal [5]......................	2.30	1.38	1.08	0.90	1.16	1.20	1.21	1.42	1.52	1.59	1.62

[1] Preliminary. [2] Derived by multiplying the price per Btu of each fossil fuel by the total Btu content of the production of each fossil fuel and dividing this accumulated value of total fossil fuel production by the accumulated Btu content of total fossil fuel production. [3] Domestic first purchase prices. [4] Wellhead prices. [5] Free-on-board (f.o.b.) rail/barge prices, which are the f.o.b. prices of coal at the point of first sale, excluding freight or shipping and insurance costs. Includes bituminous coal, subbituminous coal, and lignite.

Source: U.S. Energy Information Administration, *Annual Energy Review 2011*, September 2012. See also <http://www.eia.gov/totalenergy/>.

Table 954. Energy Consumption by Mode of Transportation: 2000 to 2011

[40 represents 40,000,000,000,000. Btu = British thermal unit. For conversion rates for each fuel type, see source]

Mode	Trillion Btu			Physical units			
	2000	2010	2011	Unit	2000	2010	2011
AIR [1]							
Aviation gasoline................................	40	27	26	mil. gal.	333	221	216
Jet fuel...	2,008	1,686	1,668	mil. gal.	14,876	12,491	12,354
HIGHWAY							
Light duty vehicle, short wheel base and motorcycle [2]............................	9,159	10,902	11,120	mil. gal.	73,275	87,215	88,962
Light duty vehicle, long wheel base [2]............	6,617	4,531	4,416	mil. gal.	52,939	36,251	35,326
Single-unit 2-axle 6-tire or more truck...........	1,195	1,887	1,773	mil. gal.	9,563	15,097	14,183
Combination truck [3]............................	3,208	3,741	3,524	mil. gal.	25,666	29,927	28,193
Bus..	139	240	242	mil. gal.	1,112	1,921	1,933
TRANSIT [4]							
Electricity...	18	22	22	mil. kWh	5,382	6,414	6,534
Diesel..	82	81	80	mil. gal.	591	633	625
Gasoline and other nondiesel fuels [5]...........	3	18	19	mil. gal.	24	98	101
Compressed natural gas........................	6	18	18	mil. gal.	44	126	128
RAIL [6]							
Distillate/diesel fuel.............................	513	485	511	mil. gal.	3,700	3,494	3,685
Electricity...	2	2	2	mil. kWh	470	559	555
WATER							
Residual fuel oil..................................	960	770	683	mil. gal.	6,410	5,143	4,560
Distillate/diesel fuel oil.........................	314	277	295	mil. gal.	2,261	1,997	2,128
Gasoline..	141	146	138	mil. gal.	1,124	1,167	1,104
PIPELINE							
Natural gas.......................................	662	695	705	mil. cu. ft.	642,210	674,124	683,715

[1] Includes general aviation and certified carriers, domestic operations only. Also includes fuel used in air taxi operations, but not commuter operations. [2] Beginning in 2010, data were calculated using a new methodology developed by FHWA. Data for 2010 are based on new categories and are not comparable to previous years. The new category "Light duty vehicle, short wheel base" includes passenger cars, light trucks, vans and sport utility vehicles with a wheelbase (WB) equal to or less than 121 inches. The new category "Light duty vehicle, long wheel base" includes large passenger cars, vans, pickup trucks, and sport/utility vehicles with wheelbases (WB) larger than 121 inches. [3] A power unit (truck tractor) and one or more trailing units (a semitrailer or trailer). [4] Includes light, heavy, and commuter rail; motor bus; trolley bus; van pools; automated guideway; and demand-responsive vehicles. [5] Gasoline and all other nondiesel fuels include gasoline, liquefied petroleum gas, liquefied natural gas, methane, ethanol, bunker fuel, kerosene, grain additive, and other fuel. [6] Includes Amtrak and freight service carriers that have an annual operating revenue of $250 million or more.

Source: U.S. Department of Transportation, Bureau of Transportation Statistics, "National Transportation Statistics," <http://www.bts.gov/publications/national_transportation_statistics/>, accessed July 2013.

Table 955. Energy Consumption by End-Use Sector: 1975 to 2012

[71.96 represents 71,960,000,000,000,000 Btu. Btu = British thermal units. For definition of Btu, see source and text, this section. Total energy consumption in the end-use sectors consists of primary energy consumption, electricity retail sales, and electrical system energy losses]

Year	Total (quad. Btu)	Residential and commercial [1] (quad. Btu)	Industrial [2] (quad. Btu)	Transportation (quad. Btu)	Percent of total		
					Residential and commercial [1]	Industrial [2]	Transportation
1975.................	71.96	24.31	29.41	18.25	33.8	40.9	25.4
1980.................	78.07	26.33	32.04	19.70	33.7	41.0	25.2
1985.................	76.39	27.49	28.82	20.09	36.0	37.7	26.3
1990.................	84.49	30.27	31.81	22.42	35.8	37.7	26.5
1995.................	91.03	33.21	33.97	23.85	36.5	37.3	26.2
2000.................	98.81	37.60	34.66	26.55	38.1	35.1	26.9
2001.................	96.17	37.18	32.72	26.28	38.7	34.0	27.3
2002.................	97.65	38.14	32.66	26.84	39.1	33.4	27.5
2003.................	97.94	38.47	32.55	26.92	39.3	33.2	27.5
2004.................	100.16	38.75	33.52	27.90	38.7	33.5	27.9
2005.................	100.28	39.48	32.45	28.35	39.4	32.4	28.3
2006.................	99.63	38.40	32.40	28.83	38.5	32.5	28.9
2007.................	101.31	39.80	32.40	29.12	39.3	32.0	28.7
2008.................	99.29	40.10	31.36	27.83	40.4	31.6	28.0
2009.................	94.60	39.00	28.49	27.11	41.2	30.1	28.7
2010.................	97.97	39.90	30.50	27.56	40.7	31.1	28.1
2011.................	97.47	39.40	30.84	27.22	40.4	31.6	27.9
2012.................	95.10	37.70	30.70	26.70	39.6	32.3	28.1

[1] Commercial sector fuel use, including that at commercial combined-heat-and-power (CHP) and commercial electricity-only plants. [2] Industrial sector fuel use, including that at industrial combined-heat-and-power (CHP) and industrial electricity-only plants.

Source: U.S. Energy Information Administration, *Monthly Energy Review*, May 2013. See also <http://www.eia.gov/totalenergy/data/monthly/>.

Table 956. Energy Consumption–End-Use Sector and Selected Source by State: 2011

[In trillions of British thermal units (97,387 represents 97,387,000,000,000,000 Btu's), except as indicated. For definition of Btu, see source and text, this section. U.S. totals may not equal sum of states due to independent rounding and/or interstate flows of electricity that are not allocated to the states. For technical notes and documentation, see source <http://www.eia.gov/state/seds/seds-technical-notes-updates.cfm>]

State	Total [1,2]	Per capita [3] (mil. Btu)	End-use sector [4] Resi-dential	Com-mercial	Indus-trial [2]	Trans-portation	Source Petro-leum [5]	Natural gas (dry) [6]	Coal	Hydro-electric power [7]	Nuclear electric power
U.S.............	97,387	313	21,374	17,952	30,924	27,137	36,562	24,921	19,664	3,103	8,269
AL.............	1,931	402	377	257	810	487	565	615	651	86	412
AK.............	638	881	54	68	315	201	270	337	15	13	–
AZ.............	1,431	221	395	346	221	470	527	294	460	89	327
AR.............	1,117	380	246	175	405	291	346	289	306	29	149
CA.............	7,858	209	1,516	1,556	1,786	3,001	3,511	2,197	55	413	384
CO.............	1,481	289	353	287	424	417	485	481	369	20	–
CT.............	742	207	239	184	80	237	330	236	6	6	167
DE.............	272	299	68	59	83	62	105	82	18	–	–
DC.............	180	291	36	120	3	22	20	34	(Z)	–	–
FL.............	4,217	221	1,231	972	477	1,538	1,680	1,237	553	2	230
GA.............	3,002	306	746	564	748	944	1,036	532	635	26	338
HI.............	286	208	35	41	64	146	251	3	16	1	–
ID.............	526	332	125	85	184	132	165	84	8	130	–
IL.............	3,978	309	980	789	1,230	979	1,241	998	1,052	1	1,003
IN.............	2,869	440	557	377	1,314	622	788	638	1,333	4	–
IA.............	1,513	494	246	208	746	313	431	310	463	9	55
KS.............	1,162	405	245	216	421	280	408	285	347	(Z)	77
KY.............	1,911	438	382	253	804	472	632	229	1,011	29	–
LA.............	4,055	886	371	281	2,680	723	1,926	1,503	270	10	174
ME.............	413	311	86	64	140	123	197	74	2	39	–
MD.............	1,426	244	418	428	146	434	498	199	241	25	151
MA.............	1,395	211	424	278	235	458	593	461	43	11	53
MI.............	2,803	284	762	610	708	722	835	787	691	13	344
MN.............	1,867	349	398	342	655	472	626	425	316	7	125
MS.............	1,163	391	229	164	411	360	420	439	108	–	108
MO.............	1,878	313	537	414	360	567	661	275	826	12	98
MT.............	398	398	87	78	113	119	175	79	166	122	–
NE.............	871	473	161	136	372	203	240	174	285	16	73
NV.............	633	233	156	120	159	197	218	256	63	21	–
NH.............	292	222	87	67	35	103	153	72	24	16	88
NJ.............	2,438	276	576	631	274	957	1,133	678	50	(Z)	352
NM.............	688	331	120	127	238	203	258	252	285	2	–
NY.............	3,615	185	1,070	1,183	347	1,015	1,304	1,247	125	272	447
NC.............	2,573	267	736	579	555	703	819	311	625	38	424
ND.............	526	768	68	73	266	118	187	78	395	25	–
OH.............	3,828	332	937	712	1,230	949	1,196	846	1,223	4	156
OK.............	1,595	421	324	248	560	463	544	677	378	15	–
OR.............	1,014	262	264	195	245	310	354	204	35	411	–
PA.............	3,725	292	924	638	1,212	952	1,256	999	1,213	31	797
RI.............	184	175	60	44	19	61	84	102	–	(Z)	–
SC.............	1,610	345	370	262	529	450	504	235	366	15	554
SD.............	382	464	71	62	153	96	120	74	32	64	–
TN.............	2,201	344	562	387	625	628	718	259	481	93	282
TX.............	12,207	476	1,746	1,556	6,088	2,818	5,934	3,757	1,695	5	415
UT.............	797	283	170	158	218	251	291	231	346	12	–
VT.............	149	238	46	29	24	50	80	9	–	14	51
VA.............	2,388	295	632	608	436	712	795	383	288	12	267
WA.............	2,080	305	510	387	586	598	751	272	57	892	50
WV.............	724	390	169	112	276	168	195	125	823	14	–
WI.............	1,789	313	426	357	582	425	540	399	447	21	121
WY.............	553	975	49	68	322	114	167	162	468	12	–

– Represents zero. Z Less than 50 billion Btu. [1] Includes other sources, not shown separately. [2] U.S. total energy and U.S. industrial sector include net imports of coal coke that are not allocated to the states. [3] Based on estimated resident population as of July 1. [4] End-use sector data include electricity sales and associated electrical system energy losses. [5] Includes fuel ethanol blended into motor gasoline. [6] Includes supplemental gaseous fuels. [7] Conventional hydroelectric power. Does not include pumped-storage hydroelectricity.

Source: U.S. Energy Information Administration, "State Energy Data System," <http://www.eia.gov/state/seds/>, accessed August 2013.

Table 957. Renewable Energy Consumption Estimates by Source: 1990 to 2012

[In trillion Btu (6,040.7 represents 6,040,700,000,000,000). For definition of Btu, see source and text, this section. Renewable energy is obtained from sources that are essentially inexhaustible, unlike fossil fuels of which there is a finite supply]

Source and sector	1990	2000	2005	2010	2011	2012
Consumption, total	**6,040.7**	**6,106.4**	**6,241.9**	**8,081.6**	**9,074.4**	**8,825.2**
Conventional hydroelectric power [1]	3,046.4	2,811.1	2,702.9	2,538.5	3,102.9	2,686.8
Geothermal energy [2]	170.7	164.4	180.7	208.0	212.3	226.6
Biomass [3]	2,735.1	3,008.2	3,116.8	4,285.7	4,420.5	4,315.6
Solar energy [4]	59.4	65.6	63.4	125.9	171.1	235.1
Wind energy [5]	29.0	57.1	178.1	923.4	1,167.6	1,361.1
Residential [6]	641.1	489.2	503.8	590.9	643.0	652.5
Wood [8]	580.0	420.0	430.0	440.0	450.0	420.0
Geothermal [2]	5.5	8.6	15.9	36.8	39.6	39.6
Solar [4]	55.6	60.6	57.9	114.1	153.4	192.9
Commercial [7]	98.2	127.7	119.6	130.4	135.9	131.2
Biomass [3]	94.0	119.1	105.1	110.9	114.6	109.3
Geothermal [2]	2.8	7.6	13.6	18.5	19.7	19.7
Hydroelectric [1]	1.4	1.0	0.9	0.8	0.2	0.4
Industrial [9]	1,717.0	1,928.1	1,873.2	2,221.1	2,282.8	2,219.5
Biomass [3]	1,684.2	1,881.5	1,836.9	2,200.6	2,261.0	2,196.9
Geothermal [2]	1.9	4.4	4.3	4.2	4.2	4.2
Hydroelectric [1]	30.9	42.2	32.0	16.3	17.5	18.0
Transportation	60.4	134.9	339.0	1,074.9	1,158.2	1,160.6
Fuel ethanol	60.4	134.9	327.4	1,041.4	1,045.0	1,049.6
Biodiesel [10]	(NA)	(NA)	11.6	33.5	113.2	111.0
Electric power [11]	3,523.9	3,426.5	3,406.3	4,064.4	4,854.5	4,661.4
Biomass [3]	316.5	452.8	405.7	459.4	436.7	428.7
Geothermal [2]	160.5	143.8	146.9	148.5	148.8	163.1
Hydroelectric [1]	3,014.0	2,767.9	2,670.1	2,521.5	3,085.1	2,668.4
Solar [4]	3.8	5.0	5.5	11.8	16.8	40.8
Wind [5]	29.0	57.1	178.1	923.3	1,167.1	1,360.3

NA Not available. [1] Power produced from natural stream flow as regulated by available storage. [2] As used at electric power plants, hot water or steam extracted from geothermal reservoirs in the Earth's crust that is supplied to steam turbines at electric power plants that drive generators to produce electricity. [3] Wood and wood-derived fuels, municipal solid waste (from biogenic sources, landfill gas, sludge waste, agricultural by products, and other biomass), fuel ethanol, and biodiesel. [4] The radiant energy of the sun, which can be converted into other forms of energy, such as heat or electricity. Solar thermal and photovoltaic electricity net generation and solar thermal direct use energy. [5] Energy present in wind motion that can be converted to mechanical energy for driving pumps, mills, and electric power generators. Wind pushes against sails, vanes, or blades radiating from a central rotating shaft. [6] Consists of living quarters for private households, but excludes institutional living quarters. [7] Consists of service-providing facilities and equipment of businesses, governments, and other private and public organizations. Includes institutional living quarters and sewage treatment facilities. Includes commercial combined-heat-and-power and commercial electricity-only plants. [8] Wood and wood-derived fuels. [9] Consists of all facilities and equipment used for producing, processing, or assembling goods. Includes industrial combined-heat-and-power and industrial electricity-only plants. [10] Any liquid biofuel suitable as a diesel fuel substitute, additive, or extender. [11] Consists of electricity-only and combined-heat-and-power plants whose primary business is to sell electricity and/or heat to the public. Includes sources not shown separately.

Source: U.S. Energy Information Administration, *Monthly Energy Review*, May 2013. See also <http://www.eia.gov/totalenergy/data/monthly/>.

Table 958. Energy Expenditures and Average Fuel Prices by Source and Sector: 1980 to 2011

[In millions of dollars (374,244 represents $374,244,000,000), except as indicated. For definition of Btu, see text, this section. End-use sector and electric utilities exclude expenditures and prices on energy sources such as hydropower, solar, wind, and geothermal. Also excludes expenditures for reported amounts of energy consumed by the energy industry for production, transportation, and processing operations]

Source and Sector	1980	1990	2000	2005	2007	2008	2009	2010	2011
EXPENDITURES (mil. dol.)									
Total [1,2,3]	374,347	474,831	687,825	1,045,907	1,234,018	1,409,325	1,063,873	1,208,424	1,394,088
Natural gas [4]	51,062	65,278	119,094	200,356	196,957	230,465	159,362	161,301	155,191
Petroleum products	237,676	237,672	359,398	596,296	740,325	871,326	580,867	711,461	897,918
Motor gasoline [5]	124,408	126,558	192,153	312,047	389,282	438,237	317,082	376,492	466,558
Coal	22,607	28,602	28,080	36,932	42,717	49,497	45,898	50,474	50,531
Retail electricity	98,095	176,691	231,578	295,787	340,925	360,570	350,438	365,900	368,009
Residential sector [6]	69,277	110,905	155,299	215,186	237,934	259,597	240,717	249,384	249,193
Commercial sector [2,3]	47,074	79,605	113,423	155,165	174,798	192,976	174,887	177,616	180,971
Industrial sector [2,3]	94,316	103,531	141,080	208,393	236,364	273,211	185,229	217,982	249,214
Transportation sector [2]	163,680	180,790	278,024	467,163	584,923	683,541	463,039	563,443	714,711
Motor gasoline [5]	121,809	123,845	189,836	304,875	381,201	430,705	311,613	369,433	457,962
Electric utilities [3]	38,027	40,627	60,054	95,975	100,719	118,571	84,508	94,603	92,509
AVERAGE FUEL PRICES (dol. per mil. Btu)									
All sectors	6.89	8.29	10.31	15.53	18.23	21.37	17.06	18.70	21.71
Residential sector [6]	7.46	11.87	14.21	19.16	21.56	23.07	22.03	22.41	22.84
Commercial sector [3]	7.83	11.87	13.90	18.59	20.73	22.44	20.67	20.91	21.17
Industrial sector [3]	4.71	5.29	6.48	10.39	11.92	14.38	11.12	11.98	13.57
Transportation sector	8.61	8.33	10.75	16.87	20.60	25.23	17.59	21.03	27.09
Electric utilities [3]	1.77	1.48	1.71	2.61	2.68	3.21	2.44	2.62	2.65

[1] Includes other sources not shown separately. [2] There is a discontinuity in this time series between 1988 and 1989 due to the expanded coverage of the use of wood and biomass waste beginning in 1989. [3] There are no direct fuel costs for hydroelectric, geothermal, wind, photovoltaic, or solar thermal energy. [4] Natural gas as it is consumed; includes supplemental gaseous fuels that are commingled with natural gas. [5] Beginning 1995, includes fuel ethanol blended into motor gasoline. [6] There are no direct fuel costs for geothermal, photovoltaic, or solar thermal energy.

Source: U.S. Energy Information Administration, "State Energy Data System (SEDS)," <http://www.eia.gov/state/seds/>, accessed August 2013.

Table 959. Fuel Ethanol and Biodiesel—Summary: 1990 to 2012

[110.9 represents 110,900,000,000,000. Data for 1990 are estimates. Beginning 1995, only feedstock data are estimates. Minus sign (-) indicates an excess of exports over imports, except where noted]

Fuel	1990	1995	2000	2005	2008	2009	2010	2011	2012 [1]
FUEL ETHANOL									
Feedstock [2] (tril. Btu)	110.9	197.7	233.1	552.4	1,299.5	1,517.5	1,839.3	1,919.1	1,825.1
Production:									
1,000 bbl	17,802	32,325	38,627	92,961	221,637	260,424	316,617	331,646	316,665
Tril. Btu	63.4	115.2	137.6	331.2	789.7	927.9	1,127.5	1,180.7	1,127.3
Net imports [3] (1,000 bbl.)	(NA)	387	116	3,234	12,610	4,720	-9,115	-24,365	-6,002
Stocks [4] (1,000 bbl.)	(NA)	2,186	3,400	5,563	14,226	16,594	17,941	18,238	20,677
Stock change [5,6] (1,000 bbl.)	(NA)	-207	-624	-439	3,691	2,368	1,347	297	2,416
Consumption:									
1,000 bbl	17,802	32,919	39,367	96,634	230,556	262,776	306,155	306,984	308,247
Tril. Btu	63.4	117.3	140.3	344.3	821.5	936.3	1,090.2	1,092.9	1,097.4
BIODIESEL									
Feedstock [7] (tril. Btu)	(NA)	(NA)	(NA)	11.7	87.7	66.7	44.4	125.2	125.4
Production:									
1,000 bbl	(NA)	(NA)	(NA)	2,162	16,145	12,281	8,177	23,035	23,082
Tril. Btu	(NA)	(NA)	(NA)	11.6	86.5	65.8	43.8	123.4	123.7
Net imports (1,000 bbl.)	(NA)	(NA)	(NA)	1	-8,626	-4,489	-1,958	-879	-2,105
Stocks [4] (1,000 bbl.)	(NA)	(NA)	(NA)	(NA)	(NA)	711	672	2,012	2,169
Stock change [5,6] (1,000 bbl.)	(NA)	(NA)	(NA)	(NA)	(NA)	711	-39	1,035	264
Consumption:									
1,000 bbl	(NA)	(NA)	(NA)	2,163	7,519	7,750	6,258	21,122	20,712
Tril. Btu	(NA)	(NA)	(NA)	11.6	40.3	41.5	33.5	113.2	111.0

NA Not available. [1] Preliminary. [2] Total corn and other biomass inputs to the production of fuel ethanol. [3] Through 2009, data are for fuel ethanol imports only; data for fuel ethanol exports are not available. Beginning in 2010, data are for fuel ethanol imports minus fuel ethanol exports. [4] Imports minus exports. Stocks are at end of year. [5] A negative number indicates a decrease in stocks. [6] Data for 2012 derived using the preliminary 2011 stock value, not the final 2011 value shown under "Stocks." [7] Total vegetable oil and other biomass inputs to the production of biodiesel.

Source: U.S. Energy Information Administration, *Monthly Energy Review*, May 2013. See also <http://www.eia.gov/totalenergy/data/monthly/>.

Table 960. Energy Expenditures—End-Use Sector and Selected Source by State: 2011

[In millions of dollars (1,394,088 represents $1,394,088,000,000). End-use sector and electric utilities exclude expenditures on energy sources such as hydroelectric, photovoltaic, solar thermal, wind, and geothermal. Also excludes expenditures for reported amounts of energy consumed by the energy industry for production, transportation, and processing operations. For technical notes and documentation, see source, <http://www.eia.gov/state/seds/seds-technical-notes-complete.cfm>]

| State | Total [1,2] | End-use sector | | | | Source | | | |
		Resi-dential	Com-mercial	Indus-trial [2]	Transpor-tation	Petroleum products [3]	Natural gas [4]	Coal	Electricity sales
U.S..............	1,394,088	249,193	180,971	249,214	714,711	897,918	155,191	50,531	368,009
AL................	24,479	4,420	2,881	4,667	12,512	14,348	3,081	2,010	7,846
AK................	7,739	803	923	800	5,214	6,468	534	56	1,005
AZ................	22,465	4,456	3,355	2,192	12,462	14,079	1,981	917	7,279
AR................	14,047	2,276	1,398	2,673	7,700	9,078	1,793	592	3,447
CA................	136,096	19,453	19,573	14,051	83,020	90,315	14,356	173	33,919
CO................	19,333	3,514	2,539	2,493	10,787	12,392	2,329	637	4,963
CT................	15,365	4,737	2,849	1,132	6,648	9,246	1,786	22	4,882
DE................	3,957	969	648	606	1,734	2,143	703	61	1,309
DC................	2,396	443	1,422	27	503	578	378	–	1,481
FL................	68,013	14,048	10,323	4,389	39,254	42,476	7,707	1,960	23,880
GA................	42,405	8,497	5,478	5,004	23,427	25,513	4,165	2,400	13,109
HI................	7,608	1,101	1,280	1,098	4,130	5,954	117	29	3,091
ID................	6,586	1,056	612	1,297	3,621	4,457	589	20	1,498
IL................	50,925	9,831	6,383	8,497	26,214	30,465	7,455	2,093	12,722
IN................	32,519	5,153	3,001	8,055	16,310	18,865	4,225	4,157	8,373
IA................	17,164	2,635	1,832	4,296	8,401	11,507	2,053	750	3,451
KS................	14,867	2,396	1,732	3,662	7,077	9,776	1,628	609	3,598
KY................	23,149	3,409	2,011	5,121	12,609	15,210	1,418	2,466	6,339
LA................	46,833	3,408	2,458	24,852	16,114	36,579	5,053	720	6,426
ME................	7,317	1,752	1,115	1,071	3,379	5,274	558	7	1,436
MD................	23,204	5,331	4,469	1,551	11,852	13,712	1,925	881	7,590
MA................	27,248	7,222	4,153	3,349	12,524	16,190	4,132	160	7,842
MI................	39,499	8,939	5,775	5,615	19,170	22,147	6,518	2,168	10,847
MN................	24,316	4,262	2,970	4,295	12,789	15,629	2,791	636	5,876
MS................	15,169	2,427	1,616	2,344	8,783	9,838	2,022	417	4,203
MO................	26,750	5,228	3,279	3,065	15,178	17,230	2,581	1,436	7,009
MT................	5,576	915	686	794	3,181	3,913	549	247	1,125
NE................	9,971	1,481	998	2,044	5,449	6,545	1,074	438	2,338
NV................	9,671	1,880	1,135	1,315	5,340	5,893	1,582	163	2,993
NH................	5,965	1,620	1,032	469	2,845	4,053	571	87	1,602
NJ................	43,214	8,257	7,527	2,855	24,575	27,450	5,805	207	10,954
NM................	8,846	1,277	1,087	1,156	5,326	6,313	895	585	1,964
NY................	65,877	18,405	17,294	3,377	26,802	34,155	11,161	448	22,889
NC................	36,102	7,609	4,744	4,304	19,445	22,432	2,547	2,283	11,332
ND................	6,409	665	636	2,167	2,941	4,734	296	767	1,021
OH................	50,996	10,091	6,372	8,421	26,112	30,360	6,554	3,382	13,856
OK................	19,766	3,142	1,984	3,103	11,536	12,744	3,494	686	4,637
OR................	14,941	2,636	1,703	1,864	8,738	9,764	1,478	65	3,793
PA................	55,164	12,920	6,637	10,067	25,540	32,695	7,433	3,685	15,383
RI................	3,818	1,153	694	275	1,696	2,319	813	–	1,008
SC................	21,175	3,950	2,371	3,152	11,702	12,823	1,439	1,411	7,081
SD................	4,547	687	477	893	2,490	3,152	451	69	940
TN................	29,699	5,261	3,678	4,203	16,557	18,358	1,835	1,425	9,278
TX................	169,290	18,809	13,486	66,867	70,127	127,656	14,692	3,213	33,065
UT................	10,431	1,460	1,187	1,125	6,658	7,327	1,215	623	2,032
VT................	3,151	885	510	306	1,450	2,238	99	–	766
VA................	33,915	6,761	4,728	3,084	19,342	21,637	2,781	1,128	9,748
WA................	27,124	4,579	3,058	2,922	16,567	18,284	2,484	133	6,295
WV................	8,888	1,581	960	2,125	4,223	5,450	624	2,227	2,431
WI................	24,356	4,925	3,321	4,053	12,058	14,332	3,028	1,169	6,944
WY................	5,406	480	593	1,733	2,601	3,823	414	710	1,118

– Represents or rounds to zero. [1] There are no direct fuel costs for hydroelectric, geothermal, wind, photovoltaic, or solar thermal energy. The U.S. total includes $342 million for coal coke net imports, which are not included in the states. [2] Includes sources not shown separately, such as electricity imports and exports and coal coke net imports, which are not allocated to the states. [3] Includes fuel ethanol blended into motor gasoline. [4] Includes supplemental gaseous fuels.

Source: U.S. Energy Information Administration, "State Energy Data System," <http://www.eia.gov/state/seds/>, accessed August 2013.

Table 961. Energy Imports and Exports by Type of Fuel: 1980 to 2011

[In quadrillion of Btu. (12.10 represents 12,100,000,000,000,000 Btu). For definition of Btu, see source and text, this section]

Type of fuel	1980	1990	1995	2000	2005	2006	2007	2008	2009	2010	2011 [1]
Net imports, total [2].........	**12.10**	**14.06**	**17.75**	**24.97**	**30.15**	**29.81**	**29.22**	**25.93**	**22.74**	**21.64**	**18.23**
Coal..................	-2.39	-2.70	-2.08	-1.21	-0.51	-0.36	-0.60	-1.22	-0.95	-1.62	-2.42
Natural gas (dry)...........	0.96	1.46	2.74	3.62	3.71	3.56	3.89	3.11	2.76	2.69	2.02
Petroleum [3].............	13.50	15.29	16.89	22.38	26.81	26.42	25.77	23.89	20.84	20.53	18.59
Other [4].....................	0.04	0.01	0.20	0.18	0.14	0.19	0.15	0.15	0.08	0.04	0.05
Imports, total..........	15.80	18.82	22.26	28.97	34.71	34.68	34.70	32.99	29.71	29.88	28.59
Coal...................	0.03	0.07	0.24	0.31	0.76	0.91	0.91	0.86	0.57	0.48	0.33
Natural gas (dry)..........	1.01	1.55	2.90	3.87	4.45	4.29	4.72	4.08	3.85	3.83	3.54
Petroleum [3].............	14.66	17.12	18.88	24.53	29.25	29.17	28.78	27.69	25.08	25.37	24.49
Other [4].................	0.10	0.08	0.24	0.26	0.25	0.31	0.29	0.37	0.21	0.19	0.23
Exports, total..............	3.69	4.75	4.51	4.01	4.56	4.87	5.48	7.06	6.96	8.23	10.36
Coal...................	2.42	2.77	2.32	1.53	1.27	1.26	1.51	2.07	1.51	2.10	2.75
Natural gas (dry).........	0.05	0.09	0.16	0.25	0.74	0.73	0.83	0.97	1.08	1.15	1.52
Petroleum................	1.16	1.82	1.99	2.15	2.44	2.75	3.01	3.80	4.24	4.84	5.90
Other [4]...................	0.07	0.07	0.05	0.08	0.11	0.13	0.14	0.22	0.13	0.15	0.18

[1] Preliminary. [2] Net imports equals imports minus exports. Minus sign (-) indicates exports are greater than imports. [3] Includes imports into the Strategic Petroleum Reserve. [4] Coal coke, small amounts of electricity transmitted across U.S. borders with Canada and Mexico, and small amounts of biodiesel.

Source: U.S. Energy Information Administration, *Annual Energy Review 2011*, September 2012. See also <http://www.eia.gov/totalenergy/>.

Table 962. U.S. Foreign Trade in Natural Gas, Crude Oil, Petroleum Products, and Coal: 1980 to 2012

[985 represents 985,000,000,000 cu. ft. Minus sign (–) indicates trade deficit]

Mineral fuel	Unit	1980	1990	1995	2000	2005	2009	2010	2011	2012 [1]
Natural gas:										
Imports........................	Bil. cu. ft.	985	1,532	2,841	3,782	4,341	3,751	3,741	3,469	3,135
Exports........................	Bil. cu. ft.	49	86	154	244	729	1,072	1,137	1,507	1,619
Net trade [2].................	Bil. cu. ft.	-936	-1,447	-2,687	-3,538	-3,612	-2,679	-2,604	-1,962	-1,516
Crude oil: [3]										
Imports [4].....................	Mil. bbl.	1,926	2,151	2,639	3,320	3,696	3,290	3,363	3,261	3,108
Exports........................	Mil. bbl.	105	40	35	18	12	16	15	17	22
Net trade [2].................	Mil. bbl.	-1,821	-2,112	-2,604	-3,301	-3,684	-3,274	-3,348	-3,244	-3,086
Petroleum products:										
Imports........................	Mil. bbl.	(NA)	(NA)	586	874	1,310	977	942	937	770
Exports........................	Mil. bbl.	(NA)	273	312	362	414	723	843	1,073	1,144
Net trade [2].................	Mil. bbl.	(NA)	(NA)	-274	-512	-896	-255	-98	135	373
Coal:										
Imports........................	Mil. sh. tons	1	3	9	13	30	23	19	13	9
Exports........................	Mil. sh. tons	92	106	89	58	50	59	82	107	126
Net trade [2].................	Mil. sh. tons	91	103	79	46	19	36	62	94	117

[1] Preliminary. [2] Exports minus imports. [3] Includes lease condensate. [4] Includes Strategic Petroleum Reserve imports.

Source: U.S. Energy Information Administration, *Monthly Energy Review*, May 2013; and "Petroleum and Other Liquids, Imports/Exports & Movements," <http://www.eia.gov/petroleum/data.cfm#imports>, accessed June 2013.

Table 963. Crude Oil Imports Into the U.S. by Country of Origin: 1980 to 2012

[In millions of barrels (1,921 represents 1,921,000,000). Barrels contain 42 gallons. Crude oil imports are reported by the Petroleum Administration for Defense (PAD) District in which they are to be processed. A PAD District is a geographic aggregation of the 50 states and D.C. into 5 districts. Includes crude oil imported for storage in the Strategic Petroleum Reserve (SPR). Total Organization of Petroleum Exporting Countries (OPEC) excludes, and non-OPEC includes, petroleum imported into the United States indirectly from members of OPEC, primarily from Caribbean and West European areas, as petroleum products that were refined from crude oil produced by OPEC]

Country of origin	1980	1990	1995	2000	2005	2007	2008	2009	2010	2011	2012
Total imports.................	**1,921**	**2,151**	**2,639**	**3,311**	**3,670**	**3,656**	**3,571**	**3,307**	**3,344**	**3,256**	**3,108**
OPEC, total [1, 2, 3, 4].............	**1,410**	**1,283**	**1,219**	**1,659**	**1,738**	**1,969**	**1,984**	**1,594**	**1,654**	**1,531**	**1,471**
Algeria............................	166	23	10	(Z)	83	162	114	101	119	65	44
Angola [2].........................	(NA)	86	131	108	164	181	184	164	139	122	81
Ecuador [3].......................	6	(NA)	35	46	101	72	78	64	71	69	64
Iraq...............................	10	188	–	226	190	177	229	164	151	168	173
Kuwait [5].........................	10	29	78	96	79	64	75	68	71	70	112
Nigeria............................	307	286	227	319	387	395	338	281	360	280	148
Saudi Arabia [5]..................	456	436	460	556	525	530	551	361	394	433	496
Venezuela........................	57	243	420	446	449	420	381	352	333	317	332
Non-OPEC, total [2, 3, 4, 6]....	**511**	**869**	**1,419**	**1,652**	**1,932**	**1,687**	**1,587**	**1,713**	**1,690**	**1,725**	**1,637**
Brazil.............................	(NA)	–	–	2	34	61	84	107	93	84	68
Canada...........................	73	235	380	492	600	681	707	707	720	806	881
Colombia.........................	(NA)	51	76	116	57	50	65	93	124	141	147
Congo, Republic of the..........	(NA)	(NA)	(NA)	(NA)	9	23	25	24	26	21	11
Mexico...........................	185	251	375	479	566	514	434	400	416	402	356
Russia............................	(NA)	(Z)	5	3	70	41	41	85	92	93	37
United Kingdom..................	63	57	124	106	80	37	27	38	44	13	7

– Represents zero. NA Not available. Z Represents less than 500,000 barrels. [1] OPEC (Organization of Petroleum Exporting Countries) includes the nations shown, as well as Iran, Libya, Qatar, United Arab Emirates, and Indonesia. [2] Angola joined OPEC at the beginning of 2007. Prior to 2007, it is included in the non-OPEC total. [3] Ecuador withdrew from OPEC on Dec. 31, 1992; therefore, it is included under OPEC prior to 1995. From 1995 through 2007, it is included in the Non-OPEC total. In Nov. 2007, Ecuador rejoined OPEC; imports for 2008 are included in the OPEC total. [4] Gabon withdrew from OPEC on Dec. 31, 1994; therefore, it is included under OPEC prior to 1995. Beginning 1995, it is included in the Non-OPEC total. [5] Imports from the Neutral Zone between Kuwait and Saudi Arabia are included in Saudi Arabia. [6] Non-OPEC total includes nations not shown.

Source: U.S. Energy Information Administration, *Petroleum Supply Monthly*, February 2013, and earlier reports. See also <http://www.eia.gov/petroleum/supply/monthly/>.

Table 964. Crude Oil and Refined Products—Summary: 1980 to 2012

[13,481 represents 13,481,000 bbl. Barrels (bbl.) of 42 gallons. Data are averages]

Year	Crude oil [1] (1,000 bbl. per day)					Refined oil products (1,000 bbl. per day)			Total oil imports [5] (1,000 bbl. per day)	Crude oil stocks [1,2] (mil. bbl.)	
	Input to refineries	Domestic production	Imports		Exports	Domestic demand	Imports	Exports		Total [6]	Strategic reserve [7]
			Total [3]	Strategic reserve [4]							
1980....	13,481	8,597	5,263	44	287	17,056	1,646	258	6,909	466	108
1985....	12,002	8,971	3,201	118	204	15,726	1,866	577	5,067	814	493
1990....	13,409	7,355	5,894	27	109	16,988	2,123	748	8,018	908	586
1995....	13,973	6,560	7,230	0	95	17,725	1,605	855	8,835	895	592
2000....	15,067	5,822	9,071	8	50	19,701	2,389	990	11,459	826	541
2005....	15,220	5,186	10,126	52	32	20,802	3,588	1,133	13,714	1,008	685
2008....	14,648	5,000	9,783	19	29	19,498	3,132	1,773	12,915	1,028	702
2009....	14,336	5,353	9,013	56	44	18,771	2,678	1,980	11,691	1,052	727
2010....	14,724	5,479	9,213	0	42	19,180	2,580	2,311	11,793	1,060	727
2011....	14,806	5,652	8,935	0	47	18,949	2,568	2,939	11,504	1,027	696
2012....	15,006	6,496	8,491	(NA)	60	18,555	2,105	3,125	10,596	1,060	695

– Represents zero. NA Not available. [1] Includes lease condensate. [2] Crude oil at end of period. Includes commercial and Strategic Petroleum Reserve stocks. [3] Includes Strategic Petroleum Reserve. [4] SPR is the Strategic Petroleum Reserve. Through 2000, includes imports by SPR only; beginning in 2004, includes imports by SPR, and imports into SPR by others. [5] Crude oil (including Strategic Petroleum Reserve imports) plus refined products. [6] Beginning in 1981, includes stocks of Alaskan crude oil in transit. [7] Crude oil stocks in the Strategic Petroleum Reserve include non-U.S. stocks held under foreign or commercial storage agreements.

Source: U.S. Energy Information Administration, "Monthly Energy Review," <http://www.eia.gov/totalenergy>, accessed August 2013.

Table 965. Petroleum and Coal Products Corporations—Sales, Net Profit, and Profit Per Dollar of Sales: 1990 to 2012

[318.5 represents $318,500,000,000. Represents SIC group 29 (NAICS group 324). Through 2000, based on Standard Industrial Classification (SIC) code; beginning 2001, based on North American Industry Classification System (NAICS). Profit rates are averages of quarterly figures at annual rates. Beginning 1987, excludes estimates for corporations with less than $250,000 in assets]

Item	Unit	1990	1995	2000	2005	2006	2007	2008	2009	2010	2011	2012
Sales............................	Bil. dol.	318.5	283.1	455.2	956.0	1,037.8	1,113.2	1,369.1	846.0	1,077.1	1,411.3	1,377.8
Net profit:												
Before income taxes...........	Bil. dol.	23.1	16.5	55.5	120.2	139.8	127.0	101.6	41.9	56.0	125.7	117.8
After income taxes.............	Bil. dol.	17.8	13.9	42.6	96.3	111.0	105.4	81.0	43.1	54.2	108.0	99.1
Depreciation [1]....................	Bil. dol.	18.7	16.7	15.5	18.6	20.0	22.6	22.9	28.0	30.8	29.4	29.1
Profits per dollar of sales:												
Before income taxes...........	Cents	7.3	5.8	12.2	12.6	13.4	11.6	5.8	5.1	5.3	8.9	8.5
After income taxes.............	Cents	5.6	4.9	9.4	10.1	10.6	9.6	4.4	5.2	5.1	7.7	7.2
Profits on stockholders' equity:												
Before income taxes...........	Percent	16.4	12.6	29.4	38.0	36.3	30.7	21.8	10.2	12.2	24.6	22.9
After income taxes..............	Percent	12.7	10.6	22.6	30.4	28.8	25.5	17.3	10.5	11.8	21.1	19.3

[1] Includes depletion and accelerated amortization of emergency facilities.

Source: U.S. Census Bureau, *Quarterly Financial Report for Manufacturing, Mining, Trade, and Selected Service Industries*. See also <http://www.census.gov/econ/qfr/>.

Table 966. Major Petroleum Companies—Financial Summary: 1980 to 2010

[32.9 represents $32,900,000,000. Data represent a composite of approximately 42 major worldwide petroleum companies aggregated on a consolidated total company basis. Minus sign (-) indicates deficit]

Item	1980	1990	1995	2000	2005	2006	2007	2008	2009	2010
FINANCIAL DATA (bil. dol.)										
Net income........................	32.9	26.8	24.3	76.4	170.6	187.6	237.6	198.1	92.6	185.0
Depreciation, depletion, etc............................	32.5	38.7	43.1	53.3	76.5	85.8	114.3	156.8	170.2	186.8
Cash flow [1].........................	65.4	65.5	67.4	129.7	239.9	261.2	327.1	440.7	279.6	362.4
Dividends paid......................	9.3	15.9	17.6	23.0	37.5	39.2	62.2	74.8	72.1	70.5
Net internal funds available for investment or debt repayment [2].....................	56.1	49.6	49.8	106.7	202.4	222.0	264.9	365.9	207.5	291.9
Capital and exploratory expenditures...............	62.1	59.6	59.8	72.8	140.4	193.1	221.7	328.0	268.0	344.3
Long-term capitalization.............................	211.4	300.0	304.3	516.9	800.4	910.6	1,211.8	1,362.0	1,449.3	1,621.1
Long-term debt......................................	49.8	90.4	85.4	112.8	165.2	177.4	240.1	299.4	365.7	444.2
Preferred stock......................................	2.0	5.2	5.7	5.4	3.5	3.4	1.9	1.4	1.2	5.0
Common stock and retained earnings [3]..........	159.6	204.4	213.2	398.7	631.7	729.8	969.8	1,061.2	1,082.4	1,171.9
Excess of expenditures over cash income [4]..	6.0	10.0	10.0	-33.9	-62.0	-28.9	-43.2	-37.9	60.5	52.4
RATIOS [5] (percent)										
Long-term debt to long-term capitalization..........	23.6	30.1	28.1	21.8	23.5	19.4	19.1	22.0	25.3	24.1
Net income to total average capital..................	17.0	9.1	8.1	15.7	23.0	22.3	21.2	15.2	6.6	10.8
Net income to average common equity.............	22.5	13.5	11.6	20.5	29.3	27.8	26.3	19.2	8.7	14.4

[1] Generally represents internally generated funds from operations: Sum of net income, changes in working capital and noncash items such as depreciation, depletion, amortization, impairments, and unrealized hedging gains/losses. [2] Cash flow minus dividends paid. [3] Includes common stock, capital surplus, and earned surplus accounts after adjustments. [4] Capital and exploratory expenditures plus dividends paid minus cash flow. [5] Represents approximate year-to-year comparisons because of changes in the makeup of the group due to mergers and other corporate changes.

Source: Carl H. Pforzheimer & Co., LLC, New York, NY, *Comparative Oil Company Statements*, annual ©.

Table 967. Nuclear Power Plants—Number, Capacity, and Generation: 1980 to 2012

[51.8 represents 51,800,000 kW]

Item	1980	1990	1995	2000	2005	2006	2007	2008	2009	2010	2011	2012[5]
Operable generating units [1,2]	71	112	109	104	104	104	104	104	104	104	104	104
Net summer capacity [2,3] (mil. kW)	51.8	99.6	99.5	97.9	100.0	100.3	100.3	100.8	101.0	101.2	101.4	101.7
Net generation (bil. kWh)	251.1	576.9	673.4	753.9	782.0	787.2	806.4	806.2	798.9	807.0	790.2	769.3
Percent of total electricity net generation	11.0	19.0	20.1	19.8	19.3	19.4	19.4	19.6	20.2	19.6	19.3	19.0
Capacity factor [4] (percent)	56.3	66.0	77.4	88.1	89.3	89.6	91.8	91.1	90.3	91.1	89.1	86.2

[1] Total of nuclear generating units holding full-power licenses, or equivalent permission to operate, at the end of the year. For example, although Browns Ferry 1 was shut down in 1985, the unit remained fully licensed and thus continued to be counted as operable. It was eventually reopened in 2007. [2] As of year-end. [3] Net summer capacity is the peak steady hourly output that generating equipment is expected to supply to system load, exclusive of auxiliary and other power plant, as demonstrated by test at the time of summer peak demand. [4] Weighted average of monthly capacity factors. Monthly factors are derived by dividing actual monthly generation by the maximum possible generation for the month (number of hours in the month multiplied by the net summer capacity at the end of the month). [5] Data for 2012 are preliminary.

Source: U.S. Energy Information Administration, *Monthly Energy Review*, May 2013. See also <http://www.eia.gov/totalenergy/data/monthly/>.

Table 968. Nuclear Power Plants—Number of Units, Net Generation, and Net Summer Capacity by State: 2011

[790,204 represents 790,204,000,000 kWh]

State	Number of units	Nuclear net generation Total (mil. kWh)	Nuclear net generation Percent of total [1]	Nuclear net summer capability Total (mil. kW)	Nuclear net summer capability Percent of total [1]	State	Number of units	Nuclear net generation Total (mil. kWh)	Nuclear net generation Percent of total [1]	Nuclear net summer capability Total (mil. kW)	Nuclear net summer capability Percent of total [1]
U.S.	**104**	**790,204**	**19.3**	**101.4**	**9.6**	MS	1	10,337	20.0	1.2	7.7
AL	5	39,356	25.2	5.0	15.5	MO	1	9,371	9.9	1.2	5.4
AZ	3	31,278	28.9	3.9	14.6	NE	2	6,933	19.2	1.2	15.2
AR	2	14,194	23.2	1.8	11.4	NH	1	8,363	41.7	1.2	29.9
CA	4	36,663	18.3	4.4	6.4	NJ	4	33,606	51.9	4.1	22.4
CT	2	15,928	47.2	2.1	23.0	NY	6	42,695	31.0	5.2	13.2
FL	5	22,015	9.9	3.9	6.6	NC	5	40,527	34.2	5.0	17.5
GA	4	32,306	25.9	4.1	10.9	OH	2	14,890	11.0	2.1	6.4
IL	11	95,823	48.0	11.5	26.2	PA	9	76,147	33.5	9.6	21.0
IA	1	5,215	9.3	0.6	3.9	SC	7	52,903	51.4	6.5	26.9
KS	1	7,319	16.1	1.2	9.2	TN	3	26,919	33.2	3.4	16.1
LA	2	16,615	15.8	2.1	8.1	TX	4	39,648	9.1	5.0	4.5
MD	2	14,397	34.4	1.7	13.6	VT	1	4,907	72.4	0.6	53.0
MA	1	5,085	13.4	0.7	5.0	VA	4	25,548	38.3	3.5	14.3
MI	4	32,889	30.1	4.0	13.2	WA	1	4,806	4.2	1.1	3.6
MN	3	11,959	22.5	1.6	10.5	WI	3	11,560	18.3	1.8	9.6

[1] For total generation and capacity, see Table 974.

Source: U.S. Energy Information Administration, *Electric Power Annual*, "Detailed State Data," <http://www.eia.gov/electricity/data/state/>, accessed September 2013.

Table 969. Uranium Concentrate—Supply, Inventories, and Average Prices: 1990 to 2011

[8.89 represents 8,890,000 pounds (lbs.). Years ending December 31. For additional data on uranium, see Section 18]

Item	Unit	1990	1995	2000	2005	2007	2008	2009	2010	2011
Production [1]	Mil. lb.	8.89	6.04	3.96	2.69	4.53	3.90	3.71	4.23	3.99
Exports [2]	Mil. lb.	2.0	9.8	13.6	20.5	14.8	17.2	23.5	23.1	16.7
Imports [2]	Mil. lb.	23.7	41.3	44.9	65.5	54.1	57.1	58.9	55.3	54.4
Electric plant purchases from domestic suppliers	Mil. lb.	20.5	22.3	24.3	27.3	18.5	20.4	17.6	16.2	19.8
Loaded into U.S. nuclear reactors [3,4]	Mil. lb.	(NA)	51.1	51.5	58.3	45.5	51.3	49.4	44.3	52.0
Inventories, total [4]	Mil. lb.	129.1	72.5	111.3	93.8	112.4	110.0	111.5	111.3	113.6
At domestic suppliers	Mil. lb.	26.4	13.7	56.5	29.1	31.2	27.0	26.8	24.7	24.1
At electric plants	Mil. lb.	102.7	58.7	54.8	64.7	81.2	83.0	84.8	86.5	89.5
Average price per pound:										
Purchased imports	Dollars	12.55	10.20	9.84	14.83	34.18	41.30	41.23	47.01	54.00
Domestic purchases	Dollars	15.70	11.11	11.45	13.98	33.13	43.43	44.53	44.88	53.41

NA Not available. [1] Data are for uranium concentrate, a yellow or brown powder obtained by the milling of uranium ore, processing of in situ leach mining solutions, or as a by-product of phosphoric acid production. [2] Includes transactions by uranium buyers (consumers). Buyer imports and exports prior to 1990 are believed to be small. [3] Does not include any fuel rods removed from reactors and later reloaded into the reactor. [4] Data for 2011 are preliminary.

Source: U.S. Energy Information Administration, *Annual Energy Review 2011*, September 2012. See also <http://www.eia.gov/totalenergy/>.

Table 970. Renewable Energy Generating Capacity and Generation: Projections 2010 to 2040

[In gigawatts, unless otherwise noted. Reference case projections are business-as-usual trend estimates, given known technology, as well as market, demographic, and technological trends. Based on results from EIA's National Energy Modeling System. Minus sign (-) indicates decrease]

Net summer capacity and generation	Reference case								Annual growth 2011-2040 (percent)
	2010	2011	2015	2020	2025	2030	2035	2040	
Electric power sector [1]									
Net summer capacity:									
Conventional hydropower......................	77.8	77.9	77.8	78.3	78.9	79.1	79.6	80.3	0.1
Geothermal [2]...............................	2.4	2.4	2.7	3.6	4.3	5.7	6.6	7.5	4.0
Municipal waste [3].........................	3.3	3.3	3.4	3.4	3.4	3.4	3.4	3.4	0.1
Wood and other biomass [4]..................	2.4	2.4	2.8	2.8	2.8	2.8	3.2	3.7	1.6
Solar thermal..............................	0.5	0.5	1.4	1.4	1.4	1.4	1.4	1.4	3.6
Solar photovoltaic [5].......................	0.4	1.0	4.7	5.4	5.9	6.8	11.8	24.5	11.6
Wind.......................................	39.4	45.7	58.1	58.8	59.6	61.3	69.1	86.8	2.2
Total electric power sector capacity.........	**126.1**	**133.1**	**150.8**	**153.8**	**156.4**	**160.5**	**175.2**	**207.6**	**1.5**
Generation (bil. kWh):									
Conventional hydropower......................	258.5	323.1	280.7	288.5	291.4	292.4	295.2	297.3	-0.3
Geothermal [2]...............................	15.2	16.7	17.8	25.3	31.0	42.0	49.4	56.4	4.3
Biogenic municipal waste [6].................	15.8	16.6	14.1	14.1	14.1	14.1	14.1	14.1	-0.6
Wood and other biomass......................	11.4	10.5	15.1	54.4	69.0	65.5	66.4	75.6	7.0
Dedicated plants............................	10.4	9.3	11.7	14.9	15.1	15.3	17.6	21.6	2.9
Cofiring....................................	1.1	1.2	3.4	39.6	53.9	50.2	48.8	54.0	14.2
Solar thermal..............................	0.8	0.8	2.7	2.7	2.7	2.7	2.7	2.7	4.3
Solar photovoltaic [5].......................	0.4	1.0	8.4	9.8	11.0	13.4	24.8	56.2	15.0
Wind.......................................	94.6	119.6	162.0	163.5	166.7	172.1	195.5	251.9	2.6
Total electric power sector generation.......	**396.7**	**488.4**	**500.7**	**558.4**	**585.9**	**602.2**	**648.1**	**754.3**	**1.5**
End-use sectors [7]									
Net summer capacity:									
Conventional hydropower [8]..................	0.3	0.3	0.3	0.3	0.3	0.3	0.3	0.3	0.0
Geothermal.................................	0.0	0.0	0.0	0.0	0.0	0.0	0.0	0.0	(X)
Municipal waste [3].........................	0.3	0.5	0.5	0.5	0.5	0.5	0.5	0.5	0.0
Biomass....................................	4.6	4.9	5.9	6.9	7.6	8.3	9.2	10.2	2.5
Solar photovoltaic [5].......................	1.8	3.0	13.2	15.6	17.0	18.9	21.5	25.1	7.6
Wind.......................................	0.2	0.2	0.7	0.9	0.9	1.1	1.2	1.5	7.1
Total end-use sector capacity.................	**7.2**	**8.9**	**20.5**	**24.2**	**26.3**	**29.1**	**32.7**	**37.5**	**5.1**
Generation (bil. kWh):									
Conventional hydropower	1.7	1.9	1.8	1.8	1.8	1.8	1.8	1.8	-0.1
Geothermal.................................	0.0	0.0	0.0	0.0	0.0	0.0	0.0	0.0	(X)
Municipal waste [3].........................	1.9	2.0	3.5	3.5	3.5	3.5	3.5	3.5	1.9
Biomass....................................	25.7	26.8	31.1	37.0	41.3	45.5	50.3	56.2	2.6
Solar photovoltaic [5].......................	2.8	4.7	20.6	24.5	26.7	29.9	34.1	40.0	7.7
Wind.......................................	0.2	0.3	1.0	1.2	1.3	1.5	1.8	2.2	7.4
Total End-Use Sector Generation.............	**32.5**	**35.7**	**58.0**	**68.1**	**74.7**	**82.3**	**91.6**	**103.7**	**3.7**
Total, all sectors									
Net summer capacity:									
Conventional hydropower......................	78.2	78.2	78.1	78.7	79.3	79.4	80.0	80.6	0.1
Geothermal.................................	2.4	2.4	2.7	3.6	4.3	5.7	6.6	7.5	4.0
Municipal waste............................	3.6	3.8	3.9	3.9	3.9	3.9	3.9	3.9	0.1
Wood and other biomass [4]..................	6.9	7.3	8.7	9.7	10.5	11.2	12.3	13.9	2.2
Solar [5]..................................	2.7	4.5	19.2	22.3	24.2	27.1	34.7	51.0	8.7
Wind.......................................	39.6	45.9	58.8	59.7	60.5	62.4	70.4	88.3	2.3
Total capacity, all sectors.....................	**133.3**	**142.1**	**171.4**	**177.9**	**182.7**	**189.7**	**207.9**	**245.2**	**1.9**
Generation (bil. kWh):									
Conventional hydropower......................	260.2	325.0	282.5	290.4	293.2	294.2	297.0	299.1	-0.3
Geothermal.................................	15.2	16.7	17.8	25.3	31.0	42.0	49.4	56.4	4.3
Municipal waste............................	17.7	18.7	17.6	17.6	17.6	17.6	17.6	17.6	-0.2
Wood and other biomass......................	37.2	37.3	46.1	91.4	110.3	111.0	116.7	131.9	4.5
Solar [5]..................................	4.1	6.5	31.7	37.1	40.4	46.0	61.6	98.9	9.8
Wind.......................................	94.8	119.9	162.9	164.7	168.0	173.6	197.2	254.1	2.6
Total generation, all sectors....................	**429.2**	**524.1**	**558.7**	**626.5**	**660.6**	**684.5**	**739.6**	**858.1**	**1.7**

X Not applicable. [1] Includes electricity-only and combined heat and power plants that have a regulatory status. [2] Includes both hydrothermal resources and near-field enhanced geothermal systems (EGS). [3] Includes municipal waste, landfill gas, and municipal sewage sludge. [4] Facilities co-firing biomass and coal are classified as coal. [5] Does not include off-grid photovoltaics (PV). [6] Includes biogenic municipal waste, landfill gas, and municipal sludge. [7] Includes combined heat and power plants and electricity-only plants in the commercial and industrial sectors and small on-site generating systems in the residential, commercial, and industrial sectors used primarily for own-use generation, but which many also sell some power to the grid.

Source: U.S. Energy Information Administration, *Annual Energy Outlook 2013*, April 2013. See also <http://www.eia.gov/forecasts/aeo/>.

Table 971. Electricity Net Generation by Sector and Fuel Type: 1990 to 2012

[3,037.8 represents 3,037,800,000,000 kWh. Data are for fuels consumed to produce electricity. Also includes fuels consumed to produce useful thermal output at a small number of electric utility combined-heat-and-power (CHP) plants]

Source and sector	Unit	1990	2000	2005	2010	2011	2012 [1]
Net generation, total...............................	**Bil. kWh.**	**3,037.8**	**3,802.1**	**4,055.4**	**4,125.1**	**4,100.7**	**4,054.5**
Electric power sector, total...............................	Bil. kWh.	2,901.3	3,637.5	3,902.2	3,972.4	3,948.7	3,898.7
Commercial sector [2]...............................	Bil. kWh.	5.8	7.9	8.5	8.6	10.1	10.6
Industrial sector [3]...............................	Bil. kWh.	130.8	156.7	144.7	144.1	141.9	145.2
Net generation by source, all sectors:							
Fossil fuels, total...............................	Bil. kWh.	2,103.6	2,692.5	2,909.5	2,883.4	2,788.9	2,782.0
Coal [4]...............................	Bil. kWh.	1,594.0	1,966.3	2,012.9	1,847.3	1,733.4	1,517.2
Petroleum [5]...............................	Bil. kWh.	126.5	111.2	122.2	37.1	30.2	22.9
Natural gas [6]...............................	Bil. kWh.	372.8	601.0	761.0	987.7	1,013.7	1,230.7
Other gases [7]...............................	Bil. kWh.	10.4	14.0	13.5	11.3	11.6	11.2
Nuclear electric power...............................	Bil. kWh.	576.9	753.9	782.0	807.0	790.2	769.3
Hydroelectric pumped storage [8]...............................	Bil. kWh.	-3.5	-5.5	-6.6	-5.5	-5.9	-4.7
Renewable energy, total...............................	Bil. kWh.	357.2	356.5	357.7	427.4	513.3	495.3
Conventional hydroelectric power...............................	Bil. kWh.	292.9	275.6	270.3	260.2	319.4	276.5
Biomass, total...............................	Bil. kWh.	45.8	60.7	54.3	56.1	56.7	57.6
Wood [9]...............................	Bil. kWh.	32.5	37.6	38.9	37.2	37.4	37.5
Waste [10]...............................	Bil. kWh.	13.3	23.1	15.4	18.9	19.2	20.0
Geothermal...............................	Bil. kWh.	15.4	14.1	14.7	15.2	15.3	16.8
Solar [11]...............................	Bil. kWh.	0.4	0.5	0.6	1.2	1.8	4.3
Wind...............................	Bil. kWh.	2.8	5.6	17.8	94.7	120.2	140.1
Other [12]...............................	Bil. kWh.	3.6	4.8	12.8	12.9	14.2	12.5
Consumption of fuels for electricity generation:							
Coal [4]...............................	Mil. sh. tons.	792.5	994.9	1,041.4	979.7	934.9	826.7
Petroleum, total...............................	Mil. bbl.	218.8	195.2	206.8	65.1	52.4	40.3
Distillate fuel oil [13]...............................	Mil. bbl.	18.1	31.7	20.7	14.1	11.2	9.2
Residual fuel oil [14]...............................	Mil. bbl.	190.7	143.4	141.5	24.0	14.3	11.7
Other liquids [15]...............................	Mil. bbl.	0.4	1.4	3.0	2.1	1.8	1.6
Petroleum coke...............................	Mil. sh. tons [16]	1.9	3.7	8.3	5.0	5.0	3.6
Natural gas [6]...............................	Bil. cu. ft.	3,691.6	5,691.5	6,036.4	7,680.2	7,883.9	9,465.2
Other gases [7]...............................	Tril. Btu.	111.8	126.0	109.9	90.1	91.3	91.0
Biomass...............................	Tril. Btu.	653.5	825.9	585.3	630.3	626.2	642.7
Wood [9]...............................	Tril. Btu.	442.3	495.8	355.3	349.5	347.6	367.1
Waste [10]...............................	Tril. Btu.	211.2	330.1	230.1	280.8	278.6	275.7
Other [12]...............................	Tril. Btu.	36.0	46.2	173.0	184.4	205.3	181.1

[1] Preliminary. [2] Commercial combined-heat-and-power (CHP) and commercial electricity-only plants. [3] Industrial CHP and industrial electricity-only plants. [4] Anthracite, bituminous coal, subbituminous coal, lignite, waste coal, and coal synfuel. [5] Distillate fuel oil, residual fuel oil, petroleum coke, jet fuel, kerosene, other petroleum, waste oil, and beginning in 2011, propane. [6] Includes a small amount of supplemental gaseous fuels that cannot be identified separately. [7] Blast furnace gas and other manufactured and waste gases derived from fossil fuels. Through 2010, also includes propane. [8] Pumped storage facility production minus energy used for pumping. [9] Wood and wood-derived fuels. [10] Municipal solid waste from biogenic sources, landfill gas, sludge waste, tires, agricultural byproducts, and other biomass. Through 2000, also includes nonrenewable waste (municipal solid waste from non-biogenic sources and tire-derived fuels). [11] Solar thermal and photovoltaic energy. [12] Batteries, chemicals, hydrogen, pitch, purchased steam, sulfur, miscellaneous technologies, and beginning 2001, nonrenewable waste (municipal solid waste from nonbiogenic sources, and tire-derived fuels). [13] Fuel oil numbers 1, 2, and 4. For 1990 through 2000, electric utility data also include small amounts of kerosene and jet fuel. [14] Fuel oil numbers 5 and 6. For 1990 through 2000, electric utility data also include a small amount of fuel oil number 4. [15] Jet fuel, kerosene, other petroleum liquids, waste oil, and beginning in 2011, propane. [16] Short tons.

Source: U.S. Energy Information Administration,"Monthly Energy Review," <http://www.eia.gov/totalenergy/data/monthly>, accessed August 2013.

Table 972. Total Electric Net Summer Capacity, All Sectors: 1990 to 2011

[In million kilowatts (734.1 represents 734,100,000). Data are at end of year. For plants that use multiple sources of energy, capacity is assigned to the predominant energy source]

Source	1990	1995	2000	2005	2007	2008	2009	2010	2011 [9]
Net summer capacity, total	**734.1**	**769.5**	**811.7**	**978.0**	**994.9**	**1,010.2**	**1,025.4**	**1,039.1**	**1,054.8**
Fossil fuels, total	527.8	554.2	598.9	757.1	764.0	770.2	774.3	782.2	790.7
Coal [1]	307.4	311.4	315.1	313.4	312.7	313.3	314.3	316.8	319.2
Petroleum [2]	77.9	66.6	61.8	58.5	56.1	57.4	56.8	55.6	55.6
Natural gas [3]	140.8	174.5	219.6	383.1	392.9	397.5	401.3	407.0	413.1
Other gases [4]	1.6	1.7	2.3	2.1	2.3	2.0	1.9	2.7	2.7
Nuclear electric power	99.6	99.5	97.9	100.0	100.3	100.8	101.0	101.2	101.4
Hydroelectric pumped storage	19.5	21.4	19.5	21.3	21.9	21.9	22.2	22.2	22.3
Renewable energy, total	86.8	93.9	94.9	98.7	108.0	116.4	127.1	132.6	139.6
Conventional hydroelectric power	73.9	78.6	79.4	77.5	77.9	77.9	78.5	78.8	78.9
Biomass, total	8.1	10.3	10.0	9.8	10.8	11.1	11.3	11.4	11.5
Wood [5]	5.5	6.7	6.1	6.2	6.7	6.9	6.9	7.0	7.1
Waste [6]	2.5	3.5	3.9	3.6	4.1	4.2	4.3	4.4	4.4
Geothermal	2.7	3.0	2.8	2.3	2.2	2.2	2.4	2.4	2.4
Solar [7]	0.3	0.3	0.4	0.4	0.5	0.5	0.6	0.9	1.5
Wind	1.8	1.7	2.4	8.7	16.5	24.7	34.3	39.1	45.2
Other [8]	0.5	0.5	0.5	0.9	0.8	0.9	0.9	0.9	0.9

[1] Anthracite, bituminous coal, subbituminous coal, lignite, waste coal, and coal synfuel. [2] Distillate fuel oil, residual fuel oil, petroleum coke, jet fuel, kerosene, other petroleum, and waste oil. [3] Includes a small amount of supplemental gaseous fuels that cannot be identified separately. [4] Blast furnace gas, propane gas, and other manufactured and waste gases derived from fossil fuels. [5] Wood and wood-derived fuels. [6] Municipal solid waste from biogenic sources, landfill gas, sludge waste, agricultural byproducts, and other biomass. Also includes nonrenewable waste (municipal solid waste from nonbiogenic sources, and tire-derived fuels). [7] Solar thermal and photovoltaic energy. [8] Batteries, chemicals, hydrogen, pitch, purchased steam, sulfur, and miscellaneous technologies. [9] Preliminary data.

Source: U.S. Energy Information Administration, *Annual Energy Review 2011*, September 2012. See also <http://www.eia.gov/totalenergy/>.

Table 973. Electricity—End Use and Average Retail Prices: 1990 to 2011

[Beginning 2003, the category "other" has been replaced by "transportation," and the categories "commercial" and "industrial" have been redefined. Data represent revenue from electricity retail sales divided by the amount of retail electricity sold (in kilowatt-hours). Prices include state and local taxes, energy or demand charges, customer service charges, environmental surcharges, franchise fees, fuel adjustments, and other miscellaneous charges applied to end-use customers during normal billing operations. Prices do not include deferred charges, credits, or other adjustments, such as fuel or revenue from purchased power, from previous reporting periods. Data are for a census of electric utilities. Beginning in 2000 data also include energy service providers selling to retail customers]

Item	1990	1995	2000	2005	2007	2008	2009	2010	2011 [1]
END USE (Billion kilowatt-hours)									
Total end use [2]	2,837.1	3,164.0	3,592.4	3,811.0	3,890.2	3,865.2	3,723.8	3,886.4	3,856.3
Direct use [3]	124.5	150.7	170.9	150.0	125.7	132.2	126.9	131.9	130.2
Retail sales, total [4]	2,712.6	3,013.3	3,421.4	3,661.0	3,764.6	3,733.0	3,596.9	3,754.5	3,726.2
Residential	924.0	1,042.5	1,192.4	1,359.2	1,392.2	1,380.0	1,364.5	1,445.7	1,423.7
Commercial [5]	838.3	953.1	1,159.3	1,275.1	1,336.3	1,336.0	1,307.2	1,330.2	1,319.3
Industrial [6]	945.5	1,012.7	1,064.2	1,019.2	1,027.8	1,009.3	917.4	970.9	975.6
Transportation [7]	4.8	5.0	5.4	7.5	8.2	7.7	7.8	7.7	7.6
AVERAGE RETAIL PRICES (Cents per kilowatt-hour)									
Total:									
Nominal	6.57	6.89	6.81	8.14	9.13	9.74	9.82	9.83	9.99
Real	9.09	8.44	7.68	8.14	8.59	8.97	8.95	8.86	8.81
Residential:									
Nominal	7.83	8.40	8.24	9.45	10.65	11.26	11.51	11.54	11.80
Real	10.84	10.29	9.29	9.45	10.03	10.37	10.49	10.40	10.41
Commercial: [8]									
Nominal	7.34	7.69	7.43	8.67	9.65	10.36	10.17	10.19	10.32
Real	10.16	9.42	8.37	8.67	9.08	9.54	9.27	9.18	9.10
Industrial: [6]									
Nominal	4.74	4.66	4.64	5.73	6.39	6.83	6.81	6.77	6.89
Real	6.56	5.71	5.23	5.73	6.02	6.29	6.21	6.10	6.08
Transportation: [7]									
Nominal	(NA)	(NA)	(NA)	8.57	9.70	10.74	10.65	10.57	10.58
Real	(NA)	(NA)	(NA)	8.57	9.13	9.89	9.71	9.52	9.33
Other: [9]									
Nominal	6.40	6.88	6.56	(X)	(X)	(X)	(X)	(X)	(X)
Real	8.86	8.43	7.39	(X)	(X)	(X)	(X)	(X)	(X)

NA Not available. X Not applicable. [1] Preliminary. [2] The sum of "total retail sales" and "direct use." [3] Use of electricity that is 1) self-generated, 2) produced by either the same entity that consumes the power or an affiliate, and 3) used in direct support of a service or industrial process located within the same facility or group of facilities that house the generating equipment. Direct use is exclusive of station use. [4] Electricity retail sales to ultimate customers reported by electric utilities and, beginning in 2000, other energy service providers. [5] Includes public street and highway lighting, interdepartmental sales, and other sales to public authorities. [6] Beginning 2003, includes agriculture and irrigation. [7] Includes sales to railroads and railways. [8] Beginning 2003, includes public street and highway lighting, interdepartmental sales, and other sales to public authorities. [9] Public street and highway lighting, interdepartmental sales, other sales to public authorities, agriculture and irrigation, and transportation including railroads and railways.

Source: U.S. Energy Information Administration, *Annual Energy Review 2011*, September 2012. See also <http://www.eia.gov/totalenergy/>.

Table 974. Electric Power Industry—Net Generation and Net Summer Capacity by State: 2000 to 2011

[3,802.1 represents 3,802,100,000,000. Capacity as of December 31. Covers utilities for public use]

State	Net generation (bil. kWh) 2000	2005	2010	2011 Total (bil. kWh)	2011 Percent from— Petroleum	Natural gas	Hydro-electric	Nuclear	Coal	Net summer capacity (mil. kW) 2010	2011
U.S....	3,802.1	4,055.4	4,125.1	4,100.7	0.7	24.7	7.8	19.3	42.3	1,039.1	1,051.3
AL........	124.4	137.9	152.2	156.3	0.1	30.5	5.7	25.2	36.3	32.4	32.6
AK........	6.2	6.6	6.8	6.9	13.8	56.9	19.6	–	9.6	2.1	2.1
AZ........	88.9	101.5	111.8	108.1	0.1	21.5	8.5	28.9	40.4	26.4	27.0
AR........	43.9	47.8	61.0	61.3	0.1	21.1	4.8	23.2	48.0	16.0	16.0
CA........	208.1	200.3	204.1	200.8	0.5	44.3	21.2	18.3	1.0	67.3	68.3
CO.......	44.2	49.6	50.7	51.4	(Z)	19.8	4.0	–	66.0	13.8	14.2
CT.......	33.0	33.5	33.3	33.7	0.5	45.0	1.7	47.2	1.6	8.3	9.1
DE.......	6.0	8.1	5.6	6.6	0.6	71.8	–	–	22.1	3.4	3.4
DC.......	0.1	0.2	0.2	0.2	64.6	35.4	–	–	–	0.8	0.8
FL........	191.8	220.3	229.1	221.9	1.5	61.5	0.1	9.9	23.4	59.2	59.6
GA.......	123.9	136.7	137.6	124.8	0.4	21.3	2.2	25.9	48.2	36.6	37.1
HI.......	10.6	11.5	10.8	10.7	73.9	–	0.9	–	13.3	2.5	2.6
ID........	11.9	10.8	12.0	16.6	(Z)	6.7	80.9	–	0.5	4.0	4.3
IL........	178.5	194.1	201.4	199.5	(Z)	3.0	0.1	48.0	45.1	44.1	43.8
IN........	127.8	130.4	125.2	122.1	1.1	8.2	0.3	–	85.3	27.0	27.4
IA........	41.5	44.2	57.5	56.4	0.3	1.8	1.6	9.3	67.8	14.6	15.3
KS........	44.8	45.9	47.9	45.4	0.1	5.6	(Z)	16.1	69.8	12.5	12.8
KY.......	93.0	97.8	98.2	98.4	1.8	1.6	3.0	–	93.2	20.5	21.1
LA........	92.9	92.6	102.9	105.5	4.5	51.5	1.0	15.8	23.3	26.7	26.2
ME.......	14.0	18.8	17.0	16.0	1.1	43.1	24.9	–	0.3	4.4	4.5
MD.......	51.1	52.7	43.6	41.8	0.5	5.5	6.1	34.4	50.4	12.5	12.6
MA.......	38.7	47.5	42.8	38.1	0.5	68.2	3.0	13.4	10.7	13.7	13.6
MI.......	104.2	121.6	111.6	109.2	0.3	11.9	1.2	30.1	54.0	29.8	29.9
MN.......	51.4	53.0	53.7	53.1	0.1	6.3	1.4	22.5	53.2	14.7	15.2
MS.......	37.6	45.1	54.5	51.6	0.1	58.1	–	20.0	18.9	15.7	15.5
MO......	76.6	90.8	92.3	94.9	0.1	4.8	1.2	9.9	82.5	21.7	22.1
MT.......	26.5	27.9	29.8	30.1	1.5	1.4	41.8	–	50.0	5.9	6.0
NE.......	29.1	31.5	36.6	36.1	0.1	1.2	4.5	19.2	71.9	7.9	8.2
NV.......	35.5	40.2	35.1	31.9	(Z)	68.4	6.9	–	16.9	11.4	11.6
NH.......	15.0	24.5	22.2	20.1	0.4	33.2	8.0	41.7	11.0	4.2	4.2
NJ.......	58.1	60.5	65.7	64.7	0.3	39.0	(Z)	51.9	6.4	18.4	18.4
NM.......	34.0	35.1	36.3	38.2	0.1	22.4	0.5	–	71.1	8.1	8.3
NY.......	138.1	146.9	137.0	137.6	0.9	36.9	20.3	31.0	6.9	39.4	39.6
NC.......	122.3	129.7	128.7	118.4	0.2	9.4	3.3	34.2	50.5	27.7	28.5
ND.......	31.3	31.9	34.7	35.1	0.1	0.1	7.4	–	77.3	6.2	6.2
OH.......	149.1	157.0	143.6	135.6	1.0	9.1	0.3	11.0	77.7	33.1	33.3
OK.......	55.6	68.6	72.3	74.6	(Z)	44.0	2.0	–	46.2	21.0	21.8
OR.......	51.8	49.3	55.1	59.7	(Z)	14.2	70.9	–	5.6	14.3	14.5
PA.......	201.7	218.1	229.8	227.6	0.2	18.4	1.4	33.5	44.2	45.6	45.8
RI.......	6.0	6.1	7.7	8.7	0.2	98.3	0.1	–	–	1.8	1.8
SC.......	93.3	102.5	104.2	103.0	0.1	12.6	1.5	51.4	33.2	24.0	24.1
SD.......	9.7	6.5	10.0	12.0	0.1	1.1	55.1	–	21.5	3.6	3.8
TN.......	95.8	97.1	82.3	81.1	0.2	4.0	11.8	33.2	50.3	21.4	21.1
TX........	377.7	396.7	411.7	435.5	0.2	46.0	0.1	9.1	36.3	108.3	109.2
UT........	36.6	38.2	42.2	40.8	0.1	12.9	3.0	–	81.1	7.5	7.6
VT.......	6.3	5.7	6.6	6.8	0.1	0.1	21.0	72.4	–	1.1	1.2
VA.......	77.2	78.9	73.0	66.7	0.8	27.5	1.8	38.3	29.8	24.1	24.7
WA......	108.2	102.0	103.5	115.3	(Z)	4.2	79.7	4.2	4.5	30.5	30.5
WV......	92.9	93.6	80.8	79.0	0.2	0.3	1.8	–	96.2	16.5	17.3
WI.......	59.6	61.8	64.3	63.3	0.9	9.9	3.4	18.3	63.1	17.8	18.3
WY.......	45.5	45.6	48.1	47.6	0.1	1.0	2.6	–	86.0	8.0	8.4

– Represents zero. Z Represents less than .05 percent of net electricity generation.

Source: U.S. Energy Information Administration, *Electric Power Annual*, "Detailed State Data," <http://www.eia.gov/electricity/data/state/>, accessed September 2013.

Table 975. Electric Power Industry—Capability, Peak Load, and Capacity Margin: 1980 to 2011

[558,237 represents 558,237,000 kW. Excludes Alaska and Hawaii. Capability represents the maximum kilowatt output with all power sources available and with hydraulic equipment under actual water conditions, allowing for maintenance, emergency outages, and system operating requirements. Capacity margin is the difference between capability and peak load. Minus sign (-) indicates decrease]

Year	Capability at the time of— Summer peak load (1,000 kW) Amount	Summer peak load Change from prior year	Winter peak load (1,000 kW) Amount	Winter peak load Change from prior year	Noncoincident peak load Summer (1,000 kW)	Noncoincident peak load Winter (1,000 kW)	Capacity margin Summer Amount (1,000 kW)	Capacity margin Summer Percent of capability	Capacity margin Winter Amount (1,000 kW)	Capacity margin Winter Percent of capability
1980	558,237	13,731	572,195	17,670	427,058	384,567	131,179	23.5	187,628	32.8
1985	621,597	17,357	636,475	14,350	460,503	423,660	161,094	25.9	212,815	33.4
1990	685,091	11,775	696,757	11,508	546,331	484,231	138,760	20.3	212,526	30.5
1991	690,915	5,824	703,212	6,455	551,418	485,761	139,497	20.2	217,451	30.9
1992	695,436	4,521	707,752	4,540	548,707	492,983	146,729	21.1	214,769	30.3
1993	694,250	-1,186	711,957	4,205	575,356	521,733	118,894	17.1	190,224	26.7
1994	702,985	8,735	715,090	3,133	585,320	518,253	117,665	16.7	196,837	27.5
1995	714,222	11,237	727,679	12,589	620,249	544,684	93,973	13.2	182,995	25.1
1996	730,376	16,154	737,637	9,958	616,790	554,081	113,586	15.6	183,556	24.9
1997	737,855	7,479	736,666	-971	637,677	529,874	100,178	13.6	206,792	28.1
1998	744,670	6,815	735,090	-1,576	660,293	567,558	84,377	11.3	167,532	22.8
1999	765,744	21,074	748,271	13,181	682,122	570,915	83,622	10.9	177,356	23.7
2000	808,054	42,310	767,505	19,234	678,413	588,426	129,641	16.0	179,079	23.3
2001	788,990	-19,064	806,598	39,093	687,812	576,312	101,178	12.8	230,286	28.6
2002	833,380	44,390	850,984	44,386	714,565	604,986	118,815	14.3	245,998	28.9
2003	856,131	22,751	882,120	31,136	709,375	593,874	146,756	17.1	288,246	32.7
2004	875,870	19,739	864,849	-17,271	704,459	618,701	171,411	19.6	246,148	28.5
2005	882,125	6,255	878,110	13,261	758,876	626,365	123,249	14.0	251,745	28.7
2006	891,226	9,101	899,551	21,441	789,475	640,981	101,751	11.4	258,570	28.7
2007	914,397	23,171	913,650	14,099	782,227	637,905	132,170	14.5	275,745	30.2
2008	909,504	-4,893	927,781	14,131	752,470	643,557	157,034	17.3	284,224	30.6
2009	916,449	6,945	920,002	-7,779	725,958	668,818	190,491	20.8	251,184	27.3
2010	923,559	7,110	935,262	15,260	767,948	651,418	155,611	16.8	283,844	30.3
2011	892,426	-31,133	893,206	-42,056	782,469	648,190	109,957	12.3	245,016	27.4

Source: Edison Electric Institute, Washington, DC, *Statistical Yearbook of the Electric Power Industry*, annual ©. See also <http://www.eei.org>.

Table 976. Electric Energy Retail Sales by Class of Service and State: 2011

[In billions of kilowatt-hours (3,749.8 represents 3,749,800,000,000). Data include both bundled and unbundled consumers]

State	Total [1]	Residential	Commercial	Industrial	State	Total [1]	Residential	Commercial	Industrial
United States	**3,749.8**	**1,422.8**	**1,328.1**	**991.3**	Missouri	84.3	35.9	31.0	17.3
Alabama	89.0	33.0	22.3	33.7	Montana	13.8	4.9	4.9	4.0
Alaska	6.3	2.1	2.9	1.3	Nebraska	29.7	9.9	9.1	10.6
Arizona	74.9	33.1	29.5	12.4	Nevada	33.9	11.5	9.0	13.4
Arkansas	47.9	18.8	12.1	17.0	New Hampshire	10.9	4.5	4.5	1.9
California	261.9	88.4	122.8	49.9	New Jersey	76.9	29.4	39.1	8.0
Colorado	53.5	18.3	19.9	15.2	New Mexico	23.0	6.9	9.3	6.9
Connecticut	29.9	12.9	13.1	3.7	New York	144.0	51.2	76.4	13.4
Delaware	11.5	4.6	4.3	2.6	North Carolina	131.1	58.1	46.5	26.6
District of Columbia	11.6	2.1	9.0	0.2	North Dakota	13.7	4.6	4.9	4.3
Florida	225.1	116.3	91.8	16.9	Ohio	154.7	53.7	47.1	53.9
Georgia	136.4	57.8	46.9	31.5	Oklahoma	59.8	24.4	19.6	15.8
Hawaii	10.0	2.9	3.4	3.7	Oregon	47.2	19.4	15.8	12.0
Idaho	23.3	8.4	6.0	8.9	Pennsylvania	148.8	54.8	43.5	49.6
Illinois	142.9	47.1	50.5	44.8	Rhode Island	7.7	3.1	3.7	0.9
Indiana	105.8	33.9	24.1	47.8	South Carolina	80.5	30.8	21.6	28.1
Iowa	45.7	14.3	12.1	19.2	South Dakota	11.7	4.6	4.4	2.6
Kansas	40.8	14.3	15.6	10.8	Tennessee	100.7	43.1	29.0	28.6
Kentucky	89.5	27.2	18.7	43.6	Texas	376.1	145.7	128.2	102.1
Louisiana	86.4	32.0	24.3	30.1	Utah	28.9	8.9	10.5	9.3
Maine	11.4	4.4	4.0	3.0	Vermont	5.6	2.1	2.0	1.4
Maryland	63.6	27.3	30.8	5.0	Virginia	110.2	45.8	47.1	17.2
Massachusetts	55.6	20.5	17.8	17.0	Washington	93.7	36.4	29.4	27.9
Michigan	105.1	34.8	38.6	31.6	West Virginia	31.2	11.7	7.8	11.7
Minnesota	68.5	22.5	22.4	23.6	Wisconsin	68.6	22.2	23.1	23.4
Mississippi	49.3	19.3	13.7	16.3	Wyoming	17.4	2.8	4.4	10.3

[1] Includes transportation, not shown separately.

Source: U.S. Energy Information Administration, "Electric Sales, Revenue, and Average Price 2011," September 2012. See also <http://www.eia.gov/electricity/>.

Table 977. Electric Energy Average Retail Price by Class of Service and State: 2011

[In cents per kilowatt-hour (kWh). Data include both bundled and unbundled consumers]

State	Total [1]	Resi-dential	Com-mercial	Indus-trial	State	Total [1]	Resi-dential	Com-mercial	Indus-trial
United States	**9.90**	**11.72**	**10.23**	**6.82**	Missouri	8.32	9.75	8.04	5.85
Alabama	9.10	11.09	10.47	6.25	Montana	8.23	9.75	9.12	5.27
Alaska	16.08	17.62	15.10	15.71	Nebraska	7.88	9.32	7.99	6.43
Arizona	9.71	11.08	9.50	6.55	Nevada	8.97	11.61	9.05	6.65
Arkansas	7.43	9.02	7.50	5.63	New Hampshire	14.74	16.52	14.04	12.27
California	13.05	14.78	13.05	10.11	New Jersey	14.30	16.23	13.47	11.43
Colorado	9.39	11.27	9.44	7.06	New Mexico	8.74	11.00	9.07	6.06
Connecticut	16.35	18.11	15.57	13.24	New York	15.89	18.26	15.81	7.83
Delaware	11.48	13.70	10.64	8.91	North Carolina	8.64	10.26	8.13	6.01
District of Columbia	12.81	13.40	12.90	6.89	North Dakota	7.50	8.58	7.61	6.24
Florida	10.61	11.51	9.85	8.55	Ohio	9.03	11.42	9.63	6.12
Georgia	9.61	11.05	9.87	6.60	Oklahoma	7.80	9.47	7.60	5.46
Hawaii	31.59	34.68	32.37	28.40	Oregon	8.04	9.54	8.15	5.47
Idaho	6.44	7.87	6.41	5.10	Pennsylvania	10.45	13.26	10.03	7.73
Illinois	8.97	11.78	8.64	6.42	Rhode Island	13.04	14.33	12.37	11.27
Indiana	8.01	10.06	8.77	6.17	South Carolina	8.80	11.05	9.30	5.94
Iowa	7.56	10.46	7.85	5.21	South Dakota	8.05	9.35	7.76	6.20
Kansas	8.89	10.65	8.78	6.71	Tennessee	9.28	9.98	10.27	7.23
Kentucky	7.17	9.20	8.49	5.33	Texas	9.00	11.08	8.83	6.24
Louisiana	7.68	8.96	8.44	5.69	Utah	7.13	8.96	7.35	5.10
Maine	12.58	15.38	12.29	8.88	Vermont	13.80	16.26	14.00	9.83
Maryland	11.93	13.31	11.28	8.76	Virginia	8.84	10.64	7.95	6.49
Massachusetts	14.11	14.67	14.33	13.38	Washington	6.78	8.28	7.49	4.09
Michigan	10.40	13.27	10.33	7.32	West Virginia	7.88	9.39	8.14	6.18
Minnesota	8.65	10.96	8.63	6.47	Wisconsin	10.21	13.02	10.42	7.33
Mississippi	8.78	10.17	9.48	6.53	Wyoming	6.58	9.11	7.72	5.41

[1] Includes transportation, not shown separately.

Source: U.S. Energy Information Administration, "Electric Sales, Revenue, and Average Price 2011," September 2012, <http://www.eia.gov/electricity/>.

Table 978. Total Electric Power Industry—Generation, Sales, Revenue, and Customers: 1990 to 2012

[2,808 represents 2,808,000,000,000 kWh. Sales and revenue are to and from ultimate customers. Commercial and Industrial are not wholly comparable on a year-to-year basis due to changes from one classification to another. For the 2005 period forward, the Energy Information Administration replaced the "Other" sector with the Transportation sector. The Transportation sector consists entirely of electrified rail and urban transit systems. Data previously reported in "Other" have been relocated to the Commercial sector, except for Agriculture (i.e., irrigation load), which have been relocated to the Industrial sector]

Class	Unit	1990	2000	2005	2007	2008	2009	2010	2011 [1]	2012 [1]
Generation [2]	Bil. kWh	2,808	3,802	4,055	4,157	4,119	3,950	4,125	4,101	4,054
Sales [3]	**Bil kWh**	**2,713**	**3,421**	**3,661**	**3,765**	**3,733**	**3,597**	**3,754**	**3,750**	**3,687**
Residential or domestic	Bil. kWh	924	1,192	1,359	1,392	1,380	1,364	1,446	1,423	1,375
Percent of total	Percent	34.1	34.9	37.1	37.0	37.0	37.9	38.5	37.9	37.3
Commercial [4]	Bil. kWh	751	1,055	1,275	1,336	1,336	1,307	1,330	1,328	1,324
Industrial [5]	Bil. kWh	946	1,064	1,019	1,028	1,009	917	971	991	981
Revenue [3]	**Bil. dol.**	**178.2**	**233.2**	**298.0**	**343.7**	**363.7**	**353.3**	**368.9**	**371.0**	**363.7**
Residential or domestic	Bil. dol.	72.4	98.2	128.4	148.3	155.4	157.0	166.8	166.7	163.4
Percent of total	Percent	40.6	42.1	43.1	43.1	42.7	44.4	45.2	44.9	44.9
Commercial [4]	Bil. dol.	55.1	78.4	110.5	128.9	138.5	132.9	135.6	135.9	133.9
Industrial [5]	Bil. dol.	44.9	49.4	58.4	65.7	68.9	62.5	65.8	67.6	65.7
Ultimate customers [3]	**Million**	**110.6**	**127.6**	**138.4**	**142.1**	**143.3**	**143.5**	**144.1**	**144.5**	**145.3**
Residential or domestic	Million	97.1	111.7	120.8	123.9	124.9	125.2	125.7	126.1	126.8
Commercial [4]	Million	12.1	14.3	16.9	17.4	17.6	17.6	17.7	17.6	17.7
Industrial [5]	Million	0.5	0.5	0.7	0.8	0.8	0.8	0.7	0.7	0.7
Avg. kWh used per customer	**1,000**	**24.5**	**26.8**	**26.5**	**26.5**	**26.1**	**25.1**	**26.0**	**25.9**	**25.4**
Residential	1,000	9.5	10.7	11.3	11.2	11.0	10.9	11.5	11.3	10.8
Commercial [4]	1,000	62.2	73.5	75.6	76.9	76.1	74.4	75.3	75.3	74.7
Avg. annual bill per customer	**Dollar**	**1,612**	**1,828**	**2,154**	**2,418**	**2,538**	**2,462**	**2,559**	**2,568**	**2,504**
Residential	Dollar	745	879	1,063	1,196	1,244	1,254	1,327	1,322	1,288
Commercial [4]	Dollar	4,562	5,464	6,551	7,418	7,884	7,570	7,670	7,706	7,557
Avg. revenue per kWh sold	**Cents**	**6.57**	**6.81**	**8.14**	**9.13**	**9.74**	**9.82**	**9.83**	**9.90**	**9.87**
Residential	Cents	7.83	8.24	9.45	10.65	11.26	11.51	11.54	11.72	11.88
Commercial [4]	Cents	7.34	7.43	8.67	9.65	10.36	10.17	10.19	10.23	10.12
Industrial [5]	Cents	4.74	4.64	5.73	6.39	6.83	6.81	6.77	6.82	6.70

[1] Preliminary. [2] "Generation" includes batteries, chemicals, hydrogen, pitch, sulfur, purchased steam, and miscellaneous technologies, which are not separately displayed. [3] Includes other types, not shown separately. Data for 1990 are as of December 31, data for following years are average yearly customers. [4] Small light and power. [5] Large light and power.

Source: Edison Electric Institute, Washington, DC, *Statistical Yearbook of the Electric Power Industry*, annual ©. See also <http://www.eei.org>.

Table 979. Revenue and Expense Statistics for Major U.S. Investor-Owned Electric Utilities: 1995 to 2011

[In millions of nominal dollars (199,967 represents $199,967,000,000). Covers investor-owned electric utilities that during each of the last 3 years met any one or more of the following conditions—1 mil. megawatt-hours of total sales, 100 megawatt-hours of sales for resale, 500 megawatt-hours of gross interchange out, and 500 megawatt-hours of wheeling for other. Missing or erroneous respondent data may result in slight imbalances in some of the expense account subtotals]

Item	1995	2000	2005	2008	2009	2010	2011
Utility operating revenues.......	**199,967**	**233,915**	**265,652**	**298,962**	**276,124**	**285,512**	**280,520**
Electric utility.....................	183,655	213,634	234,909	266,124	249,303	260,119	255,573
Other utility.....................	16,312	20,281	30,743	32,838	26,822	25,393	24,946
Utility operating expenses.......	**165,321**	**210,250**	**236,786**	**267,263**	**244,243**	**253,022**	**247,118**
Electric utility.....................	150,599	191,564	207,830	236,572	219,544	234,173	228,873
Operation..........................	91,881	132,607	150,645	175,887	154,925	166,922	161,460
Production........................	68,983	107,554	120,586	140,974	118,816	128,831	122,520
Cost of fuel....................	29,122	32,407	36,106	47,337	40,242	44,138	42,779
Purchased power..............	29,981	62,608	77,902	84,724	67,630	67,284	61,447
Other.........................	9,880	12,561	6,599	8,937	10,970	17,409	18,294
Transmission....................	1,425	2,713	5,664	6,950	6,742	6,948	6,876
Distribution.....................	2,561	3,092	3,502	3,997	3,947	4,007	4,044
Customer accounts..............	3,613	4,239	4,229	5,286	5,203	5,091	5,180
Customer service...............	1,922	1,826	2,291	3,567	3,857	4,741	5,311
Sales...........................	348	405	219	225	178	185	185
Administrative and general.....	13,028	12,768	14,130	14,718	15,991	17,120	17,343
Maintenance.......................	11,767	12,064	12,033	14,192	14,092	14,957	15,772
Depreciation......................	19,885	20,636	17,123	19,049	20,095	20,951	22,555
Taxes and other..................	27,065	24,479	26,805	26,202	29,081	31,343	29,086
Other utility.....................	14,722	18,686	28,956	30,692	24,698	18,849	18,245
Net utility operating income.....	**34,646**	**23,665**	**28,866**	**31,699**	**31,881**	**32,490**	**33,402**

Source: U.S. Energy Information Administration, "Electric Power Annual 2011," <http://www.eia.gov/electricity/annual/>, accessed March 2013, and earlier reports.

Table 980. Total Renewable Energy Net Generation of Electricity by Source and State: 2010

[In millions of kilowatt-hours (427,376 represents 427,376,000,000). For more on net generation, see Table 974]

State	Total [1]	Hydro-electric	Bio-mass [2]	Wind	Wood and derived fuels [3]	State	Total [1]	Hydro-electric	Bio-mass [2]	Wind	Wood and derived fuels [3]
U.S..........	**427,376**	**260,203**	**18,917**	**94,652**	**37,172**	MO.............	2,527	1,539	62	925	(Z)
AL............	11,081	8,704	12	(NA)	2,365	MT............	10,442	9,415	(NA)	930	97
AK............	1,452	1,433	6	13	(NA)	NE............	1,807	1,314	72	422	(NA)
AZ............	6,941	6,622	28	135	140	NV............	4,444	2,157	(NA)	(NA)	(NA)
AR............	5,283	3,659	57	(NA)	1,567	NH............	2,710	1,478	127	76	1,030
CA............	58,881	33,431	2,451	6,079	3,551	NJ............	868	18	816	13	(NA)
CO............	5,133	1,578	58	3,452	2	NM............	2,072	217	14	1,832	(NA)
CT............	1,130	391	739	(NA)	(Z)	NY............	30,286	25,472	1,671	2,596	547
DE............	138	(NA)	136	3	(NA)	NC............	6,840	4,757	195	(NA)	1,876
DC............	(NA)	(NA)	(NA)	(NA)	(NA)	ND............	6,150	2,042	12	4,096	(NA)
FL............	4,664	177	2,387	(NA)	2,019	OH............	1,129	429	276	13	399
GA............	6,502	3,322	127	(NA)	3,054	OK............	6,969	2,809	97	3,808	255
HI............	817	70	283	261	(Z)	OR............	35,299	30,542	205	3,920	632
ID............	10,168	9,154	24	441	478	PA............	6,577	2,332	1,708	1,854	675
IL............	5,257	119	670	4,454	(Z)	RI............	144	4	137	3	(NA)
IN............	3,699	454	312	2,934	(NA)	SC............	4,250	2,376	131	(NA)	1,742
IA............	10,309	948	190	9,170	(NA)	SD............	6,611	5,239	(NA)	1,372	(NA)
KS............	3,473	13	54	3,405	(NA)	TN............	9,125	8,138	33	41	914
KY............	3,020	2,580	91	(NA)	349	TX............	28,967	1,262	545	26,251	900
LA............	3,577	1,109	74	(NA)	2,393	UT............	1,476	696	56	448	(NA)
ME............	7,963	3,810	264	499	3,390	VT............	1,829	1,347	25	14	443
MD............	2,241	1,667	407	1	165	VA............	3,720	1,500	815	(NA)	1,404
MA............	2,270	996	1,125	22	125	WA............	74,905	68,288	196	4,745	1,676
MI............	4,083	1,251	802	360	1,670	WV............	2,307	1,367	(NA)	939	(NA)
MN............	7,480	840	915	4,792	933	WI............	4,586	2,112	508	1,088	878
MS............	1,504	(NA)	1	(NA)	1,503	WY............	4,271	1,024	(NA)	3,247	(NA)

NA Not available. Z Less than 500,000 million kilowatt-hours. [1] Includes types not shown separately. [2] Includes landfill gas and municipal solid waste biogenic (paper and paper board, wood, food, leather, textiles, and yard trimmings). Also includes agriculture by-products/crops, sludge waste, and other biomass solids, liquids, and gases. Excludes wood and wood waste. [3] Black liquor and wood/woodwaste solids and liquids.

Source: Energy Information Administration, "Trends in Renewable Energy Consumption and Electricity," <http://www.eia.gov/renewable/annual/trends/>, accessed February 2013.

Table 981. Major Weather-Related Power Outages by Duration: 2012

[Data shown for power outages lasting longer than 48 hours]

Type of Disturbance	Month	Area Affected	Duration	Power Loss (mega-watts)	Number of Customers Affected [1]
Severe Weather - Hurricane Sandy.....	October	Long Island, New York	337 Hours, 0 Min.	0	632,816
Fuel Supply Deficiency (Coal)...........	July	Niagara County, New York	288 Hours, 30 Min.	675	(NA)
Severe Weather - Hurricane Sandy.....	October	West Virginia	287 Hours, 59 Min.	0	208,000
Severe Weather - Hurricane Sandy.....	October	Eastern Pennsylvania	223 Hours, 48 Min.	0	270,000
Severe Weather - Hurricane Sandy.....	October	Greater New York City, New York	242 Hours, 59 Min.	0	818,000
Severe Weather - Hurricane Sandy.....	October	Maryland; West Virginia	241 Hours, 8 Min.	(NA)	150,000
Severe Weather - Thunderstorms.......	June	Maryland; West Virginia	192 Hours, 43 Min.	(NA)	145,000
Severe Weather - Hurricane Sandy.....	October	New Jersey	187 Hours, 57 Min.	(NA)	50,000
Severe Weather - Thunderstorms	June	Atlantic City Electric Service Territory New Jersey	184 Hours, 18 Min.	(NA)	205,000
Severe Weather - Hurricane Sandy.....	October	Greater Cleveland Ohio	175 Hours, 59 Min.	0	346,000
Severe Weather - Hurricane Sandy.....	October	Greater Philadelphia Pennsylvania	174 Hours, 30 Min.	(NA)	850,000
Severe Weather - Hurricane Isaac......	August	Arkansas, Louisiana, Mississippi	170 Hours, 0 Min.	(NA)	770,000
Severe Weather - Thunderstorms.......	June	West Virginia	159 Hours, 36 Min.	700	265,000
Severe Weather - Hurricane Sandy.....	October	New Jersey	159 Hours, 0 Min.	(NA)	(NA)
Severe Weather - Hurricane Sandy.....	October	New Jersey	155 Hours, 0 Min.	(NA)	217,000
Severe Weather - Hurricane Sandy.....	October	Connecticut, Western Massachusetts	148 Hours, 45 Min.	0	649,075
Severe Weather - Hurricane Sandy.....	October	Central Pennsylvania	148 Hours, 39 Min.	(NA)	400,000
Severe Weather - Hurricane Sandy.....	October	New York	136 Hours, 48 Min.	(NA)	371,000
Severe Weather - Thunderstorms.......	June	Dayton, Ohio	123 Hours, 50 Min.	500	175,000
Severe Weather - Thunderstorms.......	June	Virginia	113 Hours, 7 Min.	5,000	880,000
Severe Weather - Hurricane Sandy.....	October	Southeast New York; New Jersey	111 Hours, 59 Min.	(NA)	200,000
Severe Weather - Hurricane Sandy.....	October	Delaware, Maryland	105 Hours, 0 Min.	(NA)	70,000
Severe Weather - Winter Storm	December	Arkansas; Louisiana; Mississippi; Texas	87 Hours, 30 Min.	(NA)	242,509
Severe Weather - Nor'easter.............	October	Indiana; Kentucky; Michigan; Ohio	82 Hours, 0 Min.	(NA)	173,273
Severe Weather - Thunderstorms	June	Eastern Indiana; Northern Kentucky; Greater Cincinnati area Ohio	78 Hours, 44 Min.	2,946	4,645,572
Fuel Supply Deficiency (Water)..........	July	CAISO California	72 Hours, 0 Min.	(NA)	0
Severe Weather - Thunderstorms.......	June	Delaware; Maryland	72 Hours, 0 Min.	0	86,390
Severe Weather - Thunderstorms.......	June	Indiana; Michigan; Ohio; West Virginia	72 Hours, 0 Min.	(NA)	1,355,919
Severe Weather - Tornadoes............	April	Northern Alabama; Southeast Tennessee	71 Hours, 24 Min.	500	(NA)
Severe Weather - Thunderstorms.......	June	Greater Baltimore area, Maryland	71 Hours, 18 Min.	1,465	600,000
Severe Weather - Nor'easter.............	October	Greater Detroit Michigan	68 Hours, 0 Min.	(NA)	133,777
Severe Weather - Winter Storm.........	April	Southeastern, Michigan	67 Hours, 30 Min.	371	130,000
Severe Weather - Thunderstorms	July	Lower Valley, Central, Susquehanna Regions Pennsylvania	64 Hours, 54 Min.	(NA)	64,500
Severe Weather - Thunderstorms	June	Montgomery and Prince Georges Counties, Maryland; DC	62 Hours, 55 Min.	3,000	425,000
Severe Weather - Hurricane Sandy.....	October	Eastern Massachusetts	58 Hours, 45 Min.	(NA)	50,000
Severe Weather - High Winds...........	April	Southeast, Michigan	58 Hours, 14 Min.	218	111,393
Severe Weather - Thunderstorms.......	July	North/Central Pennsylvania	53 Hours, 9 Min.	(NA)	65,000
Severe Weather - Winter Storm.........	December	Northern California	51 Hours, 40 Min.	250	125,000
Severe Weather - Hurricane Isaac......	August	Louisiana	51 Hours, 7 Min.	(NA)	95,000
Severe Weather - Hurricane Isaac......	August	Louisiana	51 Hours, 0 Min.	300	50,000
Severe Weather - Thunderstorms.......	July	Illinois	50 Hours, 0 Min.	(NA)	320,000
Severe Weather - Thunderstorms.......	July	Central and Northern New Jersey	49 Hours, 1 Min.	(NA)	95,400
Fuel Supply Deficiency (Water)..........	June	CAISO Territory California	48 Hours, 0 Min.	(NA)	(NA)

NA Not available. [1] Number of customers affected are preliminary estimates.

Source: U.S. Energy Information Administration, *Electric Power Monthly*, May 2013. See also <http://www.eia.gov/electricity/monthly/>.

Table 982. Gas Utility Industry—Summary: 1990 to 2011

[54,261 represents 54,261,000. Covers natural, manufactured, mixed, and liquid petroleum gas. Based on a questionnaire mailed to all privately and municipally owned gas utilities in the United States, except those with annual revenues less than $25,000]

Item	Unit	1990	1995	2000	2005	2008	2009	2010	2011
End users [1]	**1,000**	**54,261**	**58,728**	**61,262**	**64,395**	**65,487**	**65,147**	**64,960**	**65,088**
Residential	1,000	49,802	53,955	56,494	59,569	60,654	60,344	60,246	60,405
Commercial	1,000	4,246	4,530	4,610	4,678	4,703	4,659	4,582	4,556
Industrial	1,000	166	181	157	145	128	142	129	125
Other	1,000	48	61	2	2	3	3	3	3
Sales [2]	**Tril. Btu** [3]	**9,842**	**9,221**	**9,232**	**8,848**	**8,594**	**8,050**	**7,980**	**7,886**
Residential	Tril. Btu	4,468	4,803	4,741	4,516	4,541	4,387	4,371	4,287
Percent of total	Percent	45	52	51	51	53	54	55	54
Commercial	Tril. Btu	2,192	2,281	2,077	2,056	2,009	1,901	1,842	1,813
Industrial	Tril. Btu	3,010	1,919	1,698	1,654	1,410	1,193	1,209	1,184
Other	Tril. Btu	171	218	715	622	635	570	558	602
Revenues [2]	**Mil. dol.**	**45,153**	**46,436**	**59,243**	**96,909**	**102,641**	**77,675**	**72,886**	**69,296**
Residential	Mil. dol.	25,000	28,742	35,828	55,680	60,195	50,500	47,231	45,046
Percent of total	Percent	55	62	60	57	59	65	65	65
Commercial	Mil. dol.	10,604	11,573	13,339	22,653	23,592	18,451	16,578	15,632
Industrial	Mil. dol.	8,996	5,571	7,432	13,751	13,205	6,171	6,437	5,867
Other	Mil. dol.	553	549	2,645	4,825	5,649	2,553	2,640	2,751
Prices per mil. Btu [3]	**Dollars**	**4.59**	**5.05**	**6.42**	**10.95**	**11.94**	**9.65**	**9.13**	**8.79**
Residential	Dollars	5.60	6.00	7.56	12.33	13.26	11.51	10.81	10.51
Commercial	Dollars	4.84	5.07	6.42	11.02	11.75	9.71	9.00	8.62
Industrial	Dollars	2.99	2.98	4.38	8.31	9.37	5.17	5.32	4.95
Gas mains mileage	**1,000**	**1,189**	**1,278**	**1,369**	**1,438**	**1,525**	**1,526**	**1,531**	**1,557**
Field and gathering	1,000	32	31	27	23	20	20	19	20
Transmission	1,000	292	297	297	297	299	297	308	305
Distribution	1,000	865	950	1,046	1,118	1,206	1,210	1,204	1,232
Construction expenditures [4]	**Mil. dol.**	**7,899**	**10,760**	**8,624**	**10,089**	**14,090**	**12,146**	**11,042**	**17,099**
Transmission	Mil. dol.	2,886	3,380	1,590	3,368	6,388	5,377	3,524	7,416
Distribution	Mil. dol.	3,714	5,394	5,437	5,129	5,427	4,948	5,674	6,988
Production and storage	Mil. dol.	309	367	138	179	174	128	151	339
General	Mil. dol.	770	1,441	1,273	1,070	1,228	1,135	1,185	1,653
Underground storage	Mil. dol.	219	177	185	343	873	559	509	703

[1] Annual average. [2] Excludes sales for resale. [3] For definition of Btu, see text, this section. [4] Includes general.

Source: American Gas Association, Washington, DC, *Gas Facts* ©, annual. See also <http://www.aga.org>.

Table 983. Gas Utility Industry—Customers, Sales, and Revenues by State: 2011

[65,088 represents 65,088,000. See headnote, Table 982. For definition of Btu, see text, this section]

State	Customers [1] (1,000) Total	Residential	Sales [2] (tril. Btu) Total	Residential	Revenues [2] (mil. dol.) Total	Residential	State	Customers [1] (1,000) Total	Residential	Sales [2] (tril. Btu) Total	Residential	Revenues [2] (mil. dol.) Total	Residential
U.S.	**65,088**	**60,405**	**7,898**	**4,296**	**69,296**	**45,046**	MO	1,483	1,343	162	106	1,765	1,233
AL	842	772	95	38	996	552	MT	293	259	35	22	296	191
AK	134	122	60	21	428	178	NE	488	447	64	36	479	306
AZ	1,203	1,146	78	40	924	580	NV	814	773	91	42	760	433
AR	620	552	58	35	583	387	NH	113	97	13	7	167	102
CA	10,968	10,543	720	520	6,530	5,003	NJ	2,718	2,514	299	209	3,127	2,380
CO	1,792	1,646	205	134	1,573	1,073	NM	617	571	53	35	432	313
CT	546	494	87	45	941	599	NY	3,812	3,553	413	294	4,925	3,855
DE	165	152	16	10	234	154	NC	1,246	1,129	118	64	1,261	774
DC	137	131	13	10	156	121	ND	144	125	33	11	214	89
FL	706	665	50	17	599	292	OH	1,440	1,352	156	121	1,509	1,205
GA	355	322	55	18	466	205	OK	1,013	922	97	63	865	634
HI	28	25	3	1	118	27	OR	767	689	89	48	899	548
ID	390	351	42	28	348	235	PA	2,639	2,443	281	206	3,248	2,492
IL	3,851	3,594	483	380	4,031	3,229	RI	247	226	24	17	346	258
IN	1,760	1,614	196	129	1,687	1,183	SC	634	577	85	28	740	347
IA	982	884	118	69	978	640	SD	194	171	25	13	187	111
KS	937	855	100	68	888	651	TN	1,220	1,089	150	69	1,305	686
KY	811	730	98	50	846	505	TX	4,645	4,326	1,311	206	6,942	2,036
LA	957	898	193	41	1,185	448	UT	893	830	113	72	869	592
ME	31	22	5	1	57	20	VT	44	39	8	3	96	52
MD	947	893	84	64	948	747	VA	1,168	1,082	119	74	1,303	908
MA	1,534	1,406	240	119	2,502	1,594	WA	1,182	1,079	146	88	1,628	1,050
MI	3,168	2,947	408	302	3,995	3,068	WV	375	342	42	26	407	274
MN	1,570	1,436	251	129	1,922	1,107	WI	1,841	1,672	240	134	2,007	1,265
MS	491	440	55	25	438	229	WY	133	118	19	10	145	88

[1] Averages for the year. [2] Excludes sales for resale.

Source: American Gas Association, Washington, DC, Gas Facts ©, annual. See also <http://www.aga.org>.

Table 984. Privately Owned Gas Utility Industry—Balance Sheet and Income Account: 1990 to 2011

[In millions of dollars (121,686 represents $121,686,000,000). The gas utility industry consists of pipeline and distribution companies. Excludes operations of companies distributing gas in bottles or tanks]

Item	1990	1995	2000	2005	2007	2008	2009	2010	2011
COMPOSITE BALANCE SHEET									
Assets, total	**121,686**	**141,965**	**165,709**	**196,215**	**205,345**	**230,002**	**219,467**	**220,860**	**234,617**
Total utility plant	112,863	143,636	162,206	207,976	213,516	237,140	235,426	239,718	248,580
Depreciation and amortization	49,483	62,723	69,366	91,794	86,244	95,211	91,958	92,012	92,423
Utility plant (net)	63,380	80,912	92,839	116,183	127,272	141,929	143,468	147,707	156,157
Investment and fund accounts	23,872	26,489	10,846	16,331	13,677	11,725	9,649	7,132	10,606
Current and accrued assets	23,268	18,564	35,691	32,325	28,871	31,960	27,703	27,288	25,766
Deferred debits [1]	9,576	13,923	24,279	29,574	34,608	42,922	37,037	37,307	40,628
Liabilities, total	**121,686**	**141,965**	**165,709**	**196,215**	**205,345**	**230,002**	**219,467**	**220,860**	**234,617**
Capitalization, total	74,958	90,581	96,079	120,949	127,609	136,108	135,797	133,414	138,254
Capital stock	43,810	54,402	47,051	62,470	71,038	74,610	74,517	74,157	77,657
Long-term debts	31,148	35,548	48,267	58,264	56,538	61,498	61,280	59,223	60,637
Current and accrued liabilities	29,550	28,272	42,312	34,936	34,017	37,450	28,711	28,564	29,864
Deferred income taxes [2]	11,360	14,393	17,157	24,937	27,009	27,637	30,236	34,401	39,034
Other liabilities and credits	5,818	8,715	10,161	15,393	16,709	28,807	24,723	24,515	27,465
COMPOSITE INCOME ACCOUNT									
Operating revenues, total	**66,027**	**58,390**	**72,042**	**102,018**	**97,195**	**109,547**	**87,419**	**82,315**	**78,750**
Minus: Operating expenses [3]	60,137	50,760	64,988	89,385	85,050	97,665	76,240	71,761	69,747
Operation and maintenance	51,627	37,966	54,602	77,673	71,011	82,386	61,865	57,758	55,200
Federal, state, and local taxes	4,957	6,182	6,163	7,513	7,803	8,477	7,889	7,569	7,988
Equals: Operating income	5,890	7,630	7,053	12,632	12,146	11,882	11,179	10,554	10,004
Utility operating income	6,077	7,848	7,166	12,812	12,472	12,293	11,428	11,045	10,463
Income before interest charges	8,081	9,484	7,589	13,972	14,329	13,313	12,232	12,368	10,991
Net income	4,410	5,139	4,245	9,777	9,758	9,067	8,458	8,619	7,308
Dividends	3,191	4,037	3,239	2,419	2,253	2,427	2,162	2,080	2,061

[1] Includes capital stock discount and expense and reacquired securities. [2] Includes reserves for deferred income taxes. [3] Includes expenses not shown separately.

Source: American Gas Association, Washington, DC, Gas Facts ©, annual. See also <http://www.aga.org>.

Table 985. Sewage Treatment Facilities: 2010 and 2011

[Based on the North American Industry Classification System (NAICS), 2007; see text, Section 15]

State	Sewage treatment facilities (NAICS 22132)				State	Sewage treatment facilities (NAICS 22132)			
	2010		2011			2010		2011	
	Number of establishments	Paid employees	Number of establishments	Paid employees		Number of establishments	Paid employees	Number of establishments	Paid employees
U.S.	**686**	**6,627**	**677**	**6,619**	MO	18	83	18	79
AL	14	206	13	182	MT	3	26	3	24
AK	1	([1])	1	([1])	NE	(NA)	(NA)	(NA)	(NA)
AZ	17	([2])	18	([2])	NV	(NA)	(NA)	(NA)	(NA)
AR	3	([1])	3	([1])	NH	10	([2])	10	([2])
CA	47	([4])	43	([4])	NJ	15	([4])	16	([3])
CO	7	64	10	75	NM	2	([1])	4	([2])
CT	12	([3])	12	108	NY	28	335	26	325
DE	3	([2])	3	([2])	NC	26	([3])	27	113
DC	(NA)	(NA)	(NA)	(NA)	ND	1	([1])	1	([1])
FL	63	464	61	505	OH	12	101	11	136
GA	8	([3])	12	([3])	OK	20	([3])	18	([3])
HI	14	([2])	14	([3])	OR	6	([2])	5	([2])
ID	8	([2])	9	33	PA	44	334	42	340
IL	30	243	29	230	RI	5	([2])	5	([2])
IN	35	424	35	432	SC	6	([2])	7	32
IA	4	([2])	4	([2])	SD	(NA)	(NA)	(NA)	(NA)
KS	2	([2])	2	([2])	TN	10	107	9	96
KY	10	([3])	10	([3])	TX	62	584	63	576
LA	29	336	27	310	UT	1	([1])	1	([1])
ME	2	([1])	1	([1])	VT	2	([1])	2	([1])
MD	7	42	7	46	VA	5	([2])	5	([2])
MA	20	([4])	19	([4])	WA	4	([2])	7	([2])
MI	22	([3])	21	([3])	WV	14	77	12	80
MN	6	([1])	6	([2])	WI	4	21	4	([1])
MS	21	538	19	549	WY	3	([1])	2	([1])

NA Not available. [1] 0 to 19 employees. [2] 20 to 99 employees. [3] 100 to 249 employees. [4] 250 to 499 employees.

Source: U.S. Census Bureau, "County Business Patterns," <http://factfinder2.census.gov>, accessed June 2013.

Table 986. Public Drinking Water Systems by Size of Community Served and Source of Water: 2011

[As of September. Covers systems that provide water for human consumption through pipes and other constructed conveyances to at least 15 service connections or serve an average of at least 25 persons for at least 180 days per year. Based on reported data in the Safe Drinking Water Information System maintained by the Environmental Protection Agency]

Type of system	Total [1]	Size of community served					Water source	
		500 or fewer persons	501 to 3,300 persons	3,301 to 10,000 persons	10,001 to 100,000 persons	100,001 persons or more	Ground water	Surface water
Total systems	**152,713**	**124,270**	**19,029**	**5,160**	**3,833**	**421**	**138,053**	**14,576**
COMMUNITY WATER SYSTEMS [2]								
Number of systems	51,356	28,462	13,737	4,936	3,802	419	39,624	11,721
Percent of systems	100	55	27	10	7	1	77	23
Population served (1,000)	299,216	4,764	19,662	28,738	108,770	137,283	86,586	212,574
Percent of population	100	2	7	10	36	46	29	71
NONTRANSIENT NONCOMMUNITY WATER SYSTEM [3]								
Number of systems	18,178	15,461	2,566	132	18	1	17,405	755
Percent of systems	100	85	14	1	–	–	96	4
Population served (1,000)	6,189	2,165	2,675	705	442	203	5,290	896
Percent of population	100	35	43	11	7	3	85	14
TRANSIENT NONCOMMUNITY WATER SYSTEM [4]								
Number of systems	83,179	80,347	2,726	92	13	1	81,024	2,100
Percent of systems	100	97	3	–	–	–	97	3
Population served (1,000)	12,652	7,171	2,631	515	335	2,000	10,086	2,562
Percent of population	100	57	21	4	3	16	80	20

– Represents zero. [1] Includes a small number of systems for which the water source (ground vs. surface) is unknown. [2] A public water system that supplies water to the same population year-round. [3] A public water system that regularly supplies water to at least 25 of the same people at least 6 months per year, but not year-round. Some examples are schools, factories, and office buildings which have their own water systems. [4] A public water system that provides water in a place such as a gas station or campground where people do not remain for long periods of time and is open at least 60 day per year.

Source: U.S. Environmental Protection Agency, *Fiscal Year 2011 Drinking Water and Ground Water Statistics*, March 2013. See also <http://water.epa.gov/drink/>.

Table 987. Public Drinking Water Systems—Number and Population Served by State: 2011

[311,101 represents 311,101,000. As of September. Covers systems supplying drinking water to at least 25 people or having 15 service connections for 180 or more days per year. Based on reported data in the Safe Drinking Water Information System maintained by the Environmental Protection Agency]

State	Number of systems	Population served (1,000)				State	Number of systems	Population served (1,000)			
		Total	Community [1]	Non-transient, non-community [2]	Transient, non-community [3]			Total	Community [1]	Non-transient, non-community [2]	Transient, non-community [3]
U.S.	**150,819**	**311,101**	**292,660**	**5,822**	**12,619**	MO	2,783	5,359	5,172	72	116
AL	611	5,554	5,517	15	6	MT	2,103	969	714	82	173
AK	1,557	778	610	62	106	NE	1,323	1,582	1,480	50	52
AZ	1,570	6,464	6,225	121	117	NV	561	2,621	2,558	42	22
AR	1,107	2,739	2,709	9	20	NH	2,427	1,169	855	92	221
CA	7,764	42,206	40,961	390	855	NJ	3,891	9,780	8,999	352	429
CO	2,053	5,711	5,386	76	248	NM	1,192	1,938	1,811	51	76
CT	2,590	2,837	2,704	114	60	NY	8,988	20,964	17,829	309	2,827
DE	493	976	900	22	54	NC	6,092	8,052	7,623	113	316
DC	6	607	607	(Z)	–	ND	542	605	581	4	20
FL	5,607	19,721	19,222	241	258	OH	4,884	11,029	10,412	213	404
GA	2,430	8,573	8,433	64	76	OK	1,669	3,625	3,567	21	37
HI	130	1,484	1,473	11	(Z)	OR	2,605	3,646	3,374	70	201
ID	1,956	1,252	1,100	52	100	PA	9,225	11,993	10,745	492	756
IL	5,596	12,609	12,129	135	345	RI	485	1,074	989	30	56
IN	4,208	5,449	4,870	195	384	SC	1,442	3,908	3,822	44	41
IA	1,917	2,867	2,742	48	77	SD	644	751	719	8	23
KS	1,022	2,702	2,677	21	4	TN	891	6,413	6,330	26	57
KY	462	4,457	4,441	11	5	TX	6,964	25,848	25,063	510	276
LA	1,403	5,026	4,922	56	48	UT	1,013	2,835	2,728	28	79
ME	1,873	913	664	66	183	VT	1,363	588	446	44	98
MD	3,504	5,623	5,194	161	267	VA	2,787	7,090	6,607	315	168
MA	1,810	9,565	9,320	75	171	WA	4,347	6,983	6,419	156	403
MI	11,246	8,957	7,616	327	1,014	WV	1,042	1,581	1,510	40	31
MN	7,118	4,875	4,263	76	535	WI	11,465	4,943	4,015	208	720
MS	1,263	3,238	3,152	75	12	WY	795	547	450	23	75

– Represents zero. Z Less than 500. [1] A public water system that supplies water to the same population year-round. [2] A public water system that regularly supplies water to at least 25 of the same people at least 6 months per year, but not year-round. Some examples are schools, factories, and office buildings which have their own water systems. [3] A public water system that provides water in a place such as a gas station or campground where people do not remain for long periods of time and is open at least 60 days per year.

Source: U.S. Environmental Protection Agency, *Fiscal Year 2011 Drinking Water and Ground Water Statistics*, March 2013. See also <http://water.epa.gov/drink/>.

Construction and Housing

This section presents data on the construction industry and on various indicators of its activity and costs; on housing units and their characteristics and occupants; and on the characteristics and vacancy rates for commercial buildings.

The principal source of these data is the U.S. Census Bureau, which issues a variety of current publications, as well as data from the decennial census. Current construction statistics compiled by the Census Bureau appear in its *New Residential Construction* and *New Residential Sales* press releases and Web sites at <www.census.gov/construction/nrc/> and <www.census.gov/construction/nrs/>. *Construction Spending* presents data on all types of construction. Reports of the censuses of construction industries (see below) are also issued on various topics.

Other Census Bureau publications include the quarterly *Housing Vacancies*, the quarterly *Survey of Market Absorption*, the biennial *American Housing Survey* (formerly *Annual Housing Survey*), and other reports of the censuses of housing and of construction industries.

Other sources include McGraw-Hill Construction, New York, NY, which presents national and state data on construction contracts; the National Association of Home Builders with data on housing starts; the NATIONAL ASSOCIATION OF REALTORS®, which presents data on existing home sales; the Bureau of Economic Analysis, which presents data on residential fixed assets; the U.S. Energy Information Administration, which provides data on commercial buildings through its periodic sample surveys; and the Federal Financial Institutions Examination Council, which provide data on home loans and home improvement loans.

Censuses and surveys—Censuses of the construction industry were first conducted by the Census Bureau for 1929, 1935, and 1939; beginning in 1967, a census has been taken every 5 years (through 2012, for years ending in "2" and "7"). The latest reports are part of the 2007 Economic Census. See text, Section 15, Business Enterprise.

The construction sector of the economic census, covers all employer establishments primarily engaged in (1) building construction by general contractors or operative builders; (2) heavy (nonbuilding) construction by general contractors; and (3) construction by special trade contractors. This sector includes construction management and land subdividers and developers. The 2007 census was conducted in accordance with the 2007 North American Industrial Classification System (NAICS). See text, Section 15, Business Enterprise.

From 1850 through 1930, the Census Bureau collected some housing data as part of its censuses of population and agriculture. Beginning in 1940, separate censuses of housing have been taken at 10-year intervals. For the 1970 and 1980 censuses, data on year-round housing units were collected and issued on occupancy and structural characteristics, plumbing facilities, value, and rent; for 1990, such characteristics were presented for all housing units.

The *American Housing Survey* (*Current Housing Reports* Series H-150 and H-170), which began in 1973, provided an annual and ongoing series of data on selected housing and demographic characteristics until 1983. In 1984, the name of the survey was changed from the *Annual Housing Survey*. Currently, national data are collected every other year, and data for selected metropolitan areas are collected on a rotating basis. All samples represent a cross section of the housing stock in their respective areas. Estimates are subject to both sampling and nonsampling errors; caution should therefore be used in making comparisons between years.

Data on residential mortgages were collected continuously from 1890 to 1970, except 1930, as part of the decennial census by the Census Bureau. Since 1973, mortgage status data, limited to single family homes on less than 10 acres with no business on the property, have been presented in the *American Housing Survey*. Data on mortgage activity are covered in Section 25, Banking and Finance.

Housing units—In general, a housing unit is a house, an apartment, a group of rooms or a single room occupied or intended for occupancy as separate living quarters; that is, the occupants live separately from any other individual in the building, and there is direct access from the outside or through a common hall. Transient accommodations, barracks for workers, and institutional-type quarters are not counted as housing units.

Statistical reliability—For a discussion of statistical collection and estimation, sampling procedures, and measures of statistical reliability applicable to Census Bureau data, see Appendix III.

Table 988. Construction—Establishments, Employees, and Payroll by Kind of Business (NAICS Basis): 2010 and 2011

[5,191 represents 5,191,000. Covers establishments with payroll. Excludes most government employees, railroad employees, and self-employed persons. Kind-of-business classification based on North American Industry Classification System (NAICS), 2007. For statement on methodology, see Appendix III]

Industry	2007 NAICS code [1]	Establishments		Paid employees [2] (1,000)		Annual payroll (mil.dol.)	
		2010	2011	2010	2011	2010	2011
Construction............................	**23**	**682,684**	**657,738**	**5,389**	**5,191**	**260,959**	**265,212**
Construction of buildings...............	236	201,877	194,451	1,163	1,100	57,525	57,674
Residential building construction..........	2361	158,241	152,254	568	534	22,564	22,524
New single-family housing construction (except operative builders)................	236115	50,138	46,678	169	152	6,252	6,137
New multifamily housing construction (except operative builders)................	236116	3,158	2,883	32	29	1,950	1,899
New housing operative builders...........	236117	17,014	15,107	101	91	5,374	5,086
Residential remodelers..................	236118	87,931	87,586	266	263	8,987	9,402
Nonresidential building construction........	2362	43,636	42,197	595	566	34,961	35,150
Industrial building construction...........	23621	3,496	3,532	76	81	4,307	4,601
Commercial and institutional building construction..........................	23622	40,140	38,665	519	484	30,654	30,549
Heavy and civil engineering construction..........	237	43,405	41,784	842	829	50,759	52,344
Utility system construction..............	2371	19,705	19,523	463	468	27,120	28,733
Water and sewer line and related structures...........	23711	12,158	11,720	148	138	7,853	7,676
Oil and gas pipeline and related structures...........	23712	1,926	2,071	127	128	8,371	8,927
Power and communication line and related structures....................	23713	5,621	5,732	188	202	10,896	12,130
Land subdivision......................	2372	7,966	7,001	41	35	2,051	1,952
Highway, street, and bridge construction....	2373	11,106	10,771	274	260	17,587	17,457
Other heavy and civil engineering construction.........	2379	4,628	4,489	64	65	4,000	4,202
Specialty trade contractors...............	238	437,402	421,503	3,384	3,262	152,676	155,194
Foundation, structure, and building exterior contractors.........................	2381	92,555	88,045	695	645	27,730	27,550
Poured concrete foundation and structures contractors.........................	23811	20,912	19,874	176	163	7,390	7,320
Structural steel and precast concrete contractors.........................	23812	3,449	3,312	54	52	2,528	2,601
Framing contractors...................	23813	11,675	10,621	62	53	1,858	1,763
Masonry contractors..................	23814	20,446	18,861	136	122	5,080	4,824
Glass and glazing contractors...........	23815	5,140	5,021	47	43	2,103	1,995
Roofing contractors...................	23816	17,730	17,694	151	145	5,949	6,158
Siding contractors....................	23817	8,031	7,551	33	31	1,173	1,151
Other foundation, structure, and building exterior contractors.................	23819	5,172	5,111	37	36	1,649	1,738
Building equipment contractors..........	2382	171,333	167,772	1,623	1,586	81,716	83,497
Electrical contractors.................	23821	70,824	68,725	669	654	33,613	34,591
Plumbing, heating, and air-conditioning contractors.........................	23822	93,761	92,370	828	807	40,696	41,310
Other building equipment contractors....	23829	6,748	6,677	126	126	7,407	7,596
Building finishing contractors............	2383	108,594	102,967	626	600	23,082	23,256
Drywall and insulation contractors.......	23831	18,388	17,275	195	179	7,627	7,318
Painting and wall covering contractors....	23832	33,435	31,739	158	161	5,598	6,113
Flooring contractors..................	23833	14,320	13,715	62	59	2,266	2,234
Tile and terrazzo contractors...........	23834	9,040	8,427	44	40	1,520	1,473
Finish carpentry contractors...........	23835	26,925	25,510	106	102	3,802	3,795
Other building finishing contractors......	23839	6,486	6,301	61	58	2,268	2,323
Other specialty trade contractors.........	2389	64,920	62,719	439	431	20,148	20,891
Site preparation contractors............	23891	35,182	33,520	259	253	12,271	12,763
All other specialty trade contractors.....	23899	29,738	29,199	180	178	7,877	8,128

[1] North American Industry Classification System code, 2007. See text, Section 15. [2] Employees on the payroll for the pay period including March 12.

Source: U.S. Census Bureau, "County Business Patterns," CB1100A11, <http://factfinder2.census.gov>, accessed May 2013.

Table 989. Value of New Construction Put in Place: 1980 to 2012

[In millions of dollars (273,936 represents $273,936,000,000). Represents value of construction put in place during year; differs from building permit and construction contract data in timing and coverage. Includes installed cost of normal building service equipment and selected types of industrial production equipment (largely site fabricated). Excludes cost of shipbuilding, land, and most types of machinery and equipment. For methodology, see Appendix III]

Year	Total	Private			Public		
		Total	Residential buildings	Non-residential	Total	Federal	State and local
1980.........	273,936	210,290	100,381	109,909	63,646	9,642	54,004
1990.........	476,778	369,300	191,103	178,197	107,478	12,099	95,379
1995.........	548,666	408,655	228,121	180,534	140,011	15,751	124,260
1996.........	599,693	453,018	257,495	195,523	146,675	15,325	131,350
1997.........	631,853	478,416	264,696	213,720	153,437	14,087	139,350
1998.........	688,515	533,737	296,343	237,394	154,778	14,318	140,460
1999.........	744,551	575,469	326,302	249,167	169,082	14,025	155,057
2000.........	802,756	621,431	346,138	275,293	181,325	14,168	167,157
2001.........	840,249	638,337	364,414	273,922	201,912	15,082	186,830
2002.........	847,874	634,435	396,696	237,739	213,438	16,578	196,860
2003.........	891,497	675,370	446,035	229,335	216,127	17,913	198,214
2004.........	991,356	771,173	532,900	238,273	220,183	18,342	201,841
2005.........	1,104,136	869,976	611,899	258,077	234,160	17,300	216,860
2006.........	1,167,222	911,837	613,731	298,105	255,385	17,555	237,831
2007.........	1,152,351	863,278	493,246	370,032	289,073	20,580	268,494
2008.........	1,067,564	758,827	350,257	408,569	308,738	23,731	285,007
2009.........	903,201	588,306	245,912	342,394	314,895	28,439	286,456
2010.........	804,561	500,595	238,819	261,776	303,966	31,133	272,833
2011.........	778,238	494,961	236,960	258,001	283,277	30,391	252,886
2012.........	854,490	578,792	275,461	303,331	275,698	25,507	250,191

Source: U.S. Census Bureau, "Construction Spending," <http://www.census.gov/construction/c30/c30index.html>, accessed June 2013.

Table 990. New Privately Owned Housing Units Authorized by State: 2011 and 2012

[624.1 represents 624,100. Based on about 20,000 places in United States having building permit systems in 2011 and 2012]

State	Housing units (1,000)			Valuation (mil. dol.)			State	Housing units (1,000)			Valuation (mil. dol.)		
	2011	2012 Total	2012 1-unit [1]	2011	2012 Total	2012 1-unit [1]		2011	2012 Total	2012 1-unit [1]	2011	2012 Total	2012 1-unit [1]
U.S......	624.1	829.7	518.7	105,269	140,425	110,661	MO.......	9.2	12.3	8.0	1,426	1,879	1,576
AL........	11.7	13.5	9.2	1,704	1,950	1,689	MT........	1.9	2.7	1.7	286	450	360
AK........	0.9	1.0	0.8	204	234	212	NE........	5.2	6.1	4.3	726	918	794
AZ........	13.0	21.7	16.2	2,580	4,457	3,844	NV........	6.2	9.1	7.4	789	1,325	1,149
AR........	6.8	8.2	5.4	861	1,132	963	NH........	2.3	2.3	1.7	432	426	364
CA........	45.5	58.5	27.7	9,639	12,727	7,840	NJ........	13.0	17.9	7.3	2,043	2,389	1,529
CO.......	13.5	23.3	12.6	2,860	4,438	3,480	NM.......	4.1	4.7	3.2	678	759	640
CT........	3.2	4.7	2.5	679	970	696	NY........	22.6	24.9	9.3	3,356	3,757	2,236
DE........	3.0	4.1	2.9	370	486	376	NC.......	32.8	48.7	29.9	5,053	7,056	5,682
DC........	4.6	3.8	0.3	609	472	49	ND.......	6.2	10.3	4.5	784	1,398	886
FL........	42.4	64.8	42.2	8,815	13,201	10,940	OH.......	13.8	16.9	10.9	2,260	2,769	2,283
GA........	18.5	24.4	17.3	2,761	3,855	3,179	OK.......	8.8	11.9	9.7	1,286	1,936	1,795
HI........	2.7	3.0	1.9	654	757	601	OR.......	7.7	10.6	6.3	1,407	1,975	1,532
ID........	3.8	6.3	5.0	733	1,124	1,038	PA.......	15.0	18.8	13.4	2,546	3,111	2,571
IL........	11.8	13.8	8.6	2,118	2,621	1,980	RI........	0.7	0.7	0.7	129	138	132
IN........	12.6	13.8	10.1	1,976	2,350	2,064	SC.......	15.5	18.7	15.3	2,760	3,443	3,188
IA........	7.5	9.5	6.8	1,246	1,641	1,349	SD.......	2.8	4.2	2.8	392	576	468
KS........	5.4	6.3	4.1	861	1,051	879	TN.......	15.0	20.1	13.9	2,353	3,114	2,628
KY........	7.8	9.7	5.5	915	1,205	947	TX.......	97.5	135.5	79.5	14,736	19,451	15,310
LA........	12.2	13.0	11.5	1,919	2,225	2,102	UT.......	10.0	13.0	10.0	1,760	2,437	2,171
ME......	2.7	3.0	2.5	436	499	459	VT........	1.3	1.3	0.9	221	219	181
MD......	13.5	15.2	9.2	2,205	2,410	1,841	VA.......	23.3	27.3	17.5	3,391	4,096	3,446
MA......	7.7	11.1	5.9	1,761	2,422	1,688	WA.......	20.9	28.1	16.5	4,036	5,649	4,112
MI.......	9.3	11.7	10.2	1,688	2,280	2,124	WV.......	2.2	2.7	1.8	306	347	289
MN......	8.9	16.1	9.2	1,764	3,007	2,220	WI........	9.9	12.0	7.7	1,606	2,017	1,618
MS......	5.3	6.0	4.9	724	836	752	WY.......	2.1	2.1	1.7	425	439	407

[1] The 1-unit structure category is a single-family home. It includes fully detached, semi-detached (semi-attached, side-by-side), row houses, and townhouses.

Source: U.S. Census Bureau, Construction Reports, "Building Permits Survey," <http://www.census.gov/construction/bps/>, accessed August 2013.

Table 991. Value of State and Local Government Construction Put in Place: 2000 to 2012

[In millions of dollars (167,157 represents $167,157,000,000)]

Type of construction	2000	2005	2006	2007	2008	2009	2010	2011	2012
Total construction [1]	**167,157**	**216,860**	**237,831**	**268,494**	**285,007**	**286,456**	**272,833**	**252,886**	**250,191**
Residential	2,962	4,047	4,349	5,094	4,894	5,772	7,576	6,221	5,007
Multifamily	2,945	3,740	3,990	4,476	4,072	4,849	6,536	5,452	4,301
Nonresidential	164,196	212,813	233,482	263,399	280,113	280,684	265,256	246,665	245,184
Office	4,494	5,211	5,588	7,249	8,515	9,170	8,317	7,429	6,128
Commercial [1]	1,820	1,882	1,567	1,777	1,965	2,003	1,456	1,797	1,547
Automotive	1,233	1,490	1,152	1,012	1,425	1,141	769	927	1,044
Parking	1,143	1,357	1,011	941	1,252	1,031	675	755	847
Warehouse	330	218	230	558	312	440	286	326	176
Health care	2,829	5,059	5,615	7,028	7,010	6,837	6,193	6,925	6,962
Hospital	1,949	3,429	4,085	5,304	5,320	5,352	4,789	5,245	5,390
Medical building	490	1,168	919	981	909	876	747	889	1,004
Special care	390	463	611	743	782	609	657	791	567
Educational [1]	46,818	65,750	69,790	78,376	84,489	83,703	71,948	67,368	65,449
Primary/secondary [1]	33,764	44,184	47,846	55,054	57,770	54,650	44,559	40,344	39,007
Elementary	12,272	14,251	13,870	16,786	18,305	17,241	13,171	10,610	11,184
Middle/junior high	5,820	9,069	10,764	11,719	10,937	10,278	7,029	8,070	7,379
High	13,326	19,892	22,631	25,887	27,985	26,729	24,055	21,204	20,070
Higher education [1]	10,749	18,033	18,961	20,556	23,542	25,081	24,384	24,120	23,440
Instructional	6,317	9,275	9,434	11,300	13,251	14,734	14,138	13,232	12,006
Parking	514	1,013	909	839	732	596	593	723	518
Administration	294	387	657	503	290	382	357	434	428
Dormitory	1,078	2,918	3,409	2,657	3,043	3,183	3,371	3,939	4,365
Library	308	588	493	700	791	871	662	569	332
Student union/cafeteria	322	880	1028	1,547	1,398	1,440	1,147	1,228	1,478
Sports/recreation	966	1,769	1,748	1,726	2,559	2,357	2,398	2,320	2,417
Infrastructure	835	1,138	1,227	1,218	1,241	1,291	1,381	1,461	1,770
Other educational [1]	1,645	2,735	2,312	1,890	2,485	3,077	2,223	1,835	2,184
Library/archive	976	2,098	1,857	1,287	1,557	1,865	1,386	1,147	1,495
Public safety [1]	5,854	6,013	6,608	8,423	9,666	9,432	7,586	7,268	7,583
Correctional	4,754	3,958	4,611	5,384	6,375	5,780	4,624	4,944	5,029
Detention	3,907	2,936	3,305	4,026	4,524	3,409	2,789	3,162	3,212
Police/sheriff	848	1,022	1,307	1,358	1,851	2,371	1,836	1,781	1,817
Other public safety	1,100	2,055	1,997	3,039	3,291	3,652	2,962	2,325	2,555
Fire/rescue	994	1,675	1,615	2,392	2,367	2,470	1,747	1,486	1,651
Amusement and recreation [1]	7,583	7,340	9,444	10,670	10,872	10,585	9,668	8,520	8,974
Sports	2,289	1,587	1,853	2,040	2,548	2,389	1,819	1,200	1,031
Performance/meeting center	2,075	1,921	2,292	1,706	1,631	1,704	1,841	1,826	1,881
Convention center	1,397	1,350	1,422	1,035	1,040	1,013	1,119	1,134	1,383
Social center	1,152	1,006	1,285	1,373	1,587	1,646	1,561	1,055	1,004
Neighborhood center	886	866	1098	1,053	1,231	1,480	1,395	887	879
Park/camp	1,930	2,728	3,887	5,255	4,975	4,733	4,259	4,254	4,954
Transportation	13,000	16,256	17,695	21,144	23,230	25,461	26,493	23,234	24,509
Air [1]	6,700	8,993	9,676	11,390	11,579	12,562	11,897	9,950	9,877
Passenger terminal	2,930	3,310	3,766	5,224	6,164	6,916	6,503	5,708	4,982
Runway	3,196	4,861	4,898	5,164	4,551	4,839	4,710	3,790	4,401
Land [1]	5,165	5,936	6,629	7,593	9,969	11,327	12,954	11,603	12,682
Passenger terminal	1,253	907	969	1,301	2,053	2,789	3,380	3,291	2,980
Mass transit	1,484	3,208	3,228	3,587	4,371	5,223	6,447	5,570	6,622
Railroad	1,471	552	320	508	585	747	751	673	855
Water [1]	1,136	1,327	1,391	2,161	1,682	1,572	1,642	1,681	1,949
Dock/marina	863	930	971	1,465	1,287	1,309	1,115	1,257	1,492
Dry dock/marine terminal	236	397	420	697	395	263	527	424	457
Power	5,501	8,320	7,766	11,449	10,992	11,775	10,770	8,644	8,950
Electrical	5,257	7,091	7,195	10,176	10,192	9,387	9,972	7,061	6,515
Distribution	2,087	1,786	2,187	2,818	3,487	3,276	3,253	1,583	1,619
Highway and street [1]	51,574	63,157	71,032	75,455	80,424	81,254	81,309	77,998	78,632
Pavement	37,929	45,177	45,933	47,679	52,837	55,186	51,433	47,542	46,716
Lighting	856	1,232	1,057	1,709	1,532	1,300	1,975	1,719	1,741
Retaining wall	1,099	675	1546	1,073	888	959	1,250	1,033	849
Tunnel	894	373	224	221	264	302	810	886	1,139
Bridge	9,302	14,244	20,057	22,827	23,690	22,075	24,222	25,596	27,036
Toll/weigh	325	320	657	421	196	268	214	262	344
Maintenance building	293	96	213	102	102	128	275	237	171
Rest facility/streetscape	878	1,042	1,347	1,424	916	1,036	1,130	725	636
Sewage and waste disposal [1]	14,000	18,336	21,524	23,323	24,102	23,455	24,555	21,024	20,705
Sewage/dry waste [1]	9,338	11,717	13,401	13,891	14,044	13,261	13,234	11,793	11,952
Plant	2,765	3,369	3,410	3,802	3,957	3,453	3,755	3,157	2,925
Line/pump station	6,326	8,243	9,820	9,784	9,823	9,494	9,375	8,540	8,915
Waste water	4,663	6,620	8,124	9,432	10,058	10,194	11,321	9,232	8,754
Plant	3,229	5,231	6,039	7,496	8,688	8,497	9,428	7,786	7,305
Line/drain	1,434	1,389	2,085	1,935	1,370	1,697	1,893	1,446	1,449
Water supply [1]	9,528	13,483	14,299	15,029	16,017	14,838	14,420	13,395	12,664
Plant	3,067	4,943	5,005	5,661	6,500	6,327	5,683	5,359	4,858
Well	378	360	623	661	460	480	383	385	357
Line	4,644	6,234	5,922	6,131	6,191	5,398	6,246	5,899	5,562
Pump station	625	776	1285	1,124	1,293	1,372	970	755	576
Reservoir	266	502	700	586	633	335	393	428	645
Tank/tower	548	668	764	867	940	926	744	570	665
Conservation and development [1]	933	1,752	2,000	2,198	2,251	2,016	2,035	2,301	2,281
Dam/levee	303	405	591	640	772	761	783	906	763
Breakwater/jetty	270	726	809	627	645	702	675	635	849
Dredging	140	211	192	204	179	248	173	210	191

[1] Includes other types of construction, not shown separately.

Source: U.S. Census Bureau, "Construction Spending," <http://www.census.gov/construction/c30/c30index.html>, accessed June 2013.

Table 992. Construction Contracts Started—Value of Construction and Floor Space of Buildings by Class of Construction: 1990 to 2012

[246.0 represents $246,000,000,000. Dollar value data includes new construction, additions and alterations. Square footage data includes new construction and additions; alterations which create no net new square footage are not included]

Year	Total	Residential buildings	Nonresidential buildings									Nonbuilding construction
			Total	Commercial [1]	Manufacturing	Education [2]	Health	Public	Religious	Social and recreational	Miscellaneous	
VALUE (bil. dol.)												
1990.............	246.0	100.9	95.4	44.8	8.4	16.6	9.2	5.7	2.2	5.3	3.1	49.7
1995.............	306.5	127.9	114.2	46.6	13.8	22.9	10.8	6.3	2.8	7.1	3.8	64.4
2000.............	472.9	208.3	173.3	80.9	8.9	40.9	12.4	7.5	4.6	13.8	4.4	91.3
2001.............	496.5	219.7	169.1	70.2	8.0	47.0	14.4	7.8	4.8	12.0	4.8	107.7
2002.............	504.0	248.7	155.1	59.6	5.5	45.3	16.1	7.3	5.1	11.5	4.7	100.2
2003.............	531.7	283.4	156.1	58.8	6.9	47.7	15.8	7.1	4.5	11.0	4.3	92.3
2004.............	593.2	333.1	164.4	67.3	8.0	44.0	17.6	7.2	4.5	11.6	4.4	95.6
2005.............	670.2	384.0	182.4	72.2	10.1	49.1	22.3	7.9	4.1	11.7	5.0	103.8
2006.............	689.5	342.1	217.3	92.9	13.7	53.8	24.3	8.2	4.1	14.3	5.9	130.1
2007.............	640.8	261.5	239.1	100.7	20.7	58.1	24.4	12.4	3.8	13.4	5.5	140.2
2008.............	558.2	160.5	243.0	81.4	31.0	63.7	30.0	13.4	3.6	13.5	6.5	154.7
2009.............	426.3	112.2	169.3	47.3	9.7	54.0	20.4	15.5	3.3	11.6	7.6	144.7
2010.............	434.8	121.7	163.7	42.0	9.5	53.4	24.8	10.6	2.4	11.2	9.8	149.4
2011.............	442.6	126.6	165.7	48.2	17.2	47.9	23.5	9.4	2.1	10.3	7.0	150.4
2012.............	476.0	165.4	155.9	53.5	12.5	42.7	22.4	8.3	1.9	8.5	6.2	154.8
FLOOR SPACE (mil. sq. ft.)												
1990.............	3,020	1,817	1,203	694	128	152	69	47	29	51	32	(X)
1995.............	3,454	2,172	1,281	700	163	186	70	40	33	56	33	(X)
1999.............	5,091	3,253	1,838	1,115	141	261	98	49	48	87	39	(X)
2000.............	4,982	3,113	1,869	1,180	111	273	88	44	49	94	29	(X)
2001.............	4,828	3,159	1,669	988	93	295	92	44	50	81	27	(X)
2002.............	4,792	3,356	1,436	810	68	277	97	37	52	71	26	(X)
2003.............	5,093	3,689	1,404	794	75	270	92	35	45	67	26	(X)
2004.............	5,518	4,061	1,457	875	86	231	94	34	43	68	27	(X)
2005.............	5,872	4,345	1,528	927	79	246	108	33	37	67	29	(X)
2006.............	5,282	3,647	1,635	1,015	83	254	110	33	35	73	33	(X)
2007.............	4,312	2,645	1,667	1,051	91	247	104	51	31	66	27	(X)
2008.............	2,952	1,573	1,379	772	80	253	109	49	28	59	28	(X)
2009.............	1,888	1,112	776	332	36	199	68	48	25	42	26	(X)
2010.............	1,844	1,164	680	279	47	175	73	34	15	35	22	(X)
2011.............	1,859	1,156	703	325	54	157	75	27	14	33	18	(X)
2012.............	2,234	1,471	763	413	58	135	70	22	13	32	19	(X)

X Not applicable. [1] Includes nonindustrial warehouses. [2] Includes science facilities.

Source: McGraw-Hill Construction, a division of McGraw-Hill Financial, New York, NY © 1-800-591-4462.

Table 993. Construction Contracts Started—Value by Region: 2008 to 2012

[In millions of dollars (558,184 represents 558,184,000,000). Includes new construction, additions and alterations]

Region	2008	2009	2010	2011	2012		
					Total [1]	Residential	Nonresidential
U.S............................	558,184	426,314	434,828	442,643	476,006	165,353	155,894
New England......................	20,550	16,876	19,890	19,774	19,660	6,081	8,397
Middle Atlantic....................	64,084	51,316	53,700	48,679	52,316	14,281	22,381
East North Central................	75,378	50,866	52,122	48,639	51,214	14,024	21,244
West North Central...............	33,428	30,960	32,190	31,377	38,129	11,719	14,322
South Atlantic.....................	114,944	86,567	80,159	87,054	106,340	40,770	28,437
East South Central...............	39,938	25,779	25,669	28,057	24,301	9,263	8,990
West South Central..............	85,805	69,226	67,583	66,699	77,300	29,869	20,907
Mountain...........................	51,087	37,874	39,266	39,198	40,157	17,454	11,799
Pacific.............................	72,969	56,850	64,249	73,165	66,591	21,891	19,417

[1] Includes nonbuilding construction, not shown separately.

Source: McGraw-Hill Construction, a division of the McGraw-Hill Financial, New York, NY © 1-800-591-4462.

Table 994. Value of Private Construction Put in Place: 2000 to 2012

[In millions of dollars (621,431 represents $621,431,000,000). Represents value of construction put in place during year; differs from building permit and construction contract data in timing and coverage. See Appendix III]

Type of construction	2000	2005	2006	2007	2008	2009	2010	2011	2012
Total construction [1]	**621,431**	**869,976**	**911,837**	**863,278**	**758,827**	**588,306**	**500,595**	**494,961**	**578,792**
Residential	346,138	611,899	613,731	493,246	350,257	245,912	238,819	236,960	275,461
New single family	236,788	433,510	415,997	305,184	185,776	105,336	112,569	108,178	129,252
New multifamily	28,259	47,297	52,803	48,959	44,338	28,538	14,686	14,772	21,348
Improvements [2]	81,091	131,092	144,931	139,103	120,144	112,038	111,564	114,010	124,862
Nonresidential	275,293	258,077	298,105	370,032	408,569	342,394	261,776	258,001	303,331
Lodging	16,304	12,666	17,624	27,481	35,364	25,388	11,201	8,217	10,433
Office [1]	52,407	37,276	45,680	53,815	55,502	37,282	24,368	22,538	26,172
General	49,637	32,962	41,085	48,945	50,137	33,346	22,203	19,984	23,701
Financial	2,689	4,285	4,542	4,785	5,054	3,720	2,122	2,324	2,038
Commercial [1]	64,055	66,584	73,368	85,858	82,654	50,460	36,504	39,972	43,924
Automotive [1]	5,967	5,614	5,528	6,281	5,640	4,535	3,546	4,308	4,962
Sales	1,629	2,834	2,285	2,571	2,430	1,564	1,355	1,874	2,174
Service/parts	3,009	1,805	2,184	2,356	1,843	2,056	1,679	1,996	2,189
Parking	1,330	975	1059	1,354	1,367	916	511	437	600
Food/beverage	8,786	7,795	7,442	8,046	8,029	4,868	4,605	5,305	5,839
Food	4,792	3,128	2,752	2,779	3,124	1,978	2,027	2,855	2,540
Dining/drinking	2,935	4,078	3,780	3,957	3,976	2,237	1,911	1,659	2,272
Fast food	1,058	590	910	1310	930	653	667	791	1,026
Multiretail [1]	14,911	22,750	29,218	34,751	31,963	18,390	12,486	13,392	15,473
General merchandise	5,100	6,740	5,699	7,572	4,373	3,976	3,794	3,377	4,070
Shopping center	6,803	12,462	18,417	22,197	22,780	11,447	6,725	6,761	8,121
Shopping mall	2,523	2,631	3,616	4,000	4,045	2,171	1,332	2,357	2,323
Other commercial [1]	13,537	11,744	10,874	13,580	12,087	6,300	4,220	3,744	3,833
Drug store	1,682	1,315	1,238	1,500	1,967	1,882	1,077	743	836
Building supply store	2,592	2,416	2,594	3,507	2,539	1,118	772	615	475
Other stores	8,136	7,075	6,135	7,744	6,552	2,528	1,741	1,701	1,851
Warehouse [1]	14,822	12,827	14,491	16,909	16,707	9,730	5,661	6,382	7,011
General commercial	13,511	11,448	13,493	15,641	15,482	8,781	5,229	6,063	6,516
Ministorage	1,263	1,311	979	1,218	1,125	873	401	227	378
Farm	5,988	5,854	5,817	6,292	8,227	6,637	5,987	6,841	6,807
Health care	19,455	28,495	32,016	35,588	38,437	35,309	29,552	28,606	29,735
Hospital	10,183	18,250	21,914	24,532	25,571	24,723	21,528	20,375	20,061
Medical building	5,066	8,031	7,165	7,981	9,242	7,531	5,276	5,339	6,043
Special care	4,206	2,213	2,937	3,074	3,625	3,055	2,748	2,893	3,632
Educational [1]	11,683	12,788	13,839	16,691	18,624	16,851	13,418	14,180	17,141
Preschool	770	516	487	704	746	716	492	342	317
Primary/secondary	2,948	2,718	3,240	3,968	3,919	3,362	2,585	2,959	2,875
Higher education [1]	6,333	6,946	7,611	9,424	11,587	10,812	8,322	8,638	11,415
Instructional	3,058	3,556	3,501	4,219	5,463	6,211	4,993	4,698	6,329
Dormitory	1,356	1,537	2,065	2,900	3,791	2,496	1,654	2,187	2,882
Sports/recreation	645	821	858	771	841	832	790	654	756
Other educational	1,318	2,294	2,090	2,167	1,965	1,643	1,687	1,851	2,082
Gallery/museum	920	1,745	1,697	1,939	1,708	1,395	1,522	1,470	1,351
Religious	8,030	7,715	7,740	7,522	7,197	6,177	5,237	4,191	3,875
House of worship	5,656	5,992	6,262	6,270	5,884	5,001	4,214	3,272	3,179
Other religious	2,347	1,723	1,478	1,252	1,313	1,176	1,023	920	696
Auxiliary building	1,280	1,251	1,219	1,099	1,122	1,031	795	649	546
Public safety [1]	423	408	419	595	623	471	241	208	116
Amusement and recreation [1]	8,768	7,507	9,326	10,193	10,508	8,402	6,483	6,984	6,644
Theme/amusement park	747	200	417	522	324	280	353	480	273
Sports	1,068	807	959	1902	2,280	2,023	1,596	1,132	1,117
Fitness	1,152	1,425	2,028	1,945	2,051	1,763	1,150	1,107	1,419
Performance/meeting center	732	1,072	737	823	1102	796	565	523	592
Social center	2,368	1,626	1,538	1,602	1,552	1,134	914	533	615
Movie theater/studio	1,461	1,248	1,309	1,159	601	338	426	531	428
Transportation [1]	6,879	7,124	8,654	9,009	9,934	9,056	9,894	9,841	10,756
Air	1,804	748	719	732	776	512	259	536	1,074
Land	4,907	6,214	7,764	8,008	9,020	8,484	9,503	9,247	9,651
Railroad	4,263	5,816	7,313	7,423	8,378	8,042	8,973	8,710	9,142
Communication	18,799	18,846	22,187	27,488	26,343	19,712	17,689	17,384	16,896
Power [1]	29,344	29,210	33,654	54,115	69,242	76,064	66,117	63,935	88,134
Electricity	23,374	22,678	26,295	41,460	52,799	60,394	48,972	52,986	74,506
Gas	4,891	5,239	5,528	7,876	10,560	10,849	8,297	7,362	6,882
Oil	1,003	1,293	1,831	4,779	5,883	4,821	8,848	3,587	6,746
Sewage and waste disposal [1]	508	240	305	408	665	468	439	563	672
Water supply [1]	714	326	477	516	466	319	717	641	414
Manufacturing	37,583	28,413	32,264	40,215	52,754	56,296	39,778	40,631	48,171
Food/beverage/tobacco	3,985	4,446	4,330	3,794	4,514	3,280	3,918	4,821	4,003
Textile/apparel/leather/furniture	413	396	133	35	260	269	579	313	188
Wood	483	933	1350	702	352	390	429	381	363
Paper	479	442	515	450	577	516	568	537	1,044
Print/publishing	848	739	670	236	243	169	53	102	77
Petroleum/coal	1,255	734	1650	5,061	14,724	23,453	11,376	5,584	4,974
Chemical	3,798	6,263	8,484	13,279	12,576	10,119	7,425	7,587	11,174
Plastic/rubber	1,645	834	812	974	1035	573	713	851	1,318
Nonmetallic mineral	1,898	1105	2,388	3,417	2,838	1,782	1,127	865	904
Primary metal	1,976	793	1327	1,558	3,329	4,682	4,642	3,261	5,115
Fabricated metal	2,148	664	517	931	1474	1,479	1,082	1,656	1,651
Machinery	864	872	862	489	917	1055	1,009	1,365	1,552
Computer/electronic/electrical	6,392	4,039	4,001	2,556	2,129	3,641	4,519	9,400	11,459
Transportation equipment	6,318	3,518	2,422	3,218	4,537	3,524	1,921	3,169	3,366

[1] Includes other types of construction, not shown separately. [2] Private residential improvement does not include expenditures on rental, vacant, or seasonal properties.

Source: U.S. Census Bureau, "Construction Spending," <http://www.census.gov/construction/c30/c30index.html>, accessed June 2013.

Table 995. New Privately Owned Housing Units Started: 1960 to 2012

[In thousands of units (1,252 represents 1,252,000). For composition of regions, see map inside front cover.]

Year	Total	1 unit	Northeast	Midwest	South	West
1960	1,252	995	221	292	429	309
1970	1,434	813	218	294	612	311
1980	1,292	852	125	218	643	306
1990	1,193	895	131	253	479	329
1996	1,477	1,161	132	321	662	361
1997	1,474	1,134	137	304	670	363
1998	1,617	1,271	148	330	743	395
1999	1,641	1,303	156	347	746	392
2000	1,569	1,231	154	318	713	383
2001	1,603	1,273	149	330	732	391
2002	1,705	1,359	158	350	781	415
2003	1,848	1,499	163	374	839	472
2004	1,956	1,610	175	356	909	516
2005	2,068	1,716	190	357	996	525
2006	1,801	1,465	167	280	910	444
2007	1,355	1,046	143	210	681	321
2008	906	622	121	135	453	196
2009	554	445	62	97	278	117
2010	587	471	72	98	298	120
2011	609	431	68	101	308	133
2012	781	535	80	128	398	175

Source: U.S. Bureau of the Census, "New Residential Construction," <http://www.census.gov/construction/nrc/historical_data/>, accessed June 2013.

Table 996. Characteristics of New Privately Owned One-Family Houses Completed: 1990 to 2012

[Percent distribution, except total houses (966 represents 966,000). Data are percent distribution of characteristics for all houses completed (includes new houses completed, houses built for sale completed, contractor-built and owner-built houses completed, and houses completed for rent). Percents exclude houses for which characteristics specified were not reported]

Characteristic	1990	2000	2010	2012	Characteristic	1990	2000	2010	2012
Total houses (1,000)	966	1,242	496	483	Bedrooms	100	100	100	100
					2 or less	15	11	13	13
Construction type	100	100	100	100	3	57	54	52	46
Site built	(NA)	94	95	96	4 or more	29	35	35	41
Modular	(NA)	3	2	2	Bathrooms	100	100	100	100
Other	(NA)	3	2	2	1-1/2 or less	13	7	8	7
Exterior wall material	100	100	100	100	2	42	39	36	32
Brick	18	20	23	24	2-1/2 or more	27	34	32	31
Wood	39	14	8	6	3 baths or more	18	20	25	30
Stucco	18	17	17	19	Heating fuel	100	100	100	100
Vinyl siding [1]	(NA)	39	36	33	Gas	59	70	54	59
Aluminum siding	5	1	(NA)	(NA)	Electricity	33	27	43	39
Fiber cement	(NA)	(NA)	13	16	Oil	5	3	1	1
Other [1]	20	8	2	2	Other	3	1	2	2
Floor area	(NA)	100	100	100	Heating system	100	100	100	100
Under 1,400 sq. ft.	(NA)	14	13	11	Warm air furnace	65	71	56	58
1,400 to 1,799 sq. ft.	(NA)	22	19	17	Electric heat pump	23	23	38	38
1,800 to 2,399 sq. ft.	(NA)	29	27	26	Other	12	6	5	5
2,400 to 2,999 sq. ft.	(NA)	17	18	19	Central air-conditioning	100	100	100	100
3,000 to 3,999 sq. ft.	(NA)	13	15	18	With	76	85	88	89
4,000 or more	(NA)	5	7	8	Without	24	15	12	11
Average (sq. ft.)	2,080	2,266	2,392	2,505					
Median (sq. ft.)	1,905	2,057	2,169	2,306	Fireplaces	100	100	100	100
Number of stories	100	100	100	100	No fireplace	34	40	51	51
1	46	47	47	44	1 or more	66	59	49	49
2 or more	49	52	46	55					
Split level	4	1	1	1					
Foundation	100	100	100	100	Parking facilities	100	100	100	100
Full or partial basement	38	37	30	30	Garage	82	89	85	87
Slab	40	46	52	54	Carport	2	1	1	1
Crawl space	21	17	18	16	No garage or carport	16	11	13	11

NA Not available. [1] Prior to 2000, "other" includes vinyl siding.

Source: U.S. Census Bureau and U.S. Department of Housing and Urban Development, "Characteristics of New Housing," <http://www.census.gov/construction/chars/>, accessed June 2013.

Table 997. Housing Starts and Average Length of Time From Start to Completion of New Privately Owned One-Unit Residential Buildings: 1980 to 2012

[852 represents 852,000. For buildings started in permit issue places]

Year	Total [1]	Purpose of construction			Region [2]			
		Built for sale	Contractor built	Owner built	North-east	Mid-west	South	West
STARTS (1,000)								
1980.	852	526	149	164	87	142	428	196
1990.	895	529	196	147	104	193	371	226
1991.	840	490	198	138	99	191	353	197
1992.	1,030	618	224	168	112	236	439	244
1993.	1,126	716	225	162	116	251	498	261
1994.	1,198	763	245	169	123	268	522	286
1995.	1,076	712	199	133	102	234	485	256
1996.	1,161	774	218	144	112	254	524	271
1997.	1,134	784	189	131	111	238	507	278
1998.	1,271	882	209	144	122	273	574	303
1999.	1,302	912	208	142	126	289	580	308
2000.	1,231	871	195	128	118	260	556	297
2001.	1,273	919	186	129	111	269	590	303
2002.	1,359	999	198	125	118	277	628	336
2003.	1,499	1,120	205	127	116	309	686	388
2004.	1,611	1,240	198	130	128	306	743	433
2005.	1,716	1,358	197	129	138	306	831	441
2006.	1,465	1,121	189	119	118	235	757	356
2007.	1,046	760	151	104	93	171	540	242
2008.	622	408	107	74	63	102	324	133
2009.	445	297	83	51	44	76	232	93
2010.	471	306	83	55	52	79	247	93
2011.	431	287	74	47	41	74	229	86
2012.	535	373	82	47	46	92	283	114
COMPLETION (months)								
1980.	6.9	6.2	5.5	10.1	7.7	8.0	6.1	7.4
1990.	6.4	5.9	5.3	10.3	9.3	5.6	5.7	6.9
1991.	6.3	5.6	5.1	10.2	8.9	5.6	5.5	6.9
1992.	5.8	5.0	5.0	9.5	7.6	5.6	5.1	6.1
1993.	5.6	4.9	5.4	9.0	7.2	5.5	5.2	6.0
1994.	5.6	4.9	5.3	9.1	7.1	5.7	5.3	5.6
1995.	5.9	5.2	5.8	9.5	7.4	6.0	5.4	6.0
1996.	6.0	5.2	5.8	9.9	8.2	6.1	5.6	5.6
1997.	6.0	5.2	5.9	9.8	7.3	6.2	5.6	5.8
1998.	6.0	5.4	6.0	9.5	7.1	6.2	5.5	6.1
1999.	6.1	5.5	6.4	9.2	7.0	6.4	5.7	6.3
2000.	6.2	5.6	6.5	9.2	7.5	6.4	5.9	6.0
2001.	6.2	5.6	7.0	9.2	7.6	6.5	5.8	6.3
2002.	6.1	5.5	6.6	9.6	7.3	6.4	5.6	6.2
2003.	6.2	5.5	6.8	9.9	7.5	6.7	5.7	6.2
2004.	6.2	5.7	7.0	9.1	7.3	6.7	5.8	6.3
2005.	6.4	5.9	7.6	9.8	7.7	6.6	6.0	6.8
2006.	6.9	6.3	7.8	10.7	8.3	7.1	6.3	7.4
2007.	7.1	6.5	7.9	10.2	8.5	7.4	6.5	8.0
2008.	7.7	6.8	8.5	11.1	8.9	8.2	6.7	9.0
2009.	7.9	6.6	8.7	11.9	10.7	8.2	6.7	9.0
2010.	6.9	5.8	7.6	11.0	10.1	7.3	5.9	7.3
2011.	6.6	5.4	7.7	10.8	8.9	6.9	5.9	6.8
2012.	6.0	4.9	7.3	10.5	8.5	6.5	5.2	6.1

[1] Includes units built for rent not shown separately. [2] For composition of regions, see map, inside front cover.

Source: U.S. Census Bureau, "New Residential Construction," <http://www.census.gov/construction/nrc/>, accessed August 2013.

Table 998. Construction Materials—Producer Price Indexes: 2005 to 2012

[1982 = 100, except as noted. This index, more formally known as the special commodity grouping index for construction materials, covers materials incorporated as integral part of a building or normally installed during construction and not readily removable. Excludes consumer durables such as kitchen ranges, refrigerators, etc. This index is not the same as the stage-of-processing index of intermediate materials and components for construction. For discussion of producer price indexes, see text, Section 14]

Commodity	2005	2006	2007	2008	2009	2010	2011	2012
Construction materials	**169.6**	**180.2**	**183.2**	**196.4**	**189.2**	**194.5**	**201.1**	**205.8**
Architectural coatings	203.3	220.2	230.5	249.0	269.7	264.1	276.3	309.5
Plastic construction products	158.8	181.8	179.2	185.6	186.2	190.9	199.0	207.1
Softwood cut stock and dimension	205.1	203.7	201.1	201.4	200.2	206.0	202.5	194.1
Softwood lumber, not edge worked [1]	115.0	105.3	92.0	81.3	72.8	85.8	85.6	92.8
Softwood lumber, made from purchased lumber [1]	111.2	112.2	117.5	121.5	109.1	111.5	112.2	115.3
Hardwood cut stock and dimension	198.4	199.1	196.6	193.6	186.0	186.2	189.2	189.1
Hardwood flooring [2]	168.0	160.3	154.1	154.2	153.2	161.2	163.4	163.2
Millwork	197.2	201.8	201.4	204.8	205.4	207.0	210.1	216.5
Softwood veneer and plywood	223.5	190.5	197.8	193.1	171.9	197.1	185.8	218.6
Hardwood veneer and plywood [3]	(NA)	101.4	102.4	103.8	103.1	103.6	103.9	106.0
Prefabricated wood buildings and components [4]	206.1	213.4	216.0	221.8	219.5	215.6	216.2	224.0
Building paper and building board mill products	184.9	173.0	155.2	163.9	156.5	168.4	163.6	187.1
Pressure and soil pipe and fittings, cast iron	240.8	259.1	273.5	333.4	335.0	348.4	373.5	394.0
Hot rolled steel sheet and strip, incl. tin mill products [5]	125.4	139.9	138.1	188.3	121.2	150.7	161.6	149.9
Hot rolled steel bars, plates, and structural shapes [5]	159.8	170.7	187.5	227.6	171.0	192.9	223.0	213.3
Aluminum extruded and drawn pipe and tube [6]	102.2	108.1	107.1	106.0	88.4	98.1	110.9	103.2
Builders' hardware [7]	179.2	187.8	198.1	215.1	217.1	219.4	230.6	234.2
Plumbing fixtures and fittings	197.6	207.2	220.6	226.7	228.9	231.4	237.0	241.5
Heating equipment	179.9	185.7	195.5	208.8	219.1	221.5	227.6	235.3
Metal doors, sash, and trim	184.9	192.9	197.3	205.6	209.2	208.1	219.0	225.9
Sheet metal products	169.4	176.1	181.2	192.5	186.8	191.0	201.6	200.4
Fabricated structural metal bar joists and concrete reinforcing bars	163.0	170.0	177.2	195.5	184.1	176.1	179.9	183.0
Fabricated metal pipe, tube, and fittings [8]	(NA)	(NA)	(NA)	(NA)	(NA)	(NA)	(NA)	100.6
Residential electric lighting fixtures, except portable [9]	106.9	110.2	113.3	117.0	121.3	121.1	124.0	125.6
Elevators, escalators, and other lifts	123.5	126.0	129.3	134.7	134.9	133.8	135.6	138.0
Air purification equipment/industrial and commercial fans and blowers	170.9	176.3	182.0	190.0	191.7	192.2	199.8	204.0
Plumbing and heating valves (low pressure) [10]	182.2	218.9	242.1	246.1	252.3	249.5	262.1	272.4
Electric switches [11]	101.9	107.8	116.3	120.7	122.1	124.4	131.6	145.0
Wire connectors for electrical circuitry [11]	106.9	111.9	117.8	123.7	127.9	132.1	133.7	135.7
Current-carrying wiring devices not elsewhere classified [12]	(NA)	(NA)	101.5	103.8	104.4	105.2	108.4	110.0
Noncurrent-carrying electrical conduit and fittings [6, 13]	106.6	116.6	112.1	123.4	114.0	119.2	128.6	133.3
Other noncurrent-carrying wiring devices [14]	102.3	108.0	114.3	123.2	126.2	126.4	130.3	131.9
Carpets and rugs	145.3	153.9	155.7	159.0	166.1	167.5	173.8	177.4
Hard surface floor coverings	169.0	175.2	179.8	192.5	198.0	203.2	216.5	227.9
Float, sheet, and plate glass	96.0	97.8	96.6	100.2	95.4	88.2	86.7	83.9
Construction sand, gravel, and crushed stone	195.8	213.9	232.4	247.7	259.1	262.2	266.5	272.8
Cement, hydraulic	176.4	199.3	209.7	209.7	206.8	193.5	187.8	190.6
Concrete products	177.2	195.1	203.5	210.6	214.0	210.6	210.8	215.0
Clay construction products excluding refractories	165.4	176.8	178.7	180.1	179.5	179.4	176.1	173.6
Prepared asphalt and tar roofing and siding products	125.0	137.0	139.7	176.7	218.1	218.9	226.0	221.2
Roofing asphalts, pitches, coatings, and cement	155.0	177.4	169.3	234.0	217.8	227.5	258.7	277.8
Gypsum products	229.6	274.9	233.0	213.2	213.8	206.6	201.9	230.3
Insulation materials	142.2	149.9	145.3	141.7	144.1	146.6	155.9	164.7
Paving mixtures and blocks	156.9	200.5	218.9	272.4	269.0	279.4	296.2	316.5
Cut stone and stone products [4]	145.1	147.5	147.8	149.3	147.9	147.8	147.8	147.9

NA Not available. [1] December 2003 = 100. [2] June 1984 = 100. [3] December 2005 = 100. [4] June 1984 = 100. [5] June 1982 = 100. [6] December 2004 = 100. [7] Includes lock units, key blanks, door and window hardware, cabinet hardware, etc. [8] December 2011 = 100. [9] June 1998 = 100. [10] December 1982 = 100. [11] December 1999 = 100. [12] June 2006 = 100. [13] Includes plastic conduit and fittings. [14] Includes boxes, covers, bar hangers, etc.

Source: U.S. Bureau of Labor Statistics, "Producer Price Indexes," <http://www.bls.gov/ppi/data.htm>, accessed June 2013.

Table 999. Price Indexes of New One-Family Houses Sold by Region: 1970 to 2012

[2005 = 100. Based on kinds of homes sold in 2005. Includes value of the lot. For composition of regions, see map, inside front cover]

Year	Total	Northeast	Midwest	South	West
1970	14.9	13.4	17.9	18.2	10.2
1980	38.9	30.2	41.2	44.4	31.9
1990	55.7	58.0	58.6	60.6	46.2
2000	75.6	73.0	83.5	80.7	64.4
2001	77.9	76.7	84.4	82.8	67.1
2002	81.4	80.2	86.1	86.3	71.5
2003	86.0	84.3	90.6	89.4	78.2
2004	92.8	91.6	96.7	94.4	88.2
2005	100.0	100.0	100.0	100.0	100.0
2006	104.7	102.6	102.9	105.4	105.2
2007	104.9	101.5	102.8	107.5	102.6
2008	99.5	100.8	98.9	103.7	92.7
2009	95.1	97.1	96.0	101.1	84.8
2010	95.0	101.1	96.9	99.5	85.4
2011	94.3	100.0	97.8	99.6	83.1
2012	97.6	102.1	101.5	102.7	86.3

Source: U.S. Census Bureau, "Construction Price Indexes," <http://www.census.gov/construction/cpi/>, accessed June 2013.

Table 1000. New Privately Owned One-Family Houses Sold by Region and Type of Financing, 1980 to 2012, and by Sales-Price Group, 2012

[In thousands (545 represents 545,000). Based on a national probability sample of monthly interviews with builders or owners of one-family houses for which building permits have been issued or, for nonpermit areas, on which construction has started. For details, see source and Appendix III. For composition of regions, see map inside front cover]

Year and sales-price group	Total sold	Region				Financing type			
		Northeast	Midwest	South	West	Conventional [1]	FHA and VA	Rural-Housing Service [2]	Cash
1980............................	545	50	81	267	145	316	196	14	32
1985............................	688	112	82	323	171	414	208	11	64
1990............................	534	71	89	225	149	347	138	10	50
1995............................	667	55	125	300	187	499	129	9	39
2000............................	877	71	155	406	244	699	138	4	40
2004............................	1,203	83	210	562	348	1,053	105	6	46
2005............................	1,283	81	205	638	358	1,151	79	1	52
2006............................	1,051	63	161	559	267	949	63	1	38
2007............................	776	65	118	411	181	695	52	2	30
2008............................	485	35	70	266	114	358	63	(NA)	23
2009............................	375	31	54	202	87	234	124	(NA)	17
2010............................	323	31	45	173	74	189	116	(NA)	18
2011............................	306	21	45	168	72	190	96	(NA)	20
2012............................	368	29	47	195	97	234	110	(NA)	24
Under $200,000..........	120	4	17	80	17	64	47	(NA)	7
$200,000 to $299,999....	120	7	16	56	41	69	44	(NA)	7
$300,000 to $499,999....	96	11	10	47	29	71	18	(NA)	7
$500,000 and over........	32	6	4	12	10	28	2	(NA)	3

NA Not available. [1] Includes houses reporting other types of financing. [2] Prior to 2000, the Farmers Home Administration.

Source: U.S. Census Bureau and U.S. Department of Housing and Urban Development, "Characteristics of New Housing," <http://www.census.gov/construction/chars/>, accessed June 2013.

Table 1001. Median Sales Price of New Privately Owned One-Family Houses Sold by Region: 1980 to 2012

[In dollars. For definition of median, see Guide to Tabular Presentation. For composition of regions, see map inside front cover. Based on a national probability sample of monthly interviews with builders or owners of one-family houses selected from building permits and a canvassing of areas not requiring permits. For more details, see source]

Year	U.S.	Northeast	Midwest	South	West	Year	U.S.	Northeast	Midwest	South	West
1980.........	64,600	69,500	63,400	59,600	72,300	2006.........	246,500	346,000	213,500	208,200	337,700
1985.........	84,300	103,300	80,300	75,000	92,600	2007.........	247,900	320,200	208,600	217,700	330,900
1990.........	122,900	159,000	107,900	99,000	147,500	2008.........	232,100	343,600	198,900	203,700	294,800
1995.........	133,900	180,000	134,000	124,500	141,400	2009.........	216,700	302,500	189,200	194,800	263,700
2000.........	169,000	227,400	169,700	148,000	196,400	2010.........	221,800	329,900	197,700	196,800	259,300
2004.........	221,000	315,800	205,000	181,100	283,100	2011.........	227,200	322,800	203,300	211,400	256,000
2005.........	240,900	343,800	216,900	197,300	332,600	2012.........	245,200	368,800	230,600	227,000	270,000

Source: U.S. Census Bureau, "New Residential Sales," <http://www.census.gov/construction/nrs/>, accessed June 2013.

Table 1002. New Manufactured (Mobile) Homes Placed for Residential Use and Average Sales Price by Region: 1985 to 2012

[283.4 represents 283,400. A mobile home is a moveable dwelling, 8 feet or more wide and 40 feet or more long, designed to be towed on its own chassis, with transportation gear integral to the unit when it leaves the factory, and without need of permanent foundation. Excluded are travel trailers, motor homes, and modular housing. Data are based on a probability sample and subject to sampling variability; see source. For composition of regions, see map inside front cover]

Year	Units placed (1,000)					Average sales price (dollars)				
	Total	Northeast	Midwest	South	West	U.S.	Northeast	Midwest	South	West
1985...............	283.4	20.2	38.6	187.6	36.9	21,800	22,700	21,500	20,400	28,700
1990...............	195.4	18.8	37.7	108.4	30.6	27,800	30,000	27,000	24,500	39,300
1995...............	319.4	15.0	57.5	203.2	43.7	35,300	35,800	35,700	33,300	44,100
1999...............	338.3	14.1	53.6	227.2	43.5	43,300	44,000	44,400	41,900	49,600
2000...............	280.9	14.9	48.7	178.7	38.6	46,400	47,000	47,900	44,300	54,100
2001...............	196.2	12.2	37.6	116.4	30.0	48,900	50,000	49,100	46,500	58,000
2002...............	174.3	11.8	34.2	101.0	27.2	51,300	53,200	51,700	48,000	62,600
2003...............	139.8	11.2	25.2	77.2	26.1	54,900	57,300	55,100	50,500	67,700
2004...............	124.4	11.0	20.6	67.4	25.5	58,200	60,200	58,800	52,300	73,200
2005...............	122.9	9.2	17.1	68.1	28.5	62,600	67,000	60,600	55,700	79,900
2006...............	112.4	7.9	14.5	66.1	23.9	64,300	65,300	59,100	58,900	83,400
2007...............	94.8	7.0	10.8	59.4	17.7	65,400	66,100	64,900	59,900	85,500
2008...............	80.5	5.0	8.2	54.0	13.3	64,700	68,400	65,700	59,600	84,900
2009...............	54.5	3.5	5.3	37.8	7.9	63,100	61,600	65,400	59,300	81,500
2010...............	50.7	3.8	5.8	34.6	6.6	62,800	65,200	60,700	60,000	79,000
2011...............	47.6	3.3	6.3	31.5	6.5	60,500	62,700	60,800	58,400	70,600
2012...............	52.1	3.8	7.8	33.8	6.6	61,900	62,800	61,200	59,700	74,600

Source: U.S. Census Bureau, "Manufactured Housing at a Glance," <http://www.census.gov/construction/mhs/mhsindex.html>, accessed June 2013.

Table 1003. Existing One-Family Homes Sold and Price by Region: 1990 to 2012

[2,914 represents 2,914,000. Includes existing detached single-family homes and townhomes; excludes condos and co-ops. Based on data (adjusted and aggregated to regional and national totals) reported by participating real estate multiple listing services. For definition of median, see Guide to Tabular Presentation. See Table 1006 for data on condos and co-ops. For composition of regions, see map inside front cover]

Year	Homes sold (1,000)					Median sales price (dollars)				
	U.S.	North-east	Mid-west	South	West	U.S.	North-east	Mid-west	South	West
1990	2,914	513	804	1,008	589	97,300	146,200	76,700	86,300	141,200
1994	3,544	618	961	1,213	752	113,500	149,300	90,900	97,200	151,900
1995	3,519	615	940	1,212	752	117,000	146,500	96,500	99,200	153,600
1996	3,797	656	986	1,283	872	122,600	147,800	102,800	105,000	160,200
1997	3,964	683	1,004	1,356	921	129,000	152,400	108,900	111,300	169,000
1998	4,495	745	1,129	1,592	1,029	136,000	157,100	116,300	118,000	179,500
1999	4,649	728	1,145	1,704	1,072	141,200	160,700	121,600	122,100	189,400
2000	4,603	715	1,116	1,707	1,065	147,300	161,200	125,600	130,300	199,200
2001	4,735	710	1,154	1,795	1,076	156,600	169,400	132,300	139,600	211,700
2002	4,974	730	1,217	1,872	1,155	167,600	190,100	138,300	149,700	234,300
2003	5,446	770	1,323	2,073	1,280	180,200	220,300	143,700	159,700	254,700
2004	5,958	821	1,389	2,310	1,438	195,200	254,400	151,500	171,800	289,100
2005	6,180	838	1,411	2,457	1,474	219,000	281,600	168,300	181,100	340,300
2006	5,677	787	1,314	2,352	1,224	221,900	280,300	164,800	183,700	350,500
2007	4,398	587	1,091	1,819	901	217,900	288,100	161,400	178,800	342,500
2008	3,665	471	882	1,439	873	196,600	271,500	150,500	169,400	276,100
2009	3,870	480	918	1,460	1,012	172,100	243,200	142,900	155,000	215,400
2010	3,708	465	859	1,426	958	173,100	243,900	140,800	153,700	220,700
2011	3,787	449	863	1,471	1,004	166,200	237,500	135,800	149,300	204,500
2012	4,128	492	1,002	1,605	1,029	177,200	237,200	143,700	158,400	234,300

Source: NATIONAL ASSOCIATION OF REALTORS ®. See also <http://www.realtor.org/research-and-statistics>.

Table 1004. Median Sales Price of Existing One-Family Homes by Selected Metropolitan Area: 2005 and 2012

[In thousands of dollars (219.0 represents $219,000). Includes existing detached single-family homes and townhouses. Areas are metropolitan statistical areas defined by Office of Management and Budget as of 2004]

Metropolitan area	2005	2012	Metropolitan area	2005	2012
United States, total	**219.0**	**177.2**	Minneapolis-St. Paul-Bloomington, MN-WI	234.8	171.8
Allentown-Bethlehem-Easton, PA-NJ	243.4	189.6	New Haven-Milford, CT	279.1	220.6
Anaheim-Santa Ana-Irvine, CA	691.9	542.7	New Orleans-Metairie-Kenner, LA	159.2	156.2
Atlanta-Sandy Springs-Marietta, GA	167.2	101.4	New York-Northern New Jersey-Long Island, NY-NJ-PA	445.2	379.3
Atlantic City, NJ	256.1	220.4	New York-Wayne-White Plains, NY-NJ	495.2	444.9
Baltimore-Towson, MD	265.3	206.0	Oklahoma City, OK	114.7	145.0
Boston-Cambridge-Quincy, MA-NH	413.2	351.2	Omaha, NE-IA	136.2	139.2
Boulder, CO	348.4	383.7	Orlando, FL	243.6	134.0
Bridgeport-Stamford-Norwalk, CT	482.4	390.5	Philadelphia-Camden-Wilmington, PA-NJ-DE-MD	215.3	213.4
Charleston-North Charleston, SC	197.0	207.5	Phoenix-Mesa-Scottsdale, AZ	247.4	147.6
Chicago-Naperville-Joliet, IL	264.2	175.3	Portland-South Portland-Biddeford, ME	246.6	219.5
Cincinnati-Middletown, OH-KY-IN	145.9	128.3	Portland-Vancouver-Beaverton, OR-WA	244.9	232.9
Cleveland-Elyria-Mentor, OH	138.9	110.0	Providence-New Bedford-Fall River, RI-MA	293.4	214.7
Colorado Springs, CO	205.9	201.6	Raleigh-Cary, NC	170.5	188.5
Dallas-Fort Worth-Arlington, TX	147.6	159.3	Reno-Sparks, NV	349.9	169.7
Deltona-Daytona Beach-Ormond Beach, FL	192.5	109.5	Richmond, VA	201.9	(NA)
Denver-Aurora, CO	247.1	252.4	Riverside-San Bernardino-Ontario, CA	374.2	189.3
Des Moines, IA	145.5	158.6	Sacramento--Arden-Arcade--Roseville, CA	375.9	176.8
Eugene-Springfield, OR	197.6	(NA)	Saint Louis, MO-IL	141.0	123.9
Hartford-West Hartford-East Hartford, CT	253.3	222.8	Salem, OR	177.7	147.7
Honolulu, HI	590.0	628.8	Salt Lake City, UT	173.9	(NA)
Houston-Baytown-Sugar Land, TX	143.0	164.8	San Diego-Carlsbad-San Marcos, CA	604.3	385.5
Indianapolis, IN	123.8	129.6	San Francisco-Oakland-Fremont, CA	715.7	543.8
Las Vegas-Paradise, NV	304.7	134.1	San Jose-Sunnyvale-Santa Clara, CA	744.5	645.0
Little Rock-N. Little Rock, AR	119.0	138.2	Seattle-Tacoma-Bellevue, WA	316.8	300.4
Los Angeles-Long Beach-Santa Ana, CA	529.0	327.5	Tampa-St. Petersburg-Clearwater, FL	205.3	133.9
Louisville, KY-IN	135.8	137.1	Trenton-Ewing, NJ	261.1	247.6
Madison, WI	218.3	210.6	Tucson, AZ	231.6	149.9
Memphis, TN-MS-AR	141.2	117.2	Virginia Beach-Norfolk-Newport News, VA-NC	197.2	187.5
Miami-Fort Lauderdale-Miami Beach, FL	363.9	203.1	Washington-Arlington-Alexandria, DC-VA-MD-WV	425.8	352.0
Milwaukee-Waukesha-West Allis, WI	215.7	187.4			

NA Not available.

Source: NATIONAL ASSOCIATION OF REALTORS ®. See also <http://www.realtor.org/research-and-statistics>.

Table 1005. Existing Home Sales by State: 2000 to 2010

[In thousands (5,174 represents 5,174,000). Includes condos and co-ops as well as single-family homes. Data shown here reflect revisions from prior estimates]

State	2000	2005	2009	2010	State	2000	2005	2009	2010
United States	**5,174**	**7,076**	**4,334**	**4,182**	Missouri	110.2	142.9	106.0	94.6
Alabama	67.0	128.0	75.0	71.6	Montana	17.4	25.4	21.7	20.4
Alaska	14.3	24.6	22.3	22.4	Nebraska	32.3	41.2	34.7	31.9
Arizona	104.8	199.2	150.8	147.5	Nevada	44.6	98.0	104.9	97.7
Arkansas	45.0	75.3	61.8	59.9	New Hampshire	26.7	(NA)	19.6	18.9
California	573.5	601.1	510.4	468.4	New Jersey	161.1	184.4	115.3	110.0
Colorado	111.5	130.4	96.1	90.5	New Mexico	29.9	57.5	32.2	30.8
Connecticut	61.5	78.0	46.5	46.2	New York	273.3	319.8	253.9	242.0
Delaware	12.9	19.3	12.5	10.9	North Carolina	134.2	215.7	136.4	135.3
District of Columbia	10.6	12.1	8.4	8.7	North Dakota	10.8	15.8	13.0	12.5
Florida	393.6	547.1	357.7	396.5	Ohio	216.4	286.9	248.7	231.9
Georgia	143.6	242.1	176.6	162.7	Oklahoma	67.3	104.6	83.4	72.6
Hawaii	22.1	36.8	18.4	20.9	Oregon	62.6	100.5	55.0	55.2
Idaho	24.1	49.8	33.8	38.8	Pennsylvania	195.9	255.2	176.5	160.2
Illinois	246.8	315.3	184.5	176.7	Rhode Island	17.0	19.8	15.4	13.6
Indiana	111.0	138.3	104.7	97.7	South Carolina	64.3	114.6	71.2	70.7
Iowa	53.3	74.9	58.0	55.7	South Dakota	12.6	18.3	17.4	14.3
Kansas	52.6	77.9	56.4	51.8	Tennessee	100.4	170.9	107.8	101.3
Kentucky	66.0	96.2	73.8	70.3	Texas	381.8	532.5	443.3	420.5
Louisiana	66.8	87.7	54.8	51.6	Utah	35.5	51.7	31.1	28.5
Maine	27.6	33.3	23.1	22.8	Vermont	12.1	15.3	11.2	11.3
Maryland	100.5	135.5	72.5	74.5	Virginia	130.0	182.5	117.0	107.9
Massachusetts	112.3	148.6	107.8	105.3	Washington	112.4	167.8	82.3	83.7
Michigan	185.0	208.6	167.1	150.8	West Virginia	22.9	38.6	27.6	26.5
Minnesota	96.3	134.9	107.5	89.7	Wisconsin	91.6	122.8	84.6	77.7
Mississippi	38.7	61.2	41.9	42.1	Wyoming	9.6	14.3	9.0	8.5

NA Not available.

Source: NATIONAL ASSOCIATION OF REALTORS ®. The National Association of Realtors state sales series was discontinued in 2011. See also <http://www.realtor.org/research-and-statistics>.

Table 1006. Existing Apartment Condos and Co-Ops—Units Sold and Median Sales Price by Region: 1990 to 2012

[272 represents 272,000. Data shown here reflect revisions from prior estimates. For definition of median, see Guide to Tabular Presentation. For composition of regions, see map inside front cover]

Year	Units sold (1,000)					Median sales price (dollars)				
	U.S.	Northeast	Midwest	South	West	U.S.	Northeast	Midwest	South	West
1990	272	73	55	80	64	86,900	107,500	70,200	64,200	114,600
1995	333	108	66	96	63	89,000	92,500	90,700	67,800	114,800
2000	571	197	106	160	108	114,000	108,500	121,700	84,200	149,100
2005	896	331	177	245	143	223,900	245,100	189,100	187,300	283,800
2006	801	299	169	211	122	221,900	249,700	190,900	184,000	264,700
2007	624	126	100	236	162	226,300	256,100	195,200	185,100	263,300
2008	459	103	71	164	121	209,800	252,500	188,200	166,800	218,500
2009	464	105	58	180	121	175,600	232,800	157,100	132,700	162,100
2010	474	95	53	202	124	171,700	242,200	150,500	118,500	154,700
2011	477	89	52	210	126	165,100	237,700	129,000	107,800	176,000
2012	528	104	66	229	129	173,700	240,100	127,800	123,900	196,700

Source: NATIONAL ASSOCIATION OF REALTORS ®. See also <http://www.realtor.org/research-and-statistics>.

Table 1007. New Unfurnished Apartments Completed and Rented in 3 Months by Region: 2000 to 2011

[226.2 represents 226,200. Structures with five or more units, privately financed, nonsubsidized, unfurnished rental apartments. Based on sample and subject to sampling variability; see source for details. For composition of regions, see map, inside front cover]

Year and rent	Number (1,000)					Percent rented in 3 months				
	U.S.	North-east	Mid-west	South	West	U.S.	North-east	Mid-west	South	West
2000	226.2	14.8	39.5	125.9	45.9	72	85	76	67	77
2005	113.0	4.7	20.5	57.8	30.0	64	75	64	62	64
2009	163.0	10.0	17.2	93.3	42.4	51	56	74	49	44
2010	89.1	5.9	16.2	42.8	24.1	61	79	68	60	55
2011	**74.7**	**10.9**	**18.6**	**38.8**	**6.4**	**59**	**67**	**53**	**60**	**54**
Less than $950	22.0	1.4	7.6	12.4	0.6	68	100	63	67	77
$950 to $1,049	10.7	0.1	4.5	5.9	0.3	41	55	24	51	71
$1,050 to $1,149	13.2	0.1	1.7	10.8	0.5	62	100	93	56	81
$1,150 to $1,249	4.7	(Z)	1.6	2.3	0.8	39	(Z)	28	47	35
$1,250 to $1,349	5.4	1.2	0.7	2.0	0.7	53	46	38	63	50
$1,350 or more	19.4	8.1	2.5	5.4	3.4	62	64	69	62	49
Median asking rent	1,084	1,350	987	1,060	1,350	(X)	(X)	(X)	(X)	(X)

X Not applicable. Z Fewer than 50 units or less than one-half of 1 percent.

Source: U.S. Census Bureau, "Survey of Market Absorption," <http://www.census.gov/housing/soma/data/annual.html>, accessed May 2013.

Table 1008. Total Housing Inventory for the United States: 1990 to 2012

[In thousands (106,283 represents 106,283,000), except percent. Based on the Current Population Survey and the Housing Vacancy Survey and subject to sampling error; see source and Appendix III for details]

Item	1990	1995	2000	2005	2007	2008	2009	2010 [2]	2011	2012
All housing units...............	**106,283**	**112,655**	**119,628**	**123,925**	**127,958**	**130,113**	**130,159**	**130,599**	**132,292**	**132,778**
Vacant.......................	12,059	12,669	13,908	15,694	17,652	18,704	18,815	18,739	18,758	18,266
Year-round vacant..................	9,128	9,570	10,439	11,916	13,276	13,936	14,143	14,294	14,239	13,800
For rent.......................	2,662	2,946	3,024	3,721	3,848	4,056	4,393	4,284	4,087	3,824
For sale only....................	1,064	1,022	1,148	1,451	2,117	2,226	2,020	1,983	1,902	1,556
Rented or sold.................	660	810	856	1,060	1,130	1,075	993	908	984	987
Held off market..............	4,742	4,793	5,411	5,684	6,181	6,579	6,737	7,120	7,266	7,433
Occasional use.............	1,485	1,667	1,892	1,884	1,993	2,071	2,068	2,241	2,268	2,285
Usual residence elsewhere.....	1,068	801	1,037	1,128	1,139	1,170	1,187	1,254	1,197	1,262
Other.......................	2,189	2,325	2,482	2,672	3,049	3,338	3,482	3,625	3,801	3,886
Seasonal [1]......................	2,931	3,099	3,469	3,778	4,376	4,768	4,673	4,444	4,519	4,466
Total occupied......................	94,224	99,985	105,720	108,231	110,306	111,409	111,344	111,860	113,534	114,513
Owner........................	60,248	64,739	71,250	74,553	75,159	75,566	75,014	74,791	75,091	74,929
Renter........................	33,976	35,246	34,470	33,678	35,147	35,843	36,330	37,069	38,443	39,583
PERCENT DISTRIBUTION										
All housing units..................	100.0	100.0	100.0	100.0	100.0	100.0	100.0	100.0	100.0	100.0
Vacant........................	11.3	11.2	11.6	12.7	13.8	14.4	14.5	14.3	14.2	13.8
Total occupied..................	88.7	88.8	88.4	87.3	86.2	85.6	85.5	85.7	85.8	86.2
Owner........................	56.7	57.5	59.6	60.2	58.7	58.1	57.6	57.3	56.8	56.4
Renter........................	32.0	31.3	28.8	27.2	27.5	27.5	27.9	28.4	29.1	29.8

[1] Includes vacant seasonal mobile homes. [2] Revised based on 2010 housing unit controls.

Source: U.S. Census Bureau, "Housing Vacancies and Home Ownership," <http://www.census.gov/housing/hvs/>, accessed March 2013.

Table 1009. Occupied Housing Inventory by Age of Householder: 1990 to 2012

[In thousands (94,224 represents 94,224,000). Based on the Current Population Survey and Housing Vacancy Survey; see source for details]

Age of householder	1990	1995	2000	2005	2007	2008	2009	2010	2011	2012
Total..................	**94,224**	**99,986**	**105,719**	**108,231**	**110,306**	**111,409**	**111,344**	**111,860**	**113,534**	**114,512**
Under 25 years old.......	5,143	5,502	6,221	6,536	6,494	6,272	6,106	6,060	6,079	6,073
25 to 29 years old.........	9,508	8,662	8,482	8,790	9,170	9,094	9,076	9,041	9,062	8,778
30 to 34 years old.........	11,213	11,206	10,219	9,583	9,349	9,343	9,331	9,477	9,957	9,969
35 to 39 years old.........	10,914	11,993	11,834	10,526	10,499	10,550	10,185	9,794	9,667	9,565
40 to 44 years old.........	9,893	11,151	12,377	11,722	11,125	10,974	10,705	10,525	10,515	10,669
45 to 49 years old.........	8,038	10,080	11,164	11,780	12,007	11,968	11,861	11,690	11,449	10,968
50 to 54 years old.........	6,532	7,882	9,834	10,595	11,082	11,415	11,605	11,721	11,784	11,845
55 to 59 years old.........	6,182	6,355	7,602	9,504	10,013	10,217	10,226	10,437	10,848	11,289
60 to 64 years old.........	6,446	5,860	6,215	7,336	8,108	8,601	8,920	9,345	9,841	9,949
65 to 69 years old.........	6,407	6,088	5,816	5,900	6,330	6,642	6,822	7,038	7,306	7,984
70 to 74 years old.........	5,397	5,693	5,567	5,016	5,063	5,114	5,288	5,449	5,556	5,813
75 years old and over....	8,546	9,514	10,388	10,943	11,065	11,219	11,220	11,285	11,468	11,613

Source: U.S. Census Bureau, "Housing Vacancies and Home Ownership," <http://www.census.gov/housing/hvs/>, accessed March 2013.

Table 1010. Vacancy Rates for Housing Units—Characteristics: 2000 to 2012

[In percent. Rate is relationship between vacant housing for rent or for sale and the total rental and homeowner supply, which comprises occupied units, units rented or sold and awaiting occupancy, and vacant units available for rent or sale. Based on the Current Population/Housing Vacancy Survey; see source for details. For composition of regions, see map inside front cover]

Characteristic	Rental Units				Homeowner units			
	2000	2010	2011	2012	2000	2010	2011	2012
Total units..................	**8.0**	**10.2**	**9.5**	**8.7**	**1.6**	**2.6**	**2.5**	**2.0**
Northeast.....................	5.6	7.6	7.3	7.3	1.2	1.7	2.2	1.9
Midwest.......................	8.8	10.8	10.2	9.3	1.3	2.6	2.6	2.0
South.........................	10.5	12.7	12.0	10.8	1.9	2.8	2.6	2.2
West..........................	5.8	8.2	7.0	6.4	1.5	2.7	2.3	1.9
Units in structure:								
1 unit.......................	7.0	9.2	8.9	8.5	1.5	2.2	2.2	1.8
2 units or more.............	8.7	11.1	10.0	9.0	4.7	9.2	8.3	7.2
5 units or more.............	9.2	11.7	10.3	9.3	5.8	9.2	8.5	6.9
Units with—								
3 rooms or less.............	10.3	13.8	12.8	11.4	10.4	14.8	15.1	14.1
4 rooms.....................	8.2	10.5	9.7	8.7	2.9	5.7	5.3	4.3
5 rooms.....................	6.9	8.9	8.2	7.9	2.0	3.0	2.8	2.2
6 rooms or more.............	5.2	7.1	6.7	6.6	1.1	1.7	1.7	1.4

Source: U.S. Census Bureau, "Housing Vacancies and Home Ownership," <http://www.census.gov/housing/hvs/>, accessed March 2013.

Table 1011. Housing Units and Tenure—States: 2011

[132,316 represents 132,316,000. The American Community Survey universe includes the household population and the population living in institutions, college dormitories, and other group quarters. Based on a sample and subject to sampling variability; see Appendix III]

State	Housing units						Housing tenure			
	Total (1,000)	Occu- pied (1,000)	Vacant (1,000)				Owner-occupied units		Renter-occupied units	
			Total	For sea- sonal use [1]	For rent	For sale	Total (1,000)	Average house- hold size	Total (1,000)	Average house- hold size
United States.............	**132,316**	**114,992**	**17,325**	**5,334**	**3,305**	**1,857**	**74,264**	**2.71**	**40,727**	**2.52**
Alabama......................	2,182	1,845	338	83	51	35	1,289	2.57	555	2.47
Alaska.......................	311	257	54	32	6	2	162	2.79	95	2.57
Arizona......................	2,864	2,356	508	211	99	60	1,502	2.67	855	2.72
Arkansas....................	1,324	1,128	197	49	42	19	751	2.58	377	2.44
California...................	13,721	12,469	1,252	353	295	149	6,843	3.00	5,625	2.91
Colorado....................	2,225	1,975	249	109	43	30	1,272	2.60	704	2.41
Connecticut.................	1,494	1,352	142	33	38	16	911	2.68	441	2.31
Delaware....................	410	333	77	45	9	6	239	2.67	95	2.59
District of Columbia........	299	269	30	2	8	3	111	2.32	158	2.03
Florida......................	9,027	7,106	1,921	887	296	179	4,741	2.61	2,365	2.64
Georgia.....................	4,103	3,495	609	105	151	95	2,257	2.75	1,238	2.70
Hawaii.......................	522	449	74	32	18	6	255	3.16	194	2.72
Idaho........................	674	580	94	48	11	10	399	2.73	181	2.58
Illinois......................	5,296	4,737	559	49	124	92	3,190	2.74	1,547	2.47
Indiana......................	2,801	2,467	334	47	71	43	1,720	2.65	747	2.37
Iowa.........................	1,341	1,217	124	18	24	17	880	2.53	336	2.18
Kansas......................	1,238	1,102	136	16	32	19	747	2.64	355	2.31
Kentucky....................	1,933	1,672	261	49	46	28	1,151	2.60	521	2.40
Louisiana...................	1,979	1,702	277	51	52	23	1,131	2.68	571	2.49
Maine........................	726	552	174	125	13	9	392	2.46	160	2.05
Maryland....................	2,392	2,135	257	55	54	31	1,437	2.76	697	2.48
Massachusetts..............	2,819	2,532	287	122	48	23	1,573	2.69	959	2.21
Michigan....................	4,526	3,772	753	288	91	81	2,706	2.63	1,066	2.37
Minnesota...................	2,354	2,096	258	126	33	23	1,525	2.59	571	2.20
Mississippi..................	1,282	1,081	201	39	50	14	755	2.67	326	2.68
Missouri.....................	2,723	2,341	382	90	68	45	1,593	2.58	748	2.30
Montana.....................	489	404	85	40	11	7	275	2.49	130	2.21
Nebraska....................	801	724	77	14	17	10	484	2.59	239	2.24
Nevada......................	1,184	982	202	47	58	24	553	2.73	429	2.74
New Hampshire.............	618	516	101	69	7	5	369	2.61	147	2.15
New Jersey..................	3,563	3,168	395	135	84	40	2,060	2.83	1,107	2.53
New Mexico.................	908	767	141	56	20	10	523	2.73	244	2.51
New York....................	8,120	7,188	932	313	158	85	3,852	2.76	3,336	2.47
North Carolina..............	4,363	3,683	680	214	129	69	2,450	2.58	1,233	2.50
North Dakota................	321	283	37	13	5	2	186	2.50	97	1.99
Ohio.........................	5,134	4,539	595	57	130	74	3,040	2.57	1,499	2.29
Oklahoma...................	1,675	1,443	232	40	45	25	967	2.59	476	2.47
Oregon......................	1,684	1,517	167	55	32	20	922	2.53	595	2.44
Pennsylvania................	5,579	4,937	642	182	100	70	3,431	2.62	1,506	2.21
Rhode Island................	465	412	52	19	10	5	250	2.59	163	2.23
South Carolina..............	2,157	1,769	388	139	76	34	1,223	2.57	545	2.55
South Dakota................	367	323	43	15	8	4	221	2.53	102	2.25
Tennessee...................	2,829	2,467	362	73	77	40	1,660	2.58	807	2.43
Texas........................	10,099	8,850	1,249	249	339	129	5,568	2.94	3,282	2.65
Utah.........................	993	884	109	53	15	16	613	3.26	271	2.85
Vermont.....................	324	257	67	50	3	4	183	2.43	74	2.11
Virginia......................	3,388	2,991	397	99	82	40	2,014	2.67	977	2.53
Washington..................	2,908	2,633	275	89	59	33	1,654	2.61	979	2.42
West Virginia................	882	735	146	44	18	14	531	2.52	204	2.29
Wisconsin...................	2,635	2,275	359	186	40	36	1,544	2.57	731	2.19
Wyoming....................	266	223	43	19	7	3	157	2.56	65	2.33

[1] For seasonal, recreational, or occasional use.

Source: U.S. Census Bureau, 2011 American Community Survey, B25002, "Occupancy Status;" B25003, "Tenure;" B25004, "Vacancy Status;" and B25010, "Average Household Size of Units by Tenure," <http://factfinder2.census.gov/>, accessed February 2013.

Table 1012. Homeownership and Rental Vacancy Rates by State: 2012

[From the Current Population Survey/Housing Vacancy Survey, and includes the civilian noninstitutionalized population, people in noninstitutional group quarters, and military households off post or with families on post (must include 1 household member who is a civilian adult). Based on a sample and subject to sampling variability, see Appendix III]

State	Homeowner vacancy rate	Rental vacancy rate	State	Homeowner vacancy rate	Rental vacancy rate	State	Homeowner vacancy rate	Rental vacancy rate
U.S.	**2.0**	**8.7**	KS	2.0	8.0			
			KY	2.0	7.2	ND	1.4	6.9
AL	2.1	11.1	LA	1.9	12.6	OH	1.7	9.3
AK	1.4	4.7	ME	1.9	5.3	OK	2.3	9.5
AZ	2.4	11.4	MD	1.9	9.3	OR	2.2	4.9
AR	3.3	10.6	MA	1.6	6.5	PA	1.7	9.1
CA	1.6	5.2	MI	1.6	11.9	RI	1.8	6.8
CO	1.7	5.8	MN	1.7	5.9	SC	2.1	9.7
CT	1.7	7.4	MS	1.7	11.0	SD	1.0	8.9
DE	2.1	9.3	MO	2.4	10.4	TN	2.6	11.6
DC	1.9	7.8	MT	1.6	5.9	TX	2.0	10.4
FL	2.2	13.1	NE	1.3	7.5	UT	1.5	7.7
GA	2.7	9.9	NV	3.4	11.9	VT	1.6	4.2
HI	2.3	10.2	NH	2.0	7.2	VA	1.9	9.5
ID	2.2	7.1	NJ	2.1	11.2	WA	2.0	5.9
IL	2.8	9.5	NM	2.1	7.0	WV	2.0	8.1
IN	2.1	12.5	NY	2.0	5.5	WI	1.5	6.3
IA	2.3	6.3	NC	2.4	11.2	WY	1.4	5.4

Source: U.S. Census Bureau, "Housing Vacancies and Home Ownership," <http://www.census.gov/housing/hvs/>, accessed March 2013.

Table 1013. Homeownership and Rental Vacancy Rates by Metropolitan Area: 2012

[Based on the Current Population Survey/Housing Vacancy Survey; see headnote Table 1012. Subject to sampling error; see source and Appendix III for details]

Metropolitan area	Homeowner vacancy rate	Rental vacancy rate	Metropolitan area	Homeowner vacancy rate	Rental vacancy rate
Inside Metropolitan Areas	**2.0**	**8.6**	Milwaukee-Waukesha-West Allis, WI	1.2	8.2
			Minneapolis-St. Paul-Bloomington, MN-WI	1.2	5.3
Akron, OH	1.4	10.0	Nashville-Davidson-Murfreesboro, TN	1.6	8.4
Albany-Schenectady-Troy, NY	0.8	9.3	New Haven-Milford, CT	2.4	8.2
Albuquerque, NM	2.2	5.1	New Orleans-Metairie-Kenner, LA	2.9	15.9
Allentown-Bethlehem-Easton, PA-NJ	2.5	6.3	New York-Northern New Jersey-Long Island, NY	2.2	6.4
Atlanta-Sandy Springs-Marietta, GA	2.6	10.6	Oklahoma City, OK	2.5	10.2
Austin-Round Rock, TX	1.3	9.6	Omaha-Council Bluffs, NE-IA	1.2	9.5
Bakersfield, CA	4.0	3.2	Orlando, FL	2.2	18.5
Baltimore-Towson, MD	2.2	9.7	Oxnard-Thousand Oaks-Ventura, CA	0.5	2.3
Baton Rouge, LA	1.1	5.6	Philadelphia-Camden-Wilmington, PA	1.9	12.6
Birmingham-Hoover, AL	1.5	10.8	Phoenix-Mesa-Scottsdale, AZ	2.7	10.3
Boston-Cambridge-Quincy, MA-NH	1.3	5.9	Pittsburgh, PA	1.3	6.4
Bridgeport-Stamford-Norwalk, CT	1.5	6.7	Portland-Vancouver-Beaverton, OR-WA	1.9	5.0
Buffalo-Cheektowaga-Tonawanda, NY	2.6	10.6	Poughkeepsie-Newburg-Middletown, NJ	0.8	4.0
Charlotte-Gastonia-Concord, NC-SC	1.3	6.4	Providence-New Bedford-Fall River RI-MA	2.9	8.0
Chicago-Naperville-Joliet, IL	2.8	9.7	Raleigh-Cary, NC	1.9	8.8
Cincinnati-Middletown, OH-KY-IN	1.8	9.3	Richmond, VA	1.4	17.5
Cleveland-Elyria-Mentor, OH	1.9	10.1	Riverside-San Bernardino-Ontario, CA	3.3	9.0
Columbia, SC	2.2	5.7	Rochester, NY	0.5	4.3
Columbus, OH	2.3	8.3	Sacramento-Arden-Arcade-Roseville, CA	2.3	5.7
Dallas-Ft. Worth-Arlington, TX	2.1	9.2	St. Louis, MO-IL	3.1	12.6
Dayton, OH	2.1	16.5	Salt Lake City, UT	0.8	7.3
Denver-Aurora, CO	1.5	4.7	San Antonio, TX	2.7	9.0
Detroit-Warren-Livonia, MI	0.9	14.8	San Diego-Carlsbad-San Marcos, CA	1.4	7.1
El Paso, TX	0.1	8.2	San Francisco-Oakland-Fremont, CA	1.0	3.2
Fresno, CA	0.8	5.6	San Jose-Sunnyvale-Santa Clara, CA	0.9	3.8
Grand Rapids-Wyoming, MI	2.4	5.6	Seattle-Bellevue-Everett, WA	2.3	5.7
Greensboro-High Point, NC	3.5	7.6	Springfield, MA	0.4	7.0
Hartford-West Hartford-East Hartford, CT	1.5	7.4	Syracuse, NY	0.8	6.3
Honolulu, HI	1.3	6.3	Tampa-St. Petersburg-Clearwater, FL	2.0	13.0
Houston-Baytown-Sugar Land, TX	1.9	11.4	Toledo, OH	3.3	5.0
Indianapolis, IN	1.8	11.1	Tucson, AZ	1.4	14.3
Jacksonville, FL	1.9	11.7	Tulsa, OK	2.4	9.5
Kansas City, MO-KS	1.6	11.2	Virginia Beach-Norfolk-Newport News, VA	2.9	8.7
Las Vegas-Paradise, NV	3.4	12.8	Washington-Arlington-Alexandria, DC-VA-MD-WV	1.3	6.4
Los Angeles-Long Beach-Santa Ana, CA	1.3	4.9	Worcester, MA	2.4	3.7
Louisville, KY-IN	2.4	7.2			
Memphis, TN-AR-MS	2.4	14.9			
Miami-Fort Lauderdale-Miami Beach, FL	0.9	8.2			

Source: U.S. Census Bureau, "Housing Vacancies and Home Ownership," <http://www.census.gov/housing/hvs/>, accessed March 2013.

Table 1014. Housing Units—Characteristics by Tenure and Region: 2011

[In thousands of units (132,419 represents 132,419,000), except as indicated. As of Fall. Based on the American Housing Survey; see Appendix III. For composition of regions, see map, inside front cover]

Characteristic	Total housing units	Sea-sonal	Year-round units Occupied Total	Owner	Renter	North-east	Mid-west	South	West	Vacant
Total units.....................	**132,419**	**4,133**	**114,907**	**76,091**	**38,816**	**21,066**	**25,682**	**42,584**	**25,575**	**13,379**
Percent distribution..................	100.0	3.1	86.8	57.5	29.3	15.9	19.4	32.2	19.3	10.1
Units in structure:										
Single family detached................	82,974	2,549	73,761	62,662	11,099	11,399	18,103	28,331	15,928	6,664
Single family attached.................	7,768	226	6,744	4,090	2,654	1,841	1,073	2,286	1,545	798
2 to 4 units...........................	10,678	187	8,956	1,419	7,537	2,847	1,971	2,162	1,976	1,535
5 to 9 units...........................	6,354	122	5,410	583	4,827	1,007	1,045	1,881	1,477	822
10 to 19 units.........................	6,028	106	5,032	518	4,514	851	979	1,908	1,294	890
20 or more units......................	9,570	316	7,815	1,142	6,672	2,523	1,423	1,961	1,906	1,439
Manufactured/mobile home [1].........	9,049	626	7,190	5,678	1,512	597	1,088	4,056	1,449	1,233
Year structure built:										
Median year..........................	1974	1976	1974	1976	1972	1959	1970	1979	1977	1973
1980 or later..........................	51,120	1,720	44,518	32,026	12,494	4,665	8,370	20,673	10,812	4,880
1970 to 1979..........................	24,755	826	21,340	12,906	8,434	2,936	4,631	8,434	5,339	2,590
1960 to 1969..........................	15,405	472	13,596	8,679	4,917	2,552	2,997	4,893	3,154	1,338
1950 and earlier.......................	41,139	1,114	35,453	22,482	12,971	10,915	9,684	8,584	6,271	4,572
Stories in structure: [2]										
1 story...............................	42,491	1,694	36,540	26,072	10,468	1,195	4,149	20,373	10,823	4,257
2 stories..............................	44,175	1,078	38,677	24,933	13,744	6,226	10,415	12,244	9,792	4,420
3 stories..............................	27,793	449	24,940	16,538	8,401	8,993	8,582	4,668	2,697	2,405
4 or more stories......................	8,911	287	7,560	2,869	4,691	4,055	1,448	1,244	814	1,063
Foundation: [3]										
Full basement.........................	28,692	418	26,288	22,987	3,301	8,801	11,314	4,083	2,089	1,986
Partial building.......................	9,299	195	8,505	7,516	990	2,343	3,364	1,597	1,202	599
Crawlspace...........................	20,437	788	17,766	14,289	3,477	688	2,553	9,204	5,321	1,884
Concrete slab.........................	30,430	980	26,663	21,013	5,651	1,310	1,751	14,993	8,610	2,787
Equipment:										
Lacking complete facilities [4].........	5,875	595	2,010	450	1,560	507	404	493	606	3,271
With complete facilities [4]............	126,544	3,538	112,898	75,642	37,256	20,559	25,278	42,091	24,970	10,108
Kitchen sink..........................	131,020	3,851	114,581	75,954	38,628	20,995	25,621	42,500	25,465	12,587
Refrigerator..........................	128,658	3,648	114,567	75,916	38,651	20,993	25,603	42,478	25,493	10,443
Cooking stove or range...............	128,898	3,651	114,079	75,796	38,283	20,932	25,531	42,275	25,341	11,168
Dishwasher...........................	85,831	2,037	77,069	57,759	19,310	12,543	16,151	29,858	18,517	6,725
Washing machine......................	103,435	2,350	95,567	73,624	21,943	15,592	21,761	37,491	20,723	5,518
Clothes dryer.........................	100,642	2,276	93,052	72,397	20,655	14,814	21,521	36,407	20,311	5,314
Disposal in kitchen sink...............	65,976	1,487	58,958	40,715	18,243	5,664	13,354	21,154	18,785	5,531
Safety Equipment:										
Smoke detector:										
Working..............................	(NA)	(NA)	106,733	70,801	35,932	20,034	24,233	38,595	23,871	(NA)
Powered by:										
Electricity........................	(NA)	(NA)	7,167	4,506	2,661	1,471	1,400	2,716	1,581	(NA)
Batteries.........................	(NA)	(NA)	64,186	40,094	24,092	12,420	15,482	22,088	14,197	(NA)
Both..............................	(NA)	(NA)	34,053	25,763	8,290	5,897	7,127	13,293	7,736	(NA)
Not working..........................	(NA)	(NA)	6,067	3,824	2,242	743	1,020	3,021	1,282	(NA)
Not reported..........................	(NA)	(NA)	2,108	1466	641	289	429	967	422	(NA)
Batteries:										
Replaced in last 6 months...........	(NA)	(NA)	72,731	48,895	23,836	14,439	17,105	25,964	15,222	(NA)
Not replaced in last 6 months.......	(NA)	(NA)	23,343	16,190	7,154	3,543	5,007	8,674	6,118	(NA)
Not reported........................	(NA)	(NA)	2,165	772	1,393	335	496	742	592	(NA)
Fire extinguisher purchased or recharged............................	(NA)	(NA)	49,486	35,985	13,501	9,318	11,149	18,920	10,099	(NA)
Sprinkler system inside home..........	(NA)	(NA)	5,791	2,125	3,666	975	905	2,053	1,859	(NA)
Working carbon monoxide detector...	(NA)	(NA)	47,841	35,215	12,626	13,840	13,862	11,567	8,573	(NA)
Main heating equipment: [5]										
Warm-air furnace.....................	83,759	1,952	73,687	51,672	22,015	9,282	21,003	26,250	17,152	8,120
Steam or hot water system...........	13,965	197	12,624	7,365	5,259	9,227	1,983	592	822	1,144
Electric heat pump....................	16,006	659	13,523	9,782	3,741	419	768	10,803	1,534	1,823
Built-in electric units.................	5,863	309	4,865	1,999	2,867	1,304	1,085	761	1,716	688
Floor, wall, or pipeless furnace.......	5,182	132	4,505	1,808	2,697	360	361	1,101	2,683	544
Room heaters with flue...............	1,102	53	932	555	377	133	101	441	257	117
Room heaters without flue............	1,291	41	1,094	629	465	28	77	929	60	156
Portable electric heaters.............	1,685	111	1,431	720	711	21	66	960	383	144
Stoves................................	1,417	226	1,067	879	188	201	158	353	355	125
Fireplaces [6].........................	337	59	239	211	27	18	46	74	101	40
None..................................	1,052	281	468	215	253	3	1	59	405	302
Main cooling equipment:										
Central air conditioning...............	92,410	2,111	82,214	60,411	21,803	7,882	19,124	40,788	14,418	8,085
One or more room units...............	28,307	565	26,034	13,824	12,210	11,103	5,792	5,189	3,951	1,708
Source of water:										
Public system or private company....	(NA)	(NA)	101,397	64,327	37,070	17,855	21,804	37,733	24,004	(NA)
Well serving 1 to 5 units..............	(NA)	(NA)	13,131	11,515	1,615	3,120	3,832	4,670	1,509	(NA)
Means of sewage disposal:										
Public sewer..........................	(NA)	(NA)	92,636	56,649	35,986	16,891	20,762	32,397	22,585	(NA)
Septic tank chemical toilet............	(NA)	(NA)	22,229	19,418	2,811	4,164	4,917	10,160	2,988	(NA)

NA Not available. [1] Includes trailers. Includes width not reported, not shown separately. [2] Excludes mobile homes; includes basements and finished attics. [3] Limited to single-family units. [4] A complete kitchen includes sink, refrigerator, oven or burners. [5] Includes other items, not shown separately. [6] With and without inserts.

Source: U.S. Census Bureau, Current Housing Reports, Series H-150, *American Housing Survey for the United States: 2011*, October 2012. See also <http://www.census.gov/housing/ahs/>.

Table 1015. Housing Units by Units in Structure and State: 2011

[In percent, except as indicated (132,316 represents 132,316,000). The American Community Survey universe includes the household population and the population living in institutions, college dormitories, and other group quarters. Based on a sample and subject to sampling variability; see Appendix III]

| Characteristic | Total housing units (1,000) | Percent of units by units in structures— ||||||||| |
		1-unit detached	1-unit attached	2 units	3 or 4 units	5 or 9 units	10 or 19 units	20 or more units	Mobile homes	Boat, RV, van, etc.
U.S.	**132,316**	**61.5**	**5.8**	**3.8**	**4.5**	**4.8**	**4.5**	**8.7**	**6.5**	**0.1**
AL	2,182	68.5	1.7	2.2	3.0	4.1	3.1	3.4	13.9	0.1
AK	311	62.6	7.0	4.9	7.5	4.7	3.4	4.3	5.4	0.1
AZ	2,864	63.2	5.2	1.5	3.5	4.3	4.8	6.8	10.4	0.4
AR	1,324	69.2	1.7	3.1	3.2	3.0	3.4	3.0	13.3	0.2
CA	13,721	58.0	7.0	2.5	5.5	6.1	5.3	11.6	3.8	0.1
CO	2,225	62.7	6.8	1.9	3.2	5.0	6.0	10.4	4.0	0.1
CT	1,494	59.2	5.3	8.0	9.1	5.6	3.8	8.2	0.9	(Z)
DE	410	58.3	15.2	1.6	2.7	3.4	5.5	4.4	8.9	(Z)
DC	299	12.2	26.1	2.7	6.9	5.8	11.7	34.4	(Z)	0.1
FL	9,027	54.1	6.3	2.2	3.8	4.9	6.0	13.4	9.1	0.1
GA	4,103	66.2	3.7	2.3	3.1	5.1	4.8	5.4	9.4	0.1
HI	522	53.8	8.9	3.0	4.1	6.1	4.9	19.1	0.2	0.1
ID	674	72.5	2.9	2.6	5.2	3.0	1.7	3.3	8.5	0.2
IL	5,296	58.4	5.9	5.7	7.1	6.0	3.9	10.4	2.6	(Z)
IN	2,801	72.7	3.5	2.8	3.7	4.4	3.9	3.9	5.1	(Z)
IA	1,341	73.8	3.6	2.4	3.6	3.7	3.9	5.1	3.9	(Z)
KS	1,238	72.2	4.7	2.7	3.5	3.9	3.6	4.5	4.9	(Z)
KY	1,933	66.7	2.3	3.2	4.3	4.4	3.1	3.2	12.7	(Z)
LA	1,979	64.3	3.4	3.8	4.3	3.2	3.1	4.1	13.8	0.1
ME	726	69.2	2.2	5.2	5.4	3.7	1.9	3.2	9.3	(Z)
MD	2,392	51.4	21.3	1.5	2.1	5.1	8.5	8.5	1.7	(Z)
MA	2,819	51.9	4.9	10.6	10.9	6.0	4.4	10.2	0.9	(Z)
MI	4,526	71.8	4.5	2.6	2.6	4.2	3.4	5.2	5.6	(Z)
MN	2,354	67.4	7.4	2.3	2.1	2.2	3.5	11.5	3.6	(Z)
MS	1,282	69.5	1.2	2.2	3.0	4.2	2.3	2.1	15.3	0.1
MO	2,723	70.0	3.4	3.5	4.7	3.9	3.4	4.6	6.3	0.1
MT	489	69.6	3.2	3.6	4.2	2.8	2.2	3.3	10.9	0.2
NE	801	72.0	4.3	2.0	2.5	3.7	5.0	6.9	3.7	(Z)
NV	1,184	58.0	4.7	1.3	6.4	9.2	5.7	8.5	6.2	0.1
NH	618	63.8	5.1	5.9	5.9	4.4	3.0	6.1	5.7	(Z)
NJ	3,563	53.5	9.3	9.6	6.5	4.7	4.9	10.5	1.0	(Z)
NM	908	63.6	3.7	2.1	3.6	3.0	2.7	4.0	17.2	0.2
NY	8,120	41.9	4.9	10.7	7.5	5.3	4.0	23.2	2.5	(Z)
NC	4,363	65.4	3.5	2.4	2.8	4.4	3.9	3.9	13.7	(Z)
ND	321	61.7	5.5	2.3	3.3	3.6	5.4	10.2	7.9	0.1
OH	5,134	68.1	4.6	4.3	4.6	4.7	4.0	5.5	4.0	(Z)
OK	1,675	72.9	2.2	2.0	2.3	3.7	3.5	3.4	9.8	0.2
OR	1,684	64.2	4.3	2.8	4.1	4.4	3.7	8.2	8.0	0.3
PA	5,579	56.7	18.4	4.6	4.2	3.5	2.5	5.8	4.2	(Z)
RI	465	54.2	3.7	11.9	12.3	5.3	3.6	8.0	1.0	(Z)
SC	2,157	62.4	2.6	2.2	2.9	4.5	3.5	4.9	16.9	(Z)
SD	367	68.1	3.9	1.7	3.4	3.8	4.3	6.3	8.5	0.1
TN	2,829	68.3	3.2	2.9	3.1	4.5	3.7	4.2	10.1	0.1
TX	10,099	65.1	2.6	2.0	3.3	4.9	6.2	8.1	7.6	0.2
UT	993	68.1	6.0	3.3	4.5	3.4	4.8	6.0	3.8	0.1
VT	324	66.8	3.2	6.6	6.2	4.5	2.0	3.6	6.9	(Z)
VA	3,388	62.3	10.5	1.6	2.8	4.5	5.7	7.1	5.5	(Z)
WA	2,908	63.3	3.6	2.8	3.8	4.8	5.0	9.6	6.9	0.2
WV	882	70.6	2.0	2.2	3.2	2.9	1.6	2.5	15.0	(Z)
WI	2,635	66.7	4.3	6.5	3.8	4.6	3.4	6.8	3.8	(Z)
WY	266	67.2	3.6	2.4	4.3	3.4	2.1	3.1	13.7	0.1

Z Less than .05 percent.

Source: U.S. Census Bureau, 2011 American Community Survey, Table B25024, "Units in Structure," <http://factfinder2.census.gov/>, accessed April 2013.

Table 1016. Housing Units—Size of Units and Lot: 2011

[In thousands (132,419 represents 132,419,000), except as indicated. As of Fall. Based on the American Housing Survey; see Appendix III. For composition of regions, see map inside front cover]

| Item | Total housing units | Sea-sonal | Year-round units Occupied | | | | | | | Vacant |
			Total	Owner	Renter	North-east	Mid-west	South	West	
Total units.............................	**132,419**	**4,133**	**114,907**	**76,091**	**38,816**	**21,066**	**25,682**	**42,584**	**25,575**	**13,379**
Rooms:										
1 room................................	601	95	391	18	374	131	62	67	131	115
2 rooms...............................	1,404	148	952	98	854	325	126	187	314	305
3 rooms...............................	11,433	584	9,107	1,033	8,074	2,341	1,816	2,582	2,368	1,742
4 rooms...............................	23,636	1,238	18,780	6,319	12,461	3,445	3,992	6,754	4,589	3,619
5 rooms...............................	30,440	1,020	25,921	17,101	8,820	3,793	5,777	10,724	5,627	3,499
6 rooms...............................	27,779	514	24,966	19,910	5,056	4,439	5,495	9,892	5,140	2,298
7 rooms...............................	17,868	264	16,613	14,705	1,908	3,075	4,094	6,006	3,439	990
8 rooms or more......................	19,257	269	18,177	16,907	1,270	3,519	4,321	6,372	3,968	810
Complete bathrooms:										
No bathrooms.........................	1,808	465	494	190	304	125	88	197	84	849
1 bathroom...........................	46,800	1,513	39,268	15,118	24,150	9,763	9,632	11,809	8,064	6,018
1 and one-half bathrooms.............	16,666	323	15,066	11,232	3,834	3,712	4,781	4,034	2,539	1,277
2 or more bathrooms..................	67,145	1,832	60,079	49,551	10,528	7,465	11,181	26,544	14,888	5,235
Square footage of unit:										
Single detached and mobile homes................................	92,023	3,175	80,951	68,340	12,611	11,996	19,191	32,387	17,377	7,897
Less than 500.........................	973	181	618	357	262	102	93	279	144	174
500 to 749............................	2,678	429	1,818	1,079	739	258	409	817	334	432
750 to 999............................	6,529	485	5,150	3,573	1,577	655	1,356	2,143	996	894
1,000 to 1,499........................	20,919	708	18,255	14,546	3,709	2,114	4,363	7,581	4,197	1,957
1,500 to 1,999........................	20,560	451	18,470	15,987	2,484	2,448	3,966	7,683	4,373	1,638
2,000 to 2,499........................	14,343	262	13,179	11,951	1,227	2,036	3,210	5,131	2,803	902
2,500 to 2,999........................	7,553	147	7,021	6,546	475	1,171	1,622	2,776	1,452	385
3,000 to 3,999........................	7,225	113	6,735	6,405	330	1,185	1,739	2,473	1,338	377
4,000 or more........................	4,479	135	4,034	3,789	245	783	980	1,540	731	310
Other [1].............................	6,762	264	5,671	4,108	1,563	1,244	1,453	1,964	1,009	827
Median square footage................	1,700	1,200	1,800	1,800	1,301	1,900	1,800	1,715	1,704	1,500
Lot size:										
Single detached and attached units and mobile homes [2]...............	96,386	3,189	84,896	70,218	14,677	13,263	19,606	33,882	18,145	8,301
Less than one-eighth acre...........	15,638	494	13,354	9,740	3,614	2,379	2,834	4,159	3,982	1,790
One-eighth to one-quarter acre......	25,011	779	21,949	17,560	4,389	2,531	5,120	7,548	6,750	2,282
One-quarter to one-half acre........	17,705	438	15,947	13,795	2,151	2,400	4,087	6,344	3,116	1,319
One-half up to one acre..............	11,321	327	10,213	8,826	1,387	1,976	2,025	4,903	1,309	781
1 up to 5 acres.......................	19,076	763	16,835	14,402	2,433	3,016	3,551	8,244	2,024	1,477
5 up to 10 acres......................	3,037	99	2,719	2,461	259	367	759	1,113	480	218
10 acres or more.....................	4,599	288	3,877	3,433	444	594	1,229	1,571	484	433
Median acreage.......................	0.25	0.32	0.26	0.30	0.19	0.32	0.27	0.34	0.18	0.25

[1] Represents units not reported or size unknown. [2] Does not include cooperatives or condominiums.

Source: U.S. Census Bureau, Current Housing Reports, Series H-150, *American Housing Survey for the United States: 2011*, October 2012. See also <http://www.census.gov/housing/ahs/>.

Table 1017. Occupied Housing Units—Tenure by Race of Householder: 1991 to 2011

[In thousands (93,147 represents 93,147,000), except percent. As of Fall. Based on the American Housing Survey; see Appendix III]

Race of householder and tenure	1991	1995	2001	2003 [1]	2005	2007	2009	2011
ALL RACES [2]								
Occupied units, total.....................	**93,147**	**97,693**	**106,261**	**105,842**	**108,871**	**110,692**	**111,806**	**114,907**
Owner-occupied.........................	59,796	63,544	72,265	72,238	74,931	75,647	76,428	76,091
Percent of occupied...................	64.2	65.0	68.0	68.3	68.8	68.3	68.4	66.2
Renter-occupied.........................	33,351	34,150	33,996	33,604	33,940	35,045	35,378	38,816
WHITE [3]								
Occupied units, total.....................	**79,140**	**81,611**	**85,292**	**87,483**	**89,449**	**90,413**	**91,137**	**92,820**
Owner-occupied.........................	53,749	56,507	62,465	63,126	65,023	65,554	65,935	65,357
Percent of occupied...................	67.9	69.2	73.2	72.2	72.7	72.5	72.3	70.4
Renter-occupied.........................	25,391	25,104	22,826	24,357	24,426	24,859	25,202	27,463
BLACK [3]								
Occupied units, total.....................	**10,832**	**11,773**	**13,292**	**13,004**	**13,447**	**13,856**	**13,993**	**14,694**
Owner-occupied.........................	4,635	5,137	6,318	6,193	6,471	6,464	6,547	6,662
Percent of occupied...................	42.8	43.6	47.5	47.6	48.1	46.7	46.8	45.3
Renter-occupied.........................	6,197	6,637	6,974	6,811	6,975	7,392	7,446	8,033
HISPANIC ORIGIN [4]								
Occupied units, total.....................	**6,239**	**7,757**	**9,814**	**11,038**	**11,651**	**12,609**	**12,739**	**13,841**
Owner-occupied.........................	2,423	3,245	4,731	5,106	5,752	6,364	6,439	6,530
Percent of occupied...................	38.8	41.8	48.2	46.3	49.4	50.5	50.5	47.2
Renter-occupied.........................	3,816	4,512	5,083	5,931	5,899	6,244	6,300	7,311

[1] Based on 2000 census controls. [2] Includes other races not shown separately. [3] The 2003 American Housing Survey (AHS) allowed respondents to choose more than one race. Beginning in 2003, data represent householders who selected this race group only and exclude householders reporting more than one race. The AHS in prior years only allowed respondents to report one race group. See also comments on race in the text for Section 1 and the below cited source. [4] Persons of Hispanic origin may be of any race.

Source: U.S. Census Bureau, Current Housing Reports, Series H-150, *American Housing Survey for the United States: 2011*, October 2012. See also <http://www.census.gov/housing/ahs/>.

Table 1018. Homeownership Rates by Age of Householder and Household Type: 1990 to 2012

[In percent. Represents the proportion of owner households to the total number of occupied households. Based on the Current Population Survey/Housing Vacancy Survey; see headnote, Table 1012, source, and Appendix III for details]

Age of householder and household type	1990	1995	2000	2005	2007	2008	2009	2010	2011	2012
United States	**63.9**	**64.7**	**67.4**	**68.9**	**68.1**	**67.8**	**67.4**	**66.9**	**66.1**	**65.4**
AGE OF HOUSEHOLDER										
Less than 25 years old	15.7	15.9	21.7	25.7	24.8	23.6	23.3	22.8	22.6	21.7
25 to 29 years old	35.2	34.4	38.1	40.9	40.6	40.0	37.7	36.8	34.6	34.3
30 to 34 years old	51.8	53.1	54.6	56.8	54.4	53.5	52.5	51.6	49.8	47.9
35 to 39 years old	63.0	62.1	65.0	66.6	65.0	64.6	63.4	61.9	59.8	56.9
40 to 44 years old	69.8	68.6	70.6	71.7	70.4	69.4	68.7	67.9	66.9	65.5
45 to 49 years old	73.9	73.7	74.7	75.0	74.0	73.6	72.3	72.0	71.0	69.9
50 to 54 years old	76.8	77.0	78.5	78.3	76.9	76.4	76.5	75.0	74.4	73.4
55 to 59 years old	78.8	78.8	80.4	80.6	79.9	79.4	78.6	77.7	77.3	76.2
60 to 64 years old	79.8	80.3	80.3	81.9	81.5	80.9	80.6	80.4	79.8	78.6
65 to 69 years old	80.0	81.0	83.0	82.8	81.7	81.6	82.0	81.6	81.7	81.1
70 to 74 years old	78.4	80.9	82.6	82.9	82.4	81.7	81.9	82.4	83.3	83.5
75 years old and over	72.3	74.6	77.7	78.4	78.7	78.6	78.9	78.9	79.3	80.0
Less than 35 years old	38.5	38.6	40.8	43.0	41.7	41.0	39.7	39.1	37.7	36.7
35 to 44 years old	66.3	65.2	67.9	69.3	67.8	67.0	66.2	65.0	63.5	61.4
45 to 54 years old	75.2	75.2	76.6	76.6	75.4	75.0	74.4	73.5	72.7	71.7
55 to 64 years old	79.3	79.5	80.3	81.2	80.6	80.1	79.5	79.0	78.5	77.3
65 years and over	76.3	78.1	80.4	80.6	80.4	80.1	80.5	80.5	80.9	81.1
TYPE OF HOUSEHOLD										
Family households:										
Married-couple families	78.1	79.6	82.4	84.2	83.8	83.4	82.8	82.1	81.5	80.8
Male householder, no spouse present	55.2	55.3	57.5	59.1	57.4	57.6	56.9	56.9	55.6	55.9
Female householder, no spouse present	44.0	45.1	49.1	51.0	49.9	49.5	49.0	48.6	48.1	46.7
Nonfamily households:										
One-person	49.0	50.5	53.6	55.6	55.2	55.0	55.1	55.3	55.0	54.5
Male householder	42.4	43.8	47.4	50.3	50.2	50.6	50.9	51.3	50.6	49.8
Female householder	53.6	55.4	58.1	59.6	59.1	58.6	58.6	58.6	58.5	58.3
Other:										
Male householder	31.7	34.2	38.0	41.7	40.0	41.3	40.2	40.7	39.5	39.8
Female householder	32.5	33.0	40.6	44.7	42.9	42.5	42.5	41.9	43.1	41.0

Source: U.S. Census Bureau, "Housing Vacancies and Home Ownership," <http://www.census.gov/housing/hvs/>, accessed March 2013.

Table 1019. Homeownership Rates by State: 1990 to 2012

[In percent. See headnote, Table 1012]

State	1990	2000	2005	2010	2011	2012	State	1990	2000	2005	2010	2011	2012
United States	**63.9**	**67.4**	**68.9**	**66.9**	**66.1**	**65.4**	Missouri	64.0	74.2	72.3	71.2	71.1	70.8
Alabama	68.4	73.2	76.6	73.2	72.9	71.9	Montana	69.1	70.2	70.4	68.1	68.4	67.8
Alaska	58.4	66.4	66.0	65.7	64.4	63.7	Nebraska	67.3	70.2	70.2	70.4	68.9	69.3
Arizona	64.5	68.0	71.1	66.6	66.0	65.3	Nevada	55.8	64.0	63.4	59.7	56.2	55.7
Arkansas	67.8	68.9	69.2	67.9	67.6	66.0	New Hampshire	65.0	69.2	74.0	74.9	74.1	74.8
California	53.8	57.1	59.7	56.1	55.3	54.5	New Jersey	65.0	66.2	70.1	66.5	66.4	66.6
Colorado	59.0	68.3	71.0	68.5	65.9	65.3	New Mexico	68.6	73.7	71.4	68.6	69.1	66.8
Connecticut	67.9	70.0	70.5	70.8	70.6	68.8	New York	53.3	53.4	55.9	54.5	53.6	53.6
Delaware	67.7	72.0	75.8	74.7	74.2	73.4	North Carolina	69.0	71.1	70.9	69.5	68.3	67.2
Dist. of Columbia	36.4	41.9	45.8	45.6	44.8	45.0	North Dakota	67.2	70.7	68.5	67.1	68.3	66.2
Florida	65.1	68.4	72.4	69.3	69.0	67.0	Ohio	68.7	71.3	73.3	69.7	68.9	67.9
Georgia	64.3	69.8	67.9	67.1	66.2	64.3	Oklahoma	70.3	72.7	72.9	69.2	69.4	68.8
Hawaii	55.5	55.2	59.8	56.1	55.4	57.2	Oregon	64.4	65.3	68.2	66.3	66.4	66.1
Idaho	69.4	70.5	74.2	72.4	72.4	73.0	Pennsylvania	73.8	74.7	73.3	72.2	71.1	71.0
Illinois	63.0	67.9	70.9	68.8	68.4	66.8	Rhode Island	58.5	61.5	63.1	62.8	63.4	62.1
Indiana	67.0	74.9	75.0	71.2	72.1	72.1	South Carolina	71.4	76.5	73.9	74.8	74.2	71.5
Iowa	70.7	75.2	73.9	71.1	71.2	70.2	South Dakota	66.2	71.2	68.4	70.6	69.3	69.2
Kansas	69.0	69.3	69.5	67.4	65.4	63.2	Tennessee	68.3	70.9	72.4	71.0	69.3	67.9
Kentucky	65.8	73.4	71.6	70.3	69.1	68.7	Texas	59.7	63.8	65.9	65.3	64.3	64.3
Louisiana	67.8	68.1	72.5	70.4	70.1	68.7	Utah	70.1	72.7	73.9	72.5	71.4	71.1
Maine	74.2	76.5	73.9	73.8	73.9	74.1	Vermont	72.6	68.7	74.2	73.6	74.6	73.4
Maryland	64.9	69.9	71.2	68.9	69.7	68.5	Virginia	69.8	73.9	71.2	68.7	67.9	67.8
Massachusetts	58.6	59.9	63.4	65.3	65.3	65.8	Washington	61.8	63.6	67.6	64.4	64.2	63.5
Michigan	72.3	77.2	76.4	74.5	74.1	74.8	West Virginia	72.0	75.9	81.3	79.0	78.7	75.8
Minnesota	68.0	76.1	76.5	72.6	71.3	72.0	Wisconsin	68.3	71.8	71.1	71.0	68.5	67.5
Mississippi	69.4	75.2	78.8	74.8	74.8	74.2	Wyoming	68.9	71.0	72.8	73.4	71.1	70.3

Source: U.S. Census Bureau, "Housing Vacancies and Home Ownership," <http://www.census.gov/housing/hvs/>, accessed March 2013.

Table 1020. Occupied Housing Units—Costs by Region: 2011

[76,091 represents 76,091,000. As of Fall. See headnote, Table 1021, for an explanation of housing costs. Based on the American Housing Survey; see Appendix III. For composition of regions, see map inside front cover]

Category	Number (1,000)					Percent distribution				
	Total units	North-east	Mid-west	South	West	Total units	North-east	Mid-west	South	West
OWNER-OCCUPIED UNITS										
Total....................................	76,091	13,480	18,032	29,119	15,460	100.0	100.0	100.0	100.0	100.0
Monthly housing costs:										
Less than $200.......................	1,879	116	401	1,039	323	2.5	0.9	2.2	3.6	2.1
$200 to $299..........................	4,463	276	1,017	2,388	782	5.9	2.0	5.6	8.2	5.1
$300 to $399..........................	5,888	536	1,593	2,797	962	7.7	4.0	8.8	9.6	6.2
$400 to $499..........................	5,180	719	1,503	2,082	876	6.8	5.3	8.3	7.1	5.7
$500 to $699..........................	8,890	1,575	2,466	3,410	1,438	11.7	11.7	13.7	11.7	9.3
$700 to $999..........................	11,400	1,982	3,082	4,699	1,637	15.0	14.7	17.1	16.1	10.6
$1,000 to $1,499......................	15,706	2,632	4,193	5,829	3,053	20.6	19.5	23.3	20.0	19.7
$1,500 to $2,499......................	14,997	3,459	2,948	4,809	3,782	19.7	25.7	16.3	16.5	24.5
$2,500 or more........................	7,690	2,187	831	2,065	2,607	10.1	16.2	4.6	7.1	16.9
Median (dol.)[1]......................	1,008	1,282	897	874	1,283	(X)	(X)	(X)	(X)	(X)
RENTER-OCCUPIED UNITS										
Total....................................	38,816	7,585	7,650	13,465	10,115	100.0	100.0	100.0	100.0	100.0
Monthly housing costs:										
Less than $200.......................	1,019	192	257	372	199	2.6	2.5	3.4	2.8	2.0
$200 to $299..........................	1,394	396	309	382	307	3.6	5.2	4.0	2.8	3.0
$300 to $399..........................	1,366	336	329	447	253	3.5	4.4	4.3	3.3	2.5
$400 to $499..........................	2,003	312	563	766	361	5.2	4.1	7.4	5.7	3.6
$500 to $699..........................	6,778	922	1,928	2,676	1,253	17.5	12.2	25.2	19.9	12.4
$700 to $999..........................	10,688	1,746	2,359	3,935	2,649	27.5	23.0	30.8	29.2	26.2
$1,000 to $1,499......................	8,787	2,074	1,129	2,787	2,796	22.6	27.3	14.8	20.7	27.6
$1,500 to $2,499......................	3,798	1,031	285	903	1,580	9.8	13.6	3.7	6.7	15.6
$2,500 or more........................	713	228	27	152	307	1.8	3.0	0.4	1.1	3.0
No cash rent..........................	2,271	351	463	1,047	409	5.9	4.6	6.1	7.8	4.0
Median (dol.)[1]......................	845	941	718	800	981	(X)	(X)	(X)	(X)	(X)

X Not applicable. [1] For explanation of median, see Guide to Tabular Presentation.

Source: U.S. Census Bureau, Current Housing Reports, Series H-150, *American Housing Survey for the United States: 2011*, October 2012. See also <http://www.census.gov/housing/ahs/>.

Table 1021. Occupied Housing Units—Financial Summary by Selected Characteristics of the Householder: 2011

[In thousands of units (114,907 represents 114,907,000), except as indicated. As of Fall. Housing costs include real estate taxes, property insurance, utilities, fuel, water, garbage collection, homeowner association fees, cooperative or condominium fees, mobile home fees, and mortgage. Based on the American Housing Survey; see Appendix III]

Characteristic	Total occupied units	Tenure		Black[1]		Hispanic origin[2]		Elderly[3]		Households below poverty level	
		Owner	Renter	Owner	Renter	Owner	Renter	Owner	Renter	Owner	Renter
Total units[4]................	114,907	76,091	38,816	6,662	8,033	6,530	7,311	20,250	4,808	7,003	11,126
Monthly housing costs:											
$199 or less.........................	2,898	1,879	1,019	211	390	148	154	935	221	566	774
$200 to $299.........................	5,857	4,463	1,394	507	359	398	233	2,337	496	884	1,003
$300 to $399.........................	7,252	5,888	1,366	505	338	485	228	2,982	362	961	637
$400 to $499.........................	7,183	5,180	2,003	402	441	341	297	2,572	369	671	769
$500 to $699.........................	15,667	8,890	6,778	801	1,501	685	1,209	3,561	818	1,097	2,310
$700 to $999.........................	22,088	11,400	10,688	1,097	2,295	947	2,211	2,984	1,003	1,051	2,635
$1,000 to $1,499.....................	24,493	15,706	8,787	1,412	1,765	1,436	1,882	2,446	637	878	1,521
$1,500 to $2,499.....................	18,796	14,997	3,798	1,254	495	1,449	778	1,653	290	608	464
$2,500 or more.......................	8,403	7,690	713	474	43	641	58	781	117	287	67
Median amount (dol.)[5].........	927	1,008	845	958	791	1,090	879	562	671	565	664
Monthly housing costs as percent of income:[6]											
Less than 5 percent.............	2,532	2,349	183	144	43	115	17	580	17	3	18
5 to 9 percent.....................	9,815	8,935	880	519	177	525	106	2,727	97	29	45
10 to 14 percent...................	12,935	10,829	2,106	724	325	628	300	3,162	163	76	51
15 to 19 percent...................	14,358	11,346	3,012	923	521	781	405	2,775	212	161	84
20 to 24 percent...................	13,657	9,955	3,701	782	649	780	627	2,160	325	236	224
25 to 29 percent...................	11,330	7,345	3,984	631	822	713	690	1,648	498	269	498
30 to 34 percent...................	8,543	5,286	3,257	506	681	521	675	1,260	463	271	447
35 to 39 percent...................	6,416	3,715	2,701	396	564	412	523	1,021	308	300	342
40 percent or more..............	30,657	15,379	15,279	1,890	3,441	1,899	3,417	4,775	2,167	4,779	7,210
Median amount (percent)[5].....	25	21	35	26	38	27	40	21	40	87	82

[1] For persons who selected this race group only. See footnote 3, Table 1017. [2] Persons of Hispanic origin may be of any race. [3] Householders 65 years old and over. [4] Include units with no cash rents, not shown separately. [5] For explanation of median, see Guide to Tabular Presentation. [6] Money income before taxes.

Source: U.S. Census Bureau, Current Housing Reports, Series H-150, *American Housing Survey for the United States: 2011*, October 2012. See also <http://www.census.gov/housing/ahs/>.

Table 1022. Owner-Occupied Housing Units—Value and Costs by State: 2011

[In percent, except as indicated (74,264 represents 74,264,000). The American Community Survey universe includes the household population and excludes the population living in institutions, college dormitories, and other group quarters. Based on a sample and subject to sampling variability; see Appendix III. For definition of median, see Guide to Tabular Presentation]

State	Total (1,000)	Percent of units with value of—			Median value (dol.)	Median selected monthly owner costs [1] (dol.)	Selected monthly owner costs as a percent income in the past 12 months			
		$99,999 or less	$100,000 to $199,999	$200,000 or more			Less than 15 percent	15.0 to 24.9 percent	25.0 to 29.9 percent	30.0 percent or more
U.S..........	74,264	24.9	31.9	43.3	173,600	1,486	17.4	33.4	12.0	36.6
AL.............	1,289	40.1	35.4	24.5	122,700	1,134	22.3	35.5	10.3	31.5
AK.............	162	12.7	24.1	63.2	238,300	1,794	17.1	38.0	12.9	32.0
AZ.............	1,502	28.6	36.4	35.0	153,800	1,365	16.1	32.8	11.4	38.9
AR.............	751	47.3	34.1	18.7	106,300	988	26.2	34.9	10.6	27.5
CA.............	6,843	8.7	15.5	75.9	355,600	2,182	11.2	26.7	12.7	48.7
CO.............	1,272	10.2	29.1	60.7	233,700	1,560	17.7	34.4	12.5	34.7
CT.............	911	4.7	22.2	73.1	278,700	2,052	14.3	32.0	12.9	40.4
DE.............	239	9.9	26.4	63.6	236,900	1,567	17.4	35.6	11.8	34.7
DC.............	111	2.6	7.4	90.0	422,400	2,224	18.6	33.5	11.9	35.5
FL.............	4,741	30.8	35.0	34.2	151,000	1,470	13.6	27.7	11.8	45.9
GA.............	2,257	30.4	37.9	31.7	147,100	1,371	17.3	33.7	11.6	36.5
HI.............	255	3.1	6.0	90.8	487,400	2,221	12.2	24.8	13.6	49.1
ID.............	399	22.5	44.5	33.0	158,800	1,212	17.6	33.3	12.1	36.7
IL.............	3,190	22.5	33.6	43.9	178,500	1,646	15.6	32.8	12.5	38.6
IN.............	1,720	37.4	42.1	20.4	122,400	1,091	24.7	38.2	10.1	26.5
IA.............	880	37.1	40.6	22.2	123,400	1,144	23.8	40.8	11.6	23.6
KS.............	747	37.9	37.6	24.5	128,300	1,252	22.0	38.1	12.6	26.8
KY.............	1,151	39.9	38.0	22.1	120,600	1,092	23.3	37.5	10.6	28.0
LA.............	1,131	35.5	37.0	27.4	139,400	1,176	25.6	34.1	10.0	29.6
ME.............	392	22.0	37.8	40.2	171,600	1,304	19.3	32.3	12.6	35.5
MD.............	1,437	6.9	19.5	73.6	287,100	1,961	16.1	34.1	12.5	36.9
MA.............	1,573	3.7	14.1	82.2	326,300	2,042	14.9	32.7	13.4	38.6
MI.............	2,706	41.3	36.9	21.8	118,100	1,275	18.4	35.6	11.8	33.7
MN.............	1,525	17.0	39.2	43.9	183,500	1,481	18.0	37.0	12.6	32.1
MS.............	755	50.1	32.2	17.8	99,900	1,048	20.2	34.3	10.5	34.1
MO.............	1,593	32.9	40.4	26.7	136,900	1,199	21.7	36.9	11.8	29.3
MT.............	275	22.2	32.7	45.1	184,100	1,256	17.6	32.4	12.7	37.1
NE.............	484	34.2	43.7	22.1	127,400	1,237	22.7	42.1	10.2	24.8
NV.............	553	25.2	39.6	35.2	158,000	1,529	14.0	30.5	12.2	42.4
NH.............	369	9.9	25.4	64.7	237,500	1,884	12.3	33.3	14.3	39.8
NJ.............	2,060	5.1	14.8	80.1	324,900	2,397	10.8	28.5	13.2	47.1
NM.............	523	28.8	34.8	36.4	159,000	1,216	21.6	32.5	10.9	34.0
NY.............	3,852	17.2	21.1	61.7	285,300	1,977	16.7	30.0	11.7	41.1
NC.............	2,450	27.8	38.6	33.6	153,700	1,246	19.4	35.1	11.2	33.7
ND.............	186	37.2	39.9	22.9	128,600	1,155	30.8	40.1	9.9	19.1
OH.............	3,040	34.2	42.7	23.0	129,600	1,243	20.0	37.3	11.6	30.7
OK.............	967	44.0	36.9	19.1	112,600	1,108	23.8	36.5	11.1	28.2
OR.............	922	11.0	28.9	60.1	232,900	1,546	13.6	31.4	13.5	41.0
PA.............	3,431	26.8	34.7	38.5	164,800	1,408	19.2	35.0	12.1	33.2
RI.............	250	4.9	26.2	68.9	245,500	1,842	13.2	31.3	14.0	41.1
SC.............	1,223	35.1	35.5	29.4	136,000	1,175	20.8	33.6	11.1	34.1
SD.............	221	34.8	41.0	24.2	131,400	1,178	21.6	41.1	11.9	24.9
TN.............	1,660	32.7	39.1	28.1	138,300	1,172	19.0	35.6	12.4	32.5
TX.............	5,568	36.8	37.8	25.4	127,700	1,398	19.9	36.6	11.3	31.4
UT.............	613	8.7	38.7	52.6	207,500	1,418	15.8	35.7	14.0	34.2
VT.............	183	12.2	33.3	54.5	213,700	1,487	14.1	34.4	14.3	36.9
VA.............	2,014	12.9	26.1	61.0	243,100	1,707	17.9	35.4	13.1	33.3
WA.............	1,654	8.8	24.9	66.3	256,300	1,733	13.8	33.0	13.5	39.2
WV.............	531	50.4	31.9	17.7	99,300	937	31.5	32.5	8.5	26.5
WI.............	1,544	19.2	44.2	36.7	166,700	1,402	15.6	37.4	13.4	33.3
WY.............	157	20.6	37.6	41.8	179,900	1,269	24.1	37.9	11.0	26.8

[1] For homes with a mortgage. Includes all forms of debt where the property is pledged as security for repayment of the debt, including deeds of trust, land contracts, home equity loans. Also includes cost of property insurance, utilities, real estate taxes, etc.

Source: U.S. Census Bureau, 2011 American Community Survey, B25075, "Value for Owner-Occupied Housing Units;" B25077, "Median Value for Owner-Occupied Housing Units;" B25088, "Median Selected Monthly Owner Costs by Mortgage Status;" and B25091, "Mortgage Status by Selected Monthly Owner Cost as a Percentage of Household Income;" <http://factfinder2.census.gov>, accessed February 2013. See also <http://www.census.gov/acs/www/>.

Construction and Housing 653

Table 1023. Renter-Occupied Housing Units—Gross Rent by State: 2011

[In percent, except as indicated (40,727 represents 40,727,000). The American Community Survey universe includes the household population, and excludes the population living in institutions, college dormitories, and other group quarters. Based on a sample and subject to sampling variability; see Appendix III]

State	Total [1] (1,000)	Percent of units with gross rent of—					Median gross rent (dol.)	Gross rent as a percent of household income in the past 12 months [2]			
		$299 or less	$300 to $499	$500 to $749	$750 to $999	$1,000 or more		Less than 15.0 percent	15.0 to 24.9 percent	25.0 to 29.0 percent	30.0 percent or more
U.S..........	40,727	4.9	8.0	22.5	23.0	36.1	871	10.3	22.1	10.6	49.3
AL..............	555	7.4	14.1	31.3	20.9	15.4	687	10.8	19.9	9.3	46.8
AK..............	95	2.0	5.4	13.0	22.2	49.5	1,049	13.7	26.0	11.3	40.6
AZ..............	855	2.3	7.7	26.1	25.4	33.2	850	10.6	22.9	10.4	47.4
AR..............	377	6.9	16.7	37.3	19.8	9.0	639	11.5	20.4	9.3	45.6
CA..............	5,625	2.8	3.6	10.1	18.8	61.3	1,174	7.9	21.1	11.1	54.5
CO..............	704	4.2	5.5	22.3	25.1	39.4	900	10.2	24.1	11.5	48.8
CT..............	441	6.0	6.0	10.9	23.2	49.7	1,021	9.9	22.1	10.1	52.0
DE..............	95	4.9	4.8	14.5	28.9	43.1	960	10.7	22.5	11.5	49.8
DC..............	158	6.4	5.2	9.1	16.0	61.0	1,216	13.1	23.0	11.6	46.3
FL..............	2,365	2.9	4.4	17.9	27.8	41.8	949	6.8	19.0	10.3	56.2
GA..............	1,238	4.2	7.8	24.5	28.2	28.9	833	9.0	21.4	10.4	49.6
HI..............	194	3.4	4.0	7.5	12.7	65.3	1,308	7.3	18.3	11.7	53.5
ID..............	181	6.3	12.9	34.4	20.7	17.2	689	11.1	21.0	11.6	46.4
IL..............	1,547	5.3	7.8	22.2	27.5	33.0	859	10.0	23.0	10.5	49.2
IN..............	747	5.4	12.0	36.7	25.7	14.8	707	11.3	22.9	9.9	47.5
IA..............	336	6.4	17.3	38.0	19.5	11.8	643	14.0	23.4	10.2	43.4
KS..............	355	5.2	14.0	32.7	23.1	18.1	709	13.0	25.2	10.8	42.8
KY..............	521	8.2	17.2	35.9	18.7	10.3	626	11.9	22.2	8.9	44.9
LA..............	571	6.2	11.4	27.4	23.7	20.4	747	11.1	18.6	8.6	47.9
ME..............	160	8.8	11.1	27.3	25.4	21.0	747	9.2	21.9	11.4	49.6
MD..............	697	4.7	4.1	8.5	18.2	60.6	1,153	9.2	23.0	11.6	50.6
MA..............	959	8.4	7.4	12.1	18.2	50.6	1,034	10.2	23.3	12.1	48.9
MI..............	1,066	5.9	10.2	32.8	25.0	20.7	739	9.9	20.6	10.3	51.0
MN..............	571	7.8	9.1	26.3	24.5	27.3	787	10.7	23.8	12.1	47.3
MS..............	326	7.8	13.6	29.7	22.3	12.9	689	9.4	19.2	8.3	46.3
MO..............	748	6.0	13.6	33.1	23.9	16.9	708	11.3	23.6	10.8	45.4
MT..............	130	7.4	16.6	33.5	17.7	15.0	650	14.6	22.7	10.4	41.6
NE..............	239	6.4	16.1	35.5	20.6	15.2	673	14.1	27.9	10.2	40.3
NV..............	429	1.7	4.0	19.9	30.3	40.8	936	9.5	24.0	11.6	49.3
NH..............	147	6.1	5.8	13.7	29.5	40.6	939	9.2	25.6	11.7	47.0
NJ..............	1,107	4.7	3.8	7.5	20.0	60.4	1,135	10.4	21.7	10.6	51.4
NM..............	244	6.2	12.1	30.6	23.6	19.9	729	11.9	20.7	9.2	47.6
NY..............	3,336	5.7	6.7	14.7	17.2	52.2	1,058	11.7	21.0	10.3	51.3
NC..............	1,233	5.0	10.1	31.7	25.3	20.3	745	10.8	22.0	9.3	47.9
ND..............	97	8.1	19.2	34.5	16.6	12.1	626	16.2	25.8	9.1	38.0
OH..............	1,499	6.9	12.9	35.4	23.8	15.4	692	11.8	21.9	10.6	47.5
OK..............	476	5.7	14.7	35.2	21.9	13.9	675	13.4	22.2	10.4	43.0
OR..............	595	3.9	6.1	26.1	29.5	29.8	840	8.7	21.6	11.3	51.8
PA..............	1,506	6.7	10.1	26.2	24.5	26.3	786	11.3	22.5	10.8	47.1
RI..............	163	9.2	7.0	17.5	26.8	36.2	875	10.3	23.2	13.1	47.9
SC..............	545	5.4	10.1	30.4	23.8	19.8	741	9.5	20.6	9.8	47.3
SD..............	102	10.7	21.1	31.6	16.6	10.8	612	19.1	23.8	11.2	35.6
TN..............	807	6.7	11.2	32.8	23.4	17.3	715	9.6	21.5	10.8	47.0
TX..............	3,282	3.7	7.3	28.3	27.1	28.0	813	11.7	24.0	10.5	46.1
UT..............	271	3.3	7.9	27.7	27.7	28.7	822	11.8	22.9	10.8	47.8
VT..............	74	5.5	7.3	23.4	25.6	31.4	849	8.6	23.3	11.2	49.2
VA..............	977	4.4	5.9	15.0	18.1	51.1	1,062	10.2	24.3	11.6	46.5
WA..............	979	4.3	5.6	19.1	25.6	41.6	930	10.0	24.5	12.3	48.0
WV..............	204	8.5	18.0	33.5	14.7	7.7	599	15.3	18.5	6.7	38.7
WI..............	731	4.6	10.5	34.3	27.7	18.5	739	12.3	24.6	11.0	46.0
WY..............	65	4.1	13.3	27.4	22.8	23.9	759	16.9	28.5	12.3	33.3

[1] Includes units with no cash rent. [2] Does not include units "not computed;" therefore, rows will not total 100 percent.

Source: U.S. Census Bureau, 2011 American Community Survey, B25063, "Gross Rent;" B25064, "Median Gross Rent;" and B25070, "Gross Rent as a Percentage of Household Income;" <http://factfinder.census.gov>, accessed February 2013.

Table 1024. Mortgage Characteristics—Owner-Occupied Units: 2011

[In thousands (76,091 represents 76,091,000). As of Fall. Based on the American Housing Survey; see Appendix III]

Mortgage characteristic	Total owner occupied units (1,000)	Housing unit characteristics		Household characteristics			
		New construc-tion [1]	Mobile homes	Black [2]	His-panic [3]	Elderly [4]	Below poverty level
ALL OWNERS							
Total...............................	**76,091**	**1,898**	**5,678**	**6,662**	**6,530**	**20,250**	**7,003**
Mortgages currently on property: [5]							
None, owned free and clear..................	25,921	324	3,356	1,985	1,914	13,155	3,787
Regular and home equity mortgages [6].............	49,735	1,574	2,306	4,637	4,567	6,678	3,133
Regular mortgage............................	47,248	1,551	2,218	4,426	4,452	5,776	2,949
Home equity lump sum mortgage..................	2,578	17	76	202	180	498	144
Home equity line of credit..................	4,762	54	50	236	249	915	163
Number of regular and home equity mortgages:							
1 mortgage..................................	43,055	1,479	2,247	4,236	4,025	6,026	2,934
2 mortgages.................................	6,553	95	59	395	537	640	194
3 mortgages or more.........................	126	–	–	5	5	13	5
Type of mortgage:							
Regular and home equity lump sum..............	1,533	6	25	84	107	150	46
With home equity line of credit..........	24	–	–	–	–	–	–
No home equity line of credit............	1,509	6	25	84	107	150	46
Regular no home equity lump sum..............	45,716	1,544	2,193	4,341	4,346	5,626	2,904
With home equity line of credit..........	3,259	41	13	142	206	357	75
No home equity line of credit............	42,456	1,503	2,180	4,199	4,140	5,269	2,829
Home equity lump sum no regular..............	1,046	10	52	118	73	348	98
With home equity line of credit..........	38	–	–	–	1	4	3
No home equity line of credit............	1,008	10	52	118	72	344	96
No regular or home equity lump sum..............	27,797	337	3,409	2,118	2,005	14,126	3,955
With home equity line of credit..........	1,441	13	37	93	42	554	85
No home equity line of credit............	26,357	324	3,372	2,025	1,963	13,572	3,870
OWNERS WITH ONE OR MORE REGULAR OR LUMP SUM HOME EQUITY MORTGAGES							
Total...............................	**48,294**	**1,561**	**2,269**	**4,544**	**4,525**	**6,124**	**3,048**
Type of primary mortgage:							
FHA..	9,039	331	199	1,453	1,172	672	544
VA...	1,674	143	59	263	130	202	69
RHS/RD.......................................	540	26	63	54	34	37	67
Other types.................................	31,901	934	1,524	2,197	2,741	4,107	1,724
Mortgage origination:							
Placed new mortgage(s).......................	48,005	1,554	2,230	4,491	4,463	6,102	3,007
Primary obtained when property acquired.........	28,829	1,292	1,887	3,129	3,110	3,121	2,171
Obtained later.............................	19,177	262	343	1,362	1,353	2,981	836
Assumed....................................	239	2	34	40	52	15	29
Wrap-around................................	40	5	5	10	9	4	9
Combination of the above...................	10	–	–	3	2	2	3
Payment plan of primary mortgage:							
Fixed payment, self amortizing..............	38,797	1,353	1,676	3,392	3,606	4,432	2,042
Adjustable rate mortgage....................	1,455	17	35	149	149	166	95
Balloon....................................	271	6	4	39	34	31	24
Graduated payment mortgage..................	117	2	7	19	11	18	12
Adjustable term mortgage....................	108	3	3	14	9	39	13
Combination of the above...................	174	4	13	18	21	35	18
Payment plan of secondary mortgage:							
Units with two or more mortgages............	3,354	53	45	258	335	275	122
Fixed payment, self amortizing..............	2,727	30	43	214	255	204	85
Adjustable rate mortgage....................	128	3	–	3	17	12	4
Adjustable term mortgage....................	45	–	–	4	1	6	5
Graduated payment mortgage..................	37	–	–	5	4	4	1
Balloon....................................	22	–	–	1	2	5	2
Other......................................	144	3	–	10	23	9	11
Combination of the above...................	44	9	–	–	5	13	1
Reason primary refinanced:							
Units with a refinanced primary mortgage [6].........	17,781	249	296	1,185	1,245	2,274	621
To get a lower interest rate................	13,747	214	158	747	805	1,611	376
To reduce monthly payment...................	5,213	87	50	413	382	640	181
To reduce payment period....................	2,816	28	36	120	161	299	51
To receive cash............................	2,543	13	79	239	252	409	97
To increase payment period..................	439	5	10	25	29	46	21
To suspend or temporarily reduce payments......	171	–	7	25	14	30	7
Other reason...............................	1,752	13	57	168	138	264	101
Cash received in primary mortgage refinance:							
Units receiving refinance cash..............	2,543	13	79	239	252	409	97
Median amount received (dol.)...............	26,000	100,000	20,000	20,000	30,000	33,415	20,000

– Represents or rounds to zero. [1] Constructed in the past 4 years. [2] For persons who selected this race group only. See footnote 3, Table 1017. [3] Persons of Hispanic origin may be of any race. [4] 65 years old and over. [5] Regular mortgages include all mortgages not classified as home-equity or reverse. [6] Figures may not add to total because more than one category may apply to a unit.

Source: U.S. Census Bureau, Current Housing Reports, Series H-150, *American Housing Survey for the United States: 2011*, October 2012. See also <http://www.census.gov/housing/ahs/>.

Table 1025. Home Purchase Loans by Race/Ethnicity and Sex: 2011

[Amount in millions of dollars (441,993 represents $441,993,000,000). Data is the final 2011 National Aggregates data]

Race and Gender [1,2,3]	Applications received		Loans originated		Applications approved not accepted		Applications denied		Applications withdrawn		Files closed for incompleteness	
	Number	Amount (million dollars)	Number	Amount (million dollars)	Number	Amount (million dollars)	Number	Amount (million dollars)	Number	Amount (million dollars)	Number	Amount (million dollars)
Total	**2,142,958**	**441,993**	**1,389,584**	**303,147**	**158,253**	**28,527**	**353,744**	**55,621**	**192,893**	**43,663**	**48,484**	**11,036**
White	1,611,085	317,014	1,081,823	223,475	113,269	19,583	246,040	37,535	138,093	29,646	31,860	6,776
Male	517,420	96,913	330,000	64,688	38,715	6,406	90,448	13,599	46,442	9,734	11,815	2,486
Female	331,112	49,039	213,015	33,662	23,318	2,925	58,925	6,731	28,837	4,614	7,017	1,107
Joint (male/female)	757,759	170,164	536,305	124,609	50,671	10,165	95,636	17,053	62,254	15,179	12,893	3,158
Black	82,244	9,966	34,095	5,034	9,262	826	30,332	2,869	6,638	949	1,917	289
Male	27,482	3,411	11,766	1,734	3,014	282	9,506	946	2,474	345	722	104
Female	35,572	3,701	14,349	1,797	3,689	289	13,963	1,175	2,775	336	796	103
Joint (male/female)	18,473	2,780	7,867	1,488	2,378	242	6,498	713	1,354	261	376	77
Hispanic or Latino	134,316	19,512	73,223	11,543	11,229	1,388	32,784	3,921	13,178	2,012	3,902	648
Male	58,163	8,547	31,366	4,986	5,141	644	14,312	1,737	5,593	872	1,751	308
Female	34,956	4,366	18,761	2,531	2,677	291	8,927	945	3,530	449	1,061	150
Joint (male/female)	40,574	6,516	22,874	3,990	3,314	446	9,325	1,213	3,985	681	1,076	186
Asian	154,150	42,900	101,694	28,610	10,918	3,134	21,815	5,520	15,236	4,292	4,487	1,344
Male	61,142	16,075	39,648	10,483	4,572	1,252	8,826	2,129	6,169	1,657	1,927	554
Female	34,209	7,794	21,747	5,013	2,474	577	5,552	1,157	3,325	767	1,111	279
Joint (male/female)	58,278	18,896	40,043	13,043	3,822	1,293	7,335	2,212	5,654	1,844	1,424	504
Native Hawaiian/Other Pacific Islander	5,482	1,105	3,244	683	386	29	1,122	192	591	131	139	27
Male	2,293	445	1,296	263	159	17	527	88	256	54	55	12
Female	1,536	270	922	170	110	25	303	45	156	32	45	6
Joint (male/female)	1,603	381	998	245	112	17	281	58	175	44	37	8
American Indian/Alaska Native	9,949	1,233	4,381	651	1,275	115	3,304	307	774	126	215	35
Male	3,917	521	1,734	269	467	47	1,322	137	299	51	95	16
Female	3,158	328	1,226	163	454	35	1,163	90	238	32	77	8
Joint (male/female)	2,246	332	1,019	186	302	29	701	70	182	38	42	10
Two or more minority races	915	200	490	124	64	10	244	39	85	21	32	7
Male	353	72	187	42	32	4	85	13	33	8	16	4
Female	307	53	140	30	19	3	107	13	30	6	11	2
Joint (male/female)	250	74	161	52	11	3	51	13	22	7	5	1
Joint [4]	30,491	8,277	20,182	5,840	2,423	551	4,670	956	2,616	753	600	177
Race not available [5]	248,642	61,298	143,675	38,730	20,656	4,236	46,217	8,203	28,860	7,747	9,234	2,383
Male	35,214	7,817	18,194	4,480	3,186	551	8,053	1,376	4,368	1,042	1,413	368
Female	21,373	3,679	10,630	2,111	1,718	232	5,649	717	2,575	474	801	144
Joint (male/female)	42,876	11,858	25,805	7,758	3,531	783	7,190	1,495	5,119	1,486	1,231	336

[1] Applicants are shown in only one race category. [2] Total includes those cases in which gender was reported and in those in which gender information was not available. [3] Applicants are shown in only one gender category. [4] "Joint" means with two applicants, one reported a single designation of "White" and the other applicant reports one or more minority racial designations. [5] "Not Available" includes situations in which information was reported as not provided or not applicable.

Source: Federal Financial Institutions Examination Council, "Home Mortgage Disclosure Act National Aggregate Report," <http://www.ffiec.gov/Hmda/default.htm>, accessed April 2013.

Table 1026. Occupied Housing Units—Neighborhood Indicators by Selected Characteristics of the Householder: 2009

[In thousands (111,806 represents 111,806,000). As of Fall. Based on the American Housing Survey; see Appendix III]

Characteristic	Total occupied units	Tenure		Black [1]		Hispanic origin [2]		Elderly [3]		Households below poverty level	
		Owner	Renter	Owner	Renter	Owner	Renter	Owner	Renter	Owner	Renter
Total units.........................	**111,806**	**76,428**	**35,378**	**6,547**	**7,446**	**6,439**	**6,300**	**18,472**	**4,623**	**6,405**	**9,334**
Street noise or traffic present:											
Bothersome street noise or heavy traffic present [4]..............	111,806	76,428	35,378	6,547	7,446	6,439	6,300	18,472	4,623	6,405	9,334
Yes....................................	25,381	15,223	10,158	1,639	2,460	1,419	1,725	3,497	1,077	1,549	3,110
No.....................................	85,122	60,264	24,858	4,836	4,895	4,972	4,545	14,744	3,498	4,692	6,119
Neighborhood crime present:											
Serious crime in past 12 months................................	111,806	76,428	35,378	6,547	7,446	6,439	6,300	18,472	4,623	6,405	9,334
Yes....................................	19,299	11,649	7,650	1,428	2,045	1,223	1,403	2,105	658	951	2,254
No.....................................	90,116	63,230	26,886	4,958	5,146	5,129	4,814	15,983	3,853	5,194	6,813
Odors present:											
Bothersome smoke, gas, or bad smell [4]................................	111,806	76,428	35,378	6,547	7,446	6,439	6,300	18,472	4,623	6,405	9,334
Yes....................................	5,434	3,278	2,156	330	614	367	359	663	164	389	727
No.....................................	105,015	72,168	32,847	6,142	6,749	6,024	5,907	17,567	4,408	5,843	8,505
Other problems:											
Noise.................................	2,950	1,733	1,217	176	296	165	217	382	95	156	340
Litter or housing deterioration......	1,691	1,101	590	196	203	85	127	266	43	121	213
Poor city or county services.......	694	440	254	80	101	49	37	70	21	72	89
People................................	4,521	2,706	1,815	298	460	269	297	510	115	249	630
Public transportation: [4]											
With public transportation.........	60,257	35,616	24,641	3,719	5,856	3,998	4,996	8,283	3,245	2,815	6,562
Household uses public transportation regularly for commuting to school or work.....................	10,212	3,817	6,395	720	1,959	569	1,682	582	564	308	2,089
Household does not use public transportation regularly for commuting to school or work...........	49,681	31,606	18,075	2,963	3,838	3,411	3,285	7,679	2,670	2,473	4,427
No public transportation.............	48,532	38,848	9,684	2,689	1,438	2,309	1,217	9,728	1,236	3,337	2,522
Not reported.........................	3,017	1,964	1,053	138	152	132	88	461	142	254	250
Police protection:											
Satisfactory..........................	101,373	69,633	31,740	5,837	6,325	5,742	5,623	16,929	4,294	5,501	8,025
Unsatisfactory.......................	7,356	4,800	2,556	516	835	568	543	1,051	193	608	990
Secured communities: [5]											
Community access secured with walls or fences.....................	10,759	5,337	5,422	367	1,371	656	1,336	1,512	827	440	1,392
Community access not secured....	100,124	70,410	29,714	6,124	6,028	5,736	4,930	16,783	3,758	5,831	7,865
Secured multiunits:											
Multiunit access secured...........	7,211	1,357	5,854	106	1,301	135	998	454	1,426	118	1,503
Multiunit access not secured.......	16,741	2,151	14,590	216	3,406	237	2,749	608	1,567	163	4,129
Senior citizen communities:											
Households with persons 55 years old and over..............	45,684	36,591	9,093	3,132	1,842	2,451	1,255	18,472	4,623	3,763	2,645
Community age restricted [6].......	3,080	1,457	1,624	89	300	71	169	1,079	1,374	194	588
Access to structure:											
Enter building from outside [4, 7].....	25,915	3,734	22,181	351	5,056	401	4,212	1,142	3,314	321	6,136
Use of steps not required.........	9,771	1,532	8,239	91	1,915	186	1,519	565	1,780	149	2,386
Use of steps required..............	16,136	2,201	13,935	260	3,141	216	2,690	577	1,529	172	3,750
Enter home from outside [8].........	85,891	72,694	13,197	6,196	2,391	6,038	2,089	17,330	1,309	6,084	3,198
Use of steps not required.........	38,011	32,654	5,357	2,706	951	3,354	950	8,253	551	2,668	1,231
Use of steps required..............	47,752	39,928	7,824	3,487	1,439	2,681	1,139	9,048	751	3,406	1,956
Community quality:											
Some or all activities present......	49,962	33,117	16,845	2,570	3,392	2,547	2,647	8,356	2,731	2,468	4,197
Community center or clubhouse...........................	24,410	14,707	9,703	1,181	2,078	1,127	1,347	4,306	1,888	1,177	2,346
Golf in the community.............	16,709	12,762	3,947	611	471	694	499	3,410	604	832	880
Trails in the community............	21,609	15,300	6,309	983	1,017	1,099	876	3,509	826	981	1,369
Shuttle bus........................	9,933	5,718	4,215	422	702	536	713	2,033	1,258	482	1,161
Daycare............................	15,883	10,633	5,249	1,157	1,297	795	934	2,392	546	822	1,568
Private or restricted beach, park, or shoreline................	21,432	15,124	6,308	925	1,053	1,158	1,145	3,327	731	964	1,466
Trash, litter, or junk on street: [9]											
None.................................	99,010	69,415	29,595	5,639	5,764	5,752	5,211	17,001	4,172	5,507	7,264
Minor accumulation.................	7,250	3,491	3,759	505	1,064	342	738	673	283	396	1,366
Major accumulation.................	2,519	1,426	1,093	201	351	193	235	318	72	187	437

[1] For persons who selected this race group only. See footnote 3, Table 1017. [2] Persons of Hispanic origin may be of any race. [3] Householders 65 years old and over. [4] Includes those not reporting. [5] Public access is restricted (walls, gates, private security). [6] At least one family member must be 55 years old or older. [7] Restricted to multiunits. [8] Restricted to single units. [9] Or on any properties within 300 feet.

Source: U.S. Census Bureau, Current Housing Reports, Series H150/09, *American Housing Survey for the United States: 2009*, March 2011. See also <http://www.census.gov/housing/ahs/>.

Table 1027. Heating Equipment and Fuels for Occupied Units: 1995 to 2011

[97,693 represents 97,693,000. As of Fall. Based on American Housing Survey. See Appendix III]

Type of equipment or fuel	Number (1,000)					Percent distribution	
	1995	2005	2007	2009	2011	2009	2011
Occupied units, total....................	**97,693**	**108,871**	**110,692**	**111,806**	**114,907**	**100.0**	**100.0**
Heating equipment:							
Warm air furnace..........................	53,165	68,275	69,582	71,141	73,687	63.6	64.1
Steam or hot water........................	13,669	12,880	12,760	12,506	12,624	11.2	11.0
Heat pumps................................	9,406	12,484	12,996	13,264	13,523	11.9	11.8
Built-in electric units.....................	7,035	4,699	4,802	4,761	4,865	4.3	4.2
Floor, wall, or pipeless furnace...........	4,963	5,102	4,994	4,802	4,505	4.3	3.9
Room heaters with flue....................	1,620	1,294	1,135	950	932	0.8	0.8
Room heaters without flue.................	1,642	1,327	1,188	1,109	1,094	1.0	1.0
Fireplaces, stoves, portable heaters or other...........	5,150	2,411	2,756	2,887	3,208	2.6	2.8
None......................................	1,044	399	478	386	468	0.3	0.4
House main heating fuel:							
Electricity.................................	26,771	34,263	36,079	37,851	40,385	33.9	35.1
Utility gas.................................	49,203	56,317	56,681	56,806	57,721	50.8	50.2
Bottled, tank, or liquid propane gas.......	4,251	6,228	6,095	5,817	5,415	5.2	4.7
Fuel oil, kerosene, etc.....................	12,029	9,929	9,317	8,813	8,599	7.9	7.5
Coal or coke..............................	210	95	91	98	79	0.1	0.1
Wood and other fuel.......................	4,186	1,640	1,487	2,035	2,240	1.8	1.9
None......................................	1,042	398	464	386	468	0.3	0.4
Cooking fuel:							
Electricity.................................	57,621	65,297	66,276	67,078	68,879	60.0	59.9
Gas [1]....................................	39,218	43,316	44,194	44,477	45,759	39.8	39.8
Other fuel.................................	566	51	26	68	92	0.1	0.1
None......................................	287	206	17	183	177	0.2	0.2

[1] Includes utility, bottled, tank, and liquid propane gas.

Source: U.S. Census Bureau, Current Housing Reports, Series H-150, *American Housing Survey for the United States: 2011*, October 2012. See also <http://www.census.gov/housing/ahs/>.

Table 1028. Occupied Housing Units—Housing Indicators by Selected Characteristics of the Householder: 2011

[In thousands of units (114,907 represents 114,907,000). As of Fall. Based on the American Housing Survey; see Appendix III]

Characteristic	Total occupied units (1,000)	Tenure		Black [1]		Hispanic origin [2]		Elderly [3]		Households below poverty level	
		Owner	Renter	Owner	Renter	Owner	Renter	Owner	Renter	Owner	Renter
Total units..........................	**114,907**	**76,091**	**38,816**	**6,662**	**8,033**	**6,530**	**7,311**	**20,250**	**4,808**	**7,003**	**11,126**
Amenities:											
Porch, deck, balcony or patio..........	97,550	69,885	27,665	5,854	5,508	5,755	4,819	18,434	3,057	6,146	7,428
Telephone available...................	112,073	74,729	37,344	6,515	7,700	6,372	6,988	19,968	4,660	6,839	10,677
Usable fireplace......................	40,371	34,700	5,672	2,317	896	2,161	856	8,649	435	1,869	931
Separate dining room..................	54,923	43,300	11,623	4,042	2,609	3,406	2,180	11,348	1,115	3,243	2,924
With 2 or more living rooms or rec. rooms................................	34,576	31,242	3,334	2,287	510	1,802	369	8,014	313	1,586	532
Garage or carport with home..........	75,431	60,389	15,042	4,347	2,109	4,942	2,939	16,441	1,647	4,620	3,228
Cars and trucks available:											
No cars, trucks, or vans..............	9,425	2,123	7,302	446	2,338	156	1,411	1,259	1,726	677	3,629
1 car with or without trucks or vans...	53,367	34,512	18,854	3,165	3,766	2,812	3,306	11,288	2,247	3,729	4,842
2 cars................................	29,620	22,808	6,811	1,750	1,032	1,822	1,322	4,607	394	1,147	1,082
3 or more cars........................	9,123	7,900	1,223	613	137	784	253	955	50	322	178
1 or more trucks or vans..............	50,275	38,853	11,422	3,029	1,769	3,718	2,607	8,382	883	3,059	2,782
Selected deficiencies:											
Signs of rats in last 12 months.......	1171	661	510	83	135	128	120	144	68	108	207
Signs of mice in last 12 months......	12,743	8,877	3,867	692	917	498	758	2,185	459	909	1,292
Holes in floors........................	1,173	566	608	65	194	58	128	121	58	140	251
Open cracks or holes..................	5,949	3,180	2,769	437	764	362	552	531	185	526	988
Paint (interior of unit).................	2,370	1,156	1,214	182	387	98	268	215	108	184	438
No electrical wiring...................	161	82	80	6	8	11	20	22	6	22	32
Exposed wiring........................	1,820	998	822	74	228	121	148	238	82	149	299
Rooms without electric outlet.........	765	387	378	44	122	30	75	80	29	75	134
Water leakage from inside structure [4]...............	9,686	5,385	4,301	603	991	448	807	1,019	321	553	1,346
Water leakage from outside structure [4]....................	12,461	8,676	3,785	990	876	567	685	1,889	339	830	1,187

[1] For persons who selected this race group only. See footnote 3, Table 1017. [2] Persons of Hispanic origin may be of any race. [3] Householders 65 years old and over. [4] During the 12 months prior to the survey.

Source: U.S. Census Bureau, Current Housing Reports, Series H-150, *American Housing Survey for the United States: 2011*, October 2012. See also <http://www.census.gov/housing/ahs/>.

Table 1029. Home Remodeling—Number of Households With Work Done by Amount Spent: 2012

[In thousands, except percent (1,430 represents 1,430,000). As of Fall 2012. For work done in the prior 12 months. Based on household survey and subject to sampling error; see source]

Remodeling project	Total households with work done [1]		Households with work done by outside contractor	Number of households by amount spent (dol.)		
	Number	Percent of households		Under $1,000	$1,000 to $2,999	Over $3,000
Conversion of garage/attic/basement into living space.	1,430	1.19	242	275	278	466
Remodel bathroom.	6,328	5.29	1,936	2,286	1,496	1,347
Remodel kitchen.	4,230	3.53	1,559	970	710	1,644
Remodel bedroom.	2,868	2.40	479	1,377	431	248
Remodel other rooms.	2,866	2.39	521	1,251	407	414
Add bathroom.	564	0.47	191	47	92	177
Add other rooms—exterior addition.	498	0.42	199	36	46	264
Add deck/porch/patio.	2,443	2.04	738	663	644	607
Roofing.	4,395	3.67	2,801	617	636	2,167
Siding—vinyl/metal.	1,249	1.04	572	326	221	348
Hardwood floors.	2,272	1.90	768	678	468	487
Laminate flooring.	2,485	2.08	821	1,094	590	286
Vinyl flooring.	1,163	0.97	309	611	170	22
Carpeting.	3,390	2.83	1,828	1,191	886	435
Kitchen cabinets.	2,253	1.88	867	556	363	609
Kitchen counter tops.	2,377	1.99	1,255	481	565	657
Concrete or masonry work.	1,955	1.63	842	677	379	368

[1] Includes no response and amount unknown.

Source: GfK Mediamark Research & Intelligence, LLC, New York, NY, Top-Line Reports ©, <http://www.gfkmri.com/>.

Table 1030. Home Improvement Loans by Race: 2011

[Applications in thousands (686.8 represents 686,800), amounts in millions of dollars (45,767.0 represents $45,767,000). Data is the final 2011 National Aggregates data]

Item	Unit	Total [1]	White, total	Black, total	Asian, total	Joint, total [2]	Race not available, total
Applications received							
Number.	1,000	686.8	498.6	68.1	14.9	7.0	87.6
Amount.	Mil. dol.	45,767.0	34,382.9	1,825.0	2,264.9	700.1	6,189.3
Loans originated							
Number.	1,000	339.4	273.9	20.1	6.9	3.7	31.8
Amount.	Mil. dol.	25,978.4	20,377.1	638.6	1,310.4	434.1	3,052.7
Applications approved but not accepted							
Number.	1,000	27.0	20.4	1.8	0.8	0.3	3.3
Amount.	Mil. dol.	2,188.8	1,620.9	73.5	131.1	34.1	310.2
Applications denied							
Number.	1,000	269.6	168.1	43.3	5.6	2.4	43.5
Amount.	Mil. dol.	10,081.3	7,036.0	840.9	419.1	121.6	1,495.3
Applications withdrawn							
Number.	1,000	37.6	27.2	2.2	1.1	0.5	6.3
Amount.	Mil. dol.	4,848.7	3,489.0	180.7	249.8	75.2	822.1
Files closed for incompleteness							
Number.	1,000	13.2	9.1	0.7	0.5	0.1	2.6
Amount.	Mil. dol.	2,669.8	1,859.9	91.3	154.5	35.1	508.9

[1] Applicants are shown in only one race category. Applicants are categorized by the race of the first person listed on the application unless the 'joint' designation applies. [2] Joint means one applicant on an application reports a single designation of "White" and the other applicant reports one or more minority racial designations.

Source: Federal Financial Institutions Examination Council, "HMDA National Aggregate Report," <http://www.ffiec.gov/hmdaadwebreport/nataggwelcome.aspx>, accessed June 2013.

Table 1031. Net Stock of Residential Fixed Assets: 1990 to 2011

[In billions of dollars (6,256 represents $6,256,000,000,000). End of year estimates]

Item	1990	1995	2000	2005	2007	2008	2009	2010	2011
Total residential fixed assets............	**6,256**	**8,009**	**10,897**	**16,862**	**18,299**	**18,017**	**17,700**	**17,772**	**17,895**
By type of owner and legal form of organization:									
Private...	6,107	7,821	10,668	16,530	17,956	17,685	17,375	17,442	17,561
Corporate.....................................	66	77	105	156	174	176	177	177	175
Noncorporate................................	6,041	7,743	10,563	16,374	17,782	17,508	17,197	17,266	17,387
Government....................................	149	188	229	332	343	333	326	330	333
Federal...	52	62	75	103	105	102	98	98	98
State and local.............................	97	127	154	229	237	231	227	232	235
By tenure group: [1]									
Owner-occupied.............................	4,512	5,975	8,327	13,276	14,445	14,195	13,919	14,003	14,153
Tenant-occupied............................	1,719	2,005	2,537	3,533	3,798	3,766	3,726	3,713	3,685

[1] Excludes stocks of other nonfarm residential assets, which consists primarily of dormitories and of fraternity and sorority houses.

Source: U.S. Bureau of Economic Analysis, Fixed Assets Accounts Tables, "Table 5.1 Current-Cost Net Stock of Residential Fixed Assets by Type of Owner, Legal Form of Organization, Industry, and Tenure Group," <http://www.bea.gov/iTable/index_FA.cfm>, accessed August 2013.

Table 1032. Commercial Buildings—Summary: 2003

[4,645 represents 4,645,000. Excludes mall buildings. Building type based on predominant activity in which the occupants were engaged. Based on a sample survey of building representatives conducted in 2003, therefore subject to sampling variability]

Characteristic	All buildings (1,000)	Total floor-space (mil. sq. ft)	Total workers in all buildings (1,000)	Mean square foot per building [1] (1,000)	Mean square foot per worker [1]	Mean operating hours per week [1]
All buildings..............................	**4,645**	**64,783**	**72,807**	**13.9**	**890**	**61**
Building floorspace (sq. ft.):						
1,001 to 5,000..........................	2,552	6,789	9,936	2.7	683	57
5,001 to 10,000.........................	889	6,585	7,512	7.4	877	61
10,001 to 25,000........................	738	11,535	10,787	15.6	1,069	67
25,001 to 50,000........................	241	8,668	8,881	35.9	976	72
50,001 to 100,000.......................	129	9,057	8,432	70.4	1,074	80
100,001 to 200,000......................	65	9,064	11,632	138.8	779	89
200,001 to 500,000......................	25	7,176	6,883	289.0	1,043	100
Over 500,000............................	7	5,908	8,744	896.1	676	115
Principal activity within building:						
Education................................	386	9,874	12,489	25.6	791	50
Food sales..............................	226	1,255	1,430	5.6	877	107
Food service............................	297	1,654	3,129	5.6	528	86
Health care.............................	129	3,163	6,317	24.6	501	59
Inpatient..............................	8	1,905	3,716	241.4	513	168
Outpatient............................	121	1,258	2,600	10.4	484	52
Lodging..................................	142	5,096	2,457	35.8	2,074	167
Retail (other than mall).................	443	4,317	3,463	9.7	1,246	59
Office...................................	824	12,208	28,154	14.8	434	55
Public assembly.........................	277	3,939	2,395	14.2	1,645	50
Public order and safety.................	71	1,090	1,347	15.5	809	103
Religious worship.......................	370	3,754	1,706	10.1	2,200	32
Service..................................	622	4,050	3,667	6.5	1,105	55
Warehouse and storage..................	597	10,078	4,369	16.9	2,306	66
Other....................................	79	1,738	1,819	21.9	956	63
Vacant..................................	182	2,567	(NA)	14.1	(NA)	(NA)
Energy sources: [2]						
Electricity..............................	4,404	63,307	72,708	14.4	871	62
Natural gas.............................	2,391	43,468	51,956	18.2	837	65
Fuel oil.................................	451	15,157	19,625	33.6	772	68
District heat............................	67	5,443	10,190	81.4	534	79
District chilled water....................	33	2,853	7,189	86.7	397	79
Propane.................................	502	7,076	5,858	14.1	1,208	60
Wood....................................	62	289	262	4.6	1,105	46

NA Not available. [1] For explanation of mean, see Guide to Tabular Presentation. [2] More than one type may apply.

Source: U.S. Energy Information Administration, *2003 Commercial Buildings Energy Consumption (CBECS)*, Detailed Tables, Table B1, "Totals and Means of Floorspace, Number of Workers, and Hours of Operation for Non-Mall Buildings." See also <http://www.eia.gov/consumption/commercial/index.cfm>.

Manufactures

This section presents summary data for manufacturing as a whole and more detailed information for major industry groups and selected products. The types of measures shown at the different levels include data for establishments, employment and payroll, value and quantity of production and shipments, value added by manufacture, inventories, and various indicators of financial status.

The principal sources of these data are U.S. Census Bureau reports of the censuses of manufactures conducted every 5 years, the *Annual Survey of Manufactures*, and *Current Industrial Reports*. Reports on current activities of industries or current movements of individual commodities are compiled by such government agencies as the Bureau of Economic Analysis; Bureau of Labor Statistics; the Department of Commerce, International Trade Administration; and by private research or trade associations.

The Quarterly Financial Report publishes up-to-date aggregate statistics on the financial results and position of U.S. corporations. Based upon a sample survey, the QFR presents estimated statements of income and retained earnings, balance sheets, and related financial and operating ratios for manufacturing corporations with assets of $250,000 or over, and mining, wholesale trade and retail trade corporations with assets of $50 million and over or above industry-specific receipt cut-off values. These statistical data are classified by industry and by asset size.

Several private trade associations provide industry coverage for certain sections of the economy.

Censuses and annual surveys—The first census of manufactures covered the year 1809. Between 1809 and 1963, a census was conducted at periodic intervals. Since 1967, it has been taken every 5 years (for years ending in "2" and "7"). Results from the 2007 census are presented in this section utilizing the North American Industry Classification System (NAICS). For additional information see text, Section 15, Business Enterprise, and the Census Bureau Web site at <http://www.census.gov/econ/census07/>. Census data, either directly reported or estimated from administrative records, are obtained for every manufacturing plant with one or more paid employees.

The *Annual Survey of Manufactures* (ASM), conducted for the first time in 1949, collects data for the years between censuses for the more general measure of manufacturing activity covered in detail by the censuses. The annual survey data are estimates derived from a scientifically selected sample of establishments. The *Annual Survey of Manufactures* is a sample survey of approximately 50,000 establishments. A new sample is selected at 5-year intervals beginning the second survey year subsequent to the Economic Census—Manufacturing. Since 2009 is the second survey year following the 2007 Economic Census, a new sample was selected based on the 2007 Economic Census—Manufacturing. The sample was supplemented by new establishments entering business in 2007 and 2008.

In 2007, there were approximately 328,500 active manufacturing establishments. For sample efficiency and cost considerations, the 2007 manufacturing population is partitioned into two groups: (1) establishments eligible to be mailed a questionnaire and (2) establishments not eligible to be mailed a questionnaire.

Establishments and classification—Each of the establishments covered in the 2007 Economic Census—Manufacturing was classified in 1 of 480 industries (473 manufacturing industries and 7 former manufacturing industries) in accordance with the industry definitions in the 2007 NAICS manual. In the NAICS system, an industry is generally defined as a group of establishments that have similar production processes. To the extent practical, the system uses supply-based or production-oriented concepts in defining industries. The resulting group of establishments must be significant in terms of number, value added by manufacture, value of shipments, and number of employees. Establishments frequently make products classified both in their industry (primary products) and other industries (secondary products). Industry statistics (employment, payroll, value added by manufacture, value of shipments, etc.) reflect the activities of the establishments, which may make both primary and secondary products. Product statistics, however, represent the output of all establishments without regard for the classification of the producing establishment. For this reason, when relating the industry statistics, especially the value of shipments, to the product statistics, the composition of the industry's output should be considered.

Establishment—An establishment is a single physical location where business is conducted or where services or industrial operations are performed. Data in this sector includes those establishments where manufacturing is performed. A separate report is required for each manufacturing establishment (plant) with one employee or more that is in operation at any time during the year. An establishment not in operation for any portion of the year is requested to return the report form with the proper notation in the "Operational Status" section of the form. In addition, the establishment is requested to report data on any employees, capital expenditures, inventories, or shipment from inventories during the year.

Durable goods—Items with a normal life expectancy of 3 years or more. Automobiles, furniture, household appliances, and mobile homes are common examples.

Nondurable goods—Items which generally last for only a short time (3 years or less). Food, beverages, clothing, shoes, and gasoline are common examples.

Statistical reliability—For a discussion of statistical collection and estimation, sampling procedures, and measures of statistical reliability applicable to Census Bureau data, see Appendix III.

Table 1033.
Table 1033. Manufacturing—Gross Domestic Product in Current and Real (2005) Dollars by Industry: 2000 to 2012

[In billions of dollars (9,951.5 represents $9,951,500,000,000). Value added GDP is the contribution of each industry's labor and capital to its gross output and to the overall gross domestic product (GDP) of the United States. Value added is equal to an industry's gross output (sales or receipts and other operating income, commodity taxes, and inventory change) minus its intermediate inputs (consumption of goods and services purchased from other industries or imported). Current-dollar value added is calculated as the sum of distributions by an industry to its labor and capital which are derived from the components of gross domestic income]

Industry	2002 NAICS code [1]	2000	2005	2009	2010	2011	2012
CURRENT DOLLARS							
Gross domestic product, total [2]	(X)	**9,951.5**	**12,623.0**	**13,973.7**	**14,498.9**	**15,075.7**	**15,684.8**
Private industries	(X)	8,736.1	11,037.1	12,056.7	12,532.3	13,081.8	13,657.6
Manufacturing	31–33	1,415.6	1,569.3	1,540.1	1,630.5	1,731.5	1,866.7
Durable goods	33, 321, 327	839.1	878.3	787.0	866.7	910.1	1,000.2
Wood products	321	28.3	33.0	20.0	22.2	22.9	(NA)
Nonmetallic mineral products	327	41.9	45.3	32.8	31.8	32.8	(NA)
Primary metals	331	46.3	53.8	35.8	42.7	49.9	(NA)
Fabricated metal products	332	120.7	120.5	113.4	115.2	122.3	(NA)
Machinery	333	110.5	109.5	108.6	117.5	131.8	(NA)
Computer and electronic products	334	172.1	183.5	208.0	235.8	227.0	(NA)
Electrical equipment, appliances, and components	335	44.1	39.9	44.4	42.3	46.8	(NA)
Motor vehicles, bodies and trailers, and parts	3361–63	117.4	112.5	27.2	64.8	76.5	(NA)
Other transportation equipment	3364–66, 69	65.8	76.3	89.0	87.1	93.9	(NA)
Furniture and related products	337	33.8	34.3	24.3	24.3	25.9	(NA)
Miscellaneous manufacturing	339	58.3	69.7	83.4	82.9	80.2	(NA)
Nondurable goods	31, 32 (except 321 and 327)	576.6	691.0	753.2	763.8	821.3	866.5
Food and beverage and tobacco products	311, 312	164.8	172.0	229.1	219.1	215.0	(NA)
Textile mills and textile product mills	313, 314	27.9	23.5	18.3	19.0	18.2	(NA)
Apparel and leather and allied products	315, 316	21.4	16.0	11.9	11.8	11.8	(NA)
Paper products	322	61.7	53.9	60.6	53.9	53.2	(NA)
Printing and related support activities	323	40.3	37.5	31.6	30.9	31.7	(NA)
Petroleum and coal products	324	43.6	139.3	101.9	126.7	169.4	(NA)
Chemical products	325	152.2	183.2	233.6	236.0	253.5	(NA)
Plastics and rubber products	326	64.6	65.7	66.3	66.4	68.6	(NA)
CHAINED (2005) DOLLARS							
Gross domestic product, total [2]	(X)	**11,216.4**	**12,623.0**	**12,757.9**	**13,063.0**	**13,299.1**	**13,593.2**
Private industries	(X)	9,786.2	11,037.1	11,026.9	11,326.9	11,557.0	11,887.2
Manufacturing	31–33	1,390.2	1,569.3	1,447.1	1,546.8	1,585.6	1,683.7
Durable goods	33, 321, 327	741.7	878.3	800.5	906.6	968.2	1,056.7
Wood products	321	32.8	33.0	27.3	29.3	32.9	(NA)
Nonmetallic mineral products	327	44.6	45.3	27.7	28.4	30.1	(NA)
Primary metals	331	62.1	53.8	43.1	39.7	40.1	(NA)
Fabricated metal products	332	129.5	120.5	90.6	99.2	105.1	(NA)
Machinery	333	111.4	109.5	93.1	106.1	120.2	(NA)
Computer and electronic products	334	78.0	183.5	303.8	357.6	361.6	(NA)
Electrical equipment, appliances, and components	335	42.6	39.9	35.9	35.7	40.1	(NA)
Motor vehicles, bodies and trailers, and parts	3361–63	93.6	112.5	23.6	64.9	84.8	(NA)
Other transportation equipment	3364–66, 69	78.5	76.3	81.4	80.2	85.5	(NA)
Furniture and related products	337	35.1	34.3	20.5	21.4	22.7	(NA)
Miscellaneous manufacturing	339	60.3	69.7	78.2	78.3	75.7	(NA)
Nondurable goods	31, 32 (except 321 and 327)	649.3	691.0	640.4	643.0	629.7	648.3
Food and beverage and tobacco products	311, 312	175.5	172.0	185.6	195.2	192.6	(NA)
Textile mills and textile product mills	313, 314	27.4	23.5	16.8	17.7	15.8	(NA)
Apparel and leather and allied products	315, 316	19.6	16.0	11.7	11.8	11.6	(NA)
Paper products	322	58.2	53.9	46.9	40.6	40.4	(NA)
Printing and related support activities	323	37.4	37.5	31.2	31.4	33.3	(NA)
Petroleum and coal products	324	74.1	139.3	107.0	103.7	95.7	(NA)
Chemical products	325	170.0	183.2	185.0	185.4	184.4	(NA)
Plastics and rubber products	326	65.7	65.7	54.7	56.5	56.4	(NA)

NA Not available. X Not applicable. [1] North American Industry Classification System, 2002; see text, Section 15. [2] Includes industries, not shown separately. For additional industries, see Table 698.

Source: U.S. Bureau of Economic Analysis, Industry Data GDP-by-industry accounts, "Value Added by Industry," and "Real Value Added by Industry," <http://www.bea.gov/iTable/index_industry.cfm>, accessed August 2013.

Table 1034. Manufacturing—Selected Industry Statistics by State: 2007

[13,333 represents 13,333,000. Based on the 2007 Economic Census and the 2007 Nonemployer Statistics. See Appendix III]

State	Employers				Nonemployers	
	Number of establishments	Number of employees (1,000)	Annual payroll (mil. dol.)	Sales, shipments, receipts or revenue (mil. dol.)	Number of establishments	Sales, shipments, receipts or revenue (mil. dol.)
U.S..............	293,919	13,333	612,474	5,339,345	328,060	16,333
AL..................	4,928	272	11,352	112,859	4,369	204
AK..................	544	13	490	8,204	1,087	33
AZ..................	5,074	172	8,774	57,978	6,524	318
AR..................	3,088	185	6,518	60,736	2,683	128
CA..................	44,296	1,448	71,247	491,372	43,798	2,817
CO..................	5,288	138	6,790	46,332	6,882	284
CT..................	4,924	191	10,345	58,405	3,776	250
DE..................	673	35	1,760	25,680	596	36
DC..................	137	2	81	333	185	8
FL..................	14,324	355	15,227	104,833	19,505	1,203
GA..................	8,699	411	16,128	144,281	8,891	425
HI..................	984	14	511	8,799	2,075	95
ID..................	1,942	65	2,829	18,011	2,499	91
IL..................	15,704	664	31,716	257,761	10,347	531
IN..................	9,015	537	24,475	221,878	6,650	295
IA..................	3,802	223	9,526	97,592	3,031	117
KS..................	3,170	178	7,983	76,752	2,739	106
KY..................	4,165	247	10,773	119,105	3,874	181
LA..................	3,442	148	7,565	205,055	4,001	190
ME..................	1,825	59	2,524	16,363	2,652	95
MD..................	3,680	128	6,454	41,456	4,031	197
MA..................	7,737	289	15,712	86,429	6,215	315
MI..................	13,675	582	29,910	234,456	11,725	547
MN..................	7,951	341	15,999	107,563	7,516	291
MS..................	2,598	159	5,757	59,869	2,347	103
MO..................	6,886	295	12,997	110,908	5,987	259
MT..................	1,324	20	808	10,638	1,959	67
NE..................	1,984	100	3,789	40,158	1,499	55
NV..................	2,035	52	2,291	15,736	2,217	138
NH..................	2,104	82	4,196	18,592	2,287	101
NJ..................	9,250	311	16,399	116,608	6,503	433
NM..................	1,574	35	1,560	17,123	3,581	103
NY..................	18,629	534	24,268	162,720	18,163	933
NC..................	10,150	506	19,590	205,867	9,828	398
NC..................	767	26	991	11,350	626	21
OH..................	16,237	760	35,485	295,891	12,782	640
OK..................	3,964	142	5,971	60,681	4,099	210
OR..................	5,717	184	8,139	66,881	6,680	258
PA..................	15,406	651	29,433	234,840	14,146	767
RI..................	1,831	54	2,375	12,062	1,290	58
SC..................	4,335	242	10,061	93,977	3,821	174
SD..................	1,052	41	1,539	13,051	877	26
TN..................	6,752	369	15,166	140,448	6,427	306
TX..................	21,115	894	42,836	593,542	28,790	1,369
UT..................	3,368	123	5,508	42,432	3,856	171
VT..................	1,108	36	1,650	10,751	1,738	54
VA..................	5,777	277	12,170	92,418	5,084	201
WA..................	7,650	270	13,275	112,053	8,599	343
WV..................	1,413	60	2,646	25,081	1,363	44
WI..................	9,659	488	21,850	163,563	6,976	312
WY..................	596	12	574	8,835	884	32

Source: U.S. Census Bureau, "2007 Economic Census, Geographic Area Series, Detailed Statistics for the State: 2007," April 2010, <http://www.census.gov/econ/census07/>, and "Nonemployer Statistics," August 2009, <http://www.census.gov/econ/nonemployer/index.html>.

Table 1035. Manufacturing—Establishments, Employees, and Annual Payroll by Industry: 2010 and 2011

[(111,970 represents 111,970,000). Excludes most government employees, railroad employees, and self-employed persons. See Appendix III]

Industry	2007 NAICS code [1]	Establishments 2010	Establishments 2011	Employees (1,000) [2] 2010	Employees (1,000) [2] 2011	Payroll (mil. dol.) 2010	Payroll (mil. dol.) 2011
All industries, total.....................	(X)	7,396,628	7,354,043	111,970	113,426	4,940,983	5,164,898
Manufacturing, total...............	31–33	**299,982**	**295,643**	**10,863**	**10,984**	**550,386**	**574,817**
Percent of all industries.............	(X)	4.1	4.0	9.7	9.7	11.1	11.1
Food.......................................	311	24,773	25,543	1,433	1,427	53,823	54,389
Beverage and tobacco products.......	312	4,646	5,059	140	146	7,141	7,422
Textile mills............................	313	2,514	2,461	109	110	4,034	4,176
Textile product mills....................	314	6,262	6,221	111	112	3,483	3,579
Apparel manufacturing.................	315	7,206	7,137	121	114	3,059	2,973
Leather and allied products............	316	1,191	1,169	27	29	915	959
Wood products...........................	321	14,387	13,859	350	344	11,985	12,120
Paper......................................	322	4,602	4,494	365	363	19,619	19,920
Printing and related support activities...................................	323	29,118	27,913	500	481	20,244	19,900
Petroleum and coal products..........	324	2,246	2,229	100	98	8,444	8,790
Chemical..................................	325	12,923	12,914	722	725	49,760	51,819
Plastics and rubber products..........	326	12,969	12,744	668	684	28,728	29,865
Nonmetallic mineral products..........	327	15,864	15,406	344	339	15,731	15,864
Primary metal............................	331	4,667	4,628	352	373	20,069	21,939
Fabricated metal products..............	332	55,946	55,491	1,276	1,332	59,653	64,400
Machinery................................	333	24,255	23,928	929	967	50,861	55,582
Computer and electronic products.....	334	13,270	13,151	878	877	63,158	66,129
Electrical equipment, appliance and components.............................	335	5,880	5,785	329	332	16,584	17,264
Transportation equipment..............	336	11,715	11,470	1,202	1,235	73,062	76,801
Furniture and related products........	337	17,468	16,494	349	335	12,234	12,295
Miscellaneous...........................	339	28,080	27,547	558	561	27,799	28,631

X Not applicable. [1] North American Industry Classification System, 2007; see text, Section 15. [2] Covers full- and part-time employees who are on the payroll in the pay period including March 12.

Source: Census Bureau, "County Business Patterns," <http://www.census.gov/econ/cbp/>, accessed September 2013.

Table 1036. Manufacturing—Establishments, Employees, and Annual Payroll by State: 2011

[(10,984 represents 10,984,000). Excludes most government employees, railroad employees, and self-employed persons. Data are for North American Industry Classification System (NAICS), 2007, codes 31–33. See Appendix III]

State	Establishments	Employees (1,000) [1]	Payroll (mil. dol.)	State	Establishments	Employees (1,000) [1]	Payroll (mil. dol.)
United States.....	**295,643**	**10,984**	**574,817**	Missouri..............	6,114	242	11,611
Alabama...............	4,269	228	10,442	Montana..............	1,210	17	697
Alaska.................	533	13	548	Nebraska.............	1,822	91	3,917
Arizona................	4,267	138	8,008	Nevada...............	1,683	39	2,011
Arkansas..............	2,689	156	6,277	New Hampshire.....	1,848	66	3,926
California..............	38,427	1,134	67,652	New Jersey..........	7,896	234	14,450
Colorado..............	4,817	118	6,379	New Mexico.........	1,392	27	1,359
Connecticut..........	4,388	151	9,628	New York............	16,653	435	22,328
Delaware.............	598	28	1,469	North Carolina.......	8,795	403	17,920
District of Columbia...	100	1	48	North Dakota........	735	23	1,033
Florida.................	12,596	276	13,483	Ohio...................	14,526	614	31,953
Georgia................	7,460	329	14,830	Oklahoma............	3,559	127	5,979
Hawaii.................	812	12	452	Oregon...............	5,232	144	7,197
Idaho..................	1,732	53	2,589	Pennsylvania........	13,958	547	27,826
Illinois.................	14,012	539	29,250	Rhode Island........	1,513	40	2,044
Indiana................	8,084	437	21,768	South Carolina.......	3,920	204	9,704
Iowa...................	3,563	200	9,715	South Dakota........	997	40	1,648
Kansas................	2,877	154	7,748	Tennessee...........	5,790	289	13,613
Kentucky..............	3,748	206	9,478	Texas.................	19,486	734	41,292
Louisiana.............	3,261	126	7,613	Utah..................	3,105	107	5,470
Maine..................	1,634	51	2,381	Vermont..............	986	31	1,600
Maryland..............	3,093	104	6,046	Virginia...............	5,105	230	11,672
Massachusetts.......	6,782	225	14,774	Washington..........	6,906	227	13,226
Michigan..............	12,334	477	26,080	West Virginia........	1,278	52	2,622
Minnesota............	7,297	291	15,623	Wisconsin............	8,939	424	21,122
Mississippi...........	2,282	138	5,753	Wyoming.............	540	10	563

[1] Covers full- and part-time employees who are on the payroll in the pay period including March 12.

Source: U.S. Census Bureau, "County Business Patterns,"<http://www.census.gov/econ/cbp/>, accessed September 2013.

Table 1037. Manufactures—Summary by Selected Industry: 2011

[Employee data in thousands (10,649.4 represents 10,649,400); financial data in millions of dollars (559,518 represents 559,518,000,000), except as noted. Based on the Annual Survey of Manufactures; see Appendix III]

Industry based on shipments	2007 NAICS code [1]	All employees			Production workers [2] (1,000)	Value added by manufactures [3] (mil. dol.)	Value of shipments [4] (mil . dol.)
		Number [2] (1,000)	Payroll				
			Total (mil. dol.)	Per employee (dol.)			
Manufacturing, total...........................	**31–33**	**10,649.4**	**559,518**	**52,540**	**7,440.1**	**2,295,220**	**5,498,599**
Food [5]..	311	1,359.0	52,828	38,873	1,072.8	264,501	710,366
Grain and oil seed milling..........................	3112	50.5	2,864	56,716	37.4	29,278	94,025
Sugar and confectionery products.................	3113	65.4	2,887	44,129	49.2	15,634	33,120
Fruit and vegetable preserving and specialty food..........	3114	160.9	6,307	39,208	133.2	29,477	65,020
Dairy products....................................	3115	130.8	6,302	48,181	95.5	32,353	106,002
Animal slaughtering and processing...............	3116	474.4	15,121	31,873	414.7	53,824	195,727
Bakeries and tortilla..............................	3118	249.0	9,177	36,858	171.7	35,154	61,051
Beverage and tobacco products....................	312	140.0	7,272	51,954	85.0	83,489	136,888
Beverage...	3121	126.2	6,360	50,403	74.3	50,621	97,867
Textile mills......................................	313	103.5	3,840	37,117	84.9	13,234	31,473
Textile product mills..............................	314	106.8	3,544	33,170	82.5	9,687	22,081
Apparel..	315	95.2	2,655	27,897	75.4	6,461	12,860
Cut and sew apparel..............................	3152	73.2	2,042	27,883	57.5	4,674	9,576
Leather and allied products........................	316	27.0	870	32,278	20.0	2,487	5,598
Wood products [5].................................	321	324.9	11,863	36,517	262.7	28,711	70,558
Sawmills and wood preservation...................	3211	73.0	2,912	39,881	61.5	7,812	21,613
Paper...	322	346.4	19,305	55,723	269.5	81,944	175,877
Pulp, paper, and paperboard mills.................	3221	107.5	7,572	70,415	85.5	41,981	82,275
Converted paper products.........................	3222	238.9	11,733	49,110	184.0	39,963	93,603
Printing and related support activities..............	323	456.9	19,727	43,176	324.9	48,601	82,707
Petroleum and coal products.......................	324	98.2	8,723	88,781	65.1	126,208	836,813
Chemical [5]......................................	325	693.6	49,818	71,829	415.3	374,940	776,817
Basic chemical....................................	3251	143.2	11,185	78,097	88.4	100,275	267,404
Pharmaceutical and medicine......................	3254	221.3	18,223	82,353	113.2	139,800	195,732
Soap, cleaning compound, and toilet preparation...	3256	88.2	5,243	59,459	57.9	52,290	94,362
Plastics and rubber products.......................	326	674.7	29,362	43,519	524.1	91,723	204,515
Plastics products.................................	3261	549.6	23,274	42,344	425.9	73,601	160,534
Rubber product...................................	3262	125.0	6,088	48,684	98.2	18,123	43,981
Nonmetallic mineral products......................	327	333.9	15,697	47,016	258.2	50,890	92,968
Glass and glass product...........................	3272	76.3	3,871	50,700	60.4	12,648	21,834
Cement and concrete products.....................	3273	152.9	6,823	44,614	118.5	19,682	38,920
Primary metal [5].................................	331	373.9	21,758	58,189	297.0	97,934	280,153
Iron and steel mills and ferroalloy.................	3311	102.1	7,363	72,099	82.8	39,770	115,365
Foundries..	3315	123.5	5,989	48,490	100.4	16,517	31,327
Fabricated metal products [5].....................	332	1,285.7	62,575	48,670	947.2	172,967	326,797
Forging and stamping.............................	3321	103.3	5,115	49,504	76.2	15,287	33,121
Architectural and structural metals.................	3323	302.2	13,912	46,029	216.7	34,162	72,187
Machine shops, turned product and screw, nut, and bolt....................................	3327	344.5	17,144	49,770	261.2	39,469	63,474
Coating, engraving, heat treating, and allied activities..	3328	113.9	5,063	44,441	87.4	16,147	27,069
Machinery [5].....................................	333	964.7	54,218	56,203	621.4	177,486	365,735
Agriculture, construction, and mining machinery.....	3331	182.0	9,987	54,888	123.7	45,504	103,090
Industrial machinery..............................	3332	102.5	6,958	67,887	55.0	19,488	35,686
HVAC and commercial refrigeration equipment.....	3334	122.2	5,552	45,429	87.6	18,088	38,678
Metalworking machinery...........................	3335	135.5	7,509	55,406	97.2	16,934	27,785
Computer and electronic products [5]...............	334	816.7	59,944	73,400	382.8	208,008	337,861
Computer and peripheral equipment................	3341	55.3	4,114	74,395	17.6	13,009	28,893
Communications equipment........................	3342	101.3	8,641	85,345	44.1	21,158	44,632
Semiconductor and other electronic component.....	3344	270.6	16,590	61,313	168.2	86,063	123,487
Navigational, measuring, medical, and control instruments......................................	3345	366.6	29,556	80,618	138.3	84,466	135,271
Electrical equipment, appliance, and component.....	335	328.4	16,961	51,639	223.7	58,536	120,023
Electrical equipment..............................	3353	114.0	6,131	53,783	72.5	19,600	38,734
Other electrical equipment and component..........	3359	129.7	7,014	54,067	86.3	24,869	51,338
Transportation equipment [5]......................	336	1,235.4	77,482	62,717	838.5	264,474	690,437
Motor vehicle.....................................	3361	148.0	9,889	66,813	126.9	54,917	233,786
Motor vehicle parts...............................	3363	404.6	20,633	50,992	309.0	62,855	184,764
Aerospace product and parts.......................	3364	402.0	32,579	81,049	207.3	105,495	183,275
Ship and boat building............................	3366	121.2	6,590	54,380	78.9	17,799	28,067
Furniture and related products [5].................	337	319.9	11,931	37,299	237.2	32,712	61,972
Miscellaneous [5].................................	339	564.7	29,147	51,614	351.9	100,226	156,101
Medical equipment and supplies...................	3391	289.6	16,915	58,415	175.4	61,932	89,519

[1] North American Industrial Classification System, 2007; see text, Section 15. [2] Includes all full-time and part-time employees on payrolls of operating manufacturing establishments. All employees represents the average of production workers plus all other employees for the payroll period ended nearest the 12th of March. Production workers represent the average of employment for payroll periods ended nearest the 12th of March, June, September, and December. [3] Adjusted value added; takes into account (a) value added by merchandising operations (that is, difference between the sales value and cost of merchandise sold without further manufacture, processing, or assembly), plus (b) net change in finished goods and work-in-process inventories between beginning and end of year. [4] This item covers the received or receivable net selling values, f.o.b. plant (exclusive of freight and taxes), of all products shipped as well as all miscellaneous receipts. In the case of multiunit companies, the manufacturer was requested to report the value of products transferred to other establishments of the same company at full economic or commercial value. [5] Includes industries not shown separately.

Source: U.S. Census Bureau, Annual Survey of Manufactures, "Statistics for Industry Groups and Industries: 2011 and 2010," <http://factfinder2.census.gov/>, accessed March 2013.

Table 1038. Manufactures—Summary by State: 2011

[10,649.4 represents 10,649,400. Data are for North American Industry Classification System (NAICS) 2007 codes 31–33. Sum of state totals may not add to U.S. total because U.S. and state figures were independently derived. See Appendix III]

State	All employees [1]			Production workers [1]		Value added by manufactures [2]		Value of shipments [3] (mil. dol.)
	Number (1,000)	Payroll		Number (1,000)	Wages (mil . dol.)	Total (mil. dol.)	Per production worker (dol.)	
		Total (mil. dol.)	Per employee (dol.)					
United States.............	10,649.4	559,518	52,540	7,440.1	313,710	2,295,220	308,491	5,498,599
Alabama......................	213.5	10,001	46,850	161.3	6,469	43,374	268,826	113,195
Alaska........................	11.1	469	42,066	9.0	329	1,740	193,334	8,323
Arizona.......................	126.8	7,829	61,720	71.5	3,185	27,192	380,100	50,048
Arkansas.....................	145.8	5,977	41,004	116.6	4,224	23,737	203,654	59,897
California.....................	1,114.2	66,869	60,015	693.6	29,834	231,029	333,100	497,755
Colorado.....................	110.2	6,068	55,068	73.8	3,191	23,270	315,441	49,230
Connecticut.................	154.6	9,488	61,381	94.7	4,510	29,885	315,524	51,946
Delaware.....................	27.2	1,452	53,295	18.7	776	7,421	396,547	20,626
District of Columbia........	1.0	41	41,648	660.0	22	104	157,435	182
Florida........................	254.7	12,893	50,628	169.7	6,489	46,016	271,226	92,182
Georgia......................	313.2	14,318	45,712	240.4	9,075	65,055	270,641	144,395
Hawaii........................	10.7	431	40,367	6.7	232	1,457	217,692	7,695
Idaho.........................	48.4	2,375	49,098	36.4	1,475	11,428	314,153	22,895
Illinois........................	535.5	29,008	54,171	366.5	15,654	115,314	314,648	275,279
Indiana.......................	428.8	21,509	50,156	321.3	14,017	100,287	312,170	232,142
Iowa..........................	192.2	9,502	49,427	140.0	5,701	39,521	282,211	102,091
Kansas.......................	151.0	7,645	50,631	107.8	4,628	31,534	292,630	84,277
Kentucky.....................	201.8	9,293	46,054	155.9	6,354	38,181	244,861	118,970
Louisiana....................	124.9	7,594	60,793	90.5	4,765	61,561	680,175	270,123
Maine.........................	47.9	2,325	48,486	33.7	1,452	7,866	233,641	15,853
Maryland.....................	104.2	5,998	57,564	65.7	2,774	23,203	353,257	41,836
Massachusetts..............	224.0	13,638	60,885	138.6	6,270	45,417	327,643	80,477
Michigan.....................	461.5	25,129	54,457	336.2	15,665	84,244	250,548	221,204
Minnesota...................	290.1	15,214	52,444	191.6	7,811	53,376	278,531	121,021
Mississippi..................	127.6	5,461	42,800	99.6	3,593	20,323	204,070	60,471
Missouri......................	230.6	11,388	49,381	170.3	7,192	45,121	264,874	107,703
Montana......................	13.2	638	48,196	9.6	403	3,354	349,474	11,706
Nebraska....................	90.2	3,817	42,301	69.1	2,630	19,174	277,322	52,946
Nevada.......................	38.5	2,080	53,978	25.8	1,062	8,172	316,727	14,923
New Hampshire.............	70.3	3,947	56,132	43.3	1,781	10,637	245,091	19,653
New Jersey..................	234.5	14,357	61,210	150.4	6,552	47,285	314,414	107,436
New Mexico..................	25.5	1,294	50,820	17.1	731	18,400	1,075,704	28,594
New York.....................	418.8	22,260	53,147	277.5	11,376	77,618	279,691	151,374
North Carolina..............	388.0	17,342	44,692	292.5	10,832	102,559	350,571	200,420
North Dakota................	21.6	968	44,761	16.3	629	4,238	260,557	13,403
Ohio..........................	598.6	30,907	51,635	432.6	18,968	118,817	274,638	292,737
Oklahoma....................	125.4	5,951	47,444	93.7	3,807	23,715	253,185	69,833
Oregon.......................	129.4	6,543	50,578	91.6	3,692	37,150	405,420	59,665
Pennsylvania...............	530.5	27,231	51,335	371.8	15,800	100,737	270,908	237,600
Rhode Island................	36.2	1,997	55,166	23.7	1,000	5,652	238,929	11,175
South Carolina..............	194.4	9,408	48,388	146.6	6,069	37,582	256,358	90,737
South Dakota...............	38.7	1,633	42,226	28.8	1,023	6,164	213,853	16,152
Tennessee...................	276.6	13,121	47,431	203.2	8,039	54,420	267,843	132,135
Texas.........................	700.8	38,534	54,988	488.8	21,946	216,794	443,491	671,372
Utah..........................	100.4	5,290	52,699	65.5	2,732	26,720	408,245	50,788
Vermont......................	28.0	1,537	54,817	18.1	748	5,017	277,224	10,550
Virginia.......................	222.0	11,189	50,400	157.6	6,476	54,557	346,143	94,688
Washington..................	230.2	13,306	57,813	152.9	7,370	52,683	344,552	115,059
West Virginia................	49.6	2,527	50,946	37.6	1,678	10,140	269,902	23,977
Wisconsin....................	427.9	21,168	49,470	309.4	12,331	72,804	235,311	163,107
Wyoming.....................	8.4	557	66,372	5.9	349	3,180	538,737	8,757

[1] Includes all full-time and part-time employees on the payrolls of operating manufacturing establishments during any part of the pay period that included the 12th of the month. Included are employees on paid sick leave, paid holidays, and paid vacations; not included are proprietors and partners of unincorporated businesses. [2] Value added is derived by subtracting the cost of materials, supplies, containers, fuel, purchased electricity, and contract work from the value of shipments (products manufactured plus receipts for services rendered). The result of this calculation is adjusted by the addition of value added by merchandising operations (i.e., the difference between the sales value and the cost of merchandise sold without further manufacture, processing, or assembly) plus the net change in finished goods and work-in-process between the beginning and end of year inventories. [3] Includes extensive and unmeasurable duplication from shipments between establishments in the same industry classification.

Source: U.S. Census Bureau, Annual Survey of Manufactures, "Geographic Area Statistics for All Manufacturing by State: 2011 and 2010," <http://factfinder2.census.gov/>, accessed March 2013.

Table 1039. Manufacturing Industries—Employees by Industry: 1990 to 2012

[Annual averages of monthly figures (109,487 represents 109,487,000). Covers all full- and part-time employees who worked during, or received pay for, any part of the pay period including the 12th of the month. Minus sign (-) indicates decrease. See also head note, Table 658]

Industry	2012 NAICS code [1]	All employees (1,000)						Percent change	
		1990	2000	2005	2010	2011	2012	1990–2000	2000–2012
All industries................................	(X)	**109,487**	**131,881**	**133,747**	**129,917**	**131,497**	**133,739**	**20.5**	**1.4**
Manufacturing..................................	31–33	17,695	17,263	14,227	11,528	11,726	11,919	-2.4	-31.0
Percent of all industries........................	(X)	16	13	11	9	9	9	(X)	(X)
Durable goods................................	(X)	10,737	10,877	8,956	7,064	7,273	7,462	1.3	-31.4
Wood products [2]........................	321	543	615	561	342	337	338	13.3	-45.1
Sawmills & wood preservation................	3211	148	134	119	82	84	84	-9.6	-37.0
Nonmetallic mineral products [2]................	327	528	554	505	371	367	364	4.9	-34.4
Cement & concrete products....................	3273	195	234	240	170	165	162	20.1	-31.0
Primary metals [2]........................	331	689	622	466	362	388	402	-9.7	-35.4
Iron & steel mills & ferroalloy production......	3311	187	135	96	87	92	94	-27.7	-30.7
Steel products from purchased steel..........	3312	70	73	61	52	57	60	4.0	-17.8
Alumina & aluminum production................	3313	108	101	73	54	57	60	-7.3	-40.8
Foundries....................................	3315	214	217	164	112	122	127	1.4	-41.5
Fabricated metal products [2]................	332	1,610	1,753	1,522	1,282	1,347	1,411	8.9	-19.5
Architectural & structural metals...........	3323	357	428	398	321	328	341	20.0	-20.3
Machine shops & threaded products..........	3327	309	365	345	313	343	362	18.4	-0.8
Coating, engraving, & heat treating metals..	3328	143	175	145	122	131	136	22.7	-22.1
Machinery [2]................................	333	1,410	1,457	1,166	996	1,056	1,098	3.3	-24.6
Agricultural, construction, & mining machinery...............	3331	229	222	208	208	227	245	-2.8	10.2
HVAC & commercial refrigeration equipment.........................	3334	165	194	154	125	130	128	17.7	-34.3
Metalworking machinery......................	3335	267	274	202	155	168	177	2.5	-35.2
Turbine & power transmission equipment.....	3336	114	111	98	92	98	102	-2.4	-8.1
Other general purpose machinery.............	3339	336	344	269	226	239	252	2.4	-26.7
Computer & electronic products [2]..............	334	1,903	1,820	1,316	1,095	1,104	1,094	-4.3	-39.9
Computer & peripheral equipment.............	3341	367	302	205	158	157	159	-17.8	-47.5
Communications equipment....................	3342	223	239	141	117	115	110	7.0	-54.1
Semiconductors & electronic components......................	3344	574	676	452	369	383	384	17.8	-43.2
Electronic instruments......................	3345	635	488	441	406	404	400	-23.2	-17.9
Electrical equipment & appliances [2].............	335	633	591	434	360	366	370	-6.7	-37.4
Electrical equipment........................	3353	244	210	152	136	139	143	-13.9	-31.9
Other electrical equipment & components........................	3359	195	191	136	119	125	127	-2.3	-33.4
Transportation equipment [2]....................	336	2,135	2,057	1,772	1,333	1,382	1,456	-3.6	-29.2
Motor vehicles..............................	3361	271	291	248	153	158	168	7.4	-42.3
Motor vehicle bodies & trailers..............	3362	130	183	171	107	114	125	40.8	-31.4
Motor vehicle parts.........................	3363	653	840	678	419	446	480	28.6	-42.9
Aerospace products & parts.................	3364	841	517	455	478	487	497	-38.5	-3.7
Ship & boat building........................	3366	174	154	154	125	123	129	-11.3	-16.1
Furniture & related products [2]..................	337	602	680	566	357	353	350	13.0	-48.5
Household & institutional furniture............	3371	398	441	381	223	219	217	10.7	-50.9
Miscellaneous manufacturing....................	339	686	728	647	567	574	580	6.2	-20.4
Medical equipment & supplies................	3391	283	305	300	303	308	311	7.7	2.1
Other miscellaneous manufacturing..........	3399	403	423	347	264	266	268	5.1	-36.6
Nondurable goods.............................	(X)	6,958	6,386	5,271	4,464	4,453	4,456	-8.2	-30.2
Food manufacturing [2].......................	311	1,507	1,553	1,478	1,451	1,459	1,469	3.0	-5.4
Fruit & vegetable preserving & specialty......	3114	218	197	174	173	173	170	-9.5	-14.0
Dairy products..............................	3115	145	136	132	130	134	136	-5.9	-0.1
Animal slaughtering & processing.............	3116	427	507	504	489	486	485	18.6	-4.4
Bakeries & tortilla manufacturing..............	3118	292	306	280	277	282	285	4.9	-7.1
Textile mills [2].............................	313	492	378	218	119	120	118	-23.1	-68.8
Fabric mills.................................	3132	270	192	104	53	56	55	-29.0	-71.2
Textile product mills [2].......................	314	236	230	176	119	118	117	-2.5	-49.2
Textile furnishings mills.....................	3141	127	129	96	57	55	52	1.3	-59.5
Apparel [2].................................	315	903	484	251	157	152	148	-46.4	-69.4
Cut & sew apparel..........................	3152	750	380	193	124	124	122	-49.3	-67.9
Paper & paper products........................	322	647	605	484	395	387	379	-6.6	-37.3
Pulp, paper, & paperboard mills..............	3221	238	191	142	112	109	108	-19.7	-43.5
Converted paper products....................	3222	409	413	343	282	278	271	1.1	-34.5
Printing & related support activities..............	323	809	807	646	488	472	462	-0.2	-42.7
Petroleum & coal products......................	324	153	123	112	114	112	113	-19.4	-8.1
Chemicals [2]...............................	325	1,036	980	872	787	784	784	-5.3	-20.1
Basic chemicals............................	3251	249	188	150	142	142	143	-24.4	-24.2
Pharmaceuticals & medicines................	3254	207	274	288	277	270	271	32.4	-1.3
Soaps, cleaning compounds, and toiletries...	3256	132	129	114	102	103	103	-2.4	-19.5
Plastics & rubber products [2]..................	326	825	951	802	625	635	645	15.3	-32.1
Plastics products...........................	3261	618	737	634	502	508	516	19.2	-30.0
Rubber products............................	3262	207	214	168	123	127	129	3.5	-39.7
Miscellaneous nondurable goods manufacturing...................	329	351	276	232	211	216	222	-21.4	-19.7
Beverages..................................	3291	173	175	167	167	171	178	1.2	1.7
Tobacco and Tobacco Products...............	3292	45	32	25	17	16	14	-28.4	-55.3
Leather & allied products......................	3293	133	69	40	28	29	29	-48.3	-57.3

X Not applicable. [1] Based on the North American Industry Classification System, 2012 (NAICS); see text, this section and Section 15. [2] Includes other industries, not shown separately.

Source: U.S. Bureau of Labor Statistics, Current Employment Statistics Program, "Employment, Hours, and Earnings—National," <http://www.bls.gov/ces/home.htm/>, accessed March 2013.

Table 1040. Manufacturing Industries—Average Weekly Hours and Average Weekly Overtime Hours of Production Workers: 1990 to 2012

[Covers all full- and part-time employees who worked during, or received pay for, any part of the pay period including the 12th of the month]

Industry	2012 NAICS code [1]	Average weekly hours of production workers					Average weekly overtime hours for production workers				
		1990	1995	2000	2005	2012	1990	1995	2000	2005	2012
Total	31–33	**40.5**	**41.3**	**41.3**	**40.7**	**41.7**	**3.9**	**4.7**	**4.7**	**3.8**	**4.2**
Durable goods	(X)	**41.1**	**42.1**	**41.8**	**41.1**	**42.0**	**3.9**	**5.0**	**4.8**	**3.8**	**4.3**
Wood products	321	40.4	41.0	41.0	40.0	41.1	3.3	3.9	4.1	3.0	3.9
Nonmetallic mineral products	327	40.9	41.8	41.6	42.2	42.2	5.0	5.7	6.1	4.7	5.1
Primary metals	331	42.1	43.4	44.2	43.1	43.8	4.6	5.7	6.5	5.7	6.2
Fabricated metal products	332	41.0	41.9	41.9	41.0	42.1	3.9	4.8	4.9	3.8	4.3
Machinery	333	42.1	43.5	42.3	42.1	42.8	4.0	5.3	5.1	3.9	4.5
Computer and electronic products	334	41.3	42.2	41.4	40.0	40.4	3.8	4.9	4.6	2.9	2.7
Electrical equipment and appliances	335	41.2	41.9	41.6	40.6	41.6	3.0	3.5	3.7	3.6	4.2
Transportation equipment [2]	336	42.0	43.7	43.3	42.4	43.8	4.5	6.5	5.5	4.7	5.2
Furniture and related products	337	38.0	38.5	39.2	39.2	40.0	2.3	2.8	3.5	2.3	3.3
Miscellaneous manufacturing	339	39.0	39.2	39.0	38.7	39.3	3.0	3.4	3.1	2.7	2.7
Nondurable goods	(X)	**39.6**	**40.1**	**40.3**	**39.9**	**41.1**	**3.9**	**4.3**	**4.5**	**3.8**	**4.1**
Food manufacturing	311	39.3	39.6	40.1	39.0	40.6	4.4	4.6	5.0	4.5	4.5
Beverages and tobacco products	312	38.9	39.3	42.0	40.1	(NA)	3.8	4.8	5.8	2.2	(NA)
Textile mills	313	40.2	40.9	41.4	40.3	42.6	4.2	5.0	4.8	3.3	3.9
Textile product mills	314	38.5	38.6	38.7	38.9	39.7	2.9	3.3	3.4	2.4	2.8
Apparel	315	34.7	35.3	35.7	35.8	37.1	2.0	2.2	2.1	1.1	2.2
Leather and allied products	316	37.4	37.7	37.5	38.4	(NA)	4.0	4.0	4.6	2.9	(NA)
Paper and paper products	322	43.6	43.4	42.8	42.5	42.9	4.9	5.5	5.7	4.9	4.6
Printing and related support activities	323	38.7	39.1	39.2	38.4	38.5	3.6	3.8	3.7	2.2	2.3
Petroleum and coal products	324	44.4	43.7	42.7	45.5	47.1	6.2	6.3	6.5	6.4	8.0
Chemicals	325	42.8	43.3	42.2	42.3	42.4	4.9	5.6	5.0	3.6	4.4
Plastics and rubber products	326	40.6	41.1	40.8	40.0	41.8	3.4	3.9	4.0	4.0	3.8

X Not applicable. NA Not available [1] Based on the North American Industry Classification System (NAICS), 2012; see text, this section and Section 15. [2] Includes railroad rolling stock manufacturing, not shown separately.

Source: U.S. Bureau of Labor Statistics, Current Employment Statistics Program, "Employment, Hours, and Earnings—National," <http://www.bls.gov/ces/home.htm/>, accessed March 2013.

Table 1041. Indexes of Employment and Hours of All Persons in Manufacturing: 1990 to 2012

[2002 = 100. Based on Current Employment Statistics and supplemented with Current Population Survey. Employment and hours of all persons include those of paid employees, the self employed (partners and proprietors), and unpaid family workers. See text, Section 12]

Industry	2007 NAICS code [1]	Employment					Hours				
		1990	2000	2005	2010	2012	1990	2000	2005	2010	2012
Food manufacturing	311	99.0	101.6	97.0	94.9	97.3	98.5	103.0	95.6	97.6	99.7
Beverage and tobacco products	312	104.3	99.1	92.2	88.8	92.5	106.0	107.6	93.9	86.6	91.3
Textile mills	313	166.1	128.0	74.2	42.6	42.4	164.4	130.3	74.0	42.8	43.4
Textile product mills	314	113.9	109.5	87.0	58.9	57.5	113.1	109.4	85.9	60.4	58.0
Apparel manufacturing	315	250.7	135.2	72.6	48.0	45.3	239.7	133.1	71.4	48.0	45.7
Leather and allied products	316	228.7	124.2	74.8	52.9	57.0	231.1	127.9	78.7	54.6	65.2
Wood product manufacturing	321	99.5	111.8	101.8	63.3	62.3	100.3	114.7	101.7	62.3	64.2
Paper manufacturing	322	118.0	110.2	88.4	72.1	69.3	121.9	112.6	89.7	73.9	70.2
Printing and related support activities	323	116.7	114.4	91.8	70.7	64.8	116.9	115.8	91.6	69.2	64.3
Petroleum and coal products	324	128.8	103.7	94.0	95.6	95.7	132.6	103.0	98.3	96.0	106.5
Chemical manufacturing	325	111.8	106.2	94.9	85.5	85.8	111.3	104.6	94.1	84.9	84.9
Plastics and rubber products	326	97.8	112.4	95.0	73.8	76.5	97.6	112.9	93.2	75.5	78.4
Nonmetallic mineral products	327	102.8	107.3	97.7	72.7	73.2	100.3	105.8	97.3	72.7	72.9
Primary metal products	331	135.7	122.0	91.8	71.4	79.3	134.7	127.2	93.8	73.5	81.8
Fabricated metal products	332	104.8	112.7	98.7	83.4	90.9	105.6	116.3	99.3	84.3	94.2
Machinery manufacturing	333	115.5	118.5	94.8	81.0	89.5	118.0	122.8	97.4	84.2	93.8
Computer and electronic products	334	126.6	121.6	87.5	73.0	72.8	132.1	126.1	88.5	75.1	74.2
Electrical equipment and appliances	335	127.7	119.0	87.9	72.6	74.6	130.9	123.4	89.1	74.4	77.5
Transportation equipment	336	116.4	112.2	96.5	72.9	79.4	115.4	114.2	96.3	73.7	81.4
Furniture and related products	337	100.3	111.1	94.9	59.7	58.3	97.3	111.0	95.3	58.0	59.7
Miscellaneous manufacturing	339	101.8	107.2	96.8	82.9	84.3	101.0	106.9	95.7	82.5	85.7

[1] North American Industry Classification System, 2007; see text, Section 15.

Source: Bureau of Labor Statistics, Labor Productivity and Costs, "Industry Employment and Hours Data Tables," June 2013, <http://www.bls.gov/lpc/iprhoursdata.htm/>.

Table 1042. Average Hourly Earnings of Production Workers in Manufacturing Industries by State: 2009 to 2012

[In dollars. Data are based on the North American Industry Classification System (NAICS), 2007. Based on the Current Employment Statistics Program. Covers full- and part-time employees who received pay for any part of the pay period including the 12th of the month. Exclude proprietors, self-employed, unpaid family or volunteer workers, farm workers, and domestic workers. See source, and Appendix III]

State	2009	2010	2011	2012	State	2009	2010	2011	2012
United States........	**18.24**	**18.61**	**18.93**	**19.08**	Missouri................	18.47	18.45	18.66	18.05
Alabama................	15.43	15.71	16.93	18.31	Montana................	16.85	17.10	18.34	17.88
Alaska..................	17.38	20.44	19.60	17.89	Nebraska...............	16.06	16.13	16.58	16.64
Arizona.................	17.14	17.00	17.60	18.17	Nevada.................	15.61	15.51	16.29	16.00
Arkansas...............	14.07	13.87	14.50	15.20	New Hampshire........	17.37	17.81	18.24	18.13
California...............	17.80	18.95	19.49	20.20	New Jersey............	18.31	18.80	19.07	19.33
Colorado...............	21.23	22.07	23.67	25.13	New Mexico............	14.59	15.76	16.22	15.70
Connecticut............	23.03	23.68	24.77	23.94	New York...............	18.54	18.39	18.44	18.54
Delaware...............	17.69	16.53	15.94	15.74	North Carolina.........	15.88	15.85	16.04	16.55
Florida.................	19.60	19.42	18.81	19.64	North Dakota..........	15.56	15.93	17.04	18.06
Georgia................	15.43	16.63	17.69	17.89	Ohio...................	18.63	18.66	19.25	19.35
Hawaii.................	19.06	18.58	18.20	19.15	Oklahoma..............	14.76	14.33	15.65	16.89
Idaho..................	20.30	20.70	20.97	20.92	Oregon................	17.69	17.60	17.96	18.67
Illinois.................	16.61	16.92	18.01	19.17	Pennsylvania..........	16.28	16.88	17.49	18.26
Indiana................	18.96	18.52	18.04	18.50	Rhode Island..........	14.12	14.71	16.29	18.26
Iowa...................	16.73	16.73	16.50	17.41	South Carolina........	16.29	16.52	16.72	17.01
Kansas................	19.09	18.87	19.52	18.46	South Dakota.........	14.82	15.28	16.34	16.95
Kentucky..............	18.11	18.94	18.90	18.43	Tennessee............	14.73	15.33	16.63	16.64
Louisiana..............	20.49	21.31	21.15	20.43	Texas.................	14.39	14.50	16.42	18.55
Maine..................	19.97	20.18	20.21	20.50	Utah...................	18.20	18.46	18.03	17.99
Maryland..............	18.77	20.06	18.60	16.64	Vermont...............	16.41	16.63	17.24	18.22
Massachusetts........	20.66	20.50	20.47	20.90	Virginia................	18.69	19.11	18.51	18.54
Michigan..............	21.58	21.79	21.11	20.71	Washington...........	23.39	23.48	23.98	24.14
Minnesota.............	18.60	18.87	19.04	19.19	West Virginia..........	18.69	18.11	18.03	18.61
Mississippi............	14.64	14.83	15.12	15.90	Wisconsin.............	18.14	18.10	17.71	18.05
					Wyoming..............	20.71	20.49	22.19	22.69

Source: U.S. Bureau of Labor Statistics, Current Employment Statistics, "Average hours and earnings of production employees on manufacturing payrolls by State," <http://www.bls.gov/ces/home.htm> accessed April 2013.

Table 1043. Manufacturing Full–Time Equivalent (FTE) Employees and Wages by Industry: 2000 to 2012

[123,384 represents 123,384,000. Based on National Income and Product Account tables. Full-time equivalent employees equals the number of employees on full-time schedules plus the number of employees for part-time schedules converted to full-time basis]

Industry	2002 NAICS code [1]	Full-time equivalent (FTE) employees (1,000)				Wage and salary accruals per (FTE) worker (dol.)			
		2000	2005	2011	2012	2000	2005	2011	2012
Domestic industries, total...........	(X)	**123,384**	**125,505**	**122,139**	**124,481**	**39,166**	**45,441**	**54,420**	**55,712**
Manufacturing............................	31–33	**16,948**	**13,954**	**11,453**	**11,663**	**43,957**	**50,908**	**61,740**	**63,057**
Percent of all industries...................	(X)	13.7	11.1	9.4	9.4	112.2	112.0	113.5	113.2
Durable goods.............................	(X)	10,713	8,820	7,129	7,349	46,573	53,118	65,510	66,429
Wood products........................	321	602	549	327	331	30,351	35,992	39,296	40,317
Nonmetallic mineral products..........	327	549	494	357	357	39,021	45,742	51,337	53,227
Primary metals........................	331	611	460	383	398	45,836	53,244	63,045	63,840
Fabricated metal products.............	332	1,735	1,499	1,312	1,382	37,766	43,658	52,642	53,638
Machinery.............................	333	1,427	1,142	1,037	1,083	46,612	53,647	65,537	66,486
Computer and electronic products......	334	1,779	1,293	1,090	1,080	70,449	78,666	99,646	102,159
Electrical equipment, appliances, and components............................	335	583	428	357	366	40,241	48,882	62,338	63,467
Motor vehicles, bodies and trailers, and parts...........................	3361–3363	1,301	1,095	715	776	48,754	54,052	60,022	59,491
Other transportation equipment........	3364–3365	740	671	654	673	53,294	65,937	83,693	84,040
Furniture and related products.........	337	671	553	345	344	29,571	34,754	40,421	41,775
Miscellaneous manufacturing...........	339	715	636	552	560	38,744	46,667	58,273	60,141
Nondurable goods........................	(X)	6,235	5,134	4,324	4,314	39,464	47,110	55,524	57,312
Food and beverage and tobacco products.............................	311–312	1,727	1,617	1,575	1,586	33,956	39,273	45,032	46,335
Textile mills and textile product mills. ..	313–314	588	372	230	225	29,013	34,263	39,544	40,727
Apparel and leather and allied products.............................	315	539	288	175	171	24,198	31,755	38,400	38,800
Paper products.........................	322	598	469	378	369	45,834	53,815	62,679	64,348
Printing and related support activities..	323	757	626	459	447	39,142	42,726	46,510	47,412
Petroleum and coal products...........	324	120	110	110	110	62,998	82,184	102,638	108,318
Chemical products.....................	325	967	862	774	774	61,314	72,955	86,069	89,665
Plastics and rubber products...........	326	938	788	622	631	35,624	41,181	48,841	50,161

X Not applicable. [1] North American Industry Classification System, 2002; see text, Section 15.

Source: U.S. Bureau of Economic Analysis, National Income and Product Accounts Tables, "Table 6.5D. Full-Time Equivalent Employees by Industry," and "Table 6.6D. Wages and Salaries Per Full-Time Equivalent Employee by Industry," <http://www.bea.gov/itable/>, accessed August 2013.

Table 1044. Manufacturers' Shipments, Inventories, and New Orders: 1997 to 2012

[In billions of dollars (3,835 represents $3,835,000,000,000), except ratio. Based on the Manufacturers' Shipments, Inventories, and Orders (M3) survey. See source for details]

Year	Shipments	Inventories (December 31) [1]	Ratio of inventories to shipments [2]	New orders	Unfilled orders (December 31)
1997..................	3,835	433	1.36	3,780	508
1998..................	3,900	439	1.37	3,808	492
1999..................	4,032	453	1.35	3,957	501
2000..................	4,209	470	1.37	4,161	545
2001..................	3,970	417	1.33	3,865	502
2002..................	3,915	412	1.30	3,819	468
2003..................	4,015	398	1.20	3,971	490
2004..................	4,309	429	1.17	4,283	537
2005..................	4,742	461	1.14	4,756	626
2006..................	5,016	509	1.22	5,078	759
2007..................	5,319	547	1.22	5,390	902
2008..................	5,468	528	1.42	5,447	995
2009..................	4,420	490	1.29	4,191	824
2010..................	4,905	537	1.27	4,876	868
2011..................	5,499	592	1.29	5,505	955
2012..................	5,733	606	1.29	5,681	991

[1] Inventories are stated at current cost. [2] Ratio based on December seasonally adjusted inventory data.

Source: Census Bureau, Manufacturers' Shipments, Inventories, and Orders, "Historical Data," <http://www.census.gov/manufacturing/m3/historical_data/index.html>, accessed September 2013.

Table 1045. Ratios of Manufacturers' Inventories to Shipments and Unfilled Orders to Shipments by Industry Group: 2000 to 2012

[Based on the Manufacturers' Shipments, Inventories, and Orders (M3) survey. See source for details]

Industry	2007 NAICS code [1]	2000	2005	2008	2009	2010	2011	2012
INVENTORIES-TO-SHIPMENTS RATIO [2]								
All manufacturing industries............................	**(X)**	**1.37**	**1.14**	**1.42**	**1.29**	**1.27**	**1.29**	**1.29**
Durable goods..	(X)	1.56	1.33	1.73	1.63	1.62	1.65	1.65
Wood products..................................	321	1.41	1.16	1.68	1.44	1.39	1.43	1.39
Nonmetallic mineral products.....................	327	1.27	1.02	1.50	1.43	1.48	1.38	1.41
Primary metals.................................	331	1.77	1.45	2.08	1.58	1.56	1.41	1.41
Fabricated metals...............................	332	1.56	1.44	1.76	1.67	1.61	1.62	1.66
Machinery......................................	333	2.05	1.66	1.99	2.01	1.82	1.88	1.96
Computers and electronic products...............	334	1.46	1.37	1.43	1.53	1.53	1.64	1.62
Electrical equipment, appliances, and components........	335	1.42	1.33	1.63	1.51	1.46	1.54	1.60
Transportation equipment.......................	336	1.43	1.11	1.77	1.60	1.66	1.75	1.70
Furniture and related products...................	337	1.37	1.14	1.20	1.18	1.17	1.12	1.11
Miscellaneous products.........................	339	1.84	1.66	1.75	1.63	1.78	1.76	1.70
Nondurable goods.....................................	(X)	1.13	0.95	1.11	0.99	0.98	0.99	0.97
Food products..................................	311	0.86	0.74	0.77	0.77	0.78	0.78	0.77
Beverages and tobacco products.................	312	1.50	1.37	1.49	1.63	1.64	1.58	1.73
Textile mills....................................	313	1.55	1.22	1.65	1.25	1.26	1.33	1.28
Textile product mills............................	314	1.88	1.19	1.75	1.47	1.71	1.58	1.55
Apparel..	315	1.93	1.48	1.72	1.53	1.54	1.70	1.88
Leather and allied products......................	316	2.01	1.80	2.37	2.05	1.78	2.05	2.22
Paper products.................................	322	1.11	1.07	1.12	0.99	0.96	1.00	1.01
Printing.......................................	323	0.79	0.81	0.86	0.78	0.80	0.82	0.84
Petroleum and coal products.....................	324	0.68	0.67	0.97	0.77	0.74	0.72	0.67
Basic chemicals................................	325	1.36	1.13	1.37	1.22	1.22	1.26	1.25
Plastics and rubber products.....................	326	1.25	1.10	1.34	1.18	1.19	1.22	1.23
UNFILLED ORDERS-TO-SHIPMENTS RATIO								
Durable goods..	(X)	4.03	4.54	7.23	6.35	6.12	6.10	6.17
Primary metals.................................	331	1.53	1.87	1.88	1.51	1.73	1.49	1.27
Fabricated metals...............................	332	2.13	2.52	2.93	2.65	2.67	2.72	2.97
Machinery......................................	333	2.65	2.78	4.26	3.63	3.76	3.91	3.31
Computers and electronic products...............	334	4.24	5.05	5.56	5.95	6.18	6.29	7.05
Electrical equipment, appliances, and components........	335	1.86	2.06	2.43	2.14	2.05	2.35	2.33
Transportation equipment.......................	336	8.13	9.24	19.18	14.59	14.15	14.88	14.51
Furniture and related products...................	337	1.29	1.29	1.44	1.49	1.42	1.40	1.34

X Not applicable. [1] Based on the North American Industry Classification System, 2007; see text, this section and Section 15. [2] Ratio based on December seasonally adjusted inventory data.

Source: Census Bureau, Manufacturers' Shipments, Inventories, and Orders, "Historical Data," <http://www.census.gov/manufacturing/m3/historical_data/index.html>, accessed September 2013.

Table 1046. Value of Manufacturers' Shipments, Inventories, and New Orders by Industry: 2000 to 2012

[In billions of dollars (4,209 represents $4,209,000,000,000). Based on the Manufacturers' Shipments, Inventories, and Orders (M3) survey. See source for details]

Industry	2007 NAICS code [1]	2000	2005	2009	2010	2011	2012
SHIPMENTS							
All manufacturing industries...................	(X)	**4,209**	**4,742**	**4,420**	**4,905**	**5,499**	**5,733**
Durable goods.........................	(X)	2,374	2,425	2,063	2,291	2,503	2,672
Wood products.........................	321	94	112	65	70	71	76
Nonmetallic mineral products........	327	97	115	90	90	93	96
Primary metals.........................	331	157	203	169	233	280	302
Fabricated metals.....................	332	268	289	281	294	327	342
Machinery...............................	333	292	303	288	318	366	399
Computers and electronic products....	334	511	373	321	331	338	343
Electrical equipment, appliances, and components....	335	125	112	105	110	120	123
Transportation equipment.............	336	640	691	540	637	690	764
Furniture and related products........	337	75	84	60	59	62	65
Miscellaneous products..............	339	115	143	144	150	156	160
Nondurable goods.....................	(X)	1,835	2,317	2,357	2,615	2,996	3,062
Food products.........................	311	435	532	627	649	710	728
Beverages and tobacco products....	312	112	124	128	131	137	142
Textile mills...........................	313	52	42	26	29	31	31
Textile product mills.................	314	34	35	21	21	22	23
Apparel.................................	315	60	31	14	13	13	13
Leather and allied products..........	316	10	6	4	5	6	6
Paper products.......................	322	165	162	162	170	176	174
Printing.................................	323	104	97	83	82	83	81
Petroleum and coal products........	324	235	476	496	627	837	881
Basic chemicals.....................	325	449	611	624	698	777	767
Plastics and rubber products........	326	178	200	171	189	205	215
INVENTORIES (December 31)							
All manufacturing industries...................	(X)	**470**	**461**	**490**	**537**	**592**	**606**
Durable goods.........................	(X)	298	276	288	314	349	364
Wood products.........................	321	10	12	8	8	9	9
Nonmetallic mineral products........	327	10	10	10	10	11	11
Primary metals.........................	331	22	26	26	31	36	36
Fabricated metals.....................	332	34	36	38	41	46	46
Machinery...............................	333	49	43	49	52	60	64
Computers and electronic products....	334	63	44	40	41	44	45
Electrical equipment, appliances, and components....	335	15	12	13	14	15	16
Transportation equipment.............	336	69	65	79	90	100	108
Furniture and related products........	337	8	8	6	6	6	6
Miscellaneous products..............	339	18	20	19	22	23	22
Nondurable goods.....................	(X)	172	185	202	222	243	242
Food products.........................	311	32	33	40	43	47	49
Beverages and tobacco products....	312	14	14	17	18	18	20
Textile mills...........................	313	6	4	3	3	3	3
Textile product mills.................	314	5	3	3	3	3	3
Apparel.................................	315	9	4	2	2	2	2
Leather and allied products..........	316	2	1	1	1	1	1
Paper products.......................	322	15	14	13	14	15	14
Printing.................................	323	6	6	5	5	5	5
Petroleum and coal products........	324	13	27	36	42	48	46
Basic chemicals.....................	325	52	59	65	72	79	77
Plastics and rubber products........	326	18	19	17	19	21	21
NEW ORDERS							
All manufacturing industries...................	(X)	**4,161**	**4,756**	**4,191**	**4,876**	**5,505**	**5,681**
Durable goods.........................	(X)	2,327	2,439	1,834	2,261	2,509	2,620
Wood products.........................	321	94	112	65	66	(NA)	(NA)
Nonmetallic mineral products........	327	97	115	90	92	(NA)	(NA)
Primary metals.........................	331	154	209	163	242	284	297
Fabricated metals.....................	332	270	298	265	301	336	348
Machinery...............................	333	295	312	261	334	383	387
Computers and electronic products....	334	436	302	256	262	262	263
Electrical equipment, appliances, and components....	335	126	115	101	111	123	123
Transportation equipment.............	336	663	750	430	643	738	806
Furniture and related products........	337	75	85	59	59	62	65
Miscellaneous products..............	339	117	142	144	151	(NA)	(NA)
Nondurable goods.....................	(X)	1,835	2,317	2,359	2,614	(NA)	(NA)

NA Not available. X Not applicable. [1] Based on the North American Industry Classification System, 2007; see text, this section and Section 15.

Source: Census Bureau, Manufacturers' Shipments, Inventories, and Orders, "Historical Data," <http://www.census.gov/manufacturing/m3/historical_data/index.html>, accessed September 2013.

Table 1047. Value of Manufacturers' Shipments, Inventories, and New Orders by Market Grouping: 2000 to 2012

[In billions of dollars (4,209 represents $4,209,000,000,000). Based on the Manufacturers' Shipments, Inventories, and Orders (M3) survey. See source for details]

Market grouping	2000	2005	2008	2009	2010	2011	2012
SHIPMENTS							
All manufacturing industries	**4,209**	**4,742**	**5,468**	**4,420**	**4,905**	**5,499**	**5,733**
Consumer goods	1,501	1,895	2,253	1,846	2,055	2,377	2,473
Consumer durable goods	391	423	359	272	329	355	394
Consumer nondurable goods	1,109	1,473	1,893	1,575	1,726	2,022	2,079
Aircraft and parts	112	114	162	151	149	158	184
Defense aircraft and parts	25	38	58	62	64	56	58
Nondefense aircraft and parts	87	76	104	89	85	102	127
Construction materials and supplies	445	510	544	426	443	476	499
Motor vehicles and parts	471	501	413	302	401	445	492
Computers and related products	110	65	66	50	38	29	30
Information technology industries	400	295	315	264	260	263	263
Nondefense capital goods	808	730	838	692	721	798	865
Excluding aircraft	758	687	772	637	667	734	778
Defense capital goods	67	92	115	123	131	120	118
INVENTORIES (December 31)							
All manufacturing industries	**470**	**461**	**528**	**490**	**537**	**592**	**606**
Consumer goods	128	140	150	153	168	183	183
Consumer durable goods	26	27	24	21	22	24	25
Consumer nondurable goods	102	113	126	132	146	159	158
Aircraft and parts	36	33	46	47	56	62	69
Defense aircraft and parts	9	12	11	12	12	13	13
Nondefense aircraft and parts	27	22	34	35	43	49	56
Construction materials and supplies	49	53	60	50	53	58	59
Motor vehicles and parts	22	23	22	19	21	24	25
Computers and related products	8	4	5	5	4	4	4
Information technology industries	51	38	37	35	35	38	38
Nondefense capital goods	127	107	130	122	135	151	161
Excluding aircraft	107	90	104	94	100	111	116
Defense capital goods	17	16	16	20	21	21	22
NEW ORDERS							
All manufacturing industries	**4,161**	**4,764**	**5,447**	**4,191**	**4,876**	**5,505**	**5,681**
Consumer goods	1,502	1,894	2,251	1,846	2,055	2,377	2,473
Consumer durable goods	393	422	358	271	329	356	394
Consumer nondurable goods	1,109	1,473	1,893	1,572	1,755	(NA)	(NA)
Aircraft and parts	131	179	212	64	157	202	225173
Defense aircraft and parts	31	36	67	51	64	58	64
Nondefense aircraft and parts	99	143	145	13	93	143	161
Construction materials and supplies	447	517	543	413	448	481	499
Motor vehicles and parts	468	503	410	300	403	447	491
Computers and related products	108	64	66	51	36	30	30
Information technology industries	410	300	315	258	264	269	270
Nondefense capital goods	831	814	878	581	742	856	891
Excluding aircraft	768	704	779	602	679	757	776
Defense capital goods	80	82	127	104	140	129	127

NA Not available.

Source: Census Bureau, Manufacturers' Shipments, Inventories, and Orders, "Historical Data," <http://www.census.gov/manufacturing/m3/historical_data/index.html>, accessed September 2013.

Table 1048. Finances and Profits of Manufacturing Corporations: 2000 to 2012

[In billions of dollars (4,548 represents $4,548,000,000,000). Data exclude estimates for corporations with less than $250,000 in assets at time of sample selection. Minus sign (-) indicates loss]

Item	2000 [1]	2001 [1]	2001 [2]	2006 [2]	2007 [2]	2008 [3]	2009 [3]	2010 [3]	2011 [3]	2012 [4]
Net sales	4,548	4,308	4,295	5,783	6,060	6,374	5,110	5,756	6,486	6,681
Net operating profit	348	185	186	405	416	358	289	420	479	508
Net profit:										
Before taxes	381	82	83	605	603	388	361	584	722	678
After taxes	275	36	36	470	443	266	286	478	594	570
Cash dividends	132	102	103	178	178	182	172	180	184	216
Net income retained in business	143	-67	-66	292	265	84	115	298	410	354

[1] Based on the Standard Industrial Classification system. [2] Based on the North American Industry Classification System, 2002. [3] Based on the North American Industry Classification System, 2007. [4] Based on the North American Industry Classification System, 2012; see text, Section 15.

Source: U.S. Census Bureau, *Quarterly Financial Report for Manufacturing, Mining, Trade, and Selected Service Industries*. See also <http://www.census.gov/econ/qfr>.

Table 1049. Manufacturing Corporations—Assets and Profits by Asset Size: 1990 to 2012

[In millions of dollars (2,629,458 represents $2,629,458,000,000). Corporations and assets as of end of 4th quarter; profits for entire year. Through 2000, based on Standard Industrial Classification code (SIC); beginning 2001, based on the North American Industry Classification System; see text, Section 15. For corporations above a certain asset value based on complete canvass. The asset value for complete canvass was raised in 1988 to $50 million and in 1995 to $250 million. Asset sizes less than these values are sampled, except as noted. For details regarding survey description, data analysis, and methodology, see source, 4th quarter report. Minus sign (-) indicates loss]

Year	Total	Asset–size class						
		Under $10 million [1]	$10 to $25 million	$25 to $50 million	$50 to $100 million	$100 to $250 million	$250 million to $1 billion	$1 billion and over
Assets:								
1990............	2,629,458	142,498	74,477	55,914	72,554	123,967	287,512	1,872,536
1995............	3,345,229	155,618	87,011	68,538	87,262	159,133	370,263	2,417,403
1999............	4,382,814	170,058	85,200	67,352	97,810	138,143	398,881	3,425,370
2000............	4,852,106	171,666	85,482	72,122	90,866	149,714	389,537	3,892,720
2001 [2]........	4,747,789	169,701	84,664	67,493	88,088	131,617	393,752	3,812,474
2002............	4,823,219	166,191	82,369	62,654	81,667	134,821	407,423	3,888,095
2003............	5,162,852	161,462	80,681	62,592	77,205	126,826	392,192	4,261,894
2004............	5,538,113	163,072	80,085	71,674	81,741	126,950	414,144	4,600,447
2005............	5,828,716	165,195	85,785	68,731	87,818	142,900	423,917	4,854,370
2006............	6,179,142	168,537	93,786	72,494	91,877	146,651	418,501	5,187,295
2007............	6,891,131	180,319	98,348	80,400	93,017	144,254	433,634	5,861,160
2008............	6,819,681	180,025	99,430	80,757	98,478	137,907	420,104	5,802,981
2009............	6,942,972	166,590	106,773	71,642	76,308	126,202	413,856	5,981,600
2010............	7,432,384	165,598	105,661	74,081	82,713	130,428	405,113	6,468,791
2011............	7,907,376	169,045	114,818	76,809	86,452	130,488	435,889	6,893,876
2012............	8,313,634	175,561	115,967	84,898	89,810	127,615	437,939	7,281,845
Net profit: [3]								
1990............	110,128	8,527	5,160	2,769	2,661	3,525	7,110	80,377
1995............	198,151	13,224	5,668	3,767	5,771	7,000	16,549	146,172
1999............	257,805	17,398	7,618	3,504	4,798	4,795	12,756	206,934
2000............	275,313	16,578	6,820	3,403	2,742	3,510	15,121	227,136
2001 [2]........	36,168	8,387	3,366	-408	403	-543	-6,782	31,746
2002............	134,686	10,003	2,784	807	1,699	3,356	-1,227	117,262
2003............	237,041	9,821	3,374	2,005	2,256	2,973	4,115	212,497
2004............	348,151	14,970	5,745	3,858	3,080	5,140	12,787	302,571
2005............	401,344	17,357	6,057	4,066	3,781	7,678	15,967	346,438
2006............	470,282	22,301	8,685	5,260	4,601	8,901	21,405	399,131
2007............	442,734	22,930	9,006	4,402	6,518	8,400	17,565	373,915
2008............	266,346	18,182	7,472	5,820	3,739	3,403	2,239	225,492
2009............	286,491	9,692	5,979	4,617	2,500	2,723	2,653	258,310
2010............	477,884	16,637	7,670	4,181	5,880	5,390	19,494	417,121
2011............	594,335	20,357	9,257	5,209	5,730	6,808	17,568	529,406
2012............	569,973	23,218	11,654	6,659	6,820	6,137	20,163	495,321

[1] Excludes estimates for corporations with less than $250,000 in assets at time of sample selection. [2] Beginning 2001, data reported based on the North American Industry Classification System. [3] After taxes.

Source: U.S. Census Bureau, *Quarterly Financial Report for Manufacturing, Mining, Trade, and Selected Service Industries*. See also <http://www.census.gov/econ/qfr>.

Table 1050. Manufacturing Corporations—Selected Finances: 1990 to 2012

[In billions of dollars (2,811 represents $2,811,000,000,000). Data are not necessarily comparable from year to year due to changes in accounting procedures, industry classifications, sampling procedures, etc.; for detail, see source. See headnote, Table 1048. Minus sign (-) indicates loss]

Year	All manufacturing corporations			Durable goods			Nondurable goods		
	Sales	Profits [1]		Sales	Profits [1]		Sales	Profits [1]	
		Before taxes	After taxes		Before taxes	After taxes		Before taxes	After taxes
1990..............	2,811	158	110	1,357	57	41	1,454	101	69
1995..............	3,528	275	198	1,808	131	94	1,721	144	104
1998..............	3,949	315	234	2,169	175	128	1,781	140	107
1999..............	4,149	355	258	2,314	199	140	1,835	157	117
2000..............	4,548	381	275	2,457	191	132	2,091	190	144
2001 [2].........	4,295	83	36	2,321	-69	-76	1,974	152	112
2002..............	4,217	196	135	2,261	45	21	1,955	149	113
2003..............	4,397	306	237	2,283	118	88	2,114	188	149
2004..............	4,934	447	348	2,537	200	157	2,397	248	192
2005..............	5,411	524	401	2,731	211	161	2,681	313	240
2006..............	5,783	605	470	2,910	249	193	2,873	356	278
2007..............	6,060	603	443	3,016	247	159	3,044	356	283
2008..............	6,374	388	266	2,970	98	43	3,405	290	223
2009..............	5,110	361	286	2,427	84	55	2,683	276	232
2010..............	5,756	584	478	2,708	287	232	3,048	297	245
2011..............	6,486	722	594	2,927	335	284	3,558	387	310
2012..............	6,681	678	570	3,111	302	263	3,570	376	307

[1] Beginning 1998, profits before and after income taxes reflect inclusion of minority stockholders' interest in net income before and after income taxes. [2] Beginning 2001, data reported based on the North American Industry Classification System.

Source: U.S. Census Bureau, *Quarterly Financial Report for Manufacturing, Mining, Trade, and Selected Service Industries*. See also <http://www.census.gov/econ/qfr>.

Table 1051. Textiles—Production and Foreign Trade: 2010

[595,198 represents 595,198,000. Fabric blends as shown in the report are reported based on the chief weight of the fiber; whereas, fabrics blends as shown for imports and exports are based on the chief value of the fiber]

Product description	Unit	Quantity (1,000)			Value ($1,000)	
		Manufac-turers' produc-tion	Exports of domestic merchan-dise [1]	Imports for con-sump-tion [2]	Exports of domestic merchan-dise [1]	Imports for con-sump-tion [2,3]
YARN						
Spun cotton yarns, carded, 85 percent or more cotton	Kilograms	595,198	309,578	19,631	808,737	91,863
Textured, crimped, twisted, or bulked filament yarns, nylon	Kilograms	641,728	28,929	60,281	147,086	253,367
Textured, crimped, twisted, or bulked filament yarns, polyester	Kilograms	287,168	28,888	40,463	98,180	97,217
BROADWOVEN FABRICS [4]						
Yarn dyed fabrics, blue denim	Sq. meters	124,273	119,894	30,057	248,802	86,954
85 percent or more spun yarn fabrics and blends (except yarn dyed), chiefly man made fiber, twills and sateens [5]	Sq. meters	168,042	(NA)	22,530	(NA)	31,204
85 percent or more filament yarn fabrics, man made, high tenacity yarn fabrics of nylon, polyester, or rayon	Sq. meters	141,686	18,163	14,426	75,034	58,408
85 percent or more filament yarn fabrics, man made, glass fiber fabrics	Sq. meters	161,877	44,480	56,564	152,206	76,699
85 percent or more filament yarn fabrics, all other man made filament fiber fabrics, including saran, olefin, and carpet backing	Sq. meters	530,281	31,519	675,795	68,777	203,430
KNIT FABRICS						
Pile fabrics	Kilograms	5,498	(S)	149,404	(S)	162,053
Elastic fabrics (over 12 inches in width) (weight 5 percent or more elastomeric yarn or rubber thread)	Kilograms	8,940	(S)	17,506	(S)	168,153
Elastic fabrics (12 inches or less in width), (weight 5 percent or more elastomeric yarn or rubber thread)	Kilograms	19,797	3,414	1,032	38,860	6,805
TOWELS						
Finished towels [6]	Dozens	1,929	341	155,616	25,845	1,823,394

NA Not available. S Withheld because estimate did not meet publication standards. [1] Source: U.S. Census Bureau report EM 545, *U.S. Exports.* [2] Source: U.S. Census Bureau report IM 145, *U.S. Imports for Consumption.* [3] Dollar value represents the c.i.f. (cost, insurance, and freight) at the first port of entry in the United States plus calculated import duty. [4] Represents production of gray broadwoven fabrics; import and export data represent gray as well as finished broadwoven fabrics. [5] Total for manmade fiber fabrics does not include chiefly manmade/wool blends. [6] Manufacturers' production of finished towels does not include washcloths, whereas the quantity and value for imports and exports does include washcloths.

Source: U.S. Census Bureau, Current Industrial Reports, "Textiles," Series MQ313A, June 2011, <http://www.census.gov/manufacturing/cir/historical_data/mq313a/index.html>.

Table 1052. Pharmaceutical Preparations—Value of Shipments: 1990 to 2010

[In millions of dollars (33,954 represents $33,954,000,000)]

Product description	Product code	1990	2000	2005	2007	2008	2009	2010
Pharmaceutical preparations, except biologicals	(X)	**33,954**	**79,262**	**118,647**	**(NA)**	**(NA)**	**(NA)**	**(NA)**
Affecting neoplasms, endocrine systems, and metabolic disease	3254121	2,743	9,784	23,779	28,497	33,260	33,340	29,557
Acting on the central nervous system and sense organs	3254124	7,219	18,508	25,627	28,714	26,430	29,158	27,998
Acting on the cardiovascular system	3254127	4,815	8,993	10,232	11,969	11,543	12,739	11,427
Acting on the respiratory system	325412A	3,724	10,179	16,367	16,177	16,573	16,357	17,980
Acting on the digestive system	325412D	4,840	10,046	16,829	9,822	9,949	10,980	10,355
Acting on the skin	325412G	1,558	2,941	3,657	3,498	3,635	3,790	4,166
Vitamin, nutrient, and hematitic preparations	325412L	2,588	5,676	7,556	8,062	8,749	8,933	9,070
Affecting parasitic and infective disease	325412P	5,411	11,037	11,228	11,014	9,403	9,636	8,727
Pharmaceutical preparations for veterinary use	325412T	1,057	2,096	3,371	3,206	3,280	2,971	2,618

NA Not available. X Not applicable.

Source: U.S. Census Bureau, Current Industrial Reports, "Pharmaceutical Preparations, Except Biologicals," Series MA325G, June 2011, <http://www.census.gov/manufacturing/cir/historical_data/ma325g/index.html>.

Table 1053. Inorganic Chemicals and Fertilizers—Production: 2000 to 2010

[In 1,000 short tons (15,809 represents 15,809,000.) 1,000 short tons = 2,000 lb.]

Product description	Product code	2000	2005	2007	2008	2009	2010
FERTILIZERS (MQ325B)							
Ammonia, synthetic anhydrous..............	3253111120	15,809	11,181	11,448	10,549	10,330	11,115
Ammonium nitrate (original melt liquor).............	3253111201	7,979	7,212	8,236	7,841	6,943	7,484
Ammonium sulfate..................	3253111240	2,808	2,906	3,145	2,783	2,499	2,740
Urea (original melt liquor) (100%)..................	3253114101	7,682	5,807	6,156	5,776	5,604	5,646
Nitric acid (100%)............................	3253111111	8,708	7,398	8,623	7,370	6,531	7,640
Phosphoric acid (100% P2O5).....................	3253121111	12,492	12,621	12,081	10,158	9,542	10,378
Sulfuric acid (100%)........................	3251881100	43,643	40,996	39,745	34,855	32,126	35,877
Superphosphates and other fertilizer materials (100% P2O5)........................	3253124102	8,899	8,141	7,241	6,014	6,142	6,897
INORGANIC CHEMICALS (MQ325A)							
Chlorine gas (100 percent) [1].......................	3251811111	14,000	10,272	11,895	10,673	9,391	10,715
Sodium hydroxide, liquid (caustic soda) (100 percent) all process: liquid [2]	3251814111	11,523	8,517	8,869	8,111	7,242	8,245
Potassium hydroxide (caustic potash) (88-92 percent) liquid [2]................	3251817111	539	527	621	582	404	481
Finished sodium bicarbonate (58 percent) NaHCO3......................	3251817131	536	581	663	682	641	686
Hydrochloric acids (100 percent) byproduct and other [3]...............	3251884131	4,717	4,619	4,331	3,902	3,584	3,907
Aluminum oxide, except natural alumina (100 percent A12O3)................	3313110100	(D)	(D)	(D)	(D)	2,918	(D)
Aluminum sulfate (commercial) (17 percent aluminum oxide) [4]..............	3251887151	1,076	967	967	(S)	831	(S)
Sodium chlorite (100 percent)...................	325188A141	940	523	617	607	420	544
Sodium silicates (soluble silicate glass, liquid and solid) (anhydrous) [5]..................	325188A181	1,136	1,309	1,182	1,106	981	1,308
Metasilicate anhydrous (100 percent)...............	325188A187	72	59	(D)	(D)	(D)	(D)
Sodium sulfate (100 percent)......................	325188A1A7	509	93	93	87	47	81
Granular carbons, activated (dry weight) [6,7].......	325998H1E4	95	(D)	27	(S)	(S)	(S)
Pulverized carbons, activated, (dry weight) [6].......	325998H1E7	71	(D)	98	(S)	(S)	(S)
Hydrogen peroxide (100 percent by weight)........	325188G181	1,083	365	429	437	377	425

D Withheld to avoid disclosing data for individual companies. S Does not meet publication standards. [1] Production includes amounts liquefied. [2] Liquid production figures represent total production, including quantities later evaporated to solid caustic. [3] Includes production from salt and acid. [4] Excludes quantities produced and consumed in municipalities. [5] Excludes amounts produced and consumed in making meta, ortho, and sesquisilicates. [6] Excludes reactivated carbon. [7] Includes pelleted carbon.

Source: U.S. Census Bureau, Current Industrial Reports, "Inorganic Chemicals," Series MQ325A, July 2010, and "Fertilizers and Related Chemicals," Series MQ325B, June 2010, <http://www.census.gov/manufacturing/cir/historical_data/mq325a/index.html> and <http://www.census.gov/manufacturing/cir/historical_data/mq325b/index.html>.

Table 1054. Metalworking Machinery—Value of Shipments: 2005 to 2010

[In thousands of dollars (2,800,272 represents $2,800,272,000)]

Product description	Product code	2005	2007	2008 [1]	2009 [1]	2010 [1]
Metalworking machinery.................................	**(X)**	**2,800,272**	**3,318,208**	**3,435,540**	**1,936,986**	**2,055,877**
Metal cutting type machine tools............................	333512 (pt)	2,079,874	2,533,389	2,650,662	1,424,012	1,519,966
Boring and drilling machines............................	333512A1	110,971	130,220	161,393	92,715	87,615
Grinding and polishing machines...........................	33351221	265,035	237,928	270,339	165,445	152,430
Lathes [2]..	33351231	248,240	375,871	396,793	204,478	207,404
Milling machines [3]................................	33351241	53,582	81,294	(D)	(D)	(D)
Machining centers..............................	33351271	619,563	807,425	(D)	(D)	(D)
Station type machines [4]..........................	33351281	104,481	(D)	(D)	117,891	43,831
Other metal cutting machine tools.......................	33351291	431,962	585,522	543,791	282,570	330,441
Remanufactured metal cutting machine tools.............	3335126111	93,404	81,004	(D)	(D)	(D)
Metal forming type machine tools.........................	333513 (pt)	720,398	784,819	784,878	512,974	535,911
Punching, shearing, bending, and forming machines..............................	33351311	344,273	409,791	391,607	256,996	263,422
Presses (excluding forging) [5]....................	33351331	139,924	135,292	142,282	75,299	93,217
All other metal forming type machines [5]...............	33351351	206,547	209,309	231,257	167,733	163,427
Remanufactured metal forming machine tools.............	3335137121	(D)	10,382	19,732	12,946	15,845

X Not applicable. D Withheld to avoid disclosing data for individual companies. [1] Data shown for years 2008-2010 do not include metal cutting and forming type machine tools valued under $3,025 each. [2] Data for product code 3335123126, "Vertical NC turning machines" are included in total "Metal cutting type," but excluded from product code 33351231. [3] Data for product code 3335124101, "All milling machines valued under $3,025 each" are included in total "Metal cutting type," but excluded from product code 33351241. [4] Data for "Station type machines" are included in total "Metal cutting type." [5] Data for product codes 3335133101 "All presses valued under $3,025 each" and 3335135101 "All other metal forming type machine tools valued under $3,025 each" are included in total "Metal forming type," but excluded from product codes 33351331 and 33351351, respectively.

Source: U.S. Census Bureau, Current Industrial Reports, "Metalworking Machinery," Series MQ333W, August 2011, <http://www.census.gov /manufacturing/cir/historical_data/mq333w/index.html>.

Table 1055. Semiconductors, Electronic Components, and Semiconductor Manufacturing Equipment—Value of Shipments: 2005 to 2010

[In millions of dollars (9,728 represents $9,728,000,000)]

Product description	Product code	2005	2007	2008	2009	2010
Semiconductor machinery..........................	3332950	9,728	13,190	9,357	4,996	9,747
Transmitting, industrial, and special purpose electron tubes [1]	3344111	652	734	806	770	788
Receiving type electron tubes [2]	3344114	621	(D)	(D)	(D)	(D)
Electron tubes and parts..........................	3344117	72	36	31	30	32
Bare printed circuit boards..........................	3344120	4,856	4,443	5,269	4,113	4,335
Integrated microcircuits [3]	3344131	61,631	49,781	51,104	40,235	49,704
Transistors..........................	3344134	603	599	409	(S)	(S)
Diodes and rectifiers..........................	3344137	372	457	458	350	545
Other semiconductor devices [4]	334413A	8,330	10,176	11,363	10,995	13,520
Capacitors for electronic circuitry..........................	3344140	1,113	945	937	736	891
Resistors for electronic circuitry..........................	3344150	653	645	622	488	563
Electronic coils, transformers, and other inductors..........................	3344160	1,216	1,393	1,380	1,076	1,099
Connectors for electronic circuitry..........................	3344170	3,589	4,189	4,065	3,088	3,720
Printed circuit assemblies, loaded boards and modules [5]	334418B	20,106	20,382	20,257	14,370	16,724
Crystals, filters, piezoelectric, and other related electronic devices [6]	3344191	779	689	656	570	544
All other miscellaneous transducers [7]	3344194	1,401	1,466	1,352	1,058	1,175
Switches, mechanical types for electronic circuitry..........................	3344197	794	662	581	396	360
Microwave components and devices [8]	334419A	1,306	1,541	1,286	1,191	1,304
All other miscellaneous electronic components..........................	334419E	4,040	4,831	4,772	3,947	4,371

D Figure withheld to avoid disclosure. S Estimates did not meet publication standards. [1] Except X-ray. [2] Including cathode ray (new and rebuilt). [3] Includes semiconductor networks, microprocessors, and MOS memories. [4] Includes semiconductor parts such as chips, wafers, and heat sinks. [5] Printed circuit boards with inserted electronic components. [6] Except microwave filters. [7] Includes electrical-electronic input/output transducers. [8] Except antennae, tubes, and semiconductors.

Source: U.S. Census Bureau, Current Industrial Reports, "Semiconductors, Electronic Components, and Semiconductor Manufacturing Equipment," Series MA334Q, September 2010, <http://www.census.gov/manufacturing/cir/historical_data/ma334q/index.html>.

Table 1056. Computers and Peripheral Equipment—Value of Shipments: 2004 to 2010

[In millions of dollars (37,895 represents $37,895,000,000)]

Product description	Product code	2004	2006	2007	2008	2009	2010
Electronic computers............................	334111	37,895	37,657	36,859	37,542	31,513	(D)
Host computers, multiusers.........................	3341111	10,993	(D)	(D)	(D)	(D)	(D)
Single user computers, microprocessor-based, capable of supporting attached peripherals............	3341117	26,309	(D)	(D)	(D)	(D)	(D)
Personal computers.........................	3341117107	15,690	(D)	(D)	(D)	(D)	(D)
Workstations.........................	3341117109	1,848	(D)	2,442	(D)	2,338	(D)
Mobile computers, including notebooks, subnotebooks, laptop, and tablet PCs.................	3341117127	8,456	(D)	(D)	(D)	(D)	(D)
Smart handheld devices.........................	3341117129	(D)	(D)	(D)	(D)	(D)	(D)
All other single user computers.........................	3341117130	(D)	(D)	25	(D)	(D)	(D)
Other computers (array, analog, hybrid, and special-use computers).........................	334111D	593	(D)	299	(S)	186	(S)
Computer storage devices (except parts, attachments, and accessories).........................	3341121	5,034	6,956	7,872	6,367	6,019	7,800
Disk subsystem and disk arrays for multiuser computer systems.........................	3341121109	1,362	(D)	2,531	(D)	(D)	(D)
Disk drives (all sizes).........................	3341121112	69	(D)	150	201	297	(S)
Storage Area Networks (SANs).........................	3341121123	(D)	(D)	2,892	(D)	2,677	(S)
Tape drives (all sizes).........................	3341121138	278	285	239	264	(D)	133
Other computer storage devices.........................	3341121150	(D)	3,795	2,061	1,321	1,090	(D)
Parts, attachments, and accessories for computer storage devices.........................	3341124	1,039	1,929	1,426	1,327	853	854
Computer terminals (except point-of-sale and funds-transfer devices, parts, attachments, and accessories).........................	3341131	274	268	331	245	267	(S)
Parts, attachments, and accessories for computer terminals (except point-of-sale and funds-transfer devices).........................	3341134	2	(D)	(D)	(D)	(D)	(D)
All other miscellaneous computer peripheral (input/output) equipment (except parts, attachments and accessories).........................	3341191	4,705	4,517	4,427	4,245	3,530	4,026
Parts, subassemblies, and accessories for computer peripheral equipment.........................	3341194	2,257	2,720	3,171	2,600	2,229	(S)
Point-of-sale terminals and funds-transfer devices........	3341197	513	621	1,034	958	343	198
Parts and attachments for point-of-sale terminals and funds-transfer devices.........................	334119D	(D)	35	12	9	(S)	(S)
Magnetic and optical recording media.........................	3346130	1,586	1,364	1,381	(S)	839	(S)

D Withheld to avoid disclosing data for individual companies. S Withheld because estimates did not meet publication standards.

Source: U.S. Census Bureau, Current Industrial Reports, Computers and Peripheral Equipment, Series MA334R (beginning with 2006, MQ334R), June 2011, <http://www.census.gov/manufacturing/cir/historical_data/mq334r/index.html>.

Table 1057. Telecommunication Equipment—Value of Shipments: 2000 to 2010

[In millions of dollars (15,174 represents $15,174,000,000)]

Product description	Product code	2000	2005	2007	2008	2009	2010
Telephone switching and switchboard equipment.........	3342101	15,174	1,576	1,959	1,674	1,068	847
Carrier line equipment and modems........................	3342104	13,112	2,824	3,512	3,137	2,851	3,035
Wire line voice and data network equipment.............	3342107	28,971	12,289	11,181	4,574	3,187	3,384
Broadcast, studio, and related electronic equipment......	3342202	4,029	3,289	3,350	4,110	4,574	4,554
Wireless networking equipment...........................	3342203	(NA)	(NA)	6,159	4,845	3,633	3,885
Radio station equipment..................................	3342205	(NA)	(NA)	17,824	16,456	16,437	15,255
Other communications systems equipment...............	3342209	(NA)	(NA)	6,355	10,882	8,970	8,301
Alarm systems [1]...	3342901	2,755	1,910	2,044	2,090	1,663	1,733
Vehicular and pedestrian traffic control equipment [2]......	3342902	838	1,020	1,239	1,231	(S)	(S)
Intercommunications systems [3]..........................	3342903	447	416	438	458	389	399
Modems, consumer type..................................	3344184	95	98	82	87	(D)	(D)

D Withheld to avoid disclosing data of individual companies. NA Not available. S Estimates did not meet publication standards. [1] Includes electric sirens and horns. [2] Includes electrical railway signals and attachments. [3] Includes inductive paging systems (selective calling), except telephone and telegraph.

Source: U.S. Census Bureau, Current Industrial Reports, "Telecommunications," Series MQ334P, 2011, <http://www.census.gov/manufacturing/cir/historical_data/mq334p/index.html>.

Table 1058. Major Household Appliances—Value of Shipments: 2000 to 2010

[In millions of dollars (2,170 represents $2,170,000,000)]

Product description	Product code	2000	2005	2007	2008	2009	2010
Electric household ranges, ovens and surface cooking units, equipment and parts.......................	3352211	2,170	2,577	2,736	2,506	2,041	2,217
Gas household ranges, ovens, and surface cooking units, equipment and parts.............................	3352213	779	1,392	1,541	1,473	1,117	1,254
Other household ranges, cooking equipment and outdoor cooking equipment [1]...........................	3352215	1,251	965	491	510	517	580
Household refrigerators, including combination refrigerator-freezers.....................................	3352221	5,396	5,405	5,440	5,891	5,188	5,466
Parts and attachments for household refrigerators and freezers...	3352223	(D)	(D)	159	107	92	96
Household laundry machines and parts..................	3352240	4,047	5,236	5,232	5,835	4,820	4,657
Water heaters, electric...................................	3352281	573	638	950	953	869	852
Water heaters, except electric...........................	3352283	844	970	1,572	1,547	1,452	1,525
Household appliances, n.e.c and parts [2].................	3352285	2,066	2,433	2,717	2,602	2,159	2,176

D Withheld to avoid disclosing data of individual companies. [1] Includes parts and accessories. [2] n.e.c. means not elsewhere classified.

Source: U.S. Census Bureau, Current Industrial Reports, "Major Household Appliances," Series MA335F, <http://www.census.gov/manufacturing/cir/historical_data/mq335f/index.html>.

Table 1059. Motor Vehicle Manufactures—Summary by Selected Industry: 2011

[34,667 represents $34,667,000,000. Based on the Annual Survey of Manufactures; see Appendix III]

Industry	2007 NAICS code [1]	All employees [2] Number	Payroll Total (mil. dol.)	Payroll per employee (dol.)	Production workers [2]	Value of shipments [3] (mil. dol.)
Motor vehicle manufacturing, total.....................	3361–3363	650,550	34,667	53,289	512,040	435,358
Motor vehicle, total..	3361	148,009	9,889	66,813	126,910	232,511
Automobile and light duty motor vehicle...................	33611	120,691	8,404	69,629	105,098	206,063
Automobile..	336111	59,808	3,937	65,829	50,111	84,460
Light truck and utility vehicle..........................	336112	60,883	4,467	73,363	54,987	121,603
Heavy duty truck...	33612	27,318	1,485	54,368	21,812	26,448
Motor vehicle body and trailer............................	3362	97,905	4,145	42,339	76,168	25,636
Motor vehicle body and trailer manufacturing.............	33621	97,905	4,145	42,339	76,168	25,636
Motor vehicle body......................................	336211	37,665	1,676	44,503	28,271	9,368
Truck trailer..	336212	22,882	916	40,028	18,597	6,660
Motor home..	336213	6,801	284	41,690	5,057	2,131
Travel trailer and camper................................	336214	30,557	1,270	41,547	24,243	7,477
Motor vehicle parts.......................................	3363	404,636	20,633	50,992	308,962	177,211
Motor vehicle gasoline engine and engine parts..........	33631	48,691	2,809	57,684	38,671	22,651
Motor vehicle electrical and electronic equipment........	33632	38,437	2,052	53,379	27,160	13,647
Motor vehicle steering and suspension...................	33633	27,398	1,366	49,858	20,704	10,151
Motor vehicle brake system..............................	33634	19,768	881	44,544	14,941	8,695
Motor vehicle transmission and power train parts.........	33635	49,184	3,181	64,684	37,615	31,652
Motor vehicle seating and interior trim...................	33636	39,247	1,641	41,814	28,591	18,070
Motor vehicle metal stamping............................	33637	73,329	3,839	52,347	58,811	26,601
Other motor vehicle parts................................	33639	108,582	4,865	44,808	82,469	45,745

[1] North American Industry Classification System, 2007; see text, Section 15. [2] Includes all full-time and part-time employees on the payrolls of operating manufacturing establishments during any part of the pay period that included the 12th of the month specified on the report form. Included are employees on paid sick leave, paid holidays, and paid vacations; not included are proprietors and partners of unincorporated businesses. [3] Includes extensive and unmeasurable duplication from shipments between establishments in the same industry classification.

Source: U.S. Census Bureau, Annual Survey of Manufactures via American FactFinder, "Statistics for Industry Groups and Industries: 2011 and 2010," <http://factfinder2.census.gov/>, accessed March 2013.

Table 1060. Motor Vehicle Manufactures—Employees, Payroll, and Shipments by Major State: 2011

[9,888,864 represents $9,888,864,000. Industry based on the 2007 North American Industry Classification System (NAICS); see text, Section 15. See footnote 3, Table 1059 for information regarding shipments. Based on the Annual Survey of Manufactures; see Appendix III]

State	Motor vehicle manufacturing (NAICS 3361)			Motor vehicle parts manufacturing (NAICS 3363)		
	Employees	Payroll (1,000 dol.)	Value of shipments (1,000 dol.)	Employees	Payroll (1,000 dol.)	Value of shipments (1,000 dol.)
United States [1]	**148,009**	**9,888,864**	**233,785,658**	**404,636**	**20,633,373**	**184,764,425**
Alabama	10,278	654,025	19,189,042	13,888	599,363	7,771,012
Arizona	–	–	–	2,186	111,805	655,071
Arkansas	–	–	–	4,418	193,620	1,234,035
California	1,944	183,669	1,143,852	15,420	690,820	5,807,730
Connecticut	–	–	–	([3])	(D)	(D)
Florida	–	–	–	2,779	123,545	838,699
Georgia	([3])	(D)	(D)	8,716	411,678	4,759,724
Illinois	6,724	499,930	10,143,958	17,305	864,721	6,193,458
Indiana	13,264	879,569	20,982,477	42,960	2,388,437	20,463,008
Iowa	–	–	–	3,396	157,865	1,233,286
Kansas	([3])	–	(D)	([2])	(D)	(D)
Kentucky	13,730	879,631	21,308,766	21,515	960,976	11,816,458
Louisiana	–	(D)	(D)	1,099	35,236	285,208
Massachusetts	–	–	–	1,655	85,133	595,116
Michigan	28,588	2,064,597	52,314,124	82,327	4,676,347	39,962,519
Minnesota	1,929	88,275	(D)	2,305	103,356	656,589
Mississippi	([3])	(D)	(D)	1,661	92,571	(D)
Missouri	([4])	(D)	(D)	8,926	398,735	3,752,005
Nebraska	–	–	–	3,338	130,683	1,083,314
New York	–	–	–	10,402	622,821	3,488,278
North Carolina	([3])	(D)	(D)	13,560	685,738	8,453,277
Ohio	19,552	1,327,667	27,199,387	54,634	3,011,748	23,030,590
Oklahoma	995	41,123	(D)	2,466	108,394	912,375
Oregon	([2])	(D)	(D)	1,412	71,730	393,750
Pennsylvania	([2])	(D)	(D)	7,016	300,392	2,459,313
South Carolina	([3])	(D)	(D)	12,791	634,988	7,432,346
South Dakota	–	–	–	1,399	62,253	474,409
Tennessee	5,161	382,334	(D)	24,578	1,155,305	13,598,152
Texas	6,879	490,121	20,792,387	11,865	545,351	4,818,806
Utah	–	–	–	3,323	172,730	(D)
Virginia	([2])	(D)	(D)	4,804	219,220	1,241,787
Washington	–	–	–	2,122	93,150	(D)
West Virginia	–	–	–	1,636	98,755	(D)
Wisconsin	([3])	(D)	(D)	9,312	380,282	3,509,505

– Represents zero. D Withheld to avoid disclosing data on individual companies. [1] Includes states not shown separately. [2] Employee class size of 1,000 to 2,499. [3] Employee class size of 2,500 to 4,999. [4] Employee class size of 5,000 to 9,999.

Source: U.S. Census Bureau, Annual Survey of Manufactures via American FactFinder, "Geographic Area Statistics: Statistics for all Manufacturing by State: 2011 and 2010," <http://factfinder2.census.gov/>, accessed March 2013.

Table 1061. Net Orders for U.S. Civil Jet Transport Aircraft: 1990 to 2012

[1990 data are net new firm orders; beginning 2000, net announced orders. Minus sign (-) indicates net cancellations. In 1997, Boeing acquired McDonnell Douglas]

Type of aircraft and customer	1990	2000	2005	2008	2009	2010	2011	2012
Total number [1]	**670**	**585**	**1,004**	**662**	**142**	**530**	**805**	**1,203**
U.S. customers	259	412	220	112	24	232	596	443
Foreign customers	411	193	811	550	118	298	209	760
Boeing 737, total	189	378	571	484	178	486	551	1,124
U.S. customers	38	302	152	107	34	206	525	407
Foreign customers	151	86	439	377	144	280	26	717
Boeing 747, total	153	24	43	3	2	-1	-1	1
U.S. customers	24	1	13	–	-2	-2	-1	–
Foreign customers	129	18	30	3	4	1	–	1
Boeing 757, total	66	43	–	–	–	–	–	–
U.S. customers	33	38	–	–	–	–	–	–
Foreign customers	33	14	–	–	–	–	–	–
Boeing 767, total	60	6	15	28	2	3	42	22
U.S. customers	23	-2	–	–	-1	–	31	19
Foreign customers	37	14	20	28	3	3	11	3
Boeing 777, total	34	113	154	54	19	46	200	68
U.S. customers	34	60	10	11	-7	3	37	4
Foreign customers	–	53	146	43	26	43	163	64
Boeing 787, total	–	–	235	93	-59	-4	13	-12
U.S. customers	–	–	45	-6	–	25	4	13
Foreign customers	–	–	190	99	-59	-29	9	-25
McDonnell Douglas MD-11, total	52	–	–	–	–	–	–	–
U.S. customers	16	–	–	–	–	–	–	–
Foreign customers	36	–	–	–	–	–	–	–
McDonnell Douglas MD-80/90, total	116	–	–	–	–	–	–	–
U.S. customers	91	–	–	–	–	–	–	–
Foreign customers	25	–	–	–	–	–	–	–
McDonnell Douglas MD-95, total	–	21	–	–	–	–	–	–
U.S. customers	–	13	–	–	–	–	–	–
Foreign customers	–	8	–	–	–	–	–	–

– Represents zero. [1] Beginning 2000, includes unidentified customers.

Source: © 2012 Aerospace Industries Association of America, Inc and Embry-Riddle Aeronautical University. See also <http://www.aia-aerospace.org/economics/aerospace_statistics/>.

Table 1062. General Aviation Airplane Shipments and Billings: 1980 to 2011

[Data are for U.S. manufactured airplanes. Totals may not add up due to rounding]

Type of Airplane	1980	1990	1995	2000	2005	2009	2010	2011
Airplane Units Shipped.............	**11,860**	**1,144**	**1,077**	**2,816**	**2,857**	**1,585**	**1,334**	**1,215**
Total piston...........................	10,756	695	576	1,913	2,095	802	746	668
Single-engine........................	8,640	608	515	1,810	2,024	770	679	617
Multi-engine.........................	2,116	87	61	103	71	32	67	51
Total turbine.........................	1,104	449	501	903	762	783	588	547
Turboprop............................	778	281	255	315	240	269	224	193
Business jet..........................	326	168	246	588	522	514	364	354
Factory Net Billings (Mil. dol.)......	**2,486**	**2,008**	**2,842**	**8,558**	**8,667**	**9,082**	**7,875**	**8,406**
Total Piston..........................	794	92	123	446	712	389	368	341
Single-engine........................	391	68	(NA)	(NA)	(NA)	(NA)	(NA)	(NA)
Multi-engine.........................	403	24	(NA)	(NA)	(NA)	(NA)	(NA)	(NA)
Total turbine.........................	1,691	1,916	2,719	8,112	7,954	8,693	7,506	8,066
Turboprop............................	875	644	653	934	749	872	724	559
Business jet..........................	816	1,272	2,066	7,178	7,205	7,821	6,782	7,507

NA Not Available.

Source: General Aviation Manufacturers Association, *2011 General Aviation Statistical Databook & Industry Outlook* ©, 2012. See also <www.gama.aero>.

Table 1063. Aerospace—Sales, New Orders, and Backlog: 2000 to 2010

[In billions of dollars (109.3 represents $109,300,000,000), except as indicated. Reported by establishments in which the principal business is the development and/or production of aerospace products]

Item	2000	2005	2006	2007	2008	2009	2010
Net sales..................................	**109.3**	**124.2**	**155.9**	**126.8**	**135.2**	**148.0**	**134.1**
U.S. Government net sales.................	41.0	62.8	69.7	48.4	59.5	59.7	58.6
Percent U.S. Government..................	37.5	50.6	44.7	38.2	44.0	40.3	43.7
Complete aircraft and parts...............	57.2	49.9	(D)	(D)	(D)	(D)	(D)
Aircraft engines and parts.................	12.5	18.5	28.6	15.5	(D)	(D)	(D)
Net, new orders...........................	**140.1**	**186.4**	**202.8**	**231.6**	**189.3**	**106.6**	**145.6**
Backlog, December 31......................	215.0	290.0	334.5	437.1	482.1	433.0	430.1

D Withheld to avoid disclosing data of individual companies.

Source: U.S. Census Bureau, Current Industrial Reports, "Civil Aircraft and Aircraft Engines; and Aerospace Industry," Series MA336G, June 2011. See also <http://www.census.gov/manufacturing/cir/historical_data/ma336g/index.html>.

Table 1064. Aerospace Industry Sales by Product Group and Customer: 2000 to 2012

[In billions of dollars (144.7 represents $144,700,000,000). Due to reporting practices and tabulating methods, figures may differ from those in Table 1061]

Group	2000	2005	2007	2008	2009	2010	2011	2012
CURRENT DOLLARS								
Total sales........................	**144.7**	**169.4**	**204.5**	**210.2**	**209.9**	**208.5**	**210.8**	**217.9**
Product group:								
Aircraft, total........................	81.6	86.6	113.0	112.2	110.7	110.0	112.8	118.8
Civil [1]............................	47.6	37.2	52.6	48.2	51.3	48.2	53.2	60.6
Military............................	34.0	49.4	60.4	64.0	59.4	61.8	59.7	58.2
Missiles.............................	9.3	20.8	22.6	24.6	24.7	23.5	23.4	23.1
Space...............................	29.7	36.7	39.9	43.2	45.0	45.4	44.6	44.9
Related products and services [2].....	24.1	25.4	29.1	30.2	29.4	29.7	30.0	31.0
Customer group:								
Aerospace products and services, total............	120.6	144.1	175.5	180.0	180.4	178.8	180.8	186.9
DOD [3]............................	47.5	80.7	94.2	101.5	99.4	101.2	99.6	96.2
NASA [4] and other agencies...........	13.4	17.3	17.8	19.5	20.8	21.1	21.2	20.3
Other customers [5]..................	59.7	46.1	63.5	59.0	60.2	56.5	60.0	70.4
Related products and services [2].....	24.1	25.4	29.1	30.2	29.4	29.7	30.0	31.0
CONSTANT (2009) DOLLARS [6]								
Total sales........................	**152.2**	**176.5**	**207.0**	**211.5**	**209.9**	**208.7**	**210.0**	**214.9**
Product group:								
Aircraft, total........................	85.8	90.2	114.3	112.9	110.7	110.1	112.4	117.2
Civil [1]............................	50.0	38.7	53.2	48.5	51.3	48.2	52.9	59.8
Military............................	35.8	51.5	61.1	64.4	59.4	61.9	59.4	57.5
Missiles.............................	9.8	21.7	22.9	24.7	24.7	23.5	23.3	22.8
Space...............................	31.2	38.2	40.4	43.5	45.0	45.4	44.4	44.3
Related products and services [3].....	25.4	26.4	29.4	30.4	29.4	29.7	29.9	30.6
Customer group:								
Aerospace products and services, total............	126.8	150.1	177.5	181.1	180.4	179.0	180.1	184.3
DOD [3]............................	49.9	84.1	95.3	102.1	99.4	101.3	99.2	94.9
NASA [4] and other agencies...........	14.1	18.0	18.0	19.6	20.8	21.1	21.1	20.0
Other customers [5]..................	62.8	48.0	64.2	59.4	60.2	56.5	59.7	69.4
Related products and services [3].....	25.4	26.4	29.4	30.4	29.4	29.7	29.9	30.6

[1] All civil sales of aircraft (domestic and export sales of jet transports, commuters, business, and personal aircraft and helicopters). [2] Electronics, software, and ground support equipment, plus sales of non-aerospace products which are produced by aerospace-manufacturing use technology, processes, and materials derived from aerospace products. [3] Department of Defense. [4] National Aeronautics and Space Administration. [5] Includes civil aircraft sales (see footnote 1), commercial space sales, all exports of military aircraft and missiles and related propulsion and parts. [6] Based on Aerospace Industry Association's aerospace composite price deflator (2009=100).

Source: © 2012 Aerospace Industries Association of America, Inc and Embry-Riddle Aeronautical University, *2013 Year-end Review and Forecast*, Dec. 2012. See also <http://www.aia-aerospace.org>.

Wholesale and Retail Trade

This section presents statistics relating to the distributive trades, specifically wholesale trade and retail trade. Data shown for the trades are classified by kind of business and cover sales, establishments, employees, payrolls, and other items. The principal sources of these data are from the U.S. Census Bureau and include the *2007 Economic Census*, annual and monthly surveys, and the *County Business Patterns* program. These data are supplemented by several tables from trade associations, such as the National Automobile Dealers Association.

Data on wholesale and retail trade also appear in several other sections. For instance, labor force employment and earnings data appear in Section 12, Labor Force, Employment, and Earnings; gross domestic product of the industry (Table 698) appears in Section 13, Income, Expenditures, Poverty, and Wealth; and financial data (several tables) from the quarterly *Statistics of Income Bulletin*, published by the Internal Revenue Service, appear in Section 15, Business Enterprise.

Censuses—Censuses of wholesale trade and retail trade have been taken at various intervals since 1929. Beginning with the 1967 census, legislation provides for a census of each area to be conducted every 5 years (for years ending in "2" and "7"). For more information on the most recent census, see the *Guide to the 2007 Economic Census* found at <http://www.census.gov/econ/census07/www/user_guide.html>. The industries covered in the censuses and surveys of business are defined in the *North American Industry Classification System*, (NAICS). Retail trade refers to places of business primarily engaged in retailing merchandise to the general public; and wholesale trade, to establishments primarily engaged in selling goods to other businesses and normally operating from a warehouse or office that have little or no display of merchandise. Many Census Bureau tables in this section utilize the 2007 NAICS codes, updating the 2002 codes, which replaced the Standard Industrial Classification (SIC) system. NAICS made substantial structural improvements and identifies over 250 new industries. At the same time, it causes breaks in time series far more profound than any prior revision of the previously used SIC system. For information on this system and how it affects the comparability of wholesale and retail statistics historically, see text, Section 15, Business Enterprise, and especially the Census Bureau Web site at <http://www.census.gov/eos/www/naics>. In general, the *2007 Economic Census* has three series of publications for these two sectors: 1) subject series with reports such as product lines and establishment and firm sizes, 2) geographic reports with individual reports for each state, and 3) industry series with individual reports for industry groups. For information on these series, see the Census Bureau Web site at <http://www.census.gov/econ/census07/>.

Current surveys—Current sample surveys conducted by the Census Bureau cover various aspects of wholesale and retail trade. Its *Monthly Retail Trade and Food Services* release at <http://www.census.gov/retail> contains monthly estimates of sales, inventories, and inventory/sales ratios for the United States, by kind of business. Annual figures on retail sales, year-end inventories, purchases, accounts receivable, and gross margins by kind of business are located on the Census Bureau Web site at <http://www.census.gov/econ/retail.html>. Additionally, annual data for accommodation and food services are located at the same site.

Statistics from the Census Bureau's monthly wholesale trade survey include national estimates of sales, inventories, and inventory/sales ratios for merchant wholesalers excluding manufacturers' sales branches and offices. Data are presented by major summary groups "durable and nondurable," and 4-digit NAICS industry groups. Merchant wholesalers excluding manufacturers' sales branches and offices are those wholesalers who take title to the goods they sell (e.g., jobbers, exporters, importers, industrial distributors). These data, based on reports submitted by a sample of firms, appear in the *Monthly Wholesale Trade Report* at <http://www.census.gov/wholesale>. This report, along with monthly sales, inventories, and inventories/sales ratios, also provides data on annual sales, inventories, and year-end inventories/sales ratios. The *Annual Wholesale Trade Survey* provides data on merchant wholesalers excluding manufacturer sales branches and offices as well as summary data for all merchant wholesalers. This report also provides separate data for manufacturer sales branches and offices, and electronic markets, agents, brokers, and commission merchants. Also included in the *Monthly Wholesale Trade Report* are data on annual sales, year-end inventories, inventories/sales ratios, operating expenses, purchases, and gross margins. Data are presented by major summary groups "durable and nondurable" and 4-digit NAICS industry groups for sales, end-of-year inventories, and operating expenses. The reports are available as documents on the Census Bureau Web site at <http://www.census.gov/econ/wholesale.html>.

E-commerce—Electronic commerce (or e-commerce) is the sale of goods and services over the Internet and extranet, electronic data interchange (EDI) network, electronic mail, or other online systems. Payment may or may not be made online. E-commerce data were collected in four separate Census Bureau surveys. These surveys used different measures of economic activity such as shipments for manufacturing, sales for wholesale and retail trade, and revenues for service industries. Consequently, measures of total economic and e-commerce activity vary by economic sector, are conceptually and definitionally different, and therefore, are not additive. This edition has several tables on e-commerce sales, such as Tables 1068, 1078, and 1079 in this section; and Table 1305 in Section 27, Accommodation, Food Services, and Other Services.

Statistical reliability—For a discussion of statistical collection and estimation, sampling procedures, and measures of statistical reliability applicable to Census Bureau data, see Appendix III.

Table 1065. Wholesale and Retail Trade—Establishments, Sales, Payroll, and Employees: 2002 and 2007

[435.5 represents 435,500. Covers establishments with payroll. For statement on methodology, see Appendix III]

Kind of business	2002 NAICS code [1]	Establishments (1,000)		Sales (bil. dol.)		Annual payroll (bil. dol.)		Paid employees (1,000)	
		2002	2007	2002	2007	2002	2007	2002	2007
Wholesale trade.................	**42**	**435.5**	**435.0**	**4,635**	**6,516**	**260**	**336**	**5,878**	**6,227**
Wholesale trade, durable goods................	423	260.4	255.0	2,171	2,898	157	207	3,357	3,619
Wholesale trade, nondurable goods.................	424	142.7	134.6	1,980	2,991	93	116	2,273	2,320
Wholesale electronic markets and agents and brokers.................	425	32.4	45.4	483	627	10	13	249	289
Retail trade.................	**44–45**	**1,114.6**	**11,281.0**	**3,056**	**3,918**	**302**	**363**	**14,648**	**15,515**
Motor vehicle and parts dealers................	441	125.1	126.8	802	891	65	73	1,845	1,914
Furniture and home furnishings stores................	442	65.2	65.1	92	108	13	15	535	557
Electronics and appliance stores................	443	46.8	50.8	82	109	9	11	391	486
Building material and garden equipment and supplies dealers................	444	(NA)	91.1	(NA)	318	(NA)	38	(NA)	1,331
Food and beverage stores................	445	148.8	146.1	457	539	49	55	2,839	2,827
Health and personal care stores................	446	81.8	88.5	178	234	20	28	1,024	1,068
Gasoline stations................	447	121.4	118.8	249	450	14	15	927	891
Clothing and clothing accessories stores.......	448	149.8	156.5	168	216	21	27	1,427	1,644
Sporting goods, hobby, book, and music stores.......	451	62.2	57.4	73	81	9	9	611	619
General merchandise stores................	452	40.7	45.9	445	577	43	54	2,525	2,763
Miscellaneous store retailers................	453	129.5	121.9	91	104	13	14	792	792
Nonstore retailers................	454	54.9	59.4	173	290	17	23	571	621

NA Not available. [1] North American Industrial Classification System; see text, Section 15.

Source: U.S. Census Bureau, 2007 Economic Census, "Economy-Wide Key Statistics," <http://factfinder2.census.gov>, accessed June 2013.

Table 1066. Wholesale Trade—Nonemployer Firms and Receipts by Industry Type: 2011

[36,220,984 represents $36,220,984,000. Includes only firms subject to federal income tax. Nonemployers are businesses with no paid employees. A firm is a single physical location where business is conducted or services or industrial operations are performed. Each distinct business income tax return filed by a nonemployer business is counted as a firm]

Industry type	2007 NAICS code [1]	Firms				Receipts ($1,000)
		Total	Corpora-tions [2]	Individual proprietor-ships [3]	Partner-ships [4]	
Wholesale trade, total.................	**42**	**403,292**	**70,163**	**307,836**	**25,293**	**36,220,984**
Durable goods merchant wholesalers................	**423**	**201,619**	**38,661**	**149,789**	**13,169**	**19,011,062**
Motor vehicle and motor vehicle parts and supplies merchant wholesalers................	4231	16,582	3,571	11,987	1,024	2,379,589
Furniture and home furnishing merchant wholesalers...........	4232	12,608	2,153	9,726	729	1,001,284
Lumber and other construction materials merchant wholesalers................	4233	8,197	1,770	5,740	687	836,594
Professional and commercial equipment and supplies merchant wholesalers................	4234	10,892	2,228	7,843	821	1,081,034
Metal and mineral (except petroleum) merchant wholesalers................	4235	3,579	772	2,554	253	472,983
Electrical and electronic goods merchant wholesalers...........	4236	11,178	3,164	7,056	958	1,238,711
Hardware and plumbing and heating equipment and supplies merchant wholesalers................	4237	4,892	1,161	3,344	387	459,280
Machinery, equipment, and supplies merchant wholesalers................	4238	18,771	5,366	11,927	1,478	2,433,978
Miscellaneous durable goods merchant wholesalers................	4239	114,920	18,476	89,612	6,832	9,107,609
Nondurable goods merchant wholesalers................	**424**	**148,405**	**25,298**	**113,301**	**9,806**	**13,511,522**
Paper and paper product merchant wholesalers................	4241	6,155	1,088	4,720	347	495,507
Drugs and druggists' sundries merchant wholesalers...........	4242	2,730	677	1,797	256	245,049
Apparel, piece goods, and notions merchant wholesalers................	4243	24,424	4,209	18,566	1,649	1,761,408
Grocery and related products merchant wholesalers................	4244	28,148	5,194	21,051	1,903	3,940,128
Farm product raw material merchant wholesalers................	4245	5,390	594	4,538	258	626,018
Chemical and allied products merchant wholesalers............	4246	3,660	1,129	2,158	373	456,963
Petroleum and petroleum products merchant wholesalers................	4247	2,235	427	1,615	193	331,215
Beer, wine, and distilled alcoholic beverage merchant wholesalers................	4248	4,995	866	3,453	676	442,162
Miscellaneous nondurable goods merchant wholesalers................	4249	70,668	11,114	55,403	4,151	5,213,072
Wholesale electronic markets and agents and brokers................	**425**	**53,268**	**6,204**	**44,746**	**2,318**	**3,698,400**
Business to business electronics markets................	42511	8,426	965	7,008	453	614,138

[1] North American Industry Classification System, 2007; see text, Section 15. [2] A legally incorporated business under state laws. [3] Also referred to as "sole proprietorship," an unincorporated business with a sole owner. Includes self-employed persons. [4] An unincorporated business where two or more persons join to carry on a trade or business with each having a shared financial interest in the business.

Source: U.S. Census Bureau, Nonemployer Statistics, "Geographic Area Series: Nonemployer Statistics by Legal Form of Organization," <http://factfinder2.census.gov>, accessed June 2013.

Table 1067. Wholesale Trade—Establishments, Employees, and Payroll: 2010 and 2011

[414.6 represents 414,600. Covers establishments with payroll. Excludes self-employed individuals, employees of private households, railroad employees, agricultural production employees, and most government employees. For statement on methodology, see Appendix III]

Kind of business	2007 NAICS code [1]	Establishments (1,000)		Employees [2] (1,000)		Payroll (bil. dol.)	
		2010	2011	2010	2011	2010	2011
Wholesale trade, total.............................	**42**	**414.6**	**411.9**	**5,599**	**5,626**	**339.1**	**357.2**
Merchant wholesalers, durable goods.............................	423	236.4	235.2	3,133	3,156	200.6	213.7
Motor vehicle/motor vehicle parts and supply merchant wholesalers.............................	4231	24.5	24.0	349	352	16.3	17.1
Furniture and home furnishing merchant wholesalers..........	4232	12.0	11.6	134	130	6.8	6.9
Lumber and other construction materials merchant wholesalers.............................	4233	18.0	17.2	198	188	9.5	9.4
Professional and commercial equipment and supplies merchant wholesalers.............................	4234	34.1	36.0	667	655	55.2	55.6
Metal and mineral (except petroleum) merchant wholesalers.............................	4235	10.6	10.3	139	144	8.0	8.8
Electrical goods merchant wholesalers.............................	4236	28.5	28.0	483	493	41.6	47.2
Hardware, plumbing and heating equipment and supplies merchant wholesalers.............................	4237	18.8	18.8	203	213	11.0	12.0
Machinery, equipment, and supplies merchant wholesalers.............................	4238	57.2	56.4	651	665	37.2	40.8
Miscellaneous durable goods merchant wholesalers...........	4239	32.7	32.9	309	315	15.1	15.8
Merchant wholesalers, nondurable goods.....................	**424**	**126.3**	**124.9**	**2,162**	**2,155**	**123.6**	**127.9**
Paper and paper product merchant wholesalers...............	4241	10.7	10.3	148	147	7.8	7.9
Drugs and druggists' sundries merchant wholesalers..........	4242	9.1	9.2	264	263	25.2	26.6
Apparel, piece goods and notions merchant wholesalers.....	4243	15.5	15.2	180	180	10.2	10.3
Grocery and related product merchant wholesalers............	4244	32.9	33.1	758	756	36.9	38.2
Farm product raw material merchant wholesalers..............	4245	6.1	6.1	63	64	3.2	3.3
Chemical and allied products merchant wholesalers...........	4246	12.4	12.2	139	145	9.6	10.3
Petroleum and petroleum products merchant wholesalers.....	4247	7.2	7.1	106	105	6.9	7.1
Beer, wine, and distilled alcoholic beverages....................	4248	4.2	4.2	176	178	9.7	10.0
Miscellaneous nondurable goods merchant wholesalers.....	4249	28.2	27.6	326	317	14.2	14.3
Wholesale electronic markets and agents and brokers.....	**425**	**51.9**	**51.8**	**304**	**315**	**14.9**	**15.5**

[1] North American Industry Classification System, 2007. See text, Section 15. [2] Covers full- and part-time employees who are on the payroll in the pay period including March 12.

Source: U.S. Census Bureau, County Business Patterns, "Geography Area Series: County Business Patterns," <http://factfinder2.census.gov>, accessed June 2013.

Table 1068. Merchant Wholesale Trade Sales—Total and E-Commerce: 2011

[4,701,976 represents $4,701,976,000,000. Covers only businesses with paid employees. Excludes manufacturers' sales branches and offices. Based on the Annual Wholesale Trade Survey, see Appendix III]

Kind of business	2007 NAICS code [1]	2011			
		Value of sales (mil. dol.)		E-commerce as percent of total sales	Percent distribution of E-commerce sales
		Total	E-commerce		
Total merchant wholesale trade........................	**42**	**4,701,976**	**836,443**	**17.8**	**100.0**
Durable goods........................	**423**	**2,152,137**	**323,159**	**15.0**	**38.6**
Motor vehicles, parts and supplies........................	4231	328,981	98,385	29.9	11.8
Furniture and home furnishings........................	4232	55,029	6,859	12.5	0.8
Lumber and other construction materials........................	4233	95,610	3,260	3.4	0.4
Professional and commercial equipment and supplies...............	4234	458,519	97,730	21.3	11.7
Computer equipment and supplies........................	42343	273,730	60,823	22.2	7.3
Metals and minerals (except petroleum)........................	4235	155,910	6,186	4.0	0.7
Electrical goods........................	4236	358,279	49,833	13.9	6.0
Hardware, plumbing and heating equipment........................	4237	102,103	10,395	10.2	1.2
Machinery, equipment and supplies........................	4238	346,444	22,301	6.4	2.7
Miscellaneous durable goods........................	4239	251,262	28,210	11.2	3.4
Nondurable goods........................	**424**	**2,549,839**	**513,284**	**20.1**	**61.4**
Paper and paper products........................	4241	85,553	21,742	25.4	2.6
Drugs, drug proprietaries and druggists' sundries...................	4242	410,085	(S)	(S)	(S)
Apparel, piece goods and notions........................	4243	137,611	30,207	22.0	3.6
Groceries and related products........................	4244	534,174	88,013	16.5	10.5
Farm product raw materials........................	4245	229,188	(S)	(S)	(S)
Chemical and allied products........................	4246	115,226	7,179	6.2	0.9
Petroleum and petroleum products........................	4247	691,282	(S)	(S)	(S)
Beer, wine, and distilled alcoholic beverages....................	4248	115,871	6,433	5.6	0.8
Miscellaneous nondurable goods........................	4249	230,849	28,195	12.2	3.4

S Figure does not meet publication standards. [1] North American Industry Classification System, 2007. See text, Section 15.

Source: U.S. Census Bureau, "E-Stats, 2011 E-commerce Multi-sector Data Tables," <http://www.census.gov/econ/estats>, accessed July 2013.

Table 1069. Merchant Wholesalers—Summary: 2000 to 2011

[In billions of dollars (2,815 represents $2,815,000,000,000), except ratios. Inventories and inventories/sales ratios, as of December, not seasonally adjusted. Excludes manufacturers' sales branches and offices. Data adjusted using final results of the 2007 Economic Census. Based on data from the Annual Wholesale Trade Survey and the Monthly Wholesale Trade Survey; see Appendix III]

Kind of business	2002 NAICS code [1]	2000	2005	2007	2008	2009	2010	2011
SALES								
Merchant wholesalers..................................	42	**2,815**	**3,629.3**	**4,201.8**	**4,459.7**	**3,726.0**	**4,181.5**	**4,702.0**
Durable goods..................................	423	**1,487**	**1,830.3**	**2,102.0**	**2,104.3**	**1,696.5**	**1,924.9**	**2,152.1**
Motor vehicles, parts, and supplies.........................	4231	222	303.8	341.2	308.1	251.3	294.7	329.0
Furniture and home furnishings.........................	4232	53	63.0	69.1	64.2	51.0	52.5	55.0
Lumber and other construction materials.........................	4233	87	139.0	126.5	116.4	90.4	92.0	95.6
Professional, commercial equipment and supplies.........	4234	282	332.8	381.8	385.7	361.7	410.5	458.5
Computer, peripheral equipment and software...........	42343	175	179.0	198.8	203.4	192.6	237.0	273.7
Metal and mineral (except petroleum)........................	4235	94	136.1	165.9	177.5	103.6	124.7	155.9
Electrical and electronic goods.........................	4236	260	284.4	349.0	354.4	310.1	346.4	358.3
Hardware, plumbing, heating equipment and supplies. . . .	4237	72	95.0	112.2	108.4	89.6	94.9	102.1
Machinery, equipment, and supplies.........................	4238	256	287.7	328.8	349.7	270.5	296.5	346.4
Miscellaneous durable goods.........................	4239	160	188.5	227.4	239.9	168.4	212.7	251.3
Nondurable goods..................................	424	**1,328**	**1,806.5**	**2,109.9**	**2,364.9**	**2,053.2**	**2,256.5**	**2,549.8**
Paper and paper products.........................	4241	78	87.2	91.3	90.5	81.3	83.5	85.6
Drugs and druggists' sundries.........................	4242	176	322.4	351.8	369.0	376.6	391.5	410.1
Apparel, piece goods, and notions.........................	4243	97	121.2	139.7	136.6	123.4	132.5	137.6
Grocery and related products.........................	4244	375	422.2	475.8	489.9	480.0	499.5	534.2
Farm product raw materials.........................	4245	103	106.0	145.8	196.4	164.6	182.8	229.2
Chemical and allied products.........................	4246	62	90.9	102.3	115.5	88.9	102.2	115.2
Petroleum and petroleum products.........................	4247	196	369.9	486.9	628.8	402.0	541.3	691.3
Beer, wine, and distilled alcoholic beverages.........................	4248	71	92.2	103.8	109.3	108.7	111.2	115.9
Miscellaneous nondurable goods.........................	4249	171	187.1	202.5	219.6	204.2	212.0	230.8
INVENTORIES								
Merchant wholesalers..................................	42	**309.7**	**369.9**	**428.7**	**445.3**	**393.8**	**436.1**	**475.3**
Durable goods..................................	423	**198.5**	**233.6**	**264.4**	**279.1**	**228.9**	**249.4**	**276.8**
Motor vehicles, parts, and supplies.........................	4231	28.8	38.2	43.4	48.2	37.5	41.1	48.9
Furniture and home furnishings.........................	4232	6.4	8.0	8.9	8.6	6.9	7.6	7.8
Lumber and other construction materials.........................	4233	8.3	13.9	13.3	12.7	10.3	10.9	11.3
Professional, commercial equipment and supplies.........	4234	27.3	27.6	31.4	31.8	29.3	32.1	33.8
Computer, peripheral equipment and software...........	42343	12.1	11.3	12.2	12.3	12.0	13.9	14.5
Metal and mineral (except petroleum)........................	4235	13.6	21.0	25.1	29.0	18.6	21.6	25.1
Electrical and electronic goods.........................	4236	31.3	30.4	35.5	36.7	29.8	32.7	35.0
Hardware, plumbing, heating equipment and supplies. . . .	4237	11.5	15.4	18.2	17.5	15.2	16.2	17.4
Machinery, equipment, and supplies.........................	4238	51.1	55.8	64.3	69.0	50.9	62.8	71.0
Miscellaneous durable goods.........................	4239	20.2	23.3	24.3	25.7	22.5	24.5	26.4
Nondurable goods..................................	424	**111.2**	**136.4**	**164.4**	**166.2**	**164.9**	**186.7**	**198.5**
Paper and paper products.........................	4241	6.7	7.1	7.2	7.5	6.5	6.9	7.2
Drugs and druggists' sundries.........................	4242	23.9	30.3	32.3	32.7	33.2	35.1	36.8
Apparel, piece goods, and notions.........................	4243	14.2	17.5	18.7	20.2	16.5	19.7	21.7
Grocery and related products.........................	4244	20.5	22.4	26.1	27.8	26.2	28.6	31.4
Farm product raw materials.........................	4245	11.5	11.6	22.3	20.0	23.3	32.9	29.9
Chemical and allied products.........................	4246	6.0	8.3	9.5	10.4	8.8	10.0	11.4
Petroleum and petroleum products.........................	4247	5.2	12.4	17.6	13.6	19.6	21.1	23.9
Beer, wine, and distilled alcoholic beverages.........................	4248	6.5	8.3	10.0	11.1	10.2	10.5	11.3
Miscellaneous nondurable goods.........................	4249	16.6	18.5	20.6	23.0	20.6	22.0	24.9
INVENTORIES/SALES RATIO								
Merchant wholesalers..................................	42	**1.10**	**1.02**	**1.02**	**1.00**	**1.06**	**1.04**	**1.01**
Durable goods..................................	423	**1.34**	**1.28**	**1.26**	**1.33**	**1.35**	**1.30**	**1.29**
Motor vehicles, parts, and supplies.........................	4231	1.30	1.26	1.27	1.57	1.49	1.40	1.49
Furniture and home furnishings.........................	4232	1.22	1.27	1.29	1.34	1.35	1.44	1.41
Lumber and other construction materials.........................	4233	0.96	1.00	1.05	1.09	1.14	1.18	1.18
Professional, commercial equipment and supplies.........	4234	0.97	0.83	0.82	0.82	0.81	0.78	0.74
Computer, peripheral equipment and software...........	42343	0.69	0.63	0.61	0.61	0.63	0.59	0.53
Metal and mineral (except petroleum)........................	4235	1.45	1.55	1.51	1.63	1.79	1.73	1.61
Electrical and electronic goods.........................	4236	1.20	1.07	1.02	1.03	0.96	0.94	0.98
Hardware, plumbing, heating equipment and supplies. . . .	4237	1.60	1.62	1.62	1.61	1.70	1.70	1.71
Machinery, equipment, and supplies.........................	4238	1.99	1.94	1.96	1.97	2.18	2.12	2.05
Miscellaneous durable goods.........................	4239	1.26	1.24	1.07	1.07	1.33	1.15	1.05
Nondurable goods..................................	424	**0.84**	**0.75**	**0.78**	**0.70**	**0.80**	**0.83**	**0.78**
Paper and paper products.........................	4241	0.87	0.81	0.79	0.82	0.80	0.83	0.85
Drugs and druggists' sundries.........................	4242	1.36	0.94	0.92	0.89	0.88	0.90	0.90
Apparel, piece goods, and notions.........................	4243	1.47	1.45	1.34	1.48	1.34	1.48	1.57
Grocery and related products.........................	4244	0.55	0.53	0.55	0.57	0.55	0.57	0.59
Farm product raw materials.........................	4245	1.12	1.09	1.53	1.02	1.41	1.80	1.31
Chemical and allied products.........................	4246	0.97	0.91	0.93	0.90	0.99	0.98	0.99
Petroleum and petroleum products.........................	4247	0.27	0.34	0.36	0.22	0.49	0.39	0.35
Beer, wine, and distilled alcoholic beverages.........................	4248	0.91	0.90	0.96	1.01	0.94	0.95	0.98
Miscellaneous nondurable goods.........................	4249	0.97	0.99	1.02	1.05	1.01	1.04	1.08

[1] North American Industry Classification System, 2007. See text, Section 15.

Source: U.S. Census Bureau, *2011 Annual Wholesale Trade Report*, February 2013. See also <http://www.census.gov/wholesale/>.

Table 1070. Wholesale and Retail Trade—Establishments, Employees, and Payroll by State: 2010 and 2011

[5,599 represents 5,599,000. Covers establishments with payroll. Excludes most government employees, railroad employees, and self-employed persons. Based on North American Industry Classification System (NAICS) 2007. See text, Section 15. For statement on methodology, see Appendix III]

State	Wholesale trade (NAICS 42)						Retail trade (NAICS 44, 45)					
	Establishments		Employees [1] (1,000)		Annual payroll (mil. dol.)		Establishments		Employees [1] (1,000)		Annual payroll (mil. dol.)	
	2010	2011	2010	2011	2010	2011	2010	2011	2010	2011	2010	2011
U.S.........	414,608	411,930	5,599	5,626	339,065	357,175	1,067,984	1,062,942	14,497	14,699	359,368	370,745
AL..........	5,335	5,314	70	70	3,443	3,541	18,484	18,275	225	226	5,139	5,229
AK..........	743	739	9	9	473	486	2,515	2,510	33	33	950	977
AZ..........	6,504	6,474	90	91	5,328	5,809	17,993	17,794	304	307	7,341	7,489
AR..........	3,386	3,403	43	43	2,093	2,180	11,006	10,843	135	137	3,060	3,158
CA..........	58,023	57,471	791	790	55,263	59,070	106,265	106,146	1,485	1,518	41,161	42,563
CO..........	7,140	7,096	91	90	5,726	5,995	18,521	18,357	240	242	6,302	6,434
CT..........	4,418	4,383	68	71	4,973	5,241	12,940	12,738	178	181	5,012	5,119
DE..........	1,023	1,058	17	16	1,355	1,449	3,654	3,623	50	52	1,252	1,297
DC..........	413	446	5	4	356	339	1,762	1,756	19	20	584	607
FL..........	30,212	30,193	277	279	14,018	14,742	70,627	70,955	913	941	22,767	23,543
GA..........	13,125	13,025	184	185	10,756	11,120	33,720	33,438	429	438	10,148	10,356
HI..........	1,749	1,732	19	18	824	814	4,694	4,678	65	67	1,710	1,799
ID..........	2,019	1,987	23	24	1,036	1,128	5,910	5,802	73	72	1,763	1,777
IL..........	19,194	19,078	299	302	19,122	20,045	40,670	40,365	589	597	14,643	14,985
IN..........	7,771	7,786	105	108	5,172	5,581	22,076	21,915	308	308	6,966	7,139
IA..........	4,801	4,799	64	65	2,951	3,098	12,343	12,215	174	174	3,772	3,916
KS..........	4,432	4,400	61	61	3,098	3,306	10,727	10,655	147	146	3,322	3,385
KY..........	4,284	4,239	68	68	3,484	3,701	15,579	15,390	218	216	5,158	5,267
LA..........	5,536	5,511	74	75	3,775	4,033	16,687	16,697	223	227	5,209	5,404
ME..........	1,591	1,582	17	17	825	812	6,513	6,396	80	80	1,881	1,907
MD..........	5,761	5,716	88	84	5,408	5,344	18,356	18,247	272	279	7,078	7,232
MA..........	8,161	8,068	130	127	10,009	9,798	24,412	24,367	344	350	9,164	9,518
MI..........	11,511	11,380	154	153	9,149	9,704	35,017	34,982	438	443	10,210	10,590
MN..........	8,249	8,176	125	126	8,495	8,962	19,547	19,368	285	286	6,785	6,946
MS..........	2,829	2,789	34	35	1,459	1,521	11,744	11,543	136	138	2,916	2,984
MO..........	7,940	7,883	119	120	5,747	6,057	21,799	21,637	306	306	7,134	7,336
MT..........	1,455	1,483	14	14	559	629	4,939	4,832	56	56	1,316	1,344
NE..........	3,024	3,047	40	40	1,935	2,012	7,417	7,338	104	107	2,360	2,480
NV..........	2,858	2,859	34	34	1,724	1,770	8,084	8,119	129	129	3,357	3,463
NH..........	1,865	1,821	24	23	1,580	1,560	6,166	6,125	95	95	2,342	2,400
NJ..........	14,871	14,642	252	250	19,689	20,651	32,408	32,053	429	434	12,094	12,373
NM..........	1,957	1,946	21	20	946	981	6,813	6,719	94	95	2,195	2,269
NY..........	32,975	32,670	347	352	21,987	22,800	76,763	77,036	865	884	23,097	24,002
NC..........	11,651	11,590	162	164	9,675	10,332	34,339	34,029	438	446	10,096	10,445
ND..........	1,500	1,535	19	20	923	1,077	3,199	3,153	45	45	1,052	1,136
OH..........	14,310	14,184	211	215	11,425	12,111	37,035	36,813	543	549	12,780	13,101
OK..........	4,594	4,501	57	57	2,764	2,976	12,964	12,979	169	171	3,854	3,995
OR..........	5,505	5,423	80	80	5,399	5,870	13,835	13,806	183	185	4,598	4,718
PA..........	15,077	14,994	234	236	14,218	14,970	44,430	44,193	645	647	15,209	15,600
RI..........	1,409	1,404	18	19	1,062	1,129	3,886	3,831	46	48	1,197	1,272
SC..........	4,899	4,812	59	63	2,919	3,257	17,708	17,553	218	219	4,866	4,937
SD..........	1,406	1,426	17	17	729	765	3,973	3,948	51	50	1,104	1,157
TN..........	6,939	6,858	113	111	6,130	6,344	22,813	22,423	302	306	7,186	7,429
TX..........	31,526	31,545	455	458	28,126	29,784	76,787	77,217	1,127	1,153	27,477	28,860
UT..........	3,522	3,550	53	52	2,564	2,792	8,816	8,908	136	135	3,293	3,329
VT..........	865	852	11	11	504	515	3,657	3,583	39	39	943	971
VA..........	7,415	7,342	102	100	5,876	6,071	27,747	27,425	401	407	9,798	10,007
WA..........	9,382	9,281	120	121	7,283	7,533	21,770	21,574	304	305	8,330	8,804
WV..........	1,552	1,544	19	19	849	891	6,557	6,460	87	86	1,880	1,942
WI..........	7,074	7,063	106	109	5,437	6,019	19,591	19,447	294	295	6,769	6,988
WY..........	827	830	8	8	424	463	2,726	2,686	31	30	751	767

[1] Covers full- and part-time employees who are on the payroll in the pay period including March 12.

Source: U.S. Census Bureau, County Business Patterns, "Geography Area Series, County Business Patterns," <http://factfinder2.census.gov/>, accessed June 2013. See also <http://www.census.gov/econ/cbp/index.html>.

Table 1071. Retail Trade—Establishments, Employees, and Payroll: 2010 and 2011

[1,068.0 represents 1,068,000. Covers establishments with payroll. Excludes most government employees, railroad employees, and self-employed persons. For statement on methodology, see Appendix III]

Kind of business	2007 NAICS code [1]	Establishments (1,000)		Employees (1,000) [2]		Payroll (bil. dol.)	
		2010	2011	2010	2011	2010	2011
Retail trade, total.....................	**44–45**	**1,068.0**	**1,062.9**	**14,497**	**14,699**	**359.4**	**370.7**
Motor vehicle and parts dealers.....................	441	117.7	116.3	1,636	1,664	63.8	68.0
Automobile dealers.....................	4411	45.4	44.9	1,039	1,057	46.3	49.8
New car dealers.....................	44111	21.9	21.3	926	938	42.5	45.6
Used car dealers.....................	44112	23.4	23.6	112	118	3.8	4.2
Other motor vehicle dealers.....................	4412	15.1	14.6	122	121	4.3	4.5
Recreational vehicle dealers.....................	44121	2.7	2.6	29	30	1.1	1.2
Motorcycle and boat and other motor vehicle dealers........	44122	12.4	12.0	93	91	3.2	3.3
Motorcycle dealers.....................	441221	5.4	5.1	52	50	1.7	1.7
Automotive parts, accessories, and tire stores.....................	4413	57.2	56.8	475	486	13.1	13.7
Automotive parts, accessories and tire stores.....................	44131	36.9	36.5	302	308	7.2	7.6
Tire dealers.....................	44132	20.3	20.4	173	178	5.9	6.1
Furniture and home furnishing stores.....................	442	54.9	52.7	429	424	11.6	11.6
Furniture stores.....................	4421	24.9	23.9	205	197	6.4	6.3
Home furnishings stores.....................	4422	30.1	28.8	224	227	5.2	5.3
Floor covering stores.....................	44221	12.3	11.9	67	62	2.3	2.2
Other home furnishings stores.....................	44229	17.8	16.9	157	165	3.0	3.1
Window treatment stores.....................	442291	2.1	2.0	7	7	0.2	0.2
Electronics and appliance stores.....................	443	48.3	49.1	412	434	11.3	12.0
Appliance, TV, and all other electronics stores.....................	44311	36.7	37.7	317	337	8.0	8.5
Household appliance stores.....................	443111	8.4	8.6	64	64	1.9	1.9
Radio, television, and other electronics stores.....................	443112	28.2	29.1	253	274	6.1	6.7
Computer and software stores.....................	44312	10.5	10.3	86	88	3.0	3.1
Building material & garden equip. & supp. dealers.....................	444	83.7	81.3	1,208	1,195	34.4	34.7
Building material & supplies dealers [3].....................	4441	64.5	62.6	1,060	1,045	30.2	30.4
Home centers.....................	44411	6.8	6.7	([4])	([4])	(D)	(D)
Hardware stores.....................	44413	15.5	15.3	133	130	3.0	3.0
Lawn & garden equip. & supplies stores [3].....................	4442	19.1	18.7	149	150	4.2	4.3
Nursery and garden centers.....................	44422	15.1	14.8	124	126	3.4	3.5
Food & beverage stores.....................	445	147.7	148.8	2,823	2,843	58.7	59.4
Grocery stores.....................	4451	92.2	93.3	2,527	2,542	53.1	53.7
Supermarkets & grocery (except convenience) stores........	44511	64.4	64.4	2,403	2,414	51.1	51.5
Convenience stores.....................	44512	27.8	28.9	124	129	2.0	2.2
Specialty food stores.....................	4452	24.0	23.6	148	152	2.6	2.7
Beer, wine, & liquor stores [4].....................	4453	31.5	31.9	148	149	2.9	3.0
Health & personal care stores [3].....................	446	90.1	92.2	1,004	986	32.4	33.2
Pharmacies & drug stores.....................	44611	42.9	44.5	736	708	25.3	25.8
Cosmetics, beauty supplies, & perfume stores.....................	44612	14.7	15.1	94	102	1.8	2.0
Optical goods stores.....................	44613	12.9	12.8	72	73	2.0	2.0
Gasoline stations.....................	447	111.7	110.8	852	848	15.3	15.3
Gasoline stations with convenience stores.....................	44711	94.1	94.0	696	699	11.9	12.0
Other gasoline stations.....................	44719	17.6	16.8	156	149	3.4	3.3
Clothing & clothing accessories stores.....................	448	147.6	148.1	1,529	1,660	26.4	28.6
Clothing stores [3].....................	4481	96.8	98.2	1,205	1,324	19.4	21.2
Men's clothing stores.....................	44811	7.4	7.4	50	52	1.2	1.3
Women's clothing stores.....................	44812	34.9	35.6	310	359	4.9	5.3
Children's & infants' clothing stores.....................	44813	7.1	7.1	89	94	1.0	1.1
Family clothing stores.....................	44814	27.7	28.1	613	667	9.7	10.8
Shoe stores.....................	4482	26.1	25.4	196	207	3.3	3.5
Jewelry, luggage, & leather goods stores.....................	4483	24.8	24.4	128	128	3.7	4.0
Jewelry stores.....................	44831	23.7	23.4	122	122	3.5	3.7
Sporting goods, hobby, book, & music stores.....................	451	52.4	50.9	548	541	9.4	9.5
Sporting goods/hobby/musical instrument stores [3].....................	4511	39.3	38.8	405	409	7.2	7.5
Sporting goods stores.....................	45111	21.4	21.2	219	220	4.2	4.4
Hobby, toy, and game stores.....................	45112	8.8	8.6	112	118	1.7	1.8
Book, periodical, & music stores [3].....................	4512	13.2	12.1	143	132	2.2	2.0
Book stores.....................	451211	8.9	8.4	113	104	1.7	1.5
Prerecorded tape, CD, & record stores.....................	45122	2.9	2.4	21	19	0.3	0.3
General merchandise stores.....................	452	46.7	47.8	2,796	2,844	59.8	60.7
Department stores.....................	4521	8.6	8.6	1,166	1,203	23.5	23.9
Other general merchandise stores.....................	4529	38.1	39.2	1,630	1,640	36.3	36.8
Warehouse clubs & superstores.....................	45291	4.5	4.6	1,335	1,313	31.3	31.6
All other general merchandise stores.....................	45299	33.5	34.6	295	327	4.9	5.2
Miscellaneous store retailers [3].....................	453	110.9	108.6	720	717	13.9	14.3
Florists.....................	4531	16.2	15.3	71	66	1.1	1.1
Office supplies, stationery, and gift stores.....................	4532	35.3	33.9	271	261	4.6	4.6
Office supplies and stationery stores.....................	45321	8.4	8.1	102	100	2.2	2.1
Gift, novelty, and souvenir stores.....................	45322	26.9	25.7	169	161	2.4	2.5
Used merchandise stores.....................	4533	17.9	18.2	144	154	2.5	2.7
Other miscellaneous store retailers [3].....................	4539	41.6	41.2	234	236	5.7	5.9
Pet and pet supplies stores.....................	45391	8.6	8.6	97	99	1.8	1.9
Nonstore retailers [3].....................	454	56.2	56.3	539	544	22.6	23.5
Electronic shopping & mail-order houses.....................	4541	22.5	23.7	312	321	14.4	15.4
Direct selling establishments.....................	4543	29.1	28.3	190	187	7.1	7.0
Fuel dealers.....................	45431	9.7	9.5	79	79	3.2	3.2

D Figure withheld to avoid disclosure. [1] Based on North American Industry Classification System, 2007. See text, Section 15. [2] See footnote 2, Table 1067. [3] Includes other kinds of business, not shown separately. [4] Includes government employees. [4] 100,000 or more employees.

Source: U.S. Census Bureau, County Business Patterns, "Geography Area Series: County Business Patterns," <http://factfinder2.census.gov>, accessed July 2013.

Table 1072. Retail Trade—Nonemployer Firms and Receipts by Industry Type: 2011

[79,730,576 represents $79,730,576,000. See headnote, Table 1066]

Industry type	2007 NAICS code [1]	Firms				Receipts ($1,000)
		Total	Corpora-tions [2]	Individual proprietor-ships [3]	Partner-ships [4]	
Retail trade, total.............................	**44–45**	**1,847,993**	**116,215**	**1,664,773**	**67,005**	**79,730,576**
Motor vehicle & parts dealers................................	441	159,208	16,157	136,394	6,657	17,718,647
Furniture & home furnishings stores........................	442	39,871	5,743	31,441	2,687	2,424,657
Electronics and appliance stores........................	443	29,514	3,870	24,313	1,331	1,505,931
Bldg material & garden equip. & supplies dealers........	444	36,731	3,934	30,929	1,868	2,307,123
Building material & supplies dealers.....................	4441	25,631	3,133	21,130	1,368	1,751,565
Food & beverage stores........................	445	103,719	12,223	84,612	6,884	8,134,874
Grocery stores............................	4451	42,926	5,154	35,474	2,298	3,890,835
Specialty food stores........................	4452	48,977	4,996	40,646	3,335	2,486,343
Health & personal care stores.....................	446	137,829	6,192	128,830	2,807	3,294,272
Gasoline stations............................	447	8,639	1,615	6,350	674	1,190,609
Clothing & clothing accessories stores.....................	448	147,986	9,530	132,050	6,406	5,446,372
Clothing stores............................	4481	96,924	6,516	85,443	4,965	3,566,996
Jewelry, luggage, and leather goods stores.............	4483	45,965	2,492	42,285	1,188	1,607,531
Sporting goods, hobby, book, & music stores...........	451	81,148	5,811	70,809	4,528	3,452,255
Book, periodical, and music stores.....................	4512	22,499	1,287	20,268	944	728,303
General merchandise stores........................	452	35,137	3,019	30,335	1,783	1,590,601
Miscellaneous store retailers........................	453	271,877	21,997	235,215	14,665	11,910,324
Office supplies, stationery, and gift stores................	4532	53,860	4,179	46,630	3,051	1,883,484
Nonstore retailers................................	454	796,334	26,124	753,495	16,715	20,754,911
Electronic shopping & mail-order houses................	4541	101,801	6,483	90,801	4,517	4,817,935
Direct selling establishments........................	4543	670,382	17,515	642,243	10,624	15,171,373

[1] North American Industry Classification System, 2007; see text, Section 15. [2] A legally incorporated business under state laws. [3] Also referred to as "sole proprietorship," an unincorporated business with a sole owner. Includes self-employed persons. [4] An unincorporated business where two or more persons join to carry on a trade or business with each having a shared financial interest in the business.

Source: U.S. Census Bureau, Nonemployer Statistics, "Geographic Area Series: Nonemployer Statistics by Legal Form of Organization," <http://factfinder2.census.gov>, accessed July 2013.

Table 1073. Retail Industries—Employees, Average Weekly Hours, and Average Hourly Earnings: 2000 to 2012

[Annual averages of monthly figures (15,280 represents 15,280,000). Covers all full- and part-time employees who worked during, or received pay for, any part of the pay period including the 12th of the month]

Industry	2012 NAICS code [1]	Employees (1,000)			Average weekly hours [2]			Average hourly earnings (dol.) [2]	
		2000	2010	2012	2000	2010	2012	2000	2012
Retail trade, total............	**44,45**	**15,280**	**14,440**	**14,875**	**30.7**	**30.2**	**30.5**	**10.87**	**13.81**
Motor vehicle and parts dealers [3].....................	441	1,847	1,629	1,732	35.9	36.5	37.7	14.94	17.84
Automobile dealers.................	4411	1,217	1,012	1,091	35.1	36.7	38.2	16.95	19.10
Auto parts, accessories, and tire stores................	4413	499	489	511	38.2	36.9	37.5	11.04	15.12
Furniture and home furnishings stores...................	442	544	438	442	31.2	29.1	29.3	12.33	15.19
Electronics and appliance stores [3].................	443	647	522	512	30.6	31.6	34.6	13.16	21.45
Electronics stores..................	443142	560	465	452	30.0	31.3	34.8	13.41	22.30
Building material and garden suply stores [3]..............	444	1,142	1,132	1,170	35.6	33.9	32.9	11.25	14.16
Building material and supplies dealers................	4441	982	1,005	1,031	36.2	34.2	32.9	11.30	14.17
Lawn and garden equipment and supplies stores.....	4442	160	127	139	32.5	31.6	33.1	10.89	14.08
Food and beverage stores [3].........	445	2,993	2,808	2,859	31.7	29.0	29.5	9.76	12.24
Grocery stores....................	4451	2,582	2,461	2,500	31.9	29.0	29.7	9.71	12.31
Supermarkets and other grocery stores..............	44511	2,438	2,323	2,357	31.9	28.9	29.6	9.84	12.42
Convenience stores................	44512	145	138	143	31.0	31.3	30.3	7.45	10.46
Specialty food stores..............	4452	270	211	219	31.6	29.7	29.1	9.97	11.36
Beer, wine, and liquor stores.......	4453	141	136	140	28.6	27.2	27.0	10.40	12.33
Health and personal care stores [3].........	446	928	981	1,003	29.8	29.4	29.8	11.68	17.20
Pharmacies and drug stores........	44611	677	715	704	29.7	29.3	29.6	11.89	17.72
Gasoline stations [3].................	447	936	819	841	31.6	30.7	30.8	8.05	10.33
Gasoline stations with convenience stores............	44711	787	719	736	31.3	30.4	30.6	7.87	10.17
Clothing and clothing accessories stores [3]..............	448	1,322	1,353	1,408	24.9	21.2	22.2	9.96	11.83
Clothing stores....................	4481	954	1,040	1,081	24.4	20.1	21.4	9.88	11.41
Shoe stores........................	4482	193	182	189	24.9	23.3	21.2	8.96	11.53
Jewelry, luggage, and leather goods stores..........	4483	175	131	138	27.7	28.1	29.6	11.48	14.67
Sporting goods, hobby, book, and music stores [3].......	451	603	579	579	26.6	23.4	23.7	9.38	11.73
Sporting goods and musical instrument stores........	4511	437	459	486	27.0	23.8	24.1	9.55	11.92
Book stores and news dealers.........................	4512	166	120	93	25.4	22.0	21.4	8.91	10.68
General merchandise stores.........	452	2,820	2,998	3,088	27.8	31.7	31.3	9.22	11.40
Miscellaneous store retailers [3].....	453	1,007	762	798	29.1	28.0	28.3	10.20	13.63
Florists............................	4531	130	69	66	29.6	22.4	26.2	8.95	11.16
Office supplies, stationary, and gift stores..............	4532	471	303	305	29.7	27.1	28.1	10.46	14.60
Used merchandise stores...........	4533	107	125	147	26.7	29.5	28.6	8.07	10.94
Other miscellaneous store retailers....................	4539	300	264	280	28.9	29.8	28.9	11.09	14.59
Pet and pet supplies stores.......	45391	72	99	106	27.0	27.4	27.3	9.78	13.48
Nonstore retailers [3]................	454	492	421	443	35.4	36.3	35.9	13.22	18.28
Electronic shopping and mail-order houses............	4541	257	247	276	36.2	35.9	35.9	13.38	19.26
Vending machine operators.........	4542	67	39	37	35.6	36.3	35.0	11.46	14.41
Direct selling establishments........	4543	169	134	131	34.1	37.0	36.2	13.70	17.34

[1] Based on the North American Industry Classification System (NAICS), 2012; see text, this section and Section 15. [2] Data shown for production and nonsupervisory employees. [3] Includes other kind of businesses, not shown separately.

Source: U.S. Bureau of Labor Statistics, Current Employment Statistics, "Employment, Hours, and Earnings—National," <http://www.bls.gov/ces/data.htm>, accessed September 2013.

Table 1074. Retail Trade and Food Services—Sales by Kind of Business: 2000 to 2011

[In billions of dollars (3,287.5 represents $3,287,500,000,000)]

Kind of Business	2007 NAICS code [1]	2000	2005	2007	2008	2009	2010	2011
Retail sales and food services, total.........	**44, 45, 722**	**3,287.5**	**4,086.6**	**4,443.8**	**4,402.5**	**4,082.1**	**4,307.9**	**4,631.1**
Retail sales, total.................................	**44, 45**	**2,983.3**	**3,690.2**	**3,999.3**	**3,946.4**	**3,630.4**	**3,841.5**	**4,136.4**
GAFO, total [2].................................	(X)	862.7	1,060.5	1,147.5	1,143.0	1,097.3	1,125.5	1,169.5
Motor vehicle and parts dealers..................	441	796.2	888.3	910.1	787.1	674.0	746.1	819.9
Automobile and other motor vehicle dealers.....	4411, 4412	732.8	818.3	835.4	710.8	599.9	668.4	737.2
Automobile dealers............................	4411	687.8	753.1	767.4	650.9	554.5	624.8	691.9
New car dealers............................	44111	630.1	681.9	687.7	576.6	488.3	551.9	613.7
Auto parts, accessories, and tire stores.........	4413	63.4	70.1	74.7	76.3	74.1	77.7	82.7
Furniture, home furnishings, electronics and appliance stores............................	442, 443	173.4	210.5	221.8	208.2	184.3	186.4	191.5
Furniture and home furnishings stores...........	442	91.2	109.1	111.1	99.6	86.3	87.3	90.1
Furniture stores............................	4421	50.6	58.7	59.3	52.9	46.2	47.2	48.3
Home furnishings stores......................	4422	40.6	50.4	51.9	46.6	40.1	40.1	41.7
Electronics and appliance stores [3].............	443	82.2	101.3	110.7	108.7	98.0	99.1	101.5
Appliances, televisions, and other electronics stores.....................	44311	58.2	78.3	86.2	84.4	75.7	73.5	74.0
Building materials, garden equipment, and supply stores [3]...............................	444	229.0	320.8	320.9	304.6	267.0	268.0	279.1
Hardware stores............................	44413	16.2	18.9	20.5	20.2	19.0	19.2	20.7
Food and beverage stores [3].....................	445	444.8	508.5	547.8	569.7	569.3	581.9	612.0
Grocery stores...............................	4451	402.5	457.7	491.4	511.4	510.3	521.2	549.1
Supermarkets and other grocery (except convenience) stores........................	44511	381.4	435.5	468.4	487.7	487.2	495.2	519.4
Beer, wine and liquor stores....................	4453	28.5	33.6	38.1	39.5	40.3	41.5	42.6
Health and personal care stores..................	446	155.2	210.1	237.2	246.8	253.2	261.1	272.1
Pharmacies and drug stores....................	44611	130.9	179.2	202.3	211.0	217.6	222.8	231.5
Gasoline stations................................	447	249.8	378.9	451.8	503.0	389.8	446.0	529.1
Clothing and clothing access, stores [3].............	448	167.7	201.0	221.2	215.8	204.8	213.7	229.3
Clothing stores [3].............................	4481	118.1	145.6	161.6	157.9	151.8	158.9	168.9
Women's clothing stores......................	44812	31.4	37.1	40.3	38.3	35.9	37.4	39.4
Shoe stores [3]................................	4482	22.9	25.3	26.8	26.7	25.1	26.4	28.1
Jewelry stores...............................	44831	24.8	28.4	30.8	29.2	26.0	26.3	29.7
Sporting goods, hobby, book & music stores [3]....	451	75.8	80.9	84.7	84.0	81.0	81.7	82.4
Sporting goods stores.........................	45111	25.3	30.7	35.8	37.1	37.1	38.3	40.3
Hobby, toy, and game stores....................	45112	16.9	16.3	16.3	16.2	15.7	16.0	16.4
General merchandise stores......................	452	404.2	528.4	578.6	596.4	591.7	608.0	630.3
Department stores (excluding L.D.) [4].............	4521	232.5	215.3	209.4	198.7	187.6	186.2	185.3
Discount department stores...................	452112	136.2	130.5	132.5	127.9	124.8	122.1	120.5
Department stores (including L.D.) [4].............	4521	239.9	220.7	213.9	202.9	190.8	189.3	188.5
Discount department stores...................	452112	139.6	133.2	134.9	130.1	126.4	123.7	122.1
Warehouse clubs and superstores..............	45291	139.6	271.9	325.0	352.1	356.5	371.0	390.6
Miscellaneous store retailers.....................	453	106.7	107.3	116.4	111.6	103.4	106.5	112.0
Office supplies, stationery, and gift stores........	4532	41.7	39.8	41.2	38.6	35.5	35.8	36.0
Office supplies and stationery stores...........	45321	22.7	22.2	23.2	21.7	20.2	19.9	19.6
Used merchandise stores........................	4533	9.8	9.3	10.9	11.0	10.4	11.1	12.2
Nonstore retailers [3]............................	454	180.5	255.6	308.8	319.3	311.9	342.0	378.7
Electronic shopping and mail-order houses......	4541	113.8	175.9	223.7	228.2	233.7	260.6	291.6
fuel dealers.................................	45431	26.7	34.3	37.4	44.2	35.1	37.9	42.9
Food services and drinking places [5]............	**722**	**304.3**	**396.5**	**444.6**	**456.1**	**451.7**	**466.5**	**494.8**

X Not applicable. [1] North American Industry Classification System, 2007; see text, Section 15. [2] GAFO (General Merchandise, Apparel, Furniture, and Office Supplies) represents stores classified in the following NAICS codes: 442, 443, 448, 451, 452, and 4532. [3] Includes other kinds of businesses, not shown separately. [4] L.D. represents leased departments. [5] See also Table 1308.

Source: U.S. Census Bureau, *2011 Annual Retail Trade Report*, March 2013. See also <http://www.census.gov/retail/index.html>.

Table 1075. Retail Trade Corporations—Sales, Net Profit, and Profit Per Dollar of Sales: 2011 and 2012

[Represents North American Industry Classification System, 2012 (NAICS) groups 44 and 45. Profit rates are averages of quarterly figures at annual rates. Covers corporations with assets of $50,000,000 or more]

Item	Unit	Total retail trade		Food and beverage stores (NAICS 445)		Clothing and general merchandise stores (NAICS 448, 452)		All other retail stores	
		2011	2012	2011	2012	2011	2012	2011	2012
Sales..	Bil. dol	2,326	2,408	425	441	799	830	1,101	1,137
Net profit:									
Before income taxes.......................	Bil. dol	106.0	108.9	8.4	10.2	48.6	52.7	49.0	46.0
After income taxes........................	Bil. dol	69.0	73.3	5.3	6.7	30.7	36.3	33.0	30.3
Profits per dollar of sales:									
Before income taxes.......................	Cents	4.5	4.5	2.0	2.3	6.0	6.3	4.4	4.0
After income taxes........................	Cents	3.0	3.0	1.3	1.5	3.8	4.3	3.0	2.7
Profits on stockholders' equity:									
Before income taxes.......................	Percent	23.6	23.5	17.8	21.3	26.3	28.5	22.5	20.0
After income taxes........................	Percent	15.4	15.8	11.4	13.8	16.6	19.6	15.2	13.2

Source: U.S. Census Bureau, *Quarterly Financial Report for Manufacturing, Mining, Trade, and Selected Service Industries*. See also <http://www.census.gov/econ/qfr/>.

Table 1076. Retail Trade and Food Services—Estimated Per Capita Sales by Selected Kind of Business: 2000 to 2011

[Estimates are shown in dollars and are based on data from the Annual Retail Trade Survey and the Census Bureau's Population Estimates Program. Based on estimated resident population estimates as of July 1. For additional information, see <http://www.census.gov/popest/>. For statement on methodology, see Appendix III]

Kind of business	2007 NAICS code [1]	2000	2005	2007	2008	2009	2010	2011
Retail and food service sales.........................	**44–45,722**	**11,651**	**13,829**	**14,752**	**14,478**	**13,306**	**13,927**	**14,863**
Retail sales, total...	**44–45**	**10,573**	**12,487**	**13,276**	**12,978**	**11,834**	**12,419**	**13,275**
Total (excluding motor vehicle and parts dealers..	*44–45 ex 441*	7,751	9,481	10,255	10,389	9,637	10,007	10,644
Motor vehicle and parts dealers............................	441	2,822	3,006	3,021	2,588	2,197	2,412	2,631
Furniture and home furnishings stores...................	442	323	369	369	327	281	282	289
Electronics and appliance stores..........................	443	291	343	367	357	320	320	326
Building material and garden equipment and supplies dealers..	444	812	1,086	1,065	1,002	870	866	896
Food and beverage stores...................................	445	1,576	1,721	1,819	1,874	1,856	1,881	1,964
Health and personal care stores...........................	446	550	711	787	812	826	844	873
Gasoline stations..	447	885	1,282	1,500	1,654	1,271	1,442	1,698
Clothing and clothing accessories stores...............	448	594	680	734	710	668	691	736
Sporting goods, hobby, book, and music stores........	451	269	274	281	276	264	264	264
General merchandise stores................................	452	1,433	1,788	1,921	1,961	1,929	1,966	2,023
Miscellaneous store retailers..............................	453	378	363	386	367	337	344	359
Nonstore retailers...	454	640	865	1,025	1,050	1,017	1,106	1,215
Food services and drinking places, total.............	**722**	**1,078**	**1,342**	**1,476**	**1,500**	**1,472**	**1,508**	**1,588**

[1] North American Industry Classification System, 2007; see text, Section 15.

Source: U.S. Census Bureau, *2011 Annual Retail Trade Survey*, March 2013. See also <http://www.census.gov/retail/>.

Table 1077. Retail Trade—Merchandise Inventories and Inventory/Sales Ratios by Kind of Business: 2000 to 2012

[Inventories in billions of dollars (405.9 represents $405,900,000,000). As of Dec. 31. Estimates exclude food services. Includes warehouses. Adjusted for seasonal variations. Sales data also adjusted for holiday and trading-day differences. Based on data from the Monthly Retail Trade Survey, Annual Retail Trade Survey, and administrative records; see Appendix III. Data have been adjusted using results of the 2007 Economic Census]

Kind of business	2007 NAICS code [1]	Inventories				Inventory/sales ratio			
		2000	2010	2011	2012	2000	2010	2011	2012
Retail Inventories, total [2].............................	**44–45**	**405.9**	**460.1**	**478.0**	**516.3**	**1.62**	**1.39**	**1.36**	**1.40**
Total excluding motor vehicle and parts dealers.....	*44–45 ex 441*	277.8	332.1	344.1	355.3	1.49	1.25	1.23	1.22
Motor vehicle and parts dealers............................	441	128.1	127.9	133.9	161.0	2.02	1.95	1.87	2.10
Furniture, home furnishings, electronics, and appliance stores..	442, 443	25.6	28.0	27.1	27.5	1.85	1.81	1.68	1.64
Building material and garden equipment and supplies dealers..	444	34.3	44.8	45.9	47.8	1.77	1.96	1.88	1.91
Food and beverage stores...................................	445	32.1	38.6	40.3	41.3	0.84	0.78	0.78	0.77
Clothing and clothing accessories stores...............	448	36.8	42.8	45.5	47.9	2.61	2.36	2.33	2.33
General merchandise stores................................	452	64.9	74.6	77.9	79.8	1.87	1.46	1.47	1.46
Department stores...	4521	42.7	31.6	31.8	30.8	2.17	2.05	2.07	2.06

[1] North American Industry Classification System, 2007; see text, Section 15. [2] Includes other kind of businesses, not shown separately.

Source: U.S. Census Bureau, "Annual Revision of Monthly Retail and Food Services: Sales and Inventories--January 1992 through March 2013," <http://www.census.gov/retail/index.html>, accessed July 2013.

Table 1078. Retail Trade Sales—Total and E-Commerce by Kind of Business: 2011

[4,136,352 represents $4,136,352,000,000. Covers retailers with and without payroll. Based on the Annual Retail Trade Survey; see Appendix III]

Kind of business	2007 NAICS code [1]	Value of sales (mil. dol.)		E-commerce as percent of total sales	Percent distribution of E-commerce sales
		Total	E-commerce		
Retail trade, total [2].....................................	**44-45**	**4,136,352**	**193,904**	**4.7**	**100.0**
Motor vehicle and parts dealers.........................	441	819,929	19,941	2.4	10.3
Electronics and appliance stores........................	443	101,455	1,309	1.3	0.7
Building material and garden equipment and supplies stores......	444	279,068	(S)	(S)	(S)
Food and beverage stores.................................	445	612,012	812	0.1	0.4
Health and personal care stores.........................	446	272,073	(S)	(S)	(S)
Clothing and clothing accessories stores.............	448	229,312	2,587	1.1	1.3
Sporting goods, hobby, book, and music stores.....	451	82,392	1,957	2.4	1.0
General merchandise stores..............................	452	630,256	39	(Z)	(Z)
Miscellaneous store retailers............................	453	111,977	1,922	1.7	1.0
Nonstore retailers..	454	378,712	163,831	43.3	84.5
Electronic shopping and mail-order houses...........	45411	291,607	163,156	56.0	84.1

S Data do not meet publication standards. Z Less than 0.05 percent. [1] North American Industry Classification System, 2007; see text, Section 15. [2] Includes other kinds of businesses, not shown separately.

Source: U.S. Census Bureau, "E-Stats, 2011 E-commerce Multi-sector Data Tables," <http://www.census.gov/econ/estats>, accessed July 2013.

Table 1079. Electronic Shopping and Mail-Order Houses—Total and E-Commerce Sales by Merchandise Line: 2010 and 2011

[260,644 represents $260,644,000,000. Represents 2007 North American Industry Classification System code 45411 which comprises establishments primarily engaged in retailing all types of merchandise using nonstore means, including catalogs, toll-free telephone numbers, or electronic media, such as interactive television or computer. Covers businesses with and without paid employees. Based on the Annual Retail Survey; see Appendix III]

Merchandise lines	2010 Value of sales (million dollars)		2010 E-commerce as percent of total sales	2011 Value of sales (million dollars)		2011 E-commerce as percent of total sales
	Total	E-commerce		Total	E-commerce	
Total..	**260,644**	**139,812**	**53.6**	**291,607**	**163,156**	**56.0**
Books and magazines............................	8,510	7,209	84.7	9,815	8,538	87.0
Clothing and clothing accessories (includes footwear)..............................	30,645	22,909	74.8	34,123	27,050	79.3
Computer hardware...............................	22,521	12,648	56.2	24,014	13,731	57.2
Computer software...............................	5,695	3,701	65.0	6,475	4,352	67.2
Drugs, health aids, beauty aids..................	76,832	10,119	13.2	85,668	10,855	12.7
Electronics and appliances......................	23,052	18,885	81.9	26,252	22,148	84.4
Food, beer, and wine............................	4,953	3,258	65.8	5,527	3,732	67.5
Furniture and home furnishings..................	13,675	10,711	78.3	16,082	12,973	80.7
Music and videos................................	6,535	5,706	87.3	7,680	6,875	89.5
Office equipment and supplies..................	6,490	5,012	77.2	6,838	5,423	79.3
Sporting goods..................................	5,396	3,701	68.6	5,908	4,377	74.1
Toys, hobby goods, and games..................	5,459	4,161	76.2	6,204	4,867	78.4
Other merchandise [1]...........................	35,591	20,929	58.8	39,746	25,297	63.6
Nonmerchandise receipts [2].....................	15,290	10,863	71.0	17,275	12,938	74.9

[1] Includes jewelry, collectibles, souvenirs, auto parts and accessories, hardware, and lawn and garden equipment and supplies. [2] Includes auction commissions, shipping and handling, customer training, customer support, and advertising.

Source: U.S. Census Bureau, "E-Stats, 2011 E-Commerce Multi-sector Data Tables," <http://www.census.gov/econ/estats/>, accessed June 2013.

Table 1080. Franchised New Car Dealerships—Summary: 1990 to 2012

[In units as indicated (316 represents $316,000,000,000)]

Item	Unit	1990	2000	2005	2006	2007	2008	2009	2010	2011	2012
Dealerships [1]................	Number	24,825	22,250	21,640	21,495	21,200	20,770	20,010	18,460	17,770	17,540
Sales........................	Bil. dol.	316	650	699	675	693	571	492	553	609	676
New cars sold [2].............	Millions	9.3	8.8	7.7	7.8	7.6	6.8	5.5	5.6	7.2	7.0
Used vehicles sold...........	Millions	14.2	20.5	19.7	19.2	18.5	15.0	14.9	15.3	15.6	17.1
Employment..................	1,000	924	1,114	1,138	1,120	1,115	1,057	913	892	934	963
Annual payroll...............	Bil. dol.	24.0	46.1	51.5	52.9	53.9	53.2	43.5	42.4	45.8	51.6
Advertising expenses.........	Bil. dol.	3.7	6.4	7.7	7.8	7.9	6.8	5.4	5.9	6.4	7.2
Dealer pretax profits as a percentage of sales..........	Percent	1.0	1.6	1.6	1.5	1.5	1.0	1.5	2.1	2.3	2.2
Inventory: [3] Domestic: [4]											
Total........................	1,000	2,537	3,183	2,991	2,943	2,712	2,478	1,697	1,687	(NA)	(NA)
Days' supply.................	Days	73	68	70	71	67	80	72	60	57	62
Imported: [4]											
Total........................	1,000	707	468	566	605	619	687	519	494	(NA)	(NA)
Days' supply.................	Days	72	50	52	51	51	65	61	55	46	52

[1] At end of year. [2] Data provided by Ward's Automotive Reports. [3] Annual average. Includes light trucks. [4] Classification based on where automobiles are produced (i.e., automobiles manufactured by foreign companies but produced in the U.S., Canada, and Mexico are classified as domestic).

Source: National Automobile Dealers Association, McLean, VA, *NADA Data: State of the Industry Report*, annual ©. See also <http://www.nada.org/Publications/NADADATA>.

Table 1081. Retail Sales and Leases of New and Used Vehicles: 1990 to 2010

[In thousands, except as noted (52,484 represents 52,484,000)]

Item	1990	2000	2004	2005	2006	2007	2008	2009	2010
Vehicle sales and leases, total (number of vehicles).............................	**52,484**	**64,320**	**62,839**	**64,626**	**62,744**	**61,562**	**52,845**	**48,545**	**51,434**
New vehicle sales and leases................	14,954	22,700	20,294	20,488	20,178	20,143	16,315	13,053	14,550
New vehicle sales.........................	13,890	17,410	16,850	16,990	16,460	16,230	13,300	10,550	11,580
New vehicle leases........................	1,064	5,290	3,444	3,498	3,718	3,913	3,015	2,503	2,970
Used vehicle sales [1].......................	37,530	41,620	42,545	44,138	42,566	41,419	36,530	35,492	36,884
Vehicle sales, total value (bil. dol.) [2]....	**447**	**736**	**765**	**776**	**786**	**774**	**643**	**575**	**635**
New vehicle sales (bil. dol.)................	227	380	407	421	445	435	351	274	311
Used vehicle sales (bil. dol.)...............	220	356	358	355	341	339	292	301	324
Average price (current dol.): [2]									
New vehicle sales.........................	16,350	21,850	24,082	24,796	26,854	26,950	26,477	26,245	26,850
Used vehicle sales........................	5,857	8,547	8,410	8,036	8,009	8,186	7,986	8,483	8,786

[1] Used car sales include sales from franchised dealers, independent dealers, and casual sales. [2] Includes leased vehicles.

Source: U.S. Bureau of Transportation Statistics, "National Transportation Statistics," <http://www.bts.gov/publications/national_transportation_statistics/>, accessed April 2012.

Table 1082. New Motor Vehicle Sales and Car Production: 1990 to 2012

[In thousands (14,137 represents 14,137,000). Data have been revised based on reclassification of the Subaru Outback from an automobile to a light truck. Data are primarily from "Ward's Automotive Reports" published by Ward's Communications, Southfield, MI]

Type of vehicle	1990	2000	2007	2008	2009	2010	2011	2012
New motor vehicle sales.....................	**14,137**	**17,812**	**16,460**	**13,493**	**10,602**	**11,772**	**13,041**	**14,788**
New-car sales..	9,300	8,778	7,562	6,769	5,402	5,636	6,090	7,244
Domestic...	6,897	6,762	5,197	4,491	3,558	3,792	4,143	5,118
Import...	2,403	2,016	2,365	2,278	1,843	1,844	1,947	2,125
New-truck sales......................................	4,837	9,034	8,898	6,724	5,201	6,137	6,951	7,544
Light...	4,560	8,572	8,527	6,426	5,001	5,919	6,645	7,198
Domestic...	3,957	7,720	7,139	5,329	4,117	5,020	5,663	6,138
Import...	603	852	1,388	1,097	884	899	983	1,061
Heavy...	278	462	371	299	200	218	306	346
Domestic-car production............................	6,231	5,471	3,867	3,731	2,196	2,731	2,977	4,106
Average expenditure per new car [1] (dol.)..........	14,371	21,041	23,892	23,441	23,276	24,296	(NA)	(NA)
Domestic (dol.)....................................	13,936	19,586	22,284	22,204	22,148	23,095	(NA)	(NA)
Import (dol.).......................................	15,510	25,965	27,465	25,903	25,499	26,808	(NA)	(NA)

NA Not available. [1] Estimate based on the manufacturer's suggested retail price.

Source: U.S. Bureau of Economic Analysis, National Economic Accounts, "Supplemental Tables: Motor Vehicles," <http://www.bea.gov/national/index.htm#supp>, accessed September 2013.

Table 1083. Food and Alcoholic Beverage Expenditures by Sales Outlet: 1990 to 2011

[In billions of dollars (569.6 represents $569,600,000,000)]

Sales outlet	1990	2000	2005	2006	2007	2008	2009	2010	2011
Food sales, total [1].............................	**569.6**	**837.0**	**1,059.7**	**1,112.7**	**1,169.9**	**1,215.4**	**1,211.8**	**1,250.7**	**1,317.8**
Food at home [2].....................................	324.6	443.2	547.9	565.6	594.8	623.7	621.1	638.7	676.6
Food stores [2].....................................	256.4	302.9	338.9	349.2	363.6	378.3	377.2	385.6	407.2
Other stores [3]....................................	25.6	74.8	133.8	142.1	149.2	159.8	160.3	167.1	177.0
Home-delivered, mail order.......................	5.3	18.7	18.5	19.2	19.7	19.6	18.4	19.0	22.0
Farmers, manufacturers, wholesalers..........	25.6	32.4	38.9	37.9	42.8	45.3	44.5	45.9	48.2
Home production and donations..................	11.7	14.4	17.8	17.2	19.5	20.7	20.6	21.3	22.2
Food away from home [4]...........................	245.2	393.8	511.7	547.1	575.1	591.7	590.8	612.0	641.2
Alcoholic beverage sales, total..............	**69.4**	**107.1**	**129.1**	**136.7**	**139.2**	**148.7**	**147.0**	**152.7**	**162.9**
Packaged alcoholic beverages....................	34.9	48.2	63.4	67.0	69.7	78.8	77.7	80.8	86.5
Liquor stores.....................................	18.6	24.4	32.1	34.6	36.8	38.1	38.7	39.9	42.5
Food stores......................................	10.8	15.8	18.6	19.0	19.5	20.3	20.3	20.7	21.9
All other...	5.4	8.0	12.7	13.4	13.3	20.4	18.7	20.1	22.1
Alcoholic drinks away from home.................	34.5	58.9	65.6	69.7	69.5	69.8	69.3	72.0	76.3
Eating and drinking places [5].....................	26.5	41.5	51.2	53.6	54.1	54.7	53.7	54.8	58.0
Hotels and motels [5]..............................	3.4	6.8	5.1	5.1	5.1	5.2	5.0	5.1	5.1
All other...	4.6	10.6	9.3	11.0	10.3	9.9	10.5	12.1	13.2

[1] Includes taxes and tips. [2] Excludes sales to restaurants and institutions. [3] Includes eating and drinking establishments, trailer parks, commissary stores, and military exchanges. [4] Includes food supplied and donated. [5] Includes tips.

Source: U.S. Department of Agriculture, Economic Research Service, "Food Expenditures," <http://www.ers.usda.gov/data-products/food-expenditures>, accessed August 2013.

This section presents data on civil air transportation, both passenger and cargo, and on water transportation, including inland waterways, oceanborne commerce, the merchant marine, cargo, and vessel tonnages.

This section also presents statistics on revenues, passenger and freight traffic volume, and employment in various revenue-producing modes of the transportation industry, including motor vehicles, trains, and pipelines. Data are also presented on highway mileage and finances, motor vehicle travel, accidents, and registrations; and characteristics of public transit, railroads, and pipelines.

Principal source of transportation data is the annual *National Transportation Statistics* publication of the U.S. Bureau of Transportation Statistics. Principal sources of air and water transportation data are the *Annual Report* issued by Airlines for America, Washington, DC and the annual *Waterborne Commerce of the United States* issued by the Corps of Engineers of the Department of Army. In addition, the U.S. Census Bureau in its Commodity Flow Survey (part of the Census of Transportation, taken every 5 years through 2007, for years ending in "2" and "7") provides data on the type, weight, and value of commodities shipped by manufacturing establishments in the United States, by means of transportation, origin, and destination. The advance reports for 2007 are part of the 2007 Economic Census. This census was conducted in accordance with the 2002 North American Industry Classification System (NAICS). See text, Section 15, Business Enterprise, for a discussion of the Economic Census and NAICS.

The Bureau of Transportation Statistics (BTS) was established within the U.S. Department of Transportation (USDOT) in 1992 to collect, report, and analyze transportation data. Today, BTS is a component of the USDOT Research and Innovative Technology Administration (RITA). BTS products include reports to Congress, the Secretary of Transportation, and stakeholders in the nation's transportation community. These stakeholders include: federal agencies, state and local governments, metropolitan planning organizations, universities, the private sector and general public. Congress requires the BTS to report (congressional mandate, laid out in 49 U.S.C. 111 (1)) on transportation statistics to the President and Congress. *The Transportation Statistics Annual Report* (TSAR), provides a data overview of U.S. transportation issues. As required by Congress, each TSAR has two essential components: a review of the state of transportation statistics with recommendations for improvements and a presentation of the data. The BTS publication *National Transportation Statistics (NTS)*, a companion report to the TSAR, has more comprehensive and longer time-series data. NTS presents information on the U.S. transportation system, including its physical components, safety record, economic performance, energy use, and environmental impacts. The BTS publication *State Transportation Statistics* presents a statistical profile of transportation in the 50 states and the District of Columbia. This profile includes infrastructure, freight movement and passenger travel, system safety, vehicles, transportation-related economy and finance, energy usage and the environment.

The principal compiler of data on public roads and on operation of motor vehicles is the U.S. Department of Transportation's (DOT) Federal Highway Administration (FHWA). These data appear in FHWA's annual *Highway Statistics* and other publications.

The U.S. National Highway Traffic Safety Administration (NHTSA), through its *Traffic Safety Facts FARS/GES Annual Report*, presents descriptive statistics about traffic crashes of all severities, from those that result in property damage to those that result in the loss of human life. The data for this report is a compilation of motor vehicle crash data from the *Fatality Analysis Reporting System (FARS)* and the *General Estimates System (GES)*. For other publications and reports, go to the National Center for Statistics and Analysis (NCSA), Publications and Data Request. The Web site is located at <http://www-nrd.nhtsa.dot.gov/CATS/>. DOT's Federal Railroad Administration (FRA), Office of Safety Analysis presents railroad safety information including accidents and incidents, inspections and highway-rail crossing data in its annual report *Railroad Safety Statistics*. The Web site is located at <http://safetydata.fra.dot.gov/officeofsafety>.

Data are also presented in many nongovernment publications. Among them are the weekly and annual *Freight Commodity Statistics* and the annual *Industry Information, Industry Statistics, Railroad Statistics*, both published by the Association of American Railroads, Washington, DC; *Public Transportation Fact Book*, containing electric railway and motorbus statistics, published annually by the American Public Transportation Association, Washington, DC.

Civil aviation—Federal promotion and regulation of civil aviation have been carried out by the Federal Aviation Administration (FAA) and the Civil Aeronautics Board (CAB). The CAB promoted and regulated the civil air transportation industry within the United States and between the United States and foreign countries. The Board granted licenses to provide air transportation service, approved or disapproved proposed rates and fares, and approved or disapproved proposed agreements and corporate relationships involving air carriers. In December 1984, the CAB ceased to exist as an agency. Some of its functions were transferred to the DOT, as outlined below. The responsibility for investigation of aviation accidents resides with the National Transportation Safety Board.

The Office of the Secretary, DOT aviation activities include: negotiation of international air transportation rights, selection of U.S. air carriers to serve capacity controlled international markets, oversight of international rates and fares, maintenance of essential air service to small communities, and consumer affairs. DOT's Bureau of Transportation Statistics (BTS) handles aviation information functions formerly assigned to CAB. Prior to BTS, the Research and Special Programs Administration handled these functions.

The principal activities of the FAA include: the promotion of air safety; controlling the use of navigable airspace; prescribing regulations dealing with the competency of airmen, airworthiness of aircraft and air traffic control; operation of air route traffic control centers, airport traffic control towers, and flight service stations; the design, construction, maintenance, and inspection of navigation, traffic control, and communications equipment; and the development of general aviation.

The CAB published monthly and quarterly financial and traffic statistical data for the certificated route air carriers. BTS continues these publications, including both certificated and noncertificated (commuter) air carriers. The FAA annually publishes data on the use of airway facilities; data related to the location of airmen, aircraft, and airports; the volume of activity in the field of nonair carrier (general aviation) flying; and aircraft production and registration.

General aviation comprises all civil flying (including such commercial operations as small demand air taxis, agriculture application, powerline patrol, etc.) but excludes certificated route air carriers, supplemental operators, large-aircraft commercial operators, and commuter airlines.

Air carriers and service—The CAB previously issued "certificates of public convenience and necessity" under Section 401 of the Federal Aviation Act of 1958 for scheduled and nonscheduled (charter) passenger services and cargo services. It also issued certificates under Section 418 of the Act to cargo air carriers for domestic all-cargo service only. The DOT Office of the Secretary now issues the certificates under a "fit, willing, and able" test of air carrier operations. Carriers operating only a 60-seat-or-less aircraft are given exemption authority to carry passengers, cargo, and mail in scheduled and nonscheduled service under Part 298 of the DOT (formerly CAB) regulations. Exemption authority carriers who offer scheduled passenger service to an essential air service point must meet the "fit, willing, and able" test.

Vessel shipments, entrances, and clearances—Shipments by dry cargo vessels comprise shipments on all types of watercraft, except tanker vessels; shipments by tanker vessels comprise all types of cargo, liquid and dry, carried by tanker vessels. A vessel is reported as entered only at the first port which it enters in the United States, whether or not cargo is unloaded at that port.

A vessel is reported as cleared only at the last port at which clearance is made to a foreign port, whether or not it takes on cargo. Army and Navy vessels entering or clearing without commercial cargo are not included in the figures.

Units of measurement—Cargo (or freight) tonnage and shipping weight both represent the gross weight of the cargo including the weight of containers, wrappings, crates, etc. However, shipping weight excludes lift and cargo vans and similar substantial outer containers. Other tonnage figures generally refer to stowing capacity of vessels, 100 cubic feet being called 1 ton. Gross tonnage comprises the space within the frames and the ceiling of the hull, together with those closed-in spaces above deck available for cargo, stores, passengers, or crew, with certain minor exceptions. Net or registered tonnage is the gross tonnage less the spaces occupied by the propelling machinery, fuel, crew quarters, master's cabin, and navigation spaces. Substantially, it represents space

available for cargo and passengers. The net tonnage capacity of a ship may bear little relation to weight of cargo. Deadweight tonnage is the weight in long tons required to depress a vessel from light water line (that is, with only the machinery and equipment on board) to load line. It is, therefore, the weight of the cargo, fuel, etc., which a vessel is designed to carry with safety.

Federal-aid highway systems—The Intermodal Surface Transportation Efficiency Act (ISTEA) of 1991 eliminated the historical Federal-Aid Highway Systems and created the National Highway System (NHS) and other federal-aid highway categories. The final NHS was approved by Congress in December of 1995 under the National Highway System Designation Act.

Functional systems—Roads and streets are assigned to groups according to the character of service intended. The functional systems are (1) arterial highways that generally handle the long trips, (2) collector facilities that collect and disperse traffic between the arterials and the lower systems, and (3) local roads and streets that primarily serve direct access to residential areas, farms, and other local areas.

Regulatory bodies— The Federal Energy Regulatory Commission (FERC) is an independent agency that regulates the interstate transmission of electricity, natural gas, and oil. FERC also reviews proposals to build liquefied natural gas (LNG) terminals and interstate natural gas pipelines as well as licensing hydropower projects. The Energy Policy Act of 2005 gave FERC additional responsibilities such as regulating the transmission and wholesale sales of electricity in interstate commerce. See source for more details.

Railroads—The Surface Transportation Board (STB) was created in the Interstate Commerce Commission Termination Act of 1995, Pub. L. No.104-88, 109 Stat. 803 (1995) (ICCTA), and is the successor agency to the Interstate Commerce Commission. The STB is an economic regulatory agency that Congress charged with the fundamental missions of resolving railroad rate and service disputes and reviewing proposed railroad mergers. The STB is decisionally independent, although it is administratively affiliated with the Department of Transportation.

The STB serves as both an adjudicatory and a regulatory body. The agency has jurisdiction over railroad rate and service issues and rail restructuring transactions (mergers, line sales, line construction, and line abandonment); certain trucking company, moving van, and noncontiguous ocean shipping company rate matters; certain intercity passenger bus company structure, financial, and operational matters; and rates and services of certain pipelines not regulated by the Federal Energy Regulatory Commission. Other ICC regulatory functions were either eliminated or transferred to the Federal Highway Administration or the Bureau of Transportation Statistics within DOT.

Class I Railroads are regulated by the STB and subject to the Uniform System of Accounts and required to file annual and periodic reports. Railroads are classified based on their annual operating revenues. The class to which a carrier belongs is determined by comparing its adjusted operating revenues for 3 consecutive years to the following scale: Class I, $250 million or more; Class II, $20 million to $250 million; and Class III, $0 to $20 million. Operating revenue dollar ranges are indexed for inflation.

Postal Service—The U.S. Postal Service provides mail processing and delivery services within the United States. The Postal Accountability and Enhancement Act of 2006 was the first major legislative change to the Postal Service since 1971 when the Postal Reorganization Act of 1970 created the Postal Service as an independent establishment of the Federal Executive Branch. The Act of 2006 changed the way the U.S. Postal Service operates and conducts business. Now annual rate increases for market dominant products are linked to the Consumer Price Index and the Postal Service has more flexibility for pricing competitive products, enabling it to respond to dynamic market conditions and changing customer needs.

Revenue and cost analysis describes the Postal Service's system of attributing revenues and costs to classes of mail and service. This system draws primarily upon probability sampling techniques to develop estimates of revenues, volumes, and weights, as well as costs by class of mail and special service. The costs attributed to classes of mail and special services are primarily incremental costs which vary in response to changes in volume; they account for roughly 60 percent of the total costs of the Postal Service. The balance represents "institutional costs." Statistics on revenues, volume of mail, and distribution of expenditures are presented in the Postal Service's annual report, *Cost and Revenue Analysis*, and its *Annual Report of the Postmaster General* and its annual *Comprehensive Statement on Postal Operations*.

Statistical reliability—For a discussion of statistical collection and estimation, sampling procedures, and measures of statistical reliability applicable to Census Bureau data, see Appendix III.

Table 1084. Transportation-Related Components of U.S. Gross Domestic Product: 2000 to 2011

[In billions of dollars (1,045.3 represents $1,045,300,000,000), except percent. For explanation of chained dollars, see Section 13 text. Minus sign (-) indicates a decrease]

Item	2000	2005	2008	2009	2010	2011
CURRENT DOLLARS						
Total transportation-related final demand [1]	**1,045.3**	**1,264.8**	**1,386.1**	**1,219.1**	**1,315.6**	**1,472.9**
Total gross domestic product (GDP)	9,951.5	12,623.0	14,291.5	13,973.7	14,498.9	15,075.7
Transportation as a percent of GDP	10.5	10.0	9.7	8.7	9.1	9.8
Personal consumption of transportation	798.4	978.0	1,029.7	879.2	960.4	1,079.4
Motor vehicles and parts	363.2	408.2	339.3	316.0	342.7	373.6
Motor vehicle fuels, lubricants, and fluids	172.9	283.8	384.5	278.7	330.1	403.8
Transportation services	262.3	286.0	305.9	284.5	287.6	302.0
Gross private domestic investment	177.6	188.8	156.8	85.0	133.1	174.5
Transportation structures	6.8	7.1	9.9	9.1	9.9	9.8
Transportation equipment	170.8	181.7	146.9	75.9	123.2	164.7
Net exports of transportation-related goods and service [2]	-109.0	-136.6	-86.7	-38.9	-79.6	-83.5
Exports (+)	179.0	216.6	271	218.7	255.8	293.0
Civilian aircraft, engines, and parts	48.1	55.9	74.0	74.8	72.0	80.2
Automotive vehicles, engines, and parts	80.4	98.4	121.5	81.7	112.0	133.1
Passenger fares	20.7	21.0	31.0	26.1	31.0	36.6
Other transportation	29.8	41.3	44.0	36.1	40.8	43.1
Imports (-)	288.0	353.2	357.2	258	335.4	376.5
Civilian aircraft, engines, and parts	26.4	25.8	35.5	30.7	31.2	35.5
Automotive vehicles, engines, and parts	195.9	239.4	233.2	159.2	225.6	255.2
Passenger fares	24.3	26.1	31.8	25.1	27.3	31.1
Other transportation	41.4	61.9	56.7	42.6	51.3	54.7
Government transportation-related purchases	178.3	234.6	286.3	293.8	301.7	302.5
Federal purchases [3]	19.3	30.1	34.7	35.7	38.6	40.6
State and local purchases [3]	150.0	188.6	230.9	235.6	238.4	238.6
Defense-related purchases [4]	9.0	15.9	20.7	22.5	24.7	23.3
CHAINED (2005) DOLLARS						
Total transportation-related final demand [1]	**1,211.9**	**1,264.8**	**1,176.3**	**1,102.1**	**1,121.3**	**1,162.5**
Total gross domestic product (GDP)	11,216.4	12,623.0	13,161.9	12,757.9	13,063.0	13,299.1
Transportation as a percent of GDP	10.8	10.0	8.9	8.6	8.6	8.7
Personal consumption of transportation	903.7	978.0	884.1	832.7	837.6	853.6
Motor vehicles and parts	356.1	408.2	346.8	322.6	329.5	347.4
Motor vehicle fuels, lubricants, and fluids	261.3	283.8	265.3	264.1	264.6	257.3
Transportation services	286.3	286.0	272.0	246.0	243.5	248.9
Gross private domestic investment	194.1	188.8	151.8	77.3	128.5	165.4
Transportation structures	7.9	7.1	9.1	8.2	8.9	8.7
Transportation equipment	186.2	181.7	142.7	69.1	119.6	156.7
Net exports of transportation-related goods and service [2]	-109.3	-136.6	-87.6	-43.3	-81.2	-82.8
Exports (+)	204.5	216.6	246.1	198.8	227.0	250.7
Civilian aircraft, engines, and parts	58.4	55.9	64.9	62.5	58.6	63.0
Automotive vehicles, engines, and parts	83.2	98.4	117.2	78.4	106.9	125.0
Passenger fares	28.6	21.0	25.8	24.8	25.4	27.0
Other transportation	34.3	41.3	38.2	33.1	36.1	35.7
Imports (-)	313.8	353.2	333.7	242.1	308.2	333.5
Civilian aircraft, engines, and parts	30.7	25.8	30.6	25.1	24.9	27.2
Automotive vehicles, engines, and parts	202.9	239.4	224.3	151.9	213.9	234.8
Passenger fares	29.1	26.1	24.5	20.9	19.9	21.2
Other transportation	51.1	61.9	54.3	44.2	49.5	50.3
Government transportation-related purchases	223.4	234.6	228.0	235.4	236.4	226.3
Federal purchases [3]	23.1	30.1	31.3	31.8	33.5	34.3
State and local purchases [3]	189.1	188.6	179.0	182.7	181.3	173.0
Defense-related purchases [4]	11.2	15.9	17.7	20.9	21.6	19.0

[1] Sum of total personal consumption of transportation, total gross private domestic investment, net exports of transportation-related goods and services, and total government transportation-related purchases. [2] Exports minus imports. [3] Federal purchases and state and local purchases are the sum of consumption expenditures and gross investment. [4] Defense-related purchases are the sum of transportation of material and travel.

Source: U.S. Bureau of Transportation Statistics, "National Transportation Statistics," <http://www.bts.gov/publications/national_transportation_statistics/>, accessed March 2013.

Table 1085. Employment in Transportation and Warehousing: 1990 to 2012

[In thousands (3,476 represents 3,476,000). Annual average of monthly figures. Based on Current Employment Statistics program; see Appendix III]

Industry	NAICS code [1]	1990	1995	2000	2005	2010	2011	2012
Transportation and warehousing	**48–49**	**3,476**	**3,838**	**4,410**	**4,361**	**4,191**	**4,302**	**4,415**
Air transportation	481	529	511	614	501	458	457	458
Rail transportation	482	272	233	232	228	216	228	230
Water transportation	483	57	51	56	61	62	61	63
Truck transportation	484	1,122	1,249	1,406	1,398	1,250	1,301	1,351
Transit and ground	485	274	328	372	389	430	440	448
Pipeline transportation	486	60	54	46	38	42	43	44
Scenic and sightseeing	487	16	22	28	29	27	28	27
Support activities	488	364	430	537	552	543	562	578
Couriers and messengers	492	375	517	605	571	528	529	533
Warehousing and storage	493	407	444	514	595	633	653	682

[1] North American Industry Classification System 2012, see text, Sections 12 and 15.

Source: U.S. Bureau of Labor Statistics, Current Employment Statistics, National, "Employment, Hours, and Earnings," <http://www.bls.gov/ces/data.htm/>, accessed March 2013.

Table 1086. Transportation and Warehousing—Establishments, Employees, and Payroll, by Kind of Business (NAICS Basis): 2009 and 2010

[Employment in thousands (4,159.6 represents 4,159,600); payroll in millions ($164,542.8 represents $164,542,800,000). Covers establishments with payroll. Excludes self-employed individuals, railroad employees, and most government employees. For statement on methodology, see Appendix III. County Business Patterns excludes rail transportation (NAICS 482) and the National Postal Service (NAICS 491)]

Industry	NAICS code [1]	Establishments		Paid employees (1,000)		Annual payroll (mil. dol.)	
		2009	2010	2009	2010	2009	2010
Transportation & warehousing.............	**48–49**	**210,088**	**208,474**	**4,159.6**	**4,012.0**	**164,542.8**	**166,790.0**
Air transportation.............................	481	5,355	5,089	438.3	420.0	23,149.2	23,476.7
Scheduled air transportation................	4811	2,897	2,700	403.2	386.8	20,778.1	21,114.8
Scheduled passenger air transportation...........	481111	2,425	2,228	383.7	367.8	19,964.2	20,202.7
Scheduled freight air transportation................	481112	472	472	(NA)	19.0	813.9	912.1
Nonscheduled air transportation.............	4812	2,458	2,389	35.1	33.2	2,371.1	2,361.9
Water transportation..........................	483	1,775	1,762	68.5	61.7	4,480.7	4,235.4
Deep sea, coastal, & Great Lakes water transportation.........................	4831	1,150	1,157	48.4	44.0	3,237.4	3,070.2
Inland water transportation.................	4832	625	605	20.1	17.7	1,243.3	1,165.2
Inland water freight transportation.........	483211	368	349	17.2	15.6	1,121.6	1,067.2
Inland water passenger transportation.......	483212	257	256	2.9	2.1	121.6	98.0
Truck transportation.........................	484	109,911	108,602	1,327.0	1,265.2	50,735.5	51,150.5
General freight trucking....................	4841	62,719	62,624	882.9	839.8	34,320.7	34,369.6
General freight trucking, local.............	48411	25,913	26,493	163.8	162.3	5,718.6	6,015.1
General freight trucking, long distance........	48412	36,806	36,131	719.1	677.5	28,602.1	28,354.5
Specialized freight trucking...............	4842	47,192	45,978	444.1	425.4	16,414.9	16,780.9
Used household & office goods moving.......	48421	7,653	7,403	86.6	83.0	2,765.0	2,707.8
Specialized freight (except used goods) trucking, local........	48422	29,269	28,391	190.5	186.0	7,079.4	7,356.8
Specialized freight (except used goods) trucking, long-distance........	48423	10,270	10,184	167.0	156.5	6,570.5	6,716.2
Transit & ground passenger transportation.............	485	18,030	18,361	437.0	441.5	10,118.5	10,437.7
Urban transit systems......................	4851	874	801	48.0	45.9	1,862.9	1,771.2
Mixed mode systems......................	485111	53	20	(NA)	2.8	(D)	107.0
Commuter rail...........................	485112	27	15	3.5	([2])	220.3	(D)
Bus and other motor vehicle mode systems.........	485113	784	750	41.1	40.0	1,526.0	1,484.3
Other...................................	485119	10	16	(NA)	0.7	(D)	31.5
Interurban & rural bus transportation..............	4852	422	382	13.4	12.2	349.3	351.4
Taxi & limousine service....................	4853	7,243	7,416	64.7	63.5	1,465.1	1,508.4
Taxi service.............................	48531	2,947	3,023	29.2	28.6	611.6	611.7
Limousine service.......................	48532	4,296	4,393	35.5	34.9	853.5	896.7
School & employee bus transportation..............	4854	4,557	4,473	213.9	214.2	4,073.5	4,149.8
Charter bus industry.......................	4855	1,327	1,319	29.2	30.7	727.6	797.7
Other transit & ground passenger transportation......	4859	3,607	3,970	67.9	74.9	1,640.2	1,859.1
Special needs transportation.............	485991	2,499	2,668	54.5	57.9	1,351.2	1,464.9
Pipeline transportation.......................	486	2,904	3,150	41.6	46.5	3,794.7	4,350.7
Pipeline transportation of crude oil..........	4861	387	421	7.1	7.8	710.5	824.2
Pipeline transportation of natural gas........	4862	1,640	1,886	24.3	29.7	2,261.2	2,776.7
Other pipeline transportation...............	4869	877	843	10.2	9.0	823.1	749.8
Scenic & sightseeing transportation..........	487	2,557	2,553	21.7	21.2	651.6	702.4
Scenic & sightseeing transportation, land...........	4871	647	673	8.8	8.8	232.0	253.2
Scenic & sightseeing transportation, water...........	4872	1,715	1,688	10.6	10.4	340.6	365.9
Scenic & sightseeing transportation, other...........	4879	195	192	2.3	2.0	78.9	83.2
Support activities for transportation..........	488	41,358	41,189	603.2	585.1	25,917.3	26,552.0
Support activities for air transportation.........	4881	5,757	5,737	163.6	159.0	6,423.1	6,350.1
Airport operations.........................	48811	2,009	1,948	80.0	80.4	2,297.9	2,295.8
Air traffic control.......................	488111	166	165	1.3	1.4	80.2	78.6
Other support activities for air transportation.........	48819	3,748	1,783	83.6	79.1	4,125.2	2,217.2
Support activities for rail transportation............	4882	1,109	1,153	25.0	25.4	1,016.8	1,167.0
Support activities for water transportation..........	4883	2,412	2,428	85.7	86.4	4,362.4	4,781.8
Port and harbor operations...............	48831	258	287	5.1	4.8	250.4	290.5
Marine cargo handling....................	48832	541	507	56.4	57.3	2,776.8	3,026.9
Navigational services to shipping..........	48833	846	847	12.7	13.5	826.4	938.0
Other...................................	48839	767	787	11.5	10.8	508.9	526.5
Support activities for road transportation..............	4884	9,978	10,063	75.0	72.6	2,189.4	2,209.2
Motor vehicle towing.....................	48841	8,263	8,260	52.3	51.2	1,551.9	1,540.3
Freight transportation arrangement..........	4885	20,583	20,282	228.9	217.5	10,729.5	10,863.2
Other support activities for transportation.........	4889	1,519	1,526	25.0	24.1	1,196.1	1,180.7
Couriers & messengers......................	492	13,774	13,445	548.6	517.2	20,784.5	20,766.6
Couriers....................................	4921	9,296	8,861	517.4	486.9	20,000.3	19,941.8
Local messengers & local delivery...........	4922	4,478	4,584	31.2	30.3	784.2	824.8
Warehousing & storage........................	493	14,424	14,323	673.7	653.6	24,910.7	25,118.0

NA Not available. D Data withheld to avoid disclosure. [1] Based on the North American Industry Classification System (NAICS), 2007. See text, Section 15. [2] 1,000 to 2,499 employees

Source: U.S. Census Bureau, "County Business Patterns," <http://www.census.gov/econ/cbp/index.html>, accessed March 2013.

Table 1087. Transportation and Warehousing—Establishments, Revenue, Payroll, and Employees by Industry: 2002 and 2007

[382,152 represents $382,152,000,000. For establishments with payroll. Based on the 2002 and 2007 Economic Censuses. Paid employees for pay period including March 12. See Appendix III]

Industry Type	NAICS code [1]	Number of establish-ments	Revenue (mil. dol.)	Annual payroll (mil. dol.)	Paid employees (1,000)
Transportation and warehousing total, 2002	**48–49**	**199,618**	**382,152**	**115,989**	**3,650.9**
Air transportation [2]	481	3,847	19,735	3,805	99.1
Water transportation	483	1,890	23,331	3,194	66.2
Truck transportation	484	112,642	164,219	47,750	1,435.2
Transit and ground passenger transportation	485	17,260	18,850	7,675	398.4
Pipeline transportation	486	2,188	22,031	2,477	36.8
Scenic and sightseeing transportation	487	2,523	1,859	526	22.5
Support activities for transportation	488	33,942	57,414	16,202	465.6
Couriers and messengers	492	12,655	58,165	17,175	561.5
Warehousing and storage	493	12,671	16,548	17,183	565.5
Transportation and warehousing total, 2007	**48–49**	**219,706**	**639,916**	**173,183**	**4,454.4**
Air transportation	481	5,661	146,612	26,120	478.2
Water transportation	483	1,721	34,447	4,544	76.0
Truck transportation	484	120,390	217,833	58,266	1,507.9
Transit and ground passenger transportation	485	17,791	26,465	9,844	444.9
Pipeline transportation	486	2,529	25,718	3,219	37.0
Scenic and sightseeing transportation	487	2,542	2,448	653	24.4
Support activities for transportation	488	42,130	86,596	24,579	608.4
Couriers and messengers	492	13,004	77,877	20,431	557.2
Warehousing and storage	493	13,938	21,921	25,526	720.5

[1] 2002 data based on the 1997 North American Industry Classification System (NAICS), 2007 data are based on the 2002 NAICS; see text, Section 15. [2] Excludes large certificated passenger carriers that do not report to the Office of Airline Information, U.S. Department of Transportation.

Source: U.S. Census Bureau, 2007 Economic Census, EC0748A2, "Transportation and Warehousing: Geographic Area Series: Comparative Statistics for the United States, (2002 NAICS Basis): 2007 and 2002," <http://factfinder.census.gov/>, accessed March 2011.

Table 1088. Transportation and Warehousing—Nonemployer Establishments and Receipts by Kind of Business: 2008 to 2010

[1,039.5 represents 1,039,500. Includes only firms subject to federal income tax. Nonemployers are businesses with no paid employees. Data originate chiefly from administrative records of the Internal Revenue Service; see Appendix III]

Kind of Business	NAICS code [1]	Establishments (1,000)			Receipts (mil. dol.)		
		2008	2009	2010	2008	2009	2010
Transportation and warehousing	**48–49**	**1,039.5**	**1,002.1**	**1,021.2**	**67,026**	**54,453**	**60,746**
Air transportation	481	20.5	19.8	19.1	1,349	1,192	1,219
Water transportation	483	6.4	6.3	6.6	538	429	490
Truck transportation	484	508.0	483.5	490.3	47,880	37,244	42,485
General freight trucking	4841	459.5	438.4	445.1	43,936	34,248	39,277
General freight trucking, local	48411	180.2	168.8	168.7	13,873	10,984	12,144
General freight trucking, long-distance	48412	279.3	269.6	276.4	30,063	23,263	27,133
Specialized freight trucking	4842	48.6	45.1	45.2	3,944	2,997	3,207
Transit and ground passenger transportation	485	207.1	210.8	218.4	7,256	6,987	7,463
Urban transit system	4851	1.2	1.1	1.1	48	39	39
Interurban and rural bus transportation	4852	1.6	1.6	1.5	78	67	67
Taxi and limousine service	4853	166.8	170.5	176.4	5,726	5,684	6,107
School and employee bus transportation	4854	6.9	6.8	6.9	214	191	191
Charter bus industry	4855	3.8	3.7	3.8	182	174	172
Other transit and ground passenger transportation	4859	26.8	27.0	28.7	1,009	832	887
Pipeline transportation	486	0.8	0.8	0.9	81	62	76
Scenic and sightseeing transportation	487	4.7	4.5	4.9	185	142	163
Support activities for transportation	488	102.2	99.6	105.2	4,821	4,203	4,624
Couriers and messengers	492	180.9	168.0	166.6	4,362	3,743	3,772
Warehousing and storage	493	8.7	8.8	9.2	553	450	455

[1] Based on the 2007 North American Industry Classification System (NAICS); see text, Section 15.

Source: Census Bureau, "Nonemployer Statistics by Legal Form of Organization: 2010," NS1000A1, <http://www.census.gov/econ/nonemployer/index.html>, accessed September 2013.

Table 1089. Transportation System Mileage Within the United States: 1980 to 2010

[3,860 represents 3,860,000. Numbers, except where indicated]

System	Unit	1980	1985	1990	1995	2000	2005	2008	2009	2010
Highway [1]	1,000	3,860	3,864	3,867	3,912	3,936	3,996	4,043	4,051	4,067
Class 1 rail [2]	Number	164,822	145,764	119,758	108,264	99,250	95,664	94,082	93,921	95,573
Amtrak	Number	24,000	24,000	24,000	24,000	23,000	22,007	21,178	21,178	21,178
Transit: [3]										
Commuter rail [4]	Number	(NA)	3,574	4,132	4,160	5,209	7,118	7,261	7,561	7,630
Heavy rail [5]	Number	(NA)	1,293	1,351	1,458	1,558	1,622	1,623	1,623	1,617
Light rail [6]	Number	(NA)	384	483	568	834	1,188	1,397	1,477	1,497
Navigable channels	Number	26,000	26,000	26,000	26,000	26,000	26,000	25,320	25,320	25,320
Oil pipeline [7, 9]	Number	(NA)	(NA)	(NA)	(NA)	(NA)	162,919	169,586	172,048	183,203
Gas pipeline [8]	1,000	1,052	1,111	1,270	1,332	1,377	1,489	1,533	1,540	1,549

NA Not available. [1] All public road and street mileage in the 50 states and the District of Columbia. Beginning in 1998, approximately 43,000 miles of Bureau of Land Management Roads are excluded. [2] Data represent miles of road owned (aggregate length of road, excluding yard tracks, sidings, and parallel lines). Portions of Class I freight railroads, Amtrak, and Commuter rail networks share common trackage. Amtrak data represent miles of road operated. [3] Transit system length is measured in directional route-miles; see source. [4] Also called metropolitan rail or regional rail. [5] Also called metro, subway, rapid transit, or rapid rail. [6] Also called streetcar, tramway, or trolley. [7] Includes trunk and gathering lines for crude-oil pipeline. [8] Excludes service pipelines. [9] Oil Pipeline data has been discontinued for years prior to 2001.

Source: U.S. Bureau of Transportation Statistics, "National Transportation Statistics," <http://www.bts.gov/publications/national_transportation_statistics>, accessed March 2013.

Table 1090. U.S. Aircraft, Vehicles, and Other Conveyances: 2000 to 2011

[Number, or in thousands (133,621 represents 133,621,000), as indicated]

System	2000	2004	2005	2006	2007	2008	2009	2010	2011
Air:									
Air carrier [1]	8,055	8,186	8,225	8,089	8,044	7,856	7,771	7,431	7,028
General aviation [2] (active fleet)	217,533	219,426	224,352	221,943	231,607	228,663	223,877	223,370	(NA)
Highway, registered vehicles (1,000):									
Light duty vehicle, short wheel base [3]	133,621	136,431	136,568	135,400	196,491	196,763	193,980	190,203	192,513
Motorcycle	4,346	5,768	6,227	6,679	7,138	7,753	7,930	8,010	8,330
Light duty vehicle, long wheel base [4]	79,085	91,845	95,337	99,125	39,187	39,685	40,488	40,242	41,328
Trucks [5]	8,023	8,171	8,482	8,819	10,752	10,873	10,973	10,770	10,271
Bus	746	795	807	822	834	843	842	846	666
Transit:									
Motor bus	58,578	61,318	62,284	64,025	63,359	63,151	63,343	63,108	59,871
Light rail cars [6]	1,306	1,622	1,645	1,801	1,802	1,948	2,059	2,096	1,969
Heavy rail cars [7]	10,311	10,858	11,110	11,052	11,222	11,377	11,461	11,510	14,942
Trolley bus	652	597	615	609	559	590	531	571	479
Commuter rail cars and locomotives	5,497	6,130	6,290	6,300	6,279	6,494	6,722	6,768	6,971
Demand response	22,087	26,333	28,346	29,406	29,433	30,773	34,235	33,555	31,846
Other [8]	7,705	10,544	11,622	12,454	12,953	14,953	17,766	18,066	20,536
Rail:									
Class I, freight cars (1,000)	560	474	475	475	460	450	416	398	381
Class I, locomotive	20,028	22,015	22,779	23,732	24,143	24,003	24,045	23,893	24,250
Nonclass I freight cars	132,448	120,169	120,195	120,688	120,463	109,487	108,233	101,755	95,972
Car companies' and shippers' freight cars	688,194	693,978	717,211	750,404	805,074	833,188	839,020	809,544	806,554
Amtrak, passenger train car	1,894	1,211	1,186	1,191	1,164	1,177	1,214	1,274	1,301
Amtrak, locomotive	378	276	258	319	270	278	274	282	287
Water:									
Non-self-propelled vessels [9]	31,360	31,296	33,152	32,211	31,654	31,238	31,008	31,412	31,498
Self-propelled vessels [10]	8,202	8,994	8,976	8,898	9,041	9,063	9,101	9,100	9,023
Ocean-going self-propelled vessels (1,000 gross tons and over) [11]	454	423	366	344	275	272	196	(NA)	(NA)
Recreational boats (1,000)	12,782	12,781	12,942	12,746	12,876	12,693	12,722	12,439	12,174

NA Not available. [1] Air carrier aircraft are those carrying passengers or cargo for hire under 14 CFR 121 and 14 CFR 135. [2] Includes air taxi aircraft. [3] Data for 2000-06 are for passenger cars. Beginning 2007, data are for Light Duty Vehicles Short Wheel Base - passenger cars, light trucks, vans and sport utility vehicles with a wheelbase of 121 inches or less. [4] Data for 2000-06 are for 2-axle, 4-tire vehicles other than passenger cars, motorcycles, and buses. Beginning 2007, data are for Light Duty Vehicles Long Wheel Base - large passenger cars, vans, pickup trucks, and sport/utility vehicles with wheelbases larger than 121 inches. [5] Includes trucks on a single frame with at least 2 axles and 6 tires, and combinations. [6] Fixed rail streetcar or trolley, for example. [7] Metro, subway, or rapid transit, for example. [8] Includes aerial tramway, automated guideway transit, cable car, ferry boat, inclined plane, monorail, and vanpool. [9] Includes dry-cargo barges, tank barges, and railroad-car floats. [10] Includes dry-cargo and/or passenger, offshore supply vessels, railroad-car ferries, tankers, and towboats. [11] 2000-06 data include private and government owned vessels of 1,000 gross tons/more. Beginning 2007, data are reported only for privately owned vessels of 1,000 gross tons/more. 2009 data include privately owned vessels of 10,000 deadweight tons/more, not including the Great Lakes vessels.

Source: U.S. Department of Transportation, Research and Innovative Technology Administration, Bureau of Transportation Statistics, *National Transportation Statistics, 2013*. See also <http://www.rita.dot.gov/bts/>.

Table 1091. Shipment Characteristics by Mode of Transportation: 2002 and 2007

[8,397,210 represents $8,397,210,000,000 (except as indicated otherwise). For business establishments in mining, manufacturing, wholesale trade, and selected retail industries. 2007 industries classified by the 2002 North American Industry Classification System (NAICS). 2002 industries classified by the 1997 NAICS. Selected auxiliary establishments are also included. Based on the 2007 Economic Census; see Appendix III]

Mode of transportation	Value (mil. dol.)		Tons (1,000)		Ton-miles (mil.)		Average miles per shipment	
	2002	2007	2002	2007	2002	2007	2002	2007
All modes....................	**8,397,210**	**11,684,872**	**11,667,919**	**12,543,425**	**3,137,898**	**3,344,658**	**546**	**619**
Single modes................	**7,049,383**	**9,539,037**	**11,086,660**	**11,698,128**	**2,867,938**	**2,894,251**	**240**	**234**
Truck [1]........................	6,235,001	8,335,789	7,842,836	8,778,713	1,255,908	1,342,104	173	206
For-hire truck..................	3,757,114	4,955,700	3,657,333	4,075,136	959,610	1,055,646	523	599
Private truck..................	2,445,288	3,380,090	4,149,658	4,703,576	291,114	286,457	64	57
Rail...........................	310,884	436,420	1,873,884	1,861,307	1,261,612	1,344,040	807	728
Water.........................	89,344	114,905	681,227	403,639	282,659	157,314	568	520
Shallow draft.................	57,467	91,004	458,577	343,307	211,501	117,473	450	144
Great Lakes..................	843	(S)	38,041	17,792	13,808	6,887	339	657
Deep draft...................	31,034	23,058	184,610	42,540	57,350	32,954	664	923
Air (includes truck and air).......	264,959	252,276	3,760	3,611	5,835	4,510	1,919	1,304
Pipeline [2].....................	149,195	399,646	684,953	650,859	(S)	(S)	(S)	(S)
Multiple modes.............	**1,079,185**	**1,866,723**	**216,686**	**573,729**	**225,715**	**416,642**	**895**	**975**
Parcel, U.S. Postal Service or courier............................	987,746	1,561,874	25,513	33,900	19,004	27,961	894	975
Truck and rail..................	69,929	187,248	42,984	225,589	45,525	196,772	1,413	1,007
Truck and water.................	14,359	58,389	23,299	145,521	32,413	98,396	1,950	1,429
Rail and water.................	3,329	13,892	105,107	54,878	114,986	47,111	957	1,928
Other multiple modes.............	3,822	45,320	19,782	113,841	13,788	46,402	(S)	1,182
Other and unknown modes...	**268,642**	**279,113**	**364,573**	**271,567**	**44,245**	**33,764**	**130**	**116**

S Data do not meet publication standards due to high sampling variability or other reasons. [1] Truck as a single mode includes shipments that went by private truck only, for-hire truck only, or a combination of private truck and for-hire truck. [2] Commodity Flow Survey data exclude shipments of crude oil.

Source: U.S. Department of Transportation, Bureau of Transportation Statistics, and U.S. Department of Commerce, Census Bureau, "2007 Commodity Flow Survey" <http://www.census.gov/econ/cfs/>, accessed October 2012.

Table 1092. Hazardous Shipments—Value, Tons, and Ton-Miles: 2002 and 2007

[660,181 represents $660,181,000,000. For business establishments in mining, manufacturing, wholesale trade, and selected retail industries. 2007 industries classified by the 2002 North American Industry Classification System (NAICS). 2002 industries classified by the 1997 NAICS. Selected auxiliary establishments are also included. Based on the 2007 Economic Census; see Appendix III]

Mode of Transportation and Class of Material	Value (mil. dol.)		Tons (1,000)		Ton-miles (mil.)		Average miles per shipment	
	2002	2007	2002	2007	2002	2007	2002	2007
All modes...........................	**660,181**	**1,448,218**	**2,191,519**	**2,231,133**	**326,727**	**323,457**	**136**	**96**
Single modes...........................	644,489	1,370,615	2,158,533	2,111,622	311,897	279,105	105	65
Truck [1]................................	419,630	837,074	1,159,514	1,202,825	110,163	103,997	86	59
For-hire truck.........................	189,803	358,792	449,503	495,077	65,112	63,288	285	214
Private truck.........................	226,660	478,282	702,186	707,748	44,087	40,709	38	32
Rail...................................	31,339	69,213	109,369	129,743	72,087	92,169	695	578
Water.................................	46,856	69,186	228,197	149,794	70,649	37,064	(S)	383
Air (includes truck and air)...........	1,643	1,735	64	(S)	85	(S)	2,080	1,095
Pipeline [2]............................	145,021	393,408	661,390	628,905	(S)	(S)	(S)	(S)
Multiple modes [3].....................	9,631	71,069	18,745	111,022	12,488	42,886	849	834
Parcel, U.S. Postal Service or courier.............	4,268	7,675	245	236	119	151	837	836
Other and unknown modes.................	6,061	6,534	14,241	8,489	2,342	1,466	57	58
Class of Material...................	**660,181**	**1,448,218**	**2,191,519**	**2,231,133**	**326,727**	**323,457**	**136**	**96**
Class 1, Explosives....................	7,901	11,754	5,000	3,047	1,568	911	651	738
Class 2, Gasses.......................	73,932	131,810	213,358	250,506	37,262	55,260	95	51
Class 3, Flammable and combustible liquid.....	490,238	1,170,455	1,788,986	1,752,814	218,574	181,615	106	91
Class 4, Flammable solid; spontaneously combustible material; dangerous when wet material...........................	6,566	4,067	11,300	20,408	4,391	5,547	158	309
Class 5, Oxidizers and organic peroxides.......	5,471	6,695	12,670	14,959	4,221	7,024	407	361
Class 6, Toxic materials and infectious substances...........................	8,275	21,198	8,459	11,270	4,254	5,667	626	467
Class 7, Radioactive materials....................	5,850	20,633	57	515	44	37	(S)	(S)
Class 8, Corrosive materials.....................	38,324	51,475	90,671	114,441	36,260	44,395	301	208
Class 9, Miscellaneous hazardous material.....	23,625	30,131	61,018	63,173	20,153	23,002	368	484

S Data do not meet publication standards due to high sampling variability or other reasons. [1] Truck as a single mode includes shipments that went by private truck only, for-hire truck only, or a combination of private truck and for-hire truck. [2] Commodity Flow Survey Data exclude shipments of crude oil. [3] Includes other modes not shown. Multimode data for 2007 and 2002 are not comparable due to methodological changes; see source.

Source: U.S. Department of Transportation, Bureau of Transportation Statistics, and U.S. Department of Commerce, Census Bureau, "2007 Commodity Flow Survey," <http://www.census.gov/econ/cfs/>, accessed October 2012.

Table 1093. Transportation Accidents, Deaths, and Injuries: 1990 to 2011

[Number, except in thousands (6,471 represents 6,471,000) as indicated]

Mode	Accidents					Deaths					Injuries				
	1990	2000	2005	2010	2011	1990	2000	2005	2010	2011, prelimi-nary	1990	2000	2005	2010	2011
Air:															
Air carrier [1]	24	56	40	29	31	39	92	22	2	–	29	29	14	16	20
Commuter [2]	15	12	6	6	4	6	5	–	–	–	11	7	–	2	2
On-demand [3]	107	80	65	31	50	51	71	18	17	41	36	12	23	3	15
General aviation	2,242	1,837	1,671	1,439	1,466	770	596	563	454	444	409	309	267	256	325
Land:															
Highway crashes (1,000) [4]	6,471	6,394	6,159	5,419	5,338	44.6	41.9	43.5	33.0	32.4	3,231	3,189	2,699	2,239	2,217
Passenger car occupants	5,561	4,926	4,499	(NA)	(NA)	24.1	20.7	18.5	12.5	12.0	2,376	2,052	1,573	1,253	1,240
Motorcyclists	103	69	101	(NA)	(NA)	3.2	2.9	4.6	4.5	4.6	84	58	87	82	81
Light truck occupants	2,152	3,208	3,382	(NA)	(NA)	8.6	11.5	13.0	9.8	9.3	505	887	872	733	728
Large truck occupants	372	438	423	(NA)	(NA)	0.7	0.8	0.8	0.5	0.6	42	31	27	20	23
Bus occupants	60	56	50	(NA)	(NA)	(Z)	(Z)	0.1	(Z)	0.1	33	18	11	17	13
Pedestrians	(NA)	(NA)	(NA)	(NA)	(NA)	6.5	4.8	4.9	4.3	4.4	105	78	64	70	69
Pedacyclists	(NA)	(NA)	(NA)	(NA)	(NA)	0.9	0.6	0.8	0.6	0.7	75	51	45	52	48
Other	(NA)	(NA)	(NA)	(NA)	(NA)	0.6	0.6	0.8	0.7	0.7	11	15	18	13	15
Railroad [5]	14,108	14,024	11,816	10,030	9,819	729	631	626	600	570	10,645	10,614	8,677	7,659	7,520
Highway-rail grade crossing [6]	691	607	571	450	443	130	119	101	125	123	221	190	180	169	215
Railroad	13,417	13,417	11,245	9,580	9,376	599	512	525	475	447	10,424	10,424	8,497	7,490	7,305
Transit [7]	13,646	14,118	6,877	8,927	6,519	125	110	57	109	106	13,646	14,118	6,877	8,927	6,519
Waterborne:															
Waterborne (vessel related) [8]	3,613	5,403	4,977	5,285	5,986	85	53	78	41	28	175	150	140	172	105
Recreational boating [9]	6,411	7,740	4,969	4,604	4,588	865	701	697	672	758	3,822	4,355	3,451	3,153	3,081
Pipeline: [10]	379	380	721	589	593	9	38	14	22	14	76	81	48	109	60
Hazard liquid	180	146	369	350	346	3	1	2	1	1	7	4	2	4	2
Gas	199	234	352	239	247	6	37	12	21	13	69	77	46	105	58
Hazardous materials [11, 12]	8,879	17,557	15,928	14,798	15,026	8	16	34	8	13	423	251	915	169	164

– Represents or rounds to zero. Z Less than 500. NA Not available. [1] See footnote 1, Table 1099. Injuries classified as serious. [2] See footnote 2, Table 1099. Injuries classified as serious. [3] See footnote 3, Table 1099. Injuries classified as serious. [4] Highway crashes often involve more than one motor vehicle, and hence "total highway crashes" is smaller than the sum of the components. Data on deaths are from U.S. National Highway Traffic Safety Administration and are based on deaths within 30 days of the accident. Includes only police reported crashes. For more details, see Table 1131. [5] Accidents and incidents resulting from freight and passenger rail operations including commuter rail. Grade crossing accidents are also included when classified as a train accident. Deaths and injuries exclude those in highway-rail grade crossing accidents involving motor vehicles. Injury figures also include occupational illness. [6] Highway-rail grade crossing fatalities and injuries, except train occupants, are also counted under highway. Fatalities and injuries involved with motor vehicles at public highway-rail grade crossings are excluded. [7] Includes motor bus, commuter rail, heavy rail, light rail, demand response, van pool, and automated guideway. Starting with 2002, only injuries requiring immediate medical treatment away from the scene now qualify as reportable. [8] Vessel-related deaths and injuries include those involving damage to vessels, such as collisions or groundings. [9] Covers occurrences involving a vessel or its equipment that results in 1) A death; 2) An injury that requires medical treatment beyond first aid; 3) Damage to a vessel and other property, totaling to more than $500 or complete loss of a vessel; or 4) The disappearance of the vessel under circumstances that indicate death or injury. Federal regulations (33 CFR 173-4) require the operator of any vessel that is numbered or used for recreational purposes to submit an accident report. [10] Beginning 1990, pipeline accidents/incidents are credited to year of occurrence; prior data are credited to the year filed. [11] Incidents, deaths, and injuries involving hazardous materials cover all types of transport. Excludes pipelines and bulk marine hazardous materials incidents (which are reported under accidents are incident numbers. [12] The data reported under accidents are incident numbers.

Source: U.S. Department of Transportation, Research and Innovative Technology Administration, Bureau of Transportation Statistics, National Transportation Statistics, 2013. See also <http://www.rita.dot.gov/bts/>.

Table 1094. U.S. Scheduled Airline Industry—Summary: 1995 to 2011

[For calendar years or as of December 31, (547.8 represents 547,800,000). For domestic and international operations. Covers carriers certificated under Section 401 of the Federal Aviation Act. Table data have been revised for 2000 through 2009. Minus sign (-) indicates loss]

Item	Unit	1995	2000	2006	2007	2008	2009	2010	2011
SCHEDULED SERVICE									
Revenue passengers enplaned....	Mil.	547.8	666.1	744.7	769.6	743.3	703.9	720.5	730.8
Revenue passenger miles..........	Bil.	540.7	692.8	797.4	829.4	812.4	769.5	798.0	814.4
Available seat miles.................	Bil.	807.1	957.0	1,006.3	1,037.7	1,021.3	957.2	972.6	992.7
Revenue passenger load factor....	Percent	67.0	72.4	79.2	79.9	79.5	80.4	82.1	82.0
Mean passenger trip length [1].......	Miles	987	1,040	1,071	1,078	1,093	1,093	1,108	1,114
Cargo ton miles.....................	Mil.	16,921	23,888	29,340	29,571	28,119	24,970	27,885	28,123
Aircraft departures..................	1,000	8,062	9,035	11,268	11,399	10,897	10,145	10,095	10,057
FINANCES [2]									
Total operating revenue [3]......	**Mil. dol.**	**95,117**	**130,248**	**165,532**	**174,696**	**186,087**	**155,051**	**174,677**	**192,362**
Passenger revenue..................	Mil. dol.	69,470	93,639	101,968	107,678	111,511	91,443	103,978	113,948
Cargo revenue.......................	Mil. dol.	8,619	12,667	21,914	24,002	29,192	23,014	17,622	(NA)
Charter revenue.....................	Mil. dol.	3,350	4,366	6,095	5,544	4,338	3,841	3,254	(NA)
Total operating expense...........	Mil. dol.	89,266	123,234	157,892	165,353	189,437	152,716	164,160	185,261
Operating profit (or loss)...........	Mil. dol.	5,852	7,014	7,640	9,344	-3,350	2,335	10,517	7,101
Interest income (or expense).......	Mil. dol.	-2,446	-2,414	-4,182	-3,915	-3,743	-4,214	-4,215	-3,982
Net profit (or loss)...................	Mil. dol.	2,314	2,533	18,186	7,691	-23,750	-2,610	3,666	1,481
Revenue per passenger mile.......	Cents	12.8	13.5	12.8	13.0	13.7	11.9	13.0	14.0
Operating profit margin.............	Percent	6.2	5.4	4.6	5.3	-1.8	1.5	6.0	3.7
Net profit margin....................	Percent	2.4	1.9	11.0	4.4	-12.8	-1.7	2.1	0.8
Adjusted net profit (or loss) [4].......	Percent	2.4	1.9	11.0	4.4	-12.8	-1.6	(NA)	(NA)
EMPLOYEES [5]									
Total.................................	1,000	546.6	679.7	565.0	576.0	559.6	526.9	531.2	538.3
Pilots and copilots.................	1,000	55.3	72.2	75.7	74.8	75.6	72.0	73.7	71.4

NA Not available. [1] For definition of mean, see Guide to Tabular Presentation. [2] 2011 data are preliminary. [3] Includes other types of revenues, not shown separately. [4] Excludes special items: bankruptcy-related reorganization charges and fresh-start accounting gains, and special goodwill charges. [5] Average full-time equivalents.

Source: Airlines for America, Washington, DC, *Economic Report*, annual ©; and Bureau of Transportation Statistics, <http://www.transtats.bts.gov/>, accessed October 2012.

Table 1095. Passenger Airline Cost Indexes: 1980 to 2011

[2000 = 100. To be included in the cost index, carriers must have met the following criteria on an annual basis: 1) must report both passenger revenue and revenue passenger miles (RPMs) and 2) passenger revenue must be greater than or equal to 25 percent of total operating revenue]

Index	1980	1990	1995	2000	2003	2004	2005	2006	2007	2008	2009	2010	2011
Composite index [1]..............	**77.4**	**101.1**	**99.0**	**100.0**	**122.8**	**149.1**	**177.9**	**195.8**	**199.8**	**262.0**	**147.4**	**160.6**	**195.0**
Labor costs...........................	52.0	73.1	91.3	100.0	122.7	122.3	117.3	119.0	119.1	119.8	127.4	135.3	136.7
Fuel..................................	113.7	98.1	69.7	100.0	107.9	144.1	206.6	242.8	258.0	374.2	233.9	269.3	350.4
Aircraft ownership [2]..............	33.5	71.1	83.0	100.0	101.8	103.4	99.1	98.9	94.3	91.0	92.8	92.9	91.9
Nonaircraft ownership..............	40.4	88.1	103.3	100.0	111.4	104.1	106.1	104.2	106.6	118.8	115.2	111.4	111.4
Professional services...............	27.0	67.5	85.4	100.0	98.4	103.4	105.5	111.2	115.8	125.4	118.5	118.5	121.4
Food and beverage..................	88.5	125.5	106.9	100.0	74.6	67.1	61.3	57.9	57.8	60.0	59.7	59.5	61.7
Landing fees.........................	49.2	81.0	95.8	100.0	130.8	131.2	130.7	135.6	136.7	148.6	158.9	169.8	166.3
Maintenance material...............	73.3	119.2	94.0	100.0	67.3	64.8	59.1	62.2	69.9	77.0	83.5	82.9	92.0
Aircraft insurance...................	246.1	161.0	341.5	100.0	180.9	174.3	157.1	181.0	152.3	124.0	150.7	164.9	163.9
Nonaircraft insurance...............	73.3	68.2	223.8	100.0	450.3	373.7	319.9	259.3	222.1	195.4	184.4	188.2	167.6
Passenger commissions............	121.5	227.0	184.8	100.0	41.9	37.2	31.6	29.2	28.2	27.0	26.7	26.4	25.7
Communication......................	50.3	85.7	86.5	100.0	82.0	76.1	73.3	68.5	71.2	79.2	77.2	75.3	80.0
Advertising and promotion.........	112.9	165.0	107.8	100.0	69.1	77.8	75.5	80.9	67.3	59.0	61.7	61.0	65.2
Utilities and office supplies........	67.9	97.7	87.0	100.0	81.0	81.3	87.6	94.3	102.2	108.8	99.8	118.4	119.2
Transportation-related expenses..	46.0	55.0	57.5	100.0	256.4	397.4	475.0	508.4	506.7	604.5	158.9	157.9	185.1
Other operating expenses..........	56.0	87.4	74.1	100.0	94.9	94.3	108.6	108.1	116.1	156.8	123.7	121.5	137.0
Interest [3]...........................	160.7	182.0	174.6	100.0	93.3	96.3	120.6	133.5	120.3	105.6	116.2	125.3	113.4

[1] Weighted average of all components, including interest. [2] Includes lease, aircraft and engine rentals, depreciation, and amortization. [3] Interest on long-term debt and capital and other interest expense.

Source: Airlines for America, Washington, DC, *U.S. Passenger Airline Cost Index* ©. See also <http://www.airlines.org/>.

Table 1096. Top 40 Airports in 2012—Passengers Enplaned: 2002 and 2012

[In thousands (622,461 represents 622,461,000), except rank. For calendar year. Intl = international. Airports ranked by total passengers enplaned by large certificated air carriers on scheduled and nonscheduled operations. Data for commuter, small-certificated and foreign-flag air carriers are not included]

Airport	2002		2012		Airport	2002		2012	
	Rank	Total	Rank	Total		Rank	Total	Rank	Total
All airports	(X)	**622,461**	(X)	**692,260**	Baltimore, MD (BWI Intl)	23	9,022	21	11,094
Total, top 40	(X)	**489,565**	(X)	**535,530**	Fort Lauderdale-Hollywood Intl, FL	28	7,706	22	10,644
Atlanta, GA (Hartsfield Intl)	1	37,099	1	45,193	Salt Lake City Intl, UT	27	7,718	23	9,579
Chicago O'Hare Intl, IL	2	28,762	2	29,984	Washington, DC (Ronald				
Dallas/Fort Worth Intl, TX	3	24,221	3	27,556	Reagan Washington Natl)	34	5,728	24	9,360
Denver Intl, CO	5	16,263	4	25,511	Chicago, IL (Midway)	25	7,839	25	9,265
Los Angeles Intl, CA	4	20,635	5	24,983	Washington, DC (Dulles Intl)	32	5,834	26	9,120
Charlotte-Douglas Intl, NC	18	10,589	6	19,928	San Diego Intl, CA	30	7,155	27	8,479
Phoenix Sky Harbor Intl, AZ	6	16,232	7	19,221	Tampa Intl, FL	29	7,329	28	8,005
San Francisco Intl, CA	13	12,406	8	18,567	Honolulu Intl, HI	26	7,769	29	7,961
Las Vegas, NV (McCarran Intl)	7	15,700	9	18,467	Portland Intl, OR	33	5,824	30	7,077
Houston, Intercontinental, TX	8	15,235	10	18,155	St. Louis, MO				
New York, NY (JFK Intl)	21	9,964	11	17,107	(Lambert-St Louis Intl)	15	11,943	31	6,179
Minneapolis-St. Paul Intl, MN	9	15,197	12	15,892	Houston, TX (William P. Hobby)	45	3,818	32	5,041
Orlando Intl, FL	14	12,175	13	15,595	Kansas City Intl, MO	35	5,115	33	4,856
Seattle-Tacoma Intl, WA	12	12,609	14	15,460	Oakland Intl, CA	31	6,005	34	4,851
Detroit, MI (Wayne County)	10	15,053	15	15,424	Nashville Intl, TN	44	3,832	35	4,777
Newark, NJ (Liberty Intl)	11	13,150	16	15,350	Austin-Bergstrom Intl, TX	48	3,171	36	4,605
Miami Intl, FL	16	11,168	17	15,316	Raleigh, NC (Raleigh-Durham Intl)	43	3,845	37	4,459
Philadelphia Intl, PA	17	10,669	18	14,361	Sacramento Intl, CA	41	4,108	38	4,326
Boston, MA (Logan Intl)	22	9,637	19	12,858	Cleveland, OH (Hopkins Intl)	37	5,063	39	4,306
New York, NY (La Guardia)	20	10,019	20	12,314	Santa Ana, CA (John Wayne)	42	3,917	40	4,301

X Not applicable.

Source: U.S. Department of Transportation, Research and Innovative Technology Administration, Bureau of Transportation Statistics, *National Transportation Statistics, 2013*. See also <http://www.rita.dot.gov/bts/>.

Table 1097. Domestic Airline Markets--Average Daily Passengers: 2011

[For calendar year. Data are for the 25 top markets and include all commercial airports in each metro area. Data represent traffic each way between origin and final destinations]

Market	Passengers	Market	Passengers
Los Angeles - New York	4,541	Honolulu - Maui	1,794
Chicago - New York	4,480	Dallas - New York	1,788
Ft. Lauderdale - New York	4,390	New York - Tampa	1,775
New York - Orlando	4,062	Boston - New York	1,758
New York - San Francisco	3,417	Chicago - Orlando	1,713
Atlanta - New York	2,800	Chicago - Las Vegas	1,699
Los Angeles - San Francisco	2,649	Chicago - Washington	1,695
Miami - New York	2,559	Las Vegas - San Francisco	1,644
Las Vegas - New York	2,146	Las Vegas - Los Angeles	1,634
Chicago - Los Angeles	2,111	Orlando - Philadelphia	1,611
Boston - Washington	1,971	Boston - Chicago	1,578
New York - West Palm Beach	1,943	Dallas - Houston	1,575
		Chicago - San Francisco	1,574

Source: Airlines for America, Washington, DC, *Annual Report*, ©.

Table 1098. U.S. Carrier Delays, Cancellations, and Diversions: 1995 to 2011

[In thousands (5,327.4 represents 5,327,400). For calendar year. See headnote, Table 1101]

Item	1995	2000	2004	2005	2006	2007	2008	2009	2010	2011
Total operations	**5,327.4**	**5,683.0**	**7,129.3**	**7,140.6**	**7,141.9**	**7,455.5**	**7,009.7**	**6,450.3**	**6,450.1**	**6,085.3**
Delays:										
Late departures [1]	827.9	1,131.7	1,187.6	1,279.4	1,424.8	1,573.0	1,327.2	1,084.3	1,111.9	1,042.4
Late arrivals [2]	1,039.3	1,356.0	1,421.4	1,466.1	1,615.5	1,804.0	1,524.7	1,218.3	1,174.9	1,109.9
Cancellations [3]	91.9	187.5	127.8	133.7	121.9	160.8	137.4	89.4	113.3	116.0
Diversions [4]	10.5	14.3	13.8	14.0	16.2	17.2	17.3	15.5	15.5	14.4

[1] Late departures comprise flights departing 15 minutes or more after the scheduled departure time. [2] Late arrivals comprise flights arriving 15 minutes or more after the scheduled arrival time. [3] A cancelled flight is one that was not operated, but was listed in a carrier's computer reservation system within seven days of the scheduled departure. [4] A diverted flight is one that left from the scheduled departure airport but flew to a destination point other than the scheduled destination point.

Source: U.S. Department of Transportation, Research and Innovative Technology Administration, Bureau of Transportation Statistics, *National Transportation Statistics, 2013*. See also <http://www.rita.dot.gov/bts/>.

Table 1099. Aircraft Accidents: 1990 to 2012

[For years ending December 31]

Item	Unit	1990	1995	2000	2005	2010	2011	2012, prel.
Air carrier accidents, all services [1]	**Number**	**24**	**36**	**56**	**40**	**29**	**31**	**27**
Fatal accidents	Number	6	3	3	3	1	–	–
Fatalities	Number	39	168	92	22	2	–	–
Aboard	Number	12	162	92	20	2	–	–
Rates per 100,000 flight hours:								
Accidents	Rate	0.198	0.267	0.306	0.206	0.163	0.173	0.151
Fatal accidents	Rate	0.049	0.022	0.016	0.015	0.006	–	–
Commuter air carrier accidents [2]	Number	15	12	12	6	6	4	4
Fatal accidents	Number	3	2	1	–	–	–	–
Fatalities	Number	6	9	5	–	–	–	–
Aboard	Number	4	9	5	–	–	–	–
Rates per 100,000 flight hours:								
Accidents	Rate	0.641	0.457	3.247	2.002	1.907	1.228	1.251
Fatal accidents	Rate	0.128	0.076	0.271	–	–	–	–
On-demand air taxi accidents [3]	Number	107	75	80	65	30	50	37
Fatal accidents	Number	29	24	22	11	6	16	9
Fatalities	Number	51	52	71	18	17	41	15
Aboard	Number	49	52	68	16	17	41	15
Rates per 100,000 flight hours:								
Accidents	Rate	4.76	3.02	2.04	1.70	0.86	1.62	1.27
Fatal accidents	Rate	1.29	0.97	0.56	0.29	0.17	0.52	0.31
General aviation accidents [4]	Number	2,242	2,056	1,837	1,670	1,440	1,470	1,471
Fatal accidents	Number	444	413	345	321	270	266	271
Fatalities	Number	770	735	596	563	457	448	432
Aboard	Number	765	728	585	558	454	437	432
Rates per 100,000 flight hours:								
Accidents	Rate	7.85	8.21	6.57	7.20	6.63	6.84	6.78
Fatal accidents	Rate	1.55	1.63	1.21	1.38	1.24	1.24	1.24

– Represents zero. [1] U.S. air carriers operating under 14 CFR 121. Beginning 2000, includes aircraft with 10 or more seats, previously operating under 14 CFR 135. [2] All scheduled service of U.S. air carriers operating under 14 CFR 135. Beginning 2000, only aircraft with fewer than 10 seats. [3] All nonscheduled service of U.S. air carriers operating under 14 CFR 135. [4] U.S. civil registered aircraft not operated under 14 CFR 121 or 135.

Source: U.S. National Transportation Safety Board, "Aviation Accident Statistics," <http://www.ntsb.gov/data/aviation_stats.html>, accessed August 2013.

Table 1100. Consumer Complaints Filed Against U.S. Airlines: 1990 to 2012

[Calendar year data. Represents complaints filed by consumers to the U.S. Department of Transportation, Aviation Consumer Protection Division, regarding service problems with air carrier personnel. See source for data on individual airlines]

Complaint category	1990	2000	2005	2007	2008	2009	2010	2011	2012
Total	**7,703**	**20,564**	**6,900**	**10,960**	**10,643**	**8,821**	**10,988**	**11,546**	**15,335**
Flight problems [1]	3,034	8,698	1,942	4,097	3,247	2,041	3,337	3,656	4,247
Baggage	1,329	2,753	1,586	2,154	2,081	1,607	1,938	1,852	2,183
Ticketing/boarding [2]	624	1,405	679	1,136	1,404	1,583	1,510	1,448	2,456
Customer service [3]	758	4,074	800	1,214	1,333	1,103	1,345	1,287	1,988
Refunds	701	803	530	745	803	669	730	985	1,184
Fares [4]	312	708	219	315	389	436	465	634	1,010
Disability [5]	(NA)	612	430	428	474	519	572	628	743
Oversales [6]	399	759	284	420	432	370	544	508	502
Discrimination [7]	(NA)	(NA)	100	82	115	131	143	128	99
Advertising	96	42	45	34	39	53	77	82	202
Tours	29	25	(8)	(8)	(8)	(8)	(8)	(8)	(8)
Animals	(NA)	1	3	7	5	5	8	9	5
Smoking	74	(9)	(9)	(9)	(9)	(9)	(9)	(9)	(9)
Credit	5	(9)	(9)	(9)	(9)	(9)	(9)	(9)	(9)
Other	342	684	282	328	321	304	319	329	716

NA Not available. [1] Cancellations, delays, and other deviations from schedule. [2] Errors in reservations and ticketing; problems in making reservations and obtaining tickets. Includes disability complaints prior to 1998. [3] Unhelpful employees, inadequate meals or cabin service, treatment of delayed passengers. [4] Incorrect or incomplete information about fares, discount fare conditions, and availability, etc. [5] Prior to 2000, included in ticketing/boarding. [6] All bumping problems, whether or not airline complied with DOT regulations. [7] Allegations of discrimination by airlines due to factors other than disability, such as race, religion, national origin or sex. [8] Included in "Other" beginning 2002. [9] Included in "Other" beginning 2000.

Source: Department of Transportation, Aviation Consumer Protection Division, *Air Travel Consumer Report*, February 2013, and earlier reports. See also <http://www.dot.gov/airconsumer>.

Table 1101. On-Time Flight Arrivals and Departures at Major U.S. Airports: 2012

[In percent. Quarterly, based on gate arrival and departure times for domestic scheduled operations of U.S. major airlines. All U.S. airlines with 1 percent or more of total U.S. domestic scheduled airline passenger revenues are required to report on-time data. A flight is considered on time if it operated less than 15 minutes after the scheduled time shown in the carrier's computerized reservation system. See source for data on individual airlines]

Airport	On-time arrivals				On-time departures			
	1st quarter	2nd quarter	3rd quarter	4th quarter	1st quarter	2nd quarter	3rd quarter	4th quarter
Total, all airports..............................	84.0	83.4	79.4	80.8	84.8	83.8	80.1	81.3
Atlanta, Hartsfield................................	85.1	86.6	81.6	85.8	85.4	85.4	80.3	84.8
Boston, Logan International....................	84.2	81.1	78.0	80.5	87.2	84.3	82.3	82.4
Baltimore/Washington International...........	88.5	84.0	77.3	76.7	86.2	79.3	73.0	72.9
Charlotte, Douglas................................	87.7	87.4	83.2	86.5	88.3	87.7	83.3	87.5
Washington, Reagan National.................	84.2	82.2	75.7	79.1	88.5	86.0	81.4	82.0
Denver International..............................	84.7	84.3	82.5	81.3	81.2	80.4	77.1	76.4
Dallas-Fort Worth International................	85.0	83.5	78.5	82.2	83.0	79.9	74.2	78.1
Detroit, Metro Wayne County.................	85.7	85.8	83.0	85.3	85.5	85.6	82.6	84.2
Newark International..............................	73.4	68.0	67.3	69.4	76.3	71.1	67.9	70.0
Fort Lauderdale-Hollywood International......	84.5	82.6	77.5	78.2	85.1	84.3	80.7	80.9
Washington/Dulles................................	82.3	79.8	74.0	80.8	81.5	78.6	72.6	78.5
Houston, George Bush..........................	79.2	80.1	76.3	84.5	76.6	77.7	73.2	81.3
New York, JFK International.....................	84.7	84.1	76.6	77.1	85.7	83.9	78.4	78.0
Las Vegas, McCarran International...........	87.3	86.1	82.6	81.9	85.0	82.0	77.8	79.0
Los Angeles International.......................	84.4	83.1	80.2	76.9	84.6	83.1	80.4	79.2
New York, La Guardia............................	82.3	78.4	74.1	72.6	88.4	84.6	79.7	77.8
Orlando International..............................	85.9	83.9	78.0	82.1	86.7	84.4	80.0	83.8
Chicago, Midway...................................	87.5	85.0	83.0	82.7	79.1	79.3	72.1	76.0
Miami International.................................	86.3	82.0	73.9	79.2	81.6	77.1	73.7	72.0
Minneapolis-St. Paul International.............	87.4	86.9	88.4	86.1	83.4	79.3	71.0	77.1
Chicago, O'Hare...................................	81.2	82.6	76.5	78.3	88.3	88.1	88.7	86.2
Portland International.............................	85.1	85.6	85.4	82.2	88.5	90.0	87.8	85.2
Philadelphia International........................	83.8	81.7	79.6	79.1	87.2	84.9	83.6	83.3
Phoenix, Sky Harbor International............	84.9	88.8	86.4	85.9	85.5	86.2	84.2	84.8
San Diego, Lindbergh Field....................	85.1	84.3	81.2	77.9	86.3	86.0	83.1	79.5
Seattle-Tacoma International...................	83.5	86.5	85.8	83.6	86.5	89.0	86.3	85.7
San Francisco International.....................	73.4	73.3	67.0	66.4	76.3	75.4	70.6	71.2
Salt Lake City International.....................	88.7	90.8	88.9	85.8	89.5	91.7	90.0	88.1
Tampa, Tampa International.....................	87.0	83.7	77.8	82.4	89.0	86.2	81.8	85.2

Source: Department of Transportation, Bureau of Transportation Statistics, "TranStats," <http://www.transtats.bts.gov/>, accessed August 2013.

Table 1102. Worldwide Airline Accidents and Fatalities by World Region: 2005 to 2011

[In thousands (27,278 represents 27,278,000)]

Year	Departures	Accidents	Accident rate [1]	Fatalities	Fatal accidents
2005...	27,278	119	4.4	824	23
2006...	27,482	112	4.1	806	15
2007...	28,911	122	4.2	645	15
2008...	28,859	138	4.8	524	17
2009...	27,870	113	4.1	670	13
2010...	29,023	121	4.2	707	19
2011...	**30,053**	**126**	**4.2**	**414**	**16**
Oceania...	855	4	4.7	55	2
North America.................................	10,979	38	3.5	–	–
Latin America and Caribbean..............	2,625	15	5.7	60	4
Europe...	7,143	39	5.5	60	4
Asia...	7,561	22	2.9	98	3
Africa...	891	7	7.9	141	3

– Represents zero. [1] Number of accidents per million departures of scheduled commercial operations that involve the transportation of passengers, cargo and mail for remuneration or hire.

Source: International Civil Aviation Organization, Montreal, Canada, "Integrated Safety Trend Analysis and Reporting System,"<http://www2.icao.int/en/ism/istars/pages2/homepage.aspx>, accessed September 2012 ©.

Table 1103. Airports, Aircraft, and Airmen: 1980 to 2011

[As of December 31 or for years ending December 31]

Item	1980	1990	1995	2000	2005	2009	2010	2011
Airports, total [1]	**15,161**	**17,490**	**18,224**	**19,281**	**19,854**	**19,750**	**19,802**	**19,782**
Public [1]	4,814	5,589	5,415	5,317	5,270	5,178	5,175	5,172
Percent—with lighted runways	66.2	71.4	74.3	75.9	76.8	(NA)	(NA)	(NA)
With paved runways	72.3	70.7	73.3	74.3	74.8	(NA)	(NA)	(NA)
Private	10,347	11,901	12,809	13,964	14,584	14,298	14,353	14,339
Percent—with lighted runways	15.2	7.0	6.4	7.2	9.2	(NA)	(NA)	(NA)
With paved runways	13.3	31.5	33.0	32.0	33.2	(NA)	(NA)	(NA)
Military	(NA)	(NA)	(NA)	(NA)	(NA)	274	274	271
Certificated [2]	730	680	667	651	575	559	551	547
Civil	(X)	(X)	572	563	(X)	(X)	(X)	(X)
Civil military	(X)	(X)	95	88	(X)	(X)	(X)	(X)
General aviation	14,431	16,810	17,557	18,630	19,279	19,191	19,251	19,235
Active air carrier fleet [3]	3,805	6,083	7,411	8,049	8,225	(NA)	(NA)	(NA)
Fixed wing	3,803	6,072	7,293	8,010	8,182	(NA)	(NA)	(NA)
Helicopter [4]	2	11	118	39	43	(NA)	(NA)	(NA)
General aviation fleet [5]	**211,043**	**198,000**	**188,089**	**217,533**	**224,352**	**223,877**	**223,370**	**(NA)**
Fixed-wing	200,094	184,500	162,342	183,276	185,373	177,446	176,272	(NA)
Turbojet	2,992	4,100	4,559	7,001	9,823	11,268	11,484	(NA)
Turboprop	4,089	5,300	4,995	5,762	7,942	9,055	9,369	(NA)
Piston	193,013	175,200	152,788	170,513	167,608	157,123	155,419	(NA)
Rotorcraft	6,001	6,900	5,830	7,150	8,728	9,984	10,102	(NA)
Other	4,945	6,600	4,741	6,700	6,454	5,480	5,684	(NA)
Gliders	(X)	(X)	2,182	2,041	2,074	1,808	1,899	(NA)
Lighter than air	(X)	(X)	2,559	4,660	4,380	3,672	3,785	(NA)
Experimental	(X)	(X)	15,176	20,407	23,627	24,419	24,784	(NA)
Airman certificates held:								
Pilot, total	**827,071**	**702,659**	**639,184**	**625,581**	**609,737**	**594,285**	**627,588**	**617,128**
Women	52,902	40,515	38,032	35,607	36,584	36,808	42,218	41,316
Student [6]	199,833	128,663	101,279	93,064	87,213	72,280	119,119	118,657
Recreational	(X)	87	232	340	278	234	212	227
Sport	(X)	(X)	(X)	(X)	134	3,248	3,682	4,066
Airplane:								
Private	357,479	299,111	261,399	251,561	228,619	211,619	202,020	194,441
Commercial	183,442	149,666	133,980	121,858	120,614	125,738	123,705	120,865
Air transport	69,569	107,732	123,877	141,596	141,992	144,600	142,198	142,511
Rotorcraft only [7]	6,030	9,567	7,183	7,775	9,518	15,298	15,377	15,220
Glider only	7,039	7,833	11,234	9,387	21,369	21,268	21,275	21,141
Flight instructor certificates	60,440	63,775	77,613	80,931	90,555	94,863	96,473	97,409
Instrument ratings	260,462	297,073	298,798	311,944	311,828	323,495	318,001	314,122
Nonpilot [8]	**368,356**	**492,237**	**651,341**	**547,453**	**644,016**	**682,315**	**686,717**	**695,515**
Mechanic	250,157	344,282	405,294	344,434	320,293	329,027	331,989	335,431
Repairmen	(X)	(X)	61,233	38,208	40,030	41,389	41,267	40,802
Parachute rigger	9,547	10,094	11,824	10,477	8,150	8,362	8,407	8,491
Ground instructor	61,550	66,882	96,165	72,326	74,378	75,461	75,205	74,586
Dispatcher	6,799	11,002	15,642	16,340	18,079	20,132	20,691	21,363
Flight navigator	1,936	1,290	916	570	298	181	174	146
Flight attendant	(X)	(X)	(X)	(X)	125,032	156,741	159,946	167,037
Flight engineer	38,367	58,687	60,267	65,098	57,756	51,022	49,038	47,659

NA Not available. X Not applicable. [1] Includes civil and joint-use civil-military airports, heliports, STOL (short takeoff and landing) ports, and seaplane bases in the United States and its territories. Sole-use military airports are included beginning in 2007. Airport-type definitions: Public--publicly owned and under control of a public agency; private--owned by a private individual or corporation. [2] Certificated airports serve air-carriers with aircraft seating more than 9 passengers. As of 2005, the Federal Aviation Administration (FAA) no longer certificates military airports. [3] Air-carrier aircraft are aircraft carrying passengers or cargo for hire under 14 CFR 121 (large aircraft—more than 30 seats) and 14 CFR 135 (small aircraft--30 seats or fewer). Beginning in 1990, the number of aircraft is the monthly average reported in use for the last three months of the year. Prior to 1990, it was the number of aircraft reported in use during December of a given year. [4] 2000 dip in helicopters due to estimating methods. [5] Beginning 1995 excludes commuters. [6] Beginning 2010, duration of validity for student pilot certificates for pilots under age 40 increased from 36 to 60 months. [7] Data for 1980 are for helicopters only. [8] All certificates on record. No medical examination required.

Source: U.S. Department of Transportation, Research and Innovative Technology Administration, Bureau of Transportation Statistics, *National Transportation Statistics, 2013*; see also <http://www.rita.dot.gov/bts/>. Airmen certificates held: U.S. Federal Aviation Administration, "U.S. Civil Airmen Statistics," <http://www.faa.gov/data_research/aviation_data_statistics/civil_airmen_statistics/>, accessed September 2013. Prior to 2000: *FAA Statistical Handbook of Aviation*, annual.

Table 1104. Commuter/Regional Airline Operations Summary: 2005 to 2011

[152.6 represents 152,600,000. Calendar year data. Commuter/regional airlines operate primarily aircraft of predominately 75 passengers or less and 18,000 pounds of payload capacity serving short haul and small community markets. Represents operations within all North America by U.S. Regional Carriers. Averages are means. For definition of mean, see Guide to Tabular Presentation]

Item	Unit	2005	2007	2009	2010	2011
Passenger carriers operating	Number	75	72	62	61	60
Passengers enplaned	Millions	152.6	159.0	159.5	163.5	160.7
Average passengers enplaned per carrier	1,000	2,034.0	2,208.5	2,572.6	2,680.3	2,678.3
Revenue passenger miles (RPM)	Billions	67.4	73.8	72.9	75.8	76.6
Average RPMs per carrier	Millions	898.8	1,024.7	1,176.0	1,243.0	1,276.6
Available seat miles	Billions	95.6	99.0	97.6	99.2	100.5
Average load factor	Percent	70.5	74.6	74.7	76.5	76.2
Departures completed	Millions	5.43	4.99	4.81	4.75	4.60
Airports served	Number	666	666	644	673	681
Average trip length	Miles	442	464	457	464	476
Average seating capacity (seats)	Number	50.0	52.4	55.0	56.0	56.0
Fleet flying hours	1,000	5,714.0	7,306.7	5,162.0	5,211.0	5,165.0

Source: Regional Airline Association, *2012 Annual Report* ©. See also <http://www.raa.org/>.

Table 1105. Freight Carried on Major U.S. Waterways: 1990 to 2011

[In millions of short tons (4.2 represents 4,200,000). One short ton equals 2,000 pounds]

Item	1990	1995	2000	2005	2008	2009	2010	2011
Atlantic Intracoastal Waterway.........	4.2	3.5	3.1	2.7	2.9	2.5	2.9	2.9
Great Lakes....................	167.1	177.8	187.5	169.4	152.4	108.7	129.5	134.7
Gulf Intracoastal Waterway............	115.4	118.0	113.8	116.1	115.9	108.1	116.2	112.6
Mississippi River system [1]............	659.1	707.2	715.5	678.0	681.6	622.1	663.2	672.5
Mississippi River main stem..........	475.3	520.3	515.6	464.6	486.8	447.7	483.2	499.0
Ohio River system [2]...................	260.0	267.6	274.4	280.1	259.2	229.5	245.2	239.6
Columbia River.....................	51.4	57.1	55.2	51.5	54.8	46.0	54.7	54.2
Snake River.........................	4.8	6.8	6.7	5.3	3.7	4.4	3.4	2.7

[1] Main channels and all tributaries of the Mississippi, Illinois, Missouri, and Ohio Rivers. [2] Main channels and all navigable tributaries and embayments of the Ohio, Tennessee, and Cumberland Rivers.

Source: U.S. Army Corps of Engineers, *Waterborne Commerce of the United States, 2011*, November 2012, and earlier reports. See also <http://www.navigationdatacenter.us/wcsc/wcsc.htm>.

Table 1106. Waterborne Commerce by Type of Commodity: 2000 to 2011

[In millions of short tons (2,424.6 represents 2,424,600,000). One short ton equals 2,000 pounds. Domestic trade includes all commercial movements between United States ports and on inland rivers, Great Lakes, canals, and connecting channels of the United States and its territories and possessions. Foreign commerce is waterborne import, export and in-transit traffic between the United States, Puerto Rico and the Virgin Islands and any foreign country; these statistics do not include traffic between any foreign country and the U.S. territories and possessions]

Commodity	2000	2005	2010	2011 Total	Domestic	Foreign imports	Foreign exports
Total...........................	2,424.6	2,527.6	2,334.4	2,367.5	887.9	869.1	610.4
Coal................................	297.0	316.6	309.6	325.6	213.3	13.4	99.0
Petroleum and petroleum products....................	1,044.0	1,111.4	1,018.8	1,003.8	303.7	551.9	148.1
Crude petroleum....................	571.4	602.7	508.5	472.5	59.4	412.8	0.3
Petroleum products [1]...................	472.4	508.8	510.4	531.3	244.2	139.2	147.8
Gasoline.........................	125.2	156.1	137.8	141.3	65.9	43.9	31.6
Distillate fuel oil...................	91.7	141.1	185.4	203.5	70.5	68.7	64.4
Residual fuel oil..................	131.6	96.1	81.1	75.2	64.1	4.6	6.5
Chemicals and related products........	172.4	174.9	180.1	186.4	73.5	48.2	64.7
Fertilizers.........................	35.1	34.5	35.8	39.2	15.4	13.1	10.7
Other chemicals and related products...........	137.3	140.4	144.3	147.2	58.0	35.2	54.0
Crude material, inedible..............	380.3	386.0	307.0	331.9	169.3	82.5	80.1
Forest products, wood and chips....................	33.1	29.4	20.8	25.0	5.3	4.4	15.2
Pulp and waste paper...............	13.6	18.7	21.4	22.6	0.1	2.1	20.5
Soil, sand, gravel, rock, and stone [1].........	165.0	177.9	120.3	121.7	90.2	28.1	3.4
Limestone......................	67.4	73.5	61.3	59.7	44.3	13.0	2.4
Phosphate rock..................	3.4	6.0	4.6	5.4	2.3	3.1	–
Sand & gravel..................	79.0	80.2	46.3	48.9	41.0	7.1	0.8
Iron ore and scrap.................	97.9	85.7	82.0	94.8	54.7	8.3	31.8
Marine shells......................	0.3	–	0.1	0.1	–	–	–
Nonferrous ores and scrap..........	29.2	29.2	23.9	26.9	6.1	16.6	4.2
Sulphur, clay, and salt.............	11.3	8.7	6.3	6.3	0.6	1.6	4.1
Slag.............................	4.0	6.0	4.3	5.1	1.9	2.9	0.3
Other nonmetal minerals.............	25.9	30.4	27.8	29.4	10.3	18.5	0.6
Primary manufactured goods........	153.0	166.4	103.7	111.1	28.8	59.8	22.5
Papers products..................	12.1	13.7	13.7	13.8	0.2	5.1	8.5
Lime, cement, and glass............	55.9	62.4	27.6	27.4	13.9	11.9	1.7
Primary iron and steel products............	57.1	52.1	33.5	42.7	12.4	27.2	3.1
Primary nonferrous metal products............	25.5	33.5	26.7	25.1	2.2	14.0	8.9
Primary wood products.............	2.5	4.8	2.2	2.2	0.1	1.7	0.5
Food and farm products...............	283.3	251.3	300.1	283.0	77.7	39.5	165.8
Fish..............................	2.4	3.0	3.1	3.3	0.2	1.9	1.2
Grain [1]............................	145.2	124.0	131.8	124.7	42.4	1.4	80.8
Wheat..........................	43.4	36.4	38.4	45.1	10.2	0.5	34.4
Corn...........................	88.2	75.2	81.8	70.3	29.6	0.1	40.6
Oilseeds [1]........................	57.6	47.2	76.9	62.8	22.8	0.4	39.7
Soybeans.....................	47.3	40.8	67.4	55.0	20.1	0.1	34.7
Vegetables products..............	8.9	8.3	12.9	13.8	1.3	5.5	7.0
Processed grain and animal feed....................	23.1	18.4	20.6	22.4	5.8	1.1	15.5
Other agricultural products.........	46.1	50.5	54.9	56.0	5.2	29.1	21.7
All manufactured equip, machinery and products.....	83.6	110.3	104.1	115.2	20.2	69.7	25.4
Waste and scrap, n.e.c. [2]............	4.3	2.0	1.3	1.5	1.5	–	–
Unknown or n.e.c. [2]....................	6.8	8.7	9.6	9.0	0.1	4.1	4.7

– Represents or rounds to zero. [1] Includes commodities not shown separately. [2] Not elsewhere classified.

Source: U.S. Army Corps of Engineers, *Waterborne Commerce of the United States, 2011*, November 2012, and earlier editions. See also <http://www.navigationdatacenter.us/wcsc/wcsc.htm>.

Table 1107. Top 30 U.S. Ports by Tons of Traffic: 2011

[In thousands of short tons (44,866 represents 44,866,000), except rank. One short ton equals 2,000 lbs. For calendar year. For the top 30 ports. Represents tons of cargo shipped from or received by the specified port. Excludes cargo carried on general ferries; coal and petroleum products loaded from shore facilities directly onto bunkers of vessels for fuel; and amounts of less than 100 tons of government-owned equipment in support of Corps of Engineers projects]

Port name	Rank	Total	Foreign Total	Foreign Inbound	Foreign Outbound	Domestic
Baltimore, MD.	16	44,866	36,765	13,223	23,543	8,100
Baton Rouge, LA.	10	57,872	22,051	15,066	6,985	35,821
Beaumont, TX.	6	73,672	47,831	38,854	8,976	25,841
Corpus Christi, TX.	7	70,538	52,934	36,354	16,579	17,604
Duluth-Superior, MN and WI.	20	35,081	7,096	604	6,492	27,985
Houston, TX.	2	237,799	167,077	88,889	78,188	70,721
Huntington - Tristate [1]	9	58,551	–	–	–	58,551
Lake Charles, LA.	13	54,247	32,911	25,800	7,110	21,336
Long Beach, CA.	4	80,276	67,050	42,696	24,354	13,227
Los Angeles, CA.	8	64,992	58,112	34,435	23,677	6,880
Mobile, AL.	12	55,552	29,646	14,710	14,937	25,906
New Orleans, LA.	5	77,175	38,234	18,486	19,748	38,941
New York, NY and NJ.	3	139,173	89,494	65,407	24,087	49,679
Newport News, VA.	28	25,201	21,777	287	21,490	3,424
Norfolk Harbor, VA.	15	47,353	40,862	9,386	31,476	6,491
Pascagoula, MS.	17	36,863	28,043	20,804	7,239	8,820
Philadelphia, PA.	23	30,632	19,621	18,867	754	11,011
Pittsburgh, PA.	21	33,819	–	–	–	33,819
Plaquemines, LA, Port of.	14	54,093	20,211	2,555	17,655	33,882
Port Arthur, TX.	24	30,275	20,070	11,937	8,133	10,205
Portland, OR.	27	25,479	17,468	3,092	14,376	8,011
Richmond, CA.	29	24,256	13,781	11,403	2,379	10,475
Savannah, GA.	19	35,459	33,108	16,720	16,388	2,352
Seattle, WA.	26	26,610	21,738	8,524	13,213	4,873
South Louisiana, LA, Port of.	1	246,509	120,845	39,711	81,134	125,664
St. Louis, MO and IL.	18	36,487	–	–	–	36,487
Tacoma, WA.	30	24,151	18,121	5,335	12,786	6,030
Tampa, FL.	22	31,408	10,452	4,851	5,601	20,956
Texas City, TX.	11	57,758	38,891	30,510	8,380	18,867
Valdez, AK.	25	29,838	–	–	–	29,838

– Represents or rounds to zero. [1] The Port of Huntington is the largest inland shipping port in the United States. Port operations occur in Ashland, KY; Ironton, OH; and Huntington, WV.

Source: U.S. Army Corps of Engineers, *Waterborne Commerce of the United States*, 2011, November 2012. See also <http://www.navigationdatacenter.us/wcsc/wcsc.htm>.

Table 1108. Top 30 U.S. Ports/Waterways Ranked by Container Traffic: 2011

[In thousands of twenty-foot equivalent units (TEUs) (32,745.6 represents 32,745,600). For calendar year. For the 30 leading ports/waterways in total TEUs. A TEU is a measure of containerized cargo capacity equal to one standard 20-foot length by 8-foot width by 8-foot, 6 inch height container]

Port/waterway name	Rank	Total loaded	Domestic loaded Total [1]	Domestic loaded Inbound	Domestic loaded Outbound	Foreign loaded Total	Foreign loaded Inbound
Total U.S. [2]	(X)	32,745.6	4,791.9	1,995.9	1,995.9	28,753.7	17,083.1
Anchorage, AK.	18	266.6	275.3	218.1	48.5	–	–
Apra Harbor, GU.	30	62.0	70.3	54.8	7.2	–	–
Baltimore, MD.	16	505.6	55.3	20.8	22.2	462.6	301.9
Boston, MA.	24	143.0	–	–	–	143.0	96.7
Camden-Gloucester, NJ.	28	85.6	53.6	16.9	36.7	32.0	27.3
Charleston, SC.	10	1,122.4	–	–	–	1,122.4	600.3
Chester, SC.	27	87.5	–	–	–	87.5	53.7
Gulfport, MS.	21	182.4	–	–	–	182.4	107.3
Honolulu, HI.	13	746.0	957.6	464.1	252.0	29.9	17.6
Houston, TX.	8	1,430.9	28.4	16.8	2.3	1,411.8	569.6
Jacksonville, FL.	12	771.2	499.2	108.7	386.5	276.1	119.1
Kahului, Maui, HI.	29	75.6	114.5	59.1	16.5	–	–
Long Beach, CA.	2	4,687.7	341.0	44.7	254.3	4,388.7	3,060.4
Los Angeles, CA.	1	5,901.9	–	–	–	5,901.9	4,015.4
Miami, FL.	14	701.8	–	–	–	701.8	346.6
Mobile, AL.	25	108.6	–	–	–	108.6	57.3
New Orleans, LA.	17	306.7	–	–	–	306.7	91.2
New York (NY and NJ).	3	4,431.1	217.4	84.6	115.1	4,231.4	2,717.2
Norfolk Harbor, VA.	7	1,527.4	71.6	32.1	23.0	1,472.3	727.5
Oakland, CA.	5	1,694.0	221.1	23.2	139.0	1,531.8	743.6
Palm Beach, FL.	26	91.0	–	–	–	91.0	28.8
Philadelphia, PA.	20	184.4	18.2	1.3	13.4	169.7	125.8
Port Everglades, FL.	15	608.4	16.5	4.8	11.1	592.4	257.5
Portland, OR.	23	156.8	9.2	5.1	-	151.8	72.1
San Juan, PR.	11	806.1	635.3	480.2	148.5	177.4	144.5
Savannah, GA.	4	2,269.2	–	–	–	2,269.2	1,077.5
Seattle, WA.	6	1,573.6	313.1	50.1	153.1	1,370.3	772.5
Tacoma, WA.	9	1,156.0	269.3	52.3	216.7	887.0	535.1
Wilmington, NC.	19	222.2	–	–	–	222.2	118.2
Wilmington, DE.	22	157.4	–	–	–	157.4	137.0

– Represents zero. X Not applicable. [1] Includes empty TEUs. [2] Includes other ports/waterways not shown separately.

Source: U.S. Army Corps of Engineers, Navigation Data Center, "U.S. Waterborne Container Traffic by Port/Waterway in 2011," <http://www.navigationdatacenter.us/wcsc/>, accessed September 2013.

Table 1109. Highway Mileage—Urban and Rural by Ownership: 1990 to 2011

[In thousands (3,880 represents 3,880,000). As of December 31. Includes Puerto Rico beginning 2000]

Type and Control of Roadways	1990	1995	2000	2006	2007	2008	2009	2010	2011
Total mileage [1]...............	**3,880**	**3,912**	**3,951**	**4,033**	**4,049**	**4,059**	**4,063**	**4,084**	**4,094**
Urban mileage [2]...................	757	819	859	1,043	1,058	1,079	1,086	1,103	1,108
Under state control.............	96	112	112	148	149	152	152	(NA)	153
Under local control [1].........	661	706	746	890	904	920	926	(NA)	945
Rural mileage......................	3,123	3,093	3,092	2,990	2,991	2,980	2,977	2,980	2,985
Under state control.............	703	691	664	636	635	633	632	(NA)	631
Under local control [1].........	2,242	2,231	2,311	2,231	2,230	2,223	2,221	(NA)	2,227
Under federal control [2].......	178	170	117	123	126	124	124	(NA)	127

[1] Includes state park, state toll, other state agency, other local agency and other roadways not identified by ownership. [2] Includes roadways in federal parks, forest, and reservations that are not part of the state and local highway system.

Source: U.S. Federal Highway Administration, "Highway Statistics 2011," and earlier reports, <http://www.fhwa.dot.gov/policyinformation/statistics.cfm>, accessed July 2013.

Table 1110. Highway Mileage by State—Functional Systems and Urban/Rural: 2011

[As of December 31. Excludes Puerto Rico. For definition of functional systems, see text, this section]

State	Total	Functional systems					Urban	Rural
		Interstate	Other freeways and expressways	Arterial	Collector	Local		
U.S................	**4,077,756**	**46,960**	**15,719**	**399,204**	**800,948**	**2,814,925**	**1,095,373**	**2,982,383**
AL...................	101,668	906	130	9,297	22,171	69,164	25,252	76,416
AK...................	16,675	1,084	–	1,575	3,282	10,733	2,688	13,987
AZ...................	65,092	1,168	204	5,818	8,097	49,804	23,498	41,594
AR...................	100,082	656	221	7,075	20,963	71,168	13,013	87,069
CA...................	172,202	2,453	1,539	27,509	32,299	108,402	90,324	81,877
CO...................	88,415	953	353	8,880	16,259	61,971	19,531	68,883
CT...................	21,445	346	279	2,725	3,207	14,888	15,193	6,252
DE...................	6,358	41	30	645	1,044	4,598	2,997	3,361
DC...................	1,501	13	17	268	156	1,046	1,501	–
FL...................	121,759	1,495	747	12,809	14,523	92,185	81,471	40,288
GA...................	123,546	1,248	147	14,136	23,072	84,943	39,998	83,548
HI...................	4,405	55	34	756	828	2,733	2,355	2,050
ID...................	48,553	612	–	4,242	10,505	33,194	5,553	43,000
IL...................	139,498	2,182	99	14,677	21,927	100,614	41,273	98,226
IN...................	97,066	1,172	170	8,523	22,447	64,754	26,895	70,171
IA...................	114,387	782	–	9,745	31,619	72,241	11,401	102,986
KS...................	140,513	874	187	9,520	33,591	96,341	12,980	127,532
KY...................	79,220	801	654	5,495	16,551	55,720	12,632	66,588
LA...................	61,635	898	52	5,607	9,983	45,096	17,169	44,466
ME...................	22,874	369	19	2,180	5,930	14,377	3,007	19,867
MD...................	32,321	481	306	3,806	5,078	22,650	17,998	14,323
MA...................	36,303	574	345	6,129	4,837	24,417	28,315	7,988
MI...................	122,086	1,244	705	14,301	24,483	81,351	35,490	86,596
MN...................	138,702	914	166	13,434	30,453	93,735	20,817	117,885
MS...................	75,119	702	71	7,546	15,559	51,240	11,011	64,107
MO...................	131,667	1,206	1,432	9,226	25,308	94,495	23,839	107,827
MT...................	74,880	1,192	–	6,038	16,193	51,457	3,182	71,698
NE...................	93,600	482	442	7,697	20,780	64,199	6,430	87,170
NV...................	36,839	571	69	3,448	5,569	27,182	8,217	28,622
NH...................	16,076	225	74	1,516	2,742	11,520	4,929	11,147
NJ...................	39,213	431	404	5,755	4,143	28,480	31,917	7,296
NM...................	68,384	1,000	–	5,142	8,556	53,686	7,904	60,480
NY...................	114,592	1,704	941	13,657	20,765	77,526	48,435	66,157
NC...................	105,869	1,174	476	9,595	17,343	77,282	35,673	70,197
ND...................	86,851	571	–	5,937	11,901	68,442	1,919	84,932
OH...................	123,247	1,574	484	10,969	22,652	87,569	45,038	78,209
OK...................	112,808	933	188	8,232	25,309	78,146	16,135	96,673
OR...................	59,148	730	57	7,053	17,699	33,610	12,911	46,237
PA...................	119,771	1,855	853	12,913	19,845	84,305	46,151	73,620
RI...................	6,485	71	88	831	887	4,609	5,260	1,225
SC...................	65,997	851	82	7,150	15,086	42,829	16,374	49,623
SD...................	82,459	679	11	6,401	19,010	56,359	2,968	79,492
TN...................	95,492	1,104	155	9,117	17,982	67,134	25,517	69,975
TX...................	312,911	3,237	1,512	31,758	65,137	211,266	99,185	213,725
UT...................	45,635	937	20	3,734	8,190	32,754	11,172	34,463
VT...................	14,290	320	18	1,303	3,110	9,539	1,465	12,824
VA...................	74,461	1,119	261	8,491	14,399	50,190	24,070	50,391
WA...................	83,743	764	1,103	7,203	17,315	57,357	23,683	60,059
WV...................	38,646	555	10	3,502	8,602	25,977	5,371	33,275
WI...................	115,018	742	562	12,181	23,405	78,127	22,481	92,537
WY...................	28,253	914	3	3,660	10,156	13,520	2,785	25,468

– Represents zero.

Source: U.S. Federal Highway Administration, "Highway Statistics 2011," and earlier reports, <http://www.fhwa.dot.gov/policyinformation/statistics.cfm>, accessed July 2013.

Table 1111. Bridge Inventory—Total Deficient and Obsolete: 2000 to 2012, and by State, 2012

[Based on the National Bridge Inventory program; for details, see source]

| State and year | Number of bridges | Deficient and obsolete | | | | | |
| | | Total number | Percent | Structurally deficient [1] | | Functionally obsolete [2] | |
				Number	Percent	Number	Percent
2000........................	587,458	167,581	28.5	86,692	14.8	80,889	13.8
2001........................	590,066	165,099	28.0	83,630	14.2	81,469	13.8
2002........................	591,220	163,010	27.6	81,437	13.8	81,573	13.8
2003........................	592,246	160,819	27.2	79,811	13.5	81,008	13.7
2004........................	593,885	158,318	26.7	77,758	13.1	80,560	13.6
2005........................	594,616	156,177	26.3	75,871	12.8	80,306	13.5
2006........................	596,842	153,990	25.8	73,764	12.4	80,226	13.4
2007........................	599,766	152,316	25.4	72,524	12.1	79,792	13.3
2008........................	601,411	151,391	25.2	71,469	11.9	79,922	13.3
2009........................	603,245	149,647	24.8	71,179	11.8	78,468	13.0
2010........................	604,474	146,633	24.3	69,223	11.5	77,410	12.8
2011........................	605,086	143,889	23.8	67,526	11.2	76,363	12.6
U.S. Total, 2012........	**607,380**	**151,497**	**24.9**	**66,749**	**11.0**	**84,748**	**14.0**
Alabama.....................	16,070	3,653	22.7	1,448	9.0	2,205	13.7
Alaska......................	1,173	275	23.4	128	10.9	147	12.5
Arizona.....................	7,835	968	12.4	247	3.2	721	9.2
Arkansas....................	12,696	2,929	23.1	898	7.1	2,031	16.0
California..................	24,812	7,156	28.8	2,978	12.0	4,178	16.8
Colorado....................	8,591	1,473	17.1	566	6.6	907	10.6
Connecticut.................	4,208	1,476	35.1	406	9.6	1,070	25.4
Delaware....................	862	175	20.3	53	6.1	122	14.2
District of Columbia........	239	185	77.4	30	12.6	155	64.9
Florida.....................	11,982	2,026	16.9	262	2.2	1,764	14.7
Georgia.....................	14,739	2,749	18.7	878	6.0	1,871	12.7
Hawaii......................	1,131	505	44.7	146	12.9	359	31.7
Idaho.......................	4,214	837	19.9	397	9.4	440	10.4
Illinois....................	26,514	4,287	16.2	2,311	8.7	1,976	7.5
Indiana.....................	18,789	4,224	22.5	2,036	10.8	2,188	11.6
Iowa........................	24,496	6,475	26.4	5,193	21.2	1,282	5.2
Kansas......................	25,176	4,617	18.3	2,658	10.6	1,959	7.8
Kentucky....................	14,031	4,463	31.8	1,244	8.9	3,219	22.9
Louisiana...................	13,175	3,815	29.0	1,783	13.5	2,032	15.4
Maine.......................	2,408	792	32.9	356	14.8	436	18.1
Maryland....................	5,294	1,467	27.7	368	7.0	1,099	20.8
Massachusetts...............	5,120	2,707	52.9	493	9.6	2,214	43.2
Michigan....................	11,000	3,026	27.5	1,354	12.3	1,672	15.2
Minnesota...................	13,121	1,613	12.3	1,190	9.1	423	3.2
Mississippi.................	17,061	3,774	22.1	2,417	14.2	1,357	8.0
Missouri....................	24,334	6,893	28.3	3,528	14.5	3,365	13.8
Montana.....................	5,120	908	17.7	399	7.8	509	9.9
Nebraska....................	15,393	3,837	24.9	2,779	18.1	1,058	6.9
Nevada......................	1,798	256	14.2	40	2.2	216	12.0
New Hampshire...............	2,429	807	33.2	362	14.9	445	18.3
New Jersey..................	6,554	2,368	36.1	651	9.9	1,717	26.2
New Mexico..................	3,924	657	16.7	307	7.8	350	8.9
New York....................	17,420	6,887	39.5	2,169	12.5	4,718	27.1
North Carolina.............	18,165	5,488	30.2	2,192	12.1	3,296	18.1
North Dakota................	4,453	993	22.3	746	16.8	247	5.5
Ohio........................	27,045	6,773	25.0	2,462	9.1	4,311	15.9
Oklahoma....................	23,781	6,986	29.4	5,382	22.6	1,604	6.7
Oregon......................	7,633	1,774	23.2	433	5.7	1,341	17.6
Pennsylvania................	22,669	9,910	43.7	5,540	24.4	4,370	19.3
Rhode Island................	757	411	54.3	156	20.6	255	33.7
South Carolina.............	9,271	1,981	21.4	1,141	12.3	840	9.1
South Dakota................	5,870	1,445	24.6	1,208	20.6	237	4.0
Tennessee...................	19,985	3,864	19.3	1,195	6.0	2,669	13.4
Texas.......................	52,260	10,052	19.2	1,372	2.6	8,680	16.6
Utah........................	2,947	469	15.9	126	4.3	343	11.6
Vermont.....................	2,727	931	34.1	288	10.6	643	23.6
Virginia....................	13,769	3,671	26.7	1,250	9.1	2,421	17.6
Washington..................	7,840	2,059	26.3	366	4.7	1,693	21.6
West Virginia...............	7,093	2,547	35.9	952	13.4	1,595	22.5
Wisconsin...................	14,057	1,936	13.8	1,157	8.2	779	5.5
Wyoming.....................	3,101	713	23.0	426	13.7	287	9.3
Puerto Rico.................	2,248	1,214	54.0	282	12.5	932	41.5

[1] Bridges are structurally deficient if they have been restricted to light vehicles, require immediate rehabilitation to remain open, or are closed. [2] Bridges are functionally obsolete if they have deck geometry, load carrying capacity, clearance or approach roadway alignment that no longer meet the criteria for the system of which the bridge is carrying a part.

Source: Federal Highway Administration, Office of Bridge Technology, "Deficient Bridges by State and Highway System 2012," December 2012, <http://www.fhwa.dot.gov/bridge/nbi.htm>.

Table 1112. Funding for Highways and Disposition of Highway–User Revenue: 1990 to 2011

[In millions of dollars (75,444 represents $75,444,000,000). Data compiled from reports of state and local authorities]

Type	1990	1995	2000	2006	2007	2008	2009	2010	2011
Total receipts.........................	**75,444**	**96,269**	**131,115**	**165,443**	**193,876**	**192,718**	**195,680**	**220,977**	**204,939**
Current income............................	69,880	87,620	119,815	147,615	168,219	172,785	169,453	187,960	177,861
Highway-user revenues.................	44,346	59,331	81,335	93,648	98,210	94,152	93,563	93,830	95,138
Other taxes and fees....................	19,827	21,732	31,137	44,455	54,189	61,163	61,562	80,220	66,968
Investment income, other receipts.....	5,707	6,557	7,342	9,512	15,820	17,471	14,328	13,910	15,754
Bond issue proceeds [1]...................	5,564	8,649	11,301	17,828	25,657	19,933	26,227	33,017	27,078
Funds drawn from or placed in reserves [2]................................	-36	-2,791	-8,418	-4,382	-12,815	-10,660	-102	-15,664	1,501
Total funds available.....................	75,408	93,478	122,697	161,061	181,061	182,058	195,578	205,313	206,440
Total disbursements..................	**75,408**	**93,478**	**122,697**	**161,061**	**181,061**	**182,058**	**195,578**	**205,313**	**206,440**
Current disbursements....................	72,457	88,994	117,592	153,413	173,095	173,869	185,843	193,034	192,727
Capital outlay.............................	35,151	44,228	61,323	78,676	90,911	91,144	94,525	100,175	101,612
Maintenance and traffic services......	20,365	24,319	30,636	40,426	44,715	44,972	49,432	48,773	46,311
Administration and research...........	6,501	8,419	10,020	13,189	14,428	14,711	15,599	16,165	16,590
Highway law enforcement and safety....................................	7,235	8,218	11,031	14,482	14,723	14,565	17,421	18,080	17,374
Interest on debt..........................	3,205	3,810	4,583	6,639	8,318	8,477	8,867	9,842	10,840
Bond retirement [1]........................	2,951	4,484	5,105	7,648	7,966	8,189	9,734	12,279	13,713

[1] Proceeds and redemptions of short-term notes and refunding issues are excluded. [2] Negative numbers indicate that funds were placed in reserves.

Source: U.S. Federal Highway Administration, "Highway Statistics 2011," and earlier reports, <http://www.fhwa.dot.gov/policyinformation/statistics.cfm>, accessed July 2013.

Table 1113. Federal Aid to State and Local Governments for Highway Trust Fund by State: 2010

[30,117 represents $30,117,000,000. Year ending Sept. 30]

State	Total (mil. dol.)	Per capita (dol.) [1]	State	Total (mil. dol.)	Per capita (dol.) [1]	State	Total (mil. dol.)	Per capita (dol.) [1]	State	Total (mil. dol.)	Per capita (dol.) [1]
U.S. [2].....	**30,117**	**97**	ID........	286	182	MO......	939	157	PA.......	1,235	97
AL.........	675	141	IL........	859	67	MT......	342	345	RI........	175	166
AK.........	352	492	IN........	722	111	NE......	131	71	SC......	456	98
AZ.........	512	80	IA........	349	114	NV......	290	107	SD......	214	262
AR.........	341	117	KS.......	398	139	NH......	161	123	TN......	660	104
CA.........	1,881	50	KY.......	497	114	NJ......	622	71	TX......	1,611	64
CO.........	416	83	LA.......	604	133	NM......	305	148	UT......	248	89
CT.........	584	163	ME......	151	114	NY......	1,632	84	VT......	163	261
DE.........	1,547	1,719	MD......	418	72	NC......	376	39	VA......	854	106
DC.........	154	255	MA......	623	95	ND......	192	284	WA......	479	71
FL.........	1,269	67	MI.......	809	82	OH......	968	84	WV......	396	213
GA.........	1,135	117	MN......	511	96	OK......	653	174	WI......	660	116
HI.........	138	102	MS......	377	127	OR......	513	134	WY......	239	423

[1] Based on estimated population as of July 1. [2] For the 50 states and the District of Columbia.

Source: U.S. Census Bureau, *Federal Aid to States for Fiscal Year 2010*, September 2011. See also <http://www.census.gov/govs/www/tools.html>.

Table 1114. State Motor Fuel Tax and Related Receipts, 2010 and 2011, and Gasoline Tax Rates, 2011

[648 represents $648,000,000. Federal tax rate is 18.4 cents a gallon. This table includes revenues from State taxes on all motor-vehicle fuels and related receipts due to motor-fuel taxation and administration. In many States, however, the tax on special fuels (fuels other than gasoline and gasohol) is applicable only to the amount used on the highways. For the States that apply the tax to all fuel sold, the revenue and refunds covering the nonhighway portion of these special fuels have been excluded]

State	Net receipts (mil. dol.) 2010	Net receipts (mil. dol.) 2011	Tax rate, [1] 2011	State	Net receipts (mil. dol.) 2010	Net receipts (mil. dol.) 2011	Tax rate, [1] 2011	State	Net receipts (mil. dol.) 2010	Net receipts (mil. dol.) 2011	Tax rate, [1] 2011
AL.........	648	650	18.00	KY.......	655	731	26.40	ND......	146	169	23.00
AK.........	25	30	8.00	LA.......	593	613	20.00	OH......	1,771	1,800	28.00
AZ.........	629	637	18.00	ME......	247	244	29.50	OK......	431	440	17.00
AR.........	482	444	21.50	MD......	721	674	23.50	OR......	610	432	30.00
CA.........	3,014	5,252	18.00	MA......	654	660	21.00	PA.......	3,341	2,100	31.20
CO.........	557	556	22.00	MI.......	945	941	19.00	RI.......	139	138	32.00
CT.........	632	629	25.00	MN......	831	842	28.00	SC......	509	515	16.00
DE.........	113	114	23.00	MS......	378	400	18.40	SD......	134	130	22.00
DC.........	21	30	23.50	MO......	684	686	17.00	TN......	825	845	20.00
FL.........	2,184	2,187	16.20	MT......	187	192	27.75	TX.......	3,061	3,085	20.00
GA.........	474	456	7.50	NE......	319	333	26.30	UT.......	338	355	24.50
HI.........	78	87	17.00	NV......	457	459	24.00	VT.......	96	99	20.00
ID.........	227	223	25.00	NH......	144	146	19.63	VA......	871	902	17.50
IL.........	1,248	1,248	19.00	NJ.......	556	556	10.50	WA......	1,180	1,194	37.50
IN.........	817	837	18.00	NM......	270	275	18.88	WV......	349	355	32.20
IA.........	429	437	21.00	NY.......	1,589	1,611	25.05	WI......	952	968	30.90
KS.........	436	425	24.00	NC......	1,541	1,652	35.25	WY......	94	96	14.00

[1] State gasoline tax rates in cents per gallon. In effect December 31.

Source: U.S. Federal Highway Administration, "Highway Statistics 2011," and earlier reports, <http://www.fhwa.dot.gov/policyinformation/statistics.cfm>, accessed July 2013.

Table 1115. Public Obligations for Highways—Changes in Indebtedness During the Year: 1995 to 2011

[In millions of dollars (37,449 represents $37,449,000,000). Table summarizes state indebtedness from all state bond issues, including the toll facility issues and the state issues for local roads. This table is compiled from reports of state authorities. Table also summarizes the change in status of the highway obligations of local governments including toll authorities]

Item	1995	2000	2005	2007	2008	2009	2010	2011
STATE GOVERNMENT								
Obligations outstanding, beginning of year.........	37,449	56,264	82,476	89,899	102,039	111,600	138,798	157,728
Obligations issued..................................	4,718	9,067	19,784	20,924	20,769	22,372	26,895	23,240
Obligations retired.................................	2,940	3,897	14,072	7,108	12,183	8,326	11,143	12,617
Obligations outstanding, end of year..............	39,228	61,434	88,187	103,715	110,625	125,646	154,550	168,351
LOCAL GOVERNMENT [1,2]								
Obligations outstanding, beginning of year.........	26,393	34,904	44,406	50,092	52,478	55,514	65,679	(NA)
Bonds outstanding, beginning of year.............	25,613	34,229	43,403	48,854	51,103	53,894	63,891	(NA)
Bonds outstanding, end of year...................	29,505	34,949	46,168	51,049	53,895	56,334	67,707	(NA)
Obligations outstanding, end of year..............	30,295	35,557	47,170	52,336	55,414	58,123	69,794	(NA)

NA Not available. [1] Short-term notes data not shown. The data are included in beginning and ending year obligations. [2] The number of local government data estimated varied year to year.

Source: U.S. Federal Highway Administration, "Highway Statistics 2011," and earlier reports, <http://www.fhwa.dot.gov/policyinformation/statistics.cfm>, accessed July 2013.

Table 1116. State Disbursements for Highways by State: 1995 to 2011

[In millions of dollars (67,615 represents $67,615,000,000). Comprise disbursements from current revenues or loans for construction, maintenance, interest and principal payments on highway bonds, transfers to local units, and miscellaneous. Includes transactions by state toll authorities. Data exclude amounts allocated for collection expenses and nonhighway purposes, and mass transit]

State	1995	2000	2006	2007	2008	2009	2010	2011
United States.................	67,615	89,832	117,048	130,306	139,584	143,767	145,944	149,959
Alabama......................	1,002	1,246	1,684	1,752	1,916	1,969	1,781	1,840
Alaska........................	438	501	654	710	730	935	756	806
Arizona.......................	1,199	2,040	2,662	2,335	2,806	2,988	2,663	2,723
Arkansas......................	666	817	1,134	1,036	1,051	1,072	1,376	1,341
California.....................	5,966	6,750	10,571	13,288	14,697	21,808	19,961	16,585
Colorado......................	922	1,392	1,490	1,601	1,695	1,906	2,249	2,577
Connecticut...................	1,153	1,304	1,223	1,265	1,370	2,175	1,761	1,733
Delaware......................	441	595	804	676	683	711	1,353	1,191
District of Columbia...........	140	244	287	334	335	469	582	413
Florida........................	3,421	4,208	7,725	8,069	8,698	7,194	7,867	6,966
Georgia.......................	1,437	1,567	2,655	2,878	3,817	3,506	2,926	3,123
Hawaii........................	360	272	323	352	444	504	460	414
Idaho.........................	350	492	622	758	802	890	959	877
Illinois........................	3,006	3,447	4,974	5,424	6,299	5,385	5,385	4,928
Indiana.......................	1,433	1,932	2,416	3,251	3,280	3,280	2,839	3,023
Iowa..........................	1,078	1,494	1,515	1,564	1,505	1,721	1,888	1,698
Kansas........................	1,019	1,206	1,521	1,414	1,487	1,464	1,571	1,478
Kentucky......................	1,397	1,651	1,635	2,194	2,404	2,522	2,528	2,073
Louisiana.....................	1,198	1,301	1,866	1,923	2,488	3,480	2,457	2,283
Maine.........................	379	488	628	584	739	652	684	705
Maryland......................	1,289	1,599	2,304	2,689	2,747	2,800	2,255	2,519
Massachusetts.................	2,501	3,524	2,723	2,815	2,898	2,810	2,923	2,923
Michigan......................	1,974	2,748	3,263	3,240	3,269	3,178	3,484	3,015
Minnesota.....................	1,210	1,692	2,143	2,168	2,352	2,365	2,625	3,336
Mississippi....................	662	1,039	1,272	1,647	1,346	1,301	1,345	1,262
Missouri......................	1,313	1,818	2,430	3,955	2,545	2,846	2,814	3,007
Montana......................	388	474	696	622	651	708	778	754
Nebraska.....................	578	745	882	1,436	1,352	1,398	1,409	1,443
Nevada.......................	484	651	1,144	1,063	906	1,221	1,007	968
New Hampshire................	328	387	524	693	681	641	793	793
New Jersey....................	2,102	4,503	5,561	4,018	3,921	4,222	5,201	6,453
New Mexico...................	535	1,162	942	942	860	1,272	1,163	1,632
New York.....................	4,584	5,307	5,659	7,459	7,537	6,977	7,711	8,516
North Carolina................	1,871	2,621	3,330	3,385	3,584	3,659	3,646	4,312
North Dakota..................	270	385	506	441	471	478	559	618
Ohio..........................	2,637	3,351	4,251	4,418	4,631	4,852	4,520	4,754
Oklahoma.....................	828	1,417	2,001	1,282	1,634	1,765	2,040	3,383
Oregon.......................	888	1,010	1,254	1,736	1,364	1,395	1,522	1,382
Pennsylvania..................	3,153	4,517	5,537	5,999	5,956	6,979	8,835	9,220
Rhode Island..................	290	256	488	494	419	389	540	480
South Carolina................	668	970	1,476	1,472	1,470	1,353	1,899	1,609
South Dakota..................	286	466	491	402	451	500	532	547
Tennessee....................	1,230	1,440	1,658	1,657	1,771	1,936	2,076	2,094
Texas.........................	3,593	5,665	9,101	13,136	15,948	9,883	9,365	11,693
Utah..........................	431	1,072	1,128	1,335	1,229	1,855	2,303	2,248
Vermont......................	194	287	335	368	395	400	436	556
Virginia.......................	2,107	2,678	3,195	3,228	3,875	3,572	3,334	3,882
Washington...................	1,909	1,871	2,656	3,057	3,901	3,807	4,149	4,937
West Virginia..................	781	1,170	1,117	1,057	1,208	1,410	1,327	1,388
Wisconsin.....................	1,252	1,663	2,161	2,279	2,392	2,549	2,702	2,892
Wyoming......................	272	396	434	484	574	611	605	564

Source: U.S. Federal Highway Administration, "Highway Statistics 2011," and earlier reports, <http://www.fhwa.dot.gov/policyinformation/statistics.cfm>, accessed July 2013.

Table 1117. State Motor Vehicle Registrations: 1990 to 2011

[In thousands (188,798 represents 188,798,000). Compiled principally from information obtained from state authorities, but it was necessary to draw on other sources and to make numerous estimates in order to complete series. Excludes motorcycles; see Table 1119]

Type	1990	1995	2000	2005	2009	2010	2011
All motor vehicles.............	**188,798**	**201,530**	**221,475**	**241,194**	**246,283**	**242,061**	**244,778**
Private and commercial............	185,541	197,941	217,567	237,140	242,058	237,784	241,068
Publicly owned......................	3,257	3,589	3,908	4,054	4,225	4,277	3,710
Automobiles [1]........................	133,700	128,387	133,621	136,568	134,880	130,892	125,657
Private and commercial............	132,164	126,900	132,247	135,192	133,438	129,434	124,136
Publicly owned......................	1,536	1,487	1,374	1,376	1,442	1,458	1,520
Buses....................................	627	686	746	807	842	846	666
Private and commercial............	275	288	314	331	351	347	312
Publicly owned......................	351	398	432	476	491	499	354
Trucks [1]..............................	54,470	72,458	87,108	103,819	110,561	110,322	118,456
Private and commercial............	53,101	70,754	85,005	101,616	108,269	108,003	116,620
Publicly owned......................	1,369	1,704	2,103	2,203	2,292	2,319	1,836

[1] Trucks include pickups, panels, and delivery vans. Beginning 1995 personal passenger vans, passenger minivans, and utility-type vehicles are no longer included in automobiles but are included in trucks.

Source: U.S. Federal Highway Administration, *Highway Statistics*, March 2013. See also <http://www.fhwa.dot.gov/policy/ohpi/hss/index.cfm>.

Table 1118. Alternative Fueled Vehicles and Estimated Consumption of Vehicle Fuels by Fuel Type: 2005 to 2011

[In thousands, (420,778 represents 420,778,000). Vehicles in use do not include concept and demonstration vehicles that are not ready for delivery to end users. Vehicles in use represent accumulated acquisitions, less retirements, as of the end of each calendar year. (g-e-g = gasoline equivalent gallons)]

Vehicles and fuel consumption	Unit	2005	2009	2010	2011
ALTERNATIVE FUELED VEHICLES IN USE					
Total............................	**Number**	**592,125**	**826,318**	**938,643**	**1,191,786**
Compressed Natural Gas (CNG).....................	Number	117,699	114,270	115,863	118,214
Electric [1]............................	Number	51,398	57,185	57,462	67,295
Ethanol, 85 percent (E85) [2, 3]........................	Number	246,363	504,297	618,506	862,837
Hydrogen............................	Number	119	357	421	527
Liquefied Natural Gas (LNG).......................	Number	2,748	3,176	3,354	3,436
Liquefied Petroleum Gas (LPG)......................	Number	173,795	147,030	143,037	139,477
Other fuels [4]........................	Number	3	3	–	–
FUEL CONSUMPTION					
Alternative fuels:.........................	1,000 gal.(g-e-g)	420,778	431,107	457,755	515,920
Compressed Natural Gas (CNG).....................	1,000 gal.(g-e-g)	166,878	199,513	210,007	220,247
Electric [1]............................	1,000 gal.(g-e-g)	5,219	4,956	4,847	7,635
Ethanol, 85 percent (E85) [2].......................	1,000 gal.(g-e-g)	38,074	71,213	90,323	137,165
Hydrogen............................	1,000 gal.(g-e-g)	25	140	152	174
Liquefied Natural Gas (LNG).......................	1,000 gal.(g-e-g)	22,409	25,652	26,072	26,242
Liquefied Petroleum Gas (LPG)......................	1,000 gal.(g-e-g)	188,171	129,631	126,354	124,457
Other fuels [4]........................	1,000 gal.(g-e-g)	2	2	–	–
Biodiesel..............................	1,000 gal.(g-e-g)	93,281	334,809	270,107	910,968
Oxygenates:					
Methyl Tertiary Butyl Ether (MTBE)....................	1,000 gal.(g-e-g)	1,654,500	(X)	(X)	(X)
Ethanol in Gasohol.........................	1,000 gal.(g-e-g)	2,756,663	7,343,133	8,527,431	8,563,841
Total alternative and replacement fuels..............	**1,000 gal.(g-e-g)**	**4,925,222**	**7,677,942**	**8,797,538**	**9,474,809**
FUEL CONSUMPTION IN NATIVE UNITS					
Alternative fuels:					
Compressed Natural Gas (CNG).....................	million cubic feet	20,106	24,038	25,302	26,536
Electric [1]..............................	1,000 kwh	173,967	165,200	161,567	254,500
Ethanol, 85 percent (E85) [2]........................	1,000 gallons	52,881	98,907	125,449	190,507
Hydrogen............................	1,000 kilograms	23	128	138	158
Liquefied Natural Gas (LNG).......................	1,000 gallons	33,953	38,867	39,503	39,761
Liquefied Petroleum Gas (LPG)......................	1,000 gallons	254,285	175,177	170,749	168,185
Biodiesel..............................	1,000 gallons	90,827	326,000	263,000	887,000
Oxygenates:					
Methyl Tertiary Butyl Ether (MTBE)....................	1,000 gallons	2,035,320	(X)	(X)	(X)
Ethanol in Gasohol.........................	1,000 gallons	4,013,679	10,753,990	12,495,404	12,548,757

– Represents zero. X Not applicable. [1] Excludes gasoline-electric and diesel-electric hybrids because the input fuel is gasoline or diesel rather than an alternative transportation fuel. [2] The remaining portion of E85 percent ethanol is gasoline. Consumption data include the gasoline portion of the fuel. [3] For 2010, the EIA estimates that the number of E85 vehicles that are capable of operating on E85, gasoline, or both, is about 8.6 million. Many of these alternative-fueled vehicles (AFVs) are sold and used as traditional gasoline-powered vehicles. In this table, AFVs in use include only those E85 vehicles believed to be used as AFVs. These are primarily fleet-operated vehicles. [4] May include P-Series fuel or any other fuel designated by the Secretary of Energy as an alternative fuel in accordance with the Energy Policy Act of 1995.

Source: U.S. Energy Information Administration, "Alternatives to Traditional Transportation Fuels," <http://www.eia.gov/renewable/data.cfm>, accessed September 2013.

Table 1119. State Motor Vehicle Registrations, 1990 to 2011; and Motorcycle Registrations and Licensed Drivers, 2011: by State

[In thousands (188,798 represents 188,798,000). Motor vehicle registrations cover publicly, privately, and commercially owned vehicles. For uniformity, data have been adjusted to a calendar-year basis as registration years in states differ; figures represent net numbers where possible, excluding reregistrations and nonresident registrations. See also Table 1117. Data for farm trucks, which are registered at a nominal fee and restricted to use in the vicinity of the owner's farm, is not included for some States. See source for details]

| State | Motor vehicle registrations [1] | | | | | | 2011 | | Motor cycle registra-tions, [2] 2011 | Licensed drivers, 2011 |
	1990	1995	2000	2005	2009	2010	Total	Auto mobiles (incl. taxis)		
U.S.........	188,798	201,530	221,475	241,194	246,283	242,061	253,216	125,657	8,410	211,875
AL...........	3,744	3,553	3,960	4,545	4,611	4,654	4,812	2,308	127	3,799
AK...........	477	542	594	673	695	710	758	216	31	521
AZ...........	2,825	2,873	3,795	3,972	4,358	4,320	5,109	2,363	179	4,592
AR [3].......	1,448	1,613	1,840	1,940	2,037	2,073	2,448	1,022	76	1,956
CA [3].......	21,926	22,432	27,698	32,487	34,433	31,014	29,177	14,550	802	23,857
CO...........	3,155	2,812	3,626	1,808	1,429	4,180	4,332	1,799	173	3,670
CT...........	2,623	2,622	2,853	3,059	3,072	3,082	2,829	1,720	98	2,986
DE...........	526	592	630	737	843	799	929	491	30	716
DC...........	262	243	242	237	218	212	316	239	4	395
FL [3].......	10,950	10,369	11,781	15,691	15,315	14,373	15,469	7,982	574	13,882
GA [3].......	5,489	6,120	7,155	8,063	8,507	7,702	7,534	3,430	200	6,506
HI...........	771	802	738	948	895	904	1,148	535	30	912
ID [3].......	1,054	1,043	1,178	1,374	1,375	1,325	1,625	611	63	1,084
IL [3].......	7,873	8,973	8,973	9,458	9,891	10,079	10,445	5,564	350	8,374
IN...........	4,366	5,072	5,571	4,955	5,848	5,698	6,133	2,882	204	6,570
IA [3].......	2,632	2,814	3,106	3,398	3,363	3,313	3,497	1,646	174	2,192
KS...........	2,012	2,085	2,296	2,368	2,425	2,436	2,446	1,142	81	2,026
KY [3].......	2,909	2,631	2,826	3,428	3,585	3,589	3,763	1,883	98	2,960
LA...........	2,995	3,286	3,557	3,819	4,033	4,086	4,053	1,801	67	3,186
ME [3].......	977	967	1,024	1,075	1,056	1,054	1,171	530	50	1,015
MD...........	3,607	3,654	3,848	4,322	4,484	4,557	3,906	2,088	120	3,857
MA [3].......	3,726	4,502	5,265	5,420	5,262	5,334	5,695	3,180	159	4,683
MI...........	7,209	7,674	8,436	8,247	7,913	9,286	9,183	4,743	308	7,060
MN [3].......	3,508	3,882	4,630	4,647	4,796	4,848	4,910	2,249	240	3,306
MS [3].......	1,875	2,144	2,289	1,978	2,026	2,016	2,037	1,051	28	1,927
MO...........	3,905	4,255	4,580	4,589	4,904	5,153	5,170	2,441	141	4,277
MT...........	783	968	1,026	1,009	925	926	1,219	436	47	752
NE [3].......	1,384	1,467	1,619	1,703	1,793	1,802	1,887	766	51	1,356
NV [3].......	853	1,047	1,220	1,349	1,397	1,362	2,152	1,079	69	1,701
NH...........	946	1,122	1,052	1,174	1,212	1,203	1,278	595	79	1,057
NJ [3].......	5,652	5,906	6,390	6,262	6,114	6,628	7,940	4,417	330	5,977
NM...........	1,301	1,484	1,529	1,548	1,621	1,612	1,772	718	65	1,419
NY...........	10,196	10,274	10,235	11,863	11,245	10,255	10,431	5,867	346	11,211
NC...........	5,162	5,682	6,223	6,148	6,047	5,743	6,250	3,264	223	6,569
ND...........	630	695	694	695	722	736	786	329	33	490
OH...........	8,410	9,810	10,467	10,634	11,022	9,801	10,217	5,412	390	7,982
OK [3].......	2,649	2,856	3,014	3,725	3,396	3,357	3,429	1,523	127	2,371
OR...........	2,445	2,785	3,022	2,897	3,046	3,050	3,128	1,472	108	2,774
PA...........	7,971	8,481	9,260	9,864	9,857	9,991	10,303	5,485	404	8,797
RI [3].......	672	699	760	812	789	782	919	528	33	750
SC...........	2,521	2,833	3,095	3,339	3,614	3,661	3,827	1,984	108	3,408
SD [3].......	704	709	793	854	926	926	995	385	69	603
TN [3].......	4,444	5,400	4,820	4,980	5,140	5,114	5,302	2,637	168	4,544
TX [3].......	12,800	13,682	14,070	17,470	18,208	17,194	19,617	8,965	439	15,123
UT...........	1,206	1,447	1,628	2,210	2,454	2,655	1,883	858	59	1,747
VT...........	462	492	515	508	557	567	605	286	30	522
VA...........	4,938	5,613	6,046	6,591	6,302	6,149	6,998	3,827	196	5,467
WA [3].......	4,257	4,503	5,116	5,598	5,581	4,683	5,881	3,037	221	5,179
WV...........	1,225	1,425	1,442	1,352	1,412	1,436	1,458	663	56	1,199
WI [3].......	3,815	3,993	4,366	4,725	4,874	4,968	5,244	2,419	317	4,147
WY [3].......	528	601	586	646	652	663	798	242	30	422

[1] Automobiles, trucks, and buses (excludes motorcycles). Excludes vehicles owned by military services. [2] Private and commercial. [3] State did not provide complete current registration data. Table displays estimates by FHWA, transaction data, or previous year data shown, see source and earlier editions for more information.

Source: U.S. Federal Highway Administration, "Highway Statistics 2011," and earlier reports, <http://www.fhwa.dot.gov/policyinformation/statistics.cfm>, accessed July 2013.

Table 1120. Motor Vehicle Distance Traveled by Type of Vehicle: 1970 to 2011

[1,110 represents 1,110,000,000,000. The travel data by vehicle type and stratification of trucks are estimated by the Federal Highway Administration (FHWA)]

Year	Vehicle—miles of travel (bil.) [1]					Average miles traveled per vehicle (1,000) [1]				
	Total [2]	Light duty vehicle short WB [3]	Buses [4]	Light duty vehicle long WB [3]	Trucks [5,6]	Total [2]	Light duty vehicle short WB [3]	Buses [4]	Light duty vehicle long WB [3]	Trucks [5,6]
1970........	1,110	920	4.5	123	62	10.0	10.0	12.0	8.7	13.6
1980........	1,527	1,122	6.1	291	108	9.5	8.8	11.5	10.4	18.7
1985........	1,775	1,256	4.5	391	124	10.0	9.4	7.5	10.5	20.6
1990........	2,144	1,418	5.7	575	146	11.1	10.3	9.1	11.9	23.6
1993........	2,296	1,385	6.1	746	160	11.6	10.5	9.4	12.4	26.3
1994........	2,358	1,416	6.4	765	170	11.7	10.8	9.6	12.2	25.8
1995........	2,423	1,438	6.4	790	178	11.8	11.2	9.4	12.0	26.5
1996........	2,486	1,470	6.6	817	183	11.8	11.3	9.4	11.8	26.1
1997........	2,562	1,503	6.8	851	191	12.1	11.6	9.8	12.1	27.0
1998........	2,632	1,550	7.0	868	196	12.2	11.8	9.8	12.2	25.4
1999........	2,691	1,569	7.7	901	203	12.2	11.9	10.5	12.0	26.0
2000........	2,747	1,967	14.8	491	262	12.2	11.0	19.8	14.6	29.1
2001........	2,796	1,987	13.0	512	272	11.9	10.7	17.3	14.7	28.9
2002........	2,856	2,036	13.3	520	276	12.2	11.1	17.5	14.3	29.4
2003........	2,890	2,051	13.4	528	286	12.2	11.1	17.2	14.8	30.3
2004........	2,965	2,083	13.5	569	284	12.2	11.0	17.0	15.2	29.7
2005........	2,989	2,096	13.2	581	285	12.1	11.0	16.3	14.8	28.8
2006........	3,014	2,048	14.0	633	301	12.0	10.5	17.1	16.3	29.1
2007........	3,031	2,104	14.5	587	304	11.9	10.7	17.4	15.0	28.3
2008........	2,977	2,025	14.8	605	311	11.6	10.3	17.6	15.3	28.6
2009........	2,957	2,016	14.4	617	288	11.6	10.4	17.1	15.2	26.3
2010........	2,967	2,026	13.8	623	287	11.9	10.7	16.3	15.5	26.6
2011........	2,946	2,043	13.8	603	267	11.6	10.6	20.7	14.6	26.0

[1] FHWA updated table VM-1 from 2000 to 2011 using an enhanced methodology implemented in March 2011. Prior to 2000, "Light Duty Vehicles Short WB" were categorized as "Cars;" and "Light Duty Vehicles Long WB" were categorized as "Vans, pickups, sport utility vehicles." [2] Motorcycles included with "Cars" through 1994; thereafter in total, not shown separately. [3] Light Duty Vehicles Short WB—passenger cars, light trucks, vans and sport utility vehicles with a wheelbase (WB) equal to or less than 121 inches. Light Duty Vehicles Long WB—large passenger cars, vans, pickup trucks, and sport/utility vehicles with WB larger than 121 inches. [4] Includes school buses. [5] Includes combinations. [6] 2000 to 2011: Single-Unit—single frame trucks that have 2-axles and at least 6 tires or a gross vehicle weight rating exceeding 10,000 lbs.

Source: U.S. Federal Highway Administration, "Highway Statistics 2011," and earlier reports, <http://www.fhwa.dot.gov/policyinformation/statistics.cfm>, accessed July 2013.

Table 1121. Domestic Motor Fuel Consumption by Type of Vehicle: 1970 to 2011

[Consumption in billions (92.3 represents 92,300,000,000 gallons). Comprises all fuel types used for propulsion of vehicles under state motor fuels laws. Excludes federal purchases for military use. Minus sign (-) indicates decrease]

Year	Annual fuel consumption (bil. gal.) [1]						Average miles per gallon [1]				
	All vehicles [2]	Annual percent change [3]	Light duty vehicle short WB [2,4]	Buses [5]	Light duty vehicle long WB [4]	Trucks [6,7]	All vehicles [2]	Light duty vehicle short WB [2,4]	Buses [5]	Light duty vehicle long WB [4]	Trucks [6,7]
1970......	92.3	4.8	67.8	0.8	12.3	11.3	12.0	13.5	5.5	10.0	5.5
1980......	115.0	-5.9	70.2	1.0	23.8	20.0	13.3	16.0	6.0	12.2	5.4
1985......	121.3	2.2	71.7	0.8	27.4	21.4	14.6	17.5	5.4	14.3	5.8
1990......	130.8	-0.8	69.8	0.9	35.6	24.5	16.4	20.3	6.4	16.1	6.0
1993......	137.3	3.3	67.2	0.9	42.9	26.2	16.7	20.6	6.6	17.4	6.1
1994......	140.8	2.5	68.1	1.0	44.1	27.7	16.7	20.8	6.6	17.3	6.1
1995......	143.8	2.1	68.1	1.0	45.6	29.0	16.8	21.1	6.6	17.3	6.1
1996......	147.4	2.5	69.2	1.0	47.4	29.6	16.9	21.2	6.6	17.2	6.2
1997......	150.4	2.0	69.9	1.0	49.4	29.9	17.0	21.5	6.7	17.2	6.4
1998......	155.4	3.3	71.7	1.1	50.5	32.0	16.9	21.6	6.7	17.2	6.1
1999......	161.4	3.9	73.2	1.1	52.8	33.9	16.7	21.4	6.7	17.0	6.0
2000......	162.5	0.7	88.9	2.2	28.9	42.0	16.9	22.1	6.7	17.0	6.2
2001......	163.5	0.6	87.8	1.9	30.1	43.0	17.1	22.6	6.8	17.0	6.3
2002......	168.7	3.2	91.5	1.9	30.8	43.3	17.0	22.3	6.9	16.9	6.4
2003......	170.0	0.8	91.6	1.9	31.3	44.8	17.0	22.4	7.1	16.9	6.4
2004......	173.5	2.1	93.4	1.9	33.8	44.4	17.1	22.3	7.1	16.9	6.4
2005......	174.8	0.7	93.2	1.9	34.4	44.5	17.2	22.5	7.1	16.9	6.4
2006......	175.0	0.1	88.6	2.0	37.0	46.4	17.2	23.1	7.1	17.1	6.5
2007......	176.2	0.7	89.6	2.0	36.9	47.2	17.2	22.9	7.2	17.1	6.4
2008......	170.8	-3.1	85.6	2.1	34.9	47.7	17.4	23.7	7.2	17.3	6.5
2009......	168.1	-1.6	85.7	2.0	35.7	44.3	17.6	23.5	7.2	17.3	6.5
2010......	170.4	1.3	86.8	1.9	36.3	45.0	17.4	23.3	7.2	17.2	6.4
2011......	168.6	-1.1	88.5	1.9	35.3	42.4	17.5	23.1	7.1	17.1	6.3

[1] See footnote 1, Table 1120. [2] Motorcycles included with "Cars" through 1994; thereafter in total, not shown separately. [3] Change from immediate prior year. [4] Light Duty Vehicles Short WB—passenger cars, light trucks, vans and sport utility vehicles with a wheelbase (WB) equal to or less than 121 inches. Light Duty Vehicles Long WB—large passenger cars, vans, pickup trucks, and sport/utility vehicles with wheelbases (WB) larger than 121 inches. [5] Includes school buses. [6] Includes combinations. [7] Beginning 2000: Single-Unit—single frame trucks that have 2-axles and at least 6 tires or a gross vehicle weight rating exceeding 10,000 lbs.

Source: U.S. Federal Highway Administration, "Highway Statistics 2011," and earlier reports, <http://www.fhwa.dot.gov/policyinformation/statistics.cfm>, accessed July 2013.

Table 1122. Fatal Motor Vehicle Accidents—National Summary: 1990 to 2011

[Based on data from the Fatality Analysis Reporting System (FARS). FARS gathers data on accidents that result in loss of human life. FARS is operated and maintained by National Highway Traffic Safety Administration's (NHTSA), National Center for Statistics and Analysis (NCSA). FARS data are gathered on motor vehicle accidents that occurred on a roadway customarily open to the public, resulting in the death of a person within 30 days of the accident. Collection of these data depend on the use of police, hospital, medical examiner/coroner, and Emergency Medical Services reports; state vehicle registration, driver licensing, and highway department files; and vital statistics documents and death certificates. See source for further detail]

Item	1990	1995	2000	2005	2008	2009	2010	2011
Fatal crashes, total	**39,836**	**37,241**	**37,526**	**39,252**	**34,172**	**30,862**	**30,296**	**29,757**
One vehicle involved	23,445	21,250	21,117	22,678	20,644	18,745	18,156	17,991
Two or more vehicles involved	16,391	15,991	16,409	16,574	13,528	12,052	12,040	11,766
Persons killed in fatal crashes [1]	**44,599**	**41,817**	**41,945**	**43,510**	**37,352**	**33,820**	**32,943**	**32,302**
Occupants	33,890	33,064	33,451	33,070	26,720	24,463	23,315	22,383
Drivers	22,854	22,370	22,914	23,237	19,279	17,670	16,864	16,430
Passengers	10,931	10,576	10,451	9,750	7,441	6,793	6,451	5,953
Other	105	118	86	83	71	63	56	65
Motorcyclists	3,244	2,227	2,897	4,576	5,312	4,469	4,518	4,612
Nonoccupants	7,465	6,526	5,597	5,864	5,320	4,888	5,110	5,307
Pedestrians	6,482	5,584	4,763	4,892	4,414	4,109	4,302	4,432
Pedalcyclists	859	833	693	786	718	628	623	677
Other	124	109	141	186	188	151	185	198
Occupants killed by vehicle type:								
Passenger cars	24,092	22,423	20,699	18,512	14,646	13,135	12,491	11,981
Mini-compact (95 inches)	3,556	2,207	1,113	452	270	212	171	185
Subcompact (95 to 99 inches)	4,753	4,584	3,660	2,536	1,667	1,333	1,252	1,166
Compact (100 to 104 inches)	5,310	6,899	7,022	6,288	4,780	4,128	3,954	3,789
Intermediate (105 to 109) inches	4,849	4,666	5,204	5,571	4,763	4,393	4,227	4,050
Full-size (110 to 114) inches	2,386	2,116	2,287	2,491	2,210	2,175	1,982	1,958
Largest (115 inches and over)	2,249	1,297	897	796	755	674	681	669
Unknown	989	654	516	378	201	180	168	164
Motorcycles and other motorized cycles	3,129	2,114	2,897	4,576	5,312	4,469	4,518	4,612
Motorcycles	3,014	2,001	2,783	4,418	5,060	4,222	4,266	4,343
Other motorized cycles	115	113	114	158	252	240	236	269
Light trucks [2]	8,601	9,568	11,526	13,037	10,816	10,312	9,782	9,272
Pickup	5,979	5,938	6,003	6,067	5,097	4,792	4,473	4,256
Utility	1,214	1,935	3,358	4,831	4,214	4,091	3,930	3,871
Van	1,154	1,639	2,129	2,112	1,492	1,394	1,342	1,128
Other	254	56	36	27	13	10	7	17
Large trucks [3]	705	648	754	804	682	499	530	635
Medium trucks	134	96	106	118	91	81	79	96
Heavy trucks	571	552	648	686	592	422	447	539
Buses	32	33	22	58	67	26	44	54
Other vehicles	296	307	401	492	523	481	451	427
Unknown	164	85	49	167	57	82	92	79
Persons involved in fatal crashes	**107,777**	**102,102**	**100,716**	**101,262**	**84,510**	**76,309**	**(NA)**	**(NA)**
Occupants	99,297	94,621	94,325	94,614	78,500	70,845	68,927	67,143
Drivers	58,893	56,164	57,280	59,220	50,416	45,337	44,599	43,668
Passengers	40,229	38,252	36,889	35,231	27,924	25,470	(NA)	(NA)
Other	175	205	156	163	160	145	(NA)	(NA)
Nonoccupants	8,480	7,481	6,391	6,648	6,010	5,464	(NA)	(NA)
Vehicle miles traveled (VMT) [4] (bil.)	2,144	2,423	2,747	2,989	2,977	2,957	2,967	2,946
Licensed drivers (1,000)	167,015	176,628	190,625	200,549	208,321	209,618	210,115	211,875
Registered vehicles (1,000)	184,275	197,065	217,993	247,031	259,360	258,958	257,312	257,512
Percent distribution of fatal accidents by the highest driver (BAC) in accident: [5]								
0.00 percent	54.0	62.1	62.7	63.3	63.1	62.3	64.0	64.0
0.01 to 0.07 percent	6.3	5.5	5.6	5.4	5.6	5.6	5.0	5.0
0.08 percent and over	39.4	32.1	31.4	31.1	31.1	31.9	31.0	31.0
Percent distribution of fatal accidents by the highest (BAC) in accident: [5]								
0.00 percent	49.5	57.7	58.7	59.5	58.6	58.0	(NA)	(NA)
0.01 to 0.07 percent	6.5	5.7	5.9	5.6	5.8	5.7	(NA)	(NA)
0.08 percent and over	44.0	36.7	35.4	34.9	35.5	36.3	(NA)	(NA)
Fatalities per 100,000 resident population								
Under 5 years old	4.90	4.30	3.70	2.94	1.95	2.02	1.99	1.79
5 to 9 years old	5.14	4.48	3.55	3.00	1.95	1.84	1.73	1.69
10 to 15 years old	7.60	7.23	5.65	4.67	3.41	3.02	2.70	2.56
16 to 20 years old	36.66	31.59	29.38	27.48	20.78	18.08	15.45	15.44
21 to 24 years old	33.47	29.68	27.02	27.73	23.25	19.11	19.43	18.69
25 to 34 years old	22.78	19.44	17.29	17.82	15.66	13.69	13.43	13.15
35 to 44 years old	16.11	15.10	15.08	15.08	12.88	11.62	11.07	10.64
45 to 54 years old	14.83	13.39	13.79	14.59	13.07	12.10	11.28	11.35
55 to 64 years old	15.00	13.92	13.61	13.88	12.03	10.87	10.90	10.45
65 to 74 years old	17.03	16.64	15.29	15.16	12.26	11.42	10.89	11.26
75 years old and over	25.45	26.09	23.29	20.47	16.56	15.52	16.70	15.18
Fatalities per 100 million VMT [4]	2.08	1.73	1.53	1.46	1.26	1.15	1.11	1.10
Fatalities per 100,000 licensed drivers	26.70	23.68	22.00	21.70	17.96	16.16	15.71	15.28
VMT [4] per registered vehicle	11,635	12,295	12,601	12,100	11,478	11,419	11,522	11,440
Fatalities per 100,000 registered vehicles	24.20	21.22	19.24	17.61	14.43	13.08	12.82	12.57
Fatal crashes per 100 million VMT [4]	1.86	1.54	1.37	1.31	1.15	1.04	1.02	1.01
Fatalities per 100,000 resident population	17.88	15.91	14.87	14.72	12.31	11.05	10.67	10.39

NA Not available. [1] Deaths within 30 days of the accident. Starting with 1995, total does not include motorcyclist data. [2] Trucks with a gross vehicle weight rating of 10,000 pounds or less, including pickups, vans, truck-based station wagons, and utility vehicles. [3] Trucks with a gross vehicle weight rating of over 10,000 pounds. [4] VMT = vehicle miles of travel. [5] BAC = blood alcohol concentration.

Source: National Highway Traffic Safety Administration, *Traffic Safety Facts, 2011*; and "Fatality Analysis Reporting System," <http://www.nhtsa.gov/FARS>, accessed September 2013.

Table 1123. Traffic Fatalities by State: 1990 to 2011

[For deaths within 30 days of the accident]

State	1990	2000	2005	2011	Fatality rate [1] 1990	Fatality rate [1] 2011	State	1990	2000	2005	2011	Fatality rate [1] 1990	Fatality rate [1] 2011
U.S.....	44,599	41,945	43,510	32,367	2.1	1.1	MO......	1,097	1,157	1,257	784	2.2	1.1
AL.......	1,121	996	1,148	894	2.6	1.4	MT......	212	237	251	209	2.5	1.8
AK.......	98	106	73	72	2.5	1.6	NE.....	262	276	276	181	1.9	1.0
AZ.......	869	1,036	1,179	825	2.5	1.4	NV.....	343	323	427	246	3.4	1.0
AR.......	604	652	654	549	2.9	1.7	NH.....	158	126	166	90	1.6	0.7
CA......	5,192	3,753	4,333	2,791	2.0	0.9	NJ.....	886	731	747	627	1.5	0.9
CO......	544	681	606	447	2.0	1.0	NM.....	499	432	488	353	3.1	1.4
CT......	385	341	278	220	1.5	0.7	NY.....	2,217	1,460	1,434	1,169	2.1	0.9
DE......	138	123	133	99	2.1	1.1	NC.....	1,385	1,557	1,547	1,227	2.2	1.2
DC......	48	48	48	27	1.4	0.8	ND.....	112	86	123	148	1.9	1.6
FL.......	2,891	2,999	3,518	2,398	2.6	1.3	OH.....	1,638	1,366	1,321	1,016	1.8	0.9
GA.......	1,562	1,541	1,729	1,223	2.2	1.1	OK.....	641	650	803	696	1.9	1.5
HI.......	177	132	140	100	2.2	1.0	OR.....	579	451	487	331	2.2	1.0
ID........	244	276	275	167	2.5	1.1	PA.....	1,646	1,520	1,616	1,286	1.9	1.3
IL........	1,589	1,418	1,363	918	1.9	0.9	RI.....	84	80	87	66	1.1	0.8
IN........	1,049	886	938	750	2.0	1.0	SC.....	979	1,065	1,094	828	2.8	1.7
IA........	465	445	450	360	2.0	1.2	SD.....	153	173	186	111	2.2	1.2
KS.......	444	461	428	386	1.9	1.3	TN......	1,177	1,307	1,270	946	2.5	1.3
KY.......	849	820	985	721	2.5	1.5	TX......	3,250	3,779	3,536	3,016	2.1	1.3
LA.......	959	938	963	675	2.5	1.5	UT.......	272	373	282	240	1.9	0.9
ME......	213	169	169	136	1.8	1.0	VT.......	90	76	73	55	1.5	0.8
MD......	707	588	614	485	1.7	0.9	VA.....	1,079	929	947	764	1.8	0.9
MA......	605	433	441	337	1.3	0.6	WA.....	825	631	649	457	1.8	0.8
MI.......	1,571	1,382	1,129	889	1.9	0.9	WV.....	481	411	374	337	3.1	1.8
MN......	566	625	559	368	1.5	0.7	WI......	769	799	815	582	1.7	1.1
MS......	750	949	931	630	3.1	1.6	WY.....	125	152	170	135	2.1	1.5

[1] Deaths per 100 million vehicle miles traveled.

Source: U.S. National Highway Traffic Safety Administration, *Traffic Safety Facts 2011*, DOT-HS-811-754, April 2013. See also <http://www.nhtsa.gov/NCSA>.

Table 1124. Motor Vehicle Occupants and Nonoccupants Killed and Injured: 1980 to 2011

[Injuries in thousands (3,231 represents 3,231,000). For deaths within 30 days of the accident]

Year	Total	Occupants Total	Passenger cars	Light trucks [1]	Large trucks [1]	Buses	Other/ unknown [2]	Motorcycle riders [3]	Nonoccupants Total	Pedestrian	Pedalcyclist	Other/ unknown [2]
KILLED												
1980................	51,091	36,783	27,449	7,486	1,262	46	540	5,144	9,164	8,070	965	129
1985................	43,825	31,479	23,212	6,689	977	57	544	4,564	7,782	6,808	890	84
1990................	44,599	33,890	24,092	8,601	705	32	460	3,244	7,465	6,482	859	124
1995................	41,817	33,064	22,423	9,568	648	33	392	2,227	6,526	5,584	833	109
2000................	41,945	33,451	20,699	11,526	754	22	450	2,897	5,597	4,763	693	141
2001................	42,196	33,243	20,320	11,723	708	34	458	3,197	5,756	4,901	732	123
2002................	43,005	34,105	20,569	12,274	689	45	528	3,270	5,630	4,851	665	114
2003................	42,884	33,627	19,725	12,546	726	41	589	3,714	5,543	4,774	629	140
2004................	42,836	33,276	19,192	12,674	766	42	602	4,028	5,532	4,675	727	130
2005................	43,510	33,070	18,512	13,037	804	58	659	4,576	5,864	4,892	786	186
2006................	42,708	32,119	17,925	12,761	805	27	601	4,837	5,752	4,795	772	185
2007................	41,259	30,527	16,614	12,458	805	36	614	5,174	5,558	4,699	701	158
2008................	37,423	26,791	14,646	10,816	682	67	580	5,312	5,320	4,414	718	188
2009................	33,883	24,526	13,135	10,312	499	26	554	4,469	4,888	4,109	628	151
2010................	32,885	23,303	12,435	9,752	529	44	543	4,502	5,080	4,280	618	182
2011................	32,367	22,448	11,981	9,272	635	54	506	4,612	5,307	4,432	677	198
INJURED (1,000)												
1990................	3,231	2,960	2,376	505	42	33	4	84	187	105	75	7
1995................	3,465	3,246	2,469	722	30	19	4	57	162	86	67	10
2000................	3,189	2,997	2,052	887	31	18	10	58	134	78	51	5
2001................	3,033	2,841	1,927	861	29	15	9	60	131	78	45	8
2002................	2,926	2,735	1,805	879	26	19	6	65	126	71	48	7
2003................	2,889	2,697	1,756	889	27	18	7	67	124	70	46	8
2004................	2,788	2,594	1,643	900	27	16	7	76	118	68	41	9
2005................	2,699	2,494	1,573	872	27	11	10	87	118	64	45	8
2006................	2,575	2,375	1,475	857	23	10	11	88	112	61	44	7
2007................	2,491	2,264	1,379	841	23	12	8	103	124	70	43	10
2008................	2,346	2,120	1,304	768	23	15	9	96	130	69	52	9
2009................	2,217	2,011	1,216	759	17	12	7	90	116	59	51	7
2010................	2,239	2,027	1,253	733	20	17	5	82	130	70	52	8
2011................	2,217	2,010	1,240	728	23	13	6	81	126	69	48	9

[1] See footnotes 2 and 3, Table 1125. [2] Includes combination trucks. [3] Includes motorcycle operators and passengers.

Source: U.S. National Highway Traffic Safety Administration, *Traffic Safety Facts 2011*, DOT-HS-811-754, April 2013. See also <http://www.nhtsa.gov/NCSA>.

Table 1125. Vehicles Involved in Crashes by Vehicle Type, Rollover Occurrence, and Crash Severity: 2011

[Excludes motorcycles]

Crash severity by vehicle type	Total	Rollover occurrence			
		Yes		No	
	Number	Number	Percent	Number	Percent
Vehicles involved in all crashes [1]	**9,312,000**	**200,000**	**2.1**	**9,112,000**	**97.9**
Passenger cars	5,328,000	78,000	1.5	5,251,000	98.5
Light trucks: [2]					
Pickup	1,353,000	45,000	3.3	1,309,000	96.7
Utility	1,689,000	56,000	3.3	1,633,000	96.7
Van	572,000	9,000	1.6	563,000	98.4
Other	10,000	(Z)	0.6	10,000	99.4
Large truck [3]	287,000	9,000	3.1	278,000	96.7
Bus	57,000	(Z)	0.4	57,000	99.6
Other/unknown	14,000	2,000	14.9	12,000	85.1
Fatal crashes	**39,196**	**7,960**	**20.3**	**31,236**	**79.7**
Passenger cars	17,442	2,673	15.3	14,769	84.7
Light trucks: [2]					
Pickup	7,764	2,044	26.3	5,720	73.7
Utility	6,753	2,121	31.4	4,632	68.6
Van	2,182	364	16.7	1,818	83.3
Other	41	13	31.7	28	68.3
Large truck [3]	3,608	490	13.6	3,118	86.4
Bus	244	13	5.3	231	94.7
Other/unknown	1,162	242	20.8	920	79.2

Z less than 500 or 0.05 percent. [1] Includes injury and property-only crashes, not shown separately. [2] Trucks of 10,000 pounds gross vehicle weight rating or less, including pickups, vans, truck-based station wagons and utility vehicles. [3] Trucks over 10,000 pounds gross vehicle weight rating.

Source: U.S. National Highway Traffic Safety Administration, *Traffic Safety Facts 2011*, DOT-HS-811-754, April 2013. See also <http://www.nhtsa.gov/NCSA>.

Table 1126. Distracted Drivers—Crashes/Road Fatalities and Injuries: 2005 to 2011

["Distraction" is defined as a specific type of inattention that occurs when drivers divert their attention from the driving task to focus on some other activity instead. "Distraction" is a subset of "inattention" (which also includes fatigue, and physical and emotional conditions of the driver). For more information, including revision in coding of "distracted driving," see appendices, source report]

Description	2005	2008	2009	2010	2011
FATAL CRASHES [1]					
Total	**39,252**	**34,172**	**30,797**	**30,196**	**29,757**
Drivers involved	59,220	50,416	45,230	44,440	43,668
Fatalities	43,510	37,423	33,808	32,885	32,367
Crashes involving driver distraction: [2]	4,026	5,307	4,898	2,843	3,020
Percent	10	16	16	9	10
Drivers involved	4,217	5,477	5,084	2,912	3,085
Percent	7	11	11	7	7
Fatalities	4,472	5,838	5,474	3,092	3,331
Percent	10	16	16	9	10
PEOPLE INJURED IN CRASHES: [3]					
Total	2,699,000	2,346,000	2,217,000	2,239,000	2,217,000
Involving driver distraction:					
Estimate	604,000	466,000	448,000	416,000	387,000
Percent of total	22	20	20	19	17

[1] Source: NHTSA's Fatality Analysis Reporting System (FARS). [2] For multi-vehicle crashes, the crash was reported as a distracted-driving crash if at least one driver was reported as distracted. In some of these multi-vehicle crashes, multiple drivers were reported as distracted. [3] Source: National Automotive Sampling System (NASS) General Estimates System (GES).

Source: U.S. National Highway Traffic Safety Administration, *Distracted Driving 2011*, April 2013, and earlier reports. See also <http://www-nrd.nhtsa.dot.gov/CATS/index.aspx> and <www.distraction.gov>.

Table 1127. Crashes by Crash Severity: 1990 to 2011

[6,471 represents 6,471,000. A crash is a police-reported event that produces injury and/or property damage, involves a vehicle in transport and occurs on a trafficway or while the vehicle is in motion after running off the trafficway. A fatal crash involves at least 1 person dying within 30 days of the crash]

Item	1990	1995	2000	2006	2007	2008	2009	2010	2011
Crashes (1,000)..................	**6,471**	**6,699**	**6,394**	**5,973**	**6,024**	**5,811**	**5,505**	**5,419**	**5,338**
Fatal..............................	39.8	37.2	37.5	38.6	37.4	34.2	30.8	30.2	29.8
Nonfatal injury...................	2,122	2,217	2,070	1,746	1,711	1,630	1,517	1,542	1,530
Property damage only...........	4,309	4,446	4,286	4,189	4,275	4,146	3,957	3,847	3,778
Percent of total crashes:									
Fatal..............................	0.6	0.6	0.6	0.6	0.6	0.6	0.6	0.6	0.6
Nonfatal injury...................	32.8	33.1	32.4	29.2	28.4	28.1	27.6	28.5	28.7
Property damage only...........	66.6	66.4	67.0	70.1	71.0	71.4	71.9	71.0	70.8

Source: U.S. National Highway Traffic Safety Administration, *Traffic Safety Facts 2011*, DOT-HS-811-754, April 2013. See also <http://www.nhtsa.gov/NCSA>.

Table 1128. Traffic Fatalities by State and Highest Driver Blood Alcohol Concentration (BAC) in the Crash: 2011

[See headnote, Table 1129. A positive blood alcohol content (BAC level .01 g/dL and higher) indicates that alcohol was consumed by the person tested, and the incident is alcohol related or alcohol involved; a BAC level of .08 g/dL or more indicates that the person was alcohol impaired]

State	Traffic fatalities, total [1]	(BAC=.00)		Alcohol involved driving fatalities (BAC=.01–.07)		Alcohol impaired driving fatalities (BAC=.08 or more)		Total fatalities involving alcohol (BAC=.01 or more)	
		Number	Percent	Number	Percent	Number	Percent	Number	Percent
United States......	**32,367**	**20,752**	**64**	**1,633**	**5**	**9,878**	**31**	**11,510**	**36**
Alabama...............	894	586	65	50	6	259	29	309	35
Alaska.................	72	47	66	3	5	21	28	24	33
Arizona...............	825	536	65	48	6	215	26	263	32
Arkansas..............	549	350	64	39	7	156	28	194	35
California.............	2,791	1,896	68	112	4	774	28	886	32
Colorado.............	447	274	61	13	3	161	36	173	39
Connecticut..........	220	121	55	7	3	92	42	99	45
Delaware.............	99	56	56	3	3	41	41	43	44
District of Columbia...	27	14	50	5	20	8	30	13	50
Florida................	2,398	1,532	64	137	6	716	30	854	36
Georgia...............	1,223	900	74	46	4	277	23	323	26
Hawaii................	100	50	50	6	6	44	44	50	50
Idaho.................	167	112	67	5	3	50	30	55	33
Illinois................	918	593	65	44	5	278	30	323	35
Indiana...............	750	506	67	36	5	207	28	243	32
Iowa..................	360	264	73	14	4	83	23	96	27
Kansas................	386	253	66	23	6	108	28	131	34
Kentucky.............	721	517	72	30	4	171	24	201	28
Louisiana.............	675	420	62	30	4	226	33	255	38
Maine.................	136	97	71	16	12	23	17	39	29
Maryland.............	485	293	60	30	6	162	33	192	40
Massachusetts........	337	204	61	15	5	114	34	130	39
Michigan..............	889	593	67	39	4	255	29	294	33
Minnesota............	368	233	63	22	6	109	30	131	36
Mississippi...........	630	467	74	14	2	149	24	163	26
Missouri..............	784	479	61	40	5	258	33	299	38
Montana..............	209	119	57	8	4	81	39	88	42
Nebraska.............	181	127	70	8	5	45	25	54	30
Nevada...............	246	155	63	21	9	70	28	91	37
New Hampshire.......	90	61	68	2	2	27	30	29	32
New Jersey...........	627	398	63	34	5	193	31	227	36
New Mexico..........	353	233	66	14	4	105	30	119	34
New York.............	1,169	781	67	72	6	315	27	387	33
North Carolina.......	1,227	807	66	52	4	365	30	417	34
North Dakota.........	148	81	55	3	2	64	43	67	45
Ohio..................	1,016	654	64	42	4	316	31	358	35
Oklahoma.............	696	448	64	29	4	220	32	249	36
Oregon...............	331	215	65	18	5	97	29	116	35
Pennsylvania.........	1,286	819	64	58	4	407	32	464	36
Rhode Island.........	66	39	59	3	4	24	37	27	41
South Carolina.......	828	448	54	65	8	315	38	379	46
South Dakota........	111	74	66	5	4	33	29	37	34
Tennessee............	946	639	68	50	5	257	27	307	32
Texas.................	3,016	1,614	54	184	6	1,213	40	1,397	46
Utah..................	240	177	74	10	4	53	22	63	26
Vermont..............	55	31	56	5	9	18	33	23	42
Virginia...............	764	488	64	50	7	224	29	274	36
Washington...........	457	275	60	26	6	156	34	182	40
West Virginia.........	337	229	68	16	5	90	27	106	32
Wisconsin.............	582	354	61	31	5	196	34	227	39
Wyoming..............	135	94	69	3	2	38	28	41	31

[1] Total fatalities include those in which there was no driver or motorcycle rider present.

Source: U.S. National Highway Traffic Safety Administration, *Traffic Safety Facts 2011*, DOT-HS-811-754, April 2013. See also <http://www.nhtsa.gov/NCSA>.

Table 1129. Fatalities by Highest Driver Blood Alcohol Concentration (BAC) in the Crash: 1990 to 2011

[A motor vehicle crash is alcohol-impaired if at least one driver involved in the crash is determined to have a BAC of .08 gram per deciliter (g/dl) or higher. Thus, any fatality that occurs in an alcohol-impaired crash is considered an alcohol-impaired-driving fatality. A person is considered to be legally impaired with a BAC of .08 g/dl or more]

Item	1990	1995	2000	2005	2008	2009	2010	2011
Total Fatalities [1].................	**44,599**	**41,817**	**41,945**	**43,510**	**37,423**	**33,883**	**32,999**	**32,367**
BAC=.00								
Number.........................	23,823	25,768	26,082	27,423	23,499	21,051	21,005	20,752
Percent.........................	53.4	61.6	62.2	63.0	62.8	62.1	64.0	64.0
BAC=.01–.07								
Number.........................	2,901	2,416	2,422	2,404	2,115	1,972	1,771	1,633
Percent.........................	6.5	5.8	5.8	5.5	5.7	5.8	5.0	5.0
Alcohol-Impaired-Driving Fatalities BAC=.08+								
Number.........................	17,705	13,478	13,324	13,582	11,711	10,759	10,136	9,878
Percent.........................	39.7	32.2	31.8	31.2	31.3	31.8	31.0	31.0

[1] Total fatalities include those in which there was no driver or motorcycle rider present.

Source: U.S. National Highway Traffic Safety Administration, *Traffic Safety Facts 2011*, DOT-HS-811-754, April 2013. See also <http://www.nhtsa.gov/NCSA>.

Table 1130. Alcohol Involvement for Drivers in Fatal Crashes: 1999 and 2011

[BAC = blood alcohol concentration. NHTSA estimates alcohol involvement when alcohol test results are unknown, see source for more information]

Age, sex, and vehicle type	1999		2011	
	Total drivers in fatal crashes	Percent with .08% BAC or greater	Total drivers in fatal crashes	Percent with .08% BAC or greater
Total drivers involved in fatal crashes [1].....................	**56,502**	**20.3**	**43,668**	**21.0**
Drivers by age group:				
Under 16 years old............	333	9.6	115	8.0
16 to 20 years old............	7,985	16.9	4,292	20.0
21 to 24 years old............	5,639	31.4	4,465	32.0
25 to 34 years old............	11,763	27.6	8,517	30.0
35 to 44 years old............	11,059	24.8	7,058	24.0
45 to 54 years old............	7,708	17.1	7,493	21.0
55 to 64 years old............	4,608	10.8	5,542	14.0
65 to 74 years old............	3,251	6.9	2,947	8.0
75 years old and over........	3,346	3.7	2,522	5.0
Drivers by sex:				
Male............................	41,012	23.4	31,809	24.0
Female.........................	14,835	11.6	11,209	14.0
Drivers by vehicle type:				
Passenger cars................	27,878	21.3	17,335	24.0
Light trucks [2]...............	19,865	22.3	16,643	21.0
Large trucks [3]...............	4,868	1.5	3,568	1.0
Motorcycles...................	2,528	32.8	4,741	29.0
Buses..........................	318	0.9	(NA)	(NA)

NA Not available. [1] Includes age and sex unknown, and other and unknown types of vehicles. [2] See footnote 2, Table 1125. [3] See footnote 3, Table 1125.

Source: U.S. National Highway Traffic Safety Administration, *Traffic Safety Facts 2011*, DOT-HS-811-754, April 2013. See also <http://www.nhtsa.gov/NCSA>.

Table 1131. Motor Vehicle Crashes—Number and Deaths: 1995 to 2011

[6,699 represents 6,699,000]

Item	Unit	1995	2000	2005	2007	2008	2009	2010	2011
CRASHES									
Total [1]	1,000	**6,699**	**6,394**	**6,159**	**6,024**	**5,811**	**5,505**	**5,419**	**5,338**
Fatal	1,000	37	38	39	37	34	31	30	30
Injury	1,000	2,217	2,070	1,816	1,711	1,630	1,517	1,542	1,530
Property Damage Only	1,000	4,446	4,286	4,304	4,275	4,146	3,957	3,847	3,778
DEATHS									
Deaths within 30 days of crash	1,000	41.8	41.9	43.5	41.3	37.4	33.9	33.0	32.4
Occupants	1,000	33.1	33.5	33.1	30.5	26.8	24.5	23.4	22.4
Passenger cars	1,000	22.4	20.7	18.5	16.6	14.6	13.1	12.5	12.0
Light trucks [2]	1,000	9.6	11.5	13.0	12.5	10.8	10.3	9.8	9.3
Large trucks [2]	1,000	0.6	0.8	0.8	0.8	0.7	0.5	0.5	0.6
Buses	1,000	0.0	0.0	0.1	0.0	0.1	0.0	0.0	0.1
Other/unknown	1,000	0.4	0.5	0.7	0.6	0.6	0.6	0.5	0.5
Motorcycle riders [3]	1,000	2.2	2.9	4.6	5.2	5.3	4.5	4.5	4.6
Nonoccupants	1,000	6.5	5.6	5.9	5.6	5.3	4.9	5.1	5.3
Pedestrians	1,000	5.6	4.8	4.9	4.7	4.4	4.1	4.3	4.4
Pedalcyclist	1,000	0.8	0.7	0.8	0.7	0.7	0.6	0.6	0.7
Other/unknown	1,000	0.1	0.1	0.2	0.2	0.2	0.2	0.2	0.2
TRAFFIC DEATH RATES [4]									
Per 100 million vehicle miles	Rate	1.7	1.5	1.5	1.4	1.3	1.2	1.1	1.1
Per 100,000 licensed drivers	Rate	23.7	22.0	21.7	20.1	18.0	16.2	15.7	15.3
Per 100,000 registered vehicles	Rate	21.2	19.3	17.7	16.0	14.4	13.1	12.8	12.6
Per 100,000 resident population	Rate	15.9	14.9	14.7	13.7	12.3	11.1	10.7	10.4

[1] Covers police-reported accidents in which at least one person dies within 30 days of the crash; or no one dies but at least one person is injured; or no one is injured but property damage has occurred. [2] See footnotes 2 and 3 in Table 1125. [3] Includes motor scooters, minibikes, and mopeds. [4] Based on 30-day definition of traffic deaths.

Source: National Highway Traffic Safety Administration, *Traffic Safety Facts, 2011*; and "Fatality Analysis Reporting System," <http://www.nhtsa.gov/FARS>, accessed September 2013.

Table 1132. Licensed Drivers and Number in Fatal Accidents by Age and Sex: 2011

[104,900 represents 104,900,000]

Age group	Licensed drivers (1,000)			Drivers in fatal accidents			Accident rates per number of drivers [2]	
	Male	Female	Both sexes	Male	Female	Both sexes [1]	Male	Female
Total	**104,900**	**106,975**	**211,875**	**31,809**	**11,209**	**43,668**	**30.3**	**10.5**
19 years old and under	4,721	4,538	9,258	2,252	1,020	3,272	47.7	22.5
Under 16 years old	180	181	361	86	29	115	47.7	16.0
16 years old	585	582	1,168	275	145	420	47.0	24.9
17 years old	986	964	1,950	413	246	659	41.9	25.5
18 years old	1,364	1,286	2,650	673	267	940	49.4	20.8
19 years old	1,605	1,525	3,130	805	333	1,138	50.1	21.8
20 to 24 years old	8,899	8,750	17,649	4,180	1,418	5,600	47.0	16.2
20 years old	1,724	1,660	3,384	829	305	1,135	48.1	18.4
21 years old	1,787	1,745	3,531	926	309	1,235	51.8	17.7
22 years old	1,790	1,760	3,551	864	289	1,153	48.3	16.4
23 years old	1,793	1,779	3,572	794	268	1,062	44.3	15.1
24 years old	1,806	1,806	3,612	767	247	1,015	42.5	13.7
25 to 29 years old	9,252	9,364	18,616	3,374	1,186	4,560	36.5	12.7
30 to 34 years old	9,052	9,225	18,277	2,952	1,005	3,957	32.6	10.9
35 to 39 years old	8,787	8,892	17,679	2,560	883	3,444	29.1	9.9
40 to 44 years old	9,599	9,661	19,260	2,706	908	3,614	28.2	9.4
45 to 49 years old	10,130	10,241	20,372	2,846	916	3,762	28.1	8.9
50 to 54 years old	10,292	10,508	20,801	2,866	865	3,731	27.8	8.2
55 to 59 years old	9,313	9,574	18,888	2,338	714	3,052	25.1	7.5
60 to 64 years old	8,132	8,378	16,510	1,904	586	2,490	23.4	7.0
65 to 69 years old	5,895	6,079	11,974	1,177	477	1,654	20.0	7.8
70 to 74 years old	4,176	4,362	8,538	928	365	1,293	22.2	8.4
75 to 79 years old	3,005	3,221	6,225	663	328	991	22.1	10.2
80 to 84 years old	2,092	2,341	4,433	543	276	819	26.0	11.8
85 and over	1,554	1,841	3,395	458	254	712	29.5	13.8

[1] Total includes 650 unknown/unreported instances. [2] Per 100,000 male/female licensed drivers. Rates for drivers 19 years old and under are likely overstated because of a higher proportion of unlicensed drivers.

Source: U.S. Federal Highway Administration, "Highway Statistics 2011," <http://www.fhwa.dot.gov/policy/ohpi/hss/index.cfm>; and National Highway Traffic Safety Administration, "Fatality Analysis Reporting System," <http://www.nhtsa.gov/FARS>; accessed July 2013.

Table 1133. Speeding-Related Traffic Fatalities by Road Type and State: 2010

[Speeding consists of exceeding the posted speed limit or driving too fast for the road conditions or any speed-related violation charged (racing, driving above speed limit, speed greater than reasonable, exceeding special speed limit)]

State	Traffic fatalities, total	Speeding-related fatalities by roadway function class							
		Total [1]	Interstate		Non-Interstate				
			Rural	Urban	Freeway and Express-way	Other Principal Arterial	Minor Arterial	Collector	Local
United States	**32,367**	**9,944**	**525**	**732**	**414**	**2,026**	**1,605**	**2,166**	**2,366**
Alabama	894	298	15	14	22	22	46	115	64
Alaska	72	26	2	2	1	4	2	4	8
Arizona	825	294	53	14	14	48	48	57	60
Arkansas	549	86	5	2	–	11	8	20	40
California	2,791	890	34	108	108	292	137	138	73
Colorado	447	183	11	5	3	49	56	36	23
Connecticut	220	73	–	12	11	14	12	7	16
Delaware	99	34	–	4	–	14	8	3	5
District of Columbia	27	10	–	2	–	–	–	–	8
Florida	2,398	296	9	27	5	60	29	2	164
Georgia	1,223	220	11	17	4	36	41	47	57
Hawaii	100	45	–	2	2	15	11	6	9
Idaho	167	45	4	–	1	12	7	8	10
Illinois	918	439	15	49	4	96	86	100	88
Indiana	750	153	14	7	–	–	14	40	78
Iowa	360	64	1	1	–	20	5	17	20
Kansas	386	109	10	–	–	23	24	19	33
Kentucky	721	141	7	5	1	25	27	57	19
Louisiana	675	214	9	15	1	38	37	59	55
Maine	136	69	1	–	–	4	20	2	42
Maryland	485	142	1	26	12	28	25	31	18
Massachusetts	337	103	1	14	11	13	10	7	41
Michigan	889	238	7	23	10	47	46	65	40
Minnesota	368	86	4	4	3	16	20	28	11
Mississippi	630	104	6	–	1	10	1	65	21
Missouri	784	310	10	22	15	42	58	101	62
Montana	209	76	11	–	–	25	12	15	12
Nebraska	181	33	4	–	–	9	5	2	13
Nevada	246	76	3	4	2	17	19	8	18
New Hampshire	90	39	4	3	–	4	1	7	20
New Jersey	627	174	6	21	19	44	33	16	34
New Mexico	353	147	19	2	–	103	–	–	17
New York	1,169	338	15	35	8	76	50	35	119
North Carolina	1,227	474	21	13	7	67	80	127	159
North Dakota	148	51	3	–	–	11	9	8	20
Ohio	1,016	299	13	21	8	43	50	88	76
Oklahoma	696	213	17	15	4	20	31	44	82
Oregon	331	103	4	1	–	29	20	35	14
Pennsylvania	1,286	615	24	38	19	124	143	140	127
Rhode Island	66	19	–	–	2	7	4	–	6
South Carolina	828	276	23	19	5	42	48	97	20
South Dakota	111	37	7	–	–	7	5	12	6
Tennessee	946	215	13	16	6	32	41	66	41
Texas	3,016	1,165	53	119	86	218	118	214	345
Utah	240	90	16	7	–	20	14	1	32
Vermont	55	20	–	1	–	3	1	10	5
Virginia	764	287	16	20	5	84	51	51	26
Washington	457	165	6	10	5	34	34	47	22
West Virginia	337	114	8	4	–	17	15	42	28
Wisconsin	582	195	4	6	9	38	37	53	48
Wyoming	135	51	5	2	–	13	6	14	11

– Represents zero. [1] Includes fatalities that occurred on roads for which the type was unknown.

Source: U.S. National Highway Traffic Safety Administration, *Traffic Safety Facts 2011*, 2013. See also <http://www.nhtsa.gov/NCSA>.

Table 1134. Roadway Traffic Congestion by Urbanized Area: 2011

[15,678 represents 15,678,000. Various federal, state, and local information sources were used to develop the database with the primary source being the Federal Highway Administration's Highway Performance Monitoring System]

Urbanized area	Freeway daily vehicle miles of travel		Annual person hours of delay		Annual congestion cost [1]		
	Total miles (1,000)	Per lane-mile of freeway	Total hours (1,000)	Per person [2]	Per person (dol.) [2]	Delay and fuel cost (mil. dol.)	Fuel wasted (gal. per person) [2]
U.S., average.............................	**15,678**	**14,931**	**47,255**	**28**	**596**	**1,024**	**13**
Akron, OH.............................	5,729	11,764	9,789	16	338	209	7
Albany-Schenectady, NY....................	7,173	9,501	13,092	21	476	293	13
Albuquerque, NM.........................	5,469	13,916	12,488	20	457	288	10
Allentown-Bethlehem, PA-NJ.................	5,096	11,375	13,247	21	460	292	10
Atlanta, GA.............................	49,501	16,667	142,041	33	719	3,135	15
Austin, TX..............................	12,650	13,274	38,307	28	602	810	13
Baltimore, MD..........................	26,805	17,172	70,263	28	617	1,557	13
Birmingham, AL.........................	10,184	12,573	20,903	24	532	458	12
Boston, MA-NH-RI........................	42,357	14,551	136,966	32	676	2,922	15
Bridgeport-Stamford, CT-NY.................	10,873	15,850	26,503	28	603	566	13
Buffalo, NY.............................	6,931	8,504	21,545	21	452	474	11
Charleston-North, Charleston, SC...........	3,754	14,007	10,885	20	449	240	10
Charlotte, NC-SC........................	12,797	13,085	28,974	27	610	653	14
Chicago, IL-IN..........................	62,791	17,940	271,718	32	722	6,214	15
Cincinnati, OH-KY-IN......................	19,370	14,264	42,785	25	552	947	12
Cleveland, OH..........................	18,569	11,753	34,980	21	433	736	10
Colorado Springs, CO....................	4,624	11,361	9,941	18	368	205	7
Columbus, OH..........................	16,466	14,915	35,689	28	584	753	12
Dallas-Fort, Worth-Arlington, TX............	62,600	17,151	167,718	32	680	3,578	14
Dayton, OH............................	7,384	10,843	12,442	17	356	265	8
Denver-Aurora, CO......................	22,205	15,178	76,154	32	687	1,612	15
Detroit, MI.............................	32,778	15,112	106,434	28	591	2,287	13
El Paso, TX-NM.........................	5,684	11,016	15,990	22	478	353	12
Fresno, CA.............................	3,857	13,629	7,376	11	239	164	5
Grand Rapids, MI.......................	5,624	10,672	10,016	16	351	215	7
Hartford, CT...........................	11,693	12,308	22,995	25	529	479	12
Honolulu, HI...........................	6,265	12,864	20,873	29	594	427	16
Houston, TX...........................	54,700	16,677	145,832	35	756	3,120	16
Indianapolis, IN........................	14,205	13,128	35,186	29	662	817	14
Jackson, MS...........................	4,664	12,404	7,535	18	430	183	9
Jacksonville, FL.........................	12,226	13,104	22,629	21	449	486	10
Kansas City, MO-KS......................	21,701	10,354	29,448	19	404	640	8
Las Vegas, NV..........................	11,980	15,973	45,419	31	645	931	15
Los Angeles-Long Beach-Santa Ana, CA. ..	137,813	23,651	501,881	38	815	10,785	17
Louisville, KY-IN........................	12,250	14,178	26,253	24	539	584	12
Memphis, TN-MS-AR......................	8,541	12,805	28,700	27	601	636	14
Miami, FL..............................	43,452	19,125	174,612	32	684	3,749	17
Milwaukee, WI..........................	11,490	13,630	27,755	19	400	599	8
Minneapolis-St Paul, MN..................	30,383	14,792	60,788	22	457	1,260	8
Nashville-Davidson, TN...................	14,974	13,903	35,781	31	700	801	16
New Haven, CT..........................	7,860	13,345	14,560	24	494	304	11
New Orleans, LA........................	4,763	12,701	19,125	18	414	441	9
New York-Newark, NY-NJ-CT...............	117,496	15,460	544,063	29	625	11,837	14
Oklahoma City, OK......................	10,647	11,523	25,182	26	552	543	12
Omaha, NE-IA..........................	5,119	11,581	10,721	17	339	219	7
Orlando, FL............................	13,353	12,889	46,607	32	699	1,031	16
Oxnard-Ventura, CA......................	7,015	17,895	12,445	18	373	265	7
Philadelphia, PA-NJ-DE-MD.................	34,246	12,797	156,027	29	629	3,387	14
Phoenix, AZ............................	29,657	17,133	82,554	22	535	1,969	13
Pittsburgh, PA..........................	11,431	8,467	46,725	27	572	1,007	12
Portland, OR-WA........................	15,084	15,599	51,987	27	587	1,130	13
Providence, RI-MA.......................	11,861	11,095	24,618	20	407	503	10
Raleigh-Durham, NC......................	12,738	12,738	17,923	16	347	396	7
Richmond, VA...........................	11,843	10,698	19,499	20	409	398	8
Riverside-San Bernardino, CA..............	22,302	21,040	51,195	25	569	1,152	10
Sacramento, CA.........................	15,556	18,630	39,138	21	440	834	9
Salt Lake City, UT.......................	8,444	13,797	21,903	21	437	449	9
San Antonio, TX.........................	19,114	15,316	39,998	26	530	825	11
San Diego, CA..........................	37,243	18,838	72,331	23	492	1,537	10
San Francisco-Oakland, CA................	51,843	20,467	155,157	38	800	3,279	16
San Jose, CA...........................	17,146	19,136	47,385	26	528	971	11
Seattle, WA............................	33,207	14,338	100,802	31	682	2,241	14
St Louis, MO-IL.........................	30,207	11,565	49,605	21	476	1,116	9
Tampa-St Petersburg, FL..................	14,360	14,134	62,876	26	554	1,325	13
Toledo, OH-MI..........................	4,013	10,290	9,195	18	391	202	8
Tucson, AZ.............................	3,793	14,702	19,078	27	649	466	17
Tulsa, OK..............................	7,634	8,558	15,500	22	462	331	10
Virginia Beach, VA.......................	13,144	13,735	46,172	30	599	932	13
Washington, DC-VA-MD....................	40,082	18,039	179,331	39	817	3,771	18
Worcester, MA..........................	5,764	10,557	10,139	23	474	212	11

[1] Value of extra time (delay) and the extra fuel consumed by vehicles traveling at slower speeds. Fuel cost per gallon is the average price for each state. [2] Per person data are based on total population.

Source: Texas A&M Transportation Institute, College Station, Texas, *2012 Urban Mobility Report*, December 2012 ©. See also <http://mobility.tamu.edu/ums/>.

Table 1135. Commuting to Work by State: 2011

[In percent, except as indicated. Workers in thousands (138,270 represents 138,270,000). For workers 16 years old and over. The American Community Survey universe includes the household population and the population living in institutions, college dormitories, and other group quarters. Based on a sample and subject to sampling variability; see Appendix III]

State	Total workers (1,000)	Percent of workers who—						Mean travel time to work (min.)
		Commuted by car, truck, or van		Used public transpor-tation [1]	Walked	Taxi, motorcycle, bicycle or other means	Worked at home	
		Drove alone	Car-pooled					
U.S.............	138,270	76.4	9.7	5.0	2.8	1.2	4.3	25.5
AL...............	1,953	84.9	9.9	0.5	1.1	0.9	2.6	23.9
AK...............	349	68.2	12.4	1.9	7.6	4.1	4.8	18.4
AZ...............	2,650	75.8	11.6	2.0	2.2	1.7	5.5	24.8
AR...............	1,216	82.7	10.3	0.4	1.9	1.1	3.3	21.3
CA...............	16,047	73.3	11.1	5.2	2.8	1.3	5.3	27.1
CO...............	2,478	75.5	9.8	3.1	2.9	1.1	6.3	24.5
CT...............	1,711	78.1	8.7	4.7	3.0	1.0	4.2	25.0
DE...............	415	81.1	8.9	3.3	2.1	0.8	3.6	25.3
DC...............	307	33.1	6.5	39.6	11.8	1.1	4.8	30.1
FL...............	7,992	79.7	9.9	2.1	1.5	1.6	4.6	25.8
GA...............	4,154	79.4	10.5	2.2	1.6	1.3	4.7	27.1
HI...............	650	67.1	14.2	5.9	4.9	2.5	4.6	25.7
ID...............	673	77.4	9.8	0.7	3.5	1.5	6.2	19.7
IL...............	5,820	73.3	8.8	9.0	3.1	1.0	4.1	28.2
IN...............	2,885	83.6	8.8	1.1	2.1	0.9	3.1	23.5
IA...............	1,513	80.5	8.9	1.1	3.5	0.9	4.6	18.8
KS...............	1,380	81.7	10.0	0.4	2.3	0.8	4.3	18.9
KY...............	1,811	83.1	9.5	1.2	2.1	1.0	2.9	22.9
LA...............	1,942	82.1	10.2	1.3	2.2	1.6	2.2	24.5
ME...............	631	78.8	9.9	0.6	3.7	1.1	5.4	23.4
MD...............	2,856	73.3	10.1	9.2	2.3	0.8	4.1	32.2
MA...............	3,216	72.2	8.2	8.9	4.6	0.9	4.5	28.0
MI...............	4,095	82.6	9.0	1.4	2.2	0.8	3.5	24.1
MN...............	2,685	77.7	9.3	3.4	2.7	0.9	5.2	23.0
MS...............	1,164	83.7	10.6	0.4	1.7	1.2	2.3	23.9
MO...............	2,705	81.4	9.7	1.4	2.0	1.0	4.2	23.1
MT...............	471	75.8	10.4	0.9	4.8	1.1	5.8	18.2
NE...............	931	81.3	9.3	0.7	2.8	0.8	4.7	18.1
NV...............	1,192	78.6	11.1	3.5	2.1	1.6	2.8	24.1
NH...............	671	80.6	8.6	0.7	2.8	1.1	5.9	26.9
NJ...............	4,060	71.8	8.5	11.0	3.1	1.4	3.8	30.5
NM...............	863	79.3	10.0	1.1	2.4	1.3	5.0	21.4
NY...............	8,775	53.9	6.7	27.0	6.6	1.4	3.9	31.5
NC...............	4,184	81.0	9.9	1.2	1.7	1.2	4.7	23.4
ND...............	369	79.1	9.5	0.4	3.9	0.7	5.7	16.9
OH...............	5,114	83.3	8.2	1.7	2.3	0.9	3.4	23.1
OK...............	1,664	81.9	10.9	0.5	1.9	1.1	3.4	21.1
OR...............	1,675	71.8	10.2	4.3	3.9	1.1	6.4	22.5
PA...............	5,728	76.6	9.1	5.3	3.9	0.9	3.8	25.9
RI...............	501	80.3	8.6	3.1	3.2	0.9	3.7	23.4
SC...............	1,958	82.3	9.3	0.7	2.3	1.3	3.8	23.6
SD...............	410	78.0	10.0	0.7	4.3	0.8	5.5	16.9
TN...............	2,738	84.0	9.4	0.9	1.4	0.8	3.3	24.2
TX...............	11,336	79.8	11.1	1.6	1.7	1.4	4.2	24.8
UT...............	1,246	76.5	12.0	2.4	2.4	1.1	4.6	21.6
VT...............	317	74.3	9.9	1.4	6.3	1.1	6.2	21.9
VA...............	3,883	78.1	9.2	4.5	2.3	1.0	4.6	27.7
WA...............	3,097	73.3	10.2	5.6	3.4	1.2	5.5	25.5
WV...............	729	82.1	10.5	0.9	2.7	0.6	3.0	25.6
WI...............	2,771	79.8	8.9	2.0	3.4	0.9	4.3	21.9
WY...............	286	77.7	10.9	1.5	3.4	1.3	4.1	18.1
PR...............	1,060	80.1	8.8	2.9	3.8	1.6	2.5	29.7

[1] Excluding taxicabs.

Source: U.S. Census Bureau, 2011 American Community Survey, B08006, "Sex of Worker by Means of Transportation to Work" and R0801, "Mean Travel Time to Work of Workers 16 Years Old and Over Who Did Not Work At Home (minutes)," <http://factfinder2.census.gov>, accessed March 2013.

Table 1136. Passenger Transit Industry—Summary: 1990 to 2011

[16,053 represents $16,053,000,000. Includes Puerto Rico. Includes aggregate information for all transit systems in the United States. Excludes nontransit services such as taxicab, school bus, unregulated jitney (a small bus or automobile that transports passengers on a route for a small fare), sightseeing bus, intercity bus, and special application mass transportation systems (e.g., amusement parks, airports, island, and urban park ferries). Includes active vehicles only]

Item	Unit	1990	1995	2000	2005	2009	2010	2011
Operating systems..................	Number	5,078	5,973	6,000	6,429	7,200	7,300	7,100
Motor bus systems................	Number	2,688	2,250	2,262	1,500	1,088	1,206	1,078
Revenue vehicles, active...........	Number	93,553	116,473	131,918	150,827	172,893	174,425	175,258
Motor bus.........................	Number	58,714	67,107	75,013	82,027	64,832	66,239	69,175
Commuter rail....................	Number	5,007	5,164	5,498	6,392	6,941	6,927	7,237
Demand response [1]...............	Number	16,471	29,352	33,080	41,958	68,957	68,621	65,336
Heavy rail........................	Number	10,419	10,157	10,591	11,110	11,461	11,510	11,342
Light rail.........................	Number	913	999	1,577	1,645	2,068	2,104	2,257
Trolley bus.......................	Number	832	885	951	615	531	571	479
Other.............................	Number	1,197	2,809	5,208	7,080	18,103	18,453	19,432
Operating funding, total............	Mil. dol.	16,053	18,241	24,243	31,708	38,918	39,117	41,310
Agency funds.....................	Mil. dol.	6,786	8,069	11,004	12,559	14,549	14,675	15,602
Passenger funding.............	Mil. dol.	5,891	6,801	8,746	10,269	12,273	12,556	13,558
Other........................	Mil. dol.	895	1,268	2,258	2,290	2,276	2,119	2,044
Government funds [2]...............	Mil. dol.	9,267	10,172	13,239	19,149	24,369	24,442	25,708
Directly generated [3]...........	Mil. dol.	([4])	1,544	1,959	2,694	2,543	2,549	2,563
Local..........................	Mil. dol.	5,327	3,981	5,319	6,658	8,763	8,458	9,069
State..........................	Mil. dol.	2,970	3,830	4,967	7,495	9,857	9,761	10,048
Federal........................	Mil. dol.	970	817	994	2,303	3,207	3,675	4,028
Operating expense.................	Mil. dol.	15,742	17,849	22,646	30,295	37,245	37,755	38,362
Vehicle operations.................	Mil. dol.	6,654	8,282	10,111	13,793	16,997	17,009	17,590
Maintenance.....................	Mil. dol.	4,631	5,047	6,445	8,259	9,693	9,797	10,015
General administration.............	Mil. dol.	3,450	2,590	3,329	4,075	5,330	5,731	5,674
Purchased transportation..........	Mil. dol.	1,008	1,930	2,761	4,168	5,225	5,218	5,083
Capital expenditures...............	Mil. dol.	(NA)	7,230	9,587	12,383	17,919	17,824	17,057
Vehicle-miles operated..............	Million	3,242	3,550	4,081	4,601	5,219	5,455	5,378
Motor bus.........................	Million	2,130	2,184	2,315	2,485	2,332	2,413	2,414
Trolley bus.......................	Million	14	14	14	13	13	12	12
Heavy rail........................	Million	537	537	595	646	685	666	655
Light rail.........................	Million	24	35	53	69	91	94	94
Commuter rail.....................	Million	213	238	271	303	344	345	347
Demand response [1]...............	Million	306	507	759	978	1,529	1,694	1,612
Other.............................	Million	18	37	74	107	227	232	244
Trips taken.......................	Million	8,799	7,763	9,363	9,815	10,381	10,218	10,319
Motor bus.........................	Million	5,677	4,848	5,678	5,855	5,452	5,256	5,234
Trolley bus.......................	Million	126	119	122	107	104	99	98
Heavy rail........................	Million	2,346	2,033	2,632	2,808	3,490	3,550	3,647
Light rail.........................	Million	175	251	320	381	465	457	479
Commuter rail.....................	Million	328	344	413	423	468	464	472
Demand response [1]...............	Million	68	88	105	125	190	190	191
Other.............................	Million	79	80	93	117	212	203	197
Avg. fare per trip..................	Cents	67	88	93	102	118	123	131
Employees, number (avg.) [5]........	1,000	273	311	360	367	403	394	397
Payroll, employee.................	Mil. dol.	7,226	8,213	10,400	12,177	14,212	14,286	14,331
Fringe benefits, employee..........	Mil. dol.	3,986	4,484	5,413	8,093	9,927	10,342	10,597

NA Not available. [1] This operation (also called paratransit or dial-a-ride) is comprised of passenger cars, vans or small buses operating in response to calls from passengers or their agents to the transit operator, who then dispatches a vehicle to pick up the passengers and transport them to their destinations. [2] Represents the sum of federal, state, and local assistance, and that portion of directly generated funds that accrue from tax collections, toll transfers from other sectors of operations, and bond proceeds. [3] These are any funds generated from taxes controlled by the transit agency. [4] Funds data are included in local government data through 1993. [5] Through 1990, represents employee equivalents of 2,080 hours = one employee; beginning 1995, equals actual employees.

Source: American Public Transportation Association, Washington, DC, *Public Transportation Fact Book*, annual ©. See also <http://www.apta.com/resources/statistics/Pages/default.aspx>.

Table 1137. Top Twenty Cities—Public Transit Savings: 2013

[Individuals who ride public transportation can save on average $10,122 annually based on the September 13, 2013 national average gas price and the national unreserved monthly parking rate. On a per month basis, transit riders can save on average $844 per month versus driving. See the monthly press release dated June 11 at <http://www.apta.com/mediacenter/pressreleases/2013/Pages/130913_Transit-Savings.aspx>. This release and other monthly "Transit Savings" releases contain information and methodology on how savings are calculated. The cities with the highest transit ridership are ranked in order of their transit savings based on the purchase of a monthly public transit pass and factoring in local gas prices for and the local monthly unreserved parking rate]

City	Savings (dollars)		City	Savings (dollars)	
	Monthly	Annual		Monthly	Annual
New York...............	1,251	15,015	Portland.................	886	10,634
San Francisco..........	1,100	13,194	Denver.................	871	10,452
Boston.................	1,095	13,136	Baltimore..............	863	10,360
Philadelphia............	1,008	12,094	Washington, D.C.......	847	10,166
Chicago................	1,001	12,014	Pittsburgh..............	829	9,944
Seattle.................	987	11,844	Cleveland..............	826	9,913
Honolulu...............	979	11,748	Miami..................	799	9,592
Los Angeles............	944	11,323	Atlanta.................	796	9,558
San Diego..............	896	10,749	Dallas..................	783	9,394
Minneapolis............	888	10,652	Las Vegas..............	766	9,188

Source: American Public Transportation Association, Media Center, Press Releases ©. See also <http://www.apta.com/mediacenter/pressreleases/2012/Pages/120906_TSR_June.aspx>.

Table 1138. Characteristics of Rail Transit by Transit Authority: 2011

Mode and transit agency	Primary city served	States served	Direc- tional route– miles [1,2]	Number of high- way- rail cross- ings [1]	Number of stations	Number of ADA acces sible stations [3]
Total [4]	**37**	**33**	**11,833.9**	**6,835**	**3,145**	**2,103**
Heavy rail	**11**	**17**	**1,596.6**	**27**	**1,025**	**514**
Chicago Transit Authority	Chicago	IL, IN	207.8	25	143	92
Greater Cleveland Regional Transit Authority	Cleveland	OH	38.1	–	18	15
L.A. County Metropolitan Transportation Authority	Los Angeles	CA	31.9	–	16	16
Maryland Transit Administration	Baltimore	MD	29.4	–	14	14
Massachusetts Bay Transportation Authority	Boston	MA, NH, RI	76.3	–	53	49
Metropolitan Atlanta Rapid Transit Authority	Atlanta	GA	96.1	–	38	38
Miami-Dade Transit Agency	Miami	FL	45.0	–	22	22
MTA New York City Transit	New York	NY, NJ, CT	487.5	–	468	87
Port Authority Trans-Hudson Corporation	New York	NY, NJ, CT	28.6	2	13	7
Port Authority Transit Corporation	Philadelphia	PA, NJ, DE	31.5	–	13	5
San Francisco Bay Area Rapid Transit District	San Francisco	CA	209.0	–	44	44
Southeastern Pennsylvania Transportation Authority	Philadelphia	PA	74.9	–	75	35
Staten Island Rapid Transit Operating Authority	New York	NY, CT	28.6	–	22	4
Washington Metropolitan Area Transit Authority	Washington	DC, MD, VA	211.8	–	86	86
Commuter rail [5]	**21**	**24**	**8,590.3**	**3,404**	**1,238**	**821**
Alaska Railroad Corporation	Anchorage	AK	959.9	133	10	10
Altamont Commuter Express	San Jose	CA	172.0	127	10	10
Capital Metropolitan Transportation	Austin	TX	64.2	–	9	9
Central Puget Sound Regional Transit Authority	Seattle	WA	146.9	101	10	10
Connecticut Department of Transportation	Hartford	CT	101.2	3	9	8
Dallas Area Rapid Transit	Dallas	TX	72.3	44	10	10
Maryland Transit Administration	Baltimore	MD	400.4	40	42	24
Massachusetts Bay Transportation Authority	Boston	MA, NH, RI	737.5	257	134	97
Metro Transit	Minneapolis	MN	77.9	36	6	6
MTA Long Island Rail Road	New York	NY, NJ, CT	638.2	343	124	103
MTA Metro-North Commuter Railroad Co	New York	NY, NJ, CT	545.7	156	111	45
New Jersey Transit Corporation	New York	NY, NJ, CT	1,001.8	330	164	72
North County Transit District	San Diego	CA	82.2	34	8	8
NE Illinois Regional Commuter Rail Corporation	Chicago	IL, WI	980.4	572	241	173
Northern Indiana Commuter Transportation District	Chicago	IL, IN	179.8	117	20	13
Northern New England Passenger Rail Authority	Boston	MA, ME, NH	230.4	65	10	10
Peninsula Corridor Joint Powers Board	San Francisco	CA	153.7	54	32	26
Pennsylvania Department of Transportation	Philadelphia	PA	144.4	4	12	5
Regional Transportation Authority	Nashville	TN	62.8	35	6	6
Rio Metro Regional Transit District	Albuquerque	NM	193.1	86	12	12
South Florida Regional Transportation Authority	Miami	FL	142.2	73	18	18
Southeastern Pennsylvania Transportation Authority	Philadelphia	PA	446.9	283	154	60
Southern California Regional Rail Authority	Los Angeles	CA	777.8	435	55	55
Tri-County Metropolitan Transportation District of Oregon	Portland	OR	29.2	27	5	5
Utah Transit Authority	Salt Lake City	UT	87.7	29	8	8
Virginia Railway Express	Washington	DC, VA, MD	161.5	20	18	18

– Represents zero. [1] Vehicles operated in maximum services (VOMS) include directly operated (DO) and Purchase Transportation (PT) by mode. [2] The mileage in each direction over which public transportation vehicles travel while in revenue service. The mileage is computed without regard to the number of traffic lanes or rail tracks existing in the right-of-way. [3] Number of stations that comply with the Americans with Disabilities Act of 1992 (ADA). Additional stations may be wheelchair accessible but not comply with other provisions of the ADA. [4] Includes light rail, not shown separately. [5] Excludes commuter-type services operated independently by Amtrak.

Source: Department of Transportation, Federal Transit Administration, National Transit Database, tables 21 "Passenger Stations" and 23 "Transit Way Mileage - Rail Modes," February 2013, <http://www.ntdprogram.gov/ntdprogram/data.htm>.

Table 1139. Transit Ridership in Selected Urbanized Areas: 2011

[Passenger trips in thousands (10,085,447 represents 10,085,447,000)]

Urbanized areas	Annual unlinked passenger trips [1] (1,000s)	Area rank based on trips per capita [2]	Unlinked passenger trips per capita	Percent distribution				
				Motor bus	Heavy rail [3]	Light rail [4]	Commuter rail [5]	Other [6]
U.S. urbanized areas................	**10,085,447**	**(X)**	**45.2**	**50.9**	**36.2**	**4.8**	**4.6**	**3.5**
Atlanta, GA........................	149,556	38	33.1	47.8	51.0	–	–	1.3
Baltimore, MD......................	110,316	18	50.1	70.4	12.7	7.9	7.5	1.5
Boston, MA-NH-RI.................	389,338	5	93.1	30.2	39.6	19.1	9.4	1.7
Chicago, IL-IN.....................	646,554	10	75.1	52.9	34.3	–	11.8	1.0
Cincinnati, OH-KY-IN..............	22,820	115	14.0	98.1	–	–	–	1.9
Cleveland, OH......................	46,960	53	26.4	80.3	12.1	5.8	–	1.7
Dallas-Fort Worth-Arlington, TX....	71,874	116	14.0	60.7	–	31.0	3.3	5.0
Denver-Aurora, CO.................	97,934	24	41.2	77.6	–	21.1	–	1.3
Detroit, MI.........................	50,669	122	13.6	91.3	–	–	–	8.7
Houston, TX........................	81,455	98	16.5	81.8	–	13.0	–	5.2
Indianapolis, IN....................	9,512	226	6.4	97.3	–	–	–	2.7
Kansas City, MO-KS...............	16,810	152	11.1	96.1	–	–	–	3.9
Las Vegas-Henderson, NV.........	56,686	43	30.1	97.9	–	–	–	2.1
Los Angeles-Long Beach-Anaheim, CA................	661,691	17	54.5	82.2	7.0	7.4	1.7	1.7
Miami, FL..........................	160,649	47	29.2	78.3	11.3	–	2.4	8.1
Milwaukee, WI.....................	46,568	36	33.8	97.7	–	–	–	2.3
Minneapolis-St. Paul, MN-WI......	93,915	35	35.4	85.9	–	11.1	0.7	2.3
New York-Newark, NY-NJ-CT......	4,099,710	1	223.4	29.1	63.2	0.5	6.3	0.9
Orlando, FL........................	28,023	82	18.6	96.3	–	–	–	3.7
Philadelphia, PA-NJ-DE-MD........	381,097	13	70.0	50.7	29.3	7.5	10.1	2.5
Phoenix-Mesa, AZ.................	68,594	79	18.9	78.5	–	18.7	–	2.9
Pittsburgh, PA.....................	65,586	29	37.8	84.6	–	10.5	–	4.8
Portland, OR-WA...................	112,004	16	60.5	58.3	–	40.5	–	1.2
Riverside-San Bernardino, CA.....	23,504	136	12.2	95.7	–	–	–	4.3
Sacramento, CA...................	30,292	90	17.6	57.0	–	41.4	–	1.6
San Antonio, TX...................	45,494	54	25.9	97.1	–	–	–	2.9
San Diego, CA.....................	98,292	37	33.2	61.4	–	34.4	1.4	2.8
San Francisco-Oakland, CA.......	423,007	2	128.9	40.2	26.3	12.1	3.0	18.5
San Jose, CA......................	42,492	55	25.5	74.5	–	23.6	–	1.9
San Juan, PR.......................	62,861	46	29.3	18.4	16.8	–	–	64.8
Seattle, WA........................	193,439	14	63.2	66.7	–	4.9	1.4	27.0
St. Louis, MO-IL...................	45,504	70	21.2	62.3	–	35.6	–	2.1
Tampa-St. Petersburg, FL.........	29,342	140	12.0	96.1	–	1.5	–	2.4
Virginia Beach, VA.................	16,543	146	11.5	95.1	–	–	–	4.9
Washington, DC-VA-MD............	478,464	3	104.3	38.5	59.9	–	1.0	0.6

– Represents zero. X Not applicable. [1] The number of times passengers board public transportation vehicles. A passenger is counted each time he or she boards a vehicle even if the boarding is part of the same journey from origin to destination. [2] As of April 1. Based on the decennial census. [3] Also called metro, subway, rapid transit, or rapid rail. [4] Also called hybrid rail, streetcar, tramway, or trolley. [5] Also called metropolitan rail or regional rail. [6] Includes such modes as trolley bus, ferry, cable car, vanpool, automated guideway, monorail, publico, inclined plane, and demand response (see footnote 1, Table 1136).

Source: U.S. Department of Transportation, Federal Transit Administration, "National Transit Database; Access NTD data, Historical Data Files and Annual Data Tables," <http://www.ntdprogram.gov/ntdprogram/data.htm>, accessed September 2013.

Table 1140. Federal Aid to State and Local Governments for Federal Transit Administration (FTA) by State: 2010

[13,041 represents $13,041,000,000. Year ending September 30]

State	Total (mil. dol.)	Per capita [1] (dol.)	State	Total (mil. dol.)	Per capita [1] (dol.)	State	Total (mil. dol.)	Per capita [1] (dol.)	State	Total (mil. dol.)	Per capita [1] (dol.)
Total [2].....	**13,041**	**42**	ID..........	23	14	MT..........	26	26	RI.........	44	42
U.S. [3]......	**12,710**	**41**	IL..........	618	48	NE..........	31	17	SC.........	50	11
AL............	57	12	IN..........	150	23	NV..........	106	39	SD.........	17	21
AK............	80	112	IA..........	70	23	NH..........	18	14	TN.........	118	19
AZ............	184	29	KS.........	36	13	NJ..........	713	81	TX.........	661	26
AR............	43	15	KY.........	86	20	NM..........	42	20	UT.........	267	96
CA............	1,553	42	LA.........	89	20	NY..........	2,684	138	VT.........	24	39
CO............	240	48	ME........	21	16	NC..........	128	13	VA.........	249	31
CT............	157	44	MD........	257	44	ND..........	17	25	WA........	427	63
DE............	26	28	MA........	302	46	OH..........	276	24	WV........	41	22
DC............	480	793	MI.........	205	21	OK..........	57	15	WI.........	108	19
FL............	357	19	MN........	247	47	OR..........	256	67	WY........	11	20
GA............	200	21	MS........	27	9	PA..........	599	47			
HI............	35	26	MO........	193	32						

[1] Based on estimated population as of July 1. [2] Includes Island Areas and undistributed funds, not shown separately. [3] For the 50 states and the District of Columbia.

Source: U.S. Census Bureau, Federal, State, and Local Governments, *Federal Aid to States for Fiscal Year, 2010*, September 2011. See <http://www.census.gov/govs/www/tools.html>.

Table 1141. Commuting Time to Work for Top Metropolitan Statistical Areas: 2012

[134,719 represents 134,719,000, except percent. For workers 16 years and over who did not work at home. By any mode of travel. Based on a sample, subject to sampling variability]

MSA	Total Com-muters	Per-cent over 35 min-utes	Less than 10 minutes	10 to 14 min-utes	15 to 19 min-utes	20 to 24 min-utes	25 to 29 min-utes	30 to 34 min-utes	35 to 44 min-utes	45 to 59 min-utes	60 or more min-utes
United States...........	134,719	22	17,886	19,214	20,853	19,973	8,219	18,496	8,719	10,244	11,115
Atlanta-Sandy Springs-Marietta, GA........	2,298	31	186	237	303	328	143	380	209	265	247
Baltimore-Towson, MD.	1,287	30	108	134	171	192	86	212	109	125	149
Boston-Cambridge-Quincy, MA-NH.........	2,261	32	236	261	284	280	125	356	198	248	273
Chicago-Joliet-Naperville, IL-IN-WI..........	4,228	34	389	475	482	546	253	666	383	491	543
Cincinnati-Middletown, OH-KY-IN.	970	19	112	136	145	167	77	145	74	67	46
Dallas-Fort Worth-Arlington, TX.	3,002	25	294	368	431	434	195	526	232	294	229
Denver-Aurora-Broomfield, CO.............	1,249	24	115	143	179	206	93	216	104	110	84
Detroit-Warren-Livonia, MI.............	1,763	24	178	216	265	276	126	281	151	156	115
Houston-Sugar Land-Baytown, TX........	2,738	28	240	304	373	393	162	489	216	291	270
Los Angeles-Long Beach-Santa Ana, CA....	5,551	28	444	653	807	824	310	986	399	501	627
Miami-Fort Lauderdale-Pompano Beach, FL........	2,456	26	176	271	337	404	152	483	208	224	200
Minneapolis-St. Paul-Bloomington, MN-WI..	1,658	20	176	214	256	286	141	246	127	122	90
New York-Northern New Jersey-Long Island, NY-NJ-PA..................	8,458	41	643	791	867	997	415	1,292	730	1,025	1,698
Orlando-Kissimmee-Sanford, FL............	967	24	71	116	148	155	78	164	76	92	67
Philadelphia-Camden-Wilmington, PA-NJ-DE-MD..................	2,629	29	268	323	354	372	164	392	211	280	265
Phoenix-Mesa-Glendale, AZ.................	1,772	23	171	228	258	287	125	302	141	154	106
Pittsburgh, PA.................	1,075	25	132	145	149	158	73	151	85	94	87
Portland-Vancouver-Hillsboro, OR-WA......	1,008	21	118	135	158	166	70	148	71	82	60
Riverside-San Bernardino-Ontario, CA.....	1,582	31	163	211	223	211	83	200	92	141	259
St. Louis, MO-IL.................	1,263	22	144	162	191	208	92	193	106	93	75
San Diego-Carlsbad-San Marcos, CA......	1,361	18	121	189	247	246	103	212	82	86	77
San Francisco-Oakland-Fremont, CA........	1,992	33	161	220	269	269	112	311	163	222	266
Seattle-Tacoma-Bellevue, WA.............	1,665	28	143	189	231	245	120	273	149	161	154
Tampa-St. Petersburg-Clearwater, FL........	1,151	23	116	146	187	187	80	172	81	106	76
Washington-Arlington-Alexandria, DC-VA-MD-WV.................	2,916	40	187	238	319	369	162	478	282	396	485

Source: Census Bureau, 2012 American Community Survey, B08134: "Means of Transportation to Work by Travel Time to Work," <http://www.census.gov/acs/www/>, accessed September 2013.

Table 1142. Commuters Who Ride Bicycles or Walk to Work by Sex—Selected Cities: 2009

[Covers cities with the highest percent of commuters who walk or bike to work, based on the National Household Travel Survey and the American Community Survey. Data are weighted 3-year averages for 2007-2009]

	Walking				Biking		
Leading Cities	Percent of commuters who walk to work	Percent male	Percent female	Leading Cities	Percent of commuters who bike to work	Percent male	Percent female
Boston, MA................	13.9	48	52	Portland, OR......................	5.5	62	38
Washington, DC............	11.4	50	50	Minneapolis, MN..................	4.1	63	37
New York, NY.............	10.3	49	51	Seattle, WA.......................	2.9	68	32
San Francisco, CA.........	10.0	54	46	San Francisco, CA...............	2.8	70	30
Seattle, WA..............	8.6	53	47	Sacramento, CA..................	2.2	67	33
Philadelphia, PA............	8.4	45	55	Oakland, CA......................	2.1	66	34
Honolulu, HI..............	8.0	53	47	Washington, DC..................	2.0	67	33
Baltimore, MD..............	6.7	46	54	Tucson, AZ.......................	1.9	71	29
Minneapolis, MN..........	6.4	58	42	Denver, CO.......................	1.8	70	30
Chicago, IL...............	5.8	48	52	Honolulu, HI......................	1.7	72	28
New Orleans, LA...........	5.8	60	40	New Orleans, LA..................	1.7	76	24
Portland, OR..............	5.2	53	47	Philadelphia, PA..................	1.6	70	30
Milwaukee, WI.............	4.6	50	50	Boston, MA.......................	1.5	67	33
Cleveland, OH.............	4.4	47	53	Albuquerque, NM.................	1.3	69	31
Oakland, CA..............	4.4	53	47	Austin, TX........................	1.2	72	28
Atlanta, GA...............	4.2	62	38	Chicago, IL.......................	1.1	76	24
Denver, CA...............	4.1	55	45	Mesa, AZ.........................	1.1	84	16
Miami, FL.................	3.8	57	43	Long Beach, CA...................	1.0	85	15
Tucson, AZ...............	3.6	54	46	Los Angeles, CA..................	0.9	80	20
Los Angeles, CA...........	3.5	52	48	San Diego, CA....................	0.9	72	28
Detroit, MI................	3.3	59	41	San Jose, CA.....................	0.9	79	21
Sacramento, CA...........	3.3	51	49	Atlanta, GA.......................	0.8	71	29
Long Beach, CA...........	3.0	55	45	Columbus, OH....................	0.8	76	24
San Diego, CA.............	2.9	53	47	Milwaukee, WI....................	0.8	73	27
Omaha, NE...............	2.7	59	41	Baltimore, MD....................	0.7	77	23

Source: Alliance for Biking and Walking, *Biking and Walking in the United States: 2012 Benchmarking Report* (copyright). See also <http://www.peoplepoweredmovement.org/>.

Table 1143. Truck Transportation, Couriers and Messengers, and Warehousing and Storage—Estimated Revenue: 2007 to 2011

[In millions of dollars (217,833 represents $217,833,000,000). For taxable employer firms. Estimates have been adjusted to the results of the 2007 Economic Census]

Kind of business	NAICS code [1]	2007	2008	2009	2010	2011
Truck transportation...............................	**484**	**217,833**	**222,109**	**180,460**	**194,616**	**215,910**
General freight trucking..................................	4841	(NA)	(NA)	(NA)	(NA)	(NA)
General freight trucking, local............................	48411	21,174	21,609	17,750	19,336	21,106
General freight trucking, long-distance...................	48412	(NA)	(NA)	(NA)	(NA)	(NA)
General freight trucking, long-distance, truckload...........	484121	83,386	86,557	70,587	77,526	87,040
General freight trucking, long-distance, less than truckload...	484122	37,948	37,925	29,484	32,019	35,877
Specialized freight trucking..............................	4842	(NA)	(NA)	(NA)	(NA)	(NA)
Used household and office goods moving...................	48421	14,549	14,226	11,891	11,940	12,371
Specialized freight (except used goods)trucking, local.........	48422	31,549	31,746	26,046	27,643	30,828
Specialized freight (except used goods) trucking, long-distance.................................	48423	29,227	30,046	24,702	26,152	28,688
Couriers and messengers............................	**492**	**77,877**	**78,836**	**69,849**	**71,622**	**78,498**
Couriers...	4921	74,392	75,594	67,145	68,799	75,427
Local messengers and local delivery......................	4922	3,485	3,242	2,704	2,823	3,071
Warehousing and storage...........................	**493**	**21,921**	**23,193**	**22,538**	**24,245**	**25,571**
General warehousing and storage.........................	49311	15,187	16,130	15,704	16,770	17,889
Refrigerated warehousing and storage.....................	49312	3,391	3,487	3,467	4,034	3,974
Farm product warehousing and storage....................	49313	864	899	801	743	855
Other warehousing and storage...........................	49319	2,479	2,677	2,566	2,698	2,853

[1] Data are based on 2007 North American Industry Classification System (NAICS); see text, this section and Section 15.

Source: Census Bureau, "Service Annual Survey: 2011, Truck Transportation, Messenger Services and Warehousing," January 2013, <http://www.census.gov/services/index.html>.

Table 1144. Truck Transportation—Summary: 2010 and 2011

[In millions of dollars (194,616 represents $194,616,000,000), except where noted. For taxable and tax-exempt employer firms. Covers NAICS 484. Estimates have been adjusted to the results of the 2007 Economic Census. Data are based on the 2007 North American Industry Classification System (NAICS); see text, this section and Section 15]

Item	2010	2011	Percent Change 2010-2011
Total operating revenue.............................	**194,616**	**215,910**	**10.9**
Total motor carrier revenue...............................	179,555	199,728	11.2
Commodities handled:			
Agricultural and fish products............................	19,115	20,851	9.1
Grains, alcohol, and tobacco products....................	8,571	8,929	4.2
Stone, nonmetallic minerals, and metallic ores............	11,347	12,386	9.2
Coal and petroleum products............................	9,755	11,245	15.3
Pharmaceutical and chemical products....................	9,339	10,104	8.2
Wood products, textiles, and leathers.....................	14,680	16,095	9.6
Base metal and machinery...............................	18,003	20,294	12.7
Electronic, motorized vehicles, and precision instruments....	9,941	10,315	3.8
Used household and office goods.........................	9,196	9,590	4.3
New furniture and miscellaneous manufactured products........	16,490	18,241	10.6
Other goods...	53,118	61,678	16.1
Hazardous materials....................................	10,898	12,760	17.1
Inventory of revenue-generating equipment (1,000):			
Trucks...	161	167	3.7
Owned and/or leased with drivers........................	147	153	4.1
Leased without drivers..................................	14	14	0.0
Truck-tractors...	653	665	1.8
Owned and/or leased with drivers........................	564	573	1.6
Leased without drivers..................................	89	92	3.4
Trailers...	1,560	1,589	1.9
Owned and/or leased with drivers........................	1,381	1,403	1.6
Leased without drivers..................................	179	186	3.9

NA Not available. [1] Local trucking is the carrying of goods within a single metro area and its adjacent nonurban areas; long-distance trucking is the carrying of goods between metro areas.

Source: Census Bureau, "Service Annual Survey, 2011: Truck Transportation, Messenger Services and Warehousing," January 2013, <http://www.census.gov/services/index.html>.

Table 1145. Railroads, Class I—Summary: 1990 to 2010

[216 represents 216,000. As of December 31, or calendar year data, except as noted. Compiled from annual reports of Class I railroads only, except where noted. Minus sign (-) indicates deficit]

Item	Unit	1990	2000	2005	2006	2007	2008	2009	2010
Class I line-hauling companies [1]	Number	14	8	7	7	7	7	7	7
Employees [2]	1,000	216	168	162	168	167	164	152	152
Compensation	Mil. dol.	8,654	9,623	10,879	11,419	11,599	11,977	10,960	11,213
Average per hour	Dollars	15.8	21.5	25.7	26.0	27.3	28.9	29.7	29.8
Average per year	Dollars	39,987	57,157	66,975	68,141	69,367	72,836	72,153	73,843
Mileage:									
Railroad line owned [3]	1,000	146	121	121	120	120	119	119	118
Railroad track owned [4]	1,000	244	205	208	207	207	206	206	214
Equipment:									
Locomotives in service	Number	18,835	20,028	22,779	23,730	24,143	24,003	24,045	23,893
Average horsepower	1,000 lb.	2,665	3,261	3,467	3,485	3,518	3,601	3,598	3,614
Cars in service:									
Freight train [5]	1,000	1,212	1,381	1,312	1,347	1,386	1,393	1,363	1,309
Freight cars [6]	1,000	659	560	475	475	460	450	416	398
Average capacity	Tons	87.5	92.3	95.1	96.0	96.7	97.7	98.0	98.6
Income and expenses:									
Operating revenues	Mil. dol.	28,370	34,102	46,118	52,152	54,600	61,243	47,849	58,406
Operating expenses	Mil. dol.	24,652	29,040	37,843	40,980	42,747	47,348	37,225	42,708
Net revenue from operations	Mil. dol.	3,718	5,062	8,275	11,172	11,852	13,895	10,624	15,698
Income before fixed charges	Mil. dol.	4,627	5,361	8,361	11,276	12,084	13,863	11,167	16,255
Provision for taxes [7]	Mil. dol.	1,088	1,430	2,224	3,643	4,108	4,645	3,576	5,731
Ordinary income	Mil. dol.	1,961	2,501	4,917	6,482	6,797	8,102	6,429	9,262
Net income	Mil. dol.	1,977	2,500	4,917	6,482	6,797	8,102	6,423	9,247
Net railway operating income	Mil. dol.	2,648	3,924	6,075	7,560	7,765	9,248	7,045	9,959
Total taxes [8]	Mil. dol.	3,780	4,379	5,176	6,830	7,272	8,069	6,519	8,924
Indus. return on net investment	Percent	8.1	6.5	8.5	10.2	9.9	10.7	8.0	10.4
Gross capital expenditures	Mil. dol.	3,591	5,290	7,068	8,159	9,853	10,189	9,701	9,618
Equipment	Mil. dol.	996	1,508	1,026	1,470	2,213	2,315	2,597	1,914
Roadway and structures	Mil. dol.	2,644	4,549	5,364	6,982	6,944	7,907	7,352	7,854
Other	Mil. dol.	-49	-767	678	-293	696	-32	-248	-150
Balance sheet:									
Total property investment	Mil. dol.	70,348	106,136	141,400	148,320	156,666	164,286	171,769	182,894
Accrued depreciation and amortization	Mil. dol.	22,222	23,989	32,508	35,763	38,702	41,187	44,195	36,140
Net investment	Mil. dol.	48,126	82,147	108,892	112,556	117,963	123,099	127,574	146,754
Shareholder's equity	Mil. dol.	23,662	32,401	55,828	58,901	59,300	62,787	67,826	96,934
Net working capital	Mil. dol.	-3,505	-5,783	-4,729	-4,461	-5,482	-3,592	-1,033	1,143
Cash dividends	Mil. dol.	2,074	819	1,267	1,089	6,427	3,345	1,377	1,989
Amtrak passenger traffic:									
Passenger revenue	Mil. dol.	941.9	1,201.6	1,461.7	1,606.0	1,774.7	1,964.7	1,819.6	1,990.3
Revenue passengers carried	1,000	22,382	22,985	25,076	24,549	26,550	28,705	27,279	29,141
Revenue passenger miles	Million	6,125	5,574	5,381	5,410	5,784	6,179	5,914	6,420
Averages:									
Revenue per passenger	Dollars	42.1	52.3	58.3	65.4	66.8	68.4	66.7	68.3
Revenue per passenger mile	Cents	15.4	21.6	27.2	27.2	30.7	31.8	30.8	31.0
Freight service:									
Freight revenue	Mil. dol.	24,471	33,083	44,457	50,315	52,932	59,409	46,127	56,310
Per ton-mile	Cents	2.7	2.3	2.6	2.8	3.0	3.3	3.0	3.3
Per ton originated	Dollar	19.3	19.0	23.4	25.7	27.3	30.7	27.7	30.4
Revenue-tons originated	Million	1,425	1,738	1,899	1,957	1,940	1,934	1,668	1,851
Revenue-tons carried	Million	2,024	2,179	2,448	2,517	2,431	2,420	2,058	2,280
Tons carried one mile	Billion	1,034	1,466	1,696	1,772	1,771	1,777	1,532	1,691
Average miles of road operated	1,000	133	121	121	120	120	119	119	121
Revenue ton-miles per mile of road	1,000	7,763	12,156	14,071	14,805	14,801	14,887	12,857	13,996
Revenue per ton-mile	Cents	3	2	3	3	3	3	3	3
Train miles	Million	380	504	548	563	543	524	436	476
Net ton-miles per train-mile [9]	Number	2,755	2,923	3,115	3,163	3,274	3,414.0	3,546.0	3,585
Net ton-miles per loaded car-mile [9]	Number	69.1	73.1	79	82	84	87	88	86
Train-miles per train-hour	Miles	24	21	19	18	19	19	21	20
Haul per ton, U.S. as a system	Miles	726	843	893	906	913	919	918	914
Accidents/incidents: [10]									
Casualties—all railroads:									
Persons killed	Number	1,297	937	884	903	851	803	696	726
Persons injured	Number	25,143	11,643	9,550	8,795	9,639	9,058	8,002	8,316
Class I railroads: [11]									
Persons killed	Number	1,166	778	745	788	714	660	587	603
Persons injured	Number	19,284	7,655	6,414	5,817	6,254	5,864	5,033	5,251

[1] See text, this section, for definition of Class I. [2] Average midmonth count. [3] Represents the aggregate length of roadway of all line-haul railroads. Excludes yard tracks, sidings, and parallel lines. (Includes estimate for Class II and III railroads). [4] Includes multiple main tracks, yard tracks, and sidings owned by both line-haul and switching and terminal. (Includes estimate for Class II and III railroads). [5] Includes cars owned by all railroads, private car companies, and shippers. [6] Class I railroads only. Excludes Canadian-owned Class I railroads Grand Trunk Corporation and Soo Line Corporation. [7] Includes state income taxes. [8] Includes payroll, income, and other taxes. [9] Revenue and nonrevenue freight. [10] Includes grade crossings and trespassers. Source for selected data prior to 2008: Federal Railroad Administration, *Railroad Safety Statistics*, <http://www.fra.dot.gov/>. [11] Includes Amtrak data. Includes highway grade crossing casualties.

Source: Except as noted, Association of American Railroads, Washington, DC, *Industry Information, Industry Statistics, Railroad Statistics*, ©. See also <http://www.aar.org/StatisticsandPublications.aspx>.

Table 1146. Railroads, Class-I Line-Haul-Revenue Freight Originated by Commodity Group: 1990 to 2011

[21,401 represents 21,401,000]

Commodity group	1990	1995	2000	2005	2007	2008	2009	2010	2011
Carloads (1,000) [1]	**21,401**	**23,726**	**27,763**	**31,142**	**31,459**	**30,625**	**26,005**	**29,209**	**29,997**
Farm products	1,690	1,692	1,437	1,510	1,681	1,726	1,531	1,758	1,719
Metallic ores	508	463	322	662	662	671	527	841	889
Coal	5,912	6,095	6,954	7,202	7,480	7,713	6,842	7,065	7,055
Nonmetallic minerals	1,202	1,159	1,309	1,488	1,398	1,325	1,054	1,217	1,263
Food and kindred products	1,307	1,377	1,377	1,448	1,493	1,501	1,462	1,619	1,585
Lumber and wood products	780	719	648	611	456	392	285	317	325
Pulp, paper, allied products	611	628	633	679	652	666	546	629	659
Chemicals, allied products	1,531	1,642	1,820	1,937	2,050	2,040	1,895	2,215	2,260
Petroleum and coal products	573	596	565	689	691	578	494	553	576
Stone, clay, and glass products	539	516	541	603	513	467	372	420	439
Primary metal products	477	575	723	680	666	634	354	521	579
Fabricated metal products	31	32	30	36	55	58	62	85	93
Machinery, exc. electrical	39	41	35	42	40	44	38	47	58
Transportation equipment	1,091	1,473	1,984	1,923	1,810	1,521	1,105	1,332	1,452
Waste and scrap materials	439	623	619	706	726	729	568	635	640
Misc. mixed shipments	3,436	4,715	6,796	8,153	8,465	8,078	6,897	7,464	7,858
Tons (mil.) [1]	**1,425**	**1,550**	**1,738**	**1,899**	**1,940**	**1,934**	**1,668**	**1,851**	**1,885**
Farm products	147	154	136	140	152	156	137	159	157
Metallic ores	47	44	32	60	59	60	44	71	76
Coal	579	627	758	804	850	879	787	814	816
Nonmetallic minerals	109	110	126	146	138	132	105	123	128
Food and kindred products	81	91	94	102	105	105	101	109	107
Lumber and wood products	53	51	49	48	36	31	22	25	25
Pulp, paper, allied products	33	36	36	38	35	34	28	31	32
Chemicals, allied products	126	138	155	165	176	175	162	186	192
Petroleum and coal products	40	43	42	57	57	46	39	43	45
Stone, clay, and glass products	44	43	48	55	48	45	35	40	42
Primary metal products	38	47	60	57	56	54	30	44	49
Fabricated metal products	1	1	1	1	1	1	1	1	1
Machinery, exc. electrical	1	1	1	1	1	1	1	1	1
Transportation equipment	23	30	42	38	34	27	19	25	27
Waste and scrap materials	28	38	40	47	48	49	37	43	43
Misc. mixed shipments	58	77	101	120	125	120	103	110	117
Gross revenue (mil. dol.) [1]	**29,775**	**33,782**	**36,331**	**46,743**	**54,637**	**60,513**	**48,041**	**57,438**	**65,258**
Farm products	2,422	3,020	2,673	3,628	4,529	5,403	4,413	5,281	5,556
Metallic ores	408	394	338	485	542	637	404	605	699
Coal	6,954	7,356	7,794	9,393	11,471	14,200	12,052	13,914	16,138
Nonmetallic minerals	885	875	969	1,293	1,527	1,749	1,320	1,817	2,340
Food and kindred products	2,188	2,464	2,424	3,253	4,041	4,610	4,261	4,794	5,133
Lumber and wood products	1,390	1,385	1,524	2,278	1,987	1,684	1,095	1,252	1,370
Pulp, paper, allied products	1,486	1,543	1,526	1,953	2,100	2,228	1,656	1,883	2,090
Chemicals, allied products	3,933	4,553	4,636	5,432	6,830	7,655	6,781	8,122	8,904
Petroleum and coal products	918	997	1,010	1,500	1,853	1,930	1,590	1,828	2,105
Stone, clay, and glass products	931	1,044	1,113	1,505	1,607	1,636	1,215	1,424	1,599
Primary metal products	979	1,199	1,371	1,734	2,267	2,572	1,312	1,966	2,381
Fabricated metal products	42	44	48	55	86	92	77	115	136
Machinery, exc. electrical	67	69	61	91	126	166	116	132	187
Transportation equipment	3,100	3,269	3,843	3,960	4,292	3,964	2,677	3,695	4,418
Waste and scrap materials	504	685	706	1,070	1,276	1,415	1,022	1,206	1,294
Misc. mixed shipments	2,728	3,768	4,927	6,998	7,863	8,184	6,240	7,121	8,245

[1] Includes commodity groups and small packaged freight shipments, not shown separately.

Source: Association of American Railroads, Washington, DC, *Freight Commodity Statistics*, annual, ©. See also <http://www.aar.org/>.

Table 1147. Railroads, Class-I Cars of Revenue Freight Loaded, 1990 to 2011, and by Commodity Group, 2010 and 2011

[In thousands (16,177 represents 16,177,000). Figures are 52-week totals. Intermodal traffic is excluded]

Year	Car-loads [1]	Commodity group	Carloads 2010 [1]	Carloads 2011 [1,2]	Commodity group	Carloads 2010 [1]	Carloads 2011 [1,2]
1990	16,177	Coal	6,675	6,700	Metals and products	457	515
2000 [1]	16,354	Metallic ores	230	265	Stone, clay, and glass products	352	370
2005 [1]	16,691	Chemicals, allied products	1,483	1,533	Crushed stone, gravel, sand	809	860
2006 [1]	16,936	Grain	1,151	1,123	Nonmetallic minerals	253	256
2007 [1]	16,564	Motor vehicles and equipment	627	688	Waste and scrap materials	410	405
2008 [1]	16,208	Pulp, paper, allied products	299	312	Lumber, wood products	132	143
2009 [1]	13,563	Primary forest products	83	77	Coke	170	171
2010 [1]	14,567	Food and kindred products	327	327	Petroleum products	333	370
2011 [1,2]	14,875	Grain mill products	515	495	All other carloads	260	268

[1] Excludes 3 Class I railroads. See text this section for definition of Class I railroads. [2] 2011 data are preliminary.

Source: Association of American Railroads, Washington, DC, *Weekly Railroad Traffic*, annual ©. See also <http://www.aar.org/>.

Table 1148. Petroleum Pipeline Companies—Characteristics: 1980 to 2012

[173 represents 173,000. Covers pipeline companies operating in interstate commerce and subject to the jurisdiction of the Federal Energy Regulatory Commission]

Item	Unit	1980	1985	1990	1995	2000	2005	2010	2011	2012
Miles of pipeline, total..........	1,000	173	171	168	177	152	131	148	150	152
Gathering lines.................	1,000	36	35	32	35	18	14	10	13	14
Trunk lines.....................	1,000	136	136	136	142	134	118	138	137	138
Total deliveries..................	Mil. Bbl.	10,600	10,745	11,378	12,862	14,450	12,732	13,518	13,568	14,136
Crude oil......................	Mil. Bbl.	6,405	6,239	6,563	6,952	6,923	6,675	7,204	7,032	7,471
Products.......................	Mil. Bbl.	4,195	4,506	4,816	5,910	7,527	6,057	6,314	6,537	6,665
Total trunk line traffic..........	Bil. Bbl. miles	3,405	3,342	3,500	3,619	3,508	3,485	3,565	3,608	3,770
Crude oil......................	Bil. Bbl. miles	1,948	1,842	1,891	1,899	1,602	1,571	1,634	1,653	1,760
Products.......................	Bil. Bbl. miles	1,458	1,500	1,609	1,720	1,906	1,914	1,931	1,955	2,009
Carrier property value..........	Mil. dol.	19,752	21,605	25,828	27,460	29,648	29,526	45,380	49,157	54,071
Operating revenues.............	Mil. dol.	6,356	7,461	7,149	7,711	7,483	7,917	11,219	12,562	14,007
Net income.....................	Mil. dol.	1,912	2,431	2,340	2,670	2,705	3,076	4,582	6,109	6,423

Source: PennWell Publishing Co., Houston, TX., *Oil & Gas Journal*, annual ©. See also <http://www.ogj.com/>.

Table 1149. U.S. Postal Service Rates for Letters and Postcards: 1991 to 2013

[In dollars. International rates exclude Canada and Mexico]

Domestic mail date of rate change	Letters — First ounce	Letters — Each added ounce	Post-cards	Express mail— first 1/2 pound	International air mail date of rate change	Letters— first ounce	Post-cards	Aero-grammes
1991 (Feb. 3).............	0.29	0.23	0.19	9.95	**First 1/2 ounce**			
1995 (Jan. 1)..............	0.32	0.23	0.20	10.75	1991 (Feb. 3).........	0.50	0.40	0.45
1999 (Jan. 10).............	0.33	0.22	0.20	11.75	1995 (July 9).........	0.60	0.40	0.45
2001 (Jan. 7).............	0.34	0.21	0.20	12.25	1999 (Jan. 10)......	0.60	0.50	0.50
2001 (July 1).............	0.34	0.23	0.21	12.45	**First ounce** [1]			
2002 (June 30)..........	0.37	0.23	0.23	13.65	2001 (Jan. 7).........	0.80	0.70	0.70
2006 (Jan. 8).............	0.39	0.24	0.24	14.40	2006 (Jan. 8).........	0.84	0.75	0.75
2007 (May 14)............	0.41	0.17	0.26	16.25	2007 (May 14).......	0.90	0.90	[2]
2008 (May 12)............	0.42	0.17	0.27	[3] 12.60	2008 (May 12).......	0.94	0.94	[2]
2009 (May 11)............	0.44	0.17	0.28	[4] 13.05	2009 (May 11)........	0.98	0.98	[2]
2010 (Jan. 4).............	0.44	0.17	0.28	[5] 13.65	2010 (no change)....	0.98	0.98	[2]
2011 (Apr. 17)............	0.44	0.20	0.29	[6] 13.25	2011 (no change)....	0.98	0.98	[2]
2012 (Jan. 22)............	0.45	0.20	0.32	[7] 12.95	2012 (Jan. 22).......	1.05	1.05	[2]
2013 (Jan. 27)............	0.46	0.20	0.33	[8] 14.10	2013 (Jan. 27).......	1.10	1.10	[2]

[1] International letter prices after the first ounce vary according to the price group that is applicable to each destination country.
[2] Aerogrammes were discontinued on May 14, 2007. [3] Zoned pricing structure initiated for Express Mail. Prices for a mail piece weighing up to a half-pound range from $12.60 to zones 1 and 2 to $19.50 to zone 8. [4] Express Mail prices increased on January 18, 2009. Prices for a mail piece weighing up to a half-pound range from $13.05 to zones 1 and 2 to $21.20 to zone 8. [5] Prices for a mail piece weighing up to a half-pound range from $13.65 to zones 1 and 2 to $22.20 to zone 8. [6] Express Mail prices changed on January 2, 2011. Prices for a mail piece weighing up to a half-pound range from $13.25 to zones 1 and 2 to $26.65 to zone 8. [7] Prices for a mail piece weighing up to a half-pound range from $12.95 to zones 1 and 2 to $28.00 to zone 8. [8] Prices for a mail piece weighing up to a half-pound range from $14.10 to zones 1 and 2 to $30.60 to zone 8.

Source: U.S. Postal Service, *Domestic Rate History* and "Price List Notice 123," <http://pe.usps.com/text/dmm300/Notice123.htm>, accessed March 2013.

Table 1150. U.S. Postal Service—Summary: 1990 to 2012

[166,301 represents 166,301,000,000 except as indicated. For years ending September 30. Includes Puerto Rico and all Island Areas]

Item	1990	1995	2000	2005	2010	2011	2012
Offices, stations, and branches	**40,067**	**39,149**	**38,060**	**37,142**	**36,222**	**35,756**	**35,369**
Number of post offices	28,959	28,392	27,876	27,385	27,077	26,927	26,755
Number of stations and branches	11,108	10,757	10,184	9,757	9,145	8,829	8,614
Delivery Points (mil.)	**(NA)**	**(NA)**	**135.9**	**144.3**	**150.9**	**151.5**	**152.1**
Residential	(NA)	(NA)	123.9	131.3	137.5	138.4	139.2
City	(NA)	(NA)	76.1	78.5	80.5	80.8	81.0
P.O. Box	(NA)	(NA)	15.9	15.6	15.7	15.9	16.0
Rural/highway contract	(NA)	(NA)	31.9	37.2	41.2	41.7	42.1
Business	(NA)	(NA)	12.1	13.0	13.3	13.1	13.0
Pieces of mail handled (mil.)	**166,301**	**180,734**	**207,882**	**211,743**	**170,859**	**168,297**	**159,859**
Domestic	165,503	179,933	206,782	210,891	167,208	164,052	155,431
First-class mail [1,2]	89,270	96,296	103,526	98,071	77,592	72,522	68,696
Priority mail [2,3,4]	518	869	1,223	888	779	790	824
Express mail [2,3,5]	59	57	71	56	43	40	40
Periodicals (formerly 2nd class)	10,680	10,194	10,365	9,070	7,269	7,077	6,741
Standard Mail (formerly Standard A) [2]	63,725	71,112	90,057	100,942	81,841	83,957	79,496
Package Services (formerly Standard B)	663	936	1,128	1,166	657	675	645
U.S. Postal Service	538	412	363	621	438	434	440
Free for the blind	35	52	47	76	68	62	58
Shipping Services Volume [2,3,6]	(X)	(X)	(X)	(X)	3,057	3,258	3,502
International economy mail (surface) [3]	166	106	79	23	([3])	([3])	([3])
International, airmail or total [3,7]	632	696	1,021	829	594	987	926
Employees, total (1,000)	**843**	**875**	**901**	**803**	**672**	**646**	**629**
Career	**761**	**753**	**788**	**705**	**584**	**557**	**528**
Headquarters	2	2	2	3	3	3	3
Headquarters support	6	4	6	4	5	4	4
Inspection Service	4	4	4	3	2	2	2
Inspector General	(X)	(X)	1	1	1	1	1
Field Career	749	743	775	693	573	547	518
Postmasters	27	27	26	25	23	22	17
Supervisors/managers	43	35	39	33	28	25	24
Professional, administrative, and technical	10	11	10	9	6	5	5
Clerks	290	274	282	222	157	150	140
Mail handlers	51	57	61	56	49	47	42
City carriers	236	240	241	228	192	184	177
Motor vehicle operators	7	8	9	9	7	7	7
Rural carriers	42	46	57	64	67	66	67
Special delivery messengers	2	2	(X)	(X)	(X)	(X)	(X)
Building and equipment maintenance	33	38	42	40	37	36	35
Vehicle maintenance	5	5	6	5	5	5	5
Other [8]	1	2	2	2	(X)	(X)	(X)
Noncareer	**83**	**122**	**114**	**98**	**88**	**89**	**101**
Casuals	27	26	30	19	7	3	6
Transitional	(X)	32	13	8	16	14	14
Rural substitutes	43	50	58	57	52	50	48
Relief/Leave replacements	12	13	12	12	11	9	9
Nonbargaining temporary	(Z)	1	1	1	2	2	4
Compensation and employee benefits (mil. dol.)	34,214	41,931	49,532	53,932	48,909	48,310	47,689
Avg. salary per employee (dol.) [9]	37,570	45,001	50,103	62,635	72,099	(NA)	(NA)
Pieces of mail per employee (1,000)	197	207	231	264	254	261	254
Total revenue (mil. dol.) [10]	**40,074**	**54,509**	**64,540**	**69,993**	**67,077**	**(NA)**	**(NA)**
Operating postal revenue	39,201	54,176	64,476	69,798	67,052	65,711	65,223
Mail revenue	**37,892**	**52,490**	**62,284**	**66,649**	**53,106**	**51,611**	**49,842**
First-class mail [1,2]	24,023	31,955	35,516	36,062	32,111	30,030	28,867
Priority mail [2,3,4]	1,555	3,075	4,837	4,634	5,455	5,636	5,940
Express mail [2,3,5]	630	711	996	872	829	800	802
Periodicals (formerly 2nd class)	1,509	1,972	2,171	2,161	1,879	1,821	1,731
Standard Mail (formerly Standard A) [2]	8,082	11,792	15,193	18,954	16,728	17,175	16,428
Package Services (formerly Standard B)	919	1,525	1,912	2,201	1,531	1,581	1,589
Shipping Services [2,3,6]	(X)	(X)	(X)	(X)	10,156	10,670	11,596
International economy mail (surface) [3]	222	205	180	134	([3])	([3])	([3])
International, airmail or total [3,7]	941	1,254	1,477	1,631	2,388	2,585	2,816
Service revenue	**1,310**	**1,687**	**2,191**	**3,150**	**3,790**	**3,430**	**3,785**
Registry [11]	174	118	98	77	48	45	39
Certified [11]	310	560	385	601	791	708	663
Insurance [11]	47	52	109	132	128	117	109
Collect-on-delivery	26	21	22	9	7	7	6
Money orders	155	196	235	208	182	172	165
Other [11]	592	737	1,342	2,122	2,635	2,381	2,803
Operating expenses (million dollars) [12]	40,490	50,730	62,992	68,283	75,426	70,634	80,964

NA Not available. X Not applicable. Z Fewer than 500. [1] Items mailed at 1st class rates and weighing 11 ounces or less. [2] Beginning 2010, Express Mail, Priority Mail, First-Class Parcels, and Standard Parcels are not included in Mail categories but reclassified under Shipping and Package Services. [3] "Volume" and "Mailing & Shipping Revenue" restructured for the "Postal Accountability and Enhancement Act (PAEA) of 2006." Some categories eliminated. [4] Provides 2 to 3 day delivery service. [5] Overnight delivery of packages weighing up to 70 pounds. [6] Beginning 2010, also includes Package Services. [7] Airmail only, for 2005 and earlier. Beginning 2010, total international, including all international revenues and pieces formerly included in First-Class Mail, Standard Mail, and Package Services. [8] Includes discontinued operations, area offices, and nurses. Beginning 2010, nurses are included with clerks, and no "other" employment is reported. [9] For career bargaining unit employees. Includes fringe benefits. [10] Net revenues after refunds of postage. Includes operating reimbursements, stamped envelope purchases, indemnity claims, and miscellaneous revenue and expenditure offsets. Shown in year which gave rise to the earnings. [11] Beginning 2000, return receipt revenue broken out from registry, certified, and insurance and included in "other." [12] Shown in year in which obligation was incurred.

Source: U.S. Postal Service, *Annual Report to Congress and Comprehensive Statement on Postal Operations*, 2012, and earlier reports; and unpublished data. See also <http://about.usps.com/strategic-planning/future-postal-service/publications.htm>.

Section 24
Information and Communications

This section presents statistics on the various information and communications media: publishing, including newspapers, periodicals, books, and software; motion pictures, sound recordings, broadcasting, and telecommunications; and information services, such as libraries. Statistics on computer use and Internet access are also included.

Information industry—The U.S. Census Bureau's *Service Annual Survey, Information Services Sector*, provides estimates of operating revenue of taxable firms and revenues and expenses of firms exempt from federal taxes for industries in the information sector of the economy. Similar estimates were previously issued in the *Annual Survey of Communications Services*. Data are based on the North American Industry Classification System (NAICS). The information sector is a newly created economic sector. It comprises establishments engaged in the following processes: (a) producing and distributing information and cultural products, (b) providing the means to transmit or distribute these products as well as data or communications, and (c) processing data. It includes establishments previously classified in the Standard Industrial Classification (SIC) in manufacturing (publishing); transportation, communications, and utilities (telecommunications and broadcasting); and services (software publishing, motion picture production, data processing, online information services, and libraries).

This new sector is comprised of industries which existed previously, were revised from previous industry definitions, or are completely new industries. Among those which existed previously are newspaper publishers, motion picture and video production, and online information services. Revised industries include book publishers, libraries, and archives.

Newly created industries include database and directory publishers, record production, music publishers, sound recording studios, cable networks, wired telecommunications carriers, paging, and satellite telecommunications.

Data from 1998 to 2003 are based on the 1997 NAICS; 2004 to 2010 data are based variously based on 2002 and 2007 NAICS; beginning in 2011, data are all based on 2007 NAICS, with data for various previous years revised to accommodate the new NAICS codes. Major revisions in many communications industries affect the comparability of these data. The following URL contains detailed information about NAICS, see <http://www.census.gov/eos/www/naics/>. See also the text in Section 15, Business Enterprise.

Several industries in the information sectors have been consolidated. Telecommunications now encompasses wired (including broadband Internet service providers), wireless (including mobile), and satellite telecommunications. Broadcasting covers radio, television, and cable and other subscription programming. Internet publishing, and broadcasting, and web search portals are now grouped together.

The 1997 Economic Census was the first economic census to cover the new information sector of the economy. The census, conducted every 5 years, for the years ending "2" and "7," provides information on the number of establishments, receipts, payroll, and paid employees for the United States and various geographic levels. The most recent reports are from the 2007 Economic Census. This census was conducted in accordance with the 2007 NAICS.

The Federal Communications Commission (FCC), established in 1934, regulates wire and radio communications. Only the largest carriers and holding companies file annual financial reports which are publically available. The FCC has jurisdiction over interstate and foreign communication services but not over intrastate or local services. Also, the gross operating revenues of the telephone carriers reporting publically available data annually to the FCC are estimated to cover about 90 percent of the revenues of all U.S. telephone companies. Data are not service comparable with Census Bureau's *Annual Survey* because of coverage and different accounting practices for those telephone companies which report to the FCC.

Reports filed by the broadcasting industry cover all radio and television stations operating in the United States. The private radio services represent the largest and most diverse group of licensees regulated by the FCC. These services provide voice, data communications, point-to-point, and point-to-multipoint radio communications for fixed and mobile communicators. Major users of these services are small businesses, the aviation industry, the maritime trades, the land transportation industry, the manufacturing industry, state and local public safety and governmental authorities, emergency medical service providers, amateur radio operators, and personal radio operations (CB and the General Mobile Radio Service). The FCC also licenses entities as private and common carriers. Private and common carriers provide fixed and land mobile communications service on a for-profit basis. Principal sources of wire, radio, and television data are the FCC's Annual Report and its annual *Statistics of Communications Common Carriers* at <http://fcc.gov/wcb/iatd/stats.html/>.

Statistics on publishing are available from the Census Bureau, as well as from various private agencies. Editor & Publisher Co., New York, NY, presents annual data on the number and circulation of daily and Sunday newspapers in its *International Year Book*. The Book Industry Study Group, New York, NY, collects data on books sold and domestic consumer expenditures. Data on academic and public libraries are collected by the Institute of Museums and Library Services. Data on Internet use by adults are collected by the Pew Internet and American Life Project, Washington, DC, and Gfk Mediamark Research and Intelligence, LLC., New York, NY.

Statistical reliability—For a discussion of statistical collection and estimation, sampling procedures, and measures of statistical reliability applicable to Census Bureau data, see Appendix III.

Table 1151. Information Industries—Type of Establishment, Employees, and Payroll: 2011

[Employees in thousands (3,121.3 represents 3,121,300); payroll in millions of dollars (234,014 represents $234,014,000,000). Excludes self-employed individuals, employees of private households, railroad employees, agricultural production employees, and most government employees. For more information see source and Appendix III]

Industry	2007 NAICS code [1]	Establishments				Employ-ees [6] (1,000)	Annual payroll (mil. dol.)
		Total [2]	Corpora-tions [3]	Sole proprietor-ships [4]	Non-profits [5]		
Information industries.........................	**51**	**134,452**	**75,771**	**3,940**	**5,066**	**3,121.3**	**234,014**
Publishing industries............................	511	27,215	13,071	1,337	809	856.7	74,849
Newspaper, periodical, book, and database publishers................................	5111	19,770	8,310	1,234	796	494.3	26,188
Newspaper publishers.............................	51111	7,671	3,689	600	169	250.6	9,979
Periodical publishers.............................	51112	6,807	2,700	349	350	114.7	7,897
Book publishers.............................	51113	2,885	929	169	244	72.0	4,730
Database and directory publishers................	51114	1,416	741	42	12	35.4	2,444
Other publishers.................................	51119	991	251	74	21	21.6	1,137
Greeting card publishers........................	511191	111	29	7	(X)	12.4	603
All other publishers............................	511199	880	222	67	21	9.2	534
Software publishers.............................	5112	7,445	4,761	103	13	362.4	48,661
Motion picture and sound recording industries.......	512	24,259	7,409	1,208	531	310.0	15,512
Motion picture and video industries................	5121	20,577	6,393	954	445	287.3	13,551
Motion picture and video production..............	51211	12,919	3,406	540	241	130.7	9,426
Motion picture and video distribution.............	51212	436	162	9	13	6.3	770
Motion picture and video exhibition...............	51213	4,819	2,153	304	180	126.8	1,419
Motion picture theaters (except drive-ins)........	512131	4,575	2,100	246	179	125.6	1,394
Drive-in motion picture theaters.................	512132	244	53	58	1	1.2	24
Post production and other motion picture and video industries.............................	51219	2,403	672	101	11	23.5	1,936
Teleproduction and other postproduction services...........................	512191	2,162	594	84	7	21.4	1,775
Other motion picture and video industries........	512199	241	78	17	4	2.1	161
Sound recording industries........................	5122	3,682	1,016	254	86	22.6	1,961
Record production.............................	51221	344	98	14	3	1.4	88
Integrated record production/distribution..........	51222	446	177	17	8	8.1	1,066
Music publishers.............................	51223	797	268	55	7	5.4	415
Sound recording studios.........................	51224	1,673	371	149	11	5.4	282
Other sound recording industries.................	51229	422	102	19	57	2.4	111
Broadcasting (except Internet)...................	515	9,814	4,841	251	1,180	263.6	19,318
Radio and television broadcasting.................	5151	9,044	4,460	229	1,028	213.6	13,364
Radio broadcasting.............................	51511	6,846	3,210	190	725	102.9	5,332
Radio networks.............................	515111	1,048	287	30	211	13.0	837
Radio stations.............................	515112	5,798	2,923	160	514	89.9	4,496
Television broadcasting.........................	51512	2,198	1,250	39	303	110.7	8,032
Cable and other subscription programming.........	5152	770	381	22	152	50.0	5,954
Telecommunications.............................	517	50,882	40,053	412	305	1,108.8	74,869
Wired telecommunications carriers.................	5171	34,995	31,752	136	258	800.5	55,304
Wireless telecommunications carriers (except satellite).............................	5172	10,145	6,221	35	8	245.9	14,965
Satellite telecommunications.....................	5174	659	301	28	10	8.4	783
Other telecommunications........................	5179	5,083	1,779	213	29	53.9	3,817
Telecommunications resellers.....................	517911	2,102	710	71	3	23.4	1,486
Data processing, hosting, and related services.............................	518	12,294	6,610	361	109	401.1	30,421
Other information services.........................	519	9,988	3,787	371	2,132	181.2	19,044
News syndicates.............................	51911	531	363	15	15	8.3	720
Libraries and archives...........................	51912	2,226	93	84	1,977	27.6	769
Internet publishing and broadcasting and Web search portals.............................	51913	6,398	3,114	230	123	135.6	16,977
All other information services.....................	51919	833	217	42	17	9.8	579

X Not applicable. [1] 2007 North American Industry Classification System; see text, this section and Section 15. [2] Includes other types of establishments, not shown separately. [3] An incorporated business that is granted a charter recognizing it as a separate legal entity having its own privileges, and liabilities distinct from those of its members. [4] An unincorporated business with a sole owner. [5] An organization that does not distribute surplus funds to its owners or shareholders, but instead uses surplus funds to help pursue its goals. Most non-profit organizations are exempt from income taxes. [6] For employees on the payroll for the pay period including March 12.

Source: U.S. Census Bureau, County Business Patterns, "Geography Area Series: County Business Patterns by Legal Form of Organization and Employment Size Class," <http://factfinder2.census.gov>, accessed June 2013.

Table 1152. Information Sector Services—Estimated Revenue and Expenses: 2009 to 2011

[In millions of dollars (1,074,959 represents $1,074,959,000,000). For all employer firms regardless of tax status. Estimates have been adjusted to the results of the 2007 Economic Census. Data released for 2011 are based on the 2007 NAICS; data for 2010 and prior have been restated to reflect comparable data on the 2007 NAICS basis. Based on the Service Annual Survey; see Appendix III]

Industry	2007 NAICS [1] code	Operating revenue			Operating expenses		
		2009	2010	2011	2009	2010	2011
Information industries..........................	**51**	**1,074,959**	**1,110,225**	**1,160,849**	**834,134**	**846,133**	**876,599**
Publishing industries (except Internet)...............	511	264,194	265,718	273,902	186,649	186,992	190,756
Newspaper publishers..........................	51111	36,358	34,695	33,164	34,380	31,489	30,868
Periodical publishers..........................	51112	39,099	38,395	39,503	29,481	28,079	28,934
Book publishers..............................	51113	27,404	28,121	27,530	16,528	16,794	16,637
Directory and mailing list publishers...............	51114	16,670	13,475	13,040	12,226	11,847	10,803
Greeting card publishers....................	511191	3,862	3,852	3,822	2,743	2,617	2,607
All other publishers..........................	511199	1,820	1,755	1,754	1,390	1,284	1,321
Software publishers..........................	5112	138,981	145,425	155,089	89,901	94,882	99,586
Motion picture and sound recording industries.......	512	90,398	95,118	95,762	74,601	76,388	77,553
Motion picture and video production and distribution [2]...............	5121x	57,910	62,567	63,840	49,647	51,551	53,283
Motion picture and video exhibition...............	51213	13,293	13,454	13,291	10,582	10,757	10,579
Teleproduction and other postproduction services...............................	512191	4,127	4,715	5,063	4,048	4,385	4,673
Other motion picture and video industries.......	512199	649	595	527	553	515	439
Record production............................	51221	425	453	495	302	303	311
Integrated record production/distribution..........	51222	8,665	8,258	7,471	6,713	6,403	5,683
Music publishers.............................	51223	4,155	3,793	3,770	1,690	1,354	1,436
Sound recording studios......................	51224	749	839	872	667	735	755
Other sound recording industries..............	51229	425	444	433	399	385	394
Broadcasting (except Internet)....................	515	98,934	107,520	112,785	73,356	78,212	80,522
Radio networks...............................	515111	4,307	4,883	5,007	4,085	4,278	4,186
Radio stations...............................	515112	11,643	12,135	12,167	9,550	9,375	9,386
Television broadcasting.......................	51512	31,553	35,334	35,293	27,665	30,240	29,835
Cable and other subscription programming.......	5152	51,431	55,168	60,318	32,056	34,319	37,115
Telecommunications..............................	517	505,503	517,507	540,040	402,672	401,776	414,729
Wired telecommunications carriers [3]...........	5171	291,054	293,929	301,674	250,218	249,733	251,943
Wireless telecommunications carriers [4] (except satellite)................................	5172	185,685	195,526	208,932	132,813	133,589	143,686
Satellite telecommunications.....................	5174	5,203	5,296	5,631	3,342	2,879	3,039
Telecommunications resellers [5].................	517911	10,044	9,817	9,749	5,736	5,383	5,399
All other telecommunications [6]................	517919	13,517	12,939	14,054	10,563	10,192	10,662
Data processing, hosting, and related services......	518	71,614	76,156	81,091	64,220	66,988	71,188
Other information services........................	519	44,316	48,206	57,269	32,636	35,777	41,851
News syndicates.............................	51911	1,953	1,960	2,164	1,661	1,635	1,798
Libraries and archives........................	51912	2,016	1,897	2,087	1,925	2,019	2,087
Internet publishing and broadcasting, and Web search portals [7].........................	51913	37,775	41,725	50,390	26,872	29,624	35,439
Other information services....................	51919	2,572	2,624	2,628	2,178	2,499	2,527

[1] North American Industry Classification System (NAICS), 2007; see text, Section 15. [2] Includes 2007 NAICS 51211 (Motion Picture and Video Production) and 2007 NAICS 51212 (Motion Picture and Video Distribution). [3] Includes 2002 NAICS 5171 (Wired Telecommunications Carriers), 2002 NAICS 5175 (Cable and Other Program Distribution), and a portion of 2002 NAICS 518111 (Internet Service Providers). [4] Includes 2002 NAICS 517211 (Paging), 2002 NAICS 517212 (Cellular and Other Wireless Telecommunications) and a portion of 2002 NAICS 518111 (Internet Service Providers). [5] Includes 2002 NAICS 5173 (Telecommunications Resellers). [6] Includes 2002 NAICS 517910 (Other Telecommunications) and a portion of 2002 NAICS 518111 (Internet Service Providers). [7] Includes 2002 NAICS 516 (Internet Publishing and Broadcasting) and 2002 NAICS 518112 (Web Search Portals).

Source: U.S. Census Bureau, Annual and Quarterly Services, "2011 Annual Services," <http://www.census.gov/services/index.html>, accessed June 2013.

Table 1153. Information Industries—Establishments, Revenue, Payroll, and Employees by Kind of Business: 2007

[For establishments with payroll (1,072,343, represents $1,072,343,000,000). Based on the 2007 Economic Census; see Appendix III]

Kind of business	2007 NAICS code [1]	Establish-ments	Receipts (mil. dol.)	Annual payroll (mil. dol.)	Paid employees (1,000)
Information industries.........................	51	**141,566**	**1,072,343**	**228,837**	**3,497**
Publishing industries (except Internet)............................	511	30,958	282,224	80,867	1,093
Newspaper, periodical, book, & directory publishers...............	5111	22,683	146,823	34,504	706
Software publishers........................	5112	8,275	135,401	46,363	387
Motion picture & sound recording industries......................	512	23,891	94,986	17,635	336
Motion picture & video industries.......................	5121	20,164	79,797	15,494	309
Sound recording industries.......................	5122	3,727	15,189	2,142	27
Broadcasting (except Internet)............................	515	10,188	99,919	18,076	295
Cable & other subscription programming...........................	5152	717	44,926	3,751	46
Telecommunications........................	517	51,999	491,124	75,401	1,251
Wired telecommunications carriers.....................	5171	33,548	290,781	54,192	885
Wireless telecommunications carriers (except satellite)...........	5172	11,973	170,584	16,201	289
Satellite telecommunications.......................	5174	823	4,450	793	10
Other telecommunications.........................	5179	5,655	25,309	4,216	67
Data processing, hosting, and related services......................	518	17,129	66,652	26,428	394
Other information services...............	519	7,401	37,438	10,428	128

[1] North American Industry Classification System, 2007; see text, this section and Section 15.

Source: U.S. Census Bureau, 2007 Economic Census, "Table EC0751A1: Geographic Area Series: Summary Statistics for the United States," <http://factfinder2.census.gov/>.

Table 1154. Information Industries—Establishments, Employees, and Payroll by State: 2011

[Annual payroll in millions of dollars (234,014 represents 234,014,000,000). Based on Census Bureau's County Business Patterns and Nonemployer Statistics programs. Data are for North American Industry Classification System (NAICS) 2007 code 51]

State	Establish-ments	Annual payroll (mil. dol)	Paid employ-ees [1]	Non-employer establish-ments	State	Establish-ments	Annual payroll (mil. dol)	Paid employ-ees [1]	Non-employer establish-ments
U.S.........	**134,452**	**234,014**	**3,121,317**	**317,803**	MO.........	2,525	3,570	60,841	4,589
AL...........	1,544	1,688	33,300	2,924	MT.........	581	396	9,261	959
AK...........	398	403	6,751	541	NE.........	907	934	18,609	1,301
AZ...........	2,044	2,964	50,521	5,592	NV.........	1,111	839	15,418	3,121
AR...........	1,017	1,262	24,099	1,701	NH.........	717	949	13,056	1,510
CA...........	20,574	49,902	497,861	56,596	NJ.........	3,759	8,170	93,646	10,230
CO...........	2,942	5,957	78,188	7,175	NM.........	750	514	12,613	1,567
CT...........	1,647	2,714	37,559	4,000	NY.........	10,983	23,389	261,730	28,706
DE...........	409	380	7,944	839	NC.........	3,438	4,608	73,347	8,067
DC...........	738	2,051	20,035	1,469	NC.........	330	364	6,971	451
FL...........	7,871	9,395	149,771	21,747	OH.........	3,836	5,256	90,329	9,142
GA...........	4,027	8,691	116,856	10,193	OK.........	1,526	1,287	27,974	2,719
HI...........	531	455	8,184	1,155	OR.........	1,926	1,983	35,295	4,633
ID...........	650	499	11,945	1,355	PA.........	4,988	8,122	124,689	10,151
IL...........	5,378	8,415	118,183	11,585	RI.........	420	401	6,790	914
IN...........	2,199	2,079	42,169	4,512	SC.........	1,386	1,642	32,719	3,296
IA...........	1,561	1,417	31,266	2,186	SD.........	421	256	6,610	573
KS...........	1,428	2,514	39,960	2,169	TN.........	2,424	2,578	48,967	6,504
KY...........	1,507	1,312	31,880	2,627	TX.........	8,912	16,620	232,005	22,324
LA...........	1,375	1,170	23,722	3,041	UT.........	1,393	2,139	33,882	3,649
ME...........	715	478	11,216	1,270	VT.........	468	256	5,270	851
MD...........	2,337	4,148	54,643	6,897	VA.........	3,852	7,935	95,525	7,795
MA...........	3,531	8,145	94,082	7,979	WA.........	3,166	13,464	115,126	6,798
MI...........	3,330	4,151	66,616	8,185	WV.........	724	448	10,768	882
MN...........	2,614	4,024	61,068	5,338	WI.........	2,303	2,923	53,964	4,065
MS...........	924	597	14,162	1,431	WY.........	315	163	3,931	499

[1] Number of paid employees for pay period including March 12.

Source: U.S. Census Bureau, County Business Patterns, "Table CB1100A11: 2011 County Business Patterns: Geography Area Series: County Business Patterns," and Nonemployer Statistics, "Table NS1100A1: 2011 Nonemployer Statistics: Geographic Area Series: Nonemployer Statistics by Legal Form of Organization: 2011," <http://factfinder2.census.gov>, accessed September 2013.

Table 1155. Utilization and Number of Selected Media: 2000 to 2011

[100.2 represents 100,200,000]

Media	Unit	2000	2003	2004	2005	2006	2007	2008	2009	2010	2011
Households with—											
Telephones [1]	Millions	100.2	107.1	106.4	107.0	108.8	112.2	112.7	114.0	114.0	114.4
Telephone service [1]	Percent	94.1	94.7	93.5	92.9	93.4	94.9	95.0	95.7	95.5	95.6
Land line households with											
wireless telephone [2]	Percent	(X)	(X)	(X)	42.4	45.6	58.9	58.5	59.4	58.1	(NA)
Wireless-only [2]	Percent	(X)	(X)	(X)	7.3	10.5	13.6	17.5	22.7	26.6	(NA)
Radio [3]	Millions	100.5	106.7	108.3	109.9	110.5	110.5	115.6	114.0	115.0	(NA)
Percent of total households	Percent	99.0	99.0	99.0	99.0	99.0	99.0	99.0	99.0	99.0	(NA)
Average number of sets	Number	5.6	8.0	8.0	8.0	8.0	8.0	8.0	8.0	8.0	(NA)
Total broadcast stations [4,5]	Number	(NA)	26,613	26,254	27,354	27,807	29,593	29,832	30,503	30,630	30,411
Radio stations	Number	(NA)	13,563	13,525	13,660	13,837	13,977	14,253	14,420	14,619	14,952
AM stations	Number	4,685	4,794	4,774	4,757	4,754	4,776	4,786	4,790	4,782	4,766
FM commercial	Number	5,892	6,217	6,218	6,231	6,266	6,309	6,427	6,479	6,526	6,542
FM educational	Number	(NA)	2,552	2,533	2,672	2,817	2,892	3,040	3,151	3,311	3,644
Television stations [4]	Number	1,663	1,733	1,748	1,750	1,756	1,759	1,759	1,782	1,781	1,783
Commercial	Number	1,288	1,352	1,366	1,370	1,376	1,379	1,378	1,392	1,390	1,387
VHF TV band	Number	567	585	589	588	587	583	582	373	368	360
UHF TV band	Number	721	767	777	782	789	796	796	1,019	1,022	1,027
Educational	Number	(NA)	381	382	380	380	380	381	390	391	396
VHF TV band	Number	(NA)	127	125	126	128	128	129	107	107	107
UHF TV band	Number	(NA)	254	257	254	252	252	252	283	284	289
Broadband subscribers: [6]											
Total fixed broadband [7]	Millions	6.8	27.7	37.4	47.8	60.2	70.2	75.7	80.0	84.5	88.3
Mobile broadband [8]	Millions	(NA)	(NA)	(NA)	(NA)	(NA)	(NA)	26.5	56.3	97.5	142.1

NA Not available. X Not applicable. [1] As of November. Based on Current Population Survey. For occupied housing units. Source: Federal Communications Commission, *Telephone Subscribership in the United States*, December 2011. See also: <www.fcc.gov/wcb/iatd/stats.html/>. [2] From January to June. Based on National Health Interview Survey for families living in the same housing unit. Source: National Center for Health Statistics, *Wireless Substitution: Early Release of Estimates From the National Health Interview Survey*, July–December 2011. See also <http://www.cdc.gov/nchs/nhis/releases.htm>. A "family" can be an individual or a group of two or more related persons living together in the same housing unit (a "household"). [3] Source: Radio Advertising Bureau, New York, NY, *Radio Marketing Guide*, annual ©. [4] As of December, 31. Source: Federal Communications Commission Encyclopedia, Broadcast Station Totals, <http://www.fcc.gov/encyclopedia/broadcast-radio-am-and-fm-application-status-lists>, accessed September 2013. [5] Includes Class A, Low Power TV, UHF and VHF Translators; FM Translators and Boosters; and Low Power FM stations. [6] As of December. Internet access over 200 kilobits per second in at least one direction. Source: Federal Communications Commission, Wireline Competition Bureau, *Internet Access Services: Status as of June 30, 2012*, May 2013. FCC Form 477 gathers standardized information about subscribership to high-speed Internet access services from telephone companies, cable system operators, terrestrial wireless service providers, satellite service providers, and other facilities-based providers of advanced telecommunications capability. [7] Includes aDSL, sDSL, cable modem, FTTP, satellite, fixed wireless, power line, and other. [8] Reporting changed between June 2008 and December 2008; see source for details.

Source: Compiled from sources mentioned in footnotes.

Table 1156. Multimedia Audiences—Summary: 2012

[In percent, except total (232,649 represents 232,649,000). As of Fall 2012. For persons 18 years old and over. Represents the percent of persons participating during the prior week, except as indicated. Based on sample and subject to sampling error; see source for details]

Item	Total population (1,000)	Television viewing	Television prime time viewing	Cable TV viewing [1]	Radio listening	Newspaper reading	Accessed Internet [2]
Total	232,649	91.65	81.57	81.26	82.08	57.93	79.47
18 to 24 years old	29,802	86.48	68.60	76.34	85.79	47.21	92.50
25 to 34 years old	41,810	86.92	74.69	75.71	86.66	48.55	91.24
35 to 44 years old	40,059	91.20	81.25	81.81	87.11	53.61	88.39
45 to 54 years old	44,215	93.59	85.87	83.41	85.94	59.58	82.22
55 to 64 years old	37,176	94.20	86.32	84.62	82.94	65.65	76.76
65 years old and over	39,407	96.45	89.72	84.73	64.14	71.25	47.52
Male	112,618	91.92	81.11	81.43	83.82	57.95	79.52
Female	119,851	91.40	82.00	81.10	80.44	57.91	79.41
White only	173,512	91.38	81.93	82.71	81.92	59.88	81.60
Black only	26,421	94.90	84.98	81.43	84.26	63.76	72.65
Other races/multiple classifications	32,536	90.42	76.91	73.39	81.12	42.82	73.61
Not high school graduate	31,082	91.88	78.94	68.16	72.95	41.90	42.88
High school graduate	70,692	92.98	83.31	82.40	80.60	59.50	70.94
Attend college	66,177	91.59	80.87	83.24	84.52	59.54	89.72
College graduate	64,519	90.13	81.67	84.28	85.59	62.28	95.92
Employed:							
Full time	111,947	91.59	80.97	83.24	89.38	57.28	90.28
Part time	27,380	88.90	76.16	79.56	84.64	58.66	86.36
Not employed	93,141	92.53	83.88	79.37	72.54	58.49	64.45
Household income:							
Less than $50,000	98,961	90.97	79.81	72.64	76.32	54.55	62.88
$50,000 to $74,999	43,960	92.18	81.80	84.71	84.43	58.93	85.78
$75,000 to $149,999	65,415	92.46	83.73	88.31	87.37	61.30	94.02
$150,000 or more	24,133	91.28	82.55	91.23	87.07	60.81	96.54

[1] In the past 7 days. [2] In the last 30 days.

Source: GfK Mediamark Research & Intelligence, LLC, New York, NY, Multimedia Audiences, Fall 2012 ©. See also <http://www.gfkmri.com>.

Table 1157. Publishing Industries—Estimated Revenue by Source and Media Type: 2010 and 2011

[In millions of dollars (265,718 represents $265,718,000,000). For all employer firms regardless of tax status. Data are based on the 2007 North American Industry Classification System (NAICS), and cover 2007 NAICS 51111, 51112, 51113, and 51114. Estimates have been adjusted to the results of the 2007 Economic Census. See text, this section and Section 15, and Appendix III]

Source of revenue and media type	2010	2011	Percent change
Publishing industries (except Internet) [1]	**265,718**	**273,902**	**3.1**
Newspaper publishers	**34,695**	**33,164**	**-4.4**
Subscription and sales	8,753	8,570	-2.1
Advertising space	21,055	19,731	-6.3
Other operating revenue	4,887	4,863	-0.5
Printing services	1,258	1,313	4.4
Distribution services	1,306	1,227	-6.0
All other	2,323	2,323	0.0
Print newspapers	27,849	26,147	-6.1
Online newspapers	1,667	1,893	13.6
Other media newspapers	292	261	-10.6
Periodical publishers	**38,395**	**39,503**	**2.9**
Subscription and sales	10,342	10,604	2.5
Advertising space	13,321	13,421	0.8
Other operating revenue	14,732	(NA)	(NA)
Printing services for others	1,276	1,248	-2.2
Licensing of rights to content	354	370	4.5
All other	13,102	(S)	(NA)
Print periodicals	19,623	19,801	0.9
Online periodicals	3,399	3,514	3.4
Other media periodicals	641	710	10.8
Book publishers	**28,121**	**27,530**	**-2.1**
Textbooks	8,759	8,354	-4.6
Children's books	3,243	3,219	-0.7
General reference books	619	651	5.2
Professional, technical, and scholarly books	5,194	5,132	-1.2
Adult trade books	6,673	6,596	-1.2
All other operating revenue	3,633	3,578	-1.5
Print books	20,150	19,240	-4.5
Online books	3,328	3,778	13.5
Other media books	1,010	934	-7.5
Directory and mailing list publishers	**13,475**	**13,040**	**-3.2**
Subscription and sales	3,673	4,178	13.7
Advertising space	9,065	8,199	-9.6
Other operating revenue	737	663	-10.0
Rental or sale of mailing lists	127	118	-7.1
All other	610	545	-10.7
Print directories, databases, and other collections of information	8,302	8,228	-0.9
Online directories, databases, and other collections of information	3,956	3,706	-6.3
Other media directories, databases, and other collections of information	480	443	-7.7

NA Not available. S Figure does not meet publication standards. [1] Includes other industries not shown separately.

Source: U.S. Census Bureau, Annual and Quarterly Services, "2011 Annual Services," <http://www.census.gov/services/index.html>, accessed June 2013.

Table 1158. Daily and Sunday Newspapers—Number and Circulation: 1970 to 2009

[Number of newspapers as of February 1 the following year. Circulation figures as of September 30 of year shown (62.1 represents 62,100,000). For English language newspapers only]

Type	1970	1980	1990	2000	2002	2003	2004	2005	2006	2007	2008	2009
NUMBER												
Daily: Total [1]	1,748	1,745	1,611	1,480	1,457	1,456	1,457	1,452	1,437	1,422	1,408	1,397
Morning	334	387	559	766	777	787	814	817	833	867	872	869
Evening	1,429	1,388	1,084	727	692	680	653	645	614	565	546	528
Sunday	586	736	863	917	913	917	915	914	907	907	902	919
NET PAID CIRCULATION (mil.)												
Daily: Total [1]	62.1	62.2	62.3	55.8	55.2	55.2	54.6	53.3	52.3	50.7	48.6	46.3
Morning	25.9	29.4	41.3	46.8	46.6	46.9	46.9	46.1	45.4	44.5	42.8	40.8
Evening	36.2	32.8	21.0	9.0	8.6	8.3	7.7	7.2	6.9	6.2	5.8	5.5
Sunday	49.2	54.7	62.6	59.4	58.8	58.5	57.8	55.3	53.2	51.2	49.1	46.8
PER CAPITA CIRCULATION [2]												
Daily: Total [1]	0.30	0.27	0.25	0.20	0.19	0.19	0.19	0.18	0.18	0.17	0.16	0.15
Morning	0.13	0.13	0.17	0.17	0.16	0.16	0.16	0.16	0.15	0.15	0.14	0.13
Evening	0.18	0.14	0.08	0.03	0.03	0.03	0.03	0.02	0.02	0.02	0.02	0.02
Sunday	0.24	0.24	0.25	0.21	0.20	0.20	0.20	0.19	0.18	0.17	0.16	0.15

[1] All-day newspapers are counted in both morning and evening columns but only once in total. Circulation is divided equally between morning and evening. [2] Based on U.S. Census Bureau estimated resident population as of July 1.

Source: Editor & Publisher Co., New York, NY, *Editor & Publisher International Year Book* ©, annual. See also <http://www.editorandpublisher.com/>.

Table 1159. Daily and Sunday Newspapers—Number and Circulation, 1991 to 2009, and by State, 2009

[Number of newspapers as of February 1 the following year. Circulation as of September 30 (60,687 represents 60,687,000). For English language newspapers only. California, New York, Massachusetts, and Virginia Sunday newspapers include national circulation]

State	Daily Number	Daily Circulation[1] Net paid (1,000)	Daily Circulation[1] Per capita[2]	Sunday Number	Sunday Net paid circulation[1] (1,000s)	State	Daily Number	Daily Circulation[1] Net paid (1,000)	Daily Circulation[1] Per capita[2]	Sunday Number	Sunday Net paid circulation[1] (1,000s)
Total, 1991	1,586	60,687	0.24	875	62,068	IA	37	518	0.17	13	553
Total, 1992	1,570	60,164	0.23	891	62,160	KS	35	331	0.12	13	297
Total, 1993	1,556	59,812	0.23	884	62,566	KY	22	486	0.11	14	528
Total, 1994	1,548	59,305	0.23	886	62,294	LA	24	530	0.12	18	579
Total, 1995	1,533	58,193	0.22	888	61,529	ME	7	186	0.14	4	151
Total, 1996	1,520	56,983	0.21	890	60,798	MD	10	390	0.07	8	527
Total, 1997	1,509	56,728	0.21	903	60,484	MA	32	1,073	0.16	16	1,026
Total, 1998	1,489	56,182	0.20	898	60,066	MI	48	1,372	0.14	28	1,660
Total, 1999	1,483	55,979	0.20	905	59,894	MN	25	754	0.14	15	926
Total, 2000	1,480	55,773	0.20	917	59,421	MS	22	293	0.10	19	305
Total, 2001	1,468	55,578	0.19	913	59,090	MO	42	747	0.12	22	1,000
Total, 2002	1,457	55,186	0.19	913	58,780	MT	11	172	0.18	7	172
Total, 2003	1,456	55,185	0.19	917	58,495	NE	15	348	0.19	6	322
Total, 2004	1,457	54,626	0.19	915	57,753	NV	6	248	0.09	5	281
Total, 2005	1,452	53,345	0.18	914	55,270	NH	9	163	0.12	8	184
Total, 2006	1,437	52,329	0.18	907	53,175	NJ	17	906	0.10	14	1,103
Total, 2007	1,422	50,742	0.17	907	51,246	NM	17	244	0.12	12	243
Total, 2008	1,408	48,598	0.16	902	49,115	NY	60	5,981	0.31	44	4,374
						NC	46	1,042	0.11	38	1,193
Total, 2009	**1,397**	**46,278**	**0.15**	**919**	**46,895**	ND	10	146	0.23	7	147
AL	24	537	0.11	20	605	OH	82	1,836	0.16	42	2,106
AK	7	87	0.12	4	89	OK	37	485	0.13	30	580
AZ	16	579	0.09	12	733	OR	18	541	0.14	12	560
AR	25	421	0.15	15	485	PA	80	2,349	0.19	43	2,600
CA	83	6,041	0.16	59	4,737	RI	6	142	0.14	3	173
CO	29	779	0.16	15	840	SC	16	499	0.11	14	585
CT	17	526	0.15	13	614	SD	11	132	0.16	4	110
DE	1	105	0.12	2	130	TN	26	731	0.12	19	851
DC	2	650	1.08	2	868	TX	81	2,105	0.08	78	2,714
FL	37	2,660	0.14	36	3,347	UT	6	307	0.11	6	355
GA	34	753	0.08	29	1,022	VT	9	104	0.17	4	82
HI	4	235	0.18	6	252	VA	26	2,937	0.37	20	861
ID	11	187	0.12	9	261	WA	22	645	0.10	17	1,303
IL	63	1,753	0.14	30	1,980	WV	20	334	0.18	15	424
IN	67	1,082	0.17	27	1,118	WI	33	724	0.13	17	870
						WY	9	82	0.15	5	67

[1] Circulation figures based on the principal community served by a newspaper which is not necessarily the same location as the publisher's office. [2] Per capita based on estimated resident population as of July 1.

Source: Editor & Publisher Co., New York, NY, *Editor & Publisher International Year Book* ©, annual. See also <http://www.editorandpublisher.com>.

Table 1160. Book Publishers' Net Shipments: 2010 to 2012

[Represents net publishers' shipments after returns. Includes all titles released by publishers in the United States and imports which appear under the imprints of American publishers. Multivolume sets, such as encyclopedias, are counted as one unit. Due to changes in methodology and scope, these data are not comparable to those previously published]

Type of publication	2010, estimated	2011, estimated	2012, estimated
Total	**2,677,545,797**	**2,394,865,436**	**2,533,773,368**
Trade[1]	2,386,111,866	2,091,763,263	2,262,004,868
Higher education	51,833,465	56,502,508	55,992,197
Elementary and high school	82,503,695	118,829,229	100,551,639
Professional	151,902,296	120,203,654	107,055,027
Scholarly	5,194,475	7,566,782	8,169,637

[1] Includes adult, juvenile, and religious.

Source: The Association of American Publishers and Book Industry Study Group, Inc., New York, NY, *BookStats*, annual © 2013. See also <http://www.bisg.org/>.

Table 1161. Software Publishers—Estimated Revenue by Type: 2007 to 2011

[In millions of dollars (135,401 represents $135,401,000,000). For all employer firms regardless of tax status. Covers NAICS 5112. Estimates have been adjusted to the results of the 2007 Economic Census. For 2009 and prior, data are based on the 2002 North American Industry Classification System (NAICS). Beginning with 2010, data are based on the 2007 NAICS. See text, this section, and Section 15, See also Appendix III]

Item	2007	2008	2009	2010	2011
Operating revenue..	**135,401**	**142,717**	**138,981**	**145,425**	**155,089**
Source of revenue:					
System software publishing [1]...	49,038	52,552	48,948	43,801	43,699
Operating system software..	17,759	18,680	17,975	17,142	16,457
Network software...	13,857	14,701	12,483	11,137	11,684
Database management software...	9,337	10,226	9,480	9,719	10,100
Development tools and programming languages software.....	2,987	3,047	3,019	2,683	2,613
Application software publishing [1]......................................	45,445	45,573	47,193	53,136	58,030
General business productivity and home use applications.....	19,311	19,868	23,111	22,656	24,277
Cross-industry application software....................................	12,949	12,264	11,383	12,103	13,647
Vertical market application software...................................	7,378	7,304	6,412	9,044	9,560
Utilities application software..	1,459	1,568	1,688	2,758	3,413
Other services [1]..	40,918	44,592	42,840	48,488	53,360
Custom application design and development [2]...................	4,077	5,259	4,656	4,175	4,598
Information technology technical consulting services...........	6,064	5,829	5,614	4,401	4,889
Application service provisioning...	(S)	(S)	(S)	(S)	(NA)
Resale of computer hardware and software.........................	3,993	4,776	4,152	2,799	3,565
Information technology-related training services..................	1,712	1,844	1,385	1,825	1,907
Breakdown of revenue by software sales type:					
System software...	49,038	52,552	48,948	43,801	43,699
Personal computer software...	17,348	18,269	17,428	13,980	(D)
Enterprise or network software..	17,644	18,329	16,575	17,216	18,894
Mainframe computer software..	9,679	10,533	9,615	9,524	8,602
Other system software...	4,367	5,421	5,330	3,081	(D)
Application software...	45,445	45,573	47,193	53,136	58,030
Personal computer software...	19,348	19,759	21,238	20,663	22,586
Enterprise or network software..	18,357	18,015	17,880	18,275	20,705
Mainframe computer software..	2,525	2,152	2,145	2,790	2,712
Other application software..	5,215	(S)	5,930	11,408	12,027

D Figure withheld to avoid disclosure of data of individual companies; data are included in higher level totals. NA Not available. S Data do not meet publication standards. [1] Includes other sources of revenue and other expenses, not shown separately. [2] For 2009 and prior, was "Customization and integration of packaged software."

Source: U.S. Census Bureau, Annual & Quarterly Services, "2011 Annual Services," <http://www.census.gov/services/index.html>, accessed June 2013.

Table 1162. Internet Publishing and Broadcasting, and Web Search Portals—Estimated Revenue and Expenses: 2010 and 2011

[In millions of dollars (41,725 represents $41,725,000,000). For all employer firms regardless of tax status. Beginning with 2010, data are based on the 2007 North American Industry Classification System (NAICS), and cover NAICS 51913. 2007 NAICS 51913 includes 2002 NAICS 516 (Internet Publishing and Broadcasting) and 2002 NAICS 518112 (Web Search Portals). Estimates have been adjusted to the results of the 2007 Economic Census. See text, Section 15, and Appendix III]

Item	2010	2011	Percent change
Operating revenue..	**41,725**	**50,390**	**20.8**
Source of revenue:			
Publishing and broadcasting of content on the Internet.........	8,312	8,954	7.7
Online advertising space..	27,519	32,559	18.3
Licensing of rights to use intellectual property...................	1,351	2,094	55.0
All other operating revenue...	4,543	6,783	49.3
Operating expenses..	**29,624**	**35,439**	**19.6**
Personnel..	14,116	17,621	24.8
Gross annual payroll...	11,786	14,747	25.1
Employer's cost for fringe benefits.....................................	1,271	1,536	20.8
Temporary staff and leased employee expense....................	1,059	1,338	26.3
Expensed materials, parts and supplies (not for resale)........	770	974	26.5
Expensed equipment...	247	284	15.0
Expensed purchase of other materials, parts and supplies....	523	690	31.9
Expensed purchased services..	3,604	4,833	34.1
Expensed purchases of software.......................................	301	306	1.7
Purchased electricity and fuels (except motor fuel)..............	200	243	21.5
Lease and rental payments..	864	994	15.0
Purchased repair and maintenance....................................	195	254	30.3
Purchased advertising and promotional services..................	2,044	3,036	48.5
Other operating expenses..	11,134	12,011	7.9
Depreciation and amortization charges...............................	2,910	3,617	24.3
Government taxes and license fees....................................	213	268	25.8
All other operating expenses..	8,011	8,126	1.4

Source: U.S. Census Bureau, Annual & Quarterly Services, "2011 Annual Services," <http://www.census.gov/services/index.html>, accessed June 2013.

Table 1163. Motion Picture and Sound Recording Industries—Estimated Revenue and Sources of Revenue: 2007 to 2011

[In millions of dollars (94,986 represents $94,986,000,000). For all employer firms regardless of tax status. Estimates have been adjusted to the results of the 2007 Economic Census. Data for 2009 and prior are based on the 2002 North American Industry Classification System (NAICS). Beginning with 2010, data are based on the 2007 NAICS. See text Section 15 and Appendix III]

Kind of business	2007	2008	2009	2010	2011
Operating revenue............	**94,986**	**95,271**	**90,398**	**88,911**	**89,244**
Motion picture and video industries............	**79,797**	**80,004**	**75,979**	**76,021**	**77,131**
Motion picture and video production and distribution [1,2]............	61,911	62,161	57,910	62,567	63,840
Domestic licensing of rights to motion picture films............	13,067	10,976	10,633	13,787	13,509
Domestic licensing of rights to television programs............	10,142	9,327	9,968	11,329	12,308
International licensing of rights to motion picture films............	6,808	7,282	6,710	9,100	8,100
International licensing of rights to television programs............	2,954	3,466	3,317	3,173	3,542
Sale of audiovisual works for wholesale, retail, and rental markets............	14,829	14,548	12,511	11,121	11,365
Motion picture and video exhibition [1]............	12,705	12,782	13,293	13,454	13,291
Feature film exhibition revenue............	8,483	8,545	8,959	9,092	8,839
Admissions to domestic films............	8,421	8,476	8,888	9,064	(NA)
Admissions to foreign films............	62	69	71	73	(NA)
Food and beverage sales............	3,711	3,722	3,825	3,797	3,862
Postproduction services and other motion picture and video industries [1]............	5,181	5,061	4,776	5,310	5,590
Audiovisual postproduction services............	2,733	2,618	2,601	3,167	3,460
Motion picture film laboratory services............	491	446	366	419	338
Duplication and copying services............	(S)	1,053	1,124	1,189	1,228
Sound recording industries............	**15,189**	**15,267**	**14,419**	**12,890**	**12,113**
Integrated record production and distribution [1]............	9,082	8,953	8,665	8,258	7,471
Licensing revenue............	1,299	1,441	1,392	1,144	(NA)
Sales of recordings............	7,454	6,914	6,493	6,506	5,802
Music publishers [1]............	4,466	4,713	4,155	3,793	3,770
Licensing of rights to use musical compositions............	(S)	2,886	2,861	2,944	2,860
Print music............	1,667	1,252	(S)	267	273
Sound recording studios [1]............	854	810	749	839	872
Studio recording............	506	497	441	594	606

NA Not available. S Data do not meet publication standards. [1] Includes other sources of revenue not shown separately. [2] Beginning 2010, includes NAICS 51211 (Motion Picture and Video Production) and NAICS 51212 (Motion Picture and Video Distribution).

Source: U.S. Census Bureau, Annual & Quarterly Services, "2011 Annual Services," <http://www.census.gov/services/index.html>, accessed June 2013.

Table 1164. Recording Media—Manufacturers' Shipments and Value: 2000 to 2012

[1,079.2 represents 1,079,200,000. Based on reports of Recording Industry Association of America member companies who distribute about 85 percent of the recorded music in the U.S. These data are supplemented by other sources]

Medium	2000	2005	2006	2007	2008	2009	2010	2011	2012
UNIT SHIPMENTS (mil.)									
Total [1]............	**1,079.2**	**1,301.8**	**1,588.5**	**1,774.3**	**1,919.2**	**1,851.8**	**1,739.6**	**1,824.9**	**1,816.5**
Physical:									
Compact disks [2]............	942.5	705.4	619.7	511.1	368.4	292.9	253.0	240.8	210.9
Music video [3]............	18.2	33.8	23.2	27.5	12.8	11.8	9.1	7.7	6.2
Singles [5]............	40.3	5.1	3.2	3.2	1.1	1.2	1.3	1.7	1.5
Other recordings [4]............	78.2	2.0	1.3	1.7	3.0	3.2	4.2	5.6	7.2
Digital:									
Download single............	(X)	366.9	586.4	809.9	1,042.7	1,138.3	1,177.4	1,332.3	1,392.2
Download album............	(X)	13.6	27.6	42.5	63.6	76.4	85.8	103.9	116.7
Kiosk [6]............	(X)	0.7	1.4	1.8	1.6	1.7	1.7	1.3	2.0
Music video............	(X)	1.9	9.9	14.2	20.8	20.4	18.4	16.3	10.5
Mobile [7]............	(X)	170.0	315.3	361.0	405.1	305.8	188.5	115.4	69.3
Subscription [8]............	(X)	1.3	1.7	1.8	1.6	1.2	1.5	1.8	3.4
VALUE (mil. dol.)									
Total [1]............	**14,323.7**	**12,296.9**	**11,758.2**	**10,372.1**	**8,768.4**	**7,683.9**	**6,995.0**	**7,133.1**	**7,065.5**
Physical:									
Compact disks [2]............	13,214.5	10,520.2	9,372.6	7,452.3	5,471.3	4,274.1	3,389.4	3,100.7	2,532.0
Music video [3]............	281.9	602.2	451.1	484.9	218.9	212.0	177.6	151.0	118.2
Singles [5]............	173.6	24.1	17.6	16.2	6.4	5.6	5.2	8.1	7.9
Other recordings [4]............	653.7	48.5	22.1	29.3	57.6	60.2	88.9	121.2	164.1
Digital:									
Download single............	(X)	363.3	580.6	801.8	1,032.2	1,220.3	1,317.4	1,522.4	1,623.6
Download album............	(X)	135.7	275.9	424.9	635.3	763.4	872.4	1,070.8	1,204.8
Kiosk [6]............	(X)	1.0	1.9	2.6	2.6	6.3	6.4	2.7	3.7
Music video............	(X)	3.7	19.7	28.2	41.3	40.6	36.6	32.4	20.8
Mobile [7]............	(X)	421.6	774.5	878.9	977.1	728.8	448.0	276.2	166.9
Subscription [8]............	(X)	149.2	206.2	200.9	221.4	213.1	212.4	359.2	570.8

X Not applicable [1] Net, after returns. [2] Prior to 2006, includes DualDisc. [3] Includes DVD video. [4] Includes LP/EP, DVD audio, and super audio CD (SACD); and prior to 2009, cassette. [5] Includes CD single and vinyl single. [6] Includes singles and albums. [7] Includes master ringtones, ringbacks, music videos, full length downloads and other mobile. [8] Weighted annual average. Number of units not included in total.

Source: Recording Industry Association of America, Washington, DC, *2012 Year-End Shipment Statistics* ©. See also <http://www.riaa.com/keystatistics.php>.

Table 1165. Radio and Television Broadcasting—Estimated Revenue and Expenses: 2010 and 2011

[In millions of dollars (4,883 represents $4,883,000,000). For all employer firms regardless of tax status. Estimates have been adjusted to the results of the 2007 Economic Census. Beginning with 2010, data are based on the 2007 North American Industry Classification System (NAICS). See text, Section 15 and Appendix III]

Item	Radio networks (NAICS 515111)		Radio stations (NAICS 515112)		TV broadcasting (NAICS 51512)	
	2010	2011	2010	2011	2010	2011
Operating revenue................................	**4,883**	**5,007**	**12,135**	**12,167**	**35,334**	**35,293**
Air time (national, regional, and local combined)...........	1,118	1,049	10,315	10,241	27,960	27,758
Other operating revenue................................	3,765	3,958	1,820	1,926	7,374	7,535
Public and noncommercial programming services..........	391	405	608	649	1,682	1,510
All other operating revenue............................	3,374	3,553	1,212	1,277	5,692	6,025
Operating expenses................................	**4,278**	**4,186**	**9,375**	**9,386**	**30,240**	**29,835**
Personnel costs.....................................	1,093	1,088	4,721	4,754	7,415	7,482
Gross annual payroll..............................	849	843	3,957	3,986	6,074	6,116
Employer's cost for fringe benefits..................	112	113	530	531	1,111	1,137
Temporary staff and leased employee expense.........	132	132	234	237	230	229
Expensed materials, parts and supplies (not for resale)......	25	22	110	115	262	257
Expensed equipment..............................	12	10	32	40	131	130
Expensed purchase of other materials, parts and supplies.........	13	12	78	75	131	127
Expensed purchased services.........................	320	327	957	962	1,651	1,712
Expensed purchases of software....................	29	29	43	45	118	130
Purchased electricity and fuels (except motor fuel).....	24	24	179	178	157	161
Lease and rental payments.........................	114	109	429	422	335	348
Purchased repair and maintenance..................	21	23	81	84	161	164
Purchased advertising and promotional services........	132	142	225	233	880	909
Other operating expenses............................	2,840	2,749	3,587	3,555	20,912	20,384
Depreciation and amortization charges...............	467	434	704	691	1,408	1,396
Governmental taxes and license fees................	17	15	122	115	122	114
Broadcast rights and music license fees.............	638	640	686	636	10,913	9,909
Network compensation fees (networks only)...........	171	140	55	52	261	249
All other operating expenses........................	1,547	1,520	2,020	2,061	8,208	8,716

Source: U.S. Census Bureau, Annual & Quarterly Services, "2011 Annual Services," <http://www.census.gov/services/index.html>, accessed June 2013.

Table 1166. Cable and Premium TV—Summary: 1980 to 2010

[17,500 represents 17,500,000. Cable TV for calendar year. Premium TV as of December 31 of year shown]

	Cable TV				Premium TV					
			Revenue [1]		Units [2]			Monthly rate [4]		
Year	Average basic sub-scribers (1,000)	Average monthly basic rate (dol.)	Total (mil. dol.)	Basic (mil. dol.)	Total premium [3] (1,000)	Premium cable (1,000)	Non-cable delivered premium (1,000)	All premium weighted average [5] (dollars)	Premium cable (dollars)	Non-cable delivered premium (dollars)
1980......	17,500	7.69	2,609	1,615	8,581	7,336	(NA)	8.91	8.62	(NA)
1985......	35,440	9.73	8,831	4,138	29,885	29,418	(NA)	10.29	10.25	(NA)
1990......	50,520	16.78	17,582	10,174	39,902	39,751	(NA)	10.35	10.30	(NA)
1995......	60,550	23.07	24,137	16,763	60,098	46,600	8,725	8.32	8.54	6.99
1997......	63,600	26.48	28,931	20,213	72,910	51,450	17,500	8.33	8.43	8.00
1998......	64,650	27.81	31,191	21,574	79,483	54,410	21,355	8.60	8.74	8.22
1999......	65,500	28.92	34,095	22,732	84,234	56,985	25,532	8.75	8.85	8.50
2000......	66,250	30.37	36,427	24,142	94,100	62,618	30,158	8.72	8.81	8.48
2001......	66,732	32.87	41,847	26,324	101,676	68,353	32,780	8.97	9.10	8.66
2002......	66,472	34.71	47,989	27,690	109,046	71,637	37,024	9.19	9.29	9.00
2003......	66,050	36.59	53,242	29,000	108,522	71,740	36,364	9.38	9.45	9.23
2004......	65,727	38.14	58,586	30,080	118,151	76,844	40,892	9.91	9.92	9.88
2005......	65,337	39.63	64,891	31,075	126,067	81,790	43,780	9.95	9.97	9.93
2006......	65,319	41.17	71,887	32,274	132,951	85,055	47,514	10.01	10.02	9.98
2007......	65,141	42.72	78,937	33,393	143,009	90,878	51,595	10.05	10.06	10.02
2008......	64,274	44.28	85,232	34,151	149,749	92,364	56,825	10.08	10.10	10.06
2009......	62,874	46.13	89,479	34,804	150,111	85,818	64,293	10.12	10.13	10.09
2010......	60,958	47.89	93,368	35,031	166,241	88,359	77,882	10.15	10.17	10.13

NA Not available. [1] Includes installation revenue, subscriber revenue, and nonsubscriber revenue; excludes telephony and high-speed access. [2] Individual program services sold to subscribers. [3] Includes multipoint distribution service (MDS), satellite TV (STV), multipoint multichannel distribution service (MMDS), satellite master antenna TV (SMATV), C-band satellite, DBS satellite and Telco Video for full- and mini-premium services. [4] Weighted average representing 8 months of unregulated basic rate and 4 months of FCC rolled-back rate. [5] Includes average premium unit price based on data for major premium movie services.

Source: SNL Kagan, a division of SNL Financial, LC. From the *Broadband Cable Financial Databook* ©, annual; the *Cable Program Investor* and *Cable TV Investor: Deals & Finance* ©, monthly newsletters; and various other SNL Kagan publications.

Table 1167. Cable and Other Subscription Programming—Estimated Revenue and Expenses: 2007 to 2011

[In millions of dollars (44,926 represents $44,926,000,000). For all taxable firms regardless of tax status. Data for 2009 and prior are based on the 2002 North American Industry Classification System (NAICS), and cover NAICS 51521. Beginning with 2010, data are based on the 2007 NAICS, and cover NAICS 5152. Estimates have been adjusted to the results of the 2007 Economic Census. See text, Section 15 and Appendix III]

Item	2007	2008	2009	2010	2011
Operating revenue	44,926	49,569	51,431	55,168	60,318
Source of revenue:					
Advertising and program revenue [1]	23,563	26,183	28,698	31,354	33,821
Air time	18,605	19,958	19,911	21,269	23,586
All other operating services revenue	2,758	3,428	2,822	2,545	2,911
Operating expenses	29,073	31,741	32,056	34,319	37,115
Personnel costs	5,592	5,956	6,204	6,754	6,945
Gross annual payroll	4,192	4,543	4,711	5,435	5,588
Employer's cost for fringe benefits	874	877	992	993	1,061
Temporary staff and leased employee expense	526	536	501	326	296
Expensed materials, parts and supplies (not for resale)	137	173	136	157	153
Expensed equipment	67	81	71	83	80
Expensed purchase of other materials, parts and supplies	70	92	65	74	73
Expensed purchased services	2,460	3,317	3,292	3,493	3,689
Expensed purchases of software	49	159	61	80	84
Purchased electricity and fuels (except motor fuel)	40	70	72	68	70
Lease and rental payments	473	556	581	615	610
Purchased repair and maintenance	64	119	124	90	100
Purchased advertising and promotional services	1,834	2,413	2,454	2,640	2,825
Other operating expenses	20,884	22,295	22,424	23,915	26,328
Depreciation and amortization charges	2,885	3,342	3,385	4,122	4,550
Government taxes and license fees	65	67	65	66	64
Program and production costs	13,804	14,411	14,739	16,551	18,126
All other operating expenses	4,130	4,475	4,235	3,176	3,588

[1] Licensing of rights to broadcast specialty programming protected by copyright.

Source: U.S. Census Bureau, Annual & Quarterly Services, "2011 Annual Services," <http://www.census.gov/services/index.html>, accessed June 2013.

Table 1168. Telecommunications Industry—Revenue by Principal Business Activity: 2010 and 2011

[Revenue in millions of dollars (214,791.6 represents $214,791,600,000). Based on carrier Form 499-Q and Form 499-A filings to the Federal Communications Commission. Data consist of total end-user and assessable carrier's carrier intrastate, interstate, and international telecommunications revenue. Excludes revenue from "international-to-international" telephone calls, which traverse U.S. territory but both originate and terminate in foreign points]

Category	Revenue (mil. dol.)	
	2010	2011
Total [1]	214,791.6	205,021.4
Total local competitors	22,040.6	22,519.6
Incumbent local exchange carriers(ILECs)	47,384.4	43,324.3
Competitive access providers (CAPs) and competitive local exchange carriers (CLECs)	11,808.4	11,520.5
Local resellers	353.0	341.3
Private service providers	642.7	678.9
Shared-tenant service providers	32.8	23.9
Interconnected Voice over Internet Protocol (VoIP) providers	9,135.8	9,887.1
Other local service providers	67.9	67.9
Fixed local service providers	69,425.2	65,843.9
Payphone service providers	162.9	139.1
Mobile service providers	111,388.3	107,375.9
Mobile telephone [2]	110,970.5	107,000.7
Paging and messaging service providers	296.9	256.5
Specialized mobile radio dispatch providers	56.6	52.8
Mobile data and other mobile service providers	64.4	65.9
Toll service providers	33,815.2	31,662.5
Interexchange carriers	23,178.2	21,230.5
Operator service providers	789.4	797.4
Prepaid calling card providers	1,412.7	1,251.5
Satellite service providers	428.2	348.2
Toll resellers	5,775.2	5,869.5
VoIP toll providers	514.8	391.4
Audio bridge service providers	976.4	1,007.1
Other toll providers	740.4	767.0

NA Not available. [1] Figures shown represent totals of all records contained in the 499-Q database, including records for filers that are not required to contribute to universal service support mechanisms and estimated amounts for companies that did not file. [2] Includes cellular personal communications service, and specialized mobile radio telephony carriers.

Source: U.S. Federal Communications Commission, Wireline Competition Bureau Statistical Reports, Local and Long Distance Telephone Industries, "Quarterly Revenue Rollup Data," <http://transition.fcc.gov/wcb/iatd/lec.html>, accessed September 2013.

Table 1169. Wired and Wireless Telecommunications Carriers— Estimated Revenue: 2010 and 2011

[In millions of dollars (293,929 represents $293,929,000,000). For all employer firms regardless of tax status. Beginning with 2010, data are based on 2007 NAICS and cover NAICS 5171 Wired Telecommunications Carriers and NAICS 5172 Cellular and Other Wireless Telecommunications. Estimates have been adjusted to the results of the 2007 Economic Census. See text, this section and Section 15, and Appendix III]

Item	2010	2011	Percent change
Wired telecommunications carriers operating revenue [1]	**293,929**	**301,674**	**2.6**
Fixed services	66,928	63,684	-4.8
Fixed local telephony	44,950	42,363	-5.8
Fixed long-distance telephony	19,338	18,702	-3.3
Fixed all distance	2,640	2,619	-0.8
Other telecommunication services	110,708	119,430	7.9
Carrier services	18,845	19,767	4.9
Private network services	21,856	20,881	-4.5
Subscriber line charges	3,391	3,926	15.8
Internet access services	52,992	59,025	11.4
Internet telephony	9,510	11,705	23.1
Telecommunications network installation services	504	480	-4.8
Reselling services for telecommunications equipment, retail	1,750	1,604	-8.3
Rental of telecommunications equipment	1,477	1,608	8.9
Repair and maintenance services for telecommunications equipment	383	434	13.3
Other revenue sources	116,293	118,560	1.9
Basic programming package	54,228	55,546	2.4
Premium programming package	21,042	23,079	9.7
Pay-per-view	3,412	3,315	-2.8
Air time (advertising and program content)	5,002	5,082	1.6
Rental and reselling services for program distribution equipment	7,329	8,432	15.0
Installation services for connections to program distribution networks	1,072	1,080	0.7
Website hosting services	225	219	-2.7
All other operating revenue	23,983	21,807	-9.1
Cellular and other wireless telecommunications operating revenue [2]	**195,526**	**208,932**	**6.9**
Mobile services	154,790	100,292	-35.2
Messaging (paging) services	4,013	4,441	10.7
Mobile telephony	58,489	58,435	-0.1
Mobile long distance	3,816	3,561	-6.7
Mobile all distance	59,650	(S)	(NA)
Internet access services	28,822	33,855	17.5
Other telecommunications services	16,903	18,622	10.2
Telecommunication network installation services	167	(S)	(NA)
Reselling services for telecommunications equipment, retail	15,123	16,844	11.4
Rental of telecommunications equipment	274	295	7.7
Repair and maintenance services for telecommunications equipment	1,339	1,483	10.8
All other operating revenue	(S)	(S)	(NA)

NA Not available. S Estimate does not meet publication standard. [1] Includes 2002 NAICS 5171 (Wired Telecommunications Carriers), 2002 NAICS 5175 (Cable and Other Program Distribution), and a portion of 2002 NAICS 518111 (Internet Service Providers). [2] Includes 2002 NAICS 517211 (Paging), 2002 NAICS 517212 (Cellular and Other Wireless Telecommunications), and a portion of 2002 NAICS 518111 (Internet Service Providers). Excludes satellite telecommunications.

Source: U.S. Census Bureau, Annual & Quarterly Services, "2011 Annual Services," <http://www.census.gov/services/index.html>, accessed June 2013.

Table 1170. Average Annual Telephone Service Expenditures by All Consumer Units: 2001 to 2011

[In dollars except percent distribution. Based on the Consumer Expenditure Survey. A consumer unit is defined as members of a household related by blood, marriage, adoption, or some other legal arrangement; a single person living alone or sharing a household with others, but who is financially independent; or two or more persons living together who share responsibility for at least two out of the three major types of expenses: food, housing, and other expenses]

Year	Average annual telephone service (dol.)				Percent distribution			
	Total telephone services [1]	Residential telephone/ pay phone	Cellular phone service	Voice over Internet Protocol	Total telephone services [1]	Residential telephone/ pay phone	Cellular phone service	Voice over Internet Protocol
2001	914	686	210	(NA)	100.0	75.0	23.0	(NA)
2002	957	641	294	(NA)	100.0	67.0	30.7	(NA)
2003	956	620	316	(NA)	100.0	64.8	33.1	(NA)
2004	990	592	378	(NA)	100.0	59.8	38.2	(NA)
2005	1,048	570	455	(NA)	100.0	54.4	43.4	(NA)
2006	1,087	542	524	(NA)	100.0	49.9	48.2	(NA)
2007	1,110	482	608	5	100.0	43.4	54.8	0.5
2008	1,127	467	643	6	100.0	41.4	57.1	0.5
2009	1,162	434	712	7	100.0	37.3	61.3	0.6
2010	1,178	401	760	9	100.0	34.1	64.5	0.7
2011	1,226	381	826	11	100.0	31.1	67.3	0.9

NA Not available. [1] Includes other items not shown separately.

Source: Bureau of Labor Statistics, Consumer Expenditure Survey, unpublished data acquired June 2013. See also <http://www.bls.gov/cex/>.

Table 1171. Cellular Telecommunications Industry: 1990 to 2012

[Calendar year data, except as noted (5,283 represents 5,283,000). Based on a survey sent to facilities-based commercial mobile radio service providers, including cellular, personal communications services, advanced wireless service, mobile WiMAX, and enhanced special mobile radio (ESMR) systems. The number of operational systems beginning 2000 differs from that reported for previous periods as a result of the consolidated operation of ESMR systems in a broader service area instead of by a city-to-city basis]

Item	Unit	1990	2000	2005	2008	2009	2010	2011	2012
Subscribers	1,000	5,283	109,478	207,896	270,334	285,646	296,286	315,964	326,475
Cell sites [1]	Number	5,616	104,288	183,689	242,130	247,081	253,086	283,385	301,779
Employees	Number	21,382	184,449	233,067	268,528	249,247	250,393	238,071	230,101
Service revenue	Mil. dol.	4,548	52,466	113,538	148,084	152,552	159,930	169,767	185,014
Roamer revenue [2]	Mil. dol.	456	3,883	3,786	3,739	3,061	3,026	3,315	(NA)
Capital investment [3]	Mil. dol.	6,282	89,624	199,025	264,761	285,122	310,015	335,332	365,426
Average monthly bill [4]	Dollars	80.90	45.27	49.98	50.07	48.16	47.21	47.00	(NA)
Average length of call [4]	Minutes	2.20	2.56	3.00	2.27	1.81	1.79	1.78	1.80
Number of text messages [5]	Billions	(NA)	(Z)	9.8	110.4	152.7	187.7	193.1	171.3
Number of MMS [5, 6]	Billions	(NA)	(NA)	0.2	1.6	5.1	4.3	5.0	7.0

NA Not available. Z Entry less than half the unit of measurement shown. [1] The basic geographic unit for wireless telecommunications coverage. [2] Service revenue generated by subscribers' calls outside of their system areas. [3] Beginning 2005, cumulative capital investment figure reached by summing the incremental capital investment in year shown with cumulative capital investment of prior year. [4] As of December 31. [5] Number of messages in final month of survey (December). [6] Multimedia Messaging Service.

Source: CTIA-The Wireless Association, Washington, DC, *Semi-Annual Wireless Industry Survey* ©.

Table 1172. Data Processing, Hosting, and Related Services--Estimated Revenue and Expenses: 2010 and 2011

[In millions of dollars (76,156 represents $76,156,000,000). For all employer firms regardless of tax status. Beginning with 2010, data are based on the 2007 North American Industry Classification System (NAICS), and cover NAICS 518. Estimates have been adjusted to the results of the 2007 Economic Census. See text, Section 15, and Appendix III]

Item	2010	2011	Percent change
Total operating revenue	**76,156**	**81,091**	**6.5**
Data processing, information technology infrastructure provisioning, and hosting services	50,199	53,379	6.3
Information technology design and development services	2,276	2,445	7.4
Information technology technical support services	3,380	3,539	4.7
Information technology technical consulting services	3,794	3,984	5.0
Information and document transformation services	2,277	2,365	3.9
Software publishing	2,527	2,842	12.5
Reselling services for computer hardware and software, retail	1,170	(S)	(NA)
All other operating revenue	10,533	11,466	8.9
Total operating expenses	**66,988**	**71,188**	**6.3**
Gross annual payroll	26,474	27,437	3.6
Employer's cost for fringe benefits	4,206	4,477	6.4
Temporary staff and leased employee expense	2,248	2,579	14.7
Expensed equipment	986	1,013	2.7
Expensed purchases of other materials, parts, and supplies	2,854	3,000	5.1
Expensed purchases of software	1,999	2,159	8.0
Purchased electricity and fuels (except motor fuels)	803	850	5.9
Lease and rental payments	2,511	2,728	8.6
Purchased repair and maintenance	831	891	7.2
Purchased advertising and promotional services	2,278	2,393	5.0
Depreciation and amortization charges	5,827	6,468	11.0
Governmental taxes and license fees	752	(S)	(NA)
All other operating expenses	15,219	16,530	8.6

NA Not available. S Data do not meet publication standards.

Source: U.S. Census Bureau, Annual & Quarterly Services, "2011 Annual Services," <http://www.census.gov/services/index.html>, accessed June 2013.

Table 1173. Household Internet Usage In and Outside of the Home by Selected Characteristics: 2011

[In thousands except percent. 119,250 represents 119,250,000. Based on the July 2011 Current Population Survey Computer and Internet Use Supplement. See text, Section 1 and Appendix III]

Characteristics	Total house-holds	In the home — Percent: All house-holds	In the home — Percent: Dial-up	In the home — Percent: Broad-band	Anywhere: Total house-holds	Anywhere: Percent of house-holds	No Internet use: Total house-holds	No Internet use: Percent of house-holds
All households.................	**119,250**	**71.70**	**2.27**	**68.57**	**93,751**	**78.62**	**25,499**	**21.38**
Age of householder:								
Under 25 years old......................	6,120	69.53	1.18	66.68	5,208	85.09	913	14.91
25 to 34 years old......................	19,922	77.75	1.36	75.33	17,402	87.35	2,520	12.65
35 to 44 years old......................	21,256	81.86	1.53	79.45	19,036	89.55	2,221	10.45
45 to 54 years old......................	24,489	77.93	2.43	74.59	20,678	84.44	3,810	15.56
55 years and older......................	47,463	61.68	3.05	58.00	31,427	66.21	16,035	33.79
Sex of householder:								
Male......................	59,917	74.57	2.33	71.38	48,280	80.58	11,637	19.42
Female......................	59,333	68.80	2.21	65.73	45,472	76.64	13,861	23.36
Race and ethnicity of householder:								
White [1]......................	83,148	76.24	2.45	72.88	67,533	81.22	15,615	18.78
Black [1]......................	14,862	56.83	1.76	54.49	10,301	69.31	4,561	30.69
American Indian/Alaskan Native [1]......	708	49.86	1.85	47.62	462	65.23	246	34.77
Asian [1]......................	4,731	82.82	1.42	80.75	4,057	85.76	674	14.24
Hispanic......................	14,222	58.32	2.08	55.27	10,113	71.11	4,109	28.89
Educational attainment of householder:								
Elementary......................	4,939	29.37	1.72	27.28	1,918	38.83	3,022	61.17
Some high school......................	9,039	41.60	2.37	38.57	4,841	53.56	4,198	46.44
High school diploma/GED...............	34,986	61.12	2.98	57.33	24,026	68.67	10,960	31.33
Some college......................	34,047	77.30	2.17	74.12	29,142	85.59	4,905	14.41
Bachelor's degree or more.............	36,238	89.93	1.73	87.31	33,824	93.34	2,414	6.66
Family income of householder:								
Less than $15,000......................	19,462	41.06	1.89	38.17	10,508	53.99	8,955	46.01
15,000 to 24,999......................	14,475	51.94	2.84	48.34	9,050	62.52	5,426	37.49
25,000 to 34,999......................	15,418	61.32	2.85	57.59	10,938	70.94	4,480	29.06
35,000 to 49,999......................	16,991	74.40	2.95	70.60	13,836	81.43	3,154	18.57
50,000 to 74,999......................	21,520	86.36	2.39	83.10	19,454	90.40	2,066	9.60
75,000 to 99,999......................	12,333	91.59	1.82	89.02	11,625	94.25	709	5.75
100,000 to 149,000......................	11,419	94.54	1.56	92.25	10,976	96.12	443	3.88
150,000 and over......................	7,632	94.62	0.95	92.72	7,366	96.51	266	3.49

[1] Non-Hispanic.

Source: U.S. Department of Commerce, National Telecommunications and Information Administration, *Exploring the Digital Nation: America's Emerging Online Experience*, June 2013. See also <http://www.ntia.doc.gov/report>.

Table 1174. Household Internet Usage by State: 2011

[In percent. Based on the July 2011 Current Population Survey Computer and Internet Use Supplement. See headnote, Table 1173]

State	Any-where	In the home: Total	In the home: Dial-up	In the home: Broad-band	No Internet use	State	Any-where	In the home: Total	In the home: Dial-up	In the home: Broad-band	No Internet use
U.S.........	**78.62**	**71.70**	**2.27**	**68.57**	**21.38**	MO............	75.01	66.04	2.42	63.33	24.99
AL..........	73.58	63.81	4.48	57.90	26.42	MT............	78.03	67.30	1.66	63.89	21.97
AK..........	86.84	76.76	3.62	71.59	13.16	NE............	79.08	71.24	2.11	68.00	20.92
AZ..........	81.97	74.47	2.34	70.62	18.03	NV............	81.66	75.44	0.94	73.16	18.34
AR..........	70.69	62.22	2.33	58.75	29.31	NH............	86.07	82.21	3.05	78.17	13.93
CA..........	81.23	74.45	1.85	71.71	18.77	NJ............	80.91	76.95	2.18	74.34	19.09
CO..........	86.19	80.09	1.35	77.61	13.81	NM............	70.96	60.31	2.02	57.39	29.04
CT..........	81.81	78.01	1.47	75.55	18.19	NY............	78.58	72.93	2.14	70.35	21.42
DE..........	77.53	72.42	2.06	69.76	22.47	NC............	75.02	68.44	1.61	66.29	24.98
DC..........	79.88	71.00	0.86	69.09	20.12	ND............	78.45	70.77	0.58	69.45	21.55
FL..........	80.60	74.87	1.33	73.23	19.40	OH............	75.02	68.52	2.38	65.28	24.98
GA..........	77.69	70.08	3.13	66.01	22.31	OK............	73.04	65.88	3.06	61.26	26.96
HI..........	76.46	71.59	1.58	68.88	23.54	OR............	85.01	78.53	2.02	74.71	14.99
ID..........	83.32	74.77	2.55	70.33	16.68	PA............	75.64	69.72	1.81	67.25	24.36
IL..........	79.47	72.55	1.80	69.82	20.53	RI............	79.34	73.38	1.56	70.76	20.66
IN..........	76.28	67.90	3.34	63.93	23.72	SC............	72.74	64.73	2.56	61.25	27.26
IA..........	78.65	71.62	3.55	67.53	21.35	SD............	79.60	71.03	2.72	67.29	20.40
KS..........	81.72	75.15	2.40	71.65	18.28	TN............	70.72	63.53	2.15	60.48	29.28
KY..........	72.98	65.64	3.37	61.27	27.02	TX............	77.24	67.19	2.91	63.29	22.76
LA..........	75.95	65.55	2.66	62.18	24.05	UT............	86.90	78.74	1.71	75.85	13.10
ME..........	80.47	74.66	3.78	69.63	19.53	VT............	80.28	74.27	3.93	69.59	19.72
MD..........	82.97	76.86	1.19	75.03	17.03	VA............	76.99	70.79	2.49	67.25	23.01
MA..........	81.94	77.37	0.92	76.03	18.06	WA............	87.33	81.94	2.43	78.43	12.67
MI..........	78.49	72.72	4.01	67.86	21.51	WV............	69.05	62.27	3.19	57.76	30.95
MN..........	84.89	78.46	2.50	74.70	15.11	WI............	80.20	74.57	2.08	71.18	19.80
MS..........	67.11	56.32	2.85	52.63	32.89	WY............	81.60	74.12	1.75	70.66	18.40

Source: U.S. Department of Commerce, National Telecommunications and Information Administration, *Exploring the Digital Nation: America's Emerging Online Experience*, June 2013. See also <http://www.ntia.doc.gov/report>.

Table 1175. Internet Access by Selected Characteristics: 2012

[In percent, except as noted (232,469 represents 232,469,000). For persons 18 years old and over. As of Fall 2012. Based on sample and subject to sampling error; see source for details]

Characteristic	Total adults	Accessed the Internet					
		At home	At work	At school or a library	At another place	Using a cellphone or smart-phone	Using WIFI or wireless connection outside of home
Total adults (1,000) [1]	232,469	170,652	86,846	24,282	54,880	107,900	61,541
PERCENT DISTRIBUTION							
Total	100.00	100.00	100.00	100.00	100.00	100.00	100.00
Age:							
18 to 34 years old	30.81	34.85	34.75	59.40	47.57	47.57	44.98
35 to 54 years old	36.25	39.15	46.70	29.15	37.01	39.57	39.60
55 years old and over	32.94	26.00	18.55	11.44	15.42	12.87	15.42
Sex:							
Male	48.44	48.45	50.71	45.55	51.34	49.39	52.66
Female	51.56	51.55	49.29	54.45	48.66	50.61	47.34
Census region: [2]							
Northeast	18.31	18.96	18.82	16.37	17.59	17.72	17.61
Midwest	37.23	35.94	36.49	36.76	37.62	37.65	36.43
South	21.79	21.68	22.09	21.49	19.47	20.29	20.73
West	22.68	23.41	22.60	25.38	25.31	24.33	25.23
Household size:							
1 to 2 persons	45.76	41.49	39.96	33.46	36.70	34.18	36.63
3 to 4 persons	36.82	40.16	43.66	44.23	44.04	44.32	43.98
5 or more persons	17.42	18.36	16.38	22.31	19.26	21.50	19.39
Any child in household	39.96	43.27	46.18	46.82	46.99	51.43	47.53
Marital status:							
Single	27.38	28.17	26.23	51.63	37.35	35.73	34.71
Married	53.55	57.54	61.12	36.45	50.30	52.37	54.47
Other	19.07	14.29	12.65	11.92	12.35	11.90	10.82
Educational attainment:							
Graduated college plus	27.75	35.23	47.02	35.56	37.17	36.71	44.10
Attended college	28.47	32.04	30.98	41.26	34.27	32.89	33.97
Did not attend college	43.78	32.73	22.00	23.17	28.56	30.40	21.93
Employed full-time	48.16	54.91	86.27	40.74	57.05	62.71	62.90
Employed part-time	11.78	12.85	13.16	21.39	14.20	13.54	13.58
Household income:							
Less than $50,000	42.57	31.32	17.27	41.47	30.84	28.91	24.48
$50,000 to $74,999	18.91	20.46	19.89	19.28	17.87	19.06	17.59
$75,000 to $149,999	28.14	34.77	43.83	27.97	33.64	35.34	38.03
$150,000 or more	10.38	13.44	19.01	11.27	17.65	16.69	19.91

[1] Includes other labor force status not shown separately. [2] For composition of regions, see map inside front cover.

Source: GfK Mediamark Research & Intelligence, LLC, New York, NY, CyberStats, Fall 2012 ©. See also <http://www.gfkmri.com>.

Table 1176. Percent of Adults Who Own Electronic Devices by Age: 2010

[In percent. Based on a telephone survey of 3,001 adults 18 and older conducted August 9-September 13, 2010, including 1,000 reached via cell phone. Interviews were conducted in English and Spanish]

Device	All Adults (18 years old and over)	18 to 34 years	35 to 46 years	47 to 56 years	57 to 65 years	66 to 74 years	75 years and over
Cell phone	85	95	92	86	84	68	48
Desktop computer	59	57	69	65	64	48	28
Laptop computer	52	70	61	49	43	30	10
iPod/MP3 music player	47	74	56	42	26	16	3
Game console	42	63	63	38	19	8	3
e-Book reader, such as Kindle or Nook	5	5	5	7	3	6	2
Tablet, like iPad	4	5	5	4	3	1	1
None of these	9	1	3	8	8	20	43

Source: Pew Research Center, Pew Internet & American Life Project, *Generations and Their Gadgets* ©. See also <http://pewinternet.org/Reports/2011/Generations-and-gadgets.aspx>.

Table 1177. Internet Activities of Adults by Geographic Community Type: 2010 to 2013

[In percent. For Internet users age 18 and over who have ever performed the activity. Based on telephone surveys of persons with land-line telephones and cell phones. In Sept 2010, 3,001 persons were interviewed, including 1,000 cell phone users. Landline sample response rate was 13.6 percent; cellular sample response rate was 17 percent. In November 2010, 2,257 persons were interviewed, including 755 cell phone users. Landline sample response rate was 13.7 percent; cellular sample response rate was 15 percent. In May 2011, 2,277 persons were interviewed, including 755 cell phone users. Landline sample response rate was 13.6 percent; cellular sample response rate was 11.5 percent. In Feb 2012, 2,253 persons were interviewed, including 901 cell phone users. Landline sample response rate was 11 percent; cellular sample response rate was 11 percent. In Dec 2012, 2,261 persons were interviewed, including 908 cell phone users. Landline sample response rate was 11 percent; cellular sample response rate was 13 percent. In May 2013, 2,252 persons were interviewed, including 1,127 cell phone users. Landline sample response rate was 10 percent; cellular sample response rate was 13 percent. Beginning in Feb 2012, interviews were conducted in English and Spanish]

Activity	Survey date (month, year)	Total adults	Internet users performing activity			
			Total	Urban	Suburban	Rural
Buy a product online	May 2011	55	71	73	72	70
Buy or make a reservation for travel	May 2011	51	65	66	66	60
Categorize or tag online content like a photo, news story or blog post	Sept. 2010	24	33	37	32	25
Create or work on your own online journal or blog	May 2011	11	14	16	13	11
Do any banking online	May 2013	51	61	62	66	42
Get news online	Dec. 2012	60	74	76	74	67
Look for health or medical information online	May 2011	55	71	72	69	81
Look for news or information about politics	Dec. 2012	50	61	63	61	57
Look online for info about a job	May 2011	44	56	63	56	45
Look for information on Wikipedia	Feb. 2012	47	58	65	57	50
Make a donation to a charity online	May 2011	19	25	31	26	15
Make a phone call online, using a service such as Skype or Vonage	Dec. 2012	24	30	33	29	26
Pay bills online	Sept. 2010	42	57	55	62	45
Pay to access or download digital content online, such as music video, or newspaper articles	Sept. 2010	32	43	47	43	35
Play online games	Sept. 2010	27	36	36	38	34
Post a comment or review online about a product you bought or a service you received	Sept. 2010	24	32	34	35	24
Rate a product, service, or person	May 2011	29	37	40	38	26
Research a product or service online	Sept. 2010	58	78	79	79	77
Search online for a map or driving directions	Sept. 2010	60	82	84	83	79
Send instant messages	Nov. 2010	34	46	49	47	42
Send or read e-mail	Nov. 2010	68	92	93	93	90
Take part in chat rooms or online discussions with other people	Sept. 2010	17	22	25	21	20
Use a search engine to find information	Feb. 2012	73	91	90	93	90
Use a social networking site like Facebook, LinkedIn or Google Plus	May 2013	61	72	74	71	69
Use Twitter	May 2013	15	18	21	18	11
Visit a local, state, or federal government web site	Dec. 2012	43	53	51	55	53
Watch a video on a video-sharing site	May 2011	55	71	72	71	68

Source: Pew Internet & American Life Project Surveys ©, <http://www.pewinternet.org>.

Table 1178. Online News Consumption by Selected Characteristics: 2000 to 2012

[[In percent. Covers Internet users age 18 and over who report getting news online "ever" or "yesterday." Based on telephone surveys of persons with land-line telephones, except as noted. In 2008, 2,251 persons were interviewed. The response rate was 25 percent. In April 2009, 2,253 persons were interviewed, including 561 cell phone users. Landline sample response rate was 20.6 percent; cellular sample response rate was 18.2 percent. In May 2010, 2,252 persons were interviewed, including 744 cell phone users. Landline sample response rate was 21.8 percent; cellular sample response rate was 19.3 percent. In May 2011, 2,277 persons were interviewed, including 755 cell phone users. Landline sample response rate was 13.6 percent; cellular sample response rate was 11.5 percent. In August 2012, 2,253 persons were interviewed, including 900 cell phone users. Landline sample response rate was 12 percent; cellular sample response rate was 11 percent. Beginning in 2011, surveys were conducted in English and Spanish.]

Characteristic	"Ever" get news online				Got news online "yesterday"			
	2000	2010	2011 [1]	2012 [1]	2000	2010	2011 [1]	2012 [1]
Total adult Internet users	**60**	**75**	**76**	**78**	**22**	**43**	**45**	**(NA)**
Age:								
18 to 29 years old	56	75	72	84	16	44	43	(NA)
30 to 49 years old	63	78	83	83	25	45	51	(NA)
50 to 64 years old	57	76	77	71	25	42	44	(NA)
65 years old and over	53	62	60	66	28	34	32	(NA)
Sex:								
Male	66	77	77	76	29	48	52	(NA)
Female	53	74	76	80	16	38	39	(NA)
Race/ethnicity:								
White, non-Hispanic	60	75	76	79	23	43	46	(NA)
Black, non-Hispanic	63	72	77	74	13	42	34	(NA)
English-speaking Hispanic	57	73	72	73	23	35	40	(NA)
Annual household income:								
Less than $30,000	55	64	65	69	21	28	31	(NA)
$30,000 to $49,999	57	74	79	80	20	35	44	(NA)
$50,000 to $74,999	63	78	82	81	22	47	52	(NA)
$75,000 or more	69	84	88	89	31	60	62	(NA)
Frequency of Internet use:								
Daily	66	82	(NA)	(NA)	33	54	(NA)	(NA)
Several times per week	59	64	(NA)	(NA)	17	14	(NA)	(NA)
Less often	51	38	(NA)	(NA)	12	5	(NA)	(NA)

NA Not available. [1] Includes interviews conducted in English and Spanish.

Source: Pew Internet & American Life Project Surveys from March 2000; May 2010; May 2011; and August 2012 ©. See also <http://www.pewinternet.org>.

Table 1179. Typical Daily Internet Activities of Adult Internet Users: 2010 to 2012

[In percent. For Internet users age 18 and over who have ever performed the activity. Based on telephone surveys of persons with land-line telephones and cell phones. In September 2010, 3,001 persons were interviewed, including 1,000 cell phone users. Landline sample response rate was 13.6 percent; cellular sample response rate was 17 percent. In November 2010, 2,257 persons were interviewed, including 755 cell phone users. Landline sample response rate was 13.7 percent; cellular sample response rate was 15 percent. In May 2011, 2,277 persons were interviewed, including 755 cell phone users. Landline sample response rate was 13.6 percent; cellular sample response rate was 11.5 percent. In February 2012, 2,253 persons were interviewed, including 901 cell phone users. Landline sample response rate was 11 percent; cellular sample response rate was 11 percent. Beginning in 2011, surveys were conducted in English and Spanish]

Activity	Survey date (month, year)	Total Internet users	Age 18 to 29 years old	Age 30 to 49 years old	Age 50 to 64 years old	Age 65 years old and over	Sex Male	Sex Female
Buy a product online	May 2011	6	7	5	7	7	7	5
Buy or make a reservation for travel	May 2011	4	4	4	3	1	4	3
Categorize or tag online content like a photo, news story or blog post	Sept. 2010	11	18	12	5	4	12	10
Create or work on your own online journal or blog	May 2011	4	4	6	3	2	6	3
Do any banking online	May 2011	24	19	28	27	15	24	23
Get news online	May 2011	45	43	51	44	32	52	39
Look for health or medical information online	May 2011	10	8	9	11	10	8	11
Look for news or information about politics	May 2011	30	27	34	34	19	36	26
Look online for info about a job	May 2011	11	15	12	9	1	11	11
Look for information on Wikipedia	Feb. 2012	16	19	15	15	11	18	13
Make a donation to a charity online	May 2011	1	1	1	2	1	1	1
Make a phone call online, using a service, such as Skype or Vonage	May 2011	5	6	5	5	2	6	4
Pay bills online	Sept. 2010	15	14	19	11	11	15	15
Pay to access or download digital content online, such as music video, or newspaper articles	Sept. 2010	10	13	9	12	3	13	8
Play online games	Sept. 2010	13	16	15	10	9	13	13
Post a comment or review online about a product you bought or a service you received	Sept. 2010	4	6	5	2	3	5	4
Rate a product, service, or person	May 2011	4	4	4	6	2	5	4
Research a product or service online	Sept. 2010	28	27	32	26	16	31	24
Search online for a map or driving directions	Sept. 2010	14	15	17	12	7	16	12
Send instant messages	Nov. 2010	18	29	17	13	4	18	18
Send or read e-mail	Nov. 2010	61	64	63	61	46	59	64
Take part in chat rooms or online discussions	Sept. 2010	7	9	9	5	2	8	6
Use a search engine to find information	Feb. 2012	59	66	65	52	38	59	60
Use a social networking site, like Facebook, LinkedIn or Google Plus	Feb. 2012	48	70	52	31	18	42	54
Use Twitter	Feb. 2012	8	17	7	4	1	8	8
Visit a local, state, or federal government Web site	May 2011	13	11	15	13	6	14	12
Watch a video on a video-sharing site	May 2011	28	47	27	20	11	32	25

Source: Pew Internet & American Life Project Surveys ©. See also <http://www.pewinternet.org>.

Table 1180. Public Libraries, Selected Characteristics: Fiscal Year 2010

[Total operating income in millions of dollars (11,300.7 represents $11,300,700,000). Based on a survey of public libraries. Data are for public libraries in the 50 states and the District of Columbia. The response rates for these items are between 97 and 100 percent. See source for details]

Population of service area	Number of— Public libraries	Number of— Stationary outlets [1]	Operating income Total [2] (mil. dol.)	Operating income Source State government (percent)	Operating income Source Local government (percent)	Paid staff [3] Total	Paid staff [3] Librarians with ALA-MLS [4]	Average number of public use Internet computers per stationary outlet [5]
Total	8,951	16,417	11,300.7	7.1	84.8	139,370	31,923	14.9
1,000,000 or more	29	1,186	1,704.2	5.3	83.6	17,312	4,672	26.8
500,000 to 999,000	55	1,102	1,640.4	7.5	85.3	18,177	4,503	24.6
250,000 to 499,999	105	1,134	1,314.4	8.1	84.6	15,378	3,828	20.8
100,000 to 249,999	350	2,051	1,859.3	7.6	85.4	23,278	5,065	19.0
50,000 to 99,999	555	1,634	1,435.4	8.4	85.1	18,164	4,259	17.9
25,000 to 49,999	973	1,735	1,429.1	6.8	86.1	18,114	4,394	16.3
10,000 to 24,999	1,756	2,251	1,179.1	6.2	85.7	16,227	3,608	13.1
5,000 to 9,999	1,486	1,634	434.3	7.3	82.6	6,871	1,129	9.5
2,500 to 4,999	1,298	1,328	175.8	5.5	79.6	3,165	320	7.0
1,000 to 2,499	1,437	1,453	99.3	5.4	77.7	2,003	129	5.2
Fewer than 1,000	907	909	29.4	7.5	76.1	684	26	4.0

[1] The sum of central and branch libraries. The total number of central libraries was 8,770; the total of branch libraries was 7,647. [2] Includes income from the federal government (0.4%) and other sources (7.9%), not shown separately. [3] Full-time equivalents. [4] Librarians with master's degrees from a graduate library education program accredited by the American Library Association (ALA). Total librarians, including those without ALA-MLS, were 46,849. [5] The average per stationary outlet was calculated by dividing the total number of public use Internet computers in central and branch outlets by the total number of such outlets.

Source: Institute of Museum and Library Services, *Public Libraries in the United States Survey: Fiscal Year 2010* (IMLS-2013–PLS-01), January 2013; and "Supplementary Tables," <http://www.imls.gov/research/publications.aspx>, accessed June 2013.

Table 1181. Number of Public Libraries and Library Services by State: Fiscal Year 2010

[1,571,048 represents 1,571,048,000. Based on a survey of public libraries. Public libraries can have one or more outlets that provide direct service to the public. The three types of outlets include central libraries, branch libraries, and bookmobiles]

State	Number of public libraries [1]	Library visits (1,000s)	Per capita visits [2]	Per capita circulation of materials [2]	Average number of public use Internet computers per stationary outlet [3]	State	Number of public libraries [1]	Library visits (1,000s)	Per capita visits [2]	Per capita circulation of materials [2]	Average number of public use Internet computers per stationary outlet [3]
U.S....	**8,951**	**1,571,048**	**5.3**	**8.3**	**14.9**	MO.......	147	31,578	6.2	10.6	12.5
AL......	212	17,082	3.7	4.6	16.5	MT........	80	4,528	5.0	7.5	8.7
AK......	75	3,419	4.8	6.3	6.7	NE.......	216	8,683	6.5	10.3	8.1
AZ......	89	29,147	4.6	8.2	20.4	NV.......	22	11,602	4.3	7.6	14.7
AR......	55	10,436	4.0	5.5	9.8	NH.......	221	8,105	8.2	12.2	5.9
CA......	181	178,979	4.6	6.3	17.0	NJ.......	284	50,167	6.1	7.6	16.5
CO......	114	33,214	6.8	13.3	17.9	NM.......	81	8,267	5.2	6.7	12.7
CT......	183	23,753	7.2	10.2	16.4	NY.......	756	117,795	6.2	8.7	15.6
DE......	21	4,493	5.8	11.5	17.0	NC.......	77	44,295	4.7	6.0	17.5
DC......	1	2,756	4.6	4.5	27.2	ND.......	73	2,436	4.2	7.2	6.9
FL......	80	87,890	4.8	7.1	29.6	OH.......	251	88,256	7.6	16.3	15.8
GA......	61	39,392	3.9	4.7	19.4	OK.......	116	15,808	5.2	7.4	11.7
HI.......	1	5,337	4.1	5.4	5.4	OR.......	126	25,033	6.8	16.2	12.9
ID.......	102	8,810	6.4	10.7	10.5	PA.......	457	47,188	3.9	5.8	11.7
IL.......	622	83,015	7.0	10.3	15.1	RI.......	48	6,279	6.0	7.4	16.7
IN.......	238	40,506	7.1	13.7	18.7	SC.......	42	18,283	4.2	6.2	18.1
IA.......	531	19,766	6.6	9.9	7.4	SD.......	102	3,959	5.5	8.2	7.2
KS.......	311	15,457	6.5	11.6	9.6	TN.......	186	21,162	3.4	4.2	14.7
KY......	117	19,764	4.6	7.0	19.4	TX.......	549	79,087	3.4	5.2	19.2
LA......	68	16,772	3.7	4.4	13.6	UT.......	72	19,463	7.0	13.7	13.9
ME.....	215	6,794	6.0	8.4	6.7	VT.......	159	3,801	7.1	8.8	5.8
MD.....	24	33,662	6.0	10.7	23.0	VA.......	91	42,597	5.5	10.0	17.2
MA.....	360	42,941	6.5	9.8	12.3	WA.......	61	45,157	6.8	13.1	16.6
MI......	384	59,470	6.0	9.0	16.1	WV.......	97	6,155	3.4	4.4	7.6
MN.....	138	28,325	5.3	11.1	14.6	WI.......	381	36,463	6.4	11.4	11.5
MS.....	50	9,847	3.3	3.0	10.3	WY.......	23	3,873	7.1	9.8	10.2

[1] Of the 8,951 public libraries, 7,204 were single outlet libraries and 1,747 were multiple outlet libraries. Single outlet libraries are a central library, bookmobile, or books by mail only outlet. Multiple outlet libraries have two or more direct service outlets including some combination of single outlet libraries. [2] Per capita rate based on total unduplicated population of legal service area given by the state library agency of each state. [3] The average per stationary outlet was calculated by dividing the total number of public use Internet computers in central and branch outlets by the total number of such outlets.

Source: Institute of Museum and Library Services, *Public Libraries in the United States Survey: Fiscal Year 2010* (IMLS-2013–PLS-01), January 2013; and "Supplementary Tables," <http://www.imls.gov/research/publications.aspx>, accessed June 2013.

Table 1182. Public Library Use of the Internet: 2010 and 2011

[In percent, except number of outlets. Based on sample survey; see source for details. Responses for the 2010 and 2011 surveys were received in the fall (September through November). Excludes Bookmobile and Books by Mail service outlets]

Item	2010 [1]				2011 [1]			
		Metropolitan status				Metropolitan status		
	Total	Urban	Suburban	Rural	Total	Urban	Suburban	Rural
Total libraries [2]..........................	16,745	2,890	5,833	8,022	16,776	2,896	5,836	8,044
Connected with public access............	99.3	99.5	99.4	99.3	100.0	100.0	100.0	99.9
Average number of workstations........	16.0	28.0	19.6	9.6	16.4	27.9	20.1	10.7
Speed of access:								
768 (Kbps) kilobits or less..............	6.4	([3])	([3])	9.2	2.8	([3])	1.1	4.8
769 Kbps to 1.4 Mbps.................	5.6	1.4	4.2	5.8	4.1	1.6	3.6	5.1
1.5 Mbps.............................	22.7	9.8	21.1	28.0	16.5	8.1	13.6	21.2
1.6 Mbps to 3 Mbps.................	12.0	11.1	9.9	13.7	12.9	4.4	11.1	16.7
3.1 Mbps to 6 Mbps.................	11.3	12.2	10.7	11.5	13.4	11.4	9.9	16.4
6.1 Mbps to 10 Mbps...............	12.1	16.3	14.6	9.0	12.2	10.6	15.0	10.9
10.1 Mbps to 20 Mbps...............	10.8	22.2	12.3	6.1	10.7	17.3	13.1	7.0
20.1 Mbps to 30 Mbps...............	2.0	2.7	2.4	1.4	5.1	8.9	6.5	3.1
30.1 Mbps to 40 Mbps...............	1.4	1.0	2.1	1.1	1.9	4.6	2.4	([3])
Greater than 40 Mbps...............	10.7	20.8	13.1	5.8	13.5	26.6	14.7	6.9
Don't know.............................	5.0	1.4	4.7	6.3	6.9	6.6	6.6	7.2
Public library availability of wireless Internet access:								
Currently available...................	85.7	91.4	89.3	81.2	90.5	96.7	93.8	86.3
Plan to make available within the next year...........................	5.9	4.9	4.4	7.2	3.9	1.7	1.9	6.0

[1] The 2010 survey had 86.5 percent response rate. The 2011 survey had 82.5 percent response rate. [2] The 2010 survey sample originated from a 2008 dataset; the 2011 survey originated from a 2009 dataset. Both datasets are from the U.S. Institute of Museum and Library Services. [3] Less than 1 percent, or insufficient data to report.

Source: Information Policy and Access Center, University of Maryland, College Park, MD, *2011-2012 Public Library Funding & Technology Access Survey: Survey Findings & Report,* by John Carlo Bertot, et al., and previous reports ©. See also <http://www.plinternetsurvey.org/>.

Table 1183. Adult Computer and Internet Users by Selected Characteristics: 2000 to 2013

[In percent. Covers persons age 18 and over who use a computer or the Internet at a workplace, school, home, or anywhere else, on at least an occasional basis. Based on telephone surveys of persons with land-line telephones unless otherwise noted. Beginning 2011, surveys include interviews conducted in English and Spanish. Data for 2013 are from May 2013 interviews with 2,252 persons, including 1,127 cellular telephone users. 2013 landline sample had 10 percent response rate; cellular sample had 13 percent response rate. Data for 2010 are from May 2010 interviews with 2,252 persons, including 744 cell phone users. 2010 landline sample had 21.8 percent response rate; cellular sample had 19.3 percent response rate. For 2000, Internet users include persons who ever go online to access the Internet or World Wide Web or to send and receive e-mail. For 2005, Internet users include those who at least occasionally use the Internet or send and receive e-mail]

Characteristic	Adult computer users				Adult Internet users				All adults, by type of home connection, 2013 [1]	
	2000	2005	2010	2013 [1]	2000	2005	2010	2013 [1]	Broad-band	Dial-up
Total adults...................	**65**	**71**	**77**	**(NA)**	**53**	**69**	**79**	**85**	**70**	**3**
Age:										
18 to 29 years old..............	82	83	89	(NA)	72	82	95	98	80	2
30 to 49 years old..............	76	81	86	(NA)	62	80	87	92	78	2
50 to 64 years old..............	61	72	78	(NA)	48	68	78	83	69	4
65 years old and over..........	21	31	42	(NA)	15	28	42	56	43	4
Sex:										
Male...........................	66	72	78	(NA)	56	70	79	85	71	3
Female.........................	64	70	76	(NA)	51	67	79	84	69	3
Race/ethnicity:										
White, non-Hispanic...........	66	72	79	(NA)	55	70	80	86	74	3
Black, non-Hispanic...........	59	60	72	(NA)	42	54	71	85	64	2
English-speaking Hispanic....	64	75	74	(NA)	48	73	82	76	53	6
Educational attainment:										
Less than high school.........	28	36	43	(NA)	19	35	52	59	37	4
High school graduate [2].......	56	63	67	(NA)	41	59	67	78	57	4
Some college..................	80	81	88	(NA)	69	80	90	92	78	2
College graduate or higher....	88	90	96	(NA)	79	88	96	96	89	2
Annual household income:										
Less than $30,000.............	48	52	58	(NA)	35	50	63	76	54	4
$30,000 to $49,999............	74	76	82	(NA)	61	74	84	88	70	4
$50,000 to $74,999............	85	88	89	(NA)	74	86	89	94	84	1
$75,000 or more...............	90	92	96	(NA)	81	91	95	96	88	2

NA Not available. [1] Beginning in 2011, surveys include interviews conducted in English and Spanish. [2] Includes those with a GED certificate.

Source: Pew Internet & American Life Project Surveys conducted September-December 2000; September and December of 2005; May 2010; and May 2013 ©. See also <http://www.pewinternet.org>.

Table 1184. Public Library Systems Operating Budget Change by Metropolitan Status: 2009 to 2012

[In percent. For fiscal year ending in year shown. Data from 2011-2012 Public Library Funding & Technology Survey, conducted by The American Library Association Office for Research & Statistics and the Information Policy & Access Center at the University of Maryland. Based upon responses from 7,260 public libraries]

Change in Budget	Urban				Suburban				Rural				All			
	2009	2010	2011	2012	2009	2010	2011	2012	2009	2010	2011	2012	2009	2010	2011	2012
Increased up to 6%....	47.3	28.2	25.2	26.1	51.1	35.1	35.3	32.0	50.6	38.8	35.8	39.0	50.5	37.0	35.0	38.4
Increased 6% or more................	10.6	5.2	4.2	1.9	9.0	5.2	5.2	4.9	9.4	7.2	5.4	4.8	9.4	6.7	5.3	4.8
Decreased less than 6%................	14.7	24.2	31.9	30.9	13.0	24.2	22.0	21.9	8.9	15.5	17.3	15.9	10.6	17.1	19.7	18.7
Decreased more than 6%................	7.4	30.4	22.6	14.7	3.6	17.4	14.2	10.2	3.3	11.0	9.6	6.7	3.7	14.3	11.9	8.3
Stayed same..........	19.9	11.4	16.2	25.6	23.3	22.7	23.2	23.3	27.8	27.5	32.0	33.7	25.9	25.0	28.2	29.7

Source: American Library Association (ALA) *Public Library Funding & Technology Access Study 2011-2012* ©, published as a supplement to *American Libraries,* Summer 2012. See also <http://www.ala.org/research/plftas/2011_2012>.

Table 1185. Public Library Holdings by Type, by State: FY2011

[In thousands (794,685 represents 794,685,000). State data comparisons should be made with caution because of differences in reporting periods and adherence to survey definitions. Data are from a census of all public libraries (over 9,000) and are not subject to sampling error; census results may contain nonsampling error]

State	Type of Holding							
	Print materials [1]	Current print serial subscriptions	Electronic books	Databases	Audio		Video	
					Physical units	Download-able titles	Physical units	Download-able titles
Total..................	794,685	1,555	35,157	435	48,199	18,365	55,308	1,105
Alabama................	9,808	10	631	16	467	103	553	4
Alaska.................	2,405	6	118	5	124	100	242	0
Arizona................	9,628	16	768	5	805	660	995	23
Arkansas...............	6,671	10	90	5	235	45	350	1
California.............	70,531	101	793	4	3,684	340	4,875	10
Colorado...............	11,454	22	289	2	948	217	1,204	22
Connecticut............	15,486	26	199	6	826	231	1,079	2
Delaware...............	1,657	7	4	1	116	0	155	0
District of Columbia....	1,466	3	15	0	87	8	130	2
Florida................	32,483	59	1,088	9	2,097	770	3,273	19
Georgia................	16,660	25	129	7	638	239	896	2
Hawaii.................	3,375	3	9	0	260	5	141	0
Idaho..................	4,370	7	25	5	228	39	274	0
Illinois...............	44,137	98	850	21	3,225	1,080	2,921	422
Indiana................	24,342	50	248	16	1,633	121	2,013	1
Iowa...................	12,268	34	298	11	685	311	816	6
Kansas.................	9,629	19	18	7	485	9	742	1
Kentucky...............	8,953	23	342	5	496	309	645	28
Louisiana..............	11,876	38	142	5	384	100	786	10
Maine..................	6,294	10	347	18	231	263	328	0
Maryland...............	12,953	28	293	1	1,019	389	1,130	4
Massachusetts..........	32,640	48	1,240	15	1,422	766	1,720	29
Michigan...............	34,098	67	625	13	1,882	445	2,178	4
Minnesota..............	15,457	33	2,389	7	906	242	914	1
Mississippi............	5,698	8	44	3	224	1	301	0
Missouri...............	17,069	44	219	3	935	47	956	1
Montana................	2,781	5	421	4	120	188	161	0
Nebraska...............	6,103	15	459	6	246	37	316	0
Nevada.................	4,523	7	136	1	438	38	553	2
New Hampshire..........	6,012	12	885	6	266	927	375	0
New Jersey.............	29,113	49	910	13	1,880	(NA)	1,857	(NA)
New Mexico.............	4,600	10	17	5	224	32	246	1
New York...............	71,909	162	2,533	20	4,295	1,475	4,243	49
North Carolina.........	16,620	28	376	5	743	175	757	9
North Dakota...........	2,421	4	119	4	92	39	113	5
Ohio...................	44,570	140	6,156	79	3,664	3,422	4,637	189
Oklahoma...............	7,394	9	72	5	414	23	353	1
Oregon.................	9,915	20	1,203	4	774	743	827	109
Pennsylvania...........	27,363	52	1,555	12	2,705	(NA)	1,676	(NA)
Rhode Island...........	4,585	6	237	3	152	285	233	4
South Carolina.........	9,480	17	69	2	443	22	616	0
South Dakota...........	3,046	5	33	5	120	7	177	2
Tennessee..............	11,445	13	48	12	560	15	637	1
Texas..................	41,367	59	555	29	2,049	183	2,404	17
Utah...................	6,800	13	63	4	636	(NA)	622	(NA)
Vermont................	3,071	6	10	3	134	20	178	0
Virginia...............	18,723	27	832	1	1,205	141	1,091	1
Washington.............	13,983	46	380	2	1,249	200	1,422	9
West Virginia..........	5,356	7	67	2	210	58	269	4
Wisconsin..............	19,648	45	6,809	19	1,384	3,355	1,772	112
Wyoming................	2,450	5	1	2	156	137	156	0

NA Not available. [1] Includes books, and non-serial government documents.

Source: Institute of Museum and Library Services, Research Data Sets, "Public Libraries in the United States Survey," <http://www.imls.gov/research/pls_data_files.aspx>, accessed July 2013.

Section 25
Banking, Finance, and Insurance

This section presents data on the nation's finances, various types of financial institutions, money and credit, securities, insurance, and real estate. The primary sources of these data are publications of several departments of the federal government, especially the U.S. Treasury Department, and independent agencies such as the Federal Deposit Insurance Corporation, the Board of Governors of the Federal Reserve System, and the Securities and Exchange Commission. National data on insurance are available primarily from private organizations, such as the American Council of Life Insurers and the National Association of Insurance Commissioners.

Financial Accounts of the United States—The Federal Reserve Board brings together statistics on all of the major forms of financial instruments to present an economy-wide view of asset and liability relationships in the Financial Accounts of the United States. The accounts relate borrowing and lending to one another and to the nonfinancial activities that generate income and production. Each claim outstanding is included simultaneously as an asset of the lender and as a liability of the debtor. The accounts also indicate the balance between asset totals and liability totals over the economy as a whole. Several publications of the Federal Reserve Board contain information on these flow of funds accounts: Summary data on flows and outstandings in the statistical release *Financial Accounts of the United States* (quarterly); and concepts and organization of the accounts in *Flow of Funds Guide* <http://www.federalreserve.gov/apps/fof/>. Data are also available on the Federal Reserve Board's Web site at <http://www.federalreserve.gov/releases/z1/>.

Survey of Consumer Finances (SCF)—The Federal Reserve Board, in cooperation with the Treasury Department, sponsors this survey, which is conducted every 3 years to provide detailed information on the finances of U.S. families. Among the topics covered are the balance sheet, pension, income, and other demographic characteristics of U.S. families. The survey also gathers information on the use of financial institutions. Since 1992, data for the SCF have been collected by the National Organization for Research at the University of Chicago. Data and information on the survey are available on the Federal Reserve Board's Web site at <http://www.federalreserve.gov/econresdata/scf/scfindex.htm>.

Banking system—Banks in this country are organized under the laws of both the states and the federal government and are regulated by several bank supervisory agencies. National banks are supervised by the Comptroller of the Currency. *Reports of Condition and Income*, commonly known as call reports, have been collected from national banks since 1863. Summaries of these reports are published in the Comptroller's *Annual Report*, which also presents data on the structure of the national banking system.

The Federal Reserve System was established in 1913 to exercise central banking functions, some of which are shared with the U.S. Treasury. It includes national banks and such state banks that voluntarily join the system. Statements of state bank members are consolidated by the Federal Reserve Board with data for national banks collected by the Comptroller of the Currency into totals for all member banks of the system. Balance sheet data for member banks and other commercial banks are available on the Federal Reserve Board's Web site at <http://www.federalreserve.gov/econresdata/statisticsdata.htm>.

The Federal Deposit Insurance Corporation (FDIC), established in 1933, insures each depositor up to $250,000. Major item balance sheet and income data for all insured financial institutions are published in the *FDIC Quarterly Banking Profile*. This publication is also available on the Internet at the following address: <http://www2.fdic.gov/qbp/>. Quarterly financial information for individual institutions is available through the FDIC and Federal Financial Institutions Examination Council Web sites at <http://www.fdic.gov> and <http://www.ffiec.gov>.

Credit unions—Federally chartered credit unions are under the supervision of the National Credit Union Administration. State-chartered credit unions are supervised by the respective state supervisory authorities. The administration publishes comprehensive program and statistical information on all federal and federally insured state credit unions in the *Annual Report of the National Credit Union Administration*.

Other credit agencies—Insurance companies, finance companies dealing primarily in installment sales financing, and personal loan companies represent important sources of funds for the credit market. Statistics on loans, investments, cash, etc., of life insurance companies are published principally by the American Council of Life Insurers in its *Life Insurers Fact Book*. Consumer credit data are available on the Federal Reserve Board's Web site at <http://www.federalreserve.gov/econresdata/statisticsdata.htm>. Government corporations and credit agencies make available credit of specified types or to specified groups of private borrowers, either by lending directly or by insuring or guaranteeing loans made by private lending institutions. Data on operations of government credit agencies, along with other government corporations, are available in reports of individual agencies.

Securities—The Securities and Exchange Commission (SEC) was established in 1934 to protect the interests of the public and investors against malpractices in the securities and financial markets and to provide the fullest possible disclosure of information regarding securities to the investing public.

Data on the securities industry and securities transactions are also available from a number of private sources. The Securities Industry and Financial Markets Association, New York, NY, <http://www.sifma.org/>, publishes the *Securities Industry Fact Book* and *Securities Industry Yearbook*. The Investment Company Institute, Washington, DC, <http://www.ici.org/>, publishes a reference book, research newsletters, and a variety of research reports that examine the industry, its shareholders, or industry issues. The annual *Investment Company Fact Book* is a guide to trends and statistics observed in the investment company industry. *Fundamentals* is a newsletter summarizing the findings of major Institute research projects. Institute research reports provide a detailed examination of shareholder demographics and other aspects of fund ownership.

Among the many sources of data on stock and bond prices and sales are the New York Stock Exchange, New York, NY, <http://www.nyse.com/>; NASDAQ, Washington, DC, <http://www.nasdaq.com/>; Global Financial Data, Los Angeles, CA, <http://www.globalfinancialdata.com/>; and Dow-Jones & Company, Inc., New York, NY, <http://www.djindexes.com>.

Insurance—Insuring companies, which are regulated by the various states or the District of Columbia, are classified as either life or property. Both life and property insurance companies may underwrite health insurance. Insuring companies, other than those classified as life, are permitted to underwrite one or more property lines provided they are so licensed and have the necessary capital or surplus. There are a number of published sources for statistics on the various classes of insurance—life, health, fire, marine, and casualty. Organizations representing certain classes of insurers publish reports for these classes. The American Council of Life Insurers publishes statistics on life insurance purchases, ownership, benefit payments, and assets in its *Life Insurers Fact Book*.

Statistical reliability—For a discussion of statistical collection, estimation, and sampling procedures and measures of reliability applicable to data from the Census Bureau and the Federal Reserve Board's Survey of Consumer Finances, see Appendix III.

Table 1186. Gross Domestic Product in Finance, Insurance, Real Estate, Rental and Leasing in Current and Chained (2005) Dollars: 2000 to 2012

[In billions of dollars, except percent (762 represents $762,000,000,000.) Represents value added by industry. Data based on the 2002 North American Classification System (NAICS). See text, Section 15. For definition of gross domestic product and explanation of chained dollars, see text, Section 13, Income]

Industry	NAICS code	Current Dollars				Chained (2005) dollars			
		2000	2010	2011	2012	2000	2010	2011	2012
Finance & insurance, total...............	**52**	**762**	**1,157**	**1,159**	**1,242**	**841**	**1,037**	**1,031**	**1,068**
Percent of gross domestic product......		7.7	8.0	7.7	7.9	7.5	7.9	7.8	7.9
Federal Reserve banks, credit inter-mediation, and related activities..........	521,522	338	559	544	(NA)	370	486	481	(NA)
Securities, commodity contracts, & investments....................	523	126	181	179	(NA)	126	173	163	(NA)
Insurance carriers & related activities......	524	274	384	398	(NA)	338	356	359	(NA)
Funds, trusts, & other financial vehicles...	525	24	34	39	(NA)	19	27	32	(NA)
Real estate & rental & leasing, total. ..	**53**	**1,236**	**1,865**	**1,899**	**1,926**	**1,422**	**1,719**	**1,735**	**1,755**
Percent of gross domestic product......		12.4	12.9	12.6	12.3	12.7	13.2	13.0	12.9
Real estate.....................	531	1,098	1,677	1,701	(NA)	1,267	1,545	1,554	(NA)
Rental & leasing services and lessors of intangible assets....................	532, 533	138	188	198	(NA)	156	174	180	(NA)

NA Not available.

Source: U.S. Bureau of Economic Analysis, "Value Added by Industry" and "Real Value Added by Industry," <http://www.bea.gov/itable/>, accessed August 2013.

Table 1187. Finance and Insurance/Real Estate and Rental and Leasing—Establishments, Revenue, Payroll, and Employees by Kind of Business (2002 NAICS Basis): 2002 and 2007

[2,804 represents $2,804,000,000,000. For establishments with payroll. Based on the 2002 and 2007 Economic Censuses; see Appendix III]

Kind of business	2002 NAICS code [1]	Number of establishments		Revenue (bil. dol.)		Annual payroll (bil. dol.)		Paid employees (1,000)	
		2002	2007	2002	2007	2002	2007	2002	2007
Finance & insurance [2].........................	**52**	**440,268**	**506,507**	**2,804**	**3,711**	**377.8**	**505.2**	**6,579**	**6,649**
Monetary authorities—central bank............	521	47	47	29	45	1.2	1.3	22	19
Credit intermediation & related activities........	522	196,451	231,439	1,056	1,343	151.2	180.9	3,300	3,280
Security, commodity contracts, & like activity...	523	72,338	85,475	316	612	103.4	166.3	832	885
Insurance carriers & related activities...........	524	169,520	184,752	1,380	1,669	120.6	153.9	2,406	2,423
Real estate & rental & leasing...............	**53**	**322,815**	**379,503**	**336**	**443**	**60.2**	**82.0**	**1,949**	**2,147**
Real estate.....................	531	256,086	311,936	224	289	41.7	58.6	1,305	1,487
Rental & leasing services.........................	532	64,344	65,120	95	122	16.9	21.1	617	630
Lessors of other nonfinancial intangible assets.............	533	2,385	2,447	17	33	1.7	2.3	27	29

[1] Based on the North American Industry Classification System (NAICS); see text, Section 15. [2] Total does not include NAICS 525, Funds, trusts, and other financial vehicles, not published in the 2007 Economic Census.

Source: U.S. Census Bureau, "2007 Economic Census, Finance and Insurance: Geographic Area Series: Comparative Statistics for the United States (2002 NAICS Basis): 2007 and 2002," and "2007 Economic Census, Real Estate and Rental and Leasing: Geographic Area Series: Comparative Statistics for the United States (2002 NAICS Basis): 2007 and 2002," <http://factfinder2.census.gov>, accessed August 2013.

Table 1188. Finance and Insurance—Nonemployer Establishments and Receipts by Kind of Business: 2009 to 2011

[733.7 represents 733,700. Includes only firms subject to federal income tax. Nonemployers are businesses with no paid employees. Data originate chiefly from administrative records of the Internal Revenue Service; see Appendix III]

Kind of business	NAICS code [1]	Establishments (1,000)			Receipts (mil. dol.)		
		2009	2010	2011	2009	2010	2011
Finance and insurance........................	**52**	**733.7**	**716.8**	**713.7**	**51,579**	**50,626**	**50,312**
Credit intermediation & related activities........................	522	63.0	53.3	48.2	3,034	2,790	2,735
Depository credit intermediation.....................	5221	6.7	6.2	6.0	180	181	183
Nondepository credit intermediation.....................	5222	25.1	21.8	20.9	1,711	1,554	1,563
Activities related to credit intermediation.....................	5223	31.2	25.3	21.3	1,143	1,056	989
Security, commodity contracts, & like activity..................	523	279.3	273.4	271.7	30,249	29,202	28,308
Securities & commodity contracts interm & brokerage.......	5231	30.5	29.8	29.4	5,345	4,969	4,689
Investment banking and securities dealing...................	52311	7.6	7.2	7.3	1,663	1,748	1,336
Securities brokerage.....................	52312	18.7	18.6	18.2	3,025	2,589	2,744
Commodity contracts dealing.....................	52313	1.2	1.1	1.1	284	236	185
Commodity contracts brokerage.....................	52314	3.0	2.9	2.8	373	397	424
Securities & commodity exchanges.....................	5232	1.9	1.9	1.9	885	660	603
Other financial investment activities.....................	5239	247.0	241.7	240.4	24,019	23,573	23,017
Insurance carriers & related activities.....................	524	391.3	390.1	393.9	18,295	18,634	19,268
Insurance carriers.....................	5241	3.2	2.7	2.6	191	185	188
Agencies & other insurance-related activities.................	5242	388.2	387.4	391.3	18,105	18,449	19,080
Insurance agencies & brokerages.....................	52421	269.7	270.5	272.8	13,572	13,854	14,198
Other insurance related activities.....................	52429	118.4	116.9	118.5	4,533	4,595	4,882

[1] Data are based on 2007 North American Industry Classification System (NAICS). For more information, see text, Section 15.

Source: U.S. Census Bureau, "Nonemployer Statistics," <http://www.census.gov/econ/nonemployer/index.html>, accessed June 2013.

Table 1189. Finance and Insurance—Establishments, Employees, and Payroll: 2010 and 2011

[473.5 represents 473,500. Covers establishments with payroll. Employees are for the week including March 12. Excludes most government employees, railroad employees, and self-employed persons. For statement on methodology, see Appendix III]

Kind of business	NAICS code [1]	Establishments (1,000)		Employees (1,000)		Payroll (bil.dol.)	
		2010	2011	2010	2011	2010	2011
Finance & insurance, total [2]	**52**	**473.5**	**467.5**	**5,929**	**5,887**	**472.4**	**493.6**
Monetary authorities—central bank	521	(Z)	0.1	18	18	1.6	1.7
Credit intermediation & related activities	522	199.1	196.2	2,757	2,759	160.2	169.1
Depository credit intermediation [2]	5221	124.4	123.6	1,982	1,994	111.6	119.8
Commercial banking	52211	92.7	92.2	1,528	1,541	91.2	98.5
Savings institutions	52212	13.8	13.7	199	201	9.8	10.4
Credit unions	52213	17.8	17.7	251	249	10.3	10.5
Nondepository credit intermediation [2]	5222	41.6	42.1	521	521	34.9	35.5
Real estate credit	522292	14.3	14.9	216	222	14.2	14.3
Activities related to credit intermediation	5223	33.1	30.5	254	244	13.7	13.9
Security, commodity contracts & like activity [2]	523	96.4	95.3	874	881	156.4	166.0
Security & commodity contracts intermediation & brokerage [2]	5231	45.4	43.7	435	425	82.0	86.1
Securities brokerage	52312	38.3	36.8	309	302	45.7	47.3
Other financial investment activities [2]	5239	50.9	51.6	434	450	73.6	79.1
Portfolio management	52392	19.1	18.9	232	229	51.0	54.4
Insurance carriers & related activities	524	176.9	175.0	2,273	2,226	153.1	156.3
Insurance carriers [2]	5241	33.3	33.3	1,421	1,384	104.7	107.4
Direct life insurance carriers	524113	8.9	10.0	360	352	28.6	30.5
Direct health & medical insurance carriers	524114	4.8	4.8	459	442	31.0	32.5
Direct property & casualty insurance carriers	524126	14.4	13.5	529	509	39.3	38.4
Agencies & other insurance-related activities [2]	5242	143.6	141.7	852	842	48.4	48.9
Insurance agencies & brokerages	52421	131.4	129.8	646	635	36.3	36.2

Z Less than 50. [1] Based on 2007 North American Industry Classification System (NAICS). For more information, see text, Section 15. [2] Includes businesses not shown separately.

Source: U.S. Census Bureau, "County Business Patterns," <http://www.census.gov/econ/cbp/index.html>, accessed June 2013.

Table 1190. Financial Accounts of the United States—Financial Assets of Financial and Nonfinancial Institutions by Holder Sector: 1990 to 2012

[In billions of dollars (35,941 represents $35,941,000,000,000). As of Dec. 31]

Sector	1990	2000	2005	2006	2007	2008	2009	2010	2011	2012
All sectors	**35,941**	**90,629**	**125,845**	**140,295**	**152,862**	**141,245**	**146,679**	**153,992**	**157,987**	**168,692**
Households [1]	14,695	33,771	44,906	49,875	52,898	43,436	46,304	50,386	51,310	55,595
Nonfinancial business	3,981	11,235	14,505	15,784	17,358	16,631	16,932	17,720	18,276	19,240
Nonfinancial noncorporate	391	1,473	2,597	3,116	3,596	3,693	3,592	3,699	3,741	3,789
Nonfinancial corporations	3,589	9,762	11,909	12,668	13,762	12,938	13,340	14,021	14,535	15,451
State and local government	1,020	1,662	2,194	2,295	2,517	2,357	2,350	2,337	2,198	2,104
Federal government	442	570	644	637	681	1,262	1,343	1,565	1,338	1,416
Monetary authority	342	636	879	908	951	2,271	2,267	2,453	2,947	2,955
Private depository institutions	4,526	7,368	10,651	11,387	12,394	14,131	13,419	13,582	14,693	15,058
U.S.-chartered depository institutions	3,957	6,100	9,106	9,798	10,545	11,663	11,266	11,295	11,712	12,056
Foreign banking offices in U.S.	367	805	818	828	1,048	1,625	1,267	1,337	1,999	1,967
Banks in U.S.-affiliated areas	26	62	106	105	105	102	95	80	76	76
Credit unions	176	401	620	656	696	741	792	871	906	959
Life insurance companies	1,351	3,136	4,351	4,685	4,950	4,515	4,824	5,176	5,340	5,613
Property-casualty insurance companies	533	858	1,246	1,336	1,386	1,306	1,377	1,374	1,396	1,445
Private pension funds	1,629	4,468	5,389	5,792	6,108	4,568	5,443	6,143	6,302	6,636
Defined benefit plans	900	1,979	2,281	2,393	2,516	1,895	2,129	2,390	2,451	2,547
Defined contribution plans	729	2,489	3,108	3,398	3,592	2,673	3,314	3,753	3,852	4,089
State and local government employee retirement funds	730	2,293	2,773	3,130	3,286	2,429	2,722	2,949	2,873	3,193
Federal government retirement funds	340	797	1,072	1,141	1,197	1,222	1,325	1,425	1,510	1,582
Money market mutual funds	493	1,812	1,993	2,296	3,033	3,757	3,259	2,755	2,643	2,650
Mutual funds	608	4,433	6,046	7,065	7,823	5,388	6,921	7,873	7,871	9,324
Closed-end funds	53	142	270	293	316	203	229	244	242	258
Exchange-traded funds	-	66	301	423	608	531	773	987	1,043	1,324
Government-sponsored enterprises (GSE)	478	1,965	2,819	2,873	3,174	3,408	3,062	6,749	6,505	6,295
Agency- and GSE-backed mortgage pools	1,020	2,493	3,548	3,841	4,464	4,961	5,377	1,139	1,305	1,437
Asset-backed securities issuers	268	1,497	3,390	4,158	4,511	4,098	3,285	2,231	1,983	1,767
Finance companies	596	1,213	1,857	1,891	1,911	1,852	1,662	1,629	1,610	1,534
Real estate investment trusts	28	65	306	345	318	251	241	283	401	559
Security brokers and dealers	262	1,221	2,127	2,742	3,092	2,217	2,084	2,075	1,950	2,068
Holding companies	325	899	1,651	1,938	2,141	2,430	3,317	3,313	3,357	4,320
Funding corporations	236	1,158	1,327	1,394	1,706	2,783	2,356	2,197	2,095	2,157
Rest of the world	1,984	6,873	11,599	14,068	16,038	15,240	15,807	17,405	18,802	20,161

– Represents zero. [1] Includes nonprofit organizations.

Source: Board of Governors of the Federal Reserve System, "Federal Reserve Statistical Release, Z.1, Financial Accounts of the United States," <http://www.federalreserve.gov/releases/z1/>, accessed June 2013.

Table 1191. Financial Accounts of the United States—Credit Market Debt Outstanding: 1990 to 2012

[In billions of dollars (13,757 represents $13,757,000,000,000). As of December 31. Excludes corporate equities and mutual fund shares. Represents credit market debt owed by sectors shown]

Item	1990	2000	2005	2006	2007	2008	2009	2010	2011	2012
Credit market debt................	**13,757**	**27,211**	**42,161**	**46,202**	**50,953**	**53,353**	**53,252**	**53,621**	**54,590**	**56,447**
Domestic nonfinancial................	10,825	18,228	27,690	30,059	32,622	34,543	35,474	36,909	38,268	40,121
Household sector [1]..................	3,572	6,964	11,716	12,833	13,689	13,669	13,397	13,060	12,864	12,819
Nonfinancial corporate business........	2,577	4,769	5,784	6,337	7,199	7,564	7,330	7,486	8,013	8,705
Nonfinancial noncorporate business......	1,191	1,912	2,898	3,313	3,775	4,093	3,973	3,940	3,952	4,024
State and local governments..........	987	1,198	2,590	2,691	2,837	2,855	2,968	3,038	2,985	2,980
Federal government................	2,498	3,385	4,702	4,885	5,122	6,362	7,805	9,386	10,454	11,594
Rest of the world..................	318	815	1,514	1,883	2,126	1,709	2,090	2,225	2,277	2,415
Financial sectors..................	2,614	8,168	12,957	14,261	16,204	17,101	15,688	14,486	14,045	13,911
U.S.-chartered depository institutions......	179	531	728	769	991	990	718	943	869	840
Foreign banking offices in U.S..........	35	2	1	–	1	–	–	–	–	–
Credit unions..................	–	3	15	19	32	41	27	26	24	25
Life insurance companies..........	–	2	11	14	29	55	48	45	47	52
Government-sponsored enterprises (GSE).....	399	1,826	2,592	2,628	2,910	3,182	2,707	6,435	6,247	6,093
Agency- and GSE-backed mortgage pools.....	1,020	2,493	3,548	3,841	4,464	4,961	5,377	1,139	1,305	1,437
Asset-backed securities issuers........	269	1,504	3,394	4,161	4,515	4,101	3,288	2,231	1,983	1,767
Finance companies................	398	807	1,109	1,144	1,280	1,200	1,044	1,281	1,263	1,209
Real estate investment trusts........	28	168	395	411	421	367	317	315	343	386
Brokers and dealers................	15	41	62	69	65	143	93	130	92	90
Holding companies................	125	288	482	559	711	808	1,254	1,237	1,221	1,419
Funding corporations................	147	503	620	645	786	1,253	817	704	652	594

– Represents or rounds to zero. [1] Includes nonprofit organizations.

Source: Board of Governors of the Federal Reserve System, "Federal Reserve Statistical Release, Z.1, Financial Accounts of the United States," June 2013, <http://www.federalreserve.gov/releases/z1/>.

Table 1192. Financial Accounts of the United States—Financial Assets and Liabilities of Foreign Sector: 1990 to 2012

[In billions of dollars (1,984 represents $1,984,000,000,000). As of December 31. Minus sign (–) indicates loss]

Type of instrument	1990	2000	2005	2006	2007	2008	2009	2010	2011	2012
Total financial assets [1]..............	**1,984**	**6,873**	**11,599**	**14,068**	**16,038**	**15,240**	**15,807**	**17,405**	**18,802**	**20,161**
Net interbank assets................	61	154	133	165	54	464	194	146	367	213
U.S. checkable deposits and currency.........	86	236	300	312	306	370	361	390	472	540
U.S. time deposits................	40	102	156	167	208	273	230	247	280	326
Money market fund shares..............	1	11	23	27	46	70	77	70	79	114
Credit market instruments..............	882	2,451	5,191	6,200	7,272	7,524	7,723	8,499	9,122	9,640
Open market paper................	11	114	240	286	278	233	192	191	192	195
Treasury securities................	438	1,021	1,984	2,126	2,376	3,253	3,671	4,467	5,071	5,526
Official..................	286	640	1,341	1,558	1,737	2,401	2,880	3,365	3,653	3,986
Private..................	152	382	644	568	640	852	791	1,102	1,418	1,540
Agency- and GSE-backed securities [2]........	49	348	1,013	1,264	1,582	1,407	1,155	1,084	1,090	1,126
Official..................	5	116	487	695	954	941	749	661	648	631
Private..................	44	232	526	568	628	466	406	423	441	495
Municipal securities................	2	8	29	34	45	51	59	72	70	65
U.S. corporate bonds [3]................	209	842	1,763	2,321	2,719	2,354	2,465	2,523	2,503	2,581
Loans to U.S. corporate business............	172	117	163	169	271	226	182	162	196	147
U.S. corporate equities................	243	1,483	2,039	2,448	2,811	1,807	2,477	2,962	2,783	3,106
Mutual fund shares..............	0	149	242	317	374	256	364	514	735	958
Trade receivables................	46	49	57	63	84	90	97	116	134	145
Miscellaneous assets................	599	2,140	3,220	3,997	4,537	4,263	4,197	4,503	4,820	5,149
Foreign direct investment in U.S. [4]...........	505	1,421	1,906	2,154	2,346	2,397	2,398	2,598	2,909	3,070
Other................	94	719	1,314	1,843	2,191	1,866	1,799	1,905	1,911	2,079
Total liabilities................	**1,454**	**3,611**	**6,158**	**7,322**	**8,704**	**8,844**	**9,079**	**9,807**	**10,081**	**10,324**
U.S. official reserve assets................	72	57	54	55	60	67	120	121	130	128
U.S. private deposits................	298	803	998	1,085	1,341	947	841	867	834	792
Credit market instruments [1]................	318	815	1,514	1,883	2,126	1,709	2,090	2,225	2,277	2,415
Commercial paper................	75	121	384	482	413	342	401	399	345	373
Bonds................	145	573	1,012	1,276	1,587	1,237	1,570	1,689	1,764	1,844
Depository institution loans n.e.c. [5]...........	19	71	84	98	103	108	97	115	144	166
Trade payables................	29	51	54	61	73	63	69	95	63	69
Miscellaneous liabilities [1]................	737	1,886	3,537	4,239	5,105	6,059	5,959	6,499	6,777	6,921
U.S. equity in IBRD, [6] etc................	20	35	43	45	47	48	50	52	55	57
U.S. direct investment abroad [3, 4]............	630	1,532	2,652	2,948	3,553	3,749	4,029	4,307	4,682	4,944
Investment by holding companies............	8	-7	27	68	111	102	125	136	166	115

[1] Includes other items not shown separately. [2] GSE = Government-sponsored enterprises. [3] Through 1992, corporate bonds include net issues by Netherlands Antillean financial subsidiaries; U.S. direct investment abroad excludes net inflows from those bond issues. [4] Direct investment is valued on a current-cost basis. [5] Not elsewhere classified. [6] International Bank for Reconstruction and Development.

Source: Board of Governors of the Federal Reserve System, "Federal Reserve Statistical Release, Z.1, Financial Accounts of the United States," June 2013, <http://www.federalreserve.gov/releases/z1/>.

Table 1193. Financial Accounts of the United States—Assets of Households and Nonprofit Organizations: 1990 to 2012

[As of December 31 (14,695 represents $14,695,000,000,000). See also Table 750]

Type of instrument	Total (billion dollars)						Percent distribution			
	1990	2000	2005	2010	2011	2012	1990	2000	2010	2012
Total financial assets.................	**14,695**	**33,771**	**44,906**	**50,386**	**51,310**	**55,595**	**100.0**	**100.0**	**100.0**	**100.0**
Deposits.........................	3,366	4,438	6,217	8,004	8,649	9,139	22.9	13.1	15.9	16.4
Foreign deposits..............	13	48	60	52	50	48	0.1	0.1	0.1	0.1
Checkable deposits and currency........	451	405	286	438	754	885	3.1	1.2	0.9	1.6
Time and savings deposits...............	2,512	3,047	4,929	6,384	6,734	7,097	17.1	9.0	12.7	12.8
Money market fund shares.............	389	937	943	1,130	1,110	1,110	2.6	2.8	2.2	2.0
Credit market instruments [1].................	1,741	2,566	4,226	5,928	5,402	5,469	11.8	7.6	11.8	9.8
Treasury securities.....................	504	579	440	1,265	816	1,198	3.4	1.7	2.5	2.2
Savings bonds.................	126	185	205	188	185	182	0.9	0.5	0.4	0.3
Bills and other Treasury securities.....	378	394	235	1,077	631	1,015	2.6	1.2	2.1	1.8
Agency and GSE-backed securities [2]....	117	589	586	390	373	97	0.8	1.7	0.8	0.2
Municipal securities........................	648	532	1,601	1,873	1,808	1,656	4.4	1.6	3.7	3.0
Corporate and foreign bonds.............	238	663	1,353	2,252	2,273	2,402	1.6	2.0	4.5	4.3
Mortgages...........................	141	103	139	90	79	66	1.0	0.3	0.2	0.1
Corporate equities [3].....................	1,961	8,140	8,179	8,844	8,866	10,178	13.3	24.1	17.6	18.3
Mutual fund shares........................	512	2,708	3,636	4,618	4,453	5,372	3.5	8.0	9.2	9.7
Security credit............................	62	412	575	694	752	776	0.4	1.2	1.4	1.4
Life insurance reserves.....................	392	819	1,083	1,137	1,204	1,186	2.7	2.4	2.3	2.1
Pension fund reserves [4]...................	3,310	9,171	11,512	13,210	13,434	14,444	22.5	27.2	26.2	26.0
Equity in noncorporate business...........	3,097	5,138	8,868	7,120	7,673	8,141	21.1	15.2	14.1	14.6
Miscellaneous assets.....................	254	379	609	831	877	889	1.7	1.1	1.6	1.6

[1] Includes other instruments not shown separately. [2] GSE = government-sponsored enterprises. [3] Only those directly held and those in closed-end and exchange-traded funds. Other equities are included in mutual funds and life insurance and pension reserves. [4] See also Table 1242.

Source: Board of Governors of the Federal Reserve System, "Federal Reserve Statistical Release, Z.1, Financial Accounts of the United States," June 2013, <http://www.federalreserve.gov/releases/z1/>.

Table 1194. Financial Assets Held by Families by Type of Asset: 2007 and 2010

[Median value in thousands of constant 2010 dollars (21.5 represents $21,500). All dollar figures are adjusted to 2010 dollars using the "current methods" version of the consumer price index for all urban consumers published by U.S. Bureau of Labor Statistics. Families include one-person units; for definition of family, see text, Section 1. Based on Survey of Consumer Finances; see Appendix III]

Age of family head and family income	Any financial asset [1]	Trans-action accounts [2]	Certifi-cates of deposit	Savings bonds	Stocks [3]	Pooled invest-ment funds [4]	Retire-ment accounts [5]	Life insur-ance [6]	Other man-aged [7]
PERCENT OF FAMILIES OWNING ASSET									
2007, total................	93.9	92.1	16.1	14.9	17.9	11.4	53.0	23.0	5.8
2010, total..............	**94.0**	**92.5**	**12.2**	**12.0**	**15.1**	**8.7**	**50.4**	**19.7**	**5.7**
Under 35 years old.......	91.3	89.0	5.7	10.0	10.1	3.6	41.1	9.6	0.9
35 to 44 years old........	92.7	90.6	5.7	11.6	12.1	7.7	52.2	12.3	2.0
45 to 54 years old........	94.2	92.5	10.0	15.0	16.0	9.6	60.0	19.8	4.5
55 to 64 years old........	95.8	94.2	14.6	14.3	19.5	11.3	59.8	25.7	7.7
65 to 74 years old........	96.2	95.8	20.6	9.1	16.1	11.1	49.0	28.4	11.4
75 years old and over....	96.4	96.4	27.2	10.1	20.1	11.9	32.8	32.4	14.1
Percentiles of income: [8]									
Less than 20..............	79.2	76.2	5.7	3.6	3.8	2.1	11.2	10.7	1.7
20 to 39.9...............	93.6	91.1	11.1	6.0	6.0	3.5	30.5	17.2	4.2
40 to 59.9...............	97.8	96.4	11.7	10.8	11.7	5.8	52.8	19.5	5.5
60 to 79.9...............	99.6	98.9	15.8	16.0	17.3	8.8	69.7	22.8	6.9
80 to 89.9...............	100.0	99.8	12.1	23.0	25.7	14.6	85.7	25.8	7.8
90 to 100................	100.0	99.9	21.5	24.4	47.8	32.1	90.1	30.9	12.3
MEDIAN VALUE [9]									
2007, total................	30.2	4.2	21.0	1.0	17.8	58.7	47.1	8.4	73.3
2010, total..............	**21.5**	**3.5**	**20.0**	**1.0**	**20.0**	**80.0**	**44.0**	**7.3**	**70.0**
Under 35 years old.......	5.5	2.1	5.2	0.5	5.4	8.5	10.5	2.1	9.0
35 to 44 years old........	14.5	2.5	7.0	1.0	10.0	41.0	31.2	5.0	10.0
45 to 54 years old........	33.7	3.5	16.0	0.8	30.0	110.0	60.0	10.0	50.0
55 to 64 years old........	55.8	5.0	20.0	1.2	35.0	110.0	100.0	9.3	65.0
65 to 74 years old........	45.2	5.7	25.0	4.0	48.0	115.0	100.0	10.0	95.0
75 years old and over....	43.8	7.2	32.2	1.0	45.0	120.0	54.0	7.0	82.0

[1] Includes other types of financial assets, not shown separately. [2] Checking, savings, and money market deposit accounts, money market mutual funds, and call accounts at brokerages. [3] Covers only those stocks and bonds that are directly held by families outside mutual funds, retirement accounts, and other managed assets. [4] Excludes money market mutual funds and indirectly held mutual funds and includes all other types of directly held pooled investment funds, such as traditional open-ended and closed-end mutual funds, real estate investment trusts, and hedge funds. [5] The tax-deferred retirement accounts consist of IRAs, Keogh accounts, and certain employer-sponsored accounts. Employer-sponsored accounts include 401(k), 403(b), and thrift saving accounts from current or past jobs; other current job plans from which loans or withdrawals can be made; and accounts from past jobs from which the family expects to receive the account balance in the future. [6] The value of such policies according to their current cash value, not their death benefit. [7] Includes personal annuities and trusts with an equity interest and managed investment accounts. [8] Percentiles of income distribution in 2010 dollars: 20th: $20,400; 40th: $35,600; 60th: $57,800; 80th: $94,600; 90th: $142,300. Percentiles of distribution of net worth in 2007 dollars: 25th: $8,300; 50th: $77,300; 75th: $301,700; 90th: $952,500. Percentile: A value on a scale of zero to 100 that indicates the percent of a distribution that is equal to or below it. [9] Median value of financial asset for families holding such assets.

Source: Board of Governors of the Federal Reserve System, "2010 Survey of Consumer Finances," June 2012; and previous editions. See <http://www.federalreserve.gov/pubs/bulletin/default.htm>.

Table 1195. Financial Accounts of the United States—Liabilities of Households and Nonprofit Organizations: 1990 to 2012

[As of December 31 (3,694 represents $3,694,000,000,000). See also Table 750]

Type of instrument	Total (bil. dol.)						Percent distribution			
	1990	2000	2005	2010	2011	2012	1990	2000	2010	2012
Total liabilities............................	**3,694**	**7,353**	**12,158**	**13,637**	**13,415**	**13,438**	**100.0**	**100.0**	**100.0**	**100.0**
Credit market instruments............................	3,572	6,964	11,716	13,060	12,864	12,819	96.7	94.7	95.8	95.4
Home mortgages [1]............................	2,489	4,814	8,907	9,895	9,666	9,432	67.4	65.5	72.6	70.2
Consumer credit............................	824	1,741	2,321	2,522	2,616	2,768	22.3	23.7	18.5	20.6
Municipal securities............................	86	138	213	263	255	241	2.3	1.9	1.9	1.8
Depository institution loans, not elsewhere classified [2]............................	14	19	-16	61	12	66	0.4	0.3	0.4	0.5
Other loans and advances............................	82	119	119	136	138	139	2.2	1.6	1.0	1.0
Commercial mortgages............................	77	133	173	182	176	173	2.1	1.8	1.3	1.3
Security credit............................	39	235	232	278	239	304	1.1	3.2	2.0	2.3
Trade payables............................	67	135	186	274	288	290	1.8	1.8	2.0	2.2
Unpaid life insurance premiums [3]............................	16	20	22	25	24	25	0.4	0.3	0.2	0.2

[1] Includes loans made under home equity lines of credit and home equity loans secured by junior liens. [2] Includes loans extended by the Federal Reserve to financial institutions such as domestic hedge funds through the Term Asset-Backed Securities Loan Facility (TALF). [3] Includes deferred premiums.

Source: Board of Governors of the Federal Reserve System, "Federal Reserve Statistical Release, Z.1, Financial Accounts of the United States," June 2013, <http://www.federalreserve.gov/releases/z1/>.

Table 1196. Financial Debt Held by Families by Type of Debt: 2007 and 2010

[Median debt in thousands of constant 2010 dollars (70.7 represents $70,700). See headnote, Table 1194]

Age of family head and family income	Any debt	Secured by residential property		Lines of credit not secured by residential property	Installment loans	Credit card balances [2]	Other [3]
		Primary residence [1]	Other				
PERCENT OF FAMILIES HOLDING DEBT							
2007, total............................	77.0	48.7	5.5	1.7	46.9	46.1	6.8
2010, total............................	**74.9**	**47.0**	**5.3**	**2.1**	**46.3**	**39.4**	**6.4**
Under 35 years old............................	77.8	34.0	2.9	1.8	61.9	38.7	5.5
35 to 44 years old............................	86.0	57.6	5.1	2.2	60.0	45.6	8.6
45 to 54 years old............................	84.1	60.4	7.6	2.7	49.8	46.2	9.7
55 to 64 years old............................	77.7	53.6	7.6	3.0	40.7	41.3	6.7
65 to 74 years old............................	65.2	40.5	5.0	1.2	30.4	31.9	2.3
75 years old and over............................	38.5	24.2	2.9	(B)	12.3	21.7	2.0
Percentiles of income: [4]							
Less than 20............................	52.5	14.8	1.3	1.2	34.1	23.2	4.2
20 to 39.9............................	66.8	29.6	1.7	2.2	40.8	33.4	4.2
40 to 59.9............................	81.8	51.6	3.5	2.1	49.9	45.0	6.8
60 to 79.9............................	86.9	65.4	6.0	1.9	56.6	53.1	7.8
80 to 89.9............................	88.9	74.5	9.1	2.0	58.8	51.0	11.8
90 to 100............................	84.5	72.8	19.4	3.7	41.8	33.6	6.6
MEDIAN DEBT [5]							
2007, total............................	67.3	107.0	100.0	3.8	13.0	3.0	5.0
2010, total............................	**70.7**	**109.6**	**98.0**	**6.0**	**12.6**	**2.6**	**4.5**
Under 35 years old............................	39.6	120.0	89.0	2.0	14.0	1.6	2.0
35 to 44 years old............................	108.0	139.9	85.0	2.5	14.7	3.5	4.4
45 to 54 years old............................	91.8	114.0	115.0	6.0	12.0	3.5	5.0
55 to 64 years old............................	76.9	97.0	98.0	11.0	11.3	2.8	6.0
65 to 74 years old............................	45.0	70.0	125.0	8.1	10.0	2.2	6.0
75 years old and over............................	30.0	52.0	74.8	(B)	7.8	1.8	13.0

B Base figure too small. [1] First and second mortgages and home equity loans and lines of credit secured. [2] Families that had an outstanding balance on any of their credit cards after paying their most recent bills. [3] Includes loans on insurance policies, loans against pension accounts, borrowing on margin accounts and unclassified loans. [4] See footnote 8, Table 1194. [5] Median amount of financial debt for families holding such debts.

Source: Board of Governors of the Federal Reserve System, "2010 Survey of Consumer Finances," June 2012, <http://www.federalreserve.gov/pubs/bulletin/default.htm>.

Table 1197. Amount of Debt Held by Families—Percent Distribution: 2007 and 2010

[See headnote, Table 1194]

Type of debt	2007	2010	Purpose of debt	2007	2010	Type of lending institution	2007	2010
Total.....................	**100.0**	**100.0**	**Total**..............	**100.0**	**100.0**	**Total**.....................	**100.0**	**100.0**
Secured by residential property:			Primary residence:			Commercial bank...............	37.3	45.1
Primary residence.........	74.7	74.1	Purchase............	69.5	69.5	Thrift institution................	4.2	4.1
Other........................	10.1	9.8	Improvement........	2.3	1.9	Credit union....................	4.2	5.1
Lines of credit not			Other residential property......................	10.8	10.5	Finance or loan company......................	3.4	4.0
secured by residential			Investments, excluding			Brokerage.......................	1.6	6.9
property......................	0.4	1.0	real estate...........	1.6	2.0	Real estate lender [1]...........	41.6	26.9
Installment loans...........	10.2	11.1	Vehicles..............	5.5	4.7	Individual lender...............	1.4	1.0
Credit card balances.......	3.5	2.9	Goods and services...	6.2	5.7	Other nonfinancial.............	2.0	2.4
Other........................	1.1	1.1	Education.............	3.6	5.2	Government....................	0.4	0.8
			Other loans...........	0.5	0.4	Credit card issuer..............	3.6	2.9
						Other type of lender...........	0.4	0.9

[1] Includes mortgage lender.

Source: Board of Governors of the Federal Reserve System, "2010 Survey of Consumer Finances," June 2012, <http://www.federalreserve.gov/econresdata/scf/scf_2010.htm#bullart>.

Table 1198. Ratios of Debt Payments to Family Income: 2004 to 2010

[In percent. All dollar figures are adjusted to 2010 dollars using the "current methods" version of the consumer price index for all urban consumers published by U.S. Bureau of Labor Statistics. Families include one-person units; for definition of family, see text, Section 1. Based on Survey of Consumer Finance; see Appendix III. For definition of median, see Guide to Tabular Presentation]

Age of family head and family income (constant [2010] dollars)	Ratio of debt payments to family income						Percent of debtors with—					
	Aggregate			Median for debtors			Ratios above 40 percent			Any payment 60 days or more past due		
	2004	2007	2010	2004	2007	2010	2004	2007	2010	2004	2007	2010
All families..........	**14.4**	**14.6**	**14.7**	**18.1**	**18.7**	**18.1**	**12.3**	**14.8**	**13.8**	**8.9**	**7.1**	**10.8**
Under 35 years old....	17.8	19.7	17.0	18.0	17.6	16.4	12.8	15.1	11.6	13.7	9.4	10.4
35 to 44 years old.....	18.3	18.6	18.4	20.6	20.3	20.9	12.4	12.8	16.4	11.7	8.6	15.7
45 to 54 years old.....	15.4	15.0	16.2	18.5	19.6	19.2	13.3	16.3	15.5	7.6	7.3	12.6
55 to 64 years old.....	11.6	12.6	12.5	15.9	17.5	17.6	10.3	14.5	13.0	4.2	4.9	8.4
65 to 74 years old.....	8.7	9.6	11.3	15.6	17.9	17.0	11.6	15.6	12.1	3.4	4.4	6.1
75 years old and over.................	7.1	4.4	6.8	12.8	13.0	14.1	10.7	13.9	11.9	3.9	1.0	3.2
Percentiles of income: [1]												
Less than 20.........	18.2	17.7	23.5	19.7	19.1	16.3	26.8	26.9	26.1	15.9	15.1	21.2
20 to 39.9............	16.7	17.2	16.9	17.4	17.1	17.5	18.6	19.5	18.6	13.8	11.5	15.2
40 to 59.9............	19.4	19.8	19.5	19.5	20.3	20.0	13.8	14.5	15.4	10.4	8.3	10.2
60 to 79.9............	18.6	21.8	19.3	20.7	21.9	20.4	7.3	12.9	11.0	7.1	4.1	8.8
80 to 89.9............	17.4	19.8	18.0	18.3	19.3	19.3	2.6	8.2	5.3	2.3	2.1	5.4
90 to 100............	9.3	8.4	9.4	12.7	12.5	13.1	1.5	3.8	2.9	0.3	0.2	2.1

[1] See footnote 8, Table 1194.

Source: Board of Governors of the Federal Reserve System, "2010 Survey of Consumer Finances," June 2012, <http://www.federalreserve.gov/pubs/bulletin/default.htm>.

Table 1199. Household Debt-Service Payments and Financial Obligations as a Percentage of Disposable Personal Income: 1990 to 2012

[As of end of year, seasonally adjusted. Household debt service ratio is an estimate of the ratio of debt payments to disposable personal income. Debt payments consist of the estimated required payments on outstanding mortgage and consumer debt. The financial obligations ratio adds automobile lease payments, rental payments on tenant-occupied property, homeowners' insurance, and property tax payments to the debt service ratio]

Year	Household debt service ratio	Financial obligations ratio			Year	Household debt service ratio	Financial obligations ratio		
		Total	Renter	Home-owner			Total	Renter	Home-owner
1990............	11.90	17.33	24.74	15.43	2008............	13.51	18.47	25.36	17.05
2000............	12.46	17.53	30.18	15.03	2009............	12.92	18.12	24.66	16.66
2005............	13.63	18.32	24.95	17.00	2010............	11.58	16.60	23.26	15.10
2006............	13.94	18.72	25.35	17.42	2011............	10.98	16.06	24.08	14.29
2007............	14.03	18.89	25.33	17.60	2012............	10.38	15.48	24.14	13.60

Source: Board of Governors of the Federal Reserve System, Data Releases, "Household Debt Service and Financial Obligations Ratios," March 2013, <http://www.federalreserve.gov/releases/housedebt/default.htm>.

Table 1200. FDIC-Insured Financial Institutions—Deposit Insurance Fund (DIF) Indicators: 1990 to 2012

[In billions of dollars, except as indicated (4,735 represents $4,735,000,000,000). As of December 31. Includes Island Areas. Includes insured branches of foreign banks. Minus sign (–) indicates decrease]

Item	1990	2000	2005	2007	2008	2009	2010	2011	2012
Number of institutions reporting.............	15,369	9,920	8,845	8,544	8,314	8,021	7,667	7,366	7,092
Assets, total [1]...........................	4,735	7,472	10,895	13,051	13,894	13,112	13,319	13,892	14,451
Domestic deposits, total [2]..............	3,415	4,212	6,230	6,922	7,505	7,705	7,888	8,782	9,475
Estimated insured deposits [3]..............	2,697	3,055	3,891	4,292	4,751	5,408	6,306	6,980	7,416
DIF balance (BIF/SAIF prior to 2006).......	4	42	49	52	17	-21	-7	12	33
Reserve ratio [4]............................	0.15	1.36	1.25	1.22	0.36	-0.39	-0.12	0.17	0.44
Number of problem institutions..............	1,496	94	52	76	252	702	884	813	651
Assets of problem institutions..............	646.8	23.8	6.6	22.2	159.4	402.8	390.0	319.4	232.7
Number of assisted institutions.............	1	–	–	–	5	8	–	–	–
Assets of assisted institutions...............	(Z)	–	–	–	1,306.0	1,917.5	–	–	–
Number of failed institutions.................	381	7	–	3	25	140	157	92	51
Assets of assisted institutions..............	146.6	0.4	–	2.6	371.9	169.7	92.1	34.9	11.6

– Represents zero. Z Less than $50 million. [1] Covers only insured commercial banks and savings institutions. Excludes U.S. branches of foreign banks. [2] Excludes foreign office deposits, which are uninsured. [3] In general, insured deposits are total domestic deposits minus estimated uninsured deposits. Prior to September 30, 2009 insured deposits included deposits in accounts of $100,000 or less; beginning September 30, 2009, insured deposits include deposits in accounts of $250,000 or less. The Dodd-Frank Wall Street Reform and Consumer Protection Act (Dodd-Frank) temporarily provided unlimited coverage for noninterest bearing transaction accounts for two years beginning December 31, 2010, and ending December 31, 2012. [4] DIF balance as percent of DIF-insured deposits.

Source: U.S. Federal Deposit Insurance Corporation, *The FDIC Quarterly Banking Profile, First Quarter 2013*, and earlier reports, <http://www2.fdic.gov/qbp/qbpSelect.asp?menuItem=QBP>.

Table 1201. FDIC-Insured Financial Institutions—Number, Assets, and Liabilities: 1990 to 2012

[In billions of dollars, except as indicated (4,649 represents $4,649,000,000,000). As of December 31. Includes Island Areas. Excludes insured branches of foreign banks. Except as noted, includes foreign branches of U.S. banks]

Item	1990	2000	2005	2007	2008	2009	2010	2011	2012
Commercial bank offices, total [1]..........	**63,232**	**73,218**	**81,049**	**86,437**	**90,028**	**89,868**	**89,082**	**89,419**	**89,805**
Number of main offices.....................	12,347	8,315	7,526	7,284	7,088	6,840	6,530	6,291	6,096
Number of branches........................	50,885	64,903	73,523	79,153	82,940	83,028	82,552	83,128	83,709
Savings institutions offices, total.........	**2,815**	**1,589**	**1,307**	**1,250**	**1,218**	**1,172**	**1,128**	**1,066**	**987**
Number of financial institutions reporting....	15,158	9,904	8,833	8,534	8,305	8,012	7,658	7,357	7,083
Assets, total [2]...........................	**4,649**	**7,462**	**10,878**	**13,034**	**13,841**	**13,087**	**13,319**	**13,892**	**14,451**
Net loans and leases........................	2,867	4,572	6,641	7,804	7,700	7,053	7,144	7,283	7,534
Real estate loans...........................	1,586	2,396	4,140	4,782	4,705	4,462	4,267	4,136	4,095
1–4 family residential mortgages..........	859	1,340	2,042	2,241	2,045	1,916	1,900	1,885	1,896
Nonfarm nonresidential....................	328	525	826	969	1,066	1,091	1,071	1,061	1,073
Construction and development...........	171	197	450	629	591	451	321	240	204
Home equity loans [3].....................	86	151	534	611	668	662	637	604	554
Multifamily residential real estate.........	98	117	188	203	206	213	213	219	234
Commercial and industrial loans............	646	1,086	1,086	1,439	1,494	1,214	1,184	1,346	1,508
Loans to individuals........................	451	672	949	1,058	1,089	1,058	1,316	1,308	1,328
Credit cards and related plans.............	142	266	396	422	445	421	702	688	696
Loans to depository institutions............	52	118	162	136	112	112	109	119	102
Lease financing receivables.................	39	167	139	131	121	109	102	100	105
Less: Reserve for losses....................	65	71	77	103	174	229	231	191	162
Securities...................................	890	1,361	1,893	1,954	2,035	2,500	2,668	2,850	3,010
Domestic office assets.......................	4,259	6,701	9,824	11,475	12,321	11,650	11,693	12,098	12,573
Foreign office assets.........................	390	760	1,054	1,559	1,520	1,437	1,626	1,794	1,878
Liabilities and capital, total [2]..........	**4,649**	**7,462**	**10,878**	**13,034**	**13,841**	**13,087**	**13,319**	**13,892**	**14,451**
Deposits...................................	3,637	4,915	7,141	8,415	9,036	9,227	9,423	10,186	10,817
Foreign office deposits.....................	293	707	921	1,503	1,539	1,530	1,550	1,428	1,370
Domestic office deposits....................	3,344	4,208	6,221	6,913	7,496	7,697	7,873	8,758	9,447
Interest-bearing deposits..................	2,846	3,437	5,004	5,718	6,073	6,144	6,184	6,493	6,906
Noninterest-bearing deposits..............	498	771	1,217	1,194	1,423	1,553	1,690	2,265	2,541
Equity capital................................	286	633	1,119	1,347	1,291	1,445	1,511	1,569	1,629

[1] Includes insured branches of foreign banks that file a Call Report. [2] Includes other items not shown separately. [3] For one- to four-family residential properties.

Source: U.S. Federal Deposit Insurance Corporation, "FDIC Quarterly Banking Profile," <www2.fdic.gov/qbp/>; and "Historical Statistics on Banking," <http://www2.fdic.gov/hsob/index.asp>; accessed August 2013.

Table 1202. FDIC-Insured Financial Institutions—Income and Selected Measures of Financial Condition: 1990 to 2012

[In billions of dollars, except as indicated (437.7 represents $437,700,000,000). Includes Island Areas. Includes foreign branches of U.S. banks. Minus sign (–) indicates decrease]

Item	1990	2000	2005	2007	2008	2009	2010	2011	2012
Interest income...........................	437.7	511.9	522.2	724.8	603.2	541.2	536.9	507.4	487.2
Interest expense...........................	295.9	276.6	205.1	372.2	245.5	143.5	106.9	84.8	65.9
Net interest income...........................	141.8	235.3	317.0	352.7	357.7	397.7	430.0	422.6	421.3
Provisions for loan losses...........................	41.4	32.1	29.8	69.3	176.2	249.7	158.0	77.5	58.3
Noninterest income...........................	62.2	165.6	223.4	233.1	207.7	260.5	235.7	230.1	248.7
Noninterest expense...........................	144.2	242.3	317.4	367.1	368.3	406.1	391.8	411.7	421.2
Income taxes...........................	9.1	43.6	64.6	46.4	6.3	6.1	38.4	50.7	58.3
Net income...........................	11.3	81.5	133.8	99.9	4.5	-10.0	85.5	118.4	141.2
PERFORMANCE RATIOS									
Return on assets [1] (percent)...........................	0.24	1.14	1.28	0.81	0.03	-0.08	0.65	0.88	1.00
Return on equity [2] (percent)...........................	3.95	13.53	12.43	7.75	0.35	-0.73	5.85	7.79	8.91
Net interest margin [3] (percent)...........................	3.47	3.77	3.47	3.29	3.16	3.49	3.76	3.60	3.42
Net charge-offs [4]...........................	34.8	26.3	31.6	44.3	100.4	188.9	187.6	113.2	82.7
Net charge-offs to loans and leases, total (percent)...........................	1.19	0.59	0.49	0.59	1.29	2.52	2.55	1.55	1.10
Net charge-off rate, credit card loans (percent)...........................	3.39	4.36	4.74	4.06	5.44	9.26	10.08	5.45	3.95
CONDITION RATIOS									
Equity capital to assets (percent)...........................	6.16	8.49	10.28	10.34	9.33	10.88	11.16	11.16	11.17
Noncurrent assets plus other real estate owned to assets [5] (percent)...........................	3.16	0.71	0.50	0.95	1.91	3.37	3.11	2.60	2.20

[1] Net income (including securities transactions and nonrecurring items) as a percentage of average total assets. [2] Net income as a percentage of average total equity capital. [3] Interest income less interest expense as a percentage of average earning assets (i.e. the profit margin a bank earns on its loans and investments). [4] Total loans and leases charged off (removed from balance sheet because of uncollectibility), less amounts recovered on loans and leases previously charged off. [5] Noncurrent assets: the sum of loans, leases, debt securities and other assets that are 90 days or more past due, or in nonaccrual status. Other real estate owned, primarily foreclosed property.

Source: U.S. Federal Deposit Insurance Corporation, "FDIC Quarterly Banking Profile," <http://www2.fdic.gov/qbp/>, accessed August 2013.

Table 1203. FDIC-Insured Financial Institutions by Asset Size: 2012

[13,391.1 represents $13,391,100,000,000. See headnote, Table 1202]

Item	Unit	Total	Less than $100 mil.	$100 mil. to $1 bil.	$1 bil. to $10 bil.	Greater than $10 bil.
COMMERCIAL BANKS						
Institutions reporting...........................	Number	6,096	1,953	3,608	446	89
Assets, total...........................	Bil. dol.	13,391.1	113.9	1,063.2	1,168.4	11,045.6
Deposits...........................	Bil. dol.	10,014.1	97.3	896.6	914.4	8,105.8
Net income...........................	Bil. dol.	130.2	0.8	8.9	13.5	107.0
Return on assets...........................	Percent	1.00	0.71	0.86	1.18	1.00
Return on equity...........................	Percent	8.91	6.15	8.07	10.09	8.89
Equity capital to assets...........................	Percent	11.11	11.63	10.64	11.72	11.08
Noncurrent assets plus other real estate owned to assets...........................	Percent	2.18	2.07	2.39	2.42	2.14
Net charge-offs to loans and leases...........................	Percent	1.11	0.43	0.63	0.78	1.22
Percentage of banks losing money...........................	Percent	10.00	13.50	8.60	7.60	2.20
SAVINGS INSTITUTIONS						
Institutions reporting...........................	Number	987	251	609	109	18
Assets, total...........................	Bil. dol.	1,059.7	14.3	211.9	286.4	547.2
Deposits...........................	Bil. dol.	803.2	11.2	169.4	218.2	404.4
Net income...........................	Bil. dol.	11.0	0.1	1.2	2.6	7.1
Return on assets...........................	Percent	1.06	0.55	0.54	0.94	1.35
Return on equity...........................	Percent	8.90	3.68	4.54	7.98	11.40
Equity capital to assets...........................	Percent	11.94	15.18	12.25	11.98	11.71
Noncurrent assets plus other real estate owned to assets...........................	Percent	2.38	2.33	2.25	2.62	2.30
Net charge-offs to loans and leases...........................	Percent	0.96	0.41	0.66	0.57	1.35
Percentage of banks losing money...........................	Percent	15.90	23.10	15.10	6.42	(NA)

NA Not available.

Source: U.S. Federal Deposit Insurance Corporation, "Quarterly Banking Profile," <http://www2.fdic.gov/qbp/> and "Statistics on Depository Institutions," <http://www2.fdic.gov/sdi/index.asp>, accessed August 2013.

Table 1204. FDIC-Insured Financial Institutions—Number and Assets by State and Island Areas: 2012

[In billions of dollars, except as indicated (14,450.8 represents $14,450,800,000,000). As of December 31. Information is obtained primarily from the Federal Financial Institutions Examination Council (FFIEC) Call Reports and the Office of Thrift Supervision's Thrift Financial Reports. Data are based on the location of each reporting institution's main office. Reported data may include assets located outside of the reporting institution's home state]

State or Island Area	Number of institutions	Assets by asset size of bank				State or Island Area	Number of institutions	Assets by asset size of bank			
		Total	Less than $100 mil.	$100 mil. to $1 bil.	Greater than $1 bil.			Total	Less than $100 mil.	$100 mil. to $1 bil.	Greater than $1 bil.
Total	**7,083**	**14,450.8**	**128.1**	**1,275.1**	**13,047.6**	NV	23	125.2	0.5	2.9	121.8
AL	140	229.4	3.0	22.8	203.5	NH	21	10.3	(Z)	6.9	3.5
AK [1]	6	5.4	(NA)	0.7	4.2	NJ	110	155.1	0.5	29.9	124.7
AZ [1]	29	12.4	0.8	4.2	7.1	NM	48	15.3	0.5	9.7	5.1
AR	126	61.3	2.3	23.1	35.9	NY	167	838.6	1.1	41.9	795.5
CA	239	508.3	1.5	53.4	453.4	NC	88	1,717.4	1.0	20.6	1,695.8
CO	104	45.7	2.1	16.5	27.1	ND	90	29.9	2.5	12.8	14.7
CT	51	81.5	0.4	15.4	65.7	OH	233	2,609.5	4.5	39.1	2,565.9
DE	23	981.6	0.1	3.7	977.8	OK	234	94.3	5.1	32.5	56.6
DC [1]	5	1.9	(NA)	1.8	(NA)	OR	32	34.6	0.4	4.6	29.6
FL	209	142.7	2.3	47.2	93.1	PA	200	216.6	1.8	57.4	157.5
GA	228	267.0	4.2	33.9	228.8	RI	13	134.1	0.1	2.8	131.2
HI [1]	9	42.7	0.1	1.2	34.8	SC	71	37.7	0.9	17.3	19.5
ID	16	6.7	0.3	5.3	1.0	SD	79	2,625.2	2.1	10.7	2,612.4
IL	560	399.4	12.8	86.8	299.7	TN	184	86.7	1.8	42.5	42.4
IN	134	68.5	1.8	26.8	39.9	TX	562	436.8	10.0	97.8	329.0
IA	338	72.6	8.0	44.0	20.7	UT	56	426.1	0.5	11.2	414.3
KS	300	63.6	8.8	32.4	22.3	VT	14	6.3	(Z)	4.5	1.7
KY	192	55.4	3.2	33.4	18.8	VA	107	634.5	0.7	26.8	607.0
LA [1]	145	70.3	1.7	26.4	36.4	WA	71	63.9	1.1	14.5	48.3
ME	28	34.5	0.3	11.0	23.1	WV [1]	61	27.5	0.8	10.6	15.3
MD	80	33.7	0.7	20.9	12.0	WI	266	98.6	5.4	49.3	43.9
MA	153	331.2	1.3	41.3	288.6	WY [1]	35	7.3	0.4	6.3	(NA)
MI	130	67.2	2.4	25.5	39.2						
MN	379	63.1	10.8	39.5	12.8	AS	1	0.1	(NA)	(NA)	(NA)
MS	87	60.1	1.3	20.0	38.8	GU [1]	3	1.7	(NA)	0.3	1.2
MO	317	151.8	7.6	46.8	97.3	FM	1	0.1	(NA)	(NA)	(NA)
MT	65	26.7	1.7	7.2	17.8	PR [1]	6	70.4	–	–	70.4
NE	213	62.5	6.0	22.6	33.9	VI	2	0.2	(NA)	(NA)	(NA)

– Represents zero. NA Not available. Z Less than $50 million. AS—American Samoa, GU—Guam, FM—Federated States of Micronesia, PR—Puerto Rico, VI—Virgin Islands. [1] Asset data by asset size not available for some institutions.

Source: U.S. Federal Deposit Insurance Corporation, "Statistics on Banking," <http://www2.fdic.gov/sdi/sob/>, accessed August 2013.

Table 1205. U.S. Banking Offices of Foreign Banks—Summary: 1990 to 2012

[In billions of dollars, except as indicated (834 represents $834,000,000,000). As of December. Covers the U.S. offices of foreign banking organizations that are located in the 50 states and the District of Columbia. Offices located in Puerto Rico, American Samoa, Guam, the Virgin Islands and other U.S.-affiliated insular areas are excluded. Foreign-owned institutions are those owned by a bank located outside of the United States and its affiliated insular areas. The U.S. offices of foreign banking organizations consist of U.S. branches and agencies of foreign banks and bank subsidiaries of foreign banking organizations. The latter are U.S. commercial banks of which more than 25 percent are owned by a foreign banking organization or where the relationship is reported as being a controlling relationship by the filer of the FR Y-10 (Report of Changes in Organizational Structure) report form]

Item	1990	2000	2005	2008	2009	2010	2011	2012	Share [1]			
									1990	2000	2010	2012
Assets	834	1,358	2,123	3,032	2,872	2,838	3,159	3,274	20.9	18.9	20.4	21.2
Loans, total	412	557	802	1,167	1,022	960	1,064	1,117	17.2	13.5	13.7	14.9
Business	199	309	276	483	384	326	372	415	27.7	25.0	25.1	24.8
Deposits	425	770	1,162	1,606	1,795	1,752	1,717	1,867	14.6	16.5	18.4	17.0

[1] Foreign owned banks plus U.S. branches and offices of foreign banks as percent of all banks in the United States.

Source: Board of Governors of the Federal Reserve System, "Share Data for U.S. Offices of Foreign Banks," March 2013, <http://www.federalreserve.gov/Releases/iba/fboshr.htm>.

Table 1206. FDIC-Insured Financial Institutions—Number of Offices and Deposits by State: 2012

[As of June 30. (8,947 represents $8.947,000,000,000). Includes insured U.S. branches of foreign banks. The term "offices" includes both main offices and branches. "Banking office" is defined to include all offices and facilities that actually hold deposits, and does not include loan production offices, computer centers, and other nondeposit installations, such as automated teller machines (ATMs). Several institutions have designated home offices that do not accept deposits; these have been included to provide a more complete listing of all offices. The figures for each geographical area only include deposits of offices located within that area. Based on the Summary of Deposits survey]

State	Number of offices	Total deposits (bil. dol.)	State	Number of offices	Total deposits (bil. dol.)	State	Number of offices	Total deposits (bil. dol.)
Total [1]	97,337	8,947	IA	1,598	73	NC	2,720	342
U.S.	96,823	8,889	KS	1,533	63	ND	439	21
AL	1,573	85	KY	1,781	71	OH	4,026	244
AK	132	10	LA	1,631	89	OK	1,397	74
AZ	1,360	87	ME	517	34	OR	1,125	66
AR	1,447	53	MD	1,752	121	PA	4,648	313
CA	7,295	953	MA	2,210	272	RI	259	45
CO	1,623	100	MI	2,949	167	SC	1,401	67
CT	1,293	103	MN	1,801	201	SD	475	315
DE	293	364	MS	1,202	46	TN	2,275	118
DC	244	33	MO	2,423	142	TX	6,854	599
FL	5,602	424	MT	394	19	UT	598	340
GA	2,651	186	NE	1,082	52	VT	257	12
HI	280	33	NV	544	113	VA	2,644	249
ID	536	19	NH	429	28	WA	1,876	113
IL	4,887	393	NJ	3,276	268	WV	671	30
IN	2,352	102	NM	512	26	WI	2,287	133
			NY	5,441	1,066	WY	228	13

[1] Includes outlying areas not shown separately.

Source: U.S. Federal Deposit Insurance Corporation, "Summary of Deposits," <http://www2.fdic.gov/sod/>, accessed August 2013.

Table 1207. Federal and State-Chartered Credit Unions—Summary: 1990 to 2012

[Except as noted, as of December 31 (36,241 represents 36,241,000). Federal data include District of Columbia, Puerto Rico, Guam, and Virgin Islands. Excludes state-insured, privately insured, and noninsured state-chartered credit unions and corporate central credit unions, which have mainly other credit unions as members]

Year	Operating credit unions		Number of failed institutions [1]	Members (1,000)		Assets (mil. dol.)		Loans outstanding (mil. dol.)		Savings (mil. dol.)	
	Federal	State		Federal	State	Federal	State	Federal	State	Federal	State
1990	8,511	4,349	164	36,241	19,454	130,073	68,133	83,029	44,102	117,892	62,082
2000	6,336	3,980	29	43,883	33,705	242,881	195,363	163,851	137,485	210,188	169,053
2005	5,393	3,302	27	47,914	36,896	377,827	300,868	249,521	208,731	321,831	255,588
2006	5,189	3,173	22	48,254	37,499	394,131	315,817	270,418	223,917	333,914	267,274
2007	5,036	3,065	12	48,474	38,363	417,578	335,885	289,169	237,755	349,101	283,298
2008	4,847	2,959	19	49,130	39,453	447,124	364,132	309,277	256,720	373,366	307,762
2009	4,714	2,840	31	49,604	40,333	482,684	402,069	311,154	261,285	408,832	343,835
2010	4,589	2,750	29	50,081	40,447	500,075	414,395	306,276	258,555	427,603	358,877
2011	4,447	2,647	16	50,743	41,093	525,633	436,121	308,845	262,640	449,316	378,093
2012	4,272	2,547	22	51,797	42,043	557,119	464,612	322,675	275,066	474,903	402,948

[1] 1990 for year ending September 30; beginning 2000, reflects calendar year. A failed institution is defined as a credit union which has ceased operation because it was involuntarily liquidated or merged with assistance from the National Credit Union Share Insurance Fund.

Source: National Credit Union Administration, *National Credit Union Administration 2012 Annual Report,* May 2013, and earlier reports. See also <http://www.ncua.gov/Legal/Pages/default.aspx>.

Table 1208. Noncash Payments by Method of Payment, and ATM Cash Withdrawals: 2006 and 2009

[95.2 represents 95,200,000,000. Based on two data collection efforts to estimate the annual number and value of significant types of noncash payments. Estimates of check payments and ATM withdrawals were based on findings from the Depository Institutions Payments Study (2010 DI study). Electronic payments volume estimates were based on findings from the Electronic Payments Study and supplemented by the 2010 DI study. The DI Payments Study collected the number and value of different types of payments from deposit accounts at a representative, random sample of depository institutions. A total of 1,311 depository institutions (commercial banks, savings institutions, and credit unions) from a stratified random sample of 2,700 institutions provided data for the survey. The Electronic Payments Study estimated the number and value of electronic payments in the U.S. for calendar year 2009. Data were collected by surveying payment networks and card issuers. Of the 116 organizations asked to participate, 94 of the largest organizations provided data. Respondents to this study collectively accounted for an estimated 95.5 percent of the electronic transactions and 99.6 percent of the electronic payments value in the U.S.]

Method of payment	Transactions (billions)		Value (trillion dollars)		Average value per transaction (dollars)	
	2006	2009	2006	2009	2006	2009
Noncash payments, total............	**95.2**	**109.0**	**75.7**	**72.2**	**796**	**663**
Checks (paid)................	30.5	24.5	41.6	31.6	1,363	1,292
Commercial checks...................	30.1	24.1	41.4	31.2	1,371	1,295
Commercial banks..................	25.1	20.7	39.0	29.2	1,550	1,414
Credit unions...................	2.7	2.1	0.8	0.7	288	352
Savings institutions.............	2.3	1.3	1.6	1.3	696	973
U.S. Treasury checks..............	0.2	0.2	0.2	0.3	1,203	1,545
Postal money orders................	0.2	0.1	(Z)	(Z)	164	183
Electronic payments..................	64.7	84.5	34.1	40.6	544	480
Automated Clearing House (ACH)......	14.6	19.1	31.0	37.2	2,122	1,946
Debit cards.................	25.0	37.9	1.0	1.4	39	38
Signature [1]...................	15.7	23.4	0.6	0.9	40	37
PIN [2]................	9.4	14.5	0.3	0.6	37	39
Credit cards [3]................	21.7	21.6	2.1	1.9	98	89
Prepaid and EBT [4]................	3.3	6.0	0.1	0.1	23	24
Memo:						
ATM cash withdrawals...............	**5.8**	**6.0**	**0.6**	**0.6**	**100**	**108**
Checks (written) [5]................	33.1	27.8	42.3	32.4	1,277	1,165
Checks converted to ACH..............	2.6	3.3	0.7	0.8	267	227

Z Less than $50 billion. [1] Signature debit card payments are made like credit card payments, but use funds from transaction deposit accounts. [2] PIN debit card payments also use funds from transaction deposit accounts and typically require the entry of the same personal identification number (PIN) used to access automated teller machines (ATMs). Excludes a portion estimated to have been returned to the customer as cash. [3] Credit cards include both general purpose and private-label cards. [4] Includes general purpose and private label prepaid cards, which use funds from a nontraditional prefunded transaction account, as well as electronic benefit transfers. [5] Includes the use of checks as source documents to initiate electronic payments.

Source: Board of Governors of the Federal Reserve System *The 2010 Federal Reserve Payments Study, Noncash Payment Trends in the United States: 2006–2009,* April 2011. See also, <http://www.frbservices.org/files/communications/pdf/research/2010_payments_study.pdf>.

Table 1209. Percentage of Households Using Selected Electronic Banking Technologies: 1995 to 2007

[Covers only those households that access services (other than by check or credit card) at a bank, thrift institution, or credit union. Based on sample surveys. For details on the Survey of Consumer Finances, see Appendix III and the Federal Reserve Board, <http://www.federalreserve.gov/econresdata/scf/scfindex.htm>. The Reuters/University of Michigan Surveys of Consumers is based on data from approximately 1,000 respondents. For details, see the University of Michigan Survey Research Center, <http://www.sca.isr.umich.edu/>]

Technology	Survey of Consumer Finances					Reuters/University of Michigan Surveys of Consumers		
	1995	1998	2001	2004	2007	1999	2003	2006
ELECTRONIC								
Direct deposit of any type..........	53	67	71	75	80	65	70	77
ATM card............................	35	55	57	65	76	59	65	69
Debit card [1]......................	20	37	50	62	71	(NA)	54	62
Preauthorized debts................	25	40	43	50	49	31	46	57
Automated phone system..........	(NA)	26	22	20	25	40	44	46
Computer banking..................	4	7	19	34	53	10	32	51
Smart card [2].....................	1	2	3	(NA)	(NA)	(NA)	6	12
Prepaid card [3]...................	(NA)	(NA)	(NA)	(NA)	(NA)	(NA)	73	73
NONELECTRONIC								
In person..........................	87	81	78	78	85	(NA)	(NA)	(NA)
Mail...............................	59	55	51	51	59	(NA)	(NA)	(NA)
Phone (talk in person).............	(NA)	43	42	42	57	(NA)	(NA)	(NA)

NA Not available. [1] A debit card is a card that automatically deducts the amount of a purchase from the money in an account. [2] A smart card is a type of payment card containing a computer chip which is set to hold a sum of money. As the card is used, purchases are subtracted from that sum. [3] Prepaid cards are cards that contain a stored value, or a value that has been paid up-front, allowing you to use the card much like cash. As you use the card, the prepaid value is drawn down. Examples are phone cards and gift cards. Smart cards are different from prepaid cards in that you can add money to the card at special machines designed for smart cards or sometimes at ATMs.

Source: Board of Governors of the Federal Reserve System, *Federal Reserve Bulletin,* July 2009, <http://www.federalreserve.gov/pubs/bulletin/2009/default.htm>; and unpublished data.

Table 1210. Percent of U.S. Households That Use Selected Payment Instruments: 2001 and 2010

[In percent. Based on Survey of Consumer Finances conducted by the Board of Governors of the Federal Reserve System; see Appendix III]

Characteristic of head of household	Any of these instruments		ATM [1]		Debit card		Direct deposit		Automatic bill paying		Software [2]	
	2001	2010	2001	2010	2001	2010	2001	2010	2001	2010	2001	2010
All households...........	**88.9**	**93.7**	**69.8**	**83.4**	**47.0**	**78.4**	**67.3**	**75.9**	**40.3**	**48.3**	**18.0**	**18.5**
Under 30 years old.........	83.8	92.2	78.1	88.7	60.6	88.5	48.8	63.2	32.1	42.9	17.0	22.3
30 to 60 years old..........	89.9	93.9	76.8	88.4	53.4	84.1	64.8	73.4	44.1	49.8	22.0	20.3
61 years old and over......	89.4	94.0	48.9	70.6	24.6	62.3	83.2	86.7	35.9	47.5	9.0	13.0
Household income: [3]												
Low income................	74.3	84.6	46.8	67.5	29.2	64.5	51.9	58.7	18.2	29.4	6.1	9.0
Moderate income.........	88.6	93.4	67.4	82.4	46.3	78.3	63.1	72.3	35.1	42.3	10.7	11.2
Middle income............	92.5	96.7	75.2	87.4	50.0	83.5	65.7	79.8	45.1	52.9	16.3	17.0
Upper income............	97.1	98.9	83.7	93.2	57.8	86.0	80.2	88.2	55.2	62.5	29.9	29.4
No college degree.........	85.1	90.9	63.7	78.1	42.3	75.0	61.8	70.4	33.7	40.8	10.9	11.2
College degree............	96.4	98.4	81.6	92.3	56.2	84.2	78.0	85.2	53.2	61.0	31.8	30.7

[1] The question on ATM cards asked whether any member of the household had an ATM card, not whether the member used it. The other questions asked about usage of other instruments. [2] The question on software asked whether the respondent or spouse/ partner uses any type of computer software to help in managing their money. [3] Low income is defined as less than 50 percent of the median household income; moderate income is 50 to 80 percent of the median; middle income is 80 to 120 percent of the median; and upper income is greater than 120 percent of the median. Each survey refers to income in the previous year. Median income was $41,990 in 2000 and $49,777 in 2009.

Source: Federal Reserve Bank of Philadelphia, Mester, Loretta J., "Changes in the Use of Electronic Means of Payment, 1995-2010," Business Review, Third Quarter 2012. See also <http://www.phil.frb.org/research-and-data/publications/business-review/>.

Table 1211. Debit Cards: Holders, Number, Transactions, and Volume, 2000 and 2010, and Projections, 2013

[160 represents 160,000,000]

Type of debit card	Cardholders (mil.)			Number of cards (mil.)			Number of point-of-sale transactions (mil.)			Purchase volume (bil. dol.)		
	2000	2010	2013, proj.	2000	2010	2013, proj.	2000	2010	2013, proj.	2000	2010	2013, proj.
Total [1].....................	**160**	**185**	**194**	**235**	**549**	**580**	**8,291**	**44,156**	**53,968**	**311**	**1,652**	**2,036**
Bank [2]......................	137	164	171	137	516	550	5,290	36,879	42,753	210	1,387	1,632
EFT Systems [3].............	159	184	192	223	281	296	2,979	7,239	11,092	100	262	395
Other [4].....................	11	13	20	11	13	20	22	39	124	1	3	8

[1] Cardholders may hold more than one type of card. Bank cards and EFT cards are the same pieces of plastic that carry multiple brands. The total card figure shown does not include any duplication. [2] Visa and MasterCard debit cards, including prepaid cards. Beginning 2010, includes Interlink & MasterCard PIN debit. [3] Cards issued by financial institution members of regional and national switches such as Star, Interlink (for 2000), Pulse, Nyce, etc. EFT = Electronic funds transfer. [4] Retail cards such as those issued by Target, Nordstrom, etc.

Source: The Nilson Report, Carpinteria, CA, Twice-monthly. (Copyright used by permission.)

Table 1212. Credit Cards: Holders, Number, Purchase Volume, and Debt, 2000 and 2010, and Projections, 2013

[159 represents 159,000,000]

Type of credit card	Cardholders (mil.)			Number of cards (mil.)			Credit card purchase volume (bil. dol.)			Credit card debt outstanding (bil. dol.)		
	2000	2010	2013, proj.	2000	2010	2013, proj.	2000	2010	2013, proj.	2000	2010	2013, proj.
Total [1].....................	**159**	**152**	**166**	**1,425**	**1,014**	**1,049**	**1,242**	**2,061**	**2,745**	**680**	**814**	**844**
Visa...........................	93	100	104	255	240	247	487	809	1,104	268	332	344
MasterCard....................	86	75	79	200	171	181	281	479	587	212	240	234
Store.........................	114	95	100	597	318	343	120	138	171	92	92	98
Oil company..................	76	56	56	98	57	56	45	47	62	5	8	11
Discover......................	36	41	47	50	55	65	69	106	132	48	50	57
American Express.............	23	34	37	33	49	55	221	476	684	50	90	98
The Rest......................	133	95	81	192	124	102	18	5	6	5	2	2

[1] Cardholders may hold more than one type of card. [2] Includes Universal Air Travel Plan (UATP), phone cards, automobile rental, and miscellaneous cards; credit card purchase volume and cardholders excludes phone cards.

Source: The Nilson Report, Carpinteria, CA, Twice-monthly. (Copyright used by permission.)

Table 1213. Usage of General Purpose Credit Cards by Families: 1995 to 2010

[General purpose credit cards include Master Card, Visa, Optima, and Discover cards. Excludes cards used only for business purposes. All dollar figures are given in constant 2010 dollars based on consumer price index data as published by U.S. Bureau of Labor Statistics. Families include one-person units; for definition of family, see text, Section 1. Based on Survey of Consumer Finances; see Appendix III. For definition of median, see Guide to Tabular Presentation]

Age of family head, family income, and housing tenure	Percent having a general purpose credit card	Median number of cards	Median new charges on last month's bill (dollars)	Percent having a balance after last month's bill	Median balance [1] (dollars)	Percent of card holding families who—		
						Almost always pay off the balance	Sometimes pay off the balance	Hardly ever pay off the balance
1995, total......................	66.4	2	200	56.0	2,000	52.4	20.1	27.5
2001, total......................	72.7	2	200	53.6	2,100	55.3	19.1	25.6
2007, total......................	70.2	2	300	58.3	3,000	55.3	19.4	25.4
2010, total.....................	**65.1**	**2**	**300**	**52.4**	**2,900**	**56.4**	**18.6**	**25.0**
Under 35 years old..............	54.1	2	200	61.1	1,700	49.5	21.6	28.9
35 to 44 years old..............	59.7	2	300	66.3	4,000	42.6	23.6	33.8
45 to 54 years old..............	67.9	2	300	60.8	3,500	47.6	22.3	30.1
55 to 64 years old..............	72.1	3	400	49.4	3,100	60.6	16.3	23.2
65 to 74 years old..............	72.9	2	400	35.5	2,200	72.4	12.2	15.4
75 years old and over..........	70.5	2	300	27.1	1,700	78.3	11.3	10.4
Less than $10,000...............	25.9	2	200	48.7	1,800	56.5	21.1	22.4
$10,000 to $24,999..............	38.6	2	100	57.2	1,100	51.2	16.9	31.8
$25,000 to $49,999..............	58.2	2	200	54.0	2,000	52.5	18.9	28.6
$50,000 to $99,999..............	80.6	2	300	59.0	3,000	51.7	21.4	26.8
$100,000 and more.............	94.8	3	1,300	40.0	6,500	68.7	15.3	15.9
Owner occupied.................	77.2	2	400	48.9	3,600	59.6	17.2	23.2
Renter occupied or other.......	40.3	2	100	66.2	1,300	43.6	24.3	32.1

[1] Among families having a balance.

Source: Board of Governors of the Federal Reserve System, unpublished data.

Table 1214. Consumer Credit Outstanding and Finance Rates: 1990 to 2012

[In billions of dollars (808 represents $808,000,000,000), except percent. Covers most short- and intermediate-term credit extended to individuals, excluding loans secured by real estate. Estimated amounts of seasonally adjusted credit outstanding as of end of year; finance rates, annual averages]

Type of credit	1990	2000	2005	2006	2007	2008	2009	2010	2011	2012
Total............................	**808**	**1,717**	**2,291**	**2,362**	**2,506**	**2,526**	**2,420**	**2,522**	**2,616**	**2,768**
Revolving...........................	239	683	830	925	1,003	1,005	917	841	842	846
Nonrevolving [1].....................	570	1,034	1,461	1,437	1,503	1,521	1,503	1,682	1,773	1,922
FINANCE RATES (percent)										
Commercial banks:										
New automobiles (48 months)..............	11.78	9.34	7.07	7.72	7.77	7.02	6.72	6.21	5.73	4.91
Other consumer goods (24 months).......	15.46	13.90	12.06	12.41	12.38	11.37	11.10	10.87	10.88	10.71
Credit card plans, all accounts.............	(NA)	15.78	12.51	13.21	13.30	12.08	13.40	13.78	12.74	12.06
Credit card plans, accounts assessed interest...........................	(NA)	14.92	14.55	14.73	14.68	13.57	14.31	14.26	13.09	12.96
Finance companies:										
New automobiles...........................	12.54	6.85	6.02	4.99	4.87	5.52	3.82	4.26	4.73	(^{2})
Used automobiles...........................	15.99	13.47	8.81	9.61	9.24	8.74	9.41	8.16	7.73	(^{2})

NA Not available. [1] Comprises automobile loans and all other loans not included in revolving credit, such as loans for mobile homes, education, boats, trailers, or vacations. These loans may be secured or unsecured. [2] Publication of these series is temporarily being suspended. The statistical foundation is in the process of being improved, and publication will resume as soon as possible.

Source: Board of Governors of the Federal Reserve System, Data Releases, Household Finances, "Consumer Credit-G.19" and "Finance Companies-G.20," <http://www.federalreserve.gov/econresdata/statisticsdata.htm>, accessed June 2013.

Table 1215. Consumer Credit by Type of Holder: 1990 to 2012

[In billions of dollars (824 represents $824,000,000,000). As of December 31. Not seasonally adjusted]

Type of holder	1990	2000	2005	2006	2007	2008	2009	2010	2011	2012
Total............................	**824**	**1,741**	**2,321**	**2,362**	**2,506**	**2,526**	**2,420**	**2,522**	**2,616**	**2,768**
Nonfinancial corporate business.........	67	81	60	53	57	56	54	46	48	49
Federal government [1].....................	–	60	90	87	93	104	179	309	417	527
U.S.-chartered depository institutions. ..	432	616	816	837	895	965	906	1,186	1,193	1,219
Credit unions...........................	92	184	229	236	237	236	237	226	223	244
Government-sponsored enterprises.....	19	37	–	–	–	–	–	–	–	–
Asset-backed securities issuers..........	77	528	610	617	653	610	572	50	46	50
Finance companies.......................	138	234	517	532	572	554	472	705	688	681

– Represents or rounds to zero. [1] Includes loans originated by the Department of Education under the Federal Direct Loan Program, as well as Federal Family Education Loan Program loans that the government purchased from depository institutions and finance companies.

Source: Board of Governors of the Federal Reserve System, "Federal Reserve Statistical Release, Z.1, Financial Accounts of the United States," June 2013, <http://www.federalreserve.gov/releases/z1>.

Table 1216. Mortgage Debt Outstanding by Type of Property and Holder: 1990 to 2012

[In billions of dollars (3,781 represents $3,781,000,000,000). As of December 31]

Type of property and holder	1990	2000	2005	2006	2007	2008	2009	2010	2011	2012
Total mortgages [1]	**3,781**	**6,769**	**12,103**	**13,512**	**14,589**	**14,656**	**14,359**	**13,739**	**13,413**	**13,154**
Home [2]	2,606	5,122	9,415	10,487	11,207	11,097	10,893	10,426	10,171	9,925
Multifamily residential	287	402	667	706	793	841	848	838	843	859
Commercial	820	1,160	1,916	2,210	2,476	2,584	2,487	2,333	2,253	2,218
Farm	68	85	105	108	113	135	131	141	146	153
Household sector	141	103	139	122	110	111	101	90	79	66
Nonfinancial noncorporate business	31	23	36	35	42	39	38	42	43	43
State and local governments	110	131	155	164	181	168	172	168	161	154
Federal government	83	76	77	80	82	96	108	107	111	112
U.S.-chartered depository institutions	1,601	2,350	4,055	4,416	4,659	4,615	4,372	4,195	4,050	3,997
Credit unions	33	120	226	253	280	312	317	317	321	328
Life insurance companies	268	236	285	304	326	342	326	317	332	344
Government-sponsored enterprises (GSE)	156	264	589	607	643	705	708	5,021	4,924	4,824
Agency- and GSE-backed mortgage pools	1,020	2,493	3,548	3,841	4,464	4,961	5,377	1,139	1,305	1,437
Asset-backed securities issuers	66	604	2,153	2,784	2,968	2,615	2,245	1,916	1,697	1,490
Finance companies	114	238	541	594	532	448	397	244	212	180
Real estate investment trusts	8	18	147	136	123	76	48	42	42	48
HOME MORTGAGES [2]										
Total [1]	**2,606**	**5,122**	**9,415**	**10,487**	**11,207**	**11,097**	**10,893**	**10,426**	**10,171**	**9,925**
Household sector	129	87	118	103	91	91	83	75	67	59
State and local governments	61	67	79	84	93	86	88	86	82	79
U.S.-chartered depository institutions	1,031	1,555	2,730	2,933	3,068	2,884	2,687	2,612	2,535	2,488
Credit unions	33	120	226	253	280	312	317	317	321	328
Government-sponsored enterprises (GSE)	119	210	454	458	448	457	445	4,699	4,596	4,485
Agency- and GSE-backed mortgage pools	991	2,426	3,446	3,749	4,372	4,864	5,267	1,069	1,217	1,322
Asset-backed securities issuers	55	385	1,647	2,170	2,210	1,897	1,574	1,299	1,106	923
Finance companies	80	187	490	538	473	375	328	170	150	133
Memo:										
Home equity loans included above [1,3]	215	408	917	1,067	1,133	1,116	1,033	928	853	769
U.S.-chartered depository institutions	175	308	701	791	873	895	841	783	723	653
Credit unions	20	41	76	87	94	99	95	88	82	76

[1] Includes other holders not shown separately. [2] Mortgages on one- to four-family properties including mortgages on farm houses. [3] Loans made under home equity lines of credit and home equity loans secured by junior liens. Excludes home equity loans held by individuals.

Source: Board of Governors of the Federal Reserve System, "Federal Reserve Statistical Release, Z.1, Financial Accounts of the United States," June 2013, <http://www.federalreserve.gov/releases/z1/>.

Table 1217. Characteristics of Conventional First Mortgage Loans for Purchase of Single-Family Homes: 2000 to 2012

[In percent, except as indicated (for purchase price, 234.9 represents $234,900). Annual averages. Covers fully amortized conventional mortgage loans used to purchase single-family nonfarm homes. Excludes refinancing loans, nonamortized and balloon loans, loans insured by the Federal Housing Administration, and loans guaranteed by the Veterans Administration. Based on a sample of mortgage lenders, including savings and loans associations, savings banks, commercial banks, and mortgage companies. Data for 2012 are unweighted]

Loan characteristics	New homes						Previously occupied homes					
	2000	2005	2009	2010	2011	2012	2000	2005	2009	2010	2011	2012
Contract interest rate,												
all loans [1]	7.4	5.9	5.0	4.7	4.5	3.6	7.9	5.8	5.1	4.8	4.6	3.7
Fixed-rate loans	8.0	6.1	5.0	4.7	4.5	3.7	8.2	6.0	5.1	4.9	4.7	3.8
Adjustable-rate loans [2]	6.5	5.3	([5])	4.3	(NA)	(NA)	7.2	5.6	([5])	4.2	(NA)	(NA)
Initial fees, charges [3]	0.69	0.54	1.00	0.82	0.73	1.14	0.66	0.33	0.55	0.71	0.89	0.99
Effective interest rate,												
all loans [4]	7.5	5.9	5.1	4.8	4.6	3.7	8.1	5.9	5.1	4.9	4.7	3.8
Fixed-rate loans	8.2	6.2	5.2	4.8	4.6	3.8	8.3	6.0	5.2	5.0	4.8	3.9
Adjustable-rate loans [2]	6.5	5.3	([5])	4.4	(NA)	(NA)	7.2	5.6	([5])	4.3	(NA)	(NA)
Term to maturity (years)	29.2	29.2	28.8	28.5	28.5	28.5	28.6	28.3	28.1	27.5	28.0	27.4
Purchase price ($1,000)	234.9	328.5	332.3	335.3	326.5	376.0	191.8	291.3	303.6	297.7	290.3	354.0
Loan-to-price ratio	77.4	75.2	73.9	73.4	77.2	76.9	77.9	74.6	74.6	74.2	76.2	75.5
Percent of loans												
with adjustable rates	40	29	([5])	3	6	9	21	30	([5])	5	13	12

NA Not available. [1] Initial interest rate paid by the borrower as specified in the loan contract. [2] Loans with a contractual provision for periodic adjustments in the contract interest rate. [3] Includes all fees, commissions, discounts, and "points" paid by the borrower, or seller, in order to obtain the loan. Excludes those charges for mortgage, credit, life, or property insurance; for property transfer; and for title search and insurance. [4] Contract interest rate plus fees and charges amortized over a ten year period. [5] Insufficient data to report meaningful numbers.

Source: U.S. Federal Housing Finance Agency, Research and Analysis, "Monthly Interest Rate Survey Data, Historical Summary Tables," <http://www.fhfa.gov/Default.aspx?Page=252>, accessed August 2013.

Table 1218. Mortgage Originations and Delinquency and Foreclosure Rates: 2000 to 2012

[In percent, except as indicated (1,139 represents $1,139,000,000,000). Covers one- to four-family residential nonfarm mortgage loans. Mortgage origination is the making of a new mortgage, including all steps taken by a lender to attract and qualify a borrower, process the mortgage loan, and place it on the lender's books. Based on the National Delinquency Survey which covers 45 million loans on one- to four-unit properties, representing between 80 to 85 percent of all 'first-lien' residential mortgage loans outstanding. Loans surveyed were reported by approximately 120 lenders, including mortgage bankers, commercial banks, and thrifts]

Item	2000	2005	2006	2007	2008	2009	2010	2011	2012
MORTGAGE ORIGINATIONS									
Total (bil. dol.)	**1,139**	**2,908**	**2,726**	**2,306**	**1,509**	**1,995**	**1,572**	**1,262**	**1,750**
Purchase (bil. dol.)	905	1,512	1,399	1,140	731	664	473	404	503
Refinance (bil. dol.)	234	1,397	1,326	1,166	777	1,331	1,099	858	1,247
DELINQUENCY RATES [1]									
Total	**4.4**	**4.5**	**4.6**	**5.4**	**6.9**	**9.4**	**9.3**	**8.0**	**7.4**
Prime conventional loans	2.3	2.3	2.4	2.9	4.3	6.5	6.5	5.3	4.6
Subprime conventional loans	11.9	10.8	12.3	15.6	19.9	25.5	25.9	23.0	20.6
Federal Housing Administration loans	9.1	12.5	12.7	12.7	13.0	14.0	12.8	12.3	11.6
Veterans Administration loans	6.8	7.0	6.7	6.4	7.2	7.9	7.5	6.8	6.4
FORECLOSURE RATES									
Total loans in foreclosure process [2]	**1.2**	**1.0**	**1.2**	**2.0**	**3.3**	**4.3**	**4.6**	**4.4**	**4.1**
Prime conventional loans	0.4	0.4	0.5	1.0	1.9	3.0	3.5	3.4	3.0
Subprime conventional loans	9.4	3.3	4.5	8.7	13.7	15.1	14.5	14.7	13.0
Federal Housing Administration loans	1.7	2.3	1.9	2.3	2.4	3.2	3.5	3.4	4.0
Veterans Administration loans	1.2	1.1	1.0	1.1	1.7	2.2	2.4	2.3	2.3
Loans entering foreclosure process [3]	**1.5**	**1.6**	**1.9**	**2.8**	**4.2**	**5.4**	**5.0**	**4.1**	**3.5**
Prime conventional loans	0.6	0.7	0.8	1.3	2.4	4.0	4.0	3.3	2.6
Subprime conventional loans	9.2	5.6	7.3	11.7	16.5	16.2	12.9	12.1	9.5
Federal Housing Administration loans	2.3	3.4	3.3	3.6	3.8	4.8	4.7	3.3	4.5
Veterans Administration loans	1.5	1.5	1.4	1.6	2.3	3.1	3.3	2.4	2.2

[1] Number of loans delinquent 30 days or more as percentage of mortgage loans serviced in survey. Annual average of quarterly figures. Delinquency rate does not include loans in the process of foreclosure. [2] Percentage of loans in the foreclosure process at year-end, not seasonally adjusted. [3] Percentage of loans entering foreclosure process at year-end, not seasonally adjusted.

Source: Mortgage Bankers Association of America, Washington, DC, "MBA Mortgage Originations Estimates," National Delinquency Survey, quarterly, <http://www.mortgagebankers.org/>; and unpublished data ©.

Table 1219. Delinquency Rates and Charge-Off Rates on Loans at Insured Commercial Banks: 1990 to 2012

[In percent. Annual averages of quarterly figures, not seasonally adjusted. Delinquent loans are those past due 30 days or more and still accruing interest as well as those in nonaccrual status. They are measured as a percentage of end-of-period loans. Charge-offs, which are the value of loans removed from the books and charged against loss reserves, are measured net of recoveries as a percentage of average loans and annualized. Includes only U.S.-chartered commercial banks]

Type of loan	1990	2000	2005	2007	2008	2009	2010	2011	2012
DELINQUENCY RATES									
Total loans	**5.34**	**2.18**	**1.57**	**2.06**	**3.67**	**6.56**	**6.96**	**5.83**	**5.02**
Real estate	6.10	1.89	1.38	2.27	4.67	8.46	9.70	8.81	8.02
Residential [1,2]	(NA)	2.11	1.55	2.56	5.01	9.14	10.82	10.41	10.37
Commercial [2,3]	(NA)	1.49	1.07	1.95	4.44	7.90	8.53	6.87	4.81
Consumer	3.83	3.55	2.81	3.14	3.76	4.70	4.15	3.23	2.79
Credit cards	(NA)	4.50	3.70	4.25	5.02	6.52	4.90	3.55	2.88
Other	(NA)	2.98	2.24	2.46	3.01	3.57	3.33	2.89	2.70
Leases	1.97	1.60	1.28	1.20	1.59	2.30	1.89	1.04	0.80
Commercial and industrial	5.35	2.22	1.51	1.22	1.88	3.91	3.46	2.00	1.33
Agricultural production	3.84	2.54	1.30	1.21	1.19	2.37	3.04	2.11	1.56
Farmland [2]	(NA)	2.20	1.59	1.50	1.75	2.88	3.57	3.50	2.88
CHARGE-OFF RATES									
Total loans	**1.43**	**0.66**	**0.54**	**0.61**	**1.41**	**2.66**	**2.66**	**1.63**	**1.13**
Real estate	0.84	0.10	0.06	0.23	1.19	2.28	2.15	1.46	1.07
Residential [1,2]	(NA)	0.12	0.08	0.26	1.28	2.36	2.12	1.58	1.36
Commercial [2,3]	(NA)	0.06	0.05	0.19	1.19	2.34	2.32	1.40	0.71
Consumer	1.81	2.36	2.74	2.50	3.52	5.50	5.90	3.62	2.58
Credit cards	3.44	4.46	4.83	4.00	5.48	9.42	9.43	5.68	4.07
Other	1.04	1.14	1.38	1.57	2.35	3.05	2.05	1.40	1.03
Leases	0.66	0.31	0.59	0.24	0.53	1.29	0.72	0.20	0.23
Commercial and industrial	1.30	0.76	0.26	0.50	0.98	2.30	1.70	0.85	0.48
Agricultural production	0.21	0.25	0.07	0.11	0.18	0.50	0.79	0.25	0.26
Farmland [2]	(NA)	0.04	0.04	0.02	0.10	0.34	0.43	0.35	0.27

NA Not available. [1] Residential real estate loans include loans secured by one- to four-family properties, including home equity lines of credit. [2] Booked in domestic offices only. [3] Commercial real estate loans include construction and land development loans, loans secured by multifamily residences, and loans secured by nonfarm, nonresidential real estate, only.

Source: Board of Governors of the Federal Reserve, Data Releases, Bank Assets and Liabilities, "Charge-Off and Delinquency Rates on Loans and Leases at Commercial Banks," <http://www.federalreserve.gov/releases/chargeoff/>, accessed May 2013.

Table 1220. Mortgaged Residential Properties in Negative Equity by State: 2012

[(48,057 represents 48,057,000), except percent. As of March. Covers 85% of all mortgages in the U.S. "Negative equity" properties, often said to be "under water" or "upside-down," have mortgages with outstanding balances exceeding the property's current value. Outstanding balances include first and second liens as well as home equity utilizations. Estimates are based on a valuation model applied to public records data]

State	Properties with a mortgage outstanding, number (1,000)			Percent in or near negative equity	State	Properties with a mortgage outstanding, number (1,000)			Percent in or near negative equity
	Total	In negative equity	Near negative equity [1]			Total	In negative equity	Near negative equity [1]	
U.S. total	**48,057**	**11,374**	**2,345**	**29**	MO	777	119	43	21
AL	352	49	21	20	MT	117	9	4	11
AK	87	5	4	10	NE	226	27	15	19
AZ	1,292	561	64	48	NV	555	340	27	66
AR	249	31	16	19	NH	218	47	12	27
CA	6,787	2,072	301	35	NJ	1,883	355	79	23
CO	1,145	237	79	28	NM	245	34	12	19
CT	822	121	30	18	NY	1,897	148	50	10
DE	182	32	9	23	NC	1,558	229	106	22
DC	100	13	4	17	ND	61	4	2	10
FL	4,220	1,902	169	49	OH	2,158	530	126	30
GA	1,601	595	101	43	OK	417	34	24	14
HI	229	24	7	14	OR	699	142	40	26
ID	245	64	13	31	PA	1,847	174	71	13
IL	2,232	625	110	33	RI	228	53	9	27
IN	638	67	27	15	SC	621	118	42	26
IA	373	39	17	15	SD	(NA)	(NA)	(NA)	(NA)
KS	302	29	14	14	TN	959	155	67	23
KY	293	30	14	15	TX	3,361	330	163	15
LA	(NA)	(NA)	(NA)	(NA)	UT	478	101	31	28
ME	(NA)	(NA)	(NA)	(NA)	VT	(NA)	(NA)	(NA)	(NA)
MD	1,354	335	66	30	VA	1,317	294	76	28
MA	1,486	250	52	20	WA	1,416	292	77	26
MI	1,351	481	67	41	WV	(NA)	(NA)	(NA)	(NA)
MN	597	108	31	23	WI	664	110	35	22
MS	(NA)	(NA)	(NA)	(NA)	WY	(NA)	(NA)	(NA)	(NA)

NA Not available, often because of insufficient public records data. [1] Mortgage holders with 0 to 5 percent positive equity in their homes.

Source: CoreLogic, Negative Equity Report (copyright), July 2012. See also <http://www.corelogic.com/about-us/research.aspx>.

Table 1221. Mortgage Loan Applications and Lender Denials by State: 2010 and 2011

[(23,264.5 represents 23,264,500). Includes loans for home purchase, home improvement, and refinancing. Covers loan processing by all lending institutions except nondepository institutions with assets of $10 million or less and depository institutions with assets of $39 million or less]

State	Applications, number (1,000)		Percent denied [1]		State	Applications, number (1,000)		Percent denied [1]	
	2010	2011	2010	2011		2010	2011	2010	2011
U.S. total [2]	**23,264.5**	**21,712.6**	**22**	**22**	MO	505.0	441.2	19	20
AL	310.6	286.3	30	32	MT	78.5	67.4	19	19
AK	49.9	44.3	20	17	NE	145.2	129.3	17	17
AZ	429.2	402.4	23	21	NV	127.5	124.5	29	24
AR	183.1	169.1	26	26	NH	131.4	116.6	21	20
CA	3,102.5	3,049.1	18	16	NJ	765.1	717.9	22	21
CO	580.0	529.5	18	18	NM	131.6	120.8	28	28
CT	317.2	281.0	19	19	NY	794.9	774.0	27	27
DE	80.7	75.0	24	23	NC	708.6	671.6	24	24
DC	59.5	62.5	16	17	ND	45.8	43.1	16	15
FL	863.7	865.9	32	29	OH	782.3	715.4	27	29
GA	574.6	577.5	27	26	OK	217.1	208.9	27	27
HI	91.3	81.4	17	16	OR	367.7	310.1	20	20
ID	124.3	106.5	23	23	PA	978.4	907.7	23	23
IL	1,135.5	994.8	18	20	RI	82.1	73.5	22	19
IN	483.4	440.8	25	25	SC	313.6	302.3	28	28
IA	261.3	235.2	16	16	SD	65.0	55.7	18	18
KS	204.5	175.9	19	19	TN	425.9	397.3	25	27
KY	313.2	293.3	26	28	TX	1,421.3	1,431.6	24	23
LA	284.6	287.2	28	29	UT	262.6	221.5	19	18
ME	116.2	101.9	23	23	VT	64.0	56.8	17	17
MD	525.0	492.7	20	20	VA	699.3	666.7	18	19
MA	775.9	696.0	14	13	WA	691.5	602.3	18	19
MI	604.3	582.0	24	24	WV	98.5	97.5	30	30
MN	502.2	431.4	17	17	WI	651.4	544.1	16	16
MS	161.5	145.8	30	29	WY	41.5	37.2	23	22

[1] Loan applications may be denied for failing to meet lender requirements for debt/income ratio, employment and credit history, collateral, cash, and application completeness. [2] Total includes unreported states as well as data for Puerto Rico.

Source: Federal Financial Institutions Examination Council, Home Mortgage Disclosure Act data. See also <http://www.ffiec.gov/hmda/>.

Table 1222. Money Stock: 1990 to 2012

[In billions of dollars (825 represents $825,000,000,000). As of December. Seasonally adjusted averages of daily figures]

Item	1990	2000	2005	2006	2007	2008	2009	2010	2011	2012
M1, total..............................	**825**	**1,088**	**1,375**	**1,367**	**1,374**	**1,605**	**1,696**	**1,837**	**2,161**	**2,446**
Currency [1]............................	247	531	724	750	760	816	864	919	1,002	1,091
Travelers' checks [2].................	8	8	7	7	6	6	5	5	4	4
Demand deposits [3]..................	277	310	325	305	302	472	443	513	743	907
Other checkable deposits [4].........	294	238	319	319	305	305	311	383	412	444
M2, total..............................	**3,273**	**4,900**	**6,657**	**7,042**	**7,451**	**8,184**	**8,487**	**8,782**	**9,638**	**10,409**
M1....................................	825	1,088	1,375	1,367	1,374	1,605	1,696	1,837	2,161	2,446
Non-M1 components of M2...............	2,448	3,813	5,282	5,676	6,076	6,579	6,792	6,946	7,477	7,963
Retail money funds.......................	352	889	682	776	930	1,021	779	674	662	640
Savings deposits (including money market deposit accounts)...............	923	1,877	3,607	3,694	3,870	4,101	4,830	5,345	6,050	6,692
Commercial banks......................	581	1,424	2,777	2,910	3,043	3,330	3,992	4,420	5,049	5,732
Thrift institutions.......................	342	454	830	783	828	771	839	926	1,002	961
Small time deposits [5]..................	1,173	1,046	994	1,206	1,276	1,457	1,182	927	765	631
Commercial banks......................	611	701	647	781	859	1,078	863	656	537	455
Thrift institutions.......................	563	345	347	425	417	379	319	271	228	176

[1] Currency outside U.S. Treasury, Federal Reserve Banks and the vaults of depository institutions. [2] Outstanding amount of U.S. dollar-denominated travelers' checks of nonbank issuers. Travelers' checks issued by depository institutions are included in demand deposits. [3] Demand deposits at domestically chartered commercial banks, U.S. branches and agencies of foreign banks, and Edge Act corporations (excluding those amounts held by depository institutions, the U.S. government, and foreign banks and official institutions) less cash items in the process of collection and Federal Reserve float. [4] Negotiable order of withdrawal (NOW) and automatic transfer service (ATS) balances at domestically chartered commercial banks, U.S. branches and agencies of foreign banks, Edge Act corporations, and thrift institutions, credit union share draft balances, and demand deposits at thrift institutions. [5] Small-denomination time deposits are those issued in amounts of less than $100,000. All Individual Retirement Account (IRA) and Keogh account balances at commercial banks and thrift institutions are subtracted from small time deposits.

Source: Board of Governors of the Federal Reserve System, Data Releases, Money Stock and Reserve Balances, "Money Stock Measures -H.6," June 2013, <http://www.federalreserve.gov/releases/h6/>.

Table 1223. Bond Yields: 2000 to 2012

[Percent per year. Annual averages of daily figures]

Type	2000	2004	2005	2006	2007	2008	2009	2010	2011	2012
U.S. Treasury, constant maturities: [1]										
1-year..	6.11	1.89	3.62	4.94	4.53	1.83	0.47	0.32	0.18	0.17
2-year..	6.26	2.38	3.85	4.82	4.36	2.01	0.96	0.70	0.45	0.28
3-year..	6.22	2.78	3.93	4.77	4.35	2.24	1.43	1.11	0.75	0.38
5-year..	6.16	3.43	4.05	4.75	4.43	2.80	2.20	1.93	1.52	0.76
7-year..	6.20	3.87	4.15	4.76	4.51	3.17	2.82	2.62	2.16	1.22
10-year..	6.03	4.27	4.29	4.80	4.63	3.66	3.26	3.22	2.78	1.80
20-year..	6.23	5.04	4.64	5.00	4.91	4.36	4.11	4.03	3.62	2.54
Municipal (Bond Buyer, 20 bonds).............	5.71	4.68	4.40	4.40	4.40	4.85	4.62	4.29	4.51	3.73
High-grade municipal bonds (Standard & Poor's) [2]...............	5.77	4.63	4.29	4.42	4.42	4.80	4.64	4.16	4.29	3.14

[1] Yields on actively traded non-inflation-indexed issues adjusted to constant maturities. Yields are based on closing indicative prices quoted by secondary market participants. Data from U.S. Treasury. [2] Source: U.S. Council of Economic Advisors, Economic Indicators, monthly.

Source: Except as noted, Board of Governors of the Federal Reserve System, "H15, Selected Interest Rates," <http://www.federalreserve.gov/releases/h15/data.htm>, accessed August 2013.

Table 1224. Volume of Debt Markets by Type of Security: 2000 to 2012

[In billions of dollars (2,489 represents $2,489,000,000,000). Covers debt markets as represented by the source]

Type of Security	2000	2005	2007	2008	2009	2010	2011	2012
NEW ISSUE VOLUME [1]								
Total	**2,489**	**5,574**	**5,989**	**4,602**	**6,679**	**6,945**	**6,018**	**6,992**
U.S. Treasury securities [2]	312	746	752	1,037	2,075	2,304	2,103	2,318
Federal agency debt [3]	447	669	942	985	1,086	1,179	839	680
Municipal	201	408	429	390	410	433	295	379
Mortgage-backed securities [4]	660	2,245	2,231	1,344	2,056	1,877	1,644	2,055
Asset-backed securities [5]	282	754	507	139	151	107	125	199
Corporate debt [6]	588	753	1,128	707	902	1,046	1,012	1,360
AVERAGE DAILY TRADING VOLUME								
Total	**357.6**	**918.6**	**1,014.9**	**1,036.1**	**817.8**	**893.7**	**847.5**	**837.0**
U.S. Treasury securities [2,7]	206.5	554.5	570.2	553.1	407.9	528.2	567.8	518.9
Federal agency debt [7]	72.8	78.8	83.0	104.5	77.7	11.2	9.6	9.7
Municipal [8]	8.8	16.9	25.1	19.4	12.5	13.3	11.3	11.3
Mortgage-backed securities [4,7]	69.5	251.8	320.1	344.9	299.9	320.6	243.3	280.4
Corporate [6]	(NA)	16.6	16.4	14.3	19.9	20.5	15.6	16.7
VOLUME OF SECURITIES OUTSTANDING								
Total	**16,925**	**26,621**	**32,220**	**33,725**	**34,743**	**36,435**	**37,045**	**38,162**
U.S. Treasury securities [2]	2,952	4,166	4,517	5,774	7,250	8,853	9,928	10,921
Federal agency debt	1,854	2,616	2,906	3,211	2,727	2,539	2,327	2,096
Municipal	1,481	3,044	3,448	3,543	3,698	3,796	3,719	3,715
Mortgage-backed securities [4]	3,566	6,160	8,161	8,391	8,503	8,475	8,339	8,168
Asset-backed securities [5]	1,052	2,112	2,952	2,624	2,348	2,053	1,834	1,701
Money market instruments [9]	2,663	3,434	4,171	3,791	3,128	2,865	2,572	2,461
Corporate debt [6]	3,358	5,090	6,065	6,391	7,089	7,854	8,325	9,101

NA Not available. [1] Covers only long-term issuance. [2] Marketable public debt. [3] Includes overnight discount notes. Beginning 2004 excludes Sallie Mae. [4] Includes only Government National Mortgage Association (GNMA), Federal National Mortgage Association (FNMA), Federal Home Loan Mortgage Corporation (FHLMC) mortgage-backed securities (MBS), and collateralized mortgage obligations (CMOs), and CMBS, and private-label MBS/CMOs. [5] Excludes mortgage-backed assets. Includes auto, credit card, home equity loans, manufacturing, student loan and other. (Collaterized debt obligations are included) [6] Includes nonconvertible corporate debt, Yankee bonds, and MTNs (Medium-Term Notes), but excludes all issues with maturities of one year or less, agency debt, and all certificates of deposit. [7] Primary dealer transactions. [8] Includes customer-to-dealer and dealer-to-dealer transactions. [9] Commercial paper, bankers acceptances, and large time deposits.

Source: The Securities Industry and Financial Markets Association, New York, NY. © Based on data supplied by Board of Governors of the Federal Reserve System, U.S. Dept. of Treasury, Thomson Reuters, FHLMC, FNMA, GNMA, Federal Home Loan Banks, Student Loan Marketing Association, Federal Farm Credit Banks, Tennessee Valley Authority, Bloomberg, Loan Performance, Dealogic and Municipal Securities Rulemaking Board. For more information: <http://www.sifma.org/>.

Table 1225. Total Returns of Stocks, Bonds, and Treasury Bills: 1980 to 2012

[In percent. Average annual percent change. Stock return data are based on the Standard & Poor's 500 index. Minus sign (-) indicates loss]

Period	Stocks				Treasury bills, total return	Bonds (10-year), total return
	Total return before inflation	Capital gains	Dividends and reinvestment	Total return after inflation		
1980 to 1989	17.55	12.59	4.40	11.85	9.13	13.01
1990 to 1999	18.21	15.31	2.51	14.85	4.95	8.02
2000 to 2009	-0.45	-2.73	2.27	-3.39	2.74	6.63
2001	-11.89	-13.04	1.32	-13.68	3.32	5.53
2002	-22.10	-23.37	1.65	-23.91	1.61	15.37
2003	28.68	26.38	1.82	26.31	1.03	0.46
2004	10.88	8.99	1.73	7.38	1.43	4.61
2005	4.91	3.00	1.85	1.45	3.30	3.09
2006	15.80	13.62	1.91	11.97	4.97	2.21
2007	5.49	3.53	1.89	1.35	4.52	10.54
2008	-37.00	-38.49	1.88	-37.10	1.24	20.23
2009	26.25	23.45	2.44	23.11	0.15	-9.50
2010	15.06	12.78	2.02	13.36	0.03	7.26
2011	2.96	0.00	2.96	0.83	0.06	16.89
2012	16.00	13.41	2.29	14.02	0.08	2.77

Source: Global Financial Data, Los Angeles, CA, "GFD Guide to Total Returns," <http://www.globalfinancialdata.com>, and unpublished data ©.

Table 1226. Equities, Corporate Bonds, and Treasury Securities— Holdings and Net Purchases by Type of Investor: 2000 to 2012

[In billions of dollars (17,575 represents $17,575,000,000,000). Holdings as of December 31. Minus sign (–) indicates net sales]

Type of investor	Holdings					Net purchases				
	2000	2005	2010	2011	2012	2000	2005	2010	2011	2012
EQUITIES [1]										
Total [2]............................	17,575	20,636	23,371	22,737	26,028	5.6	-76.7	-7.7	-218.9	-187.7
Household sector [3]..........................	8,140	8,179	8,844	8,866	10,178	-637.5	-414.4	-170.8	-122.8	-321.3
Rest of the world [4].........................	1,483	2,039	2,962	2,783	3,106	199.7	56.9	73.2	-99.3	-89.7
Life insurance companies................	892	1,162	1,403	1,390	1,545	111.3	65.9	45.6	37.7	15.3
Private pension funds....................	1,971	2,442	1,938	1,949	2,171	62.8	-42.0	25.2	-15.7	78.0
State and local government retirement funds...................................	1,299	1,629	1,778	1,702	1,993	11.6	43.3	-84.0	-69.0	53.0
Mutual funds............................	3,227	4,176	4,763	4,427	5,107	193.1	129.6	44.3	4.9	-37.2
Exchange-traded funds....................	66	286	854	864	1,093	42.4	50.0	88.3	71.6	132.9
CORPORATE & FOREIGN BONDS										
Total [2]............................	4,935	8,852	11,816	11,976	12,624	364.0	872.9	-76.6	142.6	363.0
Household sector [3]..........................	663	1,353	2,252	2,273	2,402	93.5	47.9	-323.5	53.1	25.6
Rest of the world [4].........................	842	1,763	2,523	2,503	2,581	168.2	328.5	-37.0	-68.3	-38.8
U.S.-chartered depository institutions....	311	492	549	552	551	47.6	68.1	-98.8	3.0	-1.2
Property-casualty insurance companies..............................	188	263	323	363	380	6.4	17.5	24.3	40.4	16.7
Life insurance companies................	1,215	1,825	2,030	2,124	2,167	47.9	74.7	102.9	93.4	43.8
Private pension funds....................	266	290	443	442	361	-76.3	22.2	83.4	-1.7	-81.1
State and local government retirement funds...................................	314	336	388	364	305	4.2	87.0	5.7	-24.3	-59.1
Mutual funds............................	338	660	1,243	1,413	1,719	-10.5	65.9	122.3	170.3	306.0
Funding corporations....................	25	67	760	792	922	-8.9	-29.4	51.9	32.6	129.6
TREASURY SECURITIES										
Total [2]............................	3,358	4,678	9,361	10,428	11,569	-294.9	307.3	1,579.6	1,066.8	1,140.6
Household sector [3]..........................	579	440	1,265	816	1,198	-210.8	-101.9	415.5	-256.9	370.5
State and local governments.............	310	506	540	486	478	5.5	94.3	-7.9	-53.4	-7.9
Rest of the world [4].........................	1,021	1,984	4,467	5,071	5,526	-75.2	245.1	739.8	412.1	478.4
Monetary authority.......................	512	744	1,021	1,663	1,666	33.7	26.4	244.9	642.0	2.7
Money market mutual funds..............	92	89	335	443	458	-12.5	-14.2	-71.0	107.9	14.5
Mutual funds.............................	127	156	291	361	445	10.2	6.6	43.2	70.8	83.8

[1] Excludes mutual fund shares; see Table 1240. [2] Includes other types, not shown separately. [3] Includes nonprofit organizations. [4] Holdings and net purchases of U.S. issues by foreign residents.

Source: Board of Governors of the Federal Reserve System, "Federal Reserve Statistical Release, Z.1, Financial Accounts of the United States," June 2013, <http://www.federalreserve.gov/releases/z1/>.

Table 1227. New Security Issues of Corporations by Type of Offering: 2000 to 2012

[In billions of dollars (1,075 represents $1,075,000,000,000). Represents gross proceed of issues maturing in more than one year. Figures are the principal amount or the number of units multiplied by the offering price. Excludes secondary offerings, employee stock plans, investment companies other than closed-end, intracorporate transactions, Yankee bonds, and private placements listed. Stock data include ownership securities issued by limited partnerships]

Type of Offering	2000	2010	2011	2012	Type of Offering	2000	2010	2011	2012
Total........................	1,075	1,025	1,037	1,401	Nonfinancial..........	360	498	481	663
					Financial..............	679	396	428	579
Bonds, total....................	940	894	909	1,242	Stocks, total..........	135	131	129	159
Sold in the U.S...............	827	880	881	1,205	Nonfinancial..........	118	61	59	63
Sold abroad.................	112	14	28	37	Financial..............	17	70	71	96

Source: Source: Board of Governors of the Federal Reserve System, "New Security Issues, U.S. Corporations," <http://www.federalreserve.gov/econresdata/releases/corpsecure/current.htm>, accessed August 2013.

Table 1228. U.S. Purchases and Sales of Foreign Bonds and Stocks, 2000 to 2012, and by Selected Country, 2012

[In billions of dollars (17.1 represents $17,100,000,000). Covers transactions in all types of long-term foreign securities with foreigners as reported to the Treasury International Capital Reporting System by banks, brokers, and other entities in the United States. Data cover new issues of securities, transactions in outstanding issues, and redemptions of securities. Includes transactions executed in the United States for the account of foreigners, and transactions executed abroad for the account of reporting institutions and their domestic customers. Data by country show the country of location of the foreign buyers and sellers who deal directly with reporting institutions in the United States. The data do not necessarily indicate the country of beneficial owner or issuer. The term "foreigner" covers all institutions and individuals domiciled outside the United States, including U.S. citizens domiciled abroad, and the foreign branches, subsidiaries, and other affiliates abroad of U.S. banks and businesses; the central governments, central banks, and other official institutions of foreign countries; and international and regional organizations. "Foreigner" also includes persons in the United States to the extent that they are known by reporting institutions to be acting on behalf of foreigners. Excludes acquisitions of foreign stocks through mergers that involve stock swaps. Including stock swaps, net sales of foreign securities was $21 billion in 2012. Minus sign (-) indicates net sales by U.S. investors or a net inflow of capital into the United States]

Year and country	Net purchases			Total transactions [1]			Bonds		Stocks	
	Total	Bonds	Stocks	Total	Bonds	Stocks	Purchases	Sales	Purchases	Sales
2000	17.1	4.1	13.1	5,539	1,922	3,617	963	959	1,815	1,802
2004	152.8	67.9	85.0	6,399	2,986	3,413	1,527	1,459	1,749	1,664
2005	172.4	45.1	127.3	7,572	2,965	4,608	1,505	1,460	2,367	2,240
2006	250.9	144.5	106.5	11,283	3,904	7,379	2,024	1,880	3,743	3,636
2007	229.2	133.9	95.3	16,607	6,081	10,527	3,107	2,973	5,311	5,216
2008	-74.2	-53.9	-20.2	15,356	4,489	10,866	2,218	2,272	5,423	5,443
2009	186.8	127.5	59.4	10,430	4,031	6,398	2,079	1,952	3,229	3,170
2010	115.3	54.6	60.6	14,763	7,355	7,408	3,705	3,650	3,734	3,674
2011	124.3	52.6	71.7	15,123	7,114	8,009	3,583	3,531	4,040	3,968
2012, total [2]	35.4	-4.6	40.0	14,461.7	7,706.3	6,755.4	3,850.9	3,855.5	3,397.7	3,357.7
United Kingdom	48.7	36.1	12.6	4,251.2	2,079.3	2,171.8	1,057.7	1,021.6	1,092.2	1,079.6
Cayman Islands	-14.3	-8.6	-5.7	3,558.9	2,422.1	1,136.8	1,206.8	1,215.3	565.5	571.3
Canada	9.6	8.7	0.9	1,237.0	756.7	480.3	382.7	374.0	240.6	239.7
Hong Kong	5.5	-10.2	15.7	596.0	51.0	545.1	20.4	30.6	280.4	264.7
Bermuda	-2.0	-0.5	-1.5	563.1	397.3	165.8	198.4	198.9	82.1	83.6
Japan	-0.6	-9.7	9.2	420.9	117.6	303.3	53.9	63.7	156.2	147.1
British Virgin Islands	-0.2	-1.8	1.6	313.1	150.6	162.4	74.4	76.2	82.0	80.4
France	-26.0	-26.3	0.3	277.0	123.8	153.3	48.7	75.0	76.8	76.5
Luxembourg	63.9	62.3	1.6	229.2	116.8	112.4	89.6	27.3	57.0	55.4
Australia	-18.0	-16.7	-1.3	221.4	115.4	106.0	49.3	66.1	52.4	53.7
Germany	-53.0	-51.4	-1.6	215.7	158.5	57.2	53.5	104.9	27.8	29.4
Ireland	20.3	22.8	-2.4	212.5	82.7	129.8	52.7	30.0	63.7	66.1
Anguilla	0.3	0.0	0.3	195.8	0.3	195.4	0.2	0.2	97.9	97.6
Brazil	10.7	10.2	0.5	181.2	74.8	106.4	42.5	32.3	53.4	52.9
Netherlands	-5.5	-7.7	2.3	156.3	94.9	61.4	43.6	51.3	31.8	29.6

[1] Total purchases plus total sales. [2] Includes other countries not shown separately.

Source: U.S. Department of Treasury, *Treasury Bulletin, Capital Movements Tables (Section IV)*, June 2013. See also <http://www.fms.treas.gov/bulletin/index.html>.

Table 1229. U.S. Holdings of Foreign Stocks and Bonds by Country: 2011 and 2012

[In billions of dollars (4,501.4 represents $4,501,400,000,000). See also Table 1316]

Country	Stocks		Country	Bonds	
	2011	2012		2011	2012
Total holdings	4,501.4	5,390.5	Total holdings	1,939.9	2,140.7
Europe [1]	1,955.8	2,413.2	Europe [1]	844.2	970.4
United Kingdom	691.6	822.1	United Kingdom	281.8	281.3
Switzerland	277.7	332.6	Netherlands	109.2	128.7
France	209.2	256.9	France	82.9	96.1
Germany	174.2	228.8	Belgium & Luxembourg	66.0	74.7
Netherlands	119.5	161.0	Germany	78.3	72.5
Ireland	114.2	145.1	Italy	20.8	54.4
Belgium and Luxembourg	59.1	72.3	Ireland	34.9	46.7
Sweden	53.9	66.8			
Canada	358.5	390.7	Canada	327.2	377.1
Caribbean financial centers [1]	735.4	866.4			
Cayman Islands	487.9	588.3	Caribbean financial centers [1]	257.0	210.8
Bermuda	135.1	151.0	Cayman Islands	218.1	165.5
Latin America, excluding			Bermuda	25.4	28.4
Caribbean financial centers [1]	252.0	271.1			
Brazil	154.6	149.8	Latin America, excluding		
Mexico	59.4	74.9	Caribbean financial centers [1]	139.3	195.2
Asia [1]	990.1	1,200.7	Mexico	45.5	70.2
Japan	391.3	429.4	Brazil	41.2	59.4
Korea, South	116.7	141.1			
China	74.7	131.0	Asia [1]	157.0	168.7
Hong Kong	112.3	128.4	Japan	41.0	45.7
Taiwan	71.8	88.5	Korea, South	27.6	31.3
India	55.1	75.3			
Africa [1]	69.8	86.5	Africa	17.6	21.9
South Africa	58.6	70.7			
Other countries [1]	139.9	161.8	Other countries [1]	197.7	196.6
Australia	128.6	148.4	Australia	139.1	140.6

[1] Includes other countries, not shown separately.

Source: U.S. Bureau of Economic Analysis, *Survey of Current Business*, July 2013. See also <http://www.bea.gov/scb/date_guide.asp>.

Table 1230. Foreign Purchases and Sales of U.S. Securities by Type of Security, 2000 to 2012, and by Selected Country, 2012

[In billions of dollars (457.8 represents $457,800,000,000). Covers transactions in all types of long-term domestic securities with foreigners as reported to the Treasury International Capital Reporting System by banks, brokers, and other entities in the United States (except nonmarketable U.S. Treasury notes, foreign series; and nonmarketable U.S. Treasury bonds and notes, foreign currency series). Data by country show the country of domicile of the foreign buyers and sellers of the securities; in the case of outstanding issues, this may differ from the country of the original issuer. Excludes U.S. equities acquired through mergers and reincorporations that involve stock swaps and principal repayment flows on foreign holdings of U.S. government agency and corporate asset-backed securities (ABS). Including stock swaps and accounting for ABS repayment flows, net purchases of U.S. securities was $396 billion in 2012. Minus sign (–) indicates net sales by foreigners or a net outflow of capital from the U.S.]

Year and country	Net purchases					Total transactions [1]				
	Total	Treasury bonds and notes [2]	U.S. government corporations [3] bonds	Corporate bonds [4]	Corporate stocks	Total	Treasury bonds and notes [2]	U.S. government corporations [3] bonds	Corporate bonds [4]	Corporate stocks
2000	457.8	-54.0	152.8	184.1	174.9	16,910	7,795	1,305	775	7,036
2004	916.5	352.1	226.4	309.5	28.5	29,441	17,520	2,192	2,033	7,696
2005	1,011.5	338.1	219.3	372.2	82.0	33,303	19,764	1,976	2,182	9,382
2006	1,143.2	195.5	286.5	510.8	150.4	41,011	21,720	2,858	2,846	13,587
2007	1,005.8	198.0	219.0	393.4	195.5	58,455	30,057	3,882	3,433	21,083
2008	414.9	314.9	-38.7	93.9	44.8	61,035	28,944	5,219	2,841	24,031
2009	638.9	538.4	-11.5	-40.8	152.7	40,321	22,648	2,098	2,420	13,155
2010	908.3	703.7	108.0	-13.2	109.7	49,126	31,676	2,109	1,956	13,385
2011	493.4	432.6	80.9	-45.2	25.1	55,144	35,507	2,184	2,037	15,415
2012, total [5]	624.1	405.9	141.2	-25.1	102.1	48,101	29,062	3,021	1,930	14,087
United Kingdom	129.6	98.7	11.4	-13.7	33.2	15,862	12,345	491	708	2,318
Cayman Islands	15.0	-23.1	20.8	4.3	12.9	8,992	3,682	496	402	4,412
France	93.5	84.0	-0.9	-5.5	15.9	6,852	5,344	68	35	1,406
Canada	74.2	56.3	5.1	1.7	11.2	2,757	1,394	81	128	1,154
Japan	104.2	87.3	24.7	0.2	-8.0	2,165	1,443	498	81	142
Anguilla	-2.2	-0.2	(Z)	-0.7	-1.3	1,167	20	(Z)	1	1,146
Bermuda	8.6	4.6	4.1	(Z)	-0.1	964	153	58	58	694
China	84.7	73.3	7.2	5.7	-1.5	761	334	364	19	44
British Virgin Islands	13.2	6.2	0.1	1.2	5.7	759	136	3	35	585
Ireland	-15.4	-15.0	-3.4	-4.1	7.1	730	414	211	46	60
Israel	3.1	2.7	0.3	-0.1	0.2	679	630	8	4	37
Luxembourg	-9.8	-32.3	25.0	-1.2	-1.4	463	140	174	69	80

Z Less than $50 million or $500 million. [1] Total purchases plus total sales. [2] Marketable bonds and notes. [3] Includes federally sponsored agencies. [4] Includes transactions in directly placed issues abroad by U.S. corporations and issues of states and municipalities. [5] Includes other countries, not shown separately.

Source: U.S. Department of Treasury, *Treasury Bulletin, Capital Movements Tables (Section IV)*, June 2013. See also <http://www.fms.treas.gov/index.html>.

Table 1231. Foreign Holdings of U.S. Securities by Country: 2011 and 2012

[In billions of dollars (5,006.9 represents $5,006,900,000,000). Covers only private holdings of U.S. securities, except as noted. See also Table 1316]

Country	2011	2012	Country	2011	2012
U.S. Treasury securities [1, 2]	5,006.9	5,573.8	Asia [2]	417.5	478.6
China	1,151.9	1,220.4	Japan	297.2	337.3
Japan	1,058.1	1,111.2	Taiwan	65.9	81.0
Belgium and Luxembourg	282.8	293.8	Hong Kong	18.6	16.7
Brazil	226.9	253.3	Africa	2.5	2.2
OPEC Asia [3]	212.2	222.6	Other countries [2]	40.4	37.9
Taiwan	177.3	195.4	Australia	23.1	23.4
Switzerland	142.4	195.4	Corporate stocks	3,256.9	3,842.1
Russia	149.5	161.5	Europe [2]	1,552.1	1,803.5
Hong Kong	121.7	141.9	United Kingdom	471.7	552.3
Cayman Islands	122.3	140.1	Belgium and Luxembourg	294.3	339.5
Corporate and agency bonds	2,894.6	3,062.0	Switzerland	197.3	238.7
Europe [2]	1,759.0	1,814.1	Netherlands	139.7	157.9
Belgium and Luxembourg	670.6	713.6	France	114.2	134.0
United Kingdom	532.8	491.5	Ireland	99.7	110.6
Ireland	159.6	195.6	Germany	76.6	85.2
Switzerland	129.5	118.4	Sweden	58.2	71.6
Germany	83.9	86.8	Canada	404.9	515.5
Netherlands	68.6	78.9	Caribbean financial centers [2]	666.7	774.9
France	54.9	56.7	Cayman Islands	487.7	568.1
Canada	96.8	116.7	Latin America, excluding Caribbean financial centers [2]	62.9	87.7
Caribbean financial centers [2]	552.7	587.2	Mexico	19.2	29.4
Cayman Islands	373.9	405.8	Asia [2]	453.3	526.8
Bermuda	141.4	141.5	Japan	295.0	319.8
Latin America, excluding Caribbean financial centers [2]	25.8	25.2	Africa	6.0	8.2
Mexico	5.1	4.9	Other countries [2]	111.2	125.4
			Australia	104.1	117.9

[1] Includes foreign official holdings. [2] Includes other countries not shown separately. [3] Comprises Indonesia, Iran, Iraq, Kuwait, Qatar, Saudi Arabia, and the United Arab Emirates.

Source: U.S. Bureau of Economic Analysis, *Survey of Current Business,* July 2013. See also <http://www.bea.gov/scb/date_guide.asp>.

Table 1232. Stock Prices and Yields: 2000 to 2012

[Closing values as of end of December, except as noted]

Index	2000	2005	2008	2009	2010	2011	2012
STOCK PRICES							
Standard & Poor's indices: [1]							
S&P 500 composite (1941–43 = 10)............	1,320	1,248	903	1,115	1,257	1,258	1,426
S&P 400 MidCap Index (1982 = 100)............	517	738	538	727	907	879	1,020
S&P 600 SmallCap Index (Dec. 31, 1993 = 100)...........	220	351	269	333	416	415	477
S&P 500 Citigroup Value Index (Dec. 31, 1974 = 35).........	636	648	447	525	590	573	657
S&P 500 Citigroup Growth Index (Dec. 31, 1974 = 35)........	688	597	451	582	659	678	761
Russell indices: [2]							
Russell 1000 (Dec. 31, 1986 = 130)............	700	679	488	612	697	693	790
Russell 2000 (Dec. 31, 1986 = 135)............	484	673	499	625	784	741	849
Russell 3000 (Dec. 31, 1986 = 140)............	726	723	521	653	749	743	846
N.Y. Stock Exchange common stock index:							
Composite (Dec. 31, 2002 = 5000)............	6,946	7,754	5,757	7,185	7,964	7,477	8,444
Yearly high............	7,165	7,868	9,713	7,288	7,983	8,718	8,519
Yearly low............	6,095	6,903	4,607	4,182	6,356	6,415	7,223
American Stock Exchange Composite Index (Dec. 29, 1995 = 550)............	898	1,759	1,398	1,825	2,208	2,278	2,356
NASDAQ Composite Index (Feb. 5, 1971 = 100)............	2,471	2,205	1,577	2,269	2,653	2,605	3,020
Nasdaq-100 (Jan. 31, 1985 = 125)............	2,342	1,645	1,212	1,860	2,218	2,278	2,661
Industrial (Feb. 5, 1971 = 100)............	1,483	1,860	1,191	1,748	2,184	2,168	2,595
Banks (Feb. 5, 1971 = 100)............	1,939	3,078	2,026	1,651	1,847	1,618	1,873
Computers (Oct. 29, 1993 = 200)............	1,295	992	684	1,168	1,372	1,379	1,551
Transportation (Feb. 5, 1971 = 100)............	1,160	2,438	1,885	1,951	2,562	2,173	2,281
Telecommunications (Oct. 29, 1993 = 200)............	463	184	146	217	226	197	201
Biotech (Oct. 29, 1993 = 200)............	1,085	790	730	844	970	1,085	1,431
Dow-Jones and Co., Inc.:							
Composite (65 stocks)............	3,317	3,638	3,086	3,567	4,033	4,232	4,442
Industrial (30 stocks)............	10,787	10,718	8,776	10,428	11,578	12,218	13,104
Transportation (20 stocks)............	2,947	4,196	3,537	4,100	5,107	5,020	5,307
Utility (15 stocks)............	412	405	371	398	405	465	453
COMMON STOCK YIELDS (percent)							
Standard & Poor's Composite Index (500 stocks): [3]							
Dividend-price ratio [4]............	1.15	1.83	2.37	2.01	1.81	2.07	2.29
Earnings-price ratio [5]............	3.63	5.36	3.54	4.55	5.93	6.80	6.17

[1] Standard & Poor's Indices are market-value weighted and are chosen for market size, liquidity, and industry group representation. The S&P 500 index represents 500 large publicly-traded companies. The S&P MidCap Index tracks mid-cap companies. The S&P SmallCap Index consists of 600 domestic small-cap stocks. [2] The Russell 1000 and 3000 indices show respectively the 1000 and 3000 largest capitalization stocks in the United States. The Russell 2000 index shows the 2000 largest capitalization stocks in the United States after the first 1000. [3] Source: U.S. Council of Economic Advisors, *Economic Indicators*, monthly. [4] Aggregate cash dividends (based on latest known annual rate) divided by aggregate market value based on Wednesday closing prices. Averages of monthly figures. [5] Averages of quarterly ratios which are ratio of earnings (after taxes) for 4 quarters ending with particular quarter- to-price index for last day of that quarter.

Source: Except as noted, Global Financial Data, Los Angeles, CA, ©, <http://www.globalfinancialdata.com/>.

Table 1233. Stock Ownership by Age of Head of Family and Family Income: 2004 to 2010

[Median value in thousands of constant 2010 dollars (37.7 represents $37,700). Constant dollar figures are based on consumer price index data published by U.S. Bureau of Labor Statistics. Families include one-person units; for definition of family, see text, Section 1. Based on Survey of Consumer Finance; see Appendix III. For definition of median, see Guide to Tabular Presentation]

Age of family head and family income (constant (2010) dollars)	Families having direct or indirect stock holdings [1] (percent)			Median value among families with holdings			Stock holdings share of total financial assets (percent)		
	2004	2007	2010	2004	2007	2010	2004	2007	2010
All families......................	**50.2**	**53.2**	**49.9**	**37.7**	**35.5**	**29.0**	**51.4**	**54.0**	**47.0**
Under 35 years old.................	40.8	41.6	39.8	9.2	6.8	7.0	40.4	45.6	39.3
35 to 44 years old.................	54.5	55.9	50.1	23.0	25.7	19.8	53.7	54.7	50.5
45 to 54 years old.................	56.6	63.1	58.0	57.5	47.1	37.8	53.8	54.5	48.6
55 to 64 years old.................	63.2	60.8	59.7	80.5	81.7	56.0	55.2	55.6	48.3
65 to 74 years old.................	46.9	53.1	45.6	80.5	58.1	78.1	51.5	55.6	44.2
75 years old and over.............	34.8	40.2	42.0	98.8	47.1	55.0	39.3	48.2	44.6
Percentiles of income: [2]									
Less than 20......................	11.7	14.3	12.5	8.6	6.3	5.3	32.0	39.2	40.5
20 to 39.9.........................	29.8	36.5	30.5	11.5	8.7	7.1	30.9	34.6	31.3
40 to 59.9.........................	51.9	52.9	51.7	16.9	18.3	12.0	43.4	39.5	37.5
60 to 79.9.........................	69.9	73.3	68.1	30.6	35.2	22.3	41.9	53.1	41.6
80 to 89.9.........................	83.9	86.3	82.6	65.0	66.1	57.9	48.8	50.5	44.4
90 to 100.........................	92.7	91.5	90.6	235.8	234.7	267.5	57.5	58.3	50.9

[1] Indirect holdings are those in retirement accounts and other managed assets. [2] See footnote 8, Table 1194.

Source: Board of Governors of the Federal Reserve System, *Federal Reserve Bulletin*, June 2012, <http://www.federalreserve.gov/pubs/bulletin/default.htm>.

Table 1234. Dow Jones U.S. Total Market Index by Industry: 2000 to 2011

[As of end of year]

Industry	2000	2005	2007	2008	2009	2010	2011
U.S. Total Market Index, total............	**306.88**	**302.37**	**357.48**	**219.66**	**276.57**	**316.56**	**314.50**
Basic materials.............................	154.49	205.79	307.92	147.91	239.44	309.95	259.10
Consumer goods..........................	219.82	265.88	320.39	231.71	278.07	323.20	342.44
Consumer services.......................	279.11	298.62	310.76	211.93	278.96	340.32	359.04
Oil and gas................................	272.96	422.12	679.31	429.60	494.01	580.28	593.75
Financial...................................	440.91	510.02	474.23	226.52	258.79	287.09	245.11
Health care................................	360.18	315.50	354.89	268.73	320.51	328.59	359.62
Industrials.................................	276.11	280.72	351.44	207.77	255.47	315.97	307.42
Technology................................	749.01	513.48	645.98	365.85	595.55	664.45	658.94
Telecommunications......................	210.38	126.90	179.65	115.34	119.63	133.50	132.47
Utilities....................................	177.80	152.41	204.52	137.79	148.29	153.14	175.04

Source: Dow-Jones & Company, Inc., New York, NY, *Dow-Jones Indexes* (copyright).

Table 1235. Volume of Round Lot Trading on New York Stock Exchange: 2000 to 2012

[262,478 represents 262,478,000,000. Covers round lot trades only. Beginning 2005, reflects trades of NYSE Group. Round lot: A unit of trading or a multiple thereof. On the NYSE the unit of trading is generally 100 shares in stocks. For some inactive stocks, the unit of trading is 10 shares]

Item	Unit	2000	2005	2006	2007	2008	2009	2010	2011	2012
Round lot shares traded...	**Million**	**262,478**	**516,743**	**588,127**	**664,020**	**802,170**	**738,193**	**601,275**	**534,269**	**386,174**
Average daily shares.......	Million	1,042	2,051	2,343	2,645	3,171	2,929	2,386	2,120	1,571
High day......................	Million	1,561	3,628	3,853	5,505	7,342	5,043	5,557	5,209	7,909
Low day......................	Million	403	694	797	917	849	585	849	885	571
Value of round lot shares traded..........	**Bil. dol.**	**11,060**	**17,858**	**21,790**	**28,428**	**28,080**	**17,562**	**17,852**	**18,090**	**13,301**

Source: New York Stock Exchange, Inc., New York, NY, "Facts & Figures." All rights in the "Facts & Figures" and the above table are owned exclusively by NYSE Group, Inc., © 2012 NYSE Group, Inc., All Rights Reserved. More up-to-date information may be available at <http://www.nyxdata.com/factbook>.

Table 1236. Transaction Activity in Equities, Options, and Security Futures, 2000 to 2011, and by Exchange, 2011

[In billions of dollars (36,275 represents $36,275,000,000,000). Market value of all sales of equities and options listed on an exchange or subject to last-sale reporting. Also reported are the value of such options that were exercised and the value of single-stock futures that were delivered. Excludes options and futures on indexes]

Year and exchange	Market value of sales			Option exercises and futures deliveries
	Total	Equity trading	Option trading	
2000..................................	36,275	35,557	485	233
2003..................................	22,737	22,292	164	282
2004..................................	27,876	27,158	223	495
2005..................................	34,568	33,223	350	995
2006..................................	43,941	41,798	531	1,611
2007..................................	66,136	63,064	861	2,211
2008..................................	82,012	78,653	1,096	2,264
2009..................................	59,850	57,565	710	1,574
2010..................................	64,008	61,146	725	2,137
2011, total [1]....................	**70,100**	**66,683**	**923**	**2,494**
BATS (Better Alternative Trading System) Exchange, Inc....................	6,902	6,770	36	96
Chicago Board Options Exchange, Inc...................	693	104	157	432
EDGX Exchange, Inc...................	3,807	3,807	–	–
FINRA, Inc. [2].........................	18,181	18,181	–	–
International Securities Exchange, LLC...................	493	–	135	358
NASDAQ OMX PHLX....................	1,771	668	294	809
The Nasdaq Stock Market LLC...........................	13,757	13,601	41	116
National Stock Exchange............	335	335	–	–
New York Stock Exchange, Inc.......................	8,389	8,389	–	–
NYSE Arca, Inc..........................	10,439	10,031	114	294

– Represents zero. [1] Includes other exchanges not shown separately. [2] Financial Industry Regulatory Authority.

Source: U.S. Securities and Exchange Commission, "Select SEC and Market Data 2012," <http://www.sec.gov/about.shtml>, accessed August 2013.

Table 1237. Households Owning Mutual Funds by Age and Income: 2002 and 2012

[In percent. Ownership includes money market, stock, bond, and hybrid mutual funds, variable annuities, and mutual funds owned through Individual Retirement Accounts (IRAs), Keoghs, and employer-sponsored retirement plans. In 2012, an estimated 53,800,000 households own mutual funds. A mutual fund is an open-end investment company that continuously issues and redeems shares that represent an interest in a pool of financial assets]

Age of household head [1]	Percent distribution, 2012	As a percent of all households		Household income [2]	Percent distribution, 2012	As a percent of all households	
		2002	2012			2002	2012
Total..........................	**100**	**45**	**44**	Less than $25,000..............	5	10	8
Less than 35 years old.........	17	38	34	$25,000 to $34,999.............	6	30	25
35 to 44 years old..............	20	51	52	$35,000 to $49,999.............	11	47	36
45 to 54 years old..............	24	58	53	$50,000 to $74,999.............	21	64	53
55 to 64 years old..............	22	49	52	$75,000 to $99,999.............	18	76	71
65 years old and over..........	17	30	34	$100,000 to $199,999..........	31	84	80
				$200,000 and over.............	8	76	85

[1] Age is based on the sole or co-decision maker for household saving and investing. [2] Total reported is household income before taxes in prior year.

Source: Investment Company Institute, Washington, DC, *ICI Research Perspective*, "Ownership of Mutual Funds, Shareholder Sentiment, and Use of the Internet, 2012," Vol. 18, No. 6, November 2012 ©.

Table 1238. Characteristics of Mutual Fund Owners: 2012

[In percent, except as indicated. Mutual fund ownership includes holdings of money market, stock, bond, and hybrid mutual funds; and funds owned through variable annuities, Individual Retirement Accounts (IRAs), Keoghs, and employer-sponsored retirement plans. 2012 data based on a national probability sample of 1,786 primary financial decision-makers in households with mutual fund investments. For definition of mutual fund, see headnote, Table 1239. For definition of median, see Guide to Tabular Presentation]

Characteristic	Total	Age [1]				Household income [2]			
		Under 35 years old	35 to 54 years old	55 to 64 years old	65 years old and over	Less than $50,000	$50,000 to $99,000	$100,000 to $149,000	$150,000 or more
Median age [1] (years).......................	51	31	46	59	72	53	51	50	49
Median household income [2] (dol.)............	80,000	70,000	87,500	85,700	62,500	35,000	70,000	120,000	182,000
Median household financial assets [3] (dollars).................................	190,000	50,000	150,100	350,000	350,000	62,500	100,000	250,000	500,000
Own an IRA....................................	68	59	69	71	71	60	63	75	81
Household with defined contribution retirement plan(s) [4].....................	80	85	87	83	54	66	80	89	89
401(k) plan..................................	65	69	75	69	31	50	62	74	81
403(b), state, local, or federal government plan............................	35	30	34	42	34	27	35	42	39
Median mutual fund assets (dol.)..............	100,000	28,000	100,000	200,000	150,000	40,000	70,000	150,000	300,000
Own:									
Equity funds.................................	79	79	80	82	73	65	77	84	89
Bond funds..................................	50	52	46	54	52	39	48	53	58

[1] See Table 1237, footnote 1. [2] See Table 1237, footnote 2. [3] Includes assets in employer-sponsored retirement plans but excludes value of primary residence. [4] For definition of defined contribution plan, see headnote, Table 575.

Source: Investment Company Institute, Washington, DC, *Profile of Mutual Fund Shareholders, 2012*, February 2013 ©.

Table 1239. Mutual Funds—Summary: 2000 to 2012

[Number of funds and assets as of December 31 (6,965 represents $6,965,000,000,000). A mutual fund is an open-end investment company that continuously issues and redeems shares that represent an interest in a pool of financial assets. Excludes data for funds that invest in other mutual funds. Minus sign (-) indicates net redemptions]

Type of fund	Unit	2000	2005	2006	2007	2008	2009	2010	2011	2012
Number of funds, total.....................	**Number**	**8,155**	**7,974**	**8,118**	**8,026**	**8,022**	**7,684**	**7,580**	**7,637**	**7,596**
Equity funds....................................	Number	4,372	4,571	4,750	4,742	4,802	4,616	4,547	4,581	4,514
Hybrid funds....................................	Number	519	482	495	476	483	471	475	495	540
Bond funds.....................................	Number	2,225	2,051	2,026	2,003	1,954	1,893	1,906	1,929	1,962
Money market funds, taxable [1].............	Number	704	593	573	545	534	476	442	431	400
Money market funds, tax-exempt [2]..........	Number	335	277	274	260	249	228	210	201	180
Assets, total.................................	**Bil. dol.**	**6,965**	**8,891**	**10,398**	**12,001**	**9,604**	**11,120**	**11,821**	**11,622**	**13,045**
Equity funds....................................	Bil. dol.	3,939	4,887	5,833	6,417	3,641	4,880	5,585	5,205	5,934
Hybrid funds....................................	Bil. dol.	364	610	721	807	552	695	799	839	991
Bond funds.....................................	Bil. dol.	817	1,368	1,505	1,692	1,578	2,229	2,633	2,886	3,426
Money market funds, taxable [1].............	Bil. dol.	1,611	1,690	1,969	2,618	3,339	2,917	2,474	2,400	2,406
Money market funds, tax-exempt [2]..........	Bil. dol.	234	336	369	468	494	399	330	292	287
Net new cash flow:										
Equity funds....................................	Bil. dol.	315	124	148	74	-228	(Z)	-37	-130	-153
Hybrid funds....................................	Bil. dol.	-36	37	18	42	-26	10	24	30	46
Bond funds.....................................	Bil. dol.	-50	31	60	108	30	380	241	124	304
Money market funds............................	Bil. dol.	159	62	245	654	637	-539	-525	-124	(-Z)

Z Less than $500 million. [1] Funds invest in short-term, high-grade securities sold in the money market. [2] Funds invest in municipal securities with relatively short maturities.

Source: Investment Company Institute, Washington, DC, *Investment Company Fact Book*, annual ©. For more information, see <http://www.ici.org/>.

Table 1240. Mutual Fund Shares—Holdings and Net Purchases by Type of Investor: 2000 to 2012

[In billions of dollars (4,433 represents $4,433,000,000,000). Holdings as of Dec. 31. For definition of mutual fund, see headnote, Table 1239. Excludes money market mutual funds, exchange-traded funds, and funding vehicles for variable annuities. Minus sign (−) indicates net sales]

Type of investor	Holdings					Net purchases				
	2000	2005	2010	2011	2012	2000	2005	2010	2011	2012
Total..	4,433	6,046	7,873	7,871	9,324	237.6	260.2	370.1	338.4	735.7
Households, nonprofit organizations.............	2,708	3,636	4,618	4,453	5,372	79.5	179.9	235.3	192.5	501.8
Nonfinancial corporate business..................	118	134	187	166	182	0.3	0.7	11.1	-12.8	0.3
State and local governments......................	31	32	39	37	35	1.2	0.5	-4.9	-2.0	-7.2
Rest of the world....................................	149	242	514	735	958	-9.2	32.3	111.5	147.4	153.4
U.S.-chartered depository institutions............	15	17	45	42	59	2.5	-1.8	-5.8	-0.8	8.3
Credit unions......................................	2	2	2	2	2	-0.3	-1.0	0.2	0.3	0.4
Property-casualty insurance companies.........	3	6	6	5	6	0.4	0.3	-0.1	-0.1	-0.1
Life insurance companies.........................	97	109	156	150	159	5.6	-9.9	1.0	1.1	1.3
Private pension funds..............................	1,132	1,585	2,085	2,072	2,307	107.7	70.0	35.1	27.4	71.1
State and local government retirement funds....	178	282	223	208	244	49.9	-10.8	-13.2	-14.6	6.5

Source: Board of Governors of the Federal Reserve System, "Federal Reserve Statistical Release, Z.1, Financial Accounts of the United States," June 2013, <http://www.federalreserve.gov/releases/z1/>.

Table 1241. Retirement Assets by Type of Asset: 2000 to 2012

[In billions of dollars, except as indicated (11,604 represents $11,604,000,000,000). As of December 31]

Institution	2000	2005	2007	2008	2009	2010	2011	2012
Retirement assets, total................................	11,604	14,592	17,930	14,155	16,214	17,925	17,959	19,500
IRA assets [1].....................................	2,629	3,425	4,748	3,681	4,363	4,839	4,872	5,407
Bank and thrift deposits [2]....................	250	278	340	391	431	461	482	508
Life insurance companies [3]...................	204	311	331	318	323	345	358	363
Mutual funds....................................	1,262	1,715	2,316	1,610	1,979	2,230	2,199	2,473
Securities held in brokerage accounts [1,4]...	913	1,121	1,760	1,362	1,630	1,803	1,833	2,063
Traditional [1]....................................	2,407	3,034	4,187	3,257	3,855	4,250	4,276	4,740
Roth [1]...	78	156	232	177	215	265	270	310
SEP and SAR-SEP [1,5]..........................	134	193	266	201	235	260	261	285
SIMPLE [1,6]......................................	10	42	62	46	58	64	65	72
Defined contribution plans...........................	2,867	3,575	4,354	3,378	4,018	4,545	4,594	5,057
401(k) plans....................................	1,739	2,399	2,983	2,208	2,746	3,148	3,200	3,565
403(b) plans....................................	518	620	736	620	701	759	751	795
457 plans.......................................	110	143	173	140	169	189	193	212
Other defined contribution plans [7]..........	500	413	461	411	402	449	450	485
State and local government pension plans..........	2,340	2,815	3,385	2,519	2,808	3,042	2,943	3,212
Private defined benefit plans.........................	2,020	2,262	2,646	1,979	2,228	2,481	2,418	2,556
Federal pension plans [8]............................	797	1,072	1,197	1,222	1,325	1,425	1,510	1,582
Annuities [9]...	951	1,443	1,600	1,376	1,471	1,593	1,623	1,687
Memo:								
Mutual fund retirement assets........................	2,574	3,629	4,844	3,338	4,201	4,766	4,703	5,348
Percent of total retirement assets....................	22	25	27	24	26	27	26	27
Percent of all mutual funds...........................	37	41	40	35	38	40	40	41

[1] Data for 2009 through 2012 are estimated. [2] Includes Keogh deposits. [3] Annuities held by IRAs, excluding variable annuity mutual fund IRA assets. [4] Excludes mutual fund assets held through brokerage accounts, which are included in mutual funds. [5] Simplified Employee Pension IRAs and salary reduction (SAR) (SEP) IRAs. [6] Savings Incentive Match Plan for Employees (SIMPLE) IRAs. [7] Includes Keoghs and other defined contribution plans (profit-sharing, thrift-savings, stock bonus, and money purchase) without 401(k) features. [8] Federal pension plans include U.S. Treasury security holdings of the civil service retirement and disability fund, the military retirement fund, the judicial retirement funds, the Railroad Retirement Board, and the foreign service retirement and disability fund. These plans also include securities held in the National Railroad Retirement Investment Trust and Federal Employees Retirement System (FERS) Thrift Savings Plan (TSP). [9] Annuities include all fixed and variable annuity reserves at life insurance companies less annuities held by IRAs, 403(b) plans, 457 plans, and private pension funds. Some of these annuity reserves represent assets of individuals held outside retirement plan arrangements and IRAs; however, information to separate out such reserves is not available.

Source: Investment Company Institute, "The U.S. Retirement Market, Fourth Quarter 2012" (December), <http://www.ici.org/info/ret_12_q1_data.xls.>.

Table 1242. Assets of Private and Public Pension Funds by Type of Fund: 1990 to 2012

[In billions of dollars (3,269 represents $3,269,000,000,000). As of end of year. Except for corporate equities, represents book value. Excludes social security trust funds; see Table 570]

Type of pension fund	1990	2000	2005	2007	2008	2009	2010	2011	2012
Total, all types	3,269	9,084	11,431	13,103	10,442	11,837	13,081	13,279	14,243
Private funds	2,199	5,994	7,586	8,620	6,791	7,790	8,706	8,897	9,467
Insured [1]	570	1,526	2,197	2,512	2,223	2,347	2,563	2,594	2,831
Noninsured [2, 3]	1,629	4,468	5,389	6,108	4,568	5,443	6,143	6,302	6,636
Credit market instruments [3]	464	622	700	1,043	833	843	968	1,020	983
Treasury securities	122	112	117	186	147	182	216	250	294
Corporate and foreign bonds	158	266	290	447	375	360	443	442	361
Corporate equities	606	1,971	2,442	1,936	1,380	1,647	1,938	1,949	2,171
Mutual fund shares	40	1,132	1,585	1,831	1,362	1,828	2,085	2,072	2,307
Unallocated insurance contracts [4]	215	308	338	370	279	389	399	414	383
State and local government employee retirement funds [3]	730	2,293	2,773	3,286	2,429	2,722	2,949	2,873	3,193
Credit market instruments [3]	402	743	717	850	823	737	759	761	763
Corporate and foreign bonds	142	314	336	463	485	383	388	364	305
Corporate equities	285	1,299	1,629	1,936	1,267	1,618	1,778	1,702	1,993
Mutual fund shares	8	178	282	305	167	205	223	208	244
Federal government retirement funds [5]	340	797	1,072	1,197	1,222	1,325	1,425	1,510	1,582

[1] Annuity reserves held by life insurance companies, excluding unallocated contracts held by private pension funds. [2] Private defined benefit plans and defined contribution plans (including 401(k) type plans). [3] Includes other types of assets not shown separately. [4] Assets held at life insurance companies (e.g., guaranteed investment contracts (GICs), variable annuities). [5] Includes the Federal Employees Retirement System Thrift Savings Plan, the National Railroad Retirement Investment Trust, and nonmarketable government securities held by federal government retirement funds.

Source: Board of Governors of the Federal Reserve System, "Federal Reserve Statistical Release, Z.1, Financial Accounts of the United States," June 2013, <http://www.federalreserve.gov/releases/z1/>.

Table 1243. Annual Revenues of Selected Securities Industries: 2005 to 2011

[In millions of dollars (295,806 represents $295,806,000,000). Covers taxable and tax-exempt employer firms only. Based on Service Annual Survey. Estimates have been adjusted to the results of the 2007 Economic Census. See Appendix III]

Kind of business	NAICS code [1]	2005	2007	2008	2009	2010	2011
Securities, commodity contracts, and other financial investment activities	523	(NA)	(NA)	(NA)	525,960	532,938	526,688
Securities and commodity contracts intermediation and brokerage	5231	295,806	371,500	199,367	295,424	284,557	267,166
Investment banking and securities dealing	52311	155,507	203,139	118,246	167,559	155,868	135,457
Securities brokerage	52312	131,833	155,797	68,118	115,635	114,544	117,981
Commodity contracts dealing	52313	4,941	6,981	6,114	7,025	8,748	8,122
Commodity contracts brokerage	52314	3,525	5,583	6,889	5,205	5,397	5,606
Securities and commodity exchanges	5232	(NA)	(NA)	(NA)	11,102	10,933	11,860
Other financial investment activities	5239	132,559	200,858	195,769	219,434	237,448	247,662
Miscellaneous intermediation	52391	(NA)	(NA)	(NA)	20,307	23,562	24,111
Portfolio management	52392	113,562	177,941	173,590	154,688	167,061	172,421
Investment advice	52393	18,997	22,917	22,179	22,547	22,952	25,834
All other financial investment activities	52399	(NA)	(NA)	(NA)	21,892	23,873	25,296

NA Not available. [1] Data is based on 2007 NAICS; see text, this section and Section 15.

Source: U.S. Census Bureau, Annual and Quarterly Services, "2011 Annual Services," <http://www.census.gov/services/index.html>, accessed August 2013.

Table 1244. Securities Industry—Financial Summary: 2000 to 2011

[In billions of dollars, except as indicated (349.5 represents $349,500,000,000). Minus sign (−) indicates negative loss]

Type	2000	2004	2005	2006	2007	2008	2009	2010	2011
Number of firms	7,258	6,284	6,016	5,808	5,561	5,261	5,132	4,907	4,708
Revenues, total	349.5	242.9	332.5	440.4	495.1	303.2	287.0	262.0	245.8
Commissions	54.1	47.6	46.8	49.2	54.3	56.3	49.0	47.0	47.7
Trading/investment gains	70.8	30.7	30.7	48.2	4.1	-60.0	45.3	31.2	10.2
Underwriting profits	18.7	19.1	19.9	23.6	26.5	18.7	22.6	24.4	22.9
Margin interest	24.5	7.0	13.3	23.7	32.3	18.4	4.5	5.0	6.2
Mutual fund sales	19.4	18.5	20.7	23.3	26.2	22.3	17.2	18.8	19.4
Other	161.9	120.1	201.2	272.3	351.6	247.6	148.4	135.5	139.3
Expenses, total	310.4	219.7	311.3	407.0	490.4	328.7	211.6	224.0	228.9
Interest expense	131.9	59.7	140.2	217.9	282.2	128.0	21.9	22.4	20.3
Compensation	95.2	83.5	88.8	102.2	105.7	96.1	95.4	102.1	102.4
Commissions/clearance paid	15.5	17.4	18.6	21.5	25.9	26.5	23.3	24.0	25.4
Other	67.8	59.2	63.6	63.8	76.6	78.1	71.0	75.5	80.8
Net income, pretax	39.1	23.2	21.2	33.3	4.7	-25.5	75.4	38.0	16.8
Pre-tax profit margin (percent)	11.2	9.5	6.4	7.6	0.9	-8.4	26.3	14.5	6.9
Pre-tax return on equity (percent)	31.1	15.0	13.1	21.3	2.5	-13.9	38.2	17.1	7.5
Assets	2,866	4,831	5,215	5,908	6,772	4,436	4,340	4,757	4,662
Liabilities	2,728	4,671	5,051	5,743	6,586	4,255	4,125	4,526	4,444
Ownership equity	138	160	164	165	186	181	214	231	218

Source: U.S. Securities and Exchange Commission, "Select SEC and Market Data Fiscal 2012," and earlier reports, <http://www.sec.gov/about.shtml>, accessed August 2013.

Table 1245. Life Insurance in Force and Purchases in the United States—Summary: 1990 to 2012

[As of December 31 or calendar year, as applicable (389 represents 389,000,000). Covers life insurance with life insurance companies only. Data represents all life insurance in force on lives of U.S. residents whether issued by U.S. or foreign companies]

Year	Number of policies, total (millions)	Life insurance in force			Life insurance purchases [1]					
		Value (bil. dol.)			Number (1,000)			Amount (bil. dol.)		
		Total [2]	Individual	Group	Total	Individual	Group	Total	Individual	Group
1990.......	389	9,393	5,391	3,754	28,791	14,199	14,592	1,529	1,070	459
2000.......	369	15,953	9,376	6,376	34,882	13,345	21,537	2,515	1,594	921
2005.......	373	18,399	9,970	8,263	34,519	11,407	23,112	2,836	1,796	1,040
2007.......	374	19,539	10,232	9,158	30,788	10,826	19,962	2,994	1,891	1,103
2008.......	335	19,120	10,254	8,717	28,599	10,207	18,392	2,943	1,870	1,073
2009.......	291	18,138	10,324	7,688	29,190	10,139	19,051	2,900	1,744	1,156
2010.......	284	18,426	10,484	7,831	28,621	10,123	18,498	2,809	1,673	1,135
2011.......	286	19,219	10,994	8,120	27,177	10,309	16,867	2,832	1,673	1,160
2012.......	272	19,321	11,215	8,012	27,063	10,306	16,757	2,800	1,679	1,121

[1] Excludes revivals, increases, dividend additions, and reinsurance acquired. Includes long-term credit insurance (life insurance on loans of more than 10 years' duration). [2] Includes other types of policies not shown separately.

Source: American Council of Life Insurers, Washington, DC, *Life Insurers Fact Book*, annual ©.

Table 1246. U.S. Life Insurance Companies—Summary: 2000 to 2012

[As of December 31 or calendar year, as applicable (811.5 represents $811,500,000,000). Covers domestic and foreign business of U.S. companies. Includes annual statement data for companies that primarily are health insurance companies. Beginning in 2005, includes fraternal benefit societies]

Item	Unit	2000	2005	2006	2007	2008	2009	2010	2011	2012
U.S. companies [1]............................	Number	1,269	1,119	1,072	1,009	976	946	917	895	868
Income..................................	**Bil. dol.**	**811.5**	**779.0**	**883.6**	**950.4**	**940.6**	**781.4**	**862.6**	**915.3**	**952.4**
Life insurance premiums..................	Bil. dol.	130.6	142.3	149.2	142.7	147.2	124.6	104.6	127.5	135.4
Annuity considerations [2]..................	Bil. dol.	306.7	277.1	302.7	314.2	328.1	231.6	293.6	334.9	348.1
Health insurance premiums..............	Bil. dol.	105.6	118.3	141.2	151.5	165.0	166.2	172.7	171.6	172.3
Investment and other......................	Bil. dol.	268.5	241.4	290.4	342.0	300.3	259.1	291.6	281.3	296.6
Payments under life insurance and annuity contracts....................	Bil. dol.	375.2	365.7	422.7	461.0	445.1	374.9	365.6	393.2	402.2
Payments to life insurance beneficiaries................................	Bil. dol.	44.1	53.0	55.7	58.0	59.9	59.5	58.4	62.1	63.3
Surrender values under life insurance [3]................................	Bil. dol.	27.2	39.2	38.5	47.7	58.6	48.1	35.8	33.5	31.5
Surrender values under. annuity contracts [3, 4]............................	Bil. dol.	214.0	190.3	237.8	262.3	236.7	182.7	184.1	206.2	216.8
Policyholder dividends......................	Bil. dol.	20.0	17.9	18.4	19.5	19.1	16.2	15.9	15.5	15.5
Annuity payments [4]........................	Bil. dol.	68.7	63.9	71.1	72.3	69.6	67.1	70.1	74.5	74.0
Matured endowments.......................	Bil. dol.	0.6	0.6	0.6	0.6	0.6	0.6	0.6	0.6	0.4
Other payments.............................	Bil. dol.	0.6	0.7	0.6	0.6	0.6	0.8	0.7	0.7	0.6
Health insurance benefit payments..................................	Bil. dol.	78.8	79.6	97.0	106.1	118.9	122.0	122.5	120.6	123.8
BALANCE SHEET										
Assets....................................	**Bil. dol.**	**3,182**	**4,482**	**4,823**	**5,092**	**4,648**	**4,959**	**5,311**	**5,493**	**5,777**
Mortgage-backed securities..............	Bil. dol.	(NA)	(NA)	(NA)	(NA)	633	658	631	607	583
Government bonds.........................	Bil. dol.	364	590	579	580	261	331	413	463	459
Corporate securities.......................	Bil. dol.	2,238	3,136	3,413	3,662	2,671	2,979	3,271	3,353	3,619
Bonds...................................	Bil. dol.	1,241	1,850	1,882	1,991	1,535	1,593	1,700	1,807	1,894
Stocks..................................	Bil. dol.	997	1,285	1,531	1,670	1,136	1,386	1,570	1,546	1,725
Mortgages.................................	Bil. dol.	237	295	314	336	353	336	327	343	354
Real estate................................	Bil. dol.	36	33	33	35	32	28	28	29	31
Policy loans................................	Bil. dol.	102	110	113	117	122	123	127	129	131
Other......................................	Bil. dol.	204	319	371	362	576	504	515	568	601
Interest earned on assets [5].............	Percent	7.05	4.90	5.35	5.71	5.70	4.60	4.33	4.35	4.25
Obligations and surplus funds [6].........	Bil. dol.	3,182	4,482	4,823	5,092	4,648	4,959	5,311	5,493	5,777
Policy reserves............................	**Bil. dol.**	**2,712**	**3,360**	**3,608**	**3,791**	**3,471**	**3,812**	**4,098**	**4,244**	**4,449**
Annuities [7].............................	Bil. dol.	1,875	2,189	2,345	2,476	2,150	2,438	2,660	2,729	2,920
Group..................................	Bil. dol.	960	758	807	843	716	798	863	871	958
Individual..............................	Bil. dol.	881	1,415	1,521	1,615	1,422	1,624	1,780	1,840	1,943
Supplementary contracts [8]...........	Bil. dol.	34	16	17	18	13	16	17	18	19
Life insurance...........................	Bil. dol.	742	1,029	1,110	1,148	1,134	1,178	1,224	1,286	1,302
Health insurance........................	Bil. dol.	96	141	153	166	186	196	214	229	228
Liabilities for deposit-type contracts [9]...............................	Bil. dol.	21	456	487	517	454	416	420	413	431
Capital and surplus.......................	Bil. dol.	188	256	266	282	263	301	319	321	340

NA Not available. [1] Includes life insurance companies that sell accident and health insurance. [2] Beginning 2003, excludes certain deposit-type funds from income due to codification. [3] "Surrender values" include annuity withdrawals of funds. [4] Beginning 2003, excludes payments under deposit-type contracts. [5] Net rate. [6] Includes other obligations not shown separately. [7] Beginning 2003, excludes reserves for guaranteed interest contracts (GICs). [8] Data for 2000 include reserves for contracts with and without life contingencies; beginning 2003, includes only reserves for contracts with life contingencies. [9] Policyholder dividend accumulations for all years. Beginning 2003, also includes liabilities for guaranteed interest contracts, supplementary contracts without life contingencies, and premium and other deposits.

Source: American Council of Life Insurers, Washington, DC, *Life Insurers Fact Book*, annual ©.

Table 1247. Property and Casualty Insurance—Summary: 2000 to 2012

[In billions of dollars (305.1 represents $305,100,000,000). Minus sign (−) indicates loss]

Item	2000	2005	2008	2009	2010	2011	2012
Premiums, net written [1]	305.1	427.6	440.1	422.9	426.1	441.6	456.1
Automobile, private [2]	120.0	159.6	158.6	157.4	160.3	163.3	167.7
Automobile, commercial [2]	19.8	26.8	23.8	21.9	21.1	21.0	21.9
Homeowners' multiple peril	32.7	53.0	57.4	57.7	61.3	63.4	67.4
Commercial multiple peril	(NA)	29.7	30.1	28.9	28.9	29.9	31.0
Marine, inland and ocean	8.3	11.2	12.5	11.6	10.2	11.7	12.1
Workers' compensation	26.2	39.7	36.9	32.0	31.5	35.7	37.9
Medical malpractice	(NA)	9.7	9.5	9.2	9.1	8.9	8.7
Other liability [3]	(NA)	39.4	38.6	36.0	35.7	36.3	37.7
Reinsurance	(NA)	6.6	12.7	12.6	12.3	14.0	14.7
Losses and expenses	321.3	421.4	457.6	423.3	430.4	468.8	464.0
Underwriting gain/loss	−27.3	−5.6	−21.2	−3.0	−10.5	−36.2	−16.7
Investment income	42.0	49.7	51.5	47.1	47.6	49.2	47.7
Net income after taxes	4.4	44.2	3.0	28.7	35.2	19.5	33.5

NA Not available. [1] Excludes state funds. Includes other lines of insurance not shown separately. [2] Includes premiums for automobile liability and physical damage. [3] Coverages protecting against legal liability resulting from negligence, carelessness, or failure to act.

Source: Insurance Information Institute, New York, NY, *The III Insurance Fact Book*, annual; and *Financial Services Fact Book*, annual ©. Data from ISO and SNL Financial LC. See also <http://www.iii.org>.

Table 1248. Automobile Insurance—Average Expenditures Per Insured Vehicle by State: 2000 and 2009

[In dollars. Average expenditure equals total premiums written divided by liability car-years. A car-year is equal to 365 days of insured coverage for a single vehicle. The average expenditures for automobile insurance in a state are affected by a number of factors, including the underlying rate structure, the coverages purchased, the deductibles and limits selected, the types of vehicles insured, and the distribution of driver characteristics. The NAIC does not rank state average expenditures and does not endorse any conclusions drawn from this data]

State	2000	2009	State	2000	2009	State	2000	2009	State	2000	2009
U.S.	690	785	ID	505	555	MO	612	668	PA	699	811
AL	594	652	IL	652	728	MT	530	655	RI	825	969
AK	770	897	IN	570	620	NE	533	559	SC	620	738
AZ	792	837	IA	479	532	NV	829	944	SD	482	521
AR	606	656	KS	540	578	NH	665	718	TN	592	634
CA	672	754	KY	616	699	NJ	977	1,101	TX	678	860
CO	755	741	LA	806	1,099	NM	674	713	UT	620	716
CT	871	952	ME	528	598	NY	939	1,057	VT	568	646
DE	849	1,021	MD	757	929	NC	564	610	VA	576	667
DC	996	1,128	MA	946	860	ND	477	510	WA	722	826
FL	781	1,006	MI	702	913	OH	579	616	WV	680	815
GA	674	754	MN	696	694	OK	603	680	WI	545	591
HI	702	786	MS	654	738	OR	625	723	WY	496	623

Source: National Association of Insurance Commissioners (NAIC), Kansas City, MO, Auto Insurance Database Report, annual (copyright). Reprinted with permission of the NAIC. Further reprint or distribution strictly prohibited without prior written permission of the NAIC.

Table 1249. Renters and Homeowners Insurance—Average Premiums by State: 2009

[In dollars. Average premium equals premiums divided by exposure per house-years. A house-year is equal to 365 days of insured coverage for a single dwelling and is the standard measurement for homeowners insurance. The NAIC does not rank state average expenditures and does not endorse any conclusions drawn from these data]

State	Renters [1]	Home- owners [2]	State	Renters [1]	Home- owners [2]	State	Renters [1]	Home- owners [2]
U.S.	184	880	KS	172	991	NC	127	725
AL	216	987	KY	165	711	ND	114	853
AK	181	892	LA	245	1,430	OH	173	613
AZ	201	642	ME	144	651	OK	220	1,123
AR	226	919	MD	152	779	OR	174	544
CA	218	922	MA	219	1,035	PA	143	694
CO	176	893	MI	182	740	RI	182	1,069
CT	193	1,016	MN	144	919	SC	198	970
DE	154	610	MS	251	1,185	SD	116	645
DC	169	1,069	MO	178	881	TN [3]	211	794
FL	208	1,460	MT	149	751	TX [3]	222	1,511
GA	214	787	NE	143	849	UT	155	544
HI	193	879	NV	202	703	VT	157	717
ID	158	485	NH	151	757	VA	150	734
IL	171	789	NJ	169	848	WA	173	552
IN	172	717	NM	188	751	WV	175	671
IA	135	645	NY	213	1,021	WI	125	542
						WY	159	727

[1] Based on the HO-4 renters insurance policy for tenants. Includes broad named-peril coverage for the personal property of tenants. [2] Based on the HO-3 homeowner package policy for owner-occupied dwellings, 1–4 family units. Provides "all risks" coverage (except those specifically excluded in the policy) on buildings, broad named-peril coverage on personal property, and is the most common package written. [3] The Texas Insurance Commissioner promulgates residential policy forms which are similar but not identical to the standard forms.

Source: National Association of Insurance Commissioners (NAIC), Kansas City, MO, Dwelling Fire, Homeowners Owner-Occupied, and Homeowners Tenant and Condominium/Cooperative Unit Owners Insurance (copyright). Reprinted with permission of the NAIC. Further reprint or distribution strictly prohibited without prior written permission of the NAIC.

Table 1250. Real Estate and Rental and Leasing—Nonemployer Establishments and Receipts by Kind of Business: 2009 to 2011

[2,372.9 represents 2,372,900. Includes only firms subject to federal income tax. Nonemployers are businesses with no paid employees. Data originate chiefly from administrative records of the Internal Revenue Service; see Appendix III]

Kind of business	NAICS code [1]	Establishments (1,000)			Receipts (mil. dol.)		
		2009	2010	2011	2009	2010	2011
Real estate & rental & leasing, total...............	**53**	**2,372.9**	**2,343.1**	**2,345.8**	**208,306**	**209,549**	**215,428**
Real estate.............................	531	2,290.8	2,262.2	2,265.1	201,787	203,065	208,912
Lessors of real estate.........................	5311	987.3	989.3	1,022.4	134,896	135,015	139,503
Offices of real estate agents & brokers................	5312	658.8	641.6	612.8	24,721	25,502	25,728
Activities related to real estate................	5313	644.7	631.3	629.8	42,169	42,549	43,681
Rental & leasing services.....................	532	80.1	78.9	78.6	6,328	6,288	6,311
Automotive equipment rental & leasing...............	5321	19.0	18.3	18.1	997	990	965
Consumer goods rental.................	5322	18.0	18.3	18.4	765	779	799
General rental centers................	5323	4.6	4.8	5.0	392	409	425
Commercial/industrial equipment rental & leasing...........	5324	38.6	37.5	37.0	4,175	4,109	4,121
Lessors of other nonfinancial intangible assets................	533	1.9	2.0	2.1	191	197	206

[1] Based on 2007 North American Industry Classification System (NAICS). For more information, see text, Section 15.

Source: U.S. Census Bureau, Nonemployer Statistics, "Geographic Area Series: Nonemployer Statistics for the US, States, Metropolitan Areas, and Counties," <http://factfinder2.census.gov>, accessed June 2013.

Table 1251. Real Estate and Rental and Leasing—Establishments, Employees, and Payroll: 2010 and 2011

[347.3 represents 347,300. Covers establishments with payroll. Based on the North American Industry Classification System (NAICS), 2007. Employees are for the week including March 12. Most government employees are excluded. For statement on methodology, see Appendix III]

Kind of business	NAICS code	Establishments (1,000)		Employees (1,000)		Payroll (bil. dol.)	
		2010	2011	2010	2011	2010	2011
Real estate & rental & leasing, total.......................	**53**	**347.3**	**341.7**	**1,946.4**	**1,917.6**	**80.5**	**84.0**
Real estate............................	531	287.8	285.8	1,407.9	1,397.1	58.7	60.8
Lessors of real estate........................	5311	114.4	115.8	513.3	517.2	18.7	20.1
Offices of real estate agents & brokers...............	5312	89.2	85.6	278.0	266.5	12.7	13.1
Activities related to real estate...............	5313	84.2	84.4	616.6	613.4	27.4	27.6
Rental & leasing services....................	532	57.2	53.5	509.4	491.4	19.3	20.5
Automotive equipment rental & leasing.................	5321	11.1	11.5	149.2	149.6	5.5	5.9
Passenger car rental & leasing..............	53211	5.6	6.1	([1])	([1])	3.5	3.8
Truck, utility trailer & RV rental & leasing..................	53212	5.6	5.4	46.0	48.2	2.0	2.0
Consumer goods rental [2].....................	5322	27.9	23.9	193.0	170.6	5.1	5.1
Video tape & disc rental.....................	53223	10.9	6.7	79.9	([3])	1.2	1.0
Home health equipment rental................	532291	3.8	3.8	36.6	37.1	1.6	1.6
General rental centers....................	5323	4.2	4.0	25.3	24.7	0.9	0.9
Commercial/industrial equipment rental & leasing [2]........	5324	13.9	14.1	141.8	146.5	7.9	8.7
Construction, transportation, mining equipment rental and leasing...............	53241	5.5	5.4	55.4	57.1	3.4	3.7
Lessors of other nonfinancial intangible assets...............	533	2.4	2.4	29.2	29.2	2.4	2.7

[1] Over 100,000 employees. [2] Includes industries not shown separately. [3] Between 50,000 to 99,999 employees.

Source: U.S. Census Bureau, "County Business Patterns," <http://www.census.gov/econ/cbp/index.html>, accessed August 2013.

Table 1252. Rental and Leasing Services—Revenue by Kind of Business: 2005 to 2011

[In millions of dollars (107,559 represents $107,559,000). Covers taxable and tax-exempt employer firms. Data are based on the 2007 North American Industry Classification System (NAICS); see text, this section and Section 15. Estimates have been adjusted using the results of the 2007 Economic Census. Based on Service Annual Survey; see Appendix III]

Kind of business	NAICS code	2005	2007	2008	2009	2010	2011
Rental & leasing services........................	**532**	**107,559**	**121,685**	**123,566**	**110,223**	**111,250**	**118,661**
Automotive equipment rental & leasing........................	5321	42,324	44,982	46,094	41,987	42,385	45,854
Passenger car rental & leasing........................	53211	26,305	29,222	30,299	28,537	28,922	31,459
Truck, utility trailer, & RV rental & leasing.......................	53212	16,019	15,760	15,795	13,450	13,463	14,395
Consumer goods rental [1]......................	5322	22,840	(NA)	(NA)	(NA)	21,914	21,910
Video tape & disc rental........................	53223	9,023	9,262	8,474	7,384	6,579	5,998
Home health equipment rental.......................	532291	5,073	5,877	5,921	5,534	5,673	5,766
General rental centers........................	5323	3,553	4,249	4,188	3,727	3,897	4,037
Commercial/industrial equip. rental & leasing [1].........	5324	38,842	47,704	49,141	42,409	43,054	46,860
Construction/transportation/mining equipment rental and leasing........................	53241	21,123	26,130	26,325	22,187	21,802	24,210

NA Not available. [1] Includes other kinds of business, not shown separately.

Source: U.S. Census Bureau, Annual and Quarterly Services, "2011 Annual Services," <http://www.census.gov/services/index.html>, accessed August 2013.

Arts, Recreation, and Travel

This section presents data on the arts, entertainment, and recreation economic sector of the economy, and personal recreational activities, the arts and humanities, and domestic and foreign travel.

Arts, Entertainment, and Recreation Industry—The U.S. Census Bureau surveys—*County Business Patterns, Economic Census, Nonemployer Statistics* and *Service Annual Survey*, provide data on the arts, entertainment, and recreation sector. The *County Business Patterns* annual data includes number of establishments, number of employees, first quarter and annual payrolls, and number of establishments by employment size class. The *Economic Census*, conducted every five years for the years ending '2' and '7,' provides information on the number of establishments, receipts, payroll, and paid employees for the United States and various geographic levels. Nonemployer statistics are an annual tabulation of economic data by industry for active businesses without paid employees that are subject to federal income tax. The *Service Annual Survey* provides estimates of operation revenue of taxable firms and revenues and expenses of firms exempt from federal taxes for industries in this sector of the economy. See Appendix III for more details.

Recreation and leisure activities—Data on the participation in various recreation and leisure time activities are based on several sample surveys. Data on the public's involvement with arts events and activities are published by the National Endowment for Arts (NEA). The NEA's *Survey of Public Participation in the Arts* remains the largest periodic study of arts participation in the United States. The most recent data are from the 2008 survey. Data on participation in fishing, hunting, and other forms of wildlife associated recreation are published periodically by the U.S. Department of Interior, Fish and Wildlife Service. The most recent data are from the 2006 survey. Data on participation in various sports recreation activities are published by the National Sporting Goods Association. GfK Mediamark Research and Intelligence, LLC. also conducts periodic surveys on sports and leisure activities, as well as other topics.

Parks and recreation—The Department of the Interior has responsibility for administering the national parks. The National Park Service publishes information on visits to national park areas in its annual report, *National Park Statistical Abstract. The National Parks: Index* is an annual report which contains brief descriptions, with acreage and visits for each area administered by the service, plus certain "related" areas. This information can be found at: <https://irma.nps.gov/Stats/>. Statistics for state parks are compiled by the National Association of State Park Directors.

Travel—Statistics on arrivals and departures to the United States, cities and states visited by overseas travelers, and tourism sales and employment are reported by the International Trade Administration (ITA), Office of Travel & Tourism Industries (OTTI). Data on domestic travel and travel expenditures are published by the research department of the U.S. Travel Association. Other data on household transportation characteristics are in Section 23, Transportation.

Statistical reliability—For a discussion of statistical collection and estimation, sampling procedures, and measures of statistical reliability applicable to Census Bureau data, see Appendix III.

Table 1253. Arts, Entertainment, and Recreation Services—Estimated Revenue: 2005 to 2011

[In millions of dollars (166,912 represents $166,912,000,000). For taxable and tax-exempt employer firms. Selected estimates have been adjusted using the results of the 2007 Economic Census. Based on the Service Annual Survey, see Appendix III]

Industry	NAICS Code [1]	2005	2007	2008	2009	2010	2011
Arts, entertainment, and recreation............	71	**166,912**	**189,418**	**192,584**	**188,158**	**191,982**	**199,064**
Performing arts, spectator sports, and related industries...........	711	65,405	77,772	80,075	79,940	81,581	84,288
Performing arts companies....................	7111	13,144	13,573	13,753	14,321	14,822	15,983
Spectator sports.............................	7112	24,842	30,403	31,767	31,590	32,379	33,734
Sports teams and clubs...................	711211	14,564	18,794	20,393	20,691	21,504	22,419
Racetracks...............................	711212	7,358	8,197	7,545	7,069	7,216	7,377
Other spectator sports..................	711219	2,920	3,412	3,829	3,830	3,659	3,938
Promoters of performing arts, sports, and similar events...................	7113	12,374	16,122	16,299	16,167	16,327	15,896
Agents and managers for artists, athletes, entertainers and other public figures..............	7114	4,176	4,919	5,224	5,025	4,968	5,300
Independent artists, writers, and performers......	7115	10,869	12,755	13,032	12,837	13,085	13,375
Museums, historical sites, and similar institutions. ..	712	12,471	13,286	12,382	11,588	11,736	11,806
Amusement, gambling, and recreation industries. ..	713	89,036	98,360	100,127	96,630	98,665	102,970
Amusement parks and arcades....................	7131	11,926	13,544	14,071	13,330	13,991	15,050
Amusement and theme parks....................	71311	10,491	11,890	12,268	11,589	12,197	13,254
Amusement arcades................................	71312	1,435	1,654	1,803	1,741	1,794	1,796
Gambling industries................................	7132	24,040	25,135	25,624	25,100	25,729	26,850
Casinos (except casino hotels)....................	71321	15,753	16,557	16,874	16,410	16,619	17,471
Other gambling industries.........................	71329	8,287	8,578	8,750	8,690	9,110	9,379
Other amusement and recreation industries........	7139	53,070	59,681	60,432	58,200	58,945	61,070
Golf courses and country clubs....................	71391	19,356	21,195	21,077	20,342	19,980	20,168
Skiing facilities....................................	71392	1,989	2,257	2,476	2,440	2,514	2,606
Marinas...	71393	3,561	4,042	3,774	3,303	3,461	3,581
Fitness and recreational sports centers...........	71394	18,286	21,416	22,394	21,966	22,503	23,608
Bowling centers...................................	71395	3,232	3,403	3,338	3,123	3,103	3,197
All other amusement and recreation industries. ..	71399	6,646	7,368	7,373	7,026	7,384	7,910

[1] Data for 2005 through 2010 are based on 2002 NAICS; data for 2011 and thereafter are based on 2007 NAICS; see text, this section and Section 15.

Source: U.S. Census Bureau, Annual & Quarterly Services, "2011 Annual Services," <http://www.census.gov/services.index.html>, accessed August 2013.

Table 1254. Arts, Entertainment, and Recreation—Establishments, Revenue, Payroll, and Employees by Kind of Business: 2002 and 2007

[141,904 represents $141,904,000,000. For establishments with payroll only. Definition of paid employees varies among NAICS sectors. Data are based on the 2002 and 2007 economic censuses which are subject to nonsampling error. For details on survey methodology, sampling and nonsampling errors, see Appendix III]

Kind of business	2002 NAICS code [1]	Number of establishments		Revenue (mil. dol.)		Annual payroll (mil. dol.)		Paid employees (1,000)	
		2002	2007	2002	2007	2002	2007	2002	2007
Arts, entertainment, and recreation, total........	71	**110,313**	**124,620**	**141,904**	**189,417**	**45,169**	**58,359**	**1,849**	**2,061**
Performing arts, spectator sports, and related industries [2].......	711	37,735	43,868	58,286	77,773	21,231	27,839	423	438
Performing arts companies.......................	7111	9,303	8,838	10,864	13,574	3,267	3,980	138	128
Spectator sports..........................	7112	4,072	4,237	22,313	30,403	10,206	14,136	108	121
Promoters of performing arts, sports and similar events...........	7113	5,236	6,647	12,169	16,122	2,184	2,957	102	121
Agents and managers for artists, athletes, entertainers and others.................	7114	3,262	3,534	3,602	4,919	1,251	1,694	17	19
Museums, historical sites, and similar institutions [2]........	712	6,663	7,125	8,608	13,285	2,935	3,662	123	130
Amusement, gambling, and recreation industries [2]............	713	65,915	73,627	75,010	98,359	21,002	26,859	1,303	1,494
Amusement parks and arcades.................	7131	3,015	3,145	9,443	13,544	2,069	2,802	122	134
Gambling industries..........................	7132	2,072	2,327	18,893	25,135	3,596	4,566	158	170
Other amusement and recreation services...........	7139	60,828	68,155	46,674	59,680	15,337	19,490	1,023	1,190

[1] Based on 2002 North American Industry Classification System (NAICS); see text, this section and section 15. [2] Includes other industries not shown separately.

Source: U.S. Census Bureau, 2007 Economic Census, Core Business Statistics, "Comparative Statistics 2007 and 2002, Arts, Entertainment and Recreation," <http://www.census.gov/econ/census07/>, accessed July 2012.

Table 1255. Arts, Entertainment, and Recreation—Nonemployer Establishments and Receipts by Kind of Business (NAICS Basis): 2009 to 2011

[Firms in thousands (1,124.0 represents 1,124,000); receipts in millions of dollars (25,623 represents $25,623,000,000). Includes only firms subject to federal income tax. Nonemployers are businesses with no paid employees but with annual receipts of $1,000 or more.]

Kind of business	2007 NAICS code [1]	Firms (1,000)			Receipts (mil. dol.)		
		2009	2010	2011	2009	2010	2011
Arts, entertainment, and recreation............	71	**1,124.0**	**1,154.0**	**1,188.1**	**25,623**	**26,756**	**28,194**
Performing arts, spectator sports, and related industries............	711	974.4	1,004.9	1,037.2	20,093	21,053	22,411
Performing arts companies............	7111	58.7	61.2	63.6	1,157	1,249	1,322
Spectator sports............	7112	147.1	151.9	156.6	2,466	2,515	2,648
Promoters of performing arts, sports, and similar events............	7113	42.5	45.0	48.8	1,581	1,699	1,920
Agents/managers for artists, athletes, and other public figures............	7114	35.2	36.3	38.2	1,231	1,300	1,432
Independent artists, writers, and performers............	7115	691.0	710.3	730.0	13,658	14,290	15,089
Museums, historical sites, and similar institutions............	712	6.0	5.8	5.8	95	95	99
Amusement, gambling, and recreation industries............	713	143.6	143.4	145.1	5,435	5,607	5,684
Amusement parks and arcades............	7131	4.9	4.7	4.7	250	251	243
Gambling industries............	7132	10.2	10.2	9.7	1,166	1,185	1,056
Other amusement and recreation services............	7139	128.5	128.5	130.7	4,019	4,171	4,385

[1] Data are based on 2007 NAICS; see text, Section 15.

Source: U.S. Census Bureau, Nonemployer Statistics, "Geographic Area Series: Nonemployer Statistics for the US, States, Metropolitan Areas, and Counties," <http://factfinder2.census.gov>, accessed June 2013.

Table 1256. Arts, Entertainment, and Recreation—Establishments, Employees, and Payroll by Kind of Business (NAICS Basis): 2010 and 2011

[Employee in thousands (2,003.6 represents 2,003,600); payroll in millions of dollars (62,319 represents 62,319,000,000). Covers establishments with paid employees. Excludes self-employed individuals, employees of private households, railroad employees, agricultural production employees, and most government employees. For statement on methodology, see Appendix III]

Kind of business	2007 NAICS code [1]	Establishments		Employees [2] (1,000)		Payroll (mil. dol.)	
		2010	2011	2010	2011	2010	2011
Arts, entertainment, & recreation............	71	**123,151**	**123,327**	**2,003.6**	**2,003.1**	**62,319**	**63,572**
Performing arts, spectator sports............	711	44,325	44,890	424.8	427.7	30,747	31,240
Performing arts companies............	7111	8,649	8,711	117.5	113.1	3,970	3,912
Theater companies & dinner theaters............	71111	3,266	3,290	62.2	62.3	1,972	1,945
Dance companies............	71112	682	708	9.0	9.4	231	240
Musical groups & artists............	71113	4,306	4,328	36.4	35.4	1,441	1,479
Other performing arts companies............	71119	395	385	9.9	5.9	326	248
Spectator sports............	7112	4,351	4,349	118.5	124.5	15,528	16,086
Sports teams & clubs............	711211	841	872	55.1	59.9	13,298	13,737
Racetracks............	711212	681	666	45.2	47.3	1,278	1,367
Other spectator sports............	711219	2,829	2,811	18.1	17.3	953	982
Promoters of performing arts, sports, and similar events............	7113	6,608	6,781	127.1	129.6	3,256	3,130
Promoters of performing arts, sports, & similar events with facilities............	71131	2,764	2,893	102.7	105.5	2,240	2,045
Promoters of performing arts, sports, & similar events without facilities............	71132	3,844	3,888	24.5	24.1	1,015	1,085
Agents/managers for artists, athletes, and other public figures............	7114	3,547	3,637	17.7	17.7	1,934	2,004
Independent artists, writers, & performers............	7115	21,170	21,412	44.1	42.8	6,058	6,107
Museums, historical sites, & similar institutions............	712	7,327	7,323	125.9	128.8	3,763	3,937
Museums............	71211	4,795	4,797	80.0	82.1	2,419	2,567
Historical sites............	71212	1,213	1,200	9.6	9.5	224	232
Zoos & botanical gardens............	71213	587	590	30.2	30.6	930	933
Nature parks & other similar institutions............	71219	732	736	6.1	6.5	191	204
Amusement, gambling, & recreation industries............	713	71,499	71,114	1,452.9	1,446.7	27,810	28,395
Amusement parks & arcades............	7131	3,053	3,127	146.1	144.9	2,813	2,990
Amusement & theme parks............	71311	551	564	115.9	114.0	2,428	2,584
Amusement arcades............	71312	2,502	2,563	30.2	30.9	386	406
Gambling industries............	7132	2,672	2,809	173.7	168.4	5,110	5,092
Casinos (except casino hotels)............	71321	368	392	119.6	117.9	3,654	3,717
Other gambling industries............	71329	2,304	2,417	54.2	50.5	1,456	1,376
Other amusement & recreation services............	7139	65,774	65,178	1,133.1	1,133.4	19,886	20,313
Golf courses & country clubs............	71391	11,890	11,751	296.0	289.5	8,044	7,981
Skiing facilities............	71392	382	379	81.5	81.2	724	758
Marinas............	71393	3,937	3,896	26.7	26.6	927	953
Fitness & recreational sports centers............	71394	29,913	29,506	560.6	569.7	7,292	7,638
Bowling centers............	71395	4,297	4,208	74.9	72.7	963	953
All other amusement & recreation industries............	71399	15,355	15,438	93.4	93.7	1,936	2,028

[1] 2010 and 2011 data based on 2007 NAICS; see text, this section and Section 15. [2] For employees on the payroll for the period including March 12.

Source: U.S. Census Bureau, "County Business Patterns," <http://www.census.gov/econ/cbp/index.html>, accessed June 2013.

Table 1257. Expenditures Per Consumer Unit for Entertainment and Reading: 1985 to 2011

[Data are annual averages. In dollars, except as indicated. Based on the Consumer Expenditure Survey (CES). For description of survey, see text, Section 13; also see headnote, Table 714. For composition of regions, see map, inside front cover]

Year and characteristic	Entertainment and reading		Entertainment				Reading
	Total	Percent of total expenditures	Total	Fees and admissions	Audio and visual equipment and services	Other entertainment, supplies, and equipment services [1]	
1985...............................	1,311	5.6	1,170	320	371	479	141
1990...............................	1,575	5.6	1,422	371	454	597	153
1995...............................	1,775	5.5	1,612	433	542	637	163
1996...............................	1,993	5.9	1,834	459	561	814	159
1997...............................	1,977	5.7	1,813	471	577	766	164
1998...............................	1,907	5.4	1,746	449	535	762	161
1999...............................	2,050	5.5	1,891	459	608	824	159
2000...............................	2,009	5.3	1,863	515	622	727	146
2001...............................	2,094	5.3	1,953	526	660	767	141
2002...............................	2,218	5.5	2,079	542	692	845	139
2003...............................	2,187	5.4	2,060	494	730	835	127
2004...............................	2,348	5.4	2,218	528	788	903	130
2005...............................	2,514	5.4	2,388	588	888	912	126
2006...............................	2,493	5.2	2,376	606	906	863	117
2007...............................	2,816	5.7	2,698	658	987	1,053	118
2008...............................	2,951	5.8	2,835	616	1,036	1,183	116
2009...............................	2,803	5.7	2,693	628	975	1,090	110
2010...............................	2,604	5.4	2,504	581	954	970	100
2011, total...............	**2,687**	**5.4**	**2,572**	**594**	**977**	**1,001**	**115**
Age of reference person:							
Under 25 years old.............................	1,390	4.6	1,345	264	608	473	45
25 to 34 years old.............................	2,497	5.2	2,423	501	948	974	74
35 to 44 years old.............................	3,026	5.3	2,926	810	1,101	1,015	100
45 to 54 years old.............................	3,282	5.7	3,169	808	1,111	1,250	113
55 to 64 years old.............................	2,918	5.4	2,769	571	1,055	1,144	149
65 to 74 years old.............................	2,656	5.9	2,493	548	902	1,044	163
75 years old and over.........................	1,585	4.8	1,437	224	697	516	148
Hispanic or Latino origin of reference person:							
Hispanic...	1,784	4.2	1,738	339	839	559	46
Non-Hispanic...................................	2,813	5.5	2,688	630	996	1,062	125
Race of reference person:							
White, and all other races [2].............	2,879	5.6	2,753	644	992	1,118	126
Asian...	2,412	4.0	2,301	768	868	665	111
Black...	1,480	4.0	1,432	201	909	322	48
Region of residence:							
Northeast..	2,762	5.1	2,632	710	1,033	890	130
Midwest..	2,628	5.6	2,505	583	936	987	123
South...	2,438	5.3	2,350	443	984	922	88
West..	3,090	5.6	2,950	757	959	1,234	140
Size of consumer unit:							
One person.....................................	1,612	5.3	1,522	290	672	560	90
Two or more persons..........................	3,131	5.4	3,005	721	1,103	1,181	126
Two persons..................................	3,062	5.8	2,915	608	1,017	1,290	147
Three persons................................	2,993	5.1	2,876	670	1,151	1,055	117
Four persons.................................	3,528	5.4	3,416	1,007	1,248	1,161	112
Five persons or more........................	3,049	4.9	2,957	777	1,115	1,066	92
Income before taxes:							
Quintiles of income:							
Lowest 20 percent.............................	1,031	4.7	981	145	522	314	50
Second 20 percent............................	1,694	5.3	1,622	205	744	673	72
Third 20 percent...............................	2,222	5.2	2,121	379	914	828	101
Fourth 20 percent.............................	3,242	5.6	3,107	613	1,188	1,306	135
Highest 20 percent............................	5,246	5.5	5,027	1,629	1,515	1,884	219
Education:							
Less than a high school graduate.................	1,263	4.2	1,223	127	645	452	40
High school graduate...........................	2,037	5.1	1,967	289	926	752	70
High school graduate with some college.........	2,560	5.6	2,465	462	995	1,008	95
Associate's degree.............................	2,938	5.8	2,822	510	994	1,318	116
Bachelor's degree..............................	3,671	5.6	3,499	1,027	1,142	1,330	172
Master's, professional, doctoral degree..........	4,073	5.4	3,822	1,403	1,139	1,282	251

[1] Other equipment and services include pets, toys, hobbies, and playground equipment; and other entertainment supplies, equipment, and services. [2] All other races includes Native Hawaiian or other Pacific Islander, American Indian or Alaska Native, and approximately 1 percent reporting more than one race.

Source: U.S. Bureau of Labor Statistics, Consumer Expenditure Survey, "Consumer Expenditures in 2011," <http://www.bls.gov/cex/home.htm#tables>, accessed May 2013.

Table 1258. Personal Consumption Expenditures for Recreation: 1990 to 2012

[In billions of dollars (314.7 represents $314,700,000,000), except percent. Represents market value of purchases of goods and services by individuals and nonprofit institutions]

Type of product or service	1990	2000	2005	2009	2010	2011	2012
Total recreation expenditures..................	**314.7**	**633.7**	**804.6**	**861.8**	**888.3**	**922.1**	**966.2**
Percent of total personal consumption [1]......................	8.2	9.3	9.2	8.8	8.7	8.6	8.7
Video and audio equipment, computers, and related services....	81.1	181.2	239.0	264.8	276.4	284.0	295.3
Video and audio equipment................................	43.7	79.9	101.4	99.5	99.5	101.9	104.4
Information processing equipment.....................	9.6	44.1	67.0	81.2	90.3	92.0	96.1
Services related to video and audio goods and computers......	27.8	57.2	70.6	84.1	86.6	90.1	94.8
Sports and recreational goods and related services.............	74.2	146.0	184.1	172.6	174.2	181.5	192.8
Sports and recreational vehicles.....................	16.6	34.9	49.1	37.0	35.6	37.1	39.3
Other sporting and recreational goods.................	55.4	106.8	130.0	131.4	134.2	139.8	148.8
Maintenance and repair of recreational vehicles and sports equipment...	2.1	4.2	4.9	4.2	4.4	4.6	4.7
Membership clubs, sports centers, parks, theaters, and museums..	49.7	91.9	117.9	137.9	141.8	147.6	153.7
Membership clubs and participant sports centers..............	14.3	26.4	34.3	39.1	39.5	40.2	42.4
Amusements parks, campgrounds, and related recreational services..	19.2	31.1	33.6	37.2	38.8	41.5	45.4
Admissions to specified spectator amusements.................	14.4	30.6	43.7	55.5	57.3	59.6	59.8
Motion picture theaters..............................	5.1	8.6	9.7	11.5	11.8	11.4	11.7
Live entertainment, excluding sports......................	4.5	10.4	18.3	25.2	26.3	28.2	29.4
Spectator sports.......................................	4.8	11.6	15.7	18.8	19.2	20.0	18.7
Museums and libraries.................................	1.9	3.8	6.4	6.1	6.1	6.3	6.1
Magazines, newspapers, books, and stationery...................	47.3	81.0	85.0	84.6	89.9	95.1	100.9
Gambling...	23.7	67.6	96.5	105.0	105.6	108.9	112.5
Pets, pet products, and related services......................	18.8	39.7	57.2	73.3	75.9	79.5	85.1
Photographic goods and services...........................	16.7	19.7	17.7	15.3	15.4	15.9	15.6
Package tours [2].....................................	3.2	6.7	7.2	8.3	9.1	9.7	10.3

[1] See Table 705. [2] Consists of tour operators' and travel agents' margins. Purchases of travel and accommodations included in tours are accounted for separately in other personal consumption expenditures categories.

Source: U.S. Bureau of Economic Analysis, National Income and Product Accounts, "Table 2.5.5. Personal Consumption Expenditures by Function," <http://www.bea.gov/iTable/index_nipa.cfm>, accessed August 2013.

Table 1259. Performing Arts—Selected Data: 1990 to 2011

[Sales, receipts, and expenditures in millions of dollars (282 represents $282,000,000). For season ending in year shown, except as indicated]

Item	1990	1995	2000	2005	2006	2007	2008	2009	2010	2011
Legitimate theater: [1]										
Broadway shows:										
New productions........................	40	33	37	39	39	35	36	43	39	42
Attendance (mil.)........................	8.0	9.0	11.4	11.5	12.0	12.3	12.3	12.1	11.9	12.5
Playing weeks [2, 3]......................	1,070	1,120	1,464	1,494	1,501	1,509	1,560	1,548	1,464	1,588
Gross ticket sales.......................	282	406	603	769	862	939	938	943	1,020	1,080
Broadway road tours: [4]										
Attendance (mil.)........................	11.1	15.6	11.7	18.2	17.1	16.7	15.3	14.3	15.9	13.1
Playing weeks..........................	944	1,242	888	1,389	1,377	1,400	1,138	1,112	1,242	1,003
Gross ticket sales.......................	367	548	572	707	831	833	955	881	947	803
Nonprofit professional theatres: [5]										
Companies reporting [6]....................	185	215	262	1,490	1,893	1,910	1,919	1,825	1,807	(NA)
Gross income...........................	308	444	791	1,647	1,791	1,881	1,884	1,779	1,913	(NA)
Earned income........................	188	281	466	845	923	962	955	811	964	(NA)
Contributed income....................	119	163	325	802	868	919	929	968	948	(NA)
Gross expenses........................	306	445	708	1,530	1,667	1,742	1,860	1,892	1,870	(NA)
Productions...........................	2,265	2,646	3,241	12,000	14,000	17,000	15,000	17,000	16,000	(NA)
Performances.........................	46,131	56,608	66,123	169,000	172,000	197,000	202,000	187,000	163,000	(NA)
Total attendance (mil.)...................	15.2	18.6	22.0	32.5	30.5	31.0	32.0	30.0	31.0	(NA)
OPERA America professional member companies: [7]										
Number of companies reporting [8]........	98	88	98	93	94	97	85	84	97	83
Expenses [8]............................	321	435	637	742	752	872	826	816	883	688
Performances [8]........................	2,336	2,120	1,768	1,893	1,851	1,961	1,753	1744	1,677	1,407
Total attendance (mil.) [8, 9]..............	7.5	4.1	6.2	5	5.3	5.3	5.1	4.3	6.8	6.6
Main season attendance (mil.) [8, 10]	4.1	3.9	3.8	3.3	3.4	3.6	3.1	2.9	2.2	1.8
Symphony orchestras: [11]										
Concerts..............................	18,931	29,328	33,154	37,196	36,731	37,169	33,029	32,813	35,348	35,968
Attendance (mil.).......................	24.7	30.9	31.7	26.5	29.1	28.8	28.7	25.4	26	26
Gross revenue.........................	378	536	734	812	945	1,052	992	969	1,030	1,038
Operating expenses.....................	622	859	1,126	1,513	1,603	1,808	1,862	1,864	1,849	1,822
Support..............................	258	351	521	626	713	721	785	726	695	820

NA Not Available [1] Source: The Broadway League, New York, NY. For season ending in year shown. [2] All shows (new productions and holdovers from previous seasons). [3] Eight performances constitute one playing week. [4] North American Tours include U.S. and Canadian companies. [5] Source: Theatre Communications Group, New York, NY. For years ending on or prior to August 31. [6] Beginning in 2002, nonprofit theatre data is based on survey responses and extrapolated data from IRS Form 990. [7] Source: OPERA America, © 2004, 2005, 2011 Cultural Data Project. © 2001, 2009 OPERA America. For years ending on or prior to August 31. [8] U.S. and Canadian companies for 1999 and 2009-10; U.S. companies only for all other years. [9] Includes educational performances, outreach, etc. [10] For paid performances. Data for the Metropolitan Opera are not included. [11] Source: League of American Orchestras, New York, NY. For years ending August 31. Prior to 1995, represents 254 U.S. orchestras; beginning 1995, represents all U.S. orchestras, excluding college/university and youth orchestras. Beginning 1995, data based on 1,200 orchestras.

Source: Compiled from sources listed in footnotes. See also <http://www.livebroadway.com/>; <http://www.tcg.org/>; <http://www.operaamerica.org/>; and <http://www.americanorchestras.org/>.

Table 1260. Arts and Humanities—Selected Federal Aid Programs: 1990 to 2010

[In millions of dollars (170.8 represents $170,800,000), except as indicated. For fiscal year ending September 30. FY 2009 and FY 2010 include funds from the American Recovery and Reinvestment Act]

Type of fund and program	1990	1995	2000	2005	2006	2007	2008	2009	2010
National Endowment for the Arts:									
Funds available [1]	170.8	152.1	85.2	108.8	112.8	111.7	129.3	186.8	153.1
Program appropriation [2]	152.3	138.1	79.6	99.5	100.7	100.3	119.6	178.1	138.7
Grants awarded (number) [3]	4,252	3,534	1,906	2,161	2,293	2,158	2,219	3,075	2,731
Funds obligated [4,5]	157.6	147.9	83.5	104.4	107.0	106.5	125.5	176.2	141.1
National Endowment for the Humanities:									
Funds available [1]	140.6	152.3	102.6	119.8	121.5	122.3	128.6	134.5	146.6
Program appropriation	114.2	125.7	82.7	99.9	102.2	102.2	105.7	114.7	125.7
Matching funds [6]	26.3	25.7	15.1	15.9	15.2	15.2	14.3	14.3	14.3

[1] Includes other program funds not shown separately. Excludes administrative funds. [2] FY 1990–FY 1996 include Regular Program Funds, Treasury Funds, Challenge Grant Funds, and Policy, Planning, and Research Funds. FY 1997 includes Regular Program Funds, Matching Grant Funds, and Policy, Research and Technology Funds. FY 1998–FY 2000 includes Regular Program Funds and Matching Grant Funds. [3] Excludes cooperative agreements and interagency agreements. [4] Includes obligations for new grants, supplemental awards on previous years' grants, cooperative agreements, and interagency agreements. Excludes obligations funded with administrative funds. [5] Beginning with 1997 data, the grantmaking structure changed from discipline-based categories to thematic ones. [6] Represents federal funds obligated only upon receipt or certification by endowment of matching nonfederal gifts. Funds for matching grants are not allocated by program area because they are awarded on a grant-by-grant basis.

Source: U.S. National Endowment for the Arts, unpublished data; and U.S. National Endowment for the Humanities, *Annual Report 2011,* July 2012, and earlier reports. See also <http://www.neh.gov/about/legal/reports>.

Table 1261. Total State Arts Agency Legislative Appropriations: 2012 to 2013

[In thousands of dollars (260,212 represents 260,212,000). For fiscal year ending June 30 in most states. The National Assembly of State Arts Agencies (NASAA) is the membership organization of the nations' state and jurisdictional arts agencies. Legislative appropriations include funds designated to the state arts agency by state legislatures. These include line items, which are not controlled by the agency but passed through to designated entities. State arts agencies also receive monies from other sources including other state funds, the federal government (primarily the National Endowment for the Arts), private funds, and legislative earmarks. Minus sign (-) indicates decrease in spending]

State	Legislative appropriations including line items		Percent change, 2012 to 2013	State	Legislative appropriations including line items		Percent change, 2012 to 2013	State	Legislative appropriations including line items		Percent change, 2012 to 2013
	2012, revised	2013, enacted			2012, revised	2013, enacted			2012, revised	2013, enacted	
U.S. [1]	260,212	279,418	7.4	KS [5]	–	700	(NA)	NC	7,321	7,108	-2.9
AL	3,485	3,384	-2.6	KY	3,056	2,772	-9.3	ND	682	682	–
AK	790	798	1.0	LA	3,277	2,864	-12.6	OH	7,606	9,606	26.3
AZ [2]	–	–	(NA)	ME	685	670	-2.2	OK	4,010	4,010	–
AR [3]	1,643	2,928	78.2	MD	13,169	13,164	–	OR	1,995	1,926	-3.5
CA	3,893	4,249	9.1	MA	9,200	9,528	3.6	PA	9,065	9,065	–
CO	960	1,184	23.3	MI	1,317	4,900	271.9	RI	2,109	2,425	15.0
CT	7,188	6,253	-13.0	MN	29,673	30,820	3.9	SC	1,938	1,959	1.1
DE	1,682	1,691	0.5	MS	1,663	1,662	–	SD	662	791	19.6
DC [4]	4,798	11,190	133.2	MO	7,000	5,155	-26.4	TN	8,330	8,815	5.8
FL	6,023	10,404	72.7	MT	451	448	-0.7	TX	2,543	2,843	11.8
GA	574	579	0.8	NE	1,368	1,376	0.6	UT	5,149	3,413	-33.7
HI	5,152	5,104	-0.9	NV	962	1,082	12.5	VT	508	508	–
ID	675	687	1.8	NH	335	341	1.8	VA	3,795	3,795	–
IL	8,998	8,152	-9.4	NJ	16,397	16,397	–	WA	1,103	1,086	-1.5
IN	2,722	2,640	-3.0	NM	1,478	1,469	-0.6	WV	1,215	1,159	-4.6
IA	934	1,134	21.4	NY	36,205	39,974	10.4	WI	840	784	-6.6
								WY	1,204	1,308	8.6

– Represents zero. NA Not Available [1] Includes U.S. territories. [2] Arizona: agency receives no legislative appropriation; however, it will receive $1,380,000 in other state funds from state business license revenues in FY2013, the same amount it received in FY2012. [3] Arkansas: $1.3 million of the FY2013 appropriation will be released at the governor's discretion. The same amount was appropriated but not released in FY2012. [4] DC: a proposed $6.8 million increase to the agency has yet to be finalized; the DC budget must be approved by Congress. [5] Kansas: in FY2013 a new arts agency was created, the Kansas Creative Arts Industries Commission.

Source: National Assembly of State Arts Agencies, *State Arts Agency Revenues, Fiscal Year 2013,* February 2013. See also <http://www.nasaa-arts.org/>.

Table 1262. Personal Participation in Various Arts or Creative Activities: 2008

[In percent, except as indicated (224.8 represents 224,800,000). For persons 18 years old and over. Represents participation at least once in the prior 12 months]

Item	Adult population (millions)	Classical music [1]	Paint-ing [2]	Pottery/ Jewelry	Sewing [3]	Photo-graphy	Creative writing	Pur-chased art [4]	Choir/ chorale
Total........................	**224.8**	**3.1**	**9.0**	**6.0**	**13.1**	**14.7**	**6.9**	**5.9**	**5.2**
Sex: Male.......................	108.5	3.0	7.1	4.5	2.3	13.3	6.2	5.8	3.9
Female.........................	116.3	3.2	10.7	7.4	23.2	16.1	7.5	5.9	6.3
Race and ethnicity:									
White alone....................	154.5	3.5	9.4	6.9	15.5	16.1	7.0	7.4	4.9
African American alone......	25.6	2.0	6.8	3.5	7.6	10.0	7.5	1.8	10.3
Other alone....................	14.3	4.7	11.9	6.1	10.2	16.2	8.2	2.3	5.5
Hispanic.......................	30.4	1.1	7.4	3.6	7.1	10.9	5.3	2.8	2.2
Age: 18 to 24 years old........	28.9	5.9	14.7	6.4	9.0	17.8	11.3	4.3	6.1
25 to 34 years old............	39.9	3.7	11.3	6.1	10.0	16.1	9.7	6.8	3.8
35 to 44 years old............	41.8	3.0	9.9	7.5	11.4	18.6	6.2	5.6	4.3
45 to 54 years old............	43.9	2.5	7.4	7.0	15.4	14.6	6.4	6.6	6.8
55 to 64 years old............	33.3	2.4	6.8	5.4	15.7	13.0	4.4	6.8	5.3
65 to 74 years old............	19.9	1.8	5.0	4.1	17.7	10.4	5.2	6.0	6.2
75 years old and older.......	17.1	1.4	4.4	2.1	15.4	5.5	3.1	2.9	3.6

[1] Of those who reported playing a musical instrument in the last 12 months. [2] Includes painting, drawing, sculpture, and printmaking. [3] Includes weaving, crocheting, quilting, needlepoint, and sewing. [4] Of those who reported owning original art.

Source: U.S. National Endowment for the Arts, 2008 Survey of Public Participation in the Arts, November 2009. See also <http://www.nea.gov/research/researchreports_chrono.html>.

Table 1263. Attendance/Participation Rates for Various Arts Activities: 2008

[In percent, except as indicated (224.8 represents 224,800,000). For persons 18 years old and over. Represents attending, visiting, or reading at least once in the prior twelve months. Excludes elementary and high school performances]

Item	Adult popu-lation (million)	Jazz concert	Classical music concert	Musicals	Non-musical plays	Art muse-ums/ galleries	Craft/ visual art festivals	Parks/ historic build-ings [1]	Read litera-ture [2]
Total............................	**224.8**	**7.8**	**9.3**	**16.7**	**9.4**	**22.7**	**24.5**	**24.9**	**50.2**
Sex:									
Male..........................	108.5	7.7	8.5	14.4	8.2	21.4	20.5	24.4	41.9
Female........................	116.3	7.9	10.0	18.9	10.6	24.0	28.3	25.4	58.0
Race and ethnicity:									
White alone....................	154.5	8.8	11.3	20.0	11.4	26.0	29.3	29.5	55.7
African American alone..........	25.6	8.6	4.3	8.6	5.5	12.0	12.2	12.6	42.6
Other alone.....................	14.3	4.0	8.8	13.4	6.1	23.4	17.0	20.0	43.9
Hispanic.......................	30.4	3.9	3.8	8.1	4.3	14.5	13.7	14.0	31.9
Age:									
18 to 24 years old.............	28.9	7.3	6.9	14.5	8.2	22.9	17.8	21.9	51.7
25 to 34 years old.............	39.9	7.7	7.0	16.0	9.2	24.3	22.7	25.7	50.1
35 to 44 years old.............	41.8	7.2	8.9	18.2	8.9	25.7	27.2	26.8	50.8
45 to 54 years old.............	43.9	9.8	10.2	17.4	8.7	23.3	29.1	28.0	50.3
55 to 64 years old.............	33.3	9.7	11.6	19.5	12.3	24.3	28.9	27.6	53.1
65 to 74 years old.............	19.9	6.1	12.2	18.0	11.0	19.9	24.8	24.1	49.1
75 years old and older..........	17.1	4.0	9.7	10.0	7.4	10.5	12.7	11.2	42.3
Education:									
Grade school..................	11.2	1.5	1.8	1.7	0.7	3.8	4.9	3.8	18.5
Some high school..............	22.1	2.4	2.3	5.2	2.8	9.2	11.2	9.1	34.3
High school graduate...........	68.3	3.9	3.1	8.1	4.0	9.6	17.3	14.6	39.1
Some college..................	61.4	8.1	9.1	17.1	9.0	23.8	27.5	28.4	56.2
College graduate...............	41.3	13.7	16.7	30.1	17.5	40.6	35.8	39.4	66.6
Graduate school................	20.5	17.4	27.1	37.9	24.3	52.2	41.6	48.1	71.2
Income: [3]									
Less than $10,000.............	11.6	4.3	4.0	6.6	4.2	9.4	10.7	10.3	38.6
$10,000 to $19,999...........	19.3	3.6	3.9	6.3	3.7	10.3	13.0	11.4	38.3
$20,000 to $29,999...........	23.4	4.1	4.4	7.7	4.1	11.9	15.5	13.9	41.7
$30,000 to $39,999...........	22.6	7.1	6.8	11.0	6.7	16.3	21.8	19.9	43.2
$40,000 to $49,999...........	18.8	8.9	8.7	15.4	7.4	20.2	24.7	23.2	51.9
$50,000 to $74,999...........	40.7	7.6	9.5	15.4	8.6	23.9	26.2	26.8	50.1
$75,000 to $99,999...........	27.2	8.7	11.7	21.8	13.4	31.3	33.8	32.6	59.1
$100,000 to $149,999..........	21.4	13.4	14.8	32.0	14.1	34.4	34.5	41.2	62.1
$150,000 and over..............	16.0	15.4	22.8	40.1	24.2	51.9	37.5	47.3	71.2

[1] Visiting historic parks or monuments or touring buildings or neighborhoods for the historic or design value. [2] Literature is defined as poetry, novels, short stories, or plays. [3] Excludes results for respondents who did not report income.

Source: U.S. National Endowment for the Arts, 2008 Survey of Public Participation in the Arts, November 2009. See also <http://www.nea.gov/research/researchreports_chrono.html>.

Table 1264. Attendance/Participation in Various Leisure Activities: 2008

[In percent, except as indicated (224.8 represents 224,800,000). See headnote, Table 1262]

Item	Adult popu- lation (mil.)	Attendance at—		Participation in—					
		Movies	Sports events	Exercise	Playing sports	Outdoor activities	Garden- ing	Volun- teering/ charity work	Com- munity activities
Total.........................	**224.8**	**53.3**	**30.6**	**52.9**	**26.3**	**28.2**	**41.6**	**32.0**	**27.8**
Sex:									
Male..........................	108.5	52.7	34.9	52.1	33.2	31.1	33.6	28.9	26.2
Female........................	116.3	54.0	26.6	53.6	20.0	25.4	48.9	34.9	29.3
Race and Ethnicity:									
White alone..................	154.5	55.7	34.0	57.4	29.2	16.9	47.2	35.8	31.8
African American alone......	25.6	47.4	24.5	42.6	21.0	7.2	24.4	27.0	21.9
Other alone..................	14.3	49.3	21.8	48.6	23.5	26.1	40.1	25.7	22.7
Hispanic......................	30.4	48.1	22.1	40.7	17.9	17.3	28.0	20.1	14.7
Age:									
18 to 24 years old...........	28.9	74.2	37.4	57.4	42.0	34.8	15.1	27.2	19.4
25 to 34 years old...........	39.9	64.5	37.3	57.5	34.9	35.7	34.8	29.4	23.5
35 to 44 years old...........	41.8	59.5	36.7	59.5	32.0	34.3	43.9	37.6	33.2
45 to 54 years old...........	43.9	52.6	31.3	51.8	23.9	29.0	49.1	35.7	31.8
55 to 64 years old...........	33.3	46.2	25.9	51.8	17.1	22.4	52.4	33.4	29.7
65 to 74 years old...........	19.9	31.7	18.2	47.6	13.3	17.9	54.5	30.2	30.9
75 years old and over........	17.1	18.9	10.3	30.0	6.4	6.3	41.0	23.2	21.5
Education:									
Grade school..................	11.2	15.9	6.6	21.1	6.7	8.2	30.3	11.4	8.4
Some high school.............	22.1	37.9	17.8	35.7	19.0	17.8	29.5	17.7	14.8
High school graduate........	68.3	42.5	22.8	40.0	17.4	20.8	37.7	20.9	18.3
Some college..................	61.4	60.8	33.7	58.5	29.1	30.9	43.2	35.6	29.5
College graduate.............	41.3	68.8	44.9	70.8	38.9	39.8	49.0	48.1	42.6
Graduate school..............	20.5	71.6	44.2	77.1	40.0	42.3	53.3	51.5	48.0
Income: [1]									
Less than $10,000...........	11.6	32.3	14.9	35.6	15.9	14.6	25.3	16.0	15.0
$10,000 to $19,999.........	19.3	32.4	13.4	35.3	14.5	15.3	30.4	18.8	14.8
$20,000 to $29,999.........	23.4	38.2	21.1	40.4	14.9	18.3	35.4	19.6	18.1
$30,000 to $39,999.........	22.6	48.6	22.3	46.8	23.3	24.2	37.7	29.2	22.9
$40,000 to $49,999.........	18.8	54.0	28.7	54.9	26.5	28.7	44.9	31.5	25.9
$50,000 to $74,999.........	40.7	58.5	33.3	55.6	26.0	31.6	42.8	32.2	27.5
$75,000 or more..............	27.2	67.5	42.2	66.2	37.0	40.9	50.2	42.0	35.0
$100,000 to $149,999......	21.4	71.4	46.8	73.3	39.1	39.7	54.0	49.6	47.2
$150,000 or more............	16.0	76.7	53.1	73.2	46.0	43.9	50.9	49.0	43.9

[1] Excludes results for respondents who did not report income.

Source: U.S. National Endowment for the Arts, *2008 Survey of Public Participation in the Arts,* November 2009. See also <http://www.nea.gov/research/researchreports_chrono.html>.

Table 1265. Household Pet Ownership: 2011

[In percent, except as indicated (69.9 represents 69,900,000). Based on a sample survey of 50,347 households in 2012]

Item	Unit	Dogs	Cats	Birds	Horses
2011: Total companion pet population [1].................	**Million**	**69.9**	**74.1**	**8.3**	**4.9**
Number of households owning pets...................	Million	43.3	36.1	3.7	1.8
Percent of households owning companion pets [1]................	Percent	36.5	30.4	3.1	1.5
Average number owned per household.................	Number	1.6	2.1	2.3	2.7
PERCENT OF HOUSEHOLDS OWNING PETS					
Annual household income:					
Under $20,000.................	Percent	34.5	34.1	4.3	1.4
$20,000 to $34,999..................	Percent	40.0	36.8	4.0	2.1
$35,000 to $54,999..................	Percent	42.4	35.6	3.9	1.9
$55,000 to $84,999..................	Percent	43.8	34.0	3.3	1.9
$85,000 and over..................	Percent	43.9	31.7	3.1	1.9
Household size: [1]					
One person.....................	Percent	26.8	29.8	2.6	1.3
Two persons....................	Percent	40.1	34.6	3.2	1.8
Three persons..................	Percent	50.0	38.3	4.2	2.2
Four persons...................	Percent	53.7	34.9	4.3	2.0
Five or more persons...........	Percent	54.2	38.1	6.8	2.6
VETERINARY CARE AND EXPENDITURES					
Households obtaining veterinary care [2].................	Percent	81.3	55.1	12.4	53.8
Average visits per household per year...................	Number	2.6	1.6	0.3	1.9
Expenditures per household per year (mean)..................	Dollars	378	191	33	373
Expenditures per animal (mean)...................	Dollars	227	90	14	133

[1] As of December 31, 2011. [2] During the year.

Source: American Veterinary Medical Association, Schaumburg, IL, *U.S. Pet Ownership and Demographics Sourcebook, 2012,* (copyright). See also <http://www.avma.org/reference/marketstats/sourcebook.asp>.

Table 1266. Adult Participation in Selected Leisure Activities by Frequency: 2012

[In thousands (14,227 represents 14,227,000), except percent. For Fall 2012. Percent is based on total projected population of 232,469,000. Based on sample and subject to sampling error; see source]

Activity	Participated in the last 12 months [1]		Freqency of participation							
			Two or more times a week		Once a week		Two to three times a month		Once a month	
	Number	Percent	Number	Percent	Number	Percent	Number	Percent	Number	Percent
Adult education courses.....................	14,227	6.1	2,793	1.2	1,683	0.7	678	0.3	816	0.4
Attend auto shows............................	19,761	8.5	216	0.1	217	0.1	562	0.2	1,130	0.5
Attend art galleries or shows...............	16,185	7.0	164	0.1	142	0.1	841	0.4	1,460	0.6
Attend a circus................................	6,818	2.9	(Z)	(Z)	142	0.1	96	(Z)	278	0.1
Attend classical music/opera performances................................	8,001	3.4	61	(Z)	78	(Z)	310	0.1	677	0.3
Attend country music performances.........	12,823	5.5	28	(Z)	92	(Z)	173	0.1	481	0.2
Attend dance performances.................	9,564	4.1	116	0.1	98	(Z)	153	0.1	403	0.2
Attend horse races...........................	6,253	2.7	171	0.1	225	0.1	255	0.1	260	0.1
Attend other music performances [2].......	23,135	10.0	147	0.1	313	0.1	744	0.3	1,806	0.8
Attend rock music performances...........	22,231	9.6	266	0.1	205	0.1	911	0.4	1,572	0.7
Backgammon..................................	4,070	1.8	441	0.2	199	0.1	567	0.2	290	0.1
Baking...	53,957	23.2	8,730	3.8	7,334	3.2	12,137	5.2	8,965	3.9
Barbecuing....................................	69,804	30.0	10,499	4.5	10,556	4.5	16,330	7.0	9,829	4.2
Billiards/pool..................................	17,032	7.3	1,135	0.5	1,328	0.6	1,349	0.6	2,139	0.9
Bird watching..................................	10,814	4.7	4,330	1.9	1,144	0.5	808	0.4	797	0.3
Board games..................................	29,676	12.8	1,856	0.8	2,436	1.1	4,199	1.8	5,668	2.4
Book clubs....................................	6,070	2.6	194	0.1	216	0.1	517	0.2	2,430	1.1
Chess...	6,429	2.8	812	0.4	411	0.2	557	0.2	585	0.3
Concerts on radio............................	6,016	2.6	1,013	0.4	516	0.2	571	0.3	568	0.2
Cooking for fun...............................	51,668	22.2	18,664	8.0	8,095	3.5	6,758	2.9	4,776	2.1
Crossword puzzles...........................	27,335	11.8	10,743	4.6	3,421	1.5	2,622	1.1	1,750	0.8
Dance/go dancing............................	19,148	8.2	1,628	0.7	1,471	0.6	2,238	1.0	2,141	0.9
Dining out.....................................	105,002	45.2	18,710	8.1	23,485	10.1	24,751	10.7	13,988	6.0
Entertain friends or relatives at home......	81,539	35.1	6,673	2.9	9,516	4.1	16,203	7.0	17,964	7.7
Fantasy sports league.......................	7,699	3.3	2,143	0.9	1,433	0.6	429	0.2	341	0.2
Furniture refinishing.........................	5,974	2.6	130	0.1	213	0.1	255	0.1	407	0.2
Go to bars/night clubs.......................	39,612	17.0	2,698	1.2	4,044	1.7	6,917	3.0	5,808	2.5
Go to beach...................................	55,222	23.8	2,581	1.1	2,002	0.9	4,788	2.1	4,839	2.1
Go to live theater............................	26,973	11.6	157	0.1	238	0.1	1,271	0.6	2,833	1.2
Go to museums...............................	29,708	12.8	258	0.1	237	0.1	934	0.4	2,849	1.2
Home decoration and furnishing............	20,280	8.7	764	0.3	1,197	0.5	1,643	0.7	2,686	1.2
Karaoke.......................................	7,365	3.2	191	0.1	321	0.1	743	0.3	746	0.3
Painting, drawing.............................	12,197	5.3	1,970	0.9	1,143	0.5	1,478	0.6	1,417	0.6
PC/computer games (play online with software).................	15,711	6.8	7,307	3.1	1,384	0.6	1,051	0.5	548	0.2
PC/computer games (play online without software).............	20,808	9.0	11,216	4.8	2,324	1.0	1,335	0.6	758	0.3
PC/computer games (play offline with software).................	15,739	6.8	7,397	3.2	1,211	0.5	1,593	0.7	1,000	0.4
Photo Album/Scrap book.....................	12,695	5.5	725	0.3	657	0.3	1,587	0.7	1,721	0.7
Photography...................................	22,492	9.7	3,943	1.7	2,600	1.1	3,823	1.6	3,659	1.6
Picnic..	23,847	10.3	333	0.1	612	0.3	1,780	0.8	3,601	1.6
Play bingo.....................................	9,054	3.9	770	0.3	854	0.4	632	0.3	442	0.2
Play cards.....................................	38,086	16.4	4,405	1.9	3,783	1.6	5,170	2.2	5,461	2.4
Play musical instrument......................	15,238	6.6	5,437	2.3	1,931	0.8	1,180	0.5	1,017	0.4
Reading books................................	80,550	34.7	44,906	19.3	6,509	2.8	6,574	2.8	5,089	2.2
Reading comic books.........................	5,799	2.5	1,091	0.5	484	0.2	657	0.3	457	0.2
Sodoku puzzles...............................	24,733	10.6	9,104	3.9	2,414	1.0	3,105	1.3	2,030	0.9
Trivia games..................................	11,029	4.7	2,281	1.0	928	0.4	1,460	0.6	1,123	0.5
Video/electronic games (console)..........	25,072	10.8	8,935	3.8	2,883	1.2	2,992	1.3	1,902	0.8
Video/electronic games (portable)..........	10,311	4.4	3,723	1.6	891	0.4	986	0.4	578	0.3
Woodworking..................................	9,738	4.2	1,443	0.6	1,091	0.5	936	0.4	1,061	0.5
Word games...................................	25,230	10.9	11,095	4.8	2,502	1.1	2,484	1.1	1,984	0.9
Zoo attendance...............................	27,080	11.7	164	0.1	228	0.1	425	0.2	1,553	0.7

Z Represents less than 0.05. [1] Includes those participating less than once a month not shown separately. [2] Excluding country and rock.

Source: GfK Mediamark Research & Intelligence, LLC, New York, NY, *Top-line Reports* ©. See also <http://www.gfkmri.com/>.

Table 1267. Retail Sales and Household Participation in Lawn and Garden Activities: 2005 to 2012

[(35,208 represents $35,208,000,000). For calendar year. Subject to sampling variability; see source]

Activity	Retail sales (mil. dol.)					Percent households engaged in activity				
	2005	2009	2010	2011	2012	2005	2009	2010	2011	2012
Total............................	**35,208**	**30,121**	**28,409**	**29,097**	**29,451**	**83**	**72**	**68**	**70**	**72**
Lawn care.........................	9,657	8,075	7,765	8,330	7,944	54	46	45	45	46
Indoor houseplants..............	1,464	1,081	920	991	1,008	42	30	29	29	30
Flower gardening................	3,003	2,299	1,933	2,109	2,314	41	31	28	29	31
Insect control....................	1,869	1,567	1,350	1,693	1,772	30	22	22	23	24
Shrub care.......................	1,109	623	930	1,099	942	31	21	20	23	24
Vegetable gardening............	1,154	1,762	1,701	1,630	1,769	25	27	26	25	27
Tree care.........................	2,820	1,743	2,086	2,558	2,088	26	19	16	19	21
Landscaping......................	9,078	8,418	7,232	6,250	6,280	31	27	24	26	27
Flower bulbs.....................	945	748	660	627	717	29	19	18	18	19
Fruit trees.......................	507	575	702	509	701	13	11	10	10	11
Container gardening.............	1,295	994	836	937	1,027	26	19	17	18	19
Raising transplants [1]...........	237	241	286	296	230	11	9	8	8	7
Herb gardening..................	371	423	428	442	636	17	14	15	15	16
Growing berries..................	151	229	159	168	239	8	8	8	7	8
Ornamental gardening..........	678	445	504	378	495	12	6	6	6	7
Water gardening.................	870	898	917	1,080	1,289	11	11	12	13	14

[1] Starting plants in advance of planting in ground.

Source: The National Gardening Association, Burlington, VT, *National Gardening Survey*, annual ©. See also <http://www.garden.org/>.

Table 1268. Selected Recreational Activities: 1990 to 2011

[21,000 represents 21,000,000]

Activity	Unit	1990	1995	2000	2005	2007	2008	2009	2010	2011
Golf facilities [1].....................	Number	12,846	14,074	15,489	16,052	15,970	15,979	15,979	15,890	15,753
Tennis players: [2]...................	1,000	21,000	17,820	22,900	24,720	25,130	26,880	30,130	27,810	27,050
Skiing: [3]										
Skier visits [4]......................	Million	50.0	52.7	52.2	56.9	55.1	60.5	57.4	59.8	60.5
Operating resorts...................	Number	591	520	503	492	481	473	471	471	486
Boating: [5]										
People participating in recreational boating [6]...............	Million	67.4	70.0	67.5	57.9	66.4	70.1	65.9	75.0	82.7
Retail expenditures on boating [7]....	Mil. dol.	13,731	17,226	27,065	37,317	37,416	33,809	30,821	30,434	32,271
Recreational boats in use by boat type [8]................................	Million	16.0	15.4	16.8	17.7	16.9	16.8	16.8	16.5	16.4
Outboard............................	Million	(NA)	(NA)	8.3	8.5	8.3	8.3	8.3	8.1	8.1
Inboard..............................	Million	(NA)	(NA)	1.0	1.1	1.1	1.1	1.1	1.1	1.2
Sterndrive...........................	Million	(NA)	(NA)	1.6	1.7	1.7	1.6	1.6	1.5	1.5
Personal Watercraft.................	Million	(NA)	(NA)	1.2	1.2	1.2	1.2	1.3	1.3	1.2
Sailboat.............................	Million	(NA)	(NA)	1.6	1.6	1.6	1.5	1.5	1.6	1.6
Other...............................	Million	(NA)	(NA)	3.1	3.6	3.1	3.1	3.0	3.0	2.9

NA Not available. [1] Source: National Golf Foundation, Jupiter, FL. [2] Source: Tennis Industry Association, Hilton Head, SC. Based on a nationwide telephone survey of households, in which all household members ages 6 and up are enumerated with data on tennis participation collected for each person. [3] Source: National Ski Areas Association, Kottke National End of Season Survey Report ©. [4] Represents one person visiting a ski area for all or any part of a day or night, and includes full-and half-day, night, complimentary, adult, child, season, and other types of tickets. Data are estimated and are for the season ending in the year shown. [5] Source: National Marine Manufacturers Association, Chicago, IL. ©. [6] People participating is now measured as adults 18 years and older. [7] Represents estimated expenditures for new and used boats, motors and engines, accessories, safety equipment, fuel, insurance, docking, maintenance, launching, storage, repairs, and other expenses. [8] 2011 data are estimated.

Source: Compiled from sources listed in footnotes.

Table 1269. Leisure Time Use on Weekends and Holidays by Type of Activity and Selected Demographic Characteristics: 2012

[Data are based on interviews of approximately 12,500 individuals 15 years and over who reported their activities for one 24-hour period. Respondents engaging in more than one activity at a time reported only their primary activity; except for child care, secondary activities were not reported]

Selected Characteristics	Average hours per day spent on all leisure and sports activities			Percent distribution of leisure time on weekends and holidays						
	All Days (hours)	Week-days (hours)	Weekends and Holidays (hours)	Sports, exercise, recreation	Socializing, Communicating	Watching TV	Reading	Relaxing, thinking	Playing games, using computers for leisure	Other [1]
Men	5.8	5.2	7.3	7	14	54	4	5	8	9
Women	5.0	4.5	5.9	4	19	50	7	5	6	9
Age:										
Total, 15 years and over	5.4	4.9	6.6	6	16	52	6	5	7	9
15 to 19 years	5.9	5.3	7.3	10	18	41	2	2	14	13
20 to 24 years	5.6	5.2	6.4	8	19	45	2	3	12	10
25 to 34 years	4.4	3.8	5.8	6	21	48	3	4	8	10
35 to 44 years	4.3	3.6	5.9	6	18	52	4	4	6	9
45 to 54 years	4.8	4.2	6.3	6	15	55	5	6	6	9
55 to 64 years	5.6	5.0	6.9	4	13	59	6	5	5	7
65 to 74 years	7.1	6.9	7.5	4	11	57	11	5	5	8
75 years and over	7.7	7.5	8.0	2	12	53	13	8	4	8
Race/ethnicity:										
White	5.3	4.8	6.6	6	16	51	6	4	7	9
Black	6.1	5.6	7.0	3	15	60	2	7	5	7
Hispanic origin	4.8	4.2	6.1	7	19	54	2	5	5	8
Employment status:										
Employed	4.3	3.7	5.9	6	18	51	5	4	7	10
Full-time workers	4.1	3.3	5.9	7	17	52	5	4	6	10
Part-time workers	5.1	4.7	6.1	4	19	48	4	4	9	12
Not employed	7.0	6.7	7.5	5	14	54	7	5	7	8
Weekly earnings: [2]										
$0 - $530	4.4	3.8	5.8	3	17	56	3	5	7	9
$531 - $830	4.3	3.4	6.2	7	18	52	4	5	6	8
$831 - $1,290	4.2	3.4	6.0	8	16	53	5	4	6	10
$1,291 and higher	3.8	3.0	6.0	9	18	49	6	2	5	11
Presence and age of children:										
No household children under 18	5.9	5.5	7.0	5	14	53	7	5	7	8
Household children under 18	4.5	3.9	5.8	6	20	49	3	4	7	11
Children 13 to 17 years, none younger	5.0	4.5	6.3	8	20	48	4	3	5	12
Children 6 to 12 years, none younger	4.4	3.8	5.9	5	18	50	4	4	8	11
Youngest child under 6 years	4.1	3.5	5.5	6	22	49	2	4	7	10
Educational attainment, 25 years and over:										
Less than a high school diploma	6.2	5.9	7.0	3	14	62	3	9	3	5
High school graduates, no college	5.8	5.3	7.0	4	14	58	5	6	5	8
Some college or associate degree	5.2	4.6	6.4	5	16	54	6	4	6	8
Bachelor's degree and higher	4.6	4.1	6.0	7	17	46	10	3	7	11

[1] Includes other leisure and sports activities, not elsewhere classified, and travel related to leisure and sports activities. [2] These values are based on usual weekly earnings. The earnings data are limited to wage and salary workers (both incorporated and unincorporated self-employed workers are excluded). Each earnings range represents approximately 25 percent of full-time wage and salary workers who held only one job.

Source: Bureau of Labor Statistics, *American Time Use Survey, 2012*, Bulletin USDL-13-1178, June 2013. See also <http://www.bls.gov/news.release/atus.nr0.htm>.

Table 1270. Amusement Park Attendance at Top 15 U.S. Facilities: 2008 to 2012

[In thousands (107,300 represents 107,300,000). Covers gated commercial theme parks, amusement parks, and water parks with annual attendance of one million or more]

Park Name	Location	Attendance					Percent change 2011-2012
		2008	2009	2010	2011	2012	
Total Top 15.............	(X)	**107,300**	**107,348**	**109,321**	**112,509**	**116,420**	**3.5**
Magic Kingdom, Walt Disney World.......	Lake Buena Vista, FL	17,063	17,233	16,972	17,142	17,536	2.3
Disneyland.................	Anaheim, CA	14,741	15,900	15,980	16,140	15,963	-1.1
EPCOT, Walt Disney World...............	Lake Buena Vista, FL	10,395	10,990	10,825	10,825	11,063	2.2
Disney's Animal Kingdom...............	Lake Buena Vista, FL	9,540	9,590	9,886	9,783	9,998	2.2
Disney's Hollywood Studios..............	Lake Buena Vista, FL	9,608	9,700	9,603	9,699	9,912	2.2
Universal's Islands of Adventure..........	Orlando, FL	5,207	4,627	5,949	7,674	7,981	4.0
Disney's California Adventure.............	Anaheim, CA	5,566	6,095	6,278	6,341	7,775	22.6
Universal Studios Florida.................	Orlando, FL	6,231	5,530	5,925	6,044	6,195	2.5
Universal Studios Hollywood..............	Universal City, CA	4,583	4,308	5,040	5,141	5,912	15.0
Seaworld Florida.......................	Orlando, FL	5,920	5,800	5,100	5,202	5,358	3.0
Seaworld California......................	San Diego, CA	4,147	4,200	3,800	4,294	4,444	3.5
Busch Gardens........................	Tampa, FL	4,410	4,100	4,200	4,284	4,348	1.5
Knotts Berry Farm......................	Buena Park, CA	3,565	3,333	3,600	3,654	3,508	-4.0
Cedar Point...........................	Sandusky, OH	3,198	2,942	3,051	3,143	3,221	2.5
Kings Island...........................	Kings Island, OH	3,126	3,000	3,112	3,143	3,206	2.0

X Not applicable.

Source: Themed Entertainment Association and AECOM, *2012 Theme Index: Global Attractions Attendance Report* ©, and previous reports. See also <http://www.teaconnect.org/> and <http://www.aecom.com/What+We+Do/Economics>.

Table 1271. College and Professional Football Summary: 1990 to 2011

[35,330 represents 35,330,000. For definition of median, see Guide to Tabular Presentation]

Sport	Unit	1990	1995	2000	2005	2008	2009	2010	2011
NCAA college: [1]									
Teams..............................	Number	534	600	624	618	633	633	644	638
Attendance.........................	1,000	35,330	35,638	39,059	43,487	48,839	48,285	49,671	49,699
National Football League: [2]									
Teams..............................	Number	28	30	31	32	32	32	32	32
Attendance, total [3].................	1,000	17,666	19,203	20,954	21,792	21,859	21,285	21,107	20,959
Regular season....................	1,000	13,960	15,044	16,387	17,012	17,057	16,651	16,570	16,563
Average per game..............	Number	62,321	62,682	66,078	66,455	66,629	65,043	64,978	64,699
Postseason games [4].............	1,000	848	(NA)	809	802	807	824	800	906
Players' salaries: [5]									
Average...........................	$1,000	354	584	787	1,400	1,824	1,896	2,000	2,250
Median base salary................	$1,000	275	301	441	569	788	790	906	826

NA Not available. [1] Source: National Collegiate Athletic Association, Indianapolis, IN, <http://www.ncaa.org/wps/wcm/connect/public/NCAA/Resources/Stats/> ©. [2] Source: National Football League, New York, NY, <http://www.nfl.com/>. [3] Preseason attendance data are included in totals but not shown separately. [4] Includes Pro Bowl (a nonchampionship game) and Super Bowl. [5] Source: National Football League Players Association, Washington, DC., <http://www.nflpa.org/>.

Source: Compiled from sources listed in footnotes.

Table 1272. Characteristics of Selected Spectator Sports: 1990 to 2012

[55,512 represents 55,512,000]

Sport	Unit	1990	1995	2000	2005	2008	2009	2010	2011	2012
Baseball, major leagues: [1]										
Attendance	1,000	55,512	51,289	74,340	76,286	79,975	74,823	74,508	75,504	76,675
Regular season	1,000	54,824	50,469	72,749	74,926	76,043	73,368	73,054	73,416	74,859
National League	1,000	24,492	25,110	39,851	41,644	41,579	41,128	40,890	40,741	41,475
American League	1,000	30,332	25,359	32,898	33,282	34,464	32,239	32,164	32,675	33,384
Playoffs [2]	1,000	479	533	1,314	1,191	1,167	1,166	1,210	1,745	1,646
World Series	1,000	209	286	277	168	219	289	244	343	170
Players' salaries: [3]										
Average	$1,000	598	1,111	1,896	2,476	2,926	2,996	3,015	3,095	(NA)
Basketball: [4,5]										
NCAA—Men's college:										
Teams	Number	768	866	937	984	1,017	1,033	1,027	1,030	1,040
Attendance	1,000	28,741	28,225	28,949	30,940	33,111	32,821	32,632	32,781	32,869
NCAA—Women's college:										
Teams	Number	782	864	958	1,018	1,032	1,037	1,048	1,055	1,055
Attendance [6]	1000	2,777	4,962	8,825	9,903	11,160	11,135	11,160	11,211	11,339
National Hockey League: [7]										
Regular season attendance	1,000	12,580	9,234	18,800	(NA)	21,236	21,475	20,996	20,928	(NA)
Playoffs attendance	1,000	1,356	1,329	1,525	(NA)	1,587	1,640	1,702	(NA)	(NA)
Professional rodeo: [8]										
Rodeos	Number	754	739	688	662	609	560	570	572	(NA)
Performances	Number	2,159	2,217	2,081	1,940	1,861	1,656	1,671	1,669	(NA)
Members	Number	5,693	6,894	6,255	6,127	5,825	5,653	5,323	5,137	(NA)
Permit-holders (rookies)	Number	3,290	3,835	3,249	2,701	2,233	2,042	1,881	1,883	(NA)
Total prize money	Mil. dol.	18.2	24.5	32.3	36.6	39.1	38.0	39.9	38.8	(NA)

NA Not Available. [1] Source: Major League Baseball (previously, The National League of Professional Baseball Clubs), New York, NY, ©. National League Green Book ©, and The American League of Professional Baseball Clubs, New York, NY, American League Red Book ©. [2] Beginning 1995, two rounds of playoffs were played. Prior years had one round. [3] Source: Major League Baseball Players Association, New York, NY. ©. [4] Season beginning in year shown. [5] Source: National Collegiate Athletic Association, Indianapolis, IN ©. [6] Attendance for women's basketball includes doubleheaders with men's teams beginning with the 1997 season, if attendance was taken by halftime of the women's game. [7] For season ending in year shown. Source: National Hockey League, Montreal, Quebec. ©. In September 2004, franchise owners locked out their players upon the expiration of the collective bargaining agreement. The entire season was cancelled in February 2005. [8] Source: Professional Rodeo Cowboys Association, Colorado Springs, CO, Official Professional Rodeo Media Guide, annual ©.

Source: Compiled from sources listed in footnotes.

Table 1273. Adult Attendance at Sports Events by Frequency: 2012

[In thousands (275 represents 275,000), except percent. For fall 2012. Percent is based on total projected population of 232,469,000. Data not comparable to previous years. Based on survey and subject to sampling error; see source]

Event	Attend regularly		Attend on occasion		Event	Attend regularly		Attend on occasion	
	Number	Percent	Number	Percent		Number	Percent	Number	Percent
Alpine skiing and ski jumping	275	0.12	1,116	0.48	Golf - Professional (PGA, LPGA) and other	374	0.16	2,755	1.19
Auto racing - NASCAR	370	0.16	4,995	2.15	Greyhound racing	148	0.06	958	0.41
Auto racing - Other	756	0.33	3,327	1.43	Gymnastics	338	0.15	1,139	0.49
Baseball:					High school sports	3,941	1.70	7,108	3.06
College	502	0.22	2,826	1.22	Horse racing	540	0.23	3,093	1.33
Professional (MLB)	2,350	1.01	22,125	9.52	Ice hockey -				
Basketball:					Professional (NHL)	895	0.39	6,699	2.88
College	1,315	0.57	6,551	2.82	Lacrosse - MLL	93	0.04	961	0.41
Professional (NBA, WNBA)	843	0.36	7,462	3.21	Marathon, triathlon & other endurance events	261	0.11	1,523	0.66
Beach volleyball - Professional	300	0.13	946	0.41	Mixed martial arts (MMA)	173	0.07	1,400	0.60
Bicycle racing	293	0.13	1,131	0.49	Motorcycle racing	193	0.08	1,260	0.54
Bowling	395	0.17	1,764	0.76	Olympics - Summer	146	0.06	1,199	0.52
Boxing	272	0.12	1,407	0.61	Olympics - Winter	152	0.07	1,003	0.43
Bull riding - Professional	311	0.13	1,661	0.71	Poker	217	0.09	1,015	0.44
Equestrian events	339	0.15	1,398	0.60	Rodeo	628	0.27	2,997	1.29
Extreme Sports - Summer	164	0.07	1,061	0.46	Soccer - Professional (MLS) and World Cup	334	0.14	2,246	0.97
Extreme Sports - Winter	142	0.06	920	0.40	Tennis - men's and women's	274	0.12	1,555	0.67
Figure skating	249	0.11	1,022	0.44	Track & Field	281	0.12	1,316	0.57
Fishing	966	0.42	1,838	0.79	Truck and tractor pull/ mud racing	254	0.11	1,916	0.82
Football:					Weightlifting	248	0.11	713	0.31
College	2,670	1.15	10,772	4.63	Wrestling - Professional (WWE and Other)	634	0.27	2,219	0.95
Professional (NFL) Monday or Thursday night games	1,061	0.46	5,315	2.29					
NFL weekend games	1,171	0.50	9,763	4.20					
NFL playoffs/Super Bowl	626	0.27	3,122	1.34					

Source: GfK Mediamark Research & Intelligence. LLC, New York, NY, Top-line Reports ©. See also <http://www.gfkmri.com>.

Table 1274. Participation in NCAA Sports by Sex: 2011/12

[For the academic year]

Sport	Males			Females		
	Teams	Athletes	Average squad	Teams	Athletes	Average squad
Total........................	**8,784**	**261,150**	**(X)**	**9,985**	**197,899**	**(X)**
Archery [1]....................	(X)	(X)	(X)	(X)	(X)	(X)
Badminton [1].................	(X)	(X)	(X)	(X)	(X)	(X)
Baseball.......................	927	31,999	34.5	(X)	(X)	(X)
Basketball....................	1,060	17,890	16.9	1,084	16,134	14.9
Bowling.......................	1	31	31.0	63	561	8.9
Cross country [2].............	960	13,991	14.6	1,035	15,483	15.0
Equestrian [1,2]..............	8	16	2.0	49	1,609	32.8
Fencing [2]...................	35	635	18.1	42	661	15.7
Field hockey..................	(X)	(X)	(X)	266	5,742	21.6
Football......................	651	69,643	107.0	(X)	(X)	(X)
Golf [2]......................	812	8,533	10.5	596	4,752	8.0
Gymnastics...................	17	341	20.1	83	1,440	17.3
Ice hockey...................	135	3,891	28.8	86	2,056	23.9
Lacrosse.....................	295	10,903	37.0	376	8,482	22.6
Rifle [2].....................	27	237	8.8	34	176	5.2
Rowing.......................	60	2,364	39.4	145	7,282	50.2
Rugby [1].....................	1	50	50.0	5	166	33.2
Sailing [1]...................	22	525	23.9	(X)	(X)	(X)
Skiing [2]....................	32	469	14.7	34	438	12.9
Soccer.......................	803	22,987	28.6	996	25,164	25.3
Softball......................	(X)	(X)	(X)	976	18,505	19.0
Squash [1]....................	31	474	15.3	30	458	15.3
Swimming/diving [2]..........	413	9,229	22.3	527	12,206	23.2
Synchronized swimming [1].....	(X)	(X)	(X)	1	9	9.0
Tennis.......................	765	8,177	10.7	934	8,977	9.6
Track, indoor [2].............	634	23,183	36.6	711	24,262	34.1
Track, outdoor [2]............	735	26,416	35.9	801	26,227	32.7
Volleyball....................	98	1,529	15.6	1,047	15,890	15.2
Water polo....................	43	1,015	23.6	64	1,219	19.0
Wrestling.....................	219	6,622	30.2	(X)	(X)	(X)

X Not applicable. [1] Sport recognized by the NCAA but does not have an NCAA championship. [2] Co-ed championship sport.

Source: The National Collegiate Athletic Association (NCAA), Indianapolis, IN, *NCAA Sports Sponsorship and Participation Rates Report* ©. See also <http://www.ncaapublications.com/>.

Table 1275. Participation in High School Athletic Programs by Sex: 1980 to 2013

[For academic years. Data based on number of state associations reporting and may underrepresent the number of schools with and participants in athletic programs]

Year	Participants [1]		Sex and sport	Most popular sports, 2012–2013 [2]	
	Males	Females		Schools	Participants
1980–81.......................	3,503,124	1,853,789	MALE		
1985–86.......................	3,344,275	1,807,121	Football (11-player).................	14,048	1,086,627
1990–91.......................	3,406,355	1,892,316	Track & field (outdoor)..............	16,001	580,672
1991–92.......................	3,429,853	1,940,801	Basketball...........................	17,856	538,676
1992–93.......................	3,416,389	1,997,489	Baseball.............................	15,632	474,791
1993–94.......................	3,472,967	2,130,315	Soccer...............................	11,626	410,982
1994–95.......................	3,536,359	2,240,461	Wrestling............................	10,488	270,163
1995–96.......................	3,634,052	2,367,936	Cross country........................	14,148	249,200
1996–97.......................	3,706,225	2,474,043	Tennis...............................	9,730	157,247
1997–98.......................	3,763,120	2,570,333	Golf.................................	13,415	152,584
1998–99.......................	3,832,352	2,652,726	Swimming & diving....................	7,001	138,177
1999–00.......................	3,861,749	2,675,874			
2000–01.......................	3,921,069	2,784,154			
2001–02.......................	3,960,517	2,806,998			
2002–03.......................	3,988,738	2,856,358	FEMALE		
2003–04.......................	4,038,253	2,865,299	Track & field (outdoor)..............	15,962	472,939
2004–05.......................	4,110,319	2,908,390	Basketball...........................	17,493	433,120
2005–06.......................	4,206,549	2,953,355	Volleyball...........................	15,565	420,208
2006–07.......................	4,321,103	3,021,807	Soccer...............................	11,351	371,532
2007–08.......................	4,372,115	3,057,266	Softball (fast pitch)................	15,067	362,488
2008–09.......................	4,422,662	3,114,091	Cross country........................	13,918	214,369
2009–10.......................	4,455,740	3,172,637	Tennis...............................	10,005	181,116
2010–11.......................	4,494,406	3,173,549	Swimming & diving....................	7,249	163,992
2011–12.......................	4,484,987	3,207,533	Competitive spirit squads...........	4,847	116,508
2012–13.......................	4,490,854	3,222,723	Lacrosse.............................	2,212	77,258

[1] A participant is counted in each sport participated in. [2] Ten most popular sports for each gender, ranked by number of participants.

Source: National Federation of State High School Associations, Indianapolis, IN, *The 2012–2013 High School Athletics Participation Survey* ©. Reprinted with permission of the National Federation of State High School Associations. See also <http://www.nfhs.org/>.

Table 1276. Sporting Goods Sales by Product Category: 1990 to 2011, and Projection, 2012

[In millions of dollars (50,725 represents $50,725,000,000), except percent. Data are based on an online survey of 55,000 households. Prior to 2010, Alaska and Hawaii were not included in sample. Minus sign (-) indicates decrease]

Selected product category	1990	2000	2005	2007	2008	2009	2010	2011	2012, proj.
Sales, all products	**50,725**	**74,442**	**88,434**	**91,423**	**80,431**	**71,832**	**78,691**	**81,620**	**84,180**
Annual percent change [1]	(NA)	4.6	3.1	1.1	-12.0	-12.0	9.5	3.7	3.1
Percent of retail sales	(NA)	2.5	2.4	2.3	2.0	2.0	2.0	2.0	(NA)
Athletic and sport clothing	10,130	11,030	10,898	10,834	10,113	9,246	9,399	9,661	9,985
Athletic and sport footwear [2]	11,654	13,026	15,719	17,524	17,190	17,069	17,476	18,384	19,024
Aerobic shoes	611	292	261	280	260	223	249	271	293
Basketball shoes	918	786	878	892	718	741	721	766	811
Cross training shoes	679	1,528	1,437	1,584	1,626	2,071	2,121	2,273	2,425
Golf shoes	226	226	259	244	239	202	208	216	223
Gym shoes, sneakers	2,536	1,871	2,314	2,699	2,639	3,377	3,577	3,863	3,932
Jogging and running shoes	1,110	1,638	2,157	2,193	2,301	2,363	2,316	2,464	2,612
Tennis shoes	740	533	528	452	467	396	404	421	438
Walking shoes	2,950	3,317	3,673	4,197	4,204	4,416	4,256	4,535	4,671
Athletic and sport equipment [2]	14,439	21,608	23,735	25,061	24,862	24,666	26,682	27,493	28,025
Archery	265	259	372	396	394	411	444	466	475
Baseball and softball	217	319	372	401	396	381	447	476	485
Billiards and indoor games	192	516	572	531	396	318	386	371	364
Camping	1,072	1,354	1,447	1,453	1,461	1,496	1,718	1,819	1,856
Exercise	1,824	3,610	5,177	5,500	5,328	5,319	5,446	5,582	5,694
Fishing tackle	1,910	2,030	2,139	2,247	2,067	1,859	2,059	2,101	2,122
Golf	2,514	3,805	3,466	3,722	3,495	2,927	3,198	3,309	3,356
Hunting and firearms	2,202	2,274	3,563	3,942	4,548	5,187	5,353	5,611	5,779
Optics	438	729	887	1,019	1,024	1,135	1,259	1,293	1,319
Skin diving and scuba	294	355	358	376	373	343	345	348	351
Snow skiing [3]	475	495	643	531	482	502	591	586	592
Tennis	333	383	397	440	387	368	414	419	423
Recreational transport	14,502	28,779	38,082	38,003	28,266	20,851	25,134	26,083	27,146
Bicycles and supplies	2,423	5,131	5,343	5,393	5,285	4,471	5,943	6,010	6,126
Pleasure boats, motors, accessories	7,644	13,224	17,634	17,473	13,679	10,815	10,024	10,654	11,200
Recreational vehicles	4,113	9,529	14,366	14,505	8,758	5,152	8,733	9,008	9,400
Snowmobiles	322	894	739	632	544	414	435	411	420

NA Not available. [1] Represents change from immediate prior year. [2] Includes other products not shown separately. [3] Data through 2004 categorized as "Skiing Downhill."

Source: National Sporting Goods Association, Mt. Prospect, IL, *The Sporting Goods Market in 2012* ©, and earlier reports. See also <http://www.nsga.org/i4a/pages/index.cfm?pageid=4653>.

Table 1277. Consumer Purchases of Sporting Goods by Consumer Characteristics: 2011

[Shown as percent of dollar purchases. Data are based on an online survey of 55,000 households. Because surveys prior to 2010 were conducted by mail, current data may not be fully comparable to past years]

Characteristic	Total	Footwear					Equipment				
		Aerobic shoes	Fitness shoes	Gym shoes/ sneakers	Jog-ging/ running shoes	Walking shoes	Multi purpose home gyms	Rod/ reel combi-nation	Golf club sets	Rifles	Soccer balls
Total	**100**	**100**	**100**	**100**	**100**	**100**	**100**	**100**	**100**	**100**	**100**
Age of user:											
Under 14 years old	18.8	2.4	7.1	23.4	7.1	4.3	1.8	10.7	2.8	2.9	49.8
14 to 17 years old	5.3	2.4	7.6	10.1	8.5	2.6	–	3.4	1.4	4.0	15.9
18 to 24 years old	9.8	6.7	6.3	10.5	8.9	5.0	19.3	2.5	3.9	2.4	4.8
25 to 34 years old	13.7	19.6	11.9	13.3	20.0	8.3	20.0	13.5	4.9	11.3	7.9
35 to 44 years old	13.1	20.8	20.8	12.9	23.9	13.4	27.8	12.8	19.5	30.3	9.3
45 to 64 years old	26.2	40.7	36.9	22.2	26.6	44.4	23.3	41.2	47.8	36.3	10.7
65 years old and over	13.1	7.4	9.4	7.6	5.0	22.0	7.8	16.2	19.7	12.8	1.6
Sex of user:											
Male	49.4	19.0	39.8	41.8	43.0	35.9	44.7	86.4	74.1	93.6	63.0
Female	50.6	81.0	60.2	58.2	57.0	64.1	55.3	13.6	25.9	6.4	37.0
Annual household income:											
Under $15,000	13.7	7.7	5.2	8.4	5.0	7.7	15.8	10.7	2.8	6.0	3.6
$15,000 to $24,999	12.0	8.0	5.7	10.4	6.0	9.0	5.4	11.4	5.0	6.1	6.6
$25,000 to $34,999	10.9	5.1	6.7	8.2	5.4	10.2	14.8	10.6	4.6	4.9	6.4
$35,000 to $49,999	13.9	12.0	11.7	14.3	10.8	15.4	14.8	9.6	7.8	12.6	8.5
$50,000 to $74,999	17.7	14.3	17.3	18.9	15.4	18.3	18.5	16.3	13.0	13.7	22.2
$75,000 to $99,999	11.4	14.2	14.8	12.4	17.6	13.9	15.6	14.0	14.7	21.8	15.4
$100,000 to $149,999	12.1	20.7	18.4	15.9	17.4	14.8	5.8	14.7	23.4	22.7	16.0
$150,000 and over	8.3	18.0	20.2	11.5	22.4	10.7	9.3	12.7	28.7	12.2	21.3
Education of household head:											
Less than high school	11.5	3.1	0.4	2.3	0.9	2.4	4.0	2.3	–	0.7	2.9
High school	29.8	11.4	10.5	15.8	10.2	17.3	10.8	21.3	7.4	17.3	9.9
Some college	28.6	35.7	33.6	39.2	28.1	37.6	40.6	38.9	28.1	34.4	28.2
College graduate	30.1	49.8	55.5	42.7	60.8	42.7	44.6	37.5	64.5	47.6	59.0

– Represents or rounds to zero.

Source: National Sporting Goods Association, Mt. Prospect, IL, *The Sporting Goods Market in 2012*, ©. See also <http://www.nsga.org/i4a/pages/index.cfm?pageid=4653>.

Table 1278. Participation in Selected Sports Activities: 2011

[In thousands (280,834 represents 280,834,000). Data are based on an online survey of 55,000 households. The questionnaire asked the heads of households and up to three other household members who were at least seven years of age to indicate their age, the sports in which they participated in 2011, and the number of days of participation in 2011. A participant is defined as an individual seven years of age or older who participates in a sport more than once a year. See source for methodology]

Activity	Total (Number)	Sex		Age (years)								Household income (dollars)						
		Male	Female	7–17	18–24	25–34	35–44	45–54	55–64	65–74	75 and over	Under 25,000	25,000–34,999	35,000–49,999	50,000–74,999	75,000–99,999	100,000–149,999	150,000 and over
Total Participants [1]	280,834	138,114	142,720	44,933	30,639	42,434	40,861	44,681	36,649	21,568	19,069	74,399	30,300	37,492	49,332	32,105	33,944	23,262
SERIES I SPORTS																		
Aerobic exercising [2]	41,962	13,054	28,908	4,980	5,510	8,999	7,883	6,221	4,294	2,288	1,786	8,352	3,109	5,602	7,416	5,294	6,838	5,352
Backpacking [3]	11,551	6,936	4,615	2,458	1,832	2,543	1,976	1,607	807	217	110	3,146	641	1,497	1,787	1,479	1,971	1,029
Baseball	12,292	9,658	2,634	5,827	1,665	1,950	1,449	900	315	134	52	2,518	828	1,287	2,053	1,995	1,942	1,670
Basketball	26,095	18,438	7,656	11,656	3,718	4,758	3,488	1,632	644	156	43	5,710	1,905	3,739	4,835	3,330	3,546	3,028
Bicycle riding [2]	39,147	21,384	17,763	13,804	3,276	4,513	5,220	5,759	4,157	1,624	794	7,889	3,559	4,583	6,775	5,213	6,230	4,895
Billiards/Pool	19,967	11,493	8,473	2,924	3,378	4,780	3,654	3,328	1,294	439	170	4,737	1,696	2,790	3,566	2,281	2,556	2,342
Bowling	34,868	17,322	17,545	9,849	5,680	6,942	5,479	4,064	1,798	691	363	6,702	2,844	4,680	6,339	4,922	5,639	3,741
Camping [4]	42,815	22,159	20,656	9,566	4,912	7,027	6,489	7,229	3,646	2,284	1,664	9,879	4,590	6,486	7,650	5,606	5,278	3,327
Dart throwing	9,348	5,461	3,887	1,187	1,189	2,308	2,154	1,616	644	160	89	1,875	981	1,324	1,799	1,195	940	1,234
Exercising with equipment [2]	55,455	25,474	29,981	4,981	7,153	10,178	9,785	9,522	6,733	4,299	2,804	10,136	5,067	7,015	9,796	7,542	9,121	6,778
Fishing (net)	32,356	21,608	10,748	6,384	3,430	5,013	5,216	5,765	3,644	1,947	957	7,945	2,854	4,553	5,669	4,078	4,115	3,141
Fishing—fresh water	28,012	18,512	9,500	6,000	2,913	4,194	4,540	4,937	3,083	1,515	829	6,943	2,748	3,990	4,946	3,284	3,524	2,578
Fishing—salt water	9,689	6,915	2,775	1,205	994	1,756	1,699	1,931	1,160	637	307	2,450	323	1,209	1,515	1,435	1,227	1,530
Football—tackle	9,034	7,939	1,095	5,347	1,520	1,052	605	415	66	–	28	2,288	983	790	1,944	897	840	1,293
Golf	20,928	15,888	5,040	2,339	2,141	3,178	3,304	3,892	3,111	1,864	1,100	2,514	1,212	2,723	3,654	3,108	3,994	3,724
Gymnastics	5,117	1,334	3,783	3,321	618	391	358	215	139	47	28	1,273	341	378	714	972	765	673
Hiking	39,137	19,770	19,367	5,844	4,671	7,564	6,980	6,411	4,651	1,975	1,040	8,565	3,450	4,681	6,438	4,989	5,945	5,068
Lacrosse	2,717	1,583	1,134	1,534	366	373	202	176	50	17	–	620	143	133	436	248	606	530
Running/jogging [2]	38,675	19,691	18,984	9,154	7,202	9,614	6,552	3,995	1,583	427	148	7,936	2,894	4,914	6,798	5,277	5,620	5,236
Soccer	13,941	7,846	6,095	7,971	1,863	1,844	1,424	611	171	57	–	2,852	931	1,483	2,251	2,152	2,217	2,055
Softball	10,383	5,200	5,182	3,728	1,346	2,218	1,592	991	295	168	45	2,223	529	1,131	1,973	1,419	1,769	1,340
Swimming [2]	46,028	20,607	25,421	16,144	4,826	5,914	6,436	5,929	3,668	1,840	1,272	8,835	3,418	5,556	7,569	6,574	7,758	6,318
Tennis	13,103	6,797	6,306	3,235	1,844	2,575	2,414	1,801	592	339	303	2,434	875	1,362	2,176	1,931	2,345	1,979
Volleyball [2]	10,075	3,829	6,246	4,533	1,985	1,560	906	768	205	85	34	2,484	780	1,231	1,644	1,201	1,207	1,528
Weightlifting [2]	29,137	19,177	9,960	3,530	5,032	7,022	5,300	4,405	2,277	979	592	6,083	2,226	3,794	4,595	3,961	4,780	3,697
Wrestling	3,217	2,561	655	1,319	768	519	368	150	41	25	26	1,026	194	499	440	354	293	409
Yoga	21,565	4,055	17,510	1,936	3,152	5,845	4,532	3,064	1,671	909	455	5,177	1,931	2,199	3,819	2,757	3,064	2,617
SERIES II SPORTS																		
Archery (target)	6,304	4,477	1,827	1,943	659	1,192	1,059	834	441	178	–	1,588	480	759	934	695	1,181	666
Boating-motor/power	16,668	9,930	6,738	2,748	1,683	2,291	2,683	3,395	2,147	1,188	534	2,872	1,171	1,487	2,962	2,382	3,023	2,770
Hockey (ice)	2,996	2,278	718	940	546	589	395	419	55	51	–	553	275	292	309	483	620	464
Hunting with bow & arrow	5,144	4,379	765	663	592	1,385	982	869	528	126	–	1,159	675	709	696	550	793	562
Hunting with firearms	16,371	13,970	2,401	1,703	2,117	1,983	2,634	3,240	2,803	1,209	683	3,639	1,433	3,311	3,768	1,626	1,459	1,135
In-line roller skating	6,075	2,829	3,246	2,909	901	873	657	596	90	24	26	1,530	532	911	989	781	861	471
Kayaking	7,051	3,697	3,354	1,350	949	1,219	1,230	1,159	653	314	176	1,486	438	773	878	886	1,036	1,555
Mountain biking-off road	5,952	3,788	2,164	1,177	1,057	1,209	1,147	980	277	74	32	1,340	376	609	754	878	1,224	1,239
Muzzleloading	3,056	2,571	485	572	184	472	373	584	371	391	17	706	162	411	627	304	404	585
Paintball games	5,297	4,140	1,158	2,203	993	858	584	547	59	29	–	1,330	507	451	599	626	540	1,245
Skateboarding	6,604	4,879	1,725	3,949	1,209	774	295	333	43	–	–	1,603	815	556	1,223	851	705	851
Skiing-alpine	6,855	4,005	2,850	1,712	659	1,107	1,248	1,423	506	152	48	682	247	422	937	993	1,527	2,048
Skiing-cross country	2,259	1,187	1,072	483	207	364	388	436	230	108	42	343	212	237	209	306	200	752
Snowboarding	5,131	3,324	1,807	2,710	1,123	1,234	542	424	31	8	–	634	416	546	605	560	894	477
Table tennis/ping pong	10,858	6,158	4,700	2,710	1,857	1,844	1,554	1,737	705	301	148	2,023	698	1,145	1,616	1,667	2,024	1,684
Target shooting (All gun types)	19,596	14,536	5,060	2,487	1,779	4,634	3,060	3,861	2,283	1,019	474	3,702	3,252	2,365	3,299	2,739	2,544	1,695
Target shooting-handgun	12,076	8,875	3,201	1,297	1,093	2,711	2,159	2,100	1,541	781	394	2,554	1,358	1,556	1,922	1,594	1,739	1,353
Water skiing	4,293	2,518	1,775	1,226	728	701	693	724	136	60	26	800	295	148	535	669	738	1,110

– Represents zero. [1] Includes sports not shown separately. [2] Participant engaged in activity at least six times in the year. [3] Vacation/overnight. [4] Includes wilderness camping. [5] See also <http://www.nsga.org/i4a/pages/index.cfm?pageid=4653>.

Source: National Sporting Goods Association, Mt. Prospect, IL, Sports Participation in 2011: Series 1 and Series II, ©. See also <http://www.nsga.org/i4a/pages/index.cfm?pageid=4653>.

Table 1279. National Park System—Summary: 1990 to 2012

[In units as indicated (986 represents $986,000,000). For year ending September 30, except as noted. Includes data for five areas in Puerto Rico and Virgin Islands, one area in American Samoa, and one area in Guam]

Item	1990	1995	2000	2005	2009	2010	2011	2012
FINANCES (mil. dol.): [1]								
Expenditures reported	986	1,445	1,833	2,451	2,888	3,239	3,417	3,079
Salaries and wages	459	633	799	984	1,143	1,237	1,245	1,229
Improvements, maintenance	160	234	299	361	466	531	546	537
Construction	109	192	215	381	354	443	468	288
Other	259	386	520	725	925	1,028	1,158	1,025
Funds available	1,506	2,225	3,316	4,218	5,416	5,402	5,281	4,626
Appropriations	1,053	1,325	1,881	2,425	3,467	2,848	2,823	2,783
Other [2]	453	900	1,435	1,793	1,949	2,554	2,458	1,843
Revenue from operations	79	106	234	286	352	387	360	402
RECREATION VISITS (millions): [3]								
All areas	258.7	269.6	285.9	273.5	285.6	281.3	278.9	282.8
National parks [4]	57.7	64.8	66.1	63.5	63.0	64.6	62.6	64.9
National monuments	23.9	23.5	23.8	20.9	22.6	23.0	23.0	21.8
National historical, commemorative, archaeological [5]	57.5	56.9	72.2	74.9	82.6	80.0	80.3	87.0
National parkways	29.1	31.3	34.0	31.7	29.9	28.6	29.7	29.4
National recreation areas [4]	47.2	53.7	50.0	46.8	50.9	49.0	47.4	44.7
National seashores and lakeshores	23.3	22.5	22.5	21.7	20.6	22.2	22.7	23.1
National Capital Parks	7.5	5.5	5.4	4.3	4.8	3.0	2.4	1.8
Recreation overnight stays (millions)	17.6	16.8	15.4	13.5	14.6	14.4	14.0	14.3
In commercial lodgings	3.9	3.8	3.7	3.4	3.5	3.5	4.5	4.6
In Park Service campgrounds	7.9	7.1	5.9	5.2	5.4	5.5	5.4	5.3
In backcountry	1.7	2.2	1.9	1.7	1.9	1.8	1.7	1.8
Other	4.2	3.7	3.8	3.2	3.8	3.8	2.3	2.6
LAND (1,000 acres): [6]								
Total	76,362	77,355	78,153	79,048	80,442	80,527	80,422	80,390
Parks	46,089	49,307	49,785	49,910	50,592	50,662	50,633	50,640
Recreation areas	3,344	3,353	3,388	3,391	3,414	3,418	3,420	3,420
Other	26,929	24,695	24,980	25,747	26,436	26,447	26,369	26,330
Acquisition, net	21	27	186	17	18	23	67	9

[1] Financial data are those associated with the National Park System. Certain other functions of the National Park Service (principally the activities absorbed from the former Heritage Conservation and Recreation Service in 1981) are excluded. [2] Includes funds carried over from prior years. [3] For calendar year. Includes other areas, not shown separately. [4] For 1990, combined data for North Cascades National Park and two adjacent National Recreation Areas are included in National Parks total. [5] Includes military areas. [6] Federal land only, as of December 31. Federal land acreages, in addition to National Park Service administered lands, also include lands within national park system area boundaries but under the administration of other agencies. Year-to-year changes in the federal lands figures includes changes in the acreages of these other lands and hence often differ from "net acquisition."

Source: U.S. National Park Service, *National Park Statistical Abstract 2012*, April 2013, and earlier reports; and unpublished data. See also <https://irma.nps.gov/Stats/>.

Table 1280. State Parks and Recreation Areas by State: 2012

[14,960 represents 14,960,000. For year ending June 30. Data are shown as reported by state park directors. In some states, park agency has forests, fish and wildlife areas, and/or other areas under its control. In other states, park agency is responsible for state parks only]

State	Acreage (1,000)	Visitors (1,000) [1]	Revenue Total ($1,000)	Revenue Percent of operating expenditures	State	Acreage (1,000)	Visitors (1,000) [1]	Revenue Total ($1,000)	Revenue Percent of operating expenditures
United States	14,960	741,280	1,040,749	46.0	Missouri	204	19,329	10,791	37.4
					Montana	46	1,965	1,974	23.1
Alabama	48	4,007	29,649	81.4	Nebraska	135	10,884	20,881	98.1
Alaska	3,387	5,594	2,317	24.3	Nevada	145	3,093	3,839	39.0
Arizona	64	2,156	11,812	67.8	New Hampshire	233	1,083	18,727	123.0
Arkansas	54	8,681	28,350	51.9	New Jersey	441	17,297	9,305	32.5
California	1,596	67,987	106,977	27.6	New Mexico	197	4,218	5,670	31.5
Colorado	1,046	12,236	23,048	46.5	New York	1,352	58,250	85,064	39.7
Connecticut	207	7,482	6,449	36.3	North Carolina	215	14,668	6,447	19.1
Delaware	26	4,759	13,871	56.9	North Dakota	20	1,079	2,468	46.0
Florida	785	24,983	52,512	66.0	Ohio	174	51,073	27,640	43.3
Georgia	93	8,928	32,860	67.3	Oklahoma	70	8,795	30,735	102.3
Hawaii	40	11,087	3,533	40.6	Oregon	109	42,906	18,976	36.6
Idaho	59	5,008	7,415	47.4	Pennsylvania	297	38,532	21,270	25.1
Illinois	480	41,346	7,243	15.5	Rhode Island	9	5,288	6,154	64.5
Indiana	171	16,828	47,135	82.6	South Carolina	90	7,194	21,228	83.8
Iowa	71	14,933	4,206	28.4	South Dakota	102	7,683	16,927	100.2
Kansas	33	6,404	6,350	52.9	Tennessee	190	32,373	35,679	44.1
Kentucky	45	6,977	51,398	64.7	Texas	638	8,028	39,280	60.8
Louisiana	44	2,151	10,541	35.4	Utah	151	5,051	14,334	53.9
Maine	98	2,993	3,686	48.0	Vermont	69	895	7,883	48.3
Maryland	135	11,082	17,218	47.8	Virginia	72	8,281	17,822	50.6
Massachusetts	354	30,362	12,153	19.9	Washington	120	35,338	20,291	33.9
Michigan	293	25,083	49,148	88.7	West Virginia	177	8,547	22,291	56.0
Minnesota	284	8,196	17,759	23.2	Wisconsin	146	15,887	19,372	82.1
Mississippi	25	1,125	8,411	63.0	Wyoming	120	3,159	1,663	19.0

[1] Includes overnight visitors.

Source: National Association of State Park Directors, Tucson, AZ, *Statistical Report of State Park Operations: 2011-2012, Annual Information Exchange for the Period July 1, 2011 through June 30, 2012* ©, February 2013. See also <http://www.naspd.org/>.

Arts, Recreation, and Travel 803

Table 1281. National Park Service (NPS) Visits and Acreage by State: 2012

State	Recreation visits [1]	Gross area acres	Federal land			Nonfederal land	
			NPS fee acres [2]	NPS less than fee acres [3]	Other federal fee acres [4]	Other public acres [5]	Private acres
Total [6]	282,765,682	84,422,725	79,594,996	355,419	440,002	1,367,558	2,664,750
Alabama	717,724	22,737	17,379	202	–	3,296	1,860
Alaska	2,412,524	54,654,073	52,431,052	105,505	8	372,993	1,744,514
Arizona	9,979,972	2,962,659	2,623,075	115	76,800	56,822	205,847
Arkansas	2,727,454	104,977	98,287	3,428	20	2,762	481
California	35,991,200	8,139,925	7,580,761	22,429	11,266	345,086	180,383
Colorado	5,811,546	674,723	611,044	6,855	42,451	862	13,510
Connecticut	21,465	7,782	5,719	1,055	–	874	133
District of Columbia	34,286,073	7,131	6,975	12	6	134	4
Florida	10,366,613	2,638,212	2,469,067	1,330	44,495	98,791	24,530
Georgia	7,350,309	63,326	39,781	167	1,461	16,852	5,065
Hawaii	5,119,035	369,166	357,814	1	22	11,228	100
Idaho	553,554	518,046	511,509	1,138	173	901	4,324
Illinois	295,464	115	12	–	–	17	86
Indiana	2,148,903	15,540	10,748	500	–	3,394	897
Iowa	207,352	2,713	2,708	–	–	5	1
Kansas	101,752	11,636	462	269	–	39	10,865
Kentucky	1,717,853	95,699	94,678	137	–	832	52
Louisiana	625,913	24,788	16,815	–	892	2,670	4,411
Maine	2,431,052	90,287	66,966	11,181	22	10,648	1,471
Maryland	6,658,643	73,406	40,561	5,938	480	23,796	2,630
Massachusetts	10,487,447	57,962	32,960	1,029	44	21,919	2,009
Michigan	2,192,477	718,148	631,846	728	42	58,515	27,017
Minnesota	601,274	301,333	139,573	3,193	142	98,771	59,653
Mississippi	6,449,713	118,739	104,015	5,228	–	70	9,425
Missouri	4,171,826	83,475	54,382	9,262	–	14,070	5,760
Montana	4,451,755	1,274,364	1,214,349	1,826	6,137	1,464	50,587
Nebraska	304,046	45,675	5,650	484	981	386	38,174
Nevada	4,808,929	778,512	774,751	–	2,508	81	1,172
New Hampshire	33,663	21,932	13,211	1,556	5,772	162	1,232
New Jersey	4,885,202	99,243	35,362	140	3,208	59,036	1,497
New Mexico	1,502,808	391,077	376,880	39	2,715	4,407	7,037
New York	12,633,278	72,952	33,689	3,903	164	19,913	15,284
North Carolina	17,706,032	407,066	363,503	12,272	20,782	3,289	7,220
North Dakota	669,242	72,568	71,250	256	151	55	856
Ohio	2,611,158	34,744	20,069	1,329	84	8,205	5,057
Oklahoma	1,497,654	10,241	10,008	9	189	8	27
Oregon	875,271	199,319	192,127	1,404	4,976	295	517
Pennsylvania	8,768,869	137,766	50,968	2,597	387	19,627	64,188
Rhode Island	51,944	5	5	–	–	–	–
South Carolina	1,566,756	32,618	31,972	61	5	51	530
South Dakota	3,950,666	302,969	147,028	122,326	78	78	33,537
Tennessee	8,414,094	386,457	358,797	1,679	9,629	3,616	12,735
Texas	3,939,160	1,245,833	1,202,798	85	1,013	5,087	36,851
Utah	9,503,304	2,117,043	2,097,106	833	1,142	12,803	5,160
Vermont	32,403	23,265	9,836	3,874	8,809	544	202
Virginia	23,398,517	363,312	304,508	7,018	25,049	7,101	19,635
Washington	7,529,549	1,967,532	1,834,498	2,147	100,194	12,814	17,880
West Virginia	1,543,425	92,692	65,071	369	386	6,894	19,972
Wisconsin	273,933	133,755	61,744	11,484	802	47,628	12,097
Wyoming	6,194,752	2,396,390	2,344,852	21	48,462	1,380	1,675

– Represents or rounds to zero. [1] See footnote 1, Table 1282. [2] See footnote 2, Table 1282. [3] See footnote 3, Table 1282. [4] See footnote 4, Table 1282. [5] See footnote 5, Table 1282. [6] Includes Island Areas of the U.S., not shown separately.

Source: U.S. National Park Service, Land Resources Division, unpublished data. See also <https://irma.nps.gov/Stats/>.

Table 1282. National Park Service (NPS) Visits and Acreage by Type of Area: 2012

Type of area	Recreation visits [1]	Gross area acres	Federal land			Non-federal land	
			NPS fee acres [2]	NPS less than fee acres [3]	Other federal fee acres [4]	Other public acres [5]	Private acres
Total [6]	282,765,682	84,422,725	79,594,996	355,419	440,002	1,367,558	2,664,750
National historic sites	10,139,688	34,397	21,642	765	58	960	10,972
National historical parks	28,647,174	186,355	132,651	4,174	1,327	28,926	19,276
National memorials	35,440,113	10,734	9,551	9	25	81	1,069
National monuments	21,787,708	2,027,421	1,857,189	14,759	27,460	8,058	119,955
National parks	64,879,288	52,126,767	50,366,748	226,584	46,249	559,870	927,315
National recreation areas	44,679,478	3,701,992	3,152,682	23,795	243,101	110,181	172,234
National seashores	18,877,720	596,589	404,446	14,947	61,226	106,668	9,301
National parkways	29,389,054	179,050	158,781	9,108	213	403	10,545

[1] Recreation visit represents the entry of a person onto lands or waters administered by the NPS for recreational purposes excluding government personnel, through traffic, tradespeople, and persons residing within park boundaries. [2] Complete Federal ownership of all rights in the land. [3] Federal ownership of some rights in the land. [4] Tracts under the administration of another federal agency (e.g., U.S. Forest Service, Department of the Army, etc). Bureau of Land Management tracts are also identified as Other Fee (Federal) until they are withdrawn for NPS use; then status changes to Fee (Federal). [5] Non-federal tracts owned by the state, county, and/or other municipalities, including quasi-public entities. [6] Includes other areas, not shown separately.

Source: U.S. National Park Service, Land Resources Division, and unpublished data. See also <https://irma.nps.gov/Stats/>.

Table 1283. Participants in Wildlife-Related Recreation Activities: 2011

[In thousands (37,397 represents 37,397,000). For persons 16 years old and over engaging in activity at least once in 2011. Based on survey and subject to sampling error; see source for details]

Participant	Number	Days of participation	Trips	Participant	Number	Days of participation
Total sportspersons [1].....	**37,397**	**835,725**	**711,645**	**Wildlife watchers** [1]..........	**71,776**	**(X)**
Total anglers...................	33,112	553,841	455,005	Away from home [2]............	22,496	335,625
Freshwater..................	27,547	455,862	368,805	Observe wildlife............	19,808	268,798
Excluding Great Lakes.....	27,060	443,223	353,620	Photograph wildlife.........	12,354	110,459
Great Lakes.................	1,665	19,661	15,185	Feed wildlife................	5,399	59,255
Saltwater	8,889	99,474	86,200			
				Around the home [3]..........	68,598	(X)
Total hunters..................	13,674	281,884	256,640	Observe wildlife.............	45,046	(X)
Big game......................	11,570	212,116	167,320	Photograph wildlife..........	25,370	(X)
Small game...................	4,506	50,884	43,135	Feed wildlife.................	52,817	(X)
Migratory birds...............	2,583	23,263	21,315	Visit public parks............	12,311	(X)
Other animals.................	2,168	34,434	24,869	Maintain plantings or natural areas..............	13,399	(X)

X Not applicable. [1] Detail does not add to total due to multiple responses and nonresponse. [2] Persons taking a trip of at least 1 mile from home for activity. [3] Activity within 1 mile of home.

Source: U.S. Fish and Wildlife Service, *2011 National Survey of Fishing, Hunting, and Wildlife Associated Recreation*, December 2012. See also <http://www.census.gov/prod/www/fishing.html>.

Table 1284. Expenditures for Wildlife-Related Recreation Activities: 2011

[41,789 represents $41,789,000,000. For persons 16 years old and over. Based on survey and subject to sampling error; see source for details]

Expenditure item	Fishing Expenditures (mil. dol.)	Spenders Number (1,000)	Percent	Hunting Expenditures (mil. dol.)	Spenders Number (1,000)	Percent	Wildlife watching Expenditures [1] (mil. dol.)	Spenders Number (1,000)	Percent [2]
Total, all items [3]................	**41,789**	**30,289**	**91**	**33,702**	**13,364**	**98**	**54,890**	**55,980**	**78**
Total trip-related................	21,789	29,309	89	10,421	11,914	87	17,275	19,905	88
Food and lodging..............	7,711	25,158	76	3,881	10,289	75	9,349	17,017	76
Food..........................	5,435	24,891	75	3,218	10,253	75	5,465	16,740	74
Lodging........................	2,276	5,983	18	663	1,881	14	3,884	6,851	30
Transportation..................	6,262	25,293	76	4,768	10,990	80	6,007	18,647	83
Public.........................	804	2,222	7	304	648	5	2,521	3,029	13
Private........................	5,458	24,504	74	4,464	10,885	80	6,486	17,768	79
Other trip costs...............	7,817	25,143	76	1,772	4,581	34	1,918	9,359	42
Equipment expenditures									
Equipment [4]....................	6,142	21,527	65	7,738	10,400	76	11,323	47,951	67
Auxiliary equipment...........	1,107	4,420	13	1,845	5,101	37	1,555	6,445	9
Special equipment [5]..........	8,258	2,296	7	4,389	613	4	14,272	2,219	3
Other expenditures									
Magazines and books.........	108	2,483	8	107	1,934	14	420	8,480	12
Land leasing and ownership..	3,434	924	3	7,129	2,279	17	5,677	1,233	2
Membership dues/contributions............	322	1,728	5	383	1,885	14	2,164	10,756	15
Plantings......................	(X)	(X)	(X)	703	1,273	9	2,204	8,818	12
Licenses, stamps, tags, and permits...................	629	17,166	52	986	10,214	75	(X)	(X)	(X)

X Not applicable. [1] Information on trip-related expenditures for wildlife watching was collected for away-from-home participants only. Equipment and other expenditures for wildlife watching are base on information collected from both away-fro-home and around-the-home participants. [2] Percent of wildlife-watching participants column is base on away-from-home participants for trip-related expenditures. For equipment and other expenditures the percent of wildlife-watching participants is based on total participants. [3] Total not adjusted for multiple responses or nonresponse. [4] Includes fishing, hunting, and wild-life watching. [5] Special equipment includes boats, campers, cabins, trail bikes, etc.

Source: U.S. Fish and Wildlife Service, *2011 National Survey of Fishing, Hunting, and Wildlife Associated Recreation*, December 2012. See also <http://www.census.gov/prod/2012pubs/fwh11-nat.pdf>.

Table 1285. Tribal Gaming Revenues: 2006 to 2011

[Revenue in millions of dollars (24,889 represents $24,899,000,000). For year ending September 30]

Region	2006 Number of operations	2006 Revenue	2007 Number of operations	2007 Revenue	2008 Number of operations	2008 Revenue	2009 Number of operations	2009 Revenue	2010 Number of operations	2010 Revenue	2011 Number of operations	2011 Revenue
Total [1]........	**394**	**24,889**	**391**	**26,143**	**405**	**26,739**	**419**	**26,482**	**422**	**26,503**	**421**	**27,154**
Region I........	46	2,080	46	2,264	47	2,376	49	2,521	50	2,655	49	2,764
Region II........	56	7,675	58	7,796	59	7,363	62	6,970	62	6,794	63	6,903
Region III.......	45	2,719	46	2,874	46	2,774	47	2,600	48	2,539	48	2,614
Region IV.......	122	4,070	111	4,225	115	4,402	120	4,384	119	4,452	119	4,565
Region V........	98	2,126	102	2,584	110	3,047	113	3,225	116	3,352	115	3,592
Region VI.......	27	6,219	28	6,400	28	6,776	28	6,783	27	6,711	27	6,716

[1] Portland (Region I): Alaska, Idaho, Oregon, and Washington. Sacramento (Region II): California, and Northern Nevada. Phoenix (Region III): Arizona, Colorado, New Mexico, and Southern Nevada. St. Paul (Region IV): Iowa, Michigan, Minnesota, Montana, North Dakota, Nebraska, South Dakota, Wisconsin, and Wyoming. Oklahoma City/Tulsa (Region V): Oklahoma, Texas, Kansas. Washington (Region VI): Alabama, Connecticut, Florida, Louisiana, Mississippi, North Carolina, and New York.

Source: National Indian Gaming Commission, *Gaming Revenue Reports 2007-2011*, June 2012, and earlier reports; and *Gaming Revenues by Region 2010 and 2011*, and earlier reports. See also <http://www.nigc.gov/Gaming_Revenue_Reports.aspx>.

Table 1286. Gaming Revenue by Industry: 2000 to 2009

[In millions of dollars (62,154 represents $62,154,000,000). Data shown are for gross revenue. Gross gambling revenue (GGR) is the amount wagered minus the winnings returned to players, a true measure of the economic value of gambling. GGR is the figure used to determine what an operation earns before taxes, salaries, and other expenses are paid]

Industry	2000	2003	2004	2005	2006	2007	2008	2009
Total [1]	62,154	73,036	78,589	84,433	90,931	[2]92,272	[2,3]92,157	[2,3]89,262
Card rooms	949	979	989	1,025	1,104	[3]1,180	[3]1,282	[3]1,232
Commercial casinos	26,455	[2]28,669	[2]30,595	[2]31,775	[2]34,113	[3]34,407	[2,3]33,031	[2,3]31,379
Charitable games and bingo	2,466	2,331	2,336	[3]2,338	[3]2,237	[3]2,220	[3]2,131	[3]2,067
Legal bookmaking	131	128	116	130	192	168	136	136
Lotteries	17,277	20,283	21,405	22,898	24,631	24,780	25,698	25,139
Parimutuel wagering	3,935	3,821	3,750	3,683	3,677	[3]3,529	[3]3,141	[3]2,827

[1] Includes industry not shown separately. [2] Amount includes deepwater cruise ships, cruises-to-nowhere and noncasino devices. [3] Data are estimated.

Source: Christiansen Capital Advisors, LLC. Prepared for the American Gaming Association (AGA). Industry Information, Fact Sheets, *Gaming Revenue: Current-Year Data* ©, <http://www.americangaming.org/industry-resources/research/fact-sheets> and <www.cca-i.com>.

Table 1287. North America Cruise Industry in the United States: 2008 to 2011

[Passenger data are in thousands (9,942 represents 9,942,000). Covers 20 major cruise lines that offer North American cruises with a U.S. port of call. These statistics are not directly comparable to data from the Cruise Lines International Association as published in previous editions of the Statistical Abstract. The Association defined the industry as "those cruise lines that primarily market their cruises in North America"]

Item	2008	2009	2010	2011
Vessels and Traffic:				
Number of ships	120	113	114	115
Cruises	4,239	4,126	4,216	4,222
Passengers	9,942	9,866	10,627	10,887
Passenger nights	64,344	63,874	69,827	71,821
Passenger departures by port:				
Miami, FL	2,114	2,044	2,151	1,970
Fort Lauderdale, FL	1,187	1,277	1,759	1,826
Port Canaveral, FL	1,226	1,189	1,299	1,496
New York, NY	480	406	562	612
San Juan, PR	521	507	522	522
Galveston, TX	413	386	440	462
Tampa, FL	393	401	425	458
Seattle, WA	435	430	469	439
Long Beach, CA	365	415	414	405
New Orleans, LA	185	243	261	373
Other U.S. ports	1,906	1,840	1,721	1,625
Rest of the world	310	302	334	374

Item	2008	2009	2010	2011
Passengers by destination:				
Alaska	1,015	1,011	872	884
Bahamas	1,449	1,741	1,972	2,318
Bermuda	224	264	269	338
Canada/New England	237	232	276	269
Caribbean, Western [1]	2,821	2,830	3,264	3,355
Caribbean, Eastern [2]	1,403	1,244	1,656	1,409
Caribbean, Southern [3]	869	807	820	958
Hawaii	250	193	188	215
Mexico (Pacific)	1,265	1,095	878	697
Transatlantic	173	158	158	197
Other	235	291	273	247
Passengers for top 5 cruise lines:				
Carnival Cruise Line	3,551	3,832	3,977	4,133
Royal Caribbean International	2,619	2,222	2,507	2,369
Norwegian Cruise Line	1,039	1,096	1,171	1,295
Princess Cruises	1,009	973	1,023	928
Holland America Line	627	649	654	679

[1] Area west of Haiti; includes ports in Mexico, Central America, and Colombia. [2] Area as far south as St. Martin, as far west as Haiti. [3] Area south of St. Martin to northern coast of South America as far as Aruba.

Source: Maritime Administration (MARAD), "Cruise Statistics," <http://www.marad.dot.gov/library_landing_page/data_and_statistics/Data_and_Statistics.htm>,accessed June 2012.

Table 1288. Top States and Cities Visited by Overseas Travelers: 2000 to 2012

[25,975 represents 25,975,000. Includes travelers for business and pleasure, international travelers in transit through the United States, and students. Excludes travel by international personnel and international businessmen employed in the United States. Starting with the 2006 data, the statistical policy for visitation estimates of international visitation requires a minimum sample of 400 respondents. States and cities are ranked by the latest overseas visitors data]

State and other area	Overseas visitors [1] (1,000)				City	Overseas visitors [1] (1,000)			
	2000	2005	2011	2012		2000	2005	2011	2012
Total overseas travelers [2,3]	**25,975**	**21,679**	**27,883**	**29,761**	New York, NY [4]	5,714	5,810	9,285	9,107
New York	5,922	6,092	9,508	9,315	Miami, FL	2,935	2,081	2,956	3,482
Florida	6,026	4,379	5,688	6,577	Los Angeles-Long Beach, CA	3,533	2,580	3,653	3,393
California	6,364	4,791	6,134	6,012	Orlando, FL	3,013	2,016	2,788	3,184
Hawaiian Islands	2,727	2,255	2,286	2,827	San Francisco, CA	2,831	2,124	2,872	2,798
Nevada	2,364	1,821	2,872	2,768	Las Vegas, NV	2,260	1,778	2,788	2,708
Illinois	1,377	1,149	1,255	1,399	Oahu/Honolulu, HI	2,234	1,821	1,785	2,232
Guam	1,325	1,127	1,227	1,399	Washington, DC	1,481	1,106	1,812	1,756
Massachusetts	1,429	867	1,422	1,339	Chicago, IL	1,351	1,084	1,199	1,369
Texas	1,169	954	1,283	1,339	Boston, MA	1,325	802	1,311	1,250
Pennsylvania	649	629	920	952	San Diego, CA	701	499	753	774
New Jersey	909	997	976	863	Atlanta, GA	701	564	586	655
Arizona	883	564	864	804	Houston, TX	442	(B)	586	655
Georgia	805	650	669	744	Philadelphia, PA	390	434	613	595
Utah	(B)	(B)	502	476	Flagstaff, AZ [5]	(B)	(B)	586	536
Washington	468	369	502	446	Anaheim-Santa Ana, CA	494	390	362	476
Colorado	519	(B)	446	446	Seattle, WA	416	347	474	417
Virginia	364	(B)	362	387	Dallas-Plano-Irving, TX	494	(B)	418	417
North Carolina	416	(B)	335	387	San Jose, CA	494	347	362	417

B Figure too small to meet statistical standards for reliability of a derived figure. [1] Excludes Canada and Mexico. [2] A person is counted in each area visited, but only once in the total. [3] Includes other states and cities, not shown separately. [4] Data include New York City-White Plains-Wayne, NY-NJ grouped together. [5] Data include Flagstaff, Grand Canyon and Sedona grouped together.

Source: U.S. Department of Commerce, International Trade Administration, Office of Travel and Tourism, *Overseas Visitation Estimates for U.S.: States, Cities, and Census Regions: 2012,* August 2013, and earlier reports. See also <http://www.tinet.ita.doc.gov/outreachpages/inbound.general_information.inbound_overview.html>.

Table 1289. Real Tourism Output: 2000 to 2012

[In millions of dollars (574,304 represents 574,304,000,000)]

Commodity	Direct output (current dollars)			Real output (chained 2005 dollars)		
	2000	2005	2012	2000	2005	2012
Total..	**574,304**	**701,516**	**865,375**	**640,882**	**701,516**	**703,825**
Traveler accommodations...........................	103,122	128,397	174,173	116,936	128,397	158,652
Food services and drinking places..................	86,964	115,058	135,419	100,240	115,058	109,365
Domestic passenger air transportation services..............	71,255	68,841	73,834	64,556	68,841	54,731
International passenger air transportation services..........	29,142	39,013	63,895	36,997	39,013	48,858
Passenger rail transportation services.....................	1,045	1,208	1,583	1,034	1,208	1,227
Passenger water transportation services....................	6,348	8,171	10,440	5,056	8,171	12,119
Interurban bus transportation........................	1,362	1,738	1,731	1,619	1,738	1,265
Interurban charter bus transportation.....................	1,614	1,782	1,916	1,888	1,782	1,473
Urban transit systems and other transportation services........	3,147	3,629	3,490	3,785	3,629	2,709
Taxi service.....................................	3,710	3,876	4,077	4,637	3,876	3,162
Scenic and sightseeing transportation services..............	2,549	2,876	3,772	2,980	2,876	3,311
Automotive rental.................................	25,759	28,213	35,020	28,454	28,213	28,524
Other vehicle rental...............................	622	715	860	660	715	717
Automotive repair services..........................	11,516	11,574	9,668	13,440	11,574	7,769
Parking lots and garages............................	1,262	2,094	2,401	1,579	2,094	1,711
Highway tolls.....................................	506	673	738	618	673	513
Travel arrangement and reservation services...............	29,579	32,223	41,272	28,742	32,223	37,818
Motion pictures and performing arts......................	10,332	14,049	13,951	12,233	14,049	11,939
Spectator sports..................................	5,515	7,371	7,325	6,924	7,371	5,904
Participant sports.................................	9,177	11,294	10,507	9,895	11,294	9,734
Gambling..	25,620	34,559	37,374	29,055	34,559	31,751
All other recreation and entertainment....................	13,988	17,627	18,679	16,548	17,627	16,109
Gasoline..	37,495	57,801	104,261	56,869	57,801	64,139
Nondurable PCE [1] commodities other than gasoline.........	92,675	108,731	108,987	98,346	108,731	93,209

[1] Personal consumption expenditures.

Source: U.S. Bureau of Economic Analysis, "Industry Economic Accounts, U.S. Travel and Tourism Satellite Accounts for 1998-2012," <http://www.bea.gov/industry/tourism_data.htm>, accessed July 2013.

Table 1290. Domestic and International Travel Expenditures by State: 2011

[In millions of dollars (812,651 represents $812,651,000,000). Shows aggregate spending by foreign visitors and by U.S. residents on domestic overnight trips and day trips of 50 miles or more, one way, away from home]

State	Total (mil. dol.)	Percent distribu- tion	Rank	State	Total (mil. dol.)	Percent distribu- tion	Rank	State	Total (mil. dol.)	Percent distribu- tion	Rank
U.S. total...	**812,651**	**100.0**	**(X)**	KS............	6,250	0.8	38	ND..........	2,628	0.3	47
				KY............	7,908	1.0	31	OH..........	16,214	2.0	13
AL............	8,249	1.0	30	LA............	9,923	1.2	25	OK..........	6,866	0.8	33
AK............	2,213	0.3	48	ME...........	3,231	0.4	43	OR..........	8,802	1.1	29
AZ............	15,883	2.0	16	MD...........	14,490	1.8	19	PA..........	22,835	2.8	8
AR............	5,978	0.7	37	MA...........	16,914	2.1	12	RI...........	1,771	0.2	50
CA............	105,331	13.0	1	MI............	16,194	2.0	15	SC..........	11,351	1.4	23
CO............	15,648	1.9	18	MN...........	11,706	1.4	22	SD..........	2,569	0.3	46
CT............	9,595	1.2	27	MS...........	5,838	0.7	34	TN..........	15,333	1.9	17
DE............	1,663	0.2	51	MO...........	12,210	1.5	21	TX..........	55,053	6.8	4
DC............	9,344	1.1	28	MT...........	3,701	0.5	42	UT..........	6,955	0.9	35
FL............	71,532	8.8	2	NE............	4,186	0.5	39	VT..........	2,077	0.3	49
GA............	22,734	2.8	7	NV............	29,592	3.6	6	VA..........	20,857	2.6	9
HI............	16,993	2.1	14	NH...........	3,728	0.5	41	WA..........	13,218	1.6	20
ID............	3,903	0.5	40	NJ............	19,272	2.4	10	WV..........	2,758	0.3	45
IL............	31,736	3.9	5	NM...........	6,431	0.8	36	WI..........	10,188	1.3	24
IN............	9,597	1.2	26	NY............	56,919	7.0	3	WY..........	2,921	0.4	44
IA............	7,412	0.9	32	NC...........	19,012	2.3	11	Other [1].....	24,935	3.1	(X)

X Not applicable. [1] This category includes foreign visitor spending in U.S. territories, and Canadian and Mexican visitor spending in the U.S. Those dollars are not represented in state totals.

Source: U.S. Travel Association, Washington, DC, *Impact of Travel on State Economies 2013* ©, July 2013. See also <http://www.ustravel.org/research>.

Table 1291. Travel Forecast Summary: 2009 to 2016

[In billions of dollars (12,758 represents $12,758,000,000,000)]

Measurement	Unit	2009	2010	2011	2012 [1]	2013 [2]	2014 [2]	2015 [2]	2016 [2]
Real GDP.............................	Billions	12,758	13,063	13,299	13,593	14,123	14,838	15,597.1	16,390.8
Unemployment rate...................	Percent	9.3	9.6	8.9	8.1	7.8	7.6	6.9	6.0
Consumer price index (CPI) [3]......	Percent	214.6	218.1	224.9	229.6	234.0	238.8	243.9	248.4
Travel price index (TPI) [3]............	Percent	241.5	250.7	266.9	273.0	278.5	286.0	294.5	303.5
Total travel expenditures in U.S....	Billions	699.8	747.4	812.7	855.4	889.1	928.1	972.5	1,016.3
U.S. residents......................	Billions	605.6	643.9	696.5	726.9	753.1	782.2	816.5	849.7
International visitors [4]..............	Billions	94.2	103.5	116.1	128.6	136.0	145.9	156.0	166.6
Total international visitors to the United States..............	Millions	55.0	59.8	62.7	67.0	69.6	73.4	77.5	80.7
Total domestic person trips [5]........	Millions	1,900.1	1,963.7	1,997.5	2,030.3	2,057.4	2,094.9	2,132.6	2,160.6

[1] Projected. [2] Forecast. [3] 1982 through 1984 = 100. [4] Excludes international visitors' spending on traveling to the U.S. on U.S. flag carriers, and other miscellaneous transportation. [5] One person on one trip 50 miles or more, one way, away from home or including one or more nights away from home.

Source: U.S.Travel Association, "Travel Industry Forecasts," July 2013. See also <http://www.ustravel.org/research/travel-industry-forecasts>.

Table 1292. Chain-Type Price Indexes for Direct Tourism Output: 2000 to 2012

[Index numbers, 2005=100. For explanation of chain-type price indexes, see text, Section 13]

Tourism goods and services group	2000	2004	2005	2006	2007	2008	2009	2010	2011	2012
Traveler accommodations...................	88.2	95.1	100.0	103.6	108.1	110.2	106.7	106.1	107.8	109.8
Transportation.............................	90.3	92.8	100.0	107.1	111.6	122.1	110.5	119.2	130.2	133.9
Passenger air transportation..............	99.7	93.6	100.0	106.7	109.7	120.9	109.1	118.9	127.5	133.3
All other transportation-related commodities..........................	83.9	92.2	100.0	107.4	112.9	122.9	111.3	119.2	131.9	134.3
Food services and drinking places.........	86.8	96.9	100.0	103.2	107.0	111.9	116.0	117.4	120.3	123.8
Recreation, entertainment, and shopping.......................	90.8	97.8	100.0	102.4	105.0	108.8	110.2	111.5	114.3	116.7
Recreation and entertainment.............	86.6	96.9	100.0	103.2	106.5	110.1	110.7	112.2	114.3	116.4
Shopping..................................	94.2	98.5	100.0	101.7	103.8	107.8	109.9	110.9	114.3	116.9
All tourism goods and services.............	89.6	95.3	100.0	104.5	108.4	114.5	110.5	114.3	119.9	123.0

Source: U.S. Department of Commerce, Bureau of Economic Analysis, Office of Travel and Tourism Industries, *Travel and Tourism Spending Outpaced Growth in the Overall Economy in the First Quarter of 2013*, June 2013. See also <http://bea.gov/newsreleases/industry/tourism/tournewsrelease.htm>.

Table 1293. Tourism Sales by Commodity Group and Tourism Employment by Industry Group: 2005 to 2012

[Sales in billions of dollars (702 represents $702,000,000,000). Employment in thousands (5,876 represents 5,876,000). Direct tourism-related sales comprise all output consumed directly by visitors (e.g., traveler accommodations, passenger air transportation, souvenirs). Direct tourism-related employment comprises all jobs where the workers are engaged in the production of direct tourism-related output (e.g., hotel staff, airline pilots, and souvenir sellers)]

Tourism commodity group	Direct tourism sales (bil. dol.)				Tourism industry group	Direct tourism employment (1,000)			
	2005	2010	2011	2012		2005	2010	2011	2012
All commodities [1]..............	**702**	**750**	**821**	**865**	**All industries**.................	**5,876**	**5,331**	**5,443**	**5,590**
Traveler accommodations........	128	151	162	174	Traveler accommodations......	1,345	1,302	1,344	1,370
Transportation...................	264	303	342	359	Transportation..................	1,161	1,036	1,061	1,079
Passenger air transportation....	108	124	135	138	Air transportation services....	487	450	459	462
All other transportation-related commodities....................	157	179	207	221	All other transportation-related industries..............	674	586	602	617
Food services and drinking places.............................	115	119	127	135	Food and beverage services....................	1,891	1,731	1,781	1,846
Recreation, entertainment, and shopping....................	194	177	189	197	Recreation, entertainment, and shopping.................	1,261	980	1,028	1,054
Recreation\entertainment........	85	81	85	88	Recreation\entertainment.....	650	515	551	568
Shopping.........................	109	96	104	109	Shopping.......................	611	465	478	487
					All other industries.............	253	214	229	240

[1] Commodities that are typically purchased by visitors from the producer: such as airline passenger fares, meals, or hotel services.

Source: U.S. Department of Commerce, Bureau of Economic Analysis, Office of Travel and Tourism Industries, *Travel and Tourism Spending Outpaced Growth in the Overall Economy in the First Quarter of 2013*, June 2013. See also <http://www.bea.gov/industry/index.htm#satellite>.

Table 1294. International Travelers and Payments: 1990 to 2012

[47,880 represents $47,880,000,000. For coverage, see Table 1295. Some traveler data revised since originally issued]

Year	Travel and passenger fare (mil. dol.)				U.S. net travel and passenger receipts (mil. dol.)	U.S. travelers to international countries (1,000)	International travelers to the U.S. (1,000)
	Payments by U.S. travelers		Receipts from international visitors				
	Total [1]	Travel payments [2]	Total [1]	Travel receipts [2]			
1990............	47,880	37,349	58,305	43,007	10,425	44,624	39,363
1995............	59,579	44,916	82,304	63,395	22,725	51,285	43,318
2000............	88,979	65,366	103,088	82,891	14,109	61,327	51,238
2005............	95,119	69,930	102,769	82,160	7,650	63,502	49,206
2006............	99,605	72,959	107,825	86,187	8,220	63,663	50,977
2007............	104,808	77,127	122,542	97,355	17,734	64,029	55,978
2008............	112,335	80,494	141,380	110,423	29,045	63,563	57,942
2009............	99,249	74,132	120,290	94,187	21,041	61,434	54,958
2010............	102,761	75,505	134,450	103,463	31,689	60,393	60,008
2011............	109,308	78,229	152,315	115,552	43,007	58,704	62,711
2012............	118,105	83,451	165,574	126,214	47,469	60,703	66,969

[1] Includes passenger fares, not shown separately. [2] Travel payments and receipts cover purchases of goods and services by U.S. persons traveling abroad, and by foreign travelers in the U.S. Goods and services include food, lodging, recreation, gifts, entertainment, local transportation, and other items.

Source: U.S. Department of Commerce, International Trade Administration, Office of Travel and Tourism Industries, *International Visitation to the United States: A Statistical Summary of U.S. Visitation (2012)*, June 2013; and "U.S. Travel and Tourism Statistics," <http://tinet.ita.doc.gov/outreachpages/inbound.general_information.inbound_overview.html>, accessed September 2013.

Table 1295. International Travel: 1990 to 2012

[In thousands (44,619 represents 44,619,000). U.S. travelers cover residents of the United States, its territories and possessions. International travelers to the U.S. include travelers for business and pleasure, excludes travel by international personnel and international businessmen employed in the United States. Some traveler data revised since originally issued]

Item and area	1990	1995	2000	2005	2008	2009	2010	2011	2012
U.S. travelers to international countries [1]........	**44,619**	**51,285**	**61,327**	**63,503**	**63,564**	**61,419**	**60,271**	**58,704**	**60,723**
Canada........................	12,252	13,005	15,189	14,391	12,504	11,667	11,749	11,597	11,854
Mexico.........................	16,377	18,771	19,285	20,325	20,271	19,452	20,015	20,084	20,367
Total overseas...............	15,990	19,059	26,853	28,787	30,789	30,300	28,507	27,023	28,502
Europe......................	8,043	8,596	13,373	11,976	11,238	10,635	9,806	10,826	11,245
International travelers to the U.S...................	**39,363**	**43,318**	**51,238**	**49,206**	**57,942**	**54,958**	**60,008**	**62,711**	**66,969**
Canada........................	17,263	14,663	14,667	14,862	18,915	17,977	19,964	21,337	22,699
Mexico.........................	7,041	8,016	10,596	12,665	13,686	13,229	13,469	13,491	14,509
Total overseas...............	15,059	20,639	25,975	21,679	25,341	23,756	26,363	27,883	29,761
Europe......................	6,659	8,793	11,597	10,313	12,783	11,550	11,985	12,660	12,478
Asia.........................	4,360	6,616	7,554	6,198	6,179	5,669	7,020	7,247	8,311
South America..............	1,328	2,449	2,941	1,820	2,556	2,742	3,250	3,757	4,416
Caribbean...................	1,137	1,044	1,331	1,135	1,201	1,206	1,201	1,091	1,131
Oceania.....................	662	588	731	737	852	872	1,095	1,243	1,322
Central America............	412	509	822	696	776	758	760	747	803
Middle East.................	365	454	702	527	681	666	736	811	925
Africa.......................	137	186	295	252	315	294	316	327	373

[1] A person is counted in each area visited but only once in the total.

Source: U.S. Department of Commerce, International Trade Administration, Office of Travel and Tourism, "Outbound Travel from the U.S., Monthly U.S. Outbound Air Travel to International Regions," <http://www.tinet.ita.doc.gov/outreachpages/outbound.general_information.outbound_overview.html>, accessed September 2013; and *International Visitation to the United States: A Statistical Summary of U.S. Visitation (2012)*, June 2013. See also <http://www.tinet.ita.doc.gov/outreachpages/inbound.general_information.inbound_overview.html>.

Table 1296. Top 20 U.S. Gateways for Nonstop International Air Travel: 2011

[166,398 represents 166,398,000. International passengers are residents of any country traveling nonstop to and from the United States on U.S. and foreign carriers. The data cover all passengers arriving and departing from U.S. airports on nonstop commercial international flights with 60 seats or more]

Gateway airport	Airport Code	2011	Gateway airport	Airport Code	2011
Total...........................	**(X)**	**166,398**	Washington (Dulles), DC...............	IAD	6,357
Total, top 20.....................	**(X)**	**150,544**	Dallas-Ft. Worth, TX.....................	DFW	5,232
Top 20, percentage of total...........	**(X)**	**90.5**	Honolulu, HI..............................	HNL	3,929
			Boston, MA..............................	BOS	3,906
New York (JFK), NY......................	JFK	23,472	Philadelphia, PA..........................	PHL	3,884
Miami, FL...............................	MIA	18,310	Fort Lauderdale, FL.....................	FLL	3,602
Los Angeles, CA.........................	LAX	16,284	Orlando, FL.............................	MCO	3,429
Newark, NJ.............................	EWR	11,387	Detroit, MI..............................	DTW	3,050
Chicago (O'Hare), IL.....................	ORD	10,440	Charlotte, NC............................	CLT	2,855
Atlanta, GA.............................	ATL	9,362	Seattle-Tacoma, WA.....................	SEA	2,831
San Francisco, CA.......................	SFO	8,676	Las Vegas, NV...........................	LAS	2,515
Houston (G. Bush), TX...................	IAH	8,511	Guam Island, GU........................	GUM	2,511

X Not Applicable

Source: U.S. Department of Transportation, Research and Innovative Technology Administration, Bureau of Transportation Statistics, Office of Airline Information, "T-100 International Segment data," <http://www.transtats.bts.gov/Fields.asp?Table_ID=261>, accessed September 2013.

Table 1297. Crossings for Top 5 U.S.-Canadian and U.S.-Mexican Border Land—Passenger Gateways: 2012

[33,084 represents 33,084,000]

Item and gateway	Entering the U.S. (1,000)	Item and gateway	Entering the U.S. (1,000)
All U.S.-Canadian land gateways [1]		**All U.S.-Mexican land gateways** [1]	
Personal vehicles...........................	33,084	Personal vehicles...........................	62,703
Personal vehicle passengers..........................	62,008	Personal vehicle passengers..............	115,050
Buses...	108	Buses...	212
Bus passengers...............................	2,436	Bus passengers...............................	2,867
Train passengers.............................	269	Train passengers.............................	3
Pedestrians.....................................	427	Pedestrians.....................................	41,142
Top five gateways		**Top five gateways**	
Personal vehicles:		Personal vehicles:	
Buffalo-Niagara Falls, NY...............	6,072	San Ysidro, CA..............................	11,482
Blaine, WA....................................	4,731	El Paso, TX....................................	9,462
Detroit, MI....................................	4,166	Otay Mesa, CA..............................	5,346
Port Huron, MI..............................	1,981	Hidalgo, TX....................................	4,894
Point Roberts, WA.........................	1,170	Laredo, TX.....................................	4,440
Personal vehicle passengers:		Personal vehicle passengers:	
Buffalo-Niagara Falls, NY...............	13,062	San Ysidro, CA..............................	19,945
Blaine, WA....................................	9,121	El Paso, TX....................................	15,908
Detroit, MI....................................	7,326	Hidalgo, TX....................................	9,484
Port Huron, MI..............................	3,946	Otay Mesa, CA..............................	9,298
Champlain-Rouses Pt., NY..............	2,582	Laredo, TX.....................................	8,768
Pedestrians:		Pedestrians:	
Buffalo-Niagara Falls, NY...............	291	San Ysidro, CA..............................	8,134
Sumas, WA...................................	37	El Paso, TX....................................	6,091
Point Roberts, WA.........................	21	Calexico, CA..................................	4,886
Detroit, MI....................................	16	Nogales, AZ..................................	3,239
International Falls, MN...................	16	Laredo, TX.....................................	3,206

[1] Data reflect all personal vehicles and buses, passengers, and pedestrians entering the U.S.-Canadian border and U.S.-Mexican border, regardless of nationality.

Source: U.S. Department of Transportation, Bureau of Transportation Statistics, "Border Crossing / Entry Data," <http://transborder.bts.gov/programs/international/transborder/TBDR_BC/TBDR_BC_Index.html>, accessed August 2013.

Table 1298. Foreign Visitors for Pleasure Admitted by Country of Citizenship: 2000 to 2012

[In thousands (30,511 represents 30,511,000). For years ending September 30. Represents non-U.S. citizens admitted to the country for a temporary period of time, for pleasure (tourists). Includes nonimmigrant admission classes B2 (temporary visitors for pleasure), GMT (Commonwealth of the Northern Marianas Islands visa waiver program–temporary visitors for pleasure to Guam or Northern Mariana Islands), and WT (visa waiver program–temporary visitors for pleasure)]

Country	2000 [1]	2005	2011	2012	Country	2000 [1]	2005	2011	2012
All countries [2].............	**30,511**	**23,815**	**40,579**	**42,025**	Thailand.....................	76	37	50	54
					Turkey........................	93	57	93	100
Europe [3].........................	**11,806**	**10,016**	**12,255**	**12,435**	United Arab Emirates......	36	3	11	13
Austria.......................	182	116	171	184	**Africa** [3].........................	**327**	**212**	**303**	**358**
Belgium......................	254	154	232	236	Egypt.........................	44	19	40	58
Czech Republic..............	44	26	70	74	Nigeria.......................	27	40	68	84
Denmark.....................	150	153	250	254	South Africa.................	114	64	73	79
Finland.......................	95	76	110	117	**Oceania** [3].....................	**748**	**723**	**1,253**	**1,352**
France.......................	1,113	1,007	1,493	1,560	Australia.....................	535	527	1,036	1,117
Germany.....................	1,925	1,248	1,651	1,773	New Zealand.................	170	184	202	222
Greece.......................	60	40	59	54	**North America** [3, 4]........	**6,501**	**5,546**	**14,781**	**14,469**
Hungary......................	58	30	55	56	Canada.......................	277	23	108	104
Iceland.......................	27	34	50	49	Mexico.......................	3,972	4,070	14,674	14,365
Ireland.......................	325	398	381	357	**Caribbean**....................	**1,404**	**876**	**962**	**989**
Italy..........................	626	636	991	973	Bahamas, The...............	24	257	234	234
Netherlands..................	559	483	610	612	Dominican Republic.......	195	189	222	233
Norway.......................	144	117	223	240	Haiti..........................	72	65	86	87
Poland.......................	116	119	102	97	Jamaica......................	240	152	167	174
Portugal......................	86	81	131	133	Trinidad and Tobago.......	133	106	129	139
Russia........................	74	53	179	207	**Central America**...........	**792**	**578**	**680**	**715**
Spain.........................	370	402	743	724	Costa Rica...................	172	109	152	158
Sweden......................	321	249	399	409	El Salvador..................	175	147	97	93
Switzerland..................	400	207	388	416	Guatemala...................	177	135	161	170
United Kingdom.............	4,671	4,232	3,707	3,635	Honduras....................	87	75	114	124
Asia [3]..........................	**7,853**	**5,688**	**6,705**	**7,639**	Nicaragua....................	47	33	40	43
China [5].....................	656	221	701	1,005	Panama.......................	106	64	99	108
India.........................	253	247	564	633	**South America** [3]...........	**2,867**	**1,498**	**3,367**	**3,892**
Indonesia....................	62	42	55	60	Argentina....................	515	145	467	553
Israel.........................	319	220	248	263	Bolivia........................	48	18	32	34
Japan.........................	4,946	3,758	3,164	3,515	Brazil.........................	706	385	1,277	1,526
Korea, South................	606	528	1,022	1,117	Chile..........................	194	82	150	157
Malaysia.....................	64	32	46	53	Colombia.....................	411	282	492	544
Pakistan......................	47	34	40	47	Ecuador......................	122	119	196	199
Philippines...................	163	144	181	189	Peru..........................	190	142	169	180
Saudi Arabia.................	67	10	53	79	Uruguay......................	66	24	41	48
Singapore....................	131	57	91	103	Venezuela....................	570	270	500	598
Taiwan.......................	(NA)	201	199	191					

[1] Due to the temporary expiration of the Visa Waiver Program from May through October 2000, data for business and pleasure not available separately for 2000 and 2001. [2] Total includes visitors of unknown country of citizenship. [3] Total includes other countries, not shown separately. [4] The majority of short-term admissions from Canada and Mexico are excluded. [5] Prior to 2005, data for China includes Taiwan. Beginning in 2005, data for China includes Hong Kong and Macau.

Source: U.S. Dept. of Homeland Security, Office of Immigration Statistics, *2012 Yearbook of Immigration Statistics: Supplemental Tables,* August 2013, and earlier reports. See also <http://www.dhs.gov/yearbook-immigration-statistics>.

Section 27
Accommodation, Food Services, and Other Services

This section presents statistics relating to services other than those covered in the previous sections on wholesale and retail trade, transportation, communications, financial services, and recreation services. Data shown for services are classified by kind of business and cover sales or receipts, establishments, employees, payrolls, and other items.

The principal sources of these data are from the U.S. Census Bureau and include the *2007 Economic Census*, annual surveys, and the *County Business Patterns* program. These data are supplemented by data from several sources such as the National Restaurant Association on food and drink sales (Table 1310), the American Hotel & Lodging Association on lodging (Table 1309), and Magna Global on advertising (Table 1306).

Data on these services also appear in several other sections. For instance, labor force employment and earnings data appear in Section 12, Labor Force, Employment, and Earnings; gross domestic product of the industry (Table 698) appears in Section 13, Income, Expenditures, Poverty, and Wealth; and financial data (several tables) from the quarterly *Statistics of Income Bulletin*, published by the Internal Revenue Service, appear in Section 15, Business Enterprise.

Censuses—Limited coverage of the service industries started in 1933. Beginning with the 1967 census, legislation provides for a census of each area to be conducted every 5 years (for years ending in "2" and "7"). For more information on the most current census, see the Economic Census, *Guide to Economic Census*, found at <http://www.census.gov/econ/census07/www/user_guide.html>. The industries covered in the censuses and surveys of business are defined in the

North American Industry Classification System (NAICS). For information on NAICS, see the Census Web site at <http://www.census.gov/eos/www/naics/>.

In general, the 2007 Economic Census has two final series of publications for these sectors: 1) subject series with reports such as product lines, and establishment and firm sizes and 2) geographic reports with individual reports for each state. For information on these series, see the Census Bureau Web site at <http://www.census.gov/econ/census07>.

Current surveys—The *Service Annual Survey* provides annual estimates of nationwide receipts for selected personal, business, leasing and repair, amusement and entertainment, social and health, and other professional service industries in the United States. For selected social, health, and other professional service industries, separate estimates are developed for receipts of taxable firms and revenue and expenses for firms and organizations exempt from federal income taxes. Several service sectors from this survey are covered in other sections of this publication. The estimates for tax exempt firms in these industries are derived from a sample of employer firms only. Estimates obtained from annual and monthly surveys are based on sample data and are not expected to agree exactly with results that would be obtained from a complete census of all establishments. Data include estimates for sampling units not reporting.

Statistical reliability—For a discussion of statistical collection and estimation, sampling procedures, and measures of statistical reliability applicable to Census Bureau data, see Appendix III.

Table 1299. Selected Service-Related Industries—Establishments, Sales, Payroll, and Employees by Kind of Business: 2007

[1,251,004 represents $1,251,004,000,000. Covers only establishments with payroll. For statement on methodology, see Appendix III]

Kind of business	2007 NAICS code [1]	Establishments, (number)	Sales or receipts (mil. dol.)	Annual payroll (mil. dol.)	Paid employees [2] (1,000)
Professional, scientific, and technical services............	54	**847,492**	**1,251,004**	**502,074**	**7,870**
Professional, scientific, and technical services............	541	847,492	1,251,004	502,074	7,870
Management of companies and enterprises............	55	**51,451**	**104,443**	**249,511**	**2,664**
Administrative and support and waste management and remediation services............	56	**395,292**	**630,771**	**301,450**	**10,251**
Administrative and support services............	561	373,505	555,583	284,603	9,865
Waste management and remediation services............	562	21,787	75,188	16,848	386
Accommodation and food services............	72	**634,361**	**613,796**	**170,827**	**11,601**
Accommodation............	721	62,740	180,391	46,393	1,971
Food services and drinking places............	722	571,621	433,405	124,434	9,630
Other services (except public administration)............	81	**540,148**	**405,284**	**99,123**	**3,479**
Repair and maintenance............	811	222,151	137,733	40,070	1,261
Personal and laundry services............	812	210,151	82,105	26,759	1,338
Religious, grantmaking, civic, professional, and similar organizations............	813	107,846	185,447	32,294	880

[1] North American Industrial Classification System, 2007; see text, Section 15. [2] For employees on the payroll during the pay period including March 12.

Source: U.S. Census Bureau, 2007 Economic Census, "Economy-Wide Key Statistics," <http://factfinder2.census.gov>, accessed August 2012.

Table 1300. Selected Service-Related Industries—Nonemployer Establishments and Receipts by Kind of Business: 2009 to 2011

[3,067 represents 3,067,000. Includes only firms subject to federal income tax. Nonemployers are businesses with no paid employees. Data originate chiefly from administrative records of the Internal Revenue Service; see Appendix III]

Kind of business	2007 NAICS code [1]	Firms (1,000)			Receipts (mil. dol.)		
		2009	2010	2011	2009	2010	2011
Professional, scientific, and technical services............	54	**3,067**	**3,121**	**3,164**	**123,437**	**130,613**	**136,702**
Professional, scientific, and technical services [2]............	541	3,067	3,121	3,164	123,437	130,613	136,702
Legal services............	5411	266	272	276	16,669	17,137	17,699
Accounting, tax preparation, bookkeeping, and payroll services............	5412	355	359	361	8,545	8,754	8,983
Architectural, engineering [3]............	5413	222	227	230	9,580	9,934	10,431
Management, scientific and technical consulting............	5416	654	654	654	27,869	29,778	30,900
Scientific research and development services............	5417	35	33	33	1,111	1,166	1,210
Administrative and support and waste management and remediation services............	56	**1,865**	**1,937**	**1,985**	**37,429**	**39,111**	**40,887**
Administrative and support services [2]............	561	1,845	1,917	1,965	36,130	37,694	39,427
Office administrative services............	5611	202	202	210	3,048	3,143	3,340
Business support services............	5614	214	219	222	5,448	5,648	5,882
Services to buildings and dwellings............	5617	1,142	1,205	1,233	20,431	21,305	22,165
Waste management and remediation services............	562	20	21	21	1,299	1,417	1,460
Accommodation and food services............	72	**314**	**329**	**341**	**14,015**	**14,355**	**14,863**
Accommodation............	721	53	54	56	2,827	2,894	3,018
Food services and drinking places............	722	260	275	285	11,188	11,461	11,845
Full-service restaurants............	7221	42	45	46	3,038	3,099	3,090
Limited-service eating places............	7222	48	48	49	2,934	2,930	3,042
Special food services............	7223	142	153	160	3,585	3,799	4,045
Drinking places (alcoholic beverages)............	7224	28	30	30	1,632	1,632	1,668
Other services (except public administration)............	81	**3,149**	**3,358**	**3,517**	**76,290**	**80,669**	**85,693**
Repair and maintenance [2]............	811	711	739	755	24,210	25,183	26,297
Automotive repair and maintenance............	8111	308	322	327	12,534	13,127	13,706
Personal and household goods repair [4]............	8114	303	315	325	7,884	8,131	8,480
Personal and laundry services............	812	2,233	2,414	2,556	48,955	52,320	56,247
Personal care services............	8121	1,042	1,152	1,235	22,033	23,868	25,738
Death care services............	8122	16	16	16	777	815	830
Drycleaning and laundry services............	8123	34	34	34	1,836	1,807	1,805
Other personal services............	8129	1,141	1,212	1,271	24,309	25,830	27,874
Religious, grantmaking, civic, professional, and similar organizations............	813	205	205	205	3,125	3,167	3,149

[1] North American Industry Classification System, see text, Section 15. [2] Includes other kinds of business not shown separately. [3] Includes related services. [4] Includes maintenance.

Source: U.S. Census Bureau, Nonemployer Statistics, "Geographic Area Series: Nonemployer Statistics by Legal Form of Organization," <http://factfinder2.census.gov>, accessed August 2013.

Table 1301. Selected Service-Related Industries—Establishments, Employees, and Payroll by Industry: 2010 and 2011

[852 represents 852,000, except payroll. Covers establishments with paid employees. Excludes most government employees, railroad employees, and self-employed persons. For statement on methodology, see Appendix III]

Kind of business	2007 NAICS code [1]	Establishments (1,000)		Employees [2] (1,000)		Annual payroll (bil. dol.)	
		2010	2011	2010	2011	2010	2011
Professional, scientific, & technical services	**54**	**852**	**851**	**7,822**	**7,930**	**543.1**	**568.0**
Professional, scientific, & technical services	541	852	851	7,822	7,930	543.1	568.0
Legal services	5411	188	186	1,155	1,146	89.4	91.8
Offices of lawyers	54111	173	172	1,075	1,069	85.9	88.3
Accounting, tax preparation, bookkeeping, and payroll services	5412	125	125	1,308	1,316	56.6	58.2
Tax preparation services	541213	27	27	217	202	2.1	2.2
Architectural, engineering, & related services [3]	5413	109	107	1,293	1,274	93.1	94.6
Architectural services	54131	22	21	155	148	10.1	10.1
Engineering services	54133	58	57	925	914	72.1	73.1
Specialized design services [3]	5414	30	30	106	107	5.8	6.0
Graphic design services	54143	15	15	52	50	2.5	2.7
Computer systems design & related services [3]	5415	125	126	1,426	1,445	120.6	125.3
Custom computer programming services	541511	55	59	591	644	50.0	57.0
Computer systems design services	541512	52	49	545	525	46.2	45.6
Management, scientific, technical consulting services [3]	5416	149	151	891	940	66.2	72.1
Management consulting services	54161	114	117	713	754	54.1	59.2
Environmental consulting services	54162	10	10	71	75	4.5	4.7
Scientific research & development services	5417	17	17	647	693	63.2	70.1
Research & development in the physical engineering & life sciences	54171	14	15	606	651	60.4	67.2
Advertising & related services [3]	5418	38	38	412	429	25.5	27.3
Advertising agencies	54181	13	13	149	166	11.5	13.1
Direct mail advertising	54186	3	3	55	53	2.4	2.4
Other professional, scientific, & tech services	5419	71	71	586	580	22.8	22.5
Veterinary services	54194	29	29	300	301	9.6	9.8
Management of companies and enterprises	**55**	**51**	**49**	**2,833**	**2,922**	**281.8**	**298.8**
Administrative and support and waste management and remediation services	**56**	**382**	**381**	**8,977**	**9,390**	**304.1**	**326.3**
Administrative & support services [3]	561	360	358	8,627	9,033	287.0	308.1
Employment services	5613	47	46	4,296	4,633	147.8	161.7
Temporary help services	56132	30	30	2,290	2,603	64.8	71.8
Business support services [3]	5614	35	34	767	753	23.8	23.5
Telephone call centers	56142	5	5	395	405	9.7	10.2
Collection agencies	56144	5	5	143	137	4.7	4.6
Credit bureaus	56145	1	1	20	16	1.7	1.5
Travel arrangement & reservation services	5615	21	21	228	230	11.5	11.9
Travel agencies	56151	14	14	105	105	5.4	5.5
Investigation & security services	5616	25	25	779	794	21.1	22.2
Investigation, guard, & armored car services	56161	15	15	665	679	16.1	16.9
Security systems services	56162	10	10	114	115	5.0	5.3
Services to buildings & dwellings	5617	177	177	1,629	1,636	39.7	40.8
Waste management & remediation services	562	22	23	350	357	17.1	18.1
Waste collection	5621	10	10	186	183	8.6	8.9
Waste treatment & disposal	5622	3	3	48	49	2.7	2.7
Remediation & other waste mgmt services	5629	9	10	116	126	5.8	6.5
Accommodation & food services	**72**	**644**	**649**	**11,312**	**11,556**	**185.6**	**194.2**
Accommodation	721	63	63	1,821	1,865	45.9	48.3
Traveler accommodation	7211	54	54	1,772	1,815	44.6	46.9
Hotels (except casino hotels) & motels	72111	49	49	1,369	1,410	32.1	34.0
RV (recreational vehicle) parks & recreational camps	7212	7	7	38	38	1.1	1.2
Rooming & boarding houses	7213	2	2	11	11	0.2	0.2
Food services & drinking places	722	581	586	9,491	9,692	139.7	145.9
Full-service restaurants	7221	226	227	4,490	4,570	71.0	74.3
Limited-service eating places	7222	272	276	4,021	4,106	51.3	53.3
Special food services	7223	40	40	633	668	12.7	13.3
Drinking places (alcoholic beverages)	7224	44	43	347	347	4.7	4.9
Other services (except public administration)	**81**	**725**	**722**	**5,204**	**5,182**	**140.3**	**144.2**
Repair & maintenance [3]	811	211	209	1,155	1,163	40.1	41.6
Automotive repair & maintenance	8111	157	156	791	801	24.1	25.1
Personal & household goods repair & maintenance	8114	20	20	70	68	2.0	2.0
Personal & laundry services [3]	812	208	209	1,311	1,312	27.3	28.2
Personal care services	8121	113	114	628	632	11.1	11.5
Death care services	8122	21	21	134	136	4.2	4.3
Drycleaning & laundry services	8123	37	36	307	298	7.1	7.2
Religious/grantmaking/civic/professional [4]	813	306	304	2,739	2,707	72.9	74.5
Religious organizations	8131	182	181	1,689	1,665	31.8	32.1
Grantmaking & giving services	8132	18	18	168	170	8.6	8.8
Social advocacy organizations	8133	16	16	144	148	5.8	6.1
Civic & social organizations	8134	28	27	240	236	4.4	4.4
Business/professional/labor/political [4]	8139	62	61	497	488	22.4	23.1
Labor unions [4]	81393	15	15	162	154	5.2	5.2

[1] North American Industry Classification System, 2007. See text, section 15. [2] Includes employees on the payroll for the pay period including March 12. [3] Includes other kinds of business, not shown separately. [4] And similar organizations.

Source: U.S. Census Bureau, County Business Patterns, "Geography Area Series: County Business Patterns," <http://factfinder2.census.gov>, accessed August 2013.

Table 1302. Employed Persons in Service Industries—Sex, Race, and Hispanic or Latino Origin by Industry: 2012

[16,593 represents 16,593,000. Civilian noninstitutionalized population 16 years and older. Based on the Current Population Survey (CPS); see text, Section 1, and Appendix III. For information on employees in other sectors, see Table 642 and Table 660]

Industry	2007 NAICS code [1]	Total employed (1,000)	Percent of total			
			Female	Black [2]	Asian [2]	Hispanic or Latino [3]
Professional and business services............................	(X)	**16,539**	**41.1**	**9.6**	**6.9**	**15.2**
Professional and technical services...........................	**54**	**9,913**	**43.2**	**6.4**	**9.4**	**7.5**
Legal services..	5411	1,714	56.5	6.7	5.2	9.1
Accounting, tax preparation, bookkeeping, & payroll services...................................	5412	1,044	60.4	8.0	7.1	8.6
Architectural, engineering, and related services..............	5413	1,525	25.7	6.0	5.1	6.6
Specialized design services................................	5414	371	57.9	3.8	6.4	11.0
Computer systems design & related services................	5415	2,092	24.5	5.8	20.2	5.1
Management, scientific, and technical consulting services.....	5416	1,415	41.7	7.3	7.4	5.9
Scientific research & development services....................	5417	510	48.1	6.1	13.1	8.5
Advertising and related services..........................	5418	559	50.2	6.1	7.2	7.7
Other professional, scientific, and technical services [4].....	5419	373	56.1	5.9	6.6	10.9
Veterinary services..	54194	311	77.1	5.0	2.5	10.9
Management, administrative, and waste services...........	**55–56**	**6,626**	**38.0**	**14.3**	**3.2**	**26.7**
Management of companies and enterprises...................	55	187	49.7	6.6	5.3	11.8
Employment services......................................	5613	1,037	52.1	21.2	5.1	19.5
Business support services.................................	5614	793	62.9	15.6	2.3	13.2
Travel arrangement & reservation services.................	5615	268	61.7	11.5	10.3	11.5
Investigations & security services.........................	5616	782	24.2	22.7	3.6	14.8
Services to buildings and dwellings [5]......................	5617	1,422	52.4	13.9	2.1	40.6
Landscaping services......................................	56173	1,327	7.4	6.6	1.7	42.7
Other administrative and support services...................	5611,2,9	293	38.7	9.9	5.5	14.6
Waste management and remediation services.................	562	518	14.4	14.0	1.2	20.6
Accommodation and food services..........................	**72**	**10,171**	**52.4**	**12.0**	**7.1**	**24.7**
Accommodation..	721	1,426	57.4	15.0	8.7	26.4
Traveler accommodation.................................	7211	1,332	57.6	15.7	9.1	27.7
Recreational vehicle parks and camps, and rooming and board houses.......................	7212,3	94	55.5	4.5	2.9	6.8
Food services and drinking places.........................	722	8,745	51.6	11.5	6.9	24.4
Restaurants and other food services [6]...................	722	8,484	51.5	11.7	7.0	24.9
Drinking places, alcoholic beverages.....................	7224	261	54.1	7.1	3.3	9.4
Other services...	**81**	**7,168**	**52.0**	**9.8**	**7.7**	**18.0**
Other services (except private households)...................	81	6,430	47.8	10.0	8.1	15.7
Repair and maintenance...................................	811	2,146	12.1	7.2	4.3	21.9
Automotive repair and maintenance [7]...................	8111	1,237	10.0	6.3	3.5	21.6
Car washes..	811192	171	13.5	12.0	1.8	36.8
Electronic & precision equipment repair and maintenance..	8112	179	12.2	13.4	11.7	11.2
Commercial and industrial machinery & equipment repair and maintenance..............................	8113	360	8.6	6.7	2.5	22.5
Personal and household goods repair and maintenance [8].......................................	8114	191	30.6	4.1	8.5	18.3
Footwear and leather goods repair.......................	81143	8	(Z)	(Z)	(Z)	(Z)
Personal and laundry services.............................	812	2,379	71.8	12.2	15.5	15.9
Barber shops...	812111	121	28.7	35.4	2.2	22.8
Beauty salons..	812112	987	90.0	13.2	8.4	15.0
Nail salons and other personal care services...............	812113, 81219	466	74.0	4.4	44.0	8.5
Drycleaning & laundry services...........................	8123	337	57.7	12.7	19.1	30.5
Funeral homes, cemeteries, and crematories...............	8122	124	34.0	11.0	0.2	6.8
Other personal services.................................	8129	344	59.3	11.9	3.9	15.3
Membership associations and organizations.................	813	1,904	58.0	10.4	3.1	8.6
Religious organizations.................................	8131	1,059	51.7	9.2	2.7	7.8
Civic, social, advocacy organizations, grantmaking & giving services....................................	8132,3,4	638	69.7	12.6	3.2	9.7
Business, professional, political, and similar organizations [9].........................	8139	157	61.7	7.6	4.0	7.6
Labor unions...	81393	50	32.1	16.4	7.6	16.2
Private households..	814	738	88.9	8.4	4.5	37.2

X Not applicable. Z Base less than 50,000. [1] Based on the North American Industry Classification System, 2007; see Section 15. [2] The Current Population Survey (CPS) allows respondents to choose more than one race. Data represent persons who selected this race group only and exclude persons reporting more than one race. See also comments on race in text for Section 1. [3] Persons of Hispanic or Latino ethnicity may be of any race. [4] Excludes NAICS 54194 (veterinary services). [5] Excludes NAICS 56173 (landscaping services). [6] Excludes NAICS 7224 (drinking places, alcoholic beverages). [7] Excludes NAICS 811192 (car washes). [8] Excludes NAICS 81143 (footwear and leather goods repair). [9] Excludes NAICS 81393 (labor unions).

Source: U.S. Bureau of Labor Statistics, "Labor Force Statistics from the Current Population Survey," <http://www.bls.gov/cps/tables.htm#annual>, accessed August 2013.

Table 1303. Selected Service-Related Industries—Establishments, Employees, and Annual Payroll by State: 2011

[Employees in thousands (7,930 represents 7,930,000); payroll in millions of dollars (568,030 represents $568,030,000,000). Covers establishments with paid employees. Excludes most government employees, railroad employees, and self-employed persons. For statement on methodology, see Appendix III]

| State | Professional, scientific, and technical services (NAICS 54) [1] | | | Administrative and support and waste management and remediation services (NAICS 56) [1] | | | Accommodation and food services (NAICS 72) [1] | | |
	Establishments	Employees [2] (1,000)	Annual payroll (mil. dol.)	Establishments	Employees [2] (1,000)	Annual payroll (mil. dol.)	Establishments	Employees [2] (1,000)	Annual payroll (mil. dol.)
United States........	850,903	7,930	568,030	380,671	9,390	326,264	649,011	11,556	194,214
Alabama.............	9,249	93	5,881	4,109	133	3,310	8,179	150	2,045
Alaska...............	1,920	17	1,142	1,092	20	964	2,008	26	614
Arizona..............	16,173	129	7,704	8,011	208	7,303	11,555	247	4,074
Arkansas............	5,700	34	1,585	2,590	51	1,315	5,323	92	1,171
California............	113,902	1,213	92,435	40,967	1,086	42,359	76,387	1,340	24,896
Colorado............	23,595	170	12,663	8,261	206	8,970	12,328	228	3,902
Connecticut.........	9,344	101	8,051	5,137	86	3,373	8,039	129	2,583
Delaware............	2,552	24	2,020	1,357	27	1,083	1,999	34	591
District of Columbia.....	4,997	97	10,905	1,134	34	1,441	2,308	58	1,560
Florida...............	69,381	434	25,889	32,034	1,172	43,934	36,015	758	13,256
Georgia.............	27,804	222	14,344	11,658	313	9,468	18,576	345	5,193
Hawaii..............	3,284	25	1,401	1,803	46	1,297	3,468	94	2,361
Idaho...............	4,193	31	1,648	2,113	35	948	3,515	51	697
Illinois..............	38,477	347	27,074	16,549	469	14,139	26,802	457	7,735
Indiana..............	12,836	101	5,540	7,037	167	4,713	12,747	247	3,429
Iowa................	6,216	48	2,439	3,546	70	1,925	6,869	112	1,443
Kansas..............	7,115	56	3,132	3,447	69	2,115	5,958	104	1,364
Kentucky............	8,113	64	2,953	3,979	85	2,167	7,578	153	2,074
Louisiana...........	11,580	88	4,914	4,557	101	3,191	8,807	183	2,964
Maine...............	3,517	23	1,250	1,947	22	620	3,909	46	843
Maryland............	19,542	244	19,086	7,896	178	6,712	11,036	196	3,426
Massachusetts........	21,218	250	24,160	9,706	201	7,962	16,587	259	5,046
Michigan............	21,597	240	15,953	11,303	278	8,441	19,402	328	4,626
Minnesota...........	16,433	137	9,029	7,070	140	4,899	11,090	211	3,272
Mississippi..........	4,705	30	1,368	2,251	50	1,378	5,045	114	1,789
Missouri............	13,139	141	9,007	7,253	144	4,467	12,341	236	3,412
Montana............	3,564	17	769	1,695	20	526	3,388	44	630
Nebraska...........	4,397	39	2,099	2,614	86	2,949	4,244	68	842
Nevada.............	8,089	52	3,106	4,001	87	2,678	5,719	295	8,437
New Hampshire.........	3,833	30	1,722	2,198	46	1,881	3,584	52	913
New Jersey..........	29,530	317	25,248	13,271	266	9,621	19,606	277	5,498
New Mexico..........	4,707	48	3,128	1,858	38	1,110	4,076	80	1,192
New York............	59,043	571	48,001	25,296	482	21,885	48,553	642	13,737
North Carolina........	22,624	185	12,456	11,514	249	7,411	19,224	345	5,017
North Dakota.........	1,585	11	568	950	12	346	1,841	32	446
Ohio................	24,070	237	14,492	13,151	346	9,584	23,194	424	5,656
Oklahoma...........	9,347	62	3,262	4,440	89	2,908	7,119	133	1,800
Oregon..............	11,698	80	4,749	5,171	87	2,421	10,352	145	2,392
Pennsylvania.........	29,402	310	21,630	14,765	297	9,482	27,702	431	6,639
Rhode Island.........	2,984	24	1,641	1,687	22	712	2,952	42	709
South Carolina........	9,703	81	4,472	5,340	138	3,743	9,640	178	2,584
South Dakota.........	1,808	10	433	1,056	11	295	2,331	37	539
Tennessee...........	10,886	100	5,783	6,468	199	6,060	11,710	232	3,432
Texas...............	60,651	579	42,900	25,412	859	29,673	47,009	938	14,451
Utah................	8,849	69	3,710	3,846	103	3,191	4,957	92	1,291
Vermont.............	2,169	22	1,091	1,064	7	212	1,880	30	489
Virginia.............	29,107	421	35,968	10,150	240	9,846	16,462	310	4,948
Washington..........	19,934	166	12,028	8,781	145	6,553	16,088	226	4,116
West Virginia.........	2,976	25	1,109	1,454	32	864	3,666	61	828
Wisconsin...........	11,270	107	5,654	6,725	134	3,649	14,063	217	2,809
Wyoming............	2,095	9	439	957	6	169	1,780	26	457

[1] North American Industry Classification System, 2007. See text, section 15. [2] For employees on the payroll for the pay period including March 12.

Source: U.S. Census Bureau, County Business Patterns, "Geography Area Series: County Business Patterns," <http://factfinder2.census.gov>, accessed August 2013.

Table 1304. Professional, Scientific, and Technical Services—Estimated Revenue: 2006 to 2011

[In millions of dollars (1,116,770 represents $1,116,770,000,000). For taxable employer firms. Estimates have been adjusted to the results of the 2007 Economic Census. Based on the Service Annual Survey and administrative data; see Appendix III]

Kind of business	2007 NAICS code [1]	2006	2007	2008	2009	2010	2011
Professional, scientific, and technical services (except notaries)............	**54**	**1,116,770**	**1,220,436**	**1,286,720**	**1,220,642**	**1,264,267**	**1,326,551**
Offices of lawyers...............................	54111	212,634	225,060	229,893	223,087	226,057	232,557
Other legal services............................	54119	12,321	11,629	11,741	11,167	11,231	10,824
Offices of certified public accountants.............	541211	60,244	66,588	69,233	68,915	66,509	67,938
Tax preparation services.........................	541213	4,832	5,251	5,526	5,665	5,664	5,753
Payroll services.................................	541214	25,646	28,916	31,050	28,932	29,073	31,131
Other accounting services.......................	541219	12,760	13,355	14,251	14,519	14,896	15,632
Architectural services...........................	54131	32,587	37,150	37,759	29,802	26,050	26,989
Landscape architectural services.................	54132	4,085	4,365	4,365	3,385	3,058	2,965
Engineering services............................	54133	173,861	187,532	199,943	178,375	172,403	177,703
Testing laboratories.............................	54138	10,093	12,387	13,469	12,701	13,631	14,387
Other related services [2]........................	5413x	11,670	12,767	12,379	10,697	11,057	12,019
Interior design services..........................	54141	8,899	9,799	9,290	6,814	6,394	6,992
Graphic design services.........................	54143	8,342	8,281	8,286	7,133	7,478	7,553
All other design services [3]......................	5414y	2,307	2,474	2,387	2,233	2,237	2,706
Computer systems design and related services. ...	5415	213,359	244,389	265,719	260,466	283,790	303,191
Management consulting services [4]...............	54161	108,056	115,371	121,001	109,654	118,096	125,865
Environmental consulting services................	54162	9,225	10,423	11,125	10,856	11,095	11,550
Other scientific and technical consulting services..	54169	12,209	14,011	14,870	15,215	17,148	19,272
Research and development in physical, engineering and life sciences......................	54171	60,776	65,047	73,069	75,812	84,243	92,263
Research and development in social sciences and humanities...........................	54172	1,579	1,610	1,698	1,734	1,843	1,977
Advertising agencies............................	54181	27,879	30,666	32,058	30,887	33,476	35,323
Public relations agencies........................	54182	8,630	9,279	9,247	8,855	10,004	10,316
Media buying agencies...........................	54183	3,696	4,606	4,955	4,321	4,375	4,790
Media representatives...........................	54184	3,231	3,577	3,691	3,407	3,559	3,532
Display advertising..............................	54185	7,842	9,111	9,142	7,595	7,799	8,025
Direct mail advertising...........................	54186	12,464	12,360	11,486	10,048	10,745	11,179
All other advertising [5].........................	5418y	15,365	17,835	18,621	17,405	18,886	19,667
Marketing research and public opinion polling.....	54191	14,170	15,493	16,322	15,501	16,738	17,351
Photography studios, portrait......................	541921	4,856	5,055	5,139	4,956	4,808	4,771
Commercial photography.........................	541922	1,837	1,712	1,878	1,560	1,539	1,558
Translation and interpretation services............	54193	1,502	1,895	2,122	3,069	3,276	3,154
Veterinary services..............................	54194	22,372	24,568	25,794	25,658	26,634	27,009
All other professional, scientific, and technical services..................................	54199	7,441	7,874	9,211	10,218	10,475	10,609

[1] Based on the North American Industry Classification System, 2007; see Section 15. [2] Includes NAICS 54134 (Drafting Services), NAICS 54135 (Building Inspection Services), NAICS 54136 (Geophysical Surveying and Mapping Services), and NAICS 54137 (Surveying and Mapping (except Geophysical) Services). [3] Includes NAICS 54142 (Industrial Design Services) and NAICS 54149 (Other Specialized Design Services). [4] A portion of NAICS 54161 (Management Consulting Services) moved to NAICS 56131 (Employment Placement Agencies and Executive Search Services) with the 2007 NAICS update. Historical data, 2010 and prior, have been restated to reflect comparable data on the 2007 NAICS basis. [5] Includes NAICS 54187 (Advertising Material Distribution Services) and NAICS 54189 (Other Services Related to Advertising).

Source: U.S. Census Bureau, Annual and Quarterly Services, "2011 Annual Services," <http://www.census.gov/services/index.html>, accessed August 2013.

Table 1305. Selected Service Industries—E-Commerce Revenue: 2010 and 2011

[306,501 represents $306,501,000,000. Includes data only for businesses with paid employees, except for accommodation and food services, which also includes businesses with and without paid employees. Except as noted, based on the Service Annual Survey]

Kind of business	2007 NAICS code [1]	E-commerce revenue (mil. dol.)		E-commerce as percent of total revenue, 2011	E-commerce revenue, percent distribution, 2011
		2010	2011		
Selected service industries, total [2].............	**(X)**	**306,501**	**346,060**	**3.0**	**100.0**
Selected transportation and warehousing [3]...............	4849y	73,219	87,101	11.8	25.2
Air transportation..................	481	42,046	50,758	27.5	14.7
Water transportation.................	483	2,378	2,921	8.0	0.8
Truck transportation.................	484	14,570	16,645	7.7	4.8
Information..................	51	58,789	67,998	5.9	19.6
Publishing industries (except Internet).................	511	25,527	28,213	10.3	8.2
Telecommunications.................	517	6,389	8,145	1.5	2.4
Data processing, hosting, and related services................	518	8,025	9,403	11.6	2.7
Finance and Insurance [4]................	52	60,513	63,578	1.9	18.4
Securities and commodity contracts intermediation and brokerage............	5231	15,876	16,618	6.2	4.8
Real Estate and rental and leasing................	53	15,456	19,436	4.6	5.6
Selected professional, scientific, and technical services [5]...............	54	26,974	29,962	2.2	8.7
Computer systems design and related services................	5415	8,262	9,393	3.1	2.7
Administrative and support and waste management and remediation services................	56	19,486	20,795	3.0	6.0
Travel arrangement and reservation services................	5615	10,286	11,038	28.1	3.2
Educational services [6]................	61	4,982	5,664	9.6	1.6
Health care and social assistance................	62	1,675	1,774	0.1	0.5
Arts, entertainment, and recreation................	71	5,251	5,736	2.9	1.7
Accommodation and food services [7]................	72	30,595	33,438	5.0	9.7
Other services (except public administration) [8]................	81	9,067	10,023	2.5	2.9
Repair and maintenance................	811	2,121	2,354	1.7	0.7
Religious, grantmaking, civic, professional, and similar organizations................	813	4,787	5,176	3.0	1.5

X Not applicable. [1] North American Industry Classification System (NAICS), 2007; see text Section 15. [2] Includes other kinds of business, not shown separately. [3] Excludes NAICS 482 (Rail Transportation) and NAICS 491 (Postal Service). [4] Excludes NAICS 525 (Funds, Trusts, and Other Financial Vehicles). [5] Excludes NAICS 54112 (Offices of Notaries). [6] Excludes NAICS 6111 (Elementary and Secondary Schools), NAICS 6112 (Junior Colleges), and NAICS 6113 (Colleges, Universities, and Professional Schools). [7] Estimates are based on data from the 2011 Annual Retail Trade Survey. [8] Excludes NAICS 81311 (Religious Organizations), NAICS 81393 (Labor Unions and Similar Labor Organizations), NAICS 81394 (Political Organizations), and NAICS814 (Private Households).

Source: U.S. Census Bureau, "E-Stats: 2011 E-commerce Multi-sector Data Tables," <http://www.census.gov/econ/estats/>, accessed August 2013.

Table 1306. Forecast Summary—Media Supplier Advertising Revenues: 2000 to 2010

[In millions of dollars (177,500 represents $177,500,000,000). See source for definitions of types of advertising]

Media supplier	2000	2004	2005	2006	2007	2008	2009	2010
Total supplier ad revenue................	**177,500**	**188,942**	**196,668**	**204,889**	**205,847**	**194,328**	**163,184**	**170,456**
Total [1]................	**175,535**	**186,979**	**196,398**	**202,701**	**205,523**	**191,951**	**162,744**	**167,936**
Direct................	31,108	39,688	42,477	45,882	48,680	48,190	42,444	42,484
Direct mail................	18,250	22,559	23,085	24,478	24,890	23,459	19,853	20,604
Direct online [2]................	560	4,440	6,371	8,785	11,355	13,554	13,656	15,022
Directories [3]................	12,299	12,689	13,021	12,619	12,435	11,177	8,934	6,858
National................	53,494	55,699	59,200	61,858	64,498	63,132	56,797	61,009
National television [3, 4]................	25,574	31,452	33,231	33,712	34,820	35,141	33,723	36,210
Magazines [3]................	19,025	17,961	19,351	20,373	20,975	19,533	15,554	15,623
National digital/online [5]................	5,665	3,541	3,931	5,067	6,098	6,057	5,549	7,144
Network and satellite radio................	1,065	1,175	1,161	1,178	1,226	1,220	1,100	1,145
National newspapers [3]................	2,165	1,570	1,527	1,527	1,379	1,180	873	887
Local................	90,933	91,591	94,721	94,961	92,345	80,630	63,504	64,443
Local newspapers [3]................	46,506	45,133	45,880	45,074	40,830	33,559	23,949	21,909
Local TV [3, 6]................	18,530	20,047	21,281	21,023	22,001	19,706	16,995	18,670
Local radio [3]................	18,819	18,932	19,018	19,031	18,476	16,536	13,203	13,847
Emerging outdoor................	195	377	425	545	741	914	920	1,146
Other outdoor................	5,040	5,457	5,876	6,260	6,542	6,077	4,980	4,997
Local digital/online [5]................	1,843	1,645	2,241	3,028	3,755	3,837	3,456	3,874
Political [7]................	1,180	1,259	270	1,538	324	1,777	439	2,033
Olympics [8]................	785	704	–	650	–	600	–	488

– Represents zero. [1] Excludes political and Olympic revenue. [2] Includes paid search, lead generation, and Internet yellow pages. [3] Excludes Internet-based advertising revenues. [4] Includes English and Spanish-language network TV, national cable, and national syndication. Excludes incremental olympic revenues. [5] Includes rich/online video, Internet classifieds, e-mail, digital display, and mobile. [6] Includes local broadcast and local cable TV. Excludes local political advertising revenues. [7] Total political advertising revenue on local broadcast and local cable TV. [8] Incremental advertising revenue from Olympics on network TV.

Source: MAGNAGLOBAL, New York, NY, ©. See also <http://www.magnaglobal.com>.

Table 1307. Administrative and Support and Waste Management and Remediation Services—Estimated Revenue: 2000 to 2011

[In millions of dollars (401,092 represents $401,092,000,000). For taxable and tax-exempt employer firms. Estimates have been adjusted to results of the 2007 Economic Census. Based on the Service Annual Survey and administrative data; see Appendix III]

Kind of business	2007 NAICS code [1]	2000	2005	2008	2009	2010	2011
Administrative and support and waste management and remediation services [2, 3]	**56**	**401,092**	**548,604**	**647,973**	**601,867**	**642,681**	**686,342**
Administrative and support services [2, 3]	561	349,895	483,366	569,121	529,065	560,747	601,824
Office administrative services	5611	26,288	38,143	40,970	42,558	45,520	50,405
Facilities support services	5612	13,211	18,246	28,994	29,280	29,946	31,586
Employment placement agencies and executive search services [4]	56131	9,578	14,985	19,582	16,710	17,079	19,882
Temporary help services	56132	79,622	90,654	103,792	86,111	100,689	115,010
Professional employer organizations	56133	59,635	71,741	88,657	87,609	95,099	101,208
Document preparation services	56141	1,920	2,881	3,286	2,891	2,825	2,705
Telephone answering services	561421	2,135	1,988	2,327	2,260	2,287	2,327
Telemarketing bureaus and other contact centers	561422	12,670	13,150	14,829	14,501	13,348	13,571
Private mail centers	561431	1,692	2,022	2,146	1,947	1,953	1,960
Other business service centers (including copy shops)	561439	6,565	7,940	8,177	7,220	7,071	7,086
Collection agencies	56144	7,300	11,557	11,986	11,120	11,742	12,031
Credit bureaus	56145	3,741	6,246	7,860	7,760	7,794	7,947
Repossession services	561491	418	609	810	862	764	673
Court Reporting and Stenotype Services	561492	1,250	1,953	2,207	2,205	2,233	2,254
All other business support services	561499	3,512	6,474	9,169	8,860	9,227	9,881
Travel agencies	56151	11,639	12,986	17,093	14,792	16,449	17,633
Tour operators	56152	3,564	3,818	5,279	4,887	5,283	5,618
Convention and visitors bureaus	561591	1,020	1,239	1,559	1,437	1,414	1,489
All other travel arrangement and reservation services	561599	9,896	12,935	14,075	12,747	13,851	14,522
Investigation services	561611	2,350	3,294	3,820	3,889	4,085	4,595
Security guards and patrol services	561612	13,393	17,887	19,619	19,129	18,082	17,756
Armored car services	561613	1,838	2,167	2,365	2,385	2,394	2,531
Security systems services (except locksmiths)	561621	8,683	12,474	15,624	15,312	15,822	16,842
Locksmiths	561622	1,330	1,477	1,637	1,464	1,488	1,511
Exterminating and pest control services	56171	5,723	8,118	8,936	9,135	9,543	9,764
Janitorial services	56172	24,593	29,779	34,887	32,591	33,565	35,454
Landscaping services	56173	(NA)	45,856	53,200	47,929	49,307	52,092
Carpet and upholstery cleaning services	56174	2,463	2,877	3,097	2,870	2,629	2,779
Other services to buildings and dwellings	56179	3,011	4,211	5,233	5,091	4,876	4,939
Packaging and labeling services	56191	4,432	5,097	5,188	4,874	5,309	5,526
Convention and trade show organizers	56192	8,410	10,625	11,998	9,618	10,128	11,161
All other support services	56199	18,013	19,937	20,719	19,021	18,945	19,086
Waste management and remediation services	562	51,197	65,238	78,852	72,802	81,934	84,518
Solid waste collection	562111	27,032	32,534	39,495	36,797	37,962	39,070
Hazardous waste collection	562112	1,249	1,547	1,986	1,824	1,994	2,143
Other waste collection	562119	539	855	1,795	1,428	1,417	1,635
Hazardous waste treatment and disposal	562211	3,155	4,532	5,972	5,945	6,605	7,198
Solid waste landfill	562212	5,965	5,858	5,695	4,983	5,091	5,285
Solid waste combustors and incinerators	562213	1,261	2,051	2,123	1,729	1,897	1,946
Other nonhazardous waste treatment and disposal	562219	644	663	706	554	504	514
Remediation services	56291	6,750	10,776	12,544	12,256	17,860	16,794
Materials recovery facilities	56292	1,593	2,984	4,636	3,679	4,854	5,811
Septic Tank and Related Services	562991	2,197	2,277	2,573	2,403	2,504	2,609
All other miscellaneous waste management services	562998	812	1,161	1,327	1,204	1,246	1,513

[1] North American Industry Classification System, 2007; see text, Section 15. [2] Historical data, 2010 and prior, have been restated to reflect comparable data on the 2007 NAICS basis for more detailed levels within this aggregate. [3] Prior to 2004, excludes NAICS 56173 (Landscaping services). [4] Includes 2002 NAICS 561310 (Employment Placement Agencies) and a portion of 2002 NAICS 541612 (Human Resources and Executive Search Consulting Services).

Source: U.S. Census Bureau, Annual and Quarterly Services, "2011 Annual Services," <http://www.census.gov/services/index.html>, September 2013.

Table 1308. Estimated Accommodation and Food Service Sales by Kind of Business: 2000 to 2011

[In millions of dollars (441,944 represents $441,944,000,000). Estimates are based on data from the Annual Retail Trade Survey and administrative records and have been adjusted to the final results of the 2007 Economic Census]

Kind of business	2007 NAICS code [1]	2000	2005	2007	2008	2009	2010	2011
Accommodation and food services, total	**72**	**441,944**	**558,465**	**628,055**	**639,596**	**614,054**	**630,118**	**666,926**
Accommodation	721	137,683	162,002	183,504	183,494	162,370	163,625	172,156
Traveler accommodation	7211	133,118	156,856	177,599	177,444	156,393	157,576	165,717
RV parks and recreational camps	7212	3,588	4,108	4,740	4,867	4,779	4,834	5,155
Rooming and boarding houses	7213	977	1,038	1,165	1,183	1,198	1,215	1,284
Food services and drinking places [2]	722	304,261	396,463	444,551	456,102	451,684	466,493	494,770
Full service restaurants	7221	133,579	174,119	195,505	196,641	193,017	197,446	212,479
Limited service eating places	7222	127,519	169,034	186,001	194,260	195,422	204,090	214,685
Drinking places	7224	15,330	18,053	19,888	20,232	19,969	20,205	20,719

[1] North American Industry Classification System, 2007; see text, Section 15. [2] Includes other kinds of business not shown separately.

Source: U.S. Census Bureau, "Annual Accommodation and Food Services—2011," <http://www.census.gov/retail/>, accessed August 2013.

Table 1309. Lodging Industry Summary: 1990 to 2012

Year	Average occupancy rate (percent)	Average room rate (dollars)	2012 Item	2012 Establish-ments	2012 Rooms	2012 Item	2012 Business traveler	2012 Leisure traveler
1990	63.3	57.96	Total................	52,529	4,900,642	Typical night:		
1995......	65.5	66.65				Made reservations		
2000......	63.7	85.89	By Size:			(percent).............	94	91
2005......	63.1	91.04	Under 75 rooms....	29,149	1,247,532	Amount paid (dol.).....	$133.00	$114.00
2008......	60.4	107.4	75–149 rooms......	17,299	1,817,319	Length of stay		
2009......	54.7	98.07	150–299 rooms....	4,403	881,838	(percent):		
2010......	57.6	98.06	300–500 rooms....	1,143	425,334	One night............	43	48
2011......	60.0	101.70	Over 500 rooms....	535	528,619	Two nights...........	23	27
2012......	61.4	106.15				Three or more........	34	25

Source: American Hotel & Lodging Association, Washington, DC, "Lodging Industry Profile ©," <http://www.ahla.com/content.aspx?id=32567>, accessed August 2013 .

Table 1310. Commercial and Noncommercial Services—Food and Drink Establishments and Sales: 1990 to 2013

[In millions of dollars (238,149 represents $238,149,000,000). Excludes military. Data refer to sales to consumers of food and alcoholic beverages. Sales are estimated. For details, see source]

Type of establishment	Establish-ments, 2008	Sales (mil. dol.) 1990	1995	2000	2005	2010	2012 [1]	2013 [1]
Total...............................	**957,354**	**238,149**	**294,631**	**377,652**	**486,494**	**581,065**	**633,960**	**657,956**
Commercial restaurant services [2,3].................	753,197	211,606	265,910	345,345	445,078	531,732	580,410	602,548
Eating and drinking places [2].........................	507,507	155,552	198,293	259,743	329,598	391,423	444,450	461,336
Full-service restaurants....................	222,070	77,811	96,396	133,834	165,170	188,706	202,192	208,056
Limited-service restaurants [4].....................	213,835	[5] 69,798	[5] 92,901	107,147	136,903	162,350	179,334	188,121
Snack and nonalcoholic beverage bars [5].........	53,678	([5])	([5])	12,867	17,150	25,309	27,858	29,055
Bars and taverns [6]...........................	46,624	9,533	9,948	12,412	15,002	17,722	18,875	19,458
Managed services [2]........................	23,250	14,149	18,186	24,841	32,030	40,331	43,875	45,622
Manufacturing and industrial plants..............	(NA)	3,856	4,814	6,223	6,570	6,696	7,397	7,778
Colleges and universities..........................	(NA)	2,788	3,989	5,879	9,283	13,097	14,092	14,543
Recreation and sports..........................	24,942	2,871	3,866	4,772	11,397	12,679	5,842	6,076
Lodging places...........................	11,620	13,568	15,561	19,438	23,854	27,167	31,615	33,145
Retail hosts [2,7]............................	132,792	9,513	12,589	14,869	22,502	30,774	34,009	35,210
Department store restaurants......................	2,222	876	1,038	903	490	(NA)	(NA)	(NA)
Grocery store restaurants [7]......................	54,397	5,432	6,624	7,116	12,032	(NA)	(NA)	(NA)
Gasoline service stations..................	59,087	1,718	2,520	4,693	6,137	(NA)	(NA)	(NA)
Noncommercial restaurant services [2].................	204,157	26,543	28,722	32,307	41,416	49,333	53,550	55,408
Employee restaurant services......................	3,003	1,864	1,364	986	548	406	415	431
Industrial, commercial organizations..............	765	1,603	1,129	717	260	(NA)	(NA)	(NA)
Educational restaurant services....................	106,224	7,671	9,059	9,977	11,007	12,787	14,256	14,705
Elementary and secondary schools...............	101,957	3,700	4,533	5,039	5,320	6,243	6,821	7,055
Hospitals..	5,799	8,968	9,219	9,982	12,332	15,611	16,263	16,995
Miscellaneous.......................................	52,448	2,892	3,673	4,898	9,703	11,167	(NA)	(NA)
Clubs...	29,246	1,993	2,278	3,164	7,555	9,000	9,473	9,712

NA Not available. [1] Projection. [2] Includes other groupings, not shown separately. [3] Data for establishments with payroll. [4] Fast-food restaurants. [5] Snack and nonalcoholic beverage bars included in limited service restaurants prior to 1997. [6] For establishments serving food. [7] Includes a portion of delicatessen sales in grocery stores.

Source: National Restaurant Association, Washington, DC, *Restaurant Numbers: 25 Year History, 1970–1995*, 1998 ©; *Restaurant Industry in Review* ©; and *National Restaurant Association 2013 Restaurant Industry Forecast*, 2013 ©.

Table 1311. Other Services—Estimated Revenue for Employer Firms by Kind of Business: 2000 to 2011

[In millions of dollars (302,783 represents $302,783,000,000). For taxable and tax exempt employer firms. Estimates have been adjusted to the results of the 2007 Economic Census. Based on the Service Annual Survey; see Appendix III]

Kind of business	2007 NAICS code [1]	2000	2005	2010	2011
Other services (except public administration) [2], [3]	81	**302,783**	**350,004**	**384,313**	**397,476**
Repair and maintenance	811	112,719	129,910	131,468	140,283
General automotive repair	811111	30,988	36,238	36,559	38,579
Automotive transmission repair	811113	2,773	2,709	2,199	2,296
Other automotive mechanical and electrical repair and maintenance	811118	2,984	2,411	2,298	2,385
Automotive body, paint, interior repair and maintenance	811121	22,018	25,721	25,500	27,596
Automotive glass replacement shops	811122	3,748	3,605	3,031	3,134
Automotive oil change and lubrication shops	811191	3,326	4,463	4,969	4,897
Car washes	811192	4,641	5,677	5,801	5,878
All other automotive repair and maintenance	811198	1,607	1,585	1,359	1,459
Consumer electronics repair and maintenance	811211	1,538	1,653	1,503	1,502
Computer and office machine repair and maintenance	811212	6,592	6,665	7,123	7,037
Communication equipment repair and maintenance	811213	1,756	2,648	3,024	3,164
Other electronic and precision equipment repair and maintenance	811219	4,533	6,484	7,500	8,071
Commercial and industrial machinery and equipment (except Automotive and Electronic) Repair and Maintenance	8113	16,687	21,776	24,030	27,621
Home and garden equipment and appliance repair and maintenance	81141	3,866	3,106	2,388	2,352
Reupholstery and furniture repair	81142	1,229	1,243	914	923
Other personal and household goods repair and maintenance	81149	3,109	2,770	2,319	2,437
Personal and laundry services [4]	812	67,140	78,767	82,776	85,924
Beauty shops	812112	14,445	17,981	19,507	19,067
Diet and weight reducing centers	812191	1,194	1,823	1,323	1,420
Other personal care services	812199	1,517	2,675	4,238	4,801
Funeral homes and funeral services	81221	10,279	11,830	12,566	12,871
Cemeteries and crematories	81222	3,428	4,050	2,971	3,075
Coin-operated laundries and drycleaners	81231	3,359	3,186	3,546	3,553
Dry-cleaning and laundry services (except coin-operated)	81232	7,846	7,477	7,538	7,778
Linen supply	812331	2,989	4,200	4,667	4,731
Industrial launders	812332	5,756	(S)	6,216	6,537
Pet care (except veterinary) services	81291	(NA)	1,959	2,772	2,994
Photofinishing	81292	3,809	2,441	1,907	2,190
Parking lots and garages	81293	6,389	7,827	8,388	9,053
All other personal services	81299	5,021	4,908	4,673	5,002
Religious, grantmaking, civic, professional, and similar organizations [5]	813	122,924	141,327	170,069	171,269
Grantmaking and giving services	8132	57,465	61,151	71,998	70,722
Social advocacy organizations	8133	10,852	15,393	22,676	23,740
Civic and social organizations	8134	13,703	14,917	15,042	14,917
Business, professional, labor, political, and similar organizations [6]	8139	40,904	49,866	60,353	61,890

[1] Based on the North American Industry Classification System, 2007; see Section 15. [2] Historical data, 2010 and prior, have been restated to reflect comparable data on the 2007 NAICS basis. [3] Excludes NAICS 8131 (Religious Organizations), NAICS 81393 (Labor Unions and Similar Labor Organizations), NAICS 81394 (Political Organizations), and NAICS 814 (Private Households); prior to 2004, also excludes NAICS 81291 (Pet Care Services). [4] Prior to 2004, excludes NAICS 81291 (Pet care services). [5] Excludes NAICS 8131 (Religious Organizations), NAICS 81393 (Labor Unions and Similar Labor Organizations), and NAICS 81394 (Political Organizations). [6] Excludes NAICS 81393 (Labor Unions and Similar Labor Organizations) and NAICS 81394 (Political Organizations).

Source: U.S. Census Bureau, Annual and Quarterly Services, "2011 Annual Services," <http://www.census.gov/services/index.html>, accessed September 2013.

Table 1312. National Nonprofit Associations—Number by Type: 1980 to 2012

[Data compiled during last few months of year previous to year shown and the beginning months of year shown]

Type	1980	1990	2000	2005	2007 [1]	2008	2009	2010	2011	2012
Total	**14,726**	**22,289**	**21,840**	**22,720**	**25,048**	**25,176**	**24,100**	**23,983**	**24,168**	**23,809**
Trade, business, commercial	3,118	3,918	3,880	3,789	4,072	4,003	3,840	3,761	3,792	3,715
Agriculture and environment	677	940	1,103	1,170	1,353	1,439	1,365	1,442	1,449	1,463
Legal, governmental, public admin., military	529	792	790	868	938	951	927	913	915	893
Scientific, engineering, technical	1,039	1,417	1,302	1,354	1,505	1,588	1,549	1,563	1,569	1,561
Educational	[2] 2,376	1,291	1,297	1,318	1,471	1,530	1,462	1,444	1,446	1,444
Cultural	([2])	1,886	1,786	1,733	1,881	1,896	1,761	1,717	1,721	1,677
Social welfare	994	1,705	1,829	2,072	2,307	2,582	2,531	2,673	2,727	2,805
Health, medical	1,413	2,227	2,495	2,982	3,383	3,552	3,460	3,481	3,511	3,569
Public affairs	1,068	2,249	1,776	1,854	1,951	1,842	1,769	1,734	1,749	1,697
Fraternal, nationality, ethnic	435	573	525	550	580	523	482	461	465	347
Religious	797	1,172	1,123	1,147	1,204	1,146	1,101	1,056	1,058	1,023
Veteran, hereditary, patriotic	208	462	835	774	774	645	602	585	587	565
Hobby, avocational	910	1,475	1,330	1,433	1,615	1,511	1,421	1,374	1,385	1,330
Athletic sports	504	840	717	762	960	1,008	972	946	955	931
Labor unions	235	253	232	208	227	212	195	188	190	182
Chambers of Commerce [3]	105	168	143	135	169	162	147	142	144	135
Greek and non-Greek letter societies	318	340	296	349	335	325	309	305	305	299
Fan clubs	(NA)	581	381	314	323	261	207	198	200	173

NA Not available. [1] The increase in the number of associations comes from the increase in newly discovered and established associations. [2] Data for cultural associations included with educational associations. [3] National and binational. Includes trade and tourism organizations.

Source: Gale, Cengage Learning, Farmington Hills, MI, compiled from *Encyclopedia of Associations,* annual ©.

Foreign Commerce and Aid

This section presents data on the flow of goods, services, and capital between the United States and other countries; changes in official reserve assets of the United States; international investments; and foreign assistance programs.

The Bureau of Economic Analysis publishes current figures on U.S. international transactions and the U.S. international investment position in its monthly *Survey of Current Business*. Statistics for the foreign aid programs are presented by the Agency for International Development (AID) in its annual *U.S. Overseas Loans and Grants and Assistance from International Organizations*.

The principal source of merchandise import and export data is the U.S. Census Bureau. Current data are presented monthly in *U.S. International Trade in Goods and Services Report* Series FT 900. The *Guide to Foreign Trade Statistics*, found on the Census Bureau Web site at <http://www.census.gov/foreign-trade/guide/index.html>, lists the Census Bureau's monthly and annual products and services in this field. In addition, the International Trade Administration and the Bureau of Economic Analysis present summary as well as selected commodity and country data for U.S. foreign trade on their Web sites: <http://www.trade.gov/mas/ian/tradestatistics/> and <http://www.bea.gov/international/ >, respectively. The merchandise trade data published by the Bureau of Economic Analysis in the *Survey of Current Business* and on the Web include balance of payments adjustments to the Census Bureau data. The U.S. Treasury Department's *Monthly Treasury Statement of Receipts and Outlays of the United States Government* contains information on import duties. The International Trade Commission, U.S. Department of Agriculture (agricultural products), U.S. Department of Energy (mineral fuels, like petroleum and coal), and the U.S. Geological Survey (minerals) release various reports and specialized products on U.S. trade.

International accounts—The international transactions tables (Tables 1313 to 1315) show, for given time periods, the transfer of goods, services, grants, and financial assets and liabilities between the United States and the rest of the world. The international investment position table (Table 1316) presents, for specific dates, the value of U.S. investments abroad and of foreign investments in the United States. The movement of foreign and U.S. capital as presented in the balance of payments is not the only factor affecting the total value of foreign investments. Among the other factors are changes in the valuation of assets or liabilities, including changes in prices of securities, defaults, expropriations, and write-offs.

Direct investment abroad means the ownership or control, directly or indirectly, by one person of 10 percent or more of the voting securities of an incorporated business enterprise or an equivalent interest in an unincorporated business enterprise. Direct investment position is the value of U.S. parents' claims on the equity of and receivables due from foreign affiliates, less foreign affiliates' receivables due from their U.S. parents. Income consists of parents' shares in the earnings of their affiliates plus net interest received by parents on intercompany accounts, less withholding taxes on dividends and interest.

Foreign aid—Foreign assistance is divided into three major categories—grants (military supplies and services and other grants), credits, and other assistance (through net accumulation of foreign currency claims from the sale of agricultural commodities). *Grants* are transfers for which no payment is expected (other than a limited percentage of the foreign currency "counterpart" funds generated by the grant), or which at most involve an obligation on the part of the receiver to extend aid to the United States or other countries to achieve a common objective. *Credits* are loan disbursements or transfers under other agreements which give rise to specific obligations to repay, over a period of years, usually with interest. All known returns to the U.S. government stemming from grants and credits (reverse grants, returns of grants, and payments of principal) are taken into account in net grants and net credits, but no allowance is made for interest or commissions. *Other assistance* represents the transfer of U.S. farm products in exchange for foreign currencies (plus, since enactment of Public Law 87-128, currency claims from principal and interest collected on credits extended under the farm products program), less the government's disbursements of the currencies as grants, credits, or for purchases. The net acquisition of currencies represents net transfers of resources to foreign countries under the agricultural programs, in addition to those classified as grants or credits.

In 1952, economic, technical, and military aid programs were combined under the Mutual Security Act, which in turn was followed by the Foreign Assistance Act passed in 1961. Appropriations to provide military assistance were also made in the Department of Defense Appropriation Act (rather than the Foreign Assistance Appropriation Act) beginning in 1966 for certain countries in Southeast Asia and in other legislation concerning programs for specific countries (such as Israel). Figures on activity under the Foreign Assistance Act as reported in the foreign grants and credits table (Table 1323) differ from data published by AID or its immediate predecessors, due largely to differences in reporting, timing, and treatment of particular items.

Exports—Export statistics consist of goods valued at more than $2,500 per commodity shipped by individuals and organizations (including exporters, freight forwarders, and carriers) from the U.S. to other countries. The Census Bureau compiles export data primarily from two sources: data in electronic form submitted directly by exporters and their agents (68 percent), and special computer tapes from Canada for U.S. exports to Canada (32 percent). Estimates are made for low-value exports by country of destination, and based on bilateral trade patterns. They include U.S. exports under mutual security programs and exclude shipments to U.S. Armed Forces for their own use.

The value reported in the export statistics is generally equivalent to a free alongside ship (f.a.s.) value at the U.S. port of export, based on the transaction price, including inland freight, insurance, and other charges incurred in placing the merchandise alongside the carrier at the U.S. port of exportation. This value, as defined, excludes the cost of loading merchandise aboard the exporting carrier and also excludes freight, insurance, and any other charges or transportation and other costs beyond the U.S. port of exportation. The country of destination is defined as the country of ultimate destination or country where the merchandise is to be consumed, further processed, or manufactured, as known to the shipper at the time of exportation. When ultimate destination is not known, the shipment is statistically credited to the last country to which the shipper knows the merchandise will be shipped in the same form as exported.

Statistics for U.S. exports to Canada are based on import documents filed with Canadian agencies and forwarded to the U.S. Census Bureau under a 1987 data exchange agreement. Under this agreement, each country eliminated most cross-border export documents; maintains detailed statistics on cross-border imports; exchanges monthly files of cross-border import statistics; and publishes exchanged statistics in place of previously compiled export statistics.

Prior to 1989, exports were based on Schedule B, Statistical Classification of Domestic and Foreign Commodities Exported from the United States. Beginning in 1989, Schedule B classifications are based on the Harmonized System and coincide with the Standard International Trade Classification, Revision 3. This revision will affect the comparability of most export series beginning with the 1989 data for commodities.

Imports—Import statistics consist of goods valued at more than $2,000 per commodity shipped by individuals and organizations (including importers and customs brokers) into the U.S. from other countries. The Census Bureau compiles import data from records filed with Customs and Border Protection, usually within 10 days after the merchandise enters the United States. Estimates are made for low-value shipments by country of origin, based on previous bilateral trade patterns and periodically updated. Statistics for over 99 percent of all commodity

transactions are compiled from records filed electronically with Customs and forwarded as computer tape files to the U.S. Census Bureau. Statistics for other transactions are compiled from hard-copy documents filed with Customs and forwarded on a flow basis for U.S. Census Bureau processing.

Data on import values are presented on two valuations bases in this section: The c.i.f. (cost, insurance, and freight) and the customs import value (as appraised by the U.S. Customs Service in accordance with legal requirements of the Tariff Act of 1930, as amended). This latter valuation, primarily used for collection of import duties, frequently does not reflect the actual transaction value. Country of origin is defined as country where the merchandise was grown, mined, or manufactured. If country of origin is unknown, country of shipment is reported.

Imports are classified either as "General imports" or "Imports for consumption." *General imports* are a combination of entries for immediate consumption, entries into customs bonded warehouses, and entries into U.S. Foreign Trade Zones, thus generally reflecting total arrivals of merchandise. *Imports for consumption* are a combination of entries for immediate consumption, withdrawals from warehouses for consumption, and entries of merchandise into U.S. customs territory from U.S. Foreign Trade Zones, thus generally reflecting the total of the commodities entered into U.S. consumption channels.

Beginning in 1989, import statistics are based on the Harmonized Tariff Schedule of the United States, which coincides with import Standard International Trade Classification, Revision 3. This revision will affect the comparability of most import series beginning with the 1989 data.

Area coverage—Except as noted, the geographic area covered by the export and import trade statistics is the United States Customs area (includes the 50 states, the District of Columbia, and Puerto Rico), the U.S. Virgin Islands (effective January 1981), and U.S. Foreign Trade Zones (effective July 1982).

Statistical reliability—For a discussion of statistical collection and estimation, sampling procedures, and measures of statistical reliability applicable to Census Bureau data, see Appendix III.

Table 1313. U.S. International Transactions by Type of Transaction: 1990 to 2012

[In millions of dollars (706,975 represents $706,975,000,000). Minus sign (−) indicates debits]

Type of transaction [1]	1990	1995	2000	2005	2007	2008	2009	2010	2011	2012
Exports of goods and services and income receipts	**706,975**	**1,004,631**	**1,425,260**	**1,825,596**	**2,486,810**	**2,654,418**	**2,184,786**	**2,522,520**	**2,873,654**	**2,986,949**
Exports of goods and services	535,233	794,387	1,072,782	1,288,257	1,652,859	1,840,332	1,578,187	1,844,468	2,112,825	2,210,585
Goods, balance of payments basis [2]	387,401	575,204	784,781	911,686	1,163,605	1,307,329	1,069,475	1,288,795	1,495,853	1,561,239
Services [2]	147,832	219,183	288,002	376,571	489,255	533,003	508,712	555,674	616,973	649,346
Transfers under U.S. military agency sales contracts [3,4]	9,932	14,643	6,210	12,082	17,444	14,899	16,277	14,958	18,821	18,520
Travel	43,007	63,395	82,891	82,160	97,355	110,423	94,187	103,463	115,552	126,214
Passenger fares	15,298	18,909	20,197	20,609	25,187	30,957	26,103	30,987	36,763	39,360
Other transportation	22,042	26,081	25,562	32,013	40,638	44,016	36,087	40,669	43,067	43,855
Royalties and license fees [5]	16,634	30,289	51,808	74,448	97,803	102,125	98,406	107,521	120,717	124,182
Other private services [5]	40,251	65,048	100,792	154,133	209,307	228,770	235,744	255,989	279,645	294,527
U.S. government miscellaneous services	668	818	542	1,125	1,522	1,814	1,908	2,087	2,408	2,688
Income receipts	171,742	210,244	352,478	537,339	833,951	814,086	606,599	678,051	760,829	776,364
Income receipts on U.S.-owned assets abroad	170,570	208,065	348,083	532,542	828,732	808,721	600,859	672,120	754,724	770,079
Direct investment receipts	65,973	95,260	151,839	294,538	370,758	413,739	362,520	440,906	478,803	470,233
Other private receipts	94,072	108,092	192,398	235,120	455,436	389,881	233,547	229,720	273,999	297,891
U.S. government receipts	10,525	4,713	3,846	2,884	2,538	5,101	4,792	1,494	1,923	1,954
Compensation of employees	1,172	2,179	4,395	4,796	5,219	5,364	5,740	5,931	6,105	6,286
Imports of goods and services and income payments	**-759,290**	**-1,080,124**	**-1,783,419**	**-2,465,880**	**-3,085,270**	**-3,210,575**	**-2,444,863**	**-2,844,240**	**-3,197,844**	**-3,297,677**
Imports of goods and services	-616,097	-890,771	-1,450,119	-1,996,171	-2,351,925	-2,542,634	-1,961,844	-2,343,847	-2,669,663	-2,745,240
Goods, balance of payments basis [2]	-498,438	-749,374	-1,231,722	-1,695,820	-1,986,347	-2,141,287	-1,580,025	-1,938,950	-2,239,991	-2,302,714
Services [2]	-117,659	-141,397	-218,397	-300,352	-365,577	-401,348	-381,819	-404,897	-429,672	-442,527
Direct defense expenditures [6]	-17,531	-10,043	-12,131	-25,200	-25,850	-26,193	-28,331	-28,478	-27,752	-24,734
Travel	-37,349	-44,916	-65,366	-69,930	-77,127	-80,494	-74,132	-75,505	-78,229	-83,451
Passenger fares	-10,531	-14,663	-23,613	-25,189	-27,681	-31,841	-25,117	-27,256	-31,079	-34,654
Other transportation	-24,966	-27,034	-37,209	-54,212	-55,773	-56,696	-42,601	-51,202	-54,630	-55,445
Royalties and license fees [5]	-3,135	-6,919	-16,606	-25,577	-26,479	-29,623	-31,297	-32,551	-34,786	-39,889
Other private services [5]	-22,229	-35,199	-61,085	-97,989	-150,257	-173,814	-177,212	-186,423	-199,654	-201,227
U.S. government miscellaneous services	-1,919	-2,623	-2,386	-2,255	-2,410	-2,687	-3,130	-3,483	-3,541	-3,127
Income payments	-143,192	-189,353	-333,300	-469,709	-733,345	-667,941	-483,019	-500,392	-528,181	-552,437
Income payments on foreign-owned assets in the United States	-139,728	-183,090	-322,345	-453,800	-717,623	-650,880	-468,600	-486,430	-513,997	-537,815
Direct investment payments	-3,450	-30,318	-56,910	-121,333	-126,174	-129,447	-104,828	-152,390	-168,243	-176,747
Other private payments	-95,508	-97,149	-180,918	-228,408	-426,796	-354,609	-219,417	-196,390	-213,350	-233,336
U.S. government payments	-40,770	-55,623	-84,517	-104,059	-164,653	-166,824	-144,355	-137,150	-132,404	-127,732
Compensation of employees	-3,464	-6,263	-10,955	-15,909	-15,722	-17,061	-14,418	-13,962	-14,184	-14,622
Unilateral current transfers, net [4]	**-26,654**	**-38,074**	**-58,159**	**-99,512**	**-114,929**	**-125,185**	**-121,559**	**-127,751**	**-133,535**	**-129,688**
U.S. government grants [4]	-10,359	-11,190	-16,836	-33,615	-34,567	-36,461	-42,699	-42,736	-47,350	-46,090
U.S. government pensions and other transfers	-3,224	-3,451	-4,595	-5,249	-6,694	-6,325	-6,589	-6,645	-7,837	-3,685
Private remittances and other transfers [7]	-13,070	-23,433	-36,728	-60,647	-73,668	-82,398	-72,271	-78,371	-78,349	-79,913
Capital account transactions, net	-7,220	-222	-1	13,116	384	6,010	-140	-157	-1,212	6,956
U.S.-owned assets abroad, excl. financial derivatives (increase/financial outflow (−))	-81,234	-352,264	-560,523	-546,631	-1,453,604	332,109	-128,860	-909,953	-452,304	-97,469
U.S. official reserve assets	-2,158	-9,742	-290	14,096	-122	-4,848	-52,256	-1,834	-15,877	-4,460
Special drawing rights	**-192**	**-808**	**-722**	**4,511**	**-154**	**-106**	**-48,230**	**-31**	**1,752**	**-37**
Reserve position in the International Monetary Fund	731	-2,466	2,308	10,200	1,021	-3,473	-3,357	-1,293	-18,079	-4,032
Foreign currencies	-2,697	-6,468	-1,876	-615	-989	-1,269	-669	-510	450	-391
U.S. government assets, other than official reserve assets	2,317	-984	-941	5,539	-22,273	-529,615	541,342	7,540	-103,666	85,331
U.S. credits and other long-term assets	-8,410	-4,859	-5,182	-2,255	-2,475	-2,202	-4,069	-4,976	-7,307	-8,202
Repayments on U.S. credits and other long-term assets [8]	10,856	4,125	4,265	5,603	4,104	2,354	2,133	2,408	3,333	2,546
U.S. foreign currency holdings and U.S. short-term assets	-130	-250	-24	2,191	-23,902	-529,766	543,278	10,108	-99,692	90,987
U.S. private assets	-81,393	-341,538	-559,292	-566,266	-1,431,209	866,571	-617,946	-915,659	-332,761	-178,341
Direct investment	-37,183	-98,750	-159,212	-36,235	-414,039	-329,081	-310,382	-301,080	-409,004	-388,293
Foreign securities	-28,765	-122,394	-127,908	-251,199	-366,512	197,347	-227,024	-139,084	-143,770	-144,823
U.S. claims on unaffiliated foreigners reported by U.S. nonbanking concerns [9]	-27,824	-45,286	-138,790	-71,207	-928	456,177	154,139	31,326	4,147	-25,723
U.S. claims reported by U.S. banks and securities brokers [9]	12,379	-75,108	-133,382	-207,625	-649,730	542,128	-234,679	-506,821	215,866	380,498

See footnotes at end of table.

See headnote on page 823.

Table 1313. U.S. International Transactions by Type of Transaction: 1990 to 2012-Continued.

Type of transaction [1]	1990	1995	2000	2005	2007	2008	2009	2010	2011	2012
Foreign-owned assets in the United States, excluding financial derivatives (increase/financial inflow (+))	139,357	435,102	1,038,224	1,247,347	2,064,642	431,406	315,063	1,333,921	969,006	543,884
Foreign official assets in the United States	33,910	109,880	42,758	259,268	481,043	554,634	480,286	398,309	253,816	393,922
U.S. government securities	30,243	72,712	35,710	213,334	269,897	591,381	437,324	353,294	149,101	314,660
U.S. Treasury securities	29,576	68,977	-5,199	112,841	98,432	548,653	569,893	442,012	169,813	433,155
Other	667	3,735	40,909	100,493	171,465	42,728	-132,569	-88,718	-20,712	-118,495
Other U.S. government liabilities	1,868	-105	-1,825	-421	5,436	9,029	58,206	12,442	9,563	8,241
U.S. liabilities reported by U.S. banks and securities brokers	3,385	34,008	5,746	26,260	109,019	-149,676	-68,848	-7,967	27,474	-1,572
Other foreign official assets	-1,586	3,265	3,127	20,095	96,691	103,900	53,604	40,540	67,678	72,593
Other foreign assets in the United States	105,447	325,222	995,466	988,079	1,583,599	-123,228	-165,223	935,612	715,190	149,962
Direct investment	48,494	57,776	321,274	112,638	221,166	310,092	150,442	205,851	230,224	166,411
U.S. Treasury securities	-2,534	91,544	-69,983	132,300	66,845	162,944	-15,451	298,341	188,045	156,385
U.S. securities other than U.S. Treasury securities	1,592	77,249	459,889	450,386	605,414	-165,639	1,855	140,939	-54,462	196,908
U.S. currency	16,586	8,840	-3,357	8,447	-10,675	29,187	12,632	28,319	54,996	57,141
U.S. liabilities to unaffiliated foreigners reported by U.S. nonbanking concerns	45,133	59,637	170,672	69,572	183,221	-31,475	9,536	67,985	6,053	-39,505
U.S. liabilities reported by U.S. banks and securities brokers [9]	-3,824	30,176	116,971	214,736	517,628	-428,337	-324,237	194,177	290,334	-387,378
Financial derivatives, net	(NA)	(NA)	(NA)	(NA)	6,222	-32,947	44,816	14,076	35,006	-7,064
Statistical discrepancy	28,066	30,951	-61,382	25,964	95,745	-55,235	150,757	11,585	-92,771	-5,891
Balance on goods	-111,037	-174,170	-446,942	-784,133	-822,743	-833,957	-510,550	-650,156	-744,139	-741,475
Balance on services	30,173	77,786	69,605	76,219	123,677	131,655	126,893	150,777	187,301	206,819
Balance on goods and services	-80,864	-96,384	-377,337	-707,914	-699,065	-702,302	-383,657	-499,379	-556,838	-534,656
Balance on income	28,550	20,891	19,178	67,630	100,606	146,144	123,580	177,659	232,648	223,928
Unilateral current transfers, net	-26,654	-38,074	-58,159	-99,512	-114,929	-125,185	-121,559	-127,751	-133,535	-129,688
Balance on current account	-78,968	-113,567	-416,317	-739,796	-713,389	-681,343	-381,636	-449,471	-457,725	-440,416

NA Not available. [1] Credits, +: Exports of goods and services and income receipts; unilateral current transfers to the United States; capital account transactions receipts; financial inflows—increase in foreign-owned assets (U.S. liabilities) or decrease in U.S.-owned assets (U.S. claims). Debits, –: Imports of goods and services and income payments; unilateral current transfers to foreigners; capital account transactions payments; financial outflows—decrease in foreign-owned assets (U.S. liabilities) or increase in U.S.-owned assets (U.S. c'aims). [2] Includes some goods: mainly military equipment and supplies that are commingled in the source data and cannot be separately identified. [3] Includes transfers of goods and services under U.S. military grant programs. [4] Beginning in 1999, excludes equipment and supplies exported under the U.S. Foreign Military Sales program that can be separately identified. [5] Gross basis. The definition of exports excludes U.S. parents' payments to foreign affiliates and includes U.S. affiliates' receipts from foreign parents. The definition of imports includes U.S. parents' payments to foreign affiliates and to exclude U.S. affiliates' receipts from foreign parents. [6] Beginning in 1999, excludes petroleum purchases abroad by U.S. military agencies that can be separately identified. [7] "Other transfers" component includes taxes paid by U.S. private residents to foreign governments and taxes paid by private nonresidents to the U.S. Government. [8] Includes sales of foreign obligations to foreigners. [9] Beginning in 2003, includes securities brokers' claims/liabilities on their foreign affiliates. Prior to 2003, they are included in the claims/liabilities of nonbanking concerns.

Source: U.S. Department of Commerce, Bureau of Economic Analysis, "International Economic Accounts," <http://www.bea.gov/international/index.htm>, accessed August 2013.

Table 1314. U.S. Balances on International Transactions by Area and Selected Country: 2011 and 2012

[In millions of dollars (−744,139 represents −$744,139,000,000). Country data are based on information available from U.S. reporting sources. In some instances, the statistics may not necessarily reflect the ultimate foreign transactor. Minus sign (−) indicates debits]

Area or Country	2011, balance on—				2012, balance on—			
	Goods [1]	Services	Income	Current account	Goods [1]	Services	Income	Current account
All areas...........................	**-744,139**	**187,301**	**232,648**	**-457,725**	**-741,475**	**206,819**	**223,928**	**-440,416**
Europe...........................	-121,226	53,192	67,204	-10,674	-126,041	57,056	73,121	-6,617
European Union....................	-102,462	44,086	56,302	-4,841	-117,309	46,692	65,045	-8,489
Euro Area [2].....................	-92,085	29,547	60,033	-3,793	-101,999	30,350	58,148	-16,267
Germany..........................	-50,389	-4,577	-9,129	-61,905	-60,571	-5,587	-7,519	-72,700
Italy..............................	-18,136	1,136	1,264	-16,284	-21,069	819	464	-20,444
Netherlands......................	18,268	6,605	54,982	79,818	18,251	7,219	54,999	81,096
United Kingdom..................	4,117	9,844	-3,459	9,887	-390	11,316	7,395	18,555
Canada...........................	-38,530	29,890	35,540	24,729	-35,575	31,294	31,202	25,296
Latin America, other Western Hemisphere...	-74,859	30,875	85,301	24,917	-55,844	38,121	73,367	39,713
Brazil............................	11,276	15,459	13,253	39,553	11,755	17,132	10,195	39,346
Mexico...........................	-68,963	11,897	1,805	-69,271	-66,681	12,421	1,055	-66,626
Asia and Pacific.................	-401,995	61,470	-14,718	-395,178	-440,578	65,150	-13,626	-424,377
Australia.........................	16,941	9,851	14,755	39,952	20,975	10,491	15,091	46,094
China............................	-295,329	15,616	-31,560	-314,174	-314,991	17,213	-28,271	-329,476
Hong Kong.......................	32,692	-437	1,416	33,188	32,757	-724	1,026	32,661
India.............................	-14,721	-6,099	3,605	-25,680	-18,399	-6,407	4,068	-28,975
Japan............................	-64,661	17,471	-33,476	-82,358	-77,607	17,322	-34,830	-95,640
Korea, South.....................	-12,429	5,466	2,990	-5,104	-15,226	6,506	1,556	-7,671
Singapore........................	11,292	5,987	16,609	33,809	10,102	7,388	16,648	34,120
Taiwan...........................	-14,476	4,060	-2,673	-13,313	-13,365	4,192	-3,588	-12,071
Middle East.......................	-47,909	5,771	8,333	-45,281	-49,604	9,129	7,033	-44,192
Africa............................	-59,621	3,826	9,148	-63,685	-33,833	4,802	9,570	-35,759
International organizations and unallocated..................	(X)	2,277	41,840	7,447	(X)	1,267	43,261	5,520

X Not applicable. [1] Adjusted to balance of payments basis. [2] See footnote 3, Table 1382.

Source: U.S. Bureau of Economic Analysis, "International Economic Accounts," <http://www.bea.gov/international/index.htm>, accessed August 2013.

Table 1315. Private International Service Transactions by Selected Type of Service and Selected Country: 2000 to 2012

[In millions of dollars (281,249 represents $281,249,000,000). Country data are based on information available from U.S. reporting sources. In some instances, the statistics may not necessarily reflect the ultimate foreign transactor. For all transactions, see Table 1313]

Type of Service and country	Exports				Imports			
	2000	2010	2011	2012	2000	2010	2011	2012
Private services, total........................	**281,249**	**538,629**	**595,744**	**628,138**	**203,880**	**372,936**	**398,378**	**414,666**
TYPE OF SERVICE								
Travel.............................	82,891	103,463	115,552	126,214	65,366	75,505	78,229	83,451
Passenger fares...................	20,197	30,987	36,763	39,360	23,613	27,256	31,079	34,654
Other transportation...............	25,562	40,669	43,067	43,855	37,209	51,202	54,630	55,445
Freight............................	12,791	20,453	21,733	22,293	27,885	38,000	40,418	41,873
Port services......................	12,771	20,216	21,334	21,562	9,324	13,202	14,212	13,572
Royalties and license fees.........	51,808	107,521	120,717	124,182	16,606	32,551	34,786	39,889
Other private services.............	100,792	255,989	279,645	294,527	61,085	186,423	199,654	201,227
By type:								
Financial services.............	(NA)	72,348	78,243	76,418	(NA)	15,502	17,566	16,952
Insurance services.............	3,631	14,397	14,958	16,067	11,284	61,478	55,794	52,563
Business, professional, and technical services.................	(NA)	127,393	140,974	153,093	(NA)	94,657	111,332	116,217
AREA AND COUNTRY								
Europe............................	106,296	208,030	230,385	239,208	88,741	155,029	166,981	172,397
European Union....................	93,103	175,326	194,723	199,119	76,840	128,761	140,637	143,204
Euro Area [1].....................	56,036	108,631	122,900	124,703	45,039	77,145	84,014	85,771
France...........................	10,474	16,708	18,381	18,512	10,498	15,016	16,039	15,065
Germany..........................	15,595	24,089	26,085	26,571	12,240	21,557	23,628	25,659
Italy..............................	5,403	8,491	9,464	9,496	5,059	6,733	6,996	7,354
Netherlands......................	6,975	12,919	15,176	16,196	5,559	8,004	8,518	8,952
United Kingdom..................	31,706	52,109	56,295	58,339	27,869	40,958	45,649	46,290
Canada...........................	24,613	52,452	58,445	61,213	17,875	26,460	28,422	29,779
Latin America, other Western Hemisphere.......	55,633	106,151	115,838	121,638	37,607	85,617	85,493	84,190
Brazil............................	6,236	17,237	22,285	23,864	1,946	4,379	5,308	6,862
Mexico...........................	15,532	24,356	25,617	27,350	10,780	13,591	13,905	15,128
Asia and Pacific.................	77,560	141,885	158,356	170,396	49,620	88,006	98,460	107,258
Australia.........................	5,541	13,273	16,207	17,179	3,412	5,625	6,459	6,778
China............................	5,020	21,324	27,081	30,033	3,171	9,940	11,570	12,990
Hong Kong.......................	3,794	5,595	6,402	6,357	4,129	6,414	6,811	7,048
India.............................	2,563	10,401	11,242	11,932	1,887	14,601	17,459	18,528
Japan............................	32,843	43,486	44,347	46,479	16,387	23,326	24,847	26,916
Korea, South.....................	6,924	15,014	16,371	18,082	4,587	7,715	8,577	9,357
Singapore........................	6,031	9,544	10,505	12,250	2,312	3,719	4,651	4,931
Taiwan...........................	4,616	9,151	10,527	11,311	4,154	6,019	6,556	7,391
Middle East.......................	6,753	16,760	18,625	20,741	3,380	9,630	11,114	11,838
Africa............................	4,997	10,925	11,657	12,489	2,708	7,122	7,626	7,897
International organizations and unallocated......	5,396	2,424	2,437	2,452	3,949	1,071	282	1,308

NA Not available. [1] See footnote 3, Table 1382.

Source: U.S. Bureau of Economic Analysis, "International Economic Accounts," <http://www.bea.gov/iTable/>, accessed September 2013.

Table 1316. International Investment Position by Type of Investment: 2000 to 2012

[In billions of dollars (–1,337 represents –$1,337,000,000,000). Estimates for end of year; subject to considerable error due to nature of basic data. Unless otherwise specified, types below refer to current-cost method. For information on current-cost method and market value, see source. Minus sign (-) indicates loss or deficit]

Type of investment	2000	2005	2008	2009	2010	2011	2012
Net international investment position	**-1,337**	**-1,932**	**-3,260**	**-2,275**	**-2,250**	**-3,731**	**-3,864**
Financial derivatives, net [1]	(X)	58	160	126	110	86	58
Net international investment position, excluding financial derivatives	-1,337	-1,990	-3,420	-2,402	-2,361	-3,817	-3,922
U.S.-owned assets abroad	**6,239**	**11,962**	**19,465**	**18,559**	**20,555**	**21,636**	**21,638**
Financial derivatives (gross positive fair value) [1]	(X)	1,190	6,127	3,490	3,652	4,717	3,620
U.S.-owned assets abroad, excluding financial derivatives	6,239	10,772	13,337	15,069	16,903	16,920	18,018
U.S. official reserve assets	128	188	294	404	489	537	572
Gold [2]	72	134	227	284	368	400	433
Special drawing rights	11	8	9	58	57	55	55
Reserve position in the International Monetary Fund	15	8	8	11	12	30	34
Foreign currencies	31	38	49	50	52	52	50
U.S. government assets, other than official reserve assets	85	78	624	83	75	179	94
U.S. credits and other long-term assets [3]	83	77	70	72	74	78	84
U.S. foreign currency holdings and U.S. short-term assets [4]	3	1	554	11	1	101	10
U.S. private assets	6,025	10,506	12,419	14,582	16,339	16,204	17,352
Direct investment at current cost	1,532	2,652	3,749	4,077	4,274	4,663	5,078
Foreign securities	2,426	4,329	3,986	5,566	6,632	6,441	7,531
Bonds	573	1,012	1,237	1,570	1,731	1,940	2,141
Corporate stocks	1,853	3,318	2,748	3,995	4,900	4,501	5,391
U.S. claims on unaffiliated foreigners reported by U.S. nonbanking concerns	837	1,018	931	930	880	793	845
U.S. claims reported by U.S. banks and securities brokers, not included elsewhere	1,232	2,507	3,754	4,009	4,554	4,306	3,898
Foreign-owned assets in the United States	**7,576**	**13,894**	**22,725**	**20,834**	**22,805**	**25,367**	**25,502**
Financial derivatives (gross negative fair value) [1]	(X)	1,132	5,968	3,363	3,542	4,631	3,562
Foreign-owned assets in the Unites States, excluding financial derivatives	7,576	12,762	16,757	17,470	19,263	20,736	21,940
Foreign official assets in the United States	1,037	2,313	3,944	4,403	4,913	5,256	5,692
U.S. government securities	756	1,725	3,264	3,589	3,993	4,236	4,527
U.S. Treasury securities	640	1,341	2,401	2,880	3,365	3,621	4,032
Other	116	385	864	709	629	615	495
Other U.S. government liabilities	26	23	41	99	111	120	128
U.S. liabilities reported by U.S. banks and securities brokers, not included elsewhere	153	297	256	188	180	206	204
Other foreign official assets	102	269	383	528	629	695	833
Other foreign assets	6,539	10,448	12,813	13,067	14,351	15,480	16,247
Direct investment at current cost	1,421	1,906	2,397	2,398	2,624	2,880	3,057
U.S. Treasury securities	382	644	852	791	1,094	1,386	1,542
U.S. securities other than U.S. Treasury securities	2,623	4,353	4,621	5,320	5,935	6,152	6,904
Corporate and other bonds	1,069	2,243	2,771	2,826	2,916	2,895	3,062
Corporate stocks	1,554	2,110	1,850	2,494	3,018	3,257	3,842
U.S. currency	205	280	301	314	342	397	454
U.S. liabilities to unaffiliated foreigners reported by U.S. nonbanking concerns	739	658	741	707	649	631	657
U.S. liabilities reported by U.S. banks and securities brokers, not included elsewhere	1,169	2,607	3,901	3,538	3,707	4,034	3,633
Memoranda:							
Direct investment abroad at market value	2,694	3,638	3,102	4,322	4,810	4,514	5,250
Direct investment in the United States at market value	2,783	2,818	2,486	2,995	3,422	3,510	3,924

X Not applicable. [1] A break in series in 2005 reflects the introduction of U.S. Department of the Treasury data on financial derivatives. [2] U.S. official gold stock is valued at market price. [3] Also includes paid-in capital subscriptions to international financial institutions and resources provided to foreigners under foreign assistance programs requiring repayment over several years. Excludes World War I debts that are not being serviced. [4] Beginning in 2007, includes foreign-currency-denominated assets obtained through temporary reciprocal currency arrangements between the Federal Reserve System and foreign central banks.

Source: U.S. Bureau of Economic Analysis, "International Economic Accounts: International Investment Position," <http://www.bea.gov/international/index.htm#iip>, accessed September 2013.

Table 1317. U.S. Government Reserve Assets: 1990 to 2012

[In billions of dollars (83.3 represents $83,300,000,000). As of end of year]

Type	1990	2000	2005	2007	2008	2009	2010	2011	2012
Total	83.3	67.6	65.1	70.6	77.6	130.8	132.4	148.0	150.2
Gold stock	11.1	11.0	11.0	11.0	11.0	11.0	11.0	11.0	11.0
Special drawing rights	11.0	10.5	8.2	9.5	9.3	57.8	56.8	55.0	55.1
Foreign currencies	52.2	31.2	37.8	45.8	49.6	50.5	52.1	51.9	49.9
Reserve position in IMF [1]	9.1	14.8	8.0	4.2	7.7	11.4	12.5	30.1	34.2

[1] International Monetary Fund.

Source: U.S. Department of the Treasury, Financial Management Service, *Treasury Bulletin*, June 2013 and earlier reports. See also <http://www.fms.treas.gov/bulletin/index.html>.

Table 1318. Foreign Direct Investment Position in the United States on a Historical-Cost Basis by Selected Country, 2000 to 2012, and by Industry, 2012

[In millions of dollars (1,256,867 represents $1,256,867,000,000). Foreign direct investment is defined as the ownership or control, directly or indirectly, by one foreign entity (as used here, "entity" is synonymous with "person" as the term is used in a broad legal sense including any individual, branch, partnership, association, trust, corporation, or government) of 10 percent or more of the voting interest of a U.S. business enterprise. Data are based on surveys of U.S. affiliates of foreign companies]

Country	2000	2005	2010	2011	2012			
					Total [1]	Manufac-turing	Wholesale trade	Finance [2] and insur-ance
All countries	1,256,867	1,634,121	2,280,044	2,502,628	2,650,832	898,942	292,440	365,843
Canada	114,309	165,667	192,463	210,792	225,331	39,912	5,279	64,396
Europe [3]	887,014	1,154,048	1,659,774	1,768,150	1,876,240	717,627	142,283	279,766
Austria	3,007	2,425	4,532	4,753	5,206	2,435	390	2
Belgium	14,787	10,024	69,565	80,299	88,697	55,278	16,964	(D)
Denmark	4,025	6,117	7,772	8,826	8,807	1,049	4,960	2
Finland	8,875	5,938	4,943	5,908	7,162	2,177	3,153	(Z)
France	125,740	114,260	189,763	189,629	209,121	75,775	21,408	30,093
Germany	122,412	177,176	203,077	215,250	199,006	67,429	16,628	26,126
Ireland	25,523	17,465	24,097	23,410	24,917	10,702	775	3,407
Italy	6,576	7,725	20,142	21,272	23,260	7,176	1,354	(D)
Luxembourg	58,930	79,680	170,309	192,860	202,338	73,686	(D)	45,512
Netherlands	138,894	156,602	234,408	225,703	274,904	118,268	19,514	58,144
Norway	2,665	9,810	10,478	16,088	16,432	1,277	6,199	(D)
Spain	5,068	7,472	43,095	46,177	47,352	6,247	15	3,042
Sweden	21,991	22,269	38,780	39,388	42,387	28,996	6,569	155
Switzerland	64,719	133,387	180,642	202,220	203,954	106,576	10,611	42,495
United Kingdom	277,613	371,350	400,435	461,701	486,833	137,553	26,117	67,799
Latin America and other Western Hemisphere [3]	53,691	57,175	62,130	89,135	95,642	12,290	3,609	-16,767
South and Central America [3]	13,384	22,507	17,943	25,494	25,773	8,201	3,356	721
Brazil	882	2,051	1,357	5,095	3,590	-238	2,446	(D)
Mexico	7,462	3,595	10,970	13,051	14,883	4,096	609	(D)
Venezuela	792	5,292	3,122	4,038	4,638	(D)	27	3
Other Western Hemisphere [3]	40,307	34,668	44,187	63,640	69,869	4,089	253	-17,487
Curacao	(X)	(X)	(X)	4,159	4,904	437	-36	(D)
Netherlands Antilles	3,807	5,531	2,819	(X)	(X)	(X)	(X)	(X)
U.K. Islands, Caribbean	15,191	23,063	38,477	51,012	58,584	6,192	3,838	3,324
Africa	2,700	2,341	2,265	4,285	5,338	(D)	615	(D)
Middle East [3]	6,506	8,306	16,808	20,753	20,603	(D)	7,182	(D)
Israel	3,012	4,231	8,714	10,090	9,821	(D)	254	(D)
Asia and Pacific [3]	192,647	246,585	346,605	409,512	427,679	123,401	133,471	37,402
Australia	18,775	36,392	35,632	52,522	42,685	3,839	696	3,633
China	(NA)	574	3,300	3,729	5,154	-34	509	(D)
Hong Kong	1,493	3,467	4,440	4,915	6,283	2,328	2,075	-10
India	(NA)	1,497	4,102	4,833	5,158	813	(D)	(Z)
Japan	159,690	189,851	255,012	291,053	308,253	93,398	105,933	29,499
Korea, South	3,110	6,077	15,746	19,252	24,467	3,895	16,797	175
Singapore	5,087	3,338	21,517	24,207	26,244	15,839	3,936	(D)
Taiwan	3,174	3,731	4,642	4,981	5,454	2,010	1,407	(D)

D Suppressed to avoid disclosure of data of individual companies. NA Not available. X Not applicable. Z Less than $500,000. [1] Includes other industries, not shown separately. [2] Excludes depository institutions. [3] Includes other countries, not shown separately.

Source: U.S. Bureau of Economic Analysis, "International Data: Direct Investment and Multinational Companies," <http://www.bea.gov/iTable/index_MNC.cfm>, accessed September 2013.

Table 1319. U.S. Majority-Owned Affiliates of Foreign Companies—Selected Financial and Operating Data by Industry of Affiliate: 2011

[In billions of dollars (12,334 represents $12,334,000,000,000), except as indicated. Data are preliminary. A majority-owned U.S. affiliate is a U.S. business enterprise in which a foreign entity (as used here, "entity" is synonymous with "person" as the term is used in a broad legal sense including any individual, branch, partnership, association, trust, corporation, or government) has a direct or indirect voting interest greater than 50 percent]

Industry	2007 NAICS Code	Total assets	Sales	Employ-ment (1,000)	Employee compen-sation	Gross property, plant, and equipment	Mer-chandise exports	Mer-chandise imports
All industries	(X)	12,334	3,511	5,641	438	1,684	304	636
Manufacturing [1]	31–33	1,780	1,505	2,081	175	774	188	287
Petroleum and coal products	324	281	344	53	10	217	31	94
Chemicals	325	402	301	295	37	134	41	54
Machinery	333	139	95	217	19	26	17	13
Transportation equipment	336	270	264	460	31	129	41	68
Wholesale trade	42	639	938	547	50	205	104	320
Retail trade	44–45	84	145	489	16	51	1	13
Information	51	253	118	242	23	62	2	(D)
Finance and insurance	52	8,390	353	409	67	87	–	–
Real estate and rental and leasing	53	135	25	41	3	109	(D)	(D)
Professional, scientific, and technical services	54	151	95	290	29	16	1	–
Other industries	(X)	902	332	1,542	75	380	(D)	(D)

– Represents or rounds to zero. D Suppressed to avoid disclosure of data of individual companies. X Not applicable. [1] Includes other industries not shown separately.

Source: U.S. Bureau of Economic Analysis, "Foreign Direct Investment in the United States," <http://www.bea.gov/international/di1fdiop.htm>, accessed September 2013.

Table 1320. Foreign Direct Investment in the United States—Property, Plant, and Equipment and Employment of Majority-Owned U.S. Affiliates of Foreign Companies by State: 2002 to 2011

[Gross book value of property, plant, and equipment in millions of dollars (1,035,916 represents $1,035,916,000,000); employment in thousands (5,570.4 represents 5,570,400). A U.S. majority-owned affiliate is a U.S. business enterprise in which a foreign entity (as used here, "entity" is synonymous with "person" as the term is used in a broad legal sense including any individual, branch, partnership, association, trust, corporation, or government) has a direct or indirect voting interest greater than 50 percent]

State and other area	Gross book value of property, plant, and equipment (mil. dol.)		Employment (1,000)			
	2002	2007	2002	2007	2010	2011
Total	1,035,916	1,293,735	5,570.4	5,588.2	5,435.4	5,640.7
Alabama	15,520	22,885	75.1	81.1	81.9	86.6
Alaska	30,052	34,473	12.6	11.4	14.1	14.3
Arizona	(D)	13,016	57.6	73.2	77.0	80.1
Arkansas	4,872	4,914	35.7	36.6	35.9	37.1
California	89,193	108,572	635.3	602.9	584.0	590.1
Colorado	13,026	(D)	77.7	83.5	80.9	83.3
Connecticut	(D)	13,356	(D)	103.3	100.9	102.6
Delaware	6,252	4,480	23.6	28.7	26.7	29.8
District of Columbia	5,135	5,567	17.5	16.3	22.4	21.5
Florida	28,993	35,052	258.3	248.2	232.9	238.6
Georgia	(D)	(D)	191.4	180.6	189.5	194.0
Hawaii	(D)	6,184	(D)	31.0	26.8	26.7
Idaho	2,131	2,028	12.5	14.4	13.4	13.4
Illinois	41,862	48,626	281.5	280.5	252.7	268.3
Indiana	27,991	(D)	133.3	149.1	136.0	144.9
Iowa	5,776	9,476	36.6	45.5	44.9	49.2
Kansas	5,238	7,863	34.9	58.9	54.5	58.4
Kentucky	24,091	28,188	88.4	92.9	89.2	92.2
Louisiana	26,993	31,226	50.5	49.1	56.1	57.6
Maine	5,511	6,279	31.7	29.6	30.3	30.5
Maryland	(D)	13,016	(D)	103.6	101.6	105.5
Massachusetts	(D)	26,939	(D)	183.7	187.3	188.7
Michigan	(D)	24,052	(D)	152.6	145.4	177.5
Minnesota	9,805	16,237	88.1	98.2	90.7	93.9
Mississippi	5,097	8,250	25.8	26.5	26.8	27.4
Missouri	14,484	(D)	91.5	82.4	81.7	88.3
Montana	1,824	3,366	5.9	8.1	6.3	6.1
Nebraska	1,840	(D)	18.7	23.4	23.9	25.5
Nevada	(D)	9,716	25.9	33.8	39.0	38.7
New Hampshire	(D)	5,246	(D)	38.9	39.3	39.4
New Jersey	30,956	38,425	230.1	227.4	222.9	228.6
New Mexico	(D)	4,813	13.0	17.0	15.3	16.5
New York	68,310	80,474	440.8	429.3	398.9	410.5
North Carolina	(D)	28,918	(D)	211.0	194.7	200.0
North Dakota	1,100	1,438	7.4	7.5	11.5	13.5
Ohio	32,124	43,438	214.2	238.2	210.2	220.2
Oklahoma	7,434	10,578	33.9	35.4	38.6	40.6
Oregon	(D)	9,971	51.3	45.8	43.0	46.0
Pennsylvania	(D)	39,824	(D)	264.4	261.3	267.5
Rhode Island	(D)	5,426	(D)	25.7	26.1	26.4
South Carolina	21,573	(D)	133.1	111.3	108.4	114.1
South Dakota	685	1,277	7.6	6.8	7.2	8.3
Tennessee	16,795	22,688	130.7	139.2	117.2	123.9
Texas	88,116	128,424	353.0	422.6	451.4	460.1
Utah	10,612	6,544	32.3	33.2	31.4	32.5
Vermont	1,286	1,735	11.1	10.1	11.1	11.8
Virginia	(D)	(D)	142.2	158.1	147.8	156.0
Washington	(D)	21,558	84.7	90.5	94.4	96.6
West Virginia	7,388	6,298	22.7	21.1	28.7	25.8
Wisconsin	16,103	14,560	107.1	82.0	77.5	86.0
Wyoming	10,551	11,116	8.5	8.9	7.8	8.4
Puerto Rico	2,583	2,579	19.8	20.9	21.9	22.3
Other U.S. areas	(D)	73,436	10.2	12.6	13.9	12.7
Foreign	2,328	2,162	0.3	1.0	2.3	1.9
Unspecified [1]	66,341	93,505	(NA)	(NA)	(NA)	(NA)

D Suppressed to avoid the disclosure of data of individual companies. NA Not available. [1] Includes aircraft, railroad rolling stock, satellites, undersea cable, and trucks engaged in interstate transportation.

Source: U.S. Bureau of Economic Analysis, *Survey of Current Business*, August 2012 and earlier reports; *Foreign Direct Investment in the United States: Final Results from the 2007 Benchmark Survey*, September 2011; and International Economic Accounts, "Direct Investment and Multinational Companies (MNCs)," <http://www.bea.gov/iTable/index_MNC.cfm>, accessed September 2013.

Table 1321. U.S. Direct Investment Position Abroad, Capital Outflows, and Income by Industry of Foreign Affiliates: 2000 to 2012

[In millions of dollars (1,316,247 represents $1,316,247,000,000). See headnote, Table 1322]

Industry	2000	2005	2008	2009	2010	2011	2012
DIRECT INVESTMENT POSITION ON A HISTORICAL-COST BASIS							
All industries, total [1]	1,316,247	2,241,656	3,232,493	3,565,020	3,741,910	4,084,659	4,453,307
Mining	72,111	109,280	147,496	165,674	172,819	200,883	222,401
Manufacturing [1]	343,899	430,737	474,733	501,122	518,321	569,763	637,059
Food	23,497	27,638	40,317	42,780	47,704	53,986	58,140
Chemicals	75,807	106,975	110,311	113,507	111,327	124,615	132,576
Primary and fabricated metals	21,644	23,013	18,207	18,728	18,674	21,282	23,154
Machinery	22,229	26,433	36,110	39,805	41,285	45,329	51,688
Computer and electronic products	59,909	50,773	67,859	71,811	72,935	84,980	102,084
Electrical equipment, appliances, and components	10,005	15,449	21,819	18,850	19,941	19,234	21,591
Transportation equipment	49,887	50,739	44,541	51,062	49,636	58,133	65,900
Other manufacturing	(NA)	129,716	135,569	144,579	156,819	162,205	181,925
Wholesale trade	93,936	132,915	169,970	164,117	168,722	184,547	205,054
Information	52,345	102,848	130,986	135,088	126,063	136,136	146,618
Depository institutions	40,152	66,707	128,301	124,600	118,585	113,716	119,688
Finance and insurance	217,086	463,981	686,551	722,537	734,859	737,576	775,551
Professional, scientific, and technical services	32,868	57,164	77,393	79,548	81,874	83,769	94,139
Holding companies (nonbank)	(NA)	710,386	1,198,220	1,444,844	1,584,903	1,777,198	1,948,959
Other industries	441,886	167,640	218,845	227,491	235,764	281,071	303,838
CAPITOL OUTFLOWS [INFLOWS(-)] WITHOUT CURRENT-COST ADJUSTMENT							
All industries, total [1]	142,627	15,369	308,296	287,901	277,779	386,724	366,940
Mining	2,174	12,015	25,572	12,740	11,884	32,305	27,107
Manufacturing [1]	43,002	28,121	35,866	43,832	33,320	61,081	62,064
Food	2,014	1,171	3,845	2,911	5,341	5,445	4,784
Chemicals	3,812	3,911	15,709	14,047	7,614	16,812	8,326
Primary and fabricated metals	1,233	-703	3,238	1,273	546	2,801	1,673
Machinery	2,659	2,077	6,712	3,803	4,229	7,438	5,681
Computer and electronic products	17,303	3,607	4,264	1,107	6,772	8,280	11,866
Electrical equipment, appliances, and components	2,100	1,662	3,042	574	1,743	-177	2,510
Transportation equipment	7,814	-250	-11,623	1,613	-380	8,175	6,401
Other manufacturing	(NA)	16,645	10,679	18,503	7,456	12,307	20,825
Wholesale trade	11,938	12,517	31,718	16,139	15,487	23,339	21,547
Information	16,531	2,831	7,946	11,969	8,777	10,292	9,817
Depository institutions	-1,274	-4,751	4,408	-5,786	-4,811	-8,865	3,440
Finance and insurance	21,659	13,079	58,478	46,189	21,887	19,087	20,675
Professional, scientific, and technical services	5,441	-2,055	9,444	8,500	2,774	7,234	11,252
Holding companies (nonbank)	(NA)	-66,351	118,621	130,164	169,743	209,376	177,724
Other industries	40,690	19,964	16,242	24,155	18,718	32,877	33,312
INCOME WITHOUT CURRENT-COST ADJUSTMENT [2]							
All industries, total [1]	133,692	271,877	392,954	340,039	417,605	456,523	448,880
Mining	13,164	24,559	39,822	23,699	29,138	39,278	32,080
Manufacturing [1]	42,230	46,896	60,144	40,239	61,240	70,086	65,844
Food	2,681	3,558	3,603	2,847	4,322	5,680	4,919
Chemicals	11,552	13,056	14,475	12,366	14,088	15,137	14,593
Primary and fabricated metals	1,536	1,815	1,967	719	1,349	1,853	1,553
Machinery	2,257	2,253	5,057	3,574	4,465	5,250	5,698
Computer and electronic products	8,860	7,714	11,565	6,574	11,440	11,182	10,172
Electrical equipment, appliances, and components	1,079	1,703	2,009	1,425	1,653	1,605	1,937
Transportation equipment	4,107	1,936	1,326	-826	6,471	9,548	8,077
Other manufacturing	(NA)	14,862	20,142	13,561	17,452	19,831	18,895
Wholesale trade	14,198	24,494	28,773	19,512	24,538	29,079	27,020
Information	-964	10,832	14,400	13,378	12,229	14,225	14,343
Depository institutions	2,191	164	1,013	2,120	1,328	7,261	8,526
Finance and insurance	15,210	27,911	43,618	41,237	35,143	33,435	36,980
Professional, scientific, and technical services	3,548	9,272	6,865	8,390	8,856	9,693	10,181
Holding companies (nonbank)	(NA)	109,566	179,733	170,226	220,101	228,015	225,622
Other industries	42,504	18,184	18,587	21,237	25,033	25,451	28,285

NA Not available. [1] Includes other industries, not shown separately. [2] Prior to 2008, income is shown net of withholding taxes. Beginning 2008, income is shown gross of withholding taxes.

Source: U.S. Bureau of Economic Analysis, "International Economic Accounts: Direct Investment and Multinational Companies (MNCs)," <http://www.bea.gov/iTable/index_MNC.cfm>, accessed September 2013.

Table 1322. U.S. Direct Investment Position Abroad on a Historical-Cost Basis by Selected Country: 2000 to 2012

[In millions of dollars (1,316,247 represents $1,316,247,000,000). U.S. investment abroad is the ownership or control by one U.S. person of 10 percent or more of the voting securities of an incorporated foreign business enterprise or an equivalent interest in an unincorporated foreign business enterprise. Negative position can occur when a U.S. parent company's liabilities to the foreign affiliate are greater than its equity in and loans to the foreign affiliate]

Country	2000	2005	2007	2008	2009	2010	2011	2012
All countries....................	1,316,247	2,241,656	2,993,980	3,232,493	3,565,020	3,741,910	4,084,659	4,453,307
Canada.............................	132,472	231,836	250,642	246,483	274,807	295,206	331,666	351,460
Europe [1]	687,320	1,210,679	1,682,023	1,844,182	1,991,191	2,034,559	2,247,345	2,477,040
Austria............................	2,872	11,236	14,646	13,546	10,954	11,485	13,763	15,591
Belgium...........................	17,973	49,306	62,491	65,279	46,610	43,975	50,941	53,769
Czech Republic................	1,228	2,729	4,066	5,053	5,372	5,268	5,804	6,389
Denmark..........................	5,270	6,914	8,950	10,481	13,053	11,802	15,019	15,092
Finland............................	1,342	1,950	2,202	2,012	1,659	1,597	2,184	2,013
France.............................	42,628	60,526	74,179	84,409	90,879	78,320	79,621	82,596
Germany..........................	55,508	100,473	100,601	107,833	110,149	103,319	111,088	121,184
Greece............................	795	1,884	2,179	2,092	1,919	1,775	1,189	969
Hungary..........................	1,920	2,795	6,457	3,737	4,090	4,237	5,651	6,014
Ireland............................	35,903	55,173	117,708	150,131	129,829	158,851	189,449	203,779
Italy................................	23,484	24,528	28,216	27,663	29,944	27,137	25,981	26,754
Luxembourg.....................	27,849	79,937	144,180	172,251	219,082	272,206	350,619	383,603
Netherlands.....................	115,429	240,205	412,122	423,059	497,471	514,689	573,721	645,098
Norway............................	4,379	8,533	12,188	24,706	24,238	28,541	33,283	38,803
Poland............................	3,884	5,575	15,614	12,489	13,412	13,152	13,446	14,178
Portugal..........................	2,664	2,138	2,991	3,006	2,803	2,612	2,477	2,383
Russia............................	1,147	9,363	15,029	19,777	20,763	10,040	11,658	14,066
Spain..............................	21,236	50,197	61,093	54,194	58,341	52,390	48,581	31,377
Sweden...........................	25,959	30,153	36,615	35,876	36,702	23,275	24,827	24,532
Switzerland.....................	55,377	100,692	94,675	133,222	131,707	119,891	113,715	130,315
Turkey.............................	1,826	2,563	5,584	4,542	3,675	4,155	4,851	6,028
United Kingdom................	230,762	351,513	426,357	448,412	495,382	501,247	515,991	597,813
Latin America and other Western Hemisphere............	266,576	379,582	556,160	588,992	718,478	752,788	807,362	869,268
South America [1]................	84,220	73,311	104,732	98,603	119,765	136,598	152,671	171,268
Argentina......................	17,488	10,103	13,692	12,197	12,610	11,747	13,498	14,396
Brazil..........................	36,717	30,882	48,807	43,953	55,380	66,963	73,836	79,394
Chile..........................	10,052	11,127	16,337	16,286	25,404	30,747	34,966	39,870
Colombia......................	3,693	4,292	4,552	5,028	6,050	6,181	6,475	8,434
Ecuador........................	832	941	1,007	1,098	1,339	1,283	793	851
Peru...........................	3,130	5,542	5,964	4,448	6,435	7,196	8,993	10,918
Venezuela......................	10,531	8,934	12,871	13,545	10,248	10,255	11,871	15,034
Central America [1]..............	73,841	82,496	102,472	101,291	97,127	97,752	102,991	112,729
Costa Rica......................	1,716	1,598	2,267	2,414	2,155	1,827	1,857	1,681
Honduras........................	399	821	626	809	852	936	821	881
Mexico..........................	39,352	73,687	91,046	87,443	84,047	85,751	90,795	101,030
Panama.........................	30,758	4,826	6,171	5,963	6,060	5,156	5,362	5,113
Other Western Hemisphere [1]...	108,515	223,775	348,956	389,098	501,586	518,438	551,700	585,271
Barbados.......................	2,141	3,881	2,136	3,154	5,804	7,524	11,874	13,082
Bermuda........................	60,114	113,222	211,708	207,547	287,933	265,524	280,461	304,524
Dominican Republic...........	1,143	815	712	806	1,193	1,432	1,467	1,655
U.K. Islands, Caribbean........	33,451	83,164	105,829	134,298	160,627	191,680	200,219	219,851
Africa [1]..........................	11,891	22,756	32,607	36,746	43,941	54,816	57,230	61,381
Egypt............................	1,998	5,475	7,023	7,804	10,257	12,599	14,950	17,134
Nigeria...........................	470	1,105	1,584	3,254	4,938	5,058	5,307	8,152
South Africa....................	3,562	3,969	5,240	4,999	5,447	6,017	5,830	5,502
Middle East [1]..................	10,863	21,115	28,448	31,294	33,776	34,431	34,881	42,853
Israel............................	3,735	7,978	9,487	9,444	9,018	9,464	9,271	10,208
Saudi Arabia....................	3,661	3,830	5,012	5,126	7,530	7,436	8,250	9,692
United Arab Emirates..........	683	2,285	2,967	3,337	4,118	4,935	5,864	7,826
Asia and Pacific [1].............	207,125	375,689	444,101	484,796	502,826	570,111	606,174	651,305
Australia.........................	34,838	75,669	84,331	92,668	106,212	125,421	137,261	132,825
China............................	11,140	19,016	29,710	53,927	54,069	58,996	55,304	51,363
Hong Kong.......................	27,447	36,415	40,720	40,042	50,720	41,264	39,998	47,767
India.............................	2,379	7,162	14,622	18,354	21,752	24,666	24,622	28,385
Indonesia........................	8,904	8,603	14,978	16,273	9,743	10,558	11,972	13,480
Japan............................	57,091	81,175	85,224	99,803	91,196	113,523	126,030	133,967
Korea, South....................	8,968	19,760	23,558	22,426	23,930	26,233	30,160	35,125
Malaysia.........................	7,910	11,097	12,140	12,243	9,740	11,791	12,386	15,001
New Zealand.....................	4,271	5,191	5,527	4,451	6,141	6,724	7,930	9,466
Philippines......................	3,638	6,522	6,953	5,505	4,602	5,399	4,766	4,591
Singapore.......................	24,133	76,390	93,529	83,169	87,909	102,778	118,571	138,603
Taiwan...........................	7,836	14,356	15,807	18,053	19,894	22,188	15,720	16,482
Thailand.........................	5,824	10,252	10,284	9,162	9,457	12,999	14,537	16,882

[1] Includes other countries, not shown separately.

Source: U.S. Bureau of Economic Analysis, "International Economic Accounts: Direct Investment and Multinational Companies (MNCs)," <http://www.bea.gov/iTable/index_MNC.cfm>, accessed September 2013.

Table 1323. U.S. Government Foreign Grants and Credits by Type and Country: 2000 to 2010

[In millions of dollars (1,500 represents 1,500,000,000). See text, this section. Negative figures (–) occur when the total of grant returns, principal repayments, and/or foreign currencies disbursed by the U.S. Government exceeds new grants and new credits utilized and/or acquisitions of foreign currencies through new sales of farm products]

Country	2000	2004	2005	2006	2007	2008	2009	2010
Investment in financial institutions...........	1,500	1,994	1,263	2,024	1,651	1,385	1,676	2,337
Western Europe [1]...........	**429**	**346**	**327**	**60**	**182**	**225**	**253**	**340**
Ireland...........	–	50	–	30	–	34	7	14
Spain...........	-19	-19	-19	-205	(Z)	(Z)	(Z)	(Z)
Yugoslavia [2]...........	1	13	4	-73	-2	3	-5	-2
Bosnia and Herzegovina...........	52	66	72	49	45	29	27	41
Macedonia...........	50	42	68	31	1	35	21	29
Former Yugoslavia - Regional [2]...........	63	38	66	120	45	53	168	83
Other [3] and unspecified [4]...........	478	47	29	5	5	18	4	5
Eastern Europe [1]...........	**2,270**	**1,276**	**-95**	**266**	**1,089**	**2,010**	**1,644**	**1,490**
Albania...........	26	43	54	31	43	38	32	29
Romania...........	38	35	59	42	41	9	12	24
Newly Independent States of the former Soviet Union:								
Armenia...........	20	66	85	62	74	87	71	34
Azerbaijan...........	8	47	74	51	44	36	29	34
Belarus...........	1	1	2	4	6	8	10	4
Georgia...........	36	113	131	85	104	421	232	67
Kazakhstan...........	42	57	69	41	42	44	41	158
Kyrgyzstan...........	15	39	60	50	26	40	44	41
Moldova...........	32	27	39	26	21	53	43	19
Russia...........	797	251	-681	-920	-41	403	331	223
Tajikistan...........	8	40	61	35	33	24	33	32
Turkmenistan...........	4	4	13	3	(Z)	-9	11	9
Ukraine...........	138	114	147	120	72	83	112	125
Uzbekistan...........	22	53	52	23	13	11	9	5
Former Soviet Union—Regional [4]...........	501	372	456	470	461	508	535	485
Other [3] and unspecified [4]...........	419	105	153	73	73	76	73	100
Near East and South Asia [1]...........	**3,378**	**3,135**	**5,515**	**4,767**	**9,947**	**9,038**	**11,780**	**14,413**
Afghanistan...........	5	1,382	2,304	3,807	7,541	6,125	8,555	10,862
Bangladesh...........	43	50	52	44	81	76	53	71
Egypt...........	3,139	2,689	2,827	149	1,766	1,797	1,749	1,216
Greece...........	-149	-457	-114	-103	-74	-66	-74	-76
India...........	-64	-40	-69	63	46	28	28	41
Nepal...........	15	37	51	58	64	64	80	57
Pakistan...........	366	-341	532	712	527	688	1,254	1,528
Turkey...........	-80	-298	-225	-191	-296	-43	-28	46
UNRWA [5]...........	97	27	57	137	135	–	–	–
Other and unspecified [3]...........	21	79	54	47	117	310	141	635
Africa [1]...........	**1,054**	**2,228**	**2,120**	**1,261**	**3,546**	**4,778**	**6,425**	**7,315**
Algeria...........	-53	-145	-173	-1,324	-18	-18	-11	-13
Burundi...........	3	27	6	37	18	16	32	27
Cameroon...........	1	2	7	10	5	6	7	11
Cape Verde...........	1	4	4	9	7	28	38	2
Congo, Democratic Republic of...........	(Z)	(Z)	17	1	10	11	12	7
Ethiopia...........	142	234	308	233	278	447	440	550
Ghana...........	40	67	53	57	65	87	157	123
Guinea...........	19	33	36	29	15	75	31	20
Kenya...........	44	82	96	187	179	284	390	340
Liberia...........	19	50	40	61	81	261	142	135
Madagascar...........	21	34	42	45	60	82	68	64
Malawi...........	45	54	46	68	75	88	95	92
Mali...........	50	46	55	57	55	58	114	94
Mozambique...........	119	105	65	98	111	152	192	146
Nigeria...........	-17	41	67	-178	123	200	211	255
Rwanda...........	26	36	49	55	70	93	111	103
Senegal...........	27	53	40	39	40	70	73	106
Somalia...........	7	16	10	33	40	168	108	35
South Africa...........	68	332	103	106	155	242	360	266
Sudan...........	17	120	130	390	364	529	513	521
Tanzania...........	15	66	65	76	114	129	207	215
Uganda...........	92	120	149	154	184	194	228	237
Zambia...........	44	56	91	91	119	164	151	121
Zimbabwe...........	23	31	27	32	69	141	153	113
Other and unspecified [4]...........	164	407	513	621	1,070	767	1,826	3,102
Far East and Pacific [1]...........	**551**	**-133**	**67**	**-93**	**144**	**696**	**621**	**865**
Cambodia...........	23	44	58	56	61	60	66	90
Hong Kong...........	-15	-28	-28	-28	-28	-23	-16	-15
Indonesia...........	272	-157	-3	-68	-14	-84	-46	66
Korea, South...........	-132	-110	-43	-43	-40	182	-68	-67
Laos...........	5	5	2	1	1	3	5	6
Malaysia...........	134	-45	-40	-41	-185	2	2	4
Philippines...........	22	-14	-31	-25	51	143	128	133
Thailand...........	-99	8	9	-62	1	19	8	14
Pacific Islands, Trust Territory of the Pacific Island [6].......	145	204	190	174	195	211	348	185
Other and unspecified [4]...........	19	40	47	37	182	200	215	214
Western Hemisphere [1]...........	**1,621**	**1,907**	**2,096**	**1,512**	**1,398**	**2,087**	**4,311**	**2,977**
Bolivia...........	136	217	159	142	155	135	139	79
Brazil...........	195	-136	-93	-344	-181	-166	-87	-303
Colombia...........	33	467	598	620	771	914	1,223	642
Ecuador...........	14	37	60	80	73	52	60	47
El Salvador...........	27	103	51	28	42	58	100	48
Guatemala...........	49	40	21	34	25	55	66	68
Haiti...........	63	83	118	154	164	192	232	1,047
Honduras...........	100	83	71	63	87	100	133	56

See footnotes at end of table.

Table 1323. U.S. Government Foreign Grants and Credits by Type and Country: 2000 to 2010-Continued.

See headnote on page 831.

Country	2000	2004	2005	2006	2007	2008	2009	2010
Mexico	-123	14	40	30	51	52	1,277	418
Nicaragua	53	28	37	56	75	97	91	37
Panama [7]	-13	14	8	11	6	9	7	9
Peru	87	168	127	71	-258	128	539	188
Other [8] and unspecified [4]	1,100	725	745	471	407	366	426	439
Other international organizations	**2,837**	**3,015**	**4,608**	**4,114**	**4,857**	**5,348**	**7,908**	**8,652**
Middle East	**4,345**	**8,413**	**16,705**	**10,220**	**10,195**	**10,801**	**9,608**	**9,028**
Iraq [9]	(Z)	5,040	10,857	9,157	7,039	6,228	5,269	2,942
Israel	3,932	2,163	4,953	390	2,373	2,955	1,994	2,692
Jordan	317	801	583	463	422	643	687	802
Lebanon	22	29	37	46	147	253	244	119
Yemen	16	31	25	30	40	22	31	48
West Bank-Gaza Regional	64	171	179	128	152	474	812	687

– Represents zero. Z Less than $500,000. [1] Includes other countries, not shown separately. [2] In 1992, some successor countries assumed portions of outstanding credits of the former Yugoslavia (assignment of the remaining portions is pending). Subsequent negative totals reflect payments to the United States on these assumed credits which were greater than the extension of new credits and grants to these countries. [3] Includes European Atomic Energy Community, European Coal and Steel Community, European Payments Union, European Productivity Agency, North Atlantic Treaty Organization, and Organization for European Economic Cooperation. [4] In recent years, significant amounts of foreign assistance have been reported on a regional, inter-regional, and worldwide basis. Country totals in this table may understate actual assistance to many countries. [5] United Nations Relief and Works Agency for Palestine Refugees. [6] Excludes transactions with Commonwealth of the Northern Mariana Islands after October 1986; includes transactions with Federated States of Micronesia, Republic of the Marshall Islands, and Republic of Palau. [7] Includes transfer of Panama Canal to the Republic of Panama in December 1999. [8] Includes Andean Development Corporation, Caribbean Development Bank, Central American Bank for Economic Integration, Eastern Caribbean Central Bank, Inter-American Institute of Agricultural Science, Organization of American States, and Pan American Health Organization. [9] Foreign assistance to Iraq in 1991–96 was direct humanitarian assistance to ethnic minorities of northern Iraq after the conflict in the Persian Gulf. Foreign assistance to Iraq in 2003 thru 2009 includes Iraq Reconstruction and humanitarian assistance.

Source: U.S. Bureau of Economic Analysis, press releases, and unpublished data. See also <http://www.bea.gov/scb/index.htm>.

Table 1324. U.S. Foreign Economic and Military Aid Programs: 1980 to 2011

[In millions of dollars (9,682 represents $9,682,000,000). For years ending September 30. Total aid programs are the sum of economic and military assistance. Major components in recent years include U.S. Agency for International Development (USAID), U.S. Department of Agriculture (USDA), State Department, and voluntary contributions to international financial institutions. Annual figures are in obligations]

Year and Region	Total foreign assistance	Military assistance	Economic assistance, by funding agency					
			Total	USAID	USDA	State Department	Other U.S. agencies	Multilateral organizations
1980	9,682	2,110	7,572	4,062	1,437	459	137	1,478
1985	18,107	5,780	12,327	8,132	2,052	431	164	1,548
1990	16,003	4,959	11,044	6,964	1,643	590	377	1,469
1995	15,670	4,122	11,548	7,281	1,401	132	953	1,781
2000	17,117	4,935	12,182	5,907	1,941	2,278	945	1,110
2005	37,413	7,834	29,579	10,345	2,250	5,044	10,187	1,753
2007	41,446	13,747	27,698	11,528	1,817	5,678	6,941	1,734
2008	49,013	16,135	32,878	10,051	2,896	9,758	8,284	1,889
2009	49,173	14,456	34,717	12,875	2,701	11,407	5,491	2,243
2010	51,951	14,546	37,405	13,951	2,541	12,037	5,972	2,904
2011, total	**49,593**	**17,867**	**31,726**	**10,888**	**1,962**	**12,158**	**4,065**	**2,653**
Asia	16,947	11,016	5,931	3,027	392	1,212	1,088	211
Eurasia	738	119	620	400	2	145	73	–
Eastern Europe	442	120	322	229	2	77	15	–
Latin America and Caribbean	3,639	402	3,237	1,715	154	1,025	290	54
Middle East and North Africa	8,937	5,769	3,168	1,406	61	1,593	109	–
Oceania	329	1	328	32	–	2	293	–
Sub-Saharan Africa	9,338	234	9,104	2,271	1,294	4,948	526	66
Western Europe	55	11	45	26	–	17	2	–
Canada	27	–	27	–	–	–	27	–
World, not specified	9,139	195	8,944	1,783	56	3,140	1,642	2,322

-Represents or rounds to zero.

Source: U.S. Agency for International Development (USAID), "U.S. Overseas Loans and Grants: Foreign Assistance Data," <http://gbk.eads.usaidallnet.gov/data/>, accessed August 2013. See also <http://gbk.eads.usaidallnet.gov/docs/>.

Table 1325. U.S. Foreign Economic and Military Aid by Major Recipient Country: 2000 to 2011

[In millions of dollars (17,117 represents $17,117,000,000). For years ending September 30. Annual figures are for obligations]

Region/Country	2000	2005	2009	2010	2011 Total	2011 Economic aid	2011 Military aid
Total [1]......................	17,117	37,413	49,173	51,951	49,593	31,726	17,868
Middle East & North Africa [1]...............	6,799	15,358	12,837	9,020	8,937	3,168	5,769
Egypt........................	2,076	1,567	1,790	1,699	1,471	173	1,299
Iraq..........................	1	9,711	5,773	2,142	2,148	1,184	964
Israel........................	3,863	2,714	2,423	2,837	3,026	31	2,995
Jordan.......................	448	683	812	767	851	532	319
Lebanon.....................	35	25	222	159	196	116	80
Morocco.....................	51	61	67	72	101	86	15
West Bank/Gaza [2].........	122	350	1,048	693	464	464	–
Yemen.......................	57	30	177	139	102	81	21
Sub-Saharan Africa [1]......	2,031	5,139	10,418	10,079	9,338	9,104	235
Angola.......................	105	67	58	100	88	88	–
Botswana....................	1	42	110	67	99	97	1
Burkina Faso................	18	33	509	37	42	42	–
Chad.........................	4	63	223	175	152	151	1
Congo, Democratic Republic of..........	33	121	368	376	428	406	22
Ethiopia.....................	278	688	968	989	607	606	1
Ghana.......................	67	72	177	250	164	161	3
Kenya.......................	94	263	931	826	1,032	1,030	3
Lesotho.....................	2	4	35	57	69	69	–
Liberia......................	22	149	225	288	257	243	13
Madagascar..................	27	124	60	81	78	78	–
Malawi.......................	44	84	141	210	234	234	–
Mali.........................	44	55	228	172	171	170	1
Mozambique..................	88	127	328	406	350	349	2
Namibia.....................	16	50	391	110	83	82	–
Nigeria......................	113	151	508	462	530	519	11
Rwanda......................	39	83	171	224	174	173	1
Senegal.....................	37	48	138	698	140	136	5
Somalia.....................	14	45	452	163	279	204	75
South Africa.................	57	187	574	572	757	755	2
South Sudan [3].............	–	–	–	–	388	345	43
Sudan.......................	51	1,042	1,246	928	535	535	–
Tanzania....................	45	137	381	549	560	559	1
Uganda......................	76	291	484	477	470	469	1
Zambia......................	35	144	295	338	323	323	–
Zimbabwe...................	21	61	294	225	191	191	–
Latin America & Caribbean [1]..............	2,301	2,629	3,036	4,779	3,639	3,237	402
Bolivia.......................	241	162	102	98	73	73	–
Colombia....................	1,169	824	896	855	436	276	160
El Salvador..................	35	59	152	131	109	99	10
Guatemala...................	72	96	144	171	174	154	20
Haiti.........................	85	224	372	1,410	1,263	1,262	2
Honduras....................	42	267	38	117	99	89	10
Mexico.......................	44	103	500	717	411	318	94
Peru.........................	204	179	151	212	142	129	13
Asia [1]......................	1,163	4,839	12,450	16,310	16,947	5,931	11,016
Afghanistan..................	54	2,252	8,862	11,242	12,924	2,659	10,265
Bangladesh..................	78	84	178	235	222	218	4
Cambodia....................	28	98	89	97	35	32	3
India........................	188	215	146	152	118	116	2
Indonesia....................	242	588	237	340	252	229	23
Mongolia....................	26	19	39	233	26	22	4
Nepal........................	23	73	88	80	104	102	2
Pakistan.....................	24	758	1,830	2,924	1,700	1,027	673
Philippines..................	82	167	190	238	611	585	26
Sri Lanka....................	11	160	84	111	69	67	2
Oceania [1]..................	165	162	209	214	329	328	1
Micronesia, Federated States of.........	81	94	108	91	135	135	–
Eurasia [1]..................	1,462	2,385	1,777	2,427	738	620	119
Armenia.....................	104	80	67	92	47	44	3
Georgia.....................	112	110	602	437	113	95	18
Kazakhstan..................	53	69	105	333	51	46	5
Kyrgyzstan..................	47	52	59	130	69	53	16
Moldova.....................	49	34	33	310	34	31	2
Russia.......................	709	1,603	539	506	130	89	42
Ukraine......................	200	161	187	318	111	99	11
Eastern Europe [1]..........	1,045	708	544	757	442	322	120
Kosovo......................	–	–	138	172	101	95	6
Poland......................	85	96	82	221	36	–	36
Western Europe..............	24	133	98	83	55	45	11

-Represents zero or less than $50,000. [1] Includes other countries, not shown separately. [2] See footnote 7, Table 1365. [3] South Sudan seceded from Sudan in July 2011.

Source: U.S. Agency for International Development, "U.S. Overseas Loans and Grants: Foreign Assistance Data," <http://gbk.eads.usaidallnet.gov/data/>, accessed September 2013.

Table 1326. U.S. International Trade in Goods and Services: 2000 to 2012

[In millions of dollars (–377,337 represents –$377,337,000,000). Data presented on a balance of payments basis and will not agree with the following merchandise trade tables in this section]

Category	2000	2005	2007	2008	2009	2010	2011	2012
TRADE BALANCE								
Total	**-377,337**	**-707,914**	**-699,065**	**-702,302**	**-383,657**	**-499,379**	**-556,838**	**-534,656**
Goods	-446,942	-784,133	-822,743	-833,957	-510,550	-650,156	-744,139	-741,475
Services	69,605	76,219	123,677	131,655	126,893	150,777	187,301	206,819
Travel	17,525	12,230	20,228	29,929	20,055	27,958	37,323	42,763
Passenger fares	-3,416	-4,580	-2,494	-884	986	3,731	5,684	4,706
Other transportation	-11,647	-22,199	-15,135	-12,680	-6,514	-10,533	-11,563	-11,590
Royalties, license fees	35,202	48,871	71,324	72,502	67,109	74,970	85,931	84,293
Other private services	39,707	56,144	59,050	54,956	58,532	69,566	79,991	93,300
Other [1]	-5,921	-13,118	-8,406	-11,294	-12,054	-13,520	-8,931	-6,214
U.S. govt misc. services	-1,844	-1,130	-888	-873	-1,222	-1,396	-1,133	-439
EXPORTS								
Total	**1,072,782**	**1,288,257**	**1,652,859**	**1,840,332**	**1,578,187**	**1,844,468**	**2,112,825**	**2,210,585**
Goods	784,781	911,686	1,163,605	1,307,329	1,069,475	1,288,795	1,495,853	1,561,239
Services	288,002	376,571	489,255	533,003	508,712	555,674	616,973	649,346
Travel	82,891	82,160	97,355	110,423	94,187	103,463	115,552	126,214
Passenger fares	20,197	20,609	25,187	30,957	26,103	30,987	36,763	39,360
Other transportation	25,562	32,013	40,638	44,016	36,087	40,669	43,067	43,855
Royalties, license fees	51,808	74,448	97,803	102,125	98,406	107,521	120,717	124,182
Other private services	100,792	154,133	209,307	228,770	235,744	255,989	279,645	294,527
Other [1]	6,210	12,082	17,444	14,899	16,277	14,958	18,821	18,520
U.S. govt misc. services	542	1,125	1,522	1,814	1,908	2,087	2,408	2,688
IMPORTS								
Total	**1,450,119**	**1,996,171**	**2,351,925**	**2,542,634**	**1,961,844**	**2,343,847**	**2,669,663**	**2,745,240**
Goods	1,231,722	1,695,820	1,986,347	2,141,287	1,580,025	1,938,950	2,239,991	2,302,714
Services	218,397	300,352	365,577	401,348	381,819	404,897	429,672	442,527
Travel	65,366	69,930	77,127	80,494	74,132	75,505	78,229	83,451
Passenger fares	23,613	25,189	27,681	31,841	25,117	27,256	31,079	34,654
Other transportation	37,209	54,212	55,773	56,696	42,601	51,202	54,630	55,445
Royalties, license fees	16,606	25,577	26,479	29,623	31,297	32,551	34,786	39,889
Other private services	61,085	97,989	150,257	173,814	177,212	186,423	199,654	201,227
Other [1]	12,131	25,200	25,850	26,193	28,331	28,478	27,752	24,734
U.S. govt misc. services	2,386	2,255	2,410	2,687	3,130	3,483	3,541	3,127

[1] Represents transfers under U.S. military sales contracts for exports and direct defense expenditures for imports.

Source: U.S. Census Bureau, *U.S. International Trade in Goods and Services, Annual Revision for 2012*, Series FT-900, June 2013. See also <http://www.census.gov/foreign-trade/data/index.html>

Table 1327. U.S. International Trade in Goods by Related Parties: 2000 to 2012

[In millions of dollars (1,205,339 represents $1,205,339,000,000). "Related party trade" is trade by U.S. companies with their subsidiaries abroad as well as trade by U.S. subsidiaries of foreign companies with their parent companies. Based on the North American Industry Classification System (NAICS), 2002; see text, Section 15]

Country and commodity	2002 NAICS code	2000	2005	2010	2011	2012
IMPORTS FOR CONSUMPTION						
Total imports	(X)	1,205,339	1,662,380	1,898,610	2,186,951	2,251,035
Related party trade, total [1]	**(X)**	**563,084**	**775,730**	**922,202**	**1,056,215**	**1,131,902**
Canada	(X)	100,689	127,719	138,222	162,045	173,937
Mexico	(X)	89,068	99,709	135,984	155,713	173,059
China	(X)	18,061	62,716	107,038	111,599	121,813
Japan	(X)	108,290	108,322	93,892	97,789	113,391
Germany	(X)	37,781	51,870	53,951	65,756	72,754
Computer & electronic products	334	166,279	176,719	203,900	208,047	214,767
Transportation equipment	336	161,150	188,445	179,516	200,525	239,222
Chemicals	325	45,452	84,459	134,065	152,928	150,167
Oil & gas	211	13,241	48,725	80,071	97,024	104,770
Petroleum & coal products	324	12,655	42,572	54,618	77,258	77,932
EXPORTS						
Total exports	(X)	780,418	803,992	1,277,504	1,480,552	1,546,455
Related party trade, domestic exports, total [1]	**(X)**	**196,596**	**245,712**	**314,489**	**365,014**	**381,695**
Canada	(X)	64,133	76,331	88,689	98,098	101,002
Mexico	(X)	34,249	44,570	49,313	60,515	65,352
Japan	(X)	20,313	17,427	16,718	18,673	19,327
Netherlands	(X)	6,845	9,308	15,070	17,088	16,297
China	(X)	1,552	4,909	13,436	15,325	16,556
Chemicals	325	26,376	48,121	64,548	73,517	77,735
Transportation equipment	336	46,288	52,513	55,400	65,533	69,036
Computer & electronic products	334	51,210	41,882	42,689	40,614	39,498
Petroleum & coal products	324	1,253	4,974	23,101	40,237	41,942
Machinery, except electrical	333	19,831	25,473	32,301	36,841	39,779

X Not applicable. [1] Includes other countries and other commodities, not shown separately.

Source: U.S. Census Bureau, *U.S. Goods Trade: Imports and Exports by Related-Parties 2012*, May 2013. See also <http://www.census.gov/foreign-trade/index.html>.

Table 1328. U.S. Freight Gateways—Value of Shipments: 2012

[In billions of dollars (3,821.0 represents $3,821,000,000,000), except as indicated. For the top 50 gateways ranked by value of shipments]

Port	Mode	Rank	Total trade	Exports	Imports	Exports as a percent of total
Total U.S. merchandise trade............................	**(X)**	**(X)**	**3,821.0**	**1,545.7**	**2,275.3**	**40.5**
Top 50 gateways....................................	(X)	(X)	3,146.5	1,277.6	1,868.9	40.6
As a percent of total................................	(X)	(X)	82.3	82.7	82.1	(X)
Los Angeles, CA....................................	Water	1	284.0	42.7	241.3	15.0
JFK International Airport, NY........................	Air	2	184.5	96.0	88.5	52.0
Houston, TX..	Water	3	176.6	93.2	83.4	52.8
Laredo, TX...	Land	4	168.6	76.6	92.0	45.4
Newark, NJ...	Water	5	164.8	19.6	145.1	11.9
Chicago, IL..	Air/Land	6	150.6	37.9	112.7	25.2
Detroit, MI..	Land	7	148.3	79.3	69.0	53.5
New Orleans, LA....................................	Air/Water	8	122.6	61.0	61.6	49.8
Long Beach, CA.....................................	Water	9	101.1	35.8	65.3	35.4
Port Huron, MI.....................................	Land	10	88.8	45.1	43.7	50.8
Buffalo-Niagara Falls, NY..........................	Land	11	88.8	47.5	41.2	53.6
Los Angeles International Airport, CA..............	Air	12	86.9	41.5	45.4	47.8
Savannah, GA.......................................	Water	13	76.3	33.4	42.9	43.8
Miami International Airport, FL....................	Air	14	70.7	44.8	25.9	63.3
El Paso, TX..	Land	15	66.8	29.8	37.1	44.5
Charleston, SC.....................................	Water	16	65.9	24.7	41.2	37.5
Norfolk-Newport News, VA...........................	Water	17	63.2	27.5	35.7	43.5
New York, NY.......................................	Water	18	57.4	41.2	16.2	71.7
Baltimore, MD......................................	Water	19	53.8	21.7	32.1	40.3
Anchorage, AK......................................	Air	20	51.6	15.2	36.4	29.4
Dallas-Fort Worth, TX..............................	Air	21	49.5	18.1	31.4	36.6
San Francisco International Airport, CA............	Air	22	49.3	26.2	23.1	53.1
Tacoma, WA...	Water	23	46.1	10.1	36.0	21.9
Oakland, CA..	Water	24	45.1	19.0	26.1	42.2
Cleveland, OH......................................	Air	25	42.0	24.6	17.4	58.6
Seattle, WA..	Water	26	38.9	10.5	28.4	26.9
Atlanta, GA..	Air	27	37.1	13.7	23.3	37.0
Otay Mesa Station, CA..............................	Land	28	35.8	12.3	23.4	34.5
Morgan City, LA....................................	Water	29	35.4	1.0	34.4	2.7
Philadelphia, PA...................................	Water	30	32.8	4.8	27.9	14.8
Port Arthur, TX....................................	Water	31	28.8	4.2	24.6	14.6
Corpus Christi, TX.................................	Water	32	28.5	10.6	17.8	37.4
Hildago, TX..	Land	33	26.8	10.1	16.7	37.8
Champlain-Rouses Point, NY.........................	Land	34	26.6	10.5	16.2	39.3
Gramercy, LA.......................................	Water	35	26.0	17.7	8.3	68.0
Miami, FL..	Water	36	25.6	11.9	13.7	46.4
Pembina, ND..	Land	37	25.3	14.4	10.9	57.0
Port Everglades, FL................................	Water	38	24.4	14.0	10.4	57.4
Nogales, AZ..	Land	39	24.1	9.0	15.2	37.1
Texas City, TX.....................................	Water	40	23.6	7.0	16.6	29.7
Blaine, WA...	Land	41	23.3	14.9	8.4	64.0
Jacksonville, FL...................................	Water	42	23.3	11.8	11.4	50.8
Eagle Pass, TX.....................................	Land	43	21.7	7.8	13.9	36.0
Santa Teresa, NM...................................	Land	44	20.4	8.1	12.3	39.8
Everett, WA..	Water	45	20.2	18.8	1.4	93.1
Lake Charles, LA...................................	Water	46	19.7	4.9	14.8	24.7
Seattle-Tacoma International Airport, WA...........	Air	47	19.2	14.0	5.2	72.7
Portal, ND...	Land	48	18.9	13.0	5.9	68.9
Sweetgrass, MT.....................................	Land	49	18.5	10.0	8.4	54.4
Houston Intercontinental Airport, TX..............	Air	50	18.5	10.0	8.5	54.1

X Not applicable.

Source: U.S. Census Bureau, Foreign Trade Division, USA Trade Online, <https://usatrade.census.gov/>, accessed September 2013.

Table 1329. U.S. Exports and General Imports of Merchandise by Customs District: 2005 to 2012

[In billions of dollars (901.1 represents $901,100,000,000). Exports are f.a.s. (free alongside ship) value all years; imports are on customs-value basis. These data may differ from those in Tables 1327, 1332, and 1333. For methodology, see Foreign Trade Statistics in Appendix III]

Customs district	Exports					General imports				
	2005	2009	2010	2011	2012	2005	2009	2010	2011	2012
Total [1]	**901.1**	**1,056.0**	**1,278.5**	**1,480.3**	**1,545.7**	**1,673.5**	**1,559.6**	**1,913.9**	**2,208.1**	**2,275.3**
Anchorage, AK	12.1	11.9	14.5	15.4	16.0	10.4	12.4	16.2	15.3	15.0
Baltimore, MD	9.0	11.2	14.7	20.9	22.0	29.6	21.0	28.8	32.3	33.6
Boston, MA	10.4	8.3	8.2	8.1	7.1	21.7	17.4	19.2	20.9	20.9
Buffalo, NY	35.0	35.7	40.6	47.3	47.8	42.6	31.6	39.2	41.7	42.3
Charleston, SC	16.2	16.4	19.5	22.5	24.8	31.9	26.3	29.4	36.2	39.7
Chicago, IL	29.9	31.5	35.8	36.5	38.0	78.7	96.7	125.6	140.0	149.5
Cleveland, OH	20.8	21.4	25.4	29.9	31.6	49.0	55.8	69.2	79.4	86.4
Columbia-Snake, OR	6.3	10.3	12.3	14.4	15.8	14.2	11.0	12.2	12.5	13.6
Dallas/Fort Worth, TX	17.8	17.4	18.1	18.3	19.3	31.8	30.8	38.4	45.5	48.9
Detroit, MI	106.9	89.6	113.2	124.1	128.4	123.1	81.3	106.0	120.6	124.6
Duluth, MN	1.9	2.3	2.6	3.6	4.6	9.3	5.8	6.8	8.3	8.4
El Paso, TX	19.9	19.8	29.3	34.8	38.3	28.0	30.4	44.1	47.5	52.0
Great Falls, MT	9.8	15.3	17.4	22.8	21.7	27.1	21.7	26.9	29.4	28.0
Honolulu, HI	2.4	5.8	7.4	7.4	9.8	3.7	3.8	4.6	5.7	6.5
Houston/Galveston, TX	47.0	75.1	94.5	119.5	126.8	89.4	92.4	116.9	148.6	147.1
Laredo, TX	60.5	66.8	81.4	96.0	105.3	78.7	80.0	104.2	120.2	133.9
Los Angeles, CA	78.4	86.1	105.1	121.0	121.3	215.5	196.4	242.7	266.3	282.7
Miami, FL	34.1	49.5	58.9	69.2	73.2	31.8	29.6	36.6	44.0	51.4
Milwaukee, WI	0.1	0.1	0.1	0.3	0.3	1.3	0.7	0.9	1.3	0.9
Minneapolis, MN	2.3	2.0	2.6	2.6	2.8	6.9	11.4	13.6	16.4	16.8
Mobile, AL	5.0	7.3	8.7	11.6	12.8	14.3	17.3	20.8	26.8	26.6
New Orleans, LA	32.6	57.0	69.1	84.0	93.0	97.8	94.2	125.3	150.4	150.8
New York, NY	90.9	110.9	136.3	160.7	158.4	176.7	155.6	190.6	227.2	223.5
Nogales, AZ	6.9	7.6	8.9	10.5	12.0	13.0	14.0	17.4	18.4	19.0
Norfolk, VA	16.8	19.8	21.1	24.3	27.7	23.5	21.6	23.9	25.5	28.8
Ogdensburg, NY	13.3	13.5	16.2	18.7	17.8	28.2	23.9	27.8	29.9	27.7
Pembina, ND	13.6	16.9	21.3	25.7	28.6	12.8	12.5	14.7	16.4	18.0
Philadelphia, PA	10.2	13.1	14.3	17.2	16.8	47.8	49.2	56.9	67.2	61.3
Port Arthur, TX	2.1	4.9	6.5	11.0	10.3	20.9	20.1	26.4	33.5	35.4
Portland, ME	2.8	4.2	4.4	4.7	4.9	11.2	10.0	9.8	12.2	12.0
Providence, RI	0.1	0.2	0.3	0.4	0.4	4.4	4.0	5.8	7.2	8.0
San Diego, CA	15.0	14.0	16.2	18.5	19.9	28.4	30.4	32.4	34.2	36.6
San Francisco, CA	36.6	37.0	47.1	49.9	50.5	62.4	49.7	60.6	69.7	68.7
San Juan, PR	9.7	18.8	19.7	15.8	16.3	19.5	18.9	19.4	24.6	26.0
Savannah, GA	24.7	33.8	41.0	49.6	51.8	47.9	53.4	68.0	76.8	80.6
Seattle, WA	44.1	53.9	58.5	69.7	75.9	51.7	47.7	52.6	58.9	62.8
St. Albans, VT	4.3	2.9	3.3	3.2	3.2	12.6	7.6	6.9	8.5	9.5
St. Louis, MO	1.3	1.6	1.0	0.8	0.9	9.7	10.1	11.5	19.2	21.7
Tampa, FL	10.1	10.4	14.4	17.6	17.0	19.3	13.6	16.4	18.8	20.4
Virgin Islands, U.S.	0.5	1.2	1.9	2.3	0.9	9.1	9.2	10.5	12.2	1.2
Washington, DC	3.7	6.0	6.0	5.2	5.4	3.7	10.2	8.2	9.0	6.8
Wilmington, NC	2.2	4.0	5.3	5.5	5.8	15.4	12.9	12.8	15.1	14.6

[1] Totals include the following special districts, not shown separately: vessels under their own power or afloat, low valued imports and exports, and mail shipments. Totals may also include data for two or more Customs Districts that have been combined and published under an arbitrary designation, as a solution to disclosure situations.

Source: U.S. Census Bureau, U.S. Foreign Trade Division, USA Trade Online, <https://usatrade.census.gov/>, accessed September 2013.

Table 1330. U.S. Exports of Goods by State of Origin: 2000 to 2012

[In millions of dollars (782,429 represents $782,429,000,000), except as indicated. Exports are on a f.a.s. (free along ship) value basis. Exports are based on origin of movement]

State and other areas	Exports 2000	Exports 2011	2012 Total	2012 Rank
Total	782,429	1,480,665	1,547,138	(X)
United States	712,055	1,410,410	1,475,350	(X)
Alabama	7,317	17,893	19,526	21
Alaska	2,464	5,238	4,596	40
Arizona	14,334	17,501	18,357	23
Arkansas	2,599	5,559	7,621	35
California	119,640	159,354	161,700	2
Colorado	6,593	7,334	8,164	34
Connecticut	8,047	16,198	15,866	26
Delaware	2,197	5,509	5,157	39
District of Columbia	1,003	1,055	2,015	(X)
Florida	26,543	64,756	66,398	6
Georgia	14,925	34,713	35,892	12
Hawaii	387	909	726	50
Idaho	3,559	5,899	6,113	38
Illinois	31,438	64,565	68,026	5
Indiana	15,386	32,200	34,385	13
Iowa	4,466	13,283	14,604	27
Kansas	5,145	11,572	11,660	31
Kentucky	9,612	20,066	22,092	19
Louisiana	16,814	55,124	63,156	7
Maine	1,779	3,461	3,058	44
Maryland	4,593	10,879	11,781	29
Massachusetts	20,514	27,711	25,549	16
Michigan	33,845	50,802	56,902	8
Minnesota	10,303	20,276	20,565	20
Mississippi	2,726	10,926	11,779	30
Missouri	6,497	14,145	13,910	28
Montana	541	1,581	1,573	47
Nebraska	2,511	7,578	7,449	36
Nevada	1,482	7,978	10,190	33
New Hampshire	2,373	4,294	3,485	43
New Jersey	18,638	38,241	37,035	11
New Mexico	2,391	2,090	2,980	45
New York	42,846	82,894	79,189	3
North Carolina	17,946	26,964	28,747	15
North Dakota	626	3,379	4,288	42
Ohio	26,322	46,408	48,535	9
Oklahoma	3,072	6,218	6,576	37
Oregon	11,441	18,292	18,300	24
Pennsylvania	18,792	41,030	38,869	10
Rhode Island	1,186	2,300	2,376	46
South Carolina	8,565	24,680	25,247	17
South Dakota	679	1,455	1,550	48
Tennessee	11,592	29,973	31,126	14
Texas	103,866	249,860	265,352	1
Utah	3,221	18,929	18,939	22
Vermont	4,097	4,328	4,306	41
Virginia	11,698	18,105	18,239	25
Washington	32,215	64,632	75,525	4
West Virginia	2,219	9,002	11,362	32
Wisconsin	10,508	22,049	23,097	18
Wyoming	503	1,222	1,421	49
Puerto Rico	9,735	18,653	18,663	(X)
Virgin Islands	174	2,293	870	(X)
Other [1]	60,810	49,321	52,258	(X)
Timing adjustments	-346	-12	-3	(X)

X Not applicable. [1] Includes unreported, not specified, special category, estimated shipments, and re-exports.

Source: U.S. Census Bureau, *U.S. International Trade in Goods and Services*, Series FT-900, December 2012, and previous reports. See also <http://www.census.gov/foreign-trade/data/index.html>.

Table 1331. U.S. Agricultural Exports by State: 2000 to 2011

[In millions of dollars (51,265 represents $51,265,000,000). Calendar year. Export estimates based on U.S. farm cash receipts]

State	2000	2005	2009	2010	2011
U.S.	51,265	63,182	98,454	115,820	136,374
AL	542	734	940	1,047	1,349
AK	22	9	10	12	12
AZ	695	898	1,056	1,277	1,692
AR	1,264	1,893	2,787	3,088	3,481
CA	6,713	9,467	13,042	15,021	17,844
CO	1,036	952	1,351	1,660	2,198
CT	224	182	207	206	258
DE	130	136	218	215	265
FL	1,745	1,885	2,313	2,727	3,085
GA	1,346	1,456	1,970	2,455	3,195
HI	157	222	368	434	499
ID	754	918	1,259	1,563	2,170
IL	2,857	3,428	6,427	7,206	8,238
IN	1,598	1,823	3,632	4,133	4,655
IA	3,244	4,178	8,103	9,124	10,577
KS	2,112	2,375	3,820	4,924	5,265
KY	1,405	1,466	1,948	2,144	2,434
LA	589	767	1,115	1,361	1,574
ME	122	128	153	181	215
MD	319	290	489	531	654
MA	121	118	175	188	226
MI	856	1,067	1,820	2,294	2,777
MN	2,074	2,604	4,970	5,995	6,738
MS	625	1,001	1,425	1,625	2,017
MO	1,324	1,683	2,924	3,510	3,879
MT	548	685	878	1,162	1,632
NE	2,344	2,595	5,114	5,520	6,930
NV	83	84	115	126	158
NH	31	34	50	56	64
NJ	219	259	366	422	468
NM	420	462	617	825	1,028
NY	469	566	884	1,103	1,312
NC	1,712	1,976	2,967	3,233	3,735
ND	1,249	1,641	3,013	3,616	3,948
OH	1,368	1,550	2,742	3,275	3,734
OK	922	1,109	1,261	1,721	1,987
OR	1,010	1,172	1,378	1,460	1,976
PA	640	812	1,120	1,403	1,645
RI	10	15	18	21	24
SC	374	445	656	775	959
SD	1,204	1,418	2,847	2,923	3,644
TN	592	819	1,230	1,350	1,627
TX	2,985	3,980	5,141	6,986	7,553
UT	185	241	270	359	462
VT	51	64	91	121	150
VA	525	548	758	836	1,033
WA	1,329	1,618	2,201	2,651	3,307
WV	60	63	95	102	121
WI	872	1,207	1,897	2,579	3,176
WY	186	142	224	276	404

Source: U.S. Department of Agriculture, Economic Research Service, "State Export Data," <http://www.ers.usda.gov/data-products/state-export-data.aspx>, accessed August 2013.

Table 1332. U.S. Exports, Imports, and Trade Balance by Country: 2005 to 2012

[In millions of dollars (901,082 represents $901,082,000,000). Includes silver ore and bullion. Country totals include exports of special category commodities, if any. Data include nonmonetary gold and include trade of Virgin Islands with foreign countries. For methodology, see Foreign Trade Statistics in Appendix III. Minus sign (−) denotes an excess of imports over exports]

Country	Exports, domestic and foreign					General imports					Merchandise trade balance				
	2005	2009	2010	2011	2012	2005	2009	2010	2011	2012	2005	2009	2010	2011	2012
Total[1]	901,082	1,056,043	1,278,495	1,480,290	1,545,709	1,673,455	1,559,625	1,913,857	2,208,055	2,275,320	−772,373	−503,582	−635,362	−727,765	−729,611
Afghanistan	262	1,509	2,151	2,921	1,498	67	116	85	26	37	195	1,392	2,066	2,894	1,461
Albania	19	48	46	48	54	37	15	30	26	19	−19	33	16	21	35
Algeria	1,106	1,108	1,194	1,595	1,362	10,446	10,718	14,518	14,609	9,993	−9,340	−9,610	−13,324	−13,014	−8,631
Angola	929	1,423	1,294	1,500	1,490	8,484	9,339	11,940	13,598	9,824	−7,555	−7,916	−10,646	−12,097	−8,333
Antigua and Barbuda	190	157	158	155	205	4	9	6	7	10	186	148	153	148	195
Argentina	4,122	5,569	7,392	9,881	10,268	4,584	3,890	3,803	4,503	4,350	−462	1,679	3,589	5,378	5,918
Armenia	65	77	114	94	64	46	78	76	93	89	19	—	38	2	−25
Aruba	559	446	541	713	679	2,920	1,278	20	3,262	827	−2,361	−833	521	−2,549	−148
Australia	15,589	19,599	21,805	27,545	31,151	7,342	8,012	8,583	10,243	9,549	8,246	11,588	13,222	17,302	21,602
Austria	2,544	2,537	2,429	2,888	3,419	6,103	6,379	6,835	9,483	9,449	−3,558	−3,842	−4,407	−6,595	−6,030
Azerbaijan	132	185	253	337	493	45	1,973	1,989	2,425	1,095	87	−1,787	−1,736	−2,088	−602
Bahamas, The	1,787	2,504	3,178	3,442	3,469	700	819	815	765	563	1,087	1,685	2,363	2,677	2,905
Bahrain	351	667	1,235	1,214	1,211	432	463	420	518	701	−81	204	815	695	510
Bangladesh	320	435	576	1,144	502	2,693	3,699	4,294	4,877	4,916	−2,373	−3,264	−3,718	−3,733	−4,415
Barbados	395	405	397	439	458	32	33	43	47	54	363	372	355	393	404
Belarus	35	137	133	156	102	345	574	175	363	153	−310	−437	−41	−206	−51
Belgium	18,691	21,608	25,458	29,914	29,449	13,023	13,826	15,552	17,432	17,364	5,668	7,782	9,906	12,483	12,085
Belize	218	253	289	356	266	98	100	120	191	162	119	153	169	165	104
Benin	72	397	463	617	574	—	—	1	2	3	72	397	462	615	571
Bermuda	490	807	637	667	622	87	13	23	116	84	403	794	614	551	539
Bolivia	219	431	508	611	763	293	504	680	845	1,682	−74	−73	−172	−234	−920
Botswana	67	93	49	44	48	178	132	170	293	221	−111	−39	−121	−249	−173
Brazil	15,372	26,095	35,418	42,938	43,806	24,436	20,070	23,958	31,737	32,123	−9,064	6,026	11,460	11,201	11,683
Brunei	50	100	124	184	158	563	42	12	23	86	−513	59	112	161	71
Bulgaria	268	224	171	259	249	454	228	260	416	509	−186	−4	−89	−157	−261
Cambodia	70	127	154	186	226	1,767	1,924	2,301	2,712	2,692	−1,697	−1,797	−2,147	−2,527	−2,465
Cameroon	117	154	132	221	253	158	250	297	330	308	−41	−96	−165	−110	−55
Canada	211,899	204,658	249,257	281,292	292,540	290,384	226,248	277,637	315,367	323,937	−78,486	−21,590	−28,380	−34,075	−31,397
Cayman Islands	681	643	582	616	668	53	14	11	18	15	627	630	571	598	653
Chad	54	63	90	35	37	1,498	1,984	2,044	3,174	2,660	−1,444	−1,921	−1,954	−3,139	−2,624
Chile	5,134	9,346	10,907	15,979	18,766	6,664	5,949	7,018	9,076	9,371	−1,531	−3,396	−3,889	6,903	9,395
China	41,192	69,497	91,911	103,987	110,484	243,470	296,374	364,953	399,379	425,579	−202,278	−226,877	−273,042	−295,392	−315,095
Colombia	5,462	9,451	12,068	14,321	16,355	8,849	11,323	15,659	23,114	24,620	−3,387	−1,872	−3,592	−8,793	−8,265
Congo, Rep. of.	104	277	254	227	237	1,623	3,105	3,316	2,420	1,489	−1,519	−2,828	−3,062	−2,193	−1,251
Congo, Democratic Rep. of.	65	79	93	166	200	264	331	528	606	41	−199	−251	−434	−440	159
Costa Rica	3,599	4,700	5,178	6,058	7,231	3,415	5,612	8,697	10,119	12,042	183	−912	−3,519	−4,061	−4,811
Cote d'Ivoire	124	206	163	130	188	1,198	745	1,177	1,271	1,100	−1,074	−539	−1,014	−1,140	−911
Croatia	159	202	312	511	310	364	251	336	438	444	−206	−49	−24	73	−134
Cuba	369	533	363	363	465	(X)	(X)	(X)	(X)	1	369	533	363	363	464
Curacao[2]	(X)	(X)	(X)	484	692	(X)	(X)	(X)	558	850	(X)	(X)	(X)	−74	−158
Cyprus	84	179	134	97	167	31	53	11	21	29	54	126	123	77	137
Czech Republic	1,054	970	1,411	1,681	1,832	2,193	1,933	2,450	3,344	3,931	−1,139	−964	−1,039	−1,663	−2,098
Denmark	1,918	2,056	2,132	2,243	2,221	5,144	5,511	6,012	6,760	6,776	−3,226	−3,454	−3,880	−4,517	−4,554
Djibouti	48	196	123	129	119	2	2	3	4	12	46	194	120	125	107
Dominica	62	77	73	74	79	4	3	2	2	2	58	74	71	72	77
Dominican Republic	4,719	5,269	6,579	7,318	6,974	4,604	3,329	3,672	4,199	4,365	115	1,939	2,908	3,119	2,609
Ecuador	1,964	3,938	5,409	6,066	6,692	5,759	5,273	7,451	9,622	9,485	−3,795	−1,335	−2,042	−3,557	−2,792
Egypt	3,159	5,253	6,833	6,222	5,499	2,091	2,058	2,238	2,059	3,000	1,068	3,195	4,594	4,163	2,499
El Salvador	1,854	2,019	2,434	3,369	3,096	1,989	1,822	2,206	2,485	2,587	−134	197	228	885	509
Equatorial Guinea	281	306	272	285	233	1,561	2,489	2,214	1,191	1,700	−1,280	−2,184	−1,942	−906	−1,467
Estonia	145	189	188	309	236	511	162	698	962	507	−366	27	−510	−653	−271
Ethiopia	456	267	773	690	1,275	62	113	128	144	183	394	154	645	545	1,092
Faroe Islands	3	10	2	4	2	4	62	72	106	73	−2	−52	−70	−102	−71
Fiji	28	31	44	43	56	169	144	179	132	189	−141	−113	−135	−89	−133

See footnotes at end of table.

Table 1332. U.S. Exports, Imports, and Trade Balance by Country: 2005 to 2012 —Continued.

See headnote on page 838.

Country	Exports, domestic and foreign					General imports					Merchandise trade balance				
	2005	2009	2010	2011	2012	2005	2009	2010	2011	2012	2005	2009	2010	2011	2012
Finland	2,254	1,662	2,180	3,156	2,566	4,342	3,985	3,884	4,436	5,109	-2,088	-2,323	-1,704	-1,279	-2,543
France	22,259	26,493	26,970	27,802	30,806	33,842	34,236	38,356	40,049	41,750	-11,583	-7,743	-11,386	-12,247	-10,944
French Polynesia	112	113	122	126	130	60	29	53	54	59	52	83	69	72	70
Gabon	99	171	243	204	319	2,816	1,231	2,212	4,567	1,886	-2,716	-1,060	-1,969	-4,363	-1,567
Georgia	214	364	301	579	541	194	70	198	176	226	20	294	103	403	314
Germany	34,184	43,306	48,155	49,147	48,797	84,751	71,498	82,450	98,688	108,708	-50,567	-28,192	-34,295	-49,541	-59,911
Ghana	337	716	989	1,197	1,322	158	135	273	779	291	159	581	716	418	1,031
Gibraltar	163	1,087	1,494	3,149	5,112	5	1	1	1	1	159	1,086	1,494	3,148	5,111
Greece	1,192	2,487	1,107	1,122	805	884	841	798	865	987	309	1,647	309	256	-182
Grenada	82	59	71	82	72	7	6	7	7	8	75	53	64	75	64
Guadeloupe	55	206	365	431	503	3	2	3	2	12	52	204	362	429	490
Guatemala	2,835	3,875	4,477	6,149	5,750	3,137	3,148	3,523	4,714	4,491	-302	727	954	1,435	1,259
Guinea	94	95	86	256	155	75	67	69	81	103	19	28	17	175	52
Guyana	177	260	291	364	360	120	173	299	425	523	57	87	-8	-61	-163
Haiti	710	790	1,209	1,059	1,050	447	552	551	742	775	262	238	658	317	275
Honduras	3,254	3,368	4,606	6,143	5,722	3,749	3,319	3,933	4,501	4,648	-495	48	674	1,643	1,074
Hong Kong	16,351	21,051	26,570	36,345	37,461	8,892	3,571	4,296	4,410	5,456	7,459	17,480	22,274	31,936	32,006
Hungary	1,023	1,233	1,290	1,474	1,566	2,561	2,223	2,491	2,949	3,202	-1,538	-991	-1,201	-1,474	-1,635
Iceland	512	350	325	628	371	269	179	201	216	284	243	170	124	412	87
India	7,919	16,441	19,249	21,504	22,106	18,804	21,166	29,533	36,156	40,514	-10,886	-4,725	-10,284	-14,652	-18,409
Indonesia	3,054	5,107	6,948	7,414	7,997	12,014	12,939	16,478	19,111	17,998	-8,960	-7,832	-9,531	-11,698	-10,001
Iran	96	280	211	233	251	174	65	95	1	2	-79	216	117	232	249
Iraq	1,374	1,772	1,643	2,399	2,053	9,054	9,263	12,143	16,960	19,265	-7,680	-7,491	-10,500	-14,561	-17,212
Ireland	8,447	7,465	7,276	7,646	7,392	28,733	28,101	33,848	39,375	33,327	-20,286	-20,636	-26,572	-31,729	-25,935
Israel	9,737	9,559	11,295	13,935	14,268	16,830	18,744	20,985	23,047	22,130	-7,093	-9,185	-9,690	-9,111	-7,862
Italy	11,524	12,268	14,220	15,997	16,098	31,009	26,430	28,514	33,977	36,939	-19,485	-14,162	-14,294	-17,980	-20,841
Jamaica	1,701	1,441	1,661	1,931	1,988	376	468	328	566	507	1,325	973	1,334	1,365	1,481
Japan	54,681	51,134	60,472	65,686	69,955	138,004	95,804	120,552	128,928	146,392	-83,323	-44,669	-60,080	-63,242	-76,437
Jordan	644	1,192	1,172	1,448	1,766	1,267	924	974	1,061	1,156	-623	268	198	387	611
Kazakhstan	538	603	730	826	883	1,101	1,544	1,872	1,679	1,565	-563	-940	-1,142	-853	-683
Kenya	573	654	375	461	569	348	281	311	382	390	225	373	64	80	179
Korea, South	27,572	28,612	38,821	43,400	42,284	43,781	39,216	48,875	56,661	58,896	-16,210	-10,604	-10,055	-13,262	-16,612
Kuwait	1,975	1,951	2,775	2,727	2,684	4,335	3,783	5,382	7,809	13,021	-2,360	-1,831	-2,607	-5,082	-10,337
Kyrgyzstan	31	57	79	104	146	5	6	4	3	9	27	51	76	101	136
Laos	10	20	13	26	34	4	43	59	59	25	6	-23	-47	-33	8
Latvia	178	289	345	586	515	362	142	193	363	246	-185	147	152	223	269
Lebanon	466	1,852	2,009	1,806	1,040	86	77	84	79	81	379	1,775	1,925	1,726	959
Lesotho	4	17	11	13	17	404	304	299	384	311	-400	-288	-288	-371	-294
Liberia	69	95	191	195	246	91	80	180	158	144	-22	14	11	37	101
Libya	84	666	666	307	549	1,590	1,919	2,117	645	2,493	-1,506	-1,253	-1,451	-338	-1,944
Liechtenstein	20	23	29	62	22	296	180	213	251	310	-276	-156	-183	-188	-288
Lithuania	390	399	628	1,141	757	634	590	637	1,044	1,175	-244	-191	-9	97	-418
Luxembourg	711	1,292	1,440	1,585	1,902	389	443	451	495	550	323	849	989	1,090	1,353
Macau	102	209	225	291	345	1,249	237	141	113	95	-1,147	-28	84	178	250
Macedonia	32	35	33	29	21	48	44	37	53	87	-17	-9	-4	-23	-66
Madagascar	28	106	116	56	64	324	253	108	87	110	-295	-148	8	-31	-46
Malawi	28	40	37	57	64	116	63	72	65	66	-87	-23	-35	-8	-2
Malaysia	10,461	10,403	14,080	14,245	12,841	33,685	23,283	25,901	25,777	25,933	-23,224	-12,879	-11,822	-11,532	-13,092
Malta	194	208	457	752	391	283	219	262	244	257	-89	-10	196	508	134
Marshall Islands	75	78	91	144	142	17	14	12	15	19	58	64	79	129	123
Martinique	35	263	297	340	371	22	5	23	8	26	13	258	274	332	344
Mauritania	86	56	84	243	292	1	35	53	1	1	85	22	32	242	291
Mauritius	31	70	40	46	96	222	169	196	252	260	-191	-99	-156	-206	-164
Mexico	120,248	128,892	163,665	198,069	215,931	170,109	176,654	229,986	262,874	277,570	-49,861	-47,762	-66,321	-64,805	-61,639
Mongolia	22	41	116	315	665	144	15	12	11	42	-122	26	104	304	623
Morocco	481	1,630	1,948	2,822	2,175	446	468	686	996	932	35	1,162	1,262	1,827	1,243
Mozambique	63	190	224	459	352	12	39	65	35	39	51	151	159	424	313

See footnotes at end of table.

Table 1332. U.S. Exports, Imports, and Trade Balance by Country: 2005 to 2012-Continued.

See headnote on page 838.

Country	Exports, domestic and foreign					General imports					Merchandise trade balance				
	2005	2009	2010	2011	2012	2005	2009	2010	2011	2012	2005	2009	2010	2011	2012
Namibia	112	202	110	137	185	130	329	195	436	231	-17	-126	-85	-300	-47
Nepal	25	31	28	40	37	111	55	61	77	84	-87	-24	-32	-37	-47
Netherlands	26,468	32,242	34,740	42,159	40,627	14,862	16,098	19,056	23,455	22,258	11,606	16,143	15,685	18,705	18,370
Netherlands Antilles [2]	1,138	2,056	2,943	1,187	(X)	922	476	1,026	866	(X)	215	1,580	1,917	321	(X)
New Caledonia	38	78	108	115	75	27	27	71	91	58	11	51	38	24	18
New Zealand	2,592	2,159	2,820	3,572	3,227	3,155	2,558	2,764	3,168	3,436	-563	-399	57	404	-209
Nicaragua	625	715	981	1,058	1,129	1,181	1,612	2,008	2,603	2,748	-555	-897	-1,026	-1,545	-1,619
Niger	79	58	49	48	37	66	106	27	289	82	13	-48	22	-241	-44
Nigeria	1,620	3,687	4,061	4,912	5,029	24,239	19,128	30,516	33,854	19,014	-22,620	-15,441	-26,455	-28,943	-13,986
Norway	1,942	2,790	3,100	3,623	3,501	6,776	5,688	6,950	8,305	6,566	-4,834	-2,898	-3,850	-4,682	-3,065
Oman	571	1,126	1,105	1,434	1,747	555	907	773	2,208	1,354	16	219	332	-775	393
Pakistan	1,252	1,618	1,901	1,988	1,530	3,253	3,163	3,509	3,832	3,628	-2,002	-1,545	-1,608	-1,845	-2,098
Panama	2,162	4,293	6,066	8,247	9,835	327	302	381	389	540	1,835	3,991	5,685	7,858	9,294
Papua New Guinea	55	218	186	304	391	58	103	97	142	118	-2	115	89	162	273
Paraguay	896	1,355	1,810	1,975	1,743	52	56	62	110	197	844	1,299	1,748	1,865	1,546
Peru	2,309	4,919	6,750	8,336	9,345	5,119	4,223	5,243	6,605	6,418	-2,810	696	1,506	1,731	2,927
Philippines	6,895	5,766	7,377	7,706	8,060	9,250	6,794	7,982	9,145	9,580	-2,355	-1,028	-605	-1,439	-1,519
Poland	1,268	2,302	2,983	3,137	3,344	1,949	2,038	2,964	4,379	4,621	-681	263	19	-1,241	-1,277
Portugal	1,132	1,085	1,058	1,314	1,096	2,329	1,577	2,142	2,582	2,610	-1,197	-492	-1,084	-1,269	-1,514
Qatar	987	2,713	3,160	2,803	3,577	448	506	466	1,234	1,028	539	2,207	2,693	1,570	2,549
Reunion	4	9	8	155	10	6	10	12	12	12	-2	-1	-4	143	-2
Romania	609	672	730	912	831	1,208	752	1,008	1,435	1,619	-599	-80	-278	-523	-788
Russia	3,962	5,332	5,994	8,285	10,700	15,307	18,200	25,691	34,619	29,381	-11,344	-12,868	-19,697	-26,334	-18,681
Rwanda	11	34	31	120	30	6	19	22	31	33	4	15	9	89	-3
Saudi Arabia	6,805	10,792	11,506	13,827	17,972	27,193	22,053	31,413	47,476	55,667	-20,387	-11,261	-19,907	-33,650	-37,695
Senegal	141	176	219	264	149	4	7	5	7	17	138	169	214	257	133
Serbia	(X)	113	105	126	128	(X)	62	164	134	146	(X)	51	-60	-7	-18
Sierra Leone	38	43	61	103	101	9	24	29	27	18	29	18	32	76	83
Singapore [2]	20,466	22,232	29,009	31,221	30,525	15,110	15,705	17,428	19,116	20,232	5,356	6,527	11,581	12,105	10,293
Sint Maarten [2]	(X)	(X)	(X)	398	706	(X)	(X)	(X)	24	55	(X)	(X)	(X)	374	651
Slovakia	150	210	256	302	336	961	628	1,073	1,408	1,780	-811	-418	-817	-1,106	-1,444
Slovenia	234	244	328	668	308	413	388	465	545	562	-179	-144	-137	123	-254
South Africa	3,907	4,453	5,632	7,256	7,552	5,886	5,879	8,220	9,487	8,673	-1,979	-1,426	-2,589	-2,231	-1,121
Spain	6,839	8,717	10,355	11,016	9,551	8,615	7,857	8,554	11,018	11,767	-1,776	860	1,802	-2	-2,216
Sri Lanka	198	230	179	303	224	2,083	1,593	1,748	2,086	2,257	-1,885	-1,363	-1,569	-1,783	-2,033
St. Kitts and Nevis	94	108	131	116	106	50	48	51	55	57	44	60	80	61	50
St. Lucia	135	136	402	316	377	32	18	18	18	15	103	119	384	298	362
St. Vincent and the Grenadines	45	75	86	81	99	16	1	2	2	2	30	74	84	79	96
Suriname	246	380	362	433	499	165	139	191	302	289	80	241	171	131	210
Swaziland	12	15	24	20	40	199	110	121	89	67	-187	-95	-97	-69	-27
Sweden	3,715	4,561	4,740	5,281	5,248	13,821	8,186	10,497	11,490	10,217	-10,106	-3,625	-5,758	-6,209	-4,969
Switzerland	10,718	17,504	20,704	24,369	26,390	13,000	16,053	19,137	24,362	25,673	-2,282	1,451	1,567	7	718
Syria	155	304	503	230	20	324	303	429	393	20	-169	1	74	-163	–
Taiwan	21,614	18,486	26,050	25,886	24,349	34,826	28,362	35,847	41,406	38,858	-13,211	-9,877	-9,797	-15,520	-14,509
Tajikistan	29	41	57	178	54	241	9	2	12	27	-212	33	56	166	27
Tanzania	96	158	164	258	245	34	49	43	59	115	63	109	121	199	131
Thailand	7,257	6,918	8,976	10,901	10,888	19,890	19,082	22,694	24,832	26,108	-12,633	-12,164	-13,717	-13,931	-15,220
Togo	28	125	158	210	371	6	7	9	31	52	21	118	149	179	319
Trinidad and Tobago	1,417	1,988	1,925	2,183	2,478	7,891	5,180	6,613	8,113	8,158	-6,474	-3,192	-4,688	-5,930	-5,681
Tunisia	261	501	573	588	619	264	326	406	352	738	-3	176	167	236	-119
Turkey	4,261	7,095	10,539	14,657	12,520	5,182	3,662	4,207	5,221	6,293	-943	3,433	6,331	9,436	6,227
Turkmenistan	215	294	40	71	92	135	93	48	43	90	80	201	-8	27	2
Turks and Caicos Islands	238	248	189	205	210	9	11	12	9	10	228	237	178	196	200
Uganda	63	119	94	94	100	26	31	58	46	35	37	88	36	48	66
Ukraine	533	887	1,349	2,137	1,937	1,098	495	1,078	1,457	1,350	-565	392	271	680	587
United Arab Emirates	8,120	12,211	11,663	15,900	22,546	1,468	1,498	1,145	2,440	2,253	6,651	10,713	10,517	13,460	20,293

See footnotes at end of table.

Table 1332. U.S. Exports, Imports, and Trade Balance by Country: 2005 to 2012—Continued.

See headnote on page 838.

Country	Exports, domestic and foreign					General imports					Merchandise trade balance				
	2005	2009	2010	2011	2012	2005	2009	2010	2011	2012	2005	2009	2010	2011	2012
United Kingdom..........	38,568	45,704	48,410	55,866	54,851	51,033	47,480	49,805	51,262	54,962	-12,465	-1,776	-1,395	4,604	-112
Uruguay...................	357	745	975	1,256	1,359	732	239	235	292	357	-376	506	740	965	1,002
Uzbekistan...............	74	98	101	100	285	96	89	68	51	26	-22	8	33	49	259
Venezuela................	6,421	9,315	10,645	12,358	17,516	33,978	28,059	32,707	43,257	38,724	-27,557	-18,744	-22,063	-30,899	-21,208
Vietnam...................	1,193	3,097	3,706	4,310	4,624	6,631	12,288	14,868	17,488	20,266	-5,438	-9,191	-11,162	-13,178	-15,642
Virgin Islands, British.....	125	233	146	151	172	34	6	19	6	13	91	227	127	145	159
Yemen...................	219	381	398	390	469	279	7	181	562	87	-60	374	216	-172	382
Zambia...................	29	57	56	130	147	32	9	30	47	63	7	49	27	82	84
Zimbabwe................	46	85	68	62	54	94	22	59	51	53	-15	63	9	10	1

X Not applicable. – Zero or rounds to zero. [1] Includes timing adjustment and unidentified countries, not shown separately. [2] The Netherlands Antilles dissolved on October 10, 2010. Curacao and Sint Maarten became autonomous territories of the Kingdom of the Netherlands.

Source: U.S. Census Bureau, *U.S. International Trade in Goods and Services, Annual Revision for 2012*, Series FT-900, June 2013, and earlier reports. See also <http://www.census.gov/foreign-trade/data/index.html>.

Table 1333. U.S. Exports and General Imports by Selected SITC Commodity Groups: 2000 to 2012

[In millions of dollars (781,918 represents $781,918,000,000). SITC = Standard International Trade Classification. For methodology, see Foreign Trade Statistics in Appendix III. N.e.s. = not elsewhere specified]

Selected commodity	Exports [1]				General imports [2]			
	2000	2010	2011	2012	2000	2010	2011	2012
Total..................	781,918	1,278,495	1,480,290	1,545,709	1,218,022	1,913,857	2,208,055	2,275,320
Agricultural commodities [3].........	51,296	115,790	136,346	141,252	39,186	82,018	99,135	103,230
Animal feeds..........................	3,780	8,993	9,302	10,764	597	1,349	1,929	2,522
Cereal flour..........................	1,310	3,037	3,378	3,785	1,753	4,519	5,055	5,333
Coffee................................	9	6	4	8	2,350	4,055	6,906	5,808
Corn..................................	4,695	10,166	14,035	9,816	160	300	399	948
Cotton, raw and linters..............	1,893	5,890	8,466	6,255	28	8	17	8
Meat and preparations...............	7,004	13,212	16,625	17,482	3,841	5,072	5,736	6,226
Oils/fats, vegetable.................	814	2,651	2,532	2,598	1,188	3,940	6,099	5,447
Soybeans.............................	5,284	18,636	17,607	24,639	31	220	219	328
Manufactured goods [3]...............	625,894	873,236	971,134	1,019,084	1,012,855	1,439,293	1,611,668	1,705,052
ADP equipment, office machinery.....	46,595	22,234	21,905	22,620	92,133	113,477	116,497	118,853
Airplanes, engines, and parts.......	(NA)	74,646	82,551	95,899	(NA)	22,431	25,402	29,147
Alcoholic beverage, distilled.......	424	1,125	1,285	1,418	2,946	5,609	6,257	6,504
Aluminum.............................	3,780	5,183	6,426	6,588	6,949	10,815	11,896	11,310
Artwork/antiques.....................	1,387	3,034	3,113	3,132	5,864	6,268	6,903	7,825
Basketware, etc......................	3,309	8,362	8,700	9,104	4,840	13,317	14,458	14,808
Chemicals - cosmetics...............	5,292	12,489	13,241	14,213	3,539	9,564	10,614	11,379
Chemicals - dyeing...................	4,089	7,407	8,544	7,882	2,667	3,105	3,458	3,763
Chemicals - fertilizers.............	2,249	3,725	5,133	4,497	1,684	6,647	9,165	8,759
Chemicals - inorganic...............	5,359	11,809	13,346	12,282	6,108	13,841	17,020	15,501
Chemicals - medicinal...............	12,893	41,977	40,025	42,662	14,685	65,171	69,709	68,325
Chemicals - n.e.s....................	12,264	24,054	27,100	28,813	5,725	11,301	13,304	13,950
Chemicals - organic.................	17,990	37,469	43,559	42,363	28,578	45,792	54,368	52,241
Chemicals - plastics................	19,519	42,043	46,198	45,426	10,647	17,828	20,745	21,719
Clothing.............................	8,191	3,197	3,338	3,455	64,296	78,522	85,567	84,916
Copper...............................	1,425	3,497	3,645	4,217	4,471	7,822	10,154	8,945
Cork, wood, lumber...................	4,320	4,737	5,499	5,504	8,227	4,480	4,452	5,172
Crude fertilizers....................	1,724	2,374	2,619	2,584	1,401	2,258	2,848	2,839
Electrical machinery................	89,917	77,048	77,787	77,783	108,747	119,638	137,944	144,305
Fish and preparations...............	2,806	4,224	5,278	5,165	9,907	14,577	16,522	16,564
Footwear.............................	663	729	832	825	14,842	20,903	22,654	23,886
Furniture and bedding...............	4,744	4,821	5,263	5,755	18,923	31,124	32,366	35,610
Gem diamonds.........................	1,289	2,863	3,092	3,122	12,068	18,599	22,299	20,196
General industrial machinery........	33,094	51,787	60,064	64,451	34,667	60,433	74,185	81,640
Glass................................	2,502	3,379	3,651	3,623	2,248	2,588	2,665	2,731
Gold, nonmonetary....................	5,898	17,474	33,515	36,421	2,657	13,047	16,405	17,830
Iron and steel mill products........	5,715	15,735	18,468	18,934	15,807	24,443	32,911	36,756
Jewelry..............................	1,574	4,848	5,221	5,293	6,459	10,085	11,092	10,496
Lighting, plumbing...................	1,384	2,512	2,847	3,011	5,104	7,397	8,019	9,309
Metal manufactures, n.e.s...........	13,453	17,499	20,253	21,938	16,204	25,924	29,616	33,464
Metal ores; scrap....................	4,234	28,347	32,840	28,063	3,817	7,294	9,423	9,103
Metalworking machinery..............	6,191	5,332	6,245	6,250	7,726	5,566	8,620	10,325
Nickel...............................	401	1,131	1,583	1,572	1,425	2,976	3,718	2,943
Optical goods........................	3,246	3,278	3,262	3,404	4,019	5,508	5,896	6,082
Paper and paperboard................	10,640	14,921	15,993	15,854	15,185	15,285	15,795	15,621
Photographic equipment.............	4,236	3,346	3,259	3,011	6,896	2,050	2,183	2,164
Plastic articles, n.e.s.............	7,607	9,712	10,427	11,130	8,034	16,043	17,403	18,979
Platinum.............................	888	1,370	1,036	924	5,566	4,146	5,555	4,376
Power generating machinery.........	32,743	33,015	36,314	39,162	33,773	42,503	52,101	57,819
Printed materials....................	4,776	5,881	5,859	5,853	3,680	4,586	4,514	4,521
Pulp and waste paper................	4,576	8,641	9,711	8,951	3,381	3,887	4,020	3,354
Records/magnetic media..............	5,395	4,425	4,368	4,517	5,172	5,297	5,716	5,870
Rubber articles, n.e.s..............	1,673	2,049	2,331	2,613	1,962	3,310	3,763	4,127
Rubber tires and tubes..............	2,379	4,159	5,147	5,595	4,785	10,673	13,377	14,654
Scientific instruments..............	30,984	44,287	48,255	50,214	22,007	37,796	43,532	45,870
Silver and bullion..................	227	1,673	3,093	2,500	775	4,415	8,577	6,628
Specialized industrial machinery....	30,959	46,749	51,659	53,753	22,711	30,940	41,417	44,989
Television, VCR, etc................	27,921	21,524	23,373	23,080	70,468	137,307	137,953	143,845
Textile yarn, fabric................	10,534	11,386	12,880	12,532	15,171	22,122	24,138	24,750
Toys/games/sporting goods..........	3,609	4,246	4,336	4,469	20,011	30,630	28,650	28,038
Travel goods.........................	351	463	525	541	4,430	8,013	9,034	9,996
Vehicles.............................	57,421	88,141	105,943	116,883	161,544	178,949	198,712	235,338
Wood manufactures...................	1,842	2,053	2,091	2,106	7,228	6,920	6,783	7,724
Mineral fuel [3].....................	13,179	80,625	128,873	136,023	135,367	354,982	453,872	423,591
Coal.................................	2,162	10,096	16,170	15,048	805	2,024	2,133	1,508
Crude oil............................	463	1,337	1,847	2,420	89,876	260,105	336,687	315,445
Petroleum preparations.............	5,746	53,526	90,426	101,687	25,673	67,416	92,281	89,950
Liquified propane/butane............	663	2,448	3,458	3,390	1,508	2,541	2,629	2,072
Natural gas..........................	411	5,111	6,429	4,827	12,594	17,402	13,567	8,742
Mineral fuels, other mineral........	3,734	7,442	10,113	8,351	4,911	3,410	4,548	3,942
Reexports............................	68,203	155,927	182,102	193,507	(X)	(X)	(X)	(X)

NA Not available. X Not applicable. [1] Free alongside ship (f.a.s) basis. Exports by commodity are only for domestic exports. [2] Customs value basis. [3] Includes other commodities, not shown separately.

Source: U.S. Census Bureau, *U.S. International Trade in Goods and Services, Annual Revision for 2012*, Series FT-900, June 2013, and earlier reports. See also <http://www.census.gov/foreign-trade/data/index.html>.

Table 1334. U.S. Total and Aerospace Foreign Trade: 1990 to 2012

[In millions of dollars (-101,718 represents -$101,718,000,000), except percent. Data are reported as exports of domestic merchandise, including Department of Defense shipments and undocumented exports to Canada, f.a.s. (free alongside ship) basis, and imports for consumption, customs value basis. Minus sign (-) indicates deficit]

Year	U.S. Merchandise Trade			Aerospace Trade						
	Trade balance [1]	Imports	Exports	Trade balance	Imports	Exports				
						Total	Percent of U.S. exports	Civil		Military
								Total	Transports	
1990......	-101,718	495,311	393,592	27,282	11,801	39,083	9.9	31,517	16,691	7,566
1995......	-158,801	743,543	584,742	21,562	11,509	33,071	5.7	25,079	10,606	7,991
1997......	-180,522	869,704	689,182	32,240	18,134	50,374	7.3	40,075	21,028	10,299
1998......	-229,758	911,896	682,138	40,961	23,110	64,071	9.4	51,999	29,168	12,072
1999......	-328,821	1,024,618	695,797	37,381	25,063	62,444	9.0	50,624	25,672	11,820
2000......	-436,104	1,218,022	781,918	26,735	27,944	54,679	7.0	45,566	19,615	9,113
2001......	-411,899	1,140,999	729,100	26,035	32,473	58,508	8.0	49,371	22,151	9,137
2002......	-468,263	1,161,366	693,103	29,533	27,242	56,775	8.2	47,348	21,626	9,427
2003......	-532,350	1,257,121	724,771	27,111	25,393	52,504	7.2	44,366	19,149	8,138
2004......	-654,830	1,469,704	814,875	31,002	25,815	56,817	7.0	47,772	18,577	9,045
2005......	-772,373	1,673,455	901,082	39,783	27,649	67,433	7.5	57,587	21,888	9,845
2006......	-827,971	1,853,938	1,025,967	54,809	30,453	85,262	8.3	71,857	32,897	13,404
2007......	-808,763	1,956,962	1,148,199	60,614	36,610	97,224	8.5	83,977	40,297	13,247
2008......	-816,199	2,103,641	1,287,442	57,389	37,694	95,082	7.4	82,264	33,326	12,819
2009......	-503,582	1,559,625	1,056,043	56,034	25,132	81,166	7.7	70,500	(NA)	10,666
2010......	-634,897	1,913,160	1,278,263	51,152	26,351	77,503	6.1	67,128	(NA)	10,375
2011......	-727,765	2,208,055	1,480,290	55,753	29,573	85,326	5.8	75,275	(NA)	10,051
2012......	-729,611	2,275,320	1,545,709	65,745	33,640	99,385	6.4	86,814	(NA)	12,571

NA Not available. [1] Exports minus imports.

Source: © 2012 Aerospace Industries Association of America, Inc, and Embry-Riddle Aeronautical University, *Aerospace Industry Report 2012*, (previously issued as *Aerospace Facts and Figures*). See also <http://www.aia-aerospace.org/economics/aerospace_facts_and_figures/>.

Table 1335. U.S. High Technology Exports by Industry and Selected Major Country: 2010 to 2012

[In billions of dollars (228.4 represents $228,400,000,000)]

Selected industry	2010	2011	2012	Selected country	2010	2011	2012
Total exports.............	**228.4**	**238.7**	**241.6**	**Total exports**..........	**228.4**	**238.7**	**241.6**
Computers and office equipment.....	44.0	48.3	49.4	Canada...................	29.4	32.5	32.0
Consumer electronics.................	9.6	10.2	9.9	China.....................	18.4	16.5	16.2
Communications equipment..........	34.1	38.8	40.7	Japan.....................	10.1	11.0	11.7
Electronic components................	20.0	21.3	22.1	Korea, South.............	9.8	10.2	10.9
Semiconductors......................	60.4	54.9	51.0	Malaysia.................	8.3	7.8	6.6
Industrial electronics..................	34.6	38.2	40.9	Mexico...................	36.6	40.6	42.6
Electromedical equipment............	21.6	22.6	23.3	Singapore................	9.0	8.4	7.5
Photonics............................	4.2	4.4	4.5	European Union 27 [1]. ..	40.7	41.5	39.4

[1] See footnote 3, Table 1403.

Source: TechAmerica Foundation, Washington, DC, unpublished data ©. See also <http://www.techamericafoundation.org/>.

Table 1336. U.S. Exporting Companies Profile by Employment-Size Class: 2000 and 2011

[Value in millions of dollars (668,310 represents $668,310,000,000). Based on data from export trade information and the Business Register. For information on data limitations, see Technical Documentation in source]

| Employment-size class | Number of exporters | | Known export value [1] (mil. dol.) | | Percent of— | | | |
| | | | | | Number of exporters | | Known export value | |
	2000	2011	2000	2011	2000	2011	2000	2011
All companies, total.........	**246,452**	**302,260**	**668,310**	**1,319,942**	**100.0**	**100.0**	**100.0**	**100.0**
Number of employees unknown [2]..............	74,772	117,646	47,024	127,424	30.3	38.9	7.0	9.7
1 to 19 employees.................	96,268	114,468	45,272	95,301	39.1	37.9	6.8	7.2
20 to 49 employees..............	31,362	31,655	21,262	47,225	12.7	10.5	3.2	3.6
50 to 99 employees..............	16,988	15,727	19,711	49,554	6.9	5.2	2.9	3.8
100 to 249 employees...........	13,685	11,688	32,192	70,901	5.6	3.9	4.8	5.4
250 to 499 employees...........	5,454	4,410	27,397	49,694	2.2	1.5	4.1	3.8
500 or more employees.........	7,923	6,666	475,453	879,843	3.2	2.2	71.1	66.7

[1] Known value is defined as the portion of U.S. total exports that could be matched to specific companies. Export values are on f.a.s. or "free alongside ship basis." [2] Includes missing employment data, nonemployers, and companies that reported annual payroll but did not report any employees on their payroll.

Source: U.S. Census Bureau, *Profile of U.S. Importing and Exporting Companies 2010-2011*, April 2013 and earlier reports. See also <http://www.census.gov/foreign-trade/Press-Release/edb/2011/index.html>.

Table 1337. Domestic Exports and Imports for Consumption of Merchandise by Selected NAICS Product Category: 2000 to 2012

[In millions of dollars (712,285 represents $712,285,000,000). Includes nonmonetary gold. For methodology, see Foreign Trade Statistics in Appendix III. NAICS = North American Industry Classification System; see text, Section 15]

Product category	2000	2005	2009	2010	2011	2012
Domestic exports, total	**712,285**	**798,997**	**935,698**	**1,122,416**	**1,299,301**	**1,353,897**
Agricultural, forestry, and fishery products	29,153	37,109	55,552	65,737	79,081	78,269
Agricultural products, total	23,596	30,683	49,069	58,009	69,538	68,710
Livestock and livestock products	1,255	1,118	1,409	1,540	1,918	2,339
Forestry products, not elsewhere specified	1,644	1,686	1,622	2,178	2,560	2,299
Fish, fresh or chilled, and other marine products	2,658	3,622	3,452	4,010	5,065	4,922
Mining, total	6,187	12,629	17,332	26,234	36,931	34,760
Oil and gas	1,706	4,547	6,570	9,090	11,484	10,933
Minerals and ores	4,481	8,082	10,762	17,144	25,447	23,827
Manufacturing, total	644,440	708,205	802,183	952,409	1,095,096	1,163,293
Food and kindred products	24,966	28,937	43,843	50,910	58,668	63,404
Beverages and tobacco products	5,568	3,423	4,373	5,341	6,202	6,846
Textiles and fabrics	7,010	8,483	6,434	7,832	9,063	8,574
Textile mill products	2,236	2,344	2,276	2,582	2,742	2,855
Apparel and accessories	8,104	4,075	2,812	3,071	3,203	3,289
Leather and allied products	2,322	2,300	1,876	2,420	2,838	2,833
Wood products	4,854	4,463	3,976	5,073	5,567	5,905
Paper products	15,539	16,640	19,175	22,962	24,745	24,434
Printed, publishing, & similar products	4,869	5,526	5,747	6,020	6,036	5,978
Petroleum and coal products	8,862	17,979	41,494	61,003	100,319	110,725
Chemicals	77,649	114,821	145,896	171,443	187,657	188,564
Plastics and rubber products [1]	16,970	18,784	20,340	24,255	27,133	28,560
Nonmetallic mineral products [1]	7,830	6,663	7,482	9,223	10,051	10,128
Primary metal products	20,126	27,455	38,173	49,708	65,266	73,769
Fabricated metal products	21,737	23,370	27,737	32,667	36,744	40,114
Machinery, except electrical	85,038	97,001	104,139	126,040	142,994	150,509
Computers and electronic products [1]	161,449	122,744	106,782	121,111	123,463	123,456
Electrical equipment, appliances and components [1]	25,401	26,457	26,498	30,998	34,142	36,914
Transportation equipment [1]	121,701	144,985	154,120	176,397	200,735	226,200
Furniture and fixtures	2,882	2,844	3,525	3,980	4,348	4,902
Miscellaneous manufactured commodities	19,327	28,909	35,486	39,373	43,055	44,653
Special classification provisions	32,505	41,055	59,866	77,186	88,193	77,574
Waste & scrap	4,948	10,389	21,784	29,411	39,118	27,731
Used or second-hand merchandise	1,950	2,570	6,005	4,712	5,194	4,961
Goods returned or reimported	333	65	31	29	23	26
Special classification provision, not elsewhere specified	25,274	28,030	32,046	43,034	43,858	44,856
Imports for consumption, total	**1,205,339**	**1,664,497**	**1,551,063**	**1,899,886**	**2,186,951**	**2,251,035**
Agricultural, forestry, and fishery products	24,378	30,761	36,802	42,683	51,373	50,560
Agricultural products, total	11,771	15,818	21,508	24,014	28,825	29,245
Livestock and livestock products	3,085	3,277	3,600	4,115	4,249	4,683
Forestry products, not elsewhere specified	1,409	2,250	1,773	3,356	5,402	4,117
Fish, fresh or chilled, and other marine products	8,113	9,416	9,920	11,198	12,897	12,515
Mining, total	79,841	192,115	184,585	235,394	289,077	264,567
Oil and gas	76,166	185,621	177,929	228,066	279,779	255,678
Minerals and ores	3,675	6,494	6,655	7,328	9,298	8,889
Manufacturing, total	1,040,329	1,372,004	1,260,343	1,549,521	1,767,633	1,849,273
Food and kindred products	18,944	29,779	36,131	41,037	50,118	54,170
Beverages and tobacco products	8,350	12,849	14,454	15,514	17,017	18,190
Textiles and fabrics	7,042	7,450	5,283	6,524	7,314	7,608
Textile mill products	7,347	13,508	13,227	15,824	16,943	17,233
Apparel and accessories	62,928	74,478	66,818	75,407	82,118	81,186
Leather and allied products	21,463	26,559	25,548	30,857	33,912	36,167
Wood products	15,388	23,654	9,746	11,363	11,321	13,009
Paper products	19,080	22,094	18,514	21,029	21,896	21,283
Printed, publishing, & similar products	4,197	5,599	4,890	5,323	5,242	5,266
Petroleum and coal products	40,156	81,359	75,139	102,161	141,244	135,872
Chemicals	76,606	131,936	162,366	187,631	216,035	209,868
Plastics and rubber products	17,362	28,072	27,749	34,363	39,736	43,349
Nonmetallic mineral products	14,740	18,445	13,081	16,078	17,753	18,524
Primary metal products	43,833	64,666	55,412	79,025	102,992	100,974
Fabricated metal products	27,974	41,026	39,780	46,691	53,528	59,927
Machinery, except electrical	79,366	109,619	86,832	104,797	133,770	146,947
Computers and electronic products	250,694	269,921	265,557	324,372	342,594	354,092
Electrical equipment, appliances and components	39,567	55,179	55,519	68,462	75,761	81,132
Transportation equipment	213,110	251,386	180,256	239,809	267,865	313,891
Furniture and fixtures	15,607	25,096	21,566	25,702	26,259	28,565
Miscellaneous manufactured commodities	56,577	79,329	82,475	97,552	104,216	102,022
Special classification provisions	60,791	69,617	69,301	72,253	78,869	86,636
Waste & scrap	1,875	3,207	3,459	5,260	6,659	7,300
Used or second-hand merchandise	6,345	6,026	5,205	6,403	7,082	8,070
Goods returned or reimported	33,851	37,024	38,101	40,985	44,542	51,870
Special classification provision, not elsewhere specified	18,720	23,359	22,535	19,605	20,586	19,396

[1] Due to non-disclosure requirements, certain 10-digit Schedule B commodity classifications for 2011 and 2012 are subject to suppression and require a change in aggregation.

Source: U.S. Census Bureau, *U.S. International Trade in Goods and Services*, series FT-900, December 2012, and earlier reports. See also <http://www.census.gov/foreign-trade/data/index.html>.

Table 1338. Export and Import Unit Value Indexes—Selected Countries: 2007 to 2011

[Indexes in U.S. dollars, 2000 = 100. A unit value is an implicit price derived from value and quantity data]

Country	Export unit value					Import unit value				
	2007	2008	2009	2010	2011	2007	2008	2009	2010	2011
United States	**148.7**	**166.4**	**135.1**	**163.4**	**189.3**	**160.4**	**172.3**	**127.5**	**156.3**	**179.9**
Australia	220.9	292.7	240.9	332.5	425.4	231.1	280.0	231.3	281.9	340.7
Belgium	229.0	250.1	196.2	217.3	253.3	232.1	262.3	198.8	221.9	260.2
Canada	150.6	163.5	114.3	139.6	163.3	159.0	170.5	134.8	160.2	184.8
France	171.0	187.8	147.7	160.0	182.2	186.3	211.1	165.2	180.1	210.8
Germany	239.7	261.7	202.7	228.5	267.1	212.4	238.0	186.0	212.5	252.5
Greece	200.9	224.2	173.9	184.7	265.9	234.8	276.1	207.1	191.1	180.1
Ireland	157.2	162.1	149.5	150.7	164.1	164.4	164.2	122.7	118.3	130.5
Italy	208.1	225.3	168.9	186.3	217.8	214.5	235.0	173.6	204.3	233.8
Japan	149.0	163.2	121.2	160.6	171.6	163.3	201.0	145.1	182.5	225.1
Korea, South	215.6	245.0	209.9	270.7	323.1	222.4	271.2	201.2	265.0	326.7
Netherlands	236.5	273.2	213.2	246.7	283.8	226.0	265.7	202.7	237.0	274.7
Norway	227.1	287.7	201.8	218.8	263.4	233.7	262.5	201.5	224.6	263.8
Spain	220.0	243.9	196.9	221.1	268.2	249.6	269.1	187.5	209.8	240.0
Sweden	194.0	210.1	149.9	182.2	215.0	210.5	230.8	164.2	204.7	241.7
Switzerland	213.8	249.3	214.3	243.1	292.0	195.4	222.5	188.4	213.7	252.2
United Kingdom	154.0	160.8	123.4	142.4	166.0	179.7	181.7	138.5	161.6	183.3

Source: World Bank, "World Development Indicators" database ©, <http://data.worldbank.org/>, accessed August 2013.

Table 1339. U.S. Trade with China, Leading Commodity Imports and Exports: 2008 to 2012

[In billions of dollars (337.8 represents $337,800,000,000), except as noted]

Commodity	2007 NAICS code [1]	2008	2009	2010	2011	2012	2011-2012 percent change
IMPORTS FROM CHINA							
Total imports [2]	(X)	**337.8**	**296.4**	**364.9**	**399.3**	**425.6**	**6.6**
Computer equipment	3341	45.8	44.8	59.8	68.3	68.8	0.8
Communications equipment	3342	26.6	26.4	33.5	39.8	51.9	30.3
Misc. manufactured commodities	3399	35.8	30.7	34.2	32.7	32.6	-0.1
Apparel	3152	22.6	22.7	26.6	27.6	26.9	-2.3
Semiconductors and other electronic components	3344	13.6	12.4	18.3	19.8	19.0	-4.2
Footwear	3162	14.2	13.1	15.7	16.5	16.9	2.4
Audio and video equipment	3343	19.7	18.3	19.5	15.9	15.9	0.3
Furniture and kitchen cabinets	3371	11.1	9.1	11.1	11.4	12.2	7.3
Household appliances and misc. machines	3352	8.5	7.7	9.1	9.6	10.3	7.6
Other fabricated metal products	3329	7.2	5.7	7.2	8.6	9.7	11.7
EXPORTS TO CHINA							
Total exports [2]	(X)	**67.2**	**65.1**	**85.7**	**96.9**	**103.5**	**6.8**
Oilseeds and grains	1111	7.3	9.4	11.2	11.5	16.5	43.9
Waste and scrap	9100	7.5	7.1	8.5	11.5	9.5	-17.4
Aerospace products and parts	3364	5.4	5.3	5.7	6.3	7.9	24.5
Motor vehicles	3361	1.1	1.0	3.2	5.0	5.4	7.8
Navigational, measuring, electromedical, and control instruments	3345	2.7	2.7	3.5	3.9	4.8	22.3
Basic chemicals	3251	3.1	3.4	4.1	4.6	4.7	1.3
Resin, synthetic rubber, artificial and synthetic fibers and filaments	3252	3.5	4.0	4.3	4.4	4.2	-4.6
Other agricultural products	1119	1.8	1.0	2.3	2.8	3.7	32.8
Semiconductors and other electronic components	3344	6.1	4.9	6.1	4.3	3.4	-21.0
Other general purpose machinery	3339	2.2	1.8	2.4	3.0	2.9	-2.6

X Not applicable. [1] Based on the 2007 North American Industry Classification System (NAICS). [2] Includes items not shown separately.

Source: U.S. International Trade Commission, "Interactive Tariff and Trade DataWeb," <http://dataweb.usitc.gov/>, accessed August 2013.

Table 1340. U.S. Trade in Processed Foods By Commodity: 1990 to 2012

[Includes Puerto Rico, U.S. territories, and shipments under foreign aid programs. Metric ton = 1.102 short tons or .984 long tons]

Product category	Units	1990	2000	2010	2011	2012
Processed foods imports, total [1,2]	**Metric tons**	**6,286,680**	**11,054,749**	**16,834,276**	**18,163,764**	**18,384,116**
Alcoholic beverages [2]	Kiloliters	1,277,084	2,818,882	4,115,172	4,240,281	4,443,640
Beer	Kiloliters	1,021,851	2,331,185	3,146,395	3,186,840	3,233,313
Distilled spirits	Kiloliters [3]	281,702	341,792	464,068	510,508	543,519
Wine	Kiloliters	237,065	439,989	932,137	1,009,246	1,160,475
Chocolate and confectionery	Metric tons	504,928	858,136	1,362,569	1,393,006	1,372,800
Chocolate	Metric tons	377,961	525,437	820,017	848,983	827,530
Sugar confectionery	Metric tons	107,440	293,105	499,236	503,564	507,612
Condiments and sauces	Metric tons	115,941	351,000	569,652	592,008	596,773
Fats and oils [2]	Metric tons	1,132,274	1,698,793	3,518,341	4,107,345	3,925,638
Olive oil	Metric tons	97,273	203,960	275,435	291,421	321,421
Soybean oil	1,000 kilograms	16,535	35,949	53,697	71,556	64,652
Vegetable oils (excl. soybean)	Metric tons	996,020	1,427,711	3,075,082	3,601,949	3,387,324
Food preparations [2]	Metric tons	476,332	1,111,336	2,052,421	2,196,193	2,301,305
Baking inputs, mixes, and doughs [4]	Metric tons	277,341	682,340	1,097,081	1,102,436	1,189,130
Non-alcoholic beverages [2]	Kiloliters	3,459,021	3,689,991	5,552,744	5,535,322	5,366,669
Bottled drinks [5]	Kiloliters	127,521	555,954	1,222,531	1,312,613	1,534,615
Juices	Kiloliters	3,331,499	3,134,037	4,330,213	4,222,710	3,832,053
Pasta and processed cereals [2]	Metric tons	193,034	517,471	881,572	922,990	952,884
Breakfast cereals and other breakfast products	Metric tons	34,351	113,024	277,763	296,125	291,888
Pasta	Metric tons	152,775	316,886	367,974	388,638	409,100
Prepared/preserved meats	Metric tons	216,474	197,083	143,248	145,674	138,997
Prepared/preserved seafood	Metric tons	568,051	876,402	1,283,775	1,282,187	1,230,386
Processed fruit	Metric tons	579,732	865,350	1,422,793	1,481,240	1,681,993
Processed vegetables and pulses [2]	Metric tons	836,504	1,695,961	2,455,785	2,571,019	2,633,986
Frozen potato products [6]	Metric tons	63,926	527,642	725,033	761,719	804,136
Processed/prepared dairy products [2]	Metric tons	143,662	245,530	230,269	229,311	265,366
Cheese	Metric tons	137,086	188,707	138,539	142,166	153,939
Cream	Metric tons	4,305	18,897	33,250	33,309	40,285
Ice cream	Metric tons	23	9,151	30,263	28,220	32,684
Yogurt and dairy drinks	Liters	–	23,060	11,197	84,778	731,328
Snack foods	Metric tons	208,426	627,030	1,126,307	1,179,260	1,154,859
Baked snack foods [7]	Metric tons	162,213	480,515	899,781	943,846	979,972
Mixes of nuts and fruit [8]	Metric tons	39,423	92,782	156,182	157,227	63,188
Potato chips	Metric tons	2,436	23,758	40,569	39,714	48,483
Prepared peanuts and peanut butter	Metric tons	4,354	29,976	29,774	38,474	63,217
Spices	Metric tons	113,653	192,577	300,902	317,183	326,866
Syrups and sweeteners [2]	Metric tons	874,866	1,106,543	866,613	981,121	1,036,095
Fructose and fructose syrup	Metric tons	175,714	66,513	92,496	88,439	91,914
Glucose and glucose syrup	Metric tons	44,540	113,647	217,058	218,834	216,017
Processed foods exports, total [2]	**Metric tons**	**6,028,234**	**10,908,071**	**17,719,580**	**18,326,923**	**20,603,692**
Alcoholic beverages [2]	Kiloliters	335,460	550,712	727,964	782,984	849,747
Beer	Kiloliters	232,695	262,305	320,694	361,801	444,948
Distilled spirits	Kiloliters [3]	73,373	94,719	157,857	189,915	253,775
Wine	Kiloliters	87,816	264,523	383,301	396,789	381,636
Chocolate and confectionery	Metric tons	119,104	302,600	420,212	477,007	507,905
Chocolate	Metric tons	76,174	192,742	303,757	358,168	378,322
Sugar confectionery	Metric tons	36,658	98,043	108,527	110,240	121,347
Condiments and sauces	Metric tons	119,931	363,963	638,943	681,877	725,380
Fats and oils [2]	Metric tons	1,299,208	1,998,801	3,356,665	2,655,410	2,834,966
Soybean oil	1,000 kilograms	533,388	586,786	1,656,920	1,000,171	950,978
Vegetable oils (excl. soybean)	Metric tons	575,938	1,044,199	1,066,611	999,673	1,163,261
Food preparations [2]	Metric tons	1,718,055	2,487,534	3,391,498	3,512,919	5,383,494
Baking inputs, mixes, and doughs [4]	Metric tons	1,432,974	1,904,460	2,280,017	2,359,602	4,150,635
Non-alcoholic beverages [2]	Kiloliters	937,096	1,661,547	1,617,263	1,969,845	1,697,731
Bottled drinks [5]	Kiloliters	247,244	487,448	636,964	748,841	675,834
Juices	Kiloliters	689,852	1,174,098	980,299	1,221,005	1,021,898
Pasta and processed cereals [2]	Metric tons	483,963	683,017	983,674	1,038,640	864,209
Breakfast cereals and other breakfast products	Metric tons	229,076	265,399	568,666	617,930	483,992
Pasta	Metric tons	19,061	102,295	181,765	193,640	201,092
Prepared/preserved meats	Metric tons	97,770	313,841	643,614	676,668	625,043
Prepared/preserved seafood	Metric tons	339,261	434,173	457,886	542,682	528,052
Processed fruit	Metric tons	336,563	388,844	571,165	603,877	631,919
Processed vegetables and pulses [2]	Metric tons	625,045	1,272,076	1,679,157	1,978,501	2,108,437
Frozen potato products [6]	Metric tons	214,008	568,709	790,607	916,275	1,009,421
Processed/prepared dairy products [2]	Metric tons	159,303	398,655	1,179,545	1,253,201	1,311,384
Cheese	Metric tons	11,886	47,760	173,327	224,554	259,852
Cream	Metric tons	16,768	114,847	466,853	480,524	489,875
Ice cream	Metric tons	14,548	41,652	35,680	39,026	49,535
Snack foods	Metric tons	244,468	490,079	784,168	879,011	908,058
Baked snack foods [7]	Metric tons	118,622	274,577	476,137	528,126	595,352
Mixes of nuts and fruit [8]	Metric tons	65,044	72,748	160,303	180,415	145,723
Potato chips	Metric tons	24,990	106,040	86,510	101,472	88,838
Prepared peanuts and peanut butter	Metric tons	35,812	36,713	61,218	69,000	78,145
Soups	1,000 kilograms	27,812	97,212	140,420	147,658	165,707
Syrups and sweeteners [2]	Metric tons	236,768	726,427	2,525,583	2,818,015	2,930,601
Fructose and fructose syrup	Metric tons	91,582	322,904	1,395,278	1,436,208	1,673,103
Glucose and glucose syrup	Metric tons	77,348	209,686	738,966	916,618	801,833
Molasses	Kiloliters	135,569	199,070	203,841	181,842	173,916

– Represents zero. [1] Imports for consumption. Excludes merchandise entered into bonded warehouses of Foreign Trade Zones under Customs custody; see source for details. [2] Includes commodities not shown separately. [3] Proof gallon equivalent. [4] Includes pudding. [5] Includes soda, juice mixes, beer, milk-based drinks, etc. [6] Includes French fries. [7] Pastries, pretzels, corn chips, etc. [8] Includes packaged and microwaveable popcorn.

Source: U.S. Department of Agriculture, Foreign Agricultural Service, "Global Agricultural Trade System," <http://www.fas.usda.gov/gats>, accessed July 2013.

Puerto Rico and the Island Areas

This section presents summary economic and social statistics for Puerto Rico, the U.S. Virgin Islands, Guam, American Samoa, and the Northern Mariana Islands. Primary sources include the decennial censuses of population and housing and the annual Puerto Rico Community Survey conducted by the U.S. Census Bureau; "County Business Patterns" and other Census Bureau publications and databases; other U.S. government publications, such as the National Vital Statistics Reports (NSVR) series, issued by the National Center for Health Statistics; and the annual *Economic Report for the Governor and Legislative Assembly* of the Puerto Rico Planning Board.

Jurisdiction—The United States gained jurisdiction over these areas as follows: the islands of Puerto Rico and Guam, surrendered by Spain in December 1898, were ceded to the United States by the Treaty of Paris, ratified in 1899. Puerto Rico became a commonwealth on July 25, 1952, thereby achieving a high degree of local autonomy under its own constitution. The U.S. Virgin Islands, comprising approximately 50 islands and cays, was purchased by the United States from Denmark in 1917. American Samoa, a group of seven islands, was acquired in accordance with a convention among the United States, Great Britain, and Germany, ratified in 1900 (Swains Island was annexed in 1925). By an agreement approved by the United Nations Security Council and the United States, the Northern Mariana Islands, previously under Japanese mandate, was administered by the United States between 1947 and 1986 under the United Nations trusteeship system. The Northern Mariana Islands became a U.S. commonwealth in 1986.

Censuses—Because characteristics of Puerto Rico and the island areas differ, the presentation of census data for them is not uniform. The 1960 Census of Population covered all the territories listed above except the Northern Mariana Islands (their census was conducted in April 1958 by the Office of the High Commissioner of the Trust Territory of the Pacific Islands), while the 1960 Census of Housing excluded American Samoa. The 1970, 1980, 1990, 2000, and 2010 censuses of population and housing covered all five areas. Beginning in 1967, Congress authorized the economic censuses, to be taken at 5-year intervals, for years ending in "2" and "7." Prior economic censuses were conducted in Puerto Rico for 1949, 1954, 1958, and 1963 and in Guam and the U.S. Virgin Islands for 1958 and 1963. In 1967, the census of construction industries was added for the first time in Puerto Rico; in 1972, the U.S. Virgin Islands and Guam were covered; and in 1982, the economic census was taken for the first time for the Northern Mariana Islands. Agricultural censuses have been conducted with increasing regularity in Puerto Rico since 1910, in the U.S. Virgin Islands since 1917, and in Guam and American Samoa since 1920; the first agricultural census in the Northern Mariana Islands was conducted in 1970.

Puerto Rico Community Survey—The Puerto Rico Community Survey (PRCS) began in 2005 and was an important element in the Census Bureau's re-engineered 2010 census plan. The American Community Survey (ACS) is the equivalent of the PRCS for the United States (50 states and District of Columbia). The PRCS collects and produces population and housing information every year instead of every 10 years. About 36,000 households are surveyed each year from across every municipio in Puerto Rico.

Information in other sections—In addition to the statistics presented in this section, other data on Puerto Rico and the island areas are included in many tables showing distribution by states in various sections of the *Abstract*. See "Puerto Rico" and "Island Areas of the U.S." in the Index.

Selected Island Areas of the United States

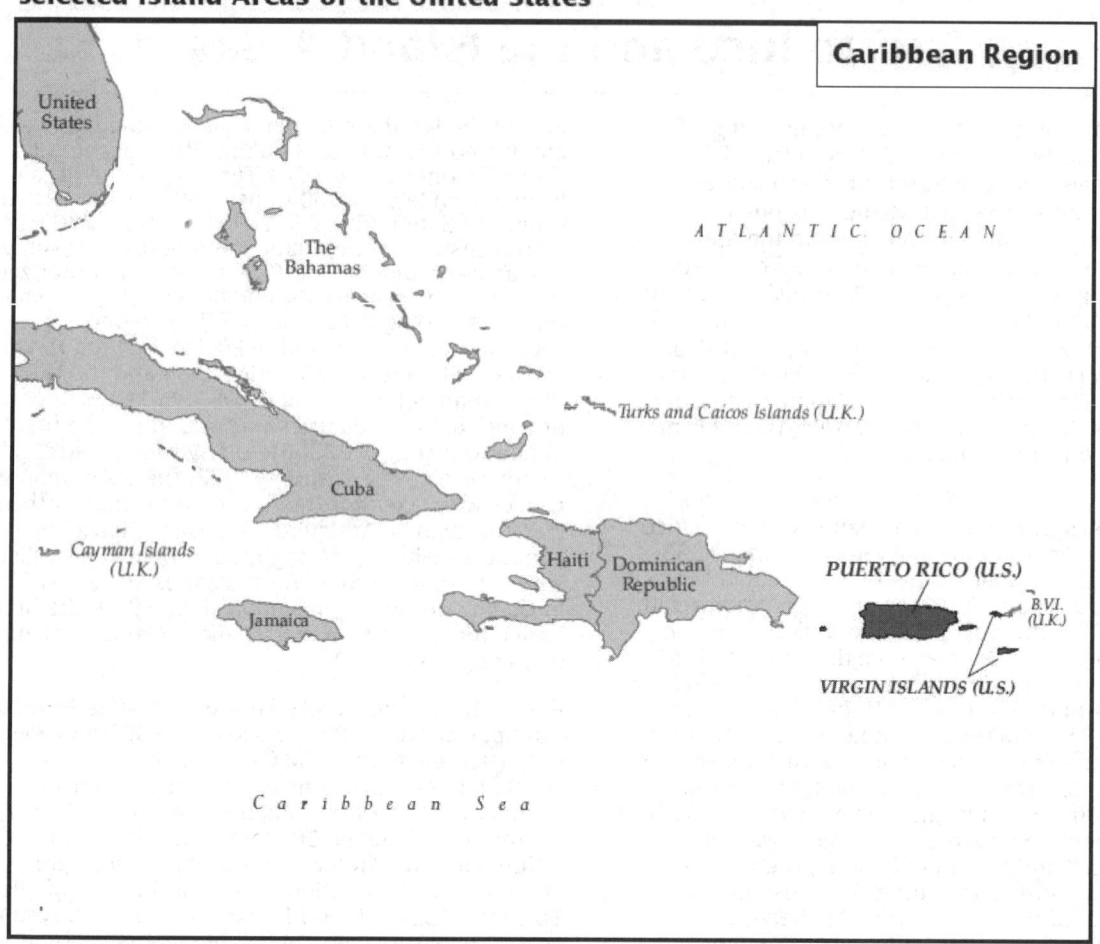

Caribbean Region

United States

ATLANTIC OCEAN

The Bahamas

Turks and Caicos Islands (U.K.)

Cuba

Cayman Islands (U.K.)

Haiti

Dominican Republic

PUERTO RICO (U.S.)

B.VI. (U.K.)

Jamaica

VIRGIN ISLANDS (U.S.)

Caribbean Sea

Pacific Region

NORTHERN MARIANA ISLANDS (U.S.)

Wake Island (U.S.)

Johnston Atoll (U.S.)

GUAM (U.S.)

PACIFIC OCEAN

Marshall Islands

Kingman Reef (U.S.)

Federated States of Micronesia

Palmyra Atoll (U.S.)

Kiribati

Nauru

Howland Island (U.S.)

Baker Island (U.S.)

Papua New Guinea

Solomon Islands

Tuvalu

Vanuatu

Coral Sea

Samoa

Australia

Fiji

AMERICAN SAMOA (U.S.)

Table 1341. Estimated and Projected Resident Population of Puerto Rico and Island Areas: 1990 to 2030

[In thousands (47 represents 47,000). Population as of July 1. Population data generally are de facto figures for the present territory. Data are adjusted to the 2010 Census of Population. See text, Section 30, for general comments regarding the data. For details of methodology, coverage, and reliability, see source]

Area	1990	2000	2005	2009	2010	2011	2012	Projected		
								2020	2025	2030
American Samoa...............	47	58	57	56	55	55	55	54	53	52
Guam......................	134	155	158	159	159	160	160	168	177	184
Northern Mariana Islands......	44	70	71	55	54	52	51	58	62	66
Puerto Rico....................	3,537	3,811	3,821	3,740	3,722	3,707	3,691	3,528	3,388	3,220
Virgin Islands..................	104	109	108	107	106	106	105	100	96	91

Source: U.S. Census Bureau, "International Data Base," <http://www.census.gov/population/international/data/idb/informationGateway.php>, accessed July 2013.

Table 1342. Births, Deaths, and Infant Deaths for Puerto Rico and the Island Areas: 2000 to 2010

[Births, deaths, and infant deaths by place of residence. Birth and death rates for 2001-2009 have been revised using population estimates based on the 2010 Census. Rates 2000 and 2010 based on population enumerated as of April 1; for other years, on population estimated as of July 1]

Area and year	Births		Deaths		Infant deaths	
	Number	Rate [1]	Number	Rate [1]	Number	Rate [2]
Puerto Rico:						
2000............................	59,333	15.6	28,365	7.4	574	9.7
2005............................	50,564	13.2	29,531	7.7	466	9.2
2007............................	46,642	12.3	29,169	7.7	394	8.5
2008............................	45,620	12.1	29,050	7.7	388	8.5
2009............................	44,773	12.0	29,005	7.8	353	7.9
2010............................	42,153	11.3	29,153	7.8	341	8.1
Guam:						
2000............................	3,766	24.2	648	4.2	22	5.8
2005............................	3,187	20.1	677	4.3	34	10.7
2007............................	3,483	21.9	778	4.9	36	10.3
2008............................	3,457	21.7	783	4.9	30	8.7
2009............................	3,417	21.4	835	5.2	36	10.5
2010............................	3,416	21.4	857	5.4	48	14.1
Virgin Islands:						
2000............................	1,564	14.4	641	5.9	21	13.4
2005............................	1,605	14.9	663	6.1	11	(B)
2007............................	1,697	15.8	703	6.5	12	(B)
2008............................	1,784	16.7	749	7.0	9	(B)
2009............................	1,687	15.8	675	6.3	11	(B)
2010............................	1,600	15.1	715	6.7	13	(B)
American Samoa:						
2000............................	1,731	30.0	219	3.8	11	(B)
2005............................	1,720	30.2	272	4.8	12	(B)
2009............................	1,340	24.0	310	5.6	15	(B)
2010............................	1,234	22.2	224	4.0	14	(B)
Northern Marianas:						
2000............................	1,431	20.5	136	2.0	11	(B)
2005............................	1,335	18.9	186	2.6	6	(B)
2009............................	1,109	20.0	203	3.7	2	(B)
2010............................	1,072	20.0	174	3.3	4	(B)

B Base figure too small to meet statistical standards of reliability. [1] Per 1,000 population. [2] Rates are infant deaths (under 1 year) per 1,000 live births.

Source: U.S. National Center for Health Statistics, National Vital Statistics Reports (NVSR), *Births: Final Data for 2010*, Vol. 61, No. 1, August 2012, and earlier reports; and *Deaths: Final Data for 2010*, Vol. 61, No. 4, May 2013, and earlier reports. See also <http://www.cdc.gov/nchs/nvss.htm>.

Table 1343. Public Elementary and Secondary Schools by Area: 2010

[Enrollment and staff are for Fall of year shown. Revenues and expenditures are for school year ending in year shown]

Item	Puerto Rico	Guam	U.S. Virgin Islands	American Samoa	Northern Marianas
Enrollment (Fall)............................	473,735	31,618	15,495	[1] 16,400	11,105
Elementary (pre-kindergarten to grade 8)........................	334,613	21,561	10,518	[1] 11,763	7,688
Secondary (grades 9 to 12)............................	139,122	10,057	4,977	[1] 4,637	3,417
Total staff (Fall)............................	59,261	3,155	2,918	[1] 1,869	1,215
School district staff............................	2,389	302	110	[1] 186	78
School staff............................	42,405	2,638	2,085	[1] 1,364	1,004
Teachers............................	36,506	1,843	1,457	[1] 971	607
Student support staff............................	3,697	47	206	[1] 218	34
Other support services staff............................	10,770	168	517	[1] 101	99
Revenues, total [3] ($1,000)............................	4,345,726	252,926	266,086	75,691	72,628
Current expenditures [4] ($1,000)............................	3,464,044	235,784	218,734	70,305	62,210
Per Pupil [4] (dollars)............................	7,807	[2] 6,781	14,285	[1] 3,481	5,812

[1] 2006 data. [2] 2005 data. [3] Includes federal, territorial, local, and private revenues. [4] Includes current expenditures only, and excludes capital expenditures, interest on school debt, community services, private school programs, adult education, and other expenditures not directly allocable to public school operations.

Source: U.S. National Center for Education Statistics, *Digest of Education Statistics*, "Advance Release of Selected 2012 Digest Tables," <http://www.nces.ed.gov/programs/digest/>, accessed June 2013.

Table 1344. Occupational Employment and Average Annual Wages in Guam, Puerto Rico, and Virgin Islands: 2012

[The Occupational Employment Survey (OES) program conducts a semiannual mail survey designed to produce estimates of employment and wages for specific occupations. For more details on the survey, see <http://www.bls.gov/oes/oes_emp.htm#scope>]

Selected occupation	SOC code [1]	Guam Employment	Guam Average annual wages [2]	Puerto Rico Employment	Puerto Rico Average annual wages [2]	Virgin Islands Employment	Virgin Islands Average annual wages [2]
Total, all occupations [3, 4]	(X)	**60,970**	**32,350**	**942,080**	**27,280**	**40,660**	**36,920**
Management occupations	11	5,300	60,340	35,580	69,890	2,500	75,340
Business and financial operations	13	2,400	48,740	40,250	37,660	1,370	50,530
Computer and mathematical	15	630	46,060	9,560	42,220	390	55,540
Architecture and engineering	17	910	56,280	13,270	50,380	210	65,430
Life, physical, and social science	19	360	46,250	6,800	43,620	390	48,990
Community and social services	21	620	36,820	18,560	27,740	430	41,650
Legal occupations	23	320	56,470	4,460	57,660	410	93,330
Education, training, and library	25	4,290	(NA)	(NA)	31,680	(NA)	(NA)
Arts, design, entertainment sports	27	630	29,430	6,320	32,190	300	41,160
Healthcare practitioner and technical	29	1,710	58,390	45,640	35,840	1,200	58,400
Healthcare support	31	720	25,190	12,300	20,240	410	26,510
Protective service	33	2,710	32,040	63,480	23,420	2,710	31,080
Food preparation and serving related	35	6,430	18,080	66,630	18,070	3,970	22,880
Buildings and grounds cleaning and maintenance	37	3,110	19,130	44,190	18,400	2,270	23,170
Personal care and service	39	1,660	22,300	13,510	18,720	950	22,550
Sales and related occupations	41	4,270	21,520	109,350	22,340	4,790	27,110
Office and administrative support	43	10,890	27,110	168,220	23,330	8,170	31,870
Farming, fishing, and forestry	45	(NA)	(NA)	1,120	24,740	(NA)	(NA)
Construction and extraction	47	5,370	28,420	37,940	20,850	1,700	(NA)
Installation, maintenance, and repair	49	3,430	30,000	30,200	28,560	2,230	42,680
Production occupations	51	1,720	27,690	64,180	22,600	1,280	(NA)
Transportation and material moving	53	3,470	29,840	53,830	21,230	2,040	28,750

NA Not available. X Not applicable. [1] Office of Management and Budget's Standard Occupational Classification (SOC) is used to define occupations. SOC categorizes workers into 1 of 801 detailed occupations and aggregates; and the detailed occupations into 23 major occupational groups. [2] Annual wages have been calculated by multiplying the hourly mean wage by a "year-round, full-time" hours figure of 2,080 hours; for those occupations where there is not an hourly mean wage published, the annual wage has been directly calculated from the reported survey data. [3] Estimates do not sum to the total because the total may include data for occupations for which separate employment estimates could not be published. See source for more information. [4] Estimates do not include self-employed workers.

Source: U.S. Bureau of Labor Statistics, "Occupational Employment Statistics," <http://www.bls.gov/oes/current/oessrcst.htm>, accessed June 2013.

Table 1345. Prisoners in Custody of Correctional Authorities in U.S. Territories and Commonwealths: 2007 and 2008

[As of December 31. Minus sign (–) indicates decrease]

Jurisdiction	Total inmates 2007	Total inmates 2008	Total inmates Percent change 2007–2008	Sentenced to more than 1 year 2007	Sentenced to more than 1 year 2008	Sentenced to more than 1 year Percent change 2007–2008	Incarceration rate, 2008 [1]
Total [2]	**14,678**	**13,576**	**-7.5**	**11,465**	**10,346**	**-9.8**	**237**
American Samoa	236	132	-44.1	122	48	-60.7	74
Guam [2]	535	578	8.1	320	304	-5.0	173
Northern Mariana Islands	137	124	-9.5	78	78	0.0	141
Puerto Rico	13,215	12,130	-8.2	10,553	9,642	-8.6	244
U.S. Virgin Islands	555	612	10.3	392	274	-30.1	249

[1] The number of prisoners with a sentence of more than 1 year per 100,000 persons in the resident population. [2] Data for Guam 2008 are estimates.

Source: U.S. Bureau of Justice Statistics, *Prisoners in 2008*, NCJ 228417, December 2009. See also <http://www.bjs.gov/index.cfm?ty=pbse&sid=40>.

Table 1346. Federal Direct Payments: 2010

[In thousands of dollars (7,951,300 represents $7,951,300,000). For fiscal years ending September 30]

Selected program payment	Puerto Rico	Guam	Virgin Islands	American Samoa	Northern Mariana Islands
Direct payments to individuals for retirement and disability [1]	7,951,300	294,106	239,101	60,683	32,971
Social security:					
Retirement insurance	3,439,821	110,217	149,834	16,732	8,840
Survivors' insurance	1,501,662	51,479	37,149	17,319	6,469
Disability insurance	2,208,140	26,131	26,871	15,258	2,208
Federal retirement and disability:					
Civilian [2]	299,200	57,295	19,140	1,882	7,841
Military	22,873	23,861	2,004	1,603	853
Veterans benefits:					
Service-connected disability	314,132	21,393	2,604	6,909	1,066
Other benefit payments	131,627	2,591	504	838	65
Other	33,846	1,138	995	142	324

[1] Includes other payments, not shown separately. [2] Includes retirement and disability payments to former U.S. Postal Service employees.

Source: U.S. Census Bureau, *Consolidated Federal Funds Report for Fiscal Year 2010*, CFFR/10, annual. See also <http://www.census.gov/govs/cffr/>.

Table 1347. Selected Social, Demographic, and Housing Characteristics in Puerto Rico: 2011

[The Puerto Rico Community Survey universe includes the household population and the population living in institutions, college dormitories, and other group quarters. Based on a sample and subject to sampling variability; see text, this section and Appendix III]

Characteristic	Estimate	Percent	Characteristic	Estimate	Percent
Total Population............	**3,706,690**	100.0	**Females 15 years and over**................	**1,587,953**	100.0
			Never married......................................	547,586	34.5
			Now married, except separated...............	576,660	36.3
SEX AND AGE			Separated..	55,714	3.5
Male..............................	1,770,224	47.8	Widowed..	167,598	10.6
Female...........................	1,936,466	52.2	Divorced..	240,395	15.1
Under 5 years...................	216,792	5.8	**HOUSEHOLDS**		
5 to 9 years.....................	227,780	6.1	**Total households**..........................	**1,256,151**	100.0
10 to 14 years..................	265,472	7.2	Family households (families)..................	903,660	71.9
15 to 19 years..................	284,644	7.7	With own children under 18 years.........	372,013	29.6
20 to 24 years..................	268,487	7.2	Married-couple families......................	520,702	41.5
25 to 34 years..................	471,617	12.7	With own children under 18 years.........	180,444	14.4
35 to 44 years..................	482,098	13.0	Male householder, no wife present..........	78,604	6.3
45 to 54 years..................	483,136	13.0	With own children under 18 years.........	37,288	3.0
55 to 59 years..................	219,782	5.9	Female householder, no husband present...	304,354	24.2
60 to 64 years..................	221,810	6.0	With own children under 18 years.........	154,281	12.3
65 to 74 years..................	326,228	8.8	Nonfamily households..........................	352,491	28.1
75 to 84 years..................	174,097	4.7	Householder living alone......................	307,888	24.5
85 years and over..............	64,747	1.7	65 years and over...........................	129,107	10.3
MARITAL STATUS			Average household size........................	2.92	(X)
Males 15 years and over....	**1,408,693**	100.0	Average family size.............................	3.50	(X)
Never married...................	583,195	41.4			
Now married, except					
separated.....................	577,252	41.0	**DISABILITY STATUS**		
Separated.......................	41,442	2.9	Total civilian		
Widowed.........................	42,659	3.0	noninstitutionalized population...............	3,680,339	100.0
Divorced.........................	164,145	11.7	With a disability................................	766,245	20.8

X Not applicable.

Source: U.S. Census Bureau, U.S. Census Bureau, 2011 Puerto Rico Community Survey, DP02PR, "Selected Social Characteristics Puerto Rico," and DP05, "Demographic and Housing Estimates," <http://factfinder2.census.gov>, accessed July 2013.

Table 1348. Owner and Renter Occupied Housing by Household Type in Puerto Rico: 2011

[The Puerto Rico Community Survey universe includes the household population and the population living in institutions, college dormitories, and other group quarters. Based on a sample and subject to sampling variability; see text, this section and Appendix III]

Household Type	Owner occupied	Renter occupied	Household Type	Owner occupied	Renter occupied
Total households...................	**876,741**	**379,410**	Householder 15 to 34 years.........	17,902	51,449
Family households......................	660,579	243,081	Householder 35 to 64 years.........	108,176	68,059
Married-couple family................	436,729	83,973	Householder 65 years and over....	49,737	9,031
Householder 15 to 34 years........	35,766	27,058	Nonfamily households....................	216,162	136,329
Householder 35 to 64 years.........	272,123	45,921	Householder living alone...............	191,086	116,802
Householder 65 years and over.....	128,840	10,994	Householder 15 to 34 years.........	7,639	18,067
Other family...........................	223,850	159,108	Householder 35 to 64 years.........	91,802	61,273
Male householder, no wife present..	48,035	30,569	Householder 65 years and over....	91,645	37,462
Householder 15 to 34 years........	5,716	13,757	Householder not living alone...........	25,076	19,527
Householder 35 to 64 years........	29,632	14,009	Householder 15 to 34 years.........	2,766	8,500
Householder 65 years and over....	12,687	2,803	Householder 35 to 64 years.........	16,573	9,428
Female householder,					
no husband present.................	175,815	128,539	Householder 65 years and over....	5,737	1,599

Source: U.S. Census Bureau, 2011 Puerto Rico Community Survey, B25011, "Tenure by Household Type and Age of Householder," <http://factfinder2.census.gov>, accessed July 2013

Table 1349. Puerto Rico— Socioeconomic Summary: 1990 to 2012

[3,512.4 represents 3,512,400, except as indicated]

Item	Unit	1990	2000	2005	2008	2009	2010	2011	2012
POPULATION									
Total [1]	1,000	3,512.4	3,808.0	3,824.0	3,772.0	3,751.0	3,731.0	3,708.0	3,681.0
Persons per family	Number	3.7	3.4	3.3	3.2	3.2	3.2	3.1	3.1
LABOR FORCE [2]									
Total [3]	1,000	1,124	1,303	1,357	1,355	1,325	1,285	1,249	1,221
Employed [4]	1,000	963	1,159	1,213	1,203	1,144	1,075	1,047	1,035
Agriculture [5]	1,000	36	24	25	15	18	17	17	17
Manufacturing	1,000	168	159	135	128	111	101	97	95
Trade	1,000	185	239	256	256	242	237	234	231
Government	1,000	222	249	268	269	259	250	230	225
Unemployed	1,000	161	143	144	152	181	210	202	185
Unemployment rate [6]	Rate	14.0	11.0	10.6	11.2	13.7	16.3	16.2	15.2
Compensation of employees	Mil. dol.	13,639	23,504	29,372	30,869	30,677	29,870	30,102	30,057
Average compensation	Dollar	14,854	20,280	24,214	25,660	26,815	27,786	28,751	29,041
Salary and wages	Mil. dol.	13,639	23,504	25,393	26,700	26,499	25,793	26,016	25,866
INCOME [7]									
Personal income:									
Current dollars	Mil. dol.	21,105	38,856	49,929	57,162	59,031	59,983	61,588	62,327
Constant (1954) dollars	Mil. dol.	5,551	8,491	10,030	10,024	9,952	9,958	10,052	9,991
Disposable personal income:									
Current dollars	Mil. dol.	19,914	36,239	46,597	54,113	56,107	57,111	59,126	59,942
Constant (1954) dollars	Mil. dol.	5,238	7,919	9,173	9,490	9,459	9,481	9,650	9,609
Average family income:									
Current dollars	Dollar	22,232	34,693	43,086	48,495	50,365	51,449	51,494	52,495
Constant (1954) dollars	Dollar	5,847	7,581	8,655	8,504	8,491	8,541	8,405	8,415
TOURISM [7]									
Number of visitors	1,000	3,426	4,566	5,073	5,213	4,415	4,379	4,214	4,197
Visitor expenditures	Mil. dol.	1,366	2,388	3,239	3,535	3,176	3,211	3,143	3,193
Average per visitor	Dollar	399	523	638	678	719	733	746	761
Net income from tourism	Mil. dol.	383	615	771	(NA)	(NA)	(NA)	(NA)	(NA)

NA Not available. [1] 1990 and 2000 enumerated as of April 1; all other years estimated as of July 1. [2] Annual average of monthly figures. For fiscal years. [3] For population 16 years old and over. [4] Includes other employment not shown separately. [5] Includes forestry and fisheries. [6] Percent unemployed of the labor force. [7] For fiscal years.

Source: Puerto Rico Planning Board, San Juan, PR, *Economic Report for the Governor and Legislative Assembly, 2012*, April 2013. See also <http://www.gdb-pur.com/economy/statistical-appendix.html>.

Table 1350. Puerto Rico—School Enrollment and Educational Attainment by Level: 2005 to 2011

[The Puerto Rico Community Survey universe includes the household population and the population living in institutions, college dormitories, and other group quarters. Based on a sample and subject to sampling variability; see text, this section and Appendix III]

Characteristic	2005	2006	2007	2008	2009	2010	2011
EDUCATIONAL ENROLLMENT							
Population 3 years and over enrolled in school	1,138,768	1,119,076	1,124,470	1,104,134	1,096,131	995,743	991,812
Nursery school, preschool	69,731	62,914	65,153	53,882	57,136	55,298	56,486
Kindergarten	52,261	51,389	46,354	47,085	46,834	45,366	45,657
Elementary school (grades 1-8)	486,546	476,075	474,355	469,220	454,396	414,233	400,439
High school (grades 9-12)	242,548	258,471	257,171	240,730	239,894	213,581	212,136
College or graduate school	287,682	270,227	281,437	293,217	297,871	267,265	277,094
EDUCATIONAL ATTAINMENT							
Population 25 years and over	2,431,653	2,501,147	2,539,282	2,571,234	2,595,507	2,444,933	2,443,515
Less than 9th grade	547,055	580,668	576,093	573,136	546,525	484,138	461,611
9th to 12th grade, no diploma	269,039	267,624	278,049	275,535	271,320	262,682	243,839
High school graduate (includes equivalency)	588,130	629,888	652,285	622,098	659,863	623,709	648,204
Some college, no degree	290,283	296,034	285,555	339,512	338,465	317,797	304,832
Associate's degree	231,848	208,153	208,037	217,084	222,600	212,186	215,478
Bachelor's degree	377,437	390,700	398,178	398,934	419,040	389,954	416,008
Graduate or professional degree	127,861	128,080	141,085	144,935	137,694	154,467	153,543
Percent high school graduate or higher	66.4	66.1	66.4	67.0	68.5	69.5	71.1
Percent bachelor's degree or higher	20.8	20.7	21.2	21.2	21.4	22.3	23.3

Source: U.S. Census Bureau, 2011 Puerto Rico Community Survey, DP02PR, "Selected Social Characteristics Puerto Rico," <http://factfinder2.census.gov>, accessed September 2013.

Table 1351. Puerto Rico—Gross Product and Net Income: 1990 to 2012

[In millions of dollars (21,619 represents $21,619,000,000). For fiscal years ending June 30. Data for 2012 are preliminary. Minus sign (–) indicates decrease]

Item	1990	2000	2008	2009	2010	2011	2012
Gross product................................	**21,619**	**41,419**	**62,703**	**63,618**	**64,295**	**65,567**	**69,462**
Agriculture..	434	407	519	567	822	796	818
Manufacturing...................................	12,126	24,489	40,234	43,872	46,577	46,832	46,114
Contract construction and mining [1]...........	720	2,157	2,032	1,777	1,518	1,462	1,471
Transportation, warehousing, and utilities............	2,468	2,579	3,097	2,862	2,923	2,941	2,759
Trade (wholesale and retail).................	4,728	6,093	7,520	7,313	7,466	7,602	7,636
Finance, insurance, and real estate...................	3,896	10,511	20,218	18,765	19,026	20,129	20,766
Services [2]...	3,015	9,987	11,571	11,703	11,993	12,459	12,650
Government.......................................	3,337	5,478	8,762	9,047	8,350	8,216	8,278
Commonwealth.................................	2,884	4,601	7,350	7,567	6,862	6,703	6,742
Municipalities..................................	453	877	1,412	1,480	1,488	1,513	1,536
Rest of the world...............................	-8,985	-20,283	-30,936	-32,768	-34,087	-34,629	-31,573
Statistical discrepancy.........................	-121	585	-312	480	-294	-238	543
Net income....................................	**17,941**	**32,610**	**50,031**	**49,986**	**50,246**	**51,536**	**55,176**
Agriculture..	486	385	519	568	824	797	819
Manufacturing...................................	11,277	22,627	37,299	40,688	43,292	43,477	42,836
Mining [1]..	26	34	36	29	21	20	20
Contract construction.........................	679	1,764	1,661	1,438	1,206	1,156	1,162
Transportation, warehousing, and utilities............	1,778	1,961	2,382	2,114	2,128	2,046	1,229
Trade (wholesale and retail).................	3,420	4,995	6,162	6,057	6,155	6,266	6,300
Finance, insurance, and real estate...................	3,280	8,175	14,943	13,422	13,099	14,450	15,603
Services [2]...	2,643	7,475	9,203	9,392	9,257	9,738	9,907
Government.......................................	3,337	5,478	8,762	9,047	8,350	8,216	8,278
Rest of the world...............................	-8,985	-20,283	-30,936	-32,768	-34,087	-34,629	-31,573

[1] Mining includes only quarries. [2] Includes all other services not elsewhere classified.

Source: Puerto Rico Planning Board, San Juan, PR, *Economic Report for the Governor and Legislative Assembly, 2012*, April 2013, and earlier reports. See also <http://www.gdb-pur.com/economy/statistical-appendix.html>.

Table 1352. Puerto Rico—Transfer Payments: 1990 to 2012

[In millions of dollars (4,871 represents $4,871,000,000). Data represent transfer payments between federal and state governments and other nonresidents. Data for 2012 are preliminary]

Item	1990	1995	2000	2005	2010	2011	2012
Total receipts................................	**4,871**	**6,236**	**8,659**	**10,551**	**16,504**	**16,854**	**17,254**
Federal government............................	4,649	5,912	7,966	9,673	15,585	15,794	16,258
Transfers to individuals [1]......................	4,577	5,838	7,868	9,547	15,352	15,580	16,013
Veterans benefits.............................	349	440	491	491	733	916	943
Medicare.......................................	368	661	1,196	1,825	2,529	2,603	2,706
Old age, disability, survivors (social security).......	2,055	2,912	3,863	5,118	7,074	7,082	7,347
Nutritional assistance........................	880	1,063	1,193	1,306	1,605	1,767	1,855
Industry subsidies............................	72	74	98	127	233	214	244
U.S. state governments.......................	18	18	15	15	29	21	20
Other nonresidents............................	205	307	679	863	890	1,040	976
Total payments..............................	**1,801**	**2,301**	**2,763**	**3,583**	**3,804**	**3,613**	**3,494**
Federal government............................	1,756	2,132	2,693	3,516	3,586	3,277	3,404
Transfers from individuals...................	817	1,052	1,326	1,792	1,862	1,505	1,564
Contribution to Medicare...................	97	162	191	303	392	401	417
Employee contribution for social security............	720	888	1,133	1,483	1,467	1,101	1,143
Transfers from industries....................	16	49	51	74	93	104	98
Unemployment insurance....................	247	184	234	221	207	208	226
Employer contribution for social security............	675	847	1,081	1,429	1,424	1,459	1,516
Other nonresidents [2]...........................	45	164	70	67	218	337	91
Net balance..................................	**3,070**	**3,935**	**5,897**	**6,968**	**12,700**	**13,241**	**13,759**
Federal government............................	2,893	3,780	5,273	6,157	11,999	12,517	12,854
U.S. state governments.......................	16	13	10	10	26	17	16
Other nonresidents............................	162	143	614	801	675	707	890

[1] Includes other receipts and payments not shown separately. [2] Includes U.S. state governments.

Source: Puerto Rico Planning Board, San Juan, PR, *Economic Report to the Governor and Legislative Assembly 2012*, April 2013. See also <http://www.gdb-pur.com/economy/statistical-appendix.html>.

Table 1353. Puerto Rico—Merchandise Imports and Exports: 1980 to 2012

[In millions of dollars (9,018 represents $9,018,000,000). Imports are imports for consumption; see text, Section 28]

Item	1980	1990	1995	2000	2005	2006	2007	2008	2009	2010	2011	2012
Imports..........	9,018	16,200	18,969	27,006	40,499	42,380	43,482	41,560	38,780	39,766	44,736	45,405
From U.S......	5,345	10,792	12,213	15,172	20,994	21,982	22,402	19,777	20,038	20,641	20,346	19,808
From other....	3,673	5,408	6,756	11,834	19,505	20,398	21,080	21,783	18,742	19,125	24,391	25,598
Exports..........	6,576	20,402	23,573	43,191	56,836	59,219	62,401	63,659	59,594	67,347	56,765	58,626
To U.S..........	5,643	17,915	20,986	38,335	47,121	47,452	47,507	46,439	40,779	47,630	40,942	42,308
To other.......	933	2,487	2,587	4,856	9,715	11,767	14,894	17,219	18,815	19,717	15,823	16,318

Source: U.S. Census Bureau, Foreign Trade Division, *U.S. Trade with Puerto Rico and U.S. Possessions* (FT 895), 2012 and earlier reports; *U.S. Merchandise Trade: Selected Highlights* (FT920), December 2011 and earlier reports; and USA Trade Online, <https://usatrade.census.gov/>, accessed September 2013.

Table 1354. Puerto Rico—Agricultural Summary: 2002 and 2007

[1 cuerda = 0.97 acre]

All farms	Unit	2002	2007	All farms	Unit	2002	2007
Farms....................	Number	17,659	15,745	Tenants...................	Number	1,636	2,425
Farm land..................	Cuerdas	690,687	557,530	Farms by type of			
Average size of farm.....	Cuerdas	39.1	35.4	organization:			
Approximate land area....	Cuerdas	2,254,365	2,254,365	Individual or family......	Number	15,843	13,958
Proportion in farms.......	Percent	30.6	24.7	Partnership..............	Number	162	49
Farms by size:				Corporation.............	Number	595	575
Less than 10 cuerdas....	Number	7,943	7,502	Other.....................	Number	1,059	1,163
10 to 19 cuerdas.........	Number	3,847	3,545	Farms by value of sales:			
20 to 49 cuerdas.........	Number	3,228	2,680	Less than $1,000.........	Number	3,977	4,442
50 to 99 cuerdas.........	Number	1,282	865	$1,000 to $2,499.........	Number	3,471	2,771
100 to 174 cuerdas......	Number	590	524	$2,500 to $4,499.........	Number	3,044	2,428
175 to 259 cuerdas......	Number	281	207	$5,000 to $7,499.........	Number	1,575	1,206
260 cuerdas or more.....	Number	488	422	$7,500 to $9,999.........	Number	1,087	882
Tenure of operator:				$10,000 to $19,999......	Number	1,781	1,497
Operators.................	Number	17,659	15,745	$20,000 to $39,999......	Number	1,062	1,030
Full owners..............	Number	13,693	11,402	$40,000 to $59,999......	Number	375	281
Part owners.............	Number	2,330	1,918	$60,000 or more..........	Number	1,287	1,208

Source: U.S. Department of Agriculture, National Agricultural Statistics Service (NASS), *2007 Census of Agriculture: Puerto Rico, Island and Municipio Data*, Geographic Area Series, Volume 1: Part 52, 2009. See also <http://www.agcensus.usda.gov/Publications/2007/Full_Report/>.

Table 1355. Puerto Rico—Farms and Market Value of Agricultural Products Sold: 2007

[For total market value, 515,686 represents $515,686,000]

Type of product	Number of farms	Market value ($1,000)	Average value per farm (dol.)	Type of product	Number of farms	Market value ($1,000)	Average value per farm (dol.)
Total.....................	**15,745**	**515,686**	**32,752**	Horticultural specialties.........	524	44,576	85,068
Crops, including horticultural				Grasses and other crops.......	256	13,372	52,236
specialties.........................	10,206	218,835	(NA)				
Coffee.........................	5,678	41,824	7,366	Livestock, poultry, and their			
Pineapples....................	53	527	9,942	products.....................	5,662	296,850	52,428
Plantains......................	3,756	44,875	11,947	Cattle and calves...............	3,568	33,005	9,250
Bananas.......................	1,980	10,082	5,092	Poultry and poultry products. ..	1,079	63,574	58,919
Grains.........................	969	1,553	1,603	Dairy products..................	354	184,543	521,307
Root crops or tubers..........	1,691	6,683	3,952	Hogs and pigs..................	1,075	6,239	5,803
Fruits and coconuts...........	2,350	19,904	8,470	Aquaculture.....................	40	833	20,818
Vegetables and melons [1].......	1,007	35,440	35,194	Other............................	787	8,657	11,000

NA Not available. [1] Includes hydroponic crops.

Source: U.S. Department of Agriculture, National Agricultural Statistics Service (NASS), *2007 Census of Agriculture: Puerto Rico, Island and Municipio Data*, Geographic Area Series, Volume 1: Part 52, 2009. See also <http://www.agcensus.usda.gov/Publications/2007/Full_Report/>.

Table 1356. Puerto Rico—Business Summary by Industry: 2011

[Payroll in thousands of dollars (16,484,993 represents $16,484,993,000). Covers establishments with payroll. Excludes self-employed individuals, employees of private households, railroad employees, agricultural production employees, and most government employees. For statement on methodology, see Appendix III]

Industry	2007 NAICS code [1]	Establishments	Employees [2]	Annual payroll (1,000)
Total, all industries.................................	**(X)**	**44,056**	**673,677**	**16,484,993**
Agriculture, forestry, fishing and hunting...........................	11	8	([3])	723
Mining, quarrying, and oil and gas extraction........................	21	48	731	14,573
Utilities..	22	25	333	18,283
Construction.......................................	23	2,130	29,663	625,110
Manufacturing......................................	31–33	1,829	83,712	2,970,240
Wholesale trade....................................	42	2,166	32,749	1,137,830
Retail trade..	44–45	10,255	131,560	2,283,871
Transportation and warehousing......................	48–49	1,001	15,376	420,142
Information...	51	555	18,739	712,574
Finance and insurance...............................	52	1,897	34,633	1,457,813
Real estate and rental and leasing....................	53	1,554	11,131	252,098
Professional, scientific, and technical services............	54	4,206	26,352	878,631
Management of companies and enterprises..............	55	90	4,224	229,952
Admin/support waste mgt/remediation services.........	56	1,807	72,513	1,371,925
Educational services.................................	61	830	38,132	820,348
Health care and social assistance.....................	62	7,293	80,391	1,845,972
Arts, entertainment, and recreation....................	71	390	3,002	63,778
Accommodation and food services.....................	72	4,354	70,173	1,004,152
Other services (except public administration)............	81	3,378	19,798	368,296
Industries not classified..............................	99	240	414	8,682

X Not applicable. [1] 2007 North American Industry Classification System. See text, section 15. [2] Covers full- and part-time employees who are on the payroll in the pay period including March 12. [3] 20 to 99 employees.

Source: U.S. Census Bureau, County Business Patterns, "Geography Area Series: County Business Patterns for Puerto Rico and the Island Areas," <http://factfinder2.census.gov/>, accessed July 2013.

Table 1357. Guam, Virgin Islands, and Northern Mariana Islands— Economic Summary by Sector: 2007

[Sales and payroll in millions of dollars (6,244 represents $6,244,000,000). Based on the 2007 Economic Census; see Appendix III]

Selected kinds of business	Guam	Virgin Islands	Northern Mariana Islands	Selected kinds of business	Guam	Virgin Islands	Northern Mariana Islands
Total:				Paid employees [2]	2,394	797	872
Establishments [1]	3,143	2,583	1,191	Retail trade:			
Sales	6,244	19,479	1,284	Establishments	660	641	255
Annual payroll	1,101	1,085	246	Sales	1,618	1,397	272
Paid employees [2]	52,394	35,300	22,622	Annual payroll	150	146	29
Construction:				Paid employees [2]	8,219	6,773	2,770
Establishments	317	195	50	Professional, scientific, and technical services:			
Sales	579	352	31	Establishments	227	257	87
Annual payroll	121	115	7	Sales	231	284	25
Paid employees [2]	6,011	3,388	528	Annual payroll	77	60	9
Manufacturing:				Paid employees [2]	2,217	1,370	404
Establishments	63	70	59	Accommodation & food services:			
Sales	167	(D)	190	Establishments	429	255	140
Annual payroll	39	(D)	57	Sales	635	461	173
Paid employees [2]	1,495	([3])	7,094	Annual payroll	155	130	45
Wholesale trade:				Paid employees [2]	11,477	6,146	4,772
Establishments	191	58	72				
Sales	800	288	143				
Annual payroll	56	25	10				

D Withheld to avoid disclosing data for individual companies; data are included in higher level totals. [1] Includes other industries, not shown separately. [2] For pay period including March 12. [3] 1,000 to 2,499 employees.

Source: U.S. Census Bureau, 2007 Economic Census of the Island Areas, Geographic Area Series, "General Statistics by Kind of Business," <http://factfinder2.census.gov/>, accessed August 2010. See also <http://www.census.gov/econ/islandareas/>.

Table 1358. Virgin Islands—Business Summary by Industry: 2011

[Payroll in thousands of dollars (1,083,493 represents $1,083,493,000). Covers establishments with payroll. Excludes self-employed individuals, employees of private households, railroad employees, agricultural production employees, and most government employees. For statement on methodology, see Appendix III]

Industry	2007 NAICS code [1]	Establishments	Employees [2]	Annual payroll (1,000)
Total, all industries	(X)	**2,725**	**32,454**	**1,083,493**
Agriculture, forestry, fishing and hunting	11	1	([3])	(D)
Mining, quarrying, and oil and gas extraction	21	2	([3])	(D)
Utilities	22	6	([4])	(D)
Construction	23	193	1,957	63,995
Manufacturing	31–33	64	([6])	(D)
Wholesale trade	42	68	779	29,061
Retail trade	44–45	597	6,492	147,252
Transportation and warehousing	48–49	117	1,770	54,288
Information	51	45	([5])	(D)
Finance and insurance	52	118	1,139	54,934
Real estate and rental and leasing	53	190	1,063	36,349
Professional, scientific, and technical services	54	257	1,153	53,003
Management of companies and enterprises	55	7	89	4,618
Admin/support waste mgt/remediation services	56	152	1,988	52,556
Educational services	61	45	914	23,027
Health care and social assistance	62	252	2,241	80,286
Arts, entertainment, and recreation	71	50	583	12,453
Accommodation and food services	72	314	6,709	152,799
Other services (except public administration)	81	233	2,294	85,147
Industries not classified	99	14	([3])	222

X Not applicable. D Withheld to avoid disclosing data for individual companies; data are included in total. [1] 2007 North American Industry Classification System. See text, section 15. [2] Covers full- and part-time employees who are on the payroll in the pay period including March 12. [3] 0 to 19 employees. [4] 100 to 249 employees. [5] 500 to 999 employees. [6] 1,000 to 2,4999 employees.

Source: U.S. Census Bureau, County Business Patterns, "Geography Area Series: County Business Patterns for Puerto Rico and the Island Areas," <http://factfinder2.census.gov/>, accessed July 2013.

Table 1359. Guam—Business Summary by Industry: 2011

[Payroll in thousands of dollars (1,286,460 represents $1,286,460,000). Covers establishments with payroll. Excludes self-employed individuals, employees of private households, railroad employees, agricultural production employees, and most government employees. For statement on methodology, see Appendix III]

Industry	2007 NAICS code [1]	Establishments	Employees [2]	Annual payroll (1,000)
Total, all industries.....	(X)	**3,379**	**53,539**	**1,286,460**
Agriculture, forestry, fishing and hunting.....	11	2	([3])	(D)
Mining, quarrying, and oil and gas extraction.....	21	1	([3])	(D)
Utilities.....	22	6	96	3,491
Construction.....	23	354	5,939	144,024
Manufacturing.....	31–33	55	1,398	37,650
Wholesale trade.....	42	216	2,610	69,215
Retail trade.....	44–45	652	8,889	184,876
Transportation and warehousing.....	48–49	99	2,697	110,960
Information.....	51	64	1,466	50,688
Finance and insurance.....	52	134	2,115	80,670
Real estate and rental and leasing.....	53	270	1,998	44,377
Professional, scientific, and technical services.....	54	246	2,422	96,093
Management of companies and enterprises.....	55	12	80	3,322
Admin/support waste mgt/remediation services.....	56	166	4,270	77,004
Educational services.....	61	53	967	20,764
Health care and social assistance.....	62	211	3,282	111,401
Arts, entertainment, and recreation.....	71	75	1,140	20,130
Accommodation and food services.....	72	460	11,635	176,322
Other services (except public administration).....	81	285	2,510	54,708
Industries not classified.....	99	18	([4])	530

X Not applicable. D Withheld to avoid disclosing data for individual companies; data are included in total. [1] 2007 North American Industry Classification System. See text, section 15. [2] Covers full- and part-time employees who are on the payroll in the pay period including March 12. [3] 0 to 19 employees. [4] 20 to 99 employees.

Source: U.S. Census Bureau, County Business Patterns, "Geography Area Series: County Business Patterns for Puerto Rico and the Island Areas," <http://factfinder2.census.gov/>, accessed July 2013.

Table 1360. Northern Marianas—Business Summary by Industry: 2011

[Payroll in thousands of dollars (153,262 represents $153,262,000). Covers establishments with payroll. Excludes self-employed individuals, employees of private households, railroad employees, agricultural production employees, and most government employees. For statement on methodology, see Appendix III]

Industry	2007 NAICS code [1]	Establishments	Employees [2]	Annual payroll (1,000)
Total, all industries.....	(X)	**1,237**	**10,450**	**153,262**
Agriculture, forestry, fishing and hunting.....	11	1	([3])	(D)
Mining, quarrying, and oil and gas extraction.....	21	2	([4])	(D)
Utilities.....	22	7	([5])	(D)
Construction.....	23	47	424	3,060
Manufacturing.....	31–33	37	405	4,970
Wholesale trade.....	42	73	505	7,249
Retail trade.....	44–45	251	1,675	22,267
Transportation and warehousing.....	48–49	38	829	13,426
Information.....	51	25	297	8,004
Finance and insurance.....	52	50	270	7,324
Real estate and rental and leasing.....	53	120	335	4,183
Professional, scientific, and technical services.....	54	87	292	8,299
Management of companies and enterprises.....	55	4	([3])	(D)
Admin/support waste mgt/remediation services.....	56	94	891	12,385
Educational services.....	61	52	220	3,358
Health care and social assistance.....	62	32	233	4,775
Arts, entertainment, and recreation.....	71	44	403	4,847
Accommodation and food services.....	72	146	2,801	29,814
Other services (except public administration).....	81	99	401	5,645
Industries not classified.....	99	28	([4])	430

X Not applicable. D Withheld to avoid disclosing data for individual companies; data are included in total. [1] 2007 North American Industry Classification System. See text, section 15. [2] Covers full- and part-time employees who are on the payroll in the pay period including March 12. [3] 0 to 19 employees. [4] 20 to 99 employees. [5] 250 to 499 employees.

Source: U.S. Census Bureau, County Business Patterns, "Geography Area Series: County Business Patterns for Puerto Rico and the Island Areas," <http://factfinder2.census.gov/>, accessed July 2013.

Table 1361. American Samoa—Business Summary by Industry: 2011

[Payroll in thousands of dollars (107,596 represents $107,596,000). Covers establishments with payroll. Excludes self-employed individuals, employees of private households, railroad employees, agricultural production employees, and most government employees. For statement on methodology, see Appendix III]

Industry	2007 NAICS code [1]	Establishments	Employees [2]	Annual payroll (1,000)
Total, all industries...................................	**(X)**	**479**	**7,369**	**107,596**
Agriculture, forestry, fishing and hunting...............................	11	3	42	380
Construction...	23	27	484	7,859
Manufacturing..	31–33	38	([7])	(D)
Wholesale trade...	42	22	294	4,465
Retail trade...	44–45	151	1,453	19,139
Transportation and warehousing..........................	48–49	26	309	4,247
Information...	51	8	131	2,505
Finance and insurance.......................................	52	9	([5])	3,030
Real estate and rental and leasing..........................	53	20	([4])	867
Professional, scientific, and technical services............	54	22	([5])	(D)
Management of companies and enterprises.................	55	3	([3])	194
Admin/support waste mgt/remediation services...........	56	19	118	1,338
Educational services...	61	8	153	1,982
Health care and social assistance.........................	62	17	([6])	(D)
Arts, entertainment, and recreation........................	71	3	([3])	(D)
Accommodation and food services.........................	72	42	504	5,675
Other services (except public administration)............	81	51	394	4,561
Industries not classified.....................................	99	10	([4])	275

X Not applicable. D Withheld to avoid disclosing data for individual companies; data are included in total. [1] 2007 North American Industry Classification System. See text, section 15. [2] Covers full- and part-time employees who are on the payroll in the pay period including March 12. [3] 0 to 19 employees. [4] 20 to 99 employees. [5] 100 to 249 employees. [6] 500 to 999 employees. [7] 1,000 to 2,499 employees.

Source: U.S. Census Bureau, County Business Patterns, "Geography Area Series: County Business Patterns for Puerto Rico and the Island Areas," <http://factfinder2.census.gov/>, accessed July 2013.

Section 30
International Statistics

This section presents statistics for the world as a whole and for many countries on a comparative basis with the United States. Data are shown for population, births and deaths, social and economic indicators, finances, agriculture, energy, climate, science and technology, communications, and military affairs.

Statistics for individual countries may be found primarily in official national publications, generally in the form of yearbooks, issued by most countries in their own national languages and expressed in their own customary units of measure. (For a listing of selected publications, see Appendix I, Guide to Foreign Statistical Abstracts.)

For international comparisons, the United Nations Statistics Division compiles data as submitted by member countries and issues a number of summary publications, generally in English and French. Among these are the annual *Statistical Yearbook; Demographic Yearbook; Population and Vital Statistics Report; International Trade Statistics Yearbook; Energy Statistics Yearbook; Industrial Commodity Statistics Yearbook; National Accounts Statistics;* and the *Monthly Bulletin of Statistics.* Specialized agencies of the United Nations also issue international summary publications on various topics, including agricultural, labor, health, and trade statistics. Among these are *Food Outlook* and the Statistical Yearbook issued by the Food and Agriculture Organization (FAO); *Global Employment Trends* issued by the International Labor Organization (ILO); *World Health Statistics* issued by the World Health Organization (WHO); and the *Handbook of Statistics* issued by the Conference on Trade and Development (UNCTAD).

The U.S. Census Bureau publishes estimates and projections of key demographic measures for countries and regions of the world in its International Data Base at <http://www.census.gov/ipc/www/idb/>.

The International Monetary Fund (IMF), the World Bank, and the Organisation for Economic Co-operation and Development (OECD) also compile international statistics. The IMF publishes a series of reports related to financial data. These include *World Economic Outlook, International Financial Statistics*, and *Balance of Payments Statistics Yearbook*. The World Bank publishes many reports on a wide range of topics related to international development. Three of their flagship statistical publications are *World Development Report, World Development Indicators*, and Global Economic Prospects. The OECD also produces numerous statistical publications in fields including economics, health, and education. Among these are the *OECD Factbook; Economic Outlook; National Accounts of OECD Countries; Science, Technology and Industry Outlook; International Migration Outlook; Employment Outlook; Health at a Glance;* and *Education at a Glance.*

Statistical coverage and country classifications— Problems of space and availability of data limit the number of countries and the extent of statistical coverage shown. The lists of countries and territories included in individual tables are generally based on source publications and databases, as cited.

In the last quarter-century, several important changes took place in the status of the world's nations. In 1991, the Soviet Union broke up into 15 independent countries: Armenia, Azerbaijan, Belarus, Estonia, Georgia, Kazakhstan, Kyrgyzstan, Latvia, Lithuania, Moldova, Russia, Tajikistan, Turkmenistan, Ukraine, and Uzbekistan.

Germany was reunified in 1990, when the German Democratic Republic (former East Germany) joined the Federal Republic of Germany (former West Germany) to form a single country. On January 1, 1993, Czechoslovakia was succeeded by two independent countries: the Czech Republic and Slovakia.

Following the breakup of the Socialist Federal Republic of Yugoslavia in 1992, the United States recognized Bosnia and Herzegovina, Croatia, Slovenia, and Macedonia as independent countries. Serbia and Montenegro, both former republics of Yugoslavia, became independent of one another on May 31, 2006. This separation is reflected in the population estimates of Table 1365, but some tables may still show both countries as combined. On February 17, 2008, Kosovo declared its independence from Serbia.

The Treaty of Maastricht created the European Union (EU) in 1992 with 12 member countries. The EU is not a state intended to replace existing states, but it is more than just an international organization. Its member states have set up common institutions to which they delegate some of their sovereignty so that decisions on specific matters of joint interest can be made democratically at a European level. This pooling of sovereignty is also called "European integration." The EU has grown in size with successive waves of accessions in 1995, 2004, 2007, and 2013. The 28 current members of the EU are: Austria, Belgium, Bulgaria, Croatia, Cyprus, Czech Republic, Denmark, Estonia, Finland, France, Germany, Greece, Hungary, Ireland, Italy, Latvia, Lithuania, Luxembourg, Malta, the Netherlands, Poland, Portugal, Romania, Slovakia, Slovenia, Spain, Sweden, and the United Kingdom.

In 1992, the EU decided to establish an economic and monetary union (EMU), with the introduction of a single European currency managed by a European Central Bank. The single currency—the euro—became a reality on January 1, 2002, when euro notes and coins replaced national currencies in 12 of the then 15 countries of the European Union (Belgium, Germany, Greece, Spain, France, Ireland, Italy, Luxembourg, the Netherlands, Austria, Portugal, and Finland). Since then, 13 additional countries have acceded to EU membership, but Slovakia, Slovenia, Malta, Cyprus, and Estonia have been the only new members of the EU to adopt the euro as the national currency.

Elsewhere in the world, Eritrea announced its independence from Ethiopia in April 1993 and was subsequently recognized as an independent nation by the United States. In the South Pacific, the Marshall Islands, Micronesia, and Palau gained independence from the United States in 1991. In May of 2002, Timor-Leste won independence from Indonesia. The Netherlands Antilles dissolved on October 10, 2010. As a result, Curaçao and Sint Maarten became autonomous territories of the Netherlands. Most recently, Sudan and South Sudan became separate countries as of July, 2011.

The population estimates and projections used in Tables 1362 through 1365, 1367, and 1368 were prepared by the U.S. Census Bureau. For each country, available data on population by age and sex, fertility, mortality, and international migration were evaluated and, where necessary, adjusted for inconsistencies and errors in the data. Comprehensive population projections were made by the cohort-component method based on an assessment of probable future trends.

Economic associations—The Organisation for European Economic Co-operation (OEEC) was originally a regional grouping of Western European countries established in 1948 for the purpose of harmonizing national economic policies and conditions. It was succeeded on September 30, 1961, by the Organisation for Economic Co-operation and Development (OECD). The current member nations of the OECD are Australia, Austria, Belgium, Canada, Chile, Czech Republic, Denmark, Estonia, Finland, France, Germany, Greece, Hungary, Iceland, Ireland, Israel, Italy, Japan, Luxembourg, Mexico, the Netherlands, New Zealand, Norway, Poland, Portugal, Slovakia, Slovenia, South Korea, Spain, Sweden, Switzerland, Turkey, the United Kingdom, and the United States.

Quality and comparability of the data—The quality and comparability of the data presented here are affected by a number of factors:

1 The year for which data are presented may not be the same for all subjects for a particular country or for a given subject for different countries, though the data shown are the most recent available. All such variations have been noted. The data shown are for calendar years except as otherwise specified.

2 The statistical bases, methods of estimating, methods of data collection, extent of coverage, precision of definition, scope of territory, and margins of error may vary for different items within a particular country, and for like items for different countries. Footnotes and headnotes to the tables describe some of the major coverage qualifications attached to the figures; considerably more detail is presented in the source publications. Many of the measures shown are merely rough indicators of magnitude.

3 Figures shown in this section for the United States may not always agree with figures shown in the preceding sections. Discrepancies may be attributable to the use of differing original sources, differences in the definition of geographic limits (the 50 states, continental U.S. only, or the U.S. including certain outlying areas and possessions), or to possible adjustments made to the U.S. figures

in order to make them more comparable with figures from other countries.

International comparisons of national accounts data—To compare national accounts data for different countries, it is necessary to convert each country's data into a common unit of currency, usually the U.S. dollar. The market exchange rates, which often are used in converting national currencies, do not necessarily reflect the relative purchasing power in the various countries. It is necessary that the goods and services produced in different countries be valued consistently if the differences observed are meant to reflect real differences in the volumes of goods and services produced. The use of purchasing power parities (see Tables 1376, 1377, and 1384) instead of exchange rates is intended to achieve this objective.

The method used to present the data shown in Table 1377 is to construct volume measures directly by revaluing the goods and services sold in different countries at a common set of international prices. By dividing the ratio of the gross domestic products of two countries expressed in their own national currencies by the corresponding ratio calculated at constant international prices, it is possible to derive the implied purchasing power parity (PPP) between the two currencies concerned. PPPs show how many units of currency are needed in one country to buy the same amount of goods and services that one unit of currency will buy in the other country. For further information, see *National Accounts, Main Aggregates, Volume I*, issued annually by the Organisation for Economic Co-operation and Development (OECD), Paris, France.

International Standard Industrial Classification—The original version of the International Standard Industrial Classification of All Economic Activities (ISIC) was adopted in 1948. A number of countries have utilized ISIC as the basis for devising their industrial classification schemes. Substantial comparability has been attained among the industrial classification schemes of many countries, including the United States, by ensuring that national classification categories correspond to ISIC categories. The United Nations, the International Labour Organization, the Food and Agriculture Organization, and other international bodies use ISIC in publishing and analyzing statistical data. Revisions of ISIC were issued in 1958, 1968, 1989, 2002, and 2008.

International Maps—A series of regional world maps is provided within this section. References are included in Table 1365 for easy location of individual countries on the maps. Map projection will be distorted due to being portrayed on a flat surface. For additional information and maps see the Central Intelligence Agency's *The World Factbook*, at <https://www.cia.gov/library/publications/the-world-factbook/.>

Political Map of the World, June 2012

AUSTRALIA Independent state
Bermuda Dependency or area of special sovereignty
Azory / AZORES Island / Island group
★ Capital

Scale: 1:36,000,000

*Lambert Conformal Conic Projection,
standard parallels 25°N and 77°N*

0   300   600 kilometers
0   300   600 miles

803541AI(G00694)6-12

CENTRAL AMERICA AND THE CARIBBEAN

North
Atlantic
Ocean

Caribbean Sea

Gulf of Mexico

North
Pacific
Ocean

Scale 1: 12,500,000

*Lambert Conformal Conic Projection,
standard parallels 7° N and 24° N*

Boundary representation is not necessarily authoritative.

Caribbean Sea

Martinique (FRANCE)
ST. LUCIA
ST. VINCENT AND
THE GRENADINES
GRENADA
BARBADOS

HONDURAS
★Tegucigalpa
NICARAGUA
★Managua

Isla de
Providencia
(COLOMBIA)
Isla de
San Andrés
(COLOMBIA)

★San José
COSTA RICA
PANAMA
Panama
City

Barranquilla
Cartagena
Maracaibo
Barquisimeto
Valencia
★Caracas
Barcelona

Port of Spain
TRINIDAD AND
TOBAGO

Aruba
(NETH.)
Curaçao
(NETH.)

Cúcuta
San
Cristóbal
VENEZUELA
Ciudad
Guayana

Georgetown
Paramaribo
Cayenne

Medellín
Bucaramanga
GUYANA
SURINAME
French
Guiana
(FRANCE)

Pereira
Ibagué
★Bogotá
Cali
COLOMBIA

Boa
Vista

Isla de Malpelo
(COLOMBIA)

Macapá

Equator

★Quito
ECUADOR
Guayaquil

Amazon
Rio Negro
Amazon
Manaus
Santarém
Belém
São Luis

Cuenca
Iquitos

North
Atlantic
Ocean

Piura
Pucallpa

Rio
Branco
Pôrto
Velho

Fortaleza
Teresina
Natal
João
Pessoa
Recife

Chiclayo
Trujillo

Huánuco
PERU
Huancayo
★Lima
Ica
Cusco

Rio Madeira
Rio Purus
Rio Juruá
Rio Tapajós
Rio Xingu
Rio Tocantins
Rio Araguaia

BRAZIL

Maceió
Aracajú
Salvador

Rio São Francisco

South
Pacific
Ocean

Arequipa
La Paz★
BOLIVIA
Cochabamba
Sucre
Potosí
Santa
Cruz
Trinidad

Cuiabá
Goiânia
★Brasília

Contagem

Arica
Iquique

Rio Paraguai

Uberlândia
Belo
Horizonte
Vitória

Antofagasta
Tropic of Capricorn

PARAGUAY
Asunción★
Ciudad
del Este

Campo
Grande

Londrina
Campinas
São Paulo
Santos
Rio de Janeiro

Isla San Félix
(CHILE)
Isla San Ambrosio
(CHILE)

Salta
San Miguel
de Tucumán
Resistencia

Rio Paraná

Curitiba
Joinvile
Florianópolis

CHILE

Córdoba
Santa
Fe
Rosario
Salto
URUGUAY

Porto
Alegre

ARCHIPIÉLAGO
JUAN FERNÁNDEZ
(CHILE)

Valparaíso
★Santiago
Mendoza
Buenos Aires★
La Plata
Montevideo★

South
Atlantic
Ocean

ARGENTINA
Concepción
Temuco

Bahía Blanca
Mar del Plata

Puerto Montt
San Carlos de
Bariloche

Scale 1:35,000,000
Azimuthal Equal-Area Projection

Comodoro
Rivadavia

0   500 Kilometers
0   500 Miles

Rio
Gallegos
Strait of
Magellan
★Stanley
Falkland Islands
(Islas Malvinas)
(administered by U.K.,
claimed by ARGENTINA)

Boundary representation is
not necessarily authoritative.

Punta Arenas
Ushuaia
Cape
Horn

South Georgia and
South Sandwich Islands
(administered by U.K.,
claimed by ARGENTINA)

803543AI (G00186) 6-12

Scale 1:19,300,000
Lambert Conformal Conic Projection,
standard parallels 40°N and 68°N

803539AI (G00772) 6-12

ROM.
Bucharest ★
Sofia ★
BULGARIA
Thessaloniki
GREECE
Athens ★
Crete

Constanța
Varna
Istanbul
Bursa
İzmir
Denizli
Antalya

Black Sea
Bosporus
Dardanelles
Aegean Sea
Nicosia ★
CYPRUS

Sevastopol'
Krasnodar
Sochi

RUSSIA
Groznyy

KAZAKHSTAN
Aqtaū
(Aktau)
Aral Sea

Nukus
UZBEKISTAN
Dasoguz
Buxoro

Samsun
Trabzon
Bat'umi
GEORGIA
Tbilisi ★
ARMENIA   AZERBAIJAN
Erzurum   Yerevan ★   Baku
Sumqayıt

TURKEY
Ankara ★
Konya
Kayseri
İçel
(Mersin)
Adana
Gaziantep
Aleppo
Latakia
SYRIA
Homs

Diyarbakır
Van
Lake Van
Tabrīz
Lake Urmia
Zanjān
Rasht

Türkmenbaşy
Balkanabat
Ashgabat
Mary
TURKMENISTAN
Türkmenabat
Mashhad
Herāt
AFG.

Mosul
Erbil
Kirkuk
Kermānshāh
Arāk
Qazvin
Qom
Tehran ★
Esfahān

Mediterranean Sea
Beirut ★
LEBANON
Damascus ★
ISRAEL
Golan Heights
Tel Aviv-Yafo
West Bank
Jerusalem ★
Amman ★
Gaza Strip
Port Said
Alexandria
Suez
JORDAN
Al Aqabah
Dead Sea

Baghdad ★
IRAQ
IRAN
An Nāşirīyah
Al Başrah
Ahvāz
Abādān
Kuwait City ★
KUWAIT
Kermān
Shīrāz
Zāhedān
PAK.

Cairo ★
Al Jīzah
EGYPT
Asyūţ
Luxor
Aswān
Tropic of Cancer

Tabūk
Ḩā'il
Buraydah
Medina
Yanbu' al Baḩr
Ḩalā'ib
Gulf of Aqaba
Administrative boundary

Ḩafar al Bāţin
Al Jubayl
Ad Dammām
Dhahran
BAHRAIN
Manama ★
QATAR
Doha ★
Abu Dhabi ★
UNITED ARAB EMIRATES
Bandar Būshehr
Persian Gulf
Strait of Hormuz
Bandar 'Abbās
OMAN
Dubai
Gulf of Oman
Muscat ★

SAUDI
ARABIA
Riyadh ★
Jeddah
Mecca

Red Sea
Port Sudan
Abhā
Jīzan

SUDAN
Omdurman   Khartoum ★
Wad Medani
Kassala
ERITREA
Asmara ★
Massawa

Salālah
Al Ghaydah
OMAN
Arabian Sea

Sanaa ★
Al Hudaydah
Ta'izz
Aden
YEMEN
Al Mukallā
Socotra
(YEMEN)

ETHIOPIA
Addis Ababa ★
T'ana Hāyk'
Desē
Dirē Dawa

Bab el Mandeb
DJIBOUTI
★ Djibouti
Gulf of Aden
Boosaaso
Berbera
Hargeysa
SOMALIA
Provisional administrative line

Scale 1:21,000,000
*Lambert Conformal Conic Projection,
standard parallels 12°N and 38°N*

0   300 Kilometers
0   300 Miles

Boundary representation is
not necessarily authoritative.

Golan Heights is Israeli-occupied Syria.

West Bank is Israeli-occupied with current status subject to
the Israeli-Palestinian Interim Agreement; permanent status
to be determined through further negotiation.

The status of the Gaza Strip is a final status issue to be
resolved through negotiations.

Israel proclaimed Jerusalem as its capital in 1950, but the
US, like nearly all other countries, maintains its Embassy in
Tel Aviv-Yafo.

803540AI (G00412) 6-12

Scale 1:48,000,000
Azimuthal Equal-Area Projection

0   800 Kilometers

0   800 Miles

Boundary representation is
not necessarily authoritative.

803537AI (G00543) 6-12

Table 1362. Total World Population: 1980 to 2050

[4,450.9 represents 4,450,900,000. As of midyear]

Year	Population (mil.)	Average annual [1] Growth rate (percent)	Average annual [1] Population change (mil.)	Year	Population (mil.)	Average annual [1] Growth rate (percent)	Average annual [1] Population change (mil.)
1980............	4,450.9	1.86	82.88	2015............	7,250.1	1.06	76.94
1985............	4,855.4	1.73	83.94	2020............	7,628.4	0.96	73.14
1990............	5,287.2	1.57	82.98	2025............	7,984.5	0.85	68.08
1995............	5,699.5	1.41	80.40	2030............	8,314.6	0.76	62.84
2000............	6,089.8	1.26	76.77	2035............	8,619.0	0.67	57.90
2005............	6,473.5	1.20	77.73	2040............	8,898.9	0.60	53.02
2010............	6,863.8	1.12	76.94	2045............	9,154.0	0.52	47.90
2012............	**7,017.5**	**1.11**	**77.67**	2050............	9,383.1	(NA)	(NA)

NA Not available. [1] Represents change from year shown to immediate succeeding year.

Source: U.S. Census Bureau, International Data Base, <http://www.census.gov/ipc/www/idb/>, accessed August 2013.

Table 1363. Population by Continent: 1980 to 2050

[In millions, except percent (4,450.9 represents 4,450,900,000). As of midyear. For geographic classification of individual countries, see source]

Year	World	Africa	North America [1]	South America	Asia	Europe	Oceania
1980............................	4,450.9	478.6	370.8	239.7	2,644.1	695.2	22.5
1990............................	5,287.2	630.1	423.6	294.9	3,189.5	722.6	26.4
2000............................	6,089.8	803.6	485.7	345.6	3,693.9	730.6	30.4
2010............................	6,863.8	1,024.4	537.2	390.0	4,138.8	738.4	34.9
2012............................	**7,017.5**	**1,073.5**	**546.5**	**398.1**	**4,223.6**	**740.0**	**35.8**
2020............................	7,628.4	1,286.5	587.9	428.0	4,542.5	744.1	39.3
2030............................	8,314.6	1,579.5	636.7	459.2	4,857.7	738.3	43.1
2040............................	8,898.9	1,898.7	679.6	480.2	5,070.2	724.1	46.1
2050............................	9,383.1	2,232.4	717.7	490.0	5,192.7	701.9	48.5
PERCENT DISTRIBUTION							
1980............................	100.0	10.75	8.33	5.39	59.41	15.62	0.51
2000............................	100.0	13.20	7.98	5.67	60.66	12.00	0.50
2012............................	**100.0**	**15.30**	**7.79**	**5.67**	**60.19**	**10.55**	**0.51**
2030............................	100.0	19.00	7.66	5.52	58.42	8.88	0.52
2050............................	100.0	23.79	7.65	5.22	55.34	7.48	0.52

[1] Data for North America include Central America and Caribbean area.

Source: U.S. Census Bureau, International Data Base, <http://www.census.gov/ipc/www/idb/>, accessed August 2013.

Table 1364. Population and Population Change by Development Status: 1950 to 2050

[2,557.6 represents 2,557,600,000. As of midyear. The "less developed" countries include all of Africa, all of Asia except Japan, the Transcaucasian and Central Asian republics, all of Latin America and the Caribbean, and all of Oceania except Australia, New Zealand, and Hawaii. For details on classification of individual countries, see source]

Year	Number (millions) World	Number (millions) Less developed countries	Number (millions) More developed countries	Percent of world Less developed countries	Percent of world More developed countries
POPULATION					
1950........................	2,557.6	1,750.6	807.1	68.44	31.56
1960........................	3,042.8	2,132.1	910.8	70.07	29.93
1970........................	3,712.3	2,708.7	1,003.6	72.97	27.03
1980........................	4,450.9	3,369.2	1,081.7	75.70	24.30
1990........................	5,287.2	4,143.1	1,144.1	78.36	21.64
2000........................	6,089.8	4,896.2	1,193.6	80.40	19.60
2010........................	6,863.8	5,628.8	1,235.0	82.01	17.99
2012........................	**7,017.5**	**5,775.5**	**1,242.0**	**82.30**	**17.70**
2020........................	7,628.4	6,356.9	1,271.5	83.33	16.67
2030........................	8,314.6	7,020.1	1,294.4	84.43	15.57
2040........................	8,898.9	7,593.5	1,305.4	85.33	14.67
2050........................	9,383.1	8,076.0	1,307.1	86.07	13.93
POPULATION CHANGE					
1950–1960....................	485.2	381.5	103.7	78.63	21.37
1960–1970....................	669.5	576.7	92.9	86.13	13.87
1970–1980....................	738.6	660.5	78.1	89.42	10.58
1980–1990....................	836.2	773.9	62.3	92.55	7.45
1990–2000....................	802.6	753.1	49.5	93.83	6.17
2000–2010....................	774.0	732.6	41.4	94.65	5.35
2010–2020....................	764.6	728.1	36.5	95.23	4.77
2020–2030....................	686.2	663.3	22.9	96.66	3.34
2030–2040....................	584.4	573.4	11.0	98.12	1.88
2040–2050....................	484.2	482.5	1.7	99.64	0.36

Source: U.S. Census Bureau, International Data Base, <http://www.census.gov/ipc/www/idb/>, accessed August 2013.

Table 1365. Population and Land Area by Country or Territory: 2000 to 2020

[6,089,811 represents 6,089,811,000. Covers countries or territories with populations of 5,000 or more in 2012. Population estimates were derived from information available as of June 2012. See text of this section for general comments concerning the data. For details of methodology, coverage, and reliability, see source. Minus sign (-) indicates decrease]

Country or territory	Map refer-ence [1]	Mid-year population (1,000) 2000	Mid-year population (1,000) 2010	Mid-year population (1,000) 2012	Mid-year population (1,000) 2020, proj.	World-wide rank, 2012	Annual growth rate [2] 2010-2020	Popula-tion per sq. mile, 2012	Land area [3] (sq. mile)
World	**S0**	**6,089,811**	**6,863,771**	**7,017,544**	**7,628,362**	**(X)**	**1.06**	**138**	**50,989,248**
Afghanistan	S6	22,461	29,121	30,420	36,644	40	2.30	121	251,827
Albania	S4	3,158	2,987	3,003	3,075	137	0.29	284	10,578
Algeria	S5	30,638	35,950	37,367	42,973	34	1.78	41	919,595
Andorra	S4	65	85	85	86	201	0.13	471	181
Angola	S5	12,683	17,043	18,056	22,484	59	2.77	38	481,354
Antigua and Barbuda	S2	75	87	89	98	200	1.24	521	171
Argentina	S3	37,336	41,343	42,192	45,379	32	0.93	40	1,056,642
Armenia	S6	3,043	2,967	2,970	3,017	138	0.17	273	10,889
Australia	S8	19,053	21,516	22,016	23,939	53	1.07	8	2,966,153
Austria	S4	8,113	8,214	8,220	8,220	94	0.01	258	31,832
Azerbaijan	S6	8,463	9,302	9,494	10,206	91	0.93	298	31,903
Bahamas, The	S2	283	310	316	338	178	0.84	82	3,865
Bahrain	S6	655	1,180	1,248	1,505	157	2.43	4,254	293
Bangladesh	S7	132,151	156,118	161,084	183,109	8	1.59	3,205	50,258
Barbados	S2	274	286	288	295	180	0.31	1,733	166
Belarus	S4	10,033	9,680	9,644	9,478	89	-0.21	123	78,340
Belgium	S4	10,264	10,423	10,438	10,465	82	0.04	893	11,690
Belize	S2	248	315	328	380	177	1.88	37	8,805
Benin	S5	6,619	9,056	9,599	11,956	90	2.78	225	42,711
Bhutan	S7	606	700	717	782	165	1.11	48	14,824
Bolivia	S3	8,195	9,947	10,290	11,640	83	1.57	25	418,265
Bosnia and Herzegovina	S4	3,806	3,885	3,879	3,836	128	-0.13	196	19,763
Botswana	S5	1,680	2,029	2,098	2,312	144	1.30	10	218,816
Brazil	S3	174,315	195,834	199,321	211,716	5	0.78	61	3,266,199
Brunei	S8	325	395	409	464	175	1.62	201	2,033
Bulgaria	S4	7,818	7,149	7,038	6,569	100	-0.85	168	41,888
Burkina Faso	S5	11,588	16,242	17,275	21,978	61	3.02	163	105,715
Burma	S7	47,439	53,414	54,585	59,126	24	1.02	216	252,321
Burundi	S5	6,823	9,863	10,557	13,429	81	3.09	1,065	9,915
Cambodia	S7	12,351	14,454	14,953	16,927	68	1.58	219	68,153
Cameroon	S5	15,343	19,294	20,130	23,471	58	1.96	110	182,514
Canada	S1	31,100	33,760	34,300	36,387	35	0.75	10	3,511,023
Cape Verde	S5	430	509	524	583	171	1.37	336	1,557
Central African Republic	S5	3,980	4,845	5,057	5,991	117	2.12	21	240,535
Chad	S5	7,943	10,543	10,976	12,756	75	1.90	23	486,180
Chile	S3	15,175	16,760	17,067	18,187	62	0.82	59	287,187
China	S7	1,263,638	1,330,141	1,343,240	1,384,545	1	0.40	364	3,694,959
Colombia	S3	38,910	44,205	45,239	49,085	29	1.05	113	401,044
Comoros	S5	545	706	737	846	164	1.81	854	863
Congo, Republic of	S5	3,104	4,126	4,366	5,444	124	2.77	33	131,854
Congo, Democratic Republic	S5	52,445	69,851	73,599	89,250	19	2.45	84	875,312
Costa Rica	S2	3,883	4,516	4,636	5,098	121	1.21	235	19,714
Cote d'Ivoire	S5	16,885	21,059	21,952	25,504	55	1.92	179	122,782
Croatia	S4	4,411	4,487	4,480	4,427	123	-0.13	207	21,612
Cuba	S2	11,072	11,098	11,075	10,932	74	-0.15	261	42,402
Cyprus	S6	920	1,103	1,138	1,267	160	1.39	319	3,568
Czech Republic	S4	10,270	10,202	10,177	10,013	84	-0.19	341	29,825
Denmark	S4	5,337	5,516	5,543	5,642	110	0.23	338	16,384
Djibouti	S5	669	741	774	922	162	2.19	87	8,950
Dominica	S2	71	73	73	74	203	0.19	252	290
Dominican Republic	S2	8,469	9,824	10,089	11,109	85	1.23	541	18,656
Ecuador	S3	12,446	14,791	15,224	16,905	67	1.34	142	106,889
Egypt	S5	65,159	80,472	83,688	96,260	15	1.79	218	384,345
El Salvador	S2	5,850	6,052	6,091	6,217	106	0.27	761	8,000
Equatorial Guinea	S5	491	651	686	836	166	2.51	63	10,831
Eritrea	S5	4,197	5,793	6,086	7,260	107	2.26	156	38,996
Estonia	S4	1,380	1,291	1,275	1,203	156	-0.71	78	16,366
Ethiopia	S5	64,365	86,043	91,196	114,640	14	2.87	236	386,102
Fiji	S8	805	876	890	936	161	0.66	126	7,056
Finland	S4	5,169	5,255	5,263	5,272	116	0.03	45	117,304
France	S4	61,255	64,941	65,631	67,848	21	0.44	265	247,270
Gabon	S5	1,236	1,545	1,608	1,877	153	1.94	16	99,486
Gambia, The	S5	1,357	1,755	1,840	2,174	149	2.14	477	3,861
Georgia	S6	4,777	4,601	4,571	4,440	122	-0.36	170	26,911
Germany [4]	S4	82,184	81,644	81,306	80,160	16	-0.18	604	134,623
Ghana	S5	18,981	23,571	24,652	29,340	48	2.19	280	87,851
Greece	S4	10,559	10,750	10,768	10,742	78	-0.01	213	50,443
Grenada	S2	102	108	109	113	191	0.48	821	133
Guatemala	S2	11,085	13,550	14,099	16,264	69	1.83	341	41,374
Guinea	S5	8,350	10,324	10,885	13,420	76	2.62	115	94,872
Guinea-Bissau	S5	1,279	1,565	1,629	1,893	152	1.90	150	10,857
Guyana	S3	786	748	742	754	163	0.08	10	76,004
Haiti	S2	8,413	9,649	9,802	10,693	88	1.03	921	10,641
Honduras	S2	6,359	7,989	8,297	9,465	93	1.69	192	43,201
Hungary	S4	10,147	9,992	9,958	9,772	87	-0.22	288	34,598
Iceland	S1	281	309	313	329	179	0.63	8	38,707
India	S7	1,006,300	1,173,108	1,205,074	1,326,093	2	1.23	1,050	1,147,956
Indonesia	S8	214,091	243,423	248,645	267,026	4	0.93	356	699,451
Iran	S6	68,652	76,923	78,869	86,543	18	1.18	133	591,352
Iraq	S6	22,679	29,672	31,129	36,889	39	2.18	184	168,868
Ireland	S4	3,822	4,623	4,722	5,177	119	1.13	178	26,596

See footnotes at end of table.

Country or territory	Map refer-ence [1]	Mid-year population (1,000)				World-wide rank, 2012	Annual growth rate [2] 2010-2020	Popula-tion per sq. mile, 2012	Land area [3] (sq. mile)
		2000	2010	2012	2020, proj.				
Israel	S6	6,115	7,354	7,591	8,479	97	1.42	967	7,849
Italy	S4	57,784	60,749	61,261	62,403	23	0.27	539	113,568
Jamaica	S2	2,616	2,847	2,889	3,051	139	0.69	691	4,182
Japan	S7	126,776	127,579	127,368	125,507	10	-0.16	905	140,728
Jordan	S6	4,688	6,407	6,509	7,278	104	1.27	190	34,287
Kazakhstan	S7	15,687	17,085	17,522	19,092	60	1.11	17	1,042,360
Kenya	S5	30,606	40,843	43,013	49,858	31	1.99	196	219,746
Kiribati	S8	85	99	102	112	197	1.17	326	313
Korea, North	S7	22,785	24,326	24,589	25,643	49	0.53	529	46,490
Korea, South	S7	46,839	48,636	48,861	49,362	25	0.15	1,306	37,421
Kosovo	S4	1,700	1,815	1,837	1,933	150	0.63	437	4,203
Kuwait	S6	1,972	2,543	2,646	2,994	140	1.63	385	6,880
Kyrgyzstan	S6	4,937	5,410	5,497	5,965	111	0.98	74	74,055
Laos	S7	5,397	6,368	6,586	7,447	102	1.57	74	89,112
Latvia	S4	2,376	2,218	2,192	2,077	142	-0.65	91	24,034
Lebanon	S6	3,791	4,125	4,140	4,243	126	0.28	1,048	3,950
Lesotho	S5	1,916	1,920	1,930	1,969	148	0.26	165	11,720
Liberia	S5	2,601	3,685	3,888	4,727	127	2.49	105	37,189
Libya	S5	5,025	6,110	5,613	6,943	109	1.28	8	679,362
Liechtenstein	S4	33	36	37	39	214	0.80	594	62
Lithuania	S4	3,654	3,545	3,526	3,435	131	-0.32	146	24,201
Luxembourg	S4	439	498	509	556	173	1.11	510	998
Macedonia	S4	2,015	2,072	2,082	2,113	145	0.19	212	9,820
Madagascar	S5	15,712	20,847	22,005	26,956	54	2.57	98	224,534
Malawi	S5	11,802	15,448	16,323	20,204	65	2.68	449	36,324
Malaysia	S8	23,151	28,275	29,180	32,652	43	1.44	230	126,895
Maldives	S7	300	396	394	392	176	-0.10	3,428	115
Mali	S5	10,788	14,583	15,494	19,623	66	2.97	33	471,118
Malta	S4	390	407	410	419	174	0.30	3,359	122
Marshall Islands	S8	53	66	68	78	209	1.68	980	70
Mauritania	S5	2,501	3,205	3,359	4,005	133	2.23	9	397,955
Mauritius	S5	1,186	1,294	1,313	1,379	155	0.64	1,675	784
Mexico	S1	99,927	112,469	114,975	124,654	11	1.03	153	750,561
Micronesia, Federated States of	S8	108	107	106	102	192	-0.45	393	271
Moldova	S4	4,180	3,732	3,657	3,364	130	-1.04	288	12,699
Monaco	S4	32	31	31	31	219	0.12	39,510	1
Mongolia	S7	2,664	3,087	3,180	3,535	135	1.36	5	599,831
Montenegro	S4	732	667	657	639	167	-0.42	127	5,194
Morocco	S5	28,113	31,627	32,309	34,956	38	1.00	188	172,317
Mozambique	S5	17,997	22,417	23,516	28,603	50	2.44	77	303,623
Namibia	S5	1,893	2,128	2,166	2,263	143	0.61	7	317,874
Nauru	S8	10	9	9	10	225	0.54	1,157	8
Nepal	S7	24,818	28,952	29,891	34,209	41	1.67	540	55,348
Netherlands	S4	15,930	16,574	16,731	17,280	63	0.42	1,278	13,086
New Zealand	S8	3,802	4,252	4,328	4,615	125	0.82	42	103,363
Nicaragua	S2	4,866	5,604	5,728	6,203	108	1.02	124	46,328
Niger	S5	10,725	15,270	16,345	21,151	64	3.26	33	489,076
Nigeria	S5	124,207	161,605	170,124	207,699	7	2.51	484	351,649
Norway	S4	4,492	4,676	4,707	4,836	120	0.34	40	117,484
Oman	S6	2,432	2,968	3,090	3,635	136	2.03	26	119,499
Pakistan	S6	152,429	184,405	190,291	213,719	6	1.48	639	297,637
Palau	S8	19	21	21	22	223	0.38	119	177
Panama	S2	2,900	3,411	3,510	3,894	132	1.33	122	28,703
Papua New Guinea	S8	4,813	6,065	6,310	7,259	105	1.80	36	174,850
Paraguay	S3	5,418	6,376	6,542	7,192	103	1.20	43	153,399
Peru	S3	25,797	28,948	29,550	31,915	42	0.98	60	494,209
Philippines	S7	81,222	99,900	103,775	119,329	12	1.78	901	115,124
Poland	S4	38,654	38,464	38,415	37,949	33	-0.13	327	117,474
Portugal	S4	10,336	10,736	10,781	10,842	77	0.10	305	35,317
Qatar	S6	640	1,719	1,952	2,444	147	3.52	436	4,473
Romania	S4	22,447	21,959	21,849	21,303	56	-0.30	246	88,761
Russia	S7	147,054	142,527	142,518	141,722	9	-0.06	23	6,323,482
Rwanda	S5	8,398	11,056	11,690	14,327	73	2.59	1,227	9,524
Saint Kitts and Nevis	S2	46	50	51	54	213	0.76	503	101
Saint Lucia	S2	153	161	162	166	189	0.34	693	234
Saint Vincent and the Grenadines	S2	108	104	104	101	195	-0.28	689	150
Samoa	S8	176	192	194	204	185	0.60	178	1,089
San Marino	S4	27	31	32	34	217	0.84	1,365	24
Sao Tome and Principe	S5	141	176	183	211	186	1.83	492	372
Saudi Arabia	S6	21,312	25,732	26,535	29,819	46	1.47	32	830,000
Senegal	S5	9,469	12,323	12,970	15,736	71	2.44	175	74,336
Serbia	S4	7,604	7,345	7,277	7,012	98	-0.46	243	29,913
Seychelles	S5	79	88	90	96	198	0.83	513	176
Sierra Leone	S5	3,809	5,246	5,486	6,625	112	2.33	198	27,653
Singapore	S8	4,063	5,140	5,353	6,210	114	1.89	20,183	265
Slovakia	S4	5,400	5,470	5,483	5,494	113	0.04	295	18,573
Slovenia	S4	2,011	2,003	1,997	1,951	146	-0.26	257	7,780
Solomon Islands	S8	434	559	585	685	168	2.03	54	10,805
Somalia	S5	7,501	9,768	10,086	11,757	86	1.85	42	242,216
South Africa	S5	45,064	49,109	48,810	48,530	26	-0.12	104	468,909
South Sudan [5]	S5	6,296	9,584	10,625	14,558	80	4.18	43	248,777
Spain	S4	40,589	46,506	47,043	50,016	27	0.73	244	192,657
Sri Lanka	S7	19,041	21,084	21,481	22,889	57	0.82	861	24,954

See footnotes at end of table.

Table 1365. Population and Land Area by Country or Territory: 2000 to 2020-Continued.

See headnote on page 871.

Country or territory	Map refer-ence [1]	Mid-year population (1,000)				World-wide rank, 2012	Annual growth rate [2] 2010-2020	Popula-tion per sq. mile, 2012	Land area [3] (sq. mile)
		2000	2010	2012	2020, proj.				
Sudan [5]	S5	27,067	32,997	34,207	39,161	36	1.71	48	718,723
Suriname	S3	464	546	560	610	170	1.10	9	60,232
Swaziland	S5	1,144	1,354	1,387	1,513	154	1.11	209	6,643
Sweden	S4	8,924	9,074	9,104	9,245	92	0.19	57	158,431
Switzerland	S4	7,277	7,770	7,926	8,404	95	0.78	513	15,443
Syria	S6	16,471	22,198	22,531	24,744	52	1.09	318	70,900
Tajikistan	S6	22,185	23,127	23,235	23,603	51	0.20	1,865	12,456
Tanzania	S5	6,230	7,487	7,768	8,874	96	1.70	142	54,637
Taiwan		33,193	44,288	46,913	58,553	28	2.79	137	342,009
Thailand	S7	61,904	66,336	67,091	69,558	20	0.47	340	197,256
Timor-Leste	S8	767	1,088	1,144	1,384	159	2.41	199	5,743
Togo	S5	4,992	6,587	6,961	8,608	101	2.68	332	20,998
Tonga	S8	100	106	106	106	194	0.04	383	277
Trinidad and Tobago	S2	1,252	1,229	1,226	1,209	158	-0.16	620	1,980
Tunisia	S5	9,508	10,525	10,733	11,494	79	0.88	179	59,985
Turkey	S6	67,329	77,804	79,749	86,757	17	1.09	268	297,157
Turkmenistan	S6	4,385	4,941	5,055	5,529	118	1.12	28	181,441
Tuvalu	S8	10	10	11	11	224	0.80	1,058	10
Uganda	S5	22,916	31,507	33,641	43,518	37	3.23	442	76,101
Ukraine	S4	49,005	45,416	44,854	42,561	30	-0.65	200	223,581
United Arab Emirates	S6	3,219	4,976	5,314	6,495	115	2.67	165	32,278
United Kingdom	S4	59,140	62,348	63,047	65,761	22	0.53	675	93,410
United States	**S1**	**282,162**	**309,330**	**313,847**	**336,836**	**3**	**0.85**	**89**	**3,531,905**
Uruguay	S3	3,220	3,301	3,316	3,388	134	0.26	49	67,574
Uzbekistan	S6	25,042	27,866	28,394	30,565	44	0.92	173	164,248
Vanuatu	S8	191	245	256	298	183	1.96	54	4,706
Venezuela	S3	23,493	27,223	28,048	31,276	45	1.39	82	340,561
Vietnam	S7	79,178	89,571	91,519	98,721	13	0.97	765	119,719
Yemen	S6	17,407	23,495	24,772	29,727	47	2.35	121	203,850
Zambia	S5	9,984	13,042	13,817	17,427	70	2.90	48	287,028
Zimbabwe	S5	11,820	11,652	12,620	15,832	72	3.07	84	149,362
TERRITORIES AND DEPENDENCIES									
American Samoa	S8	58	55	55	54	206	-0.31	715	77
Anguilla	S1	11	15	15	18	221	2.03	439	35
Aruba	S1	90	105	108	119	190	1.33	1,549	69
Bermuda	S1	63	68	69	72	202	0.50	3,313	21
Cayman Islands	S1	38	50	53	62	207	2.10	516	102
Cook Islands	S8	16	11	11	9	222	-2.93	118	91
Curacao [6]	S2	134	143	146	151	188	0.54	851	171
Faroe Islands	S4	46	49	49	52	210	0.51	92	538
French Polynesia	S8	236	269	275	295	181	0.93	186	1,478
Gaza Strip [7]	S6	1,130	1,604	1,710	2,121	151	2.79	12,304	139
Gibraltar	S4	27	29	29	30	218	0.24	11,569	3
Greenland	S1	57	58	58	58	205	0.00	(Z)	836,330
Guam	S8	155	159	160	168	187	0.54	761	210
Guernsey	S4	62	65	65	67	204	0.35	2,170	30
Hong Kong	S7	6,659	7,090	7,154	7,328	99	0.33	17,578	407
Isle of Man	S4	76	84	85	90	199	0.76	387	221
Jersey	S4	87	93	95	101	196	0.79	2,120	45
Macau	S7	432	568	578	614	169	0.79	53,088	11
Mayotte	S5	157	206	(NA)	229	184	1.03	(NA)	144
Montserrat	S2	4	5	5	5	228	0.49	131	39
New Caledonia	S8	211	252	260	290	182	1.39	37	7,056
Northern Mariana Islands	S8	70	54	51	58	208	0.75	287	179
Puerto Rico	S2	3,811	3,722	3,691	3,528	129	-0.54	1,078	3,424
Saint Barthelemy	S2	7	7	7	7	226	-0.39	904	8
Saint Helena	S5	7	8	8	8	225	0.25	65	119
Saint Martin	S2	28	30	31	33	216	0.74	1,474	21
Saint Pierre and Miquelon	S1	6	6	6	5	227	-1.06	62	93
Sint Maarten [6]	S2	31	38	39	44	212	1.46	2,977	13
Turks and Caicos Islands	S2	19	43	46	56	211	2.58	127	366
Virgin Islands, British	S2	23	30	31	37	215	2.32	534	58
Virgin Islands, U.S.	S2	109	106	105	100	193	-0.59	788	134
Wallis and Futuna	S8	15	15	15	16	220	0.33	282	55
West Bank [7]	S6	1,980	2,515	2,623	3,058	141	1.96	1,204	2,178
Western Sahara	S5	336	492	523	652	172	2.83	5	102,703

X Not applicable. NA Not available. Z Less than 0.05 percent. [1] See maps for geographic locations, as indicated. [2] Computed by the exponential method. For explanation of average annual percent change, see Guide to Tabular Presentation. [3] Data converted from square kilometers to square miles. [4] Data for 1990 are for former West Germany and East Germany combined. [5] Sudan and South Sudan became separate countries in July 2011. [6] The Netherlands Antilles dissolved on October 10, 2010. Curacao and Sint Maarten became autonomous territories of the Kingdom of the Netherlands. [7] The Gaza Strip and West Bank are Israeli occupied with interim status subject to Israeli/Palestinian negotiations. The final status is yet to be determined.

Source: U.S. Census Bureau, International Data Base, <http://www.census.gov/ipc/www/idb/>, accessed September 2013.

Table 1366. Foreign or Foreign-Born Population, Labor Force, and Net Migration in Selected OECD Countries: 2000 to 2009

[30,273 represents 30,273,000. In Australia and the United States, the data refer to residents who are foreign born. In the European countries and Japan, they represent the legal nationality or citizenship status of residents. Data are based on censuses, population registers, residence permits, and/or labor force surveys. For details about data methodology for individual countries, see source. Minus sign (-) indicates net loss]

Country	Foreign population				Foreign labor force				Average net migration 1990-2009 (per 1,000 population)
	Number (1,000)		Percent of total population		Number (1,000)				
	2000	2009	2000	2009	2000	2005	2008	2009	
United States........	**30,273**	**38,453**	**11.0**	**12.7**	**18,029**	**22,422**	**25,086**	**24,815**	**3.9**
Australia..............	4,412	5,804	23.0	26.5	2,373	2,618	3,000	3,144	6.0
Austria...............	702	895	8.8	10.7	320	374	474	479	3.8
Belgium..............	862	1,058	8.4	9.8	388	440	469	498	3.2
Denmark..............	259	330	4.8	6.0	101	115	145	(NA)	2.4
France................	(NA)	(NA)	(NA)	(NA)	1,578	1,406	1,558	1,540	1.3
Germany..............	7,297	6,695	8.9	8.2	3,546	3,823	3,893	(NA)	3.8
Italy..................	1,380	4,235	2.4	7.1	838	1,419	1,387	(NA)	3.7
Japan.................	1,686	2,185	1.3	1.7	155	180	212	213	-0.1
Luxembourg..........	165	216	37.3	43.8	153	196	233	231	10.3
Netherlands..........	668	735	4.2	4.4	300	287	(NA)	(NA)	1.8
Spain.................	1,371	5,748	(NA)	12.4	455	1,689	1,882	(NA)	7.0
Sweden...............	472	595	5.4	6.4	222	177	(NA)	(NA)	3.4
Switzerland..........	1,384	1,680	19.3	21.7	717	830	927	974	5.0
United Kingdom......	2,342	4,348	4.0	7.1	1,107	1,504	2,278	2,280	1.4

NA Not available.

Source: Organisation for Economic Co-operation and Development (OECD), 2012, "International Migration Database," OECD International Migration Statistics (database) ©, <http://dx.doi.org/10.1787/data-00342-en>; and *International Migration Outlook 2011*, OECD Publishing (2011) ©, <http://dx.doi.org/10.1787/migr_outlook-2011-55-en>; accessed August 2012.

Table 1367. Youth and Elderly Population Distribution by Country: 2012 and 2020

[Percent of total population, as of mid-year. Covers countries with 11 million or more population in 2012]

Country	2012		2020, proj.		Country	2012		2020, proj.	
	Under 15 years old	65 years old and over	Under 15 years old	65 years old and over		Under 15 years old	65 years old and over	Under 15 years old	65 years old and over
World..............	**26.2**	**8.0**	**24.8**	**9.6**	Malawi..............	44.9	2.7	43.1	2.8
					Malaysia............	29.4	5.1	26.8	6.9
Afghanistan..........	43.2	2.5	40.6	2.7	Mali.................	47.8	3.0	46.3	2.9
Algeria..............	27.8	5.0	29.6	6.2	Mexico..............	27.8	6.7	25.0	8.3
Angola...............	43.9	2.9	42.1	3.1	Morocco.............	27.4	6.2	24.9	7.5
Argentina............	25.2	11.1	23.7	12.4	Mozambique........	45.7	3.0	44.1	2.9
Australia.............	18.2	14.4	17.6	17.0	Nepal...............	33.5	4.4	27.6	5.1
Bangladesh..........	33.6	4.8	28.3	5.8	Netherlands.........	17.2	16.6	16.1	19.8
Brazil................	24.7	7.1	21.1	9.2	Niger...............	50.1	2.6	47.9	2.7
Burkina Faso........	45.7	2.5	44.3	2.4	Nigeria.............	43.9	3.0	42.2	3.1
Burma...............	27.1	5.1	24.7	6.2	Pakistan............	34.7	4.2	29.7	4.8
Cambodia............	31.9	3.8	30.2	4.6	Peru................	28.1	6.5	25.4	8.0
Cameroon............	40.3	3.4	37.4	3.7	Philippines.........	34.3	4.3	31.6	5.4
Canada...............	15.6	16.4	15.4	20.1	Poland..............	14.6	14.0	14.6	18.6
Chile................	21.4	9.4	19.8	11.8	Romania............	14.8	14.9	14.1	17.6
China................	17.4	9.1	17.0	12.4	Russia..............	15.7	13.0	17.2	15.5
Colombia............	26.2	6.3	23.3	8.4	Rwanda.............	42.6	2.4	40.0	2.9
Congo, Dem. Rep....	43.9	2.6	40.3	2.7	Saudi Arabia........	28.8	3.0	25.0	3.8
Cote d'Ivoire.........	39.3	3.1	35.6	3.7	Senegal.............	43.0	2.9	40.4	3.1
Cuba................	17.0	12.0	14.9	14.5	South Africa.........	28.4	5.9	26.9	7.4
Ecuador..............	29.5	6.6	25.8	8.1	Spain...............	15.3	17.3	15.0	18.5
Egypt................	32.5	4.7	30.3	6.0	Sri Lanka...........	24.9	8.1	23.1	10.6
Ethiopia.............	44.6	2.8	42.7	3.0	Sudan [1]...........	42.0	3.3	36.5	3.4
France...............	18.7	17.5	18.4	20.5	Syria...............	34.6	3.8	30.0	4.6
Germany.............	13.2	20.7	12.9	23.0	Taiwan..............	14.7	11.3	12.4	15.7
Ghana...............	38.9	4.0	37.4	4.4	Tanzania............	45.0	2.9	42.7	3.1
Guatemala............	37.4	4.0	33.0	4.9	Thailand............	19.5	9.5	18.1	12.4
India................	29.3	5.6	26.3	6.7	Turkey..............	26.2	6.4	23.4	8.1
Indonesia............	27.0	6.4	23.9	7.8	Uganda.............	49.1	2.1	47.4	1.9
Iran.................	23.9	5.1	23.3	6.1	Ukraine.............	13.8	15.5	14.5	17.8
Iraq.................	37.6	3.1	33.7	3.9	United Kingdom....	17.3	16.9	17.6	18.5
Italy.................	13.8	20.5	13.4	22.1	United States......	**20.0**	**13.5**	**19.8**	**16.2**
Japan................	13.5	23.9	12.5	29.2	Uzbekistan.........	25.8	4.7	23.2	5.9
Kazakhstan..........	24.4	6.7	26.1	8.4	Venezuela..........	29.0	5.6	26.1	7.4
Kenya...............	42.5	2.7	36.8	3.3	Vietnam............	24.9	5.5	22.6	6.9
Korea, North.........	22.0	9.3	20.5	9.7	Yemen..............	42.5	2.6	37.3	3.0
Korea, South........	15.1	11.9	12.6	15.6	Zambia.............	46.3	2.4	45.7	2.3
Madagascar..........	41.4	3.1	38.9	3.5	Zimbabwe..........	40.6	3.7	37.5	3.6

[1] Data for Sudan exclude South Sudan, which became an independent country in July 2011.

Source: U.S. Census Bureau, International Data Base, <http://www.census.gov/ipc/www/idb/>, accessed September 2013.

Table 1368. Births, Deaths, and Life Expectancy by Country or Territory: 2012 and 2020

[Covers countries with 12 million or more population in 2012]

Country or territory	Crude birth rate [1] 2012	Crude birth rate [1] 2020, proj.	Crude death rate [2] 2012	Crude death rate [2] 2020, proj.	Expectation of life at birth (years) 2012	Expectation of life at birth (years) 2020, proj.	Infant mortality rate [3] 2012	Infant mortality rate [3] 2020, proj.	Total fertility rate per woman [4] 2012	Total fertility rate per woman [4] 2020, proj.
World..................	19.1	17.4	7.9	7.9	67.8	69.7	38.6	31.8	2.46	2.36
Afghanistan............	39.3	36.7	14.6	12.7	49.7	52.8	121.6	104.3	5.64	4.82
Algeria.................	24.4	20.0	4.3	4.4	76.0	77.5	23.4	17.6	2.78	2.59
Angola.................	39.4	37.5	12.1	10.5	54.6	57.5	83.5	69.9	5.54	5.07
Argentina..............	17.3	15.6	7.4	7.3	77.1	78.5	10.5	8.5	2.29	2.15
Australia..............	12.3	11.9	6.9	7.5	81.9	82.5	4.6	4.1	1.77	1.76
Bangladesh............	22.5	19.5	5.7	5.6	70.1	72.4	49.0	36.8	2.55	2.24
Brazil.................	15.2	13.6	6.5	6.9	72.8	74.7	20.5	15.9	1.82	1.73
Burkina Faso..........	43.2	39.9	12.5	10.6	54.1	56.9	79.8	67.8	6.07	5.49
Burma.................	19.1	17.3	8.1	7.9	65.2	68.0	47.7	37.2	2.23	2.09
Cambodia..............	25.2	21.3	8.0	7.3	63.0	65.9	54.1	43.7	2.78	2.39
Cameroon..............	32.5	28.3	11.7	10.7	54.7	57.0	59.7	50.4	4.09	3.47
Canada................	10.3	10.1	8.1	9.0	81.5	82.2	4.9	4.4	1.59	1.61
Chile..................	14.3	13.1	5.8	6.5	78.1	79.4	7.4	6.2	1.87	1.77
China.................	12.3	11.0	7.2	8.3	74.8	76.0	15.6	12.6	1.55	1.58
Colombia..............	17.2	15.4	5.3	5.6	74.8	76.6	15.9	12.3	2.12	1.94
Congo, Democratic Republic.	37.1	31.3	10.8	9.1	55.7	58.8	76.6	63.6	5.09	3.99
Cote d'Ivoire..........	30.4	26.1	10.0	9.1	57.3	59.9	63.2	51.6	3.82	3.15
Ecuador...............	19.6	17.0	5.0	5.2	75.9	77.5	19.1	15.0	2.38	2.09
Egypt.................	24.2	20.8	4.8	4.8	72.9	74.9	24.2	17.9	2.94	2.67
Ethiopia...............	38.5	35.2	9.3	7.2	59.2	63.7	60.9	45.6	5.39	4.75
France................	12.7	11.9	8.9	9.6	81.5	82.2	3.4	3.2	2.08	2.06
Germany..............	8.3	8.6	11.0	12.1	80.2	81.1	3.5	3.3	1.41	1.47
Ghana.................	32.0	29.6	7.7	6.6	64.9	68.2	40.9	32.1	4.15	3.90
Guatemala.............	26.5	22.7	4.9	4.6	71.2	73.4	25.2	19.2	3.18	2.57
India.................	20.6	18.2	7.4	7.3	67.1	69.7	46.1	35.4	2.58	2.35
Indonesia.............	17.7	15.4	6.3	6.6	71.6	73.7	27.0	20.4	2.23	2.04
Iran..................	18.5	16.2	5.9	6.0	70.4	72.4	41.1	33.6	1.87	1.81
Iraq..................	28.2	23.4	4.7	4.3	70.9	73.1	40.3	30.3	3.58	2.96
Italy..................	9.1	8.4	9.9	10.7	81.9	82.5	3.4	3.2	1.40	1.47
Japan.................	8.4	7.3	9.2	10.2	83.9	86.0	2.2	1.9	1.39	1.43
Kazakhstan............	20.4	16.4	8.5	8.2	69.6	72.0	23.1	17.9	2.41	2.16
Kenya.................	31.9	20.8	7.3	6.6	63.1	65.1	43.6	34.0	3.98	2.57
Korea, North..........	14.5	14.5	9.1	9.4	69.2	71.6	26.2	20.0	2.01	1.92
Korea, South..........	8.4	8.2	6.4	7.6	79.3	81.1	4.1	3.6	1.23	1.29
Madagascar............	34.0	29.9	7.3	6.2	64.5	67.3	47.4	37.8	4.45	3.78
Malawi................	40.4	36.5	12.8	10.9	52.3	55.3	79.0	63.1	5.35	4.68
Malaysia..............	20.7	18.3	5.0	5.3	74.0	75.9	14.6	11.4	2.64	2.43
Mali..................	46.6	41.8	13.9	11.3	54.2	57.3	108.7	91.6	6.35	5.51
Mexico................	18.9	17.0	4.9	5.3	76.7	78.1	16.8	13.2	2.27	2.14
Morocco...............	19.0	16.9	4.8	5.0	76.1	77.7	26.5	19.5	2.19	2.07
Mozambique...........	39.3	37.2	12.8	10.9	52.0	54.8	76.9	60.5	5.40	4.90
Nepal.................	21.9	19.7	6.8	6.4	66.5	69.2	43.1	33.2	2.41	2.11
Netherlands...........	10.9	11.0	8.4	9.2	80.9	81.7	3.7	3.5	1.78	1.77
Niger.................	47.6	42.5	13.4	11.0	54.0	57.1	89.7	76.1	7.16	6.08
Nigeria...............	39.2	36.2	13.5	11.5	52.1	55.2	74.4	63.5	5.38	4.88
Pakistan..............	24.3	20.7	6.8	6.2	66.4	69.0	61.3	47.2	3.07	2.42
Peru..................	19.1	17.0	6.0	6.2	72.7	74.7	21.5	16.7	2.29	2.04
Philippines............	25.0	22.2	5.0	4.9	71.9	74.0	18.8	14.7	3.15	2.83
Poland................	10.0	8.8	10.2	10.8	76.3	77.8	6.4	5.6	1.31	1.39
Romania...............	9.5	8.5	11.8	12.0	74.2	76.0	10.7	8.7	1.30	1.38
Russia................	12.3	10.0	14.1	13.4	69.5	71.9	7.3	6.5	1.61	1.60
Saudi Arabia...........	19.2	17.8	3.3	3.4	74.4	76.1	15.6	12.0	2.26	2.04
Senegal...............	36.2	31.8	9.1	7.6	60.2	63.2	55.2	45.7	4.69	4.04
South Africa...........	19.3	18.1	17.2	17.3	49.4	51.4	42.7	36.8	2.28	2.12
Spain.................	10.4	8.7	8.9	9.3	81.3	82.0	3.4	3.2	1.48	1.51
Sri Lanka..............	17.0	14.2	6.0	6.5	75.9	77.5	9.5	7.8	2.17	2.01
Sudan [5].............	31.7	26.0	8.3	6.9	62.6	65.5	55.6	45.0	4.17	3.24
Syria.................	23.5	19.7	3.7	3.7	74.9	76.6	15.1	11.7	2.85	2.34
Taiwan................	8.7	8.0	6.7	7.9	79.6	80.6	4.6	4.2	1.10	1.14
Tanzania..............	37.7	34.6	8.6	7.1	60.3	63.9	46.5	36.4	5.08	4.59
Thailand..............	12.8	11.8	7.4	8.2	73.8	75.6	15.9	12.4	1.66	1.69
Turkey................	17.6	15.1	6.1	6.3	72.8	74.8	23.1	17.3	2.13	1.96
Uganda...............	45.8	41.1	11.6	9.4	53.5	57.2	64.2	51.8	6.14	5.44
Ukraine...............	9.6	8.5	15.8	15.4	68.7	70.7	8.4	7.3	1.29	1.35
United Kingdom........	12.3	11.9	9.3	9.5	80.2	81.1	4.6	4.1	1.91	1.86
United States..........	13.7	13.3	8.4	8.5	78.5	79.5	6.0	5.4	2.06	2.06
Uzbekistan............	17.3	16.1	5.3	5.4	72.8	74.8	21.2	16.3	1.86	1.74
Venezuela.............	19.9	18.1	5.2	5.6	74.1	75.3	20.2	17.0	2.40	2.22
Vietnam...............	16.8	14.5	6.0	6.0	72.4	74.4	20.2	15.7	1.89	1.77
Yemen................	32.6	25.6	6.8	5.7	64.1	66.9	53.5	41.9	4.45	3.20
Zambia................	43.1	40.4	13.4	11.6	51.2	53.6	70.6	56.0	5.85	5.49
Zimbabwe.............	32.2	29.9	12.4	9.8	51.8	59.3	28.2	25.3	3.61	3.40

[1] Number of births during 1 year per 1,000 persons (based on midyear population). [2] Number of deaths during 1 year per 1,000 persons (based on midyear population). [3] Number of deaths of children under 1 year of age per 1,000 live births in a calendar year. [4] Average number of children that would be born if all women lived to the end of childbearing age, based on birth rates for each specified year. [5] Data exclude South Sudan, which became a separate country in July 2011.

Source: U.S. Census Bureau, International Data Base, <http://www.census.gov/ipc/www/idb/>, accessed September 2013.

Country	Life expectancy at birth (years)				Life expectancy at age 65 (years)			
	Females		Males		Females		Males	
	2000	2011	2000	2011	2000	2011	2000	2011
United States............	**79.3**	**[1] 81.1**	**74.1**	**[1] 76.3**	**19.0**	**[1] 20.4**	**16.0**	**[1] 17.8**
Australia..................	82.0	[1] 84.2	76.6	[1] 79.7	20.4	[1] 22.0	16.9	[1] 19.1
Austria...................	81.2	83.9	75.2	78.3	19.6	21.7	16.0	18.1
Belgium..................	81.0	[1] 83.2	74.6	[1] 77.8	19.7	[1] 21.5	15.6	[1] 17.8
Brazil....................	74.1	77.0	66.4	70.1	18.1	18.9	15.7	16.1
Canada...................	81.7	(NA)	76.3	(NA)	20.2	(NA)	16.5	(NA)
Czech Republic...........	78.5	81.1	71.7	74.8	17.3	19.2	13.8	15.6
Denmark..................	79.2	81.9	74.5	77.8	18.3	(NA)	15.2	17.3
Finland...................	81.2	83.8	74.2	77.3	19.5	21.7	15.5	17.7
France....................	83.0	85.7	75.3	78.7	21.4	23.8	16.8	19.3
Germany..................	81.2	83.2	75.1	78.4	19.6	21.2	15.8	18.2
Greece...................	80.6	83.1	75.5	78.5	18.4	20.6	16.1	18.5
Hungary..................	76.2	78.7	67.5	71.2	16.7	18.3	13.0	14.3
Iceland...................	81.6	84.1	77.8	80.7	19.8	21.5	17.8	18.9
Ireland...................	79.2	82.8	74.0	78.3	18.0	20.7	14.6	17.9
Israel....................	80.9	83.6	76.7	79.9	19.0	21.2	17.0	19.0
Italy.....................	82.8	[1] 85.3	76.9	[1] 80.1	20.7	[1] 22.6	16.7	[1] 18.8
Japan....................	84.6	85.9	77.7	79.4	22.4	23.7	17.5	18.7
Korea, South.............	79.6	84.5	72.3	77.7	18.2	21.9	14.3	17.4
Mexico...................	76.1	77.2	70.5	71.2	18.4	18.5	16.5	16.7
Netherlands..............	80.7	83.1	75.6	79.4	19.3	21.2	15.4	18.1
New Zealand.............	80.8	83.0	75.9	79.4	19.8	21.3	16.5	19.0
Norway..................	81.5	83.6	76.0	79.1	19.9	21.4	16.1	18.2
Poland...................	78.0	81.1	69.6	72.6	17.5	19.9	13.5	15.4
Portugal..................	80.2	84.0	73.2	77.6	18.9	21.8	15.4	18.1
Russia...................	72.0	75.1	59.0	63.2	15.2	(NA)	11.1	(NA)
South Africa.............	57.3	53.2	52.3	52.0	15.4	(NA)	11.8	(NA)
Spain....................	82.9	85.4	75.8	79.4	20.8	22.8	16.7	18.7
Sweden..................	82.0	83.8	77.4	79.9	20.2	21.3	16.7	18.5
Switzerland..............	82.8	85.0	77.0	80.5	20.9	22.6	17.0	19.2
Turkey...................	73.1	77.1	69.0	72.0	15.1	16.1	13.4	14.1
United Kingdom.........	80.3	83.1	75.5	79.1	19.0	21.2	15.8	18.6

NA Not available. [1] Estimated.

Source: Organisation for Economic Co-operation and Development (OECD), 2013, "OECD Health Data: Health Status," OECD Health Statistics (database) ©, <http://dx.doi.org/10.1787/data-00540-en>, accessed September 2013.

Table 1370. Percentage of the Adult Population Considered to Be Obese: 2005 to 2011

[Obesity rates are defined as the percentage of the population with a Body Mass Index (BMI) over 30 kg/m^2. The BMI is a single number that evaluates an individual's weight status in relation to height (weight/height^2). Obesity estimates derived from health examinations are generally higher and more reliable than those coming from self-reports because they preclude any misreporting of people's height and weight. However, health examinations are only conducted regularly in a few countries. For more information on methods, see source]

Country	2005	2006	2007	2008	2009	2010	2011
Obese population, measured							
United States............................	**(NA)**	**35.4**	**(NA)**	**34.5**	**(NA)**	**36.5**	**(NA)**
Australia................................	(NA)	(NA)	24.6	(NA)	(NA)	(NA)	28.3
Canada.................................	23.7	(NA)	(NA)	24.2	(NA)	25.4	(NA)
Czech Republic..........................	17.0	(NA)	(NA)	22.0	(NA)	21.0	(NA)
Japan..................................	3.9	3.4	3.3	3.4	3.9	3.5	4.1
Korea..................................	3.5	(NA)	3.9	3.7	3.8	4.1	4.3
Luxembourg.............................	18.6	20.4	20.0	20.3	22.1	22.5	23.5
Mexico.................................	30.2	30.0	(NA)	(NA)	(NA)	(NA)	(NA)
New Zealand............................	(NA)	(NA)	26.5	(NA)	27.8	(NA)	(NA)
Slovak Republic.........................	17.6	(NA)	(NA)	16.9	(NA)	(NA)	(NA)
United Kingdom.........................	23.0	24.0	24.0	24.5	23.0	26.1	24.8
Obese population, self-reported							
United States............................	**25.1**	**26.0**	**26.4**	**27.6**	**27.7**	**28.1**	**28.5**
Canada.................................	15.2	(NA)	16.2	16.6	17.2	17.5	17.7
Chile...................................	(NA)	7.4	(NA)	(NA)	12.1	(NA)	(NA)
Denmark................................	11.4	(NA)	(NA)	(NA)	(NA)	13.4	(NA)
Estonia.................................	(NA)	15.9	(NA)	18.0	(NA)	16.9	(NA)
Finland.................................	14.1	14.3	14.9	15.7	14.9	15.6	16.6
France..................................	(NA)	10.5	(NA)	11.2	(NA)	12.9	(NA)
Germany................................	13.6	(NA)	(NA)	(NA)	14.7	(NA)	(NA)
Greece.................................	(NA)	16.4	(NA)	18.1	17.3	(NA)	(NA)
Iceland.................................	(NA)	(NA)	20.1	(NA)	(NA)	21.0	(NA)
Israel..................................	(NA)	12.1	(NA)	13.8	(NA)	15.7	(NA)
Italy....................................	9.9	10.2	9.9	9.9	10.3	10.3	10.0
Korea..................................	(NA)	(NA)	(NA)	1.8	2.0	2.0	2.1
Netherlands.............................	10.7	11.3	11.2	11.1	11.8	11.4	11.4
Norway.................................	9.0	(NA)	(NA)	10.0	(NA)	(NA)	(NA)
Spain...................................	(NA)	14.9	(NA)	(NA)	16.0	(NA)	16.6
Sweden.................................	10.9	9.0	10.6	10.3	10.9	11.3	11.0
Turkey..................................	(NA)	(NA)	(NA)	15.2	(NA)	16.9	(NA)

NA Not available.

Source: Organisation for Economic Co-operation and Development (OECD), 2013, "OECD Health Data: Non-medical Determinants of Health," OECD Health Statistics (database) ©, <http://dx.doi.org/10.1787/data-00546-en>, accessed September 2013.

Table 1371. Daily Tobacco Consumption by Country and Sex: 2000 to 2011

[Daily smokers as percent of population aged over 15. Includes tobacco forms consumed by smoking only]

Country	Total			Females			Males		
	2000	2010	2011	2000	2010	2011	2000	2010	2011
United States	**19.1**	**15.1**	**14.8**	**17.3**	**13.6**	**13.3**	**21.2**	**16.7**	**16.4**
Canada	(NA)	16.3	15.7	(NA)	13.7	14.0	(NA)	19.0	17.4
China	(NA)	24.1	(NA)	(NA)	2.0	(NA)	(NA)	45.4	(NA)
Denmark	30.5	20.0	(NA)	29.0	20.0	(NA)	32.0	20.0	(NA)
Estonia	30.3	26.2	(NA)	20.0	18.7	(NA)	45.0	36.8	(NA)
Finland	23.4	19.0	17.8	20.3	15.7	14.8	27.3	23.2	21.9
France	27.0	23.3	(NA)	21.0	20.7	(NA)	33.0	26.4	(NA)
Iceland	22.4	14.2	14.3	22.0	13.9	14.2	22.8	14.5	14.4
Israel	24.1	[1] 18.5	(NA)	15.4	[1] 12.6	(NA)	34.0	[1] 24.8	(NA)
Italy	24.4	23.1	22.5	17.4	17.1	16.8	31.9	29.6	28.7
Japan	27.0	19.5	20.1	11.5	8.4	9.7	47.4	32.2	32.4
Korea	(NA)	22.9	23.2	(NA)	5.2	5.1	(NA)	40.8	41.6
Luxembourg	(NA)	18.0	17.0	(NA)	16.0	16.0	(NA)	21.0	18.0
Netherlands	32.0	20.9	20.8	29.0	18.8	18.3	35.0	23.1	23.5
Norway	32.0	19.0	17.0	32.0	19.0	18.0	31.0	19.0	17.0
Russia	34.9	(NA)	(NA)	12.6	(NA)	(NA)	62.2	(NA)	(NA)
Sweden	18.9	13.6	13.1	21.0	12.5	12.4	16.8	14.7	13.9
United Kingdom	27.0	19.6	(NA)	26.0	19.1	(NA)	28.0	20.3	(NA)

NA Not available. [1] Estimated.

Source: Organisation for Economic Co-operation and Development (OECD), 2013, "OECD Health Data: Non-medical Determinants of Health," OECD Health Statistics (database) ©, <http://dx.doi.org/10.1787/data-00546-en>, accessed September 2013.

Table 1372. Road Fatalities by Country: 2000 to 2011

[Fatalities include any person killed immediately or dying within 30 days as a result of an injury accident. For countries that do not apply the threshold of 30 days, conversion coefficients are estimated so that comparisons on the basis of the 30 day-definition can be made]

Country	2000	2005	2009	2010	2011	Country	2000	2005	2009	2010	2011
United States	**(NA)**	**43,510**	**33,883**	**32,999**	**32,367**	Korea, South	10,236	6,376	5,838	5,505	5,229
Australia	(NA)	1,627	1,488	1,352	1,277	Latvia	635	442	254	218	179
Austria	976	768	633	552	523	Lithuania	641	773	370	299	296
Azerbaijan	596	1,065	930	925	1,016	Mexico	5,224	4,710	4,877	(NA)	(NA)
Belgium	1,470	1,089	943	840	858	Moldova	406	391	476	452	433
Bulgaria	1,012	957	901	776	657	Netherlands	1,160	817	720	640	661
Canada	(NA)	2,905	2,230	2,227	2,025	New Zealand	462	405	384	375	284
Croatia	655	597	538	423	416	Norway	341	224	212	208	169
Czech Republic	1,486	1,275	901	802	773	Poland	6,294	5,433	4,560	3,902	4,172
Denmark	498	331	303	255	220	Portugal	1,607	1,094	737	937	891
Estonia	197	169	100	79	101	Romania	2,499	2,461	2,987	2,377	2,018
Finland	396	379	279	272	292	Russia	29,594	33,957	27,659	26,567	27,953
France	8,172	5,318	4,264	3,986	3,963	Serbia	1,048	785	805	619	708
Germany	7,503	5,361	4,152	3,648	4,009	Slovakia	628	560	347	353	355
Greece	2,037	1,658	1,456	1,258	1,141	Slovenia	315	256	171	138	140
Hungary	1,200	1,278	822	739	638	Spain	5,776	4,442	2,714	2,478	2,056
Iceland	32	19	17	8	12	Sweden	591	440	358	266	319
Ireland	415	396	239	212	186	Switzerland	592	409	349	327	320
Italy	6,649	5,818	4,237	4,090	3,860	Turkey	5,510	4,505	4,324	4,045	3,835
Japan	10,403	7,931	5,831	5,806	5,507	United Kingdom	3,409	3,201	2,222	1,850	1,901

NA Not available.

Source: International Transport Forum (ITF) / Organisation for Economic Co-operation and Development (OECD), 2013, "Road injury accidents," Transport Statistics ©. See also <http://www.internationaltransportforum.org/>.

Table 1373. Suicide Rates by Sex and Country: 2010

[Deaths due to intentional self-harm per 100,000 persons]

Country	Total	Men	Women	Country	Total	Men	Women
United States	**12.5**	**20.4**	**5.1**	Italy	5.8	9.8	2.4
Australia	10.9	17.1	4.9	Japan	21.2	31.4	11.5
Austria	13.9	23.3	6.0	Korea, South	33.5	49.6	21.4
Brazil	5.4	9.0	2.3	Mexico	4.8	8.5	1.5
Canada [1]	11.1	17.4	5.1	Netherlands	9.2	13.3	5.4
Chile [1]	13.3	22.4	5.0	Norway	11.2	15.9	6.7
Czech Republic	13.5	23.8	4.4	Poland	15.8	28.8	4.0
Denmark	9.7	14.6	5.2	Portugal	9.3	15.9	4.2
Finland	17.3	26.8	8.3	Russia	22.5	42.3	7.2
France [1]	16.2	25.8	8.0	Slovakia	11.3	20.7	3.2
Germany	10.8	17.3	5.1	South Africa [1]	0.8	1.3	0.4
Greece	3.1	5.6	0.7	Spain	6.3	10.5	2.7
Hungary	23.4	41.1	9.2	Sweden	11.7	17.5	6.1
Ireland	11.0	17.4	4.6	Switzerland	11.9	18.1	6.5
Israel	7.4	12.6	2.6	United Kingdom	6.7	10.5	3.0

[1] 2009 data.

Source: Organisation for Economic Co-operation and Development (OECD), "OECD Health Data: Health Status," OECD Health Statistics database ©, <http://www.oecd.org/health/health-systems/oecdhealthdata.htm>, accessed September 2013.

Table 1374. Health Expenditures by Country: 1980 to 2011

[In percent. GDP = gross domestic product]

Country	Total expenditures on health (percent of GDP)					Public expenditures on health (percent of total)				
	1980	1990	2000	2010	2011	1980	1990	2000	2010	2011
United States............	**9.0**	**12.4**	**13.7**	**17.7**	**17.7**	**41.0**	**39.4**	**43.0**	**47.6**	**47.8**
Australia.....................	6.1	6.8	8.1	8.9	(NA)	62.6	66.2	66.8	67.8	(NA)
Austria.....................	7.5	8.4	10.0	11.0	10.8	68.8	72.9	75.6	75.8	76.2
Belgium....................	6.3	7.2	8.1	10.5	10.5	(NA)	(NA)	74.6	75.1	75.9
Canada.....................	7.0	8.9	8.8	11.4	11.2	75.6	74.5	70.4	70.8	70.4
Czech Republic...........	(NA)	4.4	6.3	7.4	7.5	96.8	97.4	90.3	83.8	84.2
Denmark....................	8.9	8.3	8.7	11.1	10.9	87.8	82.7	83.9	85.1	85.3
Finland.....................	6.3	7.7	7.2	9.0	9.0	79.0	80.9	71.3	74.8	75.4
France......................	7.0	8.4	10.1	11.7	11.6	80.1	76.6	79.4	76.9	76.8
Germany [1]...............	8.4	8.3	10.4	11.5	11.3	78.7	76.2	79.5	76.7	76.5
Greece.....................	5.9	6.7	8.0	9.5	9.1	55.6	53.7	60.0	66.8	65.1
Hungary....................	(NA)	(NA)	7.2	8.0	7.9	(NA)	(NA)	70.7	64.8	65.0
Iceland.....................	6.3	7.8	9.5	9.3	9.0	88.2	86.6	81.1	80.4	80.4
Ireland.....................	8.1	6.0	6.1	9.3	8.9	82.0	71.7	75.1	69.6	67.0
Italy........................	(NA)	7.7	7.9	9.4	9.2	(NA)	79.5	74.2	78.5	77.8
Japan.......................	6.4	5.8	7.6	9.6	(NA)	71.3	77.6	80.8	82.1	(NA)
Korea, South..............	3.6	3.9	4.3	7.3	7.4	22.1	39.5	50.4	56.5	55.3
Luxembourg...............	5.2	5.4	7.5	7.2	6.6	92.8	93.1	85.1	85.5	84.1
Mexico.....................	(NA)	4.4	5.1	6.2	(NA)	(NA)	40.4	46.6	47.3	(NA)
Netherlands...............	7.4	8.0	8.0	12.1	11.9	69.4	67.1	63.1	(NA)	(NA)
New Zealand..............	5.8	6.8	7.6	10.2	10.3	88.0	82.4	78.0	83.2	82.7
Norway.....................	7.0	7.6	8.4	9.4	9.3	85.1	82.8	82.5	84.7	84.9
Poland......................	(NA)	4.8	5.5	7.0	6.9	(NA)	91.7	70.0	71.2	70.3
Portugal....................	5.1	5.7	9.3	10.8	10.2	64.3	65.5	66.6	65.9	65.0
Slovakia....................	(NA)	(NA)	5.5	9.0	7.9	(NA)	(NA)	89.4	64.5	70.9
Spain.......................	5.3	6.5	7.2	9.6	9.3	79.9	78.7	71.6	74.2	73.0
Sweden.....................	8.9	8.2	8.2	9.5	9.5	92.5	89.9	84.9	81.5	81.6
Switzerland................	7.2	8.0	9.9	10.9	11.0	(NA)	52.4	55.4	65.2	64.9
Turkey......................	2.4	2.7	4.9	(NA)	(NA)	29.4	61.0	62.9	(NA)	(NA)
United Kingdom...........	5.6	5.8	7.0	9.6	9.4	89.4	83.6	79.1	83.5	82.8

NA Not available. [1] Data prior to 1991 are for former West Germany.

Source: Organisation for Economic Co-operation and Development (OECD), 2013, "OECD Health Data: Health Expenditure and Financing," OECD Health Statistics (database) ©, <http://dx.doi.org/10.1787/data-00349-en>, accessed September 2013.

Table 1375. Physicians and Inpatient Hospital Care—Selected Countries: 2000 to 2011

Country	Practicing physicians per 1,000 population				Acute inpatient hospital care							
					Beds per 1,000 population				Average length of stay (days)			
	2000	2005	2010	2011	2000	2005	2010	2011	2000	2005	2010	2011
United States........	**2.3**	**2.4**	**2.4**	**2.5**	**3.0**	**2.7**	**2.6**	**(NA)**	**5.8**	**5.6**	**5.4**	**5.4**
Australia..............	2.5	2.8	(NA)	3.3	3.6	3.5	3.4	(NA)	6.1	6.0	5.0	(NA)
Austria...............	3.9	4.3	4.8	4.8	6.2	5.8	5.5	5.4	7.6	6.9	6.6	6.5
Belgium..............	2.8	2.9	2.9	2.9	4.7	4.4	4.1	4.1	7.7	7.7	7.2	(NA)
Canada...............	(NA)	(NA)	(NA)	(NA)	3.2	2.5	1.7	(NA)	7.2	7.2	7.7	(NA)
Czech Republic......	3.4	3.6	3.6	3.6	5.7	5.3	4.9	4.7	7.9	7.1	7.0	6.8
Denmark.............	2.9	3.3	(NA)	(NA)	3.5	3.2	2.9	(NA)	3.8	3.5	(NA)	(NA)
Finland...............	2.5	2.6	(NA)	(NA)	3.5	3.3	3.0	3.0	6.9	7.1	7.0	6.9
France................	(NA)	(NA)	(NA)	3.1	4.1	3.7	3.5	3.4	5.6	5.4	5.2	5.1
Germany.............	3.3	3.4	3.7	3.8	6.1	5.6	5.3	5.3	10.1	8.8	8.1	7.9
Hungary..............	2.7	2.8	2.9	3.0	5.6	5.5	4.1	4.1	7.1	6.5	5.8	5.7
Ireland...............	(NA)	(NA)	(NA)	[1] 2.67	2.8	2.8	2.3	2.2	6.4	6.5	6.0	5.9
Israel.................	3.5	3.2	3.3	3.3	2.3	2.1	1.9	1.9	4.6	4.4	4.3	4.3
Italy..................	(NA)	(NA)	(NA)	4.1	4.1	3.3	2.9	2.8	7.0	6.7	6.7	6.8
Japan.................	1.9	(NA)	2.2	(NA)	9.6	8.2	8.0	8.0	24.8	19.8	18.2	17.9
Korea, South.........	1.3	1.6	2.0	2.0	3.9	4.6	5.5	5.9	11.0	(NA)	(NA)	(NA)
Mexico...............	1.6	1.8	2.1	2.2	1.8	1.7	1.6	1.6	(NA)	(NA)	(NA)	(NA)
Netherlands..........	(NA)	(NA)	(NA)	(NA)	3.1	2.9	3.3	3.3	9.0	7.2	5.6	5.8
New Zealand........	2.2	2.1	2.6	2.6	(NA)	(NA)	2.5	2.6	4.3	5.6	5.8	5.6
Norway...............	3.4	3.6	4.1	3.7	3.1	2.9	2.4	2.4	6.0	5.2	4.5	(NA)
Poland................	2.2	2.1	2.2	2.2	5.2	4.7	4.3	4.3	(NA)	7.9	7.3	7.1
Portugal..............	(NA)	(NA)	(NA)	(NA)	3.0	2.9	2.8	[1] 2.81	7.8	7.0	7.0	[1] 7.2
Russia................	4.2	4.2	5.0	(NA)	(NA)	(NA)	(NA)	(NA)	13.5	11.9	(NA)	(NA)
Slovak Republic......	3.2	(NA)	(NA)	(NA)	5.7	5.0	4.8	4.5	8.4	7.3	6.6	6.3
Slovenia..............	2.2	2.3	2.4	2.5	4.5	3.9	3.7	3.7	7.1	5.8	5.5	6.7
Spain.................	3.3	3.8	3.8	4.1	2.8	2.6	2.5	2.5	7.1	6.7	6.3	6.1
Sweden...............	3.1	3.5	3.9	(NA)	2.5	2.2	2.0	2.0	5.9	5.5	5.2	5.1
Switzerland...........	(NA)	(NA)	3.8	3.8	4.1	3.7	3.1	3.0	9.3	8.5	6.6	6.5
Turkey................	(NA)	(NA)	(NA)	(NA)	2.0	2.2	2.4	2.5	5.6	5.1	3.9	3.8
United Kingdom......	2.0	2.4	2.8	2.8	3.2	3.0	2.4	2.4	8.1	7.6	6.7	6.5

NA Not available. [1] Estimated.

Source: Organisation for Economic Co-operation and Development (OECD), 2013, "OECD Health Data," OECD Health Statistics (database) ©, <http://dx.doi.org/10.1787/health-data-en>, accessed September 2013.

Table 1376. Gross National Income (GNI) by Country: 2000 and 2012

[For total GNI, 32,318,399 represents $32,318,399,000,000. GNI is the sum of value added by all resident producers, plus any product taxes (less subsidies) not included in the valuation of output, plus net receipts of primary income from abroad]

Country	Gross national income [1]				GNI on purchasing power parity basis [2]			
	Total (mil. dol.)		Per capita (dol.)		Total (mil. dol.)		Per capita (dol.)	
	2000	2012	2000	2012	2000	2012	2000	2012
World [3]...................	**32,318,399**	**70,571,630**	**5,296**	**10,015**	**42,266,024**	**85,113,839**	**6,927**	**12,079**
Algeria.........................	48,963	(NA)	1,540	(NA)	156,584	(NA)	4,940	(NA)
Angola.........................	5,903	95,389	420	4,580	24,960	114,272	1,790	5,490
Argentina.....................	275,544	(NA)	7,470	(NA)	327,933	(NA)	8,890	(NA)
Australia.......................	405,058	1,351,246	21,150	59,570	488,888	979,161	25,530	43,170
Azerbaijan....................	4,922	56,269	610	6,050	16,817	87,524	2,090	9,410
Bangladesh...................	49,769	129,188	380	840	115,591	319,939	870	2,070
Belarus........................	13,773	61,755	1,380	6,530	51,380	143,909	5,140	15,210
Belgium........................	260,723	501,305	25,430	44,990	289,923	437,406	28,280	39,260
Brazil..........................	673,821	2,311,147	3,860	11,630	1,190,061	2,328,799	6,820	11,720
Cambodia......................	3,622	13,023	300	880	11,058	35,141	900	2,360
Canada........................	680,920	1,777,860	22,130	50,970	851,327	1,489,165	27,670	42,690
Chile...........................	76,111	249,455	4,920	14,280	144,663	376,989	9,360	21,590
China..........................	1,168,776	7,748,903	930	5,740	2,951,385	12,435,359	2,340	9,210
Colombia......................	93,413	333,614	2,340	6,990	228,138	482,247	5,720	10,110
Congo, Democratic Rep.. ...	4,247	14,761	90	220	10,421	24,529	220	370
Costa Rica....................	14,559	41,982	3,710	8,740	26,075	60,486	6,640	12,590
Cote d'Ivoire.................	10,783	24,249	670	1,220	24,841	38,821	1,540	1,960
Czech Republic..............	(NA)	190,597	(NA)	18,130	156,952	258,185	15,280	24,550
Denmark.......................	169,966	334,135	31,830	59,770	150,623	238,252	28,210	42,620
Dominican Republic.........	22,494	56,183	2,600	5,470	42,182	100,960	4,870	9,820
Ecuador.......................	19,446	80,469	1,550	5,190	63,459	148,518	5,060	9,590
Egypt...........................	97,275	241,819	1,470	3,000	250,856	536,276	3,790	6,640
Ethiopia.......................	8,391	37,391	130	410	30,451	104,221	460	1,140
France.........................	1,478,256	2,742,891	24,270	41,750	1,554,789	2,395,288	25,530	36,460
Germany.......................	2,079,948	3,603,895	25,300	44,010	2,095,130	3,387,574	25,480	41,370
Ghana..........................	6,467	39,349	340	1,550	17,564	49,205	930	1,940
Greece.........................	136,073	262,431	12,460	23,260	199,982	279,616	18,320	24,790
Guatemala....................	19,387	47,022	1,730	3,120	39,013	74,834	3,480	4,960
Hong Kong....................	179,503	261,599	26,930	36,560	180,539	379,564	27,090	53,050
Hungary.......................	46,722	123,233	4,580	12,390	115,307	200,822	11,290	20,200
India...........................	473,698	1,890,363	450	1,530	1,593,206	4,749,213	1,530	3,840
Indonesia......................	119,462	843,993	570	3,420	452,327	1,187,982	2,160	4,810
Iran............................	106,661	(NA)	1,620	(NA)	435,124	(NA)	6,600	(NA)
Israel..........................	112,152	(NA)	17,830	(NA)	134,992	(NA)	21,460	(NA)
Italy...........................	1,196,353	2,061,253	21,010	33,840	1,455,350	1,966,163	25,560	32,280
Japan..........................	4,445,186	6,105,798	35,040	47,870	3,335,359	4,633,143	26,290	36,320
Kazakhstan....................	18,740	163,462	1,260	9,730	66,484	200,736	4,470	11,950
Kenya..........................	13,173	36,245	420	840	35,217	76,055	1,130	1,760
Korea, South.................	465,914	1,133,791	9,910	22,670	804,280	1,544,768	17,110	30,890
Lithuania......................	11,188	41,335	3,200	13,850	29,635	67,938	8,470	22,760
Malaysia.......................	80,182	286,426	3,420	9,800	202,739	483,241	8,660	16,530
Mexico.........................	500,874	1,176,869	4,820	9,740	878,098	2,009,235	8,450	16,630
Morocco.......................	38,194	97,068	1,320	2,940	73,299	166,575	2,530	5,040
Mozambique..................	4,274	12,844	230	510	7,644	25,721	420	1,020
Netherlands...................	423,282	809,072	26,580	48,250	478,369	727,070	30,040	43,360
Nigeria.........................	33,449	241,063	270	1,430	141,138	409,083	1,150	2,420
Norway.........................	161,062	496,173	35,860	98,860	160,075	321,351	35,640	64,030
Pakistan.......................	67,667	225,432	470	1,260	233,618	543,576	1,620	3,030
Peru...........................	53,340	176,462	2,050	5,880	123,803	306,929	4,760	10,240
Philippines....................	81,319	238,713	1,050	2,470	184,935	425,233	2,380	4,400
Poland.........................	176,720	488,336	4,600	12,670	402,848	806,420	10,480	20,920
Romania.......................	38,029	179,561	1,690	8,420	126,090	347,816	5,620	16,310
Russia.........................	250,286	1,822,654	1,710	12,700	973,728	3,267,300	6,660	22,760
Saudi Arabia.................	168,133	(NA)	8,350	(NA)	362,295	(NA)	17,980	(NA)
Serbia [4].....................	10,529	38,123	1,400	5,280	43,344	80,791	5,770	11,180
Singapore.....................	98,680	250,779	24,500	47,210	135,088	324,599	33,540	61,100
South Africa..................	134,396	389,765	3,050	7,610	291,137	572,631	6,620	11,190
Spain..........................	620,843	1,391,430	15,420	30,110	850,845	1,468,598	21,130	31,780
Sri Lanka.....................	16,407	59,337	860	2,920	49,948	124,508	2,610	6,120
Sudan [5].....................	11,370	53,795	330	1,450	37,399	75,344	1,090	2,030
Sweden........................	261,623	534,959	29,490	56,210	245,910	410,775	27,720	43,160
Switzerland...................	295,689	661,591	41,160	82,730	250,382	438,803	34,850	54,870
Syria...........................	15,898	(NA)	970	(NA)	50,847	116,511	3,110	5,200
Thailand.......................	122,102	347,936	1,960	5,210	303,165	629,981	4,860	9,430
Tunisia.........................	22,073	44,765	2,310	4,150	49,091	100,882	5,130	9,360
Turkey.........................	265,345	801,097	4,200	10,830	580,475	1,294,603	9,190	17,500
Uganda........................	6,398	15,963	260	440	16,327	41,415	670	1,140
Ukraine........................	34,350	159,646	700	3,500	156,401	332,545	3,180	7,290
United Kingdom..............	1,525,743	2,418,464	25,910	38,250	1,527,127	2,263,471	25,930	35,800
United States..............	**9,845,288**	**15,734,567**	**34,890**	**50,120**	**10,070,500**	**15,887,600**	**35,690**	**50,610**
Uzbekistan....................	15,431	51,324	630	1,720	35,128	111,636	1,430	3,750
Venezuela.....................	99,739	373,481	4,090	12,470	203,835	393,045	8,350	13,120
Vietnam.......................	30,204	124,146	390	1,400	108,423	305,613	1,400	3,440
Yemen.........................	7,418	(NA)	420	(NA)	30,657	(NA)	1,750	(NA)
Zambia........................	3,136	19,060	310	1,350	8,859	22,772	880	1,620

NA Not available. [1] Gross national income calculated using the World Bank Atlas conversion factor; for details, see source. [2] For explanation of purchasing power parity (PPP), see headnote, Table 1377. [3] Includes other countries not shown separately. [4] In June 2006, Serbia and Montenegro became separate countries. Data for 2000 are for Serbia and Montenegro. Starting in 2006, data excludes Montenegro. [5] Sudan and South Sudan became separate countries in July 2011. Data for 2012 exclude South Sudan.

Source: The World Bank, Washington, DC, "World Development Indicators" database ©, <http://data.worldbank.org/data-catalog/world-development-indicators>, accessed August 2013.

Table 1377. Real Gross Domestic Product (GDP) Per Capita and Per Employed Persons by Country: 1990 to 2011

[U.S. figures based on the System of National Income and Product Accounts (NIPA) from the Bureau of Economic Analysis. All other countries, based on the 1993 United Nations System of National Accounts (SNA). Per capita data based on total resident population. Real GDP is a macroeconomic measure of the size of an economy adjusted for price changes and inflation. Employment data include people serving in the armed forces for some countries. Real dollars are calculated based on 2011 Purchasing Power Parities (PPPs). PPPs are currency conversion rates used to convert GDP expressed in different currencies to a common value (U.S. dollars in this case). PPP for a given country is the number of national currency units needed to buy the specific basket of goods and services that one dollar will buy in the United States. See text, this section]

Country	Real GDP per capita (2011 U.S. dollars)				Real GDP per employed person (2011 U.S. dollars)			
	1990	2000	2010	2011	1990	2000	2010	2011
United States.............	**36,378**	**45,026**	**47,772**	**48,282**	**75,227**	**91,921**	**105,235**	**106,541**
Canada....................	30,668	36,903	39,951	40,489	64,510	76,417	79,676	80,357
Australia..................	27,967	34,910	40,910	41,340	60,209	73,969	79,884	80,330
Japan.....................	29,679	32,322	34,519	34,294	56,912	62,703	69,087	68,537
Korea, South..............	11,985	20,575	29,411	30,254	28,409	45,717	60,984	62,119
Singapore.................	28,600	43,142	59,131	60,742	54,565	82,090	98,489	99,415
Austria...................	29,484	36,831	41,019	42,066	64,644	78,934	84,558	85,816
Belgium..................	29,276	35,427	38,269	38,767	75,776	88,274	92,844	93,317
Czech Republic...........	(NA)	18,845	25,692	26,169	(NA)	39,888	53,459	54,226
Denmark..................	32,188	40,049	40,782	40,930	63,421	78,820	81,510	82,378
Finland...................	27,201	32,128	36,802	37,636	54,680	72,512	79,526	80,779
France....................	28,546	33,207	34,734	35,133	69,831	78,808	84,122	85,152
Germany [1]...............	27,971	34,508	38,057	39,186	58,183	72,017	76,724	77,978
Ireland...................	21,551	38,429	41,371	41,537	64,348	86,202	100,162	102,983
Italy......................	27,954	32,661	32,050	32,100	70,128	81,107	78,606	78,813
Netherlands...............	30,330	38,886	42,610	42,824	69,816	78,668	84,583	85,437
Norway...................	42,626	57,922	61,782	61,869	87,816	112,140	116,190	116,251
Spain.....................	23,694	30,128	32,309	32,501	64,160	73,916	79,220	81,417
Sweden...................	28,936	34,356	40,071	41,316	53,852	70,869	83,454	84,816
United Kingdom...........	24,779	31,640	35,689	35,688	52,781	67,791	76,431	76,638

NA Not available. [1] Prior to 1991, data are for the former West Germany.

Source: U.S. Bureau of Labor Statistics, *International Comparisons of GDP per Capita and per Hour, 1960–2011*, November 2012, <http://www.bls.gov/fls/intl_gdp_capita_gdp_hour.htm>.

Table 1378. Average Annual Percent Changes in International Economic Composite Indexes by Country: 1990 to 2011

[Change from previous year; derived from indexes with base 2000 = 100. The coincident index changes are for calendar years and the leading index changes are for years ending June 30 because they lead the coincident indexes by about 6 months, on average. The G-7 countries are United States, Canada, France, Germany, Italy, United Kingdom, and Japan. Minus sign (–) indicates decrease]

Country	Leading index						Coincident index					
	1990	2000	2005	2009	2010	2011	1990	2000	2005	2009	2010	2011
Total, 13 countries......	**2.2**	**7.1**	**5.1**	**-10.8**	**8.1**	**5.0**	**5.6**	**5.2**	**1.9**	**-13.5**	**3.1**	**1.0**
12 countries, excluding U.S.........................	3.9	8.5	5.5	-6.9	4.4	5.2	8.4	5.7	1.5	-12.0	4.6	0.2
G-7 countries.............	2.1	6.7	5.0	-11.4	8.0	4.8	5.6	5.1	1.7	-14.0	2.7	0.7
North America.............	-0.8	4.9	4.3	-16.3	13.8	4.4	-0.3	5.0	2.7	-16.1	0.6	2.5
United States.............	**-0.9**	**4.7**	**4.4**	**-17.4**	**15.0**	**4.4**	**-0.3**	**4.5**	**2.6**	**-16.6**	**0.1**	**2.3**
Canada...................	-0.4	7.3	3.2	-4.7	3.0	4.4	-2.0	10.5	4.6	-11.8	5.4	3.5
Four European countries...	1.7	5.2	4.0	-7.4	6.0	5.6	6.7	10.3	1.8	-10.3	3.2	3.7
France....................	0.3	2.0	6.5	-8.0	11.9	2.6	6.5	13.2	1.8	-15.1	0.4	1.9
Germany..................	4.9	8.0	4.5	-7.4	4.1	8.4	8.5	8.8	-0.5	-7.5	7.1	7.6
Italy......................	0.6	6.2	2.2	-7.0	4.3	4.3	11.9	16.8	4.8	-15.1	-0.3	1.6
United Kingdom...........	-0.6	3.4	1.4	-7.1	4.1	5.8	0.4	4.4	3.3	-4.1	3.2	0.9
Seven Pacific region countries.................	6.1	12.1	7.1	-6.6	3.0	4.9	10.3	1.2	0.9	-12.5	5.8	-3.3
Australia..................	-2.2	8.4	5.2	-7.7	4.5	4.9	-0.4	4.7	3.5	-1.8	3.4	1.6
Taiwan....................	5.0	9.7	6.5	-0.8	10.6	6.8	5.2	4.8	5.2	-6.4	13.6	6.8
Thailand..................	12.7	10.7	5.3	-0.6	9.7	10.5	12.3	7.7	6.6	-2.2	10.7	3.8
Japan.....................	6.5	11.9	7.3	-7.5	1.4	4.3	11.0	-0.5	-0.1	-14.9	5.4	-5.2
Korea, South..............	6.0	20.7	7.6	-0.2	12.3	9.9	9.6	14.8	4.6	0.1	7.5	5.2
Malaysia..................	4.6	20.6	9.1	-3.8	17.1	12.5	9.2	11.1	3.1	-6.4	6.5	3.9
New Zealand..............	3.5	5.0	1.5	-1.9	7.1	-2.1	-1.3	3.0	6.1	-7.2	2.3	2.5

Source: Foundation for International Business and Economic Research, New York, NY, *International Economic Indicators* ©, monthly .

Table 1379. Sectoral Contributions to Gross Value Added: 2010 and 2012

[In percent. According to the 1993 System of National Accounts (SNA) and the International Standard Industrial Classification (ISIC), Revision 3 (1990). Value added is estimated at basic prices and includes financial intermediation services indirectly measured (FISIM). Value added represents an industry's contribution to national GDP and is calculated as the difference between production and intermediate inputs. Value added comprises labor costs, consumption of fixed capital, indirect taxes less subsidies, and net operating surplus and mixed income]

Country	Agriculture [1]		Industry Total [2]		Industry Manufacturing		Services	
	2010	2012	2010	2012	2010	2012	2010	2012
United States [3]	**1.2**	**(NA)**	**19.8**	**(NA)**	**12.6**	**(NA)**	**79.0**	**(NA)**
Australia	2.5	(NA)	28.7	(NA)	8.2	(NA)	68.8	(NA)
Austria	1.5	1.6	28.7	28.6	18.3	18.2	69.8	69.8
Belgium	0.8	0.8	22.5	22.2	13.8	13.3	76.7	76.9
China	10.1	(NA)	46.7	(NA)	(NA)	(NA)	43.2	(NA)
Czech Republic	1.7	2.3	37.0	37.6	23.0	24.7	61.3	60.1
Denmark	1.4	1.5	21.6	21.4	11.4	10.7	76.9	77.1
Finland	2.9	2.8	28.2	26.0	17.4	15.4	69.0	71.2
France	1.8	2.0	18.9	18.8	10.3	10.0	79.3	79.2
Germany	0.8	0.8	30.2	30.5	21.9	22.4	69.0	68.7
Greece	3.2	3.4	17.0	16.4	9.9	9.7	79.8	80.2
Hungary	3.5	3.9	30.7	31.0	22.0	23.2	65.8	65.1
Indonesia	15.3	(NA)	47.0	(NA)	24.8	(NA)	37.6	(NA)
Ireland	1.5	1.6	26.4	27.9	21.6	23.3	72.0	70.5
Italy	1.9	2.0	25.1	24.2	16.5	15.5	73.1	73.8
Japan [4]	1.2	(NA)	27.5	(NA)	19.7	(NA)	71.3	(NA)
Korea	2.6	2.6	39.3	39.7	30.3	31.1	58.0	57.7
Mexico	3.5	(NA)	34.6	(NA)	18.3	(NA)	61.9	(NA)
Netherlands	1.8	1.7	23.8	24.3	12.2	12.6	74.4	74.0
Norway	1.7	1.2	39.3	42.5	7.9	7.7	59.0	56.3
Poland	3.7	4.0	32.2	32.2	16.8	17.6	64.1	63.8
Portugal	2.3	2.2	23.9	23.4	13.4	14.3	73.8	74.4
Russia	3.9	3.9	34.7	36.0	14.8	15.2	61.4	60.1
Slovakia	2.8	3.6	35.6	35.9	20.4	22.1	61.6	60.4
South Africa	2.6	2.6	29.8	28.4	14.2	12.4	67.6	69.0
Spain	2.6	2.5	27.2	25.9	13.0	13.3	70.2	71.6
Sweden	1.7	1.6	26.9	26.0	17.0	16.0	71.4	72.3
Switzerland	0.8	(NA)	26.3	(NA)	18.6	(NA)	72.9	(NA)
Turkey	9.5	8.9	26.4	26.6	17.6	17.4	64.1	64.5
United Kingdom	0.6	0.7	22.9	22.3	10.7	10.7	76.5	77.1

NA Not available. [1] Includes forestry, fishing, and hunting sectors. [2] Includes construction, energy, and manufacturing sectors. [3] Value added is estimated at factor cost for U.S. [4] Value added is estimated approximately at market prices for Japan.

Source: Organisation for Economic Co-operation and Development (OECD), 2013, "National Accounts at a Glance," OECD National Accounts Statistics (database) ©, <http://dx.doi.org/10.1787/data-00369-en>, accessed September 2013.

Table 1380. Index of Industrial Production by Country: 1990 to 2012

[Annual averages of monthly data. Industrial production indexes generally measure output in the manufacturing, mining, electric, gas, and water utilities sectors. Minus sign (-) indicates decrease]

Country	Index (2005 = 100)								Annual percent change				
	1990	1995	2000	2005	2009	2010	2011	2012	2007 to 2008	2008 to 2009	2009 to 2010	2010 to 2011	2011 to 2012
United States	**65.2**	**75.2**	**96.6**	**100.0**	**89.8**	**94.9**	**98.1**	**101.6**	**-3.4**	**-11.3**	**5.7**	**3.4**	**3.6**
Australia	73.1	81.3	94.1	100.0	107.9	112.3	111.3	115.7	2.7	-0.3	4.1	-0.9	4.0
Austria	58.8	63.5	85.3	100.0	103.1	110.2	116.8	119.0	1.9	-11.1	7.0	5.9	1.9
Belgium	73.8	74.3	83.0	100.0	105.5	117.2	122.3	118.3	3.9	-10.1	11.1	4.4	-3.2
Brazil	70.8	78.2	85.8	100.0	104.1	115.0	115.4	112.4	3.1	-7.4	10.5	0.4	-2.6
Canada	68.3	77.7	98.9	100.0	85.4	89.6	92.8	93.8	-2.9	-10.8	4.9	3.7	1.0
Chile	(NA)	74.0	80.0	100.0	100.5	101.0	106.5	114.5	0.2	-6.7	0.5	5.4	7.5
Czech Republic	92.6	70.0	77.3	100.0	101.6	110.4	116.9	115.9	-1.8	-13.6	8.6	5.9	-0.8
Denmark	72.5	82.5	96.5	100.0	85.8	87.3	88.9	88.3	-1.1	-15.0	1.8	1.8	-0.7
Finland	58.1	66.6	91.2	100.0	94.6	100.0	101.7	99.6	0.8	-18.1	5.7	1.7	-2.1
France	91.9	90.7	100.9	100.0	84.8	88.9	90.8	88.5	-2.9	-14.1	4.9	2.0	-2.5
Germany [1]	85.1	82.0	93.9	100.0	94.0	105.0	113.5	112.8	0.2	-17.3	11.7	8.1	-0.6
Greece	83.7	82.1	100.6	100.0	89.9	84.7	78.1	75.5	-3.0	-9.7	-5.8	-7.8	-3.3
Hungary	51.9	45.6	76.0	100.0	97.6	107.9	113.9	111.9	0.0	-17.7	10.5	5.6	-1.8
India	(NA)	54.9	74.2	100.0	138.4	151.9	159.2	160.3	7.7	0.2	9.7	4.8	0.7
Ireland	23.6	37.5	74.9	100.0	101.4	109.0	109.0	107.6	-2.2	-4.5	7.5	0.0	-1.3
Italy	90.3	97.0	104.3	100.0	82.7	88.5	89.6	83.9	-3.8	-18.6	7.0	1.2	-6.3
Japan	96.9	93.9	98.3	100.0	82.0	94.3	91.5	92.1	-3.2	-21.0	15.0	-2.9	0.7
Korea, South	31.7	47.9	74.3	100.0	119.7	139.2	147.4	148.7	3.4	-0.1	16.3	5.9	0.9
Mexico [2]	66.1	69.1	98.1	100.0	99.5	105.5	109.7	113.6	-0.1	-7.7	6.1	4.0	3.6
Netherlands	78.4	84.9	95.7	100.0	99.2	106.7	106.2	105.7	0.8	-7.3	7.6	-0.5	-0.5
New Zealand	73.7	84.0	89.1	100.0	94.6	98.4	97.1	97.9	-3.2	-4.7	4.1	-1.4	0.8
Norway	74.2	93.7	104.5	100.0	93.3	88.1	83.7	85.2	0.5	-3.9	-5.6	-5.0	1.8
Poland	47.2	53.6	76.8	100.0	121.0	134.4	143.4	145.2	2.7	-3.8	11.1	6.7	1.2
Russia	(NA)	76.6	75.6	100.0	103.8	112.4	117.7	120.7	0.6	-9.3	8.3	4.8	2.5
Spain	79.1	82.0	97.8	100.0	82.8	83.5	82.3	77.3	-7.3	-15.8	0.8	-1.4	-6.0
Sweden	63.7	76.7	91.9	100.0	85.1	93.2	98.6	96.6	-2.6	-18.0	9.4	5.9	-2.1
Switzerland	78.3	81.3	99.0	100.0	110.1	117.1	118.2	(NA)	1.3	-7.9	6.3	0.9	(NA)
Turkey	56.1	65.6	79.5	100.0	102.9	116.1	127.8	131.0	-0.5	-9.9	12.8	10.1	2.5
United Kingdom	90.1	95.7	103.8	100.0	88.4	90.9	89.8	87.6	-2.9	-9.6	2.8	-1.2	-2.4

NA Not available. [1] Data prior to 1991 are for former West Germany. [2] Including construction.

Source: Organisation for Economic Co-operation and Development (OECD), 2013, "Production and Sales," Main Economic Indicators (database) ©, <http://dx.doi.org/10.1787/data-00048-en>, accessed September 2013.

Table 1381. Selected Indexes of Manufacturing Productivity by Country: 1990 to 2011

[2002 = 100. Data refer to all employed persons (including employees, self-employed, and unpaid family workers). Minus sign (–) indicates decrease]

Index	United States	Can-ada	Aust-ralia	Japan	South Korea	France	Ger-many [1]	Italy	Nether-lands	Swe-den	United King-dom
Output per hour worked:											
1990	58.1	70.6	77.9	71.6	33.4	64.8	69.7	79.0	69.4	50.1	69.7
1995	68.5	83.2	85.0	84.1	52.1	77.9	81.5	95.4	82.0	65.3	81.5
2000	88.8	100.1	93.6	99.5	90.8	95.1	97.0	100.9	96.8	91.6	94.0
2005	123.4	104.0	105.3	118.8	130.7	112.1	113.7	102.9	114.6	128.5	118.4
2010	152.7	108.5	112.0	144.5	172.7	122.4	115.0	107.7	125.9	143.8	133.6
2011	155.7	110.6	107.5	140.4	183.1	125.1	120.2	107.3	131.0	148.7	139.6
Average annual percent change:											
2000-2010	5.8	1.3	1.4	4.1	7.0	2.9	2.4	1.1	3.2	5.2	3.9
2009-2010	11.2	3.7	0.8	14.8	8.5	6.1	7.6	9.4	8.3	18.6	4.4
2010-2011	2.0	1.9	-4.0	-2.8	6.0	2.2	4.5	-0.4	4.0	3.4	4.5
Compensation per hour worked: [2][3]											
1990	62.1	68.2	64.2	77.9	24.1	64.2	59.6	61.3	63.1	61.3	59.2
1995	73.4	81.5	78.2	92.9	56.9	79.5	81.4	82.4	77.0	71.8	72.5
2000	91.3	93.6	90.5	98.6	85.2	91.9	94.9	94.3	90.7	90.8	90.6
2005	112.5	112.1	116.8	95.2	139.8	109.7	103.8	110.7	109.9	110.7	117.1
2010	130.0	121.9	140.8	96.0	187.2	126.9	114.6	128.6	125.5	126.7	143.4
2011	133.5	124.7	139.4	98.0	186.3	130.1	117.1	131.3	128.1	130.2	146.5
Average annual percent change:											
2000-2010	4.0	2.7	4.0	-0.3	8.2	3.5	2.2	3.1	3.4	3.4	4.7
2009-2010	1.1	-2.4	0.9	-1.1	7.8	1.9	-1.6	2.5	0.8	-2.1	5.1
2010-2011	2.6	2.3	-1.0	2.1	-0.4	2.5	2.2	2.1	2.1	2.8	2.1
Real hourly compensation: [4]											
1990	82.9	87.3	85.9	83.2	42.4	79.4	78.1	93.4	86.9	81.4	82.8
1995	86.0	93.4	92.3	92.8	73.9	87.6	89.7	97.9	92.2	78.4	85.6
2000	95.4	98.1	97.3	97.0	91.1	95.2	98.2	99.3	97.6	95.2	93.7
2005	103.7	104.7	108.0	95.8	126.8	103.1	99.6	103.5	104.5	107.6	107.5
2010	107.3	104.0	112.2	96.9	146.4	110.2	101.6	109.2	110.6	112.5	113.0
2011	106.8	103.3	107.2	99.3	140.1	110.6	101.5	108.5	110.3	110.4	109.7
Average annual percent change:											
2000-2010	1.5	0.6	0.8	0.0	4.9	1.6	0.7	0.9	1.4	2.1	1.9
2009-2010	-0.5	-4.2	-2.1	-0.5	4.8	0.3	-2.7	1.0	-0.4	-2.3	0.5
2010-2011	-0.5	-0.7	-4.5	2.4	-4.3	0.3	-0.1	-0.7	-0.3	-1.8	-2.9
Unit labor costs, national currency: [2][3]											
1990	107.0	96.6	82.4	108.7	72.4	99.0	85.5	77.6	91.0	122.4	85.0
1995	107.1	97.9	92.0	110.4	109.2	102.0	100.0	86.3	93.9	110.1	88.9
2000	102.8	93.5	96.8	99.1	93.8	96.6	97.8	93.4	93.8	99.0	96.4
2005	91.1	107.7	110.9	80.1	106.9	97.8	91.3	107.6	95.9	86.1	99.0
2010	85.2	112.4	125.7	66.4	108.4	103.7	99.6	119.4	99.6	88.1	107.4
2011	85.7	112.7	129.6	69.8	101.8	104.0	97.5	122.4	97.8	87.6	104.9
Average annual percent change:											
2000-2010	-1.6	1.5	2.6	-3.9	1.1	0.6	0.2	2.2	0.4	-1.0	0.8
2009-2010	-9.1	-5.8	0.0	-13.9	-0.6	-3.9	-8.6	-6.3	-6.9	-17.5	0.7
2010-2011	0.6	0.3	3.1	5.1	-6.1	0.3	-2.2	2.5	-1.9	-0.5	-2.3
Output per employed person:											
1990	58.2	69.4	77.3	77.5	34.9	70.9	72.1	80.5	70.5	45.6	71.9
1995	70.1	83.2	86.1	85.3	54.0	83.8	85.6	96.4	83.8	66.0	82.6
2000	90.5	100.7	93.7	100.2	93.3	98.7	98.9	102.1	97.5	93.9	94.2
2005	123.5	103.4	104.8	120.9	123.0	113.5	114.6	100.8	114.0	132.3	118.3
2010	155.5	106.8	109.4	143.4	160.5	122.9	113.0	100.8	125.1	145.8	132.8
2011	159.8	108.5	110.6	139.2	169.4	125.4	120.0	101.2	130.6	153.2	137.9
Average annual percent change:											
2000-2010	5.8	1.1	1.1	4.2	5.9	2.3	2.2	0.4	3.0	5.3	3.8
2009-2010	14.4	5.5	2.4	20.5	10.2	7.7	13.4	11.1	10.2	21.5	6.5
2010-2011	2.8	1.6	1.0	-2.9	5.5	2.0	6.2	0.4	4.4	5.1	3.8
Employment:											
1990	116.1	99.0	106.1	127.9	114.4	116.7	130.8	111.0	109.1	118.7	132.7
1995	113.3	91.9	100.7	119.3	109.7	103.3	105.7	100.7	101.6	98.9	118.2
2000	113.0	102.7	101.3	107.3	96.3	101.4	101.8	99.5	102.5	100.8	110.6
2005	93.5	99.2	97.0	96.2	100.1	92.6	94.2	99.0	92.2	91.9	86.0
2010	76.0	80.9	93.7	88.4	103.1	81.2	91.9	91.7	88.0	82.9	72.0
2011	77.1	81.6	90.8	87.7	104.7	80.5	93.6	92.0	87.3	83.7	70.8
Average annual percent change:											
2000-2010	-3.5	-1.7	-0.2	-1.9	1.4	-1.9	-0.8	-0.8	-1.3	-1.7	-4.2
2009-2010	-2.8	-0.2	-1.7	-1.9	4.1	-3.8	-1.9	-3.6	-3.0	-1.5	-2.5
2010-2011	1.4	0.8	-3.1	-0.7	1.6	-0.9	1.9	0.3	-0.8	1.0	-1.6
Aggregate hours worked:											
1990	116.5	97.4	105.2	138.3	119.8	127.7	135.4	113.1	110.9	107.9	136.9
1995	115.9	91.9	101.9	121.0	113.6	111.1	111.1	101.7	103.8	100.0	119.8
2000	115.1	103.2	101.5	108.1	98.8	105.2	103.8	100.6	103.3	103.3	110.9
2005	93.5	98.6	96.6	97.9	94.2	93.8	95.0	97.0	91.7	94.7	86.0
2010	77.4	79.7	91.6	87.7	95.8	81.6	90.3	85.9	87.4	84.0	71.6
2011	79.1	80.1	93.4	87.0	96.9	80.7	93.5	86.7	87.0	86.3	69.9
Average annual percent change:											
2000-2010	-3.6	-1.9	-0.5	-1.8	0.4	-2.5	-1.2	-1.5	-1.5	-1.7	-4.2
2009-2010	0.0	1.5	-0.1	3.0	5.7	-2.3	3.5	-2.1	-1.3	1.0	-0.6
2010-2011	2.2	0.5	2.0	-0.8	1.1	-1.0	3.5	1.0	-0.5	2.6	-2.3

[1] Data prior to 1991 are for the former West Germany. [2] In Australia, Canada, France, Sweden, and the United Kingdom, compensation is adjusted for employment taxes and government subsidies to estimate the actual cost to employers. [3] Indexes in national currency adjusted for changes in prevailing exchange rates. [4] Index of hourly compensation divided by the index of consumer prices to adjust for changes in purchasing power.

Source: U.S. Bureau of Labor Statistics, *International Comparisons of Manufacturing Productivity and Unit Labor Cost Trends 2011, Supplementary Tables 1950–2011*, December 2012. See also <http://www.bls.gov/ilc>.

Table 1382. Indexes of Hourly Compensation Costs for Employees in Manufacturing by Country: 2000 to 2011

[United States = 100. Compensation costs include pay for time worked, direct-pay benefits (including holiday and vacation pay and bonuses), employer social insurance expenditures, and labor-related taxes. Data are adjusted for exchange rates. Regional averages are trade-weighted to account for differences in countries' relative importance to U.S. trade in manufactured goods. See source for detail]

Area or country	2000	2005	2009	2010	2011	Area or country	2000	2005	2009	2010	2011
United States	**100.0**	**100.0**	**100.0**	**100.0**	**100.0**	Hungary	11.8	22.3	25.2	24.1	25.8
Total [1]	**62.8**	**72.2**	**74.7**	**77.6**	**82.4**	Ireland	63.1	95.0	117.2	110.0	112.1
OECD [2]	66.4	77.2	79.6	82.5	87.3	Israel	51.9	46.0	53.2	56.3	60.3
Europe	85.2	109.0	116.7	111.7	118.5	Italy	66.7	92.0	100.4	96.5	101.8
Euro Area [3]	85.7	111.1	122.5	115.7	121.7	Japan	100.2	83.8	87.8	91.2	100.5
Eastern Europe [4]	12.7	20.9	27.2	27.1	29.1	Korea, South	38.5	49.2	44.0	50.9	53.2
East Asia [5]	35.1	38.0	36.6	40.6	44.2	Mexico	18.8	18.6	16.7	17.6	18.3
Argentina	32.7	18.3	29.9	36.7	44.8	Netherlands	84.3	110.5	121.1	113.6	119.0
Australia	65.9	94.7	97.7	114.0	130.3	New Zealand	36.0	54.0	51.1	58.7	65.8
Austria	88.0	107.4	124.7	114.9	121.5	Norway	98.2	139.2	154.7	164.1	180.6
Belgium	104.7	136.0	152.9	145.7	154.2	Philippines	4.0	4.0	5.0	5.4	5.7
Brazil	17.4	16.6	23.8	29.0	32.8	Poland	13.6	18.6	22.6	23.9	24.9
Canada	73.4	87.1	86.6	99.4	102.9	Portugal	23.8	31.6	36.0	34.1	36.3
Czech Republic	13.6	24.2	33.4	33.3	37.0	Singapore	46.9	44.0	51.3	54.9	63.6
Denmark	89.0	122.9	142.1	137.7	145.4	Slovakia	10.4	19.3	32.9	30.8	33.1
Estonia	10.2	18.3	28.7	27.1	29.3	Spain	49.7	68.8	81.5	76.6	80.1
Finland	79.6	111.6	127.1	118.1	124.3	Sweden	93.7	117.4	119.7	124.9	138.3
France	85.6	108.4	118.1	112.4	118.5	Switzerland	107.9	133.1	147.8	146.8	170.0
Germany	101.8	126.2	133.9	125.9	133.4	Taiwan	29.2	26.3	22.7	24.0	26.3
Greece	39.8	50.6	66.5	64.2	61.3	United Kingdom	82.8	98.6	86.2	83.6	86.6

[1] Trade-weighted average for all 33 foreign economies listed above. [2] Organisation for Economic Co-operation and Development; see text, this section. [3] Euro area refers to European Union member countries that have adopted the Euro as their common currency as of January 1, 2011 (including Austria, Belgium, Estonia, Finland, France, Germany, Greece, Ireland, Italy, Netherlands, Portugal, Slovakia, and Spain). [4] Czech Republic, Estonia, Hungary, Poland, and Slovakia. [5] South Korea, Philippines, Singapore, and Taiwan. Excludes Japan.

Source: U.S. Bureau of Labor Statistics, *International Comparisons of Hourly Compensation Costs in Manufacturing, 2011*, December 2012. See also <http://www.bls.gov/ilc/>.

Table 1383. Annual Percent Change in Labor Productivity and Hours Worked by Country: 1996 to 2012

[Annual percent change for period shown. For all advanced economies and Eastern European countries, labor productivity growth refers to the growth in gross domestic product (GDP) per hour worked. Data are derived from The Conference Board Total Economy Database, in association with the Groningen Growth and Development Centre at the University of Groningen, Netherlands. Growth for regional aggregates is based on the weighted sum of country labor productivity growth, with the weight calculated as the two-period average of country share in nominal GDP, adjusted for purchasing power parity (PPP), plus a reallocation term. GDP for each country is measured in constant 2012 US dollars, using GDP deflator changes. Growth rates are based on the difference in the log of the levels of each variable. Minus sign (-) indicates decrease]

Country	Labor productivity		Total hours worked		Country	Labor productivity		Total hours worked	
	1996-2005	2006-2012	1996-2005	2006-2012		1996-2005	2006-2012	1996-2005	2006-2012
Advanced economies [1]	2.2	1.1	0.5	0.1	Estonia	6.8	2.5	-0.1	-0.9
United States	**2.3**	**1.0**	**1.0**	**0.1**	Hungary	3.2	0.7	0.3	-0.7
Japan	1.8	1.3	-0.8	-1.1	Latvia	5.6	4.6	1.1	-3.8
					Lithuania	5.4	2.9	0.6	-0.9
European Union (EU-15, old) [2]	1.5	0.7	0.8	-0.1	Malta	1.7	0.6	0.4	1.2
Austria	1.7	1.3	0.7	0.2	Poland	3.7	2.5	0.4	1.7
Belgium	1.3	0.3	0.9	0.8	Romania	4.2	2.2	-2.0	(Z)
Denmark	1.2	0.3	0.9	-0.1	Slovakia	4.6	3.0	-0.5	1.1
Finland	2.5	0.6	1.2	0.4	Slovenia	4.1	1.2	-0.2	-0.2
France	1.7	0.6	0.5	0.2	European Union (EU-27, enlarged) [4]	1.9	0.8	0.5	0.1
Germany	1.6	0.9	-0.4	0.6					
Greece	3.2	-0.2	0.5	-1.7	Addenda:				
Ireland	4.1	2.4	3.3	-1.8	Other Advanced Economies [1]	3.1	2.0	0.8	0.9
Italy	0.5	0.1	0.9	-0.5	Australia	2.2	1.0	1.5	1.7
Luxembourg	2.1	-0.9	2.6	2.5	Canada	1.6	0.6	1.7	0.8
Netherlands	1.7	0.4	1.0	0.7	Hong Kong	1.6	3.1	1.8	0.6
Portugal	1.1	1.0	1.4	-1.2	Iceland	3.4	0.7	1.1	0.1
Spain	0.4	1.6	3.3	-1.1	Israel	1.2	1.2	2.3	2.9
Sweden	2.8	0.7	0.3	1.1	New Zealand	1.4	0.7	1.9	0.4
United Kingdom	2.4	0.4	0.7	0.1	Norway	2.3	-0.5	0.6	1.6
European Union (EU-12, new) [3]	4.0	2.3	-0.3	0.5	Singapore	2.4	0.6	2.7	4.9
Bulgaria	3.2	3.0	-0.4	-0.7	South Korea	4.8	3.5	(Z)	(Z)
Cyprus	1.6	0.7	1.9	0.7	Switzerland	1.3	0.5	0.4	1.4
Czech Republic	3.5	1.6	-0.6	0.4	Taiwan	4.0	2.9	0.3	0.8

Z Less than 0.05 percent. [1] "Advanced" includes the U.S., EU-15, Japan, and "other advanced" economies. [2] Referring to membership of the European Union until 30 April 2004. [3] Referring to new membership of the European Union as of 1 January 2007. [4] Referring to all 27 current members of the European Union.

Source: The Conference Board, New York, NY, "The Conference Board Total Economy Database," (January 2013) ©. Reproduced with permission from The Conference Board, Inc. 2013, The Conference Board, Inc.

Table 1384. Comparative Price Levels—Selected OECD Countries: July 2013

[Purchasing power parities (PPPs) are rates of currency conversion that eliminate the differences in price levels between countries. Comparative price levels are defined as the ratios of PPPs to exchange rates. The PPPs are given in national currency units per U.S. dollar. This table should be read vertically. Each column shows the number of specified monetary units needed in each of the countries listed to buy the same representative basket of consumer goods and services. In each case the representative basket costs a hundred units in the country whose currency is specified. For example, in July 2013, an item that costs $1.00 in the United States would cost $1.17 (U.S. dollars) in Japan]

Country	United States (USD)	Canada (CAD)	Chile (Chilean peso)	France (EUR)	Germany (EUR)	Italy (EUR)	Japan (JPY)	Korea (KRW)	Mexico (MXN)	Turkey (TRY)	United Kingdom (GBP)
United States [1]	**100**	**81**	**132**	**86**	**91**	**89**	**86**	**128**	**142**	**140**	**90**
Australia	141	115	187	121	128	126	121	181	201	198	127
Austria	114	93	151	98	103	102	97	146	162	160	103
Belgium	119	97	157	102	108	106	102	152	169	167	107
Canada	123	100	163	106	112	110	105	157	175	173	111
Chile	76	61	100	65	69	67	65	97	107	106	68
Czech Republic	78	64	103	67	71	70	67	100	111	110	70
Denmark	151	123	201	130	138	135	130	194	215	213	137
Estonia	86	70	114	74	78	77	74	110	122	121	78
Finland	134	109	177	115	121	119	114	171	190	187	121
France	116	95	154	100	106	104	100	149	165	163	105
Germany	110	90	146	95	100	98	94	141	156	154	99
Greece	98	80	130	84	89	88	84	126	139	138	89
Hungary	67	55	89	58	61	60	58	86	96	95	61
Iceland	128	104	170	110	117	115	110	164	182	180	116
Ireland	122	99	162	105	111	109	105	156	174	172	110
Israel [1]	118	96	156	101	107	105	101	151	167	165	106
Italy	112	91	148	96	102	100	96	143	159	157	101
Japan	117	95	155	100	106	104	100	150	166	164	105
Korea, South	78	64	103	67	71	70	67	100	111	110	71
Luxembourg	131	106	173	112	119	117	112	167	185	183	118
Mexico	70	57	93	61	64	63	60	90	100	99	64
Netherlands	117	96	155	101	107	105	101	150	167	165	106
New Zealand [1]	125	101	165	107	113	111	107	160	177	175	113
Norway	163	132	215	140	148	145	139	208	231	228	147
Poland	62	50	82	53	56	55	53	79	87	86	56
Portugal	92	75	122	79	84	82	79	118	131	130	83
Slovakia	78	64	103	67	71	70	67	100	111	110	71
Slovenia	92	75	122	79	84	82	79	118	131	129	83
Spain	103	84	137	89	94	92	89	132	147	145	93
Sweden	136	111	180	117	124	122	117	174	194	191	123
Switzerland	162	132	215	140	147	145	139	208	230	228	146
Turkey	71	58	94	61	65	64	61	91	101	100	64
United Kingdom	111	90	147	95	101	99	95	142	157	156	100

[1] Estimates based on quarterly consumer prices.

Source: Organisation for Economic Co-operation and Development (OECD), 2013, "Prices: Comparative Price Levels," Main Economic Indicators (database) ©, <http://dx.doi.org/10.1787/data-00536-en>, accessed September 2013.

Table 1385. Indexes of Living Costs Abroad: 2013

[As of April 2013. Washington, DC=100. Indexes compare the costs in dollars of representative goods and services (excluding housing and education) purchased at the foreign location and the cost of comparable goods and services in the Washington, DC area. The indexes are place-to-place comparisons at specific times and currency exchange rates. They cannot be used for measuring cost changes over time at a foreign location. Since the indexes reflect only the expenditure pattern and living costs of American families, they are not comparable to the living costs of foreign nationals living in their own country. Survey dates show month/day/year]

Country/Territory	City	Survey date	Local index[1]	Country/Territory	City	Survey date	Local index[1]
Algeria	Algiers	2/16/2009	127	Kyrgyzstan	Bishkek	2/16/2011	157
Angola	Luanda	2/17/2011	176	Laos	Vientiane	9/21/2010	125
Argentina	Buenos Aires	2/2/2012	146	Latvia	Riga	9/22/2010	138
Armenia	Yerevan	3/14/2010	113	Lebanon	Beirut	6/24/2012	119
Australia	Canberra	3/21/2013	153	Liberia	Monrovia	8/8/2012	143
Austria	Vienna	3/23/2011	177	Libya	Tripoli	1/5/2007	116
Azerbaijan	Baku	2/1/2009	156	Lithuania	Vilnius	7/22/2012	129
Bahrain	(X)	11/3/2009	123	Luxembourg	(X)	1/24/2011	164
Bangladesh	Dhaka	2/15/2011	98	Macedonia	Skopje	4/11/2010	125
Belarus	Minsk	3/29/2011	131	Madagascar	Antananarivo	1/30/2011	139
Belgium	Brussels	3/18/2011	173	Malawi	Lilongwe	10/25/2011	154
Bermuda	(X)	5/16/2012	176	Malaysia	Kuala Lumpur	11/21/2010	133
Bolivia	La Paz	7/21/2011	120	Mali	Bamako	10/14/2010	147
Bosnia-Herzegovina	Sarajevo	4/4/2012	125	Mauritania	Nouakchott	10/17/2012	137
Botswana	Gaborone	3/11/2012	145	Mexico	Mexico City	3/6/2009	99
Brazil	Sao Paulo	1/22/2012	165	Moldova	Chisinau	5/1/2012	122
Bulgaria	Sofia	6/4/2012	126	Mongolia	Ulaanbaatar	6/2/2011	139
Burma	Rangoon	3/7/2011	153	Montenegro	Podgorica	8/7/2012	123
Burundi	Bujumbura	5/20/2012	146	Morocco	Casablanca	8/3/2011	139
Cambodia	Phnom Penh	2/7/2011	121	Mozambique	Maputo	1/26/2012	155
Cameroon	Yaounde	7/31/2012	154	Nepal	Kathmandu	9/22/2009	103
Canada	Ottawa	10/19/2012	158	Netherlands	The Hague	11/28/2011	155
Chad	Ndjamena	1/30/2012	163	New Zealand	Wellington	9/27/2010	159
Chile	Santiago	10/22/2010	135	Nicaragua	Managua	11/9/2010	111
China	Shanghai	5/11/2012	161	Niger	Niamey	11/28/2012	135
Colombia	Bogota	7/31/2012	149	Nigeria	Abuja	9/30/2010	156
Costa Rica	San Jose	12/10/2009	123	Norway	Oslo	1/26/2009	176
Cote d'Ivoire	Abidjan	1/21/2011	136	Oman	Muscat	5/17/2010	131
Croatia	Zagreb	5/14/2012	134	Pakistan	Islamabad	12/10/2004	102
Cuba	Havana	4/22/2012	131	Panama	Panama City	7/31/2008	119
Cyprus	Nicosia	1/30/2012	155	Papua New Guinea	Port Moresby	5/7/2012	146
Czech Republic	Prague	7/12/2012	140	Paraguay	Asuncion	5/5/2010	115
Congo, Dem. Rep	Kinshasa	2/16/2012	194	Peru	Lima	3/8/2012	150
Denmark	Copenhagen	3/30/2009	190	Philippines	Manila	5/4/2010	108
Djibouti	Djibouti City	2/20/2011	145	Poland	Warsaw	7/31/2012	131
Dominican Republic	Santo Domingo	11/5/2012	125	Portugal	Lisbon	2/13/2011	154
Ecuador	Quito	8/10/2009	120	Qatar	Doha	5/12/2010	149
Egypt	Cairo	3/13/2006	96	Romania	Bucharest	6/14/2012	116
El Salvador	San Salvador	3/7/2011	127	Russia	Moscow	5/8/2011	206
Equatorial Guinea	Malabo	2/18/2010	177	Rwanda	Kigali	5/2/2010	149
Estonia	Tallinn	1/9/2012	137	Saudi Arabia	Riyadh	4/9/2010	122
Ethiopia	Addis Ababa	4/17/2010	115	Senegal	Dakar	4/18/2012	150
Fiji	Suva	6/16/2010	125	Serbia	Belgrade	4/19/2011	109
Finland	Helsinki	4/14/2009	171	Sierra Leone	Freetown	1/31/2012	145
France	Paris	4/29/2012	174	Singapore	(X)	3/16/2011	152
Gabon	Libreville	8/7/2011	165	Slovakia	Bratislava	6/17/2012	135
Georgia	Tbilisi	4/14/2009	140	South Africa	Johannesburg	9/30/2010	143
Germany	Berlin	6/23/2010	168	Spain	Madrid	4/23/2012	147
Ghana	Accra	5/16/2012	163	Sri Lanka	Colombo	3/30/2012	136
Greece	Athens	12/14/2010	158	Sudan	Khartoum	10/26/2011	160
Guatemala	Guatemala City	5/17/2011	119	Sweden	Stockholm	5/13/2010	185
Guyana	Georgetown	4/13/2012	155	Switzerland	Geneva	11/15/2010	217
Haiti	Port-au-Prince	9/24/2012	145	Syria	Damascus	10/13/2010	116
Honduras	Tegucigalpa	7/18/2012	114	Taiwan	Taipei	3/26/2011	143
Hong Kong	(X)	4/26/2011	151	Tajikistan	Dushanbe	10/28/2012	111
Hungary	Budapest	6/10/2012	126	Tanzania	Dar es Salaam	5/8/2012	130
Iceland	Reykjavik	6/27/2012	150	Thailand	Bangkok	2/26/2008	126
India	New Delhi	12/1/2010	129	Tunisia	Tunis	11/13/2009	123
Indonesia	Jakarta	11/22/2011	123	Turkey	Istanbul	4/11/2011	135
Iraq	Baghdad	7/21/2004	74	Uganda	Kampala	9/23/2012	137
Ireland	Dublin	7/7/2010	164	Ukraine	Kyiv	12/21/2010	127
Israel	Tel Aviv	6/8/2010	146	United Arab Emirates	Dubai	8/24/2011	128
Italy	Rome	2/5/2012	171	United Kingdom	London	3/19/2012	208
Jamaica	Kingston	1/21/2011	123	Uruguay	Montevideo	10/31/2011	148
Japan	Tokyo City	5/12/2011	213	Uzbekistan	Tashkent	7/4/2012	135
Jordan	Amman	12/20/2010	138	Venezuela	Caracas	12/11/2011	175
Kazakhstan	Astana	11/15/2011	134	Vietnam	Hanoi	12/12/2011	112
Kenya	Nairobi	8/15/2011	155	Yemen	Sanaa	4/25/2009	92
Korea, South	Seoul	2/16/2010	140	Zambia	Lusaka	1/24/2012	144
Kuwait	Kuwait City	11/21/2009	136	Zimbabwe	Harare	6/2/2010	156

X Not applicable. [1] The local index measures living costs for private American citizens and excludes special price advantages available only to U.S. government employees. The local index is a comparison of prices at the foreign post and in Washington, DC, with the price ratios weighted by the expenditure pattern of American employees living at the foreign post. This is the index most appropriate for use by business firms and other private organizations to establish cost-of-living allowances for their American employees stationed abroad.

Source: U.S. Department of State, Bureau of Administration, "Indexes of Living Costs Abroad, Quarters Allowances, and Hardship Differentials," January and April 2013, <http://aoprals.state.gov/content.asp?content_id=186&menu_id=81>.

Table 1386. Percent of Household Final Consumption Expenditures Spent on Food, Alcohol, and Tobacco Consumed at Home by Selected Countries: 2011

Country/Territory	Food [1]	Alcoholic beverages and tobacco	Country/Territory	Food [1]	Alcoholic beverages and tobacco	Country/Territory	Food [1]	Alcoholic beverages and tobacco
United States.........	6.7	2.0	Georgia............	40.8	5.0	Peru...................	36.6	6.1
Algeria................	43.7	2.0	Germany..........	11.1	3.1	Philippines..............	36.1	1.5
Argentina..............	21.2	4.5	Greece............	17.6	4.0	Poland................	20.1	6.5
Australia..............	10.7	3.6	Guatemala........	37.9	1.5	Portugal.............	15.5	2.8
Austria................	10.9	2.9	Hong Kong........	13.6	1.0	Qatar.................	12.3	0.3
Azerbaijan.............	43.9	2.0	Hungary..........	17.8	10.0	Romania..............	29.4	3.8
Bahrain................	14.1	0.4	India..............	26.3	3.1	Russia................	31.2	7.1
Belarus................	41.4	5.7	Indonesia.........	31.9	5.6	Saudi Arabia.......	26.1	0.6
Belgium...............	14.3	3.7	Iran...............	22.9	0.5	Singapore..............	7.4	2.2
Bolivia................	28.9	1.9	Ireland............	10.2	5.5	Slovakia..............	17.7	4.2
Bosnia-Herzegovina. ..	32.6	5.5	Israel.............	17.3	1.7	Slovenia.............	14.3	4.5
Brazil.................	15.9	1.5	Italy..............	14.6	2.7	South Africa.........	19.4	4.4
Bulgaria..............	21.2	3.8	Japan..............	14.7	2.9	South Korea..........	12.6	2.3
Cameroon.............	46.9	2.0	Jordan.............	40.4	5.0	Spain................	13.0	3.2
Canada...............	9.7	3.5	Kazakhstan.......	35.7	2.6	Sweden..............	12.4	3.2
Chile..................	16.3	3.0	Kenya.............	41.3	1.6	Switzerland.........	10.2	3.2
China..................	21.3	2.2	Kuwait.............	18.6	0.5	Taiwan..............	13.1	2.2
Colombia.............	18.7	3.2	Latvia.............	17.6	7.2	Thailand.............	31.6	4.7
Costa Rica............	23.5	0.5	Lithuania.........	21.4	5.5	Tunisia..............	35.5	1.0
Croatia...............	22.6	4.3	Macedonia.........	32.7	3.8	Turkey...............	21.8	4.2
Czech Republic........	15.7	7.4	Malaysia..........	19.8	2.5	Turkmenistan........	24.6	2.0
Denmark..............	11.2	3.8	Mexico............	22.7	2.3	Ukraine..............	38.2	6.5
Dominican Republic. ..	24.8	4.2	Morocco..........	40.5	1.3	United Arab Emirates. ..	14.4	0.2
Ecuador..............	22.2	0.9	Netherlands.......	11.8	3.3	United Kingdom.........	9.4	3.5
Egypt.................	43.6	2.3	New Zealand......	14.7	2.6	Uruguay..............	18.4	3.5
Estonia...............	20.0	8.1	Nigeria............	39.6	2.5	Uzbekistan............	31.2	2.6
Finland...............	12.0	4.7	Norway............	13.1	4.1	Venezuela............	19.5	3.6
France................	13.3	3.2	Pakistan...........	41.7	1.1	Vietnam..............	21.7	3.2

[1] Includes nonalcoholic beverages.

Source: U.S. Department of Agriculture, Economic Research Service, Food Expenditure Series, "Expenditures on food and alcoholic beverages that were consumed at home by selected countries," <http://www.ers.usda.gov/data-products/food-expenditures.aspx#26654>, accessed July 2013.

Table 1387. Gross Public Debt, Expenditures, and Receipts as Percent of GDP by Country: 2000 to 2013

[Percent of nominal gross domestic product. Gross debt includes one-off revenues from the sale of the mobile telephone licenses. Expenditures and receipts refer to the general government sector, which is a consolidation of accounts for the central, state, and local governments plus social security. Expenditures, or total outlays, are defined as current outlays plus capital outlays. Receipts cover current receipts, but exclude capital receipts. Nontax receipts consist of property income (including dividends and other transfers from public enterprises), fees, charges, sales, fines, capital transfers received by the general government, etc. Minus sign (-) indicates deficit]

Country	Gross debt			Expenditures			Receipts		
	2000	2010	2013	2000	2010	2013	2000	2010	2013
United States [1]...............	1.5	-11.4	-5.4	33.9	42.7	39.1	35.4	31.3	33.7
Australia.......................	1.5	-5.2	-1.8	33.9	36.3	35.0	35.3	31.1	33.2
Austria........................	-1.8	-4.5	-2.3	52.0	52.5	51.4	50.1	48.1	49.1
Belgium.......................	-0.1	-3.9	-2.6	49.1	52.6	53.9	49.0	48.7	51.3
Canada........................	2.9	-5.2	-2.9	40.5	43.2	41.0	43.4	38.0	38.1
Czech Republic................	-3.6	-4.8	-3.3	41.6	43.9	44.9	38.0	39.1	41.5
Denmark.......................	2.2	-2.7	-1.8	53.7	57.7	58.4	55.8	55.0	56.6
Estonia........................	-0.2	0.2	0.0	36.1	40.7	40.0	35.9	40.9	40.1
Finland........................	7.0	-2.8	-2.3	48.4	55.8	56.7	55.4	53.0	54.4
France.........................	-1.5	-7.1	-4.0	51.6	56.6	57.1	50.1	49.5	53.2
Germany.......................	1.1	-4.2	-0.2	45.1	47.8	45.5	46.2	43.6	45.2
Greece........................	-3.7	-10.8	-4.1	46.7	51.4	48.3	42.9	40.6	44.1
Hungary.......................	-3.1	-4.4	-2.8	47.6	49.6	48.2	44.6	45.2	45.4
Iceland........................	1.7	-10.1	-0.2	41.9	51.6	44.0	43.6	41.5	43.8
Ireland........................	4.8	-30.8	-7.5	31.2	66.1	42.2	36.0	35.2	34.7
Israel.........................	-4.0	-4.8	-5.7	51.6	45.1	44.4	47.6	40.3	38.7
Italy..........................	-0.9	-4.3	-3.0	45.8	50.4	51.2	44.9	46.1	48.2
Japan.........................	-7.4	-8.3	-10.3	38.5	40.7	42.8	31.1	32.4	32.6
Korea.........................	5.4	1.3	1.4	22.4	30.1	31.1	27.9	31.4	32.4
Luxembourg...................	6.0	-0.9	-0.7	37.6	42.9	43.5	43.6	42.0	42.9
Netherlands....................	2.0	-5.0	-3.7	44.1	51.2	50.7	46.1	46.1	47.1
New Zealand...................	1.7	-7.5	-2.4	38.1	49.3	44.0	39.8	41.7	41.7
Norway........................	15.4	11.1	12.3	42.3	45.2	44.2	57.7	56.3	56.5
Poland.........................	-3.0	-7.9	-3.4	41.1	45.5	42.5	38.1	37.6	39.1
Portugal.......................	-3.3	-9.9	-6.4	41.6	51.5	48.1	38.3	41.7	41.7
Slovak Republic................	-12.3	-7.7	-2.6	52.1	40.0	36.9	39.9	32.3	34.3
Slovenia......................	-3.7	-5.9	-7.8	46.5	50.4	53.2	42.8	44.5	45.4
Spain..........................	-1.0	-9.7	-6.9	39.2	46.3	42.9	38.2	36.6	36.0
Sweden........................	3.6	0.0	-1.6	55.1	52.3	52.8	58.7	52.3	51.2
Switzerland....................	-0.4	0.3	0.7	35.6	33.8	34.0	35.2	34.0	34.7
United Kingdom................	3.7	-10.0	-7.1	36.5	50.3	48.4	40.3	40.3	41.3

[1] Receipts exclude the operating surpluses of public enterprises, while expenditures include them.

Source: Organisation for Economic Cooperation and Development (OECD), *2012 OECD Economic Outlook*, Vol. 2012/2 ©, OECD Publishing. See also <http://dx.doi.org/10.1787/eco_outlook-v2012-2-en>.

Table 1388. Percent Distribution of Tax Receipts by Country and Tax Type: 2000 and 2010

Country	Total [1]	Income and profits taxes [2]			Social security contributions			Taxes on goods and services [5]		
		Total [3]	Individual	Corporate	Total [4]	Employees	Employers	Total [3]	General consumption taxes [6]	Taxes on specific goods, services [7]
United States:										
2000..............	100.0	50.5	41.8	8.7	23.4	10.5	11.7	16.0	7.6	6.3
2010..............	100.0	43.6	32.8	10.8	25.7	11.3	13.0	18.0	8.1	6.9
Australia:										
2000..............	100.0	58.0	37.8	20.2	0.0	0.0	0.0	28.7	12.0	14.1
2010..............	100.0	57.1	38.6	18.5	0.0	0.0	0.0	28.4	13.8	11.9
Canada:										
2000..............	100.0	50.1	36.8	12.2	13.6	5.5	7.8	24.2	14.2	8.6
2010..............	100.0	46.8	34.9	10.7	15.3	6.1	8.7	24.3	14.0	8.7
Chile:										
2000..............	100.0	23.3	(NA)	(NA)	7.3	7.0	0.3	63.8	41.8	18.8
2010..............	100.0	38.4	(NA)	(NA)	6.9	6.6	0.3	51.3	38.7	9.8
Czech Republic:										
2000..............	100.0	22.8	12.9	9.9	44.3	10.0	28.5	31.5	18.3	11.0
2010..............	100.0	20.4	10.5	9.9	44.6	9.1	28.1	33.2	20.4	10.7
France:										
2000..............	100.0	24.9	18.0	6.9	36.1	9.0	24.8	25.8	17.1	8.0
2010..............	100.0	21.9	17.0	5.0	38.7	9.4	26.3	25.0	16.8	7.5
Germany:										
2000..............	100.0	30.1	25.3	4.8	39.0	17.2	19.2	28.1	18.4	8.8
2010..............	100.0	28.7	24.5	4.2	39.0	17.4	18.7	29.5	20.1	8.4
Italy:										
2000..............	100.0	33.2	24.8	6.9	28.5	5.4	19.9	27.9	15.4	9.6
2010..............	100.0	32.9	27.3	6.6	31.3	5.6	21.5	25.9	14.6	8.5
Japan:										
2000..............	100.0	34.8	21.1	13.8	35.2	14.7	16.4	19.3	9.1	8.0
2010..............	100.0	30.2	18.6	11.6	41.1	18.8	18.6	18.7	9.6	7.2
Korea, South:										
2000..............	100.0	28.8	14.6	14.1	16.7	6.3	6.9	38.4	17.0	19.7
2010..............	100.0	28.2	14.3	13.9	22.8	9.5	9.9	33.9	17.6	15.2
Turkey:										
2000..............	100.0	29.5	22.2	7.3	18.7	6.7	9.0	42.0	24.2	16.4
2010..............	100.0	21.7	14.3	7.4	23.7	8.8	13.1	48.4	22.1	24.5
United Kingdom:										
2000..............	100.0	39.0	29.4	9.7	17.0	6.8	9.6	31.9	18.1	12.4
2010..............	100.0	37.5	28.8	8.8	19.0	7.5	11.0	30.8	18.8	10.7

NA Not available. [1] Includes property taxes, employer payroll taxes other than social security contributions, and miscellaneous taxes not shown separately. [2] Includes taxes on capital gains. [3] Includes other taxes, not shown separately. [4] Includes contributions of self-employed persons, not shown separately. [5] Taxes on the production, sales, transfer, leasing, and delivery of goods and services and rendering of services. [6] Primarily value-added and sales taxes. [7] For example, excise taxes on alcohol, tobacco, and gasoline.

Source: Organisation for Economic Co-operation and Development (OECD), "Taxing Wages: Comparative Tables," OECD Tax Statistics database ©, <http://www.oecd.org/ctp/taxdatabase>, accessed September 2013.

Table 1389. Household Tax Burden by Country: 2012

[Percent of gross wage earnings of the average worker. The tax burden reflects income tax plus employee social security contributions less cash benefits]

Country	Single person without children	One-earner family with two children	Country	Single person without children	One-earner family with two children
OECD average [1]................	25.14	19.65	Italy.........................	30.80	24.19
United States...................	**22.73**	**10.41**	Japan........................	21.22	19.76
Australia........................	22.88	21.77	Korea, South................	12.96	10.21
Austria.........................	33.99	31.89	Luxembourg.................	27.85	17.30
Belgium........................	42.78	31.76	Mexico.......................	9.47	9.47
Canada.........................	22.58	16.05	Netherlands.................	31.94	28.73
Chile...........................	7.00	7.00	New Zealand................	16.39	16.39
Czech Republic..................	22.83	5.64	Norway......................	29.40	26.91
Denmark........................	38.89	34.81	Poland.......................	24.62	17.83
Estonia.........................	19.90	13.27	Portugal.....................	21.71	14.05
Finland.........................	29.40	29.40	Slovakia.....................	22.80	10.68
France..........................	28.32	22.25	Slovenia.....................	33.07	24.74
Germany........................	39.91	21.28	Spain........................	23.88	16.14
Greece..........................	25.37	26.68	Sweden......................	24.89	24.89
Hungary........................	35.01	26.28	Switzerland..................	16.55	10.75
Iceland.........................	29.42	20.23	Turkey.......................	27.95	26.50
Ireland.........................	17.99	10.45	United Kingdom.............	24.94	24.94
Israel..........................	15.45	15.45			

[1] The Organisation for Economic Co-operation and Development (OECD) is comprised of the 34 member countries shown above. See text, this section.

Source: Organisation for Economic Co-operation and Development (OECD), "Taxing Wages: Comparative Tables," OECD Tax Statistics database ©, <http://www.oecd.org/ctp/taxdatabase>, accessed September 2013.

Table 1390. Household Net Saving Rates by Country: 1995 to 2011

[As a percentage of household disposable income. Household savings are estimated by subtracting household consumption expenditure from household disposable income, plus the change in net equity of households in pension funds. Households include households plus nonprofit institutions serving households. Net saving rates are measured after deducting consumption of fixed capital (depreciation), with respect to assets used in enterprises operated by households, as well as owner-occupied dwellings. The household saving rate is calculated as the ratio of household savings to household disposable income (plus the change in net equity of households in pension funds). Minus sign (-) indicates an excess of expenditures over income]

Country	1995	2000	2005	2006	2007	2008	2009	2010	2011
United States	**5.7**	**3.0**	**1.7**	**2.7**	**2.4**	**5.5**	**5.0**	**5.3**	**4.4**
EU-27 [1]	(NA)	6.2	5.8	5.5	5.3	5.7	7.8	6.3	5.6
Australia [2]	5.4	2.5	1.6	3.2	3.6	10.2	8.9	9.2	(NA)
Austria	12.7	9.3	9.6	10.4	11.6	11.5	11.2	9.1	7.4
Belgium	16.4	12.5	9.9	10.7	11.4	11.5	13.3	10.1	8.8
Canada	9.4	4.8	2.2	3.6	2.9	4.0	4.7	4.9	(NA)
Czech Republic	8.1	5.8	4.8	6.1	5.7	4.8	6.8	6.2	5.1
Denmark	0.2	-4.0	-4.2	-2.3	-4.0	-3.7	-0.4	-0.2	-0.2
Finland	4.1	0.5	0.9	-1.1	-0.9	-0.3	4.2	3.6	1.3
France	12.5	11.0	11.1	11.2	11.7	11.7	12.6	12.1	12.2
Germany	11.2	9.4	10.7	10.8	11.0	11.5	10.9	10.9	10.4
Greece	(NA)	(NA)	-1.7	-1.0	2.5	-4.1	-2.9	-8.8	-12.5
Hungary	14.4	6.2	6.7	7.2	3.3	2.7	4.8	5.4	5.1
Ireland	(NA)	(NA)	1.9	-0.9	-2.2	3.7	9.8	7.0	5.6
Italy	16.6	7.9	10.2	9.5	8.9	8.5	7.1	4.9	4.1
Japan	(NA)	(NA)	1.6	1.3	1.1	0.6	2.3	2.1	2.3
Korea, South	18.5	9.3	7.2	5.2	2.9	2.9	4.6	4.3	3.5
Mexico	(NA)	(NA)	10.1	10.1	9.7	9.2	9.0	9.0	8.2
Netherlands	14.3	6.9	6.4	6.1	6.9	5.9	5.6	3.3	4.9
Norway	4.9	4.3	9.6	-0.5	0.8	3.7	6.9	5.6	7.1
Poland	14.6	10.0	5.9	6.5	4.6	-0.3	6.8	6.1	-0.2
Russia	(NA)	(NA)	11.0	12.4	12.1	10.1	13.1	15.9	(NA)
Slovenia	5.9	7.8	11.2	11.7	10.0	9.6	8.4	6.9	5.0
South Africa	1.6	1.0	0.1	-0.8	-1.2	-1.2	-0.8	-0.5	-0.2
Spain	(NA)	6.1	4.8	3.9	4.0	7.7	12.3	7.1	4.7
Sweden	7.5	3.1	4.0	4.9	7.2	9.0	11.0	8.3	10.2
Switzerland	12.1	10.6	8.8	10.7	12.5	11.7	11.4	11.4	12.8
United Kingdom	5.8	-0.3	-2.5	-3.1	-4.3	-2.7	1.8	2.0	1.9

NA Not available. [1] See footnote 4, Table 1403 for list of EU-27 countries. [2] Data refer to fiscal year.

Source: Organisation for Economic Co-operation and Development (OECD), "National Accounts at a Glance," OECD National Accounts Statistics database ©, accessed September 2013. See also <http://www.oecd-ilibrary.org/economics/national-accounts-at-a-glance_22200444>.

Table 1391. Insurance and Pensions by Country: 2011

Country	Investment assets (million U.S. dollars) [1]	Direct gross premiums (percent of GDP)	Total gross premiums (million U.S. dollars) Life	Total gross premiums (million U.S. dollars) Non-life	Gross claims payments (million U.S. dollars) Life	Gross claims payments (million U.S. dollars) Non-life	Pensions Investment assets (million U.S. dollars)	Contributions (percent of GDP) [3]	Benefits paid (percent of GDP)
United States [4]	4,586,791	11.1	799,066	1,236,495	333,218	828,168	10,607,305	3.9	4.5
Australia	94,157	5.0	47,922	36,572	46,380	39,854	1,339,959	7.5	4.5
Canada	653,519	5.0	31,990	61,964	27	29,488	1,106,091	2.9	2.9
Chile	44,892	3.9	6,067	3,633	6,026	1,362	145,512	3.7	1.1
Czech Republic	(NA)	4.0	4,079	4,706	290	221	14,019	0.8	0.5
Denmark	320,385	10.1	23,120	10,799	16,147	8,575	165,741	0.5	0.7
Estonia	1,233	1.9	223	337	160	215	1,577	5.1	(Z)
Finland	70,853	3.7	5,181	4,943	4,996	3,764	199,809	9.6	10.4
France	2,298,584	9.5	184,368	103,283	43,061	67,642	6,954	(Z)	(Z)
Germany	1,486,231	(NA)	116,693	138,807	118,559	130,144	195,358	0.3	0.2
Greece	13,581	2.3	3,010	3,878	1,509	763	102	(Z)	(Z)
Hungary	6,256	2.9	2,217	1,846	848	94	5,287	0.3	0.2
Ireland	67,210	20.2	35,293	9,263	(NA)	8,291	100,556	(NA)	(NA)
Israel	35,258	5.2	6,682	5,983	(NA)	364	120,101	2.4	1.7
Italy	573,675	7.0	105,231	51,623	43,364	7,566	106,889	0.6	0.2
Japan [5]	2,222,671	7.2	257,345	86,040	186,528	39,888	301,994	0.4	0.2
Korea, South [4]	346,009	11.2	72,003	48,866	44,636	19,670	40,146	(NA)	0.8
Luxembourg	43,427	31.6	17,317	1,843	9,909	886	1,156	0.2	0.1
Mexico	47,572	1.9	10,138	12,534	770	1,187	149,010	0.9	0.3
Netherlands	315,544	6.9	30,147	28,459	33,473	19,470	1,134,726	5.1	4.2
Norway	166,829	4.9	12,784	11,034	7,277	7,831	35,977	0.4	0.2
Poland	31,483	3.7	10,767	8,554	8,813	4,644	77,433	1.0	(Z)
Portugal	63,826	6.3	10,035	5,595	9,645	2,208	18,410	0.7	0.6
Slovak Republic	6,411	3.1	1,593	1,403	136	41	8,065	1.3	(NA)
South Africa [4]	(NA)	13.8	39,454	10,819	(NA)	(NA)	179,014	4.8	5.3
Spain	294,294	5.6	41,730	43,184	18,278	13,391	116,355	0.5	0.4
Sweden	396,887	4.9	13,947	14,165	8,248	10,552	49,635	(NA)	(NA)
Switzerland	431,125	9.9	34,552	36,853	30,693	17,944	703,448	8.4	5.1
Thailand [4]	(NA)	4.2	9,347	4,179	(NA)	(NA)	19,533	0.7	0.4
Turkey	5,235	1.3	1,887	8,397	1,160	4,775	8,569	1.0	(Z)
United Kingdom	(NA)	12.4	240,365	93,270	(NA)	(NA)	2,313,484	2.9	3.2

NA Not available or not applicable. Z Less than 0.05 percent. [1] Includes total investment assets of direct insurance companies (excludes re-insurance). [2] Includes private, autonomous pension funds of all types (occupational and personal, mandatory and voluntary). [3] Pension contributions include employee and employer contributions combined. [4] 2010 data. [5] 2005 data.

Source: Organisation for Economic Co-operation and Development (OECD), Insurance Statistics database © and Global Pension Statistics database ©, <http://www.oecd.org/daf/fin/insurance/oecdinsurancestatistics.htm> and <http://www.oecd.org/daf/fin/private-pensions/globalpensionstatistics.htm>, accessed September 2013.

Table 1392. Annual Percent Changes in Consumer Prices by Country: 2008 to 2012

[Percent change from previous year. Inflation as measured by the consumer price index reflects the annual percentage change in the cost to the average consumer of acquiring a basket of goods and services that may be fixed or adjusted at specified intervals, such as yearly. For general comments concerning the data, see text, this section. For additional qualifications of the data for individual countries, see source. Minus sign (-) indicates decrease]

Country	2008	2009	2010	2011	2012	Country	2008	2009	2010	2011	2012
World [1]	**9.0**	**2.9**	**3.6**	**5.0**	**3.8**	Kazakhstan	17.2	7.3	7.1	8.3	5.1
						Kenya	26.2	9.2	4.0	14.0	9.4
United States	**3.8**	**-0.4**	**1.6**	**3.2**	**2.1**	Korea, South	4.7	2.8	3.0	4.0	2.2
Argentina	8.6	6.3	10.8	9.5	10.0	Latvia	15.4	3.5	-1.1	4.4	2.3
Australia	4.4	1.8	2.8	3.4	1.8	Malaysia	5.4	0.6	1.7	3.2	1.7
Azerbaijan	20.8	1.4	5.9	7.8	1.1	Mexico	5.1	5.3	4.2	3.4	4.1
Bangladesh	8.9	5.4	8.1	10.7	8.7	Mongolia	25.1	6.3	10.1	9.5	15.0
Belarus	14.8	12.9	7.7	53.2	59.2	Morocco	3.7	1.0	1.0	0.9	1.3
Brazil	5.7	4.9	5.0	6.6	5.4	Myanmar	26.8	1.5	7.7	5.0	(NA)
Cambodia	25.0	-0.7	4.0	5.5	2.9	Netherlands	2.5	1.2	1.3	2.4	2.4
Canada	2.4	0.3	1.8	2.9	1.5	Pakistan	20.3	13.6	13.9	11.9	9.7
China	5.9	-0.7	3.3	5.4	2.7	Philippines	8.3	4.1	3.9	4.6	3.2
Colombia	7.0	4.2	2.3	3.4	3.2	Poland	4.3	3.8	2.7	4.2	3.7
Czech Republic	6.4	1.0	1.4	1.9	3.3	Romania	7.8	5.6	6.1	5.8	3.3
						Russian					
Egypt, Arab Rep	18.3	11.8	11.3	10.1	7.1	Federation	14.1	11.7	6.9	8.4	5.1
Ethiopia	44.4	8.5	8.1	33.2	23.4	Saudi Arabia	9.9	5.1	5.3	5.3	4.5
France	2.8	0.1	1.5	2.1	2.0	Singapore	6.5	0.6	2.8	5.3	4.5
Germany	2.6	0.3	1.1	2.1	2.0	South Africa	11.5	7.1	4.3	5.3	5.4
Ghana	16.5	19.3	10.7	8.7	9.2	Spain	4.1	-0.3	1.8	3.2	2.4
Greece	4.2	1.2	4.7	3.3	1.5	Sri Lanka	22.6	3.5	6.2	6.7	6.8
Haiti	15.5	0.0	5.7	8.4	6.3	Sweden	3.4	-0.5	1.2	3.0	0.9
						Syrian Arab					
Honduras	11.4	5.5	4.7	6.8	5.2	Republic	15.7	2.9	4.4	4.8	36.7
India	8.4	10.9	12.0	8.9	9.3	Thailand	5.4	-0.9	3.3	3.8	3.0
Indonesia	9.8	4.8	5.1	5.4	4.3	Turkey	10.4	6.3	8.6	6.5	8.9
Iran, Islamic Rep	25.5	13.5	10.1	20.6	27.3	Ukraine	25.2	15.9	9.4	8.0	0.6
Ireland	4.1	-4.5	-0.9	2.6	1.7	United Kingdom	3.6	2.2	3.3	4.5	2.8
Italy	3.4	0.8	1.5	2.7	3.0	Venezuela	(NA)	27.1	28.2	26.1	21.1
Japan	1.4	-1.3	-0.7	-0.3	0.0	Vietnam	23.1	7.1	8.9	18.7	9.1

NA Not available. [1] Includes other countries not shown separately.

Source: The World Bank, Washington, DC, World Development Indicators database, "Inflation, consumer prices" ©, <http://data.worldbank.org/data-catalog/world-development-indicators>, accessed July 2013.

Table 1393. Unemployment Rates by Country: 1990 to 2012

[Annual averages. The standardized unemployment rates shown here are calculated as the number of unemployed persons as a percentage of the civilian labor force. The unemployed are persons of working age who, in the reference period, are without work, available for work, and have taken specific steps to find work]

Country	1990	1995	2000	2005	2006	2007	2008	2009	2010	2011	2012
OECD, total [1]	(NA)	(NA)	6.1	6.6	6.1	5.6	5.9	8.1	8.3	7.9	(NA)
EU-27 [2]	(NA)	(NA)	9.2	8.9	8.2	7.1	7.0	8.9	9.6	9.6	(NA)
United States	**5.6**	**5.6**	**4.0**	**5.1**	**4.6**	**4.6**	**5.8**	**9.3**	**9.6**	**8.9**	**8.1**
Australia	6.9	8.5	6.3	5.0	4.8	4.4	4.2	5.6	5.2	5.1	5.2
Austria	3.2	3.7	3.6	5.2	4.8	4.4	3.8	4.8	4.4	4.2	4.3
Belgium	8.9	13.0	7.0	8.4	8.2	7.5	7.0	7.9	8.3	7.1	7.5
Canada	8.1	9.5	6.8	6.8	6.3	6.0	6.1	8.3	8.0	7.4	7.2
Chile	(NA)	(NA)	9.2	8.0	7.7	7.1	7.8	9.7	8.1	7.2	(NA)
Czech Republic	0.8	4.1	8.9	8.0	7.2	5.3	4.4	6.7	7.3	6.7	7.0
Denmark	8.4	7.1	4.6	5.0	4.1	4.0	3.4	6.1	7.6	7.8	(NA)
Estonia	0.7	9.7	13.6	8.0	5.9	4.7	5.6	13.8	17.0	12.5	10.2
Finland	3.2	15.4	9.8	8.4	7.7	6.9	6.4	8.3	8.4	7.8	7.7
France	7.9	10.0	8.3	8.7	8.6	7.8	7.3	9.0	9.2	9.1	(NA)
Germany	4.8	8.2	7.8	11.2	10.3	8.7	7.6	7.8	7.1	5.9	5.5
Greece	7.0	10.0	11.2	9.6	8.8	8.1	7.2	8.9	11.8	16.3	23.6
Hungary	(NA)	10.4	6.5	7.3	7.5	7.4	7.9	10.1	11.2	11.0	10.9
Iceland	1.8	4.9	2.3	2.6	2.9	2.3	3.0	7.2	7.6	7.1	6.0
Ireland	13.0	12.2	4.6	4.8	4.7	4.8	5.8	12.3	13.9	14.6	15.0
Israel	(NA)	6.9	8.8	9.0	8.4	7.3	6.1	7.5	6.6	5.6	(NA)
Italy	11.5	11.7	10.7	7.8	6.9	6.2	6.8	7.9	8.5	8.5	10.8
Japan	2.1	3.2	4.7	4.4	4.1	3.8	4.0	5.1	5.0	4.6	4.3
Korea, South	2.4	2.1	4.4	3.7	3.5	3.2	3.2	3.6	3.7	3.4	3.2
Luxembourg	1.1	2.3	1.8	3.1	2.9	2.8	2.9	4.0	4.2	4.2	(NA)
Mexico	2.7	6.9	2.6	3.5	3.2	3.4	3.5	5.2	5.2	5.2	4.9
Netherlands	7.7	7.2	2.7	4.7	3.9	3.2	2.8	3.4	4.5	4.4	5.3
New Zealand	8.0	6.4	6.2	3.8	3.8	3.7	4.2	6.2	6.5	6.5	6.9
Norway	5.3	5.0	3.5	4.6	3.5	2.5	2.6	3.2	3.6	3.3	(NA)
Poland	6.5	13.3	16.1	17.7	13.8	9.6	7.1	8.2	9.6	9.6	10.1
Portugal	4.6	7.2	4.0	7.7	7.7	8.0	7.6	9.5	10.8	12.8	15.7
Slovakia	(NA)	13.1	18.8	16.2	13.3	11.0	9.6	12.1	14.4	13.5	13.9
Spain	16.3	23.0	13.9	9.2	8.5	8.3	11.4	18.1	20.1	21.7	25.1
Sweden	1.8	9.2	5.9	7.8	7.1	6.2	6.2	8.3	8.6	7.8	8.0
Switzerland	0.5	3.2	2.5	4.2	3.8	3.4	3.2	4.1	4.2	3.8	3.9
Turkey	8.0	7.6	6.5	10.6	10.2	10.3	11.0	14.0	11.9	9.8	9.2
United Kingdom	6.9	8.6	5.5	4.7	5.4	5.3	5.3	7.7	7.8	7.9	7.9

NA Not available. [1] For complete OECD membership listing, see Section 30 introduction. [2] See footnote 4, Table 1403.

Source: Organisation for Economic Co-operation and Development (OECD), 2013, "Labour Force Statistics: Population and Labour Force," OECD Employment and Labour Market Statistics (database) ©, <http://dx.doi.org/10.1787/data-00288-en>, accessed September 2013.

Table 1394. Civilian Labor Force, Employment, and Unemployment by Country: 1970 to 2012

[For labor force and employment, 82,771 represents 82,771,000. Data based on U.S. labor force definitions (see source) except that minimum age for working-age population varies as follows: United States, Canada, France, Spain, and United Kingdom, 16 years; and Australia, Japan, Netherlands, Germany, and South Korea, 15 years. Data may not be comparable to prior years due to breaks in series resulting from changes in methodology. For specific methodological information for individual countries, see source]

Year	United States	Canada	Aus-tralia	Japan	South Korea	France	Ger-many [1]	Nether-lands	Spain	United King-dom
Civilian labor force (1,000):										
1970	82,771	8,395	5,478	50,736	10,062	20,800	26,247	(NA)	(NA)	(NA)
1980	106,940	11,725	6,693	55,738	14,431	22,719	27,256	5,870	13,279	26,762
1990	125,840	14,047	8,444	62,986	18,539	24,606	29,412	6,765	15,154	28,777
2000	142,583	15,632	9,590	66,710	[2] 22,135	25,970	39,301	[2] 8,049	17,482	28,962
2005	149,320	17,056	10,529	65,384	23,743	27,028	[2] 40,696	8,485	[2] 20,735	30,148
2010	153,889	18,263	11,806	65,521	24,749	28,043	41,495	[2] 8,697	22,941	31,405
2012	154,975	18,616	12,137	64,642	25,501	28,371	42,189	8,832	22,924	31,986
Labor force participation rate: [3]										
1970	60.4	57.8	62.1	64.5	57.6	56.2	56.9	(NA)	(NA)	(NA)
1980	63.8	65.0	62.1	62.6	59.0	56.0	54.7	55.4	50.4	62.8
1990	66.5	67.4	64.7	62.6	60.0	55.7	55.0	57.0	50.2	64.4
2000	67.1	66.0	64.4	61.7	[2] 61.2	55.4	56.7	[2] 63.4	52.3	62.8
2005	66.0	67.3	65.4	59.5	62.0	55.3	[2] 57.5	64.9	[2] 57.1	63.1
2010	64.7	67.0	66.4	59.1	61.0	55.8	58.6	[2] 64.6	59.8	63.2
2012	63.7	66.7	66.2	58.4	61.3	55.9	59.2	64.8	59.8	63.4
Civilian employment (1,000):										
1970	78,678	7,919	5,388	50,146	9,617	20,270	26,107	(NA)	(NA)	(NA)
1980	99,303	10,872	6,284	54,598	13,683	21,443	26,486	5,520	11,778	24,929
1990	118,793	12,964	7,859	61,706	18,085	22,630	27,952	6,249	12,857	26,724
2000	136,891	14,677	8,989	63,790	21,156	23,731	36,236	[2] 7,803	15,387	27,375
2005	141,730	16,032	9,998	62,908	22,856	24,596	[2] 36,123	8,044	[2] 18,823	28,681
2010	139,064	16,969	11,189	62,421	23,829	25,403	38,549	[2] 8,307	18,309	28,929
2012	142,469	17,445	11,501	62,152	24,681	25,547	39,873	8,364	17,155	29,439
Employment-population ratio: [4]										
1970	57.4	54.5	61.1	63.8	55.1	54.8	56.6	(NA)	(NA)	(NA)
1980	59.2	60.3	58.3	61.3	55.9	52.8	53.1	52.1	44.7	58.5
1990	62.8	62.2	60.2	61.3	58.6	51.3	52.3	52.7	42.6	59.8
2000	64.4	62.0	60.3	59.0	58.5	50.6	52.2	[2] 61.4	46.0	59.4
2005	62.7	63.3	62.1	57.3	59.7	50.3	[2] 51.1	61.5	[2] 51.8	60.0
2010	58.5	62.3	63.0	56.3	58.7	50.5	54.4	[2] 61.7	47.7	58.2
2012	58.6	62.5	62.7	56.1	59.4	50.3	55.9	61.4	44.8	58.3
Unemployment rate:										
1970	4.9	5.7	1.7	1.2	4.4	2.5	0.5	(NA)	(NA)	(NA)
1980	7.1	7.3	6.1	2.0	5.2	5.6	2.8	6.0	11.3	6.8
1990	5.6	7.7	6.9	2.0	2.4	8.0	5.0	7.6	15.2	7.1
2000	4.0	6.1	6.3	4.4	[2] 4.4	8.6	7.8	[2] 3.1	12.0	5.5
2005	5.1	6.0	5.0	3.8	3.7	9.0	[2] 11.2	5.2	[2] 9.2	4.9
2010	9.6	7.1	5.2	4.7	3.7	9.4	7.1	[2] 4.5	20.2	7.9
2012	8.1	6.3	5.2	3.9	3.2	10.0	5.5	5.3	25.2	8.0
Men	8.2	6.7	5.2	3.6	3.4	9.9	5.7	5.4	24.9	8.4
Women	7.9	5.8	5.3	4.2	3.0	10.0	5.2	5.2	25.5	7.4
Under 25 years old	16.2	13.0	11.7	7.5	9.0	23.9	8.2	9.6	53.7	21.2
Teenagers [5]	24.0	18.7	16.7	7.6	8.7	32.8	9.2	12.8	73.3	30.5
20 to 24 years old	13.3	10.0	8.6	7.5	9.0	21.9	7.9	7.2	49.7	16.9
25 years old and over	6.8	5.1	3.9	3.5	2.8	8.4	5.2	4.5	22.8	5.7

[1] Unified Germany for 1991 onward. Prior to 1991, data relate to the former West Germany. [2] Break in series. Data not comparable with prior years. [3] Civilian labor force as a percent of the civilian working-age population. Germany and Japan include the institutionalized population as part of the working-age population. [4] Civilian employment as a percent of the civilian working-age population. Germany and Japan include the institutionalized population as part of the working-age population. [5] 16 to 19-year-olds in the United States, Canada, France, Spain, and the United Kingdom; 15 to 19-year-olds in Australia, Japan, South Korea, Germany, and Netherlands.

Source: U.S. Bureau of Labor Statistics, *International Comparisons of Annual Labor Force Statistics, 1970–2012*, June 2013. See also <http://www.bls.gov/fls/flscomparelf.htm>.

Table 1395. Youth Educational Enrollment and Employment Status by Country: 2011

[Percent of total youth population 15 to 29 years old]

Country	15 to 19 years old — In education Total	Not in education Employed	Not in education Not employed	20 to 24 years old — In education Total	Not in education Employed	Not in education Not employed	25 to 29 years old — In education Total	Not in education Employed	Not in education Not employed
United States.....	**86.2**	**6.6**	**7.1**	**39.9**	**41.6**	**18.5**	**14.8**	**63.4**	**21.7**
Australia...........	80.0	12.2	7.8	42.1	46.2	11.7	18.9	66.6	14.6
Brazil...............	62.4	24.6	13.1	22.5	53.2	24.3	11.1	67.3	21.6
Canada.............	81.4	10.9	7.7	40.1	45.3	14.6	12.7	70.3	17.1
Chile...............	70.7	7.9	21.4	39.9	35.2	24.9	15.8	59.1	25.0
Czech Republic....	93.2	3.0	3.7	50.0	37.2	12.8	11.9	68.6	19.5
France.............	90.2	2.7	7.1	40.7	39.0	20.3	4.9	73.6	21.5
Germany...........	92.3	4.1	3.5	49.0	38.5	12.6	18.5	65.8	15.7
Greece.............	89.5	2.2	8.3	47.0	28.7	24.3	9.8	60.2	30.0
Israel...............	69.8	6.0	24.2	26.9	35.7	37.4	27.4	51.2	21.5
Italy................	84.7	3.9	11.4	41.0	30.6	28.4	16.2	55.3	28.4
Korea, South.......	88.7	2.5	8.7	42.3	34.4	23.3	8.5	66.6	24.9
Mexico.............	60.8	20.4	18.9	26.2	46.6	27.2	7.0	63.5	29.5
Netherlands.......	89.3	7.3	3.4	55.2	37.9	6.9	20.0	69.7	10.3
Norway.............	82.9	13.9	3.2	41.0	48.6	10.4	13.8	74.2	11.9
Poland.............	94.3	1.8	3.9	51.6	29.7	18.7	11.5	66.7	21.8
Spain...............	84.7	3.3	12.0	40.8	30.0	29.2	13.2	57.1	29.6
Sweden............	89.4	6.4	4.2	43.4	43.7	12.9	24.1	66.1	9.8
Switzerland........	87.9	7.1	5.0	41.5	47.8	10.7	17.7	71.4	10.9
Turkey.............	60.1	15.1	24.8	25.6	34.7	39.6	8.9	50.9	40.2
United Kingdom. ..	81.2	9.3	9.5	33.1	47.8	19.1	13.7	69.0	17.3

Source: Organisation for Economic Co-operation and Development (OECD), "Transition from school to work: Where are the 15-29 year-olds?" *Education at a Glance 2013* ©, June 2013. See also <http://www.oecd.org/edu/educationataglance2013-indicatorsandannexes.htm>.

Table 1396. Female Labor Force Participation Rates by Country: 1980 to 2012

[In percent. Female labor force of all ages divided by female population 15-64 years old]

Country	1980	1990	2000	2010	2012	Country	1980	1990	2000	2010	2012
OECD, total [1]	**(NA)**	**(NA)**	**60.4**	**63.1**	**(NA)**	Ireland...............	36.3	43.8	56.9	63.1	63.0
EU–27 [2]	(NA)	(NA)	60.3	64.7	(NA)	Italy..................	39.6	45.9	46.8	51.5	54.0
United States........	**59.5**	**68.6**	**70.8**	**68.9**	**(NA)**	Japan.................	54.8	60.3	64.0	68.6	69.5
Australia...............	52.5	62.2	66.1	72.2	73.1	Korea, South.......	46.1	51.2	54.9	58.3	59.4
Austria................	48.7	55.4	62.2	70.0	(NA)	Luxembourg.........	39.9	50.3	69.4	[4] 96.0	(NA)
Belgium...............	46.9	52.4	56.6	62.0	(NA)	Mexico...............	34.0	23.4	43.3	49.1	(NA)
Canada................	57.3	67.5	69.8	74.4	74.7	Netherlands........	35.5	52.4	65.5	72.8	(NA)
Chile..................	(NA)	(NA)	38.5	52.1	(NA)	New Zealand........	44.5	65.4	68.0	74.1	75.5
Czech Republic........	(NA)	69.1	64.2	62.3	64.4	Norway...............	62.3	71.2	76.2	77.1	(NA)
Denmark..............	[4] 71.1	78.2	75.6	76.1	(NA)	Poland...............	(NA)	(NA)	60.5	55.7	56.8
Estonia...............	(NA)	74.9	67.1	73.4	(NA)	Portugal.............	54.6	62.4	67.1	73.8	(NA)
Finland................	70.1	73.8	72.2	73.3	74.5	Slovakia.............	(NA)	(NA)	63.1	61.9	(NA)
France................	54.0	59.5	64.9	67.4	(NA)	Spain.................	32.4	41.5	52.0	66.1	68.1
Germany [3]	52.8	56.7	63.6	71.5	72.6	Sweden..............	74.3	80.9	75.0	77.5	(NA)
Greece................	33.0	43.3	49.5	56.6	(NA)	Switzerland.........	54.3	65.7	76.8	82.2	(NA)
Hungary..............	(NA)	(NA)	52.1	56.4	58.4	Turkey...............	(NA)	36.8	30.3	30.4	(NA)
Iceland...............	(NA)	(NA)	82.8	82.1	81.7	United Kingdom.....	58.2	66.4	67.8	70.5	71.4

NA Not available. [1] For complete OECD membership listing, see Section 30 introduction. [2] See footnote 4, Table 1403. [3] Prior to 1991, data are for former West Germany. [4] Estimated.

Source: Organisation for Economic Co-cooperation and Development (OECD), 2013, "Labour Market Statistics: Labour Force Statistics by Sex and Age: Indicators," OECD Employment and Labour Market Statistics (database) ©, <http://dx.doi.org/10.1787/data-00310-en>, accessed September 2013.

Table 1397. Civilian Employment-Population Ratio: 1990 to 2012

[Civilian employment as a percent of the civilian working-age population. See headnote, Table 1394]

Country	Women 1990	Women 2000	Women 2005	Women 2010	Women 2012	Men 1990	Men 2000	Men 2005	Men 2010	Men 2012
United States [1]	**54.3**	**57.5**	**56.2**	**53.6**	**53.1**	**72.0**	**71.9**	**69.6**	**63.7**	**64.4**
Canada..........................	54.1	56.0	58.1	58.5	58.5	70.6	68.2	68.6	66.2	66.6
Australia.........................	49.4	52.5	55.0	56.6	56.7	71.3	68.4	69.4	69.5	68.9
Japan............................	48.0	46.4	45.7	45.7	45.7	75.4	72.5	69.7	67.7	67.3
South Korea [1]	46.2	47.0	48.4	47.8	48.4	71.8	70.7	71.6	70.1	70.8
France...........................	42.0	44.0	45.0	46.0	46.0	61.5	58.0	56.2	55.4	55.1
Germany [1, 2, 3, 4]	40.5	44.4	44.9	48.9	50.4	65.6	60.6	57.7	60.2	61.7
Italy [1]	29.2	32.7	34.1	34.5	35.0	60.0	57.4	56.8	54.4	53.2
Netherlands [1, 3, 4]	39.4	51.8	54.1	55.7	55.9	66.5	71.4	69.2	67.9	67.1
Sweden [4]	61.8	56.1	56.0	55.2	56.7	70.6	64.2	63.8	63.3	63.5
United Kingdom..................	50.3	52.5	53.7	52.9	52.9	70.0	66.9	66.8	63.8	64.0

[1] Break in series between 1990 and 1995. [2] Unified Germany for 1991 onward. Prior to 1991, data relate to the former West Germany. [3] Break in series between 1995 and 2000. [4] Break in series between 2000 and 2010.

Source: U.S. Bureau of Labor Statistics, *International Comparisons of Annual Labor Force Statistics, 1970–2012*, June 2013. See also <http://www.bls.gov/fls/flscomparelf.htm>.

Table 1398. Civilian Employment by Sector and Country: 2000 and 2012

[136,891 represents 136,891,000. Civilian employment approximating U.S. concepts. Sectors are based on International Standard Industrial Classification (ISIC), unless otherwise indicated; see text of this section. Also see headnote, Table 1394]

Sector and Year	United States [1,2]	Canada	Australia	Japan [3]	South Korea	France [2]	Germany [2]	Italy [2]	United Kingdom
TOTAL EMPLOYMENT (1,000)									
2000, total	**136,891**	**14,677**	**8,989**	**63,790**	**21,156**	**23,731**	**36,236**	**21,358**	**27,375**
Agriculture, forestry, fishing [4]	2,464	479	442	3,070	2,243	1,097	959	1,006	330
Industry [5]	30,050	3,204	1,856	19,710	5,890	5,838	11,898	6,542	6,202
Manufacturing	19,644	2,240	1,083	13,180	4,293	4,241	8,647	4,893	4,057
Services [6]	104,377	10,994	6,691	41,010	13,023	16,796	23,379	13,809	20,843
2012, total	**142,469**	**17,445**	**11,501**	**62,152**	**24,681**	**25,547**	**39,873**	**22,620**	**29,439**
Agriculture, forestry, fishing [4]	2,186	376	334	2,270	1,528	755	620	847	349
Industry [5]	24,607	3,349	2,236	15,330	5,893	5,221	10,710	5,995	5,169
Manufacturing	14,686	1,784	967	10,300	4,105	3,321	7,915	4,206	2,890
Services [6]	115,676	13,720	8,931	44,552	17,260	19,571	28,542	15,778	23,921
PERCENT DISTRIBUTION [7]									
2000, total	**100.0**	**100.0**	**100.0**	**100.0**	**100.0**	**100.0**	**100.0**	**100.0**	**100.0**
Agriculture, forestry, fishing [4]	1.8	3.3	4.9	4.8	10.6	4.6	2.6	4.7	1.2
Industry [5]	22.0	21.8	20.6	30.9	27.8	24.6	32.8	30.6	22.7
Manufacturing	14.4	15.3	12.1	20.7	20.3	17.9	23.9	22.9	14.8
Services [6]	76.2	74.9	74.4	64.3	61.6	70.8	64.5	64.7	76.1
2012, total	**100.0**	**100.0**	**100.0**	**100.0**	**100.0**	**100.0**	**100.0**	**100.0**	**100.0**
Agriculture, forestry, fishing [4]	1.5	2.2	2.9	3.7	6.2	3.0	1.6	3.7	1.2
Industry [5]	17.3	19.2	19.4	24.7	23.9	20.4	26.9	26.5	17.6
Manufacturing	10.3	10.2	8.4	16.6	16.6	13.0	19.8	18.6	9.8
Services [6]	81.2	78.6	77.7	71.7	69.9	76.6	71.6	69.8	81.3

[1] Data for the United States and Canada are based on the North American Industry Classification System (NAICS). [2] Break in data series between 2000 and 2012. [3] Data for Japan are based on the Japanese Standard Industrial Classification System (JSIC). [4] Includes hunting. [5] Includes manufacturing, mining, and construction. [6] Transportation, communication, public utilities, trade, finance, public administration, private household services, and miscellaneous services. [7] Percent of total civilian employment.

Source: U.S. Bureau of Labor Statistics, *International Comparisons of Annual Labor Force Statistics, 1970-2012*, June 2013. See also <http://www.bls.gov/fls/flscomparelf.htm>.

Table 1399. Educational Performance and Attainment: 2009 and 2011

Country	Student mean scores in reading, science, and mathematics proficiency, 2009 [1]			Educational attainment of adult population (25 to 64 years old), 2011 (percent)		
	Reading scale	Mathematics scale	Science scale	Below upper secondary	Upper secondary and vocational	Tertiary and higher [2]
OECD average [3]	493.4	495.7	500.8	25.2	44.0	31.5
United States	**499.8**	**487.4**	**502.0**	**10.7**	**46.8**	**42.4**
Australia	514.9	514.3	527.3	25.9	35.7	38.3
Austria	470.3	495.9	494.3	17.5	63.1	19.3
Brazil	411.8	385.8	405.4	56.7	31.7	11.6
Canada	524.2	526.8	528.7	11.2	37.4	51.3
Chile	449.4	421.1	447.5	27.7	43.5	28.8
Czech Republic	478.2	492.8	500.5	7.7	74.1	18.3
France	495.6	496.8	498.2	28.4	41.8	29.8
Germany	497.3	512.8	520.4	13.7	58.7	27.6
Greece	482.8	466.1	470.1	32.9	41.1	26.1
Israel	474.0	446.9	454.9	17.0	36.6	46.4
Italy	486.1	482.9	488.8	44.0	41.1	14.9
Japan	519.9	529.0	539.4	(NA)	53.6	46.4
Korea, South	539.3	546.2	538.0	18.6	41.0	40.4
Mexico	425.3	418.5	415.9	63.7	19.0	17.3
Netherlands	508.4	525.8	522.2	27.7	40.3	32.1
Norway	503.2	498.0	499.9	18.1	43.8	38.1
Poland	500.5	494.8	508.1	10.9	65.4	23.7
Russia	459.4	467.8	478.3	5.9	40.6	53.5
Spain	481.0	483.5	488.3	46.0	22.4	31.6
Sweden	497.4	494.2	495.1	13.0	51.9	35.2
Switzerland	500.5	534.0	516.6	14.4	50.4	35.2
Turkey	464.2	445.5	453.9	67.9	18.1	14.0
United Kingdom	494.2	492.4	513.7	23.2	37.4	39.4

NA Not available. [1] Proficiency scores are based on the Program for International Student Assessment (PISA), an international standardized test which takes place in three-year cycles. PISA tests are administered to a nationally representative sample of fifteen-year-old students in each country. [2] Tertiary education entails completion of an advanced course of study or research program leading to an associate's, bachelor's, master's, or doctorate degree, usually 2 years or longer in duration. [3] For full OECD membership listing, see text this section. Brazil and Russia, which are not OECD members, are included for comparison.

Source: Organisation for Economic Co-operation and Development (OECD), *PISA 2009 Results: What Students Know and Can Do* ©, Volume I, December 2010; and *Education at a Glance 2013* ©, June 2013. See also <http://www.pisa.oecd.org> and <http://www.oecd.org/edu/educationataglance2013-indicatorsandannexes.htm>.

Table 1400. World Supply and Utilization of Major Crops and Livestock: 2005 to 2013

[In millions of units (215.9 represents 215,900,000). For major crops, data are for marketing or trade year ending in year shown, unless otherwise indicated. For livestock and dairy, data are for calendar year]

Commodity	2005	2007	2008	2009	2010	2011	2012	2013 [1]
Wheat:								
Area (hectares)	215.9	211.6	217.0	224.1	225.2	217.1	221.3	215.9
Production (metric tons)	626.7	596.3	612.4	683.7	686.7	652.3	697.2	655.6
Exports (metric tons)	113.3	115.7	116.6	143.7	135.6	134.1	153.8	143.7
Consumption (metric tons)	605.4	617.9	614.4	637.1	650.5	653.7	687.8	679.5
Ending stocks (metric tons)	156.5	134.3	128.8	168.7	201.7	199.2	199.5	180.2
Corn:								
Area (hectares)	145.4	149.4	160.6	158.8	158.7	163.8	169.6	174.4
Production (metric tons)	716.2	715.3	794.6	800.6	824.2	831.7	883.0	857.1
Exports (metric tons)	76.0	91.4	98.2	83.9	93.0	91.9	103.9	97.6
Consumption (metric tons)	688.2	725.4	773.2	782.7	818.8	850.4	862.1	871.4
Ending stocks (metric tons)	130.7	110.6	131.6	147.7	146.0	128.1	132.2	125.4
Rice, milled:								
Area (hectares)	151.8	154.5	154.9	158.2	155.9	157.8	159.2	158.2
Production (metric tons)	400.9	419.9	432.6	448.7	440.6	449.3	465.8	470.2
Exports (metric tons) [2]	29.0	31.9	29.6	29.4	31.6	36.2	39.2	38.6
Consumption (metric tons)	406.3	418.4	425.7	435.5	435.2	443.5	456.1	466.9
Ending stocks (metric tons)	74.0	75.5	80.9	92.4	94.9	98.7	105.1	105.4
Total grains: [3]								
Area (hectares)	667.1	669.9	687.9	694.7	687.9	678.2	693.4	689.6
Production (metric tons)	2,043.5	2,006.0	2,125.8	2,244.7	2,242.9	2,200.5	2,317.3	2,254.1
Exports (metric tons)	243.7	262.3	275.1	283.8	286.2	286.6	326.6	308.2
Consumption (metric tons)	1,991.7	2,048.1	2,101.6	2,161.4	2,202.0	2,228.7	2,307.5	2,281.4
Ending stocks (metric tons)	409.5	351.4	374.2	455.8	493.8	463.7	470.1	439.9
Oilseeds:								
Area (hectares)	209.4	211.3	206.1	214.2	216.2	224.1	227.0	235.0
Production (metric tons)	381.2	403.8	390.5	396.5	444.3	456.6	441.9	469.4
Exports (metric tons)	74.4	83.1	91.7	94.2	107.5	108.3	111.2	112.6
Consumption (metric tons)	366.4	392.9	400.9	401.1	421.3	443.7	460.2	461.0
Ending stocks (metric tons)	58.9	73.9	62.0	57.1	74.4	82.8	64.9	70.4
Coffee, green:								
Production (60 kg bags)	121.6	133.6	123.9	136.2	128.5	140.9	144.4	151.3
Exports (60 kg bags)	93.3	104.6	97.8	100.4	102.2	113.5	114.4	116.0
Consumption (60 kg bags)	115.8	123.0	127.7	124.6	137.2	133.1	141.0	141.4
Ending stocks (60 kg bags)	41.4	36.1	31.7	39.8	28.9	28.9	24.9	27.9
Sugar, centrifugal:								
Production (metric tons)	140.7	164.5	163.5	143.9	153.5	161.8	172.1	172.3
Exports (metric tons)	47.0	51.0	50.9	46.7	50.6	55.6	56.1	55.1
Consumption (metric tons)	141.6	149.4	150.8	153.4	154.1	154.9	159.5	162.8
Ending stocks (metric tons)	34.7	36.9	43.4	30.5	29.0	30.1	36.2	38.3
Cotton:								
Area (hectares)	35.7	34.5	32.8	30.6	30.1	33.5	35.7	34.3
Production (480 lb. bales)	121.4	122.2	119.6	107.2	102.2	116.3	125.1	120.9
Exports (480 lb. bales)	35.0	37.5	39.0	30.2	35.6	35.5	45.9	45.0
Consumption (480 lb. bales)	107.9	121.9	121.0	108.0	118.1	114.0	102.6	107.6
Ending stocks (480 lb. bales)	60.6	62.9	61.9	61.5	46.7	49.4	71.2	84.8
Beef:								
Beef cow beginning stocks (head)	218.2	216.7	217.2	210.4	200.9	202.0	203.0	203.2
Production (metric tons) [4]	56.0	58.5	58.4	57.2	57.3	57.1	57.3	57.5
Exports (metric tons) [4]	7.4	7.6	7.6	7.5	7.8	8.1	8.1	8.6
Consumption (metric tons) [4]	55.5	57.8	57.5	56.2	56.2	55.4	55.8	56.0
Ending stocks (metric tons) [4]	0.5	0.6	0.6	0.7	0.6	0.6	0.7	0.6
Pork:								
Sow beginning stocks (head)	82.1	84.3	79.6	79.2	79.2	77.3	78.5	79.6
Production (metric tons) [4]	93.7	94.2	97.9	100.6	103.0	102.0	105.5	107.4
Exports (metric tons) [4]	5.0	5.2	6.2	5.7	6.1	7.0	7.3	7.2
Consumption (metric tons) [4]	93.3	94.0	98.0	100.4	102.8	101.6	104.9	107.0
Ending stocks (metric tons) [4]	0.8	0.8	0.8	0.8	0.8	0.8	1.0	1.0
Chicken:								
Beginning stocks (metric tons)	0.6	0.6	0.5	0.6	0.5	0.5	0.5	0.6
Production (metric tons)	64.3	69.4	72.8	73.6	77.9	80.8	82.8	84.6
Exports (metric tons)	6.8	7.3	8.3	8.4	8.9	9.5	10.1	10.3
Consumption (metric tons)	63.6	69.2	71.9	72.6	76.8	79.6	81.2	83.3
Ending stocks (metric tons)	0.6	0.5	0.6	0.5	0.5	0.5	0.6	0.6
Dairy:								
Dairy cows beginning stocks (head)	242.8	248.0	249.3	246.8	246.2	246.4	247.8	249.5
Milk production (metric tons) [5]	485.4	504.6	502.5	504.6	514.4	529.8	544.8	556.1
Milk exports (metric tons) [5]	0.4	0.4	0.4	0.5	0.5	0.6	0.6	0.6
Milk consumption (metric tons) [5]	485.3	504.6	502.3	504.4	514.2	529.7	544.7	556.1

[1] Preliminary. [2] Rice export data represent Jan.-Dec. calendar years. [3] Total grains include wheat, rice, corn, sorghum, barley, oats, rye, millet, and mixed grains. [4] Carcass weight equivalent (CWE). [5] Includes milk from cows as well as other bovines.

Source: U.S. Department of Agriculture, Foreign Agricultural Service, "Production, Supply and Distribution (PS&D) Online database," <http://www.fas.usda.gov/psdonline/>, accessed May 2013.

Table 1401. World Crop Production Summary: 2011 to 2013

[In millions of metric tons (697.2 represents 697,200,000)]

Country	Wheat 2011–2012	Wheat 2012–2013 prel.	Coarse grains[1] 2011–2012	Coarse grains[1] 2012–2013 prel.	Rice (milled) 2011–2012	Rice (milled) 2012–2013 prel.	Oilseeds[2] 2011–2012	Oilseeds[2] 2012–2013 prel.	Cotton 2011–2012	Cotton 2012–2013 prel.
World	**697.2**	**655.6**	**1,154.3**	**1,128.3**	**465.8**	**470.2**	**441.9**	**469.4**	**125.1**	**120.9**
Total foreign	642.8	593.9	830.6	842.3	459.9	463.9	349.6	376.8	109.6	103.6
United States	**54.4**	**61.8**	**323.7**	**286.0**	**5.9**	**6.3**	**92.3**	**92.6**	**15.6**	**17.3**
Canada	25.3	27.2	22.9	24.3	(3)	(3)	18.9	18.3	(3)	(3)
Mexico	3.6	3.2	25.8	29.1	0.1	0.1	0.9	1.0	1.2	1.1
EU-27[4]	137.3	132.1	147.7	143.1	2.1	2.1	29.2	27.3	1.6	1.5
Russia	56.2	37.7	33.1	28.7	0.7	0.7	12.4	10.9	(3)	(3)
Ukraine	22.3	15.8	33.5	29.5	0.1	0.1	14.2	12.8	(3)	(3)
China	117.4	120.6	199.3	214.8	140.7	143.0	59.2	58.7	34.0	35.0
India	86.9	94.9	42.3	38.9	105.3	104.0	35.4	36.0	27.5	26.5
Indonesia	(3)	(3)	8.9	9.0	36.5	37.5	10.2	10.9	0.0	0.0
Pakistan	25.0	23.3	3.6	3.6	6.2	6.0	5.8	5.1	10.6	9.3
Thailand	(3)	(3)	4.4	4.7	20.5	20.2	0.6	0.6	0.0	0.0
Argentina	15.5	11.0	30.1	37.7	1.0	1.0	44.8	55.6	1.0	0.8
Brazil	5.8	4.3	75.9	78.8	7.9	8.2	70.0	86.0	8.7	5.8
Australia	29.9	22.1	12.4	10.3	0.7	0.8	5.0	4.6	5.5	4.3
South Africa	2.0	1.9	13.0	12.7	(3)	(3)	1.3	1.5	0.1	0.0
Turkey	18.8	15.5	11.3	10.6	0.5	0.5	2.1	2.1	3.4	2.6
All others	96.7	84.3	166.7	166.5	137.7	139.8	39.6	45.3	16.0	16.7

[1] Includes corn, sorghum, barley, oats, rye, millet, and mixed grain. [2] Includes soybean, cottonseed, peanut (in shell), sunflower seed, rapeseed for individual countries. Copra and palm kernel are added to world totals. [3] Indicates no reported or insignificant production. [4] See footnote 3, Table 1403.

Source: U.S. Department of Agriculture, Foreign Agricultural Service, *World Agricultural Production*, May 2013. See also <http://www.fas.usda.gov/wap_arc.asp>.

Table 1402. Meat Production by Type and Country: 2010 and 2012

[In thousands of metric tons (57,303 represents 57,303,000). Carcass weight equivalent basis for beef, veal, and pork. Chicken (16-week-old broiler) weight based on ready-to-cook equivalent]

Country	Beef and veal[1] 2010	Beef and veal[1] 2012	Country	Pork 2010	Pork 2012	Country	Chicken[2] 2010	Chicken[2] 2012
World	**57,303**	**57,257**	**World**	**102,968**	**105,519**	**World**	**77,893**	**82,774**
United States	**12,046**	**11,855**	China	51,070	52,350	**United States**	**16,563**	**16,621**
Brazil	9,115	9,307	EU-27[3]	22,571	22,630	China	12,550	13,700
EU-27[3]	8,048	7,765	**United States**	**10,186**	**10,554**	Brazil	12,312	12,645
China	5,600	5,540	Brazil	3,195	3,330	EU-27[3]	9,202	9,510
India	2,842	3,460	Russia	1,920	2,075	India	2,650	3,160
Argentina	2,620	2,620	Vietnam	1,930	2,000	Mexico	2,822	2,958
Australia	2,129	2,152	Canada	1,771	1,820	Russia	2,310	2,830
Mexico	1,745	1,820	Philippines	1,247	1,382	Argentina	1,680	1,936
Pakistan	1,470	1,400	Japan	1,292	1,297	Turkey	1,430	1,687
Russia	1,435	1,380	Mexico	1,175	1,227	Thailand	1,280	1,550
Canada	1,273	1,075	Korea, South	1,110	1,086	Indonesia	1,465	1,540
Other countries	8,980	8,883	Other countries	5,501	5,768	Other countries	13,629	14,637

[1] May include meat of other bovines. [2] Excludes chicken paws. [3] See footnote 3, Table 1403.

Source: U.S. Department of Agriculture, Foreign Agricultural Service, *Livestock and Poultry: World Markets and Trade*, semiannual, April 2013. See also <http://www.fas.usda.gov/currwmt.asp>.

Table 1403. Meat Consumption by Type and Country: 2010 and 2012

[In thousands of metric tons (56,151 represents 56,151,000). Carcass weight equivalent basis for beef, veal, and pork. Chicken (16-week-old broiler) weight based on ready-to-cook equivalent]

Country	Beef and veal[1] 2010	Beef and veal[1] 2012	Country	Pork 2010	Pork 2012	Country	Chicken[2] 2010	Chicken[2] 2012
World	**56,151**	**55,759**	**World**	**102,770**	**104,929**	**World**	**76,775**	**81,209**
United States	**12,038**	**11,744**	China	51,157	52,725	China	12,457	13,543
Brazil	7,592	7,845	EU-27[3]	20,842	20,423	**United States**	**13,470**	**13,342**
EU-27[3]	8,147	7,806	**United States**	**8,653**	**8,438**	Brazil	9,041	9,139
China	5,589	5,597	Russia	2,835	3,145	EU-27[3]	8,954	9,138
Argentina	2,346	2,458	Brazil	2,577	2,670	Mexico	3,364	3,569
Russia	2,487	2,395	Japan	2,488	2,557	Russia	2,957	3,321
India	1,925	2,049	Vietnam	1,912	1,980	India	2,648	3,151
Mexico	1,938	1,835	Mexico	1,784	1,838	Japan	2,079	2,219
Pakistan	1,436	1,367	Korea, South	1,539	1,546	South Africa	1,524	1,756
Japan	1,225	1,255	Philippines	1,405	1,518	Argentina	1,475	1,659
Canada	1,000	1,012	Taiwan	901	893	Indonesia	1,465	1,540
Other countries	10,428	10,396	Other countries	6,677	7,196	Other countries	17,341	18,832

[1] May include meat of other bovines. [2] Excludes chicken paws. [3] European Union-27: Austria, Belgium, Bulgaria, Cyprus, Czech Republic, Denmark, Estonia, Finland, France, Germany, Greece, Hungary, Ireland, Italy, Latvia, Lithuania, Luxembourg, Malta, Netherlands, Poland, Portugal, Romania, Slovakia, Slovenia, Spain, Sweden, and United Kingdom.

Source: U.S. Department of Agriculture, Foreign Agricultural Service, *Livestock and Poultry: World Markets and Trade*, semiannual, April 2013. See also <http://www.fas.usda.gov/currwmt.asp>.

Table 1404. Wheat, Rice, and Corn—Exports and Imports of Leading Countries: 2000 to 2013

[In thousands of metric tons (29,399 represents 29,399,000). Wheat data represent trade years ending in June of year shown; corn data represent trade years ending in September of year shown; rice trade data represent calender years. Countries listed are the ten leading exporters or importers in 2013]

Leading exporters	Exports			Leading importers	Imports		
	2000	2010	2013 [1]		2000	2010	2013 [1]
WHEAT				**WHEAT**			
United States.........	**29,399**	**24,172**	**28,000**	Egypt...............	5,872	10,500	8,000
EU-27 [2]...............	20,380	22,133	21,500	Brazil...............	7,298	6,694	7,500
Australia...............	17,124	13,764	19,000	Indonesia..............	3,744	5,364	6,600
Canada...............	19,373	18,992	18,500	Japan...............	5,929	5,502	6,300
Russia...............	518	18,556	10,700	Algeria [2].............	4,750	5,167	6,200
India...............	200	60	8,500	EU-27 [2].............	3,956	5,519	5,700
Argentina.............	11,039	5,255	7,500	Korea, South..........	3,811	4,470	5,500
Ukraine...............	1,952	9,337	7,000	Iran...............	7,363	3,650	5,000
Kazakhstan............	6,514	7,871	6,500	Nigeria.............	1,282	4,020	4,000
Turkey...............	1,984	4,363	3,300	Mexico............	2,632	3,196	3,900
RICE				**RICE**			
India...............	1,449	2,228	9,000	China...............	278	366	3,000
Thailand.............	6,549	9,047	8,000	Nigeria.............	1,250	2,000	2,900
Vietnam...............	3,370	6,734	7,400	Philippines.............	900	2,400	1,500
United States.........	**2,847**	**3,868**	**3,400**	Iran...............	1,100	1,520	1,500
Pakistan.............	2,026	4,000	3,200	Indonesia.............	1,500	1,150	1,500
Cambodia.............	0	750	975	Iraq...............	1,274	1,188	1,400
Uruguay.............	642	808	900	Saudi Arabia..........	992	1,069	1,225
Egypt...............	500	570	850	EU-27 [2].............	1,187	1,216	1,200
Brazil...............	26	430	850	Cote d'Ivoire...........	450	840	1,150
Burma...............	159	445	750	Malaysia.............	596	907	1,050
CORN				**CORN**			
Brazil...............	50	8,623	26,500	Japan...............	16,117	15,971	15,000
Argentina.............	8,859	16,973	22,000	EU-27 [2].............	2,384	2,931	10,500
United States.........	**49,493**	**49,721**	**19,500**	Korea, South..........	8,692	8,461	8,000
Ukraine...............	55	5,072	13,500	Mexico............	4,911	8,298	7,500
India...............	13	1,917	4,000	Taiwan.............	5,023	4,521	4,300
Paraguay.............	309	1,359	2,400	Egypt...............	4,600	5,832	4,000
Russia...............	0	427	2,300	Iran...............	1,249	4,300	3,500
South Africa...........	836	1,586	1,700	Colombia.............	2,005	3,651	3,200
EU-27 [2]...............	1,408	1,519	1,000	Malaysia.............	2,296	3,107	3,100
Canada...............	449	186	1,000	**United States.......... **	**367**	**237**	**3,000**

[1] Preliminary. [2] See footnote 3, Table 1403.

Source: U.S. Department of Agriculture, Foreign Agricultural Service (FAS), "Production, Supply and Distribution (PS&D) Online database," <http://www.fas.usda.gov/psdonline/psdhome.aspx>, accessed May 2013.

Table 1405. World Production of Major Mineral Commodities: 1990 to 2012

[Units are as noted. Th. represents thousand, mil. represents million, and bil. represents billion]

Commodity	Unit	1990	2000	2011	2012, prel.	Leading producers, 2011
MINERAL FUELS						
Coal...............	mil. short tons	5,292	5,127	8,440	(NA)	China, United States, India
Dry natural gas.............	bil. cubic feet	73,788	87,100	115,993	(NA)	United States, Russia, Iran
Natural gas plant liquids.............	mil. barrels [1]	1,696	2,327	3,146	3,304	United States, Saudi Arabia, Canada
Petroleum, crude.......................	mil. barrels [1]	22,081	25,011	27,062	27,598	Russia, Saudi Arabia, United States
NONMETALLIC MINERALS						
Cement, hydraulic.............	mil. metric tons	1,160	1,660	3,610	3,700	China, India, United States
Diamond, gem and industrial..........	mil. carats	111	122	135	(NA)	Russia, Botswana, Congo (Kinshasa)
Nitrogen in ammonia....................	mil. metric tons	97.5	108	135	137	China, India, Russia
Phosphate rock, marketable.............	mil. metric tons	162	132	198	210	China, United States, Morocco/W. Sahara
Potash, marketable....................	mil. metric tons	27.5	27.0	36.4	34.0	Canada, Russia, Belarus
Salt....................	mil. metric tons	183	195	286	280	China, United States, Germany
Sulfur, elemental basis.................	mil. metric tons	57.8	59.3	70.5	70.0	China, United States, Canada
METALS						
Aluminum [2].............	mil. metric tons	19.3	24.3	44.4	44.9	China, Russia, Canada
Bauxite, gross weight....................	mil. metric tons	113	136	262	263	Australia, China, Brazil
Chromite, gross weight.................	th. metric tons	13,200	14,700	23,300	24,000	South Africa, Kazakhstan, India
Copper, metal content [3].................	th. metric tons	8,950	13,300	16,100	17,000	Chile, Peru, China
Gold, metal content....................	metric tons	2,180	2,570	2,660	2,700	China, Australia, United States
Iron ore, gross weight [4].................	mil. metric tons	983	1,079	2,940	3,000	China, Australia, Brazil
Lead, metal content [3].................	th. metric tons	3,370	3,170	4,690	5,200	China, Australia, United States
Nickel, metal content [3].................	th. metric tons	974	1,290	1,960	2,100	Russia, Indonesia, Philippines
Steel, crude.................	mil. metric tons	771	850	1,520	1,500	China, Japan, United States
Tin, metal content [3].................	th. metric tons	221	278	244	230	China, Indonesia, Peru
Zinc, metal content.............	th. metric tons	7,180	8,770	12,800	13,000	China, Australia, Peru

NA Not available. [1] 42-gallon barrels. [2] Unalloyed ingot metal. [3] Mine output. [4] Includes iron ore concentrates and iron ore agglomerates.

Source: Mineral fuels, U.S. Energy Information Administration, "International Energy Statistics," <http://www.eia.gov/cfapps/ipdbproject/iedindex3.cfm>, accessed September 2013; Nonmetallic Minerals and Metals through 1990, U.S. Bureau of Mines, thereafter, U.S. Geological Survey, Minerals Yearbook 2011, July 2013, and earlier editions; and Mineral Commodity Summaries 2013, January 2013.

Table 1406. Net Electricity Generation by Energy Source and Country: 2010

[20,225.3 represents 20,225,300,000,000. kWh = kilowatt hours. Ranked for top 50 countries]

| Country | Total [1] (bil. kWh) | Percent distribution | | | Country | Total [1] (bil. kWh) | Percent distribution | | |
		Fossil fuels [2]	Hydro	Non-hydro renew-ables [3]			Fossil fuels [2]	Hydro	Non-hydro renew-ables [3]
World, total [4]....	**20,225.3**	**66.6**	**16.8**	**3.7**	Sweden..............	144.5	4.8	45.5	11.7
					Egypt.................	138.7	89.6	9.3	1.1
United States......	**4,112.2**	**70.1**	**6.3**	**4.1**	Norway.............	122.3	3.9	95.1	1.1
China.............	3,904.1	78.5	18.3	1.5	Argentina..........	119.3	64.8	27.9	1.9
Japan.............	1,051.8	63.1	7.7	3.2	Malaysia...........	118.2	93.5	5.4	1.1
Russia.............	983.8	66.5	16.8	0.3	Venezuela.........	115.0	33.9	66.1	–
India................	904.1	82.9	12.5	2.4	Netherlands........	111.7	85.2	0.1	11.3
					United Arab				
Canada.............	590.9	23.4	58.9	3.1	Emirates...........	91.9	100.0	–	–
Germany...........	588.0	58.9	3.4	15.2	Vietnam............	90.6	69.8	30.1	0.1
France.............	537.1	9.8	11.4	3.3	Pakistan...........	89.6	62.1	35.1	–
Brazil..............	506.9	11.9	78.8	6.6	Belgium............	88.4	40.2	0.3	8.5
Korea, South.......	467.5	68.6	0.8	0.6	Czech Republic......	80.6	59.9	3.4	3.9
United Kingdom....	353.5	76.8	1.0	6.7	Kazakhstan........	78.1	89.8	10.2	–
Spain..............	286.6	45.8	14.6	19.5	Finland.............	77.1	40.4	16.6	14.9
Italy...............	283.2	72.7	17.9	9.9	Austria.............	64.8	32.4	58.7	11.1
Mexico.............	257.3	79.4	14.3	4.1	Philippines..........	64.6	72.6	12.0	15.5
South Africa........	241.9	94.1	0.9	0.1	Switzerland........	63.6	1.6	56.1	4.0
Australia...........	228.2	90.7	5.4	3.9	Chile...............	57.9	58.4	37.1	4.5
Taiwan.............	226.8	78.8	1.8	1.9	Romania...........	57.7	45.6	34.5	0.7
Iran................	219.5	95.6	4.3	0.1	Colombia...........	55.3	27.0	72.1	1.0
Saudi Arabia........	212.3	100.0	–	–	Israel...............	55.0	99.7	0.1	0.2
Turkey.............	201.4	72.5	25.5	2.0	Greece.............	54.5	80.6	13.6	5.9
Ukraine.............	176.3	45.1	7.4	–	Kuwait.............	53.6	100.0	–	–
Indonesia...........	161.1	83.3	10.9	5.9	Paraguay...........	53.5	–	100.0	–
Poland.............	148.0	92.7	2.0	5.5	Portugal............	51.9	45.3	30.8	24.1
Thailand............	145.3	94.0	3.8	2.2	Uzbekistan.........	49.1	78.2	21.8	–

– Represents zero. [1] Electricity generated from fossil fuels, hydro, nuclear, geothermal, solar, wind, tidal, biomass, and waste resources. [2] Electricity generated from coal, oil, and gas resources. [3] Electricity generated from geothermal, solar, wind, tidal, biomass, and waste resources. [4] Includes countries not shown separately.

Source: U.S. Energy Information Administration, "International Energy Statistics Database," <http://www.eia.gov/cfapps/ipdbproject/IEDIndex3.cfm>, accessed June 2013.

Table 1407. World Primary Energy Production by Region and Type: 1980 to 2010

[In quadrillion Btu (287.3 represents 287,300,000,000,000,000). Btu = British thermal unit. For Btu conversion factors, see source]

Region and type	1980	1990	1995	2000	2005	2007	2008	2009	2010
World total.................	**287.3**	**348.6**	**361.7**	**397.1**	**456.4**	**475.2**	**488.3**	**487.3**	**508.9**
North America...............	83.2	91.8	96.1	98.8	98.4	100.7	101.4	99.6	101.9
United States [1].................	**67.2**	**70.7**	**71.2**	**71.3**	**69.4**	**71.4**	**73.2**	**72.6**	**74.8**
Central and South America............	12.1	16.7	21.1	26.0	28.0	29.0	29.6	29.4	30.4
Europe...................	40.2	46.9	49.0	50.6	48.6	46.3	46.5	44.7	45.4
Eurasia [2].................	56.5	72.1	51.9	54.1	66.3	69.6	70.3	66.9	70.3
Middle East...............	42.3	41.0	48.3	57.5	65.3	64.6	68.3	66.3	69.8
Africa...................	17.4	21.6	24.0	27.7	34.3	35.7	36.8	36.1	37.2
Asia and Oceania...............	35.8	58.5	71.2	82.4	115.4	129.3	135.5	144.3	153.9
Petroleum [3].................	133.1	136.2	141.8	156.4	168.8	167.6	169.8	166.7	171.0
Dry natural gas.................	54.8	76.1	80.4	89.6	101.7	107.5	111.2	108.7	115.8
Coal...................	71.2	89.9	86.5	93.7	122.9	135.3	140.2	144.6	151.0
Hydroelectric power...................	17.9	22.3	25.3	26.8	29.0	30.1	31.2	31.4	33.2
Nuclear electric power.................	7.6	20.4	23.3	25.7	27.5	27.1	27.1	26.7	27.3
Non-hydroelectric renewables [4].......	0.3	1.6	2.1	2.7	4.0	5.0	5.6	6.4	7.6

[1] Includes biomass, geothermal, and solar energy produced in the United States and not used for generating electricity. [2] Prior to 1992, data were for the former U.S.S.R. [3] Includes crude oil, lease condensate, and natural gas plant liquids. [4] Including biomass, geothermal, solar, wind, ocean, and wave and tidal action.

Source: U.S. Energy Information Administration, "International Energy Statistics Database," <http://www.eia.gov/cfapps/ipdbproject/IEDIndex3.cfm>, accessed June 2013.

Table 1408. World Primary Energy Consumption by Region and Type: 1980 to 2010

[In quadrillion Btu (283.2 represents 283,200,000,000,000,000). Btu = British thermal unit. For Btu conversion factors, see source]

Region and type	1980	1990	1995	2000	2005	2006	2007	2008	2009	2010
World total [1]	**283.2**	**346.0**	**362.9**	**400.1**	**459.3**	**470.1**	**482.9**	**490.7**	**487.6**	**510.6**
North America	91.6	100.1	108.5	118.5	121.2	120.8	122.9	120.1	114.6	118.3
United States [2]	**78.1**	**84.5**	**91.0**	**98.8**	**100.3**	**99.6**	**101.3**	**99.3**	**94.6**	**98.0**
Central and South America	11.5	14.5	17.6	20.8	23.2	24.3	24.7	25.7	25.3	26.9
Europe	71.7	76.3	76.7	81.5	85.8	86.3	86.7	85.6	81.2	83.8
Eurasia [3]	46.7	61.0	42.2	39.2	43.0	42.6	44.0	45.1	40.4	42.8
Middle East	5.8	11.2	13.8	17.4	22.9	23.9	23.9	26.1	27.4	28.7
Africa	6.8	9.5	10.7	12.0	14.5	14.6	15.0	16.1	15.9	16.3
Asia and Oceania	48.9	73.4	93.5	110.7	148.7	157.6	165.7	172.0	182.7	193.6
Petroleum [4]	131.1	136.2	142.5	156.1	170.8	171.0	174.2	172.8	170.2	174.9
Dry natural gas	53.9	75.4	81.1	89.8	103.2	106.1	109.3	112.8	108.6	117.1
Coal	69.9	88.1	86.3	96.7	122.2	128.4	134.2	138.3	140.8	146.7
Renewable electric power [5]	18.2	23.9	27.4	29.5	33.0	34.2	35.1	36.9	37.9	40.8

[1] Includes nuclear electric power, not shown separately. [2] Includes biomass, geothermal, and solar energy consumed in the United States and not used for generating electricity. [3] Prior to 1992, data were for the former U.S.S.R. [4] Includes all refined petroleum products. [5] Includes geothermal, solar, wind, tidal, biomass, waste, and hydroelectric power.

Source: U.S. Energy Information Administration, "International Energy Statistics Database," <http://www.eia.gov/cfapps/ipdbproject/IEDIndex3.cfm>, accessed June 2013.

Table 1409. World Daily Crude Oil Production by Major Producing Country: 1980 to 2012

[In thousands of barrels per day (59,558 barrels represents 59,558,000 barrels). Includes lease condensate. Ranked for top 30 countries as of current year]

Country	1980	1990	2000	2005	2008	2009	2010	2011	2012
World, total [1]	**59,558**	**60,497**	**68,522**	**73,644**	**73,699**	**72,307**	**74,092**	**74,140**	**75,617**
Russia	(X)	(X)	6,479	9,043	9,357	9,495	9,694	9,774	9,922
Saudi Arabia	9,900	6,410	8,404	9,550	9,261	8,250	8,900	9,458	9,832
United States	**8,597**	**7,355**	**5,822**	**5,186**	**5,000**	**5,353**	**5,479**	**5,652**	**6,498**
China	2,114	2,774	3,249	3,609	3,790	3,796	4,078	4,059	4,129
Iran	1,662	3,088	3,696	4,139	4,050	4,037	4,080	4,054	3,367
Canada	1,435	1,553	1,977	2,369	2,579	2,579	2,741	2,901	3,136
Iraq	2,514	2,040	2,571	1,878	2,375	2,391	2,399	2,626	2,983
United Arab Emirates	1,709	2,117	2,368	2,535	2,681	2,413	2,415	2,679	2,804
Kuwait	1,656	1,175	2,079	2,529	2,586	2,350	2,300	2,530	2,635
Mexico	1,936	2,553	3,104	3,423	2,839	2,646	2,621	2,600	2,593
Nigeria	2,055	1,810	2,165	2,627	2,165	2,208	2,455	2,550	2,520
Venezuela	2,168	2,137	3,155	2,565	2,464	2,319	2,216	2,300	2,300
Brazil	182	631	1,269	1,634	1,812	1,950	2,055	2,105	2,061
Angola	150	475	746	1,250	1,981	1,907	1,939	1,786	1,817
Norway	486	1,630	3,222	2,698	2,182	2,067	1,869	1,752	1,607
Algeria	1,106	1,180	1,214	1,692	1,705	1,585	1,540	1,540	1,532
Kazakhstan	(X)	(X)	718	1,288	1,345	1,455	1,525	1,553	1,514
Libya	1,787	1,375	1,410	1,633	1,736	1,650	1,650	465	1,367
Qatar	472	406	737	835	924	927	1,127	1,296	1,216
Colombia	126	440	691	526	588	671	786	914	944
Azerbaijan	(X)	(X)	280	433	870	1,006	1,035	983	922
Oman	282	685	970	774	757	813	865	886	919
United Kingdom	1,622	1,820	2,275	1,649	1,391	1,328	1,233	1,026	888
Indonesia	1,577	1,462	1,428	1,067	986	969	953	918	875
India	182	660	646	665	694	680	751	782	777
Egypt	595	873	768	623	566	587	575	566	556
Argentina	491	483	761	704	661	651	626	581	551
Malaysia	283	619	690	631	609	578	563	514	526
Ecuador	204	285	395	532	505	486	486	500	504
Australia	380	575	722	446	477	475	484	414	406

X Not applicable. [1] Includes countries not shown separately.

Source: U.S. Energy Information Administration, "International Energy Statistics Database," <http://www.eia.gov/cfapps/ipdbproject/IEDIndex3.cfm>, accessed June 2013.

Table 1410. Energy Consumption by Country: 2000 and 2010

[For total consumption, 400.1 represents 400,100,000,000,000,000. For per capita consumption, 65.7 represents 65,700,000. Total primary energy consumption includes the consumption of petroleum, dry natural gas, coal, and net nuclear, hydroelectric, and non-hydroelectric renewable electricity. See text of this section for general comments about the data. For data qualifications for countries and Btu conversion factors, see source]

Country	Total (quad. Btu) 2000	2010	Per capita (mil. Btu) 2000	2010	Country	Total (quad. Btu) 2000	2010	Per capita (mil. Btu) 2000	2010
World, total	**400.1**	**510.6**	**65.7**	**74.4**	Japan	22.4	21.8	176.8	170.7
United States	**98.8**	**98.0**	**350.2**	**316.9**	Kazakhstan	1.8	2.3	116.9	132.0
Algeria	1.2	1.8	40.4	50.0	Korea, North	0.9	0.8	37.7	33.7
Argentina	2.7	3.3	71.5	81.0	Korea, South	7.8	10.8	167.3	221.7
Australia	4.8	5.8	253.7	270.1	Kuwait	0.9	1.3	461.2	504.7
Austria	1.4	1.5	170.8	185.9	Libya	0.6	0.8	125.4	137.5
Bahrain	0.4	0.6	557.0	472.5	Malaysia	2.0	3.0	85.4	105.7
Bangladesh	0.5	1.0	3.8	6.3	Mexico	6.3	7.3	63.4	64.8
Belarus	1.1	1.1	104.9	116.9	Morocco	0.4	0.7	15.9	21.3
Belgium	2.7	2.7	266.4	263.6	Netherlands	3.8	4.3	238.1	257.4
Brazil	8.5	11.3	49.0	57.7	New Zealand	0.8	0.9	217.3	201.6
Bulgaria	0.9	0.8	111.0	107.6	Nigeria	0.8	0.7	6.5	4.5
Burma	0.2	0.2	3.5	4.5	Norway	2.0	1.9	442.6	399.5
Canada	13.3	13.0	427.8	385.1	Pakistan	1.8	2.6	12.1	13.9
Chile	1.0	1.3	66.7	79.6	Peru	0.5	0.8	20.5	29.3
China	40.9	100.9	32.4	75.8	Philippines	1.1	1.2	14.0	12.2
Colombia	1.2	1.4	30.1	30.9	Poland	3.6	4.1	93.8	105.4
Congo, Democratic Rep	0.1	0.1	1.7	1.6	Portugal	1.1	1.1	103.6	104.9
Cuba	0.5	0.4	41.5	36.0	Romania	1.6	1.4	70.7	64.9
Czech Republic	1.4	1.6	136.9	156.0	Russia	26.1	29.3	177.8	205.7
Denmark	0.9	0.8	164.2	150.6	Saudi Arabia	4.9	7.8	227.7	305.0
Ecuador	0.3	0.6	27.7	38.1	Serbia [1]	(X)	0.8	(X)	105.5
Egypt	2.0	3.3	30.8	41.1	South Africa	4.6	5.6	101.7	113.9
Finland	1.2	1.3	235.4	248.0	Spain	5.5	6.2	136.5	134.2
France	11.0	11.0	178.9	169.8	Sweden	2.3	2.2	254.5	244.9
Germany	14.4	13.9	175.3	170.7	Switzerland	1.3	1.3	178.2	162.8
Greece	1.3	1.3	126.7	124.8	Syria	0.8	1.0	47.5	46.5
Guatemala	0.2	0.2	14.2	15.7	Taiwan	3.8	4.8	171.7	208.8
Haiti	0.0	0.0	2.9	3.2	Tanzania	0.1	0.1	1.8	2.7
Hong Kong	0.8	1.3	121.0	178.1	Thailand	2.6	4.3	41.5	65.2
Hungary	1.0	1.1	100.8	105.2	Trinidad and Tobago	0.4	0.9	336.0	762.0
India	13.3	21.9	13.2	18.7	Tunisia	0.3	0.3	31.7	29.4
Indonesia	3.9	6.1	18.0	24.9	Turkey	3.2	4.5	47.0	57.7
Iran	5.0	9.1	73.2	118.4	Ukraine	5.8	5.1	117.4	112.2
Iraq	1.1	1.5	47.8	50.6	United Arab Emirates	1.9	3.5	579.7	710.7
Ireland	0.6	0.6	157.0	135.9	United Kingdom	9.7	8.9	164.5	143.0
Israel	0.8	0.9	132.7	128.6	Venezuela	2.8	3.3	117.9	122.0
Italy	7.6	7.6	131.2	125.5	Vietnam	0.7	1.9	9.3	20.8

X Not applicable. [1] Serbia and Montenegro are separate countries as of June 2006.

Source: U.S. Energy Information Administration, "International Energy Statistics Database," <http://www.eia.gov/cfapps/ipdbproject/IEDIndex3.cfm>, accessed June 2013.

Table 1411. World Energy Consumption by Region and Energy Source, 2005 to 2010, and Projections, 2020 to 2040

[In quadrillion Btu (471.1 represents 471,100,000,000,000,000). Btu = British thermal units. For Btu conversion factors, see source. Energy totals include net imports of coal coke and electricity generated from biomass in the United States. The electricity portion of the national consumption values consists of generation for domestic use plus an adjustment for electricity trade based on a fuel's share of total generation in the exporting country. OECD = Organization for Economic Co-operation and Development; see text, this section]

Region and energy source	2005	2009	2010	Projections 2020	2030	2040	Average annual percent change 2010-2040
World, total	**471.1**	**498.4**	**523.9**	**629.8**	**729.2**	**819.6**	**1.50**
OECD Americas	122.8	117.0	120.2	126.1	132.9	143.6	0.60
United States	**100.5**	**94.9**	**97.9**	**100.5**	**102.3**	**107.2**	**0.30**
OECD Europe	82.2	80.0	82.5	85.5	90.9	94.6	0.46
OECD Asia	38.8	37.7	39.6	43.0	45.4	46.4	0.53
Non-OECD Europe and Eurasia	49.5	43.7	47.2	53.3	60.8	67.1	1.18
Non-OECD Asia	113.3	148.1	159.0	230.3	290.4	337.5	2.54
Middle East	22.9	26.6	27.8	36.6	42.5	48.8	1.90
Africa	17.0	18.4	18.9	21.9	27.4	35.0	2.07
Central and South America	24.5	26.9	28.7	33.2	38.8	46.6	1.63
Liquids	170.8	171.3	176.1	194.7	210.9	232.6	0.93
Natural gas	105.0	108.7	116.8	136.0	162.6	191.3	1.66
Coal	122.3	139.1	147.4	180.3	207.9	219.5	1.34
Nuclear	27.5	26.7	27.3	37.9	49.5	57.2	2.50
Other	45.4	52.6	56.2	81.0	98.3	119.1	2.53

Source: U.S. Energy Information Administration, *International Energy Outlook 2013*, July 2013, and earlier reports. See also <http://www.eia.gov/oiaf/ieo/ieorefcase.html>.

Table 1412. World Dry Natural Gas Production by Major Producing Country: 1980 to 2011

[In billion cubic feet (53,375 represents 53,375,000,000,000). Ranked for top 30 countries, as of current year]

Country	Natural gas production								
	1980	1990	2000	2005	2007	2008	2009	2010	2011
World, total [1]	**53,375**	**73,788**	**87,100**	**98,393**	**104,047**	**107,670**	**105,168**	**111,954**	**115,993**
United States	**19,403**	**17,810**	**19,182**	**18,051**	**19,266**	**20,159**	**20,624**	**21,316**	**22,902**
Russia	(X)	(X)	19,335	21,224	21,595	21,515	19,303	21,536	22,213
Iran	250	837	2,127	3,655	3,952	4,107	4,986	5,161	5,361
Canada	2,759	3,849	6,470	6,561	6,416	6,046	5,634	5,390	5,218
Qatar	184	276	1,028	1,617	2,232	2,719	3,154	3,402	4,705
China	505	508	962	1,763	2,446	2,685	2,975	3,334	3,629
Norway	917	976	1,867	3,072	3,168	3,503	3,664	3,756	3,582
Saudi Arabia	334	1,077	1,759	2,516	2,628	2,841	2,770	3,096	3,258
Algeria	411	1,787	2,940	3,151	2,996	3,055	2,876	2,988	2,923
Netherlands	3,398	2,693	2,559	2,773	2,687	2,957	2,786	3,131	2,851
Indonesia	654	1,602	2,237	2,001	2,422	2,472	2,557	2,841	2,693
Turkmenistan	(X)	(X)	1,642	2,225	2,432	2,490	1,347	1,600	2,338
Uzbekistan	(X)	(X)	1,992	2,108	2,302	2,387	2,169	2,123	2,226
Malaysia	56	654	1,600	1,967	2,104	2,151	2,133	2,171	2,180
Egypt	30	286	646	1,501	1,642	2,083	2,214	2,166	2,163
Australia	313	723	1,159	1,440	1,354	1,405	1,575	1,733	1,970
United Arab Emirates	200	780	1,355	1,659	1,778	1,774	1,724	1,811	1,847
Mexico	900	903	1,314	1,349	1,678	1,694	1,722	1,799	1,761
India	51	399	795	1,056	1,108	1,137	1,437	1,848	1,682
United Kingdom	1,323	1,754	3,826	3,118	2,553	2,469	2,087	1,988	1,546
Trinidad and Tobago	81	177	493	1,069	1,378	1,388	1,437	1,499	1,434
Pakistan	286	482	856	1,088	1,300	1,342	1,367	1,400	1,383
Argentina	280	630	1,321	1,611	1,583	1,556	1,461	1,416	1,369
Thailand	0	208	658	837	918	1,016	1,091	1,281	1,306
Nigeria	38	131	440	791	1,148	1,159	912	1,024	1,107
Oman	28	99	322	699	849	850	875	957	937
Venezuela	517	761	961	828	732	733	651	880	887
Bangladesh	50	162	343	494	575	632	692	703	710
Ukraine	(X)	(X)	636	685	689	699	715	684	699
Azerbaijan	(X)	(X)	200	206	380	591	577	589	631

X Not applicable. [1] Includes countries not shown separately.

Source: U. S. Energy Information Administration, "International Energy Statistics Database," <http://www.eia.gov/cfapps/ipdbproject/IEDIndex3.cfm>, accessed June 2013.

Table 1413. World Coal Production by Major Producing Country: 1980 to 2011

[In millions of short tons (4,181.9 represents 4,181,900,000). Coal includes anthracite, subanthracite, bituminous, subbituminous, lignite, and brown coal. Ranked for top 30 countries, as of current year]

Country	Coal production								
	1980	1990	2000	2005	2007	2008	2009	2010	2011
World, total [1]	**4,181.9**	**5,291.6**	**5,127.2**	**6,526.9**	**7,134.9**	**7,396.9**	**7,641.6**	**7,934.3**	**8,440.3**
China	683.6	1,135.3	1,514.1	2,477.9	2,844.3	3,021.9	3,301.8	3,505.5	3,844.9
United States	**829.7**	**1,029.1**	**1,073.6**	**1,131.5**	**1,146.6**	**1,171.8**	**1,074.9**	**1,084.4**	**1,094.3**
India	125.8	247.6	370.0	473.3	531.5	568.4	613.4	611.7	639.6
Australia	115.2	225.5	338.1	410.7	441.7	437.7	453.8	467.5	456.7
Indonesia	0.6	11.6	84.5	188.0	274.3	274.2	321.0	358.3	414.8
Russia	(X)	(X)	264.9	311.8	318.6	336.2	343.7	358.9	368.0
South Africa	131.9	193.2	248.9	270.1	273.0	278.0	275.0	280.6	279.0
Germany	(X)	(X)	226.0	227.0	225.5	214.3	202.4	201.0	207.9
Poland	253.5	237.1	179.2	175.0	159.8	158.0	148.4	146.3	152.6
Kazakhstan	(X)	(X)	85.4	96.1	107.8	122.4	111.2	122.3	128.6
Colombia	4.5	22.6	42.0	65.1	77.1	81.0	80.3	82.0	94.6
Turkey	20.8	52.3	69.7	64.3	83.1	87.5	87.6	80.9	86.1
Canada	40.4	75.3	76.2	72.0	76.5	74.7	69.4	74.8	74.0
Ukraine	(X)	(X)	68.8	66.5	65.0	65.7	61.2	61.1	68.1
Greece	25.6	57.2	70.4	76.5	73.1	72.4	71.5	62.3	64.8
Czech Republic	(X)	(X)	71.8	68.4	69.0	66.4	62.2	60.9	59.9
Serbia	(X)	(X)	(X)	(X)	46.2	48.7	49.1	48.6	51.7
Vietnam	5.7	5.1	12.8	36.1	47.6	45.4	48.4	49.2	49.1
Bulgaria	33.3	34.9	29.2	27.2	31.4	31.7	30.0	32.4	41.7
Romania	38.8	42.1	32.3	34.3	39.4	39.5	37.4	34.3	38.9
Korea, North	48.6	51.0	32.8	38.2	33.4	35.6	34.8	35.2	34.8
Mongolia	5.3	7.9	5.7	8.3	10.2	11.1	15.9	28.1	34.6
Thailand	1.6	13.7	19.6	23.0	20.1	20.2	19.6	20.2	23.3
Estonia	(X)	(X)	12.9	16.1	18.2	17.8	16.5	19.8	20.7
United Kingdom	143.8	104.1	33.7	22.1	18.2	19.4	19.2	19.6	19.7
Mexico	4.0	8.6	12.5	11.9	13.8	12.6	11.6	11.1	13.7
Bosnia and Herzegovina	(X)	(X)	8.2	10.1	10.8	12.4	12.6	12.1	13.2
Hungary	28.7	19.7	15.5	10.5	10.8	10.4	9.9	10.0	10.5
Philippines	0.4	1.4	1.5	3.2	3.7	4.0	5.2	7.3	10.4
Spain	30.9	39.2	25.9	21.5	18.9	11.2	10.4	9.3	7.3

X Not applicable. [1] Includes countries not shown separately.

Source: U.S. Energy Information Administration, "International Energy Statistics Database," <http://www.eia.gov/cfapps/ipdbproject/IEDIndex3.cfm>, accessed June 2013.

Table 1414. Carbon Dioxide Emissions From Consumption of Fossil Fuels by Country: 1980 to 2011

[In million metric tons of carbon dioxide (18,433.2 represents 18,433,200,000). Ranked for top 25 countries, as of current year. Includes carbon dioxide emissions from the consumption of petroleum, natural gas, coal, and the flaring of natural gas]

Region/Country	1980	1990	2000	2005	2008	2009	2010	2011
World, total [1]	18,433.2	21,523.2	24,149.9	28,261.8	30,256.2	30,236.2	31,502.4	32,578.6
China	1,448.5	2,177.7	3,271.8	5,463.7	6,684.7	7,573.4	7,997.0	8,715.3
United States	4,775.8	5,040.4	5,863.3	5,999.2	5,844.6	5,435.3	5,636.7	5,490.6
Russia	(X)	(X)	1,498.8	1,587.5	1,645.6	1,554.6	1,642.3	1,788.1
India	291.2	578.6	991.0	1,181.4	1,471.8	1,597.8	1,601.2	1,725.8
Japan	947.0	1,047.0	1,201.4	1,241.3	1,216.3	1,104.9	1,179.8	1,180.6
Germany	(X)	(X)	854.7	847.4	823.3	772.4	793.3	748.5
Iran	116.8	202.1	321.5	451.1	512.0	562.6	564.6	624.9
Korea, South	131.7	242.1	438.7	493.8	521.8	524.4	581.1	611.0
Canada	457.4	470.6	573.3	623.8	578.2	549.7	546.7	552.6
Saudi Arabia	176.9	208.0	290.5	401.9	421.6	437.7	468.7	513.5
United Kingdom	613.6	601.8	560.3	583.1	563.9	516.2	528.9	496.8
Brazil	185.7	237.3	344.4	370.8	427.4	407.0	451.0	475.4
Mexico	240.3	302.2	382.9	397.8	452.8	421.1	432.2	462.3
South Africa	235.0	298.0	386.0	432.4	490.0	477.6	473.2	461.6
Indonesia	85.8	156.0	266.2	330.8	370.2	405.7	414.5	426.8
Italy	371.8	415.4	447.7	471.9	449.7	407.6	416.8	400.9
Australia	198.8	267.6	356.3	412.6	425.2	424.3	423.7	392.3
France	488.9	367.7	401.7	414.0	428.5	386.2	388.7	374.3
Spain	195.0	224.1	315.6	379.4	360.1	327.8	312.4	318.6
Poland	428.9	333.8	292.6	287.6	294.7	286.5	304.7	307.9
Ukraine	(X)	(X)	324.9	351.1	350.5	245.8	281.1	304.4
Turkey	68.6	129.5	201.9	230.9	272.9	269.1	269.4	296.3
Taiwan	70.6	118.3	256.1	288.8	290.4	259.6	286.9	293.3
Thailand	33.6	83.9	161.8	241.8	255.1	267.9	273.1	269.6
Netherlands	201.1	211.1	246.3	268.5	249.5	243.8	254.9	253.0

X Not applicable. [1] Includes other countries not shown separately.

Source: U.S. Energy Information Administration, "International Energy Statistics Database," <http://www.eia.gov/countries/data.cfm>, accessed June 2013.

Table 1415. Average Temperatures and Precipitation—Selected International Cities

[In degrees Fahrenheit, except as noted. Data are generally based on a standard 30-year period; for details, see source. Minus sign (−) indicates degrees below zero]

City	January Average high	January Average low	January Warmest	January Coldest	January Average precipitation (inches)	July Average high	July Average low	July Warmest	July Coldest	July Average precipitation (inches)
Amsterdam, Netherlands	41	34	57	3	3.1	69	55	90	39	2.9
Athens, Greece	55	44	70	28	1.9	89	73	108	61	0.2
Baghdad, Iraq	58	38	75	25	1.1	110	78	122	61	–
Bangkok, Thailand	89	71	95	54	0.4	90	78	99	72	6.2
Beijing, China	34	17	54	1	0.2	86	72	104	63	8.8
Berlin, Germany	35	26	58	-11	(NA)	73	56	95	41	(NA)
Bogota, Colombia	66	43	84	27	1.9	64	47	82	32	1.8
Brasilia, Brazil	81	64	95	54	(NA)	79	52	97	37	(NA)
Buenos Aires, Argentina	85	64	104	44	4.2	58	41	88	23	2.3
Cairo, Egypt	65	49	86	32	0.2	93	72	108	63	–
Frankfurt, Germany	38	30	56	-4	1.8	75	57	97	38	2.4
Geneva, Switzerland	39	29	57	-2	2.2	77	56	96	41	2.8
Hong Kong, China	67	58	79	43	1.1	89	81	97	70	14.3
Istanbul, Turkey	46	37	64	16	3.7	82	66	100	50	0.7
Jakarta, Indonesia	83	75	92	72	(NA)	88	74	92	67	(NA)
Karachi, Pakistan	76	55	93	39	0.3	89	83	109	68	3.5
Lagos, Nigeria	82	79	93	64	(NA)	79	76	88	70	(NA)
London, England	45	36	61	15	2.4	72	56	93	45	1.8
Madrid, Spain	51	32	68	14	1.8	90	61	104	46	0.4
Manila, Philippines	86	71	95	61	0.8	88	76	99	70	15.9
Mexico City, Mexico	70	45	86	26	0.3	74	56	86	37	5.1
Montreal, Canada	21	7	52	-31	2.8	79	61	93	43	3.4
Moscow, Russia	21	11	46	-33	1.4	71	55	95	41	3.2
Nairobi, Kenya	77	58	88	45	1.8	71	54	85	43	0.5
New Delhi, India	68	48	85	32	0.9	93	81	111	70	7.9
Paris, France	43	34	59	1	(NA)	75	58	95	41	(NA)
Rio De Janeiro, Brazil	91	74	109	64	5.3	81	64	102	52	1.8
Rome, Italy	55	39	64	19	3.2	83	66	100	55	0.6
Seoul, Korea	33	21	55	-1	(NA)	82	71	97	55	(NA)
Singapore, Singapore	85	73	100	66	9.4	86	76	99	70	5.9
Sydney, Australia	79	65	109	49	4.0	62	44	80	32	2.5
Tel Aviv, Israel	62	46	84	32	(NA)	87	69	100	50	(NA)
Tokyo, Japan	48	35	66	25	2.0	82	71	95	55	5.3
Toronto, Canada	28	15	59	-24	1.9	79	60	99	45	2.8

– Represents zero. NA Not available.

Source: U.S. National Oceanic and Atmospheric Administration, *Climates of the World*. See also <http://www.ncdc.noaa.gov/oa/oldpubs/>.

Table 1416. Telephones, Cellular Phones, and Internet Use by Country: 2012

[Rates per 100 inhabitants. For data qualifications for individual countries, see source]

Country	Telephone lines [1]	Cell phone subscribers [2]	Internet users [3]	Country	Telephone lines [1]	Cell phone subscribers [2]	Internet users [3]
United States............	**44.02**	**98.17**	**81.03**	Kazakhstan...............	26.50	175.39	53.32
Afghanistan...............	0.04	53.90	5.45	Kenya...............	0.59	71.89	32.10
Argentina..................	24.31	142.51	55.80	Korea, South............	61.95	110.36	84.10
Australia..................	45.69	106.19	82.35	Malaysia..................	15.65	140.94	65.80
Azerbaijan...............	18.40	107.47	54.20	Mexico...................	17.41	86.77	38.42
Bangladesh...............	0.63	63.76	6.30	Morocco..................	10.06	119.69	55.00
Brazil.....................	22.34	125.19	49.85	Myanmar.................	1.14	11.16	1.07
Canada....................	51.94	75.74	86.77	Netherlands.............	42.40	117.52	93.00
China.....................	20.60	81.26	42.30	Nigeria...................	0.25	67.68	32.88
Colombia..................	13.23	103.19	48.98	Norway...................	29.55	115.55	95.00
Congo, Dem. Rep........	0.08	28.01	1.68	Pakistan..................	3.22	66.77	9.96
Cuba......................	10.81	14.95	25.64	Panama...................	17.66	186.73	45.20
Dominican Republic......	10.46	88.75	45.00	Poland....................	15.99	132.68	65.00
Egypt.....................	10.19	115.29	44.07	Romania..................	21.88	106.14	50.00
Ethiopia..................	0.92	23.72	1.48	Russia....................	30.06	183.52	53.27
France....................	61.92	98.14	83.00	Saudi Arabia.............	16.73	184.68	54.00
Germany..................	61.84	131.30	84.00	South Africa.............	7.94	134.80	41.00
Greece....................	47.83	116.94	56.00	Spain.....................	41.09	108.32	72.00
Haiti......................	0.49	59.43	10.87	Sweden...................	45.51	122.62	94.00
Honduras..................	7.72	93.15	18.12	Switzerland..............	56.66	135.25	85.20
Hong Kong, China........	60.61	227.93	72.80	Syria......................	20.95	61.22	24.30
India......................	2.47	68.72	12.58	Thailand..................	9.14	120.29	26.50
Indonesia..................	15.52	115.20	15.36	Turkey....................	18.60	90.84	45.13
Iran.......................	38.03	76.92	26.00	Ukraine...................	27.11	132.05	33.70
Israel.....................	46.71	119.89	73.37	United Kingdom...........	52.57	130.75	87.02
Italy......................	35.52	159.48	58.00	Venezuela................	25.59	102.10	44.05
Japan.....................	50.84	109.43	79.05	Vietnam..................	11.36	149.41	39.49

[1] Includes active fixed telephone lines (those that have registered activity in the past three months) connecting the subscriber's terminal equipment to the public switched telephone network (PSTN) and having a dedicated port on a telephone exchange. Integrated services digital network (ISDN) channels and fixed wireless subscribers are included. [2] Includes subscriptions to a public mobile phone service using cellular technology, which provide access to the public switched telephone network (PSTN). Both prepaid and post-paid subscriptions are included. [3] Includes all persons with access to the Internet via fixed or mobile network, irrespective of the device used (i.e., personal computer, mobile phone, etc.).

Source: The World Bank, Washington, DC, "World Development Indicators" database ©, <http://data.worldbank.org/data-catalog/world-development-indicators>, accessed August 2013.

Table 1417. Patents by Country: 2012

[Includes only U.S. patents granted to residents of areas outside of the United States and its territories. See also Table 804 and Table 805]

Country	Total [1]	Inventions	Designs	Country	Total [1]	Inventions	Designs
Total.....................	**142,601**	**132,129**	**9,506**	Sweden..................	2,264	2,081	177
Japan.....................	52,773	50,677	1,899	Netherlands.............	2,193	1,904	117
Germany..................	15,041	13,835	1,051	Switzerland..............	2,039	1,831	200
Korea, South..............	14,168	13,233	864	Australia.................	1,786	1,525	226
Taiwan....................	11,624	10,646	953	India.....................	1,733	1,691	37
Canada....................	6,459	5,775	661	Finland...................	1,138	1,064	60
United Kingdom...........	5,876	5,213	600	Belgium...................	1,004	866	112
France....................	5,857	5,386	435	Austria...................	987	858	129
China.....................	5,341	4,637	700	Denmark..................	978	850	105
Israel.....................	2,598	2,474	86	Singapore................	841	810	30
Italy......................	2,546	2,120	412	Other countries.........	5,355	4,653	652

[1] Includes patents for botanical plants and reissues, not shown separately.

Source: U.S. Patent and Trademark Office, Patent Technology Monitoring Team, "Patent Counts, 2012, Single Year Report," <http://www.uspto.gov/web/offices/ac/ido/oeip/taf/reports_stco.htm>, accessed June 2013.

Table 1418. Global Telecommunications Indicators: 1995 to 2012

[In millions (688 represents 688,000,000), except as indicated]

Indicators	1995	2000	2005	2010	2011	2012
NUMBER (million)						
Fixed telephone lines [1]............................	688	975	1,243	1,228	1,203	(NA)
Mobile cellular subscribers [1]......................	91	738	2,205	5,312	5,957	(NA)
Internet users [1]..................................	39	396	1,022	2,012	2,264	(NA)
Fixed broadband Internet subscribers [2]..........	(NA)	16	220	527	588	(NA)
PER 100 INHABITANTS						
Fixed telephone lines [1]............................	12.05	15.96	19.46	17.83	17.28	(NA)
Mobile cellular subscriptions [1].....................	1.59	12.08	33.95	77.14	85.47	(NA)
Internet users [1]..................................	0.78	6.75	15.77	29.58	32.62	35.57
Fixed broadband Internet subscribers [2]..........	(NA)	0.36	3.45	7.70	8.61	(NA)

NA Not available. [1] See footnotes, Table 1416. [2] Includes broadband subscribers using a digital subscriber line, cable modem, or other high-speed technology.

Source: The World Bank, Washington, DC, "World Development Indicators" database ©, <http://data.worldbank.org/data-catalog/world-development-indicators>, accessed August 2013.

Table 1419. Dow Jones Global Index by Country and Industry: 2000 to 2011

[Index figures shown are as of December 31. 1991 = 100. Based on share prices denominated in U.S. dollars. Stocks in countries that impose significant restrictions on foreign ownership are included in the world index in the same proportion that shares are available to foreign investors]

Country and industry	2000	2005	2010	2011	Country and industry	2000	2005	2010	2011
World, total	**210.9**	**234.1**	**253.9**	**228.8**	Asia/Pacific	93.0	132.0	142.5	117.7
Americas	299.1	307.3	340.9	329.3	Australia	156.0	312.5	436.9	369.3
United States	**306.9**	**302.4**	**316.6**	**314.5**	Hong Kong	245.6	273.6	479.6	367.9
Canada	225.3	365.4	526.6	452.3	Indonesia	31.2	79.0	210.4	215.6
Mexico	132.2	360.1	626.8	535.2	Japan	88.3	113.5	91.8	78.4
Europe	241.2	264.8	270.2	232.0	Malaysia	88.5	119.5	254.0	248.6
Austria	86.2	335.5	277.4	176.5	New Zealand	96.7	227.3	181.9	180.1
Belgium	196.9	321.2	337.0	293.2	Singapore	135.2	176.3	327.6	263.4
Denmark	220.1	375.1	556.0	458.0	Thailand	27.2	76.7	152.1	144.1
Finland	1,537.8	948.5	936.0	624.5					
France	252.9	273.3	269.0	217.0	Basic materials	117.6	213.8	373.9	284.2
Germany	219.1	224.3	282.7	226.3	Consumer goods	183.8	241.9	318.4	308.9
Ireland	312.3	470.4	189.9	188.7	Consumer services	192.8	214.4	238.5	233.2
Italy	192.2	213.8	135.1	98.6	Oil and Gas	230.7	383.3	485.9	459.8
Netherlands	335.7	309.6	279.8	232.4	Financial	207.1	259.8	182.0	145.4
Norway	151.8	276.1	388.7	326.2	Healthcare	329.9	310.6	328.1	348.1
Spain	193.5	288.6	282.2	234.6	Industrial	167.1	192.4	228.8	200.1
Sweden	339.0	378.3	544.6	450.8	Technology	552.7	375.1	450.3	421.4
Switzerland	388.8	452.5	572.9	526.3	Telecommunications	273.3	201.6	234.5	224.5
United Kingdom	199.8	217.6	211.7	197.8	Utilities	156.0	176.9	195.1	180.0

Source: CME Group Index Services, LLC, New York, NY, Dow Jones Indexes ©. See also <http://www.djindexes.com/>.

Table 1420. Foreign Stock Market Activity—MSCI Indexes: 2000 to 2012

[Index figures shown are as of December 31. January 1, 1970 = 100, except as noted. Minus sign (–) indicates decrease. Based on share prices denominated in U.S. dollars]

Index and country	Index			Percent change [1]		Index and country	Index			Percent change [1]	
	2000	2010	2012	2010	2012		2000	2010	2012	2010	2012
ALL COUNTRY (AC) INDEXES						Hong Kong	5,475	8,724	8,860	19.7	24.4
AC World Index [2]	290	331	340	10.4	13.4	Japan	2,552	2,496	2,212	13.4	5.8
AC World Index [2] except USA [2]	194	263	250	8.4	13.3	Singapore	2,081	4,212	4,207	18.4	26.4
AC Asia Pacific [2]	90	138	129	14.3	13.6						
AC Europe [2]	377	407	401	1.6	15.4	**EMERGING MARKETS (EM)**					
European Union [2]	362	365	357	-0.2	15.0	EM Far East index [2]	128	405	399	16.1	17.5
						China [5]	23	66	63	2.3	19.0
DEVELOPED MARKETS						India [5]	115	559	430	19.4	23.9
World index	1,221	1,280	1,338	9.6	13.2	Indonesia	78	833	887	31.2	2.4
EAFE index [3]	1,492	1,658	1,604	4.9	13.6	Korea, South	79	410	429	25.3	20.2
Europe index	1,378	1,457	1,446	1.0	15.2	Malaysia	161	453	487	32.5	10.8
Pacific index	1,832	2,269	2,109	13.1	11.0	Pakistan [5]	45	98	100	19.5	23.5
Far East index	2,583	2,710	2,461	14.2	9.1	Philippines	147	351	488	30.3	43.9
						Sri Lanka [5]	36	288	211	71.9	3.2
United States	**1,250**	**1,201**	**1,362**	**13.2**	**13.5**	Taiwan	192	313	272	18.3	13.4
Canada	833	1,861	1,700	18.2	6.7	Thailand	59	340	421	50.8	30.9
Australia	318	884	876	10.0	16.4	EM Latin America index	916	4,614	3,798	12.1	5.4
New Zealand [2]	56	99	124	3.2	23.0	Argentina	1,233	3,573	1,253	70.1	-38.9
						Brazil	763	3,761	2,728	3.8	-3.5
Austria	708	1,509	1,151	7.3	22.6	Chile	605	2,910	2,395	41.8	5.6
Belgium	1,222	1,051	1,250	-2.2	36.1	Colombia [5]	42	1,113	1,360	40.8	31.6
Denmark	2,201	5,494	5,922	29.8	29.6	Mexico	1,465	6,473	7,119	26.0	27.1
Finland [2]	922	493	356	7.1	10.0	Peru [5]	125	1,817	1,598	49.2	15.5
France	1,509	1,492	1,417	-6.7	17.7	Venezuela [5]	106	(NA)	(NA)	(NA)	(NA)
Germany	1,436	1,711	1,739	6.0	27.2						
Greece [2]	476	224	81	-46.4	-0.8	EM Europe, Middle East, and Africa index [6]	100	392	(NA)	20.9	(NA)
Ireland [2]	308	106	123	-19.7	3.8	Czech Republic [7]	80	504	433	-7.4	-3.1
Italy	447	316	255	-17.6	8.6	Egypt [7]	136	860	636	9.5	44.5
Luxembourg [4]	492	(NA)	(NA)	(NA)	(NA)	Hungary [7]	234	663	514	-10.7	18.7
Netherlands	2,177	1,998	2,005	-0.6	17.2	Jordan	55	132	105	-12.0	-4.5
Norway	1,181	2,965	2,939	7.4	13.7	Morocco [7]	168	461	313	10.8	-16.5
Portugal [2]	128	125	92	-14.6	-0.7	Poland [5]	499	1,016	904	12.6	32.1
Spain	347	502	403	-25.4	-3.3	Russia [7]	155	932	808	17.2	9.6
Sweden	4,240	6,888	6,721	31.3	18.7	South Africa [5]	158	612	581	30.7	14.8
Switzerland	2,695	3,915	4,177	9.8	17.3	Turkey	248	625	634	18.4	60.5
United Kingdom	1,146	1,138	1,183	5.2	10.8						

NA Not available. [1] Percent change during calendar year (e.g., Jan. 1 through December 31). Adjusted for foreign exchange fluctuations relative to U.S. dollar. [2] January 1, 1988 = 100. [3] Europe, Australasia, Far East Index. [4] MSCI Luxembourg Index discontinued as of March 29, 2002. [5] January 1, 1993 = 100. [6] January 1, 2001 = 100 [7] January 1, 1995 = 100.

Source: MSCI <http://www.msci.com/products/indices/> ©. The MSCI data contained herein is the property of MSCI Inc. (MSCI). MSCI, its affiliates and information providers make no warranties with respect to any such data. The MSCI data contained herein is used under license and may not be further used, distributed, or disseminated without the express written consent of MSCI.

Table 1421. Foreign Stock Market Indices: 1980 to 2012

[As of year end. The DAX-30 index is a total return index which includes dividends, whereas the other foreign indices are price indices which exclude dividends]

Year	London FTSE 100	Tokyo Nikkei 225	Hong Kong Hang Seng	Germany DAX-30	Paris CAC-40	Dow Jones Europe STOXX 50
1980	647	7,116	1,477	481	(X)	(X)
1985	1,413	13,113	1,752	1,366	(X)	(X)
1990	2,144	23,849	3,025	1,398	1,518	835
1995	3,689	19,868	10,073	2,254	1,872	1,538
1999	6,930	18,934	16,962	6,958	5,958	4,742
2000	6,223	13,786	15,096	6,434	5,926	4,557
2001	5,217	10,543	11,397	5,160	4,625	3,707
2002	3,940	8,579	9,321	2,893	3,064	2,408
2003	4,477	10,677	12,576	3,965	3,558	2,660
2004	4,814	11,489	14,230	4,256	3,821	2,775
2005	5,619	16,111	14,876	5,408	4,715	3,349
2006	6,221	17,226	19,965	6,597	5,542	3,697
2007	6,457	15,308	27,813	8,067	5,614	3,684
2008	4,434	8,860	14,388	4,810	3,218	2,065
2009	5,413	10,546	21,873	5,957	3,936	2,579
2010	5,900	10,229	23,035	6,914	3,805	2,586
2011	5,572	8,455	18,434	5,898	3,160	2,370
2012	5,898	10,395	22,657	7,612	3,641	2,578

X Not applicable.

Source: Global Financial Data ©, Los Angeles, CA, <http://www.globalfinancialdata.com>, unpublished data.

Table 1422. U.S. and Foreign Stock Markets—Market Capitalization and Value of Shares Traded: 2000 to 2011

[In billions of U.S. dollars (15,104.0 represents $15,104,000,000,000). Market capitalization is the market value of all domestic listed companies at the end of the year. The market value of a company is the share price times the number of shares outstanding. Value of shares traded is the annual total turnover of listed company shares]

Country	Market capitalization				Value of shares traded			
	2000	2005	2010	2011	2000	2005	2010	2011
United States	15,104.0	16,970.9	17,139.0	15,640.7	31,862.5	21,510.0	30,454.8	30,750.6
Australia	372.8	804.1	1,454.5	1,198.2	226.3	616.1	1,221.9	1,246.4
Austria	29.9	124.4	67.7	82.4	9.4	45.9	48.1	38.7
Belgium	182.5	288.5	269.3	229.9	38.0	125.7	111.5	107.2
Brazil	226.2	474.6	1,545.6	1,229.0	101.3	154.2	901.1	961.3
Canada	841.4	1,480.9	2,160.2	1,906.6	634.7	845.0	1,365.7	1,520.0
Chile	60.4	136.4	341.6	270.3	6.1	18.9	54.3	56.9
China	581.0	780.8	4,762.8	3,389.1	721.5	586.3	8,030.0	7,671.4
Colombia	9.6	46.0	208.5	201.3	0.4	6.4	23.0	27.2
Denmark	107.7	178.0	231.7	179.5	91.6	152.0	144.6	150.5
Egypt	28.7	79.7	82.5	48.7	11.1	25.4	37.1	22.0
Finland	293.6	209.5	118.2	143.1	206.6	273.5	101.9	174.3
France	1,446.6	1,758.7	1,926.5	1,568.7	1,083.3	1,526.1	1,467.1	1,474.2
Germany	1,270.2	1,221.3	1,429.7	1,184.5	1,069.1	1,763.2	1,405.0	1,758.2
Greece	110.8	145.0	72.6	33.6	95.1	65.3	43.1	24.7
Hong Kong	623.4	693.5	1,079.6	889.6	377.9	294.1	1,597.5	1,551.6
India	148.1	553.1	1,615.9	1,015.4	509.8	433.9	1,056.8	740.2
Indonesia	26.8	81.4	360.4	390.1	14.3	41.9	129.5	139.6
Iran	34.0	38.7	86.6	107.2	5.0	8.2	17.1	20.1
Israel	64.1	120.1	218.1	145.0	23.4	59.9	133.4	117.4
Italy	768.4	798.2	318.1	431.5	778.4	1,115.2	539.3	887.5
Japan	3,157.2	4,736.5	4,099.6	3,540.7	2,693.9	4,997.4	4,280.4	4,160.5
Korea, South	171.6	718.2	1,089.2	994.3	1,067.7	1,203.0	1,626.6	2,032.9
Kuwait	20.8	130.1	119.6	100.9	4.2	94.0	41.8	21.4
Malaysia	116.9	181.2	410.5	395.1	58.5	50.0	90.2	128.9
Mexico	125.2	239.1	454.3	408.7	45.3	52.7	108.5	112.0
Netherlands	640.5	592.9	661.2	594.7	677.2	835.8	592.1	554.3
New Zealand	18.6	43.4	36.3	71.7	10.8	17.4	17.9	21.4
Norway	65.0	191.0	250.9	219.2	60.1	194.8	217.1	208.4
Philippines	51.6	40.2	157.3	165.4	8.2	7.0	26.8	32.9
Poland	31.3	93.9	190.2	138.2	14.6	30.0	77.5	95.9
Qatar	(NA)	87.3	123.6	125.4	(NA)	28.1	18.3	23.1
Russia	38.9	548.6	1,004.5	796.4	20.3	159.3	799.7	1,146.4
Saudi Arabia	67.2	646.1	353.4	338.9	17.3	1,103.5	203.2	293.0
Singapore	152.8	316.7	370.1	308.3	91.5	119.8	282.1	253.8
South Africa	205.0	565.4	1,012.5	855.7	77.5	200.7	340.0	372.2
Spain	504.2	960.0	1,171.6	1,031.0	985.9	1,557.2	1,360.9	1,419.2
Sweden	328.3	403.9	581.2	470.1	390.0	464.0	439.6	505.6
Switzerland	792.3	938.6	1,229.4	932.2	609.1	883.3	869.4	928.1
Taiwan	247.6	516.0	804.1	623.4	983.5	716.5	892.6	866.6
Thailand	29.5	124.9	277.7	268.5	23.3	89.3	217.9	232.4
Turkey	69.7	161.5	306.7	201.8	179.2	201.3	421.6	413.7
United Arab Emirates	23.3	225.6	104.7	93.8	(NA)	143.1	27.4	15.8
United Kingdom	2,580.0	3,058.2	3,107.0	2,903.2	1,835.3	4,167.0	3,006.7	2,971.8

NA Not available

Source: Standard and Poor's, New York, NY, Standard & Poor's Global Stock Markets Factbook 2012 ©. See also <http://www.standardandpoors.com>.

Table 1423. Foreign Exchange Rates: 2012

[Foreign currency units per U.S. dollar. Rates shown are annual averages, including market and official exchange rates]

Country	Currency	2012 [1]	Country	Currency	2012 [1]
Afghanistan	Afghani	51.00	Kuwait	Kuwaiti dinar	0.28
Albania	Lek	108.19	Kyrgyzstan	Som	47.01
Algeria	Algerian dinar	77.54	Laos	Kip	8,013.30
Angola	Kwanza	95.47	Latvia	Lat	0.55
Argentina	Argentine peso	4.54	Lebanon	Lebanese pound	1,507.50
Armenia	Dram	401.76	Lesotho	Loti	8.20
Australia	Australian dollar	0.97	Liberia	Liberian dollar	73.52
Austria	Euro	0.78	Libya	Libyan dinar	1.26
Azerbaijan	Manat	0.79	Lithuania	Lita	2.69
Bahrain	Bahrain dinar	0.38	Macedonia	Denar	47.89
Bangladesh	Taka	81.86	Madagascar	Malagasy ariary	2,195.00
Belarus	Belarusian ruble	8,336.90	Malawi	Kwacha	249.11
Belgium	Euro	0.78	Malaysia	Ringgit	3.09
Benin	CFA franc	510.53	Mali	CFA franc	510.53
Bhutan	Ngultrum	53.44	Mauritania	Ouguiya	296.60
Bolivia	Boliviano	6.96	Mauritius	Mauritian rupee	30.05
Bosnia/Herzegovina	Konvertibilna marka	1.52	Mexico	Peso	13.17
Botswana	Pula	7.62	Moldova	Leu	12.11
Brazil	Real	1.95	Mongolia	Togrog	1,357.60
Brunei	Brunei dollar	1.25	Morocco	Dirham	8.61
Bulgaria	Leva	1.52	Mozambique	Metical	28.38
Burkina Faso	CFA franc	510.53	Namibia	Namibia dollar	8.20
Burma	Kyat	853.48	Nepal	Nepalese rupee	85.20
Burundi	Burundi franc	1,442.51	Netherlands	Euro	0.78
Cambodia	Riel	4,033.00	New Zealand	New Zealand dollar	1.23
Cameroon	CFA franc	510.53	Nicaragua	Cordoba	23.55
Canada	Canadian dollar	1.00	Niger	CFA franc	510.53
Central African Rep	CFA franc	510.53	Nigeria	Naira	156.81
Chad	CFA franc	510.53	Norway	Krone	5.82
Chile	Chilean peso	486.49	Oman	Omani rial	0.38
China	Renminbi yuan	6.31	Pakistan	Pakistan rupee	93.40
Colombia	Colombian peso	1,798.00	Panama	Balboa	1.00
Congo, Dem. Rep	Congolese franc	920.25	Papua New Guinea	Kina	2.08
Congo, Republic of	CFA franc	510.53	Paraguay	Guarani	4,424.90
Costa Rica	Colon	502.90	Peru	Nuevo sol	2.64
Cote d'Ivoire	CFA franc	510.29	Philippines	Philippine peso	42.23
Croatia	Kuna	5.85	Poland	Zloty	3.26
Cuba	Peso	1.00	Portugal	Euro	0.78
Czech Republic	Koruna	19.58	Qatar	Riyal	3.64
Denmark	Krone	5.79	Romania	Leu	3.47
Djibouti	Djibouti franc	177.72	Russia	Ruble	30.84
Dominican Republic	Dominican peso	39.34	Rwanda	Rwandan franc	616.60
Ecuador	U.S. dollar	1.00	Saint Lucia	East Caribbean dollar	2.70
Egypt	Egyptian pound	6.06	Saudi Arabia	Riyal	3.75
El Salvador	U.S. dollar	1.00	Senegal	CFA franc	510.53
Eritrea	Nakfa	15.38	Serbia	Serbian dinar	87.99
Estonia	Euro	0.78	Sierra Leone	Leone	4,344.00
Ethiopia	Birr	17.71	Singapore	Singapore dollar	1.25
Fiji	Fijian dollar	1.79	Slovakia	Euro	0.78
Finland	Euro	0.78	Slovenia	Euro	0.78
France	Euro	0.78	Somalia	Somali shilling	1,600.00
Gabon	CFA franc	510.53	South Africa	Rand	8.20
Gambia, The	Dalasi	32.08	Spain	Euro	0.78
Georgia	Lari	1.65	Sri Lanka	Sri Lankan rupee	127.60
Germany	Euro	0.78	Sudan	Sudanese dinar	4.09
Ghana	Cedi	1.80	Suriname	Suriname dollar	3.30
Greece	Euro	0.78	Swaziland	Emalangeni	8.20
Guatemala	Quetzal	7.83	Sweden	Krona	6.77
Guinea	Guinean franc	6,986.10	Switzerland	Swiss franc	0.94
Guyana	Guyana dollar	204.36	Syria	Syrian pound	64.39
Haiti	Gourde	41.95	Taiwan	New Taiwan dollar	29.62
Honduras	Lempira	19.64	Tajikistan	Tajik somoni	4.74
Hong Kong	Hong Kong dollar	7.76	Tanzania	Tanzania shilling	1,583.00
Hungary	Forint	225.10	Thailand	Baht	31.08
Iceland	Krona	125.08	Trinidad and Tobago	Tr. and Tob. dollar	6.39
India	Rupee	53.44	Tunisia	Tunisian dinar	1.56
Indonesia	Rupiah	9,386.60	Turkey	Lira	1.80
Iran	Rial	12,175.50	Turkmenistan	Manat	2.85
Iraq	Dinar	1,166.00	Uganda	Uganda shilling	2,505.60
Ireland	Euro	0.78	Ukraine	Hryvnia	7.99
Israel	Shekel	3.86	United Arab Emirates	Dirham	3.67
Italy	Euro	0.78	United Kingdom	Pound sterling	0.63
Jamaica	Jamaican dollar	88.75	Uruguay	Uruguayan peso	20.31
Japan	Yen	79.79	Uzbekistan	Soum	1,891.10
Jordan	Jordanian dinar	0.71	Venezuela	Bolivar	4.29
Kazakhstan	Tenge	149.11	Vietnam	Dong	20,858.90
Kenya	Kenyan shilling	84.53	West Bank and Gaza	Israeli shekel	3.86
Korea, North	North Korean won	155.50	Yemen	Yemeni rial	214.35
Korea, South	Won	1,126.47	Zambia	Zambian kwacha	5.10

[1] End-of-year values were used if annual averages were unavailable. Some values were estimated using partial year data.

Source: Central Intelligence Agency, *The World Factbook*, <https://www.cia.gov/library/publications/the-world-factbook/index.html/>, accessed August 2013.

Table 1424. Research and Development (R&D) Expenditures by Sector and Country: 2011

[For total and per capita expenditures, 1,034,024 represents 1,034,024,000,000. Gross domestic expenditure on R&D (GERD) may include financing from abroad. Selected data are preliminary or estimated. For methodological information for individual countries, see source. GDP = gross domestic product]

Country	Gross domestic expenditure on R&D (GERD)			Percent of GERD performed by:			
	Total (million current PPP U.S. dollars) \1	Per capita (million current PPP U.S. dollars) \1	Percent of GDP	Government sector	Business enterprise sector	Higher education sector	Private non-profit sector
OECD total [2].........	1,034,024	834	2.4	11.7	67.0	18.7	2.6
EU-28 [2].............	320,456	631	1.9	13.1	61.9	24.1	1.1
EU-15 [3].............	299,570	749	2.1	12.3	62.9	23.8	1.2
United States [4]......	**415,193**	**1,331**	**2.8**	**12.1**	**68.3**	**15.2**	**4.3**
Argentina..............	4,641	114	0.6	42.3	24.6	31.4	1.7
Australia [5]...........	20,578	918	2.2	12.4	58.0	26.6	3.0
Austria................	9,762	1,159	2.7	5.3	68.1	26.1	0.5
Belgium...............	8,719	794	2.0	9.0	67.1	22.9	1.0
Canada...............	24,289	704	1.7	10.1	51.3	38.1	0.5
Chile [5]...............	1,331	78	0.4	8.4	38.7	30.6	22.3
China.................	208,172	155	1.8	16.3	75.7	7.9	(NA)
Czech Republic.......	5,086	485	1.8	17.5	60.3	21.6	0.5
Denmark..............	7,052	1,266	3.1	2.2	67.6	29.8	0.4
Estonia...............	710	530	2.4	8.1	63.2	27.8	0.9
Finland...............	7,635	1,417	3.8	8.8	70.5	20.0	0.7
France................	51,891	797	2.2	14.1	63.4	21.2	1.2
Germany..............	93,055	1,138	2.9	14.7	67.3	18.0	(NA)
Greece [6].............	1,867	167	0.6	20.9	28.6	49.2	1.3
Hungary..............	2,582	259	1.2	15.8	62.4	20.2	(NA)
Iceland [7].............	370	1,160	3.1	20.0	52.9	24.9	2.2
Ireland...............	3,223	704	1.7	4.9	69.0	26.1	(NA)
Israel [8]..............	9,823	1,265	4.4	3.7	80.2	12.6	3.4
Italy..................	24,812	409	1.3	13.7	54.2	28.6	3.5
Japan.................	146,537	1,146	3.4	8.4	77.0	13.2	1.5
Korea, South..........	59,890	1,203	4.0	11.7	76.5	10.1	1.6
Luxembourg...........	656	1,263	1.4	19.2	68.5	12.4	(NA)
Mexico...............	8,209	75	0.4	30.5	39.0	28.9	1.6
Netherlands [5]........	12,810	771	1.9	11.7	47.9	40.4	(NA)
New Zealand..........	1,772	401	1.3	22.7	45.4	31.8	(NA)
Norway...............	5,007	1,011	1.7	16.4	52.1	31.5	(NA)
Poland................	6,228	162	0.8	34.5	30.1	35.1	0.2
Portugal..............	4,038	379	1.5	7.5	45.9	38.3	8.3
Romania..............	1,649	77	0.5	40.7	36.0	22.9	0.4
Russia................	35,045	245	1.1	29.8	61.0	9.0	0.2
Singapore.............	7,060	1,361	2.2	10.2	62.1	27.7	(NA)
Slovakia..............	882	162	0.7	27.7	37.2	34.9	0.2
Slovenia..............	1,388	676	2.5	14.3	73.9	11.8	0.1
South Africa [7]........	4,416	89	0.9	21.6	53.2	24.3	0.9
Spain.................	19,763	428	1.3	19.5	52.1	28.2	0.2
Sweden...............	13,216	1,399	3.4	4.3	69.3	26.0	0.3
Switzerland [9].........	10,525	1,365	2.9	0.7	73.5	24.2	1.6
Taiwan................	26,493	1,141	3.0	15.1	72.7	11.9	0.3
Turkey................	10,827	146	0.9	11.3	43.2	45.5	(NA)
United Kingdom.......	39,627	632	1.8	9.3	61.5	26.9	2.4

NA Not available or not applicable. [1] Purchasing power parities (PPPs) are currency conversion rates used to convert different currencies to a common value (U.S. dollars in this case). See introductory text, this section. [2] For full membership listing of the Organisation for Economic Co-operation and Development (OECD) and the European Union-28, see introductory text, this section. [3] European Union-15: Austria, Belgium, Denmark, Finland, France, Germany, Greece, Ireland, Italy, Luxembourg, Netherlands, Portugal, Spain, Sweden, and United Kingdom. [4] Excludes all or most capital expenditures. [5] 2010 data. [6] 2007 data. [7] 2009 data. [8] Excludes defense expenditures. [9] 2008 data.

Source: Organisation for Economic Co-operation and Development (OECD), "Main Science and Technology Indicators," OECD Science, Technology and R&D Statistics database ©, <http://www.oecd.org/innovation/inno/researchanddevelopmentstatisticsrds.htm>, accessed September 2013.

Table 1425. Development Assistance Outlays by Donor Country: 2011

[133,908 represents $133,908,000,000, except percent. Official development assistance (ODA) includes concessional loans and grants made by donor governments to developing countries and to multilateral institutions such as the United Nations or the World Bank]

| Country | Official development assistance (ODA) | | | Multilateral ODA (mil. current U.S. dol.) | Net private grants (mil. current U.S. dol.) |
	Net disbursements (million current U.S. dollars)	Percent of GNI [1]	Percent of total DAC [2] ODA		
DAC countries, total [2]...........	133,908	0.31	100.0	39,754	31,969
United States.....................	**30,783**	**0.20**	**23.0**	**3,707**	**23,284**
Australia...........................	4,924	0.34	3.7	646	1,373
Austria............................	1,111	0.27	0.8	621	182
Belgium...........................	2,807	0.54	2.1	1,068	519
Canada............................	5,459	0.32	4.1	1,347	2,045
Czech Republic....................	250	0.12	0.2	174	(NA)
Denmark...........................	2,931	0.85	2.2	787	198
Finland............................	1,406	0.53	1.1	567	14
France............................	12,997	0.46	9.7	4,503	(NA)
Germany..........................	14,093	0.39	10.5	5,357	1,598
Greece............................	425	0.15	0.3	271	0
Iceland............................	26	0.21	0.0	6	-1
Ireland............................	914	0.51	0.7	310	530
Italy..............................	4,326	0.20	3.2	2,623	111
Japan.............................	10,831	0.18	8.1	3,888	497
Korea, South......................	1,325	0.12	1.0	335	175
Luxembourg.......................	409	0.97	0.3	130	7
Netherlands.......................	6,344	0.75	4.7	2,008	231
New Zealand.......................	424	0.28	0.3	95	74
Norway............................	4,756	0.96	3.6	1,194	(NA)
Portugal...........................	708	0.31	0.5	231	5
Spain.............................	4,173	0.29	3.1	1,891	(NA)
Sweden...........................	5,603	1.02	4.2	1,961	31
Switzerland........................	3,051	0.45	2.3	678	466
United Kingdom....................	13,832	0.56	10.3	5,359	631
EU institutions [3]	17,391	(NA)	(NA)	345	(NA)

NA Not available. [1] Gross national income. See headnote, Table 1376. [2] Development Assistance Committee (DAC) of the Organisation for Economic Co-operation and Development (OECD), comprised of 25 developed countries, as shown above. [3] For membership listing of the European Union (EU), see introductory text, this section.

Source: Organisation for Economic Co-operation and Development (OECD), "Detailed Aid Statistics: Official and Private Flows," OECD International Development Statistics database ©, <http://www.oecd.org/dac/stats/idsonline.htm>, accessed September 2013.

Table 1426. Net Flow of Financial Resources to Developing Countries and Multilateral Organizations, by Donor Country: 1990 to 2011

[78,197 represents $78,197,000,000. Net flow covers official and private loans, grants, development assistance, and technical assistance, minus amortization on loans. Military flows are excluded. GNI = gross national income. For explanation of GNI, see headnote, Table 1376. Minus sign (-) indicates net inflow]

| Country | Amount (million dollars) | | | | Percent of GNI | | | |
	1990	2000	2010	2011	1990	2000	2010	2011
DAC countries total [1]...............	**78,197**	**134,168**	**509,531**	**499,397**	**0.48**	**0.54**	**1.26**	**1.15**
G-7 countries total [2].................	60,802	82,122	397,307	389,642	0.44	0.39	1.24	1.14
United States......................	**11,093**	**25,252**	**214,378**	**165,085**	**0.20**	**0.25**	**1.46**	**1.09**
Australia...........................	1,548	1,891	14,531	18,463	0.55	0.51	1.23	1.27
Austria............................	367	1,135	6,372	6,101	0.23	0.61	1.70	1.47
Belgium...........................	88	2,281	7,896	1,185	0.05	1.00	1.68	0.23
Canada............................	3,464	6,483	22,642	13,548	0.62	0.95	1.46	0.79
Czech Republic....................	(NA)	(NA)	228	(NA)	(NA)	(NA)	0.13	(NA)
Denmark...........................	1,065	2,176	4,794	2,818	0.86	1.39	1.52	0.82
Finland............................	992	1,087	4,312	1,016	0.76	0.91	1.78	0.38
France............................	5,705	5,557	35,198	34,216	0.48	0.41	1.35	1.21
Germany..........................	13,560	12,331	41,637	56,202	0.90	0.66	1.24	1.54
Greece............................	(NA)	229	761	485	(NA)	0.20	0.26	0.17
Ireland............................	168	740	2,695	2,444	0.47	0.93	1.57	1.37
Italy..............................	3,223	10,846	9,608	11,912	0.30	1.01	0.47	0.55
Japan.............................	17,229	11,423	48,213	61,828	0.58	0.24	0.86	1.02
Korea.............................	324	44	11,834	12,080	0.12	0.01	1.17	1.08
Luxembourg.......................	25	129	411	417	0.21	0.73	1.07	0.99
Netherlands.......................	3,971	6,947	13,013	22,046	1.43	1.85	1.67	2.62
New Zealand.......................	108	142	426	536	0.26	0.32	0.32	0.35
Norway............................	1,194	1,437	5,876	4,755	1.16	0.87	1.41	0.96
Portugal...........................	251	4,622	162	-1,299	0.42	4.45	0.07	-0.57
Spain.............................	978	23,471	10,340	20,145	0.20	4.25	0.74	1.38
Sweden...........................	2,809	3,952	5,127	6,598	1.27	1.76	1.10	1.20
Switzerland........................	3,507	1,765	23,444	11,965	1.40	0.64	4.02	1.76
United Kingdom....................	6,527	10,230	25,632	46,851	0.68	0.72	1.12	1.91

NA Not available. [1] The OECD Development Assistance Committee (DAC) is comprised of the above-listed member countries plus the European Union. [2] Group of seven (G7) major industrialized countries: United States, Canada, France, Germany, Italy, United Kingdom, and Japan.

Source: Organisation for Economic Co-operation and Development (OECD), 2013, "Official and Private Flows," OECD International Development Statistics (database) ©, <http://dx.doi.org/10.1787/data-00063-en>, accessed September 2013.

Table 1427. External Debt by Developing Country: 1990 to 2011

[In millions of U.S. dollars (28,154 represents $28,154,000,000). Total external debt is debt owed to nonresidents repayable in foreign currency, goods, or services. Total external debt is the sum of public, publicly guaranteed, and private nonguaranteed long-term debt, use of International Monetary Fund (IMF) credit, and short-term debt. Short-term debt includes all debt having an original maturity of one year or less and interest in arrears on long-term debt]

Country	1990	2000	2010	2011	Country	1990	2000	2010	2011
Algeria	28,154	25,449	7,211	6,072	Malaysia	15,330	41,946	85,126	94,468
Angola	8,592	9,763	19,004	21,115	Mexico	104,604	152,260	243,824	287,037
Argentina	62,511	147,029	111,768	114,704	Morocco	25,027	20,790	26,299	29,049
Bangladesh	12,285	15,596	25,752	27,043	Nepal	1,627	2,878	3,797	3,956
Brazil	120,304	242,512	352,440	404,317	Nigeria	33,439	31,582	10,389	13,108
Bulgaria	10,890	12,008	49,018	39,930	Pakistan	20,589	32,954	58,488	60,182
Burma	4,684	5,832	7,789	7,765	Panama	6,506	6,606	11,382	12,583
Cameroon	6,563	10,561	3,195	3,074	Papua New Guinea	2,594	2,305	5,965	12,582
Chile	19,273	37,407	81,435	96,245	Peru	20,208	28,813	41,816	44,872
China	55,301	145,648	558,304	685,418	Philippines	30,580	58,456	73,720	76,043
Colombia	17,404	33,231	64,124	76,918	Romania	1,140	11,259	124,358	129,822
Congo, Democratic Rep.	10,259	11,805	6,204	5,448	Russia [1]	(NA)	146,547	510,152	542,977
Cote d'Ivoire	17,251	12,187	10,794	12,012	Serbia [2]	17,793	11,573	32,935	31,569
Dominican Republic	4,425	4,624	13,357	15,395	South Africa	(NA)	25,148	102,348	113,512
Ecuador	12,172	13,338	14,963	16,497	Sri Lanka	5,865	9,173	21,153	23,984
Egypt	32,963	29,172	36,427	35,001	Sudan [3]	14,762	16,085	22,233	21,169
Ethiopia	8,645	5,509	7,347	8,597	Syria	17,097	22,203	5,263	4,968
Ghana	3,734	6,261	9,318	11,289	Tanzania	6,446	7,183	8,987	10,044
Guatemala	2,910	3,948	15,039	16,286	Thailand	28,094	79,830	80,551	80,039
India	85,661	101,130	290,351	334,331	Tunisia	7,690	11,355	22,048	22,335
Indonesia	69,848	143,655	195,172	213,541	Turkey	49,424	116,787	299,859	307,007
Iran	9,020	8,024	20,041	19,113	Ukraine	(NA)	13,904	116,026	134,481
Jamaica	4,782	4,789	14,193	14,350	Uruguay	4,443	8,491	14,030	14,350
Kazakhstan	(NA)	12,890	119,190	124,437	Venezuela	33,173	42,753	61,257	67,908
Latvia	(NA)	5,012	39,741	38,255	Vietnam	23,270	12,859	49,343	57,841
Lebanon	1,787	10,250	24,591	24,767	Zimbabwe	3,279	3,841	5,866	6,275

NA Not available. [1] All outstanding external debt of the former Soviet Union is included in the Russian Federation data after 1992. Beginning in 1993, the data for the Russian Federation have been revised to include obligations to members of the former Council for Mutual Economic Assistance and other countries in the form of trade-related credits amounting to $15.4 billion as of the end of 1996. [2] Data for Serbia prior to 1993 refer to the former Yugoslavia. Data from 1993 onwards are estimates and also reflect borrowing by the former Yugoslavia not allocated to the successor republics. Data prior to 1999 include external debt obligations of Bosnia and Herzegovina, excluding World Bank, IMF, and short-term debt obligations. Data from 1999 to 2005 are for Serbia and Montenegro. In June 2006, Serbia and Montenegro became separate countries, so starting 2006, data exclude Montenegro. Data from 2008 onward exclude Kosovo, which declared independence that year. [3] Data for Sudan include South Sudan, which became an independent state in July 2011.

Source: The World Bank, Washington, DC, World Development Indicators database, "External debt stocks, total" ©, <http://data.worldbank.org/data-catalog/world-development-indicators>, accessed July 2013.

Table 1428. Foreign Direct Investment Flows in Selected Countries: 2000 to 2012

[In billions of dollars (321.3 represents $321,300,000,000). Data are converted to U.S. dollars using the yearly average exchange rate]

Country	Inflows					Outflows				
	2000	2005	2010	2011	2012 [1]	2000	2005	2010	2011	2012 [1]
United States	**321.3**	**112.6**	**205.9**	**230.2**	**166.4**	**159.2**	**36.2**	**301.1**	**409.0**	**388.3**
Australia	15.6	-24.2	35.2	64.5	55.6	4.2	-31.1	27.3	14.3	15.6
Austria	8.5	10.8	0.8	11.4	6.3	5.5	11.1	10.0	24.8	16.7
Belgium	(NA)	34.4	85.7	103.4	14.1	(NA)	32.6	43.9	82.6	27.6
Brazil	32.8	15.1	48.5	66.7	65.3	2.3	2.5	11.6	-1.0	-2.8
Canada	66.8	25.7	28.4	39.7	43.0	44.7	27.5	34.7	52.1	55.5
China	38.4	104.1	243.7	280.0	253.4	0.9	13.7	58.0	48.4	62.4
Czech Republic	5.0	11.7	6.1	2.3	10.6	(Z)	(Z)	1.2	-0.3	1.3
Denmark	33.0	12.9	-11.5	12.7	1.3	25.1	16.2	-0.1	13.3	5.4
France	43.3	84.9	33.6	38.6	25.1	177.5	114.9	64.6	59.6	37.2
Germany	198.3	47.4	57.4	49.0	6.6	56.6	75.8	121.5	52.2	67.0
Greece	1.1	0.6	0.3	1.1	2.9	2.1	1.5	1.6	1.8	(Z)
Hungary	2.8	7.7	2.2	5.8	13.1	0.6	2.2	1.1	4.7	10.6
India	3.6	7.6	27.4	36.5	24.0	0.5	3.0	15.3	12.6	8.6
Ireland	25.8	-31.7	42.8	23.6	38.3	4.6	14.3	22.3	-1.2	18.5
Italy	13.4	20.0	9.2	34.4	16.0	12.3	41.8	32.7	53.7	29.8
Japan	8.3	2.8	-1.3	-1.8	1.7	31.5	45.8	56.3	114.3	122.5
Korea, South	9.3	6.3	1.1	4.7	5.0	4.5	6.4	23.3	20.4	23.6
Mexico	18.1	24.4	21.9	21.6	13.4	(NA)	6.5	15.0	12.1	25.3
Netherlands	63.9	39.0	-7.4	17.2	-0.1	75.6	123.0	68.3	40.9	0.6
New Zealand	1.3	1.5	0.6	4.3	2.7	0.6	-1.5	0.6	2.5	-0.5
Norway	7.1	2.2	17.0	19.6	9.9	9.5	23.7	23.2	26.5	20.3
Poland	9.4	10.3	13.9	18.9	3.1	0.0	3.4	7.2	7.2	-0.6
Russia	2.7	14.4	31.7	36.9	30.3	3.2	16.7	41.1	48.6	27.7
South Africa	0.9	6.6	1.2	6.0	4.6	0.3	0.9	-0.1	2.8	4.4
Spain	39.6	25.0	39.9	26.8	27.8	58.2	41.8	37.8	36.6	-4.9
Sweden	23.4	11.6	-0.1	9.3	14.2	41.0	27.7	20.2	28.2	31.1
Switzerland	19.3	-0.9	32.6	11.8	3.6	44.7	51.0	79.3	47.3	44.3
Turkey	1.0	10.0	9.0	16.0	12.6	0.9	1.1	1.5	2.3	4.1
United Kingdom	122.0	177.9	50.6	51.1	62.4	235.5	80.0	39.5	106.7	76.5

NA Not available. Z Less than $50 million. [1] Preliminary.

Source: Organisation for Economic Co-operation and Development (OECD), 2013, "Foreign Direct Investment: Flows by Partner Country," OECD International Direct Investment Statistics (database) ©, <http://dx.doi.org/10.1787/data-00335-en>, accessed September 2013.

Table 1429. International Tourism Arrivals, Expenditures, and Receipts—Leading Countries: 1995 to 2011

[Arrivals at national borders in thousands of non-resident tourists (545,286 represents 545,286,000). Expenditures and receipts in millions of current U.S. dollars (395,126 represents 395,126,000). Receipts are money spent by foreign tourists while traveling inside the country shown and include prepayment for goods or services in destination country. Expenditures are money spent by tourists from a given country of origin while traveling outside their home country. Data exclude receipts and expenditures for international transport. Ranked for top 45 countries in tourist arrivals as of 2011. Sources and collection methods differ, thus caution should be used in comparing data across countries]

Country	Arrivals (1,000)					Expenditures (mil. dol.)					Receipts (mil. dol.)				
	1995	2000	2005	2010	2011	1995	2000	2005	2010	2011	1995	2000	2005	2010	2011
World [1]	545,286	700,658	832,133	977,972	1,025,344	395,126	451,415	655,146	859,595	954,928	421,981	493,828	709,799	953,879	1,067,070
France	60,033	77,190	74,988	77,648	81,411	16,358	22,533	31,727	38,857	44,233	27,587	32,855	43,954	46,369	54,879
United States	43,490	51,238	49,206	59,796	62,711	46,379	67,860	74,790	82,508	86,184	74,834	100,716	106,161	134,167	149,256
China	20,034	31,229	46,809	55,664	57,581	3,688	13,114	21,759	54,880	72,585	8,730	16,231	29,296	45,814	48,464
Spain	34,920	46,403	55,914	52,677	56,694	4,539	5,922	15,046	16,764	17,275	25,368	29,802	47,789	52,187	60,108
Italy	31,052	41,181	36,513	43,626	46,119	14,829	15,685	22,370	26,907	28,730	28,731	27,493	35,319	38,438	43,243
Turkey	7,083	9,586	20,273	31,396	34,038	911	1,713	2,872	4,826	4,976	4,957	7,636	18,152	20,807	23,020
United Kingdom	21,719	23,212	28,039	28,295	29,306	24,926	38,262	59,532	49,972	51,105	20,487	21,769	30,573	32,399	35,105
Germany	14,847	18,983	21,500	26,875	28,374	60,260	52,824	74,189	77,580	86,167	18,036	18,611	29,121	34,560	38,865
Russian Federation	10,290	21,169	22,201	22,281	24,932	11,599	8,848	17,314	26,587	32,466	4,312	3,429	5,870	8,830	11,398
Malaysia	7,469	10,222	16,431	24,577	24,714	2,314	2,075	3,711	7,943	10,753	3,969	5,011	8,846	18,315	19,593
Mexico	20,241	20,641	21,915	23,290	23,403	3,171	5,499	7,600	7,255	7,832	6,179	8,294	11,803	11,992	11,869
Austria	17,173	17,982	19,952	22,004	23,012	10,887	6,232	9,316	10,125	10,548	13,435	9,899	16,243	18,758	19,778
Hong Kong	(NA)	8,814	14,773	20,085	22,316	10,497	12,502	13,305	17,503	19,141	9,604	5,868	10,179	21,689	27,038
Ukraine	3,716	6,431	17,631	21,203	21,415	210	470	2,805	3,742	4,461	(NA)	394	3,125	3,788	4,294
Thailand	6,952	9,579	11,567	15,936	19,230	4,271	2,772	3,800	5,623	5,716	8,035	7,483	9,577	20,116	27,186
Saudi Arabia	3,325	6,585	8,037	10,850	17,498	(NA)	(NA)	9,087	21,135	17,271	191	(NA)	4,626	6,712	8,459
Greece	10,130	13,096	14,765	15,007	16,427	1,323	4,558	3,039	2,854	3,159	4,135	9,219	13,334	12,479	14,801
Canada	16,932	19,627	18,771	16,097	16,014	10,260	12,438	18,017	29,558	33,166	7,917	10,778	13,768	15,711	16,716
Poland	19,215	17,400	15,200	12,470	13,350	5,500	3,315	5,548	8,570	8,462	6,614	5,677	6,274	9,526	10,683
Macao	4,202	5,197	9,014	11,926	12,925	(NA)	(NA)	552	1,156	(NA)	(NA)	(NA)	7,618	27,805	(NA)
Netherlands	6,574	10,003	10,012	10,883	11,300	11,674	12,191	16,140	19,489	20,603	6,578	7,197	10,450	12,861	14,352
Singapore	6,070	6,062	7,079	9,161	10,390	4,663	4,535	10,071	18,630	21,103	7,611	5,142	6,209	14,133	17,990
Hungary	1,485	(NA)	9,979	9,510	10,250	1,498	1,651	2,277	2,404	2,485	2,928	3,733	4,120	5,339	5,629
Croatia	3,753	5,831	7,743	9,111	9,927	422	568	754	833	882	1,349	2,758	5,806	8,051	9,364
Korea, Rep.	3,753	5,322	6,023	8,798	9,795	6,341	7,132	15,406	17,669	19,463	5,150	6,834	6,851	9,765	12,304
Egypt, Arab Rep.	2,871	5,116	8,244	14,051	9,497	1,278	1,072	1,629	2,240	2,203	2,684	4,345	4,610	6,702	8,707
Morocco	2,602	4,278	5,843	9,288	9,342	302	425	612	1,203	1,363	1,296	2,039	4,813	7,121	7,321
Czech Republic	(NA)	(NA)	9,404	8,629	8,775	1,635	1,276	2,405	4,064	4,573	2,880	2,973	1,944	6,190	7,628
Syrian Arab Republic	815	2,100	3,571	8,546	(NA)	498	669	550	1,510	(NA)	1,258	1,082	550	(NA)	(NA)
Switzerland	6,946	7,821	7,229	8,628	8,534	7,420	5,419	8,782	12,528	12,657	9,459	6,652	10,041	14,978	17,650
South Africa	4,488	5,872	7,369	8,074	8,339	1,849	2,085	3,374	5,595	5,283	2,126	2,677	7,516	9,085	9,515
Indonesia	4,324	5,064	5,002	7,003	7,650	2,172	3,197	3,584	6,395	7,279	5,229	4,975	4,522	6,958	7,953
Ireland	4,818	6,646	7,333	7,134	7,630	2,034	2,525	6,074	7,071	7,023	2,211	2,615	4,782	4,086	4,593
Romania	5,445	5,264	5,839	7,498	7,611	697	425	925	1,636	1,966	590	359	1,052	1,136	1,420
Belgium	5,560	6,457	6,747	7,186	7,494	8,115	9,429	14,948	18,829	22,301	4,548	6,592	9,845	10,337	11,661
Denmark	2,124	3,535	9,178	8,744	7,363	4,288	4,669	6,850	9,082	9,840	3,691	3,671	5,293	5,704	5,993
Portugal	4,572	5,599	5,769	6,756	7,264	2,099	2,228	3,050	3,905	4,143	4,831	5,243	7,676	10,007	11,376
Bahrain	2,311	3,869	6,313	11,952	6,732	122	234	414	506	718	247	573	920	1,362	1,035
Bulgaria	3,466	2,785	4,837	6,047	6,328	195	538	1,309	1,232	1,339	473	1,074	2,412	3,571	4,021
India	2,124	2,649	3,919	5,776	6,309	996	2,690	6,187	10,549	13,722	2,582	3,460	7,493	14,160	17,518
Japan	3,345	4,757	6,728	8,611	6,219	36,764	31,884	37,565	27,950	27,262	3,224	3,373	12,430	13,224	11,000
Vietnam	1,351	2,140	3,477	5,050	6,014	(NA)	(NA)	(NA)	(NA)	(NA)	(NA)	(NA)	(NA)	(NA)	(NA)
Australia	3,726	4,931	5,499	5,885	5,875	5,165	6,387	11,253	22,241	26,949	8,130	9,289	16,850	29,839	31,456
Argentina	2,289	2,909	3,823	5,325	5,705	3,278	4,425	2,790	4,878	5,516	2,222	2,904	2,729	4,942	5,352
Brazil	1,991	5,313	5,358	5,161	5,433	3,391	3,894	4,720	16,422	21,264	972	1,810	3,861	5,919	6,555

NA Not available. [1] Includes other countries not shown separately.

Source: The World Bank, Washington, DC, "World Development Indicators" database ©, <http://data.worldbank.org/data-catalog/world-development-indicators>, accessed July 2013.

Table 1430. International Transaction Balances, Reserve Assets, and Trade in Relation to Gross Domestic Product (GDP) by Country: 2000 and 2011

[In millions of U.S. dollars (-416,343 represents -$416,343,000,000), except as noted. Minus sign (-) indicates deficit]

Country	Current account balance		Reserve assets [1]		Goods and services trade balance		Exports as percent of GDP (%)		Imports as percent of GDP (%)	
	2000	2011	2000	2011	2000	2011	2000	2011	2000	2011
United States.........	-416,343	-465,923	56,600	136,912	-382,100	-568,100	11.0	14.0	14.9	17.8
Algeria.................	(NA)	19,688	12,024	182,822	10,860	(NA)	41.2	(NA)	21.4	(NA)
Angola.................	796	13,085	1,198	28,786	2,447	22,562	89.6	65.0	62.8	43.3
Argentina..............	-8,981	-1,568	25,147	43,227	-1,801	10,223	10.9	21.8	11.5	19.5
Australia...............	-14,763	-33,753	18,118	42,783	-8,246	21,008	19.4	21.2	21.4	19.7
Austria.................	-1,339	5,519	14,319	10,987	3,356	13,874	46.2	57.3	44.5	54.0
Azerbaijan.............	-168	17,145	680	10,274	35	24,499	39.0	62.8	38.4	24.2
Bangladesh............	-306	-162	1,486	8,510	-2,473	-9,747	14.0	22.9	19.2	31.6
Belgium................	(NA)	-5,662	9,994	17,918	6,811	6,336	78.1	84.3	75.2	83.1
Brazil..................	-24,225	-52,480	32,434	350,356	-11,370	-18,163	10.0	11.9	11.7	12.6
Bulgaria...............	-703	141	3,155	15,252	-689	362	50.5	66.5	55.8	65.8
Canada................	19,622	-52,846	32,102	65,652	41,704	-21,295	45.6	30.4	39.8	31.6
Chile..................	-898	-3,283	15,035	41,932	563	8,312	29.3	37.7	28.6	34.4
China..................	20,518	136,097	168,278	3,202,789	28,873	297,805	23.3	31.4	20.9	27.3
Colombia..............	795	-9,525	8,916	31,386	-836	-2,903	15.9	18.9	16.8	19.8
Czech Republic.......	-2,690	-6,114	13,019	39,670	-1,259	8,959	60.9	72.9	63.1	68.7
Denmark...............	2,262	18,887	15,108	81,680	9,662	17,421	46.5	53.4	40.5	48.2
Dominican Republic...	-1,027	-4,499	627	4,089	-2,116	-5,774	37.0	24.9	45.9	35.3
Ecuador...............	926	-239	947	1,664	878	-1,686	32.1	31.8	27.3	34.0
Egypt, Arab Rep......	-971	-5,484	13,118	14,916	-6,605	-16,104	16.2	23.2	22.8	30.1
Finland................	10,526	-1,781	7,977	7,857	11,131	-1,935	43.6	40.8	34.4	41.5
France.................	19,674	-54,437	37,039	48,612	13,202	-82,374	28.8	26.9	27.8	29.9
Georgia................	-177	-1,839	116	2,818	-510	-2,683	23.0	36.3	39.7	54.9
Germany...............	-32,484	223,324	56,890	66,928	5,804	182,861	33.4	50.2	33.1	45.1
Ghana.................	-386	-3,501	232	5,483	-919	-5,020	48.8	38.0	67.2	50.8
Greece................	-9,820	-28,583	13,424	1,249	-17,266	-23,432	25.7	25.1	39.6	33.1
Honduras..............	-508	-1,498	1,313	2,750	-884	-3,691	54.0	47.6	66.4	68.8
Hong Kong............	6,993	14,139	107,542	285,296	7,569	7,703	141.8	224.6	137.4	221.5
Hungary...............	-4,004	1,211	11,190	48,681	-1,600	10,302	74.6	93.2	78.1	85.7
India..................	-4,601	-60,038	37,902	271,285	-4,246	-120,782	12.8	23.9	13.7	30.3
Indonesia..............	7,992	1,685	28,502	106,539	17,356	11,959	41.0	26.3	30.5	24.9
Ireland................	-356	2,514	5,360	1,399	-209	48,495	97.4	104.9	84.1	82.9
Israel..................	-2,056	3,382	23,281	74,874	-209	-2,078	37.3	36.9	37.5	37.8
Italy...................	-5,781	-67,143	25,567	49,185	10,526	-32,851	26.8	28.8	25.8	30.3
Japan..................	119,660	119,064	354,902	1,258,172	68,541	-53,670	10.9	15.1	9.4	16.1
Jordan.................	27	-3,470	3,331	11,467	-2,257	-8,156	41.8	45.6	68.5	73.9
Kazakhstan............	366	14,110	1,594	25,179	1,373	40,856	56.6	49.5	49.1	27.7
Kenya.................	-199	-3,333	898	4,264	-1,288	-5,685	21.6	29.1	31.7	46.0
Korea, South..........	14,803	26,068	96,130	304,255	15,239	22,575	38.6	56.2	35.7	54.2
Kuwait.................	14,672	70,762	7,082	25,795	9,930	79218.4	56.5	65.9	30.1	21.1
Lithuania..............	-675	-619	1,312	7,915	-718	-637	44.7	77.5	51.0	79.0
Malaysia...............	8,488	31,770	28,330	131,780	18,019	45,771	119.8	91.6	100.6	75.7
Mexico................	-18,743	-9,671	35,509	143,991	-11,595	-15,377	30.9	31.6	32.9	32.9
Morocco...............	-475	-8,000	4,823	19,526	-1,988	-13,442	28.0	34.9	33.4	48.5
Nepal..................	-131	289	945	3,631	-502	-4,539	23.3	8.9	32.4	32.8
Netherlands...........	7,264	84,590	9,643	20,264	21,360	74,714	70.1	83.0	64.5	74.1
New Zealand..........	-2,407	-6,686	3,952	17,012	861	2,206	35.0	(NA)	33.3	(NA)
Nigeria................	7,427	8,689	9,911	35,212	10,093	9,742	54.0	39.6	32.0	35.6
Norway................	25,079	66,694	27,597	49,397	28,792	65,147	46.5	41.5	29.4	28.2
Pakistan...............	-85	-2,234	1,513	14,528	-922	-10693.3	13.4	14.2	14.7	19.2
Panama................	-673	-3,826	723	2,304	320	-880	72.6	69.1	69.8	71.9
Peru...................	-1,546	-3,341	8,374	47,206	-1,148	6,943	16.0	28.7	18.2	24.8
Philippines............	-2,228	6,970	13,090	67,290	-1,613	-11,248	51.4	31.0	53.4	36.0
Poland.................	-10,343	-25,023	26,562	92,646	-10,999	4,409	27.1	(NA)	33.5	(NA)
Portugal...............	-12,189	-16,761	8,909	1,975	-12,892	-10,391	28.9	35.7	39.9	40.1
Romania...............	-1,355	-8,344	2,470	42,939	-1,930	-9,769	32.7	38.3	37.9	43.5
Russian Federation...	46,839	97,274	24,264	453,948	52,012	162,809	44.1	30.4	24.0	21.8
Saudi Arabia..........	14,317	158,545	19,585	540,677	35,333	178,672	43.7	61.6	24.9	30.6
Serbia.................	(NA)	-3,834	392	14,877	-1,012	-6,937	23.9	38.2	40.5	54.2
Singapore.............	10,244	65,323	79,961	237,527	12,327	67,670	192.3	207.2	179.5	179.6
South Africa...........	-191	-13,683	6,083	42,595	3,927	-2,481	27.9	29.3	24.9	29.9
Spain..................	-23,185	-55,066	30,989	32,843	-18,163	-11,711	29.1	30.3	32.2	31.1
Sri Lanka..............	-1,044	-4,615	1,039	6,248	-1,732	-8,613	39.0	23.1	49.6	37.6
Sudan.................	-518	710	138	193	314	1,368	16.0	18.5	13.4	16.3
Sweden................	10,074	37,969	14,863	44,025	15,711	33,483	46.5	50.0	40.2	43.8
Switzerland............	32,830	35,900	32,272	279,390	12,886	70,985	45.4	51.2	40.4	40.4
Syrian Arab Rep.......	1,061	(NA)	126	(NA)	1,316	517	35.4	(NA)	28.6	(NA)
Tanzania..............	-428	-3,951	974	3,726	-689	-4,574	13.4	31.1	20.1	50.2
Thailand...............	9,313	5,918	32,016	167,389	10,595	15,682	66.8	76.9	58.1	72.4
Tunisia................	-821	-3,386	1,811	7,454	-722	-3,248	39.5	48.9	42.9	55.8
Turkey.................	-9,920	-75,092	22,488	78,322	-7,987	-68,924	20.1	23.7	23.1	32.6
Ukraine................	1,481	-10,233	1,353	30,409	1,573	-8,921	62.4	54.4	57.4	59.8
United Kingdom.......	-38,800	-32,765	38,774	79,272	-27,163	-38,947	27.7	32.5	29.6	34.1
Venezuela.............	11,853	24,387	13,088	9,930	13,626	32,433	29.7	29.9	18.1	19.7
Vietnam...............	1,106	236	3,417	13,539	-768	-5,210	55.0	87.0	57.5	91.2

NA Not available. [1] Reserve assets are comprised of special drawing rights and reserve position in International Monetary Fund (IMF), and foreign exchange holdings. Gold holdings are excluded.

Source: The World Bank, Washington, DC, "World Development Indicators" database ©, <http://data.worldbank.org/data-catalog/world-development-indicators>, accessed July 2013.

Table 1431. Military Expenditures, 2012, and Manpower, 2010, by Country

[For manpower, 120,022 represents 120,022,000. Manpower covers males and females deemed fit for military service, ages 16–49, who are not otherwise disqualified for health reasons]

Country	Expenditures (percent of GDP [1])	Manpower (1,000)	Country	Expenditures (percent of GDP [1])	Manpower (1,000)
United States	[6] **4.6**	**120,022**	Italy	[2] 1.8	22,596
Afghanistan	10.0	7,847	Japan	1.0	43,931
Algeria	4.3	17,249	Jordan	9.5	2,824
Angola	3.0	3,039	Kazakhstan	[6] 1.1	6,438
Argentina	0.5	16,873	Kenya	1.8	12,468
Australia	3.0	8,652	Korea, South	[3] 2.7	21,033
Austria	[5] 0.8	3,134	Lebanon	2.5	1,863
Bangladesh	1.4	66,102	Libya	3.1	2,970
Brazil	1.3	83,836	Malaysia	[2] 2.0	12,423
Burma	4.8	21,633	Mexico	0.5	48,882
Cambodia	2.4	5,603	Morocco	4.8	14,403
Canada	[2] 1.1	13,023	Netherlands	[2] 1.6	6,324
Chile	2.1	7,183	Nicaragua	0.9	2,563
China	2.6	618,589	Nigeria	0.9	40,708
Colombia	3.8	19,012	Norway	[2] 1.9	1,754
Congo, Democratic Rep.	1.2	20,500	Pakistan	3.1	75,327
Cote d'Ivoire	[5] 1.5	6,556	Peru	1.0	12,354
Croatia	1.5	1,610	Poland	[2] 1.9	15,584
Cuba	[7] 3.2	4,822	Russia	[2] 3.9	46,813
Czech Republic	[7] 1.0	4,061	Saudi Arabia	9.1	13,043
Denmark	[4] 1.3	2,018	South Africa	[3] 1.7	14,093
Dominican Republic	0.7	4,279	Spain	[2] 1.2	18,721
Ecuador	2.3	6,104	Sri Lanka	2.9	8,752
Egypt	2.2	35,305	Sudan	4.2	13,316
Ethiopia	0.9	24,757	Sweden	1.5	3,359
France	[2] 2.6	23,747	Syria	[7] 3.6	9,940
Germany	[2] 1.5	29,538	Taiwan	2.2	10,025
Greece	[2] 4.3	4,049	Turkey	[2] 5.3	35,005
Honduras	1.5	3,065	Uganda	1.8	8,514
India	1.8	489,571	Ukraine	1.6	15,686
Indonesia	0.9	107,539	United Arab Emirates	6.4	3,072
Iran	[3] 2.5	39,566	United Kingdom	2.5	24,035
Iraq	[3] 8.6	13,013	Venezuela	0.7	11,690
Israel	7.4	2,964	Vietnam	[2] 2.5	41,504

[1] Spending on defense programs as percent of Gross Domestic Product (GDP), calculated on an exchange rate basis. For countries with no military forces, this figure can include expenditures on public security and police. Some data include estimates. [2] 2005 data. [3] 2006 data. [4] 2007 data. [5] 2009 data. [6] 2010 data. [7] 2011 data.

Source: Central Intelligence Agency, *The World Factbook*, <https://www.cia.gov/library/publications/the-world-factbook/index.html>, accessed August 2013.

Guide to Sources of Statistics, State Statistical Abstracts, and Foreign Statistical Abstracts

Alphabetically arranged, this guide contains references to important primary sources of statistical information for the United States and other countries. Secondary sources have been included if the information contained in them is presented in a particularly convenient form or if primary sources are not readily available. Nonrecurrent publications presenting compilations or estimates for years later than 2000, or types of data not available in regular series, are also included. Data are also available in press releases.

Valuable information may also be found in state report and foreign statistical abstracts, which are included at the end of this appendix, and in reports for particular commodities, industries, or similar segments of our economic and social structures, many of which are not included here.

Publications listed under each subject are divided into two main groups: "U.S. Government" and "Nongovernment." The location of the publisher of each report is given except for federal agencies located in Washington, DC. Most federal publications may be purchased from the Superintendent of Documents, U.S. Government Printing Office, Washington, DC, tel. 202-512-1800, or at <http://bookstore.gpo.gov>. In some cases, federal publications may be obtained from the issuing agency.

Appendix I Table: Sources of Statistics, State Statistical Abstracts, and Foreign Statistical Abstracts

Title	Frequency	Paper	Internet PDF	Internet Other Formats
U.S. GOVERNMENT				
Administrative Office of the United States Courts				
http://www.uscourts.gov				
Calendar Year Reports on Authorized Wiretaps (state and federal)	Annual		X	
Federal Court Management Statistics	Semiannual		X	X
Federal Judicial Caseload Statistics	Annual		X	
Judicial Business of the United States Courts	Annual		X	
Statistical Tables for the Federal Judiciary	Semiannual	X	X	
Agency for International Development				
http://www.usaid.gov				
U.S. Overseas Loans and Grants: Obligations and Loan Authorizations	Annual		X	X
Army Corps of Engineers				
http://www.usace.army.mil				
Waterborne Commerce of the United States (in five parts)	Annual		X	X
Board of Governors of the Federal Reserve System				
http://www.federalreserve.gov				
Assets and Liabilities of Commercial Banks in the United States H.8	Weekly	X	X	X
Consumer Credit G.19	Monthly	X	X	X
Federal Reserve Bulletin	Periodic		X	X
Financial Accounts of the United States Z.1	Quarterly	X	X	X
Foreign Exchange Rates H.10	Weekly			X
Industrial Production and Capacity Utilization G.17	Monthly	X	X	X
Money Stock Measures H.6	Weekly		X	X
Bureau of Economic Analysis				
http://www.bea.gov				
Survey of Current Business	Monthly	X	X	X
Bureau of Justice Statistics				
http://bjs.ojp.usdoj.gov				
American Indians and Crime: A BJS Statistical Profile, December 2004	Periodic	X	X	X
Background Checks for Firearm Transfers	Annual		X	X
Capital Punishment	Annual		X	X
Carjacking, 1993-2002, July 2004	Periodic		X	X
Census of Publicly Funded Forensic Crime Laboratories, 2009, August 2012	Periodic		X	X
Census of State and Federal Correctional Facilities, 2005, October 2008	Periodic		X	X
Civil Rights Complaints in U.S. District Courts, 1990-2006, August 2008	Periodic	X	X	X
Civil Trial Cases and Verdicts in Large Counties, 2001, April 2004	Periodic	X	X	X
Compendium of Federal Justice Statistics, 2004, December 2006	Periodic	X	X	X
Contacts Between Police and Public: Findings from the 2008 National Survey, October 2011	Periodic		X	X
Contract Trials and Verdicts in Large Counties, 2001, February 2005	Periodic	X	X	X
Crime and the Nation's Households, 2005, April 2007	Periodic		X	X
Crimes Against Persons Age 65 or Older, 1993-2002, January 2005	Periodic	X	X	X
Criminal Victimization	Annual		X	X
Cross-National Studies in Crime and Justice, September 2004	Periodic	X	X	X
Defense Counsel in Criminal Cases, November 2000	Periodic	X	X	X
Education and Correctional Populations, January 2003	Periodic	X	X	X
Family Violence Statistics	Periodic	X	X	X
Federal Criminal Case Processing, 2002, January 2005	Periodic	X	X	X
Federal Law Enforcement Officers, 2008, June 2012	Periodic		X	X
Felony Defendants in Large Urban Counties, 2006, May 2010	Biennial		X	X
Felony Sentences in State Courts, 2006, December 2009	Biennial		X	X
Firearm Use by Offenders, November 2001	Periodic	X	X	X

See footnotes at end of table.

Appendix I Table: Sources of Statistics, State Statistical Abstracts, and Foreign Statistical Abstracts-Continued.

See headnote on page 911.

Title	Frequency	Paper	Internet PDF	Internet Other Formats
Hepatitis Testing and Treatment in State Prisons, April 2004	Periodic	X	X	X
Hispanic Victims of Violent Crime, 1993-2000, April 2002	Periodic	X	X	X
HIV in Prisons 2007-2008	Periodic		X	X
Homicide Trends in the United States, 1980-2008	Periodic		X	X
Identity Theft Reported by Households, 2005-10, November 2011	Periodic		X	X
Immigration Offenders in the Federal Criminal Justice System, 2010, July 2012	Periodic		X	X
Incarcerated Parents and Their Children, August 2000	Periodic	X	X	X
Indicators of School Crime and Safety	Annual		X	X
Intimate Partner Violence, 1993-2010, November 2012	Periodic	X	X	X
Jail Inmates at Midyear, 2012, May 2013	Annual		X	X
Jails in Indian Country, 2012, June 2013	Annual		X	X
Justice Expenditure and Employment Extract Series, 2008, May 2012	Annual			X
Juvenile Offenders and Victims	Periodic	X	X	X
Juvenile Victimization and Offending, 1993-2003	Periodic	X	X	X
Law Enforcement Management and Administrative Statistics 2000: Data for Individual State and Local Agencies with 100 or More Officers	Periodic	X	X	X
Local Police Departments, 2007, December 2010	Periodic		X	X
Medical Malpractice Trials and Verdicts in Large Counties, April 2004	Periodic	X	X	X
Money Laundering Offenders, 1994-2001, July 2003	Periodic	X	X	X
Prevalence of Imprisonment in the U.S. Population, 1974-2001, August 2003	Periodic	X	X	X
Prisoners in 2011, December 2012	Annual		X	X
Probation and Parole in the United States	Annual		X	X
Profile of Jail Inmates, 2002, July 2004	Periodic	X	X	X
Prosecutors in State Courts, 2007, December 2011	Biennial		X	X
Rape and Sexual Assault: Reporting to Police and Medical Attention, August 2002	Periodic	X	X	X
Reentry Trends in the United States Current Data Electronic	Periodic		X	X
Sheriffs' Offices, 2007, December 2012	Periodic	X	X	X
Sourcebook of Criminal Justice Statistics	Periodic		X	X
State Court Prosecutors in Large Districts, 2001, December 2001	Periodic	X	X	X
State Court Prosecutors in Small Districts, 2001, January 2003	Periodic	X	X	X
State Court Sentencing of Convicted Felons, 2004, July 2007	Periodic		X	X
State Prison Expenditures, 2001, June 2004	Periodic	X	X	X
Summary of State Sex Offender Registries, 2001, March 2002	Periodic	X	X	X
Survey of DNA Crime Laboratories, 2001, January 2002	Periodic	X	X	X
Survey of State Criminal History Information Systems, 2010, November 2011	Biennial	X	X	X
Survey of State Procedures Related to Firearm Sales, 2005, November 2006	Periodic	X	X	X
Tort Trials and Verdicts in Large Counties, November 2004	Periodic	X	X	X
Traffic Stop Data Collection Policies for State Police, 2004, June 2005	Periodic	X	X	X
Violent Victimization of College Students, 1995-2002, January 2005	Periodic	X	X	X
Weapon Use and Violent Crime, 1993-2001, September 2003	Periodic	X	X	X
Bureau of Labor Statistics http://www.bls.gov				
100 Years of U.S. Consumer Spending: Data for the Nation, New York City, and Boston, Report 991	Periodic	X	X	
College Enrollment and Work Activity of High School Graduates	Annual		X	
Compensation and Working Conditions	Periodic		X	
Consumer Expenditure Survey, Integrated Diary and Interview Survey data	Annual		X	X
Consumer Price Index (CPI) Detailed Report	Monthly		X	X
Consumer Prices	Monthly		X	X
Employer Costs for Employee Compensation	Quarterly		X	X
Employment and Earnings	Monthly		X	X
Employment and Wages	Annual		X	X
Employment Characteristics of Families	Annual		X	X
Employment Cost Index	Quarterly		X	X
Employment Cost Indexes and Levels	Annual		X	X
The Employment Situation	Monthly		X	X
Geographic Profile of Employment and Unemployment	Annual		X	X
International Comparisons of Annual Labor Force Statistics, 16 Countries (discontinued)	Annual		X	
International Comparisons of Hourly Compensation Costs for Production Workers in Manufacturing (discontinued)	Annual		X	X
International Comparisons of Manufacturing Productivity and Unit Labor Cost Trends (discontinued)	Annual		X	X
Metropolitan Area Employment and Unemployment	Monthly		X	X
Monthly Labor Review	Monthly		X	X
National Compensation Survey	Annual		X	X
Occupational Injuries and Illnesses in the United States by Industry	Annual		X	X
Occupational Projections and Training Data	Biennial		X	X
Producer Price Index (PPI) Detailed Report	Monthly		X	X
Productivity and Costs by Industry	Periodic		X	X
Real Earnings	Monthly		X	X
Regional and State Employment and Unemployment	Monthly		X	X
Relative Importance of Components in the Consumer Price Indexes	Annual		X	X
U.S. Import and Export Price Indexes	Monthly		X	X
Union Members	Annual		X	X
Usual Weekly Earnings of Wage and Salary Workers	Quarterly		X	X
Work Experience of the Population	Annual		X	X
Bureau of Land Management http://www.blm.gov				
Public Land Statistics	Annual		X	
Census Bureau http://www.census.gov				
2002 Economic Census, Bridge Between North American Industry Classification System				

See footnotes at end of table.

Appendix I Table: Sources of Statistics, State Statistical Abstracts, and Foreign Statistical Abstracts-Continued.

See headnote on page 911.

Title	Frequency	Paper	Internet PDF	Internet Other Formats
(NAICS) and Standard Industrial Classification (SIC)	Quinquennial			X
2007 Economic Census, Company Statistics Series, Survey of Business Owners	Quinquennial			X
2007 Economic Census, Company Statistics Series, Survey of Business Owners: American Indian- and Alaska Native-Owned Firms	Quinquennial			X
2007 Economic Census, Company Statistics Series, Survey of Business Owners: Asian-Owned Firms	Quinquennial			X
2007 Economic Census, Company Statistics Series, Survey of Business Owners: Black-Owned Firms	Quinquennial			X
2007 Economic Census, Company Statistics Series, Survey of Business Owners: Hispanic-Owned Firms	Quinquennial			X
2007 Economic Census, Company Statistics Series, Survey of Business Owners: Native Hawaiian- and other Pacific Islander-Owned Firms	Quinquennial			X
2007 Economic Census, Comparative Statistics	Quinquennial			X
2007 Economic Census, Industry/Geography	Quinquennial			X
American Community Survey Annual Earnings and Poverty Report, 2007	Annual		X	
Annual Revision of Monthly Retail and Food Services: Sales and Inventories	Annual		X	
Annual Revision of Monthly Wholesale Distributors: Sales and Inventories	Annual		X	X
Annual Survey of Manufactures	Annual		X	
Census of Governments	Quinquennial		X	
Census of Governments, Volume 3, No. 2, Compendium of Public Employment	Quinquennial		X	X
Census of Housing Decennial (2010, most recent)	Decennial	X	X	X
Census of Population Decennial (2010, most recent)	Decennial	X	X	X
Consolidated Federal Funds Report (CFFR) (discontinued)	Annual	X	X	X
Consumer Income and Poverty, Alternative Poverty Estimates in the United States: 2003	Periodic	X	X	
Consumer Income and Poverty, Income, Poverty, and Health Insurance Coverage in the United States	Annual	X	X	X
Consumer Income and Poverty, P60, and Household Economic Studies, P70	Periodic	X	X	
County Business Patterns	Annual		X	X
CRRF: State and County Areas (discontinued)	Annual	X	X	X
Current Construction Reports: New Residential Construction and New Residential Sales	Monthly		X	
Current Construction Reports: Residential Improvements and Repairs, C50 (discontinued)	Monthly		X	
Current Construction Reports: Value of Construction Put in Place, C30	Monthly		X	
Current Housing Reports, American Housing Survey for Selected Metropolitan Areas, H170	Biennial	X	X	X
Current Housing Reports, American Housing Survey for the United States, H150	Biennial	X	X	X
Current Housing Reports, Characteristics of Apartments Completed, H131	Annual		X	X
Current Housing Reports, Housing Vacancies, H111	Quarterly		X	X
Current Housing Reports, Survey of Market Absorption of Apartments (SOMA)	Quarterly		X	X
Current Housing Reports, Who Can Afford to Buy a Home in 2009, H121	Occasional	X	X	X
Current Industrial Reports (discontinued)	Annual		X	
Current Population Reports (Series P20 and P23)	Periodic		X	X
Economic Census of Island Areas	Quinquennial			X
Federal Aid to States for Fiscal Year	Annual	X	X	
Global Population Profile: 2002 (Series WP)	Periodic	X	X	X
International Briefs (Series IB) (discontinued)		X	X	
International Data Base	Annual			X
International Population Reports (Series P95)	Periodic		X	
Manufacturer's Shipments, Inventories, and Orders	Monthly		X	
Manufacturer's Shipments, Inventories, and Orders: 1992-2012	Annual			X
New York City Housing and Vacancy Survey, 2011	Every 3 years			X
Nonemployer Statistics	Annual			X
Population Estimates and Projections	Annual			X
Quarterly Financial Report for Manufacturing, Mining, and Trade Corporations	Quarterly		X	
Residential Finance Survey, 2001	Every 10 years	X	X	X
Service Annual Survey Report	Annual			X
Survey of Plant Capacity Utilization	Quarterly			X
U.S. International Trade in Goods and Services: includes cumulative data	Annual		X	X
U.S. Trade with Puerto Rico and U.S. Possessions (FT 895)	Monthly		X	
Vehicle Inventory and Use Survey (discontinued)	Quinquennial	X	X	X

Centers for Disease Control and Prevention, Atlanta, Georgia
http://www.cdc.gov

Title	Frequency	Paper	Internet PDF	Internet Other Formats
CDC Injury Fact Book	Periodic	X	X	X
Morbidity and Mortality Weekly Report	Weekly	X	X	X

Centers for Medicare and Medicaid Services (CMS)
http://www.cms.gov

Title	Frequency	Paper	Internet PDF	Internet Other Formats
CMS Statistics	Annual		X	X
Data Compendium	Annual		X	X
Health Care Financing Review (discontinued)	Quarterly	X	X	
Medicare and Medicaid Research Review	Irregular		X	
Medicare and Medicaid Statistical Supplement	Annual	X	X	X
Trustees Report	Annual	X	X	X
Wallet Card	Annual	X	X	X

Central Intelligence Agency
http://www.cia.gov

Title	Frequency	Paper	Internet PDF	Internet Other Formats
World Factbook	Annual	X	X	X

Coast Guard (See Department of Homeland Security)

Comptroller of the Currency
http://www.occ.treas.gov

Title	Frequency	Paper	Internet PDF	Internet Other Formats
Quarterly Journal	Discontinued	X	X	

See footnotes at end of table.

Appendix I Table: Sources of Statistics, State Statistical Abstracts, and Foreign Statistical Abstracts-Continued.

See headnote on page 911.

Title	Frequency	Paper	Internet PDF	Internet Other Formats
Council of Economic Advisers http://www.whitehouse.gov/administration/eop/cea				
Economic Indicators	Monthly	X	X	
Economic Report of the President	Annual	X	X	X
Department of Agriculture, Economic Research Service http://www.ers.usda.gov				
Agricultural Income and Finance	Annual	X	X	X
Amber Waves	Periodic		X	
America's Diverse Family Farms	Annual	X	X	
Cotton and Wool Yearbook	Annual			X
Dairy Yearbook	Annual			X
Feed Grains Yearbook	Annual		X	X
Food Expenditures	Annual			X
Fruit and Tree Nut Yearbook	Annual		X	X
Oil Crops Yearbook	Annual			X
Poultry Yearbook	Periodic			X
Red Meat Yearbook	Periodic			X
Rice Yearbook	Annual			X
Situation and Outlook Reports. Issued for: agricultural exports, feed, fruit and tree nuts, livestock and poultry, oil crops, rice, sugar and sweeteners, vegetables, wheat, and world agriculture	Periodic	X	X	
Structure and Finances of U.S. Farms: Family Farm Report	Annual	X	X	
Sugar and Sweeteners Yearbook	Annual			X
Vegetable and Pulses Yearbook	Annual		X	X
World Agricultural Supply and Demand Estimates	Monthly	X	X	X
Department of Agriculture, Food and Nutrition Service http://www.fns.usda.gov/fns/				
Characteristics of Supplemental Nutrition Assistance Program Households	Annual	X	X	
WIC Participant and Program Characteristics	Biennial	X	X	
Department of Agriculture, Foreign Agricultural Service http://www.fas.usda.gov				
Livestock and Poultry World Markets and Trade	Semiannual	X	X	
Department of Agriculture, National Agricultural Statistics Service http://www.nass.usda.gov				
Agricultural Chemical Usage	Periodic			X
Agricultural Statistics	Annual	X	X	
Catfish Production	Semiannual	X	X	X
Cattle	Semiannual	X	X	X
Census of Agriculture	Quinquennial	X	X	X
Cherry Production	Annual	X	X	X
Chickens and Eggs	Monthly/ Annual	X	X	X
Citrus Fruits	Annual	X	X	X
Cranberries	Annual	X	X	X
Crop Production	Monthly	X	X	X
Crop Progress	Weekly	X	X	X
Crop Values	Annual	X	X	X
Dairy Products	Monthly/ Annual	X	X	X
Farm Labor	Semiannual	X	X	X
Farms, Land in Farms, and Livestock Operations	Annual	X	X	X
Floriculture Crops	Annual	X	X	X
Land Value and Cash Rents	Annual	X	X	X
Livestock Slaughter	Monthly	X	X	X
Meat Animals Production, Disposition, and Income	Annual	X	X	X
Milk Production	Monthly	X	X	X
Milk Production, Disposition, and Income	Annual	X	X	X
Noncitrus Fruits and Nuts	Semiannual	X	X	X
Poultry: Production and Value Summary	Annual	X	X	X
Stock Reports. Stocks of grain, peanuts, potatoes, and rice	Periodic	X	X	X
Trout Production	Annual	X	X	X
Turkey Hatchery	Monthly	X	X	X
Turkeys Raised	Annual	X	X	X
Usual Planting and Harvesting Dates	Periodic	X	X	X
Vegetables	Periodic	X	X	X
Weekly Weather and Crop Bulletin	Weekly	X	X	
Winter Wheat Seedlings	Annual	X	X	X
Department of Agriculture, Natural Resources and Conservation Service http://www.nrcs.usda.gov				
National Resources Inventory	Periodic	X	X	
Department of Defense http://www.defenselink.mil/pubs				
Foreign Military Sales, Foreign Military Construction Sales, and Other Security Cooperation Historical Facts	Annual	X	X	
Personnel Statistics	Periodic		X	X
Department of Education http://www.ed.gov				
Annual Report for Federal Student Aid	Annual		X	
Annual Report on Teacher Quality	Annual		X	
Federal Campus-Based Programs Data Book	Annual			X
Federal Pell Grant Program, End of Year Report	Annual		X	X

See footnotes at end of table.

Appendix I Table: Sources of Statistics, State Statistical Abstracts, and Foreign Statistical Abstracts-Continued.

See headnote on page 911.

Title	Frequency	Paper	PDF	Other Formats
Department of Health and Human Services				
http://www.hhs.gov				
Health Care Fraud and Abuse Control Program Annual Report	Annual	X	X	
Profile of Older Americans	Annual	X	X	X
Department of Homeland Security				
http://www.dhs.gov/index.shtm				
Budget in Brief	Annual	X	X	
Department of Homeland Security, Coast Guard				
http://www.uscg.mil/default.asp				
Fact File	Periodic	X	X	X
Department of Homeland Security, Office of Immigration Statistics				
http://www.dhs.gov/immigration-statistics				
Yearbook of Immigration Statistics	Annual	X	X	X
Department of Housing and Urban Development				
http://www.hud.gov				
U.S. Housing Market Conditions	Quarterly		X	
Homeless Resource Exchange	Annual		X	
Department of Justice, Bureau of Alcohol, Tobacco, Firearms and Explosives				
http://www.atf.gov/				
Firearms Commerce in the US [Annual Firearms Manufacturing and Export Report]	Annual		X	
Firearms Trace Data (by State)	Annual		X	
Department of Labor				
http://www.dol.gov				
Agency Financial Report	Annual	X	X	
Annual Performance Report	Annual	X	X	
Department of State				
http://www.state.gov				
United States Contributions to International Organizations	Annual			X
Department of Transportation				
http://www.dot.gov				
Air Travel Consumer Report	Monthly	X	X	
Airport Activity Statistics of Certified Route Air Carriers	Annual	X	X	
U.S. International Air Travel Statistics	Quarterly, Annual	X	X	X
Wage Statistics of Class I Railroads in the United States	Annual	X	X	
Department of the Treasury, Alcohol and Tobacco Tax and Trade Bureau				
http://www.ttb.gov				
Tobacco Products Monthly Statistical Releases	Monthly	X	X	
Department of the Treasury, Bureau of Public Debt				
http://www.publicdebt.treas.gov				
Monthly Statement of the Public Debt of the United States	Monthly	X	X	X
Department of the Treasury, Financial Management Services				
http://www.fms.treas.gov				
Active Foreign Credits of the United States Government (discontinued)	Quarterly	X		
Combined Statement of Receipts, Outlays, and Balances	Annual	X	X	X
Financial Report of the United States Government	Annual	X	X	X
Monthly Treasury Statement of Receipts and Outlays of the United States Government	Monthly	X	X	X
Treasury Bulletin	Quarterly	X	X	X
Department of Veterans Affairs				
http://www.va.gov				
Compensation and Pension Data by County	Annual			X
Disability Compensation, Pension, and Death Pension Data	Annual			X
Performance and Accountability Report	Annual	X	X	
Servicemembers' and Veterans' Group Life Insurance Programs Annual Report	Annual	X	X	
Drug Enforcement Administration				
http://www.justice.gov/dea				
Drug Abuse and Law Enforcement Statistics	Irregular	X	X	X
Employment and Training Administration				
http://www.doleta.gov				
Unemployment Insurance Claims	Weekly			X
Energy Information Administration				
http://www.eia.gov				
Annual Coal Report	Annual		X	X
Annual Energy Outlook	Annual	X	X	X
Annual Energy Review (suspended for 2013)	Annual	X	X	X
Electric Power Annual	Annual		X	X
Electric Power Monthly	Monthly		X	X
Electric Sales, Revenue and Retail Price	Annual		X	X
Emissions of Greenhouse Gases in the U.S. (discontinued)	Annual		X	X
International Energy Outlook	Annual	X	X	X
International Energy Statistics portal	Ongoing		X	X
Monthly Energy Review	Monthly		X	X
Performance Profiles of Major Energy Producers (discontinued)	Annual		X	X
Petroleum Marketing Annual	Monthly		X	X
Petroleum Marketing Monthly	Monthly		X	X
Petroleum Supply Annual	Annual		X	X
Petroleum Supply Monthly	Monthly		X	X

See footnotes at end of table.

Title	Frequency	Paper	Internet PDF	Internet Other Formats
Quarterly Coal Report	Quarterly		X	X
Renewable Energy Annual	Annual		X	X
Residential Energy Consumption Survey	Quadrennial		X	X
State Electricity Profiles	Annual		X	X
State Energy Data System Reports	Annual		X	X
U.S. Crude Oil, Natural Gas, and Natural Gas Liquids Reserves	Annual		X	X
Weekly Coal Production	Weekly			X
Environmental Protection Agency http://www.epa.gov				
Air Quality Data	Annual		X	X
Clean Watersheds Needs Survey	Quadrennial		X	
Drinking Water Infrastructure Needs Survey	Periodic		X	
National Water Quality Inventory	Biennial		X	X
Toxics Release Inventory	Annual		X	X
Export-Import Bank of the United States http://www.exim.gov				
Annual Report	Annual	X	X	
Report to the U.S. Congress on Export Credit Competition and the Export-Import Bank of the United States	Annual	X	X	
Farm Credit Administration http://www.fca.gov/index.html				
Annual Report on the Farm Credit System	Annual	X	X	
Federal Bureau of Investigation http://www.fbi.gov/ucr/ucr.htm				
Crime in the United States	Annual		X	X
Hate Crime Statistics	Annual		X	X
Law Enforcement Officers Killed and Assaulted	Annual		X	X
Federal Communications Commission http://www.fcc.gov				
Annual Assessment of the Status of Competition in the Market for the Delivery of Video Programming	Annual		X	X
International Telecommunications Data	Annual	X	X	X
Internet Access Services	Semi-Annual		X	X
Local Telephone Competition	Semi-Annual		X	X
Quarterly Report on Informal Consumer Inquiries and Complaints	Quarterly		X	X
Report on Cable Industry Prices	Annual		X	X
Telecommunications Industry Revenues	Annual		X	X
Trends in Telephone Service	Annual	X	X	
Federal Deposit Insurance Corporation http://www.fdic.gov				
Annual Report	Annual	X	X	X
FDIC Quarterly	Quarterly	X	X	X
Historical Statistics on Banking	Annual			X
Quarterly Banking Profile	Quarterly		X	X
Statistics on Banking	Quarterly			X
Summary of Deposits	Annual			X
Federal Highway Administration http://www.fhwa.dot.gov				
Highway Statistics	Annual	X	X	X
Federal Railroad Administration http://safetydata.fra.dot.gov/OfficeofSafety/default.aspx				
Railroad Safety Statistics	Annual	X	X	
Fish and Wildlife Service http://www.fws.gov				
Federal Aid in Fish and Wildlife Restoration	Annual		X	
National Survey of Fishing, Hunting, and Wildlife Associated Recreation	Quinquennial	X	X	
Forest Service http://www.fs.fed.us				
An Analysis of the Timber Situation in the United States 1952-2050	Periodic	X	X	
Land Areas of the National Forest System	Annual	X	X	X
RPA Assessment Tables	Periodic	X	X	X
U.S. Timber Production, Trade, Consumption, and Price Statistics 1965-2011	Biennial	X	X	
General Services Administration http://www.gsa.gov				
Federal Real Property Profile	Annual		X	X
Geological Survey http://www.usgs.gov/				
Estimated Use of Water in the United States	Quinquennial	X	X	X
Mineral Commodity Summaries	Annual	X	X	
Mineral Industry Surveys	Monthly & Quarterly		X	X
Minerals Yearbook	Annual	X	X	X
Internal Revenue Service http://www.irs.gov/uac/Tax-Stats-2				
Corporation Income Tax Returns	Annual	X	X	X
Individual Income Tax Returns	Annual	X	X	X
IRS Data Book	Annual	X	X	X
Statistics of Income Bulletin	Quarterly	X	X	X

See footnotes at end of table.

Appendix I Table: Sources of Statistics, State Statistical Abstracts, and Foreign Statistical Abstracts-Continued.

See headnote on page 911.

Title	Frequency	Paper	Internet	
			PDF	Other Formats
International Trade Administration, Office of Travel and Tourism Industries				
http://www.tinet.ita.doc.gov				
U.S. Travel and Tourism Statistics	Annual	X		X
International Trade Commission				
http://www.usitc.gov				
Recent Trends in U.S. Services Trade	Annual	X	X	
Library of Congress				
http://www.loc.gov				
Annual Report	Annual	X	X	
Maritime Administration				
http://www.marad.dot.gov				
Annual Report	Annual	X	X	
Cruise Statistics (discontinued)	Quarterly		X	X
Fleet Statistics 1,000 Gross Tons or Greater	Annual			X
U.S. Waterborne Foreign Trade	Annual			X
Vessel Calls	Annual		X	X
Mine Safety and Health Administration				
http://www.msha.gov				
Informational Reports by Mining Industry: Coal, Metallic Minerals, Nonmetallic Minerals (except stone and coal), Sand and Gravel, and Stone	Annual		X	X
Mine Injuries and Worktime	Quarterly	X	X	X
National Aeronautics and Space Administration				
http://www.nasa.gov				
Annual Procurement Report	Annual	X	X	
National Center for Education Statistics				
http://nces.ed.gov				
Academic Libraries	Biennial		X	X
Characteristics of Private Schools in the United States	Annual	X	X	X
Characteristics of Schools, Districts, Teachers, Principals, and School Libraries in the United States	Annual	X	X	X
Characteristics of the 100 Largest Public Elementary and Secondary School Districts in the United States	Annual	X	X	X
Computer and Internet Use by Students	Periodic	X	X	
The Condition of Education	Annual	X	X	X
Digest of Education Statistics	Annual	X	X	X
Enrollment in Postsecondary Institutions, Graduation Rates, and Financial Statistics	Annual		X	
Indicators of School Crime and Safety	Annual	X	X	X
The Nation's Report Card: Civics 2010	Periodic	X	X	
The Nation's Report Card: Economics 2012	Periodic	X	X	
The Nation's Report Card: Geography 2010	Periodic	X	X	
The Nation's Report Card: History 2010	Periodic	X	X	
The Nation's Report Card: Mathematics 2011	Periodic	X	X	
The Nation's Report Card: Reading 2011	Periodic	X	X	
The Nation's Report Card: Science 2011	Periodic	X	X	
The Nation's Report Card: Writing 2011	Periodic	X	X	
Projections of Education Statistics	Annual	X	X	X
Status and Trends in the Education of Racial and Ethnic Minorities	Irregular	X	X	X
Trends in High School Dropout and Completion Rates in the United States	Annual		X	X
National Center for Health Statistics				
http://www.cdc.gov/nchs/				
Health: United States	Annual	X	X	X
National Health Statistics Reports	Periodic	X	X	
National Hospital Discharge Survey: Annual Summary	Annual		X	X
National Vital Statistics Reports	Periodic	X	X	
Vital and Health Statistics:				
Series 3: Analytical and Epidemiological Studies	Irregular	X	X	
Series 10: Data from the National Health Interview Survey	Irregular	X	X	
Series 11: Health and Nutrition Examination Survey Statistics	Irregular	X	X	
Series 13: Data on Health Resources Utilization	Irregular	X	X	
Series 20: Data on Mortality	Irregular	X	X	
Series 21: Data on Natality, Marriage, and Divorce	Irregular	X	X	
Series 23: Data from the National Survey of Family Growth	Irregular	X	X	
National Credit Union Administration				
http://www.ncua.gov				
Annual Report	Annual	X	X	
Yearend Statistics for Federally Insured Credit Unions	Annual	X	X	
National Endowment for the Arts				
http://www.nea.gov				
Annual Report	Annual		X	X
Budget Request	Annual		X	
Research Notes	Periodic	X	X	
Research Reports	Periodic	X	X	
National Endowment for the Humanities				
http://www.neh.gov				
Annual Report	Annual		X	
Budget Request	Annual		X	
National Guard Bureau				
http://www.nationalguard.mil/				
Annual Review of the Chief	Annual		X	

See footnotes at end of table.

Title	Frequency	Paper	Internet PDF	Internet Other Formats
National Highway Traffic Safety Administration http://www.nhtsa.gov				
Traffic Safety Facts	Annual	X	X	
National Oceanic and Atmospheric Administration http://www.noaa.gov				
Climatic Data for the World	Monthly		X	
Comparative Climatic Data	Annual	X	X	X
Daily Normals of Temperature, Precipitation, Heating Degree Days (HDD), and Cooling Degree Days (CDD)	Periodic			X
Fisheries of the United States	Annual	X	X	
Hourly Precipitation Data. Monthly with annual summary; for each state	Monthly		X	X
Local Climatological Data. Monthly with annual summary; for major cities	Monthly		X	X
Monthly Normals of Temperature, Precipitation, Heating Degree Days (HDD), and Cooling Degree Days (CDD)	Periodic			X
Our Living Oceans	Periodic	X	X	
Storm Data	Monthly		X	
Tornado Summaries	Monthly/ Annual			X
U.S. Climate Normals	Annual	X	X	X
National Park Service http://www.nps.gov				
Federal Recreation Fee Report (discontinued)	Annual	X		
National Park Statistical Abstract	Annual	X	X	
National Science Foundation http://www.nsf.gov/statistics				
Academic Institutional Profiles	Annual			X
Academic Research and Development Expenditures	Annual		X	X
Characteristics of Doctoral Scientists and Engineers in the United States	Biennial		X	X
Characteristics of Recent Science/Engineering Graduates	Biennial		X	X
Doctorate Recipients from U.S. Universities	Annual		X	X
Federal Funds for Research and Development	Annual		X	X
Federal Research and Development Funding by Budget Function	Annual		X	X
Federal Science and Engineering Support to Universities, Colleges, and Nonprofit Institutions	Annual		X	X
Graduate Students and Postdoctorates in Science and Engineering	Annual		X	X
National Patterns of Research and Development Resources	Annual		X	X
Research and Development in Industry	Annual		X	X
Science and Engineering Degrees	Biennial		X	X
Science and Engineering Degrees, by Race/Ethnicity of Recipients	Biennial		X	X
Science and Engineering Doctorate Awards	Annual		X	X
Science and Engineering Indicators	Biennial	X	X	X
Science and Engineering State Profiles	Annual		X	X
Science Resources Statistics Info Briefs (various topics)	Frequent	X	X	X
Scientific and Engineering Research Facilities at Universities and Colleges	Biennial		X	X
Women, Minorities, and Persons with Disabilities in Science and Engineering	Biennial		X	X
National Transportation Safety Board http://www.ntsb.gov				
Review of U.S. Civil Aviation Accidents	Annual		X	
Office of Juvenile Justice and Delinquency Prevention http://ojjdp.gov				
Highlights of the National Youth Gang Survey	Annual	X	X	X
Juvenile Arrests	Annual	X	X	X
Victims of Violent Juvenile Crime	Periodic	X	X	X
Office of Management and Budget http://www.whitehouse.gov/omb				
The Budget of the United States Government	Annual	X	X	
Office of Personnel Management http://www.opm.gov				
Demographic Profile of the Federal Workforce	Biennial		X	
Employment and Trends	Bimonthly		X	X
The Fact Book	Annual		X	X
Statistical Abstract for the Federal Employee Benefit Programs	Annual			X
Work Years and Personnel Costs	Annual		X	
Office of the Clerk, U.S. House of Representatives http://clerk.house.gov				
Statistics of the Presidential and Congressional Election	Biennial		X	
Patent and Trademark Office http://www.uspto.gov				
All Technologies (Utility Patents)	Annual	X	X	X
Patent Counts by Country/State and Year	Annual	X	X	X
Patenting Trends in the United States	Annual	X		X
Technology Assessment and Forecast Reports	Periodic	X	X	X
Railroad Retirement Board http://www.rrb.gov/default.asp				
Annual Report	Annual	X	X	
Quarterly Benefit Statistics	Quarterly	X	X	
Securities and Exchange Commission http://www.sec.gov/about.shtml				
Select SEC and Market Data	Annual		X	

See footnotes at end of table.

See headnote on page 911.

Title	Frequency	Paper	Internet PDF	Internet Other Formats
Small Business Administration				
http://www.sba.gov				
Loan Program Performance Reports	Quarterly		X	
Quarterly Bulletin	Quarterly		X	X
Small Business and Micro Business Lending	Annual	X	X	X
Small Business Economy	Annual		X	X
Small Business Profiles for States and Territories	Annual		X	X
Social Security Administration				
http://www.ssa.gov				
Annual Statistical Report on the Social Security Disability Insurance Program	Annual	X	X	X
Annual Statistical Supplement to the Social Security Bulletin	Annual	X	X	X
Children Receiving Social Security Income (SSI) (discontinued)	Annual		X	X
Congressional Statistics	Annual	X	X	X
Fast Facts & Figures about Social Security	Annual	X	X	X
Income of the Population 55 and over	Biennially	X	X	X
OASDI Beneficiaries by State and County	Annual	X	X	X
Social Security Bulletin	Quarterly	X	X	X
SSI Annual Statistical Report	Annual	X	X	X
SSI Disabled Recipients Who Work (discontinued)	Annual		X	X
SSI Recipients by State and County	Annual	X	X	X
State Assistance Programs for Social Security Income (SSI) Recipients (discontinued)	Annual		X	X
Substance Abuse and Mental Health Services Administration				
http://www.samhsa.gov				
National Survey on Drug Use and Health (NSDUH)	Annual	X	X	X
National Survey on Substance Abuse Treatment Services (N-SSATS)	Annual	X	X	X
U.S. Copyright Office				
http://www.copyright.gov/				
Annual Report	Annual	X	X	
NONGOVERNMENT				
Aerospace Industries Association, Arlington, VA				
http://www.aia-aerospace.org				
Aerospace Foreign Trade: Export Activity	Annual		X	
Aerospace Foreign Trade: Import Activity	Annual		X	
Aerospace Industries Report 2012: Facts, Figures & Outlook for the Aviation and Aerospace Manufacturing Industry (Final Edition)	Annual	X	X	
Aerospace Industry Year-End Review and Forecast	Annual		X	
Manufacturing Production, Capacity, and Utilization in Aerospace and Aircraft and Parts	Quarterly		X	
Orders, Shipments, and Backlog for Large Civil Jet Transport Aircraft	Periodic		X	
Total and Production Workers Employment in the Aerospace Industry	Annual		X	
Airlines for America, Washington, DC				
http://www.airlines.org				
Airlines for America Economic Report 2011	Annual		X	
American Bureau of Metal Statistics, Inc., Chatham, NJ				
http://www.abms.com				
Non-Ferrous Metal Yearbook	Annual	X		X
American Council of Life Insurers, Washington, DC				
http://www.acli.com				
Life Insurers Fact Book	Annual		X	
American Dental Association, Chicago, IL				
http://www.ada.org				
Distribution of Dentists in the United States by Region and State 2009 (Final Edition)	Annual	X	X	
Survey of Dental Practice	Annual			X
American Forest and Paper Association, Washington, DC				
http://www.afandpa.org				
Annual Capacity and Fiber Consumption Survey	Annual		X	
Annual Statistics of Paper, Paperboard and Wood Pulp	Annual		X	
Monthly Exports/Imports Report	Monthly		X	
Monthly Statistics of Paper, Paperboard and Wood Pulp	Monthly		X	X
American Gas Association, Washington, DC				
http://www.aga.org				
Gas Facts	Annual	X	X	
American Iron and Steel Institute, Washington, DC				
http://www.steel.org				
Annual Statistical Report	Annual	X	X	
American Medical Association, Chicago, IL				
http://www.ama-assn.org				
Physician Characteristics and Distribution in the U.S.	Annual	X		X
State Medical Licensure Statistics, and License Requirements	Annual	X		X
American Osteopathic Association, Chicago, IL				
http://www.osteopathic.org/				
Osteopathic Medical Profession Report	Annual		X	
American Petroleum Institute, Washington, DC				
http://www.api.org				
Basic Petroleum Data Book	Semiannual	X	X	
Joint Association Survey on Drilling Costs	Annual	X	X	
Quarterly Well Completion Report	Quarterly	X	X	

See footnotes at end of table.

Appendix I Table: Sources of Statistics, State Statistical Abstracts, and Foreign Statistical Abstracts-Continued.

See headnote on page 911.

Title	Frequency	Paper	Internet PDF	Internet Other Formats
American Public Transportation Association, Washington, DC http://www.apta.com				
Public Transportation Fact Book	Annual		X	X
Association for Manufacturing Technology, McLean, VA http://www.amtonline.org				
2010-11 Economic Handbook of the Machine Tool Industry (Final Edition)	Annual		X	X
Machine Tool Industry Data Base	Ongoing			X
Association of American Railroads, Washington, DC http://www.aar.org				
Analysis of Class I Railroads	Annual	X	X	X
Freight Commodity Statistics	Annual	X	X	X
Railroad Facts	Annual	X	X	
Association of Racing Commissioners International, Inc., Lexington, KY http://www.arci.com				
Pari-Mutuel Racing	Annual	X		
Berman Jewish Data Bank, Storrs, CT http://www.jewishdatabank.org				
Jewish Population in the United States	Annual		X	X
Bloomberg BNA, Washington, DC http://www.bna.com				
Basic Patterns in Union Contracts	Annual	X		
BNA's Employment Outlook Report	Quarterly	X		
BNA's Job Absence and Turnover Report	Quarterly	X		
Directory of U.S. Labor Organizations	Annual	X		
National Labor Relations Board Election Statistics	Semiannual	X	x	x
Source Book on Collective Bargaining	Annual	X		
Union Membership and Earnings Data Book	Annual	X		
Book Industry Study Group, and Association of American Publishers, New York, NY http://www.bisg.org				
BookStats	Annual	X	X	X
Used-Book Sales	Periodic	X		
Boy Scouts of America, Irving, TX http://www.scouting.org				
Scouting Annual Report	Annual		X	
Chronicle of Higher Education, Inc., Washington, DC http://chronicle.com				
Almanac of Higher Education	Annual	X		X
College Board, New York, NY http://www.collegeboard.com				
College-Bound Seniors Total Group Profile Report	Annual		X	
Commodity Research Bureau, Chicago, IL http://www.crbtrader.com				
CRB Commodity Index Report	Weekly		X	X
CRB Commodity Yearbook	Annual	X		X
CRB Futures Perspective	Daily in digital only/Monthly	X	X	
CRB Infotech CD	Monthly			X
Final Markets End-of-Day Data	Daily			X
Fundamental Market Service	Daily/Weekly		X	X
Trends In Futures	Daily		X	X
Conference Board, New York, NY http://www.conference-board.org				
Business Cycle Indicators	Monthly		X	X
Corporate Contributions Report	Annual		X	
Performance: Productivity, Employment, and Growth in the World's Economies	Irregular		X	
Congressional Quarterly (CQ) Press, Washington, DC http://www.cqpress.com				
America Votes	Biennial	X		
Consumer Electronics Association, Arlington, VA http://www.ce.org				
U.S. Consumer Electronics Sales and Forecasts	Semiannual		X	
Council of State Governments, Lexington, KY http://www.csg.org				
Book of the States	Annual	X	X	
Directory I: Elective Officials	Annual	X		
Directory II: Legislative Leadership, Committees, and Staff	Annual	X		
Directory III: Administrative Officials	Annual	X		
Credit Union National Association, Madison, WI http://www.cuna.org				
Operating Ratios and Spreads	Quarterly	X	X	
Dow Jones and Company, New York, NY http://www.dj.com				
Wall Street Journal	Daily	X		X
Duncan McIntosh Company, Inc., Irvine, CA http://www.editorandpublisher.com				

See footnotes at end of table.

Appendix I Table: Sources of Statistics, State Statistical Abstracts, and Foreign Statistical Abstracts -Continued.

See headnote on page 911.

Title	Frequency	Paper	Internet PDF	Internet Other *Formats*
Editor and Publisher	Monthly	X		X
Market Guide 2010 (Final Edition)	Periodic	X		
Newspaper Databook	Annual	X		X
Edison Electric Institute, Washington, DC				
http://www.eei.org				
Statistical Yearbook of the Electric Power Industry	Annual	X	X	X
Euromonitor International, London, England				
http://www.euromonitor.com				
Consumer Americas	Annual	X	X	
Consumer Asia Pacific and Australasia	Annual	X	X	
Consumer Europe	Annual	X	X	
Consumer Middle East and North Africa	Annual	X	X	
European Marketing Data and Statistics	Annual	X	X	
International Marketing Data and Statistics	Annual	X	X	
Retail Trade International	Annual	X	X	
World Consumer Income and Expenditure Patterns	Annual	X	X	
World Consumer Lifestyles Databook	Annual	X	X	
World Economic Factbook	Annual	X	X	
World Environmental Databook	Annual	X	X	
World Health Databook	Annual	X	X	
World Retail Data and Statistics	Annual	X	X	
Federal National Mortgage Association, Washington, DC				
http://www.fanniemae.com				
Annual Report on Form 10-K	Annual		X	
Food and Agriculture Organization of the United Nations, Rome, Italy				
http://www.fao.org				
Current World Fertilizer Trends and Outlook	Annual		X	
FAO Statistical Yearbook: World Food and Agriculture	Annual	X	X	
FAO Yearbook. Fishery and Aquaculture Statistics	Periodic	X	X	
Yearbook of Forest Products	Annual	X	X	
Foundation Center, New York, NY				
http://www.foundationcenter.org				
Foundation Yearbook 2011 (Final Edition)	Annual	X		
FC Stats	Annual			X
General Aviation Manufacturers Association, Washington, DC				
http://www.gama.aero/home.php				
General Aviation Airplane Shipment Report	Quarterly		X	
General Aviation Statistical Databook & Industry Outlook	Annual		X	
Girl Scouts of the USA, New York, NY				
http://www.girlscouts.org				
Annual Report	Annual		X	
Giving USA Foundation, Chicago, IL				
http://www.givingusareports.org				
Giving USA	Annual	X	X	X
Guttmacher Institute, New York, NY				
http://www.guttmacher.org				
Perspectives on Sexual and Reproductive Health	Quarterly	X	X	
Health Forum, an American Hospital Association Company, Chicago, IL				
http://www.ahadata.com				
AHA Annual Survey Data Base	Annual			X
AHA Hospital Statistics	Annual	X		X
IHS Global, Inc., Englewood, CO				
http://www.janes.com				
IHS Jane's All the World's Aircraft: Development & Production	Annual	X		X
IHS Jane's Defence: C4ISR & Mission Systems	Annual	X		X
IHS Jane's Fighting Ships	Annual	X		X
IHS Jane's Flight Avionics	Annual	X		X
IHS Jane's Land Warfare Platforms: Armoured Fighting Vehicles	Annual	X		X
IHS Jane's Land Warfare Platforms: Logistics, Support & Unmanned	Annual	X		X
IHS Jane's Merchant Ships	Annual	X		X
IHS Jane's Simulation & Training Systems	Annual	X		X
IHS Jane's Space Systems & Industry	Annual	X		X
IHS Jane's Weapons: Air-Launched	Annual	X		X
IHS Jane's Weapons: Infantry	Annual	X		X
Independent Petroleum Association of America, Washington, DC				
http://www.ipaa.org				
IPAA Oil & Gas Producing Industry in Your State	Annual	X	X	
U.S. Petroleum Statistics	Annual	X	X	
Infobase Publishing, New York, NY				
http://www.worldalmanac.com				
The World Almanac and Book of Facts	Annual	X		
Information Today, Inc., Medford, NJ				
http://www.infotoday.com				
American Library Directory	Annual	X		
Library and Book Trade Almanac (formerly The Bowker Annual)	Annual	X		
Institute for Criminal Justice Ethics, New York, NY				
http://www.lib.jjay.cuny.edu/cje				

See footnotes at end of table.

Appendix I Table: Sources of Statistics, State Statistical Abstracts, and Foreign Statistical Abstracts-Continued.

See headnote on page 911.

Title	Frequency	Paper	Internet	
			PDF	Other *Formats*
Criminal Justice Ethics	Three Issues per Year	X	X	
Insurance Information Institute, New York, NY				
http://www.iii.org				
The Financial Services Fact Book (published jointly with the Financial Services Roundtable)	Annual	X		X
The I.I.I. Insurance Fact Book	Annual	X	X	X
Inter-American Development Bank, Washington, DC				
http://www.iadb.org				
Annual Report	Annual	X	X	
Development in the Americas	Periodic	X		
International Air Transport Association, Montreal, Canada and Geneva, Switzerland				
http://www.iata.org				
World Air Transport Statistics	Annual	X	X	X
International City Management Association, Washington, DC				
http://www.icma.org				
ICMA Chief Administrative Officers Salary & Compensation Survey	Annual		X	
Municipal Year Book	Annual	X	X	
International Labour Organization, Geneva, Switzerland				
http://www.ilo.org				
Yearbook of Labour Statistics	Annual	X		X
International Monetary Fund, Washington, DC				
http://www.imf.org				
Annual Report	Annual	X	X	X
Balance of Payments Statistics	Monthly	X	X	X
Direction of Trade Statistics	Monthly	X	X	X
Government Finance Statistics Yearbook	Annual	X	X	X
International Financial Statistics	Monthly	X	X	X
International Telecommunication Union, Geneva, Switzerland				
http://www.itu.int/home/index.html				
ITU Yearbook of Statistics	Annual	X	X	
World Telecommunication Indicators	Annual	X	X	X
Investment Company Institute, Washington, DC				
http://www.ici.org				
Investment Company Fact Book	Annual		X	X
Joint Center for Housing Studies of Harvard University, Cambridge, MA				
http://www.jchs.harvard.edu/				
The State of the Nation's Housing	Annual		X	
Joint Center for Political and Economic Studies, Washington, DC				
http://www.jointcenter.org				
Black Elected Officials: A Statistical Summary	Ongoing	X	X	
McGraw-Hill Construction Dodge, a Division of the McGraw-Hill Companies, New York, NY				
http://construction.com/dodge/dodge-reports-print.asp				
Dodge Construction Potential Bulletin	Monthly		X	
Media Source, Inc., New York, NY				
http://www.mediasourceinc.com				
Library Journal	Semimonthly	X		X
School Library Journal	Monthly	X		X
National Academy of Social Insurance, Washington, DC				
http://www.nasi.org/				
Workers Compensation: Benefits, Coverage, and Costs	Annual	X	X	
National Association of Home Builders, Washington, DC				
http://www.nahb.org				
HousingEconomics.com (online subscription)	Ongoing			X
National Association of Latino Elected and Appointed Officials, Los Angeles, CA				
http://www.naleo.org				
National Directory of Latino Elected Officials	Annual		X	X
National Association of Realtors, Chicago, IL				
http://www.realtor.org				
Economist's Commentary	Daily			X
Investment and Vacation Home Buyers Survey	Annual	X	X	
NAR Member Profile	Annual	X	X	
NAR Profile of Home Buyer and Sellers	Annual	X	X	
National Association of State Budget Officers, Washington, DC				
http://www.nasbo.org				
Fiscal Survey of the States	Semiannual	X	X	
State Expenditure Report	Annual	X	X	
National Association of State Park Directors, Raleigh, NC				
http://www.naspd.org				
Statistical Report of State Park Operations: Annual Information Exchange	Annual	X	X	
National Catholic Educational Association, Arlington, VA				
http://www.ncea.org				

See footnotes at end of table.

Appendix I Table: Sources of Statistics, State Statistical Abstracts, and Foreign Statistical Abstracts-Continued.

See headnote on page 911.

Title	Frequency	Paper	Internet PDF	Internet Other Formats
Dollars & Sense: A Report for the National Catholic Educational Association Secondary Schools Department	Biennial	X	X	
Financing the Mission: A Profile of Catholic Elementary Schools in the U.S.	Biennial	X	X	
Ganley's Catholic Schools in America	Annual	X	X	
U.S. Catholic Elementary and Secondary Schools: The Annual Statistical Report on Schools, Enrollment and Staffing	Annual	X	X	
National Council of the Churches of Christ in the USA, Washington, DC http://www.ncccusa.org				
Yearbook of American and Canadian Churches	Annual	X		X
National Education Association, Washington, DC http://www.nea.org				
Rankings & Estimates: Rankings of the States and Estimates of School Statistics	Annual	X	X	
Status of the American Public School Teacher, 2005-2006 (Final Edition)	Quinquennial	X	X	
National Fire Protection Association, Quincy, MA http://www.nfpa.org				
National Fire Protection Association (NFPA) Journal	Bimonthly	X		X
National Golf Foundation, Jupiter, FL http://www.ngf.org				
Golf Consumer Profile 2009 (Final Edition)	Periodic	X	X	
Golf Facilities in the U.S.	Annual	X	X	
National Marine Manufacturers Association, Chicago, IL http://www.nmma.org				
Recreational Boating Statistical Abstract	Annual		X	X
U.S. Recreational Boat Registration Statistics	Annual		X	
National Restaurant Association, Washington, DC http://www.restaurant.org				
Restaurant Industry 2020	Recurring		X	
Restaurant Industry Forecast	Annual		X	
Restaurant Industry Operations Report	Recurring	X	X	
Restaurant Industry Pocket Factbook	Annual	X	X	
Restaurant Performance Index	Monthly		X	
Restaurant Spending	Recurring		X	
Restaurant Trendmapper (online subscription)	Ongoing			X
National Safety Council, Itasca, IL http://www.nsc.org				
Injury Facts	Annual	X	X	X
National Sporting Goods Association, Mount Prospect, IL http://www.nsga.org				
Sporting Goods Market	Annual	X	X	
Sports Participation	Annual	X	X	
NYSE Euronext, New York, NY http://www.nyse.com				
NYSE Facts & Figures (formerly the online NYSE Fact Book)	Ongoing			X
Organization for Economic Cooperation and Development, Paris, France http://www.oecdbookshop.org/ http://www.oecd-ilibrary.org/				
Bank Profitability: Financial Statements of Banks	Biennial	X		X
Central Government Debt: Statistical Yearbook	Annual	X		X
Coal Information	Annual	X		X
CO2 Emissions From Fuel Combustion	Annual	X		X
Education at a Glance: OECD Indicators	Annual	X		X
Electricity Information	Annual	X		X
Energy Balances of Non-OECD Countries	Annual	X		X
Energy Balances of OECD Countries	Annual	X		X
Energy Prices and Taxes	Quarterly	X	X	
Energy Statistics of Non-OECD Countries	Annual	X		X
Energy Statistics of OECD Countries	Annual	X		X
Environmental Data Compendium 2007	Periodic	X	X	
Environmental Outlook	Periodic	X	X	
Financial Market Trends	Triennial	X	X	
Geographical Distribution of Financial Flows to Aid Recipients	Annual	X		
Information Technology Outlook	Biennial	X	X	X
Insurance Statistics Yearbook	Annual	X	X	X
International Development Statistics	Annual			X
International Migration Outlook	Annual	X	X	
International Trade by Commodity Statistics	Annual	X	X	
Main Economic Indicators	Monthly	X	X	
Main Science and Technology Indicators	Semiannual	X	X	
Measuring Globalisation: OECD Economic Globalisation Indicators 2010	Periodic	X	X	
Monthly Statistics of International Trade	Monthly	X	X	
National Accounts of OECD Countries	Annual	X	X	X
Volume I: Main Aggregates	Annual	X	X	X
Volume II: Detailed Tables	Annual	X	X	X
Volume IIIa: Financial Accounts	Annual	X	X	X
Volume IIIb: Financial Balance Sheets	Annual	X	X	X
Volume IV: Summary of General Aggregates and Balances	Annual	X	X	X
Natural Gas Information	Annual	X	X	
Nuclear Energy Data	Annual	X	X	
OECD Communications Outlook	Biennial	X		X

See footnotes at end of table.

Title	Frequency	Paper	Internet PDF	Internet Other Formats
OECD Economic Outlook	Semiannual	X	X	
OECD Economic Studies	Periodic	X	X	
OECD Economic Surveys	Periodic	X	X	
OECD Employment Outlook	Annual	X	X	
OECD Factbook	Annual	X	X	
OECD-FAO Agricultural Outlook	Annual	X		X
OECD Health Data	Annual			X
OECD in Figures	Periodic	X	X	
OECD Science, Technology, and Industry Outlook	Biennial	X	X	
OECD Science, Technology and R&D Statistics	Ongoing			X
OECD Territorial Reviews	Periodic	X	X	
Oil Information	Annual	X	X	
Oil, Gas, Coal, and Electricity Quarterly Statistics	Quarterly	X	X	
Quarterly National Accounts	Quarterly	X	X	
Revenue Statistics	Annual	X	X	
Review of Fisheries in Organisation for Economic Cooperation and Development (OECD) Countries-Policies and Summary Statistics	Annual	X	X	
Taxing Wages	Annual	X	X	
Uranium Resources Production and Demand	Biennial	X	X	
World Energy Outlook	Annual	X	X	
Penguin Group (USA), Inc., New York, NY http://us.penguingroup.com				
The New York Times Almanac 2011 (Final Edition)	Annual	X		
PennWell Corporation, Tulsa, OK http://www.pennwell.com				
Offshore	Monthly	X	X	X
Oil and Gas Journal	Weekly	X	X	X
Puerto Rico Planning Board, San Juan, PR http://www.jp.gobierno.pr				
Construction Industry	Periodic	X		
Economic Report to the Governor	Annual	X	X	X
External Trade Statistics, 2007	Periodic	X	X	X
Income and Product	Annual	X	X	
Statistical Appendix-Economic Report to the Governor	Annual	X	X	X
PWxyz, LLC, New York, NY http://www.publishersweekly.com				
Publishers Weekly	Weekly	X		X
Radio Advertising Bureau, Dallas, TX http://www.rab.com				
Media Facts	Ongoing			X
Why Radio: Fact Sheets	Ongoing			X
Regional Airline Association, Washington, DC http://www.raa.org				
Regional Airlines Association Annual Report	Annual			X
Securities Industry and Financial Markets Association, New York, NY http://www.sifma.org				
SIFMA Fact Book	Annual	X		X
U.S. Foreign Activity Report	Quarterly		X	X
Standard and Poor's Financial Services LLC, New York, NY http://www.standardandpoors.com				
Analyst's Handbook	Monthly	X		X
Corporation Records: Corporate Description	Monthly	X		
Corporation Records: Daily News	Daily	X		
Daily Stock Price Records	Quarterly			X
Standard and Poor's Global Stock Markets Factbook	Annual	X		
United Nations Conference on Trade and Development, Geneva, Switzerland http://www.unctad.org				
Development and Globalization: Facts and Figures	Periodic	X	X	X
Handbook of Statistics	Annual	X	X	X
United Nations Statistics Division, New York, NY http://unstats.un.org/unsd/default.htm https://unp.un.org/Default.aspx				
Demographic Yearbook (Series R)	Annual	X	X	
Energy Balances and Electricity Profiles (Series W)	Annual	X	X	
Energy Statistics Yearbook (Series J)	Annual	X	X	
Industrial Commodity Statistics Yearbook: Production Statistics	Annual	X	X	
International Trade Statistics Yearbook (Series G)	Annual	X	X	
Main Aggregates and Detailed Tables	Annual	X	X	X
Monthly Bulletin of Statistics (Series Q)	Monthly	X	X	
National Accounts Statistics: Analysis of Main Aggregates	Annual	X		
National Accounts Statistics (Series X)	Annual	X	X	
Population and Vital Statistics Report (Series A)	Quarterly	X	X	
Statistical Yearbook	Annual	X	X	
World Statistics Pocketbook (Series V)	Annual	X	X	
World's Women: Progress in Statistics	Quinquennial	X	X	
University of Michigan, Inter-University Consortium for Political and Social Research, Institute for Social Research, Ann Arbor, MI http://www.icpsr.umich.edu/icpsrweb/ICPSR/studies/8475				

See footnotes at end of table.

Appendix I Table: Sources of Statistics, State Statistical Abstracts, and Foreign Statistical Abstracts-Continued.

See headnote on page 911.

Title	Frequency	Paper	Internet PDF	Internet Other Formats
American National Election Studies Cumulative Data File	Biennial			X
Warren Communications News, Washington, DC http://www.warren-news.com Cable and TV Station Coverage Atlas	Annual			X
Television and Cable Factbook	Annual (ongoing in online format)	X		X
World Bank Group, Washington, DC http://www.worldbank.org Atlas of Global Development	Periodic	X	X	
Global Development Finance	Annual	X	X	
The Little Data Book	Annual	X	X	
World Development Indicators	Annual	X		X
World Health Organization, Geneva, Switzerland http://www.who.int/en/ Aids Epidemic Update	Periodic	X	X	
World Health Statistics Report	Annual	X	X	
World Trade Organization, Geneva, Switzerland http://www.wto.org International Trade Statistics	Annual	X	X	X
STATE STATISTICAL ABSTRACTS FROM UNIVERSITIES				
Pennsylvania State University, Pennsylvania State Data Center, Middletown, PA http://pasdc.hbg.psu.edu/ Pennsylvania Abstract: A Statistical Fact Book	Annual	X	X	X
State University of New York: Nelson A. Rockefeller Institute of Government, Albany, NY http://www.rockinst.org/ New York State Statistical Yearbook	Annual	X	X	X
University of Florida: Bureau of Economic and Business Research, Gainesville, FL http://www.bebr.ufl.edu/ Florida Statistical Abstract 2011 (Final Edition)	Annual	X	X	X
Florida Statistical Abstract Online	Ongoing			X
University of Georgia: Selig Center for Economic Growth, Athens, GA http://www.terry.uga.edu/selig/ Georgia Statistical Abstract	Biennial	X	X	X
University of Kansas: Institute for Policy and Social Research, Lawrence, KS http://www.ipsr.ku.edu/ksdata/ksah/ Kansas Statistical Abstract	Annual		X	X
University of Missouri-Columbia: Economic and Policy Analysis Research Center, Columbia, MO http://eparc.missouri.edu/ Missouri Statistical Data Archive (online)	Ongoing		X	
University of Oklahoma: Center for Economic and Management Research, Norman, OK http://www.ou.edu/content/price/cemr/ Oklahoma Statistical Abstract	Periodic	X		
STATE STATISTICAL ABSTRACT FROM AN ASSOCIATION				
Texas State Historical Association, Denton, TX https://www.tshaonline.org/publications/books/31961 Texas Almanac	Biennial	X	X	X
STATE STATISTICAL ABSTRACTS FROM STATE AGENCIES				
California Department of Finance, Economic Research Unit, Sacramento, CA http://www.dof.ca.gov/HTML/FS_DATA/STAT-ABS/Statistical_Abstract.php California Statistical Abstract	Periodic		X	
Hawaii State Department of Business, Economic Development & Tourism, Honolulu, HI http://dbedt.hawaii.gov/economic/databook/ State of Hawaii Data Book	Annual		X	
Maryland State Data Center, Maryland Department of Planning, Baltimore, MD http://www.mdp.state.md.us/msdc/ Maryland Statistical Handbook	Periodic		X	
South Carolina, Budget and Control Board, Office of Research and Statistics, Columbia, SC http://abstract.sc.gov/ South Carolina Statistical Abstract	Ongoing			X

Source: ProQuest research.

Guide to State Statistical Abstracts

This bibliography includes the most recent statistical abstracts for states published since 2000, plus those that will be issued in 2013. For some states, a near equivalent has been listed in substitution for, or in addition to, a statistical abstract. All sources contain statistical tables on a variety of subjects for the state as a whole, its component parts, or both. Internet sites also contain statistical data.

Alabama

University of Alabama, Center for Business and Economic Research, Box 870221, Tuscaloosa, AL 35487-0221. 205-348-6191. Fax: 205-348-2951. Internet site <http://cber.cba.ua.edu/>.
Alabama Economic Outlook, 2013. Annual. Print.

Alaska

Department of Commerce, Community and Economic Development, 550 West 7 th Avenue, Suite 1770, Anchorage, AK 99501. 907-269-8100. Internet site <http://commerce.alaska.gov/dnn/dcra/Home.aspx>.
The Alaska Economic Performance Report, 2009. Online.

Arizona

University of Arizona, Economic and Business Research Center, Eller College of Management, 1130 East Helen Street, McClelland Hall, Rm. 405, P.O. Box 210108, Tucson, AZ 85721-0108. 520-621-2155. Internet site <http://www.ebr.eller.arizona.edu/>.
Arizona's Economy. Quarterly. Online.

Arkansas

University of Arkansas at Little Rock, Institute for Economic Advancement, Economic Research, 2801 South University Avenue, Little Rock, AR 72204-1099. 501-569-8542. Fax: 501-569-8538. Internet site <http://www.iea.ualr.edu/resourcelinks-101/library/publications.html>.
Arkansas State and Country Economic Data, 2013. Annual. Print and Online.
Arkansas Personal Income Handbook, 2013. Annual. Print and Online.

California

Department of Finance, 915 L Street, Sacramento, CA 95814. 916-445-3878. Internet site <http://www.dof.ca.gov/HTML/FS_DATA/STAT-ABS/Statistical_Abstract.php>.
California Statistical Abstract, 2008. Online.

Colorado

University of Colorado at Boulder, Government Publications Library, University Libraries, 184 UCB, 1720 Pleasant Street, Boulder, CO 80309-0184. 303-492-7521. Internet site <http://www.colorado.edu/libraries/govpubs/online.htm>.
Colorado by the Numbers. Online.

Colorado Office of Economic Development and International Trade, 1625 Broadway, Suite 2700, Denver, CO 80202. 303-892-3840. Fax: 303-892-3848. Internet site <http://www.advancecolorado.com>.
Colorado Data Book, 2010-11. Online.

Connecticut

Connecticut Department of Economic and Community Development, 505 Hudson Street, Hartford, CT 06106-7106. 860-270-8000. Internet site <http://www.ct.gov/ecd/site/default.asp>.
Connecticut Town Profiles, 2012. Recurring. Online.

Delaware

Delaware Economic Development Office, 99 Kings Highway, Dover, DE 19901-7305. 302-739-4271. Fax: 302-739-5749. Internet site <http://dedo.delaware.gov>.
Delaware Data Book, 2013. Online.

District of Columbia

Business Resource Center, John A. Wilson Building, 1350 Pennsylvania Avenue, NW, Washington, DC 20004. 202-727-1000. Internet site <http://brc.dc.gov/resources/facts.asp>.
Market Facts and Statistics. Online.

Florida

University of Florida, Bureau of Economic and Business Research, P.O. Box 117145, 221 Matherly Hall, Gainesville, FL 32611-7145. 352-392-0171. Fax: 352-392-4739. Internet site <http://www.bebr.ufl.edu/data>.
Florida Statistical Abstract, 2011. Annual. Print and Electronic.

Georgia

University of Georgia, Terry College of Business, Selig Center for Economic Growth, Athens, GA 30602-6254. 706-542-8100. Fax: 706-542-3835 Internet site <http://www.terry.uga.edu/selig>.
Georgia Statistical Abstract, 2012-13. Biennial. Print and Online.

University of Georgia, Carl Vinson Institute of Government, 201 N. Milledge Ave., Athens, GA 30602. 706-542-2736. Fax: 706-542-9301. Internet site <http://www.georgiastats.uga.edu/>.
The Georgia County Guide, 2013. Annual. Print and Online.

Hawaii

Hawaii State Department of Business, Economic Development & Tourism, Research and Economic Analysis Division, Statistics and Data Support Branch, P.O. Box 2359, Honolulu, HI 96804. 808-586-2480. Internet site <http://dbedt.hawaii.gov/economic/databook/>.
2012 State of Hawaii Data Book. Annual. Online.

Idaho

Idaho Department of Labor, 317 West Main St., Boise, ID 83735. 208-332-3570. Fax: 208-334-6300. Internet site <http://labor.idaho.gov>.

Idaho Department of Commerce, 700 W. State St. P.O. Box 832720. 208-334-2470. Internet site <http://commerce.idaho.gov>.
Idaho at a Glance. Online.
Idaho Community Profiles. Online.

Illinois

University of Illinois, Institute of Government and Public Affairs 1007 W. Nevada Street, Urbana, IL 61801, MC-037. 217-333-3340. Fax: 217-244-4817. Internet site <http://www.igpa.uillinois.edu/>.

Indiana

Indiana University, Kelley School of Business, Indiana Business Research Center, 100 South College Avenue, Suite 240, Bloomington, IN 47404. 812-855-5507. Internet site <http://www.ibrc.indiana.edu/>.
STATS Indiana. Online.

Iowa

Iowa State University of Science and Technology: Community Indicators Program, 17 East Hall, Ames, IA 50010. 515-294-9903. Internet site <http://www.icip.iastate.edu/recap>.
Community Indicators. Online.

State Library of Iowa, State Data Center, Ola Babcock Miller Building, 1112 East Grand, Des Moines, IA 50319-0233. 800-248-4483. Fax: 515-242-6543. Internet site <http://www.iowadatacenter.org>.

Kansas

University of Kansas, Institute for Policy and Social Research, 1541 Lilac Lane, 607 Blake Hall, Lawrence, KS 66045-3129. 785-864-3701. Fax: 785-864-3683. Internet site <http://www.ipsr.ku.edu/ksdata/ksah/>.
Kansas Statistical Abstract, 2012. Online.

Kentucky

Kentucky Cabinet for Economic Development, Old Capitol Annex, 300 West Broadway, Frankfort, KY 40601. 800-626-2930. Internet site <http://www.thinkkentucky.com/>.

Louisiana

Louisiana State Census Data Center, Office of Electronic Services, 1201 N. Third Street, Suite 7-210, Baton Rouge, LA, 70802. Fax: 225-219-4027. Internet site <http://www.louisiana.gov/Explore/Demographics_and_Geography/>.

Maine

Department of Administrative and Financial Services, 78 State House Station, 19 Union Street, Augusta, ME 04333. Internet site <http://www.maine.gov/portal/facts_history/statistics.html>.

Maryland

Maryland Department of Planning, 301 W. Preston St., Baltimore, MD 21201. 410-676-4450. Internet site <http://www.mdp.state.md.us/msdc/>.
2011 Maryland Statistical Handbook. Annual. Online.

Massachusetts

MassCHIP, Massachusetts Department of Public Health, 250 Washington Street, Boston, MA 02108-4619. 617-624-6000. Internet site <http://mass.gov/dph/masschip>. Instant Topics. Online.

Michigan

Michigan Economic Development Corporation, 300 North Washington Square, Lansing, MI 48913. 1-888-522-0103. Internet site <http://www.michiganbusiness.org>.

Minnesota

Minnesota Department of Employment and Economic Development, 1st National Bank Building, 332 Minnesota Street, Suite E200, Saint Paul, MN 55101-1351. 800-657-3858. Internet site <http://www.deed.state.mn.us/facts/index.htm>.
Compare Minnesota: Profiles of Minnesota's Economy & Population. Online.

Minnesota State Demographic Center, 658 Cedar Street Room 300, Saint Paul, MN 55155, 651-296-2557. Internet site <http://www.demography.state.mn.us/>.

Mississippi

Mississippi State University, University Libraries, P.O. Box 5408, Mississippi State, MS 39762. 662-325-0810. Internet site <http://guides.library.msstate.edu/>
Mississippi Statistical Abstract, 2007. Discontinued.

Missouri

University of Missouri-Columbia, Economic and Policy Analysis Research Center, 10 Professional Building, Columbia, MO 65211. 573-882-4805. Fax: 573-882-5563. Internet site <http://eparc.missouri.edu/>.
Missouri Statistical Data Archive. Online.

Montana

Montana Department of Commerce, Census and Economic Information Center, 301 S. Park Ave., P.O. Box 200505, Helena, MT 59620-0505, 406-841-2740. Fax: 406-841-2731. Internet site <http://ceic.mt.gov/>.

Nebraska

Nebraska Department of Economic Development, P. O. Box 94666, 301 Centennial Mall South, Lincoln, NE 68509-4666. 800-426-6505. Fax: 402-471-3778. Internet site <http://info.neded.org/>.

Nevada

Nevada Department of Administration, Budget Division, 209 East Musser Street, Room 200, Carson City, NV 89701-4298. 775-684-0222. Fax: 775-684-0260. Internet site <http://www.budget.state.nv.us/>.

New Hampshire

New Hampshire Office of Energy and Planning, 107 Pleasant Street, Concord, NH 03301-8501. 603-271-2155. Fax: 603-271-2615. Internet site <http://www.nh.gov/oep/index.htm>.

New Jersey

State of New Jersey Department of Labor and Workforce Development, Bureau of Labor Market Information, P.O. Box 057 Trenton, NJ 08625-0057. 609-292-7376. Fax: 609-633-9240. Internet site <http://lwd.dol.state.nj.us/labor/lpa/LMI_index.html>.
Labor Market Information. Online.

New Mexico

University of New Mexico, Bureau of Business and Economic Research, MSC06 3510, 1 University of New Mexico, Albuquerque, NM 87131-0001. 505-277-6626. Fax: 505-277-2773. Internet site <http://bber.unm.edu/>.
New Mexico Business, Current Economic Report Monthly. Print and Online. FOR-UNM Bulletin. Quarterly. Online.

New York

Nelson A. Rockefeller Institute of Government, 411 State Street, Albany, NY 12203-1003. 518-443-5522. Fax: 518-443-5832. Internet site <http://www.rockinst.org/>.
New York State Statistical Yearbook, 2011. Annual. Print and Online.

North Carolina

Office of State Budget and Management, 116 West Jones Street, Raleigh, NC 27603-8005. 919-807-4700. Internet site <http://www.osbm.state.nc.us>.
State Comparisons. Online.

North Dakota

University of North Dakota, College of Business and Public Administration, 293 Centennial Dr., Stop 8098, Grand Forks, ND 58202-8098. 800-225-5863. Fax: 701-777-2019. Internet site <http://business.und.edu/>.

Ohio

Office of Research, Ohio Department Services Agency, 77 South High Street, P.O. Box 1001, Columbus, OH 43216-1001. 614-466-2116. Internet site <http://www.odod.state.oh.us/research>.
Research Products and Services. Updated continuously.
Ohio County Trends. Online.

Oklahoma

University of Oklahoma, Center for Economic and Management Research, Michael F. Price College of Business, 307 West Brooks, Suite 4, Norman OK 73019-4004. 405-325-2931. Fax: 405-325-7688. Internet site <http://www.ou.edu/price/cemr.html/>.
Statistical Abstract of Oklahoma, 2010. Print and Online.

Oregon

Secretary of State, Archives Division, Archives Bldg., 800 Summer Street, NE, Salem, OR 97310. 503-373-0701 ext.1. Fax: 503-378-4188. Internet site <http://arcweb.sos.state.or.us/>.
Oregon Blue Book. 2011 Centennial. Biennial. Online

Pennsylvania

Pennsylvania State Data Center, Institute of State and Regional Affairs, Penn State Harrisburg, 777 West Harrisburg Pike, Middletown, PA 17057-4898. 717-948-6336. Fax: 717-948-6754. Internet site <http://pasdc.hbg.psu.edu>.
Pennsylvania Statistical Abstract, 2013. Print and electronic.

Rhode Island

Rhode Island Economic Development Corporation, 315 Iron Horse Way, Suite 101, Providence, RI 02908. 401-278-9100. Fax: 401-273-8270. Internet site <http://www.riedc.com/>.
State and Community Profiles. Online.

South Carolina

Budget and Control Board, Office of Research and Statistics, 1919 Blanding Street, Columbia 29201. 803-898-9960. Internet site <http://abstract.sc.gov>.
South Carolina Statistical Abstract. Ongoing. Online.

South Dakota

South Dakota State University, Rural Life and Census Data Center, Box 504, Brookings, SD 57007. 605-688-4899. Fax: 605-677-5427. Internet site <http://www.sdstate.edu/soc/rlcdc/index.cfm>.
Preliminary Population Projections 2010-2035. Online.
South Dakota State and Demographic Profiles 2008. Online.

Tennessee

Tennessee State Data Center, 916 Volunteer Blvd., 716 Stokely Management Center, Knoxville, Tennessee 37996-0570. 865-974-6070. Fax: 865-974-3100. Internet site <http://tndata.utk.edu/>.

Texas

Texas State Historical Association, 1155 Union Circle #311580, Denton, TX 76203. 940-369-5243. Internet site <http://www.tshaonline.org/publications/books/3196>.
Texas Almanac, 2012-2013. Biennial. Print and Online.

Texas State Data Center and Office of the State Demographer, Institute for Demographic and Socioeconomic Research (IDSER), 501 W. César Chavez Blvd., San Antonio, TX 78207-4415. 210-458-6543. Fax: 210-458-6541. Internet site <http://osd.state.tx.us/>.

Utah

Governor's Office of Management and Budget, Demographic & Economic Analysis, Suite 150, P.O. Box 132210, Salt Lake City, UT 84114-2210. 801-538-1027. Fax: 801-538-1547. Internet site <http://www.governor.utah.gov/dea>.
2012 Economic Report to the Governor. Annual. Online.
Utah Data Guide Newsletter, 2012. Quarterly. Online.

Vermont

Department of Labor, Labor Market Information, 3 Green Mountain Drive, P.O. Box 488, Montpelier, VT 05601-0488. 802-828-4202. Fax: 802-828-4050. Internet site <http://www.vtlmi.info/>.
Vermont Economic-Demographic Profile, 2013. Annual. Online.

Virginia

University of Virginia, Weldon Cooper Center for Public Service, 2400 Old Ivy Road P.O. Box 400206, Charlottesville, VA 22904-4206. 434-982-5522. Internet site <http://www.coopercenter.org/publications>.
Stat Chat. Online.
Numbers Count. Online.

Washington

Washington State Office of Financial Management, Forecasting Division, P.O. Box 43113, Olympia, WA 98504-3113. 360-902-0555. Internet site <http://www.ofm.wa.gov/>.
Washington State Data Book, 2011. Biennial. Online.

West Virginia

West Virginia University, College of Business and Economics, Bureau of Business and Economic Research, 1601 University Ave, P.O. Box 6025, Morgantown, WV 26506-6025. 304-293-7760. Fax: 304-293-5652. Internet site <http://www.be.wvu.edu/demographics/demographicprofiles.htm>.
West Virginia Data Profile 2011. Annual. Online.
West Virginia Economic Outlook, 2013. Annual. Online.

Wisconsin

Wisconsin Legislative Reference Bureau, One East Main Street, Suite 200, Madison, WI 53703. 608-266-0341. Internet site <http://www.legis.state.wi.us/lrb/pubs/bluebook.htm/>.
2013-2014 Wisconsin Blue Book. Biennial. Online.

Wyoming

Department of Administration and Information, Economic Analysis Division, 2800 Central Avenue, Cheyenne, WY 82002-0060. 307-777-7504. Fax: 307-632-1819. Internet site <http://eadiv.state.wy.us/>.
The Equality State Almanac, 2010. Annual. Online.

Guide to Foreign Statistical Abstracts

This bibliography presents recent statistical abstracts for member nations of the Organization for Economic Cooperation and Development and Russia. All sources contain statistical tables on a variety of subjects for the individual countries. Many of the following publications provide text in English as well as in the national language(s). For further information on these publications, contact the named statistical agency responsible for editing the publication.

Australia

Australian Bureau of Statistics, Canberra. <http://www.abs.gov.au>.
Year Book Australia. Annual. 2012. (In English.)

Austria

Statistik Austria, 1110 Wien. <http://www.statistik.at/index.shtml>.
Statistisches Jahrbuch Osterreichs. Annual. 2013. With CD-ROM. (In German.) With English translations of table headings.

Belgium

Statistics Belgium, WTC III, Bd. Simon Bolivar 30, B-1000 Brussels. <http://statbel.fgov.be/en>.
Key Figures: Statistical Overview of Belgium. Annual. 2012. (In English.)

Canada

Statistics Canada, Ottawa, Ontario, KIA OT6. <http://www.statcan.ca/start-debut-eng.html>.
Canada Year book. Annual. 2012. (In English.)

Czech Republic

Cesky Statisicky Urad, Na padesatem 81, Praha 10. <http://www.czso.cz/>.
Statisticka Rocenka Ceske Republiky. Annual. 2012. With CD-ROM. (In English and Czech.)

Denmark

Danmarks Statistik, Sejrogade 11, 2100 Kobenhavn O. <http://www.dst.dk>.
Statistisk ARBOG. Annual. 2013. English version available only on internet and is free of charge at: <www.dst.dk/yearbook>. (Printed version in Danish only.)

Finland

Statistics Finland, Helsinki. <http://www.stat.fi/comment>.
Statistical Yearbook of Finland, Annual. 2012. With CD-ROM. (In English, Finnish, and Swedish.)

France

Institut National de la Statistique et des Etudes Economiques, 18, Blvd. Adolphe Pinard, 75675 Paris (Cedex 14). <http://www.insee.fr/en/>.
Tableaux de l'Economie Francaise. Annual. 2013. (In French.)

Germany

Statistiches Bundesamt, Wiesbaden. <http://www.destatis.de/contact>.
Statistisches Jahrbuch fur die Bundesrepublic Deutschland. Annual. 2012. (In German.)

Greece

Hellenic Statistical Authority. <http://www.statistics.gr/>.
Concise Statistical Yearbook 2009. (In English and Greek.)
Statistical Yearbook of Greece. Annual. 2009/2010. (In English and Greek.)

Hungary

Hungarian Central Statistical Office, 1024 Budapest. <http://www.ksh.hu>.
Statistical Yearbook of Hungary, Annual. 2012. With CD-ROM. (In English and Hungarian.)

Iceland

Statistics Iceland. Borgartuni 21a, 150 Reykjavik. <http://www.staticd.is>.
Statistical Yearbook of Iceland. Annual. 2012. (In English and Icelandic.)

Ireland

Central Statistics Office, Skehard Road, Cork. <http://www.cso.ie>.
Statistical Yearbook of Ireland. Annual. 2013. (In English.)

Italy

Istituto Nazionale di Statistica. Via Cesare Balbo 16, 00184 Roma. <http://www.istat.it>.
Annuario Statistico Italiano. Annual. 2012. With CD-ROM. (In Italian.)
Compendio Statistico Italiano. Annual. 2012. (In English and Italian.)

Japan

Statistics Bureau, Ministry of Internal Affairs and Communications, Tokyo, Japan. <http://www.stat.go.jp/english/data/index.htm>.
Japan Statistical Yearbook. Annual. 2013. (In English and Japanese.)

Korea, South

Statistics Korea, Daejeon Government, #920 Dunsan-dong Seo-gu, Daejeon, Korea 302 701. <http://korstat.go.kr/>.
Korea Statistical Yearbook. Annual. 2012. (In Korean and English.)

Luxembourg

Service Central de la Statistique et des Etudes Economiques, Luxembourg. <www.statec.lu/>.
Annuaire Statisque du Luxembourg. 2012. (In French.)

Mexico

Instituto Nacional de Estadistica y Geografia (INEGI), Av. Heroe Nacozari Num. 2301 Fracc. Jardines del Parque, CP 20270 Aguascalientes, Ags. <http://www.inegi.org.mx>.
Anuario Estadistico de los Estados Unidos Mexicanos. Annual. 2012. (In Spanish.)
Agenda Estadistica. Annual. 2010. (In Spanish.)

Netherlands

Statistics Netherlands, Henri Faasdreef 312, 2492 JP, The Hague. <http://www.cbs.nl/en/>.
Statistical Yearbook of the Netherlands. Annual. 2013. (In English.)

New Zealand

Statistics, New Zealand, Wellington. <http://www.stats.govt.nz/>.
New Zealand Official Yearbook. Annual. 2012. (In English.)

Norway

Statistics Norway, Oslo/Kongsvinger. <http://www.ssb.no/en/>.
Statistical Yearbook of Norway. Annual. 2012. (In English.)

Poland

Central Statistical Office al. Niepodleglosci 208, 00-925 Warsaw. <http://www.stat.gov.pl/english/index.htm>.
Concise Statistical Yearbook of Poland. Annual. 2013. (In Polish and English.)
Statistical Yearbook of the Republic of Poland Annual. 2012. (In Polish and English.)

Portugal

Instituto Nacional de Estatistica, Av. Antonio Jose de Almeida, P-1000-043 Lisboa. <http://www.ine.pt/index_eng.htm>.
Anuario Estatistico de Portugal. Annual. 2011. (In Portuguese and English.)

Russia

Federal State Statistics Service, Moscow. <http://www.gks.ru/>.
Russia in Figures. Annual. 2012. (In Russian.)

Slovakia

Statisticky Urad Slovenskej Republiky, Mileticova 3, 824 67 Bratislava 26. <http://portal.statistics.sk>.
Statisticka Rocenka Slovenskej Republiky. Annual. 2011. (In English and Slovak.) With CD-ROM.

Spain

Instituto Nacional de Estadistica (INE); Paseo de la Castellana, 183, 28046 Madrid. <http://www.ine.es/en/welcome_en.htm>.
Anuario Estadistico de Espana. Annual. 2013. (In Spanish.)

Sweden

Statistika Centralbyran, Box 24300, 104 51 Stockholm. <http://www.scb.se/>.
Statistik Arsbok for Sverige. Annual. 2013. (In English and Swedish.)

Switzerland

Verlag Neue Zurcher Zeitung, Zurich.
Statisches Jahrbuch der Schweiz. Annual. 2013. With CD-ROM. (In French and German.)

Turkey

Turkish Statistical Institute, Ankara. <http://www.turkstat.gov.tr>.
Turkey's Statistical Yearbook. Annual. 2012. (In English and Turkish.)
Turkey in Statistics. Annual. 2012. (In English and Turkish.)

United Kingdom

Office for National Statistics, London, <http://www.ons.gov.uk/>.
Annual Abstract of Statistics. Annual. 2010. (In English.)

Metropolitan and Micropolitan Statistical Areas: Concepts, Components, and Population

The United States Office of Management and Budget (OMB) defines metropolitan and micropolitan statistical areas according to published standards that are applied to U.S. Census Bureau data. The general concept of a metropolitan or micropolitan statistical area is that of a core area containing a substantial population nucleus, together with adjacent communities having a high degree of economic and social integration with that core. Currently defined metropolitan and micropolitan statistical areas are based on application of 2010 standards (which appeared in the Federal Register on June 28, 2010) to 2010 decennial census data. Current metropolitan and micropolitan statistical area definitions were announced by OMB effective February 2013.

Standard definitions of metropolitan areas were first issued in 1949 by the then Bureau of the Budget (predecessor of OMB), under the designation "standard metropolitan area" (SMA). The term was changed to "standard metropolitan statistical area" (SMSA) in 1959 and to "metropolitan statistical area" (MSA) in 1983. The term "metropolitan area" (MA) was adopted in 1990 and referred collectively to metropolitan statistical areas (MSAs), consolidated metropolitan statistical areas (cMSAs), and primary metropolitan statistical areas (PMSAs). The term "core-based statistical area" (CBSA) became effective in 2000 and refers collectively to metropolitan and micropolitan statistical areas.

OMB has been responsible for the official metropolitan areas since they were first defined, except for the period 1977 to 1981, when they were the responsibility of the Office of Federal Statistical Policy and Standards, U.S. Department of Commerce. The standards for defining metropolitan areas were modified in 1958, 1971, 1975, 1980, 1990, 2000, and 2010.

Defining Metropolitan and Micropolitan Statistical Areas—The 2010 standards provide that each CBSA must contain at least one urban area of 10,000 or more population. Each metropolitan statistical area must have at least one urbanized area of 50,000 or more inhabitants. Each micropolitan statistical area must have at least one urban cluster of at least 10,000 but less than 50,000 population.

Under the standards, the county (or counties) in which at least 50 percent of the population resides within urban areas of 10,000 or more population, or that contain at least 5,000 people residing within a single urban area of 10,000 or more population, is identified as a "central county" (counties). Additional "outlying counties" are included in the CBSA if they meet specified requirements of commuting to or from the central counties. Counties or equivalent entities form the geographic "building blocks" for metropolitan and micropolitan statistical areas throughout the United States and Puerto Rico.

If specified criteria are met, a metropolitan statistical area containing a single core with a population of 2.5 million or more may be subdivided to form smaller groupings of counties referred to as "metropolitan divisions."

As of February 2013, there are 381 metropolitan statistical areas and 536 micropolitan statistical areas in the United States. In addition, there are 7 metropolitan statistical areas and 5 micropolitan statistical areas in Puerto Rico.

Principal Cities and Metropolitan and Micropolitan Statistical Area Titles—The largest city in each metropolitan or micropolitan statistical area is designated a "principal city." Additional cities qualify if specified requirements are met concerning population size and employment. The title of each metropolitan or micropolitan statistical area consists of the names of up to three of its principal cities in order of descending population size and the name of each state into which the metropolitan or micropolitan statistical area extends. Titles of metropolitan divisions also typically are based on principal city names, but in certain cases consist of county names.

Defining New England City and Town Areas—In view of the importance of cities and towns in New England, the 2010 standards also provide for a set of geographic areas that are defined using cities and towns in the six New England states. The New England city and town areas (NECTAs) are defined using the same criteria as metropolitan and micropolitan statistical areas and are identified as either metropolitan or micropolitan, based, respectively, on the presence of either an urbanized area of 50,000 or more population or an urban cluster of at least 10,000 but less than 50,000 population. If the specified criteria are met, a NECTA containing a single core with a population of at least 2.5 million may be subdivided to form smaller groupings of cities and towns referred to as New England city and town area divisions.

Changes in Definitions Over Time—Changes in the definitions of these statistical areas since the 1950 census have consisted chiefly of (1) the recognition of new areas as they reached the minimum required city or urbanized area population and (2) the addition of counties (or cities and towns in New England) to existing areas as new decennial census data showed them to qualify.

In some instances, formerly separate areas have been merged, components of an area have been transferred from one area to another, or components have been dropped from an area. The large majority of changes have taken place on the basis of decennial census data. However, Census Bureau data serve as the basis for intercensal updates in specified circumstances.

Because of these historical changes in geographic definitions, users must be cautious in comparing data for these statistical areas from different dates. For some purposes, comparisons of data for areas as defined at given dates may be appropriate; for other purposes, it may be preferable to maintain consistent area definitions. Historical metropolitan area definitions are available for 1999, 1993, 1990, 1983, 1981, 1973, 1970, 1963, 1960, and 1950.

Excluding Tables 21 through 25 in the Population section; Table 622 in the Labor Force section; Table 711 in the Income section, and the tables that follow in this appendix, the tables presenting data for metropolitan areas in this edition of the Statistical Abstract are based on the 1999 or earlier metropolitan area definitions. For a list of component counties according to the 1999 definition, see Appendix II in the 2002 edition of the Statistical Abstract or <http://www.census.gov/population/www/estimates/pastmetro.html>.

Table A. Metropolitan Statistical Areas and Components—Population: 2012

[In thousands (167 represents 167,000). Population as of July 2012. Metropolitan Statistical Areas defined by the U.S. Office of Management and Budget as of February 2013. All Metropolitan Statistical Areas are arranged alphabetically]

Metropolitan Statistical Area ~~Metropolitan Division ~~~~Component county	Population, 2012 (1,000)
Abilene, TX	**167**
Callahan County, TX	14
Jones County, TX	20
Taylor County, TX	133
Akron, OH	**702**
Portage County, OH	161
Summit County, OH	541
Albany, GA	**157**
Baker County, GA	3
Dougherty County, GA	95
Lee County, GA	29
Terrell County, GA	9
Worth County, GA	22
Albany-Schenectady-Troy, NY	**875**
Albany County, NY	305
Rensselaer County, NY	160
Saratoga County, NY	222
Schenectady County, NY	155
Schoharie County, NY	32
Albuquerque, NM	**902**
Bernalillo County, NM	673
Sandoval County, NM	136
Torrance County, NM	16
Valencia County, NM	77
Alexandria, LA	**154**
Grant Parish, LA	22
Rapides Parish, LA	132
Allentown-Bethlehem-Easton, PA-NJ	**827**
Warren County, NJ	108
Carbon County, PA	65
Lehigh County, PA	355
Northampton County, PA	299
Altoona, PA	**127**
Blair County, PA	127
Amarillo, TX	**258**
Armstrong County, TX	2
Carson County, TX	6
Oldham County, TX	2
Potter County, TX	122
Randall County, TX	125
Ames, IA	**91**
Story County, IA	91
Anchorage, AK	**393**
Anchorage Municipality, AK	299
Matanuska-Susitna Borough, AK	94
Ann Arbor, MI	**351**
Washtenaw County, MI	351
Anniston-Oxford, AL	**117**
Calhoun County, AL	117
Appleton, WI	**228**
Calumet County, WI	50
Outagamie County, WI	179
Asheville, NC	**432**
Buncombe County, NC	244
Haywood County, NC	59
Henderson County, NC	108
Madison County, NC	21
Athens-Clarke County, GA	**196**
Clarke County, GA	120
Madison County, GA	28
Oconee County, GA	34
Oglethorpe County, GA	15
Atlanta-Sandy Springs-Marietta, GA	**5,458**
Barrow County, GA	70
Bartow County, GA	101
Butts County, GA	24
Carroll County, GA	112
Cherokee County, GA	221
Clayton County, GA	266
Cobb County, GA	707
Coweta County, GA	131
Dawson County, GA	22
DeKalb County, GA	707
Douglas County, GA	134
Fayette County, GA	108
Forsyth County, GA	188
Fulton County, GA	978
Gwinnett County, GA	842
Haralson County, GA	28
Heard County, GA	12
Henry County, GA	209
Jasper County, GA	14
Lamar County, GA	18
Meriwether County, GA	21
Morgan County, GA	18
Newton County, GA	102
Paulding County, GA	145
Pickens County, GA	29
Pike County, GA	18
Rockdale County, GA	86
Spalding County, GA	64
Walton County, GA	85
Atlantic City-Hammonton, NJ	**275**
Atlantic County, NJ	275
Auburn-Opelika, AL	**147**
Lee County, AL	147
Augusta-Richmond County, GA-SC	**576**
Burke County, GA	23
Columbia County, GA	132
Lincoln County, GA	8
McDuffie County, GA	22
Richmond County, GA	203
Aiken County, SC	163
Edgefield County, SC	26
Austin-Round Rock-San Marcos, TX	**1,834**
Bastrop County, TX	75
Caldwell County, TX	39
Hays County, TX	169
Travis County, TX	1,096
Williamson County, TX	456
Bakersfield-Delano, CA	**856**
Kern County, CA	856
Baltimore-Towson, MD	**2,753**
Anne Arundel County, MD	550
Baltimore County, MD	817
Carroll County, MD	167
Harford County, MD	249
Howard County, MD	299
Queen Anne's County, MD	49
Baltimore city, MD	621
Bangor, ME	**154**
Penobscot County, ME	154
Barnstable Town, MA	**215**
Barnstable County, MA	215
Baton Rouge, LA	**815**
Ascension Parish, LA	112
East Baton Rouge Parish, LA	445
East Feliciana Parish, LA	20
Iberville Parish, LA	33
Livingston Parish, LA	132
Pointe Coupee Parish, LA	23
St. Helena Parish, LA	11
West Baton Rouge Parish, LA	24
West Feliciana Parish, LA	15
Battle Creek, MI	**135**
Calhoun County, MI	135
Bay City, MI	**107**
Bay County, MI	107
Beaumont-Port Arthur, TX	**404**
Hardin County, TX	55
Jefferson County, TX	252
Newton County, TX	14
Orange County, TX	83
Beckley, WV	**125**
Fayette County, WV	46
Raleigh County, WV	79
Bellingham, WA	**205**
Whatcom County, WA	205
Bend, OR	**162**
Deschutes County, OR	162
Billings, MT	**163**
Carbon County, MT	10
Golden Valley County, MT	1
Yellowstone County, MT	152
Binghamton, NY	**249**
Broome County, NY	198
Tioga County, NY	50
Birmingham-Hoover, AL	**1,137**
Bibb County, AL	23
Blount County, AL	58
Chilton County, AL	44
Jefferson County, AL	660
St. Clair County, AL	85
Shelby County, AL	201
Walker County, AL	66
Bismarck, ND	**120**
Burleigh County, ND	86
Morton County, ND	28
Oliver County, ND	2
Sioux County, ND	4
Blacksburg-Christiansburg-Radford, VA	**179**
Floyd County, VA	15
Giles County, VA	17
Montgomery County, VA	95
Pulaski County, VA	35
Radford city, VA	17
Bloomington, IN	**162**
Monroe County, IN	141
Owen County, IN	21
Bloomington-Normal, IL	**189**
De Witt County, IL	16
McLean County, IL	172
Bloomsburg-Berwick, PA	**85**
Columbia County, PA	67
Montour County, PA	18
Boise City-Nampa, ID	**638**
Ada County, ID	409
Boise County, ID	7
Canyon County, ID	194
Gem County, ID	17
Owyhee County, ID	11
Boston-Cambridge-Quincy, MA-NH	**4,641**
Boston-Quincy, MA	**1,926**
Norfolk County, MA	682
Plymouth County, MA	500
Suffolk County, MA	744
Cambridge-Newton-Framingham, MA	**2,293**
Essex County, MA	756
Middlesex County, MA	1,537
Rockingham County-Strafford County, NH	**422**
Rockingham County, NH	298
Strafford County, NH	124
Boulder, CO	**305**
Boulder County, CO	305
Bowling Green, KY	**162**
Allen County, KY	20
Butler County, KY	13
Edmonson County, KY	12
Warren County, KY	117
Bremerton-Silverdale, WA	**255**
Kitsap County, WA	255
Bridgeport-Stamford-Norwalk, CT	**934**
Fairfield County, CT	934
Brownsville-Harlingen, TX	**416**
Cameron County, TX	416
Brunswick, GA	**113**
Brantley County, GA	19
Glynn County, GA	81
McIntosh County, GA	14
Buffalo-Niagara Falls, NY	**1,134**
Erie County, NY	919
Niagara County, NY	215
Burlington, NC	**154**
Alamance County, NC	154
Burlington-South Burlington, VT	**214**
Chittenden County, VT	159
Franklin County, VT	48
Grand Isle County, VT	7
California-Lexington Park, MD	**109**

See footnotes at end of table.

Metropolitan Statistical Area ~~Metropolitan Division ~~~~Component county	Popu- lation, 2012 (1,000)
St. Mary's County, MD	109
Canton-Massillon, OH	**403**
Carroll County, OH	29
Stark County, OH	375
Cape Coral-Fort Myers, FL	**645**
Lee County, FL	645
Cape Girardeau-Jackson, **MO-IL**	**97**
Alexander County, IL	8
Bollinger County, MO	12
Cape Girardeau County, MO	77
Carbondale-Marion, IL	**127**
Jackson County, IL	60
Williamson County, IL	67
Carson City, NV	**55**
Carson City, NV	55
Casper, WY	**79**
Natrona County, WY	79
Cedar Rapids, IA	**262**
Benton County, IA	26
Jones County, IA	21
Linn County, IA	215
Chambersburg-Waynesboro, **PA**	**151**
Franklin County, PA	151
Champaign-Urbana, IL	**234**
Champaign County, IL	203
Ford County, IL	14
Piatt County, IL	17
Charleston, WV	**226**
Boone County, WV	24
Clay County, WV	9
Kanawha County, WV	192
Charleston-North **Charleston-Summerville,** **SC**	**697**
Berkeley County, SC	190
Charleston County, SC	365
Dorchester County, SC	142
Charlotte-Gastonia-Rock Hill, **NC-SC**	**2,297**
Cabarrus County, NC	184
Gaston County, NC	208
Iredell County, NC	163
Lincoln County, NC	79
Mecklenburg County, NC	969
Rowan County, NC	138
Union County, NC	209
Chester County, SC	33
Lancaster County, SC	79
York County, SC	235
Charlottesville, VA	**223**
Albemarle County, VA	102
Buckingham County, VA	17
Fluvanna County, VA	26
Greene County, VA	19
Nelson County, VA	15
Charlottesville city, VA	44
Chattanooga, TN-GA	**538**
Catoosa County, GA	65
Dade County, GA	16
Walker County, GA	68
Hamilton County, TN	346
Marion County, TN	28
Sequatchie County, TN	14
Cheyenne, WY	**94**
Laramie County, WY	94
Chicago-Joliet-Naperville, **IL-IN-WI**	**9,522**
Chicago-Joliet-Naperville, IL	**7,318**
Cook County, IL	5,231
DeKalb County, IL	105
DuPage County, IL	928
Grundy County, IL	50
Kane County, IL	522
Kendall County, IL	118
McHenry County, IL	308
Will County, IL	683
Elgin, IL	**627**
Gary, IN	**707**
Jasper County, IN	33
Lake County, IN	494
Newton County, IN	14

Metropolitan Statistical Area ~~Metropolitan Division ~~~~Component county	Popu- lation, 2012 (1,000)
Porter County, IN	166
Lake County-Kenosha County, **IL-WI**	**870**
Lake County, IL	702
Kenosha County, WI	168
Chico, CA	**222**
Butte County, CA	222
Cincinnati-Middletown, **OH-KY-IN**	**2,129**
Dearborn County, IN	50
Ohio County, IN	6
Union County, IN	7
Boone County, KY	123
Bracken County, KY	8
Campbell County, KY	91
Gallatin County, KY	8
Grant County, KY	24
Kenton County, KY	162
Pendleton County, KY	15
Brown County, OH	44
Butler County, OH	371
Clermont County, OH	199
Hamilton County, OH	802
Warren County, OH	217
Clarksville, TN-KY	**274**
Christian County, KY	75
Trigg County, KY	14
Montgomery County, TN	184
Cleveland, TN	**118**
Bradley County, TN	101
Polk County, TN	17
Cleveland-Elyria-Mentor, OH	**2,064**
Cuyahoga County, OH	1,265
Geauga County, OH	94
Lake County, OH	230
Lorain County, OH	301
Medina County, OH	174
Coeur d'Alene, ID	**142**
Kootenai County, ID	142
College Station-Bryan, TX	**235**
Brazos County, TX	201
Burleson County, TX	17
Robertson County, TX	17
Colorado Springs, CO	**668**
El Paso County, CO	645
Teller County, CO	23
Columbia, MO	**169**
Boone County, MO	169
Columbia, SC	**785**
Calhoun County, SC	15
Fairfield County, SC	23
Kershaw County, SC	62
Lexington County, SC	270
Richland County, SC	394
Saluda County, SC	20
Columbus, GA-AL	**311**
Russell County, AL	58
Chattahoochee County, GA	13
Harris County, GA	33
Marion County, GA	9
Muscogee County, GA	198
Columbus, IN	**79**
Bartholomew County, IN	79
Columbus, OH	**1,944**
Delaware County, OH	181
Fairfield County, OH	147
Franklin County, OH	1,196
Hocking County, OH	29
Licking County, OH	168
Madison County, OH	43
Morrow County, OH	35
Perry County, OH	36
Pickaway County, OH	56
Union County, OH	53
Corpus Christi, TX	**437**
Aransas County, TX	24
Nueces County, TX	348
San Patricio County, TX	66
Corvallis, OR	**86**
Benton County, OR	86

Metropolitan Statistical Area ~~Metropolitan Division ~~~~Component county	Popu- lation, 2012 (1,000)
Crestview-Fort Walton **Beach-Destin, FL**	**248**
Okaloosa County, FL	190
Walton County, FL	58
Cumberland, MD-WV	**102**
Allegany County, MD	74
Mineral County, WV	28
Dallas-Fort Worth-Arlington, **TX**	**6,701**
Dallas-Plano-Irving, TX	**4,427**
Collin County, TX	835
Dallas County, TX	2,454
Denton County, TX	707
Ellis County, TX	154
Hunt County, TX	87
Kaufman County, TX	107
Rockwall County, TX	83
Fort Worth-Arlington, TX	**2,274**
Hood County, TX	52
Johnson County, TX	153
Parker County, TX	120
Somervell County, TX	9
Tarrant County, TX	1,880
Wise County, TX	60
Dalton, GA	**143**
Murray County, GA	39
Whitfield County, GA	103
Danville, IL	**81**
Vermilion County, IL	81
Daphne-Fairhope-Foley, AL	**191**
Baldwin County, AL	191
Davenport-Moline-Rock Island, **IA-IL**	**383**
Henry County, IL	50
Mercer County, IL	16
Rock Island County, IL	147
Scott County, IA	169
Dayton, OH	**801**
Greene County, OH	164
Miami County, OH	103
Montgomery County, OH	534
Decatur, AL	**154**
Lawrence County, AL	34
Morgan County, AL	120
Decatur, IL	**110**
Macon County, IL	110
Deltona-Daytona **Beach-Ormond Beach, FL**	**595**
Flagler County, FL	98
Volusia County, FL	497
Denver-Aurora-Broomfield, **CO**	**2,645**
Adams County, CO	460
Arapahoe County, CO	596
Broomfield County, CO	58
Clear Creek County, CO	9
Denver County, CO	634
Douglas County, CO	298
Elbert County, CO	23
Gilpin County, CO	5
Jefferson County, CO	545
Park County, CO	16
Des Moines-West Des Moines, **IA**	**589**
Dallas County, IA	72
Guthrie County, IA	11
Madison County, IA	16
Polk County, IA	444
Warren County, IA	47
Detroit-Warren-Livonia, MI	**4,292**
Detroit-Livonia-Dearborn, MI	**1,792**
Wayne County, MI	1,792
Warren-Troy-Farmington Hills, **MI**	**2,500**
Lapeer County, MI	88
Livingston County, MI	183
Macomb County, MI	847
Oakland County, MI	1,221
St. Clair County, MI	161

See footnotes at end of table.

Table A. Metropolitan Statistical Areas and Components—Population:
2012-Continued.
See headnote on page 935.

Metropolitan Statistical Area ~~Metropolitan Division ~~~~Component county	Population, 2012 (1,000)
Dothan, AL.	148
Geneva County, AL.	27
Henry County, AL.	17
Houston County, AL.	103
Dover, DE.	168
Kent County, DE.	168
Dubuque, IA.	95
Dubuque County, IA.	95
Duluth, MN-WI.	279
Carlton County, MN.	35
St. Louis County, MN.	200
Douglas County, WI.	44
Durham-Chapel Hill, NC.	523
Chatham County, NC.	66
Durham County, NC.	280
Orange County, NC.	138
Person County, NC.	39
East Stroudsburg, PA.	169
Monroe County, PA.	169
Eau Claire, WI.	164
Chippewa County, WI.	63
Eau Claire County, WI.	101
El Centro, CA.	177
Imperial County, CA.	177
Elizabethtown, KY.	150
Hardin County, KY.	107
Larue County, KY.	14
Meade County, KY.	29
Elkhart-Goshen, IN.	200
Elkhart County, IN.	200
Elmira, NY.	89
Chemung County, NY.	89
El Paso, TX.	831
El Paso County, TX.	827
Hudspeth County, TX.	3
Erie, PA.	281
Erie County, PA.	281
Eugene-Springfield, OR.	355
Lane County, OR.	355
Evansville, IN-KY.	313
Posey County, IN.	26
Vanderburgh County, IN.	181
Warrick County, IN.	60
Henderson County, KY.	47
Fairbanks, AK.	100
Fairbanks North Star Borough, AK.	100
Fargo, ND-MN.	216
Clay County, MN.	60
Cass County, ND.	156
Farmington, NM.	129
San Juan County, NM.	129
Fayetteville, NC.	375
Cumberland County, NC.	324
Hoke County, NC.	51
Fayetteville-Springdale-Rogers, AR-MO.	482
Benton County, AR.	232
Madison County, AR.	16
Washington County, AR.	211
McDonald County, MO.	23
Flagstaff, AZ.	136
Coconino County, AZ.	136
Flint, MI.	418
Genesee County, MI.	418
Florence, SC.	206
Darlington County, SC.	68
Florence County, SC.	138
Florence-Muscle Shoals, AL.	147
Colbert County, AL.	54
Lauderdale County, AL.	93
Fond du Lac, WI.	102
Fond du Lac County, WI.	102
Fort Collins-Loveland, CO.	310
Larimer County, CO.	310
Fort Smith, AR-OK.	281
Crawford County, AR.	62
Sebastian County, AR.	127
Le Flore County, OK.	50
Sequoyah County, OK.	41

Metropolitan Statistical Area ~~Metropolitan Division ~~~~Component county	Population, 2012 (1,000)
Fort Wayne, IN.	421
Allen County, IN.	360
Wells County, IN.	28
Whitley County, IN.	33
Fresno, CA.	948
Fresno County, CA.	948
Gadsden, AL.	104
Etowah County, AL.	104
Gainesville, FL.	268
Alachua County, FL.	251
Gilchrist County, FL.	17
Gainesville, GA.	185
Hall County, GA.	185
Gettysburg, PA.	101
Adams County, PA.	101
Glens Falls, NY.	128
Warren County, NY.	66
Washington County, NY.	63
Goldsboro, NC.	124
Wayne County, NC.	124
Grand Forks, ND-MN.	99
Polk County, MN.	31
Grand Forks County, ND.	67
Grand Island, NE.	83
Hall County, NE.	60
Hamilton County, NE.	9
Howard County, NE.	6
Merrick County, NE.	8
Grand Junction, CO.	148
Mesa County, CO.	148
Grand Rapids-Wyoming, MI.	1,006
Barry County, MI.	59
Kent County, MI.	614
Montcalm County, MI.	63
Ottawa County, MI.	269
Grants Pass, OR.	83
Josephine County, OR.	83
Great Falls, MT.	82
Cascade County, MT.	82
Greeley, CO.	264
Weld County, CO.	264
Green Bay, WI.	311
Brown County, WI.	253
Kewaunee County, WI.	21
Oconto County, WI.	37
Greensboro-High Point, NC.	736
Guilford County, NC.	501
Randolph County, NC.	142
Rockingham County, NC.	93
Greenville, NC.	173
Pitt County, NC.	173
Greenville-Mauldin-Easley, SC.	843
Anderson County, SC.	189
Greenville County, SC.	468
Laurens County, SC.	66
Pickens County, SC.	120
Gulfport-Biloxi, MS.	380
Hancock County, MS.	45
Harrison County, MS.	194
Stone County, MS.	140
Hagerstown-Martinsburg, MD-WV.	256
Washington County, MD.	149
Berkeley County, WV.	107
Hammond, LA.	123
Tangipahoa Parish, LA.	123
Hanford-Corcoran, CA.	151
Kings County, CA.	151
Harrisburg-Carlisle, PA.	554
Cumberland County, PA.	239
Dauphin County, PA.	270
Perry County, PA.	46
Harrisonburg, VA.	128
Rockingham County, VA.	77
Harrisonburg city, VA.	51
Hartford-West Hartford-East Hartford, CT.	1,214
Hartford County, CT.	897
Middlesex County, CT.	166

Metropolitan Statistical Area ~~Metropolitan Division ~~~~Component county	Population, 2012 (1,000)
Tolland County, CT.	152
Hattiesburg, MS.	147
Forrest County, MS.	77
Lamar County, MS.	58
Perry County, MS.	12
Hickory-Lenoir-Morganton, NC.	364
Alexander County, NC.	37
Burke County, NC.	91
Caldwell County, NC.	82
Catawba County, NC.	154
Hilton Head Island-Bluffton-Beaufort, SC.	194
Beaufort County, SC.	168
Jasper County, SC.	26
Hinesville-Fort Stewart, GA.	82
Liberty County, GA.	65
Long County, GA.	16
Homosassa Springs, FL.	139
Citrus County, FL.	139
Hot Springs, AR.	97
Garland County, AR.	97
Houma-Thibodaux, LA.	209
Lafourche Parish, LA.	97
Terrebonne Parish, LA.	112
Honolulu, HI.	976
Honolulu County, HI.	976
Houston-Sugar Land-Baytown, TX.	6,177
Austin County, TX.	29
Brazoria County, TX.	325
Chambers County, TX.	36
Fort Bend County, TX.	627
Galveston County, TX.	300
Harris County, TX.	4,254
Liberty County, TX.	77
Montgomery County, TX.	485
Waller County, TX.	44
Huntington-Ashland, WV-KY-OH.	365
Boyd County, KY.	49
Greenup County, KY.	37
Lawrence County, OH.	62
Cabell County, WV.	97
Lincoln County, WV.	22
Putnam County, WV.	56
Wayne County, WV.	42
Huntsville, AL.	431
Limestone County, AL.	88
Madison County, AL.	343
Idaho Falls, ID.	136
Bonneville County, ID.	107
Butte County, ID.	3
Jefferson County, ID.	27
Indianapolis-Carmel, IN.	1,929
Boone County, IN.	59
Brown County, IN.	15
Hamilton County, IN.	289
Hancock County, IN.	71
Hendricks County, IN.	150
Johnson County, IN.	143
Madison County, IN.	130
Marion County, IN.	919
Morgan County, IN.	69
Putnam County, IN.	38
Shelby County, IN.	44
Iowa City, IA.	158
Johnson County, IA.	136
Washington County, IA.	22
Ithaca, NY.	103
Tompkins County, NY.	103
Jackson, MI.	160
Jackson County, MI.	160
Jackson, MS.	577
Copiah County, MS.	29
Hinds County, MS.	249
Madison County, MS.	98
Rankin County, MS.	145
Simpson County, MS.	27

Metropolitan Statistical Area ~~Metropolitan Division ~~~~Component county	Population, 2012 (1,000)
Yazoo County, MS	28
Jackson, TN	**130**
Chester County, TN	17
Crockett County, TN	15
Madison County, TN	99
Jacksonville, FL	**1,378**
Baker County, FL	27
Clay County, FL	194
Duval County, FL	880
Nassau County, FL	75
St. Johns County, FL	202
Jacksonville, NC	**183**
Onslow County, NC	183
Janesville, WI	**160**
Rock County, WI	160
Jefferson City, MO	**150**
Callaway County, MO	44
Cole County, MO	76
Moniteau County, MO	16
Osage County, MO	14
Johnson City, TN	**201**
Carter County, TN	57
Unicoi County, TN	18
Washington County, TN	125
Johnstown, PA	**142**
Cambria County, PA	142
Jonesboro, AR	**124**
Craighead County, AR	100
Poinsett County, AR	24
Joplin, MO	**174**
Jasper County, MO	115
Newton County, MO	59
Kahului-Wailuku-Lahaina, HI	**158**
Kalawao County, HI	(Z)
Maui County, HI	158
Kalamazoo-Portage, MI	**330**
Kalamazoo County, MI	255
Van Buren County, MI	75
Kankakee-Bradley, IL	**113**
Kankakee County, IL	113
Kansas City, MO-KS	**2,039**
Johnson County, KS	560
Leavenworth County, KS	78
Linn County, KS	9
Miami County, KS	33
Wyandotte County, KS	159
Bates County, MO	17
Caldwell County, MO	9
Cass County, MO	100
Clay County, MO	228
Clinton County, MO	21
Jackson County, MO	677
Lafayette County, MO	33
Platte County, MO	92
Ray County, MO	23
Kennewick-Pasco-Richland, WA	**268**
Benton County, WA	182
Franklin County, WA	86
Killeen-Temple-Fort Hood, TX	**420**
Bell County, TX	323
Coryell County, TX	77
Lampasas County, TX	20
Kingsport-Bristol-Bristol, TN-VA	**309**
Hawkins County, TN	57
Sullivan County, TN	157
Scott County, VA	23
Washington County, VA	55
Bristol city, VA	18
Kingston, NY	**182**
Ulster County, NY	182
Knoxville, TN	**848**
Anderson County, TN	75
Blount County, TN	124
Campbell County, TN	40
Grainger County, TN	23
Knox County, TN	441
Loudon County, TN	50
Morgan County, TN	22
Roane County, TN	53
Union County, TN	19
Kokomo, IN	**83**
Howard County, IN	83
La Crosse, WI-MN	**135**
Houston County, MN	19
La Crosse County, WI	116
Lafayette, IN	**206**
Benton County, IN	9
Carroll County, IN	20
Tippecanoe County, IN	178
Lafayette, LA	**474**
Lafayette Parish, LA	227
Acadia Parish, LA	62
Iberia Parish, LA	74
St. Martin Parish, LA	53
Vermilion Parish, LA	59
Lake Charles, LA	**201**
Calcasieu Parish, LA	194
Cameron Parish, LA	7
Lake Havasu City-Kingman, AZ	**203**
Mohave County, AZ	203
Lakeland-Winter Haven, FL	**616**
Polk County, FL	616
Lancaster, PA	**527**
Lancaster County, PA	527
Lansing-East Lansing, MI	**466**
Clinton County, MI	76
Eaton County, MI	108
Ingham County, MI	282
Laredo, TX	**259**
Webb County, TX	259
Las Cruces, NM	**214**
Doña Ana County, NM	214
Las Vegas-Paradise, NV	**2,001**
Clark County, NV	2,001
Lawrence, KS	**113**
Douglas County, KS	113
Lawton, OK	**133**
Comanche County, OK	126
Cotton County, OK	6
Lebanon, PA	**135**
Lebanon County, PA	135
Lewiston, ID-WA	**61**
Nez Perce County, ID	40
Asotin County, WA	22
Lewiston-Auburn, ME	**108**
Androscoggin County, ME	108
Lexington-Fayette, KY	**485**
Bourbon County, KY	20
Clark County, KY	36
Fayette County, KY	305
Jessamine County, KY	50
Scott County, KY	49
Woodford County, KY	25
Lima, OH	**105**
Allen County, OH	105
Lincoln, NE	**310**
Lancaster County, NE	293
Seward County, NE	17
Little Rock-North Little Rock-Conway, AR	**718**
Faulkner County, AR	119
Grant County, AR	18
Lonoke County, AR	70
Perry County, AR	10
Pulaski County, AR	389
Saline County, AR	112
Logan, UT-ID	**128**
Franklin County, ID	13
Cache County, UT	116
Longview, TX	**217**
Gregg County, TX	123
Rusk County, TX	54
Upshur County, TX	40
Longview, WA	**102**
Cowlitz County, WA	102
Los Angeles-Long Beach-Santa Ana, CA	**13,053**
Los Angeles-Long Beach-Glendale, CA	**9,963**
Los Angeles County, CA	9,963
Santa Ana-Anaheim-Irvine, CA	**3,090**
Orange County, CA	3,090
Louisville/Jefferson County, KY-IN	**1,251**
Clark County, IN	112
Floyd County, IN	75
Harrison County, IN	39
Scott County, IN	24
Washington County, IN	28
Bullitt County, KY	76
Henry County, KY	15
Jefferson County, KY	751
Oldham County, KY	61
Shelby County, KY	44
Spencer County, KY	17
Trimble County, KY	9
Lubbock, TX	**298**
Crosby County, TX	6
Lubbock County, TX	286
Lynn County, TX	6
Lynchburg, VA	**255**
Amherst County, VA	32
Appomattox County, VA	15
Bedford County, VA	70
Campbell County, VA	55
Bedford city, VA	6
Lynchburg city, VA	77
Macon, GA	**233**
Bibb County, GA	156
Crawford County, GA	13
Jones County, GA	29
Monroe County, GA	27
Twiggs County, GA	8
Madera-Chowchilla, CA	**152**
Madera County, CA	152
Madison, WI	**621**
Columbia County, WI	57
Dane County, WI	504
Green County, WI	37
Iowa County, WI	24
Manchester-Nashua, NH	**403**
Hillsborough County, NH	403
Manhattan, KS	**98**
Pottawatomie County, KS	22
Riley County, KS	76
Mankato-North Mankato, MN	**98**
Blue Earth County, MN	65
Nicollet County, MN	33
Mansfield, OH	**123**
Richland County, OH	123
McAllen-Edinburg-Mission, TX	**807**
Hidalgo County, TX	807
Medford, OR	**206**
Jackson County, OR	206
Memphis, TN-MS-AR	**1,342**
Crittenden County, AR	50
Benton County, MS	9
DeSoto County, MS	166
Marshall County, MS	37
Tate County, MS	28
Tunica County, MS	10
Fayette County, TN	39
Shelby County, TN	941
Tipton County, TN	62
Merced, CA	**262**
Merced County, CA	262
Miami-Fort Lauderdale-Pompano Beach, FL	**5,763**
Fort Lauderdale-Pompano Beach-Deerfield Beach, FL	**1,815**
Broward County, FL	1,815
Miami-Miami Beach-Kendall, FL	**2,591**
Miami-Dade County, FL	2,591
West Palm Beach-Boca Raton-Boynton Beach, FL	**1,357**

See footnotes at end of table.

Metropolitan Statistical Area ~~Metropolitan Division ~~~~Component county	Population, 2012 (1,000)
Palm Beach County, FL	1,357
Michigan City-La Porte, IN	**111**
LaPorte County, IN	111
Midland, MI	**84**
Midland County, MI	84
Midland, TX	**152**
Martin County, TX	5.017
Midland County, TX	147
Milwaukee-Waukesha-West	
Allis, WI	**1,567**
Milwaukee County, WI	955
Ozaukee County, WI	87
Washington County, WI	133
Waukesha County, WI	392
Minneapolis-St.	
Paul-Bloomington, MN-WI	**3,422**
Anoka County, MN	336
Carver County, MN	94
Chisago County, MN	53
Dakota County, MN	405
Hennepin County, MN	1,185
Isanti County, MN	38
Le Sueur County, MN	28
Mille Lacs County, MN	26
Ramsey County, MN	520
Scott County, MN	135
Sherburne County, MN	89
Sibley County, MN	15
Washington County, MN	244
Wright County, MN	127
Pierce County, WI	41
St. Croix County, WI	85
Missoula, MT	**111**
Missoula County, MT	111
Mobile, AL	**414**
Mobile County, AL	414
Modesto, CA	**522**
Stanislaus County, CA	522
Monroe, LA	**178**
Ouachita Parish, LA	155
Union Parish, LA	22
Monroe, MI	**151**
Monroe County, MI	151
Montgomery, AL	**377**
Autauga County, AL	56
Elmore County, AL	81
Lowndes County, AL	11
Montgomery County, AL	230
Morgantown, WV	**134**
Monongalia County, WV	100
Preston County, WV	34
Morristown, TN	**115**
Hamblen County, TN	63
Jefferson County, TN	52
Mount Vernon-Anacortes, WA	**118**
Skagit County, WA	118
Muncie, IN	**117**
Delaware County, IN	117
Muskegon-Norton Shores, MI	**170**
Muskegon County, MI	170
Myrtle Beach-North Myrtle	
Beach-Conway, SC	**395**
Brunswick County, NC	112
Horry County, SC	282
Napa, CA	**139**
Napa County, CA	139
Naples-Marco Island, FL	**332**
Collier County, FL	332
Nashville-Davidson--	
Murfreesboro--Franklin, TN	**1,727**
Cannon County, TN	14
Cheatham County, TN	39
Davidson County, TN	648
Dickson County, TN	50
Hickman County, TN	24
Macon County, TN	22
Maury County, TN	82
Robertson County, TN	67
Rutherford County, TN	274
Smith County, TN	19

Metropolitan Statistical Area ~~Metropolitan Division ~~~~Component county	Population, 2012 (1,000)
Sumner County, TN	166
Trousdale County, TN	8
Williamson County, TN	193
Wilson County, TN	119
New Bern, NC	**128**
Craven County, NC	105
Jones County, NC	10
Pamlico County, NC	13
New Haven-Milford, CT	**863**
New Haven County, CT	863
New Orleans-Metairie-Kenner,	
LA	**1,227**
Jefferson Parish, LA	434
Orleans Parish, LA	369
Plaquemines Parish, LA	24
St. Bernard Parish, LA	42
St. Charles Parish, LA	53
St. James Parish, LA	22
St. John the Baptist Parish, LA	45
St. Tammany Parish, LA	239
New York-Northern New	
Jersey-Long Island,	
NY-NJ-PA	**19,832**
Nassau-Suffolk, NY	**2,849**
Nassau County, NY	1,349
Suffolk County, NY	1,499
Dutchess County-Putnam	
County, NY	**397**
Dutchess County, NY	297
Putnam County, NY	100
Newark-Union, NJ-PA	**2,489**
Essex County, NJ	788
Hunterdon County, NJ	127
Morris County, NJ	498
Somerset County, NJ	328
Sussex County, NJ	147
Union County, NJ	544
Pike County, PA	57
New York-White Plains-Wayne,	
NY-NJ	**14,098**
Bergen County, NJ	919
Hudson County, NJ	652
Middlesex County, NJ	823
Monmouth County, NJ	629
Ocean County, NJ	580
Passaic County, NJ	503
Bronx County, NY	1,408
Kings County, NY	2,566
New York County, NY	1,619
Orange County, NY	375
Queens County, NY	2,273
Richmond County, NY	471
Rockland County, NY	318
Westchester County, NY	962
Niles-Benton Harbor, MI	**156**
Berrien County, MI	156
North Port-Bradenton-	
Sarasota, FL	**720**
Manatee County, FL	334
Sarasota County, FL	386
Norwich-New London, CT	**274**
New London County, CT	274
Ocala, FL	**335**
Marion County, FL	335
Ocean City, NJ	**96**
Cape May County, NJ	96
Odessa, TX	**144**
Ector County, TX	144
Ogden-Clearfield, UT	**612**
Box Elder County, UT	50
Davis County, UT	316
Morgan County, UT	10
Weber County, UT	237
Oklahoma City, OK	**1,297**
Canadian County, OK	123
Cleveland County, OK	266
Grady County, OK	53
Lincoln County, OK	34
Logan County, OK	44
McClain County, OK	36

Metropolitan Statistical Area ~~Metropolitan Division ~~~~Component county	Population, 2012 (1,000)
Oklahoma County, OK	742
Olympia, WA	**258**
Thurston County, WA	258
Omaha-Council Bluffs, NE-IA	**886**
Harrison County, IA	15
Mills County, IA	15
Pottawattamie County, IA	93
Cass County, NE	25
Douglas County, NE	531
Sarpy County, NE	166
Saunders County, NE	21
Washington County, NE	20
Orlando-Kissimmee-Sanford,	
FL	**2,224**
Lake County, FL	303
Orange County, FL	1,202
Osceola County, FL	287
Seminole County, FL	431
Oshkosh-Neenah, WI	**169**
Winnebago County, WI	169
Owensboro, KY	**116**
Daviess County, KY	98
Hancock County, KY	9
McLean County, KY	10
Oxnard-Thousand	
Oaks-Ventura, CA	**836**
Ventura County, CA	836
Palm Bay-Melbourne-Titusville,	
FL	**547**
Brevard County, FL	547
Panama City-Lynn	
Haven-Panama City Beach,	
FL	**188**
Bay County, FL	172
Gulf County, FL	16
Parkersburg-Marietta-Vienna,	
WV-OH	**93**
Wirt County, WV	6
Wood County, WV	87
Pensacola-Ferry Pass-Brent,	
FL	**461**
Escambia County, FL	303
Santa Rosa County, FL	159
Peoria, IL	**380**
Marshall County, IL	12
Peoria County, IL	187
Stark County, IL	6
Tazewell County, IL	136
Woodford County, IL	39
Philadelphia-Camden-	
Wilmington, PA-NJ-DE-MD	**6,019**
Camden, NJ	**1,254**
Burlington County, NJ	451
Camden County, NJ	514
Gloucester County, NJ	290
Philadelphia, PA	**2,109**
Delaware County, PA	561
Philadelphia County, PA	1,548
Montgomery-Bucks-Chester,	
PA	**1,942**
Bucks County, PA	627
Chester County, PA	507
Montgomery County, PA	808
Wilmington, DE-MD-NJ	**714**
New Castle County, DE	546
Cecil County, MD	102
Salem County, NJ	66
Phoenix-Mesa-Glendale, AZ	**4,330**
Maricopa County, AZ	3,942
Pinal County, AZ	387
Pine Bluff, AR	**97**
Cleveland County, AR	9
Jefferson County, AR	75
Lincoln County, AR	14
Pittsburgh, PA	**2,361**
Allegheny County, PA	1,229
Armstrong County, PA	68
Beaver County, PA	170
Butler County, PA	185

See footnotes at end of table.

Metropolitan Statistical Area ~~Metropolitan Division ~~~~Component county	Popu- lation, 2012 (1,000)
Fayette County, PA	136
Washington County, PA	209
Westmoreland County, PA	363
Pittsfield, MA	**130**
Berkshire County, MA	130
Pocatello, ID	**84**
Bannock County, ID	84
Portland-South	
Portland-Biddeford, ME	**518**
Cumberland County, ME	284
Sagadahoc County, ME	35
York County, ME	199
Portland-Vancouver-Hillsboro,	
OR-WA	**2,290**
Clackamas County, OR	384
Columbia County, OR	49
Multnomah County, OR	759
Washington County, OR	548
Yamhill County, OR	100
Clark County, WA	438
Skamania County, WA	11
Port St. Lucie, FL	**433**
Martin County, FL	149
St. Lucie County, FL	284
Prescott, AZ	**213**
Yavapai County, AZ	213
Providence-New Bedford-Fall	
River, RI-MA	**1,601**
Bristol County, MA	551
Bristol County, RI	49
Kent County, RI	165
Newport County, RI	82
Providence County, RI	628
Washington County, RI	126
Provo-Orem, UT	**551**
Juab County, UT	10
Utah County, UT	541
Pueblo, CO	**161**
Pueblo County, CO	161
Punta Gorda, FL	**162**
Charlotte County, FL	162
Racine, WI	**195**
Racine County, WI	195
Raleigh-Cary, NC	**1,189**
Franklin County, NC	61
Johnston County, NC	175
Wake County, NC	952
Rapid City, SD	**139**
Custer County, SD	8
Meade County, SD	26
Pennington County, SD	104
Reading, PA	**413**
Berks County, PA	413
Redding, CA	**179**
Shasta County, CA	179
Reno-Sparks, NV	**434**
Storey County, NV	4
Washoe County, NV	430
Richmond, VA	**1,232**
Amelia County, VA	13
Caroline County, VA	29
Charles City County, VA	7
Chesterfield County, VA	324
Dinwiddie County, VA	28
Goochland County, VA	21
Hanover County, VA	101
Henrico County, VA	315
King William County, VA	16
New Kent County, VA	19
Powhatan County, VA	28
Prince George County, VA	37
Sussex County, VA	12
Colonial Heights city, VA	17
Hopewell city, VA	22
Petersburg city, VA	32
Richmond city, VA	210
Riverside-San	
Bernardino-Ontario, CA	**4,350**
Riverside County, CA	2,269
San Bernardino County, CA	2,081
Roanoke, VA	**310**
Botetourt County, VA	33
Craig County, VA	5

Metropolitan Statistical Area ~~Metropolitan Division ~~~~Component county	Popu- lation, 2012 (1,000)
Franklin County, VA	56
Roanoke County, VA	93
Roanoke city, VA	97
Salem city, VA	25
Rochester, MN	**210**
Dodge County, MN	20
Fillmore County, MN	21
Olmsted County, MN	147
Wabasha County, MN	21
Rochester, NY	**1,082**
Livingston County, NY	65
Monroe County, NY	748
Ontario County, NY	109
Orleans County, NY	43
Wayne County, NY	93
Yates County, NY	25
Rockford, IL	**346**
Boone County, IL	54
Winnebago County, IL	292
Rocky Mount, NC	**152**
Edgecombe County, NC	56
Nash County, NC	96
Rome, GA	**96**
Floyd County, GA	96
Sacramento--Arden-Arcade--	
Roseville, CA	**2,196**
El Dorado County, CA	181
Placer County, CA	362
Sacramento County, CA	1,450
Yolo County, CA	204
Saginaw-Saginaw Township	
North, MI	**198**
Saginaw County, MI	198
St. Cloud, MN	**190**
Benton County, MN	39
Stearns County, MN	152
St. George, UT	**145**
Washington County, UT	145
St. Joseph, MO-KS	**128**
Doniphan County, KS	8
Andrew County, MO	17
Buchanan County, MO	90
DeKalb County, MO	13
St. Louis, MO-IL [1]	**2,796**
Bond County, IL	18
Calhoun County, IL	5
Clinton County, IL	38
Jersey County, IL	23
Macoupin County, IL	47
Madison County, IL	268
Monroe County, IL	33
St. Clair County, IL	269
Franklin County, MO	101
Jefferson County, MO	220
Lincoln County, MO	53
St. Charles County, MO	369
St. Louis County, MO	1,000
Warren County, MO	33
St. Louis city, MO	318
Salem, OR	**396**
Marion County, OR	320
Polk County, OR	76
Salinas, CA	**427**
Monterey County, CA	427
Salisbury, MD	**382**
Sussex County, DE	203
Somerset County, MD	26
Wicomico County, MD	101
Salt Lake City, UT	**52**
Salt Lake County, UT	1,124
Summit County, UT	1,064
Tooele County, UT	60
San Angelo, TX	**115**
Irion County, TX	2
Tom Green County, TX	113
San Antonio-New Braunfels,	
TX	**2,234**
Atascosa County, TX	46
Bandera County, TX	21
Bexar County, TX	1,786
Comal County, TX	114

Metropolitan Statistical Area ~~Metropolitan Division ~~~~Component county	Popu- lation, 2012 (1,000)
Guadalupe County, TX	140
Kendall County, TX	36
Medina County, TX	47
Wilson County, TX	44
San Diego-Carlsbad-San	
Marcos, CA	**3,177**
San Diego County, CA	3,177
San Francisco-Oakland-	
Fremont, CA	**4,456**
Oakland-Fremont-Hayward,	
CA	**2,634**
Alameda County, CA	1,555
Contra Costa County, CA	1,080
San Francisco-San	
Mateo-Redwood City, CA	**1,565**
San Francisco County, CA	826
San Mateo County, CA	739
San Rafael, CA	**256**
Marin County, CA	256
San Jose-Sunnyvale-Santa	
Clara, CA	**1,894**
San Benito County, CA	57
Santa Clara County, CA	1,838
San Luis Obispo-Paso Robles,	
CA	**275**
San Luis Obispo County, CA	275
Santa Cruz-Watsonville, CA	**267**
Santa Cruz County, CA	267
Santa Barbara-Santa	
Maria-Goleta, CA	**431**
Santa Barbara County, CA	431
Santa Fe, NM	**146**
Santa Fe County, NM	146
Santa Rosa-Petaluma, CA	**492**
Sonoma County, CA	492
Savannah, GA	**362**
Bryan County, GA	32
Chatham County, GA	276
Effingham County, GA	53
Scranton--Wilkes-Barre, PA	**564**
Lackawanna County, PA	214
Luzerne County, PA	321
Wyoming County, PA	28
Seattle-Tacoma-Bellevue, WA	**3,552**
Seattle-Bellevue-Everett, WA	**2,740**
King County, WA	2,007
Snohomish County, WA	733
Tacoma, WA	**812**
Pierce County, WA	812
Sebastian-Vero Beach, FL	**141**
Indian River County, FL	141
Sebring, FL	**98**
Highlands County, FL	98
Sheboygan, WI	**115**
Sheboygan County, WI	115
Sherman-Denison, TX	**122**
Grayson County, TX	122
Shreveport-Bossier City, LA	**447**
Bossier Parish, LA	122
Caddo Parish, LA	257
De Soto Parish, LA	27
Webster Parish, LA	41
Sierra Vista-Douglas, AZ	**132**
Cochise County, AZ	132
Sioux City, IA-NE-SD	**169**
Plymouth County, IA	25
Woodbury County, IA	102
Dakota County, NE	21
Dixon County, NE	6
Union County, SD	15
Sioux Falls, SD	**237**
Lincoln County, SD	48
McCook County, SD	6
Minnehaha County, SD	175
Turner County, SD	8
South Bend-Mishawaka, IN-MI	**319**
St. Joseph County, IN	266
Cass County, MI	52
Spartanburg, SC	**317**
Spartanburg County, SC	289

See footnotes at end of table.

Table A. Metropolitan Statistical Areas and Components—Population: 2012-Continued.

See headnote on page 935.

Metropolitan Statistical Area ~~Metropolitan Division ~~~~Component county	Population, 2012 (1,000)
Spokane, WA	28
Spokane County, WA	532
Pend Oreille County, WA	13
Spokane County, WA	476
Stevens County, WA	44
Springfield, IL	212
Menard County, IL	13
Sangamon County, IL	199
Springfield, MA	626
Hampden County, MA	466
Hampshire County, MA	160
Springfield, MO	445
Christian County, MO	80
Dallas County, MO	17
Greene County, MO	281
Polk County, MO	31
Webster County, MO	36
Springfield, OH	137
Clark County, OH	137
State College, PA	155
Centre County, PA	155
Staunton-Waynesboro, VA	119
Augusta County, VA	74
Staunton city, VA	24
Waynesboro city, VA	21
Stockton, CA	703
San Joaquin County, CA	703
Sumter, SC	108
Sumter County, SC	108
Syracuse, NY	661
Madison County, NY	72
Onondaga County, NY	467
Oswego County, NY	122
Tallahassee, FL	375
Gadsden County, FL	47
Jefferson County, FL	14
Leon County, FL	284
Wakulla County, FL	31
Tampa-St. Petersburg-Clearwater, FL	2,843
Hernando County, FL	173
Hillsborough County, FL	1,278
Pasco County, FL	470
Pinellas County, FL	921
Terre Haute, IN	172
Clay County, IN	27
Sullivan County, IN	21
Vermillion County, IN	16
Vigo County, IN	108
Texarkana, TX-Texarkana, AR	150
Little River County, AR	13
Miller County, AR	44
Bowie County, TX	93
The Villages, FL	102
Sumter County, FL	102
Toledo, OH	609
Fulton County, OH	43
Lucas County, OH	438
Wood County, OH	128
Topeka, KS	235
Jackson County, KS	13
Jefferson County, KS	19
Osage County, KS	16
Shawnee County, KS	179
Wabaunsee County, KS	7
Trenton-Ewing, NJ	368
Mercer County, NJ	368
Tucson, AZ	992
Pima County, AZ	992
Tulsa, OK	952
Creek County, OK	71
Okmulgee County, OK	40
Osage County, OK	48
Pawnee County, OK	16

Metropolitan Statistical Area ~~Metropolitan Division ~~~~Component county	Population, 2012 (1,000)
Rogers County, OK	88
Tulsa County, OK	614
Wagoner County, OK	75
Tuscaloosa, AL	233
Hale County, AL	15
Pickens County, AL	19
Tuscaloosa County, AL	199
Tyler, TX	215
Smith County, TX	215
Utica-Rome, NY	298
Herkimer County, NY	65
Oneida County, NY	234
Valdosta, GA	144
Brooks County, GA	15
Echols County, GA	4
Lanier County, GA	10
Lowndes County, GA	115
Vallejo-Fairfield, CA	421
Solano County, CA	421
Victoria, TX	97
Goliad County, TX	7
Victoria County, TX	89
Vineland-Millville-Bridgeton, NJ	158
Cumberland County, NJ	158
Virginia Beach-Norfolk-Newport News, VA-NC	1,700
Currituck County, NC	24
Gates County, NC	12
Gloucester County, VA	37
Isle of Wight County, VA	35
James City County, VA	69
Mathews County, VA	9
York County, VA	66
Chesapeake city, VA	228
Hampton city, VA	137
Newport News city, VA	181
Norfolk city, VA	246
Poquoson city, VA	12
Portsmouth city, VA	96
Suffolk city, VA	85
Virginia Beach city, VA	447
Williamsburg city, VA	15
Visalia-Porterville, CA	452
Tulare County, CA	452
Waco, TX	256
Falls County, TX	18
McLennan County, TX	239
Walla Walla, WA	63
Columbia County, WA	4
Walla Walla County, WA	59
Warner Robins, GA	185
Houston County, GA	146
Peach County, GA	28
Pulaski County, GA	12
Washington-Arlington-Alexandria, DC-VA-MD-WV	5,860
Bethesda-Rockville-Frederick, MD	1,244
Frederick County, MD	240
Montgomery County, MD	1,005
Washington-Arlington-Alexandria, DC-VA-MD-WV	4,616
District of Columbia, DC	632
Calvert County, MD	90
Charles County, MD	151
Prince George's County, MD	881
Arlington County, VA	221
Clarke County, VA	14
Culpeper County, VA	48
Fairfax County, VA	1,119
Fauquier County, VA	67
Loudoun County, VA	337
Prince William County, VA	430

Metropolitan Statistical Area ~~Metropolitan Division ~~~~Component county	Population, 2012 (1,000)
Rappahannock County, VA	7
Spotsylvania County, VA	126
Stafford County, VA	134
Warren County, VA	38
Alexandria city, VA	146
Fairfax city, VA	23
Falls Church city, VA	13
Fredericksburg city, VA	27
Manassas city, VA	41
Manassas Park city, VA	16
Jefferson County, WV	55
Waterloo-Cedar Falls, IA	169
Black Hawk County, IA	132
Bremer County, IA	24
Grundy County, IA	12
Watertown-Fort Drum, NY	120
Jefferson County, NY	120
Wausau, WI	135
Marathon County, WI	135
Weirton-Steubenville, WV-OH	123
Jefferson County, OH	68
Brooke County, WV	24
Hancock County, WV	30
Wenatchee-East Wenatchee, WA	113
Chelan County, WA	74
Douglas County, WA	39
Wheeling, WV-OH	146
Belmont County, OH	70
Marshall County, WV	33
Ohio County, WV	44
Wichita, KS	636
Butler County, KS	66
Harvey County, KS	35
Kingman County, KS	8
Sedgwick County, KS	504
Sumner County, KS	24
Wichita Falls, TX	151
Archer County, TX	9
Clay County, TX	11
Wichita County, TX	132
Williamsport, PA	117
Lycoming County, PA	117
Wilmington, NC	263
New Hanover County, NC	209
Pender County, NC	54
Winchester, VA-WV	131
Frederick County, VA	80
Winchester city, VA	27
Hampshire County, WV	24
Winston-Salem, NC	648
Davidson County, NC	163
Davie County, NC	41
Forsyth County, NC	358
Stokes County, NC	47
Yadkin County, NC	38
Worcester, MA	924
Windham County, CT	118
Worcester County, MA	806
Yakima, WA	247
Yakima County, WA	247
York-Hanover, PA	438
York County, PA	438
Youngstown-Warren-Boardman, OH-PA	558
Mahoning County, OH	235
Trumbull County, OH	207
Mercer County, PA	116
Yuba City, CA	168
Sutter County, CA	95
Yuba County, CA	73
Yuma, AZ	200
Yuma County, AZ	200

[1] The portion of Sullivan city in Crawford County, Missouri, is legally part of the St. Louis, MO-IL Metropolitan Statistical Area. The estimate shown here for the St. Louis, MO-IL Metropolitan Statistical Area does not include this area.

Source: U.S. Census Bureau, 2012 Population Estimates, <http://www.census.gov/popest/data/metro/totals/2012/>.

Table B. Microplitan Statistical Areas and Components—Population: 2012

[In thousands (41 represents 41,000). Population as of July 2012. Micropolitan Statistical Areas defined by the U.S. Office of Management and Budget as of February 2013. All Micropolitan Statistical Areas are arranged alphabetically]

Micropolitan Statistical Area ~~Component county	Population, 2012 (1,000)	Micropolitan Statistical Area ~~Component county	Population, 2012 (1,000)	Micropolitan Statistical Area ~~Component county	Population, 2012 (1,000)
Aberdeen, SD	**41**	Independence County, AR	37	Wexford County, MI	33
Brown County, SD	37	**Bay City, TX**	**37**	**Calhoun, GA**	**56**
Edmunds County, SD	4	Matagorda County, TX	37	Gordon County, GA	56
Aberdeen, WA	**72**	**Beatrice, NE**	**22**	**Cambridge, MD**	**33**
Grays Harbor County, WA	72	Gage County, NE	22	Dorchester County, MD	33
Ada, OK	**38**	**Beaver Dam, WI**	**88**	**Cambridge, OH**	**40**
Pontotoc County, OK	38	Dodge County, WI	88	Guernsey County, OH	40
Adrian, MI	**99**	**Bedford, IN**	**46**	**Camden, AR**	**31**
Lenawee County, MI	99	Lawrence County, IN	46	Calhoun County, AR	5
Alamogordo, NM	**66**	**Beeville, TX**	**33**	Ouachita County, AR	25
Otero County, NM	66	Bee County, TX	33	**Campbellsville, KY**	**25**
Albemarle, NC	**61**	**Bellefontaine, OH**	**45**	Taylor County, KY	25
Stanly County, NC	61	Logan County, OH	45	**Cañon City, CO**	**47**
Albert Lea, MN	**31**	**Bemidji, MN**	**45**	Fremont County, CO	47
Freeborn County, MN	31	Beltrami County, MN	45	**Canton, IL**	**37**
Albertville, AL	**95**	**Bennettsville, SC**	**28**	Fulton County, IL	37
Marshall County, AL	95	Marlboro County, SC	28	**Carlsbad-Artesia, NM**	**54**
Alexandria, MN	**36**	**Bennington, VT**	**37**	Eddy County, NM	54
Douglas County, MN	36	Bennington County, VT	37	**Cedar City, UT**	**47**
Alice, TX	**42**	**Berlin, NH-VT**	**38**	Iron County, UT	47
Jim Wells County, TX	42	Coos County, NH	32	**Cedartown, GA**	**41**
Alma, MI	**42**	Essex County, VT	6	Polk County, GA	41
Gratiot County, MI	42	**Big Rapids, MI**	**43**	**Celina, OH**	**41**
Alpena, MI	**29**	Mecosta County, MI	43	Mercer County, OH	41
Alpena County, MI	29	**Big Spring, TX**	**37**	**Centralia, IL**	**39**
Altus, OK	**26**	Glasscock County, TX	1	Marion County, IL	39
Jackson County, OK	26	Howard County, TX	35	**Centralia, WA**	**76**
Americus, GA	**37**	**Big Stone Gap, VA**	**61**	Lewis County, WA	76
Schley County, GA	5	Dickenson County, VA	16	**Charleston-Mattoon, IL**	**65**
Sumter County, GA	32	Wise County, VA	41	Coles County, IL	54
Amsterdam, NY	**50**	Norton city, VA	4	Cumberland County, IL	11
Montgomery County, NY	50	**Blackfoot, ID**	**45**	**Chillicothe, OH**	**77**
Andrews, TX	**16**	Bingham County, ID	45	Ross County, OH	77
Andrews County, TX	16	**Bluefield, WV-VA**	**107**	**Claremont, NH**	**217**
Angola, IN	**34**	Tazewell County, VA	44	Grafton County, NH	89
Steuben County, IN	34	Mercer County, WV	63	Sullivan County, NH	43
Arcadia, FL	**35**	**Blytheville, AR**	**46**	Orange County, VT	29
DeSoto County, FL	35	Mississippi County, AR	46	Windsor County, VT	56
Ardmore, OK	**48**	**Bogalusa, LA**	**47**	**Clarksburg, WV**	**94**
Carter County, OK	48	Washington Parish, LA	47	Doddridge County, WV	8
Arkadelphia, AR	**23**	**Boone, IA**	**26**	Harrison County, WV	69
Clark County, AR	23	Boone County, IA	26	Taylor County, WV	17
Arkansas City-Winfield, KS	**36**	**Boone, NC**	**52**	**Clarksdale, MS**	**26**
Cowley County, KS	36	Watauga County, NC	52	Coahoma County, MS	26
Ashland, OH	**53**	**Borger, TX**	**22**	**Clearlake, CA**	**64**
Ashland County, OH	53	Hutchinson County, TX	22	Lake County, CA	64
Ashtabula, OH	**100**	**Bozeman, MT**	**93**	**Cleveland, MS**	**34**
Ashtabula County, OH	100	Gallatin County, MT	93	Bolivar County, MS	34
Astoria, OR	**37**	**Bradford, PA**	**43**	**Clewiston, FL**	**37**
Clatsop County, OR	37	McKean County, PA	43	Hendry County, FL	37
Atchison, KS	**17**	**Brainerd, MN**	**91**	**Clinton, IA**	**49**
Atchison County, KS	17	Cass County, MN	28	Clinton County, IA	49
Athens, OH	**64**	Crow Wing County, MN	63	**Clovis, NM**	**50**
Athens County, OH	64	**Branson, MO**	**85**	Curry County, NM	50
Athens, TN	**52**	Stone County, MO	32	**Coffeyville, KS**	**34**
McMinn County, TN	52	Taney County, MO	53	Montgomery County, KS	34
Athens, TX	**79**	**Breckenridge, CO**	**28**	**Coldwater, MI**	**44**
Henderson County, TX	79	Summit County, CO	28	Branch County, MI	44
Auburn, IN	**42**	**Brenham, TX**	**34**	**Columbus, MS**	**60**
DeKalb County, IN	42	Washington County, TX	34	Lowndes County, MS	60
Auburn, NY	**80**	**Brevard, NC**	**33**	**Columbus, NE**	**33**
Cayuga County, NY	80	Transylvania County, NC	33	Platte County, NE	33
Augusta-Waterville, ME	**122**	**Brookhaven, MS**	**35**	**Concord, NH**	**147**
Kennebec County, ME	122	Lincoln County, MS	35	Merrimack County, NH	147
Austin, MN	**39**	**Brookings, OR**	**22**	**Connersville, IN**	**24**
Mower County, MN	39	Curry County, OR	22	Fayette County, IN	24
Bainbridge, GA	**28**	**Brookings, SD**	**33**	**Cookeville, TN**	**107**
Decatur County, GA	28	Brookings County, SD	33	Jackson County, TN	11
Baraboo, WI	**63**	**Brownwood, TX**	**38**	Overton County, TN	22
Sauk County, WI	63	Brown County, TX	38	Putnam County, TN	73
Bardstown, KY	**44**	**Bucyrus, OH**	**43**	**Coos Bay, OR**	**63**
Nelson County, KY	44	Crawford County, OH	43	Coos County, OR	63
Barre, VT	**59**	**Burley, ID**	**43**	**Cordele, GA**	**24**
Washington County, VT	59	Cassia County, ID	23	Crisp County, GA	24
Bartlesville, OK	**52**	Minidoka County, ID	20	**Corinth, MS**	**37**
Washington County, OK	52	**Burlington, IA-IL**	**47**	Alcorn County, MS	37
Bastrop, LA	**28**	Henderson County, IL	7	**Cornelia, GA**	**44**
Morehouse Parish, LA	28	Des Moines County, IA	40	Habersham County, GA	44
Batavia, NY	**60**	**Butte-Silver Bow, MT**	**34**	**Corning, NY**	**99**
Genesee County, NY	60	Silver Bow County, MT	34	Steuben County, NY	99
Batesville, AR	**37**	**Cadillac, MI**	**48**	**Corsicana, TX**	**48**
		Missaukee County, MI	15	Navarro County, TX	48

Table B. Micropolitan Statistical Areas and Components—Population: 2012-Continued.

See headnote on page 942.

Micropolitan Statistical Area ~~Component county	Population, 2012 (1,000)	Micropolitan Statistical Area ~~Component county	Population, 2012 (1,000)	Micropolitan Statistical Area ~~Component county	Population, 2012 (1,000)
Cortland, NY	**49**	**Ellensburg, WA**	**42**	Metcalfe County, KY	10
Cortland County, NY	49	Kittitas County, WA	42	**Glenwood Springs, CO**	**74**
Coshocton, OH	**37**	**Emporia, KS**	**34**	Garfield County, CO	57
Coshocton County, OH	37	Lyon County, KS	34	Pitkin County, CO	17
Craig, CO	**13**	**Enid, OK**	**61**	**Gloversville, NY**	**55**
Moffat County, CO	13	Garfield County, OK	61	Fulton County, NY	55
Crawfordsville, IN	**38**	**Enterprise-Ozark, AL**	**51**	**Grants, NM**	**27**
Montgomery County, IN	38	Coffee County, AL	51	Cibola County, NM	27
Crescent City, CA	**28**	**Escanaba, MI**	**37**	**Great Bend, KS**	**28**
Del Norte County, CA	28	Delta County, MI	37	Barton County, KS	28
Crossville, TN	**57**	**Espanola, NM**	**40**	**Greeneville, TN**	**69**
Cumberland County, TN	57	Rio Arriba County, NM	40	Greene County, TN	69
Cullman, AL	**80**	**Eureka-Arcata-Fortuna, CA**	**135**	**Greenfield Town, MA**	**72**
Cullman County, AL	80	Humboldt County, CA	135	Franklin County, MA	72
Cullowhee, NC	**40**	**Evanston, WY**	**21**	**Greensburg, IN**	**26**
Jackson County, NC	40	Uinta County, WY	21	Decatur County, IN	26
Danville, KY	**53**	**Fairfield, IA**	**17**	**Greenville, MS**	**50**
Boyle County, KY	29	Jefferson County, IA	17	Washington County, MS	50
Lincoln County, KY	24	**Fairmont, WV**	**57**	**Greenville, OH**	**53**
Danville, VA	**106**	Marion County, WV	57	Darke County, OH	53
Pittsylvania County, VA	63	**Fallon, NV**	**24**	**Greenwood, MS**	**41**
Danville city, VA	43	Churchill County, NV	24	Carroll County, MS	10
Dayton, TN	**32**	**Faribault-Northfield, MN**	**65**	Leflore County, MS	31
Rhea County, TN	32	Rice County, MN	65	**Greenwood, SC**	**95**
Decatur, IN	**34**	**Farmington, MO**	**66**	Abbeville County, SC	25
Adams County, IN	34	St. Francois County, MO	66	Greenwood County, SC	70
Defiance, OH	**39**	**Fergus Falls, MN**	**57**	**Grenada, MS**	**22**
Defiance County, OH	39	Otter Tail County, MN	57	Grenada County, MS	22
Del Rio, TX	**49**	**Fernley, NV**	**51**	**Guymon, OK**	**21**
Val Verde County, TX	49	Lyon County, NV	51	Texas County, OK	21
Deming, NM	**25**	**Findlay, OH**	**76**	**Hailey, ID**	**28**
Luna County, NM	25	Hancock County, OH	76	Blaine County, ID	21
DeRidder, LA	**36**	**Fitzgerald, GA**	**18**	Camas County, ID	1
Beauregard Parish, LA	36	Ben Hill County, GA	18	Lincoln County, ID	5
Dickinson, ND	**27**	**Forest City, NC**	**67**	**Hannibal, MO**	**39**
Stark County, ND	27	Rutherford County, NC	67	Marion County, MO	29
Dixon, IL	**35**	**Forrest City, AR**	**28**	Ralls County, MO	10
Lee County, IL	35	St. Francis County, AR	28	**Harrison, AR**	**45**
Dodge City, KS	**35**	**Fort Dodge, IA**	**37**	Boone County, AR	37
Ford County, KS	35	Webster County, IA	37	Newton County, AR	8
Douglas, GA	**43**	**Fort Leonard Wood, MO**	**53**	**Hastings, NE**	**31**
Coffee County, GA	43	Pulaski County, MO	53	Adams County, NE	31
Dublin, GA	**58**	**Fort Madison-Keokuk, IA-MO**	**61**	**Hays, KS**	**29**
Johnson County, GA	10	Hancock County, IL	19	Ellis County, KS	29
Laurens County, GA	48	Lee County, IA	36	**Heber, UT**	**25**
DuBois, PA	**81**	Clark County, MO	7	Wasatch County, UT	25
Clearfield County, PA	81	**Fort Morgan, CO**	**28**	**Helena, MT**	**76**
Dumas, TX	**22**	Morgan County, CO	28	Jefferson County, MT	11
Moore County, TX	22	**Fort Polk South, LA**	**54**	Lewis and Clark County, MT	65
Duncan, OK	**45**	Vernon Parish, LA	54	**Helena-West Helena, AR**	**21**
Stephens County, OK	45	**Frankfort, IN**	**33**	Phillips County, AR	21
Dunn, NC	**122**	Clinton County, IN	33	**Henderson, NC**	**45**
Harnett County, NC	122	**Frankfort, KY**	**72**	Vance County, NC	45
Durango, CO	**52**	Anderson County, KY	22	**Hereford, TX**	**19**
La Plata County, CO	52	Franklin County, KY	50	Deaf Smith County, TX	19
Durant, OK	**43**	**Fredericksburg, TX**	**25**	**Hermiston-Pendleton, OR**	**88**
Bryan County, OK	43	Gillespie County, TX	25	Morrow County, OR	11
Dyersburg, TN	**38**	**Freeport, IL**	**47**	Umatilla County, OR	77
Dyer County, TN	38	Stephenson County, IL	47	**Hillsdale, MI**	**46**
Eagle Pass, TX	**55**	**Fremont, NE**	**36**	Hillsdale County, MI	46
Maverick County, TX	55	Dodge County, NE	36	**Hilo, HI**	**189**
Easton, MD	**38**	**Fremont, OH**	**61**	Hawaii County, HI	189
Talbot County, MD	38	Sandusky County, OH	61	**Hobbs, NM**	**66**
Edwards, CO	**52**	**Gaffney, SC**	**56**	Lea County, NM	66
Eagle County, CO	52	Cherokee County, SC	56	**Holland, MI**	**112**
Effingham, IL	**34**	**Gainesville, TX**	**39**	Allegan County, MI	112
Effingham County, IL	34	Cooke County, TX	39	**Hood River, OR**	**23**
El Campo, TX	**41**	**Galesburg, IL**	**52**	Hood River County, OR	23
Wharton County, TX	41	Knox County, IL	52	**Houghton, MI**	**39**
El Dorado, AR	**41**	**Gallup, NM**	**73**	Houghton County, MI	37
Union County, AR	41	McKinley County, NM	73	Keweenaw County, MI	2
Elizabeth City, NC	**64**	**Garden City, KS**	**41**	**Hudson, NY**	**62**
Camden County, NC	10	Finney County, KS	37	Columbia County, NY	62
Pasquotank County, NC	41	Kearny County, KS	4	**Huntingdon, PA**	**46**
Perquimans County, NC	14	**Gardnerville Ranchos, NV**	**47**	Huntingdon County, PA	46
Elk City, OK	**23**	Douglas County, NV	47	**Huntington, IN**	**37**
Beckham County, OK	23	**Georgetown, SC**	**60**	Huntington County, IN	37
Elkins, WV	**29**	Georgetown County, SC	60	**Huntsville, TX**	**83**
Randolph County, WV	29	**Gillette, WY**	**48**	Trinity County, TX	14
Elko, NV	**53**	Campbell County, WY	48	Walker County, TX	68
Elko County, NV	51	**Glasgow, KY**	**53**	**Huron, SD**	**18**
Eureka County, NV	2	Barren County, KY	43	Beadle County, SD	18

Micropolitan Statistical Area ~~Component county	Population, 2012 (1,000)	Micropolitan Statistical Area ~~Component county	Population, 2012 (1,000)	Micropolitan Statistical Area ~~Component county	Population, 2012 (1,000)
Hutchinson, KS	**64**	Albany County, WY	37	**Martinsville, VA**	**67**
Reno County, KS	64	**Las Vegas, NM**	**29**	Henry County, VA	53
Hutchinson, MN	**36**	San Miguel County, NM	29	Martinsville city, VA	14
McLeod County, MN	36	**Laurel, MS**	**85**	**Maryville, MO**	**23**
Indiana, PA	**88**	Jasper County, MS	17	Nodaway County, MO	23
Indiana County, PA	88	Jones County, MS	69	**Mason City, IA**	**51**
Indianola, MS	**28**	**Laurinburg, NC**	**36**	Cerro Gordo County, IA	44
Sunflower County, MS	28	Scotland County, NC	36	Worth County, IA	8
Ionia, MI	**64**	**Lawrenceburg, TN**	**42**	**Mayfield, KY**	**38**
Ionia County, MI	64	Lawrence County, TN	42	Graves County, KY	38
Iron Mountain, MI-WI	**31**	**Lebanon, MO**	**35**	**Maysville, KY**	**18**
Dickinson County, MI	26	Laclede County, MO	35	Mason County, KY	18
Florence County, WI	4	**Levelland, TX**	**23**	**McAlester, OK**	**45**
Jackson, OH	**33**	Hockley County, TX	23	Pittsburg County, OK	45
Jackson County, OH	33	**Lewisburg, PA**	**45**	**McComb, MS**	**53**
Jackson, WY-ID	**32**	Union County, PA	45	Amite County, MS	13
Teton County, ID	10	**Lewisburg, TN**	**31**	Pike County, MS	40
Teton County, WY	22	Marshall County, TN	31	**McMinnville, TN**	**40**
Jacksonville, IL	**41**	**Lewistown, PA**	**47**	Warren County, TN	40
Morgan County, IL	35	Mifflin County, PA	47	**McPherson, KS**	**29**
Scott County, IL	5	**Lexington, NE**	**26**	McPherson County, KS	29
Jacksonville, TX	**51**	Dawson County, NE	24	**Meadville, PA**	**88**
Cherokee County, TX	51	Gosper County, NE	2	Crawford County, PA	88
Jamestown, ND	**21**	**Liberal, KS**	**24**	**Menomonie, WI**	**44**
Stutsman County, ND	21	Seward County, KS	24	Dunn County, WI	44
Jamestown-Dunkirk-Fredonia, NY	**134**	**Lincoln, IL**	**30**	**Meridian, MS**	**107**
Chautauqua County, NY	134	Logan County, IL	30	Clarke County, MS	17
Jasper, IN	**55**	**Lock Haven, PA**	**40**	Kemper County, MS	10
Dubois County, IN	42	Clinton County, PA	40	Lauderdale County, MS	80
Pike County, IN	13	**Logan, WV**	**36**	**Merrill, WI**	**28**
Jefferson, GA	**61**	Logan County, WV	36	Lincoln County, WI	28
Jackson County, GA	61	**Logansport, IN**	**39**	**Mexico, MO**	**26**
Jesup, GA	**30**	Cass County, IN	39	Audrain County, MO	26
Wayne County, GA	30	**London, KY**	**127**	**Miami, OK**	**32**
Junction City, KS	**38**	Knox County, KY	32	Ottawa County, OK	32
Geary County, KS	38	Laurel County, KY	59	**Middlesborough, KY**	**28**
Juneau, AK	**33**	Whitley County, KY	35	Bell County, KY	28
Juneau City and Borough, AK	33	**Los Alamos, NM**	**18**	**Milledgeville, GA**	**55**
Kalispell, MT	**92**	Los Alamos County, NM	18	Baldwin County, GA	46
Flathead County, MT	92	**Ludington, MI**	**29**	Hancock County, GA	9
Kapaa, HI	**68**	Mason County, MI	29	**Mineral Wells, TX**	**28**
Kauai County, HI	68	**Lufkin, TX**	**88**	Palo Pinto County, TX	28
Kearney, NE	**54**	Angelina County, TX	88	**Minot, ND**	**73**
Buffalo County, NE	47	**Lumberton, NC**	**135**	McHenry County, ND	6
Kearney County, NE	6	Robeson County, NC	135	Renville County, ND	3
Keene, NH	**77**	**Macomb, IL**	**33**	Ward County, ND	65
Cheshire County, NH	77	McDonough County, IL	33	**Mitchell, SD**	**23**
Kendallville, IN	**48**	**Madison, IN**	**33**	Davison County, SD	20
Noble County, IN	48	Jefferson County, IN	33	Hanson County, SD	3
Kennett, MO	**32**	**Madisonville, KY**	**47**	**Moberly, MO**	**25**
Dunklin County, MO	32	Hopkins County, KY	47	Randolph County, MO	25
Kerrville, TX	**50**	**Magnolia, AR**	**24**	**Montrose, CO**	**41**
Kerr County, TX	50	Columbia County, AR	24	Montrose County, CO	41
Ketchikan, AK	**14**	**Malone, NY**	**52**	**Morehead City, NC**	**68**
Ketchikan Gateway Borough, AK	14	Franklin County, NY	52	Carteret County, NC	68
Key West, FL	**75**	**Malvern, AR**	**33**	**Morgan City, LA**	**54**
Monroe County, FL	75	Hot Spring County, AR	33	St. Mary Parish, LA	54
Kill Devil Hills, NC	**39**	**Manitowoc, WI**	**81**	**Moscow, ID**	**38**
Dare County, NC	35	Manitowoc County, WI	81	Latah County, ID	38
Tyrrell County, NC	4	**Marietta, OH**	**61**	**Moses Lake, WA**	**92**
Kingsville, TX	**32**	Washington County, OH	61	Grant County, WA	92
Kenedy County, TX	(Z)	**Marinette, WI-MI**	**65**	**Moultrie, GA**	**46**
Kleberg County, TX	32	Menominee County, MI	24	Colquitt County, GA	46
Kinston, NC	**59**	Marinette County, WI	42	**Mountain Home, AR**	**41**
Lenoir County, NC	59	**Marion, IN**	**69**	Baxter County, AR	41
Kirksville, MO	**30**	Grant County, IN	69	**Mountain Home, ID**	**26**
Adair County, MO	26	**Marion, NC**	**45**	Elmore County, ID	26
Schuyler County, MO	4	McDowell County, NC	45	**Mount Airy, NC**	**74**
Klamath Falls, OR	**66**	**Marion, OH**	**66**	Surry County, NC	74
Klamath County, OR	66	Marion County, OH	66	**Mount Pleasant, MI**	**71**
Laconia, NH	**60**	**Marquette, MI**	**68**	Isabella County, MI	71
Belknap County, NH	60	Marquette County, MI	68	**Mount Pleasant, TX**	**33**
La Grande, OR	**26**	**Marshall, MN**	**26**	Titus County, TX	33
Union County, OR	26	Lyon County, MN	26	**Mount Sterling, KY**	**45**
LaGrange, GA	**68**	**Marshall, MO**	**23**	Bath County, KY	12
Troup County, GA	68	Saline County, MO	23	Menifee County, KY	6
Lake City, FL	**68**	**Marshall, TX**	**67**	Montgomery County, KY	27
Columbia County, FL	68	Harrison County, TX	67	**Mount Vernon, IL**	**39**
Lamesa, TX	**14**	**Marshalltown, IA**	**41**	Jefferson County, IL	39
Dawson County, TX	14	Marshall County, IA	41	**Mount Vernon, OH**	**61**
Laramie, WY	**37**	**Martin, TN**	**35**	Knox County, OH	61
		Weakley County, TN	35	**Murray, KY**	**38**

See footnotes at end of table.

Table B. Micropolitan Statistical Areas and Components—Population: 2012-Continued.

See headnote on page 942.

Micropolitan Statistical Area ~~Component county	Population, 2012 (1,000)
Calloway County, KY............	38
Muscatine, IA......................	**43**
Muscatine County, IA..........	43
Muskogee, OK.....................	**71**
Muskogee County, OK..........	71
Nacogdoches, TX................	**66**
Nacogdoches County, TX......	66
Natchez, MS-LA..................	**52**
Concordia Parish, LA..........	20
Adams County, MS.............	32
Natchitoches, LA................	**39**
Natchitoches Parish, LA.......	39
Newberry, SC......................	**38**
Newberry County, SC..........	38
New Castle, IN....................	**49**
Henry County, IN...............	49
New Castle, PA....................	**90**
Lawrence County, PA..........	90
New Philadelphia-Dover, OH	**92**
Tuscarawas County, OH.......	92
Newport, OR......................	**46**
Lincoln County, OR............	46
Newport, TN......................	**36**
Cocke County, TN.............	36
Newton, IA........................	**37**
Jasper County, IA..............	37
New Ulm, MN.....................	**25**
Brown County, MN.............	25
Nogales, AZ.......................	**47**
Santa Cruz County, AZ.........	47
Norfolk, NE.......................	**48**
Madison County, NE...........	35
Pierce County, NE..............	7
Stanton County, NE............	6
North Platte, NE.................	**37**
Lincoln County, NE............	36
Logan County, NE..............	1
McPherson County, NE.........	1
North Vernon, IN................	**28**
Jennings County, IN............	28
North Wilkesboro, NC..........	**69**
Wilkes County, NC..............	69
Norwalk, OH......................	**59**
Huron County, OH..............	59
Oak Harbor, WA..................	**79**
Island County, WA..............	79
Ogdensburg-Massena, NY.....	**112**
St. Lawrence County, NY.......	112
Oil City, PA........................	**54**
Venango County, PA...........	54
Okeechobee, FL..................	**39**
Okeechobee County, FL.......	39
Olean, NY.........................	**79**
Cattaraugus County, NY.......	79
Oneonta, NY......................	**62**
Otsego County, NY.............	62
Ontario, OR-ID...................	**53**
Payette County, ID.............	23
Malheur County, OR...........	31
Opelousas-Eunice, LA..........	**84**
St. Landry Parish, LA...........	84
Orangeburg, SC..................	**91**
Orangeburg County, SC.......	91
Oskaloosa, IA....................	**22**
Mahaska County, IA............	22
Othello, WA......................	**19**
Adams County, WA.............	19
Ottawa, KS........................	**26**
Franklin County, KS............	26
Ottawa-Peru, IL..................	**153**
Bureau County, IL..............	34
LaSalle County, IL..............	113
Putnam County, IL.............	6
Ottumwa, IA......................	**44**
Davis County, IA................	9
Wapello County, IA............	35
Owatonna, MN...................	**36**
Steele County, MN.............	36
Owosso, MI.......................	**69**
Shiawassee County, MI........	69
Oxford, MS........................	**49**
Lafayette County, MS..........	49

Micropolitan Statistical Area ~~Component county	Population, 2012 (1,000)
Oxford, NC........................	**60**
Granville County, NC...........	60
Ozark, AL..........................	**50**
Dale County, AL.................	50
Paducah, KY-IL...................	**99**
Massac County, IL..............	15
Ballard County, KY.............	8
Livingston County, KY.........	9
McCracken County, KY........	66
Pahrump, NV.....................	**43**
Nye County, NV.................	43
Palatka, FL........................	**73**
Putnam County, FL.............	73
Palestine, TX.....................	**58**
Anderson County, TX..........	58
Pampa, TX.........................	**23**
Gray County, TX................	23
Paragould, AR....................	**43**
Greene County, AR.............	43
Paris, TN...........................	**32**
Henry County, TN..............	32
Paris, TX...........................	**50**
Lamar County, TX..............	50
Parsons, KS.......................	**21**
Labette County, KS.............	21
Payson, AZ........................	**53**
Gila County, AZ.................	53
Pecos, TX..........................	**14**
Reeves County, TX.............	14
Peru, IN............................	**36**
Miami County, IN...............	36
Picayune, MS.....................	**55**
Pearl River County, MS........	55
Pierre, SD..........................	**22**
Hughes County, SD.............	17
Stanley County, SD.............	3
Sully County, SD................	1
Pinehurst-Southern Pines, NC........................	**90**
Moore County, NC..............	90
Pittsburg, KS......................	**39**
Crawford County, KS...........	39
Plainview, TX.....................	**36**
Hale County, TX.................	36
Platteville, WI....................	**51**
Grant County, WI...............	51
Plattsburgh, NY..................	**82**
Clinton County, NY.............	82
Plymouth, IN......................	**47**
Marshall County, IN............	47
Point Pleasant, WV-OH........	**58**
Gallia County, OH..............	31
Mason County, WV.............	27
Ponca City, OK...................	**46**
Kay County, OK.................	46
Pontiac, IL.........................	**39**
Livingston County, IL...........	39
Poplar Bluff, MO.................	**43**
Butler County, MO.............	43
Portales, NM......................	**20**
Roosevelt County, NM.........	20
Port Angeles, WA................	**72**
Clallam County, WA............	72
Port Clinton, OH.................	**41**
Ottawa County, OH............	41
Port Lavaca, TX..................	**22**
Calhoun County, TX............	22
Portsmouth, OH..................	**78**
Scioto County, OH.............	78
Pottsville, PA.....................	**147**
Schuylkill County, PA...........	147
Price, UT...........................	**21**
Carbon County, UT.............	21
Prineville, OR.....................	**21**
Crook County, OR..............	21
Pullman, WA......................	**47**
Whitman County, WA..........	47
Quincy, IL-MO....................	**77**
Adams County, IL...............	67
Lewis County, MO.............	10
Raymondville, TX................	**22**
Willacy County, TX.............	22

Micropolitan Statistical Area ~~Component county	Population, 2012 (1,000)
Red Bluff, CA.....................	**63**
Tehama County, CA............	63
Red Wing, MN....................	**46**
Goodhue County, MN..........	46
Rexburg, ID.......................	**50**
Fremont County, ID............	13
Madison County, ID............	37
Richmond, IN.....................	**68**
Wayne County, IN..............	68
Richmond-Berea, KY............	**102**
Madison County, KY...........	85
Rockcastle County, KY.........	17
Rio Grande City-Roma, TX....	**62**
Starr County, TX................	62
Riverton, WY.....................	**41**
Fremont County, WY...........	41
Roanoke Rapids, NC............	**75**
Halifax County, NC.............	54
Northampton County, NC......	21
Rochelle, IL.......................	**53**
Ogle County, IL.................	53
Rockingham, NC.................	**47**
Richmond County, NC.........	47
Rock Springs, WY................	**45**
Sweetwater County, WY.......	45
Rolla, MO..........................	**45**
Phelps County, MO............	45
Roseburg, OR.....................	**107**
Douglas County, OR...........	107
Roswell, NM......................	**66**
Chaves County, NM............	66
Russellville, AR..................	**85**
Pope County, AR...............	63
Yell County, AR.................	22
Ruston, LA.........................	**47**
Lincoln Parish, LA..............	47
Rutland, VT........................	**61**
Rutland County, VT.............	61
Safford, AZ........................	**37**
Graham County, AZ............	37
St. Marys, GA.....................	**51**
Camden County, GA...........	51
Salem, OH.........................	**107**
Columbiana County, OH.......	107
Salina, KS..........................	**62**
Ottawa County, KS.............	6
Saline County, KS..............	56
Sandpoint, ID.....................	**40**
Bonner County, ID..............	40
Sandusky, OH.....................	**76**
Erie County, OH................	76
Sanford, NC.......................	**60**
Lee County, NC.................	60
Sault Ste. Marie, MI............	**39**
Chippewa County, MI..........	39
Sayre, PA..........................	**63**
Bradford County, PA...........	63
Scottsbluff, NE...................	**39**
Banner County, NE.............	1
Scotts Bluff County, NE........	37
Sioux County, NE..............	1
Scottsboro, AL....................	**53**
Jackson County, AL............	53
Searcy, AR.........................	**78**
White County, AR..............	78
Sedalia, MO.......................	**42**
Pettis County, MO.............	42
Selinsgrove, PA..................	**40**
Snyder County, PA.............	40
Selma, AL..........................	**43**
Dallas County, AL..............	43
Seneca, SC........................	**75**
Oconee County, SC............	75
Seneca Falls, NY.................	**35**
Seneca County, NY............	35
Sevierville, TN....................	**93**
Sevier County, TN..............	93
Seymour, IN.......................	**43**
Jackson County, IN.............	43
Shawano, WI......................	**46**
Menominee County, WI........	4
Shawano County, WI..........	42

See footnotes at end of table.

Table B. Micropolitan Statistical Areas and Components—Population: 2012-Continued.

See headnote on page 942.

Micropolitan Statistical Area ~~Component county	Population, 2012 (1,000)
Shawnee, OK	**71**
Pottawatomie County, OK	71
Shelby, NC	**97**
Cleveland County, NC	97
Shelbyville, TN	**46**
Bedford County, TN	46
Shelton, WA	**61**
Mason County, WA	61
Sheridan, WY	**30**
Sheridan County, WY	30
Show Low, AZ	**107**
Navajo County, AZ	107
Sidney, OH	**49**
Shelby County, OH	49
Sikeston, MO	**39**
Scott County, MO	39
Silver City, NM	**29**
Grant County, NM	29
Snyder, TX	**17**
Scurry County, TX	17
Somerset, KY	**64**
Pulaski County, KY	64
Somerset, PA	**77**
Somerset County, PA	77
Sonora, CA	**54**
Tuolumne County, CA	54
Spearfish, SD	**24**
Lawrence County, SD	24
Spencer, IA	**17**
Clay County, IA	17
Spirit Lake, IA	**17**
Dickinson County, IA	17
Starkville, MS	**48**
Oktibbeha County, MS	48
Statesboro, GA	**73**
Bulloch County, GA	73
Steamboat Springs, CO	**23**
Routt County, CO	23
Stephenville, TX	**39**
Erath County, TX	39
Sterling, CO	**23**
Logan County, CO	23
Sterling, IL	**58**
Whiteside County, IL	58
Stevens Point, WI	**70**
Portage County, WI	70
Stillwater, OK	**78**
Payne County, OK	78
Storm Lake, IA	**21**
Buena Vista County, IA	21
Sturgis, MI	**61**
St. Joseph County, MI	61
Sulphur Springs, TX	**35**
Hopkins County, TX	35
Summerville, GA	**26**
Chattooga County, GA	26
Summit Park, UT	**38**
Summit County, UT	38
Sunbury, PA	**94**
Northumberland County, PA	94
Susanville, CA	**34**
Lassen County, CA	34
Sweetwater, TX	**15**
Nolan County, TX	15
Tahlequah, OK	**48**
Cherokee County, OK	48
Talladega-Sylacauga, AL	**93**
Coosa County, AL	11
Talladega County, AL	82
Taos, NM	**33**
Taos County, NM	33
Taylorville, IL	**35**
Christian County, IL	35
The Dalles, OR	**25**
Wasco County, OR	25
Thomaston, GA	**27**
Upson County, GA	27
Thomasville, GA	**45**
Thomas County, GA	45
Tiffin, OH	**56**
Seneca County, OH	56
Tifton, GA	**41**
Tift County, GA	41

Micropolitan Statistical Area ~~Component county	Population, 2012 (1,000)
Toccoa, GA	**26**
Stephens County, GA	26
Torrington, CT	**188**
Litchfield County, CT	188
Traverse City, MI	**145**
Benzie County, MI	17
Grand Traverse County, MI	89
Kalkaska County, MI	17
Leelanau County, MI	22
Troy, AL	**33**
Pike County, AL	33
Truckee-Grass Valley, CA	**98**
Nevada County, CA	98
Tullahoma, TN	**100**
Coffee County, TN	53
Franklin County, TN	41
Moore County, TN	6
Tupelo, MS	**139**
Itawamba County, MS	23
Lee County, MS	85
Pontotoc County, MS	31
Twin Falls, ID	**101**
Jerome County, ID	22
Twin Falls County, ID	79
Ukiah, CA	**87**
Mendocino County, CA	87
Union City, TN-KY	**38**
Fulton County, KY	7
Obion County, TN	31
Urbana, OH	**40**
Champaign County, OH	40
Uvalde, TX	**27**
Uvalde County, TX	27
Valley, AL	**34**
Chambers County, AL	34
Van Wert, OH	**29**
Van Wert County, OH	29
Vermillion, SD	**14**
Clay County, SD	14
Vernal, UT	**35**
Uintah County, UT	35
Vernon, TX	**13**
Wilbarger County, TX	13
Vicksburg, MS	**57**
Claiborne County, MS	9
Warren County, MS	48
Vidalia, GA	**36**
Montgomery County, GA	9
Toombs County, GA	27
Vincennes, IN	**38**
Knox County, IN	38
Vineyard Haven, MA	**17**
Dukes County, MA	17
Wabash, IN	**32**
Wabash County, IN	32
Wahpeton, ND-MN	**23**
Wilkin County, MN	7
Richland County, ND	16

Z Less than 500

Source: U.S. Census Bureau, 2012 Population Estimates, <http://www.census.gov/popest/data/metro/totals/2012/>.

Micropolitan Statistical Area ~~Component county	Population, 2012 (1,000)
Wapakoneta, OH	**46**
Auglaize County, OH	46
Warren, PA	**41**
Warren County, PA	41
Warrensburg, MO	**54**
Johnson County, MO	54
Warsaw, IN	**78**
Kosciusko County, IN	78
Washington, IN	**32**
Daviess County, IN	32
Washington, NC	**48**
Beaufort County, NC	48
Washington Court House, OH	**29**
Fayette County, OH	29
Watertown, SD	**28**
Codington County, SD	28
Watertown-Fort Atkinson, WI	**84**
Jefferson County, WI	84
Wauchula, FL	**28**
Hardee County, FL	28
Waycross, GA	**55**
Pierce County, GA	19
Ware County, GA	36
Weatherford, OK	**29**
Custer County, OK	29
West Plains, MO	**41**
Howell County, MO	41
Whitewater, WI	**103**
Walworth County, WI	103
Williston, ND	**27**
Williams County, ND	27
Willmar, MN	**42**
Kandiyohi County, MN	42
Wilmington, OH	**42**
Clinton County, OH	42
Wilson, NC	**82**
Wilson County, NC	82
Winnemucca, NV	**17**
Humboldt County, NV	17
Winona, MN	**52**
Winona County, MN	52
Wisconsin Rapids-Marshfield, WI	**74**
Wood County, WI	74
Woodward, OK	**21**
Woodward County, OK	21
Wooster, OH	**115**
Wayne County, OH	115
Worthington, MN	**21**
Nobles County, MN	21
Yankton, SD	**23**
Yankton County, SD	23
Zanesville, OH	**86**
Muskingum County, OH	86
Zapata, TX	**14**
Zapata County, TX	14

Introduction-The data presented in this *Statistical Abstract* come from many sources. The sources include not only federal statistical bureaus and other organizations that collect and issue statistics as their principal activity, but also governmental administrative and regulatory agencies, private research bodies, trade associations, insurance companies, health associations, private organizations, and philanthropic foundations. Consequently, the data vary considerably as to reference periods, definitions of terms and, for ongoing series, the number and frequency of time periods for which data are available.

The statistics presented were obtained and tabulated by various methods. Some statistics are based on complete enumerations or censuses while others are based on samples. Some information is extracted from records kept for administrative or regulatory purposes (school enrollment, hospital records, securities registration, financial accounts, social security records, income tax returns, etc.), while other information is obtained explicitly for statistical purposes through surveys. The estimation procedures used vary from highly sophisticated scientific techniques, to crude "informed guesses."

Each set of data relates to a group of individuals or units of interest referred to as the *target universe,* or *target population*, or simply as the *universe* or *population.*

Prior to data collection, the target universe should be clearly defined. For example, if data are to be collected for the universe of households in the United States, it is necessary to define a "household." The target universe may not be completely tractable. Cost and other considerations may restrict data collection to a *survey universe* based on an available list. This list is called a *survey frame, sampling frame, or survey sample.*

The data in many tables are based on data obtained for all population units, *a census*, or on data obtained for only a portion, or *sample*, of the population units. When the data presented are based on a sample, the sample is usually a scientifically selected *probability sample.* This is a sample selected from a list or sampling frame in such a way that every possible sample has a known chance of selection and usually each unit selected can be assigned a number, greater than zero and less than or equal to one, representing its likelihood or probability of selection.

For large-scale sample surveys, the probability sample of units is often selected as a multistage sample. The first stage of a multistage sample is the selection of a probability sample of large groups of population members, referred to as primary sampling units (PSUs). For example, in a national multistage household sample, PSUs are often counties or groups of counties. The second stage of a multistage sample is the selection, within each PSU selected at the first stage, of smaller groups of population units, referred to as secondary sampling units. In subsequent stages of selection, smaller and smaller nested groups are chosen until the ultimate sample of population units is

obtained. To qualify a multistage sample as a probability sample, all stages of sampling must be carried out using probability sampling methods.

Prior to selection at each stage of a multistage (or a single stage) sample, a list of the sampling units or sampling frame for that stage must be obtained. For example, for the first stage of selection of a national household sample, a list of the counties and county groups that form the PSUs must be compiled. For the final stage of selection, lists of households, and sometimes persons within the households, have to be compiled in the field. For surveys of economic entities and for the economic censuses, the U.S. Census Bureau generally uses a frame constructed from the Bureau's Business Register. The Business Register contains all establishments with payroll in the United States including small single establishment firms as well as large multi-establishment firms.

Wherever the quantities in a table refer to an entire universe, but are constructed from data collected in a sample survey, the table quantities are referred to as *sample estimates.* In constructing a sample estimate, an attempt is made to come as close as is feasible to the corresponding universe quantity that would be obtained from a complete census of the universe. Estimates based on a sample will, however, generally differ from the hypothetical census figures. Two classifications of errors are associated with estimates based on sample surveys:

1 *sampling error*-the error arising from the use of a sample, rather than a census, to estimate population quantities and

2 *nonsampling error*-those errors arising from nonsampling sources. As discussed below, the magnitude of the sampling error for an estimate can usually be estimated from the sample data. However, the magnitude of the nonsampling error for an estimate can rarely be estimated. Consequently, actual error in an estimate exceeds the error that can be estimated.

The particular sample used in a survey is only one of a large number of possible samples of the same size which could have been selected using the same sampling procedure. Estimates derived from the different samples would, in general, differ from each other. The *standard error* (SE) is a measure of the variation among the estimates derived from all possible samples. The standard error is the most commonly used measure of the sampling error of an estimate. Valid estimates of the standard errors of survey estimates can usually be calculated from the data collected in a probability sample. For convenience, the standard error is sometimes expressed as a percent of the estimate and is called the relative standard error or *coefficient of variation* (CV). For example, an estimate of 200 units with an estimated standard error of 10 units has an estimated CV of 5 percent.

A sample estimate and an estimate of its standard error or CV can be used to construct interval estimates that have a prescribed confidence that the interval includes the average of the estimates derived from all possible samples with a known probability. To illustrate, if all possible samples were selected under essentially the same general conditions, and using the same sample design, and if an estimate and its estimated standard error were calculated from each sample, then: 1) approximately 68 percent of the intervals from one standard error below the estimate to one standard error above the estimate would include the average estimate derived from all possible samples; 2) approximately 90 percent of the intervals from 1.6 standard errors below the estimate to 1.6 standard errors above the estimate would include the average estimate derived from all possible samples; and 3) approximately 95 percent of the intervals from two standard errors below the estimate to two standard errors above the estimate would include the average estimate derived from all possible samples.

Thus, for a particular sample, one can say with the appropriate level of confidence (e.g., 90 percent or 95 percent) that the average of all possible samples is included in the constructed interval. Example of a confidence interval: An estimate is 200 units with a standard error of 10 units. An approximately 90 percent confidence interval (plus or minus 1.6 standard errors) is from 184 to 216.

All surveys and censuses are subject to nonsampling errors. Nonsampling errors are of two kinds-*random* and *nonrandom*. Random nonsampling errors arise because of the varying interpretation of questions (by respondents or interviewers) and varying actions of coders, keyers, and other processors. Some randomness is also introduced when respondents must estimate. Nonrandom nonsampling errors result from total nonresponse (no usable data obtained for a sampled unit), partial or item nonresponse (only a portion of a response may be usable), inability or unwillingness on the part of respondents to provide correct information, difficulty interpreting questions, mistakes in recording or keying data, errors of collection or processing, and coverage problems (overcoverage and undercoverage of the target universe). Random nonresponse errors usually, but not always, result in an understatement of sampling errors and thus an overstatement of the precision of survey estimates. Estimating the magnitude of nonsampling errors would require special experiments or access to independent data and, consequently, the magnitudes are seldom available.

Nearly all types of nonsampling errors that affect surveys also occur in complete censuses. Since surveys can be conducted on a smaller scale than censuses, nonsampling errors can presumably be controlled more tightly. Relatively more funds and effort can perhaps be expended toward eliciting responses, detecting and correcting response error, and reducing processing errors. As a result, survey results can sometimes be more accurate than census results.

To compensate for suspected nonrandom errors, adjustments of the sample estimates are often made. For example, adjustments are frequently made for nonresponse, both total and partial. Adjustments made for either type of nonresponse are often referred to as *imputations*. Imputation for total nonresponse is usually made by substituting for the questionnaire responses of the nonrespondents the "average" questionnaire responses of the respondents. These imputations usually are made separately within various groups of sample members, formed by attempting to place respondents and nonrespondents together that have "similar" design or ancillary characteristics. Imputation for item nonresponse is usually made by substituting for a missing item the response to that item of a respondent having characteristics that are "similar" to those of the nonrespondent.

For an estimate calculated from a sample survey, the *total error* in the estimate is composed of the sampling error, which can usually be estimated from the sample, and the nonsampling error, which usually cannot be estimated from the sample. The total error present in a population quantity obtained from a complete census is composed of only nonsampling errors. Ideally, estimates of the total error associated with data given in the *Statistical Abstract* tables should be given. However, due to the unavailability of estimates of nonsampling errors, only estimates of the levels of sampling errors, in terms of estimated standard errors or coefficients of variation, are available. To obtain estimates of the estimated standard errors from the sample of interest, see the source cited at the end of each table.

Source of Additional Material: The Federal Committee on Statistical Methodology (FCSM) is an interagency committee dedicated to improving the quality of federal statistics <http://www.fcsm.gov>.

Principal data bases-Beginning below are brief descriptions of 35 of the sample surveys and censuses that provide a substantial portion of the data contained in this *Abstract*.

U.S. DEPARTMENT OF AGRICULTURE, National Agriculture Statistics Service

Census of Agriculture

Universes, Frequency, and Types of Data: Complete count of U.S. farms and ranches conducted once every 5 years with data at the national, state, and county level. Data published on farm numbers and related items/characteristics.

Type of Data Collection Operation: Complete census for number of farms; land in farms; farm income; agriculture products sold; farms by type of organization; total cropland; irrigated land; farm operator characteristics; livestock and poultry inventory and sales; and selected crops harvested. Market value of land, buildings, and products sold, total farm production expenses, machinery and equipment, and fertilizer and chemicals.

Data Collection and Imputation Procedures: Data collection is by mailing questionnaires to all farmers and ranchers. Producers can return their forms by mail or online. Nonrespondents are contacted by telephone and correspondence follow-ups. Imputations were made for all nonresponse item/characteristics and coverage adjustments were made to account for missed farms and ranches. The response rate for the 2007 Census was 85.2 percent.

Estimates of Sampling Error: Weight adjustments were made to account for the undercoverage and whole-unit nonresponse of farms on the Census Mail List (CML). These were treated as sampling errors.

Other (nonsampling) Errors: Nonsampling errors are due to incompleteness of the census mailing list, duplications on the list, respondent reporting errors, errors in editing reported data, and in imputation for missing data. Evaluation studies are conducted to measure certain nonsampling errors such as list coverage and classification error. It is a reasonable assumption that the net effect of non measurable errors is zero (the positive errors cancel the negative errors).

Sources of Additional Material: U.S. Department of Agriculture (NASS), 2007 Census of Agriculture, Appendix A-1 Census of Agriculture Methodology, Appendix B-1 General Explanation and Census of Agriculture Report Form.

Basic Area Frame Sample

Universe, Frequency, and Types of Data: The June Agricultural Survey collects data on planted acreage and livestock inventories on all land in the 48 contiguous states and Hawaii. The survey also serves to measure list incompleteness and is subsampled for multiple frame surveys.

Type of Data Collection Operation: Stratified probability sample of about 11,000 land area units of about 1 sq. mile (range from 0.1 sq. mile in cities to several sq. miles in open grazing areas). Sample represents 42,000 operating arrangements. About 20 percent of the sample replaced annually.

Data Collection and Imputation Procedures: Data collection is by personal enumeration. Imputation is based on enumerator observation or data reported by respondents having similar agricultural characteristics.

Estimates of Sampling Error: Estimated CVs range from 1 percent to 2 percent for regional estimates to 3 percent to 6 percent for state estimates of major crop acres and livestock inventories.

Other (nonsampling) Errors: Minimized through rigid quality controls on the collection process and careful review of all reported data.

Sources of Additional Material: U.S. Department of Agriculture, National Agricultural Statistics Service, USDA's National Agricultural Statistics Service: The Fact Finders of Agriculture, March 2007.

Multiple Frame Surveys

Universe, Frequency, and Types of Data: Surveys of U.S. farm operators to obtain data on major livestock inventories, selected crop acreage and production, grain stocks, and farm labor characteristics, farm economic data, and chemical use data. Estimates are made quarterly, semi-annually, or annually depending on the data series.

Type of Data Collection Operation: Primary frame is obtained from general or special purpose lists, supplemented by a probability sample of land areas used to estimate for list incompleteness.

Data Collection and Imputation Procedures: Mail, telephone, or personal interviews used for initial data collection. Mail nonrespondent follow-up by phone and personal interviews. Imputation based on average of respondents.

Estimates of Sampling Error: Estimated CVs range from 1 percent to 2 percent at the U.S. level for crop and livestock data series and 3 to 5 percent for economic data. Regional CVs range from 3 to 6 percent, while state estimate CVs run 5 to 10 percent.

Other (nonsampling) Errors: In addition to above, replicated sampling procedures used to monitor effects of changes in survey procedures.

Sources of Additional Material: U.S. Department of Agriculture, National Agricultural Statistics Service, USDA's National Agricultural Statistics Service: The Fact Finders of Agriculture, March 2007.

Objective Yield Surveys

Universe, Frequency, and Types of Data: Monthly surveys during the growing season of corn, cotton, potatoes, soybeans, and winter wheat fields in top producing states for forecasting and estimating yield per acre.

Type of Data Collection Operation: Random location of plots in probability sample. Corn, cotton, and soybeans, are selected in June from Basic Area Frame Sample (see above). Winter wheat and potatoes are selected from March and June multiple frame surveys, respectively.

Data Collection and Imputation Procedures: Enumerators count and measure plant characteristics in sample fields. Production is measured from plots at harvest. Harvest loss is measured from post harvest gleanings.

Estimates of Sampling Error: CVs for national estimates of production are about 2 to 3 percent.

Other (nonsampling) Errors: In addition to above, replicated sampling procedures are used to monitor effects of changes in survey procedures.

Sources of Additional Material: U.S. Department of Agriculture, National Agricultural Statistics Service), USDA's National Agricultural Statistics Service: The Fact Finders of Agriculture, March 2007.

U.S. BUREAU OF JUSTICE STATISTICS (BJS)

National Crime Victimization Survey

Universe, Frequency, and Types of Data: Annual survey of U.S. household members age 12 and older to obtain data on criminal victimization for compilation of annual estimates. Survey includes nonfatal crimes and household property crimes reported and not reported to the police. The Survey does not include homicide, arson, and commercial crimes.

Type of Data Collection Operation: Data collection conducted by the Census Bureau for the Bureau of Justice Statistics. Persons interviewed are asked about the number and characteristics of victimization experiences during the prior 6 months.

Data Collection and Imputation Procedures: Interviews are conducted with household members in a nationally representative sample of approximately 169,000 persons age 12 or older. Eligible household members are interviewed every 6 months for a total of 7 interviews. Households stay in the sample for about 3 years. New households rotate into the sample on an ongoing basis. Personal interviews are used in the first interview; the intervening interviews are conducted by telephone whenever possible.

Estimates of Sampling Error: Standard of errors for 2011 victimization rates per 1,000 persons age 12/older or 1,000 households, are: .9 for all violent crimes; .1 for rape/sexual assault; .2 for robbery; .8 for assault; .4 for domestic violence; .4 for all serious violent crimes; 3.2 for all property crimes; 1.2 for household burglary; and .4 for motor vehicle theft.

Other (nonsampling) Errors: Respondent recall errors may include reporting incidents for other than the reference period; interviewer coding and processing errors; and possible mistaken reporting or classifying of events.

Sources of Additional Material: U.S. Bureau of Justice Statistics, *Criminal Victimization in the United States*, annual.

U.S. BUREAU OF LABOR STATISTICS

Consumer Expenditure Survey (CE)

Universe, Frequency and Types of Data: Consists of two continuous components: a quarterly interview survey and a weekly diary survey. These nationwide surveys collect data on consumer expenditures, income, characteristics, and assets and liabilities. Samples are national probability samples of households that are representative of the civilian noninstitutional population. The surveys have been ongoing since 1980.

Type of Data Collection Operation: The Interview Survey is a panel rotation survey. Each panel is interviewed for five quarters and then dropped from the survey. About 7,100 consumer units provide usable interviews each quarter. The Diary Survey sample is new each year and consists of about 7,100 consumer units. Data are collected on an ongoing basis in 91 PSUs.

Data Collection and Imputation Procedures: For the Interview Survey, data are collected by personal interview with each consumer unit interviewed once per quarter for five consecutive quarters. The Interview Survey is designed to collect information that respondents can recall for 3 months or longer, such as large or recurring expenditures. For the Diary Survey, respondents record all their expenditures in a self-reporting diary for two consecutive 1-week periods. The Diary Survey is designed to pick up small, frequently purchased items which can be difficult to recall over a long period of time. These items include food, beverages, and household and personal care products and services. Missing or invalid attributes, expenditures, or incomes are imputed. Assets and liabilities are not imputed. The U.S. Census Bureau collects the data for the Bureau of Labor Statistics.

Estimates of Sampling Error: Standard error tables are available since 2000.

Other (nonsampling) Errors: Includes differences in the interpretation of questions, inability or unwillingness of respondents to provide correct information, and data processing errors. They occur regardless of whether data are collected from a sample or from the entire population.

Sources of Additional Material: Bureau of Labor Statistics, see Internet site <http://www.bls.gov/cex>, and BLS Handbook of Methods, Chapter 16, see Internet site <http://www.bls.gov/opub/hom/pdf/homch16.pdf>.

Consumer Price Index (CPI)

Universe, Frequency, and Types of Data: A monthly survey of price changes of all types of consumer goods and services purchased by urban wage earners and clerical workers prior to 1978, and urban consumers thereafter. Both indexes continue to be published. The BLS calculates CPI indexes for 38 geographic areas across the U.S., and for 211 item categories called item strata, which cover all consumer purchases.

Type of Data Collection Operation: Prior to 1978, and since 1998, sample of various consumer items in 87 urban areas; from 1978-1997, in 85 PSUs, except from January 1987 through March 1988, when 91 areas were sampled.

Data Collection and Imputation Procedures: Prices of consumer items are obtained each month from about 25,500 retail outlets and from about 4,000 housing units in 87 areas. Prices of food, fuel, and a few other items are obtained monthly; prices of most other commodities and services are collected every month in the three largest geographic areas and every other month in others. Imputation is a procedure for handling missing information. The CPI uses imputation for a number of cases, including refusals, inability to collect data for some other reason (the item may be out of season), and the inability to make a satisfactory estimate of the quality change. For noncomparable substitutions, an estimate of constant-quality price change is made by imputation.

Estimates of Sampling Error: BLS calculates and publishes estimates of the 1-month, 2-month, 6-month and 12-month percent change standard errors annually, for the CPI-U. For the latest data, including information on how to use the estimates of standard error, see "Variance Estimates for Price Changes in the Consumer Price Index, January-December 2012." Information is available through the CPI home page at <http://www.bls.gov/cpi>, or <http://www.bls.gov/cpi/cpivar2012.pdf>.

Other (nonsampling) Errors: Errors result from inaccurate reporting, difficulties in defining concepts and their operational implementation, and introduction of product quality changes and new products.

Sources of Additional Material: U.S. Bureau of Labor Statistics, Internet site <http://www.bls.gov/cpi/home.htm>, and BLS Handbook of Methods, Chapter 17, see Internet site <http://www.bls.gov/opub/hom/pdf/homch17.pdf>.

Current Employment Statistics (CES) Program

Universe, Frequency, and Types of Data: Monthly survey of approximately 145,000 businesses and government agencies representing approximately 557,000 worksites throughout the U.S., clustered by unemployment insurance account number. Sample is updated twice a year, and redrawn for the 1st quarter of each year. The CES collects data on employment, hours, and earnings at detailed industry levels. The CES series are estimates of nonfarm wage and salary jobs, not of employed persons; an individual with 2 jobs is counted twice by the payroll survey. The CES excludes employees in agriculture and private households, and the self-employed.

Type of Data Collection Operation: The BLS uses various collection techniques. Data collection centers (DCCs) perform initial enrollment of each firm via telephone, collect the data for several months via Computer Assisted Telephone Interviewing (CATI), and, where possible, transfer respondents to a self-reporting mode such as touch-tone data entry (TDE), Fax, or Internet collection. Very large, multi-establishment firms are often enrolled via personal visit, and ongoing reporting is established via electronic data interchange (EDI). These firms provide electronic files to BLS that include data from all their worksites. Approximately 55,000 new sample units are enrolled in the CES survey each year. All firms with 1,000 or more employees are asked to participate in the survey, as is a sample of firms across all employment sizes. When firms are rotated into the sample, they are retained for 2 years or more. When a respondent is rotated out of the sample, BLS will not ask the firm to participate for at least 3 years.

Data Collection and Imputation Procedures: Each month, respondents extract the employment, hours, and earnings data from their payroll records and submit it to the BLS. Data are collected for the pay period that includes the 12th of each month. BLS staff prepare national estimates of employment, hours, and earnings. State agencies cooperate with the BLS to develop state and metropolitan area estimates.

Estimates of Sampling Errors: The magnitude of sampling error, or variance, is directly related to the size of the sample and the percentage of universe coverage achieved by the sample. The establishment survey sample covers over one-third of total universe employment; this yields a relatively small variance on the total nonfarm estimates.

Other (nonsampling) Errors: Estimates of employment adjusted annually to reflect complete universe. Average adjustment is 0.3 percent over the last decade, with an absolute range from than 0.1 percent to 0.7 percent.

Sources of Additional Material: U.S. Bureau of Labor Statistics, BLS Handbook of Methods, Chapter 2, see <http://www.bls.gov/opub/hom/homch2.htm>.

National Compensation Survey (NCS)

Universe, Frequency, and Types of Data: NCS collects data on occupational earnings, employment costs trends, and prevalence of employee benefits. The NCS includes establishments in private industry and in state and local government; major exclusions are workers in federal and quasi-federal agencies, military personnel, agricultural workers, workers in private households, the self-employed, and unpaid workers. The NCS produces information on workers' earnings and benefits in a variety of occupations at different work levels. NCS is responsible for two quarterly releases: the Employment Cost Index (ECI), which measures percent changes in the cost of employment, and the Employer Costs for Employee Compensation (ECEC), which measures costs per hour worked for individual benefits. The survey provides data by industry sector, industry division, occupational group, bargaining status, metropolitan area status, census region, and census division. ECEC also provides data by establishment-size class. Incidence and detailed provisions of employee benefit plans in private establishments are issued for broad occupational groups and selected industries, by establishment employment size, census division, and selected worker characteristics.

Type of Data Collection Operation: The sample of establishments is drawn by dividing the sample by industry and ownership. Each sample establishment is selected using a method of sampling called probability proportional to employment size. A probability sample of occupations within a sampled establishment is performed using a method called probability selection of occupations. The methodology and procedures used to estimate vary by product line. NCS replaces its sample on a continual basis. Private industry establishments are in the survey for approximately 5 years.

Data Collection and Imputation Procedures: A personal visit to the establishment is the initial source for collecting data. Communication via mail, fax, and telephone provide quarterly updates. Imputation is done for individual benefits. To address the problems of nonresponse and missing data, the NCS adjusts the weights of the remaining establishments and imputes missing values; missing values for an initially responding establishment are replaced by values from the original interview; missing values for an item are replaced by values derived from establishments with similar characteristics.

Estimates of Sampling Error: NCS uses standard errors to evaluate published series. These standard errors are available at <http://www.bls.gov/ncs/ect/home.htm>.

Other (nonsampling) Errors: Nonsampling errors have a number of potential sources. The primary sources are (1) survey nonresponse and (2) data collection and processing errors. Nonsampling errors are not measured. Quality assurance programs reduces the potential for nonsampling errors. These programs include the use of reinterviews, interview observations, validating data, and the systematic professional review of data. The programs also serve as a training device that provides feedback on errors for field economists (or data collectors). Quality assurance programs also provide information on sources of error. This information is used to improve procedures that result in fewer errors.

Sources of Additional Material: Bureau of Labor Statistics, BLS Handbook of Methods, Chapter 8, see <http://www.bls.gov/opub/hom//pdf/homch8.pdf>.

Producer Price Index (PPI)

Universe, Frequency, and Types of Data: Monthly survey of producing companies to determine price changes of all commodities and services produced in the United States for sale in commercial transactions. Data on agriculture, forestry, fishing, manufacturing, mining, gas, electricity, construction, public utilities, wholesale trade, retail trade, transportation, healthcare, and other services. Domestic production of goods for the military is included, as are goods shipped between establishments owned by the same company. As of

January 2009, the PPI program covered more than three-quarters of the service sector's output.

Type of Data Collection Operation: PPIs are based on selling prices reported by establishments of all sizes selected by probability sampling, with the probability of selection proportionate to size. Individual items and transaction terms from these firms also are chosen by probability proportionate to size. BLS periodically updates the PPI sample of survey respondents to better reflect current conditions when the structure, membership, technology, or product mix of an industry shifts significantly and to spread reporting burden among smaller firms. Results of these resampling efforts are incorporated into the PPI with the release of data for January and July. More than 100,000 price quotations per month are organized into three sets of PPIs: (1) Stage-of-processing indexes, (2) commodity indexes, and (3) indexes for the net output of industries and their products.

Data Collection and Imputation Procedures: BLS strongly encourages cooperating companies to supply actual transaction prices at the time of shipment to minimize the use of list prices. Prices submitted by survey respondents are effective on the Tuesday of the week containing the 13th day of the month. This survey is conducted via mail, facsimile, and the Internet. Each month approximately 100,000 prices are collected from 25,000 reporters. Missing prices are estimated by those received for similar products or services. The current standard base period for most commodity-oriented PPI series is 1982, but many indexes that began after 1982 are based on the month of their introduction. All unadjusted PPIs are routinely subject to revision only once, 4 months after their original publication, to reflect late reports and corrections by company respondents. Once revised, indexes are considered final.

Estimates of Sampling Error: Not applicable.

Other (nonsampling) Errors: Not available at present.

Sources of Additional Material: U.S. Bureau of Labor Statistics, PPI methodology, <http://www.bls.gov/ppi/methodology.htm>; and BLS Handbook of Methods, Chapter 14, <http://stats.bls.gov/opub/hom/homch14.htm>.

BOARD OF GOVERNORS OF THE FEDERAL RESERVE SYSTEM

Survey of Consumer Finances

Universe, Frequency, and Types of Data: Periodic sample survey of families. In this survey a given household is divided into a primary economic unit and other economic units. The primary economic unit, which may be a single individual, is generally chosen as the person or couple who either holds the title to the home or is listed on the lease, along with all other people in the household who are financially interdependent with that person or couple. The primary economic unit is used as the reference family. The survey collects detailed data on the composition of family balance sheets, pensions, income, the terms of loans, and relationships with financial institutions. It also gathers information on the employment history and pension rights of the survey respondent and the spouse or partner of the respondent.

Type of Data Collection Operation: The survey employs a two-part strategy for sampling families. Some families are selected by standard multistage area probability sampling methods applied to all 50 states. The remaining families in the survey are selected using statistical records derived from tax returns, under the strict rules governing confidentiality and the rights of potential respondents to refuse participation; this sample is designed to oversample wealthy households. For the 2010 SCF, the area probability sample included 5,012 families; the list sample included 1,480 families. Median interview length in the 2010 SCF was 90 minutes.

Data Collection and Imputation Procedures: National Opinion Research Center (NORC) at the University of Chicago has collected data for the survey since 1992. The majority of interviews for SCF 2010 were conducted in person. Since 1995, the survey has used computer-assisted personal interviewing. Adjustments for nonresponse are made through multiple imputation of unanswered questions and through weighting adjustments based on data used in the sample design for families that refused participation.

Estimates of Sampling Error: Because of the complex design of the survey, the estimation of potential sampling errors is not straightforward. A replicate-based procedure is available.

Other (nonsampling) Errors: The survey aims to complete 4,500 interviews, with about two thirds of that number deriving from the area-probability sample. The response rate is typically about 70 percent for the area-probability sample and about 35 percent over all strata in the tax-data sample. Proper training and monitoring of interviewers, careful design of questionnaires, and systematic editing of the resulting data were used to control inaccurate survey responses.

Sources of Additional Material: Board of Governors of the Federal Reserve System, "Changes in U.S. Family Finances from 2007 to 2010: Evidence from the Survey of Consumer Finances," *Federal Reserve Bulletin*, 2012, <http://www.federalreserve.gov/Pubs/Bulletin>.

U.S. CENSUS BUREAU

2007 Economic Census

(Industry Series, Geographic Area Series and Subject Series Reports) (for NAICS sectors 21 to 81)

Universe, Frequency, and Types of Data: Conducted every 5 years to obtain data on number of establishments, number of employees, payroll, total sales/receipts/revenue, and other industry-specific statistics. The universe is all establishments with paid employees excluding agriculture, forestry, fishing and hunting, and government. (Non-employer Statistics, discussed separately, covers those establishments without paid employees.)

Changes for 2007 included tabulations to include Census designated places (unincorporated places), expanded Survey of Business Owners data, data on franchising for more industries, and complete implementation of the North American Product Classification System (NAPCS).

Type of Data Collection Operation: All large employer firms were surveyed (i.e., all employer firms above payroll-size cutoffs established to separate large from small employers) plus, in most sectors, a sample of the small employer firms.

Data Collection and Imputation Procedures: Mail questionnaires were used with both mail and telephone follow-ups for nonrespondents. Businesses also had the option to respond electronically. Data for nonrespondents and for small employer firms not mailed a questionnaire were obtained from administrative records of other federal agencies or imputed.

Estimates of Sampling Error: Not applicable for basic data such as sales, revenue, receipts, payroll, etc. for sectors other than Construction (NAICS 23). Estimates of sampling error for construction industries are included with the data as published on the Census Bureau Web site.

Other (nonsampling) errors: Nonsampling errors may be attributed to an inability to identify all cases in the actual universe; definition and classification difficulties; differences in interpretation of questions; errors in recording or coding data; and other errors of collection, response, coverage, processing, and estimation for missing or misreported data.

Sources of Additional Material: U.S. Census Bureau, see <http://www.census.gov/econ/census07/www/methodology/>.

American Community Survey (ACS)

Universe, Frequency, and Types of Data: Nationwide survey of approximately 3 million households per year, to obtain data about demographic, social, economic, and housing characteristics of housing units and the people residing in them. It covers the household population and, beginning in 2006, also includes the group quarter population living in correctional facilities, skilled-nursing homes, military barracks, college residence halls, and other group quarters.

Type of Data Collection Operation: Housing unit address sampling is performed twice a year in both August and January. First-phase of sampling defines the universe for the second stage of sampling through two steps. First, all addresses that were eligible for the second-phase sampling within the past four years are excluded from eligibility.

This ensures that no address is in sample more than once in any 5-year period. The second step is to select a 20 percent systematic sample of "new" units, i.e. those units that have never appeared on a previous Master Address File (MAF) extract. All new addresses are systematically assigned to either the current year or to one of four back-samples. This procedure maintains five equal partitions of the universe. The second-phase sampling is done on the current year's partition and results in approximately 3,000,000 housing unit addresses in the U.S. and 36,000 in Puerto Rico (PR). **Group quarter sampling** is performed separately from the housing unit sampling. The sampling begins with separating the small (15 persons or fewer) and the large (more than 15 persons) group quarters. The target sampling rate for both groups is a 2.5% sample of the group quarters population. It results in approximately 200,000 group quarter residents being selected in the U.S., and an additional 1,000 in Puerto Rico.

Data Collection and Imputation Procedures: The American Community Survey is conducted every month on independent samples. The data collection operation for housing units (HUs) consists of three modes or phases: mail, telephone, and personal visit. For most HUs, the first phase includes a questionnaire mailed to the sample address, with a request to the household to complete the questionnaire and return it by mail. If no response is received, the Census Bureau follows up with computer-assisted telephone interviewing (CATI) when a telephone number is available. If the Census Bureau is unable to reach an occupant using CATI, or if the household refuses to participate, the address may be selected for computer-assisted personal interviewing (CAPI). Mailable addresses with neither a response to the mailout nor a telephone interview are sampled at a rate of 1 in 2, 2 in 5, or 1 in 3 based on the expected rate of completed interviews at the tract level. Unmailable addresses are sampled at a rate of 2 in 3. Those addresses selected through this process are assigned to Field Representatives (FRs), who visit the addresses, verify their existence, determine their occupancy status, and conduct interviews. **Collection of group quarters** data is conducted primarily through FR interviews. Their methods include completing the questionnaire while speaking to the resident in person or over the telephone, or leaving paper questionnaires for residents to complete for themselves and then pick them up later. This last option is used for data collection in federal prisons. If needed, a personal interview can be conducted with a proxy, such as a relative or guardian. After data collection is completed, any remaining incomplete or inconsistent information on the questionnaire are imputed during the final automated edit of the collected data.

Estimates of Sampling Error: The data in the ACS products are estimates and can vary from the actual values that would have been obtained by conducting a census of the entire population. The estimates from the chosen sample addresses can also vary from those that would have been obtained from a different set of addresses. This variation causes uncertainty, which can be measured using statistics such as standard error, margin of error, and confidence interval. All ACS estimates are accompanied by margin of errors to assist users.

Other (nonsampling) Errors: Other types of errors may occur during any of the various complex operations used to select, collect and process survey data. An important goal of the ACS is to minimize the amount of nonsampling error introduced through coverage issues in the sample list, nonresponse from sample housing units, and transcribing or editing data. One way of accomplishing this is by finding additional sources of addresses, following up on nonrespondents and maintaining quality control systems.

Sources of Additional Material: U.S. Census Bureau, American Community Survey Web site available on the Internet, <http://www.census.gov/acs/www/index.html>; U.S. Census Bureau, American Community Survey Accuracy of the Data documents available on the Internet, <http://www.census.gov/acs/www/methodology/methodology_main/>.

American Housing Survey

Universe, Frequency, and Types of Data: Conducted biennially in odd numbered years during May through September, to obtain data on occupied or vacant housing units in the United States (group quarters are excluded). Data include characteristics of occupied housing units, vacant units, new housing and mobile home units, financial characteristics, recent mover households, housing and neighborhood quality indicators, and energy characteristics. The 2011 AHS sample size was approximately 186,400 housing units (including about 8,900 ineligible); unweighted overall response rate was 87 percent, weighted overall response rate was 88 percent. The 2011 sample included an additional 5,250 subsidized housing units, and a supplemental sample of 29 metropolitan areas. The sample covered 394 primary sampling units (878 counties and cities in all States and DC).

Type of Data Collection Operation: Census Bureau interviewers visit or telephone the household occupying each housing unit in the sample. For unoccupied units, they obtain information from landlords, rental agents, or neighbors.

Data Collection and Imputation Procedures: Housing units participating in the AHS are scientifically selected to represent a cross section of all housing in the nation. The same basic sample of housing units is interviewed every two years until a new sample is selected. The U.S. Census Bureau updates the sample by adding newly constructed housing units and units discovered through coverage improvement efforts. Each housing unit in the AHS national sample is weighted and represents about 2,000 housing units in the United States. The 2011 AHS basic weight is 1,148.

Estimates of Sampling Error: Most numbers from the AHS are counts of housing units (for example, units with basements or units with an elderly person). These counts have error from sampling. As with the other types of errors, readers should be wary of numbers with large errors from sampling. For the national sample, illustrations of the Standard Error (SE) of the estimates are provided in the Appendix D of the 2011 report.

Other (nonsampling) Errors: Nonsampling errors may result from incorrect or incomplete responses, errors in coding and recording, and processing errors. Appendix D of the 2011 report has a complete discussion of the errors.

Sources of Additional Material: U.S. Census Bureau, *Current Housing Reports,* Series H-150 and H-170, *American Housing Survey* see <http://www.census.gov/hhes/www/ahs.html>.

Annual Survey of Public Employment

Universe, Frequency, and Types of Data: Covers the civilian employees of all the Federal Government agencies (except the Central Intelligence Agency, the National Security Agency, and the Defense Intelligence Agency), all agencies of the 50 state governments, and 90,690 local governments (i.e., counties, municipalities, townships, special districts, and school districts) including the District of Columbia. The survey measures the number of state, local and federal civilian government employees and their gross payrolls for the pay period including March 12. The survey is conducted annually except in years ending in '2' and '7', when a census of all state and local governments is done. The survey provides state and local government data on full-time and part-time employment, part-time hours worked, full-time equivalent

employment, and payroll statistics by governmental function. The survey provides Federal Government data on total employees, full-time employees, and total March payroll by governmental function.

Type of Data Collection Operations: Census Bureau staff compiled Federal Government data from records of the U.S. Office of Personnel Management. Forty-five of the state governments provided data from central payroll records for all or most of their agencies/institutions. Data for agencies and institutions for the remaining state governments were obtained by mail canvass questionnaires. Local governments were also canvassed using a mail questionnaire. However, elementary and secondary school system data in Florida, North Dakota, and Washington were supplied by special arrangements with the state education agency in each of these states. Additionally, in Delaware, a state government respondent supplied data for school districts. Ten counties, twelve cities, two townships and three other local school districts provided data in an electronic format. All respondents receiving the mail questionnaire had the option of completing the survey using a web-based survey instrument developed for reporting the data. The online survey instrument was completed by 21.0% of the state-level responding units and 54.6% of the local government respondents.

Editing and Imputation Procedures: Editing is a process that ensures survey data are accurate, complete, and consistent. Efforts are made at all phases of collection, processing, and tabulation to minimize errors. Although some edits are built into the Internet data collection instrument and the data entry programs, the majority of the edits are performed after the case has been loaded into the Census Bureau's database. Edits consist primarily of two types: consistency and a ratio of the current years reported value to the prior year's value. The consistency edits check the logical relationships of data items reported on the form. For example, if part-time employees and payroll are reported then part-time hours must be reported. The current year/prior year edits compare data for the number of employees, the function reported for the employees, and the average salary between reporting years. If data fall outside of acceptable tolerance levels, the item is flagged for review. Some additional checks are made comparing data from the Annual Finance Survey to data reported on the Annual Survey of Public Employment and Payroll to verify that employees reported on the Annual Survey of Public Employment and Payroll at a particular function have a corresponding expenditure on the Finance Survey. For both types of edits, the edit results are reviewed by analysts and adjusted when needed. When the analyst is unable to resolve or accept the edit failure, contact is made with the respondent to verify or correct the reported data.

Imputation: For general purpose governments and for schools, imputations were based on recent historical data from either a prior year annual survey or the most recent Census of Governments, as available. These data were adjusted by a growth rate that was determined by the growth of units that were similar (in size, geography, and type of government) to the nonrespondent. if no recent historical data were available, imputations were based on the data from a randomly selected donor that was similar to the nonrespondent. This donor's data were adjusted by dividing each data item by the population (or enrollment) of the donor and multiplying the result by the nonrespondent's population (or enrollment). For special districts, if prior year data are available, the data are brought forward with a national level growth rate applied. Otherwise, the data are imputed to be zero. In cases where good secondary data sources exist, the data from those sources were used.

Estimates of Sampling Error: For intercensal surveys, estimated coefficients of variation for all variables are given in tabulations on the Web site. For U.S. and state-and-local government-level estimates of total full-time equivalents and total payroll, most relative standard errors are generally less than 1 percent, but vary considerably for detailed characteristics.

Other (nonsampling) Errors: Sample data are subject to nonsampling errors such as inability to obtain data for every variable from all units in the sample, inaccuracies in classification, response errors, misinterpretation of questions, mistakes in keying and coding, and coverage errors. These same errors may be evident in census collections and may affect the Census of Governments data used to adjust the sample during the estimation phase and used in the imputation process.

Sources of Additional material: <http://www.census.gov/econ/overview/go1100.html> and <http://www2.census.gov/govs/apes/11_methodology.pdf>.

Annual Survey of Government Finances

Universe, Frequency, and Types of Data: The United States Census Bureau conducts an Annual Survey of Government Finances, as authorized by law under Title 13, United States Code, Section 182. Alternatively, every 5 years, in years ending in a '2' or '7', a Census of Governments, including a Finance portion, is conducted under Title 13, Section 161. The survey coverage includes all state and local governments in the United States. For both the Census and annual survey, the finance detail data is equivalent, encompassing the entire range of government finance activities-revenue, expenditure, debt, and assets.

Type of Data Collection Operations: Data for the annual survey were collected via mail canvass, Internet, and central collection from State sources. In 28 states, all or part of the general purpose finance data for local governments were obtained from cooperative arrangements between the Census Bureau and a state government agency. These usually involved a data collection effort carried out to meet the needs of both agencies-the state agency for purposes of audit, oversight, or information, and the Census Bureau for statistical purposes. Data for the balance of local governments in this annual survey were obtained via mail questionnaires sent to county, municipal, township, special district, and school district governments. School district data were collected via cooperative arrangements with state education agencies. Data for state governments were compiled by analysts of the Census Bureau, usually with the cooperation and assistance of state officials. The data were compiled from state government audits, budgets, and other financial reports, either in printed or electronic format. The

compilation generally involved recasting the state financial records into the classification categories used for reporting by the Census Bureau.

Data Collection and Imputation Procedures: Survey is conducted by mail with mail follow-ups of nonrespondents. Imputation for all nonresponse items is based on previous year reports or, for new governments, on data from similar donors. The unit response rate of the 2011 Annual Survey of Local Government Finances was 93.1 percent. The overall unit response rate of the Annual Survey of State Government Finances was 100.0 percent for 2011.

Estimates of Sampling Error: The local government statistics in the intercensal survey years are developed from a sample survey. Therefore, the local totals, as well as aggregates of state and local government data, are considered estimated amounts subject to sampling error. State government finance data are not subject to sampling. Consequently, State-local aggregates shown here have a relative standard error less than or equal to the local government estimates they include. Estimates of major United States totals for local governments are subject to a computed sampling variability of less than one-half of 1 percent. State and local government totals are generally subject to sampling variability of less than 3 percent.

Other (nonsampling) Errors: The estimates are also subject to inaccuracies in classification, response, and processing. Efforts were made at all phases of collection, processing, and tabulation to minimize errors. Data are also subject to errors from imputations for missing data, errors from misreported data, errors from miscoding, and difficulties in identifying every unit that should be included in the report. Every effort was made to keep such errors to a minimum through examining, editing, and tabulating the data reported by government officials.

Sources of Additional Material: <http://www.census.gov/govs/index.html>.

Annual Survey of Manufactures (ASM)

Universe, Frequency, and Types of Data: The Annual Survey of Manufactures is a sample survey conducted annually, except for years ending in '2' and '7,' for all manufacturing establishments having one or more paid employees. The unit response rate for the current ASM cycle is about 72 percent. The purpose of the ASM is to provide key intercensal measures of manufacturing activity, products, and location for the public and private sectors. The ASM provides statistics on employment, payroll, worker hours, payroll supplements, cost of materials, value added by manufacturing, capital expenditures, inventories, and energy consumption. It also provides estimates of value of shipments for the 471 six-digit NAICS product groups and approximately 1,384 seven-digit NAICS product classes.

Type of Data Collection Operation: The ASM is conducted on an establishment basis, selected from the census universe of 329,000 manufacturing establishments. Approximately 20,000 large establishments are selected with certainty, and the remaining 30,000 other establishments are selected with probability proportional to a composite measure of establishment size. The sample universe is updated from two sources:

Internal Revenue Service administrative records are used to include new single-unit manufacturers and the Company Organization Survey identifies new establishments of multiunit forms.

Data Collection and Imputation Procedures: Survey is conducted by mail with telephone and mail follow-ups of nonrespondents. Imputation (for all nonresponse items) is based on previous year reports, or for new establishments in survey, on industry averages.

Estimates of Sampling Error: Estimated relative standard errors for number of employees, new expenditures, and for value added totals are given in annual publications. For U.S. level industry statistics, most estimated relative standard errors are 2 percent or less, but vary considerably for detailed characteristics.

Other (nonsampling) Errors: Nonsampling errors include those due to collection, reporting, and transcription errors, many of which are corrected through computer and clerical checks.

Sources of Additional Material: <http://www.census. gov/manufacturing/asm/index.html>.

Census of Population

Universe, Frequency, and Types of Data: Complete count of U.S. population conducted every 10 years since 1790. Data obtained on number and characteristics of people in the United States.

Type of Data Collection Operation: In the 1990, 2000, and 2010 censuses the 100 percent items included: age, date of birth, sex, race, Hispanic origin, and relationship to householder. In 1980, approximately 19 percent of the housing units were included in the sample; in 1990 and 2000, approximately 17 percent.

Data Collection and Imputation Procedures: In 1980, 1990, 2000, and 2010 mail questionnaires were used extensively with personal interviews in the remainder. Extensive telephone and personal follow-up for nonrespondents was done in the censuses. Imputations were made for missing characteristics.

Estimates of Sampling Error: Sampling errors for data are estimated for all items collected by sample and vary by characteristic and geographic area. The coefficients of variation (CVs) for national and state estimates are generally very small.

Other (nonsampling) Errors: Since 1950, evaluation programs have been conducted to provide information on the magnitude of some sources of nonsampling errors such as response bias and undercoverage in each census. Results from the evaluation program for the 1990 census indicated that the estimated net undercoverage amounted to about 1.5 percent of the total resident population. For the 2010 Census, the post enumeration survey found a net overcount of 0.01 percent of the resident population.

Sources of Additional Material: U.S. Census Bureau, The Coverage of Population in the 1980 Census, PHC80-E4; *Content Reinterview Study: Accuracy of Data for Selected Population and Housing Characteristics as Measured by Reinterview*, PHC80-E2; *1980 Census of Population*, Vol. 1, (PC80-1), Appendixes B, C, and D. *Content Reinterview Survey: Accuracy of Data for Selected Population and Housing Characteristics as*

Measured by Reinterview, 1990, CPH-E-1; Effectiveness of Quality Assurance, CPH-E-2; Programs to Improve Coverage in the 1990 Census, 1990, CPH-E-3. For the 2010 Census evaluations, see <http://www.2010.census.gov/2010census/about/cpex.php>. Documentation regarding the 2010 Census is available at <http://www.census. gov/2010census/news/press-kits/ccm/ccm.html>.

County Business Patterns

Universe, Frequency, and Types of Data: County Business Patterns is an annual tabulation of basic data items extracted from the Business Register, a file of all known single- and multilocation employer companies maintained and updated by the U.S. Census Bureau. Data include number of establishments, number of employees, first quarter and annual payrolls, and number of establishments by employment size class. Data are excluded for self-employed individuals, private households, railroad employees, agricultural production workers, and most government employees.

Type of Data Collection Operation: The annual Company Organization Survey and the Economic Census provide individual establishment data for multilocation companies. Data for single establishment companies are obtained from various Census Bureau programs, such as the Annual Survey of Manufactures and Current Business Surveys, as well as from administrative records of the Internal Revenue Service, the Social Security Administration, and the Bureau of Labor Statistics.

Estimates of Sampling Error: Not applicable.

Other (nonsampling) Errors: The data are subject to nonsampling errors, such as inability to identify all cases in the universe; definition and classification difficulties; differences in interpretation of questions; errors in recording or coding the data obtained; and estimation of employers who reported too late to be included in the tabulations and for records with missing or misreported data. Employment data are missing from approximately 12 percent of incoming administrative payroll records. For these records, employment is imputed as the average employment of the two adjacent quarters, using average wage data for the prior year, or, based on average wage for the industry and geographic area. Other missing data are also imputed through various methods.

Sources of Additional Material: U. S. Census Bureau, County Business Patterns, <http://www.census.gov/ econ/cbp/index.html> and <http://www.census.gov /econ/cbp/methodology.htm>.

Current Population Survey (CPS)

Universe, Frequency, and Types of Data: Nationwide monthly sample designed primarily to produce national and state estimates of labor force and other characteristics of the civilian noninstitutionalized population 16 years of age and older.

Type of Data Collection Operation: Multistage probability sample that currently includes 60,000 households from 824 sample areas. Sample size increased in some states to improve data reliability for those areas on an annual average basis. A continual sample rotation system is used. Households are in sample 4 months, out for 8 months, and in for 4 more. Month-to-month overlap is 75 percent; year-to-year overlap is 50 percent. The CPS questionnaire is a completely computerized document that is administered by Census Bureau field representatives across the country through both personal and telephone interviews. Questions refer to respondent activities during the prior week.

Data Collection and Imputation Procedures: For first and fifth months that a household is in sample, personal interviews; other months, approximately 85 percent of the data collected by phone. Imputation is done for item nonresponse. The CPS uses 3 imputation methods: relational imputation, which infers the missing value from other characteristics on the person's record or within the household; longitudinal edits for most of the labor force edits, as appropriate; and "hot deck" allocation, a method of assigning a missing value from a record with similar characteristics, which is the hot deck. Hot decks are defined by variables such as age, race, and sex.

Estimates of Sampling Error: Sufficient sample is allocated to maintain, at most, a 1.9 percent coefficient of variation on national monthly estimates of unemployment, assuming a 6 percent unemployment rate. This translates into a change of 0.2 percentage point in the unemployment rate being significant at a 90 percent confidence level. For each of the 50 States and for the District of Columbia, the design maintains a coefficient of variation of at most 8 percent on the annual average estimate of unemployment, assuming a 6 percent unemployment rate.

Other (nonsampling) Errors: Estimates of response bias on unemployment are available. Estimates of unemployment rate from reinterviews range from -2.4 percent to 1.0 percent of the basic CPS unemployment rate (over a 30-month span from January 2004 through June 2006). Eligible CPS households are approximately 82 percent of the assigned households, with a corresponding response rate of 92 percent.

Sources of Additional Material: U.S. Census Bureau and Bureau of Labor Statistics, Current Population Survey: Design and Methodology, (Technical Paper 66), available on the Internet <http://www.census.gov/prod/2006pubs/tp-66.pdf> and the Bureau of Labor Statistics, <http://www.bls.gov/cps/> ; *BLS Handbook of Methods*, Chapter 1, available on the Internet at <http://www.bls.gov/opub/hom/homch1_a.htm>; and <http://www.census.gov/cps/methodology/>.

Foreign Trade—Export Statistics

Universe, Frequency, and Types of Data: The export statistics consist of goods valued at more than $2,500 per commodity shipped by individuals and organizations (including exporters, freight forwarders, and carriers) from the U.S. to other countries. Data are compiled in terms of commodity classification, quantities, values, shipping weights, method of transportaion (air or vessel), state of (movement) origin, customs district, customs port, country of destination, and whether contents are domestic goods or reexports. Data are continuously compiled and processed. Documents are collected as shipments depart, and processed on a flow basis. Reports summarize shipments made during calendar months, quarters, and years. Statistics are reported monthly approximately 35 days after the end of the calendar month and on a year-to-date basis.

Type of Data Collection Operation: Statistics for exported goods transactions are compiled from two sources: Electronic Export Information filed in the Automated Export System by exporters and their agents (68 percent), and electronic transmissions from Canada for U.S. exports to Canada (32 percent). Estimates are made for low-value exports by country of destination, and based on bilateral trade patterns. Statistics for U.S. exports to Canada are based on import documents filed with Canadian agencies and forwarded to the U.S. Census Bureau under a 1987 data exchange agreement. Under this agreement, each country eliminated most cross-border export documents; maintains detailed statistics on cross-border imports; exchanges monthly files of cross-border import statistics; and publishes exchanged statistics in place of previously compiled export statistics.

Estimates of Sampling Error: Not applicable.

Other (nonsampling) Errors: The goods data are a complete enumeration of EEI reported in AES and are not subject to sampling errors; but they are subject to several types of nonsampling errors. Quality assurance procedures are performed at every stage of collection, processing and tabulation; however the data are still subject to several types of nonsampling errors. The most significant of these include reporting errors, undocumented shipments, timeliness, data capture errors, and errors in the estimation of low-valued transactions.

Sources of Additional Material: Foreign Trade Statistics Overview, <http://www.census.gov/foreign-trade/about/index.html>.

Foreign Trade—Import Statistics

Universe, Frequency, and Types of Data: The import statistics consist of goods valued at more than $2,000 per commodity shipped by individuals and organizations (including importers and customs brokers) into the U.S. from other countries. Data are compiled in terms of commodity classification, quantities, values, shipping weights, methods of transportation (air or vessel), duties collected, unit prices, and market share, country of origin, customs district, customs port, import charges and duties. Data are continuously compiled and processed. Documents are collected as shipments arrive and processed on a flow basis. Reports summarize shipments made during calendar months and years. Statistics are reported monthly approximately 35 days after the end of the calendar month and on a year-to-date basis.

Type of Data Collection Operation: A full compilation (i.e., a census) is taken of import shipments, plus U.S. Census Bureau estimates of low-valued imports and BEA estimates of trade in services. Statistics for imported goods shipments are compiled from the records filed with CBP, usually within 10 days after the merchandise enters the United States. Estimates are made for low-value shipments by country of origin, based on previous bilateral trade patterns and periodically updated. Statistics for over 99 percent of all commodity transactions are compiled from records filed electronically with CBP and forwarded electronically to the U.S. Census Bureau. Statistics for other transactions are compiled from hard-copy documents filed with CBP and forwarded on a flow basis for U.S. Census Bureau processing.

Estimates of Sampling Error: Not applicable.

Other (nonsampling) Errors: The goods data are a complete enumeration of documents collected by the U.S. Customs and Border Protection and are not subject to sampling errors; but they are subject to several types of nonsampling errors. Quality assurance procedures are performed at every stage of collection, processing, and tabulation; however the data are still subject to several types of nonsampling errors. The most significant of these include reporting errors, undocumented shipments, timeliness, data capture errors, and errors in the estimation of low-valued transactions.

Sources of Additional Material: Foreign Trade Statistics Overview, <http://www.census.gov/foreign-trade/about/index.html>.

Monthly and Annual Retail Trade Survey

Universe, Frequency, and Types of Data: The size of the Monthly Retail Trade Survey (MRTS) sample is approximately 11,600 employer firms. Statistics are available at the national level only. The MRTS covers Retail Trade North American Industry Classification System (NAICS) sectors 44-45, including store and nonstore retailers; and Food Services NAICS subsector 722, including establishment preparing food and beverages for immediate on- and off-premises consumption. Covers sales at retail and food service stores, and inventories held by retail stores.

Type of Data Collection Operation: Probability sample of all firms from a list frame. The list frame is the Bureau's Business Register updated quarterly for recent birth Employer Identification (EI) Numbers issued by the Internal Revenue Service and assigned an industry classification by the Social Security Administration. The largest firms are included monthly; a sample of others is included every month also. New samples were introduced with the 2011 Annual Retail Trade Survey (ARTS) and the April 2013 Monthly Retail Trade Survey (MRTS). These samples are designed to produce estimates based on the 2007 North American Industry Classification System (NAICS). The information used to create these sampling units was extracted from data collected as part of the 2007 Economic Census and from establishment records contained on the Census Bureau's Business Register as updated to December 2010.

Data Collection and Imputation Procedures: Data are collected by mail questionnaire with telephone follow-ups and fax reminders for nonrespondents. Imputation is made for each nonresponse item and each item failing edit checks. For both unit and item nonresponse, a missing value is replaced by a predicted value obtained from an appropriate model for nonresponse. This imputation uses survey data and administrative data as input. In any given month, imputed data amount to about 27 percent of the total monthly retail and food services sales estimate and about 30 percent of the total retail end-of-month inventory estimate.

Estimates of Sampling Error: Estimated CVs and standard errors are included in monthly reports available on the Internet; see <http://www.census.gov/retail/index.html#mrts>.

Other (nonsampling) Errors: Nonsampling errors are difficult to measure and can be attributed to many sources: the inclusion of erroneous units in the survey (overcoverage), the exclusion of eligible units from the survey (undercoverage), nonresponse, misreporting, mistakes in recording and coding responses, misinterpretation of questions, and other errors of collection, response, coverage, or processing. Although nonsampling error is not measured directly, the Census Bureau employs quality control procedures throughout the process to minimize this type of error.

Sources of Additional Material: See Web sites <http://www.census.gov/retail/index.html> and <http://www.census.gov/retail/how_surveys_are_collected.html>.

Monthly Survey of Construction

Universe, Frequency, and Types of Data: Covers new, privately-owned residential buildings currently authorized by a building permit or started in areas not requiring a building permit. Data collected include start and completion dates, sales date, sales price (single-family houses only), and the physical characteristics of housing units. Survey data are available monthly and annually for housing starts since 1959, for new home sales since 1963, and for completions since 1968. Reported data are for building or sales activity taking place during the applicable reference period. Monthly data collection begins the first day after the reference month and continues through the 7th working day.

Type of Data Collection Operation: A multistage probability sample of approximately 900 of the 20,000 permit-issuing jurisdictions in the U.S. was selected. Each month in each of these permit offices, field representatives list and select a sample of permits for which to collect data. To obtain data in areas where building permits are not required, a multistage probability sample of over 70 land areas (census tracts or subsections of census tracts) was selected. All roads in these areas are canvassed and data are collected on all new residential construction found. Sampled buildings are followed up until they are completed (and sold, if for sale), or abandoned.

Data Collection and Imputation Procedures: Data are obtained by telephone inquiry and/or field visit. Nonresponse/undercoverage adjustment factors are used to account for late reported data. Each month, housing starts, completions, and sales estimates derived from this survey are adjusted by the total numbers of authorized housing units (obtained from the Building Permits Survey) to develop national and regional estimates. Estimates are adjusted to reflect variations by region and type of construction, and to account for late reports and houses started or sold before a permit has been issued. Reported data are seasonally adjusted.

Estimates of Sampling Error: Estimated CV of 5 percent to 6 percent for estimates of national totals of units started, but may be higher than 20 percent for estimated totals of more detailed characteristics, such as housing units in multiunit structures.

Other (nonsampling) Errors: Response rate is over 90 percent for most items. Nonsampling errors are attributed to definitional problems, differences in interpretation of questions, incorrect reporting, inability to obtain information about all cases in the sample, and processing errors.

Sources of Additional Material: All data are available on the Internet at <http://www.census.gov/construction/nrc/>, and <http://www.census.gov/construction/nrs/>. Further documentation of the survey is also available at those sites.

Nonemployer Statistics

Universe, Frequency, and Types of Data: Nonemployer statistics are an annual tabulation of economic data by industry for active businesses without paid employees that are subject to federal income tax. Excluded are corporations and partnerships with over $1 million in receipts (except for service-type industries, maximum is $2 million). Maximum receipts for sole proprietorshps depends on industry classification. Data showing the number of firms and receipts by industry are available for the U.S., states, counties, and metropolitan areas. Most types of businesses covered by the Census Bureau's economic statistics programs are included in the nonemployer statistics. Tax-exempt and agricultural-production businesses are excluded from nonemployer statistics.

Type of Data Collection Operation: The universe of nonemployer firms is created annually as a byproduct of the Census Bureau's Business Register processing for employer establishments. If a business is active but without paid employees, then it becomes part of the potential nonemployer universe. Industry classification and receipts are available for each potential nonemployer business. These data are obtained primarily from the annual business income tax returns of the Internal Revenue Service (IRS). The potential nonemployer universe undergoes a series of complex processing, editing, and analytical review procedures at the Census Bureau to distinguish nonemployers from employers, and to correct and complete data items used in creating the data tables.

Estimates of Sampling Error: Data are tabulated from administrative records, and are not subject to sampling error.

Other (nonsampling) Errors: The data are subject to nonsampling errors, such as industry misclassification as well as errors of response, keying, nonreporting, and coverage. The improper inclusion of possible employer establishments in the nonemployer universe is a primary source of nonsampling error. The Census Bureau takes several steps to identify and remove these establishments from the nonemployer universe.

Sources of Additional Material: U. S. Census Bureau, Nonemployer Statistics at <http://www.census.gov/econ/nonemployer/index.html>.

Service Annual Survey

Universe, Frequency, and Types of Data: The U.S. Census Bureau conducts the Service Annual Survey (SAS) to provide nationwide estimates of revenues and expenses for selected service industries. Estimates are summarized by industry classification based on the 2007 North American Industry Classification System (NAICS). The SAS was expanded in 2009. Selected service industries covered by the Service Annual Survey include all or part of the following NAICS sectors: Utilities (NAICS 22), Transportation and Warehousing (NAICS

48-49); Information (NAICS 51); Finance and Insurance (NAICS 52); Real Estate and Rental and Leasing (NAICS 53); Professional, Scientific, and Technical Services (NAICS 54); Administrative and Support and Waste Management and Remediation Services (NAICS 56); Educational Services (NAICS 61); Health Care and Social Assistance (NAICS 62); Arts, Entertainment, and Recreation (NAICS 71); and Other Services, except Public Administration (NAICS 81). Data collected include total revenue, total expenses, detailed expenses, revenue from e-commerce transactions; and for selected industries, revenue from detailed service products, revenue from exported services, and inventories. For industries with a significant nonprofit component, separate estimates are developed for taxable firms and firms and organizations exempt from federal income taxes. Questionnaires are mailed in January and request annual data for the prior year. Estimates are published approximately 12 months after the initial survey mailing.

Type of Data Collection Operation: The Service Annual Survey estimates are developed from a probability sample of employer firms and administrative records for nonemployers. Service Annual Survey questionnaires are mailed to a probability sample that is periodically reselected from a universe of firms located in the United States and having paid employees. The sample includes firms of all sizes and covers both taxable firms and firms exempt from federal income taxes. Updates to the sample are made on a quarterly basis to account for new businesses. Firms without paid employees, or nonemployers, are included in the estimates through imputation and/or administrative records data provided by other federal agencies. Links to additional information about confidentiality protection, sampling error, nonsampling error, sample design, definitions, and copies of the questionnaires may be found at <http://www.census.gov/services/index.html>.

Estimates of Sampling Error: The most recent Service Annual Survey results, including coefficients of variations (CVs), can be found at <http://www.census.gov/services/index.html>. Additional information regarding sampling error may be found at <http://www.census.gov/services/sas/sastechdoc.html>.

Other (Nonsampling) Errors: Data are imputed for unit nonresponse, item nonresponse, and for reported data that fails edits.

Sources of Additional Material: U.S. Census Bureau, Current Business Reports, *Service Annual Survey*, Census Bureau Web site: <http://www.census.gov/services/index.html>.

Survey of Business Owners (SBO)

Universe, Frequency, and Types of Data: The Survey of Business Owners (SBO), formerly known as the Surveys of Minority- and Women-Owned Business Enterprises (SMOBE/SWOBE), provides statistics that describe the composition of U.S. businesses by gender, ethnicity, race, and veteran status. Data are presented for businesses owned by American Indians and Alaska Natives, Asians, Blacks, Hispanics, Native Hawaiians and Other Pacific Islanders, Veterans, and Women. All U.S. firms operating during 2007 with receipts of $1,000 or more, with and without paid employees, which are classified by the North American Industry

Classification System (NAICS) codes 11 through 99, are represented, except for the following: NAICS 111, 112, 481111, 482, 491, 525, 813, 814, and 92. The published data include the number of firms, sales and receipts, number of paid employees, and annual payroll. Data are presented by industry classifications, geographic area (states, metropolitan and micropolitan statistical areas, counties, and corporate municipalities [places] including cities, towns, townships, villages, and boroughs), and size of firm (employment and receipts). Data are collected every 5 years, for years ending in "2" and "7."

Type of Data Collection Operation: The 2007 Survey of Business Owners (SBO) questionnaire, Form SBO-1, was mailed to a random sample of businesses. The list of all firms (or universe) was compiled from a combination of business tax returns and data collected on other economic census reports. The Survey of Business Owners (SBO) is conducted on a company or firm basis rather than an establishment basis. The survey is based on a stratified probability sample of approximately 2.3 million firms from a universe of approximately 27.1 million firms. There were 5.7 million firms with paid employees and 21.4 million firms with no paid employees.

Data Collection and Imputation Procedures: Approximately 62 percent of the 2.3 million businesses in the 2007 SBO responded to the survey. Compensation for missing data is addressed through reweighting, edit correction, and standard statistical imputation methods. Overall, imputed data accounted for approximately 47 percent of the firm count estimates by gender, ethnicity, race, and veteran status and approximately 20 percent of the estimates of sales.

Estimates of Sampling Error: Sampling error is present in these estimates because they are based on the results of a sample survey and not on an enumeration of the entire universe. Since these estimates are based on a probability sample, it is possible to estimate the sampling variability of the survey estimates. The standard error (SE) provides a measure of the variation. The relative standard error (RSE) or coefficient of variation (CV) provides a measure of the magnitude of the variation relative to the estimate and is calculated as 100 multiplied by the ratio of the estimate to the SE. The CVs for number of firms and receipts at the national level typically range from 0 to 4 percent.

Other (Nonsampling) Error: Nonsampling errors are attributed to many sources: inability to obtain information for all cases in the universe, adjustments to the weights of respondents to compensate for nonrespondents, imputation for missing data, data errors and biases, mistakes in recording or keying data, errors in collection or processing, and coverage problems. Explicit measures of the effects of these nonsampling errors are not available. However, it is believed that most of the important operational and data errors were detected and corrected through an automated data edit designed to review the data for reasonableness and consistency. Quality control techniques were used to verify that operating procedures were carried out as specified.

Sources of Additional Materials: U.S. Census Bureau, Survey of Business Owners, <http://www.census.gov/econ/sbo/>; U.S. Census Bureau, 2007

Economic Census User Guide: <http://www.census.gov/econ/census07/www/user_guide.html>

U.S. DEPARTMENT OF EDUCATION National Center for Education Statistics

Integrated Postsecondary Education Data Survey (IPEDS), Completions

Universe, Frequency, and Types of Data: Annual survey of all Title IV (federal financial aid) eligible postsecondary institutions to obtain data on enrollments; faculty and staff finances; institutional prices; financial aid; and earned degrees and other formal awards, conferred by field of study, level of degree, sex, and by racial/ ethnic characteristics (every other year prior to 1989, then annually). More than 7,500 institutions complete IPEDS surveys each year.

Type of Data Collection Operation: Complete census. The completion of all IPEDS surveys is mandatory for institutions that participate in or are applicants for participation in any federal student financial aid program (such as Pell grants and federal student loans) authorized by Title IV of the Higher Education Act of 1965.

Data Collection and Imputation Procedures: IPEDS consists of eight interrelated components that are collected over three collection periods (fall, winter, and spring) each year. Missing data are imputed by using data of similar institutions.

Estimates of Sampling Error: Not applicable.

Other (nonsampling Errors): Nonsampling errors may arise when respondents or interviewers interpret questions differently; when respondents must estimate values, or when coders, keyers, and other processors handle answers differently; when people who should be included in the universe are not; or when people fail to respond (completely or partially). Nonsampling errors usually, but not always, result in an underestimate of total survey error and thus an overestimate of the precision of survey estimates. Since estimating the magnitude of nonsampling errors often would require special experiments or access to independent data, these nonsampling errors are seldom measured. For universe surveys, an adjustment made for either type of nonresponse, total or partial, is often referred to as an imputation, which is often a substitution of the "average" questionnaire response for the nonresponse. for universe surveys, imputations are usually made separately within various groups of sample members that have similar survey characteristics.

Sources of Additional Material: U.S. Department of Education, National Center for Education Statistics, *Post-secondary Institutions and Price of Attendance in the United States: 2010-2011 and Degrees and Other Awards Conferred: 2009-10 and 12-month enrollment, 2009-10.* See <http://www.nces.ed.gov/ipeds/>.

National Household Education Surveys (NHES) Program

Universe, Frequency, and Types of Data: The National Household Education Surveys Program is a system of surveys of the noninstitutionalized civilian population of the United States. Surveys in NHES have varying universes of interest depending on the particular survey. Some surveys are recurring, others are fielded as 1-time surveys. Specific topics covered by each survey are at the NHES Web site <http://nces.ed.gov/nhes>. A list of the surveys fielded as part of NHES, each universe, and the years they were fielded is provided below.

1 Adult Education—Interviews were conducted with a representative sample of civilian, noninstitutionalized persons aged 16 and older who were not enrolled in grade 12 or below (1991, 1995, 1999, 2001, 2003, 2005).

2 Before- and After-School Programs and Activities—Interviews were conducted with parents of a representative sample of students in grades K through 8 (1999, 2001, 2005).

3 Civic Involvement—Interviews were conducted with representative samples of parents, youth, and adults (1996, 1999).

4 Early Childhood Program Participation—Interviews were conducted with parents of a representative sample of children from birth through grade 3, with the specific age groups varying by survey year (1991, 1995, 1999, 2001, 2005).

5 Household and Library Use—Interviews were conducted with a representative sample of U.S. households (1996).

6 Parent and Family Involvement in Education—Interviews were conducted with parents of a representative sample of children age three through grade 12 or in grades K through 12 depending on the survey year (1996, 1999, 2003, 2007, and 2012).

7 School Readiness—Interviews were conducted with parents of a representative sample of 3-7 year-old children (1993 and 1999) and of 3-5 year old children, not yet in kindergarten, (2007).

8 School Safety and Discipline—Interviews were conducted with a representative sample of students in grades 6-12, their parents, and the parents of a representative sample of students in grades 3-12 (1993).

Type of Data Collection Operation: Through 2007, the NHES used telephone interviews to collect data. In 2012, the NHES switched to a mail survey. The NHES 2012 sample was selected using a 2-stage address-based sampling frame. Black and Hispanic American households were sampled at a higher rate than other households. Data were collected using printed questionnaires mailed to sampled respondents.

Data Collection and Imputation Procedures: For telephone surveys, telephone numbers are selected using random digit dialing (RDD) techniques. Approximately 45,000 to 64,000 households are contacted in order to identify persons eligible for the surveys. Data are collected using computer-assisted telephone interviewing (CATI) procedures. Missing data are imputed using hot-deck imputation procedures.

Estimates of Sampling Error: Unweighted sample sizes range between 2,250 and 55,708. The average root design effects of the surveys in NHES range from 1.1 to 1.5, except for the Adult Education survey of 1991. In 1991, average root design effects for the Adult Education survey ranged from 2.3 to 4.5.

Other (nonsampling) Errors: Because of unit nonresponse and because the samples are drawn from households with telephone instead of all

households, nonresponse and/or coverage bias may exist for some estimates. However, both sources of potential bias are adjusted for in the weighting process. Analyses of both potential sources of bias in the NHES collections have been studied and no significant bias has been detected.

Sources of Additional Material: Please see the NHES Web site at <http://nces.ed.gov/nhes>; and technical notes in "Parent and Family Involvement in Education, from the National Household Education Surveys Program of 2012," NCES 2013-028, August 2013, <http://nces.ed.gov/pubs2013/2013028.pdf>.

Schools and Staffing Survey (SASS)

Universe, Frequency and Types of Data: NCES designed the SASS survey system to emphasize teacher demand and shortage, teacher and administrator characteristics, school programs, and general conditions in schools. SASS also collects data on many other topics, including principals' and teachers' perceptions of school climate and problems in their schools; teacher compensation; district hiring practices; basic characteristics of the student population; and instructional time and teacher and school performance. The SASS has four core components: the School Questionnaire, the Teacher Questionnaire, the Principal Questionnaire, and the School District Questionnaire. For the 2003-04, 2007-08, and 2011-12 SASS, public charter schools were included in the sample. Surveys have been conducted every 3 to 4 years depending on budgetary constraints. The SASS includes data from public, private, and Bureau of Indian Education (BIE) school sectors.

Type of Data Collection Operation and Imputation Procedures: The 2007-08 SASS was a mail-based survey, with telephone and field follow-up. The U.S. Census Bureau performs the data collection and begins by sending advance letters to the sampled Local Education Agencies (LEAs) and schools in August and September of collection years. Beginning in October, questionnaires are delivered by U.S. Census Bureau field representatives. The sampling frame for the public school sample is the most recent Common Core of Data (CCD) school file. CCD is a universe file that includes all elementary and secondary schools in the United States. Schools operated by the Department of Defense or those that offered only kindergarten or pre-kindergarten or adult education were excluded from the SASS sample. The list frame used for the private school sample is the most recent Private School Universe Survey (PSS) list, updated with association lists. An area frame supplement is based on the canvassing of private schools within specific geographical areas. A separate universe of schools funded by the Bureau of Indian Education (BIE) is drawn from the Program Education Directory maintained by the BIE. To avoid duplicates in the BIE files, BIE schools in the CCD school file are treated as public schools. SASS used four methods to impute values for questionnaire items that respondents did not answer. These were: (1) using data from other items on the questionnaire; (2) extracting data from a related component of SASS; (3) extracting data from the sampling frame (CCD or PSS); and (4) extracting data from the record of a sampled case with similar characteristics (commonly known as the "hot deck" method for imputing item response).

Estimates of Sampling Error: Sample errors can be calculated using replicate weights and Balanced Repeated Replication complex survey design methodology. Errors depend on cell sizes and range from less than 1 percent to over 5 percent (for reasonable cell sizes).

Other (nonsampling) Errors: Because of unit nonresponse, bias may exist in some sample cells. However, bias has been adjusted for in the weighting process. Analysis of bias has been studied and no significant bias has been detected.

Sources of Additional Material: Please see the SASS Web site at <http://nces.ed.gov/surveys/sass/>.

U.S. DEPARTMENT OF JUSTICE, FEDERAL BUREAU OF INVESTIGATION

Uniform Crime Reporting (UCR) Program

Universe, Frequency, and Types of Data: Monthly reports on the number of criminal offenses that become known to law enforcement agencies. In a given year, more than 18,000 city, university and college, county, state, tribal, and federal law enforcement agencies contribute data to the FBI. In 2012, law enforcement agencies active in the UCR Program represented more than 308 million U.S. inhabitants (98.1 percent of the total population). The coverage amounted to 98.9 percent of the population in Metropolitan Statistical Areas, 93.3 percent of the population in cities outside metropolitan areas, and 94.2 percent of the population in nonmetropolitan counties. Data are collected on crimes cleared by arrest or exceptional means; age, sex, and race of arrestees and for victims and offenders for homicides, number of law enforcement employees, on fatal and nonfatal assaults against law enforcement officers, and on hate crimes reported.

Type of Data Collection Operation: Crime statistics are based on reports of crime data submitted either directly to the FBI by contributing law enforcement agencies or through cooperating state UCR Programs. UCR program participation is voluntary. Beginning with the 2013 data collections, all data must be submitted electronically, and after July 2013, the UCR Program will no longer accept paper submissions or the electronic submission of documents (i.e., Portable Document Format files).

Data Collection and Imputation Procedures: States with UCR programs collect data directly from individual law enforcement agencies and forward reports, prepared in accordance with UCR standards, to the FBI. Accuracy and consistency edits are performed by the FBI.

Estimates of Sampling Error: Not applicable.

Other (nonsampling) Errors: Due to computer problems, changes in records management systems, personnel shortages, or a number of other reasons, some agencies cannot provide data for publication.

Sources of Additional Material: U.S. Department of Justice, Federal Bureau of Investigation, <http://www.fbi.gov/about-us/cjis/ucr/crime-in-the-u.s/2012/crime-in-the-u.s.-2012/resource-pages/about-ucr/aboutucrmain>; and *Crime in the United States*, annual, *Hate Crime Statistics*, annual,

Law Enforcement Officers Killed and Assaulted, annual, <http://www.fbi.gov/about-us/cjis/ucr/ucr>.

U.S. INTERNAL REVENUE SERVICE

Corporation Income Tax Returns

Universe, Frequency, and Types of Data: Annual study of unaudited corporation income tax returns, Forms 1120, 1120-A, 1120-F, 1120-L, 1120-PC, 1120-REIT, 1120-RIC, and 1120S, filed by corporations or businesses legally defined as corporations. The IRS Statistics of Income (SOI) Division collects data on corporations by size, industry, total assets, business receipts, deductions, liabilities, net income, income tax liability, tax credits, and other financial data. SOI aggregates these data for C corporations and passthrough entities, such as S corporations. The target population consists of all returns of active corporations organized for profit that are required to file one of the 1120 forms that are part of the SOI study.

Type of Data Collection Operation: Stratified probability sample of 108,763 returns for Tax Year 2010 (including inactive and non-eligible corporations), allocated to sample classes which are based on type of return, and either size of total assets alone or both size of total assets and a measure of income. Sampling rates for sample classes varied from 0.25 percent to 100 percent.

Data Collection and Imputation Procedures: Computer selection of sample of tax return records. Data adjusted during editing for incorrect, missing, or inconsistent entries to ensure consistency with other entries on return and to comply with statistical definitions. If the missing data items are from the balance sheet, then imputation procedures are used. If data for a whole return are missing because the return is unavailable to SOI during the data capture process, imputation procedures are also used in certain cases.

Estimates of Sampling Error: Estimated CVs for Tax Year 2010: coefficients of variation are published in the 2010 Statistics of Income Corporation Income Tax Returns, in Section 3: Description of the Sample and Limitation of the Data.

Other (nonsampling) Errors: Nonsampling errors include coverage errors, processing errors, and response errors.

Sources of Additional Material: U.S. Internal Revenue Service, *Statistics of Income, Corporation Income Tax Returns*, annual.

Individual Income Tax Returns

Universe, Frequency, and Types of Data: Annual study of unaudited individual income tax returns, Forms 1040, 1040A, and 1040EZ, filed by U.S. citizens and residents. Data provided on various financial characteristics by size of adjusted gross income, marital status, and by taxable and nontaxable returns. Data by state, based on the population of returns filed, also include returns from 1040NR, filed by nonresident aliens plus certain self employment tax returns.

Type of Data Collection Operation: Stratified probability sample of 308,946 returns for tax year 2010. The sample is classified into sample strata based on the larger of total income or total loss amounts, the size of business plus farm receipts, and other criteria such as the potential usefulness of the return for tax policy modeling. Sampling rates for sample strata varied from 0.10 percent to 100 percent.

Data Collection and Imputation Procedures: Computer selection of sample of tax return records. Data adjusted during editing for incorrect, missing, or inconsistent entries to ensure consistency with other entries on return.

Estimates of Sampling Error: Estimated CVs for tax year 2010: Adjusted gross income less deficit 0.09 percent; salaries and wages 0.17 percent; and total income tax .17 percent. (State data not subject to sampling error.)

Other (nonsampling) Errors: Processing errors and errors arising from the use of tolerance checks for the data.

Sources of Additional Material: U.S. Internal Revenue Service, *Statistics of Income, Individual Income Tax Returns*, annual, (Publication 1304).

Partnership Income Tax Returns

Universe, Frequency, and Types of Data: Annual study of preaudited income tax returns of active partnerships related to financial and tax-related activity during tax year 2010 and reported on Forms 1065 and 1065B to the IRS. Data are provided by industry, based on the NAICS industry coding used by IRS.

Type of Data Collection Operation: Stratified probability sample of 43,878 partnership returns from a population of 3.3 million filed for tax year 2010. The sample is classified based on combinations of industry code, gross receipts, net income or loss, and total assets. Sampling rates vary from 0.04 percent to 100 percent.

Data Collection and Imputation Procedures: The sample of tax return records are selected via computer after data are transcribed by IRS and placed on an administrative file. Data are manually adjusted during editing for incorrect, missing, or inconsistent entries to ensure consistency with other entries on return. Data not available due to regulations are handled with weighting adjustments.

Estimates of Sampling Error: Some of the estimated Coefficients of Variation (the estimated standard error of the total divided by the estimated total) for tax year 2010: For number of partnerships, 0.57 percent; business receipts, 0.16 percent; net income, 0.20 percent; and ordinary business income, 0.55 percent.

Other (nonsampling) Errors: The potential exists for coverage error due to unavailable returns; processing errors; and taxpayer reporting errors, since data are preaudit.

Sources of Additional Material: U.S. Internal Revenue Service, *Statistics of Income, Partnership Returns* and *Statistics of Income Bulletin*, Fall 2012.

Sole Proprietorship Income Tax Returns

Universe, Frequency, and Types of Data: Annual study of unaudited income tax returns of nonfarm sole proprietorships, Form 1040 with business schedules. Data provided on various financial characteristics by industry.

Type of Data Collection Operation: Stratified probability sample of 81,026 returns from sole proprietorships for tax year 2010. The sample is classified based on presence or absence of certain business schedules; the larger of total income or loss; size of business plus farm receipts, and other criteria such as the potential usefulness of the return for tax policy modeling. Sampling rates vary from 0.1 percent to 100 percent.

Data Collection and Imputation Procedures: Computer selection of sample of tax return records. Data adjusted during editing for incorrect, missing, or inconsistent entries to ensure consistency with other entries on return.

Estimates of Sampling Error: Estimated CVs for tax year 2010 are available. For sole proprietorships, all nonfarm industries: total business receipts, 0.58 percent; depreciation, 1.46 percent; and net income, 0.77 percent.

Other (nonsampling) Errors: Processing errors and errors arising from the use of tolerance checks for the data.

Sources of Additional Material: U.S. Internal Revenue Service, *Statistics of Income, Sole Proprietorship returns* and *Statistics of Income Bulletin*, Summer 2012.

U.S. NATIONAL CENTER FOR HEALTH STATISTICS (NCHS)

National Health Interview Survey (NHIS)

Universe, Frequency, and Types of Data: Continuous data collection covering the civilian noninstitutional population to obtain information on demographic characteristics, conditions, injuries, impairments, use of health services, health behaviors, and other health topics.

Type of Data Collection Operation: Trained interviewers from the U.S. Census Bureau visit each selected household and administer NHIS in person. Current NHIS sample design oversamples black, Hispanic, and Asian Americans. The annual NHIS questionnaire (also called the Core) consists of four main components: Household Composition, Family Core, Sample Adult Core, and Sample Child Core. The Census Bureau collects data using a computer assisted personal interviewing mode. Multistage probability sample of 49,000 households (in 198 PSUs) from 1985 to 1994; 36,000 to 40,000 households (358 design PSUs or 449 effective PSUs when divided by state boundaries) from 1995 to 2005; an estimated completed 35,000 households (428 effective PSUs) beginning in 2006. Sample size for the 2011 NHIS was 39,509 households, 101,875 persons in 40,496 families.

Data Collection and Imputation Procedures: Some missing data items (e.g., race, ethnicity) are imputed using a hot deck imputation value. Sequential regression models are used to create multiple imputation files for family income. Unit nonresponse is compensated for by an adjustment to the survey weights. Since 2004, imputation has been performed for injury and poisoning episodes for which the respondent did not provide sufficient information to determine a month, day, and year of occurrence. (Note: the NHIS questionnaire was redesigned in 1997, and a new sample design was instituted in 2006).

Estimates of Sampling Error: Because NHIS data are based on a sample of the population, they are subject to sampling error. Standard errors are reported to indicate the reliability of the estimates. Estimates and standard errors were calculated using SUDAAN software (21), which takes into account the complex sampling design of NHIS. The Taylor series linearization method was used for variance estimation in SUDAAN.

Other (nonsampling) Errors: Documentation on NHIS methods is available at <http://www.cdc.gov/nchs/nhis/methods.htm>.

Sources of Additional Material: National Center for Health Statistics, Summary Health Statistics for the U.S. Population: National Health Interview Survey, 2011, Vital and Health Statistics, Series 10, No. 255; U.S. National Center for Health Statistics, Design and Estimation for the National Health Interview Survey, 1995-2004, Vital and Health Statistics, Series 2, No. 130.

National Survey of Family Growth (NSFG)

Universe, Frequency, and Types of Data: Periodic survey of men and women 15-44 years of age in the household population of the United States. Interview topics covered include births and pregnancies, marriage, divorce, and cohabitation, sexual activity, contraceptive use, medical care, and attitudes about childbearing and parenthood. The most sensitive data—on sexual behavior related to HIV and sexually transmitted disease risk—were collected in a self-administered form in which the data are entered into a computer. Cycle 6 of the 2002 NSFG in-person interviews were completed with 12,571 respondents 15-44 years of age--7,643 females and 4,928 males. Response rate was 79 percent overall--80 percent for females and 78 percent for males. For the 2006-2010 NSFG, the NSFG interviewed a national sample of 22,682 men (75 percent response rate) and women (78 percent response rate) 15-44 years of age. Population targets included 45 percent male, 55 percent female, 20 percent Hispanic, 20 percent black, and 20 percent teenage respondents. The 2006-10 sample was drawn from 110 primary sampling units.

Type of Data Collection Operation: The 2002 and 2006-10 NSFG were conducted in conjunction with Institute for Social Research at University of Michigan. Professional female interviewers conducted in-person, face-to-face interviews using laptop computers. In the 2002 (Cycle 6) NSFG, the sample was a multistage area probability sample of men and women 15-44 years of age in the household population of the United States. Only one person 15-44 was selected from households with one or more persons 15-44. In the self-administered portion, the respondent entered his or her own answers into the computer. Hispanic and Black persons, as well as those 15-19 years of age, were sampled at higher rates than White adults. All percentages and other statistics shown for the NSFG are weighted to make national estimates. The weights adjust for the different rates of sampling for each group, and for nonresponse. The 2006–2010 NSFG used a responsive design approach to manage the field work of the survey, to control costs, to oversample teenage and minority groups, and to reduce bias in the resulting sample. This approach represented a significant change in the design, methodology, and procedures of the survey. Interviews were conducted in English and Spanish. Monetary incentives were used to promote survey participation. Signed parental consent was required for survey participants aged 15-17.

Data Collection and Imputation Procedures: For about 650 key variables, referred to as "recodes," item missing values have been replaced in the NGSF data file by predicted or imputed values. The imputed values are identified through a companion variable or "imputation flag" to indicate whether the value for a particular case was imputed or reported. The imputation rates for most of these recodes are very low—usually less than 1.0%. The highest imputation rate was for income, with 10.8% imputed. Detailed discussion of data collection and imputation procedures is available in "Responsive Design, Weighting, and Variance Estimation in the 2006–2010 National Survey of Family Growth," *Vital and Health Statistics*, Series 2, No. 158, June 2013.

Estimates of Sampling Error: Estimates are subject to error, a difference between the true population value and the value estimated from the sample. This difference may be due to systematic or fixed sources of error, such as nonresponse or noncoverage bias or due to variable sources of error, including the use of a sample to represent the population. Detailed discussion of variance estimation is available in "Responsive Design, Weighting, and Variance Estimation in the 2006–2010 National Survey of Family Growth," *Vital and Health Statistics*, Series 2, No. 158, June 2013.

Other (nonsampling) Errors: Detailed discussion of variance estimation is available in "Responsive Design, Weighting, and Variance Estimation in the 2006–2010 National Survey of Family Growth," *Vital and Health Statistics*, Series 2, No. 158, June 2013.

Sources of Additional Material: The following references can be found at <http://www.cdc.gov/nchs/nsfg.htm>. "National Survey of Family Growth, Cycle 6: Sample Design, Weighting, and Variance Estimation," *Vital and Health Statistics*, Series 2, Number 142, July 2006. "Plan and Operation of Cycle 6 of the National Survey of Family Growth," *Vital and Health Statistics*, Series 1, No. 42, August 2005. "Sexual Behavior and Selected Health Measures: Men and Women 15-44 Years of Age, United States, 2002," *Advance Data from Vital and Health Statistics*, No. 362, Sept 15, 2005. "Responsive Design, Weighting, and Variance Estimation in the 2006–2010 National Survey of Family Growth," *Vital and Health Statistics*, Series 2, No. 158, June 2013.

National Vital Statistics System

Universe, Frequency, and Types of Data: Annual data on births, deaths, marriages, divorces, and fetal deaths in the United States. Legal authority for the registration of these events resides individually with the 50 States, 2 cities (Washington, DC, and New York City), and 5 territories (Puerto Rico, the Virgin Islands, Guam, American Samoa, and the Commonwealth of the Northern Mariana Islands). These jurisdictions are responsible for maintaining registries of vital events and for issuing copies of birth, marriage, divorce, and death certificates.

Type of Data Collection Operation: Mortality data based on complete file of death records, except 1972, based on 50 percent sample. Natality statistics 1951-1971, based on 50 percent sample of birth certificates, except a 20 percent to 50 percent sample in 1967, received by NCHS.

Data Collection and Imputation Procedures: Reports based on records from registration offices of the jurisdictions listed above. Data pertaining to causes of death are classified and coded according to the International Classification of Diseases (ICD).

Estimates of Sampling Error: For recent years, there is no sampling for these files; the files are based on 100 percent of events registered.

Other (nonsampling) Errors: It is believed that more than 99 percent of the births and deaths occurring in this country are registered.

Sources of Additional Material: U.S. National Center for Health Statistics, *Vital Statistics of the United States*, Vol. I and Vol. II, annual, and the *National Vital Statistics Reports.* See the NCHS Web site at <http://www.cdc.gov/nchs/nvss.htm>.

National Highway Traffic Safety Administration (NHTSA)

Fatality Analysis Reporting System (FARS)

Universe, Frequency, and Types of Data: FARS is a census of all fatal motor vehicle traffic crashes that occur throughout the United States including the District of Columbia and Puerto Rico on roadways customarily open to the public. The crash must be reported to the state/jurisdiction, and is classified as fatal if a directly related fatality occurs within thirty days of the crash.

Type of Data Collection Operation: One or more analysts, in each state, extract data from the official documents and enter the data into a standardized electronic database.

Data Collection and Imputation Procedures: Detailed data describing the characteristics of the fatal crash, the vehicles and persons involved are from police crash reports, driver and vehicle registration records, autopsy reports, highway department, etc. Computerized edit checks monitor the accuracy and completeness of the data. The FARS incorporates a sophisticated mathematical multiple imputation procedure to develop a probability distribution of missing blood alcohol concentration (BAC) levels in the database for drivers, pedestrians, and cyclists.

Estimates of Sampling Error: Since this is census data, there are no sampling errors.

Other (nonsampling) Errors: FARS represents a census of all police-reported crashes and captures all data reported at the state level. FARS data undergo a rigorous quality control process to prevent inaccurate reporting. However, these data are highly dependent on the accuracy of the police accident reports. Errors or omissions within police accident reports may not be detected.

Sources of Additional Material: The FARS Coding and Validation Manual, ANSI D16.1 Manual on Classification of Motor Vehicle Traffic Accidents (Sixth Edition).

Weights and Measures

U.S. Customary/Metric Conversion Table

[Conversions provided in the table are approximate]

Symbol	When you know U.S. customary	Multiply by	To find metric	Symbol
in	inches	2.54	centimeters	cm
ft	feet	30.48	centimeters	cm
yd	yards	0.091	meters	m
mi	miles	1.61	kilometers	km
in^2	square inches	6.45	square centimeters	cm^2
ft^2	square feet	0.09	square centimeters	cm^2
yd^2	square yards	0.84	square meters	m^2
mi^2	square miles	2.59	square kilometers	km^2
	acre	0.41	hectare	ha
oz	ounces	28.35	grams	g
lb	pounds	0.45	kilograms	kg
oz (troy)	troy ounces	31.1	grams	g
	short tons (2,000 lb)	0.91	metric tons	t
	long tons (2,240 lb)	1.02	metric tons	t
fl oz	fluid ounces	29.57	milliliters	mL
c	cups	0.24	liters	L
pt	pints	0.47	liters	L
qt	quarts	0.95	liters	L
gal	gallons	3.78	liters	L
ft^3	cubic feet	0.03	cubic meters	m^3
yd^3	cubic yards	0.76	cubic meters	m^3
°F	degrees Fahrenheit (subtract 32)	0.55	degrees Celsius	°C

Symbol	When you know metric	Multiply by	To find U.S. customary	Symbol
cm	centimeters	0.39	inches	in
cm	centimeters	0.03	feet	ft
m	meters	1.09	yards	yd
km	kilometers	0.62	miles	mi
cm^2	square centimeters	0.015	square inches	in^2
cm^2	square centimeters	10.76	square feet	ft^2
m^2	square meters	1.2	square yards	yd^2
km^2	square kilometers	0.39	square miles	mi^2
ha	hectare	2.47	acre	
g	grams	0.04	ounces	oz
kg	kilograms	2.21	pounds	lb
g	grams	0.04	troy ounces	oz (troy)
t	metric tons	1.1	short tons (2,000 lb)	
t	metric tons	0.98	long tons (2,240 lb)	
mL	milliliters	0.03	fluid ounces	fl oz
L	liters	4.23	cups	c
L	liters	2.13	pints	pt
L	liters	1.05	quarts	qt
L	liters	0.026	gallons	gal
m^3	cubic meters	35.32	cubic feet	ft^3
m^3	cubic meters	1.32	cubic yards	yd^3
°C	degrees Celsius (after multiplying, add 32)	1.8	degrees Fahrenheit	°F

Source: National Institute of Standards and Technology (NIST), Weights and Measures Division. See <http://www.nist.gov/pml/wmd/metric/unit-conversion.cfm>

Index

Note: Index citations refer to **table** numbers, not **page** numbers

Note: Index citations refer to **table** numbers, not **page** numbers

Note: Index citations refer to **table** numbers, not **page** numbers

Note: Index citations refer to **table** numbers, not **page** numbers

---

Note: Index citations refer to **table** numbers, not **page** numbers

Note: Index citations refer to **table** numbers, not **page** numbers

Body Mass Index (BMI), 219
Bolivia. (See Foreign countries.)
Bolts, nuts, etc. (See Iron and steel products.)
Bonds:
    Foreign, 1228, 1229
    Holdings by sector, 750, 1192, 1193, 1226, 1229,
        1231
    Life insurance companies, 1226, 1246
    New issues, 1227
    Prices, yields, sales, and issues, 498, 1223, 1225,
        1228, 1230
    U.S. savings, 498, 1194
Book, periodical, and music stores, 660, 667, 1071,
    1072
Book publishing industry, 765, 1151, 1152, 1157,
    1160
Bookkeeping. (See Accounting, tax preparation,
    bookkeeping, and payroll services.)
Books (see also Book publishing industry, Libraries,
    and Reading), 1079, 1157, 1160, 1185
Boots. (See Footwear.)
Borders, Canada and Mexico, 381
Border Patrol activities, 553, 554
Boron, 929, 930,
Bosnia and Herzegovina. (See Foreign countries.)
Botox, 191
Botswana. (See Foreign countries.)
Botulism, 194
Bowling, 1268, 1273, 1274, 1278
Bowling center industry, 667, 1253, 1256
Boxing, 1273
Brazil. (See Foreign countries.)
Bread, 755, 761
Breastfeeding, 110
Bridges, 1111
Broadband, 1155, 1173, 1174, 1182, 1183, 1418
Broadcasting industry:
    Capital, 807
    Earnings, 660, 783, 1151, 1153
    Employees, 660, 783, 1151, 1153
    Establishments, 783, 1151, 1153
    Finances, 773, 1152
    Gross domestic product, 698
    Multinational companies, 822, 823
    Number of stations, 1155
    Productivity, 667
    Receipts, revenue, 773, 783, 1152, 1153
Broadway and off-Broadway shows, 1259
Broccoli, 229, 887
Broilers (see also Poultry), 765, 867, 893, 901, 902
Bromine, 929, 930
Bronchitis, 128, 208
Brunei. (See Foreign countries.)
Buddhist population. (See Religion.)
Budget, federal:
    Debt, 489
    Outlays, 488, 490, 491, 492
    Receipts, 488, 494
    Tax expenditures, 496
    Taxes, 494
Building construction:
    Earnings, 660,
    Employees, 660, 988,
    Establishments, 988,

Occupational safety, 687
Building materials, and garden supplies stores:
    Earnings, 660, 783, 1071, 1073
    Electronic commerce, 1078
    Employees, 660, 783, 1071, 1073
    Establishments, 783, 1071, 1072
    Inventories, 1047, 1077
    Nonemployers, 1072
    Price indexes, 998
    Productivity, 667
    Sales, 783, 1047, 1072, 1074, 1076, 1077
Building permits. (See Construction industry, and
    Housing and housing units.)
Buildings (see also Construction industry, and
    Housing and housing units):
    Characteristics of, 1032
    Construction value, 989, 991, 992, 994
    Federal, 521
    Fires and property loss, 372, 374, 405
    Floorspace, 521, 992, 1032
Bulgaria. (See Foreign countries.)
Bullying, 317
Burglaries, 319, 320, 321, 322, 332, 333,
Burkina Faso. (See Foreign countries.)
Burma. (See Foreign countries.)
Burundi. (See Foreign countries.)
Buses and bus transportation. (See Passenger transit
    industry and Motor vehicles.)
Business cycles, 812
Business enterprises (see also individual types of
    business and industry):
    Ages of firms, 790
    American Indian- and Alaska Native-owned
        businesses, 794, 801
    Asian-owned businesses, 794, 799
    Bankruptcies filed, 802, 803
    Births and deaths of, 791, 792
    Black-owned businesses, 794, 798
    Capital, 807
    Corporations, partnerships, and proprietorships,
        605, 771, 773, 774, 775, 776, 781, 782, 1066
    Employees, 785, 786, 787, 788, 789, 790, 792,
        821, 1302
    Establishments, 783, 785, 786, 787, 789, 790,
        792
    Expansions and contractions, 792
    Finances, 771, 774, 775, 777, 778, 818, 820, 822,
        823, 1048, 1049, 1050, 1075
    Firms, 787, 788, 789, 790, 792
    Flow of funds, 1190
    Foreign investment in the U.S., 1318, 1320
    Hispanic-owned businesses, 794, 797
    Leading indicators, 813
    Loans to minority-operated small businesses, 793
    Minority-owned, 794, 796
    Multinational companies, 821, 822, 823, 824
    Native Hawaiian and Other Pacific Islander- owned
        business, 794, 800
    Patents, 804, 805, 1417
    Payroll, 785, 786, 787, 788, 789
    Profits, 817, 818, 819, 820, 1049, 1050, 1075
    Sales, shipments, receipts, 1044, 1046, 1047,
        1050
    Small business, 788, 789, 791, 793

Note: Index citations refer to **table** numbers, not **page** numbers

---

Note: Index citations refer to **table** numbers, not **page** numbers

Expenditures for, 599, 601, 719
Tax credit, 511
Child day care services, 165, 602, 642, 660
Child support, 565, 596, 597, 599
Children (see also Births, Deaths, Marriages, Divorces, and Population):
Adopted, 600
Age and/or sex, 7, 8, 9, 10, 11, 12, 17
Aid, social welfare programs, 563, 565, 568, 589, 590, 591, 592, 594, 595, 596, 597, 598, 602, 603
AIDS, 197
Allergies, 225
American Indian, Alaska Native population, 10, 11, 12
Asian population, 10, 11, 12, 72
Asthma, 203
Attention Deficit Disorder, 198
Black, African American population, 10, 11, 12, 72
Child abuse, 361, 362
Child day care, 604, 755
Child support, 565, 596, 597, 599
Cigarette smoking, 215
Computer use, 264
Cost of raising, 719
Crime, arrests, 342, 344
Deaths and death rates, 120, 121, 122, 127, 128
Dependency ratios, 18
Disability status, 198, 199, 200, 201
Families with, 67, 68, 69, 70, 71
Food cost, 760
Food insecurity, 222
Food stamp program, 594, 595
Foreign-born population, 41, 42
Foreign country, 1367, 1368, 1399
Foster care, 600
Grandparents living with grandchildren, 73
Head Start program, 598
Health insurance coverage, 150, 153, 160, 161, 162
High school dropouts, 275, 276
High school graduates, 274, 280
Hispanic origin population, 10, 11, 12, 72
Homeschooled, 252
Homicides, school-related, 318
Hospital use, 176, 183, 184
Hunger, 222
Immigrants, 51
Immunization against diseases, 202
Income, families with children, 730
Injuries, 209
Juvenile delinquency institutions, 359
Labor force (16 to 19 years old), 614
Employed, 629, 631, 636, 638
Employment status, 623
Minimum wage workers, 681
Multiple job holders, 636
Participation rates, 624
Sex, 614, 619
Unemployed, 651, 652, 656
Language proficiency, 248
Literacy activities, skills, 246, 247
Literacy, comparative, 1399
Living arrangements, 72

Metropolitan areas, 23
Mobility status, 31
Mothers in the labor force, 97, 102, 626, 627
Native Hawaiian, Other Pacific Islander population, 10, 11, 12
Obesity, 223
Physician visits, 173, 174
Pneumonia, 184
Poverty, 740, 741
Projections, 9, 12
Races, two or more, 10, 11, 12
Respiratory infection, acute, 176
School enrollment, 232, 234, 235, 237, 238, 239, 240, 249, 254, 255, 257
School readiness, 247
Social security beneficiaries and payments, 568
Special education, 200
Stay-at-home parents, 71
Suicides, 127, 135, 318
Chile. (See Foreign countries.)
China. (See Foreign countries.)
Chiropractors, 165
Chlamydia, 194, 195
Chocolate. (See Cocoa.)
Christian population. (See Religion.)
Christmas trees,
Chromite, 1405
Chromium, 930, 936
Churches (see also Religion):
Clergy, 642
Construction value, 992
Grants, foundations, 605, 608
Membership, 82
Schools, 250
Volunteers, 610
Cigar smoking, 215
Cigarettes (see also Tobacco):
Consumption, 1371
Smokers and use, 212, 214, 215, 216
Circuit boards, 1055
Circulation of media, 1155, 1158, 1159
Circulatory diseases, 207
Cirrhosis of liver, deaths, 123, 124, 125, 126, 127, 128
Cities (see also Metropolitan statistical areas):
Climate, 410, 411, 412, 413, 1415
Commuting, 1134, 1139, 1142
Crime, 322
Cruise departure sites, 1287
Debts, 476
Employees, earnings, payrolls, 486
Finances of city governments, 475, 476
Foreign born, 40
Governmental units, 447, 448
Income, 736
Language spoken at home, 58
Officials elected, 440
Population, 28, 29, 40
Poverty, 736
Property tax rates, 467
Roadway congestion, 1134
Taxes, 466
Travel, 1288
Citizenship, 43, 50, 99

Note: Index citations refer to **table** numbers, not **page** numbers

Note: Index citations refer to **table** numbers, not **page** numbers

Note: Index citations refer to **table** numbers, not **page** numbers

Note: Index citations refer to **table** numbers, not **page** numbers

Currency:
  Foreign exchange rate, 1423
  Personal saving component, 706
  Supply, 1222
Customs and Border Protection (CBP), 553, 554, 555, 556, 558, 560
Cyber-bullying, 317
Cyprus. (See Foreign countries.)
Czech Republic. (See Foreign countries.)

D

Dairy products (see also individual products):
  Consumer expenditures, 714, 717
  Consumption, 228, 230, 1400
  Farm marketings, sales, 865, 867, 868, 899
  Foreign trade, 873, 878, 1400
  Manufacture, 667, 899, 1037
  Prices, 765, 870
  Production, 899, 1400
Dance, 1263
Data processing services. (See Computer programming and data processing services.)
Dates, 888
Day care. (See Child day care services.)
DAX, German stock index, 1421
Death care services, 660, 755, 1299, 1300, 1301, 1311
Death penalty, 366, 367, 368
Deaths, and death rates (see also Accidents and fatalities), 84
  Age and sex, 113, 115, 116, 117, 118, 127, 128, 130, 131, 132, 133, 134, 135, 136
  AIDS, 124, 125
  American Indian, Alaska Native population, 5, 115, 116, 117, 130, 133, 134, 136
  Asian population, 5, 115, 116, 117, 130, 133, 134
  Black, African American population, 5, 113, 115, 116, 117, 121, 122, 130, 133, 134, 136
  Causes of death, 123, 124, 125, 126, 127, 128, 129, 130, 131, 132, 133, 134, 136, 1093, 1145
  Fetal and neonatal, 120, 121
  Foreign countries, 1368, 1372, 1373
  Heart disease, 123, 124, 125, 126, 127, 128, 129, 130, 207
  Hispanic or Latino origin, 5, 115, 117, 118, 125, 130, 133, 134, 136
  Industrial, 687
  Infant, 84, 120, 121, 122
  Injuries, 126
  Island areas of the U.S., 122, 129, 1342
  Maternal, 121
  Military deaths, 535, 537
  Native Hawaiian, Other Pacific Islander population, 5
  Race, 5, 113, 115, 116, 117, 121, 122, 130, 133, 134
  States, 16, 119, 122, 129
  Suicide, 123, 124, 126, 127, 128, 133, 135, 537, 1373
  Traffic fatalities, 1093, 1122, 1123, 1124, 1128, 1129, 1131, 1132, 1133, 1372
  Weather related, 405, 409
  Workers' deaths, 375, 687, 688, 927

Deaths, of businesses, 791, 792
Debit cards, 1208, 1209, 1210, 1211
Debt (see also Loans and mortgages):
  City, 476
  Consumer, 1199, 1214
  County governments, 478
  Credit market, 1191
  Farm, 863
  Federal government, 489
  Foreign countries, 1427
  Households, 309, 1196
  Individual, 745
  Local government, 459, 474
  State and local government, 459, 464, 470, 472, 1115
  Student loan debt, 309, 311
Deductions, taxes, 508, 509, 510
  Business, 774, 775, 776, 780
Defense, Department of (see also Army, Air Force, Marine Corps, and Navy):
  Budget authority, outlays, 490, 492, 522, 523
  Contract and grant awards, 524, 525
  Employees, civilian, 524, 526, 527
  Expenditures, 141, 144, 492, 524, 525, 526
  Military bases, 526, 527
  Military personnel, 524, 526, 527, 528, 529, 530, 536, 537, 538
  Military reserve and National Guard, 532, 533, 534
  Military retirees, 525, 531, 565, 573
Defined contribution plans, 1190, 1241
Degrees conferred (see also individual fields), 303, 304, 305, 306, 307, 308, 837, 838, 839, 840, 841
  Salary offers, 302
Delaware. (See State data.)
Delinquency. (See Juvenile delinquency.)
Denmark. (See Foreign countries.)
Dentists, 167, 642
  Charges and expenditures for, 140, 142, 143, 148, 766
  Dental schools, students, and graduates, 308
  Medicaid payments, recipients, 156
  Offices, 165, 166
Department stores:
  Earnings, 660, 1071, 1076
  Employees, 660, 1071, Establishments, 1071
  Inventories, 1077
  Productivity, 667
  Sales, 1074, 1077, 1310
Deportations, illegal immigrants, 553, 555, 556
Deposit Insurance Fund, 1200
Deposits. (See Banks.)
Dermatologists, 169
Development aid, 1425
Diabetes, 123, 124, 125, 126, 127, 128, 129, 206
Diamonds, 930, 1405
Diatomite, 929, 930
Diesel, fuel, 954, 959
Dietitians and nutritionists, 642
Direct deposit, banking, 1209, 1210
Direct mail advertising industry, 1301, 1304, 1306
Directory and mailing list publications industry, 1151, 1152, 1157
Disabilities:

Note: Index citations refer to **table** numbers, not **page** numbers

---

Note: Index citations refer to **table** numbers, not **page** numbers

Note: Index citations refer to **table** numbers, not **page** numbers

Note: Index citations refer to **table** numbers, not **page** numbers

Note: Index citations refer to **table** numbers, not **page** numbers

Endangered species, 415
Energy (see also Electric light and power industry, and various fuel types):
  Air pollutant emissions, 390, 391, 392, 393, 394, 1414
  Commercial buildings, 1032
  Consumption, 951, 955, 956, 957, 959, 1408
    End-use sector, 955, 956
    Foreign countries, 1408, 1410, 1411
    Renewable sources, 951, 952, 957, 971, 972, 980
    Source, 951, 956
    Transportation, 954
  Electric, 949, 950, 956, 958, 960, 967, 968, 969, 971, 972, 973, 974, 975, 976, 977, 978, 979, 980
  End-use sector, 955, 956, 960
  Expenditures, 958, 960, 1032
  Federal outlays, 492
  Price indexes:
    Consumer, 753, 754, 755
    Futures, 763
    Producer, 763, 765
  Prices, 758, 973
Engineering and architectural services:
  Earnings, 660, 1301
  Employees, 660, 1300, 1301
  Establishments, 1301
  Nonemployers, 1300
  Receipts, 1300, 1304
  Research and development, 831
Engineers and scientists (see also individual fields):
  Characteristics, 842
  Degrees conferred, 305, 306, 307, 836, 838, 839, 840
  Employment, 642, 843, 844, 845
  Research and development, 828, 831, 834
  Salary, 302, 845
English, ability to speak, 56, 57, 58, 248, 258
Entertainment:
  Consumer expenditures, 716, 717, 1258
  Consumer price indexes, 755
  Gaming, 1285, 1286
  Personal expenditures, 705, 716, 717, 1258
Environment (see also Pollution):
  Charitable contributions, 605, 608
  Environmental industries, 398
  Volunteers, 610
  Wetlands, 386, 388
Environmental science, 828, 834, 836, 841
Equatorial Guinea. (See Foreign countries.)
Eritrea. (See Foreign countries.)
Eskimo population. (See American Indian, Alaska Native population.)
Establishments. (See Business enterprise, and individual industries.)
Estate and gift taxes, 499
Estonia. (See Foreign countries.)
Ethane, 934
Ethanol, 883, 959
Ethiopia. (See Foreign countries.)
Ethnicities. (See Hispanic or Latino origin population.)
Ethylene, 934

Europe. (See Foreign countries.)
European Union. (See Foreign countries.)
Exchange-traded funds, 1190, 1226
Excise taxes, 494, 499
Executions of prisoners, 367, 368
Executive Office of the President (federal), 518
Exercise program, 1264
Exercise equipment, 205, 1276, 1277
Expectation of life (average lifetime), 111, 112, 113
  Foreign countries, 1368
  Life years lost
  Projections, 112
Expenditures. (See individual subjects).
Expenditures of state and local government. (See individual governmental units.)
Expenditures of U.S. government, 450, 451, 453, 492, 704, 1113, 1323, 1324, 1325
  Aid to the arts and humanities, 1260
  Aid to Island areas, 453, 1346
  Aid to state and local government, 450, 451, 453, 1113
  Budget outlays, 488, 490, 491, 492, 493, 494
  Contract awards, 524, 525, 526
  Education. (See Federal aid to education.)
  Food programs, federal, 592, 593
  Health, 140, 141, 142, 143, 144
  Homeland security, 451, 548, 549, 550, 552
  Hospitals, 178
  Military personnel, 524, 526
  National defense, 522, 523, 767
  Outlays, 488, 489, 490, 491, 492, 493
  Payrolls, 480, 481, 515, 516, 517
  Price indexes, 767
  Public debt, 489
  Public roads, 453, 1113
  Research and development, 825, 826, 827, 829, 830
  Retirement benefits, 561
  Schools, 236
  Science/space, 846
  Veterans benefits. (See Veterans Affairs.)
Exports. (See Foreign trade.)
Express mail, 1149, 1150,

F

Fabricated metal product manufacturing:
  Capital, 807, 1321
  Earnings, 660, 1035, 1037, 1043
  Employees, 660, 1035, 1037, 1039, 1043
  Establishments, 1035
  Finance, 820, 1054
  Foreign trade, 1054, 1337
  Gross domestic product, 698, 1033
  Industrial production index, 815
  Occupational safety, 686
  Productivity, 667
  Profits, 820
  Research and development, 831
  Shipments, 1037, 1045, 1046
  Toxic chemical releases, 400
Fabrics. (See Textile mill products.)
Falls, accidental deaths, 126, 127
Families. (See Households.)

Note: Index citations refer to **table** numbers, not **page** numbers

Family and consumer sciences, degrees conferred, 305, 306, 307
Family farms, 855, 856
Farm mortgage loans, 1216
Farmers market, 891
Farms:
 Acreage, 849, 850, 851, 852, 853, 854, 856, 860, 862
  Cropland, 385, 387, 848, 882
  Crops harvested (see also individual crops), 882, 883, 884, 885, 886, 887, 1400
  Farm type, 856
  Organic, 857
 Agrichemicals, 865, 870, 876
 Agricultural products:
  Exports, 1404
  Foreign countries, production, 1401, 1402
  Market value, 848
  Prices. (See Prices received by farmers.)
  Railroad car loadings, 1146, 1147
  Waterborne commerce, 1106
  World production, 1400, 1401, 1402
 Assets and liabilities, 863, 1190
 Corporate, 851, 854, 856
 Crops (see also individual crops):
  Acreage, 882, 883, 1354
  Fruits and nuts, 888, 889, 1355
  Income, 867, 869, 1354
  Production, 877, 882, 883, 1400, 1401
  Vegetables, 887, 903
 Debt, 861, 863, 1216
 Expenses, 859, 865
 Family or individual, 851, 853, 855, 1354
 Farm land and buildings value, 853, 854, 862, 863
 Farm operators, 862
 Farm products sold, marketing receipts, 853, 854, 857, 860, 861, 862, 864, 865, 867, 868, 869
 Fertilizers:
  Farm expenditures for, 865
  Foreign trade, 876, 1333
  Prices, 765, 870
  Shipments, 1053
 Government payments to farmers, 861, 862, 864, 865, 866
 Gross farm value added, 698, 864
 Housing, rental value, 865
 Income, 855, 856, 864, 865, 866, 867, 869
 Inventories, change in, 864
 Labor expenses, 865, 870
 Machinery and motor vehicles, 863, 865
 Mortgage loans, 1216
 Number of farms, 849, 850, 851, 852, 853, 860, 861, 862
 Organic farming, 857, 891
 Parity ratio, 870
 Partnerships, 851, 853, 1354
 Prices, 870, 883, 894
 Taxes, 864, 870
 Value of land and buildings, 853, 854, 862, 863
Fats, nutrition (See also Lard, Margarine, and Oils), 231
Fatalities. (See Accidents and fatalities.)
Fatigue
Federal aid to education, 236, 451, 453, 456

Elementary and secondary education, 236
 Higher education institutions, 236
 Research and development, 825, 827, 830, 835
 Science and engineering, 834
Federal aid to state and local government, 450, 451, 453, 456
Federal budget. (See Expenditures of U.S. government.)
Federal debt, 489, 1224
Federal employees retirement trust fund. (See under Government.)
Federal funds, summary distribution by state, 497
Federal government. (See Government.)
Federal government finances. (See Receipts and Expenditures of U.S. government.)
Federal Housing Administration, mortgage loans, 1218
Federal trust funds, 495
Feed. (See Grain.)
Feedstock, 959
Feldspar, 929, 930, 933
Felony convictions, 358
Female householders. (See Households or families.)
Female population. (See Women.)
Fencing, 1274
Fertility rates, 85, 86, 88, 89
Fertilizers:
 Farm expenditures for, 865
 Foreign trade, 876, 1333
 Prices, 765, 870
 Shipments, 1053
Fetal deaths (neonatal), 120, 121
Fiber, dietary, 231
Fibers, 762, 765
Field hockey, 1274
Figs, 888
Fiji. (See Foreign countries.)
Filberts (hazelnuts), 888, 889
Filling stations. (See Gasoline stations.)
Finance and insurance industry:
 Capital, 807, 809, 811, 1227
 Earnings, 658, 660, 670, 672, 783, 795, 796, 797, 798, 799, 800, 801, 1187, 1189
 Electronic commerce, 1305
 Employees, 647, 658, 659, 660, 783, 786, 787, 795, 796, 797, 798, 799, 800, 801, 1187, 1189
 Equipment and software expenditures, 809
 Establishments, 783, 784, 786, 787, 1187, 1188, 1189
 Finances, 773, 776, 1190, 1214, 1351
 Foreign investments in U.S., 1318, Gross domestic product, 698, 700, 1186, 1351
 Hires and separations, 665, 666
 Hours, 658
 Multinational companies, 822, 823, 824
 Nonemployers, 784, 1188
 Occupational safety, 686, 687
 Profits, 818, 819
 Research and development, 831
 Sales or receipts, 773, 776, 781, 782, 783, 784, 795, 796, 797, 798, 799, 800, 801, 1187, 1188
 Union membership, 693

Note: Index citations refer to **table** numbers, not **page** numbers

Note: Index citations refer to **table** numbers, not **page** numbers

Note: Index citations refer to **table** numbers, not **page** numbers

Note: Index citations refer to **table** numbers, not **page** numbers

G

Gabon. (See Foreign countries.)
Gangs, murders, 323
Gambia, The. (See Foreign countries.)
Gambling, 1253, 1256
Games, leisure activities, 1266
Gaming, 1285, 1286
Garages. (See Gasoline stations, and Automobile
  repair and maintenance service.)
Garden activities and equipment, 205, 755, 765,
  1267
Garden supplies. (See Building materials and garden
  supplies.)
Garlic, 887
Garnet (industrial), 929, 930
Gas (see also Gas utility industry, Gasoline, and
  Petroleum):
  Liquefied petroleum gases, 934
  Natural, 926, 931, 934, 942
    Consumption, 942, 951, 954
    Energy expenditures, 958, 960
    Foreign trade, 952, 961, 962, 1337
    Offshore lease revenues, 939
    Prices, 758, 765, 766, 953
    Production and value, 934, 942, 943, 951,
      1405, 1407
    Foreign countries, 1405, 1412
    Indexes, 928
    Reserves, 938, 942, 943
    Residential, 983
    World production, 1405, 1407, 1412
    Unconventional, dry, 943
  Natural gas plant liquids, 934, 940
  Price indexes, 755
Gas utility industry (see also Utilities):
  Accidents and deaths, 1093
  Construction expenditures, 982
  Customers, 982, 983
  End users, 982
  Finances, 984
  Mains, mileage, 982
  Prices, 982
  Revenues, 950, 982, 983, 984
  Sales, 982, 983
Gasoline (see also Motor fuel):
  Consumer expenditures, 714, 715, 716, 717, 718
  Excise taxes, 1114
  Finished motor gasoline, 934, 935
  Prices, 758, 759, 766
  Transportation, 954
  Gasoline stations, retail:
    Earnings, 660, 783, 1071, 1073
    Employees, 660, 783, 1071, 1073
    Establishments, 783, 1071, 1310
    Finances, 773
    Productivity, 667
    Sales, 773, 783, 1074, 1076, 1310
Gemstones, 930
General merchandise stores:
  Earnings, 660, 783, 1071, 1073
  Electronic commerce, 1078
  Employees, 660, 783, 1071, 1073
  Establishments, 783, 1071, 1072,

Finances, 820
Inventories, 1077
Productivity, 667
Profits, 820
Sales, 783, 1072, 1074, 1076, 1078,
Geography and cartography. (See Land.)
Genetically engineered crops, 858
Georgia. (See Foreign countries and State data.).)
Geothermal energy, 957, 970, 971, 972, 1407, 1408
Germanium, 930
German stock market index (DAX), 1421
Germany. (See Foreign countries.)
Ghana. (See Foreign countries.)
Giardiasis, 194
Gift and estate taxes, 457, 499
Glass, 395, 396, 397, 765, 1333
Gold:
  Consumption, 930
  Employment, 930
  Foreign trade, 930, 1333
  Prices, 765, 930, 931
  Production and value, 928, 929, 930, 933, 1405
  Reserve assets, 1317
Golf, 1268, 1273, 1274, 1275, 1276, 1277, 1278
Golf courses, industry, 1253, 1256
Gonorrhea, 194
Government (see also Expenditures of U.S.
  government, and Receipts, and individual
  governmental units):
  Buildings, 521
  Capital stock, 751
  Consumer credit holdings, 1215
  Earnings, 485, 658, 670, 673, 674
  Employees, 483, 520, 658, 659, 660, 674, 843
    Benefits, 482
    Characteristics, 519, 520
    City government, 486
    County government, 487
    Federal, civilian, 480, 481, 516, 517, 518, 519,
      643
    Hours, 658
    Local government, 480, 481, 484, 485, 643
    Retirement systems, 565, 572, 573, 574
    State government, 480, 481, 484, 485, 643
  Employment cost index, 679
  Expenditures:
    Capital outlays, 458, 460
    City government, 476, 486
    Consumption, 704, 767
    County government, 478, 487
    Federal, 488, 490, 492, 494, 496
      Agriculture, 864, 865, 866
      Aid to state and local government, 450, 451,
        456, 1113
      Capital outlay, 458
    Local government, 458, 460, 474
    State and local government, 456, 457, 458,
      460, 462
    State government, 457, 458, 460, 465, 470,
      472
    Transfer payments, 562, 563, 564
  Federally owned land, 521
  Flow of funds, 1190, 1191
  Highways, 464, 472, 474, 1089, 1109, 1112,

Note: Index citations refer to **table** numbers, not **page** numbers

Note: Index citations refer to **table** numbers, not **page** numbers

Note: Index citations refer to **table** numbers, not **page** numbers

Note: Index citations refer to **table** numbers, not **page** numbers

Note: Index citations refer to **table** numbers, not **page** numbers

Note: Index citations refer to **table** numbers, not **page** numbers

Note: Index citations refer to **table** numbers, not **page** numbers

Note: Index citations refer to **table** numbers, not **page** numbers

Note: Index citations refer to **table** numbers, not **page** numbers

Note: Index citations refer to **table** numbers, not **page** numbers

ProQuest Statistical Abstract of the United States: 2014

Note: Index citations refer to **table** numbers, not **page** numbers

---

Note: Index citations refer to **table** numbers, not **page** numbers

Note: Index citations refer to **table** numbers, not **page** numbers

Note: Index citations refer to **table** numbers, not **page** numbers

Note: Index citations refer to **table** numbers, not **page** numbers

Note: Index citations refer to **table** numbers, not **page** numbers

Ophthalmologists, 169
Optometrists, 165
Oranges, 229, 761, 888
Oregon. (See State data.)
Ores, crude (see also individual ores), 1333
Organ transplants, 190
Organic farming, 857, 891
Osteopaths (see also Physicians), 168
Outdoor, recreation activities (see also Recreation, and specific forms of recreation), 1264, 1278, 1283
Outlays, federal budget, 488, 489, 490, 491, 492, 493, 846
Outpatient care centers industry, 165
Outpatient hospital visits, 174, 178, 179, 186
Overweight persons, 218, 219, 1370
Oysters, 922, 924, 925

P

Pain, lower back, neck, and face, 210
Pain relievers, illegal use, 215
Pakistan. (See Foreign countries.)
Palau. (See Foreign countries.)
Panama. (See Foreign countries.)
Paper and paperboard products:
  Foreign trade, 1333
  Prices, 765, 769, 917
  Production, 918, 919
  Railroad car loadings, 1146, 1147
  Recycling, 395, 396, 397
Paper products, manufacturing:
  Capital, 807
  Earnings, 660, 892, 904, 905, 908, 1035, 1037, 1043
  Employees, 660, 904, 905, 908, 1035, 1037, 1039, 1043
  Establishments, 904, 905, 1035
  Finances, 820, 892
  Foreign trade, 1337
  Gross domestic product, 698, 906, 1033
  Industrial production index, 815
  Output, 919
  Productivity, 667
  Profits, 820
  Research and development, 831
  Sales, 892, 904, 908, 1037, 1045, 1046
  Toxic chemical releases, 400
Papua New Guinea. (See Foreign countries.)
Paraguay. (See Foreign countries.)
Parent Teacher Association (PTA), 258
Parent Teacher Conferences, 258
Parent Teacher Organization (PTO), 258
Paris CAC-40 stock market index, 1421
Parkinson's disease, deaths, 126, 127
Parks, 464, 481, 1279, 1280, 1281, 1282
Parolees (see also Correctional institutions, and Prisoners), 369, 370
Parties, political. (See Political parties.)
Partnerships, establishments and finances, 771, 772, 773, 775, 776
Passenger transit industry (see also Passengers), 660, 766, 954, 1136, 1137
Passengers (see also Passenger transit industry, and various transportation modes):

Arriving from overseas, 1288, 1294, 1295, 1296
Border crossings, 558, 1297
Carrier operation, summary, 1094, 1104, 1136, 1145
Passenger traffic, volume, 558
Railroads, 1145
Patents and trademarks, 804, 805, 1417
Pathologists, 169
Payrolls. (See Earnings, and individual industries.)
Peaches, 229, 888
Peanuts, 230, 867
Pears, 229, 761, 888
Peas, green, 887
Peat, 929, 930
Pecans, 888, 889
Pedestrians, killed and injured, 1093, 1122, 1124, 1131
Pediatricians (see also Physicians), 169
Pennsylvania. (See State data.)
Pensions and retirement benefits (see also Social insurance):
  Annuities, 1241, 1246
  Expenditures, 561, 573, 714
  Foreign countries, 1391
  Funds (flow of funds), 1190, 1193, 1242
  Government employees, 565, 572, 573, 574
  Plans, 576, 588, 1241
  Railroad, 565
  Retirement and pension plans, 571, 573, 575, 588, 1226, 1240, 1241
  Veterans, 531, 565
Pentanes plus, 934
Peppers, 887
Perch, 925
Performing arts, 1253, 1256, 1259, 1263
Performing arts, spectator sports industry:
  Capital, 807
  Earnings, 660, 783, 1255
  Employees, 660, 783, 1256
  Establishments, 783, 1255, 1256
  Nonemployers, 1255
  Occupational safety, 686
  Receipts, revenue, 783,
Periodical publishing, 1151, 1152, 1157
Perlite, 929, 930
Personal and laundry services:
  Earnings, 660, 783, 1301
  Employees, 660, 783, 1301, 1302
  Establishments, 783, 1300, 1301
  Finances, 773
  Productivity, 667
  Receipts, 773, 783, 1300, 1311
Personal care, 205, 642, 755
Personal computers (PC's). (See Computers.)
Personal consumption expenditures, 695, 696, 705, 707, 766, 767, 1257
Personal health care expenditures, 142, 143, 145, 146
Personal income, 706, 708, 709, 710, 711
Personal savings, 702, 703
Peru. (See Foreign countries.)
Pesticides, 865
Pets, 755, 1071, 1258, 1265
Petroleum and coal product manufacturing:

Note: Index citations refer to **table** numbers, not **page** numbers

Note: Index citations refer to **table** numbers, not **page** numbers

Note: Index citations refer to **table** numbers, not **page** numbers

Note: Index citations refer to **table** numbers, not **page** numbers

Pulp manufacturing, 892, 905, 908
Pulpwood, 912, 913, 914, 918
Pulses, 229
Pumice and pumicite, 929, 930
Purchasing power of the dollar, 752

Q
Qatar. (See Foreign countries.)
Quarries. (See Mining industries.)
Quicksilver (mercury), 929, 930

R
Rabies, 194
Race (See individual race categories.)
Radio advertising expenditures, 1306
Radio broadcasting industry (see also Broadcasting, and Telecommunications):
  Earnings, 660, 1151, 1153
  Employees, 660, 1151, 1153
  Establishments, 1151, 1153
  Finances, 1152, 1165
  Productivity, 667
  Revenue, 1152, 1153, 1165
  Stations, 1155
Radiologists, 169
Radios, 1155, 1156
Rail transportation industry (see also Railroads):
  Capital, 807
  Earnings, 660, 1145
  Employees, 660, 1085, 1086, 1145
  Establishments, 1086
  Finances, 1145
  Gross domestic product, 698
Railroad employees' retirement funds, 561, 563
Railroads:
  AMTRAK, 954, 1145
  Carloadings, by commodity, 1146, 1147
  Energy consumption, 954
  Equipment in service, 1145
  Freight traffic, 1145, 1146, 1147
  Mileage owned and operated, 1089, 1145
  Occupational safety, 1093, 1145
  Passenger traffic and revenue, 1138, 1145, 1297
  Vehicles, 1090
Rainfall, selected cities, 1415
Raisins,
Rankings:
  Airport traffic, 1096, 1296
  Amusement parks, 1270
  Cities:
    Commuting, 1142
    Export-related jobs, 649
    Population, 28
    Residential property tax, 467
  Countries:
    Agricultural exports and imports, 1404
    Consumption of beef, pork, poultry, 1403
    Population, 1365
  Federal R&D obligations to higher education, 835
  Sports participation, 1278
  Port traffic, 1107, 1108
  State:

Domestic travel expenditures, 1290
  Exports, 1330
  Farm marketings, 869
  Foreign trade, 1330
  Government finances, 479
  Personal income per capita, 709
  Population, 15
  Public elementary/secondary school finances, 279
Rape, forcible, 319, 320, 321, 322, 327, 328, 329, 538
Raspberries, 888
Raw materials. (See Crude materials.)
Reading (see also Books, and Libraries), 716, 717, 1257, 1258, 1266, 1269
  E-book reader ownership, 1176
  Literacy, 246, 1399
Real estate (see also Housing), 746
Real estate and rental and leasing industry:
  Capital, 807, 809, 811
  Earnings, 658, 660, 670, 783, 795, 796, 797, 798, 799, 800, 801, 1187, 1251
  Employees, 642, 658, 660, 783, 786, 795, 796, 797, 798, 799, 800, 801, 1187, 1251
  Equipment and software expenditures, 809
  Establishments, 783, 784, 786, 1187, 1250, 1251
  Finances, 773, 776
  Gross domestic product, 698, 700, 1186
  Hires and separations, 665, 666
  Hours, 658
  Nonemployers, 784, 1250
  Productivity, 667
  Receipts, 773, 776, 781, 782, 783, 784, 795, 796, 797, 798, 799, 800, 801, 1187, 1250, 1252
Real estate investment trust (REITs), 1190, 1191, 1216
Receipts (see also Tax receipts, and individual industries):
  American Indian and Alaska Native-owned businesses, 801
  Asian-owned businesses, 799
  Black-owned businesses, 798
  Corporations, partnerships, and proprietorships, 771, 772, 773, 774, 775, 776, 780, 781, 782, 1066
  Hispanic- or Latino-owned businesses, 797
  International transportation, 1313
  Minority-owned businesses, 796
  Native Hawaiian and Other Pacific Islander- owned businesses, 794, 795
Revenue:
  Local governments, 457, 473
    City governments, 475
    County governments, 477
  State and local governments combined, 449, 456, 462, 463
  State governments, 457, 465, 470, 479
  Tax collections, 471
    United States government, 456, 457, 488, 494, 499
  Women-owned businesses, 795
Recreation (see also Arts, recreation, and travel, and Sports):
  Activities, 220, 1259, 1263, 1264, 1266, 1267,

Note: Index citations refer to **table** numbers, not **page** numbers

---

Note: Index citations refer to **table** numbers, not **page** numbers

Note: Index citations refer to **table** numbers, not **page** numbers

Seeds, 865
Selenium, dietary, 231
Self-employed, 631, 632, 843
Semiconductors (see also Computer and electronic product components), 1055, 1335
Senators, U.S., 426, 430, 432
Senegal. (See Foreign countries.)
Septicemia, 124, 125, 126, 127, 128
Serbia. (See Foreign countries.)
Service industries (see also specific sectors):
  Capital, 807, 809
  Earnings, 660, 670, 672, 795, 796, 797, 798, 799, 800, 801, 1299, 1301, 1357
  Electronic commerce, 1305
  Employees, 167, 647, 659, 660, 786, 795, 796, 797, 798, 799, 800, 801, 1299, 1301, 1356, 1357
  Equipment and software expenditures, 809
  Establishments, 786, 1356, 1357
  Finances, 783, 784
  Foreign trade, 1313, 1315, 1326
  Gross domestic product, 700, 1351
  Industry, 783
  Occupational safety, 686, 687
  Price indexes, 753
  Productivity, 667
  Profits, 771, 819
  Sales or receipts, 783, 784, 795, 796, 797, 798, 799, 800, 801, 1299, 1300, 1311, 1357
Service occupations:
  Benefits, 683
  Earnings, 673, 676, 678
  Employment, 642, 644, 645, 1302
  Unemployment, 654
  Union membership, 693
Service stations. (See Gasoline service stations.)
Service workers. (See Service industries, and Service occupations.)
Sewage treatment systems, 949, 950, 985
  Construction, 460, 994
  Expenditures, 456, 457, 458, 460, 464
  Prices, 755
  Residences, 1014,
Sexual activity, 103, 104
Sexual assault. (See Rape)
Sexual identity, 105
Seychelles. (See Foreign countries.
Shale gas, 943
Sheep and lambs, 867, 893, 894
Shellfish:
  Canned, quantity and value, 925
  Catch, quantity and value, 922
  Consumption, 230
  Prices, 765
  Sales, 923
Shelters, homeless, 611, 612
Shigellosis, 194
Shipments, manufacturers' (see also individual industries or products), 1037, 1038, 1046, 1047
Shipping. (See Waterborne commerce)
Ships, 765, 1287
Shoe stores, 660, 667, 1073, 1074
Shoes. (See Footwear.)
Shoplifting, 333

Shortening, 230, 761, 765
Shoreline, 378, 382
Shrimp, 922, 924, 925
Sierra Leone. (See Foreign countries.)
Silicon, 929, 930,
Silver, 929, 933, 936
  Consumption, 930
  Foreign trade, 930, 936, 1333
  Prices, 930, 931
  Production and value, 930, 933
  World production, 933
Singapore. (See Foreign countries.)
Single-parent households, 62, 67, 68, 69, 70,
Single persons. (See Marital status.)
Sinusitis, 208
Skateboarding, 315, 1278
Skiing, 1253, 1256, 1268, 1273, 1274, 1276, 1278
Slaughtering and meat-packing industry. (See Meat and meat products.)
Sleep, 226
Slovakia. (See Foreign countries.)
Slovenia. (See Foreign countries.)
Small business:
  Employees, 787, 788, 789, 791,
  Firms, 787, 788, 789, 791, 791
  Loans, 793
  Payroll, 787, 788, 789
Smart cards, 1209
Smoking, 212, 214, 215
Snow and ice pellets, selected cities, 412
Snowboarding, 1278
Snowmobiles, 1276
Soap, 765
Soccer, 1273, 1274, 1275, 1278
Social assistance industry:
  Capital, 807
  Earnings, 660, 783
  Employees, 660, 783
  Establishments, 603, 783
  Gross domestic product, 698
  Nonemployers, 603
  Receipts, 165, 602, 603, 783
Social insurance (see also Medicare, Retirement systems, and Social Security):
  Employment covered, 567
  Expenditures, 562, 563, 564
  Foreign countries, 1391
  Government insurance trust funds, 457,
    Federal receipts and expenditures, 495, 570
    State and local receipts, expenditures, 456, 464, 470, 472, 574
  Government transfer payments, 562, 563, 564
  Individual programs:
    Beneficiaries and benefits, 568, 569
    Coverage, 567, 574
    Federal retirement insurance, 572, 1190, 1242
  Old-age, survivors, disability, and health insurance:
    Contributions, 570
    Coverage, workers and earnings, 567
    Payments, 563, 568, 569, 570
    Tax collections, 499
    Trust funds, 495, 570
  Railroad insurance, 563

Note: Index citations refer to **table** numbers, not **page** numbers

---

Note: Index citations refer to **table** numbers, not **page** numbers

Note: Index citations refer to **table** numbers, not **page** numbers

Note: Index citations refer to **table** numbers, not **page** numbers

---

Note: Index citations refer to **table** numbers, not **page** numbers

Note: Index citations refer to **table** numbers, not **page** numbers

Note: Index citations refer to **table** numbers, not **page** numbers

Production, 887, 903
Vehicles. (See Motor vehicles.)
Veneer, wood products, 892, 905, 908
Venereal diseases (see also AIDS), 194
Venezuela. (See Foreign countries.)
Vermiculite, 929, 930
Vermont. (See State data.)
Vessels. (See Ships.)
Veterans:
    Business owners, 794
    Characteristics, 544
    Employment, 519, 617
    Homeless programs, 534
    Number, 542
    Pensions and other benefits:
        Service-connected compensation, 543, 546
        Disbursements, 522, 546, 561, 563
        Federal aid to state and local governments, 451
        Federal payments, 492, 493
        Veterans or dependents receiving, 543, 565
Veterans Affairs, Dept. of:
    Expenditures, 141, 144, 543, 546, 547, 562, 563, 564
    Home loans, 1218
Vetoed bills, Congressional, 434
Victimizations, criminal, 327, 328, 329, 330, 331, 332, 333, 334, 335, 338, 339
Vietnam. (See Foreign countries.)
Violent crime, (see also Crime), 319, 320, 321, 322, 323, 325, 338, 339, 342
Virgin Islands. (See Island areas of the U.S.)
Virginia. (See State data.)
Visa holders, doctorates, 837
Vital statistics. (See Births and birth rates, Deaths and death rates, Divorces, and Marriages.):
Vitamins, 231
Vocational rehabilitation, 141, 602
Volleyball, 1273, 1274, 1275, 1278
Volunteer activities, 258, 610, 1264
Votes:
    Congressional, 417, 426, 428, 429
    Gubernatorial, 436
    Presidential, 417, 421, 422, 423, 424, 425
    Votes cast, 418, 419, 420
Voting-age population, 417, 418, 419

W

Wage earners. (See Labor force and individual industries.)
Wages and wage rates. (See Earnings.)
Walnuts, 888, 889
Warehouse clubs and superstores, 1071, 1074
Warehousing and storage industry:
    Capital, 807
    Earnings, 660, 1087
    Employees, 660, 1032, 1085, 1086, 1087
    Establishments, 1032, 1086, 1087
    Gross domestic product, 698
    Revenue, 1143
Washing machines, homes with, 1014
Washington. (See State data.)
Waste management & remediation services, 783, 807, 1301, 1307
Wastepaper, 765, 917

Wastewater treatment, 949, 950, 985
Watches. (See Clocks and watches.)
Water (see also Wastewater treatment, and Water transportation industry):
    Area, 1, 376
    Consumption, 389
    Freight, 1105, 1106, 1328
    Lakes, 377, 378, 379
    Pollution, 399, 404
    Public supply, 389, 986, 987, 1014
    Vessels, 1090, 1268
Water polo, 1274
Water transportation industry:
    Capital, 807
    Earnings, 660, 1087
    Employees, 660, 1085, 1086, 1086, 1087
    Establishments, 1087
    Foreign trade, 1106
    Freight, 1105, 1106, 1328
    Fuel consumption, 954
    Gross domestic product, 698, 1328
    Occupational safety, 1093
    Outlays, 492
    Revenue
Water utility, 460, 716, 717, 755, 949, 950, 986, 987
Water, sewage and other systems, 660, 937, 949, 985, 986, 987
Waterborne commerce, 1105, 1106, 1107, 1108
Watermelons, 887
Waterways, 1105
Wealth:
    Business, 751
    Families, 748, 749
    Family farms, 855
    Government, 751
    Households, 751
    Millionaires, 747
    Persons, 745, 746, 747
Weather, 405, 408, 409, 410, 411, 412, 413, 981, 1415
Weight, 218
Weightlifting, 1273, 1278
Welfare services. (See Public aid, assistance, Social welfare, and individual programs.)
West Bank. (See Foreign countries.)
West Nile virus, 194
West Virginia. (See State data.)
Western Sahara. (See Foreign countries.)
Wetlands, 386, 388
Wheat:
    Acreage, 883, 886, 1400
    Farm marketings, sales, 867
    Farm prices, 883, 886
    Foreign trade, 875, 877, 879, 880, 883, 1400, 1404
    Price indexes, 765, 769
    Production, 877, 883, 886, 1400, 1401
    Supply and disappearance, 883
Wheat flour, 230
Whiting, 922
Wholesale trade:
    Capital expenditures, 807, 809, 811
    Earnings, 658, 660, 670, 783, 795, 796, 797, 798, 799, 800, 801, 1065, 1067, 1357

Note: Index citations refer to **table** numbers, not **page** numbers

Note: Index citations refer to **table** numbers, not **page** numbers

Note: Index citations refer to **table** numbers, not **page** numbers